# Pronunciation Key

| SYMBOL | KEY WORDS |
|---|---|
| a | **a**sk, f**a**t |
| ā | **a**pe, d**a**te |
| ä | c**a**r, l**o**t |
| e | **e**lf, t**e**n |
| er | b**er**ry, c**are** |
| ē | **e**ven, m**ee**t |
| i | **i**s, h**i**t |
| ir | m**ir**ror, h**ere** |
| ī | **i**ce, f**i**re |
| ō | **o**pen, g**o** |
| ô | l**aw**, h**o**rn |
| oi | **oi**l, p**oi**nt |
| o͝o | l**oo**k, p**u**ll |
| o͞o | **oo**ze, t**oo**l |
| yo͝o | **u**nite, c**u**re |
| yo͞o | c**u**te, f**ew** |
| ou | **ou**t, cr**ow**d |
| u | **u**p, c**u**t |
| ʉr | f**ur**, f**er**n |
| ə | **a** in ago |
|  | **e** in agent |
|  | **e** in father |
|  | **i** in unity |
|  | **o** in collect |
|  | **u** in focus |

| SYMBOL | KEY WORDS |
|---|---|
| b | **b**ed, du**b** |
| d | **d**id, ha**d** |
| f | **f**all, o**ff** |
| g | **g**et, do**g** |
| h | **h**e, a**h**ead |
| j | **j**oy, **j**ump |
| k | **k**ill, ba**k**e |
| l | **l**et, ba**ll** |
| m | **m**et, tri**m** |
| n | **n**ot, to**n** |
| p | **p**ut, ta**p** |
| r | **r**ed, dea**r** |
| s | **s**ell, pa**ss** |
| t | **t**op, ha**t** |
| v | **v**at, ha**v**e |
| w | **w**ill, al**w**ays |
| y | **y**et, **y**ard |
| z | **z**ebra, ha**z**e |
| ch | **ch**in, ar**ch** |
| ŋ | ri**ng**, si**ng**er |
| sh | **sh**e, da**sh** |
| th | **th**in, tru**th** |
| *th* | **th**en, fa**th**er |
| zh | **s** in pleasure |
| ′ | as in (ā′b′l) |

A heavy stress mark **′** is placed after a syllable that gets a strong accent, as in **con·sid·er** (kən sid**′**ər).

A light stress mark ′ is placed after a syllable that also gets an accent, but of a weaker kind, as in **dic·tion·ar·y** (dik**′**shə ner′ē).

See also the explanation of how to use the pronunciation key, beginning on page 32 of the introduction.

# NEW WORLD DICTIONARY
## *of the American Language*

DAVID B. GURALNIK
*Editor in Chief*

## *Basic School Edition*

Prentice-Hall, Inc. Englewood Cliffs, N.J.

**Webster's New World Dictionary, Basic School Edition**



**Webster's New World Dictionary, Basic School Edition,**
is based on and includes material from
Webster's New World Dictionary for Young Readers

Library of Congress Catalog Card Number: 78-59178

ISBN 529-05625-9

Printed in The United States of America

10 9 8 7 6 5 4

# CONTENTS

UNITED KINGDOM
DENMARK
Copenhagen
London
Amsterdam
NETH.
Berlin
POLAND
Warsaw
BELGIUM
Brussels
Bonn
E. GERMANY
Paris
LUX.
W. GER.
Prague
CZECHOSLOVAK
FRANCE
Bern
LIECH.
Vienna
AUS.
HUNGARY
SWITZ.
ITALY
Belgrade
ANDORRA
MONACO
SAN MARINO
Rome

# FOREWORD

The most important skill pupils can learn during their school years is how to use and understand their native language effectively. Without this skill all other learning is greatly hampered. A critical tool for use in this educational process is a dictionary especially prepared to answer clearly the questions about words that pupils will put to it, and one that will do so in an inviting and attractive way to excite the interest of its young readers.

*Webster's New World Dictionary,* Basic School Edition, is such a book. It is the first in a series of carefully coordinated dictionaries that have been prepared to serve the needs of students from the early grades through college and beyond. The vocabulary list of the Basic School Edition was selected from the vast citation file of the Webster's New World Dictionary staff on the basis of the frequency with which these words appear in the textbooks and other reading materials that pupils in grades 3 through 8 are most likely to use. To make certain that the book conforms to current practices in teaching language arts, the design and approach of the Basic School Edition was prepared in consultation with a council of skilled teachers and educators, whose welcome aid I take this opportunity of acknowledging with gratitude. I also want to thank the staff members of Prentice-Hall, Inc., whose help in designing and preparing materials for the book was invaluable.

The experience of many years that the lexicographical staff has had in preparing dictionaries was put to use in the construction of this one to make certain that the definitions and notes would be clear and readily understood, but without talking down to the users of this book. The generous use of illustration, both in words and pictures, is essential to a full exposition of the meanings of words, and this dictionary is well provided with both kinds. The thousands of verbal illustrations not only show the idiomatic way in which each of the words is used in English, but also often add additional bits of information to broaden the pupils' understanding of the terms. The lively pictures, both photographs and drawings, were designed not only to shed additional light on the definitions but to invite the kind of browsing that leads to the joy of discovery.

There are a number of special features in this work not to be found in other dictionaries at this level. The Basic School Edition uniquely identifies all the Americanisms with an open star placed before those words and meanings that originated in the United States. There are many hundreds of little word histories that help to fix the current meanings of the terms in the minds of their readers and that can also be used successfully in a classroom unit of language study. And we have included, also for the first time in a dictionary for these grades, a number of paragraphs discussing the differences in the shades of meanings of synonyms and other closely related words. All these special paragraphs, as well as notes on word usage, are set off from the definitions by the use of color tints.

Finally, the introductory essay on the American language, the special section on references following the dictionary proper, and the section on how to use the dictionary were all designed to make this the most useful one-volume work on the vocabulary of English that could be prepared for young students.

David B. Guralnik

# A Story of Some American Words

The English language is like a great tree. Its roots spread deep into history and take nourishment from many sources. Its trunk is in England, from which all the branches grew. Its many branches are the separate kinds of English spoken around the world. From England, the English language spread to Scotland, Wales, and Ireland. Explorers and colonists took English across the oceans to America, to India, to Australia and New Zealand, and to southern Africa. Today about 400 million people speak English.

One of the largest branches of this great tree is the kind of English that you speak, called *American English.* The words that make your kind of English different from others are called *Americanisms.* These are words or meanings that first came into the English language in the area you know as the United States. On these next several pages, many Americanisms are shown in heavy type. Most of them can be found in this dictionary as entries or meanings with a little star before them.

Such everyday words as **report card, bathtub,** and **radio** were born in **America.** Many Americanisms you use may puzzle speakers of Australian English or British English. Likewise, many of their words may puzzle you. For example, when talking about parts of an **automobile,** you would use the words **hood** and **trunk.** A speaker of British English would use *bonnet* and *boot* for those same parts. Today many new Americanisms are quickly taken into the other kinds of English spoken around the world.

The growth of American English is related closely to the growth of our country. Like the people who make up our country, our words come from many different origins.

The many Native Americans had their own languages to describe their world. The first explorers of America were amazed to find a country filled with many new and strange plants and animals. These explorers and the **colonists** who followed them began giving names to what they saw. They borrowed some names from the native people. Our name for the **hickory** tree comes from the Indian word *pawcohiccora.* The names of many animals are originally Indian words. Among them are **moose, skunk, coyote,** and **raccoon.** Other names for the new plants and animals were invented from combinations of familiar English words, such as **jack-in-the-pulpit** and **Venus' flytrap,** and **bullfrog** and **hummingbird.**

☆ **raccoon**

☆ **sequoia**

The name **raccoon** originally meant "scratcher" in the Algonquian language. ■

The first explorers to see the giant **sequoias** of California did not know they were looking at some of the oldest and biggest living things in the world. Some sequoias are over seventy-five meters high and may be as much as 3,500 years old. Scientists named this tree in 1847 in honor of Sequoya (c. 1760-1843), a Cherokee. In order to record his people's history and culture, Sequoya developed a system for writing the Cherokee language. ■

The explorers also gave names to the unfamiliar land formations. British settlers made up the word **backwoods.** And they later used the word **palisades** to describe the cliffs along the Hudson River. The Spanish of **the Southwest** gave us the words **canyon** and **mesa.** The French along the Mississippi River gave us the word **prairie.**

☆ **palisades**

☆ **scow**

As the colonies and, later, the United States spread, American English grew. In 1664 the British took over New Amsterdam from the Dutch and renamed it New York. They also took over some Dutch words and made them their own. **Kill,** meaning *stream,* survives in such place names as Catskill and Fishkill. Another Dutch word, **scow,** describes a kind of flat-bottomed boat with square ends. The first British settlers in New York used scows to carry firewood and other cargo along the Hudson River and nearby waterways. **Sleighs** were used in winter when snow covered the road between New York City and Albany.

When the United States took over Florida from the Spanish, the word **everglades** was invented to describe the lush swamps there. And when the Southwest became part of the United States, American settlers saw **mustangs.** These were small, wild horses descended from the horses left by the Spanish conquerors 300 years before.

The settlers of the **western frontier** added many words to our language, such as **buckboard, stampede, prospector,** and **maverick.**

☆ **cowboy**

When you think of the word **cowboy,** you probably think of the **Wild West.** But during the Revolutionary War, this word referred to British loyalists. These "cowboys" hid in the brush and clanked cowbells to ambush hungry American patriots in search of food. Today's meaning for *cowboy* came into our language after this time. ■

☆ **electrician**

☆ **belittle**

Benjamin Franklin and Thomas Jefferson helped American English grow. During his experiments with electricity, Franklin invented the word **electrician.** Jefferson was the first to use the word **belittle.** Both words are used widely today. ■

American democracy was new in a world that had been used to the governments of kings and queens. The new country needed words and meanings to describe its system of government. As political parties were formed, the words **Federalist, Democrat,** and **Republican** took on new meanings. People seeking **terms** in **Congress** as **Representatives** would announce their **candidacy.** Then they would **campaign** for votes in their **Congressional districts.**

☆ **buncombe**

The slang word **bunk,** meaning "talk that is empty and only for show," comes from the older word **buncombe.** This word was first used at the 16th Congress (1819-1821) to describe any of the long, boring speeches of Felix Walker, a **Congressman** from Buncombe County, North Carolina. ■

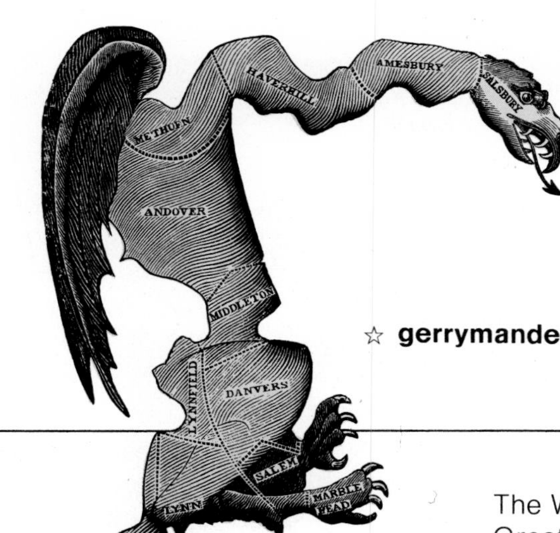


☆ **gerrymander**

Another Americanism that had its beginning in politics is **gerrymander.** The word refers to the dividing of a voting area so as to give one political party a lead. In 1812, while Elbridge Gerry was governor, Essex County, Massachusetts, was divided for such a political purpose. On a map the new area almost had the shape of a salamander. The names *Gerry* and *salamander* were combined to form the new word. ■

The War of 1812 was a test for the young nation. By then Great Britain and France had been at war for almost twenty years. Certain British laws aimed against France were hurting American shipping and trade. Politicians called **war hawks** urged Congress to declare war against Great Britain.

Although the Americans won several battles, the British were better prepared for war. In 1814 British troops entered Washington, D.C. and burned the **Capitol,** the **White House,** and other government buildings. Soon after a peace treaty ended the war. Neither side was victorious.

☆ **Christmas tree**

The term **Christmas tree** is an Americanism that has been part of our language since about 1838. The custom of trimming trees for Christmas was brought to this country by German immigrants. ■

☆ **clipper**

Swift ships called **clippers** were used in the California **Gold Rush** in the late 1840s. They sailed from New York to San Francisco, carrying supplies and fortune hunters. The trip around the tip of South America took over three months. ■

Many new words and phrases entered our language during the Civil War. Several are still in use today. Others appear only in history books.

☆ **boys in blue**

The Civil War set the **boys in blue** of **the Union** against **Johnny Reb** of **the Confederacy.** These words now have only historical meaning. However, another word from the period, **draftee,** has remained active in our language up to now. When the Union army ran out of volunteers, Congress began to draft able-bodied men. Since then, draftees have served in every major American war.

As part of the war against **the South,** the Union blockaded **Southern** ports. The South used fast ships, called **blockade runners,** to slip through the enemy's line of ships and bring needed supplies from Europe. Like *draftee,* this term has been used at other times since the Civil War.

---

☆ **sleeper (a)**
☆ **Pullman (b)**
☆ **boxcar (c)**
☆ **gondola (d)**
☆ **caboose (e)**

To develop **the West,** Congress supported the building of railroads. The first **transcontinental** railroad was completed in 1869. Many of the words of railroading, such as **boxcar, Pullman, gondola, sleeper,** and **caboose,** are Americanisms. ■

---

**Sideburns** are named after Ambrose Everett Burnside (1824-1881), a Union General in the Civil War, who wore his beard in this fashion. ■

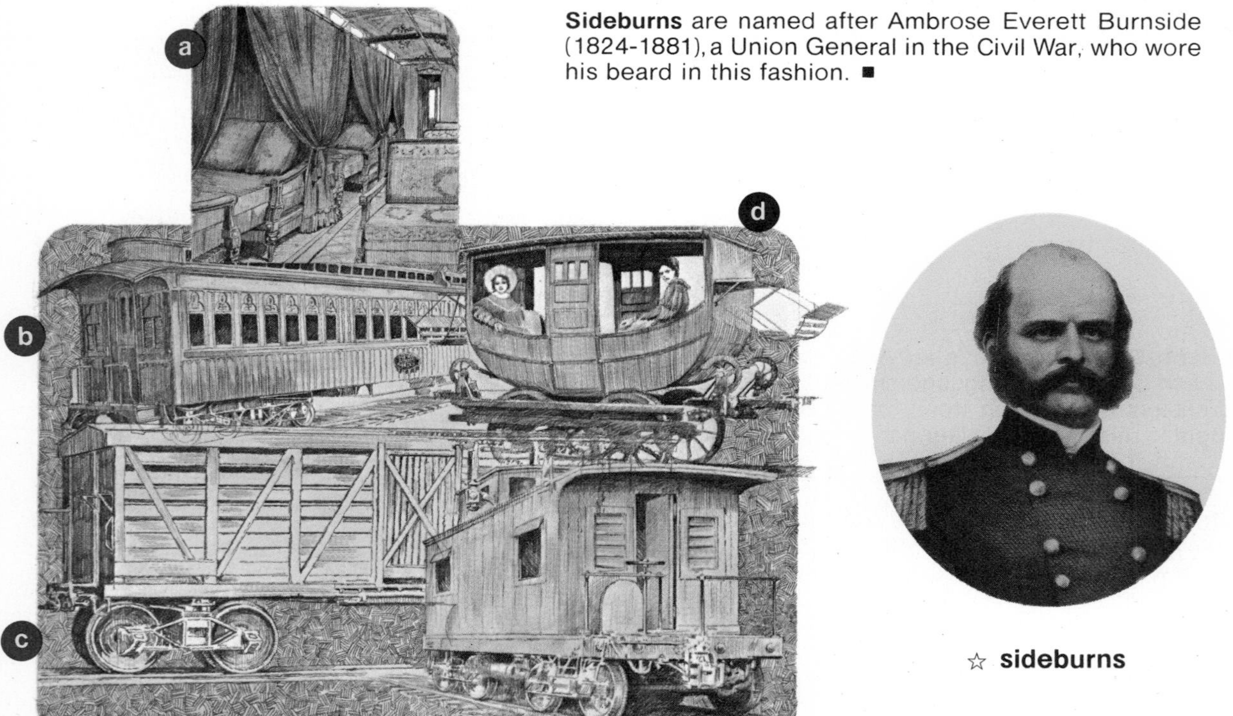


☆ **sideburns**

☆ **parka**

When the United States bought Alaska from Russia in 1867, new words came into American English. One was **mukluk,** describing a type of sealskin boot worn by Eskimos. Another was **parka,** describing a kind of hooded coat. Today, parkas filled with down are popular with skiers. ■

The period following the Civil War is called **Reconstruction.** During this time **the North** controlled the ruined political, economic, and social life of the South. It was a difficult time for many people. Dishonesty and racial conflict were common. Some white **Southerners** worked with the **Northern** politicians and tried to control the votes of the former slaves. These whites were hated by other white Southerners and called **scalawags. Northerners** who went South after the war in search of a quick fortune and political power were called **carpetbaggers.** When Reconstruction ended in 1877, it had solved few of the problems dividing the North and the South.

☆ **carpetbagger**

☆ **sharecropper** ☆ **shack**

Earning a living in the South after the Civil War was hard for poor whites and especially so for blacks. Landlords, hoping to rebuild their plantations, began a **sharecrop system.** Under it, the poor became tenant farmers and worked the landlords' land. Most **sharecroppers** lived in simple **shacks.** They earned no money for their labor, only a share of the crop they raised. ■

Non-English-speaking **immigrants** came to the United States both before and after the Civil War. With them came many words that soon found a place in American English.

The Germans gave us such words as **delicatessen, meld,** and **pretzel.** From the Chinese, who helped build the first transcontinental railroad, came **chow** and **gung-ho.** From the Yiddish-speaking Jews came **kibitzer** and **schmaltz.** The lists of each group and their contributions could go on and on.

☆ **immigrant**

☆ **restaurant**

Many immigrants to America settled in large cities. Today our cities show this rich and varied cultural influence. For example, a city dweller can enjoy many different foods at ethnic **restaurants.** The names for many of these foods are now American English. From the Mexicans we have **taco, tortilla,** and **enchilada;** from the Japanese, **sukiyaki;** from the Chinese, **chow mein;** from the Jews, **blintz;** from the Italians, **pizza;** and from the Swedes, **smorgasbord.** ■

☆ **tortilla**

☆ **smorgasbord**

Many inventors, including Thomas A. Edison and Alexander Graham Bell, were active in the United States in the late 1800s. New inventions needed new words to describe them. **Typewriter, barbed wire, telephone, phonograph,** and **zipper** are among the many words that entered our language at this time.

☆ **skyscraper**

The first **skyscraper** to appear above the rooftops of American cities was built in 1884 in Chicago. It was ten stories high. ■

The late 1800s was a **boom time,** a period of great growth in business. While **tycoons** were building fortunes, **labor unions** were **organizing** industries to get workers better wages and working conditions.

It was also a time of political scandals, of **bossism, bandwagons,** and **mugwumps.** This last word was used to describe people who refused to vote for the candidate of the party they belonged to. It originally came from an Indian word for "chief."

☆ **bandwagon**

**Bandwagons** were popular in circus parades. In politics, to be **on the bandwagon** means to be on the popular or winning side of an election. ■

During the 1890s Americans first enjoyed a new sport, called **basketball.** They rode the first **Ferris wheel** in 1893. They read **best sellers** and **dime novels.** And they went to theaters charging five-cent admission, called **nickelodeons.**

☆ **assembly line**

During the twentieth century, the United States was developing into a major industrial and world power. American society was now changing faster than ever before. At the same time our language was also growing and changing faster. Hundreds of new words and meanings began entering our language every year.

After industry perfected the **assembly line, automobiles** soon began to crowd American roads. With the automobile came many new words and meanings to describe America on wheels. **Gas station, jaywalk, hitchhike, windshield, bumper,** and **freeway** are just a few.

☆ **bread line**

In 1929 a **depression** began that put millions of Americans out of work. **Bread lines,** in which hungry people waited for food, became a common sight. ■

In 1930 **airlines** began commercial service between New York and California. The flight took 36 hours with an overnight stop in Kansas City. ■

☆ **airline**

☆ **radar**

**Radar** helped the Allies win World War II. This Americanism, like many recent American words, is an **acronym.** Such words are made up from the first, or first few, letters of a series of words. *Radar* comes from *ra*dio *d*etecting *a*nd *r*anging. ■

During World War II, such words as **walkie-talkie, jeep,** and **GI** became household words. By the end of the war in 1945, the world had entered the **Atomic Age.**

☆ **abstract expressionism**

Many famous people in the arts and sciences fled to America from war-torn Europe. The influence of European artists led to the development in the late 1940s of the kind of art pictured here, called **abstract expressionism.** ■

---

**Rock-and-roll** music spread across America during the 1950s. It survives today in the form of **rock.** This music developed from other types of American music: **jazz, the blues,** and folk and country music. ■

☆ **rock-and-roll**

The United States today seems to be a nation in a hurry to meet its future. Our language and **life styles** reflect this haste. Americans eat **TV dinners** and go to **fast-food restaurants.** In cities they go to work on **rapid transit** systems. At their jobs many Americans use **digital computers** and other high-speed machines.

☆ **jumbo jet**

☆ **jumbo**

**Jumbo jets** are among the largest aircraft. The Americanism **jumbo,** meaning "very large," began among black Americans who lived on the islands off the coast of South Carolina and Georgia. Their African word *jamba* meant "elephant." ■

☆ **space shuttle**

In space, our **probes** are racing toward the outer planets of the solar system. Also in this quest for more knowledge, scientists are studying **quasars** and **neutron stars** at the far reaches of the universe. **Space shuttles** will soon be building stations in space. From them a new kind of American pioneer will venture forth.

With each step in our history, American English will continue to change. Some words will grow old and drop from our language like dried leaves from a tree. At the same time, many other words will flourish to help us explain the complex world in which we will be living.

# How to use your DICTIONARY

## What You Can Find in Your Dictionary

Are you sometimes puzzled by a word that you may have never seen or heard before? Can you tell when a word you already know is being used in a different way? What do you do if there are no clues to help you find out a word's meaning? Do you ever have trouble spelling or pronouncing a word? When you are writing, do you sometimes reach the end of a line and wonder where to divide a word? Have you ever wondered about where a word came from and whether it is still in use today?

The book you are now holding can help you solve these problems, and more. It is a dictionary and it was prepared especially for you. It gives the meanings of the words you hear most often in your classroom, and on radio and television, and of the words you see most often in newspapers, magazines, and books. It shows how words are used. It can help you to improve your writing by showing you how to spell a word or use it correctly.

Your dictionary is the most important reference book in your classroom. Your dictionary is a guidebook. It tells you how words are used by most people. Thus, you may find in it two ways of spelling one word, as *theater* and *theatre.* Both spellings can be found in magazines and books and both are, therefore, considered to be correct. You may also find two pronunciations, as for *news,* since some people pronounce it one way (nōōz) and some pronounce it another way (nyōōz).

You need a guidebook because our language is always changing. New words are added, like *aerospace, defoliate,* and *hertz.* Familiar words used in combinations take on new meanings, such as *tape recorder, paperback, spaceship, drive-in, audio-visual,* and *chalkboard.* Some older words such as *steed* and *troth* are now seldom used. Your dictionary will tell you how to use all of these words correctly.

You may sometimes hear or read an especially hard word or a technical word that is not explained in this dictionary. Then you will need to look in a larger, more advanced dictionary, where such words may be found.

# *Locating Words in Your Dictionary*

## Entry Words

Below is a section from your dictionary. The words that are shown in heavy black type are called "entry words" or "main entries." All the information about an entry word, including the word itself, is called an "entry." Notice that entry words start a little to the left of each column so that you can find them more easily. How many entry words are shown?

---

**ag·ate** (ag′ət) ***n.*** **1** a hard stone with striped or clouded coloring, used in jewelry. **2** a small glass ball that looks like this, used in playing marbles.

**a·ga·ve** (ə gä′vē) ***n.*** an American desert plant, as the century plant, with thick, fleshy leaves. Fiber for making rope is got from some kinds of agave. *See the picture.*

**agcy.** *abbreviation for* **agency**.

---

## Alphabetical Order

To find any word in the dictionary, you need to know how the words are arranged. The entry words are arranged in the same order as the letters in the alphabet. Most of the entry words are single words. Some, however, are compound words, some are abbreviations, and some are parts of words, such as prefixes and suffixes. All entry words are listed in alphabetical order.

You can locate words quickly if you know how to use alphabetical order. When all the words in a group begin with the same letter, you must look for the first letter that is different.

| It may be the second letter, | or the third letter, |
|---|---|
| a**b**acus | ba**c**khand |
| A**n**des | ba**d**minton |
| A**r**abic numerals | Ba**l**boa |
| -a**t**ion | ba**r**rel |
| A**v**e. | ba**t**tleship |
| a**z**ure | ba**y** window |

| or the fourth letter, | or the fifth letter. |
|---|---|
| dis**a**ppear | crow**d** |
| dis**h**cloth | crow**n** |
| dis**q**ualify | or |
| dis**t**ant | crue**l** |
| | crue**t** |

Sometimes you may run out of letters to compare. Remember that the shorter word comes first. If you were looking up the following two words, which one would come first?

complain
complaint

*Complain* is found first in the dictionary. It has only eight letters, while *complaint* has nine.

On a piece of paper write each of the following three lists of words in alphabetical order. Check your lists by looking for the words in your dictionary.

| | | |
|---|---|---|
| bevy | Fort Worth | posture |
| banner | F.O.B. | position |
| black | found | possessive |
| bi- | fox | postal card |
| Bonn | follow | posy |
| bricklayer | -fold | Poseidon |

**Sections of a Dictionary**

Words that are at the beginning or end of the alphabet are easy to locate in the dictionary. What if the word you are looking for comes somewhere in the middle of the alphabet? Here is a hint that will help you find that word more quickly. Think of your dictionary as being divided into four nearly equal parts. If each part, or quarter, were about the same number of pages, then the letters would come out as follows:

First Quarter: ABCD
Second Quarter: EFGHIJKL
Third Quarter: MNOPQR
Fourth Quarter: STUVWXYZ

Did you know that our English language has more words that begin with the letter *C* or *D* than it does with the letters *X, Y,* and *Z?* Look at the number of pages in the dictionary that have words beginning with the letter *S.* Now compare this number to the number of pages with *K* words. Which letter has more pages? You can now see why each quarter section of the dictionary has a different number of letters.

If you wanted to look up the word *frugal,* you might think that *F* was in the first quarter, as it comes early in the alphabet. However, you need to look at the beginning of the second quarter to find words that begin with the letter *F.*

**Letter Tabs**

Your dictionary has extra helpers to aid you in locating words. These are called letter tabs. The letter tabs can be found in the margin, next to the pronunciation key, near the bottom of each right-side page. Look at pages 1 to 50. Notice that the right-side pages all have *A* on the tabs. This shows that only main entries that begin with the letter *A* are found on these pages.

## Guide Words

The two words in color at the top of each page in your dictionary are "guide words." A slanting line separates the first from the second guide word. The first guide word tells you the first entry word that appears on that page. The second guide word tells you the last entry word on that page. All the other entry words come in alphabetical order between these two words.

Suppose the guide words on a page were *misty/mobile.* You know that the first entry word on the page would be *misty* and the last entry word would be *mobile.* If you were looking up the word *mitten,* would you find it on that page? Yes, because alphabetically *mitten* comes between *misty* and *mobile.*

Remember to use the first letter of the word you are looking up to decide which quarter of the dictionary contains that word. Turn to that quarter and use the letter tabs to find where the entry words beginning with that letter are located. Then use the guide words to find the exact page on which your word is listed. Keep in mind what you know about alphabetical order as you look for your word.

Here are two guide words: *pelican/penicillin.* Decide which of the words below would appear on the page with these guide words. Write those words in alphabetical order.

| | | |
|---|---|---|
| pen | person | penguin |
| peel | pattern | perfect |

## Entries You Will Find in Your Dictionary

You have already learned that most entry words are single words. However, an abbreviation can be an entry word, as can compound words, suffixes, prefixes, and so forth.

**Compound Entries** Main entry words made up of more than one word are called compound entries. They are arranged in the same order as single-word entries.

**com·mon·er** (käm′ən ər) ***n.*** any person who is not a member of the nobility.
**common fraction** a fraction with the numerator separated from the denominator by a diagonal or horizontal line, as 5/11 or 3/4.
**com·mon·ly** (käm′ən lē) ***adv.*** as a general rule; usually; ordinarily.

Compound entries are combinations of words that have a special meaning when they are used together. Suppose you saw the term *air pocket.* You probably know what a *pocket* looks like, and you know what *air* is. But what do the two words mean when they are used together? Your dictionary tells you that an air pocket is "a condition of the air that causes an airplane to make sudden, short drops." When a combination of words like this puzzles you, look to see if the combined form is an entry word.

Not all word combinations are included as main entries. Some combinations can be figured out by looking up the separate words. You won't find combinations like "birthday cake" as compound entries in your dictionary because you can understand what they mean by looking up each word.

Here are pairs of word combinations. On a sheet of paper copy each pair. Then decide which one of each pair you think has a special meaning and might be found as a compound entry in a dictionary. Check the dictionary to see if your answer is correct.

| | | |
|---|---|---|
| rock bottom | soda cracker | double portion |
| large rock | chocolate soda | double talk |

**Abbreviations** Another kind of entry word found in your dictionary is the abbreviation. An abbreviation is a shortened form of a word or phrase. *Min.* stands for *minute,* and *USA* stands for *United States of America.* Abbreviations are listed alphabetically, as though they were whole words.

**dam·son** (dam′z'n) ***n.*** **1** a small, purple plum. **2** the tree it grows on.
**Dan.** *abbreviation for* **Danish.**
**dance** (dans) ***v.*** **1** to move the body and feet in some kind of rhythm, usually to music [to *dance* a waltz or a minuet]. **2** to jump or bob up and down lightly or excitedly [waves *dancing* in the moonlight; children *dancing* with joy]. —**danced, danc′ing** ◆***n.*** **1** the act of dancing, or one round of dancing [May I have the next *dance* with you?] **2** the special steps of a particular kind of dancing [My favorite *dance* is the polka.] **3** a party for dancing. **4** a piece of music for dancing.

Look up the following abbreviations in the dictionary. On a piece of paper write the abbreviation and next to it write the whole word or phrase that the abbreviation stands for.

| | | | |
|---|---|---|---|
| FM | bu. | A.M. | CA |
| Lat. | pkg. | Tues. | secy. |

**Contractions** Contractions are shortened forms of a word or phrase. They are listed in their correct alphabetical order along with the two words that form the contraction.

**-ism** (iz'm) *a suffix meaning:* **1** doctrine, theory, or belief [*Liberalism* is a belief in liberal ideas.] **2** the act or result of [*Criticism* is the act of or result of criticizing.] **3** the condition, conduct, or qualities of [*Patriotism* is the conduct of a patriot.] **4** an example of [A *witticism* is an example of a witty saying.]

**is·n't** (iz″nt) is not.

**i·so·bar** (ī′sə bär) ***n.*** a line on a weather map connecting places where the air pressure is the same. *See the picture.*

**Prefixes** A prefix is a syllable or a group of syllables joined to the beginning of a word to form a related word. One common prefix is *bi-*.

**bi-** *a prefix meaning:* **1** having two [A *bicuspid* tooth has two points on its crown.] **2** happening every two [A *biennial* election takes place every two years.] **3** happening twice during every [*Biannual* meetings are held twice a year.]

In this dictionary, most common prefixes are listed as main entries. You can find the meaning of many words formed with prefixes by adding the meaning of the prefix to the meaning of the root word. In this way you can understand the meaning of *nonabsorbent* even though it is not a main entry in your dictionary. If you look up the prefix *non-,* you will see that it means "not." The dictionary defines *absorbent* as "able to absorb moisture, light, etc." If you put the two meanings together, you know the word means "not able to absorb moisture, light, etc."

Words whose meanings are not easily understood, even if you know the meaning of the root word and prefix, are usually given as main entries in the dictionary. For example, *antifreeze,* which is formed from *anti-* and *freeze,* is a main entry because the meaning of the prefix when added to the meaning of the root word does not tell you that *antifreeze* is a *liquid* that prevents freezing.

**Suffixes** Many words are formed by adding an ending to another word. Endings like *-ly* and *-ness* are called suffixes and are usually added to a root word. For example, *sadness* is formed by adding the suffix *-ness* to the root word *sad.* In this dictionary, the common suffixes are listed as main entries.

**-ness** (nis *or* nəs) *a suffix meaning:* **1** the condition or quality [*Sadness* is the condition of being sad.] **2** an act or thing that is; an example of being [A *rudeness* is a rude act.]

To find the meaning of a word formed by adding a suffix, look for the root word first. Suppose you don't know the meaning of *rashness.* When you look for this word in the dictionary, you find it listed in the entry for *rash:*

**rash**[1] (rash) ***adj.*** too hasty or reckless; risky [It would be *rash* to quit your job before you know of a new one.] —**rash'ly** ***adv.*** —**rash'ness** ***n.***

Your next step is to find the meaning of the suffix *-ness:*

**-ness** (nis *or* nəs) *a suffix meaning:* **1** the condition or quality [*Sadness* is the condition of being sad.] **2** an act or thing that is; an example of being [A *rudeness* is a rude act.]

From these two entries, you learn the meaning of *rashness:* "the condition or quality of being too hasty or reckless."

Some of the words formed by adding suffixes are listed as main entries, as, for example, *hopeful.* Others, whose meanings can be easily understood, are shown at the end of an entry, as *hopefulness.* Notice in the following example that each word formed with a suffix is followed by a part-of-speech label that tells you how the word is to be used.

**hope·ful** (hōp'fəl) ***adj.*** **1** feeling or showing hope [a *hopeful* smile]. **2** causing or giving hope [a *hopeful* sign]. —**hope'ful·ness** ***n.***

*Exercise*

All of the following words have either a prefix or suffix attached to a root word. On a sheet of paper, copy the words and next to each write the root word you would look up in your dictionary.

| | | |
|---|---|---|
| glumly | precook | unhappy |
| rework | wasteful | enjoyment |

**Inflected Forms**

Sometimes the word you want to find is not listed as a main entry in the same way that such words as *pelican* and *freeze* are. In that case, you need to do a little detective work. For example, to find the word *hopping,* you will have to look up the entry word *hop.* Such words formed from entry words are usually listed after definitions for the entry word.

**hop**[1] (häp) ***v.*** **1** to make a short leap or leaps on one foot. **2** to jump over [to *hop* a fence]. **3** to move by jumps, as a bird or frog. ☆**4** to get aboard [to *hop* a bus]. **5** to move or go briskly: *used only in everyday talk* [I *hopped* out of bed to answer the phone.] —**hopped, hop′ping** ◆***n.*** **1** the act of hopping. ☆**2** a bounce, as of a baseball. **3** a short flight in an airplane: *used only in everyday talk.*

These changed forms of a root word are called inflected forms. Now let's look at the various kinds of inflected forms more closely.

**Plurals** A word is a noun if it names a person, place, thing, or idea. If it names only one, it is called a *singular* noun. If a noun names more than one, it is a *plural* noun.

The plurals of most nouns are formed by adding *-s* or *-es* to the singular. For instance, the plural of *boy* is *boys* and the plural of *glass* is *glasses.* Plurals formed in this regular way are not shown in the dictionary, unless they have a special use or meaning. In the entries for words like *bird, moon,* and *stadium,* the plural is not given because it is formed by merely adding the plural ending *-s.*

The plurals of some nouns are not formed by adding *-s* or *-es.* For these words, the plural form is given in the entry with the abbreviation *pl.*

**ox** (äks) ***n.*** **1** a castrated male of the cattle family, used for pulling heavy loads. **2** any animal of a group that chew their cud and have cloven hoofs, including the buffalo, bison, etc. —*pl.* **ox·en** (äk′s'n)

These plurals are listed after the noun meanings of the entry word. In a few instances, the plural is also listed as a main entry.

**chil·dren** (chil′drən) ***n.*** *plural of* **child.**

Sometimes the plural form of a word has a special meaning. For example, the fourth meaning in the entry for *bearing* is a special meaning of the plural form *bearings.*

**bear·ing** (ber′iŋ) ***n.*** **1** the way one stands or walks; carriage [the upright *bearing* of a soldier]. **2** the way one behaves; manner [a kindly *bearing*]. **3** the fact of having something to do with; connection [The price of feed has a direct *bearing* on the cost of beef.] **4 bearings,** *pl.* direction or position in relation to something else [The ship lost her *bearings* in the fog.] *See the picture.* **5** a part of a machine on which another part turns or slides so that there is little friction: *see* **ball bearing.**

Sometimes, as in the entry for *arms,* the entry word is in the plural form, with its special meanings given.

> **arms** (ärmz) ***n.pl.*** **1** tools used for fighting; weapons. **2** fighting; warfare. **3** the designs and figures on a coat of arms: *see* **coat of arms.** —**bear arms,** to serve as a soldier, sailor, etc. —**take up arms,** to go to war or get ready to fight. —**up in arms,** angry and ready to fight.

## *Exercise*

Write the words below on a piece of paper. Next to each word write the plural form. Use your dictionary if you need help. If you don't find the inflected or changed form in the entry, then all you need to do is add an *-s* or *-es.*

| | | |
|---|---|---|
| table | chief | village |
| deer | penny | ox |
| lady | wolf | mouse |

**Comparative and Superlative Forms** Many adjectives have a comparative form and a superlative form. The adjective *small,* for example, has the comparative form *smaller* to describe something that is "more small." You would say, *A pony is smaller than a horse.* The superlative form *smallest* is used to describe something that is "most small." *Our kitten is the smallest one in the litter.* When these forms are made in a regular way, by adding *-er* or *-est,* they are not shown in the dictionary.

Some adverbs, which are words that tell how, where, or when something is done, have comparative and superlative forms. The same rule is followed for them. For example, the adverb *soon* is changed to *sooner* and *soonest.*

Comparative and superlative forms that are made in a way that is *not* regular are shown in the dictionary after the meanings. Such forms are also shown if the spelling of the root word is changed when *-er* and *-est* are added.

Look at the word *big* below. Notice that another *g* is written before *-er* or *-est* is added.

> **big** (big) ***adj.*** **1** of great size; large [a *big* cake; a *big* city]. *See* SYNONYMS *at* **great. 2** great in force [a *big* wind]. **3** important; outstanding [a *big* day in my life]. **4** showy or boastful [a lot of *big* talk]. ☆**5** noble; generous [a *big* heart]. —**big'ger, big'gest** ◆***adv.*** in a showy or boastful way [to talk *big*]; also, in a broad way; showing imagination: *used only in everyday talk* [Think *big!*] —**big'ness** ***n.***

Some longer words would be too big if the comparative and superlative forms were made by adding *-er* and *-est*. Instead, the words *more* and *most* are used, as in *more beautiful* and *most beautiful.* In order to tell which words fall into this group, say the words out loud. You can usually tell from the way they sound which words need *more* or *most* and not the ending *-er* or *-est.*

## Exercise

On a piece of paper copy the following root words. Write the comparative and superlative forms next to each. Use your dictionary if you need help. If the inflected form is not given, remember to just add *-er* and *-est* to the root word or use *more* and *most* with words of three or more syllables.

| | | |
|---|---|---|
| old | fast | hungry |
| pale | early | well |
| green | fat | intelligent |

**Principal Parts of Verbs** Most verbs are words that show action. Like adjectives and adverbs, verbs have inflected endings. These verb endings are added to help show the different times an action can take place. The following sentences show how the verb endings *-ed* and *-ing* are added to the verb *ask.*

| **Present Tense** | **Past Tense** |
|---|---|
| We *ask* questions. | We *asked* questions. |
| We are *asking* questions. | We had *asked* questions. |

The principal parts of most verbs, such as *ask,* are formed in a regular way. You add *-ed* to form the past tense, *-ed* to form the past participle, and *-ing* to form the present participle.

| | **Past Tense** | **Past Participle** | **Present Participle** |
|---|---|---|---|
| ask | asked | asked | asking |
| walk | walked | walked | walking |

Your dictionary includes *ask* and *walk* as main entries. It does not show their principal parts because they are regular.

The principal parts of many verbs, however, are not formed in the regular way. One or more principal parts may be quite different from the main entry, or a spelling change may be necessary before the endings are added. The principal parts for such verbs are usually given after the meanings, as in the following.

**be·gin** (bi gin′) ***v.*** to start being, doing, acting, etc.; get under way [Work *begins* at 8:00 A.M. My cold *began* with a sore throat.] **—be·gan′, be·gun′, be·gin′ning**

The principal parts of *educate* are shown because of their spelling change. In *educate* you drop the final *e* before you add *-ing* or *-ed.*

**ed·u·cate** (ej′ə kāt) ***v.*** to teach or train a person, especially in a school or college; develop the mind of. — **ed′u·cat·ed, ed′u·cat·ing**

**Geographical Entries**

Your dictionary lists the names of many well-known cities, rivers, mountains, and countries. It also has entries for the continents and oceans. These are listed in their alphabetical place in the dictionary. The *Amazon River* is in the *A's. Rocky Mountains* is under *R.* However, *Mount Everest* will be found in the *E's,* under *Everest.*

**Biographical Entries**

Famous people are also listed in your dictionary. They are listed alphabetically, by their last names. *George Washington* is listed in the *W's,* as **Washington, George.** *Harriet Tubman* is listed in the *T's* as **Tubman, Harriet.**

**Spelling**

Often someone will say, "How can I find a word in the dictionary if I don't know how to spell it?" That is a common problem with many English words. There are many words in our language that are not spelled as they sound. For instance, the word *knee* was at an earlier time pronounced with the sound of *k* at the beginning. We no longer use the *k* in pronouncing the word, but we still spell it *knee.*

Another reason for these spelling problems is that many letters stand for more than one sound. For example, the letter *a* stands for different sounds in the words *ate, cat,* and *father.* Notice that the letter *o* in *both* does not stand for the same sound as the *o* in *hot* or the *o* in *form.* The *o* in *people* or the *o* in *leopard* does not stand for a sound at all. Our language is full of surprises like these. You must be prepared for them as you read and as you write.

Also, the same sound can have a number of different spellings. Think of how you would go about finding out how to spell the word *choir* if you had only heard it spoken. You might think that it is spelled *kwire.* If you looked in the *K* section of the dictionary, you would not find such a word. By using the Word Finder Table, you will learn the various letter combinations that may be used in spelling the common sounds of English.

To use the Word Finder Table you need to start with the beginning sound of the word you are trying to find. If the beginning sound is a consonant, you use the table for Consonant Sounds. For example, the beginning sound of "choir" is *k* as in *keep.* Find that sound in the first column. Then go across to the second column. There you will find nine letter combinations that stand for this sound. Using these letter combinations in place of the letter "k" will help you to locate the word. If you find the page in your dictionary that has entry words beginning with the letters *ch,* you will soon find the word *choir.* After you find the correct letter combinations for the beginning sounds of a word, you should then be able to find the word. Use the Word Finder Table to help you. If the word you are looking for begins with a consonant sound, use the table labeled Consonant Sounds. If the word begins with a vowel sound, use the table labeled Vowel Sounds.

## WORD FINDER TABLE

### Consonant Sounds

| 1. If the sound is like the letter— | 2. try spelling with letters— | 3. as in the words— |
|---|---|---|
| b as in *bed* | b,bb | ru**b**, ru**bb**er |
| ch as in *chin* | ch,tch,te,ti,tu | **ch**air, ca**tch**, righ**te**ous, ques**ti**on, na**tu**re |
| d as in *did* | d,dd,ed | no**d**, ri**dd**le, call**ed** |
| f as in *fall* | f,ff,gh,ph,lf | **f**ix, di**ff**erent, lau**gh**, **ph**one, ca**lf** |
| g as in *get* | g,gg,gh,gu | **g**ive, e**gg**, **gh**ost, **gu**ard |
| h as in *he* | h,wh | **h**er, **wh**o |
| j as in *jump* | j,g,gg,d,di,dg,dj | **j**am, **g**em, exa**gg**erate, gra**d**uate, sol**di**er, ju**dg**ment, a**dj**ust |
| k as in *keep* | k,lk,c,cc,ch,ck,cqu,cu,qu | **k**ite, wa**lk**, **c**an, a**cc**ount, **ch**rome, lu**ck**, la**cqu**er, bis**cu**it, li**qu**or |
| l as in *let* | l,ll,sl | **l**eave, ca**ll**, i**sl**and |
| m as in *met* | m,mm,mb,mn,lm | dru**m**, dru**mm**er, li**mb**, hy**mn**, ca**lm** |
| n as in *not* | n,nn,gn,kn,pn | **n**ear, di**nn**er, **gn**ome, **kn**eel, **pn**eumonia |
| ng as in *ring* | ng,n,ngue | lo**ng**, thi**n**k, to**ngue** |
| p as in *put* | p,pp | ho**p**, di**pp**er |
| r as in *red* | r,rr,rh,wr | **r**iver, be**rr**y, **rh**yme, **wr**ong |
| s as in *sell* | s,ss,sc,c,ps,sch | **s**it, mi**ss**, **sc**ience, **c**ent, **ps**ychology, **sch**ism |
| sh as in *she* | sh,s,ss,sch,sci,si,ssi,ce,ch,ci,ti | **sh**are, **s**ure, i**ss**ue, **sch**wa, con**sci**ence, man**si**on, mi**ssi**on, o**ce**an, ma**ch**ine, fa**ci**al, na**ti**on |
| t as in *top* | t,th,tt,ght,ed | **t**ear, **Th**omas, be**tt**er, bou**ght**, walk**ed** |
| v as in *vat* | v,lv,f | do**v**e, sa**lv**e, o**f** |
| w as in *will* | w,o,u | **w**ait, ch**o**ir, q**u**iet |
| y as in *yet* | y,i,j | **y**ellow, on**i**on, hallelu**j**ah |
| z as in *zebra* | z,zz,s,ss,x | **z**one, bu**zz**er, bu**s**y, sci**ss**ors, **x**ylophone |
| zh as in *pleasure* | z,ge,s,si,zi | a**z**ure, gara**ge**, lei**s**ure, confu**si**on, gla**zi**er |

### Vowel Sounds

| 1. If the sound is like the letter— | 2. try spelling with letters— | 3. as in the words— |
|---|---|---|
| a as in *cat* | a,ai | ask, plaid |
| a as in *cake* | a,ai,au,ay,ea,ei,ey,et | ate, rain, gauge, pay, break, veil, obey, sachet |
| a as in *care* | a,ai,ay,e,ea,ei | dare, air, prayer, there, wear, their |
| ah as in *father* | a,ea,o | far, hearth, stop |
| aw as in *saw* | aw,au,a,o,oa,ou | awful, autumn, all, order, broad, ought |
| e as in *ten* | e,ea,eo,ie,a,ae,ai,ay,u | every, heavy, leopard, friend, any, aerate, said, says, bury |
| e as in *even* | e,ee,ea,ei,eo,ey,i,ie,ae,oe | equal, eel, eat, receive, people, key, machine, field, algae, phoebe |
| i as in *hit* | i,ie,ee,o,u,ui,y | ill, sieve, been, women, busy, build, hymn |
| i as in *kite* | i,ie,ei,ey,ai,uy,y | ice, tie, height, eye, aisle, buy, fly |
| o as in *go* | o,oa,oe,ou,ow,au,eau,ew | open, oat, toe, soul, grow, mauve, beau, sew |
| oo as in *tool* | oo,o,oe,u,ue,ui,eu,ew,ough | moose, move, shoe, rule, blue, fruit, maneuver, threw, through |
| oo as in *book* | oo,o,ou,u | wood, wolf, would, pull |
| ow as in *now* | ow,ou,ough | crowd, out, bough |
| oy as in *boy* | oy,oi | toy, boil |
| uh as in *cuff* | u,o,oo,oe,ou | summer, son, flood, does, double |
| ur as in *hurt* | er,ear,ar,ir,or,our,ur,yr | germ, heard, forward, bird, work, courage, turn, myrtle |
| u as in *fuse* | u,ue,ui,eau,eu,ew,iew,yu,you | use, cue, suit, beauty, feud, few, view, yule, youth |
| a as in the first syllable of *asleep* | a,e,i,o,u, and many combinations of these letters | ago, agent, unity, collect, focus |

## *Exercise*

1. If you are looking for a word that sounds like *bow,* as in "bow and arrow," but means "a man who is courting a woman," use the Vowel Sounds chart to help you find the correct spelling. Remember to check your dictionary.

Which one of these spellings is correct?

b*o, boa, boe, bou, bow, bau, beau, bew*

2. If you are looking for a word that sounds like *faze* but means "any stage in a series of changes," use the Consonant Sounds chart to help you find the correct spelling. Remember to check your dictionary.

Which one of these spellings is correct?

*faze, ffaz, ghass, phase, lfax*

## Variant Spellings

Some words may be spelled in more than one way. Different spellings of the same word are called *variant* spellings. When a variant spelling appears at the end of an entry, it usually means that this spelling is used less often. The spelling *judgement* is less common than the spelling *judgment.* When no special pronunciation is shown for the variant spelling, then both spellings are pronounced the same way, as are *judgment* and *judgement.*

**judg·ment** (juj′mənt) ***n.*** **1** a judging or deciding. **2** a decision given by a judge or a law court [The *judgment* was for the defendant.] **3** an opinion; the way one thinks or feels about something [In my *judgment,* she will win the election.] **4** criticism or blame [to pass *judgment* on another]. **5** a being able to decide what is right, good, practical, etc.; good sense [a person of clear *judgment*]. *Sometimes spelled* **judgement.**

If the spellings are almost the same and both spellings are very common, they are placed together in heavy black type at the head of the entry. Neither spelling is considered more correct, but the one given first is usually the one used more often.

**the·a·ter** or **the·a·tre** (thē′ə tər) ***n.*** **1** a place where plays, movies, etc. are shown. **2** any place like this, with rows of seats, as for those watching surgery in a hospital. **3** any place where certain things happen [She served in the European *theater* in World War II.] **4** the art or business of acting or of producing plays; drama. **5** all the people who write, produce, or act in plays.

If the spellings are different enough so that the entry words are some distance apart, as in the words *aeon* and *eon,* the definition is given under the spelling that is most commonly used.

**ae·on** (ē′ən *or* ē′än) ***n. same as*** **eon.**
**e·on** (ē′ən *or* ē′än) ***n.*** a very long period of time; thousands and thousands of years [The first human beings lived *eons* ago.]

## *Exercise*

Each of the following words has more than one spelling. Look up each word in your dictionary. On a piece of paper, write the word, and next to it write its variant spelling. Remember, the spelling shown here is the spelling that is used more often and therefore will appear as the entry word.

| ketchup | savior | orangutan | marvelous |
|---|---|---|---|
| gasoline | fiber | ax | enthrall |

## Word Division for Writing

When you are writing sentences, you sometimes find that you cannot fit a whole word at the end of a line. If the word has more than one syllable, you must decide where to divide it.

There is no easy rule for dividing words into syllables, but your dictionary can help you. Each entry word of more than one syllable is shown in this way.

**el·e·phant** **ab·bre·vi·a·tion**

The small center dot separates the word into syllables. You may divide a word at any place where a dot appears. Try not to divide short words. Also, a syllable of one or two letters on a line by itself might be hard to read. Words of one syllable, like *blue* or *dog,* are not to be broken up when writing.

No center dots are shown in the separate words of compound entries like *double boiler.* If you need to divide the word *double* or *boiler,* the syllable division has already been given in the entries for each of these words.

Remember that when you divide a word at the end of a line, you have to put a hyphen after the word part to show there is more to come on the next line.

## Exercise

Copy each of the following words on a sheet of paper. Next to each one, write the word as it appears in your dictionary, showing each syllable separated by a dot.

| | | | |
|---|---|---|---|
| lyric | stalagmite | simultaneous | scholastic |
| impatient | registration | manufacture | emblem |

## Steps to Remember

When you are looking for a word in the dictionary, you will save time and effort if you follow these steps.

1. Decide which quarter of the dictionary would contain the first letter of the word.
2. Turn to the letter tabs that show the section of the dictionary containing that letter.
3. Use the guide words to find the page on which the word is listed.
4. Look first at the main entries. Use alphabetical order to find the word quickly.
5. If you find the word, but the meanings do not seem right, look at the next main entry. Sometimes two or more main entries are spelled the same way but have different meanings.
6. If you do not find the word listed as a main entry, look at the word again. Is there a word from which this word could have been formed? Look up the root word and check the words printed in dark bold type at the end of that entry.
7. Make sure you are thinking of the correct spelling. Use the Word Finder Table to help you find the correct spelling.

# *Going from the Entry Word to the Entry Itself*

If someone asked you what language you speak, you would probably answer, "English." A better answer would be "American English," for the way you speak differs somewhat from the way people in England speak. You can understand them, of course, but many of their words would sound different.

People in the Midwest, in New England, and in the South all speak the "American English" language. Yet, like the English people, they pronounce many words differently. These differences are not important. For example, the dialect or speech of a person from the South is no better or more correct than that of a person from the Midwest. The way most people talk in the greater part of the United States used to be called General American English. Today it is called the Midland dialect. This dictionary shows you how words are pronounced by people who speak this dialect. You may live in a region where certain words are pronounced differently. For example, people who live in New England tend to drop the "r" sound in such words as *father*. You will naturally use the same pronunciation as your parents, teachers, and most of the people in your region.

## Pronunciation Symbols

After each entry word in your dictionary, you will see the word rewritten with special symbols and enclosed in parentheses. This respelling gives you the most common pronunciation or pronunciations of the word in the Midland dialect.

**dem·on·stra·tion** (dem′ən strā′shən) ***n.*** **1** the act or means of demonstrating something; a showing, proving, or explaining [a *demonstration* of grief; a *demonstration* of an automobile]. **2** a meeting or parade of many people to show publicly how they feel about something.

Most of the pronunciation symbols used in this dictionary are formed from letters of the alphabet. You will notice that some of these letters have special marks above them. These marks are called *diacritical* marks. All the diacritical marks used with vowel letters are shown below. With each is the name used when referring to the diacritical mark.

long mark or macron *a, e, i, o*
ā as in *cake* (kāk)
ē as in *beat* (bēt)
ī as in *ice* (īs)
ō as in *go* (gō)

two-dot *a*
ä as in *far* (fär)
circumflex *o*
ô as in *long* (lông)
ʉ as in *turn* (tʉrn)

**Pronunciation Key**

A list of all the symbols used in the pronunciations is called the "Pronunciation Key." Each symbol is followed by key words that show the sound each symbol stands for. This key appears on the inside of the front and back covers of this dictionary.

**Abbreviated Pronunciation Key**

There is an abbreviated pronunciation key at the bottom of each right-hand page in your dictionary. This gives you a quick way to check the sound of a certain symbol. Each symbol is shown with a key word. The key word *ape,* for example, gives you the sound of the symbol (ā). The key word *horn* gives you the sound of the symbol (ô). Sometimes you may need to refer to the complete Pronunciation Key in the front or back of the dictionary.

**Special Symbols**

The dictionary has some special symbols that are not made up of regular letters of the alphabet.

**Schwa (ə)** Say in a natural way, "He is about ten years old." Notice that you did not pronounce the word *about* with a long *a* (ā bout′) or a two-dot *a* (ä bout′) or a short *a* (a bout′). You used a soft "uh" sound. The pronunciation of the word is (ə bout′). The symbol for this soft sound is called the schwa (ə). When a vowel occurs in an unstressed syllable, it may not have its usual sound. The schwa stands for the soft or neutral vowel sound heard in unstressed syllables.

**ŋg Symbol** The (ŋg) symbol stands for the sound at the end of such words as *sing* and *wing.* In this dictionary, it is also used to show the sound of *n* when followed by *g,* as in *finger* (fiŋg′gər) and the sound of *n* when followed by *k,* as in *drink* (driŋgk).

**Apostrophe (')** Another symbol is the apostrophe ('), which you will find only before the sounds of *l, m,* or *n* when they appear in an unstressed syllable. When you say the word *apple,* for example, you may pronounce the second syllable with almost no vowel sound between the letters *p* and *l,* as in (ap′'l). The apostrophe is used to take the place of a vowel sound in the respelling. Some people do put a vowel sound in the word *apple* as in (ap′əl). In this dictionary, you will find only the first of these two possible pronunciations, as also in *rhythm* (rith′'m) and in *cotton* (kät′'n).

**Consonant Digraphs** When you say the word *blend,* you blend the sounds represented by the letters *b* and *l.* There are some consonant clusters in which you do not hear each consonant sound. You hear a completely new sound. "*Th*" is this kind of consonant cluster. When you say the word *think,* you do not hear the *t* sound and the *h* sound. The combined letters *th* have a new sound. When consonant letters combine to form a new sound, they are called digraphs.

*sh* as in *sh*ell
*ch* as in *ch*eese

A special symbol is used to show that these sounds are different from consonant blends. You can see from the following examples that the consonant letters are shown as joined in the respelling.

change (chānj)
show (shō)

**Vowel Sounds Followed by r**

When you say a word, you do not pronounce each sound separately. You blend the sounds together. When *r* follows a vowel, the sound of the vowel changes a little. This change is so slight, however, that the same symbol for the vowel sound is used.

| | | | |
|---|---|---|---|
| calm | (cälm) | mitt | (mit) |
| car | (cär) | mirror | (mir′ər) |
| bet | (bet) | cost | (kôst) |
| berry | (ber′ē) | cord | (kôrd) |

Remember that the same sound may be represented in spelling by different letter combinations.

The *ir* sound as in *mirror* can also be represented by the following letters.

*ere* as in h*ere* (hir)
*ear* as in b*ear*d (bird)
*eer* as in ch*eer* (chir)

The *er* sound in *berry* can also be represented by the following letters.

*air* as in f*air* (fer)
*are* as in c*are* (ker)

The ʉ sound in *her* can also be represented by the following letters.

*ur* as in f*ur* (fʉr)
*ir* as in f*ir* (fʉr)
*ear* as in *lear*n (lʉrn)
*or* as in w*or*m (wʉrm)
*ir* as in squ*ir*m (skwʉrm)

The ô sound in *cord* can also be represented by the following letters.

*ar* as in w*ar* (wôr)
*oar* as in c*oar*se (kôrs)
*oor* as in d*oor* (dôr)
*our* as in c*our*se (kôrs)

**Word Division for Pronunciation**

Each respelling is shown in parentheses following the entry word. These respellings are divided into syllables. The word division shown in the respelling helps you to pronounce the word. You know that each syllable must have one vowel sound.

Spaces are used between the syllables in the respellings to show where words are divided for pronunciation. In some words the division of syllables for pronunciation is the same as the division of syllables for writing shown in the main entry.

dis·tance (dis′təns)  or·der (ôr′dər)

However, sometimes the word division for writing and the word division for pronunciation are not the same.

act·ing (ak′tiŋ)  neg·lect (ni glekt′)

Remember, you use the word division shown for the entry word when deciding how to divide the word when writing. The word division shown in the respelling will help you in pronouncing the word.

**Accents**

In saying most words of more than one syllable, you put a heavier accent, or stress, on one of the syllables than on the others. Say aloud the words *picture* and *above.* Did you notice how you accented the first syllable in *picture* and the second syllable in *above?* In this dictionary, a dark accent mark (′) is placed after the syllable that is stressed, as in (pik′chər), (ə buv′).

In many words of more than two syllables one syllable will be marked with a heavy stress, and another syllable will be marked with a lighter stress. Say the word *dictionary.* Notice that the first syllable received the most stress. This is called the primary stress or accent. The third syllable receives some stress but less than the first syllable. This syllable receives the secondary stress or accent. This lighter stress is shown by a light accent mark after the third syllable, as in *dic·tion·ar·y* (dik′shə ner′ē).

Many words of three syllables, especially verbs such as *aggravate* and *supervise,* have a primary stress on the first syllable and a much lighter accent on the last syllable. In such three-syllable words it is not necessary to show this secondary stress: (ag′rə vāt), (so͞o′pər vīz).

Some words of two syllables have two equally heavy stresses. This happens most often with compound words written with a hyphen. In such cases, a heavy accent mark is shown after each stressed syllable, as in *good-sized* (go͝od′sīzd′).

Sometimes a word will be stressed one way when it is used as one part of speech, and some other way when it is used as another part of speech. The syllable that is stressed depends upon the meaning of the word. Read the following sentences.

That object is a can opener.  (äb′jikt)
I object to your leaving now.  (əb jekt′)

In the first sentence, *object* is a noun. In the second sentence, *object* is a verb. Look for the word *object* in your dictionary. You will find the pronunciation (äb′jikt) and the meanings for *object* used as a noun. In the second part of the entry, you will find the pronunciation (əb jekt′) and the meanings for *object* used as a verb.

In checking pronunciations, always read the entire entry. There may be special ways to pronounce the word when it is used as different parts of speech or when it has a special meaning.

## Exercise

Read the list of words after this paragraph. Think where you would put the stress marks. Then copy the words on a sheet of paper and place the accent marks where they should go. Some words will need both a primary and secondary accent. Be sure to make a heavier mark for the primary accent. Use the dictionary to check your work.

| | |
|---|---|
| in•stant (in stənt) | dis•turb (di sturb) |
| caf•e•te•ri•a (kaf ə tir ē ə) | sus•pend•ers (sə spen dərz) |
| pro•pel•ler (prə pel ər) | e•lec•tric•i•ty (i lek tris ə tē) |
| mos•qui•to (mə skē tō) | tem•po•rar•y (tem pə rer ē) |

### More Than One Pronunciation

You already know that many words can have different accents, depending upon the meaning of the words. Also, many words are pronounced differently even by people who speak the same dialect of English. For example, the word *either* can be pronounced (ē′*th*ər) or (ī′*th*ər). For the word *duty* some people say (do͞o′tē) while others say (dyo͞o′tē).

When two or more pronunciations are given for the same word, any of them may be used. The fact that one is given first does not mean that it is "better" than another. It simply means that the first one seems to be used more often than the other or others.

### Order of Meaning

Every main entry in the dictionary is followed by one or more meanings. Your dictionary usually gives the most common meaning first. The next meaning or two may be closely related to the first one. Other less common meanings are listed next. After these come the meanings used only in special subjects or fields, such as science, business, poetry, or sports. Next you may find a meaning that was once common but is now rare. Last of all come the meanings that are heard only in everyday talk and the meanings that are considered slang. Each meaning is given a number to set it off from the others. A new series of numbers is used for each part of speech. Here is a dictionary entry for a word with many different meanings.

| | |
|---|---|
| **Most common meaning** | **kick** (kik) ***v.*** **1** to strike out with the foot or feet, as in striking something or in dancing, swimming, etc. **2** to move by striking with the foot [to *kick* a football]. **3** to spring back suddenly, as a gun does when fired. **4** to complain or grumble: *used only in everyday talk.* |
| **Special label** | ☆**5** to get rid of: *slang in this meaning* [to *kick* a habit]. ◆***n.*** **1** a blow with the foot. **2** a way of kicking. **3** a springing back suddenly, as a gun does when fired; recoil. ☆**4** a complaint or protest: *used only in everyday talk.* ☆**5** a thrill, or excited feeling: *used only in everyday talk.* —☆**kick in,** to pay, as one's share: *a slang phrase.* —**kick off, 1** to put a football into play with a place kick. ☆**2** to start, as a campaign. |
| **Special label** | ☆**3** to die: *slang in this meaning.* —**kick out,** to get rid of or put out: *used only in everyday talk.* —**kick'er** ***n.*** |

## Context Clues

When you use a dictionary to find a meaning of an unfamiliar word, it is helpful to know the sentence or paragraph in which the word is used. This is called the context of the word. The words that come just before and just after a particular word in a sentence or paragraph form the context of that word. After you find the entry for the word in the dictionary, read each meaning. Then use the context of your word to check which meaning fits. Always read all the meanings of a word before you decide that you have chosen the right meaning.

## Exercise

Read the sentences below, noting the italicized word in each sentence. Each of the italicized words has more than one meaning. Look up each word in your dictionary. On a piece of paper, write the definition that best fits the context of the word.

1. Would you write an *outline* of your report?
2. The president gave Mrs. Travis the *floor* to make her speech.
3. What was the *message* of the book you just read?
4. Carlos had a very *thick* milk shake.
5. The ship pulled into its *berth.*

## Homographs

Sometimes you may find that none of the meanings in an entry seem right for the context of the word. Perhaps you are looking at the wrong entry. There may be another entry or entries spelled and pronounced exactly the same but with different meanings.

Words that are spelled alike but have different meanings are called homographs. They are listed alphabetically, just as all entry words are, and each is marked with a small number just after the boldface spelling.

Suppose you were reading about walking on the "port" side of an airplane. You know that *port* means a harbor for ships, but that definition would not make sense in this context. If you look up the word *port* in your dictionary, you will find the following four separate entries for this word. After reading the definitions, you will see that the third entry for *port* (**port³**) has a meaning that fits the context of this sentence.

**port**[1] (pôrt) ***n.*** **1** *another word for* **harbor**. **2** a city with a harbor where ships can load and unload.
**port**[2] (pôrt) ***n.*** a sweet, dark-red wine.
**port**[3] (pôrt) ***n.*** the left-hand side of a ship or airplane as one faces forward, toward the bow. ***◆adj.*** of or on this side.
**port**[4] (pôrt) ***n.*** **1** *same as* **porthole**. **2** the covering for a porthole. **3** an opening, as in an engine, for letting steam, gas, etc. in or out.

## Part-of-Speech Labels

Many words may be used in more than one way. Notice the way the word *change* is used in each of these sentences.

I must *change* my shirt.
Do you have *change* for a dollar?

In the first sentence, *change* is used as a verb. In the second sentence, it is used as a noun. In your dictionary, the meanings for each part of speech are grouped together. The noun meanings are grouped together after ***n.,*** the abbreviation for *noun.* The verb meanings are grouped together after ***v.,*** the abbreviation for *verb.*

Look at the following entry for *change.* The meanings for the word *change* used as a verb are given first because these meanings are more common. A heavy, dark diamond (◆) is used to signal the next part of speech, or the use of the word *change* as a noun.

**change** (chānj) ***v.*** **1** to make or become different in some way; alter [Time *changes* all things. His voice began to *change* at the age of thirteen.] **2** to put or take one thing in place of another; substitute [to *change* one's clothes; to *change* jobs]. **3** to give or take one thing in return for another; substitute [Let's *change* seats. Can you *change* this dollar bill for four quarters?] **4** to get off one train, bus, or plane and get on another [The passengers *change* at Chicago.] —**changed, chang'ing** ***◆n.*** **1** the act of changing in some way [There will be a *change* in the weather tomorrow.] **2** something put in place of something else [a fresh *change* of clothing]. **3** the money returned when one has paid more than the amount owed [If it costs 70 cents and you pay with a dollar, you get back 30 cents as *change.*] **4** a number of coins or bills whose total value equals a single larger coin or bill [I have *change* for your $10 bill.] **5** small coins [The *change* jingled in my pocket.] —**change off,** to take turns.

The following abbreviations are used in your dictionary for part-of-speech labels. They are usually shown in dark italic type.

| | | | |
|---|---|---|---|
| ***n.*** | noun | ***adv.*** | adverb |
| ***v.*** | verb | ***prep.*** | preposition |
| ***pron.*** | pronoun | ***conj.*** | conjunction |
| ***adj.*** | adjective | ***interj.*** | interjection |

Look up the following words in your dictionary. On a sheet of paper, copy the word and next to it write its part of speech or parts of speech. Then write a sentence using each word as the parts of speech shown. You will write 15 sentences.

| | | | |
|---|---|---|---|
| minor | from | oh | how |
| pinch | flashy | mushroom | that |

**Illustrative Phrases and Sentences**

Your dictionary uses many examples to show you exactly how a word is used. The examples may be phrases or sentences. These phrases and sentences provide meaningful contexts for the meanings of words. Every example is put into brackets [ ]. Look at the examples for the word *long.* Notice that the word itself is printed in italic type.

> **long**[1] (lôŋ) ***adj.*** **1** measuring much from end to end or from beginning to end; not short [a *long* board; a *long* trip; a *long* wait]. **2** reaching over a certain distance; in length [a rope six feet *long*]. **3** large; big [She took a *long* chance.] **4** taking a longer time to say than other sounds [The "a" in "cave" and the "i" in "hide" are *long*.] ◆***adv.*** **1** for a long time [Don't be gone *long*.] **2** from the beginning to the end [all summer *long*]. **3** at a far distant time [They lived *long* ago.] —**as long as** or **so long as, 1** during the time that. **2** seeing that; since. **3** on the condition that. —**before long,** soon.

**Variant Terms**

Look at the entry for the word *platypus.* A platypus is also called a *duckbill.* When two or more words have exactly the same meaning, the word that is used most often is shown as the main entry. The variant term or terms are shown at the end of the entry. The phrase *also called* is used to signal the variant terms.

> **plat·y·pus** (plat′ə pəs) ***n.*** a small water animal of Australia that has webbed feet, a tail like a beaver's, and a bill like a duck's. It lays eggs, but suckles its young. *Also called* **duckbill** or **duckbill platypus.** *See the picture. —pl.* **plat′y·pus·es** or **plat·y·pi** (plat′ə pī′)

## Cross References

Instead of repeating information given elsewhere in the dictionary, an entry will sometimes tell you to turn to another entry, often for the meaning of a word, sometimes for additional information about that word. The directions *see, see also, same as,* or *another word for* mean that you should turn to the other entry for the meaning that will help you.

> **Armistice Day** *see* **Veterans Day.**
>
> ☆**Veterans Day** November 11, a legal holiday honoring all veterans of the armed forces. This holiday was formerly called Armistice Day, which celebrated the armistice of World War I.

The word you should look up is called the cross reference and is in heavy black type.

## Exercise

Copy on a sheet of paper the list of words given below. Look up each word in your dictionary. Write next to each word the main entry under which you will find the definition.

| | | |
|---|---|---|
| Rumania | ameba | Iscariot |
| Odysseus | moving picture | Bonaparte |

## Common Idioms

An idiom is "a phrase or expression that has a meaning different from what the words suggest in their usual meaning."

> Bob was down *in the dumps* because he didn't make the team. He had *set his heart on* it. Carl was *in the same boat.* Their only hope was that the coach might have *a change of heart* and give them one more chance to *try out.*

When you read the above paragraph, you knew that Bob was not really in a place where rubbish is dumped, nor was Carl in a real boat. If you did not know the meanings of the idioms, you would have trouble understanding the paragraph.

In this dictionary, you will find a great many idioms. When you are looking for an idiom, look under what seems to be the most important word in the idiom. This is not always the first word. Idioms are listed after the meanings of the entry word.

> **boat** (bōt) ***n.*** **1** a small vessel for traveling on water, such as a rowboat, sailboat, lifeboat, or motorboat. In popular use, but not by sailors, a ship of any size is sometimes called a boat. **2** a dish shaped a little like a boat [a gravy *boat*]. ◆***v.*** to row or sail in a boat [We went *boating* on the river.] —**in the same boat,** facing the same kind of problem.

Read the following idioms. Look up each one in your dictionary. Choose any five, and on a piece of paper, write a sentence using each idiom.

| | | |
|---|---|---|
| go Dutch | as the crow flies | make no bones about |
| cry wolf | pave the way | wash one's hands of |
| up a tree | eat one's words | turn over a new leaf |

**Americanisms**

An Americanism is a word or usage of a word that was born in this country. An open star before an entry word means that the word is an Americanism. When you see the star in front of an entry word, it means that every meaning and every form of that word given is an Americanism. If a star is placed before a single definition or part of a definition, only that definition or part is an Americanism.

> ☆**bas·ket·ball** (bas′kit bôl) ***n.*** **1** a game played between two teams of five players each, usually indoors. Points are scored by tossing a ball through a raised, open net, hanging from a metal ring. There is a basket at either end of the playing court. **2** the large, round, leather ball used in this game. It is filled with air.

**Reading, Writing, and Speaking**

The dictionary uses special labels to give you additional information about many words.

**Subject Labels** In this dictionary, you will find many notes about the ways in which words are used or about meanings that are special to a particular kind of work. You will find two notes of this sort in the entry for *cover.*

> **cov·er** (kuv′ər) ***v.*** **1** to place one thing over another; spread over [*Cover* the bird cage at night. *Cover* the wall with white paint. Water *covered* the fields.] **2** to keep from being seen or known; hide [He tried to *cover* up the scandal.] **3** to protect, as from harm or loss [Are you *covered* by insurance?] **4** to provide for; take care of [Is this case *covered* by the rules?] **5** to have to do with; be about; include [This book *covers* the Civil War.] **6** to go; travel [The camel *covered* 65 miles that day.] **7** to keep a gun aimed at [*Cover* him while I call the police.] ☆**8** to get the news or pictures of: *used by newspaper and TV people* [Many reporters *covered* the airplane crash.] ☆**9** to guard or defend: *used in sports* [*Cover* first base.] ◆***n.*** **1** anything that covers, as a lid, a blanket, the binding of a book, etc. **2** anything that hides or protects [under *cover* of darkness]. —☆**cover for,** to provide an alibi or excuse for another person. —**take cover,** to seek shelter.

**Everyday Talk — Slang** When you say, "It was a *lovely* party," or "I'm *mighty* hungry," you are using the words *lovely* and *mighty* in a special way – as you would in everyday talk at home or with your friends. This is informal language. You may not hear such words in a serious lecture or see them in most of your schoolbooks.

When a word has an informal meaning, a special note in italic type follows that meaning. You will notice that in the following entries a colon (:) comes before the note. The other uses and meanings can be used in all kinds of speaking and writing.

---

**love·ly** (luv′lē) ***adj.*** **1** very pleasing in looks or character; beautiful [a *lovely* person]. **2** very enjoyable: *used only in everyday talk* [We had a *lovely* time.] **—love′li·er, love′li·est —love′li·ness *n.***

---

Many slang words become popular but are in use for only a short time. Since you will need to understand or want to use today's slang at certain times, a few slang words and meanings that are widely used are included in this dictionary. They are followed by a special label in italic type.

---

**chow** (chou) ***n.*** **1** a dog that was first bred in China, with a thick, brown or black coat and a black tongue. *See the picture.* ☆**2** food or mealtime: *slang in this meaning.*

---

**Regional Differences** Just as there are differences in pronunciations between one region and another, there are also differences in the words that are used in speaking of the same thing. As you travel around this country, you will hear *lug* and *tote,* as well as *carry.* You will hear *skillet* and *spider,* as well as *frying pan.* Do you know what a *critter* is? Or a *poke* of candy? Such words are included in this dictionary with a special note.

---

**crit·ter** (krit′ər) ***n.*** *another word for* **creature**: *used only in some regions.*

---

These words are perfectly correct in the parts of the country where they are commonly used. The notes in the dictionary simply remind you that such words may not be understood by people in other regions.

If you travel to other countries where English is spoken, you will also hear and read words not commonly used in the United States. In England, for example, you hear *lift* for *elevator* and *lorry* for *truck.* Some of the words that are used mainly in Great Britain are also used in Canada. Special notes are included in an entry to tell you in what country these words are common. The following entries will show you some of these special notes.

**gaol** (jāl) ***n.*** *British spelling of* **jail.** —**gaol'er** ***n.***
**draughts** (drafts) ***n.pl.*** the game of checkers: *the British name.*
**ken** (ken) ***n.*** knowledge or understanding [Nuclear physics is beyond my *ken.*] ◆***v.*** to know: *used mainly in Scotland.* —**kenned, ken'ning**

**Usage Note** Your language is constantly changing as new words come into use and some of the old words go out of use. You can see this change by comparing the language of today with the language of poems and stories written long ago. Many of the older words that you may need to know are listed in this dictionary. A special note is included in italic type to tell you if the word is no longer used or is seldom used.

**meet²** (mēt) ***adj.*** fitting or proper: *no longer much used.*
**thou** (*th*ou) ***pron.*** *an older form of* **you** *(in the singular), used as the subject of a verb, as in the Bible.*

Sometimes you will find a special usage note following the entry. These notes may tell about a special meaning or about the ways in which a word is used. These notes are highlighted by a colored tint over them. Look at the note after the entry for **a.**

**a** (ə *or* ā) ***adj.*** **1** one; one sort of [I picked *a* rose.] **2** each; any one [*A* dog that bites should be tied up.] **A** is also called an *indefinite article. See also* **the.** **3** in or for each [It costs fifty cents *a* box.]

**A** is used before all words beginning with a consonant sound [*a* bell, *a* house, *a* unicorn (yo͞o'nə kôrn)]. **An** is used before a vowel sound [*an* orange, *an* honor, *an* usher].

## *Exercise*

Look up the italicized words in your dictionary. On a piece of paper, write each word and then write the special note included in the entry.

1. *Belay* there! Give your name before you come aboard.
2. The tenants walked upstairs because the *lift* was broken.
3. Let me give you the *lowdown* about the surprise party.
4. The McDonalds have a new, wee *bairn.*
5. The *lorry* was carrying a load of newspapers.
6. The shopkeeper deposited the *cheque* in the bank.

**Etymologies**

The words in use today have come into our language over a period of thousands of years. Most of them come from languages that existed long before the time that English began to be thought of as a separate language. Our words have come from many sources. A large number of our words were borrowed from the Latin and Greek languages and from earlier forms of French and German. *Circus* was once a Latin word. *Theater* comes from the French language. The French borrowed the word from ancient Greek. *Algebra* comes from an Arabic word. This dictionary shows the history of some entry words in a special note, called an *etymology* (et′ə mäl′ə jē). These etymologies are highlighted by a colored tint over them. An etymology will help you to have a better understanding of the meaning of a word and show you how it came to have that meaning.

**an·thol·o·gy** (an thäl′ə jē) ***n.*** a collection of poems, stories, or other writings. —*pl.* **an·thol′o·gies**
**Anthology** comes from an ancient Greek word meaning "a garland of flowers." It was made up of *anthos,* meaning "flower," and *legein,* meaning "to gather." An anthology can be thought of as a bouquet of fine writings.

The answers to the following questions can be found by looking up each italicized word and reading the etymology. Write the answers on a sheet of paper.

1. What famous Greek philosopher taught his students in an *academy?*
2. If a person wanted the gift of *blarney,* what should that person do?
3. Which is considered the more polite term, *Asian* or *Asiatic?*
4. What were the first *barricades* made from?
5. What was the original color of *baize?*
6. From what ancient language does the word *apostle* come?
7. What word is related to *aggravate?*

## Synonyms

At the end of some entries you will find a group of words that begins with the heading SYNONYMS. Synonyms are words that are closely related in meaning, such as *break, smash,* and *crush.* Often there are slight differences in meaning. Usually there are short phrases and sentences to show the synonyms in use.

SYNONYMS: **Break** means to divide something into pieces by using force, pressure, etc. **Smash** means to break something or hit something suddenly, violently, and noisily [The car *smashed* into the wall.] **Crush** means to press so hard on something that it folds up or breaks into bits [I *crushed* the empty carton under my foot.]

There are cross references to the synonyms to make them easier to find. For example, in the entries for *smash* and *crush,* there is a cross reference to *break* that reads "*See* SYNONYMS *at* **break**."

Write the following words on a piece of paper. Look up each word, and next to it write a synonym that is given in your dictionary.

| | | |
|---|---|---|
| frank | thin | animal |
| decline | pleasant | scream |
| look | hungry | weak |

**Illustrations**

Your dictionary provides pictures to help you to understand some of the definitions better. These pictures can show you how things look or how they are used. A caption is given to identify each picture. Many captions also give additional information about the entry. For instance, a caption may include the size of an animal. In addition, there is a note in the entry telling you to *see the picture.* When you are skimming or browsing through your dictionary, some pictures may catch your interest. If you want additional information, look at the main entry.

**Abbreviations Used in Webster's New World Dictionary**

| | | | |
|---|---|---|---|
| A.D. | of the Christian era | n. | noun |
| adj. | adjective | pl. | plural |
| adv. | adverb | prep. | preposition |
| B.C. | before Christ | pron. | pronoun |
| conj. | conjunction | sing. | singular |
| etc. | and so forth | v. | verb |
| interj. | interjection | | |

A dictionary can tell you many things about how words and phrases are used. Words are very important. You use them to pass on information and to express your feelings. You need them if you are to understand others. You use them at work and at play. They are tools of communication and sources of pleasure. You find them on the labels of cans and in the lyrics of popular songs. You shout them at baseball games. You tell jokes and make puns with them. People running for office use them to get your vote. Writers use them to tell you their stories. Without them you would be unable to think, write, and talk. They are as much a part of your life as the air you breathe and the food you eat. Use your dictionary to explore the exciting world of words.

1. Guide Words
2. Main Entry
3. Syllable Division
4. Pronunciation
5. Parts of Speech
6. Definition
7. Derived Form
8. Usage Label
9. Word History
10. Americanism
11. Biographical Entry
12. Variant Terms
13. Variant Spelling
14. Usage Note
15. Compound Entry
16. Synonyms
17. Homographs

## bade/bead

**bade** (bad) *a past tense of* **bid.**

**badg·er** (baj′ər) ***n.*** **1** an animal with a broad back, thick fur, and short legs. It lives in holes which it digs in the ground. **2** the fur of this animal. ◆***v.*** to annoy; pester [The speaker was *badgered* by interruptions.]

**baf·fle** (baf″l) ***v.*** **1** to confuse so as to keep from understanding or solving; puzzle [The crime has *baffled* the police for months.] **2** to interfere with; hold back; hinder [The drapes *baffle* the sound.] —**baf′fled, baf′fling** ◆***n.*** a wall, screen, etc. that holds back or turns to one side the flow of a liquid, heat, or sound waves.

**ba·gel** (bā′g'l) ***n.*** a hard bread roll shaped like a doughnut.

**bag·gy** (bag′ē) ***adj.*** hanging loosely and bulging in places [*baggy* trousers]. —**bag′gi·er, bag′gi·est** —**bag′gi·ness *n.***

**bairn** (bern) ***n.*** a child: *a Scottish word.*

**baize** (bāz) ***n.*** thick woolen cloth, usually dyed green, used to cover a billiard table.

> **Baize** comes from the Latin word *badius,* meaning "reddish brown." From this we learn that the cloth, now usually dyed green, was originally another color. The word is related to **bay**[5].

☆**bak·er·y** (bāk′ər ē) ***n.*** a place where bread, cakes, etc. are baked or sold. —*pl.* **bak′er·ies**

**Bal·bo·a** (bal bō′ə), **Vas·co de** (väs′kō de) 1475?–1517?; Spanish explorer. In 1513, he became the first European to see the Pacific Ocean.

**Bal·kans** (bôl′kənz) the countries on a peninsula (**Balkan Peninsula**) in southeastern Europe; Yugoslavia, Romania, Bulgaria, Albania, Greece, and part of Turkey: *also called* **Balkan States.** *See the map.*

**ban·do·leer** or **ban·do·lier** (ban′də lir′) ***n.*** a broad belt worn over one shoulder and across the chest, with pockets for carrying ammunition.

**bar·racks** (bar′əks) ***n.pl.*** a building or group of buildings where soldiers live: *used with either a singular or plural verb* [This *barracks* is old. These *barracks* are old.]

**barrel organ** a large music box usually played by turning a handle; hand organ.

**ba·sis** (bā′sis) ***n.*** the thing or part on which something rests or depends; support. —*pl.* **ba·ses** (bā′sēz)

> SYNONYMS: **Basis, base**[1], and **foundation** all carry the idea of a part that supports or underlies something that rests or depends on it. **Base**[1] and **foundation** usually suggest a physical structure, while **basis** suggests a structure that is not physical [the *base* of a lamp; the *foundation* of a building; a story with no *basis* in fact]. **Foundation** also suggests something stable and permanent [A good education gives us a good *foundation* for our adult lives.]

**bass**[1] (bās) ***n.*** **1** the lowest kind of man's singing voice. **2** a singer with such a voice. **3** an instrument with the lowest range of tones; especially, the **double bass. 4** the lowest part of harmony in a piece of music. ◆***adj.*** **1** of or for a bass. **2** having low, deep sounds or tones [a *bass* drum].

**bass**[2] (bas) ***n.*** a fish with spiny fins, found in both fresh and salt water and used for food. —*pl.* **bass** or **bass′es**

**bas·soon** (bə so͞on′) ***n.*** a woodwind musical instrument with deep, low tones. Its long, curved mouthpiece has two reeds. *See the picture.*

**bass viol** (bās) *same as* **double bass.**

**bat**[1] (bat) ***n.*** **1** a wooden club used in hitting the ball in baseball. **2** any strong, sturdy stick. ☆**3** a turn in batting in baseball [Pat got three hits in four times at *bat.*] **4** a hard blow or hit: *used only in everyday talk.* ◆***v.*** **1** to hit with a bat or something like a bat. **2** to take a turn at batting in baseball. **—bat′ted, bat′ting** —☆**off the bat** or ☆**right off the bat,** right away; immediately: *used only in everyday talk.*

**bat**[2] (bat) ***n.*** a furry animal that looks like a mouse but has wings of stretched skin. Bats usually fly at night. *See the picture.* **—blind as a bat,** completely blind. Bats do not see well but find their way by sending out sound waves, which bounce off obstacles and come back as echoes.

**batch** (bach) ***n.*** **1** the amount of something made at one time [a *batch* of cookies; wool yarn from different *batches*]. **2** an amount of something to be used or worked on at one time [a *batch* of dishes to wash and dry].

**ba·tiste** (ba tēst′) ***n.*** a light, thin linen or cotton cloth, used for shirts, dresses, etc.

**Ba·ton Rouge** (bat′′n ro͞ozh′) the capital of Louisiana, on the Mississippi River.

**bbl.** *abbreviation for* **barrel.** *—pl.* **bbls.**

**be-** *a prefix meaning:* **1** around [To *beset* is to set around, or surround.] **2** completely [To *besmear* is to smear completely.] **3** away [To *betake* oneself is to take oneself away.] **4** about [To *bemoan* someone is to moan about someone.] **5** to make [To *becalm* is to make calm.] **6** to furnish or cover with [To *begrime* is to cover with grime.]

**bead** (bēd) ***n.*** **1** a small, usually round piece of glass, metal, etc. with a small hole in it so that it can be put on a string [She wore a string of *beads* around her neck.] **2** a drop or bubble [He has *beads* of sweat on his face.] ◆***v.*** to decorate or cover with beads [a *beaded* handbag]. —☆**draw a bead on,** to take careful aim at.

18. Illustration
19. Cross Reference
20. Inflected Forms
21. Idiom
22. Geographical Entry
23. Abbreviation
24. Prefix
25. Sentence or Phrase
26. Pronunciation Key and Letter Tab

| | | | |
|---|---|---|---|
| **a** fat | **ir** here | **ou** out | **zh** leisure |
| **ā** ape | **ī** bite, fire | **u** up | **ng** ring |
| **ä** car, lot | **ō** go | **ur** fur | a *in* ago |
| **e** ten | **ô** law, horn | **ch** chin | e *in* agent |
| **er** care | **oi** oil | **sh** she | **ə** = i *in* unity |
| **ē** even | **oo** look | **th** thin | o *in* collect |
| **i** hit | **o͞o** tool | ***th*** then | u *in* focus |

**b**

# Pronunciation Key

| SYMBOL | KEY WORDS | SYMBOL | KEY WORDS |
|---|---|---|---|
| a | **a**sk, f**a**t | b | **b**ed, du**b** |
| ā | **a**pe, d**a**te | d | **d**id, ha**d** |
| ä | c**a**r, l**o**t | f | **f**all, o**ff** |
| | | g | **g**et, do**g** |
| e | **e**lf, t**e**n | h | **h**e, a**h**ead |
| er | b**err**y, c**are** | j | **j**oy, **j**ump |
| ē | **e**ven, m**ee**t | k | **k**ill, ba**k**e |
| | | l | **l**et, ba**ll** |
| i | **i**s, h**i**t | m | **m**et, tri**m** |
| ir | m**irr**or, h**ere** | n | **n**ot, to**n** |
| ī | **i**ce, f**i**re | p | **p**ut, ta**p** |
| | | r | **r**ed, dea**r** |
| ō | **o**pen, g**o** | s | **s**ell, pa**ss** |
| ô | l**a**w, h**o**rn | t | **t**op, ha**t** |
| ơi | **oi**l, p**oi**nt | v | **v**at, ha**v**e |
| ơo | l**oo**k, p**u**ll | w | **w**ill, al**w**ays |
| ōō | **oo**ze, t**oo**l | y | **y**et, **y**ard |
| yơo | **u**nite, c**u**re | z | **z**ebra, ha**z**e |
| yōō | c**u**te, f**ew** | | |
| ơu | **ou**t, cr**ow**d | ch | **ch**in, ar**ch** |
| | | ŋ | ri**ng**, si**ng**er |
| u | **u**p, c**u**t | sh | **sh**e, da**sh** |
| ʉr | f**ur**, f**er**n | th | **th**in, tru**th** |
| | | *th* | **th**en, fa**th**er |
| ə | **a** in **a**go | zh | **s** in plea**s**ure |
| | **e** in ag**e**nt | | |
| | **e** in fath**e**r | ' | as in (ā'b'l) |
| | **i** in un**i**ty | | |
| | **o** in c**o**llect | | |
| | **u** in foc**u**s | | |

A heavy stress mark **'** is placed after a syllable that gets a strong accent, as in **con·sid·er** (kən sid**'**ər).

A light stress mark ' is placed after a syllable that also gets an accent, but of a weaker kind, as in **dic·tion·ar·y** (dik**'**shən er'ē).

See also the explanation of how to use the pronunciation key, beginning on page 32

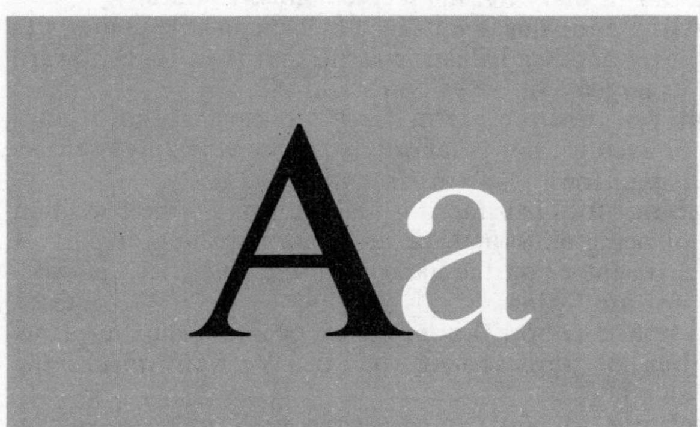

**A, a** (ā) ***n.*** the first letter of the English alphabet. *—pl.* **A's, a's** (āz)

**A** (ā) ***n.*** the highest grade, as in some schools, meaning "excellent" or "best."

**a** (ə *or* ā) ***adj.*** **1** one; one sort of [I picked *a* rose.] **2** each; any one [*A* dog that bites should be tied up.] **A** is also called an *indefinite article. See also* **the.** **3** in or for each [It costs fifty cents *a* box.]

> **A** is used before all words beginning with a consonant sound [*a* bell, *a* house, *a* unicorn (yōō′nə kôrn)]. **An** is used before a vowel sound [*an* orange, *an* honor, *an* usher].

**AA** or **A.A.** **1** Alcoholics Anonymous. **2** antiaircraft.

**AAA** American Automobile Association.

**Aar·on** (er′ən) in the Bible, the older brother of Moses. Aaron was the first high priest of the Hebrews.

**A.B.** Bachelor of Arts.

**ab** or **a.b.** (times) at bat (in baseball).

**a·back** (ə bak′) ***adv.*** backward; back.

> This word is now seldom used except in the phrase **taken aback,** which means "surprised and confused."

**ab·a·cus** (ab′ə kəs) ***n.*** a frame with groups of beads sliding back and forth on wires. The abacus is used for doing arithmetic quickly without writing. *See the picture. —pl.* **ab′a·cus·es**

**a·ban·don** (ə ban′dən) ***v.*** **1** to give up completely [Don't *abandon* hope of being saved.] **2** to leave; desert [The crew *abandoned* the burning ship.] *See* SYNONYMS *at* **desert.** ◆***n.*** freedom of actions or feelings, with no control [to dance with wild *abandon*]. —**a·ban′don·ment** ***n.***

**a·base** (ə bās′) ***v.*** to make lower in position or more humble [She would not *abase* herself before the tyrant.] —**a·based′, a·bas′ing —a·base′ment** ***n.***

**a·bash** (ə bash′) ***v.*** to make someone feel embarrassed or uneasy; make ill at ease [No amount of criticism could *abash* him.]

**a·bate** (ə bāt′) ***v.*** to make or become less or weaker; diminish; decrease [The hurricane winds *abated.*] —**a·bat′ed, a·bat′ing —a·bate′ment** ***n.***

**ab·bess** (ab′is) ***n.*** a woman who is head of an abbey of nuns.

**ab·bey** (ab′ē) ***n.*** the place where a group of monks or nuns live and work. It is headed by an abbot or abbess.

**ab·bot** (ab′ət) ***n.*** a man who is head of an abbey of monks.

> **Abbot** comes from a very old Aramaic word, *abba,* that means "father."

**ab·bre·vi·ate** (ə brē′vē āt) ***v.*** to make shorter by cutting out part [The word "Street" is often *abbreviated* to 1
"St."] —**ab·bre′vi·at·ed, ab·bre′vi·at·ing**

**ab·bre·vi·a·tion** (ə brē′vē ā′shən) ***n.*** **1** a shortened form of a word or phrase, as *n.* for *noun* or *U.S.A.* for *United States of America.* **2** the act of making or becoming shorter.

**ABC**[1] (ā′bē′sē′) ***n.*** **1** the alphabet: *usually in plural,* **ABC's.** **2** the simplest facts of a subject or the basic skills of an activity [We learned the *ABC's* of tennis at camp.]

**ABC**[2] American Broadcasting Company.

**ab·di·cate** (ab′də kāt) ***v.*** to give up some high position, office, or power; especially, to resign as king or queen. —**ab′di·cat·ed, ab′di·cat·ing —ab′di·ca′tion** ***n.***

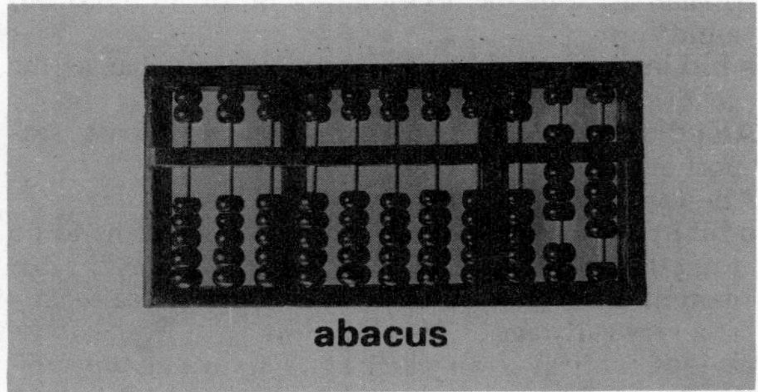

abacus

| | | | |
|---|---|---|---|
| **a** fat | **ir** here | **ou** out | **zh** leisure |
| **ā** ape | **ī** bite, fire | **u** up | **ng** ring |
| **ä** car, lot | **ō** go | **ur** fur | a *in* ago |
| **e** ten | **ô** law, horn | **ch** chin | e *in* agent |
| **er** care | **oi** oil | **sh** she | **ə** = i *in* unity |
| **ē** even | **oo** look | **th** thin | o *in* collect |
| **i** hit | **ōō** tool | ***th*** then | u *in* focus |

**ab·do·men** (ab′də mən *or* ab dō′mən) ***n.*** **1** the part of the body between the chest and hips; belly. It contains the stomach, intestines, liver, etc. **2** the part of an insect's body farthest back. *See the picture.*

**ab·dom·i·nal** (ab däm′ə n'l) ***adj.*** of, in, or for the abdomen [*Abdominal* pains may be caused by hunger.]

**ab·duct** (ab dukt′) ***v.*** to take a person away unlawfully and by force; kidnap. —**ab·duc′tion** ***n.*** —**ab·duc′tor** ***n.***

**A·bel** (ā′b'l) in the Bible, the second son of Adam and Eve. He was killed by his brother, Cain.

**Ab·er·deen** (ab ər dēn′) a city in eastern Scotland, on the North Sea.

**ab·er·ra·tion** (ab′ə rā′shən) ***n.*** **1** a turning aside from what is right, true, etc. [Stealing is an *aberration* in conduct.] **2** an act or condition that is not normal [An abnormal fear is a kind of mental *aberration.*] **3** the failure of light rays from one point to meet at a single focus. **4** a fault in a lens or mirror that keeps such light rays from meeting and causes a blurred image. *See the picture.*

**a·bet** (ə bet′) ***v.*** to urge on or help, especially in doing something wrong [She was found guilty of *abetting* the thief because she had hidden him.] —**a·bet′ted, a·bet′ting**

**a·bey·ance** (ə bā′əns) ***n.*** a stopping for a while, as during some activity [The game was held in *abeyance* while the rules were checked.]



**ab·hor** (əb hôr′) ***v.*** to feel great fear, disgust, or hatred for; hate very much [Frank *abhors* fighting.] —**ab·horred′, ab·hor′ring**

**ab·hor·rence** (əb hôr′əns) ***n.*** **1** a feeling of hatred [I have an *abhorrence* of bullies.] **2** something feared, hated, or considered disgusting [Cruelty is an *abhorrence* to us all.]

**ab·hor·rent** (əb hôr′ənt) ***adj.*** causing fear, disgust, hatred, etc. [Kidnapping is an *abhorrent* crime.]

**a·bide** (ə bīd′) ***v.*** **1** to remain; go on being; stay; dwell. *The word is now seldom used with this meaning except in poetry, the Bible, etc.* [*Abide* with me.] **2** to put up with; bear; stand [I can't *abide* tight collars.] —**abide by, 1** to remain true to a promise, etc. [to *abide by* an agreement]. **2** to give in to and carry out [I shall *abide by* the decision.] —**a·bode′** or **a·bid′ed, a·bid′ing**

**a·bid·ing** (ə bīd′iŋ) ***adj.*** lasting without change [the *abiding* love of parents for their child].

**Ab·i·djan** (ab i jän′) the capital of Ivory Coast; seaport on the Atlantic.

**Ab·i·lene** (ab′ə lēn) a city in central Texas.

**a·bil·i·ty** (ə bil′ə tē) ***n.*** **1** the power or means to do something [Does he have the *ability* to pay?] **2** a natural skill or talent [Mozart showed musical *ability* at a very early age.] —*pl.* **a·bil′i·ties**

**ab·ject** (ab′jekt *or* ab jekt′) ***adj.*** **1** causing unhappiness; wretched; miserable [*abject* poverty]. **2** lacking self-respect; mean [an *abject* coward]. —**ab·ject′ly** ***adv.***

**a·blaze** (ə blāz′) ***adj.*** **1** burning with flames [The barn was *ablaze.*] **2** shining brightly [The courtyard was *ablaze* in the noonday sun.]

**a·ble** (ā′b'l) ***adj.*** **1** having the means or power to do something [She is *able* to take care of herself.] **2** having the skill or talent that is needed [an *able* mechanic]. —**a′bler, a′blest**

> SYNONYMS: A person who is **able** has the power to do something [a baby not yet *able* to walk] or may have a special skill [an *able* guitarist]. A **capable** person has the ability to do something well [a *capable* typist], while one who is **qualified** has passed certain tests or met special conditions [a *qualified* science teacher].

**-a·ble** (ə b'l) *a suffix meaning:* **1** that can be [A *drinkable* liquid is one that can be drunk.] **2** tending to [*Peaceable* people tend to live in peace.]

**a·ble-bod·ied** (ā′b'l bäd′ēd) ***adj.*** healthy and strong.

**a·bly** (ā′blē) ***adv.*** in an able manner; skillfully.

**ABM** antiballistic missile, a ballistic missile used to destroy another ballistic missile that is in flight toward its target.

**ab·nor·mal** (ab nôr′m'l) ***adj.*** not normal; not regular or average; not usual or typical [Snow in July is *abnormal* in Iowa.] —**ab·nor′mal·ly** ***adv.***

**ab·nor·mal·i·ty** (ab′nôr mal′ə tē) ***n.*** **1** the condition of being abnormal. **2** an abnormal thing or part [A sixth finger on the hand is an *abnormality.*] —*pl.* **ab′-nor·mal′i·ties**

**a·board** (ə bôrd′) ***adv.*** on, in, or into a ship, airplane, bus, or train. ◆***prep.*** on; in [We went *aboard* the ship.]

**a·bode** (ə bōd′) *a past tense and past participle of* **abide.** ◆***n.*** a place where one lives; home [Log cabins were the *abode* of many early settlers.]

**a·bol·ish** (ə bäl′ish) ***v.*** to do away with completely; get rid of [Congress may *abolish* a law.]

**ab·o·li·tion** (ab′ə lish′ən) ***n.*** the act of doing away with something completely [the *abolition* of slavery].

**ab·o·li·tion·ist** or **Ab·o·li·tion·ist** (ab′ə lish′ən ist) ***n.*** any of the people who wanted to put an end to slavery in the United States before the Civil War.

**A-bomb** (ā′bäm′) ***n.*** *same as* **atomic bomb.**

**a·bom·i·na·ble** (ə bäm′ə nə b'l) ***adj.*** **1** nasty and disgusting; hateful [an *abominable* crime]. **2** very unpleasant; disagreeable [That TV program is *abominable.*] —**a·bom′i·na·bly** ***adv.***

> **Abominable** comes from a Latin word that means "from a bad omen." A bad omen is a sign that something unpleasant or disagreeable may happen.

**Abominable Snowman** a large, hairy creature that looks human and that some people claim to have seen living in the Himalayas.

**ab·o·rig·i·nes** (ab′ə rij′ə nēz′) ***n.pl.*** the first people known to have lived in a certain place; natives [The Indians are the *aborigines* of America.] —*sing.* **ab′o-rig′i·ne′**

**a·bort** (ə bôrt′) ***v.*** to cut short an action or operation that has already started [When the spacecraft went off course, its flight was *aborted.*]

**a·bor·tion** (ə bôr′shən) ***n.*** the bringing out of an embryo or fetus from the womb before it is developed enough to live.

**a·bor·tive** (ə bôr′tiv) ***adj.*** failing to succeed; having no results [an *abortive* plan].

**a·bound** (ə bound′) ***v.*** **1** to exist in large numbers or amounts [Insects *abound* in a jungle.] **2** to have plenty; be filled [The park *abounds* with birds.]

**a·bout** (ə bout′) ***adv.*** **1** on every side; all around

[Look *about.*] **2** here and there; in all directions [Birds fly *about.*] **3** near [It is somewhere *about.*] **4** in or to the opposite direction [Turn yourself *about.*] **5** nearly; more or less [*about* ten years old]. **6** almost: *used only in everyday talk* [I'm just *about* ready.] ◆***adj.*** active; awake or recovered [At dawn I was up and *about.*] ◆***prep.*** **1** around; on all sides of [Waves rose *about* the boat.] **2** here and there in; everywhere in [Stop running *about* the house.] **3** near to [born *about* 1920]. **4** with [You have your wits *about* you.] **5** taking care of [Go *about* your business.] **6** almost ready [I am *about* to cry.] **7** having to do with [a book *about* ships].

**a·bout-face** (ə bout′fās′) ***n.*** **1** a facing in the opposite direction. **2** a change to the opposite opinion or attitude [The mayor did an *about-face* in deciding to support the levy.] ◆***v.*** (ə bout′fās′) to face in the opposite direction. —**a·bout′-faced′, a·bout′-fac′ing**

**a·bove** (ə buv′) ***adv.*** **1** in or at a higher place; up [Birds are flying *above.*] **2** before or earlier in a book or paragraph [our goal, as stated *above*]. ◆***prep.*** **1** higher than; over [We flew *above* the clouds.] **2** better than [*above* the average]. **3** more than [It cost *above* a dollar.] ◆***adj.*** found or mentioned above or earlier [The *above* facts prove it.] —**above all,** most of all; mainly.

**a·bove·board** (ə buv′bôrd′) ***adv., adj.*** hiding nothing; open and honest; straightforward.

> **Aboveboard** was first used in card games. Players who keep their cards above the board, or table, are not likely to cheat by switching cards.

**ab·ra·ca·dab·ra** (ab′rə kə dab′rə) ***n.*** **1** a word supposed to have magic powers, used in casting spells. **2** foolish talk; nonsense.

**A·bra·ham** (ā′brə ham) in the Bible, the first patriarch and ancestor of the Jews.

**ab·ra·sion** (ə brā′zhən) ***n.*** **1** a scraping off of skin. **2** a wearing away by rubbing or scraping [the *abrasion* of rock by wind or water]. **3** a spot where the skin or surface has been scraped off.

**ab·ra·sive** (ə brā′siv) ***adj.*** **1** causing abrasion; scraping or rubbing. **2** making people angry or annoyed; irritating. ◆***n.*** something that grinds or polishes, as sandpaper.

**a·breast** (ə brest′) ***adv., adj.*** side by side, as in moving forward; in line. *See the picture.*

**a·bridge** (ə brij′) ***v.*** **1** to make shorter, smaller, or fewer; especially, to shorten a talk, book, etc. by using fewer words. **2** to take away [Congress shall make no law *abridging* freedom of speech.] —**a·bridged′, a·bridg′ing**

**a·bridg·ment** or **a·bridge·ment** (ə brij′mənt) ***n.*** **1** the act of abridging [Such a law would be an *abridgment* of freedom of speech.] **2** a shortened form or version [an *abridgment* of a novel].

**a·broad** (ə brôd′) ***adv.*** **1** in many places; widely [A report went *abroad* that the president was ill.] **2** outdoors [Couples strolled *abroad* in the park.] **3** outside one's own country [going *abroad* to Europe]. —**from abroad,** from a foreign land or lands.

**ab·ro·gate** (ab′rə gāt) ***v.*** to put an end to; repeal; cancel [to *abrogate* a law]. —**ab′ro·gat·ed, ab′ro·gat·ing**

**a·brupt** (ə brupt′) ***adj.*** **1** coming or happening suddenly, without warning [to make an *abrupt* stop]. **2** very blunt or gruff [He answered with an *abrupt* "No!"] **3** very steep [an *abrupt* cliff]. —**a·brupt′ly** ***adv.*** —**a·brupt′ness** ***n.***

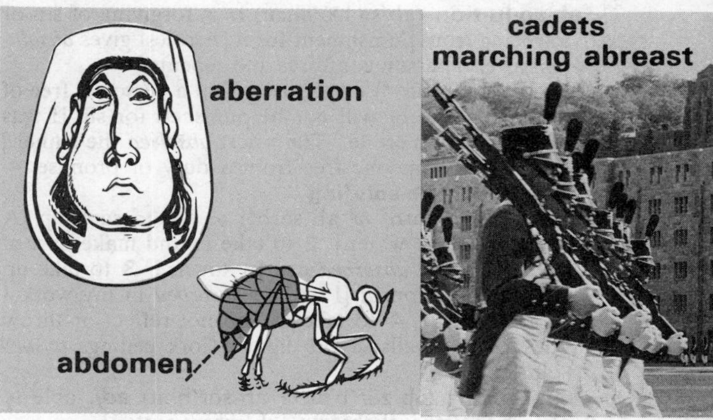


**ab·scess** (ab′ses) ***n.*** a sore, swollen, infected place in the body, filled with pus.

**ab·scessed** (ab′sest) ***adj.*** having an abscess.

**ab·scond** (əb skänd′) ***v.*** to run away and hide, especially in order to escape the law.

**ab·sence** (ab′s′ns) ***n.*** **1** the fact of being absent [During my *absence,* you do the dishes.] **2** the fact of being without; lack [In the *absence* of proof, she could not be held guilty.]



**ab·sent** (ab′s′nt) ***adj.*** **1** not present; away [No one in the class was *absent* that day.] **2** lacking or missing [If calcium is *absent* from the diet, the bones will become soft.] **3** not showing interest or attention [listening with an *absent* look on the face]. ◆***v.*** (ab sent′) to keep oneself away [to *absent* oneself from classes].

**ab·sen·tee** (ab′s′n tē′) ***n.*** a person who is absent, as from school, work, etc. ◆***adj.*** living far away from land or a building that one owns [an *absentee* landlord].

**ab·sent·ly** (ab′s′nt lē) ***adv.*** in an absent way; not paying attention [She smiled *absently.*]

**ab·sent-mind·ed** (ab′s′nt mīn′did) ***adj.*** **1** thinking or dreaming of something else and not paying attention. **2** always forgetting things.

**ab·so·lute** (ab′sə lo͞ot) ***adj.*** **1** perfect; complete; whole [It's hard to have *absolute* silence.] **2** not mixed; pure [*absolute* alcohol]. **3** not limited by any rules or conditions [Dictators are *absolute* rulers.] **4** positive; definite [an *absolute* certainty]. —**ab′so·lute·ly** ***adv.***

**absolute zero** the temperature at which it is believed that a substance would have no movement of its molecules and no heat. On the Celsius scale, absolute zero is about 273° below zero, and on the Fahrenheit scale it is nearly 460° below zero.

**ab·so·lu·tion** (ab′sə lo͞o′shən) ***n.*** a forgiving of sin or a freeing from punishment for it [A priest gives *absolution* after a person confesses and repents.]

**ab·solve** (əb zälv′) ***v.*** **1** to say that a person is free of guilt or blame or will not be punished for sin [I was *absolved* of the crime. The priest *absolved* the sinner.] **2** to make someone free from a duty or promise. —**ab·solved′, ab·solv′ing**

**ab·sorb** (əb zôrb′ *or* ab sôrb′) ***v.*** **1** to suck up [A sponge *absorbs* water.] **2** to take in and make part of itself [The city *absorbed* nearby towns.] **3** to take up the full attention of [I was so *absorbed* in my work I forgot to eat.] **4** to take in and not reflect or throw back [Black walls *absorb* light. Cork ceilings *absorb* sound.]

**ab·sorb·ent** (əb zôr′b′nt *or* ab sôr′b′nt) ***adj.*** able to absorb moisture, light, etc. [*absorbent* cotton].

**ab·sorb·ing** (əb zôr′biŋ *or* ab sôr′biŋ) ***adj.*** very interesting [She told an *absorbing* story.]

**ab·sorp·tion** (əb zôrp′shən *or* ab sôrp′shən) ***n.*** **1** an absorbing or being absorbed [The walls are insulated to lessen the *absorption* of heat.] **2** great interest or full attention [His *absorption* in the book made him late.]

**ab·stain** (əb stān′) ***v.*** to do without willingly; hold oneself back [to *abstain* from meat during Lent].

**ab·sten·tion** (əb sten′shən) ***n.*** the act of abstaining, or holding back [An *abstention* in voting is a refusal to vote either "yes" or "no."]



**ab·sti·nence** (ab′stə nəns) ***n.*** doing without some or all food, drink, or other pleasures willingly.

The word *abstinence* sometimes has the particular meaning of doing without alcoholic liquor.

**ab·stract** (ab strakt′ *or* ab′strakt) ***adj.*** **1** thought of apart from a particular act or thing [A just trial is a fair one, but justice itself is an *abstract* idea.] **2** hard to understand [That explanation is too *abstract*.] **3** formed with designs taken from real things, but not actually like any real object or being [an *abstract* painting]. *See the picture.* ◆***n.*** (ab′strakt) a shortened version of an article, speech, etc. ◆***v.*** (ab strakt′) to make a shortened version of; summarize [to *abstract* the record of a court trial].

**ab·stract·ed** (ab strak′tid) ***adj.*** thinking of something else; absent-minded.

**ab·strac·tion** (ab strak′shən) ***n.*** **1** an abstract idea, word, etc. ["Beauty" and "honesty" are *abstractions*.] **2** an abstract picture or piece of sculpture. **3** the act of thinking of other things; absent-mindedness [I was lost in *abstraction* and did not notice how much time had passed.]

**abstract sculpture**

**acacia**

**ab·struse** (ab stro͞os′) ***adj.*** hard to understand [Dictionary definitions should not be *abstruse*.]

**ab·surd** (əb surd′ *or* ab zurd′) ***adj.*** so clearly untrue or unreasonable as to be something to laugh at or make fun of [It is *absurd* to eat peas with a knife.] —**ab·surd′ly *adv.***

**ab·surd·i·ty** (əb sur′də tē *or* ab zur′də tē) ***n.*** the condition of being absurd; foolishness; nonsense [When you think about most superstitions, you can see the *absurdity* of them.] —*pl.* **ab·surd′i·ties**

**a·bun·dance** (ə bun′dəns) ***n.*** a great supply; an amount more than enough [Where there is an *abundance* of goods, prices are supposed to go down.]

**a·bun·dant** (ə bun′dənt) ***adj.*** **1** very plentiful; more than enough [The farmers had an *abundant* crop of grain last year.] **2** rich; well-supplied [a lake *abundant* in fish].

**a·buse** (ə byo͞oz′) ***v.*** **1** to use in a wrong or improper way [They never *abuse* the privilege of lunching in the classroom by leaving litter about.] **2** to hurt by treating badly; mistreat [It would be wrong to *abuse* animals in trying to train them.] **3** to scold or speak harshly about or to. —**a·bused′, a·bus′ing** ◆***n.*** (ə byo͞os′) **1** wrong, bad, or unjust use or practice [We object to any *abuse* of voting rights.] **2** unkind, cruel, or unfair treatment. **3** insulting or harshly scolding language.

**a·bu·sive** (ə byo͞os′iv) ***adj.*** **1** abusing; mistreating [an *abusive* guard]. **2** harshly scolding; insulting [*abusive* language].

**a·but** (ə but′) ***v.*** to touch at one end; border [Our pasture *abuts* their farm.] —**a·but′ted, a·but′ting**

**a·but·ment** (ə but′mənt) ***n.*** something that abuts or borders upon something else; especially, a part on the ground that supports an arch or the end of a bridge.

**a·bys·mal** (ə biz′m′l) ***adj.*** of or like an abyss; too deep to measure [*abysmal* poverty, *abysmal* ignorance]. —**a·bys′mal·ly *adv.***

**a·byss** (ə bis′) ***n.*** **1** a great, deep crack or gap in the earth; chasm. **2** anything too deep to measure [an *abyss* of shame].

**Ab·ys·sin·i·a** (ab′ə sin′ē ə) *the former name of* **Ethiopia.** —**Ab′ys·sin′i·an *adj., n.***

**AC, A.C., a.c.** *abbreviation for* **alternating current.**

**a·ca·cia** (ə kā′shə) ***n.*** **1** a tree or shrub of warm regions. It has feathery leaves and clusters of yellow or white flowers. *See the picture.* **2** *another name for* **locust tree.**

**ac·a·dem·ic** (ak′ə dem′ik) ***adj.*** **1** having to do with schools, colleges, or teaching [the *academic* life of a college professor]. **2** having to do with general education, especially the kind that prepares students who plan to go to college [Literature, languages, and social studies are included in an *academic* course.] **3** not practical; only in theory [an *academic* discussion about life on Venus]. *Also* **ac′a·dem′i·cal** —**ac′a·dem′i·cal·ly *adv.***

**a·cad·e·my** (ə kad′ə mē) ***n.*** **1** a private high school. **2** any school for special training, as in music, art, or military science. **3** a society of scholars, writers, artists, etc. working in the interests of the arts or sciences. —*pl.* **a·cad′e·mies**

**Academy** comes from the Greek name for a grove of trees near Athens. Plato, an ancient Greek philosopher and teacher, taught his students in that grove. The Greeks thought that it had once belonged to a hero in Greek legend named *Akademos*.

**A·ca·pul·co** (ak′ə po͞ol′kō *or* äk′ə po͞ol′kō) a seaport in southwestern Mexico, on the Pacific Ocean. It is a famous resort.

**ac·cede** (ak sēd′) ***v.*** **1** to begin to carry out the duties of a position or office [Elizabeth II *acceded* to the British throne in 1952.] **2** to give one's consent; agree [We are *acceding* to their request.] —**ac·ced′ed, ac·ced′ing**

**ac·cel·er·ate** (ək sel′ə rāt) ***v.*** **1** to increase the speed of; make run or work faster [The driver *accelerated* the engine.] **2** to hasten or bring about sooner [New pupils are *accelerating* the growth of the school.] —**ac·cel′er·at·ed, ac·cel′er·at·ing**

**ac·cel·er·a·tion** (ək sel′ə rā′shən) ***n.*** **1** the act of accelerating; increase in speed. **2** the rate at which speed is increased [New spark plugs improved the *acceleration* of the engine.]

**ac·cel·er·a·tor** (ək sel′ə rāt′ər) ***n.*** a thing that accelerates an action; especially, the foot pedal that can make an automobile go faster by feeding the engine more gasoline.

**ac·cent** (ak′sent) ***n.*** **1** extra force, or stress, given to some syllables or words in speaking [The *accent* in "accident" is on the first syllable.] **2** a mark used to show such stress, either as strong (′) or weak (′) [Note the strong and weak *accents* in "ac·cel′er·a′tor."] **3** the special way of pronouncing used by people from a certain region or country [My mother speaks English with an Irish *accent*.] **4** extra force given to certain beats in music to make rhythm. ◆***v.*** (*also* ak sent′) **1** to pronounce with special stress [*Accent* the second syllable of "Detroit."] **2** to mark with an accent. **3** to emphasize.

**ac·cen·tu·ate** (ak sen′cho͞o wāt) ***v.*** **1** to pronounce or mark with an accent or stress. **2** to make more likely to be noticed; emphasize [The low windows *accentuated* the height of the room.] —**ac·cen′tu·at·ed, ac·cen′tu·at·ing** —**ac·cen′tu·a′tion** ***n.***

**ac·cept** (ək sept′) ***v.*** **1** to take what is offered or given [Will you *accept* $20 for that old bicycle?] **2** to receive with favor; approve [We *accepted* the driver's apology.] **3** to agree to; consent to [Dale will not *accept* defeat.] **4** to answer "yes" to [We *accept* your invitation.] **5** to believe to be true [to *accept* a theory]. *See* SYNONYMS *at* **receive.**

**ac·cept·a·ble** (ək sep′tə b'l) ***adj.*** worth accepting; good enough; satisfactory; proper [an *acceptable* answer]. —**ac·cept′a·bly** ***adv.***

**ac·cept·ance** (ək sep′təns) ***n.*** **1** an accepting or being accepted [the *acceptance* of an award]. **2** approval or belief [That theory now has the *acceptance* of most scientists.]

**ac·cess** (ak′ses) ***n.*** **1** a way of approach [The *access* to the park is by this road.] **2** the right or ability to approach, enter, or use [Do the students have *access* to a good library?]

**ac·ces·si·ble** (ak ses′ə b'l) ***adj.*** **1** that can be approached or entered [The cafeteria is *accessible* only to employees.] **2** that can be got; obtainable [Fresh fruit is now *accessible* all winter long.] —**ac·ces′si·bil′i·ty** ***n.***

**ac·ces·sion** (ak sesh′ən) ***n.*** **1** a coming to the throne, power, etc. [the *accession* of Queen Victoria in 1837]. **2** increase by something added [The United States expanded west by the *accession* of a vast region in 1803.] **3** something added [The museum's new *accession* is a Picasso painting.]

**ac·ces·so·ry** (ək ses′ər ē) ***n.*** **1** something extra; thing added, as for convenience, comfort, or decoration [A radio and air conditioner are *accessories* on a car. A purse and gloves are *accessories* to an outfit.] **2** a person who helps another to break the law, although absent at the time of the crime [The doorkeeper became an *accessory* by helping the murderer escape.] —*pl.* **ac·ces′so·ries** ◆***adj.*** being something extra or added to help the more important thing [The vacuum cleaner has *accessory* attachments.]

**ac·ci·dent** (ak′sə dənt) ***n.*** **1** a happening that is not expected or planned [Our meeting was a happy *accident*.] **2** an unfortunate happening or instance of bad luck that causes damage or injury [I've had three *accidents* driving a car.] **3** fortune; chance [Some discoveries are made by *accident*.]

**ac·ci·den·tal** (ak′sə den′t'l) ***adj.*** happening by chance [Goodyear's discovery of how to vulcanize rubber was *accidental*.] —**ac′ci·den′tal·ly** ***adv.***

**ac·claim** (ə klām′) ***v.*** **1** to greet with loud applause or strong approval [The audience *acclaimed* the soprano for her brilliant solo.] **2** to announce or recognize by clapping hands, cheering, or some other show of approval [The crowd *acclaimed* the new president.] ◆***n.*** loud praise, approval, or welcome [The winning team returned to much *acclaim*.]



**ac·cla·ma·tion** (ak′lə mā′shən) ***n.*** **1** loud applause or strong approval [The champion was welcomed with wild *acclamation*.] **2** a vote made by voice that need not be counted because all or most of those voting clearly approve [The leader was elected by *acclamation*.]

**ac·cli·mate** (ak′lə māt *or* ə klī′mət) ***v.*** to get used to a new climate or different surroundings [to become *acclimated* to a new school]. *Also* **ac·cli·ma·tize** (ə klī′mə tīz) —**ac′cli·mat·ed, ac′cli·mat·ing**

**ac·co·lade** (ak′ə lād *or* ak ə lād′) ***n.*** something done or given as a sign of great respect [Applause from one's own orchestra is a high *accolade* for a soloist.]

**ac·com·mo·date** (ə käm′ə dāt) ***v.*** **1** to make fit; adjust [She *accommodated* her walk to the slow steps of her grandfather.] **2** to do a favor for [Chris *accommodated* Pat with a loan.] **3** to find room or lodging for [This motel will *accommodate* 250 people.] **4** to become adjusted in focusing [My eyes have trouble *accommodating* to faraway objects.] —**ac·com′mo·dat·ed, ac·com′mo·dat·ing**

**ac·com·mo·dat·ing** (ə käm′ə dāt′iŋ) ***adj.*** willing to please; ready to help; obliging [The *accommodating* driver helped us into the taxi.]

| | | | | | | | |
|---|---|---|---|---|---|---|---|
| **a** | fat | **ir** | here | **ou** | out | **zh** | leisure |
| **ā** | ape | **ī** | bite, fire | **u** | up | **ŋ** | ring |
| **ä** | car, lot | **ō** | go | **ur** | fur | | a *in* ago |
| **e** | ten | **ô** | law, horn | **ch** | chin | | e *in* agent |
| **er** | care | **oi** | oil | **sh** | she | **ə =** | i *in* unity |
| **ē** | even | **o͝o** | look | **th** | thin | | o *in* collect |
| **i** | hit | **o͞o** | tool | ***th*** | then | | u *in* focus |

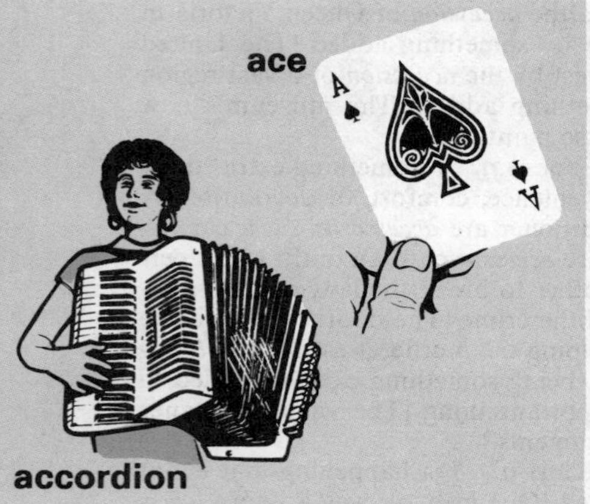

**ac·com·mo·da·tion** (ə käm′ə dā′shən) ***n.*** **1** a change so as to fit new conditions; adjustment [the *accommodation* of courses to the students' needs]. **2** a help or convenience [Free delivery is an *accommodation* to those who shop at our store.] **3 accommodations,** *pl.* lodgings or space for travelers, as in a hotel or ship [The *accommodations* at the inn were very comfortable.]

**ac·com·pa·ni·ment** (ə kum′pə ni mənt) ***n.*** something that goes along with another thing; especially, music played along with a solo part [the piano *accompaniment* to a song].



**ac·com·pa·nist** (ə kum′pə nist) ***n.*** a person who plays a musical accompaniment.

**ac·com·pa·ny** (ə kum′pə nē) ***v.*** **1** to go along with; be together with [At this movie, children must be *accompanied* by adults. Rain *accompanied* the high winds.] **2** to play a musical accompaniment for or to [Will you *accompany* my singing on your guitar?] —**ac·com′pa·nied, ac·com′pa·ny·ing**

SYNONYMS: **Accompany** means to go along with as a companion or friend [Please *accompany* me home.] **Escort** means to accompany someone so as to protect or be helpful [An usher *escorted* us down the aisle.] **Attend** means to be with someone so as to serve [a rich man *attended* by his valet].

**ac·com·plice** (ə käm′plis) ***n.*** a person who helps another break the law [The driver of the car was an *accomplice* in the robbery.]

**ac·com·plish** (ə käm′plish) ***v.*** to do; carry out [The task was *accomplished* in one day.]

**ac·com·plished** (ə käm′plisht) ***adj.*** **1** done; completed [an *accomplished* project]. **2** trained; skilled [an *accomplished* pianist].

**ac·com·plish·ment** (ə käm′plish mənt) ***n.*** **1** an accomplishing; completion. **2** a task that has been successfully completed; achievement [Digging the Panama Canal was a great *accomplishment*.] **3** an art or skill that has been learned [One of my cousin's *accomplishments* is cooking.]

**ac·cord** (ə kôrd′) ***v.*** **1** to give, grant, or award [The poet was *accorded* many honors.] **2** to be in agreement or harmony [The story you tell does not *accord* with the facts.] ◆***n.*** agreement; harmony [The three judges were in *accord* concerning the winner.] —**of one's own accord,** willingly, without being asked [Jane and Dan washed the dishes *of their own accord*.]

**ac·cord·ance** (ə kôrd′′ns) ***n.*** agreement; harmony [It was built in *accordance* with the plans.] —**ac·cord′ant** ***adj.***

**ac·cord·ing** (ə kôrd′iŋ) ***adj.*** agreeing; in harmony: *now used only in the following phrase.* —**according to, 1** in agreement with [The bus left *according to* schedule.] **2** in the order of [The plants were arranged *according to* height.] **3** as stated or reported by [*According to* the newspaper, the fire caused great damage.]

**ac·cord·ing·ly** (ə kôrd′iŋ lē) ***adv.*** **1** in a way that is fitting and proper [They were guests and were treated *accordingly*.] **2** therefore [We forgot to close the door; *accordingly,* the cat got out.]

**ac·cor·di·on** (ə kôr′dē ən) ***n.*** a musical instrument with keys, metal reeds, and a bellows. It is played by pulling out and pressing together the bellows to force air through the reeds, which are opened by fingering the keys. *See the picture.*

**ac·cost** (ə kôst′) ***v.*** to come close to and speak to, especially in an unfriendly way [Beggars *accosted* the tourists and demanded money.]

**ac·count** (ə kount′) ***v.*** **1** to consider or judge to be [Our team is *accounted* likely to win.] **2** to give a detailed record of money handled [Our treasurer can *account* for every penny spent.] **3** to give a satisfactory reason; explain [How do you *account* for your absence from school?] **4** to be the reason or cause [Carelessness *accounts* for many accidents.] ◆***n.*** **1** *often* **accounts,** *pl.* a statement of money received, paid, or owed; record of business dealings. **2** worth; importance [a thing of little *account*]. **3** an explanation [There is no satisfactory *account* of the cause of the disease.] **4** a report or story [The book is an *account* of their travels.] —**call to account,** to demand an explanation from. —**on account of,** because of. —**on no account,** not under any circumstances. —**on someone's account,** for someone's sake [I hope she did not agree to go just *on my account*.] —**take into account** or **take account of,** to allow for or consider. —**turn to account,** to get use or profit from.

**ac·count·a·ble** (ə koun′tə b′l) ***adj.*** **1** expected to account for what one does; responsible [In a democracy the government is *accountable* for its actions.] **2** that can be accounted for; explainable [Her anger is *accountable*.]

**ac·count·ant** (ə kount′′nt) ***n.*** a person whose work is keeping or examining accounts, or business records.

**ac·count·ing** (ə koun′tiŋ) ***n.*** **1** the system or work of keeping accounts, or business records. **2** a report on how accounts have been settled or balanced.

**ac·cou·ter** (ə ko͞ot′ər) ***v.*** to dress or outfit [The knights were *accoutered* in armor.]

**ac·cou·ter·ments** (ə ko͞ot′ər mənts) ***n.pl.*** **1** clothes; dress. **2** a soldier's equipment except clothes and weapons.

**Ac·cra** (ə krä′) the capital of Ghana, on the Atlantic Ocean.

**ac·cred·it** (ə kred′it) ***v.*** **1** to give someone the official power to act; authorize [She is an *accredited* agent for the company.] **2** to approve of as coming up to the required standards [an *accredited* college]. **3** to think of as belonging to; attribute [discoveries *accredited* to him].

**ac·cre·tion** (ə krē′shən) ***n.*** a coming or joining together of separate particles or parts [Limestone is formed by *accretion.*]

**ac·crue** (ə kro͞o′) ***v.*** **1** to come as a natural result or as an advantage [Power *accrues* to the wealthy.] **2** to be added at certain times as an increase [Interest *accrues* to your savings account daily.] —**ac·crued′, ac·cru′ing**

**ac·cu·mu·late** (ə kyo͞om′yə lāt) ***v.*** to pile up, collect, or gather over a period of time [Junk has *accumulated* in the garage. Our school has *accumulated* a large library.] —**ac·cu′mu·lat·ed, ac·cu′mu·lat·ing**

> **Accumulate** comes from a Latin verb meaning "to heap up." That verb comes from *cumulus,* the Latin word for "a heap or pile." We use the word *cumulus* also for a kind of cloud formed of round masses that pile up on each other.

**ac·cu·mu·la·tion** (ə kyo͞om′yə lā′shən) ***n.*** **1** the act of accumulating or collecting. **2** a collection of things [an *accumulation* of records].

**ac·cu·ra·cy** (ak′yər ə sē) ***n.*** the fact of being accurate, or without mistakes; precision; exactness.

**ac·cu·rate** (ak′yər it) ***adj.*** careful and exact; correct; without mistakes or errors [an *accurate* report; an *accurate* worker; an *accurate* clock]. —**ac′cu·rate·ly *adv.***

**ac·curs·ed** (ə kur′sid *or* ə kurst′) ***adj.*** **1** under a curse; sure to end badly. **2** very bad, unpleasant, or annoying [When will we see an end to this *accursed* rain?]

**ac·cu·sa·tion** (ak′yə zā′shən) ***n.*** a claim or charge that a person is guilty of doing wrong or of breaking the law [He denied her *accusation* that he had lied.]

**ac·cu·sa·tive** (ə kyo͞o′zə tiv) ***adj.*** showing the direct object of a verb or the object of a preposition. ◆***n.*** the accusative case.

> In Latin and some other languages, nouns, pronouns, and adjectives have special endings to show that they are in the **accusative** case. In English the objective case is sometimes called the accusative case, and only a few pronouns, as *him* and *them,* have these special endings.

**ac·cuse** (ə kyo͞oz′) ***v.*** **1** to charge someone with doing wrong or breaking the law [He is *accused* of robbing the store.] **2** to find fault with; blame [They *accused* her of being lazy.] —**ac·cused′, ac·cus′ing** —**ac·cus′er *n.***

**ac·cus·tom** (ə kus′təm) ***v.*** to make familiar by habit or use [I'll try to *accustom* myself to the new furniture.]

**ac·cus·tomed** (ə kus′təmd) ***adj.*** customary; usual [She greeted us with her *accustomed* charm.] —**accustomed to,** used to; in the habit of [He is *accustomed to* staying up late.]

**ace** (ās) ***n.*** **1** a playing card or a face of dice marked with one spot. *See the picture.* **2** an expert in some activity [an *ace* at selling cars]. **3** in tennis and some other games, a score made by a serve that is not returned. ◆***adj.*** expert; first-rate: *used only in everyday talk* [an *ace* mechanic].

**ac·e·tate** (as′ə tāt) ***n.*** a salt of acetic acid [Cellulose *acetate,* formed from acetic acid and cellulose, is used in making rayon, plastics, etc.]

**a·ce·tic acid** (ə sēt′ik) a sour, colorless liquid that has a sharp smell. It is found in vinegar.

**a·cet·y·lene** (ə set′′l ēn) ***n.*** a colorless, poisonous gas that burns brightly with a hot flame. It is used in blowtorches for welding or cutting metal.

**ache** (āk) ***v.*** **1** to have or give a dull, steady pain [My head *aches.*] **2** to want very much; long: *used only in everyday talk* [She is *aching* to take a trip.] —**ached, ach′ing** ◆***n.*** a dull, steady pain.

**a·chieve** (ə chēv′) ***v.*** **1** to do; succeed in doing; accomplish [He *achieved* very little while he was mayor.] **2** to get or reach by trying hard; gain [She *achieved* her ambition to be a lawyer.] —**a·chieved′, a·chiev′ing** *See* SYNONYMS *at* **reach.**

**a·chieve·ment** (ə chēv′mənt) ***n.*** **1** the act of achieving something [his *achievement* of a lifelong dream]. **2** something achieved by skill, work, courage, etc. [The landing of spacecraft on the moon was a remarkable *achievement.*]

**A·chil·les** (ə kil′ēz) a hero of Greek legend, a leader of the Greeks in the Trojan War. He was killed by an arrow that struck his heel, the only part of his body that could be injured.

**ac·id** (as′id) ***n.*** a chemical compound that contains hydrogen and forms a salt when combined with a base. Acids dissolve in water, taste sour, and make blue litmus turn red. ◆***adj.*** **1** of or like an acid. **2** sour; sharp and biting to the taste [A lemon is an *acid* fruit.] **3** very sarcastic [an *acid* remark]. *See* SYNONYMS *at* **sour.**



> **Acid** comes from *acidus,* the Latin word for "sour," which is related to *acus,* the Latin word for "needle." A needle has a sharp point, and an acid has a sharp taste.

**a·cid·i·ty** (ə sid′ə tē) ***n.*** the quality or condition of being acid; sourness.

**ac·knowl·edge** (ək näl′ij) ***v.*** **1** to admit to be true [I *acknowledge* that you are right.] **2** to recognize the authority of [They *acknowledged* him as their king.] **3** to recognize and answer or express one's thanks for [She *acknowledged* my greeting by smiling. Have you written to your uncle to *acknowledge* his gift?] —**ac·knowl′edged, ac·knowl′edg·ing**

**ac·knowl·edg·ment** or **ac·knowl·edge·ment** (ək näl′ij mənt) ***n.*** **1** the act of acknowledging. **2** something given or done in acknowledging.

**ACLU** American Civil Liberties Union.

**ac·me** (ak′mē) ***n.*** the highest point; peak [Skating in the Olympics was the *acme* of her career.]

**ac·ne** (ak′nē) ***n.*** a common skin disease of young people in which pimples keep appearing on the face, back, and chest. It happens when oil glands in the skin become clogged and swollen.

**ac·o·lyte** (ak′ə līt) ***n.*** someone who assists a priest at Mass, as an altar boy. *See the picture.*

| | | | | | | | |
|---|---|---|---|---|---|---|---|
| **a** | fat | **ir** | here | **ou** | out | **zh** | leisure |
| **ā** | ape | **ī** | bite, fire | **u** | up | **ng** | ring |
| **ä** | car, lot | **ō** | go | **ur** | fur | | a *in* ago |
| **e** | ten | **ô** | law, horn | **ch** | chin | | e *in* agent |
| **er** | care | **oi** | oil | **sh** | she | **ə =** | i *in* unity |
| **ē** | even | **o͝o** | look | **th** | thin | | o *in* collect |
| **i** | hit | **o͞o** | tool | ***th*** | then | | u *in* focus |

**ac·o·nite** (ak′ə nīt) ***n.*** **1** a poisonous plant with flowers shaped like hoods. **2** a medicine that was made from the roots of one kind of aconite but is no longer much used.

**a·corn** (ā′kôrn) ***n.*** the nut, or fruit, of the oak tree. *See the picture.*

**a·cous·tic** (ə ko͞os′tik) or **a·cous·ti·cal** (ə ko͞os′ti k'l) ***adj.*** having to do with hearing or with sound [An *acoustic* guitar is not amplified by electricity. The *acoustical* tile on the walls muffles the noise in the room.]

**a·cous·tics** (ə ko͞os′tiks) ***n.pl.*** **1** the qualities of a theater, room, etc. that have to do with how clearly sounds can be heard in it. **2** the science that deals with sound: *used with a singular verb.*

**ac·quaint** (ə kwānt′) ***v.*** **1** to let know; make aware; inform [*Acquaint* yourself with the facts.] **2** to cause to know personally; make familiar [Are you *acquainted* with Lou?]

**ac·quaint·ance** (ə kwānt′'ns) ***n.*** **1** knowledge of a thing or person got from one's own experience [She has some *acquaintance* with modern art.] **2** a person one knows but not as a close friend. **—make someone's acquaintance,** to become an acquaintance of someone.

**ac·qui·esce** (ak′wē es′) ***v.*** to agree without arguing; give in quietly [He *acquiesced* in our decision.] **—ac′qui·esced′, ac′qui·esc′ing**

**ac·qui·es·cence** (ak′wē es′'ns) ***n.*** the act of acquiescing, or agreeing without arguing. **—ac′qui·es′cent *adj.***

**ac·quire** (ə kwīr′) ***v.*** to get as one's own; become the owner of [The museum *acquired* an Egyptian mummy for its collection.] **—ac·quired′, ac·quir′ing** *See* SYNONYMS *at* **get.**

**ac·quire·ment** (ə kwīr′mənt) ***n.*** **1** the act of acquiring. **2** something acquired, as a skill gained by learning [Among her *acquirements* is the ability to play the guitar.]

**ac·qui·si·tion** (ak′wə zish′ən) ***n.*** **1** the act of acquiring. **2** something acquired [Our library's new *acquisitions* include an encyclopedia.]

**ac·quis·i·tive** (ə kwiz′ə tiv) ***adj.*** eager to get and keep things; greedy [an *acquisitive* collector of paintings].

**ac·quit** (ə kwit′) ***v.*** **1** to rule that a person accused of something is not guilty [The judge *acquitted* the suspect.] **2** to conduct oneself; behave [The players *acquitted* themselves very well, in spite of being booed.] **—ac·quit′ted, ac·quit′ting**

**ac·quit·tal** (ə kwit′'l) ***n.*** the freeing of an accused person by a ruling of "not guilty."

**a·cre** (ā′kər) ***n.*** **1** a measure of land equal to 43,560 square feet. **2 acres,** *pl.* lands or fields [golden *acres* of grain].

> **Acre** meant "field" in Old English. It is related to *ager,* the Latin word for "field," and to the word **agriculture.**

**a·cre·age** (ā′kər ij) ***n.*** the number of acres in a piece of land [What is the *acreage* of your uncle's farm?]

**ac·rid** (ak′rid) ***adj.*** **1** sharp, bitter, or irritating to the taste or smell [the *acrid* smell of ammonia]. **2** bitter or sarcastic in speech ["Of course you're always right," was his *acrid* comment.]

**ac·ri·mo·ni·ous** (ak′rə mō′nē əs) ***adj.*** bitter or sharp in manner or speech [an *acrimonious* quarrel].

**ac·ri·mo·ny** (ak′rə mō′nē) ***n.*** bitterness or sharpness of manner or speech.

**ac·ro·bat** (ak′rə bat) ***n.*** a performer who does tricks in tumbling or on the trapeze, tightrope, etc. *See the picture.*

**ac·ro·bat·ic** (ak′rə bat′ik) ***adj.*** **1** of an acrobat. **2** like an acrobat or an acrobat's tricks [an *acrobatic* dancer].

**ac·ro·bat·ics** (ak′rə bat′iks) ***n.pl.*** **1** an acrobat's tricks. **2** any hard tricks [mental *acrobatics*].

☆**ac·ro·nym** (ak′rə nim) ***n.*** a word that is formed from the first letters, or first syllables, of two or more words ["Comsat" is an *acronym* formed from "communication satellite."]

**A·crop·o·lis** (ə kräp′ə lis) the hill in Athens on top of which the Parthenon was built. *See the picture.*

**a·cross** (ə krôs′) ***adv.*** from one side to the other [The new bridge makes it easy to get *across* in a car.] ◆***prep.*** **1** from one side to the other of [We swam *across* the river.] **2** on the other side of [They live *across* the street.] **3** into contact with [I came *across* an old friend today.]

**a·cryl·ic fiber** (ə kril′ik) a fiber made of chemicals, that is used in making fabrics.

**act** (akt) ***n.*** **1** a thing done; deed [an *act* of bravery]. **2** an action; a doing of something [caught in the *act* of stealing]. **3** a law; decree [an *act* of Congress]. **4** one of the main divisions of a play, opera, etc. [The first *act* takes place in a palace.] **5** any of the separate performances on a variety program [The clown *act* came next.] **6** a showing of some emotion that is not real or true [Bill's anger was just an *act.*] ◆***v.*** **1** to play the part of, as on a stage [She *acted* Juliet.] **2** to behave like [Don't *act* the fool.] **3** to seem or pretend to be [He *acted* worried.] **4** to do something [We must *act* now if we want tickets.] **5** to have an effect [Acids *act* on metal.] —☆**act up,** to behave playfully or to misbehave: *used only in everyday talk.*

**act·ing** (ak′tiŋ) ***adj.*** taking over another's duties for a while [Who is the *acting* manager when the usual one is absent?]

**ac·tion** (ak′shən) ***n.*** **1** the doing of something [An emergency calls for quick *action.*] **2** an act or thing done. **3 actions,** *pl.* behavior [the *actions* of a coward]. **4** the effect produced by something [the *action* of a drug]. **5** the way of moving, working, etc. [the *action* of a washing machine]. **6** a lawsuit. **7** combat in war; battle [He was wounded in *action.*] —**in action,** active; in motion. **—take action, 1** to become active. **2** to start a lawsuit.

**ac·ti·vate** (ak′tə vāt) ***v.*** to make active; put into action [You can *activate* a power saw by turning on the switch.] **—ac′ti·vat·ed, ac′ti·vat·ing —ac′ti·va′tion *n.***

**ac·tive** (ak′tiv) ***adj.*** **1** acting; working [an *active* volcano]. **2** full of action; lively; busy; quick [She's an *active* child.] **3** having the verb in the form (called *voice*) that shows its subject as doing the action: opposite of *passive* [In the sentence "we ate the cake," the verb "ate" is in the *active* voice.] **—ac′tive·ly *adv.***

> SYNONYMS: **Active** is used of someone or something that is normal in action or operation or very lively or quick [an *active* golfer throughout

her life]. **Energetic** suggests the use of much energy or effort [Running gives them an *energetic* workout.] **Vigorous** means forceful, healthy, and strong [a *vigorous* tomato plant].

**ac·tiv·i·ty** (ak tiv′ə tē) ***n.*** **1** the condition of being active; action; motion [There was not much *activity* in the shopping mall today.] **2** normal power of mind or body; liveliness; alertness [His mental *activity* at age eighty was remarkable.] **3** something that one does besides one's regular work [We take part in many *activities* after school.] —*pl.* **ac·tiv′i·ties**

**ac·tor** (ak′tər) ***n.*** a person who acts in plays, movies, television shows, etc.

**ac·tress** (ak′tris) ***n.*** a woman or girl who acts in plays, movies, television shows, etc.

**ac·tu·al** (ak′cho͞o wəl) ***adj.*** as it really is; in fact; real; true [The *actual* cost was higher than we expected. Who is the *actual* ruler of that country?] *See* SYNONYMS *at* **true.**

**ac·tu·al·i·ty** (ak′cho͞o wal′ə tē) ***n.*** actual fact or condition; reality [In *actuality*, this clean-looking water is polluted.]

**ac·tu·al·ly** (ak′cho͞o wəl ē *or* ak′chə lē) ***adv.*** really; in fact [We *actually* had no money.]

**ac·tu·ate** (ak′cho͞o wāt) ***v.*** **1** to put into action [The clothes washer is *actuated* by pushing a button.] **2** to cause to take action [They were *actuated* by a wish to be helpful.] —**ac′tu·at·ed, ac′tu·at·ing**

**a·cu·men** (ə kyo͞o′mən) ***n.*** keenness and quickness in understanding and dealing with a situation; shrewdness [It took political *acumen* to get the law passed.]

**ac·u·punc·ture** (ak′yoo puŋk′chər) ***n.*** a way of treating some illnesses or of lessening pain by putting thin needles into certain parts of the body for a time. This method has been used by the Chinese for many centuries.

**a·cute** (ə kyo͞ot′) ***adj.*** **1** having a sharp point [a leaf with an *acute* tip]. **2** very keen and sensitive; sharp and quick [*acute* eyesight or hearing]. **3** very strong and deep [*acute* pain; *acute* jealousy]. **4** severe and serious, but only for a short time; not chronic [an *acute* disease]. **5** very severe and causing a problem [an *acute* shortage of gasoline]. **6** less than 90 degrees: said of an angle. —**a·cute′ly** ***adv.*** —**a·cute′ness** ***n.***

**acute accent** a mark (´) placed over a certain letter or syllable.

An **acute accent** may be used to show the sound of a vowel, as over an *e* in French (*divorcée*) or to show heavy stress on a syllable, as in Spanish (*capón*).

**ad** (ad) ***n.*** *a short form of* **advertisement.**

**A.D.** of the Christian era; from the year in which Jesus Christ is believed to have been born.

**A.D.** is an abbreviation of *Anno Domini,* Latin for "in the year of the Lord." The Roman emperor Augustus lived from 63 B.C. to 14 A.D.

**ad·age** (ad′ij) ***n.*** an old saying that has been accepted as wise or true ["Where there's smoke, there's fire" is an *adage*.]

**a·da·gi·o** (ə dä′jō *or* ə dä′jē ō) ***adj., adv.*** slow or slowly. This is an Italian word used in music to tell how fast a piece should be played.

**Ad·am** (ad′əm) in the Bible, the first man and the husband of Eve.

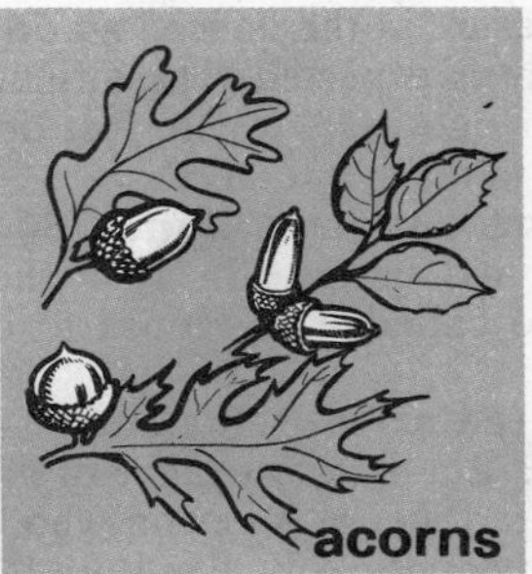

Adam's apple

acorns

acrobats

Acropolis

**ad·a·mant** (ad′ə mənt) ***adj.*** not giving in easily; firm; not yielding [They were *adamant* in their refusal to help.]

**Ad·ams** (ad′əmz), **John** 1735–1826; the second president of the United States, from 1797 to 1801.

**Adams, John Quin·cy** (kwin′sē) 1767–1848; the sixth president of the United States, from 1825 to 1829. He was the son of John Adams.

**Adams, Samuel** 1722–1803; American statesman. He was a leader of the American Revolution.

**Adam's apple** a bulge in the throat, seen especially in men. It is formed by a cartilage of the upper end of the windpipe, or trachea. *See the picture.*

**a·dapt** (ə dapt′) ***v.*** **1** to change so as to make fit or usable [A sliding curtain rod can be *adapted* for windows of various widths.] **2** to change oneself to fit new conditions [The colonists had to *adapt* themselves to the new land.] —**a·dapt′er** or **a·dap′tor** ***n.***

**a·dapt·a·ble** (ə dap′tə b′l) ***adj.*** **1** that can be adapted or made to fit. **2** able to adapt oneself easily to changes.

**ad·ap·ta·tion** (ad′əp tā′shən) ***n.*** **1** the act of adapting or changing so as to fit or become suitable. **2** a thing adapted from something else, as a play from a novel.

**ADC** or **A.D.C.** Aid to Dependent Children.

**add** (ad) ***v.*** **1** to put or join something to another thing so that there will be more or so as to mix into one thing [We *added* some books to our library. *Add* two cups of sugar to the batter.] **2** to say further [Jane agreed to go but *added* that she would be late.] **3** to join numbers so as to get a total, or sum [*Add* 3 and 5.] **4** to cause an increase [Live music *added* to



| | | | | | | | |
|---|---|---|---|---|---|---|---|
| **a** | fat | **ir** | here | **ou** | out | **zh** | leisure |
| **ā** | ape | **ī** | bite, fire | **u** | up | **ŋ** | ring |
| **ä** | car, lot | **ō** | go | **ʉr** | fur | | a *in* ago |
| **e** | ten | **ô** | law, horn | **ch** | chin | | e *in* agent |
| **er** | care | **oi** | oil | **sh** | she | ə = | i *in* unity |
| **ē** | even | **oo** | look | **th** | thin | | o *in* collect |
| **i** | hit | **o͞o** | tool | ***th*** | then | | u *in* focus |

our pleasure at the dance.] —**add up,** **1** to equal the sum that is expected [These figures don't *add up.*] **2** to seem right [His excuse just doesn't *add up.*] —**add up to,** to reach a total of.

**Ad·dams** (ad′əmz), **Jane** 1860–1935; U.S. social worker and writer. In 1889 she opened a place in Chicago called Hull-House to offer services to the poor.

**ad·der** (ad′ər) ***n.*** **1** a small, poisonous snake of Europe. **2** a harmless snake of North America.

**ad·dict** (ad′ikt) ***n.*** a person who has a habit so strong that he cannot easily give it up [a drug *addict*]. ➜***v.*** (ə dikt′) to give oneself up to some strong habit [Some people are *addicted* to watching television.] —**ad·dic′tion** ***n.***

☆**adding machine** a machine that prints numbers and then adds them up when one presses certain keys. Some adding machines can also subtract, divide, and multiply.

**Ad·dis A·ba·ba** (ä′dis ä′bə bə *or* ə bä′bə) the capital of Ethiopia.

**ad·di·tion** (ə dish′ən) ***n.*** **1** an adding of numbers to get a sum or total. **2** a joining of one thing to another thing [The lemonade was improved by the *addition* of sugar.] **3** a thing or part added [The gymnasium is a new *addition* to our school.] —**in addition to,** besides [*In addition to* playing the flute, Sue is on the swimming team.]



**ad·di·tion·al** (ə dish′ən əl) ***adj.*** more; extra; added [We ordered an *additional* supply of pencils.] —**ad·di′tion·al·ly** ***adv.***

**ad·di·tive** (ad′ə tiv) ***n.*** a substance added to another in small amounts for a special reason, as a chemical added to food to keep it from spoiling.

**ad·dle** (ad′'l) ***v.*** **1** to make or become confused [The wine *addled* his mind.] **2** to make or become rotten: said of an egg. —**ad′dled, ad′dling**

**ad·dle·brained** (ad′'l brānd′) ***adj.*** having a confused mind; mixed up.

**ad·dress** (ə dres′) ***v.*** **1** to speak to or write to; direct one's words to [Please *address* your remarks to me. The principal will *address* our first assembly.] **2** to write on a letter or package the name, street number, city, etc. of the one to whom it is being sent. **3** to use the right form in speaking or writing to [How does one *address* the mayor?] **4** to get oneself working [We must *address* ourselves to the problem.] ➜***n.*** **1** a written or spoken speech. **2** (ə dres′ *or* ad′res) the place to which mail or goods can be sent to one; place where one lives or works.

adobe

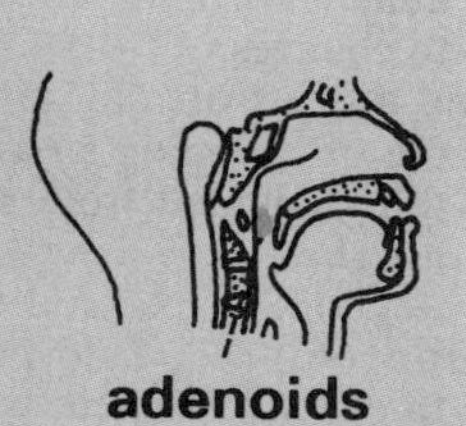

adenoids

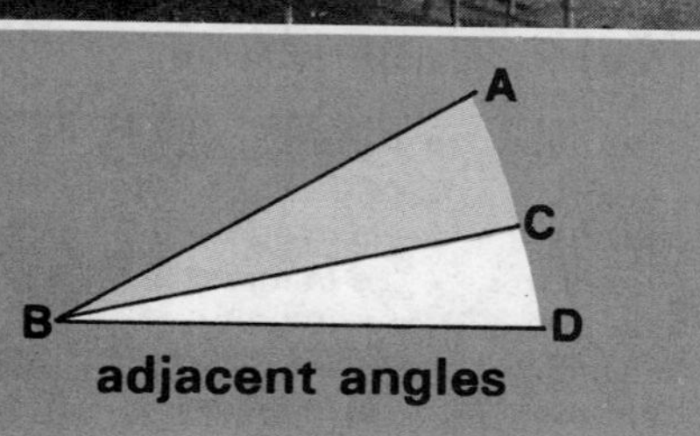


adjacent angles

adjutant stork
1.5 m (5 ft) high

**ad·duce** (ə do͞os′ *or* ə dyo͞os′) ***v.*** to give as a reason or proof [To show that the earth is not flat he *adduced* the fact that ships disappear below the horizon.] —**ad·duced′, ad·duc′ing**

**A·den** (äd′'n, ād′'n) a seaport in southwestern Arabia, on the Arabian Sea. It is the capital of one of the two countries called Yemen.

**ad·e·noids** (ad′'n oidz) ***n.pl.*** growths of tissue in the upper part of the throat, behind the nose. Adenoids sometimes swell up and make it hard to breathe and speak. *See the picture.*

**a·dept** (ə dept′) ***adj.*** highly skilled; expert [He's quite *adept* at making people feel at home.]

**ad·e·qua·cy** (ad′ə kwə sē) ***n.*** the fact of being enough or good enough for what is needed [the *adequacy* of their diet].

**ad·e·quate** (ad′ə kwət) ***adj.*** enough or good enough for what is needed; sufficient; suitable [an *adequate* supply of food; *adequate* skills]. —**ad′e·quate·ly** ***adv.***

**ad·here** (əd hir′) ***v.*** **1** to stick and not come loose; stay attached [This stamp won't *adhere* to the envelope.] **2** to stay firm in supporting or approving [to *adhere* to a plan; to *adhere* to a leader]. —**ad·hered′, ad·her′ing**

**ad·her·ence** (əd hir′əns) ***n.*** a supporting or approving of a person, idea, etc.

**ad·her·ent** (əd hir′ənt) ***n.*** a supporter of a person, idea, etc. ➜***adj.*** sticking fast; attached.

**ad·he·sion** (əd hē′zhən) ***n.*** the act of sticking to something or of being stuck together.

**ad·he·sive** (əd hēs′iv) ***adj.*** **1** sticking and not coming loose; clinging. **2** having a sticky surface [*Adhesive* tape is used to hold bandages in place.] ➜***n.*** a sticky substance [Glue is an *adhesive.*]

**a·dieu** (ə dyo͞o′ *or* ə do͞o′) ***interj., n.*** goodbye.

☆**a·di·os** (a′dē ōs′) ***interj.*** goodbye. *This word is from Spanish.*

**Ad·i·ron·dacks** (ad′ə rän′daks) a mountain range in northeastern New York State: *also called* **Adirondack Mountains.**

**adj.** *abbreviation for* **adjective.**

**ad·ja·cent** (ə jās′ənt) ***adj.*** near or next [The playground is *adjacent* to the school.]

**adjacent angles** two angles having the same vertex and a side in common. *See the picture.*

**ad·jec·tive** (aj′ik tiv) ***n.*** a word used with a noun or pronoun to tell which, what kind of, how many, or whose [In the sentence "Every egg was fresh," the words "every" and "fresh" are *adjectives.*] —**ad·jec·ti·val** (aj′ik tī′v'l) ***adj.***

**ad·join** (ə join′) ***v.*** **1** to be next to [The garage *adjoins* the house.] **2** to be next to each other; be side by side [The houses *adjoin.*] —**ad·join′ing** ***adj.***

**ad·journ** (ə jurn′) ***v.*** **1** to close a session or meeting for the day or for a time [Congress has *adjourned* for two weeks.] **2** to change the place of meeting: *used* only in everyday talk [Let's adjourn to the lounge.] — **ad·journ'ment** *n.*

**ad·judge** (ə juj') **v.** **1** to decide or declare after much thought [The prisoner was *adjudged* innocent.] **2** to give or award by law [A sum of $9,000 was *adjudged* to the accident victim.] —**ad·judged', ad·judg'ing**

**ad·junct** (aj'uŋkt) ***n.*** a less important thing added to something more important [We planted an orchard as an *adjunct* to our farm.]

**ad·jure** (ə joor') **v.** to command or ask earnestly or solemnly [The judge *adjured* the witness to tell all he knew.] —**ad·jured', ad·jur'ing** —**ad·ju·ra·tion** (aj'oo rā'shən) ***n.***

**ad·just** (ə just') **v.** **1** to change or move so as to make fit [You can *adjust* the piano bench to suit your size.] **2** to arrange the parts of to make work correctly; regulate [My watch needs *adjusting.*] **3** to settle or put in order [We *adjust* our accounts at the end of the month.] **4** to get used to one's surroundings [They could not *adjust* to life on the farm.]

**ad·just·a·ble** (ə jus'tə b'l) ***adj.*** that can be adjusted [This chair is *adjustable* for reclining.]

**ad·just·er** or **ad·jus·tor** (ə jus'tər) ***n.*** a person or thing that adjusts something [An insurance *adjuster* decides how much to pay in a claim.]

**ad·just·ment** (ə just'mənt) ***n.*** **1** a changing or settling of things to bring them into proper order or relation [She made a quick *adjustment* to her new job.] **2** a way or device by which parts are adjusted [An *adjustment* on our television set can make the picture brighter.]

**ad·ju·tant** (aj'ə tənt) ***n.*** **1** an assistant; especially, an army officer who serves as a secretary to the commanding officer. **2** a large stork of India and Africa: *its full name is* **adjutant stork**. *See the picture.*

**ad-lib** (ad'lib') **v.** to make up and put in words, gestures, etc. not in the script as one is performing: *used only in everyday talk* [Good actors learn to *ad-lib* when they forget their lines.]—**ad'-libbed', ad'-lib'bing**

> **Ad-lib** is a shortened form of a Latin phrase *ad libitum,* meaning "as one pleases," that is used in music to mark a part that performers can change or leave out as they please.

**Adm.** *abbreviation for* **Admiral.**

☆**ad·man** (ad'man') ***n.*** a man whose work or business is advertising. —*pl.* **ad·men** (ad'men')

**ad·min·is·ter** (əd min'ə stər) **v.** **1** to manage or direct [The principal *administers* the school.] **2** to give or carry out [The courts *administer* justice.] **3** to give or apply medicine, treatment, etc. [We were trained to *administer* first aid to injured persons.] **4** to direct the taking of an oath [The Chief Justice *administers* the oath of office to a president-elect.] **5** to give help [She *administers* to the sick.]

**ad·min·is·trate** (əd min'ə strāt) **v.** *same as* **administer.** —**ad·min'is·trat·ed, ad·min'is·trat·ing**

**ad·min·is·tra·tion** (əd min'ə strā'shən) ***n.*** **1** an administering; management; direction. **2** *often* **Administration,** the president and the other people who work in the executive branch of a government [The *Administration* was criticized for its foreign policy.] **3** their term of office [Johnson was vice-president during Kennedy's *administration.*] **4** the people who manage a company, school, or other organization. — **ad·min'is·tra'tive** ***adj.***

**ad·min·is·tra·tor** (əd min'ə strāt'ər) ***n.*** a person who administers or directs something; executive; manager.

**ad·mi·ra·ble** (ad'mər ə b'l) ***adj.*** deserving to be admired or praised; excellent [an *admirable* student]. — **ad'mi·ra·bly** ***adv.***

**ad·mi·ral** (ad'mər əl) ***n.*** **1** the commanding officer of a navy or of a fleet of ships. **2** a naval officer of the highest rank.

**ad·mi·ral·ty** (ad'mər əl tē) ***n.*** **1** the British department of the navy. **2** the branch of law that deals with ships and shipping. —*pl.* **ad'mi·ral·ties**

**ad·mi·ra·tion** (ad'mə rā'shən) ***n.*** **1** a feeling of delight and pleased approval at anything fine, skillful, beautiful, etc. [The pitcher won the *admiration* of his teammates.] **2** a thing or person bringing about such feelings [Their new kitchen is the *admiration* of all their neighbors.]

**ad·mire** (əd mīr') **v.** to regard with wonder, delight, and pleased approval [Her statue was *admired* by everyone.] —**ad·mired', ad·mir'ing** —**ad·mir'er** ***n.*** — **ad·mir'ing·ly** ***adv.***

**ad·mis·si·ble** (əd mis'ə b'l) ***adj.*** that can be admitted, accepted, or allowed [A witness's opinions are not *admissible* evidence in a trial.]

**ad·mis·sion** (əd mish'ən) ***n.*** **1** the act of admitting or of being admitted. **2** the right of entering [The reporter was refused *admission* to the meeting.] **3** the price paid for entering [*Admission* to the movie was three dollars.] **4** an admitting of the truth of something; confession [His silence was an *admission* of guilt.] 11

**ad·mit** (əd mit') **v.** **1** to permit or give the right to enter [One ticket *admits* two persons.] **2** to have room for [The hall *admits* 500 people.] **3** to take or accept as being true; confess [Lucy will not *admit* her mistake.] —**ad·mit'ted, ad·mit'ting**

**ad·mit·tance** (əd mit''ns) ***n.*** the right to enter [Is there *admittance* to the library on Sunday?]

**ad·mit·ted·ly** (əd mit'id lē) ***adv.*** by one's own admission or confession [I am *admittedly* afraid to enter the old house at night.]

**ad·mix·ture** (ad miks'chər) ***n.*** **1** a mixture. **2** a thing added in mixing.

**ad·mon·ish** (əd män'ish) **v.** **1** to warn a person to correct some fault [The judge *admonished* her to drive more slowly.] **2** to criticize in a mild way [Bill was *admonished* for coming home late.]

**ad·mo·ni·tion** (ad'mə nish'ən) ***n.*** **1** a warning to correct some fault. **2** mild criticism.

**a·do** (ə dōō') ***n.*** fuss; trouble [Much *ado* was made about her going away for a week.]

☆**a·do·be** (ə dō'bē) ***n.*** **1** brick made of clay dried in the sun instead of baked by fire. **2** the clay of which such brick is made. **3** a building made of adobe. *See the picture.*

| | | | | | | | |
|---|---|---|---|---|---|---|---|
| **a** | fat | **ir** | here | **ou** | out | **zh** | leisure |
| **ā** | ape | **ī** | bite, fire | **u** | up | **ŋ** | ring |
| **ä** | car, lot | **ō** | go | **ur** | fur | | a *in* ago |
| **e** | ten | **ô** | law, horn | **ch** | chin | | e *in* agent |
| **er** | care | **oi** | oil | **sh** | she | **ə =** | i *in* unity |
| **ē** | even | **oo** | look | **th** | thin | | o *in* collect |
| **i** | hit | **ōō** | tool | ***th*** | then | | u *in* focus |

**ad·o·les·cence** (ad′ə les″ns) ***n.*** the time of life between childhood and adulthood; youth.

**ad·o·les·cent** (ad′ə les″nt) ***adj.*** **1** growing up; developing from a child to an adult. **2** of or like an adolescent; not yet grown up. ✦***n.*** a boy or girl between childhood and adulthood; teen-age person.

**a·dopt** (ə däpt′) ***v.*** **1** to choose and take into one's family by a legal process [They *adopted* their daughter when she was four months old.] **2** to take and use as one's own [He *adopted* her teaching methods for his own classroom.] **3** to choose or follow [We must *adopt* a new plan of action.] —**a·dop′tion** ***n.***

**a·dor·a·ble** (ə dôr′ə b′l) ***adj.*** very attractive and likable; delightful; charming: *used only in everyday talk* [What an *adorable* cottage!]

**ad·o·ra·tion** (ad′ə rā′shən) ***n.*** **1** the act of worshiping. **2** great love and respect.



**a·dore** (ə dôr′) ***v.*** **1** to worship as divine ["O come let us *adore* Him."] **2** to love greatly or honor highly [He *adored* his wife.] **3** to like very much: *used only in everyday talk* [She *adored* the hat.] —**a·dored′, a·dor′ing**

**a·dorn** (ə dôrn′) ***v.*** to add beauty or splendor to; decorate [A gold vase *adorned* the table.]

**a·dorn·ment** (ə dôrn′mənt) ***n.*** **1** the act of adorning [Men wear ties for *adornment*.] **2** something that adorns; decoration; ornament [Paintings and other *adornments* covered the walls.]

**A·dri·at·ic** (ā′dri at′ik) a sea between Italy and Yugoslavia, that is an arm of the Mediterranean: *also called* **Adriatic Sea**.

**a·drift** (ə drift′) ***adv., adj.*** **1** floating freely without being steered; drifting [The boat was *adrift* in the ocean.] **2** without any clear aim or purpose [Having no work, he felt *adrift* in life.]

**a·droit** (ə droit′) ***adj.*** skillful and clever [It will take *adroit* handling to keep them both satisfied.] —**a·droit′ly** ***adv.*** —**a·droit′ness** ***n.***

**ad·u·la·tion** (aj′ə lā′shən) ***n.*** greater flattery or praise than is proper or deserved [The singer was greeted by the *adulation* of thousands of fans.]

**a·dult** (ə dult′ *or* ad′ult) ***adj.*** **1** grown up; having reached full size and strength [an *adult* person or plant]. **2** of or for grown men or women [an *adult* novel or play]. ✦***n.*** **1** a man or woman who is fully grown up; mature person. **2** an animal or plant that is fully developed. —**a·dult′hood** ***n.***

**a·dul·ter·ate** (ə dul′tər āt) ***v.*** to make impure or of poorer quality by adding a harmful or unnecessary substance [milk *adulterated* with water]. —**a·dul′ter·at·ed, a·dul′ter·at·ing** —**a·dul′ter·a′tion** ***n.***

**a·dul·ter·ous** (ə dul′tər əs) ***adj.*** guilty of adultery.

**a·dul·ter·y** (ə dul′tər ē) ***n.*** the act of breaking the marriage vows by having sex with someone not one's husband or wife. —*pl.* **a·dul′ter·ies**

**adv.** *abbreviation for* **adverb**.

**ad·vance** (əd vans′) ***v.*** **1** to go or bring forward; move ahead [On first down they *advanced* the football two yards.] **2** to suggest; offer [A new plan has been *advanced*.] **3** to help to grow or develop; promote [This law *advances* the building of new homes.] **4** to cause to happen earlier [The test date was *advanced* from May 10 to May 5.] **5** to make or become higher; increase [Prices continue to *advance*.] **6** to lend [Writers are often *advanced* money before they finish writing their books.] **7** to get a higher or more important position [She *advanced* all the way to principal of the school.] —**ad·vanced′, ad·vanc′ing** ✦***n.*** **1** a moving forward or ahead; progress [new *advances* in science]. **2** a rise in value or cost [The *advance* in prices was greater than in wages.] **3** a payment made before it is due, as of wages. **4 advances,** ***pl.*** attempts to gain favor or become friendly [Try to encourage your neighbors' *advances*.] ✦***adj.*** **1** in front [an *advance* guard]. **2** ahead of time [*advance* information]. —**in advance, 1** in front. **2** before due; ahead of time [Must we pay the rent *in advance*?]

SYNONYMS: **Advance** means to help hurry along the progress of something [a theory that *advanced* science]. **Promote** means to help in the setting up or bringing about of something [acts that *promote* peace]. **Further** suggests a bringing closer something that is wanted or needed [actions taken to *further* full employment].

**ad·vanced** (əd vanst′) ***adj.*** **1** in advance; in front. **2** far on in life; old [She started a new career at an *advanced* age.] **3** ahead of the times or of other people [*advanced* ideas]. **4** at a higher level; not at the beginning [*advanced* studies].

**ad·vance·ment** (əd vans′mənt) ***n.*** **1** an advancing, or moving forward. **2** the fact of being promoted to a higher position. **3** the act of getting or making better [We must work for the *advancement* of human beings.]

**ad·van·tage** (əd van′tij) ***n.*** **1** a more favorable position; better chance [My speed gave me an *advantage* over them.] **2** a thing, condition, or event that can help one; benefit [What are the *advantages* of a smaller school?] —**take advantage of,** to make use of for one's own benefit.

**ad·van·ta·geous** (ad′vən tā′jəs) ***adj.*** giving advantage; favorable; helpful [an *advantageous* position].

**Ad·vent** (ad′vent) ***n.*** **1** the period including the four Sundays just before Christmas. **2** Christ's birth. **3 advent,** a coming or arrival [the *advent* of spring].

**ad·ven·ture** (əd ven′chər) ***n.*** **1** an exciting and dangerous happening [He told of his *adventures* in the jungle.] **2** an unusual experience that is remembered [Going to a circus is an *adventure* for a child.]

**ad·ven·tur·er** (əd ven′chər ər) ***n.*** **1** a person who has or looks for adventures. **2** a person who tries to become rich in a dishonest or tricky way.

**ad·ven·tur·ous** (əd ven′chər əs) ***adj.*** **1** liking adventure; willing to take risks [an *adventurous* explorer]. *Also* **ad·ven′ture·some**. **2** full of danger; risky [an *adventurous* journey].

**ad·verb** (ad′vʉrb) ***n.*** a word used with a verb, adjective, or another adverb to tell when, where, how, what kind, or how much. *Quickly* tells how in "run *quickly*"; *always* tells when in "*always* sad"; *bright* tells what kind in "*bright* red dress"; *very* tells how much in "run *very* quickly." —**ad·ver·bi·al** (ad vur′bē əl) ***adj.***

**ad·ver·sar·y** (ad′vər ser′ē) ***n.*** a person who is against another; enemy or opponent. —*pl.* **ad′ver·sar′ies**

**ad·verse** (ad vurs′ *or* ad′vərs) ***adj.*** **1** coming against someone or something; opposed [*adverse* river currents; *adverse* criticism]. **2** not helpful; harmful [the *adverse* effects of a dry spell on crops]. —**ad·verse′ly** ***adv.***

**ad·ver·si·ty** (ad vur′sə tē) ***n.*** misfortune; bad luck; trouble. —*pl.* **ad·ver′si·ties**

**ad·ver·tise** (ad′vər tīz) ***v.*** **1** to tell about a product in public and in such a way as to make people want to buy it [to *advertise* cars on television and in magazines]. **2** to announce or ask for publicly, as in a newspaper [to *advertise* a house for rent; to *advertise* for a sales clerk]. —**ad′ver·tised, ad′ver·tis·ing** —**ad′ver·tis′er** ***n.***

**Advertise** comes from a word in Latin which means "to turn to." Advertising is meant to turn our attention to something so that we will want to use or buy it.

**ad·ver·tise·ment** (ad′vər tīz′mənt *or* əd vur′tiz mənt) ***n.*** a public announcement, as in a newspaper, advertising something.

**ad·ver·tis·ing** (ad′vər tī′ziŋ) ***n.*** **1** an advertisement or advertisements. **2** the work of preparing advertisements and getting them printed or on radio and TV [*Advertising* is a major industry in this country.]

**ad·vice** (əd vīs′) ***n.*** opinion given as to what to do or how to do something [We followed her *advice* in selecting a new home.]

**ad·vis·a·ble** (əd vī′zə b'l) ***adj.*** being good advice; wise; sensible [It is *advisable* to use the seat belts in a car.] —**ad·vis′a·bil′i·ty** ***n.***

**ad·vise** (əd vīz′) ***v.*** **1** to give advice or an opinion to [The doctor *advised* me to have an operation.] **2** to offer something as advice; recommend [I *advised* a long vacation.] **3** to notify; inform [The letter *advised* us of the time of the meeting.] —**ad·vised′, ad·vis′ing**

**ad·vise·ment** (əd vīz′mənt) ***n.*** careful thought; consideration [They will take our suggestion under *advisement* before making a decision.]

**ad·vis·er** or **ad·vi·sor** (əd vī′zər) ***n.*** a person who advises or gives an opinion.

**ad·vi·so·ry** (əd vī′zər ē) ***adj.*** advising or able to advise [*advisory* experts]. ◆***n.*** a warning that bad weather is on the way. —*pl.* **ad·vi′so·ries**

**ad·vo·ca·cy** (ad′və kə sē) ***n.*** the act of advocating; a speaking or writing in support of something.

**ad·vo·cate** (ad′və kāt) ***v.*** to speak or write in support of; be in favor of [The senator *advocated* a new housing bill.] —**ad′vo·cat·ed, ad′vo·cat·ing** ◆***n.*** (ad′və kit *or* ad′və kāt) **1** a person who speaks or writes in favor of something. **2** a person who argues another's case; especially, a lawyer.

**advt.** *abbreviation for* **advertisement.** —*pl.* **advts.**

**adz** or **adze** (adz) ***n.*** a tool that is a little like an ax, but has a curved blade. It is used for trimming and smoothing wood. *See the picture.*

**A.E.C.** or **AEC** Atomic Energy Commission.

**Ae·ge·an** (ē jē′ən) a sea between Greece and Turkey, that is an arm of the Mediterranean: *also called* **Aegean Sea.**

**ae·gis** (ē′jis) ***n.*** sponsorship or support [He spoke under the *aegis* of the university.]

**Ae·ne·as** (i nē′əs) a famous Trojan warrior of Greek and Roman legend. The Roman poet Virgil tells of Aeneas and his adventures after the Trojan War in a long poem called the **Ae·ne·id** (i nē′əd).

**ae·on** (ē′ən *or* ē′än) ***n.*** *same as* **eon.**

**aer·ate** (er′āt) ***v.*** **1** to place out in the open air. **2** to force air or gas into [If you *aerate* water with carbon dioxide, you have soda water.] —**aer′at·ed, aer′at·ing**

**aer·i·al** (er′ē əl) ***adj.*** **1** of or in the air. **2** of or for aircraft or flying [*aerial* maps]. ◆***n.*** an antenna for radio or television.

**aer·i·al·ist** (er′ē əl ist) ***n.*** an acrobat who does stunts as on a trapeze or high wire.

**aer·ie** or **aer·y** (er′ē *or* ir′ē) ***n.*** the nest of an eagle or other bird of prey, built in a high place. *See the picture.* —*pl.* **aer′ies**

**aer·o·nau·tics** (er′ə nô′tiks) ***n.pl.*** the science of making and flying aircraft: *used with a singular verb.* —**aer′o·nau′ti·cal** or **aer′o·nau′tic** ***adj.***

☆**aer·o·space** (er′ō spās′) ***n.*** the earth's atmosphere and all the space outside it.

**Ae·sop** (ē′säp *or* ē′səp) a Greek writer of fables, who is thought to have lived in the 6th century B.C.

**aes·thet·ic** (es thet′ik) ***adj.*** **1** of beauty or the study of beauty. **2** very sensitive to art and beauty; artistic. —**aes·thet′i·cal·ly** ***adv.***

**a·far** (ə fär′) ***adv.*** at or to a distance: *now seldom used except in poetry.* —**from afar,** from a distance [We heard the barking *from afar.*]

**af·fa·ble** (af′ə b'l) ***adj.*** pleasant and easy to talk to; friendly. —**af′fa·bil′i·ty** ***n.*** —**af′fa·bly** ***adv.***

**af·fair** (ə fer′) ***n.*** **1** a happening or event; occurrence [The meeting will be a long, tiresome *affair.*] **2 affairs,** *pl.* matters of business [Who will take care of your *affairs* while you are away?]

**af·fect**[1] (ə fekt′) ***v.*** **1** to bring about a change in; have an effect on [Bright light *affects* the eyes.] **2** to make feel sad or sympathetic [The child's accident *affected* us deeply.]

**af·fect**[2] (ə fekt′) ***v.*** **1** to like to have, use, wear, etc. [She *affects* plaid coats.] **2** to pretend to be, have, feel, like, etc. [Although he disliked sports, he *affected* an interest in baseball.]

**af·fec·ta·tion** (af′ek tā′shən) ***n.*** unnatural behavior that is meant to impress others [Ed's use of long words is just an *affectation.*]

**af·fect·ed**[1] (ə fek′tid) ***adj.*** **1** injured or diseased [She rubbed salve on the affected part of the skin.] **2** feel-

| | | | | | | | |
|---|---|---|---|---|---|---|---|
| **a** | fat | **ir** | here | **ou** | out | **zh** | leisure |
| **ā** | ape | **ī** | bite, fire | **u** | up | **ŋ** | ring |
| **ä** | car, lot | **ō** | go | **ur** | fur | | a *in* ago |
| **e** | ten | **ô** | law, horn | **ch** | chin | | e *in* agent |
| **er** | care | **oi** | oil | **sh** | she | **ə =** | i *in* unity |
| **ē** | even | **oo** | look | **th** | thin | | o *in* collect |
| **i** | hit | **ōō** | tool | ***th*** | then | | u *in* focus |

ing sad or sympathetic [The president's death left them deeply *affected.*]

**af·fect·ed²** (ə fek′tid) ***adj.*** unnatural in a way meant to impress people [*affected* politeness].

**af·fect·ing** (ə fek′tiŋ) ***adj.*** making one feel sympathy or pity [The book "Oliver Twist" is an *affecting* story of an orphan.]

**af·fec·tion** (ə fek′shən) ***n.*** **1** a fond or tender feeling; warm liking [The *affection* one feels for a pet is not the same as love.] *See* SYNONYMS *at* **love. 2** a disease or sickness [an *affection* of the liver].

**af·fec·tion·ate** (ə fek′shən it) ***adj.*** gentle and loving [an *affectionate* pat on the arm]. **—af·fec′tion·ate·ly *adv.***

**af·fi·da·vit** (af′ə dā′vit) ***n.*** a statement written by a person who swears that it is the truth [He signed an *affidavit* saying that he had paid the debt.]

**af·fil·i·ate** (ə fil′ē āt) ***v.*** to take in or be taken in as a member or another part; join [Our store has become *affiliated* with a large supermarket chain.] **—af·fil′i·at·ed, af·fil′i·at·ing** ◆***n.*** (ə fil′ē it) an affiliated person or organization [a local *affiliate* of a national group]. **—af·fil′i·a′tion *n.***

> **Affiliate** comes from a Latin verb meaning "to adopt as a son." When people become affiliated with a group, it is as though they are being adopted.

**af·fin·i·ty** (ə fin′ə tē) ***n.*** **1** close relationship or kinship [Folk ballads show the close *affinity* of music with poetry.] **2** the special attraction that one person has for another. *—pl.* **af·fin′i·ties**

**af·firm** (ə furm′) ***v.*** to say something and be willing to stand by its truth; declare positively [I cannot *affirm* that Smith is guilty of any crime.] **—af·fir·ma·tion** (af′ər mā′shən) ***n.***

**af·firm·a·tive** (ə fur′mə tiv) ***adj.*** saying that something is true; answering "yes" [an *affirmative* reply]. ◆***n.*** **1** a word, phrase, or action showing that one approves or agrees [She nodded her head in the *affirmative.*] **2** the side that favors or agrees with the point being debated [There were more votes in the negative than in the *affirmative.*]

**af·fix** (ə fiks′) ***v.*** **1** to fasten; attach; stick [*Affix* a label to the jar.] **2** to add at the end [You must *affix* your signature to the contract.] ◆***n.*** (af′iks) a prefix or suffix.

**af·flict** (ə flikt′) ***v.*** to cause pain or suffering to; trouble [She is *afflicted* with a skin rash.]

**af·flic·tion** (ə flik′shən) ***n.*** pain; trouble; suffering or the cause of suffering [the *afflictions* that war brings].

**af·flu·ence** (af′loo wəns *or now also* af lo͞o′əns) ***n.*** great plenty; especially, riches, or wealth.

**af·flu·ent** (af′loo wənt *or now also* af lo͞o′ənt) ***adj.*** having all the money or wealth needed; prosperous; rich.

**af·ford** (ə fôrd′) ***v.*** **1** to have money enough to spare for: *usually used with* can *or* be able [Can we *afford* a new car?] **2** to be able to do something without taking great risks [I can *afford* to speak frankly.] **3** to give; furnish [Music *affords* her much pleasure.]

**af·front** (ə frunt′) ***v.*** to insult right to one's face and on purpose [He *affronted* us by yawning in a bored way.] ◆***n.*** speech or conduct that is meant to be rude or to hurt someone; deliberate insult [Her criticism of the food was an *affront* to the cook.]

**af·ghan** (af′gan) ***n.*** a soft, crocheted or knitted blanket or shawl.

**Af·ghan·i·stan** (af gan′ə stan) a country in southwestern Asia, between Iran and Pakistan.

**a·field** (ə fēld′) ***adv.*** away from home; astray [They wandered far *afield* and became lost.]

**a·flame** (ə flām′) ***adv., adj.*** **1** in flames; burning. **2** glowing [fields *aflame* with sunlight].

**AFL-CIO** American Federation of Labor and Congress of Industrial Organizations, a large organization of labor unions.

**a·float** (ə flōt′) ***adj., adv.*** **1** floating on the surface [toy boats *afloat* in the pond]. **2** flooded [The ship sprang a leak and soon the lower decks were *afloat.*] **3** heard from many people; circulating [Rumors were *afloat.*]

**a·foot** (ə foot′) ***adv.*** **1** on foot; walking [They set out *afoot* for the beach.] **2** going on or being made; in progress; astir [There is trouble *afoot.*]

**a·fore·men·tioned** (ə fôr′men′shənd) ***adj.*** mentioned before in what was said or written.

**a·fore·said** (ə fôr′sed′) ***adj.*** spoken of before.

**a·foul** (ə foul′) ***adv., adj.*** in a mess or tangle. **—run afoul of,** to get into trouble with [They *ran afoul of* the law.]

**Afr.** *abbreviation for* **Africa** *or* **African.**

**a·fraid** (ə frād′) ***adj.*** feeling fear; frightened [*afraid* of the dark]. *Afraid* is often used in everyday talk to show regret [I'm *afraid* I can't go with you.]

**a·fresh** (ə fresh′) ***adv.*** again; anew [She tore up the note and started writing *afresh.*]

**Af·ri·ca** (af′ri kə) the second largest continent. It is south of Europe, between the Atlantic and Indian oceans.

**Af·ri·can** (af′ri kən) ***adj.*** of Africa, its people, their cultures, etc. ◆***n.*** a person born or living in Africa; sometimes, especially, a member of any of the dark-skinned peoples of Africa.

☆**Af·ro** (af′rō) ***n.*** a full, puffed-out hair style, especially as worn by some blacks. *See the picture. —pl.* **Af′ros**

**aft** (aft) ***adj., adv.*** at, near, or toward the stern of a ship or the rear of an aircraft.

**af·ter** (af′tər) ***adv.*** **1** behind; coming next [You go on ahead, and we'll follow *after.*] **2** following in time; later [They came at noon and left three hours *after.*] ◆***prep.*** **1** behind [The soldiers marched one *after* the other.] **2** in search of [What are you *after*?] **3** later than [It's ten minutes *after* four.] **4** as a result of; because of [*After* what has happened, he won't go.] **5** in spite of [*After* all his bad luck, he is still cheerful.] **6** next to in rank or importance [A captain comes *after* a major.] **7** in the style of; imitating [They copied their capitol *after* the one in Washington.] **8** for; in honor of [a child named *after* Lincoln]. **9** about; concerning [She asked *after* you.] ◆***conj.*** following the time when [They left the party *after* we did.]

**af·ter·ef·fect** (af′tər ə fekt′) ***n.*** an effect coming later, or as a result of a main effect [a drug with harmful *aftereffects*].

**af·ter·glow** (af′tər glō) ***n.*** the glow that is left after a light has gone, as after a sunset.

**af·ter·im·age** (af′tər im′ij) ***n.*** an image of something seen that continues on the retina for a while even when the eyes are closed.

**af·ter·math** (af′tər math) ***n.*** something following as a result, especially something bad [Disease and hunger are usually the *aftermath* of war.]

**af·ter·noon** (af tər no͞on′) ***n.*** the time of day from noon to evening.

**af·ter·thought** (af′tər thôt) ***n.*** a thought or idea that comes to the mind later, often too late to be helpful [The day following the test, I had some *afterthoughts* about my answers.]

**af·ter·ward** (af′tər wərd) or **af·ter·wards** (af′tər wərdz) ***adv.*** at a later time; later [We had dinner and went for a walk *afterward.*]

**Ag** *the symbol for the chemical element* silver.

**a·gain** (ə gen′) ***adv.*** **1** once more; a second time [If you don't understand the sentence, read it *again.*] **2** back; as before [He is home *again.*] **3** on the other hand [She may, and then *again* she may not.] —**again and again,** often; many times. —**as much again,** twice as much.

**a·gainst** (ə genst′) ***prep.*** **1** opposite or opposed to [the fight *against* disease; a vote *against* the bill]. **2** toward so as to strike [Throw the ball *against* the wall.] **3** opposite to the direction of [Walk *against* the traffic.] **4** so as to be prepared for [We provided *against* a poor crop.] **5** as a charge on [The bill was entered *against* his account.]

**a·gape** (ə gāp′) ***adv., adj.*** gaping; with the mouth wide open, as in surprise or wonder [We stared at the strange sight *agape.*]

**ag·ate** (ag′ət) ***n.*** **1** a hard stone with striped or clouded coloring, used in jewelry. **2** a small glass ball that looks like this, used in playing marbles.

**a·ga·ve** (ə gä′vē) ***n.*** an American desert plant, as the century plant, with thick, fleshy leaves. Fiber for making rope is got from some kinds of agave. *See the picture.*

**agcy.** *abbreviation for* **agency.**

**age** (āj) ***n.*** **1** the time that a person or thing has existed from birth or beginning [He left school at the *age* of fourteen.] **2** a stage of life [She is at an awkward *age.*] **3** the fact of being old [Gray hair comes with *age.*] **4** a generation [Future *ages* will read her books.] **5** a period of time in history [the Stone *Age*]. *See* SYNONYMS *at* **period.** **6** *usually* **ages,** *pl.* a long time: *used only in everyday talk* [It's been *ages* since I've seen my cousin.] ◆***v.*** to grow old or make old [The dog is *aging* rapidly. Hard work has *aged* the gardener.] —**aged, ag′ing** —**of age,** having reached the time of life when one has the full legal rights of an adult.

**-age** (ij) *a suffix meaning:* **1** the act or result of [*Marriage* is the act of marrying.] **2** amount or number of [*Acreage* is the number of acres.] **3** cost of [*Postage* is the cost of posting a letter.] **4** group of [*Peerage* is a group of peers.] **5** home of [A *hermitage* is the home of a hermit.]

**a·ged** (ā′jid) ***adj.*** **1** grown old [my *aged* aunt]. **2** (ājd) of the age of [a pupil *aged* ten].

**a·gen·cy** (ā′jən sē) ***n.*** **1** the means by which something is done [Electricity is the *agency* by which our homes are lighted.] **2** the work or office of a person or company that acts for someone else [an insurance *agency*]. **3** a division of government or some other organization that offers a special kind of help [a social *agency*]. —*pl.* **a′gen·cies**

Afro

agave

**a·gen·da** (ə jen′də) ***n.*** a list of things to be done or talked about, as at a meeting [The *agenda* for this evening was mailed to you last week.] —*pl.* **a·gen′das**

**a·gent** (ā′jənt) ***n.*** **1** a person or thing that brings about a certain result [Education is a powerful *agent* in helping people to understand one another.] **2** a person or company that acts for another [Most actors have *agents* to handle their business.]

**ag·gran·dize** (ə gran′dīz *or* ag′rən dīz) ***v.*** to make more powerful, richer, etc. [Some public officials used their office to *aggrandize* themselves.] —**ag·gran′dized, ag·gran′diz·ing** —**ag·gran·dize·ment** (ə gran′diz mənt) ***n.***

**ag·gra·vate** (ag′rə vāt) ***v.*** **1** to make worse; make more troublesome [You will *aggravate* your sprained ankle by walking.] **2** to make impatient; annoy; bother: *used only in everyday talk* [The talking in the audience began to *aggravate* us.] —**ag′gra·vat·ed, ag′gra·vat·ing** —**ag′gra·va′tion** ***n.***

> **Aggravate** comes from a Latin word which means "to make heavier" and is related to the word **gravity.** When a problem is aggravated, it is made heavier or greater than it was.

**ag·gre·gate** (ag′rə gət) ***adj.*** gathered into a whole; thought of as a group; total [the *aggregate* number of unemployed]. ◆***n.*** a group of things gathered into a total or whole [The *aggregate* of books in the library amounts to over 10,000.]

**ag·gre·ga·tion** (ag′rə gā′shən) ***n.*** a number of separate things brought together into a single group.

**ag·gres·sion** (ə gresh′ən) ***n.*** **1** the starting of a fight or war by a person or nation; especially, any warlike act by one country against another without just cause. **2** the habit of fighting or quarreling.

**ag·gres·sive** (ə gres′iv) ***adj.*** **1** ready to start fights or quarrels [an *aggressive* bully]. **2** bold and active; full of energy and ideas [an *aggressive* leader]. —**ag·gres′sive·ly** ***adv.*** —**ag·gres′sive·ness** ***n.***

> SYNONYMS: **Aggressive,** in a good sense, suggests that someone is ready and willing to take action in order to reach a goal, and in a bad sense,

| | | | |
|---|---|---|---|
| **a** fat | **ir** here | **ou** out | **zh** leisure |
| **ā** ape | **ī** bite, fire | **u** up | **ng** ring |
| **ä** car, lot | **ō** go | **ur** fur | a *in* ago |
| **e** ten | **ô** law, horn | **ch** chin | e *in* agent |
| **er** care | **oi** oil | **sh** she | **ə** = i *in* unity |
| **ē** even | **oo** look | **th** thin | o *in* collect |
| **i** hit | **o͞o** tool | ***th*** then | u *in* focus |

suggests a willingness to control and hurt others while reaching that goal. **Assertive** implies that a person is confident and firm in speaking or giving opinions.

**ag·gres·sor** (ə gres′ər) ***n.*** a person or country that starts a fight or war.

**ag·grieve** (ə grēv′) ***v.*** to make feel hurt or insulted; offend [The colonists were much *aggrieved* by the tax on tea.] —**ag·grieved′, ag·griev′ing**

**a·ghast** (ə gast′) ***adj.*** feeling great shock or horror; horrified [*aghast* at the sight of blood].

**ag·ile** (aj′'l) ***adj.*** moving with quickness and ease; active; nimble [an *agile* jumper]. *See* SYNONYMS *at* **nimble.** —**ag′ile·ly** ***adv.***

**a·gil·i·ty** (ə jil′ə tē) ***n.*** the ability to move with quickness and ease [Tennis requires *agility*.]

**ag·i·tate** (aj′ə tāt) ***v.*** **1** to stir or shake up; move violently [A washing machine *agitates* the clothes.] **2** to excite or disturb the feelings of [News of the disaster *agitated* them.] **3** to stir up interest and support through speeches and writing so as to cause change [They *agitated* for better working conditions.] —**ag′i·tat·ed, ag′i·tat·ing**

**ag·i·ta·tion** (aj′ə tā′shən) ***n.*** **1** the act of stirring or shaking violently. **2** a disturbing or exciting of the feelings. **3** talk or writing meant to stir up people and produce changes.

**ag·i·ta·tor** (aj′ə tāt′ər) ***n.*** a person or thing that agitates. *See the picture.*



**a·glow** (ə glō′) ***adv., adj.*** flushed with color, as from excitement; glowing [a face *aglow* with joy].

**ag·nos·tic** (ag näs′tik) ***n.*** a person who believes that it is impossible to know whether or not there is a God.

**a·go** (ə gō′) ***adj.*** gone by; past [They were married ten years *ago*.] ◆***adv.*** in the past [long *ago*].

**a·gog** (ə gäg′) ***adv., adj.*** full of excitement or interest [The children are all *agog* over the puppy.]

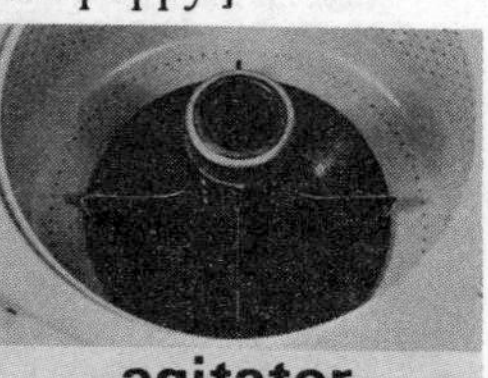


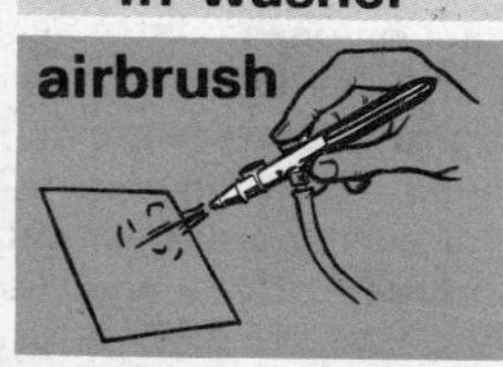

**ag·o·nize** (ag′ə nīz) ***v.*** to suffer or make suffer very great pain in the body or mind [*agonizing* over making a decision]. —**ag′o·nized, ag′o·niz·ing**

**ag·o·ny** (ag′ə nē) ***n.*** very great pain in the body or mind [The victims of the fire were in *agony*.] —*pl.* **ag′o·nies**

**a·grar·i·an** (ə grer′ē ən) ***adj.*** **1** having to do with land as it is owned for farming [The large estates were divided among the peasants to solve the *agrarian* problem.] **2** of farming or farmers; agricultural.

**a·gree** (ə grē′) ***v.*** **1** to say "yes"; consent [The detective *agreed* to investigate the case.] **2** to have the same opinion [The waiter *agreed* that the steak was overdone. My parents *agree* in their choice for mayor.] **3** to be alike or similar; be in accord [Our tastes in art *agree*.] **4** to be healthful or proper: *followed by* with [This climate *agrees* with me.] **5** in grammar, to have the same number, person, case, or gender [The verb *agrees* with its subject in number and person.] —**a·greed′, a·gree′ing**

**a·gree·a·ble** (ə grē′ə b'l) ***adj.*** **1** pleasing or pleasant [an *agreeable* odor]. **2** willing or ready to say "yes" [The principal was *agreeable* to our plan.] —**a·gree′a·bly** ***adv.***

**a·gree·ment** (ə grē′mənt) ***n.*** **1** the fact of agreeing or being similar [The news report was not in *agreement* with the facts.] **2** a fixing of terms between two or more people, countries, etc., as in a treaty [The U.S. has trade *agreements* with many nations.]

**ag·ri·cul·tur·al** (ag′ri kul′chər əl) ***adj.*** of agriculture; having to do with farming.

**ag·ri·cul·ture** (ag′ri kul′chər) ***n.*** the science and work of growing crops and raising livestock; farming.

**a·ground** (ə ground′) ***adv., adj.*** on or onto the shore, the bottom, a reef, etc. [The ship ran *aground* in the shallow bay.] *See the picture.*

**a·gue** (ā′gyo͞o) ***n.*** **1** a disease, especially malaria, in which the patient has both fever and chills, one after the other. **2** a chill; fit of shivering.

**ah** (ä) ***interj.*** a sound made in various ways to show pain, delight, regret, disgust, surprise, etc.

**a·ha** (ä hä′) ***interj.*** a sound made to show satisfaction, pleasure, triumph, etc., sometimes in a mocking way.

**a·head** (ə hed′) ***adv., adj.*** in or to the front; forward [The lighthouse was directly *ahead* of the ship. Our horse moved *ahead* in the last lap of the race.] —**ahead of,** in advance of; before [We arrived *ahead of* the other guests.] —**get ahead of,** to do better than; outdo.

**a·hem** (ə hem′) ***interj.*** a cough or slight noise in the throat made to get someone's attention, give a warning, show doubt, etc.

**a·hoy** (ə hoi′) ***interj.*** a call used by sailors in hailing a person or ship [Ship *ahoy!*]

**aid** (ād) ***v.*** to give help to; assist [The cane *aided* the patient in walking.] ◆***n.*** **1** help; assistance [A compass is an *aid* to navigation.] *See* SYNONYMS *at* **help.** **2** a helper; assistant [a nurse's *aid*].

**aide** (ād) ***n.*** **1** an assistant. **2** an officer in the army, navy, etc. who is an assistant to an officer of higher rank: *the full title is* **aide-de-camp** (ād′də kamp′), *pl.* **aides-de-camp** (ādz′də kamp′).

**ail** (āl) ***v.*** **1** to cause pain to; trouble; distress [What *ails* you to make you so cross?] **2** to be ill; feel sick [Grandfather is *ailing* today.]

**ai·le·ron** (ā′lə rän) ***n.*** a hinged flap on the back edge of the wing of an airplane. It is moved up or down in keeping the plane steady or in making a turn in the air. *See the picture.*

**ail·ment** (āl′mənt) ***n.*** an illness; sickness.

**aim** (ām) ***v.*** **1** to point a gun, missile, etc. or direct a blow or remark [*Aim* the dart at the target's center. That criticism was *aimed* at us.] **2** to have as one's goal or purpose [We *aim* to please.] ◆***n.*** **1** the aiming of a weapon at a target [My *aim* was blocked by a tree.] **2** intention, object, or purpose [Her chief *aim* in life is to help others.] —**take aim,** to point at a target; direct a bullet, blow, remark, etc.

**aim·less** (ām′lis) ***adj.*** having no aim or purpose [Some people seem to lead *aimless* lives.]

**ain't** (ānt) a shortened everyday form of *am not, is not, are not, has not,* or *have not.*

> **Ain't** is not now usually thought of as standard English, although it once was and is still regarded by some as a useful contraction of *am not* in asking a question [I'm going too, *ain't* I?]

**air** (er) ***n.*** **1** the mixture of gases that is all around the earth. Air cannot be seen, but it can spread to fill a space and it can move in currents. It consists mainly of nitrogen and oxygen, but also contains hydrogen, carbon dioxide, and other gases. **2** space above the earth; sky [The lark flew into the *air.*] **3** the feeling one gets from someone or something [An *air* of luxury fills the room. The stranger had an *air* of mystery.] **4** a melody or tune; song. ◆***adj.*** having to do with airplanes, air forces, etc. [*air* power]. ◆***v.*** **1** to let air into or through in order to dry, cool, or freshen [*Air* the room to let out the smoke.] **2** to make widely known [I wish our classmates wouldn't *air* their quarrels.] —**on the air,** broadcasting over radio or TV. —**put on airs,** to act as if one were better than others. —**up in the air,** not settled; not decided. —**walk on air,** to feel very happy or lively.

☆**air bag** a large bag that is supposed to inflate at once in a car in case of a collision, to protect riders from being thrown forward.

**air base** an airport for military airplanes.

☆**air·brush** (er′brush) ***n.*** a device used to shoot a spray of paint, ink, or other liquid onto a surface. *See the picture.*

☆**air-con·di·tion** (er′kən dish′ən) ***v.*** to provide with air conditioning. —**air′-con·di′tioned** ***adj.***

☆**air conditioning** a system for cleaning the air in a building, car, or the like and making it cooler and drier. —**air conditioner**

**air·craft** (er′kraft) ***n.*** any machine or machines for flying [Airplanes, dirigibles, and helicopters are all *aircraft.*] —*pl.* **air′craft**

**aircraft carrier** a warship that carries airplanes. It has a large, flat deck for taking off and landing. *See the picture.*

**Aire·dale** (er′dāl) ***n.*** a large terrier having a hard, wiry, tan coat with black markings. *See the picture.*

> **Airedale** dogs originally came from the valley of the Aire River in Yorkshire, England. "Dale" is another word for "valley."

**air·field** (er′fēld) ***n.*** a field where aircraft can take off or land.

**air force** the branch of the armed forces of a country in charge of the aircraft for air warfare.

**air·i·ly** (er′ə lē) ***adv.*** in an airy or light manner; jauntily [He spoke *airily* of the danger.]

**air·ing** (er′iŋ) ***n.*** **1** the condition of being left open to the air for drying, freshening, etc. [These blankets need *airing.*] **2** a making known to the public [The newspapers gave the scandal an *airing.*] **3** a walk or ride outdoors.

**air·less** (er′lis) ***adj.*** without air; especially, without fresh air [a musty, *airless* attic].

☆**air·line** (er′līn) ***n.*** **1** a system or company for moving freight and passengers by aircraft. **2** a route for travel by air.

**air·lin·er** (er′lī′nər) ***n.*** a large passenger airplane.

**air·mail** (er′māl) ***n.*** **1** mail carried by aircraft. **2** the system of carrying mail by aircraft. Today much regular mail is carried by aircraft and there is no longer a special airmail system except for overseas mail.

**air·man** (er′mən) ***n.*** **1** a pilot or crew member of an aircraft. **2** an enlisted person in the U.S. Air Force. —*pl.* **air′men**

**air·plane** (er′plān) ***n.*** an aircraft that is kept up by the force of air upon its wings and is driven forward by a jet engine or propeller.

**air pocket** a condition of the air that causes an airplane to make sudden, short drops.

**air·port** (er′pôrt) ***n.*** a place where aircraft can land to get fuel, be repaired, take on passengers, etc.

**air raid** an attack by aircraft, usually bombers.



☆**air rifle** a rifle in which the force of air under pressure is used to shoot BB's, etc.

**air·ship** (er′ship) ***n.*** any aircraft that is filled with a gas lighter than air and that can be steered, as a dirigible or blimp.

**air·sick** (er′sik) ***adj.*** feeling sick or vomiting from traveling in an aircraft.

**air·space** (er′spās) ***n.*** the space over the surface of the earth; especially, the space over a country, thought of as being under that country's control.

**air·strip** (er′strip) ***n.*** an airfield prepared quickly, as for use in warfare.

**air·tight** (er′tīt′) ***adj.*** **1** closed so tightly that air cannot get in or out [an *airtight* can of coffee]. **2** that cannot be criticized or proved to be false [an *airtight* alibi].

**air·y** (er′ē) ***adj.*** **1** open to the air; breezy [an *airy* room]. **2** flimsy as air; not practical [*airy* schemes]. **3** light as air; delicate [*airy* music]. **4** of or in the air [the *airy* heights of the Alps]. —**air′i·er, air′i·est**

**aisle** (īl) ***n.*** **1** an open way for passing between sections of seats, as in a theater. **2** a part of a church along the inside wall, set off by a row of pillars.

**a·jar** (ə jär′) ***adv., adj.*** slightly open [The door stood *ajar.*]

**AK** *abbreviation for* **Alaska.**

| | | | | | | | |
|---|---|---|---|---|---|---|---|
| **a** | fat | **ir** | here | **ou** | out | **zh** | leisure |
| **ā** | ape | **ī** | bite, fire | **u** | up | **ŋ** | ring |
| **ä** | car, lot | **ō** | go | **ur** | fur | | a *in* ago |
| **e** | ten | **ô** | law, horn | **ch** | chin | | e *in* agent |
| **er** | care | **oi** | oil | **sh** | she | **ə =** | i *in* unity |
| **ē** | even | **oo** | look | **th** | thin | | o *in* collect |
| **i** | hit | **ōō** | tool | ***th*** | then | | u *in* focus |

alcove

man with arms akimbo

alfalfa

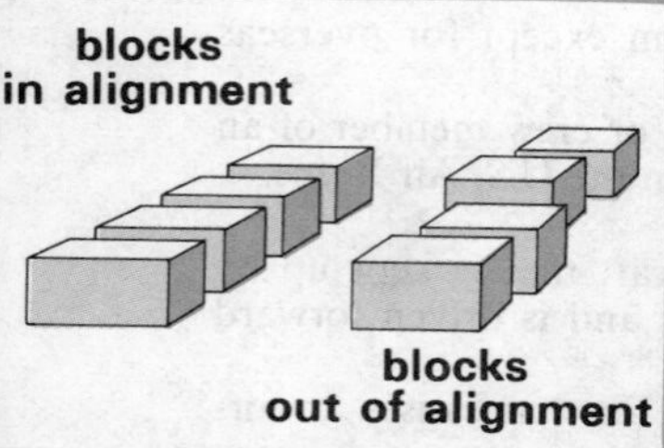
blocks in alignment

blocks out of alignment

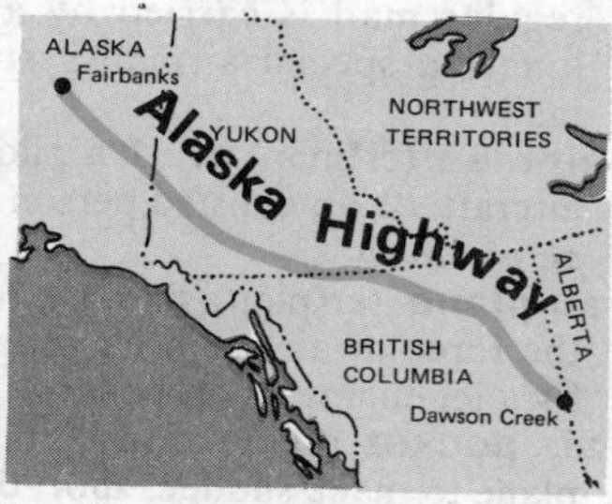




**a.k.a.** also known as. The initials are used especially in police records before a false or made-up name [Lou Morgan *a.k.a.* Lou Murphy].

**a·kim·bo** (ə kim′bō) ***adv., adj.*** with the hands on the hips and the elbows bent outward. *See the picture.*

**a·kin** (ə kin′) ***adj.*** **1** of the same family or kin; related. **2** somewhat alike; similar [The lemon and lime are *akin* in taste.]

**Ak·ron** (ak′rən) a city in northeastern Ohio.

**-al** (əl) *a suffix meaning:* **1** of, like, or suitable for [*Musical* sounds are sounds of or like music.] **2** the act or process of [*Denial* is the act of denying.]

**Al** *the symbol for the chemical element* aluminum.

**Al·a·bam·a** (al′ə bam′ə) a State in the southeastern part of the U.S.: abbreviated **Ala., AL**

**al·a·bas·ter** (al′ə bas′tər) ***n.*** a smooth, white stone that is carved into statues, vases, etc. ◆***adj.*** smooth and white like alabaster.

**a la carte** (ä′lə kärt′) with a separate price for each dish on the menu instead of a single price for a whole meal [Dinners served *a la carte* are usually more expensive.]

**a·lack** (ə lak′) ***interj.*** an exclamation used in olden times to show regret, surprise, etc.

**a·lac·ri·ty** (ə lak′rə tē) ***n.*** quick, lively action; eager quickness [Sal ran to the door with *alacrity*.]

**A·lad·din** (ə lad″n) a boy in *The Arabian Nights* who found a magic lamp and a magic ring. Whenever he rubbed these, a jinni would appear to do whatever he asked.

**Al·a·mo** (al′ə mō) a mission, later a fort, at San Antonio, Texas. Mexican troops captured it from the Texans in 1836.

**a la mode** or **à la mode** (ä′lə mōd′) **1** made or served in a certain style; especially, served with ice cream [pie *a la mode*]. **2** in the fashion; stylish.

**a·larm** (ə lärm′) ***n.*** **1** a signal that is a warning of danger [The bugle was blown to sound the *alarm*.] **2** a bell, siren, etc. that gives such a warning [a fire *alarm*]. **3** sudden fear caused by possible danger [The town was filled with *alarm* when the river started to flood.] ◆***v.*** to make suddenly afraid or anxious [We were *alarmed* to find the house empty.]

> **Alarm** comes from an old Italian phrase *all' arme,* a cry meaning "to arms." It was shouted to soldiers when an enemy was about to attack, warning them to take up their arms, or weapons, and prepare to fight.

**alarm clock** a clock that can be set to ring or buzz at any particular time, as to awaken a person from sleep. Alarm clocks for the deaf flash a light.

**a·larm·ing** (ə lärm′iŋ) ***adj.*** that can make one suddenly afraid or anxious; frightening [There is an *alarming* increase in lung cancer.] **—a·larm′ing·ly** ***adv.***

**a·larm·ist** (ə lärm′ist) ***n.*** a person who is easily frightened and warns others to expect the worst.

**a·las** (ə las′) ***interj.*** an exclamation showing sorrow, pity, regret, or fear.

**A·las·ka** (ə las′kə) a State of the U.S. in northwestern North America, separated from Asia by the Bering Strait: abbreviated **Alas., AK —A·las′kan** ***adj., n.***

**Alaska Highway** a highway extending from British Columbia, Canada, to central Alaska. *See the map.*

**alb** (alb) ***n.*** a long, white linen robe, worn by a priest at Mass.

**al·ba·core** (al′bə kôr) ***n.*** a kind of tuna that lives in warm waters.

**Al·ba·ni·a** (al bā′nē ə) a country in southern Europe. **—Al·ba′ni·an** ***adj., n.***

**Al·ba·ny** (ôl′bə nē) the capital of New York State, on the Hudson River.

**al·ba·tross** (al′bə trôs) ***n.*** a large sea bird with long, narrow wings, webbed feet, and a large, hooked beak.

**al·be·it** (ôl bē′it) ***conj.*** although; even though [an uneducated person, *albeit* no fool].

**Al·bert** (al′bərt), Prince, 1819–1861; husband of Queen Victoria of England.

**Al·ber·ta** (al bur′tə) a province of southwestern Canada.

**al·bi·no** (al bī′nō) ***n.*** **1** a person whose skin, hair, and eyes lack normal coloring. Albinos have a pale skin, whitish hair, and pink eyes. **2** an animal or plant lacking normal coloring. *—pl.* **al·bi′nos**

**al·bum** (al′bəm) ***n.*** **1** a book with blank pages for collecting pictures, clippings, stamps, etc. **2** a booklike holder for phonograph records, or a set of such records. **3** a single, long-playing record not part of a set.

**al·bu·men** (al byo͞o′mən) ***n.*** **1** the white of an egg. **2** *another spelling of* **albumin.**

**al·bu·min** (al byo͞o′mən) ***n.*** a protein found in egg white, milk, muscle, blood, and in many plant tissues and fluids.

**Al·bu·quer·que** (al′bə kur′kē) a city in central New Mexico.

**al·che·mist** (al′kə mist) ***n.*** a person who studied or worked in alchemy.

**al·che·my** (al′kə mē) ***n.*** **1** an early form of chemistry, often mixed with magic, studied in the Middle Ages. The chief aims of alchemy were to change iron or lead into gold and to find a drink that would keep people young forever. **2** a way of changing one thing into something better.

**al·co·hol** (al′kə hôl) ***n.*** **1** a colorless, strong-smelling liquid that evaporates easily and burns with a hot flame. It is got by fermenting grain, fruit, etc. and is used in industry and medicine. It is the substance in whiskey, beer, wine, etc. that makes people drunk. **2** any liquor that has alcohol in it.

**al·co·hol·ic** (al′kə hôl′ik) ***adj.*** of or containing alcohol. ◆***n.*** a person suffering from alcoholism.

**al·co·hol·ism** (al′kə hôl′iz′m) ***n.*** an illness in which there is a strong desire to continue drinking alcoholic liquor; also, the diseased condition caused by drinking too much liquor.

**Al·cott** (ôl′kət), **Louisa May** 1832–1888; American writer of novels.

**al·cove** (al′kōv) ***n.*** a small part of a room that is set back from the main part [The *alcove* off the kitchen serves as a breakfast nook.] *See the picture.*

**Al·den** (ôl′d'n), **John** 1599?–1687; a Pilgrim settler in the colony at Plymouth. He is one of the characters in Longfellow's poem "The Courtship of Miles Standish."

**al·der** (ôl′dər) ***n.*** a small tree like the birch. It has woody cones and grows in wet soils.

**al·der·man** (ôl′dər mən) ***n.*** in some cities, a member of the city council. *—pl.* **al′der·men** —**al·der·man·ic** (al′dər man′ik) ***adj.***

**ale** (āl) ***n.*** a drink very much like beer, made from malt and hops.

**a·lert** (ə lurt′) ***adj.*** **1** watchful and ready [an *alert* guard]. **2** quick in thought or action; active; nimble [My neighbor is very *alert* for a person who is eighty.] ◆***n.*** **1** a warning signal, as of an expected tornado. **2** the time from such a warning until the danger is over. ◆***v.*** to warn to be ready [The town was *alerted* to the danger of a flood.] —**on the alert,** watchful and ready. —**a·lert′ly** ***adv.*** —**a·lert′ness** ***n.***

**A·leu·tian Islands** (ə lo͞o′shən) a part of Alaska which is a chain of islands off the southwest coast.

**Al·ex·an·der the Great** (al′ig zan′dər) 356–323 B.C.; king of Macedonia who conquered Egypt, Persia, and many other lands between the Mediterranean and India.

**Al·ex·an·dri·a** (al′ig zan′drē ə) a seaport in Egypt, on the Mediterranean.

**al·fal·fa** (al fal′fə) ***n.*** a plant with purple, cloverlike flowers and long, deep roots. It is grown as food for cattle, horses, etc. *See the picture.*

**Al·fred the Great** (al′frid) 849–900?; an early king of part of England.

**al·gae** (al′jē) ***n.pl.*** a group of simple plants that have no true root, stem, or leaf and often grow in colonies in water or on damp surfaces. Most seaweeds are algae.

**al·ge·bra** (al′jə brə) ***n.*** a form of mathematics that uses letters as well as numbers in formulas, equations, etc. to solve problems. Example: if $2x^2 + 3x + 15 = 29$, then $x = 2$.

**Algebra** comes from an Arabic word, *al-jabr,* that means "the putting together of broken parts." An algebra problem deals with a number of elements that are "put together" in the solution.

**al·ge·bra·ic** (al′jə brā′ik) ***adj.*** of, like, or used in algebra. —**al′ge·bra′i·cal·ly** ***adv.***

**Al·ger** (al′jər), **Ho·ra·ti·o** (hə rā′shē ō) 1832–1899; American writer of stories for boys.

**Al·ge·ri·a** (al jir′ē ə) a country in northern Africa, formerly under French control. —**Al·ge′ri·an** ***adj., n.***

**Al·giers** (al jirs′) the capital of Algeria.

**Al·gon·qui·an** (al gäŋ′kē ən *or* al gäŋ′kwē ən) ***adj.*** of or having to do with a large group of North American Indian tribes. ◆***n.*** **1** the family of languages spoken by these tribes. **2** a member of any of these tribes.

**Al·gon·quin** (al gäŋ′kin *or* al gäŋ′kwin) ***n.*** **1** a member of a tribe of Algonquian Indians of southeastern Canada. **2** the language that they speak.

**a·li·as** (ā′lē əs) ***n.*** a name that is not one's true name, used to hide who one really is. *See* SYNONYMS *at* **pseudonym.** ◆***adv.*** having the alias of [John Bell *alias* Paul Jones.]

**A·li Ba·ba** (ä′lē bä′bə *or* al′ē bab′ə) in *The Arabian Nights,* a poor woodcutter who finds the treasure of forty thieves in a cave. He makes the door of the cave open by saying "Open sesame!"

**al·i·bi** (al′ə bī) ***n.*** **1** the plea that a person accused of a crime was not at the scene of the crime when it took place. ☆**2** any excuse: *used only in everyday talk* [What's your *alibi* for not finishing the work?] *—pl.* **al′i·bis** ◆☆***v.*** to give an excuse: *used only in everyday talk.* —**al′i·bied, al′i·bi·ing**

**Alibi** is a Latin word formed from a phrase meaning "somewhere else." A person offering an alibi often says, "I was somewhere else when the crime was committed."

**al·ien** (āl′yən) ***adj.*** **1** belonging to another country or people; foreign [*alien* customs]. **2** strange; not natural [Such foods were *alien* to their diet.] ◆***n.*** **1** a foreigner. **2** a person living in a country but not a citizen of it.

**al·ien·ate** (āl′yən āt) ***v.*** to make lose the friendship or love once felt; make unfriendly [His thoughtless remarks *alienated* her.] —**al′ien·at·ed, al′ien·at·ing** —**al′ien·a′tion** ***n.***

**a·light**[1] (ə līt′) ***v.*** **1** to get down or off; dismount [Kit *alighted* from the horse.] **2** to come down after flight; settle [The bird *alighted* on the ground.] —**a·light′ed** or **a·lit′, a·light′ing**

**a·light**[2] (ə līt′) ***adj.*** lighted up; glowing [a face *alight* with joy].

**a·lign** (ə līn′) ***v.*** **1** to put or come into a straight line [*Align* the chairs along the wall.] **2** to adjust the parts of something, as the wheels of a car, so that they work well together. **3** to get into agreement, close cooperation, etc. [The Senator is *aligned* with the conservatives.]

**a·lign·ment** (ə līn′mənt) ***n.*** **1** arrangement in a straight line. *See the picture.* **2** the condition of being adjusted to work well together [The front wheels are

| | | | | | | | |
|---|---|---|---|---|---|---|---|
| **a** | fat | **ir** | here | **ou** | out | **zh** | leisure |
| **ā** | ape | **ī** | bite, fire | **u** | up | **ŋ** | ring |
| **ä** | car, lot | **ō** | go | **ur** | fur | | a *in* ago |
| **e** | ten | **ô** | law, horn | **ch** | chin | | e *in* agent |
| **er** | care | **oi** | oil | **sh** | she | **ə =** | i *in* unity |
| **ē** | even | **oo** | look | **th** | thin | | o *in* collect |
| **i** | hit | **o͞o** | tool | ***th*** | then | | u *in* focus |

out of *alignment.*] **3** a condition of close cooperation [an *alignment* of European nations].

**a·like** (ə līk′) ***adj.*** like one another; similar [He and his mother look *alike.*] ◆***adv.*** in the same way; similarly [They dress *alike.* Treat them *alike.*]

**al·i·men·ta·ry** (al′ə men′tər ē) ***adj.*** having to do with food or digestion [The *alimentary* canal is the passage from the mouth through the stomach and intestines.]

**al·i·mo·ny** (al′ə mō′nē) ***n.*** money that a court orders one to pay regularly to support the person from whom one has been divorced.

**a·line** (ə līn′) ***v.*** *another spelling of* **align. —a·lined′, a·lin′ing —a·line′ment *n.***

**a·live** (ə līv′) ***adj.*** **1** having life; living. *See* SYNONYMS *at* **living. 2** going on; in action; not ended or destroyed [to keep old memories *alive*]. **3** lively; alert. **—alive with,** full of living or moving things [a garden *alive with* insects].

**al·ka·li** (al′kə lī) ***n.*** any chemical substance, such as soda or potash, that neutralizes acids and forms salts with them. Alkalies dissolved in water have a soapy feel and taste. *—pl.* **al′ka·lies** or **al′ka·lis**

**al·ka·line** (al′kə lin *or* al′kə līn) ***adj.*** of, like, or containing an alkali [Lime is an *alkaline* substance used to neutralize acid soil.] **—al·ka·lin·i·ty** (al′kə lin′ə tē) ***n.***

**al·ka·loid** (al′kə loid) ***n.*** any of a group of bitter compounds, such as caffeine, morphine, and quinine, which are found mostly in plants. Alkaloids have many uses in medicine.

**all** (ôl) ***adj.*** **1** the whole thing or the whole amount of [in *all* England; *all* the gold]. **2** every one of [*All* people must eat.] **3** as much as possible [My apology was made in *all* sincerity.] **4** any; any whatever [true beyond *all* question]. **5** alone; only [Life is not *all* pleasure.] ◆***pron.*** **1** everyone: *used with a plural verb* [*All* of us are here.] **2** everything; the whole matter [*All* is over between them.] **3** every part or bit [*All* of the candy is gone.] ◆***n.*** **1** everything one has [The workers gave their *all* to the cause.] **2** the whole amount [That's *all* you're going to get.] ◆***adv.*** **1** completely; entirely [*all* worn out; *all* through the night]. **2** each; apiece [The score is ten *all.*] **—above all,** before all other things. **—after all,** in spite of everything. **—all but, 1** all except. **2** almost. **—all in,** very tired: *used only in everyday talk.* **—all in all, 1** keeping everything in mind. **2** as a whole. **—all over, 1** ended. **2** everywhere [Have you looked *all over?*] **—at all, 1** to the smallest amount [I don't mind *at all.*] **2** in any way. **3** under any conditions [I would not go *at all.*] **—for all,** in spite of. **—in all,** altogether.

**Al·lah** (al′ə *or* ä′lə) the Muslim name for God.

☆**all-A·mer·i·can** (ôl′ə mer′ə kən) ***adj.*** **1** made up entirely of Americans [an *all-American* group of scientists]. **2** chosen as one of the best college athletes of the year in the United States [an *all-American* football player].

☆**all-a·round** (ôl′ə round′) ***adj.*** able to do many things or be used for many purposes [A tractor is a piece of *all-around* farm machinery.]

**al·lay** (ə lā′) ***v.*** **1** to put to rest; quiet; calm [Your quiet manner helped to *allay* their fears.] **2** to make lighter or less; relieve, as pain or grief.

**al·le·ga·tion** (al′ə gā′shən) ***n.*** **1** the act of alleging. **2** a positive statement, often one without proof [a false *allegation* of bribery].

**al·lege** (ə lej′) ***v.*** **1** to say firmly, usually without proof [The pilot *alleged* that she had seen a flying saucer.] **2** to give as an excuse or reason [In his defense, Jones *alleged* insanity at the time of the crime.] **—al·leged′, al·leg′ing**

**Al·le·ghe·ny** (al′ə gā′nē) a river in western Pennsylvania. It joins the Monongahela at Pittsburgh to form the Ohio River.

**Allegheny Mountains** a mountain range in central Pennsylvania, Maryland, West Virginia, and Virginia: *also called* **the Al′le·ghe′nies**

**al·le·giance** (ə lē′jəns) ***n.*** **1** the fact of being loyal to one's country or ruler [We pledge *allegiance* to the flag as a symbol of our country.] **2** loyalty or devotion, as to friends or a cause.

> SYNONYMS: **Allegiance** is the duty one has to support and serve one's country, and may also mean the duty one feels toward a leader or cause. **Loyalty** is thought of as the steady devotion one feels toward family, friends, or country.

**al·le·go·ry** (al′ə gôr′ē) ***n.*** a story used to teach or explain an idea or moral rule. In allegories people, animals, and things have hidden meanings beside the ones that are easily seen [Aesop's fables are short *allegories.*] *—pl.* **al′le·go′ries —al′le·gor′i·cal *adj.***

**al·le·gro** (ə leg′rō *or* ə lā′grō) ***adj., adv.*** fast; lively. It is an Italian word used in music to tell how fast a piece should be played.

**al·le·lu·ia** (al′ə lo͞o′yə) ***interj., n.*** *same as* **hallelujah.**

**Al·len** (al′ən), **E·than** (ē′thən) 1738–1789; American soldier in the American Revolution. He led a group of soldiers, called the *Green Mountain Boys,* who captured a British fort in northeastern New York.

**Al·len·town** (al′ən toun) a city in eastern Pennsylvania.

☆**al·ler·gic** (ə lur′jik) ***adj.*** **1** of or caused by an allergy [an *allergic* reaction]. **2** having an allergy [The baby is *allergic* to cow's milk.]

☆**al·ler·gy** (al′ər jē) ***n.*** a condition in which one becomes sick, gets a rash, etc. by breathing in, touching, eating, or drinking something that is not harmful to most people [Hay fever is usually caused by an *allergy* to certain pollens.] *—pl.* **al′ler·gies**

**al·le·vi·ate** (ə lē′vē āt) ***v.*** to make easier to bear; lighten or relieve [Drugs are sometimes used to *alleviate* pain.] **—al·le′vi·at·ed, al·le′vi·at·ing —al·le′vi·a′tion *n.***

**al·ley**[1] (al′ē) ***n.*** **1** a narrow street or walk between or behind buildings. **2** a long, narrow lane of polished wood, along which the balls are rolled in bowling. **3** a place that has several such lanes for bowling. *—pl.* **al′leys —up one's alley,** just right for one's tastes or skills: *a slang phrase.*

**al·ley**[2] (al′ē) ***n.*** a fine, large marble used as the shooter in playing marbles. *—pl.* **al′leys**

**All Fools' Day** *same as* **April Fools' Day.**

**al·li·ance** (ə lī′əns) ***n.*** **1** a joining or coming together for some purpose; uniting of families by marriage, of nations by treaty, etc. **2** the agreement made for such a uniting. **3** the nations or persons united in such a way.

**al·lied** (ə līd′ *or* al′īd) ***adj.*** **1** united by treaty, agreement, etc. **2** closely related [Spanish and Portuguese are *allied* languages.]

**al·lies** (al′īz) ***n.*** *plural of* **ally.** The nations who joined to fight against Germany in World Wars I and II were called **the Allies.**

**al·li·ga·tor** (al′ə gāt′ər) ***n.*** **1** a large lizard like the crocodile, found in warm rivers and marshes of the U.S. and China. *See the picture.* **2** a scaly leather made from its hide.

**alligator pear** *another name for* **avocado.**

**all-im·por·tant** (ôl′im pôr′t′nt) ***adj.*** very important.

**al·lit·er·a·tion** (ə lit′ə rā′shən) ***n.*** a repeating of the same sound at the beginning of two or more words, as in a line of poetry [There is an *alliteration* of *s* in "Sing a song of sixpence."]

**al·lo·cate** (al′ə kāt) ***v.*** **1** to set aside for a special purpose [Congress *allocates* funds for national parks.] **2** to divide in shares or according to a plan; allot [They *allocated* their time between work and play.] —**al′lo·cat·ed, al′lo·cat·ing —al′lo·ca′tion *n.***

**al·lot** (ə lät′) ***v.*** **1** to divide or give out in shares or by lot [The land was *allotted* equally to the settlers.] **2** to give to a person as a share [Each speaker is *allotted* five minutes.] —**al·lot′ted, al·lot′ting**

**al·lot·ment** (ə lät′mənt) ***n.*** **1** an allotting, or giving out in shares. **2** a thing allotted; share.

**all-out** (ôl′out′) ***adj.*** complete or wholehearted [an *all-out* effort].

**al·low** (ə lou′) ***v.*** **1** to let be done; permit; let [*Allow* us to pay. No smoking *allowed.*] *See* SYNONYMS *at* **let. 2** to let have [She *allows* herself no sweets.] **3** to let enter or stay [Dogs are not usually *allowed* on buses.] **4** to admit to be true or right [His claim for $50 was *allowed.*] **5** to give or keep an extra amount so as to have enough [*Allow* an inch for shrinkage.] —**allow for,** to keep in mind [*Allow for* the difference in their ages.]

**al·low·a·ble** (ə lou′ə b′l) ***adj.*** that can be allowed; permissible.

**al·low·ance** (ə lou′əns) ***n.*** **1** an amount of money, food, etc. given regularly to a child or to anyone who depends on others for support. **2** an amount added or taken off to make up for something [We give an *allowance* of $5 on your used tire when you buy a new one.] —**make allowance for, 1** to keep in mind things that will help explain or excuse something. **2** to leave room, time, etc. for; allow for.

**al·loy** (al′oi *or* ə loi′) ***n.*** **1** a metal that is a mixture of two or more metals, or of a metal and something else [Bronze is an *alloy* of copper and tin.] **2** a common metal, as copper, mixed with a precious metal, as gold, often to give hardness. ◆***v.*** (ə loi′) to mix metals into an alloy.

**all right 1** good enough; satisfactory; adequate [Your work is *all right.*] **2** yes; very well [*All right,* I'll do it.] **3** certainly: *used only in everyday talk* [They finished off the pie, *all right.*]

> Although the one-word spelling *alright* is sometimes seen, it is still thought to be wrong by most careful writers.

**all-round** (ôl′round′) ***adj.*** *same as* **all-around.**

**all·spice** (ôl′spīs) ***n.*** **1** the berry of a West Indian tree. **2** the spice made from this berry. Its flavor is like that of several spices mixed together.

almond

alligator

☆**all-star** (ôl′stär′) ***adj.*** made up of outstanding or star performers [an *all-star* team].

**all-time** (ôl′tīm′) ***adj.*** that is the best or greatest up to the present time [an *all-time* record].

**al·lude** (ə lo͞od′) ***v.*** to mention without going into any detail; refer in a general way [He *alluded* to secrets which he could not reveal.] —**al·lud′ed, al·lud′ing**

**al·lure** (ə loor′) ***v.*** to tempt with something desirable; attract; entice. —**al·lured′, al·lur′ing** ◆***n.*** the power to attract; fascination [the *allure* of faraway places].

**al·lure·ment** (ə loor′mənt) ***n.*** **1** fascination; charm. **2** something that allures.

**al·lur·ing** (ə loor′ing) ***adj.*** tempting strongly; highly attractive [an *alluring* offer].

**al·lu·sion** (ə lo͞o′zhən) ***n.*** a brief mention without going into details [The poem contains several *allusions* to Greek mythology.]



**al·lu·vi·al** (ə lo͞o′vē əl) ***adj.*** made up of the sand or clay washed down by flowing water [*alluvial* deposits at the mouth of the river].

**al·ly** (ə lī′) ***v.*** **1** to join together by agreement; unite for a special purpose [Nations often *ally* themselves by treaty.] **2** to relate by close likenesses [The onion is *allied* to the lily.] —**al·lied′, al·ly′ing** ◆***n.*** (al′ī) a country or person joined with another for a special purpose [England was our *ally* during World War II.] —*pl.* **al′lies**

**al·ma ma·ter** (al′mə mät′ər *or* mā′tər) **1** the college or school that one attended. **2** its official song.

**al·ma·nac** (ôl′mə nak) ***n.*** **1** a yearly calendar with notes about the weather, tides, etc. **2** a book published each year with information and charts on many subjects.

**al·might·y** (ôl mīt′ē) ***adj.*** having power with no limit; all-powerful. —**the Almighty,** God.

**al·mond** (ä′mənd *or* am′ənd) ***n.*** **1** an oval nut that is the seed of a fruit which looks like a small peach. *See the picture.* **2** the small tree that this fruit grows on.

**al·most** (ôl′mōst) ***adv.*** not completely but very nearly [He tripped and *almost* fell. Sue is *almost* ten.]

**alms** (ämz) ***n.*** money, food, etc. given to help poor people: *used with either a singular or plural verb.*

**al·oe** (al′ō) ***n.*** **1** a plant of South Africa with fleshy

| | | | | | | | |
|---|---|---|---|---|---|---|---|
| **a** | fat | **ir** | here | **ou** | out | **zh** | leisure |
| **ā** | ape | **ī** | bite, fire | **u** | up | **ng** | ring |
| **ä** | car, lot | **ō** | go | **ur** | fur | | a *in* ago |
| **e** | ten | **ô** | law, horn | **ch** | chin | | e *in* agent |
| **er** | care | **oi** | oil | **sh** | she | **ə =** | i *in* unity |
| **ē** | even | **oo** | look | **th** | thin | | o *in* collect |
| **i** | hit | **o͞o** | tool | ***th*** | then | | u *in* focus |

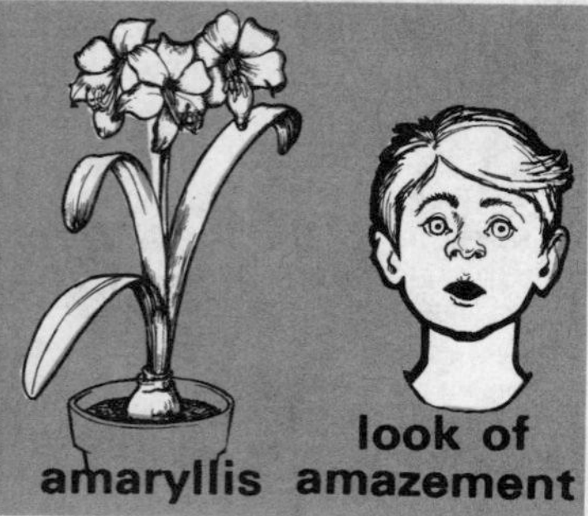
amaryllis look of amazement

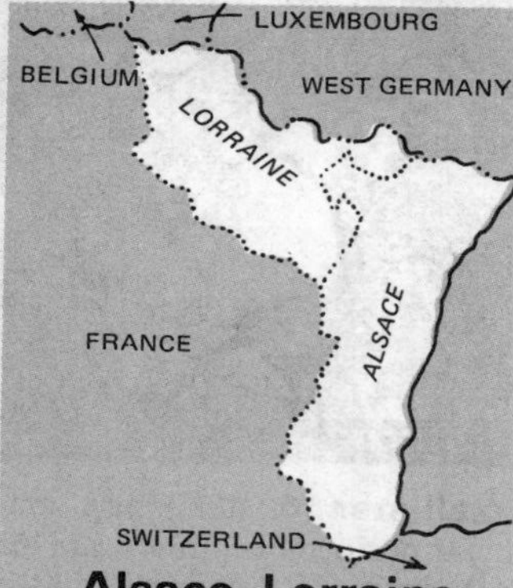

Alsace–Lorraine

alpaca
90 cm (3 ft.) high at shoulder

alternate leaves

leaves. **2 aloes,** *pl.* a bitter drug made from the juice of some aloe leaves and used as a laxative: *used with a singular verb.*



**a·loft** (ə lôft′) ***adv.*** **1** high up; far above the ground [The ape swung *aloft* into the upper branches of the tree.] **2** in the air; flying. **3** high above the deck of a ship; near the top of the mast.

☆**a·lo·ha** (ə lō′ə *or* ä lō′hä) ***n., interj.*** a Hawaiian word that means "love" and is used for "hello" or "goodbye."

**a·lone** (ə lōn′) ***adj., adv.*** **1** away from anything or anyone else [The hut stood *alone* on the prairie.] **2** without any other person [The writer worked *alone.*] **3** without anything else; only [The carton *alone* weighs two pounds.] —**let alone, 1** not to bother or interfere with. **2** not to speak of [I haven't a dime, *let alone* a dollar.] —**let well enough alone,** to be satisfied with things as they are.

SYNONYMS: **Alone** simply suggests the fact of being by oneself or itself. **Lonely** gives a strong feeling of being sad about being alone. **Lonesome** suggests a longing for company, often a certain person [a child *lonesome* for its mother].

**a·long** (ə lông′) ***prep.*** on or beside the length of [Put these planks *along* the wall.] ◆***adv.*** **1** forward or onward [The policeman told us to move *along.*] **2** as a companion [Come *along* with us.] **3** with one [Take your camera *along.*] —**all along,** from the very beginning [Our secret was known *all along.*] —**along with, 1** together with. **2** in addition to. —**get along, 1** to go forward. **2** to manage [Can they *get along* on $110 a week?] **3** to succeed. **4** to be on friendly terms; agree [We can't *get along.*]

**a·long·side** (ə lông′sīd′) ***prep.*** at the side of; side by side with [You'll find the car *alongside* the building.] —**alongside of,** at the side of; beside.

**a·loof** (ə lo͞of′) ***adj., adv.*** keeping oneself apart or at a distance; showing no interest or sympathy [They stood *aloof* and did not even listen.]

**Aloof** comes from a Dutch word that means "windward" and is related to our word **luff.** A sailboat is often turned windward to steer clear of the shore. A person who is aloof "steers clear of" other people.

**a·loud** (ə loud′) ***adv.*** **1** loudly [to cry *aloud* for help]. **2** with the normal voice [Read the letter *aloud.*]

**al·pac·a** (al pak′ə) ***n.*** **1** a sheeplike animal of South America related to the llama. *See the picture.* **2** its soft wool. **3** a cloth woven from this wool. **4** a shiny cloth of wool and cotton, used for linings, suits, etc.

**al·pha** (al′fə) ***n.*** **1** the first letter of the Greek alphabet. **2** the first or the beginning of anything.

**al·pha·bet** (al′fə bet) ***n.*** **1** the letters of a language, given in the regular order [The English *alphabet* goes from A to Z.] **2** any system of symbols used in writing [the Braille *alphabet*].

The word **alphabet** was formed by joining the names of the first two letters of the Greek alphabet, *alpha* and *beta.*

**al·pha·bet·i·cal** (al′fə bet′i k'l) ***adj.*** **1** of the alphabet. **2** arranged in the regular order of the alphabet [Entries in a dictionary are in *alphabetical* order.] *Also* **al′pha·bet′ic** —**al′pha·bet′i·cal·ly** ***adv.***

**al·pha·bet·ize** (al′fə bə tīz′) ***v.*** to arrange in alphabetical order. —**al′pha·bet·ized′, al′pha·bet·iz′·ing**

**Al·pine** (al′pīn) ***adj.*** **1** of the Alps or the people who live there. **2** of or like high mountains.

**Alps** (alps) a mountain system in Europe, with ranges in France, Switzerland, Germany, Italy, Austria, and Yugoslavia.

**al·read·y** (ôl red′ē) ***adv.*** **1** by or before this time [When we arrived, dinner had *already* begun.] **2** even now [I am *already* ten minutes late.]

**al·right** (ôl rīt′) *see the note at* **all right.**

**Al·sace-Lor·raine** (al sās′lô rān′) a region in northeastern France. It was under German rule from 1871 to 1919 and from 1940 to 1944. *See the map.*

**al·so** (ôl′sō) ***adv.*** in addition; too; besides [Welles directed the film and *also* acted in it.]

**Alta.** *abbreviation for* **Alberta.**

**al·tar** (ôl′tər) ***n.*** **1** a high place on which sacrifices or offerings are made to a god. **2** a table, stand, etc. used for certain religious rituals as in a church [The bride and groom knelt before the *altar.*]

**al·ter** (ôl′tər) ***v.*** to change; make or become different in part [Some customs *alter* as time goes on. The tailor *altered* the legs of the pants.] —**al′ter·a·ble** ***adj.***

**al·ter·a·tion** (ôl′tə rā′shən) ***n.*** an altering; change.

**al·ter·ca·tion** (ôl′tər kā′shən) ***n.*** a noisy quarrel.

**al·ter·nate** (ôl′tər nit) ***adj.*** **1** coming by turns; first one and then the other [*alternate* stripes of blue and yellow]. *See the picture.* **2** every other [We take piano lessons on *alternate* Tuesdays.] ◆***n.*** a person ready to take the place of another if needed; substitute. ◆***v.*** (ôl′tər nāt) **1** to do, use, act, happen, etc. by turns [Good times *alternate* with bad.] **2** to take turns [The fifth and sixth grades *alternate* in using the gymnasium.] —**al′ter·nat·ed, al′ter·nat·ing** —**al′ter·nate·ly** ***adv.*** —**al′ter·na′tion** ***n.***

**alternating current** an electric current that reverses its direction at regular intervals.

**al·ter·na·tive** (ôl tur′nə tiv) ***adj.*** allowing a choice between two, or sometimes more than two, things [There are *alternative* routes to our farm.] ◆***n.*** **1** a choice between two or more things. **2** any one of the things that can be chosen. —**al·ter′na·tive·ly** ***adv.***

**al·though** (ôl *thō*′) ***conj.*** in spite of the fact that; even if; though: *sometimes spelled* **altho** [*Although* the sun is shining, it may rain later.]

**al·tim·e·ter** (al tim′ə tər) ***n.*** an instrument for measuring altitude, especially one that shows how high an airplane is flying.

**al·ti·tude** (al′tə to͞od *or* al′tə tyo͞od) ***n.*** **1** height; especially, the height of a thing above the earth's surface or above sea level. **2** a high place.

**al·to** (al′tō) ***n.*** **1** the lowest kind of singing voice of women, girls, or young boys. **2** a singer with such a voice. **3** an instrument with the second highest range in a family of instruments [*alto* saxophone]. —*pl.* **al′tos** ◆***adj.*** of or for an alto.

**al·to·geth·er** (ôl′tə ge*th*′ər) ***adv.*** **1** to the full extent; wholly; completely [You're not *altogether* wrong.] **2** in all; all being counted [They read six books *altogether.*] **3** when everything is kept in mind; on the whole [The concert was *altogether* a success.]

**al·tru·ism** (al′tro͞o iz′m) ***n.*** the act of putting the good of others ahead of one's own interests; unselfish action. —**al′tru·ist** ***n.***

**al·tru·is·tic** (al′tro͞o is′tik) ***adj.*** putting the good of others ahead of one's own interests; unselfish. —**al′tru·is′ti·cal·ly** ***adv.***

**al·um** (al′əm) ***n.*** a mineral salt used in making baking powders, dyes, and paper. It is also used to stop bleeding from small cuts.

**a·lu·mi·num** (ə lo͞o′mə nəm) ***n.*** a silvery, lightweight metal that is a chemical element. It does not rust. ◆***adj.*** of or containing aluminum.

☆**a·lum·na** (ə lum′nə) ***n.*** a woman or girl alumnus [She is an *alumna* of Yale.] —*pl.* **a·lum·nae** (ə lum′nē)

**a·lum·nus** (ə lum′nəs) ***n.*** a person, especially a man or boy, who has gone to or is a graduate of a particular school or college [He is an *alumnus* of Harvard.] —*pl.* **a·lum·ni** (ə lum′nī)

**al·ways** (ôl′wiz *or* ôl′wāz) ***adv.*** **1** at all times; at every time [*Always* be courteous.] **2** all the time; continually; forever [Oxygen is *always* present in the air.]

**am** (am) *the form of the verb* **be** *that is used to show the present time with* I [I *am* happy. *Am* I late?]

**AM** amplitude modulation: a method of radio broadcasting in which the strength of the radio wave changes according to the signal being sent. AM broadcasts travel farther than FM. *See also* **FM**.

**A.M.** Master of Arts.

**A.M.** or **a.m.** in the time from midnight to noon. *A.M.* is the abbreviation of *ante meridiem,* a Latin phrase meaning "before noon" [Be here at 8:30 *A.M.*]

**AMA** or **A.M.A.** American Medical Association.

**a·mal·gam** (ə mal′gəm) ***n.*** **1** a mixture of mercury with another metal or other metals [Silver *amalgam* is used to fill teeth.] **2** any mixture or blend.

**a·mal·ga·mate** (ə mal′gə māt) ***v.*** to join together into one; mix; combine [Five companies were *amalgamated* to form the corporation.] —**a·mal′ga·mat·ed, a·mal′ga·mat·ing** —**a·mal′ga·ma′tion** ***n.***

**Am·a·ril·lo** (am′ə ril′ō) a city in northwestern Texas.

**am·a·ryl·lis** (am′ə ril′əs) ***n.*** a plant that grows from a bulb, with several flowers that look like lilies, growing on a single stem. *See the picture.*

**a·mass** (ə mas′) ***v.*** to pile up; collect or gather together [to *amass* much money].

**am·a·teur** (am′ə chər *or* am′ə to͝or) ***n.*** **1** a person who does something for the pleasure of it rather than for money; one who is not a professional. **2** a person who does something without much skill. ◆***adj.*** **1** of or done by amateurs [an *amateur* performance]. **2** being an amateur [an *amateur* athlete].

**am·a·teur·ish** (am′ə cho͝or′ish *or* am′ə to͝or′ish) ***adj.*** like an amateur; unskillful; not expert.

**a·maze** (ə māz′) ***v.*** to cause to feel great surprise or sudden wonder; astonish [They were *amazed* at the great height of the waterfall.] —**a·mazed′, a·maz′ing**

**a·maze·ment** (ə māz′mənt) ***n.*** great surprise or wonder; astonishment. *See the picture.*

**a·maz·ing** (ə māz′ing) ***adj.*** causing amazement; astonishing. —**a·maz′ing·ly** ***adv.***

**Am·a·zon** (am′ə zän) a river in South America, flowing across Brazil into the Atlantic. It is over 3,000 miles long and is the longest river in South America. ◆***n.*** **1** in Greek myths, any member of a race of women warriors. **2** **amazon,** any large, strong woman.

> The **Amazon** River was so named by Spanish explorers, who thought that women warriors like those in the Greek myths lived along its shores.

**am·bas·sa·dor** (am bas′ə dər) ***n.*** **1** an official of highest rank sent by a country to represent it in another country. **2** any person sent as a representative or messenger [the U.S. *ambassador* to the UN].

**am·ber** (am′bər) ***n.*** **1** a brownish-yellow substance found along some seacoasts and used in jewelry, etc. It is the hardened resin of pine trees that grew millions of years ago. **2** the color of amber. ◆***adj.*** **1** made of amber. **2** having the color of amber.

**am·ber·gris** (am′bər grēs *or* am′bər gris) ***n.*** a grayish, waxy substance that comes from the intestines of certain whales. It is used in making some perfumes.

**am·bi·dex·trous** (am′bə dek′strəs) ***adj.*** able to use the right or left hand with equal ease, as in writing or throwing.

**am·bi·gu·i·ty** (am′bə gyo͞o′ə tē) ***n.*** **1** the condition of being ambiguous; a being unclear or indefinite. **2** an ambiguous word or remark. —*pl.* **am′bi·gu′i·ties**

**am·big·u·ous** (am big′yoo wəs) ***adj.*** **1** having two or more possible meanings ["A funny person" is *ambiguous* as it can mean that the person is either comical or strange.] **2** not clear; not definite [Don't be so *ambiguous* in your answers.] —**am·big′u·ous·ly** ***adv.***

**am·bi·tion** (am bish′ən) ***n.*** **1** strong desire to be successful or to gain fame, power, or wealth. **2** the thing that one desires so strongly [Her *ambition* is to be a lawyer.]

| | | | | | | | |
|---|---|---|---|---|---|---|---|
| **a** fat | **ir** here | **ou** out | **zh** leisure | | | | |
| **ā** ape | **ī** bite, fire | **u** up | **ng** ring | | | | |
| **ä** car, lot | **ō** go | **ur** fur | a *in* ago | | | | |
| **e** ten | **ô** law, horn | **ch** chin | e *in* agent | | | | |
| **er** care | **oi** oil | **sh** she | **ə** = i *in* unity | | | | |
| **ē** even | **oo** look | **th** thin | o *in* collect | | | | |
| **i** hit | **o͞o** tool | ***th*** then | u *in* focus | | | | |

**am·bi·tious** (am bish′əs) ***adj.*** **1** full of or showing ambition [A senator *ambitious* to be president.] **2** needing great effort, skill, etc. [an *ambitious* program]. —**am·bi′tious·ly** ***adv.***

SYNONYMS: **Ambitious** suggests a great effort to get a higher position, wealth, fame, etc., and can be used in either an approving or disapproving way. **Aspiring** suggests an effort to reach a high goal that may be too hard to reach.

**am·ble** (am′b'l) ***v.*** **1** to move at a smooth, easy pace by raising first both legs on one side, then both legs on the other: said of horses, camels, etc. **2** to walk in a slow, relaxed manner. —**am′bled, am′bling** •***n.*** **1** a horse's ambling gait. **2** a slow, relaxed walking pace.

**am·bro·sia** (am brō′zhə) ***n.*** **1** the food of the ancient Greek and Roman gods. **2** anything that tastes or smells very delicious. —**am·bro′sial** ***adj.***

**am·bu·lance** (am′byə ləns) ***n.*** a special automobile or wagon for carrying sick or injured people.

**am·bush** (am′boosh) ***n.*** **1** a group, as of soldiers, waiting in hiding to make a surprise attack. **2** the place of hiding. •***v.*** to attack from hiding [The patrol was *ambushed* and captured in the jungle.]

**a·me·ba** (ə mē′bə) ***n.*** *another spelling of* **amoeba.** —*pl.* **a·me′bas** or **a·me·bae** (ə mē′bē)

**a·mel·io·rate** (ə mēl′yə rāt) ***v.*** to make or become better; improve [The workers sought to *ameliorate* their working conditions.] —**a·mel′io·rat·ed, a·mel′io·rat·ing** —**a·mel′io·ra′tion** ***n.***



**a·men** (ā′men′ *or* ä′men′) ***interj.*** a Hebrew word meaning "may it be so!" or "so it is": *used after a prayer or to show that one agrees.*

**a·me·na·ble** (ə mē′nə b'l *or* ə men′ə b'l) ***adj.*** willing to be controlled or to take advice; responsive [I'm *amenable* to any reasonable suggestion].

**a·mend** (ə mend′) ***v.*** **1** to change or revise [Some selfish groups get laws *amended* to favor themselves.] **2** to make better; improve [Try to *amend* your ways.]

**a·mend·ment** (ə mend′mənt) ***n.*** a change in or addition to a bill, law, constitution, etc. [The first ten *amendments* to the Constitution are called the Bill of Rights.]

amphibious vehicle

amphitheater

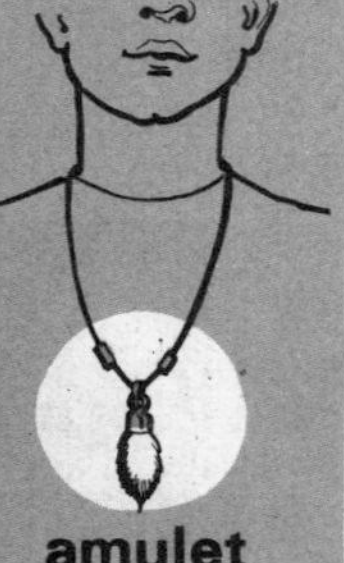
amulet

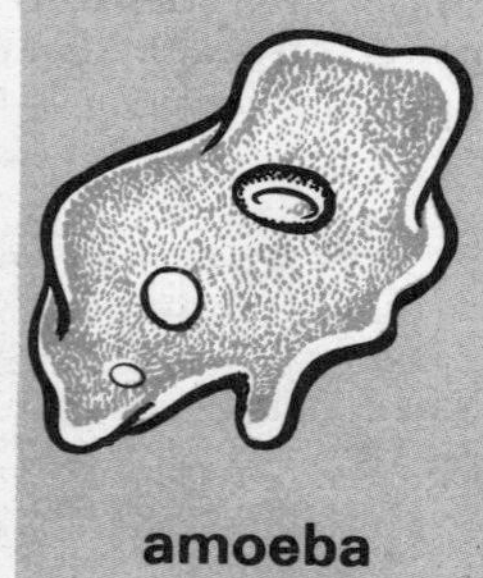
amoeba

anachronism

**a·mends** (ə mendz′) ***n.pl.*** something given or done to make up for an injury, insult, or loss that one has caused; compensation [She tried to make *amends* for her rudeness by apologizing to him.]

**a·men·i·ty** (ə men′ə tē) ***n.*** **1** anything that adds to one's comfort; convenience [The town had *amenities* such as swimming pools and skating rinks.] **2 ameni·ties,** *pl.* the polite and thoughtful ways in which people are supposed to behave. —*pl.* **a·men′i·ties**

**A·mer·i·ca** (ə mer′ə kə) **1** either North America or South America. **2** North America and South America together. ☆**3** the United States of America.

**A·mer·i·can** (ə mer′ə kən) ***adj.*** **1** of or in America [the *American* Indians]. ☆**2** of or in the United States [*American* foreign policy]. •***n.*** **1** a person born or living in America. ☆**2** a citizen of the United States.

☆**A·mer·i·can·ism** (ə mer′ə kən iz'm) ***n.*** **1** a word or phrase of American English that was first used in the United States or in the American colonies ["Jukebox" and "squaw" are *Americanisms,* and so is "Americanism" itself.] **2** loyalty to the United States or to its customs, beliefs, etc.

☆**A·mer·i·can·ize** (ə mer′ə kə nīz′) ***v.*** to make or become American in customs, speech, beliefs, etc. —**A·mer′i·can·ized′, A·mer′i·can·iz′ing** —**A·mer′i·can·i·za′tion** ***n.***

**American Revolution** the revolution from 1763 to 1783 by which the American colonies won their independence from England. It became the Revolutionary War in 1775.

**American Samoa** *see* **Samoa.**

**am·e·thyst** (am′ə thist) ***n.*** **1** a purple stone, especially a kind of quartz, that is used as a jewel. **2** purple or violet.

**Amethyst** comes from a Greek word meaning "not drunk." The ancient Greeks believed that someone wearing an amethyst would not get drunk from drinking alcoholic liquor.

**a·mi·a·ble** (ā′mē ə b'l) ***adj.*** pleasant and friendly; good-natured [an *amiable* companion; an *amiable* remark]. —**a′mi·a·bly** ***adv.***

**am·i·ca·ble** (am′i kə b'l) ***adj.*** friendly in feeling; peaceable [an *amicable* debate]. —**am′i·ca·bly** ***adv.***

**amid** (ə mid′) ***prep.*** among; in the middle of [Weeds grew *amid* the flowers.]

**a·mid·ships** (ə mid′ships) ***adv.*** in or toward the middle of the ship [The other vessel struck us *amidships.*]

**a·midst** (ə midst′) ***prep.*** *same as* **amid.**

☆**a·mi·go** (ə mē′gō) ***n.*** friend: *a Spanish word.* —*pl.* **a·mi′gos**

**a·miss** (ə mis′) ***adv., adj.*** in a wrong way; out of order; faulty or faultily; wrong [If nothing goes *amiss,* they will return on Monday.]

**am·i·ty** (am′ə tē) ***n.*** friendly, peaceful relations, as between nations or groups; friendship.

**Am·man** (äm′än) the capital of Jordan.

**am·mo·nia** (ə mōn′yə) ***n.*** **1** a colorless gas that is made up of nitrogen and hydrogen and has a very sharp smell. It is used in making fertilizers. **2** a liquid made by dissolving this gas in water, used as a cleaning fluid: *also called* **ammonia water.**

**am·mu·ni·tion** (am′yə nish′ən) ***n.*** **1** anything that is hurled by a weapon or is exploded as a weapon, such as bullets, bombs, rockets, etc. **2** anything that can be used in attack or defense [The article gave her *ammunition* for her argument.]

**am·ne·sia** (am nē′zhə) ***n.*** the condition of suddenly forgetting all or some of the past, as because of brain injury or shock.

**am·nes·ty** (am′nəs tē) ***n.*** a general pardon or forgiveness for political acts against a government [The president granted *amnesty* to the rebels living in exile.] —*pl.* **am′nes·ties**

**a·moe·ba** (ə mē′bə) ***n.*** a tiny animal made up of just one cell, found in the ground and in water. It can be seen only through a microscope and it moves by changing its shape. *See the picture.* —*pl.* **a·moe′bas** or **a·moe·bae** (ə mē′bē)

**a·mok** (ə muk′) ***adj., adv.*** in a mad rage to kill. —**run amok,** to rush about in a mad rage.

**a·mong** (ə muŋ′) ***prep.*** **1** in the company of; together with [You are *among* friends.] **2** from place to place in [They passed *among* the crowd.] **3** in the number or class of [They are *among* the richest people in town.] **4** with a share for each of [The estate was divided *among* the relatives.] **5** with one another [Don't quarrel *among* yourselves.] *See* **between.**

**a·mongst** (ə muŋst′) ***prep.*** *same as* **among.**

**am·o·rous** (am′ər əs) ***adj.*** **1** full of or showing love; loving [*amorous* words; an *amorous* suitor]. **2** in love. —**am′o·rous·ly** ***adv.***

**a·mor·phous** (ə môr′fəs) ***adj.*** **1** not having a definite form or shape [The amoeba is a tiny, *amorphous* animal.] **2** of no definite type or kind [an *amorphous* collection of books]. **3** solid but not made up of crystals [an *amorphous* lump of charcoal].

**A·mos** (ā′məs) **1** a Hebrew prophet in the Bible. **2** a book of the Bible with his prophecies.

**a·mount** (ə mount′) ***v.*** **1** to add up; total [The bill *amounts* to $4.50.] **2** to be equal in meaning or effect [Her failure to reply *amounts* to a refusal.] ◆***n.*** **1** the sum; total [The bill was $50, but he paid only half that *amount*.] **2** a quantity [a small *amount* of rain].

**am·pere** (am′pir) ***n.*** a unit for measuring the strength of an electric current. It is the amount of current sent by one volt through a resistance of one ohm.

**am·phib·i·an** (am fib′ē ən) ***adj.*** **1** belonging to a group of coldblooded animals with a backbone, that live both on land and in water. **2** *same as* **amphibious.** ◆***n.*** **1** any amphibian animal, as the frog, which has lungs but begins life in water as a tadpole with gills. **2** any amphibious animal, as the seal or beaver. **3** an airplane that can take off from or come down on either land or water. **4** a tank, truck, etc. that can travel on either land or water.

**am·phib·i·ous** (am fib′ē əs) ***adj.*** **1** that can live both on land and in water [an *amphibious* plant]. **2** that can operate or travel on both land and water [an *amphibious* truck]. *See the picture.*

**am·phi·the·a·ter** or **am·phi·the·a·tre** (am′fə thē′ə tər) ***n.*** a round or oval building having rising rows of seats around an open space in which sports events, plays, etc. are held. *See the picture.*

**am·ple** (am′p'l) ***adj.*** **1** having plenty of space; roomy; large [an *ample* kitchen for a large family]. **2** more than enough; abundant [From his *ample* funds he gave to many in need.] **3** enough; adequate [Our oil supply is *ample* for the winter.]

**am·pli·fi·ca·tion** (am′plə fi kā′shən) ***n.*** **1** an amplifying, or making larger or stronger; increase. **2** more details [Your report needs *amplification*.]

**am·pli·fi·er** (am′plə fī′ər) ***n.*** **1** a person or thing that amplifies. **2** a device, especially one with vacuum tubes or semiconductors, used to make electric or radio waves stronger before they are changed into sounds, as in a phonograph or radio.

**am·pli·fy** (am′plə fī) ***v.*** **1** to make larger, stronger, louder, etc. **2** to give more details about [The point was *amplified* in debate.] —**am′pli·fied, am′pli·fy·ing**

**am·pli·tude** (am′plə to͞od *or* am′plə tyo͞od) ***n.*** **1** great size or extent; largeness. **2** an ample or great amount; abundance. **3** the range of something that swings back and forth, as a pendulum, from the middle position to either end.

**am·ply** (am′plē) ***adv.*** in an ample manner; fully [You will be *amply* rewarded.]

**am·pu·tate** (am′pyə tāt) ***v.*** to cut off, especially by surgery [The doctor *amputated* the leg below the knee.] —**am′pu·tat·ed, am′pu·tat·ing** —**am′pu·ta′tion** ***n.***

**Am·ster·dam** (am′stər dam) a seaport in the Netherlands. It is the official capital. *See also* The **Hague.**

☆**Am·trak** (am′trak) ***n.*** a railroad system for carrying passengers throughout the United States.

**a·muck** (ə muk′) ***adj., adv.*** *another spelling of* **amok.**

**am·u·let** (am′yə lit) ***n.*** something worn on the body because it is supposed to have magic to protect against harm or evil; a charm. *See the picture.* 

**A·mund·sen** (ä′moon sən), **Ro·ald** (rō′äl) 1872–1928; Norwegian explorer. He was the first person to reach the South Pole, in 1911.

**a·muse** (ə myo͞oz′) ***v.*** **1** to keep busy or interested with something pleasant or enjoyable; entertain [We *amused* ourselves with games.] *See* SYNONYMS *at* **entertain.** **2** to make laugh or smile by being comical or humorous [Her jokes always *amuse* me.] —**a·mused′, a·mus′ing**

**a·muse·ment** (ə myo͞oz′mənt) ***n.*** **1** the condition of being amused. **2** something that amuses or entertains.

☆**amusement park** an outdoor place with rides and other things to amuse people. Such parks may have a merry-go-round, roller coaster, games, refreshment stands, etc.

**a·mus·ing** (ə myo͞oz′iŋ) ***adj.*** causing laughter or smiles. *See* SYNONYMS *at* **funny.** —**a·mus′ing·ly** ***adv.***

**an** (ən *or* an) ***adj.*** **1** one; one sort of [Will you bake *an* apple pie?] **2** each; any one [Pick *an* apple from the tree.] **3** in or for each [I earn three dollars *an* hour.] *See the note at* **a.**

**-an** (ən) *a suffix meaning:* **1** of, in, or having to do with [A *suburban* home is in a suburb.] **2** born in or living in [An *Asian* is a person born or living in Asia.]

**a·nach·ro·nism** (ə nak′rə niz'm) ***n.*** **1** the connecting

| | | | | | | | |
|---|---|---|---|---|---|---|---|
| **a** | fat | **ir** | here | **ou** | out | **zh** | leisure |
| **ā** | ape | **ī** | bite, fire | **u** | up | **ŋ** | ring |
| **ä** | car, lot | **ō** | go | **ur** | fur | | a *in* ago |
| **e** | ten | **ô** | law, horn | **ch** | chin | | e *in* agent |
| **er** | care | **oi** | oil | **sh** | she | **ə =** | i *in* unity |
| **ē** | even | **oo** | look | **th** | thin | | o *in* collect |
| **i** | hit | **o͞o** | tool | ***th*** | then | | u *in* focus |

of a person, thing, or happening with another that came later in history *[Shakespeare was guilty of an* *anachronism* when he had a clock striking in a play about ancient Rome.*]* **2.** anything that is or seems to be out of its proper time in history *[*A horse in a city is an *anachronism* today.*] See the picture on page 24.*

**an·a·con·da** (an'ə kän'də) ***n.*** a very long, heavy snake of South America. Anacondas kill their prey by crushing it in their coils. *See the picture.*

**an·aes·the·sia** (an'əs thē'zhə) ***n.*** *another spelling of* **anesthesia.** —**an'aes·thet'ic *adj., n.***

**an·a·gram** (an'ə gram) ***n.*** **1** a word or phrase made from another word or phrase by changing the order of the letters ["Dare" is an *anagram* of "read."] **2 anagrams,** *pl.* a game played by forming words from letters picked from a pile.

**An·a·heim** (an'ə hīm) a city in southwestern California.

**an·al·ge·sic** (an''l jē'zik) ***adj.*** stopping or easing pain. ◆***n.*** a drug that eases pain, as aspirin.

**a·nal·o·gous** (ə nal'ə gəs) ***adj.*** alike or the same in some ways [A computer is *analogous* to the brain.]

**a·nal·o·gy** (ə nal'ə jē) ***n.*** likeness in some ways between things that are otherwise unlike; resemblance in part [How a jet airplane flies can be explained by showing an *analogy* with air escaping fast from a toy balloon.] —*pl.* **a·nal'o·gies**

**a·nal·y·sis** (ə nal'ə sis) ***n.*** a separating or breaking up of something into its parts so as to examine them and see how they fit together [A chemical *analysis* of a substance will tell what elements are in it. The *analysis* of a problem will help tell what caused it.] —*pl.* **a·nal·y·ses** (ə nal'ə sēz)

**an·a·lyst** (an'ə list) ***n.*** **1** a person who analyzes. **2** *a shorter form of* **psychoanalyst.**

**an·a·lyt·i·cal** (an'ə lit'i k'l) or **an·a·lyt·ic** (an'ə lit'ik) ***adj.*** **1** having to do with analysis [an *analytical* process]. **2** good at analyzing [an *analytical* person]. —**an'a·lyt'i·cal·ly *adv.***

**an·a·lyze** (an'ə līz) ***v.*** to separate or break up any thing or idea into its parts so as to examine them and see how they fit together [to *analyze* the causes of war]. —**an'a·lyz'er *n.***

**an·ar·chism** (an'ər kiz'm) ***n.*** the belief that all forms of government act in an unfair way against the liberty of the individual and should be done away with.

> **Anarchism** comes from a Greek word meaning "without a leader." Anarchists want no monarch or president over them.

**an·arch·ist** (an'ər kist) ***n.*** **1** a person who believes in anarchism. **2** a person who brings about disorder, as by ignoring rules, duties, etc.

**an·arch·y** (an'ər kē) ***n.*** **1** the complete absence of government and law. **2** a condition of disorder or confusion. —**an·ar·chic** (an är'kik) ***adj.***

**a·nath·e·ma** (ə nath'ə mə) ***n.*** **1** a terrible curse against a person or thing, often one putting a person out of a church. **2** a person or thing that is hated or put under a curse.

**an·a·tom·i·cal** (an'ə täm'i k'l) ***adj.*** of or having to do with anatomy.

**a·nat·o·mist** (ə nat'ə mist) ***n.*** a person who is skilled in anatomy.

**a·nat·o·my** (ə nat'ə mē) ***n.*** **1** a cutting apart of an animal or plant in order to study its parts. **2** the study of the form or structure of animals or plants. Anatomy deals with the different tissues, parts, and organs of a body. **3** the structure of the body [The *anatomy* of a frog is in many ways like that of a person.]

**-ance** (əns) *a suffix meaning:* **1** the act of [*Assistance* is the act of assisting.] **2** the state of being [*Vigilance* is the state of being vigilant.] **3** a thing that [A *conveyance* is a thing that conveys.]

**an·ces·tor** (an'ses tər) ***n.*** **1** a person who comes before one in a family line, especially someone earlier than a grandparent; forefather [Their *ancestors* came from Poland.] **2** an early kind of animal from which later kinds have developed [The *ancestor* of the elephant was the mammoth.]

**an·ces·tral** (an ses'trəl) ***adj.*** of or inherited from an ancestor or ancestors [an *ancestral* farm].

**an·ces·try** (an'ses'trē) ***n.*** all one's ancestors; one's past family [a person of African *ancestry*]. —*pl.* **an'ces·tries**

**an·chor** (aŋ'kər) ***n.*** **1** a heavy object let down into the water by a chain to keep a ship from drifting. It is usually a metal piece with hooks that grip the ground at the bottom of the water. *See the picture.* **2** anything that keeps something else steady or firm [In time of trouble, faith was the old folks' *anchor.*] ◆***v.*** **1** to keep from drifting or coming loose by using an anchor. **2** to attach or fix firmly [The shelves are *anchored* to the wall.] —**weigh anchor,** to pull up the anchor.

**an·chor·age** (aŋ'kər ij) ***n.*** **1** a place to anchor ships. **2** a strong support that keeps something steady. **3** the act of anchoring.

**An·chor·age** (aŋ'kər ij) a seaport in southern Alaska.

**an·cho·rite** (aŋ'kə rīt) ***n.*** a hermit; especially, one who lives alone for religious reasons.

**anchor man** **1** the last runner on a relay team, the last bowler on a bowling team, etc. **2** the chief member of a team of newscasters.

**an·cho·vy** (an'chō vē *or* an chō'vē) ***n.*** a very small fish of the herring family. Anchovies are usually salted and canned in oil, or made into a salty paste. —*pl.* **an'cho·vies**

**an·cient** (ān'shənt) ***adj.*** **1** of times long past; belonging to the early history of people, before about 500 A.D. **2** having lasted a long time; very old [their *ancient* quarrel]. —**the ancients,** the people who lived in ancient times.

**an·cient·ly** (ān'shənt lē) ***adv.*** in ancient times.

**-an·cy** (ən sē) *same as* **-ance.**

**and** (and *or* ənd *or* ən) ***conj.*** **1** also; in addition; as well as [They picked *and* preserved plums *and* pears.] **2** plus; added to [6 *and* 2 equals 8]. **3** as a result [Help me *and* I'll be grateful.] **4** to: *used only in everyday talk* [Try *and* get it.]

**an·dan·te** (än dän'tā *or* an dan'tē) ***adj., adv.*** rather slow. It is an Italian word used in music to tell how fast a piece should be played.

> **Andante** comes from the Italian word *andare,* meaning "to walk." Music played andante moves along at a moderate pace, not fast like music played presto.

**An·der·sen** (an′dər s′n), **Hans Christian** 1805–1875; Danish writer of fairy stories.

**An·der·son** (an′dər s′n), **Marian** 1902?– ; American concert singer.

**An·des** (an′dēz) a mountain system along the length of western South America.

**and·i·ron** (an′dī′ərn) ***n.*** either one of a pair of metal supports on which to rest logs in a fireplace. *See the picture.*

**An·dor·ra** (an dôr′ə) a tiny republic between Spain and France, in the Pyrenees. —**An·dor′ran** ***adj., n.***

**an·droid** (an′droid) ***n.*** in science fiction, an automaton made to look like a human being; mechanical person.

**an·ec·dote** (an′ik dōt) ***n.*** a short, interesting or amusing story of some happening or about some person [I told my *anecdote* about the first time I tried to ski.] —**an′ec·dot′al** ***adj.***

**a·ne·mi·a** (ə nē′mē ə) ***n.*** a condition in which a person's blood does not have enough red corpuscles or hemoglobin so that it does not carry a normal amount of oxygen. The person becomes pale and tired.

**a·ne·mic** (ə nē′mik) ***adj.*** of or having anemia.

**an·e·mom·e·ter** (an′ə mäm′ə tər) ***n.*** a device for measuring the speed of wind.

**a·nem·o·ne** (ə nem′ə nē) ***n.*** **1** a plant with white, pink, red, or purple flowers, that are shaped like small cups. **2** *same as* **sea anemone.**

**an·es·the·sia** (an′əs thē′zhə) ***n.*** a condition in which one has no feeling of pain, heat, touch, etc. in all or part of the body.

**an·es·the·si·ol·o·gist** (an′əs thē′zē äl′ə jist) ***n.*** a doctor who specializes in the science of anesthetics.

☆**an·es·thet·ic** (an′əs thet′ik) ***adj.*** taking away any feeling of pain, heat, touch, etc. [an *anesthetic* drug]. ◆***n.*** a drug, gas, etc. used to bring about anesthesia, as before surgery. A **local anesthetic** causes numbness in just a part of the body, while a **general anesthetic** can make one completely unconscious.

**an·es·the·tist** (ə nes′thə tist) ***n.*** a person trained to give anesthetics during surgical operations.

**an·es·the·tize** (ə nes′thə tīz) ***v.*** to bring about a loss of pain or feeling or to make unconscious, especially by giving anesthetics. —**an·es′the·tized, an·es′the·tiz·ing**

**a·new** (ə nōō′ *or* ə nyōō′) ***adv.*** once more; again, especially in a new way [They tore down the slums and began to build *anew.*]

**an·gel** (ān′j'l) ***n.*** **1** a being that is supposed to live in heaven and have more power and goodness than human beings. Angels are often mentioned in the Bible as messengers of God. They are usually pictured as having a human form, wings, and a halo. *See the picture.* **2** a person thought of as being as beautiful or as good as an angel. **3** a helping or guiding spirit.

☆**angel cake** or **angel food cake** a light, spongy, white cake made without shortening or egg yolks, but with many egg whites.

**an·gel·ic** (an jel′ik) or **an·gel·i·cal** (an jel′i k'l) ***adj.*** **1** of the angels; heavenly. **2** as beautiful, good, or innocent as an angel [a child with an *angelic* smile].

**An·ge·lus** or **an·ge·lus** (an′jə ləs) ***n.*** **1** a prayer said at morning, noon, and evening in the Roman Catholic Church. **2** the bell rung to tell the time for this prayer.

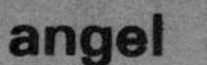

angel

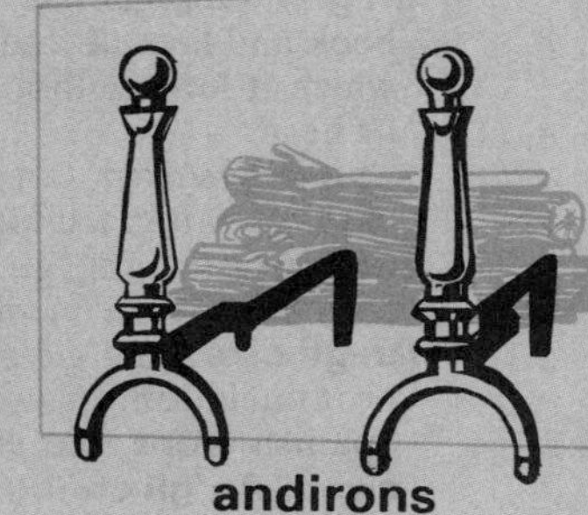

andirons

**anaconda** 9 m (30 ft.) long

**anchors**

**an·ger** (aŋ′gər) ***n.*** a feeling of being very annoyed and wanting to fight back at a person or thing that hurts one or is against one; wrath; rage. ◆***v.*** to make angry [The tourist's rudeness *angered* us.] 

SYNONYMS: **Anger** is the general word for the feeling of displeasure mixed with a desire to fight back. **Rage** means a sudden, strong outburst of anger when one's self-control seems lost. **Fury** means a rash, wildly excited anger when one becomes completely unreasonable.

**an·gle**[1] (aŋ′g'l) ***n.*** **1** the shape made by two straight lines meeting in a point, or by two surfaces meeting along a line. **2** the space between such lines or surfaces. It is measured in degrees. **3** the way one looks at something; point of view [Consider the problem from all *angles.*] **4** a tricky way of getting what one wants: *used only in everyday talk* [He's always looking for an *angle* in the deals he makes.] ◆***v.*** **1** to move or bend at an angle. **2** to tell or write a story or report in a way that tries to make others have certain feelings about it: *used only in everyday talk* [The news story was *angled* to make the suspect look guilty.] —**an′gled, an′gling**

**an·gle**[2] (aŋ′g'l) ***v.*** **1** to fish with a hook and line. **2** to use tricks or schemes to get something [to *angle* for a compliment by flattering others]. —**an′gled, an′gling**

| | | | | | | | |
|---|---|---|---|---|---|---|---|
| **a** | fat | **ir** | here | **ou** | out | **zh** | leisure |
| **ā** | ape | **ī** | bite, fire | **u** | up | **ŋ** | ring |
| **ä** | car, lot | **ō** | go | **ur** | fur | | a *in* ago |
| **e** | ten | **ô** | law, horn | **ch** | chin | | e *in* agent |
| **er** | care | **oi** | oil | **sh** | she | **ə =** | i *in* unity |
| **ē** | even | **oo** | look | **th** | thin | | o *in* collect |
| **i** | hit | **ōō** | tool | ***th*** | then | | u *in* focus |

a

**an·gler** (aŋ′glər) ***n.*** **1** a person who fishes using a hook and line. **2** a saltwater fish that eats smaller fish which it lures with a long, threadlike rod growing on its head.

☆**an·gle·worm** (aŋ′g'l wurm′) ***n.*** an earthworm, used for bait in fishing.

**An·gli·can** (aŋ′gli kən) ***adj.*** of the Church of England. ◆***n.*** a member of the Church of England.

**An·gli·cize** (aŋ′glə sīz) ***v.*** to make English in form, pronunciation, customs, manner, etc. ["Patio" is a Spanish word that has been *Anglicized.*] —**An′gli·cized, An′gli·ciz·ing**

**an·gling** (aŋ′gliŋ) ***n.*** the act of fishing with a hook and line.

**An·glo-** (aŋ′glō) a word root meaning "English" or "England" [An *Anglo*-American agreement is an agreement between England and America.]

**An·glo-Sax·on** (aŋ′glō sak′s'n) ***n.*** **1** a member of the Germanic peoples who invaded England and were living there at the time of the Norman Conquest. **2** their language: *now usually called* **Old English**. **3** an English person or one whose ancestors were English. ◆***adj.*** **1** of the Anglo-Saxons, their language, etc. **2** having English ancestors.

**An·go·la** (aŋ gō′lə) a country on the southwestern coast of Africa.

**An·go·ra** (aŋ gôr′ə) ***n.*** **1** a kind of cat with long, silky fur. **2** a kind of goat with long, silky hair. This hair, called **Angora wool**, is used in making mohair. **3** a long-eared rabbit (**Angora rabbit**) with long, silky hair. This hair is used to make a soft yarn which is woven into sweaters, mittens, etc.



**an·gri·ly** (aŋ′grə lē) ***adv.*** in an angry manner.

**an·gry** (aŋ′grē) ***adj.*** **1** feeling or showing anger [*angry* words; an *angry* crowd]. **2** wild and stormy [an *angry* sea]. **3** inflamed and sore [an *angry* wound]. —**an′gri·er, an′gri·est**

**an·guish** (aŋ′gwish) ***n.*** great suffering, as from worry, grief, or pain; agony [They were in *anguish* until their child was cured of her illness.] —**an′guished** ***adj.***

animated cartoon

ant

Annunciation

annex

**an·gu·lar** (aŋ′gyə lər) ***adj.*** **1** having angles or sharp corners [an *angular* building]. **2** measured by an angle [the *angular* motion of a pendulum]. **3** with bones that jut out; gaunt [an *angular* face].

**an·gu·lar·i·ty** (aŋ′gyə lar′ə tē) ***n.*** **1** the condition of being angular or having angles. **2** a sharp corner; angle. —*pl.* **an′gu·lar′i·ties**

**an·i·line** (an′'l in *or* an′'l ēn′) ***n.*** a poisonous, oily liquid that is made from benzene and is used in making dyes. ◆***adj.*** made from aniline [*aniline* dyes].

**an·i·mal** (an′ə m'l) ***n.*** **1** any living being that can move about by itself, has sense organs, and does not make its own food as plants do from inorganic matter [Insects, snakes, fish, birds, cattle, and people are all *animals.*] **2** any such being other than a human being; especially, any four-footed creature; beast. **3** a person who is like a beast or brute. ◆***adj.*** **1** of or from an animal [*animal* fats]. **2** like an animal or beast; coarse, wild, etc. [to live an *animal* existence].

SYNONYMS: An **animal** is any kind of living being that can move about [An insect is a tiny *animal.*] A **beast** is thought of as any animal except man, especially a large, four-footed animal [Donkeys are *beasts* of burden.] **Brute** is usually used when one wishes to stress the wildness or strength of an animal or that it cannot reason or speak [The cat, poor *brute,* could not tell me of its suffering.]

**an·i·mate** (an′ə māt) ***v.*** **1** to give life, liveliness, or spirit to [A smile *animated* the child's face.] **2** to cause to act; inspire [A nurse is *animated* by the desire to help others.] —**an′i·mat·ed, an′i·mat·ing** ◆***adj.*** (an′ə mit) living; having life [*animate* beings].

**an·i·mat·ed** (an′ə māt′id) ***adj.*** vigorous; lively [an *animated* conversation]. —**an′i·mat′ed·ly** ***adv.***

☆**animated cartoon** a motion picture made by filming a series of drawings, each changed slightly from the one before. The drawn figures seem to move when the drawings are shown on a screen, one quickly after the other. *See the picture.*

**an·i·ma·tion** (an′ə mā′shən) ***n.*** **1** life. **2** liveliness; vigor; spirit [They spoke with *animation* of their trip to Mexico.] **3** the art or work of making animated cartoons.

**an·i·mos·i·ty** (an′ə mäs′ə tē) ***n.*** a feeling of strong dislike or hatred; ill will [Making fun of people can arouse their *animosity.*] —*pl.* **an′i·mos′i·ties**

**an·ise** (an′is) ***n.*** **1** a plant of the parsley family, whose seeds have a strong, pleasant smell. **2** this seed, used for flavoring and in medicine.

**An·ka·ra** (aŋ′kər ə) the capital of Turkey.

**an·kle** (aŋ′k'l) ***n.*** the joint that connects the foot and the leg.

**an·klet** (aŋ′klit) ***n.*** **1** a band worn around the ankle, usually as an ornament. **2** a short sock.

**an·nals** (an′'lz) ***n.pl.*** **1** a record of events year by year, put down in the order in which they happened. **2** a history [Joan of Arc holds a special place in the *annals* of France.]

**An·nap·o·lis** (ə nap′ə lis) the capital of Maryland, on Chesapeake Bay. The U.S. Naval Academy is there.

**an·neal** (ə nēl′) ***v.*** to make glass or metal less brittle by heating it and then cooling it slowly.

**an·nex** (ə neks′) ***v.*** to add on or attach a smaller thing to a larger one [Texas was *annexed* to the Union in 1845.] ◆***n.*** (an′eks) something added on; especially, an extra part built on or near a building to give more space. *See the picture.* —**an′nex·a′tion** ***n.***

**an·ni·hi·late** (ə nī′ə lāt) ***v.*** to destroy completely; put out of existence; wipe out [An atomic bomb can *annihilate* a city.] —**an·ni′hi·lat·ed, an·ni′hi·lat·ing** —**an·ni′hi·la′tion** ***n.***

**an·ni·ver·sa·ry** (an′ə vur′sər ē) ***n.*** **1** the date on which something happened in an earlier year [June 14 will be the tenth *anniversary* of their wedding.] **2** the celebration of such a date. ◆***adj.*** of or celebrating an anniversary. —*pl.* **an′ni·ver′sa·ries**

**an·no·tate** (an′ə tāt) ***v.*** to add notes that explain something or give one's opinions [Scholars *annotate* the plays of Shakespeare.] —**an′no·tat·ed, an′no·tat·ing**

**an·no·ta·tion** (an′ə tā′shən) ***n.*** **1** the act of annotating. **2** a note or notes added to explain something or offer opinions.

**an·nounce** (ə nouns′) ***v.*** **1** to tell the public about; proclaim [to *announce* the opening of a new store]. **2** to say; tell [Mother *announced* she wasn't going with us.] **3** to say that someone has arrived [Will you please *announce* me to Mrs. Lopez?] **4** to make known or clear [Footsteps *announced* the scout's return.] —**an·nounced′, an·nounc′ing**

**an·nounce·ment** (ə nouns′mənt) ***n.*** **1** an announcing of something that has happened or will happen. **2** something announced, often in the form of a written or printed notice [The wedding *announcements* are here.]

**an·nounc·er** (ə nouns′ər) ***n.*** a person who announces; especially, one who introduces radio or television programs, reads the news and commercials, etc.

**an·noy** (ə noi′) ***v.*** to irritate, bother, or make slightly angry [Their loud talk *annoyed* the librarian.] —**an·noy′ing** ***adj.***

> SYNONYMS: Something that **annoys** causes one to be disturbed for a time [The teacher was *annoyed* to be out of chalk.] To **irk** means to wear down one's patience by repeatedly annoying [Their constant whining is beginning to *irk* me.] To **tease** is to annoy on purpose, especially in a playful way [They *teased* Dale for wearing orange socks.]

**an·noy·ance** (ə noi′əns) ***n.*** **1** the act of annoying or the fact of being annoyed [He showed his *annoyance* by frowning.] **2** a thing or person that annoys [A barking dog is an *annoyance* to neighbors.]

**an·nu·al** (an′yoo wəl) ***adj.*** **1** that comes or happens once a year; yearly [an *annual* summer vacation]. **2** for a year's time, work, etc. [an *annual* wage]. **3** living or lasting for only one year or season [The marigold is an *annual* plant.] ◆***n.*** **1** a book or magazine published once a year. **2** a plant that lives only one year or season.

**an·nu·al·ly** (an′yoo wəl ē) ***adv.*** each year; every year.

**an·nu·i·ty** (ə nōō′ə tē *or* ə nyōō′ə tē) ***n.*** **1** a kind of insurance from which a person gets regular payments of money after reaching a certain age. **2** a yearly payment of money. —*pl.* **an·nu′i·ties**

**an·nul** (ə nul′) ***v.*** to do away with; put an end to; make no longer binding under the law; cancel [The marriage was *annulled* after a week.] —**an·nulled′, an·nul′ling** —**an·nul′ment** ***n.***

**An·nun·ci·a·tion** (ə nun′sē ā′shən) ***n.*** **1** in the Bible, the angel Gabriel's announcement to Mary that she was to give birth to Jesus. **2** a church festival on March 25 in memory of this. *See the picture.*

**an·ode** (an′ōd) ***n.*** **1** the pole or piece by which positive electricity enters an electron tube; positive electrode. **2** in a battery that supplies electric current, the negative electrode.

**a·noint** (ə noint′) ***v.*** **1** to rub oil or ointment on. **2** to put oil on in a ceremony of making holy or placing in a high office [David was *anointed* king of Israel by Samuel.]

**a·nom·a·lous** (ə näm′ə ləs) ***adj.*** not following the usual rule or pattern; abnormal [The penguin is an *anomalous* bird because it cannot fly.]

**a·nom·a·ly** (ə näm′ə lē) ***n.*** anything anomalous [The platypus, which lays eggs, is an *anomaly* among mammals.] —*pl.* **a·nom′a·lies**

**a·non** (ə nän′) ***adv.*** **1** in a short time; soon. **2** at another time [I leave now, but I shall see you *anon.*] *This word is now seldom used.*

**anon.** *abbreviation for* **anonymous.**

**an·o·nym·i·ty** (an′ə nim′ə tē) ***n.*** the condition of being anonymous.

**a·non·y·mous** (ə nän′ə məs) ***adj.*** **1** whose name is not known [an *anonymous* writer]. **2** written, given, etc. by a person whose name is kept secret [an *anonymous* letter; an *anonymous* gift]. —**a·non′y·mous·ly** ***adv.***



**an·oth·er** (ə nu*th*′ər) ***adj.*** **1** one more [Have *another* cup of tea.] **2** a different; not the same [Exchange the book for *another* one.] **3** one of the same sort as [A child may dream of being *another* Curie.] ◆***pron.*** **1** one more [I've had a cookie, but I'd like *another.*] **2** a different one [If one store doesn't have it, try *another.*]

**an·swer** (an′sər) ***n.*** **1** something said, written, or done in return to a question, argument, letter, action, etc.; reply; response [The only *answers* required for the test were "true" or "false." His *answer* to the insult was to turn his back.] **2** a solution to a problem, as in arithmetic. ◆***v.*** **1** to give an answer; reply or react, as to a question or action. **2** to serve or be usable for [A small tack will *answer* my purpose.] **3** to be responsible [You must *answer* for the children's conduct.] **4** to match or agree with [That house *answers* to the description.]

**an·swer·a·ble** (an′sər ə b'l) ***adj.*** **1** responsible; obliged to give an accounting or explanation [I know I am *answerable* for my actions.] **2** that can be answered or shown to be wrong [an *answerable* argument].

**ant** (ant) ***n.*** a small insect, usually without wings, that lives in or on the ground, in wood, etc. Ants live together in large, organized groups called colonies. *See the picture.*

| | | | |
|---|---|---|---|
| **a** fat | **ir** here | **ou** out | **zh** leisure |
| **ā** ape | **ī** bite, fire | **u** up | **ng** ring |
| **ä** car, lot | **ō** go | **ur** fur | a *in* ago |
| **e** ten | **ô** law, horn | **ch** chin | e *in* agent |
| **er** care | **oi** oil | **sh** she | **ə** = i *in* unity |
| **ē** even | **oo** look | **th** thin | o *in* collect |
| **i** hit | **ōō** tool | ***th*** then | u *in* focus |

**-ant** (ənt) *a suffix meaning:* **1** that has, shows, or does [A *defiant* person is one who shows defiance.] **2** a person or thing that [An *irritant* is something that irritates.]

**ant.** *abbreviation for* **antonym.**

**ant·ac·id** (ant′as′id) ***adj.*** that neutralizes or weakens acids. ◆***n.*** an antacid substance [Baking soda is an *antacid.*]

**an·tag·o·nism** (an tag′ə niz′m) ***n.*** the condition of being against or feeling unfriendly toward.

**an·tag·o·nist** (an tag′ə nist) ***n.*** a person who opposes, fights, or competes with another; opponent; rival.

**an·tag·o·nis·tic** (an tag′ə nis′tik) ***adj.*** being or acting against another; opposing; hostile. —**an·tag′o·nis′ti·cal·ly *adv.***

**an·tag·o·nize** (an tag′ə nīz) ***v.*** to make someone dislike or be against oneself; make an enemy of [Rudeness will *antagonize* customers.] —**an·tag′o·nized, an·tag′o·niz·ing**

**ant·arc·tic** (ant ärk′tik *or* ant är′tik) ***adj.*** or or near the South Pole or the region around it. ◆***n.*** the region around the South Pole.

**Ant·arc·ti·ca** (ant ärk′ti kə *or* ant är′ti kə) a large area of land, completely covered with ice, around the South Pole: *also called* **Antarctic Continent.**

**Antarctic Ocean** the ocean around Antarctica.

**ante-** *a prefix meaning* before [To *antedate* something is to come before it in time.]



**ant·eat·er** (ant′ēt′ər) ***n.*** an animal with a long snout and a long, sticky tongue. It feeds mainly on ants.

**an·te·ced·ent** (an′tə sēd′ənt) ***adj.*** coming or happening before; previous [The pilot told of the storm *antecedent* to the crash.] ◆***n.*** **1** a thing or happening coming before something else. **2** one's ancestry, past life, etc. **3** the word or group of words to which a pronoun refers [In "the guide who led us," "guide" is the *antecedent* of "who."]

**an·te·date** (an′ti dāt) ***v.*** **1** to come or happen before [The American Revolution *antedated* the French Revolution.] **2** to give an earlier date to [You *antedate* a check written on May 3 if you put May 1 on it.] —**an′te·dat·ed, an′te·dat·ing**

**an·te·di·lu·vi·an** (an′ti də lo͞o′vē ən) ***adj.*** **1** of the time before the Flood mentioned in the Bible. **2** very old or old-fashioned [*antediluvian* ideas]. ◆***n.*** an antediluvian person or thing.

**an·te·lope** (an′tə lōp) ***n.*** a swift, graceful animal that is a little like a deer. Antelopes have horns and are related to oxen and goats. *See the picture.*

**an·ten·na** (an ten′ə) ***n.*** **1** either of a pair of slender feelers on the head of an insect, crab, lobster, etc. —*pl.* **an·ten·nae** (an ten′ē) or **an·ten′nas** **2** a wire or set of wires used in radio and television to send and receive signals; aerial. —*pl.* **an·ten′nas**

**an·te·ri·or** (an tir′ē ər) ***adj.*** **1** at or toward the front; forward. **2** coming before; earlier.

**an·te·room** (an′ti ro͞om) ***n.*** a room leading to a larger or more important room; waiting room.

**an·them** (an′thəm) ***n.*** **1** the official song of a country, school, etc. [The national *anthem* of the United States is "The Star-Spangled Banner."] **2** a religious song or hymn, usually with words from the Bible.

**an·ther** (an′thər) ***n.*** the part of a flower's stamen that holds the pollen. Anthers are the small heads on the slender stems that grow at the center of a flower. *See the picture.*

**ant hill** a heap of dirt carried by ants from their underground nest and piled around its entrance.

**an·thol·o·gy** (an thäl′ə jē) ***n.*** a collection of poems, stories, or other writings. —*pl.* **an·thol′o·gies**

> **Anthology** comes from an ancient Greek word meaning "a garland of flowers." It was made up of *anthos,* meaning "flower," and *legein,* meaning "to gather." An anthology can be thought of as a bouquet of fine writings.

**An·tho·ny** (an′thə nē), **Susan B.** 1820–1906; American teacher who was a leader in the movement to help women gain the right to vote.

**an·thra·cite** (an′thrə sīt) ***n.*** hard coal, which burns with much heat and little smoke.

**an·thrax** (an′thraks) ***n.*** a disease of cattle, sheep, etc. that is caused by bacteria and can be passed on to human beings.

**an·thro·poid** (an′thrə poid) ***adj.*** like a human being in form; manlike [The gorilla, chimpanzee, and orangutan are *anthropoid* apes.] ◆***n.*** any anthropoid ape.

**an·thro·pol·o·gist** (an′thrə päl′ə jist) ***n.*** an expert in anthropology.

**an·thro·pol·o·gy** (an′thrə päl′ə jē) ***n.*** the science that studies human beings, especially their origin, development, divisions, and customs. —**an′thro·po·log′i·cal *adj.***

**anti-** *a prefix meaning:* **1** against, opposed to [*Antislavery* means opposed to slavery.] **2** that acts against [An *antitoxin* is a substance that acts against the toxin of a disease.]

☆**an·ti·bi·ot·ic** (an′ti bī ät′ik) ***n.*** a chemical substance produced by bacteria, fungi, etc., that can kill, or stop the growth of, germs. Antibiotics, such as penicillin, are used in treating diseases.

☆**an·ti·bod·y** (an′ti bäd′ē) ***n.*** a protein that is formed in the body to react to foreign substances, such as toxins or bacteria. In this way the body becomes immune to certain diseases. —*pl.* **an′ti·bod′ies**

**an·tic** (an′tik) ***adj.*** odd and funny; laughable. ◆***n.*** a playful or silly act, trick, etc.; prank [The children laughed at the clown's *antics.*]

**An·ti·christ** (an′ti krīst) ***n.*** in the Bible (I John 2:18), the great opponent of Christ.

**an·tic·i·pate** (an tis′ə pāt) ***v.*** **1** to look forward to; expect [We *anticipate* a pleasant trip.] **2** to be aware of or take care of ahead of time [Our hosts *anticipated* our every wish.] **3** to be ahead of in doing or achieving [Some think that the vikings *anticipated* Columbus in discovering America.] —**an·tic′i·pat·ed, an·tic′i·pat·ing** —**an·tic′i·pa′tion *n.***

**an·ti·cli·mac·tic** (an′ti klī mak′tik) ***adj.*** that is, has, or is like an anticlimax.

**an·ti·cli·max** (an′ti klī′maks) ***n.*** a dropping from the important or serious to the unimportant or silly [Last week she wrecked her car, broke her leg, and then, as an *anticlimax,* caught cold.]

**an·ti·dote** (an′tə dōt) ***n.*** **1** a substance that is taken to work against the effect of a poison. **2** anything that works against an evil or unwanted condition [The party was a good *antidote* to the sadness we felt.]

**An·tie·tam** (an tēt′əm) a creek in western Maryland, where a battle of the Civil War was fought in 1862.

anvil

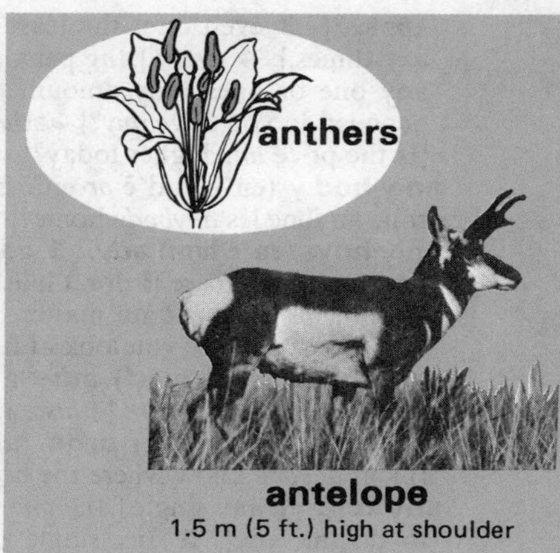
anthers

antelope
1.5 m (5 ft.) high at shoulder

☆**an·ti·freeze** (an′ti frēz) ***n.*** a liquid with a low freezing point, such as alcohol, put in the water of automobile radiators to prevent freezing.

☆**an·ti·gen** (an′tə jən) ***n.*** a foreign substance in the body, such as a toxin or enzyme, that causes antibodies to form.

**An·ti·gua** (an tē′gə *or* an tē′gwə) an island in the West Indies, that is partly under British protection.

**an·ti·his·ta·mine** (an′ti his′tə mēn) ***n.*** a medicine used to relieve asthma, hay fever, and, sometimes, the common cold.

☆**an·ti·knock** (an′ti näk) ***n.*** a substance added to gasoline to do away with noise caused by too fast combustion in an engine.

**An·til·les** (an til′ēz) the main group of islands of the West Indies.

**an·ti·mo·ny** (an′tə mō′nē) ***n.*** a silvery-white, brittle metal that is a chemical element. It is used in alloys to harden them and in certain medicines and pigments.

**An·ti·och** (an′tē äk′) a city in southern Turkey, that was once the capital of ancient Syria.

**an·ti·pas·to** (an′ti pas′tō *or* an′ti päs′tō) ***n.*** a dish of various appetizers, such as fish, meat, olives, etc.

**an·tip·a·thy** (an tip′ə thē) ***n.*** **1** great dislike; strong feeling against [The hiker had a strong *antipathy* to stray dogs.] **2** the thing for which one feels such dislike. *—pl.* **an·tip′a·thies**

**an·ti·per·spir·ant** (an′ti pur′spər ənt) ***n.*** a substance used on the skin to reduce sweating.

**an·tip·o·des** (an tip′ə dēz) ***n.pl.*** a region on the other side of the earth: *used with a plural or singular verb* [The British call New Zealand and Australia the *antipodes.*]

**Antipodes** comes from a Greek word that means "with the feet opposite." People on the other side of the earth do indeed have their feet directly opposite our own.

**an·ti·quat·ed** (an′tə kwāt′id) ***adj.*** no longer used; old-fashioned; out-of-date [*antiquated* styles; *antiquated* ideas].

**an·tique** (an tēk′) ***adj.*** very old; of former times; made or used a long time ago. ◆***n.*** a piece of furniture or silverware, a tool, etc. made many years ago [They sell *antiques* of colonial America.]

**an·tiq·ui·ty** (an tik′wə tē) ***n.*** **1** the early period of history, especially before the Middle Ages; ancient times [the legends of *antiquity*]. **2** great age; oldness [The pyramids are of great *antiquity.*] **3** the people, works of art, customs, etc. of ancient times: *usually used in plural* [a student of Roman *antiquities*]. *—pl.* **an·tiq′ui·ties**

**an·ti-Sem·i·tism** (an′ti sem′ə tiz′m) ***n.*** **1** prejudice against Jews. **2** unfair or cruel treatment of Jews.— **an·ti-Se·mit·ic** (an′ti sə mit′ik) ***adj.***

**an·ti·sep·tic** (an′ti sep′tik) ***adj.*** **1** preventing infection by killing germs. **2** free from living germs; sterile [an *antiseptic* room]. ◆***n.*** any substance used to kill germs or stop their growth, as alcohol or iodine.

☆**an·ti·slav·er·y** (an′ti slā′vər ē) ***adj.*** against slavery.

**an·ti·so·cial** (an′ti sō′shəl) ***adj.*** **1** not liking to be with other people [Are you so *antisocial* that you never have visitors?] **2** harmful to society in general [All crimes are *antisocial* acts.]

**an·tith·e·sis** (an tith′ə sis) ***n.*** **1** the exact opposite [Joy is the *antithesis* of sorrow.] **2** an opposing of things or ideas, as in the sentence "You are going; I am staying." *—pl.* **an·tith·e·ses** (an tith′ə sēz)

**an·ti·tox·in** (an′ti täk′sin) ***n.*** a substance formed in the body which acts against a disease, such as tetanus. An antitoxin formed in the blood of a diseased animal is sometimes injected into human beings to keep them from getting the disease.

☆**an·ti·trust** (an′ti trust′) ***adj.*** working to prevent or control trusts, or large businesses that are monopolies.

**ant·ler** (ant′lər) ***n.*** **1** the horn of any animal of the deer family. Antlers are grown and shed once every year. **2** a branch of such a horn. **—ant′lered *adj.***

**Antoinette, Marie** *see* **Marie Antoinette.**

**An·to·ny** (an′tə nē), **Mark** 83?–30 B.C.; Roman general and statesman, who was a follower of Julius Caesar.

**an·to·nym** (an′tə nim) ***n.*** a word opposite in meaning to another word ["Sad" is an *antonym* of "happy."]

**Ant·werp** (an′twərp) a seaport in northern Belgium.

**a·nus** (ā′nəs) ***n.*** the opening in the body through which waste matter leaves the intestines.

**an·vil** (an′vəl) ***n.*** an iron or steel block on which heated metal objects, such as horseshoes, are hammered into shape. *See the picture.*

**anx·i·e·ty** (aŋ zī′ə tē) ***n.*** **1** the condition of feeling uneasy or worried about what may happen; concern [She waited with *anxiety* to hear what the doctor would say.] **2** an eager but often uneasy desire [He fumbled the ball in his *anxiety* to do well.] *—pl.* **anx·i′e·ties**

**anx·ious** (aŋk′shəs) ***adj.*** **1** having anxiety; uneasy in mind; worried [Were you *anxious* during the flight?] **2** full of anxiety [an *anxious* hour]. **3** eagerly wishing [*anxious* to do well]. **—anx′ious·ly *adv.***

**an·y** (en′ē) ***adj.*** **1** one, no matter which one, of more than two [*Any* pupil may answer.] **2** some, no matter how much, how many, or what kind [Do you have *any*



| | | | | | | | |
|---|---|---|---|---|---|---|---|
| **a** | fat | **ir** | here | **ou** | out | **zh** | leisure |
| **ā** | ape | **ī** | bite, fire | **u** | up | **ŋ** | ring |
| **ä** | car, lot | **ō** | go | **ur** | fur | | a *in* ago |
| **e** | ten | **ô** | law, horn | **ch** | chin | | e *in* agent |
| **er** | care | **oi** | oil | **sh** | she | **ə =** | i *in* unity |
| **ē** | even | **oo** | look | **th** | thin | | o *in* collect |
| **i** | hit | **ōō** | tool | ***th*** | then | | u *in* focus |

apples?] **3** even one; the least number of [I haven't *any* dimes.] **4** every [*Any* person knows this.] ◆***pron.*** any one or ones; any amount or number [I lost my pencils; do you have *any*?] ◆***adv.*** to any degree; at all [Is the price *any* higher today?]

**an·y·bod·y** (en′ē bud′ē *or* en′ē bäd′ē) ***pron.*** any person; anyone [Is *anybody* home?]

**an·y·how** (en′ē hou) ***adv.*** **1** no matter what else may be true; in any case [I don't like the color, and *anyhow* it's not my size.] **2** no matter in what way [That's a fine report *anyhow* you look at it.]

**an·y·more** (en′ē môr′) ***adv.*** now; nowadays [They don't live here *anymore.*] : *also written* **any more.**

**an·y·one** (en′ē wun) ***pron.*** any person; anybody [Does *anyone* know where the house is?]

**any one** **1** any single [*Any one* worker should be able to do the job.] **2** any single person or thing [Take one; *any one* you want.]

☆**an·y·place** (en′ē plās) ***adv.*** in or to any place; anywhere: *used only in everyday talk.*

**an·y·thing** (en′ē thiŋ) ***pron.*** any object, event, fact, etc. [Did *anything* important happen today?] ◆***n.*** a thing, no matter of what kind [That shop has *anything* and everything for sale.] ◆***adv.*** in any way; at all [That hat isn't *anything* like yours.] —**anything but,** not at all [I'm *anything but* lonely.]

**an·y·way** (en′ē wā) ***adv.*** nevertheless; anyhow.

**an·y·where** (en′ē hwer) ***adv.*** **1** in, at, or to any place [Leave it *anywhere* in my office. You may go *anywhere* you wish.] **2** at all; to any extent: *used only in everyday talk* [The cabin isn't *anywhere* near the lake.] —**get anywhere,** to have any success: *used only in everyday talk.*



**a·or·ta** (ā ôr′tə) ***n.*** the main artery of the body. It carries blood from the heart to all parts and organs. —*pl.* **a·or′tas** or **a·or·tae** (ā ôr′tē)

**a·pace** (ə pās′) ***adv.*** at a fast rate; swiftly [The plans went forward *apace.*]

**A·pach·e** (ə pach′ē) ***n.*** a member of a tribe of Indians of northern Mexico and the southwestern United States. —*pl.* **A·pach′es** or **A·pach′e**

**a·part** (ə pärt′) ***adv.*** **1** separately or away in place or time [We were born two years *apart.* I cannot get these pages *apart.*] **2** in or to pieces [The ship was blown *apart* by a bomb. She took the motor *apart.*] ◆***adj.*** separated; not together [We were *apart* for three months last year.] —**apart from,** except for; other than [*Apart from* newspapers he reads very little.]

**a·part·ment** (ə pärt′mənt) ***n.*** a group of rooms, or a single large room, to live in. It is usually a single suite in a building (called an **apartment house**) of several or many suites.

**ap·a·thet·ic** (ap′ə thet′ik) ***adj.*** not interested; having no strong feeling; indifferent [Many people remained *apathetic* about the problem of the polluted lake.] —**ap′a·thet′i·cal·ly** ***adv.***

**ap·a·thy** (ap′ə thē) ***n.*** a lack of strong feeling or of interest or concern [Because of public *apathy* the vote was very light.]

**ape** (āp) ***n.*** **1** a large monkey that has no tail and can walk in an almost upright position [The gorilla and chimpanzee are *apes.*] **2** any monkey. **3** a person who imitates or mimics another. ◆***v.*** to imitate or mimic. —**aped, ap′ing**

**Ap·en·nines** (ap′ə nīnz) a mountain range in central Italy.

**ap·er·ture** (ap′ər chər) ***n.*** an opening or hole [Light enters a camera through the *aperture* when the shutter is opened.]

**a·pex** (ā′peks) ***n.*** the highest point of anything; peak [the *apex* of a pyramid; the *apex* of a career]. —*pl.* **a′pex·es** or **ap·i·ces** (ap′ə sēz)

**a·phid** (ā′fid *or* af′id) ***n.*** an insect that lives on plants by sucking their juice. *See the picture.*

**aph·o·rism** (af′ə riz′m) ***n.*** a short, clear statement telling a general truth ["A book you haven't read is a new book" is an *aphorism.*]

**a·pi·ar·y** (ā′pē er′ē) ***n.*** a place where bees are kept for their honey, usually a collection of hives. —*pl.* **a′pi·ar′ies**

**a·piece** (ə pēs′) ***adv.*** for each one; each [These apples are twenty cents *apiece.*]

**APO** Army Post Office.

**A·poc·a·lypse** (ə päk′ə lips) ***n.*** the last book of the New Testament; book of Revelation.

**A·poc·ry·pha** (ə päk′rə fə) ***n.pl.*** certain books that are included in the Roman Catholic version of the Bible but are not accepted in the Protestant versions or in Jewish Scriptures.

**a·poc·ry·phal** (ə päk′rə f'l) ***adj.*** **1** coming from a source that is unknown or not sure, and therefore probably false [The story of George Washington and the cherry tree is *apocryphal.*] **2** **Apocryphal,** of or like the Apocrypha.

**A·pol·lo** (ə päl′ō) the Greek and Roman god of music, poetry, and medicine, and later of the sun.

**a·pol·o·get·ic** (ə päl′ə jet′ik) ***adj.*** making an apology or showing that one is sorry for doing something wrong. —**a·pol′o·get′i·cal·ly** ***adv.***

**a·pol·o·gist** (ə päl′ə jist) ***n.*** a person who defends a certain idea, religion, action, etc.

**a·pol·o·gize** (ə päl′ə jīz) ***v.*** to make an apology; say that one is sorry for doing something wrong or being at fault [They *apologized* for being late.] —**a·pol′o·gized, a·pol′o·giz·ing**

**a·pol·o·gy** (ə päl′ə jē) ***n.*** a statement that one is sorry for doing something wrong or being at fault [Please accept my *apology* for sending you the wrong book.] —*pl.* **a·pol′o·gies**

**ap·o·plec·tic** (ap′ə plek′tik) ***adj.*** **1** of or like apo-

**aphid**

**appendix**

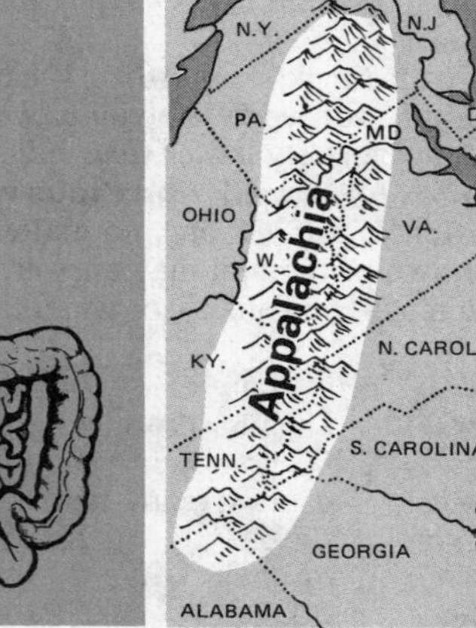

plexy [an *apoplectic* fit]. **2** seeming as though about to have apoplexy [*apoplectic* with rage].

**ap·o·plex·y** (ap′ə plek′sē) ***n.*** a condition in which one is suddenly unable to move, think, or feel, as a result of the breaking or blocking of a blood vessel in the brain.

**a·pos·ta·sy** (ə päs′tə sē) ***n.*** a turning away from the religion, faith, principles, etc. that one used to believe in.

**a·pos·tate** (ə päs′tāt) ***n.*** a person who has turned away from the religion, faith, principles, etc. in which that person once believed.

**a·pos·tle** (ə päs″l) ***n.*** **1** *usually* **Apostle,** any of the twelve disciples chosen to spread the teachings of Jesus. **2** any early Christian missionary. **3** any leader of a new movement to bring about reform [Susan B. Anthony was an *apostle* of the women's movement.]

> **Apostle** comes from an ancient Greek word meaning "to send out." The twelve Apostles were sent out to spread the teachings of Jesus.

**ap·os·tol·ic** (ap′əs täl′ik) ***adj.*** **1** having to do with the Apostles, their teachings, or their times. **2** *often* **Apostolic,** of or from the Pope [an *Apostolic* letter].

**a·pos·tro·phe** (ə päs′trə fē) ***n.*** the mark (′) used: **1** in a shortened word or phrase to show that a letter or letters have been left out [*ne'er* for *never*; *I'll* for *I will*]. **2** to show the possessive case [the *soldier's* uniform; the *teachers'* lounge]. **3** to form certain plurals [five *6's*; to dot the *i's*].

**a·poth·e·car·y** (ə päth′ə ker′ē) ***n.*** a person who makes and sells drugs and medicines; druggist; pharmacist. —*pl.* **a·poth′e·car′ies**

**Ap·pa·la·chi·a** (ap′ə lā′chə *or* ap′ə lā′chē ə *or* ap′ə lach′ə) a region of the eastern U.S. that includes the central and southern Appalachian Mountains. *See the map.*

**Ap·pa·la·chi·an Mountains** (ap′ə lā′chən *or* ap′ə lā′chē ən *or* ap′ə lach′ən) a mountain system in eastern North America, reaching from Canada to Alabama: *also called* **the Appalachians.**

**ap·pall** or **ap·pal** (ə pôl′) ***v.*** to cause to feel shock or be greatly upset; dismay [We were *appalled* at the conditions in which they live.] —**ap·pal′ling** ***adj.***

**ap·pa·ra·tus** (ap′ə rat′əs *or* ap′ə rāt′əs) ***n.*** **1** the tools, instruments, or equipment needed to do a certain job, experiment, etc. [Test tubes and gas burners are the *apparatus* of the chemist.] **2** any complicated system of parts [The stomach and intestines are part of the digestive *apparatus*.] —*pl.* **ap′pa·ra′tus** or **ap′pa·ra′tus·es**

**ap·par·el** (ə per′əl) ***n.*** clothing; garments; dress [They sell only children's *apparel*.] ◆***v.*** to dress; clothe [The king was *appareled* in purple robes.] —**ap·par′eled** or **ap·par′elled, ap·par′el·ing** or **ap·par′el·ling**

**ap·par·ent** (ə per′ənt) ***adj.*** **1** easy to see or understand; obvious; clear [Poor attendance at the play makes it *apparent* that it will fail.] **2** that appears to be, but is perhaps not really so; seeming [an *apparent* lack of interest]. —**ap·par′ent·ly** ***adv.***

**ap·pa·ri·tion** (ap′ə rish′ən) ***n.*** a strange figure appearing suddenly and thought to be a ghost.

**ap·peal** (ə pēl′) ***v.*** **1** to ask earnestly for help, an opinion, etc. [They *appealed* to the bank for a loan.] **2** to be interesting or attractive [a movie that *appeals* to everyone]. **3** to ask that a decision in a law case be reviewed by a higher court. ◆***n.*** **1** an earnest request for help, sympathy, etc. **2** a quality that makes someone or something interesting or attractive [Mystery stories have a great *appeal* to many people.] **3** a request to have a decision in a law case reviewed by a higher court; also, the right to make such a request.

> SYNONYMS: **Appeal** suggests an earnest, sometimes urgent request and when used in law a request that a higher court review a decision. **Plead,** when used in law, suggests a formal answer to a charge that something wrong has been done, and in general use, it suggests that an urgent request is being supported by reasons for it.

**ap·pear** (ə pir′) ***v.*** **1** to come into sight or into being [A ship *appeared* on the horizon. Leaves *appear* on the tree every spring.] **2** to become understood [It *appears* I'm right.] **3** to seem; look [He *appears* to be in good health.] **4** to present oneself [I must *appear* in court today.] **5** to come before the public [The actor will *appear* on television. The magazine *appears* monthly.]

**ap·pear·ance** (ə pir′əns) ***n.*** **1** the act of appearing. **2** the way a person or thing looks [From his *appearance*, we knew he was angry.] **3** a false or wrong impression [She gave the *appearance* of being busy.]

**ap·pease** (ə pēz′) ***v.*** to satisfy or make calm by giving what is wanted [Water *appeases* thirst. In earlier times people tried to *appease* their gods by making sacrifices.] —**ap·peased′, ap·peas′ing** —**ap·pease′ment** ***n.***



**ap·pel·late** (ə pel′it) ***adj.*** that is appealed to [An *appellate* court is one that can hear appeals and change the decisions of lower courts.]

**ap·pend** (ə pend′) ***v.*** to add or attach as an extra part [*Append* to your report a list of books you used.]

**ap·pend·age** (ə pen′dij) ***n.*** a thing that is attached or grows out as a natural, but less important part [A branch of a tree and the tail of a dog are both *appendages*.]

☆**ap·pen·dec·to·my** (ap′ən dek′tə mē) ***n.*** an operation by which a surgeon removes a person's appendix. —*pl.* **ap′pen·dec′to·mies**

☆**ap·pen·di·ci·tis** (ə pen′də sīt′əs) ***n.*** a diseased condition of a person's appendix in which it becomes red and swollen.

**ap·pen·dix** (ə pen′diks) ***n.*** **1** an extra section added at the end of a book [The *appendix* to a book often has notes of explanation.] **2** a small closed tube growing out of the large intestine. It has no known purpose. *See the picture.* —*pl.* **ap·pen′dix·es** or **ap·pen·di·ces** (ə pen′də sēz)

**ap·per·tain** (ap ər tān′) ***v.*** to belong naturally or be a part; have to do with [Scientists are working on problems that *appertain* to space travel.]

**ap·pe·tite** (ap′ə tīt) ***n.*** **1** a desire or wish for food

| | | | | | | | |
|---|---|---|---|---|---|---|---|
| **a** | fat | **ir** | here | **ou** | out | **zh** | leisure |
| **ā** | ape | **ī** | bite, fire | **u** | up | **ng** | ring |
| **ä** | car, lot | **ō** | go | **ur** | fur | | a *in* ago |
| **e** | ten | **ô** | law, horn | **ch** | chin | | e *in* agent |
| **er** | care | **oi** | oil | **sh** | she | **ə =** | i *in* unity |
| **ē** | even | **oo** | look | **th** | thin | | o *in* collect |
| **i** | hit | **ōō** | tool | ***th*** | then | | u *in* focus |

apse

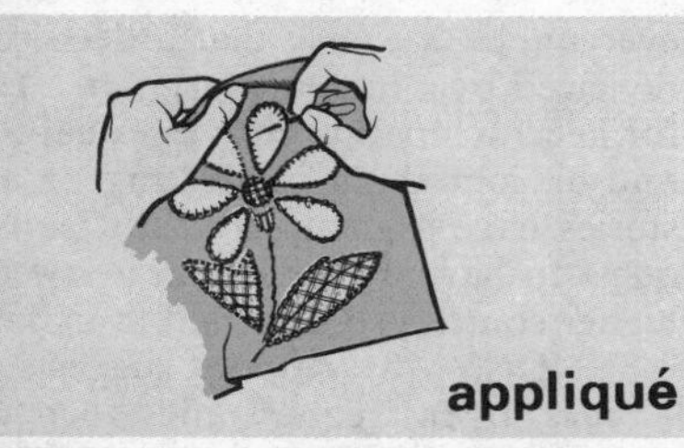
appliqué

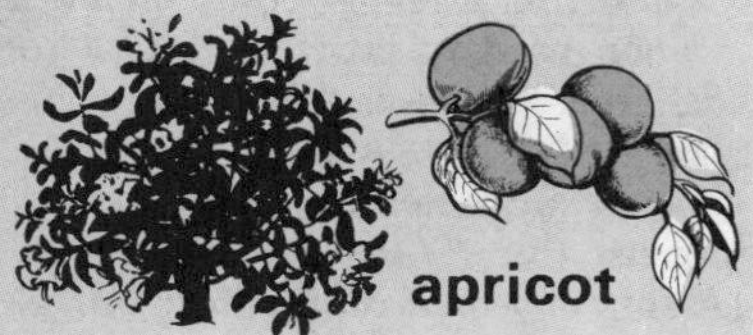
apricot

[Exercise gave her a strong *appetite.*] **2** any strong desire [He has an *appetite* for good books.]

**ap·pe·tiz·er** (ap′ə tī′zər) ***n.*** a small bit of a tasty food or a drink for giving one a bigger appetite at the beginning of a meal [Olives, tomato juice, etc. are used as *appetizers.*]

**ap·pe·tiz·ing** (ap′ə tī′ziŋ) ***adj.*** that gives one a bigger appetite; tasty [What an *appetizing* smell!]

**ap·plaud** (ə plôd′) ***v.*** to show that one enjoys or approves of something, especially by clapping one's hands.

**ap·plause** (ə plôz′) ***n.*** the act of showing that one enjoys or approves of something, especially by clapping one's hands.

**ap·ple** (ap′'l) ***n.*** **1** a round, firm fruit with juicy flesh, a green, yellow, or red skin, and small seeds. **2** the tree this fruit grows on. —**apple of one's eye,** a person or thing that is especially dear to one.

☆**apple butter** a kind of jam made from apples cooked with spices.

**ap·ple·sauce** (ap′'l sôs) ***n.*** a food made by cooking pieces of apple in water until they become a soft, pulpy mass.

**Ap·ple·seed** (ap′'l sēd), **Johnny** 1775–1845; American pioneer who planted apple trees throughout the Midwest. His real name was *John Chapman.*

**ap·pli·ance** (ə plī′əns) ***n.*** a machine or device for doing a certain task, especially one that is worked mechanically or by electricity [Stoves, refrigerators, irons, etc. are household *appliances.*]

**ap·pli·ca·ble** (ap′li kə b'l) ***adj.*** that can be applied or used; suitable [Your suggestion is not *applicable* to the problem.] —**ap′pli·ca·bil′i·ty** ***n.***

**ap·pli·cant** (ap′li kənt) ***n.*** a person who applies or asks for something [*applicants* for a job].

**ap·pli·ca·tion** (ap′lə kā′shən) ***n.*** **1** the act of applying or putting something on [the *application* of paint to a wall]. **2** the act of putting something to use [This job calls for the *application* of many skills.] **3** a thing that is applied, especially a remedy or medicine [*applications* of salve to treat a rash]. **4** a way of applying or being used [a scientific discovery having many *applications* in industry]. **5** the act of asking for something; request [an *application* for employment]. **6** a form on which questions must be answered when applying for something, as for a job. **7** continued effort of the mind or body; the act of paying close attention [She became an honor student by *application* to her studies.]

**ap·plied** (ə plīd′) ***adj.*** put to a practical use [An *applied* science is one that uses known facts to get something done.]

**ap·pli·qué** (ap lə kā′) ***n.*** a decoration made of one material, sewed or pasted to another material. *See the picture.*

**ap·ply** (ə plī′) ***v.*** **1** to put or spread on [*Apply* glue to the surface.] **2** to put into use [*Apply* your knowledge to this problem.] **3** to work hard and steadily [He *applied* himself to his studies.] **4** to ask in a formal way [I *applied* for permission to leave early.] **5** to have to do with or be suitable to [This rule *applies* to all of us.] —**ap·plied′, ap·ply′ing**

**ap·point** (ə point′) ***v.*** **1** to fix or set; decide upon [Let's *appoint* a time for our meeting.] **2** to name or choose for an office or position [Federal judges are *appointed* by the President.]

**ap·point·ee** (ə poin′tē′) ***n.*** a person who has been appointed to some position.

**ap·poin·tive** (ə poin′tiv) ***adj.*** to which one is appointed rather than elected [an *appointive* office].

**ap·point·ment** (ə point′mənt) ***n.*** **1** the act of appointing or the fact of being appointed [the *appointment* of Jones as supervisor]. **2** a position held by an appointed person [She accepted the *appointment* in the State Department.] **3** an arrangement to meet someone or be somewhere at a certain time [an *appointment* for lunch]. **4 appointments,** *pl.* furniture [a hotel with fine *appointments*].

**Ap·po·mat·tox** (ap′ə mat′əks) a former village in central Virginia where Lee surrendered to Grant in 1865, ending the Civil War.

**ap·por·tion** (ə pôr′shən) ***v.*** to divide and give out in shares [The money will be *apportioned* to various charities.] —**ap·por′tion·ment** ***n.***

**ap·prais·al** (ə prā′z'l) ***n.*** **1** the act of appraising or the fact of being appraised. **2** the value decided on in appraising.

**ap·praise** (ə prāz′) ***v.*** **1** to set a price for; decide how much something is worth [The agent *appraised* the house at $50,000.] **2** to judge how good or useful something is [A literary critic *appraises* books.] —**ap·praised′, ap·prais′ing —ap·prais′er** ***n.***

**ap·pre·cia·ble** (ə prē′shə b'l) ***adj.*** enough to be seen or noticed; noticeable [an *appreciable* difference in their sizes]. —**ap·pre′cia·bly** ***adv.***

**ap·pre·ci·ate** (ə prē′shē āt) ***v.*** **1** to think well of; understand and enjoy [I now *appreciate* modern art.] **2** to recognize and be grateful for [We *appreciate* all you have done for us.] **3** to be fully aware of [I can *appreciate* your problems.] ☆**4** to make or become more valuable [Our house will *appreciate* with the addition of a fireplace.] —**ap·pre′ci·at·ed, ap·pre′ci·at·ing —ap·pre′ci·a′tion** ***n.***

SYNONYMS: **Appreciate** suggests that someone is able to see the value of something or to enjoy it [I *appreciate* good music.] To **value** something is to think highly of it because of what it is worth to one [I *value* your friendship.] To **prize** something is to value it highly or feel great pleasure about it [We *prize* our city art museum.]

**ap·pre·cia·tive** (ə prē′shə tiv) ***adj.*** feeling or showing that one appreciates something [The *appreciative* audience cheered.]

**ap·pre·hend** (ap′rə hend′) ***v.*** **1** to capture or arrest [The police *apprehended* the burglar.] **2** to catch the meaning of; understand [I don't fully *apprehend* your last remark.] **3** to expect anxiously or with fear; dread [We *apprehended* disaster in the snowstorm ahead.]

**ap·pre·hen·sion** (ap′rə hen′shən) ***n.*** **1** the act of capturing or arresting [the *apprehension* of a criminal]. **2** understanding [Do you have any *apprehension* of my meaning?] **3** an anxious feeling that something bad will happen; dread [I opened the telegram with *apprehension.*]

**ap·pre·hen·sive** (ap′rə hen′siv) ***adj.*** feeling anxious or fearful about what may happen; uneasy [Talk about war made us *apprehensive.*]

**ap·pren·tice** (ə pren′tis) ***n.*** **1** a person who is learning a trade by helping a worker skilled in that trade. In earlier times, an apprentice was bound by law to work for a master a certain number of years to pay for the training. **2** any beginner or learner. ♦***v.*** to place or take on as an apprentice [Benjamin Franklin was *apprenticed* to a printer at an early age.] —**ap·pren′ticed, ap·pren′tic·ing**

**ap·pren·tice·ship** (ə pren′tis ship) ***n.*** the condition or period of being an apprentice.

**ap·prise** or **ap·prize** (ə prīz′) ***v.*** to let know; inform; notify [Please *apprise* me of any change in plans.] —**ap·prised′** or **ap·prized′, ap·pris′ing** or **ap·priz′ing**

**ap·proach** (ə prōch′) ***v.*** **1** to come closer or draw nearer [We saw three riders *approaching*. Vacation time *approaches.*] **2** to be like or similar to [That green paint *approaches* what we want.] **3** to go to someone with a plan or request [Have you *approached* the bank about a loan?] ♦***n.*** **1** a coming closer or drawing nearer [The first robin marks the *approach* of spring.] **2** a path or road that leads to some place [The *approaches* to the city are clogged with traffic.] —**ap·proach′a·ble** ***adj.***

**ap·pro·pri·ate** (ə prō′prē āt) ***v.*** **1** to set aside for a special use [Congress has *appropriated* money for building roads.] **2** to take for one's own use, especially without permission [Who *appropriated* my umbrella?] —**ap·pro′pri·at·ed, ap·pro′pri·at·ing** ♦***adj.*** (ə prō′pri it) just right for the purpose; suitable [songs *appropriate* to the holiday season]. —**ap·pro′pri·ate·ly** ***adv.***

**ap·pro·pri·a·tion** (ə prō′prē ā′shən) ***n.*** **1** the act of appropriating. **2** a sum of money set aside for a special use.

**ap·prov·al** (ə prōōv′'l) ***n.*** **1** the thought or feeling that someone or something is good or worthwhile [The audience showed its *approval* by applauding.] **2** permission given because of such feeling [The letter was sent with my *approval.*] —**on approval,** for the customer to examine and decide whether to buy or return. [They sent us the chair *on approval.*]

**ap·prove** (ə prōōv′) ***v.*** **1** to think or say to be good, worthwhile, etc.; be pleased with: *often used with* of [She doesn't *approve* of smoking.] **2** to give one's consent to [Has the mayor *approved* the plans?] —**ap·proved′, ap·prov′ing**

**ap·prox·i·mate** (ə präk′sə mit) ***adj.*** **1** very much like; close to [The painting is an *approximate* copy.] **2** more or less correct or exact [The *approximate* area of the U.S. is 3,600,000 square miles.] ♦***v.*** (ə präk′sə māt) to be or make almost the same as or very much like [These artificial flavors do not even *approximate* real fruit flavors.] —**ap·prox′i·mat·ed, ap·prox′i·mat·ing** —**ap·prox′i·mate·ly** ***adv.***

**ap·prox·i·ma·tion** (ə präk′sə mā′shən) ***n.*** **1** an approximating, or coming close. **2** an estimate or guess that is nearly correct or exact [Give us an *approximation* of the cost of the repairs.]

**a·pri·cot** (ap′rə kät *or* ā′prə kät) ***n.*** **1** a pale orange fruit that is a little like a peach, but smaller. *See the picture.* **2** the tree it grows on. **3** a pale orange color.

**A·pril** (ā′prəl) ***n.*** the fourth month of the year, which has 30 days: abbreviated **Apr.**

**April Fools' Day** April 1. On this day it is a custom to play harmless tricks on people.

**a·pron** (ā′prən) ***n.*** **1** a garment of cloth, leather, etc. worn over the front part of the body, to cover and protect one's clothes. **2** a wide part of a driveway, as where it joins the street. **3** the part of a stage in front of the curtain.

> The word **apron** was originally written *napron* and comes from the same root as *napkin.* In early times some people thought they were hearing "an apron" when someone said "a napron" and so the word gradually changed in spelling.

**ap·ro·pos** (ap rə pō′) ***adj.*** just right for what is being said or done; suitable; apt [an *apropos* suggestion]. —**apropos of,** in connection with; regarding [*Apropos of* your remark, here is what I suggest.]

**apse** (aps) ***n.*** a part of a church that is set back, usually at the east end of the nave. It is generally in the shape of a half circle that has a domed roof. *See the picture.*

**apt** (apt) ***adj.*** **1** likely or almost certain; inclined [It is *apt* to rain today.] **2** just right for what is being said or done; appropriate; fitting [an *apt* remark]. **3** quick to learn or understand [an *apt* student]. —**apt′ly** ***adv.*** —**apt′ness** ***n.***

**apt.** *abbreviation for* **apartment.** —*pl.* **apts.**

**ap·ti·tude** (ap′tə tōōd *or* ap′tə tyōōd) ***n.*** **1** an ability that one has naturally; talent [an *aptitude* for teaching]. *See* SYNONYMS *at* **talent.** **2** quickness to learn or understand [a scholar of great *aptitude*].

**Aq·ua-lung** (ak′wə luŋ) *a trademark for* a kind of scuba.

**aq·ua·ma·rine** (ak′wə mə rēn′) ***n.*** **1** a clear, pale blue-green mineral, used in jewelry. **2** a pale blue-green color. ♦***adj.*** blue-green.

☆**aq·ua·naut** (ak′wə nôt) ***n.*** a person who is trained to live and do scientific work in a watertight chamber deep in the ocean.

**a·quar·i·um** (ə kwer′ē əm) ***n.*** **1** a glass tank or bowl in which living fishes, water animals, and water plants

| | | | | | | | |
|---|---|---|---|---|---|---|---|
| **a** | fat | **ir** | here | **ou** | out | **zh** | leisure |
| **ā** | ape | **ī** | bite, fire | **u** | up | **ŋ** | ring |
| **ä** | car, lot | **ō** | go | **ur** | fur | | a *in* ago |
| **e** | ten | **ô** | law, horn | **ch** | chin | | e *in* agent |
| **er** | care | **oi** | oil | **sh** | she | **ə** = | i *in* unity |
| **ē** | even | **oo** | look | **th** | thin | | o *in* collect |
| **i** | hit | **ōō** | tool | ***th*** | then | | u *in* focus |

are kept. **2** a building where collections of such animals and plants are shown to the public. *—pl.* **a·quar′i·ums** or **a·quar·i·a** (ə kwer′ē ə)

**A·quar·i·us** (ə kwer′ē əs) the eleventh sign of the zodiac, for the period from January 21 to February 19: *also called* the Water Carrier. *See the picture at* **zodiac.**

**a·quat·ic** (ə kwät′ik *or* ə kwat′ik) ***adj.*** **1** growing or living in or upon water [*aquatic* plants]. **2** done in or upon the water [*aquatic* sports].

**aq·ue·duct** (ak′wə dukt) ***n.*** **1** a large pipe or channel for bringing water from one place to another. Aqueducts are usually sloped a little so that the water will flow down. **2** a high structure like a bridge, for carrying such a pipe across a river or valley.

**a·que·ous** (ā′kwē əs *or* ak′wē əs) ***adj.*** containing water or like water; watery [an *aqueous* solution].

**aq·ui·line** (ak′wə līn *or* ak′wə lən) ***adj.*** **1** of or like an eagle. **2** curved or hooked like an eagle's beak [an *aquiline* nose].

**A·qui·nas** (ə kwī′nəs), Saint **Thomas** 1225?–1274; Italian philosopher and writer on religious matters.

**Ar** *the symbol for the chemical element* argon.

**AR** *abbreviation for* **Arkansas.**

**Ar·ab** (ar′əb) ***n.*** any member of a people living in Arabia or in lands near Arabia and in northern Africa. Many tribes of Arabs are nomads who roam the deserts. ◆***adj.*** of or having to do with the Arabs.

**ar·a·besque** (ar ə besk′) ***n.*** **1** a complicated design of flowers, leaves, lines, circles, etc. twisted together. **2** a position in ballet dancing in which one leg is stretched straight back. *See the picture.* ◆***adj.*** of or done in arabesque [an *arabesque* pattern in a rug].

**A·ra·bi·a** (ə rā′bē ə) a large peninsula in southwestern Asia. It is mostly a desert region.

**A·ra·bi·an** (ə rā′bē ən) ***adj.*** of Arabia or the Arabs. ◆***n.*** a person born or living in Arabia.

**Arabian Nights, The** a collection of very old stories from Arabia, India, Persia, etc. The stories of Ali Baba, Sinbad the Sailor, and Aladdin are in this collection.

arch

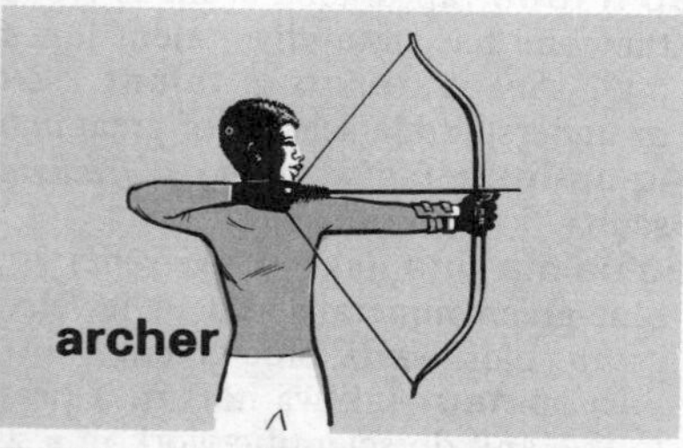
archer

arabesque

arbor

**Arabian Sea** a part of the Indian Ocean between India and Arabia.

**Ar·a·bic** (ar′ə bik) ***adj.*** of Arabia, the Arabs, or their language. ◆***n.*** the language of the Arabs. It is related to Hebrew and Aramaic.

**Arabic numerals** the figures 1, 2, 3, 4, 5, 6, 7, 8, 9, and the 0 (zero). They were first taught to Europeans by the Arabs, but were originally used in India and are sometimes called *Hindu-Arabic numerals.*

**ar·a·ble** (ar′ə b′l) ***adj.*** in a fit condition for plowing [The flooded land is no longer *arable.*]

**a·rach·nid** (ə rak′nid) ***n.*** any of a large group of animals related to the insects. They have eight legs and a body that is usually divided into two sections [Spiders and scorpions are *arachnids.*]

**Ar·a·ma·ic** (ar′ə mā′ik) ***n.*** a language spoken in Biblical times. It is related to Hebrew and Arabic.

**Ar·a·rat** (ar′ə rat) a mountain in eastern Turkey. Noah's Ark is supposed to have landed there.

**ar·bi·ter** (ar′bə tər) ***n.*** **1** a person who has the power to judge or decide [The *arbiter* in a baseball game is the umpire.] **2** *same as* **arbitrator.**

The judge who arbitrates a quarrel is called an **arbiter.** This Latin word is made up of two others that mean "to go to see." In ancient Rome, an arbiter went to see for himself what the thing was all about before making up his mind.

**ar·bi·trar·y** (är′bə trer′ē) ***adj.*** based only on what one wants or thinks; ignoring rules or others' opinions [an *arbitrary* decision; an *arbitrary* ruler]. **—ar′bi·trar′i·ly** ***adv.***

**ar·bi·trate** (är′bə trāt) ***v.*** **1** to settle an argument by choosing someone to hear both sides and make a decision [Labor and management have decided to *arbitrate* their dispute over wages.] **2** to give a decision as an arbitrator [The court will *arbitrate* in the border dispute.] **—ar′bi·trat·ed, ar′bi·trat·ing —ar′bi·tra′tion** ***n.***

**ar·bi·tra·tor** (är′bə trāt′ər) ***n.*** **1** a person chosen to judge a dispute. **2** *same as* **arbiter.**

**ar·bor** (är′bər) ***n.*** a place shaded by trees or bushes or by vines on a trellis; bower. *See the picture.*

**ar·bo·re·al** (är bôr′ē əl) ***adj.*** **1** of or like trees. **2** living in trees [Squirrels are *arboreal* animals.]

**ar·bor·vi·tae** (är′bər vī′tē) ***n.*** a small evergreen tree with flattened sprays of leaves that look like scales.

**ar·bu·tus** (är byo͞ot′əs) ***n.*** an evergreen plant that trails along the ground and has clusters of white or pink flowers that bloom in the spring.

**arc** (ärk) ***n.*** **1** a part of the line that forms a circle or any curve. **2** the streak of bright light made by an electric current passing between two electrodes. ◆***v.*** to move in an arc, or curved line. **—arced** or **arcked, arc′ing** or **arck′ing**

**ar·cade** (är kād′) ***n.*** **1** a covered passageway, as through a building, often with an arched roof; especially, such a passage with small shops on both sides. **2** a row of arches supported by columns.

**arch**[1] (ärch) ***n.*** **1** a curved part of a structure that holds up the weight of material over an open space. Arches are used in doors, windows, bridges, etc. *See the picture.* **2** anything shaped like an arch [the *arch* of the foot]. ◆***v.*** **1** to curve into an arch [The cat *arched* its back.] **2** to form an arch [The bridge *arches* over the river.]

**arch**[2] (ärch) ***adj.*** **1** main; chief [the *arch* villain]. **2** playful or full of mischief; pert [an *arch* smile].

**arch-** *a prefix meaning* main or chief [An *archangel* is a chief angel.]

**ar·chae·ol·o·gy** (är'kē äl'ə jē) ***n.*** the study of ancient times and ancient peoples. Such study is carried on by digging up what is left of ancient cities, buildings, tombs, etc. —**ar·chae·o·log·i·cal** (är'kē ə läj'i k'l) ***adj.*** —**ar'chae·ol'o·gist** ***n.***

**ar·cha·ic** (är kā'ik) ***adj.*** **1** belonging to an earlier time; ancient or old-fashioned [a yard with an *archaic* iron fence]. **2** that is now seldom used except in poetry, the Bible, etc. ["Thou art" is an *archaic* form of "you are."]

**arch·an·gel** (ärk'ān'jəl) ***n.*** a chief angel, or angel of the highest rank.

**arch·bish·op** (ärch'bish'əp) ***n.*** a bishop of the highest rank.

**arch·duch·ess** (ärch'duch'is) ***n.*** the wife or widow of an archduke.

**arch·duke** (ärch'do͞ok' *or* ärch'dyo͞ok') ***n.*** a prince of the family that used to rule Austria.

**ar·che·ol·o·gy** (är'kē äl'ə jē) ***n.*** *another spelling of* **archaeology**.

**arch·er** (är'chər) ***n.*** a person who shoots with bow and arrow. *See the picture.*

**arch·er·y** (är'chər ē) ***n.*** **1** the skill or sport of shooting with bow and arrow. **2** the bows, arrows, and other equipment of an archer. **3** archers as a group.

**ar·che·type** (är'kə tīp) ***n.*** the first one, that serves as a model for others [The Constitution of the U.S. has been the *archetype* for many constitutions.]

**Ar·chi·me·des** (är'kə mē'dēz) 287?–212 B.C.; Greek mathematician and inventor.

**ar·chi·pel·a·go** (är'kə pel'ə gō) ***n.*** a group or chain of many islands in a sea. —*pl.* **ar'chi·pel'a·goes** or **ar'chi·pel'a·gos**

**ar·chi·tect** (är'kə tekt) ***n.*** a person who works out the plans for buildings, bridges, etc. and sees that these plans are carried out by the builders.

**ar·chi·tec·ture** (är'kə tek'chər) ***n.*** **1** the science or work of planning and putting up buildings. **2** a style or special way of building [Gothic *architecture* uses pointed arches.] —**ar'chi·tec'tur·al** ***adj.*** —**ar'chi·tec'tur·al·ly** ***adv.***

**ar·chives** (är'kīvz) ***n.pl.*** **1** a place where old public records and papers of historical interest are kept. **2** such records and papers.

**arch·ly** (ärch'lē) ***adv.*** in a playful or mischievous way; pertly [He smiled at her *archly*.]

**arch·way** (ärch'wā) ***n.*** a passage or entrance under an arch.

**arc·tic** (ärk'tik *or* är'tik) ***adj.*** of or near the North Pole or the region around it. ◆***n.*** the region around the North Pole.

**Arctic Ocean** the ocean around the North Pole.

**ar·dent** (är'd'nt) ***adj.*** full of eagerness; very enthusiastic; passionate. —**ar'dent·ly** ***adv.***

> **Ardent** comes from a Latin word that means "burning." An ardent worker for a cause is one who is burning, or excited, with enthusiasm.

**ar·dor** (är'dər) ***n.*** very warm feeling; passion; eagerness; enthusiasm [Patrick Henry spoke with *ardor* in the fight for liberty.] *The usual British spelling is* **ardour**.

**ar·du·ous** (är'jo͝o wəs) ***adj.*** **1** hard to do; difficult [*arduous* work]. **2** using much energy; strenuous [*arduous* efforts]. —**ar'du·ous·ly** ***adv.***

**are**[1] (är) *the form of the verb* **be** *used to show the present time with* you, we, *and* they, *and with plural nouns* [*Are* we late? You *are*.]

**are**[2] (er *or* är) ***n.*** a unit of measuring land in the metric system, equal to 100 square meters.

**ar·e·a** (er'ē ə) ***n.*** **1** the amount or size of a surface, measured in square units [If a floor is 10 meters wide and 20 meters long, its *area* is 200 square meters.] **2** a part of the earth's surface; region [Our family lives mostly in rural *areas*.] **3** a space used for a special purpose [a picnic *area*]. **4** a place or range of action; field [What is her *area* of work?]

☆**area code** a group of three numerals that is the first part of a long-distance telephone number and that shows what area that telephone is in. There are over 120 area codes in the United States and Canada.

**a·re·na** (ə rē'nə) ***n.*** **1** the open field in the middle of a Roman amphitheater, where gladiators fought. **2** a building with an open space in the middle used for sports, concerts, etc. **3** any place or area of conflict or struggle [the *arena* of politics].

**are·n't** (ärnt) are not [They *aren't* going.]

> **Aren't** is sometimes used in place of *am not* in questions by those who do not like to use *ain't* [I'm going too, *aren't* I?]

**Ar·gen·ti·na** (är'jən tē'nə) a country in southern South America.

**ar·gon** (är'gän) ***n.*** a chemical element that is a gas without color or smell. It is found in the air in small amounts and is used in electric light bulbs, radio tubes, etc.

**ar·gue** (är'gyo͞o) ***v.*** **1** to give reasons for or against something [to *argue* against a bill in Congress]. **2** to have a disagreement; quarrel [The children were *arguing* about whose turn it was.] **3** to seem to prove; show; indicate [Her polite manners *argue* a good upbringing.] **4** to make do something by giving reasons [They *argued* me into going with them.] —**ar'gued**, **ar'gu·ing**

**ar·gu·ment** (är'gyə mənt) ***n.*** **1** the act of arguing; discussion in which people disagree; dispute. **2** a reason given for or against something [What are your *arguments* for wanting to study mathematics?] **3** a brief report of the main points of a book, article, etc.

> SYNONYMS: An **argument** is a disagreement in which each side tries to use reason and logic and bring out facts that prove or disprove points to be made. A **dispute** is a disagreement in which each side may become angry and excited in trying to prove the other wrong. A **controversy** is a disagreement over a serious matter that goes on for a long time [the *controversy* over State lotteries].

| | | | | | | | |
|---|---|---|---|---|---|---|---|
| **a** | fat | **ir** | here | **ou** | out | **zh** | leisure |
| **ā** | ape | **ī** | bite, fire | **u** | up | **ng** | ring |
| **ä** | car, lot | **ō** | go | **ur** | fur | | a *in* ago |
| **e** | ten | **ô** | law, horn | **ch** | chin | | e *in* agent |
| **er** | care | **oi** | oil | **sh** | she | ə = | i *in* unity |
| **ē** | even | **o͝o** | look | **th** | thin | | o *in* collect |
| **i** | hit | **o͞o** | tool | ***th*** | then | | u *in* focus |

**ar·gu·men·ta·tive** (är′gyə men′tə tiv) ***adj.*** always ready to argue; quarrelsome.

**a·ri·a** (är′ē ə *or* er′ē ə) ***n.*** a song in an opera or oratorio, that is sung by one person accompanied by musical instruments.

**ar·id** (ar′id) ***adj.*** **1** not having enough water for things to grow; dry and barren [A desert is an *arid* region.] *See* SYNONYMS *at* **dry.** **2** not interesting; dull [an *arid* talk]. —**a·rid·i·ty** (ə rid′ə tē) ***n.*** —**ar′id·ly** ***adv.***

**Ar·i·es** (er′ēz *or* er′i ēz) the first sign of the zodiac, for the period from March 21 to April 19: *also called* the Ram. *See the picture at* **zodiac.**

**a·right** (ə rīt′) ***adv.*** correctly; rightly [Did I hear you *aright?*]

**a·rise** (ə rīz′) ***v.*** **1** to get up, as from sleeping or sitting; rise. **2** to move upward; ascend [Clouds of dust *arose* from the dry plains.] **3** to begin to be; start [Many new businesses have *arisen* in the town.] **4** to come as a result [Prejudice *arises* from ignorance.] *See* SYNONYMS *at* **rise.** —**a·rose′, a·ris·en** (ə riz′'n), **a·ris·ing** (ə rīz′iŋ)

**ar·is·toc·ra·cy** (ar′ə stäk′rə sē) ***n.*** **1** an upper or ruling class of society who were born into families having wealth and high social position. **2** government by such a class. **3** those thought to be the best in some way [an *aristocracy* of scientists]. *—pl.* **ar′is·toc′ra·cies**



**Aristocracy** comes from Greek words that mean "rule by the best people." The original idea of a small group of citizens trained and educated to govern changed to the idea of a small ruling class of people who had inherited their wealth and position.

**a·ris·to·crat** (ə ris′tə krat) ***n.*** **1** a member of the aristocracy, or upper class. **2** a person who acts, thinks, or believes like people of the upper class.

**a·ris·to·crat·ic** (ə ris′tə krat′ik) ***adj.*** **1** belonging to the aristocracy. **2** like an aristocrat; proud, noble, etc. (*in a good sense*) or haughty, snobbish, etc. (*in a bad sense*). —**a·ris′to·crat′i·cal·ly** ***adv.***

**Ar·is·tot·le** (ar′is tät′'l) 384–322 B.C.: Greek philosopher, who was a student of Plato.

**a·rith·me·tic** (ə rith′mə tik) ***n.*** the science or art of using numbers, especially in adding, subtracting, multiplying, and dividing. —**ar·ith·met·i·cal** (ar′ith met′i k'l) ***adj.***

**Ar·i·zo·na** (ar′ə zō′nə) a State in the southwestern part of the U.S.: abbreviated **Ariz., AZ**

**ark** (ärk) ***n.*** **1** in the Bible, the ship in which Noah, his family, and two of every kind of animal lived during the great flood. **2** the chest holding the two stone tablets on which the Ten Commandments were inscribed. It was kept in the holiest part of the ancient Jewish Temple. *Its full name was the* **ark of the covenant.** **3** the place in a synagogue where the Torahs are kept. *See the picture.*

**Ar·kan·sas** (är′k'n sô) a State in the south central part of the U.S.: abbreviated **Ark., AR**

**Ar·ling·ton** (är′liŋ tən) a county in Virginia near Washington, D.C. A national cemetery is located there.

**arm**[1] (ärm) ***n.*** **1** the part of the body between the shoulder and the hand; an upper limb. **2** anything thought of as being like an arm, as the raised side of a chair, the sleeve of a coat, an inlet of the sea, or a branch of government. ☆**3** the ability to pitch or throw a ball [Our catcher has a good *arm.*] —**arm in arm,** with arms joined, as two people walking together. —**with open arms,** in a warm and friendly way [We were greeted *with open arms.*]

**arm**[2] (ärm) ***n.*** any weapon: *see* **arms.** ◆***v.*** **1** to furnish with a weapon or weapons. **2** to furnish with some kind of protection [I was *armed* against the cold with a heavy coat.]

**ar·ma·da** (är mä′də) ***n.*** **1** a fleet of warships [The Spanish *Armada* sent against England in 1588 was defeated.] **2** a fleet of warplanes.

**ar·ma·dil·lo** (är′mə dil′ō) ***n.*** a burrowing animal with an armor of bony plates around its back and head. Armadillos are found in Texas, Central America, and South America. Some kinds can roll up into a ball when in danger. *See the picture. —pl.* **ar′ma·dil′los**

**ar·ma·ment** (är′mə mənt) ***n.*** **1** *often* **armaments,** *pl.* all the guns, bombs, ships, planes, etc. for waging war. **2** all the weapons of a warship, warplane, tank, etc.

**ar·ma·ture** (är′mə chər) ***n.*** **1** that part of an electric generator in which the current is brought into being; also, that part of a motor in which the movement is produced. In both cases, it is an iron core wound around with wire, and it is usually a rotating part. **2** a soft iron bar placed across the poles of a magnet. **3** the part moved by a magnet in an electric relay or bell. **4** a framework on which the clay is put in making a piece of sculpture.

**arm·band** (ärm′band) ***n.*** a cloth band worn around the upper arm to show sorrow over someone's death.

**arm·chair** (ärm′cher) ***n.*** a chair with supports at the sides for the arms or elbows.

**armed forces** (ärmd) all the military, naval, and air forces of a country.

**Ar·me·ni·a** (är mē′nē ə) a former country in southwestern Asia, now divided between the Soviet Union, Turkey, and Iran. —**Ar·me′ni·an** ***adj., n.***

**arm·ful** (ärm′fo͝ol) ***n.*** as much as the arms or one arm can hold. *—pl.* **arm′fuls**

**arm·hole** (ärm′hōl) ***n.*** an opening for the arm in a shirt, coat, etc.

**ar·mis·tice** (är′mə stis) ***n.*** an agreement to stop fighting for a time, as before getting together to draw up a peace treaty; truce.

**Armistice Day** *see* **Veterans Day.**

**ar·mor** (är′mər) ***n.*** **1** covering worn to protect the body against weapons [The knight's suit of *armor* was made of metal plate.] *See the picture.* **2** any covering that protects, as the shell of a turtle or the metal plates on a warship. *The usual British spelling is* **armour.**

**ar·mored** (är′mərd) ***adj.*** **1** covered with armor [an *armored* car]. **2** supplied with tanks and other armored vehicles [an *armored* division of an army].

**ar·mor·er** (är′mər ər) ***n.*** a soldier or sailor whose job is to take care of the small guns of a company, warship, etc.

**ar·mor·y** (är′mər ē) ***n.*** **1** a place where weapons are stored; arsenal. ☆**2** a building where a National Guard unit drills. ☆**3** a factory where pistols, rifles, etc. are made. *—pl.* **ar′mor·ies**

**arm·pit** (ärm′pit) ***n.*** the hollow place under the arm where it joins the shoulder.

**arm·rest** (ärm′rest) ***n.*** a support on which to rest one's arm, as on the inside of a car door.

**arms** (ärmz) ***n.pl.*** **1** tools used for fighting; weapons. **2** fighting; warfare. **3** the designs and figures on a coat of arms: *see* **coat of arms.** —**bear arms,** to serve as a soldier, sailor, etc. —**take up arms,** to go to war or get ready to fight. —**up in arms,** angry and ready to fight.

**Arm·strong** (ärm′strông), **Louis** 1900–1971; American jazz musician.

**Armstrong, Neil** 1930– ; American astronaut. He was the first person to step on the moon.

**ar·my** (är′mē) ***n.*** **1** a large group of soldiers trained for war, especially on land; also, all the soldiers of a country. **2** a large group of persons organized to work for some cause [the Salvation *Army*]. **3** any large group of persons or animals [An *army* of workers was building the bridge.] —*pl.* **ar′mies**

**Ar·nold** (är′nəld), **Benedict** 1741–1801; American general in the Revolution who became a traitor.

**a·ro·ma** (ə rō′mə) ***n.*** a pleasant smell, as of a plant or of something cooking.

**ar·o·mat·ic** (ar′ə mat′ik) ***adj.*** having a pleasant, often spicy, smell; fragrant [*aromatic* herbs].

**a·rose** (ə rōz′) *the past tense of* **arise.**

**a·round** (ə round′) ***adv.*** **1** in a circle [The wheel turned *around.*] **2** in circumference [A baseball measures about nine inches *around.*] **3** on all sides [The valley is hemmed *around* by mountains.] **4** in or to the opposite direction [We turned *around* and went back home.] **5** in various places; here and there [The coach is looking *around* for new players.] **6** for everyone [There's not enough cake to go *around.*] **7** near by: *used only in everyday talk* [Stay *around* in case we need you.] ◆***prep.*** **1** in a circle that surrounds [Pine trees grew *around* the lake.] **2** on all sides of [the suburbs *around* the city]. **3** here and there in; about [Toys were scattered *around* the room.] ☆**4** close to; about [It cost *around* four dollars.] ◆***adj.*** **1** on the move; about [She's up and *around* now.] **2** existing; living [when dinosaurs were *around*].

In the United States, **around** is used for the meanings given above, but in Great Britain, the word **round** is used for most meanings of *around* as an adverb and preposition.

**a·rouse** (ə rouz′) ***v.*** **1** to awaken, as from sleep. **2** to work up; bring into being; excite [His tear-stained face *aroused* our pity.] —**a·roused′, a·rous′ing**

**ar·raign** (ə rān′) ***v.*** to bring before a law court to answer a charge with either "guilty" or "not guilty." —**ar·raign′ment** ***n.***

**ar·range** (ə rānj′) ***v.*** **1** to put in a certain order [to *arrange* furniture in a room]. **2** to make plans; prepare [We *arranged* to meet at the theater.] **3** to change so as to fit; adapt; adjust [This violin solo has been *arranged* for the guitar.] —**ar·ranged′, ar·rang′ing**

**ar·range·ment** (ə rānj′mənt) ***n.*** **1** the act of arranging or putting in order. **2** the way in which something is arranged [a new *arrangement* of pictures on the wall]. **3** a preparation; plan: *usually used in pl.,* **arrangements** [*Arrangements* have been made for the party.]

ark in a synagogue

**ar·rant** (ar′ənt) ***adj.*** that is very plainly such; absolute; complete [an *arrant* fool].

**ar·ray** (ə rā′) ***v.*** **1** to put in the proper order [The troops were *arrayed* for battle.] **2** to dress in fine clothes [*arrayed* in an elegant silk gown]. ◆***n.*** **1** arrangement in the proper order [soldiers in battle *array*]. **2** a large display [an *array* of fine china]. **3** fine clothes; finery.

**ar·rears** (ə rirz′) ***n.pl.*** money owed or work to be done that is not yet taken care of; unfinished business [*arrears* of unpaid bills]. —**in arrears,** behind in paying a debt or in one's work.



**ar·rest** (ə rest′) ***v.*** **1** to stop from growing or spreading [A coat of paint will *arrest* the rust.] **2** to catch and hold [The large sign *arrested* her attention.] **3** to seize or take to jail on a charge of breaking the law [The policeman *arrested* him for careless driving.] ◆***n.*** the act of arresting by the police. —**under arrest,** held as a prisoner on a charge of breaking the law.

**ar·rest·ing** (ə res′ting) ***adj.*** getting people's interest or attention; striking [an *arresting* picture].

**ar·riv·al** (ə rī′v′l) ***n.*** **1** the act of arriving [to welcome the *arrival* of spring]. **2** a person or thing that has arrived [They are recent *arrivals* to the U.S. from South America.]

**ar·rive** (ə rīv′) ***v.*** **1** to come to a place after a journey [When does the bus from Chicago *arrive* here?] **2** to come [The time has *arrived* to say goodbye.] **3** to get success or fame [The pianist had *arrived* by the age of 25.] —**ar·rived′, ar·riv′ing** —**arrive at,** **1** to reach by traveling. **2** to reach by work, thinking, etc. [Have you *arrived* at a decision?]

**ar·ro·gance** (ar′ə gəns) ***n.*** a feeling of too great pride or confidence in oneself that makes a person ignore what others think or want; haughtiness.

**ar·ro·gant** (ar′ə gənt) ***adj.*** having or showing arrogance; haughty. *See* SYNONYMS *at* **proud.** —**ar′ro·gant·ly** ***adv.***

| | | | |
|---|---|---|---|
| **a** fat | **ir** here | **ou** out | **zh** leisure |
| **ā** ape | **ī** bite, fire | **u** up | **ng** ring |
| **ä** car, lot | **ō** go | **ur** fur | a *in* ago |
| **e** ten | **ô** law, horn | **ch** chin | e *in* agent |
| **er** care | **oi** oil | **sh** she | **ə** = i *in* unity |
| **ē** even | **oo** look | **th** thin | o *in* collect |
| **i** hit | **ōō** tool | ***th*** then | u *in* focus |

**ar·row** (ar′ō) ***n.*** **1** a slender rod that is shot from a bow. Arrows usually have a point at the front end and feathers at the back end. *See the picture.* **2** anything that looks or is used like an arrow; especially, a sign (←) used to point out a direction or place.

**ar·row·head** (ar′ō hed′) ***n.*** the pointed tip of an arrow.

**ar·row·root** (ar′ō ro͞ot′ *or* ar′ō ro͝ot′) ***n.*** **1** a starch from the roots of a tropical plant, used as food. **2** this plant.

> The **arrowroot** got its name from the fact that Indians in the West Indies used the starch from its roots as a medicine on wounds caused by poisoned arrows.

☆**ar·roy·o** (ə roi′ō) ***n.*** a small river or stream, or a gully where a stream has dried up: *this word is used in the Southwest.* —*pl.* **ar·roy′os**

**ar·se·nal** (är′s'n əl) ***n.*** a place where guns and ammunition are made or stored.

**ar·se·nic** (är′s'n ik) ***n.*** a silvery-white metal, a chemical element sometimes found in the form of a powder. It is very poisonous and is used in powders and sprays for killing insects, rats, and mice.

**ar·son** (är′s'n) ***n.*** the crime of setting fire to a building or other property on purpose.

**art** (ärt) ***n.*** **1** the making or doing by people of things that have form and beauty [Drawing, painting, sculpture, architecture, music, literature, drama, and the dance are *arts.*] *See also* **fine arts.** **2** paintings, drawings, statues, or other things made by artists. **3** any of certain areas of learning, as literature, languages, history, philosophy, music, etc.: *usually used in pl.,* **arts**: *in this meaning the* **arts** *are thought of as separate from the* **sciences.** **4** the ability to make or do things; skill [the *art* of cooking]. **5** any craft or profession [the *art* of healing]. **6** a sly or cunning trick; wile [the *arts* of a successful politician].



> SYNONYMS: **Art** is the ability to make or do something, especially something beautiful, in an original way. **Skill** is the ability of an expert at doing something, especially something that is useful or practical. **Craft** is the ability to do something that takes skill, but not as much imagination as art [Painting portraits is an *art.* Repairing plumbing is a *skill.* Weaving baskets is a *craft.*]

**ar·te·ri·al** (är tir′ē əl) ***adj.*** **1** of or like an artery or arteries. **2** having to do with the blood in the arteries [*Arterial* blood is a brighter blood than the blood in the veins because it has taken up oxygen from the lungs.]

**ar·ter·y** (är′tər ē) ***n.*** **1** any of the tubes that carry blood from the heart to all parts of the body. *See also* **vein.** **2** a main road or channel [a railroad *artery*]. —*pl.* **ar′ter·ies**

**ar·te·sian well** (är tē′zhən) a deep well in which the water gushes up because of the pressure under the ground. *See the picture.*

**art·ful** (ärt′f'l) ***adj.*** **1** skillful or clever [*artful* reasoning]. **2** sly or cunning; crafty [an *artful* swindle]. —**art′ful·ly** ***adv.***

**ar·thri·tis** (är thrīt′is) ***n.*** a disease in which the joints of the body swell up and become sore and stiff. —**ar·thrit·ic** (är thrit′ik) ***adj.***

**ar·thro·pod** (är′thrə päd) ***n.*** any one of a large group of animals that have legs with several joints and a body divided into two or more parts [Insects, spiders, crabs, and lobsters are all *arthropods.*]

**Ar·thur** (är′thər) a king of Britain in legends, who led the knights of the Round Table. Such a king may have lived in the 6th century A.D.

**Arthur, Chester Alan** 1830–1886; 21st president of the United States, from 1881 to 1885.

**ar·ti·choke** (är′tə chōk) ***n.*** **1** a plant that looks like a large thistle. **2** its flower head, which is cooked and eaten as a vegetable. *See the picture.*

**ar·ti·cle** (är′ti k'l) ***n.*** **1** a thing of a certain kind; separate thing [A shirt is an *article* of clothing.] **2** a section that deals with a separate point in a constitution, treaty, contract, etc. **3** a complete piece of writing on a single subject, as in a newspaper or magazine. **4** any of the words *a, an,* or *the.*

> *A* and *an* are the **indefinite articles** and *the* is the **definite article.** "The house" is a definite, particular house; "a house" is not.

**ar·tic·u·late** (är tik′yə lit) ***adj.*** **1** spoken in such a way that all the sounds and words are clear and distinct [an *articulate* reply]. **2** able to speak in this way; also, able to tell one's thoughts clearly so they are understood [an *articulate* speaker]. **3** having joints [The legs are *articulate* limbs.] ✦***v.*** (är tik′yə lāt) **1** to say in a clear, distinct way. **2** to put or come together by means of a joint [The arm *articulates* with the body at the shoulder.] —**ar·tic′u·lat·ed, ar·tic′u·lat·ing**

**ar·tic·u·la·tion** (är tik′yə lā′shən) ***n.*** **1** way of talking or pronouncing. **2** the way parts are joined together. **3** a joint, as between bones.

**ar·ti·fact** (är′tə fakt) ***n.*** a thing made by human work or skill, especially a simple tool, weapon, container, etc.

**ar·ti·fice** (är′tə fis) ***n.*** a clever method or sly trick [He used every *artifice* to avoid capture.]

**ar·ti·fi·cial** (är′tə fish′əl) ***adj.*** **1** made by a human being, not by nature; not natural [*artificial* flowers made of plastic]. **2** put on just for an effect; not sincere; false [an *artificial* smile]. —**ar·ti·fi·ci·al·i·ty** (är′tə fish′ē al′ə tē) ***n.*** —**ar′ti·fi′cial·ly** ***adv.***

**artificial respiration** the act of trying to start or keep a person breathing by forcing air into and out of the lungs, as in cases of drowning, shock, etc.

**ar·til·ler·y** (är til′ər ē) ***n.*** large guns, too heavy to carry; mounted guns, as cannons. —**the artillery,** the branch of an army that uses such guns.

**ar·ti·san** (är′tə z'n) ***n.*** a worker who is skilled in some trade; craftsman.

**art·ist** (är′tist) ***n.*** **1** a person who works in any of the fine arts, especially in painting, drawing, sculpture, etc. **2** a person who does anything very well [Our cook is an *artist* with pastries.]

**ar·tis·tic** (är tis′tik) ***adj.*** **1** of art or artists. **2** done with skill and a good sense of color, form, design, etc. [an *artistic* job of redecorating]. **3** knowing and enjoying what is beautiful. —**ar·tis′ti·cal·ly** ***adv.***

**art·ist·ry** (är′tis trē) ***n.*** artistic work or skill.

**art·less** (ärt′lis) ***adj.*** **1** without art or skill; clumsy. **2** without tricks or lies; simple; natural [an *artless* way of speaking].

**-ar·y** (er′ē *or* ər ē) *a suffix meaning:* **1** having to do with [The word *customary* means having to do with customs.] **2** a person or thing connected with [A *missionary* is a person connected with missions.]

**as** (az) ***adv.*** **1** to the same amount or degree; equally [Are you *as* tall as your cousin?] **2** for instance; for example [Some plants, *as* corn and potatoes, are native to America.] ◆***conj.*** **1** to the same amount or degree that [It flew straight *as* an arrow. I'm as hungry *as* you are.] **2** in the way that [Do *as* I tell you.] **3** at the same time that; while [She wept *as* she spoke.] **4** because; since [*As* I am tired, I'll stay home.] **5** that the result was [She was so brave *as* to put us all to shame.] **6** though [Full *as* he was, he kept on eating.] ◆***pron.*** a fact that [I'm tired, *as* anyone can see.] ◆***prep.*** in the role or manner of [He poses *as* a friend. That table can serve *as* a desk.] —**as for** or **as to,** in regard to; concerning [*As* for me, I'll have milk.] —**as if** or **as though,** as it (or one) would if [They acted *as if* they were tired. It looks *as though* it will rain.] —☆**as is,** just as it is; without changing it: *used only in everyday talk* [This used car costs $800 *as is.*] —☆**as of,** up to, on, or from (a certain time) [You can reach me at this number *as of* next Friday.] —**the same as,** like; resembling [Your hat is *the same as* mine.]

**As** *the symbol for the chemical element* arsenic.

**as·bes·tos** (as bes′təs *or* az bes′təs) ***n.*** a grayish mineral found in long fibers which can be made into a kind of cloth or paper. Asbestos will not burn, and so it is used in fireproof curtains, insulation, etc.

**as·cend** (ə send′) ***v.*** to go up; move upward; rise; climb [The procession *ascended* the hill.]

**as·cend·an·cy** or **as·cend·en·cy** (ə sen′dən sē) ***n.*** the condition of having control or power; domination [For centuries ancient Rome held *ascendancy* over Europe.]

**as·cend·ant** or **as·cend·ent** (ə sen′dənt) ***adj.*** **1** rising; ascending. **2** in control; dominant. —**in the ascendant,** becoming more powerful or important.

**as·cen·sion** (ə sen′shən) ***n.*** a rising; ascent. —**the Ascension,** in the Bible, the ascent of Jesus into heaven after rising from the dead.

**as·cent** (ə sent′) ***n.*** **1** an ascending or rising; climbing [an *ascent* in a balloon; a rapid *ascent* to leadership]. **2** a way leading up; slope.

**as·cer·tain** (as′ər tān) ***v.*** to find out in such a way as to be sure [We *ascertained* the facts about the case by reading through old newspapers.] —**as′cer·tain′a·ble** ***adj.*** —**as′cer·tain′ment** ***n.***

**as·cet·ic** (ə set′ik) ***n.*** a person who chooses to live without the usual comforts and pleasures of life; especially, one who lives this way for religious reasons. ◆***adj.*** of or like ascetics or their way of life. —**as·cet′i·cism** ***n.***

> **Ascetic** comes from a Greek word meaning "to train the body." Ascetics try to get control over the body by fasting or giving themselves pain.

**a·scor·bic acid** (ə skôr′bik) vitamin C, which is found in citrus fruits, tomatoes, etc. and is very important in the diet.

**as·cribe** (ə skrīb′) ***v.*** **1** to think to be the result of: *used with* to [She *ascribed* her poor work to worry over money matters.] **2** to think of as belonging to or coming from; attribute: *used with* to [The poems are *ascribed* to Homer.] —**as·cribed′, as·crib′ing** —**as·crip·tion** (ə skrip′shən) ***n.***

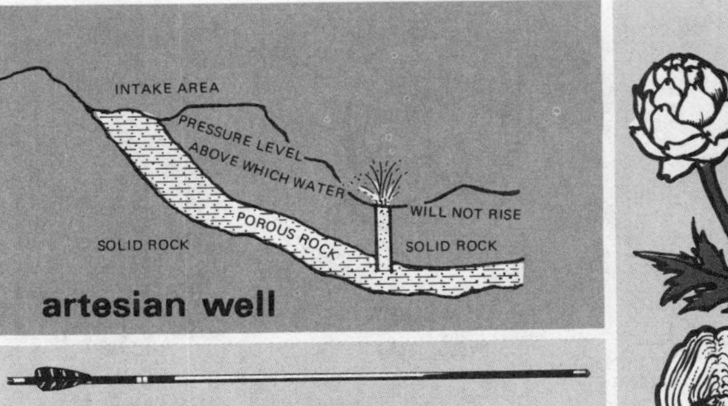

**artesian well**

**arrows**

**artichoke**

**ash**[1] (ash) ***n.*** the grayish powder left after something has burned. *See also* **ashes.**

**ash**[2] (ash) ***n.*** a shade tree whose tough wood has a straight, close grain.

**a·shamed** (ə shāmd′) ***adj.*** **1** feeling shame because something bad, wrong, or foolish was done [They were *ashamed* of having broken the window.] **2** not willing because of a fear that one will feel shame or be embarrassed [I am *ashamed* to ask for help.]

**ash·en**[1] (ash′ən) ***adj.*** **1** of ashes. **2** like ashes, especially in color; pale [an *ashen* face].

**ash·en**[2] (ash′ən) ***adj.*** of the ash tree or its wood. 

**ash·es** (ash′iz) ***n.pl.*** **1** the grayish powder or fine dust that is left after something has been burned. **2** the body of a dead person, especially what is left after it has been cremated.

**a·shore** (ə shôr′) ***adv., adj.*** to or on the shore [They jumped overboard and swam *ashore.*]

**ash·tray** (ash′trā) ***n.*** a container into which smokers drop tobacco ashes: *also written* **ash tray.**

**Ash Wednesday** the Wednesday that is the first day of Lent. In some churches on this day ashes are put on the forehead to show sorrow for having sinned.

**ash·y** (ash′ē) ***adj.*** **1** full of or covered with ashes. **2** having the gray color of ashes; pale.

**A·sia** (ā′zhə) the largest continent, about 17,000,000 square miles in area. The Pacific Ocean is on its east and it is separated from northern Europe by the Ural Mountains.

**Asia Minor** a peninsula in western Asia, between the Black Sea and the Mediterranean, including most of Turkey.

**A·sian** (ā′zhən) or **A·si·at·ic** (ā′zhē at′ik) ***adj.*** having to do with Asia or its people. ◆***n.*** a person born or living in Asia.

> Although *Asiatic* used to be the more common term, it is nowadays thought to be less polite, and *Asian* is the term more often used.

| | | | | | | | |
|---|---|---|---|---|---|---|---|
| **a** | fat | **ir** | here | **ou** | out | **zh** | leisure |
| **ā** | ape | **ī** | bite, fire | **u** | up | **ng** | ring |
| **ä** | car, lot | **ō** | go | **ur** | fur | | a *in* ago |
| **e** | ten | **ô** | law, horn | **ch** | chin | | e *in* agent |
| **er** | care | **oi** | oil | **sh** | she | **ə** = | i *in* unity |
| **ē** | even | **oo** | look | **th** | thin | | o *in* collect |
| **i** | hit | **ōō** | tool | ***th*** | then | | u *in* focus |

a

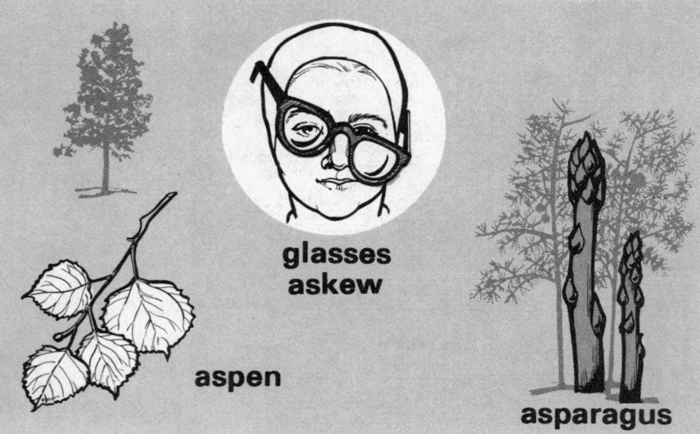


**a·side** (ə sīd′) ***adv.*** **1** on or to one side [Kim pulled the curtain *aside.*] **2** away; for use later [Put a cookie *aside* for me.] ☆**3** apart; out of one's thoughts [All joking *aside,* I mean what I said.] ◆***n.*** words spoken by an actor or actress to the audience, supposedly not heard by the other players. —☆**aside from** except for [*Aside from* history, she likes school.]

**as·i·nine** (as′ə nīn) ***adj.*** stupid, silly, or foolish [an *asinine* suggestion].

**ask** (ask) ***v.*** **1** to use words in trying to find out; seek the answer to [We *asked* how much it cost. Why do you *ask* so many questions?] **2** to put a question to; seek information from [*Ask* her where she's going.] **3** to tell what is wanted; make a request [We *asked* the bank for a loan. Vic *asked* to be excused from school.] **4** to demand or expect as a price [They are *asking* too much for the house.] **5** to invite [We weren't *asked* to the party.] **6** to act in such a way as to bring on [I think you're *asking* for trouble.]



**a·skance** (ə skans′) ***adv.*** **1** sidewise; with a glance to the side. **2** with doubt or suspicion [They looked *askance* at the plan for moving.]

**a·skew** (ə skyo͞o′) ***adv., adj.*** on or to one side; not straight [The captain's hat was knocked *askew.*] *See the picture.*

**a·slant** (ə slant′) ***adv., adj.*** on a slant; in a slanting direction. ◆***prep.*** on a slant across.

**a·sleep** (ə slēp′) ***adj.*** **1** sleeping; in a state of sleep. **2** numb except for a prickling feeling [I sat on my foot and now it is *asleep.*] ◆***adv.*** into a sleeping condition [to fall *asleep*].

**asp** (asp) ***n.*** a small, poisonous snake found in Africa and Europe.

**as·par·a·gus** (ə spar′ə gəs) ***n.*** a plant with small leaves that look like scales. Its young shoots are cooked and eaten as a vegetable. *See the picture.*

**A.S.P.C.A.** American Society for the Prevention of Cruelty to Animals.

**as·pect** (as′pekt) ***n.*** **1** look or appearance [In the shadows his face had a frightening *aspect.*] **2** a way that one may look at or think about something [Have you considered all the *aspects* of the problem?] **3** the side facing in a particular direction [the eastern *aspect* of the house].

**as·pen** (as′pən) ***n.*** a kind of poplar tree whose leaves flutter in the lightest breeze. *See the picture.*

**as·per·i·ty** (as per′ə tē) ***n.*** **1** roughness or harshness, as of weather. **2** sharpness of temper.

**as·per·sion** (ə spur′zhən) ***n.*** a false or unfair remark that can hurt someone; slander [to cast *aspersions* on a person's character].

**as·phalt** (as′fôlt) ***n.*** **1** a dark, sticky substance like tar, that is found in the ground. **2** a mixture of this with sand or gravel, used mainly to pave roads.

**as·phyx·i·ate** (as fik′sē āt) ***v.*** to make unconscious by cutting down the supply of oxygen in the blood [A person who suffocates, as in drowning, has been *asphyxiated.*] —**as·phyx′i·at·ed, as·phyx′i·at·ing** —**as·phyx′i·a′tion** ***n.***

**as·pic** (as′pik) ***n.*** a jelly of meat juice, tomato juice, etc., molded, often with meat or seafood, and eaten as a relish.

**as·pir·ant** (as′pər ənt *or* ə spīr′ənt) ***n.*** a person who is trying to get honors or a high position.

**as·pi·rate** (as′pə rāt) ***v.*** to pronounce with the sound of *h* [The *h* in "home" is *aspirated;* the *h* in "honor" is not.] —**as′pi·rat·ed, as′pi·rat·ing** ◆***n.*** (as′pər it) the sound of *h* in *home.* ◆***adj.*** (as′pər it) pronounced with this sound.

**as·pi·ra·tion** (as′pə rā′shən) ***n.*** **1** a strong wish, hope, or ambition [She has *aspirations* to become a doctor.] **2** the act of breathing; breath. **3** the act of pronouncing with the sound of *h.*

**as·pire** (ə spīr′) ***v.*** to be ambitious to get or do something; seek [Napoleon *aspired* to create a French empire.] —**as·pired′, as·pir′ing**

**as·pi·rin** (as′pər in) ***n.*** a medicine used to lessen pain or to bring down fever. It is a white powder that is usually pressed into tablets.

**as·pir·ing** (ə spīr′iŋ) ***adj.*** trying to reach some high goal [an *aspiring* concert pianist]. *See* SYNONYMS *at* **ambitious.**

**ass** (as) ***n.*** **1** a donkey. **2** a stupid or silly person; fool.

**as·sail** (ə sāl′) ***v.*** **1** to attack by hitting, punching, etc. **2** to attack with questions, arguments, etc. —**as·sail′a·ble** ***adj.***

**as·sail·ant** (ə sāl′ənt) ***n.*** a person who assails; attacker.

**as·sas·sin** (ə sas′′n) ***n.*** a murderer, especially one who kills a government leader or other important person, usually for political reasons.

> **Assassin** comes from the Arabic word *hashshashin,* which means "a person who uses a drug called *hashish.*" The word was first used of members of a secret group of Muslims who killed Crusaders while under the influence of hashish.

**as·sas·si·nate** (ə sas′′n āt) ***v.*** to murder; especially, to murder a government leader or other important person, usually for political reasons. —**as·sas′si·nat·ed, as·sas′si·nat·ing** —**as·sas′si·na′tion** ***n.***

**as·sault** (ə sôlt′) ***n.*** **1** a sudden attack with great force [The soldiers made an *assault* on the fortress.] **2** a direct threat to harm someone. The carrying out of such a threat is called **assault and battery.** ◆***v.*** to make a violent attack upon.

**as·say** (as′ā) ***n.*** the testing of an ore, alloy, etc., as to find out how much of a certain metal is in it. ◆***v.*** to make an assay of; test; analyze. —**as·say′er** ***n.***

**as·sem·blage** (ə sem′blij) ***n.*** **1** a group of persons or things gathered together; gathering or collection [an *assemblage* of musicians]. **2** a fitting together of parts, as in a modern kind of sculpture.

**as·sem·ble** (ə sem′b'l) ***v.*** **1** to gather together into a group; collect [The members of the family *assembled* for a reunion.] ☆**2** to put together the parts of [My hobby is *assembling* model ships.] *See* SYNONYMS *at* **gather.** —**as·sem′bled, as·sem′bling**

**as·sem·bly** (ə sem′blē) ***n.*** **1** a gathering together of people [The Bill of Rights includes the right of peaceful *assembly.*] **2** a group of persons gathered together; meeting. **3 Assembly,** the lower branch of the legislature in some States. **4** a fitting together of parts, as in making automobiles. **5** the parts so fitted together [the tail *assembly* of an airplane]. **6** a signal on a bugle or drum for soldiers to come together in formation. —*pl.* **as·sem′blies**

**as·sent** (ə sent′) ***v.*** to say "yes"; give one's consent; agree [to *assent* to a request]. ◆***n.*** consent or agreement [Please give your *assent* to our plan.]

**as·sert** (ə surt′) ***v.*** **1** to say in a clear, sure way; declare [The doctors *assert* that his health is good.] **2** to insist on or defend, as one's rights or a claim. —**assert oneself,** to insist on one's rights.

SYNONYMS: To **assert** is to say something with confidence [The judge *asserted* that human nature will never change.] To **declare** is to assert something openly, often knowing it will be opposed [The colonies *declared* their independence in 1776.]

**as·ser·tion** (ə sur′shən) ***n.*** **1** the act of asserting something. **2** a strong or positive statement [Do you believe her *assertion* that she is innocent?]

**as·ser·tive** (ə sur′tiv) ***adj.*** sure of oneself; bold and positive. *See* SYNONYMS *at* **aggressive.** —**as·ser′tive·ly *adv.*** —**as·ser′tive·ness *n.***

**as·sess** (ə ses′) ***v.*** **1** to say how much a property is worth in order to figure the tax on it [A city official *assessed* the house at $45,000.] **2** to decide what the amount of a fine or tax should be. **3** to put a tax, fine, or charge on [The club *assessed* each member $100 for dues.]

**as·sess·ment** (ə ses′mənt) ***n.*** **1** the act of assessing. **2** the amount that is assessed.

**as·ses·sor** (ə ses′ər) ***n.*** a person who assesses property in order to figure the tax on it.

**as·set** (as′et) ***n.*** **1** anything owned that has value [The *assets* of the company include its land, buildings, machinery, stock, cash, and money owed to it.] **2** a fine or valuable thing to have [Good health can be your greatest *asset.*]

**as·sid·u·ous** (ə sij′oo wəs) ***adj.*** working hard and steadily; diligent [an *assiduous* student]. —**as·sid′u·ous·ly *adv.***

**as·sign** (ə sīn′) ***v.*** **1** to set apart for a special purpose; designate [Let's *assign* a day for the trip.] **2** to place at some task or work [Two pupils were *assigned* to write the report.] **3** to give out as a task; allot [The teacher *assigned* some homework.] **4** to give or hand over to another [All rights to the book were *assigned* to the college.]

**as·sign·ment** (ə sīn′mənt) ***n.*** **1** the act of assigning. **2** something assigned, as a lesson.

**as·sim·i·late** (ə sim′ə lāt) ***v.*** **1** to take something in and make it part of oneself; absorb [The body *assimilates* food. Did you *assimilate* what you just read? America has *assimilated* people of many nations.] **2** to make or become like or alike [The immigrants *assimilated* their ways to those of the new land.] —**as·sim′i·lat·ed, as·sim′i·lat·ing** —**as·sim′i·la′tion *n.***

**as·sist** (ə sist′) ***v.*** to help; aid [Please *assist* me in preparing the program.] *See* SYNONYMS *at* **help.** ◆***n.*** an act of helping, as a play in baseball that helps another fielder make a putout.

**as·sist·ance** (ə sis′təns) ***n.*** help; aid.

**as·sist·ant** (ə sis′tənt) ***n.*** a person who assists or helps another; helper; aid [an *assistant* to the president]. ◆***adj.*** assisting or helping the person under whom one works [an *assistant* principal].

**as·siz·es** (ə sīz′əz) ***n.pl.*** court sessions held at regular times in each county of England.

**Assn.** *abbreviation for* **Association.**

**as·so·ci·ate** (ə sō′shē āt *or* ə sō′sē āt) ***v.*** **1** to connect in one's mind; think of together [We *associate* the taste of something with its smell.] **2** to bring or come together as friends or partners [Don't *associate* with people who gossip.] —**as·so′ci·at·ed, as·so′ci·at·ing** ◆***n.*** (ə sō′shē it *or* ə sō′sē it) a person with whom one is joined in some way; friend, partner, or fellow worker. ◆***adj.*** (ə sō′shē it *or* ə sō′sē it) **1** joined with others in some way [an *associate* justice of the Supreme Court]. **2** having less than full rank; of a lower position [an *associate* professor].

**as·so·ci·a·tion** (ə sō′sē ā′shən *or* ə sō′shē ā′shən) ***n.*** **1** a group of people joined in some way or for some purpose; society. **2** fellowship or partnership. **3** the act of joining or connecting. **4** a connection in the mind of one idea or feeling with another [the *association* of the color blue with coolness].



**as·sort·ed** (ə sôr′tid) ***adj.*** **1** of different sorts; of various kinds; miscellaneous [a box of *assorted* candies]. **2** matched [a poorly *assorted* pair].

**as·sort·ment** (ə sôrt′mənt) ***n.*** **1** the act of sorting or arranging into groups. **2** a collection of various sorts; variety [an *assortment* of books].

**asst.** *abbreviation for* **assistant.**

**as·suage** (ə swāj′) ***v.*** to make easier or calmer; lessen; lighten [Kind words help to *assuage* grief.] —**as·suaged′, as·suag′ing**

**as·sume** (ə sōōm′ *or* ə syōōm′) ***v.*** **1** to take on a certain look, form, or role [In a Greek myth, Zeus *assumes* the form of a bull.] **2** to take upon oneself; take over [to *assume* an obligation; to *assume* control]. **3** to suppose something to be a fact; take for granted [Let's *assume* our guests will be on time.] **4** to pretend to have; put on [Although afraid, he *assumed* an air of bravery.] —**as·sumed′, as·sum′ing**

**as·sump·tion** (ə sump′shən) ***n.*** **1** the act of assuming [the *assumption* of power]. **2** anything taken for granted [I acted on the *assumption* that they would be on time.] **3 Assumption,** in Roman Catholic belief,

| | | | | | | | |
|---|---|---|---|---|---|---|---|
| **a** | fat | **ir** | here | **ou** | out | **zh** | leisure |
| **ā** | ape | **ī** | bite, fire | **u** | up | **ng** | ring |
| **ä** | car, lot | **ō** | go | **ur** | fur | | a *in* ago |
| **e** | ten | **ô** | law, horn | **ch** | chin | | e *in* agent |
| **er** | care | **oi** | oil | **sh** | she | ə = | i *in* unity |
| **ē** | even | **oo** | look | **th** | thin | | o *in* collect |
| **i** | hit | **ōō** | tool | ***th*** | then | | u *in* focus |

the taking up of the Virgin Mary's body and soul into heaven after her death; also, the church festival on August 15 celebrating this.

**as·sur·ance** (ə shoor′əns) ***n.*** **1** the fact of being sure about something; confidence [I have no *assurance* that we will win.] **2** something said or done to make one feel confident [The flood victims received *assurances* of government aid.] **3** self-confidence; belief in one's own abilities [The young lawyer gained *assurance* as she got more experience.] **4** *the British word for* **insurance.**

**as·sure** (ə shoor′) ***v.*** **1** to make a person sure of something; convince [What can we do to *assure* you of our friendship?] **2** to tell or promise positively [I *assure* you I'll be there.] **3** to make a doubtful thing certain; guarantee [Their gift of money *assured* the success of our campaign.] —**as·sured′, as·sur′ing**

**as·sured** (ə shoord′) ***adj.*** **1** made sure; guaranteed [an *assured* income]. **2** confident; sure of oneself [an *assured* manner]. —**as·sur·ed·ly** (ə shoor′id lē) ***adv.***

**As·syr·i·a** (ə sir′ē ə) an ancient empire in western Asia. It reached its height in the seventh century B.C. *See the map.* —**As·syr′i·an** ***adj., n.***

**as·ter** (as′tər) ***n.*** a plant with purple, pink, or white flowers. The simple kinds look like daisies, but some asters are large and have many petals.

**as·ter·isk** (as′tər isk) ***n.*** a sign in the shape of a star (*) used in printing and writing to call attention to a footnote or other explanation or to show that something has been left out.

**a·stern** (ə sturn′) ***adv.*** **1** behind a ship or aircraft. **2** at or toward the back part of a ship or aircraft. **3** backward.

**as·ter·oid** (as′tə roid) ***n.*** any of the many small planets that move in orbits around the sun between the orbits of Mars and Jupiter.

**asth·ma** (az′mə) ***n.*** a disease in which there are attacks of wheezing, coughing, and hard breathing. It is usually caused by an allergy.

**a·stig·ma·tism** (ə stig′mə tiz′m) ***n.*** a fault in the lens of the eye, which keeps the light rays from coming to a focus. Astigmatism makes things look blurred or twisted out of shape.

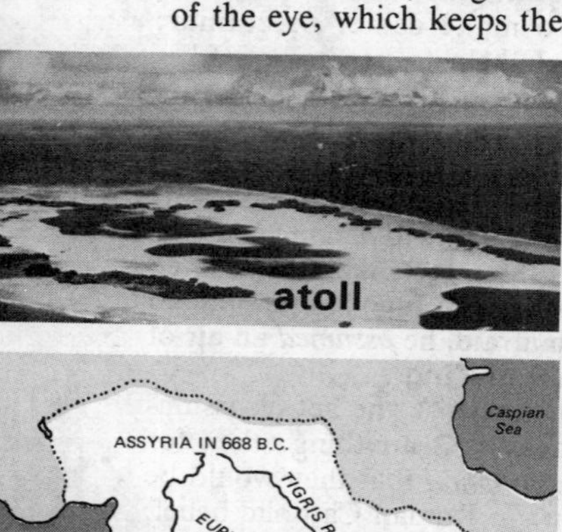

atoll

Assyria

atomizer

Athena



**a·stir** (ə stur′) ***adv., adj.*** moving about; in motion; active [The town is *astir* with visitors.]

**as·ton·ish** (ə stän′ish) ***v.*** to surprise greatly; fill with wonder; amaze. —**as·ton′ish·ing** ***adj.*** —**as·ton′ish·ment** ***n.***

**as·tound** (ə stound′) ***v.*** to surprise so greatly as to make confused or unable to speak [She stood there *astounded* by their praise.] —**as·tound′ing** ***adj.***

**a·stray** (ə strā′) ***adv.*** **1** off the right path [The cows went *astray* and trampled the garden.] **2** so as to be in error [I was led *astray* by getting wrong figures.]

**a·stride** (ə strīd′) ***adv.*** with one leg on each side [She sits *astride* when riding horseback.] ◆***prep.*** with one leg on each side of [He sat *astride* the bench.]

**as·trin·gent** (ə strin′jənt) ***n.*** a lotion or medicine that tightens up body tissues. Astringents are used to stop bleeding in small cuts or to give the skin a fresh, tingling feeling. ◆***adj.*** that acts as an astringent.

**as·trol·o·gy** (ə sträl′ə jē) ***n.*** a false science based on a belief that the stars, planets, and moon affect people's lives and that one can tell the future by studying the stars. —**as·trol′o·ger** ***n.*** —**as·tro·log·i·cal** (as′trə läj′i k'l) ***adj.***

**as·tro·naut** (as′trə nôt) ***n.*** a person trained to make rocket flights in outer space.

> An **astronaut** can be thought of as a sailor among the stars. *Astronaut* comes from a French word, and that in turn comes from the Greek words *astron,* meaning "star," and *nautes,* meaning "sailor."

**as·tro·nau·tics** (as′trə nôt′iks) ***n.pl.*** the science that studies the problems of traveling in outer space: *used with a singular verb.*

**as·tron·o·mer** (ə strän′ə mər) ***n.*** an expert in astronomy.

**as·tro·nom·i·cal** (as′trə näm′i k'l) ***adj.*** **1** having to do with astronomy. **2** extremely great [The distances between stars are measured in *astronomical* figures.]

**as·tron·o·my** (ə strän′ə mē) ***n.*** the science that studies the motion, size, and makeup of the stars, planets, comets, etc.

**as·tute** (ə stoot′ *or* ə styoot′) ***adj.*** having or showing a clever or sharp mind; keen. —**as·tute′ly** ***adv.***

**A·sun·ción** (ä soon syōn′) the capital of Paraguay.

**a·sun·der** (ə sun′dər) ***adv.*** into pieces or bits; apart [The boat hit the rock and was broken *asunder*.]

**As·wan** (äs′wän *or* as′wän) a city in southeastern Egypt. There is a large dam on the Nile near this city.

**a·sy·lum** (ə sī′ləm) ***n.*** **1** a place where one is safe and secure; refuge. **2** a place that is a home for large groups of helpless people, such as orphans or those who are very old or mentally ill [Today, foster homes, mental hospitals, nursing homes, etc. take the place of the old-fashioned *asylums*.]

**at** (at) ***prep.*** **1** on; in; near; by [Are they *at* home?] **2** to or toward [Look *at* her. Aim *at* the target.] **3** attending [Clem was *at* the party.] **4** busy with [people *at* work]. **5** in a condition of [England and France were *at* war.] **6** in the manner of [The players ran out *at* a trot.] **7** because of [terrified *at* the sight]. **8** in the amount, rate, or price of [*at* ten cents each]. **9** on or close to the age of [Her father died *at* 69.]

**ate** (āt) *past tense of* **eat.**

**-ate** (āt) *a suffix meaning:* **1** to make, become, or form [To *invalidate* is to make invalid. To *ulcerate* is to form an ulcer.] **2** to treat with [To *vaccinate* is to treat with vaccine.] **3** (it) of or like [*Collegiate* activities are activities of college students.]

**a·the·ist** (ā′thē ist) ***n.*** a person who believes that there is no God. —**a′the·ism *n.*** —**a′the·is′tic *adj.***

**A·the·na** (ə thē′nə) or **A·the·ne** (ə thē′nē) the Greek goddess of wisdom and skills. *See the picture.* The Romans called this goddess *Minerva.*

**A·the·ni·an** (ə thē′nē ən) ***adj.*** of Athens or its people. ◆***n.*** a person born or living in Athens; especially, a citizen of ancient Athens.

**Ath·ens** (ath′ənz) the capital of Greece, in the southeastern part. In ancient times this city was the center of Greek culture.

**ath·lete** (ath′lēt) ***n.*** a person who is skilled at games, sports, or exercises in which one needs strength, skill, and speed.

> Athletes in the Olympic games try to win medals. The word **athlete** comes from a Greek word that means "one who tries to win a prize in a contest."

**athlete's foot** a skin disease of the feet in which little blisters form and there is itching. It is caused by a tiny fungus.

**ath·let·ic** (ath let′ik) ***adj.*** **1** of or for athletes or athletics. **2** like an athlete; physically strong and active. —**ath·let′i·cal·ly *adv.***

**ath·let·ics** (ath let′iks) ***n.pl.*** games and sports in which one needs strength, skill, and speed: *sometimes used with a singular verb.*

**a·tin·gle** (ə ting′g'l) ***adj.*** tingling, as with excitement.

**-a·tion** (ā′shən) *a suffix meaning:* **1** the act of [*Multiplication* is the act of multiplying.] **2** the condition of being [*Gratification* is the condition of being gratified.] **3** the result of [A *complication* is the result of complicating.]

**-a·tive** (āt′iv *or* ə tiv) *a suffix meaning* of, serving to, or tending to [An *informative* talk is one that serves to inform. A *talkative* person is one who tends to talk too much.]

**At·lan·ta** (ət lan′tə) the capital of Georgia, in the northern part.

**At·lan·tic** (at lan′tik) the ocean lying between the American continents to the west and Europe and Africa to the east. ◆***adj.*** of, in, on, or near this ocean.

**Atlantic City** a city and resort in southeastern New Jersey, on the Atlantic Ocean.

**At·lan·tis** (at lan′tis) an island or continent told about in legends. It was supposed to have sunk into the Atlantic Ocean.

**At·las** (at′ləs) a giant in Greek myths who held up the heavens on his shoulders.

**at·las** (at′ləs) ***n.*** a book of maps.

> A book of maps came to be called an **atlas** because in earlier days this kind of book often had on the first page a drawing of Atlas holding a globe on his shoulders.

**at·mos·phere** (at′məs fir) ***n.*** **1** all the air around the earth. **2** the gases around any planet or star. **3** the air in any particular place. **4** the general feeling or spirit of a place or thing [The gaily painted room had a cheerful *atmosphere.*]

**at·mos·pher·ic** (at′məs fer′ik) ***adj.*** **1** of or in the atmosphere [Lightning is an *atmospheric* disturbance.] **2** having to do with the atmosphere [*Atmospheric* pressure at sea level is equal to 14.69 pounds per square inch.]

**at. no.** *abbreviation for* **atomic number.**

**at·oll** (a′tôl *or* ā′täl) ***n.*** a coral island that is shaped like a ring around a lagoon. *See the picture.*

**at·om** (at′əm) ***n.*** **1** any of the tiny particles of which the chemical elements are made. Atoms, which combine to form molecules, are themselves made up of various smaller particles [An *atom* of helium consists of a nucleus with two electrons revolving around it.] **2** a tiny particle of anything [There isn't an *atom* of truth in that story.]

**atom bomb** *same as* **atomic bomb.**

**a·tom·ic** (ə täm′ik) ***adj.*** **1** of an atom or atoms. **2** using atomic energy [an *atomic* submarine]. **3** using atomic bombs [*atomic* warfare]. **4** very small; tiny. —**a·tom′i·cal·ly *adv.***

☆**atomic bomb** a very destructive kind of bomb in which the nuclei of atoms of plutonium or uranium are split, releasing energy in an explosion with enormous force and heat. *See also* **hydrogen bomb.**

**atomic energy** the energy released when the nuclei of atoms are split or fused.

**atomic number** a number showing the position of a chemical element in a table (called the **periodic table**) in which all the elements are arranged according to their characteristics. The atomic number is the number of protons in the nucleus of an atom [The *atomic number* of hydrogen is 1; that of gold is 79.]

**atomic weight** a number showing the weight of an atom of an element as compared with carbon (having a number set at 16) [The *atomic weight* of hydrogen is 1.008; that of gold is 196.967.]

**at·om·iz·er** (at′ə mī′zər) ***n.*** a device used to shoot out a fine spray, as of medicine or perfume. *See the picture.*

**a·tone** (ə tōn′) ***v.*** to make up for having done something wrong or harmful; make amends [Is there any way I can *atone* for my unkind words?] —**a·toned′, a·ton′ing**

**a·tone·ment** (ə tōn′mənt) ***n.*** **1** the act of atoning. **2** something done to make up for having done something wrong or harmful; amends.

**a·top** (ə täp′) ***prep.*** on the top of [a feather *atop* his hat].

**a·tri·um** (ā′trē əm) ***n.*** **1** the main room of an ancient Roman house. **2** either of the two top sections of the heart. The blood flows into these from the veins. —*pl.* **a·tri·a** (ā′trē ə)

**a·tro·cious** (ə trō′shəs) ***adj.*** **1** very cruel or evil ["Uncle Tom's Cabin" tells of Simon Legree's *atrocious* treatment of slaves.] **2** very bad or unpleasant: *used only in everyday talk* [What *atrocious* weather!] —**a·tro′cious·ly *adv.***

| | | | | | | | |
|---|---|---|---|---|---|---|---|
| **a** | fat | **ir** | here | **ou** | out | **zh** | leisure |
| **ā** | ape | **ī** | bite, fire | **u** | up | **ng** | ring |
| **ä** | car, lot | **ō** | go | **ur** | fur | | a *in* ago |
| **e** | ten | **ô** | law, horn | **ch** | chin | | e *in* agent |
| **er** | care | **oi** | oil | **sh** | she | **ə =** | i *in* unity |
| **ē** | even | **oo** | look | **th** | thin | | o *in* collect |
| **i** | hit | **ōō** | tool | ***th*** | then | | u *in* focus |

**a·troc·i·ty** (ə träs′ə tē) ***n.*** **1** great cruelty or wickedness. **2** a cruel or wicked act [the *atrocities* of the Nazi concentration camps]. **3** a very bad or unpleasant thing: *used only in everyday talk.* —*pl.* **a·troc′i·ties**

**at·ro·phy** (a′trə fē) ***n.*** a wasting away or shrinking up, as of a muscle. ◆***v.*** to waste away or fail to grow [Muscles can *atrophy* from lack of use and so can the mind.] —**at′ro·phied, at′ro·phy·ing**

**at·tach** (ə tach′) ***v.*** **1** to fasten or join together, as by sticking or tying [*Attach* a stamp to the envelope.] **2** to bring close together by feelings of love or affection [Most people become *attached* to their pets.] **3** to add at the end; affix [Will you *attach* your signature to this petition?] **4** to think of as belonging to; ascribe [I *attach* great importance to this bit of news.] **5** to assign to some position [Captain Lopez has been *attached* to our division.] **6** to take property from a person by order of a court of law [We had to *attach* Smith's salary to collect the money owed to us.]

**at·ta·ché** (at′ə shā′) ***n.*** a person with special duties on the staff of an ambassador or minister to another country [a press *attaché*].

**attaché case** a flat case for carrying papers, etc. *See the picture.*

**at·tach·ment** (ə tach′mənt) ***n.*** **1** the act of attaching something. **2** anything used for attaching; fastening. **3** strong liking or love; friendship; affection. **4** anything added or attached [This sewing machine has an *attachment* for making buttonholes.]



**at·tack** (ə tak′) ***v.*** **1** to start a fight with; strike out at; make an assault [The prisoner *attacked* the guard. The regiment will *attack* at dawn.] **2** to speak or write against; oppose [The senator *attacked* the proposed law with strong words.] **3** to begin working on with energy [to *attack* a problem]. **4** to begin acting upon harmfully [The disease *attacked* the old dog suddenly.] ◆***n.*** **1** the act of attacking [the enemy's *attack;* an *attack* on someone's character]. **2** a sudden beginning as of a disease [an *attack* of flu].

**at·tain** (ə tān′) ***v.*** **1** to get by working hard; gain; achieve [to *attain* success]. **2** to reach or come to [She *attained* the age of 90.] *See* SYNONYMS *at* **reach.** —**at·tain′a·ble *adj.***

**at·tain·der** (ə tān′dər) ***n.*** a taking away of the property and civil rights of a person who has been sentenced to death [The U.S. Constitution forbids the passing of a *bill of attainder,* that would set such additional punishment.]

**at·tain·ment** (ə tān′mənt) ***n.*** **1** the act of attaining [the *attainment* of one's ambitions]. **2** something that has been attained, especially a skill or knowledge; accomplishment [a doctor famous for great *attainments* in surgery].

**at·tar** (at′ər) ***n.*** a perfume made from the petals of flowers, especially of roses.

**at·tempt** (ə tempt′) ***v.*** to try, or to try to do or get [to *attempt* to swim the English Channel; to *attempt* a hard task]. *See* SYNONYMS *at* **try.** ◆***n.*** **1** a try [a successful *attempt* to reach the top]. **2** an attack [An *attempt* was made on his life.]

**at·tend** (ə tend′) ***v.*** **1** to be present at [We *attend* school five days a week.] **2** to take care of; wait upon [She was *attended* by a doctor and a nurse.] **3** to go with or follow [Success *attended* our efforts.] **4** to give care or attention [I'll *attend* to the matter soon.]

**at·tend·ance** (ə ten′dəns) ***n.*** **1** the act of attending. **2** people present [The *attendance* at the ball game was 36,000.] —**take attendance,** to find out who is present.

**at·tend·ant** (ə ten′dənt) ***adj.*** **1** attending or taking care [an *attendant* nurse]. **2** that goes along; joined with; accompanying [Every job has its *attendant* problems.] ◆***n.*** a person who attends, or serves; servant, keeper, etc. [an *attendant* at the zoo; the queen and her *attendants*].

**at·ten·tion** (ə ten′shən) ***n.*** **1** the act of keeping one's mind closely on something, or the ability to do this; heed; notice [The speaker had everyone's *attention.*] **2** notice or observation [Your smile caught my *attention.*] **3** a kind act or thoughtful behavior; courtesy [We are grateful for letters and other *attentions* from home.] **4** a position of standing straight and still, as in waiting for a command [The soldiers stood at *attention.*]

**at·ten·tive** (ə ten′tiv) ***adj.*** **1** that pays attention, or listens closely [A performer likes an *attentive* audience.] **2** kind, thoughtful, courteous, etc. [The Lees are *attentive* hosts.] —**at·ten′tive·ly *adv.*** —**at·ten′tive·ness *n.***

**at·ten·u·ate** (ə ten′yoo wāt) ***v.*** **1** to make thin or slender [a vase *attenuated* at its mouth]. **2** to weaken; take away the force of [The power of King John was *attenuated* by the Magna Charta.] —**at·ten′u·at·ed, at·ten′u·at·ing** —**at·ten′u·a′tion *n.***

**at·test** (ə test′) ***v.*** **1** to declare that something is true or genuine [The purity of the diamond was *attested* by the jeweler.] **2** to be a witness; testify [I can *attest* that she arrived at noon.]

**at·tic** (at′ik) ***n.*** the room or space just below the roof of a house; garret.

**At·ti·la** (at′'l ə *or* ə til′ə) 406?–453 A.D.; king of the Huns, from about 433 to 453 A.D.

**at·tire** (ə tīr′) ***v.*** to dress, especially in very fine clothes; dress up; array [a monarch *attired* in purple]. —**at·tired′, at·tir′ing** ◆***n.*** clothes, especially very fine clothes.

**at·ti·tude** (at′ə to͞od *or* at′ə tyo͞od) ***n.*** **1** the position of the body in doing a particular thing [We knelt in an *attitude* of prayer.] **2** a way of acting or behaving that shows what one is thinking or feeling [a friendly *attitude*].

**Attn.** or **attn.** *abbreviation for* **attention.**

**at·tor·ney** (ə tur′nē) ***n.*** **1** a person who has been given the right to act for another, as in business dealings. This right is called a **power of attorney.** **2** a lawyer. —*pl.* **at·tor′neys**

> An **attorney** is someone you turn to when you have a legal problem. The word comes from an old French verb which means just that, "to turn to someone."

**attorney general** the chief law officer of a country or State [The U.S. *Attorney General* is the head of the Justice Department.] —*pl.* **attorneys general** or **attorney generals**

**at·tract** (ə trakt′) ***v.*** **1** to make come closer; pull toward oneself [A magnet *attracts* iron.] **2** to be admired or noticed by [a beautiful park that *attracts* many visitors].

SYNONYMS: **Attract** suggests that some power such as magnetism is pulling a person or thing that is quite easily pulled [Candy *attracts* those with a sweet tooth.] **Charm** suggests that a kind of magic spell has been put on a person by something or someone who is very pleasant [The speaker *charmed* the audience with his funny tales.]

**at·trac·tion** (ə trak′shən) ***n.*** **1** the act or power of attracting [Money has a great *attraction* for some people.] **2** anything that attracts [A fine beach was one of the *attractions* of the resort.]

**at·trac·tive** (ə trak′tiv) ***adj.*** that attracts or is able to attract, as by being pleasing, charming, pretty, etc. [an *attractive* dress].

**at·trib·ut·a·ble** (ə trib′yo͞o tə b'l) ***adj.*** that can be attributed [errors *attributable* to carelessness].

**at·trib·ute** (ə trib′yo͞ot) ***v.*** to think of something as belonging to or coming from a particular person or thing [There have been many plays *attributed* to Shakespeare.] —**at·trib′ut·ed, at·trib′ut·ing** ◆***n.*** (at′rə byo͞ot) **1** a quality that is thought of as a natural part of some person or thing; characteristic [Friendliness is an *attribute* of a good neighbor.] **2** an object used as a symbol [Cupid's *attribute* is the bow and arrow.] —**at′tri·bu′tion *n.***

**at·tri·tion** (ə trish′ən) ***n.*** a wearing down or weakening little by little [The long siege turned into a war of *attrition*.]

**at·tune** (ə to͞on′ *or* ə tyo͞on′) ***v.*** to bring into harmony or agreement; adjust [Their ways are not *attuned* to the times.] —**at·tuned′, at·tun′ing**

**atty.** *abbreviation for* **attorney.**

**at. wt.** *abbreviation for* **atomic weight.**

**Au** *the symbol for the chemical element* gold.

**au·burn** (ô′bərn) ***adj., n.*** reddish brown.

**Auck·land** (ôk′lənd) a seaport in northern New Zealand.

**auc·tion** (ôk′shən) ***n.*** a public sale at which each thing is sold to the person offering to pay the highest price. ◆***v.*** to sell at an auction.

**auc·tion·eer** (ôk shə nir′) ***n.*** a person whose work is selling things at auctions.

**au·da·cious** (ô dā′shəs) ***adj.*** **1** bold or daring; fearless. **2** too bold; not showing respect; impudent. —**au·da′cious·ly *adv.***

**au·dac·i·ty** (ô das′ə tē) ***n.*** **1** bold courage; daring. **2** too much boldness; impudence.

**au·di·ble** (ô′də b'l) ***adj.*** that can be heard; loud enough to be heard [an *audible* whisper]. —**au′di·bil′i·ty *n.*** —**au′di·bly *adv.***

**au·di·ence** (ô′dē əns) ***n.*** **1** a group of persons gathered together to hear and see a speaker, a play, a concert, etc. **2** all those persons who are tuned in to a radio or TV program. **3** an interview with a person of high rank [an *audience* with the Pope].

**Audience** comes from a Latin word meaning "to hear." All the words in this dictionary that begin with *audi-* come from the same word and have something to do with hearing.

**au·di·o** (ô′dē ō) ***adj.*** having to do with the part that is heard on a telecast. *See also* **video.**

**au·di·o-vis·u·al** (ô′dē ō vizh′o͞o wəl) ***adj.*** involving both hearing and sight [Motion pictures and recordings are *audio-visual* aids used in teaching.]

**au·dit** (ô′dit) ***n.*** an examination of the accounts or records of a business to see that they are right. ◆***v.*** to make such an examination.

auger

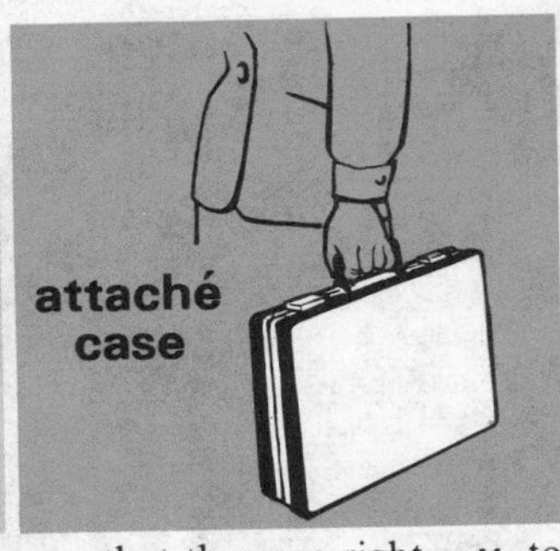


**au·di·tion** (ô dish′ən) ***n.*** a hearing in which an actor or musician who is being tested for a job gives a short performance. ◆☆***v.*** **1** to give an audition to. **2** to perform in an audition.

**au·di·tor** (ô′də tər) ***n.*** **1** a listener or hearer. **2** a person whose work is auditing accounts.

**au·di·to·ri·um** (ô′də tôr′ē əm) ***n.*** a building or room where an audience can gather.

**au·di·to·ry** (ô′də tôr′ē) ***adj.*** having to do with the sense of hearing [the *auditory* nerve].

**Au·du·bon** (ôd′ə bän), **John James** 1785–1851; American naturalist, famous for his paintings of birds.

**Aug.** *abbreviation for* **August.**

**au·ger** (ô′gər) ***n.*** a tool for boring holes, as in wood or in the earth. *See the picture.* 

**aught** (ôt) ***n.*** **1** anything at all [She will never come, for *aught* I know.] **2** a zero; ought.

**aug·ment** (ôg ment′) ***v.*** to make or become greater [to *augment* one's income by selling insurance].

**aug·men·ta·tion** (ôg′men tā′shən) ***n.*** **1** the act of augmenting. **2** an addition; increase.

**au·gur** (ô′gər) ***n.*** **1** a priest in ancient Rome who claimed to foretell the future by explaining certain omens and signs. **2** any fortuneteller. ◆***v.*** to be a sign of something that will happen [Cloudy skies *augur* rain.] —**augur well** (or **augur ill**), to be a sign that something good (or something bad) will happen.

**au·gu·ry** (ô′gyər ē) ***n.*** **1** the practice of trying to foretell the future from omens or signs. **2** an omen or sign. —*pl.* **au′gu·ries**

**Au·gust** (ô′gəst) ***n.*** the eighth month of the year, which has 31 days: abbreviated **Aug.**

**au·gust** (ô gust′) ***adj.*** causing one to feel awe and respect [an *august* assembly of scholars].

**Au·gus·ta** (ô gus′tə) **1** the capital of Maine. **2** a city in eastern Georgia.

**Au·gus·tine** (ô′gəs tēn *or* ô gus′t'n), Saint 354–430 A.D.; an early leader of the Christian Church.

**au jus** (ō zho͞o′ *or* ō zho͞os′) served in its own juice or gravy: said of meat. *Au jus* is a French phrase which means "with the juice."

| | | | | | | | |
|---|---|---|---|---|---|---|---|
| **a** | fat | **ir** | here | **ou** | out | **zh** | leisure |
| **ā** | ape | **ī** | bite, fire | **u** | up | **ng** | ring |
| **ä** | car, lot | **ō** | go | **ur** | fur | | a *in* ago |
| **e** | ten | **ô** | law, horn | **ch** | chin | | e *in* agent |
| **er** | care | **oi** | oil | **sh** | she | **ə** = | i *in* unity |
| **ē** | even | **o͝o** | look | **th** | thin | | o *in* collect |
| **i** | hit | **o͞o** | tool | ***th*** | then | | u *in* focus |

a

**auk** (ôk) ***n.*** a diving bird of the northern seas, with webbed feet and short wings. The **great auk**, which is now extinct, could not fly. *See the picture.*

**aunt** (ant *or* änt) ***n.*** **1** a sister of one's mother or father. **2** the wife of one's uncle.

**au·ra** (ôr′ə) ***n.*** a special feeling that seems to come from and surround some person or thing [There was an *aura* of gentleness about the teacher.]

**au re·voir** (ō′rə vwär′) until we meet again: *a French phrase used for* "goodbye."

**au·ri·cle** (ôr′ə k'l) ***n.*** **1** the outer part of the ear. **2** *another word for* **atrium** (of the heart).

**au·ro·ra bo·re·a·lis** (ô rôr′ə bôr′ē al′is) bright bands of light sometimes seen at night in the sky of the Northern Hemisphere; northern lights.

**aus·pi·ces** (ôs′pə sēz) ***n.pl.*** approval and help; support [a plan under government *auspices*].

**aus·pi·cious** (ôs pish′əs) ***adj.*** seeming to show that success will follow; favorable [Her score on the first test was an *auspicious* beginning for the school year.] **—aus·pi′cious·ly *adv.***

**Aus·ten** (ôs′tən), **Jane** 1775–1817; English writer of novels.

**aus·tere** (ô stir′) ***adj.*** **1** very strict or stern in the way one looks or acts. **2** very simple and plain; without decoration or luxury [Pioneers usually lead an *austere* life.] *See the picture.* **—aus·tere′ly *adv.*** **—aus·ter·i·ty** (ô ster′ə tē) ***n.***

**Aus·tin** (ôs′tən) the capital of Texas.

**Aus·tin** (ôs′tən), **Stephen** 1793–1836; American pioneer. He founded the first American colony in Texas.

**Aus·tral·ia** (ô strāl′yə) **1** an island continent in the Southern Hemisphere, southeast of Asia. **2** a country made up of this continent and Tasmania. **—Aus·tral′ian *adj., n.***

**Aus·tri·a** (ôs′trē ə) a country in central Europe. **—Aus′tri·an *adj., n.***

**au·then·tic** (ô then′tik) ***adj.*** **1** that can be believed; reliable; true [an *authentic* news report]. **2** that is genuine; real [an *authentic* antique]. **—au·then′ti·cal·ly *adv.***

**au·then·ti·cate** (ô then′tə kāt) ***v.*** to prove that something is genuine or real [Have they *authenticated* the will?] **—au·then′ti·cat·ed, au·then′ti·cat·ing**

**au·then·tic·i·ty** (ô′thən tis′ə tē) ***n.*** the fact of being authentic; genuineness.

**au·thor** (ô′thər) ***n.*** **1** a person who writes something, as a book or story [The Brontë sisters were the *authors* of novels.] **2** a person who makes or begins something; creator [the *author* of a new plan for peace]. ◆***v.*** to be the author of.

**au·thor·i·ta·tive** (ə thôr′ə tāt′iv) ***adj.*** **1** having or showing authority; official [She spoke in an *authoritative* manner.] **2** that can be trusted because it comes from an expert or authority [an *authoritative* opinion]. **—au·thor′i·ta′tive·ly *adv.***

**au·thor·i·ty** (ə thôr′ə tē) ***n.*** **1** the right to give orders, make decisions, or take action [Do you have the *authority* to spend the money?] *See* SYNONYMS *at* **power**. **2** a person or agency that has the right to govern or the power to enforce laws [The city *authorities* have approved the plan.] **3** a person, book, etc. that can be trusted to give the right information or advice [an *authority* on rare diseases]. *—pl.* **au·thor′i·ties**

**au·thor·i·za·tion** (ô′thər i zā′shən) ***n.*** **1** the act of authorizing something. **2** the right or permission given [You have my *authorization* to send the letter.]

**au·thor·ize** (ô′thə rīz) ***v.*** **1** to give permission for something [The city *authorized* a housing project.] **2** to give someone the right or power to do something [The President *authorized* him to sign the treaty.] **—au′thor·ized, au′thor·iz·ing**

**au·thor·ship** (ô′thər ship) ***n.*** the origin of a book, idea, etc. [a story of unknown *authorship*].

☆**au·to** (ôt′ō) ***n.*** an automobile. *—pl.* **au′tos**

**auto-** *a prefix meaning:* **1** of or for oneself. **2** by oneself or itself. *See the words that follow below.*

**au·to·bi·og·ra·phy** (ôt′ə bī äg′rə fē) ***n.*** the story of one's own life written by oneself. *—pl.* **au′to·bi·og′ra·phies —au·to·bi·o·graph·i·cal** (ôt′ə bī′ə graf′i k'l) or **au′to·bi′o·graph′ic *adj.***

**au·toc·ra·cy** (ô täk′rə sē) ***n.*** government in which one person has all the power. *—pl.* **au·toc′ra·cies**

**au·to·crat** (ôt′ə krat) ***n.*** **1** a ruler who has complete power; dictator. **2** a person who forces others to do as that person wishes.

**au·to·crat·ic** (ôt′ə krat′ik) ***adj.*** of or like an autocrat; having complete power over others; dictatorial. **—au′to·crat′i·cal·ly *adv.***

**au·to·graph** (ôt′ə graf) ***n.*** something written in a person's own handwriting, especially that person's name. *See the picture.* ◆***v.*** to write one's name on [Please *autograph* this baseball.]

**au·to·mat·ic** (ôt′ə mat′ik) ***adj.*** **1** done without thinking about it, as though by a machine; unconscious [Breathing is usually *automatic.*] **2** moving or working by itself [*automatic* machinery]. ◆***n.*** a pistol or rifle that keeps firing shots rapidly until the trigger is released. **—au′to·mat′i·cal·ly *adv.***

☆**au·to·ma·tion** (ôt′ə mā′shən) ***n.*** a system in which the operations are done automatically and are controlled by machines instead of by people.

**au·tom·a·ton** (ô tämʹə tän) ***n.*** **1** a machine that can move or act by itself. **2** a person who acts in an automatic way, like a machine.

☆**au·to·mo·bile** (ôtʹə mə bēlʹ *or* ôtʹə mə bēlʹ) ***n.*** a car moved by an engine that is part of it, used for traveling on streets or roads; motorcar.

**au·to·mo·tive** (ôtʹə mōtʹiv) ***adj.*** **1** having to do with automobiles [the *automotive* industry]. **2** able to move by its own power [an *automotive* vehicle].

**au·ton·o·mous** (ô tänʹə məs) ***adj.*** ruling or managing itself; having self-government; independent [an *autonomous* nation]. —**au·tonʹo·mous·ly** ***adv.***

**au·ton·o·my** (ô tänʹə mē) ***n.*** self-government; independence [a town with local *autonomy*].

**au·top·sy** (ôʹtäp sē) ***n.*** an examination of a dead body to find the cause of death or the damage done by a disease. —*pl.* **auʹtop·sies**

**Autopsy** comes from a Greek word meaning "a seeing for oneself." When the reason for a death is not clear, it becomes necessary to look inside the dead body to find the cause.

**au·tumn** (ôtʹəm) ***n.*** the season of the year that comes between summer and winter; fall. ◆***adj.*** of or like autumn. —**au·tum·nal** (ô tumʹn'l) ***adj.***

**aux·il·ia·ry** (ôg zilʹyər ē) ***adj.*** that helps or aids; acting as an extra help [*auxiliary* police]. ◆***n.*** an auxiliary person, group, or thing [Our church has a women's *auxiliary*.] —*pl.* **aux·ilʹia·ries**

**auxiliary verb** a verb that is used to form tenses, moods, or voices of other verbs.

*Have, be, may, can, must, do, shall, will* are used as auxiliary verbs. In the sentence "He will be late, but she may not be," *will* and *may* are auxiliary verbs.

**av.** or **avdp.** *abbreviations for* **avoirdupois.**

**a·vail** (ə vālʹ) ***v.*** to be of use, help, or advantage to [Will force alone *avail* us?] ◆***n.*** use or help; advantage [I tried, but to no *avail*.] —**avail oneself of,** to take advantage of, as an opportunity.

**a·vail·a·ble** (ə vāʹlə b'l) ***adj.*** that can be got, used, or reached [This style is *available* in three colors.] —**a·vailʹa·bilʹi·ty** ***n.***

**av·a·lanche** (avʹə lanch) ***n.*** **1** a large mass of snow, ice, rocks, etc. sliding swiftly down a mountain. *See the picture.* **2** anything that comes suddenly and in large numbers [an *avalanche* of mail; an *avalanche* of blows].

**av·a·rice** (avʹə ris) ***n.*** too great a desire to have wealth; greed for riches.

**av·a·ri·cious** (avʹə rishʹəs) ***adj.*** too eager to have wealth; greedy for riches. —**avʹa·riʹcious·ly** ***adv.***

**Ave.** or **ave.** *abbreviation for* **avenue.**

**A·ve Ma·ri·a** (äʹvā mə rēʹə) **1** "Hail, Mary," the first words of a Latin prayer to the Virgin Mary used in the Roman Catholic Church. **2** this prayer.

**a·venge** (ə venjʹ) ***v.*** to get revenge for; get even for a wrong or injury [to *avenge* an insult]. —**a·vengedʹ, a·vengʹing** —**a·vengʹer** ***n.***

**av·e·nue** (avʹə no͞o *or* avʹə nyo͞o) ***n.*** ☆**1** a street, especially a wide one. **2** a road, path, or drive, often with trees along both sides. **3** a way to something [Books are *avenues* to knowledge.]

**Avenue** comes from a Latin verb *advenire,* meaning "to come, or arrive." We come to a place by means of such a street or road.

**a·ver** (ə vurʹ) ***v.*** to state as the truth; declare positively [They *averred* their innocence all the way to prison.] —**a·verredʹ, a·verʹring**

**av·er·age** (avʹrij *or* avʹər ij) ***n.*** **1** the number got by dividing the sum of two or more quantities by the number of quantities added [The *average* of 7, 9, and 17 is 11 (7 + 9 + 17 = 33 ÷ 3 = 11).] **2** the usual kind or amount; that which is found most often [*intelligence* above the average]. ◆***adj.*** **1** being the average [The *average* test score was 82.] **2** of the usual kind; normal; ordinary [an *average* student]. ◆***v.*** **1** to figure the average of [*Average* these prices for me.] **2** to be, do, have, etc. as an average [I *average* eight hours of sleep a day.] —**avʹer·aged, avʹer·ag·ing** —**on the average,** as an average amount, rate, etc. [They earn $200 a week *on the average*.]

SYNONYMS: **Average** is the number got by dividing a sum by the number of quantities added [The *average* of 7, 9, and 17 is 11.] **Mean** is the figure halfway between two extremes [The *mean* temperature for a day with a high of 24° and a low of 12° is 18°.] The **median** is the middle number in a series arranged from high to low [The *median* grade in the group 93, 88, 79, 75, and 71 is 79.]

**a·verse** (ə vursʹ) ***adj.*** not willing; opposed [He is *averse* to lending money.]

**a·ver·sion** (ə vurʹzhən) ***n.*** **1** a strong dislike [She has an *aversion* to parties.] **2** a thing that is strongly disliked [Coffee is my chief *aversion*.]



**a·vert** (ə vurtʹ) ***v.*** **1** to turn away [to *avert* one's eyes]. **2** to keep from happening; prevent [I apologized to *avert* trouble.]

**avg.** *abbreviation for* **average.**

**a·vi·ar·y** (āʹvē erʹē) ***n.*** a large cage or building for keeping many birds. —*pl.* **aʹvi·arʹies**

**a·vi·a·tion** (āʹvē āʹshən) ***n.*** the science, skill, or work of flying airplanes.

**a·vi·a·tor** (āʹvē ātʹər) ***n.*** a person who flies airplanes; pilot.

**av·id** (avʹid) ***adj.*** very eager or greedy [an *avid* reader of books; *avid* for power]. —**avʹid·ly** ***adv.***

**a·vid·i·ty** (ə vidʹə tē) ***n.*** great eagerness or greed.

☆**av·o·ca·do** (avʹə käʹdō *or* ävʹə käʹdō) ***n.*** **1** a tropical fruit that is shaped like a pear and has a thick, green or purplish skin and a single large seed. Its yellow, buttery flesh is used in salads, sauces, dips, etc. *See the picture.* **2** the tree that it grows on. —*pl.* **avʹo·caʹdos**

**av·o·ca·tion** (avʹə kāʹshən) ***n.*** something one does besides one's regular work, often just for pleasure; hobby [My teacher's *avocation* is making furniture.]

**a·void** (ə voidʹ) ***v.*** **1** to keep away from; get out of the way of; shun [to *avoid* crowds]. **2** to keep from happening [Try to *avoid* spilling the milk.] —**a·voidʹa·ble** ***adj.*** —**a·voidʹance** ***n.***

| | | | |
|---|---|---|---|
| **a** fat | **ir** here | **ou** out | **zh** leisure |
| **ā** ape | **ī** bite, fire | **u** up | **ng** ring |
| **ä** car, lot | **ō** go | **ur** fur | a *in* ago |
| **e** ten | **ô** law, horn | **ch** chin | e *in* agent |
| **er** care | **oi** oil | **sh** she | **ə** = i *in* unity |
| **ē** even | **oo** look | **th** thin | o *in* collect |
| **i** hit | **o͞o** tool | ***th*** then | u *in* focus |

**av·oir·du·pois weight** (av′ər də poiz′) a system of weights used in England and America. The basic unit is the pound, which has sixteen ounces. *See also* **troy weight.**

**A·von** (ā′vən *or* ā′vän) a river in southwestern England.

**a·vow** (ə vou′) ***v.*** to say or admit openly or frankly [to *avow* an error or fault]. —**a·vow′al *n.***

**a·vowed** (ə voud′) ***adj.*** openly declared or admitted; confessed [Robin Hood was an *avowed* opponent of injustice.] —**a·vow·ed·ly** (ə vou′id lē) ***adv.***

**a·wait** (ə wāt′) ***v.*** **1** to wait for; expect [We are *awaiting* your arrival.] **2** to be ready for; be in store for [A surprise *awaits* you.]

**a·wake** (ə wāk′) ***v.*** **1** to bring or come out of sleep; wake. **2** to make or become active; stir up [to *awake* old memories]. —**a·woke′** or **a·waked′**, **a·waked′**, **a·wak′ing** ◆***adj.*** **1** not asleep. [The coffee kept her *awake.*] **2** active; alert. [We must stay *awake* to the danger of our position.]

**a·wak·en** (ə wāk′′n) ***v.*** to awake; rouse.

**a·wak·en·ing** (ə wāk′′n iŋ) ***n.*** a waking up; rousing.

**a·ward** (ə wôrd′) ***v.*** **1** to give by the decision of a judge [The court *awarded* her $8,000 in damages.] **2** to give as the result of judging in a contest [His essay was *awarded* first prize.] ◆***n.*** **1** a decision, as by a judge. **2** something awarded; prize.

**a·ware** (ə wer′) ***adj.*** knowing or understanding; conscious; informed [Are you *aware* of the problem facing us?] —**a·ware′ness *n.***



**a·way** (ə wā′) ***adv.*** **1** to another place [Tom Sawyer ran *away* from home.] **2** in the proper place [Put the tools *away.*] **3** far [*away* behind]. **4** off; aside [Please clear the snow *away.*] **5** from one's keeping [Don't give *away* the secret.] **6** out of hearing or out of sight [The sound faded *away.*] **7** at once [Fire *away*!] **8** without stopping [He worked *away* all night.] ◆***adj.*** **1** not here; absent; gone [She is *away* for the day.] **2** at a distance [ten miles *away*]. ◆***interj.*** go away! begone! —**away with,** take away [*Away with* the fool!] —**do away with,** to get rid of; put an end to. [They have *done away with* the old dress code.]

**awe** (ô) ***n.*** deep respect mixed with fear and wonder [The starry sky filled them with *awe.*] ◆***v.*** to make have a feeling of awe [They were *awed* by the Grand Canyon.] —**awed, aw′ing** —**stand in awe of** or **be in awe of,** to respect and fear.

**awe·some** (ô′səm) ***adj.*** **1** causing one to feel awe [The burning building was an *awesome* sight.] **2** showing awe [He had an *awesome* look on his face.]

**awe-struck** (ô′struk′) ***adj.*** filled with awe or wonder: also **awe-strick·en** (ô′strik′′n)

**aw·ful** (ô′fəl) ***adj.*** **1** making one feel awe or dread; causing fear [an *awful* scene of destruction]. **2** very bad, ugly, great, etc.: *used only in everyday talk* [an *awful* joke; an *awful* fool].

**aw·ful·ly** (ô′fə lē *or* ô′flē) ***adv.*** **1** in an awful way. ☆**2** very; extremely: *used only in everyday talk* [I'm *awfully* glad you came.]

**a·while** (ə wīl′) ***adv.*** for a while; for a short time [Sit down and rest *awhile.*]

**awk·ward** (ôk′wərd) ***adj.*** **1** not having grace or skill; clumsy; bungling [an *awkward* dancer; an *awkward* writing style]. **2** hard to use or manage; not convenient [The long handle makes this an *awkward* tool.] **3** uncomfortable; cramped [sitting in an *awkward* position]. *See the picture.* **4** embarrassed or embarrassing [an *awkward* remark]. —**awk′ward·ly *adv.*** —**awk′ward·ness *n.***

**awl** (ôl) ***n.*** a small, pointed tool for making holes in wood or leather. *See the picture.*

**awn·ing** (ô′niŋ) ***n.*** a covering made of canvas, metal, or wood fixed to a frame over a window, door, etc. to keep off the sun and rain.

**a·woke** (ə wōk′) *the usual past tense of* **awake.**

**A·WOL** or **a·wol** (ā′wôl) ***adj.*** absent without leave: said of a military person who is away from duty without permission.

**a·wry** (ə rī′) ***adv., adj.*** **1** twisted to one side; askew [The curtains were blown *awry* by the wind.] **2** wrong; amiss [Our plans went *awry.*]

**ax** or **axe** (aks) ***n.*** a tool for chopping or splitting wood. It has a long wooden handle and a metal head with a sharp blade. —*pl.* **ax′es**

**ax·i·al** (ak′sē əl) ***adj.*** of, like, or around an axis [*axial* rotation].

**ax·i·om** (ak′sē əm) ***n.*** a statement that needs no proof because its truth can be plainly seen [It is an *axiom* that no one lives forever.]

**ax·i·o·mat·ic** (ak′sē ə mat′ik) ***adj.*** of or like an axiom; plainly true. —**ax′i·o·mat′i·cal·ly *adv.***

**ax·is** (ak′sis) ***n.*** **1** a real or imaginary straight line about which something turns [The *axis* of the earth passes through the North and South poles.] **2** a central line around which the parts of a thing are arranged in a balanced way [the *axis* of a picture]. —*pl.* **ax·es** (ak′sēz) —**the Axis,** Germany, Italy, and Japan as allies in World War II.

**ax·le** (ak′s'l) ***n.*** **1** a rod on which a wheel turns, or one connected to a wheel so that they turn together. **2** the bar joining two opposite wheels, as of an automobile: *also called* **ax·le·tree** (ak′s'l trē)

azalea

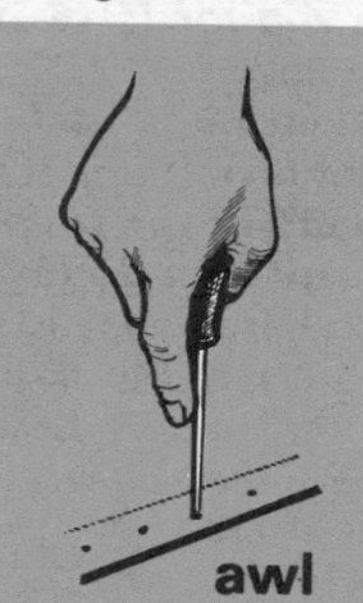

awl

baboon
1.5 m (5 ft.) long, including tail

Aztec

awkward position

**aye** or **ay** (ī) ***adv.*** yes. ◆***n.*** a vote of "yes."
**AZ** *abbreviation for* **Arizona.**
**a·zal·ea** (ə zāl′yə) ***n.*** a shrub having narrow, pointed leaves that are shed each season, and flowers of various colors. *See the picture.*

The **azalea** got its name from a Greek word meaning "dry" because the plant grows best in soil that is not too wet.

**A·zores** (ā′zôrz) a group of Portuguese islands west of Portugal.
**A·zov** (ā′zôf), **Sea of** the northern section of the Black Sea, in the southwestern U.S.S.R.
**Az·tec** (az′tek) ***n.*** **1** a member of a people who lived in Mexico and had a highly developed civilization before they were conquered by Spain in 1519. *See the picture.* **2** their language. ◆***adj.*** of the Aztecs.
**az·ure** (azh′ər) ***n.*** the blue color of a clear sky; sky blue. ◆***adj.*** of this color.

# Bb

**B, b** (bē) ***n.*** the second letter of the English alphabet. —*pl.* **B's, b's** (bēz)
**B** ***n.*** **1** *the symbol for the chemical element* boron. ☆**2** a grade, as in some schools, meaning "good" or "better than average."
**Ba** *the symbol for the chemical element* barium.
**B.A.** Bachelor of Arts.
**baa** (bä) ***n.*** the sound made by a sheep or goat. ◆***v.*** to make this sound; bleat.
**bab·ble** (bab′'l) ***v.*** **1** to make sounds like a baby trying to talk. **2** to talk or say fast or foolishly; blab. **3** to make a low, bubbling sound, as a brook does when running over stones. —**bab′bled, bab′bling** ◆***n.*** **1** jumbled speech sounds. **2** foolish or silly talk. **3** a low, bubbling sound [the *babble* of the stream]. —**bab′bler** ***n.***
**babe** (bāb) ***n.*** a baby; infant.
**Ba·bel** (bā′b'l *or* bab′'l) in the Bible, a city where the people tried to build a tower to reach heaven. They were stopped by God, who caused them to speak in different languages and scattered them over the earth. ◆***n.*** *also* **babel,** noisy confusion, as of many people talking at once.
**ba·boon** (ba bo͞on′) ***n.*** a fierce monkey of Africa and Arabia with a large head shaped like a dog's. *See the picture.*
**ba·bush·ka** (bə boosh′kə) ***n.*** a scarf worn on the head by a woman or girl and tied under the chin.
**ba·by** (bā′bē) ***n.*** **1** a very young child; infant. **2** a person who seems helpless, cries easily, etc. like a baby. **3** the youngest or smallest in a group. —*pl.* **ba′bies** ◆***adj.*** **1** of or for a baby [*baby* food]. **2** very young or small [a *baby* fox]. **3** like a baby; childish [*baby* talk]. ◆***v.*** **1** to treat like a baby; pamper. ☆**2** to handle very carefully: *used only in everyday talk* [to *baby* a new car]. —**ba′bied, ba′by·ing**
**ba·by·hood** (bā′bē hood) ***n.*** the time or stage when one is a baby.
**ba·by·ish** (bā′bē ish) ***adj.*** like a baby; helpless, timid, etc.
**Bab·y·lon** (bab′ə lən) the ancient capital of Babylonia, known for its wealth and wickedness.
**Bab·y·lo·ni·a** (bab′ə lō′nē ə) an ancient, powerful empire of southwestern Asia. —**Bab′y·lo′ni·an** ***adj., n.***
☆**ba·by-sit** (bā′bē sit′) ***v.*** to act as a baby sitter. —**ba′by-sat′, ba′by-sit′ting**
**baby sitter** a person hired to take care of a child or children, as when the parents are away for the evening.
**Bac·chus** (bak′əs) an ancient Greek and Roman god of wine and merrymaking.
**Bach** (bäk), **Jo·hann Se·bas·tian** (yō′hän si bas′chən) 1685–1750; German composer. 51
**bach·e·lor** (bach′'l ər *or* bach′lər) ***n.*** **1** a man who has not married. **2** a person who has received the first degree from a college or university for completing a four-year course [Graduates who major in the humanities receive a *Bachelor* of Arts degree. Those who major in science receive a *Bachelor* of Science degree.]

**Bachelor** comes from a Latin word for a young nobleman who was trying to become a knight during the Middle Ages. Such a young man was unmarried.

**bachelor's button** a plant with flowers shaped a little like buttons and usually blue.
**ba·cil·lus** (bə sil′əs) ***n.*** any of the bacteria that are shaped like a rod. Some bacilli cause diseases, such as tuberculosis. —*pl.* **ba·cil·li** (bə sil′ī)
**back** (bak) ***n.*** **1** the part of the body that is opposite to the chest and belly. In most animals other than human beings, it is the part opposite the underside. **2** the backbone or spine [I hurt my *back* when I fell.] **3** the part of a chair or seat that supports one's back. **4** the part of something behind or opposite the front [the *back* of the room; the *back* of a leg]. **5** the side of something that is less often used or seen; reverse [the *back* of the hand; the *back* of a rug]. **6** a football player whose position is behind the line. ◆***adj.*** **1** at

| | | | |
|---|---|---|---|
| **a** fat | **ir** here | **ou** out | **zh** leisure |
| **ā** ape | **ī** bite, fire | **u** up | **ng** ring |
| **ä** car, lot | **ō** go | **ur** fur | a *in* ago |
| **e** ten | **ô** law, horn | **ch** chin | e *in* agent |
| **er** care | **oi** oil | **sh** she | **ə** = i *in* unity |
| **ē** even | **oo** look | **th** thin | o *in* collect |
| **i** hit | **o͞o** tool | ***th*** then | u *in* focus |

the rear or back; behind [the *back* wheel of a bicycle]. **2** of or for a time in the past [a *back* copy of a newspaper; *back* pay]. **3** in the opposite direction; reversed [the *back* stroke of a piston]. ◆***adv.*** **1** at or to the back; backward [Please move *back* in the bus.] **2** to the place that it came from [Throw the ball *back*.] **3** to an earlier condition or time [They nursed her *back* to health.] **4** in return [I paid *back* the money I borrowed.] ◆***v.*** **1** to move backward or to the rear [The truck *backed* up to the platform.] **2** to help or support [We all *backed* the plan.] **3** to put something on the back of [The rug is *backed* with rubber.] —**back and forth,** backward and forward or from side to side. —☆**back down,** to give up doing something that one has started. —**back out** or **back out of,** to refuse to do something one has promised to do. —**behind one's back,** without one's knowing or allowing it. —☆**get off one's back,** to stop nagging one: *a slang phrase.* —☆**go back on,** to refuse to do something one has promised to do: *used only in everyday talk.* —☆**in back of,** at or to the rear of; behind.

**back·bite** (bak′bīt) ***v.*** to say unkind or untrue things about a person who is absent. —**back′bit, back′bitten** or **back′bit, back′bit·ing**

**back·bone** (bak′bōn) ***n.*** **1** the long row of connected bones in the back of human beings and many animals; spine. **2** the main support of anything [The steel industry is the *backbone* of the nation's economy.] **3** willpower, courage, determination, etc. [It takes *backbone* to be a pioneer.]



**back·er** (bak′ər) ***n.*** a person who gives help or support; supporter; sponsor.

☆**back·field** (bak′fēld) ***n.*** in football, the players whose usual position is behind the line; especially, the offensive players who carry the ball.

**back·fire** (bak′fīr) ***n.*** an explosion of gas that takes place at the wrong time in the cylinder of an engine, as of an automobile; also, one that occurs in the wrong place, as in the exhaust pipe, making a loud noise. ◆***v.*** **1** to have a backfire [The truck *backfired* twice.] **2** to have a bad or unexpected result [His plan *backfired*.] —**back′fired, back′fir·ing**

**back·gam·mon** (bak′gam′ən) ***n.*** a game played on a special board by two people. The players have fifteen pieces each, which they move after throwing dice to get a number. *See the picture.*

> **Backgammon** is just another, earlier way of saying "back game." This game, which is more than 1,000 years old, is so called because sometimes pieces that have been removed are put back on the board.

**back·ground** (bak′ground) ***n.*** **1** the part of a scene or picture that is or seems to be toward the back. **2** a surface against which something is shown or seen [The flag has white stars on a blue *background*.] **3** a less important position where one is not likely to be noticed [The candidate's rich backer stayed in the *background*.] **4** a person's training and experience [She has the right *background* for the job.] **5** the events that came before; causes [The book tells about the *background* of the Civil War.]

**back·hand** (bak′hand) ***n.*** a kind of stroke, as in tennis, in which the back of the hand swings out toward the ball. *See the picture.* ◆***adj.*** made or done with such a stroke [a *backhand* swing]. ◆***adv.*** with a backhand stroke. ◆***v.*** ☆to catch a ball with the back of the hand turned inward and the arm reaching across the body.

**back·hand·ed** (bak′han′did) ***adj.*** **1** *same as* **backhand. 2** finding fault while seeming to praise; not sincere ["You don't look nearly so fat in that dress" is a *backhanded* compliment.]

**back·ing** (bak′iŋ) ***n.*** **1** anything placed in back for support or strength [The photograph has a *backing* of cardboard.] **2** support or aid [The plan has the *backing* of the President.]

**back·lash** (bak′lash) ***n.*** **1** a quick, sharp recoil. **2** any sudden or violent reaction, as a group of people who fear or resent any protest or demonstration by another group.

☆**back·log** (bak′lôg) ***n.*** a piling up, as of work to be done or orders to be filled.

☆**back·pack** (bak′pak) ***n.*** a knapsack, often tied to a lightweight frame, worn by campers and hikers. *See the picture.* ◆***v.*** to hike wearing a backpack.

**back·slide** (bak′slīd) ***v.*** to go back to wrong ways of believing or acting; often, to lose religious faith. —**back′slid, back′slid** or **back′slid·den, back′slid·ing** —**back′slid·er *n.***

**back·stage** (bak′stāj′) ***adv., adj.*** in or to the part of the theater where the actors get ready to go on stage, where the sets are kept, etc.

**back·stroke** (bak′strōk) ***n.*** **1** a backhand stroke. **2** a stroke made by a swimmer lying face upward and stretching the arms alternately over the head. *See the picture.*

**back talk** impolite answers that show a lack of respect: *used only in everyday talk.*

**back-to-back** (bak′tə bak′) ***adj.*** ☆one right after another: *used only in everyday talk.*

☆**back·track** (bak′trak) ***v.*** to go back by the same way that one has come.

**back·up** or **back-up** (bak′up) ***adj.*** **1** standing by ready to help or be used [a *backup* pilot]. **2** supporting [a *backup* effort]. ◆***n.*** **1** a piling up because of a stoppage. **2** a support or help.

**back·ward** (bak′wərd) ***adv.*** **1** toward the back; behind [to look *backward*]. **2** with the back toward the front [If a man rides *backward,* he can see where he has been.] **3** in a way opposite to the usual way [Noel is Leon spelled *backward*.] **4** from a better to a worse condition. ◆***adj.*** **1** turned toward the back or in an opposite way [a *backward* glance]. **2** not eager; bashful; shy. **3** making progress slowly; retarded [*backward* children; *backward* nations].

**back·wards** (bak′wərdz) ***adv.*** *same as* **backward.**

**back·wa·ter** (bak′wôt′ər) ***n.*** **1** water moved backward or held back, as by the tide or by a dam. **2** a place where there is no progress.

☆**back·woods** (bak′woodz′) ***n.pl.*** wild land covered with forests, far from towns or cities.

☆**back·woods·man** (bak′woodz′mən) ***n.*** a man who lives in the backwoods. —*pl.* **back′woods′men**

**ba·con** (bā′k′n) ***n.*** salted and smoked meat from the sides and back of a hog.

**Ba·con** (bā′k′n), **Francis** 1561–1626; English philosopher and writer of essays.

**bac·te·ri·a** (bak tir′ē ə) ***n.pl.*** living things that have only one cell and are so small that they can be seen only with a microscope. Some bacteria cause diseases, and others make milk turn sour, cause cheese to ripen, or help make plant food from nitrogen in the air. *See the picture.* —*sing.* **bac·te·ri·um** (bak tir′ē əm) —**bac·te′ri·al** ***adj.***

**bac·te·ri·ol·o·gy** (bak tir′ē äl′ə jē) ***n.*** the science or study of bacteria.

**bad** (bad) ***adj.*** **1** not good; not what it should be; poor; unfit [*bad* lighting; *bad* workmanship]. **2** not pleasant; not what one would like [*bad* news]. **3** rotten; spoiled [a *bad* apple]. **4** in error; wrong; faulty [*bad* spelling]. **5** wicked; evil [a *bad* man]. **6** causing injury; harmful [Reading in poor light is *bad* for the eyes.] **7** serious; severe [a *bad* mistake; a *bad* storm]. **8** in poor health; ill. **9** sorry; unhappy [Pat felt *bad* about losing the money.] —The comparative of *bad* is **worse,** the superlative is **worst.** ◆***adv.*** badly: *used only in everyday talk* [The team played *bad.*] ◆***n.*** **1** a bad thing or condition [to go from *bad* to worse]. **2** those who are wicked [In fairy tales the *bad* are always punished.] —**not bad,** fairly good: *used only in everyday talk.*

SYNONYMS: **Bad** can mean anything from "not pleasing or satisfactory" to "completely corrupt," when one is speaking of doing something wrong. **Evil** and **wicked** are used of people who do something wrong or break a law on purpose, but **evil** is used especially of people who really want to harm or hurt others while **wicked** is sometimes used playfully of people who like to play jokes or tricks on others [*evil* thoughts; a *wicked* little boy].

**bade** (bad) *a past tense of* **bid.**

☆**bad egg** a mean or dishonest person. *A slang term.*

**badge** (baj) ***n.*** **1** a pin, emblem, or ribbon worn to show that one belongs to a certain group or has done something special [a police *badge*; a girl scout's *badge*]. **2** any sign or symbol [A battle wound is sometimes called a red *badge* of courage.]

**badg·er** (baj′ər) ***n.*** **1** an animal with a broad back, thick fur, and short legs. It lives in holes which it digs in the ground. **2** the fur of this animal. ◆***v.*** to annoy; pester [The speaker was *badgered* by interruptions.]

☆**bad·lands** (bad′landz) ***n.pl.*** any land without trees or grass, where the wind and rain have worked the soil and soft rocks into strange shapes.

**bad·ly** (bad′lē) ***adv.*** **1** in a bad way; harmfully, unpleasantly, incorrectly, wickedly, etc. **2** very much; greatly: *used only in everyday talk* [I want a new bicycle *badly.*]

**bad·min·ton** (bad′min t′n) ***n.*** a game like tennis, in which a cork with feathers in one end is batted back and forth across a high net by players using light rackets.

**Badminton** was the name of the estate of an English duke where the game, which had been brought from India, was first played in 1873.

☆**bad-mouth** (bad′mouth) ***v.*** to talk about in an unkind, disapproving way; criticize: *a slang word.*

**bad-tem·pered** (bad′tem′pərd) ***adj.*** having a bad temper; getting angry easily; irritable.

**baf·fle** (baf′'l) ***v.*** **1** to confuse so as to keep from understanding or solving; puzzle [The crime has *baffled* the police for months.] **2** to interfere with; hold back; hinder [The drapes *baffle* the sound.] —**baf′fled, baf′fling** ◆***n.*** a wall, screen, etc. that holds back or turns to one side the flow of a liquid, heat, or sound waves.

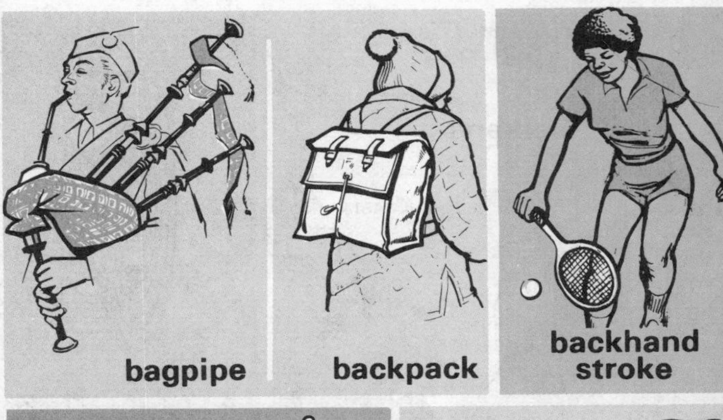
bagpipe — backpack — backhand stroke

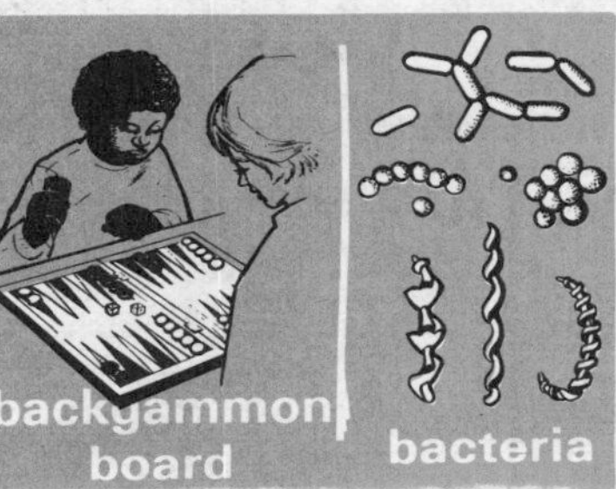
backgammon board — bacteria

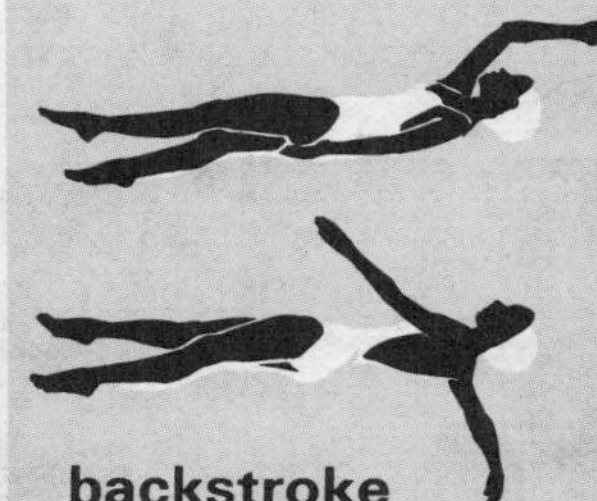
backstroke

**bag** (bag) ***n.*** **1** paper, cloth, or other soft material made up so as to have a closed bottom and sides, used for holding or carrying things [Unlike a box, a *bag* can take the shape of what it is holding.] **2** a suitcase, woman's purse, etc. **3** anything shaped or bulging like a bag [*bags* under the eyes]. **4** game that a hunter catches and kills. **5** in baseball, a base. ☆**6** one's special interest, concern, talent, etc.: *slang in this meaning.* ◆***v.*** **1** to put into a bag. **2** to bulge like a full bag [His trousers *bag* at the knees.] **3** to catch or kill in hunting [The hunter *bagged* two ducks.] —**bagged, bag′ging**

**ba·gel** (bā′g'l) ***n.*** a hard bread roll shaped like a doughnut.

**bag·gage** (bag′ij) ***n.*** the trunks, suitcases, etc. that a person takes on a trip; luggage.

**bag·gy** (bag′ē) ***adj.*** hanging loosely and bulging in places [*baggy* trousers]. —**bag′gi·er, bag′gi·est** —**bag′gi·ness** ***n.***

**Bagh·dad** or **Bag·dad** (bag′dad) the capital of Iraq.

**bag·pipe** (bag′pīp) ***n.*** *often* **bagpipes,** *pl.* a musical instrument with a leather bag into which the player blows air. The air is then forced with the arm through several pipes to make shrill tones. Bagpipes are now played mainly in Scotland. *See the picture.*

| | | | | | | | |
|---|---|---|---|---|---|---|---|
| **a** fat | **ir** here | **ou** out | **zh** leisure | | | | |
| **ā** ape | **ī** bite, fire | **u** up | **ŋ** ring | | | | |
| **ä** car, lot | **ō** go | **ʉr** fur | a *in* ago | | | | |
| **e** ten | **ô** law, horn | **ch** chin | e *in* agent | | | | |
| **er** care | **oi** oil | **sh** she | ə = i *in* unity | | | | |
| **ē** even | **oo** look | **th** thin | o *in* collect | | | | |
| **i** hit | **o͞o** tool | ***th*** then | u *in* focus | | | | |

**bah** (bä *or* ba) ***interj.*** a sound made to show a feeling of disgust or scorn.



**Ba·ha·mas** (bə hä′məz) a country on a group of islands in the West Indies, southeast of Florida.

**Bah·rain** or **Bah·rein** (bä rān′) a country on a group of islands in the Persian Gulf, off the coast of Arabia.

**bail**[1] (bāl) ***n.*** money left with a law court as a guarantee that an arrested person will appear for trial. If the person fails to appear, the court keeps the money. ◆***v.*** to have an arrested person set free by giving bail; also, to set free from some difficulty [My friends *bailed* me out.] —**go bail for,** to furnish bail for.

**bail**[2] (bāl) ***v.*** to take water out of a boat, as by dipping with a bucket. —**bail out,** to make a parachute jump from an aircraft.

**bail**[3] (bāl) ***n.*** a curved handle, as on a bucket.

**bail·iff** (bā′lif) ***n.*** **1** a sheriff's assistant. **2** an officer who has charge of prisoners and jurors in a court.

**bairn** (bern) ***n.*** a child: *a Scottish word.*

**bait** (bāt) ***n.*** **1** food put on a hook or trap to attract and catch fish or animals. **2** anything used to tempt or attract a person. ◆***v.*** **1** to put bait on a hook or trap. **2** to set attacking dogs against [People used to *bait* chained bears for amusement.] **3** to torment or tease by saying annoying or cruel things [They *baited* me by calling me "Fatty."]

**baize** (bāz) ***n.*** thick woolen cloth, usually dyed green, used to cover a billiard table.

> **Baize** comes from the Latin word *badius,* meaning "reddish brown." From this we learn that the cloth, now usually dyed green, was originally another color. The word is related to **bay**[5].

**bake** (bāk) ***v.*** **1** to cook in an oven, with little or no water or other liquid [I *baked* a cake. The potatoes *baked* for an hour.] **2** to make or become dry and hard by heat [to *bake* bricks in a kiln]. —**baked, bak′ing**

**bak·er** (bāk′ər) ***n.*** a person whose work or business is baking bread, cakes, and pastry.

**baker's dozen** thirteen. At one time bakers added an extra roll to each dozen they sold.

☆**bak·er·y** (bāk′ər ē) ***n.*** a place where bread, cakes, etc. are baked or sold. —*pl.* **bak′er·ies**

☆**bak·ing powder** (bāk′iŋ) a white powder containing baking soda and an acid substance, used in cakes, biscuits, etc. to make them rise.

☆**baking soda** a white powder that neutralizes acids and is also used in or like baking powder.

**bal·a·lai·ka** (bal′ə līk′ə) ***n.*** a Russian stringed instrument somewhat like a guitar but having a triangular body and usually three strings.

**bal·ance** (bal′əns) ***n.*** **1** equality in amount, weight, value, or importance, as between two things or the parts of a single thing [the *balance* of two children on a seesaw; the *balance* of light and dark in a painting]. **2** the ability to keep one's body steady without falling [She lost her *balance* when she looked down from the ladder.] **3** one's normal, steady state of mind. **4** an equal condition between the amount of money that one owes and the amount that is owed to one. **5** the amount of money one has in a bank account. **6** the amount still owed after part of a bill has been paid. **7** the part left over; remainder: *used only in everyday talk* [If you'll carry some of these bags, I'll carry the *balance.*] **8** a device for weighing, having two shallow pans hanging from the ends of a bar supported in the middle. *See the picture.* **9** a wheel that controls the speed of moving parts, as in a clock: *also called* **balance wheel.** ◆***v.*** **1** to compare two things to see which is heavier, better, or more important. **2** to keep oneself or something else from falling, by holding steady [The seal *balanced* the ball on its nose. The dancer *balanced* on her toes.] **3** to make two things or parts equal in weight, value, or importance [If you and I sit in the front and Lou in the back, we can *balance* the boat.] **4** to make up for by acting in an opposite way; counteract [His rough manner is *balanced* by his many kind acts.] **5** to find the difference, if any, between the amount of money that one has or that is owed to one and the amount one owes or has spent; also, to make these amounts equal [to *balance* a checking account]. —**bal′anced, bal′anc·ing** —**in the balance,** not yet settled or decided.

**Bal·bo·a** (bal bō′ə), **Vas·co de** (väs′kō de) 1475?–1517?; Spanish explorer. In 1513, he became the first European to see the Pacific Ocean.

**bal·co·ny** (bal′kə nē) ***n.*** **1** a platform with a low wall or railing, that juts out from the side of a building. **2** an upper floor of rows of seats in a theater or auditorium. It often juts out over the main floor. —*pl.* **bal′co·nies**

**bald** (bôld) ***adj.*** **1** having no hair on all or part of the scalp [Many men become *bald,* but few women do.] **2** not covered by natural growth [a *bald,* rocky hill]. **3** plain and frank [the *bald* facts]. —**bald′ly *adv.*** —**bald′ness *n.***

☆**bald eagle** a large, strong eagle of North America, which has a white-feathered head and neck when it is full-grown. It is the eagle shown on the coat of arms of the United States. *See the picture for* **eagle.**

**bal·der·dash** (bôl′dər dash) ***n.*** talk or writing that is nonsense.

**bald·faced** (bôld′fāst) ***adj.*** ☆brazen; shameless [a *baldfaced* lie].

**bal·dric** (bôl′drik) ***n.*** a belt worn over one shoulder and across the chest to hold a sword, bugle, etc.

**bale** (bāl) ***n.*** a large bundle of tightly packed cotton, hay, straw, etc., wrapped up for shipping. ◆***v.*** to make into bales [to *bale* hay]. —**baled, bal′ing**

**bale·ful** (bāl′fəl) ***adj.*** harmful or evil; sinister [a *baleful* glance]. —**bale′ful·ly *adv.*** —**bale′ful·ness *n.***

**balk** (bôk) ***v.*** **1** to stop and stubbornly refuse to move or act. **2** to bring to a stop; block [The project was *balked* by a lack of funds.] ◆***n.*** **1** something that blocks or hinders. **2** in baseball, the action by a pitcher of starting a pitch but not finishing it. This allows any base runners to move up one base.

**Bal·kan** (bôl′kən) ***adj.*** of the Balkans or their people.

**Bal·kans** (bôl′kənz) the countries on a peninsula (**Balkan Peninsula**) in southeastern Europe; Yugoslavia, Romania, Bulgaria, Albania, Greece, and part of Turkey: *also called* **Balkan States**. *See the map.*

**balk·y** (bôk′ē) ***adj.*** in the habit of balking [a *balky* mule]. —**balk′i·er, balk′i·est**

**ball**[1] (bôl) ***n.*** **1** any round object; sphere [a meat *ball;* a *ball* of yarn]. **2** a solid or hollow object, round or egg-shaped, used in playing various games [a golf *ball;* a foot*ball*]. **3** a game played with a ball, especially baseball [Let's play *ball.*] **4** the throw, pitch, or flight of a ball [to throw a fast *ball;* to hit a long *ball*]. ☆**5** in baseball, a pitch that is not a strike and is not swung at by the batter. Four balls allow the batter to go to first base. **6** a round shot for a rifle or cannon. ◆***v.*** to form into a ball.

**ball**[2] (bôl) ***n.*** **1** a large, formal dancing party. **2** a very pleasant time: *slang in this meaning.*

**bal·lad** (bal′əd) ***n.*** **1** a song or poem that tells a story in short verses. **2** a popular love song.

☆**ball and chain** a heavy metal ball fastened by a chain to a prisoner's body to keep him from escaping.

**bal·last** (bal′əst) ***n.*** **1** heavy material, such as metal or sand, carried in a ship, balloon, etc. to keep it steady. **2** crushed rock or gravel used to make a firm bed for railroad tracks. **3** anything that makes a person or personal relationships more stable or firm. ◆***v.*** to make steady by adding ballast.

**ball bearing** **1** a part of a machine in which the moving parts revolve or slide on rolling metal balls so that there is very little friction. *See the picture.* **2** any of these metal balls. —**ball′-bear′ing *adj.***

**bal·le·ri·na** (bal′ə rē′nə) ***n.*** a woman ballet dancer.

**bal·let** (bal′ā *or* ba lā′) ***n.*** **1** a dance performed on a stage, usually by a group of dancers in costume. It often tells a story by means of its graceful, fixed movements. **2** a group of such dancers.

**bal·lis·tics** (bə lis′tiks) ***n.pl.*** the science that has to do with the shooting of bullets, rockets, etc.: *used with a singular verb.* —**bal·lis′tic *adj.***

**bal·loon** (bə lo͞on′) ***n.*** **1** a large bag that floats high above the ground when filled with a gas lighter than air. Balloons are now often used to carry instruments for studying the upper air. **2** a small rubber bag blown up with air or gas and used as a toy. ◆***v.*** to swell like a balloon.

**bal·lot** (bal′ət) ***n.*** **1** a piece of paper on which a person marks a choice in voting. **2** the act or a way of voting. ◆***v.*** to vote by ballot.

> **Ballot** comes from an Italian word meaning "small ball." At one time small black and white balls, instead of pieces of paper, were used in voting. A *black ball* was used as a vote against someone or something. From this practice, we get the verb **blackball**.

☆**ball-point** or **ball·point** (bôl′point′) ***n.*** *same as* **ball point pen**.

☆**ball point pen** a kind of fountain pen whose writing point is a tiny ball that rolls the ink onto the writing surface.

**ball·room** (bôl′ro͞om) ***n.*** a large room or hall for dancing.

**balm** (bäm) ***n.*** **1** a sweet-smelling oil that is gotten from certain trees and is used as an ointment. **2** any salve or lotion used for healing or for relieving pain. **3** anything that soothes [Sleep was a *balm* to her troubled mind.]

**balm·y** (bäm′ē) ***adj.*** like balm; soothing, mild, or pleasant [a *balmy* day]. —**balm′i·er, balm′i·est** —**balm′i·ness *n.***

☆**ba·lo·ney** (bə lō′nē) ***n.*** **1** *same as* **bologna**. **2** nonsense; foolishness: *slang in this meaning.*

☆**bal·sa** (bôl′sə) ***n.*** **1** a tree growing in tropical America that has a very lightweight wood used in making airplane models, rafts, etc. **2** this wood.

**bal·sam** (bôl′səm) ***n.*** **1** *same as meaning* 1 *of* **balm**. **2** any tree or plant from which balm is got; especially, a kind of fir tree.

**Bal·tic** (bôl′tik) a sea in northern Europe bounded on the west by Sweden and leading into the North Sea: *the full name is* **Baltic Sea**. ◆***adj.*** of or on the Baltic Sea [Lithuania, Latvia, and Estonia are sometimes called the *Baltic* States.]

**Bal·ti·more** (bôl′tə môr) a seaport in northern Maryland, on Chesapeake Bay.

☆**Baltimore oriole** a black and orange songbird of North America. *See the picture for* **oriole**.

**bal·us·ter** (bal′əs tər) ***n.*** any of the small posts that support the upper rail of a railing, as on a staircase. *See the picture.*

**bal·us·trade** (bal′ə strād) ***n.*** a railing held up by balusters, as on a staircase. *See the picture.*

**Bal·zac** (bôl′zak), **Ho·no·ré de** (ä nä rā′ də) 1799–1850; French writer of novels.

**bam·boo** (bam bo͞o′) ***n.*** a tropical plant with woody stems that are hollow and jointed. It is a kind of grass that grows as tall as trees, and its stems are used in making canes, furniture, fishing poles, etc.

**bam·boo·zle** (bam bo͞o′z'l) ***v.*** **1** to trick or cheat. **2** to confuse or puzzle [The riddle has us *bamboozled.*] —**bam·boo′zled, bam·boo′zling**

**ban** (ban) ***v.*** to have a rule against doing, saying, using, etc.; forbid [Some doctors *ban* smoking in their waiting rooms.] *See* SYNONYMS *at* **forbid**. —**banned,**

| | | | | | | | |
|---|---|---|---|---|---|---|---|
| **a** | fat | **ir** | here | **ou** | out | **zh** | leisure |
| **ā** | ape | **ī** | bite, fire | **u** | up | **ng** | ring |
| **ä** | car, lot | **ō** | go | **ur** | fur | | a *in* ago |
| **e** | ten | **ô** | law, horn | **ch** | chin | | e *in* agent |
| **er** | care | **oi** | oil | **sh** | she | **ə** = | i *in* unity |
| **ē** | even | **oo** | look | **th** | thin | | o *in* collect |
| **i** | hit | **o͞o** | tool | ***th*** | then | | u *in* focus |

55

b

**ban′ning** ◆***n.*** **1** an official order forbidding something [The city placed a *ban* on the burning of rubbish.] **2** a curse.

**ba·nal** (bā′n′l) ***adj.*** said or told so often that it has become dull or stale; trite [His speech was full of *banal* jokes.]

**ba·nan·a** (bə nan′ə) ***n.*** **1** a large tropical plant with long, broad leaves and a large bunch of fruit growing on a single stalk. *See the picture.* **2** its narrow, slightly curved fruit. It has a sweet, creamy flesh covered by a yellow or reddish skin.

**band** (band) ***n.*** **1** a cord or wire, or a strip of some material, used to encircle something or to bind something together [The iron *bands* around the barrel broke. A wedding ring is sometimes called a *band*.] **2** a stripe of some different color or material [a *band* of chrome along the side of the car]. **3** any of the separate divisions on a long-playing record. **4** a range of frequencies for radio broadcasting [a shortwave *band*]. **5** a group of people joined together to do something [a *band* of explorers]. **6** a group of musicians playing together, especially on wind instruments and drums [a dance *band;* a marching *band*]. ◆***v.*** **1** to put a band on or around. ☆**2** to mark with a band [The pigeons were *banded* on the leg.] **3** to join together or unite [The neighbors *banded* together to build the barn.]

**band·age** (ban′dij) ***n.*** a strip of cloth, gauze, etc. used to cover a sore or wound or to bind up an injured part of the body. ◆***v.*** to bind or cover with a bandage. —**band′aged, band′ag·ing**

☆**Band-Aid** (ban′dād) *a trademark for* a small bandage of gauze and adhesive tape.

**ban·dan·na** or **ban·dan·a** (ban dan′ə) ***n.*** a large, colored handkerchief, usually with a pattern printed on it. Bandannas are often worn around the neck or head.

> **Bandanna** comes to us from the Sanskrit word for "tying." In India, the cloth to be dyed is tied so that some parts take up the dye and other parts do not. We call this method **tie-dyeing.**

**band·box** (band′bäks) ***n.*** a light cardboard box for holding hats, collars, etc.

**ban·deau** (ban dō′) ***n.*** a narrow ribbon worn around the head to hold the hair in place. —*pl.* **ban·deaux** (ban dōz′)

**ban·dit** (ban′dit) ***n.*** a robber, especially one who robs travelers on the road.

**band·mas·ter** (band′mas′tər) ***n.*** the leader of a band of musicians.

**ban·do·leer** or **ban·do·lier** (ban′də lir′) ***n.*** a broad belt worn over one shoulder and across the chest, with pockets for carrying ammunition.

☆**band saw** a saw whose blade is a long, narrow loop of metal that runs over pulleys. It is usually worked by electricity.

**band shell** an outdoor platform for musical concerts. At the back of the platform is a large shell that has the shape of half of a hollow sphere, for reflecting the sound.

**band·stand** (band′stand) ***n.*** **1** a platform from which a band of musicians can give a concert outdoors. It usually has a roof, but is open on all sides. *See the picture.* **2** any platform for a band of musicians, as in a ballroom.

☆**band·wag·on** (band′wag′ən) ***n.*** a gaily decorated wagon for a band of musicians to ride in, as in a parade. —**on the bandwagon,** on the winning or popular side, as in an election: *used only in everyday talk.*

**ban·dy**[1] (ban′dē) ***v.*** to toss or pass back and forth; give and get back [to *bandy* gossip]. —**ban′died, ban′dy·ing —bandy words,** to have an argument.

**ban·dy**[2] (ban′dē) ***adj.*** bending outward at the knees; bowed [*bandy* legs].

**ban·dy·leg·ged** (ban′dē leg′id *or* ban′dē legd′) ***adj.*** having bandy legs; bowlegged.

**bane** (bān) ***n.*** something that causes worry, ruin, or death. —**bane′ful *adj.***

**bang**[1] (baŋ) ***v.*** **1** to hit hard and make a noise [She *banged* her fist on the door. The shutters *banged* against the house.] **2** to shut hard and make a noise [Don't *bang* the door!] **3** to make a loud noise [The drums were *banging*. We heard a gun *bang* twice.] ◆***n.*** **1** a hard blow or loud knock [a *bang* on the door]. **2** a sudden loud noise [Bombs go off with a *bang*.] ◆***adv.*** hard, noisily, and suddenly [The car went *bang* into the wall.] —**bang up,** to hurt or damage.

☆**bang**[2] (baŋ) ***v.*** to cut hair short and straight across. ◆***n.*** *usually* **bangs,** *pl.* banged hair worn across the forehead.

**Bang·kok** (baŋ′käk) the capital of Thailand.

**Ban·gla·desh** (bäŋ′glə desh′) a country in southern Asia, northeast of India.

**ban·gle** (baŋ′g′l) ***n.*** **1** a bracelet or anklet worn as an ornament. **2** a hanging disk-shaped ornament, as on a bracelet or tambourine.

**bang-up** (baŋ′up′) ***adj.*** very good; excellent: *used only in everyday talk.*

**ban·ish** (ban′ish) ***v.*** **1** to force a person to leave his country as a punishment; exile. **2** to put away; get rid of [She tried to *banish* all thoughts of her troubles.] —**ban′ish·ment *n.***

**ban·is·ter** (ban′əs tər) ***n.*** **1** *often* **banisters,** *pl.* a railing held up by a row of small posts (*balusters*), as along a staircase. **2** the railing itself.

☆**ban·jo** (ban′jō) ***n.*** a stringed musical instrument with a long neck and a round body covered on top with tightly stretched skins. It has, usually, four or five strings that are plucked with the fingers or a pick. *See the picture.* —*pl.* **ban′jos** or **ban′joes —ban′jo·ist *n.***

**bank**[1] (baŋk) ***n.*** **1** a place of business for keeping, exchanging, or lending money. Banks make a profit by charging interest for the money they lend. **2** a place for keeping a supply of something for use later on [a blood *bank*]. —☆**bank on,** to depend on: *used only in everyday talk.*

**bank**[2] (baŋk) ***n.*** **1** a large or long mound or pile [a *bank* of earth; a *bank* of clouds]. **2** the land along the sides of a river or stream. **3** a shallow place in a sea or lake [The ship ran aground on the sand *bank*.] ◆***v.*** **1** to pile up so as to form a bank [The snow was *banked* along the driveway.] **2** to slope a road where it goes around a curve. **3** to tilt an airplane while making a turn so that the wing on the inside of the turn is lower. **4** to cover a fire with ashes or more fuel so that it will burn slower.

**bank**³ (baŋk) ***n.*** **1** a row or tier of oars, as in an ancient galley. **2** a row or tier of objects [a *bank* of lights; a *bank* of keys on an organ].

**bank·er** (baŋ′kər) ***n.*** a person who owns or manages a bank.

**bank·ing** (baŋ′kiŋ) ***n.*** the work of a banker; the business of managing a bank.

☆**bank·roll** (baŋk′rōl) ***n.*** a supply of money. ◆***v.*** to supply with money: *used only in everyday talk.*

**bank·rupt** (baŋk′rupt) ***adj.*** **1** not able to pay one's debts and freed by law from the need for doing so [Any property a *bankrupt* person may still have is usually divided among those to whom the person owes money.] **2** that has failed completely [The school's policy on this matter seems *bankrupt.*] ◆***n.*** a person who is bankrupt. ◆***v.*** to make bankrupt.

**Bankrupt** comes from two Italian words meaning "broken bench." Moneylenders used to carry on their business at a bench or table. They would be put out of business if the bench were broken, just as nowadays people are put out of business if they cannot pay their debts.

**bank·rupt·cy** (baŋk′rupt sē) ***n.*** **1** the condition of being bankrupt. **2** a case of someone's being bankrupt. **3** complete failure. —*pl.* **bank′rupt·cies**

**ban·ner** (ban′ər) ***n.*** **1** a piece of cloth with an emblem or words on it [The *banner* behind the President's desk bears the seal of the U.S.] **2** a flag [the Star-Spangled *Banner*]. **3** a headline across a newspaper page. ◆***adj.*** top; leading [Our company had a *banner* year in sales.]

**banns** (banz) ***n.pl.*** a public announcement in church that two persons are soon to be married.

**ban·quet** (baŋ′kwit) ***n.*** a formal dinner or feast for many people. Banquets, during which speeches are made, are often held to celebrate something or to raise money. ◆***v.*** **1** to have a banquet for. **2** to dine at a banquet; feast.

**ban·shee** or **ban·shie** (ban′shē) ***n.*** in Irish and Scottish folk tales, a female spirit who is supposed to wail or shriek as a sign that someone in a family is about to die.

**ban·tam** (ban′təm) ***n.*** **1** *often* **Bantam,** a breed of chicken of small size. **2** a small person who is a fighter.

**ban·ter** (ban′tər) ***n.*** playful teasing or joking. ◆***v.*** to joke or tease in a playful way.

**Ban·tu** (ban′to͞o) ***n.*** **1** any member of a group of Negroid tribes in central and southern Africa. **2** any of the group of languages of these peoples. —*pl.* **Ban′tus** or **Ban′tu** ◆***adj.*** of the Bantus or their languages.

**ban·yan** (ban′yən) ***n.*** a fig tree of the East Indies whose branches take root in the ground, forming many new trunks. *See the picture.*

**bap·tism** (bap′tiz′m) ***n.*** **1** the religious ceremony of taking persons into a Christian church by dipping them in water or sprinkling water on them. **2** a first experience, especially one that is hard or severe [The new troops received their *baptism* when they were fired upon.] —**bap·tis′mal** ***adj.***

**Bap·tist** (bap′tist) ***n.*** **1** a member of a Christian church which believes that baptism should be given only to believers (not to infants) and only by dipping the entire body in water. **2** a person who baptizes [John the *Baptist*].

bandstand

banyan

**bap·tis·ter·y** or **bap·tis·try** (bap′tis trē) ***n.*** a place used for baptism, usually in a church. —*pl.* **bap′tis·ter·ies** or **bap′tis·tries**

**bap·tize** (bap′tīz *or* bap tīz′) ***v.*** **1** to take a person into a Christian church by baptism. **2** to give a name to at baptism; christen. —**bap′tized, bap′tiz·ing**

**bar** (bär) ***n.*** **1** a long, fairly narrow piece of wood, metal, etc. Bars are often used to block the way, to fasten something, or as a lever [The prison has *bars* on the windows. He pried open the box with a steel *bar.*] **2** a solid piece of something, having an even shape [a *bar* of soap; a chocolate *bar*]. **3** anything that prevents or stands in the way [The sand *bar* blocked the river channel. Foreign birth is a *bar* to becoming president.] **4** a stripe or band of color or light [*Bars* of sunlight came through the clouds.] **5** a law court [They were called before the *bar* to answer for their crimes.] **6** anything that acts like a law court in judging a person [the *bar* of public opinion]. **7** lawyers as a group [Which judges does the *bar* support for reelection?] **8** the profession of a lawyer [She is studying for the *bar.*] **9** a counter or place at which drinks and, sometimes, food are served. **10** any of the lines that run from top to bottom of a musical staff, dividing it into equal groups of beats, called measures; also, any of these measures [The band played the opening *bars* of "America."] ◆***v.*** **1** to fasten with a bar [The door is *barred* and bolted.] **2** to block; shut off; obstruct [A fallen tree *bars* the path.] **3** to stand in the way; prevent; forbid [State law *bars* convicts from voting.] **4** to keep out; refuse to let in [The dog was *barred* from the house.] **5** to mark with stripes or bands. —**barred, bar′ring** ◆***prep.*** except; leaving out: *now*



| | | | |
|---|---|---|---|
| **a** fat | **ir** here | **ou** out | **zh** leisure |
| **ā** ape | **ī** bite, fire | **u** up | **ŋ** ring |
| **ä** car, lot | **ō** go | **ur** fur | a *in* ago |
| **e** ten | **ô** law, horn | **ch** chin | e *in* agent |
| **er** care | **oi** oil | **sh** she | ə = i *in* unity |
| **ē** even | **oo** look | **th** thin | o *in* collect |
| **i** hit | **o͞o** tool | ***th*** then | u *in* focus |

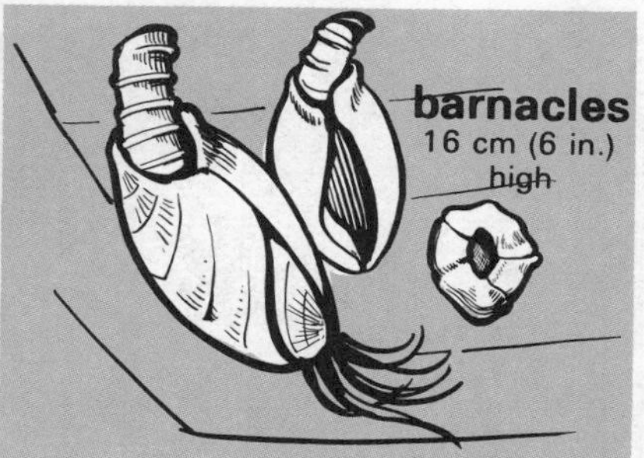


*used only in the phrase* **bar none,** *meaning* "with no exception."

**barb** (bärb) ***n.*** a sharp point sticking out in an opposite direction from the main point of a fishhook, arrow, etc. *See the picture.* **◆v.** to put a barb or barbs on.



**Bar·ba·dos** (bär bā′dōz *or* bär bā′dōs) a country that is the easternmost island of the West Indies.

**bar·bar·i·an** (bär ber′ē ən) ***n.*** **1** a person living in a savage or primitive society. **2** a crude or cruel person; brute. **◆adj.** **1** not civilized; savage; primitive. **2** cruel; brutal.

**bar·bar·ic** (bär ber′ik) ***adj.*** of or like barbarians; not civilized; wild; crude.

**bar·bar·ism** (bär′bər iz′m) ***n.*** **1** an action or behavior that is brutal or savage. **2** a word or phrase that is not in good use ["Youse" is a *barbarism* for "you."]

**bar·bar·i·ty** (bär ber′ə tē) ***n.*** **1** brutal or savage act or behavior; cruelty. **2** a crude or coarse style or taste. *—pl.* **bar·bar′i·ties**

**bar·ba·rous** (bär′bər əs) ***adj.*** **1** not civilized; primitive. **2** cruel, savage, or brutal. **3** crude or coarse [a *barbarous* style or taste]. **4** using words or phrases that are not thought to be in good use. **—bar′ba·rous·ly *adv.***

> **Barbarous** comes from a Greek word meaning "foreign, strange, and ignorant." The Greek word is related to a Sanskrit word meaning "stammering." If we meet a foreigner, we may think he is strange and ignorant because we do not understand his language or speech. It is really we who are ignorant, because we do not know his language.

**Bar·ba·ry** (bär′bər ē) a region in northern Africa, between Egypt and the Atlantic Ocean. The coast of this region was in earlier times a center for pirates.

**bar·be·cue** (bär′bə kyo͞o) ***n.*** **1** a hog, ox, etc. roasted whole on a spit over an open fire. **2** any meat roasted over an open fire. ☆**3** a picnic or party at which such meat is served. **4** a stove or pit for cooking outdoors. **◆v.** **1** to roast on a spit over an open fire. **2** to broil or roast meat or fish in a highly seasoned sauce (called **barbecue sauce**). **—bar′be·cued, bar′be·cu·ing**

**barbed** (bärbd) ***adj.*** **1** having a barb or barbs. **2** sharp and painful [*barbed* remarks].

☆**barbed wire** wire with sharp points all along it. It is used for fences or barriers.

**bar·bell** (bär′bel) ***n.*** a metal bar to which different sizes of flat, round weights can be attached at each end, used in lifting weights.

**bar·ber** (bär′bər) ***n.*** a person whose work is cutting hair, shaving beards, etc.

**bar·ber·ry** (bär′ber′ē) ***n.*** **1** a shrub with small thorns and small, red berries. **2** this berry. *—pl.* **bar′ber′ries**

☆**bar·ber·shop** (bär′bər shäp) ***n.*** the place where a barber works.

**bar·bi·tu·rate** (bär bich′ər it) ***n.*** any of various drugs taken to make one sleep.

**Bar·ce·lo·na** (bär′sə lō′nə) a seaport in Spain, on the Mediterranean.

**bard** (bärd) ***n.*** **1** a person who wrote and sang poems in ancient times. **2** a poet.

**bare**[1] (ber) ***adj.*** **1** not covered or clothed; naked; stripped [*bare* legs; a *bare* spot in the lawn]. **2** not furnished; empty [a *bare* room]. **3** simple; plain [the *bare* facts]. **4** no more than; mere [a *bare* ten inches away]. **◆v.** to make bare; uncover; expose. **—bared, bar′ing —lay bare,** to make clear; expose; reveal.

> SYNONYMS: Something is **bare** when its usual or natural covering is missing or has been removed [the *bare* boughs of the oaks in winter]. **Bare** is usually used of a part of the body that is not covered, while **naked** and **nude** are usually used of the entire body when it is not clothed [a *bare* midriff; *naked* in the bathtub; a model posing *nude* for an artist]. **Naked** is sometimes used like **bare** [a *naked* sword] and **nude** is usually thought to be a nicer word than **naked** [a *nude* statue].

**bare**[2] (ber) *a former past tense of* **bear**[1].

**bare·back** (ber′bak) ***adv., adj.*** on a horse with no saddle [to ride *bareback*].

**bare·faced** (ber′fāst) ***adj.*** feeling or showing no shame; impudent; bold [a *barefaced* lie].

**bare·foot** (ber′fo͝ot) ***adj., adv.*** with bare feet; without shoes and stockings.

**bare·foot·ed** (ber′fo͝ot′id) ***adj.*** *same as* **barefoot.**

**bare·head·ed** (ber′hed′id) ***adj., adv.*** wearing no hat or other covering on the head.

**bare·ly** (ber′lē) ***adv.*** **1** only just; no more than; scarcely [It is *barely* a year old.] **2** in a bare way; meagerly [a *barely* furnished room, with only a bed in it].

**Bar·ents Sea** (ber′ənts) part of the Arctic Ocean, north of Europe.

**bar·gain** (bär′g′n) ***n.*** **1** an agreement to give or do something in return for something else [Let's make a *bargain* to help each other with our chores.] **2** something offered or gotten for less than the usual cost [This coat was a *bargain* at only $20.00.] **◆v.** to talk over a sale or trade, trying to get the best possible terms [We *bargained* with the salesman for an hour before buying the car.] **—bargain for,** to expect; be ready for [more trouble than she had *bargained for*]. **—into the bargain,** in addition; as well.

**barge** (bärj) ***n.*** **1** a large boat with a flat bottom, for carrying goods on rivers or canals. *See the picture.* **2**

any large or clumsy looking boat of this kind. ✦*v.* to enter in a clumsy or rude way [They *barged* in without knocking.] —**barged, barg′ing**

**bar·i·tone** (bar′ə tōn) ***n.*** **1** a man's voice that is lower than a tenor but higher than a bass. **2** a singer with such a voice, or an instrument with a range like this. ✦***adj.*** of or for a baritone.

**bar·i·um** (ber′ē əm) ***n.*** a chemical element that is a silver-white metal. Its salts are used in medicine and in making paints.

**bark**[1] (bärk) ***n.*** the outside covering of the trunk and branches of a tree. ✦***v.*** **1** to peel the bark from. **2** to scrape some skin off [Don't *bark* your shins on that low table.]

**bark**[2] (bärk) ***v.*** **1** to make the short, sharp cry of a dog. **2** to make a sound like this [The rifles *barked.*] **3** to speak or shout sharply [to *bark* orders]. ✦***n.*** the sound made in barking.

**bark**[3] (bärk) ***n.*** **1** a sailing ship with three masts. **2** a small sailing boat: *used formerly, especially in poetry.*

**bark·er** (bär′kər) ***n.*** a person in front of a theater, carnival tent, or sideshow who tries to get people to go inside by talking in a loud and lively way.

**bar·ley** (bär′lē) ***n.*** **1** a cereal grass whose seed, or grain, is used in making malt, soups, etc. **2** this grain.

**bar·ley·corn** (bär′lē kôrn′) ***n.*** barley grass or its grain.

**barn** (bärn) ***n.*** a farm building for sheltering cows, farm machines, etc. and for storing crops.

**bar·na·cle** (bär′nə k′l) ***n.*** a small sea animal with a shell, which fastens itself to rocks, the bottoms of ships, etc. *See the picture.*

☆**barn dance** a party, sometimes held in a barn, where people do square dances.

**barn owl** a brown and gray owl with a spotted white breast. It often builds its nest in deserted barns.

**barn·storm** (bärn′stôrm) ***v.*** to go about the country from one small town to another acting in plays, giving concerts, etc.

**barn·yard** (bärn′yärd) ***n.*** the yard or ground near a barn, often with a fence around it.

**ba·rom·e·ter** (bə räm′ə tər) ***n.*** **1** an instrument that measures the pressure of the air around us. It is used in forecasting changes in the weather and finding the height above sea level. **2** anything that shows changes in conditions [The stock market is a *barometer* of business.] —**bar·o·met·ric** (bar′ə met′rik) ***adj.***

**bar·on** (bar′ən) ***n.*** **1** a British nobleman of the lowest rank in the House of Lords. **2** a nobleman in a few other countries.

**bar·on·ess** (bar′ə nis) ***n.*** **1** a baron's wife or widow. **2** a woman with a baron's rank.

**bar·on·et** (bar′ə nit) ***n.*** a man with the rank of a British nobleman below a baron but above a knight.

**ba·ro·ni·al** (bə rō′nē əl) ***adj.*** of or fit for a baron [a *baronial* mansion].

**ba·roque** (bə rōk′) ***adj.*** **1** having many decorations and fancy, curved designs [a *baroque* cathedral of the 16th century]. **2** having complicated melodies with fugues and counterpoint [the *baroque* music of Bach]. **3** having gaudy decorations and too many of them.

**bar·racks** (bar′əks) ***n.pl.*** a building or group of buildings where soldiers live: *used with either a singular or plural verb* [This *barracks* is old. These *barracks* are old.]

**bar·ra·cu·da** (bar′ə ko͞o′də) ***n.*** a large, fierce fish found in warm seas. —*pl.* **bar′ra·cu′da** or **bar′ra·cu′das**

**bar·rage** (bə räzh′) ***n.*** **1** the continued shooting of many cannons or machine guns against a part of the enemy's line. It protects one's own troops when moving forward or retreating. **2** any heavy attack.

**bar·rel** (bar′əl) ***n.*** **1** a large, round container that has bulging sides and a flat top and bottom. It is usually made of wooden slats bound together by metal hoops. **2** the amount a barrel will hold: the standard barrel in the U.S. holds 31 1/2 gallons (119.2275 liters). **3** the straight tube of a gun through which the bullet or shell is shot. ✦***v.*** **1** to put in barrels. ☆**2** to move fast; speed: *slang in this meaning.* —**bar′reled** or **bar′relled, bar′rel·ing** or **bar′rel·ling**

**barrel organ** a large music box usually played by turning a handle; hand organ.

**bar·ren** (bar′ən) ***adj.*** **1** unable to have children [a *barren* woman]. **2** not producing crops or fruit [*barren* soil; a *barren* tree]. **3** not bringing useful results; not worthwhile [a *barren* plan]. **4** not having any; empty [a person *barren* of charm]. ✦***n.*** an area of barren land. —**bar′ren·ness** ***n.***

**bar·rette** (bə ret′) ***n.*** a clasp for holding a girl's or woman's hair in place. *See the picture.*

**bar·ri·cade** (bar′ə kād *or* bar ə kād′) ***n.*** **1** a pile of things built up quickly to block a road or entrance, especially in order to hold off an attack. **2** anything that blocks the way; barrier. ✦***v.*** **1** to put up barricades in; block [The streets were *barricaded* with posts and barbed wire.] **2** to keep out or shut in with a barricade [She *barricaded* herself in her room.]

> The word **barricade,** which comes to us from French, is probably related to **barrel.** The first barricades were made of barrels filled with dirt and stones and piled together.

**bar·ri·er** (bar′ē ər) ***n.*** **1** a fence, wall, or other thing that blocks the way or keeps one from going on. **2** anything that keeps people apart or prevents progress [The caste system of India created many *barriers.*]

**bar·ring** (bär′iŋ) ***prep.*** unless there should be; excepting [*Barring* rain, we leave tonight.]

**bar·ris·ter** (bar′is tər) ***n.*** in England, a lawyer who pleads cases in court.

☆**bar·room** (bär′ro͞om) ***n.*** a room with a bar or a counter at which alcoholic drinks are sold.

**bar·row**[1] (bar′ō) ***n.*** **1** *same as* **wheelbarrow.** **2** a small cart with two wheels, pushed by hand.

**bar·row**[2] (bar′ō) ***n.*** a heap of earth or rocks used in olden times to mark a grave.

☆**bar·tend·er** (bär′ten′dər) ***n.*** a person who serves alcoholic drinks at a bar.

**bar·ter** (bär′tər) ***v.*** to pay for goods with other goods instead of with money; trade [I'll *barter* my catcher's



| | | | | | | | |
|---|---|---|---|---|---|---|---|
| **a** | fat | **ir** | here | **ou** | out | **zh** | leisure |
| **ā** | ape | **ī** | bite, fire | **u** | up | **ŋ** | ring |
| **ä** | car, lot | **ō** | go | **ʉr** | fur | | a *in* ago |
| **e** | ten | **ô** | law, horn | **ch** | chin | | e *in* agent |
| **er** | care | **oi** | oil | **sh** | she | **ə** = | i *in* unity |
| **ē** | even | **oo** | look | **th** | thin | | o *in* collect |
| **i** | hit | **o͞o** | tool | ***th*** | then | | u *in* focus |

mitt for your fielder's glove.] *See* SYNONYMS *at* **sell.** ◆*n.* the act of bartering. —**bar'ter·er** *n.*

**Bar·tók** (bär'tôk), **Bé·la** (bā'lä) 1881–1945; Hungarian composer.

**Bar·ton** (bär't'n), **Clara** 1821–1912; American nurse. She organized the American Red Cross in 1881.

**bas·al** (bā's'l) *adj.* basic or fundamental.

**ba·salt** (bə sôlt' *or* bās'ôlt) *n.* a hard, dark rock found in lava that has cooled and hardened.

**base**[1] (bās) *n.* **1** the thing or part on which something rests; lowest part or bottom; foundation [A cement slab forms the *base* of the statue.] **2** the main part, on which the rest depends; basis [A worker's *base* pay is the rate paid for each hour or each week that is worked, not counting overtime, bonuses, etc.] *See* SYNONYMS *at* **basis.** **3** any of the four goals which a baseball player must safely reach one after the other before scoring a run. **4** any goal or safety point in certain other games. **5** a center or headquarters; especially, the place from which troops, planes, ships, or explorers set out or from which they get their orders and supplies. **6** a chemical substance that acts on an acid to form a salt [Sodium hydroxide, a *base,* acts with hydrochloric acid to form sodium chloride, or common table salt.] **7** *same as meaning* 6 *of* **root.** ◆*v.* to put or rest on a base or on something that acts as a support [love *based* on respect]. —**based, bas'·ing**



**base**[2] (bās) *adj.* **1** not having or showing much honor, courage, or decency; not noble; mean [a *base* coward; *base* ingratitude]. **2** of a low class or kind [*base* servitude]. **3** low in value as compared to others [Iron is a *base* metal; gold is a precious one.] —**base'ly** *adv.* —**base'ness** *n.*

**base·ball** (bās'bôl) *n.* ☆**1** a game played with a ball and bat by two teams of nine players each. It is played on a field with four bases laid out in a diamond with squared sides. ☆**2** the ball used in this game.

☆**base·board** (bās'bôrd) *n.* a narrow board covering the edge of a wall next to the floor.

**base·less** (bās'lis) *adj.* not based on fact or truth; without good reason [*baseless* fears].

**base·man** (bās'mən) *n.* a baseball player whose position is at first base, second base, or third base. —*pl.* **base'men**

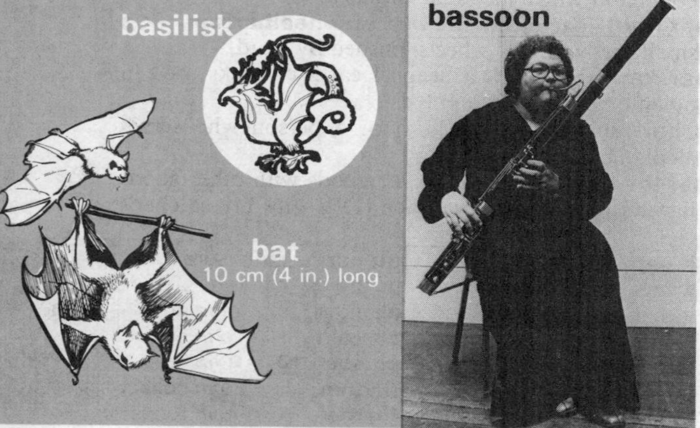


**base·ment** (bās'mənt) *n.* the cellar or lowest rooms of a building, below the main floor and at least partly below the surface of the ground.

**bash** (bash) *v.* to hit or damage with a blow; smash: *used only in everyday talk.*

**bash·ful** (bash'fəl) *adj.* timid and shy when among people. —**bash'ful·ly** *adv.* —**bash'ful·ness** *n.*

**bas·ic** (bā'sik) *adj.* **1** at the base; being the base or basis; fundamental; main [the *basic* rules of the game]. **2** of or containing a chemical base; alkaline. —**bas'i·cal·ly** *adv.*

**bas·il** (baz''l *or* bā'z'l) *n.* a plant with a pleasant smell. Its leaves are used as a seasoning in cooking.

**ba·sil·i·ca** (bə sil'i kə) *n.* in ancient Rome, a building consisting of a long room with a part shaped like a half circle at the far end. It had a row of columns along each side.

**bas·i·lisk** (bas'ə lisk) *n.* a monster like a lizard, told about in myths. Its breath and glance were supposed to kill people. *See the picture.*

**ba·sin** (bās''n) *n.* **1** a wide, shallow bowl for holding a liquid. **2** a washbowl or sink. **3** a bay or sheltered part of a sea or lake [a yacht *basin*]. **4** all the land drained by a river and its branches.

**ba·sis** (bā'sis) *n.* the thing or part on which something rests or depends; support. —*pl.* **ba·ses** (bā'sēz)

SYNONYMS: **Basis, base**[1], and **foundation** all carry the idea of a part that supports or underlies something that rests or depends on it. **Base**[1] and **foundation** usually suggest a physical structure, while **basis** suggests a structure that is not physical [the *base* of a lamp; the *foundation* of a building; a story with no *basis* in fact]. **Foundation** also suggests something stable and permanent [A good education gives us a good *foundation* for our adult lives.]

**bask** (bask) *v.* **1** to warm oneself pleasantly, as in the sunlight. **2** to enjoy any kind of warm and pleasant feeling [He *basked* in her favor.]

**bas·ket** (bas'kit) *n.* **1** a container made by weaving together cane, rushes, wood strips, etc. It often has a handle or handles [a bushel *basket;* a clothes *basket*]. **2** the amount a basket holds [How much a *basket* do these apples cost?] **3** anything that looks like a basket or is used as one [a wastepaper *basket* made of metal]. ☆**4** the open net, hanging from a metal ring, through which the ball is tossed in basketball; also, a goal scored by tossing the ball through this ring and net.

☆**bas·ket·ball** (bas'kit bôl) *n.* **1** a game played between two teams of five players each, usually indoors. Points are scored by tossing a ball through a raised, open net, hanging from a metal ring. There is a basket at either end of the playing court. **2** the large, round, leather ball used in this game. It is filled with air.

The nets used in **basketball** today do not look much like baskets, but when Dr. James Naismith invented the game in 1891, he used real peach baskets from which the bottoms had been cut away.

**Basque** (bask) *n.* any member of a group of people living in the western Pyrenees Mountains of Europe.

**bas-re·lief** (bä'rə lēf') *n.* sculpture in which figures are carved in a flat surface so that they stand out a little from the background [Lincoln's head on the penny is like a *bas-relief.*]

**bass**[1] (bās) ***n.*** **1** the lowest kind of man's singing voice. **2** a singer with such a voice. **3** an instrument with the lowest range of tones; especially, the **double bass.** **4** the lowest part of harmony in a piece of music. ◆***adj.*** **1** of or for a bass. **2** having low, deep sounds or tones [a *bass* drum].

**bass**[2] (bas) ***n.*** a fish with spiny fins, found in both fresh and salt water and used for food. —*pl.* **bass** or **bass'es**

**bass clef** (bās) a sign on a musical staff showing that the notes on the staff are below middle C.

**bas·set** (bas'it) ***n.*** a hunting dog with a long body, short legs, and long ears. *Its full name is* **basset hound.**

**bas·si·net** (bas'ə net') ***n.*** a large basket used as a baby's bed, often with a hood at one end.

**bas·soon** (bə sōōn') ***n.*** a woodwind musical instrument with deep, low tones. Its long, curved mouthpiece has two reeds. *See the picture.*

**bass viol** (bās) *same as* **double bass.**

☆**bass·wood** (bas'wood) ***n.*** **1** a kind of linden tree. **2** its soft, but strong wood.

**bast** (bast) ***n.*** a strong fiber gotten from plants and used in making ropes and mats.

**bas·tard** (bas'tərd) ***n.*** **1** a child born to a woman who is not married to the child's father. **2** a person who is treated with contempt or pity. *It is now thought to be vulgar or unkind to use this word.*

**baste**[1] (bāst) ***v.*** to sew with long, loose stitches so as to hold the parts in place until the final sewing is done. After a hem or seam is properly sewn, these stitches are pulled out. —**bast'ed, bast'ing**

**baste**[2] (bāst) ***v.*** to keep meat juicy during roasting by pouring juices or melted fats over it. —**bast'ed, bast'ing**

**Bas·tille** (bas tēl') a famous prison in Paris that was destroyed by mobs on July 14, 1789. This action was the beginning of the French Revolution. ◆***n.*** **bastille,** any prison.

**bas·tion** (bas'chən) ***n.*** **1** a part of a fort that juts out to give the defenders a better place to shoot from. **2** any strong defense.

**bat**[1] (bat) ***n.*** **1** a wooden club used in hitting the ball in baseball. **2** any strong, sturdy stick. ☆**3** a turn in batting in baseball [Pat got three hits in four times at *bat.*] **4** a hard blow or hit: *used only in everyday talk.* ◆***v.*** **1** to hit with a bat or something like a bat. **2** to take a turn at batting in baseball. —**bat'ted, bat'ting** —☆**off the bat** or ☆**right off the bat,** right away; immediately: *used only in everyday talk.*

**bat**[2] (bat) ***n.*** a furry animal that looks like a mouse but has wings of stretched skin. Bats usually fly at night. *See the picture.* —**blind as a bat,** completely blind. Bats do not see well but find their way by sending out sound waves, which bounce off obstacles and come back as echoes.

**batch** (bach) ***n.*** **1** the amount of something made at one time [a *batch* of cookies; wool yarn from different *batches*]. **2** an amount of something to be used or worked on at one time [a *batch* of dishes to wash and dry].

**bat·ed** (bāt'id) ***adj.*** held in: *now mainly in the phrase* **with bated breath,** in a frightened or excited way, as if holding one's breath.

**bath** (bath) ***n.*** **1** a washing or dipping of something in a liquid; especially, a washing of the body with water [Give the dog a *bath.*] **2** water or other liquid for bathing, or for dipping or soaking anything [The *bath* is too hot. The hot metal was dipped in an oil *bath.*] **3** a bathtub. **4** a bathroom. **5** a building where people go to take baths. —*pl.* **baths** (ba*th*z)

**bathe** (bā*th*) ***v.*** **1** to take a bath or give a bath to; wash. **2** to put into or cover with a liquid; wet or soak [to *bathe* a wound in alcohol]. **3** to go swimming [to *bathe* in the sea]. **4** to cover or fill with a liquid or something spoken of as if it were a liquid [Sweat *bathed* our brows. The trees were *bathed* in moonlight.] —**bathed, bath'ing** —**bath'er** ***n.***

**bath·house** (bath'hous) ***n.*** ☆a building where people change clothes before swimming.

**bathing cap** a tightfitting cap of rubber or plastic for keeping the hair dry while bathing or swimming.

**bathing suit** a garment worn for swimming.

**bath·mat** (bath'mat) ***n.*** a mat used in a bathtub or next to a bathtub, as to keep a person from slipping.

☆**bath·robe** (bath'rōb) ***n.*** a long, loose garment worn to and from the bath or while relaxing.

**bath·room** (bath'rōōm) ***n.*** a room with a bathtub, toilet, washstand, etc.

☆**bath·tub** (bath'tub) ***n.*** a large tub in which a person takes a bath. Nowadays it is usually fastened to water pipes in a bathroom.

**ba·tiste** (ba tēst') ***n.*** a light, thin linen or cotton cloth, used for shirts, dresses, etc.

**ba·ton** (bə tän') ***n.*** **1** a slender stick used by a conductor in directing an orchestra. **2** a short staff that is the sign of authority of an officer or official [a marshal's *baton*]. ☆**3** a metal rod twirled in a showy way by a drum major or drum majorette.

**Ba·ton Rouge** (bat''n rōōzh') the capital of Louisiana, on the Mississippi River.

**bat·tal·ion** (bə tal'yən) ***n.*** **1** a large group of soldiers, especially the basic unit of a division, made up of several companies or batteries. **2** any large group joined together in doing something [A *battalion* of ants invaded our summer cottage.]

**bat·ten** (bat''n) ***n.*** **1** a strip of wood put over a seam between boards. **2** a strip used to fasten canvas over a ship's hatches, as in a storm. ◆***v.*** to fasten with battens [The sailors *battened* down the hatches.]

**bat·ter**[1] (bat'ər) ***v.*** **1** to beat with blow after blow; pound noisily [The waves *battered* the rocks on the shore.] **2** to break to pieces by pounding [The firemen *battered* down the door.] **3** to damage or wear out by rough use [The furniture was *battered.*] ◆***n.*** a thin, flowing mixture of flour, milk, eggs, etc. beaten together for making such things as cakes, waffles, and cookies.

**bat·ter**[2] (bat'ər) ***n.*** the player whose turn it is to bat in baseball or cricket.

| | | | | | | | |
|---|---|---|---|---|---|---|---|
| **a** | fat | **ir** | here | **ou** | out | **zh** | leisure |
| **ā** | ape | **ī** | bite, fire | **u** | up | **ng** | ring |
| **ä** | car, lot | **ō** | go | **ur** | fur | | a *in* ago |
| **e** | ten | **ô** | law, horn | **ch** | chin | | e *in* agent |
| **er** | care | **oi** | oil | **sh** | she | **ə** = | i *in* unity |
| **ē** | even | **oo** | look | **th** | thin | | o *in* collect |
| **i** | hit | **ōō** | tool | ***th*** | then | | u *in* focus |

**bat·ter·ing ram** (bat′ər iŋ ram′) a heavy, wooden beam, used for battering down gates, doors, and walls. As used in ancient warfare, it sometimes had an iron ram's head at one end. *See the picture.*

**bat·ter·y** (bat′ər ē) ***n.*** **1** a set of things connected or used together [A *battery* of microphones surrounded the mayor.] **2** an electric cell or a group of connected cells that furnishes an electric current [*Batteries* are used in automobiles and flashlights.] **3** a beating: *see* **assault.** **4** a number of heavy guns, or cannons, used together in warfare. **5** the group of soldiers manning these. ☆**6** in baseball, the pitcher and catcher as a unit. —*pl.* **bat′ter·ies**

**bat·ting** (bat′iŋ) ***n.*** **1** the act of a person who bats in baseball or cricket. ☆**2** a sheet or wad of cotton or wool fiber used in bandages, quilts, etc.

**bat·tle** (bat′'l) ***n.*** **1** a particular fight between armed forces during a war [The naval *battle* lasted two days.] **2** armed fighting generally; warfare [He limps from a wound received in *battle.*] **3** any fight or struggle; conflict [a *battle* of ideas]. ◆***v.*** to fight or struggle [The little ship *battled* against the storm.] —**bat′tled, bat′tling** —**give battle** or **do battle,** to take part in a battle; fight. —**bat′tler *n.***

**bat·tle-ax** or **bat·tle-axe** (bat′'l aks) ***n.*** a heavy ax used in the past as a weapon of war.

**battle cry** a cry or slogan used to encourage those in a battle or struggle.

62 **bat·tle·dore** (bat′'l dôr) ***n.*** the racket used to hit the shuttlecock in a game (called **battledore and shuttlecock**) like badminton.

**bat·tle·field** (bat′'l fēld) ***n.*** the place where a battle is fought or was fought.

**bat·tle·ground** (bat′'l ground) ***n.*** *same as* **battlefield.**

**bat·tle·ment** (bat′'l mənt) ***n.*** **1** a low wall on a tower, with open spaces to shoot through. *See the picture.* **2** decoration like this on any building.

☆**bat·tle·ship** (bat′'l ship) ***n.*** a large warship with big guns and very heavy armor.

**bau·ble** (bô′b'l) ***n.*** a bright, showy thing that has little value; trinket.

**baux·ite** (bôk′sīt *or* bō′zīt) ***n.*** the claylike ore from which aluminum is gotten.

**Ba·var·i·a** (bə ver′ē ə) a state in southern Germany. —**Ba·var′i·an *adj., n.***

**bawd·y** (bô′dē) ***adj.*** not decent or proper; vulgar; obscene. —**bawd′i·er, bawd′i·est**

**bawl** (bôl) ***v.*** **1** to call out in a loud, rough voice; bellow ["Forward march!" *bawled* the sergeant.] **2** to weep and wail loudly, as a child does. —**bawl out,** to scold angrily: *a slang phrase.*

**bay**[1] (bā) ***n.*** a part of a sea or lake that cuts into a coastline to form a hollow curve.

**bay**[2] (bā) ***n.*** **1** a part of a room or building that is partly set off from the rest of the building, as by pillars or screens [Tools and lumber are kept in different *bays* in the warehouse.] **2** a part of a room built out from the wall line, forming an alcove inside: *see also* **bay window.**

**bay**[3] (bā) ***v.*** to bark or howl with long, deep sounds [The hound *bayed* at the moon.] ◆***n.*** **1** the sound of baying. **2** the condition of a hunted animal that has been cornered and is forced to turn and fight [The deer was brought to *bay* at the end of the canyon.] **3** the condition of being held off by a cornered animal [The deer kept the hunters at *bay* with its antlers.]

**bay**[4] (bā) ***n.*** an evergreen tree with tough, shiny leaves; laurel tree. The sweet-smelling leaf (**bay leaf**) is dried and used for flavor in cooking.

**bay**[5] (bā) ***n.*** **1** a reddish-brown color. **2** a horse, etc. of this color. ◆***adj.*** having this color.

**bay·ber·ry** (bā′ber′ē) ***n.*** ☆**1** a shrub that bears gray berries with a waxy coating that is used in making some candles. ☆**2** any of these berries. —*pl.* **bay′ber′ries**

**bay·o·net** (bā′ə nit) ***n.*** a blade like a dagger that can be put on the front end of a rifle. ◆***v.*** to stab or kill with a bayonet. —**bay′o·net·ed** or **bay′o·net·ted, bay′o·net·ing** or **bay′o·net·ting**

☆**bay·ou** (bī′o͞o) ***n.*** in the southern United States, a slow-moving, marshy body of water, often one that joins a river or lake with a gulf.

**bay window** a window or set of windows in a bay that is built out from the wall of a building. *See the picture.*

**ba·zaar** (bə zär′) ***n.*** **1** a sale of many kinds of articles, usually to raise money for a club, church, or charity. **2** in Oriental countries, a market or a street where there are many shops.

☆**ba·zoo·ka** (bə zo͞ok′ə) ***n.*** a rocket gun that can be carried, first used in World War II.

> In the 1930's, a radio comedian named Bob Burns used to play a comic horn which he had made out of pieces of gas pipe and which he called a **bazooka**. The rocket gun, which looks a little like that horn, was named after it.

**bb** or **b.b.** base on balls (in baseball).

☆**BB** (bē′bē) ***n.*** a tiny metal ball to be shot from an air rifle (**BB gun**). —*pl.* **BB's**

**BBC** British Broadcasting Corporation.

**bbl.** *abbreviation for* **barrel.** —*pl.* **bbls.**

**B.C.** **1** before Christ; before the year in which Jesus Christ was believed to have been born [Julius Caesar died in 44 *B.C.*] **2** *abbreviation for* **British Columbia.**

**be** (bē) ***v.*** *Be* is used to join a subject with a word or words that tell something about it. It is also used to tell that something exists or takes place, and as a helping verb with other verb forms. **1** *Be* may join a subject with a noun, adjective, or pronoun [Ed and Lois *are* students. Mary *is* tall. Who *is* he?] **2** *Be* may mean "to live," "to happen or take place," or "to stay or continue" [Lincoln *is* no more. The wedding will *be* next Saturday. I will *be* here until Monday.] **3** *Be* may be used as a helping verb with a past participle, a present participle, or an infinitive [Bill *is* gone. Jane *is* going. Leon *is* to go later.] —**was** or **were, been, be′ing**

> In the present tense *be* has these forms: I *am;* he, she, or it *is;* we, you, or they *are.*

**be-** *a prefix meaning:* **1** around [To *beset* is to set around, or surround.] **2** completely [To *besmear* is to smear completely.] **3** away [To *betake* oneself is to take oneself away.] **4** about [To *bemoan* someone is to moan about someone.] **5** to make [To *becalm* is to make calm.] **6** to furnish or cover with [To *begrime* is to cover with grime.]

**Be** *the symbol for the chemical element* beryllium.

**beach** (bēch) ***n.*** a smooth, sloping stretch of sand and pebbles at the edge of a sea or lake. ◆***v.*** to run aground onto a beach [to *beach* a boat].

**beach·head** (bēch′hed) ***n.*** an area controlled by troops that have invaded an enemy shore.

**bea·con** (bēk′′n) ***n.*** **1** a light for warning or guarding, as a bonfire set burning on a hill as a signal. **2** a tower which sends out beams of light or radio waves to guide ships or airplanes at night and in stormy or foggy weather.

**bead** (bēd) ***n.*** **1** a small, usually round piece of glass, metal, etc. with a small hole in it so that it can be put on a string [She wore a string of *beads* around her neck.] **2** a drop or bubble [He has *beads* of sweat on his face.] ◆***v.*** to decorate or cover with beads [a *beaded* handbag]. —☆**draw a bead on**, to take careful aim at.

**Bead** comes from an Old English word meaning "to pray or ask." A string of beads, called a rosary, is used by Roman Catholics to keep count while saying prayers.

**bead·ing** (bēd′iŋ) ***n.*** **1** a trimming or design made of beads. **2** a molding or edge made to look like a row of beads.

**bea·dle** (bē′d′l) ***n.*** in earlier times, a church officer whose duty was to keep order in church.

**bead·y** (bē′dē) ***adj.*** small, round, and sparkling [the *beady* eyes of a snake].

**bea·gle** (bē′g′l) ***n.*** a small hunting dog with a smooth coat, short legs, and drooping ears.

**beak** (bēk) ***n.*** **1** a bird's bill, especially the sharp, hooked bill of the eagle, hawk, owl, etc. **2** a part or thing that is like a beak.

**beak·er** (bēk′ər) ***n.*** **1** a large cup or goblet. **2** a wide glass with a lip for pouring, used by chemists and druggists. *See the picture.*

**beam** (bēm) ***n.*** **1** a long, thick piece of wood or metal, used in buildings and ships as horizontal supports for roofs, floors, and decks. **2** the distance from one side of a ship to the other at its widest place. **3** the crossbar of a balance, with a scale hanging from each end. **4** a ray or stream of light. **5** a bright, joyful look or smile. **6** a stream of radio or radar signals sent out to guide airplanes or ships in their course. ◆***v.*** **1** to shine brightly [A light *beamed* from the window.] **2** to show one's pleasure with a bright look or smile. **3** to aim a radio signal, radio program, etc. [to *beam* the program to France]. —**on the beam**, **1** following the guiding beam, as an airplane. ☆**2** doing things exactly right: *used only in everyday talk.*

**bean** (bēn) ***n.*** **1** the smooth, hard seed taken from the pods of certain plants for use as food. Kidney beans and lima beans are seeds of this kind. **2** a pod with such seeds. String beans are cooked and eaten as a green vegetable, pod and all. **3** any plant that bears beans. **4** any seed or fruit that looks like a bean [coffee *bean*].

☆**bean·bag** (bēn′bag) ***n.*** a small cloth bag filled with dried beans and used in certain games.

**bean·stalk** (bēn′stôk) ***n.*** the main stem of a bean plant.

**bear**[1] (ber) ***v.*** **1** to take from one place to another; carry [The guests arrived *bearing* gifts.] **2** to have or show [She *bears* a resemblance to you. The letter *bore* his signature.] **3** to hold up [The walls *bear* the weight of the roof.] **4** to give birth to [She has *borne* three children.] **5** to bring into being; produce [Our pear tree *bore* no fruit.] **6** to hold or behave oneself in a certain way [She *bears* herself with dignity.] **7** to be able to stand something painful or annoying; put up with; endure [I can't *bear* this heat.] **8** to take care of; pay for [She *bore* all the expenses.] **9** to keep hold of [I can *bear* a grudge for a long time.] **10** to carry or move along [The current *bore* the boat toward the falls.] **11** to call for; need [This situation will *bear* watching.] —*The past tense is* **bore**, *the past participle is* **borne** (see also **born**), *the present participle is* **bear′ing**. —**bear down**, **1** to press or push down. **2** to try hard. —**bear on**, to have to do with; apply to [Her story *bears on* the crime.] —**bear out**, to show to be true; prove. —**bear up**, to hold up, as under a strain; keep one's spirits up. —**bear with**, to put up with; endure [*Bear with* me while I explain.] —**bear′a·ble** ***adj.*** —**bear′er** ***n.***

battlement

battering ram

beaker

bay window



**bear**[2] (ber) ***n.*** **1** a large, heavy animal with shaggy fur and a very short tail. Common kinds of bear are the brown bear, grizzly bear, and polar bear. **2** a person who is clumsy, rude, and rough. —**bear′ish** ***adj.***

**beard** (bird) ***n.*** **1** the hair growing on the lower part of a man's face; whiskers. **2** any growth like a beard, as the hair on a goat's chin or the stiff fibers on a spike of wheat. ◆***v.*** to come face to face with in a brave way. —**beard′ed** ***adj.***

**bear·er** (ber′ər) ***n.*** **1** a person or thing that bears or carries something [a *bearer* of good news]. **2** the person who presents a check, note, or money order for payment.

| | | | |
|---|---|---|---|
| **a** fat | **ir** here | **ou** out | **zh** leisure |
| **ā** ape | **ī** bite, fire | **u** up | **ŋ** ring |
| **ä** car, lot | **ō** go | **ʉr** fur | a *in* ago |
| **e** ten | **ô** law, horn | **ch** chin | e *in* agent |
| **er** care | **oi** oil | **sh** she | **ə** = i *in* unity |
| **ē** even | **oo** look | **th** thin | o *in* collect |
| **i** hit | **ōō** tool | ***th*** then | u *in* focus |

b

beef cuts

beaver

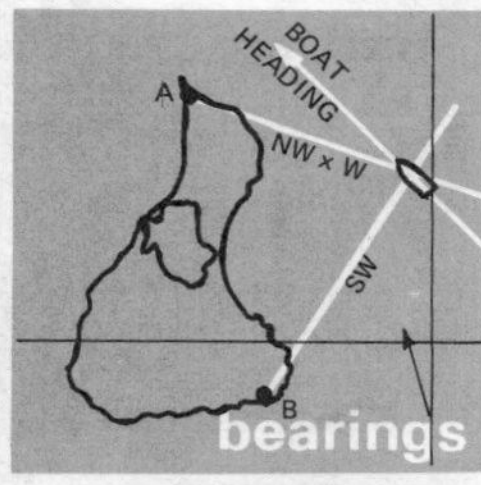

bearings

beetling cliff

**bear·ing** (ber′iŋ) ***n.*** **1** the way one stands or walks; carriage [the upright *bearing* of a soldier]. **2** the way one behaves; manner [a kindly *bearing*]. **3** the fact of having something to do with; connection [The price of feed has a direct *bearing* on the cost of beef.] **4 bear·ings,** *pl.* direction or position in relation to something else [The ship lost her *bearings* in the fog.] *See the picture.* **5** a part of a machine on which another part turns or slides so that there is little friction: *see* **ball bearing.**



**beast** (bēst) ***n.*** **1** any large, four-footed animal [A horse is a *beast* of burden (used for carrying things). A lion is a *beast* of prey (that kills other animals for food).] *See* SYNONYMS *at* **animal. 2** a cruel or stupid person.

**beast·ly** (bēst′lē) ***adj.*** **1** like a beast; cruel, stupid, etc. **2** not to one's liking; unpleasant; disagreeable: *used only in everyday talk* [*beastly* weather]. —**beast′li·er, beast′li·est**

**beat** (bēt) ***v.*** **1** to hit or strike again and again; pound [Stop *beating* that drum. Rain was *beating* on the roof.] **2** to punish by hitting or whipping [We don't approve of *beating* children.] **3** to mix by stirring strongly with a fork, spoon, or beater [*Beat* the whites of two eggs.] **4** to move up and down; flap [The bird *beat* its wings against the window.] **5** to make by pounding, tramping, etc. [We *beat* a path through the tall grass.] **6** to force or push [They *beat* their way through the crowd.] **7** to move or sound in an even, regular way; throb [He could feel his heart *beat*.] **8** to make a sound when struck [We heard war drums *beating*.] **9** to mark time in music, as by tapping. **10** to win over; defeat [Our team *beat* the West High team.] **11** to confuse or puzzle: *used only in everyday talk* [It *beats* me how they get so much done.] —**beat, beat′en, beat′ing** ◆***n.*** **1** a beating or throbbing, as of the heart. **2** a blow, stroke, etc. made again and again [the *beat* of the hail on the window]. **3** a route followed in one's work [a reporter's regular *beat*]. **4** the unit of rhythm or accent in music [Waltz time has three *beats* in each measure.] ◆***adj.*** tired out; exhausted: *slang in this meaning.* —**beat back** or **beat off,** to drive or force back.

SYNONYMS: To **beat** something is to hit it again and again with the hands, feet, or something held in the hand [The child *beat* on the pan with a spoon.] To **pound** is to hit harder than in beating, or to hit with something heavier [She *pounded* the nails in with a hammer.]

**beat·en** (bēt′'n) *past participle of* **beat.** ◆***adj.*** **1** that has been hit with many blows [He cringed like a *beaten* dog.] **2** made flat by being much walked on [a *beaten* path through the fields]. **3** shaped or made thin by hammering [*beaten* gold]. **4** that has lost; defeated.

**beat·er** (bēt′ər) ***n.*** a thing that is used for beating [an egg *beater*].

**be·a·tif·ic** (bē′ə tif′ik) ***adj.*** full of happiness or joy [a *beatific* smile].

**be·at·i·fy** (bē at′ə fī) ***v.*** **1** to make blessed or full of happiness. **2** in the Roman Catholic Church, to say that a certain dead person is among the blessed in heaven. —**be·at′i·fied, be·at′i·fy·ing —be·at·i·fi·ca·tion** (bē at′ə fi kā′shən) ***n.***

**be·at·i·tude** (bē at′ə to͞od *or* bē at′ə tyo͞od) ***n.*** complete happiness; bliss. —**the Beatitudes,** the part of the Sermon on the Mount, in the book of Matthew, which begins "Blessed are the poor in spirit."

☆**beat-up** (bēt′up′) ***adj.*** in a worn-out condition; broken down; shabby: *a slang word* [a *beat-up* automobile].

**beau** (bō) ***n.*** a man who is courting a woman; sweetheart. —*pl.* **beaus** or **beaux** (bōz)

**Beau·mont** (bō′mänt) a city in southeastern Texas.

**beau·te·ous** (byo͞ot′ē əs) ***adj.*** *same as* **beautiful.**

**beau·ti·ful** (byo͞ot′ə fəl) ***adj.*** very pleasant to look at or hear; giving delight to the mind [a *beautiful* face]. —**beau′ti·ful·ly *adv.***

**beau·ti·fy** (byo͞ot′ə fī) ***v.*** to make beautiful or more beautiful. —**beau′ti·fied, beau′ti·fy·ing —beau·ti·fi·ca·tion** (byo͞ot′ə fi kā′shən) ***n.***

**beau·ty** (byo͞ot′ē) ***n.*** **1** that quality in a person or thing which makes it pleasant for one to look at, hear, or think about [the *beauty* of a sunset]. **2** a beautiful thing. **3** a beautiful woman. —*pl.* **beau′ties**

☆**beauty shop** or **beauty salon** a place where women can go to have their hair cut, styled, or tinted, their nails manicured, etc.

**bea·ver**[1] (bē′vər) ***n.*** **1** an animal that has soft, brown fur and a flat, broad tail, and can live on land and in water. It cuts down trees with its teeth and builds dams across rivers. *See the picture.* **2** the fur of a beaver. ☆**3** a person who works hard: *used only in everyday talk.*

**bea·ver**[2] (bē′vər) ***n.*** a part of a helmet used in the Middle Ages, that could be moved down to protect the mouth and chin.

**be·calmed** (bi kämd′) ***adj.*** not able to move because there is no wind [The sailboat was *becalmed* in the still lagoon.]

**be·came** (bi kām′) *past tense of* **become.**

**be·cause** (bi kôz′) ***conj.*** for the reason that; since [I'm late *because* I overslept.] —**because of,** on account of; as a result of [He was absent from school *because of* illness.]

**beck** (bek) ***n.*** a movement of the hand or head that

tells someone to come closer. —**at the beck and call of,** obeying every order of.

**Beck·et** (bek′ət), Saint **Thomas à** 1118?–1170; English churchman; archbishop of Canterbury.

**beck·on** (bek′′n) ***v.*** to call closer by a motion of the head or hand.

**be·come** (bi kum′) ***v.*** **1** to come to be [I *became* ill last week. Her baby brother had *become* a young man.] **2** to be right or suitable for; make attractive [That hat *becomes* you.] —**be·came′, be·come′, be·com′ing** —**become of,** to happen to [What *became of* that movie star?]

**be·com·ing** (bi kum′iŋ) ***adj.*** right or suitable; attractive [a *becoming* gown].

**bed** (bed) ***n.*** **1** a piece of furniture for sleeping or resting on. **2** any place or thing used for sleeping or resting [A park bench was the hobo's *bed.*] **3** sleep [It's time for *bed.*] **4** a piece of ground where plants are grown [a flower *bed*]. **5** the ground at the bottom of a river, lake, etc. **6** any flat base or foundation [They placed the printing press on a *bed* of concrete.] **7** a layer of something in the ground [a *bed* of coal]. ◆***v.*** to go or put to sleep; prepare a place for sleeping [We'll *bed* down here in the woods.] —**bed′ded, bed′ding** —**bed and board,** a place to sleep and meals.

**bed·bug** (bed′bug) ***n.*** a small, flat, biting insect that is sometimes found in beds.

**bed·cham·ber** (bed′chām′bər) ***n.*** *same as* **bedroom.**

**bed·clothes** (bed′klōz *or* bed′klōthz) ***n.pl.*** sheets, pillows, blankets, etc. used on a bed.

**bed·ding** (bed′iŋ) ***n.*** **1** mattresses and bedclothes. **2** straw, leaves, etc. for animals to sleep on.

**be·deck** (bi dek′) ***v.*** to decorate or adorn.

**bed·fel·low** (bed′fel′ō) ***n.*** a person who shares one's bed.

**bed·lam** (bed′ləm) ***n.*** a place or condition of noise and confusion [The classroom became a *bedlam* when a bird flew in the window.]

> "Bedlam" is the British pronunciation of *Bethlehem,* the short name of a place in London (*St. Mary of Bethlehem*) where the mentally ill were once kept locked up, and where there was much noise and confusion.

**Bed·ou·in** (bed′oo win) ***n.*** an Arab who belongs to any of the tribes that wander in the deserts of Arabia, Syria, or North Africa. —*pl.* **Bed′ou·ins** or **Bed′ou·in**

**be·drag·gled** (bi drag′′ld) ***adj.*** wet and dirty, as with mud; untidy; messy.

**bed·rid·den** (bed′rid′′n) ***adj.*** having to stay in bed for a long time because of sickness.

☆**bed·roll** (bed′rōl) ***n.*** a roll of bedding carried by campers for sleeping outdoors.

**bed·room** (bed′rōōm) ***n.*** a room with a bed, for sleeping in.

**bed·side** (bed′sīd) ***n.*** the space beside a bed [A nurse was at her *bedside.*]

☆**bed·spread** (bed′spred) ***n.*** a cover spread over a bed when it is not being slept in.

☆**bed·spring** (bed′spriŋ) ***n.*** a framework of springs in a bedstead on which a mattress lies.

**bed·stead** (bed′sted) ***n.*** the frame of a bed, holding the bedspring and mattress.

**bed·time** (bed′tīm) ***n.*** the time when one usually goes to bed.

**bee** (bē) ***n.*** **1** a hairy insect that has four wings and feeds on the nectar of flowers. Some bees live together in colonies or hives and make honey and wax. **2** a meeting of people for working at something together [a sewing *bee*].

**beech** (bēch) ***n.*** **1** a tree with smooth bark, dark-green leaves, and nuts that may be eaten. **2** the hard wood of this tree. —**beech′en *adj.***

**beech·nut** (bēch′nut) ***n.*** the small three-cornered nut of the beech tree.

**beef** (bēf) ***n.*** **1** meat from a steer, cow, or bull. *See the picture.* **2** a full-grown steer, cow, or bull, raised for its meat. —*pl.* **beeves** or **beefs**

**beef·steak** (bēf′stāk) ***n.*** a thick slice of beef to be broiled or fried.

**beef·y** (bēf′ē) ***adj.*** fleshy and solid; having much muscle [a *beefy* football player]. —**beef′i·er, beef′i·est**

**bee·hive** (bē′hīv) ***n.*** **1** a box or other shelter for a colony of bees, in which they make and store honey. **2** any place where there is much activity.

☆**bee·line** (bē′līn) ***n.*** a straight line from one place to another; direct route.

**been** (bin) *past participle of* **be.**

**beer** (bir) ***n.*** **1** an alcoholic drink made of malt and water, and flavored with hops. **2** a drink that is not alcoholic, flavored with certain roots and plants [root *beer;* ginger *beer*].

**bees·wax** (bēz′waks) ***n.*** the wax that some bees make for building their honeycomb. It is used in making candles and polishes.



**beet** (bēt) ***n.*** a plant with a thick, fleshy root. One kind has a round, red root, which is eaten as a cooked vegetable. Another kind has a long white root from which sugar is made.

**Bee·tho·ven** (bā′tō vən), **Lud·wig van** (lōōt′vik vän) 1770–1827; German composer.

**bee·tle** (bēt′′l) ***n.*** an insect that has two pairs of wings. The hard front wings cover the thin hind wings when the hind wings are folded.

**bee·tling** (bēt′liŋ) ***adj.*** sticking out; overhanging [*beetling* eyebrows]. *See the picture.*

**beeves** (bēvz) ***n.*** *a plural of* **beef.**

**be·fall** (bi fôl′) ***v.*** to happen to [What *befell* them?] —**be·fell′, be·fall·en** (bi fôl′ən), **be·fall′ing**

**be·fit** (bi fit′) ***v.*** to be right or proper for. —**be·fit′ted, be·fit′ting**

**be·fog** (bi fôg′ *or* bi fäg′) ***v.*** **1** to cover with fog; make foggy. **2** to confuse; muddle [My mind was *befogged* by lack of sleep.] —**be·fogged′, be·fog′ging**

**be·fore** (bi fôr′) ***prep.*** **1** ahead of [The valley stretched *before* us.] **2** in front of [We paused *before* the door.] **3** earlier than; previous to [Will you finish *before* noon?] **4** rather than; instead of [I'd choose death *before* dishonor.] ◆***adv.*** **1** in the past; earlier

| | | | | | | | |
|---|---|---|---|---|---|---|---|
| **a** | fat | **ir** | here | **ou** | out | **zh** | leisure |
| **ā** | ape | **ī** | bite, fire | **u** | up | **ŋ** | ring |
| **ä** | car, lot | **ō** | go | **ʉr** | fur | | a *in* ago |
| **e** | ten | **ô** | law, horn | **ch** | chin | | e *in* agent |
| **er** | care | **oi** | oil | **sh** | she | **ə =** | i *in* unity |
| **ē** | even | **oo** | look | **th** | thin | | o *in* collect |
| **i** | hit | **ōō** | tool | ***th*** | then | | u *in* focus |

[I've heard that song *before.*] **2** at an earlier time; sooner [Come to see me at ten, not *before.*] **3** ahead; in front [They marched off, the banners going *before.*] ◆***conj.*** **1** earlier than the time that [Think *before* you speak.] **2** sooner than; rather than [I'd die *before* I'd tell.]

**be·fore·hand** (bi fôr′hand′) ***adv., adj.*** ahead of time [Let's arrange the seating *beforehand.*]

**be·friend** (bi frend′) ***v.*** to act as a friend to.

**be·fud·dle** (bi fud′'l) ***v.*** to confuse; make dull or stupid [The wine *befuddled* me.] —**be·fud′dled, be·fud′dling**

**beg** (beg) ***v.*** **1** to ask for as charity or as a gift [He *begged* a dollar from me.] **2** to ask as a favor; ask seriously or humbly [She *begged* us not to tell the secret.] **3** to ask for in a polite way [I *beg* your pardon.] —**begged, beg′ging** —**beg off,** to ask to be excused from doing something. —**go begging,** to be unwanted [The tasteless food *went begging.*]

**be·gan** (bi gan′) *past tense of* **begin.**

**be·get** (bi get′) ***v.*** **1** to be the father of [God told Jacob he would *beget* many children.] **2** to cause to be; produce [Poverty *begets* crime.] —**be·got′** or in earlier times **be·gat** (bi gat′), **be·got′ten** or **be·got′, be·get′ting**

**beg·gar** (beg′ər) ***n.*** **1** a person who begs, especially one who lives by begging. **2** a person who is very poor. ◆***v.*** **1** to make a beggar of; make poor. **2** to make seem poor or useless [The building's beauty *beggars* description.]



**be·gin** (bi gin′) ***v.*** to start being, doing, acting, etc.; get under way [Work *begins* at 8:00 A.M. My cold *began* with a sore throat.] —**be·gan′, be·gun′, be·gin′ning**

**be·gin·ner** (bi gin′ər) ***n.*** a person who is just beginning to learn something; novice.

**be·gin·ning** (bi gin′iŋ) ***n.*** a start or starting; first part or first action [We came in just after the *beginning* of the movie. Going to the dance together was the *beginning* of our friendship.]

**be·gone** (bi gôn′) ***interj.*** go away! get out!

**be·go·nia** (bi gōn′yə) ***n.*** a plant with showy red, white, or pink flowers and large leaves. *See the picture.*

**be·got** (bi gät′) *the past tense and a past participle of* **beget.**

**be·got·ten** (bi gät′'n) *a past participle of* **beget.**

begonia

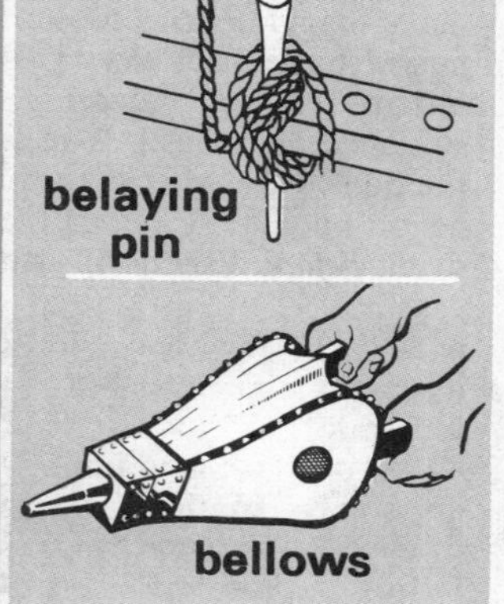
belaying pin

bellows

**be·grime** (bi grīm′) ***v.*** to cover with grime or dirt; make dirty; soil. —**be·grimed′, be·grim′ing**

**be·grudge** (bi gruj′) ***v.*** **1** to feel envy or bitterness because of something another has or enjoys [You shouldn't *begrudge* him his good luck.] **2** to give without wanting to; complain while giving [He *begrudges* me every cent of my allowance.] —**begrudged′, be·grudg′ing**

**be·guile** (bi gīl′) ***v.*** **1** to cheat or trick into doing or believing something wrong [Delilah *beguiled* Samson into telling her the secret of his strength.] **2** to pass time pleasantly [She *beguiled* her days with reading.] **3** to please greatly; charm [Her singing *beguiled* us.] —**be·guiled′, be·guil′ing**

**be·gun** (bi gun′) *past participle of* **begin.**

**be·half** (bi haf′) ***n.*** support or interest [Many of his friends spoke in his *behalf.*] —**on behalf of, 1** in the interest of. **2** speaking or acting for; representing.

**be·have** (bi hāv′) ***v.*** **1** to act in a certain way; to conduct oneself [They *behaved* badly at the picnic.] **2** to act in a proper way; do the right things [Try to *behave* yourself in public.] —**be·haved′, be·hav′ing**

**be·hav·ior** (bi hāv′yər) ***n.*** the way a person or thing behaves, or acts; conduct or action [His *behavior* at the dance was rude. The Curies studied the *behavior* of radium.]

**be·head** (bi hed′) ***v.*** to cut off the head of.

**be·held** (bi held′) *past tense and past participle of* **behold.**

**be·he·moth** (bi hē′məth) ***n.*** in the Bible, a very large animal. Many scholars think that it was the hippopotamus.

**be·hest** (bi hest′) ***n.*** an order or command [I have come at the *behest* of the queen.]

**be·hind** (bi hīnd′) ***adv.*** **1** in or to the rear or back [The children trailed *behind.*] **2** in an earlier time or condition [My happy days lie *behind.*] **3** late or slow in action or progress [We fell *behind* in our work.] ◆***prep.*** **1** in the rear of; in back of [Sit *behind* me.] **2** lower in position than [They are two grades *behind* me in school.] **3** later than [The train was *behind* schedule.] **4** supporting; in favor of [Congress is *behind* the plan.] ◆***adj.*** that is to the rear or in back of [Pass it to the person *behind.*] ◆***n.*** the lower back part of the body; rump: *used only in everyday talk.*

**be·hold** (bi hōld′) ***v.*** to look at; see [They never *beheld* a sadder sight.] —**be·held′, be·hold′ing** ◆***interj.*** look! see!

**be·hold·en** (bi hōl′d'n) ***adj.*** obliged to feel grateful; owing thanks [I am *beholden* to you for your advice.]

**be·hoove** (bi ho͞ov′) ***v.*** to be necessary for; be the duty of [It *behooves* you to think for yourself.] —**behooved′, be·hoov′ing**

**beige** (bāzh) ***n., adj.*** the color of sand; grayish tan.

**be·ing** (bē′iŋ) *present participle of* **be.** ◆***n.*** **1** existence or life [Our club came into *being* last year.] **2** a living creature [a human *being*]. —**for the time being,** for now.

**Bei·rut** (bā ro͞ot′) the capital of Lebanon; seaport on the Mediterranean Sea.

**be·la·bor** (bi lā′bər) ***v.*** **1** to attack with words; scold. **2** to spend too much time or effort on [He *belabored* the point.]

**be·lat·ed** (bi lāt′id) ***adj.*** too late; not on time [a *belated* birthday greeting]. —**be·lat′ed·ly *adv.***

**be·lay** (bi lā′) ***v.*** to make a rope hold tight by winding it around a pin (called **belaying pin**). *See the picture.* —**be·layed′, be·lay′ing** ◆***interj.*** stop!: *a sailor's word* [*Belay* there!]

**belch** (belch) ***v.*** **1** to let gas from the stomach out through the mouth, usually with a noise. **2** to throw out with force [The volcano *belched* flame.] ◆***n.*** **1** the act of belching. **2** the thing belched.

**be·lea·guer** (bi lē′gər) ***v.*** to besiege; surround as with an attacking army.

**Bel·fast** (bel′fast) a seaport and the capital of Northern Ireland.

**bel·fry** (bel′frē) ***n.*** a tower or the part of a tower in which a bell or bells are hung. —*pl.* **bel′fries**

**Belg.** *abbreviation for* **Belgian** *or* **Belgium.**

**Bel·gian** (bel′jən) ***adj.*** of Belgium or its people. ◆***n.*** a person born or living in Belgium.

**Bel·gium** (bel′jəm) a country in western Europe, on the North Sea.

**Bel·grade** (bel′grād) the capital of Yugoslavia.

**be·lie** (bi lī′) ***v.*** **1** to give a false idea of; hide [Her smile *belies* her anger.] **2** to show to be false [His cruelty *belied* his kind words.] —**be·lied′, be·ly′ing**

**be·lief** (bə lēf′) ***n.*** **1** a believing or feeling that certain things are true or real; faith [You cannot destroy my *belief* in the honesty of most people.] **2** trust or confidence [I have *belief* in Pat's ability.] **3** anything believed or accepted as true; opinion [What are your religious *beliefs*?]

SYNONYMS: **Belief** means acceptance of something as true even though one cannot be absolutely certain that it is true [I have a firm *belief* that there is more good than evil in the world.] **Faith** means unshakable, trusting belief in something that cannot be proved, especially by reasoning [She has *faith* that she will be cured.]

**be·lieve** (bə lēv′) ***v.*** **1** to accept as true or real [Can we *believe* that story?] **2** to have religious faith [to *believe* in life after death]. **3** to have trust or confidence [I know you will win; I *believe* in you.] **4** to suppose; guess. —**be·lieved′, be·liev′ing** —**be·liev′a·ble *adj.*** —**be·liev′er *n.***

☆**be·lit·tle** (bi lit′'l) ***v.*** to make seem little or unimportant [She *belittled* his winning the prize by saying he was just lucky.] —**be·lit′tled, be·lit′tling**

**Be·lize** (bə lēz′) a British territory in Central America, on the Carribbean.

**bell** (bel) ***n.*** **1** a hollow, metal object that rings when it is struck. The common bell is shaped like an upside-down cup, with a clapper hanging inside. **2** the sound made by a bell. **3** anything shaped like a common bell [a *bell* of a trumpet]. **4** a stroke of a bell rung every half hour on shipboard to mark the periods of a watch [Eight *bells* mark the end of each four-hour watch.] ◆***v.*** **1** to put a bell on [to *bell* a cow]. **2** to flare out like a bell.

**Bell** (bel), **Alexander Graham** 1847–1922; American scientist who invented the telephone.

**bel·la·don·na** (bel′ə dän′ə) ***n.*** **1** a poisonous plant with reddish flowers and black berries. **2** a drug made from this plant.

**Belladonna** comes from an Italian phrase meaning "beautiful lady." The drug belladonna makes the pupils of the eyes larger and was used by some women years ago as a kind of cosmetic.

**belle** (bel) ***n.*** a pretty woman or girl; often, the one who is the prettiest or the most popular [the *belle* of the ball].

**bel·li·cose** (bel′ə kōs) ***adj.*** eager to fight or quarrel; warlike.

**bel·lig·er·ent** (bə lij′ər ənt) ***adj.*** **1** at war; engaged in a war. **2** showing a readiness to fight or quarrel [a *belligerent* gesture or tone]. ◆***n.*** a person or nation that is fighting or at war. —**bel·lig′er·ence** or **bel·lig′er·en·cy *n.*** —**bel·lig′er·ent·ly *adv.***

**bell·man** (bel′mən) ***n.*** ☆a person whose work in a hotel is to carry luggage and do errands: *sometimes also called* **bell·boy** (bel′boi) *or* **bell·hop** (bel′häp) —*pl.* **bell′men**

**bel·low** (bel′ō) ***v.*** **1** to roar loudly as a bull does. **2** to shout out, as in anger or pain. ◆***n.*** the sound of bellowing; roar.

**Bel·low** (bel′ō), **Saul** 1915– ; American writer of novels.

**bel·lows** (bel′ōz) ***n.*** **1** a device that blows out air when its sides are squeezed together. It is used especially to make fires burn strongly. *See the picture.* **2** anything like a bellows, as the folding part of some cameras. —*pl.* **bel′lows**

**bel·ly** (bel′ē) ***n.*** **1** the lower front part of the human body, between the chest and thighs; abdomen. **2** the underside of an animal's body. **3** the stomach. **4** the part deep inside [the *belly* of a ship]. **5** a bulging part [the *belly* of a sail]. —*pl.* **bel′lies** ◆***v.*** to swell out; bulge [The sails *bellied* out in the wind.] —**bel′lied, bel′ly·ing**

**bel·ly·ache** (bel′ē āk′) ***n.*** pain in the abdomen or bowels. ◆☆***v.*** to grumble or complain: *a slang word.* —**bel′ly·ached′, bel′ly·ach′ing**

**bel·ly·but·ton** (bel′ē but′'n) ***n.*** *another word for* **navel**: *used only in everyday talk.*

**be·long** (bi lông′) ***v.*** **1** to have its proper place [This chair *belongs* in the corner.] **2** to be part of something; be connected [That belt *belongs* to these pants.] **3** to be owned by someone [This book *belongs* to you.] **4** to be a member of something [He *belongs* to the Scouts.]

**be·long·ings** (bi lông′ingz) ***n.pl.*** those things that belong to a person; possessions.

**be·lov·ed** (bi luv′id, bi luvd′) ***adj.*** much loved [my *beloved* cousin]. ◆***n.*** a beloved person.

**be·low** (bi lō′) ***adv., adj.*** in or to a lower place; beneath [I'll take the upper bunk and you can sleep *below*.] ◆***prep.*** lower than in place, position, price, rank, etc. [the people living *below* us; a price *below* $25].

**belt** (belt) ***n.*** **1** a strip of leather, cloth, etc. worn around the waist to hold up clothing or as an ornament. **2** a strap looped around two or more wheels. When one wheel turns, it moves the strap, which turns

| | | | | | | | |
|---|---|---|---|---|---|---|---|
| a | fat | ir | here | ou | out | zh | leisure |
| ā | ape | ī | bite, fire | u | up | ng | ring |
| ä | car, lot | ō | go | ur | fur | | a *in* ago |
| e | ten | ô | law, horn | ch | chin | | e *in* agent |
| er | care | oi | oil | sh | she | ə = | i *in* unity |
| ē | even | oo | look | th | thin | | o *in* collect |
| i | hit | ōō | tool | *th* | then | | u *in* focus |

the other wheel or wheels. *See the picture.* **3** an area or zone different in some way from others [Corn is grown in the corn *belt*.] ◆*v.* **1** to put a belt on. **2** to strike hard: *used only in everyday talk.*

**be·moan** (bi mōn′) *v.* to moan or cry about; lament [to *bemoan* one's fate].

**bench** (bench) *n.* **1** a long, hard seat for several persons, with or without a back. **2** a strong table on which work with tools is done [a carpenter's *bench*]. **3** the place where judges sit in a courtroom. **4** *sometimes* **Bench,** the work or position of a judge; also, judges as a group [a member of the *Bench*]. ☆**5** a seat where sports players sit when not on the field. ◆*v.* ☆to keep from playing in a game [The coach *benched* the player for fighting.]

**bend** (bend) *v.* **1** to pull or press something hard or stiff into a curve or angle [*Bend* the branch down so we can reach the plums.] **2** to be curved in this way [The trees *bent* under the weight of the snow.] **3** to turn in a certain direction [He *bent* his steps toward home.] **4** to give in or make give in [I'll *bend* to your wishes.] **5** to stoop [*Bend* over and touch your toes.] —**bent, bend′ing** ◆*n.* **1** the act of bending. **2** a bent or curving part.

SYNONYMS: A **bend** is an angle or curve caused by a changing or putting pressure on something that is usually straight [a *bend* in the road; a *bend* in a wire]. A **curve** is a line that looks like the arc of a circle [A boomerang travels in a *curve*.]



**bend·ed** (ben′did) *adj.* that is bent [on *bended* knee].

**be·neath** (bi nēth′) *adv., adj.* in a lower place; below or just below; underneath [Look *beneath* the table. The cups are on the shelf *beneath*.] ◆*prep.* **1** lower than; below or just below; under [*beneath* sunny skies; the ground *beneath* my feet; a rank *beneath* that of colonel]. **2** not worthy of [She felt it was *beneath* her to cheat.]

**Ben·e·dic·tine** (ben′ə dik′tin *or* ben′ə dik′tēn) *adj.* having to do with the religious order founded by Saint Benedict, an Italian monk of the 6th century. ◆*n.* a Benedictine monk or nun.

**ben·e·dic·tion** (ben′ə dik′shən) *n.* **1** an asking for God's blessing, as by a minister at the end of a church service. **2** a blessing.

**ben·e·fac·tion** (ben′ə fak′shən) *n.* the act of doing good or giving help to those in need [The family's *benefactions* included a $500 gift to the clinic.]

**ben·e·fac·tor** (ben′ə fak′tər) *n.* a person who has given money or other help to someone in need.

**be·nef·i·cence** (bə nef′ə səns) *n.* **1** a being kind or doing good; charity. **2** something given or done to help others; kind act or gift. —**be·nef′i·cent** *adj.*

**ben·e·fi·cial** (ben′ə fish′əl) *adj.* being of help or use; helpful; favorable [*beneficial* advice].

**ben·e·fi·ci·ar·y** (ben′ə fish′ē er′ē *or* ben′ə fish′ər ē) *n.* **1** a person who gets benefit. **2** a person who gets money or property from a will or insurance policy. —*pl.* **ben′e·fi′ci·ar′ies**

**ben·e·fit** (ben′ə fit) *n.* **1** help or advantage; also, anything that helps [Speak louder for the *benefit* of those in the rear.] **2** *often* **benefits,** *pl.* money paid by an insurance company, the government, etc. as during old age or sickness, or for death. **3** any public event put on to raise money for a certain person, group, or cause [The show is a *benefit* for crippled children.] ◆*v.* **1** to do good for; aid; help [The new tax law *benefits* big businesses.] **2** to be helped; profit [You'll *benefit* from exercise.]

**be·nev·o·lence** (bə nev′ə ləns) *n.* a wanting to do good; kindliness; generosity [The townspeople showed their *benevolence* by giving money for a new hospital.]

**be·nev·o·lent** (bə nev′ə lənt) *adj.* doing or wanting to do good; kind; generous.

**Ben·gal** (ben gôl′ *or* beng gôl′) a region in the northeastern part of the peninsula of India. Part of the region is in the country of India and part is in Bangladesh.

**Bengal, Bay of** a part of the Indian Ocean between India and Burma.

**Ben·gha·zi** (ben gä′zē) a seaport on the coast of Libya. It is one of the two capitals of Libya.

**be·night·ed** (bi nīt′id) *adj.* being in darkness or ignorance; backward; ignorant [a poor, *benighted* people, held back by superstition].

Originally **benighted** was used to describe travelers who were overtaken by the darkness of night. Now we use the word to describe someone who is overtaken by the darkness of ignorance.

**be·nign** (bi nīn′) *adj.* **1** good-natured; kindly [a *benign* smile]. **2** doing good; helpful [The sickly child was taken to a more *benign* climate.] **3** doing little or no harm; not likely to cause death [a *benign* tumor]. —**be·nign′ly** *adv.*

**be·nig·nant** (bi nig′nənt) *adj.* **1** kindly or gracious. **2** beneficial; helpful.

**Be·nin** (be nēn′) a country in western Africa, on the Atlantic Ocean.

**ben·i·son** (ben′ə z′n) *n.* a blessing; benediction.

**Ben·ja·min** (ben′jə mən) **1** in the Bible, the youngest son of Jacob. **2** the tribe of Israel descended from him.

**bent** (bent) *past tense and past participle of* **bend.** ◆*adj.* **1** made curved or crooked; not straight [I used a *bent* pin for a fishhook.] **2** wanting very much; determined [She is *bent* on going.] ◆*n.* a natural liking or skill [a *bent* for working with numbers].

**be·numb** (bi num′) *v.* to make numb; cause to be unable to think or feel normally [The poor widow was *benumbed* by grief.]

**ben·zene** (ben′zēn) *n.* a clear liquid gotten from coal tar. It is a compound of carbon and hydrogen, used in making varnishes and dyes.

**ben·zine** (ben′zēn) *n.* a clear liquid that burns easily, gotten from petroleum. It is used in dry cleaning and as a motor fuel.

**ben·zol** (ben′zōl) *n. another word for* **benzene.**

**be·queath** (bi kwēth′ *or* bi kwēth′) *v.* **1** to leave one's money, etc. to another when one dies [He *bequeathed* his fortune to his niece.] **2** to leave behind; pass on [The artist *bequeathed* her talent to her son.]

**be·quest** (bi kwest′) *n.* a bequeathing or something bequeathed [I got a *bequest* of $5,000 from my aunt.]

**be·rate** (bi rāt′) *v.* to scold in a harsh way. —**be·rat′ed, be·rat′ing**

**be·reave** (bi rēv′) *v.* to take away something or someone dear to one; leave sad and lonely [I was *bereaved* by my friend's death.] —**be·reaved′** or **be·reft′, be·reav′ing** —**be·reave′ment** *n.*

**be·reft** (bi reft′) *a past tense and past participle of* **bereave.** ✦***adj.*** left sad, lonely, or empty by having had something taken away [*Bereft* of all power, Napoleon was exiled to St. Helena.]

**be·ret** (bə rā′) ***n.*** a flat, round cap of a soft material, such as felt or wool. *See the picture.*

**berg** (bŭrg) ***n.*** *same as* **iceberg.**

**ber·i·ber·i** (ber′ē ber′ē) ***n.*** a disease in which the body grows weak and crippled. It is caused by a lack of vitamin $B_1$ in the diet.

**Ber·ing Sea** (ber′iŋ *or* bir′iŋ) the northern part of the Pacific Ocean.

**Bering Strait** the narrow waterway between Siberia and Alaska, in the Bering Sea.

**Berke·ley** (bŭr′klē) a city on the coast of central California, near Oakland.

**Ber·lin** (bər lin′) a city in eastern Germany. It is divided into an eastern district (the capital of East Germany) and a western district. *See the map.*

**berm** or **berme** (bŭrm) ***n.*** ☆a shoulder or ledge, as along the edge of a paved road.

**Ber·mu·da** (bər myōō′də) a group of British islands in the Atlantic, east of South Carolina.

**Bern** or **Berne** (bŭrn) the capital of Switzerland.

**Bern·hardt** (bŭrn′härt), **Sarah** 1844–1923; French actress: famous for her performances in tragic plays.

**ber·ry** (ber′ē) ***n.*** any small, juicy fruit with seeds and a soft pulp, as a strawberry, blackberry, or blueberry. In scientific use, many fleshy fruits having a skin are classed as berries, for example, the tomato, banana, and grape. —*pl.* **ber′ries** —**go berrying,** to look for and pick berries.

**ber·serk** (bər sŭrk′) ***adj., adv.*** in or into a mad rage or frenzy [The frightened horse went *berserk* and kicked the trainer.]

> **Berserk** comes from an Old Norse word for the bearskin worn by warriors. In Norse myths, certain warriors would go into a mad frenzy in battle.

**berth** (bŭrth) ***n.*** **1** a bed or bunk along a wall, on a ship, train, etc. **2** a place where a ship anchors or ties up to a dock. **3** a position or job [He applied for a *berth* as chief engineer.] —**give a wide berth to,** to stay a safe distance away from.

**ber·yl** (ber′əl) ***n.*** a very hard, bright mineral, often bluish-green, as the emerald.

**be·ryl·li·um** (bə ril′ē əm) ***n.*** a chemical element that is a grayish, lightweight metal. It is used in making strong alloys.

**be·seech** (bi sēch′) ***v.*** to ask in a pleading way; implore. —**be·sought′** or **be·seeched′, be·seech′ing**

**be·set** (bi set′) ***v.*** to attack from all sides; surround [The tourist was *beset* with worries.] —**be·set′, be·set′ting**

**be·side** (bi sīd′) ***prep.*** **1** by or at the side of; close to [The garage is *beside* the house.] **2** compared with [My share seems small *beside* yours.] **3** in addition; besides. —**beside oneself,** wild or upset because of anger or worry.

**be·sides** (bi sīdz′) ***adv.*** in addition; as well; furthermore [We'll have games and dancing and food *besides.*] ✦***prep.*** in addition to; as well as [Will anyone be there *besides* you?]

**be·siege** (bi sēj′) ***v.*** **1** to surround a place with soldiers and keep it under attack so as to force a surrender. **2** to crowd around or make many demands on someone [The fans *besieged* the star for autographs.] —**be·sieged′, be·sieg′ing**

**be·smear** (bi smir′) ***v.*** to smear over; smudge.

**be·smirch** (bi smŭrch′) ***v.*** to make dirty; soil [a name *besmirched* by scandal].

**be·som** (bē′zəm) ***n.*** a broom made of a bunch of twigs tied to a handle. *See the picture.*

**be·sot·ted** (bi sät′id) ***adj.*** dull or dazed, as from drinking liquor.

**be·sought** (bi sôt′) *a past tense and past participle of* **beseech.**

**be·span·gle** (bi spaŋ′g′l) ***v.*** to decorate with spangles. —**be·span′gled, be·span′gling**

**be·spat·ter** (bi spat′ər) ***v.*** to spatter over, as with spots of mud.

**be·speak** (bi spēk′) ***v.*** **1** to make plain or clear; be a sign of; show [Their large mansion *bespeaks* their wealth.] **2** to order ahead of time; reserve [Are these seats *bespoken?*] —**be·spoke** (bi spōk′), **be·spo·ken** (bi spō′k′n) or **be·spoke′, be·speak′ing**

**Bes·se·mer process** (bes′ə mər) a method of making steel by forcing air through melted iron.

**best** (best) ***adj.*** **1** above all others in worth or ability; most excellent, most fit, most desirable, etc. [Joan is the *best* player on the team. When is the *best* time to plant tulips?] **2** being the most; almost all [Gym class takes the *best* part of an hour.] —*Best* is the superlative of **good.** ✦***adv.*** **1** in a way that is best or most excellent, fit, etc. [Which choir sang *best?*] **2** more than any other; most [Of all your books, I like that one *best.*] —*Best* is the superlative of **well²**. ✦***n.*** **1** a person or thing that is most excellent, most fit, etc. [That doctor is among the *best* in the profession.



| | | | | | | | |
|---|---|---|---|---|---|---|---|
| **a** | fat | **ir** | here | **ou** | out | **zh** | leisure |
| **ā** | ape | **ī** | bite, fire | **u** | up | **ŋ** | ring |
| **ä** | car, lot | **ō** | go | **ur** | fur | | a *in* ago |
| **e** | ten | **ô** | law, horn | **ch** | chin | | e *in* agent |
| **er** | care | **oi** | oil | **sh** | she | **ə =** | i *in* unity |
| **ē** | even | **oo** | look | **th** | thin | | o *in* collect |
| **i** | hit | **ōō** | tool | ***th*** | then | | u *in* focus |

bib

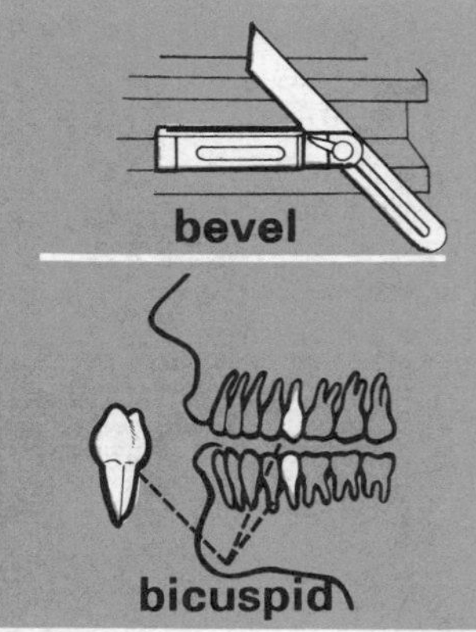
bevel

bicuspid

When I buy shoes, I buy the *best*.] **2** the most that can be done; utmost [We did our *best* to win.] ◆***v.*** to win out over; defeat [We *bested* them at tennis.] —**all for the best,** turning out to be good or fortunate after all. —**at best,** as the most that can be expected; at most. —**get the best of,** to defeat. —**had best,** ought to; should. —**make the best of,** to do as well as one can with.

**bes·tial** (bes′chəl) ***adj.*** like a beast; brutal or cruel. —**bes·ti·al·i·ty** (bes′chē al′ə tē) ***n.***

**be·stir** (bi stur′) ***v.*** to stir up; make busy [He *bestirred* himself and made lunch.] —**be·stirred′, be·stir′ring**



☆**best man** the man who stands with the bridegroom at a wedding and hands him the ring.

**be·stow** (bi stō′) ***v.*** to give as a gift or as charity [Andrew Carnegie *bestowed* millions of dollars on libraries.] —**be·stow′al** ***n.***

**be·strew** (bi stro͞o′) ***v.*** to scatter or be scattered over [a lawn *bestrewed* with leaves]. —**be·strewed′, be·strewed′** or **be·strewn** (bi stro͞on′), **be·strew′ing**

**be·stride** (bi strīd′) ***v.*** to sit on something, or stand over something, with one leg on each side [to *bestride* a horse or ditch]. —**be·strode** (bi strōd′), **be·strid·den** (bi strid″n), **be·strid′ing**

☆**best seller** a book, phonograph record, etc. that is being sold in larger amounts than most others.

**bet** (bet) ***n.*** **1** an agreement between two persons that the one who is proved wrong about something must pay or do something [Let's make a *bet* about who will finish first.] **2** the thing to be paid or done [The *bet* will be one candy bar.] ☆**3** someone or something likely to bring about what is wanted [Gerry is the best *bet* for this job.] ◆***v.*** **1** to risk something in a bet [I'll *bet* one candy bar that I finish first.] **2** to make a bet or be willing to make a bet [I *bet* we'll be late.] —**bet** or **bet′ted, bet′ting** —☆**you bet!** certainly! *used in everyday talk.*

**be·ta** (bāt′ə) ***n.*** the second letter of the Greek alphabet.

**be·take** (bi tāk′) ***v.*** to take oneself; go [The knight *betook* himself to the castle.] —**be·took′, be·tak′en, be·tak′ing**

**be·think** (bi thiŋk′) ***v.*** to think or remind [I suddenly *bethought* myself of what I had come for.] —**be·thought** (bi thôt′), **be·think′ing**

**Beth·le·hem** (beth′lə hem′, beth′lē əm) an ancient town in Judea (now in western Jordan) where Jesus was born.

**be·tide** (bi tīd′) ***v.*** to happen to; befall.

> **Betide** is now used mainly in the phrase **woe betide someone,** meaning "May bad luck happen to someone."

**be·times** (bi tīmz′) ***adv.*** early [We awoke *betimes* to journey forth before daylight.]

**be·to·ken** (bi tō′k'n) ***v.*** to be a sign of; show [This ring *betokens* our friendship.]

**be·took** (bi to͝ok′) *past tense of* **betake.**

**be·tray** (bi trā′) ***v.*** **1** to help the enemy of one's country, side, or friends; be a traitor to [Benedict Arnold planned to *betray* the Colonies in 1780.] **2** to fail to keep a promise, secret, agreement, etc.; be unfaithful [My cousin *betrayed* my trust by wasting my money.] **3** to make plain to see; show signs of [His shaky voice *betrayed* his fear.] —**be·tray′al** ***n.***

**be·troth** (bi trōth′ *or* bi trôth′) ***v.*** to promise in marriage [to *betroth* a daughter].

**be·troth·al** (bi trōth′əl *or* bi trôth′əl) ***n.*** a betrothing; engagement to be married.

**be·trothed** (bi trōthd′ *or* bi trôtht′) ***n.*** the person to whom one is engaged to be married.

**bet·ter**[1] (bet′ər) ***adj.*** **1** above another, as in worth or ability; more excellent, more fit, more desirable, etc. [Grace is a *better* player than Chris. I have a *better* idea.] **2** being more than half [It takes the *better* part of a day to get there.] **3** not so sick; more healthy than before. —*Better* is the comparative of **good.** ◆***adv.*** **1** in a way that is better or more excellent, fit, etc. [They will sing *better* with more practice.] **2** more [I like the orange drink *better* than the lime.] —*Better* is the comparative of **well²**. ◆***n.*** **1** a person or thing that is more excellent, more fit, etc. [This ball is the *better* of the two.] **2** a person with more authority [Obey your *betters*.] ◆***v.*** to make or become better; improve; surpass [The runner has *bettered* the record for the mile run by two seconds.] *See* SYNONYMS *at* **improve.** —**better off,** in a better or improved condition. —**for the better,** to a better or improved condition [Terry's work has changed *for the better*.] —**get the better of,** to defeat. —**had better,** ought to; should.

**bet·ter·ment** (bet′ər mənt) ***n.*** a making or being made better; improvement.

**bet·tor** or **bet·ter²** (bet′ər) ***n.*** one who bets.

**be·tween** (bi twēn′) ***prep.*** **1** in the space, time, or degree that separates [a lake *between* the U.S. and Canada; office hours *between* one and five o'clock; a color *between* blue and green]. **2** having to do with; involving [the war *between* the North and the South]. **3** that connects [a road *between* Reno and Yuma; a bond *between* friends]. **4** with a part for or from each of. **5** one or the other of [You must choose *between* love and duty.] **6** because of both [*Between* work and study, Phil had no time for play.] —**between you and me,** as a secret that you and I share. —**in between, 1** in a middle position. **2** in the midst of.

> **Between** and **among** are sometimes used in place of each other, in meanings 4 and 5, but **between** is usually used of only two and **among** of more than two. [*Between* them the two partners finished the report in two hours. The six investors have $5,000 *among* them.]

**be·twixt** (bi twikst′) ***prep., adv.*** between: *now seldom used except in the phrase* **betwixt and between,** meaning "not completely one or the other."

**bev·el** (bev′'l) ***n.*** **1.** a sloping part or surface, as the angled edge of plate glass. **2.** a tool used for measuring and marking angles. *See the picture.* ◆***v.*** to cut or grind so as to give a slope or angle to *[Bevel* the edges of the mirror.*]* —**bev′eled** or **bev′elled, bev′el·ing** or **bev′el·ling** ◆***adj.*** sloped; beveled *[a bevel* edge*]*.

**bev·er·age** (bev′rij *or* bev′ər ij) ***n.*** any kind of drink (except water), as milk, coffee, or lemonade.

**bev·y** (bev′ē) ***n.*** **1** a group, as of women or girls. **2** a flock, especially of quail. —*pl.* **bev′ies**

> **Bevy** comes from an old French word meaning "to drink" and is related to the words *beverage* and *imbibe,* and also to the **bib** that sops up a baby's spilled drink. Originally a bevy was a group of drinkers, but later it came to mean any small group, especially of birds or women.

**be·wail** (bi wāl′) ***v.*** to weep over; complain about [to *bewail* one's bad luck].

**be·ware** (bi wer′) ***v.*** to be careful; be on one's guard against [*Beware* of ice on the sidewalks.]

**be·wil·der** (bi wil′dər) ***v.*** to make confused; puzzle very much [The winding streets *bewildered* us.] —**be·wil′der·ment** ***n.***

**be·witch** (bi wich′) ***v.*** **1** to use magic on; put a spell on [Circe *bewitched* Ulysses' companions and turned them into pigs.] **2** to charm and delight; fascinate [The youth was *bewitched* by her beauty.] —**be·witch′ing** ***adj.***

**be·yond** (bi yänd′) ***prep.*** **1** on the far side of; farther away than [The town is just *beyond* the hill.] **2** later than [I stayed up *beyond* midnight.] **3** outside the reach or power of [They are *beyond* help.] **4** more or better than [Our trip was *beyond* my fondest hopes.] ◆***adv.*** farther away [The field is behind the house; the woods lie *beyond.*] —**the beyond** or **the great beyond,** whatever follows death.

**bg.** *abbreviation for* **bag.** —*pl.* **bgs.**

**Bhu·tan** (bo͞o tän′) a country in the Himalayas, northeast of the country of India.

**bi-** *a prefix meaning:* **1** having two [A *bicuspid* tooth has two points on its crown.] **2** happening every two [A *biennial* election takes place every two years.] **3** happening twice during every [*Biannual* meetings are held twice a year.]

**Bi** *the symbol for the chemical element* bismuth.

**bi·an·nu·al** (bī an′yo͞o wəl) ***adj.*** coming twice a year. —**bi·an′nu·al·ly** ***adv.***

**bi·as** (bī′əs) ***n.*** **1** a slanting line cut or sewn across the weave of cloth. **2** a leaning in favor of or against something or someone; partiality or prejudice. *See* SYNONYMS *at* **prejudice.** ◆***v.*** to cause to have a bias in thinking; prejudice; influence [The jury had been *biased* by news stories.] —**bi′ased** or **bi′assed, bi′as·ing** or **bi′as·sing** —**on the bias,** diagonally across the weave [cloth cut *on the bias*].

**bib** (bib) ***n.*** **1** a cloth tied around a child's neck at meals to protect the clothing. *See the picture.* **2** the part of an apron or overalls above the waist.

**Bib.** *abbreviation for* **Bible.**

**bibb lettuce** lettuce that has loose heads of very crisp, dark-green leaves.

**Bi·ble** (bī′b'l) ***n.*** **1** the collection of writings (Old Testament) which became the sacred book of the Jewish religion, or these writings together with the New Testament, which became the sacred book of the Christian religion. **2** the sacred book of any religion [The Koran is the Muslim *Bible.*] —**Bib·li·cal** or **bib·li·cal** (bib′li k'l) ***adj.***

> **Bible** comes from a Greek word that meant both "book" and "papyrus," the plant once used for making a kind of paper. The word **paper** comes from another Greek word for papyrus. Many people still call the Bible "the Book" or "the Good Book."

**bib·li·og·ra·phy** (bib′lē äg′rə fē) ***n.*** a list of writings about a certain subject or by a certain author. —*pl.* **bib′li·og′ra·phies** —**bib·li·o·graph·i·cal** (bib′lē ə graf′i k'l) ***adj.***

**bi·cam·er·al** (bī kam′ər əl) ***adj.*** having two groups in the lawmaking body [The *bicameral* U.S. Congress is made up of the Senate and House of Representatives.]

**bi·car·bon·ate of soda** (bī kär′bə nit) *another name for* **baking soda.**

**bi·ceps** (bī′seps) ***n.*** the large muscle in the front of the upper arm.

**bick·er** (bik′ər) ***v.*** to have a small quarrel over an unimportant matter; squabble.

**bi·cus·pid** (bī kus′pid) ***n.*** a tooth with two points on its top surface [An adult has eight *bicuspids.*] *See the picture.* 71

**bi·cy·cle** (bī′si k'l) ***n.*** a vehicle to ride on that has two wheels, one behind the other. It is moved by foot pedals and steered by a handlebar. ◆***v.*** to ride a bicycle. —**bi′cy·cled, bi′cy·cling** —**bi·cy·clist** (bī′si klist) ***n.***

**bid** (bid) ***v.*** **1** to command or ask [Do as you are *bidden.*] **2** to tell [I *bade* my friend farewell.] **3** to offer as the price for something [Will you *bid* $10 for the chair at the auction?] —**bade** or **bid, bid·den** (bid′'n) or **bid, bid′ding** For meaning 3, only *bid* is used as the past tense and past participle. ◆***n.*** **1** a bidding of an amount; the amount bid [The builder whose *bid* for the work is the lowest will win the contract.] **2** an attempt or try [a *bid* for fame].

**bid·der** (bid′ər) ***n.*** a person who bids, as at an auction.

**bide** (bīd) ***v.*** **1** to stay or wait. **2** to dwell; live. —**bode** or **bid′ed, bid′ed, bid′ing**

> **Bide** is a word that is not much used today except in the phrase **bide one's time,** meaning "to wait patiently for a chance." The past tense used for this phrase is always *bided.*

**bi·en·ni·al** (bī en′ē əl) ***adj.*** **1** happening once every two years [a *biennial* meeting]. **2** lasting for two years [a *biennial* plant]. ◆***n.*** a plant that lives for two years, as the pansy. It usually produces its flowers in the second year.

**bier** (bir) ***n.*** a stand on which a coffin or dead body is placed before or during a funeral.

☆**bi·fo·cals** (bī′fō k′lz) ***n.pl.*** eyeglasses in which each lens has two parts, one for seeing close things, as in reading, and the other for seeing things far away. *See the picture.*

**big** (big) ***adj.*** **1** of great size; large [a *big* cake; a *big* city]. *See* SYNONYMS *at* **great. 2** great in force [a *big* wind]. **3** important; outstanding [a *big* day in my life]. **4** showy or boastful [a lot of *big* talk]. ☆**5** noble; generous [a *big* heart]. —**big′ger, big′gest** ◆***adv.*** in a showy or boastful way [to talk *big*]; also, in a broad way; showing imagination: *used only in everyday talk* [Think *big!*] —**big′ness *n.***

**big·a·my** (big′ə mē) ***n.*** the crime of marrying someone while one is still married to another person. —**big′a·mist *n.*** —**big′a·mous *adj.***

**big·heart·ed** (big′här tid) ***adj.*** quick to give or forgive.

☆**big·horn** (big′hôrn) ***n.*** a wild sheep with long, curved horns, found in the Rocky Mountains. *See the picture.*

**bight** (bīt) ***n.*** **1** a loop in a rope. **2** a curve in a river or coastline. **3** a bay.

**big·ot** (big′ət) ***n.*** a person who stubbornly and without thinking holds to certain opinions and will not listen to other views; prejudiced and narrow-minded person. —**big′ot·ed *adj.***

**big·ot·ry** (big′ə trē) ***n.*** the condition of being a bigot; blind, stubborn prejudice.

☆**big top** **1** the main tent of a circus. **2** the life lived by circus performers *This word is used only in everyday talk.*

☆**bike** (bīk) ***n., v.*** *same as* **bicycle** *or* **motorcycle**: *used only in everyday talk.* —**biked, bik′ing**

**bi·ki·ni** (bə kē′nē) ***n.*** **1** a very brief, two-piece bathing suit for women. **2** very brief, legless underpants or trunks.

birch

bighorn sheep
1.2 m (4 ft.) high at shoulder

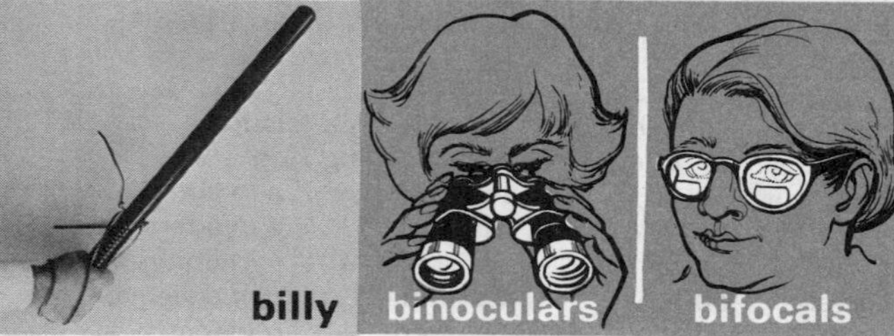
billy
binoculars
bifocals

**bi·lat·er·al** (bī lat′ər əl) ***adj.*** **1** of, on, or having two sides. **2** by or for two sides or parties [a *bilateral* treaty]. —**bi·lat′er·al·ly *adv.***

**bile** (bīl) ***n.*** **1** the bitter, yellowish or greenish fluid that is made by the liver and stored in the gall bladder. It helps in digestion. **2** bad temper; anger.

**bilge** (bilj) ***n.*** **1** the rounded, lower part of a ship's hold. **2** the stale, dirty water that gathers there: *also* **bilge water. 3** nonsense: *slang in this meaning.*

**bil·ious** (bil′yəs) ***adj.*** **1** having something wrong with the bile or liver. **2** bad-tempered; cross. —**bil′ious·ness *n.***

**bilk** (bilk) ***v.*** to cheat or swindle. —**bilk′er *n.***

**bill**[1] (bil) ***n.*** **1** a listing of money owed for certain goods or services [a grocery *bill*]. **2** a list of things offered, as a menu or a theater program [a *bill* of fare]. **3** an advertising poster or a handbill. ☆**4** a piece of paper money [a dollar *bill*]. **5** a proposed law that is to be voted on by a group of lawmakers [A *bill* to provide health insurance is before Congress.] ◆***v.*** **1** to send a bill to, showing money owed [That store *bills* us on the first of the month.] **2** to list or advertise in a performance [They were *billed* as stars in the movie.]

> **Bill**[1] comes from the Latin word *bulla,* which in its first use meant "bubble." Then the word came to mean the bubble of wax that was used to seal a letter. Later that word and the English word **bill** that comes from it were used for the letter itself, and finally for the things written in a letter, such as a listing of money owed. **Bull**[2] also comes from Latin *bulla.*

**bill**[2] (bil) ***n.*** **1** the horny jaws of a bird, usually coming out to a point; beak. **2** a part like this, as a turtle's mouth. ◆***v.*** to show affection: *now used only in the phrase* **bill and coo,** meaning "to kiss, talk softly, etc. in a loving way."

☆**bill·board** (bil′bôrd) ***n.*** a large board outdoors, on which advertisements are posted.

**bil·let** (bil′it) ***v.*** to give soldiers lodging in private homes by military order [The troops were *billeted* in farms along the border.] ◆***n.*** lodging got by military order.

☆**bill·fold** (bil′fōld) ***n.*** a thin, flat case for carrying paper money in the pocket; wallet.

**bil·liards** (bil′yərdz) ***n.*** a game played with hard balls on a special table covered with green felt and having cushioned edges. The balls are struck with a long stick called a cue.

**bil·lion** (bil′yən) ***n., adj.*** a thousand millions (1,000,000,000).

☆**Bill of Rights** the first ten amendments to the Constitution of the United States, which protect such rights as freedom of speech and religion.

**bill of sale** a paper showing that something has been sold by one person to another.

**bil·low** (bil′ō) ***n.*** **1** a large ocean wave. **2** anything that sweeps along and swells like a wave [Great *billows* of smoke poured from the chimney.] ◆***v.*** to swell out in billows [The sails *billowed* in the wind.] —**bil′low·y *adj.***

**bil·ly** (bil′ē) ***n.*** a short, heavy stick carried by some police officers. *See the picture.* —*pl.* **bil′lies**

**billy goat** a male goat.

**bi·month·ly** (bī munth′lē) ***adj., adv.*** **1** once every two months [A *bimonthly* magazine comes out six times a year.] **2** twice a month: *in this meaning,* **semimonthly** *is the preferred word.*

**bin** (bin) ***n.*** an enclosed space for storing things, such as flour, coal, or tools.

**bi·na·ry** (bī′nər ē) ***adj.*** **1** made up of two parts. **2** describing or of a system of numbers in which the base used is two. Each number is shown as a power of two by using only two digits, as 0 and 1.

**bind** (bīnd) ***v.*** **1** to tie together, as with rope; tie tightly [*Bind* these logs together to make a raft.] **2** to stick or fasten by sticking; hold together [The swallow uses mud to *bind* its nest.] **3** to bring or keep together by a feeling of love or duty [Sharing a common meal *binds* our little club together.] **4** to hold or keep; tie down [What *binds* you to your job?] **5** to force to do something because of a promise, law, or contract [The witness is *bound* by his oath to tell the truth.] **6** to put a bandage on [The nurse will *bind* up your wounds.] **7** to fasten printed sheets together and put them between covers, thus making a book. **8** to decorate or make stronger with a band, as of tape [*Bind* the edges of the rug to keep them from raveling.] **9** to constipate. —**bound, bind′ing** ◆***n.*** ☆a difficult situation: *used only in everyday talk* [She's in a *bind.*]

SYNONYMS: **Bind** can often be used in place of **tie,** and **tie** in place of **bind** [to *tie* or *bind* tomato plants to stakes]. But usually **tie** suggests fastening one thing to another by means of a rope or string that can be knotted [to *tie* shoe laces], while **bind** suggests the use of a band put around two or more things to hold them closely together [to *bind* someone's legs with straps].

**bind·er** (bīn′dər) ***n.*** **1** a person who works in a bindery. **2** a material that binds things together [Tar is used as a *binder* for gravel in paving.] **3** a folder for holding sheets of paper together. ☆**4** the part of a reaper that ties the grain into bundles; also, a machine that both cuts and binds grain.

☆**bind·er·y** (bīn′dər ē) ***n.*** a place where books are bound. —*pl.* **bind′er·ies**

**bind·ing** (bīn′diŋ) ***adj.*** that holds one to a promise or agreement [a *binding* contract]. ◆***n.*** **1** the covers and backing of a book. **2** the work done in a bindery. **3** a tape used in sewing to make seams and edges stronger.

☆**bin·go** (biŋ′gō) ***n.*** a gambling game played with cards having rows of numbered squares. Each player has a card or cards with different numbers. Counters are used to cover the numbered squares that match numbers called out by someone who draws numbered disks from a box. The first to cover a row wins.

**bin·na·cle** (bin′ə k′l) ***n.*** a box that holds a ship's compass, located near the helm (or steering wheel).

**bin·oc·u·lars** (bi näk′yə lərz) ***n.pl.*** a pair of small telescopes fastened together for use with both eyes [Field glasses and opera glasses are two kinds of *binoculars.*] *See the picture.*

**bi·o·chem·is·try** (bī′ō kem′is trē) ***n.*** the science that studies the chemistry of plant and animal life.

**bi·o·de·grad·a·ble** (bī′ō di grā′də b′l) ***adj.*** that is easily decomposed, especially by the action of bacteria [a *biodegradable* detergent].

**bi·o·feed·back** (bī′ō fēd′bak) ***n.*** a method of trying to control one's feelings, especially worry or nervousness, by training oneself, with the help of certain electric devices, to change one's heartbeat, blood pressure, etc.

**biog.** *abbreviation for* **biographical** *or* **biography.**

**bi·og·ra·pher** (bī äg′rə fər) ***n.*** a person who writes a biography or biographies.

**bi·og·ra·phy** (bī äg′rə fē) ***n.*** the story of a person's life written by another person. —*pl.* **bi·og′ra·phies** —**bi·o·graph·i·cal** (bī′ə graf′i k′l) ***adj.***

**bi·o·log·i·cal** (bī′ə läj′i k′l) ***adj.*** having to do with biology. —**bi′o·log′i·cal·ly** ***adv.***

**bi·ol·o·gy** (bī äl′ə jē) ***n.*** the science of plants and animals; the study of living things and the way they live and grow. —**bi·ol′o·gist** ***n.***

☆**bi·on·ic** (bī än′ik) ***adj.*** **1** describing an artificial replacement for a part of the body. **2** supplied with such a part or parts, as in science fiction, so that one's strength and abilities are greatly improved.

**bi·op·sy** (bī′äp′sē) ***n.*** the taking out of bits of living tissue or fluids from the body in order to study them, as under a microscope. —*pl.* **bi′op′sies**

**bi·par·ti·san** (bī pär′tə z′n) ***adj.*** made up of or by two political parties [a *bipartisan* foreign policy].

**bi·ped** (bī′ped) ***n.*** any animal with only two legs [Birds and human beings are *bipeds.*]

**bi·plane** (bī′plān) ***n.*** the earlier type of airplane with two main wings, one above the other.

**birch** (burch) ***n.*** **1** a tree that has a thin, smooth bark that is easily peeled in papery strips from the trunk. *See the picture.* **2** its hard wood, used in making furniture. **3** a birch rod or a bunch of birch twigs, used for whipping. ◆***v.*** to whip with a birch.



**bird** (burd) ***n.*** **1** a warmblooded animal that has a backbone, two feet, and wings, and is covered with feathers. Birds lay eggs and can usually fly. **2** a shuttlecock, used in playing badminton. ☆**3** a person; especially, an odd sort of person: *slang in this meaning.* —**birds of a feather,** people with the same tastes and interests.

☆**bird·bath** (burd′bath) ***n.*** a basin of water set on a stand outdoors, for birds to bathe in.

☆**bird dog** a dog trained to hunt birds.

**bird·ie** (bur′dē) ***n.*** **1** a small bird: *a child's word.* ☆**2** in the game of golf, a score of one stroke less than par for any hole.

**bird of paradise** a brightly colored bird of New Guinea, with long, lacy tail feathers.

**bird of prey** a bird that kills other animals for food, as the eagle or hawk.

**bird's-eye** (burdz′ī) ***adj.*** seen from high above [We get a *bird's-eye* view from the tower.]

**Bir·ming·ham** (bur′miŋ ham) **1** a city in north central Alabama. **2** (bur′miŋ əm) a city in central England.

**birth** (burth) ***n.*** **1** the act of being born [the anniversary of Queen Victoria's *birth*]. **2** origin or back-

| | | | | | | | |
|---|---|---|---|---|---|---|---|
| **a** | fat | **ir** | here | **ou** | out | **zh** | leisure |
| **ā** | ape | **ī** | bite, fire | **u** | up | **ŋ** | ring |
| **ä** | car, lot | **ō** | go | **ur** | fur | | a *in* ago |
| **e** | ten | **ô** | law, horn | **ch** | chin | | e *in* agent |
| **er** | care | **oi** | oil | **sh** | she | ə = | i *in* unity |
| **ē** | even | **oo** | look | **th** | thin | | o *in* collect |
| **i** | hit | **ōō** | tool | ***th*** | then | | u *in* focus |

ground [She was a princess by *birth.*] **3** the beginning of something new [1957 marks the *birth* of the Space Age]. —**give birth to,** to bring into being [The cow gave *birth* to a calf. Edison gave *birth* to many inventions.]

**birth·day** (burth′dā) ***n.*** **1** the day on which a person is born or something is begun. **2** the anniversary of this day.

**birth·mark** (burth′märk) ***n.*** a mark or spot found on the skin at birth.

**birth·place** (burth′plās) ***n.*** the place where a person was born or a thing had its beginning.

**birth·rate** (burth′rāt) ***n.*** the number of births during a year for each thousand of the total number of people in any country, area, or group: *also written* **birth rate.**

**birth·right** (burth′rīt) ***n.*** the rights that a person has by being born in a certain family or place; also, the rights of a firstborn son [Freedom of speech is part of our American *birthright.* Esau sold his *birthright* to his younger brother, Jacob.]

**bis·cuit** (bis′kit) ***n.*** ☆**1** a small bread roll made of dough quickly raised with baking powder. **2** a cracker or cookie: *mainly a British meaning.*

**bi·sect** (bī sekt′ *or* bī′sekt) ***v.*** **1** to cut into two parts [Budapest is *bisected* by the Danube River.] **2** to divide into two equal parts [A circle is *bisected* by its diameter.]



**bish·op** (bish′əp) ***n.*** **1** a minister or priest of high rank, who is the head of a church district or diocese. **2** a chess piece that can move diagonally across any number of empty squares.

> **Bishop** comes from a Latin word *episcopus,* meaning "overseer." A bishop oversees the churches in his district. The word *episcopal* comes from the same Latin word, and Episcopal churches are governed by bishops.

**bish·op·ric** (bish′ə prik) ***n.*** **1** the church district controlled by a bishop; diocese. **2** the position or rank of a bishop.

**Bis·marck** (biz′märk) the capital of North Dakota.

**Bis·marck** (biz′märk), **Otto von** 1815–1898; German statesman. He organized the German states into the German Empire of which he was chancellor from 1871 to 1890.

**bis·muth** (biz′məth) ***n.*** a chemical element that is a brittle, grayish-white metal. Bismuth is used in alloys that have a low melting point, and its salts are used in medicine.

**bi·son** (bīs′′n *or* bī′z′n) ***n.*** a wild animal of the ox family, with a shaggy mane, short, curved horns, and a humped back. The American bison is often called a *buffalo. See the picture. —pl.* **bi′son**

**bit**[1] (bit) ***n.*** **1** a metal bar that is the part of a bridle that fits in a horse's mouth. It is used for controlling the horse. **2** the cutting part of a drilling or boring tool. *See the picture of* **brace and bit. 3** the part of a key that turns the lock.

**bit**[2] (bit) ***n.*** **1** a small piece or amount [a *bit* of candy; torn to *bits*]. **2** a short time; moment [wait a *bit*]. **3** a small extent: often used with *a* and like an adverb [a *bit* bored]. ◆***adj.*** very small [a *bit* part in a movie]. —**bit by bit,** little by little; gradually. —**every bit,** entirely. —☆**two bits,** twenty-five cents (*four bits* is fifty cents, and so on): *used only in everyday talk.*

**bitch** (bich) ***n.*** a female dog, wolf, fox, etc.

**bite** (bīt) ***v.*** **1** to seize, snap at, or cut with the teeth or with parts like jaws [The dog *bit* the mail carrier's leg. The trap *bit* into the rabbit's foot. Don't *bite* off such large pieces.] **2** to sting, as a mosquito or bee does. **3** to hurt in a sharp, stinging way [The cold wind *bites* my face.] **4** to press hard into something; grip [The wheels of the car *bit* into the snow.] **5** to be tricked into swallowing bait [The fish won't *bite.*] —**bit** (bit), **bit′ten** or **bit, bit′ing** ◆***n.*** **1** the act of biting [The *bite* of a dog can be dangerous.] **2** a wound or sting from biting [arms covered with mosquito *bites*]. **3** a stinging or painful feeling [the *bite* of a cold wind]. **4** a mouthful [Don't take such big *bites.*] **5** a light meal or snack. **6** the way the upper and lower teeth come together [I wear braces on my teeth to correct my *bite.*] —**bite the bullet,** to be very brave in a painful situation.

> Before pain-killing drugs were developed, a wounded soldier was often told to **bite the bullet** put in his mouth, to help him bear the pain during surgery.

**bit·ing** (bīt′iŋ) ***adj.*** sharp, stinging, or cutting [a *biting* wind; a *biting* criticism].

**bit·ten** (bit′′n) *a past participle of* **bite.**

**bit·ter** (bit′ər) ***adj.*** **1** having a strong, often unpleasant taste [The seed in a peach pit is *bitter.*] **2** full of sorrow, pain, or discomfort [Poor people often suffer *bitter* hardships.] **3** sharp or stinging [a *bitter* wind]. **4** with strong feelings of hatred or dislike [*bitter* enemies]. ◆***adv.*** in a bitter or unpleasant way [The night was *bitter* cold.] —**bit′ter·ly** ***adv.*** —**bit′ter·ness** ***n.***

**bit·tern** (bit′ərn) ***n.*** a bird that looks like a small heron and lives in marshes. It has a loud, deep, hollow cry. *See the picture.*

**bit·ter·sweet** (bit′ər swēt) ***n.*** **1** a poisonous vine with purple flowers and red berries that taste bitter and sweet. ☆**2** a woody vine with bright orange seedcases that split open to show red seeds. ◆***adj.*** both bitter and sweet; also, both sad and happy.

**bi·tu·men** (bi to͞o′mən *or* bī tyo͞o′mən) ***n.*** a mineral that burns easily and is found in nature as asphalt. It can also be made from petroleum or coal.

**bi·tu·mi·nous coal** (bi to͞o′mə nəs *or* bī tyo͞o′mə nəs) soft coal, which burns easily and with more smoke than hard coal (anthracite).

**bi·valve** (bī′valv) ***n.*** a water animal whose soft, boneless body is inside a shell of two parts hinged together, as a clam or oyster.

**biv·ou·ac** (biv′wak *or* biv′o͝o wak′) ***n.*** a camp of soldiers outdoors with little or no shelter, set up for a short time. ◆***v.*** to camp outdoors. —**biv′ou·acked, biv′ou·ack·ing**

**bi·week·ly** (bī wēk′lē) ***adj., adv.*** once every two weeks.

**bi·zarre** (bi zär′) ***adj.*** very odd or unusual; queer; fantastic; grotesque.

**bk.** *abbreviation for* **bank** *or* **book.** *—pl.* **bks.**

**blab** (blab) ***v.*** **1** to tell a secret; tattle. **2** to gossip. —**blabbed, blab′bing**

**black** (blak) ***adj.*** **1** opposite of white; of the color of coal or pitch. Although we speak of black as a color, it is really the absence of all color. A surface is black only when it absorbs all the light rays that make color and reflects none back. **2** without any light [a *black* and moonless night]. **3** having to do with or belonging to the group of people in Africa or from Africa whose members generally have a dark skin and black hair; Negro. **4** of or for black people [*black* studies]. **5** marking the highest degree of skill [a *black* belt in karate]. **6** full of sorrow or suffering; sad; unhappy; gloomy [*black* thoughts; a *black* day]. **7** evil; wicked [*black* deeds]. **8** angry or sullen [*black* looks]. ◆*n.* **1** black color, black paint, black dye, etc. **2** black clothes, especially when worn in mourning. **3** *sometimes* **Black,** a black person; Negro. ☆**4** a condition of financial success, of making a profit [Our business will get into the *black* this year.] ◆*v.* **1** to make black; blacken. **2** to polish with blacking. —**black out, 1** to put out all lights, as at the end of a theatrical skit. **2** to become unconscious. —**black′ness** *n.*

**black-and-blue** (blak′ən blo͞o′) *adj.* discolored or turned dark, as by a bruise or bruises: said of skin.

**black and white** **1** writing or print [to put it in *black and white*]. **2** any picture, TV image, or reproduction done in black and white or in black, white, and gray. **3** a strict standard of right and wrong. —**black-and-white** (blak′ən hwīt′) *adj.*

**black·ball** (blak′bôl) *v.* to vote against letting someone join one's club or social group.

At one time a black ball was used in voting against someone or something. The use of black and white balls dropped into a container was a way of voting secretly. Now we use ballots or pull levers to do so. *See also* **ballot.**

**Black·beard** (blak′bird) English pirate. His real name was *Edward Teach* or *Edward Thatch;* he died in 1718.

**black·ber·ry** (blak′ber′ē) *n.* **1** the small, dark purple or black fruit of a prickly bush or vine. **2** this bush or vine. —*pl.* **black′ber′ries**

**black·bird** (blak′burd) *n.* any of various birds such as the cowbird and the red-winged blackbird. All male blackbirds have black feathers.

**black·board** (blak′bôrd) *n.* a chalkboard, especially one made of black slate.

**black·en** (blak′ən) *v.* **1** to make or become black; darken [Rain clouds *blackened* the sky.] **2** to hurt or damage by telling bad things about [Their good name was *blackened* by gossip.]

**black eye** a bruise on the flesh around the eye, as from a hard blow.

**black-eyed Su·san** (blak′īd so͞o′z′n) ☆a plant having yellow, daisylike flowers, with a dark-brown center.

**Black Forest** a wooded mountain region in southwestern Germany.

**black·guard** (blag′ərd *or* blag′ärd) *n.* a wicked person; scoundrel; villain.

**black·head** (blak′hed) *n.* a pimple with a black tip, caused by a bit of fatty matter clogging a pore.

**Black Hills** a mountainous region in southwestern South Dakota and northeastern Wyoming.

**black·ing** (blak′ing) *n.* a black polish.

**black·jack** (blak′jak) *n.* ☆**1** a short, thick club that is covered with leather and has a flexible handle. It is used for hitting people. ☆**2** a card game in which each player tries to get cards that add up to 21 points. ◆☆*v.* to hit with a blackjack.

**bittern**
75 cm (30 in.) including bill

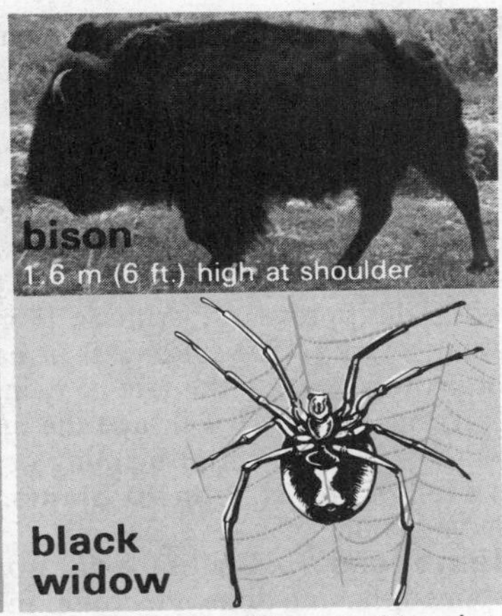

**bison**
1.6 m (6 ft.) high at shoulder

**black widow**

**black·list** (blak′list) *n.* a list of people that one does not like or that are to be punished in some way. ◆*v.* to put on a blacklist.

**black lung disease** a disease of the lungs caused by breathing in coal dust.

**black·mail** (blak′māl) *n.* **1** the crime of threatening to tell something harmful about someone unless he pays some money. **2** money got in this way. ◆*v.* to get or try to get such money from someone.



**black·out** (blak′out) *n.* **1** the act of putting out or hiding all lights that might be seen by an enemy at night. **2** the fact of becoming unconscious.

**Black Sea** a sea south of the U.S.S.R. and north of Turkey.

**black sheep** a person who is thought by his or her family to be no good or to have a bad reputation.

**black·smith** (blak′smith) *n.* a person who makes or fixes iron things by heating them in a forge and then hammering them on an anvil. A blacksmith often makes and fits horseshoes.

☆**black·snake** (blak′snāk) *n.* a harmless, dark-colored snake found in North America.

**black·thorn** (blak′thôrn) *n.* **1** a shrub that grows in Europe and has thorns and white flowers. Its purple fruit looks like a plum and is called a *sloe.* **2** a cane or stick made from its stem.

**black·top** (blak′täp) *n.* an asphalt mixture for paving roads. ◆*v.* to cover with blacktop. —**black′topped, black′top·ping**

☆**black widow** a black spider with red marks on its belly. The female is poisonous and eats its mate. *See the picture.*

**blad·der** (blad′ər) *n.* **1** a bag inside the body that is an organ to hold a fluid; especially, such a bag that collects the urine coming from the kidneys. **2** something like this bag [a football *bladder*].

| | | | | | | | |
|---|---|---|---|---|---|---|---|
| **a** | fat | **ir** | here | **ou** | out | **zh** | leisure |
| **ā** | ape | **ī** | bite, fire | **u** | up | **ng** | ring |
| **ä** | car, lot | **ō** | go | **ur** | fur | | a *in* ago |
| **e** | ten | **ô** | law, horn | **ch** | chin | | e *in* agent |
| **er** | care | **oi** | oil | **sh** | she | **ə =** | i *in* unity |
| **ē** | even | **oo** | look | **th** | thin | | o *in* collect |
| **i** | hit | **o͞o** | tool | ***th*** | then | | u *in* focus |

**blade** (blād) ***n.*** **1** a broad, flat part of something [the *blade* of an oar; the shoulder *blade*]. **2** the sharp, cutting part of a knife, saw, sword, etc. **3** a sword or a swordsman. **4** a lively young man. **5** the leaf of grass or of a cereal. **6** the broad, flat part of any leaf.

**blame** (blām) ***v.*** **1** to say or think that someone or something is the cause of what is wrong or bad [Don't *blame* others for your own mistakes.] **2** to find fault with; disapprove of; criticize [I can't *blame* you for being angry.] *See* SYNONYMS *at* **criticize.** —**blamed, blam′ing** ◆***n.*** **1** the fact of being the cause of what is wrong or bad [I will take the *blame* for the broken window.] **2** the act of blaming or finding fault [a letter full of *blame*]. —**be to blame,** to be at fault; deserve blame.

**blame·less** (blām′lis) ***adj.*** not deserving to be blamed; having done no wrong; innocent.

**blame·wor·thy** (blām′wur′thē) ***adj.*** deserving to be blamed; having done wrong.

**blanch** (blanch) ***v.*** **1** to turn pale; lose color in the face [to *blanch* with fear]. **2** to make lighter in color; whiten [Gardeners *blanch* celery by covering the stalks with soil.] **3** to remove the skins of with boiling water [to *blanch* almonds].

**bland** (bland) ***adj.*** **1** pleasant and polite [His *bland* manner charmed us.] **2** smooth and mild; not sharp [Custard is a *bland* food.] **3** dull or uninteresting [a *bland,* somewhat boring book]. —**bland′ly *adv.*** —**bland′ness *n.***



**blan·dish·ment** (blan′dish mənt) ***n.*** flattery or coaxing to get what one wants [Politicians use *blandishments* on the voters to get reelected.]

**blank** (blangk) ***adj.*** **1** not marked or written on [a *blank* sheet of paper]. **2** showing no expression or interest [I kept a *blank* look on my face.] **3** empty of any thought [It is hard to keep your mind *blank.*] ◆***n.*** **1** a paper with empty spaces to be written in [an application *blank*]. **2** an empty space on such a paper [Fill in all the *blanks.*] **3** a cartridge that has no bullet, fired only to make a noise: *the full name is* **blank cartridge.** —**blank′ly *adv.*** —**blank′ness *n.***

**blan·ket** (blang′kit) ***n.*** **1** a large, soft piece of cloth used as a covering for warmth, especially in bed. **2** any covering that is spread out [a *blanket* of snow]. ◆***adj.*** taking care of a number of things; general [The principal gave us *blanket* instructions for the fire drill.] ◆***v.*** to cover with a blanket [Leaves *blanketed* the lawn.]

**blare** (bler) ***v.*** to sound out with loud, harsh tones [Car horns *blared.*] —**blared, blar′ing** ◆***n.*** such a loud, harsh sound.

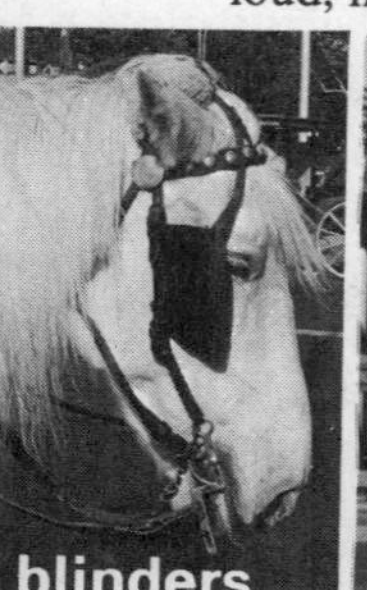
blinders

bleachers

**blar·ney** (blär′nē) ***n.*** smooth talk used in flattering or coaxing.

> **Blarney** comes from the name of a castle in Ireland. Some people say that those who are able to hang from a window of that castle and kiss a certain stone receive the gift of blarney.

**bla·sé** (blä zā′) ***adj.*** bored with having enjoyed too many pleasures; never surprised or pleased.

**blas·pheme** (blas fēm′) ***v.*** to show lack of respect for God or for anything thought to be sacred; curse or swear. —**blas·phemed′, blas·phem′ing**

**blas·phe·my** (blas′fə mē) ***n.*** words or action showing lack of respect for God or for anything thought to be sacred. —*pl.* **blas′phe·mies** —**blas′phe·mous *adj.***

> SYNONYMS: **Blasphemy** is any strong speech meant to show contempt for God or for anything holy. The use of **profanity** shows lack of respect and awe for any holy person or thing. **Swearing** and **cursing** make use of profane language and oaths, but **cursing** also makes use of prayers that ask for evil or harmful things to happen to others.

**blast** (blast) ***n.*** **1** a strong rush of air or gust of wind. **2** the sound of a rush of air, as through a trumpet or whistle. **3** an explosion, as of dynamite. ◆***v.*** **1** to blow up with an explosive [to *blast* rock]. **2** to blight or destroy [Frost *blasted* the fruit crop.] —**at full blast,** at full speed or in full operation. —**blast off,** to take off with an explosion and begin its flight, as a rocket does.

**blast furnace** a tall furnace for smelting ore, in which a blast of air is used to produce the very high heat needed.

**bla·tant** (blāt′'nt) ***adj.*** very loud and noisy.

**blaze**[1] (blāz) ***n.*** **1** a bright flame or fire. **2** any bright light [the *blaze* of searchlights]. **3** a sudden or showy outburst; flash [a *blaze* of glory]. **4** a bright display [The garden was a *blaze* of color.] ◆***v.*** **1** to burn brightly. *See* SYNONYMS *at* **glow. 2** to shine brightly [At night the carnival *blazed* with lights.] **3** to burst out with strong feeling [to *blaze* with anger]. —**blazed, blaz′ing**

**blaze**[2] (blāz) ***n.*** **1** a white spot on the face of an animal. ☆**2** a mark made on a tree by cutting off a piece of bark [Mark your trail by cutting *blazes* as you go.] ◆☆***v.*** to mark a tree or trail with blazes.

**blaz·er** (blā′zər) ***n.*** a lightweight sports jacket, in a solid, often bright color or with stripes.

**bla·zon** (blā′z'n) ***v.*** **1** to decorate in a showy way. **2** to make known all over [TV ads *blazon* this breakfast food.]

**bldg.** *abbreviation for* **building.**

**bleach** (blēch) ***v.*** to make or become white or pale by means of chemicals or by the action of sunshine. ◆***n.*** any chemical used in bleaching, as peroxide.

☆**bleach·ers** (blēch′ərz) ***n.pl.*** a section of seats, usually bare benches without a roof, for watching outdoor sports. *See the picture.*

**bleak** (blēk) ***adj.*** **1** open to wind and cold; not sheltered; bare [the *bleak* plains]. **2** cold and cutting; harsh [a *bleak* wind]. **3** not cheerful; gloomy [a *bleak* future]. —**bleak′ly *adv.*** —**bleak′ness *n.***

**blear** (blir) ***v.*** to make dim or blurred.

**blear·y** (blir′ē) ***adj.*** made dim or blurred [Her eyes were *bleary* from lack of sleep.] —**blear′i·er, blear′i·est**

**bleat** (blēt) ***v.*** **1** to make the sound of a sheep, goat, or calf. **2** to talk or say in a weak, trembling voice. ◆***n.*** the sound made in bleating.
**bled** (bled) *past tense and past participle of* **bleed.**
**bleed** (blēd) ***v.*** **1** to lose blood [The wound stopped *bleeding.*] **2** to feel pain, grief, or sympathy [My heart *bleeds* for the widow.] **3** to draw blood from [Doctors used to try to cure illnesses by *bleeding* their patients.] **4** to get money from, as by blackmail: *used only in everyday talk.* —**bled, bleed′ing**
**blem·ish** (blem′ish) ***n.*** a mark that spoils or damages; flaw; defect [skin *blemishes;* a *blemish* in her character]. ◆***v.*** to put a blemish on.
**blench** (blench) ***v.*** to shrink back, as in fear.
**blend** (blend) ***v.*** **1** to mix different kinds together in order to get a certain flavor, color, etc. [to *blend* tea or paint]. **2** to come together or mix so that the parts are no longer distinct [The sky *blended* with the sea at the horizon.] **3** to go well together; be in harmony [Her blue sweater *blends* well with her gray skirt.] *See* SYNONYMS *at* **mix.** ◆***n.*** a mixture of different kinds [a *blend* of coffee]. —**blend′er** ***n.***
**bless** (bles) ***v.*** **1** to make holy; consecrate [*Bless* this food to our use.] **2** to ask God's favor for [The rabbi *blessed* the congregation.] **3** to bring happiness or good fortune to [God *bless* you!] **4** to praise or glorify [Let us *bless* the Lord!] **Bless** is often used when exclaiming to show mild surprise. [*Bless* me if it isn't Jan!] —**blessed** (blest) or **blest, bless′ing**

> **Bless** comes from the Old English word for "blood." The Anglo-Saxons would make an altar holy by sprinkling it with blood.

**bless·ed** (bles′id *or* blest) ***adj.*** **1** holy; sacred. **2** full of bliss; fortunate [*blessed* in having two fine children]. —**bless′ed·ness** ***n.***
**bless·ing** (bles′iŋ) ***n.*** **1** a prayer asking God's favor for something. **2** good wishes or approval [The parents gave the engaged couple their *blessing.*] **3** anything that brings joy or comfort [Rain now would be a *blessing.*]
**blest** (blest) *a past tense and past participle of* **bless.**
**blew** (blo͞o) *past tense of* **blow**[1] *and* **blow**[2].
**blight** (blīt) ***n.*** **1** any disease that hurts or kills plants. **2** anything that hurts or destroys [Slums are a *blight* on a city.] ◆***v.*** to damage or destroy; ruin [Our hopes were *blighted.*]
**blimp** (blimp) ***n.*** a small, egg-shaped airship: *used only in everyday talk.*
**blind** (blīnd) ***adj.*** **1** not able to see; having no sight. **2** not able to notice, understand, or judge [Her parents were *blind* to her faults.] **3** hidden from sight [a *blind* stitch]. **4** having no opening [a *blind* wall]. **5** closed at one end [a *blind* alley]. **6** done by instruments only [*blind* flying in a fog]. ◆***v.*** **1** to make blind; make unable to see. **2** to make unable to understand or judge well [Her desire to perform on the trampoline *blinded* her to its dangers.] ◆***n.*** **1** a window shade of stiffened cloth, metal slats, etc. **2** a person or thing that is made use of in order to mislead others. —**blind′ly** ***adv.*** —**blind′ness** ***n.***
**blind·ers** (blīn′dərz) ***n.pl.*** two leather flaps on a bridle that keep a horse from seeing to the sides. *See the picture.*
**blind·fold** (blīnd′fōld) ***v.*** to cover someone's eyes, as by tying a cloth around the head. ◆***adj.*** with the eyes covered; not seeing. ◆***n.*** a cloth used to cover the eyes.
**blind·man's buff** (blīnd′manz buf′) a game in which a blindfolded player has to catch another player and then tell who it is: *also* **blind′man's bluff′** (bluf′)
**blink** (bliŋk) ***v.*** **1** to keep closing and opening the eyes rapidly. *See* SYNONYMS *at* **wink. 2** to flash off and on. ◆***n.*** a brief flash of light. —**on the blink,** not working right: *a slang phrase.*
**blink·er** (bliŋk′ər) ***n.*** ☆something that blinks; especially, a flashing signal that warns.
**bliss** (blis) ***n.*** great joy or happiness. —**bliss′ful** ***adj.*** —**bliss′ful·ly** ***adv.***
**blis·ter** (blis′tər) ***n.*** **1** a small swollen place on the skin, filled with watery matter and caused by a burn or by rubbing. **2** any part that swells like a blister [*blisters* in a coat of paint]. ◆***v.*** **1** to make blisters on [The sun *blistered* my nose.] **2** to form blisters [Old paint may *blister.*]
**blithe** (blīth *or* blīth) ***adj.*** cheerful; gay; carefree [Shelley called the skylark a "*blithe* spirit."] —**blithe′ly** ***adv.***
**blithe·some** (blīth′səm *or* blīth′səm) ***adj.*** blithe; gay.
☆**bliz·zard** (bliz′ərd) ***n.*** a heavy snowstorm with very strong, cold winds.

> **Blizzard** is an American word, probably made up from such words as *blow, bluster,* and *dazzle.* It became popular when it was used in newspapers to describe terrible storms in the winter of 1880.



**bloat** (blōt) ***v.*** to puff up as when swollen with air or water. —**bloat′ed** ***adj.***
**blob** (bläb) ***n.*** a small lump of something soft and moist [a *blob* of jelly or paint].
**bloc** (bläk) ***n.*** a group of people or nations working together for some common purpose or to help one another.
**block** (bläk) ***n.*** **1** a thick piece of wood, stone, or metal, often having flat surfaces [a butcher's *block;* a set of toy *blocks*]. ☆**2** the platform used at an auction. **3** a mold on which things are shaped [a hat *block*]. **4** anything that stops movement or progress [A *block* behind the back wheels will keep the car from moving. Laziness is a *block* to success.] **5** a number of things thought of as a single unit [We have reserved a *block* of seats for the play.] ☆**6** the square or rectangle formed by four streets [The city hall takes up the whole *block.*]; also, the area along one of the streets [They live in our *block.*] **7** a pulley in a frame. ◆***v.*** **1** to stop movement or progress [The fallen tree *blocked* the path.] **2** to shape [*Block* the sweater after you wash it.] —**block out,** to plan an outline. —**block up,** to fill up so that nothing can pass through. —**block′er** ***n.***
**block·ade** (blä kād′) ***n.*** **1** a shutting off of a port or other place by enemy troops or warships to keep peo-

| | | | | | | | |
|---|---|---|---|---|---|---|---|
| **a** | fat | **ir** | here | **ou** | out | **zh** | leisure |
| **ā** | ape | **ī** | bite, fire | **u** | up | **ŋ** | ring |
| **ä** | car, lot | **ō** | go | **ur** | fur | | a *in* ago |
| **e** | ten | **ô** | law, horn | **ch** | chin | | e *in* agent |
| **er** | care | **oi** | oil | **sh** | she | ə = | i *in* unity |
| **ē** | even | **oo** | look | **th** | thin | | o *in* collect |
| **i** | hit | **o͞o** | tool | ***th*** | then | | u *in* focus |

blockhouse

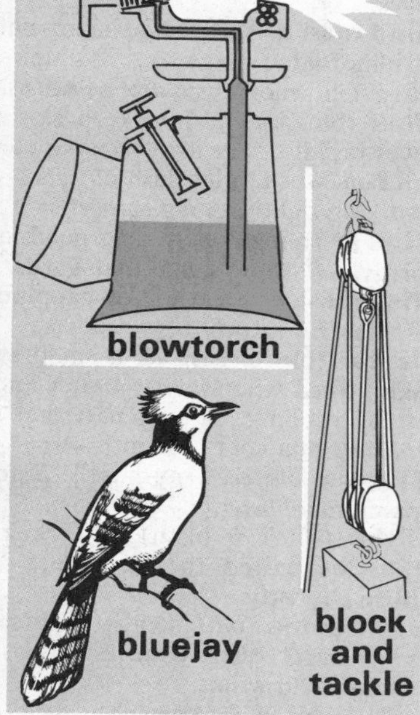
blowtorch

bloodhounds

bluejay

block and tackle

ple or supplies from moving in or out. **2** any obstacle or barrier. ◆*v.* to put under a blockade. —**block·ad′ed, block·ad′ing**

**block and tackle** pulley blocks and ropes, used for lifting large, heavy objects. *See the picture.*

**block·head** (bläk′hed) *n.* a stupid person.

**block·house** (bläk′hous) *n.* a strong wooden fort with openings in the walls to shoot from and a second story that sticks out. *See the picture.*

**blond** or **blonde** (bländ) *adj.* **1** having light-colored, especially yellow, hair and a very light skin. **2** light-colored [*blond* hair; *blond* furniture]. ◆*n.* a blond person. —**blond′ness** or **blonde′ness** *n.*

**blood** (blud) *n.* **1** the red liquid that is pumped through the arteries and veins by the heart. The blood carries oxygen and cell-building material to the body tissues and carries carbon dioxide and waste material away from them. **2** family line or ancestors; descent. This meaning is based on the false idea that the blood of one family or race has something special that makes it different from the blood of another family or race [They are of the same *blood.*] —**bad blood,** anger; hatred. —**in cold blood,** on purpose and cruelly, but without anger or any sign of feeling [to kill *in cold blood*].

**blood bank** **1** a place where whole blood or blood plasma is stored, according to the type of blood. **2** any reserve of blood for use in giving transfusions.

**blood bath** a massacre; slaughter.

**blood·cur·dling** (blud′kʉrd′liŋ) *adj.* very frightening [a *bloodcurdling* scream].

**blood·hound** (blud′hound) *n.* a large dog with a wrinkled face and long, drooping ears. Bloodhounds have a keen sense of smell and are often used in tracking escaped prisoners. *See the picture.*

**blood·less** (blud′lis) *adj.* **1** without blood or without enough blood; pale [*bloodless* cheeks]. **2** without life; dead. **3** without killing [a *bloodless* revolution].

**blood poisoning** a diseased condition of the blood caused by germs or toxins.

**blood pressure** the pressure of the blood against the walls of the arteries and other blood vessels. It changes according to one's health, age, etc.

**blood·shed** (blud′shed) *n.* the shedding of blood; killing [War brings much *bloodshed.*]

**blood·shot** (blud′shät) *adj.* red because the small blood vessels are swollen or broken [*bloodshot* eyes].

**blood·suck·er** (blud′suk′ər) *n.* a leech or other animal that sucks blood.

**blood·thirst·y** (blud′thʉr′stē) *adj.* eager to hurt or kill; murderous.

**blood vessel** any of the many tubes in the body through which the blood flows; any artery, vein, or capillary.

**blood·y** (blud′ē) *adj.* **1** full of or covered with blood [a *bloody* nose]. **2** with much killing or wounding [a *bloody* battle]. **3** bloodthirsty. —**blood′i·er, blood′i·est** ◆*v.* to cover or smear with blood. —**blood′ied, blood′y·ing**

**bloom** (blo͞om) *n.* **1** a flower or blossom. **2** the time or condition of bearing blossoms [The lilies are in *bloom.*] **3** a time or condition of beauty, freshness, or vigor [She was in the *bloom* of girlhood.] **4** the healthy glow of youth [the *bloom* on her cheeks]. **5** the powdery coating on certain fruits, as the plum or grape. ◆*v.* **1** to bear blossoms [Tulips *bloom* in the spring.] **2** to be healthy and fresh; be at one's best [The children *bloomed* at camp this summer.]

☆**bloom·ers** (blo͞om′ərz) *n.pl.* **1** short baggy pants fitting snugly at the waist and thighs, worn by girls and women for sports. **2** an undergarment somewhat like this.

**Bloomers** take their name from Amelia Jenks Bloomer, a hard worker for women's rights in the 19th century. Mrs. Bloomer said that women and girls should wear such pants to make it easier for them to ride bicycles and take part in sports.

**blos·som** (bläs′əm) *n.* **1** a flower, especially of a plant that bears fruit [apple *blossoms*]. **2** a condition or time of flowering [The pear trees are in *blossom.*] ◆*v.* **1** to bear blossoms; bloom. **2** to unfold or develop [She has *blossomed* into a fine lady.]

**blot** (blät) *n.* **1** a spot or stain, especially of ink. **2** anything that spoils or mars [That shack is a *blot* on the landscape.] ◆*v.* **1** to make blots on; spot; stain [The pen leaked and *blotted* his shirt.] **2** to erase, hide, or get rid of [These memories were soon *blotted* from her mind.] **3** to dry by soaking up the wet liquid [You can *blot* ink with a piece of soft paper.] —**blot′ted, blot′ting**

**blotch** (bläch) *n.* **1** any spot or patch that spoils the even color or smoothness of the skin. **2** any large spot or stain. ◆*v.* to mark with blotches.

**blot·ter** (blät′ər) *n.* **1** a piece of thick, soft paper used to blot ink dry. ☆**2** a book for writing down things as they happen [A police *blotter* is a record of arrests and charges.]

**blouse** (blous) *n.* **1** a loose outer garment like a shirt, worn by women and children. **2** the jacket of a military uniform.

**blow**[1] (blō) *v.* **1** to move with some force, as air

[There is a wind *blowing*.] **2** to force air out, as from the mouth [*Blow* on your hands to warm them.] **3** to force air into or through in order to clear [to *blow* one's nose]. **4** to breathe hard and fast; pant. **5** to make sound by blowing or being blown [*Blow* your trumpet. The noon whistle is *blowing*.] **6** to be carried by the wind [My hat suddenly *blew* off.] **7** to drive by blowing [The fan *blew* the paper out the window.] **8** to form or cause to swell by forcing in air or gas [to *blow* bubbles]. **9** to melt [to *blow* a fuse]. —**blew, blown, blow'ing** ◆***n.*** **1** the act of blowing. **2** a strong wind; gale. —**blow out, 1** to put out, as a flame, by blowing. **2** to burst suddenly, as a tire. **3** to melt, as a fuse, from too much electric current. —**blow over, 1** to move away, as rain clouds. **2** to pass over; be forgotten. —**blow up, 1** to fill with air or gas [to *blow up* a balloon]. **2** to burst or explode. **3** to lose one's temper: *used only in everyday talk.*

**blow**[2] (blō) ***n.*** **1** a hard hit, as with the fist. **2** a sudden attack [One swift *blow* can win the battle.] **3** a sudden misfortune; shock [His death was a great *blow* to her.] —**come to blows,** to begin fighting.

**blow-dry** (blō'drī') ***v.*** to dry wet hair with an electric device (**blow'-dry'er**) that is made to be held in the hand and that sends out a strong stream of heated air. —**blow'-dried', blow'-dry'ing**

**blow·er** (blō'ər) ***n.*** **1** a person who blows [a glass *blower*]. **2** a fan for blowing air, as from a furnace through a house.

☆**blow·gun** (blō'gun) ***n.*** a long tube through which darts are blown by mouth.

**blown** (blōn) *past participle of* **blow**[1].

**blow·out** (blō'out) ***n.*** the bursting of a tire.

☆**blow·torch** (blō'tôrch) ***n.*** a small torch that shoots out a hot flame. It is used to melt metal, burn off old paint, etc. *See the picture.*

**blub·ber** (blub'ər) ***n.*** the fat of whales and other sea animals, from which an oil is gotten. ◆***v.*** to weep loudly.

**bludg·eon** (bluj''n) ***n.*** a short club with a thick, heavy end. ◆***v.*** **1** to hit with a bludgeon. **2** to threaten or bully.

**blue** (blo͞o) ***adj.*** **1** having the color of the clear sky or the deep sea. **2** feeling sad or gloomy; in low spirits. —**blu'er, blu'est** ◆***n.*** **1** the color of the clear sky or the deep sea. **2** any blue paint or dye. **3** anything colored blue, as the sky or the sea. —**out of the blue,** suddenly and without being expected; as if from the sky. —☆**the blues, 1** a sad, gloomy feeling: *used only in everyday talk.* **2** a type of folk song with a slow jazz rhythm and sad words, first developed by American blacks.

**blue·bell** (blo͞o'bel) ***n.*** any of several plants that have blue flowers shaped like bells.

**blue·ber·ry** (blo͞o'ber'ē) ***n.*** ☆**1** a small, round, dark blue berry that is eaten. ☆**2** the shrub on which it grows. —*pl.* **blue'ber'ries**

**blue·bird** (blo͞o'burd) ***n.*** ☆a small songbird of North America that has a blue back and wings.

**blue·bon·net** (blo͞o'bän'it) ***n.*** ☆a small wildflower of the pea family, having blue blossoms.

**blue·bot·tle** (blo͞o'bät''l) ***n.*** a large, hairy fly with a shiny blue body.

☆**blue·fish** (blo͞o'fish) ***n.*** a silvery-blue sea fish that is used for food.

☆**blue·grass** (blo͞o'gras) ***n.*** **1** a grass with bluish-green stems. **2** Southern string-band folk music.

**blue·ing** (blo͞o'iŋ) ***n.*** *same as* **bluing.**

**blue·jack·et** (blo͞o'jak'it) ***n.*** a sailor in the navy.

☆**blue jay** a bird with a blue back and a crest of feathers on its head. It has a loud, rough call: *also written* **blue·jay** (blo͞o'jā) ***n.*** *See the picture.*

☆**blue laws** strict, harsh laws like those passed by the Puritans; especially, laws that forbid dancing, shows, sports, etc. on Sunday.

**blue·print** (blo͞o'print) ***n.*** a photographic copy of the plans for a building, bridge, etc. It has white lines and letters on a blue background.

**blue ribbon** first prize in a competition.

**blu·et** (blo͞o'it) ***n.*** ☆a small plant that grows in low tufts and has blue flowers.

☆**bluff**[1] (bluf) ***v.*** to fool or try to fool by acting very sure of oneself. ◆***n.*** **1** an act of bluffing [His threat is just a *bluff*.] **2** a person who bluffs.

**bluff**[2] (bluf) ***n.*** ☆a high, steep bank or cliff. ◆***adj.*** **1** having a broad, flat front that slopes steeply [*bluff* river banks]. **2** rough and frank; blunt.

☆**blu·ing** (blo͞o'iŋ) ***n.*** a blue liquid or powder put into the rinse water when doing laundry. It keeps white fabrics from turning yellow.

**blu·ish** (blo͞o'ish) ***adj.*** somewhat blue.

**blun·der** (blun'dər) ***n.*** a foolish or stupid mistake. ◆***v.*** **1** to make such a mistake. **2** to move clumsily or carelessly; stumble.



**Blunder** comes from an Old Norse word meaning "to shut the eyes." A person may stumble when his eyes are shut. **Blunderbuss** has nothing to do with this word. It is a mistaken spelling of the Dutch word *donderbus,* which means "thunder box" and which was probably a good description of the noisy gun.

**blun·der·buss** (blun'dər bus) ***n.*** a short gun with a wide muzzle, used about 300 years ago.

**blunt** (blunt) ***adj.*** **1** having a dull edge or point; not sharp [a *blunt* ax]. **2** speaking plainly and honestly, without trying to be polite [Her *blunt* reply was "I don't like you."] ◆***v.*** to make dull [The knife was *blunted* from long use.] —**blunt'ly *adv.*** —**blunt'ness *n.***

**blur** (blur) ***v.*** **1** to make less clear or sharp; confuse [The face in the picture is *blurred*.] **2** to smear or smudge [The children's greasy fingerprints *blurred* the windowpane.] —**blurred, blur'ring** ◆***n.*** **1** the state of being blurred or unclear; dim or confused condition. **2** a stain or blot.

**blurt** (blurt) ***v.*** to say suddenly without stopping to think [to *blurt* out a secret].

**blush** (blush) ***v.*** to become red in the face, as from shyness or shame [Helen *blushed* at the compliment.] ◆***n.*** **1** a reddening of the face, as from shyness or

| | | | | | | | |
|---|---|---|---|---|---|---|---|
| **a** | fat | **ir** | here | **ou** | out | **zh** | leisure |
| **ā** | ape | **ī** | bite, fire | **u** | up | **ŋ** | ring |
| **ä** | car, lot | **ō** | go | **ur** | fur | | a *in* ago |
| **e** | ten | **ô** | law, horn | **ch** | chin | | e *in* agent |
| **er** | care | **oi** | oil | **sh** | she | **ə =** | i *in* unity |
| **ē** | even | **oo** | look | **th** | thin | | o *in* collect |
| **i** | hit | **o͞o** | tool | ***th*** | then | | u *in* focus |

shame. **2** a rosy color [the *blush* of dawn]. —**at first blush,** without stopping to think further.

**blus·ter** (blus′tər) ***v.*** **1** to blow in a stormy way [*blustering* winds]. **2** to speak in a noisy, boastful, or bullying way. ◆***n.*** **1** stormy noise. **2** noisy or boastful talk. —**blus′ter·y** ***adj.***

**Blvd.** or **blvd.** *abbreviation for* **boulevard.**

**BO** or **B.O.** **1** body odor. **2** box office.

**bo·a** (bō′ə) ***n.*** **1** a very large tropical snake that winds about its prey and crushes it to death [The python is a kind of *boa*.] **2** a long, fluffy scarf of feathers, fur, etc., worn by women.

**boa con·stric·tor** (kən strik′tər) a kind of boa that reaches a length of 10 to 15 feet.

**boar** (bôr) ***n.*** **1** a male pig. **2** a wild pig of Europe, Africa, and Asia.

**board** (bôrd) ***n.*** **1** a long, flat, broad piece of sawed wood, used in building. **2** a flat piece of wood or other hard material made for a special use [a checker*board;* a bulletin *board;* an ironing *board*]. **3** a table at which meals are eaten. **4** food served at a table; especially, meals given regularly for pay. **5** a group of people who manage or control a business, school, department, etc. [*board* of education]. **6** the side of a ship [to jump over*board*]. ◆***v.*** **1** to cover up with boards [The windows of the old house were *boarded* up.] **2** to give or get meals, or room and meals, regularly for pay. **3** to get on a ship, airplane, bus, etc. —

**on board,** on a ship, airplane, bus, etc.

**board·er** (bôr′dər) ***n.*** a person who lives, or eats meals, in another's home for pay.

**board·ing·house** (bôrd′iŋ hous′) ***n.*** a house where meals, or room and meals, can be had for pay: *also written* **boarding house.**

**boarding school** a school where the pupils live during the school year.

☆**board·walk** (bôrd′wôk) ***n.*** a walk made of thick boards, especially along a beach.

**boast** (bōst) ***v.*** **1** to talk about with too much pride and pleasure; praise too highly; brag [We tired of hearing him *boast* of his bravery.] **2** to be proud of having [Our city *boasts* a fine new zoo.] ◆***n.*** **1** the act of boasting or bragging. **2** something that one can boast of [It was her *boast* that she had never been late to school.] —**boast′er** ***n.***

**boast·ful** (bōst′fəl) ***adj.*** boasting; always ready to brag. —**boast′ful·ly** ***adv.*** —**boast′ful·ness** ***n.***

**boat** (bōt) ***n.*** **1** a small vessel for traveling on water, such as a rowboat, sailboat, lifeboat, or motorboat. In popular use, but not by sailors, a ship of any size is sometimes called a boat. **2** a dish shaped a little like a boat [a gravy *boat*]. ◆***v.*** to row or sail in a boat [We went *boating* on the river.] —**in the same boat,** facing the same kind of problem.

**boat·swain** (bō′s′n) ***n.*** a petty officer on a ship who directs the work of the crew.

**bob** (bäb) ***n.*** **1** to move with short, jerky motions [Our heads *bobbed* up and down as our car bounced over the ruts.] **2** to cut off short [to *bob* a dog's tail]. —**bobbed, bob′bing** ◆***n.*** **1** a short, jerky movement [She greeted us with a *bob* of her head.] **2** a style of short haircut for women or girls. **3** a hanging weight at the end of a plumb line. **4** a cork on a fishing line.

**bob·bin** (bäb′in) ***n.*** a kind of spool around which thread or yarn is wound. Bobbins are used in weaving, on sewing machines, etc.

**bob·by** (bäb′ē) ***n.*** a policeman: *a British slang word.* —*pl.* **bob′bies**

☆**bobby pin** a small metal hairpin with the sides pressing close together.

☆**bobby socks** or **bobby sox** girls' socks that reach just above the ankle: *used only in everyday talk.*

☆**bob·cat** (bäb′kat) ***n.*** *same as meaning* 1 *of* **wildcat.**

☆**bob·o·link** (bäb′ə liŋk′) ***n.*** a North American songbird related to the blackbird.

> The names of several birds were meant to imitate their calls. **Bobolink** is such a name, and so are *bobwhite, whippoorwill,* and *pewee.*

☆**bob·sled** (bäb′sled) ***n.*** a long sled ridden in races down a slide by a team of two or four persons. It has a steering wheel and a brake. *See the picture.*

**bob·tail** (bäb′tāl) ***n.*** **1** a tail that has been cut short. **2** an animal with its tail cut short. ◆***adj.*** having its tail cut short [a *bobtail* cat].

☆**bob·white** (bäb hwīt′) ***n.*** a small North American quail with brown and white markings on a gray body. *See the note at* **bobolink.**

**Boc·cac·ci·o** (bō kä′chē ō′), **Gio·van·ni** (jô vän′nē) 1313–1375; Italian writer. His famous book is the *Decameron.*

**bode** (bōd) ***v.*** to be a sign or omen of [That black cloud *bodes* rain.] —**bod′ed, bod′ing** —**bode ill,** to be a bad sign. —**bode well,** to be a good sign.

**bod·ice** (bäd′is) ***n.*** **1** the tightly fitting upper part of a woman's dress. **2** a kind of vest worn by women and girls, usually laced down the front.

**bod·ied** (bäd′ēd) ***adj.*** having a certain kind of body [able-*bodied*].

**bod·i·ly** (bäd′′l ē) ***adj.*** of, in, by, or to the body [*bodily* labor; *bodily* harm]. *See* SYNONYMS *at* **physical.** ◆***adv.*** as a single body; in a whole group.

**bod·y** (bäd′ē) ***n.*** **1** the whole physical part of a person or animal [Athletes have strong *bodies.*] **2** the main part of a person or animal, not including the head, legs, and arms [The boxer received many blows to the *body.*] **3** the main or central part of anything, as the trunk of a tree or the part of a car that holds the passengers. **4** a separate portion of matter; mass [An island is a *body* of land. The stars are heavenly *bodies.*] **5** a group of people or things thought of as a single unit [a *body* of soldiers; a *body* of facts]. **6** a person: *used only in everyday talk* [What more can a *body* do?] —*pl.* **bod′ies**

> SYNONYMS: A **body** is the whole physical person or animal, with all its parts, alive or dead. A **corpse** is the dead body of a human being. A **carcass** is the dead body of an animal or, sometimes, in showing contempt, the dead body of a human being.

**bod·y·guard** (bäd′ē gärd′) ***n.*** a person or group of persons whose work is to guard someone.

**Boer** (bôr) ***n.*** a South African whose ancestors were Dutch colonists. ◆***adj.*** of the Boers.

**bog** (bäg *or* bôg) ***n.*** wet, spongy ground; a small marsh or swamp. ◆***v.*** to sink or become stuck, as in a bog. —**bogged, bog′ging** —**bog′gy** ***adj.***

**bo·gey** (bō′gē) ***n.*** *another spelling for* **bogy.** —*pl.* **bo′geys**

**bog·gle** (bäg′'l) ***v.*** **1** to be startled at something. **2** to confuse or be confused by something that is surprising, vast, or very hard to understand [Such an expanse *boggles* the mind. My mind *boggles* at the thought of how large the universe is.] —**bog′gled, bog′gling**

**Bo·go·tá** (bō gə tä′) the capital of Colombia.

☆**bo·gus** (bō′gəs) ***adj.*** not genuine; false; counterfeit [a *bogus* dollar bill].

**bo·gy** (bō′gē *or* boog′ē) ***n.*** **1** an imaginary evil spirit; goblin. **2** a person or thing that causes unnecessary fear. —*pl.* **bo′gies**

**Bo·he·mi·a** (bō hē′mē ə) a region in western Czechoslovakia, once a kingdom. *See the map.*

**Bo·he·mi·an** (bō hē′mē ən) ***n.*** **1** a person born or living in Bohemia. **2** the language of Bohemia; Czech. **3** an artist, writer, musician, etc. who feels free to live according to rules and morals that are different from those of most people. ◆***adj.*** **1** of Bohemia, its people, or their language. **2** of or like a Bohemian (*in meaning* 3); unconventional.

**boil¹** (boil) ***v.*** **1** to bubble up and become steam or vapor by being heated [Water *boils* at 100°C.] **2** to heat a liquid until it bubbles up in this way [to *boil* water]. **3** to cook in a boiling liquid [to *boil* potatoes]. **4** to be stirred up, as with rage. ◆***n.*** the condition of boiling [Bring the soup to a *boil.*] —**boil down, 1** to make less by boiling. **2** to make shorter by using fewer words; abridge.

**boil²** (boil) ***n.*** a painful, red swelling on the skin. Boils are filled with pus and caused by infection.

**boil·er** (boil′ər) ***n.*** **1** a pot or tub in which things are boiled. **2** a tank in which water is heated until it becomes steam, which is then used for heating or power. **3** a tank for heating and storing hot water.

**Boi·se** (boi′sē *or* boi′zē) the capital of Idaho.

**bois·ter·ous** (bois′tər əs) ***adj.*** **1** rough and stormy. **2** noisy and lively [a *boisterous* party].

**bold** (bōld) ***adj.*** **1** ready to take risks or face danger; daring; fearless [a *bold* explorer]. *See* SYNONYMS *at* **brave. 2** too free in manner; not polite or respectful; impudent. **3** so sharp or clear as to stand out [*bold* handwriting]. —**bold′ly *adv.*** —**bold′ness *n.***

**bole** (bōl) ***n.*** the trunk of a tree.

**bo·le·ro** (bə ler′ō) ***n.*** **1** a Spanish dance with a lively rhythm. **2** the music for this. **3** a short, open vest, often with sleeves. —*pl.* **bo·le′ros**

**Bo·lí·var** (bō lē′vär), **Si·món** (sē mōn′) 1783–1830; Venezuelan general. He was a leader in the fight to free South America from Spanish rule.

**Bo·liv·i·a** (bə liv′ē ə) a country in western South America. —**Bo·liv′i·an *adj., n.***

**boll** (bōl) ***n.*** the seed pod of certain plants, especially of cotton, which contains the fiber.

☆**boll weevil** a small, gray beetle whose larvae hatch in cotton bolls and damage the cotton.

**bo·lo·gna** or **bo·lo·ney** (bə lō′nē) ***n.*** a large sausage made of various meats.

**Bol·she·vik** (bōl′shə vik *or* bäl′shə vik) ***n.*** **1** a member of the political party that came into power after the revolution of 1917 in Russia. It became the Communist Party of the Soviet Union. **2** a radical in politics. —*pl.* **Bol′she·viks** or **Bol·she·vi·ki** (bōl′shə vē′kē)

**bol·ster** (bōl′stər) ***n.*** a long, narrow pillow or cushion.

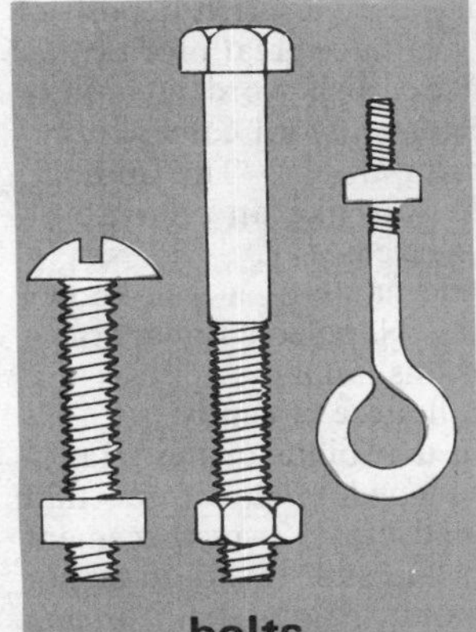
bolts

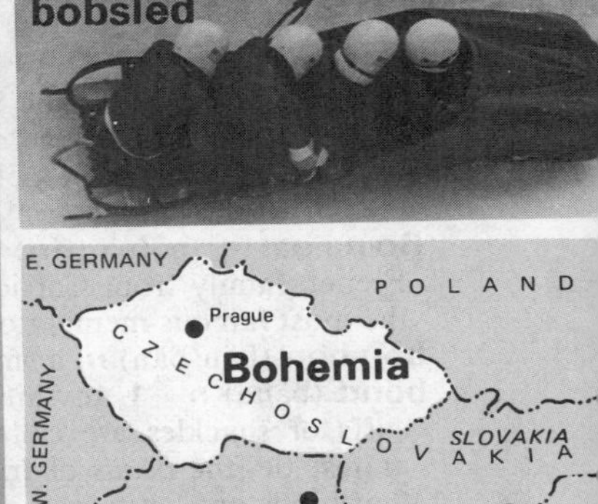

bobsled

◆***v.*** to prop up, as if with a bolster; support [The coach's talk *bolstered* up our spirits.]

**bolt¹** (bōlt) ***n.*** **1** a heavy metal pin that is threaded like a screw. It is used with a nut to hold parts together. *See the picture.* **2** a metal bar that slides into a part, as across a door for keeping it shut. **3** the part of a lock that is moved by the key. **4** a large roll of cloth. **5** a flash of lightning. **6** a short arrow shot from a crossbow. **7** the act of one who bolts [She made a sudden *bolt* from the room.] ◆***v.*** **1** to fasten with a bolt. **2** to run out or run away suddenly [The horse *bolted* through the gate.] **3** to swallow quickly; gulp down [to *bolt* one's food]. ☆**4** to stop being a member or supporter of [to *bolt* a political party]. —**a bolt from the blue,** a sudden surprise. —**bolt upright,** straight up; very erect.



**bolt²** (bōlt) ***v.*** to sift through a sieve.

**bomb** (bäm) ***n.*** **1** a hollow case filled with an explosive, a harmful gas, etc. Bombs are blown up by a fuse or timing device or by being dropped or thrown against something with force. ☆**2** a complete failure: *slang in this meaning.* ◆***v.*** **1** to attack or destroy with bombs. **2** to fail completely: *slang in this meaning.*

**bom·bard** (bäm bärd′) ***v.*** **1** to attack with artillery; shell. **2** to keep on directing questions or requests at. —**bom·bard′ment *n.***

**bom·bar·dier** (bäm bə dir′) ***n.*** the member of a bomber crew who releases the bombs.

**bom·bast** (bäm′bast) ***n.*** talk or writing that sounds grand and important but has little meaning. —**bom·bas′tic *adj.*** —**bom·bas′ti·cal·ly *adv.***

**Bom·bay** (bäm bā′) a city in western India.

**bomb·er** (bäm′ər) ***n.*** **1** an airplane made for dropping bombs in warfare. **2** a person who bombs.

**bomb·shell** (bäm′shel) ***n.*** **1** a bomb. **2** a sudden or shocking surprise.

**bo·na fi·de** (bō′nə fīd′ *or* bän′ə fīd′ *or* bō′nə fī′dē) in good faith; genuine [a *bona fide* contract].

| | | | | | | | |
|---|---|---|---|---|---|---|---|
| **a** fat | **ir** here | **ou** out | **zh** leisure | | | | |
| **ā** ape | **ī** bite, fire | **u** up | **ng** ring | | | | |
| **ä** car, lot | **ō** go | **ur** fur | a *in* ago | | | | |
| **e** ten | **ô** law, horn | **ch** chin | e *in* agent | | | | |
| **er** care | **oi** oil | **sh** she | ə = i *in* unity | | | | |
| **ē** even | **oo** look | **th** thin | o *in* collect | | | | |
| **i** hit | **ōō** tool | ***th*** then | u *in* focus | | | | |

**b**

☆**bo·nan·za** (bə nan′zə) ***n.*** **1** a very rich deposit of ore. **2** anything that gives wealth or great profit.

**Bonanza** is originally a Spanish word meaning "fair weather," and the Spanish word comes from a Latin word meaning "calm at sea." The finding of a rich deposit of gold was like an enjoyable calm after a hard, stormy search.

**Bo·na·parte** (bō′nə pärt) the name of a well-known French family from Corsica. Napoleon Bonaparte is the most famous member of this family.

**bon·bon** (bän′bän) ***n.*** a small piece of candy.

**bond** (bänd) ***n.*** **1** anything that binds or ties [Handcuffs or shackles are called *bonds.*] **2** a force that unites; tie [the *bonds* of friendship]. **3** an agreement that binds one, as to pay certain sums or to do or not do certain things. **4** an amount paid as bail: *usually called* **bail bond.** **5** a certificate sold by a government or business as a way of raising money. It promises to return the money to the buyer by a certain date, along with interest [The city issued *bonds* to build a subway.] **6** something, as glue, solder, or a chain, that holds things together. ◆***v.*** **1** to fasten with a bond. **2** to furnish a bond or bonds for.

**bond·age** (bän′dij) ***n.*** the condition of being a slave; slavery.

**bond·ed** (bän′did) ***adj.*** **1** insured or protected by bonds. **2** stored in a warehouse (called a **bonded warehouse**) under government care, until taxes are paid [*bonded* whiskey].



**bond·man** (bänd′mən) ***n.*** a slave or serf. *—pl.* **bond′-men**

**bonds·man** (bändz′mən) ***n.*** **1** a person who becomes responsible for another by furnishing a bond (*in meaning* 3 *or* 4). **2** a slave or serf. *—pl.* **bonds′-men**

**bond·wom·an** (bänd′woom′ən) ***n.*** a woman who is a slave or serf. *—pl.* **bond′wom′en**

**bone** (bōn) ***n.*** **1** any of the hard pieces that are joined together to form the skeleton of a person or animal [There are about 200 *bones* in the human body.] **2** the material of which these are formed [Calcium helps build *bone.*] **3** a substance like bone or a thing made of bone [Ivory is often called *bone.*] ◆***v.*** to take the bones out of [to *bone* fish]. —**boned, bon′-ing** —**make no bones about,** to admit freely: *used only in everyday talk.*

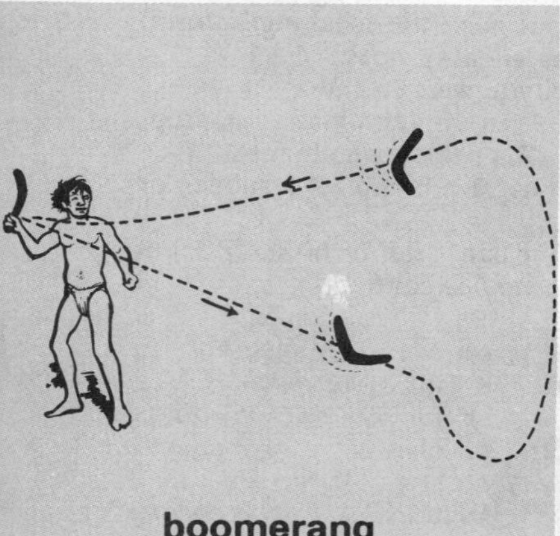
boomerang

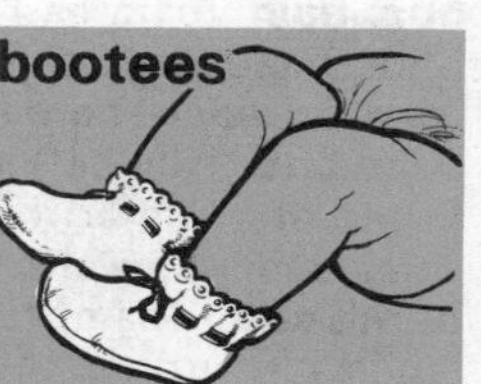
bootees

bonnet

☆**bon·er** (bōn′ər) ***n.*** a silly or stupid mistake: *a slang word.*

**bon·fire** (bän′fīr) ***n.*** a fire built outdoors.

☆**bon·go** (bäŋ′gō) ***n.*** either of a pair of small drums, played with the hands. *—pl.* **bon′gos**

**bo·ni·to** (bə nēt′ō) ***n.*** a large ocean fish related to the mackerel and tuna. Its flesh is often canned. *—pl.* **bo-ni′tos** or **bo·ni′toes**

**Bonn** (bän) the capital of West Germany.

**bon·net** (bän′it) ***n.*** **1** a hat for women and children that is held in place by a ribbon tied under the chin. *See the picture.* **2** a flat, brimless cap worn by men and boys in Scotland.

**bon·ny** or **bon·nie** (bän′ē) ***adj.*** handsome or pretty, with a healthy, cheerful glow: *used mainly in Scotland and parts of England.* —**bon′ni·er, bon′ni·est**

**bon·sai** (bän sī′) ***n.*** a tiny tree or shrub that has been pruned to keep it small and artistic in shape. *—pl.* **bon·sai′**

**bo·nus** (bō′nəs) ***n.*** anything given in addition to what is due or expected; gift of something extra. *—pl.* **bo-nus·es** (bō′nəs iz)

**bon voy·age** (bän′ voi äzh′) a pleasant journey: a phrase used in French to say goodbye to a traveler.

**bon·y** (bō′nē) ***adj.*** **1** of or like bone [The skull is a *bony* structure.] **2** full of bones [a *bony* piece of fish]. **3** having bones that stick out; thin; lean [Lincoln's *bony* face.] —**bon′i·er, bon′i·est** —**bon′i·ness** ***n.***

**boo** (bōō) ***interj., n.*** a long, drawn-out sound made in showing dislike or scorn; also, a short sound like this made to startle a person. *—pl.* **boos** ◆***v.*** to shout "boo" at in showing dislike. —**booed, boo′ing**

**boo·by** (bōō′bē) ***n.*** **1** a stupid or foolish person. **2** a large, heavy sea bird. *—pl.* **boo′bies**

☆**booby prize** a silly prize given in fun to the person with the lowest score in a game, race, etc.

**booby trap** **1** a hidden bomb that is fixed to some harmless-looking object so that it will explode when someone touches or lifts the object. **2** any hidden trick or trap.

**boo·hoo** (bōō hōō′) ***n.*** noisy weeping. *—pl.* **boo·hoos′** ◆***v.*** to weep in a noisy way. —**boo·hooed′, boo-hoo′ing**

**book** (book) ***n.*** **1** printed sheets of paper fastened together at one side, between protective covers; volume [Our library has 40,000 *books.*] **2** a long piece of writing such as a novel, a history, a long poem, etc. [Smith's *book* will be published in two volumes.] **3** a main part of a long piece of writing ["Genesis" is the first *book* of the Bible.] **4** a number of blank pages bound together between covers [an account *book;* a note*book*]. **5** a number of small things bound together in a cover [a *book* of matches; a *book* of tickets]. ◆***v.*** **1** to write down in a book or record; list [The police *book* people who are arrested and brought into the station.] **2** to engage ahead of time, as rooms or transportation, by having one's name put on a list [to *book* passage on a ship]. —**an open book,** something plain to see or understand. —**by the book,** according to the rules. —**keep books,** to keep accounts or business records. —**know like a book,** to know very well. —**the Book** or **the Good Book,** the Bible.

**Book** comes from the Old English word for "beech." In early times, writing was sometimes done by carving on boards of beech.

**book·case** (book′kās) ***n.*** a set of shelves or a cabinet for holding books.

**book·end** (book′end) ***n.*** a fancy weight or bracket put at the end of a row of books to keep them standing.

**book·ish** (book′ish) ***adj.*** **1** spending much time reading or studying. **2** too formal; dull; dry [a *bookish* style of writing].

**book·keep·er** (book′kēp′ər) ***n.*** a person whose work is to keep accounts for a business.

**book·keep·ing** (book′kēp′ing) ***n.*** the work of keeping business accounts.

**book·let** (book′lit) ***n.*** a little book, often with paper covers.

**book·mark** (book′märk) ***n.*** anything slipped between the pages of a book to mark a place.

☆**book·mo·bile** (book′mō bēl′) ***n.*** a traveling library in a truck, van, etc. that goes to places which do not have a regular library.

**book·shelf** (book′shelf) ***n.*** a shelf on which books may be kept. —*pl.* **book′shelves**

☆**book·store** (book′stôr) ***n.*** a store where books are sold.

**book·worm** (book′wurm) ***n.*** **1** an insect larva that bores holes in books. **2** anyone who reads or studies a great deal.

**boom**[1] (bo͞om) ***v.*** to make a deep, hollow sound like a bass drum. ◆***n.*** such a sound.

**boom**[2] (bo͞om) ***n.*** **1** a pole that comes out from a mast to keep the bottom of a sail stretched out. **2** a beam that comes out from a derrick for lifting and guiding a load. **3** a heavy chain or other barrier put in a harbor or river to keep ships out or to keep floating logs in.

☆**boom**[3] (bo͞om) ***v.*** to grow suddenly or swiftly; thrive [Industry *boomed* after the war.] ◆***n.*** a sudden, rapid growth; especially, a time of business prosperity.

**boom·er·ang** (bo͞om′ə rang) ***n.*** **1** a flat, curved stick that can be thrown so it will come back to the thrower. It is used as a weapon by the natives of Australia. *See the picture.* **2** something said or done to harm a person that turns out to hurt the one who started it. ◆***v.*** to act as a boomerang.

**boon** (bo͞on) ***n.*** **1** a welcome gift; blessing [The early spring was a *boon* to the farmers.] **2** a favor; request: *now seldom used in this meaning* [Grant me a *boon.*]

**boon companion** a close friend who often joins one in seeking fun and pleasure.

**boon·docks** (bo͞on′däks) ***n.pl.*** **1** a jungle or wild, wooded area. ☆**2** any faraway, rural or unsettled region; hinterland. *This word is used with* the *and only in everyday talk.*

**Boone** (bo͞on), **Daniel** 1734–1820; American pioneer and explorer.

**boor** (boor) ***n.*** a person who has bad manners and is very rude to others. —**boor′ish *adj.***

☆**boost** (bo͞ost) ***v.*** **1** to raise by pushing from below; push up [Can you *boost* the child into the tree?] **2** to make higher or greater [to *boost* taxes; to *boost* electric current]. **3** to urge others to support [Let's form a club to *boost* the football team.] ◆***n.*** a pushing up; a raise or help [Lower prices resulted in a *boost* in sales.] —**boost′er *n.***

**boot**[1] (bo͞ot) ***n.*** **1** a covering of leather, rubber, etc. for the foot and part of the leg. **2** a kick with the foot. ◆***v.*** to kick. —**to get the boot,** to be fired from one's job: *a slang phrase.*

**boot**[2] (bo͞ot) ***v.*** to benefit or profit: *now seldom used* [It *boots* us little to object.] —**to boot,** in addition; besides [We ate up the cake and a pie *to boot.*]

**boot·black** (bo͞ot′blak) ***n.*** a person whose work is shining boots and shoes.

☆**boot·ee** (bo͞ot′ē) ***n.*** a baby's soft shoe, knitted or made of cloth. *See the picture.*

**booth** (bo͞oth) ***n.*** a small space all or partly closed off so as to form a stall or shed [a *booth* at a market; a voting *booth;* a telephone *booth;* a restaurant *booth*].

☆**boot·leg** (bo͞ot′leg) ***v.*** to sell alcoholic liquor when it is against the law, as during Prohibition. —**boot′legged, boot′leg·ging —boot′leg·ger *n.***

> At one time, when people wanted to carry about things that were illegal, they would hide them in the legs of their high boots. Such people were called **bootleggers.**

**boot·less** (bo͞ot′lis) ***adj.*** doing no good; useless [a *bootless* effort].

**boo·ty** (bo͞ot′ē) ***n.*** **1** goods taken from the enemy in war. **2** any goods taken by force or robbery; plunder. **3** any gifts, prizes, etc.: *used in a joking way.*

**bo·rax** (bôr′aks) ***n.*** a white salt used in making glass, enamel, and soaps.

**Bor·deaux** (bôr dō′) a seaport in southwestern France. ◆***n.*** a white or red wine originally from France.



**bor·der** (bôr′dər) ***n.*** **1** a line that divides one country or state from another; frontier. **2** an edge or a narrow strip along an edge; margin [a red tablecloth with a blue *border;* a *border* of flowers around the yard]. ◆***v.*** **1** to put a border on [The pillowcase is *bordered* with lace.] **2** to lie along the edge of [Lilies *border* the path.] —**border on** or **border upon,** to be next to; be close to [Canada *borders on* the United States. Her grief *borders on* madness.]

**bor·der·land** (bôr′dər land) ***n.*** **1** the land near a border between countries. **2** an uncertain condition that is not quite one thing or the other [the *borderland* between waking and sleeping].

**bor·der·line** (bôr′dər līn) ***n.*** a border or boundary between countries or states. ◆***adj.*** **1** on a border or boundary [a *borderline* town]. **2** not quite one thing or the other; uncertain; doubtful [a *borderline* type of mental illness].

**bore**[1] (bôr) ***v.*** **1** to make a hole by digging or drilling [A tunnel was *bored* through the mountain.] **2** to make tired by being dull or uninteresting [The speaker *bored* the crowd with old jokes.] —**bored, bor′ing** ◆***n.*** **1** the hollow part inside a tube or pipe [This gun has a narrow *bore.*] **2** a hole made by boring. **3** a dull or uninteresting person or thing.

**bore**[2] (bôr) *past tense of* **bear**[1].

| | | | | | | | |
|---|---|---|---|---|---|---|---|
| **a** | fat | **ir** | here | **ou** | out | **zh** | leisure |
| **ā** | ape | **ī** | bite, fire | **u** | up | **ng** | ring |
| **ä** | car, lot | **ō** | go | **ur** | fur | | a *in* ago |
| **e** | ten | **ô** | law, horn | **ch** | chin | | e *in* agent |
| **er** | care | **oi** | oil | **sh** | she | **ə =** | i *in* unity |
| **ē** | even | **oo** | look | **th** | thin | | o *in* collect |
| **i** | hit | **o͞o** | tool | ***th*** | then | | u *in* focus |

**bore·dom** (bôr′dəm) ***n.*** the condition of being bored by something dull or uninteresting.

**bor·er** (bôr′ər) ***n.*** **1** a tool for boring. **2** an insect or worm that bores holes in fruit, trees, etc.

**bo·ric acid** (bôr′ik) a white powder dissolved in water for use as a mild antiseptic.

**born** (bôrn) *a past participle of* **bear[1]**, meaning "given birth to" [The twins were *born* an hour apart.] ◆***adj.*** **1** brought into life or being [a newly *born* idea]. **2** as if from the time of birth; natural [The child is a *born* musician.]

**borne** (bôrn) *the usual past participle of* **bear[1]** [She has *borne* a child. He has *borne* much pain.]

**Bor·ne·o** (bôr′nē ō) a large island in the East Indies, southwest of the Philippines.

**bo·ron** (bôr′än) ***n.*** a chemical element that is found only in certain compounds, such as borax. It is used in making glass, metal alloys, etc.

**bor·ough** (bur′ō) ***n.*** **1** a town or village that has a charter to govern itself. **2** one of the five main divisions of New York City.

**bor·row** (bär′ō *or* bôr′ō) ***v.*** **1** to get to use something for a while by agreeing to return it later [You can *borrow* that book from the library.] **2** to take another's word, idea, etc. and use it as one's own [The Romans *borrowed* many of their myths from the Greeks.] —☆**borrow trouble,** to worry before anything has gone wrong.



**bosh** (bäsh) ***n., interj.*** nonsense: *used only in everyday talk.*

**bos·om** (booz′əm) ***n.*** **1** a person's breast [Rest your head on my *bosom.*] **2** the breast thought of as the place where feelings begin [Deep within my *bosom,* I knew I was wrong.] **3** the inside; central part [in the *bosom* of her family]. **4** the part of a garment that covers the breast. ◆***adj.*** very close and dear [a *bosom* friend].

**Bos·po·rus** (bäs′pər əs) a strait in northwestern Turkey, joining the Black Sea and the Sea of Marmara.

☆**boss[1]** (bôs) ***n.*** **1** a person who is in charge of workers, as an employer, a manager, or a foreman. **2** a person who controls a political group, as in a county. ◆***v.*** **1** to act as boss of. **2** to act bossy toward: *used only in everyday talk* [He *bossed* them around.]

**boss[2]** (bôs) ***n.*** a small knob or stud sticking out as a decoration. ◆***v.*** to decorate with bosses.

☆**boss·y** (bôs′ē) ***adj.*** acting like a boss; fond of giving orders: *used only in everyday talk.*

**Bos·ton** (bôs′t'n) a seaport that is the capital of Massachusetts. —**Bos·to·ni·an** (bôs tō′nē ən) ***adj., n.***

**bo·sun** (bōs′'n) ***n.*** *another spelling for* **boatswain.**

**bot.** *abbreviation for* **botanical** *or* **botany.**

**bo·tan·i·cal** (bə tan′i k'l) ***adj.*** having to do with botany [Plants are raised in a *botanical* garden so that they can be studied and exhibited.] *Also written* **bo·tan′ic.**

**bot·a·ny** (bät′'n ē) ***n.*** the science that studies plants and how they grow. —**bot′a·nist** ***n.***

**botch** (bäch) ***v.*** to fix or patch in a clumsy way; to spoil by poor or careless work; bungle [She failed to match the color and so *botched* the paint job.] ◆***n.*** a poor or careless piece of work.

**both** (bōth) ***adj., pron.*** the two, or the two of them [*Both* birds are small, and *both* sing well.] ◆***conj., adv.*** equally; as well; not only: *used in phrases with* and [I am *both* tired and hungry.]

**both·er** (bäth′ər) ***v.*** **1** to annoy; cause worry or trouble to; pester [Does the noise *bother* you?] **2** to take the time or trouble [Don't *bother* to answer this letter.] ◆***n.*** something that annoys or causes worry or trouble [Flies are a *bother.*]

**both·er·some** (bäth′ər səm) ***adj.*** annoying.

**Bot·swa·na** (bät swä′nə) a country in southern Africa, north of South Africa.

**bot·tle** (bät′'l) ***n.*** **1** a container, especially for liquids, usually made of glass or plastic. Bottles generally have a narrow neck and no handles. **2** the amount that a bottle holds [The baby drank a *bottle* of milk.] ◆***v.*** **1** to put into a bottle. **2** to store under pressure in a tank [*bottled* gas]. —**bot′tled, bot′tling** —**bottle up,** to hold back; restrain [to *bottle up* the enemy].

**bot·tle·neck** (bät′'l nek) ***n.*** anything that slows up something moving along, work being done, etc. [This narrow street is a *bottleneck* during rush hours.]

**bot·tom** (bät′əm) ***n.*** **1** the lowest part [Sign your name at the *bottom* of this paper.] **2** the part on which a thing rests; base [Any side on which a crate rests becomes its *bottom.*] **3** the seat of a chair. **4** the ground under a body of water [The ship sank to the *bottom.*] ☆**5** *often* **bottoms,** *pl.* low land along a river. **6** the true facts or the main reason; basis or cause [Get to the *bottom* of the problem.] ◆***adj.*** of or at the bottom; lowest [the *bottom* shelf].

☆**bottom land** low land that has a river flowing through it.

**bot·tom·less** (bät′əm lis) ***adj.*** so deep that it seems to have no bottom [a *bottomless* lake].

**bou·doir** (bo͞od′wär) ***n.*** a woman's bedroom or dressing room.

> **Boudoir** is a French word whose original meaning was "pouting room." In earlier times, if a young lady was sulky, she was sent to her boudoir where she could pout in private.

**bouf·fant** (bo͞o fänt′) ***adj.*** puffed out; full, as some skirts, hair styles, etc. *See the picture.*

**bough** (bou) ***n.*** a large branch of a tree.

**bought** (bôt) *past tense and past participle of* **buy.**

**bouil·lon** (bool′yän) ***n.*** a clear soup.

**boul·der** (bōl′dər) ***n.*** any large rock made round and smooth by weather and water.

**boul·e·vard** (bool′ə värd) ***n.*** ☆a wide street, often lined with trees: abbreviated **blvd.**

**bounce** (bouns) ***v.*** **1** to hit against a surface so as to spring back; bound or rebound [to *bounce* a ball against a wall; to *bounce* up and down on a sofa]. **2** to move suddenly; jump; leap [I *bounced* out of bed when the alarm went off.] —**bounced, bounc′ing** ◆***n.*** **1** a springing or bounding; leap. **2** the ability to bound or rebound [This ball has lost its *bounce.*]

**bounc·ing** (boun′siŋ) ***adj.*** big, healthy, strong, etc. [It's a *bouncing* baby boy.]

**bound[1]** (bound) ***v.*** **1** to move with a leap or leaps [The dog came *bounding* to meet her.] **2** to spring back from a surface; rebound; bounce. ◆***n.*** **1** a jump; leap [He reached the door with one *bound.*] **2** a bounce.

**bound²** (ound) *past tense and past participle of* **bind**. ◆***adj.*** **1** sure; certain [She's *bound* to lose.] **2** having a binding or cover [a *bound* book]. **3** having one's mind set; resolved: *used only in everyday talk* [The team is *bound* and determined to win.] —**bound up in,** very busy with [She is *bound up in* her work.]

**bound³** (bound) ***adj.*** ready to go or going; headed [We are *bound* for home.] This word is sometimes used as a suffix, as in *northbound*.

**bound⁴** (bound) ***n.*** a boundary line or limit. ◆***v.*** to form a boundary of [The Ohio River *bounds* Indiana on the south.] —**out of bounds, 1** outside the playing limits, as of a football field. **2** not to be entered or used; forbidden.

SYNONYMS: **Bound⁴** means to put a boundary around something [The playground is *bounded* by a fence.] **Limit** means to set or fix a point in space or time beyond which one cannot go or is not allowed to go [*Limit* your visit to ten minutes.]

**bound·a·ry** (boun′drē *or* boun′dər ē) ***n.*** a line or thing that marks the outside edge or limit [The Delaware River forms the eastern *boundary* of Pennsylvania.] —*pl.* **bound′a·ries**

**bound·en** (boun′dən) ***adj.*** that one is bound by; that one must do [a *bounden* duty].

**bound·less** (bound′lis) ***adj.*** having no bounds or limits [the *boundless* skies].

**boun·te·ous** (boun′tē əs) ***adj.*** *same as* **bountiful**.

**boun·ti·ful** (boun′tə f′l) ***adj.*** **1** giving much gladly; generous [a *bountiful* patron]. **2** more than enough; plentiful [a *bountiful* harvest]. —**boun′ti·ful·ly** ***adv.***

**boun·ty** (boun′tē) ***n.*** **1** any action of giving much gladly; generosity. **2** something given freely; generous gift. **3** a reward given by a government, as for killing harmful animals. —*pl.* **boun′ties**

**bou·quet** (bō kā′ *or* bo͞o kā′) ***n.*** **1** a bunch of flowers. **2** (bo͞o kā′) a fragrant smell.

**Bour·bon** (boor′bən) the name of the former ruling family of France, of Spain, and of several other countries and states in Europe.

**bour·bon** (bur′bən *or* boor′bən) ***n.*** ☆a whiskey made chiefly from corn: *sometimes written* **Bourbon**.

**bour·geois** (boor zhwä′) ***n.*** a person of the middle class, or bourgeoisie. —*pl.* **bour·geois′** ◆***adj.*** of or like the middle class or its way of life: *now usually used to mean* respectable, ordinary, smugly comfortable, etc.

**bour·geoi·sie** (boor′zhwä zē′) ***n.*** the social class between the working class and the very wealthy; middle class: *used with a singular or plural verb.*

**bout** (bout) ***n.*** **1** a contest; fight [a boxing *bout*]. **2** a period of time when one is ill or doing something; spell [a *bout* of the flu].

**bou·tique** (bo͞o tēk′) ***n.*** a small shop where expensive articles or clothes are sold.

**bo·vine** (bō′vīn) ***adj.*** **1** of an ox or cow. **2** like an ox or cow; slow, dull, without feeling, etc.

**bow¹** (bou) ***v.*** **1** to bend the head or body in respect, worship, greeting, etc. **2** to give up or yield [I shall *bow* to your wishes.] **3** to bend or weigh down [The worker's back was *bowed* down by the load.] ◆***n.*** a bending of the head or body, as in respect, greeting, etc. —**take a bow,** to come back on stage in answer to applause.

**bow²** (bō) ***n.*** **1** a weapon for shooting arrows, made of a curved strip of wood with a cord tied to both ends. *See the picture for* **archer**. **2** a slender stick with horsehairs tied along its length. It is drawn across the strings of a violin, cello, etc. to play music. **3** anything curved or bent [a rain*bow*]. **4** a knot tied with loops in it [Shoelaces are tied with a *bow*.] ◆***v.*** **1** to bend or curve [The wall *bowed* outward.] **2** to play a violin, etc. with a bow.

bowlegged man

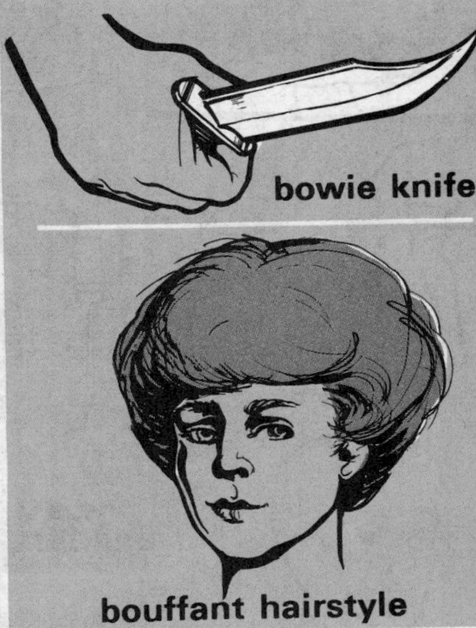
bowie knife

bouffant hairstyle



**bow³** (bou) ***n.*** the front part of a ship, boat, etc.

**bow·els** (bou′əlz) ***n.pl.*** **1** the intestines, especially of a human being. **2** the part deep inside [the *bowels* of the earth].

**bow·er** (bou′ər) ***n.*** a place shaded by trees or bushes or by vines on a trellis; arbor.

☆**bow·ie knife** (bo͞o′ē *or* bō′ē) a long knife with a single edge, used by hunters. *See the picture.*

**bowl¹** (bōl) ***n.*** **1** a deep, rounded dish. **2** as much as a bowl will hold [She ate two *bowls* of soup.] **3** a thing or part shaped like a bowl [Tobacco is put in the *bowl* of a pipe.] ☆**4** a stadium or amphitheater.

**bowl²** (bōl) ***n.*** **1** the heavy ball used in the game of bowls. **2** a rolling of the ball in bowling. ◆***v.*** **1** to play at bowling or take a turn at bowling. **2** to move swiftly and smoothly [The car *bowled* along the highway.] —**bowl over, 1** to knock over. **2** to surprise very much; shock: *used only in everyday talk.* —**bowl′er** ***n.***

**bow·leg·ged** (bō′leg′id *or* bō′legd) ***adj.*** having legs that are bowed outward. *See the picture.*

**bowl·ing** (bō′liŋ) ***n.*** **1** a game in which each player rolls a heavy ball along a wooden lane (**bowling alley**), trying to knock down ten wooden pins at the far end. **2** *same as* **bowls.**

| | | | |
|---|---|---|---|
| **a** fat | **ir** here | **ou** out | **zh** leisure |
| **ā** ape | **ī** bite, fire | **u** up | **ŋ** ring |
| **ä** car, lot | **ō** go | **ur** fur | a *in* ago |
| **e** ten | **ô** law, horn | **ch** chin | e *in* agent |
| **er** care | **oi** oil | **sh** she | **ə** = i *in* unity |
| **ē** even | **oo** look | **th** thin | o *in* collect |
| **i** hit | **o͞o** tool | ***th*** then | u *in* focus |

b

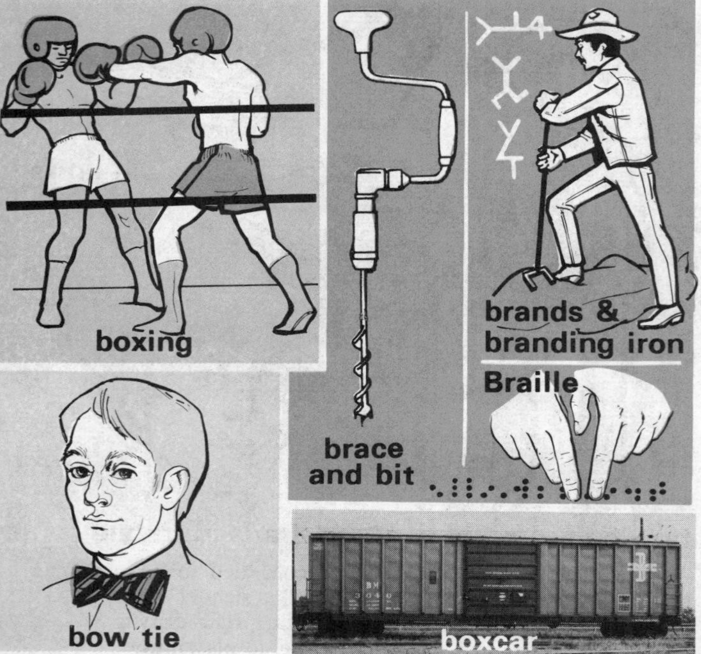




**bowls** (bōlz) ***n.*** an old game played on a smooth lawn (**bowling green**) with a heavy wooden ball. Each player tries to roll a ball as close as possible to another ball at the far end.

**bow·sprit** (bou′sprit *or* bō′sprit) ***n.*** a large pole sticking out forward from the bow of a ship. Ropes from the front mast and sails are tied to it.

**bow·string** (bō′string) ***n.*** the string of an archer's bow.

**bow tie** (bō) a necktie tied in a bow. *See the picture.*

**box**[1] (bäks) ***n.*** **1** a container to hold or carry things in, made of stiff material like cardboard or wood. It usually has four sides, a bottom, and a lid on top. **2** as much as a box will hold [I ate two whole *boxes* of popcorn.] **3** anything that is more or less like a box, as an enclosed place with seats for a jury, a booth, etc. ☆**4** the marked-off place where the batter or the pitcher must stand in baseball. ◆***v.*** to put into a box [*Box* the oranges for shipping.] —**box in** or **box up,** to shut in or keep in.

**box**[2] (bäks) ***n.*** a blow or slap with the hand or fist, especially on the ear. ◆***v.*** **1** to hit with such a blow or slap. **2** to fight with the fists: *see* **boxing.**

**box**[3] (bäks) ***n.*** an evergreen shrub or small tree with leathery leaves: *also called* **box′wood.**

☆**box·car** (bäks′kär) ***n.*** a railroad car for carrying freight, with a roof and closed sides. *See the picture.*

**box·er** (bäk′sər) ***n.*** **1** a man who boxes. **2** a large dog with a stocky body and small ears.

**box·ing** (bäk′sing) ***n.*** the skill or sport of fighting with the fists, especially in padded leather mittens (**boxing gloves**). *See the picture.*

**box office** a place where tickets are sold, as in a theater.

**boy** (boi) ***n.*** **1** a male child before he becomes a man. **2** any man; fellow: *used only in everyday talk* [The *boys* at the office formed a bowling team.] **3** a man servant, porter, etc.: *now thought to be unfriendly or insulting.* ◆☆***interj.*** an exclamation used to show pleasure, surprise, etc.

**boy·cott** (boi′kät) ***v.*** to join together in refusing to buy, sell, or use something or to have any dealings with someone [We all *boycotted* the ice cream store because it was dirty.] ◆☆***n.*** the act of boycotting a business, etc.

> The word **boycott** comes from the name of Captain Charles C. Boycott, who collected rent for a landlord in Ireland. After he raised the rents of his neighbors in 1880, they had no more to do with him. They wouldn't even sell him groceries.

☆**boy·friend** (boi′frend) ***n.*** **1** a sweetheart of a girl or woman. **2** a boy who is one's friend. *This word is used only in everyday talk.*

**boy·hood** (boi′hood) ***n.*** the time of being a boy [He delivered papers in his *boyhood.*]

**boy·ish** (boi′ish) ***adj.*** of, like, or fit for a boy [a *boyish* prank]. —**boy′ish·ly *adv.***

**boy scout** a member of the **Boy Scouts,** a club for boys that teaches outdoor skills and service to others.

☆**boy·sen·ber·ry** (boi′z'n ber′ē) ***n.*** a large, purple berry, probably a cross of the raspberry, loganberry, and blackberry. —*pl.* **boy′sen·ber′ries**

**Br** *the symbol for the chemical element* bromine.

**Br.** *abbreviation for* **Britain** *or* **British.**

**bra** (brä) ***n.*** an undergarment worn by women to support the breasts.

**brace** (brās) ***v.*** **1** to make stronger by propping up [*Brace* the shelf by nailing a wedge under it.] **2** to make ready for a jolt, shock, etc. [I *braced* myself for the crash.] **3** to give energy to; stimulate [The cool, fresh air will *brace* you.] —**braced, brac′ing** ◆***n.*** **1** a pair or couple [a *brace* of pistols]. **2** a thing for supporting a weak part or for keeping parts in place [A timber propping up floorboards, a stiff frame for supporting a weak leg, etc., and a metal band on the teeth to straighten them are all called *braces.*] **3 braces,** *pl.* suspenders: *used in Great Britain.* **4** either of the signs { }, used to group together words, lines, or staves of music. **5** a tool for drilling: *see* **brace and bit.** —☆**brace up,** to become strong or brave again after defeat, disappointment, etc.

**brace and bit** a tool for boring holes, which has a removable drill (*bit*) in a handle (*brace*) that turns around and around. *See the picture.*

**brace·let** (brās′lit) ***n.*** a band or chain worn as an ornament around the wrist or arm.

**brac·ing** (brās′ing) ***adj.*** filling with energy; refreshing [the *bracing* air at the seashore].

**brack·et** (brak′it) ***n.*** **1** a support fastened to a wall for holding up a shelf, balcony, etc. **2** a shelf or fixture sticking out from a wall. **3** either of the signs [ ], used to enclose words, figures, etc. that are put in to explain something or make a comment [In this dictionary examples showing how words are used are in *brackets.*] **4** a grouping into classes according to a system [the $5,000 to $10,000 income *bracket*]. ◆***v.*** **1** to fasten or support with brackets. **2** to put a word or words between brackets. **3** to group or think of together [Grant and Lee are *bracketed* in history.]

**brack·ish** (brak′ish) ***adj.*** **1** a little salty, as the water of some marshes near the sea. **2** having an unpleasant taste.

**bract** (brakt) ***n.*** a leaf that grows at the base of a flower or on the flower stem. Bracts usually look like small scales.

**brad** (brad) ***n.*** a thin nail with a small head.

**brae** (brā) ***n.*** a hillside: *a Scottish word.*

**brag** (brag) ***v.*** to boast. —**bragged, brag'ging** ◆***n.*** boastful talk.

**brag·gart** (brag'ərt) ***n.*** a person who is always boasting.

**Brah·ma** (brä'mə) in the Hindu religion, the god who created the universe.

**Brah·man** or **Brah·min** (brä'mən) ***n.*** a member of the highest caste of Hindus. It is the social caste of priests and scholars.

**Brah·ma·pu·tra** (brä'mə po͞o'trə) a river in northern India. It joins the Ganges at the Bay of Bengal.

**Brahms** (brämz), **Jo·han·nes** (yō hän'əs) 1833–1897; German composer.

**braid** (brād) ***v.*** **1** to weave together three or more strands of hair, straw, ribbon, etc. **2** to make by weaving such strands [to *braid* a rug]. ◆***n.*** **1** a length of braided hair. **2** a band of braided cloth, ribbon, etc. used for trimming or decoration.

**Braille** or **braille** (brāl) ***n.*** a system of printing and writing for blind people. The letters, numbers, etc. are formed by patterns of raised dots which are felt with the fingers. *See the picture.*

> Louis **Braille** was a French teacher of the blind. He himself had been blinded in 1812, when he was still a little boy. He thought up the system, later named after him, to help blind people read and write.

**brain** (brān) ***n.*** **1** the gray and white tissue inside the skull of a person or of any animal with a backbone. It is the main part of the nervous system, by which one thinks and feels. **2** *often* **brains,** *pl.* intelligence; understanding [Use your *brains.*] **3** a very intelligent person: *used only in everyday talk.* ◆***v.*** to hit hard on the head: *slang in this meaning.* —**beat one's brains,** to try hard to remember, understand, etc.

**brain·less** (brān'lis) ***adj.*** foolish; stupid.

**brain·power** (brān'pou'ər) ***n.*** ability to think and use one's brain.

☆**brain·storm** (brān'stôrm) ***n.*** a sudden, brilliant idea: *used only in everyday talk.*

**brain·wash** (brān'wôsh) ***v.*** ☆to teach a set of ideas to so thoroughly as to change a person's beliefs and attitudes completely: *used only in everyday talk.*

**brain·y** (brān'ē) ***adj.*** having a good mind; intelligent: *used only in everyday talk.*—**brain'i·er, brain'i·est**

**braise** (brāz) ***v.*** to brown in fat and then cook over a low fire in a covered pan with a little liquid [to *braise* meat]. —**braised, brais'ing**

**brake**[1] (brāk) ***n.*** a large, coarse fern.

**brake**[2] (brāk) ***n.*** a device used to slow down or stop a car, machine, etc. It is often a block or band that is pressed against a wheel or other moving part. ◆***v.*** to slow down or stop with a brake. —**braked, brak'ing**

**brake**[3] (brāk) ***n.*** a thick growth of bushes, tall grasses, etc.; thicket.

☆**brake·man** (brāk'mən) ***n.*** a railroad worker who operated the brakes on a train, but is now usually assistant to the conductor. —*pl.* **brake'men**

**bram·ble** (bram'b'l) ***n.*** any prickly shrub, as the raspberry or blackberry.

**bran** (bran) ***n.*** the husks of ground wheat, rye, etc. that are left after sifting the flour.

**branch** (branch) ***n.*** **1** any part of a tree growing from the trunk or from a main limb. **2** anything coming out like a branch from the main part [the *branch* of a river]. **3** a division or part [Chemistry is a *branch* of science.] **4** a part that is away from the main unit [Our public library has *branches* in the suburbs.] ◆***v.*** to divide into branches [The road *branches* two miles east of town.] —**branch off,** to go off in another direction. —**branch out,** to make one's interests or activities greater or broader.

**brand** (brand) ***n.*** **1** a piece of burning wood. **2** a mark burned on the skin with a hot iron [*Brands* are put on cattle to show who owns them.] *See the picture.* **3** the iron so used: *also called* **branding iron**. **4** a mark of shame [He bore the *brand* of a traitor.] **5** a mark or name put on the goods of a particular company; trademark. **6** a particular kind or make [a new *brand* of toothpaste]. ◆***v.*** **1** to mark as with a brand [a scene *branded* in my memory]. **2** to set apart as something shameful [They *branded* him a liar.]

**bran·dish** (bran'dish) ***v.*** to shake or wave in a threatening way [to *brandish* a sword].

**brand-new** (bran'no͞o' *or* brand'nyo͞o') ***adj.*** entirely new; never used before.

> Something that is **brand-new** is as fresh and bright as a metal object that has just come from a smith's forge. The "brand-" in this word is the same as the *brand* that means "a branding iron."

**bran·dy** (bran'dē) ***n.*** **1** an alcoholic liquor made from wine. **2** an alcoholic liquor made from fruit juice. —*pl.* **bran'dies**

**brash** (brash) ***adj.*** **1** acting too quickly; rash. **2** bold in a rude way; impudent. —**brash'ly *adv.***

**Bra·sí·lia** (brä zē'lyä) the capital of Brazil.

**brass** (bras) ***n.*** **1** a yellow metal that is an alloy of copper and zinc. **2** *often* **brasses,** *pl.* brass-wind musical instruments. **3** rude boldness: *used only in everyday talk.* **4** any officers or officials of high rank: *slang in this meaning, often used with a plural verb.*

**bras·siere** or **bras·sière** (brə zir') ***n.*** *same as* **bra.**

**brass winds** musical instruments made of coiled metal tubes and having a cup-shaped mouthpiece, as the trumpet and tuba. —**brass'-wind' *adj.***

**brass·y** (bras'ē) ***adj.*** **1** of or like brass. **2** bold in a rude way; impudent. **3** loud and blaring [a *brassy* voice]. —**brass'i·er, brass'i·est** —**brass'i·ness *n.***

**brat** (brat) ***n.*** a child who does not behave or is hard to control: *sometimes used in a joking way.*

**bra·va·do** (brə vä'dō) ***n.*** a pretending to be brave or bold when one is really afraid.

**brave** (brāv) ***adj.*** **1** willing to face danger, pain, or trouble; not afraid; full of courage. **2** fine, grand, or splendid [a *brave* new world]. —**brav'er, brav'est**



| | | | | | | | |
|---|---|---|---|---|---|---|---|
| a | fat | ir | here | ou | out | zh | leisure |
| ā | ape | ī | bite, fire | u | up | ng | ring |
| ä | car, lot | ō | go | ur | fur | | a *in* ago |
| e | ten | ô | law, horn | ch | chin | | e *in* agent |
| er | care | oi | oil | sh | she | ə = | i *in* unity |
| ē | even | oo | look | th | thin | | o *in* collect |
| i | hit | o͞o | tool | *th* | then | | u *in* focus |

◆*n.* a North American Indian warrior. ◆*v.* to face without fear; defy [We *braved* the storm.] —**braved, brav'ing** —**brave'ly** ***adv.*** —**brave'ness** ***n.***

SYNONYMS: To be **brave** is to show no fear in facing danger or trouble. To be **courageous** is to be always ready to deal fearlessly with any dangerous situation because one has a strong will and spirit. To be **bold** is to have a daring character, whether shown in a courageous, rude, or defiant way.

**brav·er·y** (brā'vər ē) ***n.*** the quality of being brave; courage.

**bra·vo** (brä'vō) ***interj., n.*** a word shouted to mean "very good! well done! excellent!" [The audience shouted "*Bravo*!" when the pianist finished the étude.] —*pl.* **bra'vos**

**brawl** (brôl) ***n.*** a rough, noisy quarrel or fight. ◆***v.*** to quarrel or fight noisily. —**brawl'er** ***n.***

**brawn** (brôn) ***n.*** big, strong muscles, or muscular strength [The bully was all *brawn* and no brain.]

**brawn·y** (brôn'ē) ***adj.*** strong and muscular. —**brawn'i·er, brawn'i·est** —**brawn'i·ness** ***n.***

**bray** (brā) ***n.*** **1** the loud, harsh cry that a donkey makes. **2** a sound like this. ◆***v.*** to make a cry or noise of this kind.

**bra·zen** (brā'z'n) ***adj.*** **1** of or like brass. **2** showing no shame; bold; impudent [a *brazen* lie]. —**brazen it out,** to act boldly as if one does not have to be ashamed [Although caught cheating, she tried to *brazen it out.*] —**bra'zen·ly** ***adv.***



**bra·zier** (brā'zhər) ***n.*** a metal pan for holding burning coals or charcoal.

**Bra·zil** (brə zil') a country in central and northeastern South America. —**Bra·zil·ian** (brə zil'yən) ***adj., n.***

**Brazil nut** a three-sided nut that is the seed of a tree growing in South America. It has a dark shell and a white, oily kernel, and grows in a hard shell that holds a number of such nuts. *See the picture.*

**Braz·za·ville** (brä'zə vil), the capital of the Congo.

**breach** (brēch) ***n.*** **1** a failing to keep a promise, to obey a law, etc. [*breach* of contract]. **2** an opening made by breaking through [The troops forced a *breach* in the enemy's lines.] **3** a break in friendly relations [a *breach* between friends]. ◆***v.*** to make a breach in; to break through.

**breach of promise** a breaking of a promise to marry.

**bread** (bred) ***n.*** **1** a common food baked from a dough made with flour or meal, water, yeast, etc. **2** any baked goods like bread but made with a batter [quick *breads*; corn*bread*]. **3** food or the means of living [to earn one's *bread*]. **4** money: *slang in this meaning.* ◆***v.*** to cover with bread crumbs before cooking [*breaded* pork chops]. —**break bread,** to eat, especially to eat with someone else. —**know which side one's bread is buttered on,** to know what is best for oneself.

**bread·fruit** (bred'fro͞ot) ***n.*** the large, round fruit of a tree growing in tropical areas. It has a starchy pulp which becomes like bread when baked.

**breadth** (bredth) ***n.*** **1** the distance from side to side of a thing; width. **2** lack of narrowness [*breadth* of knowledge].

**bread·win·ner** (bred'win'ər) ***n.*** a person who works to earn money to support a family or other dependents.

**break** (brāk) ***v.*** **1** to come or make come apart by force; split or crack sharply into pieces [*Break* an egg into the bowl. The rusty hinge *broke.*] **2** to force one's way [The firemen *broke* through the door.] **3** to get out of working order; make or become useless [You can *break* your watch by winding it too tightly.] **4** to cut open the surface of [to *break* ground for a new building]. **5** to make something fail by using force [The company *broke* the workers' strike.] **6** to tame by using force [The cowboys *broke* the wild ponies.] **7** to do better than; outdo [He *broke* the record for running the mile.] **8** to upset the order of [The soldiers *broke* ranks and ran.] **9** to fail to carry out or follow [to *break* an agreement; to *break* the law] **10** to end, stop, or interrupt [The net *broke* the acrobat's fall. The fuse melted and *broke* the electric circuit.] **11** to make poor or bankrupt [Another such loss will *break* me.] **12** to change suddenly or become choked [His voice *broke* as he sobbed out his sad story.] **13** to begin or come suddenly [Dawn was *breaking.*] **14** to become known or make known [The news story *broke* today. Who will *break* the sad news to her?] ☆**15** to curve suddenly near the plate: said of a pitched baseball. —**broke, bro'ken, break'ing** ◆***n.*** **1** a breaking open or apart. ☆**2** a sudden move; dash [We made a *break* for the door.] **3** a broken place [The X-ray showed a *break* in the bone.] **4** a beginning [We rose at the *break* of day.] **5** an interruption [Recess is a relaxing *break* in our school day.] ☆**6** an escape, as from jail. ☆**7** a chance: *slang in this meaning* [Give me a *break*. That was a lucky *break*.] —**break away,** to leave suddenly. —**break down,** **1** to lose control of oneself; begin to cry. **2** to go out of working order. **3** to separate into parts for study. —**break in,** **1** to enter by force. **2** to interrupt. **3** to train a beginner. —**break into,** **1** to enter by force. **2** to begin suddenly to speak or perform. **3** to interrupt. —**break off,** **1** to stop suddenly. **2** to stop being friendly. —**break out,** **1** to develop a rash on the skin. **2** to begin suddenly. **3** to escape suddenly. —**break up,** **1** to take apart or fall apart; wreck. **2** to stop; put an end to. **3** to end a friendship: *used only in everyday talk.* ☆**4** to make feel upset; disturb: *used only in everyday talk.* —**break with,** to stop being friendly with.

SYNONYMS: **Break** means to divide something into pieces by using force, pressure, etc. **Smash** means to break something or hit something suddenly, violently, and noisily [The car *smashed* into the wall.] **Crush** means to press so hard on something that it folds up or breaks into bits [I *crushed* the empty carton under my foot.]

**break·a·ble** (brāk'ə b'l) ***adj.*** that can be broken or that is likely to break.

**break·age** (brāk'ij) ***n.*** **1** the act of breaking. **2** things or amount broken. **3** loss or damage by breaking [*Breakage* on the shipment amounted to $100.]

**break·down** (brāk'doun) ***n.*** **1** a getting out of working order, or a falling apart [*breakdown* of a machine]. **2** a becoming sick in body or mind [a nervous *breakdown*]. **3** a separating into parts; analysis [a *breakdown* of costs].

**break·er** (brāk′ər) ***n.*** a person or thing that breaks, as a wave that breaks on the shore.

**break·fast** (brek′fəst) ***n.*** the first meal of the day. ◆***v.*** to eat breakfast.

> When you eat **breakfast**, you are doing just what the spelling of the word says. You are "breaking a fast" after not eating all night.

**break·neck** (brāk′nek) ***adj.*** likely to cause an accident; unsafe [driving at *breakneck* speed].

**break·wa·ter** (brāk′wôt′ər) ***n.*** a wall built to break the force of waves, as near a harbor or beach. *See the picture.*

**bream** (brēm) ***n.*** **1** a freshwater fish related to the minnows. **2** any of several saltwater fishes. —*pl.* **bream** or **breams**

**breast** (brest) ***n.*** **1** the upper, front part of the body, between the neck and the belly. **2** either of the two glands on this part of a woman's body, from which babies get milk. **3** the breast thought of as the center of feelings [Anger raged in his *breast.*] —**make a clean breast of,** to confess everything.

**breast·bone** (brest′bōn) ***n.*** the thin, flat bone to which most of the ribs are joined in the front of the chest; sternum.

**breast·plate** (brest′plāt) ***n.*** a piece of armor for protecting the breast.

**breast stroke** a stroke in which the swimmer faces the water and pushes both arms out sideways from a position in front of the head while the legs are drawn up and then kicked quickly backward.

**breath** (breth) ***n.*** **1** air taken into the lungs and then let out. **2** easy or natural breathing [Wait until I get my *breath* back.] **3** life or spirit [While there is *breath* in me, I will resist.] **4** a slight breeze [There's not a *breath* of air.] —**below one's breath** or **under one's breath,** in a whisper. —**catch one's breath,** **1** to gasp or pant. **2** to pause or rest. —**in the same breath,** at almost the same moment. —**out of breath,** breathless; panting, as from hard work. —**save one's breath,** to keep quiet when talk would be useless. —**take one's breath away,** to fill one with wonder; thrill.

**breathe** (brē*th*) ***v.*** **1** to take air into the lungs and then let it out. **2** to live [While I *breathe,* you are safe.] **3** to speak quietly; whisper [Don't *breathe* a word of it to anyone.] **4** to stop for breath; rest [to *breathe* a horse after a long run]. —**breathed, breath′ing**

**breath·er** (brē′*th*ər) ***n.*** a pause for rest: *used only in everyday talk.*

**breath·less** (breth′lis) ***adj.*** **1** breathing hard; panting [She was *breathless* after the long run.] **2** not breathing for a moment because of excitement, fear, etc. **3** without breath.

**breath·tak·ing** (breth′tāk′iŋ) ***adj.*** very exciting; thrilling [a *breathtaking* sight].

**bred** (bred) *past tense and past participle of* **breed.**

**breech** (brēch) ***n.*** a lower, back part; especially, the part of a gun behind the barrel.

**breech·es** (brich′iz) ***n.pl.*** **1** short trousers reaching just below the knees. *See the picture.* **2** any trousers: *used only in everyday talk.*

**breed** (brēd) ***v.*** **1** to give birth to young; hatch; reproduce [Mosquitoes *breed* in swamps.] **2** to keep and raise animals in pairs, so that they will have young. **3** to raise flowers, vegetables, etc. and try to develop new or better varieties. **4** to cause or produce [Poverty *breeds* crime.] **5** to bring up, or train [born and *bred* to be a farmer]. —**bred, breed′ing** ◆***n.*** a special type of some animal or plant; race; stock [Spaniels and poodles are *breeds* of dogs.] —**breed′er *n.***

breakwater

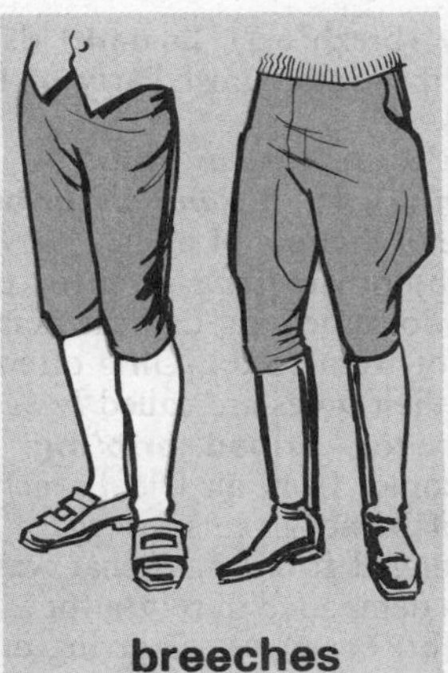
breeches

Brazil nuts

**breeze** (brēz) ***n.*** **1** a light and gentle wind. **2** a thing easy to do: *used only in everyday talk* [The test was a *breeze.*] ◆***v.*** to move or go quickly, briskly, etc.: *slang in this meaning.* —**breezed, breez′ing**

☆**breeze·way** (brēz′wā) ***n.*** a covered passageway, as between a house and garage. 

**breez·y** (brēz′ē) ***adj.*** **1** with breezes blowing; slightly windy [a *breezy* day]. **2** light and happy [*breezy* talk]. —**breez′i·er, breez′i·est** —**breez′i·ly *adv.*** —**breez′i·ness *n.***

**Bre·men** (brā′mən *or* brem′ən) a seaport in northern West Germany.

**breth·ren** (breth′rən) ***n.pl.*** brothers.

> Nowadays **brethren** is not much used. However, members of some churches use the word in talking to or about their fellow members.

**bre·vi·ar·y** (brē′vē er′ē) ***n.*** a book containing the daily prayers, hymns, etc. to be said by a Roman Catholic priest. —*pl.* **bre′vi·ar·ies**

**brev·i·ty** (brev′ə tē) ***n.*** the quality of being brief; shortness [the *brevity* of a speech].

**brew** (brōō) ***v.*** **1** to make by steeping, boiling, and fermenting malt and hops [to *brew* beer]. **2** to make by steeping in boiled water [to *brew* tea]. **3** to plan or scheme [They are *brewing* mischief.] **4** to begin to form [A storm is *brewing.*] ◆***n.*** a drink that has been brewed.

**brew·er** (brōō′ər) ***n.*** a person whose work or business is brewing beer and ale.

**brew·er·y** (brōō′ər ē) ***n.*** a place where beer and ale are brewed. —*pl.* **brew′er·ies**

| | | | | | | | |
|---|---|---|---|---|---|---|---|
| **a** | fat | **ir** | here | **ou** | out | **zh** | leisure |
| **ā** | ape | **ī** | bite, fire | **u** | up | **ŋ** | ring |
| **ä** | car, lot | **ō** | go | **ʉr** | fur | | a *in* ago |
| **e** | ten | **ô** | law, horn | **ch** | chin | | e *in* agent |
| **er** | care | **oi** | oil | **sh** | she | **ə =** | i *in* unity |
| **ē** | even | **oo** | look | **th** | thin | | o *in* collect |
| **i** | hit | **ōō** | tool | ***th*** | then | | u *in* focus |

**Brezh·nev** (brezh′nef), **Le·o·nid** (lā′ô net′) 1906– ; leader of the Communist Party of the Soviet Union, from 1964.

**bri·ar**[1] (brī′ər) ***n.*** *same as* **brier**[1].

**bri·ar**[2] (brī′ər) ***n.*** **1** *same as* **brier**[2]. **2** a tobacco pipe made of the root of brier.

**bribe** (brīb) ***n.*** anything given or promised to get a person to do something that the person should not do or does not want to do [Gifts offered to Senators to influence their votes are called *bribes*.] ◆***v.*** to offer or give a bribe to. —**bribed, brib′ing**

> **Bribe** comes from an Old French word meaning "a bit of bread given to beggars." The meaning later changed from a gift that was begged to one that was demanded in return for a favor.

**brib·er·y** (brī′bər ē) ***n.*** the giving or taking of bribes. —*pl.* **brib′er·ies**

**bric-a-brac** (brik′ə brak′) ***n.*** small objects placed about a room for decoration, as little china figures, small vases, etc.

**brick** (brik) ***n.*** **1** a block of baked clay, used in building. **2** bricks as material [a house built of *brick*]. **3** anything shaped like a brick [a *brick* of ice cream]. ◆***adj.*** built of brick [a *brick* wall]. ◆***v.*** to build, line, or pave with brick. —**brick up** or **brick in,** to close or wall in with brick.

**brick·bat** (brik′bat) ***n.*** **1** a piece of brick thrown as a weapon. **2** a faultfinding remark.

☆**brick cheese** a somewhat hard American cheese shaped like a brick and having many small holes.

**brick·lay·er** (brik′lā′ər) ***n.*** a person whose work is building with bricks. —**brick′lay′ing *n.***

**brick·work** (brik′wurk) ***n.*** a thing or part built of bricks.

**brid·al** (brīd′'l) ***adj.*** of a bride or wedding [a *bridal* gown; a *bridal* feast].

**bride** (brīd) ***n.*** a woman who has just been married or is about to be married.

**bride·groom** (brīd′gro͞om) ***n.*** a man who has just been married or is about to be married.

**brides·maid** (brīdz′mād) ***n.*** one of the young women who attend the bride at a wedding.

**bridge**[1] (brij) ***n.*** **1** something built over a river, railroad, etc. to serve as a road or path across. **2** something that is a means of connecting or contacting [Our common language is a *bridge* between the Canadians and us.] **3** the upper, bony part of the nose. **4** the part of a pair of eyeglasses that fits over the nose. **5** the thin, curved piece over which the strings of a violin, cello, etc. are stretched. **6** the high platform on a ship from which the officer in charge controls it. **7** a small frame for false teeth, that is fastened to a real tooth or teeth: *also called* **bridge′work**. *See the picture.* ◆***v.*** to make or be a bridge over [to *bridge* a river]. —**bridged, bridg′ing**

**bridge**[2] (brij) ***n.*** a card game played by two pairs of players.

**bridge·head** (brij′hed) ***n.*** a strong position taken by an attacking army on the enemy's side of a bridge, river, etc.

**Bridge·port** (brij′pôrt) a seaport in southwestern Connecticut, on Long Island Sound.

**bri·dle** (brīd′'l) ***n.*** the part of a horse's harness for the head. It has a bit for the mouth to which the reins are fastened. *See the picture.* ◆***v.*** **1** to put a bridle on. **2** to hold back or control as with a bridle [You must *bridle* your anger.] **3** to pull one's head back quickly with the chin drawn in, as in showing anger at an insult. —**bri′dled, bri′dling**

**bridle path** a path for horseback riding.

**brief** (brēf) ***adj.*** **1** not lasting very long; short in time [a *brief* visit]. **2** using just a few words; not wordy; concise [a *brief* news report]. ◆***n.*** a statement giving the main points of a law case, for use in court. ◆***v.*** to give the main points or necessary facts to [to *brief* pilots before a flight]. —**hold a brief for,** to argue in favor of. —**in brief,** in a few words. —**brief′ly *adv.*** —**brief′ness *n.***

**brief·case** (brēf′kās) ***n.*** a flat case, usually of leather, for carrying papers, books, etc.

**bri·er**[1] (brī′ər) ***n.*** any prickly or thorny bush, as the wild rose.

**bri·er**[2] (brī′ər) ***n.*** **1** a low shrub of Europe whose root is used in making tobacco pipes. **2** this root.

**brig** (brig) ***n.*** **1** a ship with two masts and square sails. ☆**2** the prison on a warship. ☆**3** the guardhouse; prison: *soldiers' slang in this meaning.*

**bri·gade** (bri gād′) ***n.*** **1** a unit of the U.S. Army made up of two or more battalions. **2** any group of people who work together as a unit [a fire *brigade*].

**brig·a·dier general** (brig ə dir′) a military officer who ranks just above a colonel.

**brig·and** (brig′ənd) ***n.*** a bandit, especially one of a group that moves around.

**brig·an·tine** (brig′ən tēn) ***n.*** a kind of brig that has square sails on the foremast only.

**bright** (brīt) ***adj.*** **1** shining; giving light; full of light [a *bright* star; a *bright* day]. **2** very strong or brilliant in color or sound [a *bright* red; the *bright* tones of a cornet]. **3** lively; cheerful [a *bright* smile]. **4** having a quick mind; clever [a *bright* child]. **5** full of hope; cheerful [a *bright* future]. ◆***adv.*** in a bright manner [stars shining *bright*]. —**bright′ly *adv.*** —**bright′ness *n.***

> SYNONYMS: Something is **bright** if it gives forth or reflects light or is filled with light [a *bright* day; a *bright* star]. Something is **shining** if it has a steady brightness that goes on and on [the *shining* sun]. Something is **brilliant** if it has a strong or flashing brightness [*brilliant* sunlight; *brilliant* diamonds].

**cat bristling**

**bridge of false teeth**

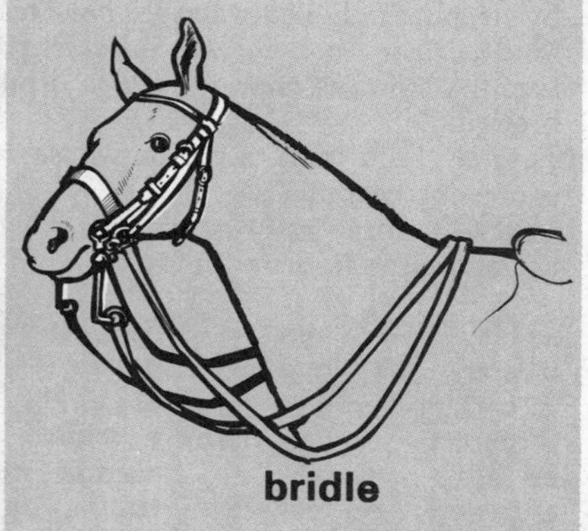

**bridle**

**bright·en** (brīt′'n) ***v.*** **1** to make or become bright or brighter [The new lamps *brighten* up the room.] **2** to make or become happy or happier; cheer [Your smile has *brightened* my day.]

**Brigh·ton** (brīt′'n) a city in southern England, on the English Channel.

**bril·liance** (bril′yəns) or **bril′lian·cy** (bril′yən sē) ***n.*** the fact of being brilliant; great brightness, splendor, intelligence, etc.

**bril·liant** (bril′yənt) ***adj.*** **1** very bright; glittering or sparkling [the *brilliant* sun on the water]. **2** very splendid or distinguished [a *brilliant* performance]. **3** very clever or intelligent [a *brilliant* student; a *brilliant* discovery]. *See* SYNONYMS *at* **bright** *and* **intelligent.** ◆***n.*** a diamond or other gem cut in such a way that it will sparkle. —**bril′liant·ly** ***adv.***

**brim** (brim) ***n.*** **1** the top rim of a cup, bowl, etc. [filled to the *brim*]. **2** a rim or edge that sticks out [the *brim* of a hat]. ◆***v.*** to fill or be full to the brim [eyes *brimming* over with tears]. —**brimmed, brim′ming**

**Brim** comes from an Old English word meaning "the edge of the sea." Later it came to mean the edge around anything that holds a liquid, and finally, any edge that sticks out, as from a hat.

**brim·ful** (brim′fool′) ***adj.*** full to the brim.

**brim·stone** (brim′stōn) ***n.*** *same as* **sulfur.**

**brin·dle** (brin′d'l) ***adj.*** *same as* **brindled.** ◆***n.*** **1** a brindled color. **2** a brindled animal.

**brin·dled** (brin′d'ld) ***adj.*** having a gray or tan coat streaked or spotted with a darker color [a *brindled* cow].

**brine** (brīn) ***n.*** **1** water full of salt, as for use in pickling meat, etc. **2** the ocean.

**bring** (briŋ) ***v.*** **1** to carry or lead here or to the place where the speaker will be [*Bring* it to my house tomorrow.] **2** to cause to happen or come [War *brings* death and hunger.] **3** to persuade or influence [I can't *bring* myself to sell my old desk.] **4** to sell for [Coffee *brings* a high price today.] —**brought, bring′ing** —**bring about,** to cause; make happen. —**bring around** or **bring round, 1** to persuade by arguing, urging, etc. **2** to bring back to consciousness. —**bring forth, 1** to give birth to. **2** to make known. —**bring forward,** to introduce or show. —**bring off,** to make happen; carry out. —**bring on,** to cause to begin or happen. —**bring out, 1** to make known or make clear. **2** to publish a book or bring a play, person, etc. before the public. —**bring over,** to convince or persuade. —**bring to, 1** to bring back to consciousness. **2** to stop, as a ship. —**bring up, 1** to take care of during childhood; raise; rear. **2** to mention or suggest in a discussion. **3** to cough up or vomit. **4** to cause to stop suddenly.

**brink** (briŋk) ***n.*** **1** the edge, especially at the top of a steep place. **2** the point just short of [on the *brink* of discovery; at the *brink* of war].

**brin·y** (brīn′ē) ***adj.*** of or like brine; very salty. —**brin′i·er, brin′i·est**

**Bris·bane** (briz′bān) seaport on the eastern coast of Australia.

**brisk** (brisk) ***adj.*** **1** quick and full of energy [a *brisk* pace]. **2** cool, dry, and refreshing [a *brisk* October morning]. —**brisk′ly** ***adv.*** —**brisk′ness** ***n.***

**bris·ket** (bris′kit) ***n.*** meat cut from the breast of a beef. *See the picture for* **beef.**

**bris·tle** (bris′'l) ***n.*** **1** any short, stiff, prickly hair, especially of a hog. **2** such a hair, or an artificial hair like it, used for brushes. ◆***v.*** **1** to stand up stiffly, like bristles [The hair on the cat's back *bristled* as the dog came near.] *See the picture.* **2** to become tense with anger; be ready to fight back [She *bristled* at the insult.] **3** to be thickly covered with [The battlefield *bristled* with guns.] —**bris′tled, bris′tling** —**bris·tly** (bris′lē) ***adj.***

**Bris·tol** (bris′t'l) a seaport in southwestern England.

**Brit.** *abbreviation for* **Britain** *or* **British.**

**Brit·ain** (brit′'n) *same as* **Great Britain.**

**Brit·ish** (brit′ish) ***adj.*** of Great Britain or its people. —**the British,** the people of Great Britain.

**British Columbia** a province of Canada, on the Pacific Ocean.

**British Isles** a group of islands northwest of France, including Great Britain, Ireland, and several smaller islands.

**Brit·on** (brit′'n) ***n.*** **1** a person born or living in Great Britain. **2** one of the native Celtic people living in southern Britain before it was invaded by the Anglo-Saxons.

**Brit·ta·ny** (brit′'n ē) a region in France, on a peninsula in the northwestern part.

**brit·tle** (brit′'l) ***adj.*** easily broken because it is hard and not flexible [The bones of an old person are usually *brittle.*] ◆☆***n.*** a brittle, crunchy candy with nuts in it [peanut *brittle*]. 91

**bro.** *abbreviation for* **brother.** —*pl.* **bros.**

**broach** (brōch) ***v.*** **1** to start talking about [I'll *broach* the subject to them at dinner.] **2** to make a hole in so as to let out liquid; tap [to *broach* a cask of wine].

**broad** (brôd) ***adj.*** **1** large from side to side; wide [a *broad* room]. **2** clear and open [*broad* daylight]. **3** easy to understand; not subtle; obvious [a *broad* hint; *broad* humor]. **4** wide in range; not limited [a *broad* variety; a *broad* education]. **5** broad-minded; tolerant or liberal. **6** main or general [the *broad* outlines of a subject]. —**broad′ly** ***adv.***

SYNONYMS: **Broad** and **wide** both are used when talking about how large something is from side to side. **Wide** is usually used when speaking of measurement or distance between sides or ends [two feet *wide;* a *wide* opening]. **Broad** is used when speaking of the full area or surface between sides or limits [*broad* hips; *broad* plains].

**broad·cast** (brôd′kast) ***v.*** **1** to send over the air by means of radio or television [to *broadcast* a program]. —**broad′cast** or **broad′cast·ed, broad′cast·ing** **2** to scatter or spread widely. —**broad′cast, broad′cast·ing** ◆***n.*** **1** the act of broadcasting. **2** a radio or television program [the six o'clock news *broadcast*]. ◆***adv.*** scattered about; far and wide [Seed may be sown *broadcast* or in rows.]

| | | | |
|---|---|---|---|
| **a** fat | **ir** here | **ou** out | **zh** leisure |
| **ā** ape | **ī** bite, fire | **u** up | **ŋ** ring |
| **ä** car, lot | **ō** go | **ʉr** fur | a *in* ago |
| **e** ten | **ô** law, horn | **ch** chin | e *in* agent |
| **er** care | **oi** oil | **sh** she | ə = i *in* unity |
| **ē** even | **oo** look | **th** thin | o *in* collect |
| **i** hit | **ōō** tool | ***th*** then | u *in* focus |

brownie

Brussels sprouts

broccoli

brontosaurus
23 m (75 ft.) long

**broad·cloth** (brôd′klôth) ***n.*** **1** a fine, smooth cotton or silk cloth, used for shirts, pajamas, etc. **2** a fine, smooth woolen cloth.

**broad·en** (brôd′'n) ***v.*** to make or become broad or broader; widen.

**broad jump** *an earlier name for* **long jump.**

**broad·loom** (brôd′lo͞om) ***adj.*** woven on a wide loom [*broadloom* rugs and carpets].

**broad-mind·ed** (brôd′mīn′did) ***adj.*** keeping one's mind open to others' beliefs, to different ways of life, etc.; not having prejudice; tolerant. **—broad′-mind′-ed·ness** ***n.***

**broad·side** (brôd′sīd) ***n.*** **1** the entire side of a ship above the waterline. **2** the firing at one time of all the guns on one side of a ship. **3** a sheet of paper printed on one side, as with advertising. **4** a strong or insulting attack in words. ◆***adv.*** **1** directly in the side [The train rammed the car *broadside*.] **2** without choosing targets [The teacher criticized the class *broadside*.]

**broad·sword** (brôd′sôrd) ***n.*** a sword with a broad blade, for slashing rather than thrusting.

**Broad·way** (brôd′wā) a street in New York City known as the main area of theater and entertainment.

**bro·cade** (brō kād′) ***n.*** a rich cloth with a raised design woven into it.

**broc·co·li** (bräk′ə lē) ***n.*** a vegetable whose tender shoots and loose heads of tiny green buds are cooked for eating. *See the picture.*

**bro·chure** (brō sho͝or′) ***n.*** a pamphlet, now especially one that advertises something.

**bro·gan** (brō′g'n) ***n.*** a heavy work shoe, fitting high on the ankle.

**brogue**[1] (brōg) ***n.*** the way the people of a particular region pronounce words; especially, the way English is spoken by the Irish.

**brogue**[2] (brōg) ***n.*** a heavy oxford shoe.

**broil** (broil) ***v.*** **1** to cook or be cooked close to a flame or other high heat [to *broil* steaks over charcoal]. **2** to make or be very hot [a *broiling* summer day]. ◆***n.*** the act or state of broiling.

**broil·er** (broil′ər) ***n.*** **1** a pan or grill for broiling. **2** the part of a stove used for broiling. **3** a young chicken for broiling.

**broke** (brōk) *past tense of* **break.** ◆***adj.*** having no money; bankrupt: *used only in everyday talk.*

**bro·ken** (brō′kən) *past participle of* **break.** ◆***adj.*** **1** split or cracked into pieces [a *broken* dish; a *broken* leg]. **2** not in working condition [a *broken* watch]. **3** not kept or carried out [a *broken* promise]. **4** interrupted; not even [*broken* sleep]. **5** not following the usual rules of grammar or word order [They speak *broken* English.] **6** sick or beaten [a *broken* spirit].

**bro·ken-down** (brō′kən doun′) ***adj.*** **1** sick or worn out, as by old age or disease. **2** out of order; useless [a *broken-down* automobile].

**bro·ken·heart·ed** (brō′kən här′tid) ***adj.*** full of sorrow or despair; very unhappy.

**bro·ker** (brō′kər) ***n.*** a person who buys and sells stocks, real estate, etc. for others.

> **Broker** comes from an Old French word meaning "to tap a cask of wine." A broker used to be a person who sold wine. The word later came to mean someone who bought and sold other things.

**bro·ker·age** (brō′kər ij) ***n.*** the business of a broker.

**bro·mide** (brō′mīd) ***n.*** **1** a salt containing bromine. Some bromides are used as a drug to calm the nerves. **2** a popular saying used so often that it has become stale and dull. Example: "Every cloud has its silver lining."

**bro·mine** (brō′mēn) ***n.*** a reddish-brown liquid that gives off a strong vapor. It is one of the chemical elements.

**bron·chi** (bräng′kī) ***n.pl.*** the two main branches of the windpipe. *—sing.* **bron·chus** (bräng′kəs)

**bron·chi·al** (bräng′kē əl) ***adj.*** having to do with the bronchi or with the smaller tubes leading from the bronchi into the lungs [a *bronchial* cold].

**bron·chi·tis** (bräng kī′tis) ***n.*** an illness in which the lining of the bronchial tubes is inflamed and there is painful coughing.

☆**bron·co** or **bron·cho** (bräng′kō) ***n.*** a wild or only partly tamed horse or pony of the western U.S. *—pl.* **bron′cos** or **bron′chos**

**Bron·të** (brän′tē), **Charlotte** 1816–1855; English writer of novels. She wrote *Jane Eyre.*

**Brontë, Emily** 1818–1848; English writer of novels and a sister of Charlotte. She wrote *Wuthering Heights.*

☆**bron·to·sau·rus** (brän′tə sôr′əs) ***n.*** a huge American dinosaur that ate plants. *See the picture. —pl.* **bron′to·sau′rus·es** or **bron·to·sau·ri** (brän′tə sôr′ī)

**Bronx** (brängks) a borough of New York City.

**bronze** (bränz) ***n.*** **1** a metal that is an alloy of copper and tin. **2** a statue or other work of art made of bronze ["The Thinker" is a famous *bronze*.] **3** a reddish-brown color like that of bronze. ◆***adj.*** of or like bronze. ◆***v.*** to give a bronze color to. **—bronzed, bronz′ing**

**brooch** (brōch *or* bro͞och) ***n.*** a large pin with a clasp, worn as an ornament on a woman's dress.

**brood** (bro͞od) ***n.*** **1** a group of birds hatched at one time and cared for together. **2** all the children in a family. ◆***v.*** **1** to sit on and hatch eggs. **2** to keep thinking in a worried or troubled way [She *brooded* over the loss of her money.]

**brood·er** (bro͞od′ər) ***n.*** **1** a person or animal that broods. ☆**2** a heated shelter for raising young chicks, ducklings, etc.

**brook**[1] (bro͝ok) ***n.*** a small stream.

**brook**[2] (bro͝ok) ***v.*** to put up with; stand for; bear; endure [The speaker *brooked* no interruptions.]

**Brook·lyn** (bro͝ok′lən) a borough of New York City.

**broom** (bro͞om) ***n.*** **1** a brush with a long handle, used for sweeping. **2** a shrub with small leaves, slender branches, and yellow flowers.

**broom·stick** (bro͞om′stik) ***n.*** the handle of a broom.

**bros.** *abbreviation for* **brothers.**

**broth** (brôth) ***n.*** water in which meat or a vegetable has been boiled; a thin, clear soup.

**broth·er** (bru*th*′ər) ***n.*** **1** a boy or man as he is related to the other children of his parents. **2** a person who is close to one in some way; especially, a fellow member of the same race, religion, club, etc. —*pl.* **broth′ers** —**breth′ren** *is an older pl.*

**broth·er·hood** (bru*th*′ər ho͝od) ***n.*** **1** the tie between brothers or between people who feel they all belong to one big family [the *brotherhood* of man]. **2** a group of men joined together in some interest, work, belief, etc.

**broth·er-in-law** (bru*th*′ər in lô′) ***n.*** **1** the brother of one's husband or wife. **2** the husband of one's sister. —*pl.* **broth′ers-in-law′**

**broth·er·ly** (bru*th*′ər lē) ***adj.*** **1** of or like a brother. **2** friendly, loyal, kindly, etc. [*brotherly* advice]. —**broth′er·li·ness** ***n.***

**brougham** (bro͞om) ***n.*** a closed carriage with the driver's seat outside.

**brought** (brôt) *past tense and past participle of* **bring.**

**brow** (brou) ***n.*** **1** the eyebrow. **2** the forehead. **3** the top edge of a steep hill or cliff.

**brow·beat** (brou′bēt) ***v.*** to frighten a person into doing something by using rough talk and stern looks; bully. —**brow′beat, brow′beat·en, brow′beat·ing**

**brown** (broun) ***n.*** the color of chocolate or coffee, a mixture of red, black, and yellow. ◆***adj.*** having this color. ◆***v.*** to make or become brown [The turkey is *browning* in the oven.]

**Brown** (broun), **John** 1800–1859; an American who fought slavery. He led a raid on a U.S. arsenal to get weapons for slaves to use in revolting. He was hanged for treason.

☆**brown-bag** (broun′bag′) ***v.*** to carry one's lunch to school or work, as in a brown paper bag. —**brown′-bagged′, brown′-bag′ging**

**brown·ie** (broun′ē) ***n.*** **1** a small elf in folk tales who does good deeds for people at night. *See the picture.* ☆**2** a small, flat bar of chocolate cake that has nuts in it. **3 Brownie,** a member of the Girl Scouts in the youngest group, seven and eight years old.

**Brown·ing** (broun′iŋ), **Elizabeth Bar·rett** (bar′it) 1806–1861; English poet. She was the wife of Robert Browning.

**Browning, Robert** 1812–1889; English poet.

**brown·ish** (broun′ish) ***adj.*** somewhat brown.

**brown rice** rice that has not been polished.

**brown sugar** sugar that has not been refined or is only partly refined. It is brown in color.

**browse** (brouz) ***v.*** **1** to nibble at leaves, twigs, shoots, etc. [deer *browsing* in the forest]. **2** to look through a book or books, stopping to read a bit here and there. **3** to look casually over things for sale. —**browsed, brows′ing**

**bru·in** (bro͞o′ən) ***n.*** a bear: *a name used in children's tales.*

**bruise** (bro͞oz) ***v.*** **1** to hurt a part of the body, as by a blow, without breaking the skin [Her *bruised* knee turned black-and-blue.] **2** to hurt the outside of [Some peaches fell and were *bruised.*] **3** to cause pain or injury to [Your unkind comments *bruised* her feelings.] —**bruised, bruis′ing** ◆***n.*** an injury to the outer part or flesh that does not break the skin but darkens it in color.

**bruit** (bro͞ot) ***v.*** to make widely known, as by rumor [It is *bruited* about that they are engaged.]

**brunch** (brunch) ***n.*** breakfast and lunch eaten as one meal late in the morning.

**bru·nette** or **bru·net** (bro͞o net′) ***adj.*** having black or dark-brown hair, dark eyes, and a dark skin. ◆***n.*** a brunette person.

**brunt** (brunt) ***n.*** the heaviest or hardest part [to bear the *brunt* of the blame].

**brush** (brush) ***n.*** **1** a bunch of bristles, hairs, or wires fastened into a hard back or handle. Brushes are used for cleaning, polishing, grooming, painting, etc. **2** the act of rubbing with a brush. **3** a light, grazing stroke [a *brush* of the hand]. **4** a bushy tail. **5** low, shrubby growth; brushwood [The wounded bird hid in the *brush.*] ☆**6** land grown over with brush, where few people live. **7** a short, sharp fight or quarrel [The gang had several *brushes* with the police.] ◆***v.*** **1** to use a brush on; clean, polish, paint, smooth, etc. with a brush [*Brush* your shoes. *Brush* the paint on evenly.] **2** to touch or graze in passing [The tire of the car *brushed* against the curb.] **3** to remove by a stroke, as of the hand [*Brush* the flies away from the cake.] —☆**brush off,** to get rid of; dismiss: *a slang phrase.* —**brush up,** to study something again so as to refresh one's memory about it.



☆**brush·off** (brush′ôf) ***n.*** the act of getting rid of someone abruptly or rudely: *a slang word.* It is used especially in the phrases **give the brushoff** and **get the brushoff.**

**brush·wood** (brush′wo͝od) ***n.*** **1** tree branches that have been chopped or broken off. **2** a thick growth of small trees and shrubs; underbrush.

**brusque** (brusk) ***adj.*** rough and abrupt in manner or speech [The captain gave *brusque* orders to his crew.] —**brusque′ly** ***adv.*** —**brusque′ness** ***n.***

**Brus·sels** (brus′′lz) the capital of Belgium.

**Brussels sprouts** **1** a vegetable with green buds like tiny cabbage heads growing on its stem. *See the picture.* **2** these buds, cooked for eating.

**bru·tal** (bro͞ot′′l) ***adj.*** like a brute; cruel and without feeling; savage or violent. —**bru′tal·ly** ***adv.***

**bru·tal·i·ty** (bro͞o tal′ə tē) ***n.*** **1** the fact of being brutal; cruelty. **2** a brutal or savage act. —*pl.* **bru·tal′i·ties**

| | | | |
|---|---|---|---|
| **a** fat | **ir** here | **ou** out | **zh** leisure |
| **ā** ape | **ī** bite, fire | **u** up | **ŋ** ring |
| **ä** car, lot | **ō** go | **ur** fur | a *in* ago |
| **e** ten | **ô** law, horn | **ch** chin | e *in* agent |
| **er** care | **oi** oil | **sh** she | **ə** = i *in* unity |
| **ē** even | **o͝o** look | **th** thin | o *in* collect |
| **i** hit | **o͞o** tool | ***th*** then | u *in* focus |

Buddha

buggy

bucksaw

bugle

**bru·tal·ize** (brōōt′'l īz) ***v.*** **1** to make or become brutal. **2** to treat in a brutal way. —**bru′tal·ized, bru′tal·iz·ing**

**brute** (brōōt) ***n.*** **1** a beast. *See* SYNONYMS *at* **animal. 2** a person who is brutal or stupid, coarse, and crude. ◆***adj.*** of or like a beast; without reasoning; brutal, savage, stupid, etc. [War is the use of *brute* force to get one's way.] —**brut′ish** ***adj.***



**Bru·tus** (brōōt′əs) 85?–42 B.C.; a Roman statesman. He was one of the murderers of Julius Caesar.

**B.S.** or **B.Sc.** Bachelor of Science.

**Btu** or **b.t.u.** *abbreviation for* **British thermal unit,** which is a unit for measuring heat. It is often used to show how much heat an air conditioner can remove from a given area.

**bu.** *abbreviation for* **bushel** *or* **bushels.**

**bub·ble** (bub′'l) ***n.*** **1** a very thin film of liquid forming a ball around air or gas [soap *bubbles*]. **2** a tiny ball of air or gas in a liquid [The *bubbles* in soda water tickle my nose.] **3** any plan or idea that bursts or falls apart as easily as a bubble. ◆***v.*** **1** to make bubbles; foam [Boiling water *bubbles.*] **2** to make a boiling or gurgling sound [a *bubbling* brook]. —**bub′bled, bub′bling** —**bubble over,** to be very enthusiastic.

☆**bubble chamber** a container filled with a very hot liquid in which atomic particles that are charged with electricity can be studied. Photographs are taken of the bubbles that form along the paths made by the particles.

**bu·bon·ic plague** (byōō bän′ik) a deadly disease that spreads rapidly and is carried to human beings by fleas from rats. In the Middle Ages it killed millions of people and was called the Black Death.

**buc·ca·neer** (buk ə nir′) ***n.*** a pirate, or sea robber.

> The first French settlers in Haiti used to hunt wild oxen and smoke the meat just like the native Indians did on a grill that the Indians called a *boucan.* These settlers were therefore called **buccaneers** and since many of them were pirates, the name soon came to mean "pirate."

**Bu·chan·an** (byōō kan′ən), **James** 1791–1868; the 15th president of the United States, from 1857 to 1861.

**Bu·cha·rest** (bōō kə rest′) the capital of Romania.

**buck** (buk) ***n.*** **1** the male of certain animals, especially of the deer, goat, or rabbit. ☆**2** a dollar: *slang in this meaning.* ◆***v.*** ☆**1** to jump upward quickly, with the head down and the back curved, as a horse does when it tries to throw its rider. **2** to plunge forward with the head down, as a goat. ☆**3** to resist in a stubborn way: *used only in everyday talk.* —☆**buck up,** to cheer up; brace up: *used only in everyday talk.* —☆**pass the buck,** to try to make someone else take the blame or responsibility: *used only in everyday talk.*

☆**buck·board** (buk′bôrd) ***n.*** a light, open carriage with a single seat placed on a platform that rests right on the two axles.

**buck·et** (buk′it) ***n.*** **1** a round container with a flat bottom and a curved handle, used to hold or carry water, coal, etc.; pail. **2** a thing like a bucket, as the scoop on a steam shovel. **3** a bucketful.

**buck·et·ful** (buk′it fool) ***n.*** as much as a bucket can hold. —*pl.* **buck′et·fuls**

☆**buck·eye** (buk′ī) ***n.*** **1** a tree related to the horse chestnut. **2** its large, brown, glossy seed, contained in a bur.

**buck·le**[1] (buk′'l) ***n.*** **1** a clasp on one end of a strap or belt for fastening the other end in place. **2** an ornament like a clasp, as on a shoe. ◆***v.*** to fasten with a buckle. —**buck′led, buck′ling** —☆**buckle down,** to set to work with real effort.

**buck·le**[2] (buk′'l) ***v.*** to bend, warp, or crumple [The bridge began to *buckle* under the weight of the truck.] —**buck′led, buck′ling** ◆***n.*** a part that is buckled.

**buck·ler** (buk′lər) ***n.*** a small, round shield worn on the arm.

**buck·ram** (buk′rəm) ***n.*** a coarse, stiff cloth used in binding books or as lining in clothes.

☆**buck·saw** (buk′sô) ***n.*** a saw set in a frame and held with both hands in cutting wood. *See the picture.*

☆**buck·shot** (buk′shät) ***n.*** a large lead shot for shooting deer and other large animals.

**buck·skin** (buk′skin) ***n.*** **1** a soft, strong, tan leather made from the skins of deer or sheep. **2 buckskins,** *pl.* clothes or shoes of buckskin.

**buck·toothed** (buk′tōōtht′) ***adj.*** having large front upper teeth that stick out.

**buck·wheat** (buk′hwēt) ***n.*** **1** a plant grown for its black, three-cornered seeds. **2** this seed, which is used as fodder and is ground into a dark flour. ☆**3** this flour, used in pancakes.

> **Buckwheat** has no connection with the word **buck.** The first part of the name comes from the Old English word for "beech" because buckwheat seeds look like tiny beechnuts.

**bu·col·ic** (byōō käl′ik) ***adj.*** **1** of shepherds; pastoral [the *bucolic* poems of Virgil]. **2** of country life or farms; rural [a quiet, *bucolic* scene].

**bud** (bud) ***n.*** **1** a small swelling on a plant, from which a shoot, a flower, or leaves will grow. **2** an early stage of growth or blossoming [Our lilacs are in *bud.*] ◆***v.*** **1** to begin to show buds. **2** to begin to grow or blossom [Mozart was a *budding* genius when he was only three.] —**bud′ded, bud′ding** —**nip in the bud,** to stop something before it can develop fully.

**Bu·da·pest** (bo͞o′də pest) the capital of Hungary, on the Danube River.

**Bud·dha** (bood′ə) 563?–483? B.C.; a religious leader of India, who founded Buddhism. *See the picture.*

**Bud·dhism** (bood′iz′m) ***n.*** a religion of Asia, founded by Buddha. It teaches that by right living and right thinking the soul is freed from pain, sorrow, and desire. —**Bud′dhist *adj., n.***

☆**bud·dy** (bud′ē) ***n.*** a close friend; comrade: *used only in everyday talk.* —*pl.* **bud′dies**

**budge** (buj) ***v.*** to move even a little [Two strong people could not *budge* the boulder.] —**budged, budg′ing**

**budg·et** (buj′it) ***n.*** a careful plan for spending the money that is received in a certain period. ◆***v.*** **1** to plan the spending of money; make a budget. **2** to plan in detail how to spend [I *budget* my time as well as my money.]

**Bue·nos Ai·res** (bwā′nəs er′ēz *or* ī′rēz) the capital of Argentina, a seaport.

**buff** (buf) ***n.*** **1** a heavy, soft, dark-yellow leather made from the skin of a buffalo or ox. **2** a stick or wheel covered with leather, used for cleaning and shining. **3** a dark-yellow color. ◆***adj.*** dark-yellow. ◆***v.*** to clean or shine, as with a buff.

**Buf·fa·lo** (buf′ə lō) a city in western New York State, on Lake Erie.

**buf·fa·lo** (buf′ə lō) ***n.*** a wild ox, sometimes tamed as a work animal, as the water buffalo of India. The American bison is also commonly called a *buffalo.* —*pl.* **buf′fa·loes** or **buf′fa·los** or **buf′fa·lo** ◆☆***v.*** to baffle, bewilder, or bluff: *slang in this meaning.* —**buf′fa·loed, buf′fa·lo·ing**

**Buffalo Bill** *the nickname of* **William Cody**.

**buff·er** (buf′ər) ***n.*** **1** a person who buffs. **2** a wheel or stick for buffing. **3** anything that cushions the shock of a blow or bump. **4** any person, country, etc. that comes between two others that are likely to fight.

**buf·fet**[1] (buf′it) ***n.*** **1** a slap or punch. **2** any blow or shock [The poor really feel the *buffets* of misfortune.] ◆***v.*** to hit, punch, slap, etc. [The strong winds *buffeted* the old oak tree.]

**buf·fet**[2] (bə fā′ *or* boo fā′) ***n.*** **1** a piece of furniture with drawers and cupboards in which silverware, table linens, etc. are stored. **2** platters of food on a buffet or table from which people serve themselves.

**buf·foon** (bə fo͞on′) ***n.*** a person who is always clowning and trying to be funny; clown.

**buf·foon·er·y** (bə fo͞on′ər ē) ***n.*** the jokes and tricks of a buffoon; clowning.

**bug** (bug) ***n.*** **1** a crawling insect with sucking mouthparts. In common talk, any insect is often called a *bug.* **2** a germ that causes disease: *used only in everyday talk.* ☆**3** a tiny microphone hidden to record conversation secretly: *slang in this meaning.* ☆**4** a defect, as in a machine: *slang in this meaning.* ◆☆***v.*** **1** to hide a microphone in a room so as to record conversation secretly. **2** to annoy, bother, etc. **3** to open wide or bulge, as one's eyes when one is amazed. *All the meanings of the verb are slang.* —**bugged, bug′ging**

**bug·a·boo** (bug′ə bo͞o) ***n.*** *another name for* **bugbear**. —*pl.* **bug′a·boos**

**bug·bear** (bug′ber) ***n.*** **1** a frightening person or thing made up in stories to scare children into being good. **2** a thing that one keeps being afraid of for no good reason.

**bug·gy** (bug′ē) ***n.*** **1** a light carriage with one seat, pulled by one horse. *See the picture.* ☆**2** a baby carriage. —*pl.* **bug′gies**

**bu·gle** (byo͞o′g′l) ***n.*** a type of small trumpet, usually without keys or valves. Bugles are used mainly for sounding calls and signals, as in the army. *See the picture.* —**bu·gler** (byo͞o′glər) ***n.***

> **Bugle** comes from the Latin word *buculus,* meaning "young ox." Long ago the horns of wild oxen, called *buglehorns,* were used as trumpets in battle. Later the name was shortened to **bugle** and the trumpets began to be made of metal.

**build** (bild) ***v.*** **1** to make by putting together materials or parts; construct [to *build* a house]. **2** to bring into being; create, develop, etc. [to *build* a business; a theory *built* on facts]. —**built** *or older* **build′ed, build′ing** ◆***n.*** the way something is built or shaped; figure [He has a stocky *build.*]

**build·er** (bil′dər) ***n.*** one that builds; especially, a person whose business is putting up houses and other buildings.

**build·ing** (bil′diŋ) ***n.*** **1** anything that is built with walls and a roof; a structure, as a house, factory, or school. **2** the act or work of one who builds.

**built** (bilt) *a past tense and past participle of* **build**.

☆**built-in** (bilt′in′) ***adj.*** made as part of the building; not movable [*built-in* cabinets].



**bulb** (bulb) ***n.*** **1** the round, fleshy, underground growth of the onion, lily, etc., made up of layers of scales. It is the bud from which the stem and roots grow. **2** an underground stem, as a corm or tuber, that looks like a bulb [A crocus *bulb* is not a true *bulb.*] **3** anything shaped like a bulb [an electric light *bulb*].

**bul·bous** (bul′bəs) ***adj.*** **1** growing from bulbs. **2** shaped like a bulb [a *bulbous* nose].

**Bul·gar·i·a** (bul ger′ē ə) a country in southeastern Europe, on the Black Sea. —**Bul·gar′i·an *adj., n.***

**bulge** (bulj) ***n.*** a part that swells out [The marbles make a *bulge* in your pocket.] ◆***v.*** to swell outward [The mail carrier's bag *bulged* with mail.] —**bulged, bulg′ing**

**bulk** (bulk) ***n.*** **1** a greatness of size or mass [The empty cardboard box was hard to carry because of its *bulk.*] **2** the largest or main part [The *bulk* of her fortune is in land.] ◆***v.*** to seem large or important. —**in bulk,** not put up in small packages [We saved money by buying the rice *in bulk.*]

> SYNONYMS: **Bulk, mass,** and **volume** are all used of a body or whole made up of a certain quantity of something or of a collection of units of something. **Bulk** is used of a body that is very large or heavy or numerous [We children were

| | | | | | | | |
|---|---|---|---|---|---|---|---|
| **a** | fat | **ir** | here | **ou** | out | **zh** | leisure |
| **ā** | ape | **ī** | bite, fire | **u** | up | **ŋ** | ring |
| **ä** | car, lot | **ō** | go | **ʉr** | fur | | a *in* ago |
| **e** | ten | **ô** | law, horn | **ch** | chin | | e *in* agent |
| **er** | care | **oi** | oil | **sh** | she | ə = | i *in* unity |
| **ē** | even | **oo** | look | **th** | thin | | o *in* collect |
| **i** | hit | **o͞o** | tool | ***th*** | then | | u *in* focus |

dwarfed by the *bulk* of the elephant. The *bulk* of humanity is found in Asia.] **Mass** is used of a body that is unified or solid [a molten *mass* of iron]. **Volume** is used of a mass that is moving or flowing [*Volumes* of smoke poured from the chimney.]

**bulk·head** (bulk′hed) ***n.*** any of the strong walls that divide a ship or airplane into sections. They keep water or fire from spreading in case of an accident.

**bulk·y** (bul′kē) ***adj.*** having great bulk; especially, so big as to be awkward to handle [a *bulky* container]. —**bulk′i·er, bulk′i·est —bulk′i·ness** ***n.***

**bull**[1] (bool) ***n.*** **1** the full-grown male of cattle, buffalo, etc. **2** the full-grown male of some other large animals, as the elephant, moose, or whale. ◆***adj.*** male [a *bull* moose].

**bull**[2] (bool) ***n.*** an official letter or order of the Pope.

**bull·dog** (bool′dôg) ***n.*** a short-haired, stocky dog that has a square jaw and a stubborn grip with its teeth. *See the picture.* ◆☆***v.*** to throw a steer by taking hold of its horns and twisting its neck. —**bull′dogged, bull′dog·ging**

☆**bull·doze** (bool′dōz) ***v.*** **1** to frighten by using force or threats; bully: *used only in everyday talk.* **2** to level off or move with a bulldozer. —**bull′dozed, bull′doz·ing**

☆**bull·doz·er** (bool′dō′zər) ***n.*** **1** a person who bulldozes. **2** a large blade like a shovel on the front of a tractor, for pushing earth or rubble; also, a tractor with such a blade. *See the picture.*



**bul·let** (bool′it) ***n.*** a small ball or cone of metal for shooting from a firearm.

**bul·le·tin** (bool′ət ′n) ***n.*** **1** a short, up-to-date report [a recent *bulletin* on the flood]. **2** a magazine or paper published regularly for a certain group.

☆**bulletin board** a board or wall space on which bulletins or notices are put up.

buoys

bulldog

bur

bun

bulldozer

**bull·fight** (bool′fīt) ***n.*** a public show in which a bull is first stirred up to anger and is then, usually, killed with a sword by a matador. —**bull′fight·er** ***n.***

**bull·finch** (bool′finch) ***n.*** a small songbird of Europe and Asia, with a short, rounded beak.

☆**bull·frog** (bool′frôg) ***n.*** a large frog that has a deep, loud croak.

**bull·head** (bool′hed) ***n.*** ☆a North American freshwater fish with a large head and no scales.

☆**bull·horn** (bool′hôrn) ***n.*** an electronic device for making the voice sound very loud. It is carried around like a megaphone.

**bul·lion** (bool′yən) ***n.*** bars of gold or silver before they have been made into coins.

**bull·ock** (bool′ək) ***n.*** a castrated bull; steer.

**Bull Run** a small stream in northeastern Virginia. Two Civil War battles were fought nearby, in 1861 and in 1862. Confederate forces won each battle.

**bull's-eye** (boolz′ī) ***n.*** **1** the round center of a target. **2** a shot that hits this mark.

**bul·ly** (bool′ē) ***n.*** a person who likes to hurt or frighten those who are smaller or weaker. —*pl.* **bul′lies** ◆***v.*** to hurt or frighten as a bully does; browbeat; bulldoze. —**bul′lied, bul′ly·ing** ◆***adj., interj.*** ☆very good; fine: *used only in everyday talk.*

**bul·rush** (bool′rush) ***n.*** a tall plant that grows in shallow water and marshy places.

**bul·wark** (bool′wərk) ***n.*** **1** a wall of earth, stone, etc. for defending against an enemy. **2** a person or thing that is a defense or protection [The Bill of Rights is a *bulwark* of our civil liberties.] **3 bulwarks,** *pl.* the part of a ship's side above the deck.

☆**bum** (bum) ***n.*** a person who does no work but spends much time loafing; a useless person; vagrant. ◆***v.*** **1** to loaf; idle away time. **2** to beg for [to *bum* a ride]. —**bummed, bum′ming** ◆***adj.*** bad; not good. —**bum′mer, bum′mest** *The word* bum *is slang in all its meanings.*

**bum·ble·bee** (bum′b′l bē′) ***n.*** a large, hairy, yellow-and-black bee that buzzes loudly.

**bump** (bump) ***v.*** **1** to knock against something; hit with a jolt [The bus *bumped* the car ahead of it. Don't *bump* into the wall.] **2** to move with jerks or jumps; jolt [The car *bumped* over the railroad tracks.] ◆***n.*** **1** a knock or blow; light jolt. **2** a part that bulges out, causing an uneven surface. **3** a swelling caused by a blow.

**bump·er** (bum′pər) ***n.*** ☆**1** a bar across the front or back of a car or truck to give it protection if it bumps into something. **2** a cup or glass filled to the brim. ◆***adj.*** very large or full [a *bumper* crop].

**bump·kin** (bump′kin) ***n.*** a person from the country who does not have city manners.

**bump·y** (bum′pē) ***adj.*** full of bumps; rough [a *bumpy* road]. —**bump′i·er, bump′i·est —bump′i·ness** ***n.***

**bun** (bun) ***n.*** **1** a small bread roll, often sweetened. **2** hair worn in a twisted knot or roll. *See the picture.*

**bunch** (bunch) ***n.*** **1** a group of things of the same kind growing or placed together [a *bunch* of bananas; a *bunch* of keys]. **2** a group of people: *used only in everyday talk* [A whole *bunch* of us are going.] ◆***v.*** to gather into a bunch [Passengers *bunched* up at the front of the bus.]

**bun·dle** (bun′d′l) ***n.*** **1** a group of things tied up or wrapped up together [a *bundle* of old clothes]. **2** any package or parcel. ✦v. **1** to wrap or tie together into a bundle [*Bundle* your old newspapers together.] **2** to send or go quickly [The children were *bundled* off to bed.] —**bun′dled**, **bun′dling** —**bundle up**, to put on plenty of warm clothing.

SYNONYMS: A **bundle** is a number of things bound together so as to be easily carried or stored [a *bundle* of sticks]. A **parcel** or **package** is something wrapped in paper or put in a box so that it can be easily carried, mailed, etc. A **pack**[1] is a package of a standard size or containing a specified number or amount [a *pack* of cigarettes]. **Pack**[1] is also used of a compact bundle carried on the back, as in hiking.

**bung** (buŋ) *n.* **1** a cork or other stopper for the hole in a barrel or cask. **2** such a hole, through which liquid can be drawn out: *its full name is* **bunghole**. ✦v. to close with a bung; stop up.

**bun·ga·low** (buŋ′gə lō) *n.* a small house with one story and an attic.

**Bungalow** comes from a Hindu word meaning "of Bengal," because such small houses were often seen in that part of India.

**bun·gle** (buŋ′g′l) *v.* to spoil by clumsy work; botch [They *bungled* the repair job on our TV.] —**bun′gled**, **bun′gling** ✦*n.* **1** the act of bungling. **2** a bungled piece of work. —**bun′gler** *n.*

**bun·ion** (bun′yən) *n.* a red, painful swelling at the base of the big toe, with a thickening of the skin.

**bunk**[1] (buŋk) *n.* **1** a bed that sticks out from the wall like a shelf. **2** any narrow bed. ✦☆*v.* **1** to sleep in a bunk. **2** to use a makeshift sleeping place [Pat and I *bunked* in the barn.]

☆**bunk**[2] (buŋk) *n.* talk that is silly or misleading; nonsense; humbug: *a slang word.*

**bunk·er** (buŋ′kər) *n.* **1** a large bin, as for storing fuel on a ship. **2** a hollow or a mound of earth making an obstacle on a golf course.

**Bunker Hill** a hill in Boston, Massachusetts. In 1775 a battle of the American Revolution was fought nearby. The British defeated American colonial forces.

**bun·ny** (bun′ē) *n.* a rabbit: *a pet name used by children.* —*pl.* **bun′nies**

**bunt** (bunt) *v.* ☆to bat a pitched baseball lightly so that it does not go out of the infield. ✦*n.* ☆**1** the act of bunting. ☆**2** a bunted ball.

**bun·ting**[1] (bun′tiŋ) *n.* **1** a thin cloth used in making flags. **2** flags or pieces of cloth in the colors and patterns of the flag, used as decorations. ☆**3** a closed, warm blanket for a baby, open at one end with a hood for the head.

**bun·ting**[2] (bun′tiŋ) *n.* a small, brightly colored bird with a short, stout bill.

**buoy** (bōō′ē *or* boi) *n.* **1** an object floating in water and held in place by an anchor to warn of danger or to mark a channel. It often has a light or bell. *See the picture.* **2** a life preserver: *the full name is* **life buoy**. ✦*v.* **1** to keep afloat. **2** to lift up or keep up in spirits; encourage [Her pep talk *buoyed* up the members of her sales staff.]

**buoy·an·cy** (boi′ən sē *or* bōō′yən sē) *n.* **1** the power to float or rise in liquid or air [Balsa wood is used in rafts because of its great *buoyancy*.] **2** the power to keep something afloat [Blimps cannot fly high where the air is thin and has little *buoyancy*.] **3** a cheerful spirit not easily kept down.

**buoy·ant** (boi′ənt *or* bōō′yənt) *adj.* **1** able to float or rise in liquid or air. **2** able to keep things afloat [The Great Salt Lake in Utah is more *buoyant* than the ocean.] **3** cheerful and lively [*buoyant* spirits]. —**buoy′ant·ly** *adv.*

**bur** or **burr** (bur) *n.* **1** a seedcase that is rough and prickly on the outside. *See the picture.* **2** a plant with burs. **3** a thing that sticks like a bur. *See also* **burr.**

**bur.** *abbreviation for* **bureau.**

**Bur·bank** (bur′baŋk) a city in southwestern California. It is a suburb of Los Angeles.

**Bur·bank** (bur′baŋk), **Luther** 1849–1926; U.S. scientist who bred many new kinds of fruits, flowers, and vegetables.

**bur·den**[1] (burd′′n) *n.* **1** anything that is carried; load [a light *burden*]. **2** anything one has to bear or put up with; heavy load [a *burden* of sorrow]. ✦*v.* to put a burden on; load; weigh down [Don't *burden* me with your troubles.] —**burden of proof**, the obligation to prove something.

**bur·den**[2] (burd′′n) *n.* **1** the chorus of a song. **2** the main or central idea; theme.

**bur·den·some** (burd′ən səm) *adj.* hard to bear; troublesome [a *burdensome* duty].

**bur·dock** (bur′däk) *n.* a plant with burs, large leaves, and a strong smell.

**bu·reau** (byoor′ō) *n.* ☆**1** a chest of drawers for holding clothes. It usually has a mirror. **2** an office, as for a certain part of a business [an information *bureau*]. ☆**3** a department of the government [The *Bureau* of Internal Revenue is in charge of collecting Federal taxes.] —*pl.* **bu′reaus** or **bu·reaux** (byoor′ōz)

**Bureau** comes from the Old French name for a kind of cloth once used to cover desks. It then became the word for such a desk or for an office, and later for a chest of drawers. The word **bureaucracy** (see the next entry) is made up of **bureau** and the suffix **-cracy**, meaning "government." So we see that a **bureaucracy** is government by people working at desks.

**bu·reauc·ra·cy** (byoo rä′krə sē) *n.* **1** government by appointed officials who follow all rules without question and without exceptions. **2** such officials, as a group, or the way they govern. —*pl.* **bu·reauc′ra·cies**

**bu·reau·crat** (byoor′ə krat) *n.* **1** an official in a bureaucracy. **2** any official who follows rules and routines blindly without thinking. —**bu′reau·crat′ic** *adj.*

**burg** (burg) *n.* ☆a city, town, or village: *used only in everyday talk.*

☆**bur·ger** (bur′gər) *a suffix meaning:* **1** a sandwich with a patty of ground meat, fish, etc. [turkey*burger*]. **2** hamburger and [cheese*burger*].

**bur·gess** (bur′jis) *n.* ☆a member of the lower house

| | | | | | | | |
|---|---|---|---|---|---|---|---|
| **a** | fat | **ir** | here | **ou** | out | **zh** | leisure |
| **ā** | ape | **ī** | bite, fire | **u** | up | **ŋ** | ring |
| **ä** | car, lot | **ō** | go | **ur** | fur | | a *in* ago |
| **e** | ten | **ô** | law, horn | **ch** | chin | | e *in* agent |
| **er** | care | **oi** | oil | **sh** | she | ə = | i *in* unity |
| **ē** | even | **oo** | look | **th** | thin | | o *in* collect |
| **i** | hit | **ōō** | tool | ***th*** | then | | u *in* focus |

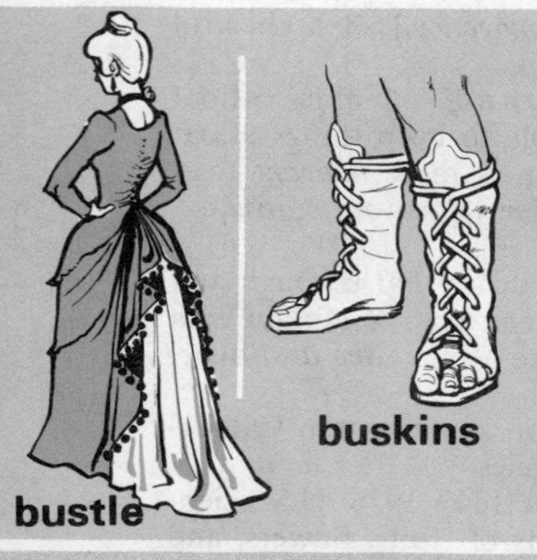


butte

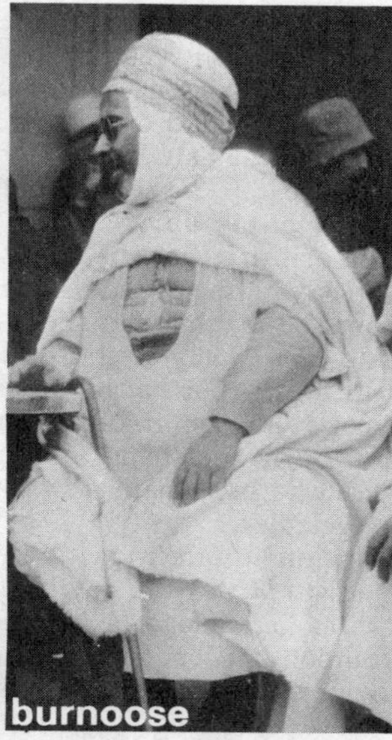


of the legislature of Maryland or Virginia before the American Revolution.

**bur·glar** (bʉr′glər) ***n.*** a person who breaks into a building, especially in order to steal.

☆**bur·glar·ize** (bʉr′glə rīz) ***v.*** to break into a building and steal as a burglar does: *used only in everyday talk.* —**bur′glar·ized, bur′glar·iz·ing**



**bur·gla·ry** (bʉr′glər ē) ***n.*** the act of breaking into a building, especially at night in order to steal. —*pl.* **bur′gla·ries**

**bur·go·mas·ter** (bʉr′gə mas′tər) ***n.*** the mayor of a city or town in certain European countries.

**Bur·gun·dy** (bʉr′gən dē) a district of eastern France that was once a kingdom. ✦***n.*** a red or white wine, originally from Burgundy.

**bur·i·al** (ber′ē əl) ***n.*** the act of burying a dead body in a grave, a tomb, or the sea.

**burial ground** a cemetery.

**bur·lap** (bʉr′lap) ***n.*** a coarse cloth made of jute or hemp, used for making bags, etc.

**bur·lesque** (bər lesk′) ***n.*** ☆**1** a stage show consisting of songs, dances, and comic skits, usually of a vulgar kind. **2** a funny or sarcastic imitation of something serious [This musical comedy is a *burlesque* of a tragic Italian opera.] ✦***v.*** to imitate in a funny or sarcastic way. —**bur·lesqued′, bur·lesqu′ing**

**bur·ly** (bʉr′lē) ***adj.*** big and strong; husky. —**bur′li·er, bur′li·est**

**Bur·ma** (bʉr′mə) a country in southeastern Asia, on the Indian Ocean. —**Bur·mese** (bər mēz′) ***adj., n.***

**burn**[1] (bʉrn) ***v.*** **1** to be on fire; blaze [The candle *burned* for a long time.] **2** to set on fire in order to give heat or light [They *burn* gas in their furnace.] **3** to destroy or be destroyed by fire [Our rubbish is *burned* at the dump.] **4** to injure or be injured by fire or heat, or by something that has the same effect, as acid or friction; scorch, singe, scald, etc. **5** to make by fire, acid, etc. [The spark *burned* a hole in his coat.] **6** to make feel hot [Pepper *burns* the throat.] **7** to feel hot [My head is *burning* with fever.] **8** to excite or be excited, as with anger, curiosity, or desire. —**burned** or **burnt, burn′ing** ✦***n.*** an injury or damage caused by fire, heat, wind, acid, etc.

SYNONYMS: **Burn** is the basic word meaning to destroy or injure by flames or extreme heat [The house *burned* down. She was sun*burned*.] **Scorch** means to damage the surface of material such as wood or cloth by burning slightly [He *scorched* the wood while burning off old paint with a blowtorch.] **Singe** means to burn slightly around the edges or tips [His eyebrows were *singed* when he got too close to the bonfire.]

**burn**[2] (bʉrn) ***n.*** a brook: *a Scottish word.*

**burn·a·ble** (bʉrn′ə b′l) ***adj.*** that can be burned. ✦***n.*** something that can be burned, especially rubbish.

**burn·er** (bʉr′nər) ***n.*** **1** the part of a stove, furnace, etc. from which the flame comes. **2** a stove, furnace, etc. [an oil *burner*].

**bur·nish** (bʉr′nish) ***v.*** to make or become shiny by rubbing; polish [*burnished* gold]. ✦***n.*** a gloss or polish.

**bur·noose** (bər no͞os′ *or* bʉr′no͞os) ***n.*** a long cloak with a hood, worn by Arabs and Moors. *See the picture.*

**Burns** (bʉrnz), **Robert** 1759–1796; Scottish poet.

**burnt** (bʉrnt) *a past tense and past participle of* **burn**[1]. ✦***adj.*** that has been burned, scorched, etc.

☆**burp** (bʉrp) ***n.*** belch: *used only in everyday talk.* ✦***v.*** **1** to belch: *used only in everyday talk.* **2** to cause a baby to get rid of gas in its stomach, as by patting its back.

**burr** (bʉr) ***n.*** **1** a rough edge left on metal, etc. after it has been cut or drilled. **2** a strong rolling of the sound of the letter *r* [a Scottish *burr*]. **3** a whirring sound. *See also* **bur.**

**Burr** (bʉr), **Aaron** 1756–1836; American political leader. He killed Alexander Hamilton in a duel.

**bur·ro** (bʉr′ō) ***n.*** a donkey, especially one used as a pack animal in the southwestern U.S. —*pl.* **bur′ros**

**bur·row** (bʉr′ō) ***n.*** a hole or tunnel dug in the ground by an animal [Woodchucks live in *burrows*.] ✦***v.*** **1** to dig a burrow. **2** to crawl into or hide as in a burrow. **3** to search or work hard, as if by digging.

**bur·si·tis** (bər sīt′əs) ***n.*** a condition of a body joint in which it becomes painful and inflamed. The shoulder and the hip are the joints most often affected.

**burst** (bʉrst) ***v.*** **1** to break open suddenly with force, especially because of pressure from the inside; fly into pieces; explode [A balloon will *burst* if you blow too much air into it.] **2** to go, come, start, or appear suddenly and with force [She *burst* into the room. He *burst* into laughter.] **3** to be as full or as crowded as possible [a room *bursting* with people; people *bursting* with joy]. —**burst, burst′ing** ✦***n.*** **1** a sudden outbreak; explosion [The President was greeted with a *burst* of cheers.] **2** a sudden, forceful effort or action; spurt [a *burst* of speed].

**Bu·run·di** (bo͝o ro͝on′dē) a country in east central Africa.

**bur·y** (ber′ē) ***v.*** **1** to put a dead body into the earth, a tomb, or the sea [The Egyptians *buried* the Pharaohs in pyramids.] **2** to cover up so as to hide [He *buried* his face in his hands.] **3** to put away and forget [Let's *bury* our feud.] **4** to put oneself deeply into [She *buried* herself in her work.] —**bur′ied, bur′y·ing**

**bus** (bus) ***n.*** a large motor coach for carrying many passengers, usually along a regular route. —*pl.* **bus′es**

or bus'ses ◆*v.* to go or carry by bus. —**bused** or **bussed, bus'ing** or **bus'sing**

**Bus** is shortened from *omnibus,* the original name for such a motor coach. *Omnibus* is a Latin word meaning "for everybody." So a **bus** is a coach on which everybody can ride.

**bus·boy** (bus'boi) ***n.*** a waiter's assistant who sets and clears tables, brings water, etc.

**bus·by** (buz'bē) ***n.*** a tall fur hat worn as part of the uniform of a drum major, drum majorette, guardsman, etc. —*pl.* **bus'bies**

**bush** (boosh) ***n.*** **1** a woody plant, smaller than a tree and having many stems branching out low instead of one main stem or trunk; shrub. ☆**2** wild land that has not been cleared and settled [The hunting party was lost in the *bush.*] ◆***v.*** to spread or grow out like a bush. —**beat around the bush,** to talk around a subject without getting to the point.

**bushed** (boosht) ***adj.*** very tired; worn-out: *used only in everyday talk.*

**bush·el** (boosh''l) ***n.*** **1** a measure of volume for grain, fruit, vegetables, etc. It is equal to 4 pecks, or 32 quarts. **2** a basket or other container that holds a bushel.

**bush·ing** (boosh'ing) ***n.*** a metal lining used to keep moving parts of a machine from wearing down. It can be replaced when it is worn out.

**bush·mas·ter** (boosh'mas'tər) ***n.*** a large, poisonous snake of South America.

☆**bush·whack** (boosh'hwak) ***v.*** to attack someone from hiding. —**bush'whack·er** ***n.***

**bush·y** (boosh'ē) ***adj.*** **1** thick and spreading out like a bush [*bushy* eyebrows]. **2** overgrown with bushes [*bushy* land]. —**bush'i·er, bush'i·est**

**bus·i·ly** (biz'ə lē) ***adv.*** in a busy way.

**busi·ness** (biz'nis) ***n.*** **1** what one does for a living; one's work or occupation [Shakespeare's *business* was writing plays.] **2** what one has a right or duty to do [You had no *business* telling her I was here.] **3** a matter or affair [Let's settle the *business* of what I'm to do.] **4** the buying and selling of goods and services; commerce; trade. **5** a place where things are made or sold; store or factory [Pat owns three *businesses.*] ◆***adj.*** of or for business [a *business* office; *business* hours]. —**mean business,** to be in earnest: *used only in everyday talk.*

**busi·ness·like** (biz'nis līk') ***adj.*** working with care and good system; efficient.

**busi·ness·man** (biz'nis man') ***n.*** a man who works in a business, especially as an owner or manager. —*pl.* **busi'ness·men'**

☆**busi·ness·wom·an** (biz'nis woom'ən) ***n.*** a woman who works in a business, especially as an owner or manager. —*pl.* **busi'ness·wom'en**

**bus·ing** or **bus·sing** (bus'ing) ***n.*** ☆the carrying of children by bus to schools outside of their neighborhoods, so that classes will be made up of pupils of different races.

**bus·kin** (bus'kin) ***n.*** a kind of boot worn long ago. The laced buskin worn by actors in ancient times is a symbol of tragedy. *See the picture.*

**bus·ses** (bus'iz) ***n.*** *a plural of* **bus.**

**bust¹** (bust) ***n.*** **1** a piece of sculpture showing the head and upper chest of a person. **2** the bosom of a woman.

**bust²** (bust) ***v.*** **1** to burst or break. ☆**2** to move to a lower rank. ☆**3** to hit. ☆**4** to tame, as a bronco. ☆**5** to arrest. ◆***n.*** ☆**1** a total failure. ☆**2** an arrest. *This is a slang word in all its meanings.*

**bus·tle¹** (bus''l) ***v.*** to hurry busily or with much fuss and bother. —**bus'tled, bus'tling** ◆***n.*** busy and noisy activity; commotion [the *bustle* of traffic in rush hour].

**bus·tle²** (bus''l) ***n.*** a padding or frame worn at the back by women to puff out the skirt. *See the picture.*

**bus·y** (biz'ē) ***adj.*** **1** doing something; active; at work; not idle [The students are *busy* at their desks.] **2** full of activity; with much action or motion [a *busy* morning; a *busy* store]. **3** being used [Short buzzes on the phone tell that the line is *busy.*] —**bus'i·er, bus'i·est** ◆***v.*** to make or keep busy [The cooks *busied* themselves in the kitchen.] —**bus'ied, bus'y·ing** —**bus'y·ness** ***n.***

**bus·y·bod·y** (biz'ē bäd'ē) ***n.*** a person who mixes into other people's business; meddler. —*pl.* **bus'y·bod'ies**

**but** (but) ***prep.*** except; other than [Nobody came *but* me.] ◆***conj.*** **1** yet; however [The story is long, *but* it is never dull.] **2** on the contrary [I am old, *but* you are young.] **3** unless; if not [It never rains *but* it pours.] **4** that [I don't question *but* you're correct.] ◆***adv.*** **1** only [if I had *but* known]. **2** no more than; merely [She is *but* a child.] —**but for,** if it were not for.

**bu·tane** (byoo'tān) ***n.*** a kind of gas used as a fuel.

**butch·er** (booch'ər) ***n.*** **1** a person whose work is killing animals for use as food. **2** a person who cuts up meat for sale. **3** a cruel person who causes many deaths or much suffering. ◆***v.*** **1** to kill animals for use as food. **2** to kill in a cruel, senseless way; slaughter [The army *butchered* the helpless civilians.] **3** to mess up; botch.

The word **butcher** comes from an Old French word, *bouchier,* which meant "one who kills and sells male goats." The word for "male goat" was *bouc,* which is related to our word **buck.**

**butch·er·y** (booch'ər ē) ***n.*** cruel slaughter.

**but·ler** (but'lər) ***n.*** a man servant, usually in charge of the other servants.

**butt¹** (but) ***n.*** **1** the thick end of anything [a rifle *butt*]. **2** the end left after something is used [a cigar *butt*]. **3** a person who is made fun of or teased [The boy with the crew cut was the *butt* of their jokes.]

**butt²** (but) ***v.*** to strike or push with the head; ram [Goats *butt.*] ◆***n.*** a push with the head. —☆**butt in** or **butt into,** to mix into someone else's business: *a slang phrase.*

**butt³** (but) ***n.*** a large cask for wine or beer.

**butte** (byoot) ***n.*** a steep hill standing alone in a plain, especially in the western U.S.; small mesa. *See the picture.*

| | | | | | | | |
|---|---|---|---|---|---|---|---|
| **a** | fat | **ir** | here | **ou** | out | **zh** | leisure |
| **ā** | ape | **ī** | bite, fire | **u** | up | **ng** | ring |
| **ä** | car, lot | **ō** | go | **ur** | fur | | a *in* ago |
| **e** | ten | **ô** | law, horn | **ch** | chin | | e *in* agent |
| **er** | care | **oi** | oil | **sh** | she | ə = | i *in* unity |
| **ē** | even | **oo** | look | **th** | thin | | o *in* collect |
| **i** | hit | **ōō** | tool | ***th*** | then | | u *in* focus |

**but·ter** (but′ər) ***n.*** **1** the yellow fat gotten by churning cream. It is used as a spread on bread and in cooking. **2** a spread or other substance somewhat like butter [peanut *butter*]. ◆***v.*** to spread with butter [*Butter* the toast.]

**but·ter·cup** (but′ər kup) ***n.*** a plant with yellow, cup-shaped flowers, growing in fields.

**but·ter·fat** (but′ər fat) ***n.*** the fatty part of milk, from which butter is made.

**but·ter·fly** (but′ər flī) ***n.*** an insect with a slender body and four broad wings, usually brightly colored. —*pl.* **but′ter·flies**

**but·ter·milk** (but′ər milk) ***n.*** the sour liquid left after churning butter from milk.

☆**but·ter·nut** (but′ər nut) ***n.*** **1** the oily nut of the white walnut tree. **2** this walnut tree.

☆**butternut squash** a small, bell-shaped, smooth winter squash, with yellowish flesh.

**but·ter·scotch** (but′ər skäch) ***n.*** a hard, sticky candy made from brown sugar and butter. ◆***adj.*** having the flavor of butterscotch [*butterscotch* sauce].

**but·ter·y** (but′ər ē) ***adj.*** **1** like butter. **2** having butter in it or having butter spread on it.

**but·tocks** (but′əks) ***n.pl.*** the fleshy parts at the back of the hips; rump.

**but·ton** (but′ən) ***n.*** **1** a small disk or knob sewed to a garment. It is pushed through a buttonhole to fasten parts together or is just a decoration. **2** a small knob that is pushed or turned to work a bell, light, machine, etc. ◆***v.*** to fasten or close with a button or buttons [*Button* up your overcoat.]

**but·ton·hole** (but′′n hōl) ***n.*** a slit in a garment through which a button can be fastened. ◆***v.*** to make a person listen to one, as if by grasping the person's coat by a buttonhole. —**but′ton·holed, but′ton·hol·ing**

**but·tress** (but′ris) ***n.*** **1** a support built against a wall to make it strong. *See the picture.* **2** any support or prop. ◆***v.*** to prop up or support [to *buttress* a wall; to *buttress* an argument].

**bux·om** (buk′səm) ***adj.*** plump, healthy, and good-natured [Only women are called *buxom*.]

**buy** (bī) ***v.*** **1** to get by paying money or something else [The Dutch *bought* Manhattan Island for about $24.] ☆**2** to accept as true, practical, agreeable, etc.: *slang in this meaning* [I can't *buy* his excuse.] —**bought, buy′ing** ◆***n.*** the value of a thing compared with its price [Turnips are your best *buy* in January vegetables.] —**buy off,** to bribe. —**buy out,** to buy all the stock or business rights of. —**buy up,** to buy all of something that can be gotten. —**buy′er** ***n.***

**buzz** (buz) ***v.*** **1** to make a humming sound like a long, steady *z* [Bees *buzz* in flight.] **2** to talk in low, excited tones [The town *buzzed* with the news.] **3** to fly an airplane low over [A pilot was fined for *buzzing* the tower.] **4** to signal with a buzzer. ◆***n.*** **1** a humming sound like a long, steady *z.* **2** a confused sound, as of many excited voices. **3** a telephone call: *used only in everyday talk.* [Give me a *buzz* tonight.] —**buzz about** or **buzz around,** to scurry around.

**buz·zard** (buz′ərd) ***n.*** **1** a kind of hawk that is slow and heavy in flight. ☆**2** *a shorter name for* **turkey buzzard.**

**buzz·er** (buz′ər) ***n.*** an electrical device that makes a buzzing sound used as a signal.

**B.V.M.** Blessed Virgin Mary.

**by** (bī) ***prep.*** **1** near or beside [Sit *by* the fire.] **2** in or during [We traveled *by* night.] **3** for a fixed time [paid *by* the hour]. **4** not later than [Be back *by* ten o'clock.] **5** going through; via [to New Jersey *by* the Holland Tunnel]. **6** past; beyond [He walked right *by* me.] **7** in the interest of; for [She did well *by* her children.] **8** through the means or work of [books *by* Alcott; to travel *by* car]. **9** according to [to play *by* ear]. **10** in [It grows dark *by* degrees.] **11** with permission of [*by* your leave]. **12** in the amount of [cheaper *by* the dozen; cloth *by* the yard]. ◆***adv.*** **1** near; close at hand [Stand *by!*] **2** away; aside [Put some money *by* for a rainy day.] **3** past [We watched the parade go *by.*] —**by and by,** after a while. —**by and large,** ☆on the whole; considering everything. —**by oneself,** **1** without any other person; alone. **2** without any help. —**by the by,** by the way.

**by-** *a prefix meaning:* **1** close by; near [A *bystander* stands near the scene of action.] **2** on the side of; of lesser importance [A *byproduct* is less important than the main product.]

**by-and-by** (bī′′n bī′) ***n.*** a future time.

**bye-bye** (bī′bī *or* bī bī′) ***n., interj.*** *same as* **goodbye.**

**Bye·lo·rus·sia** (bye′lō rush′ə) a republic in the western part of the Soviet Union. —**Bye′lo·rus′sian** ***adj., n.***

**by·gone** (bī′gôn) ***adj.*** past; gone by. ◆***n.*** anything that is gone or past. —**let bygones be bygones,** let the past be forgotten.

**by·law** (bī′lô) ***n.*** a rule passed by a club, a board of directors, etc. for use in its own meetings.

☆**by·line** (bī′līn) ***n.*** a line printed above or after a newspaper or magazine article telling who wrote it.

**by·pass** (bī′pas) ***n.*** a road, pipe, etc. that leaves the main route in order to get around an obstacle [Route 2A is a *bypass* around the town.] ◆***v.*** **1** to go around instead of through. **2** to ignore, fail to consult, etc.

**by·path** or **by-path** (bī′path) ***n.*** side path; path away from the main road, especially one that is not used very much.

**by·play** (bī′plā) ***n.*** action going on aside from the main action, as in a scene of a play.

**by·prod·uct** or **by-prod·uct** (bī′präd′əkt) ***n.*** anything made from the things left over in making a main product [Glue is a *byproduct* of meatpacking.]

**by·road** (bī′rōd) ***n.*** a side road; bypath.

**By·ron** (bī′rən), **Lord** 1788–1824; English poet. His full name was **George Gordon Byron.**

**by·stand·er** (bī′stan′dər) ***n.*** a person who stands near but does not take part in what is happening; onlooker.

**by·way** (bī′wā) ***n.*** a side path or road; bypath.

**by·word** (bī′wurd) ***n.*** **1** a common saying; proverb ["Waste not, want not" is a *byword* with her.] **2** a person or thing considered typical of something bad [The Huns' cruelty made them a *byword.*]

**By·zan·tine** (biz′′n tēn *or* biz′′n tīn) ***adj.*** having to do with the eastern part of the later Roman Empire (395–1453 A.D.). Byzantine architecture had round arches, mosaic art work, and domes over square areas.

**By·zan·ti·um** (bi zan′shē əm *or* bi zan′tē əm) an ancient city where Istanbul now stands.

**C, c** (sē) ***n.*** the third letter of the English alphabet. —*pl.* **C's, c's** (sēz)

**C** (sē) ***n.*** **1** the Roman numeral for 100. **2** a grade, as in some schools, meaning "fair" or "average."

**C** *the symbol for the chemical element* carbon.

**C, C.** *abbreviation for* **Celsius** *or* **centigrade.**

**C., c.** *abbreviation for* **cent** *or* **cents, centimeter, century, chapter, copyright, cup.**

**CA** *abbreviation for* **California.**

**Ca** *the symbol for the chemical element* calcium.

**cab** (kab) ***n.*** **1** a carriage or automobile **(taxicab)** that can be hired along with its driver. **2** the place in a locomotive, truck, crane, etc. where the driver or engineer sits.

**ca·bal** (kə bal′) ***n.*** **1** a small group of persons who are joined in a secret scheme or plot. **2** the scheme or plot of such a group.

**ca·ba·na** (kə bän′ə *or* kə ban′ə *or* kə bän′yə) ***n.*** **1** a cabin or hut. **2** a small shelter where one can change one's clothes to go swimming.

**cab·a·ret** (kab ə rā′) ***n.*** a restaurant with dancing and singing as entertainment.

**cab·bage** (kab′ij) ***n.*** a vegetable with thick leaves folded tightly over each other to form a hard, round head. The leaves are cooked or eaten raw.

**cab·in** (kab′in) ***n.*** **1** a small house built in a simple, rough way, usually of wood [Lincoln was born in a log *cabin.*] **2** a room on a ship, especially one with berths for sleeping. **3** the space in an airplane where the passengers ride.

**cab·i·net** (kab′ə nit) ***n.*** **1** a case or cupboard with drawers or shelves for holding or storing things [a china *cabinet;* a medicine *cabinet*]. ☆**2** *often* **Cabinet,** a group of officials who act as advisers to the head of a nation. Our President's cabinet is made up of the heads of the departments of our government.

**cab·i·net·mak·er** (kab′ə nit māk′ər) ***n.*** a skilled worker who makes fine furniture or woodwork.

**ca·ble** (kā′b′l) ***n.*** **1** a thick, heavy rope, now usually made of wires twisted together [The bridge is supported by *cables.*] *See the picture.* **2** a bundle of insulated wires through which electric current can be sent [Telephone and telegraph *cables* are often laid under the ground or on the ocean floor.] ☆**3** *a shorter word for* **cablegram.** ◆***v.*** to send a cablegram to. —**ca′bled, ca′bling**

☆**ca·ble·gram** (kā′b′l gram) ***n.*** a message sent across an ocean by telegraph cable.

**cable TV** *same as* **CATV.**

**ca·boose** (kə bo͞os′) ***n.*** ☆a car for the crew on a freight train. It is usually the last car.

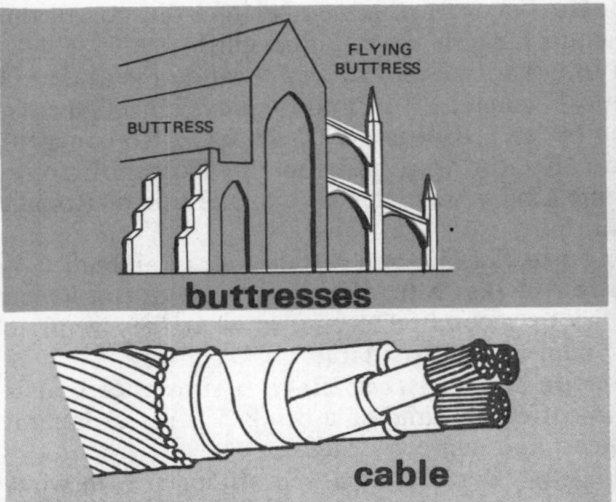

buttresses

cable

cactus

**Cab·ot** (kab′ət), **John** 1450?–1498?; Italian explorer who discovered the coast of North America in 1497 while sailing in the service of England.

**ca·ca·o** (kə kā′ō *or* kə kä′ō) ***n.*** **1** a small tropical tree from whose seeds cocoa and chocolate are made. **2** these seeds. —*pl.* **ca·ca′os**

**cache** (kash) ***n.*** **1** a place for hiding or storing something, as food or supplies. **2** anything so hidden. ◆***v.*** to hide or store in a cache. —**cached, cach′ing**

**cack·le** (kak′′l) ***v.*** **1** to make the shrill, broken sounds of a hen. **2** to laugh or talk in a shrill way. —**cack′led, cack′ling** ◆***n.*** the act or sound of cackling.



**cac·tus** (kak′təs) ***n.*** a plant with fleshy stems that bear spines or scales instead of leaves. Cactuses grow in hot, dry places and often have showy flowers. *See the picture.* —*pl.* **cac′tus·es** or **cac·ti** (kak′tī)

**cad** (kad) ***n.*** a man who treats others in a way that is not right or fair.

**cad·die** or **cad·dy**[1] (kad′ē) ***n.*** a person whose work is helping golfers by carrying the clubs, finding lost balls, etc. —*pl.* **cad′dies** ◆***v.*** to do the work of a caddie. —**cad′died, cad′dy·ing**

**cad·dy**[2] (kad′ē) ***n.*** a small can or box, especially one for holding tea. —*pl.* **cad′dies**

**ca·dence** (kād′′ns) ***n.*** **1** flow or rhythm with a regular beat [to march in fast *cadence;* the *cadence* of waves breaking on the shore]. **2** the rise or fall of the voice or the tone of the voice in speaking. **3** the final chords or other ending of a section of music.

**ca·det** (kə det′) ***n.*** **1** a student in training to become an officer in the army, navy, or air force. **2** a student at any military school. **3** any person in training, as a practice teacher.

> **Cadet** is the French word for "younger son." In earlier times, the oldest son of a family inherited the father's property. A younger son, having no property, often chose the army as a career.

| | | | | | | | |
|---|---|---|---|---|---|---|---|
| **a** | fat | **ir** | here | **ou** | out | **zh** | leisure |
| **ā** | ape | **ī** | bite, fire | **u** | up | **ng** | ring |
| **ä** | car, lot | **ō** | go | **ur** | fur | | a *in* ago |
| **e** | ten | **ô** | law, horn | **ch** | chin | | e *in* agent |
| **er** | care | **oi** | oil | **sh** | she | **ə =** | i *in* unity |
| **ē** | even | **oo** | look | **th** | thin | | o *in* collect |
| **i** | hit | **o͞o** | tool | ***th*** | then | | u *in* focus |

☆**Ca·dette** (kə det′) ***n.*** a member of a division of the Girls Scouts for girls aged 12 through 14.

**cad·mi·um** (kad′mē əm) ***n.*** a blue-white metal that is a chemical element. It is used in alloys and pigments.

**Cae·sar** (sē′zər), **Julius** 100?–44 B.C.; Roman general and dictator who built up the Roman Empire. The name *Caesar* was later used as the title of Roman emperors.

**ca·fé** or **ca·fe** (ka fā′) ***n.*** a restaurant or barroom.

☆**caf·e·te·ri·a** (kaf′ə tir′ē ə) ***n.*** a restaurant in which people go to a counter to choose what they want to eat and then carry it to a table.

**caf·feine** or **caf·fein** (kaf′ēn) ***n.*** a substance that is found in coffee, tea, and cola drinks. It is a stimulant to the heart and nervous system.

**cage** (kāj) ***n.*** **1** a box or closed-off space with wires or bars on the sides, in which to keep birds or animals. ☆**2** a screen used in baseball batting practice. ◆***v.*** to shut up in a cage. —**caged, cag′ing**

☆**ca·gey** or **ca·gy** (kā′jē) ***adj.*** sly, tricky, or cunning: *used only in everyday talk.* —**ca′gi·er, ca′gi·est**

**Cain** (kān) in the Bible, the oldest son of Adam and Eve. He killed his brother Abel. —☆**raise Cain,** to make much noise, trouble, etc.: *a slang phrase.*

**cairn** (kern) ***n.*** a pile of stones in the form of a cone, set up as a tomb or landmark.

**Cai·ro** (kī′rō) the capital of Egypt, on the Nile River.

**cais·son** (kā′sän) ***n.*** **1** a trailer cart for carrying ammunition for cannon. **2** a watertight box inside of which people work when building under water.



**ca·jole** (kə jōl′) ***v.*** to make a person do what one wants by flattery or false promises; wheedle. —**ca·joled′, ca·jol′ing —ca·jol′er·y *n.***

**cake** (kāk) ***n.*** **1** a mixture of flour, eggs, milk, sugar, etc., baked in a loaf and often covered with icing. **2** a small, flat mass of batter or of some hashed food, that is fried or baked [a griddle*cake;* a fish *cake*]. **3** any solid mass with a definite shape [a *cake* of soap]. ◆***v.*** to form into a hard mass [The old paint had *caked* in the can.] —**caked, cak′ing**

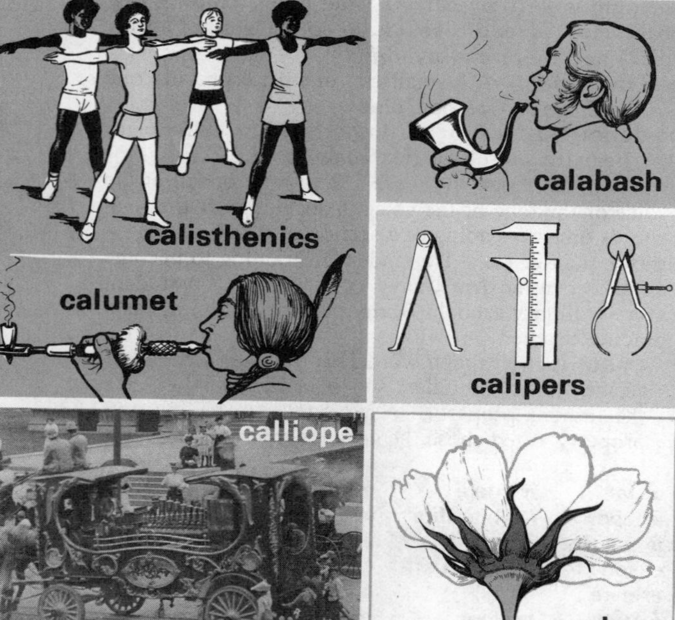


**Cal.** or **cal.** *abbreviation for* **calorie** *or* **calories.**

**cal·a·bash** (kal′ə bash) ***n.*** **1** a tropical American tree with a fruit that looks like a gourd. **2** this fruit. **3** a bowl, tobacco pipe, etc. made from the dried shell of this fruit. *See the picture.*

**cal·a·mine** (kal′ə mīn) ***n.*** a zinc compound that is used in skin lotions and salves.

**ca·lam·i·tous** (kə lam′ə təs) ***adj.*** bringing calamity or disaster [a *calamitous* winter].

**ca·lam·i·ty** (kə lam′ə tē) ***n.*** **1** deep trouble or misery [the *calamity* of war]. **2** a terrible happening that brings great sorrow; disaster. —*pl.* **ca·lam′i·ties**

**cal·ci·fy** (kal′sə fī) ***v.*** to turn hard and stony from deposits of lime or calcium salts. —**cal′ci·fied, cal′ci·fy·ing**

**cal·ci·mine** (kal′sə mīn) ***n.*** a white or colored, watery liquid used as a thin paint for plastered ceilings or walls. ◆***v.*** to cover with calcimine. —**cal′ci·mined, cal′ci·min·ing**

**cal·cine** (kal′sīn) ***v.*** to heat or burn something until it dries out and turns into powder or ashes. —**cal′cined, cal′cin·ing**

**cal·ci·um** (kal′sē əm) ***n.*** a chemical element that is a soft, silver-white metal. It is found combined with other elements in the bones and teeth of animals and in limestone, marble, chalk, etc.

**cal·cu·late** (kal′kyə lāt) ***v.*** **1** to find out by using arithmetic; compute [*Calculate* the amount of cloth you will need for the skirt.] **2** to find out by reasoning; estimate [Try to *calculate* the effect of your decision.] **3** to plan or intend [The joke was *calculated* to shock us.] —**cal′cu·lat·ed, cal′cu·lat·ing**

SYNONYMS: **Calculate** means to use arithmetic or, often, higher mathematics such as algebra or calculus [The astronauts *calculated* the distance to the moon.] **Compute** means to use simple arithmetic to get an exact result [to *compute* the volume of a cylinder].

**cal·cu·lat·ing** (kal′kyə lāt′iŋ) ***adj.*** full of sly schemes; shrewd or cunning.

**cal·cu·la·tion** (kal′kyə lā′shən) ***n.*** **1** the act of calculating. **2** the answer found by calculating. **3** careful or shrewd thought or planning.

**cal·cu·la·tor** (kal′kyə lāt′ər) ***n.*** **1** a person who calculates. **2** a machine that adds, subtracts, etc. rapidly, now often by electronic means.

**cal·cu·lus** (kal′kyə ləs) ***n.*** a kind of mathematics used to solve hard problems in science and statistics.

**Calculus** is a Latin word meaning "pebble." The early Romans used little stones for counting or "calculating" in doing arithmetic.

**Cal·cut·ta** (kal kut′ə) a seaport in northeastern India.

**cal·dron** (kôl′drən) ***n.*** a large pot or kettle.

**cal·en·dar** (kal′ən dər) ***n.*** **1** a system for arranging time into days, weeks, months, and years [Most countries now use the Gregorian *calendar.*] **2** a table or chart showing such an arrangement, usually for a single year [an old 1970 *calendar*]. **3** a list or schedule [A court *calendar* lists the cases to be heard.]

**cal·en·der** (kal′ən dər) ***n.*** a machine with rollers for giving paper or cloth a smooth or glossy surface. ◆***v.*** to press in such a machine.

**calf**[1] (kaf) ***n.*** **1** a young cow or bull. **2** a young elephant, whale, hippopotamus, seal, etc. **3** *a shorter word for* **calfskin.** *—pl.* **calves**

**calf**[2] (kaf) ***n.*** the fleshy back part of the leg between the knee and the ankle. *—pl.* **calves**

**calf·skin** (kaf′skin) ***n.*** **1** the skin of a young cow or bull. **2** a soft, flexible leather made from this.

**cal·i·ber** or **cal·i·bre** (kal′ə bər) ***n.*** **1** the size of a bullet or gun shell as measured by its diameter [A bullet of .45 *caliber* is 45/100 inch in diameter.] **2** the diameter of the inside of a gun barrel or other tube [A gun of .45 *caliber* fires a .45 caliber bullet.] **3** ability or quality [a diplomat of high *caliber*].

**cal·i·brate** (kal′ə brāt) ***v.*** **1** to find out the caliber of. **2** to check or correct the markings for the degrees on a measuring instrument, as a thermometer. **—cal′i·brat·ed, cal′i·brat·ing —cal′i·bra′tion *n.* —cal′i·bra′tor *n.***

**cal·i·co** (kal′ə kō) ***n.*** a cotton cloth that is usually printed with a colored pattern. *—pl.* **cal′i·coes** or **cal′i·cos** ◆***adj.*** **1** made of calico. **2** spotted like calico [a *calico* cat].

**Cal·i·for·nia** (kal′ə fôr′nyə) a State in the southwestern part of the U.S., on the Pacific Coast: abbreviated **Calif., CA —Cal′i·for′nian *adj., n.***

**cal·i·pers** (kal′ə pərz) ***n.pl.*** an instrument made up of a pair of hinged legs, for measuring the thickness or diameter of a thing. *See the picture.*

**ca·liph** or **ca·lif** (kā′lif) ***n.*** supreme ruler: the title taken by some of the heads of Muslim states in past times.

**cal·is·then·ics** (kal′əs then′iks) ***n.pl.*** exercises, such as push-ups, that are done to develop a strong, trim body. *See the picture.*

**calk** (kôk) ***v.*** *another spelling of* **caulk.**

**call** (kôl) ***v.*** **1** to say or read in a loud voice; shout [*Call* the roll.] **2** to ask or order to come; summon [Please *call* a taxi for us.] **3** to bring together persons for [to *call* a meeting]. **4** to give a name to [Let's *call* the baby Leslie.] **5** to telephone. **6** to awaken [*Call* me at six.] **7** to think of as being [I *call* that a shame.] ☆**8** to stop [The game was *called* because of rain.] ☆**9** to declare to be [The umpire *called* him out.] ◆***n.*** **1** the act of calling; shout or cry [a *call* for help]. **2** an order to come; summons. **3** the power to attract [the *call* of the wild]. **4** need or necessity [There's no *call* for tears.] **5** a signal [a bugle *call*]. **6** the act of telephoning [I put in a *call* to Chicago.] **7** the special cry or sound of an animal or bird. **8** a short visit [a doctor's house *call*]. **9** a ruling by an official [That was a good *call* by the referee.] **—call for, 1** to demand or need. **2** to come and get; stop for. **—call forth,** to bring into action or being [*Call forth* your courage.] **—call off, 1** to order away [*Call off* the dog.] **2** to read out loud from a list [*Call off* the roll.] **3** to decide not to have an event that was supposed to take place. **—call on, 1** to visit for a short time. **2** to ask a person to speak. **—call out,** to speak in a loud voice; shout. **—call up, 1** to bring back to mind; recall. **2** to order to come, especially for duty in the armed forces. **3** to telephone. **—on call,** ready when called for. **—call′er *n.***

**cal·la** (kal′ə) ***n.*** a plant with a large, white leaf that looks like a flower surrounding a long, yellow spike that is the true flower: *also called* **calla lily.**

**call·ing** (kôl′iŋ) ***n.*** **1** the action of one that calls. **2** one's trade, occupation, or profession.

**cal·li·o·pe** (kə lī′ə pē *or* kal′ē ōp) ***n.*** a musical instrument with a series of steam whistles. It is played like an organ. *See the picture.*

> The **calliope** was named after the Greek Muse of poetry and singing. Her name came from two Greek words meaning "beautiful voice." Some people wonder why this instrument with its harsh tones was given such a name.

**cal·lis·then·ics** (kal′əs then′iks) ***n.pl.*** *another spelling of* **calisthenics.**

**cal·lous** (kal′əs) ***adj.*** **1** having a callus or calluses. **2** not having any feeling for the suffering of others; unfeeling ["Who cares?" was her *callous* remark.] ◆***v.*** to make or become callous.

**cal·low** (kal′ō) ***adj.*** young and without experience; immature [a *callow* youth].

**cal·lus** (kal′əs) ***n.*** a hardened, thickened place on the skin. *—pl.* **cal′lus·es**

**calm** (käm) ***adj.*** not disturbed, excited, or stirred up; quiet; still [a *calm* sea; a *calm* mind; a *calm* answer]. ◆***n.*** a lack of wind or motion; stillness; quiet [the *calm* after a storm]. ◆***v.*** to make or become calm. [The puppy will *calm* down after a while.] **—calm′ly *adv.* —calm′ness *n.***

**cal·o·mel** (kal′ə mel) ***n.*** a white, tasteless powder that is a compound of mercury. It used to be given as a medicine to make the bowels move. 

**ca·lor·ic** (kə lôr′ik) ***adj.*** **1** of heat. **2** of calories [Nuts have a high *caloric* content.]

**cal·o·rie** (kal′ə rē) ***n.*** **1** the unit for measuring heat. It is the amount of heat needed to raise the temperature of one gram of water one degree Celsius. **2** a unit for measuring the energy that food supplies to the body [One large egg supplies about 100 *calories.*]

**cal·u·met** (kal′yoo met) ***n.*** a pipe smoked by American Indians as a sign of peace. *See the picture.*

**cal·um·ny** (kal′əm nē) ***n.*** a false and mean statement that is made to hurt someone's reputation; slander. *—pl.* **cal′um·nies**

**Cal·va·ry** (kal′və rē) in the Bible, the place near Jerusalem where Jesus was put to death.

**calves** (kavz) ***n.*** *plural of* **calf.**

**Cal·vin** (kal′vin), **John** 1509–1564; French Protestant leader.

**Cal·vin·ism** (kal′vin iz′m) ***n.*** the religious system of John Calvin, which teaches that God has decided the fate of each person. **—Cal′vin·ist *adj., n.***

**ca·lyp·so** (kə lip′sō) ***n.*** a kind of song popular in the West Indies. Calypsos have a strong rhythm and often deal in a humorous way with current events. *—pl.* **ca·lyp′sos**

**ca·lyx** (kā′liks) ***n.*** the outer ring of leaves, or sepals, growing at the base of a flower. *See the picture.* It

| | | | | | | | |
|---|---|---|---|---|---|---|---|
| a | fat | ir | here | ou | out | zh | leisure |
| ā | ape | ī | bite, fire | u | up | ŋ | ring |
| ä | car, lot | ō | go | ur | fur | | a *in* ago |
| e | ten | ô | law, horn | ch | chin | | e *in* agent |
| er | care | oi | oil | sh | she | ə = | i *in* unity |
| ē | even | oo | look | th | thin | | o *in* collect |
| i | hit | ōō | tool | *th* | then | | u *in* focus |

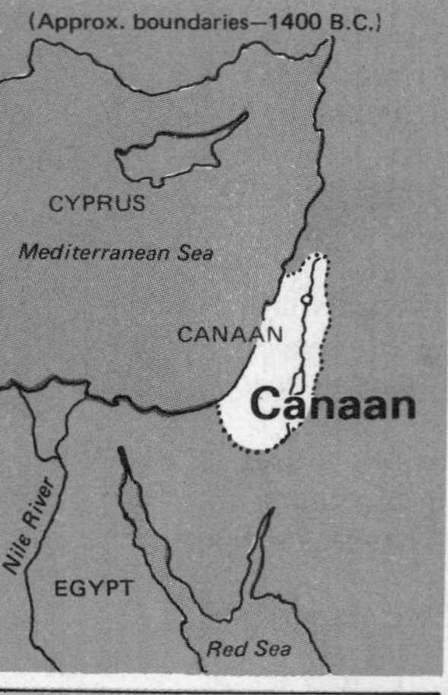

Canaan

camouflaged lizard

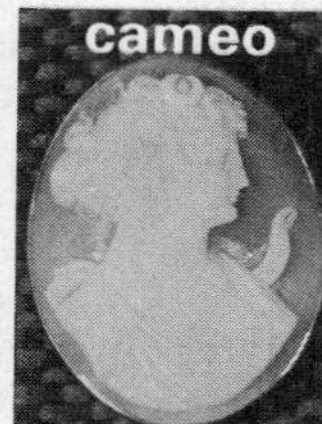
cameo

cancelled stamp

campanile

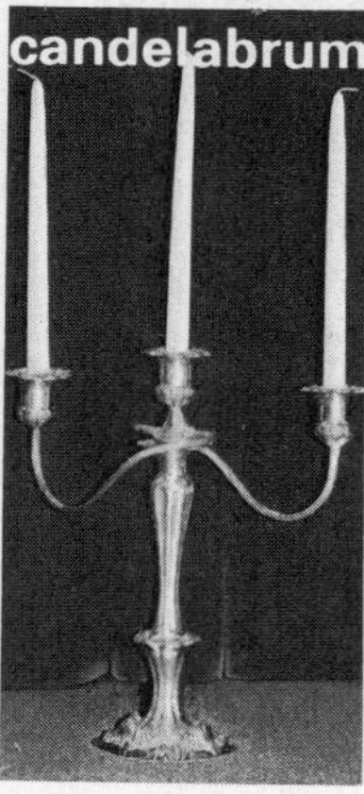
candelabrum

forms the outer cover of the unopened bud. *—pl.* **ca′lyx·es** or **ca·ly·ces** (kā′lə sēz *or* kal′ə sēz)

104 **cam** (kam) ***n.*** a wheel that is not a circle or that has a part sticking out, so that it gives an irregular motion to another wheel or to a shaft moving along its edge. Cams are used to change circular motion to a back-and-forth motion.

**ca·ma·ra·de·rie** (käm′ə räd′ər ē) ***n.*** the warm friendship that comrades feel for one another.

**cam·ber** (kam′bər) ***n.*** **1** a slight arch in a surface, as of a road or airplane wing. **2** a slight tilt given to a pair of automobile wheels so that they are a little closer at the bottoms than at the tops.

**cam·bi·um** (kam′bē əm) ***n.*** a layer of soft tissue between the wood and bark in woody plants, from which new wood and bark grow.

**Cam·bo·di·a** (kam bō′dē ə) a country in a large peninsula south of central China. The official name since 1976 is *Kampuchea.*

**cam·bric** (kām′brik) ***n.*** a thin, fine, light cloth of linen or cotton.

**Cam·bridge** (kām′brij) **1** a city in England, home of Cambridge University. **2** a city in Massachusetts.

**came** (kām) *past tense of* **come.**

**cam·el** (kam″l) ***n.*** a large, cud-chewing animal with a humped back, that is commonly used for riding and for carrying goods in Asian and North African deserts. When food and drink are scarce, it can keep going for a few days on the fat and water stored in its body tissue. The **Arabian camel** has one hump and the **Bac·tri·an** (bak′trē ən) **camel** has two.

**ca·mel·lia** (kə mēl′yə) ***n.*** a plant with shiny evergreen leaves and flowers that look like roses.

**Cam·e·lot** (kam′ə lät) in British legend, the city where King Arthur held court.

**cam·e·o** (kam′ē ō) ***n.*** a gem or shell with a figure carved in it. Its two layers are usually of different colors, so that when the top is carved, the bottom serves as a background. *See the picture. —pl.* **cam′e·os**

**cam·er·a** (kam′ər ə) ***n.*** **1** a closed box for taking pictures. The light that enters when a lens or hole at one end is opened by a shutter forms an image on the film or plate at the other end. **2** that part of a TV transmitter which picks up the picture to be sent and changes it to electrical signals.

> **Camera** is a Latin word meaning "room" or "chamber." The full name of the box for taking pictures was once **camera obscura,** which meant "dark chamber" and described the closed part in which the image is formed on the film by the lens.

**Ca·me·roon** (kam′ə ro͞on′) a country in western Africa, on the Atlantic Ocean.

**cam·ou·flage** (kam′ə fläzh) ***n.*** **1** the act of hiding soldiers, guns, vehicles, etc. from the enemy by making them look like part of the landscape, as by painting them or covering them with leaves and branches. **2** a disguise of this kind in nature, as the green color of insects that live on leaves and grass. **3** anything used to disguise or mislead [Her smile was only *camouflage* covering hurt feelings.] ◆***v.*** to disguise in order to hide. *See the picture.* **—cam′ou·flaged, cam′ou·flag·ing**

**camp** (kamp) ***n.*** **1** a group of tents, huts, or other rough shelters to live in for a time. **2** a place with barracks or tents where soldiers, sailors, etc. live while they are being trained or when they are not in combat. **3** a place in the country where people, especially children, can have an outdoor vacation. ◆***v.*** **1** to set up a camp [Let's *camp* by the river tonight.] **2** to live in a camp or in the outdoors for a time [We'll be *camping* in Michigan this summer.] **—break camp,** to take down a camp and go away.

**cam·paign** (kam pān′) ***n.*** **1** a series of battles or other military actions having a special goal [Napoleon's Russian *campaign* ended in his defeat.] **2** a series of planned actions for getting something done [a *campaign* to get someone elected]. ◆***v.*** to take part in a campaign. **—cam·paign′er *n.***

**cam·pa·ni·le** (kam′pə nē′lē) ***n.*** a tower with bells in it, especially one that stands apart from another building. *See the picture.*

**camp·er** (kamp′ər) ***n.*** **1** a person who vacations at a camp. ☆**2** a motor vehicle or trailer having the special things needed for camping.

**camp·fire** (kamp′fīr) ***n.*** **1** an outdoor fire, as at a camp. **2** a party or meeting around such a fire.

☆**Camp Fire Girls** a national club for girls that seeks to help them become healthy women of good character.

**cam·phor** (kam′fər) ***n.*** a substance with a strong smell, that comes from the wood of an Asian tree. It is used in skin ointments and to keep moths away from clothes.

☆**camp·site** (kamp′sīt) ***n.*** any place for a camp or for camping.

☆**cam·pus** (kam′pəs) ***n.*** the grounds, and sometimes the buildings as well, of a school or college.

**can**[1] (kan) *a helping verb used with other verbs and meaning:* **1** to know how to [I *can* read French and Italian.] **2** to be able to [The baby *can* walk.] **3** to be likely to [*Can* that be true?] **4** to have the right to [You *can* vote at eighteen.] **5** to have permission to;

may: *used only in everyday talk* [*Can* I go out to play?] The past tense is **could**.

SYNONYMS: In formal use, **can** means "to be able to do something" and **may** means "to be allowed to do something." **Can** is often used in place of **may** in everyday talk, especially in asking questions or saying "no" [*Can't* I go? You *cannot*.]

**can**[2] (kan) ***n.*** **1** a metal container of various kinds [a milk *can;* a *can* of shoe polish]. ☆**2** an airtight metal container in which foods are sealed to keep them from spoiling for some time. **3** as much as a can holds; contents of a full can. ***•v.*** **1** to put into airtight cans or jars so as to keep in good condition for later use. **2** to fire from a job: *slang in this meaning.* —**canned, can′ning** —**can′ner** ***n.***

**Can.** *abbreviation for* **Canada.**

**Ca·naan** (kā′nən) in the Bible, the land promised by God to Abraham and his descendants, between the Jordan River and the Mediterranean. *See the map.*

**Ca·naan·ite** (kā′nən īt) ***n.*** a person who lived in Canaan before the Israelites settled there.

**Canad.** *abbreviation for* **Canadian.**

**Can·a·da** (kan′ə də) a country in the northern part of North America.

**Canada goose** a large wild goose of North America. It is gray, with a black head and neck.

**Ca·na·di·an** (kə nā′dē ən) ***adj.*** of Canada or its people. ***•n.*** a person born or living in Canada.

**ca·nal** (kə nal′) ***n.*** **1** a channel dug and filled with water to allow ships to cross a stretch of land. Canals are also used to carry water for irrigating crops. **2** a tube in the body [the alimentary *canal*].

**Canal Zone** the strip of land ten miles wide in Central America that surrounds the Panama Canal. It is governed by the United States.

**ca·na·pé** (kan′ə pē) ***n.*** a cracker or bit of toast spread with cheese, spiced meat, fish, etc. and served as an appetizer.

**ca·nard** (kə närd′) ***n.*** a false, harmful rumor made up and spread on purpose.

**ca·nar·y** (kə ner′ē) ***n.*** **1** a small, yellow songbird kept as a pet in a cage. *—pl.* **ca·nar′ies** **2** a light yellow: *also called* **canary yellow.**

The **canary** gets its name from the Canary Islands where this bird was first found. The islands got their name from the Latin word *canis,* meaning "dog," from which we also get the word **canine.** There were once many wild dogs on these islands.

**Canary Islands** a group of islands off the northwest coast of Africa, belonging to Spain.

**ca·nas·ta** (kə nas′tə) ***n.*** a card game like rummy but played with two decks of cards.

**Ca·na·ver·al** (kə nav′ər əl), **Cape,** a cape on the eastern coast of Florida, where missiles and spacecraft are tested and launched.

**Can·ber·ra** (kan′bər ə) the capital of Australia, in the southeastern part.

**can·cel** (kan′s'l) ***v.*** **1** to cross out with lines or mark in some other way [Postage stamps and checks are *canceled* to show that they have been used.] *See the picture.* **2** to do away with; wipe out; say that it will no longer be [to *cancel* an order]. **3** to balance something so that it has no effect [My gains and losses *cancel* each other.] —**can′celed** or **can′celled, can′celing** or **can′cel·ling**

**can·cel·la·tion** (kan′s'l ā′shən) ***n.*** **1** the act of canceling. **2** something canceled. **3** a mark that cancels, as on a postage stamp.

**can·cer** (kan′sər) ***n.*** **1** a disease in which certain cells grow wild and spread throughout the body. **2** a growth made up of such cells. **3** anything harmful that spreads and destroys. —**can′cer·ous *adj.***

**Can·cer** (kan′sər) the fourth sign of the zodiac, for the period from June 22 to July 21: *also called* the Crab. *See also* **moon child,** *the picture for* **zodiac,** and **Tropic of Cancer.**

**can·de·la·bra** (kan′də lä′brə *or* kan′də lab′rə) ***n.*** *same as* **candelabrum.** *—pl.* **can′de·la′bras**

**can·de·la·brum** (kan′də lä′brəm *or* kan′də lab′rəm) ***n.*** a large candlestick with branches for several candles. *See the picture. —pl.* **can′de·la′bra** or **can′de·la′brums**

**can·did** (kan′did) ***adj.*** **1** saying what one honestly thinks; frank, honest, and fair [a *candid* opinion]. *See* SYNONYMS *at* **frank. 2** not formal or posed [a *candid* photograph]. —**can′did·ly *adv.***

☆**can·di·da·cy** (kan′də də sē) ***n.*** the fact of being a candidate [Her *candidacy* for the Senate was announced.] *—pl.* **can′di·da·cies**

**can·di·date** (kan′də dāt) ***n.*** a person who seeks, or who has been suggested for, an office or award [a *candidate* for mayor].

A person running for political office in ancient Rome usually wore a white toga to show how pure or sincere he was. Such a person was called *candidatus,* meaning "dressed in white." Both **candidate** and **candid** come from this Latin word.



**can·died** (kan′dēd) ***adj.*** **1** cooked in or glazed with sugar [*candied* apples]. **2** partly or wholly turned to sugar [*candied* syrup].

**can·dle** (kan′d'l) ***n.*** a stick or piece of tallow or wax with a wick through it, which gives light when burned. ***•v.*** to examine eggs for freshness by holding in front of a light. —**can′dled, can′dling** —**not hold a candle to,** to be not nearly so good as [She *can't hold a candle to* her father in chess.]

**can·dle·light** (kan′d'l līt) ***n.*** the soft light given off by candles [We dined by *candlelight.*]

**can·dle·pow·er** (kan′d'l pou′ər) ***n.*** a measure of how strong a light is, based on the light given off by a candle of a standard size.

**can·dle·stick** (kan′d'l stik) ***n.*** a device with a small cup or spike for holding a candle.

**can·dor** (kan′dər) ***n.*** an open, honest, and fair way of saying what one thinks; frankness.

**C & W** Country and Western (music).

**can·dy** (kan′dē) ***n.*** **1** a sweet food made from sugar or syrup, with flavor, coloring, fruits, nuts, etc. added. **2** a piece of such food. *—pl.* **can′dies** ***•v.*** **1** to preserve by cooking with sugar [to *candy* orange peel].

| | | | | | | | |
|---|---|---|---|---|---|---|---|
| **a** | fat | **ir** | here | **ou** | out | **zh** | leisure |
| **ā** | ape | **ī** | bite, fire | **u** | up | **ng** | ring |
| **ä** | car, lot | **ō** | go | **ur** | fur | | a *in* ago |
| **e** | ten | **ô** | law, horn | **ch** | chin | | e *in* agent |
| **er** | care | **oi** | oil | **sh** | she | **ə** = | i *in* unity |
| **ē** | even | **oo** | look | **th** | thin | | o *in* collect |
| **i** | hit | **ōō** | tool | ***th*** | then | | u *in* focus |

2 to form into crystals of sugar [The syrup has *candied.*] —**can′died, can′dy·ing**

**cane** (kān) ***n.*** **1** the hollow, jointed stem of some plants, as bamboo or rattan. **2** a plant with such a stem, as sugar cane. **3** a stick carried when walking. **4** thin strips of rattan used in weaving baskets, chair seats, etc. ◆***v.*** **1** to beat with a cane. **2** to make or fix with cane [to *cane* a chair seat]. *See the picture.* —**caned, can′ing**

**ca·nine** (kā′nīn) ***adj.*** of or like a dog or the family of animals that includes dogs [Wolves and foxes are *canine* animals.] ◆***n.*** **1** a dog. **2** a sharp-pointed tooth on either side of the upper jaw and lower jaw, next to the incisors: *the full name is* **canine tooth.**

**can·is·ter** (kan′is tər) ***n.*** a box or can with a lid, for keeping coffee, tea, etc.

**can·ker** (kaŋ′kər) ***n.*** **1** an open sore in the mouth or on a lip. **2** any bad influence that slowly destroys something [Idleness can be a *canker* eating away at ambition.] —**can′ker·ous *adj.***

☆**canned** (kand) ***adj.*** put into airtight cans or jars so as to keep in good condition [*canned* milk].

☆**can·ner·y** (kan′ər ē) ***n.*** a factory where foods are canned. —*pl.* **can′ner·ies**

**Cannes** (kan *or* kän) a city in southeastern France.

**can·ni·bal** (kan′ə b′l) ***n.*** **1** a person who eats human flesh. **2** any animal that eats its own kind. —**can′ni·bal·ism *n.*** —**can′ni·bal·is′tic *adj.***



**can·non** (kan′ən) ***n.*** a large gun mounted on some base; piece of artillery. —*pl.* **can′nons** or **can′non**

**can·non·ade** (kan′ə nād′) ***n.*** a steady firing of cannon.

**can·non·ball** (kan′ən bôl) ***n.*** a type of heavy metal ball that used to be fired from cannons.

**can·not** (kan′ät *or* kə nät′) *the usual way of writing* can not. —**cannot but,** have no choice except to [I *cannot but* believe that you will be elected.]

**can·ny** (kan′ē) ***adj.*** shrewd and careful, as in making deals [a *canny* buyer]. —**can′ni·er, can′ni·est** —**can′ni·ly *adv.***

**ca·noe** (kə nōō′) ***n.*** a narrow, light boat with its sides meeting in a sharp edge at each end. It is moved by one or more paddles. *See the picture.* ◆***v.*** ☆to ride in a canoe. —**ca·noed′, ca·noe′ing**

**can·on** (kan′ən) ***n.*** **1** a law or all the laws of a church [the Roman Catholic *canon*]. **2** a rule, principle, or standard [That remark went against all the *canons* of good taste.] **3** an official list, as of saints or of those books of the Bible which are accepted by a particular church. **4** a clergyman who is on the staff of a cathedral. —**ca·non·i·cal** (kə nän′i k′l) ***adj.***

**ca·ñon** (kan′yən) ***n.*** *another spelling of* **canyon.**

**can·on·ize** (kan′ə nīz) ***v.*** to say that a certain dead person is among the saints in heaven [St. Francis was *canonized* by the Roman Catholic Church in 1228.] —**can′on·ized, can′on·iz·ing** —**can′on·i·za′tion *n.***

**can·o·py** (kan′ə pē) ***n.*** **1** a cloth or other covering fastened as a roof above a throne, bed, etc., or held on poles over a person or sacred thing. *See the picture.* **2** anything that seems to cover like a canopy [We walked through the woods beneath a *canopy* of leaves.] —*pl.* **can′o·pies** ◆***v.*** to put or form a canopy over. —**can′o·pied, can′o·py·ing**

**canst** (kanst) *the older form of* **can[1]** *used with* thou, *as in the Bible.*

**cant[1]** (kant) ***n.*** **1** the special words and phrases used by a particular group or class of people; jargon [Thieves have a *cant* of their own.] **2** talk in which the speaker pretends to be good, religious, etc. although not really so.

**cant[2]** (kant) ***n.*** a tilt or slant. ◆***v.*** to tilt, slant, or tip.

**can′t** (kant) cannot.

**can·ta·loupe** or **can·ta·loup** (kan′tə lōp) ***n.*** a muskmelon, especially a kind that has a hard, rough skin and sweet, juicy, orange-colored flesh.

**can·tan·ker·ous** (kan taŋ′kər əs) ***adj.*** having a bad temper; ready to quarrel.

**can·ta·ta** (kən tät′ə) ***n.*** a piece of music sung by soloists and a chorus. A cantata tells a story, like an opera, but is not acted on a stage with scenery.

**can·teen** (kan tēn′) ***n.*** **1** a store, as in an army camp or factory, where food, drink, and personal supplies are sold. **2** a place where people can gather for refreshments and social activities [a youth *canteen*]. **3** a small container for carrying drinking water, as on a hike.

**can·ter** (kan′tər) ***n.*** a slow, easy gallop [The horse went at a *canter.*] ◆***v.*** to ride or go at an easy gallop.

> **Canter** is shortened from the phrase "Canterbury gallop." The pilgrims who used to visit the cathedral at Canterbury many years ago would take their time getting there, riding at a slow, easy pace.

**can·ti·cle** (kan′ti k′l) ***n.*** a song or hymn with words from the Bible.

**can·ti·le·ver** (kan′t′l ē′vər *or* kan′t′l ev′ər) ***n.*** a beam or support that is fastened to a wall or pier at only one end. *See the picture.*

**can·to** (kan′tō) ***n.*** any of the main sections of a long poem. —*pl.* **can′tos**

**Can·ton** **1** (kan tän′) *the former name of* **Kwangchow. 2** (kan′tən) a city in eastern Ohio.

**can·ton** (kan′tən *or* kan tän′) ***n.*** any of the states of Switzerland.

**Can·ton·ese** (kan tə nēz′) ***adj.*** of Canton, China, or its people [*Cantonese* cooking is popular in America.] ***n.*** the dialect of Chinese spoken in the area of Canton.

**can·tor** (kan′tər) ***n.*** a singer who leads the congregation in prayer in a synagogue or Jewish temple.

**can·vas** (kan′vəs) ***n.*** **1** a strong, heavy cloth of hemp, cotton, or linen, used for tents, sails, oil paintings, etc. **2** an oil painting on canvas. —**under canvas, 1** in tents [a circus *under canvas*]. **2** with sails unfurled.

☆**can·vas·back** (kan′vəs bak) ***n.*** a wild duck of North America with a brownish head and grayish back.

**can·vass** (kan′vəs) ***v.*** **1** to go among people asking for votes, opinions, donations, etc. or trying to sell something. **2** to examine or discuss in detail [The club will *canvass* ways of raising money.] ◆***n.*** the act of canvassing, as in trying to figure out how an election will turn out. —**can′vass·er *n.***

☆**can·yon** (kan′yən) ***n.*** a long, narrow valley with high cliffs on each side. It usually has a stream running through it.

**cap** (kap) ***n.*** **1** a covering for the head, that fits closely and has only a visor or no brim at all. Some caps show the rank or work of the wearer [a cardinal's *cap;* a nurse's *cap;* a fool's *cap*]. **2** anything like a cap, as a cover, lid, or top [a bottle *cap;* the *cap* of a mushroom; mountain *caps*]. **3** a dot of gunpowder set in paper for firing in a toy gun. ⬥***v.*** **1** to put a cap on [*Cap* that bottle.] **2** to cover the top of [Snow *capped* the hills.] **3** to do as well as or better than [The other runners could not *cap* Leslie's winning time.] **4** to bring to a high point of excitement [The concert was *capped* by the surprise appearance of their favorite singer.] —**capped, cap′ping**

**CAP** or **C.A.P.** Civil Air Patrol.

**cap.** *abbreviation for* **capital.** *—pl.* **caps.**

**ca·pa·bil·i·ty** (kā′pə bil′ə tē) ***n.*** the power to do something; ability [She has the *capability* to become a lawyer.] *—pl.* **ca′pa·bil′i·ties**

**ca·pa·ble** (kā′pə b'l) ***adj.*** able to do things well; fit or skilled [a *capable* teacher]. *See* SYNONYMS *at* **able.** —**capable of, 1** able or ready to [*capable of* telling a lie]. **2** having what is necessary for [a table *capable of* seating ten]. —**ca′pa·bly *adv.***

**ca·pa·cious** (kə pā′shəs) ***adj.*** able to hold much; spacious; roomy [a *capacious* trunk].

**ca·pac·i·tor** (kə pas′ə tər) ***n.*** a device used for storing an electric charge.

**ca·pac·i·ty** (kə pas′ə tē) ***n.*** **1** the amount of space that can be filled; room for holding [a jar with a *capacity* of 2 quarts; a stadium with a seating *capacity* of 80,000]. **2** the ability to be, learn, become, etc.; skill or fitness [the *capacity* to be an actor]. **3** position or office [He made the decision in his *capacity* as president.] *—pl.* **ca·pac′i·ties**

**cape**[1] (kāp) ***n.*** a garment without sleeves that is fastened at the neck and hangs over the back and shoulders. *See the picture.*

**cape**[2] (kāp) ***n.*** a piece of land that sticks out into a lake or sea.

**ca·per**[1] (kā′pər) ***v.*** to skip about in a playful way. ⬥***n.*** **1** a playful skip or leap. **2** a playful or silly trick; prank. **3** a criminal act, especially a robbery: *slang in this meaning.* —**cut a caper, 1** to caper. **2** to play tricks.

**ca·per**[2] (kā′pər) ***n.*** **1** a Mediterranean bush whose tiny green flower buds are pickled and used as a flavoring. **2** any of these buds.

**Cape Town** a seaport city in South Africa, where the legislature meets: *also written* **Cape·town** (kāp′toun′)

**cap·il·lar·y** (kap′ə ler′ē) ***n.*** **1** a tube that is very narrow inside [The ordinary thermometer is a *capillary.*] **2** any of the tiny blood vessels joining the arteries and the veins. *—pl.* **cap′il·lar′ies** ⬥***adj.*** of or like a capillary.

**cap·i·tal** (kap′ə t'l) ***adj.*** **1** that can be punished by death [a *capital* crime]. **2** most important; chief [a *capital* virtue]. **3** where the government is located [a *capital* city]. **4** very fine; excellent [a *capital* idea]. *See also* **capital letter.** ⬥***n.*** **1** *same as* **capital letter. 2** a city or town where the government of a state or nation is located. **3** money or property, especially when used in business to make more money. **4** the top part of a column. *See the picture.* —**make capital of,** to make the most of; get advantage from.

**cap·i·tal·ism** (kap′ə t'l iz'm) ***n.*** a system in which the land, factories, etc. used in making goods are owned and operated privately for profit.

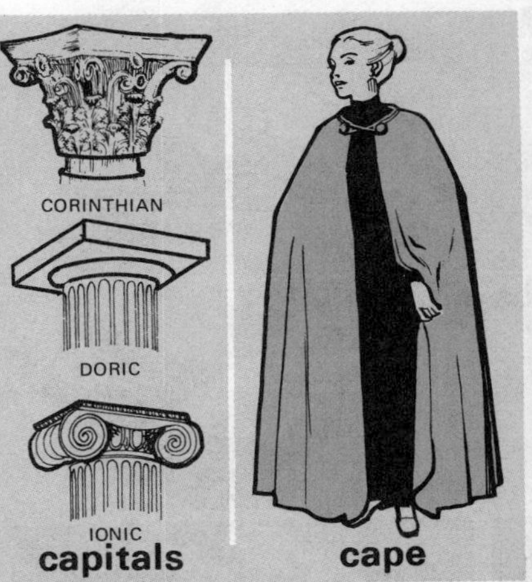

capitals
cape

bed with a canopy
caned seat

cantilever

canoe

**cap·i·tal·ist** (kap′ə t'l ist) ***n.*** a person who has capital; owner of much wealth used in business.

☆**cap·i·tal·is·tic** (kap′ə t'l is′tik) ***adj.*** of or like capitalists, or being in favor of capitalism. 

**cap·i·tal·i·za·tion** (kap′ə t'l ə zā′shən) ***n.*** **1** the act of capitalizing. **2** the stocks and bonds that stand for the total capital of a business.

**cap·i·tal·ize** (kap′ə t'l īz′) ***v.*** ☆**1** to begin with a capital letter or write in capital letters [We usually *capitalize* proper nouns.] **2** to change into capital, or wealth, that can be used in a business. **3** to use something for one's own advantage or profit [to *capitalize* on another's error]. —**cap′i·tal·ized, cap′i·tal·iz·ing**

**capital letter** the form of a letter that is used to begin a sentence or a name [THIS IS PRINTED IN CAPITAL LETTERS.]

**capital punishment** the killing of someone by law as punishment for a crime.

**Cap·i·tol** (kap′ə t'l) ☆the building in which the U.S. Congress meets, at Washington, D.C. ⬥***n.*** ☆*usually* **capitol,** the building in which a State legislature meets.

**ca·pit·u·late** (kə pich′ə lāt) ***v.*** to surrender or give up to an enemy on certain conditions. —**ca·pit′u·lat·ed, ca·pit′u·lat·ing** —**ca·pit′u·la′tion *n.***

**ca·pon** (kā′pän) ***n.*** a rooster with its sex glands removed, fattened for eating.

**ca·price** (kə prēs′) ***n.*** a sudden change in the way one

| | | | |
|---|---|---|---|
| **a** fat | **ir** here | **ou** out | **zh** leisure |
| **ā** ape | **ī** bite, fire | **u** up | **ng** ring |
| **ä** car, lot | **ō** go | **ur** fur | a *in* ago |
| **e** ten | **ô** law, horn | **ch** chin | e *in* agent |
| **er** care | **oi** oil | **sh** she | **ə** = i *in* unity |
| **ē** even | **oo** look | **th** thin | o *in* collect |
| **i** hit | **ōō** tool | ***th*** then | u *in* focus |

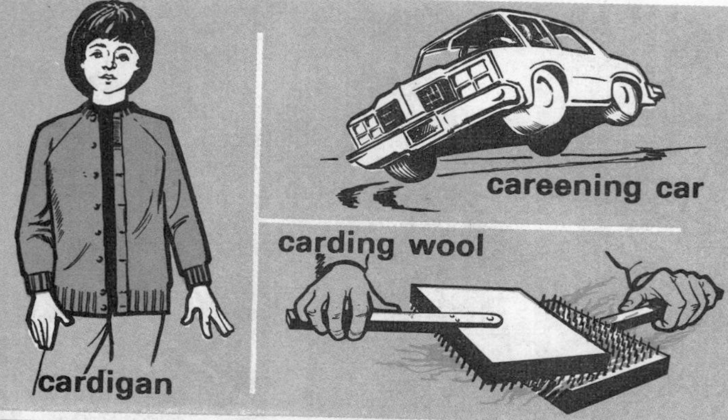


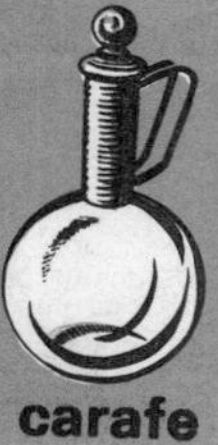
carafe

careworn face

capstan

thinks or acts that seems to be without reason [It was mere *caprice* that made him quit his job.]



**ca·pri·cious** (kə prish′əs) ***adj.*** likely to change suddenly and for no reason plain to see; flighty [a *capricious* child; a *capricious* breeze].

**Cap·ri·corn** (kap′rə kôrn) the tenth sign of the zodiac, for the period from December 22 to January 20: *also called* the Goat. *See the picture for* **zodiac.** *See also* **Tropic of Capricorn.**

**cap·size** (kap′sīz) ***v.*** to overturn or upset [The lifeboat *capsized* in the stormy sea.] —**cap′sized, cap′siz·ing**

**cap·stan** (kap′stən) ***n.*** an upright drum, as on a ship, around which a cable is wound so as to pull up an anchor, etc. Capstans are turned by a bar or bars at the top or, now usually, by a motor. *See the picture.*

**cap·sule** (kap′s'l *or* kap′syo͞ol) ***n.*** ☆**1** a small container holding a dose of medicine. A capsule is made of gelatin and dissolves quickly after being swallowed. **2** a case containing the seeds of some plants. ☆**3** the enclosed part of a spacecraft, that holds the people and instruments. It can be separated from the rocket as for the return to earth.

**Capt.** *abbreviation for* **Captain.**

**cap·tain** (kap′t'n) ***n.*** **1** a chief or leader of some group or activity [a police *captain;* the *captain* of a football team]. **2** a U.S. Army, Air Force, or Marine Corps officer who ranks just above a first lieutenant. **3** a U.S. Navy officer who ranks just above a commander. **4** the person in charge of a ship. ◆***v.*** to be captain of [Who will *captain* the chess team?] —**cap′tain·cy *n.***

**cap·tion** (kap′shən) ***n.*** ☆a title at the head of an article or below a picture, as in a newspaper.

**cap·tious** (kap′shəs) ***adj.*** **1** eager to point out others' mistakes; quick to find fault. **2** made only in order to argue or find fault [*captious* criticism].

**cap·ti·vate** (kap′tə vāt) ***v.*** to be highly interesting or pleasing to; fascinate [He was *captivated* by her lovely voice.] —**cap′ti·vat·ed, cap′ti·vat·ing**

**cap·tive** (kap′tiv) ***n.*** a person caught and held prisoner, as in war. ◆***adj.*** **1** held as a prisoner. ☆**2** forced to listen, whether wanting to or not [a *captive* audience].

**cap·tiv·i·ty** (kap tiv′ə tē) ***n.*** the condition of being held as a prisoner [the largest lion in *captivity*].

**cap·tor** (kap′tər) ***n.*** a person who takes another as a prisoner.

**cap·ture** (kap′chər) ***v.*** **1** to catch and hold by force or skill [to *capture* enemy troops; to *capture* the attention]. **2** to show or picture in a real way [You haven't quite *captured* her spirit in your painting.] *See* SYNONYMS *at* **catch.** —**cap′tured, cap′tur·ing** ◆***n.*** **1** a capturing or being captured [*Capture* of the spy is certain.] **2** something that has been captured.

**car** (kär) ***n.*** **1** anything that moves on wheels, for carrying people or things; especially, an automobile. ☆**2** any of the parts of a train [a sleeping *car;* a box*car*]. ☆**3** that part of an elevator in which people ride.

**ca·ra·bao** (kär′ə bou′) ***n.*** *another name for* **water buffalo.** —*pl.* **ca′ra·baos′**

**Ca·ra·cas** (kə räk′əs) capital of Venezuela, in the northern part.

**car·a·cul** (kar′ə kəl) ***n.*** *another spelling of* **karakul.**

**ca·rafe** (kə raf′) ***n.*** a glass bottle for holding water, coffee, etc. *See the picture.*

**car·a·mel** (kar′ə m'l *or* kär′m'l) ***n.*** **1** burnt sugar used to color or flavor food or drink. **2** a chewy candy made from sugar, milk, etc.

**car·at** (kar′ət) ***n.*** **1** the unit used for weighing gems. It is equal to 1/5 of a gram. **2** *another spelling of* **karat.**

**car·a·van** (kar′ə van) ***n.*** **1** a group of people, as merchants, traveling together for safety, especially through a desert. **2** a large covered wagon or car for carrying people, animals, etc.; van [a circus *caravan*].

**car·a·way** (kar′ə wā) ***n.*** **1** a plant with spicy, strong-smelling seeds. **2** these seeds, used to flavor bread, cakes, cheese, etc.

**car·bine** (kär′bīn *or* kär′bēn) ***n.*** a small, light kind of rifle.

**car·bo·hy·drate** (kär′bə hī′drāt) ***n.*** any of a group of substances made up of carbon, hydrogen, and oxygen, including the sugars and starches. Carbohydrates are an important part of our diet.

**car·bol·ic acid** (kär bäl′ik) a poisonous acid made from coal tar, that was once commonly used as an antiseptic.

**car·bon** (kär′bən) ***n.*** **1** a chemical element that is not a metal, found in all plant and animal matter. Diamonds and graphite are pure carbon, while coal and charcoal are forms of impure carbon. **2** a sheet of carbon paper. **3** a copy made with this: *the full name is* **carbon copy.**

**car·bon·ate** (kär′bə nāt) ***n.*** a salt of carbonic acid. ◆***v.*** to put carbon dioxide in so as to make bubble [Soda pop is a *carbonated* drink.] —**car′bon·at·ed, car′bon·at·ing —car′bon·a′tion *n.***

**carbon dioxide** a gas made up of carbon and oxygen, that has no color and no smell and is heavier than air. It is breathed out of the lungs and is taken in by plants, which use it to make their food.

**car·bon·ic acid** (kär bän′ik) a weak acid formed by dissolving carbon dioxide in water.
**car·bon·ize** (kär′bə nīz) ***v.*** **1** to change into carbon, as by burning. **2** to coat or combine with carbon. —**car′bon·ized, car′bon·iz·ing**
**carbon monoxide** a very poisonous gas that has no color and no smell. It is formed when carbon is not fully burned, as in an automobile engine.
**carbon paper** very thin paper coated on one side with a carbon substance. It is put between sheets of paper, and typing or writing on the upper sheet makes a copy on the lower ones.
**car·bun·cle** (kär′buŋ k'l) ***n.*** a red swelling beneath the skin, filled with pus and caused by infection. It is larger and more painful than a boil.
**car·bu·ret·or** (kär′bə rāt′ər) ***n.*** the part of a gasoline engine that mixes air with gasoline spray to make the mixture that explodes in the cylinders.
**car·cass** (kär′kəs) ***n.*** **1** the dead body of an animal. **2** a human body: *used in a joking or mocking way.* **3** a framework or shell [the *carcass* of a ship]. *See* SYNONYMS *at* **body**.
**card**[1] (kärd) ***n.*** **1** a flat piece of cardboard or stiff paper, often with something printed on it [A calling *card* carries a person's name, address, etc. Greeting *cards* are sent on holidays, birthdays, etc. A score *card* is used to keep track of the score of a game.] *See also* **playing cards** *and* **post card**. **2** a comical person: *used only in everyday talk.* —**in the cards**, that seems likely to happen. —**put** (or **lay**) **one's cards on the table**, to be frank in telling one's plans, etc.
**card**[2] (kärd) ***n.*** a tool like a metal comb or wire brush used to separate fibers of wool or cotton before spinning. ◆***v.*** to use such a tool on. *See the picture.*
**card·board** (kärd′bôrd) ***n.*** a thick, stiff kind of paper used for making cards, light boxes, etc.
**car·di·ac** (kär′dē ak′) ***adj.*** of the heart.
**car·di·gan** (kär′də gən) ***n.*** a sweater that has long sleeves and that buttons down the front. *See the picture.*
**car·di·nal** (kär′d'n əl) ***adj.*** **1** of most importance; chief [The *cardinal* points of the compass are north, south, east, and west.] **2** bright-red. ◆***n.*** **1** one of the Roman Catholic officials whom the Pope appoints to his council. When the Pope dies, the cardinals elect a new pope. ☆**2** an American songbird that is bright red and has a black face.

> **Cardinal** comes from a Latin word meaning "hinge." A door depends on its hinge for turning. Something that is cardinal is important because other things hinge, or depend, on it. A cardinal in the church, a most important official, wears red garments. The songbird is called a cardinal because of its bright-red color.

**cardinal number** any number used in counting or in showing how many [Three, sixty, and 169 are *cardinal numbers.*] *See also* **ordinal number**.
**cards** (kärdz) ***n.pl.*** a game, such as bridge or poker, played with cards. *See* **playing cards**.
**care** (ker) ***n.*** **1** the condition of being troubled by fear or worry [His mind was filled with *care* for their safety.] **2** a watching over or tending; protection [The books were left in my *care*.] **3** serious attention or interest; regard [She did her homework with *care*.] **4** something to worry about or watch over [A sick pet is such a *care!*] ◆***v.*** **1** to feel an interest, worry, regret, etc. [Do you *care* if I go? I didn't *care* that I lost.] **2** to wish or want [Do you *care* to come along?] **3** to watch over or take charge of something [Will you *care* for my canary while I'm gone?] **4** to feel a liking [I don't *care* for dancing.] —**cared, car′ing** —**care of,** in the charge of or at the address of: abbreviated **c/o** or **c.o.** [Send the letter *care of* my parents.] —**take care,** to be careful; watch out. —☆**take care of, 1** to watch over; protect [*Take care of* the baby.] **2** to look after; do what needs to be done about [I *took care of* that matter quickly.]
**ca·reen** (kə rēn′) ***v.*** **1** to lean or tip to one side, as a sailing ship under a strong wind. **2** to lean or roll from side to side while moving fast [The car *careened* down the bumpy hill.] *See the picture.*
**ca·reer** (kə rir′) ***n.*** **1** the way one earns one's living; profession or occupation [Have you thought of teaching as a *career?*] **2** one's progress through life or in one's work [a long and successful *career* in politics]. ◆☆***adj.*** making a career of what is usually a temporary job [a *career* soldier]. ◆***v.*** to move at full speed; rush wildly.
**care·free** (ker′frē) ***adj.*** without care or worry.
**care·ful** (ker′fəl) ***adj.*** **1** taking care so as not to have mistakes or accidents; cautious [Be *careful* in crossing streets.] **2** done or made with care [*careful* work]. —**care′ful·ly *adv.*** —**care′ful·ness *n.***
**care·less** (ker′lis) ***adj.*** **1** not paying enough attention; not thinking before one acts or speaks [*Careless* drivers cause accidents.] **2** done or made without care; full of mistakes [*careless* writing]. **3** without worry; carefree [those *careless,* happy days]. —**care′less·ly *adv.*** —**care′less·ness *n.***
**ca·ress** (kə res′) ***v.*** to touch or stroke in a loving or gentle way [He *caressed* his cat fondly. The breeze *caressed* the trees.] ◆***n.*** a loving or gentle touch, kiss, or hug.
**car·et** (kar′it *or* ker′it) ***n.*** the mark ∧, used to show where something is to be added in a written or printed line.
**care·tak·er** (ker′tāk′ər) ***n.*** a person whose work is to take care of some thing or place; custodian [the *caretaker* of an estate].
**care·worn** (ker′wôrn) ***adj.*** worn out by troubles and worry [a *careworn* face]. *See the picture.*
**car·go** (kär′gō) ***n.*** the load of goods carried by a ship, airplane, truck, etc. —*pl.* **car′goes** or **car′gos**
**Car·ib·be·an Sea** (kar′ə bē′ən *or* kə rib′ē ən) a sea bounded by the West Indies, Central America, and South America. It is a part of the Atlantic Ocean.
☆**car·i·bou** (kar′ə bo͞o) ***n.*** a large deer of North America closely related to the reindeer.
**car·i·ca·ture** (kar′ə kə chər) ***n.*** **1** a picture or imitation of a person or thing in which certain features or



| | | | | | | | |
|---|---|---|---|---|---|---|---|
| **a** | fat | **ir** | here | **ou** | out | **zh** | leisure |
| **ā** | ape | **ī** | bite, fire | **u** | up | **ŋ** | ring |
| **ä** | car, lot | **ō** | go | **ʉr** | fur | | a *in* ago |
| **e** | ten | **ô** | law, horn | **ch** | chin | | e *in* agent |
| **er** | care | **oi** | oil | **sh** | she | ə = | i *in* unity |
| **ē** | even | **oo** | look | **th** | thin | | o *in* collect |
| **i** | hit | **o͞o** | tool | ***th*** | then | | u *in* focus |

parts are exaggerated in a joking or mocking way. *See the picture.* **2** the skill or work of making such pictures, etc. **⬥v.** to make or be a caricature of [Cartoonists often *caricature* the President.] —**car'i·ca·tured, car'i·ca·tur·ing** —**car'i·ca·tur·ist** **n.**

**car·ies** (ker'ēz) **n.** decay of teeth or bones [Tooth cavities are caused by *caries.*]

**car·il·lon** (kar'ə län) **n.** a set of bells on which melodies can be played, now usually from a keyboard.

☆**car·load** (kär'lōd) **n.** a load that fills a car [The train included 50 *carloads* of coal.]

**Car·lyle** (kär līl'), **Thomas** 1795–1881; Scottish writer of essays and of history.

**car·mine** (kär'min *or* kär'mīn) **n.** a red or purplish-red color. **⬥adj.** red or purplish-red.

**car·nage** (kär'nij) **n.** a bloody killing of many people, especially in battle; slaughter.

**car·nal** (kär'n'l) **adj.** of the flesh or body, not of the spirit; worldly [*carnal* desires].

**car·na·tion** (kär nā'shən) **n.** a plant with white, pink, or red flowers that smell like cloves.

**Car·ne·gie** (kär'nə gē), **Andrew** 1835–1919; U.S. steel manufacturer, who was born in Scotland. He gave much money to public libraries, schools, etc.

**car·ni·val** (kär'nə v'l) **n.** **1** an entertainment that travels from place to place, with sideshows, amusement rides, refreshments, etc. **2** feasting and merrymaking with many people joining in parades, dances, and masquerades; especially, such a festival in the week before Lent.



> **Carnival** comes from a Latin phrase meaning "to take away meat." During the period of Lent, many Christians fast by not eating any meat.

**car·niv·o·rous** (kär niv'ə rəs) **adj.** feeding on flesh [Lions are *carnivorous* animals.]

**car·ol** (kar'əl) **n.** a song of joy or praise, especially a Christmas song. **⬥v.** to sing in joy; especially, to sing Christmas carols. —**car'oled** or **car'olled, car'ol·ing** or **car'ol·ling**

**Car·o·li·na** (kar'ə lī'nə) North Carolina or South Carolina.

**ca·rouse** (kə rouz') **v.** to join with others in drinking and having a noisy, merry time. —**ca·roused', ca·rous'ing** **⬥n.** a noisy, merry drinking party: *also* **ca·rous·al** (kə rou'zəl).

**carp**[1] (kärp) **n.** a freshwater fish with soft fins and large scales, that is used for food. —*pl.* **carp** or **carps**

**carp**[2] (kärp) **v.** to look for little faults in other people; complain in a nagging way. —**carp'er** **n.**

**Car·pa·thi·an Mountains** (kär pā'thē ən) mountain ranges reaching into parts of Czechoslovakia, Poland, the Ukraine, and Romania.

**car·pel** (kär'p'l) **n.** the part of a flower in which the seeds grow. The pistil is formed of one or more carpels. *See the picture.*

**car·pen·ter** (kär'pən tər) **n.** a worker who builds and repairs wooden things, especially the wooden parts of buildings, ships, etc.

**car·pen·try** (kär'pən trē) **n.** the work or trade of a carpenter.

**car·pet** (kär'pit) **n.** **1** a thick, heavy fabric used to cover floors. **2** anything that covers like a carpet [a *carpet* of snow]. **⬥v.** to cover as with a carpet [The lawn was *carpeted* with leaves.] —**on the carpet,** being, or about to be, scolded or criticized.

**car·pet·bag** (kär'pit bag') **n.** an old-fashioned kind of traveling bag, made of carpeting.

☆**car·pet·bag·ger** (kär'pit bag'ər) **n.** a Northerner who went into the South just after the Civil War to make money by taking advantage of the confusion there.

**car·pet·ing** (kär'pit iŋ) **n.** carpets or the fabrics used for carpets.

☆**car pool** a system in which the members of a group take turns in using their cars to drive the group to work, their children to school, etc.

☆**car·port** (kär'pôrt) **n.** a shelter for an automobile, built against the side of a building, usually with two or three sides left open.

**car·riage** (kar'ij) **n.** **1** a vehicle with wheels, usually one drawn by horses, for carrying people. **2** a frame on wheels for carrying something heavy [a gun *carriage*]. **3** a light vehicle for wheeling a baby about; buggy. **4** a moving part of a machine for carrying something along [The *carriage* of a typewriter holds the paper.] **5** the way one stands or walks; posture; bearing.

**car·ried** (kar'ēd) *past tense and past participle of* **carry.**

**car·ri·er** (kar'ē ər) **n.** **1** a person or thing that carries [a mail *carrier;* an aircraft *carrier*]. **2** a company that is in the business of moving goods or passengers. Railroad, bus, and truck companies are called **common carriers.** **3** a person or animal that can pass on a disease germ even though immune to that germ.

**car·ri·on** (kar'ē ən) **n.** the rotting flesh of a dead body.

**Car·roll** (kar'əl), **Lewis** 1832–1898; the English author who wrote *Alice's Adventures in Wonderland.* His real name was Charles L. Dodgson.

**car·rot** (kar'ət) **n.** a plant with a long, thick, orange-red root that is eaten as a vegetable.

**car·rou·sel** (kar ə sel') **n.** ☆a merry-go-round.

**car·ry** (kar'ē) **v.** **1** to take from one place to another; transport or conduct [Please help me *carry* these books home. The large pipe *carries* water. Air *carries* sounds.] **2** to cause to go; lead [A love of travel *carried* them around the world.] **3** to bring over a figure from one column to the next in adding a row of figures. **4** to win [Perkins *carried* the election.] **5** to hold or support; bear [These beams *carry* the weight of the roof.] **6** to have in; contain [The letter *carried* a threat.] **7** to sit, stand, or walk in a certain way [The ambassador *carried* herself with dignity.] ☆**8** to have for sale [Does this store *carry* toys?] **9** to be able to reach over a distance [His voice *carries* well.] **10** to sing or play the notes of correctly [I just can't *carry* a tune.] —**car'ried, car'ry·ing** **⬥n.** the act of carrying something [The football player averaged five yards per *carry.*] —*pl.* **car'ries** —**be** or **get carried away,** to be filled with such strong feelings that one does not think clearly. —**carry off, 1** to kill [The disease *carried off* thousands.] **2** to win a prize. **3** to deal with a matter in a successful way. —**carry on, 1** to do or manage, as a business. **2** to go on as before. **3** to behave in a wild or silly way: *used only in everyday talk.* —**carry out,** to get done; accomplish; bring to a finish [to *carry out* a threat].

☆**car·ry·out** (kar'ē out') ***adj.*** that is a kind of service by which prepared food and drink can be bought and taken out to eat somewhere else.

**car·sick** (kär'sik) ***adj.*** sick from riding in a car, so that one feels like vomiting.

**Car·son** (kär's'n), **Kit** 1809–1868; American frontiersman who served as a scout in the West. His formal name was Christopher Carson.

**cart** (kärt) ***n.*** a small wagon, often with only two wheels, moved by hand or drawn by an animal [a pony *cart;* a grocery *cart*]. *See the picture.* ◆***v.*** to carry in a cart, truck, etc. —**put the cart before the horse,** to do things in the wrong order. —**cart'er** ***n.***

**cart·age** (kär'tij) ***n.*** **1** the work of delivering goods. **2** the charge for this.

**carte blanche** (kärt' blänsh') full freedom to do as one thinks best [She has *carte blanche* in shopping.]

**car·tel** (kär tel') ***n.*** a group of companies joined together to have complete control over the production and prices of certain products; trust or monopoly [an international *cartel* of oil producers].

**Car·ter** (kär'tər), **Jimmy** 1924– ; 39th president of the United States, from 1977. His full legal name is **James Earl Carter.**

**Car·thage** (kär'thij) an ancient city and state in northern Africa, near where Tunis now is. It was destroyed by the Romans in 146 B.C. —**Car·tha·gin·i·an** (kär'thə jin'ē ən) ***adj., n.***

**Car·tier** (kär tyā'), **Jacques** (zhäk) 1491–1557; French explorer in northeastern North America.

**car·ti·lage** (kärt''l ij) ***n.*** a tough, flexible tissue that is connected with the bones and forms parts of the skeleton; gristle [The tough part of the outer ear is *cartilage.*] —**car·ti·lag·i·nous** (kärt''l aj'ə nəs) ***adj.***

**car·ton** (kärt''n) ***n.*** a box or other container made of cardboard, plastic, etc. [A milk *carton* is made of stiff, waxed paper.]

**car·toon** (kär to͞on') ***n.*** **1** a drawing, as in a newspaper or magazine, that shows how the editor or artist feels about some person or thing in the news. It is often a caricature that criticizes or praises. **2** a humorous drawing. ☆**3** *same as* **comic strip.** ☆**4** *same as* **animated cartoon.** ◆☆***v.*** to draw cartoons. —**car·toon'ist** ***n.***

**car·tridge** (kär'trij) ***n.*** **1** the metal or cardboard tube that holds the gunpowder and the bullet or shot for use in a firearm. **2** a small container used in a larger device, as one holding ink for a pen. **3** a roll of camera film in a case. **4** a unit holding the needle for a phonograph.

**cart·wheel** (kärt'hwēl) ***n.*** a handspring done sidewise. *See the picture.*

**Ca·ru·so** (kə ro͞o'sō), **En·ri·co** (en rē'kō) 1873–1921; Italian opera singer. He was a tenor.

**carve** (kärv) ***v.*** **1** to make by cutting or as if by cutting [to *carve* a statue in marble; to *carve* out a career for oneself]. **2** to cut into slices or pieces [to *carve* a turkey]. —**carved, carv'ing** —**carv'er** ***n.***

**Car·ver** (kär'vər), **George Washington** 1864–1943; American scientist who developed many products from peanuts, soybeans, and other plants.

**carv·ing** (kär'viŋ) ***n.*** **1** the work or art of one who carves. **2** a carved figure or design.

**Cas·a·blan·ca** (kas'ə blaŋ'kə) a city that is a large seaport in northwestern Morocco.

caricature of Benjamin Franklin

casement

carpel

cart

cartwheel

**cas·cade** (kas kād') ***n.*** **1** a small, steep waterfall. **2** something like this, as sparks falling in a shower. ◆***v.*** to fall in a cascade. —**cas·cad'ed, cas·cad'ing**



**case**[1] (kās) ***n.*** **1** a single example or happening [a *case* of carelessness; four *cases* of measles]. **2** a person being treated or helped, as by a doctor or social worker. **3** any matter being watched or studied, as by the police [ten *cases* of robbery]. **4** a matter to be decided by a court of law; lawsuit [Two attorneys will handle the *case.*] **5** the real facts or condition [I'm sorry, but that's not the *case.*] **6** in grammar, the form of a noun, pronoun, or adjective that shows how it is related to the other words around it [In the sentence "He hit me," the subject *he* is in the nominative *case* and the object *me* is in the objective *case.*] —**in any case,** no matter what else may be true; anyhow. —**in case,** if it should be that; if [Remind me *in case* I forget.] —**in case of,** if there should happen to be. —**in no case,** not under any conditions; never.

**case**[2] (kās) ***n.*** **1** a container for holding and protecting something [a watch*case;* a seed*case;* a violin *case*]. **2** as much as a case will hold [A *case* of root beer is 24 bottles.] **3** a frame, as for a window. ◆***v.*** to put or hold in a case. —**cased, cas'ing**

**ca·se·in** (kā'sē in *or* kā'sēn) ***n.*** the main protein of milk that is left when the water, butterfat, and sugar are removed. It is used in making plastics, glues, etc.

**case·ment** (kās'mənt) ***n.*** a window frame that opens on hinges along the side, like a door. *See the picture.*

| | | | |
|---|---|---|---|
| **a** fat | **ir** here | **ou** out | **zh** leisure |
| **ā** ape | **ī** bite, fire | **u** up | **ŋ** ring |
| **ä** car, lot | **ō** go | **ʉr** fur | a *in* ago |
| **e** ten | **ô** law, horn | **ch** chin | e *in* agent |
| **er** care | **oi** oil | **sh** she | **ə** = i *in* unity |
| **ē** even | **oo** look | **th** thin | o *in* collect |
| **i** hit | **o͞o** tool | ***th*** then | u *in* focus |

**case·work** (käs′wurk) ***n.*** social work in which the worker deals with a person's or family's problems and tries to help solve them. —**case′work·er** ***n.***

**cash** (kash) ***n.*** **1** money that one actually has, in coins or bills. **2** money or a check paid at the time of buying something [I always pay *cash* and never charge things.] ◆***v.*** to give or get cash for [to *cash* a check]. ◆***adj.*** of or for cash [a *cash* sale]. —☆**cash in on,** to get profit from.

**cash·ew** (kash′o͞o) ***n.*** **1** a soft, curved nut that is the seed of a tropical evergreen tree. **2** this tree.

**cash·ier** (ka shir′) ***n.*** a person who handles the money in a bank, store, restaurant, etc.

**cash·mere** (kazh′mir *or* kash′mir) ***n.*** **1** a very fine, soft wool, especially that from goats of Kashmir and Tibet. **2** a soft cloth made of this wool or wool like it. **3** a shawl or sweater made of cashmere.

☆**cash register** a machine used in business, that shows the amount of each sale and records it on a strip of paper. It usually has a drawer for holding the money. *See the picture for* **register.**

**cas·ing** (kās′ing) ***n.*** **1** a covering that protects, as the outer part of an automobile tire or the skin of a sausage. ☆**2** the framework around a window or door.

**ca·si·no** (kə sē′nō) ***n.*** **1** a room or building for entertainment, now especially for gambling. **2** *another spelling of* **cassino.** —*pl.* **ca·si′nos**



**cask** (kask) ***n.*** **1** a barrel for holding liquids. **2** as much as a cask will hold.

**cas·ket** (kas′kit) ***n.*** **1** a small box for holding valuable things, as jewelry. **2** a coffin.

**Cas·pi·an Sea** (kas′pē ən) an inland sea between the Caucasus and Asia.

**Cas·satt** (kə sat′), **Mary** 1845–1926; U.S. painter.

**cas·sa·va** (kə sä′və) ***n.*** a tropical plant whose starchy roots are used in making tapioca.

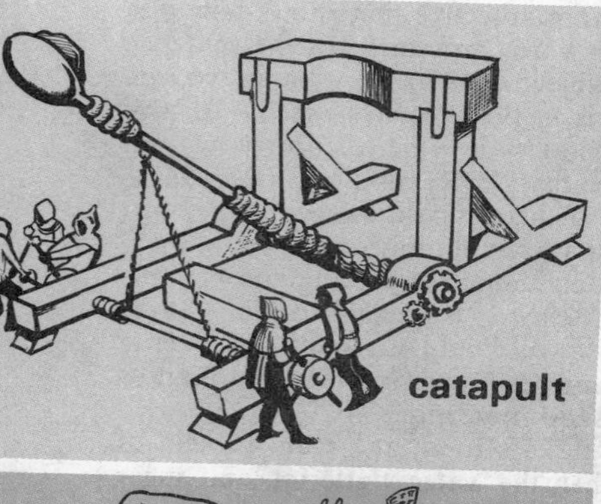

catapult

cassette for recorder

castanets

catalpa

casters

**cas·se·role** (kas′ə rōl) ***n.*** **1** a covered baking dish in which food can be cooked and then served. **2** the food baked and served in such a dish.

**cas·sette** (ka set′) ***n.*** **1** a case with a roll of film in it, for loading a camera quickly and easily. **2** a case with recording tape in it, for quick, easy use in a tape recorder. *See the picture.*

**cas·sia** (kash′ə) ***n.*** **1** the bark of a tree of southeastern Asia, used to make a kind of cinnamon. **2** this tree. **3** a tropical plant whose pods and leaves are used in medicines that make the bowels move.

**cas·si·no** (kə sē′nō) ***n.*** a card game in which the players win cards by matching them with others in their hand.

**cas·sock** (kas′ək) ***n.*** a long, usually black robe worn by some clergymen.

**cas·so·war·y** (kas′ə wer′ē) ***n.*** a bird of Australia and New Guinea that cannot fly. It is like the ostrich, only smaller. —*pl.* **cas′so·war′ies**

**cast** (kast) ***v.*** **1** to throw out or down; toss; fling; hurl [to *cast* stones into the water; to *cast* a line in fishing]. **2** to let fall; turn or direct [to *cast* one's eyes or attention on a thing; to *cast* light on a mystery]. **3** to throw off; shed [The snake *cast* its skin.] **4** to deposit a ballot or vote. **5** to shape melted metal, plastic, etc. by pouring or pressing into a mold and letting it harden; also, to make by this method [to *cast* a pair of bookends]. **6** to choose actors for a play or movie [The director had difficulty *casting* all the parts. Pat was *cast* in the leading role.] ◆***n.*** **1** the act of casting or throwing; a throw. **2** a way of casting or how far something is thrown. **3** something formed in a mold or as a mold [a bronze *cast* of a statue; a *cast* of a footprint]. **4** a stiff plaster form for keeping a broken arm or leg in place while it is healing. **5** the set of actors in a play. **6** a condition in which the eye is turned a little out of focus; squint. **7** a form or appearance [a face having a handsome *cast*]. **8** a slight coloring; tinge [The water is blue with a greenish *cast.*] —**cast, cast′ing** —**cast about, 1** to look; search [They're *casting about* for a shortstop.] **2** to make plans. —**cast aside** or **cast away,** to throw away or get rid of; discard. —**cast off, 1** to get rid of; discard. **2** to free a ship from a dock, as by untying the lines.

**cas·ta·nets** (kas tə nets′) ***n.pl.*** a pair of small, hollowed pieces of hard wood or ivory that are held in the hand and clicked together to beat time to music. They are used especially in Spanish dances. *See the picture.*

> **Castanet** comes from a Spanish word, and that word comes from the Latin name for "chestnut." Castanets look a little like chestnuts.

**cast·a·way** (kast′ə wā) ***n.*** a shipwrecked person. ◆***adj.*** **1** thrown away; discarded. **2** stranded, especially because of a shipwreck.

**caste** (kast) ***n.*** **1** any of the social classes into which Hindus are born. At one time Hindus of one caste could not mix with those of another. **2** any system in which people are separated into classes because of their rank, wealth, etc.; also, any such class.

**cast·er** (kas′tər) ***n.*** **1** a person or thing that casts. **2** a small wheel on a swivel. One is attached to each leg or corner of a piece of furniture so that it can be moved easily. *See the picture.*

**cas·ti·gate** (kas′tə gāt) ***v.*** to punish harshly, especially by criticizing in public. —**cas′ti·gat·ed, cas′ti·gat·ing** —**cas′ti·ga′tion** ***n.*** —**cas′ti·ga·tor** ***n.***

**Cas·tile** (kas tēl′) a region in central and northern Spain that was once a kingdom.

**Cas·til·ian** (kas til′yən) ***adj.*** having to do with Castile or its people [*Castilian* Spanish is the standard form of the language in Spain.] ◆***n.*** **1** a person born or living in Castile. **2** Castilian Spanish.

**cast·ing** (kas′tiŋ) ***n.*** anything cast in a mold, especially something cast in metal.

**cast-i·ron** (kast′ī′ərn) ***adj.*** **1** made of cast iron. **2** hard, strong, and able to take rough treatment, like cast iron [a *cast-iron* stomach].

**cast iron** hard, brittle iron shaped by casting.

**cas·tle** (kas′'l) ***n.*** **1** a large building or group of buildings that was the home of a king or noble in the Middle Ages. Castles had thick walls, moats, etc. to protect them against attack. **2** a piece used in playing chess, that is shaped like a castle tower. It is also called a **rook**.

**castle in the air** something that one imagines and wants but is not likely to get; daydream: *also called* **castle in Spain.**

**cast·off** (kast′ôf) ***adj.*** thrown away; discarded; abandoned. ◆***n.*** a person or thing cast off.

**cas·tor** (kas′tər) ***n.*** *another spelling of* **caster** *in meaning* 2.

**cas·tor oil** (kas′tər) a thick oil squeezed from the bean of a tropical plant. It is used as a medicine to make the bowels move.

**cas·trate** (kas′trāt) ***v.*** to remove the male sex glands of [A capon is a *castrated* rooster.] —**cas′trat·ed, cas′trat·ing**

**Cas·tro** (kas′trō), **Fi·del** (fē del′) 1927?– ; Cuban leader of a revolution in 1959 and political leader of Cuba since then.

**cas·u·al** (kazh′oo wəl) ***adj.*** **1** happening by chance; not planned [a *casual* visit]. **2** not having any particular purpose [a *casual* glance; a *casual* remark]. **3** not regular; occasional [*casual* labor]. **4** for wear at times when dressy clothes are not needed [*casual* sports clothes]. —**cas′u·al·ly** ***adv.*** —**cas′u·al·ness** ***n.***

**cas·u·al·ty** (kazh′əl tē *or* kazh′oo wəl tē) ***n.*** **1** an accident, especially one that causes death. **2** anyone hurt or killed in an accident. **3** a soldier, sailor, etc. who has been killed, wounded, or captured or who is missing. —*pl.* **cas′u·al·ties**

**cas·u·ist·ry** (kazh′oo wis trē) ***n.*** the deciding of questions of right or wrong in conduct; now, often, the use of clever but false reasoning to prove that one is right. —**cas′u·ist** ***n.***

**cat** (kat) ***n.*** **1** a small animal with soft fur, often kept as a pet or for killing mice. **2** any larger animal related to this, as the lion, tiger, or leopard. —**let the cat out of the bag,** to let a secret be found out.

**cat·a·clysm** (kat′ə kliz'm) ***n.*** any sudden and violent change, as a great flood, earthquake, war, or revolution. —**cat′a·clys′mic** ***adj.***

**cat·a·combs** (kat′ə kōmz) ***n.pl.*** a group of connected rooms underground for burying dead people. The Catacombs of Rome were used by the early Christians as a place to hide.

**cat·a·log** or **cat·a·logue** (kat′'l ôg) ***n.*** ☆**1** a card file in alphabetical order giving a complete list of things in a collection, as of all the books in a library. **2** a book or paper listing all the things for sale or on display. ◆***v.*** to make a list of or put into a list. —**cat′a·loged** or **cat′a·logued, cat′a·log·ing** or **cat′a·logu·ing**

☆**ca·tal·pa** (kə tal′pə) ***n.*** a tree with large, heart-shaped leaves and long, slender pods. *See the picture.*

**cat·a·lyst** (kat′'l ist) ***n.*** a substance that causes a chemical change when added to something but is not changed itself. —**cat·a·lyt·ic** (kat′'l it′ik) ***adj.***

**cat·a·ma·ran** (kat′ə mə ran′) ***n.*** **1** a boat with two hulls side by side. **2** a narrow raft made of logs.

**cat·a·pult** (kat′ə pult) ***n.*** **1** a large weapon that worked like a slingshot, used in olden times to throw spears, arrows, rocks, etc. at the enemy. *See the picture.* **2** a modern machine for launching an airplane from the deck of a ship. ◆***v.*** **1** to throw from or as if from a catapult. **2** to move suddenly and quickly, as if thrown from a catapult [Armstrong *catapulted* to fame by being the first person on the moon.]

**cat·a·ract** (kat′ə rakt) ***n.*** **1** a large waterfall. **2** any strong flood or rush of water. **3** an eye disease in which the lens becomes clouded, causing a gradual loss of sight.

**ca·tarrh** (kə tär′) ***n.*** *an old-fashioned name for* a condition in which there is a thick flow of mucus from the nose and throat, as in a cold.

**ca·tas·tro·phe** (kə tas′trə fē) ***n.*** a sudden happening that causes great loss, suffering, or damage; terrible disaster [The Chicago fire was a great *catastrophe.*] —**cat·a·stroph·ic** (kat′ə sträf′ik) ***adj.***



☆**cat·bird** (kat′burd) ***n.*** a gray American songbird whose call sounds like the mewing of a cat.

**cat·boat** (kat′bōt) ***n.*** a sailboat with a single sail on a mast set forward in the bow.

**cat·call** (kat′kôl) ***n.*** a hooting or whistling sound made as a rude way of showing that one does not like a certain speaker, actor, etc.

**catch** (kach) ***v.*** **1** to take hold of, as after a chase; capture [to *catch* a thief]. **2** to get by a hook, trap, or the like [to *catch* fish; to *catch* mice]. **3** to stop by grasping with the hands or arms [to *catch* a ball]. **4** to become held or entangled; snag [My sleeve *caught* on the nail.] **5** to get to in time [to *catch* a bus]. **6** to become sick or infected with [to *catch* the flu]. **7** to get by seeing, hearing, or thinking [to *catch* sight of a thing; to *catch* what a person says or means]. **8** to come upon or see by surprise; discover [She *caught* him reading a comic book in study hall.] **9** to strike suddenly [The blow *caught* him by surprise. Her poem *caught* my fancy.] **10** to take hold and spread [The dry grass *caught* fire from a spark.] ☆**11** to act as a catcher in baseball [You pitch and I'll *catch.*] —**caught, catch′ing** ◆***n.*** **1** the act of catching a ball, etc. [The outfielder made a running *catch.*] **2** any-

| | | | |
|---|---|---|---|
| **a** fat | **ir** here | **ou** out | **zh** leisure |
| **ā** ape | **ī** bite, fire | **u** up | **ŋ** ring |
| **ä** car, lot | **ō** go | **ur** fur | a *in* ago |
| **e** ten | **ô** law, horn | **ch** chin | e *in* agent |
| **er** care | **oi** oil | **sh** she | ə = i *in* unity |
| **ē** even | **oo** look | **th** thin | o *in* collect |
| **i** hit | **ōō** tool | ***th*** then | u *in* focus |

thing that is caught [a *catch* of 14 fish]. **3** a thing that catches or fastens [Fix the *catch* on the cupboard door.] **4** a musical round. **5** a break in the voice, as when speaking with deep feeling. ☆**6** a hidden or tricky part: *used only in everyday talk* [There's a *catch* in the advertiser's offer.] —**catch it,** to get a scolding or other punishment: *used only in everyday talk.* —☆**catch on, 1** to become popular. **2** to understand. —**catch up, 1** to come up even, as by hurrying or by doing extra work. **2** to take up suddenly; snatch. —**catch up on,** to do more work, get more sleep, etc. so as to make up for time that was lost.

SYNONYMS: **Catch** is a general word that means to seize or take a person or thing that is moving [The cat *caught* the mouse. Can you *catch* the key if I throw it?] **Capture** means to catch something or someone with difficulty, and usually by using force or cleverness [The soldiers *captured* the fort. Police *captured* the murderer.]

**catch·er** (kach′ər) ***n.*** **1** one who catches. ☆**2** in baseball, the player behind home plate, who catches pitched balls that are not hit away by the batter. *See the picture.*

**catch·ing** (kach′iŋ) ***adj.*** easily passed on to another; contagious [Measles are *catching.* Her joy is *catching.*]

**catch·up** (kech′əp, kach′əp) ***n.*** *another spelling of* **ketchup.**

**catch·y** (kach′ē) ***adj.*** **1** pleasing and easy to remember [a *catchy* tune]. **2** tricky or difficult [That question's *catchy.*] —**catch′i·er, catch′i·est**



**cat·e·chism** (kat′ə kiz'm) ***n.*** **1** a set of questions and answers used in teaching religion. **2** any long set of questions asked of someone, as in testing. —**cat·e·chist** (kat′ə kist) ***n.***

**cat·e·gor·i·cal** (kat′ə gôr′ə k'l) ***adj.*** without any conditions; without an "if" or "maybe"; absolute [a *categorical* refusal]. —**cat′e·gor′i·cal·ly** ***adv.***

**cat·e·go·ry** (kat′ə gôr′ē) ***n.*** a division of a main subject or group; class [Biology is divided into two *categories,* zoology and botany.] —*pl.* **cat′e·go′ries**

**ca·ter** (kā′tər) ***v.*** **1** to provide food and service [Smith's business is *catering* for large parties.] **2** to try to please by doing or giving what is wanted [This store *caters* to young people.] —**ca′ter·er** ***n.***

**cat·er·pil·lar** (kat′ər pil′ər) ***n.*** the larva of the moth or butterfly, that looks like a hairy worm. It hatches from an egg and later becomes the pupa.

**Caterpillar** comes from an old French word, and that word comes from two Latin words, *catta* meaning "cat" and *pilosa* meaning "hairy." Some caterpillars look a little like hairy cats.

**cat·er·waul** (kat′ər wôl) ***n.*** the howling or screeching sound sometimes made by a cat. ◆***v.*** to make such a sound.

**cat·fish** (kat′fish) ***n.*** ☆a fish without scales, and with feelers about the mouth that are a little like a cat's whiskers. *See the picture.*

**cat·gut** (kat′gut) ***n.*** a tough cord made from the dried intestines of sheep, etc. It is used to sew up wounds in surgery and to make the strings for musical instruments, tennis rackets, etc.

**ca·thar·tic** (kə thär′tik) ***n.*** a strong medicine to make the bowels move, as castor oil.

**ca·the·dral** (kə thē′drəl) ***n.*** **1** the main church of a bishop's district, containing his throne. **2** any large, important church.

**Cath·er·ine the Great** (kath′rin *or* kath′ər in) 1729–1796; empress of Russia, from 1762 to 1796.

**cath·ode** (kath′ōd) ***n.*** **1** the pole or piece from which electrons are given off in an electron tube. **2** the positive electrode of a storage battery.

**cath·o·lic** (kath′ə lik) ***adj.*** **1** including many or all kinds; broad; liberal [You seem to have *catholic* tastes in art.] **2 Catholic,** having to do with the Christian church whose head is the Pope; Roman Catholic. ◆***n.*** **Catholic,** a member of the Roman Catholic Church. —**Ca·thol·i·cism** (kə thäl′ə siz'm) ***n.***

**cat·kin** (kat′kin) ***n.*** the blossom of certain trees, as the willow, consisting of a cluster of small flowers along a drooping spike. *See the picture.*

☆**cat·nap** (kat′nap) ***n.*** a short, light sleep.

☆**cat·nip** (kat′nip) ***n.*** a plant of the mint family, with downy leaves. Cats like its smell.

**cat-o′-nine-tails** (kat′ə nīn′tālz) ***n.*** a whip made of nine knotted cords fixed to a handle. It was once used for punishment. —*pl.* **cat-o′-nine-tails**

**cat's cradle** a game in which a string is looped over the fingers and passed back and forth between the players. Each time a different design is made. *See the picture.*

**Cats·kill Mountains** (kat′skil) a mountain range in southern New York: *also called* **the Catskills.** It is famous as a vacation area.

**cat's-paw** (kats′pô′) ***n.*** a person who is talked into doing something wrong or dangerous for someone else.

The word **cat's-paw** comes from a story about a monkey who talked a cat into raking hot chestnuts out of a fire with its paw for the monkey.

**cat·sup** (kech′əp, kat′səp) ***n.*** *another spelling of* **ketchup.**

**cat·tail** (kat′tāl) ***n.*** a tall plant that grows in marshes and swamps. It has long, flat leaves and long, brown, fuzzy spikes.

**cat·tle** (kat′'l) ***n.pl.*** animals of the cow family that are raised on farms and ranches, as cows, bulls, steers, and oxen.

In earlier times **cattle** was used to mean all kinds of farm animals. Nowadays farm animals in general are called livestock. The word **cattle** has no singular form.

☆**cat·tle·man** (kat′'l mən) ***n.*** a person who raises cattle for the market. —*pl.* **cat′tle·men**

**cat·ty** (kat′ē) ***adj.*** **1** of or like a cat. **2** saying mean things about others. —**cat′ti·er, cat′ti·est**

☆**CATV** a television system that uses a single, high antenna to pick up signals from distant stations. It then sends those signals by direct cable to the homes of people who pay to get them. The initials CATV stand for **community antenna television.**

**cat·walk** (kat′wôk) ***n.*** a narrow path or platform, as along the edge of a bridge.

**Cau·ca·sian** (kô kā′zhən) ***adj.*** **1** of the Caucasus. **2** *an earlier word for* **Caucasoid.**

**Cau·ca·soid** (kôk′ə soid) ***adj.*** belonging to the group of human beings that is loosely called the "white race," although it includes many people with dark skin. The group includes most of the peoples of

Europe, North Africa, the Near East, India, etc. ◆*n.* a member of this group.

**Cau·ca·sus** (kô′kə səs) a mountain range in the U.S.S.R., between the Black and Caspian seas. *See the map.*

☆**cau·cus** (kôk′əs) ***n.*** a private meeting of the leaders or of a committee of a political party to pick candidates or make plans to be presented at the main meeting. ◆***v.*** to hold a caucus. —**cau′cused** or **cau′cussed, cau′cus·ing** or **cau′cus·sing**

**cau·dal** (kôd′′l) ***adj.*** **1** that is a tail or is like a tail [the *caudal* fin of a fish]. **2** at or near the tail.

**caught** (kôt) *past tense and past participle of* **catch.**

**caul·dron** (kôl′drən) ***n.*** *another spelling of* **caldron.**

**cau·li·flow·er** (kôl′ə flou′ər *or* käl′ə flou′ər) ***n.*** a kind of cabbage with a head of white, fleshy flower clusters growing tightly together. It is eaten as a vegetable. *See the picture.*

**caulk** (kôk) ***v.*** to fill up cracks or seams with putty, tar, etc. [Boats are *caulked* to make them watertight.] *Also spelled* **calk.**

**cause** (kôz) ***n.*** **1** a person or thing that brings about some action or result [A spark from the wire was the *cause* of the fire.] **2** a reason for some action, feeling, etc. [We had *cause* to admire the coach.] **3** a purpose or goal that a number of people are interested in and work for; movement [This group works for the *cause* of peace.] ◆***v.*** to be the cause of; make happen; bring about [The icy streets *caused* some accidents.] —**caused, caus′ing —cause′less *adj.***

**cause·way** (kôz′wā) ***n.*** **1** a raised road or path, as across a marsh. **2** a highway.

**caus·tic** (kôs′tik) ***adj.*** **1** that can burn or eat away living tissue by chemical action [Lye is a *caustic* substance.] **2** very sarcastic; sharp or biting [*caustic* comments]. ◆***n.*** a caustic substance.

**cau·ter·ize** (kôt′ər īz) ***v.*** to burn with a hot iron or needle, or with a caustic substance [Warts can be removed by *cauterizing* them.] —**cau′ter·ized, cau′ter·iz·ing**

**cau·tion** (kô′shən) ***n.*** **1** the act of being careful not to get into danger or make mistakes [Use *caution* in crossing streets.] **2** a warning [Let me give you a word of *caution.*] ◆***v.*** to warn; tell of danger [The sign *cautioned* us to slow down.]

**cau·tious** (kô′shəs) ***adj.*** careful not to get into danger or make mistakes [a *cautious* chess player]. —**cau′tious·ly *adv.***

**cav·al·cade** (kav′′l kād) ***n.*** **1** a parade of people on horseback, in carriages, etc. **2** any long series of things [a *cavalcade* of events].

**cav·a·lier** (kav′ə lir′) ***n.*** **1** a horseman; especially, a knight. **2** a man who is very polite and respectful, especially to women. ◆***adj.*** free and easy, or not caring, sometimes in a haughty way [a *cavalier* answer to a serious question].

**cav·al·ry** (kav′′l rē) ***n.*** soldiers who fight on horseback or, now usually, in armored vehicles.

**cave** (kāv) ***n.*** a hollow place inside the earth, often an opening in a hillside. —**cave in,** to fall in or sink in; collapse [The heavy rain made the tunnel *cave in.*] —**caved, cav′ing**

**cave man** a human being of the time when people lived in caves, many thousands of years ago.

**cav·ern** (kav′ərn) ***n.*** a cave, especially a large cave.

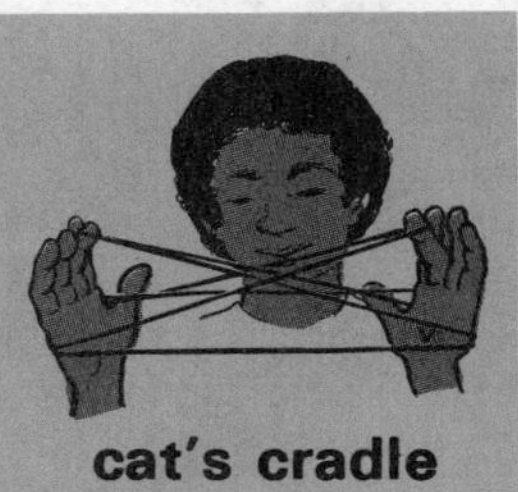

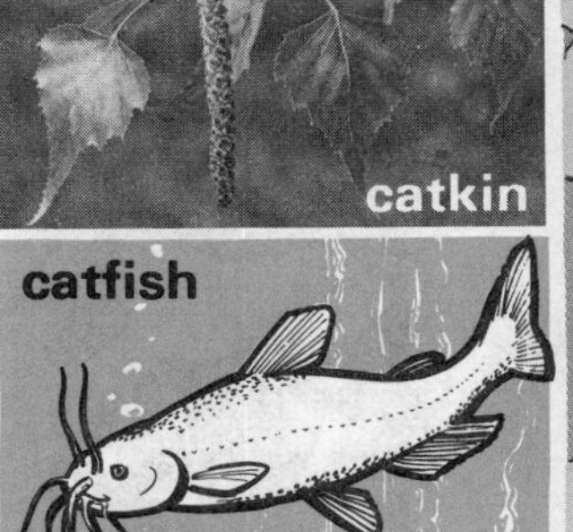


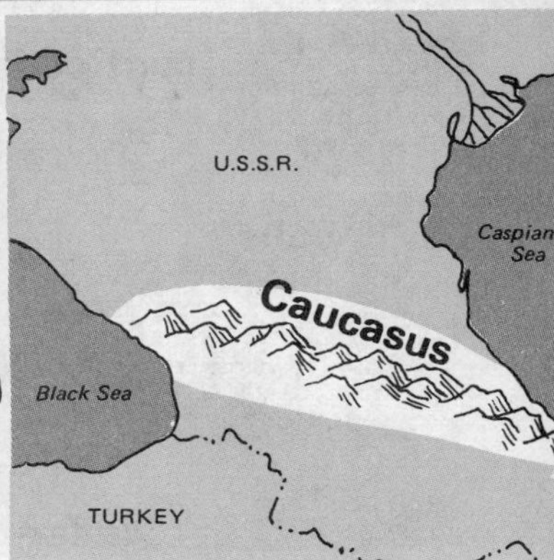


**cav·ern·ous** (kav′ər nəs) ***adj.*** **1** like a cavern; hollow or deep [*cavernous* cheeks]. **2** full of caverns [*cavernous* hills]. 115

**cav·i·ar** or **cav·i·are** (kav′ē är′) ***n.*** the salted eggs of sturgeon or of certain other fish, eaten as an appetizer.

**cav·il** (kav′′l) ***v.*** to object when there is little reason to do so; criticize unimportant things —**cav′iled** or **cav′illed, cav′il·ing** or **cav′il·ling** ◆***n.*** unnecessary criticism of minor things.

**cav·i·ty** (kav′ə tē) ***n.*** **1** a hollow place, such as one caused by decay in a tooth. **2** a natural hollow space in the body [the chest *cavity*]. —*pl.* **cav′i·ties**

☆**ca·vort** (kə vôrt′) ***v.*** to leap about in a playful way; romp; frolic.

**caw** (kô) ***n.*** the loud, harsh cry of a crow or raven. ◆***v.*** to make this sound.

**cay·enne** (kī en′ *or* kā en′) ***n.*** a very hot red pepper made from the dried seeds or fruit of a certain kind of pepper plant.

**cay·use** (kī yo͞os′) ***n.*** a small horse used by cowboys.

**CB** *abbreviation for* **citizens' band.**

**CBS** Columbia Broadcasting System.

**cc.** or **c.c.** *abbreviation for* **carbon copy** *or for* **cubic centimeter** *or* **cubic centimeters.**

**Cd** *the symbol for the chemical element* cadmium.

**cease** (sēs) ***v.*** to bring or come to an end; stop [*Cease* firing!] —**ceased, ceas′ing**

**cease-fire** (sēs′fīr′) ***n.*** a stopping of a war for a time when both sides agree to it.

| | | | |
|---|---|---|---|
| **a** fat | **ir** here | **ou** out | **zh** leisure |
| **ā** ape | **ī** bite, fire | **u** up | **ng** ring |
| **ä** car, lot | **ō** go | **ur** fur | a *in* ago |
| **e** ten | **ô** law, horn | **ch** chin | e *in* agent |
| **er** care | **oi** oil | **sh** she | ə = i *in* unity |
| **ē** even | **oo** look | **th** thin | o *in* collect |
| **i** hit | **o͞o** tool | ***th*** then | u *in* focus |

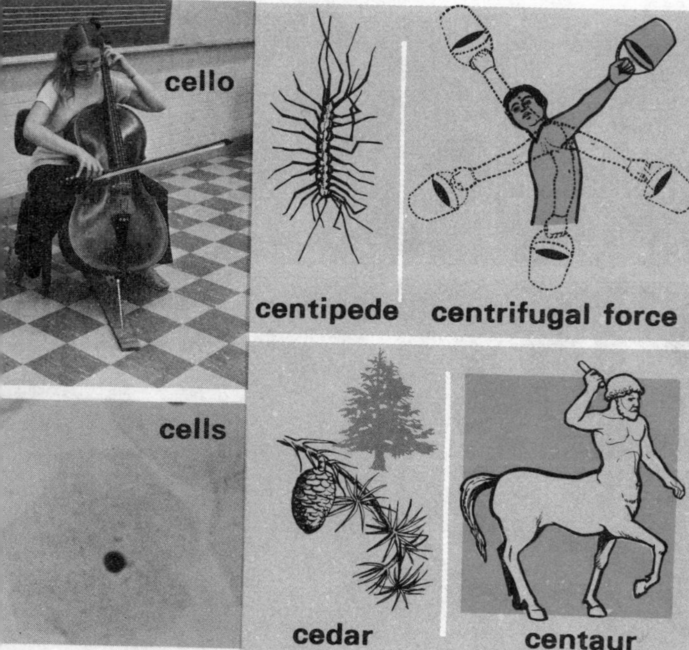


**cease·less** (sēs′lis) ***adj.*** going on and on; continuous [the *ceaseless* sound of the surf]. —**cease′less·ly *adv.***

 **ce·dar** (sē′dər) ***n.*** **1** an evergreen tree having clusters of leaves shaped like needles, small cones, and sweet-smelling, reddish wood. *See the picture.* **2** this wood, which is used to make chests and closets for storing clothes.

**cede** (sēd) ***v.*** to give up one's rights in; surrender [Spain *ceded* Puerto Rico to the U.S. in 1898.] —**ced′ed, ced′ing**

**ceil·ing** (sēl′iŋ) ***n.*** **1** the inside top part of a room, opposite the floor. **2** a limit set on how high something may go [a *ceiling* on prices]. **3** the distance up that one can see, as limited by the lowest covering of clouds. —**hit the ceiling,** to become very angry; *a slang phrase.*

**cel·e·brate** (sel′ə brāt) ***v.*** **1** to honor a victory, the memory of something, etc. in some special way [to *celebrate* a birthday with a party; to *celebrate* the Fourth of July with fireworks.] **2** to honor or praise widely [Aesop's fables have been *celebrated* for centuries.] **3** to perform a ceremony in worshiping [to *celebrate* Mass]. **4** to have a good time: *used only in everyday talk* [Let's *celebrate* when we finish painting the garage.] —**cel′e·brat·ed, cel′e·brat·ing** —**cel′e·bra′tion *n.***

**cel·e·brat·ed** (sel′ə brāt′id) ***adj.*** famous; well-known [a *celebrated* pianist].

**ce·leb·ri·ty** (sə leb′rə tē) ***n.*** **1** a famous person [The scientist Curie became a *celebrity.*] —*pl.* **ce·leb′ri·ties** **2** fame; renown [She seeks no *celebrity.*]

**ce·ler·i·ty** (sə ler′ə tē) ***n.*** swiftness; speed.

**cel·e·ry** (sel′ər ē) ***n.*** a plant whose crisp, long stalks are eaten as a vegetable.

**ce·les·tial** (sə les′chəl) ***adj.*** **1** of the heavens or sky [The stars are *celestial* bodies.] **2** of the finest or highest kind; perfect [*celestial* bliss].

**cel·i·ba·cy** (sel′ə bə sē) ***n.*** the condition of staying unmarried, especially because of a religious vow.

**cel·i·bate** (sel′ə bət) ***n.*** a person who is not married, especially a priest, monk, etc. who has vowed not to marry. ◆***adj.*** unmarried.

**cell** (sel) ***n.*** **1** a small, plainly furnished room, as in a prison or a monastery. **2** any one of a number of small, hollow, connected spaces, as in a honeycomb. **3** the basic unit of living matter, or tissue, usually very small. A cell is made up of protoplasm, usually with a nucleus, and is enclosed by a membrane or wall [All plants and animals are made up of one or more *cells.*] *See the picture.* **4** a container holding metal or carbon pieces in a liquid or paste, for making electricity by chemical action [A battery is made up of one or more *cells.*]

**cel·lar** (sel′ər) ***n.*** a room or rooms underground, usually beneath a building, for storing things.

**cel·list** (chel′ist) ***n.*** a person who plays the cello.

**cel·lo** (chel′ō) ***n.*** a musical instrument like a violin but larger and having a deeper tone. *Its full name is* **violoncello.** *See the picture.* —*pl.* **cel′los** or **cel·li** (chel′ē)

**cel·lo·phane** (sel′ə fān) ***n.*** a material made from cellulose in thin, clear, waterproof sheets. It is used for wrapping food and other things.

**cel·lu·lar** (sel′yoo lər) ***adj.*** of, like, or containing cells [*cellular* tissue].

☆**cel·lu·loid** (sel′yoo loid) ***n.*** a substance made from cellulose and camphor, that was once much used for making camera film, combs, toys, etc.

**cel·lu·lose** (sel′yoo lōs) ***n.*** the main substance in the woody part of plants and trees. It is used in making paper, rayon, and explosives.

**Cel·si·us** (sel′sē əs) ***adj.*** of or describing a thermometer on which the freezing point of pure water is 0° and the boiling point is 100°: *also called* **centigrade.**

**Celt** (selt *or* kelt) ***n.*** a member of a people speaking a Celtic language.

**Cel·tic** (sel′tik *or* kel′tik) ***n.*** a family of languages that includes those spoken by the Britons and Gauls in ancient times and modern Welsh, Irish, and Scottish. ◆***adj.*** of the Celts or their languages.

**ce·ment** (si ment′) ***n.*** **1** a powder made of lime and clay, mixed with water and sand to make mortar or with water, sand, and gravel to make concrete. It hardens like stone when it dries. **2** any soft substance that fastens things together when it hardens, as paste or glue ◆***v.*** **1** to fasten together or cover with cement [to *cement* the pieces of a broken cup]. **2** to make stronger [to *cement* a friendship].

**cem·e·ter·y** (sem′ə ter′ē) ***n.*** a place for burying the dead; graveyard. —*pl.* **cem′e·ter′ies**

**cen·ser** (sen′sər) ***n.*** a container in which incense is burned, as in some church services. *See the picture for* **altar boy.**

**cen·sor** (sen′sər) ***n.*** **1** an official who has the power to examine books, news stories, mail, movies, etc. and to remove or change anything the government does not wish people to see or hear. **2** an official in ancient Rome who took the census and watched over the conduct of the people. ◆***v.*** to examine books, letters, movies, etc. and to remove or hold back anything thought not right for people to see or hear. —**cen′sor·ship *n.***

**cen·so·ri·ous** (sen sôr′ē əs) ***adj.*** always finding fault; criticizing. —**cen·so′ri·ous·ly *adv.***

**cen·sure** (sen′shər) ***n.*** a blaming or finding fault; disapproval. ◆***v.*** to blame or find fault with; criticize harshly [The newspapers *censured* the mayor for taking bribes.] —**cen′sured, cen′sur·ing**

**cen·sus** (sen′səs) ***n.*** an official counting of all the people in a country or area to find out how many there are and of what sex, ages, occupations, etc. [The U.S. *census* is taken every ten years.]

**cent** (sent) ***n.*** ☆a 100th part of a dollar, or a coin worth one cent; penny.

**cent.** *abbreviation for* **central, century.**

**cen·taur** (sen′tôr) ***n.*** a creature in Greek myths that was part man and part horse. *See the picture.*

**cen·te·nar·y** (sen ten′ər ē *or* cen′tə ner′ē) ***n.*** **1** a period of 100 years; century. **2** *another word for* **centennial.** —*pl.* **cen·te′nar·ies**

**cen·ten·ni·al** (sen ten′ē əl) ***adj.*** **1** of or lasting for 100 years. **2** happening once in 100 years. **3** of a 100th anniversary. ◆***n.*** a 100th anniversary or its celebration [Our nation's *centennial* was in 1876.]

**cen·ter** (sen′tər) ***n.*** **1** a point inside a circle or sphere that is the same distance from all points on the circumference or surface. *See* SYNONYMS *at* **middle. 2** the middle point or part; place at the middle [A vase of flowers stood at the *center* of the table.] **3** a person or thing at the middle point [The *center* in basketball is at the middle of the floor when play begins. The *center* in football is at the middle of the front line.] **4** a main point or place, where there is much activity or attention [a shopping *center;* a *center* of interest]. ◆***v.*** **1** to place in or at the center [Try to *center* the design on the page.] **2** to collect in one place; concentrate [We *centered* all our attention on the baby.]

**center of gravity** that point in a thing around which its weight is evenly balanced.

**cen·ter·piece** (sen′tər pēs) ***n.*** a bowl of flowers or other decoration put at the center of a table.

**cen·ti·grade** (sen′tə grād) ***adj., n.*** *same as* **Celsius.**

**cen·ti·gram** (sen′tə gram) ***n.*** a unit of weight, equal to 1/100 gram. *An earlier British spelling is* **cen′ti·gramme.**

**cen·time** (sän′tēm) ***n.*** the 100th part of the French franc and of certain other money units.

**cen·ti·me·ter** (sen′tə mēt′ər) ***n.*** a unit of measure, equal to 1/100 meter. *The usual British spelling is* **cen′ti·me′tre.**

**cen·ti·pede** (sen′tə pēd) ***n.*** a small animal like a worm with many pairs of legs along its body. The two front legs are poison fangs. *See the picture.*

**cen·tral** (sen′trəl) ***adj.*** **1** in or at the center; forming the center [the *central* part of Ohio]. **2** at about the same distance from different points [We chose a *central* meeting place.] **3** most important; main; principal [the *central* plot in a novel]. —**cen′tral·ly *adv.***

**Central African Empire** a country in central Africa.

**Central America** the narrow part of America between Mexico and South America. It includes Guatemala, Nicaragua, Panama, Costa Rica, etc.

**cen·tral·ize** (sen′trə līz) ***v.*** to bring or come to a center; especially, to bring under one control [All government powers were *centralized* under a dictator.] —**cen′tral·ized, cen′tral·iz·ing** —**cen′tral·i·za′tion *n.***

☆**Central Standard Time** *see* **Standard Time.**

**cen·tre** (sen′tər) ***n., v.*** *the usual British spelling of* **center.** —**cen′tred, cen′tring**

**cen·trif·u·gal force** (sen trif′yə gəl) the force that pulls a thing outward when it is spinning rapidly around a center.

> If you swing a pail of water quickly in a circle, the **centrifugal force** of the pail's weight will keep the water from spilling out. The **centripetal force** of your hand holding the pail will keep the pail from flying away. *See the picture.*

**cen·trip·e·tal force** (sen trip′ə təl) the force that pulls a thing inward when it is spinning rapidly around a center. *See the note at* **centrifugal force.**

**cen·tu·ri·on** (sen tyoor′ē ən *or* sen toor′ē ən) ***n.*** the commander of a group of about 100 soldiers in ancient Rome.

**cen·tu·ry** (sen′chər ē) ***n.*** **1** any of the 100-year periods counted forward or backward from the beginning of the Christian Era [From 500 to 401 B.C. was the fifth *century* B.C. From 1901 to 2000 is the twentieth *century* A.D.] **2** any period of 100 years [Mark Twain was born over a *century* ago.] —*pl.* **cen′tu·ries**

☆**century plant** a desert plant that is a kind of agave.

> The **century plant** blooms only once, when it is from 10 to 30 years old, and then dies. It got its name from the mistaken idea that it blooms only once a century.



**ce·phal·ic** (sə fal′ik) ***adj.*** of, in, or near the head or skull.

**ce·ram·ics** (sə ram′iks) ***n.pl.*** **1** the art or work of making objects of baked clay, as pottery, porcelain, etc.: *used with a singular verb.* **2** objects made of baked clay. —**ce·ram′ic *adj.***

**Cer·ber·us** (sur′bər əs) in Greek and Roman myths, a dog with three heads, that guarded the entrance to Hades.

**ce·re·al** (sir′ē əl) ***n.*** **1** any grass that bears seeds used for food [Rice, wheat, and oats are common *cereals.*] **2** the seeds of such a grass; grain. ☆**3** food made from grain, especially breakfast food, as oatmeal or cornflakes. ◆***adj.*** of or having to do with grain or the grasses bearing it.

**cer·e·bel·lum** (ser′ə bel′əm) ***n.*** the part of the brain behind and below the cerebrum.

**cer·e·bral** (ser′ə brəl *or* sə rē′brəl) ***adj.*** having to do with the brain or with the cerebrum.

**cerebral palsy** a condition caused by injury to the brain, usually before or during birth, in which there is some difficulty in moving or speaking.

**cer·e·brum** (ser′ə brəm *or* sə rē′brəm) ***n.*** the upper, main part of the brain.

**cer·e·ment** (ser′ə mənt) ***n.*** the shroud or garment in which a dead person is buried.

| | | | | | | | |
|---|---|---|---|---|---|---|---|
| **a** | fat | **ir** | here | **ou** | out | **zh** | leisure |
| **ā** | ape | **ī** | bite, fire | **u** | up | **ng** | ring |
| **ä** | car, lot | **ō** | go | **ur** | fur | | a *in* ago |
| **e** | ten | **ô** | law, horn | **ch** | chin | | e *in* agent |
| **er** | care | **oi** | oil | **sh** | she | **ə =** | i *in* unity |
| **ē** | even | **oo** | look | **th** | thin | | o *in* collect |
| **i** | hit | **ōō** | tool | ***th*** | then | | u *in* focus |

**cer·e·mo·ni·al** (ser′ə mō′nē əl) ***adj.*** of or for a ceremony [The queen was crowned in her *ceremonial* robes.] ◆***n.*** **1** a system of rules for a ceremony, as in religion [a *ceremonial* for baptism]. **2** a ceremony.

**cer·e·mo·ni·ous** (ser′ə mō′nē əs) ***adj.*** **1** full of ceremony. **2** very polite and formal [a *ceremonious* bow]. —**cer′e·mo′ni·ous·ly** ***adv.***

**cer·e·mo·ny** (ser′ə mō′nē) ***n.*** **1** an act or set of acts done in a special way, with all the right details [a wedding *ceremony* in church; the *ceremony* of inaugurating the President]. **2** very polite behavior that follows strict rules; formality [The special dinner was served with great *ceremony*.] —*pl.* **cer′e·mo′nies** —**stand on ceremony**, to follow the rules of polite behavior strictly.

SYNONYMS: **Ceremony** means an act that is done according to strict rules and in a serious way [a graduation *ceremony*.] **Rite** is used for a religious act having strict rules of form [burial *rites*]. **Ritual** means a group of rites or ceremonies, especially the rites of a certain religion [the *ritual* of Catholicism].

**Ce·res** (sir′ēz) the Roman goddess of plants and farming. The Greeks called her *Demeter*.

**ce·rise** (sə rēs′ *or* sə rēz′) ***n., adj.*** bright red.

**cer·tain** (sʉrt′'n) ***adj.*** **1** without any doubt or question; sure; positive [Are you *certain* of your facts?] **2** bound to happen; not failing or missing [to risk *certain* death; the soldier's *certain* aim]. **3** not named or described, though perhaps known [It happened in a *certain* town out west.] **4** some, but not much [to a *certain* extent]. —**for certain**, surely; without doubt [Do you know *for certain*?]

**cer·tain·ly** (sʉrt′'n lē) ***adv.*** without any doubt; surely [I shall *certainly* be there.]

**cer·tain·ty** (sʉrt′'n tē) ***n.*** **1** the condition of being certain; sureness [The weather cannot be predicted with *certainty*.] **2** anything that is certain; positive fact [I know for a *certainty* that they are related.] —*pl.* **cer′tain·ties**

**cer·tif·i·cate** (sʉr tif′ə kit) ***n.*** a written or printed statement that can be used as proof of something because it is official [A birth *certificate* proves where and when someone was born.]

**cer·ti·fy** (sʉr′tə fī) ***v.*** **1** to say in an official way that something is true or correct; verify [The doctor's letter *certified* that her absence was due to illness.] **2** to guarantee; vouch for [A *certified* check is one that the bank guarantees to be good.] **3** to give a certificate to [A *certified* public accountant has a certificate of approval from the State.] —**cer′ti·fied, cer′ti·fy·ing** —**cer′ti·fi·ca′tion** ***n.***

**ce·ru·le·an** (sə ro͞o′lē ən) ***adj.*** sky-blue.

**Cer·van·tes** (sər van′tēz), **Mi·guel de** (mē gel′ dā) 1547–1616; Spanish writer who wrote *Don Quixote*.

**ce·si·um** (sē′zē əm) ***n.*** a soft, silvery metal that is a chemical element. It is used in electric eyes.

**ces·sa·tion** (se sā′shən) ***n.*** a ceasing or stopping, either forever or for some time [There was a *cessation* of work during the holidays.]

**ces·sion** (sesh′ən) ***n.*** a ceding or giving up of rights or land [The *cession* of Guam to the U.S. by Spain took place in 1898.]

**cess·pool** (ses′po͞ol) ***n.*** a tank or deep hole in the ground for collecting the waste matter from the sinks and toilets of a house.

**Cey·lon** (sə län′) *an older name for* **Sri Lanka**.

**Ce·zanne** (sā zän′), **Paul** 1839–1906; French artist.

**cf** or **c.f.** center field (in baseball).

**cf.** compare: *cf.* is the abbreviation of *confer*, the Latin word for "compare."

**cg, cg., cgm, cgm.** *abbreviations for* **centigram** *or* **centigrams.**

**Ch.** or **ch.** *abbreviation for* **chaplain, chapter, chief, church.**

**Chad** (chad) a country in north-central Africa.

**chafe** (chāf) ***v.*** **1** to rub so as to make warm [to *chafe* one's hands]. **2** to make or become sore by rubbing [The stiff collar *chafed* my neck.] **3** to make or become angry or annoyed [The delay *chafed* her. He *chafed* at his loss.] —**chafed, chaf′ing** —**chafe at the bit**, to be impatient or annoyed, as from having to wait.

**chaff** (chaf) ***n.*** **1** the husks of wheat or other grain, separated from the seed by threshing. **2** a worthless thing. **3** friendly teasing or joking; banter. ◆***v.*** to tease or make fun of in a friendly way [His friends *chaffed* him for missing the bus.]

**chaf·finch** (chaf′finch) ***n.*** a small songbird of Europe. It is often kept in a cage as a pet.

**chaf·ing dish** (chāf′iŋ) a pan placed in a frame over a small heating device. It is used to cook food at the table or to keep food hot. *See the picture.*

**Cha·gall** (shä gäl′), **Marc** 1889– ; Russian artist living most of the time in France.

**cha·grin** (shə grin′) ***n.*** a feeling of being embarrassed and annoyed because one has failed or has been disappointed. ◆***v.*** to embarrass and annoy [Our hostess was *chagrined* when the guest of honor failed to appear.] —**cha·grined′, cha·grin′ing**

**chain** (chān) ***n.*** **1** a number of links or loops joined together in a line that can be bent [a *chain* of steel; a *chain* of daisies]. **2 chains**, *pl.* anything that binds or holds someone prisoner, as bonds or shackles. **3** a series of things joined together [a mountain *chain;* a *chain* of events]. ☆**4** a number of stores, restaurants, etc. owned by one company. **5** a chain of metal links used for measuring length [A surveyor's *chain* is 66 feet long.] ◆***v.*** **1** to fasten or bind with chains [The prisoner was *chained* to the wall.] **2** to hold down; bind [I was *chained* to my job.]

**chain mail** armor that is made of small metal links joined together, so that it will bend.

**chain reaction** a series of actions or happenings, each of which in turn starts another. Atomic energy is produced by a chain reaction in which some particles of atoms are set free to strike other atoms in a mass, setting free more particles that strike still other atoms, and so on.

☆**chain saw** a power saw that cuts with teeth moving on an endless chain. *See the picture.*

☆**chain store** any of a group of stores owned and run by the same company.

**chair** (cher) ***n.*** **1** a piece of furniture that has a back and is a seat for one person. **2** an important or official position [Professor Lane holds a *chair* in history at the college.] **3** the chairman [The *chair* recognizes Ms. Chen.]

☆**chair·lift** (cher′lift) ***n.*** a line of seats hanging from a cable moved by a motor. It is used especially to carry skiers up a slope. *See the picture.*

**chair·man** (cher′mən) ***n.*** a person who is in charge of a meeting or is the head of a committee or board. *Many people prefer to use the word* **chair·per·son** (cher′pur′s'n) *—pl.* **chair′men —chair′man·ship *n.***

**chaise** (shāz) ***n.*** **1** a light carriage, especially one with two wheels and a folding top. **2** *same as* **chaise longue.**

**chaise longue** (shāz′lông′) a chair built like a couch, having a seat long enough to hold the outstretched legs of the person sitting: *now sometimes called* **chaise lounge** (shāz′lounj′). *See the picture.*

**Chal·de·a** or **Chal·dae·a** (kal dē′ə) an ancient land in a region that is now the southern part of Iraq.

**cha·let** (sha lā′) ***n.*** **1** a kind of Swiss house built of wood. It has balconies and a sloping overhanging roof. **2** any house like this.

**chal·ice** (chal′is) ***n.*** a drinking cup; especially, the wine cup used in the Communion service.

**chalk** (chôk) ***n.*** **1** a whitish limestone that is soft and easily crushed into a powder. It is made up mainly of tiny sea shells. **2** a piece of chalk or of material like it, for writing on chalkboards. ◆***v.*** to mark with chalk. **—chalk up, 1** to score, as points in a game. **2** to charge or credit [*Chalk* it *up* to experience.] **—chalk′y *adj.***

**chalk·board** (chôk′bôrd) ***n.*** a large piece of smooth, dark material for writing or drawing on with chalk. It is usually green or black.

**chal·lenge** (chal′ənj) ***v.*** **1** to question the right or rightness of; refuse to believe unless proof is given [to *challenge* a claim; to *challenge* something said or the person who says it]. **2** to call to take part in a fight or contest; dare [He *challenged* her to a game of chess.] **3** to refuse to let pass unless a certain sign is given [The sentry waited for the password after *challenging* the soldier.] **4** to call for skill, effort, or imagination [That puzzle will really *challenge* you.] **—chal′lenged, chal′leng·ing** ◆***n.*** **1** the act of challenging [I accepted his *challenge* to a race.] **2** something that calls for much effort; hard task [Climbing Mt. Everest was a real *challenge*.]

**cham·ber** (chām′bər) ***n.*** **1** a room, especially a bedroom. **2 chambers,** *pl.* a group of connected rooms or offices [a judge's *chambers*]. **3** a large hall or meeting room. **4** a number of people working together as a group for some purpose [A *chamber* of deputies is a legislature. A *chamber* of commerce tries to help business interests.] **5** an enclosed space in the body of a plant or animal [a *chamber* of the heart]. **6** the part of a gun that holds the cartridge or shell.

**cham·ber·lain** (chām′bər lin) ***n.*** **1** an officer in charge of the household of a ruler or lord. **2** a high official in certain royal courts.

**cham·ber·maid** (chām′bər mād) ***n.*** a woman whose work is taking care of bedrooms, as in a hotel.

**chamber music** music that is meant to be played by small groups in small halls [Sonatas, trios, and quartets are forms of *chamber music*.]

☆**cham·bray** (sham′brā) ***n.*** a smooth cotton cloth made by weaving white threads across colored ones.

**cha·me·le·on** (kə mēl′yən *or* kə mē′lē ən) ***n.*** **1** a small lizard that can change the color of its skin to match its background. *See the picture.* **2** a person who keeps changing opinions and attitudes.

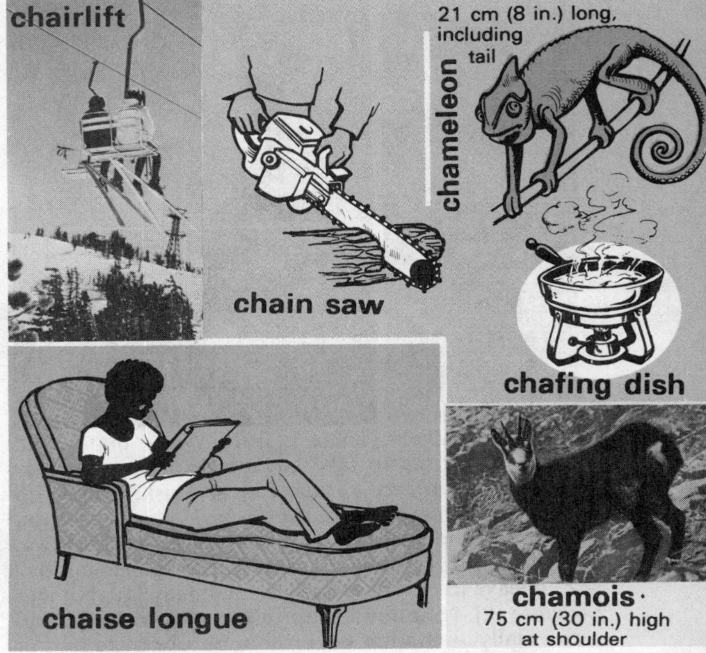


**cham·ois** (sham′ē) ***n.*** **1** a small antelope like a goat, found in the mountains of Europe and southwestern Asia. *See the picture.* **2** a soft leather made from its skin or from the skin of sheep, deer, or goats [Pieces of *chamois* are often used as polishing cloths.] *—pl.* **cham′ois**

**champ**[1] (champ) ***v.*** to chew hard and noisily. **—champ at the bit, 1** to keep biting its bit in a restless way: said of a horse. **2** to be restless.

**champ**[2] (champ) ***n.*** a champion: *a slang word.*

**cham·pagne** (sham pān′) ***n.*** a pale yellow wine that bubbles like soda water.

**cham·paign** (sham pān′) ***n.*** flat, open country.

**cham·pi·on** (cham′pē ən) ***n.*** **1** a person or thing that wins first place or is judged to be best, as in a contest or sport [a spelling *champion;* a tennis *champion*]. **2** a person who fights for another or for a cause; defender [a *champion* of the poor]. ◆***adj.*** winning over all others; being the best of its kind [a *champion* bull]. ◆***v.*** to fight for or defend [Carrie Chapman Catt *championed* women's right to vote.]

**cham·pi·on·ship** (cham′pē ən ship′) ***n.*** **1** the position or title of a champion; first place. **2** the act of championing, or defending.

**chance** (chans) ***n.*** **1** the way things turn out; happening of events by accident [They left it to *chance* when they would meet again.] **2** the fact of being



| | | | | | | | |
|---|---|---|---|---|---|---|---|
| **a** | fat | **ir** | here | **ou** | out | **zh** | leisure |
| **ā** | ape | **ī** | bite, fire | **u** | up | **ng** | ring |
| **ä** | car, lot | **ō** | go | **ur** | fur | | a *in* ago |
| **e** | ten | **ô** | law, horn | **ch** | chin | | e *in* agent |
| **er** | care | **oi** | oil | **sh** | she | **ə =** | i *in* unity |
| **ē** | even | **oo** | look | **th** | thin | | o *in* collect |
| **i** | hit | **ōō** | tool | ***th*** | then | | u *in* focus |

possible or likely [There is little *chance* that it will rain.] **3** a time to take advantage of; opportunity [This is your *chance* to succeed.] **4** a risk; gamble [to take a *chance* on winning]. ◆***adj.*** happening by chance; accidental [a *chance* meeting of friends]. ◆***v.*** **1** to happen by chance [I *chanced* to be passing by.] **2** to leave to chance; risk [This plan may fail, but let's *chance* it.] —**chanced, chanc'ing** —**by chance,** accidentally. —**chance on** or **chance upon,** to find or meet by chance.

**chan·cel** (chan's'l) ***n.*** the part of a church around the altar, used by the clergy and choir.



**chan·cel·lor** (chan'sə lər) ***n.*** a high official, as the prime minister in some countries, the chief judge in some law courts, or the head of some universities.

**chanc·y** (chan'sē) ***adj.*** not certain; risky. —**chanc'i·er, chanc'i·est**

**chan·de·lier** (shan də lir') ***n.*** a lighting fixture hanging from the ceiling with branches for several lights. *See the picture.*

**chan·dler** (chand'lər) ***n.*** a person who sells supplies or goods of a certain kind [A ship *chandler* sells provisions for ships.]

> **Chandler** comes from the old French word for "candle." Originally a chandler was a person who sold candles. The word **chandelier** comes from the same French word, since the earliest chandeliers held candles instead of electric lights.

**change** (chānj) ***v.*** **1** to make or become different in some way; alter [Time *changes* all things. His voice began to *change* at the age of thirteen.] **2** to put or take one thing in place of another; substitute [to *change* one's clothes; to *change* jobs]. **3** to give or take one thing in return for another; substitute [Let's *change* seats. Can you *change* this dollar bill for four quarters?] **4** to get off one train, bus, or plane and get on another [The passengers *change* at Chicago.] —**changed, chang'ing** ◆***n.*** **1** the act of changing in some way [There will be a *change* in the weather tomorrow.] **2** something put in place of something else [a fresh *change* of clothing]. **3** the money returned when one has paid more than the amount owed [If it costs 70 cents and you pay with a dollar, you get back 30 cents as *change.*] **4** a number of coins or bills whose total value equals a single larger coin or bill [I have *change* for your $10 bill.] **5** small coins [The *change* jingled in my pocket.] —**change off,** to take turns.

**change·a·ble** (chān'jə b'l) ***adj.*** changing often or likely to change [*changeable* weather].

**change·less** (chānj'lis) ***adj.*** not changing; remaining the same; constant [a *changeless* love].

**change·ling** (chānj'liŋ) ***n.*** a child secretly put in the place of another; especially, in folk tales, one exchanged in this way by fairies.

**chan·nel** (chan''l) ***n.*** **1** the bed of a river or stream. **2** the deeper part of a river, harbor, etc. **3** a body of water joining two larger bodies of water [The English *Channel* links the Atlantic Ocean to the North Sea.] **4** any tube or groove through which a liquid flows. **5** any means by which something moves or passes [We get news through newspapers, TV, and other *channels.*] **6** the band of frequencies on which a single radio or television station sends out its programs. ◆***v.*** **1** to make a channel in. **2** to send through a channel. [*Channel* your questions through the principal's office.] —**chan'neled** or **chan'nelled, chan'nel·ing** or **chan'nel·ling**

**Channel Islands** a group of British islands in the English Channel, including Jersey and Guernsey.

**chant** (chant) ***n.*** **1** a song, especially one in which strings of words or syllables are sung in the same tone [*Chants* are used in some church services.] **2** a singsong way of speaking [the *chant* of an auctioneer]. ◆***v.*** to sing or say in a chant [to *chant* a prayer]. —**chant'er *n.***

**chan·tey** or **chan·ty** (shan'tē *or* chan'tē) ***n.*** a song that sailors sing in rhythm with their motions while working. —*pl.* **chan'teys** or **chan'ties**

**Chan·ti·cleer** (chan'tə klir') a name for the rooster in folk tales and poems.

**Cha·nu·kah** (khä'noo kä') *another spelling of* **Hanuka.**

**cha·os** (kā'äs) ***n.*** the greatest confusion and disorder [The winning team's locker room was in a state of *chaos* after the game.]

> **Chaos** is a Greek word meaning "space." The Greeks in olden times thought that before the universe came into being, there was an endless space having things in it that had no form or order.

**cha·ot·ic** (kā ät'ik) ***adj.*** in the greatest confusion or disorder. —**cha·ot'i·cal·ly *adv.***

**chap**[1] (chap) ***n.*** a man or boy; fellow: *used only in everyday talk.*

**chap**[2] (chap) ***v.*** to crack open; make or become rough [The cold wind *chapped* my skin.] —**chapped, chap'ping**

**chap.** *abbreviation for* **chapter.**

**chap·el** (chap''l) ***n.*** **1** a place where Christians worship, that is smaller than a church. **2** a small room in a church, having its own altar. **3** any room or building for holding religious services, as in a hospital, college, or army camp.

**chap·er·on** or **chap·er·one** (shap'ə rōn) ***n.*** an older person who goes along with young, unmarried people to a party, dance, etc. to see that they behave properly. ◆***v.*** to be a chaperon to. —**chap'er·oned, chap'er·on·ing**

**chap·lain** (chap'lən) ***n.*** a minister, priest, or rabbi serving in the armed forces or in a hospital, prison, etc.

**chap·let** (chap′lit) ***n.*** **1** a wreath for the head. **2** a string of beads, especially a short rosary.

☆**chaps** (chaps) ***n.pl.*** leather coverings worn over the legs of trousers by cowboys to protect their legs from thorny bushes. *See the picture.*

**chap·ter** (chap′tər) ***n.*** **1** any of the main parts into which a book is divided. **2** a thing like a chapter; part; episode [a *chapter* of one's life]. ☆**3** a branch of a club or society that has a number of branches.

**char** (chär) ***v.*** **1** to change to charcoal by burning. **2** to burn slightly; scorch [They liked their steaks *charred.*] —**charred, char′ring**

**char·ac·ter** (kar′ik tər) ***n.*** **1** all the things that a person does, feels, and thinks by which that person is judged as being good or bad, strong or weak, etc. [That insulting remark showed her true *character.*] **2** these things when thought of as being especially good or strong [Persons of *character* are needed in high positions.] **3** all those things that make one person or thing different from others; special quality; nature [The fields and woods around the school gave it a rural *character.*] **4** any letter, figure, or symbol used in writing and printing. **5** a person in a story or play. **6** an odd or unusual person: *used only in everyday talk.* —**in character,** that seems to fit the person's character. —**out of character,** that does not seem to fit the person's character.

**char·ac·ter·is·tic** (kar′ik tər is′tik) ***adj.*** that helps make up the special character of some person or thing; typical; like no other [the *characteristic* tail feathers of the peacock]. ✦***n.*** something that makes a person or thing different from others; special part or quality [The pointed arch is a *characteristic* of Gothic style.] —**char′ac·ter·is′ti·cal·ly** ***adv.***

SYNONYMS: **Characteristic** is used to describe a special quality of a person or thing that helps us to know what that person or thing is [his *characteristic* honesty; the *characteristic* taste of honey]. **Individual** and **distinctive** are used of a quality that something has that makes it different from other similar things, and **distinctive** often suggests an excellent quality of this kind [She has an *individual,* or *distinctive,* writing style.]

**char·ac·ter·ize** (kar′ik tə rīz′) ***v.*** **1** to describe or show as having certain characteristics [Tennyson *characterized* King Arthur as wise and brave.] **2** to be characteristic or typical of [Bright colors *characterized* her paintings.] —**char′ac·ter·ized′, char′ac·ter·iz′ing** —**char′ac·ter·i·za′tion** ***n.***

**cha·rades** (shə rādz′) ***n.pl.*** a game in which players try to guess the word or phrase that another player is acting out without speaking, often syllable by syllable: *used with a singular verb.*

**char·coal** (chär′kōl) ***n.*** **1** a form of carbon made by heating wood to a high degree in a closed container without air. It is used as a fuel, filter, crayon, etc. **2** a very dark gray or brown, almost black.

**charge** (chärj) ***v.*** **1** to load or fill [to *charge* a gun with ammunition]. ☆**2** to supply with electrical energy [to *charge* a battery]. **3** to give a task, duty, etc. to; make responsible for [The nurse was *charged* with the care of the child.] **4** to give instructions to [A judge *charges* a jury.] **5** to accuse of doing wrong; blame [The prisoner was *charged* with murder.] **6** to set as a price; ask for payment [Barbers once *charged* a quarter for a haircut. We do not *charge* for gift wrappings.] **7** to write down as something owed, to be paid for later [The store will *charge* your purchase.] **8** to rush at with force; attack [Our troops *charged* the enemy.] —**charged, charg′ing** ✦***n.*** **1** the thing or amount used to load or fill something, as a gun. **2** the amount of electrical energy, as in a battery. **3** a person or thing that one must take care of; responsibility [The children were the nurse's *charges.*] **4** instruction or order [The judge gave her *charge* to the jury.] **5** a claim that someone has done wrong; accusation [a *charge* of cruelty]. **6** price or cost [Is there any *charge* for delivering?] **7** *a shorter form of* **charge account;** also, a single entry in a charge account. **8** an attack, as by soldiers. **9** the signal for such an attack [The bugler sounded the *charge.*] —**charge off, 1** to put down as a loss. **2** to think of as due to a certain cause [*Charge off* that mistake to lack of experience.] —**in charge,** having the responsibility or control. —**charge′a·ble** ***adj.***

☆**charge account** a plan by which a customer may buy things from a store or business and pay for them at a later time.

**charg·er** (chär′jər) ***n.*** **1** a horse ridden in battle or on parade. **2** a device used to charge batteries.

**char·i·ly** (cher′ə lē) ***adv.*** in a chary way; with care, caution, shyness, etc.

**char·i·ot** (char′ē ət) ***n.*** an open cart with two wheels, drawn by horses. It was used in ancient times in battles, races, etc. *See the picture.*

**char·i·ot·eer** (char′ē ə tir′) ***n.*** the driver of a chariot.

**cha·ris·ma** (kə riz′mə) ***n.*** a special quality in a person that causes others to admire or have respect for that person as a leader. —**char·is·mat·ic** (kar′iz mat′ik) ***adj.***

**char·i·ta·ble** (char′ə tə b'l) ***adj.*** **1** kind and generous in giving money or other help to people in need; benevolent. **2** for the poor, the sick, and others needing help [a *charitable* institution]. **3** kind and forgiving in judging other people [It was *charitable* of you not to mention my mistake.] —**char′i·ta·bly** ***adv.***

**char·i·ty** (char′ə tē) ***n.*** **1** a giving of money or help to people in need. **2** an institution, fund, etc. for giving such help [give to the *charity* of your choice]. **3** kindness in judging other people. **4** love or good will to all other people ["faith, hope, and charity"]. —*pl.* **char′i·ties**

**char·la·tan** (shär′lə t'n) ***n.*** a person who pretends to be an expert in something or to have more skill than is really the case; quack; fake.

**Char·le·magne** (shär′lə mān′) 742–814 A.D.; king of the Franks and the first emperor of the Holy Roman Empire.

**Charles I** (chärlz) king of England from 1625 to 1649. He was beheaded for treason.



| | | | | | | | |
|---|---|---|---|---|---|---|---|
| **a** | fat | **ir** | here | **ou** | out | **zh** | leisure |
| **ā** | ape | **ī** | bite, fire | **u** | up | **ng** | ring |
| **ä** | car, lot | **ō** | go | **ur** | fur | | a *in* ago |
| **e** | ten | **ô** | law, horn | **ch** | chin | | e *in* agent |
| **er** | care | **oi** | oil | **sh** | she | **ə =** | i *in* unity |
| **ē** | even | **oo** | look | **th** | thin | | o *in* collect |
| **i** | hit | **ōō** | tool | ***th*** | then | | u *in* focus |

**Charles·ton** (chärl′stən) **1** the capital of West Virginia. **2** a seaport in South Carolina.

☆**char·ley horse** (chär′lē) a cramp in muscles of the leg or arm: *used only in everyday talk*.

**charm** (chärm) ***n.*** **1** an act, thing, word, or phrase that is supposed to have magic power to help or hurt. **2** any small object worn as a decoration on a bracelet, necklace, etc. **3** a quality or feature in someone or something that attracts or pleases greatly [His greatest *charm* is his smile.] ◆***v.*** **1** to act on or protect as if by magic [She led a *charmed* life.] **2** to attract or please greatly; fascinate; delight [The singer *charmed* the audience.] *See* SYNONYMS *at* **attract.**

**charm·er** (chärm′ər) ***n.*** a delightful, attractive, or fascinating person.

**charm·ing** (chär′miŋ) ***adj.*** very pleasing; attractive; delightful. —**charm′ing·ly** ***adv.***

**Cha·ron** (ker′ən) ***n.*** the boatman in Greek myths who carried the souls of the dead across the river Styx to Hades.

**chart** (chärt) ***n.*** **1** a map, especially one for use in steering a ship or guiding an aircraft [A sailor's *chart* shows coastlines, depths, currents, etc.] **2** a group of facts about something set up in the form of a diagram, graph, table, etc. ◆***v.*** **1** to make a map of. **2** to show on a chart [to *chart* the weather].

**char·ter** (chär′tər) ***n.*** **1** an official paper in which certain rights are given by a government to a person or business [a royal *charter* to settle a colony; a city *charter* to operate a bus line]. **2** an official paper telling the aims and principles of a group [the *Charter* of the United Nations]. **3** an official paper from a society giving a group permission to organize a chapter of the society. ◆***v.*** **1** to give a charter to. **2** to hire or lease for the special use of a group [to *charter* a bus].



**char·treuse** (shär trōōz′ *or* shär trōōs′) ***n.*** pale, yellowish green.

**char·wom·an** (chär′woom′ən) ***n.*** a woman whose work is cleaning or scrubbing offices or public buildings. —*pl.* **char′wom′en**

**char·y** (cher′ē) ***adj.*** **1** not taking chances; careful; cautious [Be a little more *chary* of offending them.] **2** not giving freely; sparing [He was *chary* of his favors to friends.] —**char′i·er, char′i·est**

**Cha·ryb·dis** (kə rib′dis) a whirlpool off the coast of Sicily. *See* **Scylla.**

**chase** (chās) ***v.*** **1** to go after or keep following in order to catch or harm [The fox was *chasing* a rabbit.] **2** to drive away [She waved her hand to *chase* the flies away.] —**chased, chas′ing** ◆***n.*** **1** the act of chasing; pursuit. **2** the act of hunting animals, especially as a sport: *often called* **the chase.** —**give chase,** to chase or pursue. —**chas′er** ***n.***

checkered shirt

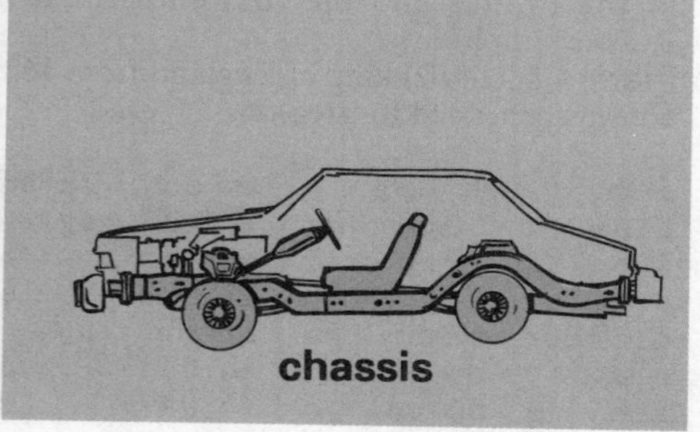
chassis

**chasm** (kaz′′m) ***n.*** **1** a deep crack in the earth; narrow gorge. **2** a wide difference in ideas or beliefs that keeps people or groups apart.

**chas·sis** (chas′ē *or* shas′ē) ***n.*** **1** the framework of an automobile, including all parts except the engine and body. *See the picture.* **2** the framework that holds the working parts of a radio or television set. —*pl.* **chas·sis** (chas′ēz *or* shas′ēz)

**chaste** (chāst) ***adj.*** **1** behaving in a moral way, especially in sexual matters. **2** pure and simple in style or design; not fancy.

**chas·ten** (chās′′n) ***v.*** **1** to punish in order to make better [to *chasten* a disobedient child]. **2** to make less lively, wild, spirited, etc.

**chas·tise** (chas tīz′) ***v.*** to punish, especially by beating. —**chas·tised′, chas·tis′ing** —**chas·tise′ment** ***n.***

**chas·ti·ty** (chas′tə tē) ***n.*** the quality of being chaste, moral, or pure.

**chat** (chat) ***v.*** to talk in an easy, relaxed way. —**chat′·ted, chat′ting** ◆***n.*** an easy, relaxed talk or conversation.

**cha·teau** (sha tō′) ***n.*** a castle or large country house, especially in France. —*pl.* **cha·teaux** (sha tōz′)

**Chat·ta·noo·ga** (chat′ə nōō′gə) a city in southeastern Tennessee.

**chat·tel** (chat′′l) ***n.*** a piece of property that can be moved [Land and buildings are not *chattels*; furniture, automobiles, livestock, etc. are *chattels.*]

**chat·ter** (chat′ər) ***v.*** **1** to make short, quick sounds that seem almost like talk [Birds and apes *chatter.*] **2** to talk fast and in a foolish way, without stopping. **3** to make fast clicking sounds with the teeth, when the lower jaw trembles because of fear or cold. ◆***n.*** **1** the noise of chattering. **2** fast, foolish talk. —**chat′ter·er** ***n.***

**chat·ty** (chat′ē) ***adj.*** **1** always ready to chat [a *chatty* neighbor]. **2** full of easy, friendly talk [a *chatty* letter]. —**chat′ti·er, chat′ti·est**

**Chau·cer** (chô′sər), **Geof·frey** (jef′rē) 1340?–1400; English poet who wrote *The Canterbury Tales.*

**chauf·feur** (shō′fər *or* shō fur′) ***n.*** a person whose work is to drive an automobile for another person. ◆***v.*** to work or serve as a chauffeur .

> **Chauffeur** is a French word that comes from the French verb *chauffer,* meaning "to heat." Some early automobiles were driven by steam, and the driver had to stoke the furnace that heated the water. Such drivers were called **chauffeurs,** or "stokers."

**cheap** (chēp) ***adj.*** **1** low in price [Vegetables are *cheaper* in summer than in winter.] **2** charging low prices [a *cheap* hotel]. **3** worth more than it costs [That suit would be *cheap* at twice the price.] **4** got with not much work or trouble; easily got [a *cheap* victory]. **5** of low value or of poor quality [a radio made of *cheap* parts that will wear out]. **6** not worth having respect for [Don't make yourself *cheap* by getting rowdy.] **7** stingy; not willing to spend money: *used only in everyday talk.* ◆***adv.*** at a low cost [I bought these shoes *cheap* at a sale.] —**cheap′ly** ***adv.*** —**cheap′ness** ***n.***

SYNONYMS: **Cheap** and **inexpensive** both mean low in cost or price. **Inexpensive** usually suggests that the thing bought is well worth the cost [a good, *inexpensive* frying pan]. **Cheap** often suggests that while the price is low, so is the quality [*cheap* shoes that wore out quickly].

**cheap·en** (chēp′'n) ***v.*** to make or become cheap or cheaper.

☆**cheap·skate** (chēp′skāt) ***n.*** a person who does not like to spend money; stingy person: *a slang word.*

**cheat** (chēt) ***v.*** **1** to act in a way that is not fair or honest in order to get what one wants [to *cheat* a person out of money; to *cheat* on a test]. **2** to escape by tricks or by good luck [to *cheat* death]. ◆***n.*** **1** a person who cheats: *also* **cheat′er.** **2** an act of cheating; a trick, fraud, or swindle.

**check** (chek) ***n.*** **1** a person or thing that holds back or controls [High tariffs act as a *check* on trade.] **2** a sudden stop [Let's put a *check* to so much tardiness.] **3** a test to find out if something is as it should be [Add the column of numbers again as a *check* on your answer.] **4** the mark ✓, used to show that something is right, or to call attention to something. ☆**5** a ticket or other token that shows one's right to claim an article left in a checkroom, etc. [a hat *check;* baggage *check*]. ☆**6** a piece of paper telling how much one owes, as for a meal at a restaurant. **7** a written order to a bank to pay a certain amount of money from one's account to a certain person. **8** a pattern of small squares like a checkerboard; also, any of the squares in such a pattern. **9** in chess, the condition of a king that is in danger and must be put into a safe position. ◆***v.*** **1** to stop suddenly [An alert guard *checked* the escape of the thief.] **2** to hold back or control [to *check* one's anger]. ☆**3** to prove to be right or find what is wanted by examining, comparing, etc. [These figures *check* with mine. *Check* the records for this information.] **4** to mark with a check (*see meaning* 4 *of the noun*). **5** to mark with a pattern of squares [a *checked* suit]. **6** to put in a checkroom for a time [to *check* a coat during a concert]. **7** in chess, to place an opponent's king in check (*see meaning* 9 *of the noun*). ◆***interj.*** I agree! I shall do it! Right!: *used only in everyday talk.* —☆**check in,** to write one's name on a list as a guest at a hotel, convention, etc. —☆**check out,** **1** to settle one's bill and leave a hotel. **2** to add up the prices of things bought, as in a supermarket, and collect the amount owed. **3** to turn out to be right or true [Did his story *check out?*] —☆**check up on,** to try to learn the facts about; investigate. —**in check,** under control [Try to keep your temper *in check.*] —**check′er** ***n.***

☆**check·book** (chek′bo͝ok) ***n.*** a book that holds forms for writing checks (*meaning* 7).

**check·er** (chek′ər) ***n.*** **1** a small square, as on a checkerboard. **2** one of the flat, round pieces used in playing checkers. ◆***v.*** to mark off in squares of different colors or shades [Orchards and farm fields *checker* the landscape.]

**check·er·board** (chek′ər bôrd) ***n.*** a board divided into 64 squares of two colors, with no square the same color as the one next to it. It is used in the games of checkers and chess.

**check·ered** (chek′ərd) ***adj.*** **1** having a pattern of squares. *See the picture.* **2** broken up into many parts, some of them unpleasant; full of ups and downs [a *checkered* career].

**check·ers** (chek′ərz) ***n.pl.*** a game played on a checkerboard by two players, each of whom tries to capture all 12 pieces of the other player: *used with a singular verb.*

**check·mate** (chek′māt) ***n.*** **1** the winning move in chess that ends the game by putting the opponent's king in a position where it cannot be saved; also, such a position. **2** a condition in which one is completely stopped or defeated. ◆***v.*** to place in checkmate; defeat completely. —**check′mat·ed, check′mat·ing**

Chess was probably first played in India, but it spread quickly to other countries, including Persia. **Checkmate** comes from two Persian words meaning "the king is dead."

☆**check·out** (chek′out) ***n.*** the act or place of checking out, as in a supermarket.

**check·point** (chek′point) ***n.*** a place where traffic is stopped, as for checking by the police.

☆**check·room** (chek′ro͞om) ***n.*** a room where hats, coats, baggage, etc. may be left in safekeeping for a time.

☆**check·up** (chek′up) ***n.*** an examination of something to find out its condition, especially a complete medical examination of a person.

**cheek** (chēk) ***n.*** **1** the side of the face between the nose and the ear and below the eye. **2** the kind of boldness that shows no respect; impudence: *used only in everyday talk* [They had the *cheek* to push into line ahead of us.]



**cheep** (chēp) ***n.*** the short, high, thin sound of a young bird; peep. ◆***v.*** to make such a sound.

**cheer** (chir) ***n.*** **1** a glad, excited shout of welcome, joy, or approval [The crowd gave the team three *cheers.*] **2** good or glad feelings; joy, hope, etc. [a visit that brought *cheer* to the invalid]. ◆***v.*** **1** to make or become glad or hopeful [Things are getting better, so *cheer* up!] **2** to urge on or applaud with cheers. —**be of good cheer,** to be glad or hopeful.

**cheer·ful** (chir′fəl) ***adj.*** **1** full of cheer; glad; joyful [a *cheerful* smile]. **2** bright and gay [a *cheerful* room]. **3** willing; glad to help [a *cheerful* worker]. —**cheer′ful·ly** ***adv.*** —**cheer′ful·ness** ***n.***

☆**cheer·lead·er** (chir′lē′dər) ***n.*** a person who leads others in cheering, as for a football team.

**cheer·less** (chir′lis) ***adj.*** not cheerful; sad; dreary [a *cheerless,* rainy Monday]. —**cheer′less·ly** ***adv.***

**cheer·y** (chir′ē) ***adj.*** cheerful; lively and happy [They gave us a *cheery* welcome.] —**cheer′i·er, cheer′i·est** —**cheer′i·ly** ***adv.*** —**cheer′i·ness** ***n.***

**cheese** (chēz) ***n.*** a solid food made by pressing together curds of soured milk.

**cheese·cloth** (chēz′klôth) ***n.*** a thin cotton cloth with a very loose weave.

| | | | |
|---|---|---|---|
| **a** fat | **ir** here | **ou** out | **zh** leisure |
| **ā** ape | **ī** bite, fire | **u** up | **ng** ring |
| **ä** car, lot | **ō** go | **ur** fur | a *in* ago |
| **e** ten | **ô** law, horn | **ch** chin | e *in* agent |
| **er** care | **oi** oil | **sh** she | ə = i *in* unity |
| **ē** even | **oo** look | **th** thin | o *in* collect |
| **i** hit | **o͞o** tool | ***th*** then | u *in* focus |

**chee·tah** (chē′tə) ***n.*** an animal found in Africa and southern Asia that is like the leopard but smaller. It can be trained to hunt. *See the picture.*



**chef** (shef) ***n.*** **1** a head cook, as in a restaurant. **2** any cook.

**Che·khov** (chek′ôf), **An·ton** (än tôn′) 1860–1904; Russian writer of plays and short stories.

**chem.** *abbreviation for* **chemical** *or* **chemistry.**

**chem·i·cal** (kem′i k'l) ***adj.*** **1** of or in chemistry [a *chemical* process]. **2** made by or used in chemistry [*chemical* compounds]. ◆***n.*** any substance used in chemistry or got by a chemical process [Various *chemicals* are used in making plastics.] —**chem′i·cal·ly** ***adv.***

**che·mise** (shə mēz′) ***n.*** a kind of loose undergarment like a slip, that women used to wear.

**chem·ist** (kem′ist) ***n.*** **1** an expert in chemistry. **2** a druggist: *a British meaning.*

**chem·is·try** (kem′is trē) ***n.*** the science in which substances are examined to find out what they are made of, how they act under different conditions, and how they are combined or separated to form other substances.

**chem·o·ther·a·py** (kē′mō ther′ə pē *or* kem′ə ther′ə pē) ***n.*** the use of chemical drugs to treat certain illnesses or diseases.

**cheque** (chek) ***n.*** *the British spelling of* **check** (*in meaning* 7).

**cher·ish** (cher′ish) ***v.*** **1** to treat with love or care; hold dear; take good care of [to *cherish* one's family; to *cherish* one's rights]. **2** to keep firmly in the mind; cling to the idea or feeling of [I *cherish* the hope that they will be friends again.]

**Cher·o·kee** (cher′ə kē) ***n.*** a member of a tribe of Indians most of whom were moved from the southeastern U.S. to Oklahoma. —*pl.* **Cher′o·kees** or **Cher′o·kee**

**cher·ry** (cher′ē) ***n.*** **1** a small, round fruit with sweet flesh covering a smooth, hard seed. Cherries are bright red, dark red, or yellow. **2** the tree that this fruit grows on. **3** the wood of this tree. **4** bright red. —*pl.* **cher′ries**

**cher·ub** (cher′əb) ***n.*** **1** a kind of angel mentioned in the Bible. A cherub is usually shown in pictures as a chubby child with little wings. **2** any child with a sweet, innocent face. —*pl.* **cher′ubs** or, for meaning 1, usually **cher·u·bim** (cher′ə bim)

**che·ru·bic** (chə rōō′bik) ***adj.*** of or like a cherub; plump and sweet-looking [a *cherubic* face].

**Ches·a·peake Bay** (ches′ə pēk) a bay of the Atlantic Ocean that reaches into Maryland and Virginia.

**Chesh·ire cat** (chesh′ir) a grinning cat in *Alice's Adventures in Wonderland,* that fades away leaving only its grin. *See the picture.*

**chess** (ches) ***n.*** a game played on a chessboard by two players. Each has 16 pieces (called **chess′men**) which are moved in trying to capture the other's pieces and checkmate the other's king.

**chess·board** (ches′bôrd) ***n.*** the board used in playing chess. It is the same as a checkerboard.

**chest** (chest) ***n.*** **1** a heavy box with a lid, for storing or shipping things. **2** a piece of furniture with drawers; bureau: *also called* **chest of drawers.** **3** the part of the body inside the ribs; also, the outside front part of this [a cold in the *chest;* a bruise on the child's *chest*].

**chest·nut** (ches′nut) ***n.*** **1** a dark-brown nut with a smooth, thin shell and a prickly husk. It is usually eaten cooked or roasted. *See the picture.* **2** the tree of the beech family that this nut grows on. **3** the wood of this tree. **4** reddish brown. ☆**5** an old, stale joke, story, etc.: *used only in everyday talk.*

**chev·i·ot** (shev′ē ət) ***n.*** a rough woolen cloth that is woven with raised diagonal lines.

**chev·ron** (shev′rən) ***n.*** a piece of cloth shaped like an upside-down V, sewn on the sleeve of a military or police uniform to show rank.

**chew** (chōō) ***v.*** **1** to bite and grind up with the teeth. **2** to think or talk about for a while [We *chewed* the problem over.] ◆***n.*** something chewed or for chewing. —☆**chew out,** to scold sharply: *a slang phrase.*

☆**chewing gum** a gummy substance, such as chicle, flavored and sweetened for chewing.

☆**che·wink** (chi wiŋk′) ***n.*** a small North American bird that nests on the ground and has a cry that sounds like its name.

**chew·y** (chōō′ē) ***adj.*** needing much chewing [*chewy* candy]. —**chew′i·er, chew′i·est**

**Chey·enne**[1] (shī en′ *or* shī an′) ***n.*** a member of a tribe of Indians from the area of Minnesota, now living mainly in Montana and Oklahoma. —*pl.* **Chey·ennes′** or **Chey·enne′**

**Chey·enne**[2] (shī an′ *or* shī en′) the capital of Wyoming.

**chg.** *abbreviation for* **charge.** —*pl.* **chgs.**

**chgd.** *abbreviation for* **charged.**

**chic** (shēk) ***adj.*** stylish in a pleasing way; up-to-date and attractive [a *chic* new gown].

**Chi·ca·go** (shə kä′gō *or* shə kô′gō) a city in northeastern Illinois, on Lake Michigan.

**chi·can·er·y** (shi kān′ər ē) ***n.*** the use of clever but tricky talk or acts to fool or confuse people.

☆**Chi·ca·no** (chi kä′nō) ***n.*** an American whose family is Mexican but who lives in the U.S. —*pl.* **Chi·ca′nos**

**chick** (chik) ***n.*** **1** a young chicken. **2** any young bird.

☆**chick·a·dee** (chik′ə dē) ***n.*** a small, gray bird with a black cap and throat. *See the picture.*

**chick·en** (chik′ən) ***n.*** **1** a common farm bird raised for its eggs and flesh; hen or rooster, especially a young one. **2** the flesh of a chicken. **3** a timid or cowardly person: *slang in this meaning.* ◆***adj.*** afraid or cowardly: *slang in this meaning.*

**chick·en-heart·ed** (chik′ən här′tid) ***adj.*** afraid to take a chance; timid or cowardly.

**chicken pox** a children's disease in which there is a mild fever and small blisters form on the skin.

**chick·weed** (chik′wēd) ***n.*** a common weed with small, oval leaves and tiny, white flowers.

☆**chic·le** (chik′'l) ***n.*** a gummy substance made from the sap of a tropical American tree. It is used in making chewing gum.

**chic·o·ry** (chik′ə rē) ***n.*** **1** a plant with blue flowers and with leaves that look like those of the dandelion. **2** the root of this plant, which is sometimes roasted, ground, and mixed with coffee.

**chide** (chīd) ***v.*** to scold, especially in a mild way [He *chided* the children for being messy.] —**chid′ed** or **chid** (chid), **chid′ing**

**chief** (chēf) ***n.*** the leader or head of some group [an Indian *chief;* the *chief* of a hospital staff]. ◆***adj.*** **1** having the highest position [the *chief* foreman]. **2** main; most important [Jill's *chief* interest is golf.] —**in chief,** in the highest position; with the most authority [commander *in chief*].

☆**Chief Executive** the President of the U.S.

**chief justice** the judge who is in charge of a court made up of several judges [The *Chief Justice* of the U.S. is the judge in charge of the Supreme Court.]

**chief·ly** (chēf′lē) ***adv.*** most of all; mainly; mostly [A watermelon is *chiefly* water.]

**chief·tain** (chēf′tən) ***n.*** a leader or chief, especially of a clan or tribe.

**chif·fon** (shi fän′) ***n.*** a thin, soft cloth as of silk or nylon. ◆***adj.*** made light and fluffy by adding beaten egg whites [a lemon *chiffon* pie].

**chig·ger** (chig′ər) ***n.*** the tiny, red larva of certain mites, or a kind of flea, that gets under the skin and causes itching.

**Chi·hua·hua** (chi wä′wä) ☆***n.*** a very small dog with large, pointed ears. The breed originally came from Mexico. *See the picture.*

**chil·blain** (chil′blān) ***n.*** a painful, red swelling on the feet or hands that a person sometimes gets from being out too long in freezing weather.

**child** (chīld) ***n.*** **1** a baby; infant. **2** a young boy or girl. **3** a son or daughter [Their *children* are all grown up.] —*pl.* **chil′dren** —**child's play,** a very simple thing to do. —**child′less *adj.***

**child·birth** (chīld′burth) ***n.*** the act of giving birth to a child.

**child·hood** (chīld′hood) ***n.*** the time of being a child [I've known her since my *childhood.*]

**child·ish** (chīld′ish) ***adj.*** **1** of or fit for a child [*childish* games]. **2** more like a child's than a grown-up's; foolish, too simple, etc. [What a *childish* reason for wanting to leave!] —**child′ish·ly *adv.*** —**child′ish·ness *n.***

**child·like** (chīld′līk) ***adj.*** like a child, especially in being innocent, trusting, etc. [a *childlike* pleasure in simple things].

**chil·dren** (chil′drən) ***n.*** *plural of* **child.**

**Chil·e** (chil′ē) a country on the southwestern coast of South America. —**Chil′e·an *adj., n.***

☆**chil·i** (chil′ē) ***n.*** **1** the dried pod of red pepper, used as a very hot seasoning. —*pl.* **chil′ies** **2** *same as* **chili con carne.** *Also spelled* **chil′e.**

☆**chil·i con car·ne** (chil′ē kən kär′nē) a Mexican food made with ground beef, red peppers, spices, and usually beans: *also spelled* **chile con carne.**

☆**chili sauce** a sauce of chopped tomatoes, green and red sweet peppers, spices, etc.

**chill** (chil) ***n.*** **1** a feeling of coldness that makes one shiver. **2** a coolness that is uncomfortable [There's a *chill* in the air.] ◆***adj.*** *same as* **chilly.** ◆***v.*** **1** to make or become cool or cold [Melons taste better if they are *chilled.*] **2** to cause a chill in [The evening breeze *chilled* us.]

**chil·ly** (chil′ē) ***adj.*** **1** so cool as to be uncomfortable; rather cold [a *chilly* room]. **2** not friendly [a *chilly* smile]. —**chil′li·er, chil′li·est**

> SYNONYMS: **Chilly, cold,** and **frigid** all refer to low temperatures, but **cold** suggests a lack of warmth that makes one uncomfortable [a sunny but *cold* January day], while **chilly** suggests only slight coolness that causes a little discomfort [It's *chilly* in the shade.] **Frigid** refers to freezing temperatures that cause numbness or pain [the *frigid* waters of the icy lake].



**chime** (chīm) ***n.*** **1** a bell or metal tube that is part of a set of bells or tubes on which tunes can be played. **2 chimes,** *pl.* the sounds made by such bells or tubes. **3** a single bell struck by a small hammer, as in a clock. ◆***v.*** to ring, as a chime or chimes. —**chimed, chim′ing** —**chime in, 1** to join in. **2** to agree.

**Chi·me·ra** (ki mir′ə *or* kī mir′ə) ***n.*** **1** a monster in Greek myths that breathed fire and was part lion, part goat, and part serpent. *See the picture.* **2 chimera,** any imaginary monster or any foolish or wild idea. —**chi·mer·i·cal** (ki mir′i k'l *or* ki mer′i k'l) ***adj.***

**chim·ney** (chim′nē) ***n.*** **1** a pipe or shaft going up through a roof to carry off smoke from a furnace, fireplace, or stove. Chimneys are usually enclosed with brick or stone. **2** a glass tube around the flame of a lamp. —*pl.* **chim′neys**

**chim·pan·zee** (chim′pan zē′ *or* chim pan′zē) ***n.*** an ape of Africa that is smaller than a gorilla and is a very intelligent animal: *the word is often shortened to* **chimp** (chimp). *See the picture on page 127.*

**chin** (chin) ***n.*** the part of the face below the lower lip; front part of the lower jaw. ◆***v.*** ☆to pull oneself up,

| | | | | | | | |
|---|---|---|---|---|---|---|---|
| **a** | fat | **ir** | here | **ou** | out | **zh** | leisure |
| **ā** | ape | **ī** | bite, fire | **u** | up | **ng** | ring |
| **ä** | car, lot | **ō** | go | **ur** | fur | | a *in* ago |
| **e** | ten | **ô** | law, horn | **ch** | chin | | e *in* agent |
| **er** | care | **oi** | oil | **sh** | she | **ə** = | i *in* unity |
| **ē** | even | **oo** | look | **th** | thin | | o *in* collect |
| **i** | hit | **ōō** | tool | ***th*** | then | | u *in* focus |

**C**

while hanging by the hands from a bar, until the chin is just above the bar. *See the picture.* —**chinned, chin′ning**

**Chin.** *abbreviation for* **China** *or* **Chinese.**

**Chi·na** (chī′nə) a country in eastern Asia. It has the most people of any country in the world.

**chi·na** (chī′nə) ***n.*** **1** a fine kind of porcelain that was first made in China. **2** dishes or ornaments made of this. **3** any dishes made of earthenware. *Also called* **chi·na·ware** (chī′nə wer).

☆**chinch bug** (chinch) a small, black bug with white wings that damages grain plants.

**chin·chil·la** (chin chil′ə) ***n.*** **1** a small, ratlike animal found in the Andes Mountains in South America. **2** its soft, gray fur, which is very expensive. **3** a heavy wool cloth with a rough surface, used for making coats.

**Chi·nese** (chī nēz′) ***n.*** **1** a member of a people whose native country is China. *—pl.* **Chi·nese′** **2** the language of China. ◆***adj.*** of China, its people, language, or culture.

**Chinese checkers** a game like checkers for two to six players. It is played on a board with a star-shaped pattern of holes in which marbles are placed and then moved from hole to hole.

**Chinese lantern** a lantern made of brightly colored paper. It can be folded flat when not in use.

**chink**[1] (chiŋgk) ***n.*** a narrow opening; crack. ◆***v.*** to fill the chinks in.

**chink**[2] (chiŋgk) ***n.*** a sharp, clinking sound like that made by coins striking together. ◆***v.*** to make this sound or cause to make this sound.

**chi·no** (chē′nō) ***n.*** **1** a strong cotton cloth used for work clothes or sports clothes. **2 chinos,** *pl.* pants made of chino. *—pl.* **chi′nos**

☆**chi·nook** (shi no͞ok′ *or* chi no͞ok′) ***n.*** **1** a warm, moist wind that blows in from the sea onto the coast of Oregon and Washington. **2** a dry wind that comes down the eastern slope of the Rocky Mountains.

**chintz** (chints) ***n.*** a cotton cloth printed in colors and usually having a firm, glossy surface.

> **Chintz** comes from a word in Sanskrit, a very old language of India. The Sanskrit word means "spotted" or "bright." The cloth is brightly colored and covered with flower designs or other patterns.

**chip** (chip) ***v.*** **1** to break or cut a small piece or thin slice from [Who *chipped* that cup?] **2** to break off into small pieces [This glass *chips* easily.] **3** to make by cutting or chopping as with an ax or chisel [*Chip* a hole in the ice.] —**chipped, chip′ping** ◆***n.*** **1** a small, thin piece broken or cut off [Potato *chips* are thin slices of potato fried until they are crisp.] **2** a place where a small piece has been chipped off [a *chip* in the edge of a plate]. **3** a small, round disk used in gambling games in place of money. —☆**chip in,** to share in giving money or help: *used only in everyday talk.* —**chip off the old block,** a person who looks or acts much like one of his or her parents. —☆**chip on one's shoulder,** a readiness to fight or quarrel: *used only in everyday talk.*

**chip·munk** (chip′muŋgk) ***n.*** a small squirrel of North America with striped markings on its head and back. Chipmunks live in holes in the ground. *See the picture.*

**chip·per** (chip′ər) ***adj.*** feeling healthy and cheerful: *used only in everyday talk.*

**chi·rop·o·dist** (kə räp′ə dist) ***n.*** *an earlier name for* **podiatrist.**

☆**chi·ro·prac·tor** (kī′rə prak′tər) ***n.*** a person who practices a system of treating diseases by pressing and moving the spine and the joints of the body with the hands.

**chirp** (churp) ***v.*** to make the short, shrill sound of some birds or insects. ◆***n.*** this sound.

**chis·el** (chiz″l) ***n.*** a tool having a strong blade with a sharp edge for cutting or shaping wood, stone, or metal. *See the picture.* ◆***v.*** **1** to cut or shape with a chisel. **2** to get something by cheating: *used only in everyday talk.* —**chis′eled** or **chis′elled, chis′el·ing** or **chis′el·ling** —**chis′el·er** or **chis′el·ler** ***n.***

**chit·chat** (chit′chat) ***n.*** light talk about common, everyday things; small talk.

**chit·ter·lings** (chit′lənz) ***n.pl.*** the small intestines of pigs prepared as food, usually by frying: *also sometimes spelled* **chit′lins** or **chit′lings.**

**chiv·al·rous** (shiv″l rəs) ***adj.*** helping the weak and showing great courtesy to women as the knights of old were supposed to do; gallant, polite, kind, etc. —**chiv′al·rous·ly *adv.***

**chiv·al·ry** (shiv″l rē) ***n.*** **1** the way of life followed by the knights of the Middle Ages. **2** the noble qualities a knight was supposed to have, such as courage, honor, and a readiness to help the weak and protect women.

**chives** (chīvz) ***n.pl.*** a plant related to the onion, having slender, hollow leaves that are chopped up and used for flavoring. *See the picture.*

☆**chlor·dane** (klôr′dān) ***n.*** an oily chemical that is a strong poison and is used to kill insects, especially grubs in the soil.

**chlo·ride** (klôr′īd) ***n.*** a chemical compound of chlorine and another element or elements [Sodium *chloride,* formed of sodium and chlorine, is common table salt.]

**chlo·ri·nate** (klôr′ə nāt) ***v.*** to add chlorine to in order to make pure [to *chlorinate* drinking water]. —**chlo′ri·nat·ed, chlo′ri·nat·ing**

**chlo·rine** (klôr′ēn) ***n.*** a greenish-yellow, poisonous gas that is a chemical element. It is used in bleaches and for making water pure.

**chlo·ro·form** (klôr′ə fôrm) ***n.*** a sweetish, colorless liquid that changes into a vapor quickly and easily. In earlier times, it was used by doctors to make a patient unconscious, as before an operation. ◆***v.*** **1** to make unconscious by giving chloroform. **2** to kill with chloroform [to *chloroform* butterflies before putting them into a collection].

**chlo·ro·phyll** or **chlo·ro·phyl** (klôr′ə fil) ***n.*** the green coloring matter in plants. Sunlight causes it to change carbon dioxide and water into the carbohydrates that are the food of the plant.

**chock** (chäk) ***n.*** a block or wedge placed under a wheel, barrel, etc. to keep it from rolling. ◆***v.*** to hold steady with a chock.

**chock-full** (chäk′fool′ *or* chuk′fool′) ***adj.*** as full as possible [a carton *chock-full* of books].

**choc·o·late** (chôk′lət *or* chäk′ə lət) ***n.*** **1** a paste, powder, syrup, or bar made from cacao seeds that have been roasted and ground. **2** a drink made of chocolate, sugar, and milk or water. **3** a candy made of chocolate or covered with chocolate. **4** reddish brown. ◆***adj.*** made of or flavored with chocolate.

**choice** (chois) ***n.*** **1** the act of choosing or picking; selection [You may have a dessert of your own *choice.*] **2** the right or chance to choose [You have no *choice* in the matter since seats will be assigned.] **3** a person or thing chosen [Green is my *choice* for mayor.] **4** a group of things from which to choose [We have a *choice* of three movies to see.] ◆***adj.*** **1** very good; of the best kind [*choice* fruits]. **2** describing a grade of meat that is lower than prime [*choice* beef]. —**choic′er, choic′est**

SYNONYMS: **Choice** refers to a person's right or chance to pick out whatever is wanted from a number of things [It was your own *choice;* no one forced you to go.] **Option** refers to a right to choose that is given to a person by someone in authority [The judge gave the guilty person the *option* of going to jail or paying a large fine.]

**choir** (kwīr) ***n.*** **1** a group of people trained to sing together, especially as part of a church service. **2** the part of a church where the choir sits or stands.

**choke** (chōk) ***v.*** **1** to keep from breathing by blocking the windpipe or squeezing the throat; strangle; suffocate. **2** to have a hard time breathing [The thick smoke made me *choke.*] **3** to block up a passage; clog [Heavy traffic *choked* the main roads.] **4** to hold back the growth or action of; smother [Weeds are *choking* the grass in the lawn.] **5** to cut off some air from a carburetor so as to make a richer gasoline mixture, as in cold weather. ☆**6** to hold a bat, golf club, etc. away from the end and closer toward the middle of the handle. —**choked, chok′ing** ◆***n.*** **1** the act or sound of choking. **2** the valve that chokes a carburetor. —**choke back,** to hold back, as sobs or tears. —**choke down,** to swallow with difficulty [to *choke down* a medicine]. —**choke off,** to bring to an end; stop. —**choke up, 1** to block up; clog. **2** to be unable to speak or act normally, as because of fear, sadness, or nervousness: *used only in everyday talk.*

**chok·er** (chōk′ər) ***n.*** **1** a thing that chokes. **2** a necklace that fits closely around the neck. *See the picture.*

**chol·er** (käl′ər) ***n.*** great anger: *an old-fashioned word.*

**chol·er·a** (käl′ər ə) ***n.*** a deadly disease that spreads quickly, as a plague, especially in places where sanitation is poor.

**chol·er·ic** (käl′ər ik *or* kə ler′ik) ***adj.*** easily made angry; having a quick temper.

**cho·les·ter·ol** (kə les′tə rōl) ***n.*** a waxy substance found in the body and in certain foods. When there is much of it in the blood, it is thought to cause hardening of the arteries.

**chomp** (chämp) ***v.*** to chew hard and noisily.

**choose** (cho͞oz) ***v.*** **1** to pick out one or more from a number or group [*Choose* a subject from this list.] **2** to make up one's mind; decide or prefer [She *chose* to stay home.] —**chose, cho′sen, choos′ing**

☆**choos·y** or **choos·ey** (cho͞o′zē) ***adj.*** very careful or fussy in choosing: *used only in everyday talk.* —**choos′i·er, choos′i·est**

**chop** (chäp) ***v.*** **1** to cut by strokes with an ax or

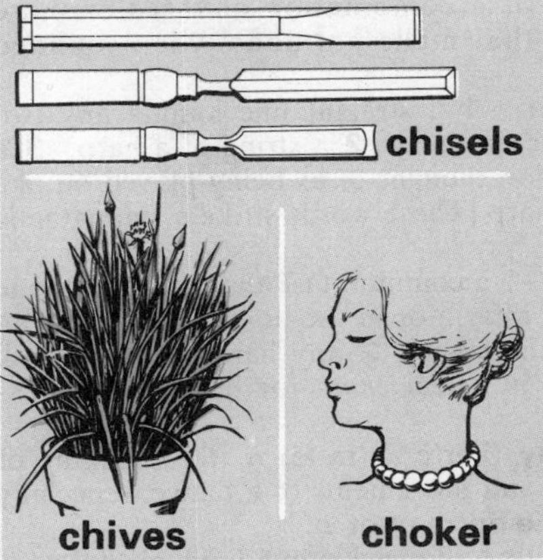

chisels

chives

choker

girl chinning herself

chimpanzee

1.4 m (4 1/2 ft.) tall

chipmunk

23 cm (9 in.) long, including tail

other sharp tool [to *chop* down a tree]. **2** to make a short, quick stroke [The batter *chopped* at the ball.] **3** to cut into small bits [to *chop* up an onion]. —**chopped, chop′ping** ◆***n.*** **1** a short, quick stroke or blow [a karate *chop*]. **2** a slice of lamb, pork, or veal cut with a piece of bone from the rib, loin, or shoulder. *See the picture on page 129.*

**Cho·pin** (shō′pan), **Frédéric** (fred′ər ik) 1810–1849; a Polish composer and pianist who lived in France.

**chop·per** (chäp′ər) ***n.*** **1** a person or thing that chops. ☆**2** a helicopter: *used only in everyday talk.*

**chop·py** (chäp′ē) ***adj.*** **1** having many small, rough waves [A strong wind made the lake *choppy.*] **2** short and quick; not smooth and graceful; jerky [He runs with a *choppy* stride.] —**chop′pi·er, chop′pi·est**

**chops** (chäps) ***n.pl.*** the flesh around the mouth [The dog licked its *chops* after eating.]

**chop·sticks** (chäp′stiks) ***n.pl.*** a pair of small sticks used as in some Asian countries to lift food to the mouth. *See the picture on page 129.*

☆**chop su·ey** (chäp′ so͞o′ē) a mixture of bits of meat, bean sprouts, mushrooms, etc. cooked in a sauce and served with rice. Chop suey was first made by Chinese in America.

**cho·ral** (kôr′əl) ***adj.*** **1** of or for a choir or chorus. **2** sung or recited by a choir or chorus.

**cho·rale** or **cho·ral** (kə ral′ *or* kô ral′) ***n.*** **1** a simple hymn tune or a choral work based on such a tune. **2** a group of singers; choir.

| | | | | | | | |
|---|---|---|---|---|---|---|---|
| **a** | fat | **ir** | here | **ou** | out | **zh** | leisure |
| **ā** | ape | **ī** | bite, fire | **u** | up | **ng** | ring |
| **ä** | car, lot | **ō** | go | **ur** | fur | | a *in* ago |
| **e** | ten | **ô** | law, horn | **ch** | chin | | e *in* agent |
| **er** | care | **oi** | oil | **sh** | she | **ə** = | i *in* unity |
| **ē** | even | **oo** | look | **th** | thin | | o *in* collect |
| **i** | hit | **o͞o** | tool | ***th*** | then | | u *in* focus |

**C**

**chord**[1] (kôrd) ***n.*** a combination of three or more musical tones that make harmony when sounded together.

**chord**[2] (kôrd) ***n.*** **1** a straight line joining any two points on an arc or circle. **2** a string of a harp. **3** a feeling or emotion thought of as being played on like the string of a harp [Those words strike a sympathetic *chord* in me.]

**chore** (chôr) ***n.*** **1** a common task that has to be done regularly, as on a farm or in the home [Her *chores* include mowing the lawn.] **2** any hard or boring task [Writing letters is a real *chore* for him.] *See* SYNONYMS *at* **task**.

**chor·e·og·ra·phy** (kôr'ē äg'rə fē) ***n.*** the planning of the dance steps and movements of a dance, especially a ballet. —**chor'e·og'ra·pher** ***n.***

**chor·tle** (chôr't'l) ***v.*** to chuckle in a loud, gleeful way. —**chor'tled, chor'tling**

Lewis Carroll, the author of *Alice's Adventures in Wonderland,* realized that people sometimes show delight by making a sound that is part chuckle and part snort. There was no name for that sound, so he took letters from the words *chuckle* and *snort* and made up the word **chortle.**

**chor·us** (kôr'əs) ***n.*** **1** a group of people trained to speak or sing together [Ancient Greek plays usually had a *chorus* which explained what the actors were doing.] **2** music to be sung by a chorus ["The Anvil *Chorus*" is a famous song from an Italian opera]. **3** singers and dancers who work together as a group and not as soloists, as in a musical show. **4** a number of voices speaking at once [The teacher was answered by a *chorus* of eager replies.] **5** the part of a song that is repeated after each verse; refrain [The *chorus* of "The Battle Hymn of the Republic" begins "Glory, glory, hallelujah!"] •***v.*** to speak or sing together or at the same time [The Senators *chorused* their approval.] —**in chorus,** all at once; together.



**chose** (chōz) *past tense of* **choose.**

**cho·sen** (chō'z'n) *past participle of* **choose.** •***adj.*** picked out carefully, as for a special purpose [A *chosen* few soldiers formed the king's guard.]

**chow** (chou) ***n.*** **1** a dog that was first bred in China, with a thick, brown or black coat and a black tongue. *See the picture.* ☆**2** food or mealtime: *slang in this meaning.*

☆**chow·der** (chou'dər) ***n.*** a thick soup made of fish or clams with onions, potatoes, milk or tomatoes, etc.

☆**chow mein** (chou mān') a mixture of bits of meat, onions, celery, bean sprouts, etc. cooked in a sauce and served with fried noodles. Chow mein was first made by Chinese in America.

**Christ** (krīst) Jesus of Nazareth, regarded by Christians as the Messiah.

The title **Christ** is from the Greek word for "messiah," which comes from a Hebrew word. Both the Greek and Hebrew words actually mean "the anointed one." Kings of ancient Israel were anointed in a ceremony when they began to rule.

**chris·ten** (kris''n) ***v.*** **1** to baptize or give a name to at baptism [The baby was *christened* Leslie.] **2** to give a name to [We *christened* the boat Speedwell II.] —**chris'ten·ing** ***n.***

**Chris·ten·dom** (kris''n dəm) ***n.*** **1** all the Christian people. **2** those parts of the world where Christianity is the most common religion.

**Chris·tian** (kris'chən) ***n.*** a person who believes in Jesus as the Messiah and in the religion based on the teachings of Jesus. •***adj.*** **1** of Jesus or his teachings. **2** belonging to the religion based on these teachings. **3** having the qualities that Christians are supposed to have, as kindness, charity, and humbleness.

**Chris·ti·an·i·ty** (kris'chē an'ə tē) ***n.*** **1** the Christian religion. **2** all the Christian people.

**Chris·tian·ize** (kris'chə nīz) ***v.*** to make Christian. —**Chris'tian·ized, Chris'tian·iz·ing**

**Christian name** the name given at baptism, to go with the family name; first name.

**Christian Science** a religion and system of healing founded by Mary Baker Eddy in 1866. It teaches that sin, disease, and death are errors of the mind which proper thinking will correct.

**chris·tie** or **chris·ty** (kris'tē) ***n.*** a turn at high speed made by skiers to change direction or stop. —*pl.* **chris'ties**

**Christ·like** (krīst'līk) ***adj.*** like Jesus Christ, especially in character or spirit.

**Christ·mas** (kris'məs) ***n.*** a holiday on December 25 celebrating the birth of Jesus Christ.

☆**Christmas tree** an evergreen tree decorated with ornaments and lights at Christmas time.

**Chris·to·pher** (kris'tə fər), Saint a Christian martyr believed to have lived in the third century A.D. He has been thought of as the patron saint of travelers.

**chro·mat·ic** (krō mat'ik) ***adj.*** **1** of color or having color or colors. **2** in music, with a half tone between each note [There are 13 half tones in an octave of the *chromatic* scale.]

**chrome** (krōm) ***n.*** chromium, especially when it is used to plate steel or other metal.

**chro·mi·um** (krō'mē əm) ***n.*** a very hard metal that is a chemical element. It does not rust easily and is used in steel alloys and as a plating for metals. Chromium compounds are used in paints and dyes.

**chro·mo·some** (krō'mə sōm) ***n.*** any of certain tiny particles in the nucleus of cells. Chromosomes contain DNA and carry the genes that pass on the inherited characteristics of an animal or plant.

**chron·ic** (krän'ik) ***adj.*** **1** going on for a long time or coming back again and again [a *chronic* disease]. **2** having been one for a long time; constant or habitual [a *chronic* complainer; a *chronic* invalid]. —**chron'i·cal·ly** ***adv.***

**chron·i·cle** (krän'i k'l) ***n.*** a history or story; especially, a record of happenings in the order in which they happened. •***v.*** to tell or write the history of; record [to *chronicle* a voyage]. —**chron'i·cled, chron'i·cling** —**chron'i·cler** ***n.***

**Chron·i·cles** (krän'i k'lz) either of two books of the Bible.

**chron·o·log·i·cal** (krän'ə läj'i k'l) ***adj.*** **1** arranged in the order in which things happened [a *chronological* chart of English history]. **2** of chronology. —**chron'o·log'i·cal·ly** ***adv.***

**chro·nol·o·gy** (krə näl'ə jē) ***n.*** **1** the science of measuring time and of finding the correct dates for happenings. **2** arrangement of happenings in the order in which they happened. —*pl.* **chro·nol'o·gies**

**chro·nom·e·ter** (krə näm′ə tər) ***n.*** a very accurate clock or watch, as for scientific use.

**chrys·a·lis** (kris′'l əs) ***n.*** **1** the form of a butterfly when it is in a cocoon, between the time when it is a larva and the time when it is a winged adult. **2** the cocoon.

**chrys·an·the·mum** (kri san′thə məm) ***n.*** **1** a plant with round flowers that bloom in the late summer and fall. It is grown in a variety of sizes and colors, such as yellow, white, red, or purple. **2** any of these flowers. *See the picture.*

**Chrysanthemum** comes from a Greek word meaning "golden flower." It seems clear that the original plant must have had gold-colored blossoms.

**chrys·o·lite** (kris′ə līt) ***n.*** a green or yellow stone sometimes used as a gem.

**chub·by** (chub′ē) ***adj.*** round and plump. *See the picture.* —**chub′bi·er, chub′bi·est** —**chub′bi·ness *n.***

**chuck**[1] (chuk) ***v.*** **1** to tap or pat under the chin in a gentle, playful way. **2** to throw with a quick, short toss. **3** to get rid of: *used only in everyday talk.* ◆***n.*** **1** a gentle tap under the chin. **2** a toss. **3** food: *used chiefly in the West.*

**chuck**[2] (chuk) ***n.*** a cut of beef from the shoulder, between the neck and the ribs.

**chuck·le** (chuk′'l) ***v.*** to laugh softly in a low tone. *See* SYNONYMS *at* **laugh.** —**chuck′led, chuck′ling** ◆***n.*** a soft laugh.

☆**chuck wagon** a wagon with kitchen equipment for serving food to cowboys or other outdoor workers.

☆**chug** (chug) ***n.*** a short, exploding sound, such as that made by steam escaping from a steam engine. ◆***v.*** to move while making such sounds [The train *chugged* up the hill.] —**chugged, chug′ging**

**chum** (chum) ***n.*** a close friend. ◆***v.*** to go about together, as close friends do. —**chummed, chum′ming** *This word is used only in everyday talk.*

In British boarding schools of the 17th century, students who roomed together were called "chamber mates." In student slang the word was shortened to *cham,* and from that comes the word **chum.**

**chum·my** (chum′ē) ***adj.*** very friendly; like a chum: *used only in everyday talk.* —**chum′mi·er, chum′mi·est** —**chum′mi·ness *n.***

**Chung·king** (choong′king′) a city in central China, on the Yangtze River.

**chunk** (chungk) ***n.*** a short, thick piece [a *chunk* of meat]. —☆**chunk′y *adj.* chunk′i·er, chunk′i·est**

**church** (church) ***n.*** **1** a building for holding religious services, especially one for Christian worship. **2** religious services [*Church* will be at 11 on Sunday.] **3** all Christians as a group. **4** a particular group of Christians who have the same beliefs and forms of worship [the Methodist *Church*].

**Church·ill** (chur′chil), Sir **Win·ston** (win′stən) 1874–1965; the British prime minister from 1940 to 1945 and from 1951 to 1955.

**church·man** (church′mən) ***n.*** **1** a clergyman. **2** a church member. —*pl.* **church′men**

**Church of England** the Episcopal Church of England, that has the British monarch as its head.

**church·yard** (church′yärd) ***n.*** the yard around a church, often used as a burial ground.

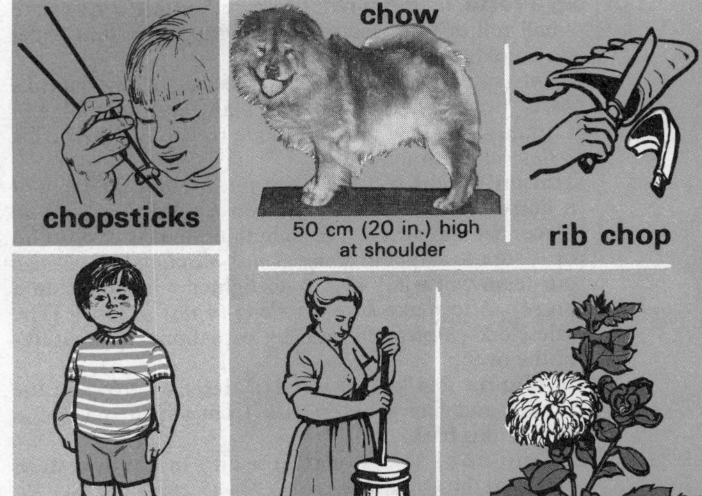


**churl** (churl) ***n.*** **1** a person of the lowest class in England long ago; peasant or rustic. **2** a person who is rude and bad-tempered. —**churl′ish *adj.*** —**churl′ish·ness *n.***



**churn** (churn) ***n.*** a container in which milk or cream is stirred hard or shaken to make butter. *See the picture.* ◆***v.*** **1** to stir or shake milk or cream in a churn so as to make butter. **2** to stir or move about with much force [The motorboats *churned* up the water of the lake.]

☆**chute**[1] (shōōt) ***n.*** **1** a part of a river where the water moves swiftly; also, a waterfall. **2** a tube or slide in which things are dropped or slid down to a lower place [We have a laundry *chute* going from the bedroom to the basement.]

**chute**[2] (shōōt) ***n.*** *a shortened form of* **parachute**: *used only in everyday talk.* —**chut′ist *n.***

**CIA** *abbreviation for* **Central Intelligence Agency.**

**ci·ca·da** (si kā′də) ***n.*** an insect that is like a large fly with transparent wings. The male makes a loud, shrill sound with a special organ on its underside.

**Cic·er·o** (sis′ə rō) 106–43 B.C.; a Roman statesman who was a famous orator.

**-cide** (sīd) *a suffix meaning* killer or killing [*Suicide* is the act of killing oneself.]

**ci·der** (sī′dər) ***n.*** juice pressed from apples, used as a drink or made into vinegar.

**ci·gar** (si gär′) ***n.*** a tight roll of tobacco leaves for smoking.

| | | | | | | | |
|---|---|---|---|---|---|---|---|
| a | fat | ir | here | ou | out | zh | leisure |
| ā | ape | ī | bite, fire | u | up | ng | ring |
| ä | car, lot | ō | go | ur | fur | | a *in* ago |
| e | ten | ô | law, horn | ch | chin | | e *in* agent |
| er | care | oi | oil | sh | she | ə = | i *in* unity |
| ē | even | oo | look | th | thin | | o *in* collect |
| i | hit | ōō | tool | *th* | then | | u *in* focus |

**cig·a·rette** or **cig·a·ret** (sig′ə ret′ *or* sig′ə ret) ***n.*** a small roll of finely cut tobacco wrapped in thin paper for smoking.

**cil·i·a** (sil′ē ə) ***n.pl.*** **1** the eyelashes. **2** fine hairlike parts growing out from some plant and animal cells. Certain one-celled animals move by waving their cilia. —*sing.* **cil·i·um** (sil′ē əm)

☆**cinch** (sinch) ***n.*** **1** a band put around the belly of a horse or other animal to keep a saddle or pack in place. *See the picture.* **2** something that is easy to do or is sure to happen: *slang in this meaning* [It's a *cinch* our team will win.] ◆***v.*** **1** to tighten a cinch, as on a horse. **2** to make sure of: *slang in this meaning* [The salesclerk *cinched* the sale by explaining the features of the oven.]

**cin·cho·na** (sin kō′nə) ***n.*** **1** a tree that grows in the tropics and has a bitter bark from which quinine is got. **2** this bark.

**Cin·cin·nat·i** (sin′sə nat′ē) a city in southwestern Ohio, on the Ohio River.

**cinc·ture** (singk′chər) ***n.*** a belt or girdle.

**cin·der** (sin′dər) ***n.*** **1** a tiny bit of partly burned coal, wood, or the like [The wind blew a *cinder* in his eye.] **2 cinders,** *pl.* the ashes from coal or wood.

**Cin·der·el·la** (sin′də rel′ə) a girl in a fairy tale who works hard in the house of her stepmother until her fairy godmother helps her to meet a prince, who marries her.

 **cin·e·ma** (sin′ə mə) ***n.*** **1** a movie; motion picture. **2** a movie theater. **3** the art or business of making movies. *Mainly a British word.*

**cin·na·mon** (sin′ə mən) ***n.*** **1** a light brown spice made from the inner bark of a tree that grows in the East Indies. **2** this bark or the tree it comes from. **3** a light yellowish or reddish brown.

**ci·pher** (sī′fər) ***n.*** **1** a zero; the symbol 0. **2** a person or thing that has no importance. **3** secret writing that can be understood only by those who have the key to it; code. **4** the key to such a code. ◆***v.*** to do arithmetic: *the verb is not much used today.*

**cir·ca** (sur′kə) ***prep.*** about: *used with figures or dates* [Euclid lived *circa* 300 B.C.]

**Cir·ce** (sur′sē) a witch in Homer's *Odyssey* who turns men into pigs.

**cir·cle** (sur′k′l) ***n.*** **1** a closed curved line forming a perfectly round, flat figure. Every point on this line is the same distance from a point inside called the center. *See the picture.* **2** the figure formed by such a line. **3** anything round like a circle or ring [a *circle* of children playing a game]. **4** any series that ends the way it began or is repeated over and over; cycle [Wash dishes, dirty them, wash them again—it's a tiresome *circle*.] **5** a group of people joined together by the same interests [a reading *circle* that studies great books]. ◆***v.*** **1** to form a circle around [The bystanders *circled* the flagpole.] **2** to move around, as in a circle [The planets *circle* the sun.] —**cir′cled, cir′cling**

**cir·clet** (sur′klit) ***n.*** **1** a small circle. **2** a round band worn as an ornament, especially on the head.

**cir·cuit** (sur′kit) ***n.*** **1** the act of going around something; course or journey in a circle [The moon's *circuit* of the earth takes about 28 days.] **2** the regular journey through a district of a person doing certain work; also, such a district [a judge's *circuit*]. **3** the line or distance around some area. **4** a group of theaters under the same owner or manager, at which movies, plays, etc. are shown first at one then at another. **5** the complete path of an electric current; also, any hookup, wiring, etc. that is connected into this path.

**cir·cu·i·tous** (sər kyoo′ə təs) ***adj.*** not straight or direct; roundabout [a *circuitous* explanation].

**cir·cu·lar** (sur′kyə lər) ***adj.*** **1** having the shape of a circle; round [a *circular* saw]. **2** moving in a circle [a *circular* railway]. ◆***n.*** a letter or advertisement that is prepared in many copies for sending to many people.

**cir·cu·late** (sur′kyə lāt) ***v.*** **1** to move in a regular course and return to the same point [Blood *circulates* through the body from the heart.] **2** to move or send about from person to person or place to place [That rumor has been *circulating* through the town.] —**cir′cu·lat·ed, cir′cu·lat·ing**

**cir·cu·la·tion** (sur′kyə lā′shən) ***n.*** **1** free movement around from place to place [The fan kept the air in *circulation*.] **2** the movement of blood through the veins and arteries. **3** the passing of something from person to person or place to place [Gold money is not in *circulation* in the U.S.] **4** the average number of copies of a magazine or newspaper sent out or sold in a certain period [Our school paper has a weekly *circulation* of 630.]

**cir·cu·la·to·ry** (sur′kyə lə tôr′ē) ***adj.*** having to do with circulation, as of the blood.

**circum-** *a prefix meaning* around, about, on all sides [To *circumnavigate* the earth means to sail or fly around it.]

**cir·cum·cise** (sur′kəm sīz) ***v.*** to cut off the foreskin of, either as a religious ceremony or for reasons of hygiene. —**cir′cum·cised, cir′cum·cis·ing** —**cir·cum·ci·sion** (sur′kəm sizh′ən) ***n.***

**cir·cum·fer·ence** (sər kum′fər əns) ***n.*** **1** the line that bounds a circle or other rounded figure or area. *See*

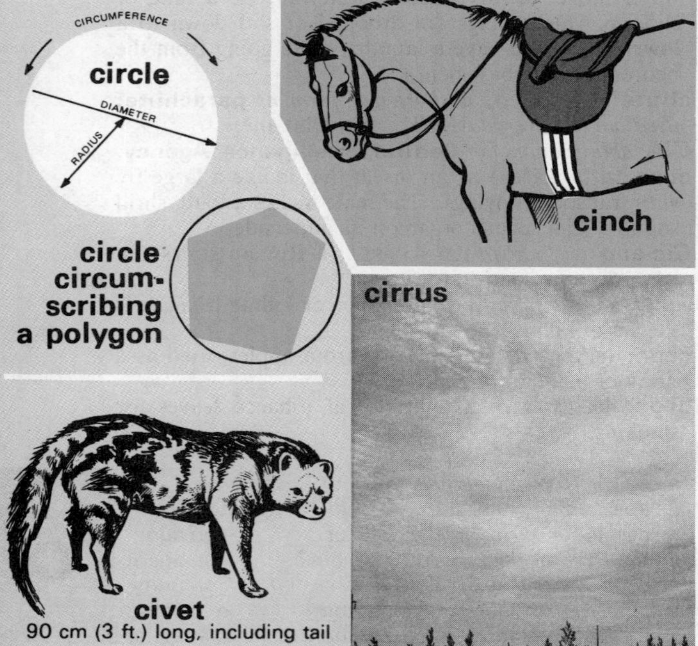

90 cm (3 ft.) long, including tail

*the picture for* **circle**. **2** the length of such a line [The *circumference* of the pool is 70 feet.]

**cir·cum·flex** (sur′kəm fleks) ***n.*** the mark ˆ, used in some French words to show the sound of a vowel. It is also used as a pronunciation mark in this dictionary, as in *story* (stôr′ē).

**cir·cum·lo·cu·tion** (sur′kəm lō kyo͞o′shən) ***n.*** a roundabout or long way of saying something ["To become the recipient of" is a *circumlocution* for "to get."]

**cir·cum·nav·i·gate** (sur′kəm nav′ə gāt) ***v.*** to sail or fly around [to *circumnavigate* the earth]. —**cir′cum·nav′i·gat·ed, cir′cum·nav′i·gat·ing** —**cir′cum·nav′i·ga′tion *n.***

**cir·cum·scribe** (sur′kəm skrīb) ***v.*** **1** to draw a line around or encircle; especially, to draw a figure around another figure so that they touch at as many points as possible [to *circumscribe* a circle with a pentagon]. *See the picture.* **2** to hold in closely; confine or restrict [Her interests were very *circumscribed* until she went to college.] —**cir′cum·scribed, cir′cum·scrib·ing**

**cir·cum·spect** (sur′kəm spekt) ***adj.*** careful to consider everything before acting, deciding, etc.; cautious; prudent [Be *circumspect* in choosing a partner.] —**cir′cum·spec′tion *n.***

**cir·cum·stance** (sur′kəm stans) ***n.*** **1** a fact or event connected in some way with a situation [What were the *circumstances* that led up to Smith's arrest?] **2** formal acts and showy display; ceremony [pomp and *circumstance*]. **3 circumstances,** *pl.* the condition in which one lives, especially with regard to money [They are in comfortable *circumstances*.] —**under no circumstances,** never; under no conditions. —**under the circumstances,** if one considers the special facts of the case.

**cir·cum·stan·tial** (sur′kəm stan′shəl) ***adj.*** based on certain circumstances or facts [The fingerprints on the gun are *circumstantial* evidence.]

**cir·cum·vent** (sur′kəm vent′) ***v.*** to get the better of a person or prevent a plan by using tricks or cleverness. —**cir′cum·ven′tion *n.***

**cir·cus** (sur′kəs) ***n.*** **1** a traveling show held in tents or in a hall, with clowns, trained animals, acrobats, etc. ☆**2** a very funny or entertaining person or thing: *used only in everyday talk.* **3** a stadium or arena in ancient Rome, where games or races were held.

When we speak of the center ring of a **circus,** we are repeating ourselves. The Greek word *kirkos,* from which we got **circus,** simply means "ring" or "circle." The words **circle** and **circulate** and the prefix **circum-** all come from the same Greek word.

**cir·rus** (sir′əs) ***n.*** a kind of cloud that looks like thin strips of woolly curls. *See the picture.* —*pl.* **cir′rus**

**cis·tern** (sis′tərn) ***n.*** a tank for storing water, especially rain water.

**cit·a·del** (sit′ə d′l *or* sit′ə del) ***n.*** **1** a fort on a high place, for defending a town. **2** a place of safety; refuge. [A free press is the *citadel* of democracy.]

**ci·ta·tion** (sī tā′shən) ***n.*** **1** an order to come to a law court [A traffic ticket for speeding is a *citation*.] **2** a telling or quoting of something written in a book, article, etc.; also, the piece of writing quoted. ☆**3** an official mention that praises [to receive a *citation* from the President for bravery in war].

**cite** (sīt) ***v.*** **1** to order to come to a law court [Jones was *cited* for bad brakes.] **2** to mention or quote [We are *citing* four books to prove our point.] ☆**3** to mention for praise [The brave Army nurse was *cited* in official reports.] —**cit′ed, cit′ing**

**cit·i·zen** (sit′ə zən) ***n.*** **1** a person who is a member of a country or state either because of being born there or having been made a member by law. Citizens have certain duties to their country and are entitled to certain rights. **2** a person who lives in a particular city or town [the *citizens* of Atlanta].

**cit·i·zen·ry** (sit′ə zən rē) ***n.*** all citizens as a group.

☆**citizens' band** a band of shortwave radio for use over short distances by private persons.

**cit·i·zen·ship** (sit′ə zən ship′) ***n.*** the condition of being a citizen; also, the rights and duties of a citizen [*Citizenship* includes the right to vote and the duty to serve on a jury.]

**cit·ric** (sit′rik) ***adj.*** having to do with, or coming from, citrus fruit [*Citric* acid is a weak acid found in oranges, lemons, etc.]

**cit·ron** (sit′rən) ***n.*** **1** a fruit that is like a large lemon with a thick skin. **2** the thorny tree that it grows on. **3** the candied peel of this fruit, used in cakes, puddings, etc.

**cit·ron·el·la** (si′trə nel′ə) ***n.*** a strong-smelling oil that changes into vapor easily. It is used in perfume, soap, insect sprays, etc.

**cit·rus** (sit′rəs) ***n.*** **1** any fruit of the family that includes oranges, lemons, limes, citrons, and grapefruit. **2** a tree on which such a fruit grows. ◆***adj.*** of these trees or fruits. *The adj. is sometimes spelled* **citrous.**

**cit·y** (sit′ē) ***n.*** **1** a large, important town, especially, in the United States, one having a population over a certain number and holding a charter from the State in which it is located. **2** all the people of a city. —*pl.* **cit′ies**

☆**city hall** **1** a building in which the offices of a city government are located. **2** the government of a city.

☆**city manager** a person appointed by a city council to manage the affairs of the city.

**civ·et** (siv′it) ***n.*** **1** an animal of Africa and Asia that looks like a small hyena: *also called* **civet cat.** *See the picture.* **2** a substance with a strong smell, that comes from the glands of this animal. It is used in making some perfumes.

**civ·ic** (siv′ik) ***adj.*** **1** of a city [plans for *civic* development]. **2** of citizens or citizenship [Voting is a *civic* duty.]

☆**civ·ics** (siv′iks) ***n.pl.*** the study of how one's government works and of one's duties and rights as a citizen: *used with a singular verb.*

**civ·il** (siv′′l) ***adj.*** **1** of a citizen or citizens [*civil* rights]. **2** of or within a country or its government [*civil* service; *civil* war]. **3** not rude; polite [Stop

| | | | | | | | |
|---|---|---|---|---|---|---|---|
| **a** | fat | **ir** | here | **ou** | out | **zh** | leisure |
| **ā** | ape | **ī** | bite, fire | **u** | up | **ng** | ring |
| **ä** | car, lot | **ō** | go | **ur** | fur | | a *in* ago |
| **e** | ten | **ô** | law, horn | **ch** | chin | | e *in* agent |
| **er** | care | **oi** | oil | **sh** | she | **ə =** | i *in* unity |
| **ē** | even | **oo** | look | **th** | thin | | o *in* collect |
| **i** | hit | **o͞o** | tool | ***th*** | then | | u *in* focus |

shouting and give me a *civil* answer.] **4** not having to do with the military or with religion [a *civil* marriage].

SYNONYMS: A **civil** person is one who is merely not rude [Keep a *civil* tongue in your head.] A **polite** person follows the rules of proper social behavior [It is not *polite* to interrupt.] A **courteous** person is one who shows kindness and thoughtfulness [Always be *courteous* to strangers.]

**civil engineering** the planning and building of highways, bridges, harbors, and the like. —**civil engineer**

**ci·vil·ian** (sə vil′yən) ***n.*** a person who is not a member of the armed forces. ◆***adj.*** of or for civilians; not military.

**ci·vil·i·ty** (sə vil′ə tē) ***n.*** politeness or a polite act; courtesy. —*pl.* **ci·vil′i·ties**

**civ·i·li·za·tion** (siv′ə lə zā′shən) ***n.*** **1** the stage in the progress of human beings when they are no longer savages and when arts, sciences, government, etc. are developed [*Civilization* came to Asia before it appeared in Europe.] **2** the countries and peoples that are civilized [The explorer returned to *civilization* after a year in the jungle.] **3** the way of life of a people, nation, or period [the *civilization* of the Middle Ages].

**civ·i·lize** (siv′ə līz) ***v.*** to make no longer savage and ignorant and give training in the arts, sciences, government, etc. —**civ′i·lized, civ′i·liz·ing**

**civil liberties** the freedom that one has by law to think, speak, and act as one likes so long as one does not harm others.



**civ·il·ly** (siv″l ē), ***adv.*** in a polite or courteous way; politely.

**civil rights** the rights of all citizens, regardless of race, religion, sex, etc., to enjoy life, liberty, property, and the equal protection of the law. The 13th, 14th, 15th, 19th, 23d, 24th, and 26th Amendments to the Constitution guarantee these rights in the U.S.

**civil service** all those people who work for the government except in the armed forces or in certain other posts; especially, a system under which government jobs are got by those who score highest on examinations open to everyone.

**civil war** war between sections or groups of the same nation. —**the Civil War,** the war from 1861 to 1865 between the North and the South in the U.S. It is sometimes called the *War between the States.*

**Cl** *the symbol for the chemical element* chlorine.

**clack** (klak) ***v.*** **1** to make a sudden, sharp sound or cause to make this sound [Spanish dancers *clack* their heels on the floor.] **2** to chatter. ◆***n.*** a sudden, sharp sound [The door closed with a *clack.*]

**clad** (klad) *a past tense and past participle of* **clothe.** ◆***adj.*** clothed; dressed [a poorly *clad* child].

**claim** (klām) ***v.*** **1** to demand or ask for something that one thinks one has a right to [He *claimed* the package at the post office.] **2** to call for; need; deserve [This problem *claims* our attention.] ☆**3** to state as a fact something that may or may not be true [She *claimed* that she had been cheated.] ◆***n.*** **1** a demand for something that one thinks one has a right to [to present a *claim* for damages done to one's car]. **2** a right or title to something [a *claim* to the throne]. **3** something claimed, as a piece of land staked out by a settler. ☆**4** something said as a fact that may or may not be true [False *claims* are sometimes made about used cars.] —**lay claim to,** to say that one has a right or title to.

**Claim** comes from the Latin word *clamare,* that means "to call out loudly." A person who claims something is likely to do so in a loud voice.

**claim·ant** (klā′mənt) ***n.*** a person who makes a claim.

**clair·voy·ance** (kler voi′əns) ***n.*** the supposed ability to see things that are not in sight [Our neighbor claimed to find the lost object by *clairvoyance.*]

**clair·voy·ant** (kler voi′ənt) ***adj.*** seeming to have clairvoyance. ◆***n.*** a person who seems to have clairvoyance.

**clam** (klam) ***n.*** a shellfish with a soft body enclosed in two hard shells hinged together. Clams live in sand at the edge of a sea or lake. Some kinds are used as food. *See the picture.* ◆***v.*** to dig for clams. —**clammed, clam′ming** —☆**clam up,** to keep silent or refuse to talk: *used only in everyday talk.*

☆**clam·bake** (klam′bāk) ***n.*** a picnic at which clams steamed or baked with chicken, corn, etc. are served.

**clam·ber** (klam′bər) ***v.*** to climb with effort, especially by using the hands as well as the feet [to *clamber* up the side of a cliff].

**clam·my** (klam′ē) ***adj.*** moist and cold [His hands become *clammy* when he is frightened.] —**clam′mi·er, clam′mi·est** —**clam′mi·ness** ***n.***

**clam·or** (klam′ər) ***n.*** a loud, continued noise or uproar, as of a crowd demanding something or complaining. ◆***v.*** to cry out or demand noisily [The audience *clamored* for more songs.] *The British spelling is* **clamour.** —**clam′or·ous** ***adj.***

**clamp** (klamp) ***n.*** a device for holding things together; especially, a device with two parts that are brought together by a screw so that they grip something. *See the picture.* ◆***v.*** to grip or fasten with a clamp. —☆**clamp down,** to become more strict.

**clan** (klan) ***n.*** **1** a group of families who claim to be descended from the same ancestor. **2** a group of people who have the same interests; clique; set.

**clan·des·tine** (klan des′t′n) ***adj.*** kept secret because of guilty feelings [a *clandestine* meeting]. *See* SYNONYMS *at* **secret.** —**clan·des′tine·ly** ***adv.***

**clang** (klaŋ) ***n.*** a loud, ringing sound, as of a large bell. ◆***v.*** to make such a sound.

**clan·gor** (klaŋ′ər) ***n.*** a continued clanging [the *clangor* of church bells].

**clank** (klaŋk) ***n.*** a sound like a clang but not so ringing [The hammer hit the anvil with a *clank.*] ◆***v.*** to make such a sound [She dragged the *clanking* pipe along the ground.]

**clan·nish** (klan′ish) ***adj.*** **1** of a clan. **2** sticking closely to one's own group and staying away from other people [We refused to join the club because its members were so *clannish.*]

**clans·man** (klanz′mən) ***n.*** a member of a clan. —*pl.* **clans′men**

**clap** (klap) ***v.*** **1** to make the sudden, loud sound of two flat surfaces being struck together **2** to strike the palms of the hands together, as in applauding. **3** to strike with the palm of the hand ["Good work!" he said, *clapping* me on the shoulder.] **4** to put or bring swiftly [The thief was *clapped* into jail.] —**clapped, clap′ping** ◆***n.*** **1** the sudden, loud sound of clapping [a *clap* of thunder]. **2** a sharp blow; slap.

**clap·board** (klab′ərd *or* klap′bôrd) ***n.*** ☆a thin board with one edge thicker than the other, used for siding on the outside of a wooden house.

**Clapboard** comes from an old Dutch word that meant "a board that fits." Clapboards are made with one edge thinner than the other so that one can overlap another with a tight fit.

**clap·per** (klap′ər) ***n.*** one that claps; especially, the tongue of a bell.

**clar·et** (klar′ət) ***n.*** **1** a dry red wine. **2** purplish red.

**clar·i·fy** (klar′ə fī) ***v.*** **1** to make or become clear and pure [Strain the liquid to *clarify* it.] **2** to make or become easier to understand [She *clarified* the problem by drawing a diagram.] —**clar′i·fied, clar′i·fy·ing** —**clar′i·fi·ca′tion** ***n.***

**clar·i·net** (klar ə net′) ***n.*** a woodwind musical instrument whose mouthpiece has one reed and whose lower end is shaped like a bell. It is played by opening and closing holes with the fingers or keys. *See the picture.*

**clar·i·on** (klar′ē ən) ***adj.*** clear, sharp, and shrill [the *clarion* sounds of a trumpet].

**clar·i·ty** (klar′ə tē) ***n.*** clearness.

**Clark** (klärk), **William** 1770–1838; American explorer: *see the entry for* Meriwether **Lewis.**

**clash** (klash) ***n.*** **1** a loud, harsh noise, as of metal striking against metal with great force [the *clash* of a sword on a shield]. **2** a sharp disagreement; conflict [a *clash* of ideas]. ➡***v.*** **1** to strike with a clash [He *clashed* the cymbals together.] **2** to go against each other; be not in harmony; disagree sharply [Their ideas for the new school *clashed.* The red chair *clashed* with the orange drapes.]

**clasp** (klasp) ***n.*** **1** a fastening, as a hook or catch, for holding two things or parts together [The *clasp* on my pocketbook is loose.] *See the picture.* **2** a holding in the arms; embrace. **3** a holding with the hand; grip. ➡***v.*** **1** to fasten with a clasp. **2** to hold tightly in the arms [The baby fell asleep *clasping* a doll.] **3** to grip with the hand [I *clasped* his hand in greeting.]

**class** (klas) ***n.*** **1** a number of people or things thought of as a group because they are alike in certain ways [Whales belong to the *class* of mammals. She is a member of the working *class.*] ☆**2** a group of students meeting together to be taught; also, a meeting of this kind [My English *class* is held at 9 o'clock.] ☆**3** a group of students who are or will be graduating together [the *class* of 1981]. **4** a division or grouping according to grade or quality [to travel first *class*]. **5** very fine style or appearance; excellence: *slang in this meaning* [a golfer with a lot of *class*]. ➡***v.*** to put in a class; classify [My teacher *classes* me with his best students.]

**clas·sic** (klas′ik) ***adj.*** **1** of the highest quality or rank; that is a model of its kind [a *classic* example of good writing]. **2** of the art, literature, and culture of the ancient Greeks and Romans. **3** having a formal style that is simple, neat, and balanced [the *classic* lines of the building]. **4** famous because it is typical and has become a tradition [Turkey is the *classic* dish for Thanksgiving dinner.] ➡***n.*** **1** a book, painting, symphony, etc. of the highest excellence. **2** a person who creates such works. ☆**3** a famous event that is held regularly [The World Series is baseball's fall *classic.*] —**the classics,** the literature of the ancient Greeks and Romans.

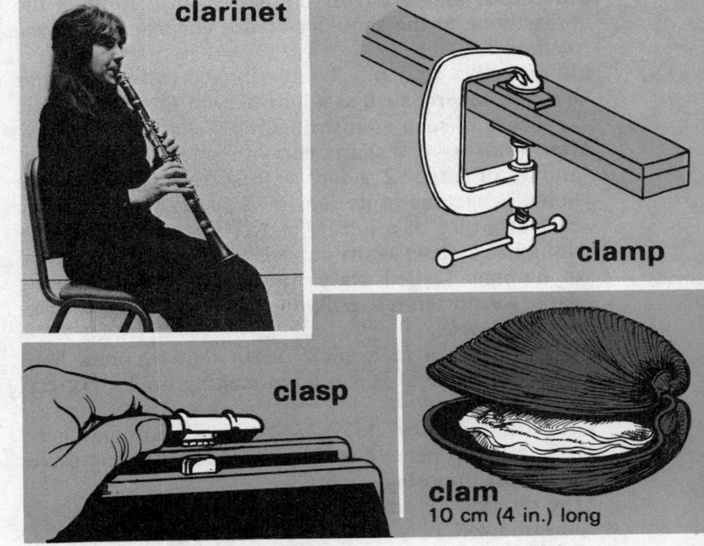

10 cm (4 in.) long

**clas·si·cal** (klas′i k'l) ***adj.*** **1** *same as meanings* 1, 2, *and* 3 *of* **classic. 2** describing a kind of music that is not simple in form and that requires much study and training to write and perform [Symphonies, concertos, sonatas, etc. are called *classical* music.] —**clas′si·cal·ly** ***adv.*** 133

**clas·si·fi·ca·tion** (klas′ə fi kā′shən) ***n.*** **1** the act of arranging things into classes or groups according to some system. **2** any of these classes or groups.

**clas·si·fy** (klas′ə fī) ***v.*** to arrange by putting into classes or groups according to some system [Plants and animals are *classified* into various orders, families, species, etc.] —**clas′si·fied, clas′si·fy·ing**

☆**class·mate** (klas′māt) ***n.*** a member of the same class at a school or college [Maria and Bill are *classmates.*]

☆**class·room** (klas′ro͞om) ***n.*** a room in a school or college where classes meet to be taught.

**clat·ter** (klat′ər) ***n.*** **1** a series of sharp, clashing sounds [the *clatter* of feet running through the halls]. **2** a noisy chatter; hubbub. ➡***v.*** to make a clatter or move with a clatter.

**clause** (klôz) ***n.*** **1** a group of words that includes a subject and verb, but that forms only part of a sentence. In the sentence "She will visit us if she can," *She will visit us* is a clause that could be a complete sentence, and *if she can* is a clause that depends on the first clause. **2** any of the separate points or articles in a law, contract, treaty, etc.

**claus·tro·pho·bi·a** (klôs′trə fō′bē ə) ***n.*** a very great fear of being in a small, enclosed space.

| | | | |
|---|---|---|---|
| **a** fat | **ir** here | **ou** out | **zh** leisure |
| **ā** ape | **ī** bite, fire | **u** up | **ng** ring |
| **ä** car, lot | **ō** go | **ur** fur | a *in* ago |
| **e** ten | **ô** law, horn | **ch** chin | e *in* agent |
| **er** care | **oi** oil | **sh** she | **ə** = i *in* unity |
| **ē** even | **oo** look | **th** thin | o *in* collect |
| **i** hit | **o͞o** tool | ***th*** then | u *in* focus |

**clav·i·cle** (klav′ə k'l) ***n.*** the narrow bone joining the breastbone to the shoulder blade; collarbone. *See the picture.*

**cla·vier** (klə vir′) ***n.*** **1** any stringed instrument that has a keyboard, such as a harpsichord or piano. **2** the keyboard of such an instrument.

**claw** (klô) ***n.*** **1** a sharp, curved nail on the foot of an animal or bird. **2** a foot with such nails [The eagle holds its victims in its *claws.*] **3** the grasping part on each front leg of a lobster, crab, or scorpion. **4** anything like a claw, as the curved, forklike part on a type of hammer (called **claw hammer**) used for pulling nails. ◆***v.*** to scratch, pull, dig, or tear with claws or as if with claws.

**clay** (klā) ***n.*** a stiff, sticky earth that becomes hard when it is baked. It is used in making bricks, pottery, tile, and china.

**Clay** (klā), **Henry** 1777–1852; a U.S. statesman, who tried to keep peace between the States holding slaves and those opposing slavery.

**clay·ey** (klā′ē) ***adj.*** **1** of, like, or full of clay. **2** smeared with clay. —**clay′i·er, clay′i·est**

**clean** (klēn) ***adj.*** **1** without dirt or impure matter [*clean* dishes; *clean* oil]. **2** without evil or wrongdoing [to lead a *clean* life]. **3** neat and tidy [to keep a *clean* desk]. **4** done in a skillful, exact way [a *clean* dive into the pool]. **5** having no flaws or weak spots [a *clean* record]. **6** complete or thorough [a *clean* shave;

a *clean* sweep]. ◆***adv.*** **1** so as to be clean [He swept the room *clean.*] **2** completely; entirely [She has gone *clean* out of her mind.] ◆***v.*** to make clean. [Please *clean* the oven.] —**clean out, 1** to empty so as to make clean. **2** to empty. **3** to use up the money of: *used only in everyday talk.* —**clean up, 1** to make clean or neat. **2** to take care of; finish: *used only in everyday talk.* —**clean′ness *n.***

**clean-cut** (klēn′kut′) ***adj.*** **1** having a clear, sharp outline; distinct. **2** having a healthy, trim, neat look [a *clean-cut* young fellow].

**clean·er** (klēn′ər) ***n.*** **1** a person whose work is cleaning. **2** a tool or substance used for cleaning.

**clean·ly**[1] (klen′lē) ***adj.*** always keeping clean or kept clean. —**clean′li·ness *n.***

**clean·ly**[2] (klēn′lē) ***adv.*** in a clean manner.

**cleanse** (klenz) ***v.*** to make clean or pure [to feel *cleansed* of sin]. —**cleansed, cleans′ing**

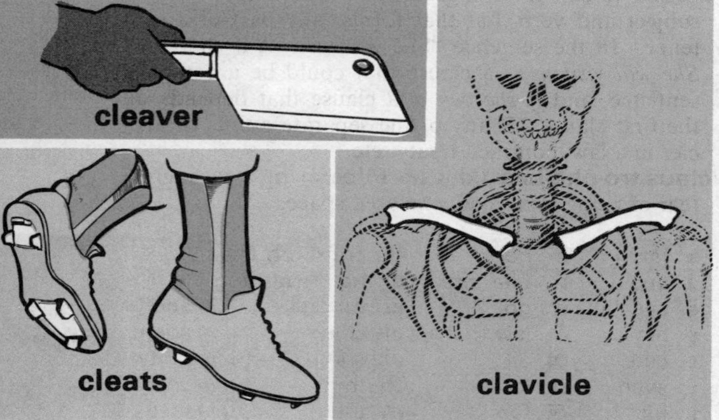


**cleans·er** (klen′zər) ***n.*** a substance used for cleansing, such as scouring powder.

**clear** (klir) ***adj.*** **1** bright or sunny; without clouds or mist [a *clear* day]. **2** that can be seen through; transparent [*clear* glass]. **3** having no spots, scars, or flaws [a *clear* skin]. **4** sharp and distinct; not dim or blurred [a *clear* outline; a *clear* tone]. **5** able to see or think well [*clear* vision; a *clear* mind]. **6** easy to understand; not confusing [a *clear* explanation]. **7** plain; obvious [a *clear* case of carelessness]. **8** complete or certain [a *clear* majority of votes; a *clear* title to property]. **9** not guilty; innocent [a *clear* conscience]. **10** left over after expenses or charges are paid [a *clear* profit of $10,000]. **11** without anything in the way; not blocked; open [a *clear* view; a *clear* passage]. ◆***adv.*** **1** in a clear manner; clearly [The bells rang out *clear.*] **2** all the way [It sank *clear* to the bottom.] ◆***v.*** **1** to make or become clear [The sky *cleared* after the storm. They filtered the water to *clear* it.] **2** to empty or remove [*Clear* the snow from the sidewalk. Help me *clear* the table of dishes.] **3** to open or unblock [Lye will *clear* those pipes.] **4** to free from guilt or blame [to *clear* a suspect of a crime]. **5** to pass over, under, or by with space to spare [The horse leaped and *cleared* the fence by a few inches. The tugboat barely *cleared* the bridge.] **6** to make as a profit [We *cleared* $50 on the rummage sale.] —**clear away** or **clear off,** to take away so as to leave a cleared space. —**clear out, 1** to empty. ☆**2** to go away: *used only in everyday talk.* —**clear up, 1** to make or become clear. **2** to explain. **3** to cure or become cured. —**in the clear, 1** in the open; not shut in, blocked, or hidden by anything. **2** not suspected of being guilty: *used only in everyday talk.* —**clear′ly *adv.*** —**clear′ness *n.***

SYNONYMS: The air, a liquid, or a piece of glass is **clear** when there is nothing in it to make it colored, dirty, cloudy, muddy, or hazy. Something, as a window pane, is **transparent** when it is so clear that objects on the other side can be seen distinctly.

**clear·ance** (klir′əns) ***n.*** **1** the act of clearing. **2** the clear space between a moving thing and that which it passes through, under, or over.

**clear-cut** (klir′kut′) ***adj.*** **1** having a clear, sharp outline. **2** distinct; definite; not doubtful [a *clear-cut* victory].

**clear·ing** (klir′iŋ) ***n.*** ☆a piece of land from which the trees have been cleared.

**clear·sight·ed** (klir′sīt′id) ***adj.*** **1** seeing clearly. **2** understanding or thinking clearly.

**cleat** (klēt) ***n.*** **1** a piece of metal or wood fastened to something to make it stronger or to prevent slipping. Cleats are used under shelves, on the soles of shoes, etc. *See the picture.* **2** a wooden or metal piece on which ropes are fastened on a ship.

**cleav·age** (klē′vij) ***n.*** the act of splitting in two or the way in which something splits; division [a *cleavage* in rock].

**cleave**[1] (klēv) ***v.*** to divide by a sharp blow; split [Lightning can *cleave* a tree.] —**cleaved** or **cleft** or **clove, cleaved** or **cleft** or **clo′ven, cleav′ing**

**cleave**[2] (klēv) ***v.*** to cling closely; stick [barnacles *cleaving* to a rock; to *cleave* to a belief]. —**cleaved, cleav′ing**

**cleav·er** (klēv′ər) ***n.*** a heavy cutting tool with a broad blade, used by butchers. *See the picture.*

**clef** (klef) ***n.*** a sign at the beginning of a musical staff that shows the pitch of the notes on the staff [The notes in the treble or G *clef* are mainly above middle C. The notes in the bass or F *clef* are mainly below middle C.]

**cleft** (kleft) *a past tense and past participle of* **cleave.** ◆***adj.*** split open; divided [A *cleft* palate is a split in the roof of the mouth that some people are born with.] ◆***n.*** an opening or hollow made by or as if by splitting [a passage through a *cleft* in the rocks; a *cleft* in the chin].

**clem·a·tis** (klem′ə tis *or* klə mat′is) ***n.*** a climbing plant, or vine, with brightly colored flowers.

**clem·en·cy** (klem′ən sē) ***n.*** **1** kindness in judging or punishing someone; mercy [The judge showed *clemency* because the prisoner was ill.] **2** mildness, as of the weather.

**Clem·ens** (klem′ənz), **Samuel Lang·horne** (laŋ′hôrn) *the real name of* **Mark Twain.**

**clem·ent** (klem′ənt) ***adj.*** **1** showing mercy; merciful. **2** pleasant or mild [*clement* weather].

**clench** (klench) ***v.*** **1** to close or press tightly together [to *clench* the fist; to *clench* the teeth]. **2** to grip firmly. ◆***n.*** a firm grip.

**Cle·o·pa·tra** (klē′ə pat′rə) 69?–30 B.C.; queen of Egypt who was loved by Julius Caesar and by Mark Antony.

**cler·gy** (klur′jē) ***n.*** all ministers, priests, rabbis, etc. as a group. *—pl.* **cler′gies**

**cler·gy·man** (klur′jē mən) ***n.*** a minister, priest, rabbi, etc. *—pl.* **cler′gy·men**

**cler·ic** (kler′ik) ***n.*** *another word for* **clergyman.**

**cler·i·cal** (kler′i k′l) ***adj.*** **1** having to do with a clergyman or the clergy [Some priests and ministers wear a *clerical* collar.] **2** having to do with office clerks or their work [I'm looking for a *clerical* job.]

**clerk** (klurk; *the British pronounce it* klärk) ***n.*** **1** an office worker who keeps records, types letters, etc. [Some *clerks,* as a *clerk* of courts or a city *clerk,* have special duties.] ☆**2** a person who sells in a store; salesperson.

**Cleve·land** (klēv′lənd) a city in northeastern Ohio.

**Cleve·land** (klēv′lənd), **Gro·ver** (grō′vər) 1837–1908; 22d president of the United States, from 1885 to 1889, and the 24th president, from 1893 to 1897.

**clev·er** (klev′ər) ***adj.*** **1** quick in thinking or learning; smart; intelligent. *See* SYNONYMS *at* **intelligent. 2** skillful [Watchmakers are *clever* with their hands.] **3** showing skill or fine thinking [a *clever* move in chess]. —**clev′er·ly *adv.*** —**clev′er·ness *n.***

**clew** (klo͞o) ***n.*** **1** a ball of thread or yarn. **2** *another spelling of* **clue. 3** a metal loop in the corner of a sail for holding ropes by which the sail is raised or lowered.

A man named Theseus in a Greek legend found his way out of a maze by following a thread from a **clew.** We now use that word, usually spelled **clue,** for any hint that helps someone solve a problem.

**cli·ché** (klē shā′) ***n.*** an expression or idea that has become stale from too much use ["As old as the hills" is a *cliché.*]

**click** (klik) ***n.*** a slight, sharp sound like that of a lock snapping into place. ◆***v.*** **1** to make or cause to make a click. **2** to be a success or get along well: *used only in everyday talk.*

**cli·ent** (klī′ənt) ***n.*** **1** a person or company for whom a lawyer, accountant, etc. is acting. **2** a customer.

**cli·en·tele** (klī′ən tel′) ***n.*** all of one's clients or customers as a group.

**cliff** (klif) ***n.*** a high, steep face of rock that goes down sharply with little or no slope.

**cli·mac·tic** (klī mak′tik) ***adj.*** of or forming a climax [the *climactic* act of a play]. —**cli·mac′ti·cal·ly *adv.***

**cli·mate** (klī′mət) ***n.*** **1** the average weather conditions of a place over a period of years [Arizona has a mild, dry *climate,* but its weather last week was stormy.] **2** a region with particular weather conditions [They went south to a warmer *climate.*] **3** the general feeling or spirit of a place [a town with an intellectual *climate*].

**cli·mat·ic** (klī mat′ik) ***adj.*** of climate [*climatic* conditions]. —**cli·mat′i·cal·ly *adv.***

**cli·max** (klī′maks) ***n.*** the final and strongest idea or event in a series; highest point of interest or excitement [The *climax* of the movie came when the children were saved from the fire.]

SYNONYMS: A **climax** is the highest point in a series in which each point is more interesting or exciting than the one before. A **summit** is the topmost point, as of a hill, or the highest level that can be reached. A **peak** is the highest of a number of high points, as in a mountain range or in a graph.

**climb** (klīm) ***v.*** **1** to go up, or sometimes down, by using the feet and often the hands [to *climb* the stairs; to *climb* up or down a tree]. **2** to rise to a higher position [She has *climbed* to fame. The airplane *climbed* to 30,000 feet.] **3** to grow upward on some support [The ivy *climbed* the wall.] ◆***n.*** **1** the act of climbing; rise; ascent [a tiring *climb*]. **2** a thing to be climbed [That hill is quite a *climb.*] —**climb′er *n.***

**clime** (klīm) ***n.*** a region or place with a certain climate: *used mostly in old poems.*

**clinch** (klinch) ***v.*** **1** to fasten a nail that has been driven through something by hammering down the end that sticks out. **2** to settle definitely; fix [The extra offer of $100 *clinched* the deal.] ☆**3** to hold on tight in boxing so as to keep one's opponent from punching. ◆***n.*** the act of clinching. —**clinch′er *n.***

**cling** (kliŋ) ***v.*** to hold on tightly; stick; adhere [The child *clung* to her father's hand. The vine *clings* to the wall.] —**clung, cling′ing**

**clin·ic** (klin′ik) ***n.*** **1** a place where patients are examined or treated by a group of doctors who are specialists. **2** a place in a hospital or medical school where poor people can come for free treatment or advice. **3**

| | | | | | | | |
|---|---|---|---|---|---|---|---|
| **a** | fat | **ir** | here | **ou** | out | **zh** | leisure |
| **ā** | ape | **ī** | bite, fire | **u** | up | **ŋ** | ring |
| **ä** | car, lot | **ō** | go | **ur** | fur | | a *in* ago |
| **e** | ten | **ô** | law, horn | **ch** | chin | | e *in* agent |
| **er** | care | **oi** | oil | **sh** | she | **ə** = | i *in* unity |
| **ē** | even | **oo** | look | **th** | thin | | o *in* collect |
| **i** | hit | **o͞o** | tool | ***th*** | then | | u *in* focus |

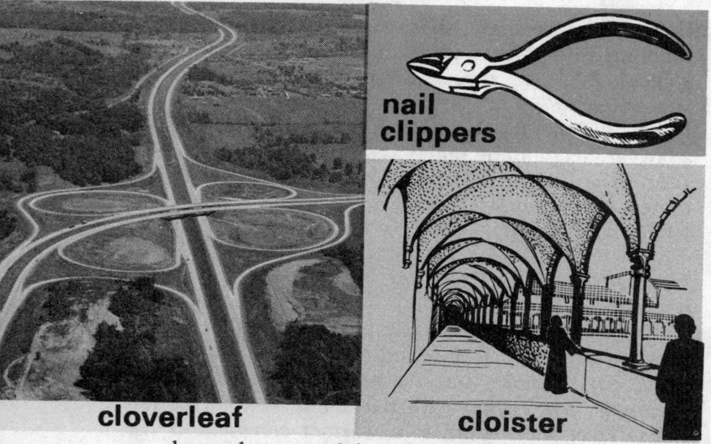

nail clippers

cloverleaf

cloister

a place where special problems are studied or treated [a hearing and speech *clinic*]. **4** the teaching of medicine by examining and treating patients while students watch. —**clin'i·cal** ***adj.***

**clink** (kliŋk) ***n.*** a short, tinkling sound, as of coins struck together. ◆***v.*** to make such a sound or cause to make such a sound.

**clink·er** (kliŋk'ər) ***n.*** a stony mass formed in a coal fire from the impure parts of the coal.

**clip**[1] (klip) ***v.*** **1** to cut off or cut out as with shears or scissors [to *clip* wool from a sheep; to *clip* pictures from a magazine]. **2** to cut the hair or wool of [We had our dog *clipped*.] **3** to make shorter as by cutting [The word "omnibus" has been *clipped* to "bus."] **4** to move with speed [The car *clipped* right along.] **5** to hit with a quick, sharp punch or blow: *used only in everyday talk.* **6** to cheat as by charging too much: *slang in this meaning.* —**clipped, clip'ping** ◆***n.*** **1** the act of clipping. **2** a high rate of speed [to move at a *clip*]. **3** a quick, sharp punch or blow: *used only in everyday talk.*



**clip**[2] (klip) ***n.*** anything that is used to hold or fasten two or more things together [a paper *clip*]. ◆***v.*** to fasten with a clip. —**clipped, clip'ping**

☆**clip·board** (klip'bôrd) ***n.*** a small writing board with a hinged clip at the top for holding papers.

**clip·per** (klip'ər) ***n.*** **1** a person who clips. **2** *often* **clippers,** *pl.* a tool for clipping or shearing [a *clipper* for trimming hedges; a barber's *clippers*]. *See the picture.* ☆**3** a sailing ship with a sharp bow and narrow width, built for speed. Many clippers were built in the middle 19th century.

**clip·ping** (klip'iŋ) ***n.*** **1** a piece cut off or out of something [a *clipping* from a plant]. ☆**2** an item cut out of a newspaper or magazine.

**clique** (klēk *or* klik) ***n.*** a small group of people who are friendly only with one another and have little to do with outsiders.

**cloak** (klōk) ***n.*** **1** a loose outer garment, usually without sleeves. **2** something that covers or hides [The fog formed a *cloak* over the valley.] ◆***v.*** **1** to cover as with a cloak. **2** to conceal; hide [She *cloaked* her anger by joking.]

**cloak·room** (klōk'ro͞om) ***n.*** a room in a school, theater, etc. where coats, hats, etc. may be left for a time.

☆**clob·ber** (kläb'ər) ***v.*** to hit many times; maul: *a slang word.*

**clock** (kläk) ***n.*** a device for measuring and showing the time, as by means of pointers moving around a dial or by showing a changing series of digits on the face of the clock. Clocks, unlike watches, are not meant to be worn or carried. ◆***v.*** to measure the time of a race or runner.

**clock·wise** (kläk'wīz) ***adv., adj.*** in the direction in which the hands of a clock move [When you turn the knob *clockwise,* the radio goes on.]

**clock·work** (kläk'wurk) ***n.*** the springs, gears, and wheels of a clock, or of anything that works like a clock. —**like clockwork,** very regularly and exactly. [His daily schedule runs *like clockwork*.]

**clod** (kläd) ***n.*** **1** a lump of earth or clay. **2** a dull, stupid person.

**clog** (kläg) ***n.*** **1** anything that blocks up or gets in the way. **2** a heavy shoe, usually with a wooden sole. ◆***v.*** **1** to slow up or stop movement. **2** to block up or become blocked up [Thick grease *clogged* the drainpipe. The large crowd *clogged* the entrances to the ball park.] —**clogged, clog'ging**

**clois·ter** (klois'tər) ***n.*** **1** a place where monks or nuns live; monastery or convent. **2** any peaceful place where one can get away from people. **3** a covered walk along an inside wall, as of a convent, that borders on a courtyard. *See the picture.* ◆***v.*** to shut away as in a cloister. —**clois'tered** ***adj.***

**clomp** (klämp) ***v.*** to walk in a heavy, noisy way.

☆**clon·ing** (klō'niŋ) ***n.*** a way of producing a plant or animal that is exactly like another by replacing the nucleus of an unfertilized germ cell with the nucleus of a body cell from the original plant or animal.

**close**[1] (klōs) ***adj.*** **1** with not much space between; near [The old houses are too *close* to each other.] **2** having parts near together; compact; dense [a *close* weave]. **3** as near to the surface as possible [a *close* shave]. **4** very near in relationship; very dear [a *close* friend]. **5** very nearly like the original [a *close* copy]. **6** thorough or careful [Pay *close* attention.] **7** nearly equal or even [a *close* contest]. **8** shutting in with not much free space; confining [*close* quarters]. **9** carefully guarded [a *close* secret]. **10** not frank or open; secretive [He is very *close* about his business dealings.] **11** like a miser; stingy [She is *close* with her money.] **12** stuffy and full of stale air [a *close* room]. —**clos'er, clos'est** ◆***adv.*** so as to be close or near; closely [Follow *close* behind the leader.] —**close'ly** ***adv.*** —**close'ness** ***n.***

**close**[2] (klōz) ***v.*** **1** to make no longer open; shut [*Close* the door.] **2** to fill up or stop up [to *close* a hole]. **3** to bring or come to a finish; end [to *close* a speech]. **4** to stop from carrying on its work [Is the library *closed* on Saturday?] **5** to bring or come together [to *close* ranks]. —**closed, clos'ing** ◆***n.*** an end; finish. —**close down,** ☆to shut or stop entirely. —**close in,** to draw near from different directions, cutting off escape. —☆**close out,** to sell goods at a low price, so as to get rid of the whole stock. —**close up, 1** to draw nearer together. **2** to shut or stop up entirely.

☆**close call** (klōs) a narrow escape from danger: *also called* **close shave**: *used only in everyday talk.*

**closed circuit** a system of sending television signals

by cable to just a certain number of receiving sets for some special purpose.

**close·fist·ed** (klōs′fis′tid) ***adj.*** stingy; miserly.

**close·mouthed** (klōs′mouthd′) ***adj.*** not talking much; telling little: *also* **close·lipped** (klōs′lipt′).

**clos·et** (kläz′it) ***n.*** **1** a small room or cupboard for clothes, linens, supplies, etc. **2** a small private room where one can be alone: *no longer much used in this meaning.* ◆***v.*** to shut up in a room for a private talk [The president was *closeted* with his close advisers.]

☆**close-up** (klōs′up′) ***n.*** a picture taken with the camera very close to the subject.

**clo·sure** (klō′zhər) ***n.*** **1** the act of closing or the fact of being closed. **2** *same as* **cloture.**

**clot** (klät) ***n.*** a lump formed when matter in a liquid thickens [a blood *clot*]. ◆***v.*** to form a clot or clots. —**clot′ted, clot′ting**

**cloth** (klôth) ***n.*** **1** a material made from threads of cotton, silk, wool, nylon, etc., especially by weaving or knitting. **2** a piece of such material for a particular use [a table*cloth;* a wash*cloth*]. —*pl.* **cloths** (klôthz *in the meaning* "pieces of cloth"; klôths *in the meaning* "kinds of cloth") —**the cloth,** the clergy.

**clothe** (klōth) ***v.*** **1** to put clothes on; dress. **2** to get clothes for [It costs a lot to *clothe* a large family.] **3** to cover or surround [hills *clothed* in snow; a hero *clothed* in glory]. —**clothed** or **clad, cloth′ing**

**clothes** (klōz *or* klōthz) ***n.pl.*** **1** cloth or other material made up in different shapes and styles to wear on the body; dresses, suits, hats, underwear, etc.; garments. **2** *a shorter form of* **bedclothes.**

**clothes·horse** (klōz′hôrs *or* klōthz′hôrs) ***n.*** **1** a frame on which clothes are hung for airing or drying. **2** a person who pays too much attention to clothes and new fashions: *slang in this meaning.*

**clothes·line** (klōz′līn) ***n.*** a rope or wire on which clothes are hung for drying or airing.

☆**clothes·pin** (klōz′pin) ***n.*** a small clip of wood or plastic for holding clothes on a line.

**cloth·ier** (klōth′yər) ***n.*** a person who makes or sells clothes.

**cloth·ing** (klō′thing) ***n.*** clothes or garments.

**clo·ture** (klō′chər) ***n.*** a way of ending debate in a legislature so that the matter can be put to a vote.

**cloud** (kloud) ***n.*** **1** a mass of fine drops of water or tiny crystals of ice floating in the air above the earth. **2** a mass of smoke, dust, or steam. **3** a great number of things moving in a solid mass [a *cloud* of locusts]. **4** any dark marking or mass, as in marble or in a liquid. **5** anything that threatens or makes gloomy [They are under a *cloud* of suspicion.] ◆***v.*** **1** to cover or make dark as with clouds [The sun is *clouded* over. His reputation is *clouded* with gossip.] **2** to make or become gloomy or troubled [Her face *clouded* with worry.] **3** to make or become muddy or foggy [The water *clouded.*] —**in the clouds, 1** high up in the sky. **2** not practical; fanciful. **3** having a daydream.

☆**cloud·burst** (kloud′burst) ***n.*** a sudden, very heavy rain.

**cloud·less** (kloud′lis) ***adj.*** free from clouds; clear; bright [a *cloudless* sky].

**cloud·y** (kloud′ē) ***adj.*** **1** covered with clouds; overcast. **2** marked with spots or streaks, as marble. **3** not clear; muddy, foggy, vague, dim, etc. [*cloudy* water; *cloudy* ideas]. —**cloud′i·er, cloud′i·est**

**clout** (klout) ***n.*** **1** a hard blow or rap. ☆**2** power or influence: *used only in everyday talk* [She used her *clout* to get him a job.] ◆***v.*** to strike or hit hard: *used only in everyday talk.*

**clove**[1] (klōv) ***n.*** the dried flower bud of a tropical evergreen tree, used as a spice.

**clove**[2] (klōv) ***n.*** a section of a bulb, as of garlic.

**clove**[3] (klōv) *a past tense of* **cleave**[1].

**clo·ven** (klō′v'n) *a past participle of* **cleave**[1]. —***adj.*** divided; split [a *cloven* hoof].

**clo·ver** (klō′vər) ***n.*** a low-growing plant with leaves in three parts and small, sweet-smelling flowers. *Red clover* is grown for fodder; *white clover* is often found in lawns. —**in clover,** living a pleasant, easy life.

> Once in a while a clover with leaves in four parts will be found. There is a popular superstition that such a four-leaf clover brings good luck to the finder.

**clo·ver·leaf** (klō′vər lēf) ***n.*** ☆a place where highways meet, with one going under the other and with curving ramps, so that traffic can move easily and smoothly. *See the picture.* —*pl.* **clo′ver·leafs**

**clown** (kloun) ***n.*** **1** a person who entertains, as in a circus, by doing comical tricks and silly stunts; jester; buffoon. **2** a person who likes to make jokes or act in a comical way [the *clown* of our family]. **3** a rude or clumsy person; boor. ◆***v.*** **1** to perform as a clown. **2** to play practical jokes and act silly. —**clown′ish *adj.***

**cloy** (kloi) ***v.*** to make weary or displeased by too much of something good [The rich desserts began to *cloy* our appetites.]

**club** (klub) ***n.*** **1** a heavy wooden stick, used as a weapon. **2** any stick made for some special purpose [a golf *club*]. **3** the mark ♣, used on a black suit of playing cards; also, a card of this suit. **4** a group of people who meet together for pleasure or for some special purpose [a bridge *club;* an athletic *club*]. **5** the building or place where they meet. ◆***v.*** **1** to hit as with a club. **2** to join together for some purpose. —**clubbed, club′bing**

**club·house** (klub′hous) ***n.*** **1** a building used by a club. ☆**2** the locker room used by a sports team.

☆**club sandwich** a sandwich made with three or more slices of toast and fillings of chicken, bacon, lettuce, tomato, etc.

**club soda** *another name for* **soda water.**

**cluck** (kluk) ***v.*** to make a low, sharp, clicking sound, like that made by a hen calling her chickens. ◆***n.*** this sound or a sound like it.

**clue** (klo͞o) ***n.*** a fact or thing that helps to solve a puzzle or mystery [Muddy footprints were a *clue* to the man's guilt.] *See the note at* **clew.**

**clump** (klump) ***n.*** **1** a group of things close together; cluster [a *clump* of trees]. **2** a mass or lump [a *clump*

| | | | | | | | |
|---|---|---|---|---|---|---|---|
| a | fat | ir | here | ou | out | zh | leisure |
| ā | ape | ī | bite, fire | u | up | ng | ring |
| ä | car, lot | ō | go | ur | fur | | a *in* ago |
| e | ten | ô | law, horn | ch | chin | | e *in* agent |
| er | care | oi | oil | sh | she | ə = | i *in* unity |
| ē | even | oo | look | th | thin | | o *in* collect |
| i | hit | o͞o | tool | *th* | then | | u *in* focus |

of dirt]. **3** the sound of heavy footsteps. ◆*v.* to walk heavily.

**clum·sy** (klum′zē) ***adj.*** **1** not having good control, as of one's hands or feet; awkward [The *clumsy* boy dropped his fork.] **2** badly made or done; crude [a *clumsy* shed made of old boards]. —**clum′si·er, clum′si·est** —**clum′si·ly** ***adv.*** —**clum′si·ness** ***n.***

> **Clumsy** comes from an early English word meaning "numb with cold." When one's hands and feet are numb with cold, one moves in an awkward or clumsy way.

**clung** (kluŋ) *past tense and past participle of* **cling.**

☆**clunk·er** (kluŋk′ər) ***n.*** an old, noisy automobile in bad condition: *a slang word.*

**clus·ter** (klus′tər) ***n.*** a number of things growing together or seen together [a *cluster* of grapes; a *cluster* of stars]. ◆*v.* to grow or gather together [Pigeons *clustered* around her.]

**clutch** (kluch) ***v.*** **1** to grasp or hold tightly [The old man was *clutching* her hand as they crossed the street.] **2** to reach or grab for; snatch [As she stumbled she *clutched* at the railing.] ◆*n.* **1** the grasp of a hand or claw; a clutching [The thief made a *clutch* at her handbag.] **2 clutches,** *pl.* power or control [The heroine was in the *clutches* of the villain.] **3** a device in an automobile, etc. that puts moving parts into gear or takes them out of gear.

**clut·ter** (klut′ər) ***n.*** a number of things scattered in an
138 untidy way; disorder [the *clutter* in an attic]. ◆*v.* to make untidy and confused [a desk *cluttered* up with papers and books].

**cm** or **cm.** *abbreviation for* **centimeter** *or* **centimeters.**

**co-** *a prefix meaning:* **1** together with [A *co*-worker is a person who works together with another.] **2** equally; to the same extent [A *co*-owner is a person who owns something equally with another.]

**Co** *the symbol for the chemical element* cobalt.

**CO** *abbreviation for* **Colorado.**

**CO** or **C.O.** **1** commanding officer. **2** conscientious objector.

**Co.** or **co.** *abbreviation for* **company, county.**

**c/o** or **c.o.** *an abbreviation meaning* "in care of" *or* "at the address of" [Send me the box *c/o* my mother.]

**coach** (kōch) ***n.*** **1** a large, closed carriage drawn by horses, with the driver's seat outside. *See the picture.* ☆**2** a railroad car with seats for passengers. **3** a bus. **4** a class of seats on an airplane that are less expensive than those in the first-class section. **5** a person who teaches and trains students, athletes, singers, etc. [a football *coach*]. ◆*v.* to teach, train, or tutor [Will you *coach* me for the test in history?]

**coach·man** (kōch′mən) ***n.*** the driver of a coach or carriage. —*pl.* **coach′men**

**co·ag·u·late** (kō ag′yoo lāt) ***v.*** to turn into a soft, thick mass, as blood does in a wound; clot. —**co·ag′u·lat·ed, co·ag′u·lat·ing** —**co·ag′u·la′tion** ***n.***

**coal** (kōl) ***n.*** **1** a black, solid substance that is dug up from the ground for use as a fuel. Coal is mostly carbon, formed from decaying plant matter that has been pressed together for millions of years. **2** a piece of glowing or charred coal, wood, etc.; ember. ◆*v.* **1** to supply with coal. **2** to take in a supply of coal.

**co·a·lesce** (kō ə les′) ***v.*** to grow or come together into one mass or body; unite [Several political groups *coalesced* in 1854 to form the Republican Party.] —**co·a·lesced′, co·a·lesc′ing** —**co·a·les′cence** ***n.***

**co·a·li·tion** (kō′ə lish′ən) ***n.*** a joining together of persons or groups, as for a political purpose.

☆**coal oil** *another name for* **kerosene.**

**coal tar** a black, thick liquid formed when soft coal is heated in a closed container without air [Dyes, medicines, and explosives have been developed from *coal tar*.]

**coarse** (kôrs) ***adj.*** **1** made up of rather large particles; not fine [*coarse* sand]. **2** rough or harsh to the touch [*coarse* cloth]. **3** not polite or refined; vulgar; crude [a *coarse* joke]. —**coarse′ly** ***adv.*** —**coarse′ness** ***n.***

> SYNONYMS: **Coarse** is used of something said or done that is not polite or refined and that seems wrong or unpleasant to some people [He told several *coarse* jokes.] **Vulgar** is used to show that good taste or culture are thought to be missing from a person's background [Their mansion was decorated in a *vulgar,* showy way.]

**coars·en** (kôr′s′n) ***v.*** to make or become coarse [Outdoor life *coarsened* his skin.]

**coast** (kōst) ***n.*** **1** land along the sea; seashore. ☆**2** a slide or ride downhill, as on a sled. ◆*v.* **1** to sail along a coast. ☆**2** to ride or slide downhill, as on a sled. ☆**3** to keep on moving after the driving power is cut off [We ran out of gas, but the car *coasted* into the gas station.]

**coast·al** (kōs′t′l) ***adj.*** of, near, or along a coast [a *coastal* city].

**coast·er** (kōs′tər) ***n.*** **1** a person or thing that coasts. **2** a ship that sails from port to port along a coast. ☆**3** a sled or wagon for coasting. ☆**4** a small tray or disk placed under a glass or bottle to protect a table top, etc.

**Coast Guard** a branch of the U.S. armed forces whose work is to defend the coasts, stop smuggling, help ships in trouble, etc. It is under the control of the Department of Transportation or, in wartime, of the Department of the Navy.

**coast·line** (kōst′līn) ***n.*** the outline or shape of a coast.

**coat** (kōt) ***n.*** **1** an outer garment with sleeves, that opens down the front [an over*coat;* the *coat* of a suit]. **2** the natural covering of an animal, as of skin or fur [Our dog has a curly, black *coat*.] **3** any outer covering or layer [The house needs two *coats* of paint.] ◆*v.* to cover with a coat or layer of something [The street is *coated* with ice.]

**co·a·ti** (kō ät′ē) ***n.*** a small animal that lives in trees in Mexico and Central and South America. It is like the raccoon but has a longer snout. —*pl.* **co·a′tis** *Also called* **co·a·ti·mun·di** (kō ät′ē mun′dē).

**coat·ing** (kōt′iŋ) ***n.*** **1** a layer of something covering a surface [a *coating* of enamel]. **2** cloth for making coats.

**coat of arms** a group of designs and figures arranged as on a shield, to serve as the special mark of some person, family, or institution. *See the picture.*

**coat of mail** a suit of armor that was made of metal rings linked together or of small metal plates overlapping one another.

**co·au·thor** (kō ô′thər) ***n.*** an author who works with another author in writing something, as a book.

**coax** (kōks) ***v.*** to keep on asking for something in a pleasant and gentle way [She *coaxed* her parents to let her go swimming.]

**co·ax·i·al cable** (kō ak′sē əl) a specially insulated cable for sending telephone, telegraph, or television signals.

**cob** (käb) ***n.*** **1** *same as* **corncob**. **2** a male swan. **3** a short, stout horse.

**co·balt** (kō′bôlt) ***n.*** a hard, shiny, gray metal that is a chemical element. It is used in alloys and in making paints, inks, etc., especially blue ones.

> **Cobalt** comes from a German word meaning "goblin." In earlier times, miners regarded cobalt as worthless and thought that goblins had put it in the mines in place of valuable silver. *See also the word history at* **nickel**.

**cob·ble** (käb′'l) ***v.*** to mend, especially shoes or boots. **—cob′bled, cob′bling**

**cob·bler**[1] (käb′lər) ***n.*** a person whose work is mending shoes or boots.

☆**cob·bler**[2] (käb′lər) ***n.*** a fruit pie with no bottom crust and a top crust of biscuit dough.

**cob·ble·stone** (käb′'l stōn) ***n.*** a rounded stone. At one time cobblestones were much used for paving streets.

**co·bra** (kō′brə) ***n.*** a very poisonous snake of Asia and Africa. When it is excited, the skin around its neck swells into a hood. *See the picture.*

**cob·web** (käb′web) ***n.*** a web spun by a spider.

> Since cobwebs are often found in quiet, undisturbed places, the word is often used in a figure of speech about things that are not much used or not very active [I tried to blow the *cobwebs* from my brain and remember where I had put the picture.]

**co·caine** or **co·cain** (kō kān′) ***n.*** a drug that deadens the nerves. It was once much used in dentistry and medicine to lessen pain, but it is habit-forming and so other drugs are now used.

**coc·cus** (käk′əs) ***n.*** any of a group of round or oval bacteria [Scarlet fever is caused by a bacterium called strepto*coccus*.] *—pl.* **coc·ci** (käk′sī)

**cock**[1] (käk) ***n.*** **1** a male bird; especially, a rooster. **2** a faucet or valve used to control the flow of a liquid or gas. **3** the hammer of a gun; also, its position when set for firing. ◆***v.*** **1** to tip to one side; tilt [He *cocked* his hat over his ear.] **2** to turn up or toward something [The dog *cocked* its ear.] **3** to set the hammer of a gun in firing position.

**cock**[2] (käk) ***n.*** a small pile of hay or straw, shaped like a cone.

**cock·ade** (kä kād′) ***n.*** a knot of ribbon or other decoration, worn on a hat as a badge.

**cock-a-doo·dle-doo** (käk′ə do͞o′d'l do͞o′) ***n.*** an imitation of the sound made by a rooster.

> In other languages other imitations are used for that sound. For example, in French the word is *cocorico* and in Spanish it is *quiquiriquí*.

**cock·a·too** (käk′ə to͞o) ***n.*** a parrot of Australia, etc., that has a high crest and white feathers with a tinge of yellow or pink. *—pl.* **cock′a·toos**

**cock·a·trice** (käk′ə tris) ***n.*** a serpent in legends that was supposedly able to kill just by looking.

**cock·er·el** (käk′ər əl) ***n.*** a young rooster.

**cobra**
1.8 m (6 ft.) long

**coach**

**coat of arms**

**cockroach**

**cock·er spaniel** (käk′ər) a small dog with long, drooping ears, long, silky hair, and short legs.

**cock·eyed** (käk′īd) ***adj.*** **1** cross-eyed. **2** crooked or lopsided; off at an angle: *slang in this meaning* [Her hat is on *cockeyed*.] **3** silly or ridiculous: *slang in this meaning* [a *cockeyed* idea or plan].

**cock·fight** (käk′fīt) ***n.*** a fight between gamecocks. 

**cock·le** (käk′'l) ***n.*** **1** a shellfish that is used for food and has two hinged shells with ridges. **2** one of these shells: *also called* **cock′le·shell**. **3** a wrinkle or pucker. **—warm the cockles of one's heart**, to make one feel pleased or cheerful.

**cock·ney** (käk′nē) ***n.*** **1** a person who comes from the East End of London, England, and speaks the kind of English that is heard in that district. *—pl.* **cock′neys** **2** this kind of English [In *cockney*, the "h" sound is often dropped, so that "his" is spoken as "is."] ◆***adj.*** of or like cockneys or their speech.

**cock·pit** (käk′pit) ***n.*** in a small airplane, the space where the pilot and passengers sit. In a large plane, it is the space for the pilot and copilot.

**cock·roach** (käk′rōch) ***n.*** an insect with long feelers, and a flat, soft, brown or black body. It is a common pest in some kitchens. *See the picture.*

**cocks·comb** (käks′kōm) ***n.*** **1** the red, fleshy growth on the head of a rooster. **2** a plant with red or yellow flowers that look like this.

**cock·sure** (käk′shoor′) ***adj.*** absolutely sure; especially, sure of oneself in a stubborn way.

**cock·tail** (käk′tāl) ***n.*** ☆**1** an alcoholic drink made by mixing liquor with certain wines, fruit juices, etc. ☆**2** an appetizer served at the beginning of a meal, such as tomato juice, or seafood in a sharp sauce.

| | | | |
|---|---|---|---|
| **a** fat | **ir** here | **ou** out | **zh** leisure |
| **ā** ape | **ī** bite, fire | **u** up | **ng** ring |
| **ä** car, lot | **ō** go | **ur** fur | a *in* ago |
| **e** ten | **ô** law, horn | **ch** chin | e *in* agent |
| **er** care | **oi** oil | **sh** she | **ə** = i *in* unity |
| **ē** even | **o͝o** look | **th** thin | o *in* collect |
| **i** hit | **o͞o** tool | ***th*** then | u *in* focus |

**C**

**cock·y** (käk′ē) ***adj.*** sure of oneself in a rude and bold way; conceited: *used only in everyday talk.* —**cock′i·er, cock′i·est** —**cock′i·ly** ***adv.*** —**cock′i·ness** ***n.***

**co·co** (kō′kō) ***n.*** **1** *a shorter name for* **coconut palm. 2** a coconut. —*pl.* **co′cos**

**co·coa** (kō′kō) ***n.*** **1** a powder made from roasted cacao seeds, used in making chocolate. **2** a drink made from this powder by adding sugar and hot water or milk. **3** a light, reddish brown.

**co·co·nut** or **co·coa·nut** (kō′kə nut) ***n.*** the large, round fruit of a tall, tropical palm tree (called the **coconut palm** or **coco palm**). Coconuts have a thick, hard, brown shell that has an inside layer of sweet white matter used as a food. The hollow center is filled with a sweet, milky liquid.

**co·coon** (kə ko͞on′) ***n.*** the silky case that caterpillars spin to shelter themselves while they are changing into butterflies or moths. *See the picture.*

**cod** (käd) ***n.*** an important large food fish found in northern seas. —*pl.* **cod** or **cods**

**C.O.D.** or **c.o.d.** collect on delivery [When goods are sent *C.O.D.*, the receiver must pay for them when they are delivered.]

**Cod, Cape** (käd) a peninsula in southeastern Massachusetts.

**cod·dle** (käd′′l) ***v.*** **1** to cook, especially eggs, gently in water that is very hot but not boiling. **2** to treat tenderly, as a baby or a sick person; pamper. —**cod′dled, cod′dling**



**code** (kōd) ***n.*** **1** a set of laws, as of a nation, city, or organization, arranged in a clear, orderly way. **2** any set of rules for proper behavior [a moral *code*]. **3** a set of signals used in sending messages, as by telegraph or flags [the Morse *code*]. **4** a system of secret writing in which words, letters, figures, etc. are given special meanings [Wartime messages are often sent in *code* so that the enemy will not understand them.] ◆***v.*** to put a message into the signals or secret letters of a code. —**cod′ed, cod′ing**

**co·deine** (kō′dēn) ***n.*** a drug got from opium and used in medicine to lessen pain and in cough medicines.

**cod·fish** (käd′fish) ***n.*** *same as* **cod.**

**codg·er** (käj′ər) ***n.*** an odd or queer fellow, especially an older one.

**cod·i·fy** (käd′ə fī *or* kō′də fī) ***v.*** to put in the form of a code; arrange in an orderly way [Justinian *codified* Roman law in the 6th century.] —**cod′i·fied, cod′i·fy·ing** —**cod′i·fi·ca′tion** ***n.***

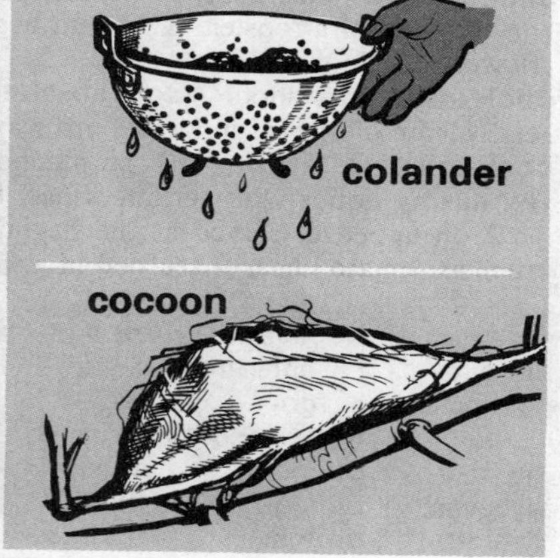


**cod·ling moth** (käd′ling) a small moth whose larvae ruin various fruits [The worm you find in an apple is the larva of the *codling moth.*]

**cod-liv·er oil** (käd′liv′ər) oil that is got from the livers of cod and certain other fish. It is rich in vitamins A and D.

**Co·dy** (kō′dē), **William Frederick** 1846–1917; American army scout, who was famous for his shooting and riding skills. He performed in shows under the name of **Buffalo Bill.**

☆**co·ed** or **co-ed** (kō′ed) ***n.*** a woman or girl student at a coeducational college. *This word is no longer much used.*

☆**co·ed·u·ca·tion·al** (kō′ej ə kā′shən ′l) ***adj.*** that is or has to do with a school or college in which both boys and girls or men and women are in the same classes together.

**coe·la·canth** (sē′lə kanth) ***n.*** a large fish of earliest times, from which land animals may have developed. There are only a few coelacanths alive today.

**co·erce** (kō ʉrs′) ***v.*** to force into doing something; compel [He was *coerced* by threats into helping them.] —**co·erced′, co·erc′ing** —**co·er·cion** (kō ʉr′shən) ***n.***

**co·ex·ist** (kō′ig zist′) ***v.*** **1** to go on living or existing together at the same time. **2** to live together in a peaceful way even though there are political or other differences. —**co′ex·ist′ence** ***n.***

**cof·fee** (kôf′ē) ***n.*** **1** a dark-brown drink made by brewing the roasted and ground seeds of a tropical plant in boiling water. **2** these seeds (*also called* **coffee beans**) or the plant on which they grow. *See the picture.*

☆**coffee break** a short rest from work, when coffee or other refreshment may be taken.

**cof·fee·pot** (kôf′ē pät′) ***n.*** a pot with a lid and spout, in which coffee is made.

**coffee shop** a restaurant, as in a hotel, where refreshments and light meals are served.

☆**coffee table** a low table on which refreshments can be served, as in a living room.

**cof·fer** (kôf′ər) ***n.*** **1** a box or chest in which money or valuables are kept; money box. **2 coffers,** *pl.* a treasury; funds [The city emptied its *coffers* to pay for the new park.]

**cof·fin** (kôf′in) ***n.*** the case or box into which a dead person is put to be buried.

**cog** (käg) ***n.*** **1** any one of a row of teeth on the rim of a wheel, which fit between the teeth on another wheel so that one wheel can turn the other. **2** a person thought of as just one small part in the working of a business, etc.: *used only in everyday talk.*

**co·gent** (kō′jənt) ***adj.*** strong and to the point; convincing [a *cogent* reason or argument]. —**co′gen·cy** ***n.*** —**co′gent·ly** ***adv.***

**cog·i·tate** (käj′ə tāt) ***v.*** to think hard; consider with care. —**cog′i·tat·ed, cog′i·tat·ing** —**cog′i·ta′tion** ***n.***

**co·gnac** (kōn′yak *or* kän′yak) ***n.*** a French brandy.

**cognate** (käg′nāt) ***adj.*** related by coming from the same source [English and Swedish are *cognate* languages.] ◆***n.*** something, especially a word, that is cognate with something else [The words "guard" and "warden" are *cognates* because they come from the same Germanic root.]

**cog·ni·zance** (käg′nə zəns) *n.* the fact of being aware or knowing; knowledge. —**take cognizance of,** to pay attention to; notice. —**cog′ni·zant** *adj.*

**co·here** (kō hir′) *v.* **1** to stick together, as parts of a mass. **2** to be connected in a natural or logical way [The ideas in a report should *cohere.*] —**co·hered′, co·her′ing**

**co·her·ent** (kō hir′ənt) *adj.* **1** sticking together [a *coherent* blob of jelly]. **2** having all parts connected in a proper way; clear [She told a rambling story that was not very *coherent.*] **3** speaking or thinking in a way that makes sense [He was terrified and no longer *coherent.*] —**co·her′ence** *n.* —**co·her′ent·ly** *adv.*

**co·he·sion** (kō hē′zhən) *n.* the act of sticking together; also, the power to stick together. —**co·he·sive** (kō hēs′iv) *adj.*

**co·ho** (kō′hō) *n.* a small salmon of the Pacific Ocean that has been brought into fresh waters of the northern U.S. for fishermen to catch. —*pl.* **co′ho** or **co′hos**

**co·hort** (kō′hôrt) *n.* **1** a group of from 300 to 600 soldiers in ancient Rome. There were ten cohorts in a legion. **2** any group moving or working together [Brigham Young led a *cohort* of Mormons to Utah.] **3** a fellow worker; associate [The mayor came with several *cohorts.*]

**coif** (koif) *n.* a cap that fits the head closely. Coifs were once worn by knights under their helmets.

**coif·fure** (kwä fyoor′) *n.* a style in which the hair is worn.

**coil** (koil) *v.* to wind around and around in circles or in a spiral [The sailors *coiled* the ropes on the deck of the ship. The vine *coiled* around the tree.] ◆*n.* **1** anything wound in circles or in a spiral [a *coil* of wire]. **2** each turn of something wound in this way [This spring has weak *coils.*]

**coin** (koin) *n.* **1** a piece of metal money having a certain value. **2** metal money in general [The U.S. Mint produces *coin.*] ◆*v.* **1** to make metal into coins. **2** to make up or invent [The word "gas" was *coined* by a Belgian chemist in the 17th century.]

**coin·age** (koi′nij) *n.* **1** the act of coining [the *coinage* of money; the *coinage* of new words]. **2** coins; metal money [The U.S. no longer issues gold *coinage.*] **3** a word or expression that has been made up or invented ["Laser" and "rock-and-roll" are American *coinages*].

**co·in·cide** (kō′in sīd′) *v.* **1** to be exactly alike in shape and size [If one circle fits exactly over another, they *coincide.*] **2** to happen at the same time [Our birthdays *coincide.*] **3** to agree; be the same [Our interests do not *coincide.*] —**co′in·cid′ed, co′in·cid′ing**

> SYNONYMS: **Coincide** tells us that the things being talked about are exactly alike [It is good that our vacation plans for this summer *coincide.*] **Agree** suggests that things fit or go together easily [The stories of the witnesses do not exactly *agree.*]

**co·in·ci·dence** (kō in′sə dəns) *n.* **1** a happening of events that seem to be connected but are not actually; accidental happening [It is just a *coincidence* that both roommates are named Jones.] **2** the fact of coinciding [the *coincidence* of two triangles].

**co·in·ci·dent** (kō in′sə dənt) *adj.* **1** happening at the same time; coinciding [Winter in the U.S. is *coincident* with summer in Australia.] **2** exactly alike in shape and size [*coincident* circles].

**co·in·ci·den·tal** (kō in′sə den′t'l) *adj.* being a coincidence; happening by accident and not really connected [Our meeting in Paris was *coincidental.*]

**coke** (kōk) *n.* coal from which most of the gases have been removed by heating. It burns with great heat and little smoke. It is used as a fuel in blast furnaces.

**Col.** *abbreviation for* **Colonel.**

**co·la** (kō′lə) *n.* a sweet drink made of soda water with a flavoring that comes from the nut of an African tree.

**col·an·der** (kul′ən dər *or* käl′ən dər) *n.* a pan with holes in the bottom for draining off liquids, as in washing vegetables. *See the picture.*

**cold** (kōld) *adj.* **1** having a temperature much lower than that of the human body; very chilly; frigid [a *cold* day; a *cold* drink]. *See* SYNONYMS *at* **chilly. 2** without the proper heat or warmth [Your bath will get *cold.*] **3** feeling chilled [If you are *cold,* put on your coat.] **4** without any feeling; unkind, unfriendly, or gloomy [a *cold* welcome; a *cold* stare]. **5** still far from what one is trying to find out [Guess again, you're *cold.*] ☆**6** unconscious: *slang in this meaning* [The punch knocked him *cold.*] ☆**7** in all details; thoroughly: *slang in this meaning* [I've got all the plays down *cold.*] ◆*n.* **1** a lack of heat or warmth [the intense *cold* of the arctic regions]. **2** a common illness in which there is sneezing and coughing and a running nose. —**catch cold,** to become ill with a cold. —**get cold feet,** to become timid or afraid: *used only in everyday talk.* —**throw cold water on,** to discourage. —**cold′ly** *adv.* —**cold′ness** *n.*

**cold·blood·ed** (kōld′blud′id) *adj.* **1** having a body temperature that becomes colder or warmer as the air or water around the animal changes [Fishes and snakes are *coldblooded* animals.] **2** not having normal human feelings of kindness and pity; cruel [a *coldblooded* murderer].

**cold cream** a creamy substance used to make the skin clean and soft.

**cold·heart·ed** (kōld′här′tid) *adj.* not feeling sympathy or kindness; unkind.

**cold sore** a sore made up of little blisters that form about the mouth when one has a cold or fever.

**cold war** strong disagreement between nations in political or economic matters, but without actual warfare.

**Cole·ridge** (kōl′rij), **Samuel Taylor** 1772–1834; English poet.

☆**cole·slaw** (kōl′slô) *n.* a salad made of shredded raw cabbage, often mixed with salad dressing and seasoning: *also written* **cole slaw.**

> **Coleslaw** comes from two Dutch words, *kool,* which means "cabbage," and *sla,* which means "salad." Because it is served cold, some people by mistake call it "cold slaw."

**col·ic** (käl′ik) *n.* sharp pain in the bowels.



| | | | | | | | |
|---|---|---|---|---|---|---|---|
| **a** | fat | **ir** | here | **ou** | out | **zh** | leisure |
| **ā** | ape | **ī** | bite, fire | **u** | up | **ng** | ring |
| **ä** | car, lot | **ō** | go | **ur** | fur | | a *in* ago |
| **e** | ten | **ô** | law, horn | **ch** | chin | | e *in* agent |
| **er** | care | **oi** | oil | **sh** | she | **ə** = | i *in* unity |
| **ē** | even | **oo** | look | **th** | thin | | o *in* collect |
| **i** | hit | **ōō** | tool | ***th*** | then | | u *in* focus |

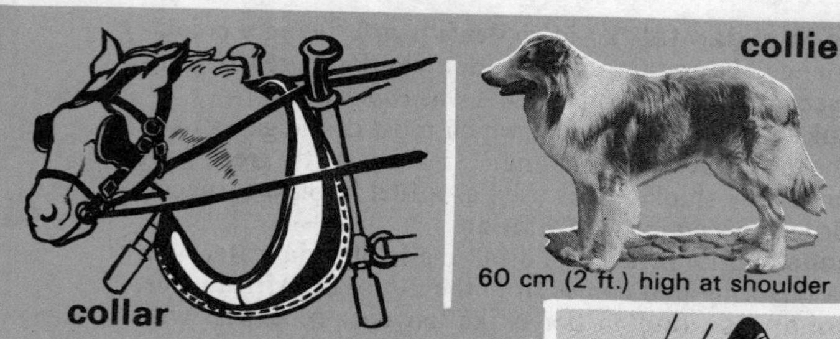
collar

collie

60 cm (2 ft.) high at shoulder

Colosseum

colonnade

**Col·i·se·um** (käl'ə sē'əm) ***n.*** **1** *another spelling of* **Colosseum. 2 coliseum,** a large building or stadium for sports events, shows, etc.

**col·lab·o·rate** (kə lab'ə rāt) ***v.*** **1** to work together in preparing something [Charles and Mary Lamb *collaborated* in writing "Tales from Shakespeare."] **2** to help or work with an enemy that has invaded one's country. —**col·lab'o·rat·ed, col·lab'o·rat·ing** —**col·lab'o·ra'tion** ***n.*** —**col·lab'o·ra·tor** ***n.***



**col·lapse** (kə laps') ***v.*** **1** to fall down or fall to pieces, as when the sides fail to hold [The bridge *collapsed* when the flood waters weakened its piers.] **2** to break down or lose strength suddenly; fail [Our hope has *collapsed.* The wounded soldier *collapsed* from loss of blood.] **3** to fold together neatly in a small space [The beach chair *collapses* for easy carrying.] —**col·lapsed', col·laps'ing** ◆***n.*** the act of collapsing; a falling in, breakdown, failure, etc. [the *collapse* of a burning building; a nervous *collapse*]. —**col·laps'i·ble** ***adj.***

**col·lar** (käl'ər) ***n.*** **1** the part of a garment that fits around the neck. It is sometimes a separate piece or a band that is folded over. **2** a band of leather or metal for a dog's or cat's neck. **3** the part of a horse's harness that fits around its neck. *See the picture.* **4** a metal ring or band that is used to connect pipes or rods or to keep some part of a machine steady. ◆***v.*** **1** to put a collar on. **2** to grab as by the collar; seize [The police *collared* the thief.]

**col·lar·bone** (käl'ər bōn) ***n.*** *another name for* **clavicle.**

**col·lat·er·al** (kə lat'ər əl) ***adj.*** **1** that goes along with the main thing, but in a less important way; additional or secondary [*collateral* evidence]. **2** having the same ancestors but in a different branch of the family [Your cousins are your *collateral* relatives.] ◆***n.*** ☆stocks, bonds, or other property that is given to a lender of money to hold as a pledge that the loan will be repaid.

**col·league** (käl'ēg) ***n.*** a person who works in the same office, the same profession, etc.; fellow worker.

**col·lect** (kə lekt') ***v.*** **1** to gather in one place; assemble [*Collect* the rubbish and burn it. Water *collects* around the sink drain.] *See* SYNONYMS *at* **gather. 2** to gather things as a hobby [She has been *collecting* stamps for years.] **3** to call for and get money owed [The building manager *collects* the rent.] ◆***adj., adv.*** ☆with payment to be made by the person receiving [Telephone me *collect.*]

**col·lect·ed** (kə lek'tid) ***adj.*** **1** gathered together in one book or set [the *collected* works of Shakespeare]. **2** in full control of oneself; not upset [Try to stay calm and *collected* during the discussion.] *See* SYNONYMS *at* **cool.**

**col·lec·tion** (kə lek'shən) ***n.*** **1** the act of gathering [Rubbish *collection* is on Friday.] **2** things collected [a *collection* of coins]. **3** something gathered into a mass or pile [a *collection* of dust]. **4** money collected [a *collection* for a church].

**col·lec·tive** (kə lek'tiv) ***adj.*** **1** of or as a group; of or by all in the group [The team made a *collective* effort to win.] **2** worked on, managed, or owned by a group [a *collective* farm]. **3** that is singular in form but is the name for a group of individual persons or things [Army, orchestra, and crowd are *collective* nouns.] —**col·lec'tive·ly** ***adv.***

A **collective** noun usually takes a singular verb if it is thought of as a single unit. Example: The orchestra is playing a Mozart symphony. If the noun is thought of as a group of individuals, it can take a plural verb. Example: The orchestra are tuning up their instruments.

**col·lec·tor** (kə lek'tər) ***n.*** a person or thing that collects [a coin *collector;* a bill *collector*].

**col·leen** (käl'ēn) ***n.*** a girl: *this is an Irish word.*

**col·lege** (käl'ij) ***n.*** **1** a school that one can go to after high school for higher studies. Colleges give degrees to students when they graduate. A college is often a part of a university, which may have a number of special colleges, as of law or medicine. **2** a school where one can get training in some special work [a business *college*]. **3** a group of persons having certain powers and duties [the electoral *college*].

**col·le·gian** (kə lē'jən) ***n.*** a college student.

**col·le·giate** (kə lē'jət) ***adj.*** of or like a college or college students [*collegiate* life].

**col·lide** (kə līd') ***v.*** **1** to come together with force; bump into [The car *collided* with a train.] **2** to be opposed; disagree; clash [Our views *collide* on the subject.] —**col·lid'ed, col·lid'ing**

**col·lie** (käl'ē) ***n.*** a large dog with long hair and a narrow head, often used to herd sheep. *See the picture.*

**col·lier** (käl'yər) ***n.*** **1** a coal miner. **2** a ship for carrying coal.

**col·lier·y** (käl'yər ē) ***n.*** a coal mine and its buildings, equipment, etc. —*pl.* **col'lier·ies**

**col·li·sion** (kə lizh'ən) ***n.*** **1** the act of coming together with force; crash [an automobile *collision*]. **2** a clash of ideas, interests, etc.

**col·loid** (käl'oid) ***n.*** a thick substance formed when very fine particles that cannot be dissolved stay evenly scattered throughout a liquid, gas, or solid. —**col·loi·dal** (kə loi'd'l) ***adj.***

**col·lo·qui·al** (kə lō'kwē əl) ***adj.*** being or containing the words and phrases that are used only in everyday talk, or in writing that is like everyday talk ["My buddy flunked the exam" is a *colloquial* way of saying "My close friend failed the examination."] —**col·lo'qui·al·ly** ***adv.***

**col·lo·qui·al·ism** (kə lō'kwē əl iz'm) ***n.*** a colloquial word or phrase.

**col·lu·sion** (kə lo͞o'zhən) ***n.*** a secret agreement for a wrong or unlawful purpose [The cashier had worked in *collusion* with the thieves.]

**Colo.** *abbreviation for* **Colorado.**

**Co·logne** (kə lōn') a city in western West Germany, on the Rhine.

**co·logne** (kə lōn') ***n.*** a sweet-smelling liquid like perfume, but not so strong.

**Co·lom·bi·a** (kə lum'bē ə) a country in northwestern South America.

**co·lon**[1] (kō'lən) ***n.*** a punctuation mark (:) used before a long quotation, example, series, etc. It is also used after the greeting of a formal letter [Dear Ms. Franklin:].

**co·lon**[2] (kō'lən) ***n.*** the main part of the large intestine, that leads to the rectum.

**colo·nel** (kur'n'l) ***n.*** an army or air force officer ranking just above a lieutenant colonel.

> At one time the word **colonel** was written *coronel.* The spelling was later changed to bring it closer to the Italian word *colonello* from which we got it. That word came from the Latin word *columna,* meaning "column." A **colonel** leads a column of soldiers. Even though the spelling was changed, we still pronounce the word as though it is spelled with an "r."

**co·lo·ni·al** (kə lō'nē əl) ***adj.*** **1** of or living in a colony or colonies. **2** *often* **Colonial,** of or in the thirteen British colonies in North America that became the United States. ➛***n.*** a person who lives in a colony.

☆**col·o·nist** (käl'ə nist) ***n.*** **1** one of the first settlers of a colony. **2** a person who lives in a colony.

**col·o·nize** (käl'ə nīz) ***v.*** **1** to start a colony or colonies in [Spain was the first nation to *colonize* the New World.] **2** to settle in a colony. —**col'o·nized, col'o·niz·ing** —**col'o·ni·za'tion** ***n.***

**col·on·nade** (käl ə nād') ***n.*** a row of columns as along the side of a building. *See the picture.*

**col·o·ny** (käl'ə nē) ***n.*** **1** a group of people who settle in a distant land but are still under the rule of the country from which they came. **2** the place where they settle [the Pilgrim *colony* at Plymouth]. **3** a land that is ruled by a country some distance away [Java was once a Dutch *colony.*] **4** a group of people who live together in a city and have the same interests or background [an artists' *colony;* the Chinese *colony* in San Francisco]. **5** a group of animals or plants living or growing together [a *colony* of ants]. —*pl.* **col'o·nies** —**the Colonies,** the thirteen British colonies in North America that won their independence and became the United States.

**col·or** (kul'ər) ***n.*** **1** the effect that light rays of different wavelengths have on the eyes [The *colors* of the rainbow lie in bands shading from red (formed by the longest rays), through orange, yellow, green, blue, and violet (formed by the shortest rays).] **2** anything used to produce color; dye; pigment; paint. Black, white, and gray are often called colors, but see the entries for **black, white,** and **gray. 3 colors,** *pl.* a flag or banner. **4** look, appearance, or sound [writings that have the *color* of truth]. **5** an interesting quality or character [She is a speaker with a lot of *color.*] ➛***v.*** **1** to give color to or change the color of [*Color* the drawings with crayons. Fever *colored* his cheeks.] **2** to take on a color or to change color. **3** to change or affect in some way [Her opinions *color* her reports.] —**call to the colors,** to call or order to serve in the armed forces. —**change color, 1** to become pale. **2** to blush or flush. —**show one's colors,** to show what one really is or what one really feels. —**with flying colors,** with great success.

> SYNONYMS: **Color** is the general word for the effect of different light rays on the eyes. **Shade** is used to describe any of the small differences in the darkness or lightness of a color [a light *shade* of green]. **Tint** is used to describe the amount of white in a color and suggests that the color is pale or delicate [pastel *tints*].

**Col·o·rad·o** (käl'ə rad'ō *or* käl'ə rä'dō) **1** a State in the southwestern part of the U.S.: abbreviated **Colo., CO 2** a river flowing southwest through Colorado.

**col·or·a·tion** (kul'ə rā'shən) ***n.*** the way in which a thing is colored; coloring.

**col·or·blind** (kul'ər blīnd) ***adj.*** not able to see the differences between certain colors, as between red and green, or, sometimes, not able to see the differences between any colors. —**col'or·blind'ness** ***n.***

**col·ored** (kul'ərd) ***adj.*** **1** having color [*colored* paper; a green-*colored* tie]. **2** belonging to any of the groups of human beings other than the whites; especially, being black, or Negro: *no longer much used with this meaning.* 143

**col·or·ful** (kul'ər fəl) ***adj.*** **1** full of color; bright [*colorful* wallpaper]. **2** full of variety or interest; vivid; picturesque [The circus is a *colorful* setting for a novel.]

**col·or·ing** (kul'ər iŋ) ***n.*** **1** the act or art of adding colors. **2** anything used to color; dye; pigment; paint. **3** the way in which a thing is colored [the bright *coloring* of tropical birds].

**col·or·less** (kul'ər lis) ***adj.*** **1** without color [*colorless* glass]. **2** not lively or interesting; dull [a *colorless* piece of music].

**co·los·sal** (kə läs''l) ***adj.*** very large or very great; enormous or immense.

**Col·os·se·um** (käl'ə sē'əm) a stadium in Rome which was built in the first century A.D. A large part of it is still standing. *See the picture.*

**co·los·sus** (kə läs'əs) ***n.*** a very large or important person or thing. The **Colossus of Rhodes** was a huge statue of Apollo built at Rhodes by the Greeks in the third century B.C. —*pl.* **co·los·si** (kə läs'ī) or **co·los'sus·es**

**col·our** (kul'ər) ***n., v.*** *British spelling of* **color.**

**colt** (kōlt) ***n.*** a young male horse, donkey, etc.

| | | | | | | | |
|---|---|---|---|---|---|---|---|
| **a** | fat | **ir** | here | **ou** | out | **zh** | leisure |
| **ā** | ape | **ī** | bite, fire | **u** | up | **ŋ** | ring |
| **ä** | car, lot | **ō** | go | **ur** | fur | | a *in* ago |
| **e** | ten | **ô** | law, horn | **ch** | chin | | e *in* agent |
| **er** | care | **oi** | oil | **sh** | she | **ə =** | i *in* unity |
| **ē** | even | **oo** | look | **th** | thin | | o *in* collect |
| **i** | hit | **o͞o** | tool | ***th*** | then | | u *in* focus |

☆**Co·lum·bi·a** (kə lum′bē ə) **1** the United States: *a name used in poetry.* **2** the capital of South Carolina. **3** a river rising in British Columbia and flowing between Washington and Oregon to the Pacific.

**col·um·bine** (käl′əm bīn) ***n.*** a plant having showy flowers with spurs on them.

**Co·lum·bus** (kə lum′bəs) the capital of Ohio.

**Co·lum·bus** (kə lum′bəs), **Christopher** 1451?–1506; the Italian explorer who discovered America in 1492 while sailing in the service of Spain.

**Columbus Day** the second Monday in October, a legal holiday celebrating the discovery of America by Christopher Columbus in 1492.

**col·umn** (käl′əm) ***n.*** **1** a long, generally round, upright support; pillar. Columns usually stand in groups to hold up a roof or other part of a building, but they are sometimes used just for decoration. *See the picture.* **2** any long, upright thing like a column [a *column* of water; the spinal *column*]. **3** any of the long sections of print lying side by side on a page and separated by a line or blank space [Each page of this book has two *columns.*] **4** any of the articles by one writer or on a special subject, that appear regularly in a newspaper or magazine [a chess *column*]. **5** a group of soldiers, ships, etc. placed in a row, one behind another.

☆**col·um·nist** (käl′əm nist) ***n.*** a person who writes a column, as in a newspaper [a sports *columnist*].

**com-** *a prefix meaning* with *or* together [To *compress* a mass is to press it together.]



**co·ma** (kō′mə) ***n.*** a condition like a deep, long sleep, often caused by injury or disease.

**Co·man·che** (kə man′chē) ***n.*** a member of a tribe of American Indians who used to live in the Western plains but now live mainly in Oklahoma.

**comb** (kōm) ***n.*** **1** a thin strip of hard rubber, plastic, metal, etc. with teeth. A comb is passed through the hair to arrange or clean it, or is put in the hair to hold it in place. **2** a tool like this, used for cleaning and straightening wool or flax. **3** the red, fleshy growth on the head of a rooster, etc. **4** *a shorter form of* **honeycomb.** ◆***v.*** **1** to smooth, arrange, or clean with a comb. **2** to search carefully through [I *combed* the house for that book.]

**com·bat** (kəm bat′ *or* käm′bat) ***v.*** to fight or struggle; oppose [They are bringing out new drugs to *combat* disease.] —**com·bat′ed** or **com·bat′ted, com·bat′ing** or **com·bat′ting** ◆***n.*** (käm′bat) **1** battle [He was wounded in *combat.*] **2** a struggle or conflict.

**com·bat·ant** (käm′bə tənt *or* kəm bat′'nt) ***adj.*** fighting or ready to fight. ◆***n.*** a person who is fighting; fighter.

**com·bat·ive** (kəm bat′iv *or* käm′bə tiv) ***adj.*** fond of fighting; ready or eager to fight.

**comb·er** (kōm′ər) ***n.*** **1** a person or machine that combs wool or flax. ☆**2** a large wave that breaks on a beach.

**com·bi·na·tion** (käm′bə nā′shən) ***n.*** **1** the act of combining or joining [He succeeded by a *combination* of hard work and luck.] **2** a thing made by combining other things [This green paint is a *combination* of blue and yellow.] **3** a number of people united together for some purpose. **4** the series of numbers or letters that must be turned to in the right order to open a kind of lock called a ☆**combination lock** [Most safes have a *combination lock.*] **5** in mathematics, any of the subsets into which a set of units may be arranged, paying no attention to order [Some *combinations* of 123 are 231, 321, and 123.]

**com·bine** (kəm bīn′) ***v.*** to come or bring together; join; unite [to *combine* work with pleasure; to *combine* chemical elements]. —**com·bined′, com·bin′ing** ◆***n.*** (käm′bīn) ☆**1** a machine that gathers grain and threshes it at the same time. *See the picture.* ☆**2** a group of people or businesses joined together, usually for an improper or selfish purpose.

**combining form** a word form or part of a word that is combined with other forms or with affixes to form a word ["Hydro-" is a *combining form,* as in "hydrophobia."]

**com·bus·ti·ble** (kəm bus′tə b'l) ***adj.*** **1** that catches fire and burns easily [Be careful of *combustible* cleaning fluids.] **2** easily excited [She has a *combustible* temper.]

**com·bus·tion** (kəm bus′chən) ***n.*** the act or process of burning [An internal-*combustion* engine is one in which the fuel is burned within the engine itself.]

**come** (kum) ***v.*** **1** to move from "there" to "here" [*Come* to me. Will you *come* to our party?] **2** to arrive or appear [Help will *come* soon.] **3** to be in a certain order [After 9 *comes* 10.] **4** to be descended [She *comes* from a large family.] **5** to be caused; result [Poor grades may *come* from lack of study.] **6** to get to be; become [The string around the package *came* loose.] **7** to be made or sold [This dress *comes* in four colors.] **8** to add up; amount [Your grocery bill *comes* to $20.78.] **9** to reach; extend [These shorts *come* to the knees.] **Come** is often used as an exclamation to show that one is angry, impatient, suspicious, etc. [*Come, come!* You can't play ball in here.] —**came, come, com′ing** —**come about,** to happen; occur. —**come across** or **come upon,** to meet or find by accident. —**come at,** to approach angrily, as if to attack. —**come back,** to return. —**come between,** to separate or make unfriendly. [Don't let a little quarrel *come between* us.] —**come by,** to get; gain [This rare stamp is hard to *come by.*] —**come in, 1** to enter. **2** to arrive. **3** to begin to be used; become fashionable. **4** to finish in a contest [She *came in* first.] —**come into, 1** to join. **2** to get or inherit [He *came into* a fortune.] —**come off, 1** to become separated or unfastened. **2** to take place; happen [The rummage sale *came off* well.] —**come out, 1** to be shown or told [Your secret will *come out.*] **2** to be offered for sale [This book *came out* last month.] **3** to end up. —**come over,** to happen to [What's *come over* you?] —**come to,** to become conscious again. —**come up,** to be mentioned, as in a discussion. —**come upon,** to find by chance. —**come up to,** to equal. —☆**come up with,** to find or produce [Try to *come up with* an answer.] —☆**how come?** how is it that? why?: *used only in everyday talk.*

**co·me·di·an** (kə mē′dē ən) ***n.*** an actor who plays comic parts, or one who tells jokes and does funny things to make people laugh.

**co·me·di·enne** (kə mē′dē en′) ***n.*** a woman who is a comedian.

**com·e·dy** (käm′ə dē) ***n.*** **1** a play or movie that is more or less humorous and has a happy ending. **2** a comical happening in real life [The mix-up with the twins was quite a *comedy*.] —*pl.* **com′e·dies**

The ancient Greeks would sometimes hold a banquet or festival that they called a *komos*. There would be much singing and dancing. The chief singer, called a *komoidos*, would often tell funny stories. From that title we get our word **comedy**.

**come·ly** (kum′lē) *adj.* pleasant to look at; pretty [a *comely* woman]. —**come′li·er, come′li·est**

**com·er** (kum′ər) *n.* a person who comes [The contest is open to all *comers*.]

**com·et** (käm′ət) *n.* a heavenly body that has a bright center and, usually, a fiery tail, and that moves in a regular course around the sun.

**com·fort** (kum′fərt) *v.* to make feel less sad or sorrowful; ease the pain of; soothe [How can we *comfort* the children who lost their dog?] ◆*n.* **1** the condition of having one's pain or sorrow made easier [Your kind words have given me *comfort*.] **2** someone or something that brings such comfort or cheer [The blind man's radio was a great *comfort* to him.] **3** the condition of not having hardships, worry, pain, etc. [to live in *comfort*].

SYNONYMS: We can **comfort** someone who is miserable or unhappy by cheering him or her up and making it easier to bear pain or sorrow [Your cards and visits *comforted* me in the hospital.] We can **console** someone who has suffered a loss or disappointment by offering sympathy and help that makes troubles seem less hard to bear [Your many kindnesses *consoled* me when my grandmother died.]

**com·fort·a·ble** (kumf′tər b′l *or* kum′fər tə b′l) *adj.* **1** giving comfort or ease; not giving pain [a *comfortable* pair of shoes]. **2** feeling comfort; not uneasy [Are you *comfortable* in that chair?] —**com′fort·a·bly** *adv.*

**com·fort·er** (kum′fər tər) *n.* **1** a person or thing that brings comfort. ☆**2** a quilted bed covering.

**com·ic** (käm′ik) *adj.* **1** having to do with comedy. **2** funny or amusing; making one laugh. ◆*n.* **1** *same as* **comedian**. ☆**2 comics**, *pl.* a section of comic strips, as in a newspaper.

**com·i·cal** (käm′i k′l) *adj.* funny or amusing [The clown was a *comical* fellow.]

☆**comic book** a paper booklet of comic strips.

☆**comic strip** a series of cartoons or drawings that tells a comical or exciting story.

**com·ing** (kum′iŋ) *adj.* that will come; approaching; on the way [Let's go this *coming* Friday.] ◆*n.* arrival; approach [Cold mornings warn of the *coming* of winter.]

**com·ma** (käm′ə) *n.* a punctuation mark (,) used to show a pause that is shorter than the pause at the end of a sentence [The *comma* is often used between clauses or after the opening phrase of a sentence. Words, numbers, or phrases in a series are separated by *commas*.]

**com·mand** (kə mand′) *v.* **1** to give an order to; direct [I *command* you to halt!] **2** to be in control of [Captain Stone *commands* Company B.] **3** to deserve to have [Her courage *commands* our respect.] ◆*n.* **1** an order or direction [He obeyed the queen's *commands*.] **2** the power or ability to control or command; control [Who is in *command* here? He has no *command* of his temper.] **3** a military force, a district, etc. under someone's control [The general took charge of his new *command*.]

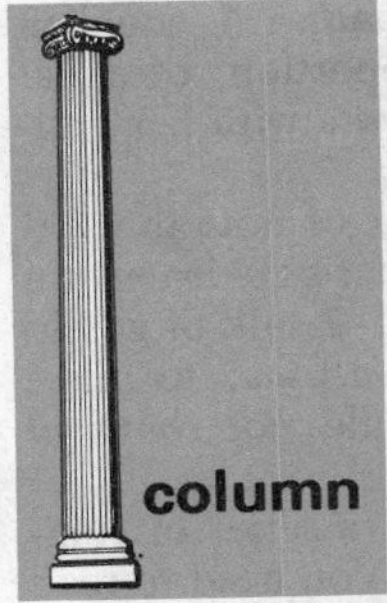
column

combine

**com·man·dant** (käm′ən dant *or* käm′ən dänt) *n.* an officer in charge of a command; commander.

**com·man·deer** (käm ən dir′) *v.* to take by force or by authority, especially for military use [The army *commandeered* the school for use as a hospital.]

**com·mand·er** (kə man′dər) *n.* **1** a person who commands, especially one in charge of a military force. **2** an officer in the navy who ranks just under a captain.

**commander in chief** the top commander of the armed forces of a nation [In the U.S., the President is the *Commander in Chief*.] —*pl.* **commanders in chief**

**com·mand·ing** (kə man′diŋ) *adj.* **1** in command or control [a *commanding* officer]. **2** that has or seems to have authority [a *commanding* voice].

**com·mand·ment** (kə mand′mənt) *n.* a law or order; especially, in the Bible, any of the ten laws (**Ten Commandments**) that God gave to Moses.



**com·man·do** (kə man′dō) *n.* any member of a small group of specially trained soldiers who make surprise raids behind enemy lines. —*pl.* **com·man′dos** or **com·man′does**

**com·mem·o·rate** (kə mem′ə rāt) *v.* to honor or keep alive the memory of [The Washington Monument *commemorates* our first President.] —**com·mem′o·rat·ed, com·mem′o·rat·ing**

**com·mem·o·ra·tion** (kə mem′ə rā′shən) *n.* **1** the act of commemorating. **2** a celebration or ceremony in memory of someone or something. —**in commemoration of**, in honor of the memory of.

**com·mence** (kə mens′) *v.* to begin or start. —**commenced′, com·menc′ing**

**com·mence·ment** (kə mens′mənt) *n.* **1** a beginning or start. **2** the graduation ceremony of a school or college, when graduates receive their degrees or diplomas.

**com·mend** (kə mend′) *v.* **1** to mention with approval; praise [a ballet company *commended* by all the dance critics]. **2** to put in someone's care or keeping; commit. —**com·men·da·tion** (käm′ən dā′shən) *n.*

**com·mend·a·ble** (kə men′də b′l) *adj.* deserving to be praised [a *commendable* effort].

| | | | | | | | |
|---|---|---|---|---|---|---|---|
| **a** | fat | **ir** | here | **ou** | out | **zh** | leisure |
| **ā** | ape | **ī** | bite, fire | **u** | up | **ŋ** | ring |
| **ä** | car, lot | **ō** | go | **ur** | fur | | a *in* ago |
| **e** | ten | **ô** | law, horn | **ch** | chin | | e *in* agent |
| **er** | care | **oi** | oil | **sh** | she | **ə** = | i *in* unity |
| **ē** | even | **oo** | look | **th** | thin | | o *in* collect |
| **i** | hit | **ōō** | tool | ***th*** | then | | u *in* focus |

**com·men·su·rate** (kə men′shər it) ***adj.*** **1** equal in measure or size. **2** in the right proportion; of equal value [She wants a salary *commensurate* with her ability.]

**com·ment** (käm′ent) ***n.*** **1** a remark or note that explains or gives an opinion [The teacher's *comments* on the poem helped us to understand it.] **2** talk or gossip [Your absence caused much *comment*.] ◆***v.*** to make comments or remarks [Doctors should not *comment* on their patients to others.]

**com·men·tar·y** (käm′ən ter′ē) ***n.*** **1** a series of comments or notes on a book, play, etc. [You need to read *commentaries* in order to understand Shakespeare's plays.] **2** something serving like a comment or illustration [This political scandal is a *commentary* on our corrupt society.] —*pl.* **com′men·tar′ies**

**com·men·tate** (käm′ən tāt) ***v.*** **1** to write or give a commentary on. **2** to perform as a commentator as on radio or TV. —**com′men·tat·ed, com′men·tat·ing**

**com·men·ta·tor** (käm′ən tāt′ər) ***n.*** **1** a person who writes a commentary on a book, etc. **2** a person whose work is reporting and also commenting on the news, as on radio or TV.

**com·merce** (käm′ərs) ***n.*** the buying and selling of goods, especially when done on a large scale between cities, states, or countries; trade.

146 **com·mer·cial** (kə mʉr′shəl) ***adj.*** **1** having to do with commerce or trade [*commercial* relations between countries]. **2** in, for, or concerned with the making of profit [Their new restaurant is a great *commercial* success.] ◆***n.*** a paid advertisement on radio or TV. —**com·mer′cial·ly *adv.***

**com·mer·cial·ize** (kə mʉr′shəl īz) ***v.*** to make into a business matter, especially in order to make a profit [All the ads on TV make it highly *commercialized*.] —**com·mer′cial·ized, com·mer′cial·iz·ing —com·mer′cial·ism *n.***

**com·min·gle** (kə miŋ′g'l) ***v.*** to mingle or mix together; blend —**com·min′gled, com·min′gling**

**com·mis·er·ate** (kə miz′ə rāt) ***v.*** to feel or show sorrow or pity for another's troubles; sympathize [We *commiserated* with the victims of the flood.] —**com·mis′er·at·ed, com·mis′er·at·ing —com·mis′er·a′tion *n.***

**com·mis·sar** (käm′ə sär) ***n.*** at one time, the head of any of the government departments in the U.S.S.R. Since 1946 the name has been *minister*.

**com·mis·sar·y** (käm′ə ser′ē) ***n.*** ☆a store, as in a military camp or lumber camp, where food and supplies can be bought. —*pl.* **com′mis·sar′ies**

**com·mis·sion** (kə mish′ən) ***n.*** **1** the right to perform certain duties or to have certain powers; also, a paper giving this right [Officers in the U.S. armed forces hold their rank by a *commission* from the President.] **2** a thing that a person is given the power to do for another. **3** a group of people chosen to do a certain thing [A *commission* was appointed to study the traffic problem.] **4** the act of committing, or doing [the *commission* of a crime]. **5** a part of the money taken in on sales that is paid to the person making the sale [She received 10% of the price as her *commission*.] ◆***v.*** **1** to give a commission to [Generals, colonels, majors, captains, and lieutenants are called *commissioned* officers.] **2** to give the right to do something; authorize. **3** to put a ship into service. —**in commission, 1** in use. **2** in fit condition for use. —**out of commission, 1** not in use. **2** not in fit condition for use.

**com·mis·sion·er** (kə mish′ə nər) ***n.*** **1** a member of a commission. **2** the head of a government commission or department [a water *commissioner*].

**com·mit** (kə mit′) ***v.*** **1** to give in charge; place as a trust [to *commit* a patient to a mental hospital]. **2** to do or perform something bad or wrong [to *commit* a crime; to *commit* suicide]. **3** to put someplace or set apart for some purpose [We *committed* the empty bottles to the trash can. She *commits* much of her time to church work.] **4** to do or say something that will involve or pledge one [If you join that book club, you *commit* yourself to buying four books.] —**com·mit′ted, com·mit′ting —commit to memory,** to memorize.

SYNONYMS: When we **commit** someone to the care of others, we put that person into their keeping. When we **entrust** someone to the care of others, we are committing that person with the hope and trust that he or she will be kept safely and cared for properly.

**com·mit·ment** (kə mit′mənt) ***n.*** **1** a committing or being committed. **2** a promise; pledge.

**com·mit·tee** (kə mit′ē) ***n.*** a group of people chosen to study some matter or to do a certain thing [a *committee* to plan the party].

**com·mode** (kə mōd′) ***n.*** **1** a chest of drawers. **2** a small, low table with drawers or cabinet space. **3** a washstand. **4** a toilet.

**Commode** comes from a French word meaning "convenient" and the French word from a Latin word meaning "suitable." [*Commodes* have a suitable design to make them convenient to use.] **Commodious** comes from the same Latin word. [A *commodious* apartment has a suitable design to make it roomy.]

**com·mo·di·ous** (kə mō′dē əs) ***adj.*** having plenty of room; roomy; not crowded. *See note at* **commode**.

**com·mod·i·ty** (kə mäd′ə tē) ***n.*** anything that is bought and sold; article of trade or commerce. —*pl.* **com·mod′i·ties**

**com·mo·dore** (käm′ə dôr) ***n.*** **1** at one time, an officer in the navy who ranked just above a captain. **2** a title given to the president of a yacht club, etc.

**com·mon** (käm′ən) ***adj.*** **1** belonging equally to each or all [England, Canada, and the U.S. share a *common* language.] **2** belonging to all the people; public [a *common* park]. **3** of, from, by, or to all [the *common* good]. **4** often seen or heard; widespread; usual [Squirrels are *common* in these woods. That's a *common* saying.] **5** of the usual kind; ordinary; not outstanding [the *common* man]. **6** having no rank [Privates are *common* soldiers.] **7** coarse or crude; vulgar [She has rather *common* manners.] ◆***n.*** *often* **commons,** *pl.* ☆land that is owned or used by all the people of a town or village; public land. —**in common,** owned, used, or shared equally by all. —**com′mon·ness *n.***

SYNONYMS: Whatever is **common** is found in all or most places or is shared by all or most members of a group [a *common* sight; a *common* meal].

Whatever is **general** extends widely through all or nearly all those included in a certain kind, class, or group [There is *general* poverty among the people in that neighborhood.]

**common cold** *same as* **cold** *n. in meaning* 2.

**common denominator** **1** a number that can be divided without a remainder by each denominator of two or more fractions [The *common denominator* of 1/2 and 3/5 is 10; 1/2 becomes 5/10 and 3/5 becomes 6/10.] **2** something held in common or shared by two or more people or things [The *common denominator* of the group is the school that they all went to.]

**com·mon·er** (käm′ən ər) ***n.*** any person who is not a member of the nobility.

**common fraction** a fraction with the numerator separated from the denominator by a diagonal or horizontal line, as 5/11 or 3/4.

**com·mon·ly** (käm′ən lē) ***adv.*** as a general rule; usually; ordinarily.

**common market** an association of countries formed to bring about a closer union in trade and commerce, especially by lowering or doing away with tariffs among themselves. The European Economic Community is also called the **Common Market**.

**common noun** any noun that is not the name of a particular person or thing and is not begun with a capital letter [Some *common nouns* are "man," "car," "cat," and "sea."] *See also* **proper noun**.

**com·mon·place** (käm′ən plās) ***adj.*** not new or interesting; ordinary. ◆***n.*** a common or ordinary thing, idea, remark, etc. [Travel by jet airplane is now a *commonplace*.]

**com·mons** (käm′ənz) ***n.pl.*** all the people who do not belong to the nobility; the common people [The House of *Commons* is the group of elected representatives in the British parliament.]

**common sense** ordinary good sense; intelligence that comes from experience [It's *common sense* to be careful with matches.]

**com·mon·weal** (käm′ən wēl) ***n.*** the public good; the general welfare.

**com·mon·wealth** (käm′ən welth) ***n.*** **1** the people of a nation or state. **2** a nation or state in which the people hold the ruling power; democracy or republic. ☆**3** sometimes, any State of the United States. —**the Commonwealth**, a group of independent nations, including the United Kingdom, Australia, Canada, India, etc., joined together under the British monarch.

**com·mo·tion** (kə mō′shən) ***n.*** a noisy rushing about; confusion [There was a great *commotion* as the ship began to sink.]

**com·mu·nal** (käm′yoon 'l *or* kə myōōn′'l) ***adj.*** **1** of or belonging to the community; public [This park is *communal* property.] **2** of a commune. —**com·mu′nal·ly *adv.***

**com·mune**[1] (kə myōōn′) ***v.*** to meet or deal with in close understanding [Walking in the woods, they *communed* with nature.] —**com·muned′, com·mun′ing**

**com·mune**[2] (käm′yōōn) ***n.*** **1** the smallest district that has a local government in France, Belgium, and some other countries in Europe. ☆**2** a small group of people living together and sharing their earnings, the work to be done, etc.

**com·mu·ni·ca·ble** (kə myōō′ni kə b'l) ***adj.*** that can be passed along from person to person [*communicable* ideas; a *communicable* disease].

**com·mu·ni·cant** (kə myōō′ni kənt) ***n.*** a person who receives or who may receive Holy Communion.

**com·mu·ni·cate** (kə myōō′nə kāt) ***v.*** **1** to pass along; transmit [Copper wire can *communicate* electricity.] **2** to make known; give or exchange information [to *communicate* by telephone; to *communicate* ideas by the written word]. **3** to be connected [The living room *communicates* with the dining room.] —**com·mu′ni·cat·ed, com·mu′ni·cat·ing**

**com·mu·ni·ca·tion** (kə myōō′nə kā′shən) ***n.*** **1** the act of communicating [the *communication* of disease; the *communication* of news]. **2** a way or means of communicating [The hurricane broke down all *communication* between the two cities.] **3** information, message, letter, etc. [They received the news in a *communication* from their lawyer.]

**com·mu·ni·ca·tive** (kə myōō′nə kāt′iv *or* kə myōō′ni kə tiv) ***adj.*** willing to talk or tell something; talkative.

**com·mun·ion** (kə myōōn′yən) ***n.*** **1** a sharing of things in common [These poets had a *communion* of interests.] **2** a close relationship with deep understanding; fellowship [Camping outdoors gave us a feeling of *communion* with nature.] **3** a group of Christians having the same faith and rites. **4 Communion**, the act of sharing in, or celebrating, Holy Communion.

**com·mu·ni·qué** (kə myōō′nə kā′) ***n.*** an official message or bulletin, as of military plans. 

**com·mu·nism** (käm′yə niz'm) ***n.*** **1** a system in which the means of producing goods are owned by the community, and all of the people share in the work and the goods produced. **2 Communism**, a political movement for setting up such a system.

**com·mu·nist** (käm′yə nist) ***n.*** **1** a person who favors or supports communism. **2 Communist**, a member of a political party that seeks to set up communism. ◆***adj.*** **1** of, like, or supporting communism. **2 Communist**, of or having to do with a political party that seeks to set up communism. —**com′mu·nis′tic *adj.***

**com·mu·ni·ty** (kə myōō′nə tē) ***n.*** **1** all the people who live in a particular district, city, etc. [The new swimming pool is for the use of the entire *community*.] **2** a group of people living together and having similar interests and work [a college *community*]. **3** a sharing in common [a *community* of interests]. —*pl.* **com·mu′ni·ties**

☆**community college** a junior college set up to serve a certain community and partly supported by it.

**com·mute** (kə myōōt′) ***v.*** ☆**1** to travel as a commuter. **2** to change a punishment, duty, etc. to one that is less harsh [to *commute* a prisoner's sentence from five to three years]. —**com·mut′ed, com·mut′ing** —**com·mu·ta·tion** (käm′yə tā′shən) ***n.***

| | | | |
|---|---|---|---|
| **a** fat | **ir** here | **ou** out | **zh** leisure |
| **ā** ape | **ī** bite, fire | **u** up | **ng** ring |
| **ä** car, lot | **ō** go | **ur** fur | a *in* ago |
| **e** ten | **ô** law, horn | **ch** chin | e *in* agent |
| **er** care | **oi** oil | **sh** she | ə = i *in* unity |
| **ē** even | **oo** look | **th** thin | o *in* collect |
| **i** hit | **ōō** tool | ***th*** then | u *in* focus |

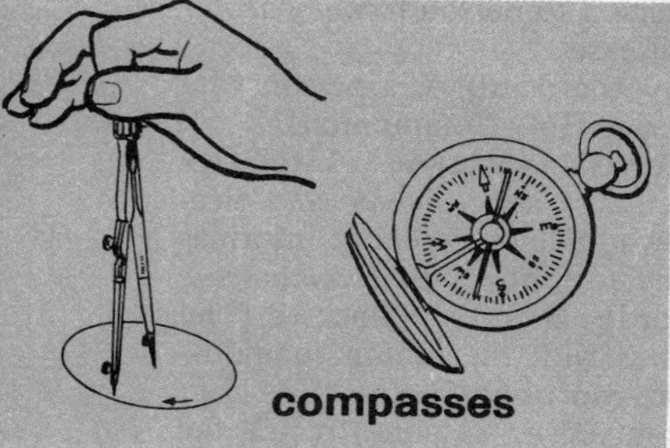
compasses

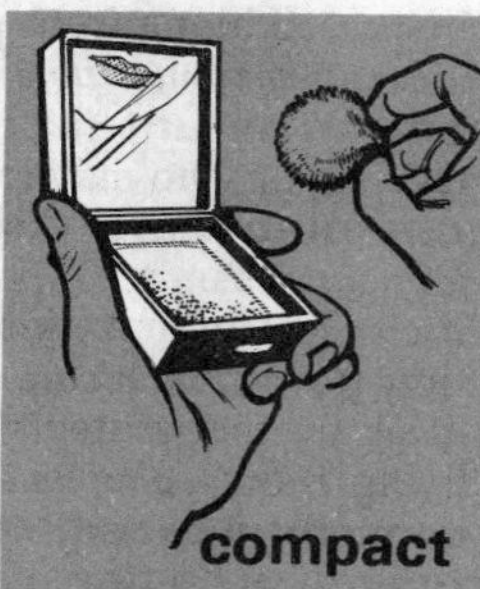
compact

☆**com·mut·er** (kə myo͞ot′ər) ***n.*** a person who travels daily by train, bus, car, etc. between home and work or school.

**comp.** *abbreviation for* **companion, compare, composer, compound.**

**com·pact** (kəm pakt′ *or* käm′pakt) ***adj.*** **1** closely and firmly packed together [Tie the clothes in a neat, *compact* bundle.] **2** having parts fitted together so as not to waste space [a *compact* kitchen]. **3** having no unnecessary words; brief [a *compact* report]. ◆***n.*** (käm′pakt) **1** a small case containing a mirror and face powder. *See the picture.* **2** an agreement [a secret *compact* among the companies to keep prices up]. ☆**3** a model of automobile smaller and cheaper than the standard model.

☆**com·pac·tor** (kəm pak′tər) ***n.*** a machine for pressing trash tightly into small bundles that can be got rid of easily.



**com·pan·ion** (kəm pan′yən) ***n.*** **1** a person who goes along with another; especially, one who often shares or supports the other's activities; comrade; associate. **2** either one of a pair of matched things [Where is the *companion* to this glove?]

> **Companion** comes from the Latin words for "with" and "bread." The ancient Romans thought of a *companion* as a person that you would eat bread with.

**com·pan·ion·a·ble** (kəm pan′yən ə b'l) ***adj.*** easy to be friends with; friendly; sociable.

**com·pan·ion·ship** (kəm pan′yən ship) ***n.*** the state of being companions; fellowship.

**com·pan·ion·way** (kəm pan′yən wā) ***n.*** a stairway leading from deck to deck on a ship.

**com·pa·ny** (kum′pə nē) ***n.*** **1** a group of people; especially, a group joined together in some work or activity [a *company* of actors; a business *company*]. **2** a group of soldiers that is usually under the command of a captain. **3** the state of being companions; companionship [We enjoy each other's *company*.] **4** friends or companions [One is judged by the *company* one keeps.] **5** a guest or guests [We invited *company* for dinner.] —*pl.* **com′pa·nies** —**keep company, 1** to go together, as a couple that plans to marry. **2** to be a companion to [I'll stay to *keep* you *company*.]

**com·pa·ra·ble** (käm′pər ə b'l *or* kəm par′ə b'l) ***adj.*** **1** that can be compared; of more or less the same kind [Rugby is a game *comparable* with football.] **2** worthy to be compared [Few are *comparable* to her in wealth.] —**com′pa·ra·bly *adv.***

**com·par·a·tive** (kəm par′ə tiv) ***adj.*** **1** that compares [*Comparative* anatomy studies and compares the differences in the structure of human beings and the lower animals.] **2** judged by comparison with others; relative [Our book sale was a *comparative* success.] **3** being the form of adjectives and adverbs that shows a greater but not the greatest degree in meaning ["Better" is the *comparative* degree of "good" and "well."] ◆***n.*** the comparative degree ["Softer" and "more thoughtful" are the *comparatives* of "soft" and "thoughtful."] —**com·par′a·tive·ly *adv.***

**com·pare** (kəm per′) ***v.*** **1** to describe as being the same; liken [The sound of thunder can be *compared* to the roll of drums.] **2** to examine certain things in order to find out how they are alike or different [How do the two cars *compare* in size and price?] **3** to equal or come close to by comparison [Few dogs can *compare* with the Great Dane in size.] **4** to form the positive, comparative, and superlative degrees of an adjective or adverb. —**com·pared′, com·par′ing** —**beyond compare,** without equal.

**com·par·i·son** (kəm par′ə s'n) ***n.*** **1** a comparing or being compared. **2** enough likeness or similarity to make comparing worthwhile [There's no *comparison* between the two players when it comes to batting.] **3** the change in an adjective or adverb to show the positive, comparative, and superlative degrees [The degrees of *comparison* of "long" are "long," "longer," "longest."] —**in comparison with,** compared with.

**com·part·ment** (kəm part′mənt) ***n.*** **1** any of the parts into which a space is divided by sides or walls. **2** a separate part or section.

**com·pass** (kum′pəs) ***n.*** **1** an instrument for showing direction, especially one with a moving needle that always points to magnetic north. *See the picture.* **2** *often* **compasses,** *pl.* an instrument with two hinged legs, used for drawing circles or measuring distances. *See the picture.* **3** boundary; circumference [He lived most of his life within the *compass* of this little town.] **4** the full range or extent; reach [within the *compass* of its influence; the *compass* of a singer's voice]. ◆***v.*** **1** to go round; form a circle around; surround. **2** to accomplish or gain [to *compass* one's goals]. **3** to grasp with the mind; understand [We can hardly *compass* their grand scheme.]

**com·pas·sion** (kəm pash′ən) ***n.*** a feeling of being sorry for others and wanting to help them; deep sympathy; pity. *See* SYNONYMS *at* **pity.**

**com·pas·sion·ate** (kəm pash′ən it) ***adj.*** feeling or showing compassion; full of sympathy. —**com·pas′sion·ate·ly *adv.***

**com·pat·i·ble** (kəm pat′ə b'l) ***adj.*** able to live or be together; getting along well together; in agreement [The two girls were *compatible* roommates.] —**com·pat′i·bil′i·ty *n.*** —**com·pat′i·bly *adv.***

**com·pa·tri·ot** (kəm pā′trē ət) ***n.*** a person who comes from the same country as another.

**com·peer** (käm′pir *or* kəm pir′) ***n.*** **1** a person of the same rank; equal; peer. **2** a companion.

**com·pel** (kəm pel′) ***v.*** to make do something; force [Many men were *compelled* by the draft to serve in the armed forces.] —**com·pelled′, com·pel′ling**

**com·pen·sate** (käm′pən sāt) ***v.*** to make up for; take the place of; pay or repay [He worked late to *compensate* for time off. She was *compensated* for her injuries.] —**com′pen·sat·ed, com′pen·sat·ing**

**com·pen·sa·tion** (käm′pən sā′shən) ***n.*** **1** the act of compensating. **2** something given or done to make up for something else [She was given an expensive gift as extra *compensation* for her services.]

**com·pete** (kəm pēt′) ***v.*** to take part in a contest; be a rival for something [Two hundred students *competed* for the scholarship.] —**com·pet′ed, com·pet′ing**

**com·pe·tence** (käm′pə təns) or **com·pe·ten·cy** (käm′pə tən sē) ***n.*** enough skill or intelligence to do something; ability.

**com·pe·tent** (käm′pə tənt) ***adj.*** having enough ability to do what is needed; capable [a *competent* typist]. —**com′pe·tent·ly *adv.***

**com·pe·ti·tion** (käm′pə tish′ən) ***n.*** the act of competing; contest or rivalry.

**com·pet·i·tive** (kəm pet′ə tiv) ***adj.*** having to do with competition or based on competition [*competitive* sports]. —**com·pet′i·tive·ly *adv.***

**com·pet·i·tor** (kəm pet′ə tər) ***n.*** a person who competes; rival [business *competitors*].

**com·pi·la·tion** (käm′pə lā′shən) ***n.*** something that is compiled [A dictionary is a *compilation* of facts about words.]

**com·pile** (kəm pīl′) ***v.*** to bring together in an orderly way, as facts, writings, statistics, etc. [Each student *compiled* a book of favorite quotations.] —**com·piled′, com·pil′ing**

**com·pla·cent** (kəm plās′'nt) ***adj.*** satisfied with the way one is or with what one has done [*Complacent* students avoid doing any extra work.] —**com·pla′cen·cy** or **com·pla′cence *n.***

**com·plain** (kəm plān′) ***v.*** **1** to find fault with something or show pain or displeasure [Everyone *complained* about the poor food in the cafeteria.] **2** to make a report about something bad [We *complained* to the police about the noisy party next door.]

**com·plain·ant** (kəm plān′ənt) ***n.*** a person who brings charges in a law case.

**com·plaint** (kəm plānt′) ***n.*** **1** the act of complaining or finding fault. **2** something to complain about [The tenants gave a list of their *complaints* to the landlord.] **3** an illness [They have the aches and pains and other *complaints* of old age.]

**com·plai·sant** (kəm plā′z'nt) ***adj.*** willing to please; obliging. —**com·plai′sance *n.***

☆**com·plect·ed** (kəm plek′tid) ***adj.*** *another word for* **complexioned**: *used only in everyday talk.*

**com·ple·ment** (käm′plə mənt) ***n.*** **1** something that completes a whole or makes perfect [The sharp cheese was a delicious *complement* for the apple pie.] **2** the full number needed [This ship has a *complement* of 300 men.] **3** the word or words that complete a predicate [In "We made him our captain," "our captain" is a *complement*.] ◆***v.*** (käm′plə ment) to make complete or perfect by supplying what is needed [A bright scarf would *complement* your black dress.]

**com·ple·men·ta·ry** (käm′plə men′tər ē) ***adj.*** supplying what is missing in another; completing [Any two colors that combine to form white light are called *complementary* colors.]

**com·plete** (kəm plēt′) ***adj.*** **1** having no parts missing; full; whole [a *complete* deck of cards]. *See* SYNONYMS *at* **full**. **2** finished; ended [No one's education is ever really *complete*.] **3** thorough; perfect [I have *complete* confidence in my doctor.] ◆***v.*** to make complete; finish or make whole, full, perfect, etc. [When will the new road be *completed?*] —**com·plet′ed, com·plet′ing** —**com·plete′ly *adv.***

**com·ple·tion** (kəm plē′shən) ***n.*** a making or being completed, full, perfect, etc.; finishing.

**com·plex** (kəm pleks′ *or* käm′pleks) ***adj.*** made up of different parts connected in a way that is hard to understand; not simple; intricate [A computer is a *complex* machine. Unemployment is a *complex* problem.] ◆***n.*** (käm′pleks) **1** a group of connected ideas, things, etc. that form a single whole [the *complex* of roads in a State]. **2** a mixed-up feeling about something that makes one show fear, dislike, etc. [an inferiority *complex;* a *complex* about traveling in airplanes].

> SYNONYMS: **Complex** is used in talking about something that is made up of many connected parts, so that much study or skill is needed to understand or operate it [A television set is a *complex* device.] **Complicated** is used in talking about something that is very complex and so is very difficult to understand or solve [We had some *complicated* problems in arithmetic.]

**com·plex·ion** (kəm plek′shən) ***n.*** **1** the color and appearance of the skin, especially of the face. **2** the general look or nature [The *complexion* of our lives is changed by war.]

**com·plex·ioned** (kəm plek′shənd) ***adj.*** having a certain kind of complexion [light-*complexioned*].

**com·plex·i·ty** (kəm plek′sə tē) ***n.*** **1** the quality of being complex or intricate. **2** something that is complex or intricate. —*pl.* **com·plex′i·ties** 

**complex sentence** a sentence made up of a main clause and one or more dependent clauses.

**com·pli·ance** (kəm plī′əns) ***n.*** **1** a complying, or giving in to a request or demand. **2** the condition of being too ready to give in to others. —**in compliance with,** in agreement with or obedient to. —**com·pli′ant *adj.***

**com·pli·cate** (käm′plə kāt) ***v.*** to make difficult, mixed-up, or involved [Heavy debts have *complicated* my life.] —**com′pli·cat·ed, com′pli·cat·ing**

> **Complicate** comes from a Latin word that means "woven together." When things become complicated for us, it is as if the many threads of our lives have been woven together into a carpet with a pattern that is hard to figure out.

**com·pli·cat·ed** (käm′plə kāt′id) ***adj.*** not simple; hard to untangle, solve, understand, etc. [a *complicated* jigsaw puzzle]. *See* SYNONYMS *at* **complex**.

**com·pli·ca·tion** (käm′plə kā′shən) ***n.*** **1** a complicated or mixed-up condition; confusion or intricacy. **2** a happening that makes something more complicated or involved [the *complications* of a plot; a disease with *complications*].

**com·plic·i·ty** (kəm plis′ə tē) ***n.*** the fact of being involved with another person in doing something wrong

| | | | | | | | |
|---|---|---|---|---|---|---|---|
| **a** | fat | **ir** | here | **ou** | out | **zh** | leisure |
| **ā** | ape | **ī** | bite, fire | **u** | up | **ng** | ring |
| **ä** | car, lot | **ō** | go | **ur** | fur | | a *in* ago |
| **e** | ten | **ô** | law, horn | **ch** | chin | | e *in* agent |
| **er** | care | **oi** | oil | **sh** | she | **ə =** | i *in* unity |
| **ē** | even | **oo** | look | **th** | thin | | o *in* collect |
| **i** | hit | **ōō** | tool | ***th*** | then | | u *in* focus |

or unlawful [Helping a robber escape makes one guilty of *complicity* in a crime.]

**com·pli·ment** (käm′plə mənt) ***n.*** **1** something said when one wants to praise, approve, or admire. **2** a polite or respectful act [The audience paid the pianist the *compliment* of listening quietly.] **3 compliments,** *pl.* polite greetings; respects [Please give your mother my *compliments.*] ◆***v.*** (käm′plə ment) to pay a compliment to; congratulate [We *complimented* the actors on their performance.]

**com·pli·men·ta·ry** (käm′plə men′tər ē) ***adj.*** **1** paying a compliment; giving praise or admiring [*complimentary* remarks]. **2** given free [a *complimentary* ticket to a play].

**com·ply** (kəm plī′) ***v.*** to do what is asked or demanded; yield; submit to [They wouldn't *comply* with the rules of the game.] —**com·plied′, com·ply′ing**

**com·po·nent** (kəm pō′nənt) ***n.*** any of the main parts of a whole; constituent; ingredient [the *components* of a high-fidelity sound system]. ◆***adj.*** helping to form a whole [*component* parts].

**com·port** (kəm pôrt′) ***v.*** **1** to behave in a certain way [You should *comport* yourself properly.] **2** to agree or fit in [The comic remarks did not *comport* with the seriousness of the situation.]

**com·pose** (kəm pōz′) ***v.*** **1** to make by combining [Mortar is *composed* of lime, sand, and water.] **2** to put together in proper order [The figures in this paint-

150 ing are well *composed.*] **3** to create or write [to *compose* a song or poem]. **4** to adjust or settle [They tried to *compose* their differences.] **5** to put into a calm condition; quiet [Try to *compose* yourself before you speak.] **6** to put together pieces of type for printing. —**com·posed′, com·pos′ing**

**com·posed** (kəm pōzd′) ***adj.*** calm; peaceful; not excited, confused, etc. *See* SYNONYMS *at* **cool.**

**com·pos·er** (kəm pō′zər) ***n.*** a person who composes, especially one who composes music.

**com·pos·ite** (kəm päz′it) ***adj.*** made up of distinct parts; compound [The head of a *composite* flower, as the aster, is made up of many small flowers.] ◆***n.*** a thing made up of distinct parts [The picture is a *composite* of two photographs.] *See the picture.*

**com·po·si·tion** (käm′pə zish′ən) ***n.*** **1** the act, work, or style of composing something. **2** something composed, as a piece of writing or a musical work. **3** the parts or materials of a thing and the way they are put together [We shall study the *composition* of this gas.] **4** a mixture [a *composition* of various metals].

**com·post** (käm′pōst) ***n.*** a mixture of rotten vegetable matter, manure, etc. for fertilizing soil.

**com·po·sure** (kəm pō′zhər) ***n.*** calmness of mind; self-control; serenity.

**com·pound** (käm′pound) ***n.*** **1** anything made up of two or more parts or materials; mixture. **2** a chemical substance formed by combining two or more elements [Water ($H_2O$) is a *compound.*] ◆***adj.*** made up of two or more parts ["Handbag" is a *compound* word.] ◆***v.*** (käm pound′) **1** to combine or make by combining [Pharmacists *compound* medical prescriptions.] **2** to make greater by adding anything new [Having an extra guest *compounded* the problem of seating people.]

**compound fracture** a bone fracture in which broken ends of bone have broken through the skin.

**compound sentence** a sentence made up of two or more main clauses. Example: "The sun is shining and the birds are singing."

**com·pre·hend** (käm′prə hend′) ***v.*** **1** to understand [I cannot *comprehend* this book.] *See* SYNONYMS *at* **understand. 2** to take in; include [All the new rules are *comprehended* in this booklet.]

**com·pre·hen·si·ble** (käm′prə hen′sə b'l) ***adj.*** that can be understood; understandable.

**com·pre·hen·sion** (käm′prə hen′shən) ***n.*** the act of understanding or the power to understand [The course gave us a good *comprehension* of science.]

**com·pre·hen·sive** (käm′prə hen′siv) ***adj.*** **1** including much; covering many details [a *comprehensive* survey]. **2** understanding fully [a *comprehensive* mind]. —**com′pre·hen′sive·ly *adv.***

**com·press** (kəm pres′) ***v.*** to press or squeeze closely together; press into a smaller space [The air in a tire is *compressed.*] ◆***n.*** (käm′pres) a pad of folded cloth, often wet, for putting heat, cold, pressure, etc. on a part of the body. *See the picture.* —**com·pres·sion** (kəm presh′ən) ***n.*** —**com·pres′sor *n.***

**com·prise** (kəm prīz′) ***v.*** to consist of; be made up of; contain [a library that *comprises* 2,000 books]. —**com·prised′, com·pris′ing**

**com·pro·mise** (käm′prə mīz) ***n.*** a settling of an argument or dispute in which each side gives up part of what it wants. ◆***v.*** **1** to settle by a compromise [They *compromised* by taking turns on the bicycle.] **2** to put in danger of being criticized or disgraced [Do not *compromise* your reputation by cheating.] —**com′promised, com′pro·mis·ing**

**comp·trol·ler** (kən trō′lər) ***n.*** *another spelling for meaning* 1 *of* **controller.**

**com·pul·sion** (kəm pul′shən) ***n.*** a forcing or being forced to do something [Only *compulsion* can make them agree.] —**com·pul′sive *adj.***

**com·pul·so·ry** (kəm pul′sər ē) ***adj.*** that must be done; required [*compulsory* training].

**com·punc·tion** (kəm puŋk′shən) ***n.*** a feeling sorry or guilty about doing something [They had no *compunctions* about being late.]

**com·pute** (kəm pyo͞ot′) ***v.*** to figure something by arithmetic; calculate [to *compute* the tax]. *See* SYNONYMS *at* **calculate.** —**com·put′ed, com·put′ing** —**com·pu·ta·tion** (käm′pyoo tā′shən) ***n.***

**com·put·er** (kəm pyo͞ot′ər) ***n.*** **1** a person who computes. **2** an electronic device used as a calculator or to store and select data.

☆**com·put·er·ize** (kəm pyo͞ot′ər īz) ***v.*** to equip with or operate by electronic computers [a bank's *computerized* accounting system]. —**com·put′er·ized, com·put′er·iz·ing**

**com·rade** (käm′rad) ***n.*** a close friend; companion or fellow worker. —**com′rade·ship *n.***

**Com·sat** (käm′sat) *a trademark for* a man-made satellite in space for receiving and passing on telephone messages, television programs, etc. by means of microwaves.

**con**[1] (kän) ***adv.*** in a way that is against: *now only in the phrase* **pro and con,** meaning "for and against" [We discussed the matter *pro and con.*] ◆***n.*** a reason or vote against [the pros and *cons* of the plan].

☆**con²** (kän) ***v.*** to trick a person out of money or property by first gaining that person's trust: *a slang word.* —**conned, con′ning**

**con-** the form of the prefix **com-** that is used before the consonants *c, d, g, j, n, q, s, t,* and *v.*

**Conan Doyle,** Sir **Arthur** *see* **Doyle.**

**con·cave** (kän kāv′ *or* kän′kāv) ***adj.*** hollow and rounded like the inside of a bowl. *See the picture.* —**con·cave′ly *adv.*** —**con·cav·i·ty** (kän kav′ə tē) ***n.***

**con·ceal** (kən sēl′) ***v.*** to hide or keep secret; put or keep out of sight [I *concealed* my amusement. The thief *concealed* the stolen jewelry in a pocket.] *See* SYNONYMS *at* **hide¹.**

**con·ceal·ment** (kən sēl′mənt) ***n.*** **1** the act of hiding or keeping secret. **2** a hiding place.

**con·cede** (kən sēd′) ***v.*** **1** to admit to be true or certain; say that it is so [They *conceded* that we had won the game.] **2** to let have; grant [They *conceded* us the victory.] —**con·ced′ed, con·ced′ing**

**con·ceit** (kən sēt′) ***n.*** too high an opinion of oneself; vanity [His *conceit* shows when he talks about how bright he is.] —**con·ceit′ed *adj.***

**con·ceiv·a·ble** (kən sēv′ə b′l) ***adj.*** that can be imagined or thought of [They had no *conceivable* reason for lying.] —**con·ceiv′a·bly *adv.***

**con·ceive** (kən sēv′) ***v.*** **1** to form or develop in the mind; think of; imagine [I have *conceived* a plan for making a fortune.] **2** to understand [It is difficult to *conceive* how this motor works.] **3** to become pregnant. —**con·ceived′, con·ceiv′ing**

**con·cen·trate** (kän′sən trāt) ***v.*** **1** to gather all one's thoughts or efforts [I must *concentrate* on this problem.] **2** to bring or come closely together in one place [The troops are *concentrated* at the border.] **3** to make or become stronger or thicker [You can *concentrate* the jam by boiling off some of the water.] —**con′cen·trat·ed, con′cen·trat·ing** ✦***n.*** a substance that has been concentrated, as evaporated milk.

**con·cen·tra·tion** (kän′sən trā′shən) ***n.*** **1** a gathering or being gathered together. **2** careful, close attention [Chess requires great *concentration.*] **3** strength or thickness [the *concentration* of an acid].

**concentration camp** a prison camp for holding people who are thought to be dangerous to the ruling group. These camps were much used in Nazi Germany.

**con·cen·tric** (kən sen′trik) ***adj.*** having the same center [*concentric* circles]. *See the picture.*

**Con·cep·ción** (kən sep′sē ōn′) a seaport on the south-central coast of Chile.

**con·cept** (kän′sept) ***n.*** an idea or thought; especially, a general idea of what a thing or class of things is [Jefferson's *concept* of democracy differed from Hamilton's.]

**con·cep·tion** (kən sep′shən) ***n.*** **1** the act of conceiving or forming an idea [You will get credit for the *conception* of this plan.] **2** a general idea; concept [A baby has almost no *conception* of time.] **3** the start of pregnancy.

**con·cern** (kən surn′) ***v.*** **1** to have a relation to; be important to; involve [This matter *concerns* all of us.] **2** to make anxious or uneasy; trouble [Don't let the loss of the game *concern* you.] ✦***n.*** **1** something that is important to one [The way I dress is no one's *concern* but my own.] **2** worry or anxiety [He felt great

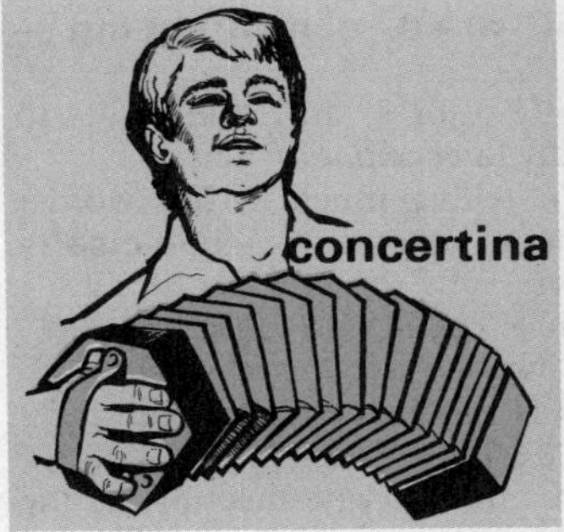
concertina

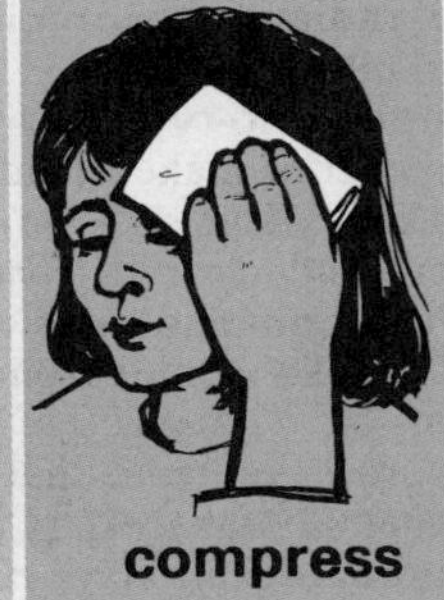
compress

concave lenses

concentric circles

composite picture

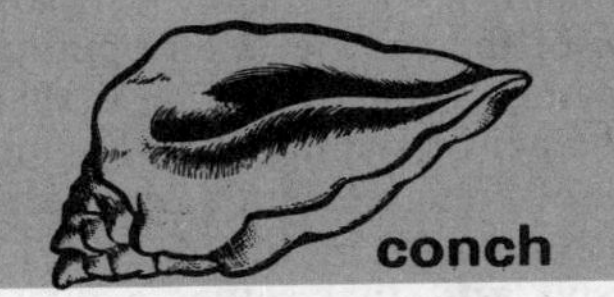
conch

*concern* over his wife's health.] **3** a business or company [a manufacturing *concern*]. —**as concerns,** in regard to; about.

**con·cerned** (kən surnd′) ***adj.*** **1** interested or involved [a *concerned* citizen]. **2** worried or anxious.

**con·cern·ing** (kən sur′niŋ) ***prep.*** having to do with; relating to; about.

**con·cert** (kän′sərt) ***n.*** a musical program, especially one in which a number of musicians perform together. —**in concert,** with all in agreement, or acting together as one ["Yes!" they shouted *in concert.*]

**con·cert·ed** (kən sur′tid) ***adj.*** planned or agreed upon by all; combined [We made a *concerted* effort to get there on time.]

**con·cer·ti·na** (kän′sər tē′nə) ***n.*** a musical instrument like a small accordion. *See the picture.*

**con·cer·to** (kən cher′tō) ***n.*** a piece of music for a solo instrument or instruments with an orchestra. It usually has three movements. —*pl.* **con·cer′tos** or **con·cer·ti** (kən cher′tē)

**con·ces·sion** (kən sesh′ən) ***n.*** **1** an act of conceding or giving in. **2** a thing conceded [We shall need to make *concessions* in order to get the contract.] **3** a right or lease given by a government, company, etc. [the refreshment *concession* at the ball park].

**conch** (käŋk *or* känch) ***n.*** **1** a sea mollusk with a large spiral shell. **2** this shell. *See the picture.*

**con·cil·i·ate** (kən sil′ē āt) ***v.*** to win over by friendly acts; make friendly [Some colonists tried to *conciliate*



| | | | | | | | |
|---|---|---|---|---|---|---|---|
| **a** | fat | **ir** | here | **ou** | out | **zh** | leisure |
| **ā** | ape | **ī** | bite, fire | **u** | up | **ŋ** | ring |
| **ä** | car, lot | **ō** | go | **ur** | fur | | a *in* ago |
| **e** | ten | **ô** | law, horn | **ch** | chin | | e *in* agent |
| **er** | care | **oi** | oil | **sh** | she | **ə =** | i *in* unity |
| **ē** | even | **oo** | look | **th** | thin | | o *in* collect |
| **i** | hit | **ōō** | tool | ***th*** | then | | u *in* focus |

the Indians.] —**con·cil′i·at·ed, con·cil′i·at·ing** —**con·cil′i·a′tion** ***n.***

**con·cil·i·a·to·ry** (kən sil′ē ə tôr′ē) ***adj.*** that serves to win over or make friendly [a *conciliatory* act].

**con·cise** (kən sīs′) ***adj.*** telling much in few words; short and clear [a *concise* statement]. —**con·cise′ly** ***adv.*** —**con·cise′ness** ***n.***

> **Concise** comes from a Latin word meaning "to cut off." A piece of writing is concise when any word or sentence that is not needed is cut out and when no unnecessary details are added.

**con·clave** (kän′klāv) ***n.*** **1** a private meeting, as the one held by cardinals to elect a pope. **2** a meeting of people for some purpose; conference.

**con·clude** (kən klo͞od′) ***v.*** **1** to come or bring to an end [I *concluded* my speech with a call for peace.] **2** to settle or arrange [to *conclude* an agreement]. **3** to decide; make up one's mind [I *concluded* that they were right.] —**con·clud′ed, con·clud′ing**

**con·clu·sion** (kən klo͞o′zhən) ***n.*** **1** the end; last part [We left at the *conclusion* of the show.] **2** an opinion reached by thinking; judgment [My *conclusion* is that you are both right.] **3** the act of settling or arranging something [the *conclusion* of an agreement]. —**in conclusion,** finally; as a last statement.

**con·clu·sive** (kən klo͞o′siv) ***adj.*** that settles a question; convincing [His fingerprint would be *conclusive* evidence that he did it.] —**con·clu′sive·ly** ***adv.***

 **con·coct** (kən käkt′) ***v.*** to make up, prepare, or invent [to *concoct* a new recipe; to *concoct* an excuse].

> **Concoct** comes from a Latin word meaning "to boil together" or "to cook together." Then in English it came to mean "to make something by putting together various things," as when a cook concocts a stew out of leftovers. And now it means "to make up or prepare anything."

**con·coc·tion** (kən käk′shən) ***n.*** **1** the act of concocting. **2** something concocted.

**con·com·i·tant** (kən käm′ə tənt) ***adj.*** going along with; accompanying [*concomitant* events]. ◆***n.*** something that goes along; accompaniment [Coughing is often a *concomitant* to smoking.]

**Con·cord** (käŋ′kərd) **1** the capital of New Hampshire. **2** a town in eastern Massachusetts, where an early battle of the American Revolution was fought on April 19, 1775.

**con·cord** (käŋ′kôrd) ***n.*** harmony; peaceful agreement [*concord* between nations].

**con·cord·ance** (kən kôr′d'ns) ***n.*** **1** concord; agreement [I must act in *concordance* with the rules.] **2** a kind of index that lists the words used by an author or in a book, and tells where they appear [a Bible *concordance*].

**con·course** (kän′kôrs) ***n.*** **1** a coming or flowing together [a *concourse* of rivers]. **2** a crowd of people. ☆**3** a large, open place where crowds gather, as in an airport terminal. **4** a broad boulevard.

**con·crete** (kän′krēt *or* kän krēt′) ***n.*** a hard substance made of cement, sand, gravel, and water. It is used for making roads, bridges, buildings, etc. ◆***adj.*** **1** real or exact; not imaginary or vague [to offer *concrete* help; to give a *concrete* example]. **2** made of concrete.

**con·cu·bine** (käŋ′kyə bīn′) ***n.*** a woman who lives with a man but is not actually his wife. Among some peoples, a man could have several wives and concubines.

**con·cur** (kən kur′) ***v.*** **1** to agree in an opinion or decision [Dr. Smith *concurred* with Dr. Black in the diagnosis.] **2** to act or happen together. —**con·curred′, con·cur′ring**

**con·cur·rence** (kən kur′əns) ***n.*** **1** agreement [We are in complete *concurrence.*] **2** an acting or happening together [a *concurrence* of events].

**con·cur·rent** (kən kur′ənt) ***adj.*** **1** acting or happening together [*concurrent* causes]. **2** in agreement.

**con·cus·sion** (kən kush′ən) ***n.*** **1** a shaking with great force; shock [An earthquake can cause *concussion* miles away.] **2** an injury to the brain from a blow on the head.

**con·demn** (kən dem′) ***v.*** **1** to say that a person or thing is wrong or bad [We *condemn* cruelty to animals.] **2** to declare to be guilty; convict [A jury tried and *condemned* them.] **3** to give as punishment; sentence [The judge *condemned* the murderer to life imprisonment.] ☆**4** to take property by law for public use [The land was *condemned* for use as a school.] **5** to declare to be unfit for use [The old school was *condemned* for lack of fire escapes.] —**con·dem·na·tion** (kän′dem nā′shən) ***n.***

**con·den·sa·tion** (kän′den sā′shən) ***n.*** **1** the act of condensing. **2** the condition of being condensed. **3** something condensed [This book is a *condensation* of the novel.]

**con·dense** (kən dens′) ***v.*** **1** to make or become thicker, denser, or more closely packed together [Milk is *condensed* by evaporation. Steam *condenses* to water when it strikes a cold surface.] **2** to put into fewer words [The book was *condensed* into an article.] —**con·densed′, con·dens′ing**

**con·dens·er** (kən den′sər) ***n.*** **1** a person or thing that condenses. **2** *another name for* **capacitor.**

**con·de·scend** (kän də send′) ***v.*** **1** to act too proud or haughty while doing a favor; be patronizing [The actor *condescended* to sign just a few autographs.] **2** to be politely willing to do something thought to be beneath one's dignity [The judge *condescended* to join in the game.] —**con·de·scen·sion** (kän′də sen′shən) ***n.***

**con·di·ment** (kän′də mənt) ***n.*** a seasoning for food, as salt, pepper, mustard, etc.

**con·di·tion** (kən dish′ən) ***n.*** **1** the particular way a person or thing is [What is the *condition* of the patient? Weather *conditions* won't allow us to go.] *See* SYNONYMS *at* **state. 2** the right or healthy way to be [The whole team is in *condition.*] **3** an illness: *used only in everyday talk* [a lung *condition*]. **4** anything which must be or must happen before something else can take place [Her parents made it a *condition* that she had to do her homework before she could watch TV.] ◆***v.*** **1** to bring into fit condition [Spring training helps to *condition* baseball players.] **2** to form a habit in; accustom [My dog is *conditioned* to bark at strangers.] **3** to be a condition of; determine [the things that *condition* our happiness].

**con·di·tion·al** (kən dish′ən 'l) ***adj.*** **1** depending on a condition [Your trip is *conditional* on your good behavior.] **2** telling of a condition ["If Jane arrives on time" is a *conditional* clause.] —**con·di′tion·al·ly** ***adv.***

☆**con·do** (kän′dō) ***n.*** *a short form of* **condominium.** *—pl.* **con′dos**

**con·dole** (kən dōl′) ***v.*** to show sympathy with someone in sorrow [Friends came to *condole* with her when her grandfather died.] —**con·doled′, con·dol′ing**

**con·do·lence** (kən dō′ləns) ***n.*** a showing of sympathy with someone in sorrow.

**con·do·min·i·um** (kän′də min′ē əm) ***n.*** ☆an apartment building or a group of houses joined together. The people living in a condominium own the units in which they live and together own the area around the buildings.

**con·done** (kən dōn′) ***v.*** to forgive or overlook a wrong done [Many parents *condone* the mistakes of their own children.] —**con·doned′, con·don′ing**

**con·dor** (kän′dər) ***n.*** a large vulture with a bare head and neck, found in the Andes Mountains and in California. *See the picture.*

**con·duce** (kən do͞os′ *or* kən dyo͞os′) ***v.*** to help to bring about; contribute [Eating the right foods *conduces* to good health.] —**con·duced′, con·duc′ing**

**con·du·cive** (kən do͞o′siv *or* kən dyo͞o′siv) ***adj.*** helping to bring about; contributing [Soft music is often *conducive* to sleep.]

**con·duct** (kän′dukt) ***n.*** **1** the way one acts or behaves; behavior [The teacher praised the students for their good *conduct* in class.] **2** way of handling or managing; management [The *conduct* of the war is in the hands of the President.] ➧***v.*** (kən dukt′) **1** to lead or guide [The waiter *conducted* us to our table.] **2** to manage; direct; be the leader of [to *conduct* a meeting; to *conduct* an orchestra]. **3** to behave [They *conducted* themselves like adults.] **4** to be a means for carrying; transmit [Copper *conducts* electricity.]

**con·duc·tion** (kən duk′shən) ***n.*** the passing along or letting through, as of liquid in a pipe or electricity in a wire.

**con·duc·tiv·i·ty** (kän′duk tiv′ə tē) ***n.*** the ability to conduct heat, electricity, or sound.

**con·duc·tor** (kən duk′tər) ***n.*** **1** a person who conducts; director [the *conductor* of an orchestra]. ☆**2** the person in charge who collects fares on a train, streetcar, etc. **3** something that conducts electricity, heat, or sound [Air is a good *conductor* of heat.]

**con·duit** (kän′dit *or* kän′do͝o wit) ***n.*** **1** a pipe or passage for carrying fluids, as a gas pipe, gutter, or sewer. **2** a tube for protecting electric wires or cables.

**cone** (kōn) ***n.*** **1** a solid object that narrows evenly from a flat circle at one end to a point at the other. *See the picture.* **2** anything shaped like this, as a shell of pastry for holding ice cream. **3** the fruit of some evergreen trees, containing the seeds.

☆**Con·es·to·ga wagon** (kän′ə stō′gə) a covered wagon with broad wheels used by American pioneers crossing the prairies.

**con·fec·tion** (kən fek′shən) ***n.*** any kind of candy or other sweet thing like candy.

**con·fec·tion·er** (kən fek′shən ər) ***n.*** a person who makes or sells candies and other sweets.

**con·fec·tion·er·y** (kən fek′shən er′ē) ***n.*** **1** candies and other sweets. **2** a shop where candies, etc. are sold. *—pl.* **con·fec′tion·er′ies**

**con·fed·er·a·cy** (kən fed′ər ə sē) ***n.*** a union of people, groups, or states for a certain purpose; league. *—pl.* **con·fed′er·a·cies** —☆**the Confederacy,** the eleven Southern States that seceded from the U.S. in 1860 and 1861: *also called* **Confederate States of America.**

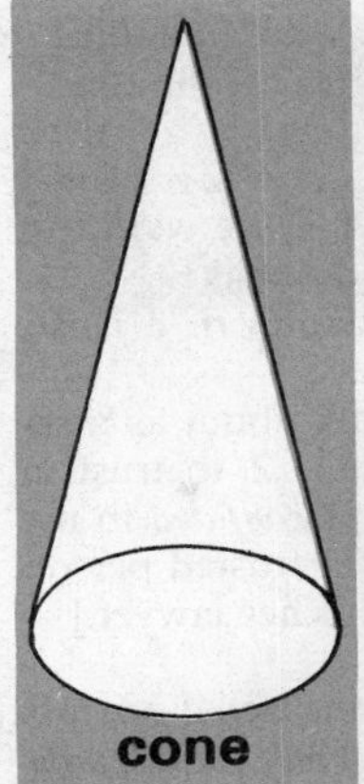
cone

condor 3 m (10 ft.) wingspread

confetti

**con·fed·er·ate** (kən fed′ər it) ***adj.*** **1** joined in a confederacy. ☆**2 Confederate,** of the Confederacy. ➧***n.*** **1** a person who joins with others, especially to do something not lawful; ally or accomplice. ☆**2 Confederate,** a supporter of the Confederacy. ➧***v.*** (kən fed′ər āt) to join together in a confederacy. —**con·fed′er·at·ed, con·fed′er·at·ing**

**con·fed·er·a·tion** (kən fed′ə rā′shən) ***n.*** **1** a uniting or being united in a league or alliance. **2** nations or states joined in a league, as for defense; alliance.



**con·fer** (kən fʉr′) ***v.*** **1** to give or grant [They *conferred* a medal upon the hero.] **2** to meet for a discussion; have a talk [The mayor will *confer* with the city council.] —**con·ferred′, con·fer′ring**

**con·fer·ence** (kän′fər əns) ***n.*** **1** a meeting of people to discuss something [A *conference* on education was held in Washington.] **2** an association, as of college athletic teams.

**con·fess** (kən fes′) ***v.*** **1** to tell what one has done that is bad; admit a fault or crime [Will you *confess* that you started the fight?] **2** to tell what one really thinks; acknowledge [I *confess* that opera bores me.] **3** to tell one's sins to God or to a priest. **4** to listen to a person's confession of sins, as a priest does.

**con·fes·sion** (kən fesh′ən) ***n.*** **1** the act of confessing; telling of one's faults, sins, etc. **2** something confessed.

**con·fes·sion·al** (kən fesh′ən ′l) ***n.*** the place in a church where a priest hears confessions.

**con·fes·sor** (kən fes′ər) ***n.*** **1** a person who confesses. **2** a priest who hears confessions.

**con·fet·ti** (kən fet′ē) ***n.pl.*** bits of colored paper thrown about at carnivals, parades, etc.: *used with a singular verb* [*Confetti* was all over the street.] *See the picture above and the note on the next page.*

| | | | | | | | |
|---|---|---|---|---|---|---|---|
| **a** | fat | **ir** | here | **ou** | out | **zh** | leisure |
| **ā** | ape | **ī** | bite, fire | **u** | up | **ng** | ring |
| **ä** | car, lot | **ō** | go | **ʉr** | fur | | a *in* ago |
| **e** | ten | **ô** | law, horn | **ch** | chin | | e *in* agent |
| **er** | care | **oi** | oil | **sh** | she | **ə =** | i *in* unity |
| **ē** | even | **o͝o** | look | **th** | thin | | o *in* collect |
| **i** | hit | **o͞o** | tool | ***th*** | then | | u *in* focus |

**Confetti** comes from an Italian word meaning "candies." At one time little candies or imitation candies made of plaster were thrown at one another by people at carnivals. But now we throw handfuls of little pieces of paper when we want to have fun at carnivals, weddings, and the like.

**con·fi·dant** (kän′fə dant *or* kän fə dänt′) ***n.*** a close, trusted friend to whom one tells secrets.

**con·fide** (kən fīd′) ***v.*** **1** to tell or talk about as a secret [She *confided* her troubles to me.] **2** to trust in someone who can keep one's secrets [I *confided* in my sister.] **3** to give into the keeping of a trusted person [She *confided* the care of her fortune to her lawyer.] —**con·fid′ed, con·fid′ing**

**con·fi·dence** (kän′fə dəns) ***n.*** **1** strong belief or trust in someone or something; reliance [They have *confidence* in my skill.] **2** a belief in oneself; self-confidence [I began to play the piano with *confidence.*] **3** trust in another to keep one's secret [She told it to him in strict *confidence.*] **4** a secret [Don't burden me with your *confidences.*]

**con·fi·dent** (kän′fə dənt) ***adj.*** full of confidence; sure; certain; assured [*confident* of victory; a *confident* manner]. —**con′fi·dent·ly** ***adv.***

**con·fi·den·tial** (kän′fə den′shəl) ***adj.*** **1** told in confidence; secret [a *confidential* report]. **2** trusted with private or secret matters [a *confidential* agent]. —**con′fi·den′tial·ly** ***adv.***

 **con·fig·u·ra·tion** (kən fig′yə rā′shən) ***n.*** the shape, form, or outline of a thing.

**con·fine** (kən fīn′) ***v.*** **1** to keep within limits; restrict [Please *confine* your talk to five minutes.] **2** to keep shut up, as in prison, or in bed because of illness. —**con·fined′, con·fin′ing** ◆***n.*** (kän′fīn) a boundary or limit: *usually used in the plural,* **confines** [the *confines* of a town]. —**con·fine′ment** ***n.***

**con·firm** (kən furm′) ***v.*** **1** to make sure or firm by agreeing or approving [The Senate *confirmed* the treaty.] **2** to prove to be true; verify [to *confirm* a rumor]. —**be confirmed,** to take part in the religious ceremony of confirmation.

**con·fir·ma·tion** (kän′fər mā′shən) ***n.*** **1** the act of confirming, or making sure. **2** something that confirms or proves. **3** a Christian ceremony in which a person is made a full member in a church. ☆**4** a Jewish ceremony in which young people reaffirm their belief in basic concepts of Judaism.

**con·firmed** (kən furmd′) ***adj.*** **1** set in one's ways or habits [a *confirmed* bachelor]. **2** proved to be true [a *confirmed* theory].

**con·fis·cate** (kän′fə skāt) ***v.*** to seize with authority [to *confiscate* smuggled goods]. —**con′fis·cat·ed, con′fis·cat·ing** —**con′fis·ca′tion** ***n.***

**con·fla·gra·tion** (kän′flə grā′shən) ***n.*** a big fire that does great damage.

**con·flict** (kän′flikt) ***n.*** **1** a fight or battle. **2** a clash or sharp disagreement, as of interests or ideas. ◆***v.*** (kən flikt′) to be or act against; be opposed to [Their ideas *conflict* with mine.]

**conflict of interest** a conflict between one's duty to the public and one's own interests, as when an elected official of the government owns stock in a company that wants to get government contracts.

**con·flu·ence** (kän′flo͞o əns) ***n.*** **1** a flowing together as of two streams. *See the picture.* **2** a coming together, as of people. —**con′flu·ent** ***adj.***

**con·form** (kən fôrm′) ***v.*** **1** to make or be the same or similar [Their thinking *conformed* with ours.] **2** to be or act in the required way; be in agreement with [to *conform* to rules]. —**con·form′a·ble** ***adj.*** —**con·form′ist** ***n.***

**con·for·ma·tion** (kän′fôr mā′shən) ***n.*** the way in which a thing is formed or shaped; arrangement of parts; structure [An earthquake changed the *conformation* of the land.]

**con·form·i·ty** (kən fôr′mə tē) ***n.*** **1** the condition or fact of being in agreement [in *conformity* with the law]. **2** a following of rules, orders, customs, or accepted ideas [Extreme *conformity* often prevents original thought.] —*pl.* **con·form′i·ties**

**con·found** (kən found′) ***v.*** to mix up or confuse; bewilder [*Confounded* by all the winding streets, they became lost.]

**con·front** (kən frunt′) ***v.*** **1** to meet face to face, especially in a bold way; stand up against [to *confront* an enemy]. **2** to bring face to face [She confessed when *confronted* with the facts.]

**con·fron·ta·tion** (kän′frən tā′shən) ***n.*** a face-to-face meeting, as of two persons who hold opposite views on some matter.

**Con·fu·cius** (kən fyo͞o′shəs) 551?–479? B.C.; a Chinese philosopher and teacher.

**con·fuse** (kən fyo͞oz′) ***v.*** **1** to mix up, especially in the mind; put into disorder; bewilder [You will *confuse* us with so many questions.] **2** to fail to see or remember the difference between; mistake [You are *confusing* me with my twin.] —**con·fused′, con·fus′ing** —**con·fus·ed·ly** (kən fyo͞oz′id lē) ***adv.***

**con·fu·sion** (kən fyo͞o′zhən) ***n.*** **1** disorder or bewilderment; a being confused [There was *confusion* in the room when fire broke out.] **2** a confusing or failing to see the difference [His *confusion* of the color red and the color green comes from color blindness.]

**Cong.** *abbreviation for* **Congress.**

**con·geal** (kən jēl′) ***v.*** to make or become solid or thick, as by cooling or freezing; thicken [Melted fat *congeals* as it cools.]

**con·gen·ial** (kən jēn′yəl) ***adj.*** **1** able to get along well together; having the same interests [*congenial* friends]. **2** fitting one's needs or mood; agreeable [*congenial* surroundings].

**con·gen·i·tal** (kən jen′ə t'l) ***adj.*** present from the time of birth [a *congenital* disease].

**con·gest** (kən jest′) ***v.*** **1** to fill up with too much blood or other fluid [The heart is *congested* after a heart attack. Your nose is *congested* from your cold.]

confluence of rivers

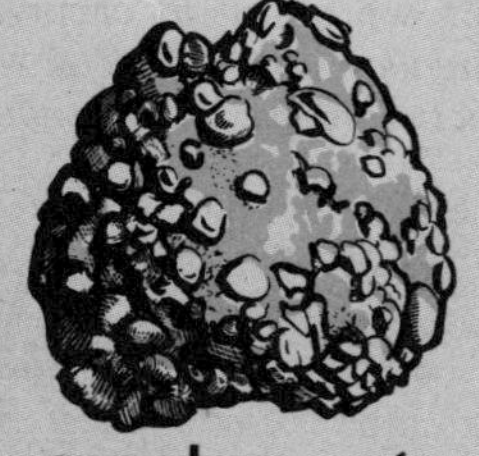
conglomerate rock

**2** to fill too full; clog; make crowded [The parking lot is *congested.*] —**con·ges′tion** ***n.***

**con·glom·er·ate** (kən gläm′ə rāt) ***v.*** to form or collect into a rounded mass. —**con·glom′er·at·ed, con·glom′er·at·ing** ✦***adj.*** (kən gläm′ər it) made up of separate parts or materials formed into one mass [A *conglomerate* rock is made up of pebbles and stones cemented together in hard clay and sand.] ✦***n.*** (kən gläm′ər it) **1** a conglomerate mass or rock. *See the picture.* ☆**2** a large corporation made up of a number of companies dealing in different products or services. —**con·glom′er·a′tion** ***n.***

**Con·go** (käng′gō) **1** a river in central Africa, flowing into the Atlantic. **2** a country in west central Africa, west of Zaire.

**con·grat·u·late** (kən grach′ə lāt) ***v.*** to tell a person that one is happy for his or her success or good luck [I *congratulate* you on your marriage.] —**con·grat′u·lat·ed, con·grat′u·lat·ing**

**con·grat·u·la·tion** (kən grach′ə lā′shən) ***n.*** **1** the act of congratulating. **2** *usually* **congratulations,** *pl.* words that tell of one's happiness at another's success or good luck [Let's send *congratulations* to the winner.]

**con·gre·gate** (käng′grə gāt) ***v.*** to come together; assemble [We *congregated* around the piano.] —**con′gre·gat·ed, con′gre·gat·ing**

**Congregate** comes from Latin words that mean "to gather together into a flock." The members of a church's congregation are sometimes called a flock.

**con·gre·ga·tion** (käng′grə gā′shən) ***n.*** **1** a gathering, especially of a group of people. **2** a group of people meeting for a religious service. **3** the members of a particular place of worship.

**con·gre·ga·tion·al** (käng′grə gā′shən ′l) ***adj.*** **1** of or like a congregation. **2 Congregational,** of a Protestant faith in which each member congregation governs itself. —**Con′gre·ga′tion·al·ist** ***n., adj.***

**con·gress** (käng′grəs) ***n.*** **1** a coming together; meeting; convention. ☆**2 Congress,** the group of elected officials in the United States government that makes the laws. It consists of the Senate and the House of Representatives.

☆**con·gres·sion·al** (kən gresh′ən ′l) ***adj.*** having to do with a congress or with Congress.

☆**Congressional district** any of the districts into which a State is divided for electing Congressmen. Each district elects a member of the House of Representatives.

☆**con·gress·man** (käng′grəs mən) ***n.*** a member of Congress, especially of the House of Representatives. —*pl.* **con′gress·men**

☆**con·gress·wom·an** (käng′grəs woom′ən) ***n.*** a woman member of Congress, especially of the House of Representatives. —*pl.* **con′gress·wom′en**

**con·gru·ent** (käng′groo wənt) ***adj.*** in agreement or harmony; corresponding.

**con·gru·ous** (käng′groo wəs) ***adj.*** **1** *same as* **congruent.** **2** fitting in a proper way; suitable.

**con·i·cal** (kän′i k′l) ***adj.*** **1** shaped like a cone. **2** having to do with a cone. —**con′i·cal·ly** ***adv.***

**co·ni·fer** (kän′ə fər *or* kō′nə fər) ***n.*** a tree or shrub that bears cones, as the pine, spruce, etc. —**co·nif·er·ous** (kə nif′ər əs) ***adj.***

**conj.** *abbreviation for* **conjunction.**

**con·jec·ture** (kən jek′chər) ***n.*** a guess or guessing; opinion formed without sure facts [What we know of Shakespeare's life is based mainly on *conjecture.*] ✦***v.*** to make a conjecture. —**con·jec′tured, con·jec′tur·ing** —**con·jec′tur·al** ***adj.***

**con·join** (kən join′) ***v.*** to join together; unite. —**con·joint′** ***adj.*** —**con·joint′ly** ***adv.***

**con·ju·gal** (kän′jə gəl) ***adj.*** of marriage.

**con·ju·gate** (kän′jə gāt) ***v.*** to list the different forms of a verb in person, number, and tense [*Conjugate* "to be," beginning "I am, you are, he is."] —**con′ju·gat·ed, con′ju·gat·ing** —**con′ju·ga′tion** ***n.***

**con·junc·tion** (kən jungk′shən) ***n.*** **1** a joining together; combination [High winds, in *conjunction* with rain, made travel difficult.] **2** a word used to join other words, phrases, or clauses [*And, but, or, if,* etc. are *conjunctions.*]

**con·jure** (kän′jər *or* kun′jər) ***v.*** **1** to practice magic or witchcraft, as in supposedly making evil spirits come to do one's bidding. **2** (kən joor′) to beg or plead with in a very serious way —**con′jured, con′jur·ing** —**conjure up,** to make appear as if by magic [The music *conjured up* memories.]

**con·jur·er** or **con·ju·ror** (kän′jər ər *or* kun′jər ər) ***n.*** a magician.

**conk** (kängk *or* kôngk) ***v.*** to hit on the head: *a slang word.* —**conk out,** **1** to stop working, as a motor [The old car's engine *conked out* going up the hill.] **2** to become very tired and fall asleep [Leslie *conked out* after working hard all day.] *A slang phrase.*

**con·nect** (kə nekt′) ***v.*** **1** to join together; unite [Many bridges *connect* Ohio and Kentucky.] *See* SYNONYMS *at* **join.** **2** to relate in some way; think of together [Do you *connect* Bill's silence with Ann's arrival?] ☆**3** to meet so that passengers can change to another train, plane, bus, etc. [Does the flight from Boston *connect* with the flight to Chicago?] **4** to plug into an electrical circuit.

**Con·nect·i·cut** (kə net′ə kət) a New England State of the U.S.: abbreviated **Conn., CT**

**con·nec·tion** (kə nek′shən) ***n.*** **1** a joining or being joined; union. **2** a part or thing that connects. **3** the condition of being related in some way; relationship [What is the *connection* between lightning and thunder?] **4** a person with whom one is associated in some way [She has some important *connections.*] ☆**5** *usually* **connections,** *pl.* the act of changing from one bus, airplane, etc. to another [If you don't make your *connections* in Chicago, you will have to wait six hours.] **6** an electrical circuit. —**in connection with,** **1** together with. **2** referring to.

**con·nec·tive** (kə nek′tiv) ***adj.*** that connects; connecting. ✦***n.*** a word that connects others, as a conjunction or preposition.

| | | | |
|---|---|---|---|
| **a** fat | **ir** here | **ou** out | **zh** leisure |
| **ā** ape | **ī** bite, fire | **u** up | **ng** ring |
| **ä** car, lot | **ō** go | **ur** fur | a *in* ago |
| **e** ten | **ô** law, horn | **ch** chin | e *in* agent |
| **er** care | **oi** oil | **sh** she | **ə** = i *in* unity |
| **ē** even | **oo** look | **th** thin | o *in* collect |
| **i** hit | **ōō** tool | ***th*** then | u *in* focus |

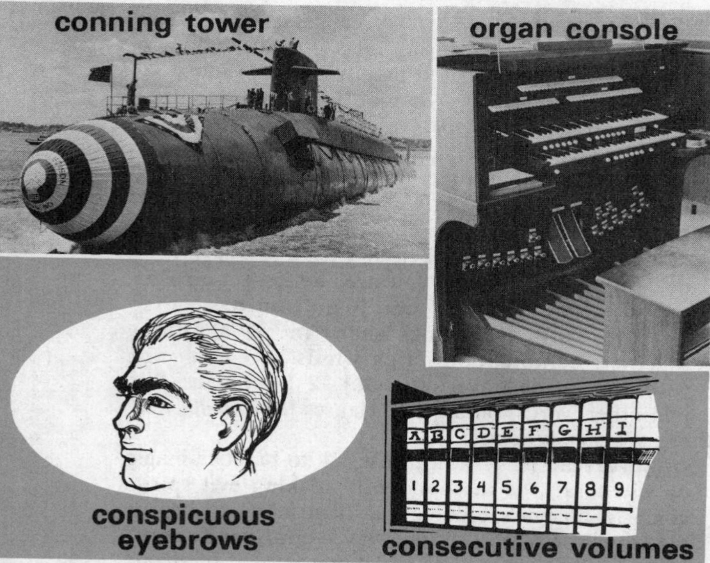


conning tower

organ console

conspicuous eyebrows

consecutive volumes

**conn·ing tower** (kän′iŋ) a low tower on a submarine, used as a place for observation. It is also used as an entrance to the interior. *See the picture.*

**con·niv·ance** (kə nī′vəns) ***n.*** the act of conniving.

**con·nive** (kə nīv′) ***v.*** **1** to pretend not to see something wrong or evil, so that one seems to be giving consent. **2** to help someone secretly in wrongdoing; conspire. —**con·nived′, con·niv′ing —con·niv′er *n.***



**con·nois·seur** (kän ə sur′) ***n.*** a person who has much knowledge and good taste in some fine art [a *connoisseur* of music].

**con·no·ta·tion** (kän′ə tā′shən) ***n.*** something connoted; idea associated with a word or phrase in addition to its actual meaning.

**con·note** (kə nōt′) ***v.*** to suggest some idea or feeling in addition to the actual meaning [The word "snake" means "a crawling reptile," but it usually *connotes* sneakiness and meanness.] —**con·not′ed, con·not′ing**

**con·quer** (käŋ′kər) ***v.*** **1** to get or gain by using force, as by winning a war [The Spaniards *conquered* Mexico.] **2** to overcome by trying hard; get the better of; defeat [She *conquered* her bad habits.] —**con′quer·or *n.***

**con·quest** (käŋ′kwest) ***n.*** **1** the act of conquering. **2** something conquered, as a country.

**con·quis·ta·dor** (kän kwis′tə dôr) ***n.*** any of the early Spanish conquerors of Mexico, Peru, etc.

**Con·rad** (kän′rad), **Joseph** 1857–1924; an English novelist. He was born in Poland.

**con·science** (kän′shəns) ***n.*** a sense of right and wrong; feeling that keeps one from doing bad things [My *conscience* bothers me after I tell a lie.] —**on one's conscience,** making one feel guilty.

**con·sci·en·tious** (kän′shē en′shəs) ***adj.*** **1** always trying to do the right thing [a *conscientious* worker]. **2** made or done with care in a way one knows is right [*conscientious* work]. —**con′sci·en′tious·ly *adv.***

**conscientious objector** ☆a person who will not take part in war because of a strong belief that war is wrong.

**con·scious** (kän′shəs) ***adj.*** **1** aware of one's own feelings or of things around one [*conscious* of a slight noise; *conscious* of having a fever]. **2** able to feel and think; in the normal waking state [One usually becomes *conscious* again a few minutes after fainting.] **3** done or doing with awareness or on purpose [*conscious* humor]. —**con′scious·ly *adv.***

**con·scious·ness** (kän′shəs nis) ***n.*** **1** a being conscious; awareness. **2** all the thoughts and feelings a person has when awake [The memory of the accident was gone from the driver's *consciousness.*]

☆**con·script** (kən skript′) ***v.*** to force to serve in the armed forces; draft. ◆***n.*** (kän′skript) a person forced to serve in the armed forces; draftee. —**con·scrip′tion *n.***

**con·se·crate** (kän′sə krāt) ***v.*** **1** to set apart as holy; make sacred for religious use [The priest *consecrated* the water.] **2** to give up to a purpose; devote [They *consecrated* their lives to helping the poor.] —**con′se·crat·ed, con′se·crat·ing —con′se·cra′tion *n.***

**con·sec·u·tive** (kən sek′yə tiv) ***adj.*** coming in regular order without a break [It snowed for three *consecutive* days.] *See the picture.* —**con·sec′u·tive·ly *adv.***

**con·sen·sus** (kən sen′səs) ***n.*** agreement of all or most in some opinion [It was the *consensus* of the parents that a new school should be built.]

**con·sent** (kən sent′) ***v.*** to agree or give approval [Will you *consent* to serve as president?] ◆***n.*** agreement or approval [May I have your *consent* to leave early?]

> **Consent** comes from Latin words that mean "to feel with." When a person consents to do something suggested by another, then each feels the same way that the other does.

**con·se·quence** (kän′sə kwens) ***n.*** **1** a result or outcome [What were the *consequences* of your decision?] **2** importance [a matter of great *consequence*]. —**take the consequences,** to accept the results of one's actions.

**con·se·quent** (kän′sə kwent) ***adj.*** coming as a result; resulting [the robber's trial and *consequent* imprisonment].

**con·se·quen·tial** (kän′sə kwen′shəl) ***adj.*** **1** following as a result. **2** important.

**con·se·quent·ly** (kän′sə kwent lē) ***adv.*** as a result; therefore [The frost spoiled the crops and *consequently* prices rose.]

**con·ser·va·tion** (kän′sər vā′shən) ***n.*** a protecting, or conserving from loss, waste, or harm [The *conservation* of forests and rivers is important to our well-being.]

**con·ser·va·tism** (kən sur′və tiz'm) ***n.*** a feeling or working against changes and reform, especially in political and social matters.

**con·ser·va·tive** (kən sur′və tiv) ***adj.*** **1** wanting to keep things as they are and being against change and reform [One of the political parties of Great Britain is the *Conservative* Party.] ☆**2** cautious or safe; not risky [a *conservative* taste in music; a *conservative* estimate of costs]. ◆***n.*** a conservative person.

**con·ser·va·to·ry** (kən sur′və tôr′ē) ***n.*** **1** a small, private greenhouse. **2** a school of music, art, etc. —*pl.* **con·ser′va·to′ries**

**con·serve** (kən surv′) ***v.*** to keep from being hurt, lost, or wasted [to *conserve* one's energy]. —**con·served′, con·serv′ing** ◆***n.*** (kän′sərv) a kind of jam made of two or more fruits.

**con·sid·er** (kən sid′ər) ***v.*** **1** to think about in order to make up one's mind [Please *consider* my suggestions.] **2** to keep in mind; take into account [Her health is good, if you *consider* her age.] **3** to be thoughtful about [to *consider* the feelings of others]. **4** to think to be; believe [I *consider* you an expert.]

> SYNONYMS: To **consider** is to think over something in order to understand it or make a decision [Please *consider* my poem for publication.] To **weigh** is to balance in the mind facts or opinions that conflict with each other [The jury will *weigh* the defendant's story against that of her accuser.] To **reflect** is to think about something in a quiet, serious way [Reading Plato makes us *reflect* on ideas of love and truth.]

**con·sid·er·a·ble** (kən sid′ər ə b'l) ***adj.*** much or large [They had *considerable* success.]

**con·sid·er·a·bly** (kən sid′ər ə blē) ***adv.*** much; a great deal [I feel *considerably* better.]

**con·sid·er·ate** (kən sid′ər it) ***adj.*** thoughtful of other people's feelings; kind [It was *considerate* of you to invite her too.] *See* SYNONYMS *at* **thoughtful.** —**con·sid′er·ate·ly *adv.***

**con·sid·er·a·tion** (kən sid′ə rā′shən) ***n.*** **1** the act of considering; careful thought [After long *consideration,* I decided to buy the house.] **2** a reason for doing something [Her sense of duty was her chief *consideration* in agreeing to help her brother.] **3** something paid for a favor or service [Jan repairs clocks for a *consideration.*] **4** the quality of being thoughtful about other people's feelings; kindness. —**in consideration of, 1** because of. **2** in return for. —**take into consideration,** to keep in mind; take into account. —**under consideration,** being thought over.

**con·sid·ered** (kən sid′ərd) ***adj.*** decided after careful thought [It was his *considered* judgment that she should sell her house.]

**con·sid·er·ing** (kən sid′ər iŋ) ***prep.*** keeping in mind; taking into account [The director has done well, *considering* all that has happened.]

**con·sign** (kən sīn′) ***v.*** **1** to give over; entrust [I'll *consign* my books to your care.] **2** to send or address [This shipment is *consigned* to our New York office.]

**con·sign·ment** (kən sīn′mənt) ***n.*** **1** the act of giving over, or consigning. **2** something consigned [We have shipped you a *consignment* of TV sets.]

**con·sist** (kən sist′) ***v.*** **1** to be made up of; contain [Bronze *consists* of copper and tin.] **2** to be contained in as a cause or quality [Being good does not *consist* in just doing what is expected of one.]

**con·sis·ten·cy** (kən sist′ən sē) ***n.*** **1** thickness or firmness [Flour is added to gravy to give it *consistency.*] **2** the quality of being consistent; action that is always the same or suitable [She is unpredictable because she lacks *consistency.*]

**con·sis·tent** (kən sist′ənt) ***adj.*** **1** acting or thinking always in the same way [Parents should be *consistent* in their discipline.] **2** in agreement or harmony; suitable [His words are not *consistent* with his acts.] —**con·sis′tent·ly *adv.***

**con·sis·to·ry** (kən sis′tər ē) ***n.*** a church council or court. —*pl.* **con·sis′to·ries**

**con·so·la·tion** (kän′sə lā′shən) ***n.*** **1** the act of consoling. **2** something that consoles, or makes one less sad or troubled; comfort.

**consolation prize** a prize given to a person taking part in a contest who does well but does not win.

**con·sole**[1] (kən sōl′) ***v.*** to make less sad or troubled; comfort [A toy *consoled* the lost child.] *See* SYNONYMS *at* **comfort.** —**con·soled′, con·sol′ing**

**con·sole**[2] (kän′sōl) ***n.*** **1** the part of an organ at which the player sits, containing the keyboard, pedals, etc. *See the picture.* **2** a radio, phonograph, or television cabinet that stands on the floor. ☆**3** an instrument panel for controls of an aircraft, computer, etc.

**con·sol·i·date** (kən säl′ə dāt) ***v.*** **1** to join together into one; unite; merge [The corporation was formed by *consolidating* many companies.] **2** to make or become strong or firm [The troops *consolidated* their position by bringing up heavy guns.] —**con·sol′i·dat·ed, con·sol′i·dat·ing** —**con·sol′i·da′tion *n.***

☆**consolidated school** a public school attended by pupils from several neighboring districts, especially in a rural area.

**con·som·mé** (kän sə mā′) ***n.*** a clear meat soup that is served hot or cold.

**con·so·nance** (kän′sə nəns) ***n.*** agreement or harmony.

**con·so·nant** (kän′sə nənt) ***adj.*** in harmony or agreement [Your actions were *consonant* with your principles.] ◆***n.*** **1** a speech sound made by stopping or partly stopping the breath with the tongue, teeth, or lips. **2** any of the letters used to show these sounds [The letters of the alphabet except *a, e, i, o,* and *u* are usually *consonants; w* and *y* are sometimes *consonants.*]

**con·sort** (kän′sôrt) ***n.*** a wife or husband, especially of a ruling king or queen. ◆***v.*** (kən sôrt′) to spend much time; associate [She *consorts* with snobs.]

**con·spic·u·ous** (kən spik′yoo wəs) ***adj.*** **1** easy to see; plainly seen [a *conspicuous* sign]. *See the picture.* **2** getting attention by being unusual; remarkable [They received medals for *conspicuous* bravery.] —**con·spic′u·ous·ly *adv.***

**con·spir·a·cy** (kən spir′ə sē) ***n.*** **1** a secret plan by two or more people to do something bad or unlawful; plot [a *conspiracy* to kill the king]. **2** a working or joining together [A *conspiracy* of events kept me from the party.] —*pl.* **con·spir′a·cies**

**con·spir·a·tor** (kən spir′ə tər) ***n.*** a person who takes part in a conspiracy; plotter.

**con·spire** (kən spīr′) ***v.*** **1** to plan together secretly, as to commit a crime. **2** to join or act together toward some result [Rain and cold *conspired* to spoil our vacation.] —**con·spired′, con·spir′ing**

> **Conspire** comes from a Latin word that means "to breathe together." Conspirators are often pictured with their heads together, whispering or talking under their breath.

| | | | | | | | |
|---|---|---|---|---|---|---|---|
| **a** | fat | **ir** | here | **ou** | out | **zh** | leisure |
| **ā** | ape | **ī** | bite, fire | **u** | up | **ŋ** | ring |
| **ä** | car, lot | **ō** | go | **ʉr** | fur | | a *in* ago |
| **e** | ten | **ô** | law, horn | **ch** | chin | | e *in* agent |
| **er** | care | **oi** | oil | **sh** | she | ə = | i *in* unity |
| **ē** | even | **oo** | look | **th** | thin | | o *in* collect |
| **i** | hit | **ōō** | tool | ***th*** | then | | u *in* focus |

**con·sta·ble** (kän′stə b'l) ***n.*** a policeman of a town or village.

**Constable** comes from Latin words that mean "count of the stable." In earlier times, he was in charge of the grooms taking care of a stable of horses.

**con·stab·u·lar·y** (kən stab′yə ler′ē) ***n.*** a police force.

**con·stan·cy** (kän′stən sē) ***n.*** a staying the same; faithfulness or firmness.

**con·stant** (kän′stənt) ***adj.*** **1** not changing; staying the same; fixed [To be a pilot is Neal's *constant* goal.] **2** loyal; faithful [a *constant* friend]. **3** going on all the time; never stopping [I'm tired of our visitor's *constant* complaints.] ◆***n.*** something that never changes [Pi is a *constant* used in figuring measurements of all circles.] —**con′stant·ly** ***adv.***

**Con·stan·tine** (kän′stən tēn *or* kän′stən tīn) 280?–337 A.D.; emperor of Rome from 306 to 337 A.D. He was the first Roman emperor to become a Christian.

**Con·stan·ti·no·ple** (kän′stan tə nō′p'l) *the old name for* Istanbul, a city in Turkey.

**con·stel·la·tion** (kän′stə lā′shən) ***n.*** a group of stars, usually named after something that it is supposed to suggest [Orion is a *constellation* seen in the winter sky.] *See the picture.*

**con·ster·na·tion** (kän′stər nā′shən) ***n.*** great fear that makes one feel helpless; dismay [The earthquake filled us with *consternation.*]



**con·sti·pate** (kän′stə pāt) ***v.*** to cause constipation in. —**con′sti·pat·ed, con′sti·pat·ing**

**con·sti·pa·tion** (kän′stə pā′shən) ***n.*** a condition in which waste matter from the bowels does not empty easily or often enough.

**con·stit·u·en·cy** (kən stich′oo wən sē) ***n.*** **1** all the voters of a particular district. **2** the district itself. —*pl.* **con·stit′u·en·cies**

**con·stit·u·ent** (kən stich′oo wənt) ***adj.*** **1** needed to form a whole; used in making a thing [a *constituent* part]. **2** having the right to vote or elect. **3** having the power to make or change a constitution [a *constituent* assembly]. ◆***n.*** **1** one of the parts that make up a whole [Oxygen is one of the *constituents* of air.] **2** any of the voters represented by a particular official.

**con·sti·tute** (kän′stə to͞ot *or* kän′stə tyo͞ot) ***v.*** **1** to make up; form; compose [Twelve people *constitute* a jury.] **2** to set up; establish [A committee was *constituted* to study the problem.] **3** to give a certain right or duty to; appoint [We *constitute* you our leader.] —**con′sti·tut·ed, con′sti·tut·ing**

**con·sti·tu·tion** (kän′stə to͞o′shən *or* kän′stə tyo͞o′shən) ***n.*** **1** the act of setting up, forming, establishing, etc. **2** the way in which a person or thing is formed; makeup; structure [My strong *constitution* keeps me from catching cold.] **3** the system of basic laws or rules of a government, society, etc. **4** a document in which these laws and rules are written down [The *Constitution* of the U.S. is the supreme law here.]

**con·sti·tu·tion·al** (kän′stə to͞o′shən 'l *or* kän′stə tyo͞o′shən 'l) ***adj.*** **1** of or in the makeup of a person or thing; basic [a *constitutional* weakness]. **2** of or in agreement with a nation's constitution [Freedom of speech is one of our *constitutional* rights.] ◆***n.*** a walk taken as exercise. —**con′sti·tu′tion·al·ly** ***adv.***

**con·sti·tu·tion·al·i·ty** (kän′stə to͞o′shə nal′ə tē *or* kän′stə tyo͞o′shə nal′ə tē) ***n.*** the fact of being in agreement with a nation's constitution [Our case will test the *constitutionality* of this law in court.]

**con·strain** (kən strān′) ***v.*** to hold in or keep back by force or strain; force; compel [We felt *constrained* to agree. She gave a *constrained* laugh.]

**con·straint** (kən strānt′) ***n.*** **1** force; a constraining or being constrained. **2** the holding in of one's feelings [She spoke of her sorrow with *constraint.*]

**con·strict** (kən strikt′) ***v.*** to make smaller or narrower by pressing together; squeeze; contract [The tight collar *constricted* my neck.] —**con·stric′tion** ***n.*** —**con·stric′tive** ***adj.*** —**con·stric′tor** ***n.***

**con·struct** (kən strukt′) ***v.*** to make or build with a plan [to *construct* a house or a theory].

**con·struc·tion** (kən struk′shən) ***n.*** **1** the act of constructing or building. **2** the way in which something is constructed or put together [a house of brick *construction*]. **3** something built; structure [The Gateway Arch of St. Louis is a remarkable *construction.*] **4** an explanation or meaning [Don't put the wrong *construction* on what I said.] **5** the arrangement of words in a sentence ["Of what is it made?" is a more formal *construction* than "What's it made of?"]

**con·struc·tive** (kən struk′tiv) ***adj.*** able or helping to construct or build up; making suggestions [*Constructive* criticism helps us to correct our mistakes.]

**con·strue** (kən stro͞o′) ***v.*** **1** to explain the meaning of; interpret [We *construed* her silence to mean that she agreed.] **2** to find out or show how the parts of a sentence are related. —**con·strued′, con·stru′ing**

**con·sul** (kän′s'l) ***n.*** **1** a government official appointed by a country to look after its interests and help its citizens in a foreign city. **2** either of the two chief officials of the ancient Roman republic. —**con·su·lar** (kän′s'l ər) ***adj.***

**con·sul·ate** (kän′s'l it) ***n.*** **1** the position and duties of a consul. **2** the building where a consul works and often lives.

**con·sult** (kən sult′) ***v.*** **1** to go to for information or advice [If your coughing continues, *consult* a doctor.] **2** to talk things over in order to decide [I must *consult* with my wife about that.] **3** to keep in mind; consider [*Consult* your own wishes in the matter.]

**con·sult·ant** (kən sul′t'nt) ***n.*** an expert who is called on for special advice or services.

**con·sul·ta·tion** (kän′səl tā′shən) ***n.*** **1** a meeting to talk over some problem. **2** the act of consulting.

**con·sume** (kən so͞om′ *or* kən syo͞om′) ***v.*** **1** to destroy, as by fire. **2** to use up; spend or waste [The meeting *consumed* most of the day.] **3** to drink up or eat up [The family *consumed* a gallon of milk.] —**consumed′, con·sum′ing —consumed with,** filled with [to be *consumed with* envy].

**con·sum·er** (kən so͞o′mər *or* kən syo͞o′mər) ***n.*** a person or thing that consumes; especially, a person who buys goods for his own needs and not to sell to others or to use in making other goods for sale.

**con·sum·er·ism** (kən so͞o′mər iz'm *or* kən syo͞o′mər iz'm) ***n.*** a way of protecting the public by letting people know about goods that are unsafe, poorly made, falsely advertised, etc.

**con·sum·mate** (kän′sə māt) ***v.*** to make complete; finish; fulfill [to *consummate* a project]. —**con′sum·mat·ed, con′sum·mat·ing** ◆***adj.*** (kən sum′it) **1** complete; absolute [*consummate* happiness]. **2** very skillful [a *consummate* liar]. —**con′sum·ma′tion** ***n.***

**con·sump·tion** (kən sump′shən) ***n.*** **1** a consuming or using up. **2** the amount used up [What is the annual *consumption* of paper in the U.S.?] **3** tuberculosis of the lungs: *an old-fashioned word.*

**cont.** *abbreviation for* **containing, contents, continent, continued, control.**

**con·tact** (kän′takt) ***n.*** **1** a touching or meeting [The light is turned on by the *contact* of the switch with the wire.] **2** the condition of being in touch or associating [I come into *contact* with many people.] **3** connection, communication, etc. [The pilot made *contact* with the airport.] ☆**4** an acquaintance who is influential [a *contact* at city hall]. ◆***v.*** ☆to get in touch with; communicate with.

**contact lens** a tiny, thin lens of glass or plastic placed in the fluid over the cornea of the eye in order to correct a vision defect.

**con·ta·gion** (kən tā′jən) ***n.*** **1** the spreading of disease from one person to another by contact. **2** any disease spread in this way. **3** the spreading of a feeling or idea from person to person [the *contagion* of mirth in a theater].

**con·ta·gious** (kən tā′jəs) ***adj.*** **1** spread by contact [a *contagious* disease]. **2** quickly spreading from person to person [*contagious* laughter].

**con·tain** (kən tān′) ***v.*** **1** to have in it; hold; enclose or include [This bottle *contains* cream. Your list *contains* 25 names.] **2** to be able to hold; be equal to [This jug *contains* a gallon. A gallon *contains* four quarts.] **3** to hold back; control or restrain [Try to *contain* your anger.]

**con·tain·er** (kən tān′ər) ***n.*** a thing for holding something; box, can, bottle, pot, etc.

**con·tam·i·nate** (kən tam′ə nāt) ***v.*** to make dirty, impure, or infected by touching or mixing with; pollute; corrupt [You might be *contaminated* if you kiss someone who has the flu.] —**con·tam′i·nat·ed, con·tam′i·nat·ing** —**con·tam′i·na′tion** ***n.***

SYNONYMS: To **contaminate** is to make something impure or unfit for use by bringing it into contact with something else that is dirty or corrupting [The canned goods were *contaminated* by bacteria from unclean canning methods.] To **pollute** is to make something completely foul or poisoned by contaminating it [Exhaust fumes *pollute* our air.]

**contd.** *abbreviation for* **continued.**

**con·tem·plate** (kän′təm plāt) ***v.*** **1** to look at or think about carefully or seriously; study; consider [He *contemplated* the problem for a long time.] **2** to have as a plan; expect; intend [I *contemplate* going to Mexico next summer.] —**con′tem·plat·ed, con′tem·plat·ing** —**con′tem·pla′tion** ***n.***

**con·tem·pla·tive** (kən tem′plə tiv *or* kän′təm plāt′iv) ***adj.*** thoughtful; contemplating.

**con·tem·po·ra·ne·ous** (kən tem′pə rā′nē əs) ***adj.*** existing or happening in the same period of time [*contemporaneous* events]. —**con·tem′po·ra′ne·ous·ly** ***adv.***

**con·tem·po·rar·y** (kən tem′pə rer′ē) ***adj.*** existing or happening in the same period of time. ◆***n.*** a person living in the same period as another [The painters Mary Cassatt and Edgar Degas were *contemporaries.*] —*pl.* **con·tem′po·rar′ies**

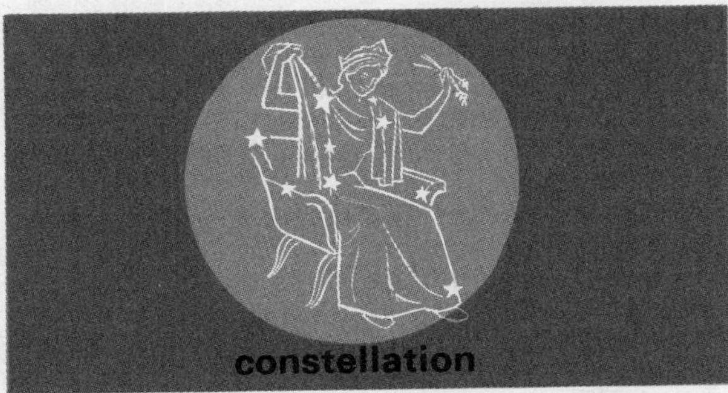
**constellation**

**con·tempt** (kən tempt′) ***n.*** **1** the feeling one has toward someone or something one considers low, worthless, or evil; scorn [to feel *contempt* for a cheat]. **2** the condition of being despised or scorned [to be held in *contempt*]. **3** the act of showing a lack of respect for a court or legislature, as by refusing to obey a lawful order [to be fined for *contempt* of court].

**con·tempt·i·ble** (kən temp′tə b′l) ***adj.*** that should be treated with contempt; deserving scorn [a *contemptible* liar].

**con·temp·tu·ous** (kən temp′chōō wəs) ***adj.*** full of contempt; scornful [a *contemptuous* smile].

**con·tend** (kən tend′) ***v.*** **1** to fight or struggle [to *contend* with greed and envy]. **2** to strive in a contest; compete [Jones will *contend* for the prize.] **3** to argue; hold to be a fact [We *contend* that he is guilty.] —**con·tend′er** ***n.***

**con·tent**[1] (kən tent′) ***adj.*** happy with what one has or is; not wanting anything else; satisfied [Are you *content* with the food here?] ◆***v.*** to satisfy; make content [I must *content* myself with reading about travel.] *See* SYNONYMS *at* **satisfy.** ◆***n.*** the condition of being satisfied or contented [a sigh of *content*].

**con·tent**[2] (kän′tent) ***n.*** **1** the amount held or contained [The *content* of that jar is one liter. Cast iron has a high carbon *content*.] **2 contents,** *pl.* all that is contained; everything inside [the *contents* of a trunk]. **3** *often* **contents,** *pl.* the things dealt with in a piece of writing, etc. [a table of *contents* in a book].

**con·tent·ed** (kən ten′tid) ***adj.*** satisfied.

**con·ten·tion** (kən ten′shən) ***n.*** **1** the act of contending; argument, struggle, or strife [*contention* about a point of law]. **2** something that one argues for as right or true [It was my *contention* that we should all pay.]

**con·ten·tious** (kən ten′shəs) ***adj.*** always ready to argue; quarrelsome.

**con·tent·ment** (kən tent′mənt) ***n.*** the condition of being contented; feeling of quiet satisfaction.



| | | | |
|---|---|---|---|
| **a** fat | **ir** here | **ou** out | **zh** leisure |
| **ā** ape | **ī** bite, fire | **u** up | **ŋ** ring |
| **ä** car, lot | **ō** go | **ur** fur | a *in* ago |
| **e** ten | **ô** law, horn | **ch** chin | e *in* agent |
| **er** care | **oi** oil | **sh** she | **ə** = i *in* unity |
| **ē** even | **oo** look | **th** thin | o *in* collect |
| **i** hit | **ōō** tool | ***th*** then | u *in* focus |

**con·test** (kən test′) ***v.*** **1** to try to prove that something is not true, right, or lawful; dispute [to *contest* a will]. **2** to fight for; struggle to win or keep [to *contest* a prize]. ◆***n.*** (kän′test) **1** a fight, struggle, or argument. **2** a race, game, etc. in which there is a struggle to be the winner.

**con·test·ant** (kən tes′tənt) ***n.*** a person who takes part in a contest.

**con·text** (kän′tekst) ***n.*** the words just before and after a certain word or sentence that help make clear what it means [A remark taken out of *context* may be misunderstood.]

**con·tig·u·ous** (kən tig′yoo wəs) ***adj.*** **1** touching along all or most of one side [The U.S. is *contiguous* with Canada.] **2** lying near; neighboring [*contiguous* houses].

**con·ti·nence** (känt′′n əns) ***n.*** control of oneself and one's appetites; not eating, drinking, etc. too much. —**con′ti·nent** ***adj.***

**con·ti·nent** (känt′′n ənt) ***n.*** any of the main large land areas of the earth. The continents are Africa, Asia, Australia, Europe, North America, South America, and, sometimes, Antarctica. —**the Continent,** all of Europe except the British Isles.

**con·ti·nen·tal** (känt′′n en′t'l) ***adj.*** **1** of or like a continent. **2 Continental,** of or having to do with the continent of Europe [taking a *Continental* tour]. **3 Continental,** of the American colonies at the time of the American Revolution [the *Continental* Congress]. ◆***n.*** **Continental, 1** a person living on the continent of Europe; European. **2** a soldier of the American Revolutionary army. *See the picture.*



**con·tin·gen·cy** (kən tin′jən sē) ***n.*** **1** the condition of being uncertain or dependent on chance [The *contingency* of future events makes planning ahead hard.] **2** a chance happening; uncertain event; accident [We must be ready for any *contingency*.] —*pl.* **con·tin′gen·cies**

**con·tin·gent** (kən tin′jənt) ***adj.*** **1** that may or may not happen; possible [*contingent* events]. **2** depending on something uncertain; conditional [Promotion to the next grade is *contingent* on passing the final exams.] ◆***n.*** **1** a chance happening; accident. **2** a group forming a part of a larger one; especially, one's share of workers, delegates, etc. [the Chicago *contingent* at the convention].

contour farming

Continental soldier

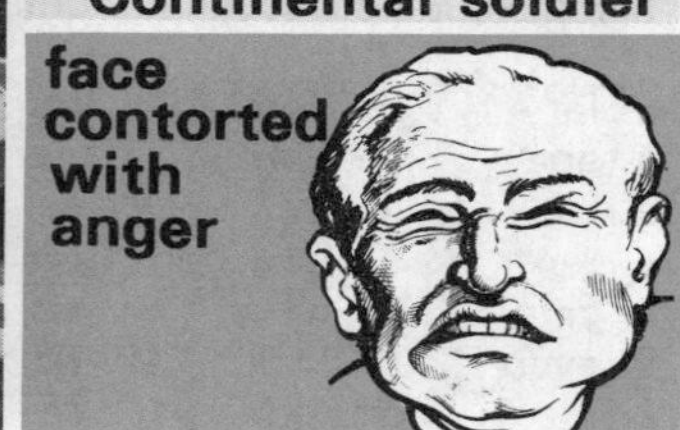
face contorted with anger

**con·tin·u·al** (kən tin′yoo wəl) ***adj.*** **1** happening over and over again; repeated often [the *continual* banging of the door]. **2** continuous; going on without stopping [the *continual* roar of the waterfall]. —**con·tin′u·al·ly** ***adv.***

SYNONYMS: **Continual** refers to something that takes place, or is repeated, again and again over a long period of time [The *continual* interruptions made it hard to concentrate.] **Continuous** applies to something that goes on without a pause for a long time or stretches out over a long distance without any break [in almost *continuous* pain; a *continuous* line of cars barely moving along the highway].

**con·tin·u·ance** (kən tin′yoo wəns) ***n.*** **1** a continuing; keeping up or going on [The treaty provides for a *continuance* of trade.] **2** the putting off of something to a later time [The lawyer asked for a *continuance* of the trial.]

**con·tin·u·a·tion** (kən tin′yoo wā′shən) ***n.*** **1** a keeping up or going on without stopping. **2** a taking up or beginning again after stopping. **3** a part or thing added on, as a sequel to a story.

**con·tin·ue** (kən tin′yoo̅) ***v.*** **1** to keep on being or doing [The rain *continued* for five days.] **2** to stay in the same place or position [The chairman will *continue* in office for another year.] **3** to go on or start again after a stop; resume [After a sip of water, the speaker *continued*.] **4** to go on or extend; stretch [This road *continues* to the main highway.] **5** to put off to a later time [The trial will be *continued* until Monday.] —**con·tin′ued, con·tin′u·ing**

**con·ti·nu·i·ty** (kän′tə no̅o̅′ə tē) ***n.*** **1** the condition of being continuous [the logical *continuity* of the lecture, which never wandered from the subject]. **2** the remarks made by an announcer, etc. that tie together the parts of a radio or TV program.

**con·tin·u·ous** (kən tin′yoo wəs) ***adj.*** going on without a stop or break; connected [one huge, *continuous* area of concrete]. *See* SYNONYMS *at* **continual.** —**con·tin′u·ous·ly** ***adv.***

**con·tort** (kən tôrt′) ***v.*** to twist or force out of its usual form [a face *contorted* with pain]. *See the picture.*

**con·tor·tion** (kən tôr′shən) ***n.*** a contorting or being contorted, as of the face or body.

**con·tor·tion·ist** (kən tôr′shən ist) ***n.*** a person, as a circus acrobat, whose body is limber enough to be twisted into unusual positions.

**con·tour** (kän′toor) ***n.*** the outline of something, or a line drawn to represent this. ◆***adj.*** **1** made so as to fit the shape of something [*contour* sheets for a bed]. **2** being or having to do with farming in which land is plowed along the natural lines of ridges, slopes, etc. in order to stop erosion [*contour* farming]. *See the picture.*

**con·tra·band** (kän′trə band) ***n.*** things that it is against the law to bring into or take out of a country; smuggled goods.

**con·tra·cep·tion** (kän′trə sep′shən) ***n.*** the use of special devices, drugs, etc. to keep the human ovum from being fertilized. —**con′tra·cep′tive** ***adj., n.***

**con·tract** (kän′trakt) ***n.*** **1** an agreement, especially a written agreement that one can be held to by law [a *contract* to build a house]. **2** a form of bridge, the card game. ◆***v.*** (kən trakt′) **1** to get; come to have [to *contract* a disease]. **2** to make or become smaller;

draw together; shrink [Cold *contracts* metals. The judge's brows were *contracted* in a frown.] **3** (kän'-trakt) to make a contract to do, buy, or sell something.

**con·trac·tion** (kən trak'shən) ***n.*** **1** a contracting or being contracted [the *contraction* of a gas when it is cooled]. **2** a shortened form of a word or phrase, as *I'm* for *I am.*

**con·trac·tor** (kän'trak tər) ***n.*** a person or company that contracts to do certain work or to supply certain materials, especially one that does so in the building trades.

**con·tra·dict** (kän trə dikt') ***v.*** **1** to say the opposite of; deny the things said by someone [The witness *contradicted* the story told by the suspect. Stop *contradicting* me.] **2** to be opposite to or different from; go against [The facts *contradict* your theory.]

> **Contradict** comes from a Latin word that means "to speak against." In English to contradict someone means "to deny what someone else has said," which is one way of speaking against that person.

**con·tra·dic·tion** (kän'trə dik'shən) ***n.*** **1** a contradicting or being contradicted [the child's innocent *contradiction* of what we had just said]. **2** a remark or act that contradicts another [The report contains a direct *contradiction* of the rumors.]

**con·tra·dic·to·ry** (kän'trə dik'tər ē) ***adj.*** not in agreement; saying the opposite; contrary [the *contradictory* use of words in the phrase "square circle"].

☆**con·trail** (kän'trāl) ***n.*** a white trail of condensed water vapor that sometimes forms in the sky behind an airplane.

**con·tral·to** (kən tral'tō) ***n.*** **1** the lowest kind of woman's singing voice. **2** a singer with such a voice. —*pl.* **con·tral'tos** ◆***adj.*** of or for a contralto.

**con·trap·tion** (kən trap'shən) ***n.*** any strange-looking device or machine that one does not fully understand; gadget: *used only in everyday talk.*

**con·trar·i·wise** (kän'trer ē wīz') ***adv.*** as opposed to what has been said; on the contrary.

**con·trar·y** (kän'trer ē) ***adj.*** **1** opposite; completely different [to hold *contrary* opinions]. **2** opposed; being or acting against [*contrary* to the rules]. **3** (*often* kən trer'ē) opposing in a stubborn way; perverse [such a *contrary* child, always saying "No!"]. ◆***n.*** the opposite [Just the *contrary* of what you say is true.] —**on the contrary,** as opposed to what has been said.

**con·trast** (kən trast') ***v.*** **1** to compare in a way that shows the differences [to *contrast* France and England]. **2** to show differences when compared [Golf *contrasts* sharply with tennis as a sport.] ◆***n.*** (kän'trast) **1** a difference between things being compared [the *contrast* between air and rail travel]. **2** something showing differences when compared with something else [Reading a novel is quite a *contrast* to seeing a movie based on the novel.]

**con·trib·ute** (kən trib'yo͞ot) ***v.*** **1** to give together with others [I *contribute* to my church.] **2** to write an article, poem, etc. as for a magazine or newspaper. —**con·trib'ut·ed, con·trib'ut·ing** —**contribute to,** to have a part in bringing about [Good luck *contributed to* our success.]

**con·tri·bu·tion** (kän'trə byo͞o'shən) ***n.*** **1** the act of contributing. **2** something contributed, as money to a charity or a poem to a magazine.

**con·trib·u·tor** (kən trib'yoo tər) ***n.*** a person or thing that contributes.

**con·trib·u·to·ry** (kən trib'yoo tôr'ē) ***adj.*** having a part in bringing something about; contributing [a *contributory* factor to our victory].

**con·trite** (kən trīt' *or* kän'trīt) ***adj.*** **1** feeling very sorry for having done something. **2** showing such feeling [a *contrite* apology]. —**con·tri·tion** (kən trish'ən) ***n.***

> The word **contrite** comes from a Latin word meaning "worn out" or "ground to pieces." A person who is contrite and feels very sorry for having done something wrong may come to feel worn out, as if ground into pieces.

**con·triv·ance** (kən trī'vəns) ***n.*** **1** the act or a way of contriving. **2** something contrived, as an invention or mechanical device.

**con·trive** (kən trīv') ***v.*** **1** to think up; plan; devise [Let's *contrive* a way to help her.] **2** to build in a skillful or clever way [He *contrived* a new kind of car.] **3** to bring about, as by a clever or tricky plan; manage [We *contrived* to get into the locked room.] —**con·trived', con·triv'ing**

**con·trived** (kən trīvd') ***adj.*** not coming about in an easy, natural way [The ending to the play seems *contrived.*]

**con·trol** (kən trōl') ***v.*** **1** to have the power of ruling, guiding, or managing [A thermostat *controls* the heat.] **2** to hold back; curb [*Control* your temper!] —**con·trolled', con·trol'ling** ◆***n.*** **1** power to direct or manage [He's a poor coach, with little *control* over the team.] **2** the condition of being directed; restraint [The car went out of *control.*] **3** a part or thing that controls a machine [the *controls* of an airplane]. —**con·trol'la·ble** ***adj.***

**con·trol·ler** (kən trōl'ər) ***n.*** **1** a person in charge of spending, as for a company or government. **2** a person or thing that controls.

**con·tro·ver·sial** (kän'trə vur'shəl) ***adj.*** that is or can be much argued about; debatable [a *controversial* book]. —**con'tro·ver'sial·ly** ***adv.***

**con·tro·ver·sy** (kän'trə vur'sē) ***n.*** argument or debate. *See* SYNONYMS *at* **argument.** —*pl.* **con'tro·ver'sies**

**con·tu·sion** (kən to͞o'zhən) ***n.*** a bruise; injury in which the skin is not broken.

**co·nun·drum** (kə nun'drəm) ***n.*** a riddle whose answer contains a pun. Example: "What is the difference between a jeweler and a jailer?" "One sells watches and the other watches cells."

**con·va·lesce** (kän və les') ***v.*** to get back health and strength after an illness. —**con·va·lesced', con·va·lesc'ing**

**con·va·les·cence** (kän'və les''ns) ***n.*** the act or time of convalescing.

| | | | |
|---|---|---|---|
| **a** fat | **ir** here | **ou** out | **zh** leisure |
| **ā** ape | **ī** bite, fire | **u** up | **ng** ring |
| **ä** car, lot | **ō** go | **ur** fur | a *in* ago |
| **e** ten | **ô** law, horn | **ch** chin | e *in* agent |
| **er** care | **oi** oil | **sh** she | **ə** = i *in* unity |
| **ē** even | **oo** look | **th** thin | o *in* collect |
| **i** hit | **o͞o** tool | ***th*** then | u *in* focus |

**con·va·les·cent** (kän′və les′'nt) ***adj.*** getting back health and strength after illness. ◆***n.*** a convalescent person.

**con·vec·tion** (kən vek′shən) ***n.*** a carrying or passing along, as of heat in air, gas, or liquid currents [In a house heated by *convection,* hot air or water moves through pipes from the furnace to the rooms.]

**con·vene** (kən vēn′) ***v.*** to come or call together for a meeting; assemble [Congress regularly *convenes* in January, but in a crisis the President can *convene* Congress for a special session.] —**con·vened′, con·ven′·ing**

**con·ven·ience** (kən vēn′yəns) ***n.*** **1** a being convenient or making things easier [We enjoy the *convenience* of living near a shopping center.] **2** personal comfort or advantage [The store has a telephone for the *convenience* of customers.] **3** anything that adds to one's comfort or saves work [freezers, dryers, and other modern *conveniences*]. —**at one's convenience,** at a time or in a way that suits one.

**con·ven·ient** (kən vēn′yənt) ***adj.*** adding to one's comfort; making things easier; handy [a *convenient* place for a meeting]. —**con·ven′ient·ly** ***adv.***

**con·vent** (kän′vent) ***n.*** a group of nuns living together under strict religious vows, or the place where they live.

**con·ven·tion** (kən ven′shən) ***n.*** **1** a meeting of members or delegates from various places, held every



year or every few years [a political *convention;* a national *convention* of English teachers]. **2** an agreement between persons or nations. **3** a custom or way of behaving that most people follow [It is a *convention* to say "How do you do?" on being introduced to someone.]

**con·ven·tion·al** (kən ven′shən 'l) ***adj.*** **1** that is a convention or custom; usual or customary ["Yours truly" is a *conventional* closing to a letter.] **2** behaving in the way that most people do or in ways that most people approve of [Don't be so *conventional*—show some spirit and imagination!] —**con·ven·tion·al·i·ty** (kən ven′shə nal′ə tē) ***n.*** —**con·ven′tion·al·ly** ***adv.***

**con·verge** (kən vurj′) ***v.*** to come together or seem to come together at a point; move toward the same place [Railroad tracks *converge* as they extend into the distance. Crowds *converged* on the stadium.] *See the picture.* —**con·verged′, con·verg′ing**

**con·ver·gence** (kən vur′jəns) ***n.*** a coming together or seeming to come together, or the place at which this takes place. —**con·ver′gent** ***adj.***

**con·ver·sant** (kən vur′s'nt) ***adj.*** knowing about through study or experience; familiar or acquainted [He is *conversant* with the subject.]

**con·ver·sa·tion** (kän′vər sā′shən) ***n.*** a talk or a talking together.

**con·ver·sa·tion·al** (kän′vər sā′shən 'l) ***adj.*** of, for, or like conversation [This author writes in a relaxed, *conversational* style.]

**con·verse**[1] (kən vurs′) ***v.*** to talk; have a conversation. —**con·versed′, con·vers′ing** ◆***n.*** (kän′vərs) talk; conversation.

**con·verse**[2] (kän′vərs) ***adj.*** turned about; opposite or contrary. ◆***n.*** the opposite ["Wet" is the *converse* of "dry."] —**con·verse′ly** ***adv.***

**con·ver·sion** (kən vur′zhən) ***n.*** **1** a converting or being converted; change [An atomic explosion is based on the *conversion* of matter into energy.] **2** a change from one belief or religion to another.

**con·vert** (kən vurt′) ***v.*** **1** to change from one form or use to another; transform [The mill *converts* grain into flour.] *See* SYNONYMS *at* **transform. 2** to change from one belief or religion to another [Missionaries tried to *convert* them to Christianity.] **3** to exchange for something of equal value [The bank will *convert* your dollars into English pounds.] ☆**4** to score an extra point or points after a touchdown in football. ◆***n.*** (kän′vərt) a person who has changed from one religion or belief to another. —**con·vert′er** ***n.***

**con·vert·i·ble** (kən vur′tə b'l) ***adj.*** that can be converted [Matter is *convertible* into energy.] ◆***n.*** ☆an automobile with a top that can be folded back.

**con·vex** (kän veks′ *or* kän′veks) ***adj.*** curving outward like the outside of a ball [a *convex* lens]. *See the picture.* —**con·vex′i·ty** ***n.*** —**con·vex′ly** ***adv.***

**con·vey** (kən vā′) ***v.*** **1** to take from one place to another; carry or transport [The cattle were *conveyed* in trucks to the market.] **2** to be the means through which something moves or flows; transmit [a pipeline to *convey* oil]. **3** to make known; give [Please *convey* my best wishes to them.] **4** to hand over, as land, from one owner to another.

**con·vey·ance** (kən vā′əns) ***n.*** **1** the act of conveying. **2** anything used for conveying, as a truck or car.

**con·vey·or** or **con·vey·er** (kən vā′ər) ***n.*** a person or thing that conveys; especially, a moving endless chain or belt (called, in full, **conveyor belt**).

**con·vict** (kən vikt′) ***v.*** to judge and find guilty, as in a court trial [The jury *convicted* him of robbery.] ◆***n.*** (kän′vikt) a person who is serving a sentence in prison.

**con·vic·tion** (kən vik′shən) ***n.*** **1** a convicting or being convicted of a crime. **2** a fixed idea or strong belief [It is my *conviction* that democracy is the best form of government.]

**con·vince** (kən vins′) ***v.*** to make feel sure; persuade [I'm *convinced* they are telling the truth.] —**con·vinced′, con·vinc′ing**

**con·vinc·ing** (kən vin′siŋ) ***adj.*** causing one to feel sure or to agree [She gave *convincing* reasons for staying up late.]

**con·viv·i·al** (kən viv′ē əl) ***adj.*** enjoying a good time, as at parties; loving fun; sociable.

**con·vo·ca·tion** (kän′və kā′shən) ***n.*** a meeting called for some purpose [a college *convocation* at which some students received honors and awards].

**con·vo·lu·tion** (kän′və lo͞o′shən) ***n.*** a twist, coil, or fold [The surface of the brain has *convolutions.*] *See the picture.*

**con·voy** (kän′voi) ***v.*** to go along with as an escort or in order to protect [a tanker *convoyed* by two destroyers]. ◆***n.*** a group of ships, vehicles, etc. traveling together in order to protect one another.

**con·vulse** (kən vuls′) ***v.*** **1** to shake or disturb violently. **2** to cause to shake, as with laughter or grief. —**con·vulsed′, con·vuls′ing**

**con·vul·sion** (kən vul′shən) ***n.*** **1** a sudden, sharp tightening or twitching of the muscles, as in certain diseases. **2** any strong disturbance, as an earthquake or a riot.

**con·vul·sive** (kən vul′siv) ***adj.*** convulsing or like a convulsion [*convulsive* laughter].

**coo** (ko͞o) ***n.*** the soft, murmuring sound made by doves and pigeons. ◆***v.*** **1** to make this sound. **2** to speak or say in a soft, loving way.

**cook** (ko͝ok) ***v.*** **1** to prepare food by heating; boil, roast, bake, etc. **2** to be cooked [The roast should *cook* longer.] ◆***n.*** a person who prepares food for eating. —**cook up,** to think up: *used only in everyday talk* [We *cooked up* an excuse for not going.] —☆**what's cooking?** what's going on?: *a slang phrase.*

**Cook** (ko͝ok), **James** 1728–1779; English navy officer. He explored Australia, New Zealand, etc.

**cook·er** (ko͝ok′ər) ***n.*** a container in which food is cooked [a pressure *cooker*].

**cook·ie** or **cook·y** (ko͝ok′ē) ***n.*** ☆a small, flat, sweet cake. —*pl.* **cook′ies**

☆**cook·out** (ko͝ok′out) ***n.*** a meal cooked and eaten outdoors.

**cool** (ko͞ol) ***adj.*** **1** not warm but not very cold. **2** not too hot; comfortable [*cool* clothes]. **3** calm; not excited [Keep *cool* in an emergency.] **4** not friendly or interested; showing dislike [She greeted me with a *cool* "hello."] **5** not suggesting warmth [Blue and green are *cool* colors.] ☆**6** very good: *slang in this meaning* [That new movie is really *cool.*] ◆***n.*** a place, time, etc. that is cool [in the *cool* of the evening]. ◆***v.*** **1** to become cool [Let the cake *cool* before you ice it.] **2** to make cool [blowing on the soup to *cool* it]. —**cool off, 1** to calm down. **2** to lose interest. —**cool′ly** ***adv.*** —**cool′ness** ***n.***

> SYNONYMS: **Cool** is used of a person who keeps calm and is able to think clearly even in a situation which would upset and excite most people. **Composed** suggests the calm, dignified manner of a person with so much self-control that it is not easily lost whatever may happen. **Collected** is used of a person who can control his feelings in a difficult situation by using will power and good sense.

**cool·ant** (ko͞ol′ənt) ***n.*** a fluid used to remove heat, as from an automobile engine.

**cool·er** (ko͞ol′ər) ***n.*** a container or room in which things are cooled or kept cool.

**Coo·lidge** (ko͞o′lij), **(John) Calvin** 1872–1933; the 30th president of the United States, from 1923 to 1929.

**coo·lie** (ko͞o′lē) ***n.*** a laborer living in China, India, etc., especially in former times, and having no special skills.

☆**coon** (ko͞on) ***n.*** *a shorter form of* **raccoon.**

**coop** (ko͞op) ***n.*** a cage or pen for chickens, ducks, etc. or small animals. ◆***v.*** to shut up in a coop or small space [We felt *cooped* up in the tiny apartment.]

**co-op** (kō′äp) ***n.*** a cooperative store, group, etc.: *used only in everyday talk.*

**Coop·er** (ko͞op′ər), **James Fen·i·more** (fen′ə môr) 1789–1851; U.S. novelist.

**co·op·er·ate** (kō äp′ə rāt) ***v.*** to work together to get something done [If we all *cooperate,* we can finish sooner.] —**co·op′er·at·ed, co·op′er·at·ing** —**co·op′-er·a′tion** ***n.***

**co·op·er·a·tive** (kō äp′ər ə tiv *or* kō äp′rə tiv) ***adj.*** **1** willing to cooperate; helpful. **2** that is or belongs to a group whose members produce goods together or sell them and share the profits [Local farmers have started a *cooperative* store.] ◆***n.*** a cooperative group, store, etc.

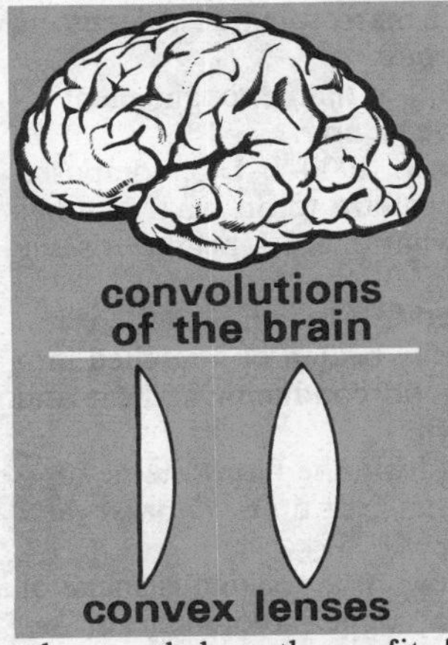

convolutions of the brain

convex lenses

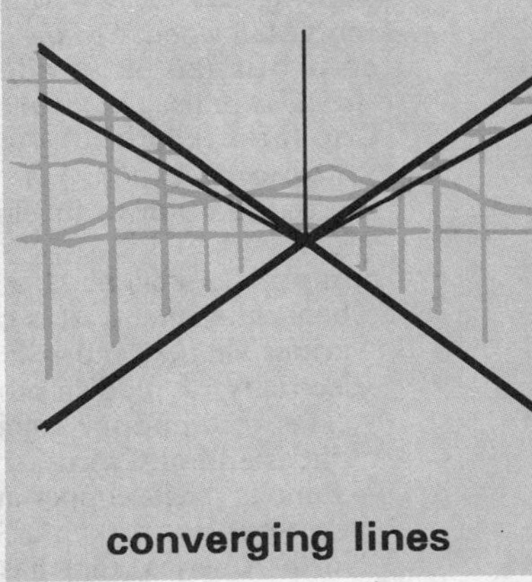

converging lines

**co-opt** (kō äpt′) ***v.*** **1** to get a person with different views to join one's own group, political party, etc. **2** to add a person to a group by a vote of the members.

**co·or·di·nate** (kō ôr′d'n it) ***adj.*** of equal importance [In the phrase "a young, healthy dog," "young" and "healthy" are *coordinate* adjectives.] ◆***v.*** (kō ôr′də nāt) to bring together in the proper relation; make work well together [She was able to *coordinate* the efforts of dozens of volunteers.] —**co·or′di·nat·ed, co·or′di·nat·ing**

**co·or·di·na·tion** (kō ôr′d'n ā′shən) ***n.*** a working together smoothly, or a causing to work together smoothly [*Coordination* of both hands is important in playing the piano.]

**coot** (ko͞ot) ***n.*** a water bird with short wings, that swims and dives like a duck.

**cop** (käp) ☆***n.*** a policeman: *a slang word.* —☆**cop out, 1** to fail to do what one has promised or agreed to do. **2** to give up; quit. *This is a slang phrase.* —**copped, cop′ping**

**cope** (kōp) ***v.*** to deal with a problem; take care of successfully [The police were barely able to *cope* with the unruly crowds.] —**coped, cop′ing**

**Co·pen·hag·en** (kō′pən hā′gən) a seaport and the capital of Denmark.

**Co·per·ni·cus** (kō pur′ni kəs), **Nic·o·la·us** (nik′ə lā′əs) 1473–1543; Polish astronomer, who taught that the planets move around the sun. —**Co·per′ni·can** ***adj., n.***

**cop·i·er** (käp′ē ər) ***n.*** **1** one who copies. **2** a duplicating machine.

**co·pi·lot** (kō′pī lət) ***n.*** the assistant pilot of an airplane.

**cop·ing** (kō′piŋ) ***n.*** the sloping top layer of a stone or brick wall.

| | | | | | | | |
|---|---|---|---|---|---|---|---|
| **a** | fat | **ir** | here | **ou** | out | **zh** | leisure |
| **ā** | ape | **ī** | bite, fire | **u** | up | **ŋ** | ring |
| **ä** | car, lot | **ō** | go | **ur** | fur | | a *in* ago |
| **e** | ten | **ô** | law, horn | **ch** | chin | | e *in* agent |
| **er** | care | **oi** | oil | **sh** | she | **ə =** | i *in* unity |
| **ē** | even | **o͝o** | look | **th** | thin | | o *in* collect |
| **i** | hit | **o͞o** | tool | ***th*** | then | | u *in* focus |

**coping saw** a saw with a narrow blade for cutting curves in wood. *See the picture.*
**co·pi·ous** (kō′pē əs) ***adj.*** more than enough; plentiful [*copious* praise]. —**co′pi·ous·ly** ***adv.***
**Cop·land** (kōp′lənd), **Aaron** 1900– ; U.S. composer.
☆**cop-out** (käp′out) ***n.*** a failure to do what one has agreed to do or to finish what one has begun: *a slang word.*
**cop·per** (käp′ər) ***n.*** **1** a reddish-brown metal that is a chemical element. It is easily beaten or stretched into various shapes, and is a good conductor of heat and electricity. **2** reddish brown.

The word **copper** comes from the Greek name for the island of Cyprus. In ancient times Cyprus was famous for its copper mines.

☆**cop·per·head** (käp′ər hed) ***n.*** a poisonous snake of North America, that has a copper-colored head. *See the picture.*
**cop·pice** (käp′is) ***n.*** *same as* **copse.**
**cop·ra** (käp′rə) ***n.*** dried coconut meat.
**copse** (käps) ***n.*** a group of small trees or shrubs growing close together; thicket.
☆**cop·ter** (käp′tər) ***n.*** *shorter form of* **helicopter.**
**cop·y** (käp′ē) ***n.*** **1** a thing made just like another; imitation or likeness [four carbon *copies* of a letter]. **2** any one of a number of books, magazines, pictures, etc. with the same printed matter [a library with six *copies* of *Tom Sawyer*]. **3** a piece of writing that is to be set in type for printing [Reporters must write clear *copy.*] —*pl.* **cop′ies** ◆***v.*** **1** to make a copy or copies of [*Copy* the questions that are on the chalkboard.] **2** to act or be the same as; imitate. *See* SYNONYMS *at* **imitate.** —**cop′ied, cop′y·ing**
☆**cop·y·cat** (käp′ē kat) ***n.*** a person who copies or imitates others: *a child's word.*
**cop·y·right** (käp′ē rīt) ***n.*** the legal right to be the only publisher, producer, or seller of a particular piece of writing, art, or music. ◆***v.*** to protect by copyright [Books are not *copyrighted* until they are published.]
**co·quette** (kō ket′) ***n.*** a vain girl or woman who tries to get men to notice and admire her; flirt.
**cor·al** (kôr′əl) ***n.*** **1** a hard, stony substance made up of the skeletons of many tiny sea animals. Reefs of coral are found in tropical seas. *See the picture.* **2** a piece of coral. **3** yellowish red. ◆***adj.*** **1** made of coral. **2** yellowish-red in color.
**cord** (kôrd) ***n.*** **1** a thick string or thin rope. **2** any part of the body that is like a cord [the spinal *cord;* vocal *cords*]. **3** a wire or wires covered with rubber or other insulation and used to carry electricity from an outlet to a lamp, appliance, etc. **4** a raised ridge on certain kinds of cloth, as on corduroy; also, such a cloth. **5** **cords,** *pl.* corduroy trousers. **6** a measure of cut firewood. A cord is a pile 8 feet long, 4 feet wide, and 4 feet high.
**cor·dial** (kôr′jəl) ***adj.*** deeply felt; hearty; sincere [a *cordial* welcome]. ◆***n.*** a sweet and rather thick alcoholic drink. —**cor′dial·ly** ***adv.***
**cor·di·al·i·ty** (kôr′jē al′ə tē) ***n.*** a cordial quality; warm, friendly feeling.
☆**cord·less** (kôrd′lis) ***adj.*** operated by a battery and not by a cord going to an electric outlet [a *cordless* electric shaver].



**cor·don** (kôr′d'n) ***n.*** a line or circle, as of police or ships, placed around an area to guard it ◆***v.*** to put a cordon around [Police *cordoned* off the shopping center where the explosion took place.]
**cor·do·van** (kôr′də vən) ***n.*** a soft, colored leather, usually made from horsehide.
**cor·du·roy** (kôr′də roi) ***n.*** **1** a heavy cotton cloth having a soft, velvety surface with raised ridges. **2** **corduroys,** *pl.* trousers made of this cloth ◆***adj.*** **1** of or like corduroy. ☆**2** made of logs laid crosswise [a *corduroy* road].
**cord·wood** (kôrd′wood) ***n.*** firewood sold in cords.
**core** (kôr) ***n.*** **1** the hard center of some fruits, as the apple or pear, containing the seeds. **2** the central part of anything. **3** the most important part [the *core* of the problem]. ◆***v.*** to cut out the core of a fruit. —**cored, cor′ing**

Experts on the history of words are not certain how **core** came into the language. But it seems likely that it came to us, through French, from the Latin word for the heart, that all-important blood-pumping muscle which is located near the center of the body.

**CORE** (kôr) Congress of Racial Equality.
**Cor·inth** (kôr′inth) an ancient city in Greece.
**Co·rin·thi·an** (kə rin′thē ən) ***adj.*** **1** of Corinth. **2** describing a highly decorated style of ancient Greek architecture in which the columns have fancy carvings of leaves at the top.
**Co·rin·thi·ans** (kə rin′thē ənz) either of two books of the Bible, written by the Apostle Paul.
**cork** (kôrk) ***n.*** **1** the thick outer bark of a kind of oak tree that grows in the Mediterranean area. Cork is very light and tough and is used for various purposes. **2** a piece of cork, especially one used as a stopper for a bottle or cask. **3** a stopper made of any material, as of rubber. ◆***v.*** to stop or shut up, as with a cork [to *cork* a bottle].
**cork·screw** (kôrk′skro͞o) ***n.*** a tool for pulling corks out of bottles. *See the picture.*
**corm** (kôrm) ***n.*** an underground stem of certain plants, that looks like a bulb [The crocus grows from a *corm.*]
**cor·mo·rant** (kôr′mə rənt) ***n.*** a large sea bird with webbed toes and a long, hooked beak.
**corn**[1] (kôrn) ***n.*** **1** a kind of grain that grows in kernels on large ears. Some kinds of corn are ground into meal, while others are cooked and eaten as a vegetable. Corn is also an important feed for farm animals. **2** any kind of grain [In England, *corn* usually means "wheat."]
**corn**[2] (kôrn) ***n.*** a hard, thick, painful growth of skin on a toe, usually caused by a tight shoe.
☆**corn bread** bread made with cornmeal.
☆**corn·cob** (kôrn′käb) ***n.*** the hard, woody part of an ear of corn, on which the kernels grow.
**cor·ne·a** (kôr′nē ə) ***n.*** the clear outer layer of the eyeball, covering the iris and the pupil.
**corned** (kôrnd) ***adj.*** kept from spoiling by the use of salt or strong salt water [*corned* beef].
**cor·ner** (kôr′nər) ***n.*** **1** the place where two lines or surfaces come together to form an angle. **2** the space between such lines or surfaces [a lamp in the *corner* of a room]. **3** the place where two streets meet. **4** a place or region; quarter [every *corner* of America].

☆**5** the act of buying up all or most of a certain stock or item for sale so as to raise its price [to have a *corner* in cotton]. ◆***v.*** ☆**1** to drive or force into a corner or difficult position from which it is hard to escape. ☆**2** to get a corner in some stock or item for sale. **3** to turn corners [This car *corners* easily.] ◆***adj.*** at, on, or in a corner [a *corner* table]. —☆**cut corners, 1** to take a shorter route by going across corners. **2** to cut down on expenses, time, labor, etc.

**Corner** comes from a Latin word meaning "horn." A corner has a shape that sticks out so that it comes to a point in the same way that a horn does.

**cor·ner·stone** (kôr′nər stōn) ***n.*** **1** a stone at the corner of a building; especially, such a stone laid at a ceremony at the time building is begun. **2** the most important part; foundation [The Bill of Rights is often called the *cornerstone* of our liberties.]

**cor·net** (kôr net′) ***n.*** a musical instrument like a trumpet, but with a shorter tube.

☆**corn·flakes** (kôrn′flāks) ***n.pl.*** a breakfast cereal of crisp flakes made from corn and served cold, as with milk: *also written* **corn flakes.**

**corn·flow·er** (kôrn′flou′ər) ***n.*** a plant with white, pink, or blue flowers.

**cor·nice** (kôr′nis) ***n.*** a molding that sticks out along the top of an outside or inside wall.

**Cor·nish** (kôr′nish) ***adj.*** of Cornwall or its people.

**corn·meal** (kôrn′mēl) ***n.*** ☆meal ground from kernels of corn.

☆**corn pone** (pōn) a kind of corn bread baked in small, oval loaves: *chiefly a Southern term.*

**corn·starch** (kôrn′stärch) ***n.*** a fine, starchy flour made from corn and used in cooking.

☆**corn syrup** a syrup made from cornstarch.

**cor·nu·co·pi·a** (kôr′nə kō′pē ə) ***n.*** **1** a painting or sculpture of a horn overflowing with fruits, flowers, and grain; horn of plenty. *See the picture.* **2** an amount that is full and overflowing. **3** any container shaped like a cone.

**Corn·wall** (kôrn′wôl) a county in the southwestern tip of England.

**Corn·wal·lis** (kôrn wôl′is), **Charles** 1738–1805; English general. He commanded the British forces during the American Revolution.

**corn·y** (kôr′nē) ***adj.*** ☆old-fashioned, stale, or sentimental in a foolish way: *used only in everyday talk.* —**corn′i·er, corn′i·est**

**co·rol·la** (kə räl′ə) ***n.*** the petals of a flower.

**cor·ol·lar·y** (kôr′ə ler′ē) ***n.*** something that can be taken for granted once another thing has been proved or has become a fact [If two angles of a triangle are equal, it follows as a *corollary* that two of its sides are equal.] —*pl.* **cor′ol·lar′ies**

**co·ro·na** (kə rō′nə) ***n.*** the ring of light seen around the sun during a total eclipse.

☆**cor·o·nar·y throm·bo·sis** (kôr′ə ner′ē thräm bō′sis) the blocking by a blood clot of any branch of the two arteries (**coronary arteries**) that feed blood to the heart muscle.

**cor·o·na·tion** (kôr′ə nā′shən) ***n.*** the crowning of a king or queen.

**cor·o·ner** (kôr′ə nər) ***n.*** an official whose duty is to find out the cause of any death that does not seem to be due to natural causes.

**copperhead**
75 cm (2 1/2 ft.) long

**coral**

**coping saw**

**corkscrew**

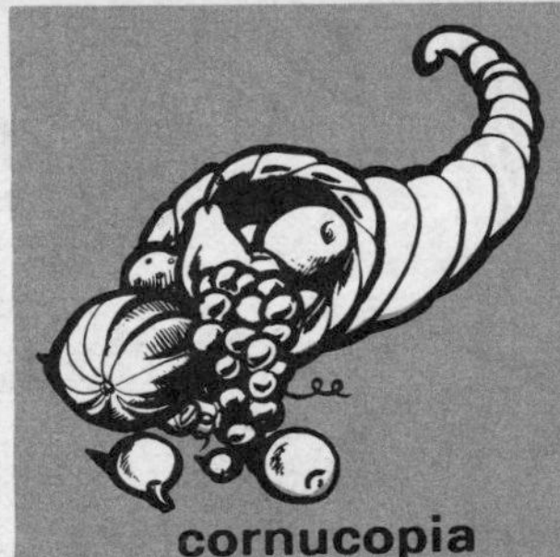
**cornucopia**

**cor·o·net** (kôr′ə net) ***n.*** **1** a small crown worn by princes and others of high rank. **2** a band of jewels, flowers, etc. worn around the head.

**Corp.** *abbreviation for* **Corporal, Corporation.**

**corp.** or **corpn.** *abbreviation for* **corporation.**

**cor·po·ral**[1] (kôr′pər əl) ***n.*** a noncommissioned officer in the armed forces below a sergeant.

**cor·po·ral**[2] (kôr′pər əl) ***adj.*** of the body; bodily [A whipping is *corporal* punishment.]

**cor·po·rate** (kôr′pər it) ***adj.*** **1** formed into a corporation; incorporated. **2** of a corporation [*corporate* debts]. **3** shared by all members of a group; common [*corporate* blame].

**cor·po·ra·tion** (kôr′pə rā′shən) ***n.*** a group of people who get a charter that gives the group some of the legal powers and rights that one person has [Cities and colleges, as well as businesses, can be organized as *corporations.*]

**cor·po·re·al** (kôr pôr′ē əl) ***adj.*** of, for, or like the body; not spiritual; bodily [*corporeal* appetites].

**corps** (kôr) ***n.*** **1** a section or a special branch of the armed forces [the Signal *Corps;* the Marine *Corps*]. **2** a group of people who are joined together in some work, organization, etc. [a diplomatic *corps;* a press *corps*]. —*pl.* **corps** (kôrz)

**corpse** (kôrps) ***n.*** the dead body of a person. *See* SYNONYMS *at* **body.**

**cor·pu·lent** (kôr′pyoo lənt) ***adj.*** fat and fleshy; stout in build. —**cor′pu·lence** ***n.***

| | | | | | | | |
|---|---|---|---|---|---|---|---|
| **a** | fat | **ir** | here | **ou** | out | **zh** | leisure |
| **ā** | ape | **ī** | bite, fire | **u** | up | **ng** | ring |
| **ä** | car, lot | **ō** | go | **ur** | fur | | a *in* ago |
| **e** | ten | **ô** | law, horn | **ch** | chin | | e *in* agent |
| **er** | care | **oi** | oil | **sh** | she | **ə** = | i *in* unity |
| **ē** | even | **oo** | look | **th** | thin | | o *in* collect |
| **i** | hit | **ōō** | tool | ***th*** | then | | u *in* focus |



C

corral

corsage

cotter pin

cougar
2.4 m (8 ft.) long, including tail

corrugated surface



**Cor·pus Christ·i** (kôr′pəs kris′tē) a city in southeastern Texas.

**cor·pus·cle** (kôr′pəs ′l) ***n.*** any of the red cells or white cells that float in the blood [Red *corpuscles* carry oxygen to the body tissues. Certain white *corpuscles* kill harmful germs.]

**corr.** *abbreviation for* **correction, corresponding.**

☆**cor·ral** (kə ral′) ***n.*** a place fenced in for holding horses, cattle, sheep, etc. *See the picture.* ◆***v.*** **1** to round up or shut up, as in a corral. **2** to get control of; take: *slang in this meaning.* —**cor·ralled′, cor·ral′ling**

**cor·rect** (kə rekt′) ***v.*** **1** to make right; get rid of mistakes in [*Correct* your spelling before turning in your papers.] **2** to point out the mistakes of; sometimes, to punish or scold for such mistakes [to *correct* a child's behavior]. ◆***adj.*** **1** without a mistake; right; true [a *correct* answer]. **2** agreeing with what is thought to be proper [*correct* behavior]. —**cor·rect′ly *adv.*** —**cor·rect′ness *n.***

**cor·rec·tion** (kə rek′shən) ***n.*** **1** the act of correcting. **2** a change that corrects a mistake; change from wrong to right [Write your *corrections* in the margin.] **3** punishment or scolding to correct faults. —**cor·rec′tion·al *adj.***

**cor·rec·tive** (kə rek′tiv) ***adj.*** that corrects or is meant to correct [a *corrective* device].

**cor·re·late** (kôr′ə lāt) ***v.*** to bring things into proper relation with one another; connect related things [We *correlated* the results of our experiments.] —**cor′re·lat·ed, cor′re·lat·ing**

**cor·re·la·tion** (kôr′ə lā′shən) ***n.*** the relation or connection between things [the high *correlation* between ignorance and prejudice].

**cor·rel·a·tive** (kə rel′ə tiv) ***adj.*** having a relation with one another; especially, describing either of a pair of words that show such a relation [In "Neither the teacher nor the students will go," "neither" and "nor" are *correlative* conjunctions.]

**cor·re·spond** (kôr ə spänd′) ***v.*** **1** to be in agreement with; match [Their opinions *correspond* with mine.] **2** to be the same or equal to [A general in the army *corresponds* to an admiral in the navy.] **3** to write letters to and receive letters from someone [I have been *corresponding* with ten people.]

**cor·re·spond·ence** (kôr′ə spän′dəns) ***n.*** **1** the fact of corresponding; agreement or sameness. **2** the writing and receiving of letters [to engage in *correspondence*]. **3** the letters written or received [The *correspondence* concerning the new contract is in the file.]

**cor·re·spond·ent** (kôr′ə spän′dənt) ***n.*** **1** a person with whom one corresponds in letter writing. **2** a person hired by a newspaper to send news regularly from a distant city or country.

**cor·ri·dor** (kôr′ə dər) ***n.*** a long hall or passageway, especially one into which rooms open.

**cor·rob·o·rate** (kə räb′ə rāt) ***v.*** to make more sure; add proof to; confirm [Two witnesses *corroborated* my story.] —**cor·rob′o·rat·ed, cor·rob′o·rat·ing** —**cor·rob′o·ra′tion *n.***

**cor·rode** (kə rōd′) ***v.*** to eat into or wear away slowly, as by the action of acid or rust. —**cor·rod′ed, cor·rod′ing** —**cor·ro·sion** (kə rō′zhən) ***n.***

**cor·ro·sive** (kə rōs′iv) ***adj.*** corroding or causing corrosion [a *corrosive* acid]. ◆***n.*** something that corrodes things.

**cor·ru·gate** (kôr′ə gāt) ***v.*** to put grooves and ridges in, so as to make look wavy; make wrinkles in [*corrugated* paper]. *See the picture.* —**cor′ru·gat·ed, cor′ru·gat·ing** —**cor′ru·ga′tion *n.***

**cor·rupt** (kə rupt′) ***adj.*** changed from good to bad; having become evil, rotten, dishonest, incorrect, etc. [*corrupt* officials; *corrupt* business practices; a *corrupt* version of a book]. ◆***v.*** to make or become corrupt. —**cor·rupt′ly *adv.***

**cor·rupt·i·ble** (kə rup′tə b′l) ***adj.*** that can be corrupted. —**cor·rupt′i·bil′i·ty *n.***

**cor·rup·tion** (kə rup′shən) ***n.*** **1** a change from good to bad. **2** evil or wicked ways. **3** bribery or other dishonest dealings [*corruption* in government]. **4** decay; rottenness.

**cor·sage** (kôr säzh′ *or* kôr säj′) ***n.*** ☆a small bunch of flowers for a woman to wear, as at the waist or shoulder. *See the picture.*

**cor·sair** (kôr′ser) ***n.*** **1** a pirate. **2** a pirate ship.

**cor·set** (kôr′sit) ***n.*** an undergarment that fits tightly around the waist and hips. It is worn mainly by women, to support or shape the body.

**Cor·si·ca** (kôr′si kə) a French island in the Mediterranean, southeast of France.

**cor·tege** or **cor·tège** (kôr tezh′ *or* kôr tāzh′) ***n.*** **1** a solemn parade or procession, as at a funeral. **2** a number of followers or attendants; retinue.

**Cor·tés** or **Cor·tez** (kôr tez′), **Her·nan·do** (hər nan′dō) 1485–1547; Spanish soldier. He and his men conquered Mexico.

**cor·tex** (kôr′teks) ***n.*** **1** the layer of gray matter covering most of the brain. **2** the bark of a plant. —*pl.* **cor·ti·ces** (kôr′tə sēz)

☆**cor·ti·sone** (kôrt′ə sōn *or* kôrt′ə zōn) ***n.*** a hormone that comes from the adrenal glands or is man-made. It is used in treating allergies, arthritis, etc.

**Cos.** or **cos.** *abbreviation for* **Companies, Counties.**
**cos·met·ic** (käz met′ik) ***n.*** any substance used to make the skin or hair beautiful [Hair lotion and lipstick are *cosmetics.*] ***✦adj.*** for improving the looks; beautifying.
**cos·mic** (käz′mik) ***adj.*** **1** having to do with the whole universe. **2** huge; enormous; vast.
**cosmic rays** streams of atomic particles that keep striking the earth from outer space.
**cos·mo·naut** (käz′mə nôt) ***n.*** *another name for* **astronaut.**

> **Cosmonaut** is the word the Russians use just as we use *astronaut*. Cosmonaut comes from two Greek words that mean "sailor in the cosmos, or universe."

**cos·mo·pol·i·tan** (käz′mə päl′ə t′n) ***adj.*** **1** having to do with the world as a whole. **2** interested in and liking the people and cultures of all countries; feeling at home anywhere. ***✦n.*** a cosmopolitan person.
**cos·mos** (käz′məs) ***n.*** **1** the universe as a system with order. **2** any whole system with order. **3** a tropical plant with slender leaves and white or colored flowers.
**Cos·sack** (käs′ak) ***n.*** a member of a people of southern Russia, famous as horsemen.
**cost** (kôst) ***v.*** **1** to be priced at; be sold for [It *costs* a dime.] **2** to cause the giving up of or loss of [The flood *cost* many lives.] —**cost, cost′ing** ***✦n.*** **1** amount of money, time, work, etc. asked or paid for something; price [the high *cost* of meat]. **2** loss or sacrifice [They eat no fruits or vegetables, at the *cost* of their health.] **3 costs,** *pl.* expenses of a law trial, usually paid by the loser. —**at all costs** or **at any cost,** by any means needed.
**Cos·ta Ri·ca** (käs′tə rē′kə) a country in Central America. —**Cos′ta Ri′can**
**cost·ly** (kôst′lē) ***adj.*** costing much; expensive or valuable [a *costly* error; *costly* clothes]. —**cost′li·er, cost′li·est** —**cost′li·ness** ***n.***

> SYNONYMS: Something is **costly** if it costs much and is rare and looks rich and beautiful [*costly* diamonds]. Something is often thought to be **costly** if it would cost much in effort or money to correct or replace [a *costly* mistake]. Something is **expensive** if it has a price that is greater than the thing is worth or more than a person can pay [an *expensive* coat].

**cost of living** the average cost of the necessities of life, as food, clothing, and shelter.
**cos·tume** (käs′to͞om *or* käs′tyo͞om) ***n.*** **1** the way or style of dressing of a certain place or time or for a certain purpose [a Japanese *costume;* an eighteenth-century *costume;* a riding *costume*]. **2** clothing worn by an actor in a play or by a person at a masquerade [a pirate *costume*]. ***✦v.*** to supply a costume to. —**cos′tumed, cos′tum·ing**
☆**cos·tum·er** (käs′to͞om ər *or* käs′tyo͞om ər) ***n.*** a person who makes, sells, or rents costumes.
**co·sy** (kō′zē) ***adj., n.*** *another spelling of* **cozy.** —**co′si·er, co′si·est** —*pl.* **co′sies**
**cot**[1] (kät) ***n.*** a narrow bed, as one made of canvas on a frame that can be folded up.
**cot**[2] (kät) ***n.*** **1** *same as* **cottage. 2** a covering for a hurt finger.
**cote** (kōt) ***n.*** a small shelter for sheep, doves, etc.
**co·te·rie** (kōt′ər ē) ***n.*** a close circle of friends or fellow workers; clique.
**cot·tage** (kät′ij) ***n.*** a small house [a peasant's *cottage;* a summer *cottage* at the beach].
☆**cottage cheese** a soft, white cheese made from the curds of sour milk.
**cot·ter** or **cot·tar** (kät′ər) ***n.*** a Scottish farmer who rents land and a cottage from a large landholder.
**cotter pin** a split pin used to hold parts together. Its ends are spread apart after it is fitted into a slot or hole. *See the picture.*
**cot·ton** (kät′′n) ***n.*** **1** the soft, white fibers that grow around the seeds of a shrubby plant. **2** this plant. **3** thread or cloth made of these fibers. ***✦adj.*** of cotton [a *cotton* field; a *cotton* shirt].
☆**cotton gin** a machine for pulling cotton fibers away from the seeds.
☆**cot·ton·mouth** (kät′′n mouth) ***n.*** *another name for* **water moccasin.**
**cot·ton·seed** (kät′′n sēd) ***n.*** the seed of the cotton plant, from which an oil (**cottonseed oil**) is pressed for use in margarine, cooking oil, etc.
☆**cot·ton·tail** (kät′′n tāl) ***n.*** the common American rabbit with a short, white, fluffy tail.
**cot·ton·wood** (kät′′n wood) ***n.*** **1** a poplar tree that has seeds covered with cottonlike hairs. **2** its wood.
**cot·y·le·don** (kät′′l ēd′′n) ***n.*** the first leaf, or either of the pair of first leaves, growing out of a seed.
**couch** (kouch) ***n.*** **1** a piece of furniture for sitting or lying on; sofa. **2** any resting place [A pile of hay was my *couch.*] ***✦v.*** **1** to place as if on a couch [They were *couched* in comfort.] **2** to bring down to a position for attacking [to *couch* a spear]. **3** to put into words [Her speech was *couched* in flowery language.]
**cou·gar** (ko͞o′gər) ***n.*** a large animal of the cat family, with a slender, tan body and a long tail. *See the picture.*
**cough** (kôf) ***v.*** **1** to force air from the lungs with a sudden, loud noise, as to clear the throat. **2** to get out of the throat by coughing [to *cough* up phlegm]. ***✦n.*** **1** the act or sound of coughing. **2** a condition of coughing often [I have a bad *cough.*]
**could** (kood) *past tense of* **can** [At one time you *could* buy a hamburger for five cents.]

> **Could** is also used as a helping verb with about the same meaning as *can,* but showing less force or sureness [You *could* be right. I *could* do it tomorrow.]

**could·n't** (kood′′nt) could not.
**coun·cil** (koun′s′l) ***n.*** **1** a group of people meeting together to plan or decide something or to give advice. **2** a group of people elected to make the laws for a city or town.
**coun·cil·man** (koun′s′l mən) ***n.*** a member of a council, as of a city. —*pl.* **coun′cil·men**



| | | | | | | | | | | |
|---|---|---|---|---|---|---|---|---|---|---|
| **a** | fat | **ir** | here | **ou** | out | **zh** | leisure | | | |
| **ā** | ape | **ī** | bite, fire | **u** | up | **ng** | ring | | | |
| **ä** | car, lot | **ō** | go | **ur** | fur | | | | a *in* ago | |
| **e** | ten | **ô** | law, horn | **ch** | chin | | | | e *in* agent | |
| **er** | care | **oi** | oil | **sh** | she | | | ə = | i *in* unity | |
| **ē** | even | **oo** | look | **th** | thin | | | | o *in* collect | |
| **i** | hit | **o͞o** | tool | ***th*** | then | | | | u *in* focus | |

**coun·ci·lor** (koun′sə lər) ***n.*** a member of a council.

**coun·sel** (koun′s'l) ***n.*** **1** a talking together in order to exchange ideas or opinions; discussion [They took *counsel* before making the decision.] **2** advice or opinion [What is your *counsel* in this matter?] **3** the lawyer or lawyers who are handling a case. ◆***v.*** **1** to give advice to; advise. **2** to recommend; urge [They *counseled* caution in dealing with the matter.] —**coun′seled** or **coun′selled**, **coun′sel·ing** or **coun′sel·ling**

**coun·se·lor** or **coun·sel·lor** (koun′sə lər) ***n.*** **1** a person who advises; adviser. **2** a lawyer. **3** a person in charge of children at a camp.

**count**[1] (kount) ***v.*** **1** to name numbers in a regular order [I'll *count* to five.] **2** to add up so as to get a total [*Count* the people here.] **3** to take account of; include [There are ten here, *counting* you.] **4** to be taken into account; have importance, value, etc. [Every bit of help *counts.*] **5** to believe to be; consider [I *count* myself lucky.] **6** to have a certain value [A touchdown *counts* for six points.] ◆***n.*** **1** a counting or adding up. **2** the total number counted. **3** any of the crimes that a person is charged with [She is guilty on two *counts.*] —**count off**, to separate into equal groups by counting [*Count off* by groups of four.] —**count on**, to depend on [You can *count on* us to help.]

**count**[2] (kount) ***n.*** a nobleman in some European countries.



☆**count·down** (kount′doun) ***n.*** the schedule of things that take place in planned order just before the firing of a rocket, the setting off of a nuclear explosion, etc.; also, the counting backward in units of time while these things take place.

**coun·te·nance** (koun′tə nəns) ***n.*** **1** the look on a person's face that shows that person's nature or feelings [a friendly *countenance*]. **2** the face [A smile spread over his *countenance.*] **3** approval or support [to give *countenance* to a plan]. ◆***v.*** to approve or support [I will not *countenance* such rudeness.] —**coun′te·nanced**, **coun′te·nanc·ing**

counterclockwise direction

tennis court

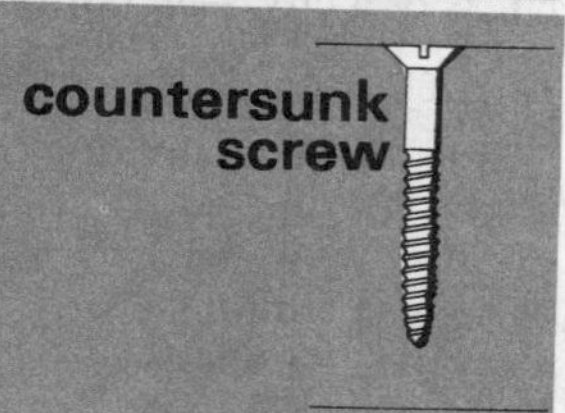
countersunk screw

railroad–car coupling

**count·er**[1] (koun′tər) ***n.*** **1** a person or thing that counts. **2** a small piece for keeping count, as in games. **3** a long table in a store or restaurant for serving customers, showing goods, etc.

**coun·ter**[2] (koun′tər) ***adv.*** in the opposite direction or way; contrary [The vote went *counter* to my wishes.] ◆***adj.*** being or acting in the opposite direction or way; contrary; opposed [a *counter* blow]. ◆***v.*** to act or do counter to; oppose; give another in return [to *counter* one plan with another; to *counter* a punch in boxing].

**counter-** *a prefix meaning* opposite, against, *or* in return [To *counteract* something is to act against it. A *counterattack* is an attack in return for another attack.]

**coun·ter·act** (koun tər akt′) ***v.*** to act against; to stop or undo the effect of [The rains will help *counteract* the dry spell.]

**coun·ter·at·tack** (koun′tər ə tak′) ***n.*** an attack made in return for another attack. ◆***v.*** to attack so as to answer the enemy's attack.

**coun·ter·bal·ance** (koun′tər bal′əns) ***n.*** a weight, power, force, etc. that balances or acts against another ◆***v.*** (koun′tər bal′əns) to be a counterbalance to.—**coun′ter·bal′anced**, **coun′ter·bal′anc·ing**

**coun·ter·claim** (koun′tər klām) ***n.*** an opposing claim in answer to a claim against one.

**coun·ter·clock·wise** (koun′tər kläk′wīz) ***adj.***, ***adv.*** in a direction opposite to that in which the hands of a clock move. *See the picture.*

**coun·ter·cul·ture** (koun′tər kul′chər) ***n.*** the way of life of the young people of the 1960's and 1970's which was opposed to the way most people lived.

**coun·ter·feit** (koun′tər fit) ***adj.*** made in imitation of the real thing so as to fool or cheat people [*counterfeit* money]. *See* SYNONYMS *at* **false**. ◆***n.*** a thing that is counterfeit. ◆***v.*** **1** to make an imitation of in order to cheat [to *counterfeit* money]. **2** to pretend; feign [to *counterfeit* sorrow]. —**coun′ter·feit·er** ***n.***

**coun·ter·mand** (koun tər mand′) ***v.*** to take back a command, as by giving an opposite one.

**coun·ter·pane** (koun′tər pān) ***n.*** *another word for* **bedspread**.

**coun·ter·part** (koun′tər pärt) ***n.*** **1** a person or thing that is very much like another [He is his father's *counterpart.*] **2** a thing that goes with another thing to form a set [This cup is the *counterpart* to that saucer.]

**coun·ter·point** (koun′tər point) ***n.*** the art or way of putting two or more melodies together so that they fit together in harmony [You can hear *counterpoint* if two people sing "Swanee River" and "Humoresque" together at the same time.]

**coun·ter·poise** (koun′tər poiz) ***n.*** **1** *another word for* **counterbalance**. **2** the condition of being in balance. ◆***v.*** *another word for* **counterbalance**. —**coun′ter·poised**, **coun′ter·pois·ing**

**coun·ter·rev·o·lu·tion** (koun′tər rev′ə lo͞o′shən) ***n.*** a movement to overthrow a government that was set up by a revolution.

**coun·ter·sign** (koun′tər sīn) ***n.*** a secret signal or password that must be given to a guard or sentry by someone who wishes to pass. ◆***v.*** to sign a paper already signed by someone else, in order to confirm it.

**coun·ter·sink** (koun′tər siŋk) ***v.*** **1** to widen the top part of a hole for a bolt or screw so that the head will not stick out from the surface. **2** to fit a bolt or screw into such a hole. *See the picture.* —**coun·ter·sunk** (koun′tər sungk), **coun′ter·sink·ing**

**count·ess** (koun′tis) ***n.*** **1** the wife or widow of a count or earl. **2** a woman with the rank of a count or earl.

**count·less** (kount′lis) ***adj.*** too many to count; innumerable [the *countless* stars].

**coun·tri·fied** (kun′tri fīd) ***adj.*** looking or acting like plain people from the country.

**coun·try** (kun′trē) ***n.*** **1** an area of land; region [wooded *country*]. **2** the whole land of a nation [The *country* of Japan is made up of islands.] **3** the people of a nation [The speech was broadcast to the whole *country*.] **4** the nation to which one belongs ["My *country*, 'tis of thee"]. **5** land with farms and small towns; land outside of cities [Let's drive out to the *country*.] —*pl.* **coun′tries** ◆***adj.*** of, in, from, or like the country; rural ["To home" is *country* talk for "at home."]

> **Country** comes from a Latin word meaning "that which is beyond." If you live in a city or town, you think of the country as the land that lies beyond the limits of your city or town.

**coun·try·man** (kun′trē mən) ***n.*** a man of one's own country. —*pl.* **coun′try·men**

**coun·try·side** (kun′trē sīd′) ***n.*** **1** the country, or land outside of cities; rural area. **2** the people who live in the country.

**coun·ty** (koun′tē) ***n.*** ☆**1** in the U.S., any of the sections into which a State is divided. Each county has its own officials. **2** any of the districts into which Great Britain and Ireland are divided. **3** the people of a county. —*pl.* **coun′ties**

**coup** (ko͞o) ***n.*** a sudden, bold, and clever move that brings about some striking change, as in a government. —*pl.* **coups** (ko͞oz)

**coup d'é·tat** (ko͞o′dā tä′) the sudden overthrow of a government by a military or political group using force. *This is a French phrase.*

**coupe** (ko͞op) ***n.*** an automobile with two doors and a closed body that is smaller than that of a sedan.

**cou·pé** (ko͞o pā′) ***n.*** **1** a closed carriage that seats two riders and has a raised seat outside for the driver. **2** *same as* **coupe.**

**cou·ple** (kup′'l) ***n.*** **1** two things of the same kind that go together; pair [a *couple* of book ends]. *See* SYNONYMS *at* **pair.** **2** a man and woman who are married, engaged, or partners, as in a dance. **3** a few; several: *used only in everyday talk* [I've got only a *couple* of dollars left after paying for dinner.] ◆***v.*** to join together; unite; connect [to *couple* railroad cars]. —**cou′pled, cou′pling**

**cou·plet** (kup′lit) ***n.*** two lines of poetry that go together and are usually rhymed. Example:

He that fights and runs away
May live to fight another day.

**cou·pling** (kup′ling) ***n.*** **1** the act of joining together. **2** a device for joining parts or things together [a *coupling* for railroad cars; a *coupling* for pipes]. *See the picture.*

**cou·pon** (ko͞o′pän *or* kyo͞o′pän) ***n.*** **1** a ticket or part of a ticket that gives the holder certain rights [The *coupon* on the cereal box is worth 10¢ toward buying another box.] **2** a part of a bond which is cut off at certain times and turned in for payment of interest. **3** a part of a printed advertisement that can be used for ordering goods, samples, etc.

**cour·age** (kur′ij) ***n.*** the quality of being able to control one's fear and so to face danger, pain, or trouble willingly; bravery.

**cou·ra·geous** (kə rā′jəs) ***adj.*** having or showing courage; brave. *See* SYNONYMS *at* **brave.**

**cou·ri·er** (koor′ē ər *or* kur′ē ər) ***n.*** a messenger sent in a hurry with an important message.

**course** (kôrs) ***n.*** **1** a going on from one point to the next; progress in space or time [the *course* of history; the *course* of a journey]. **2** a way or path along which something moves; channel, track, etc. [a golf *course;* race*course*]. **3** the direction taken [The ship's *course* was due south.] **4** a way of acting or proceeding [The law must take its *course*.] **5** a number of like things in regular order; series [a *course* of exercises to build the muscles]. **6** a part of a meal served at one time [The main *course* was roast beef.] **7** a complete series of studies [I took a business *course* in high school.] **8** any of these studies [a mathematics *course*]. **9** a single row of bricks or stones in a wall. ◆***v.*** to run; race through or after [blood *coursing* through the veins; hounds *coursing* rabbits]. —**coursed, cours′ing** —**in the course of,** during. —**of course, 1** as one expects; naturally. **2** without doubt; certainly.

**court** (kôrt) ***n.*** **1** an open space with buildings or walls around it; courtyard. **2** a short street, often closed at one end. **3** a space marked out for playing some game [a basketball *court;* a handball *court*]. *See the picture.* **4** the palace of a king or other ruler. **5** the family, advisers, and attendants who gather at a ruler's court. **6** a formal meeting held by a ruler. **7** courtship. **8** a person or persons who examine and decide cases of law; judge or judges. **9** a place where law trials are held. **10** a meeting of all the persons who are to seek justice in a law case, including the judge or judges, the lawyers, and the jury [The *court* will convene at nine tomorrow morning.] ◆***v.*** **1** to pay attention to or try to please in order to get something [Politicians usually *court* the voters before an election.] **2** to try to get the love of in order to marry; woo [He's been *courting* her for five years.] **3** to try to get or seem to be trying to get [to *court* praise; to *court* danger].

**cour·te·ous** (kur′tē əs) ***adj.*** polite and kind; thoughtful of others. *See* SYNONYMS *at* **civil.**

**cour·te·sy** (kur′tə sē) ***n.*** **1** courteous or polite behavior; good manners [Thank you for your *courtesy* in writing to me.] **2** a polite act or remark. —*pl.* **cour′te·sies**

**court·house** (kôrt′hous) ***n.*** **1** a building in which law courts are held. ☆**2** a building that contains the offices of a county government.



| | | | |
|---|---|---|---|
| **a** fat | **ir** here | **ou** out | **zh** leisure |
| **ā** ape | **ī** bite, fire | **u** up | **ng** ring |
| **ä** car, lot | **ō** go | **ur** fur | a *in* ago |
| **e** ten | **ô** law, horn | **ch** chin | e *in* agent |
| **er** care | **oi** oil | **sh** she | ə = i *in* unity |
| **ē** even | **oo** look | **th** thin | o *in* collect |
| **i** hit | **o͞o** tool | ***th*** then | u *in* focus |

**cour·ti·er** (kôr′tē ər) ***n.*** an attendant at the court of a king or queen.

**court·ly** (kôrt′lē) ***adj.*** polite and dignified in a way thought proper for the court of a king or queen [*courtly* manners]. —**court′li·ness** ***n.***

**court-mar·tial** (kôrt′mär′shəl) ***n.*** **1** a court of persons in the armed forces for the trial of those accused of breaking military law. —*pl.* **courts′-mar′tial** **2** a trial by a court-martial. —*pl.* **court′-mar′tials** ◆***v.*** to try by a court-martial. —**court′-mar′tialed** or **court′-mar′tialled**, **court′-mar′tial·ing** or **court′-mar′tial·ling**

**court·room** (kôrt′ro͞om) ***n.*** a room in which a law court is held.

**court·ship** (kôrt′ship) ***n.*** the courting of a woman in order to marry her.

**court·yard** (kôrt′yärd) ***n.*** an open space with buildings or walls around it.

**cous·in** (kuz′′n) ***n.*** **1** the son or daughter of one's uncle or aunt: *also called* **first cousin**. You are a *second cousin* to the children of your parents' first cousins, and you are a *first cousin once removed* to the children of your first cousins. **2** a distant relation.

**cove** (kōv) ***n.*** a small bay or inlet.

**cov·e·nant** (kuv′ə nənt) ***n.*** a serious agreement between persons, groups, or nations. ◆***v.*** to make such an agreement.

**Cov·en·try** (kuv′ən trē) a city in central England. —**send someone to Coventry**, to refuse to have anything to do with someone.



**cov·er** (kuv′ər) ***v.*** **1** to place one thing over another; spread over [*Cover* the bird cage at night. *Cover* the wall with white paint. Water *covered* the fields.] **2** to keep from being seen or known; hide [He tried to *cover* up the scandal.] **3** to protect, as from harm or loss [Are you *covered* by insurance?] **4** to provide for; take care of [Is this case *covered* by the rules?] **5** to have to do with; be about; include [This book *covers* the Civil War.] **6** to go; travel [The camel *covered* 65 miles that day.] **7** to keep a gun aimed at [*Cover* him while I call the police.] ☆**8** to get the news or pictures of: *used by newspaper and TV people* [Many reporters *covered* the airplane crash.] ☆**9** to guard or defend: *used in sports* [*Cover* first base.] ◆***n.*** **1** anything that covers, as a lid, a blanket, the binding of a book, etc. **2** anything that hides or protects [under *cover* of darkness]. —☆**cover for**, to provide an alibi or excuse for another person. —**take cover**, to seek shelter.

☆**cov·er·age** (kuv′ər ij) ***n.*** the amount or extent covered by something.

**cov·er·alls** (kuv′ər ôlz) ***n.pl.*** a one-piece work garment with sleeves and legs, worn by mechanics, trash collectors, etc. *See the picture.*

☆**covered wagon** a large wagon with an arched cover of canvas, used in pioneer days.

**cov·er·ing** (kuv′ər iŋ) ***n.*** anything that covers.

**cov·er·let** (kuv′ər lit) ***n.*** *another word for* **bedspread**.

**cov·ert** (kuv′ərt *or* kō′vərt) ***adj.*** done in a hidden or secret way [He took a *covert* look at his neighbor's exam.] *See* SYNONYMS *at* **secret**. ◆***n.*** a sheltered place; especially, underbrush where animals can hide. —**cov′ert·ly** ***adv.***

**cov·er-up** (kuv′ər up) ***n.*** something used or done to hide what one is really doing, as a crime; front.

**cov·et** (kuv′it) ***v.*** to want greedily something belonging to another ["You shall not *covet* your neighbor's house . . . ."]

**cov·et·ous** (kuv′it əs) ***adj.*** wanting greedily what belongs to another. —**cov′et·ous·ly** ***adv.*** —**cov′et·ous·ness** ***n.***

**cov·ey** (kuv′ē) ***n.*** **1** a small flock of birds, especially partridges or quail. **2** a small group of people. —*pl.* **cov′eys**

**cow**[1] (kou) ***n.*** **1** the full-grown female of any animal of the ox family; especially, the common farm animal kept for its milk. **2** the female elephant, seal, whale, etc.

**cow**[2] (kou) ***v.*** to make afraid or meek; intimidate.

**cow·ard** (kou′ərd) ***n.*** a person who is unable to control his fear and so shrinks from danger or trouble.

> In old French the word for **coward** also had the meaning "with the tail between the legs." It came from the Latin word for "tail." Most of us have seen a dog that is afraid put its tail between its legs and slink away.

**cow·ard·ice** (kou′ərd is) ***n.*** the way a coward acts or feels; lack of courage.

**cow·ard·ly** (kou′ərd lē) ***adj.*** of or like a coward. ◆***adv.*** in the manner of a coward.

☆**cow·bird** (kou′burd) ***n.*** a small blackbird that often lays its eggs in other birds' nests.

**cow·boy** (kou′boi) ***n.*** ☆**1** a ranch worker, usually on horseback, who herds or tends cattle. ☆**2** in stories, movies, etc., any Western character who rides a horse and carries a gun.

**cow·er** (kou′ər) ***v.*** to bend over or tremble, as from fear or cold; crouch or cringe.

☆**cow·hand** (kou′hand) ***n.*** *same as meaning* 1 *of* **cowboy**.

**cow·herd** (kou′hurd) ***n.*** a person who tends cattle that are grazing.

**cow·hide** (kou′hīd) ***n.*** **1** the hide of a cow. **2** leather made from it. ☆**3** a whip made from this leather, often a braided whip.

**cowl** (koul) ***n.*** **1** a monk's hood, usually fastened to a cloak. *See the picture.* **2** the top front part of an automobile body, to which the windshield and dashboard are fastened. **3** *same as* **cowling**.

**cow·lick** (kou′lik) ***n.*** a tuft of hair that cannot easily be combed flat.

**cowl·ing** (kou′liŋ) ***n.*** a metal covering for an airplane engine.

**cow·pox** (kou′päks) ***n.*** a disease of cows. People were once vaccinated with a mild virus of cowpox to keep them from getting smallpox.

☆**cow·punch·er** (kou′pun′chər) ***n.*** *same as* **cowboy**: *used only in everyday talk.*

**cow·slip** (kou′slip) ***n.*** a wildflower with yellow blossoms.

**cox·comb** (käks′kōm) ***n.*** a vain, conceited fellow who keeps showing off himself and his clothes.

**cox·swain** (käk′s′n *or* käk′swān) ***n.*** the person who steers a small boat or a racing shell.

**coy** (koi) ***adj.*** shy or bashful, or pretending to be so, often in a flirting way. —**coy′ly** ***adv.***

☆**coy·o·te** (kī ōt′ē *or* kī′ōt) ***n.*** a small wolf of the western prairies of North America.

**coz·en** (kuz′'n) ***v.*** to cheat or fool. —**coz′en·age *n.***

**co·zy** (kō′zē) ***adj.*** warm and comfortable; snug [We were *cozy* in our sleeping bags.] —**co′zi·er, co′zi·est** ◆***n.*** a padded cover for a teapot, to keep the tea hot. —*pl.* **co′zies** —**co′zi·ly *adv.*** —**co′zi·ness *n.***

**CPA** or **C.P.A.** *abbreviation for* Certified Public Accountant.

**Cpl** or **Cpl.** *abbreviation for* **Corporal.**

**CQ** (sē′kyōō′) a signal used by radio amateurs, inviting others to start talking.

**Cr** *the symbol for the chemical element* chromium.

**crab**[1] (krab) ***n.*** a broad, flat shellfish with four pairs of legs and a pair of claws. Some kinds are used as food. *See the picture.*

**crab**[2] (krab) ***n.*** **1** *same as* **crab apple.** **2** a person who is always cross and complaining. ◆***v.*** to complain or find fault: *used only in everyday talk* [The prisoners *crabbed* about their food.] —**crabbed, crab′bing**

**crab apple** **1** a small, very sour apple, used for making jellies and preserves. **2** the tree it grows on.

**crab·bed** (krab′id) ***adj.*** **1** crabby; peevish. **2** hard to read or make out [*crabbed* handwriting].

**crab·by** (krab′ē) ***adj.*** cross and complaining; hard to please; peevish. —**crab′bi·er, crab′bi·est** —**crab′bi·ly *adv.*** —**crab′bi·ness *n.***

**crab grass** a coarse grass that spreads quickly and can spoil the looks of a lawn.

**crack** (krak) ***v.*** **1** to make or cause to make a sudden, sharp noise, as of something breaking [The lion tamer *cracked* his whip.] **2** to break or split, with or without the parts falling apart [The snowball *cracked* the window. *Crack* the coconut open.] **3** to become harsh or change pitch suddenly [Her voice *cracked* when she sang the highest note.] **4** to hit with a sudden, sharp blow: *used only in everyday talk* [I *cracked* my knee against the desk.] **5** to break down; lose control of oneself: *used only in everyday talk* [He *cracked* under the strain.] **6** to break into: *used only in everyday talk* [The burglar *cracked* the safe.] **7** to say or tell in an amusing way: *slang in this meaning* [to *crack* jokes]. ◆***n.*** **1** a sudden, sharp noise, as of something breaking [The can hit the pavement with a loud *crack.*] **2** a break, usually with the parts still holding together [a *crack* in a cup]. ☆**3** a narrow opening; crevice [I peered through a *crack* in the fence.] **4** a sudden, sharp blow: *used only in everyday talk* [a *crack* on the head]. **5** a try: *used only in everyday talk* [Let me have a *crack* at that puzzle.] **6** a joking or mocking remark: *slang in this meaning.* ◆***adj.*** excellent; first-rate: *used only in everyday talk* [a *crack* reporter]. —☆**crack down on,** to become strict or stricter with. —☆**cracked up to be,** thought or said to be: *used only in everyday talk.* —**crack up, 1** to crash, as an airplane. **2** to have a breakdown in health: *used only in everyday talk.* **3** to have a fit of laughing or crying: *used only in everyday talk.*

**cracked** (krakt) ***adj.*** **1** having cracks in it. **2** sounding harsh [a *cracked* voice]. **3** crazy; insane: *used only in everyday talk.*

**crack·er** (krak′ər) ***n.*** **1** a thin, crisp biscuit made of dough that does not rise; wafer. **2** *same as* **firecracker.**

**crack·le** (krak′'l) ***v.*** to make sharp, snapping sounds [The dry wood *crackled* as it burned.] —**crack′led, crack′ling** ◆***n.*** **1** a number of such sounds. **2** fine, irregular cracks on the surface of some kinds of pottery, china, etc.

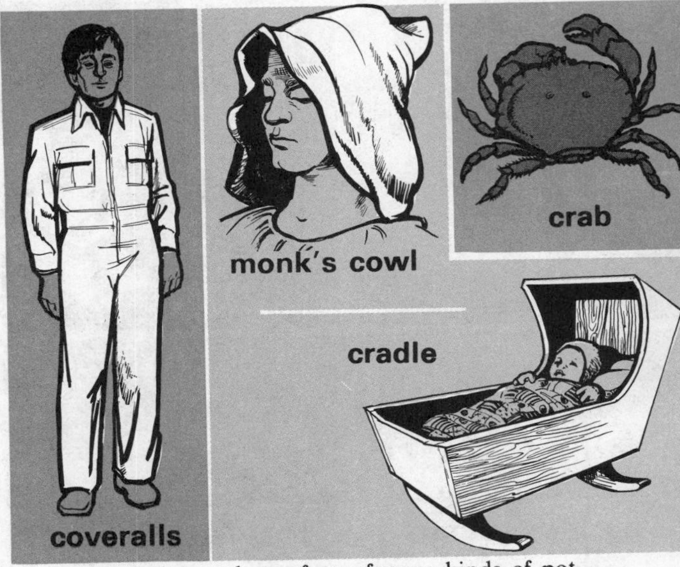


**crack·ling** (krak′liŋ) ***n.*** **1** a series of sharp, snapping sounds. **2** the crisp rind of roast pork. **3** the crisp part left after frying hog fat.

**crack·up** (krak′up′) ***n.*** **1** a crash, as of an airplane. **2** a breakdown of body or mind: *used only in everyday talk.* 



**-cra·cy** (krə sē) *a suffix meaning* government [*Democracy* is government by the people.]

**cra·dle** (krā′d'l) ***n.*** **1** a baby's small bed, usually on rockers. *See the picture.* **2** the place where something began [Boston is often called the *cradle* of the American Revolution.] **3** anything that looks like a cradle or that is used for holding, rocking, etc. [the *cradle* for holding a telephone receiver]. **4** a frame on a scythe for laying the cut grain evenly. ◆***v.*** to rock or hold as in a cradle. —**cra′dled, cra′dling**

**craft** (kraft) ***n.*** **1** special skill or ability. *See* SYNONYMS *at* **art. 2** work that takes special skill, especially with the hands [the *craft* of weaving]. **3** the members of a skilled trade. **4** skill in fooling or tricking others; slyness. **5** a boat, ship, or aircraft: **craft** is the *pl.* for this meaning.

**crafts·man** (krafts′mən) ***n.*** a worker in a skilled trade. —*pl.* **crafts′men**

**craft·y** (kraf′tē) ***adj.*** skillful in fooling or tricking others; sly; cunning. —**craft′i·er, craft′i·est** —**craft′i·ly *adv.*** —**craft′i·ness *n.***

**crag** (krag) ***n.*** a steep, rugged rock that rises above or juts out from others.

**crag·gy** (krag′ē) ***adj.*** having many crags; steep and rugged. —**crag′gi·er, crag′gi·est** —**crag′gi·ness *n.***

| | | | |
|---|---|---|---|
| **a** fat | **ir** here | **ou** out | **zh** leisure |
| **ā** ape | **ī** bite, fire | **u** up | **ŋ** ring |
| **ä** car, lot | **ō** go | **ur** fur | a *in* ago |
| **e** ten | **ô** law, horn | **ch** chin | e *in* agent |
| **er** care | **oi** oil | **sh** she | ə = i *in* unity |
| **ē** even | **oo** look | **th** thin | o *in* collect |
| **i** hit | **ōō** tool | ***th*** then | u *in* focus |

**C**

crane

craters of the moon

creel

baby creeping

baby crawling

**cram** (kram) ***v.*** **1** to pack full or too full [Her suitcase is *crammed* with clothes.] **2** to stuff or force [He *crammed* the papers into a drawer.] **3** to study many facts in a hurry, as for a test. —**crammed, cram′ming**

**cramp** (kramp) ***n.*** **1** a sharp, painful tightening of a muscle, as from a chill or strain. **2 cramps,** *pl.* sharp pains in the belly. **3** a metal bar with both ends bent, used for holding together blocks of stone or timbers. ◆***v.*** **1** to cause a cramp in. **2** to keep from moving or acting freely; hamper. **3** to turn the front wheels of a car sharply.



☆**cran·ber·ry** (kran′ber′ē) ***n.*** **1** a hard, sour, red berry used in sauces and jellies. **2** the marsh plant it grows on. —*pl.* **cran′ber′ries**

**crane** (krān) ***n.*** **1** a large wading bird with very long legs and neck, and a long, straight bill. **2** a machine for lifting or moving heavy weights. One kind uses a long, movable arm; another kind uses a beam that travels on an overhead support. *See the picture.* ◆***v.*** to stretch the neck, as in trying to see over something. —**craned, cran′ing**

**Crane** (krān), **Stephen** 1871–1900; U.S. writer.

**cra·ni·um** (krā′nē əm) ***n.*** the skull, especially the part containing the brain. —*pl.* **cra′ni·ums** or **cra′ni·a** (krā′nē ə) —**cra′ni·al *adj.***

**crank** (krangk) ***n.*** **1** a handle or arm that is bent at right angles and connected to a shaft of a machine in order to turn it. ☆**2** a person who has odd, stubborn notions about something: *used only in everyday talk.* **3** a cross, complaining person: *used only in everyday talk.* ◆***v.*** to start or work by turning a crank.

**crank·case** (krangk′kās) ***n.*** the metal case enclosing a crankshaft, as in an automobile.

**crank·shaft** (krangk′shaft) ***n.*** a shaft that turns a crank or is turned by a crank, as in an automobile engine.

**crank·y** (krang′kē) ***adj.*** cross or complaining. —**crank′i·er, crank′i·est —crank′i·ness *n.***

**cran·ny** (kran′ē) ***n.*** a small, narrow opening; chink or crack, as in a wall. —*pl.* **cran′nies**

**crape** (krāp) ***n.*** **1** *another spelling of* **crepe** (*meaning* 1). **2** a piece of black crepe used as a sign of mourning, sometimes worn as a band around the arm.

**crash** (krash) ***v.*** **1** to fall, hit, or break with force and with a loud, smashing noise. **2** to fall to the earth so as to be damaged or smashed [The airplane *crashed.*] ☆**3** to get into a party, theater, etc. without an invitation or ticket: *used only in everyday talk.* ◆***n.*** **1** a loud, smashing noise. **2** the crashing of a car, airplane, etc. **3** a sudden failure or ruin, as of a business firm or of business in general.

**crass** (kras) ***adj.*** very stupid and coarse [a *crass* insult]. —**crass′ly *adv.*** —**crass′ness *n.***

**crate** (krāt) ***n.*** a box made of wooden slats, for packing things. ◆☆***v.*** to pack in a crate. —**crat′ed, crat′ing**

**cra·ter** (krāt′ər) ***n.*** **1** a hollow that is shaped like a bowl, as at the mouth of a volcano or on the surface of the moon. *See the picture.* **2** any hollow like this, as one made by a bomb explosion.

**cra·vat** (krə vat′) ***n.*** *another word for* **necktie.**

**crave** (krāv) ***v.*** **1** to long for very much; want badly [to *crave* food]. **2** to beg for [to *crave* pardon]. —**craved, crav′ing**

**cra·ven** (krā′vən) ***adj.*** very cowardly. ◆***n.*** a complete coward. —**cra′ven·ly *adv.*** —**cra′ven·ness *n.***

**crav·ing** (krā′ving) ***n.*** a strong longing or appetite [Some people have a *craving* for sweets.]

**craw** (krô) ***n.*** **1** the crop of a bird. **2** the stomach of any animal.

**craw·fish** (krô′fish) ***n.*** *same as* **crayfish.**

**crawl** (krôl) ***v.*** **1** to move slowly by dragging the body along the ground as a worm does. *See the picture.* **2** *another word for* **creep** *in meaning 1.* **3** to move slowly [The truck *crawled* up the steep hill.] **4** to be full of crawling things [The rotten log was *crawling* with worms.] **5** to feel as if insects were crawling on the skin [It makes my flesh *crawl* to hear ghost stories.] ◆***n.*** **1** a crawling; slow, creeping movement. **2** a swimming stroke with the face down in the water, except for breathing, and with the legs kicked up and down without stopping.

**cray·fish** (krā′fish) ***n.*** ☆**1** a small, freshwater shellfish that looks like a small lobster. **2** a sea shellfish that is like the lobster, but does not have large claws.

**cray·on** (krā′ən *or* krā′än) ***n.*** a small stick of chalk, charcoal, or colored wax, used for drawing or writing. ◆***v.*** to draw with crayons.

**craze** (krāz) ***v.*** **1** to make sick in the mind, or insane [*crazed* by grief]. **2** to make fine cracks or crackle in the glaze of pottery, china, etc. —**crazed, craz′ing** ◆***n.*** something that is the fashion for a short while; fad.

**cra·zy** (krā′zē) ***adj.*** **1** mentally ill; insane. **2** very foolish or mad [a *crazy* idea]. **3** very eager or enthusiastic: *used only in everyday talk* [I'm *crazy* about the movies.] ☆**4** wonderful, thrilling, etc.: *slang in this meaning.* —**cra′zi·er, cra′zi·est —cra′zi·ly *adv.*** —**cra′zi·ness *n.***

☆**crazy quilt** a quilt made of pieces of cloth of various colors, sizes, and shapes.

**creak** (krēk) ***v.*** to make a harsh, squeaking sound, as rusted hinges or old floorboards. ◆***n.*** such a sound. —**creak′y *adj.***

**cream** (krēm) ***n.*** **1** the oily, yellowish part of milk that rises to the top and contains the butterfat. **2** any food that is made of cream or is like cream [ice *cream*]. **3** a smooth, oily substance used to clean and soften the skin. **4** the best part [the *cream* of the crop]. **5** yellowish white. ◆*v.* **1** to beat, as butter and sugar, until creamy. **2** to form a creamy foam on top. ☆**3** to beat or defeat soundly: *slang in this meaning.*

**cream cheese** a soft, white cheese made of cream or of milk and cream.

**cream·er** (krēm′ər) ***n.*** ☆a small pitcher for cream.

☆**cream·er·y** (krēm′ər ē) ***n.*** **1** a place where milk and dairy products are prepared. **2** a store where these are sold. —*pl.* **cream′er·ies**

**cream·y** (krēm′ē) ***adj.*** of, like, or full of cream; smooth and rich. —**cream′i·er, cream′i·est**

**crease** (krēs) ***n.*** **1** a line or ridge made by folding or pressing [the *crease* in trousers]. **2** a fold or wrinkle [the *creases* in an old man's face]. ◆*v.* to make a crease or creases in. —**creased, creas′ing**

**cre·ate** (krē āt′) ***v.*** to bring into being; cause to be; bring about; make; form; produce [Rembrandt *created* many fine paintings. More cars on the road *create* more traffic problems.] —**cre·at′ed, cre·at′ing**

SYNONYMS: To **create** something is to make or form something for the first time by using some special skill or art [Louisa May Alcott *created* interesting characters.] To **invent** something is to make or produce something for the first time, often as a result of doing experiments [Alexander Graham Bell *invented* the telephone.] To **discover** something is to be the first to see or know about it [Balboa was the first European to *discover* the Pacific Ocean.]

**cre·a·tion** (krē ā′shən) ***n.*** **1** the act of creating. **2** the whole world and everything in it; universe. **3** anything created or brought into being.

**cre·a·tive** (krē ā′tiv) ***adj.*** creating or able to create; inventive; having imagination and ability. —**cre·a·tiv·i·ty** (krē′ā tiv′ə tē) ***n.***

**cre·a·tor** (krē āt′ər) ***n.*** a person that creates. —**the Creator,** God; the Supreme Being.

**crea·ture** (krē′chər) ***n.*** a living being; any person or animal.

**cre·dence** (krēd′′ns) ***n.*** belief or trust in what someone says [Be slow to give *credence* to rumors.]

**cre·den·tials** (kri den′shəlz) ***n.pl.*** a letter or paper carried by a person to show that he can be trusted, or to prove his right to do something.

**cred·i·ble** (kred′ə b′l) ***adj.*** that can be believed; believable [a *credible* statement]. —**cred·i·bil·i·ty** (kred′ə bil′ə tē) ***n.*** —**cred′i·bly *adv.***

**cred·it** (kred′it) ***n.*** **1** belief; trust [I give little *credit* to what he says.] **2** praise or approval [I give her *credit* for trying.] **3** official recognition in a record [You will receive *credit* for your work on this project.] **4** a person or thing that brings praise [She is a *credit* to the team.] **5** trust that a person will be able and willing to pay later [That store doesn't give *credit,* so you have to pay cash.] **6** amount of money in someone's account [Depositing the check gave him a *credit* of $80.00.] ◆*v.* **1** to accept as true; believe [She wouldn't *credit* his excuse.] **2** to add to a person's account [*Credit* him with $10.00.] —**credit someone with,** to believe that someone has or give recognition to someone for [to *credit someone with* honesty]. —**do credit to,** to bring honor to. —**on credit,** by agreeing to pay later [to buy a car *on credit*]. —**to one's credit,** bringing honor to one.

**cred·it·a·ble** (kred′it ə b′l) ***adj.*** deserving credit or praise. —**cred′it·a·bly *adv.***

**credit card** a card that gives to the owner of it the right to charge bills at certain stores, hotels, gas stations, restaurants, etc.

**cred·i·tor** (kred′i tər) ***n.*** a person to whom one owes something.

**cre·du·li·ty** (krə dōō′lə tē *or* krə dyōō′lə tē) ***n.*** a willingness to believe, even without proof.

**cred·u·lous** (krej′oo ləs) ***adj.*** willing to believe things, even without proof; easily fooled.

**creed** (krēd) ***n.*** **1** a statement of the main beliefs of a religion. **2** any belief or set of beliefs that guide a person.

**creek** (krēk *or* krik) ***n.*** **1** a small stream, a little larger than a brook. **2** a narrow inlet or bay: *now mainly a British meaning.*

**creel** (krēl) ***n.*** a basket for holding fish, often worn on the back by a person when fishing. *See the picture.*

**creep** (krēp) ***v.*** **1** to move along with the body close to the ground, as a baby on hands and knees. *See the picture at* **crawl.** **2** to move in a slow or sneaking way [The cars *crept* along in the heavy traffic. The thieves *crept* into the store at night.] **3** to come on almost without being noticed [Old age *crept* up on her.] **4** to grow along the ground or a wall, as ivy. —**crept, creep′ing** ◆*n.* the act of creeping. —**make one's flesh creep,** to make one feel fear or disgust, as if insects were creeping on one's skin. —**the creeps,** a feeling of fear or disgust: *used only in everyday talk.*

**creep·er** (krēp′ər) ***n.*** **1** a person or thing that creeps. **2** any plant that grows along the ground or a wall.

**creep·y** (krēp′ē) ***adj.*** having or causing a feeling of fear or disgust, as if insects were creeping on one's skin. —**creep′i·er, creep′i·est** —**creep′i·ness *n.***

**cre·mate** (krē′māt) ***v.*** to burn a dead body to ashes. —**cre′mat·ed, cre′mat·ing** —**cre·ma′tion *n.***

**Cre·ole** (krē′ōl) ***n.*** **1** a person descended from the original French settlers of Louisiana. **2** the French language that these people speak. ◆*adj.* **1** of or having to do with Creoles. **2** *usually* **creole,** made of sautéed tomatoes, green peppers, onions, etc. and spices [*creole* sauce].

The word **Creole** comes to us through Spanish and French from a Portuguese word meaning "born at home." Whether one is a Creole depends on where one was born or where one's ancestors were born.

**cre·o·sote** (krē′ə sōt) ***n.*** an oily liquid with a sharp smell, made from wood tar or coal tar and used on wood to keep it from rotting.

| | | | |
|---|---|---|---|
| **a** fat | **ir** here | **ou** out | **zh** leisure |
| **ā** ape | **ī** bite, fire | **u** up | **ng** ring |
| **ä** car, lot | **ō** go | **ur** fur | a *in* ago |
| **e** ten | **ô** law, horn | **ch** chin | e *in* agent |
| **er** care | **oi** oil | **sh** she | **ə** = i *in* unity |
| **ē** even | **oo** look | **th** thin | o *in* collect |
| **i** hit | **ōō** tool | ***th*** then | u *in* focus |

**crepe** or **crêpe** (krāp) ***n.*** **1** a thin, crinkled cloth. **2** *same as meaning* 2 *of* **crape.** **3** *same as* **crepe paper.** **4** *same as* **crepe rubber.** **5** (krāp *or* krep) a very thin pancake, rolled up or folded with a filling: *usually* **crêpe.**

**crepe paper** thin paper crinkled like crepe.

**crepe rubber** soft rubber in sheets with a wrinkled surface, used for shoe soles.

**crept** *past tense and past participle of* **creep.**

**cre·scen·do** (krə shen′dō) ***adj., adv.*** gradually becoming louder or stronger: *a direction in music shown by the sign* < . ◆***n.*** a gradual increase in loudness. —*pl.* **cre·scen′dos**

**cres·cent** (kres′'nt) ***n.*** **1** the shape of the moon in its first or last quarter. *See the picture.* **2** anything shaped like this, as a curved bun or roll. ◆***adj.*** shaped like a crescent.

**cress** (kres) ***n.*** a small plant whose sharp-tasting leaves are used in salads.

**crest** (krest) ***n.*** **1** a tuft of feathers or fur, on the head of certain birds and animals. **2** a plume of feathers or other decoration worn on a helmet. **3** a design, as of a crown or an eagle's head, placed at the top of a coat of arms, or used as a family mark on silverware, stationery, etc. **4** the top of anything [the *crest* of a wave; a mountain *crest*].

**crest·ed** (kres′tid) ***adj.*** having a crest.

**crest·fall·en** (krest′fôl′ən) ***adj.*** having lost one's spirit or courage; made sad or humble [The players trooped into the locker room, *crestfallen* at losing the game.]



**Crete** (krēt) a Greek island in the eastern Mediterranean. —**Cre′tan *adj., n.***

**cre·tonne** (krē′tän *or* kri tän′) ***n.*** a heavy cotton or linen cloth with patterns printed in colors, used for curtains, chair covers, etc.

**cre·vasse** (kri vas′) ***n.*** a deep crack or crevice, especially in a glacier.

**crev·ice** (krev′is) ***n.*** a narrow opening caused by a crack or split, as in rock.

**crew**[1] (kro͞o) ***n.*** **1** all the persons working on a ship, aircraft, etc. [A ship's *crew* is usually thought of apart from its officers.] **2** any group of people working together [a road *crew;* a gun *crew*]. **3** a group or gang; mob. **4** a rowing team. ◆***v.*** to serve as a crew member.

**crew**[2] (kro͞o) *a past tense of* **crow**[2].

☆**crew cut** a style of man's haircut in which the hair is cut very close to the head. *See the picture.*

**crib** (krib) ***n.*** **1** a small bed with high sides, for a baby. **2** a box or trough for feeding animals. **3** a structure made of slats and used for storing grain. **4** notes, a translation, etc. used in a dishonest way to do schoolwork: *used only in everyday talk.* ◆***v.*** to use a crib to do schoolwork; also, to pass off another's ideas as one's own: *used only in everyday talk.* —**cribbed, crib′bing**

**crib·bage** (krib′ij) ***n.*** a card game in which the score is kept by moving pegs on a small board.

**crick** (krik) ***n.*** a painful cramp, as in the neck.

**crick·et**[1] (krik′it) ***n.*** a leaping insect related to the grasshopper. Male crickets make a chirping noise by rubbing the wings together.

**crick·et**[2] (krik′it) ***n.*** **1** an outdoor game played with a ball, bats, and wickets, by two teams of eleven players each. Cricket is played mainly in England. **2** fair play; sportsmanship: *used only in everyday* talk. —**crick′et·er *n.***

**cried** (krīd) *past tense and past participle of* **cry.**

**cri·er** (krī′ər) ***n.*** **1** a person who cries or shouts. **2** a person whose work was shouting out public announcements, news, etc. through the streets. *See the picture.*

**cries** (krīz) **1** *the form of the verb* **cry** *used in the present with* he, she, *or* it. **2** *the plural of the noun* **cry.**

**crim.** *abbreviation for* **criminal.**

**crime** (krīm) ***n.*** **1** the doing of something that is against the law; serious wrongdoing that breaks the law. **2** an evil or foolish act; sin [It would be a *crime* to waste this food.]

**Cri·me·a** (krī mē′ə) a peninsula in the Soviet Union, jutting into the Black Sea. *See the map.* —**Cri·me′an *adj.***

**crim·i·nal** (krim′ə n'l) ***adj.*** **1** being a crime; that is a crime [a *criminal* act]. **2** having to do with crime [*criminal* law]. ◆***n.*** a person guilty of a crime. —**crim′i·nal·ly *adv.***

**crimp** (krimp) ***v.*** **1** to press into narrow, even folds; pleat [The lace ruffles were *crimped.*] **2** to make hair wavy or curly. ◆***n.*** **1** the act of crimping. **2** a crimped fold or pleat.

**crim·son** (krim′z'n) ***adj., n.*** deep red [Blood is *crimson.*] ◆***v.*** to make or become crimson.

**cringe** (krinj) ***v.*** to draw back, bend over, or tremble with fear [The dog *cringed* and put its tail between its legs.] —**cringed, cring′ing**

**crin·kle** (kriŋ′k'l) ***v.*** **1** to make or become full of wrinkles or creases [Old paper money is usually *crinkled* from use.] **2** to make a sound like that of paper being crushed. —**crin′kled, crin′kling** —**crin′kly *adj.***

**crin·o·line** (krin′'l in) ***n.*** **1** a coarse, stiff cloth used as a lining or in petticoats for puffing out skirts. **2** *another name for* **hoop skirt.**

**crip·ple** (krip′'l) ***n.*** a person or animal that is lame or injured so as to be unable to move in a normal way. ◆***v.*** **1** to make a cripple of; lame [*crippled* with a broken leg]. *See* SYNONYMS *at* **maim.** **2** to hurt or weaken [The snowstorm *crippled* bus service.] —**crip′pled, crip′pling**

> **Cripple** is related to the word "creep," which comes from an Old English word meaning "to go bent down."

**cri·sis** (krī′sis) ***n.*** **1** the turning point in a disease that shows whether the patient will get well or die. **2** any turning point, as in history. **3** a time of great danger or trouble. —*pl.* **cri·ses** (krī′sēz)

**crisp** (krisp) ***adj.*** **1** hard or firm, but easily broken or snapped [*crisp* bacon; *crisp* lettuce]. **2** sharp, clear, lively, etc.; not dull or slow [a *crisp* way of speaking]. **3** fresh and bracing [*crisp* air]. **4** tightly curled and wiry [*crisp* hair]. ◆***v.*** to make or become crisp. —**crisp′ly *adv.*** —**crisp′ness *n.***

**crisp·y** (kris′pē) ***adj.*** *same as* **crisp.** —**crisp′i·er, crisp′i·est**

**criss·cross** (kris′krôs) ***adj.*** marked with or moving in crossing lines [a *crisscross* pattern]. ◆***v.*** to move crosswise or mark with crossing lines [Railroad tracks *criss-cross* the valley.]

**cri·te·ri·on** (krī tir′ē ən) ***n.*** a rule or test by which something can be judged; measure of value [Low cost was her only *criterion* in buying her car.] —*pl.* **cri·te·ri·a** (krī tir′ē ə) or **cri·te′ri·ons**

**crit·ic** (krit′ik) ***n.*** **1** a person who forms judgments of people or things; especially, one whose work is to write such judgments of books, music, plays, etc., as for a newspaper or magazine. **2** a person who is quick to find fault.

**crit·i·cal** (krit′i k'l) ***adj.*** **1** tending to find fault or to disapprove [You're too *critical* of other people.] **2** based on sound, careful judgment [a *critical* opinion]. **3** having to do with critics or criticism. **4** dangerous or risky; causing worry [If the levy doesn't pass, the schools will be in a *critical* financial situation.] **5** of or forming a crisis [the *critical* stage of a disease]. —**crit′i·cal·ly *adv.***

**crit·i·cism** (krit′ə siz'm) ***n.*** **1** the forming of judgments, especially about books, music, etc. **2** a piece of writing by a critic; review. **3** the act of finding fault; disapproval.

**crit·i·cize** (krit′ə sīz) ***v.*** **1** to judge as a critic. **2** to find fault with; disapprove of [The boss *criticizes* everything I do.] —**crit′i·cized, crit′i·ciz·ing**

SYNONYMS: **Criticize** is the general term for finding fault with a person or thing [The motorists *criticized* the way the road was built.] To **blame** is to point out who or what is at fault for causing a mistake, error, etc. [I *blame* myself for the accident.]

**cri·tique** (kri tēk′) ***n.*** **1** a piece of writing that gives a careful judgment of a book, play, etc. **2** the art of a critic; criticism.

**crit·ter** (krit′ər) ***n.*** *another word for* **creature**: *used only in some regions.*

**croak** (krōk) ***v.*** **1** to make a deep, hoarse sound in the throat [Frogs and ravens *croak*.] **2** to say in a deep, hoarse voice [The messenger, tired from running, *croaked* a warning.] ◆***n.*** a croaking sound.

**Cro·a·tia** (krō ā′shə) a state in northwestern Yugoslavia. —**Cro·a′tian *adj., n.***

**cro·chet** (krō shā′) ***n.*** a kind of needlework done with one hooked needle (**crochet hook**). ◆***v.*** to do or to make something by doing this kind of needlework. —**cro·cheted** (krō shād′), **cro·chet·ing** (krō shā′ing) —**cro·chet′er *n.***

**crock** (kräk) ***n.*** a pot or jar made of baked clay.

**crock·er·y** (kräk′ər ē) ***n.*** pots, jars, and dishes made of baked clay; earthenware.

**croc·o·dile** (kräk′ə dīl) ***n.*** a large lizard like the alligator, that lives in and near tropical rivers. It has a thick, tough skin, a long tail, large jaws, and pointed teeth. *See the picture.*

**cro·cus** (krō′kəs) ***n.*** a small plant that grows from a corm and has a yellow, purple, or white flower. It is one of the first plants to bloom in the spring. —*pl.* **cro′cus·es** or **cro·ci** (krō′sī)

**Croe·sus** (krē′səs) a very rich king in Asia Minor in the 6th century B.C.

**crois·sant** (krə sänt′) ***n.*** a rich, flaky bread roll made in the form of a crescent.

**Cro-Ma·gnon** (krō mag′nən) ***adj.*** of a race of tall men who lived in Europe in the Stone Age.

UKRANIAN S.S.R.
Odessa
Crimea
Yalta
BLACK SEA

crocodile
up to 6 m (20 ft.) long

crook

crew cut

crescent

town crier

**Crom·well** (kräm′wel), **Oliver** 1599–1658; English general who ruled the country after Charles I was beheaded. 175

**crone** (krōn) ***n.*** a wrinkled old woman; hag.

**cro·ny** (krō′nē) ***n.*** a close friend or companion. —*pl.* **cro′nies**

**crook** (kro͝ok) ***n.*** **1** a thing or part that is bent or curved [the *crook* of one's arm; a *crook* in the road]. **2** a shepherd's staff with a hook at the end. *See the picture.* ☆**3** a person who steals or cheats: *used only in everyday talk.* ◆***v.*** to bend or curve [to *crook* one's arm].

**crook·ed** (kro͝ok′id) ***adj.*** **1** not straight; bent, curved, or twisted [a *crooked* road]. ☆**2** not honest; cheating.

**croon** (kro͞on) ***v.*** to sing or hum in a low, gentle tone [to *croon* lullabies].

**crop** (kräp) ***n.*** **1** any farm product grown in the soil, as wheat, cotton, fruit, etc.; also, the amount of such a product grown at one time. **2** a group of things or persons [a new *crop* of students; a *crop* of complaints]. **3** a pouch in a bird's gullet where food is softened for digestion. **4** the handle of a whip. **5** a short whip with a loop at the end, used in horseback riding. **6** hair cut very short [a close *crop*]. ◆***v.*** **1** to cut or bite off the tops or ends of [The goat *cropped* the grass.] **2** to cut short; trim [to *crop* hair]. —**cropped, crop′ping** —**crop out** or **crop up,** to come up in a way that is not expected.

| | | | |
|---|---|---|---|
| **a** fat | **ir** here | **ou** out | **zh** leisure |
| **ā** ape | **ī** bite, fire | **u** up | **ng** ring |
| **ä** car, lot | **ō** go | **ur** fur | a *in* ago |
| **e** ten | **ô** law, horn | **ch** chin | e *in* agent |
| **er** care | **oi** oil | **sh** she | ə = i *in* unity |
| **ē** even | **oo** look | **th** thin | o *in* collect |
| **i** hit | **o͞o** tool | ***th*** then | u *in* focus |

**crop·per** (kräp′ər) ***n.*** a person or thing that crops. —**come a cropper,** **1** to fall headlong. **2** to fail or be ruined. *This phrase is used only in everyday talk.*

**cro·quet** (krō kā′) ***n.*** an outdoor game in which the players use mallets to drive a wooden ball through hoops in the ground.

**cro·quette** (krō ket′) ***n.*** a little ball of chopped meat, fish, etc. fried in deep fat.

**cro·sier** (krō′zhər) ***n.*** the staff of a bishop or abbot, that is a symbol of his office.

**cross** (krôs) ***n.*** **1** an upright post with a bar across it near the top, on which the ancient Romans put criminals to death. **2** the figure of a cross used as a symbol of the crucifixion of Jesus and of the Christian religion. **3** any trouble that one has to bear [A sick child has been Jan's *cross.*] **4** any design or mark made by crossing lines. *See the picture.* **5** a mixing of different breeds of animals or plants. **6** the result of such mixing [A bull terrier is a *cross* between a bulldog and a terrier.] ◆***v.*** **1** to make the sign of the cross over, as a religious act [to *cross* oneself]. **2** to place across or crosswise [*Cross* your fingers.] **3** to draw a line or lines across [*Cross* your t's.] **4** to go from one side to the other of; go or extend across [She *crossed* the ocean. The bridge *crosses* the river.] **5** to pass each other while moving in opposite directions [Our letters *crossed* in the mail.] **6** to go against; oppose; hinder [No one likes to be *crossed.*] **7** to mix different breeds



of animals or plants. ◆***adj.*** **1** lying or passing across; crossing [a *cross* street]. **2** cranky or irritable; having a bad temper. —**cross off** or **cross out,** to do away with or cancel as by drawing lines across. —**cross one's mind,** to come to one's mind; occur to one. —**cross one's path,** to meet one. —**cross′ly** ***adv.*** —**cross′ness** ***n.***

**cross·bar** (krôs′bär) ***n.*** a bar or line placed crosswise, as a bar between goal posts.

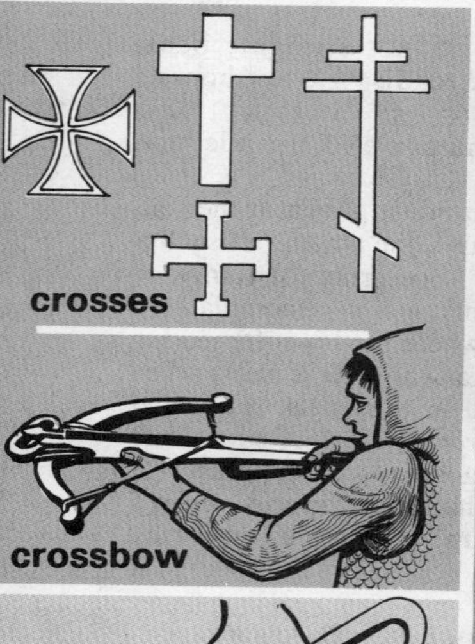

crosses

crossbow

crowbar

crow's–nest

cross section of an apple

**cross·bones** (krôs′bōnz) ***n.*** the figure of two bones placed across each other, under a skull, used as a sign of death or deadly danger.

**cross·bow** (krôs′bō) ***n.*** a weapon of the Middle Ages, consisting of a bow set across a wooden stock. The stock had a groove that held the arrow and a trigger that released the bowstring. *See the picture.* A modern type of crossbow is being used by some hunters today.

**cross·breed** (krôs′brēd) ***v.*** to mix different breeds of animals or kinds of plants; hybridize. —**cross·bred** (krôs′bred), **cross′breed·ing** ◆***n.*** an animal or plant produced by crossbreeding.

**cross-coun·try** (krôs′kun′trē) ***adj., adv.*** **1** across open country or fields instead of on roads [a *cross-country* race]. **2** across a country [a *cross-country* flight].

**cross·cut** (krôs′kut) ***adj.*** made or used for cutting across [A *crosscut* saw cuts wood across the grain.] ◆***n.*** a cut or way across. ◆***v.*** to cut across. —**cross′-cut, cross′cut·ting**

**cross-ex·am·ine** (krôs′ig zam′in) ***v.*** to question again, as a witness already questioned by the other side during a trial, in order to check the earlier answers or to get more information. —**cross′-ex·am′-ined, cross′-ex·am′in·ing** —**cross′-ex·am′i·na′tion** ***n.***

**cross-eyed** (krôs′īd′) ***adj.*** having the eyes turned toward each other.

**cross·ing** (krôs′iŋ) ***n.*** **1** the act of one that crosses. **2** the place where lines, streets, etc. cross each other. **3** a place where a street or river may be crossed.

**cross·piece** (krôs′pēs) ***n.*** a piece, as of wood or metal, lying across something else.

**cross-pur·pose** (krôs′pur′pəs) ***n.*** an opposing purpose. —**at cross-purposes,** having a mistaken idea as to each other's purposes.

**cross-ref·er·ence** (krôs′ref′ər əns *or* krôs′ref′rəns) ***n.*** a notice to look in another part of a book, list, etc. for more information.

Sometimes a **cross-reference** in this dictionary tells the reader to look at the more common spelling of the word to find its meaning. Others invite the reader to look at a list of synonyms in another part of the book, or at a picture helping to explain the word being defined.

**cross·road** (krôs′rōd) ***n.*** **1** a road that crosses another road. **2** *usually* **crossroads,** *pl.* the place where roads cross each other.

**cross section** **1** the act of cutting something straight across. **2** a piece cut off in this way. *See the picture.* **3** a sample that has enough of each kind in it to show what the whole is like [The newspaper polled a *cross section* of the city's voters.]

☆**cross·walk** (krôs′wôk) ***n.*** a lane marked off for people to use in walking across a street.

**cross·wise** (krôs′wīz) ***adv.*** so as to cross; across: *also* **cross·ways** (krôs′wāz)

☆**cross·word puzzle** (krôs′wurd) a puzzle that consists of a square made up of blank spaces, which are to be filled with letters that form certain words. Clues to these words are given with the square.

**crotch** (kräch) ***n.*** **1** a place where branches fork from the trunk of a tree. **2** the place where the legs fork from the human body. **3** the seam or place where the legs of a pair of pants meet.

**crotch·et** (kräch′it) ***n.*** a peculiar whim or stubborn notion. —**crotch′et·y** ***adj.***

**crouch** (krouch) ***v.*** to stoop with the legs bent close to the ground, as an animal about to leap. ◆***n.*** the act or position of crouching.

**croup**[1] (kro͞op) ***n.*** a children's disease that causes hoarse coughing and hard breathing. —**croup′y** ***adj.***

**croup**[2] (kro͞op) ***n.*** the rump of a horse.

**crou·ton** (kro͞o′tän) ***n.*** any of the small, crisp, toasted pieces of bread often served in soup, salads, etc.

**crow**[1] (krō) ***n.*** a large black bird known for its harsh cry or caw. —**as the crow flies,** in a straight line between two places.

**crow**[2] (krō) ***v.*** **1.** to make the shrill cry of a rooster. —**crowed** *or mainly in British use* **crew, crow′ing 2.** to make loud sounds like this, as in happiness, delight, or boasting. —**crowed, crow′ing** ◆***n.*** the shrill cry of a rooster.

**crow·bar** (krō′bär) ***n.*** a long metal bar with one end like a chisel, for prying things. *See the picture.*

**crowd** (kroud) ***n.*** **1** a large group of people together [*crowds* of Christmas shoppers]. **2** the common people; the masses. ☆**3** a group of people having something in common; set: *used only in everyday talk* [My brother's *crowd* is too old for me.] ◆***v.*** **1** to push or squeeze [Can we all *crowd* into one car?] **2** to come together in a large group [People *crowded* to see the show.] **3** to pack or fill too full.

**crown** (kroun) ***n.*** **1** a headdress of gold, jewels, etc., worn by a king or queen. **2** the power of being the ruler [The nobles fought for the *crown.*] **3** *often* **Crown,** the king or queen [arrested by order of the *Crown*]. **4** a wreath worn on the head as a sign of honor or victory. **5** first place in a contest; championship [The boxer won the heavyweight *crown.*] **6** anything like a crown; especially, the top part [a *crown* of golden hair; the *crown* of a hill; the *crown* of a hat]. **7** the top part of the head. **8** the part of a tooth that sticks out from the gum. ◆***v.*** **1** to make a king or queen by putting a crown on [Elizabeth I was *crowned* in 1558.] **2** to honor or reward [The victor was *crowned* with glory.] **3** to be at the top of [Woods *crowned* the hill.] **4** to cover the crown of a tooth with gold or porcelain to protect it. **5** to complete or end [Success *crowned* his effort.] **6** to hit over the head: *slang in this meaning.*

**crow's-foot** (krōz′foot′) ***n.*** *usually* **crow's-feet,** *pl.* any of the wrinkles that often develop at the outer corners of the eyes of older people. —*pl.* **crow's-feet**

**crow's-nest** (krōz′nest′) ***n.*** a small box or platform near the top of a ship's mast, where the lookout stands. *See the picture.*

**cru·cial** (kro͞o′shəl) ***adj.*** of the most importance; that decides something [The final examination is the *crucial* test.] —**cru′cial·ly** ***adv.***

**cru·ci·ble** (kro͞o′sə b′l) ***n.*** a pot or vat in which ores and metals are melted.

**cru·ci·fix** (kro͞o′sə fiks) ***n.*** a Christian symbol that is a cross with the figure of Jesus on it.

**cru·ci·fix·ion** (kro͞o′sə fik′shən) ***n.*** **1** the act of crucifying. **2 the Crucifixion,** the crucifying of Jesus, or a picture or painting of this.

**cru·ci·fy** (kro͞o′sə fī) ***v.*** **1** to put to death by nailing or tying to a cross. **2** to treat in a cruel way; torture or abuse. —**cru′ci·fied, cru′ci·fy·ing**

**crude** (kro͞od) ***adj.*** **1** looking or acting rough or clumsy [a *crude* drawing; a *crude* backwoodsman]. **2** in its natural or raw condition, before it has been prepared for use [*crude* oil]. —**crude′ly** ***adv.*** —**crude′ness** ***n.***

**cru·el** (kro͞o′əl) ***adj.*** **1** liking to make others suffer; having no mercy or pity [The *cruel* Pharaoh made slaves of the Israelites.] **2** causing pain and suffering [*cruel* insults; a *cruel* winter]. —**cru′el·ly** ***adv.***

**cru·el·ty** (kro͞o′əl tē) ***n.*** **1** the quality of being cruel. **2** a cruel action, remark, etc. —*pl.* **cru′el·ties**

**cru·et** (kro͞o′it) ***n.*** a small glass bottle for serving oil, vinegar, etc. at the table. *See the picture on page 179.*

**cruise** (kro͞oz) ***v.*** **1** to sail or drive about from place to place, as for pleasure or in searching for something. **2** to move smoothly at a speed that is not strained [The airplane *cruised* at 300 miles per hour.] —**cruised, cruis′ing** ◆***n.*** a ship voyage from place to place for pleasure.

**cruis·er** (kro͞oz′ər) ***n.*** **1** a fast warship smaller than a battleship. **2** anything that cruises, as a police car, motorboat, etc.

☆**crul·ler** (krul′ər) ***n.*** a kind of twisted doughnut made with a rich dough.

**crumb** (krum) ***n.*** **1** a tiny piece broken off, as of bread or cake. **2** any bit or scrap [*crumbs* of knowledge]. ◆***v.*** **1** to coat meat, croquettes, etc. with crumbs in order to prepare for cooking. **2** to take the crumbs off a table.



**crum·ble** (krum′b′l) ***v.*** to break into crumbs or small pieces [*Crumble* the crackers into your soup. The old plaster walls *crumbled.*] —**crum′bled, crum′bling**

**crum·bly** (krum′blē) ***adj.*** likely to crumble; easily crumbled [*crumbly* rocks; *crumbly* cake]. —**crum′bli·er, crum′bli·est**

**crum·my** (krum′ē) ***adj.*** cheap, worthless, inferior, etc.: *a slang word.* —**crum′mi·er, crum′mi·est**

**crum·pet** (krum′pit) ***n.*** a small, unsweetened cake baked on a griddle. It is usually toasted before serving.

**crum·ple** (krum′p′l) ***v.*** **1** to crush together into creases; wrinkle [*Crumple* the paper in your hand. This fabric *crumples.*] **2** to fall or break down. —**crum′pled, crum′pling**

**crunch** (krunch) ***v.*** **1** to chew with a noisy, crackling sound [to *crunch* raw carrots]. **2** to grind or move over with a noisy, crushing sound [The wheels *crunched* the pebbles in the driveway.] ◆***n.*** **1** the act or sound of crunching. **2** a tight situation; pinch: *slang in this sense.*

**crunch·y** (krunch′ē) ***adj.*** making a crunching sound [*crunchy* celery]. —**crunch′i·er, crunch′i·est**

**crup·per** (krup′ər) ***n.*** **1** a leather strap fastened to a harness and passed under a horse's tail. **2** the rump of a horse.

| | | | | | | | |
|---|---|---|---|---|---|---|---|
| **a** | fat | **ir** | here | **ou** | out | **zh** | leisure |
| **ā** | ape | **ī** | bite, fire | **u** | up | **ng** | ring |
| **ä** | car, lot | **ō** | go | **ur** | fur | | a *in* ago |
| **e** | ten | **ô** | law, horn | **ch** | chin | | e *in* agent |
| **er** | care | **oi** | oil | **sh** | she | **ə =** | i *in* unity |
| **ē** | even | **oo** | look | **th** | thin | | o *in* collect |
| **i** | hit | **o͞o** | tool | ***th*** | then | | u *in* focus |

**cru·sade** (kro͞o sād′) ***n.*** **1** *sometimes* **Crusade,** any of the wars which Christians from the West fought in the 11th, 12th, and 13th centuries to capture the Holy Land from the Muslims. **2** any fight for a cause thought to be good or against something thought to be bad [a *crusade* for better housing; a *crusade* against cancer]. ◆***v.*** to take part in a crusade. —**cru·sad′ed, cru·sad′ing —cru·sad′er *n.***

**cruse** (kro͞oz *or* kro͞os) ***n.*** a small jar for water, oil, etc. *This word is now seldom used.*

**crush** (krush) ***v.*** **1** to press or squeeze with force so as to break, hurt, or put out of shape [She *crushed* the flower in her hand. His hat was *crushed* when he sat on it.] *See* SYNONYMS *at* **break. 2** to grind or pound into bits [This machine *crushes* rocks.] **3** to bring to an end by force; subdue; suppress [The government *crushed* the revolt.] **4** to become crumpled or wrinkled [That cotton scarf *crushes* easily.] ◆***n.*** **1** a crushing or squeezing; strong pressure. **2** many people or things crowded together [We were caught in a *crush* of people leaving the stadium.] ☆**3** a strong attraction toward someone: *used only in everyday talk* [John has a *crush* on Mary.]

**Cru·soe** (kro͞o′sō), **Rob·in·son** (räb′in sən) the hero of Daniel Defoe's novel, *Robinson Crusoe,* who is shipwrecked on a desert island.

**crust** (krust) ***n.*** **1** the hard, crisp, outer part of bread; also, a piece of this. **2** any dry, hard piece of bread. **3** the shell or cover of a pie, made of flour and shortening. **4** any hard covering or top layer, as of snow or soil. ◆***v.*** to cover or become covered with a crust [The roofs were *crusted* with ice and snow.]



**crus·ta·cean** (krus tā′shən) ***n.*** an animal with a hard outer shell, that usually lives in water [Shrimps, crabs, and lobsters are *crustaceans.*]

**crust·y** (krus′tē) ***adj.*** **1** having a crust or like a crust [*crusty* snow]. **2** having a bad temper; rude and impolite. —**crust′i·er, crust′i·est —crust′i·ly *adv.***

**crutch** (kruch) ***n.*** **1** a support used under the arm by a lame person to help in walking. *See the picture.* **2** any kind of support or help.

**crux** (kruks) ***n.*** the most important or deciding point [The *crux* of the matter is that we have no money for a new car.]

**cry** (krī) ***v.*** **1** to make a loud sound with the voice; call out or shout [Lou *cried* out in fright when a face appeared at the window.] **2** to show sorrow, pain, etc. by sobbing or shedding tears. **3** to say loudly; shout; exclaim ["Help! Help!" the victim *cried.*] —**cried, cry′ing** ◆***n.*** **1** a loud sound made by the voice; shout or call [I heard your *cry* for help.] **2** a call or slogan that is supposed to rouse people [a battle *cry*]. **3** a fit of sobbing and weeping [I had a good *cry* and fell asleep.] **4** the sound an animal makes [the *cry* of a lost sheep]. —*pl.* **cries —a far cry,** something much different [What the politicians promise is *a far cry* from what they do.] —**cry for, 1** to plead for. **2** to need greatly. —**cry one's eyes out,** to weep much and bitterly.

☆**cry·ba·by** (krī′bā′bē) ***n.*** **1** a child who cries often without much reason. **2** a person who complains when he fails to win or get his own way. —*pl.* **cry′ba′bies**

**cry·ing** (krī′iŋ) ***adj.*** that must be taken care of [a *crying* need].

**cry·o·gen·ics** (krī′ə jen′iks) ***n.pl.*** the science that deals with the production of very low temperatures and the effects they have on things.

**crypt** (kript) ***n.*** an underground room, especially one under a church, for burying the dead.

**cryp·tic** (krip′tik) ***adj.*** having a hidden or difficult meaning; secret; mysterious [a *cryptic* answer]. —**cryp′ti·cal·ly *adv.***

**cryp·to·gram** (krip′tə gram) ***n.*** something written in a code or secret writing.

**crys·tal** (kris′t'l) ***n.*** **1** a clear, transparent quartz that looks like glass. **2** a very clear, sparkling glass. **3** something made of such glass, as a goblet or bowl. ☆**4** the glass or plastic cover over the face of a watch. **5** any of the regularly shaped pieces into which many substances are formed when they become solids. A crystal has a number of flat surfaces in an orderly arrangement [Salt, sugar, and snow are made up of *crystals.*] *See the picture.* ◆***adj.*** **1** made of crystal. **2** clear as crystal [the *crystal* waters of a stream].

**crystal ball** a large glass ball in which fortunetellers pretend to see what will happen in the future.

**crys·tal·line** (kris′tə lin) ***adj.*** **1** made of crystal. **2** clear as crystal. **3** formed of crystals or like a crystal.

**crys·tal·lize** (kris′tə līz) ***v.*** **1** to form crystals [Boil the maple syrup until it *crystallizes.*] **2** to take on or give a definite form [Their customs were *crystallized* into law.] —**crys′tal·lized, crys′tal·liz·ing —crys′tal·li·za′tion *n.***

**CSC** Civil Service Commission.

**CST, C.S.T.** Central Standard Time.

**CT** *abbreviation for* **Connecticut.**

**ct.** *abbreviation for* **cent.** —*pl.* **cts.**

**ctr.** *abbreviation for* **center.**

**Cu** *the symbol for the chemical element* copper.

**cu.** *abbreviation for* **cubic.**

**cub** (kub) ***n.*** **1** the young of certain animals, such as the bear, lion, and whale. **2** a person who is a beginner in some work or activity.

**Cu·ba** (kyo͞o′bə) a country on an island in the West Indies. —**Cu′ban *adj., n.***

**cub·by·hole** (kub′ē hōl′) ***n.*** **1** a small, snug room, closet, or compartment. **2** a pigeonhole in a desk, secretary, etc.

**cube** (kyo͞ob) ***n.*** **1** a solid with six square sides, all the same size. **2** anything with more or less this shape [an ice *cube*]. **3** the result got by multiplying a number by itself and then multiplying the product by the same number [The *cube* of 3 is 27 (3 x 3 x 3 = 27).] ◆***v.*** **1** to get the cube of a number [5 *cubed* is 125]. **2** to cut into cubes [I *cubed* the fruit for salad.] —**cubed, cub′ing**

**cube root** the number of which a given number is the cube [The *cube root* of 8 is 2.]

**cu·bic** (kyo͞o′bik) ***adj.*** **1** having the shape of a cube. **2** having measure in three directions [A *cubic* foot is the volume of a cube that is one foot long, one foot wide, and one foot high.]

**cu·bi·cle** (kyo͞o′bi k'l) ***n.*** a small, separate room or compartment, as for study or sleep.

**cub·ism** (kyo͞o′biz'm) ***n.*** a form of art in the early 20th century in which whatever was done as a painting or sculpture was made to look as if made up of cubes, squares, spheres, triangles, etc. —**cub′ist** ***n., adj.*** —**cu·bis′tic** ***adj.***

**cu·bit** (kyo͞o′bit) ***n.*** a measure of length used in ancient times, about 18 to 22 inches.

> **Cubit** comes from the Latin word for "elbow." In ancient times people had crude but simple ways of measuring things. At first a cubit was the length of the arm from the end of the middle finger to the elbow. One could use one's arm in measuring some things. The human arm varies in length, and later the measure came to be 18 to 22 inches.

**Cub Scout** a member of a division of the Boy Scouts for boys eight through ten years old.

**cuck·oo** (ko͞o′ko͞o *or* ko͝ok′o͞o) ***n.*** **1** a dull-brown bird with a long, slender body. The European cuckoo lays its eggs in the nests of other birds. **2** the cry of a cuckoo, which sounds a little like its name. —*pl.* **cuck′oos** ◆***adj.*** crazy or silly: *slang in this meaning.*

**cu·cum·ber** (kyo͞o′kum bər) ***n.*** **1** a long vegetable with green skin and firm, white flesh. It is used in salads and made into pickles. *See the picture.* **2** the vine that it grows on. —**cool as a cucumber,** calm; not excited.

**cud** (kud) ***n.*** a mouthful of swallowed food that cattle, sheep, goats, etc. bring back up from the first stomach to chew again slowly a second time.

**cud·dle** (kud′'l) ***v.*** **1** to hold lovingly and gently in one's arms [to *cuddle* a baby]. **2** to lie close and snug; nestle [to *cuddle* up in bed]. —**cud′dled, cud′dling**

**cudg·el** (kuj′əl) ***n.*** a short, thick stick or club. ◆***v.*** to beat with such a club. —**cudg′eled** or **cudg′elled, cudg′el·ing** or **cudg′el·ling** —**cudgel one's brains,** to think hard.

**cue**[1] (kyo͞o) ***n.*** **1** the last few words in an actor's speech that are a signal to another actor to enter or to speak. **2** a few notes of music that are a signal to another musician or to a singer to begin. **3** any signal, hint, or suggestion [If you are not sure which fork to use, take a *cue* from your hostess.] ◆***v.*** to give a cue to. —**cued, cu′ing** or **cue′ing**

> **Cue** comes from the letter *Q* or *q* used in printed play scripts of the 16th and 17th centuries to mark when an actor was supposed to come onto the stage. It is probably an abbreviation for some Latin word, perhaps *quando,* meaning "when."

**cue**[2] (kyo͞o) ***n.*** **1** a long stick used in pool and billiards to strike the ball. **2** *same as* **queue.**

**cuff**[1] (kuf) ***n.*** **1** a band at the wrist of a sleeve, either fastened to the sleeve or separate. **2** a fold turned up at the bottom of a trouser leg. **3** a handcuff.

**cuff**[2] (kuf) ***v.*** to hit with the open hand; slap. ◆***n.*** a slap.

**cuff link** a pair of linked buttons or the like for keeping a shirt cuff closed.

**cui·sine** (kwi zēn′) ***n.*** **1** style of cooking [a Swedish cuisine]. **2** the food prepared, as at a restaurant.

**cu·li·nar·y** (kyo͞o′lə ner′ē) ***adj.*** having to do with cooking or cookery.

**cull** (kul) ***v.*** **1** to pick out; select and gather. **2** to look over in order to choose those wanted [to *cull* a cornfield for ripe ears]. ◆***n.*** a thing taken out as not being good enough.

**cul·mi·nate** (kul′mə nāt) ***v.*** to reach its highest point [My career *culminated* in being elected mayor.] —**cul′mi·nat·ed, cul′mi·nat·ing** —**cul′mi·na′tion** ***n.***

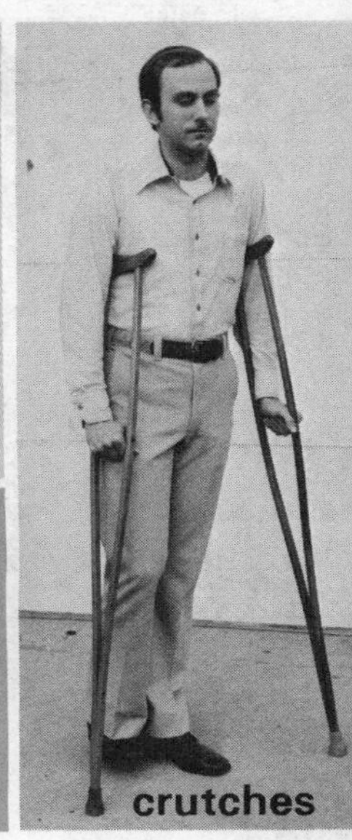


**cul·pa·ble** (kul′pə b'l) ***adj.*** deserving blame; guilty. —**cul′pa·bil′i·ty** ***n.*** —**cul′pa·bly** ***adv.***

**cul·prit** (kul′prit) ***n.*** **1** a person who is guilty of a crime or wrongdoing. **2** a person accused of a crime in court.

**cult** (kult) ***n.*** **1** a way of worshiping; system of religious rites [a *cult* of snake worshipers]. **2** a fashion or belief that a number of people are enthusiastic about [the *cult* of sun bathing].



**cul·ti·vate** (kul′tə vāt) ***v.*** **1** to prepare and use land for growing crops; till. **2** to grow plants or crops. **3** to break up the soil around plants in order to kill weeds and help the plants grow. **4** to help to grow by care, training, or study [*Cultivate* your mind.] **5** to try to become friendly with, as in order to get or learn something [to *cultivate* a person]. —**cul′ti·vat·ed, cul′ti·vat·ing**

**cul·ti·va·tion** (kul′tə vā′shən) ***n.*** **1** the cultivating of land or plants. **2** the improving of something through care, training, or study. **3** the result of improving one's mind, tastes, and manners; culture; refinement.

**cul·ti·va·tor** (kul′tə vāt′ər) ***n.*** **1** a person who cultivates. **2** a tool or machine for loosening the earth and killing weeds around plants.

**cul·ture** (kul′chər) ***n.*** **1** the cultivation of soil. **2** the raising or improving of some plant, animal, etc. [bee *culture*]. **3** a growth of bacteria specially made, as for medical research. **4** improvement by study or training, especially of the mind, manners, and taste; refinement. **5** the ideas, skills, arts, tools, and way of life of a certain people in a certain time; civilization [the *culture* of the Aztecs]. —**cul′tur·al** ***adj.*** —**cul′tur·al·ly** ***adv.***

| | | | |
|---|---|---|---|
| **a** fat | **ir** here | **ou** out | **zh** leisure |
| **ā** ape | **ī** bite, fire | **u** up | **ng** ring |
| **ä** car, lot | **ō** go | **ur** fur | a *in* ago |
| **e** ten | **ô** law, horn | **ch** chin | e *in* agent |
| **er** care | **oi** oil | **sh** she | **ə** = i *in* unity |
| **ē** even | **o͝o** look | **th** thin | o *in* collect |
| **i** hit | **o͞o** tool | ***th*** then | u *in* focus |

48 cm (19 in.) long, including bill

**cul·tured** (kul′chərd) ***adj.*** **1** produced by cultivation. **2** having culture or refinement.



**cultured pearl** a pearl grown inside a mollusk, as by putting inside it a bead of mother-of-pearl around which the pearl will form.

**cul·vert** (kul′vərt) ***n.*** a drain or waterway passing under a road, railroad track, etc. *See the picture.*

**cum·ber** (kum′bər) ***v.*** to hinder, burden, or trouble; encumber.

**cum·ber·some** (kum′bər səm) ***adj.*** hard to handle or deal with, as because of size, weight, or many parts; clumsy; unwieldy.

**cu·mu·la·tive** (kyōōm′yə lāt′iv) ***adj.*** growing stronger, larger, etc. by being added to [The evidence against the thief has been *cumulative.*]

**cu·mu·lus** (kyōōm′yə ləs) ***n.*** a kind of cloud in which round masses are piled up on each other.

**cu·ne·i·form** (kyōō nē′ə fôrm) ***adj.*** shaped like a wedge; especially, describing the characters used in the writings of ancient Assyria, Persia, etc. ◆***n.*** cuneiform characters. *See the picture.*

**cun·ning** (kun′iŋ) ***adj.*** **1** skillful in cheating or tricking; crafty; sly. ☆**2** pretty in a sweet or delicate way [a *cunning* child]. ◆***n.*** skill in cheating or tricking. —**cun′ning·ly** ***adv.***

**cup** (kup) ***n.*** **1** a small container for drinking from, in the shape of a bowl and often with a handle. **2** as much as a cup will hold; cupful [I drank two *cups* of tea.] **3** anything shaped like a cup, as a silver bowl given as a prize. **4** one's share [a full *cup* of happiness]. **5** the hole on a golf green into which the ball is hit. ◆***v.*** to shape like a cup [*Cup* your hands.] —**cupped, cup′ping**

**cup·bear·er** (kup′ber′ər) ***n.*** a person who served cups of wine at banquets in ancient times.

**cup·board** (kub′ərd) ***n.*** a closet or cabinet with shelves for holding dishes, food, etc.

☆**cup·cake** (kup′kāk) ***n.*** a small cake, sometimes baked in a paper cup.

**cup·ful** (kup′fool) ***n.*** as much as a cup will hold. A standard measuring cup holds eight ounces. —*pl.* **cup′fuls**

**Cu·pid** (kyōō′pid) the Roman god of love. He is usually pictured as a small boy with wings who carries a bow and arrow.

**cu·pid·i·ty** (kyōō pid′ə tē) ***n.*** strong desire, especially for wealth; greed.

**cu·po·la** (kyōō′pə lə) ***n.*** **1** a rounded roof or ceiling. **2** a small dome on a roof. *See the picture.*

**cur** (kur) ***n.*** **1** a dog of mixed breed; mongrel. **2** a mean, cowardly person.

**cur·a·ble** (kyoor′ə b′l) ***adj.*** that can be cured.

**cu·rate** (kyoor′it) ***n.*** a clergyman who helps a vicar or rector.

**cur·a·tive** (kyoor′ə tiv) ***adj.*** curing or helping to cure. ◆***n.*** a thing that cures; remedy.

**cu·ra·tor** (kyoo rāt′ər *or* kyoor′āt ər) ***n.*** a person in charge of a museum, library, etc.

**curb** (kurb) ***n.*** **1** a chain or strap passed around a horse's jaw and attached to the bit. It holds back the horse when the reins are pulled. **2** anything that checks or holds back [Fear of punishment is often a *curb* to wrongdoing.] **3** the stone or concrete edging along a street. ◆***v.*** to hold back; keep in check [to *curb* one's appetite].

**curd** (kurd) ***n.*** *often* **curds,** *pl.* the thick, clotted part of soured milk, used for making cheese.

**cur·dle** (kur′d′l) ***v.*** to form into curd or clots. —**cur′dled, cur′dling** —**curdle one's blood,** to frighten very much.

**cure** (kyoor) ***n.*** **1** anything that makes a sick person well; remedy [Penicillin is a *cure* for pneumonia.] **2** a healing or being healed. **3** a way of making well or healing [There is no *cure* for my sadness.] ◆***v.*** **1** to make well; heal [to *cure* a sick person or a disease]. **2** to stop or get rid of something bad [Low grades *cured* me of neglecting my homework.] **3** to keep meat, fish, etc. from spoiling, as by salting or smoking. —**cured, cur′ing**

**cu·ré** (kyoo rā′) ***n.*** a parish priest: *a French word.*

**cure-all** (kyoor′ôl′) ***n.*** ☆something supposed to cure all illness or all bad conditions.

**cur·few** (kur′fyōō) ***n.*** a time in the evening beyond which certain persons or all people must not be on the streets [Our town has a nine o'clock *curfew* for children.]

> **Curfew** comes from an old French word meaning "to cover a fire." In the Middle Ages, a "curfew" was a time for ringing a bell that told people to cover their fires, put out their lights, and go to bed.

**Cu·rie** (kyoo rē′), **Marie,** 1867–1934; Polish scientist in France. She and her husband discovered radium.

**Cu·rie** (kyoo rē′), **Pierre,** 1859–1906; French scientist. Pierre was the husband of Marie.

**cu·ri·o** (kyoor′ē ō′) ***n.*** any unusual or rare article [We brought back painted scrolls and other *curios* from Japan.] —*pl.* **cu′ri·os**

**cu·ri·os·i·ty** (kyoor′ē äs′ə tē) ***n.*** **1** a strong feeling of wanting to know or learn [*Curiosity* is a child's best teacher.] **2** such a feeling about something that is not one's business [Control your *curiosity;* don't ask how much they paid for it.] **3** a strange or unusual thing

[A fire engine pulled by horses is now a *curiosity*.] —*pl.* **cu′ri·os′i·ties**

**cu·ri·ous** (kyoor′ē əs) ***adj.*** **1** wanting very much to learn or know [a *curious* student.] **2** wanting to know something that is not one's business [I'm *curious* to know how much money the doctor makes.] **3** strange or unusual [*curious* spellings on an old map]. —**cu′ri·ous·ly *adv.***

**curl** (kurl) ***v.*** **1** to twist into ringlets or coils [to *curl* hair]. **2** to move in circles or rings [The fog *curled* around our feet.] **3** to curve or bend around; roll up [Heat *curled* the pages of the book. I *curled* up on the sofa.] ◆***n.*** **1** a little coil of hair. **2** anything curled or curved [a *curl* of smoke from the chimney].

**cur·lew** (kur′lo͞o) ***n.*** a large brownish bird with long legs that lives on the shore. *See the picture.*

**curl·i·cue** (kur′li kyo͞o) ***n.*** a fancy curve or twist, as in a design or in handwriting.

**curl·y** (kur′lē) ***adj.*** **1** curled or curling [long, *curly* wood shavings]. **2** full of curls [*curly* hair]. —**curl′i·er, curl′i·est** —**curl′i·ness *n.***

**cur·rant** (kur′ənt) ***n.*** **1** a small, sweet, black raisin, used in cooking. **2** a small, sour berry used in jams and jellies; also, the bush it grows on.

**Currant** comes from a French phrase meaning "raisins from Corinth." Raisins were first brought into England from Corinth in the Middle Ages.

**cur·ren·cy** (kur′ən sē) ***n.*** ☆**1** the money in common use in any country; often, paper money. **2** general use; popularity [Slang words usually lose *currency* quickly.] —*pl.* **cur′ren·cies**

**cur·rent** (kur′ənt) ***adj.*** **1** of the present time; now going on; most recent [the *current* decade; *current* events]. **2** commonly known, used, or accepted [*current* gossip; a belief *current* in earlier times]. ◆***n.*** **1** a flow of water or air in a definite direction; stream. **2** the flow of electricity in a wire or other conductor. **3** the general movement or drift, as of opinion. —**cur′rent·ly *adv.***

**cur·ric·u·lum** (kə rik′yə ləm) ***n.*** the course or plan of study in a school [Is French in the *curriculum* at your school?] —*pl.* **cur·ric·u·la** (kə rik′yoo lə) or **cur·ric′u·lums**

**cur·ry**[1] (kur′ē) ***v.*** to rub down and clean an animal's coat with a currycomb or brush. —**cur′ried, cur′ry·ing** —**curry favor,** to try to win favor from someone by flattery.

**cur·ry**[2] (kur′ē) ***n.*** **1** a spicy powder or sauce made with many herbs and seasonings. **2** food flavored with this. —*pl.* **cur′ries**

**cur·ry·comb** (kur′ē kōm) ***n.*** a comb with rows of teeth or ridges, to curry a horse. *See the picture.*

**curse** (kurs) ***n.*** **1** a calling on God or the gods to bring evil on some person or thing. *See* SYNONYMS *at* **blasphemy. 2** a word or words used in swearing at someone. **3** a cause of evil or trouble; misfortune [Is atomic power a blessing or a *curse?*] ◆***v.*** **1** to call on God or the gods to harm or punish; damn. **2** to swear at; use bad or profane language. **3** to bring evil or trouble on; afflict [*cursed* with illness]. —**cursed, curs′ing**

**curs·ed** (kur′sid *or* kurst) ***adj.*** **1** under a curse. **2** deserving to be cursed; evil; hateful [this *cursed* cold].

**cur·sive** (kur′siv) ***adj.*** written with the strokes of the letters joined in each word.

**cur·so·ry** (kur′sər ē) ***adj.*** done in a hurry and without attention to details; superficial [The teacher gave the book a *cursory* reading.] —**cur′so·ri·ly *adv.***

**curt** (kurt) ***adj.*** so short or abrupt as to seem rude; brusque [a *curt* dismissal; a *curt* reply]. —**curt′ly *adv.*** —**curt′ness *n.***

**cur·tail** (kər tāl′) ***v.*** to cut short; reduce [to *curtail* expenses]. —**cur·tail′ment *n.***

**cur·tain** (kur′t′n) ***n.*** **1** a piece of cloth or other material hung at a window, in front of a stage, etc. to decorate or to cover, hide, or shut off. **2** anything that hides, covers, or shuts off [a *curtain* of fog]. ◆***v.*** to furnish or hide as with a curtain [Her life was *curtained* in secrecy.]

**curt·sy** or **curt·sey** (kurt′sē) ***n.*** a bow of greeting or respect that women and girls make by bending the knees and lowering the body a little. It is not often done today. *See the picture.* —*pl.* **curt′sies** or **curt′seys** ◆***v.*** to make a curtsy. —**curt′sied** or **curt′seyed, curt′sy·ing** or **curt′sey·ing**

**cur·va·ture** (kur′və chər) ***n.*** a curving or a curve [*curvature* of the spine].

**curve** (kurv) ***n.*** **1** a line that has no straight part; bend with no angles [A circle is a continuous *curve.* Their house is on a *curve* in the road.] *See* SYNONYMS *at* **bend.** ☆**2** a baseball pitched with a spin so that it curves to one side before crossing the plate. ◆***v.*** **1** to turn or bend so as to form a curve [The trail *curves* to the left.] **2** to move in a curved path [The next pitch *curved* in to the batter.] —**curved, curv′ing**

**cush·ion** (koosh′ən) ***n.*** **1** a pillow or soft pad for sitting on or leaning against [the *cushions* of a sofa]. **2** something soft or springy like a cushion, as the rim of a billiard table, where the ball hits. **3** anything that makes pain, worry, etc. less or provides comfort. ◆***v.*** **1** to furnish with a cushion [a *cushioned* seat]. **2** to protect from shock by means of a cushion [Grass *cushioned* my fall.]

**cush·y** (koosh′ē) ***adj.*** easy; comfortable: *a slang word* [a *cushy* job]. —**cush′i·er, cush′i·est**

**cusp** (kusp) ***n.*** any of the high points on the chewing part of a tooth.

**cus·pid** (kus′pid) ***n.*** a tooth with one cusp; canine tooth.

☆**cus·pi·dor** (kus′pə dôr) ***n.*** a container to spit into; spittoon.

**cuss** (kus) ***n., v.*** *same as* **curse:** *used only in everyday talk.*

**cuss·ed** (kus′id) ***adj.*** **1** cursed. **2** stubborn. *This word is used only in everyday talk.*

**cus·tard** (kus′tərd) ***n.*** **1** a soft food made of eggs, milk, and sugar, either boiled or baked. **2** a similar mixture frozen like ice cream: *the full name is* **frozen custard.**

**Cus·ter** (kus′tər), **George Armstrong** 1839–1876;

| | | | |
|---|---|---|---|
| **a** fat | **ir** here | **ou** out | **zh** leisure |
| **ā** ape | **ī** bite, fire | **u** up | **ng** ring |
| **ä** car, lot | **ō** go | **ur** fur | a *in* ago |
| **e** ten | **ô** law, horn | **ch** chin | e *in* agent |
| **er** care | **oi** oil | **sh** she | ə = i *in* unity |
| **ē** even | **oo** look | **th** thin | o *in* collect |
| **i** hit | **o͞o** tool | ***th*** then | u *in* focus |

U.S. army officer. He was killed in a battle with the Sioux Indians.

**cus·to·di·an** (kəs tō′dē ən) ***n.*** **1** a person who is the keeper or guardian of something [the *custodian* of a private library]. **2** a person whose work is to take care of a building; janitor.

**cus·to·dy** (kus′tə dē) ***n.*** a guarding or keeping safe; care [The tax records are in the *custody* of the county auditor.] —**in custody,** in the keeping of the police; in jail or prison. —**take into custody,** to arrest.

**cus·tom** (kus′təm) ***n.*** **1** a usual thing to do; habit [It is my *custom* to have tea after dinner.] **2** something that has been done for a long time and so has become the common or regular thing to do [the *custom* of eating turkey on Thanksgiving]. **3 customs,** *pl.* taxes collected by a government on goods brought in from other countries; also, the government agency that collects these taxes. **4** the support given to a business by buying regularly from it [That baker has had our family's *custom* for many years.] ***•adj.*** **1** made or done to order [*custom* shoes]. **2** making things to order [a *custom* tailor].

SYNONYMS: **Custom** is used in talking about any way of doing something that has become accepted among a group of people [The *custom* of shaking hands began in ancient times.] **Habit** is used to suggest something done so often by a person that it is done without thinking about it [He has a *habit* of tugging at his ear when he is nervous.] **Practice** also suggests that something is done often but done in a conscious, deliberate way [It is her *practice* to read in bed.]



**cus·tom·ar·y** (kus′tə mer′ē) ***adj.*** in keeping with custom; usual [It is *customary* to tip a waiter or waitress.] *See* SYNONYMS *at* **usual.** —**cus′tom·ar′i·ly** ***adv.***

**cus·tom·er** (kus′tə mər) ***n.*** **1** a person who buys, especially one who buys regularly [I have been a *customer* of that shop for many years.] **2** any person with whom one has dealings: *used only in everyday talk* [a rough *customer*].

**cus·tom·house** (kus′təm hous) ***n.*** a building or office where customs are paid to the government: *also written* **cus′toms·house.**

☆**cus·tom·ize** (kus′təm īz) ***v.*** to make or build according to the orders of a particular person. —**cus′tom·ized, cus′tom·iz·ing**

☆**cus·tom-made** (kus′təm mād′) ***adj.*** made especially for a certain customer; made to order.

**cut** (kut) ***v.*** **1** to make an opening in with a knife or other sharp tool; pierce; gash [Andy *cut* his chin while shaving.] **2** to divide into parts with such a tool; sever [Will you *cut* the cake?] **3** to make by cutting [They *cut* a path through the underbrush.] **4** to make shorter by trimming [to *cut* one's hair]. **5** to make less; reduce; decrease [Prices were *cut*.] **6** to hurt as if with sharp strokes [*Cut* by the cold wind.] **7** to take cutting [This wood *cuts* easily.] **8** to go through or across, usually to make a shorter way [The path *cuts* across the meadow. The tunnel *cuts* through the mountain.] **9** to grow a new tooth that makes its way through the gum. **10** to hit a ball so that it spins or glances off. ☆**11** to make a recording on a phonograph record. **12** to pretend not to know a person; snub: *used only in everyday talk.* **13** to stay away from a school class without being excused: *used only in everyday talk.* —**cut, cut′ting** ***•n.*** **1** a cutting or being cut. **2** a stroke or blow that is sharp or cutting. **3** an opening made by a knife or other sharp tool. **4** a piece cut off [a *cut* of beef]. ☆**5** a making less; reduction [a *cut* in pay]. **6** the shortest way across: *usually* **short cut.** **7** the style in which a thing is cut; fashion [the *cut* of a suit]. **8** something said or done that hurts one's feelings. **9** a block or plate engraved for printing; also, a picture, etc. made from this. ☆**10** the fact of being away from school without being excused: *used only in everyday talk.* ☆**11** a share, as of profits: *slang in this meaning.* —**cut and dried,** planned ahead of time. —**cut back,** to make shorter as by cutting off the end. —**cut down, 1** to cause to fall by cutting. **2** to make less; reduce. —**cut in, 1** to move in suddenly [A car *cut in* ahead of ours.] **2** to break in on; interrupt. —**cut off, 1** to separate from other parts by cutting. **2** to stop suddenly; shut off. —**cut out, 1** to remove by cutting. **2** to remove; leave out; omit. **3** to make by cutting. ☆**4** to stop; discontinue: *used only in everyday talk.* —**cut out for,** suited for. —**cut short,** to stop suddenly before the end. —**cut up, 1** to cut into pieces. ☆**2** to joke; clown: *slang in this meaning.*

**cut·back** (kut′bak) ***n.*** a reduction or decrease in the amount of goods produced, the number of employees, etc.

☆**cute** (kyo͞ot) ***adj.*** **1** clever or shrewd [a *cute* trick]. **2** pretty or pleasing, especially in a dainty way. *This word is used only in everyday talk.* —**cut′er, cut′est** —**cute′ly** ***adv.*** —**cute′ness** ***n.***

**cut·i·cle** (kyo͞ot′i k′l) ***n.*** **1** the outer layer of the skin. **2** hardened skin, as at the base and sides of a fingernail.

**cut·lass** or **cut·las** (kut′ləs) ***n.*** a short, curved sword with a sharp edge on one side. *See the picture.*

**cut·ler** (kut′lər) ***n.*** a person who makes, sells, or repairs knives or other cutting tools.

**cut·ler·y** (kut′lər ē) ***n.*** **1** cutting tools such as knives and scissors. **2** such things used in preparing and eating food.

**cut·let** (kut′lit) ***n.*** a small slice of meat from the ribs or leg, for frying or broiling.

**cut·off** (kut′ôf) ***n.*** **1** a road that is a short cut. **2** a valve or other part that shuts off a flow of steam, water, etc.

☆**cut-rate** (kut′rāt′) ***adj.*** selling or on sale at a lower price [*cut-rate* drugs].

**cut·ter** (kut′ər) ***n.*** **1** a person or thing that cuts, as a person who cuts cloth into the sections that form a garment. **2** a small, swift boat or ship, as an armed ship used by the coast guard. ☆**3** a small, light sleigh, usually pulled by one horse.

**cut·throat** (kut′thrōt) ***n.*** a murderer. ***•adj.*** without mercy; ruthless [*cutthroat* competition].

**cut·ting** (kut′ing) ***n.*** **1** the act of one that cuts. **2** a piece cut off, as a shoot cut from a plant for starting a new plant. ***•adj.*** **1** that cuts; sharp [a *cutting* edge]. **2** chilling or piercing [a *cutting* wind]. **3** hurting the feelings [a *cutting* remark].

**cut·tle·bone** (kut′'l bōn) ***n.*** the hard inside shell of the cuttlefish. It is used as a bird food.

**cut·tle·fish** (kut′'l fish) ***n.*** a sea animal with ten arms and a hard inside shell. Some cuttlefishes squirt out a black fluid when in danger. *See the picture.*

**cut·worm** (kut′wurm) ***n.*** a caterpillar that feeds on young plants, as cabbage or corn, which it cuts off near the ground.

**Cuz·co** (ko͞os′kō) a city in southern Peru. It was the capital of the Inca empire from the twelfth to sixteenth century.

**cwt.** *abbreviation for* **hundredweight.**

**-cy** (sē) *a suffix meaning:* **1** quality or condition of being [*Hesitancy* is the quality of being hesitant.] **2** position or rank of [*Captaincy* is the rank of captain.]

**cy·a·nide** (sī′ə nīd) ***n.*** any of certain highly poisonous compounds. They smell like bitter almonds.

☆**cy·ber·net·ics** (sī′bər net′iks) ***n.pl.*** the study of the way electronic computers work compared with the way the human nervous system works: *used with a singular verb.*

**cy·cla·men** (sī′klə mən *or* sik′lə mən) ***n.*** a plant with heart-shaped leaves and white, pink, or red flowers.

**cy·cle** (sī′k'l) ***n.*** **1** a complete set of events that keep coming back in the same order; also, the time it takes for one complete set to take place [the life *cycle* of a frog; the yearly *cycle* of the seasons]. **2** a bicycle, tricycle, or motorcycle. **3** a complete set of stories, songs, or poems about a certain hero or event. ✦***v.*** to ride a bicycle, motorcycle, etc. —**cy′cled, cy′cling**

**cy·clic** (sī′klik *or* sik′lik) ***adj.*** of or like a cycle; happening in cycles.

**cy·clist** (sī′klist) ***n.*** a person who rides a bicycle, tricycle, or motorcycle.

**cy·clone** (sī′klōn) ***n.*** a storm with very strong winds moving around a center of low pressure.

> **Cyclone** comes from a Greek word meaning "to circle around" or "to whirl." Cyclones have winds that move around a center in either a clockwise or counterclockwise direction.

**cy·clon·ic** (sī klän′ik) ***adj.*** of or like a cyclone.

**cy·clo·pe·di·a** or **cy·clo·pae·di·a** (sī′klə pē′dē ə) ***n.*** *same as* **encyclopedia.**

**Cy·clops** (sī′kläps) ***n.*** any of a race of giants in Greek myths, who had only one eye, in the middle of the forehead. —*pl.* **Cy·clo·pes** (sī klō′pēz)

☆**cy·clo·tron** (sī′klə trän) ***n.*** a large device for giving such high speed to atomic particles that they will break into other atoms and cause changes in the nuclei.

**cyg·net** (sig′nət) ***n.*** a young swan.

**cyl·in·der** (sil′ən dər) ***n.*** **1** a round figure with two flat ends that are parallel circles. *See the picture.* **2** anything shaped like this, as the part of a revolver that holds the cartridges, or the chamber in which a piston of an engine moves up and down.

**cy·lin·dri·cal** (sə lin′dri k'l) ***adj.*** having the shape of a cylinder.

**cym·bal** (sim′b'l) ***n.*** a round brass plate, used in orchestras and bands, that makes a sharp, ringing sound when it is hit. Cymbals can be used in pairs that are struck together. *See the picture.*

**cyn·ic** (sin′ik) ***n.*** a person who is cynical.

**cyn·i·cal** (sin′i k'l) ***adj.*** **1** doubting that people are ever sincere, honest, or good. **2** gloomy and bitter about life; sarcastic, sneering, etc. —**cyn′i·cal·ly** ***adv.***

**cyn·i·cism** (sin′ə siz'm) ***n.*** **1** the feelings or beliefs of a cynical person. **2** a cynical idea or remark.

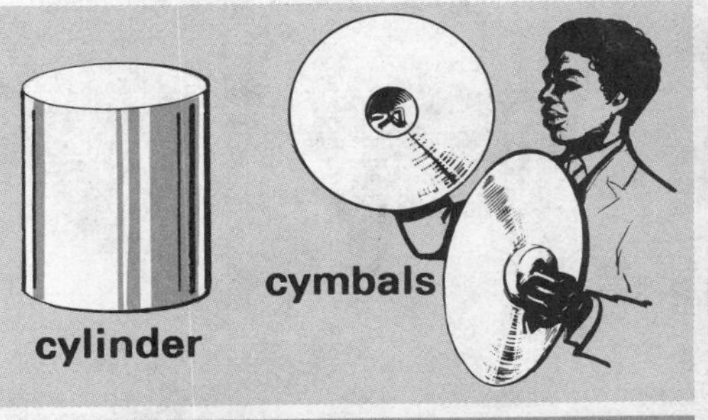


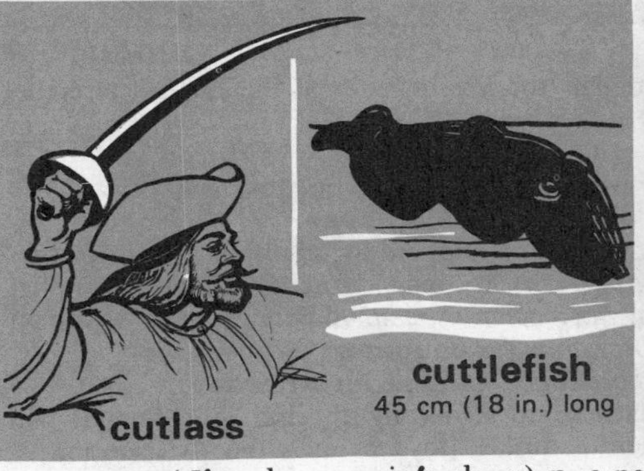

**cy·no·sure** (sī′nə sho͝or *or* sin′ə sho͝or) ***n.*** a person or thing that is a center of attention [The winner of the beauty contest was the *cynosure* of all eyes.]



**cy·press** (sī′prəs) ***n.*** **1** an evergreen tree with cones and dark leaves. *See the picture.* **2** the hard wood of this tree.

**Cy·prus** (sī′prəs) a country on an island in the Mediterranean, south of Turkey. —**Cyp·ri·ot** (sip′rē ət) ***adj., n.***

**Cy·rus** (sī′rəs) ?–529 B.C.; king of Persia and founder of the Persian Empire.

**cyst** (sist) ***n.*** a small bag or pouch growing in some part of the body, especially one filled with fluid or hard matter.

**C.Z.** *abbreviation for* **Canal Zone.**

**czar** (zär) ***n.*** the title of any of the former emperors of Russia.

**cza·ri·na** (zä rē′nə) ***n.*** the wife of a czar.

**Czech** (chek) ***n.*** **1** a person born or living in Czechoslovakia, especially a Slav of the western part. **2** the Slavic language of the Czechs. ✦***adj.*** of Czechoslovakia or its people.

**Czech·o·slo·vak** (chek′ə slō′väk) ***adj.*** of Czechoslovakia or its people. ✦***n.*** a person born or living in Czechoslovakia.

**Czech·o·slo·va·ki·a** (chek′ə slō vä′kē ə) a country in central Europe

**Czech·o·slo·va·ki·an** (chek′ə slō vä′kē ən) ***adj., n.*** *same as* **Czechoslovak.**

| | | | |
|---|---|---|---|
| **a** fat | **ir** here | **ou** out | **zh** leisure |
| **ā** ape | **ī** bite, fire | **u** up | **ng** ring |
| **ä** car, lot | **ō** go | **ur** fur | a *in* ago |
| **e** ten | **ô** law, horn | **ch** chin | e *in* agent |
| **er** care | **oi** oil | **sh** she | **ə** = i *in* unity |
| **ē** even | **oo** look | **th** thin | o *in* collect |
| **i** hit | **o͞o** tool | ***th*** then | u *in* focus |

**D, d** (dē) ***n.*** the fourth letter of the English alphabet. *—pl.* **D's, d's** (dēz)

**D** (dē) ***n.*** the Roman numeral for 500.

**d.** *abbreviation for* **date, daughter, day, dead, degree, diameter, dollar, dose.**

**d.** was used in England as an abbreviation for the old **penny** or **pence.** It actually stands for the Latin word *denarius,* a small coin of ancient Rome.

**da.** *abbreviation for* **daughter, day** *or* **days.**

**D.A.** *abbreviation for* **District Attorney.**

**dab** (dab) ***v.*** to stroke lightly and quickly; pat with soft, gentle strokes [to *dab* one's face with lotion; to *dab* paint on a surface]. **—dabbed, dab′bing ◆*n.*** **1** a light, quick stroke; tap; pat. **2** a small bit of something soft or moist [a *dab* of butter].



**dab·ble** (dab′'l) ***v.*** **1** to dip the hands lightly in and out of water, as in play. **2** to do something lightly or playfully, not in a serious or thorough way [We formed a little group that *dabbles* in music.] **—dab′bled, dab′bling —dab′bler *n.***

**Dac·ca** (dak′ə *or* däk′ə) the capital of Bangladesh.

**dace** (dās) ***n.*** a small fish related to the carp, found in fresh water. *—pl.* **dace** or **dac′es**

dam

**dachshund**

23 cm (9 in.) high at shoulder

**daffodil**

**damper**

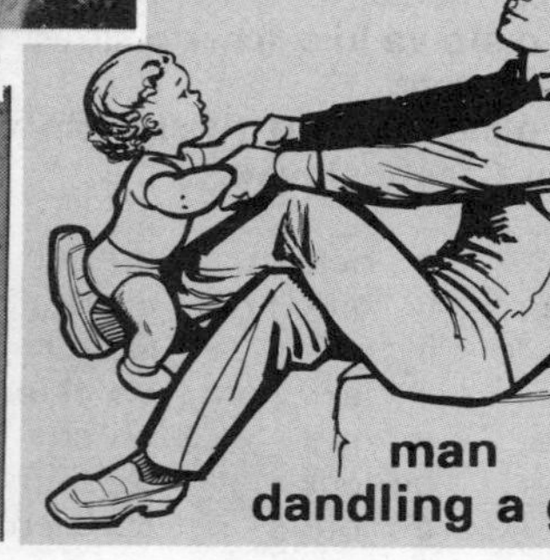

**man dandling a girl**

**dachs·hund** (däks′hoond *or* däks′hoont) ***n.*** a small dog with a long body and very short legs. *See the picture.*

☆**Da·cron** (dā′krän *or* dak′rän) *a trademark for* a synthetic fiber or a fabric made from this that is washable and does not wrinkle easily.

**dac·tyl·ic** (dak til′ik) ***adj.*** describing poetry made up of measures of three syllables each, with the accent on the first syllable ["Higgledy-piggledy" is a *dactylic* line.]

**dad** (dad) ***n.*** father: *used only in everyday talk.*

**dad·dy** (dad′ē) ***n.*** father: *mainly a child's word. —pl.* **dad′dies**

**dad·dy-long·legs** (dad′ē lông′legz) ***n.*** *another name for* **harvestman.** *—pl.* **dad′dy-long′legs**

**daf·fo·dil** (daf′ə dil) ***n.*** a plant that grows from a bulb and has long, narrow leaves and yellow flowers. *See the picture.*

**daf·fy** (daf′ē) ***adj.*** crazy; foolish; silly: *used only in everyday talk.* **—daf′fi·er, daf′fi·est —daf′fi·ness *n.***

**daft** (daft) ***adj.*** silly, foolish, crazy, etc.

**dag·ger** (dag′ər) ***n.*** **1** a weapon with a short, pointed blade, used for stabbing. **2** the mark †, used in printing to call attention, as to a footnote. **—look daggers at,** to look at in an angry way.

☆**da·guerre·o·type** (də ger′ə tīp) ***n.*** an old kind of photograph made on a chemically treated metal or glass plate.

**dahl·ia** (dal′yə) ***n.*** a tall plant having large, showy flowers in various bright colors.

**dai·ly** (dā′lē) ***adj.*** **1** done, happening, or published every day or every weekday. **2** calculated by the day [a *daily* rate]. **◆☆*n.*** a daily newspaper. *—pl.* **dai′lies ◆*adv.*** every day; day after day.

☆**daily dozen** a group of setting-up exercises (originally twelve) that one does every day: *used only in everyday talk.*

**dain·ty** (dān′tē) ***adj.*** **1** pretty or lovely in a delicate way [a *dainty* lace handkerchief]. *See* SYNONYMS *at* **delicate. 2** showing a delicate or fussy taste [a *dainty* appetite]. **3** delicious and choice [The dessert was a *dainty* dish.] **—dain′ti·er, dain′ti·est ◆*n.*** a food of the best kind; delicacy. *—pl.* **dain′ties — dain′ti·ly *adv.* —dain′ti·ness *n.***

**dair·y** (der′ē) ***n.*** **1** a building where milk and cream are kept and butter and cheese are made. **2** a farm (**dairy farm**) on which milk, butter, cheese, etc. are produced. **3** a store that sells milk, butter, cheese, etc. *—pl.* **dair′ies**

**dair·y·maid** (der′ē mād) ***n.*** a girl or woman who works in a dairy.

**dair·y·man** (der′ē mən) ***n.*** **1** a man who works in or for a dairy. **2** a man who owns or manages a dairy. *—pl.* **dair′y·men**

**da·is** (dā′is) ***n.*** a platform at one end of a room [The throne stood on a *dais.*] *—pl.* **da′is·es**

**dai·sy** (dā′zē) ***n.*** ☆**1** a common plant with flowers that have white or pink petals around a yellow center. **2** such a flower. *—pl.* **dai′sies**

**Daisy** comes from two words in Old English that mean "day's eye." In the evening, the petals of the daisy close around the yellow disk in the center. In the morning, the petals open up again. The daisy is the eye of the day, closed at night and open during the day.

**Da·kar** (dä kär′) seaport and capital of Senegal.
**Da·ko·ta** (də kō′tə) the U.S. territory from which North Dakota and South Dakota were formed.
**dale** (dāl) ***n.*** *another name for* **valley.**
**Da·li** (dä′lē), **Sal·va·dor** (sal′və dôr) 1904– ; Spanish painter, in the U.S. since 1940.
**Dal·las** (dal′əs) a city in northeastern Texas.
**dal·li·ance** (dal′ē əns) ***n.*** the act of dallying; flirting, toying, trifling, etc.
**dal·ly** (dal′ē) ***v.*** **1** to deal with in a light and playful way; toy; flirt; trifle [to *dally* with an idea]. **2** to waste time; loiter [Don't *dally* after the show.] —**dal′lied, dal′ly·ing**
**Dal·ma·tia** (dal mā′shə) a region of Yugoslavia along the Adriatic Sea.
**Dal·ma·tian** (dal mā′shən) ***n.*** a large dog with short hair and a black-and-white coat.
**dam**[1] (dam) ***n.*** a wall built to hold back flowing water, or the water held back in this way. *See the picture.* ◆***v.*** to hold back as by a dam; keep back the flow of [to *dam* a river; to *dam* up one's energy]. —**dammed, dam′ming**
**dam**[2] (dam) ***n.*** the female parent of a horse, cow, sheep, etc.
**dam·age** (dam′ij) ***n.*** **1** the hurting or breaking of a thing so as to make it of less value [The storm caused some *damage* to the barn.] **2 damages,** *pl.* money asked or paid to make up for harm or damage done [The victim of the accident sued for $10,000 in *damages.*] ◆***v.*** to do damage to [The frost *damaged* the crops.] *See* SYNONYMS *at* **injure.** —**dam′aged, dam′ag·ing**
**Da·mas·cus** (də mas′kəs) the capital of Syria. It is one of the oldest cities in the world.
**Damascus steel** a hard steel decorated with wavy lines, once used for making swords: *also called* **damask steel.**
**dam·ask** (dam′əsk) ***n.*** **1** a rich, shiny cloth, as of silk or linen, decorated with woven designs and used for tablecloths, furniture covering, etc. **2** a deep pink or rose color. **3** *same as* **Damascus steel.** ◆***adj.*** **1** of or like damask. **2** deep-pink or rose.
**dame** (dām) ***n.*** **1** a lady: *an old word, not much used now.* **2** a title of honor held by some British women. **3** any woman: *slang in this meaning.*
**damn** (dam) ***v.*** **1** to say strongly that something is very bad [All critics *damned* the play.] **2** to doom to endless punishment [Their own sins have *damned* them.] **3** to condemn to an unhappy fate [They seem *damned* to a life of poverty.] **4** to swear at by saying "damn"; curse. —**damned** (damd), **damn′ing** ◆***n.*** the saying of "damn" as a curse, or to show anger, etc. —**dam·na·tion** (dam nā′shən) ***n.***
**dam·na·ble** (dam′nə b′l) ***adj.*** deserving to be damned; very bad, hateful, outrageous, etc. [a *damnable* villain]. —**dam′na·bly *adv.***
**Dam·o·cles** (dam′ə klēz) a man in Greek legend who was given a lesson in the dangers of a ruler's life when the king seated him at a feast under a sword hanging by a single hair.
**damp** (damp) ***adj.*** slightly wet; moist [*damp* clothes; *damp* weather]. *See* SYNONYMS *at* **wet.** ◆***n.*** **1** a slight wetness; moisture [Rains caused *damp* in the basement.] **2** a harmful gas sometimes found in mines. ◆***v.*** **1** to make damp. **2** to check or partly smother [to *damp* a fire]. —**damp′ly *adv.*** —**damp′ness *n.***
**damp·en** (dam′pən) ***v.*** **1** to make or become slightly wet or moist [*Dampen* the curtains before ironing them.] **2** to make low or dull; deaden; check [Lou's cold reply *dampened* our enthusiasm.]
**damp·er** (dam′pər) ***n.*** **1** a plate in a flue, as of a furnace or stove, that can be turned to control the draft. *See the picture.* **2** anything that dulls or deadens.
**dam·sel** (dam′z′l) ***n.*** a girl or maiden: *now seldom used.*
**dam·son** (dam′z′n) ***n.*** **1** a small, purple plum. **2** the tree it grows on.
**Dan.** *abbreviation for* **Danish.**
**dance** (dans) ***v.*** **1** to move the body and feet in some kind of rhythm, usually to music [to *dance* a waltz or a minuet]. **2** to jump or bob up and down lightly or excitedly [waves *dancing* in the moonlight; children *dancing* with joy]. —**danced, danc′ing** ◆***n.*** **1** the act of dancing, or one round of dancing [May I have the next *dance* with you?] **2** the special steps of a particular kind of dancing [My favorite *dance* is the polka.] **3** a party for dancing. **4** a piece of music for dancing.
**danc·er** (dan′sər) ***n.*** a person who dances.
**dan·de·li·on** (dan′də lī′ən) ***n.*** a common weed with yellow flowers on long, hollow stems and jagged leaves that can be eaten.

> **Dandelion** comes from old French *dent de lion,* meaning "tooth of the lion." It is called this because the plant's jagged leaves have the outline of sharp teeth.



**dan·der** (dan′dər) ***n.*** **1** tiny particles, as from feathers, skin, or hair, that may cause allergies. ☆**2** anger or temper: *used only in everyday talk.* —**get one's dander up,** to make or become angry: *used only in everyday talk.*
**dan·dle** (dan′d′l) ***v.*** to dance a child up and down playfully, as on the knee. *See the picture.* —**dan′dled, dan′dling**
**dan·druff** (dan′drəf) ***n.*** small, light flakes of dead skin formed on the scalp.
**dan·dy** (dan′dē) ***n.*** **1** a man who is very fussy about his clothes and looks. **2** something that is very good: *used only in everyday talk.* —*pl.* **dan′dies** ◆***adj.*** ☆very good; fine: *used only in everyday talk.* —**dan′di·er, dan′di·est**
**Dane** (dān) ***n.*** a person born or living in Denmark.
**dan·ger** (dān′jər) ***n.*** **1** a condition in which there could be harm, trouble, loss, etc.; risk; peril [to live in constant *danger*]. **2** something that may cause harm [Jungle explorers face many *dangers.*]
**dan·ger·ous** (dān′jər əs) ***adj.*** full of danger; likely to cause injury, pain, etc.; unsafe [This shaky old bridge is *dangerous.*] —**dan′ger·ous·ly *adv.***

| | | | | | | | |
|---|---|---|---|---|---|---|---|
| **a** | fat | **ir** | here | **ou** | out | **zh** | leisure |
| **ā** | ape | **ī** | bite, fire | **u** | up | **ng** | ring |
| **ä** | car, lot | **ō** | go | **ur** | fur | | a *in* ago |
| **e** | ten | **ô** | law, horn | **ch** | chin | | e *in* agent |
| **er** | care | **oi** | oil | **sh** | she | **ə =** | i *in* unity |
| **ē** | even | **oo** | look | **th** | thin | | o *in* collect |
| **i** | hit | **ōō** | tool | ***th*** | then | | u *in* focus |

**dan·gle** (daŋ′g'l) ***v.*** **1** to hang loosely so as to swing back and forth [A long tail *dangled* from the kite.] *See the picture.* **2** to hold so that it dangles [The child *dangled* the doll by one arm.] —**dan′gled, dan′gling**

**Dan·iel** (dan′yəl) **1** a Hebrew prophet in the Bible who was saved from a den of lions by his faith in God. **2** a book of the Bible with his prophecies.

**Dan·ish** (dā′nish) ***adj.*** of Denmark or the Danes. ◆***n.*** **1** the language of the Danes. **2** a rich pastry of raised dough filled with fruit and iced: *the full name is* **Danish pastry** or **danish pastry.**

**dank** (daŋk) ***adj.*** unpleasantly damp; moist and chilly [a *dank* dungeon]. —**dank′ness *n.***

**Dan·te** (dän′tā *or* dan′tē) 1265–1321; Italian poet. He wrote *The Divine Comedy.* His full name is **Dante A·li·ghie·ri** (ä′li gyer′ē).

**Dan·ube** (dan′yo͞ob) a river in southern Europe, flowing from southwestern Germany eastward into the Black Sea. *See the map.*

**dap·per** (dap′ər) ***adj.*** **1** neat, trim, and dressed with care. **2** small and active [The *dapper* jockey mounted his horse.]

**dap·ple** (dap′'l) ***adj.*** marked with spots; mottled [a *dapple* horse]. ◆***v.*** to mark with spots or patches [Clumps of daisies *dappled* the meadow.] —**dap′pled, dap′pling**

**Dar·da·nelles** (där də nelz′) the strait joining the Aegean Sea and the Sea of Marmara.

186 **dare** (der) ***v.*** **1** to be brave or bold enough to do a certain thing [I wouldn't *dare* to oppose the officer.] **2** to face bravely or boldly; defy [The hunter *dared* the dangers of the jungle.] **3** to call on someone to do a certain thing in order to show courage; challenge [She *dared* me to swim across the lake.] —**dared, dar′ing** ◆***n.*** a challenge to prove that one is not afraid [I accepted her *dare* to swim across the lake.] —**dare say,** to think it very likely.

**dare·dev·il** (der′dev′'l) ***n.*** a bold, reckless person. ◆***adj.*** bold and reckless.

**Dar es Sa·laam** (där′es sə läm′) the capital of Tanzania.

**dar·ing** (der′iŋ) ***adj.*** bold enough to take risks; fearless. ◆***n.*** bold courage.

**Da·ri·us I** (də rī′əs) 550?–486? B.C.; king of Persia from 521 to 486 B.C.

**dark** (därk) ***adj.*** **1** having little or no light [a *dark* room; a *dark* night]. **2** closer to black than to white; deep in shade; not light [*dark* green]. **3** hidden; full of mystery [a *dark* secret]. **4** gloomy or hopeless [Things look *dark* for Lou.] **5** with little or no learning; ignorant [The Middle Ages are sometimes called the *Dark* Ages.] ◆***n.*** **1** a being dark; darkness, as of night [Are you afraid of the *dark?*] **2** a dark color or shade [the contrast of lights and *darks* in a picture]. —**in the dark,** not knowing or informed; ignorant [I'm *in the dark* about your plans.] —**dark′ly *adv.*** —**dark′ness *n.***

**dark·en** (där′kən) ***v.*** to make or become dark.

**dark horse** one who wins or may win a contest without being expected to: *used only in everyday talk.*

**dar·ling** (där′liŋ) ***n.*** a person whom one loves very much [People in love often call each other "*Darling.*"] ◆***adj.*** **1** very dear; beloved [Tracy is my *darling* child.] **2** attractive; cute: *used only in everyday talk* [That's a *darling* dress.]

**darn** (därn) ***v.*** to mend a hole or tear in cloth by sewing stitches back and forth over it ◆***n.*** a place that has been darned.

**dart** (därt) ***n.*** **1** a short arrow with a sharp point that is thrown as a weapon, or at a target in games. *See the picture.* **2** a sudden, quick move [The child made a *dart* into the street.] **3** a short, stitched fold to make a garment fit more closely. ◆***v.*** **1** to send out suddenly and fast [She *darted* a look at the pie.] **2** to move suddenly and fast [birds *darting* through the trees].

☆**Dar·von** (där′vän) *a trademark for* a drug used to lessen pain.

**Dar·win** (där′win), **Charles Robert** 1809–1882; English scientist and writer who is known for his theory of evolution.

**dash** (dash) ***v.*** **1** to throw so as to break; smash [He *dashed* the bottle to the floor.] **2** to hit roughly [The high wind *dashed* the boat on the rocks.] **3** to splash [We *dashed* some water in his face.] **4** to put an end to; destroy [Her hopes are *dashed.*] **5** to do or write something quickly [I'll *dash* off a note to Agnes.] **6** to move quickly; rush [The thief *dashed* down the alley.] ◆***n.*** **1** a heavy blow; smash [the *dash* of the waves on the beach]. **2** a little bit; pinch [Put a *dash* of salt in the salad.] ☆**3** a short, fast run or race [a 100-yard *dash*]. **4** energy or liveliness [Leslie always adds *dash* to a party.] **5** *a shorter form of* **dashboard. 6** the mark (—), used in printing or writing to show a break in a sentence, or to show that something has been left out. **7** a mark like this that stands for the long click used in forming letters in the Morse code.

**dash·board** (dash′bôrd) ***n.*** the panel in a motor vehicle, boat, etc. that has the controls and gauges on it.

☆**da·shi·ki** (dä shē′kē) ***n.*** a loose-fitting, usually brightly colored robe or tunic modeled after an African tribal garment.

**dash·ing** (dash′iŋ) ***adj.*** **1** full of dash or energy; lively [a *dashing* young artist]. **2** colorful or showy [a *dashing* costume].

**das·tard·ly** (das′tərd lē) ***adj.*** sneaky or mean, like a coward.

**da·ta** (dāt′ə *or* dat′ə) ***n.pl.*** facts or figures from which something can be learned: *used with either a singular or plural verb* [This *data* is listed in tables. These *data* are listed in tables.] —*sing.* **da′tum**

**data processing** the recording or handling of information by mechanical or electronic equipment.

**date**[1] (dāt) ***n.*** **1** the time at which a thing happens [The *date* of Lincoln's birth was February 12, 1809.] **2** the day of the month [What's the *date* today?] **3** the words or figures on a coin, letter, etc. that tell when it was made. ☆**4** an agreement to meet at a certain time, as between a couple going out together; also, the person with whom one goes out. ◆***v.*** **1** to mark with a date [The letter is *dated* May 15.] **2** to find out or give the date or age of [A tree can be *dated* by counting the rings in the trunk.] **3** to be dated; belong to a particular time [a painting that *dates* from an artist's earliest work]. ☆**4** to have a date with [Sarah is *dating* Joe tonight.] —**dat′ed, dat′ing** —**out of date,** no longer in use; old-fashioned. —**up to date,** keeping up with the latest ideas, facts, styles, etc.; modern. —**date′less *adj.***

**date²** (dāt) ***n.*** the sweet, fleshy fruit of a tall palm tree (**date palm**). The fruit has a long, hard seed. *See the picture.*

**da·tum** (dāt′əm *or* dat′əm) ***n.*** *singular of* **data.**

**daub** (dôb) ***v.*** **1** to cover or smear with sticky, soft stuff [She *daubed* salve on his burned finger.] **2** to paint in a sloppy way. ◆***n.*** **1** something daubed on [*daubs* of plaster]. **2** a poorly painted picture. —**daub′er *n.***

**daugh·ter** (dôt′ər) ***n.*** **1** a girl or woman as she is related to a parent or to both parents. **2** a girl or woman who is influenced by something in the way that a child is by a parent [a *daughter* of France].

**daugh·ter-in-law** (dôt′ər in lô′) ***n.*** the wife of one's son. —*pl.* **daugh′ters-in-law′**

**Dau·mier** (dō myā′), **Ho·no·ré** (ô nô rā′) 1809–1879; French painter and caricaturist.

**daunt** (dônt) ***v.*** to make afraid or discouraged [She was never *daunted* by misfortune.]

**daunt·less** (dônt′lis) ***adj.*** that cannot be frightened or discouraged; fearless [The *dauntless* rebels fought on.] —**daunt′less·ly *adv.***

**dau·phin** (dô′fin) ***n.*** in earlier times, the title of the oldest son of the king of France.

**dav·en·port** (dav′ən pôrt) ***n.*** ☆a large sofa.

**Da·vid** (dā′vid) the second king of Israel, whose story is told in the Bible.

**da Vin·ci** (də vin′chē), **Le·o·nar·do** (lē′ə när′dō) 1452–1519; Italian artist and scientist.

**Da·vis** (dā′vis), **Jefferson** 1808–1889; the president of the Confederacy from 1861 to 1865.

**dav·it** (dav′it) ***n.*** either of a pair of posts on a ship, which support a small boat and are used in lowering it into the water. *See the picture.*

**Da·vy Jones** (dā′vē jōnz′) the spirit of the sea: *a joking name used by sailors.*

> **Davy Jones' locker** is the bottom of the sea, thought of as the grave of those drowned or buried at sea.

**daw** (dô) ***n.*** *a shorter form of* **jackdaw.**

**daw·dle** (dôd′'l) ***v.*** to waste time by being slow; idle; loiter. —**daw′dled, daw′dling** —**daw′dler *n.***

**dawn** (dôn) ***v.*** **1** to begin to grow light as the sun rises [Day is *dawning.*] **2** to come into being; begin to develop [With the discovery of electricity, a new age *dawned.*] **3** to begin to be understood or felt [The meaning suddenly *dawned* on me.] ◆***n.*** **1** the beginning of day; daybreak. **2** the beginning of anything [the *dawn* of the Space Age].

**day** (dā) ***n.*** **1** the time of light between sunrise and sunset. **2** a period of 24 hours, measured from midnight to midnight. This is nearly equal to the time that it takes the earth to revolve once on its axis. **3** a period or time [the best writer of our *day*]. **4** time of power, glory, or success [I have had my *day.*] **5** the day's battle or contest [They won the *day.*] **6** the time one works each day [an eight-hour *day*]. **7 days,** *pl.* life or lifetime [You spend your *days* in study.] —**call it a day,** to stop working for the day: *used only in everyday talk.* —**day by day,** each day. —**day in, day out,** every day.

**day·break** (dā′brāk) ***n.*** the time in the morning when light begins to show; dawn.

**day-care** (dā′ker′) ***adj.*** of or describing a place where very young children, not yet in school, may be cared for and trained during the day while their parents are working. Such a place is often called a **day-care** 187
**center** or ☆**day nursery.**

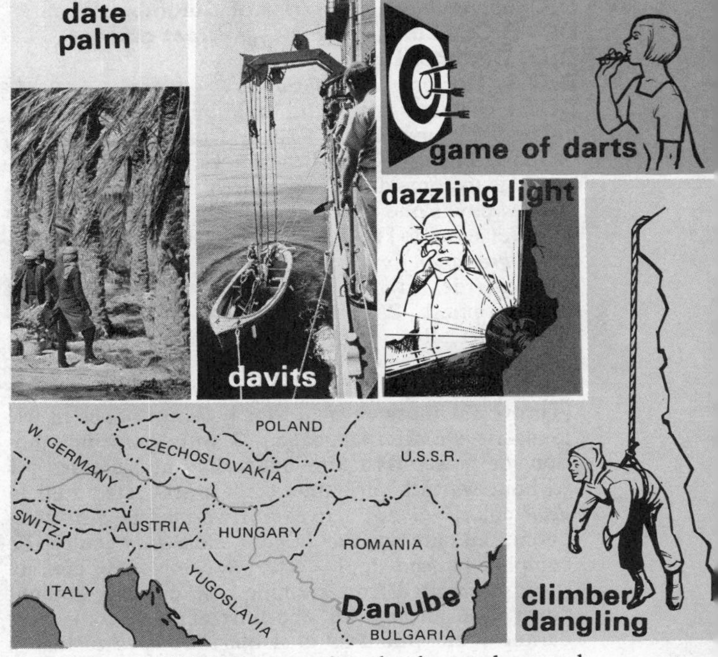

date palm

davits

game of darts

dazzling light

Danube

climber dangling

**day·dream** (dā′drēm) ***n.*** pleasant, dreamy thinking or wishing. ◆***v.*** to have daydreams.

**day laborer** an unskilled worker who is paid by the day.

**day·light** (dā′līt) ***n.*** **1** the light of day; sunlight. **2** dawn; daybreak. **3** daytime.

**day·light-sav·ing time** (dā′līt′sā′viŋ) time that is one hour later than standard time, generally used in the summer [9 p.m. *daylight-saving time* is 8 p.m. standard time].

**day·time** (dā′tīm) ***n.*** the time of daylight, between dawn and sunset.

**Day·ton** (dāt′'n) a city in southwestern Ohio.

**daze** (dāz) ***v.*** to stun or bewilder, as by a shock or blow [I was *dazed* by the news of the accident.] —**dazed, daz′ing** ◆***n.*** a dazed condition; bewilderment.

**daz·zle** (daz′'l) ***v.*** **1** to make nearly blinded, as with great brightness [I was *dazzled* by the headlights of approaching cars.] *See the picture.* **2** to be so brilliant or splendid as to overcome the mind or cause admiration [the *dazzling* skill of the pianist]. —**daz′zled, daz′zling** ◆***n.*** a dazzling, or a thing that dazzles.

**db** *abbreviation for* **decibel** *or* **decibels.**

**dbl.** *abbreviation for* **double.**

| | | | | | | | |
|---|---|---|---|---|---|---|---|
| **a** | fat | **ir** | here | **ou** | out | **zh** | leisure |
| **ā** | ape | **ī** | bite, fire | **u** | up | **ŋ** | ring |
| **ä** | car, lot | **ō** | go | **ʉr** | fur | | a *in* ago |
| **e** | ten | **ô** | law, horn | **ch** | chin | | e *in* agent |
| **er** | care | **oi** | oil | **sh** | she | **ə =** | i *in* unity |
| **ē** | even | **oo** | look | **th** | thin | | o *in* collect |
| **i** | hit | **ōō** | tool | ***th*** | then | | u *in* focus |

d

**D.C.** *abbreviation for* **District of Columbia.**

**DC, D.C., d.c.** *abbreviation for* **direct current.**

**D.D.** Doctor of Divinity.

**D.D.S.** Doctor of Dental Surgery.

**DDT** a chemical compound for killing insects.

**de-** *a prefix meaning:* **1** away from; off [A train is *derailed* when it goes off the tracks.] **2** down [To *descend* is to come down.] **3** entirely; completely [A *despoiled* city is one that is completely plundered.] **4** do in reverse; undo [To *defrost* food is to unfreeze it.]

**DE** *abbreviation for* **Delaware.**

**dea·con** (dēk′'n) ***n.*** **1** a clergyman who ranks just below a priest. **2** a church officer who helps the minister, especially in matters not having to do with worship.

**dead** (ded) ***adj.*** **1** no longer living; without life [Throw out those *dead* flowers.] **2** no longer in use [Sanskrit is a *dead* language.] **3** without feeling, motion, or power [His arm hung *dead* at his side.] **4** without warmth, brightness, sharpness, etc.; dull [a *dead* color]. **5** not active; not working [a *dead* telephone]. **6** sure or exact [a *dead* shot; *dead* center]. **7** complete [a *dead* stop]. ◆***adv.*** **1** completely; entirely [I am *dead* tired from running.] **2** directly; straight [Steer *dead* ahead.] ◆***n.*** the time of most cold, most darkness, etc. [the *dead* of winter; the *dead* of night]. —**the dead,** those who have died.

SYNONYMS: **Dead** is used of someone or something that was alive but is no longer so. **Deceased** is a legal term for one who has recently died [The property of the *deceased* is left to the church.] **Late** is used before the name of a person who is dead [the *late* Babe Ruth].



**dead·beat** (ded′bēt) ☆***n.*** **1** a person who tries to get out of paying for things that should be paid for. **2** a lazy, idle person.

**dead·en** (ded′'n) ***v.*** **1** to take away feeling; make numb [The dentist *deadens* the nerve before drilling a tooth.] **2** to dull or weaken [Heavy curtains will *deaden* street noises.]

**dead end** a street, alley, etc. closed at one end. —**dead′-end′** ***adj.***

**dead letter** a letter that is not claimed or delivered, as because of a wrong address.

**dead·line** (ded′līn) ***n.*** ☆the latest time by which something must be done or finished.

**dead·lock** (ded′läk) ***n.*** a halt in a struggle because both sides are equally strong and neither will give in [The Vice President's vote breaks the *deadlock* of a tie in Senate voting.] ◆***v.*** to bring or come to a deadlock.

**dead·ly** (ded′lē) ***adj.*** **1** causing death; that can kill [The cobra is a *deadly* snake.] **2** full of hate or violence [*deadly* combat; *deadly* enemies]. **3** as in death [a *deadly* paleness]. **4** very boring or dull. —**dead′li·er, dead′li·est** ◆***adv.*** **1** as if dead [He looks *deadly* pale.] **2** very; extremely [The principal was *deadly* serious.] —**dead′li·ness** ***n.***

**dead reckoning** a way of figuring the position of a ship by means of the compass and ship's log, rather than by the sun or stars.

**Dead Sea** a salt lake between Israel and Jordan.

**dead·wood** (ded′wood) ***n.*** ☆a person or thing that is useless or a burden.

**deaf** (def) ***adj.*** **1** not able to hear or not able to hear well. **2** not willing to hear; not paying attention [The president was *deaf* to our plea for money.] —**deaf′ness** ***n.***

**deaf·en** (def′'n) ***v.*** **1** to make deaf. **2** to make so much noise that it becomes hard to hear.

**deaf-mute** (def′myōōt′) ***n.*** a person who is deaf from birth and cannot talk because of never hearing the sounds of words. Most deaf-mutes can now be taught to talk.

**deal** (dēl) ***v.*** **1** to have to do with; handle, take care of, give attention to, etc. [Science *deals* with facts.] **2** to act or behave [The leader *dealt* fairly with me.] **3** to do business; trade [to *deal* with the corner grocer; to *deal* in rare books]. **4** to give; deliver [The officer *dealt* the thief a blow on the head.] **5** to pass out playing cards to the players. —**dealt, deal′ing** ◆***n.*** **1** an agreement, as in business; sale, contract, or bargain [They made a *deal* to rent the house. The senator made a *deal* to get extra votes.] ☆**2** any arrangement or plan [The New *Deal* was the government's plan to end the depression in the 1930's.] **3** the act of dealing playing cards, or the cards dealt. **4** an amount; quantity. —**a good deal** or **a great deal,** very much [I have *a good deal* of time. You must walk *a great deal* faster.]

**deal·er** (dēl′ər) ***n.*** **1** a person in business; one who buys and sells [a hardware *dealer*]. **2** the one who passes out the cards in a card game.

**deal·ing** (dēl′iŋ) ***n.*** *usually* **dealings,** *pl.* way of acting toward others; relations [In her *dealings* with friends, she is fair; in business *dealings,* she is dishonest.]

**dealt** (delt) *past tense and past participle of* **deal.**

**dean** (dēn) ***n.*** ☆**1** an official in a school or college who is in charge of the students or teachers. **2** a clergyman in charge of a cathedral. **3** the member of a group who has been in it the longest [the *dean* of American poets].

**dear** (dir) ***adj.*** **1** much loved; beloved [a *dear* friend]. **2** much valued; highly thought of: *used in letters to show politeness* [*Dear* Senator]. **3** costing much; high in price; expensive [Meat is too *dear* for us to buy much.] **4** earnest [our *dearest* wish]. ◆***adv.*** at a high cost [You'll pay *dear* for saying that.] ◆***n.*** a person whom one loves; darling [Her father said, "Let's go home, *dear*."] ◆***interj.*** a word said to show surprise, pity, etc. [Oh, *dear!* What shall I do?] —**dear′ly** ***adv.*** —**dear′ness** ***n.***

**dearth** (durth) ***n.*** a too small supply; scarcity [a *dearth* of good books].

**dear·y** or **dear·ie** (dir′ē) ***n.*** dear; darling: *used only in everyday talk, often in a humorous way.* —*pl.* **dear′ies**

**death** (deth) ***n.*** **1** the act or fact of dying; ending of life. **2** any end that is like dying [the *death* of our hopes]. **3** the condition of being dead [as still as *death*]. **4** the cause of death [Smallpox used to be *death* to thousands.] —**put to death,** to kill; execute. —**to death,** very much [He worried her *to death.*]

**death·bed** (deth′bed) ***n.*** the bed on which a person dies, or the last hours of one's life.

**death·less** (deth′lis) ***adj.*** that can never die; immortal [the poet's *deathless* words].

**death·like** (deth′līk) ***adj.*** like death or as in death [a *deathlike* calm].

**death·ly** (deth′lē) ***adj.*** **1** causing death; deadly [a *deathly* poison]. **2** like death or as in death [a *deathly* stillness]. ◆***adv.*** to a deadly degree; extremely [She is *deathly* ill.]

**death rate** the number of deaths among a certain number of people over a certain period of time; usually, the average number of deaths for every thousand people during a year.

**death's-head** (deths′hed′) ***n.*** a human skull as a symbol of death. *See the picture.*

☆**death·trap** (deth′trap) ***n.*** a building, automobile, etc. that is not safe.

**Death Valley** a dry, hot desert region in eastern California and southern Nevada. It is 282 ft. below sea level.

**de·ba·cle** (di bäk″l *or* dā bak″l) ***n.*** a sudden great disaster or upset [Napoleon's invasion of Russia was a *debacle* that ended in his defeat.]

**Debacle** comes from a French word that means "to break up." In English it was first used of "a breaking up of ice in a river," then of "a rush of flood water filled with debris." When ice breaks up in a river and causes a flood, it may bring a sudden great disaster to many people.

**de·bar** (dē bär′) ***v.*** to keep from some right or privilege [The newcomer was *debarred* from voting.] —**de·barred′, de·bar′ring**

**de·base** (di bās′) ***v.*** to make lower in value or character; cheapen [to *debase* oneself by lying; to *debase* money by raising the price of gold]. —**de·based′, de·bas′ing —de·base′ment *n.***

**de·bat·a·ble** (di bāt′ə b′l) ***adj.*** that can be debated; that has strong points on both sides [a *debatable* question].

**de·bate** (di bāt′) ***v.*** **1** to give reasons for or against; argue about something, especially in a formal contest between two opposite sides [The Senate *debated* the question of foreign treaties.] **2** to consider reasons for and against [I *debated* the problem in my own mind.] —**de·bat′ed, de·bat′ing** ◆***n.*** the act of debating something; discussion or formal argument. —**de·bat′er *n.***

SYNONYMS: A **debate** is a formal argument on a public question, often in the form of a contest with a team on each side [Our high school held a *debate* with Roosevelt High School on disarmament.] A **dispute** is an angry, heated argument between people who disagree on some matter [The neighbors had a *dispute* over the boundary line.]

**de·bauch** (di bôch′) ***v.*** to lead into bad or evil ways; lead astray; corrupt.

**de·bauch·er·y** (di bôch′ər ē) ***n.*** the satisfying of one's desires and appetites in a bad or wild way; dissipation. —*pl.* **de·bauch′er·ies**

**de·bil·i·tate** (di bil′ə tāt) ***v.*** to weaken [Too much bed rest after surgery can be *debilitating* to the body.] —**de·bil′i·tat·ed, de·bil′i·tat·ing**

**de·bil·i·ty** (di bil′ə tē) ***n.*** weakness; feebleness.

**deb·it** (deb′it) ***n.*** an entry in an account book of money owed. ◆***v.*** to enter as a debit in an account book.

**deb·o·nair** or **deb·o·naire** (deb′ə ner′) ***adj.*** cheerful and pleasant in a carefree way.

**de·brief** (dē brēf′) ***v.*** to question someone who has ended a mission, to get information.

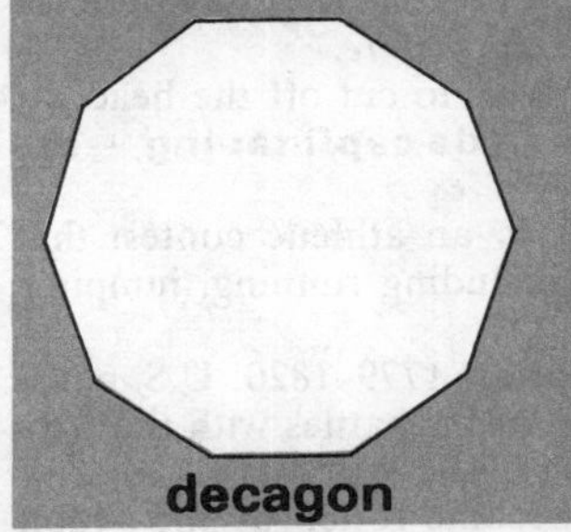

decagon

death's–head

**de·bris** or **dé·bris** (də brē′ *or* dā′brē) ***n.*** broken, scattered remains; rubbish [the *debris* from an explosion; the *debris* on picnic grounds].

**debt** (det) ***n.*** **1** something that one owes to another [a *debt* of $25; a *debt* of gratitude]. **2** the condition of owing [I am greatly in *debt* to you.]

**debt·or** (det′ər) ***n.*** one who owes a debt.

**de·bug** (dē bug′) ***v.*** to find and remove hidden listening devices from a room or building: *a slang term.* —**de·bugged′, de·bug′ging**

☆**de·bunk** (di buŋk′) ***v.*** to show how false something really is: *used only in everyday talk.*

**De·bus·sy** (deb′yoo sē′ *or* də byōō′sē), **(Achille) Claude** 1862–1918; French composer.

**de·but** or **dé·but** (di byōō′ *or* dā′byōō) ***n.*** **1** a first appearance before the public, as of a performer. **2** the entering of a girl into high society, usually by means of a formal party.

**deb·u·tante** (deb′yoo tänt′) ***n.*** a girl making her debut into high society.

**Dec.** *abbreviation for* **December.**

**dec.** *abbreviation for* **deceased, decrease.**

**deca-** or **dec-** *a prefix meaning* ten [A *decagon* is a plane figure with ten sides.]

**dec·ade** (dek′ād) ***n.*** a period of ten years.

**dec·a·dence** (dek′ə dəns *or* di kād′əns) ***n.*** a becoming bad, immoral, or impure [A love of cruel sports showed the *decadence* of Nero's court.] —**dec′a·dent *adj.***

**dec·a·gon** (dek′ə gän) ***n.*** a plane figure with ten sides and ten angles. *See the picture.*

**de·cal** (di kal′) ***n.*** a picture or design that is transferred from a specially prepared paper onto glass, wood, etc. *This word is a shortened form of* **de·cal·co·ma·ni·a** (di kal′kə mā′nē ə)

**Dec·a·logue** or **Dec·a·log** (dek′ə lôg) ***n.*** *another name for* **Ten Commandments.**

**de·camp** (di kamp′) ***v.*** **1** to pack up and leave a camp. **2** to leave suddenly and secretly [The treasurer *decamped* with the tax money.]

**de·cant** (di kant′) ***v.*** to pour off carefully, as into another bottle, without stirring up the sediment [to *decant* wine].



| | | | | | | | |
|---|---|---|---|---|---|---|---|
| a | fat | ir | here | ou | out | zh | leisure |
| ā | ape | ī | bite, fire | u | up | ng | ring |
| ä | car, lot | ō | go | ur | fur | | a *in* ago |
| e | ten | ô | law, horn | ch | chin | | e *in* agent |
| er | care | oi | oil | sh | she | ə = | i *in* unity |
| ē | even | oo | look | th | thin | | o *in* collect |
| i | hit | ōō | tool | *th* | then | | u *in* focus |

**de·cant·er** (di kan′tər) ***n.*** a decorative glass bottle for serving wine or liquor. *See the picture.*

**de·cap·i·tate** (di kap′ə tāt) ***v.*** to cut off the head of; behead. **—de·cap′i·tat·ed, de·cap′i·tat·ing —de·cap′i·ta′tion *n.***

**de·cath·lon** (di kath′län) ***n.*** an athletic contest that tests skills in ten events, including running, jumping, and throwing.

**De·ca·tur** (di kāt′ər), **Stephen** 1779–1820; U.S. naval officer. He is best known for his battles with the Barbary pirates and the British in the War of 1812.

**de·cay** (di kā′) ***v.*** **1** to become rotten by the action of bacteria [The fallen apples *decayed* on the ground.] **2** to fall into ruins; become no longer sound, powerful, rich, beautiful, etc. [Spain's power *decayed* after its fleet was destroyed.] **3** to break down so that there are fewer radioactive atoms. **◆*n.*** **1** a rotting or falling into ruin. **2** the breaking down of radioactive material so that there are fewer radioactive atoms.

**de·cease** (di sēs′) ***n.*** death [My cousin will inherit the estate upon the *decease* of my aunt.]

**de·ceased** (di sēst′) ***adj.*** dead. *See* SYNONYMS *at* **dead. —the deceased,** the dead person or dead persons.

**de·ceit** (di sēt′) ***n.*** **1** a deceiving or lying. **2** a lie or a dishonest act or acts.

**de·ceit·ful** (di sēt′fəl) ***adj.*** full of deceit; lying or misleading. **—de·ceit′ful·ly *adv.* —de·ceit′ful·ness *n.***



**de·ceive** (di sēv′) ***v.*** to make someone believe what is not true; fool or trick; mislead [The queen *deceived* Snow White by pretending to be her friend.] **—de·ceived′, de·ceiv′ing —de·ceiv′er *n.***

**De·cem·ber** (di sem′bər) ***n.*** the last month of the year, which has 31 days: abbreviated **Dec.**

**de·cen·cy** (dē′sən sē) ***n.*** the quality of being decent; proper behavior, modesty, courtesy, etc. [He did have the *decency* to thank her.] *—pl.* **de′cen·cies**

**de·cent** (dē′sənt) ***adj.*** **1** proper and fitting; not to be ashamed of; respectable [*decent* manners; *decent* language]. **2** fairly good; satisfactory [a *decent* wage]. **3** kind; generous; fair [It was *decent* of you to lend me your car.] **—de′cent·ly *adv.***

**de·cen·tral·ize** (dē sen′trə līz) ***v.*** to turn over power from a main center, as a national government, to local groups or branches. **—de·cen′tral·ized, de·cen′tral·iz·ing —de·cen′tral·i·za′tion *n.***

decorations

decanter

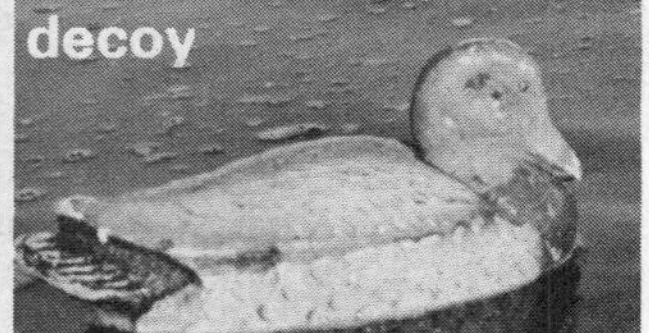

decoy

**de·cep·tion** (di sep′shən) ***n.*** **1** a deceiving or fooling. **2** something that fools, as a fraud.

SYNONYMS: **Deception** means anything that deceives, whether it is done by plan or brought about by illusion [The visitor's claim of being a duchess was a *deception.* A mirage in the desert is a *deception* to the eye.] **Fraud** means a deliberate deception to cheat someone of rights, property, etc. [Selling cut glass as diamonds is a *fraud.*]

**de·cep·tive** (di sep′tiv) ***adj.*** deceiving; not what it seems to be. **—de·cep′tive·ly *adv.***

**dec·i·bel** (des′ə bel) ***n.*** a unit for measuring the relative loudness of sound.

**de·cide** (di sīd′) ***v.*** **1** to choose after some thought; make up one's mind [I can't *decide* what suit to wear.] **2** to end a contest or argument by giving one side the victory; settle [A jury will *decide* the case.] **—de·cid′ed, de·cid′ing**

**de·cid·ed** (di sīd′id) ***adj.*** **1** clear and sharp; definite [a *decided* change in the weather]. **2** sure or firm; without doubt. [Clem has very *decided* ideas on the subject.] **—de·cid′ed·ly *adv.***

**de·cid·u·ous** (di sij′oo wəs) ***adj.*** **1** falling off at a certain time of the year, as the leaves of some trees. **2** shedding its leaves every year; not evergreen. [Elms are *deciduous* trees.]

**dec·i·gram** (des′ə gram) ***n.*** a unit of weight, equal to 1/10 gram.

**dec·i·li·ter** (des′ə lēt′ər) ***n.*** a unit of volume, equal to 1/10 liter.

**dec·i·mal** (des′ə m′l) ***adj.*** of or based upon the number ten; counted by tens [The metric system of measure is a *decimal* system.] **◆*n.*** a fraction with a denominator of 10, or of 100 or 1,000, etc. It is shown by a point (**decimal point**) before the numerator, as .5 (5/10) or .63 (63/100).

**dec·i·mate** (des′ə māt) ***v.*** to destroy or kill one tenth of or, now, any large part of [The city was *decimated* by earthquake.] **—dec′i·mat·ed, dec′i·mat·ing —dec′i·ma′tion *n.***

**dec·i·me·ter** (des′ə mēt′ər) ***n.*** a measure of length, equal to 1/10 meter.

**de·ci·pher** (di sī′fər) ***v.*** **1** to translate from secret writing or code into ordinary language. **2** to make out the meaning, as of scrawled or blurred writing.

**de·ci·sion** (di sizh′ən) ***n.*** **1** the act of deciding or settling something, or the opinion or choice decided on [The *decision* of the judges will be final.] **2** firmness of mind; determination [a person of *decision*].

**de·ci·sive** (di sī′siv) ***adj.*** **1** that settles or could settle a question or argument [a *decisive* battle in a war]. **2** showing firmness or determination [a *decisive* tone of voice].

**deck** (dek) ***n.*** **1** any of the floors of a ship, reaching from side to side. The main deck is usually a roof over the ship's hold. **2** a pack of playing cards. **◆*v.*** to dress or adorn with fine clothes or decoration [to *deck* oneself in expensive jewels]. **—clear the decks,** to get ready for action.

**de·claim** (di klām′) ***v.*** to speak loudly and with strong feeling, as some orators do in trying to sway an audience.

**dec·la·ma·tion** (dek′lə mā′shən) ***n.*** **1** the act or skill of declaiming. **2** a speech, poem, etc. that is or can be declaimed.

**de·clam·a·to·ry** (di klam′ə tôr′ē) ***adj.*** **1** of or fit for declaiming [a *declamatory* poem]. **2** speaking loudly and with great feeling.

**dec·la·ra·tion** (dek′lə rā′shən) ***n.*** **1** a declaring or being declared [The *declaration* of a holiday is always good news.] **2** a public statement; proclamation [the *Declaration* of Independence].

**Declaration of Independence** the statement written by Thomas Jefferson and adopted July 4, 1776, by the Second Continental Congress, declaring the thirteen American colonies free and independent of Great Britain.

**de·clar·a·tive** (di klar′ə tiv) ***adj.*** making a statement; asserting something ["I shall go away" is a *declarative* sentence.]

**de·clare** (di kler′) ***v.*** **1** to make known; say or announce openly [Let us *declare* war on cancer. "I'm leaving for good!" he *declared.*] *See* SYNONYMS *at* **assert.** **2** to tell what taxable goods one is bringing into a country [At the customs office, we *declared* the camera we bought in Canada.] —**de·clared′, de·clar′ing** —**I declare!** I am surprised, startled, etc.

**de·clas·si·fy** (dē klas′ə fī) ***v.*** ☆to make available to the public governmental documents or reports that have been classified as secret. —**de·clas′si·fied, de·clas′si·fy·ing**

**de·clen·sion** (di klen′shən) ***n.*** **1** a class of nouns, pronouns, and adjectives that have the same endings or other changes to show case, or how they are used in a sentence. **2** the changing of the forms of such words. English has declension only for pronouns, as *he, him, his.*

**de·cline** (di klīn′) ***v.*** **1** to bend or slope downward [The lawn *declines* to the sidewalk.] **2** to become less, as in health, power, or value; decay [A person's strength usually *declines* in old age.] **3** to refuse something, especially in a polite way [I am sorry I must *decline* your invitation.] **4** to give the different case forms of a noun, pronoun, or adjective in order. —**de·clined′, de·clin′ing** ◆***n.*** **1** a becoming less, smaller, or weaker; decay [a *decline* in prices]. **2** the last part [the *decline* of day]. **3** a downward slope [We slid down the *decline.*]

> SYNONYMS: To **decline** an invitation, offer, or proposal is to state in a very polite way that one cannot accept it [She *declined* the nomination.] To **refuse** is to say "no" in a definite, direct, often blunt way [They *refused* to meet our demands.] To **reject** is to refuse in a negative and hostile way to accept, use, believe, etc. [The workers *rejected* the new contract.]

**de·cliv·i·ty** (di kliv′ə tē) ***n.*** a downward slope of the ground. —*pl.* **de·cliv′i·ties**

**de·code** (dē kōd′) ***v.*** to figure out the meaning of something written in code. —**de·cod′ed, de·cod′ing**

**de·com·pose** (dē kəm pōz′) ***v.*** **1** to rot or decay. **2** to break up into its separate basic parts [Water can be *decomposed* into hydrogen and oxygen.] —**de·com·posed′, de·com·pos′ing** —**de·com·po·si·tion** (dē′-käm pə zish′ən) ***n.***

**de·con·gest·ant** (dē′kən jes′tənt) ***n.*** a medicine used to relieve congestion, as in the nose when one has a cold, hay fever, etc.

**de·con·tam·i·nate** (dē′kən tam′ə nāt) ***v.*** to rid something of a harmful or polluting substance, as poison or radioactive material. —**de′con·tam′i·nat·ed, de′-con·tam′i·nat·ing**

**dé·cor** or **de·cor** (dā kôr′ *or* dā′kôr) ***n.*** **1** decoration. **2** the scheme for decorating a room, stage set, etc.

**dec·o·rate** (dek′ə rāt) ***v.*** **1** to add something so as to make prettier or more pleasing; ornament; adorn [to *decorate* a blouse with embroidery]. **2** to plan and arrange the colors and furnishings of a room or house. **3** to give a medal, ribbon, or other sign of honor to [The general *decorated* the soldier for bravery.] —**dec′o·rat·ed, dec′o·rat·ing**

**dec·o·ra·tion** (dek′ə rā′shən) ***n.*** **1** the act of decorating. **2** anything used for decorating; ornament [*decorations* for the Christmas tree]. **3** a medal, ribbon, etc. given as a sign of honor. *See the picture.*

☆**Decoration Day** *another name for* **Memorial Day.**

**dec·o·ra·tive** (dek′ə rə tiv *or* dek′ə rā′tiv) ***adj.*** that serves to decorate; ornamental.

**dec·o·ra·tor** (dek′ə rā′tər) ***n.*** a person who decorates; especially, one whose work is decorating and furnishing rooms.

**dec·o·rous** (dek′ə rəs) ***adj.*** having or showing dignity and good taste; behaving properly. —**dec′o·rous·ly** ***adv.***

**de·co·rum** (di kôr′əm) ***n.*** that which is suitable or fitting; proper and dignified behavior, speech, etc. [Loud laughter in the library shows a lack of *decorum.*] 191

**de·coy** (di koi′ *or* dē′koi) ***n.*** **1** an artificial bird or animal used to attract wild birds or animals to a place where they can be shot or trapped; also, a live bird or animal used in the same way. *See the picture.* **2** a thing or person used to lure someone into a trap. ◆***v.*** (di koi′) to lure into a trap or danger.

**de·crease** (di krēs′ *or* dē′krēs) ***v.*** to make or become gradually less or smaller [She has *decreased* her weight by dieting. The pain is *decreasing.*] —**de·creased′, de·creas′ing** ◆***n.*** **1** a decreasing or growing less [a *decrease* in profits]. **2** the amount of decreasing [The sales *decrease* last month was $400.] —**on the decrease,** decreasing.

**de·cree** (di krē′) ***n.*** an official order or decision, as of a government or court. ◆***v.*** to order or decide by decree [The governor *decreed* a special holiday.] —**de·creed′, de·cree′ing**

**de·crep·it** (di krep′it) ***adj.*** broken down or worn out by old age or long use.

> **Decrepit** comes from a Latin word that means "to creak or rattle." When we say a car is *decrepit,* we are saying it is an old car whose parts have begun to creak and rattle.

**de·crep·i·tude** (di krep′ə to͞od *or* di krep′ə tyo͞od) ***n.*** the condition of being decrepit; feebleness or weakness caused by old age or long use.

| | | | |
|---|---|---|---|
| **a** fat | **ir** here | **ou** out | **zh** leisure |
| **ā** ape | **ī** bite, fire | **u** up | **ng** ring |
| **ä** car, lot | **ō** go | **ur** fur | a *in* ago |
| **e** ten | **ô** law, horn | **ch** chin | e *in* agent |
| **er** care | **oi** oil | **sh** she | **ə** = i *in* unity |
| **ē** even | **oo** look | **th** thin | o *in* collect |
| **i** hit | **o͞o** tool | ***th*** then | u *in* focus |

d

**de·cre·scen·do** (dē′krə shen′dō) ***adj., adv.*** gradually becoming softer: *a direction in music usually shown by the sign* >. ◆***n.*** a decrease in loudness. *—pl.* **de′cre·scen′dos**

☆**de·crim·i·nal·ize** (dē krim′ə n′l īz′) ***v.*** to do away with or lessen the legal penalties for a certain crime. —**de·crim′i·nal·ized′, de·crim′i·nal·iz′ing**

**de·cry** (di krī′) ***v.*** to speak out against strongly and openly; condemn [to *decry* the wasteful spending of tax money]. —**de·cried′, de·cry′ing**

**ded·i·cate** (ded′ə kāt) ***v.*** **1** to set aside for a special purpose [The church was *dedicated* to the worship of God. The doctor has *dedicated* her life to cancer research.] **2** to say at the beginning of a book, etc. that it was written in honor of, or out of affection for, a certain person [He *dedicated* his novel to his wife.] —**ded′i·cat·ed, ded′i·cat·ing** —**ded′i·ca′tion** ***n.***

**ded·i·ca·to·ry** (ded′i kə tôr′ē) ***adj.*** of or as a dedication [a *dedicatory* speech].

**de·duce** (di do͞os′ *or* di dyo͞os′) ***v.*** to figure out by reasoning from known facts or general principles; infer [The existence of the planet Neptune was *deduced* before its actual discovery.] —**de·duced′, de·duc′ing**

**Deduce** comes from a Latin word meaning "to lead down." We deduce something when we see that one set of facts can lead us down to another set.



**de·duct** (di dukt′) ***v.*** to take away; subtract [If I trade in the old one, they'll *deduct* $50.00 from the price of the new one.]

**de·duc·tion** (di duk′shən) ***n.*** **1** the act of deducting; subtraction. **2** the amount deducted. **3** reasoning from known facts or general principles to a logical conclusion [Detectives in stories solve crimes by *deduction.*] **4** a conclusion reached in this way. —**de·duc′tive** ***adj.***

**deed** (dēd) ***n.*** **1** a thing done; act; action ["*Deeds* speak louder than words."] **2** a paper drawn up according to law that hands over a property to someone. ◆***v.*** to hand over a property by such a paper.

**deem** (dēm) ***v.*** to think, believe, or judge [She was *deemed* worthy of the honor.]

**deep** (dēp) ***adj.*** **1** reaching far down, far in, or far back [a *deep* lake; a *deep* wound; a *deep* closet]. **2** reaching a certain distance down, in, or back [This pot is only five inches *deep.*] **3** having a low tone or tones [a *deep* groan; a *deep* bass voice]. **4** hard to understand [a *deep* subject]. **5** great, heavy, or serious [*deep* disgrace; a *deep* sleep]. **6** strongly felt [*deep* love]. **7** dark and rich [*deep* colors]. **8** very much taken up; greatly involved [*deep* in thought; *deep* in debt]. ◆***n.*** **1** a deep place. **2** the middle or darkest part [the *deep* of the night]. ◆***adv.*** far down, far in, or far back [to dig *deep*]. —**in deep water,** in trouble or in a difficult situation. —**the deep** the sea or ocean: *used mainly in poetry.* —**deep′ly** ◆***adv.*** —**deep′ness** ***n.***

**deep·en** (dēp′'n) ***v.*** to make or become deeper.

**deep-root·ed** (dēp′ro͞ot′id) ***adj.*** **1** having deep roots. **2** firmly fixed; hard to remove [*deep-rooted* love].

**deep-seat·ed** (dēp′sēt′id) ***adj.*** firmly fixed; hard to remove; deep-rooted.

**deer** (dir) ***n.*** a swift-running, hoofed animal that chews its cud. The male usually has antlers that are shed every year. *See the picture. —pl.* **deer**

**deer·skin** (dir′skin) ***n.*** **1** the hide of a deer. **2** leather made from this hide.

**de·face** (di fās′) ***v.*** to spoil the looks of; mar [to *deface* an oil painting by slashing it with a knife]. —**defaced′, de·fac′ing**

**def·a·ma·tion** (def′ə mā′shən) ***n.*** a defaming or being defamed; slander or libel.

**de·fam·a·to·ry** (di fam′ə tôr′ē) ***adj.*** defaming; hurting a person's reputation.

**de·fame** (di fām′) ***v.*** to say false and harmful things so as to hurt the reputation of; slander or libel. —**defamed′, de·fam′ing** —**de·fam′er** ***n.***

**de·fault** (di fôlt′) ***n.*** **1** failure to do what one should do or be where one should be [When the other team did not arrive, we won the game by *default.*] **2** failure to pay money owed. ◆***v.*** to fail to do or pay what or when one should.

**de·feat** (di fēt′) ***v.*** **1** to win victory over; overcome; beat [to *defeat* an opponent]. **2** to bring to nothing; make fail; balk [His hopes were *defeated* by a stroke of bad luck.] ◆***n.*** **1** a being defeated; failure to win [Germany's *defeat* in World War II]. **2** a defeating; victory over [the Allies' *defeat* of Germany].

**de·feat·ist** (di fēt′ist) ***n.*** a person who gives up a fight before it is lost. ◆***adj.*** of or like a defeatist. —**defeat′ism** ***n.***

**def·e·cate** (def′ə kāt) ***v.*** to get rid of waste matter from the bowels. —**def′e·cat·ed, def′e·cat·ing**

**de·fect** (dē′fekt *or* di fekt′) ***n.*** a fault or flaw; imperfect part; weakness [a *defect* in a diamond; a *defect* in one's hearing]. ◆***v.*** (di fekt′) to desert one's cause or group so as to join the other side; forsake. —**de·fec′tion** ***n.*** —**de·fec′tor** ***n.***

**de·fec·tive** (di fek′tiv) ***adj.*** having a defect or defects; imperfect; faulty.

**de·fence** (di fens′) ***n.*** *British spelling of* **defense.**

**de·fend** (di fend′) ***v.*** **1** to keep safe from harm or danger; guard; protect [She learned karate to *defend* herself.] **2** to uphold something that is under attack; especially, to be the lawyer for a person accused or sued in a law court. **3** to make an excuse for; justify [Can you *defend* your rudeness?] —**de·fend′er** ***n.***

SYNONYMS: To **defend** someone or something is to turn aside or hold off any attack or invasion [They have watchdogs to *defend* their property.] To **protect** someone or something is to put up a barrier that will keep harm and injury away [A fence helps to *protect* the garden from rabbits.]

**de·fend·ant** (di fen′dənt) ***n.*** the person in a law court who is being accused or sued.

**de·fense** (di fens′ *or* dē′fens) ***n.*** **1** a defending against attack [They fought in *defense* of their country.] **2** something that defends; means of protecting [Forts were built as *defenses* along the frontier.] **3** arguments given to support or uphold something under attack. ☆**4** a defendant and his or her lawyers.

**de·fense·less** (di fens′lis) ***adj.*** having no defense; not able to protect oneself.

**de·fen·si·ble** (di fen′sə b'l) ***adj.*** that can be defended or shown to be right.

**de·fen·sive** (di fen′siv) ***adj.*** protecting from attack; defending [The army set up *defensive* barricades.] ◆***n.***

a defensive position or act [The weaker team was soon on the *defensive*.] —**de·fen′sive·ly** *adv.*

**de·fer**[1] (di fur′) *v.* to put off until a later time; postpone [The judge *deferred* the trial until the following week.] —**de·ferred′, de·fer′ring —de·fer′ment** *n.*

**de·fer**[2] (di fur′) *v.* to give in to the wishes or opinion of another, as in showing respect [She *deferred* to her daughter's wishes.] —**de·ferred′, de·fer′ring**

**def·er·ence** (def′ər əns) *n.* polite respect for the wishes or opinion of another. —**in deference to,** out of respect for.

**def·er·en·tial** (def′ə ren′shəl) *adj.* showing deference; very respectful.

**de·fi·ance** (di fī′əns) *n.* the act of defying or opposing a powerful person or thing [He showed his *defiance* of custom by not wearing a necktie.] —**in defiance of, 1** defying. **2** in spite of.

**de·fi·ant** (di fī′ənt) *adj.* full of defiance; bold [The *defiant* tenants refused to pay their rent until repairs were made.] —**de·fi′ant·ly** *adv.*

**de·fi·cien·cy** (di fish′ən sē) *n.* an amount short of what is needed; shortage [A *deficiency* of vitamin C causes scurvy.] —*pl.* **de·fi′cien·cies**

**de·fi·cient** (di fish′ənt) *adj.* not having enough; lacking [a country *deficient* in natural resources].

**def·i·cit** (def′ə sit) *n.* a shortage in the amount of money needed [With the budget set at $50,000 and an income of only $30,000, the *deficit* is $20,000.]

**de·file**[1] (di fīl′) *v.* to make dirty or impure [The water in the spring was *defiled* with garbage.] —**de·filed′, de·fil′ing —de·file′ment** *n.*

**de·file**[2] (di fīl′) *v.* to march in single file. —**de·filed′, de·fil′ing** ◆*n.* a steep valley or narrow pass, through which soldiers must go in single file. *See the picture.*

**de·fine** (di fīn′) *v.* **1** to tell the meaning or meanings of; explain [The dictionary *defines* "deficient" as "not having enough."] **2** to describe in detail; make clear [Can you *define* your duties as a secretary?] **3** to mark clearly the outline or limits of [to *define* a boundary]. —**de·fined′, de·fin′ing**

**def·i·nite** (def′ə nit) *adj.* **1** having exact limits [a *definite* boundary]. **2** clear and exact in meaning [*definite* orders]. **3** certain; positive [It's *definite* that she has a broken arm.] —**def′i·nite·ly** *adv.*

**definite article** *see the note at* **article.**

**def·i·ni·tion** (def′ə nish′ən) *n.* **1** a defining or being defined. **2** a statement that tells what a thing is or what a word means. **3** the clearness or sharpness of an outline. *See the picture.*

**de·fin·i·tive** (di fin′ə tiv) *adj.* that is positive and final; that decides [a *definitive* answer].

**de·flate** (di flāt′) *v.* **1** to make smaller or flatter by letting out air or gas [to *deflate* a tire]. **2** to make smaller or less important [I felt *deflated* when no one said "Hello."] —**de·flat′ed, de·flat′ing**

**de·fla·tion** (di flā′shən) ◆*n.* **1** a deflating or being deflated. **2** a lessening of the amount of money in circulation, making it more valuable.

**de·flect** (di flekt′) *v.* to turn or make go to one side [The bowling ball was *deflected* by an uneven spot in the alley.] —**de·flec′tion** *n.*

**De·foe** (di fō′), **Daniel** 1660?–1731; English writer who wrote *Robinson Crusoe.*

☆**de·fo·li·ant** (dē fō′lē ənt) *n.* a chemical spray that strips growing plants of their leaves.

deer

definition definition

defile

**de·fo·li·ate** (dē fō′lē āt) *v.* to remove the leaves from plants, especially trees, as by spraying them with a defoliant. —**de·fo′li·at·ed, de·fo′li·at·ing —de·fo′li·a′tion** *n.*

**de·for·est** (dē fôr′ist) *v.* to remove the trees or forests from a piece of land.

**de·form** (di fôrm′) *v.* to spoil the form or look of; disfigure [a tree *deformed* by heavy snows and storms].

**de·form·i·ty** (di fôr′mə tē) *n.* **1** the condition of being deformed. **2** a part that is deformed. —*pl.* **de·form′i·ties**

**de·fraud** (di frôd′) *v.* to take away money, rights, etc. from by cheating or tricking. 

**de·fray** (di frā′) *v.* to pay or supply the money for [extra pay to *defray* expenses]. —**de·fray′al** *n.*

**de·frost** (di frôst′) *v.* **1** to get rid of frost or ice from [to *defrost* a refrigerator]. **2** to cause to become unfrozen [to *defrost* frozen foods].

**de·frost·er** (di frôst′ər) *n.* any device used to melt ice and frost, as from a windshield.

**deft** (deft) *adj.* quick but sure; skillful [the *deft* strokes of an artist's brush]. —**deft′ly** *adv.*

**de·funct** (di fuŋkt′) *adj.* no longer living or existing; dead; extinct [That magazine is now *defunct.*]

**de·fy** (di fī′) *v.* **1** to stand up against or oppose boldly and openly [They *defied* their leader.] **2** to resist completely in a baffling way [This problem *defies* solution.] **3** to dare or challenge [I *defy* you to prove me wrong.] —**de·fied′, de·fy′ing**

**De·gas** (də gä′), **Ed·gar** (ed gär′) 1834–1917; French painter.

**de Gaulle** (də gôl′), **Charles** 1890–1970; French general. He was president of France from 1959 to 1969.

**de·gen·er·a·cy** (di jen′ər ə sē) *n.* the fact of being or becoming degenerate.

**de·gen·er·ate** (di jen′ər it) *adj.* having sunk into a lower or worse condition [the *degenerate* life of the

| | | | | | | | |
|---|---|---|---|---|---|---|---|
| **a** | fat | **ir** | here | **ou** | out | **zh** | leisure |
| **ā** | ape | **ī** | bite, fire | **u** | up | **ŋ** | ring |
| **ä** | car, lot | **ō** | go | **ur** | fur | | a *in* ago |
| **e** | ten | **ô** | law, horn | **ch** | chin | | e *in* agent |
| **er** | care | **oi** | oil | **sh** | she | **ə =** | i *in* unity |
| **ē** | even | **oo** | look | **th** | thin | | o *in* collect |
| **i** | hit | **ōō** | tool | ***th*** | then | | u *in* focus |

d

delta of a river

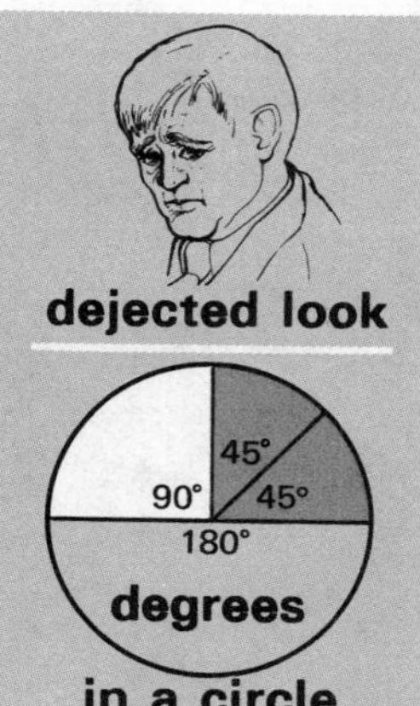
dejected look

degrees in a circle

Roman emperor Nero]. ◆*n.* a degenerate person, especially one who does not know right from wrong and does evil things. ◆*v.* (di jen′ər āt) to become degenerate; sink into a bad or low condition. —**de·gen′er·at·ed, de·gen′er·at·ing —de·gen′er·a′tion** *n.*

**de·grade** (di grād′) *v.* **1** to bring down to a lower rank, as in punishing; demote. **2** to make lower or worse; make lose self-respect; disgrace [Officials who take bribes *degrade* themselves.] —**de·grad′ed, de·grad′ing —deg·ra·da·tion** (deg′rə dā′shən) *n.*

**de·gree** (di grē′) *n.* **1** a step in a series; stage in the progress of something [He advanced by *degrees* from office boy to president.] **2** a unit used in measuring temperature that is shown by the symbol °. The boiling point of water is 100° Celsius or 212° Fahrenheit. **3** a unit used in measuring angles and arcs of circles [There are 360 *degrees* in the circumference of a circle.] *See the picture.* **4** rank or position in life or in some group [a lady of high *degree*]. **5** a rank given by a college to a student who has satisfactorily completed a course of study, or to an outstanding person as an honor [a B.A. *degree*]. **6** amount or extent [A burn of the third *degree* is one that does the greatest amount of damage to the skin and flesh.] **7** any of the three forms that an adjective or adverb takes when it is compared [The positive *degree* is "dark," the comparative *degree* is "darker," and the superlative *degree* is "darkest."] —**by degrees,** in a gradual way; step by step.



**de·hu·mid·i·fi·er** (dē′hyo͞o mid′ə fī′ər) *n.* a device that removes moisture from the air.

**de·hy·drate** (dē hī′drāt) *v.* **1** to remove water from; dry [Powdered milk is milk that has been *dehydrated.*] **2** to lose water; become dry. —**de·hy′drat·ed, de·hy′drat·ing —de′hy·dra′tion** *n.*

**de·i·fy** (dē′ə fī) *v.* to make a god of; worship as a god [The Romans *deified* their emperors.] —**de′i·fied, de′i·fy·ing —de′i·fi·ca′tion** *n.*

**deign** (dān) *v.* to think of as not being beneath one's dignity; condescend; lower oneself [The famous star wouldn't deign to shake hands with us.]

**de·ist** (dē′ist) *n.* a person who believes that God made the world but takes no further part in controlling it. —**de′ism** *n.* —**de·is′tic** *adj.*

**de·i·ty** (dē′ə tē) *n.* **1** a god or goddess [the *deities* of ancient Greece]. **2** the condition of being a god [a tribe that believed in the *deity* of animals]. —*pl.* **de′i·ties —the Deity,** God.

**de·ject·ed** (di jek′tid) *adj.* in low spirits; sad; discouraged. *See the picture.* —**de·ject′ed·ly** *adv.*

**de·jec·tion** (di jek′shən) *n.* lowness of spirits; sadness; discouragement.

**del.** *abbreviation for* **delegate, delegation.**

**Del·a·ware** (del′ə wer) **1** a State on the eastern coast of the U.S.: abbreviated **Del., DE** **2** a river flowing between Pennsylvania and New Jersey into the Atlantic.

**de·lay** (di lā′) *v.* **1** to put off to a later time; postpone [The bride's illness will *delay* the wedding.] **2** to make late; hold back; keep from going on [We were *delayed* by the storm.] ◆*n.* a delaying or being delayed [Engine trouble caused a *delay* in the plane's takeoff.]

SYNONYMS: To **delay** is to hold someone back or cause something to be postponed [We were *delayed* in getting to school when the school bus broke down.] To **hinder** is to make it hard for someone to begin or to make progress [She was *hindered* by lack of education.]

**de·lec·ta·ble** (di lek′tə b′l) *adj.* very pleasing; delightful [*delectable* to the taste].

**de·lec·ta·tion** (dē′lek tā′shən) *n.* delight; enjoyment; great pleasure [a program for the *delectation* of opera lovers].

**del·e·gate** (del′ə gāt *or* del′ə git) *n.* a person sent to speak and act for his group or branch; representative [Our club will send a *delegate* to the State convention.] ◆*v.* (del′ə gāt) **1** to send or appoint as a delegate. **2** to give over a right or duty to another; entrust [The people *delegate* to a legislature the power to make laws.] —**del′e·gat·ed, del′e·gat·ing**

**del·e·ga·tion** (del′ə gā′shən) *n.* **1** a delegating or being delegated [the *delegation* of certain duties to one's assistant]. **2** a group of delegates [The Iowa *delegation* voted as a unit.]

**de·lete** (di lēt′) *v.* to take out or cross out something printed or written [Her name has been *deleted* from the list of members.] —**de·let′ed, de·let′ing —de·le·tion** (di lē′shən) *n.*

**del·e·te·ri·ous** (del′ə tir′ē əs) *adj.* harmful to health or well-being; injurious.

**Delft** (delft) a city in western Netherlands.

**delft·ware** (delft′wer) *n.* a kind of earthenware that is glazed and is usually blue and white. It was first made in Delft.

**Del·hi** (del′ē) a city in northern India: *see also* **New Delhi.**

☆**del·i** (del′ē) *n. a shorter form of* **delicatessen.**

**de·lib·er·ate** (di lib′ər it) *adj.* **1** carefully thought out and made or done on purpose [a *deliberate* refusal]. **2** careful in making up one's mind; not hasty [She was very *deliberate* in choosing a career.] **3** slow; unhurried [Take *deliberate* aim.] ◆*v.* (di lib′ər āt) to think or discuss carefully in order to make up one's mind [The jury *deliberated* for six hours before reaching a verdict.] —**de·lib′er·at·ed, de·lib′er·at·ing —de·lib′er·ate·ly** *adv.*

**Deliberate** comes from a Latin word meaning "to weigh carefully," which comes from the Latin word for a scales, in which things are weighed. A matter being deliberated is weighed very carefully in a person's mind.

**de·lib·er·a·tion** (di lib′ə rā′shən) ***n.*** **1** a careful thinking through [Choose now, as there is no time for *deliberation.*] **2** *often* **deliberations,** *pl.* a talking about or debating of some problem before deciding [There are serious *deliberations* before drawing up a treaty between countries.]

**del·i·ca·cy** (del′i kə sē) ***n.*** **1** the condition of being delicate; fineness in skill or work; fragile beauty, sensitiveness, weakness, etc. [the *delicacy* of spun glass or of a rose petal; *delicacy* in dealing with risky matters; *delicacy* in health]. **2** a choice food [smoked oysters and other *delicacies*]. —*pl.* **del′i·ca·cies**

**del·i·cate** (del′i kit) ***adj.*** **1** pleasing in its lightness, mildness, or softness [a *delicate* flavor, odor, or color]. **2** beautifully fine in quality or form [*delicate* linen; *delicate* workmanship]. **3** slight and not easily felt or seen [a *delicate* difference]. **4** easily hurt or spoiled; not strong; frail or fragile [*delicate* glassware; *delicate* health]. **5** needing careful handling [a *delicate* problem]. **6** having a quick and sensitive reaction to small differences or details [a *delicate* ear for music; a *delicate* gauge]. —**del′i·cate·ly** ***adv.***

SYNONYMS: Anything **delicate** or **dainty** is very pleasing to sensitive and refined people. But **delicate** suggests something very fine, fragile, or subtle, like an aroma or lace, while **dainty** suggests something small, graceful, or choice, as a little cake or a tiny foot.

☆**del·i·ca·tes·sen** (del′i kə tes″n) ***n.*** **1** a store that sells prepared foods, such as cooked meats, cheeses, salads, relishes, etc. **2** the foods sold in such a store.

**de·li·cious** (di lish′əs) ***adj.*** very pleasing, especially to the taste or smell; delightful. —**de·li′cious·ly** ***adv.***

**de·light** (di līt′) ***v.*** **1** to give great pleasure to [The fine food *delighted* us all.] **2** to be greatly pleased; rejoice [We *delighted* in our good fortune.] ◆***n.*** **1** great joy or pleasure [a child's *delight* with a new toy]. **2** something giving great joy or pleasure [Their garden is a real *delight* to them.]

**de·light·ful** (di līt′fəl) ***adj.*** giving delight or pleasure; very pleasing [a *delightful* party]. —**de·light′ful·ly** ***adv.***

**de·lin·e·ate** (di lin′ē āt) ***v.*** **1** to draw or sketch; portray. **2** to describe or picture in words [The hero is *delineated* in the story as a very brave man.] —**de·lin′e·at·ed, de·lin′e·at·ing** —**de·lin′e·a′tion** ***n.***

**de·lin·quen·cy** (di liŋ′kwən sē) ***n.*** **1** failure to do what is needed; neglect of duty. ☆**2** the doing of bad or unlawful things [juvenile *delinquency*]. —*pl.* **de·lin′quen·cies**

**de·lin·quent** (di liŋ′kwənt) ***adj.*** **1** failing to do what is needed [*delinquent* in paying a bill]. ☆**2** overdue [The taxes on their house are *delinquent.*] ◆***n.*** *a shorter form of* **juvenile delinquent.**

**de·lir·i·ous** (di lir′ē əs) ***adj.*** **1** in a delirium; raving [*delirious* from a high fever]. **2** wildly excited [*delirious* with joy]. —**de·lir′i·ous·ly** ***adv.***

**Delirious** comes from a Latin word meaning "to turn the furrow the wrong way in plowing." A person who plows in a crazy way might be thought to be delirious or raving mad.

**de·lir·i·um** (di lir′ē əm) ***n.*** **1** a condition of the mind, as during a fever or insanity, in which one is very restless and excited, has strange visions, and keeps talking wildly. **2** any very great excitement.

**de·liv·er** (di liv′ər) ***v.*** **1** to bring or carry and hand over; transfer [*Deliver* the groceries to my house. I *delivered* your message by phone.] **2** to take something around and leave it at the proper places; distribute [The postal service delivers packages.] **3** to speak or read aloud [to *deliver* a speech]. **4** to strike [to *deliver* a blow]. **5** to set free or rescue [He has *delivered* us from evil.] **6** to help a mother give birth to a baby [The doctor *delivered* the twins.]

**de·liv·er·ance** (di liv′ər əns) ***n.*** a freeing or being freed; rescue.

**de·liv·er·y** (di liv′ər ē) ***n.*** **1** the act of delivering; a transferring or distributing [daily *deliveries* to customers; the *delivery* of a prisoner into custody]. **2** the way in which a person speaks [the fast *delivery* of a TV announcer]. **3** the act of giving birth to a child. **4** the act of throwing, striking, etc. or the way this is done [the pitcher's *delivery* of the ball]. —*pl.* **de·liv′er·ies**

**dell** (del) ***n.*** a small valley or sheltered low place, usually with trees in it.

**Del·phi** (del′fī) an ancient Greek city on the slopes of Mount Parnassus.

**Del·phic oracle** (del′fik) the oracle of Apollo at Delphi in ancient times. The oracle, when questioned, gave answers that were hard to understand.

**del·phin·i·um** (del fin′ē əm) ***n.*** a plant with spikes of tubelike flowers, usually blue, on tall stalks.

**del·ta** (del′tə) ***n.*** **1** the fourth letter of the Greek alphabet, shaped like a triangle. **2** the triangle-shaped piece of land formed when sand and soil are deposited at the mouth of a large river. *See the picture.*



**de·lude** (di lo͞od′) ***v.*** to fool, as by false promises; mislead; trick. —**de·lud′ed, de·lud′ing**

**del·uge** (del′yo͞oj) ***n.*** **1** a great flood. **2** a heavy rain; downpour. **3** a rush or flood of anything [A *deluge* of questions followed her talk.] ◆***v.*** to flood or overflow. —**del′uged, del′ug·ing** —**the Deluge,** the great flood told about in the story of Noah.

**de·lu·sion** (di lo͞o′zhən) ***n.*** **1** a deluding or misleading. **2** a false or mistaken belief, especially when it is a sign of mental illness.

**de·lu·sive** (di lo͞os′iv) ***adj.*** misleading; false [They have a *delusive* hope of suddenly becoming rich.]

**de·luxe** (di luks′ *or* di lo͝oks′) ***adj.*** of extra fine quality; luxurious [The *deluxe* model of the car has leather seats.] ◆***adv.*** in a deluxe manner; luxuriously.

**delve** (delv) ***v.*** to search for facts [to *delve* into books; to *delve* into the past]. —**delved, delv′ing**

**Dem.** *abbreviation for* **Democrat** *or* **Democratic.**

**dem·a·gogue** or **dem·a·gog** (dem′ə gôg) ***n.*** a person who stirs up the feelings and prejudices of people to win them over quickly and use them to get power.

**Demagogue** comes from a Greek word meaning "a leader of the people." In ancient Greece a demagogue could have been an honest man who

| | | | | | | | |
|---|---|---|---|---|---|---|---|
| **a** | fat | **ir** | here | **ou** | out | **zh** | leisure |
| **ā** | ape | **ī** | bite, fire | **u** | up | **ŋ** | ring |
| **ä** | car, lot | **ō** | go | **ʉr** | fur | | a *in* ago |
| **e** | ten | **ô** | law, horn | **ch** | chin | | e *in* agent |
| **er** | care | **oi** | oil | **sh** | she | ə = | i *in* unity |
| **ē** | even | **o͝o** | look | **th** | thin | | o *in* collect |
| **i** | hit | **o͞o** | tool | ***th*** | then | | u *in* focus |

had won the respect of the people. In modern times a demagogue is thought to be a dishonest person who does not deserve respect.

**dem·a·gog·y** (dem′ə gō′jē) ***n.*** the ways of a demagogue.

**de·mand** (di mand′) ***v.*** **1** to ask for as a right, or as if one had the right; ask with authority [We *demanded* the money we had been promised.] **2** to call for; need [This work *demands* great care.] ◆***n.*** **1** a demanding or the thing demanded. **2** a claim or need [This job makes great *demands* on my time.] **3** the desire for a certain product by buyers who are ready to buy at the stated price [The *demand* for new cars is less this year than it was last year.] —**in demand,** wanted.

**de·mar·ca·tion** (dē′mär kā′shən) ***n.*** **1** the setting and marking of limits or boundaries. **2** a limit or boundary.

**de·mean**[1] (di mēn′) ***v.*** to make low or cheap; degrade [You *demean* yourself when you tell a lie.]

**de·mean**[2] (di mēn′) ***v.*** to behave [He *demeaned* himself like a gentleman.]

**de·mean·or** (di mēn′ər) ***n.*** behavior or conduct [She has a quiet, gentle *demeanor.*]

**de·ment·ed** (di men′tid) ***adj.*** sick in the mind; insane.

**de·mer·it** (di mer′it) ***n.*** **1** a fault or failing. ☆**2** a mark put down against a person, as for poor work or conduct.



**de·mesne** (di mān′ *or* di mēn′) ***n.*** **1** a lord's mansion and the land around it. **2** a region or domain.

**De·me·ter** (di mēt′ər) the Greek goddess of plants and farming.

**dem·i·god** (dem′ē gäd′) ***n.*** in Greek and Roman myths, a being who was part god and part human.

**dem·i·john** (dem′ē jän′) ***n.*** a large bottle or jug with a narrow neck and a wicker cover. *See the picture.*

**de·mil·i·ta·rize** (dē mil′ə tə rīz′) ***v.*** to take away the army and the power to wage war [to *demilitarize* a captured country]. —**de·mil′i·ta·rized′, de·mil′i·ta·riz′ing —de·mil′i·ta·ri·za′tion *n.***

**de·mise** (di mīz′) ***n.*** a ceasing to exist; death.

**dem·i·tasse** (dem′ē tas′) ***n.*** a small cup for serving black coffee after dinner.

**de·mo·bi·lize** (dē mō′bə līz) ***v.*** to release soldiers, sailors, etc. from military service, as at the end of a war. —**de·mo′bi·lized, de·mo′bi·liz·ing —de·mo′bi·li·za′tion *n.***

**de·moc·ra·cy** (di mäk′rə sē) ***n.*** **1** government in which the people hold the ruling power, usually giving it over to representatives whom they elect to make the laws and run the government. **2** a country, state, etc. with such government. **3** equal rights, opportunity, and treatment for all [The student council wants more *democracy* in our school.] —*pl.* **de·moc′ra·cies**

**dem·o·crat** (dem′ə krat) ***n.*** **1** a person who believes in and supports democracy; believer in rule by the people, equal rights for all, etc. ☆**2 Democrat,** a member of the Democratic Party.

**dem·o·crat·ic** (dem′ə krat′ik) ***adj.*** **1** of, belonging to, or supporting democracy. **2** treating people of all classes in the same way [a *democratic* employer]. ☆**3 Democratic,** of or belonging to the Democratic Party. —**dem′o·crat′i·cal·ly *adv.***

☆**Democratic Party** one of the two major political parties in the U.S.

**de·moc·ra·tize** (di mäk′rə tīz) ***v.*** to make or become democratic. —**de·moc′ra·tized, de·moc′ra·tiz·ing**

**de·mol·ish** (di mäl′ish) ***v.*** to tear down; smash; destroy or ruin [The tornado *demolished* the barn. Our hopes were *demolished* by his refusal.]

**dem·o·li·tion** (dem′ə lish′ən *or* dē′mə lish′ən) ***n.*** the act of demolishing or wrecking; often, destruction by explosives.

**de·mon** (dē′mən) ***n.*** **1** a devil; evil spirit. **2** a very evil or cruel person or thing [the *demon* of jealousy]. —**de·mon·ic** (di män′ik) ***adj.***

**de·mo·ni·a·cal** (dē′mə nī′ə k′l) ***adj.*** of or like a demon; fiendish; frenzied: *also* **de·mo·ni·ac** (dē mō′nē ak).

**de·mon·ism** (dē′mən iz′m) ***n.*** **1** belief in demons. **2** the worship of demons.

**de·mon·stra·ble** (di män′strə b′l) ***adj.*** that can be demonstrated or proved. —**de·mon′stra·bly *adv.***

**dem·on·strate** (dem′ən strāt) ***v.*** **1** to show or prove by facts, actions, feelings, etc. [I *demonstrated* my desire for an education by working my way through college.] **2** to explain by the use of examples or experiments [We can *demonstrate* the laws of heredity by breeding fruit flies.] **3** to show how something works or is used, especially in an effort to sell it [The sales person *demonstrated* the vacuum cleaner.] **4** to show one's feelings by taking part in a public meeting, parade, etc. [Thousands joined in the march to *demonstrate* for peace.] —**dem′on·strat·ed, dem′on·strat·ing**

**dem·on·stra·tion** (dem′ən strā′shən) ***n.*** **1** the act or means of demonstrating something; a showing, proving, or explaining [a *demonstration* of grief; a *demonstration* of an automobile]. **2** a meeting or parade of many people to show publicly how they feel about something.

**de·mon·stra·tive** (di män′strə tiv) ***adj.*** **1** showing one's feelings in a very open way [a *demonstrative* child]. **2** that points out ["That" and "these" are *demonstrative* pronouns.]

**dem·on·stra·tor** (dem′ən strāt′ər) ***n.*** **1** a person or thing that demonstrates, as a person who takes part in a public demonstration. ☆**2** a product, as an automobile, used for demonstration, in an effort to sell the product.

☆**de·mor·al·ize** (di môr′ə līz) ***v.*** to weaken the spirit or discipline of [The soldiers were *demoralized* by a lack of supplies.] —**de·mor′al·ized, de·mor′al·iz·ing —de·mor′al·i·za′tion *n.***

**De·mos·the·nes** (di mäs′thə nēz) 384?–322 B.C.; a famous Greek orator.

☆**de·mote** (di mōt′) ***v.*** to put in a lower grade or rank [The soldier was *demoted* from sergeant to private.] —**de·mot′ed, de·mot′ing —de·mo′tion *n.***

**de·mur** (di mur′) ***v.*** to be unwilling to do something; object [I want to help, but I *demur* at doing all the work.] —**de·murred′, de·mur′ring**

**de·mure** (di myoor′) ***adj.*** modest and shy or pretending to be modest and shy. —**de·mure′ly *adv.***

**den** (den) ***n.*** **1** a cave or other place where a wild animal makes its home; lair. *See the picture.* **2** a secret place where criminals meet. **3** a small, cozy room where one can be alone to read, work, etc.

**de·na·ture** (dē nā′chər) ***v.*** to change the nature of; especially, to make alcohol unfit for drinking without spoiling it for other uses. —**de·na′tured, de·na′tur·ing**

**den·drite** (den′drīt) ***n.*** the branched part of a nerve cell that carries impulses toward the cell body.

**de·ni·al** (di nī′əl) ***n.*** **1** the act of saying "no" to a request; refusal. **2** a statement that something is not true or right [a *denial* of the police officer's charges]. **3** the act of taking away or holding back [a *denial* of privileges]. **4** a refusal to recognize as one's own [a *denial* of one's family].

**den·im** (den′im) ***n.*** a coarse cotton cloth that will take hard wear and is used for work clothes or play clothes.

**den·i·zen** (den′i z'n) ***n.*** a person, animal, or plant that lives in a certain place [*denizens* of the city; winged *denizens* of the air].

**Den·mark** (den′märk) a country in northern Europe, on a peninsula and on several islands in the North and Baltic seas.

**de·nom·i·na·tion** (di näm′ə nā′shən) ***n.*** **1** a class or kind of thing with a particular name or value [coins of different *denominations*]. **2** a religious sect or group [Protestant *denominations,* as Lutheran and Baptist]. —**de·nom′i·na′tion·al *adj.***

**de·nom·i·na·tor** (di näm′ə nāt′ər) ***n.*** the number or quantity below or to the right of the line in a fraction. It shows the number of equal parts into which the whole has been divided [In the fraction 2/5, 5 is the *denominator.* John ate 2/5 of a pie, or 2 of the 5 equal parts.]

**de·no·ta·tion** (dē′nō tā′shən) ***n.*** **1** a denoting; indication. **2** the exact meaning of a word, without the added ideas that it may have taken on: *see also* **connotation.**

**de·note** (di nōt′) ***v.*** **1** to be a sign of; show [Dark clouds *denote* rain.] **2** to mean; stand for; be the name of [The words "metaphor" and "simile" *denote* two different figures of speech.] —**de·not′ed, de·not′ing**

**de·nounce** (di nouns′) ***v.*** **1** to speak out against in a strong way; say that something is bad [to *denounce* dishonesty in government]. **2** to give information against someone, as to the police; inform against. —**de·nounced′, de·nounc′ing**

**dense** (dens) ***adj.*** **1** having its parts close together; crowded; thick [a *dense* woods; a *dense* fog]. *See the picture.* **2** slow in understanding; stupid. —**dense′ly *adv.*** —**dense′ness *n.***

**den·si·ty** (den′sə tē) ***n.*** **1** the condition of being dense, thick, or crowded. **2** the quantity or mass of something for each unit of area or volume [the *density* of population per square mile; the *density* of a gas]. —*pl.* **den′si·ties**

**dent** (dent) ***n.*** a slight hollow made in a hard surface by a blow or by pressure. ◆***v.*** **1** to make a dent in. **2** to become dented.

**den·tal** (den′t'l) ***adj.*** having to do with the teeth or with a dentist's work.

☆**dental floss** thin, strong thread pulled between the teeth to remove tiny pieces of food.

☆**dental hygienist** a dentist's assistant, who cleans teeth, takes X-rays of the teeth, etc.

**den·ti·frice** (den′tə fris) ***n.*** any paste, powder, or liquid used to clean the teeth.

den
demijohn
denture
dense woods

**den·tin** (den′tin) or **den·tine** (den′tēn *or* den′tin) ***n.*** the hard, bony material forming the main part of a tooth, under the enamel. *See the picture for* **tooth.**

**den·tist** (den′tist) ***n.*** a doctor whose work is preventing and taking care of diseased or crooked teeth, or replacing them with artificial teeth.

**den·tist·ry** (den′tist rē) ***n.*** the work or profession of a dentist.



**den·ture** (den′chər) ***n.*** a set, or partial set, of artifical teeth made to fit into the mouth. *See the picture.*

**de·nude** (di no͞od′ *or* di nyo͞od′) ***v.*** to make bare or naked; strip [land *denuded* of trees]. —**de·nud′ed, de·nud′ing**

**de·nun·ci·a·tion** (di nun′sē ā′shən) ***n.*** the act of denouncing; a condemning, informing against, etc.

**Den·ver** (den′vər) the capital of Colorado.

**de·ny** (di nī′) ***v.*** **1** to say that something is not true or right; contradict [They *denied* that they had broken the window.] **2** to refuse to grant or give [We were *denied* permission to see the movie.] **3** to refuse to recognize as one's own; disown [He *denied* his father.] **4** to refuse the use of [The rules of the club *deny* lockers to all except members.] —**de·nied′, de·ny′ing** —**deny oneself,** to do without things that one wants.

**de·o·dor·ant** (dē ō′dər ənt) ***adj.*** that stops or covers up bad smells. ◆***n.*** a deodorant salve, liquid, spray, etc. used on the body.

**de·o·dor·ize** (dē ō′dər īz) ***v.*** to remove or cover up the smell of. —**de·o′dor·ized, de·o′dor·iz·ing**

**de·part** (di pärt′) ***v.*** **1** to go away; set out; leave [The train will *depart* on time.] **2** to turn aside; change [They *departed* from custom and ate out on Thanksgiving.] **3** to die.

| | | | |
|---|---|---|---|
| **a** fat | **ir** here | **ou** out | **zh** leisure |
| **ā** ape | **ī** bite, fire | **u** up | **ng** ring |
| **ä** car, lot | **ō** go | **ur** fur | a *in* ago |
| **e** ten | **ô** law, horn | **ch** chin | e *in* agent |
| **er** care | **oi** oil | **sh** she | **ə** = i *in* unity |
| **ē** even | **oo** look | **th** thin | o *in* collect |
| **i** hit | **o͞o** tool | ***th*** then | u *in* focus |

**de·part·ed** (di pär′tid) ***adj.*** dead [our *departed* ancestors]. —**the departed,** the dead person or persons.

**de·part·ment** (di pärt′mənt) ***n.*** a separate part or branch, as of a government or business [the police *department;* the shipping *department;* the *department* of mathematics in a college]. —**de·part·men·tal** (di pärt′men′t'l *or* dē′pärt men′t'l) ***adj.***

☆**department store** a large store with separate departments for selling many kinds of goods.

**de·par·ture** (di pär′chər) ***n.*** **1** a departing; going away. **2** a turning aside, or changing to something new [Office work is a new *departure* for me.]

**de·pend** (di pend′) ***v.*** **1** to be controlled or decided by [The attendance at the game *depends* on the weather.] **2** to put one's trust in; be sure of [You can't *depend* on the weather.] **3** to rely for help or support [They *depend* on their parents for money.] *See* SYNONYMS *at* **rely.**

**de·pend·a·ble** (di pen′də b'l) ***adj.*** that can be depended on; reliable [a *dependable* friend]. —**de·pend′a·bil′i·ty** ***n.***

**de·pend·ence** (di pen′dəns) ***n.*** **1** the condition of being controlled or decided by something else. **2** a depending on another for help or support. **3** trust; reliance [They place *dependence* on my word.]

**de·pend·en·cy** (di pen′dən sē) ***n.*** **1** *same as* **dependence. 2** a land or country that is controlled by another country. —*pl.* **de·pend′en·cies**

198 **de·pend·ent** (di pen′dənt) ***adj.*** **1** controlled or decided by something else [The size of my allowance was *dependent* on our family income.] **2** relying on another for help or support [A baby is completely *dependent* on its parents.] ◆***n.*** a person who depends on someone else for support.

**dependent clause** *another name for* **subordinate clause.**

**de·pict** (di pikt′) ***v.*** **1** to be a picture of; portray [This painting *depicts* a London street.] **2** to picture in words; describe [The novel *depicts* life in a small town.] —**de·pic′tion** ***n.***

**de·pil·a·to·ry** (di pil′ə tôr′ē) ***adj.*** that is used to remove unwanted hair. ◆***n.*** a cream or other substance or a device used to remove unwanted hair. —*pl.* **de·pil′a·to′ries**

**de·plane** (dē plān′) ***v.*** to get out of an airplane after it lands. —**de·planed′, de·plan′ing**

**de·plete** (di plēt′) ***v.*** to empty or use up; exhaust [Lack of rain will soon *deplete* our water supply. My energy was *depleted.*] —**de·plet′ed, de·plet′ing** —**de·ple′tion** ***n.***

**de·plor·a·ble** (di plôr′ə b'l) ***adj.*** that can or should be deplored; regrettable; very bad [a *deplorable* error; *deplorable* slums]. —**de·plor′a·bly** ***adv.***

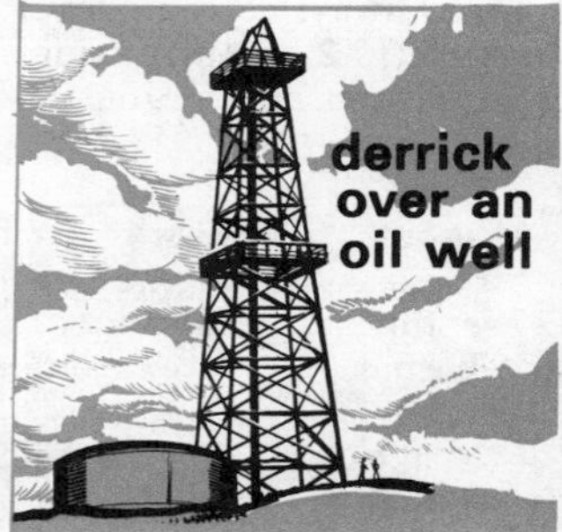

**de·plore** (di plôr′) ***v.*** to be sorry about; feel or show deep regret about [The editorial *deplored* the lack of playgrounds in the city.] —**de·plored′, de·plor′ing**

**de·pop·u·late** (dē päp′yə lāt) ***v.*** to lessen the number of people in [A plague *depopulated* Europe in the 14th century.] —**de·pop′u·lat·ed, de·pop′u·lat·ing** —**de·pop′u·la′tion** ***n.***

**de·port** (di pôrt′) ***v.*** **1** to force to leave a country by official order; banish [They were *deported* for having entered the country illegally.] **2** to behave in a certain way [The members of the class *deported* themselves like adults.]

SYNONYMS: To **deport** is to send persons who are not citizens out of the country either because they entered illegally or because the government thinks they are undesirable to have in the country. To be **exiled** is to be forced to leave one's own country because the government has ordered it or because staying there might be dangerous or unpleasant.

**de·por·ta·tion** (dē′pôr tā′shən) ***n.*** a deporting or being deported from a country.

**de·port·ment** (di pôrt′mənt) ***n.*** the way a person behaves; good or bad manners; behavior.

**de·pose** (di pōz′) ***v.*** **1** to remove from a position of power, especially from a throne. **2** to state or testify under oath but out of court. —**de·posed′, de·pos′ing**

**de·pos·it** (di päz′it) ***v.*** **1** to place for safekeeping, as money in a bank. **2** to give as part payment or as a pledge [They *deposited* $500 on a new car.] **3** to lay down [I *deposited* my books on the chair. The river *deposits* tons of mud at its mouth.] ◆***n.*** **1** something placed for safekeeping, as money in a bank. **2** the state of being so placed [I have $200 on *deposit.*] **3** money given as a pledge or part payment. **4** something left lying, as sand, clay, or minerals deposited by the action of wind, water, or other forces of nature.

**dep·o·si·tion** (dep′ə zish′ən) ***n.*** **1** the act of removing someone from a position of power [the *deposition* of a king]. **2** the written statement of a witness, made under oath but not in court, to be used later at a trial.

**de·pos·i·tor** (di päz′ə tər) ***n.*** a person who deposits something, especially money in a bank.

**de·pos·i·to·ry** (di päz′ə tôr′ē) ***n.*** a place where things are put for safekeeping; storehouse. —*pl.* **de·pos′i·to′ries**

**de·pot** (dē′pō) ***n.*** **1** a storehouse or warehouse. ☆**2** a railroad or bus station. **3** (dep′ō) a place for storing military supplies.

**de·prave** (di prāv′) ***v.*** to make bad, wicked, or corrupt [They had become *depraved* by living in prison.] —**de·praved′, de·prav′ing**

**Deprave** comes from a Latin word meaning "to make crooked." Being depraved means going away from what is thought to be the straight or proper way of behaving.

**de·prav·i·ty** (di prav′ə tē) ***n.*** a depraved condition or act; wickedness. —*pl.* **de·prav′i·ties**

**dep·re·cate** (dep′rə kāt) ***v.*** **1** to feel or show disapproval of [The speaker *deprecated* our lack of interest.] **2** to make seem unimportant; belittle [to be self-*deprecating*]. —**dep′re·cat·ed, dep′re·cat·ing** —**dep′re·ca′tion** ***n.***

**dep·re·ca·to·ry** (dep′rə kə tôr′ē) ***adj.*** that deprecates, shows disapproval, or makes seem unimportant [a *deprecatory* remark].

**de·pre·ci·ate** (di prē′shē āt) ***v.*** **1** to make or become less in value [An automobile *depreciates* with age.] **2** to make seem unimportant; belittle [I don't like to hear you *depreciate* yourself.] —**de·pre′ci·at·ed, de·pre′ci·at·ing** —**de·pre′ci·a′tion** ***n.***

**dep·re·da·tion** (dep′rə dā′shən) ***n.*** a robbing, plundering, or destroying, as by enemy troops.

**de·press** (di pres′) ***v.*** **1** to make sad or gloomy; discourage. **2** to press down; lower [*Depress* the gas pedal slowly.] **3** to make less active; weaken [The high cost of materials has *depressed* the building industry.]

**de·pres·sion** (di presh′ən) ***n.*** **1** sadness; gloominess [to suffer from a fit of *depression*]. **2** a pressing down, or lowering. **3** a hollow or low place [Water collected in the *depressions* in the ground.] ☆**4** a period during which there is less business and many people lose their jobs.

**de·prive** (di prīv′) ***v.*** **1** to take away from by force; dispossess [The Indians were *deprived* of their lands.] **2** to keep from having or enjoying [I hope this won't *deprive* me of your company.] —**de·prived′, de·priv′ing** —**dep·ri·va·tion** (dep′rə vā′shən) ***n.***

**dept.** *abbreviation for* **department.**

**depth** (depth) ***n.*** **1** the fact of being deep, or how deep a thing is; deepness [the *depth* of the ocean; a closet five feet in *depth;* the *depth* of a color; the great *depth* of their love]. **2** the middle part [the *depth* of winter]. **3** *usually* **depths,** *pl.* the part farthest in; also, the deep or deepest part [the *depths* of a wood; from the *depths* of one's heart]. —**out of one's depth** or **beyond one's depth,** beyond what one can do or understand.

**dep·u·ta·tion** (dep′yoo tā′shən) ***n.*** a group of persons sent to act for others; delegation [Our neighborhood sent a *deputation* to the mayor to ask for street repairs.]

**de·pute** (di pyōōt′) ***v.*** to choose a person to take one's place or to do one's work [Early painters often *deputed* helpers to finish their paintings.] —**de·put′ed, de·put′ing**

**dep·u·tize** (dep′yə tīz) ***v.*** to make a person one's deputy. —**dep′u·tized, dep′u·tiz·ing**

**dep·u·ty** (dep′yə tē) ***n.*** a person chosen to take the place of or help another [a sheriff's *deputy*]. —*pl.* **dep′u·ties**

**de·rail** (di rāl′) ***v.*** to go or cause to go off the rails [to *derail* a train]. —**de·rail′ment** ***n.***

**de·range** (di rānj′) ***v.*** **1** to make a person insane. **2** to upset the order or working of; mix up [Our routine was *deranged* by their visit.] —**de·ranged′, de·rang′ing** —**de·range′ment** ***n.***

**Der·by** (dur′bē) ***n.*** **1** any of certain famous horse races [the Kentucky *Derby*]. —*pl.* **Der′bies** ☆**2 derby,** a stiff felt hat with a round crown. *See the picture.* —*pl.* **der′bies**

☆**de·reg·u·late** (dē reg′yə lāt) ***v.*** to do away with the regulations concerning [Should the government *deregulate* the price of natural gas?] —**de·reg′u·lat·ed, de·reg′u·lat·ing**

**der·e·lict** (der′ə likt) ***adj.*** **1** that has been deserted and given up as lost [a *derelict* ship at sea]. ☆**2** not doing what one should do; neglectful [to be *derelict* in one's duty]. ◆***n.*** **1** a ship deserted at sea. **2** a poor, homeless person without friends or a job.

**der·e·lic·tion** (der′ə lik′shən) ***n.*** **1** an abandoning or being abandoned: *now seldom used.* **2** a failing to do one's duty [guilty of a *dereliction*].

**de·ride** (di rīd′) ***v.*** to make fun of; laugh at in a scornful way; ridicule. —**de·rid′ed, de·rid′ing**

**de·ri·sion** (di rizh′ən) ***n.*** a deriding; jeering or ridicule.

**de·ri·sive** (di rī′siv) ***adj.*** deriding, or making fun; ridiculing. —**de·ri′sive·ly** ***adv.***

**der·i·va·tion** (der′ə vā′shən) ***n.*** **1** a deriving or developing from some source. **2** the source or origin of anything [a Roman myth of Greek *derivation*]. **3** the way in which a word has developed from some source [This dictionary gives the *derivations* as well as the meanings for many words.]

**de·riv·a·tive** (də riv′ə tiv) ***adj.*** derived from something else; not original [*derivative* art]. ◆***n.*** something derived from something else [Certain medicines are *derivatives* of coal tar.]

**de·rive** (di rīv′) ***v.*** **1** to get or receive from a source [We *derive* gasoline from petroleum. Many English words are *derived* from Latin. I *derive* enjoyment from music.] **2** to come from a certain source [Our laws *derive* from those of England.] —**de·rived′, de·riv′ing**

**der·ma** (dur′mə) or **der·mis** (dur′mis) ***n.*** the layer of skin just below the outer skin. 

**der·ma·ti·tis** (dur′mə tīt′is) ***n.*** a condition of the skin in which it becomes inflamed.

**de·rog·a·to·ry** (di räg′ə tôr′ē) ***adj.*** meant to make someone or something seem lower or of less value; belittling [*derogatory* remarks].

**der·rick** (der′ik) ***n.*** **1** a large machine for lifting and moving heavy things. It has a long beam that is supported and moved by ropes and pulleys. ☆**2** a tall framework, as over an oil well, that holds machinery for drilling or pumping, etc. *See the picture.*

**der·vish** (dur′vish) ***n.*** a member of any of various Muslim religious groups which live a life of poverty.

☆**de·sal·i·na·tion** (dē sal′ə nā′shən) ***n.*** the removal of salt from sea water to make it drinkable: *also* **de·sal′i·ni·za′tion.**

**de·scend** (di send′) ***v.*** **1** to move down to a lower place [to *descend* from a hilltop; to *descend* a staircase]. **2** to become lesser or smaller [Prices have *descended* during the past month.] **3** to come from a certain source [They are *descended* from pioneers.] **4** to be passed on to an heir [This house will *descend* to my children.] **5** to lower oneself in dignity [She has *descended* to begging for money.] **6** to make a sudden attack [The troops *descended* upon the enemy camp.]

**de·scend·ant** (di sen′dənt) ***n.*** a person who is descended from a certain ancestor.

| | | | | | | | |
|---|---|---|---|---|---|---|---|
| **a** | fat | **ir** | here | **ou** | out | **zh** | leisure |
| **ā** | ape | **ī** | bite, fire | **u** | up | **ng** | ring |
| **ä** | car, lot | **ō** | go | **ur** | fur | | a *in* ago |
| **e** | ten | **ô** | law, horn | **ch** | chin | | e *in* agent |
| **er** | care | **oi** | oil | **sh** | she | **ə =** | i *in* unity |
| **ē** | even | **oo** | look | **th** | thin | | o *in* collect |
| **i** | hit | **ōō** | tool | ***th*** | then | | u *in* focus |

destroyer

detached garage

**de·scent** (di sent′) ***n.*** **1** a descending, or moving down to a lower place. **2** a way or slope downward [a steep *descent* down the mountain]. **3** a sudden attack. **4** a becoming lower; decline; fall [a sharp *descent* in prices]. **5** a family from which one descends; ancestry [someone of French *descent*].

**de·scribe** (di skrīb′) ***v.*** **1** to tell or write about in some detail [to *describe* a trip one has taken]. **2** to trace or form the outline of [His hand *described* a circle in the air.] —**de·scribed′**, **de·scrib′ing** —**de·scrib′a·ble** ***adj.***



**de·scrip·tion** (di skrip′shən) ***n.*** **1** the act of describing something or words that describe [The ad had a *description* of the lost dog.] **2** sort or kind [books of every *description*].

**de·scrip·tive** (di skrip′tiv) ***adj.*** describing; that describes [*descriptive* writing].

**de·scry** (di skrī′) ***v.*** to catch sight of something far away or hard to see [We suddenly *descried* land straight ahead.] —**de·scried′**, **de·scry′ing**

**des·e·crate** (des′ə krāt) ***v.*** to use something sacred in a wrong or bad way; treat as not sacred [to *desecrate* a Bible by marking it up]. —**des′e·crat·ed**, **des′e·crat·ing** —**des′e·cra′tion** ***n.***

**de·seg·re·gate** (dē seg′rə gāt) ***v.*** to stop the practice of keeping people of different races separate, as in public schools. —**de·seg′re·gat·ed**, **de·seg′re·gat·ing** —**de·seg′re·ga′tion** ***n.***

**de·sert**¹ (di zʉrt′) ***v.*** **1** to go away from someone or something that one ought not to leave; abandon [to *desert* one's wife]. **2** to leave a military post without permission and with no idea of coming back. —**de·sert′er** ***n.*** —**de·ser′tion** ***n.***

SYNONYMS: To **desert** is to run away on purpose from someone or something one is bound to by duty or a promise [Thousands of men *deserted* from the army.] To **abandon** is to leave someone or something because it is necessary to do so [to *abandon* a sinking ship] or because one has no sense of responsibility [to *abandon* kittens along the highway].

**des·ert**² (dez′ərt) ***n.*** a dry sandy region with little or no plant life. ◆***adj.*** **1** of or like a desert. **2** wild and not lived in [a *desert* island].

**de·sert**³ (di zʉrt′) ***n.*** what a person deserves, either as reward or punishment: *often used in the plural,* **deserts** [The villains in fairy tales usually get their just *deserts*.]

**de·serve** (di zʉrv′) ***v.*** to have a right to; be one that ought to get [This matter *deserves* thought. You *deserve* a scolding.] —**de·served′**, **de·serv′ing** —**de·serv′ed·ly** ***adv.***

**de·serv·ing** (di zʉr′viŋ) ***adj.*** that ought to get help or a reward [a *deserving* student].

**des·ic·cate** (des′i kāt) ***v.*** to dry completely [Prunes are *desiccated* plums.] —**des′ic·cat·ed**, **des′ic·cat·ing**

**de·sign** (di zīn′) ***v.*** **1** to think up and draw plans for [to *design* a new model of a car]. **2** to arrange the parts, colors, etc. of [Who *designed* this book?] **3** to set apart for a certain use; intend [This chair was not *designed* for hard use.] ◆***n.*** **1** a drawing or plan to be followed in making something [the *designs* for a house]. **2** the arrangement of parts, colors, etc.; pattern or decoration [the *design* in a rug]. **3** a plan or purpose [It was my *design* to study law.] **4 designs,** *pl.* a secret plan, usually a dishonest or selfish one [They had *designs* on my money.] —**by design,** on purpose.

**des·ig·nate** (dez′ig nāt) ***v.*** **1** to point out; show [Cities are *designated* on this map by dots.] **2** to choose or appoint [We have *designated* Smith to be chief delegate.] **3** to give a name to; call [The highest rank in the army is *designated* "general."] —**des′ig·nat·ed**, **des′ig·nat·ing** —**des′ig·na′tion** ***n.***

**designated hitter** a baseball player in the regular batting order whose only action in the game is to bat in place of the pitcher.

**de·sign·er** (di zī′nər) ***n.*** a person who designs or makes original plans [a dress *designer*].

**de·sign·ing** (di zī′niŋ) ***adj.*** **1** that designs or makes plans or patterns. **2** plotting or scheming. ◆***n.*** the art or work of making designs.

**de·sir·a·ble** (di zīr′ə b′l) ***adj.*** worth wanting or having; pleasing, excellent, beautiful, etc. —**de·sir′a·bil′i·ty** ***n.*** —**de·sir′a·bly** ***adv.***

**de·sire** (di zīr′) ***v.*** **1** to wish or long for; want strongly [to *desire* fame]. **2** to ask for; request [The principal *desires* to see you in her office.] —**de·sired′**, **de·sir′ing** ◆***n.*** **1** a strong wish. **2** the thing wished for.

SYNONYMS: **Desire** can be used in place of **wish** or **want** to mean "to long for," but carries a stronger feeling [to *desire* success]. **Wish** is sometimes used when one longs for something that is not likely to be fulfilled [They *wished* summer were here.] **Want** is used when one longs for something lacking or needed, and is less formal than **wish** [I *want,* or *wish,* to go with them.]

**de·sir·ous** (di zīr′əs) ***adj.*** desiring; wanting [to be *desirous* of learning].

**de·sist** (di zist′) ***v.*** to stop doing something; cease [*Desist* from fighting.]

**desk** (desk) ***n.*** a piece of furniture with a smooth top at which one can write, draw, or read. It often has drawers for storing things.

**Des Moines** (də moin′) the capital of Iowa.

**des·o·late** (des′ə lit) ***adj.*** **1** left alone; lonely; forlorn [The father was *desolate* without his children.] **2** not lived in; deserted [a *desolate* wilderness]. **3** ruined or destroyed [the *desolate* farms in a drought area]. **4** very unhappy; miserable [The death of their friend left them *desolate.*] ◆*v.* (des′ə lāt) **1** to make unfit for life; ruin; destroy [The tornado *desolated* many towns.] **2** to leave alone; forsake; abandon. **3** to make unhappy or miserable [We were *desolated* by the robbery.] —**des′o·lat·ed, des′o·lat·ing —des′o·la′·tion *n.***

**De So·to** (di sōt′ō), **Her·nan·do** (hər nan′dō) 1500?–1542; Spanish explorer who discovered the Mississippi River.

**de·spair** (di sper′) ***n.*** **1** a giving up or loss of hope [Sam is in *despair* of ever getting a vacation.] **2** a person or thing that causes one to lose hope [That student is the *despair* of all the teachers.] ◆*v.* to lose or give up hope [The prisoner *despaired* of ever being free again.]

**des·per·a·do** (des′pə rä′dō *or* des′pə rā′dō) ***n.*** a dangerous, reckless criminal; bold outlaw. —*pl.* **des′per·a′does** or **des′per·a′dos**

**des·per·ate** (des′pər it) ***adj.*** **1** reckless because one has lost hope [This *desperate* criminal has broken out of jail.] **2** having a very great desire, need, etc. [*desperate* for love]. **3** making one lose hope; very dangerous or serious [a *desperate* illness]. **4** very great [in *desperate* need]. —**des′per·ate·ly *adv.***

**des·per·a·tion** (des′pə rā′shən) ***n.*** **1** the condition of being desperate. **2** recklessness that comes from despair [In *desperation* the hunted deer leaped across the chasm.]

**des·pi·ca·ble** (des′pik ə b′l *or* di spik′ə b′l) ***adj.*** that deserves to be despised; contemptible [a *despicable* bully]. —**des′pi·ca·bly *adv.***

**de·spise** (di spīz′) ***v.*** to dislike strongly and feel scorn for [I *despise* cheaters.] —**de·spised′, de·spis′ing**

**de·spite** (di spīt′) ***prep.*** in spite of; regardless of [We started out *despite* the storm.]

**de·spoil** (di spoil′) ***v.*** to rob or plunder [The museum was *despoiled* of its treasures.]

**de·spond·ent** (di spän′dənt) ***adj.*** having lost one's hope or courage; discouraged [He is *despondent* over the loss of his job.] —**de·spond′en·cy** or **de·spond′·ence *n.***

**des·pot** (des′pət) ***n.*** a person who has complete control over a group of people; especially, a cruel and unjust ruler; tyrant. —**des·pot·ic** (de spät′ik) ***adj.*** —**des′pot·ism *n.***

**des·sert** (di zʉrt′) ***n.*** ☆something sweet served at the end of a meal, as fruit, pie, or cake.

**des·ti·na·tion** (des′tə nā′shən) ***n.*** the place that a person or thing is going to [We shall visit Belgium, but our *destination* is Paris.]

**des·tine** (des′tin) ***v.*** to head toward some goal or end, as if led by fate [The play seemed *destined* to succeed.] —**des′tined, des′tin·ing —destined for, 1** intended for [She seems *destined for* a career as a singer.] **2** bound for; headed for [We were *destined for* home.]

**des·tin·y** (des′tə nē) ***n.*** **1** that which is bound to happen; one's fate [Was it my *destiny* to become a teacher?] **2** that which seems to make things happen the way they do; fate [*Destiny* brought us here.] —*pl.* **des′tin·ies**

**des·ti·tute** (des′tə to͞ot *or* des′tə tyo͞ot) ***adj.*** **1** having no money or means by which to live; very poor. **2** not having; being without; lacking [The desert is *destitute* of trees.]

**des·ti·tu·tion** (des′tə to͞o′shən *or* des′tə tyo͞o′shən) ***n.*** the condition of being destitute or very poor; complete poverty.

**de·stroy** (di stroi′) ***v.*** to put an end to by breaking up, tearing down, ruining, or spoiling [The flood *destroyed* 300 homes.]

**de·stroy·er** (di stroi′ər) ***n.*** **1** a person or thing that destroys. **2** a small, fast warship. *See the picture.*

**de·struc·tion** (di struk′shən) ***n.*** the act of destroying or the condition of being destroyed; ruin [The forest fire caused much *destruction.*]

**de·struc·tive** (di struk′tiv) ***adj.*** destroying or likely to destroy [a *destructive* windstorm].

**des·ul·to·ry** (des″l tôr′ē) ***adj.*** passing from one thing to another in an aimless way [Their talk at lunch was *desultory*.]

**de·tach** (di tach′) ***v.*** **1** to unfasten and take away; disconnect [Five cars were *detached* from the train.] **2** to choose and send on a special task [Soldiers were *detached* to guard the President's train.] —**de·tach′a·ble *adj.***

**de·tached** (di tacht′) ***adj.*** **1** separate; not connected [a *detached* garage]. *See the picture.* **2** not taking sides or having feelings one way or the other; aloof [a *detached* observer].

**de·tach·ment** (di tach′mənt) ***n.*** **1** a detaching; separation. **2** troops or ships chosen and sent on a special task [a *detachment* of guards]. **3** the state of being detached or aloof [Try to look at your troubles with *detachment.*]



**de·tail** (di tāl′ *or* dē′tāl) ***n.*** **1** any of the small parts that go to make up something; item [Tell us all the *details* of your plan. You must use care on the *details* of your painting.] *See* SYNONYMS *at* **item. 2** a dealing with things item by item [Don't go into *detail* about your trip.] **3** a small group of soldiers or sailors chosen for a special task; also, the special task [A *detail* was sent to blow up the bridge.] ◆*v.* **1** to give all the details of [The mechanic had to *detail* all costs of repairs on the bill.] **2** to choose for a special task [*Detail* someone for sentry duty.] —**in detail,** item by item; leaving out no detail.

> **Detail** comes from a French word meaning "to cut up." **Tailor** comes from the same word. A tailor cuts up a larger piece of cloth into smaller pieces which he then sews together so that they make up something, as a suit. A good tailor is careful about details.

**de·tain** (di tān′) ***v.*** **1** to keep from going on; hold back [A long freight train *detained* us.] **2** to keep for a while in jail; confine [They were *detained* by the police for questioning.]

**de·tect** (di tekt′) ***v.*** to discover something hidden or not easily noticed [to *detect* a slight flaw]. —**de·tec′·tion *n.***

| | | | |
|---|---|---|---|
| **a** fat | **ir** here | **ou** out | **zh** leisure |
| **ā** ape | **ī** bite, fire | **u** up | **ng** ring |
| **ä** car, lot | **ō** go | **ʉr** fur | a *in* ago |
| **e** ten | **ô** law, horn | **ch** chin | e *in* agent |
| **er** care | **oi** oil | **sh** she | **ə** = i *in* unity |
| **ē** even | **oo** look | **th** thin | o *in* collect |
| **i** hit | **o͞o** tool | ***th*** then | u *in* focus |

**de·tec·tive** (di tek′tiv) ***n.*** a person, usually on a police force, whose work is trying to solve crimes, getting secret information, etc. ◆***adj.*** of detectives and their work.

**de·tec·tor** (di tek′tər) ***n.*** a person or thing that detects; especially, a device used to show that something is present.

**de·ten·tion** (di ten′shən) ***n.*** a detaining or being detained; forced delay or confinement [his long *detention* in the county jail].

**de·ter** (di tur′) ***v.*** to keep a person from doing something through fear, doubt, etc.; discourage [Does the death penalty *deter* crime?] —**de·terred′, de·ter′ring**

**de·ter·gent** (di tur′jənt) ***adj.*** that cleans [a *detergent* wax that cleans and polishes]. ◆***n.*** a substance used for cleaning, especially one that looks and acts like soap but is made from certain chemicals, not from fats and lye.

**de·te·ri·o·rate** (di tir′ē ə rāt′) ***v.*** to make or become worse; turn bad [The neglected old house has *deteriorated* in recent years.] —**de·te′ri·o·rat′ed, de·te′ri·o·rat′ing** —**de·te′ri·o·ra′tion** ***n.***

**de·ter·mi·nant** (di tur′mi nənt) ***adj.*** that determines or decides. ◆***n.*** a thing that determines; deciding factor.

**de·ter·mi·na·tion** (di tur′mə nā′shən) ***n.*** **1** a deciding or finding out for sure. **2** firmness of purpose; fixed aim [Our team's *determination* to win never weakened.]



**de·ter·mine** (di tur′mən) ***v.*** **1** to settle or decide on [I haven't *determined* whether to go to college.] **2** to set one's mind on something; resolve [She is *determined* to be a lawyer.] **3** to find out exactly [First *determine* the area of the floor.] **4** to be the thing that decides; have an important effect on [One's hobbies often *determine* what one chooses to do for a living.] —**de·ter′mined, de·ter′min·ing**

**de·ter·mined** (di tur′mənd) ***adj.*** **1** having one's mind set; decided; resolved [*Determined* to pass the course, we studied hard.] **2** firm and unwavering [a *determined* knock on the door].

**de·ter·rent** (di tur′ənt) ***adj.*** that deters. ◆***n.*** a thing that deters [Is the chance of going to prison a *deterrent* to crime?]

**de·test** (di test′) ***v.*** to dislike with strong feeling; hate; abhor. —**de·test′a·ble** ***adj.*** —**de·tes·ta·tion** (dē′tes tā′shən) ***n.***

**de·throne** (dē thrōn′) ***v.*** to remove from a throne or from any high position. —**de·throned′, de·thron′ing**

**det·o·nate** (det′′n āt) ***v.*** to explode with much noise. —**det′o·nat·ed, det′o·nat·ing** —**det·o·na·tion** (det′′n ā′shən) ***n.***

**det·o·na·tor** (det′′n āt′ər) ***n.*** a fuse or the like for setting off an explosive.

**de·tour** (dē′to͞or) ***n.*** **1** a turning aside from the direct or regular route. **2** a route used when the regular route is closed to traffic. ◆***v.*** to go or send by a detour.

**de·tract** (di trakt′) ***v.*** to take away something, especially something worthwhile or attractive [Weeds *detract* from the beauty of a lawn.] —**de·trac′tion** ***n.*** —**de·trac′tor** ***n.***

**det·ri·ment** (det′rə mənt) ***n.*** damage or harm, or something that causes this [She watches TV all evening to the *detriment* of her studies.] —**det′ri·men′tal** ***adj.***

**De·troit** (di troit′) a city in southeastern Michigan.

**deuce**[1] (do͞os *or* dyo͞os) ***n.*** **1** a playing card with two spots. *See the picture.* **2** a tie score of 40 points each or 5 games each in tennis.

**deuce**[2] (do͞os *or* dyo͞os) ***n., interj.*** the devil or bad luck: *used as a mild curse to show that one is annoyed, surprised, etc.*

**Deu·ter·on·o·my** (do͞ot′ər än′ə mē *or* dyo͞ot′ər än′ə mē) the fifth book of the Bible.

**De Va·ler·a** (dev′ə ler′ə), **Ea·mon** (ā′mən) 1882–1975; a prime minister of Ireland and then, from 1959 to 1973, the president of Ireland.

**dev·as·tate** (dev′ə stāt) ***v.*** to ruin or destroy completely; make waste [A nuclear war could *devastate* the world.] —**dev′as·tat·ed, dev′as·tat·ing** —**dev′as·ta′tion** ***n.***

**de·vel·op** (di vel′əp) ***v.*** **1** to make or become larger, fuller, better, etc.; grow or expand [The seedling *developed* into a tree. Reading *develops* one's knowledge.] **2** to bring or come into being and work out gradually; evolve [Dr. Salk *developed* a vaccine for polio. Mold *developed* on the cheese.] **3** to treat an exposed photographic film or plate with chemicals, so as to show the picture. **4** to become known [It *developed* that Pat had the highest batting average.]

**de·vel·op·ment** (di vel′əp mənt) ***n.*** **1** the act of developing; a causing to grow, expand, improve, etc. **2** a thing that is developed, as a tract of land with newly built homes, etc. **3** a happening; event [an unexpected *development* in a case]. —**de·vel·op·men·tal** (di vel′əp men′t′l) ***adj.***

**de·vi·ate** (dē′vē āt) ***v.*** to turn aside from the usual or expected way, goal, rule, standard, etc. [The story of the witness never *deviated* from the truth.] —**de′vi·at·ed, de′vi·at·ing** —**de′vi·a′tion** ***n.***

**de·vice** (di vīs′) ***n.*** **1** something made or invented for some special use; tool, machine, etc. [A windmill is a *device* for putting wind power to work.] **2** a plan that has been worked out to bring about a certain result; scheme [Sending him on an errand was a *device* to get him out of the house.] **3** a design or emblem, as on a shield or badge. —**leave to one's own devices,** to allow to do as one wishes.

**dev·il** (dev′′l) ***n.*** **1** any of the evil spirits of hell in religious belief and in folk tales; especially, **the Devil,** the chief evil spirit, who is also called Satan. He is usually shown as a man with horns, a forked tail, etc. **2** an evil or cruel person or spirit. **3** a person who is very lively, playful, daring, etc. **4** a very unhappy or unlucky person. **5** a printer's helper. ◆***v.*** to annoy or tease. —**dev′iled** or **dev′illed, dev′il·ing,** or **dev′il·ling** —**dev′il·ish** ***adj.***

**dev·iled** or **dev·illed** (dev′′ld) ***adj.*** chopped up fine and highly seasoned [*deviled* ham].

**dev·il·fish** (dev′′l fish) ***n.*** **1** the largest kind of ray, a fish with a broad, flat body and a long tail. *See the picture.* **2** *another name for* **octopus.**

**dev·il-may-care** (dev′′l mā ker′) ***adj.*** reckless or careless; happy-go-lucky.

**dev·il·ment** (dev′′l mənt) ***n.*** mischief or mischievous action.

☆**dev·il's-food cake** (dev′'lz fo͞od′) a rich chocolate cake.

**dev·il·try** (dev′'l trē) ***n.*** reckless mischief, fun, etc.

**de·vi·ous** (dē′vē əs) ***adj.*** **1** not in a straight path; roundabout; winding [We approached by a *devious* trail that followed a creek.] **2** that strays from what is right or usual; not frank [*devious* behavior]. —**de′vi·ous·ly** ***adv.***

**de·vise** (di vīz′) ***v.*** **1** to work out; think up; plan or invent something [to *devise* a scheme to make money]. **2** to give or leave in a will. —**de·vised′, de·vis′ing**

**de·void** (di void′) ***adj.*** without any; empty [a person *devoid* of pity; a room *devoid* of color].

**de·volve** (di välv′) ***v.*** to be passed on [When the president is away, the duties *devolve* on the vice-president.] —**de·volved′, de·volv′ing**

**de·vote** (di vōt′) ***v.*** to give up to some purpose, activity, or person [They *devote* many hours to helping others.] —**de·vot′ed, de·vot′ing**

**de·vot·ed** (di vōt′id) ***adj.*** very loving or loyal [a *devoted* father; a *devoted* supporter].

**dev·o·tee** (dev ə tē′ *or* dev ə tā′) ***n.*** a person who is strongly devoted to something or someone [a *devotee* of the theater].

**de·vo·tion** (di vō′shən) ***n.*** **1** a devoting or being devoted [his *devotion* to his wife; her *devotion* to the cause]. **2 devotions,** *pl.* prayers, especially when done in private. —**de·vo′tion·al** ***adj.***

**de·vour** (di vour′) ***v.*** **1** to eat up in a hungry or greedy way. **2** to ruin or destroy [The little town was *devoured* by the landslide.] **3** to take in greedily with the eyes or ears [My cousin *devours* comic books.] **4** to swallow up; absorb [She was *devoured* by curiosity.]

**de·vout** (di vout′) ***adj.*** **1** very religious; pious. *See* SYNONYMS *at* **pious. 2** serious and with deep feeling; sincere [a *devout* admirer]. —**de·vout′ly** ***adv.*** —**de·vout′ness** ***n.***

**dew** (do͞o *or* dyo͞o) ***n.*** **1** water from the air that forms in little drops on cool surfaces at night. **2** anything like dew, as droplets of sweat. —**dew′y** ***adj.***

**dew·drop** (do͞o′dräp *or* dyo͞o′dräp) ***n.*** a drop of dew.

**Dew·ey** (do͞o′ē *or* dyo͞o′ē), **John** 1859–1952; U.S. philosopher and educator.

**dew·lap** (do͞o′lap *or* dyo͞o′lap) ***n.*** a fold of skin hanging under the throat of cattle, etc. *See the picture.*

☆**DEW line** (do͞o *or* dyo͞o) a line of radar stations in the far north of North America, that can give warning of enemy air attack. The letters DEW come from the words *Distant Early Warning.*

**dex·ter·i·ty** (dek ster′ə tē) ***n.*** skill in the use of one's hands, body, or mind [The barber shows *dexterity* with the scissors. He has the *dexterity* of a diplomat.]

**dex·ter·ous** (dek′strəs *or* dek′stər əs) ***adj.*** skillful in the use of the hands, body, or mind; deft or clever [a *dexterous* surgeon]. —**dex′ter·ous·ly** ***adv.***

**dex·trose** (dek′strōs) ***n.*** a sugar found in plants and animals; glucose.

**dex·trous** (dek′strəs) ***adj.*** *same as* **dexterous.**

**dh** or **d.h.** *abbreviation for* **designated hitter.**

**di-** *a prefix meaning* two *or* double [Carbon *dioxide* has two atoms of oxygen per molecule.]

**dia-** *a prefix meaning* through *or* across [A *diagonal* line slants across a figure.]

**di·a·be·tes** (dī′ə bēt′is *or* dī′ə bēt′ēz) ***n.*** a sickness in which the body produces little or no insulin to break down and use the sugar eaten. It can be controlled by taking prepared insulin regularly. *It is often called* **sugar diabetes.**

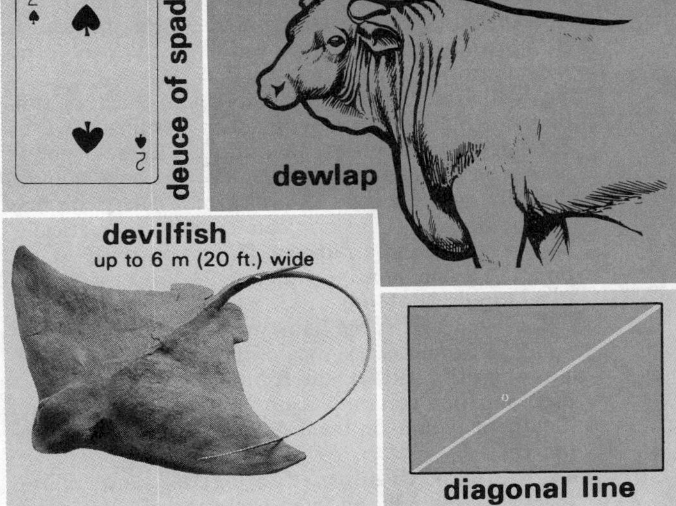


**di·a·bet·ic** (dī′ə bet′ik) ***adj.*** of or having diabetes. ◆***n.*** a person who has diabetes.

**di·a·bol·ic** (dī′ə bäl′ik) or **di·a·bol·i·cal** (dī′ə bäl′i k'l) ***adj.*** of or like a devil; very wicked or cruel; fiendish; devilish [a *diabolic* scheme]. —**di′a·bol′i·cal·ly** ***adv.***



**di·a·crit·ic** (dī′ə krit′ik) ***n.*** *same as* **diacritical mark.**

**di·a·crit·i·cal mark** (dī′ə krit′i k'l) a mark added to a letter to show how to pronounce it. Examples: ä, ā, ô.

**di·a·dem** (dī′ə dem) ***n.*** **1** a crown. **2** an ornamental cloth headband worn as a crown.

**di·ag·nose** (dī əg nōs′) ***v.*** to make a diagnosis of. —**di·ag·nosed′, di·ag·nos′ing**

**di·ag·no·sis** (dī′əg nō′sis) ***n.*** **1** the act or practice of examining a patient and studying the symptoms to find out what disease the patient has. **2** a careful examination of all the facts in a situation to find out how it has been brought about [a *diagnosis* of the last election]. **3** the decision or opinion that results from such examinations. —*pl.* **di·ag·no·ses** (dī′əg nō′sēz)

**di·ag·nos·tic** (dī′əg näs′tik) ***adj.*** of, being, or having to do with a diagnosis [a *diagnostic* test].

**di·ag·o·nal** (dī ag′ə n'l) ***adj.*** **1** slanting from one corner to the opposite corner, as of a square. *See the picture.* **2** going in a slanting direction [a tie with *diagonal* stripes]. ◆***n.*** a diagonal line, plane, course, or part. —**di·ag′o·nal·ly** ***adv.***

**di·a·gram** (dī′ə gram) ***n.*** a drawing, plan, or chart that helps explain a thing by showing all its parts, how it is put together, how it works, etc. [a *diagram* show-

| | | | | | | | |
|---|---|---|---|---|---|---|---|
| **a** | fat | **ir** | here | **ou** | out | **zh** | leisure |
| **ā** | ape | **ī** | bite, fire | **u** | up | **ŋ** | ring |
| **ä** | car, lot | **ō** | go | **ʉr** | fur | | a *in* ago |
| **e** | ten | **ô** | law, horn | **ch** | chin | | e *in* agent |
| **er** | care | **oi** | oil | **sh** | she | **ə =** | i *in* unity |
| **ē** | even | **oo** | look | **th** | thin | | o *in* collect |
| **i** | hit | **o͞o** | tool | ***th*** | then | | u *in* focus |

ing how to assemble a radio set; a *diagram* of all the rooms in a museum]. ◆**v.** to show or explain by means of a diagram; make a diagram of. —**di'a·gramed** or **di'a·grammed, di'a·gram·ing** or **di'a·gram·ming** —**di'a·gram·mat'ic** ***adj.***

**di·al** (dī'əl) ***n.*** **1** the face of a watch, clock, or sundial. **2** the face of certain other instruments, as a compass, gauge, meter, or radio or TV set, having marks on which a moving pointer can show amount, direction, place, etc. ☆**3** a disk on a telephone that can be turned for making connections automatically. ◆**v.** **1** to tune in a radio or TV station. ☆**2** to call on a telephone by using a dial. —**di'aled** or **di'alled, di'al·ing** or **di'al·ling**

**Dial** comes from the Latin word for day. The dial of a clock tells us the time of day.

**di·a·lect** (dī'ə lekt) ***n.*** the form of a language that is used only in a certain place or among a certain group [Southern *dialect* or Irish *dialect* of English]. —**di'a·lec'tal** ***adj.***

**di·a·logue** or **di·a·log** (dī'ə lôg) ***n.*** **1** a talking together, especially an open exchange of ideas, as in an effort to understand each other's views. **2** the parts of a play, novel, radio or television program, etc. that are conversation.

**di·am·e·ter** (dī am'ət ər) ***n.*** **1** a straight line passing through the center of a circle or sphere, from one side to the other. *See the picture for* **circle.** **2** the length



of such a line [The *diameter* of the moon is about 2,160 miles.]

**di·a·met·ri·cal** (dī'ə met'ri k'l) ***adj.*** **1** of or along a diameter. **2** directly opposite. —**di'a·met'ri·cal·ly** ***adv.***

**di·a·mond** (dī'mənd *or* dī'ə mənd) ***n.*** **1** a very precious stone, usually colorless, formed of nearly pure carbon. It is the hardest known mineral and is used as a gem, as the tip of a phonograph needle, and in the cutting edge of tools. *See the picture.* **2** a figure shaped like this: ◇ . **3** a playing card of a suit marked with this figure in red. ☆**4** the infield of a baseball field or the whole playing field.

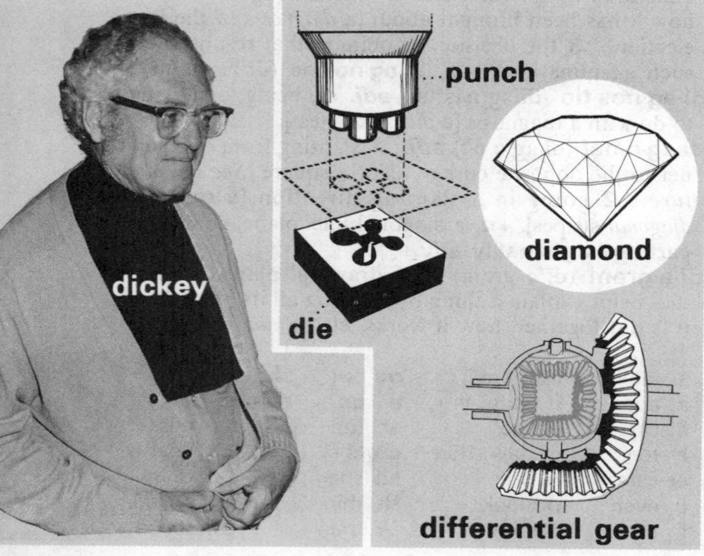


**di·a·mond·back** (dī'mənd bak) ***n.*** ☆**1** a large, poisonous rattlesnake with diamond-shaped markings on its back, found in the southern U.S. ☆**2** a turtle with diamond-shaped markings on its shell, found along the coast from Cape Cod to Mexico: *its full name is* **diamondback terrapin.**

**Di·an·a** (dī an'ə) the Roman goddess of the moon and of hunting.

**di·a·pa·son** (dī'ə pāz''n) ***n.*** **1** the whole range of a voice or musical instrument. **2** one of the principal stops of an organ covering the organ's complete range.

**di·a·per** (dī'pər *or* dī'ə pər) ***n.*** a soft cloth arranged between the legs and around the waist of a baby. ◆**v.** to put a fresh diaper on.

**di·a·phragm** (dī'ə fram) ***n.*** **1** the wall of muscles and tendons between the cavity of the chest and the cavity of the abdomen. **2** a vibrating disk that makes or receives sound waves, as in a telephone receiver or mouthpiece, a loudspeaker, etc. **3** a disk with a center hole to control the amount of light that goes through a camera lens.

**di·ar·rhe·a** or **di·ar·rhoe·a** (dī'ə rē'ə) ***n.*** a condition in which bowel movements come too often and are too loose.

**di·a·ry** (dī'ə rē) ***n.*** **1** a record written day by day of some of the things done, seen, or thought by the writer. **2** a book for keeping such a record. —*pl.* **di'a·ries**

**Diary** comes from a Latin word that means "daily allowance of food" or "the record kept of such an allowance." *Diary* still means "a daily record."

**di·a·ther·my** (dī'ə thur'mē) ***n.*** a medical treatment in which the tissues under the skin are given heat by means of a high-frequency electric current.

**di·a·tribe** (dī'ə trīb) ***n.*** a speech or writing that attacks some person or thing in a very harsh way.

**dice** (dīs) ***n.pl.*** small cubes marked on each side with a different number of dots (from one to six). Dice are used, usually in pairs, in various games of chance. —*sing.* **die** or **dice** ◆**v.** to cut into small cubes [to *dice* beets]. —**diced, dic'ing**

**dick·ens** (dik''nz) ***n., interj.*** *a mild word used in everyday talk instead of* **devil** [What the *dickens!*]

**Dick·ens** (dik''nz), **Charles** 1812–1870; English novelist. —**Dick·en·si·an** (di ken'zē ən) ***adj.***

☆**dick·er** (dik'ər) ***v.*** to try to buy or sell something by bargaining; haggle.

**dick·ey** (dik'ē) ***n.*** a kind of shirt front with a collar but no sleeves, which can be worn under a sweater, shirt, etc. *See the picture.* —*pl.* **dick'eys**

**Dick·in·son** (dik'in s'n), **Emily** 1830–1886; U.S. poet.

**dick·y** (dik'ē) ***n.*** *another spelling of* **dickey.** —*pl.* **dick'ies**

**di·cot·y·le·don** (dī'kät 'l ēd''n) ***n.*** a flowering plant with two cotyledons, or seed leaves, in the embryo. All flowering plants are either dicotyledons or monocotyledons.

**dict.** *abbreviation for* **dictator, dictionary.**

☆**Dic·ta·phone** (dik'tə fōn) *a trademark for* a machine that makes a record of words spoken into it so that they can be played back. It is used in offices for dictating letters, etc. to be typed.

**dic·tate** (dik'tāt) ***v.*** **1** to speak or read something aloud for someone else to write down [to *dictate* a letter to a secretary]. **2** to say or tell with authority;

command or order [Do what your conscience *dictates.*] —**dic′tat·ed, dic′tat·ing** ◆*n.* an order or command given with authority [They follow the *dictates* of fashion.]

**dic·ta·tion** (dik tā′shən) *n.* **1** the dictating of words for another to write down [rapid *dictation*]. **2** the words dictated [a notebook filled with *dictation*]. **3** the giving of orders or commands with authority [to rebel against *dictation* by one's elders].

**dic·ta·tor** (dik′tāt ər) *n.* **1** a ruler who has complete power over a country. **2** any person with much power, whose every word is obeyed [As a dress designer, he is a *dictator* of fashion.] **3** a person who dictates words for another to write down. —**dic·ta′tor·ship** *n.*

**dic·ta·to·ri·al** (dik′tə tôr′ē əl) *adj.* of or like a dictator; overbearing; tyrannical [a *dictatorial* boss].

**dic·tion** (dik′shən) *n.* **1** the way in which something is put into words; choice and arrangement of words [The *diction* of everyday talk is different from the *diction* of a formal essay.] **2** a way of speaking or pronouncing words; enunciation [A good actor should have *diction* that is clearly understood.]

**dic·tion·ar·y** (dik′shə ner′ē) *n.* **1** a book in which some or most of the words of a language, or of some special field, are listed in alphabetical order with their meanings, pronunciations, etc. [a school *dictionary;* a medical *dictionary*]. **2** a book like this in which words of one language are explained in words of another language [a Spanish-English *dictionary*]. —*pl.* **dic′tion·ar′ies**

**dic·tum** (dik′təm) *n.* a saying; especially, an opinion given with authority [the *dictums* of a music critic]. —*pl.* **dic′tums** or **dic·ta** (dik′tə)

**did** (did) *past tense of* **do**[1].

**di·dac·tic** (dī dak′tik) *adj.* **1** used for teaching, or meant to teach a lesson [Many of Aesop's fables are *didactic.*] **2** too willing to teach others [He is very *didactic* and can show you the right way to do everything.] —**di·dac′ti·cal·ly** *adv.*

**did·n't** (did′′nt) did not.

**didst** (ditst) *the older form of* **did** *used with* thou, *as in the Bible.*

**die**[1] (dī) *v.* **1** to stop living; become dead. **2** to stop going, moving, acting, etc. [The motor sputtered and *died.*] **3** to lose force; become weak, faint, etc. [The sound of music *died* away.] **4** to want greatly: *used only in everyday talk* [She's *dying* to know my secret.] —**died, dy′ing** —**die off,** to die one by one until all are gone.

**die**[2] (dī) *n.* **1** either of a pair of dice: *see* **dice.** —*pl.* **dice** (dīs) **2** a tool or device used to give a certain form to some object [*Dies* are used to punch holes in metal, cut threads on screws, stamp the design on coins, etc.] *See the picture.* —*pl.* **dies** (dīz) —**the die is cast,** the decision has been made and there is no turning back from it.

**die casting** **1** the process of making a casting by forcing molten metal into a die, or mold made of metal, under great pressure. **2** a casting made in this way.

**die-hard** or **die·hard** (dī′härd′) *n.* a person who is stubborn and does not easily give up old ways of thinking or of doing things.

**die·sel** (dē′z'l *or* dē′s'l) *n. often* **Diesel** **1** a kind of internal-combustion engine that burns fuel oil by using heat produced by compressing air: *also called* **diesel engine** *or* **diesel motor**. **2** a locomotive or motor vehicle with such an engine.

**di·et**[1] (dī′ət) *n.* **1** what a person or animal usually eats or drinks; usual food [Rice is a basic food in the *diet* of many Asian peoples.] **2** a special choice as to kinds and amounts of food eaten, as for one's health or to gain or lose weight [a sugar-free *diet;* a reducing *diet*]. ◆*v.* to eat certain kinds and amounts of food, especially in order to lose weight.

**di·et**[2] (dī′ət) *n.* a formal meeting for discussion; especially, the lawmaking assembly of certain countries [the Japanese *Diet*].

**di·e·tar·y** (dī′ə ter′ē) *adj.* having to do with a food diet [the *dietary* laws of the Muslims].

**di·e·tet·ic** (dī′ə tet′ik) *adj.* of or for a food diet.

**di·e·tet·ics** (dī′ə tet′iks) *n.pl.* the study of the kinds and amounts of food needed for good health: *used with a singular verb.*

☆**di·e·ti·tian** or **di·e·ti·cian** (dī′ə tish′ən) *n.* a person whose work is planning diets that will give people the kinds and amounts of food that they need.

**dif·fer** (dif′ər) *v.* **1** to be not the same; be unlike [Our tastes in music *differ.*] **2** to have unlike or opposite opinions or ideas; disagree [We *differed* about the merits of the candidates.]

**dif·fer·ence** (dif′ər əns *or* dif′rəns) *n.* **1** the state of being different or unlike [the *difference* between right and wrong]. **2** a way in which people or things are unlike [a *difference* in size]. **3** a differing in opinions; disagreement or argument [They are friends in spite of their *differences* over politics.] **4** the amount by which one quantity is greater or less than another [The *difference* between 11 and 7 is 4.] —**make a difference,** to have some effect or importance; to matter.

**dif·fer·ent** (dif′ər ənt *or* dif′rənt) *adj.* **1** not alike; unlike [Cottage cheese is quite *different* from Swiss cheese.] **2** not the same; separate; distinct [There are three *different* colleges in the city.] **3** not like most others; unusual [Their house is really *different.*] —**dif′fer·ent·ly** *adv.*

> We say "This is *different from* that" or, in everyday talk, "This is *different than* that." The British say "This is *different to* that."

**dif·fer·en·tial** (dif′ə ren′shəl) *adj.* that differ according to conditions [*differential* rates]. ◆*n.* **1** a difference in rates, charges, or the like. **2** an arrangement of gears, as in the rear axle of an automobile, which lets the outside wheel turn faster around curves than the inside wheel: *the full name is* **differential gear**. *See the picture.*

**dif·fer·en·ti·ate** (dif′ə ren′shē āt) *v.* **1** to tell or see the difference [Some colorblind people can't *differentiate* between red and green.] **2** to be or make different



| | | | |
|---|---|---|---|
| **a** fat | **ir** here | **ou** out | **zh** leisure |
| **ā** ape | **ī** bite, fire | **u** up | **ng** ring |
| **ä** car, lot | **ō** go | **ur** fur | a *in* ago |
| **e** ten | **ô** law, horn | **ch** chin | e *in* agent |
| **er** care | **oi** oil | **sh** she | **ə** = i *in* unity |
| **ē** even | **oo** look | **th** thin | o *in* collect |
| **i** hit | **ōō** tool | ***th*** then | u *in* focus |

[What *differentiates* the polar bear from other bears?] —**dif'fer·en'ti·at·ed, dif'fer·en'ti·at·ing —dif'fer·en'ti·a'tion** ***n.***

**dif·fi·cult** (dif'i kəlt) ***adj.*** **1** hard to do, make, or understand; that takes much trouble, thought, or skill [This arithmetic problem is *difficult.*] **2** hard to please; not easy to get along with [a *difficult* employer].

**dif·fi·cul·ty** (dif'i kul'tē) ***n.*** **1** how difficult, or hard to deal with, a thing is [These lessons are arranged in order of their *difficulty.*] **2** something that is difficult [The astronauts overcame many *difficulties* to land on the moon.] **3** trouble or the cause of trouble [Did you have *difficulty* in doing your homework?] —*pl.* **dif'fi·cul'ties**

SYNONYMS: A **difficulty** is any problem or trouble, whether great or small, that one has to deal with [a slight *difficulty;* an immense *difficulty*]. A **hardship** brings suffering or trouble that is very difficult or hard to bear [the *hardships* of the poor].

**dif·fi·dent** (dif'i dənt) ***adj.*** not sure of oneself; bashful or shy. —**dif'fi·dence** ***n.*** —**dif'fi·dent·ly** ***adv.***

**dif·frac·tion** (di frak'shən) ***n.*** the breaking up of a ray of light into dark or light bands or into the colors of the spectrum.

**dif·fuse** (di fyo͞os') ***adj.*** **1** spread out; not centered in one place [This lamp gives *diffuse* light.] **2** using more words than are needed; wordy [a *diffuse* style of



writing]. ◆***v.*** (di fyo͞oz') **1** to spread out in every direction; scatter widely [to *diffuse* light, heat or information]. **2** to mix together, as gases or liquids; intermingle. —**dif·fused', dif·fus'ing —dif·fuse'ly** ***adv.*** —**dif·fu·sion** (di fyo͞o'zhən) ***n.***

**dig** (dig) ***v.*** **1** to turn up or remove ground with a spade, the hands, claws, etc. [The children are *digging* in the sand.] **2** to make by digging [to *dig* a well]. **3** to make a way by digging [The miners are *digging* through a wall of clay.] **4** to get out by digging [to *dig* potatoes from the garden]. ☆**5** to find out, as by careful study [to *dig* out the truth]. **6** to jab or poke [to *dig* someone in the ribs]. ☆**7** to work or study hard: *used only in everyday talk.* ☆**8** to understand; also, to approve of: *slang in these meanings.* —**dug** *or in older use* **digged, dig'ging** ◆***n.*** **1** a jab or poke. **2** an insulting or sneering remark: *used only in everyday talk.*

dike

dinosaur
10 m (33 ft.) long, including tail

dimples

dilapidated barn

**dig.** *abbreviation for* **digest.**

**di·gest** (di jest' *or* dī jest') ***v.*** **1** to change food in the stomach and intestines into a form that can be used by the body [Small babies cannot *digest* solid food.] **2** to be digested [Some foods do not *digest* easily.] **3** to think over so as to understand fully [Read and *digest* that article.] ◆***n.*** (dī'jest) a short account or report of a longer story, article, etc.; summary [a *digest* of recent law cases].

**di·gest·i·ble** (di jes'tə b'l *or* dī jes'tə b'l) ***adj.*** that can be digested.

**di·ges·tion** (di jes'chən *or* dī jes'chən) ***n.*** **1** the act or process of digesting food. **2** the ability to digest food. —**di·ges'tive** ***adj.***

**dig·ger** (dig'ər) ***n.*** a person or thing that digs, especially a tool or machine made for digging.

**dig·it** (dij'it) ***n.*** **1** any number from 0 through 9. **2** a finger or toe.

**dig·it·al** (dij'it 'l) ***adj.*** **1** of or like a digit, especially a finger. **2** having or using digits, or numbers that are digits. **3** showing the time, temperature, etc. by a row of digits rather than by numbers on a dial, etc. [a *digital* clock; a *digital* thermometer].

**dig·i·tal·is** (dij'ə tal'is) ***n.*** a medicine made from the dried leaves of the purple foxglove. It is used in treating heart disease to speed up the action of the heart.

**dig·ni·fied** (dig'nə fīd) ***adj.*** having dignity; noble, proper, self-respecting, etc.

**dig·ni·fy** (dig'nə fī) ***v.*** to give dignity or honor to; make seem worthy or noble [to *dignify* a custodian by calling him a superintendent]. —**dig'ni·fied, dig'ni·fy·ing**

**dig·ni·tar·y** (dig'nə ter'ē) ***n.*** a person holding a high position, as in a government or church. —*pl.* **dig'ni·tar'ies**

**dig·ni·ty** (dig'nə tē) ***n.*** **1** the quality of being worthy or noble; real worth [We should respect the *dignity* of all persons.] **2** a noble or stately appearance or manner [the *dignity* with which swans move in water]. **3** high rank or position that deserves respect [We must uphold the *dignity* of our courts.] **4** proper pride and self-respect [It was beneath her *dignity* to accept any more help from her parents.] —*pl.* **dig'ni·ties**

**di·gress** (də gres' *or* dī gres') ***v.*** to wander from the subject that one has been talking or writing about. —**di·gres'sion** ***n.***

**Digress** comes from a Latin word that means "to go apart or walk away." A person who digresses seems to be walking away from what is being talked about.

**dike** (dīk) ***n.*** a wall or dam built to keep a sea or river from flooding over land. *See the picture.* ◆***v.*** to protect with a dike. —**diked, dik'ing**

**di·lap·i·dat·ed** (di lap'ə dāt'id) ***adj.*** falling to pieces; broken down; shabby and neglected [a *dilapidated* barn]. *See the picture.*

**di·lap·i·da·tion** (di lap'ə dā'shən) ***n.*** a dilapidated or run-down condition; ruin.

**di·late** (dī lāt' *or* di lāt') ***v.*** to make or become wider or larger; expand; swell [The pupils of the eyes become *dilated* in the dark.] **—di·lat'ed, di·lat'ing —di·la'tion *n.***

**dil·a·to·ry** (dil'ə tôr ē) ***adj.*** slow or late in doing things; delaying [I am *dilatory* in answering letters.]

**di·lem·ma** (di lem'ə) ***n.*** a situation in which one must choose between things that are equally unpleasant or dangerous; difficult choice.

**dil·et·tante** (dil ə tant' *or* dil'ə tän'tē) ***n.*** a person who loves the fine arts; now especially, one who is interested in art, literature, etc., but not in a deep or serious way. *—pl.* **dil·et·tantes'** or **dil·et·tan·ti** (dil'ə tän'tē)

**dil·i·gence** (dil'ə jəns) ***n.*** careful and steady work or effort; industry.

**dil·i·gent** (dil'ə jənt) ***adj.*** doing one's work in a careful, steady way; working hard; industrious. **—dil'i·gent·ly *adv.***

**dill** (dil) ***n.*** a plant whose spicy seeds and stems are used to flavor pickles, etc.

**dil·ly·dal·ly** (dil'ē dal'ē) ***v.*** to waste time by not making up one's mind; loiter or dawdle. **—dil'ly·dal'lied, dil'ly·dal'ly·ing**

**di·lute** (di lo͞ot' *or* dī lo͞ot') ***v.*** **1** to thin out or weaken by adding water or other liquid [to *dilute* condensed milk]. **2** to weaken by mixing with something else [She *diluted* her praise with a little faultfinding.] **—di·lut'ed, di·lut'ing** ◆***adj.*** diluted [*dilute* acid]. **—di·lu'tion *n.***

**dim** (dim) ***adj.*** **1** not bright or clear; somewhat dark; shadowy; gloomy [the *dim* twilight; a *dim* view of the future]. **2** not clear to the hearing or mind; faint; indistinct [a *dim* sound in the distance; a *dim* recollection]. **3** not seeing or understanding clearly [*dim* vision; a mind *dim* with age]. **—dim'mer, dim'mest** ◆***v.*** to make or grow dim [Approaching cars should *dim* their headlights.] **—dimmed, dim'ming —dim'ly *adv.* —dim'ness *n.***

**dim.** *abbreviation for* **dimension, diminutive.**

**dime** (dīm) ***n.*** ☆a coin of the U.S. and of Canada equal to ten cents: one-tenth of a dollar.

**di·men·sion** (də men'shən) ***n.*** **1** a measurement of something in length, width, or height [The *dimensions* of the box are 40 inches in length, 30 inches in height, and 24 inches in width.] **2** *often* **dimensions,** *pl.* size or importance [a project of vast *dimensions*].

**di·men·sion·al** (də men'shən 'l) ***adj.*** **1** of dimension. **2** having a certain number of dimensions [a three-*dimensional* figure].

**di·min·ish** (də min'ish) ***v.*** to make or become smaller in size or less in force, importance, etc. [Overpopulation *diminishes* the world food supply. Danger of frost *diminishes* in April.]

**di·min·u·en·do** (də min'yoo wen'dō) ***adj., adv., n.*** *same as* **decrescendo.** *—pl.* **di·min'u·en'dos**

**dim·i·nu·tion** (dim'ə nyo͞o'shən *or* dim'ə no͞o'shən) ***n.*** a lessening in size, amount, etc.

**di·min·u·tive** (də min'yoo tiv) ***adj.*** **1** very small; tiny. **2** showing that something is smaller [The word "booklet" is formed by adding the *diminutive* suffix "-let" to "book."] ◆***n.*** a word formed by adding a diminutive suffix.

**dim·i·ty** (dim'ə tē) ***n.*** a thin cotton cloth used for dresses and curtains. *—pl.* **dim'i·ties**

**dim·ple** (dim'p'l) ***n.*** **1** a small hollow spot, as on the cheek or chin. *See the picture.* **2** any slight hollow, as in the surface of water. ◆***v.*** to form dimples [Her cheeks *dimple* when she smiles.] **—dim'pled, dim'pling**

**din** (din) ***n.*** a loud, steady noise; confused uproar [the *din* of a boiler factory]. *See* SYNONYMS *at* **noise.** ◆***v.*** **1** to make a din. **2** to keep repeating; say again and again [He *dinned* the warning into my ears.] **—dinned, din'ning**

**dine** (dīn) ***v.*** **1** to eat dinner. **2** to give a dinner to [to *dine* a visitor]. **—dined, din'ing**

**din·er** (dī'nər) ***n.*** **1** a person eating dinner. ☆**2** a railroad car in which meals are served to passengers: *also* **dining car.** ☆**3** a small restaurant built to look like a dining car.

☆**din·ette** (dī net') ***n.*** a small room or an alcove, used as a dining room.

**ding** (diŋ) ***n.*** the sound of a bell. ◆***v.*** to make this sound.

**ding-dong** (diŋ'dôŋ') ***n.*** the sound of a bell struck again and again.

**din·ghy** (diŋ'gē) ***n.*** a small boat, usually a rowboat. *—pl.* **din'ghies**

**din·gy** (din'jē) ***adj.*** having a dull, dirty look; not bright or clean [a *dingy* room]. **—din'gi·er, din'gi·est —din'gi·ness *n.***

**dining room** a room where meals are eaten.

**din·ner** (din'ər) ***n.*** **1** the main meal of the day, whether eaten in the evening or about noon. **2** a banquet in honor of some person or event. 207

**di·no·saur** (dī'nə sôr) ***n.*** any of a group of reptiles that lived millions of years ago. Dinosaurs had four legs and a long, tapering tail, and some were almost 100 feet long. *See the picture.*

> The word **dinosaur** was put together from two Greek words meaning "terrible" and "lizard." If there were lizards or reptiles today as large as dinosaurs, they could be terrifying.

**dint** (dint) ***n.*** strength or power; force [By *dint* of persuasion the teacher got John to work.]

**di·oc·e·san** (dī äs'ə s'n) ***adj.*** of a diocese. ◆***n.*** the bishop of a diocese.

**di·o·cese** (dī'ə sis *or* dī'ə sēs') ***n.*** the church district under the control of a bishop.

**Di·og·e·nes** (dī äj'ə nēz) 412?–323? B.C.; Greek philosopher. According to legend, he went about with a lantern looking for an honest person.

**di·ox·ide** (dī äk'sīd) ***n.*** an oxide containing two atoms of oxygen in each molecule.

**dip** (dip) ***v.*** **1** to put into a liquid and quickly pull out again [to *dip* a brush into paint]. **2** to go down into a liquid and quickly come out again [The oars of the galley *dipped* in rhythm.] **3** to lower and quickly raise or rise again [The airplane *dipped* its right wing. The treetops *dipped* in the wind.] **4** to slope downward, as a road. **5** to take out by scooping up with a dipper,

| | | | | | | | |
|---|---|---|---|---|---|---|---|
| **a** | fat | **ir** | here | **ou** | out | **zh** | leisure |
| **ā** | ape | **ī** | bite, fire | **u** | up | **ŋ** | ring |
| **ä** | car, lot | **ō** | go | **ur** | fur | | a *in* ago |
| **e** | ten | **ô** | law, horn | **ch** | chin | | e *in* agent |
| **er** | care | **oi** | oil | **sh** | she | **ə =** | i *in* unity |
| **ē** | even | **oo** | look | **th** | thin | | o *in* collect |
| **i** | hit | **o͞o** | tool | ***th*** | then | | u *in* focus |

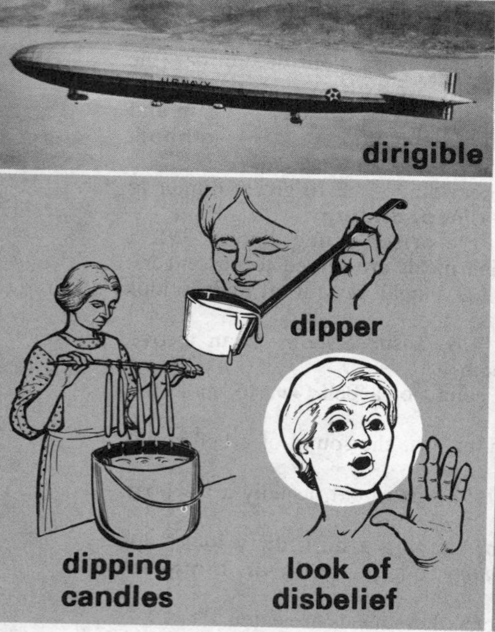
dirigible

dipper

dipping candles

look of disbelief

clothes in disarray

the hand, etc. [to *dip* water from a bucket]. **6** to make a candle by putting a wick into melted tallow or wax again and again. *See the picture.* **7** to look into or study for a little while [to *dip* into a book]. —**dipped, dip′ping** ✦*n.* **1** a dipping or being dipped; a plunge into water, a quick drop, a downward slope, etc. **2** something dipped or scooped out [a *dip* of ice cream]. **3** a liquid into which things are dipped, as in cleaning or dyeing. ☆**4** a thick, creamy sauce, in which crackers are dipped to be eaten as appetizers.



**diph·the·ri·a** (dif thir′ē ə *or* dip thir′ē ə) ***n.*** a disease of the throat that is spread by a germ, causes fever and soreness, and makes breathing difficult.

**diph·thong** (dif′thông *or* dip′thông) ***n.*** a sound made by pronouncing two vowels one right after the other without stopping [The "ou" in "mouse" is a *diphthong* formed by the vowel sounds ä and o͞o.]

**di·plo·ma** (di plō′mə) ***n.*** a certificate given to a student by a school or college to show that the student has completed a required course of study.

**di·plo·ma·cy** (di plō′mə sē) ***n.*** **1** the carrying on of relations between nations, as in building up trade, making treaties, etc. **2** skill in dealing with people so as to get their help and keep them friendly; tact. —*pl.* **di·plo′ma·cies**

**dip·lo·mat** (dip′lə mat) ***n.*** **1** a person in a government whose work is dealing with other nations. **2** a person who has tact in dealing with others.

**dip·lo·mat·ic** (dip′lə mat′ik) ***adj.*** **1** having to do with diplomacy. **2** tactful [a *diplomatic* salesperson]. —**dip′lo·mat′i·cal·ly** ***adv.***

**dip·per** (dip′ər) ***n.*** **1** a person or thing that dips. ☆**2** a cup with a long handle, used for scooping up liquids; ladle. ☆**3** either of two groups of stars in the shape of a dipper. One is called the **Big Dipper,** the other the **Little Dipper.**

**dip·stick** (dip′stik) ***n.*** a metal rod for measuring how much there is of something in a container, as of oil in an automobile crankcase.

**dire** (dīr) ***adj.*** very bad; dreadful; terrible [*dire* misfortune]. —**dir′er, dir′est**

**di·rect** (di rekt′) ***adj.*** **1** by the shortest way; without turning or stopping; straight [a *direct* route home]. **2** honest and to the point; frank [a *direct* question]. **3** with no one or nothing between; immediate [The wire was in *direct* contact with the ground.] **4** traced from parent to child to grandchild, etc. [a *direct* descendant]. **5** exact; complete [the *direct* opposite]. **6** in the exact words used by the speaker [a *direct* quotation]. ✦***v.*** **1** to be in charge of; manage; control [to *direct* the building of a bridge; to *direct* a choir; to *direct* a play]. **2** to command or order [You are *directed* to appear in court.] **3** to tell someone the way to a place [Can you *direct* me to the office?] **4** to aim or steer; point [The counselor's remarks were *directed* at me.] ✦***adv.*** directly [Go *direct* to your house.] —**di·rect′ness** ***n.***

**direct current** an electric current that flows in one direction only.

**di·rec·tion** (də rek′shən) ***n.*** **1** a directing or managing; control [The choir is under the *direction* of Ms. Jones.] **2** an order or command. **3** *usually* **directions,** *pl.* instructions on how to get to some place or how to do something [*directions* for driving to Omaha; *directions* for building a model boat]. **4** the point toward which something faces or the line along which something moves or lies ["North," "up," "forward," and "left" are *directions*.] **5** the line along which something develops [to plan in the *direction* of a longer school year]. —**di·rec′tion·al** ***adj.***

**di·rec·tive** (də rek′tiv) ***n.*** an order or instruction coming from a central office.

**di·rect·ly** (də rekt′lē) ***adv.*** **1** in a direct line or way; straight [Come *directly* home after school. The town lies *directly* to the north.] **2** with nothing coming between; immediately [He is *directly* responsible to me.] **3** exactly; completely [*directly* opposite].

**direct object** the word in a sentence that tells who or what receives the action of the verb [In "Chris wrote a story," "story" is the *direct object*.] *See also* **indirect object.**

**di·rec·tor** (di rek′tər) ***n.*** **1** a person who directs or manages the work of others [the *director* of a play, a band, a government bureau]. **2** a member of a group chosen to direct the affairs of a business. —**di·rec′tor·ship** ***n.***

**di·rec·to·ry** (də rek′tə rē) ***n.*** a book or list of names, addresses, etc. [a telephone *directory,* an office *directory*]. —*pl.* **di·rec′to·ries**

**dirge** (dʉrj) ***n.*** a slow, sad piece of music showing grief for the dead, as at a funeral.

**dir·i·gi·ble** (dir′i jə b′l) ***n.*** a large, long airship that can be steered. *See the picture.*

> **Dirigible** comes from a Latin word meaning "to direct" or "to keep straight." Both dirigibles and blimps are airships that can be directed or steered or kept straight on their course. Blimps are smaller.

**dirk** (dʉrk) ***n.*** a short dagger.

**dirt** (dʉrt) ***n.*** **1** mud, dust, soot, or other matter that makes things unclean; filth. **2** earth or soil. **3** indecent talk, writing, or action.

**dirt·y** (durt′ē) ***adj.*** **1** having dirt on or in it; not clean; soiled. **2** foul or indecent; not nice; mean [a *dirty* trick]. **3** muddy or clouded in color [a *dirty* yellow]. **4** rough or stormy [*dirty* weather]. **—dirt′i·er, dirt′i·est** ◆***v.*** to make or become dirty; soil. **—dirt′-ied, dirt′y·ing —dirt′i·ness *n.***

**dis-** *a prefix meaning:* **1** away, away from, or out of [*Displace* means to move away from its place.] **2** the opposite of [*Dishonest* means the opposite of honest.] **3** to fail, stop, or refuse to [*Disagree* means to fail to agree.]

**dis.** *abbreviation for* **discount, distance.**

**dis·a·bil·i·ty** (dis′ə bil′ə tē) ***n.*** **1** the condition of not being able or fit to do something. **2** something that disables, as an illness or injury. *—pl.* **dis′a·bil′i·ties**

**dis·a·ble** (dis ā′b′l) ***v.*** to make unable to move, act, or work in a normal way; cripple [She is *disabled* by arthritis.] **—dis·a′bled, dis·a′bling**

**dis·a·buse** (dis ə byo͞oz′) ***v.*** to free from false ideas; put right [The teacher *disabused* the students of their belief in fairies.] **—dis·a·bused′, dis·a·bus′ing**

**dis·ad·van·tage** (dis′əd van′tij) ***n.*** **1** anything that stands in the way of success; handicap; drawback [A trick knee is a *disadvantage* to a baseball player.] **2** loss or harm [This decision will work to your *disadvantage*.] **—dis·ad·van·ta·geous** (dis ad′vən tā′jəs) ***adj.***

**dis·ad·van·taged** (dis′əd van′tijd) ***adj.*** kept from having decent living conditions, an education, etc. because of being poor.

**dis·af·fect·ed** (dis′ə fek′tid) ***adj.*** no longer friendly or loyal; discontented [The *disaffected* sailors talked of mutiny.] **—dis′af·fec′tion *n.***

**dis·a·gree** (dis ə grē′) ***v.*** **1** to differ in opinion; often, to quarrel or argue [to *disagree* on politics]. **2** to be different; differ [His story of the accident *disagreed* with hers.] **3** to be harmful or unpleasant to [Corn *disagrees* with me.] **—dis·a·greed′, dis·a·gree′-ing**

**dis·a·gree·a·ble** (dis′ə grē′ə b′l) ***adj.*** **1** not pleasing to one; unpleasant; offensive [a *disagreeable* odor]. **2** hard to get along with; bad-tempered; cross. **—dis′a-gree′a·bly *adv.***

**dis·a·gree·ment** (dis′ə grē′mənt) ***n.*** **1** a quarrel or argument. **2** a difference of opinion. **3** a being unlike; difference.

**dis·ap·pear** (dis ə pir′) ***v.*** to stop being seen or to stop existing; vanish [The car *disappeared* around a curve. Dinosaurs *disappeared* millions of years ago.] **—dis′-ap·pear′ance *n.***

> SYNONYMS: To **disappear** is to pass out of sight or existence either suddenly or gradually [Old customs sometimes *disappear*.] To **vanish** is to disappear suddenly, completely, and often mysteriously [My pen *vanished* from my desk. The snake *vanished* into the grass.] To **fade** is to disappear slowly and often remain to some extent [The color in this rug has *faded*.]

**dis·ap·point** (dis ə point′) ***v.*** to fail to give or do what is wanted, expected, or promised; leave unsatisfied [I am *disappointed* in the weather. You promised to come, but *disappointed* us.]

**dis·ap·point·ment** (dis′ə point′mənt) ***n.*** **1** a disappointing or being disappointed [one's *disappointment* over not winning]. **2** a person or thing that disappoints [The team is a *disappointment* to us.]

**dis·ap·prov·al** (dis′ə pro͞ov′′l) ***n.*** a refusing to approve; opinion or feeling against something [The crowd showed its *disapproval* by booing.]

**dis·ap·prove** (dis ə pro͞ov′) ***v.*** to refuse to approve; have an opinion or feeling against; think to be wrong [The Puritans *disapproved* of dancing.] **—dis·ap-proved′, dis·ap·prov′ing —dis′ap·prov′ing·ly *adv.***

**dis·arm** (dis ärm′) ***v.*** **1** to take away weapons from [The police *disarmed* the robbers.] **2** to reduce or get rid of a nation's armed forces or its weapons of war [When all nations *disarm*, there will be peace.] **3** to make harmless or friendly [the *disarming* manner of a small child].

**dis·ar·ma·ment** (dis är′mə mənt) ***n.*** the act of getting rid of or reducing a nation's armed forces or weapons of war.

**dis·ar·range** (dis ə rānj′) ***v.*** to upset the order or arrangement of; make less neat [Do not *disarrange* the papers on my desk.] **—dis·ar·ranged′, dis·ar·rang′-ing —dis′ar·range′ment *n.***

**dis·ar·ray** (dis ə rā′) ***n.*** an untidy condition; disorder or confusion. *See the picture.*

**dis·as·sem·ble** (dis′ə sem′b′l) ***v.*** ☆to take apart [to *disassemble* a motor]. **—dis′as·sem′bled, dis′as-sem′bling**

**dis·as·ter** (di zas′tər) ***n.*** a happening that causes much damage or suffering, as a flood or earthquake; catastrophe. **—dis·as′trous *adj.*** 209

**dis·a·vow** (dis ə vou′) ***v.*** to say that one knows nothing about or does not approve of; disclaim [She will never be able to *disavow* that letter she wrote.] **—dis′-a·vow′al *n.***

**dis·band** (dis band′) ***v.*** to break up as a group or organization [The school board *disbanded* all fraternities and sororities at our school.]

**dis·bar** (dis bär′) ***v.*** to take away from a lawyer the right to practice law. **—dis·barred′, dis·bar′ring — dis·bar′ment *n.***

**dis·be·lief** (dis bə lēf′) ***n.*** the state of not believing; lack of belief [The guide stared at me in *disbelief*.] *See the picture.*

**dis·be·lieve** (dis bə lēv′) ***v.*** to refuse to believe; have no belief in; reject as untrue. **—dis·be·lieved′, dis-be·liev′ing**

**dis·burse** (dis burs′) ***v.*** to pay out, especially from public funds. **—dis·bursed′, dis·burs′ing —dis-burse′ment *n.***

**disc** (disk) ***n.*** **1** *another spelling of* **disk**. **2** a phonograph record. **3** a thin, flat, round plate for storing computer data. ☆**4** a blade on a disc harrow.

> **Disc** and **disk** are different spellings of the same word. There is no rule to follow about which spelling to use, and either may be used. **Disc** is the usual spelling for phonograph record and in

| | | | | | | | |
|---|---|---|---|---|---|---|---|
| **a** | fat | **ir** | here | **ou** | out | **zh** | leisure |
| **ā** | ape | **ī** | bite, fire | **u** | up | **ng** | ring |
| **ä** | car, lot | **ō** | go | **ur** | fur | | a *in* ago |
| **e** | ten | **ô** | law, horn | **ch** | chin | | e *in* agent |
| **er** | care | **oi** | oil | **sh** | she | **ə** = | i *in* unity |
| **ē** | even | **oo** | look | **th** | thin | | o *in* collect |
| **i** | hit | **o͞o** | tool | ***th*** | then | | u *in* focus |

**disc brake** and **disc harrow**. **Disk** is usually used in medical and scientific terms, as the *disk* between vertebrae, the *disk* of the sunflower, and the moon's *disk*.

**dis·card** (dis kärd′) ***v.*** **1** to throw away or get rid of something that is no longer wanted. **2** in playing cards, to remove an unwanted card from one's hand. ***•n.*** (dis′kärd) **1** the act of discarding or condition of being discarded. **2** something that is discarded.

**disc brake** an automobile brake that works by two friction pads pressing on either side of a disc that rotates along with the wheel.

**dis·cern** (di surn′ *or* di zurn′) ***v.*** to see or make out clearly; recognize [Can you *discern* a sail on the horizon? I cannot *discern* what reason she had for quitting.] **—dis·cern′i·ble** ***adj.*** **—dis·cern′ment** ***n.***

**dis·cern·ing** (di surn′ing *or* di zurn′ing) ***adj.*** having good judgment or understanding.

**dis·charge** (dis chärj′) ***v.*** **1** to release from something that controls or holds in [to *discharge* a soldier from the army, a patient from a hospital, or a prisoner from jail]. **2** to dismiss from a job; fire. **3** to remove a burden or load; unload [The boat *discharged* its cargo.] **4** to give forth or let out [The steam is *discharged* through this pipe.] **5** to pay a debt or perform a duty [I have *discharged* all my obligations.] **6** to shoot or fire, as a gun. ☆**7** to use up the electricity in [to *discharge* a battery]. **—dis·charged′, dis·charg′ing** ***•n.*** (*usually* dis′chärj) **1** a discharging or being discharged. **2** a certificate that discharges [an honorable *discharge* from the army]. **3** something discharged [The coat was stained by the *discharge* from the wound.]

The Latin word from which **discharge** comes means "to unload," and came from two other Latin words meaning "from" and "wagon or car." To take from a wagon or car something it carries is to unload it. One sense of *discharge* still carries this meaning, when we say that a bus discharges its passengers.

☆**disc harrow** a harrow with sharp discs that turn to break up the soil. *See the picture.*

**dis·ci·ple** (di sī′p'l) ***n.*** **1** a pupil or follower of a teacher or leader, as in religion, art, etc. **2** any of the early followers of Jesus.

**dis·ci·pli·nar·i·an** (dis′ə pli ner′ē ən) ***n.*** a person who believes in and enforces strict discipline.

**dis·ci·pli·nar·y** (dis′ə pli ner′ē) ***adj.*** of or for discipline [to take *disciplinary* action].

**dis·ci·pline** (dis′ə plin) ***n.*** **1** training that teaches one to obey rules and control one's behavior [the strict *discipline* of army life]. **2** the result of such training; self-control; orderliness [The pupils showed perfect *discipline.*] **3** punishment [cruel prison *discipline*]. ***•v.*** **1** to train in discipline [Regular chores help to *discipline* children.] **2** to punish. *See* SYNONYMS *at* **punish. —dis′ci·plined, dis′ci·plin·ing**

man throwing discus

disc harrow

☆**disc jockey** a person who broadcasts a radio program of popular music on records.

**dis·claim** (dis klām′) ***v.*** to deny that one has any claim to or connection with; refuse to admit or accept; deny [to *disclaim* one's right to property; to *disclaim* knowledge of a crime].

**dis·close** (dis klōz′) ***v.*** **1** to bring into view; uncover [I opened my hand and *disclosed* the new penny.] **2** to make known; reveal [to *disclose* a secret]. *See* SYNONYMS *at* **reveal. —dis·closed′, dis·clos′ing**

**dis·clo·sure** (dis klō′zhər) ***n.*** **1** a disclosing. **2** a thing disclosed [The newspaper printed startling *disclosures* about prison conditions.]

☆**dis·co** (dis′kō) ***n.*** *a shorter form of* **discothèque.** —*pl.* **dis′cos**

**dis·col·or** (dis kul′ər) ***v.*** to change in color by fading, streaking, or staining [The strong soap *discolored* his socks.] **—dis·col′or·a′tion** ***n.***

**dis·com·fit** (dis kum′fit) ***v.*** to make confused, as by spoiling plans; upset or embarrass.

**dis·com·fort** (dis kum′fərt) ***n.*** **1** lack of comfort; being uneasy in body or mind. **2** anything that causes this.

**dis·com·pose** (dis kəm pōz′) ***v.*** to make nervous and ill at ease; fluster; upset [Unexpected guests always *discompose* me.] **—dis·com·posed′, dis·com·pos′ing —dis′com·po′sure** ***n.***

**dis·con·cert** (dis kən surt′) ***v.*** to bring confusion or disorder to, as by surprising; upset [We were *disconcerted* by the sudden change in plans.]

**dis·con·nect** (dis kə nekt′) ***v.*** to undo the connection of; separate; unfasten [*Disconnect* the record player by pulling the plug from the socket.] **—dis·con·nec′tion** ***n.***

**dis·con·so·late** (dis kän′sə lit) ***adj.*** so sad or unhappy that nothing will comfort [The students were *disconsolate* over the loss of the final game.]

**dis·con·tent** (dis kən tent′) ***n.*** a feeling of not being satisfied and of wanting something different: *also* **dis′con·tent′ment.**

**dis·con·tent·ed** (dis′kən tent′id) ***adj.*** wanting things different from what they are; not satisfied.

**dis·con·tin·ue** (dis′kən tin′yo͞o) ***v.*** to stop doing, using, etc.; give up [to *discontinue* a subscription to a magazine]. **—dis′con·tin′ued, dis′con·tin′u·ing**

**dis·con·tin·u·ous** (dis′kən tin′yoo wəs) ***adj.*** not continuous; full of interruptions or gaps.

**dis·cord** (dis′kôrd) ***n.*** **1** a failing to get along well together; lack of agreement; conflict [*Discord* among nations may lead to war.] **2** a harsh, unpleasant sound. **3** a sounding together of musical notes that do not harmonize.

SYNONYMS: **Discord** means disagreement, and may stand for quarreling between persons, clashing qualities in things, or sounds out of harmony [the *discord* between the beliefs of the two religious sects]. **Strife** emphasizes the struggle to win out where there is conflict or disagreement [*strife* between members of the two rival unions].

**dis·cord·ant** (dis kôr′dənt) ***adj.*** **1** not agreeing or going well together; conflicting [The senators had *discordant* ideas.] **2** not in harmony; clashing. **—dis·cord′ance *n.* —dis·cord′ant·ly *adv.***

☆**dis·co·thèque** (dis′kə tek) ***n.*** a nightclub or other public place for dancing to recorded popular music.

**dis·count** (dis′kount) ***n.*** an amount taken off a price, bill, or debt [He got a 10% *discount* by paying cash, so the radio cost $90 instead of $100.] **◆*v.*** **1** to take off a certain amount as a discount from a price, bill, etc. **2** to allow for exaggeration; believe only in part [You'd better *discount* that story of hers.]

**dis·cour·age** (dis kur′ij) ***v.*** **1** to prevent by disapproving or interfering [We *discouraged* her from buying the bike. The storm *discouraged* our hike.] **2** to cause to lose hope or confidence [The singer was *discouraged* by the lack of applause.] **—dis·cour′aged, dis·cour′ag·ing —dis·cour′age·ment *n.***

**dis·course** (dis′kôrs) ***n.*** **1** talk or conversation. **2** a formal speech or writing on a serious subject. **◆*v.*** (dis kôrs′) to give a long or formal talk. **—dis·coursed′, dis·cours′ing**

**dis·cour·te·ous** (dis kur′tē əs) ***adj.*** not polite; rude. *See* SYNONYMS *at* **rude. —dis·cour′te·ous·ly *adv.***

**dis·cour·te·sy** (dis kur′tə sē) ***n.*** **1** rudeness; impolite behavior. **2** a rude act or remark. *—pl.* **dis·cour′te·sies**

**dis·cov·er** (dis kuv′ər) ***v.*** **1** to be the first to find, see, or learn about [Marie and Pierre Curie *discovered* radium.] *See* SYNONYMS *at* **create. 2** to come upon, learn, or find out about [I *discovered* my name on the list.] **3** to be the first person who is not a native to come to or see a continent, river, etc.

**dis·cov·er·y** (dis kuv′ər ē) ***n.*** **1** a finding out, learning, seeing for the first time, etc. **2** a thing that is discovered. *—pl.* **dis·cov′er·ies**

**dis·cred·it** (dis kred′it) ***v.*** **1** to give or be a reason for not believing or trusting [Her earlier lies *discredit* anything she may say.] **2** to make seem not reliable or honest; hurt the reputation of [The judge has been *discredited* by the newspapers.] **◆*n.*** **1** doubt or lack of belief [These facts throw *discredit* on his story.] **2** disgrace or dishonor [He ran away, much to his *discredit*.]

**dis·cred·it·a·ble** (dis kred′it ə b′l) ***adj.*** that discredits or brings disgrace or dishonor.

**dis·creet** (dis krēt′) ***adj.*** careful about what one says or does; prudent. **—dis·creet′ly *adv.***

**dis·crep·an·cy** (dis krep′ən sē) ***n.*** a difference or disagreement [There are several *discrepancies* in their report.] *—pl.* **dis·crep′an·cies**

**dis·cre·tion** (dis kresh′ən) ***n.*** **1** carefulness in what one says or does; prudence [A person should use *discretion* in dealing with strangers.] **2** judgment or opinion [Use your own *discretion* in choosing a topic.]

**dis·cre·tion·ar·y** (dis kresh′ən er′ē) ***adj.*** left to one's own free judgment or choice [*discretionary* powers].

**dis·crim·i·nate** (dis krim′ə nāt) ***v.*** **1** to see the difference between; distinguish [Some colorblind persons cannot *discriminate* between red and green.] **2** to show prejudice by treating in a less favorable way [Some businesses *discriminate* against older persons in hiring.] **—dis·crim′i·nat·ed, dis·crim′i·nat·ing**

**dis·crim·i·na·tion** (dis krim′ə nā′shən) ***n.*** **1** the act of discriminating or distinguishing [*discrimination* between right and wrong]. **2** the practice of treating persons or things in different ways because of prejudice [*discrimination* against minority groups]. **3** good judgment [to show *discrimination* in buying clothes].

**dis·crim·i·na·to·ry** (dis krim′ə nə tôr′ē) ***adj.*** practicing discrimination, or showing prejudice.

**dis·cur·sive** (dis kur′siv) ***adj.*** going from one topic to another in a rambling way [a *discursive* speech].

**dis·cus** (dis′kəs) ***n.*** a heavy disk of metal and wood that is thrown in an athletic contest as a test of strength and skill. *See the picture.*

**dis·cuss** (dis kus′) ***v.*** to talk or write about, with various opinions and ideas being given [Let us *discuss* modern art.] **—dis·cus·sion** (dis kush′ən) ***n.***

A group of people discussing something might be described as scattering ideas around. **Discuss** comes from a Latin word that means "to scatter."

**dis·dain** (dis dān′) ***v.*** to look down on with scorn; act as though something were beneath one's dignity [Lou *disdained* their insulting remarks.] **◆*n.*** scorn for a person or thing one considers beneath one. **—dis·dain′ful *adj.***

**dis·ease** (di zēz′) ***n.*** a condition of not being healthy; sickness; illness [Chicken pox is a common childhood *disease*. Some fungi cause *disease* in animals and plants.] **—dis·eased′ *adj.***

**dis·em·bark** (dis′im bärk′) ***v.*** to put or go ashore from a ship; land. **—dis·em·bar·ka·tion** (dis′em bär kā′shən) ***n.***



**dis·em·bod·ied** (dis′im bäd′ēd) ***adj.*** separated from the body [*disembodied* spirits].

**dis·en·chant** (dis′in chant′) ***v.*** to free from a false idea; make see the truth about something [I was *disenchanted* when I found out that she cheated in order to win.] **—dis′en·chant′ment *n.***

**dis·en·cum·ber** (dis′in kum′bər) ***v.*** to free from something that burdens or troubles.

**dis·en·gage** (dis′in gāj′) ***v.*** to free from something that holds, binds, or connects; unfasten; detach [to *disengage* oneself from a pledge; to *disengage* troops from battle; to *disengage* gears]. **—dis′en·gaged′, dis′en·gag′ing —dis′en·gage′ment *n.***

**dis·en·tan·gle** (dis′in taŋ′g′l) ***v.*** to free from tangles or confusion; straighten out [*Disentangle* the yarn. We tried to *disentangle* the truth in his story from the lies.] **—dis′en·tan′gled, dis′en·tan′gling —dis′en·tan′gle·ment *n.***

**dis·fa·vor** (dis fā′vər) ***n.*** **1** a feeling against; disapproval; dislike [I look on daylight-saving time with *disfavor*.] **2** the condition of being disliked or disapproved of [to fall into *disfavor*].

**dis·fig·ure** (dis fig′yər) ***v.*** to spoil the looks of as by marking up; deface; mar [Severe burns have *disfigured* her hands.] **—dis·fig′ured, dis·fig′ur·ing —dis·fig′ure·ment *n.***

| | | | |
|---|---|---|---|
| **a** fat | **ir** here | **ou** out | **zh** leisure |
| **ā** ape | **ī** bite, fire | **u** up | **ŋ** ring |
| **ä** car, lot | **ō** go | **ur** fur | a *in* ago |
| **e** ten | **ô** law, horn | **ch** chin | e *in* agent |
| **er** care | **oi** oil | **sh** she | **ə** = i *in* unity |
| **ē** even | **oo** look | **th** thin | o *in* collect |
| **i** hit | **ōō** tool | ***th*** then | u *in* focus |

disorderly desk

girl in disguise

dislocated hip

disheveled hair

**dis·fran·chise** (dis fran′chīz) ***v.*** to take away a right from someone, especially the right of a citizen to vote. —**dis·fran′chised, dis·fran′chis·ing** —**dis·fran·chise·ment** (dis fran′chiz mənt) ***n.***

**dis·gorge** (dis gôrj′) ***v.*** to throw up something inside; vomit or discharge [The whale *disgorged* Jonah. The volcano *disgorged* lava.] —**dis·gorged′, dis·gorg′ing**



**dis·grace** (dis grās′) ***n.*** **1** loss of favor, respect, or honor; dishonor; shame [She is in *disgrace* for cheating on the test.] **2** a person or thing bringing shame [Slums are a *disgrace* to a city.] ◆***v.*** to bring shame or dishonor upon; hurt the reputation of [My cousin's crime has *disgraced* our family.] —**dis·graced′, dis·grac′ing**

**dis·grace·ful** (dis grās′fəl) ***adj.*** causing disgrace; shameful. —**dis·grace′ful·ly *adv.***

**dis·grun·tle** (dis grun′t'l) ***v.*** to displease and make sulky; make peevish and discontented. —**dis·grun′tled, dis·grun′tling**

**dis·guise** (dis gīz′) ***v.*** **1** to make seem so different as not to be recognized [to *disguise* oneself with a false beard; to *disguise* one's voice]. **2** to hide so as to keep from being known [She *disguised* her dislike of him by being very polite.] —**dis·guised′, dis·guis′ing** ◆***n.*** **1** any clothes, makeup, way of acting, etc. used to hide who or what one is. *See the picture.* **2** a disguising or being disguised [Come to the masquerade in *disguise.*]

**dis·gust** (dis gust′) ***n.*** a strong dislike that makes one feel sick [The smell of garbage filled me with *disgust.*] ◆***v.*** to cause disgust in. —**dis·gust′ing *adj.*** —**dis·gust′ing·ly *adv.***

**dish** (dish) ***n.*** **1** any of the plates, bowls, saucers, etc. used to serve food at the table. **2** an amount of food served in a dish [She ate a *dish* of ice cream.] **3** a kind of food [Hash is his favorite *dish.*] ◆***v.*** to serve in a dish [*Dish* up the beans.] —**dish′ful *adj.***

**dish·cloth** (dish′klôth) ***n.*** a cloth used for washing dishes.

**dis·heart·en** (dis här′t'n) ***v.*** to make lose hope; discourage. —**dis·heart′en·ing *adj.***

**di·shev·eled** or **di·shev·elled** (di shev′'ld) ***adj.*** not in neat order; mussed or rumpled; untidy [*disheveled* hair; a *disheveled* look]. *See the picture.*

**dis·hon·est** (dis än′ist) ***adj.*** not honest; lying, cheating, stealing, etc. —**dis·hon′est·ly *adv.*** —**dis·hon′es·ty *n.***

**dis·hon·or** (dis än′ər) ***n.*** **1** loss of honor or respect; shame; disgrace [There is no *dishonor* in losing if you do your best.] **2** a person or thing that causes dishonor; discredit. ◆***v.*** to bring shame upon; disgrace or insult.

**dis·hon·or·a·ble** (dis än′ər ə b'l) ***adj.*** bringing dishonor; disgraceful. —**dis·hon′or·a·bly *adv.***

☆**dish·pan** (dish′pan) ***n.*** a pan in which dishes, cooking utensils, etc. are washed.

☆**dish·wash·er** (dish′wôsh′ər *or* dish′wäsh′ər) ***n.*** **1** a machine for washing dishes, cooking utensils, etc. **2** a person who washes dishes, etc., especially in a restaurant.

**dis·il·lu·sion** (dis′i lo͞o′zhən) ***v.*** to free from a false idea or an illusion [Janet *disillusioned* Timmy about Santa Claus.] ◆***n.*** *same as* **disillusionment.**

**dis·il·lu·sion·ment** (dis′i lo͞o′zhən mənt) ***n.*** the act of freeing or state of being freed from a false idea.

**dis·in·clined** (dis′in klīnd′) ***adj.*** not eager or willing; reluctant [A good driver is *disinclined* to take risks.] —**dis·in·cli·na·tion** (dis′in klə nā′shən) ***n.***

**dis·in·fect** (dis′in fekt′) ***v.*** to kill disease germs in or on [to *disinfect* water with chlorine].

**dis·in·fect·ant** (dis′in fek′tənt) ***n.*** anything that disinfects, or kills disease germs, as alcohol.

**dis·in·her·it** (dis′in her′it) ***v.*** to take away the right to inherit; keep from being an heir [Parents sometimes *disinherit* a child who marries someone they do not like.]

**dis·in·te·grate** (dis in′tə grāt) ***v.*** to break up into parts or pieces; separate entirely [The bomb explosion *disintegrated* the building. The Roman Empire began to *disintegrate* in the 4th century.] —**dis·in′te·grat·ed, dis·in′te·grat·ing** —**dis·in′te·gra′tion *n.***

**dis·in·ter** (dis′in tʉr′) ***v.*** to dig up from a grave or take from a tomb. —**dis′in·terred′, dis′in·ter′ring**

**dis·in·ter·est·ed** (dis in′trist id *or* dis in′tər ist id) ***adj.*** **1** not having a selfish interest in the matter; impartial [A *disinterested* judge picked the winner.] **2** not interested; uninterested: *an older meaning that is being used again. See* SYNONYMS *at* **indifferent.**

**dis·joint** (dis joint′) ***v.*** to cut or tear apart at the joints [The cook *disjointed* the roast chicken.]

**dis·joint·ed** (dis joint′id) ***adj.*** not connected in thought; not clear or orderly; broken up [speaking in short, *disjointed* sentences].

**disk** (disk) ***n.*** **1** any thin, flat, round thing. **2** anything like this in form [the moon's *disk*]. *See the note at* **disc.**

**dis·like** (dis līk′) ***v.*** to have a feeling of not liking; be opposed to [I *dislike* people I can't trust.] —**dis·liked′, dis·lik′ing** ◆***n.*** a feeling of not liking; distaste [The gardener felt a strong *dislike* for toads.]

**dis·lo·cate** (dis′lō kāt) ***v.*** **1** to put a bone out of its proper place at a joint [to *dislocate* one's hip]. *See the picture.* **2** to put into disorder [to *dislocate* traffic]. —**dis′lo·cat·ed, dis′lo·cat·ing** —**dis′lo·ca′tion *n.***

**dis·lodge** (dis läj′) ***v.*** to force or be forced from a position or place where resting, hiding, etc. [A big rock was *dislodged* by the landslide.] —**dis·lodged′, dis·lodg′ing**

**dis·loy·al** (dis loi′əl) ***adj.*** not loyal or faithful; faithless. —**dis·loy′al·ty *n.***

**dis·mal** (diz′m′l) ***adj.*** **1** causing gloom or misery; sad [a *dismal* story]. **2** dark and gloomy [a *dismal* room]. —**dis′mal·ly *adv.***

**Dismal** comes from two Latin words meaning "evil days." In the Middle Ages certain days of the year were thought to be unlucky or evil. These "evil days" made people sad. In time, anything that made people sad could be called dismal.

**dis·man·tle** (dis man′t′l) ***v.*** **1** to make bare by removing furniture, equipment, etc. [to *dismantle* an old ship]. **2** to take apart [to *dismantle* a derrick in order to move it]. —**dis·man′tled, dis·man′tling**

**dis·may** (dis mā′) ***v.*** to fill with fear or dread so that one is not sure of what to do [We were *dismayed* at the sight of the destruction.] ◆***n.*** loss of courage or confidence when faced with trouble or danger [The doctor's report filled her with *dismay*.]

**dis·mem·ber** (dis mem′bər) ***v.*** to tear or cut to pieces; divide up [to *dismember* a body; to *dismember* a conquered country]. —**dis·mem′ber·ment *n.***

**dis·miss** (dis mis′) ***v.*** **1** to send away; tell or allow to leave [The teacher *dismissed* the class.] **2** to remove from a job or position; discharge; fire. **3** to put out of one's mind [*Dismiss* your fears.] **4** to turn down a plea, claim, etc. in a law court. —**dis·miss′al *n.***

**dis·mount** (dis mount′) ***v.*** **1** to get off or put off a horse, bicycle, motorcycle, etc. **2** to take from its mounting or support [The mechanic *dismounted* the motor to work on it.]

**Dis·ney** (diz′nē), **Walt(er)** 1901–1966; U.S. producer of movies, especially of animated cartoons.

**dis·o·be·di·ence** (dis′ə bē′dē əns) ***n.*** a refusing to obey; lack of obedience. —**dis′o·be′di·ent *adj.***

**dis·o·bey** (dis ə bā′) ***v.*** to fail to obey or refuse to obey.

**dis·or·der** (dis ôr′dər) ***n.*** **1** lack of order; jumble; confusion [The troops retreated in *disorder*.] **2** a riot or commotion [There were public *disorders* in the troubled country.] **3** a sickness; ailment [a nervous *disorder*]. ◆***v.*** to cause disorder in.

**dis·or·der·ly** (dis ôr′dər lē) ***adj.*** **1** not orderly or neat; untidy; messy [a *disorderly* desk]. *See the picture.* **2** that disturbs peace and quiet [arrested for *disorderly* conduct]. —**dis·or′der·li·ness *n.***

**dis·or·gan·ize** (dis ôr′gə nīz) ***v.*** to make confused or disordered; break up the system of [The unexpected guests *disorganized* the party.] —**dis·or′gan·ized, dis·or′gan·iz·ing** —**dis·or′gan·i·za′tion *n.***

**dis·own** (dis ōn′) ***v.*** to say that one will have nothing further to do with; refuse to accept as one's own [to *disown* one's family].

**dis·par·age** (dis par′ij) ***v.*** to speak of as having little importance or worth; belittle [Her envious friend *disparaged* her high grades.] —**dis·par′aged, dis·par′ag·ing** —**dis·par′age·ment *n.***

**dis·par·i·ty** (dis par′ə tē) ***n.*** a difference or lack of equality [There was a great *disparity* in the pay the two workers received.] —*pl.* **dis·par′i·ties**

**dis·pas·sion·ate** (dis pash′ən it) ***adj.*** not filled with emotion or prejudice; calm and impartial [A judge should be *dispassionate*.] —**dis·pas′sion·ate·ly *adv.***

**dis·patch** (dis pach′) ***v.*** **1** to send out promptly to a certain place or to do a certain job [We've *dispatched* someone to repair the break in the wire.] **2** to kill or put to death. **3** to finish quickly [to *dispatch* one's business]. ◆***n.*** **1** speed; promptness [He worked with great *dispatch*.] **2** a message, especially an official one [a *dispatch* from the general ordering an attack]. **3** a news story sent to a newspaper, radio or TV station, etc. [A *dispatch* from Japan told of floods there.]

**dis·patch·er** (dis pach′ər) ***n.*** ☆a person who sends out trains, buses, etc. on a schedule.

**dis·pel** (dis pel′) ***v.*** to scatter and drive away; make disappear [Wind *dispelled* the fog.] —**dis·pelled′, dis·pel′ling**

**dis·pen·sa·ry** (dis pen′sə rē) ***n.*** a room or place, as in a school, where a person can get medicines or first-aid treatment. —*pl.* **dis·pen′sa·ries**

**dis·pen·sa·tion** (dis′pən sā′shən) ***n.*** **1** a dispensing or giving out; distribution. **2** a managing or controlling of affairs [They believe in a divine *dispensation* of the universe.] **3** a religious system [the Christian *dispensation*]. **4** permission, as by a church, to ignore a rule.

**dis·pense** (dis pens′) ***v.*** **1** to give out; distribute [The agency *dispensed* clothing to the refugees.] **2** to prepare and give out [A pharmacist *dispenses* medicines.] —**dis·pensed′, dis·pens′ing** —**dispense with,** to do without; get along without [to *dispense with* rules].



SYNONYMS: To **dispense** something is to give it out after carefully measuring it [to *dispense* drugs]. To **distribute** something is to give out shares or spread about units of something among a number of people [to *distribute* pamphlets].

**dis·pen·ser** (dis pen′sər) ***n.*** a container that dispenses its contents in handy units or amounts.

**dis·perse** (dis purs′) ***v.*** to break up and scatter; spread in all directions [The crowd began to *disperse* after the game was over. The wind *dispersed* the clouds.] —**dis·persed′, dis·pers′ing** —**dis·per′sal** or **dis·per′sion *n.***

**dis·pir·it** (di spir′it) ***v.*** to make sad or discouraged; depress. —**dis·pir′it·ed *adj.***

**dis·place** (dis plās′) ***v.*** **1** to move from its usual or proper place [The storm *displaced* the telephone wires.] **2** to take the place of; replace [A ship *displaces* a certain amount of water.] —**dis·placed′, dis·plac′ing**

**displaced person** a person forced from his or her own country, as because of war, and left homeless in another country.

**dis·place·ment** (dis plās′mənt) ***n.*** **1** a moving or being moved from its proper place. **2** the amount of water that a ship displaces.

**dis·play** (dis plā′) ***v.*** **1** to put or spread out so as to be seen; exhibit [to *display* a collection of stamps].

| | | | | | | | |
|---|---|---|---|---|---|---|---|
| **a** | fat | **ir** | here | **ou** | out | **zh** | leisure |
| **ā** | ape | **ī** | bite, fire | **u** | up | **ng** | ring |
| **ä** | car, lot | **ō** | go | **ur** | fur | | a *in* ago |
| **e** | ten | **ô** | law, horn | **ch** | chin | | e *in* agent |
| **er** | care | **oi** | oil | **sh** | she | **ə =** | i *in* unity |
| **ē** | even | **oo** | look | **th** | thin | | o *in* collect |
| **i** | hit | **ōō** | tool | ***th*** | then | | u *in* focus |

*See* SYNONYMS *at* **show.** **2** to do something that is a sign or example of; show; reveal [to *display* one's courage]. ◆***n.*** **1** a displaying or showing; exhibition [a *display* of jewelry; a *display* of strength]. **2** a mere show of something that is not genuine [a *display* of sympathy].

**dis·please** (dis plēz′) ***v.*** to make angry or not satisfied; annoy. **—dis·pleased′, dis·pleas′ing**

**dis·pleas·ure** (dis plezh′ər) ***n.*** the condition of being annoyed or not satisfied.

**dis·port** (dis pôrt′) ***v.*** to play or amuse oneself [The children were *disporting* themselves in the pool.]

**dis·pos·a·ble** (dis pō′zə b'l) ***adj.*** that can be thrown away after use [*disposable* bottles].

**dis·pos·al** (dis pō′z'l) ***n.*** the act of disposing; a getting rid of, arranging, settling, etc. [the *disposal* of garbage and rubbish; the *disposal* of a lawsuit]. **—at one's disposal,** for one's use or service; as one wishes; at one's command.

**dis·pose** (dis pōz′) ***v.*** **1** to put in a certain order; arrange [to *dispose* the chairs in a circle]. **2** to make willing or ready [I am not *disposed* to agree.] **3** to make likely to be or do [Hot weather *disposes* me to laziness.] **—dis·posed′, dis·pos′ing —dispose of, 1** to get rid of, as by giving or throwing away, using up, or selling [*Dispose of* those apples before they rot.] **2** to take care of; settle [to *dispose of* a problem].

**dis·pos·er** (dis pō′zər) ***n.*** a device in the drain of a kitchen sink that grinds up garbage which is then flushed down the drain.

**dis·po·si·tion** (dis′pə zish′ən) ***n.*** **1** a putting in order or being put in order; arrangement [the *disposition* of the troops]. **2** a getting rid of something [the *disposition* of garbage]. **3** an inclination or willingness [a *disposition* to be helpful]. **4** one's general nature or mood; temperament [a kind *disposition*].

**dis·pos·sess** (dis pə zes′) ***v.*** to force by law to give up property [The bank *dispossessed* them of their house.] **—dis′pos·ses′sion *n.***

**dis·proof** (dis pro͞of′) ***n.*** **1** the act of disproving. **2** facts that disprove something.

**dis·pro·por·tion** (dis′prə pôr′shən) ***n.*** the state of being out of proportion, or unequal.

**dis·pro·por·tion·ate** (dis′prə pôr′shə nit) ***adj.*** too great or too small in proportion to others. *See the picture.*

**dis·prove** (dis pro͞ov′) ***v.*** to show to be false or incorrect [to *disprove* a theory]. **—dis·proved′, dis·prov′ing**

**dis·pu·tant** (dis pyo͞ot′'nt *or* dis′pyoo tənt) ***n.*** a person who disputes or argues.

**dis·pu·ta·tion** (dis′pyoo tā′shən) ***n.*** *another word for* **dispute.**

**dis·pute** (dis pyo͞ot′) ***v.*** **1** to argue or discuss a question; debate or quarrel. **2** to question or deny the truth of [The U.S. *disputed* Spain's claim to Cuba.] **3** to fight for; contest [The retreating army *disputed* every foot of ground.] **—dis·put′ed, dis·put′ing** ◆***n.*** a disputing; argument, debate, etc. *See* SYNONYMS *at* **argument** *and* **debate.**

**dis·qual·i·fy** (dis kwäl′ə fī) ***v.*** to make unfit or to say that someone is unfit, as for a position or to take part in some contest [The Constitution *disqualifies* a foreign-born person from becoming President.] **—dis·qual′i·fied, dis·qual′i·fy·ing**

**dis·qui·et** (dis kwī′ət) ***v.*** to make uneasy or anxious; disturb [The deadly silence was *disquieting*.] ◆***n.*** a disturbed or uneasy feeling; anxiety.

**dis·qui·e·tude** (dis kwī′ə to͞od *or* dis kwī′ə tyo͞od) ***n.*** a disturbed or uneasy condition; restlessness; anxiety.

**dis·qui·si·tion** (dis′kwə zish′ən) ***n.*** a long, serious speech or writing on some subject.

**Dis·rae·li** (diz rā′lē), **Benjamin** 1804–1881; English statesman and writer.

**dis·re·gard** (dis′ri gärd′) ***v.*** to pay no attention to; ignore [to *disregard* a warning]. ◆***n.*** lack of attention; an ignoring [He acted with a total *disregard* for his safety.]

**dis·re·pair** (dis′ri per′) ***n.*** the condition of needing repairs [an old house in *disrepair*].

**dis·rep·u·ta·ble** (dis rep′yoo tə b'l) ***adj.*** having or causing a bad reputation; not respectable [*disreputable* companions].

**dis·re·pute** (dis′ri pyo͞ot′) ***n.*** the condition of no longer having a good reputation; disfavor.

**dis·re·spect** (dis′ri spekt′) ***n.*** lack of respect or politeness; rudeness. **—dis′re·spect′ful *adj.* —dis′re·spect′ful·ly *adv.***

**dis·robe** (dis rōb′) ***v.*** to undress. **—dis·robed′, dis·rob′ing**

**dis·rupt** (dis rupt′) ***v.*** **1** to break apart. **2** to disturb the orderly course of [A few noisy members *disrupted* the meeting.] **—dis·rup′tion *n.***

**dis·sat·is·fac·tion** (dis sat′is fak′shən) ***n.*** the condition of being dissatisfied; discontent.

**dis·sat·is·fy** (dis sat′is fī) ***v.*** to fail to satisfy; leave wanting something more or different; make discontented. **—dis·sat′is·fied, dis·sat′is·fy·ing**

**dis·sect** (di sekt′) ***v.*** **1** to cut apart carefully, as in order to examine the parts [We *dissect* frogs in biology class.] **2** to study carefully every part of; analyze [The senators *dissected* the budget report.] **—dis·sec′tion *n.***

**dis·sem·ble** (di sem′b'l) ***v.*** to hide one's real feelings or ideas by pretending to have different ones [to *dissemble* fear by smiling]. **—dis·sem′bled, dis·sem′bling**

**dis·sem·i·nate** (di sem′ə nāt) ***v.*** to scatter or spread far and wide [Books *disseminate* ideas.] **—dis·sem′i·nat·ed, dis·sem′i·nat·ing —dis·sem′i·na′tion *n.***

> **Disseminate** comes from a Latin word that means "to scatter seed." Disseminating ideas or information is like sowing seeds in the minds of people. Some of the seeds grow, and some do not.

**dis·sen·sion** (di sen′shən) ***n.*** a dissenting; disagreement or, especially, violent quarreling.

**dis·sent** (di sent′) ***v.*** to differ in opinion; disagree [Several of us *dissented* from the majority vote.] ◆***n.*** a disagreement; difference of opinion. **—dis·sent′er *n.***

**dis·ser·ta·tion** (dis′ər tā′shən) ***n.*** a long, serious report on some subject, especially one written to get a degree from a university.

**dis·ser·vice** (dis sur′vis) ***n.*** an unkind or harmful act [The story about her in the newspaper did her a *disservice*.]

**dis·sev·er** (di sev′ər) ***v.*** to cut off or cut apart; sever.

**dis·si·dent** (dis′ə dənt) ***adj.*** not agreeing; dissenting. ◆***n.*** a dissident person. **—dis′si·dence *n.***

**dis·sim·i·lar** (di sim′ə lər) ***adj.*** not alike; different. —**dis·sim·i·lar·i·ty** (di sim′ə lar′ə tē) ***n.***

**dis·sim·u·late** (di sim′yə lāt) ***v.*** to hide one's real feelings by pretending to have different ones; dissemble. —**dis·sim′u·lat·ed, dis·sim′u·lat·ing** —**dis·sim′u·la′tion** ***n.***

**dis·si·pate** (dis′ə pāt) ***v.*** **1** to break up and disappear or make disappear [to *dissipate* smoke; to *dissipate* sorrow]. **2** to spend or use foolishly; waste [to *dissipate* one's wealth]. **3** to spend much time in wild or harmful pleasure. —**dis′si·pat·ed, dis′si·pat·ing** —**dis′si·pa′tion** ***n.***

**dis·so·ci·ate** (di sō′shē āt) ***v.*** to break the connection between; cut off association with; separate [to *dissociate* two ideas]. —**dis·so′ci·at·ed, dis·so′ci·at·ing** —**dis·so′ci·a′tion** ***n.***

**dis·so·lute** (dis′ə lo͞ot) ***adj.*** living a wild, immoral life; dissipated.

**dis·so·lu·tion** (dis′ə lo͞o′shən) ***n.*** **1** a dissolving or a breaking up; disintegration [the *dissolution* of an empire]. **2** an ending; finish [the *dissolution* of a friendship].

**dis·solve** (di zälv′) ***v.*** **1** to make or become liquid, as by melting in a liquid [to *dissolve* sugar in coffee]. **2** to break up and disappear or make disappear [Our courage *dissolved* in the face of danger.] **3** to bring or come to an end; finish [They *dissolved* their partnership.] —**dis·solved′, dis·solv′ing**

**dis·so·nance** (dis′ə nəns) ***n.*** **1** a sounding together of musical notes that do not harmonize; discord. **2** any lack of harmony or agreement. —**dis′so·nant** ***adj.***

**dis·suade** (di swād′) ***v.*** to convince a person not to do something [Try to *dissuade* them from going.] —**dis·suad′ed, dis·suad′ing** —**dis·sua·sion** (di swā′zhən) ***n.***

**Dist., dist.** *abbreviations for* **district.**

**dis·taff** (dis′taf) ***n.*** a stick from which flax or wool is unwound while it is being spun into thread on a spindle. *See the picture.* ◆***adj.*** female; especially, describing the mother's side of a family.

**dis·tance** (dis′təns) ***n.*** **1** the length of a line between two points [The *distance* between New York and Chicago is 713 miles.] **2** the condition of being far apart in space or time; remoteness ["*Distance* lends charm." There was quite a *distance* between their views.] **3** a place far away [viewing things from a *distance*]. ◆***v.*** to leave behind; do better than; pass [He *distanced* all his competition.] —**dis′tanced, dis′tanc·ing** —**keep at a distance,** to be cool or unfriendly to. —**keep one's distance,** to stay aloof or be unfriendly.

**dis·tant** (dis′tənt) ***adj.*** **1** far apart in space or time; remote [a *distant* country; a *distant* age]. **2** away [The next bus stop is a half mile *distant.*] **3** aloof or unfriendly. **4** not closely related [*distant* relatives]. —**dis′tant·ly** ***adv.***

**dis·taste** (dis tāst′) ***n.*** dislike; aversion.

**dis·taste·ful** (dis tāst′fəl) ***adj.*** not to one's taste or liking; disagreeable; unpleasant. —**dis·taste′ful·ly** ***adv.***

**dis·tem·per** (dis tem′pər) ***n.*** a disease of young dogs in which there is fever and weakness.

**dis·tend** (dis tend′) ***v.*** to swell or expand [The pelican's pouch was *distended* with fish.]

**dis·till** or **dis·til** (dis til′) ***v.*** **1** to heat, especially a liquid, so that it gives off vapor which is then cooled so that it becomes a purer liquid [to *distill* ocean water for drinking]. **2** to get by distilling [to *distill* alcohol from fermented grain]. **3** to draw out the part that is basic, pure, etc. [to *distill* the meaning of a poem]. —**dis·tilled′, dis·till′ing**

**Distill** comes from the Latin word for "icicle." When something is distilled, it drips down like water from a melting icicle.

**dis·til·la·tion** (dis′tə lā′shən) ***n.*** **1** a distilling, as of crude oil to get gasoline, kerosene, etc. *See the picture.* **2** anything got by distilling.



**dis·till·er** (dis til′ər) ***n.*** a person or company that distills alcoholic liquors.

**dis·till·er·y** (dis til′ər ē) ***n.*** a place where alcoholic liquors are distilled. —*pl.* **dis·till′er·ies**

**dis·tinct** (dis tiŋkt′) ***adj.*** **1** not alike; different [My twin sisters have *distinct* personalities.] **2** not the same; separate [Her lecture was divided into four *distinct* parts.] **3** clearly seen, heard, felt, etc. [a *distinct* smell of perfume in the room]. **4** very definite; positive [a *distinct* improvement]. —**dis·tinct′ly** ***adv.*** —**dis·tinct′ness** ***n.***

**dis·tinc·tion** (dis tiŋk′shən) ***n.*** **1** the act of keeping distinct or separate [This school is open to all, without *distinction* of race or religion.] **2** a way in which things differ [We can see the *distinctions* between two breeds of dog.] **3** a being better than average; excellence [She served with *distinction* in the Senate.] **4** the condition of being honored; fame; honor [to earn *distinction* as a scholar].

**dis·tinc·tive** (dis tiŋk′tiv) ***adj.*** making distinct or different from others; characteristic [the *distinctive* markings of a skunk]. *See* SYNONYMS *at* **characteristic.** —**dis·tinc′tive·ly** ***adv.***

**dis·tin·guish** (dis tiŋ′gwish) ***v.*** **1** to set apart as different; be the difference in [What *distinguishes* human

| | | | | | | | |
|---|---|---|---|---|---|---|---|
| a | fat | ir | here | ou | out | zh | leisure |
| ā | ape | ī | bite, fire | u | up | ŋ | ring |
| ä | car, lot | ō | go | ʉr | fur | | a *in* ago |
| e | ten | ô | law, horn | ch | chin | | e *in* agent |
| er | care | oi | oil | sh | she | ə = | i *in* unity |
| ē | even | oo | look | th | thin | | o *in* collect |
| i | hit | o͞o | tool | *th* | then | | u *in* focus |

beings from the apes?] **2** to see the difference in [to *distinguish* right from wrong]. **3** to see, hear, taste, etc. clearly [I could *distinguish* no odor of gas in the room.] **4** to make famous or outstanding [The Brontë sisters *distinguished* themselves as writers.] **—dis·tin′guish·a·ble** ***adj.***

**dis·tin·guished** (dis tiŋ′gwisht) ***adj.*** **1** famous; outstanding [a *distinguished* poet]. **2** having the look of a distinguished person [a diplomat with a *distinguished* air].

**dis·tort** (dis tôrt′) ***v.*** **1** to twist out of its usual shape or look [The old mirror gave a *distorted* reflection.] *See the picture.* **2** to change so as to give a false idea [The facts were *distorted.*] **3** to make a sound or signal sound different when reproduced [The sound of music is *distorted* on my new radio.] **—dis·tor′tion** ***n.***

**dis·tract** (dis trakt′) ***v.*** **1** to draw one's thoughts or attention to something else; divert [The movie *distracted* her from her worries.] **2** to make unable to think clearly; confuse; bewilder [I get *distracted* when two people talk to me at once.]

**dis·trac·tion** (dis trak′shən) ***n.*** **1** a distracting or drawing away of one's attention. **2** anything that distracts in either a pleasant or an unpleasant way [The man's coughing was a *distraction* to the audience. Chess was their favorite *distraction* after work.] **3** a confused state of mind; bewilderment [Their shrieking is driving me to *distraction.*]



**dis·traught** (dis trôt′) ***adj.*** very confused or troubled, as by worry or grief.

**dis·tress** (dis tres′) ***v.*** to cause pain, sorrow, or worry to; make suffer; trouble [The bad news *distressed* us.] **•*n.*** **1** pain, sorrow, or worry; suffering. **2** anything causing this. **3** a state of danger or trouble [a ship in *distress*]. **—dis·tress′ful** ***adj.***

**dis·tressed** (dis trest′) ***adj.*** **1** full of distress or pain; worried, anxious, suffering, etc. **2** of or describing an area where many people are unemployed, poor, etc.

**dis·trib·ute** (dis trib′yoot) ***v.*** **1** to give out in shares; deal out [Food was *distributed* to the starving.] *See* SYNONYMS *at* **dispense.** **2** to spread out or scatter [*Distribute* the paint evenly over the surface.] **3** to sort out or arrange according to a plan [Shrubs were *distributed* in rows along the driveway.] **—dis·trib′ut·ed, dis·trib′ut·ing**

**dis·tri·bu·tion** (dis′trə byōō′shən) ***n.*** the act or way of distributing something [a *distribution* of funds; a fair *distribution*]. **—dis·trib·u·tive** (dis trib′yoo tiv) ***adj.***

**dis·trib·u·tor** (dis trib′yoo tər) ***n.*** ☆**1** a person or company that distributes goods to customers. ☆**2** a device for distributing electricity to the spark plugs of a gasoline engine. *See the picture.*

**dis·trict** (dis′trikt) ***n.*** **1** any of the parts into which a country, city, etc. is divided for some special purpose [a school *district;* a Congressional *district*]. **2** any region; part of a country, city, etc. [the business *district* of Cleveland].

☆**district attorney** a lawyer who works for the State or Federal government in some district by handling cases against those accused of breaking the law.

**District of Columbia** a Federal district in the eastern United States on the Potomac River, occupied entirely by Washington, the capital: abbreviated **D.C.**

**dis·trust** (dis trust′) ***n.*** a lack of trust; doubt; suspicion. **•*v.*** to have no trust in; doubt. **—dis·trust′ful** ***adj.***

**dis·turb** (dis turb′) ***v.*** **1** to break up the quiet or calm of [The roar of motorcycles *disturbed* the peace.] **2** to make worried or uneasy; upset [They are *disturbed* by their parents' divorce.] **3** to put into disorder; mix up [Someone *disturbed* the books on my shelf.] **4** to break in on; bother or interrupt [Don't *disturb* me while I'm working.]

**dis·turb·ance** (dis turb′əns) ***n.*** **1** a disturbing or being disturbed. **2** anything that disturbs. **3** noisy confusion; uproar; disorder.

**dis·un·ion** (dis yōōn′yən) ***n.*** **1** a breaking up; separation. **2** a failing to work together in harmony; disagreement.

**dis·u·nite** (dis′yoo nīt′) ***v.*** to break up; separate or divide. **—dis′u·nit′ed, dis′u·nit′ing —dis·u·ni·ty** (dis yōō′nə tē) ***n.***

**dis·use** (dis yōōs′) ***n.*** lack of use [Skills can be forgotten through *disuse.*]

**ditch** (dich) ***n.*** a long, narrow opening dug in the earth, as for carrying off water; trench [a *ditch* along the road]. **•*v.*** **1** to dig a ditch in or around. **2** to throw into a ditch. **3** to get rid of: *slang in this meaning.*

**dith·er** (dith′ər) ***n.*** an excited and confused condition.

**dit·to** (dit′ō) ***n.*** **1** the same as what was just said or written. **2** the mark ", used to show that what is written above it is to be repeated. *—pl.* **dit′tos**

Example: 2 pairs of shoes at $17.00 a pair
5 " " socks " $1.50 " "

**•*adv.*** as said before.

**dit·ty** (dit′ē) ***n.*** a short, simple song. *—pl.* **dit′ties**

**di·ur·nal** (dī ur′n′l) ***adj.*** **1** happening every day; daily. **2** of the daytime.

**di·van** (dī′van *or* di van′) ***n.*** a large, low couch, usually without armrests or back.

**dive** (dīv) ***v.*** **1** to plunge into water, usually headfirst. **2** to plunge into anything, as with the hand, body, or mind [The soldiers *dived* into their foxholes.

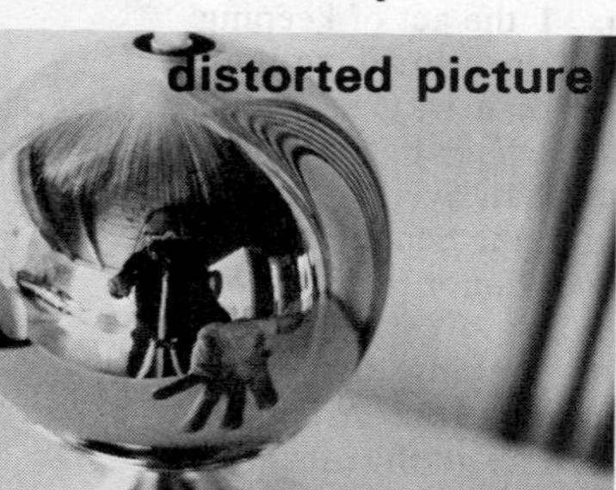
distorted picture

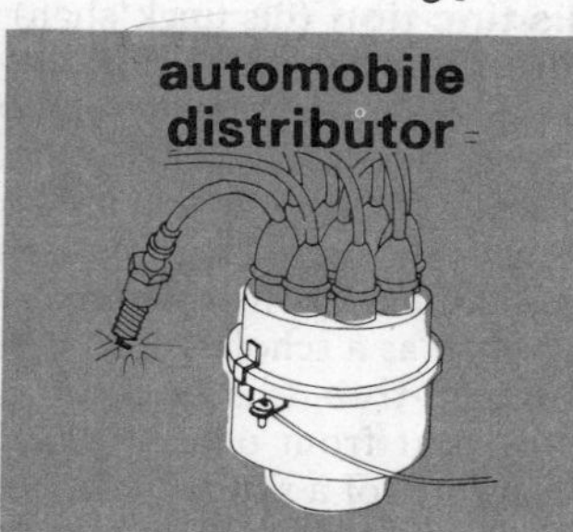
automobile distributor

diving board

divers

I *dived* into my homework right after dinner.] **3** to make a steep plunge downward, as an airplane. —**dived** or **dove, dived, div′ing** ◆*n.* **1** the act of diving into water. **2** any sudden plunge [an airplane *dive*]. ☆**3** a low, cheap bar, nightclub, etc.: *used only in everyday talk.*

**di·ver** (dīv′ər) *n.* **1** a person who dives. **2** a person who works under water, usually wearing a special suit and a helmet through which air is supplied. *See the picture.* **3** a bird that dives into water for its food, as the loon.

**di·verge** (də vurj′) *v.* **1** to branch off and move farther away from one another [The single path became two paths that *diverged*.] **2** to differ, as in opinion. —**di·verged′, di·verg′ing**

**di·ver·gence** (də vur′jəns) *n.* **1** a diverging or branching off. **2** a difference, as in opinion. —**di·ver′gent** *adj.*

**di·verse** (dī vurs′ *or* dī′vurs) *adj.* not alike; different [The customs of France and Italy are quite *diverse*.]

**di·ver·si·fy** (də vur′sə fī) *v.* **1** to make different; vary [Farmers *diversify* crops to keep the soil healthy.] **2** to expand a business by adding different kinds of products, services, etc. —**di·ver′si·fied, di·ver′si·fy·ing**

**di·ver·sion** (də vur′zhən) *n.* **1** a diverting, or turning aside [The dam caused a *diversion* of the stream.] **2** anything to which one turns for fun or relaxation; pastime [In a small town, the circus is a welcome *diversion*.]

**di·ver·si·ty** (də vur′sə tē) *n.* **1** the condition of being different or varied; difference [The male and female cardinal show a *diversity* in plumage.] **2** variety [a *diversity* of opinions]. —*pl.* **di·ver′si·ties**

**di·vert** (də vurt′) *v.* **1** to turn aside [to *divert* enemy troops; to *divert* one's attention]. **2** to entertain or amuse [The fiddlers *diverted* King Cole.]

**di·vest** (də vest′) *v.* **1** to take off; strip [The prisoner was *divested* of all clothing.] **2** to take away from; make give up; deprive [The officer was *divested* of his rank.]

**di·vide** (də vīd′) *v.* **1** to separate into parts; split up [a classroom *divided* by a movable wall]. **2** to separate into equal parts by arithmetic [If you *divide* 12 by 3, you get 4.] **3** to put into separate groups; classify [Living things are *divided* into plants and animals.] **4** to make separate or keep apart [A stone wall *divides* their farms.] **5** to give out in shares; portion out [*Divide* the cake among them.] **6** to disagree or cause to disagree [The members are *divided* on the tax issue.] —**di·vid′ed, di·vid′ing** ◆*n.* ☆a ridge that separates two areas drained by rivers flowing in opposite directions.

**div·i·dend** (div′ə dend) *n.* **1** the number into which another number is divided [In 6 ÷ 3 = 2, the number 6 is the *dividend*.] **2** an amount of money from profits that a company divides, especially among those who own stock in it; also, a single share of this.

**di·vid·er** (də vīd′ər) *n.* **1** a screen, set of shelves, etc. placed so as to separate a room into different areas. **2** **dividers,** *pl. same as* **compass** (*in meaning* 2).

**div·i·na·tion** (div′ə nā′shən) *n.* **1** a trying or pretending to tell the future by means of magic, the stars, or other mysterious means. **2** something told in this way; prophecy.

**di·vine** (də vīn′) *adj.* **1** of or like God or a god [a *divine* power]. **2** coming from God; holy [*divine* scripture]. **3** devoted to God; religious [*divine* worship]. **4** very pleasing or attractive: *used only in everyday talk* [The pie was *divine*.] ◆*n.* a clergyman or other person trained in theology. ◆*v.* **1** to try or pretend to tell the future; prophesy. **2** to guess or sense what another is thinking or feeling [I *divined* the purpose of her visit from the happy look she wore.] —**di·vined′, di·vin′ing** —**di·vine′ly** *adv.* —**di·vin′er** *n.*

☆**diving board** a springboard from which swimmers can dive into a pool or lake. *See the picture.*

**di·vin·i·ty** (də vin′ə tē) *n.* **1** the condition of being a god or like a god. **2** a god or goddess. **3** the study of religion; theology. —*pl.* **di·vin′i·ties** —**the Divinity,** God.

**di·vis·i·ble** (də viz′ə b′l) *adj.* that can be divided; especially, that can be divided without having anything left over [The number 6 is *divisible* by either 2 or 3.] —**di·vis′i·bil′i·ty** *n.*

**di·vi·sion** (də vizh′ən) *n.* **1** a dividing or being divided. **2** the process in arithmetic of finding out how many times one number is contained in another. **3** a sharing or giving out in portions; distribution [the *division* of profits among partners]. **4** a difference in opinion; disagreement. **5** anything that divides, as a line or wall. **6** a section, department, or part [the sales *division* of a company; the children's *division* of a library]. **7** an army unit larger than a regiment and smaller than a corps. —**di·vi′sion·al** *adj.*



**di·vi·sive** (də vī′siv) *adj.* causing division; especially, causing disagreement.

**di·vi·sor** (də vī′zər) *n.* the number by which another number is divided [In 6 ÷ 3 = 2, the number 3 is the *divisor*.]

**di·vorce** (də vôrs′) *n.* **1** the ending of a marriage by an act of law. **2** complete separation [to favor the *divorce* of church and state]. ◆*v.* **1** to end one's marriage by an act of law. **2** to keep apart; separate [She *divorced* herself from the pleasures of life.] —**di·vorced′, di·vorc′ing**

**di·vor·cee** (də vôr′sā′) *n.* a divorced woman.

**di·vulge** (də vulj′) *v.* to make known; reveal [Do not *divulge* the contents of this letter.] —**di·vulged′, di·vulg′ing**

**Dix·ie** (dik′sē) the Southern States of the United States; the South.

**diz·zy** (diz′ē) *adj.* **1** having a whirling or spinning feeling that makes one lose one's balance; giddy; unsteady [Riding on the merry-go-round made us *dizzy*.] **2** that makes one feel dizzy [a *dizzy* height]. —**diz′zi·er, diz′zi·est** —**diz′zi·ly** *adv.* —**diz′zi·ness** *n.*

**DJ** (dē′jā) *abbreviation for* **disc jockey.** —*pl.* **DJ's**

**Dji·bou·ti** (ji bo͞ot′ē) **1** a country in eastern Africa. **2** its capital.

| | | | | | | | |
|---|---|---|---|---|---|---|---|
| **a** | fat | **ir** | here | **ou** | out | **zh** | leisure |
| **ā** | ape | **ī** | bite, fire | **u** | up | **ng** | ring |
| **ä** | car, lot | **ō** | go | **ur** | fur | | a *in* ago |
| **e** | ten | **ô** | law, horn | **ch** | chin | | e *in* agent |
| **er** | care | **oi** | oil | **sh** | she | **ə** = | i *in* unity |
| **ē** | even | **oo** | look | **th** | thin | | o *in* collect |
| **i** | hit | **o͞o** | tool | ***th*** | then | | u *in* focus |

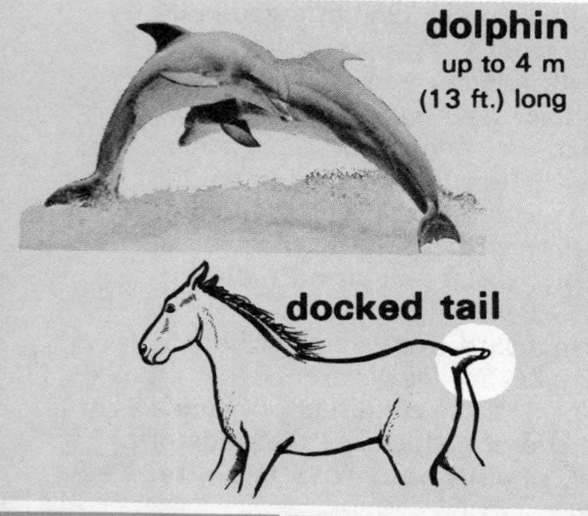

**DNA** an essential part of all living matter and a basic material in the chromosomes of the cell. It carries the pattern of inherited characteristics. *See the picture.*



**Dne·pr** or **Dnie·per** (nē′pər) a river in the western U.S.S.R., flowing into the Black Sea.

**do**[1] (do͞o) ***v.*** **1** to work at or carry out an action; perform [What do you *do* for a living? I'll *do* the job.] **2** to finish [Dinner has been *done* for an hour.] **3** to bring about; cause [The storm *did* a lot of damage.] **4** to put forth; exert [She *did* her best.] **5** to take care of; attend to [Who will *do* the dishes?] **6** to be right for the purpose; fit [Will this dress *do* for the party?] **7** to get along; fare [The patient is *doing* well.] **8** to move along at a speed of [Her car will *do* 100 miles an hour.] **9** to give [to *do* honor to a famous person]. *Do* is also used to ask a question [*Do* you want some candy?], to give force to what one is saying [I *do* have to go. *Do* stay for dinner. I *do* not believe you.], and to take the place of another verb [He'll go if you *do.*] —**did, done, do′ing** —**do up,** to make ready or wrap up: *used only in everyday talk.* —**have to do with,** to be related; have connection with. —**make do,** to manage or get along with what one has.

**do**[2] (dō) ***n.*** the first or last note of a musical scale.

**do.** *abbreviation for* **ditto.**

**DOA** or **D.O.A.** dead on arrival.

**dob·bin** (däb′in) ***n.*** a gentle, plodding horse.

**Do·ber·man pin·scher** (dō′bər mən pin′shər) a large dog with smooth, dark hair, tan markings, and a short tail.

☆**doc** (däk) ***n.*** doctor: *a slang word.*

**doc·ile** (däs′′l) ***adj.*** easy to handle or train; tame; obedient [a *docile* horse]. —**doc′ile·ly *adv.*** —**do·cil·i·ty** (dä sil′ə tē) ***n.***

**dock**[1] (däk) ***n.*** ☆**1** a long platform built out over water as a landing place for ships; pier; wharf. *See the picture.* **2** the water between two docks. **3** *shorter form of* **dry dock.** ☆**4** a platform at which trucks or freight cars are loaded or unloaded. ◆***v.*** **1** to bring a ship to a dock [Tugs help to *dock* ocean liners.] **2** to come into a dock [The ship *docks* at Pier 9.] ☆**3** to join vehicles together in outer space.

**dock**[2] (däk) ***n.*** the place in a court of law where the accused person stands or sits.

**dock**[3] (däk) ***n.*** a common weed with small, green flowers and large, smooth leaves.

**dock**[4] (däk) ***n.*** the solid part of an animal's tail. ◆***v.*** **1** to cut off the end of; bob [to *dock* a horse's tail]. *See the picture.* **2** to cut or take some part from [They will *dock* your wages if you are absent.]

**dock·et** (däk′it) ***n.*** ☆**1** a list of the cases to be tried by a law court. **2** any list of things to be done or considered; agenda. ◆***v.*** ☆ to put on a docket.

**dock·yard** (däk′yärd) ***n.*** a place along a waterfront where ships are built or repaired.

**doc·tor** (däk′tər) ***n.*** **1** a person trained to heal the sick; especially, a physician or surgeon. **2** a person who has received the highest degree given by a university [*Doctor* of Philosophy]. ◆***v.*** **1** to try to heal [to *doctor* oneself]. **2** to change secretly; tamper with [The lawyer *doctored* the evidence by destroying certain letters.] *The verb is used only in everyday talk.*

**doc·trine** (däk′trin) ***n.*** something that is taught as a belief or principle of a religion, political party, scientific group, etc. —**doc′trin·al *adj.***

SYNONYMS: A **doctrine** is a belief that has been carefully thought out and is taught and supported by those who believe it [the political *doctrines* of democracy]. A **dogma** is a belief or doctrine that some person or group in a position of power hands down, often in an arrogant way, as something that is true and not to be questioned [a religion with few *dogmas*].

**doc·u·ment** (däk′yə mənt) ***n.*** **1** any printed or written record used to prove something, as a birth certificate or a deed to property. **2** anything used as proof [Brady's photographs are useful *documents* of the Civil War.] ◆***v.*** (däk′yə ment) to furnish or prove with documents.

**doc·u·men·ta·ry** (däk′yə men′tə rē) ***adj.*** **1** made up of documents [You must show *documentary* proof of age.] **2** that shows or presents news events, social conditions, etc. in a story based mainly on facts [a *documentary* film]. ◆***n.*** a documentary film, TV show, etc. —*pl.* **doc′u·men′ta·ries**

**doc·u·men·ta·tion** (däk′yə mən tā′shən) ***n.*** the use of documents as proof, or such documents.

**dod·der** (däd′ər) ***v.*** to tremble or move in an unsteady way, as a very old person does.

**dodge** (däj) ***v.*** **1** to move quickly to one side, as to get out of the way of a person or thing [to *dodge* a blow]. **2** to get away from or avoid by tricks or cleverness [to *dodge* a question]. —**dodged, dodg′ing** ◆***n.*** **1** the act of dodging. **2** a trick used in cheating or in avoiding something. —**dodg′er *n.***

**do·do** (dō′dō) ***n.*** a large bird that had small wings and could not fly. Dodos lived on an island in the Indian Ocean and were all killed off by the year 1700. *See the picture.* —*pl.* **do′dos** or **do′does**

**doe** (dō) ***n.*** the female of the deer, antelope, rabbit, etc. —*pl.* **does** or **doe**

**do·er** (do͞o′ər) ***n.*** **1** a person who does something [a *doer* of good]. **2** a person who gets things done [a *doer,* not a talker].

**does** (duz) *the form of the verb* **do** *showing the present time with singular nouns and with* he, she, *or* it.

**doe·skin** (dō′skin) ***n.*** **1** a soft leather made from the skin of a female deer or, now usually, from lambskin. **2** a soft, smooth woolen cloth.

**does·n't** (duz′′nt) does not.

**doff** (däf) ***v.*** to take off, as one's hat or coat.

**dog** (dôg) ***n.*** **1** a flesh-eating animal related to the fox and wolf, that is raised as a pet or for use in hunting or herding. **2** a device for holding or gripping something. ☆**3 dogs,** *pl.* feet: *slang in this meaning.* **4** an unattractive person: *slang in this meaning.* ◆***v.*** to follow or hunt like a dog [The child *dogged* her father's footsteps.] —**dogged, dog′ging**

**dog days** the uncomfortably hot part of summer.

**doge** (dōj) ***n.*** the chief official in the former republics of Venice and Genoa.

**dog·ear** (dôg′ir) ***n.*** a turned-down corner of the leaf of a book. *See the picture.* —**dog′eared *adj.***

**dog·fish** (dôg′fish) ***n.*** a small kind of shark.

**dog·ged** (dôg′id) ***adj.*** refusing to give up; steady and determined [Lincoln's *dogged* efforts to get an education.] —**dog′ged·ly *adv.***

**dog·ger·el** (dôg′ər əl) ***n.*** poetry of a poor kind; also, light or comic verses with a regular rhythm and simple ideas.

**dog·gy** or **dog·gie** (dôg′ē) ***n.*** a little dog: *a child's word.* —*pl.* **dog′gies**

☆**do·gie** or **do·gy** (dō′gē) ***n.*** a stray or motherless calf: *used in the western U.S.* —*pl.* **do′gies**

**dog·ma** (dôg′mə) ***n.*** **1** a belief that a church holds and teaches to be truth, not to be doubted; also, all such beliefs of any particular church. **2** any belief held as a truth not to be questioned [a matter of scientific *dogma*]. *See* SYNONYMS *at* **doctrine.**

**dog·mat·ic** (dôg mat′ik) ***adj.*** **1** having to do with dogma. **2** giving an opinion in a too positive or self-assured way, but without proof [a *dogmatic* person]. —**dog·mat′i·cal·ly *adv.***

**dog·ma·tism** (dôg′mə tiz′m) ***n.*** the giving of an opinion in a dogmatic way.

**dog·trot** (dôg′trät) ***n.*** a slow, easy trot.

**dog·wood** (dôg′wood) ***n.*** a tree whose blossom is surrounded by four white or pink leaves that look like petals.

**doi·ly** (doi′lē) ***n.*** a small mat, as of lace or paper, often placed under a vase, dish, etc. as a decoration or to protect the top of the table. —*pl.* **doi′lies**

**do·ings** (do͞o′iŋz) ***n.pl.*** things done; actions or activities.

**dol·drums** (däl′drəmz *or* dōl′drəmz) ***n.pl.*** **1** the parts of the ocean near the equator where the winds are light or do not blow at all. **2** a condition of feeling sad, bored, etc.

**dole** (dōl) ***n.*** **1** the giving out of money or food to people in great need; relief. **2** anything given out in this way. ◆***v.*** to give out in small amounts [He *doled* out the peanuts to his playmates one by one.] —**doled, dol′ing**

**dole·ful** (dōl′fəl) ***adj.*** very sad; sorrowful; mournful. —**dole′ful·ly *adv.***

**doll** (däl) ***n.*** **1** a toy that is a small figure of a person, especially of a baby or child. **2** a pretty child or young woman. **3** any attractive person: *slang in this meaning.* ◆***v.*** to dress in a showy or stylish way: *used only in everyday talk* [They *dolled* up for the party.]

**dol·lar** (däl′ər) ***n.*** ☆**1** a United States coin or piece of paper money, equal to 100 cents. The dollar is our basic unit of money; its symbol is $. **2** a unit of money in certain other countries, as Canada.

**dol·ly** (däl′ē) ***n.*** **1** a doll: *a child's word.* ☆**2** a low frame on wheels, for moving heavy things around, as in a factory. —*pl.* **dol′lies**

**do·lor** (dō′lər) ***n.*** deep sorrow or sadness; grief: *used mainly in poetry.*

**dol·or·ous** (dō′lər əs *or* däl′ər əs) ***adj.*** very sorrowful or sad; mournful [*dolorous* weeping; the *dolorous* news of the plane crash]. —**dol′or·ous·ly *adv.***

**dol·phin** (däl′fən) ***n.*** a water animal related to the whale but smaller. The common dolphin has a long snout and many teeth. *See the picture.*

**dolt** (dōlt) ***n.*** a stupid, slow-thinking person. —**dolt′ish *adj.***

**-dom** (dəm) *a suffix meaning:* **1** the position or domain of [A *kingdom* is the domain of a king.] **2** the condition of being [*Wisdom* is the condition of being wise.] **3** the whole group of [*Officialdom* is the whole group of officials.]

**dom.** *abbreviation for* **domestic, dominion.**

**do·main** (dō mān′) ***n.*** **1** all the land controlled by a certain government or ruler [the queen's *domain*]. **2** a field of activity or thought [the *domain* of science].

**dome** (dōm) ***n.*** **1** a round roof shaped more or less like half a globe. **2** anything shaped like a dome [the *dome* of the mountain].

**do·mes·tic** (də mes′tik) ***adj.*** **1** of the home or family [*domestic* joys; *domestic* chores]. **2** of or made in one's own country [*domestic* olives grown in California]. **3** not wild; tame; used to living with people [Dogs, horses, cows, etc. are *domestic* animals.] **4** enjoying the home and family life [a *domestic* young married couple]. ◆***n.*** a maid, cook, butler, or other house servant. —**do·mes′ti·cal·ly *adv.***

**do·mes·ti·cate** (də mes′tə kāt) ***v.*** **1** to tame an animal or cultivate a plant for use by human beings. **2** to make happy or content with the home and family life [a *domesticated* couple who seldom go out]. —**do·mes′ti·cat·ed, do·mes′ti·cat·ing** —**do·mes′ti·ca′tion *n.***

**do·mes·tic·i·ty** (dō′mes tis′ə tē) ***n.*** **1** life with one's family around the home. **2** a liking for home life.

**dom·i·cile** (däm′ə sīl) ***n.*** one's house or home; residence. ◆***v.*** to put in a domicile. —**dom′i·ciled, dom′i·cil·ing**

**dom·i·nant** (däm′ə nənt) ***adj.*** most important or most powerful; ruling, controlling, etc. [a nation *dominant* in the world; the *dominant* idea of a speech]. —**dom′i·nance *n.***

| | | | | | | | |
|---|---|---|---|---|---|---|---|
| **a** fat | **ir** here | **ou** out | **zh** leisure | | | | |
| **ā** ape | **ī** bite, fire | **u** up | **ŋ** ring | | | | |
| **ä** car, lot | **ō** go | **ur** fur | a *in* ago | | | | |
| **e** ten | **ô** law, horn | **ch** chin | e *in* agent | | | | |
| **er** care | **oi** oil | **sh** she | ə = i *in* unity | | | | |
| **ē** even | **oo** look | **th** thin | o *in* collect | | | | |
| **i** hit | **o͞o** tool | ***th*** then | u *in* focus | | | | |

d

**dom·i·nate** (däm′ə nāt) ***v.*** **1** to control or rule; be most important or powerful [A desire to win *dominates* all her actions. The colonies were *dominated* by the mother country.] **2** to tower over; rise high above [These tall buildings *dominate* the city.] —**dom′i·nat·ed, dom′i·nat·ing** —**dom′i·na′tion** ***n.***

**Dominate** comes from the Latin word for "master," *dominus,* and so do the words **domineer** and **dominion.**

**dom·i·neer** (däm ə nir′) ***v.*** to rule over in a harsh or bullying way [Their older sister *domineered* over them.] —**dom·i·neer′ing** ***adj.***

**Do·min·i·can** (də min′i kən) ***adj.*** **1** having to do with the religious order founded in 1215 by Saint Dominic, a Spanish priest. **2** of the Dominican Republic. ◆***n.*** **1** a Dominican friar or nun. **2** a person born or living in the Dominican Republic.

**Dominican Republic** a country in the eastern part of Hispaniola, in the West Indies.

**do·min·ion** (də min′yən) ***n.*** **1** the power of governing; rule. **2** a territory or country ruled over.

**dom·i·no** (däm′ə nō) ***n.*** **1** a small, oblong piece of wood, plastic, etc. marked with dots on one side. A set of these pieces is used in playing the game called **dominoes,** in which the halves are matched. *See the picture.* **2** a mask for the eyes; also, a masquerade costume consisting of a loose, hooded cloak and such a mask. —*pl.* **dom′i·noes** or **dom′i·nos**

220 **Don**[1] (dän) a river in the western U.S.S.R., flowing into the Black Sea.

**Don**[2] (dän) ***n.*** a Spanish title of respect used before the first name of a man [*Don* Juan].

**don** (dän) ***v.*** to put on, as one's hat or coat. —**donned, don′ning**

☆**do·nate** (dō′nāt) ***v.*** to give to some cause, fund, charity, etc.; contribute [to *donate* money to the scholarship fund]. —**do′nat·ed, do′nat·ing** —**do·na′tion** ***n.***

**done** (dun) *past participle of* **do**[1]. ◆***adj.*** **1** finished; completed. **2** cooked.

**Don Ju·an** (dän jo͞o′ən *or* dän wän) a nobleman of Spanish legend, who had many love affairs.

**don·key** (däŋ′kē *or* dôŋ′kē) ***n.*** an animal like a horse but smaller and with longer ears. *See the picture.* —*pl.* **don′keys**

**do·nor** (dō′nər) ***n.*** a person who donates or gives something [a blood *donor*].

**Don Quix·o·te** (dän′kē hōt′ē *or* dän′kwik′sət) the mad but harmless hero of a book by the Spanish writer Cervantes. In his desire to help those in need and to fight evil, he does foolish things.

**don′t** (dōnt) do not.

**doo·dle** (do͞o′d′l) ***v.*** ☆to scribble in an aimless way, especially when thinking about something else. —**doo′dled, doo′dling** ◆***n.*** ☆a design, mark, etc. made in this way. —**doo′dler** ***n.***

**doom** (do͞om) ***n.*** **1** one's fate or destiny, especially when bad or tragic; ruin or death [The first time our dog chased a car, its *doom* was sealed.] **2** a judgment that someone is guilty and must be punished [She gasped when the judge pronounced her *doom.*] ◆***v.*** to destine or sentence to some bad or tragic end [*doomed* to die].

**dooms·day** (do͞omz′dā) ***n.*** *another name for* **Judgment Day.**

**door** (dôr) ***n.*** **1** a frame, as of boards or panels, for closing or opening an entrance to a building, room, cupboard, etc. Doors usually swing on hinges or slide in grooves. **2** the room or building into which a door leads [I live two *doors* down the hall.] **3** any opening with a door in it; doorway. —**out of doors,** *same as* **outdoors.** —**show someone the door,** to ask someone to leave.

**door·man** (dôr′man′) ***n.*** a man whose work is opening the door of a building for those who enter or leave, hailing taxicabs, etc. —*pl.* **door′men′**

**door·mat** (dôr′mat) ***n.*** a mat for people to wipe their shoes on before entering a house, room, etc.

**door·step** (dôr′step) ***n.*** the step or steps in front of an outside door.

**door·way** (dôr′wā) ***n.*** **1** an opening in a wall that can be closed by a door. **2** a way of getting in or to [Hard work is the *doorway* to success.]

☆**dope** (dōp) ***n.*** **1** any thick liquid or other material used to lubricate or absorb something. **2** a narcotic drug. **3** a stupid person. **4** any sort of information. *Slang in meanings* 2, 3, 4. ◆***v.*** to give a narcotic drug to. —**doped, dop′ing** —**dop′ey** or **dop′y** ***adj.***

**Dor·ic** (dôr′ik) ***adj.*** describing the oldest and plainest style of Greek architecture. The columns have no fancy carving at the top.

☆**dorm** (dôrm) ***n.*** *a shorter form of* **dormitory**: *used only in everyday talk.*

**dor·mant** (dôr′mənt) ***adj.*** **1** not moving or growing, as if asleep [Many trees are *dormant* in winter.] **2** not active; quiet [a *dormant* volcano].

**dor·mer** (dôr′mər) ***n.*** **1** a part that is built out from a sloping roof, containing an upright window. *See the picture.* **2** such a window: *also* **dormer window.**

**dor·mi·to·ry** (dôr′mə tôr′ē) ***n.*** **1** a large room with beds for a number of people. **2** a building with many rooms for sleeping and living in, as at a college. —*pl.* **dor′mi·to′ries**

**dor·mouse** (dôr′mous) ***n.*** a European animal like a small squirrel. —*pl.* **dor·mice** (dôr′mīs)

The **dormouse** is an animal that hibernates in the winter. Its name comes from an old French word meaning "sleepy." The dormouse at Alice's tea party in Wonderland is always falling asleep.

**dor·sal** (dôr′s′l) ***adj.*** of, on, or near the back [the *dorsal* fin of a sailfish].

**do·ry** (dôr′ē) ***n.*** a small fishing boat with a flat bottom and high sides. —*pl.* **do′ries**

**dos·age** (dōs′ij) ***n.*** **1** the system that is to be followed in taking doses [The recommended *dosage* is 1/2 teaspoon every 4 hours.] **2** a dose of a medicine.

**dose** (dōs) ***n.*** the amount of a medicine to be taken at one time. ◆***v.*** to give a dose of medicine to. —**dosed, dos′ing**

**dot** (dät) ***n.*** **1** a tiny mark or spot, as made by a pencil [Put a *dot* over every "i" and "j."] **2** a small, round spot [a tie with polka *dots*]. **3** a mark like a period that stands for the short click used in forming letters in the Morse code. ◆***v.*** to mark with a dot or cover as with dots [Islands *dotted* the bay.] —**dot′ted, dot′ting** —**on the dot,** at the exact time: *used only in everyday talk.*

**DOT** Department of Transportation.

**dot·age** (dōt′ij) ***n.*** the condition of a very old person who is childish and feeble.

**dot·ard** (dōt′ərd) ***n.*** a very old person who is childish and feeble.

**dote** (dōt) ***v.*** **1** to be childish or weak-minded because of very old age. **2** to be fond or loving in a blind, foolish way [to *dote* on one's children]. —**dot′ed, dot′ing**

**doth** (duth) *the older form of* **does** *used with* thou, *as in the Bible.*

**dou·ble** (dub′′l) ***adj.*** **1** having two parts that are alike [a *double* house; a *double* door; gun with a *double* barrel]. **2** being of two kinds [Sometimes a word is used in a joke because it has a *double* meaning and can be understood in two different ways.] **3** twice as much, as many, as great, as fast, etc. [a *double* portion; *double* time]. **4** made for two [a *double* bed; a *double* garage]. **5** having more than the usual number of petals [a *double* daffodil]. ◆***adv.*** **1** with twice the amount, size, speed, etc.; doubly. **2** two at one time; in a pair [to ride *double* on a bicycle]. ◆***n.*** **1** an amount twice as great. **2** a person or thing that looks very much like another; duplicate [The girl is a *double* of her mother.] ☆**3** a hit in baseball on which the batter gets to second base. **4 doubles,** *pl.* a game of tennis, badminton, etc. with two players on each side. ◆***v.*** **1** to make or become twice as large, as strong, as fast, etc. [*Double* the recipe. The population of the city has *doubled.*] **2** to fold over or up [Make a hem by *doubling* over the edge of the cloth. He *doubled* his fist.] **3** to make a sharp turn and go back [to *double* on one's tracks]. **4** to be used for more than one purpose [The bedroom *doubles* as a study.] ☆**5** to hit a double in baseball. **6** to sail around [The ship *doubled* the Cape.] —**dou′bled, dou′bling** —**double up, 1** to fold or bend over [to *double up* with laughter]. **2** to share a room, etc. with someone else. —**on the double,** quickly: *used only in everyday talk.*

**double bass** (bās) a woodwind musical instrument that looks like a huge violin and has deep, low tones.

☆**double boiler** two pots, one fitting partly into the other. Water is boiled in the bottom pot in order to cook food placed in the top one. *See the picture.*

**dou·ble-breast·ed** (dub′′l bres′tid) ***adj.*** overlapping so that there is a double thickness of material across the breast, as a style of coat.

**dou·ble-cross** (dub′′l krôs′) ***v.*** to trick or betray by doing the opposite of what one has promised: *used only in everyday talk.* —**dou′ble-cross′er** ***n.***

☆**double date** a date in which two couples go out together: *used only in everyday talk.*

☆**dou·ble-date** (dub′′l dāt′) ***v.*** to go out with someone on a double date: *used only in everyday talk.* —**dou′ble-dat′ed, dou′ble-dat′ing**

**dou·ble-deal·ing** (dub′′l dēl′iŋ) ***n.*** a dealing with others in a tricky or dishonest way.

☆**double feature** two movies on the same program.

☆**dou·ble-head·er** (dub′′l hed′ər) ***n.*** two games, especially baseball games, played one right after the other on the same playing field, usually by the same teams.

**dou·ble-joint·ed** (dub′′l joint′tid) ***adj.*** having joints that let the fingers, legs, etc. bend at unusual angles.

**dou·ble-knit** (dub′′l nit′) ***adj.*** knit with a double stitch, so that the fabric is extra thick.

**donkey**

1.2 m (4 ft.) high at shoulder

☆**dou·ble-park** (dub′′l pärk′) ***v.*** to park a motor vehicle right beside another one parked alongside a curb.



☆**double play** in baseball, a single play in which two players are put out.

**dou·ble-quick** (dub′′l kwik′) ***adj.*** very quick. ◆***n.*** a very quick marching pace, almost a run.

**dou·blet** (dub′lit) ***n.*** a short jacket worn by men from the 14th to the 16th centuries. *See the picture.*

☆**double talk** meaningless talk or sounds intended to confuse someone.

**dou·bloon** (du blo͞on′) ***n.*** an old Spanish coin that was made of gold.

**dou·bly** (dub′lē) ***adv.*** twice or twice as much [*doubly* careful].

**doubt** (dout) ***v.*** to think that something may not be true or right; be unsure of; question [I *doubt* that those are the correct facts. Never *doubt* my love.] ◆***n.*** **1** a doubting; being unsure of something [I have no *doubt* that you will win.] **2** a condition of being uncertain or not yet decided [The time of the dance is still in *doubt.*] *See* SYNONYMS *at* **uncertainty.** —**beyond doubt** or **without doubt,** surely. —**no doubt, 1** surely. **2** probably. —**doubt′er** ***n.***

**doubt·ful** (dout′fəl) ***adj.*** feeling or causing doubt; not sure; not decided [I'm *doubtful* about our chances of winning.] —**doubt′ful·ly** ***adv.***

**doubt·less** (dout′lis) ***adv.*** **1** without doubt; certainly. **2** probably.

| | | | |
|---|---|---|---|
| **a** fat | **ir** here | **ou** out | **zh** leisure |
| **ā** ape | **ī** bite, fire | **u** up | **ŋ** ring |
| **ä** car, lot | **ō** go | **ur** fur | a *in* ago |
| **e** ten | **ô** law, horn | **ch** chin | e *in* agent |
| **er** care | **oi** oil | **sh** she | **ə =** i *in* unity |
| **ē** even | **o͝o** look | **th** thin | o *in* collect |
| **i** hit | **o͞o** tool | ***th*** then | u *in* focus |

**dough** (dō) ***n.*** **1** a mixture of flour, liquid, etc. worked into a soft, thick mass for baking into bread, pastry, etc. ☆**2** money: *slang in this meaning.*

**dough·nut** (dō′nut) ***n.*** a small, sweet cake fried in deep fat, usually shaped like a ring.

**dough·ty** (dou′tē) ***adj.*** bold and strong: *no longer much used.* —**dough′ti·er, dough′ti·est**

**dough·y** (dō′ē) ***adj.*** of or like dough; pasty. —**dough′i·er, dough′i·est**

**Doug·lass** (dug′ləs), **Frederick** 1817?–1895; U.S. Negro leader and writer.

**dour** (door *or* door) ***adj.*** unfriendly or gloomy in looks or manner; glum; sullen.

**douse** (dous) ***v.*** **1** to plunge quickly into a liquid [I *doused* the washcloth into the hot water.] **2** to pour liquid over; drench [I *doused* cold water on my face.] **3** to put out a light or a fire: *used only in everyday talk.* —**doused, dous′ing**

**dove**[1] (duv) ***n.*** a pigeon, especially any of the smaller kinds. The dove is often used as a symbol of peace.

**dove**[2] (dōv) *a past tense of* **dive.**

**dove·cote** (duv′kōt) or **dove·cot** (duv′kät) ***n.*** a small box for pigeons to build their nests in. It is usually set on a pole.

**Do·ver** (dō′vər) **1** the capital of Delaware. **2** a strait between England and France. **3** an English seaport on this strait.



**dove·tail** (duv′tāl) ***v.*** **1** to fasten two pieces together by fitting parts cut out in one piece into notches cut out of the other. **2** to fit facts, plans, etc. together in a sensible way. ◆***n.*** a joint made by dovetailing. *See the picture.*

**dow·a·ger** (dou′ə jər) ***n.*** **1** a widow with a title or property received from her dead husband. **2** any elderly woman who is rich and dignified.

**dow·dy** (dou′dē) ***adj.*** not neat or not stylish in looks or dress. —**dow′di·er, dow′di·est**

dragon

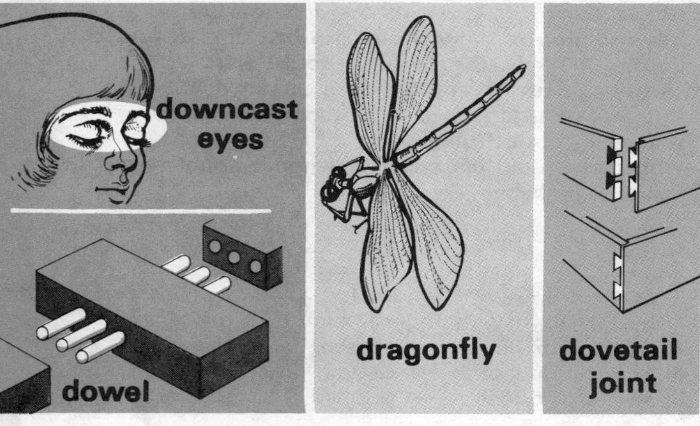

downcast eyes

dowel

dragonfly

dovetail joint

**dow·el** (dou′əl) ***n.*** a peg of wood, metal, etc. that fits into opposite holes in two pieces to join them together. *See the picture.*

**dow·er** (dou′ər) ***n.*** **1** that part of a man's property which his widow inherits for life. **2** *another word for* **dowry. 3** a natural skill, gift, or talent. ◆***v.*** to give a dower to.

**down**[1] (doun) ***adv.*** **1** to, in, or on a lower place [to tumble *down;* to lie *down*]. **2** in or to a place thought of as lower [The sun goes *down* in the evening. That song has gone *down* in popularity.] **3** from an earlier to a later time [*down* through the years; passed *down* from mother to daughter]. **4** in or to a worse condition [to break *down* in body or mind]. **5** to a smaller amount, size, etc. [to come *down* in price; to boil *down* maple syrup]. **6** to a more quiet or serious condition [to settle *down* to work]. **7** to the greatest amount; completely [loaded *down*]. **8** in cash [Pay $5 *down* and $5 a week.] **9** in writing [Take *down* her name.] ◆***adj.*** **1** put, brought, going, or gone down [There is no *down* payment. The boxer is *down.* The sun is *down.* The piston rattles on the *down* stroke.] **2** ill [He is *down* with the flu.] **3** sad or discouraged. ◆***prep.*** down to, toward, along, through, into, among, or upon [The bus rolled *down* the hill. I live *down* this street.] ◆***v.*** to put, throw, or swallow down [The fighter *downed* his opponent. She *downed* a glass of milk.] ◆***n.*** **1** a piece of bad luck [to have one's ups and *downs*]. ☆**2** in football, one of four plays in a row during which time a team must either score or gain ten yards, or give up the ball to the other team. —☆**down and out,** without money, friends, health, etc. —**down on,** angry with: *used only in everyday talk.* —**down with!** away with! get rid of!

**Down** comes from an Old English word meaning "from the hill." When one comes from a hill, one goes to a lower place.

**down**[2] (doun) ***n.*** **1** soft, fluffy feathers, as on a young bird. **2** soft, fuzzy hair.

**down·cast** (doun′kast) ***adj.*** **1** looking downward [*downcast* eyes]. *See the picture.* **2** very unhappy; sad [We were *downcast* at losing the game.]

**down·fall** (doun′fôl) ***n.*** **1** a sudden loss of wealth or power; ruin [the *downfall* of a tyrant]. **2** a heavy fall of rain or snow.

☆**down·grade** (doun′grād) ***n.*** a downward slope, as of a road. ◆***v.*** **1** to put in a less important job. **2** to speak of slightingly. —**down′grad·ed, down′grad·ing** —**on the downgrade,** becoming lower, weaker, or less important.

**down·heart·ed** (doun′här′tid) ***adj.*** sad or discouraged.

**down·hill** (doun′hil′) ***adv.*** **1** toward the bottom of a hill. **2** to a lower, weaker, or less important condition. ◆***adj.*** **1** going downward. **2** having to do with skiing downhill.

**down·pour** (doun′pôr) ***n.*** a heavy rain.

**down·right** (doun′rīt) ***adv.*** very; really; extremely [a *downright* good book]. ◆***adj.*** absolute; complete [That speeder is a *downright* fool.]

**down·stairs** (doun′sterz′) ***adv., adj.*** to or on a lower floor [to go *downstairs;* a *downstairs* room]. ◆***n.*** a lower floor or floors.

**down·stream** (doun′strēm′) ***adv., adj.*** in the direction in which a stream is flowing.

☆**down·town** (doun′toun′) ***adj., adv.*** in or toward the lower part or the main business section of a city or town. ◆***n.*** this section of a city or town.

**down·trod·den** (doun′träd′′n) ***adj.*** forced by those in power to live in poverty, slavery, etc.; oppressed.

**down·ward** (doun′wərd) ***adv., adj.*** **1** toward a lower place or position. **2** from an earlier to a later time.

**down·wards** (doun′wərdz) ***adv.*** *same as* **downward.**

**down·y** (doun′ē) ***adj.*** of or like down, or covered with down; soft and fuzzy. —**down′i·er, down′i·est**

**dow·ry** (dou′rē) ***n.*** the property that a bride brings to her husband when she is married. —*pl.* **dow′ries**

**dox·ol·o·gy** (däk säl′ə jē) ***n.*** a hymn of praise to God. —*pl.* **dox·ol′o·gies**

**Doyle** (doil), Sir **Arthur Co·nan** (kō′nən) 1859–1930; English novelist. He wrote the *Sherlock Holmes* stories.

**doz.** *abbreviation for* **dozen** *or* **dozens.**

**doze** (dōz) ***v.*** to sleep lightly; nap. —**dozed, doz′ing** ◆***n.*** a nap. —**doze off,** to fall into a light sleep.

**doz·en** (duz′′n) ***n.*** a group of twelve. —*pl.* **doz′ens** or, *especially after a number,* **doz′en.**

**DP** *abbreviation for* **displaced person.**

**Dr.** *abbreviation for* **Doctor, Drive.**

**dr.** *abbreviation for* **debtor, dram** *or* **drams.**

**drab** (drab) ***n.*** a dull, yellowish-brown color. ◆***adj.*** **1** dull yellowish-brown. **2** dull; not bright or attractive. —**drab′ber, drab′best** —**drab′ly *adv.*** —**drab′ness *n.***

**draft** (draft) ***n.*** **1** a movement of air, as in a room or chimney. **2** a part for controlling the movement of air, as in a furnace. **3** a drink. **4** a choosing or taking of a person or persons for some special purpose, especially for service in the armed forces. ☆**5** persons chosen for military service. **6** a plan or drawing of a work to be done. **7** an outline or trial copy of a piece of writing [the first *draft* of a speech]. **8** a written order for the payment of money by a bank; check [a *draft* for $50]. **9** a drawing or hauling, as of a load. **10** the depth to which a ship sinks when it is loaded. ◆***v.*** **1** to choose or take for some special work or position, especially military service, by drawing from a group. **2** to make a plan, outline, etc. ◆***adj.*** **1** used for pulling loads [a *draft* animal]. **2** drawn from a cask on order [*draft* beer].

☆**draft·ee** (draf tē′) ***n.*** a person drafted to serve in the armed forces.

**drafts·man** (drafts′mən) ***n.*** a person who prepares drawings or sketches for buildings, machinery, etc. —*pl.* **drafts′men**

**draft·y** (draf′tē) ***adj.*** letting in or having a draft of air [a *drafty* room]. —**draft′i·er, draft′i·est**

**drag** (drag) ***v.*** **1** to pull in a slow, hard way, especially along the ground; haul [He *dragged* the sled up the hill.] **2** to be pulled along the ground, floor, etc. [Her skirt *dragged* in the mud.] **3** to move or pass too slowly [Time *dragged* as we waited for recess.] **4** to search for something in a river, lake, etc. by dragging a net or hooks along the bottom. —**dragged, drag′ging** ◆***n.*** **1** something that works by being dragged along, as a harrow, grapnel, or dragnet. **2** anything that holds back or slows down [Poor training is a *drag* on any career.] ☆**3** influence that gains special favors. ☆**4** a puff on a cigarette. ☆**5** a dull or boring person or situation. *Meanings* 3, 4, 5 *of the noun are slang.*

SYNONYMS: **Drag** means to pull slowly something heavy [to *drag* a desk across the room]. To **haul** is to transport something heavy [A truck *hauled* the new gym bleachers to the school.] To **tow** is to pull by means of a rope or cable [to *tow* a stalled car].

**drag·net** (drag′net) ***n.*** **1** a net dragged along the bottom of a river, lake, etc. for catching fish. ☆**2** any system set up for catching criminals or other wanted people.

**drag·on** (drag′ən) ***n.*** a make-believe monster in stories, that looks like a giant lizard, usually with wings and claws, breathing out fire and smoke. *See the picture.*

**drag·on·fly** (drag′ən flī) ***n.*** an insect with a long, slender body and four delicate wings. It does not sting and feeds mostly on flies and mosquitoes while in flight. *See the picture.* —*pl.* **drag′on·flies**

**dra·goon** (drə gōōn′) ***n.*** in earlier times, a soldier who fought on horseback. ◆***v.*** to force to do something [Peasants were *dragooned* into building a fort.]

The French soldier of days gone by who was called a **dragoon** carried a short musket called a *dragoon* (or *dragon*) because it "breathed fire," as did the dragons in stories.

☆**drag race** a race between hot-rod cars to test how fast they can gain speed from a complete stop.



**drain** (drān) ***v.*** **1** to make flow away [*Drain* the water from the potatoes.] **2** to draw off water or other liquid from; make empty [to *drain* a swamp; to *drain* one's glass]. **3** to flow off [Water won't *drain* from a flat roof.] **4** to become empty or dry [Our bathtub *drains* slowly.] **5** to flow into [The Ohio River *drains* into the Mississippi.] **6** to use up slowly; exhaust [Hard work *drains* her energy.] ◆***n.*** **1** a pipe or channel for carrying off water, sewage, etc. [a bathtub *drain*]. **2** something that drains or uses up slowly [War is a *drain* on a nation's youth.]

**drain·age** (drān′ij) ***n.*** **1** a draining, or the way in which something is drained off. **2** a liquid that is drained off.

**drake** (drāk) ***n.*** a male duck.

**dram** (dram) ***n.*** **1** a small weight, equal to 1/8 ounce in apothecaries' weight or 1/16 ounce in avoirdupois weight. **2** a small drink.

**dra·ma** (drä′mə *or* dram′ə) ***n.*** **1** a story that is written to be acted out, as on a stage; play. **2** the art of writing or performing plays. **3** a series of interesting or exciting events [the *drama* of the American Revolution].

☆**Dram·a·mine** (dram′ə mēn) *a trademark for* a white powder taken to keep one from feeling sick at the stomach or vomiting, as during an airplane flight.

| | | | | | | | |
|---|---|---|---|---|---|---|---|
| **a** | fat | **ir** | here | **ou** | out | **zh** | leisure |
| **ā** | ape | **ī** | bite, fire | **u** | up | **ng** | ring |
| **ä** | car, lot | **ō** | go | **ur** | fur | | a *in* ago |
| **e** | ten | **ô** | law, horn | **ch** | chin | | e *in* agent |
| **er** | care | **oi** | oil | **sh** | she | **ə** = | i *in* unity |
| **ē** | even | **oo** | look | **th** | thin | | o *in* collect |
| **i** | hit | **ōō** | tool | ***th*** | then | | u *in* focus |

**dra·mat·ic** (drə mat′ik) ***adj.*** **1** of or having to do with drama or the theater. **2** like a drama or play; interesting and exciting [a *dramatic* baseball game]. —**dra·mat′i·cal·ly *adv.***

**dra·mat·ics** (drə mat′iks) ***n.pl.*** the art of acting in or producing plays: *used with a singular verb.*

**dram·a·tist** (dram′ə tist) ***n.*** a person who writes plays; playwright.

**dram·a·tize** (dram′ə tīz) ***v.*** **1** to make into a drama, or play [The life of Cleopatra was *dramatized* in a movie.] **2** to be very dramatic about; make seem very exciting or tense [He *dramatizes* his troubles.] —**dram′a·tized, dram′a·tiz·ing** —**dram′a·ti·za′tion *n.***

**drank** (draŋk) *past tense of* **drink.**

**drape** (drāp) ***v.*** **1** to cover or decorate with cloth hanging in loose folds [The windows were *draped* with red velvet.] **2** to arrange or hang in graceful folds [She *draped* the shawl about her shoulders.] *See the picture.* —**draped, drap′ing** ◆***n.*** cloth hanging in loose folds; especially, a curtain; drapery: *usually used in the plural.*

**drap·er·y** (drā′pər ē) ***n.*** a curtain or other cloth hanging in loose folds. —*pl.* **drap′er·ies**

**dras·tic** (dras′tik) ***adj.*** acting with force; having a strong effect; harsh [*drastic* punishment]. —**dras′ti·cal·ly *adv.***

**draught** (draft) ***n., v., adj.*** *British spelling of* **draft.**

224 **draughts** (drafts) ***n.pl.*** the game of checkers: *the British name.*

**draw** (drô) ***v.*** **1** to make move toward one or along with one; pull; haul [The mules *drew* the wagon.] **2** to pull up, down, back, across, in, or out [to *draw* the drapes; to *draw* a cork from a bottle]. **3** to take out; get [to *draw* money from a bank; to *draw* a conclusion]. **4** to come as a regular addition [bank savings *draw* interest]. **5** to get the attention of; attract [to *draw* a large audience]. **6** to come or move [We *drew* near the town. The train *drew* away from the station.] **7** to bring about; result in [Her question *drew* no reply.] **8** to make a picture, design, etc., as with a pencil or pen. **9** to describe [He *drew* a glowing picture of the future.] **10** to write a check or bank draft. **11** to stretch [to *draw* a rope tight]. **12** to distort [a face *drawn* with fear]. **13** to inhale [*Draw* a deep breath.] **14** to allow air or smoke to move through [This chimney *draws* well.] **15** to sink to a certain depth in water [This ship *draws* 30 feet.] —**drew, drawn, draw′ing** ◆***n.*** **1** a drawing or being drawn. **2** something drawn. **3** a contest in which the final scores are the same; tie. **4** a thing or event that attracts interest, audiences, etc. **5** a gully or ravine. —**draw away,** to move away or ahead. —**draw out, 1** to lengthen [Grandpa *draws out* his stories.] **2** to get a person to talk. —**draw up, 1** to put in the proper written form [to *draw up* a contract]. **2** to stop [The car *drew up* next to ours.]

**draw·back** (drô′bak) ***n.*** a condition that acts against one; hindrance; disadvantage.

**draw·bridge** (drô′brij) ***n.*** a bridge that can be raised, lowered, or drawn aside, as to allow ships to pass or to keep someone from crossing. *See the picture.*

**draw·er** (drô′ər) ***n.*** **1** a person or thing that draws. **2** (drôr) a box that slides in and out of a table, chest, desk, etc.

**drawers** (drôrz) ***n.pl.*** a piece of underwear with legs, for the lower part of the body. Drawers can be short or long.

**draw·ing** (drô′iŋ) ***n.*** **1** the making of pictures, designs, etc., as with a pencil or pen. **2** such a picture, design, etc. **3** a lottery.

**drawing room** a room where guests are received and entertained; parlor. *This term is no longer much used.*

**drawl** (drôl) ***v.*** to speak in a slow way, drawing out the syllables. ◆***n.*** speech that is drawled.

**drawn** *past participle of* **draw.** ◆***adj.*** having a worn-out look, as from pain.

**dray** (drā) ***n.*** a wagon for heavy loads, having sides that can be taken off.

**dread** (dred) ***v.*** to look forward to with great fear or worry [I *dread* giving a speech.] ◆***n.*** great fear, especially of something about to happen [to live in *dread* of the future]. ◆***adj.*** causing great fear [Cancer can be a *dread* disease.]

**dread·ful** (dred′fəl) ***adj.*** **1** causing dread; fearful [the *dreadful* threat of war]. **2** very bad, unpleasant, unhappy, etc.: *used only in everyday talk.* —**dread′ful·ly *adv.***

**dread·nought** or **dread·naught** (dred′nôt) ***n.*** a large battleship with many big guns.

> **Dreadnought** was first used of a heavy cloth for coats. If one were warmly clothed, one would dread "nought" (nothing). The cloth was used as lining for rooms where gunpowder was stored aboard battleships. In 1906, a very large and heavy British battleship was named "Dreadnought."

**dream** (drēm) ***n.*** **1** a series of thoughts, pictures, or feelings that passes through the mind of a sleeping person. **2** a pleasant idea that one imagines or hopes for; daydream [to have *dreams* of glory]. ◆***v.*** **1** to have a dream or dreams. **2** to have daydreams. **3** to imagine as possible; have any idea of [I wouldn't *dream* of going without you.] —**dreamed** or **dreamt** (dremt), **dream′ing** —**dream′er *n.***

**dream·y** (drē′mē) ***adj.*** **1** fond of daydreaming or of imagining things; not practical. **2** like something in a dream; not clear; misty, soft, etc. [*dreamy* music]. —**dream′i·er, dream′i·est** —**dream′i·ly *adv.***

**drear·y** (drir′ē) ***adj.*** without happiness or cheer; gloomy, sad, or dull [a long, *dreary* tale]. —**drear′i·er, drear′i·est** —**drear′i·ly *adv.*** —**drear′i·ness *n.***

> **Dreary** is a much milder word than it used to be. In olden days it meant "sad," but before that it meant "bloody or gory," from the Old English word for "blood."

**dredge**[1] (drej) ***n.*** **1** a machine for scooping or sucking up mud, sand, etc. as from a harbor or river bed. *See the picture.* **2** a kind of net dragged along the bottom of a river, bay, etc. to gather shellfish. ◆***v.*** to clear, gather, etc. with a dredge. —**dredged, dredg′ing**

**dredge**[2] (drej) ***v.*** to coat or sprinkle with [*Dredge* the chicken with flour before frying.] —**dredged, dredg′ing**

**dregs** (dregz) ***n.pl.*** **1** solid bits that settle to the bottom in a liquid; sediment. **2** the most worthless part [the *dregs* of society].

**Drei·ser** (drī′sər *or* drī′zər), **Theodore** 1871–1945; U.S. novelist.

**drench** (drench) ***v.*** to make wet all over; soak [The garden was *drenched* by the rain.] *See* SYNONYMS *at* **soak.**

**Dres·den** (drez′dən) a city in central East Germany, noted for its fine chinaware.

**dress** (dres) ***n.*** **1** the common outer garment worn by girls and women. It is usually of one piece with a skirt. **2** clothes in general [native *dress;* formal *dress*]. ***•v.*** **1** to put clothes on; clothe. **2** to arrange the hair in a certain way. **3** to put medicine and bandages on a wound or sore. **4** to make ready for use; prepare [to *dress* a chicken; to *dress* leather]. **5** to arrange in an attractive way [to *dress* a store window]. **6** to get or put in a straight line, as soldiers. ***•adj.*** **1** of or for dresses [*dress* material]. **2** worn on formal occasions [a *dress* suit]. **3** requiring formal clothes [The dinner is a *dress* affair.]

**dress·er** (dres′ər) ***n.*** ☆**1** a chest of drawers for a bedroom, often with a mirror. **2** a person or thing that dresses.

**dress·ing** (dres′iŋ) ***n.*** **1** a bandage or medicine for a wound or sore. **2** a sauce, as of oil, vinegar, and seasoning, added to salads and other dishes. **3** a stuffing, as of bread and seasoning, for roast chicken, turkey, etc.

**dressing gown** a loose robe worn by a person who is not fully dressed.

**dress·mak·er** (dres′māk′ər) ***n.*** a person whose work is making dresses and other clothes for girls and women. **—dress′mak′ing *n.***

**dress·y** (dres′ē) ***adj.*** **1** fancy or showy in dress or looks [Those shoes are too *dressy* for school.] **2** in the latest fashion; stylish; smart. **—dress′i·er, dress′i·est —dress′i·ness *n.***

**drew** (dro͞o) *past tense of* **draw.**

**drib·ble** (drib′'l) ***v.*** **1** to flow or let flow in drops or in a trickle [Water *dribbled* from the pipe. Contributions *dribbled* in.] **2** to let saliva drip from the mouth; drool. **3** in basketball or soccer, to control the ball while moving, by using short bounces or short, light kicks. *See the picture.* **—drib′bled, drib′bling *•n.*** **1** a small drop or a flowing in small drops. **2** a very small amount. **3** the act of dribbling a ball.

**drib·let** (drib′lit) ***n.*** a small amount; bit.

**dried** (drīd) *past tense and past participle of* **dry.**

**dri·er** (drī′ər) ***adj.*** more dry. *This word is the comparative of* **dry. *•n.*** **1** a liquid put in paint or varnish to make it dry fast. **2** *another spelling of* **dryer.**

**dries** (drīz) *the form of* **dry** *showing the present time with singular nouns and* he, she, *or* it.

**dri·est** (drī′ist) ***adj.*** most dry. *This word is the superlative of* **dry.**

**drift** (drift) ***v.*** **1** to be carried along by a current of water or air [The raft *drifted* downstream. The leaves *drifted* to the ground.] **2** to go along in an aimless way [The guitarist *drifted* from job to job.] **3** to pile up in heaps by the force of wind [The snow *drifted* against the door.] ***•n.*** **1** the act of being driven or carried along. **2** the amount or direction of drifting. **3** a pile formed by the force of wind or water [a *drift* of sand along the shore]. **4** a trend or tendency [the nation's *drift* toward war]. **5** general meaning [I got the *drift* of her speech.]

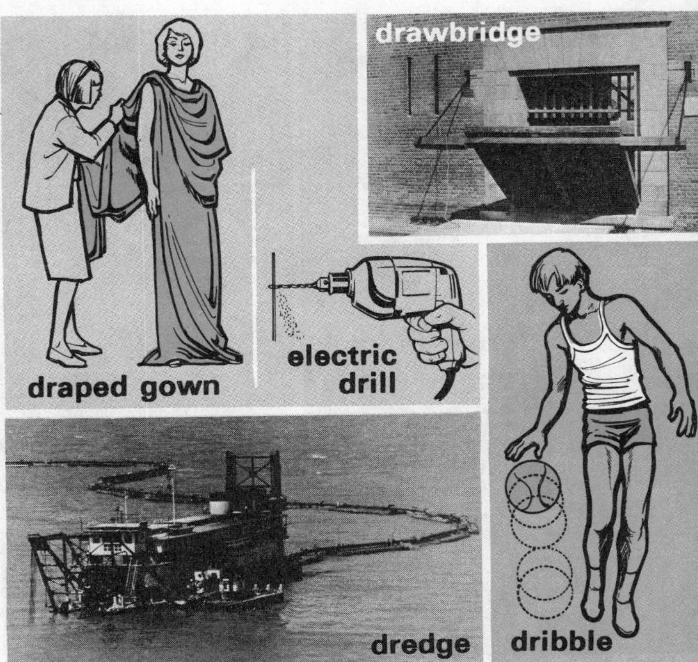


**drift·wood** (drift′wood) ***n.*** wood drifting in the water or washed ashore.

**drill¹** (dril) ***n.*** **1** a tool with a sharp point that is turned in wood, metal, etc. to make holes. *See the picture.* **2** the training of soldiers in marching, handling guns, etc. **3** a practicing of something over and over in order to learn it. ***•v.*** **1** to make a hole with a drill. **2** to teach or train by having someone practice the same thing over and over [Will you help *drill* the class in spelling?] **3** to train soldiers in marching and other exercises.



**drill²** (dril) ***n.*** a machine for making holes or furrows and planting seeds in them.

**dri·ly** (drī′lē) ***adv.*** *another spelling of* **dryly.**

**drink** (driŋk) ***v.*** **1** to swallow a liquid [to *drink* water]. **2** to soak up or draw in [The dry soil quickly *drank* up the rain.] **3** to take in eagerly with the mind or senses [to *drink* in knowledge]. **4** to drink alcoholic liquor. **—drank, drunk, drink′ing *•n.*** **1** any liquid that one drinks. **2** alcoholic liquor. **—drink to,** to drink a toast to.

**drink·a·ble** (driŋk′ə b'l) ***adj.*** fit for drinking.

**drip** (drip) ***v.*** **1** to fall in drops [Sweat *dripped* from his brow.] **2** to let drops of liquid fall [That faucet *drips.*] **—dripped, drip′ping *•n.*** **1** a falling in drops. **2** liquid falling in drops.

**drip-dry** (drip′drī′) ***adj.*** describing fabrics or garments that dry quickly when hung soaking wet and that need little or no ironing.

| | | | | | | | |
|---|---|---|---|---|---|---|---|
| **a** | fat | **ir** | here | **ou** | out | **zh** | leisure |
| **ā** | ape | **ī** | bite, fire | **u** | up | **ŋ** | ring |
| **ä** | car, lot | **ō** | go | **ur** | fur | | a *in* ago |
| **e** | ten | **ô** | law, horn | **ch** | chin | | e *in* agent |
| **er** | care | **oi** | oil | **sh** | she | **ə =** | i *in* unity |
| **ē** | even | **oo** | look | **th** | thin | | o *in* collect |
| **i** | hit | **o͞o** | tool | ***th*** | then | | u *in* focus |

dry dock

drive–in bank

drumsticks

dropper

hair dryer

**drip·pings** (drip′iŋz) ***n.pl.*** the fat and juices that drip from roasting meat.



**drive** (drīv) ***v.*** **1** to control the movement of an automobile, horse and wagon, bus, etc. **2** to move or go [The truck *drove* slowly up the hill.] **3** to go or take in an automobile, etc. [Shall we *drive* to Akron? Our neighbor *drives* us to school.] **4** to make move or go [They *drove* the cattle along the trail. This engine is *driven* by steam.] **5** to move by hitting [to *drive* a nail; to *drive* a golf ball]. **6** to force into a certain condition or act [They're *driving* me mad.] **7** to force to work hard. **8** to use effort in bringing about [to *drive* a bargain]. —**drove, driv′en, driv′ing** ◆***n.*** **1** a trip in an automobile, etc. **2** a street, road, or driveway. ☆**3** a rounding up of animals, as for branding. **4** a hard, swift blow, hit, thrust, etc. [The golfer hit a 200-yard *drive.*] **5** an arrangement of gears that lets a car move forward [I put the car into *drive.*] ☆**6** a group effort to get something done; campaign [a *drive* to collect money for charity]. ☆**7** the power or energy to get things done [Her *drive* made her a success.] —**drive at,** to have in mind; mean. —**drive in,** ☆in baseball, to cause a runner to score or a run to be scored, as by getting a hit.

☆**drive-in** (drīv′in′) ***adj.*** of or having to do with a restaurant, bank, movie theater, etc. designed to serve people who drive up and remain seated in their cars. ◆***n.*** such a restaurant, theater, bank, etc. *See the picture.*

**driv·el** (driv′'l) ***v.*** **1** to talk in a foolish, childish way. **2** to let saliva drip from the mouth. —**driv′eled** or **driv′elled, driv′el·ing** or **driv′el·ling** ◆***n.*** foolish talk; nonsense. —**driv′el·er** or **driv′el·ler *n.***

**driv·en** (driv′'n) *past participle of* **drive.**

**driv·er** (drī′vər) ***n.*** **1** a person or thing that drives. **2** a golf club with a wooden head, used in hitting the ball from the tee: *also called* **number one wood.**

☆**drive·way** (drīv′wā′) ***n.*** a path for cars, leading from a street or road to a garage, house, etc.

**driz·zle** (driz′'l) ***v.*** to rain lightly in fine drops. —**driz′zled, driz′zling** —**driz′zly *adj.***

**droll** (drōl) ***adj.*** comical in a strange or odd way [a *droll* clown]. —**droll′ness *n.*** —**drol′ly *adv.***

**Droll** comes from the French word *drôle,* which means "clown" or "jester." The French got their word from an old Dutch word that meant either "a short, stout fellow" or "a bowling pin."

**drom·e·dar·y** (dräm′ə der′ē) ***n.*** the one-humped, or Arabian, camel. It is trained for fast riding. —*pl.* **drom′e·dar′ies**

**drone** (drōn) ***n.*** **1** a male honeybee. It has no sting and does no work. **2** an idle person who lives by the work of others. **3** a humming or buzzing. ◆***v.*** **1** to make a humming or buzzing sound [The planes *droned* overhead.] **2** to talk on and on in a dull way. —**droned, dron′ing**

**drool** (dro͞ol) ***v.*** to drip saliva, etc. from the mouth; drivel.

**droop** (dro͞op) ***v.*** **1** to sink, hang, or bend down [The heavy snow made the branches *droop.*] **2** to become weak, sad, tired, etc. [The team's spirit *drooped* after the defeat.] ◆***n.*** a drooping or hanging down [the *droop* of his shoulders]. —**droop′y *adj.***

**drop** (dräp) ***n.*** **1** a bit of liquid that is rounded in shape, as when falling [*drops* of rain]. **2** anything like this in shape [a chocolate *drop*]. **3** a very small amount [He hasn't a *drop* of courage.] **4** a sudden fall or decrease [a *drop* in attendance]. **5** the distance down [a *drop* of five feet]. ◆***v.*** **1** to fall or let fall in drops [Tears *dropped* from the actor's eyes.] **2** to fall or let fall [Ripe fruit *dropped* from the trees. He *dropped* his lunch in the mud.] **3** to fall dead or wounded; also, to kill or wound. **4** to pass into a certain condition [to *drop* off to sleep]. **5** to stop, end, or let go [Let's *drop* this argument. He was *dropped* from his job.] **6** to make or become lower or less, as temperature or price. **7** to make less loud [They *dropped* their voices as they went into the library.] **8** to send or say in an offhand way [to *drop* someone a note; to *drop* a hint]. **9** to leave out [She *dropped* a chapter when she rewrote the book.] **10** to leave at a certain place: *used only in everyday talk* [The taxi *dropped* us at our hotel.] —**dropped** or *sometimes* **dropt, drop′ping** —**drop back** or **drop behind,** to fall behind; lag. —**drop in** or **drop by,** to make an unexpected or informal visit. —**drop off,** to become fewer or less; decrease; decline. —**drop out,** to stop taking part; stop being a member.

☆**drop·cloth** (dräp′klôth) ***n.*** a large piece of cloth, plastic, etc. used to cover something and protect it from dripping paint.

**drop·let** (dräp′lit) ***n.*** a very small drop.

☆**drop·out** (dräp′out) ***n.*** a student who leaves school before graduating.

**drop·per** (dräp′ər) ***n.*** ☆a small glass tube with a hollow rubber bulb on one end, used to measure out a liquid in drops. *See the picture.*

**drop·sy** (dräp′sē) ***n.*** *an earlier name for* **edema.**

**dross** (drôs) ***n.*** **1** a scum on top of molten metal. **2** worthless stuff.

**drought** (drout) or **drouth** (drouth) ***n.*** a long period of dry weather, with little or no rain.

**drove**[1] (drōv) ***n.*** **1** a group of cattle, sheep, etc. driven along together; herd; flock. **2** a moving crowd of people.
**drove**[2] (drōv) *past tense of* **drive.**
**dro·ver** (drō′vər) ***n.*** a person who herds droves of animals, especially to market.
**drown** (droun) ***v.*** **1** to die or kill by keeping under water, where the lungs can get no air to breathe. **2** to be so loud as to overcome some other sound [Cheers *drowned* out the speaker.]
**drowse** (drouz) ***v.*** to be half asleep; doze. —**drowsed, drows′ing**
**drow·sy** (drou′zē) ***adj.*** **1** sleepy or half asleep. **2** making one feel sleepy [*drowsy* music]. —**drow′si·er, drow′si·est** —**drow′si·ly *adv.*** —**drow′si·ness *n.***
**drub** (drub) ***v.*** to beat as with a stick or club. —**drubbed, drub′bing**
**drudge** (druj) ***n.*** a person who does hard and tiresome work. ◆***v.*** to work as a drudge does. —**drudged, drudg′ing**
**drudg·er·y** (druj′ər ē) ***n.*** hard and tiresome work. —*pl.* **drudg′er·ies**
**drug** (drug) ***n.*** **1** any substance used as or in a medicine. **2** a substance used to make one sleep or to lessen pain; a narcotic, especially one that is habit-forming and is taken to give one visions, hallucinations, etc. ◆***v.*** **1** to give drugs to, especially so as to put to sleep or make unconscious. **2** to put a harmful drug into food, a drink, etc. **3** to make feel dull or dazed. —**drugged, drug′ging** —**drug on the market,** a product which few or none want to buy.
**drug·gist** (drug′ist) ***n.*** a person who sells drugs, medical supplies, etc., especially one who has a license to fill doctors' prescriptions; pharmacist.
☆**drug·store** (drug′stôr) ***n.*** a store where medicines are sold and often prepared. Most drugstores today also sell a variety of other things.
**dru·id** or **Dru·id** (dro͞o′id) ***n.*** one of the priests of the Celtic religion in ancient Britain, Ireland, and France.
**drum** (drum) ***n.*** **1** a rhythm instrument that is usually a hollow cylinder with skin stretched tightly over one or both ends. It is played by beating. **2** a sound like that made by beating a drum. **3** a container or other object shaped like a drum [an oil *drum*]. ◆***v.*** **1** to beat or play on a drum. **2** to keep on beating or tapping, as with the fingers. **3** to make remember by repeating again and again [The teacher *drummed* the multiplication table into us.] —**drummed, drum′ming** —**drum up** to get by trying [to *drum up* new business].
**drum major** a person who twirls a baton at the head of a marching band.
☆**drum ma·jor·ette** (mā jə ret′) a girl who twirls a baton at the head of a marching band.
**drum·mer** (drum′ər) ***n.*** a person who plays a drum.
**drum·stick** (drum′stik) ***n.*** **1** a stick used in playing a drum. **2** the lower half of the leg of a cooked fowl. *See the picture.*
**drunk** (drungk) *past participle of* **drink.** ◆***adj.*** having lost control of oneself from drinking alcoholic liquor; intoxicated. ◆***n.*** a drunkard: *slang in this meaning.*
**drunk·ard** (drung′kərd) ***n.*** a person who is often drunk.
**drunk·en** (drung′kən) *an old past participle of* **drink.** ◆***adj.*** **1** drunk; intoxicated [a *drunken* person]. **2** brought on by being drunk [a *drunken* sleep]. —**drunk′en·ly *adv.*** —**drunk′en·ness *n.***
**dry** (drī) ***adj.*** **1** not under water [*dry* land]. **2** not wet or damp; without moisture. **3** having little or no rain or water [a *dry* summer]. **4** with all its water or other liquid gone [a *dry* fountain pen; *dry* bread; a *dry* well]. **5** not shedding tears [*dry* eyes]. **6** thirsty. **7** not giving milk [a *dry* cow]. **8** not having butter, jam, etc. spread on it [*dry* toast]. **9** not bringing up mucus [a *dry* cough]. **10** funny in a quiet but sharp way [*dry* humor]. **11** dull; boring [a *dry* lecture]. **12** plain or bare [*dry* facts]. **13** not sweet [a *dry* wine]. ☆**14** not allowing alcoholic liquor to be sold [a *dry* county]. —**dri′er, dri′est** ◆***v.*** to make or become dry. —**dried, dry′ing** —**dry up, 1** to make or become thoroughly dry. ☆**2** to stop talking: *slang in this meaning.* —**dry′ly *adv.*** —**dry′ness *n.***

SYNONYMS: Something is **dry** if it has little or no water or moisture [The climate is *dry* where there is little rainfall. During the drought, the river bed was *dry*.] Something is **arid** if there is almost no water in the air or soil [an *arid* wasteland where no plants grow].

**dry·ad** or **Dry·ad** (drī′əd) ***n.*** a nymph of the woods in Greek myths.
**dry cell** an electric battery cell with its chemicals in paste form or with a material to soak up the liquid chemicals so they cannot spill.
**dry-clean** (drī′klēn′) ***v.*** to clean clothing or fabrics with some liquid other than water, as naphtha. —**dry cleaner** —**dry cleaning**
**dry dock** a dock from which the water can be emptied, used in building or repairing ships. *See the picture.*
**dry·er** (drī′ər) ***n.*** **1** a machine for drying things by heating or blowing air [clothes *dryer;* hair *dryer*]. *See the picture.* **2** *another spelling of* **drier.**
**dry goods** cloth, clothing, thread, etc.
☆**dry ice** carbon dioxide in a solid form, used for cooling things or keeping them cold. It evaporates instead of melting.
**dry measure** a system of measuring the volume of dry things, as grain, vegetables, etc., especially the system in which 2 pints = 1 quart, 8 quarts = 1 peck, and 4 pecks = 1 bushel. In the metric system, one quart equals 1.1 liters.
**dry wall** ☆a wall made of wallboard, plasterboard, etc. without using wet plaster.
**D.S.** or **D.Sc.** Doctor of Science.
**DST, D.S.T.** *abbreviation for* **daylight-saving time.**
**Du.** *abbreviation for* **Dutch.**
**du·al** (do͞o′əl) ***adj.*** of, having, or being two; double [The actor played a *dual* role.]
**du·al·ism** (do͞o′əl iz′m) ***n.*** **1** the state of being dual. **2** the belief that the world is made up of just two



| | | | | | | | |
|---|---|---|---|---|---|---|---|
| **a** | fat | **ir** | here | **ou** | out | **zh** | leisure |
| **ā** | ape | **ī** | bite, fire | **u** | up | **ng** | ring |
| **ä** | car, lot | **ō** | go | **ur** | fur | | a *in* ago |
| **e** | ten | **ô** | law, horn | **ch** | chin | | e *in* agent |
| **er** | care | **oi** | oil | **sh** | she | **ə** = | i *in* unity |
| **ē** | even | **oo** | look | **th** | thin | | o *in* collect |
| **i** | hit | **o͞o** | tool | ***th*** | then | | u *in* focus |

d

things, as mind and matter. **3** the religious belief that good and evil are always at war in the universe.

**dub**[1] (dub) ***v.*** **1** to give a man the rank of knight by tapping him on the shoulder with a sword. **2** to give a name, nickname, or title to [Tom's friends *dubbed* him "Slim."] **3** to make smooth by hammering, scraping, or rubbing. —**dubbed, dub′bing**

☆**dub**[2] (dub) ***v.*** to put music or speech on the sound track of a film, TV program, etc. [The Italian film was *dubbed* in English.] —**dubbed, dub′bing**

**du·bi·ous** (do͞o′bē əs *or* dyo͞o′bē əs) ***adj.*** **1** full of doubt; not sure [I feel *dubious* about trusting Lou.] **2** causing doubt; not clear in meaning [a *dubious* answer]. **3** probably not good, right, moral, etc.; questionable [a person of *dubious* character]. —**du′bi·ous·ly *adv.***

**Dub·lin** (dub′lən) the capital of Ireland.

**Du Bois** (do͞o bois′), **W(illiam) E(dward) B(urghardt)** 1868–1963; U.S. historian and Negro leader.

**du·cal** (do͞o′k'l *or* dyo͞o′k'l) ***adj.*** of a duke or dukedom.

**duc·at** (duk′ət) ***n.*** any of several gold or silver coins once used in countries of Europe.

**Du·champ** (do͞o shän′), **Mar·cel** (mär sel′) 1887–1968; U.S. painter, born in France.

**duch·ess** (duch′is) ***n.*** **1** the wife or widow of a duke. **2** a woman who has the rank of a duke and rules a duchy.



**duch·y** (duch′ē) ***n.*** the land ruled by a duke or duchess. —*pl.* **duch′ies**

**duck**[1] (duk) ***n.*** **1** a swimming bird with a flat bill, short legs, and webbed feet; especially, the female of this bird. The male is called a *drake*. **2** the flesh of a duck eaten as food.

**duck**[2] (duk) ***v.*** **1** to dive or dip under water for a very short time. **2** to lower or move the head or body quickly, as in getting away from a blow or in hiding. **3** to avoid a task, person, etc.: *used only in everyday talk.* ◆***n.*** the act of ducking.

**duck**[3] (duk) ***n.*** a linen or cotton cloth like canvas but finer and lighter in weight [Doctors' uniforms are often made of white *duck*.]

**duck·bill** (duk′bil) ***n.*** *another name for* **platypus.**

**duck·ling** (duk′ling) ***n.*** a young duck.

**duct** (dukt) ***n.*** **1** a tube or channel through which a gas or liquid moves [air *ducts* from a furnace]. **2** a tube in the body through which a liquid flows [tear *ducts* of the eyes].

> **Duct** comes from the same Latin word as **duke** does; the Latin word *ducere* means "to lead." Dukes used to lead men into battle; a duct leads a fluid from one place to another.

**duc·tile** (duk′t'l) ***adj.*** **1** that can be drawn out into wire or hammered thin [Copper is a *ductile* metal.] **2** that can be molded or shaped, as clay. —**duc·til·i·ty** (duk til′ə tē) ***n.***

**duct·less gland** (dukt′lis) a gland, as the thyroid, that has no ducts but sends its fluid directly into the blood or lymph.

**dud** (dud) ***n.*** **1** a bomb or shell that fails to explode. **2** a person or thing that fails to do what is expected. *This word is used only in everyday talk.*

☆**dude** (do͞od) ***n.*** **1** a man who is very fussy about his clothes and looks; dandy. **2** a person from the city, especially one from the East, who is vacationing on a ranch: *a Western slang meaning.* **3** a man or boy: *slang in this meaning.*

**dudg·eon** (duj′ən) ***n.*** anger; hurt feelings: *used mainly in the phrase* **in high dudgeon,** very angry.

**due** (do͞o *or* dyo͞o) ***adj.*** **1** owed as a debt; payable [Our gas bill of $9 is *due* today.] **2** that is right and fitting; proper; suitable [to act with all *due* respect; to use *due* care]. **3** expected to come or be done at a certain time [The plane is *due* at noon.] ◆***adv.*** in a straight line; exactly [Their farm is *due* west of the town.] ◆***n.*** **1** anything due, as recognition [to give a man his *due*]. **2 dues,** *pl.* money paid regularly for being a member in a club, etc. —☆**due to, 1** caused by [Her absence was *due to* illness.] **2** because of: *used only in everyday talk* [The bus is late *due to* the storm.]

**du·el** (do͞o′əl *or* dyo͞o′əl) ***n.*** **1** a fight according to set rules between two people armed with weapons and watched by witnesses. **2** any contest like this, as a debate. ◆***v.*** to fight a duel. —**du′eled** or **du′elled, du′el·ing** or **du′el·ling** —**du′el·ist** or **du′el·list *n.***

**du·et** (do͞o et′ *or* dyo͞o et′) ***n.*** **1** a piece of music for two voices or two instruments. **2** the two people who sing or play it.

**dug** (dug) *past tense and past participle of* **dig.**

☆**dug·out** (dug′out) ***n.*** **1** a boat made by hollowing out a log. **2** a shelter dug in the ground or in a hillside. **3** a covered shelter near a baseball diamond, where the players of a team sit when not at bat or in the field.

**duke** (do͞ok *or* dyo͞ok) ***n.*** **1** a prince who is the ruler of a duchy. **2** a nobleman of the highest rank, just below a prince. —**duke′dom *n.***

**dul·cet** (dul′sit) ***adj.*** pleasant to hear; sweet-sounding; melodious [a *dulcet* voice].

**dul·ci·mer** (dul′sə mər) ***n.*** **1** a musical instrument with metal strings. It is played by striking the strings with two small hammers. **2** a musical instrument shaped like a violin. It is played, especially in the southern Appalachians, by plucking with a wooden plectrum or a goose quill. *See the picture.*

**dull** (dul) ***adj.*** **1** not having a sharp edge or point; blunt [a *dull* knife]. **2** not feeling or felt in a sharp way; weak [a *dull* sense of hearing; a *dull* pain]. **3** slow in thinking or learning; stupid. **4** not active or lively; sluggish or listless [a *dull* period for sales]. **5** not interesting; boring [a long, *dull* book]. **6** not bright; dim [a *dull* color]. **7** not clear; muffled [a *dull* thud]. ◆***v.*** to make or become dull. —**dull′ness *n.*** —**dul′ly *adv.***

**dull·ard** (dul′ərd) ***n.*** a stupid person.

**Du·luth** (də lo͞oth′) a city in eastern Minnesota, on Lake Superior.

**du·ly** (do͞o′lē *or* dyo͞o′lē) ***adv.*** as due; in a way or at a time that is right or fitting [Are you *duly* grateful? Their rent was *duly* paid.]

**dumb** (dum) ***adj.*** **1** not having the power to speak; mute [a *dumb* beast]. **2** not speaking for a time; speechless [struck *dumb* with fear]. ☆**3** stupid: *used only in everyday talk.* —**dumb′ly *adv.*** —**dumb′ness *n.***

**dumb·bell** (dum′bel) ***n.*** **1** a short bar with round weights at the ends, usually used in pairs to exercise the muscles. *See the picture.* ☆**2** a stupid person: *slang in this meaning.*

**dumb·found** or **dum·found** (dum′found′) ***v.*** to make unable to speak, as by shocking.

**dumb·wait·er** (dum′wāt′ər) ***n.*** ☆a small elevator for sending food, etc. from one floor to another.

**dum·my** (dum′ē) ***n.*** **1** an imitation of something, as a figure made to look like a person and used to display clothing. **2** a player in some card games, as bridge, whose cards are laid face up on the table and are played by his or her partner. **3** a stupid person: *slang in this meaning.* —*pl.* **dum′mies** ◆***adj.*** **1** imitation or sham [a *dummy* drawer]. **2** secretly acting for another or controlled by another [a *dummy* corporation].

**dump** (dump) ***v.*** **1** to unload in a pile or heap, as sand. **2** to throw away or get rid of. ◆***n.*** ☆**1** a place where rubbish is dumped. **2** a place where military supplies are stored. ☆**3** a place that is dirty, rundown, etc.: *slang in this meaning.* —**in the dumps,** feeling sad.

**dump·ling** (dump′liŋ) ***n.*** **1** a small ball of dough, cooked and served with meat or soup. **2** a crust of baked dough filled with fruit.

☆**dump truck** a truck with a back end that can be tilted to dump a load. *See the picture.*

**dump·y** (dum′pē) ***adj.*** **1** short and fat; plump. **2** ugly and run-down: *slang in this meaning.* —**dump′i·er, dump′i·est**

**dun**[1] (dun) ***adj., n.*** dull grayish brown.

**dun**[2] (dun) ***v.*** to ask again and again for money owed. —**dunned, dun′ning** ◆***n.*** a demand that a debt be paid.

**Dun·bar** (dun′bär), **Paul Laurence** 1872–1906; U.S. poet.

**Dun·can** (duŋ′kən), **Is·a·dor·a** (iz′ə dôr′ə) 1878–1927; U.S. dancer.

**dunce** (duns) ***n.*** a stupid person or one who learns slowly.

**dune** (do͞on *or* dyo͞on) ***n.*** a rounded hill or ridge of sand heaped up by the wind.

**dung** (duŋ) ***n.*** the waste matter dropped by animals; manure.

**dun·ga·ree** (duŋ gə rē′) ***n.*** **1** a coarse cotton cloth, especially blue denim. **2 dungarees,** *pl.* work pants or overalls made of this cloth.

**Dungaree** is the spelling in English of a Hindi word for a coarse cotton cloth, or calico, brought from India.

**dun·geon** (dun′jən) ***n.*** a dark room underground, used as a prison.

☆**dunk** (duŋk) ***v.*** **1** to dip bread, cake, etc. into coffee or other liquid before eating it. **2** to put a basketball in a basket with a dunk shot.

☆**dunk shot** a field goal made in basketball by leaping up and thrusting the ball down into the basket.

**dupe** (do͞op *or* dyo͞op) ***n.*** a person who is easily fooled or cheated. ◆***v.*** to fool or cheat. —**duped, dup′ing**

**du·plex** (do͞o′pleks *or* dyo͞o′pleks) ***adj.*** having two parts or units; double [a *duplex* house]. ◆☆***n.*** *a shorter form of* **duplex house.**

☆**duplex house** a house that has two separate units, so that a different family can live in each unit. *See the picture.*

dulcimer

duplex house

dumbbell

dump truck

**du·pli·cate** (do͞o′plə kit *or* dyo͞o′plə kit) ***adj.*** **1** exactly like another or like each other [*duplicate* keys]. **2** double. ◆***n.*** a thing exactly like another; an exact copy [The typist made a *duplicate* of the letter.] ◆***v.*** (do͞o′plə kāt *or* dyo͞o′plə kāt) to make an exact copy or copies of. —**du′pli·cat·ed, du′pli·cat·ing** —**in duplicate,** in two copies that are exactly alike. —**du′pli·ca′tion *n.*** 

**duplicating machine** a machine for making exact copies of a letter, photograph, drawing, etc.

**du·plic·i·ty** (do͞o plis′ə tē *or* dyo͞o plis′ə tē) ***n.*** a dealing with others in a tricky or dishonest way. —*pl.* **du·plic′i·ties**

**du·ra·ble** (door′ə b'l *or* dyoor′ə b'l) ***adj.*** lasting in spite of hard wear or much use. —**du′ra·bil′i·ty *n.*** —**du′ra·bly *adv.***

**du·ra·tion** (doo rā′shən *or* dyoo rā′shən) ***n.*** the time that something lasts or continues [We will eat lunch in the cafeteria for the *duration* of the year.]

**Dur·ban** (dur′bən) a seaport in eastern South Africa.

**Dü·rer** (dyo͞or′ər), **Al·brecht** (äl′brekt) 1471–1528; German painter and wood engraver.

**du·ress** (doo res′ *or* dyoo res′) ***n.*** the use of force or threats to make someone do something [The contract was not binding because she signed it under *duress.*]

**dur·ing** (door′iŋ *or* dyoor′iŋ) ***prep.*** **1** throughout the whole time of; all through [Food was hard to get *during* the war.] **2** at some time in the course of [We left *during* the performance of the play.]

**dusk** (dusk) ***n.*** the dim part of twilight that comes before the dark of night.

**dusk·y** (dus′kē) ***adj.*** dim, dark, or gloomy; shadowy. —**dusk′i·er, dusk′i·est** —**dusk′i·ness *n.***

| | | | |
|---|---|---|---|
| **a** fat | **ir** here | **ou** out | **zh** leisure |
| **ā** ape | **ī** bite, fire | **u** up | **ŋ** ring |
| **ä** car, lot | **ō** go | **ur** fur | a *in* ago |
| **e** ten | **ô** law, horn | **ch** chin | e *in* agent |
| **er** care | **oi** oil | **sh** she | **ə** = i *in* unity |
| **ē** even | **oo** look | **th** thin | o *in* collect |
| **i** hit | **o͞o** tool | ***th*** then | u *in* focus |

**Düs·sel·dorf** (dyo͞os′əl dôrf) a city in western West Germany.

**dust** (dust) ***n.*** **1** fine, powdery earth or other material that floats in the air and settles on surfaces. **2** the human body after death. ◆***v.*** **1** to wipe the dust from [*Dust* the table with this cloth.] **2** to sprinkle with a dust or fine powder [*Dust* the cake with powdered sugar.] —**bite the dust,** to be killed, especially in battle. —**shake the dust off one's feet,** to leave in anger or scorn. —**throw dust in someone's eyes,** to fool or mislead someone.

**dust·er** (dust′ər) ***n.*** **1** a cloth or brush used for getting dust off. ☆**2** a short, lightweight housecoat.

**dust·pan** (dust′pan) ***n.*** a pan like a small shovel, into which dirt from the floor is swept. *See the picture.*

**dust·y** (dus′tē) ***adj.*** **1** covered or filled with dust [*dusty* tables]. **2** like dust or powder [the *dusty* scales of a moth's wing]. **3** of the color of dust; grayish. —**dust′i·er, dust′i·est** —**dust′i·ness** ***n.***

**Dutch** (duch) ***adj.*** **1** of the Netherlands, its people, language, etc. **2** of the Pennsylvania Dutch. ◆***n.*** the language of the Netherlands. —☆**go Dutch,** to have each person pay his or her own expenses: *used only in everyday talk.* —☆**in Dutch,** in trouble: *used only in everyday talk.* —**the Dutch,** **1** the people of the Netherlands. ☆**2** the Pennsylvania Dutch.

**Dutch·man** (duch′mən) ***n.*** a person born or living in the Netherlands. —*pl.* **Dutch′men**

230 **Dutch oven** a heavy metal pot with a domelike lid, for cooking pot roasts.

☆**Dutch treat** a dinner, party, or other entertainment at which each person pays his or her own expenses: *used only in everyday talk.*

**du·te·ous** (do͞ot′ē əs *or* dyo͞ot′ē əs) ***adj.*** dutiful or obedient. —**du′te·ous·ly** ***adv.***

**du·ti·ful** (do͞ot′ə fəl *or* dyo͞ot′ə fəl) ***adj.*** doing or ready to do one's duty; having a proper sense of duty [a *dutiful* parent]. —**du′ti·ful·ly** ***adv.***

**du·ty** (do͞ot′ē *or* dyo͞ot′ē) ***n.*** **1** what a person should do because it is thought to be right, just, or moral [It is the *duty* of every citizen to vote.] **2** any of the things that are supposed to be done as part of a person's work [the *duties* of a secretary]. **3** the respect that one should show toward one's parents, older people, etc. **4** a tax paid to the government, especially on goods brought in from other countries. —*pl.* **du′ties**

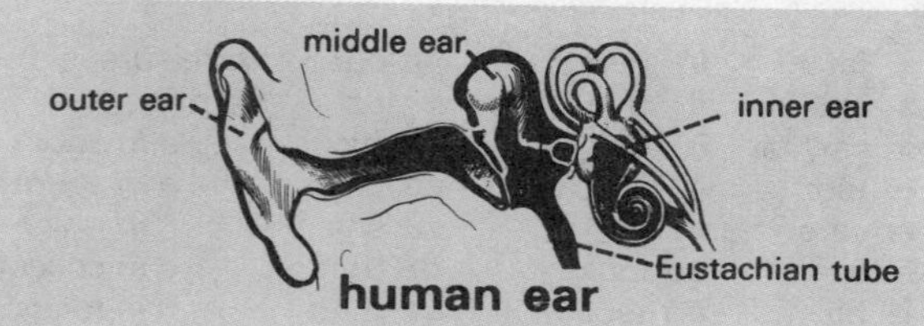

**human ear**

**Dvo·řák** (dvôr′zhäk), **An·ton** (än′tôn) 1841–1904; Czech composer.

**dwarf** (dwôrf) ***n.*** **1** a person, animal, or plant that is much smaller than most others of its kind. **2** a little man in fairy tales who is supposed to have magic powers. ◆***v.*** **1** to make something seem small in comparison; tower over [The redwood *dwarfs* other trees.] **2** to keep small; stunt the growth of [Bonsai trees are *dwarfed* by pruning.] ◆***adj.*** smaller than others of its kind [the *dwarf* salmon]. —**dwarf′ish** ***adj.***

SYNONYMS: A **dwarf** is a person much smaller than other people and is sometimes deformed. A **midget** is also quite small but has a normally formed body.

**dwell** (dwel) ***v.*** to make one's home; live: *now found mainly in older writings.* —**dwelt** (dwelt) or **dwelled, dwell′ing** —**dwell on** or **dwell upon,** to go on thinking or talking about for a long time. —**dwell′er** ***n.***

**dwell·ing** (dwel′iŋ) ***n.*** a house or home: *also* **dwelling place.**

**DWI** or **D.W.I.** driving while intoxicated.

**dwin·dle** (dwin′d′l) ***v.*** to keep on becoming smaller or less; diminish [Her savings had *dwindled* away.] —**dwin′dled, dwin′dling**

**dye** (dī) ***n.*** **1** a substance dissolved in water and used to color cloth, hair, leather, etc. **2** the color produced in cloth, etc. by dyeing. ◆***v.*** to color as with a dye. —**dyed, dye′ing** —**dy′er** ***n.***

**dye·stuff** (dī′stuf) ***n.*** any substance used as a dye or from which a dye is got.

**dy·ing** (dī′iŋ) *present participle of* **die.**

**dy·nam·ic** (dī nam′ik) ***adj.*** **1** having to do with energy or force in action. **2** full of energy or power; forceful; vigorous [a *dynamic* person]. —**dy·nam′i·cal·ly** ***adv.***

**dy·nam·ics** (dī nam′iks) ***n.pl.*** **1** the science that has to do with the motions of bodies under the influence of certain forces. **2** all the forces that are at work in any activity [the *dynamics* of politics].

**dy·na·mite** (dī′nə mīt) ***n.*** a powerful explosive made of nitroglycerin and a material, as wood pulp, that soaks it up. ◆***v.*** to blow up with dynamite. —**dy′na·mit·ed, dy′na·mit·ing**

The Swedish inventor Alfred Nobel invented a powerful explosive, and he also invented the word for it, **dynamite.** He used the Greek word for power, *dynamis,* in making up the new word.

**dy·na·mo** (dī′nə mō) ***n.*** **1** a machine for changing mechanical energy into electrical energy: *now called* **generator.** **2** a very forceful, energetic person. —*pl.* **dy′na·mos**

**dy·nas·ty** (dī′nəs tē) ***n.*** **1** a family of rulers following one after another. **2** the period of time during which such a family rules. —*pl.* **dy′nas·ties** —**dy·nas·tic** (dī nas′tik) ***adj.***

**dys·en·ter·y** (dis″n ter′ē) ***n.*** a disease of the intestines, in which there are loose bowel movements containing blood and mucus.

**dys·pep·si·a** (dis pep′shə *or* dis pep′sē ə) ***n.*** digestive trouble; indigestion.

**dys·pep·tic** (dis pep′tik) ***adj.*** **1** having indigestion. **2** grouchy or gloomy.

**dz.** *abbreviation for* **dozen** *or* **dozens.**

**E, e** (ē) ***n.*** the fifth letter of the English alphabet. *—pl.* **E's, e's** (ēz)

**E** error *or* errors (in baseball).

**E, E., e, e.** *abbreviations for* **east** *or* **eastern.**

**ea.** *abbreviation for* **each.**

**each** (ēch) ***adj., pron.*** every one of two or more, thought of separately [*Each* pupil will receive a book. *Each* of the books is numbered.] ◆***adv.*** for each; apiece [The tickets cost $5.00 *each.*] **—each other,** each one the other [You and I should help *each other.*]

**ea·ger** (ē'gər) ***adj.*** wanting very much; anxious to do or get [*eager* to win; *eager* for praise]. **—ea'ger·ly** ***adv.*** **—ea'ger·ness** ***n.***

**ea·gle** (ē'g'l) ***n.*** a large, strong bird that captures and eats other birds and animals and has sharp eyesight. The **bald eagle** is the symbol of the U.S. *See the picture.*

**ea·gle-eyed** (ē'g'l īd) ***adj.*** having sharp eyesight.

**ea·glet** (ē'glit) ***n.*** a young eagle.

**ear**[1] (ir) ***n.*** **1** either of two organs in the head through which sound is heard. *See the picture.* **2** the part of the ear that sticks out from the head. **3** anything like an ear [the *ear* of a cream pitcher]. **4** the sense of hearing [She has a good *ear* for music.] **5** attention or heed [Give *ear* to my plea.] **—be all ears,** to listen in an eager way. **—fall on deaf ears,** to be unheeded. —☆**keep an ear to the ground,** to pay close attention to what people are thinking. **—play by ear,** to play music without reading notes. **—play it by ear,** to act as the situation calls for, without planning ahead: *used only in everyday talk.* **—turn a deaf ear,** to refuse to listen or heed.

**ear**[2] (ir) ***n.*** the part of a cereal plant on which the grain grows [an *ear* of corn].

**ear·ache** (ir'āk) ***n.*** a pain in the ear.

**ear·drum** (ir'drum) ***n.*** the thin, tight skin inside the ear that vibrates when sound waves strike it.

**Ear·hart** (er'härt), **Amelia** 1898–1937; early U.S. airplane pilot who set records for long-distance flying.

**earl** (ʉrl) ***n.*** a British nobleman ranking just below a marquess.

**ear·ly** (ʉr'lē) ***adv., adj.*** **1** near the beginning; soon after the start [in the *early* afternoon; *early* in his career]. **2** before the usual or expected time [The bus arrived *early.*] **—ear'li·er, ear'li·est —ear'li·ness** ***n.***

**ear·mark** (ir'märk) ***n.*** **1** a notch or other mark made on the ear of a cow, horse, etc. to show who owns it. **2** a trait or quality that tells what a person or thing is or can be [This student has all the *earmarks* of a fine engineer.] ◆***v.*** **1** to put an earmark on [to *earmark* cattle]. **2** to set aside for a special purpose [That money is *earmarked* for a new car.]

☆**ear·muffs** (ir'mufs) ***n.pl.*** cloth or fur coverings worn over the ears to keep them warm in cold weather.

**earn** (ʉrn) ***v.*** **1** to get as pay for work done [She *earns* $10 an hour.] **2** to get or deserve because of something one has done [At the Olympics he *earned* a gold medal for swimming.] **3** to get as profit [Your savings *earn* 5% interest.]

**ear·nest** (ʉr'nist) ***adj.*** not light or joking; serious or sincere [an *earnest* wish]. **—in earnest,** serious or determined [Are you *in earnest* about helping us?] **—ear'nest·ly** ***adv.*** **—ear'nest·ness** ***n.***

**earn·ings** (ʉr'niŋz) ***n.pl.*** money earned; wages, salary, or profits.

**ear·phone** (ir'fōn) ***n.*** a receiver held to the ear, for listening to a telephone, radio, etc.

**ear·ring** (ir'riŋ) ***n.*** an ornament worn on or in the lobe of the ear.

**ear·shot** (ir'shät) ***n.*** the distance within which a person's voice or other sound can be heard; range of hearing [He shouted for help but we were out of *earshot.*]

**earth** (ʉrth) ***n.*** **1** the planet that we live on. It is the fifth largest planet and the third in distance away from the sun. **2** the dry part of the earth's surface, that is not the sea. **3** soil or ground [a flowerpot filled with good, rich *earth*]. **—down to earth,** practical or realistic. **—on earth,** of all possible persons, things, etc.: *used to give force to what one is saying* [Who *on earth* told you that?] **—run to earth,** to hunt down.

**earth·en** (ʉr'thən) ***adj.*** **1** made of earth [an *earthen* floor]. **2** made of baked clay [*earthen* jars].

**earth·en·ware** (ʉr'thən wer) ***n.*** the coarser sort of dishes, vases, jars, etc. made of baked clay.

**earth·ly** (ʉrth'lē) ***adj.*** **1** having to do with the earth, or this world, and not with heaven [*earthly* possessions]. **2** possible [This advice was of no *earthly* use.]

> SYNONYMS: **Earthly** has to do with the present life here on earth, as opposed to the idea of a heavenly life to come [*earthly* delights]. **Worldly** has to do with ordinary life, in which more attention is paid to material things that are needed or wanted than to spiritual matters [*worldly* concerns].

**earth·quake** (ʉrth'kwāk) ***n.*** a shaking or trembling of the ground, caused by the shifting of underground rock or by the action of a volcano.

**earth·work** (ʉrth'wʉrk) ***n.*** a wall made by piling up earth, as around a fort.

**earth·worm** (ʉrth'wʉrm) ***n.*** a round worm that lives in the earth and helps keep the soil loose.

**earth·y** (ʉr'thē) ***adj.*** **1** of or like earth or soil [an *earthy* smell]. **2** simple, or coarse, and natural; not refined [*earthy* humor]. **—earth'i·er, earth'i·est**

| | | | | | | | |
|---|---|---|---|---|---|---|---|
| **a** | fat | **ir** | here | **ou** | out | **zh** | leisure |
| **ā** | ape | **ī** | bite, fire | **u** | up | **ŋ** | ring |
| **ä** | car, lot | **ō** | go | **ʉr** | fur | | a *in* ago |
| **e** | ten | **ô** | law, horn | **ch** | chin | | e *in* agent |
| **er** | care | **oi** | oil | **sh** | she | **ə** = | i *in* unity |
| **ē** | even | **oo** | look | **th** | thin | | o *in* collect |
| **i** | hit | **ōō** | tool | ***th*** | then | | u *in* focus |

**ease** (ēz) ***n.*** **1** the condition of not needing to try too hard [She swam a mile with *ease.*] **2** a calm condition or relaxed position [to put a person at *ease;* to stand at *ease*]. **3** the condition of being without worry, pain, or trouble; comfort or luxury [They lived a life of *ease.*] ◆***v.*** **1** to make feel less worry, pain, or trouble; comfort. **2** to make less painful [The pills *eased* my headache.] **3** to take away some of the strain or pressure on; loosen: *often used with* up [*Ease* up on that rope.] **4** to move slowly and carefully [The movers *eased* the piano through the door.] —**eased, eas′ing**

> **Ease** comes from a Latin word meaning "lying nearby." Anything lying nearby is easy to reach. And having things easy to reach, get, or do brings ease to a person.

**ea·sel** (ē′z'l) ***n.*** a standing frame for holding an artist's canvas, a chalkboard, etc. *See the picture.*

**eas·i·ly** (ē′z'l ē) ***adv.*** **1** without trying too hard; with no trouble [I can do ten push-ups *easily.*] **2** without a doubt; by far [Our team is *easily* the best.] **3** very likely; probably [We may *easily* be an hour late getting there.]

**eas·i·ness** (ē′zē nis) ***n.*** the fact or condition of being easy.

**east** (ēst) ***n.*** **1** the direction toward the point where the sun rises. **2** a place or region in or toward this direction. ◆***adj.*** **1** in, of, to, or toward the east [the *east* bank of the river]. **2** from the east [an *east* wind]. **3** **East,** that is the eastern part of [*East* Germany]. ◆***adv.*** in or toward the east [Go *east* ten miles.] —**the East,** ☆**1** the eastern part of the U.S., especially the northern part east of the Alleghenies. **2** Asia or the Orient.

**East Berlin** the capital of East Germany.

**East·er** (ēs′tər) ***n.*** a Christian festival held on a Sunday early in spring to celebrate the resurrection of Jesus.

**east·er·ly** (ēs′tər lē) ***adj., adv.*** **1** in or toward the east. **2** from the east.

**east·ern** (ēs′tərn) ***adj.*** **1** in, of, or toward the east [the *eastern* sky]. **2** from the east [an *eastern* wind]. **3** **Eastern,** of the East.

**Eastern Church** *another name for* **Orthodox Eastern Church.**

**East·ern·er** (ēs′tərn ər) ***n.*** a person born or living in the East [A native of New England is called an *Easterner.*]

**Eastern Hemisphere** the half of the earth that includes Europe, Africa, Asia, and Australia.

**east·ern·most** (ēs′tərn mōst) ***adj.*** farthest east.

☆**Eastern Standard Time** *see* **Standard Time.**

**East Germany** a country in north-central Europe.

**East Indies** the Malay Archipelago; especially, the islands of Indonesia. At an earlier time, the East Indies also included India, the Indochinese Peninsula, and the Malay Peninsula.

**east·ward** (ēst′wərd) ***adv., adj.*** toward the east. ◆***n.*** an eastward direction or place.

**east·wards** (ēst′wərdz) ***adv.*** *same as* **eastward.**

**eas·y** (ē′zē) ***adj.*** **1** not hard to do, learn, get, etc. [an *easy* job; an *easy* book]. **2** without worry, pain, or trouble [an *easy* life]. **3** restful or comfortable [an *easy* chair]. **4** not stiff or awkward; relaxed and pleasant [an *easy* manner]. **5** not hard to put up with; not strict [*easy* punishment; an *easy* boss]. **6** not rushed [an *easy* pace]. —**eas′i·er, eas′i·est** ◆***adv.*** easily: *used only in everyday talk* [The car rides *easy.*] —**easy does it,** be careful. —**take it easy,** to keep from being rushed, hasty, angry, etc.: *used only in everyday talk.*

**eas·y·go·ing** (ē′zē gō′iŋ) ***adj.*** not worried, rushed, or strict about things.

**eat** (ēt) ***v.*** **1** to take food into the mouth, chew, and swallow it. **2** to have a meal [Who is *eating* with us tonight?] **3** to use up; consume [Medical bills *ate* up their savings.] **4** to destroy by wearing away [car fenders *eaten* away by rust]. **5** to make as by eating [The acid *ate* holes in the cloth.] —**ate, eat·en** (ēt′'n), **eat′ing** —**eat one's words,** to admit that what one said was wrong. —**eat′er** ***n.***

**eat·a·ble** (ēt′ə b'l) ***adj.*** fit to be eaten; edible. ◆***n.*** *usually* **eatables,** *pl.* things to be eaten; food.

**eaves** (ēvz) ***n.pl.*** the edge or edges of a roof hanging over the side of a building. *See the picture.*

**eaves·drop** (ēvz′dräp) ***v.*** to listen to others talking when they do not know they are being overheard. —**eaves′dropped, eaves′drop·ping**

**ebb** (eb) ***n.*** **1** the flow of water back toward the sea as the tide falls. **2** the fact of becoming weaker or less [the *ebb* of one's hopes]. ◆***v.*** **1** to fall, as the tide. **2** to become weaker or less [Our hopes for victory *ebbed.*] *See* SYNONYMS *at* **wane.**

**ebb tide** the tide flowing back toward the sea.

**eb·on·y** (eb′ə nē) ***n.*** the black, hard wood of certain tropical trees. ◆***adj.*** **1** made of ebony. **2** black or dark.

**e·bul·lient** (i bo͝ol′yənt *or* i bul′yənt) ***adj.*** bubbling or overflowing, as with joy or enthusiasm.

**ec·cen·tric** (ik sen′trik) ***adj.*** **1** not usual or normal in the way one behaves; odd or queer [an *eccentric* old hermit]. **2** not having the same center, as two circles one inside the other. *See the picture.* **3** having its axis not in the center [*Eccentric* wheels are used to change circular motion into back-and-forth motion.] *See the picture.* ◆***n.*** an eccentric person. —**ec·cen′tri·cal·ly** ***adv.***

**ec·cen·tric·i·ty** (ek′sen tris′ə tē) ***n.*** unusual or odd behavior, or a queer habit or action. —*pl.* **ec′cen·tric′i·ties**

**Ec·cle·si·as·tes** (i klē′zē as′tēz) a book of the Bible, said to have been written by Solomon.

**ec·cle·si·as·tic** (i klē′zē as′tik) ***n.*** a minister or priest. ◆***adj.*** *same as* **ecclesiastical.**

**ec·cle·si·as·ti·cal** (i klē′zē as′ti k'l) ***adj.*** having to do with the church or the clergy.

**ech·e·lon** (esh′ə län) ***n.*** **1** a formation of troops, ships, or airplanes arranged like steps. *See the picture.* **2** a particular part or level of a military force [a *rear* echelon; higher *echelons*].

**ech·o** (ek′ō) ***n.*** **1** sound heard again when sound waves bounce back from a surface. —*pl.* **ech′oes** **2** **Echo,** a nymph of Greek myths who pined away for Narcissus until only her voice was left. ◆***v.*** **1** to be filled with echoes [The long hall *echoed.*] **2** to be repeated as an echo [Her shout *echoed* in the empty theater.] **3** to repeat the words or actions of another person ["It's true," she said. "It's true," he *echoed.*] —**ech′oed, ech′o·ing**

**é·clair** (ā kler′ *or* ē kler′) ***n.*** an oblong shell of pastry filled with custard or whipped cream.

**e·clipse** (i klips′) ***n.*** **1** a hiding of all or part of the sun by the moon when it passes between the sun and the earth (called a **solar eclipse**); also, a hiding of the moon by the earth's shadow (called a **lunar eclipse**). **2** a becoming dim or less brilliant [Her fame went into an *eclipse.*] ◆***v.*** **1** to cause an eclipse of; darken. **2** to make seem less brilliant by being even more so [Their latest recording has *eclipsed* all their earlier ones.] —**e·clipsed′, e·clips′ing**

**ec·o·log·i·cal** (ek′ə läj′i k′l *or* ē′kə läj′i k′l) ***adj.*** of ecology [*ecological* problems].

**e·col·o·gy** (ē käl′ə jē) ***n.*** the science that deals with the relations between all living things and the conditions that surround them. —**e·col′o·gist** ***n.***

**e·co·nom·ic** (ē′kə näm′ik *or* ek′ə näm′ik) ***adj.*** **1** having to do with the managing of money in a home, business, or government [the President's *economic* advisers]. **2** having to do with economics [the *economic* development of a country].

**e·co·nom·i·cal** (ē′kə näm′i k′l *or* ek′ə näm′i k′l) ***adj.*** not wasting money, time, material, etc.; thrifty [an *economical* person; an *economical* car]. —**e′co·nom′i·cal·ly** ***adv.***

**e·co·nom·ics** (ē′kə näm′iks *or* ek′ə näm′iks) ***n.pl.*** the science that deals with the way in which goods and wealth are produced, distributed, and used: *used with a singular verb.* —**e·con·o·mist** (i kän′ə mist) ***n.***

**e·con·o·mize** (i kän′ə mīz) ***v.*** to be economical or to cut down on expenses. [She *economized* by riding a bus to work.] —**e·con′o·mized, e·con′o·miz·ing**

**e·con·o·my** (i kän′ə mē) ***n.*** **1** the managing of money earned and spent in a home, business, etc. **2** a careful managing of money, materials, etc. so that there is no waste. —*pl.* **e·con′o·mies**

> **Economy** comes from the Greek word for "manager," which comes from the Greek word for "house." An economical person is a careful manager at home.

**e·co·sys·tem** (ē′kō sis′təm *or* ek′ō sis′təm) ***n.*** all the animals, plants, and bacteria that make up a particular community living in a certain environment.

**ec·ru** (ek′ro͞o) ***adj., n.*** light tan.

**ec·sta·sy** (ek′stə sē) ***n.*** a strong feeling of joy or delight; rapture [The thought of a camping trip in the Rockies threw them into *ecstasy.*] —*pl.* **ec′sta·sies**

**ec·stat·ic** (ek stat′ik) ***adj.*** **1** full of ecstasy [an *ecstatic* mood]. **2** causing ecstasy; thrilling [*ecstatic* music]. —**ec·stat′i·cal·ly** ***adv.***

**Ec·ua·dor** (ek′wə dôr) a country on the northwestern coast of South America.

**ec·u·men·i·cal** (ek′yoo men′i k′l) ***adj.*** seeking to bring better understanding among religious groups, especially among the different Christian churches.

**ec·ze·ma** (ek′sə mə *or* ig zē′mə) ***n.*** a condition of the skin in which it becomes red, scaly, and itchy.

**-ed** (id *or* əd; d *or* t) **1** *a suffix used to form the past tense and past participle of many verbs* [*hated; walked*]. The past participle may often be an adjective as well [*boiled* meat]. **2** *a suffix meaning* having [The *moneyed* class is those people having much money.]

**ed.** *abbreviation for:* **1 edition** *or* **editor.** —*pl.* **eds. 2 education.**

airplanes flying in echelon

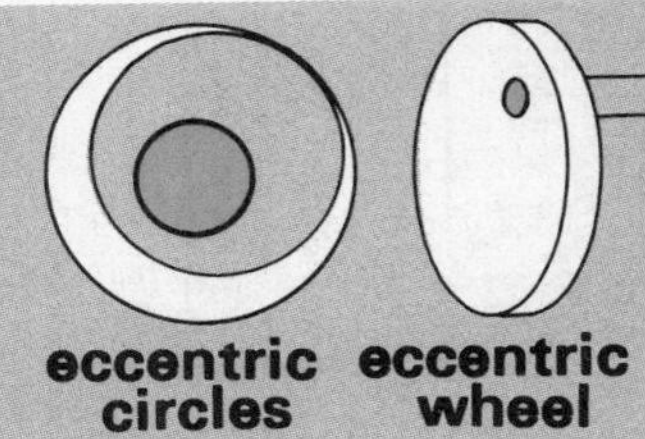

eccentric circles eccentric wheel

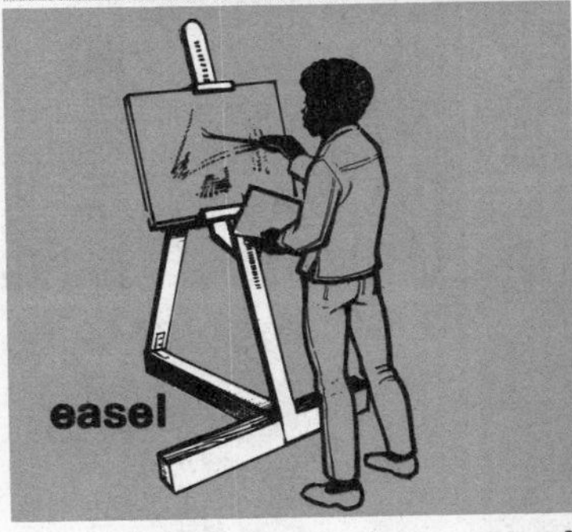

easel

eaves

**ed·dy** (ed′ē) ***n.*** a little current of air, water, etc. moving in circles against the main current. —*pl.* **ed′dies** ◆***v.*** to move in an eddy [The water *eddied* as it hit the rocks.] —**ed′died, ed′dy·ing**

**Ed·dy** (ed′ē), **Mary Baker** 1821–1910; the U.S. founder of Christian Science.

**e·del·weiss** (ā′d′l vīs) ***n.*** a small plant, found espe- 233
cially in the Alps, with white leaves and flowers that look somewhat like wool.

**e·de·ma** (i dē′mə) ***n.*** a condition in which much fluid collects in parts of the body, causing swelling.

**E·den** (ē′d′n) in the Bible, the garden where Adam and Eve first lived. ◆***n.*** any place of great happiness or delight.

**edge** (ej) ***n.*** **1** the sharp, cutting part [the *edge* of a knife]. **2** the line or part where something begins or ends; border or margin [the *edge* of a plate; the *edge* of the forest]. **3** the brink [on the *edge* of disaster]. ☆**4** an advantage: *used only in everyday talk* [His height gave him an *edge* over the others.] ◆***v.*** **1** to form or put an edge on [a pocket *edged* with braid]. **2** to move with the side forward, as through a crowd. **3** to move in a slow and careful way [I *edged* away from the dog.] —**edged, edg′ing** —**on edge, 1** very tense or nervous. **2** impatient.

**edge·ways** (ej′wāz) ***adv.*** with the edge forward: *also* **edge·wise** (ej′wīz).

**edg·ing** (ej′iŋ) ***n.*** something that forms an edge or is placed along the edge; border.

**edg·y** (ej′ē) ***adj.*** very nervous and tense; on edge. —**edg′i·er, edg′i·est**

**ed·i·ble** (ed′ə b′l) ***adj.*** fit to be eaten [Are these berries *edible?*]

| | | | |
|---|---|---|---|
| **a** fat | **ir** here | **ou** out | **zh** leisure |
| **ā** ape | **ī** bite, fire | **u** up | **ŋ** ring |
| **ä** car, lot | **ō** go | **ur** fur | a *in* ago |
| **e** ten | **ô** law, horn | **ch** chin | e *in* agent |
| **er** care | **oi** oil | **sh** she | **ə** = i *in* unity |
| **ē** even | **oo** look | **th** thin | o *in* collect |
| **i** hit | **o͞o** tool | ***th*** then | u *in* focus |

eerie house

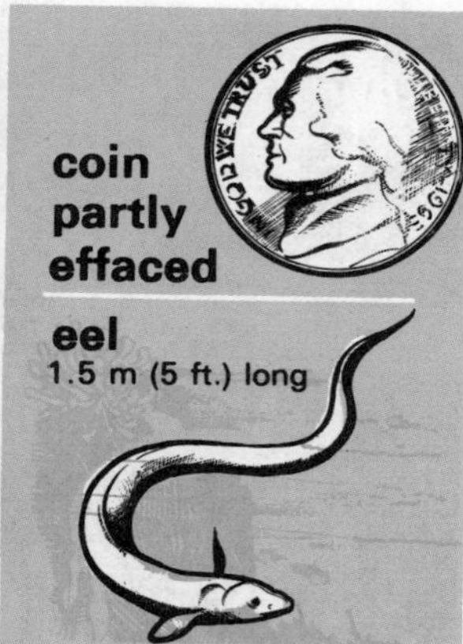
coin partly effaced

eel
1.5 m (5 ft.) long

egret
60 cm (24 in.) long, including bill

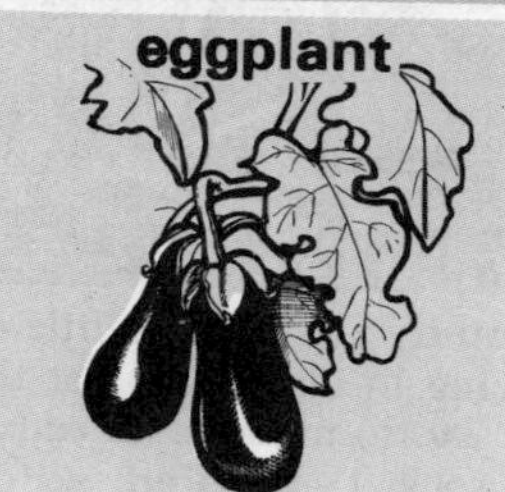
eggplant

**e·dict** (ē′dikt) ***n.*** an order given by a ruler or other high official, which must be obeyed as a law.

**ed·i·fice** (ed′ə fis) ***n.*** a building, especially one that is large or looks important.

**ed·i·fy** (ed′ə fī) ***v.*** to teach, especially so as to make better or more moral [an *edifying* book]. —**ed′i·fied, ed′i·fy·ing** —**ed′i·fi·ca′tion *n.***

**Ed·in·burgh** (ed″n bur′ə) the capital of Scotland, in the southeastern part.

**Ed·i·son** (ed′ə s′n), **Thomas A.** 1847–1931; a U.S. inventor of many things.

**ed·it** (ed′it) ***v.*** **1** to get a piece of writing ready to be published, by arranging, correcting, or changing the material. **2** to be in charge of a newspaper, magazine, etc. and decide what is to be printed in it. ☆**3** to get a film, tape, or recording ready by choosing and putting together the parts.

**e·di·tion** (i dish′ən) ***n.*** **1** the size or form in which a book is published [a paperback *edition* of a novel]. **2** all the copies of a book, newspaper, etc. printed at about the same time; also, any one of these copies [the first *edition* of a book].

**ed·i·tor** (ed′ə tər) ***n.*** **1** a person who edits. ☆**2** the head of a department of a newspaper, magazine, etc.

**ed·i·to·ri·al** (ed′ə tôr′ē əl) ***adj.*** of or by an editor [*editorial* offices]. ◆☆***n.*** an article in a newspaper or magazine, or a talk on radio or TV, that openly gives the opinion of the editor, publisher, or owner. —**ed′i·to′ri·al·ly *adv.***

**Ed·mon·ton** (ed′mən tən) the capital of Alberta, Canada.

**ed·u·ca·ble** (ej′ə kə b′l) ***adj.*** able to be educated.

**ed·u·cate** (ej′ə kāt) ***v.*** to teach or train a person, especially in a school or college; develop the mind of. —**ed′u·cat·ed, ed′u·cat·ing**

**ed·u·ca·tion** (ej′ə kā′shən) ***n.*** **1** the act or work of educating or training people; teaching [a career in *education*]. **2** the things a person learns by being taught; schooling or training [a high-school *education*].

**ed·u·ca·tion·al** (ej′ə kā′shən ′l) ***adj.*** **1** having to do with education [*educational* theories]. **2** that teaches or gives information [an *educational* film].

**ed·u·ca·tor** (ej′ə kāt′ər) ***n.*** **1** a teacher. **2** a person who trains others to be teachers.

**-ee** (ē) *a suffix meaning:* **1** a person to whom something is given or done [An *appointee* is a person who is appointed.] **2** a person in a particular condition [An *employee* is a person in the employ of another.]

**eel** (ēl) ***n.*** a fish that has a long, slippery body and looks like a snake. *See the picture.*

**-eer** (ir) *a suffix meaning:* **1** a person who has something to do with [An *auctioneer* is in charge of auctions. A *profiteer* makes unfair profits.] **2** to do something in connection with [To *electioneer* is to campaign in an election.]

**ee·rie** or **ee·ry** (ir′ē) ***adj.*** giving one a feeling of fear or mystery; weird [an *eerie* house that looked haunted]. *See the picture.* —**ee′ri·er, ee′ri·est**

**ef·face** (i fās′) ***v.*** to rub out or wipe out; erase [The date on the coin was *effaced.* Time has *effaced* his memory.] *See the picture.* —**ef·faced′, ef·fac′ing** —**efface oneself,** to keep oneself from being noticed; stay in the background.

**ef·fect** (ə fekt′) ***n.*** **1** anything that is caused by some other thing; result [Candy can have a bad *effect* on the teeth.] **2** the power to bring about results; influence [Scolding has no *effect* on them.] **3** an impression made on the mind [The angry words were just for *effect.* The artist created a clever *effect* through the use of color.] **4 effects,** *pl.* goods or belongings [Her personal *effects* are in the blue suitcase.] ◆***v.*** to make happen; bring about [The treatment *effected* a cure.] —**give effect to,** to put into action. —**in effect, 1** really; in fact. **2** in force or operation, as a law. —**take effect,** to begin to have results.

**ef·fec·tive** (ə fek′tiv) ***adj.*** **1** making a certain thing happen; especially, bringing about the result wanted [an *effective* remedy]. **2** in force or operation; active [The law becomes *effective* Monday.] **3** making a strong impression on the mind; impressive [an *effective* speaker]. —**ef·fec′tive·ly *adv.***

**ef·fec·tu·al** (ə fek′choo wəl) ***adj.*** that brings or can bring the result that is wanted [an *effectual* plan; an *effectual* cure].

**ef·fem·i·nate** (i fem′ə nit) ***adj.*** having the looks or ways that have been thought of as belonging more to women than to men; not manly [an *effeminate* boy]. —**ef·fem·i·na·cy** (i fem′ə nə sē) ***n.***

**ef·fer·vesce** (ef ər ves′) ***v.*** **1** to give off bubbles as soda water does; bubble. **2** to be lively and full of high spirits. —**ef·fer·vesced′, ef·fer·vesc′ing** —**ef·fer·ves′cence *n.*** —**ef·fer·ves′cent *adj.***

**ef·fete** (e fēt′) ***adj.*** no longer able to produce; worn out or weak, especially because of a lack of self-control [The culture of ancient Rome became *effete.*]

**ef·fi·ca·cious** (ef′ə kā′shəs) ***adj.*** that brings about the result wanted; effective [an *efficacious* drug]. —**ef′fi·ca′cious·ly *adv.***

**ef·fi·ca·cy** (ef′i kə sē) ***n.*** the power to bring about the result wanted; effectiveness.

**ef·fi·cient** (ə fish′ənt) ***adj.*** bringing about the result or effect wanted with the least waste of time, effort, or materials [an *efficient* method of production; an *efficient* manager]. —**ef·fi′cien·cy** ***n.***

**ef·fi·gy** (ef′ə jē) ***n.*** a statue or other image of a person; often, a crude figure of a person who is hated. —*pl.* **ef′fi·gies**

> Sometimes a crowd will make an effigy of a hated person and burn it or hang it to show their anger. That is called **burning in effigy** or **hanging in effigy**.

**ef·fort** (ef′ərt) ***n.*** **1** the use of energy to get something done; a trying hard with the mind or body [It took great *effort* to climb the mountain.] **2** a try or attempt [They made no *effort* to be friendly.] **3** something done with effort [My early *efforts* at poetry were not published.]

**ef·fort·less** (ef′ərt lis) ***adj.*** using or seeming to use very little effort [an *effortless* swing at the ball]. —**ef′fort·less·ly** ***adv.***

**ef·fron·ter·y** (e frun′tər ē) ***n.*** boldness that shows no shame; audacity [After losing my baseball, Jack had the *effrontery* to ask me for another.]

**ef·ful·gence** (e ful′jəns) ***n.*** shining brightness; radiance. —**ef·ful′gent** ***adj.***

**ef·fu·sion** (e fyo͞o′zhən) ***n.*** **1** a pouring forth of liquid. **2** a pouring out of feeling, words, etc. [an *effusion* of joy].

**ef·fu·sive** (e fyo͞o′siv) ***adj.*** overflowing with words or feeling; gushing [*Effusive* praise seldom seems sincere.] —**ef·fu′sive·ly** ***adv.***

**e.g.** for example.

> **E.g.** is the abbreviation of the Latin phrase *exempli gratia,* which means "for the sake of example."

**egg**[1] (eg) ***n.*** **1** the oval or round body that is laid by a female bird, fish, reptile, insect, etc. and from which a young bird, fish, etc. is later hatched. It has a brittle shell or tough outer skin. **2** the cell formed by a female, that will make a new plant or animal of the same kind if it is fertilized; ovum. **3** a hen's egg, raw or cooked.

**egg**[2] (eg) ***v.*** to urge to do something; incite [The girls *egged* Jill on to climb the wall.]

☆**egg·nog** (eg′näg) ***n.*** a drink made of beaten eggs, milk, and sugar, often containing rum, whiskey, etc.

**egg·plant** (eg′plant) ***n.*** **1** a large vegetable that is shaped like a pear and has a purple skin. It is cooked and eaten. *See the picture.* **2** the plant that it grows on.

☆**egg roll** a Chinese-American dish that is made by wrapping thin egg dough around minced vegetables, shrimp, etc. to form a small roll. It is then fried in deep fat.

**egg·shell** (eg′shel) ***n.*** the thin shell covering a bird's egg. ◆***adj.*** yellowish-white.

**e·gis** (ē′jis) ***n.*** *another spelling of* **aegis.**

**eg·lan·tine** (eg′lən tīn) ***n.*** a wild rose that has pink flowers, sweet-smelling leaves, and a prickly stem; sweetbrier.

**e·go** (ē′gō) ***n.*** a person as aware of himself or herself; the self. —*pl.* **e′gos**

**e·go·ism** (ē′gō iz′m) ***n.*** **1** a thinking mainly of oneself and of one's own interests; selfishness. **2** *another word for* **egotism.** —**e′go·ist** ***n.***

**e·go·tism** (ē′gə tiz′m) ***n.*** **1** a thinking or talking about oneself too much. **2** too high an opinion of oneself; conceit. —**e′go·tist** ***n.*** —**e′go·tis′tic** or **e′go·tis′ti·cal** ***adj.***

**e·gre·gious** (i grē′jəs) ***adj.*** standing out sharply as wrong or bad [That ugly lamp is an *egregious* example of bad taste.]

**e·gress** (ē′gres) ***n.*** **1** the act of going out [The blockade prevented the *egress* of ships from the harbor.] **2** a way to go out; exit [There is another *egress* at the rear of the building.]

**e·gret** (ē′gret) ***n.*** a kind of bird that lives along the shore. It has long white plumes that were once used in women's hats. *See the picture.*

**E·gypt** (ē′jipt) a country in northeastern Africa on the Mediterranean and Red seas.

**E·gyp·tian** (i jip′shən) ***adj.*** of Egypt, its people, or their culture. ◆***n.*** **1** a person born or living in Egypt. **2** the language of the ancient Egyptians. Modern Egyptians speak Arabic.

**eh** (ā) ***interj.*** a sound made to show doubt or surprise. It often means "What did you say?" or "Don't you agree?"

**ei·der** (ī′dər) ***n.*** **1** a large sea duck of the northern regions. **2** *a shorter word for* **eiderdown.**

**ei·der·down** (ī′dər doun) ***n.*** **1** the soft breast feathers, or down, of eiders, used for stuffing quilts and pillows. **2** a quilt stuffed with this.

**eight** (āt) ***n., adj.*** one more than seven; the number 8.

**eight·een** (ā′tēn′) ***n., adj.*** eight more than ten; the number 18. 

**eight·eenth** (ā′tēnth′) ***adj.*** coming after seventeen others; 18th in order. ◆***n.*** **1** the eighteenth one. **2** one of eighteen equal parts of something; 1/18.

**eighth** (ātth) ***adj.*** coming after seven others; 8th in order. ◆***n.*** **1** the eighth one. **2** one of eight equal parts of something; 1/8.

**eighth note** a note in music that is held for one eighth as long a time as a whole note.

**eight·i·eth** (āt′ē ith) ***adj.*** coming after seventy-nine others; 80th in order. ◆***n.*** **1** the eightieth one. **2** one of eighty equal parts of something; 1/80.

**eight·y** (āt′ē) ***n., adj.*** eight times ten; the number 80. —*pl.* **eight′ies** —**the eighties,** the numbers or years from 80 through 89.

**Ein·stein** (īn′stīn), **Albert** 1879–1955; a famous scientist who was born in Germany and became a U.S. citizen. He developed the theory of relativity.

**Eir·e** (er′ə) *the Gaelic name for* **Ireland.**

**Ei·sen·how·er** (ī′z′n hou′ər), **Dwight** (dwīt) **D.** 1890–1969; the 34th president of the United States, from 1953 to 1961.

**ei·ther** (ē′thər *or* ī′thər) ***adj.*** **1** one or the other of two [Use *either* exit.] **2** both one and the other; each [She had a tool in *either* hand.] ◆***pron.*** one or the other of two [*Either* of the suits will fit you.] ◆***conj.***

| | | | | | | | |
|---|---|---|---|---|---|---|---|
| **a** | fat | **ir** | here | **ou** | out | **zh** | leisure |
| **ā** | ape | **ī** | bite, fire | **u** | up | **ŋ** | ring |
| **ä** | car, lot | **ō** | go | **ʉr** | fur | | a *in* ago |
| **e** | ten | **ô** | law, horn | **ch** | chin | | e *in* agent |
| **er** | care | **oi** | oil | **sh** | she | **ə =** | i *in* unity |
| **ē** | even | **oo** | look | **th** | thin | | o *in* collect |
| **i** | hit | **o͞o** | tool | ***th*** | then | | u *in* focus |

according to the first of two choices: *a word used to show a choice between two things joined by* or [*Either* come with me or stay home.] ◆**adv.** any more than the other; also [If I don't go, you won't *either*.]

**e·jac·u·late** (i jak′yə lāt) **v.** to say suddenly and sharply; cry out; exclaim ["Stop that!" he *ejaculated*.] —**e·jac′u·lat·ed, e·jac′u·lat·ing —e·jac′u·la′tion n.**

**e·ject** (i jekt′) **v.** to force out; throw out; expel [The chimney *ejects* smoke. The heckler was *ejected* from the meeting.] —**e·jec′tion n.**

SYNONYMS: **Eject** usually suggests a throwing out from within [to *eject* saliva from the mouth]. **Expel** suggests a forcing out, especially a forcing out of a country, group, etc., often with shame [*expelled* from school]. **Oust** refers to a getting rid of something unwanted, as by using force or by the action of law [to *oust* a dishonest mayor].

**eke** (ēk) **v.** **1** to be barely able to get or make: *used with* out [to *eke* out a living]. **2** to add to so as to have enough: *used with* out [She *eked* out her income by working at a second job.] —**eked, ek′ing**

**e·lab·o·rate** (i lab′ər it) **adj.** worked out in a very careful way, with many details; complicated [an *elaborate* plan; an *elaborate* costume]. *See the picture.* ◆**v.** (i lab′ə rāt) **1** to work out in a very careful and detailed way [to *elaborate* a theory]. **2** to give more details [Please *elaborate* on your answer.] —**e·lab′o·rat·ed, e·lab′o·rat·ing —e·lab′o·ra′tion n.**

 **e·lapse** (i laps′) **v.** to slip by; pass by, as time does [An hour *elapsed* before their return.] —**e·lapsed′, e·laps′ing**

**e·las·tic** (i las′tik) **adj.** **1** able to spring back into shape or position after being stretched or squeezed; springy [an *elastic* rubber ball]. **2** that can easily be changed to fit conditions; adaptable [*elastic* rules]. ◆**n.** any cloth or tape with rubber or rubberlike threads running through it to make it elastic. —**e·las′ti·cal·ly adv.**

**e·las·tic·i·ty** (i las′tis′ə tē) **n.** the condition of being elastic [the *elasticity* of a rubber band].

**e·late** (i lāt′) **v.** to make very proud, happy, or joyful [We're *elated* by their success.] —**e·lat′ed, e·lat′ing**

**e·la·tion** (i lā′shən) **n.** a feeling of great joy or pride; high spirits [The news that she had won filled him with *elation*.]

**El·ba** (el′bə) an Italian island between Corsica and Italy. Napoleon was exiled there from 1814 to 1815.

**el·bow** (el′bō) **n.** **1** the joint where the forearm and upper arm meet; the outer part of the angle made by bending the arm. **2** anything bent like an elbow, as a pipe used in plumbing. *See the picture.* ◆**v.** to push or shove as with the elbows [He *elbowed* his way into the locker room.]

Weavers used to measure cloth by holding it along the arm from the bending joint to the end of the finger. That distance was called an "ell" (*see the entry for* **ell**) and the bend in the arm was the "ell bow," or **elbow** as we now write it.

**elbow grease** hard work or effort: *used only in everyday talk.*

**el·bow·room** (el′bō ro͞om′) **n.** enough room to move around in or work in.

**el·der**[1] (el′dər) **adj.** older [the *elder* son]. ◆**n.** **1** an older person [We can learn much from our *elders*.] **2** any of certain church officials.

**el·der**[2] (el′dər) **n.** a shrub or tree with small, white flowers and red or purple berries.

**el·der·ber·ry** (el′dər ber′ē) **n.** **1** *same as* **elder**[2]. **2** the berry of the elder. —*pl.* **el′der·ber′ries**

**eld·er·ly** (el′dər lē) **adj.** somewhat old.

**eld·est** (el′dist) **adj.** oldest [the *eldest* daughter].

**El Do·ra·do** or **El·do·ra·do** (el′də rä′dō) an imaginary place that is supposed to be filled with wealth. Early Spanish explorers in America were seeking such a place.

**e·lect** (i lekt′) **v.** **1** to choose for some office by voting [to *elect* a student council]. **2** to choose or decide [We *elected* to stay.] ◆**adj.** elected but not yet holding office [the president-*elect*]. —**the elect,** persons belonging to a group that has special privileges.

**e·lec·tion** (i lek′shən) **n.** the act of choosing or the fact of being chosen, especially by voting.

**e·lec·tion·eer** (i lek′shə nir′) **v.** to try to get people to vote for a candidate, etc.

**e·lec·tive** (i lek′tiv) **adj.** **1** filled by election [The presidency is an *elective* office.] **2** chosen by vote; elected [Some judges are *elective* officials and some are appointed.] **3** that may be chosen but need not be [Music and art are usually *elective* subjects in high school.] ◆☆**n.** an elective subject in a school or college.

**e·lec·tor** (i lek′tər) **n.** **1** a person who has the right to vote in an election. **2** a member of the electoral college. —**e·lec′tor·al adj.**

**electoral college** ☆a group of persons elected by the voters to choose the president and vice-president of the United States. The electors of each State are expected to vote for the candidates who won the election in their State.

**e·lec·tor·ate** (i lek′tər it) **n.** all the persons who have the right to vote in an election.

**e·lec·tric** (i lek′trik) **adj.** **1** of or having to do with electricity [*electric* current; *electric* wire]. **2** making or made by electricity [an *electric* generator; *electric* lighting]. **3** worked by electricity [an *electric* toothbrush]. **4** very tense or exciting [an *electric* situation].

**e·lec·tri·cal** (i lek′tri k′l) **adj.** **1** *same as* **electric.** **2** having to do with the science of electricity [an *electrical* engineer].

**e·lec·tri·cal·ly** (i lek′trik lē *or* i lek′tri k′l ē) **adv.** by the use of electricity.

☆**electric chair** a chair in which a person sentenced to die is strapped and killed with charges of electricity.

**electric eel** a large fish of South America that looks like an eel and has special organs that can give sharp electric shocks.

☆**electric eye** *another name for* **photoelectric cell.**

**electric guitar** a guitar whose tones are changed into electrical signals, which are changed back to louder tones by an amplifier and sent out through a loudspeaker. *See the picture.*

☆**e·lec·tri·cian** (i lek′trish′ən) **n.** a person whose work is setting up or fixing electrical equipment.

The word **electrician** was made up by Benjamin Franklin, who was one of the first people to study and experiment with electricity.

**e·lec·tric·i·ty** (i lek′tris′ə tē) **n.** a form of energy that comes from the movement of electrons and protons.

It can be produced by friction (as by rubbing wax with wool), by chemical action (as in a storage battery), or by induction (as in a dynamo or generator). Electricity is used to produce light, heat, power, etc. Electricity moving in a stream, as through a wire, is called **electric current.**

**e·lec·tri·fy** (i lek′trə fī) ***v.*** **1** to charge with electricity. **2** to bring the use of electric power into [Most farms have now been *electrified.*] **3** to give a shock of excitement to; thrill [The good news *electrified* the students.] —**e·lec′tri·fied, e·lec′tri·fy·ing** —**e·lec′tri·fi·ca′tion** ***n.***

**electro-** *a prefix meaning:* **1** electric [An *electromagnet* is an electric magnet.] **2** electricity [To *electrocute* is to kill by electricity.]

**e·lec·tro·car·di·o·gram** (i lek′trō kär′dē ə gram′) ***n.*** a tracing made by a machine (called an **e·lec′tro·car′di·o·graph′**) that shows the electrical action of the heart. It is used to help find out whether the heart is diseased.

☆**e·lec·tro·cute** (i lek′trə kyo͞ot) ***v.*** to kill by electricity, as through accident or in carrying out a death sentence by law. —**e·lec′tro·cut·ed, e·lec′tro·cut·ing** —**e·lec′tro·cu′tion** ***n.***

**e·lec·trode** (i lek′trōd) ***n.*** any terminal that conducts an electric current into or out of a battery, arc lamp, etc. or that collects and controls electrons, as in an electron tube.

**e·lec·trol·y·sis** (i lek′träl′ə sis) ***n.*** **1** the breaking up of a dissolved chemical compound into its parts by passing an electric current through it [When copper sulfate is broken up by *electrolysis,* the copper is deposited on a piece of metal.] **2** the removal of unwanted hair from the body by destroying the hair roots with an electrified needle.

**e·lec·tro·lyte** (i lek′trə līt) ***n.*** any dissolved compound that can carry an electric current and be broken up into its parts by the current. —**e·lec·tro·lyt·ic** (i lek′trə lit′ik) ***adj.***

**e·lec·tro·mag·net** (i lek′trō mag′nit) ***n.*** a piece of soft iron with a coil of wire around it, that becomes a magnet when an electric current passes through the wire. *See the picture.* —**e·lec·tro·mag·net·ic** (i lek′trō mag net′ik) ***adj.***

**e·lec·tro·mo·tive** (i lek′trə mōt′iv) ***adj.*** producing an electric current.

**e·lec·tron** (i lek′trän) ***n.*** any of the particles with a negative electric charge that move around the nucleus of an atom. *See also* **proton.**

**e·lec·tron·ic** (i lek′trän′ik) ***adj.*** **1** of electrons. **2** working or produced by the action of electrons.

**e·lec·tron·ics** (i lek′trän′iks) ***n.pl.*** the science dealing with the action of electrons and with the use of electron tubes, transistors, etc.: *used with a singular verb.*

**electron tube** a sealed glass or metal container with two or more electrodes and a gas or a vacuum inside through which electrons can flow. Electron tubes are used in electronic equipment.

**e·lec·tro·plate** (i lek′trə plāt) ***v.*** to put a coating of silver, copper, nickel, etc. on by electrolysis. —**e·lec′tro·plat·ed, e·lec′tro·plat·ing**

**el·e·gant** (el′ə gənt) ***adj.*** **1** rich-looking and attractive in a dignified or refined way [an *elegant* dress]. **2** showing good taste, politeness, etc. [*elegant* manners]. —**el′e·gance** ***n.***

elaborate design

electric guitar

electromagnet

elbow

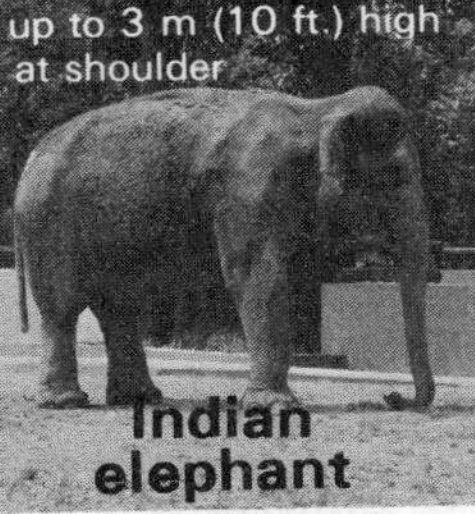

up to 3 m (10 ft.) high at shoulder

Indian elephant

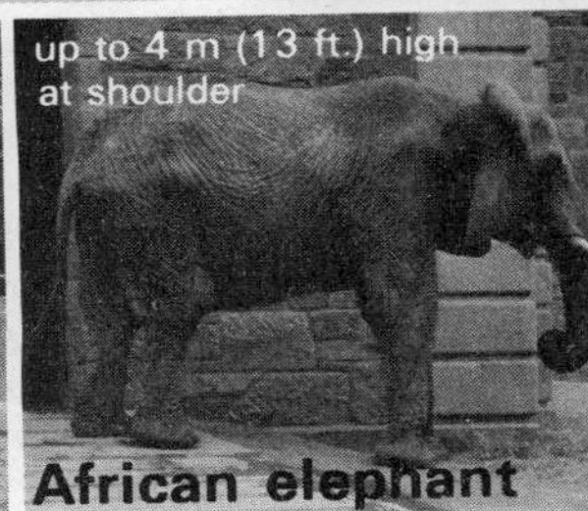

up to 4 m (13 ft.) high at shoulder

African elephant

**el·e·gy** (el′ə jē) ***n.*** a serious or sad poem, usually honoring a dead person. —*pl.* **el′e·gies**

**el·e·ment** (el′ə mənt) ***n.*** **1** any of the parts or qualities of a thing, especially a necessary or basic part [The story has an *element* of suspense. She taught us the *elements* of grammar.] **2** the natural setting or situation for a person or thing [He's in his *element* when he is in the woods.] **3** any substance that cannot be broken down into different substances except by splitting its atom. All matter is made up of such chemical elements, of which there are more than 100. **4** the wire, coil, etc. that becomes glowing hot, as in an electric oven. —**the elements,** wind, rain, and the other forces of nature that make the weather. —**el·e·men·tal** (el′ə men′t′l) ***adj.*** 

**el·e·men·ta·ry** (el′ə men′tər ē) ***adj.*** having to do with the first or simplest things to be learned about something; basic [*elementary* arithmetic].

**elementary school** a school of the first six grades (sometimes, first eight grades), where basic subjects are taught.

**el·e·phant** (el′ə fənt) ***n.*** a huge animal with a thick skin, two ivory tusks, and a long snout, or trunk. It is found in Africa and India and is the largest of the four-legged animals. *See the picture.*

**el·e·vate** (el′ə vāt) ***v.*** to lift up; raise; make higher [The platform was *elevated* above the ground. The play *elevated* our spirits. The bishop was *elevated* to a cardinal.] — **el′e·vat·ed, el′e·vat·ing**

| | | | | | | | |
|---|---|---|---|---|---|---|---|
| **a** | fat | **ir** | here | **ou** | out | **zh** | leisure |
| **ā** | ape | **ī** | bite, fire | **u** | up | **ng** | ring |
| **ä** | car, lot | **ō** | go | **ur** | fur | | a *in* ago |
| **e** | ten | **ô** | law, horn | **ch** | chin | | e *in* agent |
| **er** | care | **oi** | oil | **sh** | she | **ə** = | i *in* unity |
| **ē** | even | **oo** | look | **th** | thin | | o *in* collect |
| **i** | hit | **o͞o** | tool | ***th*** | then | | u *in* focus |

**el·e·va·tion** (el′ə vā′shən) ***n.*** **1** a raising up or being raised up [her *elevation* to the position of principal]. **2** a higher place or position [The house is on a slight *elevation.*] **3** height above the surface of the earth or above sea level [The mountain has an *elevation* of 20,000 feet.]

**el·e·va·tor** (el′ə vāt′ər) ***n.*** ☆**1** a platform or cage for carrying people and things up and down in a building, mine, etc. It is attached by cables to a machine that moves it. ☆**2** a building for storing grain. **3** a part of the tail of an airplane that can be moved to make the airplane go up or down.

**e·lev·en** (i lev″n) ***n., adj.*** one more than ten; the number 11.

**e·lev·enth** (i lev′ənth) ***adj.*** coming after ten others; 11th in order. ◆***n.*** **1** the eleventh one. **2** one of the eleven equal parts of something; 1/11.

**elf** (elf) ***n.*** a small fairy in folk tales, often one that is full of mischief; sprite. —*pl.* **elves** (elvz)

**elf·in** (el′fin) ***adj.*** of or like an elf; full of strange charm [*elfin* laughter]. ◆***n.*** an elf.

**elf·ish** (el′fish) ***adj.*** like an elf; full of mischief; impish [*elfish* pranks].

**El Grec·o** (el grek′ō) 1541?–1614?; a painter in Italy and Spain, who was born in Crete.

**e·lic·it** (i lis′it) ***v.*** to draw out; bring forth [The comedian's jokes *elicited* laughter.]

**el·i·gi·ble** (el′i jə b′l) ***adj.*** having the qualities or conditions that are required; qualified [Is the caretaker *eligible* for a pension?] —**el′i·gi·bil′i·ty** ***n.***

**E·li·jah** (i lī′jə) in the Bible, a Hebrew prophet of the 9th century B.C.

**e·lim·i·nate** (i lim′ə nāt) ***v.*** to get rid of; take out or leave out; remove or omit [a building program to *eliminate* slums; to *eliminate* waste matter from the body]. —**e·lim′i·nat·ed, e·lim′i·nat·ing** —**e·lim′i·na′tion** ***n.***

**Eliminate** comes from a Latin word meaning "to turn out of doors," and that word is made up from two Latin words, *ex,* meaning "out" and *limen,* meaning "threshold." When you **eliminate** something, it is as though you throw it out over your threshold.

**El·i·ot** (el′ē ət), **George** 1819–1880; the pen name of Mary Ann Evans, an English writer of novels.

**e·lite** or **é·lite** (i lēt′ *or* ā lēt′) ***n.*** the group thought of as being the finest or best.

**e·lix·ir** (i lik′sər) ***n.*** **1** a substance for turning cheap metals into gold, or one for keeping people alive forever, that alchemists of the Middle Ages kept trying to find. **2** a medicine made of drugs mixed with alcohol and usually sweetened.

**E·liz·a·beth I** (i liz′ə bəth) 1533–1603; the queen of England from 1558 to 1603.

**Elizabeth II** born in 1926; the queen of England since 1952.

**E·liz·a·be·than** (i liz′ə bē′thən) ***adj.*** of the time when Elizabeth I was queen of England (1558 to 1603). ◆***n.*** an English person of that time, especially a writer.

**elk** (elk) ***n.*** ☆**1** a large deer of North America with branching antlers; the wapiti. *See the picture.* **2** a large deer of northern Europe and Asia that looks like a moose. —*pl.* **elk** or **elks**

**ell** (el) ***n.*** an old measure of length that in England was equal to 45 inches.

**el·lipse** (i lips′) ***n.*** a closed curve that is shaped like an egg, but with equal ends; perfect oval. *See the picture.*

**el·lip·ti·cal** (i lip′ti k′l) or **el·lip·tic** (i lip′tik) ***adj.*** shaped like an ellipse; oval.

**elm** (elm) ***n.*** **1** a tall shade tree with spreading branches. *See the picture.* **2** its hard wood.

**el·o·cu·tion** (el′ə kyōō′shən) ***n.*** a style of giving talks or readings in public, especially an older style now thought of as showy and not natural. —**el′o·cu′tion·ist** ***n.***

**e·lon·gate** (i lông′gāt) ***v.*** to make or become longer; lengthen. —**e·lon′gat·ed, e·lon′gat·ing** —**e·lon′ga′tion** ***n.***

**e·lope** (i lōp′) ***v.*** to run away secretly in order to get married. —**e·loped′, e·lop′ing** —**e·lope′ment** ***n.***

**el·o·quence** (el′ə kwəns) ***n.*** strong, graceful speech or writing that can stir people's feelings or make them think a certain way.

**el·o·quent** (el′ə kwənt) ***adj.*** **1** having eloquence; stirring people's feelings or having an effect on how they think [an *eloquent* plea to a jury]. **2** showing much feeling [an *eloquent* sigh of relief]. —**el′o·quent·ly** ***adv.***

**El Pas·o** (el pas′ō) a city in northwestern Texas, on the Rio Grande.

**El Sal·va·dor** (el sal′və dôr) a country in western Central America.

**else** (els) ***adj.*** **1** not the same; different; other [I thought you were someone *else.*] **2** that may be added; more [Do you want anything *else?*] ◆***adv.*** **1** in a different time, place, or way [Where *else* did you go?] **2** if not; otherwise [Study or *else* you will fail.]

The adjective **else** comes after the word it modifies. In the possessive case, *else* is the word put in the possessive form, not the pronoun that it follows [Has anybody *else's* book arrived?]

**else·where** (els′hwer) ***adv.*** in, at, or to some other place; somewhere else [Look for it *elsewhere.*]

**e·lu·ci·date** (i lo͞o′sə dāt) ***v.*** to make clear; explain [I will try to *elucidate* the meaning of that poem.] —**e·lu′ci·dat·ed, e·lu′ci·dat·ing —e·lu′ci·da′tion *n.***

**e·lude** (i lo͞od′) ***v.*** **1** to escape or get away from by being quick or clever; evade [The convict *eluded* the police for a week.] **2** to keep from being seen, understood, or remembered by [Your name *eludes* me.] —**e·lud′ed, e·lud′ing**

**e·lu·sive** (i lo͞o′siv) ***adj.*** **1** that keeps eluding or escaping [an *elusive* criminal]. **2** hard to understand or keep clearly in mind; puzzling [an odd, *elusive* tune].

**elves** (elvz) ***n.*** *the plural of* **elf.**

**E·ly·sian** (i lizh′ən) ***adj.*** of or like Elysium; happy; blissful; delightful.

**E·ly·si·um** (i lizh′ē əm *or* i liz′ē əm) ***n.*** **1** the place in Greek myths where good people went after death. **2** any place or condition of complete happiness.

**′em** (əm) ***pron.*** them: *used only in everyday talk.*

**em-** *the same as the prefix* **en-**: *used before* p, b, *or* m, *as in* empower *or* embrace.

**e·ma·ci·ate** (i mā′shē āt) ***v.*** to make very thin; make lose much weight [The cattle were *emaciated* after the long drought.] *See the picture.* —**e·ma′ci·at·ed, e·ma′ci·at·ing —e·ma′ci·a′tion *n.***

**em·a·nate** (em′ə nāt) ***v.*** to come out; proceed; issue [A delicious smell *emanated* from the kitchen. The order *emanated* from headquarters.] —**em′a·nat·ed, em′a·nat·ing —em′a·na′tion *n.***

**e·man·ci·pate** (i man′sə pāt) ***v.*** to set free from slavery or strict control [Lincoln *emancipated* the black slaves.] —**e·man′ci·pat·ed, e·man′ci·pat·ing —e·man′ci·pa′tion *n.* —e·man′ci·pa·tor *n.***

> **Emancipate** comes from a Latin word meaning "to take away the hand." In ancient Rome, the buyer of a slave would put a hand on that person to show that he was the master. So when a slave is emancipated, it is as though the owner has taken away his hand.

☆**Emancipation Proclamation** a proclamation by President Lincoln stating that from January 1, 1863, all slaves in territory still at war with the Union would be free.

**e·mas·cu·late** (i mas′kyə lāt) ***v.*** **1** to remove the male sex glands of. **2** to take away the force or strength of [The law against gambling was *emasculated* by lowering the fine.] —**e·mas′cu·lat·ed, e·mas′cu·lat·ing —e·mas′cu·la′tor *n.***

**em·balm** (im bäm′) ***v.*** to treat a dead body with chemicals to keep it from decaying for a while.

**em·bank·ment** (im baŋk′mənt) ***n.*** a long mound or wall of earth, stone, etc. used to keep back water, hold up a roadway, etc. *See the picture.*

**em·bar·go** (im bär′gō) ***n.*** **1** a government order that forbids certain ships to leave or enter its ports. **2** any government order that stops or hinders trade. —*pl.* **em·bar′goes** ◆***v.*** to put an embargo upon. —**em·bar′goed, em·bar′go·ing**

**em·bark** (im bärk′) ***v.*** **1** to go on board a ship or put on a ship [We *embarked* at San Francisco for Japan.] **2** to start out; begin [to *embark* on an adventure]. —**em·bar·ka·tion** (em′bär kā′shən) ***n.***

**em·bar·rass** (im ber′əs) ***v.*** **1** to make feel uncomfortable or self-conscious [There are some people who feel *embarrassed* when someone pays them a compliment.] **2** to cause to be in trouble; hinder; worry [To be in debt is to be financially *embarrassed.*] —**em·bar′rass·ment *n.***

> SYNONYMS: To be **embarrassed** is to feel nervous and uneasy when others are aware of one's errors or lack of ability [I was *embarrassed* when my mistake in addition was pointed out.] To be **humiliated** is to lose dignity or self-respect when one is regarded with contempt [Jane was *humiliated* when Jim falsely accused her of lying.]

**em·bas·sy** (em′bə sē) ***n.*** **1** the building where an ambassador lives and works. **2** an ambassador together with the staff. **3** the work, duties, or mission of an ambassador. —*pl.* **em′bas·sies**

**em·bat·tled** (im bat′'ld) ***adj.*** in position for battle; ready to fight [The invaders attacked the *embattled* town.]

**em·bed** (im bed′) ***v.*** **1** to set firmly in some substance [to *embed* tiles in cement]. **2** to fix firmly in the mind [The first landing on the moon is an event that is *embedded* in the memories of millions.] —**em·bed′ded, em·bed′ding**

**em·bel·lish** (im bel′ish) ***v.*** to decorate or improve by adding something [to *embellish* a talk with details]. —**em·bel′lish·ment *n.***

**em·ber** (em′bər) ***n*** a piece of coal, wood, etc. still glowing in the ashes of a fire.

**em·bez·zle** (im bez′'l) ***v.*** to steal money that has been placed in one's care [The bank teller *embezzled* $20,000.] —**em·bez′zled, em·bez′zling —em·bez′zle·ment *n.* —em·bez′zler *n.*** 

**em·bit·ter** (im bit′ər) ***v.*** to make bitter; make feel angry or hurt [He was *embittered* by her remark.]

**em·bla·zon** (im blā′z'n) ***v.*** **1** to decorate with bright colors or in a rich, showy way [The bandstand was *emblazoned* with bunting.] **2** to mark with an emblem [The shield was *emblazoned* with a golden lion.]

**em·blem** (em′bləm) ***n.*** a thing that stands for another thing or for an idea; sign or symbol [The bald eagle is the *emblem* of the U.S.]

**em·blem·at·ic** (em′blə mat′ik) ***adj.*** of or serving as an emblem; symbolic [The color green is *emblematic* of Irish nationalism.]

**em·bod·y** (im bäd′ē) ***v.*** **1** to put an idea or quality into a definite form that can be seen; make real in any way [The Constitution *embodies* Jefferson's ideas on government.] **2** to bring together into a single thing or system [The laws of a State are *embodied* in its legal code.] **3** to make part of some thing or system; incorporate [The latest findings are *embodied* in the scientist's new book.] —**em·bod′ied, em·bod′y·ing —em·bod′i·ment *n.***

**em·bold·en** (im bōl′d'n) ***v.*** to make bold or bolder; give courage to.

| | | | | | | | |
|---|---|---|---|---|---|---|---|
| **a** | fat | **ir** | here | **ou** | out | **zh** | leisure |
| **ā** | ape | **ī** | bite, fire | **u** | up | **ŋ** | ring |
| **ä** | car, lot | **ō** | go | **ur** | fur | | a *in* ago |
| **e** | ten | **ô** | law, horn | **ch** | chin | | e *in* agent |
| **er** | care | **oi** | oil | **sh** | she | **ə** = | i *in* unity |
| **ē** | even | **oo** | look | **th** | thin | | o *in* collect |
| **i** | hit | **o͞o** | tool | ***th*** | then | | u *in* focus |

e

**em·bo·lism** (em′bə liz'm) ***n.*** the stopping up of a vein or artery, as by a blood clot.

**em·boss** (im bôs′) ***v.*** **1** to decorate with patterns that stand out from the surface [wallpaper *embossed* with a leaf design]. **2** to make stand out from the surface [Lincoln's head is *embossed* on the penny.]

**em·brace** (im brās′) ***v.*** **1** to hold closely in one's arms in showing fondness or love; hug [The groom *embraced* his bride.] **2** to hug each other [The bride and groom *embraced.*] **3** to take up in an eager or serious way [to *embrace* a religion, an idea, or a career]. **4** to surround or enclose [a coral isle *embraced* by the sea]. **5** to include or contain [Biology *embraces* both botany and zoology.] —**em·braced′, em·brac′ing** ◆***n.*** the act of embracing; hug.

**em·broi·der** (im broi′dər) ***v.*** **1** to make fancy designs on cloth with needlework [to *embroider* letters on a sampler]. **2** to add imaginary details to a story to make it more interesting.

**em·broi·der·y** (im broi′dər ē) ***n.*** **1** the art or work of embroidering. **2** an embroidered decoration. *See the picture.* —*pl.* **em·broi′der·ies**

**em·broil** (im broil′) ***v.*** to draw into a quarrel or fight; involve [I said nothing as I didn't want to become *embroiled* in their argument.]

**em·bry·o** (em′brē ō) ***n.*** **1** an animal in the first stages of its growth, while it is in the egg or in the uterus. *See the picture.* **2** the part of a seed from
240 which a plant develops. **3** an early stage of development [Our plans are still in *embryo.*] —*pl.* **em′bry·os**

**em·bry·on·ic** (em′brē än′ik) ***adj.*** **1** of an embryo. **2** not fully developed [*embryonic* ideas].

☆**em·cee** (em′sē′) ***n.*** a master of ceremonies. ◆***v.*** to act as a master of ceremonies. *This word is used only in everyday talk.*

> **Emcee** is just a way of writing the pronunciation of "M.C.," the initials of the phrase "Master of Ceremonies."

**e·mend** (i mend′) ***v.*** to correct an error or fault, as in a piece of writing. —**e·men·da·tion** (ē′mən dā′shən) ***n.***

**em·er·ald** (em′ər əld) ***n.*** **1** a clear, bright-green jewel. **2** bright green.

**e·merge** (i murj′) ***v.*** **1** to come out so as to be seen; appear [A bear *emerged* from the woods.] **2** to become known [Slowly the true story *emerged.*] **3** to develop as something new or improved [A strong breed *emerged.*] —**e·merged′, e·merg′ing** —**e·mer·gence** (i mur′jəns) ***n.***

**e·mer·gen·cy** (i mur′jən sē) ***n.*** a sudden happening that needs action or attention right away [the *emergency* created by a hurricane]. —*pl.* **e·mer′gen·cies**

**e·mer·i·tus** (i mer′ə təs) ***adj.*** retired from work, but keeping one's rank or title as a special honor [a professor *emeritus*].

**Em·er·son** (em′ər sən), **Ralph Wal·do** (wôl′dō) 1803–1882; a U.S. writer and philosopher.

**em·er·y** (em′ər ē) ***n.*** a dark, very hard mineral, crushed to a powder which is used on grinding wheels, polishing cloths, small strips of cardboard for filing the nails, etc.

**e·met·ic** (i met′ik) ***adj.*** that makes one vomit. ◆***n.*** a medicine that makes one vomit.

**em·i·grant** (em′ə grənt) ***n.*** one who emigrates.

**em·i·grate** (em′ə grāt) ***v.*** to leave one country or region to settle in another [Many people have *emigrated* from Ireland to the U.S.] *See* SYNONYMS *at* **migrate.** —**em′i·grat·ed, em′i·grat·ing** —**em′i·gra′tion *n.***

**é·mi·gré** or **e·mi·gré** (em′ə grā *or* ā mə grā′) ***n.*** an emigrant, especially one forced to leave a country for political reasons.

**em·i·nence** (em′ə nəns) ***n.*** **1** a place above most others in rank, worth, fame, etc.; greatness [Emily Dickinson's *eminence* in poetry.] **2** a high place, as a hill. **3 Eminence,** a title of honor for a cardinal in the Roman Catholic Church.

**em·i·nent** (em′ə nənt) ***adj.*** standing above most others in rank, worth, fame, etc.; very famous [an *eminent* scientist]. —**em′i·nent·ly *adv.***

**e·mir** (i mir′) ***n.*** in certain Muslim countries, a ruler, prince, or commander.

**em·is·sar·y** (em′ə ser′ē) ***n.*** a person sent on a special mission, often in secret. —*pl.* **em′is·sar′ies**

**e·mis·sion** (i mish′ən) ***n.*** **1** the act of emitting. **2** something emitted; discharge.

**e·mit** (i mit′) ***v.*** to send out or give forth [The owl *emitted* a screech. A volcano *emits* lava. Plutonium *emits* harmful rays.] —**e·mit′ted, e·mit′ting**

**e·mo·tion** (i mō′shən) ***n.*** **1** strong feeling [a voice choked with *emotion*]. **2** any particular feeling, such as love, hate, joy, or fear.

> SYNONYMS: **Emotion** is used of any of the ways in which one reacts to something without careful thinking [My *emotion* changed from pity to disgust.] **Feeling** is a less formal word meaning the same thing, but can also suggest a sharing of another's emotion [The actors played the scene with deep *feeling.*] **Passion** refers to a very strong emotion, especially love or anger.

**e·mo·tion·al** (i mō′shən 'l) ***adj.*** **1** having to do with the emotions or feelings [*emotional* problems]. **2** full of emotion or strong feeling [an *emotional* look; an *emotional* speech]. **3** having feelings that are easily stirred; quick to cry, be angry, etc. [an *emotional* person]. —**e·mo′tion·al·ly *adv.***

**em·pa·thy** (em′pə thē) ***n.*** the ability to share another's emotions or feelings.

**em·per·or** (em′pər ər) ***n.*** a man who rules an empire.

**em·pha·sis** (em′fə sis) ***n.*** **1** special attention given to something so as to make it stand out; importance; stress [That college puts too much *emphasis* on sports.] **2** special force given to certain syllables or words in speaking. —*pl.* **em·pha·ses** (em′fə sēz)

**em·pha·size** (em′fə sīz) ***v.*** to give special force or attention to; stress [I want to *emphasize* the importance of honesty.] —**em′pha·sized, em′pha·siz·ing**

**em·phat·ic** (im fat′ik) ***adj.*** **1** said or done with emphasis, or special force [She agreed with an *emphatic* nod.] **2** without doubt; definite [an *emphatic* defeat]. —**em·phat′i·cal·ly *adv.***

**em·phy·se·ma** (em′fə sē′mə) ***n.*** a disease of the lungs that makes it hard for a person to breathe.

**em·pire** (em′pīr) ***n.*** **1** a group of countries or territories under the control of one government or ruler [Much of Europe was once a part of the Roman *Empire.*] **2** any government whose ruler has the title of emperor or empress. **3** a large business or group of businesses controlled by one person, family, or group.

**em·pir·i·cal** (em pir′i k'l) ***adj.*** based mainly on practical experience or on experiment and not on theory [*empirical* knowledge].

**em·place·ment** (im plās′mənt) ***n.*** the platform from which a heavy gun or cannon is fired.

**em·ploy** (im ploi′) ***v.*** **1** to hire and pay for the work or services of; have working for one [That company *employs* 50 people.] **2** to use [The baby *employed* clever tricks to get attention.] **3** to keep busy; occupy [Idle people need something to *employ* their minds.] ◆***n.*** the condition of being employed [Phil is no longer in our *employ*.]

**em·ploy·ee** or **em·ploy·e** (im ploi′ē *or* em′ploi ē′) ***n.*** a person who works for another in return for pay.

**em·ploy·er** (im ploi′ər) ***n.*** a person or company for whom other people work for pay.

**em·ploy·ment** (im ploi′mənt) ***n.*** **1** the condition of being employed. **2** one's work, trade, or profession. **3** the number or percentage of persons employed.

**em·po·ri·um** (em pôr′ē əm) ***n.*** a large store that has many different things for sale: *an old-fashioned word.* —*pl.* **em·po′ri·ums** or **em·po·ri·a** (em pôr′ē ə)

**em·pow·er** (im pou′ər) ***v.*** to give certain power or rights to; authorize [The warrant *empowered* the police to search the house.]

**em·press** (em′pris) ***n.*** **1** a woman who rules an empire. **2** the wife of an emperor.

**emp·ty** (emp′tē) ***adj.*** **1** having nothing or no one in it; not occupied; vacant [an *empty* jar; an *empty* house]. **2** without real meaning or worth; vain [*empty* pleasures; *empty* promises]. **3** hungry: *used only in everyday talk.* —**emp′ti·er, emp′ti·est** ◆***v.*** **1** to make or become empty [The auditorium was *emptied* in ten minutes.] **2** to take out or pour out [*Empty* the dirty water in the sink.] **3** to flow out; discharge [The Amazon *empties* into the Atlantic.] —**emp′tied, emp′ty·ing** ◆***n.*** an empty bottle, box, truck, freight car, etc. —*pl.* **emp′ties** —**emp′ti·ly** ***adv.*** —**emp′ti·ness** ***n.***

**emp·ty-hand·ed** (emp′tē han′did) ***adj.*** bringing or carrying away nothing [Don't go to the party *empty-handed.*]

**em·py·re·an** (em′pī rē′ən *or* em pir′ē ən) ***n.*** **1** the highest heaven. **2** the sky.

**e·mu** (ē′myo͞o) ***n.*** a large Australian bird like the ostrich but smaller. Emus cannot fly. *See the picture.*

**em·u·late** (em′yə lāt) ***v.*** to try to be as good as or better than [He will do well if he *emulates* his parents.] —**em′u·lat·ed, em′u·lat·ing** —**em′u·la′tion** ***n.***

**em·u·lous** (em′yə ləs) ***adj.*** wanting to be as good as or better than another.

**e·mul·si·fy** (i mul′sə fī) ***v.*** to form into an emulsion. —**e·mul′si·fied, e·mul′si·fy·ing**

**e·mul·sion** (i mul′shən) ***n.*** a mixture of liquids, as oil and water, in which very fine drops of one stay evenly scattered throughout the other [Homogenized milk is an *emulsion.*]

**en-** *a prefix meaning:* **1** to put into or on [*Enthrone* means to put on a throne.] **2** to make [*Enrich* means to make rich.] **3** in or into [*Entangle* means to tangle in.] *En-* is often added to a word to make it stronger in meaning [*Enliven* means to liven very much.] Many words beginning with *en-* are also spelled *in-*.

emu 1.5 m (5 ft.) high

embryo of a rabbit

**-en** (ən) *a suffix meaning:* **1** to make or become [*Darken* means to make or become dark.] **2** to get or give [*Strengthen* means to get or give strength.] **3** made of [*Woolen* means made of wool.] The suffix *-en* is also used to form the past participle of some verbs (as *fallen)* and the plural of some nouns (as *oxen).*

**en·a·ble** (in ā′b'l) ***v.*** to make able; give the means or power to [A loan *enabled* Lou to go to college.] —**en·a′bled, en·a′bling**

**en·act** (in akt′) ***v.*** **1** to make into a law [Congress *enacted* a bill raising tariffs.] **2** to act out, as in a play [to *enact* the part of a doctor].



**en·act·ment** (in akt′mənt) ***n.*** **1** the act of making a law. **2** a law.

**en·am·el** (i nam′'l) ***n.*** **1** a glassy substance baked onto metal, etc., as in pans, sinks, stoves, or jewelry, to form a coating that protects or decorates. **2** the hard, glossy coating of the teeth. **3** a paint that leaves a hard, glossy surface when it dries. ◆***v.*** to coat or decorate with enamel. —**en·am′eled** or **en·am′elled, en·am′el·ing** or **en·am′el·ling**

**en·am·or** (in am′ər) ***v.*** to fill with love; charm; captivate [He is much *enamored* of her.]

**en·camp** (in kamp′) ***v.*** to set up a camp [The army *encamped* in the valley.] —**en·camp′ment** ***n.***

**en·cap·su·late** (in kap′sə lāt *or* in kap′syo͞o lāt) ***v.*** to enclose in a capsule or in something like a capsule. —**en·cap′su·lat·ed, en·cap′su·lat·ing**

**en·case** (in kās′) ***v.*** **1** to put into a case or cases. **2** to cover completely [a turtle *encased* in its shell]. —**en·cased′, en·cas′ing** —**en·case′ment** ***n.***

**-ence** (əns) *a suffix meaning* act, condition, *or* quality [*Indulgence* is the act of indulging. *Permanence* is the condition or quality of being permanent.]

**en·ceph·a·li·tis** (en sef′ə līt′is) ***n.*** a disease in which the brain becomes inflamed.

**en·chant** (in chant′) ***v.*** **1** to cast a magic spell over; bewitch. **2** to delight; charm greatly [I'm *enchanted*

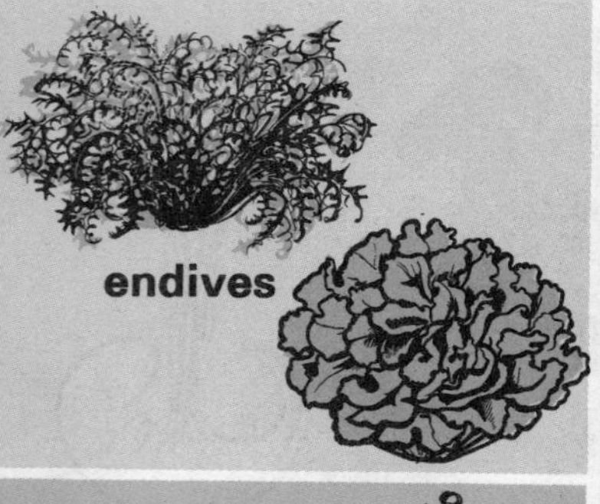

endives

engaged gears

enclosure

encumbered hiker

by the rose garden.] —**en·chant'er** *n.* —**en·chant'ing** *adj.*

**en·chant·ment** (in chant'mənt) *n.* **1** the act of enchanting, as by a magic spell. **2** something that charms or delights greatly. **3** great delight or pleasure.



**en·chant·ress** (in chant'ris) *n.* **1** a woman who casts magic spells; sorceress; witch. **2** a fascinating or charming woman.

☆**en·chi·la·da** (en'chə lä'də) *n.* a tortilla rolled with meat inside and served with a chili sauce.

**en·cir·cle** (in sʉr'k'l) *v.* **1** to form a circle around; surround [Hills *encircle* the valley.] **2** to move in a circle around [The moon *encircles* the earth.] —**en·cir'cled, en·cir'cling** —**en·cir'cle·ment** *n.*

**en·close** (in klōz') *v.* **1** to shut in all around; surround [High walls *enclose* the prison.] **2** to put inside a container, often along with something else [Please *enclose* the check in the envelope with your letter.] —**en·closed', en·clos'ing**

**en·clo·sure** (in klō'zhər) *n.* **1** the act of enclosing. **2** a space that is enclosed [The dog is kept in an *enclosure.*] *See the picture.* **3** anything put into an envelope along with a letter. **4** something that encloses, as a fence.

**en·code** (in kōd') *v.* to put a message into a code. —**en·cod'ed, en·cod'ing** —**en·cod'er** *n.*

**en·com·pass** (in kum'pəs) *v.* **1** to surround on all sides; enclose or encircle. **2** to have in it; contain or include [A dictionary *encompasses* much information.]

**en·core** (äŋ'kôr) *interj.* again! once more!: a call by an audience for a performer to repeat a song, piece, etc. or give an extra one. ◆*n.* a song, etc. added in answer to applause by an audience.

**en·coun·ter** (in koun'tər) *v.* **1** to meet by chance or unexpectedly [I *encountered* an old friend on my vacation.] **2** to come up against [to *encounter* trouble]. **3** to meet in battle. ◆*n.* **1** a meeting by chance. **2** a battle or fight.

**en·cour·age** (in kʉr'ij) *v.* **1** to give courage or hope to; make feel more confident [Praise *encouraged* her to go on with the project.] **2** to give help to; aid; promote [Warm weather *encourages* the sale of cold drinks.] —**en·cour'aged, en·cour'ag·ing** —**en·cour'age·ment** *n.*

**en·croach** (in krōch') *v.* **1** to go beyond the usual limits [The lake has *encroached* upon the shoreline.] **2** to push into the property or rights of another; trespass, especially in a gradual or sneaking way [Over the years, campers had been *encroaching* on the farmer's land.] —**en·croach'ment** *n.*

**en·crust** (in krust') *v. another spelling of* **incrust.** —**en'crus·ta'tion** *n.*

**en·cum·ber** (in kum'bər) *v.* to load down or burden so as to make it hard to move or act [a hiker *encumbered* with a heavy backpack; a business *encumbered* with debt]. *See the picture.* —**en·cum'brance** *n.*

**-en·cy** (ən sē) *a suffix, like* **-ence,** *meaning* act, condition, *or* quality [*Efficiency* is the quality or condition of being efficient.]

**ency.** or **encycl.** *abbreviations for* **encyclopedia.**

**en·cyc·li·cal** (in sik'li k'l) *n.* a letter from the Pope to the bishops of the Roman Catholic Church.

**en·cy·clo·pe·di·a** or **en·cy·clo·pae·di·a** (in sī'klə pē'dē ə) *n.* a book or set of books that gives information on all branches of knowledge or, sometimes, on just one branch of knowledge. It is made up of articles usually in alphabetical order.

The Greek word from which we get **encyclopedia** is made up of three words, *en* meaning "in," *kyklos* meaning "a circle," and *paidea* meaning "education." An **encyclopedia** is, therefore, a work that deals with all subjects that lie within the circle of education.

**en·cy·clo·pe·dic** or **en·cy·clo·pae·dic** (in sī'klə pē'dik) *adj.* of or like an encyclopedia; having information on many subjects.

**end** (end) *n.* **1** the last part; finish; conclusion [the *end* of the day; the *end* of a story]. **2** the place where something begins or stops; farthest part [the west *end* of town; the *end* of a rope]. **3** death or destruction [He met his *end* in battle.] **4** what one hopes to get or do; aim; goal [to achieve one's *ends*]. **5** a piece left over; remnant [a sale of odds and *ends*]. ☆**6** the player at either end of the line in football. ◆*v.* to bring or come to an end; finish; stop [When will the meeting *end?*] ◆*adj.* at the end; final [an *end* product]. —**make ends meet,** to just manage to live on one's income. —**on end, 1** standing straight up. **2** with no interruption [They traveled for days *on end.*] —**to end,** that is the best, greatest, etc. of [a trip *to end* all trips].

**en·dan·ger** (in dān'jər) *v.* to put in danger or peril [to *endanger* one's life].

**en·dear** (in dir') *v.* to make beloved or well liked [Her smile *endeared* her to us all.]

**en·dear·ment** (in dir'mənt) *n.* **1** warm liking; affection. **2** a word or act showing love or affection.

**en·deav·or** (in dev'ər) *v.* to try hard; make an effort; strive. ◆*n.* an effort or try.

**en·dem·ic** (en dem'ik) *adj.* commonly found in a particular place or region [an *endemic* disease].

**end·ing** (en'diŋ) *n.* the last part; end; finish [The story had a happy *ending.*]

**en·dive** (en'dīv *or* än'dēv) *n.* a plant with ragged, curly leaves that are used in salads. *See the picture.*

**end·less** (end′lis) ***adj.*** **1** having no end; going on forever [*endless* space]. **2** lasting too long; seeming never to end [their *endless* chatter]. **3** with the ends joined to form a closed ring [an *endless* belt]. —**end′less·ly** ***adv.***

**en·do·crine gland** (en′də krin) a gland that produces a secretion which goes straight into the blood or lymph. It is then carried to some part of the body where it has its effect [The thyroid, adrenal, and pituitary glands are *endocrine glands.*]

**en·dorse** (in dôrs′) ***v.*** **1** to sign one's name on the back of a check, note, etc., in order to cash it or pass it on to another person. **2** to give support to; approve of; favor [The newspaper *endorsed* our candidate.] —**en·dorsed′, en·dors′ing** —**en·dorse′ment** ***n.*** —**en·dors′er** ***n.***

**en·dow** (in dou′) ***v.*** **1** to provide with some quality or thing [a person *endowed* with musical talent; a land *endowed* with natural resources]. **2** to provide a gift of money to a college, hospital, museum, etc., that will bring a regular income to help support it. —**en·dow′ment** ***n.***

**en·dur·ance** (in door′əns *or* in dyoor′əns) ***n.*** the ability to hold up or last, especially under strain or suffering [Boxing takes *endurance.*] *See* SYNONYMS *at* **patience.**

**en·dure** (in door′ *or* in dyoor′) ***v.*** **1** to hold up under pain, weariness, etc.; put up with; bear; stand [to *endure* torture; to *endure* insults]. **2** to go on for a long time; last; remain [The story of Cinderella has *endured* for ages.] —**en·dured′, en·dur′ing** —**en·dur′a·ble** ***adj.***

**end·ways** (end′wāz) ***adv.*** **1** standing on end; upright. **2** with the end forward [Bring the desk in *endways.*] **3** with the ends meeting; end to end. *Another form of the word is* **end·wise** (end′wīz).

**en·e·ma** (en′ə mə) ***n.*** a method of making the bowels move by bringing water or other liquid into the colon through a tube in the rectum.

**en·e·my** (en′ə mē) ***n.*** **1** a person, group, or country that hates another or fights against another; foe. **2** one who hates or fights against an idea, cause, conditions, etc. [John Brown was an *enemy* of slavery.] **3** anything that harms [She is her own worst *enemy.*] —*pl.* **en′e·mies**

**en·er·get·ic** (en′ər jet′ik) ***adj.*** full of energy; active or ready to act; forceful [an *energetic* athlete]. *See* SYNONYMS *at* **active.** —**en′er·get′i·cal·ly** ***adv.***

**en·er·gize** (en′ər jīz) ***v.*** to put energy into; make active [The fresh air *energized* us.] —**en′er·gized, en′er·giz·ing**

**en·er·gy** (en′ər jē) ***n.*** **1** power to work or be active; force; vigor [Eleanor Roosevelt was a woman of great *energy.*] **2** the power of certain forces in nature to do work [Electricity and heat are forms of *energy.*] —*pl.* **en′er·gies**

SYNONYMS: **Energy** refers to power that is waiting and can be used [nuclear *energy*]. **Strength** suggests the ability to act upon something, or to hold out or last [Do you have enough *strength* to lift this box? The cables for the bridge have great *strength.*] **Power** is a more general word used to mean the ability to do something either in a physical way or with the mind [the *power* of the press; water *power*].

**en·er·vate** (en′ər vāt) ***v.*** to take away the strength or energy of; weaken [Lack of exercise has *enervated* me.] —**en′er·vat·ed, en′er·vat·ing** —**en′er·va′tion** ***n.***

**en·fee·ble** (in fē′b′l) ***v.*** to make feeble. —**en·fee′bled, en·fee′bling**

**en·fold** (in fōld′) ***v.*** **1** to wrap up; cover with folds of something [*enfolded* in layers of cloth]. **2** to hold closely; embrace [He *enfolded* the baby in his arms.]

**en·force** (in fôrs′) ***v.*** **1** to force people to pay attention to; make people obey [to *enforce* traffic laws]. **2** to bring about by using force or being strict [He is unable to *enforce* his views on others.] —**en·forced′, en·forc′ing** —**en·force′ment** ***n.***

**en·fran·chise** (in fran′chīz) ***v.*** **1** to free, as from slavery. **2** to give the right to vote to [Women in the U.S. were *enfranchised* in 1920.] —**en·fran′chised, en·fran′chis·ing** —**en·fran′chise·ment** ***n.***

**Eng.** *abbreviation for* **England** *or* **English.**

**en·gage** (in gāj′) ***v.*** **1** to promise to marry [Harry is *engaged* to Grace.] **2** to promise or undertake to do something [She *engaged* to tutor the child after school.] **3** to get the right to use something or the services of someone; hire [to *engage* a hotel room; to *engage* a lawyer]. **4** to take part or be active [I have no time to *engage* in dramatics.] **5** to keep busy or use up [Tennis *engages* all her spare time.] **6** to draw into; involve [She *engaged* him in conversation.] **7** to get and hold [I'm trying to *engage* Lou's attention.] **8** to meet in battle with [to *engage* enemy forces]. **9** to fit or lock together, as the teeth of gears. *See the picture.* —**en·gaged′, en·gag′ing** 243

**en·gage·ment** (in gāj′mənt) ***n.*** **1** a promise to marry. **2** an appointment to meet someone or go somewhere [Sorry, I have an earlier *engagement* for lunch.] **3** the condition of being hired for some job, especially in show business. **4** a battle. **5** the act of engaging.

**en·gag·ing** (in gāj′iŋ) ***adj.*** charming or attractive [an *engaging* smile].

**en·gen·der** (in jen′dər) ***v.*** to bring into being; produce [Friction *engenders* heat.]

**en·gine** (en′jən) ***n.*** **1** a machine that uses energy of some kind to create motion and do work [An automobile *engine* uses the energy of hot gases formed by exploding gasoline.] **2** a railroad locomotive. **3** any machine or mechanical device [*engines* of warfare].

**en·gi·neer** (en′jə nir′) ***n.*** **1** a person who is trained in some branch of engineering. **2** a person who runs an engine, as the driver of a railroad locomotive. **3** a soldier whose special work is the building or wrecking of roads, bridges, etc. ◆***v.*** ☆**1** to plan, direct, or build as an engineer. ☆**2** to plan or manage skillfully [to *engineer* a drive to raise money for charity].

**en·gi·neer·ing** (en′jə nir′iŋ) ***n.*** the science or work of planning and building machinery, roads, bridges,

| | | | | | | | |
|---|---|---|---|---|---|---|---|
| **a** | fat | **ir** | here | **ou** | out | **zh** | leisure |
| **ā** | ape | **ī** | bite, fire | **u** | up | **ŋ** | ring |
| **ä** | car, lot | **ō** | go | **ʉr** | fur | | a *in* ago |
| **e** | ten | **ô** | law, horn | **ch** | chin | | e *in* agent |
| **er** | care | **oi** | oil | **sh** | she | **ə =** | i *in* unity |
| **ē** | even | **oo** | look | **th** | thin | | o *in* collect |
| **i** | hit | **ōō** | tool | ***th*** | then | | u *in* focus |

buildings, etc. There are many different branches of engineering, as civil, electrical, mechanical, and chemical engineering.

**Eng·land** (iŋ′glənd) the largest part of Great Britain, south of Scotland. It is a division of the United Kingdom.

**Eng·lish** (iŋ′glish) ***adj.*** of England, its people, language, etc. **◆*n.*** **1** the language spoken in England, the U.S., Canada, Australia, New Zealand, Liberia, etc. **2** a course in school for studying the English language or English literature. ☆**3** *sometimes* **english,** a spinning motion given to a ball, as in billiards or bowling. —**the English,** the people of England.

**English Channel** the part of the Atlantic Ocean between England and France.

**English horn** a woodwind instrument with a double reed, that is like an oboe but a little larger and lower in pitch. *See the picture.*

**Eng·lish·man** (iŋ′glish mən) ***n.*** a person, especially a man, born or living in England. —*pl.* **Eng′lish·men**

☆**English muffin** a flat, round roll, often baked on a griddle. It is usually split and toasted for serving.

**Eng·lish·wom·an** (iŋ′glish wo͝om′ən) ***n.*** a woman born or living in England. —*pl.* **Eng′lish·wom′en**

**en·gorge** (in gôrj′) ***v.*** **1** to eat greedily. **2** to cause a blood vessel or body tissue to become filled up with too much blood or other fluid. —**en·gorged′, en·gorg′ing**

244 **en·grave** (in grāv′) ***v.*** **1** to carve or etch letters, designs, etc. on [a date *engraved* on a building]. **2** to cut or etch a picture, lettering, etc. into a metal plate, wooden block, etc. to be used for printing; also, to print from such a plate, block, etc. [an *engraved* invitation]. **3** to fix in the mind [That song is *engraved* in my memory.] —**en·graved′, en·grav′ing —en·grav′er *n.***

**en·grav·ing** (in grāv′iŋ) ***n.*** **1** the art or work of making metal plates, wooden blocks, etc. for printing. **2** a picture, design, etc. printed from such a plate or block.

**en·gross** (in grōs′) ***v.*** to interest so much that other things are forgotten or not noticed; absorb [to be *engrossed* in a fascinating book].

**en·gulf** (in gulf′) ***v.*** to cover completely; swallow up [A huge wave *engulfed* the swimmer.]

**en·hance** (in hans′) ***v.*** to make better, greater, etc. [Adding a garage *enhanced* the value of the house.] —**en·hanced′, en·hanc′ing**

**e·nig·ma** (ə nig′mə) ***n.*** anyone or anything that is hard to understand or explain; puzzle.

> **Enigma** comes from a Greek word meaning "to speak in riddles." It is hard to understand someone who speaks in riddles.

**en·ig·mat·ic** (en′ig mat′ik) ***adj.*** of or like an enigma; puzzling; mysterious [an *enigmatic* smile]. *See the picture. Also* **en′ig·mat′i·cal. —en′ig·mat′i·cal·ly *adv.***

**en·join** (in join′) ***v.*** **1** to order or command [We were *enjoined* to be quiet in the library.] **2** to forbid or prohibit [The court *enjoined* the union from picketing.]

**en·joy** (in joi′) ***v.*** **1** to get joy or pleasure from [We *enjoyed* the baseball game.] **2** to have the use of or have as a benefit [The book *enjoyed* large sales.] —**enjoy oneself,** to have a good time; have fun. —**en·joy′ment *n.***

**en·joy·a·ble** (in joi′ə b'l) ***adj.*** giving joy or pleasure; delightful [What an *enjoyable* concert!]

**en·large** (in lärj′) ***v.*** to make or become larger [She has greatly *enlarged* her stamp collection.] —**en·larged′, en·larg′ing —enlarge on** or **enlarge upon,** to give more details about.

**en·large·ment** (in lärj′mənt) ***n.*** **1** a making or becoming larger. **2** something that has been made larger; especially, an enlarged copy of a photograph.

**en·light·en** (in līt′'n) ***v.*** to get someone to have knowledge or know the truth; get rid of ignorance or false beliefs; inform. —**en·light′en·ment *n.***

**en·list** (in list′) ***v.*** **1** to join or get someone to join; especially, to join some branch of the armed forces [She *enlisted* in the navy. This office *enlisted* ten new recruits.] **2** to get the support of [Try to *enlist* your parents' help.] —**en·list′ment *n.***

**enlisted man** a man in the armed forces who is not a commissioned officer or a warrant officer.

**enlisted woman** a woman in the armed forces who is not a commissioned officer or a warrant officer.

**en·liv·en** (in lī′v'n) ***v.*** to make lively, interesting, bright, etc.; liven up [A magician *enlivened* the party by doing magic tricks.]

**en masse** (en mas′ *or* än mas′) all together, as a group [The players left the field *en masse.*]

**en·mesh** (en mesh′) ***v.*** to tangle up, as if in the meshes of a net [*enmeshed* in troubles].

**en·mi·ty** (en′mə tē) ***n.*** the bitter feeling that an enemy or enemies have; hatred. —*pl.* **en′mi·ties**

**en·no·ble** (i nō′b'l) ***v.*** to make noble; make a person better or finer; uplift. —**en·no′bled, en·no′bling**

**en·nui** (än′wē) ***n.*** a feeling of being very bored and tired of everything.

**e·nor·mi·ty** (i nôr′mə tē) ***n.*** **1** great wickedness [the *enormity* of a crime]. **2** a very wicked crime. —*pl.* **e·nor′mi·ties**

> At one time **enormity** was also used to mean "enormous size." Although some people still use it that way, it is now generally thought to be a careless or improper use.

**e·nor·mous** (i nôr′məs) ***adj.*** much larger than usual; huge [an *enormous* stadium]. —**e·nor′mous·ly *adv.*** —**e·nor′mous·ness *n.***

> SYNONYMS: Anything **enormous** goes far beyond the normal size or amount [*enormous* ears; *enormous* cost]. Anything **immense** is very large or much larger than usual, but still normal [the *immense* redwood trees]. Anything **huge** is immense and also has great bulk or mass [a *huge* building; a *huge* harvest].

**e·nough** (i nuf′) ***adj.*** as much or as many as needed or wanted; sufficient [There is *enough* food for all.] **◆*n.*** the amount needed or wanted [I have heard *enough* of that music.] **◆*adv.*** **1** as much as needed; to the right amount [Is your steak cooked *enough?*] **2** fully; quite [Oddly *enough,* she never asked me.]

**en·quire** (in kwīr′) ***v.*** *another spelling of* **inquire.** —**en·quired′, en·quir′ing**

**en·quir·y** (in kwīr′ē *or* in′kwə rē) ***n.*** *another spelling of* **inquiry.** —*pl.* **en·quir′ies**

**en·rage** (in rāj′) ***v.*** to make very angry; put into a rage; infuriate. —**en·raged′, en·rag′ing**

**en·rap·ture** (in rap′chər) ***v.*** to fill with great delight; enchant [They were *enraptured* by the sight of the garden.] —**en·rap′tured, en·rap′tur·ing**

**en·rich** (in rich′) ***v.*** to make richer in value, quality, etc. [Music *enriches* one's life. This bread is *enriched* with vitamins.] —**en·rich′ment *n.***

**en·roll** or **en·rol** (in rōl′) ***v.*** **1** to write one's name in a list, as in becoming a member; register [New students must *enroll* on Monday.] **2** to make someone a member [We want to *enroll* you in our swim club.] —**en·rolled′, en·roll′ing**

**en·roll·ment** or **en·rol·ment** (in rōl′mənt) ***n.*** **1** the act of enrolling. **2** the number of people enrolled.

**en route** (än ro͞ot′) on the way [The plane stops in Chicago *en route* to Los Angeles.]

**en·sconce** (in skäns′) ***v.*** to settle in a snug, safe, or hidden place [Our cat is *ensconced* in the easy chair.] —**en·sconced′, en·sconc′ing**

**en·sem·ble** (än säm′b'l) ***n.*** **1** all the parts taken as a whole; whole effect. **2** a complete costume; articles of clothing that match and are worn together [Blue shoes and gloves completed her *ensemble.*] **3** a small group of musicians playing or singing together [a string *ensemble*].

**en·shrine** (in shrīn′) ***v.*** **1** to put in a shrine [Washington's body is *enshrined* at Mount Vernon.] **2** to keep with love and respect; cherish [His memory is *enshrined* in our hearts.] —**en·shrined′, en·shrin′ing**

**en·shroud** (in shroud′) ***v.*** to cover so as to hide [towers *enshrouded* in fog].

**en·sign** (en′sīn) ***n.*** **1** a flag or banner, especially a national flag. ☆**2** (en′s'n) a U.S. Navy officer of the lowest rank.

**en·si·lage** (en′s'l ij) ***n.*** green or fresh fodder for cattle, etc., that is stored in a silo.

**en·slave** (in slāv′) ***v.*** **1** to make a slave of; put into slavery. **2** to keep complete control over, as though by force [She felt *enslaved* by housework.] —**en·slaved′, en·slav′ing —en·slave′ment *n.***

**en·snare** (in sner′) ***v.*** to catch in a snare or trap; trap. —**en·snared′, en·snar′ing**

**en·sue** (in so͞o′ *or* in syo͞o′) ***v.*** **1** to come after; follow [What *ensued* after I left the room?] **2** to happen as a result; result [the damage that *ensued* from the flood]. —**en·sued′, en·su′ing**

**en·sure** (in shoor′) ***v.*** **1** to make sure or certain [Good weather will *ensure* a large attendance.] **2** to make safe; protect [Seat belts help to *ensure* you against injury in a car accident.] *See also* **insure.** —**en·sured′, en·sur′ing**

**-ent** (ənt) *a suffix meaning:* **1** that is or acts a certain way [A *persistent* person is one who persists.] **2** a person or thing that [A *president* is a person who presides.]

**en·tail** (in tāl′) ***v.*** **1** to make necessary; require; involve [This project will *entail* much work.] **2** to leave property to a certain line of heirs, so that none of them may sell it or give it away. ◆***n.*** property entailed or the line of heirs to which it must go.

**en·tan·gle** (in tang′g'l) ***v.*** **1** to catch or trap in a tangle [Our fishing lines became *entangled.* Flies get *entangled* in a spider's web.] **2** to get mixed up, as in some trouble [They *entangled* him in a dishonest business deal.] —**en·tan′gled, en·tan′gling —en·tan′gle·ment *n.***

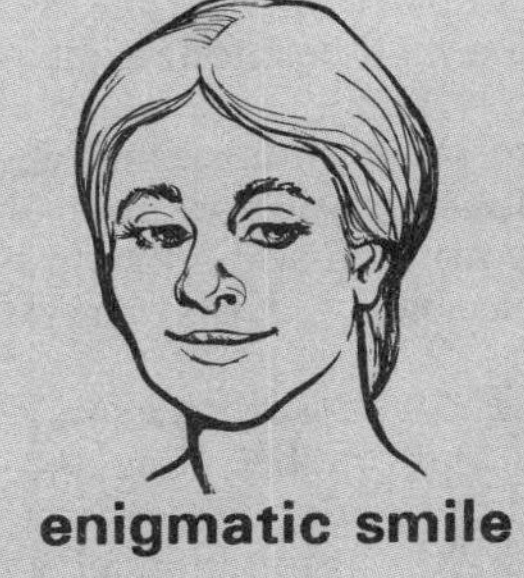

enigmatic smile

English horn

**en·tente** (än tänt′) ***n.*** **1** an understanding or agreement between nations or persons. **2** the nations or persons having such an understanding.

**en·ter** (en′tər) ***v.*** **1** to come or go in or into [to *enter* a room]. **2** to force a way into; pierce [The bullet *entered* his leg.] **3** to become a member of; join [to *enter* the navy]. **4** to start or begin [to *enter* a career]. **5** to cause to join or be let in [to *enter* a horse in a race]. **6** to write down in a list [Her name was *entered* on the honor roll.] **7** to put on record before a law court [He *entered* a plea of innocent.] —**enter into, 1** to take part in [to *enter into* a conversation]. **2** to form a part of [That possibility never *entered into* my planning.] —**enter on** or **enter upon,** to start; begin.

**en·ter·prise** (en′tər prīz) ***n.*** **1** any business or undertaking, especially one that takes daring and energy. **2** willingness to undertake new or risky projects [They succeeded because of their *enterprise.*]



**en·ter·pris·ing** (en′tər prī′zing) ***adj.*** willing to start or try new things; bold and active.

**en·ter·tain** (en tər tān′) ***v.*** **1** to keep interested and give pleasure to [She *entertained* us by playing the organ.] **2** to have as a guest; be a host to [to *entertain* friends at dinner]. **3** to have guests [It's expensive to *entertain* these days.] **4** to have in mind; consider [We *entertained* the idea of leaving.] —**en·ter·tain′ing *adj.***

SYNONYMS: We are **amused** when someone or something appeals to our sense of humor or makes us laugh [an *amusing* clown]. We are **entertained** by something planned to give us pleasure or joy by appealing to the senses or the mind [an *entertaining* play].

**en·ter·tain·er** (en′tər tān′ər) ***n.*** a person who entertains, especially one whose work is singing, dancing, etc., as on television or in nightclubs.

**en·ter·tain·ment** (en′tər tān′mənt) ***n.*** **1** the act of entertaining. **2** something that entertains, as a show or concert.

**en·thrall** or **en·thral** (in thrôl′) ***v.*** **1** to hold as if in a spell; fascinate; charm [We were *enthralled* by his exciting story.] **2** to make a slave of; enslave. —**en·thralled′, en·thrall′ing**

| | | | | | | | |
|---|---|---|---|---|---|---|---|
| **a** | fat | **ir** | here | **ou** | out | **zh** | leisure |
| **ā** | ape | **ī** | bite, fire | **u** | up | **ng** | ring |
| **ä** | car, lot | **ō** | go | **ur** | fur | | a *in* ago |
| **e** | ten | **ô** | law, horn | **ch** | chin | | e *in* agent |
| **er** | care | **oi** | oil | **sh** | she | **ə =** | i *in* unity |
| **ē** | even | **oo** | look | **th** | thin | | o *in* collect |
| **i** | hit | **o͞o** | tool | ***th*** | then | | u *in* focus |

**en·throne** (in thrōn′) **v.** **1** to place on a throne, as a king or queen. **2** to place in a high position; exalt. —**en·throned′, en·thron′ing**

☆**en·thuse** (in thōōz′) **v.** to show enthusiasm: *used only in everyday talk.* —**en·thused′, en·thus′ing**

**en·thu·si·asm** (in thōō′zē az′m) **n.** a strong liking or interest [an *enthusiasm* for baseball]. *See* SYNONYMS *at* **passion.**

**Enthusiasm** comes from a Greek word meaning "inspired by a god." Poets and prophets long ago were thought to be inspired by a god. The earliest meaning of *enthusiasm* was "the inspiration of a poet or prophet."

**en·thu·si·ast** (in thōō′zē ast) **n.** a person who is full of enthusiasm.

**en·thu·si·as·tic** (in thōō′zē as′tik) **adj.** full of enthusiasm; showing great interest or liking [an *enthusiastic* follower; *enthusiastic* applause]. —**en·thu′si·as′ti·cal·ly adv.**

**en·tice** (in tīs′) **v.** to tempt by offering something that is wanted [She *enticed* the bird to eat from her hand.] —**en·ticed′, en·tic′ing** —**en·tice′ment n.**

**en·tire** (in tīr′) **adj.** **1** including all the parts; whole; complete [I've read the *entire* book.] **2** not broken, not weakened, not lessened, etc. [We have his *entire* support.] —**en·tire′ly adv.**

**en·tire·ty** (in tīr′tē) **n.** wholeness; completeness. —**in its entirety,** as a whole, not only in parts [They approved our plan *in its entirety.*]



**en·ti·tle** (in tīt′'l) **v.** **1** to give a right or claim to [The ticket *entitled* me to a free seat.] **2** to give a name or title to [Harriet Beecher Stowe's famous book was *entitled* "Uncle Tom's Cabin."] —**en·ti′tled, en·ti′tling**

**en·ti·ty** (en′tə tē) **n.** something that really exists as a single, actual thing [A person is an *entity.* A nation is an *entity.*] —*pl.* **en′ti·ties**

**en·tomb** (in tōōm′) **v.** to put in a tomb or grave; bury. —**en·tomb′ment n.**

**en·to·mol·o·gy** (en′tə mäl′ə jē) **n.** the science that studies insects. —**en·to·mo·log·i·cal** (en′tə mə läj′i k'l) **adj.** —**en′to·mol′o·gist n.**

**en·trails** (en′trālz) **n.pl.** the parts inside an animal's body, especially the intestines.

**en·trance**[1] (en′trəns) **n.** **1** the act of entering. **2** a place for entering; door, gate, etc. **3** the right to enter [The sign at the drive read "No *entrance.*"]

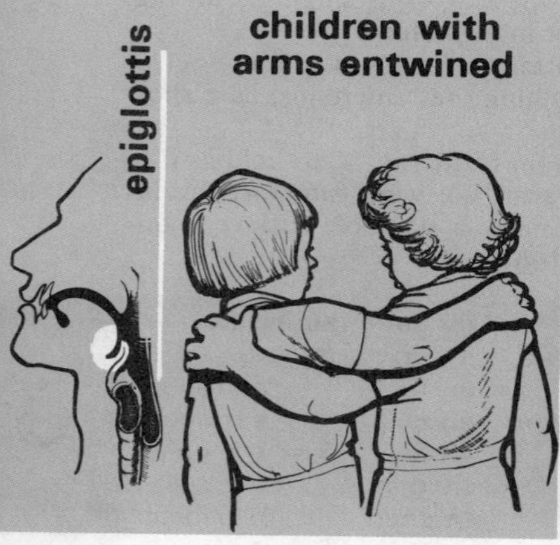

children with arms entwined

epaulet

**en·trance**[2] (in trans′) **v.** **1** to put into a trance. **2** to fill with joy or delight; enchant [We were *entranced* by the sunset.] —**en·tranced′, en·tranc′ing**

**en·trant** (en′trənt) **n.** a person who enters, especially one who enters a contest.

**en·trap** (in trap′) **v.** **1** to catch in a trap. **2** to get someone into trouble by using tricks [to *entrap* a witness into telling a lie]. —**en·trapped′, en·trap′ping**

**en·treat** (in trēt′) **v.** to plead with or beg [We *entreated* her to stay longer.]

**en·treat·y** (in trēt′ē) **n.** a pleading or begging; strong request. —*pl.* **en·treat′ies**

**en·tree** or **en·trée** (än′trā) **n.** **1** the right to enter [Everyone has *entree* into a public library.] **2** the main dish of a meal [For the *entree,* we had a choice of fried chicken or baked ham.]

**en·trench** (in trench′) **v.** **1** to surround or protect with trenches [Enemy troops were *entrenched* across the river.] **2** to fix in a firm, sure way [an official *entrenched* in office]. —**en·trench′ment n.**

**en·trust** (in trust′) **v.** **1** to put in charge of; give a duty to [She *entrusted* her secretary with answering her mail.] **2** to turn over for safekeeping [*Entrust* your key to me.] *See* SYNONYMS *at* **commit.**

**en·try** (en′trē) **n.** **1** the act of entering. **2** a way or passage by which to enter. **3** each separate thing put down in a list, diary, etc. [Each word printed in heavy type in this dictionary is an *entry.*] **4** a person or thing entered in a contest. —*pl.* **en′tries**

**en·twine** (in twīn′) **v.** to twine together or around [a fence *entwined* with ivy; children with their arms *entwined*]. *See the picture.* —**en·twined′, en·twin′ing**

**e·nu·mer·ate** (i nōō′mə rāt *or* i nyōō′mə rāt) **v.** to count or name one by one; list [The agent *enumerated* all the features of the tour.] —**e·nu′mer·at·ed, e·nu′mer·at·ing** —**e·nu′mer·a′tion n.**

**e·nun·ci·ate** (i nun′sē āt) **v.** **1** to speak or pronounce words [A telephone operator must *enunciate* clearly.] **2** to state clearly; announce [to *enunciate* a theory]. —**e·nun′ci·at·ed, e·nun′ci·at·ing** —**e·nun′ci·a′tion n.**

**en·vel·op** (in vel′əp) **v.** to cover on all sides; wrap up or wrap in [Darkness *enveloped* the camp.] —**en·vel′oped, en·vel′op·ing** —**en·vel′op·ment n.**

**en·ve·lope** (en′və lōp *or* än′və lōp) **n.** **1** a folded paper cover in which letters are sealed for mailing [The address goes on the front of the *envelope.*] **2** any wrapper or covering [a seed *envelope*].

**en·ven·om** (in ven′əm) **v.** **1** to put poison in [They *envenomed* their arrows with a deadly juice.] **2** to fill with hate, bitterness, etc. [He was *envenomed* by their cruelty toward him.]

**en·vi·a·ble** (en′vē ə b'l) **adj.** good enough to be envied or wished for [She sang with *enviable* skill.]

**en·vi·ous** (en′vē əs) **adj.** full of envy or showing envy [an *envious* look]. —**en′vi·ous·ly adv.**

**en·vi·ron·ment** (in vī′rən mənt) **n.** the things that surround anything; especially, all the conditions that surround a person, animal, or plant and affect growth, actions, character, etc. [Removing pollution from water and air will improve our *environment.*] —**en·vi′ron·men′tal adj.**

☆**en·vi·ron·men·tal·ist** (in vī′rən men′t'l ist) **n.** a person who works to protect the conditions of living things, as by controlling pollution and the careless use of natural resources.

**en·vi·rons** (in vī′rənz) ***n.pl.*** the districts that surround a place; suburbs or outskirts.

**en·vis·age** (en viz′ij) ***v.*** to form a picture of in the mind; imagine [The sculptor *envisaged* the statue she would chisel.] —**en·vis′aged, en·vis′ag·ing**

**en·voy** (en′voi *or* än′voi) ***n.*** **1** a messenger. **2** a person sent by his or her government to represent it in a foreign country. An envoy ranks just below an ambassador.

**en·vy** (en′vē) ***n.*** **1** jealousy and dislike felt toward another having some thing, quality, etc. that one would like to have [He glared at the winner with a look of *envy*.] **2** the person or thing one has such feelings about [Their new car is the *envy* of the neighborhood.] —*pl.* **en′vies** ✦***v.*** to feel envy toward or because of [to *envy* a person for her wealth]. —**en′vied, en′vy·ing**

**en·zyme** (en′zīm) ***n.*** a substance produced in plant and animal cells that causes a chemical change in other substances but is not changed itself [Pepsin is an *enzyme* in the stomach that helps to digest food.]

**e·o·hip·pus** (ē′ō hip′əs) ***n.*** the small ancestor of the horse, that lived millions of years ago. It was about the size of a fox.

**e·on** (ē′ən *or* ē′än) ***n.*** a very long period of time; thousands and thousands of years [The first human beings lived *eons* ago.]

**EPA** Environmental Protection Agency.

**ep·au·let** or **ep·au·lette** (ep′ə let) ***n.*** a decoration worn on the shoulder of a uniform. *See the picture.*

> **Epaulet** comes from the French word for shoulder and that word comes from the Latin word *spatula,* meaning "flat blade." We sometimes call the flat bone in the back of the shoulder the "shoulder blade."

**e·phem·er·al** (i fem′ər əl) ***adj.*** lasting only one day or a very short time; short-lived [*ephemeral* insects; *ephemeral* pleasures].

**E·phe·sians** (i fē′zhənz) a book of the New Testament, written by the Apostle Paul.

**epi-** *a prefix meaning* on, over, *or* outside [The *epidermis* is the outside layer of skin.]

**ep·ic** (ep′ik) ***n.*** **1** a long, serious poem that tells the story of a hero or heroes [Homer's "Odyssey" is an *epic* about the wanderings of Ulysses.] **2** a story, play, etc. thought of as having the greatness and splendor of an epic. ✦***adj.*** of or like an epic; grand, heroic, etc. [the *epic* western march of the pioneers].

**ep·i·cure** (ep′i kyoor) ***n.*** a person who knows and cares much about fine foods, wines, etc.

**ep·i·cu·re·an** (ep′i kyoo rē′ən) ***adj.*** fond of eating and drinking good things and having pleasures. ✦***n.*** an epicurean person.

**ep·i·dem·ic** (ep′ə dem′ik) ***n.*** the rapid spreading of a disease to many people at the same time [an *epidemic* of flu in the city]. ✦***adj.*** widespread, as a disease.

**ep·i·der·mis** (ep′ə dur′mis) ***n.*** the outer layer of the skin of animals. It has no blood vessels.

**ep·i·glot·tis** (ep′ə glät′is) ***n.*** a little piece of cartilage that covers the windpipe when a person swallows. It keeps food from getting into the lungs. *See the picture.*

**ep·i·gram** (ep′ə gram) ***n.*** a short saying that makes its point in a witty or clever way ["Experience is the name everyone gives to his mistakes" is an *epigram.*] —**ep·i·gram·mat·ic** (ep′i grə mat′ik) ***adj.***

**ep·i·lep·sy** (ep′ə lep′sē) ***n.*** a disorder of the nervous system that can cause sudden attacks of tightening of the muscles, fainting, etc. from time to time.

**ep·i·lep·tic** (ep′ə lep′tik) ***adj.*** of epilepsy or having epilepsy. ✦***n.*** a person who has epilepsy.

**ep·i·logue** or **ep·i·log** (ep′ə lôg) ***n.*** a part added at the end of a play, novel, etc., in which the author makes some comment; especially, a closing speech to the audience by one of the actors in a play.

**E·piph·a·ny** (i pif′ə nē) ***n.*** a Christian festival on January 6 celebrating the visit of the Wise Men to worship the infant Jesus as the Christ.

**e·pis·co·pal** (i pis′kə pəl) ***adj.*** of or governed by bishops. The word **Episcopal** is sometimes used in the names of Protestant churches that are governed by bishops, as the Protestant Episcopal Church.

**E·pis·co·pa·lian** (i pis′kə pāl′yən) ***adj.*** *another word for* **Episcopal.** ✦***n.*** ☆a member of the Protestant Episcopal Church, the church in the U.S. that follows the practices of the Church of England.

**ep·i·sode** (ep′ə sōd) ***n.*** any happening or incident that forms part of a whole story, life, history, etc. [The surrender at Appomattox was the last *episode* of the Civil War.]

**e·pis·tle** (i pis′'l) ***n.*** **1** a letter: *now used in a joking way.* **2 Epistle,** any of the letters written by the Apostles and included as books of the New Testament.

**ep·i·taph** (ep′ə taf) ***n.*** words carved on a tomb in memory of the person buried there.

**ep·i·thet** (ep′ə thet) ***n.*** a word or phrase that describes a person or thing by naming some quality or feature, as America *the Beautiful.*

> **Epithet** comes from a Greek word meaning "something that is put on, or added." An epithet is a description that is added to the regular name.

**e·pit·o·me** (i pit′ə mē) ***n.*** **1** a person or thing that shows all the typical qualities of something [He is the *epitome* of kindness.] **2** a short report of the main points of a book, article, etc.; summary.

**e·pit·o·mize** (i pit′ə mīz) ***v.*** to be an epitome, or typical example, of [Daniel Boone *epitomizes* the frontiersman.] —**e·pit′o·mized, e·pit′o·miz·ing**

**e plu·ri·bus u·num** (ē′ ploor′ə bəs yoo′nəm) out of many, one: *this Latin phrase is the motto of the United States.*

**ep·och** (ep′ək) ***n.*** **1** a period of time thought of in connection with the important happenings, changes, etc. in it [The first earth satellite marked a new *epoch* in the study of the universe.] **2** a period in the history of the earth [The recent *epoch* in geology began about 12,000 years ago.] —**ep′och·al** ***adj.***

**ep·ox·y** (e päk′sē) ***adj.*** that contains a resin which gives it a strong, hard, sticking quality [an *epoxy* glue; an *epoxy* enamel].

| | | | | | | | |
|---|---|---|---|---|---|---|---|
| **a** | fat | **ir** | here | **ou** | out | **zh** | leisure |
| **ā** | ape | **ī** | bite, fire | **u** | up | **ng** | ring |
| **ä** | car, lot | **ō** | go | **ur** | fur | | a *in* ago |
| **e** | ten | **ô** | law, horn | **ch** | chin | | e *in* agent |
| **er** | care | **oi** | oil | **sh** | she | **ə =** | i *in* unity |
| **ē** | even | **oo** | look | **th** | thin | | o *in* collect |
| **i** | hit | **ōō** | tool | ***th*** | then | | u *in* focus |

**Ep·som salts** or **Ep·som salt** (ep′səm) a white powder in the form of crystals, that is a salt of magnesium. It is dissolved in water and used as a medicine to make the bowels move.

**eq·ua·ble** (ek′wə b'l) ***adj.*** **1** changing very little or not at all; steady; even [an *equable* climate]. **2** not easily stirred up or troubled; calm [an *equable* temper]. —**eq′ua·bly *adv.***

**e·qual** (ē′kwəl) ***adj.*** **1** of the same amount, size, or value [The horses were of *equal* height.] **2** having the same rights, ability, or position [All persons are *equal* in a court of law in a just society.] ◆***n.*** any person or thing that is equal [As a sculptor, she has few *equals.*] ◆***v.*** **1** to be equal to; match [His long jump *equaled* the school record. Six minus two *equals* four.] **2** to do or make something equal to [You can *equal* my score easily.] —**e′qualed** or **e′qualled, e′qual·ing** or **e′qual·ling** —**equal to,** having enough power, skill, or courage for [I'm not *equal to* running five miles.] —**e′qual·ly *adv.***

**e·qual·i·ty** (i kwäl′ə tē) ***n.*** the condition of being equal, especially of having the same political, social, and economic rights and duties.

**e·qual·ize** (ē′kwə līz) ***v.*** to make equal or even [Be sure to *equalize* the portions.] —**e′qual·ized, e′qual·iz·ing** —**e′qual·i·za′tion *n.*** —**e′qual·iz·er *n.***

**equal sign** or **equal mark** the sign or mark = , used in arithmetic to show that amounts or figures are equal, as 2 + 2 = 4.



**e·qua·nim·i·ty** (ek′wə nim′ə tē *or* ē′kwə nim′ə tē) ***n.*** the quality of being calm and not easily troubled or made angry; evenness of temper.

**e·quate** (i kwāt′) ***v.*** to think of or deal with as being equal or closely related [Many people *equate* wealth with happiness.] —**e·quat′ed, e·quat′ing**

**e·qua·tion** (i kwā′zhən) ***n.*** **1** a statement showing that two quantities are equal by putting an equal sign (=) between them [4 + 8 = 6 x 2 is an *equation.*] **2** the act of equating things, or making them equal.

**e·qua·tor** (i kwāt′ər) ***n.*** an imaginary circle around the middle of the earth, at an equal distance from the North Pole and South Pole. *See the picture.*

**e·qua·to·ri·al** (ē′kwə tôr′ē əl) ***adj.*** **1** of or near the equator [*equatorial* regions]. **2** like the conditions near the equator [*equatorial* heat].

**e·ques·tri·an** (i kwes′trē ən) ***adj.*** **1** of horses or horseback riding. **2** on horseback [an *equestrian* statue]. ◆***n.*** a rider on horseback, as in a circus.

**e·ques·tri·enne** (i kwes′trē en′) ***n.*** a woman rider on horseback, as in a circus.

**equi-** *a prefix meaning* equal *or* equally [An *equilateral* triangle has all sides equal.]

**e·qui·dis·tant** (ē′kwə dis′tənt) ***adj.*** at an equal distance [Parallel lines are *equidistant* from each other at all points.]

**e·qui·lat·er·al** (ē′kwə lat′ər əl) ***adj.*** having all sides equal in length.

**e·qui·lib·ri·um** (ē′kwə lib′rē əm) ***n.*** the condition in which opposite weights, forces, etc. are in balance. *See the picture.*

**e·quine** (ē′kwīn *or* ek′wīn) ***adj.*** of or like a horse.

**e·qui·noc·tial** (ē′kwə näk′shəl) ***adj.*** of, or happening at the time of, an equinox [an *equinoctial* storm].

**e·qui·nox** (ē′kwə näks) ***n.*** either of the two times of the year when the sun crosses the equator, about March 21 and September 22. At these times night and day are equal all over the earth.

**e·quip** (i kwip′) ***v.*** to provide with what is needed; outfit [The soldiers were *equipped* for battle. The car is *equipped* with power brakes.] —**e·quipped′, e·quip′ping**

**eq·ui·page** (ek′wə pij) ***n.*** **1** equipment, as of an army. **2** a carriage, especially one with its horses, coachmen, and other servants.

**e·quip·ment** (i kwip′mənt) ***n.*** **1** the special things needed for some purpose; outfit, supplies, etc. [fishing *equipment*]. **2** the act of equipping.

**e·qui·poise** (ek′wə poiz) ***n.*** **1** perfect balance of weights or forces. **2** a weight or force that balances another.

**eq·ui·ta·ble** (ek′wit ə b'l) ***adj.*** fair or just [an *equitable* share]. —**eq′ui·ta·bly *adv.***

**eq·ui·ty** (ek′wət ē) ***n.*** **1** fairness or justice. **2** the value of a piece of property after subtracting the amount owed on it, as in mortgages.

**e·quiv·a·lent** (i kwiv′ə lənt) ***adj.*** equal or the same in amount, value, meaning, etc. ◆***n.*** something that is equal or the same [Three teaspoonfuls are the *equivalent* of one tablespoonful.] —**e·quiv′a·lence *n.***

**e·quiv·o·cal** (i kwiv′ə k'l) ***adj.*** **1** having more than one meaning so as to be confusing or misleading [An *equivocal* answer is one that avoids answering the question directly.] **2** undecided or doubtful [an *equivocal* outcome]. **3** that can be questioned; suspicious [*equivocal* conduct in politics]. —**e·quiv′o·cal·ly *adv.***

**e·quiv·o·cate** (i kwiv′ə kāt) ***v.*** to use words that have more than one meaning in order to confuse or mislead. —**e·quiv′o·cat·ed, e·quiv′o·cat·ing** —**e·quiv′o·ca′tion *n.***

**-er** (ər) *a suffix meaning:* **1** a person or thing that [A *catcher* is a person or thing that catches.] **2** a person living in [A *Vermonter* is a person living in Vermont.] **3** a person having to do with [A *hatter* is a person who makes hats.] **4** more [A *pleasanter* day is a day that is more pleasant.]

**e·ra** (ir′ə *or* er′ə) ***n.*** **1** a period of time measured from some important event [The Christian *Era* is dated from the birth of Jesus.] **2** a period of history having some special characteristic [We have entered the *era* of space travel.] **3** any of the five main divisions of time in geology. *See* SYNONYMS *at* **period.**

**ERA** **1** earned run average (in baseball). **2** Equal Rights Amendment.

**e·rad·i·cate** (i rad′ə kāt) ***v.*** to uproot or remove completely; get rid of; wipe out [to *eradicate* a disease]. —**e·rad′i·cat·ed, e·rad′i·cat·ing** —**e·rad′i·ca′tion *n.***

**e·rase** (i rās′) ***v.*** **1** to rub out; scrape away [to *erase* writing]. **2** to remove something from; wipe clean [to *erase* a chalkboard; to *erase* a magnetic tape]. **3** to remove from the mind or memory. —**e·rased′, e·ras′ing**

In olden times, before there were pens and paper, people would write on wax tablets. If they made a mistake, they would scratch or scrape the wax to remove the error. From the Latin word *erasus,* meaning "that has been scratched out," we get our word **erase.**

**e·ras·er** (i rā′sər) ***n.*** a thing that erases, as a piece of rubber used to rub out pencil marks or a felt pad used to wipe chalk marks from a chalkboard.

**e·ra·sure** (i rā′shər) ***n.*** **1** the act of erasing or rubbing out. **2** an erased word, mark, etc. **3** the space on a surface where something has been erased.

**ere** (er) ***prep., conj.*** before: *no longer much used* [They left *ere* break of day.]

**e·rect** (i rekt′) ***adj.*** straight up; not bending or leaning; upright [The guard stood *erect* at the gate.] ◆***v.*** **1** to put up or put together; build; construct [to *erect* a house]. **2** to set in an upright position [to *erect* a telephone pole]. —**e·rec′tion** ***n.***

**erg** (ʉrg) ***n.*** a unit of work or energy in physics.

**er·go** (ʉr′gō) ***conj., adv.*** therefore: *a Latin word.*

**Er·ics·son** or **Er·ic·son** (er′ik sən), **Leif** (lēf *or* lāf) a Norwegian explorer who lived about 1000 A.D. He is thought to be the first European to land in America.

**Er·ie** (ir′ē), **Lake** one of the Great Lakes, between Lake Huron and Lake Ontario.

**Er·in** (er′in) *a poetic name for* **Ireland**.

**er·mine** (ʉr′mən) ***n.*** **1** a weasel that lives in northern regions. Its fur is brown in summer, but turns white with a black-tipped tail in winter. *See the picture.* **2** the white fur of this animal, used especially on royal robes and on the robes of some European judges.

**e·rode** (i rōd′) ***v.*** to wear away; eat away or into [Rust *eroded* the iron fence. The hillside was *eroded* by heavy rains.] —**e·rod′ed, e·rod′ing**

**E·ros** (er′äs *or* ir′äs) the Greek god of love. The Romans called this god *Cupid.*

**e·ro·sion** (i rō′zhən) ***n.*** an eroding or wearing away [the *erosion* of soil by water and wind].

**err** (ʉr *or* er) ***v.*** **1** to be wrong; make a mistake [The speaker *erred* in calling Columbus a Spaniard.] **2** to do wrong; sin ["To *err* is human, to forgive divine."]

**er·rand** (er′ənd) ***n.*** **1** a short trip to do a thing, often for someone else [I'm going downtown on an *errand* for my sister.] **2** the thing to be done on such a trip [What is your *errand?*]

**er·rant** (er′ənt) ***adj.*** **1** roaming about in search of adventure [a knight-*errant*]. **2** turning from what is right; erring.

**er·rat·ic** (i rat′ik) ***adj.*** **1** not regular in action; likely to change and, therefore, not to be depended on [an *erratic* watch]. **2** queer or odd [*erratic* notions]. —**er·rat′i·cal·ly** ***adv.***

**er·ro·ne·ous** (ə rō′nē əs) ***adj.*** not correct; wrong [an *erroneous* idea]. —**er·ro′ne·ous·ly** ***adv.***

**er·ror** (er′ər) ***n.*** **1** a belief, answer, act, etc. that is untrue, incorrect, or wrong; mistake [an *error* in multiplication]. **2** the condition of being wrong or incorrect [You are in *error* if you think I don't care.] ☆**3** a play by a baseball fielder which is poorly made, but which would have resulted in an out if it had been properly made.

SYNONYMS: **Error** is the general word used for anything said, done, or believed that is not accurate, true, or right [an *error* in judgment]. A **mistake** is an error that has happened because of carelessness or misunderstanding [a *mistake* in spelling].

**erst·while** (ʉrst′hwīl) ***adj.*** former; of an earlier time [my *erstwhile* friend].

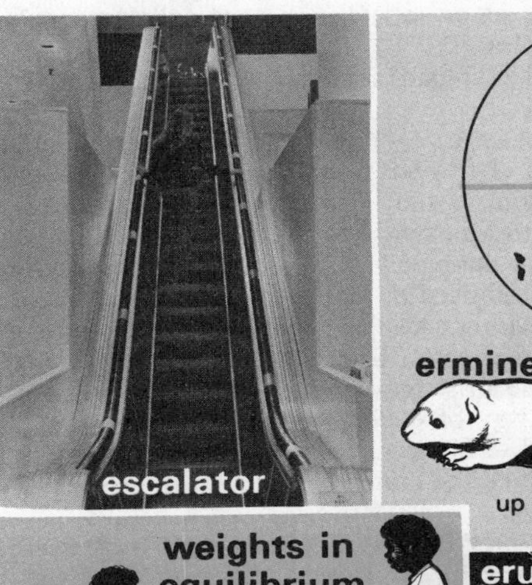


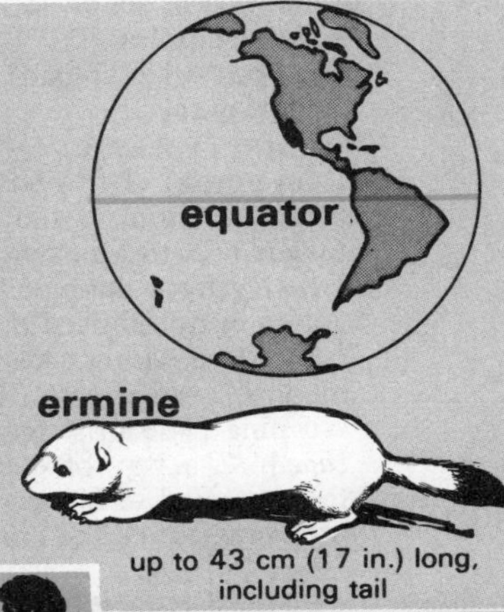


ermine

up to 43 cm (17 in.) long, including tail

**er·u·dite** (er′yoo dīt *or* er′oo dīt) ***adj.*** having or showing much knowledge; scholarly; learned. —**er′u·dite·ly** ***adv.***

**er·u·di·tion** (er′yoo dish′ən *or* er′oo dish′ən) ***n.*** wide knowledge that comes from reading and study; scholarship; learning.

**e·rupt** (i rupt′) ***v.*** **1** to burst forth [Lava *erupted* from the volcano.] **2** to throw forth lava, water, etc. [The volcano *erupted.*] **3** to break out in a rash.

**e·rup·tion** (i rup′shən) ***n.*** **1** a bursting or throwing forth, as of lava from a volcano. *See the picture.* **2** a breaking out in a rash; also, a rash [Measles causes an *eruption.*]

**-er·y** (ər ē) *a suffix meaning:* **1** a place to [A *brewery* is a place to brew.] **2** a place for [A *nunnery* is a place for nuns.] **3** the practice or work of [*Surgery* is the work of a surgeon.] **4** the product of [*Pottery* is the product of a potter.] **5** a collection of [*Crockery* is a collection of crocks and earthenware.] **6** the condition of [*Slavery* is the condition of a slave.]

**E·sau** (ē′sô) in the Bible, Isaac's older son, who sold his birthright to his brother, Jacob.

☆**es·ca·late** (es′kə lāt) ***v.*** **1** to rise as on an escalator. **2** to keep getting larger, greater, more serious, etc. [The price of oil keeps *escalating.*] —**es′ca·lat·ed, es′ca·lat·ing**

☆**es·ca·la·tor** (es′kə lāt′ər) ***n.*** a stairway whose steps are part of an endless moving belt, for carrying people up or down. *See the picture.*



| | | | | | | | |
|---|---|---|---|---|---|---|---|
| **a** | fat | **ir** | here | **ou** | out | **zh** | leisure |
| **ā** | ape | **ī** | bite, fire | **u** | up | **ng** | ring |
| **ä** | car, lot | **ō** | go | **ʉr** | fur | | a *in* ago |
| **e** | ten | **ô** | law, horn | **ch** | chin | | e *in* agent |
| **er** | care | **oi** | oil | **sh** | she | **ə =** | i *in* unity |
| **ē** | even | **oo** | look | **th** | thin | | o *in* collect |
| **i** | hit | **ōō** | tool | ***th*** | then | | u *in* focus |

**es·cal·lop** or **es·cal·op** (e skäl′əp *or* e skal′əp) ***n., v.*** *same as* **scallop.**

**es·ca·pade** (es′kə pād) ***n.*** a daring or reckless adventure or prank.

**es·cape** (ə skāp′) ***v.*** **1** to break loose; get free, as from prison. **2** to keep from getting hurt, killed, etc.; keep safe from; avoid [Very few people *escaped* the plague.] **3** to leak out; flow or drain away [Gas was *escaping* from the pipe.] **4** to slip away from; be forgotten or not noticed by [The name *escaped* me.] **5** to come from without being intended [A scream *escaped* his lips.] —**es·caped′, es·cap′ing** ◆***n.*** **1** the act of escaping [The prisoners made their plans for an *escape.*] **2** a way of escaping [The fire closed in and there seemed to be no *escape.*] **3** any way of putting problems out of the mind for a while [Movies are my *escape.*]

**Escape** comes from two Latin words, *ex cappa,* meaning "out of the cape." When a thief was caught and held, he might try to escape by slipping out of his cape, or cloak, and running away.

**es·cape·ment** (ə skāp′mənt) ***n.*** **1** the part of a watch or clock that keeps the action regular. It consists of a notched wheel that turns as the wheel is released, one notch at a time, by a catch. *See the picture.* **2** the part of a typewriter that lets the carriage move in an even, regular way.

**es·carp·ment** (e skärp′mənt) ***n.*** **1** a high, steep cliff.
250 **2** a bank of earth with a steep slope, made as part of a fortification.

**es·chew** (es choo′) ***v.*** to stay away from; shun; avoid [to *eschew* all evil].

**es·cort** (es′kôrt) ***n.*** **1** one or more persons, ships, automobiles, etc. that go along with another or others in order to give protection or pay honor. **2** a man who accompanies a woman, as to a party. ◆***v.*** (i skôrt′) to go along with or accompany as an escort. *See* SYNONYMS *at* **accompany.**

**es·crow** (es′krō) ***n.*** the state of a deed, bond, etc. held by a third person until certain conditions are carried out [A bank may hold a deed in *escrow* until the sale of a house is completed.]

**es·cutch·eon** (i skuch′ən) ***n.*** a shield on which a coat of arms is shown. *See the picture.*

**-ese** (ēz *or* ēs) *a suffix meaning* of a certain country or place [*Chinese* is the language of China.]

**Es·ki·mo** (es′kə mō) ***n.*** **1** any member of a group of people who live mainly in the arctic regions of the Western Hemisphere. —*pl.* **Es′ki·mos** or **Es′ki·mo** **2** the language of the Eskimos. ◆***adj.*** of the Eskimos.

**Eskimo dog** a strong dog with a bushy tail and gray shaggy fur, used for pulling sleds in the Arctic.

**e·soph·a·gus** (i säf′ə gəs) ***n.*** the tube through which food passes from the throat to the stomach.

**es·o·ter·ic** (es′ə ter′ik) ***adj.*** understood or known by only a few people; of a secret kind that has been taught only to certain chosen persons [the *esoteric* rites of some religions].

**ESP** the ability that some people seem to have to see, hear, or know things without using the normal senses of sight, hearing, etc. The letters ESP come from the words "*e*xtra*s*ensory *p*erception."

**esp.** *abbreviation for* **especially.**

**es·pe·cial** (ə spesh′əl) ***adj.*** more than ordinary; outstanding; special [of *especial* interest to you].

**es·pe·cial·ly** (ə spesh′əl ē) ***adv.*** mainly; in particular; specially [I like all fruit, but I am *especially* fond of pears.]

**Es·pe·ran·to** (es′pə rän′tō) ***n.*** a language that was made up in 1887, using word roots from various European languages. It is meant to be used as an international language.

**es·pi·o·nage** (es′pē ə näzh′ *or* es′pē ə nij) ***n.*** the act of spying on the secrets of others; especially, the use of spies by a government to learn the military secrets of other nations.

**es·pous·al** (i spou′z′l) ***n.*** the act of espousing or supporting a cause, plan, or idea.

**es·pouse** (i spouz′) ***v.*** to take up and support a cause, plan, or idea; advocate [My parents *espoused* the cause of women's rights.] —**es·poused′, es·pous′ing**

**es·prit** (es prē′) ***n.*** spirit or bright wit.

**es·prit de corps** (es prē′ də kôr′) a feeling of pride and honor in the group to which one belongs.

**es·py** (ə spī′) ***v.*** to manage to get a look at; catch sight of [We *espied* the snake half hidden in the tall grass.] —**es·pied′, es·py′ing**

**es·quire** (es′kwīr *or* ə skwīr′) ***n.*** **1** in England, a man who ranks just below a knight. **2** **Esquire,** a polite title used instead of *Mr.*

The title **Esquire** is more commonly used in England than in the U.S. It is usually abbreviated **Esq.** and placed after the name: example, "Samuel Johnson, *Esq.*"

**-ess** (is *or* əs) *a suffix meaning* female [A *lioness* is a female lion.] *Words ending in* **-ess** *but describing people, such as* **poetess** *and* **sculptress,** *are no longer much used.*

**es·say** (es′ā) ***n.*** **1** a short piece of writing on some subject, giving the writer's personal ideas. **2** an attempt to do something; a try. ◆***v.*** (e sā′) to try; attempt [to *essay* a task].

**es·say·ist** (es′ā ist) ***n.*** a writer of essays.

**Es·sen** (es′'n) a city in western West Germany.

**es·sence** (es′'ns) ***n.*** **1** that which makes something what it is; most important or basic quality of a thing [The *essence* of law is justice.] **2** a substance that keeps in a strong, pure form the special taste, smell, or other quality of the plant, drug, etc. from which it is taken [*essence* of wintergreen]. **3** a perfume.

**es·sen·tial** (ə sen′shəl) ***adj.*** **1** that is a most typical or basic part [Friendliness was an *essential* part of his character.] **2** most important or necessary; vital [It is *essential* for guards on duty to stay awake.] ◆***n.*** something that is most important or necessary [A good sense of rhythm is an *essential* for a drummer.] —**es·sen′tial·ly** ***adv.***

**-est** (ist *or* əst) *a suffix used to form:* **1** the superlative of many adjectives and adverbs [*Greatest* means "most great."] **2** the present tense of verbs used with *thou* ["Thou *goest*" is an older way of saying "you go."]

**EST, E.S.T.** *abbreviation for* **Eastern Standard Time.**

**est.** *abbreviation for* **established, estimated.**

**es·tab·lish** (ə stab′lish) ***v.*** **1** to put in a condition that is not easily changed; settle; fix [to *establish* a habit]. **2** to cause to be; bring about [to *establish* good relations]. **3** to put into an office or position [Queen Elizabeth II was *established* on the throne in 1952.] **4** to begin or found a government, nation, company, etc. [Ghana was *established* in 1957.] **5** to show to be true; prove [The suspect was released when she *established* an alibi.]

**es·tab′lish·ment** (ə stab′lish mənt) ***n.*** **1** the act of establishing or the fact of being established. **2** something established, as a business, household, army, church, etc. —**the Establishment,** the group of people who have the power to control the affairs of a nation or society.

**es·tate** (ə stāt′) ***n.*** **1** everything a person owns, including money, land, and other property [She left her entire *estate* to her nephew.] **2** a large piece of land with a large home on it [They have a city house and a country *estate*.]

**es·teem** (ə stēm′) ***v.*** **1** to have a good opinion of; regard as valuable; respect [I *esteem* his praise above all other.] *See* SYNONYMS *at* **regard. 2** to think of; consider; deem [We *esteem* it an honor to be your hosts.] ◆***n.*** good opinion; high regard; respect [to hold someone in high *esteem*].

**es·ter** (es′tər) ***n.*** an organic chemical substance containing carbon and formed by combining an acid and an alcohol.

**Es·ther** (es′tər) **1** in the Bible, the Jewish wife of a Persian king. She saved her people from slaughter. **2** the book of the Bible that tells her story.

**es·thet·ic** (es thet′ik) ***adj.*** *another spelling of* **aesthetic.**

**es·ti·ma·ble** (es′tə mə b′l) ***adj.*** that deserves to get esteem or respect; worthy [an *estimable* book].

**es·ti·mate** (es′tə māt) ***v.*** to make a general but careful guess about the size, value, cost, etc. [We *estimated* the size of the audience to be 500.] —**es′ti·mat·ed, es′ti·mat·ing** ◆***n.*** **1** a general guess about size, value, cost, etc. [an *estimate* of $250 to repair your car]. **2** opinion or judgment [Was that a good movie in your *estimate*?]

**es·ti·ma·tion** (es′tə mā′shən) ***n.*** **1** the act of making an estimate. **2** opinion or judgment; estimate. **3** good opinion; esteem; respect [You are held in high *estimation* by all your fellow workers.]

**Es·to·ni·a** (es tō′nē ə) a republic of the Soviet Union in northeastern Europe. —**Es·to′ni·an *adj., n.***

**es·trange** (ə strānj′) ***v.*** to make no longer friendly; make stay away [You have *estranged* your friends by gossiping.] —**es·tranged′, es·trang′ing** —**es·trange′ment *n.***

**es·tu·ar·y** (es′choo wer′ē) ***n.*** an arm of the sea; especially, a wide mouth of a river where the tide flows in. —*pl.* **es′tu·ar′ies**

**-et** (it) *a suffix meaning* small [An *eaglet* is a small eagle.]

**etc.** *abbreviation for* **et cetera.**

**et cet·er·a** (et set′ər ə) and others; and so forth.

> **Et cetera** is usually abbreviated *etc.* and is used after a list of things to show that other similar things not mentioned could be included [Vitamin C is found in oranges, lemons, *etc.*]

**etch** (ech) ***v.*** to engrave a design on metal or glass by coating the surface with a substance such as wax, on which the design is drawn with a sharp needle. Acid is then used to eat into the open parts of the surface, leaving the covered parts raised. Ink can then be put on the finished plate to print the design.

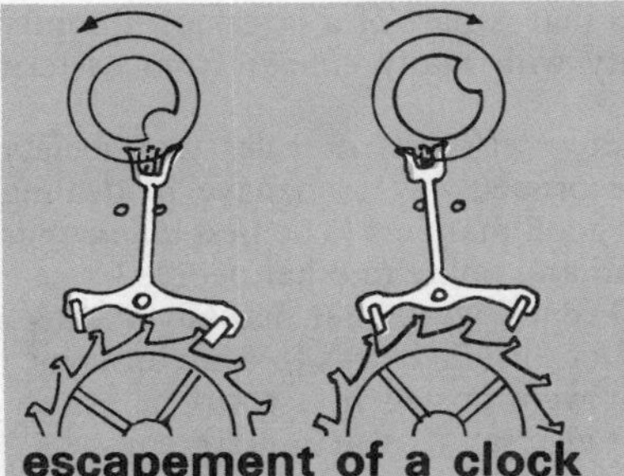
escapement of a clock

escutcheon

**etch·ing** (ech′iŋ) ***n.*** **1** a plate or design that is etched. **2** a print made from an etched plate. **3** the art of making such designs or prints.

**e·ter·nal** (i tur′n′l) ***adj.*** **1** lasting forever; without a beginning or end. **2** seeming to have no end; continual [Stop your *eternal* arguments!] **3** always the same [*eternal* truth]. —**the Eternal,** God. —**e·ter′nal·ly *adv.***

**e·ter·ni·ty** (i tur′nə tē) ***n.*** **1** all time, without beginning or end; endless time. **2** a long period of time that seems to have no end [It seemed an *eternity* before they arrived.] **3** the endless time after death.

**-eth**[1] *see* **-th**[1].

**-eth**[2] (əth) an old-fashioned ending for the present tense of verbs used with *he, she,* or *it* ["She *asketh*" is an older way of saying "she asks."]

**e·ther** (ē′thər) ***n.*** **1** a colorless liquid used to make a person unconscious, as during an operation in a hospital. **2** an invisible substance that was once supposed to fill all space not filled by a solid, liquid, or gas. **3** the clear sky above the clouds: *used mainly in older poetry.*

**e·the·re·al** (i thir′ē əl) ***adj.*** **1** like the clear sky; light; airy; delicate [*ethereal* music]. **2** not of the earth; heavenly.

**eth·i·cal** (eth′i k′l) ***adj.*** **1** having to do with ethics or morals [*ethical* standards]. *See* SYNONYMS *at* **moral. 2** that is right according to some system of morals [*ethical* behavior]. —**eth′i·cal·ly *adv.***

**eth·ics** (eth′iks) ***n.pl.*** **1** the study of right and wrong in the way people behave; science of morals: *used with a singular verb.* **2** rules of right and wrong behavior [According to legal *ethics,* a lawyer must not reveal the secrets of a client.]

**E·thi·o·pi·a** (ē′thē ō′pē ə) a country in eastern Africa, south of Egypt. It was once called **Abyssinia.** —**E′thi·o′pi·an *adj., n.***

**eth·nic** (eth′nik) ***adj.*** having to do with any of the different groups of people as based on their customs, languages, cultures, or history [Our city has many different *ethnic* restaurants.] ◆***n.*** a person who belongs

| | | | | | | | |
|---|---|---|---|---|---|---|---|
| **a** | fat | **ir** | here | **ou** | out | **zh** | leisure |
| **ā** | ape | **ī** | bite, fire | **u** | up | **ŋ** | ring |
| **ä** | car, lot | **ō** | go | **ur** | fur | | a *in* ago |
| **e** | ten | **ô** | law, horn | **ch** | chin | | e *in* agent |
| **er** | care | **oi** | oil | **sh** | she | **ə =** | i *in* unity |
| **ē** | even | **oo** | look | **th** | thin | | o *in* collect |
| **i** | hit | **ōō** | tool | ***th*** | then | | u *in* focus |

to an ethnic group that is part of a larger community [Cleveland is a city with many *ethnics* from eastern Europe.]

**et·i·quette** (et′i kət *or* et′i ket) ***n.*** rules that society has set up for the proper way to behave in dealing with other people; good manners [The best *etiquette* is based on being kind and polite to other people.]

> **Etiquette** is a French word that actually means "ticket," "label," or "list." It was first used of the lists of rules that were posted in a court or army camp. We might also say that **etiquette** can be a "ticket" that allows a person to enter polite society.

**Et·na** (et′nə) a volcano in eastern Sicily.

**E·ton** (ēt′'n) a town in south-central England. A famous private school for boys is located there.

**E·tru·ri·a** (i troor′ē ə) an ancient country in what is now western Italy.

**E·trus·can** (i trus′kən) ***adj.*** of Etruria, the people who lived there, or their culture. ◆***n.*** **1** any of the people who lived in Etruria. **2** their language.

**-ette** (et) *a suffix meaning:* **1** small [A *kitchenette* is a small kitchen.] ☆**2** girl or woman [A drum *majorette* is a girl drum major.] **3** used in place of [*Leatherette* is used in place of leather.]

**é·tude** (ā′tōōd *or* ā′tyōōd) ***n.*** a piece of music written mainly to give players practice in certain skills on some instrument [piano *études*].



**ETV** educational television.

**et·y·mol·o·gy** (et′ə mäl′ə jē) ***n.*** **1** the history of a word, which shows where it came from and how it has changed into its present spelling and meaning [The *etymologies* of some words are given in this dictionary in colored blocks after the definitions.] **2** the science that studies such word histories. *—pl.* **et′y·mol′o·gies** **—et·y·mo·log·i·cal** (et′ə mə läj′i k'l) ***adj.***

**eu-** *a prefix meaning* good, well, or pleasant [*Euphony* is pleasant sound.]

**eu·ca·lyp·tus** (yōō′kə lip′təs) ***n.*** an evergreen tree that grows in hot, moist regions near the tropics. It is valuable for its gum, oil, and wood. At one time these trees grew mainly in Australia. *See the picture. —pl.* **eu′ca·lyp′tus·es** or **eu·ca·lyp·ti** (yōō′kə lip′tī)

**Eu·cha·rist** (yōō′kə rist) ***n.*** **1** *another name for* **Holy Communion.** **2** the sacred bread and wine used in this rite. **—Eu′cha·ris′tic** ***adj.***

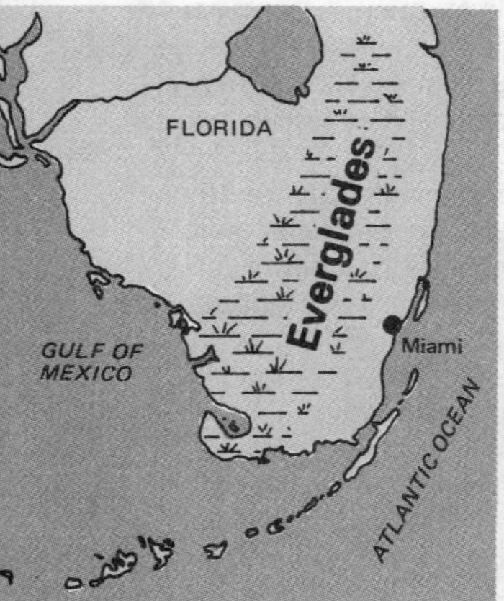

runner evading a tackler

eucalyptus

**Eu·clid** (yōō′klid) a Greek mathematician who lived about 300 B.C. and wrote a famous book on geometry.

**eu·lo·gize** (yōō′lə jīz) ***v.*** to say very good things about; praise highly; extol. **—eu′lo·gized, eu′lo·giz·ing —eu′lo·gis′tic** ***adj.***

**eu·lo·gy** (yōō′lə jē) ***n.*** a speech or writing praising a person or thing; often, a formal speech praising a person who has just died. *—pl.* **eu′lo·gies**

**eu·nuch** (yōō′nək) ***n.*** a man whose sex glands have been removed; castrated man [*Eunuchs* once served as guards in a sultan's harem.]

**eu·phe·mism** (yōō′fə miz'm) ***n.*** **1** a word or phrase that is used in place of another that is thought to be too strong or unpleasant ["Remains" is a *euphemism* for "corpse."] **2** the use of such words or phrases. **—eu′phe·mis′tic** ***adj.***

**eu·pho·ni·ous** (yoo fō′nē əs) ***adj.*** having a pleasant sound or a pleasant combination of sounds.

**eu·pho·ny** (yōō′fə nē) ***n.*** pleasant sound; especially, a pleasant combining of sounds in music or speaking.

**Eu·phra·tes** (yoo frāt′ēz) a river that flows southward through eastern Turkey, Syria, and Iraq, into the Persian Gulf.

**Eur.** *abbreviation for* **Europe** *or* **European.**

**Eur·a·sia** (yoo rā′zhə) a land mass made up of the continents of Europe and Asia.

**Eur·a·sian** (yoo rā′zhən) ***n.*** a person with one European parent and one Asian parent.

**eu·re·ka** (yoo rē′kə) ***interj.*** I have found it!: a shout of surprise or pleasure upon finding something one is looking for.

> **Eureka** comes from the Greek word meaning "I have found it." It is said that the mathematician Archimedes was once asked to find out whether the king's crown was truly all gold. While Archimedes was bathing one day, it occurred to him that a body must displace its own weight in water, and that this might be a way to test the purity of gold. He leaped out of his bath shouting "Eureka!"

**Eu·rip·i·des** (yoo rip′ə dēz) a Greek writer of tragic plays. He lived in the 5th century B.C.

**Eu·rope** (yoor′əp) the continent between Asia and the Atlantic Ocean.

**Eu·ro·pe·an** (yoor′ə pē′ən) ***adj.*** of Europe, its people, or their culture. ◆***n.*** a person born or living in Europe.

**Eu·sta·chi·an tube** (yoo stā′shən *or* yoo stā′kē ən) a thin tube leading into the middle ear, that makes the air pressure equal on both sides of the eardrum. *See the picture for* **ear.**

**e·vac·u·ate** (i vak′yoo wāt) ***v.*** **1** to remove; take away [to *evacuate* troops from a region; to *evacuate* air from a jar]. **2** to move out of; leave [*Evacuate* the building in case of fire.] **3** to make empty; take out the contents of [to *evacuate* the stomach]. **—e·vac′u·at·ed, e·vac′u·at·ing —e·vac′u·a′tion** ***n.***

**e·vade** (i vād′) ***v.*** to keep away from or avoid by using tricks or cleverness; elude [The running back *evaded* the tackler by dodging. Are you trying to *evade* my question?] *See the picture.* **—e·vad′ed, e·vad′ing**

**e·val·u·ate** (i val′yoo wāt) ***v.*** to find or try to find the value or worth of; judge [Critics *evaluate* new books as they are published.] —**e·val'u·at·ed, e·val'u·at·ing** —**e·val'u·a'tion** *n.*

**e·van·gel·i·cal** (ē'van jel'i k'l *or* ev'ən jel'i k'l) ***adj.*** **1** having to do with the four Gospels or the New Testament. **2** of those Protestant churches which believe that the soul is saved only through faith in Jesus.

**e·van·gel·ism** (i van'jə liz'm) ***n.*** a preaching of the gospel, as at revival meetings.

**e·van·gel·ist** (i van'jə list) ***n.*** **1** anyone who preaches the gospel; especially, a preacher who travels about from place to place holding religious meetings. **2 Evangelist,** any of the four writers of the Gospels; Matthew, Mark, Luke, or John. —**e·van'gel·is'tic *adj.***

**e·vap·o·rate** (i vap'ə rāt) ***v.*** **1** to change into vapor [Heat *evaporates* water. The perfume in the bottle has *evaporated.*] **2** to disappear like vapor; vanish [Our courage *evaporated* when we saw the lion.] **3** to make thicker by heating so as to take some of the water from [to *evaporate* milk]. —**e·vap'o·rat·ed, e·vap'o·rat·ing** —**e·vap'o·ra'tion** *n.*

☆**evaporated milk** milk that is made thick by evaporation and then put in cans.

**e·va·sion** (i vā'zhən) ***n.*** the act of evading; especially, an avoiding of a duty, question, etc. by using tricks or cleverness [His wordy answer was really an *evasion* of my charge.]

**e·va·sive** (i vā'siv) ***adj.*** trying to evade; not direct or frank [an *evasive* answer to a question]. —**e·va'sive·ly *adv.***

**Eve** (ēv) in the Bible, the first woman and the wife of Adam.

**eve** (ēv) ***n.*** **1** *often* **Eve,** evening, especially the evening or day before a holiday [People often have parties on New Year's *Eve.*] **2** the period just before something [on the *eve* of victory].

**e·ven**[1] (ē'vən) ***adj.*** **1** flat, level, or smooth [an *even* surface]. **2** regular or steady; not changing [an *even* flow of air]. **3** on the same level; to the same height [The water was *even* with the rim.] **4** that can be divided by two without leaving a remainder [The *even* numbers are 2, 4, 6, 8, etc.] **5** the same in number or amount; equal [Divide the candy in *even* shares.] **6** owing nothing and being owed nothing [We owe each other a dollar and so we're *even.*] **7** calm; not easily excited [an *even* temper]. **8** exact [an *even* mile]. ✦***adv.*** **1** though it may seem unlikely; indeed [*Even* a child could do it. They didn't *even* look.] **2** by comparison; still [an *even* better meal]. **3** exactly; just [It happened *even* as I expected.] **4** at the same time; while [*Even* as she spoke, the bell rang.] ✦***v.*** to make or become even or level [*Even* off the ends of the logs. His home run *evened* the score.] —☆**break even,** to finish as neither a winner nor a loser: *used only in everyday talk.* —**even if,** in spite of the fact that; though. —**get even with,** to have revenge upon. —**e'ven·ly *adv.*** —**e'ven·ness *n.***

**e·ven**[2] (ē'vən) ***n.*** evening: *no longer much used.*

**eve·ning** (ēv'niŋ) ***n.*** the close of the day and early part of the night; the time from sunset to bedtime.

**evening star** a bright planet, usually Venus, seen in the western sky soon after sunset.

**e·vent** (i vent') ***n.*** **1** a happening; especially, an important happening [The annual circus was a great *event* in our lives.] **2** any of the contests in a sports program [The final *event* in the track meet was the pole vault.] —**in any event,** no matter what happens. —**in the event of,** if there should happen to be; in case of.

**e·vent·ful** (i vent'fəl) ***adj.*** **1** full of important happenings [an *eventful* life]. **2** having an important result [an *eventful* talk]. —**e·vent'ful·ly *adv.***

**e·ven·tide** (ē'vən tīd) ***n.*** evening: *no longer much used.*

**e·ven·tu·al** (i ven'choo wəl) ***adj.*** coming at the end or as a result [Quarrels led to *eventual* war.]

**e·ven·tu·al·i·ty** (i ven'choo wal'ə tē) ***n.*** a possible happening [Be prepared for any *eventuality.*] —*pl.* **e·ven'tu·al'i·ties**

**e·ven·tu·al·ly** (i ven'choo wəl ē) ***adv.*** in the end; finally [We *eventually* became friends.]

**ev·er** (ev'ər) ***adv.*** **1** at any time [Have you *ever* seen a falling star?] **2** at all times; always [They lived happily *ever* after.] **3** truly; indeed: *used only in everyday talk* [Was I *ever* tired!] —**ever so,** very; extremely: *used only in everyday talk* [You've been *ever so* kind.]

**Ev·er·est, Mount** (ev'ər ist) a mountain in southeastern Asia, between Tibet and Nepal. It is the highest mountain in the world, a little over 8,845 meters (or 29,000 feet).

☆**ev·er·glade** (ev'ər glād) ***n.*** a large swamp. —**the Everglades,** a large area of swampland in southern Florida. *See the map.*

**ev·er·green** (ev'ər grēn) ***adj.*** having green leaves all through the year. ✦***n.*** an evergreen tree or bush [Pines and spruces are *evergreens.*]

**ev·er·last·ing** (ev'ər las'tiŋ) ***adj.*** **1** lasting forever; never ending; eternal. **2** going on too long; seeming as though it will never end [Stop your *everlasting* complaints.] —**the Everlasting,** God.

**ev·er·more** (ev ər môr') ***adv.*** forever; always [I promise to *evermore* be true.] —**for evermore,** always.

**ev·er·y** (ev'rē) ***adj.*** **1** all the group of which the thing named is one; each [*Every* student must take the test. She has read *every* book on the list.] **2** all that there could be [You've been given *every* chance.] **3** each time after a certain period has passed [Take a pill *every* three hours.] —**every now and then** or **every so often,** from time to time; once in a while: *used only in everyday talk.* —**every other,** with one between; skipping one, as the first, third, fifth, etc. in a series, or the second, fourth, sixth, etc. —☆**every which way,** in every direction; in complete disorder: *used only in everyday talk.*

**ev·er·y·bod·y** (ev'rē bäd'ē *or* ev'rē bud'ē) ***pron.*** every person; everyone [*Everybody* loves a good story.]

**ev·er·y·day** (ev'rē dā) ***adj.*** **1** happening each day; daily [Car accidents have become an *everyday* occurrence.] **2** fit for usual or common use [*Everyday* talk



| | | | | | | | |
|---|---|---|---|---|---|---|---|
| **a** | fat | **ir** | here | **ou** | out | **zh** | leisure |
| **ā** | ape | **ī** | bite, fire | **u** | up | **ŋ** | ring |
| **ä** | car, lot | **ō** | go | **ur** | fur | | a *in* ago |
| **e** | ten | **ô** | law, horn | **ch** | chin | | e *in* agent |
| **er** | care | **oi** | oil | **sh** | she | **ə** = | i *in* unity |
| **ē** | even | **oo** | look | **th** | thin | | o *in* collect |
| **i** | hit | **ōō** | tool | ***th*** | then | | u *in* focus |

is ordinary common speech, as it is different from formal talk or writing.]

**ev·er·y·one** (ev′rē wən) ***pron.*** every person.

The word **everyone** is used to mean "everybody" or "every person." If you mean "every person or thing of those mentioned," then the term is written and pronounced as two words, **every one** [*Every one* of the students will be there.]

**ev·er·y·thing** (ev′rē thing) ***pron.*** **1** every thing that there is; all things [Did you remember to bring *everything* for the picnic?] **2** the most important thing [His daughter is *everything* to him.]

**ev·er·y·where** (ev′rē hwer) ***adv.*** in or to every place [*Everywhere* I go I meet friends.]

**e·vict** (i vikt′) ***v.*** to force a person by law to move from a rented place, as for not paying the rent. —**e·vic′tion *n.***

**ev·i·dence** (ev′ə dəns) ***n.*** something that shows or proves, or that gives reason for believing; proof or indication [The footprint was *evidence* that someone had been there. Clear skin gives *evidence* of a good diet.] *See* SYNONYMS *at* **proof.** ◆***v.*** to show clearly; make plain [His smile *evidenced* his joy.] —**ev′i·denced, ev′i·denc·ing** —**in evidence,** easily seen; in plain sight.

**ev·i·dent** (ev′ə dənt) ***adj.*** easy to see or understand; clear; plain [It was *evident* that she had won.] —**ev′i·dent·ly *adv.***

254 **e·vil** (ē′v′l) ***adj.*** **1** bad or wrong on purpose; wicked [to lead an *evil* life]. *See* SYNONYMS *at* **bad. 2** causing pain or trouble; harmful [Those years were *evil* times.] ◆***n.*** **1** something bad or wrong done on purpose; wickedness; sin ["The *evil* that men do lives after them."] **2** anything that causes harm, pain, or suffering [War is a great *evil*.] —**e′vil·ly *adv.*** —**e′vil·ness *n.***

**e·vil·do·er** (ē′v′l do͞o′ər) ***n.*** a person who does evil; wicked person.

**e·vince** (i vins′) ***v.*** to show plainly; make clear [She *evinced* a strong interest in science.] —**e·vinced′, e·vinc′ing**

**e·voke** (i vōk′) ***v.*** to bring forth or produce [Those cookies *evoke* memories of my childhood.] —**e·voked′, e·vok′ing**

**ev·o·lu·tion** (ev′ə lo͞o′shən) ***n.*** **1** the gradual changes that take place as something develops into a different or more complicated form [the *evolution* of the automobile from the buggy; the *evolution* of the frog from the tadpole]. **2** the theory that all plants and animals have developed from earlier forms by changes that took place over periods of many years and were passed on from one generation to the next. —**ev′o·lu′tion·ar′y *adj.***

excavation

ewer

**e·volve** (i välv′) ***v.*** to develop by gradual changes; unfold [to *evolve* a new theory]. —**e·volved′, e·volv′ing**

**ewe** (yo͞o) ***n.*** a female sheep.

**ew·er** (yo͞o′ər) ***n.*** a large water pitcher that has a wide mouth. *See the picture.*

**ex-** **1** *a prefix seen in words that come from Latin or Greek, meaning* out, from, out of, *or* beyond [To *exhale* is to breathe out. To *exceed* is to go beyond a limit.] **2** *a prefix meaning* former *or* earlier, *written with a hyphen* [An *ex-judge* is a former judge.]

**ex.** *abbreviation for* **example, except, extra.**

**ex·act** (ig zakt′) ***adj.*** **1** not having any mistakes; strictly correct; accurate [*exact* measurements; her *exact* words]. **2** very strict [He was *exact* in enforcing the rules.] ◆***v.*** to demand and get [to *exact* a high fee; to *exact* obedience]. —**ex·act′ness *n.***

**ex·act·ing** (ig zak′ting) ***adj.*** **1** demanding much; strict [an *exacting* employer]. **2** that needs great skill and care [an *exacting* job].

**ex·ac·tion** (ig zak′shən) ***n.*** **1** the act of exacting, or demanding. **2** something that is exacted, as a fee or tax.

**ex·ac·ti·tude** (ig zak′tə to͞od *or* ig zak′tə tyo͞od) ***n.*** the quality of being exact; exactness.

**ex·act·ly** (ig zakt′lē) ***adv.*** **1** in an exact way; precisely [That's *exactly* the bike I want.] **2** quite true; I agree: *used as an answer to something said by another.*

**ex·ag·ger·ate** (ig zaj′ə rāt) ***v.*** to make seem larger or greater than it really is [He always *exaggerates* when he tells of his adventures.] —**ex·ag′ger·at·ed, ex·ag′ger·at·ing** —**ex·ag′ger·a′tion *n.***

**Exaggerate** comes from a Latin word meaning "to heap up." Heaping something up into a tall pile tends to make it look larger.

**ex·alt** (ig zôlt′) ***v.*** **1** to praise or worship [to *exalt* God]. **2** to make higher in rank, power, dignity, etc. **3** to fill with happiness, pride, etc. [They were *exalted* by the music.]

**ex·al·ta·tion** (eg′zôl tā′shən) ***n.*** **1** the act of exalting. **2** a feeling of great joy or pride.

**ex·am** (ig zam′) ***n.*** an examination: *used only in everyday talk.*

**ex·am·i·na·tion** (ig zam′ə nā′shən) ***n.*** **1** an examining or being examined. **2** a test to find out how much someone knows or has learned [Did you pass the *examination* in arithmetic?]

**ex·am·ine** (ig zam′ən) ***v.*** **1** to look at closely in order to find out the facts about or the condition of; inspect [to *examine* the sky for signs of rain; to *examine* a person's eyes]. **2** to ask questions in order to find out how much someone knows or has learned [to *examine* a witness in court]. —**ex·am′ined, ex·am′in·ing** —**ex·am′in·er *n.***

**ex·am·ple** (ig zam′p′l) ***n.*** **1** something chosen to show what the rest are like or to explain a general rule; sample; instance [This painting is a good *example* of her work.] **2** a model or pattern that is to be copied [Dr. King's life was an *example* of courage to us all.] *See* SYNONYMS *at* **model. 3** a warning or caution [The judge fined the speeder as an *example* to others.] —**set an example,** to behave in such a way as to be a model for others.

**ex·as·per·ate** (ig zas′pə rāt) ***v.*** to make angry; annoy very much; irritate [It *exasperates* me that he is never on time.] —**ex·as′per·at·ed, ex·as′per·at·ing —ex·as′per·a′tion *n.***

**ex·ca·vate** (eks′kə vāt) ***v.*** **1** to dig a hole or opening in [to *excavate* a hill in building a tunnel]. **2** to make by digging; dig [to *excavate* the basement for a house]. **3** to take out by digging; dig out [to *excavate* a ton of earth]. **4** to uncover by digging [to *excavate* the ruins of a temple]. —**ex′ca·vat·ed, ex′ca·vat·ing —ex′ca·va·tor *n.***

**ex·ca·va·tion** (eks′kə vā′shən) ***n.*** **1** the act of excavating. **2** a hole or hollow made by digging, as in looking for ruins. *See the picture.*

**ex·ceed** (ik sēd′) ***v.*** **1** to go beyond what is allowed [to *exceed* the speed limit]. **2** to be more or better than [The success of our sale *exceeded* our hopes.]

**ex·ceed·ing** (ik sēd′iŋ) ***adj.*** more than usual; extreme [*Exceeding* pride can make one rude at times.]

**ex·ceed·ing·ly** (ik sēd′iŋ lē) ***adv.*** very; extremely [They are *exceedingly* rich.]

**ex·cel** (ik sel′) ***v.*** to be better or greater in a certain way [Rudy *excels* us all at chess.] —**ex·celled′, ex·cel′ling**

**ex·cel·lence** (ek′s′l əns) ***n.*** the fact of being better or greater; extra goodness [We all praised the *excellence* of their singing.]

**Ex·cel·len·cy** (ek′s′l ən sē) ***n.*** a title of honor given to certain persons of high position, as ambassadors, bishops, or governors [An ambassador is addressed as "Your *Excellency.*"] —*pl.* **Ex′cel·len·cies**

**ex·cel·lent** (ek′s′l ənt) ***adj.*** better than others of its kind; very good [Their cakes are fairly good, but their pies are *excellent.*] —**ex′cel·lent·ly *adv.***

☆**ex·cel·si·or** (ek sel′sē ôr′) ***adj., interj.*** always upward; higher: *a Latin word used as a motto or as an exclamation.* ◆***n.*** (ik sel′sē ər) thin, curly shavings of wood used for packing breakable things or for stuffing some furniture.

**ex·cept** (ik sept′) ***prep.*** leaving out; other than; but [Everyone *except* you liked the movie.] ◆***v.*** to leave out; omit; exclude [Only a few of the students were *excepted* from her criticism.] ◆***conj.*** were it not that; only: *used only in everyday talk* [I'd go with you *except* I'm tired.]

**ex·cept·ing** (ik sep′tiŋ) ***prep.*** *same as* **except** [This ticket may be used any evening *excepting* Saturday.]

**ex·cep·tion** (ik sep′shən) ***n.*** **1** the act of excepting, or leaving out [Everyone must attend, with the *exception* of Don.] **2** a person or thing that is different from others of its kind; case to which certain rules or principles do not apply [Most mammals do not lay eggs, but the platypus is an *exception.*] —**take exception, 1** to object. **2** to resent something; feel hurt [I *take exception* to that remark.]

**ex·cep·tion·al** (ik sep′shən ′l) ***adj.*** that is an exception; different or unusual, either because much better than the average [an *exceptional* pianist] or because of needing special attention [a class for *exceptional* children]. —**ex·cep′tion·al·ly *adv.***

**ex·cerpt** (ek′surpt) ***n.*** a section copied or quoted from a book, article, etc.; extract. ◆***v.*** (ik surpt′) to take out or quote from a book, article, etc.; extract.

**ex·cess** (ik ses′ *or* ek′ses) ***n.*** **1** more than what is needed or proper; too much [Eating an *excess* of candy will harm the teeth.] **2** the amount by which one quantity is greater than another [After paying all my bills, I had an *excess* of $50 last month.] ◆***adj.*** (*usually* ek′ses) more than the usual limit; extra [Airlines charge for *excess* luggage.] —**in excess of,** more than. —**to excess,** too much [to eat *to excess*].

**ex·ces·sive** (ik ses′iv) ***adj.*** that is too much or too great [*excessive* fees]. —**ex·ces′sive·ly *adv.***

**ex·change** (iks chānj′) ***v.*** **1** to give in return for something else; trade [She *exchanged* the bicycle for a larger one.] **2** to give each other similar things [The bride and groom *exchanged* rings during the ceremony.] —**ex·changed′, ex·chang′ing** ◆***n.*** **1** a giving of one thing in return for another; trade [I'll give you my pen in *exchange* for that book.] **2** a giving to one another of similar things [Our club has a gift *exchange* at Christmas time.] **3** a place where business or trading is carried on [a stock *exchange*]. ☆**4** a central system for connecting telephones serving a certain area.

**ex·cheq·uer** (iks chek′ər) ***n.*** **1** a treasury, as of a country or an organization. **2 Exchequer,** the department of the British government that is in charge of the national funds.

> **Exchequer** comes from an old French word for the table or board on which the games of chess and checkers were played. Such a table marked with squares was also used for keeping track of money accounts, using colored counters. Later the king's assistants who kept track of the money came to be called the royal **exchequer**.



**ex·cise**[1] (ek′sīz) ***n.*** a tax on the making, selling, or using of certain goods, as tobacco, within a country: *also* **excise tax.**

**ex·cise**[2] (ik sīz′) ***v.*** to cut out; remove [The surgeon *excised* the tumor.] —**ex·cised′, ex·cis′ing —ex·ci·sion** (ik sizh′ən) ***n.***

**ex·cit·a·ble** (ik sīt′ə b′l) ***adj.*** easily excited. —**ex·cit′a·bil′i·ty *n.***

**ex·cite** (ik sīt′) ***v.*** **1** to stir into motion; make active; stimulate [Some medicines *excite* the heart and make it beat faster.] **2** to call forth; bring out [His sad story *excited* our pity.] **3** to cause strong feeling in; stir up; arouse [The sight of men landing on the moon *excited* the whole world.] —**ex·cit′ed, ex·cit′ing**

**ex·cit·ed** (ik sīt′id) ***adj.*** having strong feelings; stirred up. —**ex·cit′ed·ly *adv.***

**ex·cite·ment** (ik sīt′mənt) ***n.*** **1** the condition of being excited [The hotel fire caused great *excitement* in the town.] **2** anything that excites.

**ex·cit·ing** (ik sīt′iŋ) ***adj.*** causing excitement; stirring; thrilling [an *exciting* story].

**ex·claim** (iks klām′) ***v.*** to speak out suddenly and with strong feeling, as in surprise, anger, etc. ["I won't go!" she *exclaimed.*]

| | | | |
|---|---|---|---|
| **a** fat | **ir** here | **ou** out | **zh** leisure |
| **ā** ape | **ī** bite, fire | **u** up | **ŋ** ring |
| **ä** car, lot | **ō** go | **ur** fur | a *in* ago |
| **e** ten | **ô** law, horn | **ch** chin | e *in* agent |
| **er** care | **oi** oil | **sh** she | **ə** = i *in* unity |
| **ē** even | **oo** look | **th** thin | o *in* collect |
| **i** hit | **o͞o** tool | ***th*** then | u *in* focus |

exhibitionist

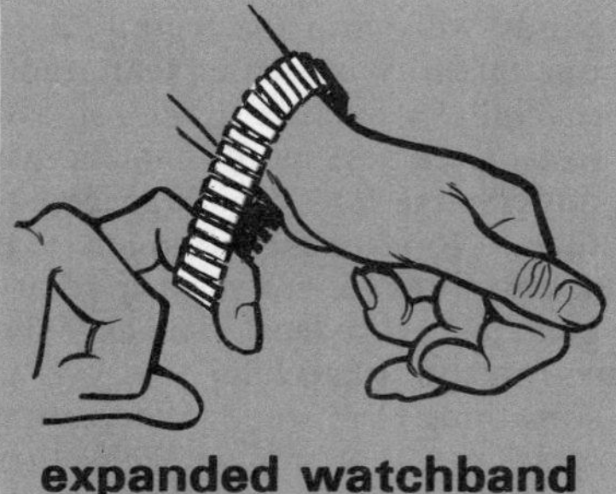

expanded watchband

**ex·cla·ma·tion** (eks′klə mā′shən) ***n.*** **1** the act of exclaiming. **2** a word or phrase that is exclaimed to show strong feeling; interjection ["Oh!" and "Help!" are *exclamations.*]

☆**exclamation mark** or **exclamation point** the mark (!) used after a word or sentence to show surprise, anger, or other strong feeling.

**ex·clam·a·to·ry** (iks klam′ə tôr′ē) ***adj.*** showing or using exclamation [an *exclamatory* sentence].

**ex·clude** (iks klo͞od′) ***v.*** to keep out or shut out; refuse to let in, think about, include, etc.; bar [They *excluded* John from their club. Don't *exclude* the possibility of defeat.] —**ex·clud′ed, ex·clud′ing**

**ex·clu·sion** (iks klo͞o′zhən) ***n.*** the act of excluding or the fact of being excluded.

**ex·clu·sive** (iks klo͞o′siv) ***adj.*** **1** given or belonging



to no other; not shared; sole [That store has the *exclusive* right to sell this Swedish glassware.] **2** keeping out certain people, especially those who are not wealthy or against whom there is prejudice; not open to the public [an *exclusive* club]. **3** shutting out all other interests, thoughts, activities, etc. [an *exclusive* interest in sports]. —**exclusive of,** not including; leaving out [The workers get two weeks of vacation, *exclusive of* holidays.] —**ex·clu′sive·ly *adv.***

**ex·com·mu·ni·cate** (eks′kə myo͞o′nə kāt) ***v.*** to punish by taking away the right to take part in the rituals of a church. —**ex′com·mu′ni·cat·ed, ex′com·mu′ni·cat·ing —ex′com·mu′ni·ca′tion *n.***

**ex·cre·ment** (eks′krə mənt) ***n.*** waste matter from the bowels.

**ex·cres·cence** (iks kres′'ns) ***n.*** a thing growing out of something else in a way that is not normal, as a wart.

**ex·crete** (iks krēt′) ***v.*** to get rid of waste matter from the body. —**ex·cret′ed, ex·cret′ing**

**ex·cre·tion** (iks krē′shən) ***n.*** **1** an excreting. **2** waste matter excreted; sweat, urine, etc.

**ex·cru·ci·at·ing** (iks kro͞o′shē āt′iŋ) ***adj.*** causing great pain; torturing; agonizing.

**ex·cur·sion** (ik skur′zhən) ***n.*** **1** a short trip taken for pleasure. **2** a round trip on a bus, train, etc. at a special lower rate.

**ex·cus·a·ble** (ik skyo͞o′zə b'l) ***adj.*** that can or should be excused [an *excusable* error].

**ex·cuse** (ik skyo͞oz′) ***v.*** **1** to be a proper reason or explanation for [That was a selfish act that nothing will *excuse.*] **2** to think of a fault or wrongdoing as not important; overlook; forgive; pardon [Please *excuse* this interruption.] **3** to set free from some duty or promise; release [The busy teacher was *excused* from serving on the jury.] **4** to allow to leave or go [You may be *excused* from the table.] —**ex·cused′, ex·cus′ing** ◆***n.*** (ik skyo͞os′) **1** a reason given to explain some action or behavior; apology [Ignorance of the law is no *excuse* for wrongdoing.] **2** a freeing from a duty or promise [May I have an *excuse* from art class?] **3** anything that serves as an excuse [Her sprained ankle was Mae's *excuse* for staying home.] **4** a reason that one has made up to explain one's actions; pretext [I shall invent some *excuse* for not going.] —**excuse oneself, 1** to apologize. **2** to ask for permission to leave.

**ex·e·cute** (ek′si kyo͞ot) ***v.*** **1** to carry out; do; perform [to *execute* a plan]. **2** to put a law or order into operation; administer [The President promises to *execute* the laws passed by Congress.] **3** to put to death in a way that is ordered by law [to *execute* a criminal]. *See* SYNONYMS *at* **kill. 4** to make a work of art according to a plan or design [to *execute* a statue]. **5** to make a contract, will, etc. legal, as by signing it. —**ex′e·cut·ed, ex′e·cut·ing**

**ex·e·cu·tion** (ek′sə kyo͞o′shən) ***n.*** **1** the act of executing, or carrying out something [The plan was a good one, and her *execution* of it was perfect.] **2** the act of putting someone to death as ordered by law. **3** the way in which something is done or performed [the *execution* of a painting; the *execution* of a solo passage on a violin]. **4** the act of making legal, as by signing one's name [the *execution* of a contract].

**ex·e·cu·tion·er** (ek′sə kyo͞o′shən ər) ***n.*** a person who kills those sentenced by law to die.

**ex·ec·u·tive** (ig zek′yə tiv) ***n.*** **1** any of the persons who manage the affairs of an organization, as the officers of a business. **2** any of the persons who see that the laws of a nation or state are carried out [The Constitution makes the President our chief *executive.*] ◆***adj.*** **1** having to do with managing; of or like an executive [A mayor should have *executive* ability.] **2** having the power and the duty to see that the laws of a nation or state are carried out [the *executive* branch of a government].

**ex·ec·u·tor** (ig zek′yə tər) ***n.*** a person who has been named to carry out the terms of another person's will.

**ex·em·pla·ry** (ig zem′plə rē) ***adj.*** **1** that is a model or example; worth imitating [Mary's record as a committee member has been *exemplary.*] **2** meant to be a warning [*exemplary* punishment].

**ex·em·pli·fy** (ig zem′plə fī) ***v.*** to show by giving or being an example of [The judge *exemplified* fairness and honesty.] —**ex·em′pli·fied, ex·em′pli·fy·ing** —**ex·em·pli·fi·ca·tion** (ig zem′plə fi kā′shən) ***n.***

**ex·empt** (ig zempt′) ***v.*** to set free from a rule or duty that others must follow; excuse [He was *exempted* from military service because of poor eyesight.] ◆***adj.*** freed from a usual rule or duty [goods that are *exempt* from payment of tax].

**ex·emp·tion** (ig zemp′shən) ***n.*** **1** the act of exempting. **2** a certain sum of money earned, on which income tax is not paid [An *exemption* is given for each person supported, for old age, etc.]

**ex·er·cise** (ek′sər sīz) ***n.*** **1** the act of using; use [the *exercise* of a skill]. **2** active use of the body in order to make it stronger or healthier [Long walks are good outdoor *exercise.*] **3** *usually* **exercises,** *pl.* a series of movements done regularly to make some part of the body stronger or to develop some skill [These *exercises* will strengthen your legs.] **4** a problem to be studied and worked on by a student in order to get more skill [piano *exercises*]. ☆**5 exercises,** *pl.* a program of speeches, songs, etc. at some ceremony [Who will be the main speaker at our graduation *exercises?*] ◆***v.*** **1** to put into action; use [*Exercise* caution in crossing the street.] **2** to put into use or do certain regular movements, in order to develop or train [*Exercise* your weak ankle. I *exercise* every morning.] *See* SYNONYMS *at* **practice.** —**ex'er·cised, ex'er·cis·ing**

> **Exercise** comes from a Latin word meaning "to drive farm animals out to work." Originally the verb was always used to mean "to make somebody else work." Now, of course, we exercise ourselves and our own bodies.

**ex·ert** (ig zurt') ***v.*** to put into use; use [He *exerted* all his strength.] —**exert oneself,** to try hard.

**ex·er·tion** (ig zur'shən) ***n.*** **1** the act of exerting, or using [She succeeded by the *exertion* of all her skill.] **2** the use of power and strength; effort [The swimmer was worn out by his *exertions*.]

**ex·hale** (eks hāl') ***v.*** **1** to breathe out [Take a deep breath, then *exhale*.] **2** to give off a gas or vapor, or pass off as a vapor. —**ex·haled', ex·hal'ing** —**ex·ha·la·tion** (eks'hə lā'shən) ***n.***

**ex·haust** (ig zôst') ***v.*** **1** to use up completely [Our drinking water was soon *exhausted*.] **2** to let out the contents of; make completely empty [The leak soon *exhausted* the gas tank.] **3** to use up the strength of; tire out; weaken [They are *exhausted* from playing tennis.] *See* SYNONYMS *at* **tired.** **4** to study or deal with in a complete or thorough way [This book *exhausts* the subject of owls.] ◆***n.*** **1** the used steam or gas that comes from the cylinders of an engine; especially, the fumes from the gasoline engine in an automobile. **2** the forcing out of such steam or gas. **3** a pipe through which such steam or gas is forced out: *also* **exhaust pipe.**

**ex·haust·i·ble** (ig zôs'tə b'l) ***adj.*** that can be exhausted, or used up [The nation's supply of oil is *exhaustible*.] —**ex·haust'i·bil'i·ty** ***n.***

**ex·haus·tion** (ig zôs'chən) ***n.*** **1** the act of exhausting, or using up. **2** the condition of being very tired or weakened; great weariness.

**ex·haus·tive** (ig zôs'tiv) ***adj.*** leaving nothing out; complete; thorough [an *exhaustive* search].

**ex·hib·it** (ig zib'it) ***v.*** **1** to show or display to the public [to *exhibit* stamp collections]. **2** to show or reveal [Such an act *exhibits* great courage.] ◆***n.*** **1** something exhibited to the public [an art *exhibit*]. **2** something shown as evidence in a court of law.

**ex·hi·bi·tion** (ek'sə bish'ən) ***n.*** **1** the act of exhibiting, or showing. **2** a public showing, as of a collection of things.

**ex·hi·bi·tion·ist** (ek'sə bish'ən ist) ***n.*** a person who shows off in such a way as to make people look. *See the picture.*

**ex·hib·i·tor** or **ex·hib·it·er** (ig zib'ə tər) ***n.*** a person, company, etc. that exhibits something at a public showing, as at a fair.

**ex·hil·a·rate** (ig zil'ə rāt) ***v.*** to make feel cheerful and lively [I was *exhilarated* by the fresh air.] —**ex·hil'a·rat·ed, ex·hil'a·rat·ing** —**ex·hil'a·ra'tion** ***n.***

**ex·hort** (ig zôrt') ***v.*** to urge or advise strongly [She *exhorted* us to try harder.] —**ex'hor·ta'tion** ***n.***

**ex·hume** (ig zyōōm' *or* iks hyōōm') ***v.*** to remove from a grave. —**ex·humed', ex·hum'ing**

**ex·i·gen·cy** (ek'sə jən sē) ***n.*** **1** a situation calling for quick action. **2 exigencies,** *pl.* the needs created by such a situation. —*pl.* **ex'i·gen·cies**

**ex·ile** (eg'zīl *or* ek'sīl) ***v.*** to force a person to leave his or her own country and live somewhere else; banish. *See* SYNONYMS *at* **deport.** —**ex'iled, ex'il·ing** ◆***n.*** **1** the condition of being exiled; banishment. **2** a person who is exiled.

**ex·ist** (ig zist') ***v.*** **1** to be; have actual being [The unicorn never really *existed*.] **2** to occur or be found [Tigers do not *exist* in Africa.] **3** to live [Fish cannot *exist* long out of water.]

**ex·ist·ence** (ig zis'təns) ***n.*** **1** the condition of being; an existing. **2** an occurring. **3** life or a way of life [a happy *existence*]. —**ex·ist'ent** ***adj.***

**ex·it** (eg'zit *or* ek'sit) ***n.*** **1** a place for going out; door or passage out. **2** the act of going out; departure [We made a quick *exit*.]

> **Exit** is a Latin word meaning "he (or she) goes out." It was orginally used as a direction to an actor to go off the stage [*Exit* Hamlet.]

**Ex·o·dus** (ek'sə dəs) **1** the going out of the Israelites from Egypt, as told in the Bible. **2** the second book of the Bible, telling of this.

**ex·o·dus** (ek'sə dəs) ***n.*** any going out by many people; departure [the *exodus* from the city to the suburbs].



**ex·on·er·ate** (ig zän'ə rāt) ***v.*** to prove to be not guilty; declare to be innocent [The prisoner was *exonerated* by what the witnesses said.] —**ex·on'er·at·ed, ex·on'er·at·ing** —**ex·on'er·a'tion** ***n.***

**ex·or·bi·tant** (ig zôr'bə tənt) ***adj.*** too much or too great; not reasonable or not fair [an *exorbitant* price]. —**ex·or'bi·tance** ***n.***

**ex·or·cise** or **ex·or·cize** (ek'sôr sīz) ***v.*** to drive out a supposed evil spirit by saying prayers or making a magic sign. —**ex'or·cised** or **ex'or·cized, ex'or·cis·ing** or **ex'or·ciz·ing** —**ex'or·cist** ***n.***

**ex·ot·ic** (ig zät'ik) ***adj.*** strange, different, or foreign, especially in a fascinating way [*exotic* plants]. —**ex·ot'i·cal·ly** ***adv.***

**ex·pand** (ik spand') ***v.*** **1** to make or grow bigger or wider, as by unfolding, puffing out, or spreading; enlarge [Take a deep breath to *expand* your chest. The peacock *expanded* its tail.] *See the picture.* **2** to tell or develop the details of [to *expand* an idea into a short story].

> SYNONYMS: Something **expands** when it grows larger or is made larger, as by opening up, spreading out, or puffing up [You *expand* your hand by stretching out the fingers.] Something **swells** when it expands beyond its normal size [Her sprained ankle *swelled*.]

| | | | | | | | |
|---|---|---|---|---|---|---|---|
| a | fat | ir | here | ou | out | zh | leisure |
| ā | ape | ī | bite, fire | u | up | ng | ring |
| ä | car, lot | ō | go | ur | fur | | a *in* ago |
| e | ten | ô | law, horn | ch | chin | | e *in* agent |
| er | care | oi | oil | sh | she | ə = | i *in* unity |
| ē | even | oo | look | th | thin | | o *in* collect |
| i | hit | ōō | tool | *th* | then | | u *in* focus |

**ex·panse** (ik spans′) ***n.*** a large, open area or surface [an *expanse* of desert].

**ex·pan·sion** (ik span′shən) ***n.*** **1** the act of expanding or the fact of being expanded [the *expansion* of the village into a large city]. **2** the amount or part that is expanded [Plans for the school include a six-room *expansion.*]

**ex·pan·sive** (ik span′siv) ***adj.*** **1** that can expand [Gases are *expansive.*] **2** spread over a wide area; broad; extensive [the *expansive* wheat fields of the Middle West]. **3** showing a frank and open manner, especially in a warm and friendly way [Grandpa grew *expansive* as he talked of his childhood.] —**ex·pan′sive·ly** ***adv.***

**ex·pa·ti·ate** (ik spā′shē āt) ***v.*** to speak or write in great detail [She *expatiated* on her recent travels.] —**ex·pa′ti·at·ed, ex·pa′ti·at·ing**

**ex·pa·tri·ate** (eks pā′trē āt) ***v.*** to force a person to leave his or her own country; exile. —**ex·pa′tri·at·ed, ex·pa′tri·at·ing** ◆***n.*** (eks pā′trē it) an expatriated person; one who leaves one's own country to live in another. —**ex·pa′tri·a′tion** ***n.***

**ex·pect** (ik spekt′) ***v.*** **1** to think that something will happen or come; look forward to [I *expect* to hear from Jane soon.] **2** to look for as proper or due [He *expected* a reward for finding it.] **3** to guess or suppose: *used only in everyday talk* [I *expect* you'll be wanting dinner.]

**ex·pect·an·cy** (ik spek′tən sē) ***n.*** **1** the act of expecting; expectation [The children awaited the party in happy *expectancy.*] **2** that which is expected [Babies today have a longer life *expectancy* than those born a hundred years ago.] —*pl.* **ex·pect′an·cies**

**ex·pect·ant** (ik spek′tənt) ***adj.*** waiting for something to happen; expecting [The children waited with happy, *expectant* faces for the show to begin.] —**ex·pect′ant·ly** ***adv.***

**ex·pec·ta·tion** (ek′spek tā′shən) ***n.*** **1** the act of expecting, or looking forward to something [He sat on the edge of his seat in *expectation.*] **2** *often* **expectations,** *pl.* something expected, or looked forward to, especially with good reason [She has *expectations* of being promoted to a better job.]

**ex·pec·to·rate** (ik spek′tə rāt) ***v.*** to cough up mucus, etc. from the throat and spit it out. —**ex·pec′to·rat·ed, ex·pec′to·rat·ing** —**ex·pec′to·ra′tion** ***n.***

> **Expectorate** is sometimes also used as a joking or fancy substitute for the word **spit** itself, or it is used by those who consider the word **spit** to be an unpleasant one.

**ex·pe·di·en·cy** (ik spē′dē ən sē) ***n.*** **1** the condition of being right or useful for some purpose; fitness [As a matter of *expediency,* we will fly there rather than drive.] **2** the doing of something that is selfish rather than right [His seeming friendliness is based more on *expediency* than on a wish to be helpful.] *Also* **ex·pe′di·ence.** —*pl.* **ex·pe′di·en·cies**

**ex·pe·di·ent** (ik spē′dē ənt) ***adj.*** **1** wise or useful for some purpose; convenient [Would it be *expedient* to deliver this letter in person?] **2** helpful to oneself, but not really right or proper [The mayor opposed the school levy as an *expedient* way of getting reelected.] ◆***n.*** something useful for a certain purpose [The guard kept awake by the *expedient* of drinking coffee.] —**ex·pe′di·ent·ly** ***adv.***

**ex·pe·dite** (ek′spə dīt) ***v.*** to make move or act in an easier or faster way; speed up; hasten [We can *expedite* the loading by adding two workers to the crew.] —**ex′pe·dit·ed, ex′pe·dit·ing** —**ex′pe·dit·er** ***n.***

> **Expedite** comes from a Latin word meaning "to free someone who is caught by the feet." A person can move in an easier or faster way if the feet are free.

**ex·pe·di·tion** (ek′spə dish′ən) ***n.*** **1** a long journey or voyage by a group of people, as to explore a region or to take part in a battle. **2** the people, ships, etc. making such a trip. **3** speed or quickness with little effort or waste [We finished our task with *expedition.*] —**ex′pe·di′tion·ar′y** ***adj.***

**ex·pe·di·tious** (ek′spə dish′əs) ***adj.*** with great speed; quick and efficient [to work in an *expeditious* manner].

**ex·pel** (ik spel′) ***v.*** **1** to drive out or throw out with force; eject [a tea kettle *expelling* steam through its spout]. *See* SYNONYMS *at* **eject. 2** to send away or make leave as a punishment [Paul was *expelled* from the club because he failed to pay his dues.] —**ex·pelled′, ex·pel′ling**

**ex·pend** (ik spend′) ***v.*** to use up or spend.

**ex·pend·a·ble** (ik spen′də b'l) ***adj.*** that can be used up or spent; especially, in warfare, worth sacrificing in order to gain some end.

**ex·pend·i·ture** (ik spen′də chər) ***n.*** **1** the act of using up or spending money, time, energy, etc. **2** the amount used up or spent.

**ex·pense** (ik spens′) ***n.*** **1** the act of spending money, time, etc. **2** *also* **expenses,** *pl.* the amount of money spent; often, money spent or needed for carrying out a job [Many salespersons are paid a salary, plus traveling *expenses.*] **3** something that causes spending [Owning a car is a great *expense.*] **4** loss or sacrifice [The battle was won at terrible *expense.*]

**ex·pen·sive** (ik spen′siv) ***adj.*** costing much; having a high price [She wears *expensive* clothes.] *See* SYNONYMS *at* **costly.** —**ex·pen′sive·ly** ***adv.***

**ex·pe·ri·ence** (ik spir′ē əns) ***n.*** **1** the fact of living through a happening or happenings [*Experience* teaches us many things.] **2** something that one has done or lived through [This trip was an *experience* that I'll never forget.] **3** skill that one gets by training, practice, and work [a lawyer with much *experience*]. ◆***v.*** to have the experience of [to *experience* success]. —**ex·pe′ri·enced, ex·pe′ri·enc·ing**

**ex·pe·ri·enced** (ik spir′ē ənst) ***adj.*** having had experience or having learned from experience [an *experienced* mechanic or doctor].

**ex·per·i·ment** (ik sper′ə mənt) ***n.*** a test or tests to find out something or to see whether a theory is correct [an *experiment* to measure the effects of a medicine]. ◆***v.*** to make experiments. —**ex·per·i·men·ta·tion** (ik sper′ə mən tā′shən) ***n.***

**ex·per·i·men·tal** (ik sper′ə men′t'l) ***adj.*** **1** based on or having to do with experiment [an *experimental* science]. **2** being an experiment; testing; trial [a baby's first, *experimental* steps]. —**ex·per′i·men′tal·ly** ***adv.***

**ex·pert** (ek′spərt *or* ik spurt′) ***adj.*** **1** having much special knowledge and experience; very skillful [an *expert* golfer]. **2** of or from an expert [*expert* advice].

◆*n.* (ek′spərt) an expert person; authority [an *expert* in art].

**ex·pert·ise** (ek′spər tēz′) ***n.*** the special skill or knowledge that an expert has [an architect's *expertise* in the materials used for building].

**ex·pi·ate** (ek′spē āt) ***v.*** to make up for doing something wrong or bad; make amends for [She *expiated* her crime by helping the victim.] **—ex′pi·at·ed, ex′pi·at·ing —ex′pi·a′tion *n.***

**ex·pi·ra·tion** (ek′spə rā′shən) ***n.*** **1** the fact of coming to an end; close [the *expiration* of a term of office]. **2** a breathing out, as of air from the lungs.

**ex·pire** (ik spīr′) ***v.*** **1** to come to an end; stop [The lease *expires* next month.] **2** to die. **3** to breathe out. **—ex·pired′, ex·pir′ing**

**ex·plain** (ik splān′) ***v.*** **1** to make clear or plain; give details of [He *explained* how the engine works.] **2** to give the meaning of [The teacher *explained* the story.] **3** to give reasons for [Can you *explain* your absence?]

**ex·pla·na·tion** (eks′plə nā′shən) ***n.*** **1** the act of explaining [This plan needs *explanation.*] **2** something that explains [This long nail is the *explanation* for the flat tire.] **3** a meaning given in explaining [different *explanations* of the same event].

**ex·plan·a·to·ry** (ik splan′ə tôr′ē) ***adj.*** that explains; explaining [an *explanatory* letter].

**ex·ple·tive** (eks′plə tiv) ***adj.*** **1** an oath or exclamation ["Gosh" and "oh" are *expletives.*] **2** a word that has no particular meaning but is used to fill out a phrase [In the phrase "it is raining," the word "it" is an *expletive.*]

**ex·plic·it** (ik splis′it) ***adj.*** so clear and plain that there can be no doubt as to the meaning; definite [The doctor gave her *explicit* orders to stay in bed and rest.] **—ex·plic′it·ly *adv.***

**ex·plode** (ik splōd′) ***v.*** **1** to blow up or burst with a loud noise and force [The firecracker *exploded.* The engineer *exploded* the dynamite.] **2** to show to be false or foolish [Science has helped to *explode* many superstitions.] **3** to burst forth angrily [She *exploded* with anger.] **—ex·plod′ed, ex·plod′ing**

> **Explode** originally meant "to chase an unpopular actor off the stage by clapping and hooting." Later it came to mean "to make any loud noise," such as that made when a bomb goes off.

**ex·ploit** (eks′ploit) ***n.*** a daring act or bold deed [the *exploits* of Robin Hood]. ◆***v.*** (ik sploit′ *or* eks′ploit) **1** to make full and proper use of [to *exploit* the water power of a river]. **2** to use in a selfish way; take unfair advantage of [Children were *exploited* when they had to work in factories.] **—ex′ploi·ta′tion *n.***

**ex·plore** (ik splôr′) ***v.*** **1** to travel in a region that is unknown or not well known, in order to find out more about it [to *explore* a wild jungle]. **2** to look into or examine carefully [to *explore* a problem]. **—ex·plored′, ex·plor′ing —ex′plo·ra′tion *n.* —ex·plor′er *n.***

**ex·plo·sion** (ik splō′zhən) ***n.*** **1** the act of exploding, or blowing up with a loud noise [the *explosion* of a bomb]. **2** any noisy outburst [an angry *explosion* of temper]. **3** a rapid and great increase [the population *explosion*].

**ex·plo·sive** (ik splō′siv) ***adj.*** **1** that can cause an explosion [an *explosive* substance]. **2** like an explosion [an *explosive* clap of thunder]. **3** that might explode suddenly [Riots had caused an *explosive* situation.] ◆***n.*** a substance that can explode [dynamite and other *explosives*].

**ex·po·nent** (ik spō′nənt) ***n.*** **1** a person who explains and makes clear [an *exponent* of modern music]. **2** a person or thing that is an example or symbol of something [The singer Caruso was an *exponent* of grand opera.] **3** a small figure or symbol placed at the upper right of another figure or symbol to show how many times that other figure or symbol is to be used as a factor. Example: $b^3$ is equal to b x b x b.

**ex·port** (ik spôrt′ *or* eks′pôrt) ***v.*** to send goods from one country for sale in another [Japan *exports* many radios.] ◆***n.*** (eks′pôrt) **1** the act of exporting [Brazil raises coffee for *export.*] **2** something exported [Oil is Venezuela's chief *export.*] **—ex′por·ta′tion *n.* —ex·port′er *n.***

**ex·pose** (ik spōz′) ***v.*** **1** to put in a position of danger; leave unprotected [People on a golf course during a thunderstorm are *exposed* to lightning.] **2** to put something where it can be worked on or changed by outside action [Copper that is *exposed* to the weather will turn green.] **3** to let be seen; display [She removed the bandage and *exposed* the wound.] **4** to make known; reveal [to *expose* a crime]. **5** to let light fall on the film or plate in a camera, and in this way cause a picture to be recorded. **—ex·posed′, ex·pos′ing**

**ex·po·si·tion** (eks′pə zish′ən) ***n.*** **1** a large show or fair that is open to the public [Chicago held a great *exposition* in 1893.] **2** explanation, or some writing or speaking that explains something [Your *exposition* of the play was helpful.]



**ex·pos·i·to·ry** (ik späz′ə tôr′ē) ***adj.*** that explains something; explanatory [*expository* writing].

**ex·pos·tu·late** (ik spas′chə lāt) ***v.*** to argue with a person seriously against something that person has done or means to do [The players *expostulated* in vain with the umpire.] **—ex·pos′tu·lat·ed, ex·pos′tu·lat·ing —ex·pos′tu·la′tion *n.***

**ex·po·sure** (ik spō′zhər) ***n.*** **1** the act of exposing [the *exposure* of a plot]. **2** the fact of being exposed [tanned by *exposure* to the sun]. **3** the position of a house, etc., described by the direction from which it is exposed to sun and wind [Our kitchen has a southern *exposure.*] **4** the time during which film in a camera is exposed to light; also, a section of film that can be made into one picture [Give this film a short *exposure.* There are twelve *exposures* on this film.]

**ex·pound** (ik spound′) ***v.*** to explain, especially by giving many details [to *expound* a theory].

**ex·press** (ik spres′) ***v.*** **1** to put into words; state [It is hard to *express* my feelings.] **2** to give or be a sign of; show [a frown that *expressed* doubt]. ☆**3** to send goods by a fast way. ◆***adj.*** **1** clearly said or meant;

| | | | | | | | |
|---|---|---|---|---|---|---|---|
| **a** | fat | **ir** | here | **ou** | out | **zh** | leisure |
| **ā** | ape | **ī** | bite, fire | **u** | up | **ŋ** | ring |
| **ä** | car, lot | **ō** | go | **ur** | fur | | a *in* ago |
| **e** | ten | **ô** | law, horn | **ch** | chin | | e *in* agent |
| **er** | care | **oi** | oil | **sh** | she | ə = | i *in* unity |
| **ē** | even | **oo** | look | **th** | thin | | o *in* collect |
| **i** | hit | **ōō** | tool | ***th*** | then | | u *in* focus |

definite; explicit [I came for the *express* purpose of seeing you.] **2** taking the shortest and fastest route; not making many stops [an *express* train or bus]. **3** for fast driving [an *express* highway]. ◆***n.*** **1** a train, bus, etc. that takes the shortest and fastest route, not making many stops. ☆**2** a way of sending goods or packages that is faster than other ways. Express usually costs more. ☆**3** goods sent by express. ◆***adv.*** by express [The package came *express*.] —**express oneself,** to tell in words what one thinks or how one feels.

**ex·pres·sion** (ik spresh′ən) ***n.*** **1** an expressing, or putting into words [This note is an *expression* of my gratitude.] **2** a way of speaking, singing, or playing something that gives it real meaning or feeling [to read with *expression*]. **3** a word or phrase ["You bet" is an everyday *expression* meaning "certainly."] **4** the act of showing how one feels, what one means, etc. [Laughter is an *expression* of joy.] **5** a look that shows how one feels, what one means, etc. [a sad *expression* on the face]. **6** a symbol or set of symbols that tell some fact in mathematics.

**ex·pres·sive** (ik spres′iv) ***adj.*** **1** that expresses or shows [a smile *expressive* of joy]. **2** full of meaning or feeling [an *expressive* nod]. —**ex·pres′sive·ly** ***adv.***

**ex·press·ly** (ik spres′lē) ***adv.*** **1** in a plain or definite way [I told you *expressly* not to go.] **2** for the purpose; especially [He went to college *expressly* to become a teacher.]



☆**ex·press·way** (ik spres′wā) ***n.*** a wide highway divided into a number of lanes, meant for fast traffic. It is usually entered or left by means of cloverleafs.

**ex·pul·sion** (ik spul′shən) ***n.*** the act of expelling, or forcing out, or the condition of being expelled [the *expulsion* of hot gases from a rocket].

**ex·punge** (ik spunj′) ***v.*** to erase or remove completely [to *expunge* names from a record]. —**ex·punged′, ex·pung′ing**

**ex·pur·gate** (eks′pər gāt) ***v.*** to clean up by taking out words or sentences thought to be indecent [to *expurgate* a book]. —**ex′pur·gat·ed, ex′pur·gat·ing**

**ex·qui·site** (eks′kwi zit *or* ik skwiz′it) ***adj.*** **1** done with great care and skill [*exquisite* carvings]. **2** very beautiful [an *exquisite* sunset]. **3** of the best quality; excellent [an *exquisite* performance]. **4** very great or sharp [*exquisite* joy or pain]. —**ex′qui·site·ly** ***adv.***

**ex·tant** (ek′stənt *or* ik stant′) ***adj.*** still existing [Only a few copies of the book are still *extant*.]

**ex·tem·po·ra·ne·ous** (ik stem′pə rā′nē əs) ***adj.*** done or spoken without much planning, especially without being written down [an *extemporaneous* speech].

**ex·tem·po·rize** (ik stem′pə rīz) ***v.*** to say, do, or make something without much planning [Upon receiving the award, she *extemporized* a speech of thanks.] —**ex·tem′po·rized, ex·tem′po·riz·ing**

**ex·tend** (ik stend′) ***v.*** **1** to make longer; stretch out [Careful cleaning *extends* the life of a rug.] **2** to lie or stretch [The fence *extends* along the meadow.] **3** to make larger or more complete; enlarge; increase [to *extend* one's power]. **4** to offer or give [May I *extend* congratulations to the winner?] **5** to straighten or stretch out [*Extend* your arm for the tetanus shot.] —**ex·tend′ed** ***adj.***

**ex·ten·sion** (ik sten′shən) ***n.*** **1** the act of extending; a stretching out, enlarging, increasing, etc. [May I have an *extension* of time for paying what I owe you?] **2** something that extends, or makes larger; addition [We are building an *extension* to the library.] **3** an extra telephone on the same line as the main telephone. ◆☆***adj.*** that is or has a part that can be extended, or stretched out [an *extension* ladder]. *See the picture.*

**ex·ten·sive** (ik sten′siv) ***adj.*** **1** being large, great, widespread, etc. [the *extensive* jungles of Brazil]. **2** applying to many things; having a great effect; far-reaching [to make *extensive* changes in a program]. —**ex·ten′sive·ly** ***adv.***

**ex·tent** (ik stent′) ***n.*** **1** the size, amount, length, etc. to which something extends [The *extent* of knowledge has increased over the centuries.] **2** degree or limit [To a certain *extent* he is right.] **3** a large area [They own a vast *extent* of woodland.]

**ex·ten·u·ate** (ik sten′yoo wāt) ***v.*** to make a wrongdoing seem less serious by being or giving an excuse [The heavy snowfall was given as an *extenuating* factor for their absence.] —**ex·ten′u·at·ed, ex·ten′u·at·ing** —**ex·ten′u·a′tion** ***n.***

**ex·te·ri·or** (ik stir′ē ər) ***adj.*** **1** of or on the outside; outer [The *exterior* trim of the house is gray.] **2** coming from the outside [*exterior* forces]. ◆***n.*** the outside or outer part.

**ex·ter·mi·nate** (ik stur′mə nāt) ***v.*** to kill or destroy completely; wipe out [That company's work is *exterminating* rats.] —**ex·ter′mi·nat·ed, ex·ter′mi·nat·ing** —**ex·ter′mi·na′tion** ***n.*** —**ex·ter′mi·na·tor** ***n.***

**ex·ter·nal** (ik stur′n′l) ***adj.*** **1** on the outside; outer [Red spots are an *external* sign of an allergy.] **2** on the outside of the body [a medicine for *external* use only]. **3** that comes from the outside [an *external* force]. **4** merely seeming to be so [*external* politeness]. **5** having to do with foreign countries [a nation's *external* affairs]. ◆***n.*** an external thing or appearance. —**ex·ter′nal·ly** ***adv.***

**ex·tinct** (ik stiŋkt′) ***adj.*** **1** no longer living; having died out [Dinosaurs are *extinct*.] **2** no longer burning or active [an *extinct* volcano].

**ex·tinc·tion** (ik stiŋk′shən) ***n.*** **1** the fact of becoming extinct, or dying out [The California condor faces *extinction*.] **2** a putting an end to or wiping out [the *extinction* of all debts]. **3** an extinguishing, or putting out [the *extinction* of a fire].

**ex·tin·guish** (ik stiŋ′gwish) ***v.*** **1** to put out; quench [to *extinguish* a fire or light]. **2** to put an end to; destroy [to *extinguish* all hope].

**ex·tin·guish·er** (ik stiŋ′gwish ər) ***n.*** a person or thing that extinguishes; especially, a device for putting out a fire by spraying a liquid or gas on it. *See the picture.*

**ex·tol** or **ex·toll** (ik stōl′) ***v.*** to say very good things about; praise highly [His performance on the harp was *extolled* by the critics.] —**ex·tolled′, ex·tol′ling**

**ex·tort** (ik stôrt′) ***v.*** to get money, a confession, etc. from someone by using force or threats.

**ex·tor·tion** (ik stôr′shən) ***n.*** **1** the act of extorting money, etc., as by using threats. **2** something that has been extorted. —**ex·tor′tion·ist** ***n.***

**ex·tra** (eks′trə) ***adj.*** more than is usual, expected, or necessary; in addition [Remember to carry *extra* water. There is an *extra* charge for this service.] ◆**n.** **1** an extra person, thing, charge, etc. [The store hired *extras* to work before Christmas.] ☆**2** a special edition of a newspaper to tell an important news story. Such editions are now seldom published. **3** an actor in a motion picture who is hired from day to day to play a small part, often as a member of a crowd. ◆**adv.** more than it usually is; especially [an *extra* long meeting].

**ex·tract** (ik strakt′) **v.** **1** to pull out something by trying hard [to *extract* a tooth; to *extract* a promise]. **2** to get by squeezing, pressing, etc. [to *extract* orange juice]. **3** to manage to get [to *extract* the meaning of a remark]. **4** to take a section from a piece of writing, as in order to quote it. ◆**n.** (eks′trakt) **1** a strong substance that has been extracted from something, for use as a flavoring or food [vanilla *extract*]. **2** a section of a book, etc. that has been chosen as for quoting.

**ex·trac·tion** (ik strak′shən) **n.** **1** the act of extracting, or pulling out by effort. **2** the people from whom a person is descended; origin; descent [a person of Mexican *extraction*].

☆**ex·tra·cur·ric·u·lar** (eks′trə kə rik′yə lər) **adj.** not part of the required course of study in a school or college [Football and student council are *extracurricular* activities.]

**ex·tra·dite** (eks′trə dīt) **v.** to hand over a person accused of a crime or an escaped prisoner to another country or State that claims that person. —**ex′tra·dit·ed, ex′tra·dit·ing** —**ex·tra·di·tion** (eks′trə dish′ən) **n.**

**ex·tra·ne·ous** (ik strā′nē əs) **adj.** coming from outside; not really belonging; foreign [The milk is strained to remove *extraneous* material.]

> SYNONYMS: **Extraneous** is used of something which, although it is not truly a part of something else, can be worked into it [The artist added some *extraneous* details to the picture.] **Foreign** is used of something that is so different from something else that it cannot be made a part of it [She removed the *foreign* particle from his eye.]

**ex·traor·di·nar·y** (ik strôr′d'n er′ē) **adj.** much different from the ordinary; very unusual; remarkable [*extraordinary* skill]. —**ex·traor′di·nar′i·ly adv.**

**ex·trav·a·gant** (ik strav′ə gənt) **adj.** **1** spending more than one can afford or more than is necessary; wasteful [The *extravagant* shopper bought four suits at one time.] **2** going beyond what is proper; too much [*extravagant* praise]. —**ex·trav′a·gance n.** —**ex·trav′a·gant·ly adv.**

**ex·treme** (ik strēm′) **adj.** **1** to the greatest degree; very great [*extreme* pain]. **2** farthest away; most remote [the *extreme* limits of outer space]. **3** far from what is usual; also, very far from the center of opinion [She holds *extreme* political views.] ◆**n.** either of two things that are as different or as far from each other as possible [the *extremes* of laughter and tears]. —**go to extremes,** to do or say more than is necessary or proper. —**ex·treme′ly adv.**

**ex·trem·ist** (ik strēm′ist) **n.** a person who goes to extremes or who holds extreme ideas.

**ex·trem·i·ty** (ik strem′ə tē) **n.** **1** the farthest point or part; end [the eastern *extremity* of the island]. **2 extremities,** *pl.* the hands and feet. **3** the greatest degree [an *extremity* of grief]. **4** great need, danger, etc. [The surrounded troops realized the *extremity* of their position.] **5** a strong or severe action [driven to *extremities* in an emergency]. —*pl.* **ex·trem′i·ties**

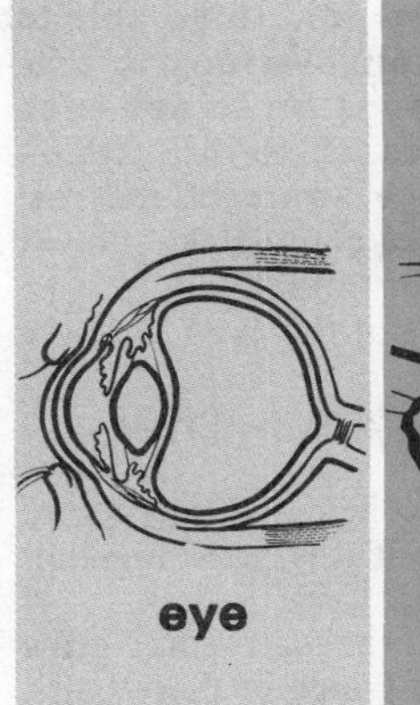

eye

fire extinguisher

extension ladder

**ex·tri·cate** (eks′trə kāt) **v.** to set free from some danger or difficulty; release [The boy tried to *extricate* his foot from the crevice.] —**ex′tri·cat·ed, ex′tri·cat·ing** —**ex′tri·ca′tion n.**

**ex·trin·sic** (ek strin′sik) **adj.** not really belonging to the thing with which it is connected; external [Your comments are *extrinsic* to the matter we are discussing.]

**ex·tro·vert** (eks′trə vurt) **n.** one who is interested in other people and things rather than just in one's own thoughts and feelings. —**ex′tro·vert·ed adj.** 

**ex·u·ber·ant** (ig zo͞o′bər ənt *or* ig zyo͞o′bər ənt) **adj.** healthy and lively; full of good humor [I always feel *exuberant* in the spring.] —**ex·u′ber·ance n.**

**ex·ude** (ig zo͞od′ *or* ig zyo͞od′) **v.** to come or pass out in drops, as through the pores or a cut; ooze [Maple trees *exude* sap in the spring.] —**ex·ud′ed, ex·ud′ing**

**ex·ult** (ig zult′) **v.** to be very proud and happy; rejoice [to *exult* in victory].

**ex·ult·ant** (ig zult″nt) **adj.** exulting; full of happiness and pride [an *exultant* smile].

**ex·ul·ta·tion** (eg′zul tā′shən) **n.** an exulting; a feeling of great joy and pride.

**eye** (ī) **n.** **1** the part of the body with which a human being or animal sees. *See the picture.* **2** the iris of the eye [blue *eyes*]. **3** *often* **eyes,** *pl.* the ability to see; sight; vision [weak *eyes*]. **4** a look; glance [Cast an *eye* over here.] **5** the ability to judge by looking [a good *eye* for distances]. **6** *often* **eyes,** *pl.* judgment; opinion [In her *eyes,* he is perfect.] **7** something that reminds one of an eye, as a bud of a potato or the hole in a needle. ◆**v.** to look at; observe [We *eyed* the stranger suspiciously.] —**eyed, ey′ing** —**all eyes,** paying very close attention. —**catch one's eye,** to get one's attention. —**feast one's eyes on,** to look

| | | | | | | | |
|---|---|---|---|---|---|---|---|
| **a** | fat | **ir** | here | **ou** | out | **zh** | leisure |
| **ā** | ape | **ī** | bite, fire | **u** | up | **ng** | ring |
| **ä** | car, lot | **ō** | go | **ur** | fur | | a *in* ago |
| **e** | ten | **ô** | law, horn | **ch** | chin | | e *in* agent |
| **er** | care | **oi** | oil | **sh** | she | **ə =** | i *in* unity |
| **ē** | even | **oo** | look | **th** | thin | | o *in* collect |
| **i** | hit | **o͞o** | tool | ***th*** | then | | u *in* focus |

at with pleasure. —**have an eye for,** to be able to notice and appreciate. —**keep an eye on,** to take care of; watch carefully. —**lay eyes on** or **set eyes on,** to see; look at. —**make eyes at,** to flirt with. —**open one's eyes,** to make one aware of the real facts. —**see eye to eye,** to agree completely. —**shut one's eyes to,** to refuse to see or think about.

**eye·ball** (ī'bôl) ***n.*** the whole part of the eye inside the socket.

**eye·brow** (ī'brou) ***n.*** the curved, bony part over each eye, or the hair growing on it.

**eye·glass** (ī'glas) ***n.*** **1** a lens to help one see better. **2 eyeglasses,** *pl.* a pair of such lenses fitted together in a frame.

**eye·lash** (ī'lash) ***n.*** **1** any of the hairs that grow along the edge of the eyelid. **2** a fringe of these hairs.

**eye·less** (ī'lis) ***adj.*** without eyes; blind.

**eye·let** (ī'lit) ***n.*** **1** a small hole for a cord, lace, or hook to go through. *See the picture.* **2** a metal ring placed in such a hole to make it stronger.

**eye·lid** (ī'lid) ***n.*** either of the two folds of skin that cover and uncover the eyeball.

**eye·piece** (ī'pēs) ***n.*** the lens in a microscope, telescope, etc. that is held nearest the eye.

**eye·sight** (ī'sīt) ***n.*** **1** the ability to see; sight; vision [keen *eyesight*]. **2** the distance a person can see [Keep within *eyesight!*]

**eye·sore** (ī'sôr) ***n.*** an unpleasant thing to look at [A lawn full of weeds is an *eyesore.*]

**eye·strain** (ī'strān) ***n.*** a tired condition of the eye muscles, as from too much use or an incorrect use of the eyes.

**eye·tooth** (ī'to͞oth) ***n.*** either of the two canine teeth in the upper jaw, the third tooth from the center on each side. —*pl.* **eye'teeth**

**eye·wit·ness** (ī'wit'nis) ***n.*** a person who actually saw something happen, not one who was told of it by someone else.

**ey·rie** or **ey·ry** (er'ē *or* ir'ē) ***n.*** *another spelling of* **aerie.** —*pl.* **ey'ries**

**E·zek·i·el** (i zē'kē əl) **1** a Hebrew prophet of the 6th century B.C. **2** a book of the Bible with his prophecies.

**Ez·ra** (ez'rə) **1** a Hebrew prophet of the 5th century B.C. **2** a book of the Bible telling of his life and teachings.

**F,f** (ef) ***n.*** the sixth letter of the English alphabet. —*pl.* **F's, f's** (efs)

**F** **1** *the symbol for the chemical element* fluorine. **2** the lowest grade, as in some schools, meaning "failing."

**F** or **F.** *abbreviation for* **Fahrenheit.**

**F.** or **f.** *abbreviation for* **fathom, female, following, forte** (in music), **franc** or **francs.**

**fa** (fä) ***n.*** the fourth note of a musical scale.

**FAA** Federal Aviation Agency.

**fa·ble** (fā'b'l) ***n.*** **1** a very short story that teaches a lesson. It is usually about animals who act and talk like people [Aesop's *fable* "The Grasshopper and the Ant" teaches the need to work hard and be thrifty.] **2** a story that is not true.

**fa·bled** (fā'b'ld) ***adj.*** told about in fables or legends [the *fabled* beauty of Helen of Troy].

**fab·ric** (fab'rik) ***n.*** **1** a material made from fibers or threads by weaving, knitting, etc., as any cloth, felt, lace, etc. **2** anything made of parts put together, or the way in which it is put together; structure [the *fabric* of our society].

**fab·ri·cate** (fab'rə kāt) ***v.*** **1** to make or build by putting parts together; manufacture. **2** to make up; invent [He *fabricated* an excuse for being late. In other words, he told a lie.] —**fab'ri·cat·ed, fab'ri·cat·ing** —**fab'ri·ca'tion *n.*** —**fab'ri·ca'tor *n.***

**fab·u·lous** (fab'yoo ləs) ***adj.*** **1** hard to believe; astounding; very unusual [They spent a *fabulous* amount of money.] **2** very good; wonderful: *used only in everyday talk* [We had a *fabulous* vacation.] —**fab'u·lous·ly *adv.***

**fa·çade** or **fa·cade** (fə säd') ***n.*** **1** the front of a building. *See the picture.* **2** a grand or fine front that is meant to conceal something not at all grand.

**face** (fās) ***n.*** **1** the front part of the head, including the eyes, nose, and mouth. **2** a look that shows meaning or feeling [a sad *face*]. **3** surface or side; especially, the main, top, or front side [the *face* of the earth; the *face* of a playing card]. **4** dignity or reputation [to lose *face*]. ◆***v.*** **1** to turn toward or have the face turned toward [Please *face* the class. Our house *faces* a park.] **2** to meet or oppose with boldness or courage [to *face* danger]. **3** to put another material on the surface of [The courthouse is *faced* with marble.] —**faced, fac'ing** —**face to face, 1** with each facing the other. **2** very close. —**in the face of, 1** in the presence of. **2** in spite of. —**make a face,** to twist the face; make a grimace. —**on the face of it,** as far as can be seen; apparently. —**to one's face,** openly; in front of one.

**face card** any king, queen, or jack in a deck of cards.

**fac·et** (fas'it) ***n.*** **1** any of the many polished sides of a cut gem, as a diamond. *See the picture.* **2** any of the various sides or appearances [the many *facets* of someone's personality].

**fa·ce·tious** (fə sē'shəs) ***adj.*** joking or trying to be funny, especially at the wrong time. —**fa·ce′tious·ly** ***adv.*** —**fa·ce′tious·ness** ***n.***

**face value** **1** the value printed on money, a bond, etc. **2** the seeming value [I took Lynn's promise at *face value.*]

**fa·cial** (fā′shəl) ***adj.*** of or for the face. ✦☆***n.*** a treatment intended to make the skin of the face look better, as by massage and putting on creams and lotions.

☆**facial tissue** a sheet of soft tissue paper used for cleansing, or as a handkerchief, etc.

**fac·ile** (fas″l) ***adj.*** **1** not hard to do; easy [a *facile* job]. **2** acting, working, or done easily, or in a quick, smooth way [a *facile* mind; a *facile* style of writing]. **3** not sincere or serious; superficial [a *facile* answer to a difficult question]. —**fac′ile·ly** ***adv.***

**fa·cil·i·tate** (fə sil′ə tāt) ***v.*** to make easier; help [This new machine will *facilitate* your work.] —**fa·cil′i·tat·ed, fa·cil′i·tat·ing** —**fa·cil′i·ta′tion** ***n.***

**fa·cil·i·ty** (fə sil′ə tē) ***n.*** **1** ease or skill in working or acting [She reads French with great *facility.*] **2** *usually* **facilities,** *pl.* a thing that helps one do something [The apartment has its own laundry *facilities.*] **3** a building or room for some activity [This added wing is a new *facility* for the nursery school.] —*pl.* **fa·cil′i·ties**

**fac·ing** (fās′iŋ) ***n.*** **1** a lining or trimming sewn on a collar, cuff, etc., often for decoration. **2** a covering of another material, used to decorate or protect a surface [a marble *facing* on a building].

**fac·sim·i·le** (fak sim′ə lē) ***n.*** something made to look just like another thing; exact copy [You may send a label or a *facsimile* of it.] *See the picture.*

**fact** (fakt) ***n.*** **1** a thing that has actually happened or that is really true [I can't deny the *fact* that I was late.] **2** realness or truth [Can you tell what is *fact* and what is fiction in her story?] **3** something said to have happened or supposed to be true [Check the accuracy of your *facts.*] —**as a matter of fact** or **in fact,** really; actually.

**fac·tion** (fak′shən) ***n.*** **1** a group of people inside a political party, club, government, etc. working together against other such groups for its own ideas or goals. **2** an arguing or quarreling among the members of a group [bitter *faction* in the Senate over taxes]. —**fac′tion·al** ***adj.***

**fac·tious** (fak′shəs) ***adj.*** **1** tending to cause faction, or arguing. **2** full of or caused by faction.

**fac·ti·tious** (fak tish′əs) ***adj.*** not real or natural; forced [These ads for toys create *factitious* needs in children.]

**fac·tor** (fak′tər) ***n.*** **1** any one of the causes or happenings that together bring about a result [The hot climate was a *factor* in my decision to move north.] **2** any of the numbers or symbols that are multiplied together to form a product [2, 5, and 10 are *factors* of 100.] **3** a person who acts for another in a business deal; agent.

**fac·to·ry** (fak′tə rē) ***n.*** a building or group of buildings where goods are made, especially by machinery. —*pl.* **fac′to·ries**

**fac·to·tum** (fak tōt′əm) ***n.*** a person hired to do all sorts of odd jobs.

**fac·tu·al** (fak′choo wəl) ***adj.*** containing or based on facts; real; true [a *factual* account]. —**fac′tu·al·ly** ***adv.***

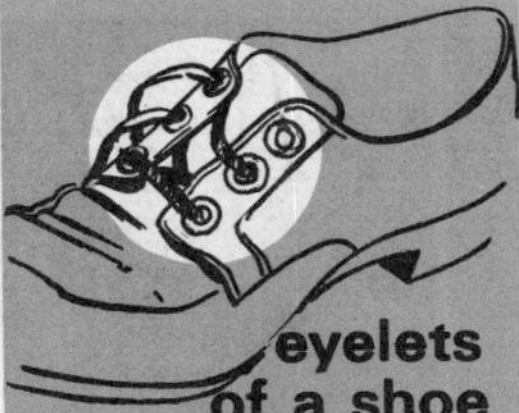
eyelets of a shoe

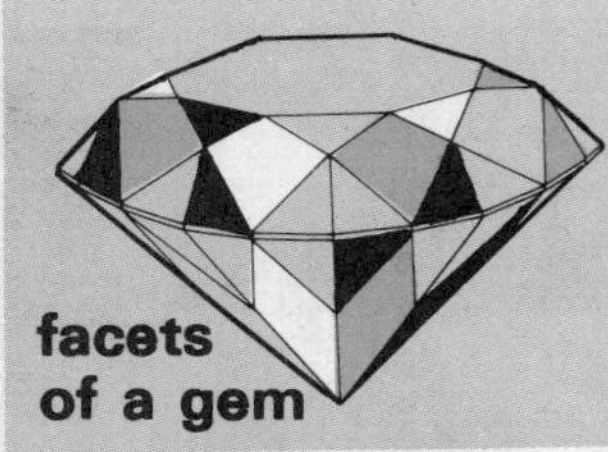
facets of a gem

façade

**fac·ul·ty** (fak″l tē) ***n.*** **1** any of the natural powers of the body; sense [the *faculty* of speech]. **2** a special skill or talent; knack [the *faculty* of remembering names]. ☆**3** all the teachers of a school, college, or university or of one of its departments [our high-school *faculty;* the medical *faculty*]. —*pl.* **fac′ul·ties**



**fad** (fad) ***n.*** a custom, style, etc. that many people are interested in for a short time; passing fashion [Many people thought TV was a *fad* in the 1940's.]

**fade** (fād) ***v.*** **1** to make or become less bright; lose or take away color [Sunlight may *fade* your curtains. The painting had *faded* with age.] **2** to become less fresh or strong; wither [The roses *faded* and their petals fell.] **3** to disappear slowly; die out [The music *faded* away.] *See* SYNONYMS *at* **disappear.** —**fad′ed, fad′ing**

**Fade** comes from an old French word meaning "pale." When something fades in color, it becomes pale or less bright.

**fag** (fag) ***v.*** to make tired by hard work [I was *fagged* out after cutting the grass.] —**fagged, fag′ging**

**fag end** **1** the worn-out or untwisted end of a piece of rope or cloth. **2** the last and worst part [tired at the *fag end* of the day].

**fag·ot** or **fag·got** (fag′ət) ***n.*** a bundle of sticks or twigs tied together for use as fuel.

**Fahr·en·heit** (fer′ən hīt) ***adj.*** of or describing a thermometer on which the boiling point of water is 212 degrees and the freezing point is 32 degrees above zero.

**fail** (fāl) ***v.*** **1** to not do what one tried to do or what one should have done; not succeed; miss or neglect [She *failed* as a singer. He *failed* to keep his promise.]

| | | | | | | | |
|---|---|---|---|---|---|---|---|
| **a** | fat | **ir** | here | **ou** | out | **zh** | leisure |
| **ā** | ape | **ī** | bite, fire | **u** | up | **ŋ** | ring |
| **ä** | car, lot | **ō** | go | **ur** | fur | | a *in* ago |
| **e** | ten | **ô** | law, horn | **ch** | chin | | e *in* agent |
| **er** | care | **oi** | oil | **sh** | she | **ə =** | i *in* unity |
| **ē** | even | **oo** | look | **th** | thin | | o *in* collect |
| **i** | hit | **ōō** | tool | ***th*** | then | | u *in* focus |

fairway

falcon
41 cm (16 in.) long

**2** to give or get a grade that shows one has not passed a test, a school course, etc. **3** to be of no help to; disappoint [Don't *fail* me in my hour of need.] **4** to not be present when needed or called upon; leave [Our courage *failed* us when we saw the shark.] **5** to lose strength; weaken [The cancer patient was *failing* fast.] **6** to stop working [The brakes *failed.*] **7** to become bankrupt [Many banks *failed* in 1933.] —**without fail,** surely; positively.

**fail·ing** (fāl′iŋ) ***n.*** **1** a fault or weakness [My worst *failing* is that I talk too much.] **2** a failure. ◆***prep.*** without; lacking [*Failing* some rain soon, the crops will wither.]

**fail-safe** (fāl′sāf) ***adj.*** describing a complicated system of devices designed to prevent any accidental operation of something, especially of aircraft armed with nuclear weapons.



**fail·ure** (fāl′yər) ***n.*** **1** the act of failing, or not succeeding [the *failure* of a plan]. **2** the fact of losing strength or weakening [the *failure* of eyesight]. **3** the act of not doing; neglect [Her *failure* to answer my letter worried me.] **4** the fact or state of becoming bankrupt. **5** a failing to pass to a higher grade in school. **6** a person or thing that fails.

**faint** (fānt) ***adj.*** **1** weak; not strong or clear; dim or feeble [a *faint* whisper; a *faint* odor; *faint* shadows]. **2** weak and dizzy, as if about to swoon. **3** not very certain; slight [a *faint* hope]. ◆***n.*** a condition in which one becomes unconscious because not enough blood reaches the brain, as in sudden shock. ◆***v.*** to fall into a faint; swoon. —**faint′ly** ***adv.***

**faint·heart·ed** (fānt′här′tid) ***adj.*** cowardly or timid.

**fair**[1] (fer) ***adj.*** **1** beautiful [your *fair* city]. **2** clean, spotless, without error, etc. [a *fair* copy of a letter; a *fair* name]. **3** light in color; blond [*fair* hair; *fair* skin]. **4** clear and sunny [*fair* weather]. **5** just and honest; according to what is right [a *fair* price; *fair* play]. *See* SYNONYMS *at* **just**. **6** neither very bad nor very good; average [We have a *fair* chance of winning.] ☆**7** in baseball, describing a batted ball that is not foul. ◆***adv.*** in a fair manner [Play *fair.*] —**fair′ness** ***n.***

**fair**[2] (fer) ***n.*** ☆**1** a gathering of people held every so often for the buying and selling of goods, the showing of things made, work done, animals and crops raised, etc. Prizes are often awarded and amusements and sideshows are often found at a fair [a county *fair;* a world's *fair*]. **2** a carnival where there is entertainment and things are sold in order to raise money, as for a charity.

**fair·ly** (fer′lē) ***adv.*** **1** in a just and honest way. **2** to a fair degree; neither very much nor very little; somewhat [It is *fairly* hot.] **3** completely; really [His voice *fairly* rang.]

**fair·way** (fer′wā) ***n.*** that part of a golf course where the grass is cut short, but not including the putting greens. *See the picture.*

**fair·y** (fer′ē) ***n.*** a tiny, graceful being in folk tales and legends. Fairies were supposed to have magic powers and to look like little people with wings. —*pl.* **fair′ies** ◆***adj.*** **1** of fairies. **2** like a fairy; graceful; delicate.

**fair·y·land** (fer′ē land′) ***n.*** **1** the imaginary land where fairies live. **2** a lovely and enchanting place.

**fairy tale** **1** a story about fairies and their magic deeds. **2** any untrue story or lie.

**faith** (fāth) ***n.*** **1** belief or trust that does not question or ask for proof [They have great *faith* in their doctor.] *See* SYNONYMS *at* **belief**. **2** belief in God and religion [Job kept his *faith* in spite of his troubles.] **3** a particular religion [the Jewish *faith;* the Christian *faith*]. **4** state of being loyal; allegiance [The knights pledged their *faith* to the king.] **5** a promise [to keep one's *faith*]. —**bad faith,** a state of being dishonest and not sincere. —**good faith,** a state of being honest and sincere. —**in faith,** indeed; really.

**faith·ful** (fāth′fəl) ***adj.*** **1** remaining loyal; constant [*faithful* friends]. **2** showing a strong sense of duty or responsibility [*faithful* attendance]. **3** accurate; exact [a *faithful* account of the accident]. —**the faithful,** the true believers or loyal followers of some religion, cause, etc. —**faith′ful·ly** ***adv.*** —**faith′ful·ness** ***n.***

SYNONYMS: Someone who is **faithful** is steady and dependable in staying true to a person or thing that one is bound to by an oath, duty, promises, etc. [a *faithful* husband or wife]. One who is **loyal** gives complete support to a person, cause, etc. that one feels is right, worthwhile, or good [a *loyal* follower].

**faith·less** (fāth′lis) ***adj.*** not deserving trust; disloyal or dishonest. —**faith′less·ly** ***adv.***

**fake** (fāk) ***v.*** to make something seem real or genuine in order to fool or deceive [I *faked* a cold and stayed home.] —**faked, fak′ing** ◆***n.*** a person or thing that is not really what it is supposed to be; fraud [That doctor is a *fake.*] ◆***adj.*** not genuine or real; false; sham [to cry *fake* tears; a *fake* diamond]. *See* SYNONYMS *at* **false**. —**fak′er** ***n.***

**fa·kir** (fə kir′) ***n.*** a Muslim or Hindu holy man who makes his living by begging.

**fal·con** (fal′kən *or* fôl′kən) ***n.*** any of various hawks with long, pointed wings and a short, curved beak, especially one trained to hunt and kill small birds and animals. *See the picture.*

**fal·con·ry** (fal′kən rē *or* fôl′kən rē) ***n.*** the training of falcons to hunt, or the sport of hunting with them.

**fall** (fôl) ***v.*** **1** to drop to a lower place; come down [Rain is *falling.* Apples *fell* from the tree.] **2** to come down suddenly from an upright position; tumble or collapse [The runner stumbled and *fell.* The old bridge *fell* into the river.] **3** to take a downward direction [Her glance *fell.* The land *falls* away to the river.] **4** to become lower, less, weaker, etc. [Prices are *falling.* Her voice *fell.*] **5** to hit or land [The arrow *fell* wide of its mark.] **6** to be wounded or killed in battle [Thousands *fell* at Gettysburg.] **7** to be conquered [Berlin *fell* to the Allies.] **8** to lose power, position, etc. [The government *fell*.] **9** to pass into a certain condition; become [to *fall* asleep; to *fall* into a rage]. **10** to take on a sad look [His face *fell*.] **11** to take place; happen [The meeting *falls* on a Friday.] **12** to come as by chance, inheritance, etc. [Her wealth will *fall* to her son.] **13** to come at a certain place [The accent *falls* on the first syllable.] **14** to be divided [His dramas *fall* into two types.] —**fell, fall′en, fall′ing** ◆*n.* **1** a dropping or coming down [a steady *fall* of rain; a *fall* on the ice]. **2** a downward direction or slope. **3** *usually* **falls,** *pl.* a waterfall. **4** something that has fallen, or the amount that has fallen [a six-inch *fall* of snow]. **5** the distance that something falls [a *fall* of 50 feet]. **6** the time of year when leaves fall from the trees, between summer and winter; autumn. **7** overthrow or ruin; downfall [the *fall* of Rome]. **8** a becoming less; decrease [a *fall* in the temperature]. —**fall back,** to retreat or withdraw. —**fall back on,** to turn, or return, to for help. —**fall behind, 1** to drop back. **2** to not pay in time. —**fall flat,** to be a complete failure. —☆**fall for, 1** to fall in love with: *used only in everyday talk.* **2** to be fooled by: *used only in everyday talk.* —**fall in, 1** to get into line, as soldiers. **2** to meet or join with others. **3** to agree. —**fall off, 1** to drop. **2** to become smaller, less, worse, etc. —**fall on** or **fall upon, 1** to attack. **2** to be the duty of. —**fall out, 1** to drop out of line. **2** to quarrel. —**fall through,** to fail; come to nothing. —**fall to, 1** to begin. **2** to start eating. —**fall under,** to come under.

**fal·la·cious** (fə lā′shəs) *adj.* mistaken or misleading in ideas, opinions, etc. —**fal·la′cious·ly** *adv.*

**fal·la·cy** (fal′ə sē) *n.* **1** a false or mistaken idea, opinion, etc. **2** false reasoning. —*pl.* **fal′la·cies**

**fall·en** (fôl′ən) *adj.* **1** thrown or dropped down; lying on the ground [*fallen* apples]. **2** overthrown or ruined [the *fallen* city]. **3** dead.

**fal·li·ble** (fal′ə b′l) *adj.* liable to be wrong or to make mistakes. —**fal′li·bil′i·ty** *n.*

**falling star** *same as* **meteor.**

☆**fall·off** (fôl′ôf) *n.* the act of becoming less or worse; decline.

**fall·out** (fôl′out′) *n.* ☆**1** the falling to earth of radioactive particles after a nuclear explosion. ☆**2** these particles.

**fal·low** (fal′ō) *adj.* plowed but left unplanted during the growing season [Farmers let the land lie *fallow* at times to kill weeds, make the soil richer, etc.] ◆*n.* land that lies fallow.

**false** (fôls) *adj.* **1** not true or right; wrong [a *false* idea]. **2** not honest; lying [The witness gave *false* testimony.] **3** not loyal or faithful [a *false* friend]. **4** not real or genuine; often, meant to fool or mislead [a *false* clue; a *false* alarm; *false* teeth]. **5** based on wrong or foolish ideas [*false* pride]. —**fals′er, fals′est** ◆*adv.* in a false way. —**play a person false,** to fool, cheat, or betray a person. —**false′ly** *adv.* —**false′ness** *n.*

SYNONYMS: **False** is used of anything that is not what it pretends to be and that may or may not be meant to fool people [*false* hair]. Something **counterfeit** is a carefully made copy meant to fool or cheat people [*counterfeit* money]. **Fake** is used of any person or thing that is not genuine or real [*fake* pearls; a *fake* doctor].

**false·face** (fôls′fās) *n.* a mask, especially a mask that is meant to be comical or frightening.

**false·hood** (fôls′hood) *n.* a lie or the telling of lies.

**fal·set·to** (fôl set′ō) *n.* a way of singing in a voice that is much higher than the usual voice. It is used mainly by tenors. —*pl.* **fal·set′tos** ◆*adj.* of or singing in falsetto. ◆*adv.* in falsetto.

**fal·si·fy** (fôl′sə fī) *v.* **1** to make false by giving an untrue idea of or by changing [to *falsify* one's feelings; to *falsify* records]. **2** to tell lies. —**fal′si·fied, fal′si·fying** —**fal′si·fi·ca′tion** *n.*

**fal·si·ty** (fôl′sə tē) *n.* **1** the fact of being false; a being wrong, dishonest, disloyal, etc. **2** a lie or error. —*pl.* **fal′si·ties**

**fal·ter** (fôl′tər) *v.* **1** to move in a shaky or unsteady way; stumble. **2** to speak in a broken or stumbling way; stammer [She *faltered* as she told of the tragedy.] **3** to act in an unsure way; hesitate; waver [The army *faltered* under enemy fire.] ◆*n.* a faltering.

**fame** (fām) *n.* the condition of being well known or much talked about; great reputation [Marie Curie's scientific research brought her much *fame*.]

**famed** (fāmd) *adj.* well-known; famous.

**fa·mil·ial** (fə mil′yəl) *adj.* of or involving a family.

**fa·mil·iar** (fə mil′yər) *adj.* **1** friendly; intimate; well-acquainted [a *familiar* face in the crowd]. **2** too friendly; intimate in a bold way [We were annoyed by the *familiar* manner of our new neighbor.] **3** knowing about; acquainted with [Are you *familiar* with this book?] **4** well-known; common; ordinary [Car accidents are a *familiar* sight.] ◆*n.* a close friend. 

**Familiar** comes from the Latin word for "family." Members of a family are very well acquainted. They speak and act in a familiar way with one another.

**fa·mil·iar·i·ty** (fə mil′yar′ə tē) *n.* **1** very close friendship or acquaintance; intimacy. **2** friendliness or intimacy that is too bold or not wanted. **3** the fact of having close knowledge of or experience with [*familiarity* with poverty]. —*pl.* **fa·mil′iar′i·ties**

**fa·mil·iar·ize** (fə mil′yə rīz) *v.* **1** to make familiar or well acquainted [He *familiarized* himself with the city.] **2** to make widely known [This song has been *familiarized* by much playing.] —**fa·mil′iar·ized, fa·mil′iar·iz·ing**

**fam·i·ly** (fam′ə lē) *n.* **1** a group made up of two parents and all of their children. **2** the children alone [a widow who raised a large *family*]. **3** a group of people who are related by marriage or a common ancestor; relatives; clan. **4** a large group of related plants or animals [The robin is a member of the thrush *family*.] **5** a group of related things [a *family* of languages]. —*pl.* **fam′i·lies**

☆**family style** a way of serving food so that people at the table serve themselves from large dishes.

| | | | | | | | | |
|---|---|---|---|---|---|---|---|---|
| **a** | fat | **ir** | here | **ou** | out | **zh** | leisure | |
| **ā** | ape | **ī** | bite, fire | **u** | up | **ng** | ring | |
| **ä** | car, lot | **ō** | go | **ur** | fur | | | a *in* ago |
| **e** | ten | **ô** | law, horn | **ch** | chin | | | e *in* agent |
| **er** | care | **oi** | oil | **sh** | she | **ə** = | | i *in* unity |
| **ē** | even | **oo** | look | **th** | thin | | | o *in* collect |
| **i** | hit | **o͞o** | tool | ***th*** | then | | | u *in* focus |

**fam·ine** (fam′ən) ***n.*** **1** a great lack of food that causes starving throughout a wide region. **2** a great lack of anything [the steel *famine* during the war].

**fam·ish** (fam′ish) ***v.*** to make or be very hungry [We were *famished* after the hard day's work.] *See* SYNONYMS *at* **hungry.**

**fa·mous** (fā′məs) ***adj.*** much talked about as being outstanding; very well known.

**fan**[1] (fan) ***n.*** **1** a thing used to stir up the air for a cooling or freshening effect. Simple fans are waved in the hand and some can be folded together when not in use. Electric fans have blades that are turned by a motor. *See the picture.* **2** anything shaped like a hand fan when it is open [The turkey spread its tail into a *fan.*] ◆***v.*** **1** to stir up the air as with a fan. **2** to blow air toward as with a fan [She *fanned* herself with the program. The wind *fanned* the flames.] **3** to spread out like an open fan [The police *fanned* out to search the field.] —**fanned, fan′ning**

☆**fan**[2] (fan) ***n.*** a person who is greatly interested in some sport or hobby, or is a great admirer of some famous performer [a football *fan*].

**fa·nat·ic** (fə nat′ik) ***n.*** a person who carries his interest or belief in something to a point that is no longer reasonable [a religious *fanatic* who spends all his time in prayer]. ◆***adj.*** madly enthusiastic: *also* **fa·nat′i·cal.** —**fa·nat′i·cal·ly** ***adv.***

**fa·nat·i·cism** (fə nat′ə siz′m) ***n.*** the mad enthusiasm of a fanatic.



**fan·ci·er** (fan′sē ər) ***n.*** a person with a strong interest in something, especially in the breeding of some plant or animal [a cat *fancier*].

**fan·ci·ful** (fan′si fəl) ***adj.*** **1** full of fancy; having or showing a quick and playful imagination [*fanciful* costumes for the Halloween party]. **2** not real; imaginary [a *fanciful* idea that horseshoes bring luck].

**fan·cy** (fan′sē) ***n.*** **1** the power of picturing in the mind things that are not real, especially in a light and playful way; imagination ["Alice's Adventures in Wonderland" is the product of Lewis Carroll's *fancy.*] **2** anything imagined; an idea, notion, whim, etc. [He had a sudden *fancy* to go swimming at midnight.] **3** a liking [She has taken a *fancy* to him.] —*pl.* **fan′cies** ◆***adj.*** **1** having much design and decoration; not plain; elaborate [a *fancy* tie]. *See the picture.* **2** of better quality than the usual; special [a *fancy* grade of canned pears]. **3** needing more skill or grace than usual [*fancy* diving]. **4** very high or too high [*fancy* prices for new cars]. —**fan′ci·er, fan′ci·est** ◆***v.*** **1** to form an idea of; imagine [I can't *fancy* you as a ballet dancer.] **2** to have a liking for [He *fancies* Swiss chocolate.] **3** to believe something without being sure; suppose [She is, I *fancy,* still bowling on Mondays.] —**fan′cied, fan′cy·ing**

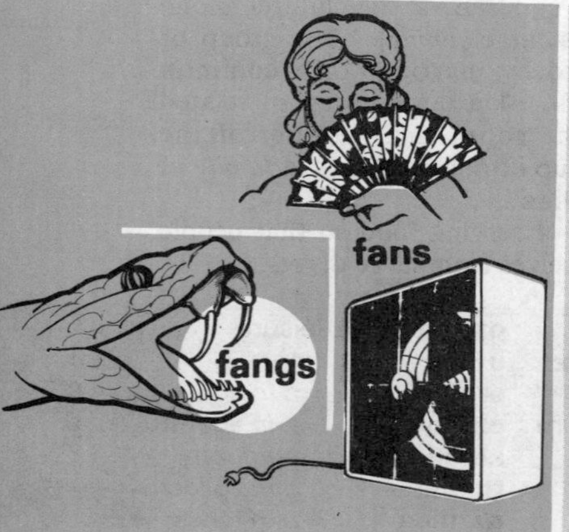

**fan·fare** (fan′fer) ***n.*** **1** a loud, showy musical phrase played on trumpets [A *fanfare* announced the entrance of the queen.] **2** any showy display [to do one's duty without any *fanfare*].

**fang** (faŋ) ***n.*** **1** one of the long, pointed teeth with which meat-eating animals seize and tear their prey. **2** one of the long, hollow teeth through which poisonous snakes shoot their poison. *See the picture.*

**fan·tail** (fan′tāl) ***n.*** **1** a tail that spreads out like an open fan. **2** a pigeon, goldfish, etc. with such a tail.

**fan·ta·size** (fan′tə sīz) ***v.*** to have fantasies or have daydreams about. —**fan′ta·sized, fan′ta·siz·ing**

**fan·tas·tic** (fan tas′tik) ***adj.*** **1** very strange and unreal; fanciful in a wild way; weird [the *fantastic* costumes in the Mardi Gras parade]. **2** seeming to be beyond belief [the *fantastic* spaceflights to the moon]. *Also* **fan·tas′ti·cal.** —**fan·tas′ti·cal·ly** ***adv.***

**fan·ta·sy** (fan′tə sē) ***n.*** **1** imagination or fancy. *See* SYNONYMS *at* **imagination. 2** a play, story, daydream, etc. that is full of imagination and very unreal ["Peter Pan" is a *fantasy.*] —*pl.* **fan′ta·sies**

**far** (fär) ***adj.*** **1** not near or close; a long way off; distant [a *far* land; the *far* past]. **2** more distant [Go to the *far* side of the room.] —**far′ther, far′thest** ◆***adv.*** **1** to or from a great distance [She has traveled *far.*] **2** to a certain distance or degree [How *far* have you read in this book?] **3** a great deal; very much [She is a *far* better player than I am.] —**far′ther, far′thest** —**as far as** or **so far as,** to the distance or degree that. —**by far** or **far and away,** very much. —**far and near** or **far and wide,** everywhere. —**so far,** up to this place, time, or degree. —**so far, so good,** up to this point everything is all right.

**Far·a·day** (far′ə dā), **Michael** 1791–1867; English scientist, who did important work in electricity and magnetism.

**far·a·way** (fär′ə wā) ***adj.*** **1** distant; far [a *faraway* place]. **2** seeming to be distant or away; withdrawn [a *faraway* look on his face].

**farce** (färs) ***n.*** **1** a humorous play with ridiculous things in it that are meant to make people laugh. **2** any ridiculous action; especially, a pretending that is ridiculous because no one is fooled by it [Her concern for us was a *farce.*]

> **Farce** comes from a Latin word meaning "to stuff." In ancient Rome, farces were put on to fill up the time between the acts of a play.

**far·ci·cal** (fär′si k′l) ***adj.*** of or like a farce; ridiculous; absurd.

**fare** (fer) ***v.*** **1** to get along; do or be [We *fared* well on our trip.] **2** to happen or result [How did it *fare* with her?] —**fared, far′ing** ◆***n.*** **1** money paid for a trip on a bus, plane, etc. [How much is the *fare* on the subway?] **2** a passenger who has paid a fare. **3** food [to live on simple *fare*].

**Far East** the countries of eastern Asia, including China, Japan, Korea, etc.

**fare·well** (fer'wel') ***interj.*** goodbye. ◆***n.*** a leaving or going away; also, good wishes said when leaving. ◆***adj.*** last; final [a *farewell* wave].

**far·fetched** (fär'fecht') ***adj.*** not natural; forced [an example so *farfetched* we couldn't believe it].

**far-flung** (fär'flung') ***adj.*** covering a wide area [Rome controlled a *far-flung* empire.]

**fa·ri·na** (fə rē'nə) ***n.*** flour or meal made from cereal grains, especially whole wheat, or from potatoes, nuts, etc. and eaten as a cooked cereal.

**farm** (färm) ***n.*** **1** a piece of land used to raise crops or animals; also, the house, barn, orchards, etc. on such land. **2** any place where certain things are raised [An area of water for raising fish is a fish *farm*.] ◆***v.*** to use land to raise crops or animals [He *farmed* ten acres.] —**farm out, 1** to rent land, a business, etc. for a fee. **2** to send out work from a shop or office to workers on the outside.

**farm·er** (fär'mər) ***n.*** a person who owns or works on a farm.

**farm·house** (färm'hous) ***n.*** a house on a farm.

**farm·ing** (fär'ming) ***n.*** the work of running a farm; the raising of crops, animals, etc.

**farm·stead** (färm'sted) ***n.*** the land and buildings of a farm.

**farm·yard** (färm'yärd) ***n.*** the yard around the buildings of a farm.

**far-off** (fär'ôf') ***adj.*** distant; faraway.

**far-out** (fär'out') ***adj.*** ☆very new, unusual, advanced, experimental, etc.: *used only in everyday talk.*

**far-reach·ing** (fär'rēch'ing) ***adj.*** having a wide influence on many people [The invention of radio had *far-reaching* effects.]

**far·row** (far'ō) ***n.*** a litter of pigs. ◆***v.*** to give birth to a litter of pigs.

**far·see·ing** (fär'sē'ing) ***adj.*** *same as* **farsighted** (*in meanings* 1 *and* 2).

**far·sight·ed** (fär'sīt'id) ***adj.*** **1** able to see far. **2** able to look ahead and plan for the future. **3** able to see things that are far away more clearly than those that are close. —**far'sight'ed·ness** ***n.***

**far·ther** (fär'*th*ər) *the comparative of* **far.** ◆***adj.*** **1** more distant [My home is *farther* from school than yours.] **2** more; added. ◆***adv.*** **1** at or to a greater distance [I can swim *farther* than you can.] **2** to a greater extent; more. **3** in addition; moreover; besides.

> When we are speaking of actual distance, **farther** is the word generally used [The library is *farther* away than the school.] When we are adding to the thought that has been stated, we use **further** [I have something *further* to say to you.]

**far·ther·most** (fär'*th*ər mōst) ***adj.*** most distant; farthest.

**far·thest** (fär'*th*ist) *the superlative of* **far.** ◆***adj.*** most distant [the *farthest* parts of the State]. ◆***adv.*** at or to the greatest distance [Who threw the ball *farthest?*]

**far·thing** (fär'*th*ing) ***n.*** a small British coin worth less than a penny, and no longer in use.

**fas·ci·nate** (fas'ə nāt) ***v.*** **1** to hold the attention of by being interesting or delightful; charm [The puppet show *fascinated* the children.] **2** to hold still without the power to move or act, as by terrifying. —**fas'ci·nat·ed, fas'ci·nat·ing** —**fas'ci·na'tion** ***n.***

**fas·cism** (fash'iz'm) ***n.*** *sometimes* **Fascism,** a system of government in which the country is ruled by a dictator, and in which minority groups have no rights, war is glorified, etc. Fascism came to power in Italy under Mussolini and in Germany under Hitler. —**fas'cist** ***adj., n.***

**fash·ion** (fash'ən) ***n.*** **1** the popular or up-to-date way of dressing, speaking, or behaving; style [It was once the *fashion* to wear powdered wigs.] **2** the way in which a thing is done, made, or formed [tea served in the Japanese *fashion*]. ◆***v.*** to make, form, or shape [Bees *fashion* honeycombs out of wax.] —**after a fashion** or **in a fashion,** in some way; not too well.

**fash·ion·a·ble** (fash'ən ə b'l) ***adj.*** following the latest fashions or styles; stylish [a *fashionable* hat]. —**fash'ion·a·bly** ***adv.***

**fast**[1] (fast) ***adj.*** **1** moving, working, etc. at high speed; rapid; quick; swift [a *fast* pace; a *fast* reader]. **2** that makes high speed possible [a *fast* highway]. **3** that takes a short time [a *fast* lunch]. **4** showing a time that is ahead of the real time [Your watch is *fast*.] **5** close and true; loyal [*fast* friends]. **6** that will not fade [*fast* colors]. **7** fastened in a firm way; fixed [Make sure the bulb is *fast* in the socket.] **8** wild and reckless [a *fast* life]. ◆***adv.*** **1** at a high speed; swiftly; rapidly [arrested for driving too *fast*]. **2** in a firm or fixed way; firmly [The boat was stuck *fast* on the sand bar.] **3** in a complete way; soundly; thoroughly [*fast* asleep]. **4** ahead of time [The buses are running *fast*.] 267

> SYNONYMS: **Fast** and **rapid** both suggest moving or acting at high speed, but usually **fast** is used of a person or thing [a *fast* train] while **rapid** is used of the action [*rapid* transportation]. **Quick** suggests something that happens promptly or in a brief period [a *quick* answer].

**fast**[2] (fast) ***v.*** to go without any food or certain foods, as in following the rules of one's religion. ◆***n.*** **1** a fasting. **2** a day or period of fasting.

☆**fast·back** (fast'bak) ***n.*** an automobile body whose roof forms an unbroken curve from windshield to rear bumper.

**fas·ten** (fas''n) ***v.*** **1** to join or become joined; attach [The collar is *fastened* to the shirt.] **2** to make stay closed or in place, as by locking or shutting [*Fasten* the door.] **3** to direct and hold; fix [*Fasten* your attention on the game.] **4** to cause to be connected [to *fasten* a crime on someone]. —**fas'ten·er** ***n.***

**fas·ten·ing** (fas''n ing) ***n.*** anything used to fasten, as a bolt, lock, button, etc.

☆**fast-food** (fast'fo͞od') ***adj.*** describing a business, as a hamburger stand, that offers food cooked and served quickly.

**fas·tid·i·ous** (fas tid'ē əs) ***adj.*** not easy to please; very particular and sensitive [She is *fastidious* about her personal grooming.] —**fas·tid'i·ous·ly** ***adv.***

| | | | | | | | |
|---|---|---|---|---|---|---|---|
| **a** fat | **ir** here | **ou** out | **zh** leisure | | | | |
| **ā** ape | **ī** bite, fire | **u** up | **ng** ring | | | | |
| **ä** car, lot | **ō** go | **ur** fur | a *in* ago | | | | |
| **e** ten | **ô** law, horn | **ch** chin | e *in* agent | | | | |
| **er** care | **oi** oil | **sh** she | ə = i *in* unity | | | | |
| **ē** even | **oo** look | **th** thin | o *in* collect | | | | |
| **i** hit | **o͞o** tool | ***th*** then | u *in* focus | | | | |

f

**fast·ness** (fast′nis) ***n.*** **1** the quality of being fast. **2** a strong, safe place; stronghold.

☆**fast time** *another term for* **daylight-saving time.**

**fat** (fat) ***n.*** **1** a yellow or white substance found in animal bodies and in plant seeds. It is oily or greasy and is used in cooking and frying. **2** the richest or best part [to live off the *fat* of the land]. ◆***adj.*** **1** covered with much fat or flesh; plump or too plump [*fat* cheeks; a *fat* chicken]. **2** full of fat; oily or greasy [Butter is a *fat* food.] **3** thick or broad [a *fat* book]. **4** bringing much profit [a *fat* contract]. **5** well supplied or filled [a *fat* purse]. —**fat′ter, fat′test** ◆***v.*** to make or become fat: *the usual word now is* **fatten.** —**fat′ted, fat′ting** —☆**a fat chance,** very little or no chance: *a slang phrase.* —**fat′ness** ***n.***

**fa·tal** (fāt′'l) ***adj.*** **1** causing death [a *fatal* disease]. **2** causing ruin; disastrous [a *fatal* blow to their hopes]. **3** important in its outcome; decisive [This is the *fatal* day!] —**fa′tal·ly** ***adv.***

**fa·tal·ist** (fāt′'l ist) ***n.*** a person who believes that fate decides everything and that no one can control one's fate. —**fa′tal·is′tic** ***adj.***

**fa·tal·i·ty** (fə tal′ə tē) ***n.*** **1** any death caused by a disaster, as in an accident, war, etc. [The earthquake caused many *fatalities.*] **2** a tendency to cause death; deadliness [The new vaccine has reduced the *fatality* of the disease.] —*pl.* **fa·tal′i·ties**

**fate** (fāt) ***n.*** **1** a power that is supposed to settle ahead of time how things will happen [She believed that *fate* had destined her to be famous.] **2** the things that happen as though controlled by this power; one's lot or fortune [Was it his *fate* to be President?] **3** the way things turn out in the end; outcome [What was the *fate* of the ship in the storm?] —**the Fates,** the three goddesses in Greek and Roman myths who control human life.

**fat·ed** (fāt′id) ***adj.*** fixed by fate; destined or doomed [lovers *fated* to die young].

**fate·ful** (fāt′fəl) ***adj.*** **1** telling what is to come; prophetic [the *fateful* words of the oracle]. **2** having most important results [a *fateful* decision]. **3** controlled as if by fate. **4** bringing death or destruction [the *fateful* explosion]. —**fate′ful·ly** ***adv.***

**fa·ther** (fä′*th*ər) ***n.*** **1** a man as he is related to his child or children; a male parent. **2 Father,** God. **3** an ancestor. **4** a person important to the beginning of something; founder; creator [George Washington is called the *Father* of his country.] **5 fathers,** *pl.* the leaders of a city, country, etc. **6** a priest. ◆***v.*** **1** to be the father of; beget [He *fathered* two daughters.] **2** to care for as a father does. **3** to bring into being; create; invent [to *father* an idea]. —**fa′ther·hood** ***n.*** —**fa′ther·less** ***adj.***

**fa·ther-in-law** (fä′*th*ər ən lô′) ***n.*** the father of one's wife or husband. —*pl.* **fa′thers-in-law′**

**fa·ther·land** (fä′*th*ər land) ***n.*** one's country; especially, the country where one was born.

**fa·ther·ly** (fä′*th*ər lē) ***adj.*** of or like a father [*fatherly* care]. —**fa′ther·li·ness** ***n.***

☆**Father's Day** the third Sunday in June, a day set aside (in the U.S.) in honor of fathers.

**fath·om** (fa*th*′əm) ***n.*** a length of six feet, used as a unit of measure for the depth of water. ◆***v.*** **1** to measure the depth of. **2** to understand completely [I can't *fathom* the mystery.]

**Fathom** comes from an Old English word meaning "the two arms outstretched to measure something." A tall person with arms outstretched at the sides would measure about six feet from right hand to left hand, the same length as a fathom.

**fath·om·less** (fa*th*′əm lis) ***adj.*** **1** too deep to measure. **2** too mysterious to understand.

**fa·tigue** (fə tēg′) ***n.*** a tired feeling, as from hard work or not enough rest; weariness. ◆***v.*** to tire out; make weary; exhaust. —**fa·tigued′, fa·tigu′ing**

**fat·ten** (fat′'n) ***v.*** to make or become fat.

**fat·ty** (fat′ē) ***adj.*** **1** containing or made of fat [*fatty* tissue]. **2** like fat; greasy; oily. —**fat′ti·er, fat′ti·est**

**fat·u·ous** (fach′o͞o wəs) ***adj.*** stupid or foolish in a smug way. —**fat′u·ous·ly** ***adv.***

**fau·cet** (fô′sit) ***n.*** a device with a valve which can be turned on or off to control the flow of a liquid, as from a pipe; tap; cock. *See the picture.*

**Faulk·ner** (fôk′nər), **William** 1897–1962; U.S. novelist.

**fault** (fôlt) ***n.*** **1** a thing that keeps something from being perfect; defect; flaw [His main *fault* is that he's lazy.] **2** an error; mistake. **3** blame; responsibility [It isn't my *fault* that we're late.] —**at fault,** deserving blame. —**find fault,** to look for faults; complain. —**find fault with,** to criticize.

**fault·find·ing** (fôlt′fīn′diŋ) ***adj.*** finding fault; calling attention to defects. —**fault′find′er** ***n.***

**fault·less** (fôlt′lis) ***adj.*** not having a fault; perfect. —**fault′less·ly** ***adv.***

**fault·y** (fôlt′ē) ***adj.*** having a fault or faults; imperfect. —**fault′i·er, fault′i·est** —**fault′i·ly** ***adv.***

**faun** (fôn) ***n.*** in Roman myths, a minor god who had the head and body of a man, and the horns, pointed ears, tail, and hind legs of a goat. *See the picture for* **Pan.**

**fau·na** (fô′nə) ***n.*** all the animals of a particular place or time [the *fauna* of Iceland].

**Faust** (foust) a man in an old legend who sold his soul to the devil in return for knowledge and power.

**fa·vor** (fā′vər) ***n.*** **1** a helpful and kind action [I did my sick friend the *favor* of shopping for her.] **2** liking or approval [The waiter tried to win our *favor.*] **3** a small gift or souvenir [Every guest at the party received a pen as a *favor.*] ◆***v.*** **1** to like or approve of [We *favor* any plan for lower taxes.] **2** to help or aid [The dark night *favored* his escape.] **3** to prefer or help in an unfair way [The umpire seemed to *favor* the other team.] **4** to look like [The baby *favors* her mother.] **5** to use gently so as to keep from hurting [He *favors* his injured leg.] —**in favor of, 1** supporting or approving. **2** to the advantage of. —**in one's favor,** to one's advantage.

**fa·vor·a·ble** (fā′vər ə b'l) ***adj.*** **1** helpful [*favorable* winds]. **2** supporting or approving [a *favorable* opinion]. **3** pleasing or desirable [She made a *favorable* impression on the critics.] —**fa′vor·a·bly** ***adv.***

**fa·vor·ite** (fā′vər it) ***n.*** **1** the person or thing liked better than others. **2** the one who is thought most likely to win a contest. ◆***adj.*** best liked; preferred [Pie is my *favorite* food.]

**fa·vor·it·ism** (fā′vər it iz'm) ***n.*** the act of showing unfair liking for one over others.

**fa·vour** (fā′vər) ***n., v.*** *the British spelling of* **favor.**

**fawn**[1] (fôn) ***v.*** **1** to show pleasure by wagging its tail, licking hands, etc. [Dogs *fawn.*] **2** to try to gain favor by acting humble, flattering, etc. [He *fawns* on his rich relatives.]

**fawn**[2] (fôn) ***n.*** **1** a young deer, less than one year old. *See the picture.* **2** a pale, yellowish brown.

**faze** (fāz) ***v.*** to disturb or upset: *used only in everyday talk.* —**fazed, faz′ing**

**FBI** or **F.B.I.** *abbreviation for* ☆**Federal Bureau of Investigation,** which is a branch of the U.S. Department of Justice. The duty of the FBI is to investigate crimes against Federal law.

**FCC** or **F.C.C.** Federal Communications Commission.

**F.D.** Fire Department.

**FDA** or **F.D.A.** Food and Drug Administration.

**Fe** *the symbol for the chemical element* iron.

**fe·al·ty** (fē′əl tē) ***n.*** loyalty; especially, the loyalty owed by a vassal to his feudal lord.

**fear** (fir) ***n.*** **1** the feeling one has when danger, pain, or trouble is near; feeling of being worried or excited or of wanting to run and hide [Jungle animals have a natural *fear* of lions.] **2** a feeling of being uneasy [I have no *fear* that it will rain.] **3** something that causes fear [The chance of failure is a common *fear.*] ◆***v.*** **1** to feel fear of; be afraid of; dread [Even brave people can *fear* real danger.] **2** to feel uneasy or anxious [I *fear* that I'll miss the bus.]

**fear·ful** (fir′fəl) ***adj.*** **1** causing fear; terrifying [a *fearful* danger]. **2** feeling fear; afraid [*fearful* of the dark]. **3** caused by fear [a *fearful* cry]. **4** very bad, great, etc.: *used only in everyday talk* [a *fearful* liar]. —**fear′ful·ly *adv.***

**fear·less** (fir′lis) ***adj.*** having no fear; not afraid; brave. —**fear′less·ly *adv.***

**fear·some** (fir′səm) ***adj.*** causing fear; frightening.

**fea·si·ble** (fē′zə b'l) ***adj.*** **1** that can be done with conditions as they are; possible [Your plan is not *feasible* because it costs too much.] *See* SYNONYMS *at* **possible. 2** that is likely or within reason; probable [Is it *feasible* that John is wrong?] **3** usable or suitable [land *feasible* for growing grapes]. —**fea′si·bil′i·ty *n.***

**feast** (fēst) ***n.*** **1** a large meal with many courses; banquet. **2** a happy religious celebration; festival. ◆***v.*** **1** to eat a big or rich meal. **2** to make a feast for. **3** to cause delight or pleasure to [She *feasted* her eyes on the jewels.]

**feat** (fēt) ***n.*** something done that shows great courage, skill, or strength; remarkable deed.

**feath·er** (fe*th*′ər) ***n.*** **1** any of the parts that grow out of the skin of birds, covering the body and filling out the wings and tail. Feathers are soft and light. *See the picture.* **2** anything like a feather in looks, lightness, etc. **3** the same class or kind [birds of a *feather*]. ◆***v.*** **1** to cover or become covered with feathers. **2** to turn the blade of an oar or propeller so that the edge is foremost. —**feather in one's cap,** an achievement one can be proud of. —**in fine feather,** in good humor or health. —**feath′er·y *adj.***

**feather bed** a strong cloth container thickly filled with feathers or down and used as a mattress.

**feath·er·weight** (fe*th*′ər wāt) ***n.*** **1** a boxer who weighs over 118 but not over 126 pounds. **2** a wrestler who weighs over 123 but not over 134 pounds.

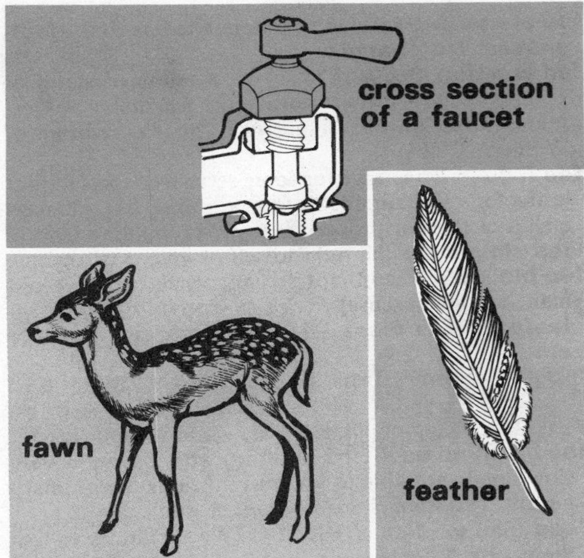


**fea·ture** (fē′chər) ***n.*** **1** any part of the face, as the nose, eyes, mouth, chin, etc. [a girl with lovely *features*]. **2** a separate or special part or quality [Geysers are a *feature* of Yellowstone National Park. The sales tax has some bad *features.*] ☆**3** a main attraction at a show, sale, etc.; especially, a full-length movie. ☆**4** a special article or column in a newspaper or magazine. ◆***v.*** ☆**1** to be or make a feature of [A magician was *featured* on the program.] ☆**2** to think of; imagine: *slang in this meaning* [I can't *feature* her doing that.] —**fea′tured, fea′tur·ing**



**Feb·ru·ar·y** (feb′rə wer′ē *or* feb′yoo wer′ē) ***n.*** the second month of the year. It usually has 28 days but in leap year it has 29 days: abbreviated **Feb.**

**fe·ces** (fē′sēz) ***n.pl.*** waste matter that comes from the bowels; excrement. —**fe·cal** (fē′kəl) ***adj.***

**fe·cund** (fē′kənd *or* fek′ənd) ***adj.*** bringing much or many into being; fruitful or fertile. —**fe·cun·di·ty** (fi kun′də tē) ***n.***

**fed** (fed) *past tense and past participle of* **feed.** —**fed up,** disgusted or bored: *used only in everyday talk.*

**Fed.** *abbreviation for* **Federal, Federated, Federation.**

**fed·er·al** (fed′ər əl) ***adj.*** **1** of or describing a union of states having a central government. **2** of such a central government [a *federal* constitution]. ☆**3** *usually* **Federal,** of the central government of the U.S. [the *Federal* courts]. ☆**4 Federal,** of or supporting an early American political party (**Federalist Party**) that was in favor of strong federal power. ☆**5 Federal,** of or supporting the Union in the Civil War. ◆***n.*** ☆**Federal,** a supporter of the Union in the Civil War. —**fed′er·al·ist *adj., n.***

| | | | | | | | |
|---|---|---|---|---|---|---|---|
| a | fat | ir | here | ou | out | zh | leisure |
| ā | ape | ī | bite, fire | u | up | ng | ring |
| ä | car, lot | ō | go | ur | fur | | a *in* ago |
| e | ten | ô | law, horn | ch | chin | | e *in* agent |
| er | care | oi | oil | sh | she | ə = | i *in* unity |
| ē | even | oo | look | th | thin | | o *in* collect |
| i | hit | ōō | tool | *th* | then | | u *in* focus |

**fed·er·ate** (fed'ə rāt) ***v.*** to join in a federation. —**fed'er·at·ed, fed'er·at·ing**

**fed·er·a·tion** (fed'ə rā'shən) ***n.*** a union of states or groups under a central power [the *federation* of German states under Bismarck; the *Federation* of Women's Clubs].

**fee** (fē) ***n.*** **1** a charge for some service or special right [a doctor's *fee;* admission *fees;* a license *fee*]. **2** ownership of land or property. A person holding land in **fee simple** has the right to sell or give it to anyone.

**fee·ble** (fē'b'l) ***adj.*** not strong; weak [a *feeble* old man; a *feeble* excuse]. *See* SYNONYMS *at* **weak.** —**fee'bler, fee'blest** —**fee'ble·ness** ***n.*** —**fee'bly** ***adv.***

**Feeble** comes from a Latin word meaning "to weep." A person who is too feeble to cope with the problems of life may break down and weep.

**fee·ble·mind·ed** (fē'b'l mīn'did) ***adj.*** having a very slow mind; not able to learn as much as the ordinary person. *This word is no longer much used.*

**feed** (fēd) ***v.*** **1** to give food to [We should try to *feed* the poor.] **2** to serve as food [to *feed* oats to horses]. **3** to eat [The cattle are *feeding.*] **4** to supply something that is needed for the working or growth of [We *fed* the stove with wood. His continued rudeness *fed* her anger.] —**fed, feed'ing** ◆***n.*** **1** food for animals; fodder. **2** a meal: *used only in everyday talk.* —**feed'er** ***n.***

270 **feed·back** (fēd'bak) ***n.*** a process in which factors that produce a result are themselves changed, corrected, etc. by that result.

**feel** (fēl) ***v.*** **1** to touch in order to find out something [*Feel* the baby's bottle to see if the milk is warm.] **2** to be aware of through the senses or the mind [He *felt* rain on his face. Do you *feel* pain in this tooth?] **3** to be aware of being; be [I *feel* sad.] **4** to have grief, pity, etc. because of [He *felt* her death deeply.] **5** to be or seem to the sense of touch [The water *feels* cold.] **6** to think or believe [She *feels* that we should go.] **7** to try to find by touching; grope [He *felt* his way through the dark tunnel.] —**felt, feel'ing** ◆***n.*** **1** the act of feeling. **2** the way a thing feels to the touch [It seems to be all wool by the *feel* of it.] —☆**feel like,** to have a desire for: *used only in everyday talk* [I don't *feel like* talking.] —**feel up to,** to feel able to: *used only in everyday talk.*

fern

fencing

Ferris wheel

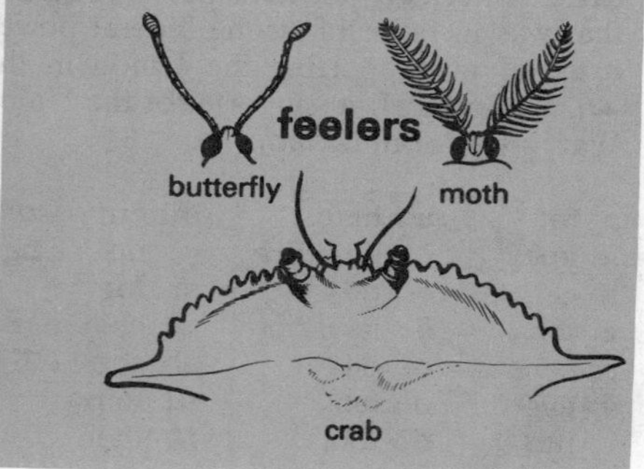


feelers

**feel·er** (fēl'ər) ***n.*** **1** a slender part growing out from an animal or insect, by which it can touch and feel; antenna. *See the picture.* **2** a person or thing that feels. **3** something asked or said to find out what a person thinks.

**feel·ing** (fēl'iŋ) ***n.*** **1** the sense of touch, by which one can tell whether something is rough or smooth, hot or cold, etc. **2** the condition of being aware; consciousness [a *feeling* of pain]. **3** what is felt deeply inside one, as love, hate, joy, anger, or fear; emotion [to control one's *feelings*]. *See* SYNONYMS *at* **emotion.** **4** pity or sympathy [She spoke with *feeling* of their suffering.] **5** an opinion or belief [I have a *feeling* that Lou is right.] ◆***adj.*** sensitive and full of sympathy [He made a sincere and *feeling* tribute to her memory.] —**to hurt one's feelings,** to make one unhappy or angry; offend. —**feel'ing·ly** ***adv.***

**feet** (fēt) ***n.*** *plural of* **foot.**

**feign** (fān) ***v.*** **1** to make up something that is not true [to *feign* an excuse]. **2** to pretend [to *feign* illness].

**feint** (fānt) ***n.*** **1** a pretended blow or attack meant to put one's opponent off guard against the real one that follows. **2** a false show; sham [to make a *feint* of working]. ◆***v.*** to make a feint, as in boxing.

☆**feist·y** (fīs'tē) ***adj.*** **1** lively; energetic. **2** ready and willing to fight; quarrelsome. *This word is used only in everyday talk.* —**feist'i·er, feist'i·est**

**feld·spar** (feld'spär) ***n.*** a hard, glassy kind of rock, containing aluminum.

**fe·lic·i·tate** (fə lis'ə tāt) ***v.*** to wish joy to; congratulate. —**fe·lic'i·tat·ed, fe·lic'i·tat·ing** —**fe·lic'i·ta'tion** ***n.***

**fe·lic·i·tous** (fə lis'ə təs) ***adj.*** just right for the occasion; fitting; apt [a *felicitous* remark].

**fe·lic·i·ty** (fə lis'ə tē) ***n.*** **1** happiness; bliss. **2** anything that brings happiness. **3** a way of writing or speaking, or a remark, that is pleasing and just right for the occasion [He expressed his thanks with *felicity.*] —*pl.* **fe·lic'i·ties**

**fe·line** (fē'līn) ***adj.*** **1** of a cat or the cat family. **2** like a cat. ◆***n.*** any member of the cat family, as the leopard, lion, tiger, etc.

**fell**[1] (fel) *past tense of* **fall.**

**fell**[2] (fel) ***v.*** **1** to make fall; knock down [The boxer *felled* his opponent.] **2** to cut down [to *fell* a tree].

**fell**[3] (fel) ***adj.*** fierce; cruel [a *fell* blow].

**fel·low** (fel'ō *or* fel'ə) ***n.*** **1** man or boy: *used only in everyday talk.* **2** a partner, helper, or associate [*fellows* in crime]. **3** either one of two things that go together [I can't find the *fellow* to this shoe.] **4** a student who has a fellowship at a university or college. **5** a member of any of various scholarly societies. ◆***adj.*** in the same situation; associated [my *fellow* students].

**fel·low·ship** (fel'ō ship' *or* fel'ə ship) ***n.*** **1** friendship; companionship. **2** a group of people having the same activities or interests. **3** money given to a student at a university or college to help him or her study for a higher degree.

**fel·on**[1] (fel′ən) ***n.*** a person guilty of a serious crime, such as murder; criminal.

**fel·on**[2] (fel′ən) ***n.*** a painful infection near a fingernail or toenail.

**fel·o·ny** (fel′ə nē) ***n.*** a serious crime, such as murder or kidnapping, that brings severe punishment, usually a prison sentence. *—pl.* **fel′o·nies** —**fe·lo·ni·ous** (fə lō′nē əs) ***adj.***

**felt**[1] (felt) ***n.*** a heavy material made of wool, fur, or hair pressed together under heat. ◆***adj.*** made of felt [a *felt* hat].

**felt**[2] (felt) *past tense and past participle of* **feel.**

**fem.** *abbreviation for* **feminine.**

**fe·male** (fē′māl) ***adj.*** **1** belonging to the sex that bears the young or produces eggs [A *female* fox is called a "vixen."] **2** of or for women or girls [*female* clothing]. ◆***n.*** a female person, animal, or plant. *See* SYNONYMS *at* **woman.**

SYNONYMS: **Female** stands for the members of the sex that is different from the male sex and is used of plants and animals as well as human beings. **Feminine** refers to those qualities thought of as making up the special character of women and girls, such as gentleness. **Womanly** suggests the noble qualities of a woman who has poise and maturity.

**fem·i·nine** (fem′ə nin) ***adj.*** **1** of or having to do with women or girls [*feminine* traits]. **2** having those qualities that women and girls have been thought of as having. *See* SYNONYMS *at* **female.** **3** of a class of words in grammar that refer to females or to things thought of as female. —**fem·i·nin·i·ty** (fem′ə nin′ə tē) ***n.***

**fem·i·nism** (fem′ə niz′m) ***n.*** **1** the principle that women should have equal rights with men. **2** the movement to win such rights. —**fem′i·nist** ***n.***

**fe·mur** (fē′mər) ***n.*** the bone in the thigh; thighbone. It is the largest bone in the body.

**fen** (fen) ***n.*** a swamp; marsh.

**fence** (fens) ***n.*** **1** a railing or wall, as of posts, rails, or wire, put around a field or yard to keep something in or out or to mark a boundary. **2** a person who buys and sells stolen goods. ◆***v.*** **1** to close in or hem in as with a fence. **2** to deal in stolen goods. **3** to fight with foils or other swords. —**fenced, fenc′ing** —☆**on the fence,** not decided; not taking one side or the other. —**fenc′er** ***n.***

**fenc·ing** (fen′siŋ) ***n.*** **1** the art or sport of fighting with foils or other swords; swordplay. *See the picture.* **2** material for making fences.

**fend** (fend) ***v.*** to keep off or turn aside [to *fend* off danger; to *fend* off a blow]. —**fend for oneself,** to get along without help from others.

**fend·er** (fen′dər) ***n.*** ☆**1** a metal piece over the wheel of a car to keep off splashing mud. **2** a metal piece at the front of a locomotive to throw off things that are hit. **3** a low screen or frame in front of an open fireplace.

**fen·nel** (fen′əl) ***n.*** a tall herb that has yellow flowers and seeds that are used as a seasoning and in medicine.

**FEP** Fair Employment Practices.

**fer·ment** (fər ment′) ***v.*** **1** to cause a slow chemical change to take place in a substance by means of yeast, bacteria, etc. Fermenting changes apple juice to vinegar, grape juice to wine, starch to sugar, and malt to beer. **2** to undergo this change [The milk *fermented* and became sour.] **3** to make or become excited or stirred up. ◆***n.*** (fʉr′ment) **1** a substance that causes fermenting. **2** fermentation. **3** a state of excitement; commotion [the *ferment* of war].

**fer·men·ta·tion** (fʉr′mən tā′shən) ***n.*** the chemical change in a substance that is caused by a ferment, as yeast or bacteria.

**Fer·mi** (fer′mē), **En·ri·co** (en rē′kō) 1901–1954; Italian scientist, in the U.S. after 1938. He helped develop the atomic bomb.

**fern** (fʉrn) ***n.*** a plant that does not bear flowers but instead has special seeds (called **spores**) that grow on the backs of its feathery leaves. Ferns grow in shady and moist places. *See the picture.*

**fe·ro·cious** (fə rō′shəs) ***adj.*** **1** cruel or fierce in a wild way; savage. **2** very great: *used only in everyday talk* [a *ferocious* appetite]. —**fe·ro′cious·ly** ***adv.***

**fe·roc·i·ty** (fə räs′ə tē) ***n.*** wild force or cruelty; fierceness.

**fer·ret** (fer′it) ***n.*** a small animal like a weasel, that can be tamed for use in hunting rabbits, rats, etc. ◆***v.*** **1** to force out of a hiding place by using a ferret. **2** to search for and force out [to *ferret* out the truth].

**fer·ric** (fer′ik) or **fer·rous** (fer′əs) ***adj.*** having to do with or containing iron.



☆**Fer·ris wheel** (fer′is) a very large wheel that turns in an upright position and has seats hanging from the rim. It is used as an amusement ride. *See the picture.*

The first **Ferris wheel** was made by George Washington Gale Ferris for a World's Fair in Chicago in 1893. It was very large, with 36 cars holding 40 persons in each. Most Ferris wheels have swinging seats that hold just two or three persons.

**fer·rule** (fer′əl *or* fer′ool) ***n.*** a metal ring or cap put on the end of a handle, cane, etc. to keep it from splitting or to make it stronger.

**fer·ry** (fer′ē) ***v.*** **1** to take or go across a river, bay, etc. in a boat or raft. **2** to deliver an airplane by flying it to the place where it will be used. **3** to transport by airplane. —**fer′ried, fer′ry·ing** ◆***n.*** **1** a boat used in ferrying: *also* **fer′ry·boat.** **2** the place where ferrying is done. **3** the regular ferrying of people, cars, etc. as across a river. *—pl.* **fer′ries**

**fer·tile** (fʉr′t′l) ***adj.*** **1** producing much fruit or large crops; rich [*fertile* soil]. **2** able to produce offspring, seeds, or fruit [a *fertile* orchard; *fertile* cattle]. **3** able to develop into a new plant or animal [*fertile* seeds; *fertile* eggs]. **4** bringing forth many ideas; inventive [a *fertile* imagination]. —**fer·til·i·ty** (fər til′ə tē) ***n.***

| | | | | | | | |
|---|---|---|---|---|---|---|---|
| **a** | fat | **ir** | here | **ou** | out | **zh** | leisure |
| **ā** | ape | **ī** | bite, fire | **u** | up | **ŋ** | ring |
| **ä** | car, lot | **ō** | go | **ʉr** | fur | | a *in* ago |
| **e** | ten | **ô** | law, horn | **ch** | chin | | e *in* agent |
| **er** | care | **oi** | oil | **sh** | she | ə = | i *in* unity |
| **ē** | even | **oo** | look | **th** | thin | | o *in* collect |
| **i** | hit | **ōō** | tool | ***th*** | then | | u *in* focus |

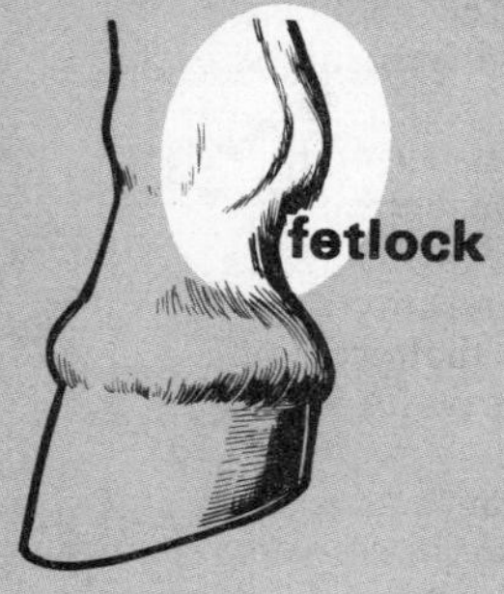


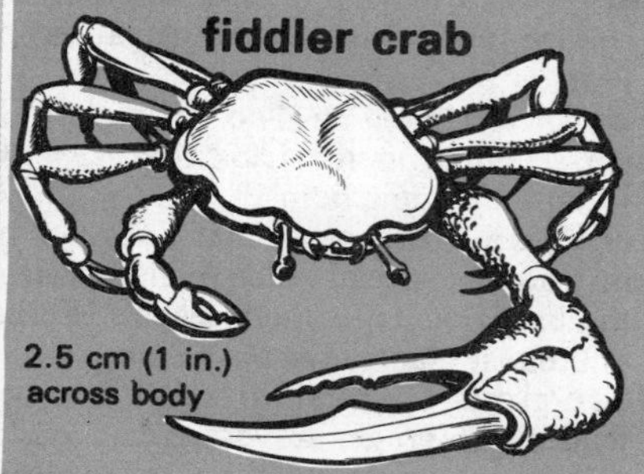


**fer·til·ize** (fur′t'l īz) ***v.*** **1** to make fertile, especially by adding fertilizer to [*Fertilize* your lawn in the spring.] **2** to bring a male germ cell to a female egg cell so as to cause a new animal or plant to develop [Bees *fertilize* flowers by carrying pollen from one to another.] —**fer′til·ized, fer′til·iz·ing** —**fer′til·i·za′-**

 **tion** ***n.***

**fer·til·iz·er** (fur′t'l ī′zər) ***n.*** manure or certain chemicals put in the soil as a food for plants.

**fer·ule** (fer′əl *or* fer′ool) ***n.*** a flat stick or ruler used for punishing children.

**fer·vent** (fur′vənt) ***adj.*** **1** showing very warm or strong feeling; intense; ardent [a *fervent* appeal for help]. **2** hot; glowing [*fervent* rays of the sun]. —**fer′ven·cy** ***n.*** —**fer′vent·ly** ***adv.***

**fer·vid** (fur′vid) ***adj.*** full of fervor or passion [*fervid* hatred].

**fer·vor** (fur′vər) ***n.*** **1** great warmth of feeling; ardor; zeal. **2** great heat. *The usual British spelling is* **fervour.**

**fes·tal** (fes′t'l) ***adj.*** of or like a festival or holiday; joyous [Graduation was a *festal* event.]

**fes·ter** (fes′tər) ***v.*** **1** to become filled with pus [The cut on his arm *festered.*] **2** to cause angry or bitter feelings [Her envy *festered* in her.] ✦***n.*** a sore that fills up with pus.

**fes·ti·val** (fes′tə v'l) ***n.*** **1** a day or time of feasting or celebrating; happy holiday [The Mardi Gras in New Orleans is a colorful *festival.*] **2** a time of special celebration or entertainment [Our town holds a maple sugar *festival* every spring.] ✦***adj.*** of or for a festival [*festival* music].

**fes·tive** (fes′tiv) ***adj.*** of or for a festival; merry; joyous [*festive* decorations].

**fes·tiv·i·ty** (fes tiv′ə tē) ***n.*** **1** merrymaking and celebrating [a time of *festivity*]. **2 festivities,** *pl.* things done as part of a happy celebration [the *festivities* of graduation week]. —*pl.* **fes·tiv′i·ties**

**fes·toon** (fes to͞on′) ***n.*** a decoration of flowers, leaves, paper, etc. arranged to hang in loops. *See the picture.* ✦***v.*** to decorate with festoons.

**fet·a cheese** (fet′ə) a white, soft cheese made in Greece from ewe's milk or goat's milk.

**fetch** (fech) ***v.*** **1** to go after and bring back; get [The dog *fetched* my slippers.] **2** to bring forth; draw [She *fetched* a sigh.] **3** to sell for [The sofa should *fetch* $50.]

**fetch·ing** (fech′iŋ) ***adj.*** attractive or charming [Carlotta has a *fetching* smile.]

**fete** or **fête** (fāt) ***n.*** a festival or party, especially one held outdoors. ✦***v.*** to honor with a fete; entertain [The performers were *feted* many times on their tour.] —**fet′ed** or **fêt′ed, fet′ing** or **fêt′ing**

**fet·id** (fet′id *or* fēt′id) ***adj.*** having a bad smell; stinking.

**fet·ish** (fet′ish *or* fēt′ish) ***n.*** **1** any object that is believed to have magical power [Primitive people wear *fetishes* to protect themselves from harm.] **2** anything to which a person is devoted in a way that is too strong [He makes a *fetish* of watching football on TV.]

**fet·lock** (fet′läk) ***n.*** a tuft of hair on the back of a horse's leg just above the hoof; also, this part of the horse's leg. *See the picture.*

**fet·ter** (fet′ər) ***n.*** **1** a shackle or chain for the feet. **2** anything that keeps one from moving or acting in a free way. ✦***v.*** to bind as with fetters [They are *fettered* by debts.]

**fet·tle** (fet′'l) ***n.*** condition of body and mind [Our team is in fine *fettle* for the game.]

**fe·tus** (fēt′əs) ***n.*** a human being or an animal in the later stages of its growth inside the uterus or egg. —*pl.* **fe′tus·es**

**feud** (fyo͞od) ***n.*** a bitter quarrel, especially one between two families. ✦***v.*** to carry on a feud.

**feu·dal** (fyo͞od′'l) ***adj.*** of or having to do with feudalism.

**feu·dal·ism** (fyo͞od′'l iz'm) ***n.*** the way of life in Europe during the Middle Ages, when land was owned by the king or lords, but held by vassals in return for help in war and other services. The land was worked by serfs.

**fe·ver** (fē′vər) ***n.*** **1** a body temperature that is higher than normal, as in some sicknesses. **2** a sickness in which there is a high fever [yellow *fever;* scarlet *fever*]. **3** a condition of nervousness or excitement [the *fever* of city life].

**fe·vered** (fē′vərd) ***adj.*** **1** having a fever. **2** excited or nervous.

**fe·ver·ish** (fē′vər ish) ***adj.*** **1** having a fever, especially a slight fever. **2** caused by fever [*feverish* raving]. **3** causing fever [a *feverish* climate]. **4** excited or nervous [*feverish* plans for escape]. —**fe′ver·ish·ly** ***adv.***

**few** (fyo͞o) ***adj.*** not many; a small number of [Christmas comes a *few* days before New Year's.] ✦***pron., n.*** not many; a small number [Many left, *few* stayed. A *few* of the men wore hats.] —☆**quite a few,** a rather large number: *used only in everyday talk.* —**the few,** a small select group. —**few′ness** ***n.***

> **Few** is used in speaking of things that can be counted [*few* cars; a *few* people], while **less** is used of an abstract quality or idea or of something that cannot be counted [*less* courage; *less* noise; *less* butter].

**fey** (fā) ***adj.*** strange, as in being peculiar, full of mischief, fanciful, etc.

**fez** (fez) ***n.*** a brimless felt cap that was once worn by Turkish men. It was usually red and had a black tassel. *See the picture.* —*pl.* **fez'zes**

**ff.** and the following pages ["The article is found on pages 39 *ff.*" means that it begins on page 39 and continues on the following pages.]

**FHA** or **F.H.A.** Federal Housing Administration.

**fi·an·cé** (fē'än sā') ***n.*** the man who is engaged to marry a certain woman.

**fi·an·cée** (fē'än sā') ***n.*** the woman who is engaged to marry a certain man.

**fi·as·co** (fē as'kō) ***n.*** something that ends as a complete or foolish failure [Our scheme to get rich ended in a *fiasco.*] —*pl.* **fi·as'coes** or **fi·as'cos**

**fi·at** (fī'at) ***n.*** an order given by a person who has authority; decree.

**fib** (fib) ***n.*** a lie about something not very important. ◆***v.*** to tell such a lie. —**fibbed, fib'bing** —**fib'ber *n.***

**fi·ber** or **fi·bre** (fī'bər) ***n.*** **1** any of the thin parts like threads that form the tissue of animals and plants [Cotton *fibers* are spun into yarn.] **2** the tissue formed of such fibers [muscle *fiber*]. **3** the way a person thinks and acts; character; nature [a leader of strong moral *fiber*].

**fi·ber·board** (fī'bər bôrd) ***n.*** **1** a boardlike material made from pressed fibers of wood, etc. It bends easily and is used in building. **2** a piece of this material.

☆**fi·ber·fill** (fī'bər fil) ***n.*** a lightweight, fluffy filling for quilts, pillows, jackets, etc., made of synthetic fibers.

**fi·brin** (fī'brən) ***n.*** a substance formed in blood clots that helps the action of clotting.

**fi·broid** (fī'broid) ***adj.*** formed of tissue that is made up of fibers [a *fibroid* tumor].

**fib·u·la** (fib'yoo lə) ***n.*** the long, thin outer bone of the human leg, between the knee and the ankle. —*pl.* **fib·u·lae** (fib'yoo lē) or **fib'u·las**

**Fibula** is the Latin word for a clasp or pin. The outer leg bone together with the larger inner bone in human beings looks like a clasp.

**-fi·ca·tion** (fi kā'shən) a suffix used to form nouns from many verbs that end with the suffix *-fy.* It means "the act or condition of" [*Glorification* means the act or condition of glorifying.]

**fick·le** (fik''l) ***adj.*** changing often in one's feelings or interests; inconstant [a *fickle* sweetheart]. —**fick'le·ness *n.***

**fic·tion** (fik'shən) ***n.*** **1** a piece of writing about imaginary people and happenings, as a novel, play, or story; also, such writings as a group. **2** something made up or imagined [What she said about her uncle is just a *fiction.*] —**fic'tion·al *adj.***

**fic·tion·al·ize** (fik'shən 'l īz) ***v.*** to deal with real events or people's lives as if they were fiction. —**fic'tion·al·ized, fic'tion·al·iz·ing**

**fic·ti·tious** (fik tish'əs) ***adj.*** of or like fiction; not real; made-up [a *fictitious* character in a play].

**fic·tive** (fik'tiv) ***adj.*** **1** of fiction or the writing of fiction. **2** not real; imaginary.

**fid·dle** (fid''l) ***n.*** a violin: *now used mostly in an informal way.* ◆***v.*** **1** to play on the violin: *used only in an informal way.* **2** to move the fingers in a nervous or restless way; toy or play [Stop *fiddling* with your pen.] —**fid'dled, fid'dling** —**fit as a fiddle,** in excellent health. —**fid'dler *n.***

☆**fiddler crab** a small, burrowing crab, the male of which has one claw much larger than the other. *See the picture.*

**fid·dle·sticks** (fid''l stiks') ***interj.*** nonsense!

**fi·del·i·ty** (fə del'ə tē *or* fī del'ə tē) ***n.*** **1** the quality of being true to one's promise, duty, etc.; loyalty; faithfulness. **2** exactness in copying or translating.

**fidg·et** (fij'it) ***v.*** to move about in a nervous or restless way [to *fidget* in one's seat]. —**the fidgets,** restless or nervous feelings or movements.

**fidg·et·y** (fij'it ē) ***adj.*** nervous or restless.

**fie** (fī) ***interj.*** for shame! shame on you!: *now often used in a joking way.*

**fief** (fēf) ***n.*** land held from a feudal lord in return for help in war and other services.

**field** (fēld) ***n.*** **1** a wide piece of open land without many trees; especially, a piece of land for growing crops, grazing animals, etc. **2** a piece of land having a special use or producing a certain thing [a landing *field;* an oil *field*]. **3** a battlefield. **4** a wide, flat space [a *field* of ice]. **5** the space within which something is active, can be seen, etc. [*field* of vision; magnetic *field*]. **6** a branch of learning or of special work [the *field* of science; the *field* of industry]. **7** the background, as on a flag or coin [Our flag has 50 stars on a blue *field.*] **8** an area where games or athletic events are held; also, the part of such an area where such events as high jump, long jump, pole vault, shot put, etc. are held. **9** all the people entered in a contest. ◆***adj.*** of, in, or on a field. ◆***v.*** **1** to stop or catch and return a batted ball. **2** to put a player or team into active play. —☆**play the field,** to explore every chance one has. —**take the field,** to go into action at the start of a game, battle, etc.



**field·er** (fēl'dər) ***n.*** a player in the field in baseball, cricket, etc.

**field glasses** a pair of powerful binoculars.

☆**field goal** **1** a goal kicked from the field in football, scoring three points. **2** a basket toss made from play in basketball, scoring two points.

**field hockey** *same as* **hockey** *in meaning* 2.

**field marshal** in some armies, an officer of the highest rank.

**fiend** (fēnd) ***n.*** **1** an evil spirit; devil; demon. **2** a very evil or cruel person. ☆**3** a person who is too strongly devoted to a habit or interest: *used only in everyday talk* [a fresh-air *fiend*]. —**fiend'ish *adj.***

**Fiend** comes from an Old English word that means "the one who hates." **The Fiend** is sometimes used to mean the Devil, or Satan, the chief evil spirit.

**fierce** (firs) ***adj.*** **1** wild or cruel; violent; raging [a *fierce* dog; a *fierce* wind]. **2** very strong or eager [a *fierce* effort]. —**fierc'er, fierc'est** —**fierce'ly *adv.*** —**fierce'ness *n.***

| | | | | | | | |
|---|---|---|---|---|---|---|---|
| **a** | fat | **ir** | here | **ou** | out | **zh** | leisure |
| **ā** | ape | **ī** | bite, fire | **u** | up | **ng** | ring |
| **ä** | car, lot | **ō** | go | **ur** | fur | | a *in* ago |
| **e** | ten | **ô** | law, horn | **ch** | chin | | e *in* agent |
| **er** | care | **oi** | oil | **sh** | she | **ə =** | i *in* unity |
| **ē** | even | **oo** | look | **th** | thin | | o *in* collect |
| **i** | hit | **ōō** | tool | ***th*** | then | | u *in* focus |

**fi·er·y** (fī′ər ē) ***adj.*** **1** of or filled with fire; flaming [the dragon's *fiery* breath]. **2** like fire; very hot [Pepper has a *fiery* taste.] **3** full of strong feeling; excited [*fiery* words; a *fiery* nature]. —**fi′er·i·er, fi′er·i·est** —**fi′er·i·ness** ***n.***

☆**fi·es·ta** (fē es′tə) ***n.*** a holiday or time of feasting and merrymaking; festival.

**fife** (fīf) ***n.*** a small flute that has a high, shrill tone. It is used mainly with drums in playing marches. *See the picture.* ◆***v.*** to play on a fife. —**fifed, fif′ing**

**fif·teen** (fif′tēn′) ***n., adj.*** five more than ten; the number 15.

**fif·teenth** (fif′tēnth′) ***adj.*** coming after fourteen others; 15th in order. ◆***n.*** **1** the fifteenth one. **2** one of fifteen equal parts of something; 1/15.

**fifth** (fifth) ***adj.*** coming after four others; 5th in order. ◆***n.*** **1** the fifth one. **2** one of five equal parts of something; 1/5.

**fif·ti·eth** (fif′tē ith) ***adj.*** coming after forty-nine others; 50th in order. ◆***n.*** **1** the fiftieth one. **2** one of fifty equal parts of something; 1/50.

**fif·ty** (fif′tē) ***n., adj.*** five times ten; the number 50. —*pl.* **fif′ties** —**the fifties**, the numbers or years from 50 through 59.

☆**fif·ty-fif·ty** (fif′tē fif′tē) ***adj., adv.*** in two equal shares: *used only in everyday talk.*

**fig** (fig) ***n.*** **1** a sweet fruit shaped like a small pear and filled with a soft pulp containing many seeds. Figs are often dried for eating. **2** the tree on which this fruit grows. *See the picture.* **3** the smallest amount [not worth a *fig*].



**fig.** *abbreviation for* **figure.**

**fight** (fīt) ***v.*** **1** to use fists, weapons, or other force in trying to beat or overcome someone or something; battle; struggle [to *fight* hand to hand; to *fight* a war]. **2** to work hard in trying to overcome [to *fight* against fear]. —**fought, fight′ing** ◆***n.*** **1** the use of force to beat or overcome someone or something; battle. **2** any contest or struggle [the *fight* against poverty]. **3** strength or desire for fighting [I still have some *fight* left in me.] —**fight off**, to struggle to avoid. —**fight′er** ***n.***

**fig·ment** (fig′mənt) ***n.*** something imagined or made up in the mind.

**fig·ur·a·tive** (fig′yər ə tiv) ***adj.*** giving a meaning that is different from the exact meaning, but that forms a sharp picture in the mind [In "screaming headlines," the word "screaming" is a *figurative* use.] —**fig′ur·a·tive·ly** ***adv.***

**fig·ure** (fig′yər) ***n.*** **1** shape, outline, or form [A square is a *figure* with four sides. Lou has a slim *figure.*] *See* SYNONYMS *at* **form.** **2** a picture or diagram, as in a book of instructions. **3** a design or pattern, as in cloth or wallpaper. **4** a person thought of in a certain way [She is an important *figure* in world affairs. He is a sorry *figure* of a man.] **5** a number [the *figure* 8]. **6 figures,** *pl.* arithmetic [He is good at *figures.*] **7** a sum of money [Gold sells at a high *figure.*] **8** a set of movements in dancing or skating. **9** a form of speech in which words are used out of their usual meaning to form a sharp picture in the mind: *also called* **figure of speech** ["Cool as a cucumber" is a *figure of speech.*] ◆***v.*** **1** to find an answer by using arithmetic [*Figure* how much I owe you.] ☆**2** to think or believe: *used only in everyday talk* [I *figure* it will rain.] **3** to have something to do with [Poor food *figured* in his ill health.] ☆**4** to be just as expected: *used only in everyday talk* [That *figures.*] —**fig′ured, fig′ur·ing** —☆**figure on,** to plan or depend on. —☆**figure out,** to find the answer to; understand.

**fig·ured** (fig′yərd) ***adj.*** decorated with figures or designs [a *figured* necktie].

**fig·ure·head** (fig′yər hed) ***n.*** **1** a carved figure on the bow of a ship for decoration. *See the picture.* **2** a person who holds a high position but has no real power.

**fig·u·rine** (fig yə rēn′) ***n.*** a small statue made of china, metal, etc.; statuette.

**Fi·ji** (fē′jē) a country on a group of islands in the South Pacific.

**fil·a·ment** (fil′ə mənt) ***n.*** a very slender thread, fiber, or wire [the *filaments* of a spider's web or inside an electric light bulb].

**fil·bert** (fil′bərt) ***n.*** *another name for* **hazelnut.**

**filch** (filch) ***v.*** to steal something small and of little value; pilfer.

**file**[1] (fīl) ***n.*** **1** a folder, box, or cabinet for keeping papers in order. **2** a number of papers, cards, magazines, etc. kept in an orderly way. **3** an orderly line of persons or things. ◆***v.*** **1** to arrange papers, cards, etc. in order [*File* these letters according to the dates on which they were received.] **2** to put into official records [to *file* a claim for a piece of land]. **3** to move in a line [The children *filed* out of the school.] —**filed, fil′ing** —**in file,** in line, one behind another. —**on file,** kept in order so that it can be referred to.

> **File** comes from an old French word that means "to string papers on a thread." One way to file or arrange papers in order would be to string them on a thread. The old French word goes back to the Latin word for thread.

**file**[2] (fīl) ***n.*** a steel tool with a rough, ridged surface for smoothing or grinding down something. *See the picture.* ◆***v.*** to smooth or grind down with a file [to *file* one's fingernails]. —**filed, fil′ing**

**fi·let** (fi lā′ *or* fil′ā) ***n.*** **1** a kind of net or lace. **2** *same as* **fillet** *in meaning* 2.

**fi·let mi·gnon** (fi lā′ min yōn′ *or* fi lā′ min yän′) a thick, round cut of lean beef tenderloin broiled, usually with mushrooms and bacon.

**fil·i·al** (fil′ē əl) ***adj.*** that should be expected from a son or daughter [*filial* devotion].

**fil·i·bus·ter** (fil′ə bus′tər) ***v.*** ☆to try to keep a bill from being passed in a legislature, by making long speeches or talking about other things. ◆***n.*** ☆**1** the act of filibustering. ☆**2** a member of a legislature who filibusters: *also* **fil′i·bus′ter·er.**

**fil·i·gree** (fil′ə grē) ***n.*** delicate, lacy work, as of gold or silver wire, used for decoration. ◆***adj.*** like or made of filigree. *See the picture.* ◆***v.*** to decorate with filigree. —**fil′i·greed, fil′i·gree·ing**

**fil·ing** (fīl′ing) ***n.*** any of the tiny bits scraped off with a file [metal *filings*].

**Fil·i·pi·no** (fil′ə pē′nō) ***n.*** a person born in the Philippines. —*pl.* **Fil′i·pi′nos** ◆***adj.*** *another word for* **Philippine.**

**fill** (fil) ***v.*** **1** to put as much as possible into; make full [to *fill* a pail with water]. **2** to take up all the space in; occupy all of [The crowd *filled* the hall.] **3** to spread throughout [Smoke *filled* the house.] **4** to become full [Pat's eyes *filled* with tears.] **5** to hold, or put someone into, a certain job or office; occupy [Can you *fill* the position of treasurer?] ☆**6** to supply the things needed in [to *fill* an order; to *fill* a prescription]. **7** to close up by stuffing something in [to *fill* holes or cracks with putty]. **8** to satisfy the hunger of [The cookies *filled* them.] **9** to swell out, as the sails of a boat. ◆***n.*** **1** all that is needed to make full or satisfy [to drink one's *fill*]. ☆**2** anything used to fill a space or hole [The gravel will be used as *fill* in the driveway.] —**fill in, 1** to make complete by adding something. ☆**2** to be a substitute. —**fill out, 1** to make or become larger, rounder, etc. ☆**2** to write the information asked for, as in a form. —**fill up,** to make or become completely full.

**fill·er** (fil′ər) ***n.*** **1** a person or thing that fills. **2** something used for filling, as a substance for filling cracks or paper for filling a loose-leaf notebook.

**fil·let** (fil′it) ***n.*** **1** a narrow band worn around the head as a decoration, etc. **2** (fil′ā *or* fi lā′) a lean piece of fish or meat without bones. ◆***v.*** (fil′ā *or* fi lā′) to remove the bones from and slice meat or fish.

**fill·ing** (fil′iŋ) ***n.*** a thing used to fill something, as metal that a dentist puts into a tooth cavity or the food put into a pastry shell.

**fil·lip** (fil′əp) ***n.*** **1** a sharp tap made by snapping a finger from the end of the thumb. *See the picture.* **2** anything that stirs or livens up; stimulus [Relishes give a *fillip* to a meal.] ◆***v.*** to toss with a fillip.

**Fill·more** (fil′môr), **Mill·ard** (mil′ərd) 1800–1874; the 13th president of the United States, from 1850 to 1853.

**fil·ly** (fil′ē) ***n.*** a young female horse; young mare. —*pl.* **fil′lies**

**film** (film) ***n.*** **1** a thin skin or coating [a *film* of ice on the pond]. **2** a sheet or roll of material covered with a chemical substance that is changed by light, used for taking photographs or making movies. **3** a haze or blur [a *film* over the eyes]. **4** a movie. ◆***v.*** **1** to cover or become covered with a film. **2** to make a movie of [to *film* a stage play].

**film·strip** (film′strip) ***n.*** a strip of film having still photographs, often of charts, diagrams, etc., which can be shown one after another on a screen and used as an aid in teaching.

**film·y** (fil′mē) ***adj.*** like a film or covered with a film. —**film′i·er, film′i·est** —**film′i·ness *n.***

**fil·ter** (fil′tər) ***n.*** **1** a device for making water, air, or other fluid clean or pure by passing it through sand, charcoal, cloth, etc. **2** the sand, charcoal, etc. used in this device. **3** anything that acts like a filter [A color *filter* for a camera lens lets only certain light rays through.] ◆***v.*** **1** to pass or put through a filter [to *filter* smoke; water *filtering* through gravel]. **2** to act as a filter for. **3** to remove with a filter. **4** to pass slowly [The news *filtered* through town.]

**filth** (filth) ***n.*** **1** waste matter, garbage, etc. that is disgusting [Sewers carry away *filth*.] **2** anything that is thought of as very disgusting or not decent.

**filth·y** (fil′thē) ***adj.*** full of filth; disgusting. —**filth′i·er, filth′i·est** —**filth′i·ly *adv.*** —**filth′i·ness *n.***

**fil·tra·tion** (fil trā′shən) ***n.*** the act of filtering or the process of being filtered.

fig tree and fruit

filigree necklace

figurehead

fillip

file

fife

**fin** (fin) ***n.*** **1** any of the parts like a blade or fan that stick out from the body of a fish and are used in swimming and balancing. *See the picture on page 276.* **2** anything like a fin, as certain parts for balancing an airplane or rocket. 275

**fi·na·gle** (fə nā′g'l) ***v.*** to get or arrange by being clever, crafty, or tricky [He *finagled* a pay raise for himself.] —**fi·na′gled, fi·na′gling**

**fi·nal** (fī′n'l) ***adj.*** **1** coming at the end; last; concluding [the *final* chapter in a book]. *See* SYNONYMS *at* **last. 2** allowing no further change; deciding [The decision of the judges is *final*.] ◆***n.*** **1** anything final. **2 finals,** *pl.* the last set in a series of games, tests, etc. —**fi′nal·ly *adv.***

**fi·na·le** (fə nä′lē) ***n.*** **1** the closing part of a piece of music, a musical show, etc. **2** the close or end, as of a career.

**fi·nal·ist** (fī′n'l ist) ***n.*** a person taking part in the final, deciding contest of a series.

**fi·nal·i·ty** (fī nal′ə tē) ***n.*** **1** the fact of being final [the *finality* of a court decision]. **2** a final action, remark, etc. —*pl.* **fi·nal′i·ties**

**fi·nal·ize** (fī′n'l īz) ***v.*** to make final or complete; finish [We must *finalize* that agreement.] —**fi′nal·ized, fi′nal·iz·ing** —**fi′nal·i·za′tion *n.***

**fi·nance** (fə nans′ *or* fī′nans) ***n.*** **1 finances,** *pl.* all the money or income that a government, company, person, etc. has ready for use. **2** the managing of money matters [Bankers are often experts in *finance*.]

| | | | | | | | |
|---|---|---|---|---|---|---|---|
| **a** | fat | **ir** | here | **ou** | out | **zh** | leisure |
| **ā** | ape | **ī** | bite, fire | **u** | up | **ŋ** | ring |
| **ä** | car, lot | **ō** | go | **ur** | fur | | a *in* ago |
| **e** | ten | **ô** | law, horn | **ch** | chin | | e *in* agent |
| **er** | care | **oi** | oil | **sh** | she | ə = | i *in* unity |
| **ē** | even | **oo** | look | **th** | thin | | o *in* collect |
| **i** | hit | **ōō** | tool | ***th*** | then | | u *in* focus |

**f**

**◆v.** to give or get money for [loans to *finance* new business]. —**fi·nanced′, fi·nanc′ing**

**fi·nan·cial** (fə nan′shəl) ***adj.*** having to do with money matters [*financial* problems]. —**fi·nan′cial·ly *adv.***

**fin·an·cier** (fin ən sir′) ***n.*** **1** an expert in money matters, as a banker or stockbroker. **2** a person who spends or invests large sums of money in business dealings.

**finch** (finch) ***n.*** a songbird that has a short beak and eats seeds, as the sparrow and canary.

**find** (fīnd) ***v.*** **1** to come upon by chance; discover [I sometimes *find* violets in the woods.] **2** to get by searching [The prospectors *found* gold. We *found* the answer.] **3** to get back something that has been lost; recover [We *found* the missing book.] **4** to learn about; come to know [I *find* that I was wrong.] **5** to feel or think [I *find* pleasure in music. They *find* TV boring.] **6** to declare after careful thought [The jury *found* them guilty.] **7** to get to; reach [The arrow *found* its mark.] —**found, find′ing ◆n.** something found, especially something of value. —**find out,** to learn; discover [to *find out* a secret].

**find·er** (fīn′dər) ***n.*** **1** a person or thing that finds or discovers. **2** a camera lens that shows just what will appear in the picture.

**find·ing** (fīn′diŋ) ***n.*** **1** the act of one who finds; discovery. **2** something found. **3** *often* **findings,** *pl.* a decision reached by a judge, scholar, etc. after thinking carefully about the facts.



**fine¹** (fīn) ***adj.*** **1** very good; better than average; excellent [a *fine* report card]. **2** not having impurities; refined [*fine* gold]. **3** clear and bright [a *fine* fall day]. **4** having small particles or grains [*fine* sand]. **5** very thin or small [*fine* thread; *fine* print]. **6** delicate; carefully made [*fine* china]. **7** sharp; keen [a knife with a *fine* edge]. **8** having to do with small, slight differences [the *fine* distinction between sympathy and pity]. **9** calling for great accuracy [a *fine* adjustment]. —**fin′er, fin′est ◆*adv.*** very well: *used only in everyday talk.* —**fine′ly *adv.*** —**fine′ness *n.***

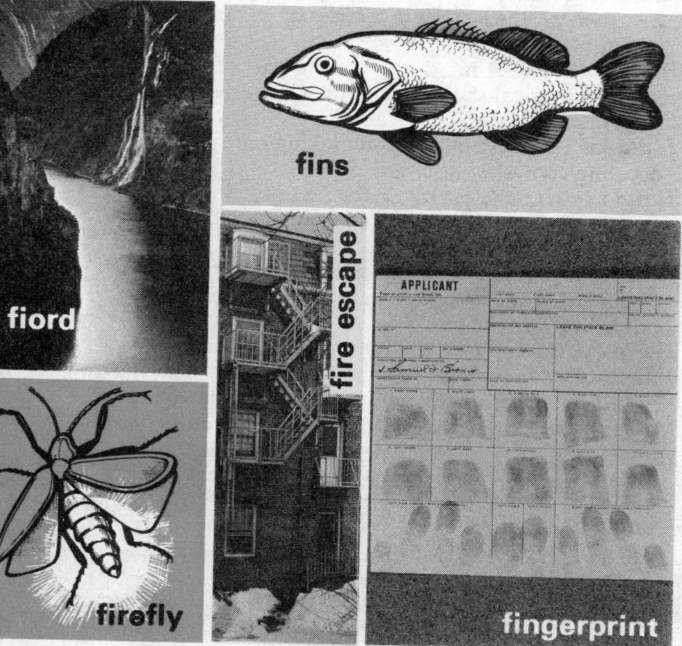
fiord
fins
fire escape
firefly
fingerprint

**fine²** (fīn) ***n.*** money paid as punishment for breaking a law or rule [a traffic *fine;* a library *fine*]. **◆v.** to order to pay a fine [She was *fined* five dollars for speeding.] —**fined, fin′ing**

**fine arts** such arts as drawing, painting, sculpture, etc., and also, sometimes, music, literature, dancing, etc.

**fin·er·y** (fīn′ər ē) ***n.*** showy or fancy clothes and jewelry. —*pl.* **fin′er·ies**

**fi·nesse** (fi nes′) ***n.*** **1** skill in taking care of difficult or touchy problems without causing anger [to show *finesse* in dealing with customers]. **2** delicate or skillful work [the *finesse* with which the artist drew a portrait].

**fin·ger** (fiŋ′gər) ***n.*** **1** any of the five parts at the end of the hand, especially any of these besides the thumb. **2** the part of a glove that covers a finger. **3** anything shaped or used like a finger. **◆v.** **1** to touch with the fingers [Don't *finger* the toys on the counter.] **2** to play by using certain fingers on the strings or keys of a musical instrument. [How would you *finger* this chord?]

**fin·ger·board** (fiŋ′gər bôrd) ***n.*** **1** a strip of hard wood in the neck of a violin or other stringed instrument against which the strings are pressed with the fingers to make the desired tones. **2** a keyboard of a piano, organ, etc.

**fin·ger·nail** (fiŋ′gər nāl) ***n.*** the hard, tough cover at the top of each finger tip.

☆**finger painting** the act or method of painting by using the fingers or hand to spread paints made of starch, glycerin, and pigments (**finger paints**) on wet paper. —**fin′ger-paint′ *v.***

**fin·ger·print** (fiŋ′gər print) ***n.*** the mark made by pressing the tip of a finger against a flat surface. The fine lines and circles form a pattern that can be used to identify a person. *See the picture.* **◆v.** to take the fingerprints of someone by pressing the finger tips on an inked surface and then on paper.

**fin·ick·y** (fin′i kē) ***adj.*** too particular; fussy [You are too *finicky* about what you eat.]

**fi·nis** (fin′is *or* fī′nis) ***n.*** the end; finish: *the word* **finis** *is sometimes put at the end of a book or movie.*

**fin·ish** (fin′ish) ***v.*** **1** to bring or come to an end; complete or become completed [Did you *finish* your work? The game *finished* early.] **2** to give a certain surface to, as by polishing or painting. **3** to give final touches to; perfect [We *finished* the room by putting up molding.] **4** to use up; consume completely [*Finish* your milk.] **5** to make useless, helpless, etc. [The long hike almost *finished* me.] **◆n.** **1** the last part; end [The audience stayed to the *finish*.] **2** polish or perfection, as in one's manners. **3** the kind of surface a thing has [an oil *finish* on wood]. —**finish off,** **1** to end. **2** to kill or destroy. —**finish up,** **1** to end. **2** to use all of. —**finish with,** **1** to end. **2** to stop dealing with. —**fin′ished *adj.***

**Finish** comes from a Latin word which means a kind of post placed in the ground to show the boundary of a piece of land. The post placed on a person's land showed where it came to an end.

**fi·nite** (fī′nīt) ***adj.*** having definite limits; that can be measured [*finite* distances].

☆**fink** (fiŋk) ***n.*** a person thought of as disgusting and deserving contempt. *This is a slang word.*

**Fin·land** (fin′lənd) a country in northern Europe, east of Sweden.

**Finn** (fin) ***n.*** a person born or living in Finland.

**Finn·ish** (fin′ish) ***adj.*** of Finland, its people, etc. ✦***n.*** the language of the Finns.

**fin·ny** (fin′ē) ***adj.*** **1** having fins. **2** like a fin. **3** of or full of fish.

**fiord** (fyôrd) ***n.*** a narrow inlet of the sea between steep cliffs, especially in Norway. *See the picture.*

**fir** (fur) ***n.*** **1** an evergreen tree of the pine family, having woody cones. **2** its wood.

**fire** (fīr) ***n.*** **1** the heat and light of something burning. **2** something burning, as in a stove or furnace. **3** anything bright or hot like a fire [the *fire* of a diamond]. **4** a burning that destroys things [a forest *fire*]. **5** strong feeling; excitement [a speech full of *fire*]. **6** the shooting of guns [under enemy *fire*]. **7** a great number of questions, complaints, etc. [He resigned under the *fire* of criticism.] ✦***v.*** **1** to set fire to; make burn: *now seldom used except in connection with the stirring up of feeling, thought, or action* [to *fire* one's imagination; to *fire* a revolt]. **2** to keep burning; tend the fire of [to *fire* a furnace]. **3** to bake in a kiln [to *fire* bricks]. **4** to shoot, as a gun or bullet. **5** to throw or direct with force and suddenness [The shortstop *fired* the ball to first base. The reporters *fired* questions at the mayor.] ☆**6** to send away from a job or position; discharge. —**fired, fir′ing** —**catch fire** or **catch on fire,** to begin burning. —**fire up,** to start a fire, as in a boiler. —**on fire,** **1** burning. **2** very excited. —**open fire,** to begin to shoot. —**play with fire,** to do something risky. —**set fire to,** to make burn. —**take fire,** **1** to begin to burn. **2** to become excited. —**under fire,** **1** under attack. **2** being criticized.

**fire·arm** (fīr′ärm) ***n.*** any weapon that shoots bullets or shells and that is small enough to carry, as a rifle or pistol.

**fire·bomb** (fīr′bäm) ***n.*** a bomb intended to start a fire. ✦***v.*** to attack with a firebomb or firebombs.

**fire·brand** (fīr′brand) ***n.*** **1** a piece of burning wood. **2** a person who stirs up a revolt.

☆**fire·crack·er** (fīr′krak′ər) ***n.*** a roll of paper with gunpowder inside. It is exploded with a loud noise by lighting a fuse.

**fire·damp** (fīr′damp) ***n.*** a gas in coal mines that can explode when mixed with air.

**fire engine** **1** a motor truck with equipment for spraying water or chemicals to put out a fire. **2** any motor truck for carrying firefighters to a fire.

**fire escape** a ladder, stairway, etc. by which one can escape from a burning building. *See the picture.*

**fire extinguisher** a device for putting out a fire by spraying liquid or gas on it. *See the picture for* **extinguisher.**

**fire·fight·er** (fīr′fīt′ər) ***n.*** a person who helps fight fires, especially a member of a company of people whose work is fighting fires.

**fire·fly** (fīr′flī) ***n.*** a small, flying beetle whose lower body glows with a light that goes off and on at night. *See the picture.* —*pl.* **fire′flies**

☆**fire·house** (fīr′hous) ***n.*** *another name for* **fire station.**

**fire·light** (fīr′līt) ***n.*** light from an open fire.

**fire·man** (fīr′mən) ***n.*** **1** a man who is a firefighter. **2** a person who tends the fire in a furnace, locomotive engine, etc. —*pl.* **fire′men**

**fire·place** (fīr′plās) ***n.*** an open place for a fire, especially one inside a house, built of brick or stone and connected to a chimney.

**fire·plug** (fīr′plug) ***n.*** *another name for* **hydrant.**

**fire·proof** (fīr′proof) ***adj.*** that does not burn or is not easily destroyed by fire [a *fireproof* carpet]. ✦***v.*** to make fireproof, as by treating with chemicals.

**fire·side** (fīr′sīd) ***n.*** **1** the part of a room near a fireplace; hearth. **2** home or home life.

**fire station** a place where fire engines are kept and where firefighters stay when on duty.

**fire·trap** (fīr′trap) ***n.*** a building that would not be safe if it caught on fire because it will burn easily or because it does not have enough exits.

**fire·wood** (fīr′wood) ***n.*** wood for burning in a fireplace, campfire, etc.

**fire·works** (fīr′wurks) ***n.pl.*** things made with gunpowder, etc. that are burned or exploded to make loud noises or a fancy show of lights at night, often used in celebrations [Rockets, sparklers, and firecrackers are *fireworks.*] *Sometimes used in the singular,* **firework.**

**firm**[1] (furm) ***adj.*** **1** that does not easily give way when pressed; solid [*firm* muscles]. **2** that cannot be moved easily; fixed; stable [He stood as *firm* as a rock.] **3** that stays the same; not changing; constant [a *firm* friendship]. **4** strong and steady; not weak; determined [a *firm* command]. —**firm′ly *adv.*** —**firm′ness *n.***

> SYNONYMS: **Firm** is used when talking about something whose parts hold together so tightly that it does not give way easily under pressure or springs back into shape after being pressed [a *firm* mattress]. **Hard** is used for that which is so firm that it is not easily cut into or crushed [*hard* as rock].

**firm**[2] (furm) ***n.*** a business company, especially one in which there are two or more partners.

**fir·ma·ment** (fur′mə mənt) ***n.*** the sky, written of by poets as if it were a solid blue arch.

**first** (furst) ***adj.*** **1** before another or before all others in time, order, quality, etc.; earliest, foremost, etc. [the *first* snow of winter; the *first* door to the right; *first* prize; fruit of the *first* quality]. **2** playing or singing the highest part [*first* violin; *first* tenor]. ✦***adv.*** **1** before anything or anyone else [*First* we had soup. Guests are served *first.*] **2** for the first time [When did you *first* meet them?] **3** more willingly; rather [When told to beg, she said she'd starve *first.*] ✦***n.*** **1** the one that is first [to be the *first* to succeed]. **2** the beginning; start [At *first,* I believed him.] **3** the first day of the month [We left on the *first.*] **4** a first happening



| | | | | | | | |
|---|---|---|---|---|---|---|---|
| a | fat | ir | here | ou | out | zh | leisure |
| ā | ape | ī | bite, fire | u | up | ŋ | ring |
| ä | car, lot | ō | go | ur | fur | ə = | a *in* ago |
| e | ten | ô | law, horn | ch | chin | | e *in* agent |
| er | care | oi | oil | sh | she | | i *in* unity |
| ē | even | oo | look | th | thin | | o *in* collect |
| i | hit | ōō | tool | *th* | then | | u *in* focus |

120 cm (4 ft.) high at shoulder

or a first thing of its kind [Going to the opera was a *first* for us.]

**first aid** the help given to an injured or sick person while waiting for regular medical help. —**first′-aid′** ***adj.***

**first·born** (furst′bôrn′) ***adj.*** born first in a family; oldest. ⬥***n.*** the firstborn child.



**first-class** (furst′klas′) ***adj.*** best of its kind; of the highest quality or most expensive [a *first-class* restaurant; a *first-class* cabin on a ship]. ⬥***adv.*** in a first-class cabin, etc. [to travel *first-class*].

**first cousin** the son or daughter of one's aunt or uncle.

**first·hand** (furst′hand′) ***adj., adv.*** straight from the source; not from a second person or thing; direct [a *firsthand* report].

☆**first lady** *often* **First Lady,** the wife of the president of the United States.

**first person** that form of a pronoun or verb which refers to the speaker or speakers ["I," "me," "we," "us," etc. are in the *first person.*]

**first-rate** (furst′rāt′) ***adj.*** of the highest class or quality; very good; excellent [a *first-rate* novel]. ⬥***adv.*** very well: *used only in everyday talk* [It works *first-rate.*]

**firth** (furth) ***n.*** a narrow inlet or arm of the sea.

**fis·cal** (fis′kəl) ***adj.*** having to do with money matters; financial. —**fis′cal·ly** ***adv.***

☆**fiscal year** any period of twelve months used for figuring financial accounts. The U.S. government fiscal year legally ends June 30.

**fish** (fish) ***n.*** **1** an animal that lives in water and has a backbone, fins, and gills for breathing. Most fish are covered with scales. **2** the flesh of a fish used as food. —*pl.* **fish** (or when different kinds are meant, **fishes**) [She caught three *fish.* The aquarium exhibits many *fishes.*] ⬥***v.*** **1** to catch or try to catch fish. **2** to search or feel about for, find, and pull out [He *fished* a dime out of his pocket.] **3** to try to get something in a roundabout way [He is always *fishing* for a compliment.]

**fish and chips** fillets of fish that are coated with batter, fried, and served with French fried potatoes: *mainly a British term.*

**fish·er** (fish′ər) ***n.*** **1** a person who fishes. **2** an animal related to the marten, like a weasel but larger.

**fish·er·man** (fish′ər mən) ***n.*** a person who fishes either for sport or for a living. —*pl.* **fish′er·men**

**fish·er·y** (fish′ər ē) ***n.*** **1** the business of catching fish. **2** a place where fish are caught. **3** a place for breeding fish. —*pl.* **fish′er·ies**

**fish·hook** (fish′hook) ***n.*** a hook with a barb or barbs for catching fish.

**fish·ing** (fish′iŋ) ***n.*** the catching of fish for sport or for a living.

**fishing rod** a long pole with a line, hook, and sometimes a reel, used in fishing. *See the picture.*

**fish·mon·ger** (fish′muŋ′gər *or* fish′mäŋ′gər) ***n.*** a person who sells fish: *chiefly a British word.*

☆**fish stick** a small oblong fillet or cake of fish breaded and fried.

**fish·y** (fish′ē) ***adj.*** **1** full of fish. **2** tasting or smelling of fish. **3** dull or without expression [a *fishy* stare]. **4** that makes one feel doubt; not likely: *used only in everyday talk* [a *fishy* story]. —**fish′i·er, fish′i·est**

**fis·sion** (fish′ən) ***n.*** **1** a splitting apart; dividing into parts. **2** *same as* **nuclear fission.**

**fis·sure** (fish′ər) ***n.*** a crack or split, as in a rock.

**fist** (fist) ***n.*** a hand with the fingers closed tightly into the palm [*Fists* are used in boxing.]

**fist·i·cuffs** (fis′ti kufs) ***n.pl.*** the act or skill of fighting with the fists; boxing.

**fit**[1] (fit) ***v.*** **1** to be the right size or shape for [Does this coat *fit* you?] **2** to make or change so as to be the right size or shape [His new suit has to be *fitted.*] **3** to be right or suitable to [Let the punishment *fit* the crime.] **4** to make right or suitable [to *fit* words to music]. **5** to put something into something else; insert [to *fit* a key into a lock]. **6** to furnish with what is needed or wanted; outfit: *often used with* out [to *fit* out a ship for a voyage]. —**fit′ted** or **fit, fit′ted, fit′ting** ⬥***adj.*** **1** suitable or suited to someone or something [a meal *fit* for a king]. **2** proper or right [It is not *fit* for you to be so rude.] **3** healthy; in good physical condition [She feels *fit* again after her illness.] —**fit′ter, fit′test** ⬥***n.*** the way something fits [This coat is a tight *fit.*] —**fit′ly** ***adv.*** —**fit′ness** ***n.***

SYNONYMS: **Fit** is used of something that has the special qualities needed for some situation or purpose [This meat is not *fit* to eat.] **Suitable** is used for something that is right or useful in a certain situation [a car *suitable* for mountain driving].

**fit**[2] (fit) ***n.*** **1** a sudden attack or outburst that is hard to control [a *fit* of coughing; a *fit* of anger]. **2** a sudden attack in which one becomes unconscious or has convulsions or both. —**by fits and starts,** from time to time; not in a regular way.

**fit·ful** (fit′fəl) ***adj.*** happening or done only from time to time; not regular or steady [a *fitful* sleep]. —**fit′ful·ly** ***adv.*** —**fit′ful·ness** ***n.***

**fit·ted** (fit′id) ***adj.*** made so as to fit closely the shape of that which it covers [*fitted* bed sheets].

**fit·ting** (fit′iŋ) ***adj.*** right, proper, or suitable [a *fitting* tribute to a wonderful woman]. ⬥***n.*** **1** the act of trying on clothes, etc. to see that they fit. **2** a part used to join or adapt other parts, as on pipes.

**Fitz·ger·ald** (fits jer′əld), **F. Scott** 1896–1940; U.S. writer of novels and stories.
**five** (fīv) ***n., adj.*** one more than four; the number 5.
**fix** (fiks) ***v.*** **1** to make stay in place; fasten firmly [a flagpole *fixed* in concrete; an idea *fixed* in the mind]. **2** to direct and hold [to *fix* one's eyes on something]. **3** to make stiff or rigid [a jaw *fixed* in determination]. **4** to decide on; settle; set definitely [to *fix* the date of a wedding]. **5** to set right or set in order; adjust [to *fix* one's hair]. **6** to make whole again; repair or mend [I *fixed* the broken chair.] **7** to get ready; prepare [to *fix* dinner]. **8** to treat with a chemical so as to keep from fading [to *fix* photographic film]. ☆**9** to get the result wanted by bribery, trickery, etc.: *used only in everyday talk* [to *fix* an election]. ☆**10** to get even with; punish: *used only in everyday talk.* ◆***n.*** ☆an unpleasant or difficult situation; predicament: *used only in everyday talk.* —**fix on** or **fix upon,** to choose. —**fix up, 1** to repair; mend. **2** to arrange properly. **3** to take care of. *This phrase is used only in everyday talk.* —**fixed *adj.*** —**fix·ed·ly** (fik′sid lē) ***adv.***
**fix·a·tion** (fik sā′shən) ***n.*** a very strong interest or concern [She has a *fixation* about germs.]
**fixed star** a star so far from the earth that it seems not to move in relation to other stars.
**fix·ings** (fik′siŋgz) ***n.pl.*** ☆all the things that go with the main thing; trimmings: *used only in everyday talk* [a turkey and all the *fixings*].
**fix·ture** (fiks′chər) ***n.*** **1** any of the fittings that are fastened to a building in such a way as to be considered a part of it [bathroom *fixtures;* a light *fixture*]. **2** any person or thing that has been in some position or place so long as to seem fixed there [Dr. Lander is a *fixture* at the hospital.]
**fizz** (fiz) ***n.*** a hissing or sputtering sound, as of soda water. ◆***v.*** to make this sound.
**fiz·zle** (fiz′'l) ***v.*** **1** to make a hissing or sputtering sound. **2** to fail, especially after a good start: *used only in everyday talk.* —**fiz′zled, fiz′zling** ◆***n.*** **1** a hissing or sputtering sound. **2** a thing that ends in failure: *used only in everyday talk.*
**fjord** (fyôrd) ***n.*** *another spelling of* **fiord.**
**FL** or **Fla.** *abbreviations for* **Florida.**
**fl.** *abbreviation for* **fluid.**
**flab·ber·gast** (flab′ər gast) ***v.*** to surprise so greatly that one is speechless; amaze.
**flab·by** (flab′ē) ***adj.*** soft and limp; not firm and strong [*flabby* muscles]. —**flab′bi·er, flab′bi·est** —**flab′bi·ness *n.***
**flac·cid** (flak′sid *or* flas′id) ***adj.*** soft and limp; flabby. —**flac′cid·ly *adv.***
**flag**[1] (flag) ***n.*** a piece of cloth with certain colors and designs, used as a symbol of a country, State, organization, etc. or as a signal. ◆***v.*** **1** to signal with a flag. **2** to signal to stop: *often used with* down [The stranded motorist *flagged* down a passing car.] —**flagged, flag′ging**
**flag**[2] (flag) ***n.*** the iris, a plant with sword-shaped leaves and blue, white, or yellow flowers.
**flag**[3] (flag) ***v.*** to become limp, weak, or tired; droop [The hikers began to *flag* after the tenth mile.] —**flagged, flag′ging**
**flag·el·late** (flaj′ə lāt) ***v.*** to whip or flog. —**flag′el·lat·ed, flag′el·lat·ing** —**flag′el·la′tion *n.***
**flag·on** (flag′ən) ***n.*** a kind of pitcher with a handle, a spout, and, often, a lid.
**flag·pole** (flag′pōl) ***n.*** a pole on which a flag is raised and flown: *also* **flag·staff** (flag′staf).
**fla·grant** (flā′grənt) ***adj.*** clearly bad or wicked; outrageous [a *flagrant* crime]. —**fla′grant·ly *adv.***
**flag·ship** (flag′ship) ***n.*** the main ship of a fleet, on which the commander stays.
**flag·stone** (flag′stōn) ***n.*** any of the flat stones used in making a walk or terrace.
**flail** (flāl) ***n.*** a farm tool used to beat grain in order to separate it from its husk. It has a long handle, with a shorter stick attached so that it will swing freely. *See the picture.* ◆***v.*** **1** to beat, as with a flail. **2** to wave the arms about [The young children were kicking and *flailing* about in the water.]
**flair** (fler) ***n.*** **1** a natural skill; talent [a *flair* for music]. **2** an understanding of what is stylish [You dress with great *flair.*]
**flak** (flak) ***n.*** **1** the fire of antiaircraft guns. **2** loud and strong criticism, disapproval, etc.
**flake** (flāk) ***n.*** a small, thin piece or chip [a *flake* of snow or dried paint]. ◆***v.*** to come off in flakes [plaster *flaking* off the walls]. —**flaked, flak′ing**
**flak·y** (flāk′ē) ***adj.*** **1** of or made up of flakes. **2** breaking easily into flakes. ☆**3** strange or odd, as in behavior: *slang in this meaning.* —**flak′i·er, flak′i·est** —**flak′i·ness *n.***
**flam·boy·ant** (flam boi′ənt) ***adj.*** too showy or fancy [a *flamboyant* costume]. —**flam·boy′ance *n.*** —**flam·boy′ant·ly *adv.***
**flame** (flām) ***n.*** **1** the burning gas of a fire seen as a flickering light; blaze. **2** the condition of burning with a blaze [to burst into *flame*]. **3** anything as hot or bright as a flame. ◆***v.*** **1** to burn with a flame; blaze. **2** to burst out like a flame [to *flame* with anger]. —**flamed, flam′ing**
**fla·men·co** (flə meŋ′kō) ***n.*** **1** the energetic dancing or music of Spanish gypsies. **2** any of their songs or dances. —*pl.* **fla·men′cos**
**fla·min·go** (flə miŋ′gō) ***n.*** a wading bird that has a very long neck and legs, and pink or red feathers. It lives in tropical regions. *See the picture.* —*pl.* **fla·min′gos** or **fla·min′goes**
**flam·ma·ble** (flam′ə b'l) ***adj.*** easily set on fire. —**flam′ma·bil′i·ty *n.***

Containers of gasoline and other substances which can easily catch on fire were once labeled "inflammable." Nowadays, in business and industry, **flammable** is usually used.

**Flan·ders** (flan′dərz) a region in Europe in western Belgium and northern France. It was once a country.
**flange** (flanj) ***n.*** a flat edge that stands out from the rim of a wheel, pipe, etc. to hold it in place, guide it, etc. *See the picture.*

| | | | | | | | |
|---|---|---|---|---|---|---|---|
| **a** | fat | **ir** | here | **ou** | out | **zh** | leisure |
| **ā** | ape | **ī** | bite, fire | **u** | up | **ŋ** | ring |
| **ä** | car, lot | **ō** | go | **ʉr** | fur | | a *in* ago |
| **e** | ten | **ô** | law, horn | **ch** | chin | | e *in* agent |
| **er** | care | **oi** | oil | **sh** | she | **ə** = | i *in* unity |
| **ē** | even | **oo** | look | **th** | thin | | o *in* collect |
| **i** | hit | **ōō** | tool | ***th*** | then | | u *in* focus |

**flank** (flangk) ***n.*** **1** the side of an animal between the ribs and the hip. *See the picture for* **beef**. **2** the side of anything [the right *flank* of an army]. ◆***v.*** **1** to be at the side of [Fountains *flank* the statue on either side.] **2** to go around the side of enemy troops, etc.

**flan·nel** (flan′'l) ***n.*** **1** a soft cloth with a nap, made usually of wool or cotton. **2 flannels,** *pl.* trousers, etc. made of flannel.

**flap** (flap) ***n.*** **1** anything flat and broad that hangs loose or covers an opening [the *flap* of a pocket or an envelope]. **2** the motion or slapping sound of a swinging flap [the *flap* of an awning]. **3** a commotion or fuss: *slang in this meaning.* ◆***v.*** **1** to move with a slapping sound [The flag *flapped* in the wind.] **2** to move up and down or back and forth [The bird *flapped* its wings.] —**flapped, flap′ping**

**flap·jack** (flap′jak) ***n.*** *another word for* **pancake**.

**flare** (fler) ***v.*** **1** to blaze up with a bright flame or burn with a flame that is whipped about [The torch *flared* in the wind.] **2** to spread outward like a bell [The lower end of a clarinet *flares* out.] —**flared, flar′ing** ◆***n.*** **1** a short burst of bright light. **2** a very bright light used as a distress signal, etc. **3** a sudden short outburst [a *flare* of temper]. **4** a spreading outward like a bell, or the part that spreads out [the *flares* in a skirt]. —**flare up, 1** to burst into flame. **2** to become suddenly angry, excited, etc.

**flare-up** (fler′up) ***n.*** **1** a sudden outburst of flame.

280 **2** a sudden, brief outburst of anger, trouble, etc.

**flash** (flash) ***v.*** **1** to send out a short and bright burst of light [Electric signs *flashed* all along the street.] **2** to sparkle or gleam [Her eyes *flashed* with anger.] **3** to come, move, or send swiftly or suddenly [The train *flashed* by. The news was *flashed* to Paris by radio.] **4** to show briefly or so as to impress others: *used only in everyday talk* [He *flashed* a roll of money.] ◆***n.*** **1** a short burst of light or of something bright [a *flash* of lightning; a *flash* of wit, hope, etc.] **2** a very short time; moment [I'll be there in a *flash*.] ☆**3** a bit of late news sent by telegraph, radio, etc.

**flash·bulb** (flash′bulb) ***n.*** a light bulb that gives a short, bright light for taking photographs.

☆**flash·cube** (flash′kyo͞ob) ***n.*** a cube with a flashbulb in each one of four sides. It rotates after each bulb flashes, making the next bulb ready for flashing. *See the picture.*

☆**flash flood** a sudden, violent flood, as after a heavy rain.

**flash·ing** (flash′ing) ***n.*** sheets of metal or other material used to seal joints or edges, especially of a roof. *See the picture.*

**flash·light** (flash′līt) ***n.*** an electric light that uses batteries and is small enough to carry.

**flash·y** (flash′ē) ***adj.*** too showy or fancy [*flashy* clothes]. —**flash′i·er, flash′i·est**

**flask** (flask) ***n.*** a small bottle with a narrow neck, used by chemists, etc. *See the picture.*

**flat**[1] (flat) ***adj.*** **1** smooth and level [a *flat* stretch of land]. **2** lying spread out at full length; horizontal [to lie *flat* on the floor]. **3** not very thick or deep [A penny is *flat*.] **4** definite; positive [a *flat* refusal]. **5** not changing; always the same [a *flat* rate]. **6** without much taste or sparkle [This ginger ale is *flat*.] ☆**7** having lost air [a *flat* tire]. **8** not shiny or glossy [a *flat* paint]. **9** in music, below the true pitch; also, lower in pitch by a half tone. —**flat′ter, flat′test** ◆***adv.*** **1** in a flat way; flatly [to fall *flat* on the floor; to sing *flat*]. **2** exactly [He ran the race in ten seconds *flat*.] ◆***n.*** **1** a flat part [the *flat* of the hand]. **2** a stretch of flat land. **3** a shallow box, as for carrying seedlings. **4** a musical tone or note one half step below another; also, the sign (♭) used to mark such a note. ◆***v.*** to make or become flat [to *flat* a note]. —**flat′ted, flat′ting** —**fall flat,** to fail to have the effect that is wanted [Her joke fell *flat*.] —**flat′ly *adv.*** —**flat′ness *n.***

**flat**[2] (flat) ***n.*** an apartment of rooms on one floor.

**flat·bed** or **flat-bed** (flat′bed) ***adj.*** ☆describing or of a truck, trailer, etc. having a bed or platform without sides or stakes. ◆***n.*** ☆a flatbed truck, trailer, etc.

**flat·boat** (flat′bōt) ***n.*** a boat with a flat bottom, for carrying heavy loads, especially on rivers.

☆**flat·car** (flat′kär) ***n.*** a railroad car without sides or a roof, for carrying certain kinds of freight. *See the picture.*

**flat·fish** (flat′fish) ***n.*** a fish with a flat body and both eyes on the top side, as the flounder, halibut, sole, etc.

**flat·foot** (flat′fo͝ot) ***n.*** a condition in which the bottom of the foot is flat instead of being curved by the arch. —**flat′-foot′ed *adj.***

**flat·i·ron** (flat′ī′ərn) ***n.*** an iron for pressing clothes.

**flat·ten** (flat′'n) ***v.*** to make or become flat.

**flat·ter** (flat′ər) ***v.*** **1** to praise too much or without meaning it, as in order to win favor. **2** to make seem better or more attractive than is really so [This picture *flatters* me.] **3** to make feel pleased or honored [I'm *flattered* that you remember me.] —**flatter oneself,** to hold the pleasing belief that [Don't *flatter yourself* that you will be forgiven.] —**flat′ter·er *n.***

> **Flatter** comes from an old French word meaning "to smooth" or "to touch gently with the hand." When people flatter us, we may feel as if we are being caressed or gently touched.

**flat·ter·y** (flat′ər ē) ***n.*** too much praise, or praise that is not really meant. —*pl.* **flat′ter·ies**

**flaunt** (flônt) ***v.*** to show off in a bold way [to *flaunt* one's wealth].

**fla·vor** (flā′vər) ***n.*** **1** the special quality of something that is a mixing of its taste and smell [the *flavor* of chocolate]. **2** taste in general [a soup lacking *flavor*]. ◆***v.*** to give flavor to. *The usual British spelling is* **flavour**.

**fla·vor·ing** (flā′vər ing) ***n.*** something added to give a certain flavor [vanilla *flavoring*].

**flaw** (flô) ***n.*** **1** a break, scratch, crack, etc. that spoils something; blemish [There is a *flaw* in this diamond.] **2** any fault or error [a *flaw* in one's reasoning]. —**flaw′less *adj.*** —**flaw′less·ly *adv.***

**flax** (flaks) ***n.*** **1** a slender plant with blue flowers and narrow leaves. The fibers from its stem are spun into linen thread and its seeds are used to make linseed oil. **2** the fibers of this plant.

**flax·en** (flak′s'n) ***adj.*** **1** of flax. **2** like flax in color; pale-yellow [*flaxen* hair].

**flay** (flā) ***v.*** **1** to strip off the skin of, as by whipping. **2** to scold in a harsh way.

**flea** (flē) ***n.*** a small jumping insect that has no wings.

It bites animals and people and feeds on their blood. *See the picture.*

**flea market** an outdoor sale, mainly of cheap or secondhand goods, with many people buying and selling.

**fleck** (flek) ***n.*** a spot of color, dirt, etc.; speck. ◆***v.*** to cover or sprinkle with flecks; speckle [brown cloth *flecked* with green].

**fled** (fled) *past tense and past participle of* **flee.**

**fledg·ling** (flej′ling) ***n.*** **1** a young bird that has grown the feathers it needs for flying. **2** a young person who has had little or no experience.

**flee** (flē) ***v.*** **1** to run away from danger or from something unpleasant; escape [We *fled* when we heard the flood warnings.] **2** to move swiftly away [The years *flee* by.] —**fled, flee′ing**

**fleece** (flēs) ***n.*** **1** the coat of wool on a sheep or on a goat, llama, etc. **2** a soft, warm, napped fabric. ◆***v.*** **1** to clip the fleece from. **2** to take money from by trickery; swindle. —**fleeced, fleec′ing**

**fleec·y** (flēs′ē) ***adj.*** of or like fleece; soft and light [*fleecy* clouds]. —**fleec′i·er, fleec′i·est**

**fleet**[1] (flēt) ***n.*** **1** a group of warships under one command [our Pacific *fleet*]. **2** the entire navy of a country [the British *fleet*]. **3** any group of ships, trucks, buses, etc. moving together or under one control.

**fleet**[2] (flēt) ***adj.*** moving swiftly; swift.

**fleet·ing** (flēt′ing) ***adj.*** passing swiftly; not lasting [a *fleeting* glimpse].

**Flem·ing** (flem′ing) ***n.*** **1** a person born in Flanders. **2** a Belgian who speaks Flemish.

**Flem·ish** (flem′ish) ***adj.*** of Flanders, its people, etc. ◆***n.*** the language of Flanders, which is a kind of German. —**the Flemish,** the people of Flanders.

**flesh** (flesh) ***n.*** **1** the soft parts of the body, especially the parts between the skin and the bones. **2** these parts of an animal used as food; meat. **3** the human body [more than *flesh* can bear]. **4** all human beings [the way of all *flesh*]. **5** the pulpy part of fruits and vegetables. —**in the flesh, 1** in person; really present. **2** alive. —**one's own flesh and blood,** one's close relatives.

**flesh·ly** (flesh′lē) ***adj.*** having to do with the body, its weaknesses, appetites, etc.

**flesh·y** (flesh′ē) ***adj.*** having much flesh; plump. —**flesh′i·er, flesh′i·est**

**fleur-de-lis** (flur′də lē′) ***n.*** a design that looks a little like a lily or iris. It was an emblem of French kings. *See the picture.* —*pl.* **fleurs-de-lis** (flur′də lēz′)

**flew** (flo͞o) *past tense of* **fly**[1].

**flex** (fleks) ***v.*** **1** to bend [to *flex* an arm]. **2** to make tighter and harder; contract [to *flex* a muscle].

**flex·i·ble** (flek′sə b′l) ***adj.*** **1** that bends easily without breaking [a *flexible* rubber hose]. **2** easily changed or managed [Our doctor has *flexible* office hours.] —**flex′i·bil′i·ty *n.***

**flick** (flik) ***n.*** **1** a light, quick stroke, as with a whip; snap. **2** a light, snapping sound. ◆***v.*** to give a light, quick stroke to, as with a whip or the fingernail [I *flicked* the ant off the table.]

**flick·er**[1] (flik′ər) ***v.*** **1** to burn or shine in a way that is not clear or steady; waver [The candles *flickered* in the wind.] **2** to move in a quick, light, unsteady way [*flickering* shadows]. ◆***n.*** **1** a flickering light or flame. **2** a look or feeling that comes and goes quickly [A *flicker* of fear crossed her face.]

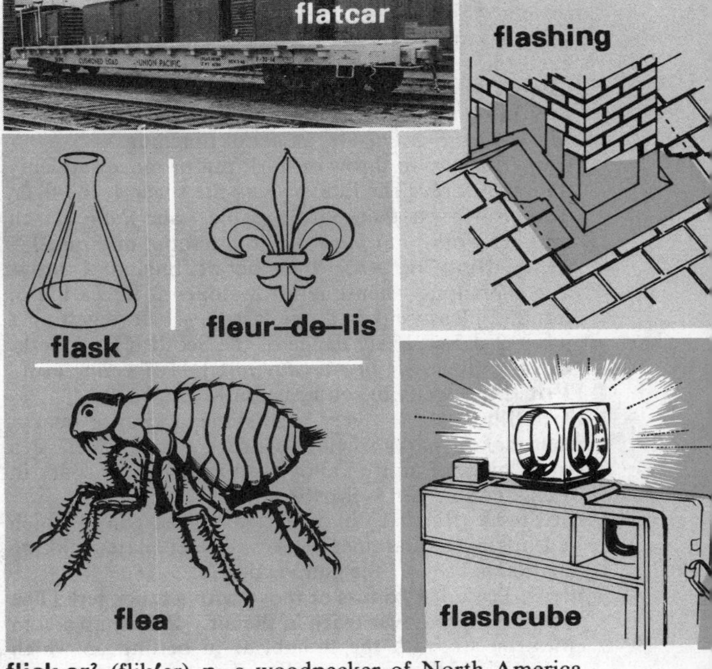


**flick·er**[2] (flik′ər) ***n.*** a woodpecker of North America with a red mark on the back of the head and wings colored golden on the underside. *See the picture on page 282.*



**flied** (flīd) *a past tense and past participle of* **fly**[1], *in its meaning in baseball.*

**fli·er** (flī′ər) ***n.*** **1** a thing that flies. **2** a person who flies an airplane; aviator. ☆**3** a bus or train that travels very fast. ☆**4** a small handbill. ☆**5** a reckless gamble: *used only in everyday talk. This word is also spelled* **flyer,** *especially in meanings* 2, 3, *and* 5.

**flies** (flīz) **1** *the form of the verb* **fly**[1], *used in the present with* he, she, *or* it. **2** *the plural of* **fly**[1] *and* **fly**[2].

**flight**[1] (flīt) ***n.*** **1** the act or way of flying or moving through space. **2** a trip through the air, as by an airplane, bird, etc. [a 500-mile *flight*]. **3** a group of things flying together [a *flight* of wild swans]. **4** a going above or beyond the usual limits [a *flight* of the imagination]. **5** a set of stairs, as between landings or floors.

**flight**[2] (flīt) ***n.*** a fleeing or running away. —**put to flight,** to make run away.

☆**flight bag** **1** a small, lightweight piece of luggage designed to fit under the passenger seat in an airplane. **2** a small bag with a zipper top for carrying personal things as on an airplane.

**flight·y** (flīt′ē) ***adj.*** not taking things seriously; frivolous. —**flight′i·er, flight′i·est**

| | | | | | | | |
|---|---|---|---|---|---|---|---|
| **a** | fat | **ir** | here | **ou** | out | **zh** | leisure |
| **ā** | ape | **ī** | bite, fire | **u** | up | **ng** | ring |
| **ä** | car, lot | **ō** | go | **ur** | fur | | a *in* ago |
| **e** | ten | **ô** | law, horn | **ch** | chin | | e *in* agent |
| **er** | care | **oi** | oil | **sh** | she | **ə =** | i *in* unity |
| **ē** | even | **o͝o** | look | **th** | thin | | o *in* collect |
| **i** | hit | **o͞o** | tool | ***th*** | then | | u *in* focus |

**flim·sy** (flim′zē) ***adj.*** easily broken or damaged; not solid or strong; weak [a *flimsy* cardboard box; a *flimsy* excuse]. —**flim′si·er, flim′si·est** —**flim′si·ness *n.***

**flinch** (flinch) ***v.*** to draw back from a blow or from anything difficult or painful [The soldier never *flinched* from duty.] ◆***n.*** an act of flinching.

**fling** (fliŋ) ***v.*** to throw or hurl; put or move suddenly and with force [The hunter *flung* the spear at the tiger. The crowd was *flung* into a panic. She *flung* herself into her work. Pat *flung* out of the room in a rage.] —**flung, fling′ing** ◆***n.*** **1** the act of flinging; a throw. **2** a short time when one throws oneself into a life of fun and pleasure [I had one last *fling* before getting a job.] **3** a fast, lively dance of the Scottish Highlands. **4** a try: *used only in everyday talk* [Have a *fling* at it.]

**Flint** (flint) a city in southeastern Michigan.

**flint** (flint) ***n.*** **1** a very hard stone, a kind of quartz, that makes sparks when it is struck against steel. **2** a small piece of an iron alloy used to strike the spark in a cigarette lighter. —**flint′y *adj.***

**flint·lock** (flint′läk) ***n.*** an old-fashioned gun in which a flint in the hammer strikes a steel plate, making sparks that set off the gunpowder.

**flip**[1] (flip) ***v.*** **1** to toss or move with a quick jerk [The acrobat *flipped* over twice in the air.] **2** to snap a coin into the air, with the thumb, as in betting on which side will land uppermost. *See the picture.* **3** to turn over quickly [*flipping* pages in a book]. ☆**4** to lose self-control because one is excited, angry, etc.: also **flip out, flip one's lid**: *this meaning and these phrases are slang.* —**flipped, flip′ping** ◆***n.*** the act of flipping; snap, toss, etc.



**flip**[2] (flip) ***adj.*** flippant, saucy, or impudent: *used only in everyday talk.* —**flip′per, flip′pest**

**flip·pant** (flip′ənt) ***adj.*** joking or trying to be funny when one should be more serious or show more respect. —**flip′pan·cy *n.*** —**flip′pant·ly *adv.***

flippers of a seal

flounce

flicker
30 cm (1 ft.) long

flipping a coin



writing with flourishes

**flip·per** (flip′ər) ***n.*** **1** any of the broad, flat limbs on seals, whales, etc., used for swimming. *See the picture.* ☆**2** a paddlelike rubber piece worn on each foot as a help in swimming.

**flirt** (flʉrt) ***v.*** **1** to act in a playful or bold way in trying to attract someone and begin a love affair. **2** to think about or have to do with, but not in a serious way; toy [Joe *flirted* with the idea of studying law.] **3** to move back and forth quickly [The bird *flirted* its tail.] ◆***n.*** **1** a person who flirts with others. **2** a flirting motion.

> **Flirt** may come from an old French word meaning "to move from flower to flower." A bee might seem to flirt with flowers, not taking any of them seriously enough to stay very long.

**flir·ta·tion** (flər tā′shən) ***n.*** the act of flirting, or playing at love. —**flir·ta′tious *adj.***

**flit** (flit) ***v.*** to fly or move in a quick and light way; dart [butterflies *flitting* from blossom to blossom; memories *flitting* through the mind]. —**flit′ted, flit′ting**

**float** (flōt) ***v.*** **1** to rest on top of water or other liquid and not sink [Ice *floats.*] **2** to move or drift slowly, as on a liquid or through the air [Clouds *floated* overhead.] **3** to cause to float [You may *float* your boats in this pond.] **4** to get started; set going; launch [to *float* a loan]. ◆***n.*** **1** something that floats on a liquid or keeps something else afloat, as a raft, a cork on a fishing line, or a hollow tank on an airplane wing to allow landing on water. **2** a hollow metal ball that floats on the liquid in a tank and shuts off the valve controlling the liquid when it reaches a certain level. **3** a platform on wheels that carries a display or exhibit in a parade. —**float′er *n.***

**floating ribs** the eleventh and twelfth pairs of ribs, not attached to the breastbone or to other ribs but only to the vertebrae.

**flock** (fläk) ***n.*** **1** a group of animals or birds that feed or travel together [a *flock* of sheep; a *flock* of geese]. **2** any group of people or things, as the members of a church. ◆***v.*** to come or travel together in a group ["Birds of a feather *flock* together."]

**floe** (flō) ***n.*** a large sheet of floating ice.

**flog** (fläg *or* flôg) ***v.*** to beat, as with a whip or stick; thrash. —**flogged, flog′ging**

**flood** (flud) ***n.*** **1** an overflowing of water on land next to a river, lake, etc. **2** the flowing in of the tide. **3** any great flow or outburst [a *flood* of tears, words, etc.] ◆***v.*** **1** to flow over its banks onto nearby land. **2** to flow, cover, or fill like a flood [The sound of music *flooded* the room.] **3** to put much or too much water, fuel, etc. on or in [to *flood* a carburetor].

**flood·gate** (flud′gāt) ***n.*** a gate that controls the flow of water, as in a canal.

**flood·light** (flud′līt) ***n.*** **1** a lamp that sends out a broad beam of bright light. **2** such a beam of light. ◆***v.*** to light by such a lamp.

**floor** (flôr) ***n.*** **1** the bottom part of a room, hall, etc., on which to walk. **2** the bottom surface of anything [the ocean *floor*]. **3** a story of a building [an office on the fifth *floor*]. ☆**4** the right to speak at a meeting [You can ask the chairman for the *floor*.] ◆***v.*** **1** to cover with a floor. **2** to knock down to the floor. ☆**3** to make unable to act, as by shocking, confusing, etc.: *used only in everyday talk* [Her answer *floored* me.]

**floor·board** (flôr′bôrd) ***n.*** **1** a board in a floor. **2** the floor of an automobile.

**floor·ing** (flôr′iŋ) ***n.*** **1** a floor or floors. **2** material for making floors.

**flop** (fläp) ***v.*** **1** to move or flap about in a loose or clumsy way [The fish *flopped* about in the bottom of the boat.] **2** to fall or drop in this way [She *flopped* into a chair.] **3** to fail: *used only in everyday talk* [Our school play *flopped.*] —**flopped, flop′ping** ◆***n.*** **1** the act or sound of flopping. **2** a failure: *used only in everyday talk.*

**flop·py** (fläp′ē) ***adj.*** flopping or tending to flop: *used only in everyday talk* [a *floppy* hat]. —**flop′pi·er, flop′pi·est**

**flo·ra** (flôr′ə) ***n.*** all the plants of a particular place or time [the *flora* of Alaska].

**flo·ral** (flôr′əl) ***adj.*** of or like flowers [a *floral* design on cloth].

**Flor·ence** (flôr′əns) a city in central Italy. —**Flor·en·tine** (flôr′ən tēn) ***adj., n.***

**flor·id** (flôr′id) ***adj.*** **1** flushed with red or pink; ruddy [a *florid* face]. **2** too full of decoration; very showy [a *florid* piece of music]. —**flor′id·ly *adv.*** —**flor′id·ness *n.***

> **Florid** comes from a Latin word meaning "flower." Many flowers are very colorful or showy.

**Flor·i·da** (flôr′ə də) a State in the southeastern part of the U.S.: abbreviated **Fla., FL**

**flor·in** (flôr′in) ***n.*** any of certain gold or silver coins used at various times in some European countries.

**flo·rist** (flôr′ist) ***n.*** a person whose business is selling flowers, house plants, etc.

**floss** (flôs) ***n.*** **1** soft and light bits of silky fiber. **2** loosely twisted thread of soft silk, used in embroidery. **3** a thin, strong thread used for cleaning between the teeth. *The full name is* **dental floss.** ◆***v.*** to clean between the teeth with dental floss. —**floss′y *adj.***

**flo·til·la** (flō til′ə) ***n.*** **1** a small fleet. **2** a fleet of boats or small ships.

**flot·sam** (flät′səm) ***n.*** parts of a wrecked ship or its cargo found floating on the sea: *see also* **jetsam.**

**flounce**[1] (flouns) ***v.*** to move or turn quickly, flinging the arms or body about, as in anger [The customer *flounced* out of the store.] —**flounced, flounc′ing** ◆***n.*** the act of flouncing.

**flounce**[2] (flouns) ***n.*** a wide ruffle sewed on by its upper edge to a skirt, sleeve, etc. *See the picture.* ◆***v.*** to trim with a flounce or flounces. —**flounced, flounc′ing**

**floun·der**[1] (floun′dər) ***v.*** **1** to struggle in a clumsy way in moving through mud, snow, etc. **2** to speak or act in a clumsy or confused way [to *flounder* through a speech].

**floun·der**[2] (floun′dər) ***n.*** a kind of flatfish caught for food.

**flour** (flour) ***n.*** wheat or other grain that has been ground into a fine powder, or meal. It is used for making bread, cakes, etc. ◆***v.*** to put flour on or in. —**flour′y *adj.***

**flour·ish** (flur′ish) ***v.*** **1** to grow strongly; be successful or healthy; prosper [The arts *flourished* in ancient Greece.] **2** to wave in the air [The crowd greeted the president by *flourishing* small flags.] ◆***n.*** **1** a sweeping movement [The hostess entered the room with a *flourish.*] **2** a fancy line or curve added to writing as a decoration. *See the picture.* **3** a loud, showy burst of music; fanfare [a *flourish* of trumpets].

**flout** (flout) ***v.*** to pay no attention to in an insulting or mocking way; treat with scorn [to *flout* someone's advice].

**flow** (flō) ***v.*** **1** to move in a stream as water does [Oil *flows* through the pipeline.] **2** to move in a smooth and easy way [The crowds *flowed* by. The talk *flowed* on for hours.] **3** to come from as a source; spring ["Praise God from whom all blessings *flow.*"] **4** to hang loose [with hair *flowing* down the back]. ◆***n.*** **1** the act, way, or amount of flowing. **2** anything that moves along in a steady way; stream or current [a *flow* of mail]. **3** the rising of the tide.

**flow·er** (flou′ər) ***n.*** **1** the part of a plant that bears the seed and usually has brightly colored petals; blossom or bloom. **2** a plant grown for its blossoms. **3** the best or finest part [the *flower* of a nation's youth]. **4** the best time or finest period [in the *flower* of one's life]. ◆***v.*** **1** to come into bloom; bear flowers. **2** to reach its best or finest period [Your musical talent *flowered* early.]

**flow·ered** (flou′ərd) ***adj.*** decorated with flowers or a design like flowers [a *flowered* dress].

**flowering crab** a small tree that has many large, red to pink flowers.

**flow·er·pot** (flou′ər pät) ***n.*** a pot to hold earth for a plant to grow in. 

**flow·er·y** (flou′ər ē) ***adj.*** **1** covered or decorated with flowers [a *flowery* field]. **2** of or like flowers [a *flowery* design]. **3** full of fine words or fancy language [a *flowery* speech]. —**flow′er·i·ness *n.***

**flown** (flōn) *past participle of* **fly**[1].

**flt.** *abbreviation for* **flight.**

**flu** (flo͞o) ***n.*** *a shorter word for* **influenza.**

☆**flub** (flub) ***v.*** to make a botch of a job, a chance, etc. —**flubbed, flub′bing** ◆***n.*** a mistake or blunder. *This word is used only in everyday talk.*

**fluc·tu·ate** (fluk′cho͞o āt) ***v.*** to rise and fall; keep changing or wavering [The price of eggs *fluctuates.*] —**fluc′tu·at·ed, fluc′tu·at·ing** —**fluc′tu·a′tion *n.***

**flue** (flo͞o) ***n.*** a tube for allowing smoke, hot air, etc. to go out, as in a chimney.

**flu·en·cy** (flo͞o′ən sē) ***n.*** the quality of being fluent, especially in writing or speaking.

**flu·ent** (flo͞o′ənt) ***adj.*** **1** moving easily and smoothly [*fluent* verse]. **2** able to write or speak easily and clearly [She is *fluent* in two languages.] —**flu′ent·ly *adv.***

**fluff** (fluf) ***n.*** downy bits of feathers, cotton, fur, etc., or a soft mass of such bits. ◆***v.*** **1** to shake or pat until soft and fluffy [to *fluff* a pillow]. **2** to make a mistake in speaking: *used only in everyday talk* [The actor *fluffed* a line.]

| | | | | | | | |
|---|---|---|---|---|---|---|---|
| **a** | fat | **ir** | here | **ou** | out | **zh** | leisure |
| **ā** | ape | **ī** | bite, fire | **u** | up | **ŋ** | ring |
| **ä** | car, lot | **ō** | go | **ur** | fur | | a *in* ago |
| **e** | ten | **ô** | law, horn | **ch** | chin | | e *in* agent |
| **er** | care | **oi** | oil | **sh** | she | ə = | i *in* unity |
| **ē** | even | **oo** | look | **th** | thin | | o *in* collect |
| **i** | hit | **o͞o** | tool | ***th*** | then | | u *in* focus |

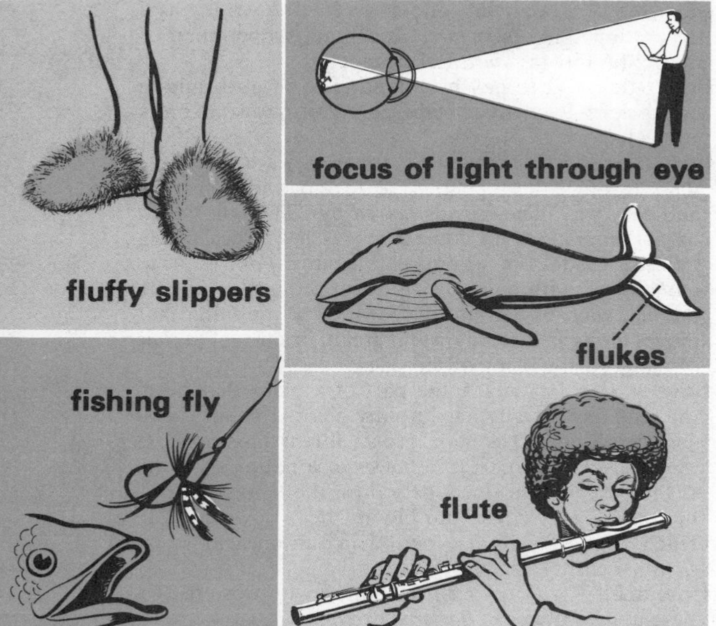


**fluff·y** (fluf'ē) ***adj.*** **1** soft and light like fluff. **2** covered with fluff. *See the picture.* —**fluff'i·er, fluff'i·est** —**fluff'i·ness** ***n.***



**fluid** (flōō'id) ***n.*** any substance that flows, as water, air, molten metal, etc.; any liquid or gas. ◆***adj.*** **1** that can flow. **2** like a fluid; moving or changing; not fixed [*fluid* beliefs].

**fluid dram** a liquid measure equal to 1/8 fluid ounce.

**fluid ounce** a liquid measure equal to 8 fluid drams, 1/16 pint, or 0.0296 liter.

**fluke**[1] (flōōk) ***n.*** **1** any of the pointed parts of an anchor that catch in the ground. ☆**2** the barb of an arrow, spear, or harpoon. **3** either of the rounded parts of a whale's tail. *See the picture.*

**fluke**[2] (flōōk) ***n.*** a strange bit of luck, good or bad: *used only in everyday talk.*

**flume** (flōōm) ***n.*** ☆**1** a sloping chute in which water is run down, as for moving logs, supplying power, etc. ☆**2** a deep, narrow ravine with a stream at the bottom.

**flung** (flung) *past tense and past participle of* **fling.**

☆**flunk** (flungk) ***v.*** to fail, as in schoolwork: *used only in everyday talk.*

**flun·ky** or **flun·key** (flung'kē) ***n.*** **1** a person who obeys the orders of another in the way that a servant would. ☆**2** a person who has very unimportant or humble work. —*pl.* **flun'kies** or **flun'keys**

**flu·o·res·cent** (floo res''nt *or* flōō'ə res''nt) ***adj.*** that gives off cool light while being acted on by some form of energy, such as X-rays and ultraviolet rays. —**flu'o·res'cence** ***n.***

**fluorescent lamp** a glass tube coated on the inside with a substance that gives off cool light when mercury vapor in the tube is acted on by an electric current.

☆**fluor·i·date** (flôr'ə dāt *or* floor'ə dāt) ***v.*** to add fluorides to drinking water in trying to prevent tooth decay. —**fluor'i·dat·ed, fluor'i·dat·ing** —**fluor'i·da'tion** ***n.***

**flu·o·ride** (floor'īd *or* flōō'ə rīd) ***n.*** a salt containing fluorine.

**flu·o·rine** (floor'ēn *or* flōō'ə rēn) ***n.*** a greenish-yellow, poisonous gas that is a chemical element. It is very active chemically.

☆**fluor·o·scope** (floor'ə skōp *or* flôr'ə skōp) ***n.*** a machine for examining the inner parts of something, as the body. X-rays are passed through the object, casting shadows of the parts on a fluorescent screen.

**flur·ry** (flur'ē) ***n.*** ☆**1** a sudden, short rush of wind, or a sudden, light fall of rain or snow. **2** a sudden, brief excitement or confusion. —*pl.* **flur'ries** ◆***v.*** to confuse or excite [New drivers get *flurried* when they are in heavy traffic.] —**flur'ried, flur'ry·ing**

**flush** (flush) ***v.*** **1** to make or become red in the face; blush [Fever had *flushed* her cheeks. He *flushed* with anger.] **2** to make happy or excited [Our team was *flushed* with victory.] **3** to empty out with a sudden flow of water [to *flush* a toilet]. **4** to rise or make rise suddenly from a hiding place [The dog *flushed* a pheasant in the tall grass.] ◆***n.*** **1** a sudden flow, as of water. **2** a blush. **3** a sudden, strong feeling [the *flush* of pleasure]. **4** a sudden, strong growth [the first *flush* of youth]. ◆***adj.*** **1** having plenty of something, especially money. **2** being even or on the same line or plane with; making an even line or surface [a door that is *flush* with the wall]. **3** direct or exact; straight [The blow was *flush* on the chin.] ◆***adv.*** **1** so as to form an even surface or line [Storm doors close *flush* with the door frame.] **2** directly; squarely [The snowball hit me *flush* in the face.]

**flus·ter** (flus'tər) ***v.*** to make or become excited or confused. ◆***n.*** a flustered condition.

**flute** (flōōt) ***n.*** **1** a musical wind instrument with a high pitch. It is a long, thin tube that is played by blowing across a hole at one end and opening or closing a series of holes along the side with the fingers or with keys. *See the picture.* **2** a long, rounded groove, as in a column. ◆***v.*** **1** to play on a flute, or to sound like a flute. **2** to make long, rounded grooves in a column. —**flut'ed, flut'ing**

**flut·ing** (flōōt'ing) ***n.*** a series of long, rounded grooves, as in a column.

**flut·ist** (flōōt'ist) ***n.*** a flute player.

**flut·ter** (flut'ər) ***v.*** **1** to flap the wings without flying [The sick bird *fluttered* helplessly.] **2** to wave rapidly [The flag *fluttered* in the breeze.] **3** to move about in a restless way. **4** to tremble; quiver [Our hearts *fluttered* when the car skidded.] ◆***n.*** **1** a fluttering movement. **2** a state of excitement or confusion [parents in a *flutter* over a wedding].

**flutter kick** a swimming stroke in which the legs are moved up and down in short, rapid, steady strokes.

**flux** (fluks) ***n.*** **1** a flowing or flow. **2** constant changing [Fashions for clothes are always in a state of *flux.*] **3** a substance, such as borax or rosin, used to help metals melt together, as in soldering. **4** a passing of fluid from the body in a way that is not normal, especially from the bowels.

**fly**[1] (flī) ***v.*** **1** to move through the air by using wings, as a bird. **2** to travel or carry through the air, as in an aircraft. **3** to pilot an aircraft. **4** to wave or float in the air, or cause to float in the air, as a flag or kite. **5**

to move swiftly [The door *flew* open. Time *flies*.] **6** to run away from danger; flee. ☆**7** to hit a fly in baseball. —**flew, flown, fly'ing** *The past tense and past participle for meaning* 7 *is* **flied.** ◆*n.* **1** a flap of cloth covering buttons, a zipper, etc. in a garment. ☆**2** a baseball batted high in the air inside the foul lines. —*pl.* **flies** —☆**fly out,** to be put out in baseball by hitting a fly that is caught. —**let fly,** to hurl or attack. —**on the fly, 1** while flying. **2** while in a hurry: *used only in everyday talk.*

**fly**[2] (flī) *n.* **1** a flying insect having one pair of wings, as the housefly and gnat. Some insects with two pairs of wings are called flies, as the mayfly. **2** an object used in fishing, made of bright feathers, silk, etc. tied to a fishhook to look like a fly. *See the picture.* —*pl.* **flies**

**fly·catch·er** (flī'kach'ər) *n.* a small bird that catches insects while flying.

**fly·er** (flī'ər) *n. another spelling of* **flier.**

**flying fish** a fish of warm seas that has a pair of fins like wings. It can leap out of the water and glide through the air with these.

☆**flying saucer** *another name for* **UFO.**

☆**flying squirrel** a squirrel that has winglike folds of skin attached to its legs and body. It can use these to make long, gliding leaps.

**fly·leaf** (flī'lēf) *n.* an extra leaf, usually blank, at the very beginning or the very end of a book. —*pl.* **fly·leaves** (flī'lēvz)

**fly·speck** (flī'spek) *n.* **1** a tiny spot made by a fly. **2** any tiny spot. **3** any very small or unimportant mistake.

**fly·wheel** (flī'hwēl) *n.* a heavy wheel on a machine, for keeping its motion smooth and steady.

**FM** frequency modulation: a way of sending out radio waves which cannot be picked up very far away. The sound of FM is richer and clearer than AM. *See also* **AM.**

**foal** (fōl) *n.* a very young horse, mule, donkey, etc. ◆*v.* to give birth to a foal.

**foam** (fōm) *n.* **1** a white mass of bubbles formed on liquids, as when they are shaken. **2** something like foam, as frothy saliva. **3** a spongy material made by spreading gas bubbles in liquid rubber, plastic, etc. ◆*v.* to form or collect foam; froth [The mad dog *foamed* at the mouth.]

**foam rubber** rubber made in the form of firm sponge, used in seats, mattresses, etc.

**foam·y** (fōm'ē) *adj.* foaming, full of foam, or like foam [the *foamy* water in the rapids]. —**foam'i·er, foam'i·est** —**foam'i·ness** *n.*

**fob** (fäb) *n.* ☆a short chain or ribbon attached to a watch and hanging out of a small pocket in the front of trousers, often with an ornament at the end.

**F.O.B.** or **f.o.b.** free on board: this abbreviation after a price means that it includes free delivery from the factory to the train, ship, etc. but that the buyer must pay all further transportation costs.

**fo·cal** (fō'k'l) *adj.* of or at a focus.

**fo·cus** (fō'kəs) *n.* **1** a point where rays of light, heat, etc. come together or from which they spread; especially, the point where rays of light meet after being reflected by a mirror or refracted by a lens. *See the picture.* **2** the distance from the center of a lens to the point where light rays passing through it meet. **3** an adjustment of this distance to make a clear image [She brought the camera into *focus*.] **4** any center of activity or interest [The baby was a *focus* of attention.] —*pl.* **fo'cus·es** or **fo·ci** (fō'sī) ◆*v.* **1** to bring to a focus [to *focus* light rays]. **2** to adjust the eye or a lens in order to make a clear image [Glasses help him to *focus* his eyes on small print.] **3** to fix or settle on some one thing; center [When the TV is off, I can *focus* my attention on my homework.] —**fo'cused** or **fo'cussed, fo'cus·ing** or **fo'cus·sing** —**in focus,** clear; distinct. —**out of focus,** not clear; blurred.

> **Focus** is also a Latin word meaning "fireplace." A fireplace, in earlier times, was the center of a house, from which people got light and heat.

**fod·der** (fäd'ər) *n.* coarse food for cattle, horses, etc., such as cornstalks, hay, and straw.

**foe** (fō) *n.* an enemy or opponent.

**foe·tus** (fē'təs) *n. another spelling of* **fetus.**

**fog** (fôg *or* fäg) *n.* **1** a large mass of tiny drops of water, near the earth's surface; thick mist that makes it hard to see. *See* SYNONYMS *at* **mist. 2** a condition of being confused or bewildered. ◆*v.* **1** to cover with a fog. **2** to make or become blurred; confuse [Poor focusing *fogged* the photograph. Illness may *fog* the mind.] —**fogged, fog'ging**

**fo·gey** (fō'gē) *n. another spelling of* **fogy.** —*pl.* **fo'geys**

**fog·gy** (fôg'ē *or* fäg'ē) *adj.* **1** having fog [a *foggy* day]. **2** mixed up; confused [a *foggy* idea]. —**fog'gi·er, fog'gi·est** —**fog'gi·ly** *adv.* —**fog'gi·ness** *n.*



**fog·horn** (fôg'hôrn *or* fäg'hôrn) *n.* a horn blown during a fog to warn ships of danger.

**fo·gy** (fō'gē) *n.* a person who sticks to old-fashioned ideas or ways. —*pl.* **fo'gies**

**foi·ble** (foi'b'l) *n.* a small fault or weakness in a person's character.

**foil**[1] (foil) *v.* to keep from doing something; thwart; stop [Their evil plans were *foiled* again.]

**foil**[2] (foil) *n.* **1** a very thin sheet of metal [aluminum *foil*]. **2** something that makes another thing seem better by contrast [Bill's funny questions served as a *foil* for Anita's witty answers.] **3** a long, thin sword used in fencing, with a button on the point to prevent injury.

**foist** (foist) *v.* to cheat or use tricks in passing something off as a fine or genuine thing [to *foist* a false diamond on someone].

**fold**[1] (fōld) *v.* **1** to bend something over upon itself so that one part is on top of another [You *fold* a letter before putting it in an envelope.] **2** to bring together and twist around one another [to *fold* the arms]. **3** to clasp or embrace [He *folded* his baby girl in his arms.] **4** to wrap up [*Fold* your lunch in this newspaper.] ☆**5** to fail or give in: *used only in everyday talk* [Their business *folded*. The team *folded* under pressure.] ◆*n.*

| | | | |
|---|---|---|---|
| **a** fat | **ir** here | **oi** out | **zh** leisure |
| **ā** ape | **ī** bite, fire | **u** up | **ŋ** ring |
| **ä** car, lot | **ō** go | **ur** fur | a *in* ago |
| **e** ten | **ô** law, horn | **ch** chin | e *in* agent |
| **er** care | **oi** oil | **sh** she | ə = i *in* unity |
| **ē** even | **oo** look | **th** thin | o *in* collect |
| **i** hit | **ōō** tool | ***th*** then | u *in* focus |

1 a layer made in folding [The handkerchief has eight *folds*.] 2 a crease made by folding.

**fold²** (fōld) ***n.*** 1 a pen in which sheep are kept. 2 the members of a church.

**-fold** (fōld) *a suffix meaning* a certain number of parts or times [A *tenfold* division is a division into ten parts or a dividing ten times.]

☆**fold·a·way** (fōld′ə wā) ***adj.*** that can be folded together and stored away [a *foldaway* cot].

**fold·er** (fōl′dər) ***n.*** 1 a folded piece of heavy paper or cardboard, for holding papers. ☆2 a booklet made of folded sheets. 3 a person or thing that folds.

**fo·li·age** (fō′lē ij) ***n.*** the leaves of a tree or plant, or of many trees or plants.

**fo·li·o** (fō′lē ō) ***n.*** 1 a sheet of paper folded once so that it forms four pages of a book. 2 a book of the largest size, originally made of sheets folded in this way. 3 the number of a page in a book. —*pl.* **fo′li·os**

**folk** (fōk) ***n.*** 1 a people or nation. 2 **folk** or **folks,** *pl.* people or persons [The farmer disliked city *folk*. *Folks* differ in their hobbies.] —*pl.* **folk** or **folks** ◆***adj.*** of the common people [a *folk* saying]. —**one's folks,** one's family or relatives: *used only in everyday talk.*

**folk dance** a dance that the common people of a country have danced over a long period of time.

**folk·lore** (fōk′lôr) ***n.*** the stories, beliefs, customs, etc. handed down among a people.

**folk music** music made and handed down among the common people, especially folk songs.



**folk song** 1 a song made and handed down among the common people. 2 a song composed to sound like such a song. —**folk singer**

☆**folk·sy** (fōk′sē) ***adj.*** friendly in a simple, direct way, or too friendly in a way that seems insincere: *used only in everyday talk.* —**folk′si·er, folk′si·est**

**folk tale** a story made and handed down by word of mouth among the common people: *also* **folk story.** *See* SYNONYMS *at* **myth.**

**fol·li·cle** (fäl′i k′l) ***n.*** a tiny opening or sac, as in the skin [Hairs grow from *follicles*.]

**fol·low** (fäl′ō) ***v.*** 1 to come or go after [The lamb *followed* Mary to school. Monroe *followed* Madison as President.] 2 to come as a result of [A good performance *followed* her long hours of practice.] 3 to travel along [*Follow* this road for two miles.] 4 to watch or listen to closely [to *follow* the TV news]. 5 to understand [I can't *follow* your reasoning.] 6 to take as one's work [He *followed* the plumber's trade.] 7 to be guided or led by; obey [to *follow* rules, a leader, advice, etc.] —**as follows,** as will next be told or explained. —**follow out** or **follow up,** to carry out fully. —**follow through,** to continue a stroke after hitting a ball, as in golf.

**fol·low·er** (fäl′ə wər) ***n.*** 1 a person or thing that follows, especially one who follows another's teachings. 2 a servant or other attendant.

**fol·low·ing** (fäl′ə wing) ***adj.*** going or coming after; next after [the *following* week]. ◆***n.*** people who follow; followers. ◆***prep.*** after [*Following* dinner we played cards.] —**the following,** the persons or things to be mentioned next.

**fol·ly** (fäl′ē) ***n.*** 1 the condition of being foolish. 2 any foolish action, belief, etc. —*pl.* **fol′lies**

**fo·ment** (fō ment′) ***v.*** to excite or stir up trouble of some sort [to *foment* a riot].

**fond** (fänd) ***adj.*** 1 loving and tender [*fond* parents; *fond* words]. 2 held dear; cherished [a *fond* hope]. —**fond of,** having a liking for. —**fond′ly *adv.*** —**fond′ness *n.***

**fon·dant** (fän′dənt) ***n.*** a soft, creamy candy made of sugar, often used as a filling for other candies.

**fon·dle** (fän′d′l) ***v.*** to stroke or handle in a tender and loving way; caress [to *fondle* a doll]. —**fon′dled, fon′dling**

**fon·due** or **fon·du** (fän do͞o′ *or* fän′do͞o) ***n.*** 1 a dish made by melting cheese in wine, with a little brandy and seasoning added, used as a dip for cubes of bread. 2 a dish in which cubes of meat are dipped in simmering oil until cooked. 3 cheese soufflé with bread crumbs.

**font** (fänt) ***n.*** 1 a basin for holding holy water or water for baptizing. *See the picture.* 2 a spring or source.

**food** (fo͞od) ***n.*** 1 anything that is taken in by a plant or animal to keep up its life and growth; what is eaten or drunk by an animal or absorbed by a plant. 2 such a thing in solid form [*food* and drink]. 3 anything that helps another thing to develop [*food* for thought].

**food poisoning** sickness caused by eating food that is poisonous, as certain mushrooms, or from eating food that is poisonous because it has harmful chemicals or harmful bacteria in it.

☆**food stamp** any of the stamps issued by the U.S. government and sold at less than face value to certain persons who are poor or out of work for them to use in buying food.

**food·stuff** (fo͞od′stuf) ***n.*** any material that is used as food.

**fool** (fo͞ol) ***n.*** 1 a person who does silly or senseless things or who is easily tricked. 2 a man kept by a nobleman or king in earlier times to amuse by joking and clowning; jester. ◆***v.*** 1 to get someone to believe something that is not true; trick; deceive [He *fooled* his mother by pretending to be asleep.] 2 to act like a fool; joke or clown. —**fool with,** to meddle with or toy with: *used only in everyday talk.*

> **Fool** comes from a Latin word meaning "windbag" or "bellows." A person who talks too much is sometimes called a windbag and thought to be a fool.

**fool·har·dy** (fo͞ol′här′dē) ***adj.*** bold or daring in a foolish way; rash [He was *foolhardy* to try to climb the mountain alone.] —**fool′har′di·ness *n.***

**fool·ish** (fo͞ol′ish) ***adj.*** without good sense; silly. —**fool′ish·ly *adv.*** —**fool′ish·ness *n.***

☆**fool·proof** (fo͞ol′pro͞of) ***adj.*** so simple, safe, etc. that nothing can go wrong [a *foolproof* plan].

**fools·cap** (fo͞olz′kap) ***n.*** a large size of writing paper, about 13 by 16 inches.

☆**fool's gold** *another name for* **pyrite.**

**foot** (foot) ***n.*** 1 the end part of the leg, on which a person or animal stands or moves. 2 the lowest part; base or bottom [the *foot* of a page; the *foot* of a mountain]. 3 the part farthest from the head or beginning [the *foot* of a bed; the *foot* of the line]. 4 the part that covers the foot [the *foot* of a stocking]. 5 a measure of length, equal to 12 inches or 0.3048 meter. 6 one of the parts into which a line of poetry is divided by the rhythm ["Jack/and Jill/went up/the hill" contains four *feet*.] —*pl.* **feet** ◆**v.** ☆to pay: *used only in everyday talk* [to *foot* the bill]. —**foot it,** to dance, walk, or run: *used only in everyday talk.* —**on foot,** walking or running. —**put one's foot down,** to be firm: *used only in everyday talk.* —**under foot,** in the way.

**foot·ball** (foot′bôl) **n.** **1** a leather ball with a bladder inside blown up with air, used in certain games. The American football is oval in shape. **2** a game played with such a ball by two teams on a long field with a goal at each end.

**foot·bridge** (foot′brij) **n.** a narrow bridge for use only by people walking.

**foot·fall** (foot′fôl) **n.** the sound of a footstep.

☆**foot·hill** (foot′hil) **n.** a low hill at or near the bottom of a mountain or mountain range.

**foot·hold** (foot′hōld) **n.** **1** a place to put a foot down securely [We climbed the cliff by finding *footholds*.] **2** a secure place from which one cannot easily be moved.

**foot·ing** (foot′ing) **n.** **1** a firm placing of the feet [She lost her *footing* on the gravel path and fell.] **2** a foothold [There's no *footing* on that ice.] **3** the way things are set, arranged, etc.; condition or relationship [to put a business on a sound *footing;* to be on a friendly *footing* with one's neighbors].

**foot·lights** (foot′līts) **n.pl.** a row of lights along the front of a stage floor. *See the picture.*

**foot·loose** (foot′lōōs) **adj.** free to go wherever one likes or to do as one likes.

**foot·man** (foot′mən) **n.** a man servant who helps the butler in a large household. —*pl.* **foot′men**

**foot·note** (foot′nōt) **n.** a note at the bottom of a page that explains something on the page.

**foot·pad** (foot′pad) **n.** a robber who attacks people on streets or highways.

**foot·path** (foot′path) **n.** a narrow path for use only by people walking.

**foot·print** (foot′print) **n.** a mark made by a foot or shoe, as in sand.

**foot·race** (foot′rās) **n.** a race between runners on foot.

**foot·rest** (foot′rest) **n.** something solid to rest the feet on.

**foot soldier** a soldier who moves and fights for the most part on foot; infantryman.

**foot·sore** (foot′sôr) **adj.** having sore or tired feet, as from much walking.

**foot·step** (foot′step) **n.** **1** a step in walking, or the distance covered by this. **2** the sound of a step. **3** a footprint. —**follow in someone's footsteps,** to be or try to be like someone who has gone before.

**foot·stool** (foot′stōōl) **n.** a low stool used as a rest for the feet when one is sitting. *See the picture.*

☆**foot·wear** (foot′wer) **n.** shoes, boots, slippers, etc.

**foot·work** (foot′wurk) **n.** the way of moving or using the feet, as in dancing, boxing, walking, etc.

**fop** (fäp) **n.** a man who is very fussy about his clothes and looks; dandy. —**fop′pish adj.**

**for** (fôr *or* fər) **prep.** **1** in place of; instead of [to use paper plates *for* china]. **2** on the side of; in favor or support of [to fight *for* freedom; to vote *for* a levy]. **3** in honor of [The baby was named *for* her aunt.] **4** in order to be, keep, have, get, reach, etc. [He swims *for*

font

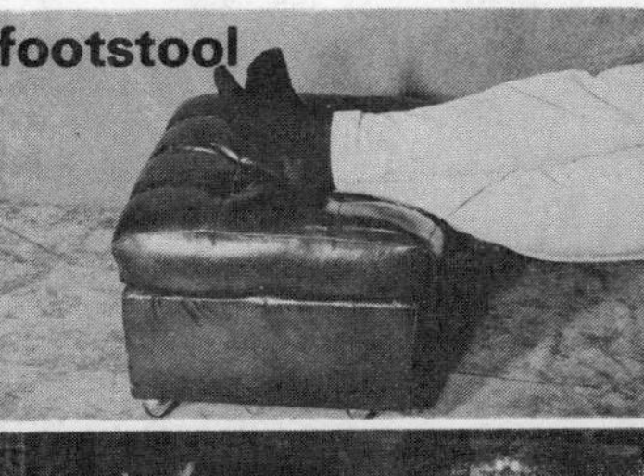
footstool

footlights

exercise. She left *for* home. I asked *for* Mae.] **5** in search of [looking *for* berries]. **6** meant to be received or used by or in [dresses *for* young girls; money *for* paying bills]. **7** with regard to; as regards; concerning [a need *for* improvement; an ear *for* music]. **8** as being [We know that *for* a fact.] **9** if one considers; considering [She's tall *for* her age.] **10** because of [He was praised *for* his honesty.] **11** in spite of [*For* all his studying, he got a low grade.] **12** as compared with; to balance or equal [Our goal is to save one dollar *for* every ten dollars we earn.] **13** equal to; in the amount of [a bill *for* $60.00]. **14** at the price of [Jane sold her bicycle *for* $20.00.] **15** to the distance of; as far as [We walk every day *for* two miles.] **16** through the time of; as long as [The movie lasts *for* an hour.] **17** at a certain time [I have an appointment *for* one o'clock.] ◆**conj.** because; since [Comfort her, *for* she is sad.] —**O! for,** I wish that I had [*O! for* a glass of cold water.]

**for·age** (fôr′ij) **n.** food for cows, horses, etc.; fodder. ◆**v.** **1** to go about looking for food [The sheep were *foraging* in the meadow.] **2** to look about for what one needs or wants [I *foraged* in the attic for some old magazines.] **3** to steal or take food or supplies from by force; plunder, as armies do in war. —**for′aged, for′ag·ing** —**for′ag·er n.**

**for·ay** (fôr′ā) **n.** a sudden attack or raid in order to seize or steal things. ◆**v.** to make a foray; raid.

**for·bade** or **for·bad** (fər bad′) *past tense of* **forbid.**

**for·bear**[1] (fôr ber′) **v.** **1** to hold back from doing or saying something [The other children were teasing the dog, but Jim *forbore*.] **2** to keep one's feelings under control. —**for·bore** (fôr bôr′), **for·borne** (fôr bôrn′), **for·bear′ing**

**for·bear**[2] (fôr′ber) **n.** *another spelling of* **forebear.**

**for·bear·ance** (fôr ber′əns) **n.** the act of forbearing; especially, the showing of self-control or patience [We listened to the boring talk with *forbearance*.]

| | | | | | | | |
|---|---|---|---|---|---|---|---|
| a | fat | ir | here | ou | out | zh | leisure |
| ā | ape | ī | bite, fire | u | up | ng | ring |
| ä | car, lot | ō | go | ur | fur | | a *in* ago |
| e | ten | ô | law, horn | ch | chin | | e *in* agent |
| er | care | oi | oil | sh | she | ə = | i *in* unity |
| ē | even | oo | look | th | thin | | o *in* collect |
| i | hit | ōō | tool | *th* | then | | u *in* focus |

**for·bid** (fər bid′) ***v.*** to order that something not be done; not allow; prohibit [The law *forbids* you to park your car there. Talking out loud is *forbidden* in the library.] —**for·bade′** or **for·bad′, for·bid′den, for·bid′ding**

SYNONYMS: To **forbid** something is to order that it not be done. To **prohibit** something is to forbid it by law or by official order. To **ban** something is to prohibit it and also strongly condemn it.

**for·bid·ding** (fər bid′iŋ) ***adj.*** looking as if it may be harmful or unpleasant; frightening [Those storm clouds are *forbidding.*]

**force** (fôrs) ***n.*** **1** power or energy that can do or make something [Electricity is a powerful natural *force.* The *force* of the high winds broke the windows.] **2** power or strength used against a person or thing [The police used *force* to scatter the crowd.] **3** the power to make someone think or act in a certain way [the *force* of logic; the *force* of threats]. **4** the power to cause motion or to stop or change motion [the *force* of gravity]. **5** a group of people working together for some special purpose [a sales *force;* a military *force*]. ◆***v.*** **1** to make do something by using strength or power of some kind [You shouldn't *force* a child to eat. The blizzard *forced* us to stay home.] **2** to break open or through by using strength [He *forced* the lock with a pick.] **3** to get or put by using

strength [Can you *force* the lid off this jar? She *forced* another cookie into her mouth.] **4** to produce by trying hard or straining [Ruth *forced* a smile through her tears.] **5** to make a plant, fruit, etc. grow faster than is natural [Gardeners *force* tomatoes in a greenhouse by giving them extra heat and light.] ☆**6** in baseball, to cause a base runner to run to the next base and be put out there. —**forced, forc′ing —in force, 1** having effect; operating [Is this law still *in force?*] **2** with full strength.

**force·ful** (fôrs′fəl) ***adj.*** having much force; strong; powerful; vigorous [a *forceful* speech]. —**force′ful·ly *adv.***

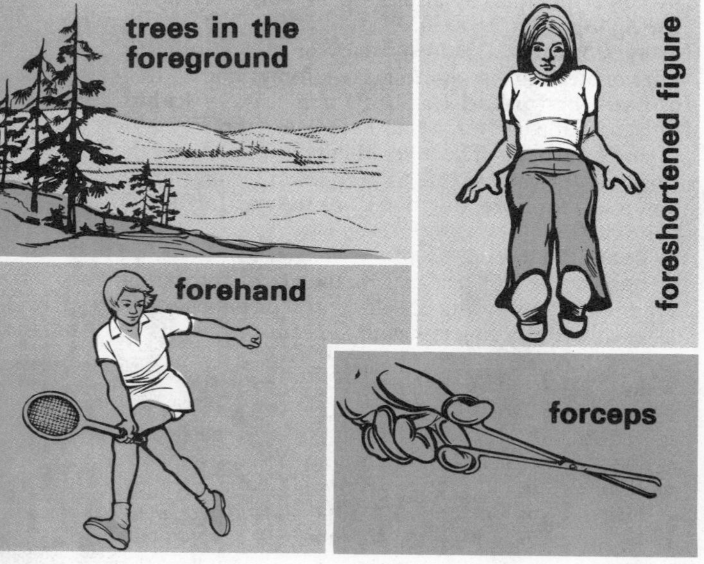


**for·ceps** (fôr′səps) ***n.*** small tongs or pincers for pulling or grasping, used by dentists, surgeons, etc. *See the picture.* —*pl.* **for′ceps**

**for·ci·ble** (fôr′sə b′l) ***adj.*** **1** done or made by force [The robbers made a *forcible* entry into the bank.] **2** having force; forceful [*forcible* arguments in favor of reform]. —**for′ci·bly *adv.***

**ford** (fôrd) ***n.*** a shallow place in a river or stream where one can walk or ride across. ◆***v.*** to cross a stream or river in this way.

**Ford** (fôrd), **Gerald R., Jr.** 1913– ; the 38th president of the United States, from 1974 to 1977.

**Ford, Henry** 1863–1947; U.S. manufacturer of automobiles.

**fore** (fôr) ***adv., adj.*** at, in, or toward the front part, as of a ship; forward. ◆***n.*** the front part. ◆***interj.*** a warning shouted by someone about to drive a golf ball. —**to the fore,** to the front; into view.

**fore-** *a prefix meaning:* **1** before [*Forenoon* is the time before noon.] **2** the front or front part [A *foreleg* is a front leg.]

**fore and aft** from the bow to the stern of a ship; lengthwise [sails rigged *fore and aft*]. —**fore′-and-aft′ *adj.***

**fore·arm**[1] (fôr′ärm) ***n.*** the part of the arm between the elbow and the wrist.

**fore·arm**[2] (fôr ärm′) ***v.*** to arm beforehand; get ready for trouble before it comes.

**fore·bear** (fôr′ber) ***n.*** a person who comes before one in a family line; ancestor.

**fore·bode** (fôr bōd′) ***v.*** to be a sign of something bad about to happen; warn of [Their angry words *forebode* a fight.] —**fore·bod′ed, fore·bod′ing**

**fore·bod·ing** (fôr bōd′iŋ) ***n.*** a warning or a feeling of something bad about to happen [Heavy spring rains are a *foreboding* of floods.]

**fore·cast** (fôr′kast) ***v.*** to tell or try to tell how something will turn out; predict [Rain is *forecast* for tomorrow.] *See* SYNONYMS *at* **foretell. —fore′cast** or **fore′cast·ed, fore′cast·ing** ◆***n.*** a telling of what will happen; prediction [a weather *forecast*]. —**fore′cast·er *n.***

**fore·cas·tle** (fōk′s′l *or* fôr′kas ′l) ***n.*** **1** the upper deck of a ship in front of the foremast. **2** the front part of a merchant ship, where the sailors eat and sleep.

**fore·close** (fôr klōz′) ***v.*** to end a mortgage and become the owner of the mortgaged property [A bank can *foreclose* a mortgage if payments on its loan are not made in time.] —**fore·closed′, fore·clos′ing —fore·clo·sure** (fôr klō′zhər) ***n.***

**fore·fa·ther** (fôr′fä′*th*ər) ***n.*** a person who comes before one in a family line; ancestor.

**fore·fin·ger** (fôr′fiŋ′gər) ***n.*** the finger nearest the thumb; index finger.

**fore·foot** (fôr′foot) ***n.*** either of the front feet of an animal. —*pl.* **fore′feet**

**fore·front** (fôr′frunt) ***n.*** **1** the part at the very front. **2** the most active or important position [in the *forefront* of the political campaign].

**fore·go**[1] (fôr gō′) ***v.*** to go before; precede. —**fore·went′, fore·gone′, fore·go′ing**

**fore·go**[2] (fôr gō′) ***v.*** *another spelling of* **forgo.**

**fore·go·ing** (fôr′gō′iŋ) ***adj.*** going or coming before; just mentioned. —**the foregoing,** the persons or things mentioned just before.

**fore·gone** (fôr gôn′) ***adj.*** that could be known before or foretold [a *foregone* conclusion].

**fore·ground** (fôr′ground) ***n.*** the part of a scene or picture that is or seems to be nearest to the one looking at it. *See the picture.*

**fore·hand** (fôr′hand) ***n.*** a kind of stroke, as in tennis, made with the palm of the hand turned forward. *See the picture.* ◆***adj.*** done with such a stroke [a *forehand* swing]. ◆***adv.*** with a forehand swing.

**fore·head** (fôr′id) ***n.*** the part of the face above the eyebrows.

**for·eign** (fôr′in) ***adj.*** **1** that is outside one's own country, region, etc. [a *foreign* land]. **2** of, from, or dealing with other countries [*foreign* trade; *foreign* languages; *foreign* policy]. **3** not belonging; not a natural or usual part [conduct *foreign* to one's nature; *foreign* matter in the eye]. *See* SYNONYMS *at* **extraneous.**

> **Foreign** comes from a Latin word meaning "out-of-doors." The meaning broadened from "outside one's house" to "outside one's country."

**for·eign·er** (fôr′in ər) ***n.*** a person from another country, thought of as an outsider.

**fore·knowl·edge** (fôr′näl′ij) ***n.*** knowledge of something before it happens.

**fore·leg** (fôr′leg) ***n.*** either of the front legs of an animal.

**fore·lock** (fôr′läk) ***n.*** a lock of hair growing just above the forehead.

**fore·man** (fôr′mən) ***n.*** **1** a person in charge of a group of workers, as in a factory. **2** the person on a jury who serves as its leader and speaks for the jury in court. —*pl.* **fore′men**

**fore·mast** (fôr′mast) ***n.*** the mast nearest the front or bow of a ship.

**fore·most** (fôr′mōst) ***adj.*** first, as in place, time, importance, etc. [the *foremost* writers of their time; to keep something *foremost* in mind]. ◆***adv.*** before all else [She is first and *foremost* a dancer.]

**fore·noon** (fôr′no͞on) ***n.*** the time from sunrise to noon; especially, the late morning.

**fo·ren·sic** (fə ren′sik) ***adj.*** of or used in a law court or debate [*Forensic* medicine is the practice of medicine as it has to do with the law.]

**fore·or·dain** (fôr′ôr dān′) ***v.*** to order or decide beforehand what will happen.

**fore·paw** (fôr′pô) ***n.*** a front paw.

**fore·run·ner** (fôr′run′ər) ***n.*** **1** a messenger sent ahead to announce that someone is coming; herald. **2** a sign of something to follow [A sore throat is often the *forerunner* of a cold.]

**fore·sail** (fôr′sāl *or* fôr′səl) ***n.*** **1** the lowest sail on the foremast of a ship rigged with square sails. **2** the main triangular sail on the foremast of a schooner.

**fore·see** (fôr sē′) ***v.*** to see or know beforehand [to *foresee* the future]. —**fore·saw′**, **fore·seen′**, **fore·see′ing**

**fore·shad·ow** (fôr shad′ō) ***v.*** to be a sign of something to come.

**fore·short·en** (fôr shôr′t′n) ***v.*** to shorten some lines in drawing something so as to make some parts seem farther from the eye than others. *See the picture.*

**fore·sight** (fôr′sīt) ***n.*** **1** a foreseeing. **2** the power to foresee. **3** a looking forward. **4** a looking ahead and planning for the future.

**fore·skin** (fôr′skin) ***n.*** the fold of skin that covers the end of the penis. The fold is often removed by circumcision.

**for·est** (fôr′ist) ***n.*** many trees growing closely together over a large piece of land; large woods. ◆***v.*** to plant with trees.

**fore·stall** (fôr stôl′) ***v.*** to get ahead of or keep from happening by doing something first [to *forestall* an argument by changing the subject].

☆**for·est·a·tion** (fôr′is tā′shən) ***n.*** the planting or care of forests.

**for·est·er** (fôr′is tər) ***n.*** a person who takes care of forests, fights forest fires, etc.

**for·est·ry** (fôr′is trē) ***n.*** the science and work of planting and taking care of forests.

**fore·taste** (fôr′tāst) ***n.*** a taste or sample of what can be expected [Her summer job on the newspaper was a *foretaste* of a career as a reporter.]

**fore·tell** (fôr tel′) ***v.*** to tell or show what will take place in the future; predict. —**fore·told′**, **fore·tell′ing**

> SYNONYMS: To **foretell** is to tell what will happen. To **predict** is to tell what will happen on the basis of facts, especially scientific facts. To **forecast** is to predict how things will probably be or go [to *foretell* the future; to *predict* an eclipse; to *forecast* the weather].

**fore·thought** (fôr′thôt) ***n.*** a thinking or planning ahead of time.



**for·ev·er** (fər ev′ər) ***adv.*** **1** for all time; without ever coming to an end [No person lives *forever.*] **2** always; at all times [The phone was *forever* ringing.]

**for·ev·er·more** (fər ev′ər môr′) ***adv.*** *same as* **forever** *in meaning* 1.

**fore·warn** (fôr wôrn′) ***v.*** to warn ahead of time [We were *forewarned* we wouldn't get tickets later.]

**fore·went** (fôr went′) *past tense of* **forego.**

**fore·word** (fôr′wurd) ***n.*** a piece of writing at the beginning of a book that tells something about it; introduction or preface.

**for·feit** (fôr′fit) ***v.*** to give up or lose something because of what one has done or has failed to do [Because our team was late in arriving, we had to *forfeit* the game.] ◆***n.*** **1** the thing that is forfeited; penalty. **2** the act of forfeiting [the *forfeit* of a right].

**for·fei·ture** (fôr′fə chər) ***n.*** **1** the act of forfeiting. **2** the thing forfeited.

**for·gath·er** (fôr gath′ər) ***v.*** to come together; assemble; meet.

**for·gave** (fər gāv′) *past tense of* **forgive.**

**forge**[1] (fôrj) ***n.*** **1** a furnace for heating metal so that it can be pounded into the shape wanted. **2** a place where such work with metal is done, as a blacksmith's shop. ◆***v.*** **1** to shape on a forge by heating and pounding. **2** to make something false to be passed off

| | | | | | | | |
|---|---|---|---|---|---|---|---|
| **a** | fat | **ir** | here | **ou** | out | **zh** | leisure |
| **ā** | ape | **ī** | bite, fire | **u** | up | **ŋ** | ring |
| **ä** | car, lot | **ō** | go | **ur** | fur | | a *in* ago |
| **e** | ten | **ô** | law, horn | **ch** | chin | | e *in* agent |
| **er** | care | **oi** | oil | **sh** | she | **ə =** | i *in* unity |
| **ē** | even | **oo** | look | **th** | thin | | o *in* collect |
| **i** | hit | **o͞o** | tool | ***th*** | then | | u *in* focus |

fossils of trilobites

forklift truck

as true or real; especially, to commit the crime of copying another's signature on a bank check. —**forged, forg'ing**

**forge²** (fôrj) *v.* to move with difficulty or with sudden speed and energy [Joe *forged* ahead and won the race.] —**forged, forg'ing**

**forg·er** (fôr'jər) *n.* **1** a person who forges metal. **2** a person guilty of forgery.

**for·ger·y** (fôr'jər ē) *n.* **1** the crime of copying another's signature, or of making a false piece of writing, in order to pass it off as the real thing. **2** something that has been forged [This letter, supposedly written by Abraham Lincoln, is a *forgery*.] —*pl.* **for'ger·ies**

**for·get** (fər get') *v.* **1** to be unable to remember; lose from the mind [I have *forgotten* Joan's address.] **2** to fail to do, bring, etc., as because of carelessness; neglect [You *forgot* to lock the door. I *forgot* my books again.] —**for·got', for·got'ten** or **for·got', for·get'ting** —**forget oneself**, to behave in a way that is not proper.



**for·get·ful** (fər get'fəl) *adj.* **1** always forgetting things; having a poor memory. **2** careless or neglectful. —**for·get'ful·ness** *n.*

**for·get-me-not** (fər get'mē nät') *n.* a low-growing plant bearing small blue flowers.

**for·give** (fər giv') *v.* to give up feeling angry or wanting to punish; show mercy to; excuse or pardon [She *forgave* him for his unkindness to her.] —**for·gave', for·giv'en, for·giv'ing** —**for·giv'a·ble** *adj.*

**for·give·ness** (fər giv'nis) *n.* **1** the act of forgiving or being forgiven; pardon. **2** the quality of being ready to forgive.

**for·go** (fôr gō') *v.* to do without; give up [I *forgo* all desserts when I'm dieting.] —**for·went', for·gone', for·go'ing**

**fork** (fôrk) *n.* **1** a tool with a handle at one end and two or more points or prongs at the other, used to pick up something. Small forks are used in eating, and large forks, as pitchforks, are used for tossing hay and manure on a farm. **2** anything with points like a fork's [a *fork* of lightning]. ☆**3** the point where something divides into two or more branches [the *fork* of a road or of a tree]. **4** any of the branches [Follow the left *fork* into town.] ◆*v.* **1** to divide into branches [Go left where the road *forks*.] **2** to pick up with a fork [*Fork* some hay into the stalls.] —☆**fork over** or **fork out**, to hand over or pay out: *used only in everyday talk.*

**forked** (fôrkt) *adj.* shaped like a fork; divided into branches.

☆**fork·lift** (fôrk'lift) *n.* a device, often on a truck (**forklift truck**), for lifting, moving, or stacking heavy objects. It has prongs that stick out and can be slid under the load and then raised or lowered. *See the picture.*

**for·lorn** (fər lôrn') *adj.* sad or unhappy, as because of loneliness or being uncared for; pitiful; wretched [a *forlorn*, lost child].

**form** (fôrm) *n.* **1** a shape or outline; figure [I saw a dark *form* against the sky.] **2** a mold used to give a certain shape to something [Cement is poured in wooden *forms* to make slabs for sidewalks.] **3** the way in which something is put together to make it what it is; kind; sort [a *form* of government; a *form* of poetry]. **4** a way of doing something [Her *form* in golf is awkward.] **5** a way of acting or behaving [It is good *form* to write your hostess a thank-you note.] **6** a printed paper that has blank spaces to be filled in [an order *form*; an application *form*]. **7** the condition of one's health, spirits, etc. [The boxer was in good *form* for the fight.] **8** any of the ways in which a word is changed for different uses ["Am" is a *form* of "be."] ◆*v.* **1** to give a certain shape to [The children *formed* the wet sand into a castle.] **2** to train [These daily tasks helped to *form* my character.] **3** to build up or develop [She has *formed* good habits.] **4** to come together in order to make [Let's *form* a hiking club.] **5** to make up out of separate parts [The United States is *formed* of 50 States.]

SYNONYMS: The **form** of something is the way it looks because of the way it is put together. A **figure** is the way a physical form looks because of the lines and surfaces that limit or outline it. The **shape** of something is also related to its outline and usually suggests something that has bulk, weight, or mass.

**for·mal** (fôr'məl) *adj.* **1** following the rules or customs in an exact way [*formal* manners; a *formal* wedding]. **2** not relaxed or familiar; stiff [a *formal* welcome]. **3** made to be worn at ceremonies and fancy parties [*formal* dress]. **4** arranged in a regular, orderly way [*formal* gardens]. ◆*n.* **1** a formal dance. **2** a woman's long evening dress. —**for'mal·ly** *adv.*

**form·al·de·hyde** (fôr mal'də hīd') *n.* a colorless gas with a strong smell. It is usually dissolved in water for killing germs and for preserving animal parts in a laboratory.

**for·mal·i·ty** (fôr mal'ə tē) *n.* **1** the condition of being formal; especially, the following of rules or customs in an exact way. **2** a formal act or ceremony [the *formalities* of graduation exercises]. —*pl.* **for·mal'i·ties**

**for·ma·tion** (fôr mā'shən) *n.* **1** a forming or being formed [the *formation* of coal beds in the earth]. **2** the way something is formed or put together; arrangement [a solid *formation* of rock; soldiers lined up in close *formation*].

**form·a·tive** (fôr'mə tiv) *adj.* of formation, growth, or development [the *formative* years of one's life].

**for·mer** (fôr'mər) *adj.* **1** coming before; earlier; past [in *former* times; a *former* senator]. **2** being the first of two just mentioned: *often used as a noun with* the [In the contest between Carter and Ford, the *former* was elected.]

**for·mer·ly** (fôr'mər lē) *adv.* at an earlier time; in the past [Iran was *formerly* called Persia.]

☆**For·mi·ca** (fôr mīk′ə) *a trademark for* a plastic that resists heat and is glued in sheet form to the tops of tables, sinks, etc.

**for·mi·da·ble** (fôr′mə də b'l) ***adj.*** **1** causing fear or dread [The tiger has a *formidable* look.] **2** hard to do or take care of [a *formidable* task]. —**for′mi·da·bly *adv.***

**form·less** (fôrm′lis) ***adj.*** having no definite form or plan; shapeless.

**for·mu·la** (fôr′myə lə) ***n.*** **1** a phrase that is used over and over in a certain way so that its actual meaning is nearly lost ["Yours truly" is a common *formula* for ending a letter.] **2** a set of directions for doing or making something [a *formula* for the baby's milk]. **3** a group of symbols or figures that show some rule or fact in mathematics [The *formula* $A = \pi r^2$ shows how to find the area of a circle.] **4** a group of symbols and figures showing the elements in a chemical compound [The *formula* for water is $H_2O$.]

**for·mu·late** (fôr′myə lāt) ***v.*** to put together and express in a clear and orderly way [to *formulate* a theory]. —**for′mu·lat·ed, for′mu·lat·ing** —**for′mu·la′tion *n.***

**for·sake** (fər sāk′) ***v.*** to go away from or give up; leave; abandon [She will never *forsake* a friend in trouble.] —**for·sook** (fər sook′), **for·sak′en, for·sak′ing**

**for·sooth** (fər sōōth′) ***adv.*** in truth; no doubt; indeed: *now used only in a joking way.*

**for·swear** (fôr swer′) ***v.*** **1** to swear or promise to give up something [to *forswear* smoking]. **2** to swear falsely that something is true; perjure oneself. —**for·swore** (fôr swôr′), **for·sworn** (fôr swôrn′), **for·swear′ing**

**for·syth·i·a** (fər sith′ē ə) ***n.*** a shrub with yellow flowers that bloom in early spring.

**fort** (fôrt) ***n.*** a building with strong walls, guns, etc., for defending against an enemy.

**forte**¹ (fôrt) ***n.*** a thing that one does especially well [Skin diving is his *forte.*]

**for·te**² (fôr′tā *or* fôr′tē) ***adj., adv.*** loud. This is an Italian word used in music to tell how loud a piece should be played.

**forth** (fôrth) ***adv.*** **1** forward or onward [She never left the house from that day *forth.*] **2** out; into view [The bears came *forth* from their den.] —**and so forth,** and others: *see* **et cetera.**

**forth·com·ing** (fôrth′kum′ing) ***adj.*** **1** about to take place, come out, etc. [the author's *forthcoming* book]. **2** ready when needed [The help they had promised was not *forthcoming.*]

**forth·right** (fôrth′rīt′) ***adj.*** frank and open; direct, not hinted at [her *forthright* reviews of movies].

**forth·with** (fôrth with′) ***adv.*** immediately; at once [Give us your answer *forthwith.*]

**for·ti·eth** (fôr′tē ith) ***adj.*** coming after thirty-nine others; 40th in order. ✦***n.*** **1** the fortieth one. **2** one of forty equal parts of something; 1/40.

**for·ti·fi·ca·tion** (fôr′tə fi kā′shən) ***n.*** **1** a fortifying or making strong. **2** something used in fortifying, as a fort. **3** a fortified place.

**for·ti·fy** (fôr′tə fī) ***v.*** **1** to make strong or stronger; strengthen [to *fortify* concrete with steel rods; to *fortify* an argument with many facts]. **2** to strengthen against attack, as by building forts, walls, etc. **3** to add vitamins or minerals to [milk *fortified* with vitamin D]. —**for′ti·fied, for′ti·fy·ing**

**for·tis·si·mo** (fôr tis′ə mō) ***adj., adv.*** very loud. This is an Italian word used in music to tell how loud a piece should be played.

**for·ti·tude** (fôr′tə tōōd *or* fôr′tə tyōōd) ***n.*** courage to bear up calmly under pain or trouble. *See* SYNONYMS *at* **grit.**

**fort·night** (fôrt′nīt) ***n.*** two weeks: *used mainly in Great Britain.* —**fort′night·ly *adj., adv.***

> **Fortnight** comes from an Old English word that means "fourteen nights." There are fourteen nights in two weeks.

**for·tress** (fôr′trəs) ***n.*** *another word for* **fort.**

**for·tu·i·tous** (fôr tōō′ə təs *or* fôr tyōō′ə təs) ***adj.*** happening by chance; accidental [a *fortuitous* meeting].

**for·tu·nate** (fôr′chə nit) ***adj.*** lucky; having, bringing, or coming by good luck [a *fortunate* man]. —**for′tu·nate·ly *adv.***

**for·tune** (fôr′chən) ***n.*** **1** the supposed power that brings good or bad to people; luck; chance. **2** one's future; what is going to happen to a person [The gypsy said she would tell his *fortune.*] **3** good luck; success. **4** a large sum of money; wealth [to inherit a *fortune*].

**for·tune·tell·er** (fôr′chən tel′ər) ***n.*** a person who pretends to tell what is going to happen in people's lives, as by reading cards.

**Fort Worth** (fôrt′ wurth′) a city in northern Texas. 291

**for·ty** (fôr′tē) ***n., adj.*** four times ten; the number 40. —*pl.* **for′ties** —**the forties,** the numbers or years from 40 through 49.

**fo·rum** (fôr′əm) ***n.*** **1** the public square of an ancient Roman city, where the lawmakers and courts met. **2** a meeting of people to discuss public matters, problems, etc.

**for·ward** (fôr′wərd) ***adj.*** **1** at, toward, or of the front. **2** ahead of others in ideas, growth, progress, etc.; advanced. **3** ready or eager; prompt [She was *forward* in helping.] **4** too bold or free in manners; rude or impudent. ✦***adv.*** **1** to the front; ahead [We moved slowly *forward* in the ticket line.] **2** toward the future [He looks *forward* to old age.] ✦***n.*** any of certain players in a front position, as in basketball or hockey. ✦***v.*** **1** to help move forward; advance; promote [to *forward* the interests of business]. **2** to send on, as to a new address [*Forward* her mail to Paris.] —**for′ward·ness *n.***

**for·wards** (fôr′wərdz) ***adv.*** *same as* **forward.**

**fos·sil** (fäs′'l) ***n.*** **1** any hardened remains or prints, as in rocks or bogs, of plants or animals that lived many years ago. *See the picture.* **2** a person who is very set or old-fashioned in his or her ideas or ways. ✦***adj.*** **1** of or like a fossil. **2** taken from the earth [Coal and oil are *fossil* fuels.]

| | | | | | | | |
|---|---|---|---|---|---|---|---|
| **a** | fat | **ir** | here | **ou** | out | **zh** | leisure |
| **ā** | ape | **ī** | bite, fire | **u** | up | **ng** | ring |
| **ä** | car, lot | **ō** | go | **ur** | fur | | a *in* ago |
| **e** | ten | **ô** | law, horn | **ch** | chin | | e *in* agent |
| **er** | care | **oi** | oil | **sh** | she | **ə** = | i *in* unity |
| **ē** | even | **oo** | look | **th** | thin | | o *in* collect |
| **i** | hit | **ōō** | tool | ***th*** | then | | u *in* focus |

**fos·sil·ize** (fäs′ə līz) ***v.*** **1** to change into a fossil or fossils. **2** to make or become out-of-date, rigid, or unable to change. —**fos′sil·ized, fos′sil·iz·ing**

**fos·ter** (fôs′tər) ***v.*** **1** to bring up with care; nourish. **2** to help grow or develop; promote [to *foster* peace among nations]. **3** to cling to in one's mind; cherish [to *foster* a hope]. ◆***adj.*** having the standing of a certain member of the family, but not by birth or adoption [a *foster* parent; a *foster* child; a *foster* sister].

**Fos·ter** (fôs′tər), **Stephen Col·lins** (käl′inz) 1826–1864; U.S. composer of songs.

**foster home** a home in which a child is brought up by people who are not his or her parents either by birth or by adoption.

**fought** (fôt) *past tense and past participle of* **fight**.

**foul** (foul) ***adj.*** **1** dirty, smelly, rotten, etc.; disgusting [a *foul* pigsty]. **2** blocked up, as with dirt [Water barely trickled through the *foul* pipes.] **3** very wicked; evil [a *foul* crime]. **4** stormy; not clear [*foul* weather]. **5** not decent; coarse or profane [*foul* language]. **6** tangled or snarled [*foul* rope]. ☆**7** not fair [A *foul* play, blow, etc. in sports is one that is against the rules. A *foul* ball in baseball is a batted ball that falls outside the *foul* lines running through first base or third base.] **8** not good; unpleasant: *used only in everyday talk* [We had a *foul* time at the picnic when it rained.] ◆***n.*** **1** an act that is against the rules of a game [Pushing is a *foul* in basketball.] *See the picture.*
292 ☆**2** a foul ball in baseball. ◆***v.*** **1** to make or become dirty, smelly, etc. [The city sewers have *fouled* the lake.] **2** to make or become blocked up; clog [Rust has *fouled* the pipes.] **3** to make or become tangled [*fouled* yarn]. **4** to make a foul against, as in a game [The boxer *fouled* his opponent by hitting below the belt.] ☆**5** to bat a baseball foul. —☆**foul out,** to be put out in baseball by the catch of a foul ball. —☆**foul up,** to make a mess of; bungle: *used only in everyday talk.* —**run foul of,** to get in trouble with. —**foul′ly *adv.*** —**foul′ness *n.***

**fou·lard** (fo͞o lärd′) ***n.*** **1** a thin, light material of silk, rayon, etc., usually printed with a small design. **2** a necktie, scarf, etc. made of this material.

**found**[1] (found) *past tense and past participle of* **find**.

**found**[2] (found) ***v.*** **1** to set up; establish [to *found* a new college]. **2** to set for support; base [an argument *founded* on facts].

framework of a house

40 cm (16 in.) high at shoulder

fox

foul in football

**Found**[2] comes from a Latin word meaning "bottom." In putting up a building, there must be a solid foundation at the bottom. In setting up, or "founding," a business, college, etc., there must be a foundation of money, ideas, and goals at the bottom.

**found**[3] (found) ***v.*** to make by pouring molten metal into a mold; cast.

**foun·da·tion** (foun dā′shən) ***n.*** **1** the part at the bottom that supports a wall, house, etc.; base. **2** the basis on which an idea, belief, etc. rests. *See* SYNONYMS *at* **basis**. **3** a founding or being founded; establishment. **4** a fund set up by gifts of money for helping others, paying for research, etc. **5** an organization that manages such a fund.

**found·er**[1] (foun′dər) ***n.*** a person who founds, or establishes [the *founder* of a city].

**found·er**[2] (foun′dər) ***n.*** a person who founds, or casts, metals.

**foun·der**[3] (foun′dər) ***v.*** **1** to fill with water and sink [The ship struck a reef and *foundered.*] **2** to stumble, fall, or break down.

**found·ling** (found′liŋ) ***n.*** a baby found after it has been abandoned by its parents, who are not known.

**found·ry** (foun′drē) ***n.*** a place where molten metal is cast in molds. —*pl.* **found′ries**

**fount** (fount) ***n.*** **1** a fountain or spring. **2** a source.

**foun·tain** (foun′t'n) ***n.*** **1** a place in the earth from which water flows; spring. **2** a thing built for a stream of water to rise and fall in [a drinking *fountain;* a decorative *fountain* in a garden]. **3** a source [A library is a *fountain* of knowledge.] **4** *same as* **soda fountain**.

**foun·tain·head** (foun′t'n hed) ***n.*** the main source of something.

**fountain pen** a pen that carries a supply of ink which flows to the writing point.

**four** (fôr) ***n., adj.*** one more than three; the number 4. —**on all fours, 1** on all four feet. **2** on hands and knees.

**four-foot·ed** (fôr′foot′id) ***adj.*** having four feet [The bear is a *four-footed* animal.]

☆**Four-H club** or **4-H club** (fôr′āch′) a national club for young people living in farm areas. It gives training in farming and home economics.

**four·score** (fôr′skôr′) ***adj., n.*** four times twenty; 80 ["*Fourscore* and seven years ago . . ."]

**four·some** (fôr′səm) ***n.*** a group of four people, as four people playing golf together.

**four·square** (fôr′skwer′) ***adj.*** **1** perfectly square. **2** frank; honest [a *foursquare* answer].

**four·teen** (fôr′tēn′) ***n., adj.*** four more than ten; the number 14.

**four·teenth** (fôr′tēnth′) ***adj.*** coming after thirteen others; 14th in order. ◆***n.*** **1** the fourteenth one. **2** one of fourteen equal parts of something; 1/14.

**fourth** (fôrth) ***adj.*** coming after three others; 4th in order. ◆***n.*** **1** the fourth one. **2** one of four equal parts of something; 1/4.

**fourth dimension** a dimension in addition to the three ordinary dimensions of length, width, and depth. In the theory of relativity, time is thought of as the fourth dimension.

☆**Fourth of July** *see* **Independence Day**.

**fowl** (foul) ***n.*** **1** any bird [wild *fowl*]. **2** any of the larger birds raised for food, as the chicken, turkey, or duck. **3** the flesh of such a bird used as food.

**fowl·er** (foul′ər) ***n.*** one who hunts wild birds.

**fox** (fäks) ***n.*** **1** a small, wild animal of the dog family, with pointed ears, a bushy tail, and, usually, reddish-brown fur. *See the picture.* **2** its fur. **3** a foxy person.

**fox·glove** (fäks′gluv) ***n.*** a tall plant with clusters of flowers shaped like thimbles.

**fox·hole** (fäks′hōl) ***n.*** a hole dug in the ground as protection for one or two soldiers.

**fox·hound** (fäks′hound) ***n.*** a strong, fast hound trained to hunt foxes.

**fox terrier** a small, lively dog with a smooth or wire-haired coat.

☆**fox trot** **1** a popular dance for couples, with some fast steps and some slow steps. **2** the music for this dance.

**fox·y** (fäk′sē) ***adj.*** sly and cunning; tricky. —**fox′i·er, fox′i·est**

**foy·er** (foi′ər *or* foi′ā) ***n.*** a lobby or entrance hall, as in a theater or hotel.

**FPO** Fleet Post Office (in the U.S. Navy).

**Fr.** *abbreviation for* **Father, France** *or* **French, Friar.**

**fr.** *abbreviation for* **franc** *or* **francs.**

**fra·cas** (frā′kəs *or* frak′əs) ***n.*** a noisy fight or loud quarrel; brawl.

**frac·tion** (frak′shən) ***n.*** **1** a quantity less than a whole, or one; one or more equal parts of a whole [Some *fractions* are 1/2, 3/4, and 19/25.] **2** any quantity written with a numerator and denominator [5/4 is a *fraction.*] **3** a small part or amount [She can save only a *fraction* of the money she earns.] —**frac′tion·al *adj.***

**Fraction** comes from a Latin word meaning "to break." A fraction is one of the parts broken from a whole.

**frac·tious** (frak′shəs) ***adj.*** hard to manage; unruly, cross, fretful, etc.

**frac·ture** (frak′chər) ***n.*** **1** a breaking or being broken. **2** a break or crack, especially in a bone. ◆***v.*** to break or crack [an arm *fractured* in a fall]. —**frac′tured, frac′tur·ing**

**frag·ile** (fraj′'l) ***adj.*** easily broken or damaged; delicate [a *fragile* teacup; *fragile* health]. —**fra·gil·i·ty** (frə jil′ə tē) ***n.***

SYNONYMS: Anything **fragile** or **frail** can be easily broken, but something **fragile** is usually delicate and weak, while something **frail** is usually weak and slender [a *fragile* crystal goblet; a flower on a *frail* stem].

**frag·ment** (frag′mənt) ***n.*** **1** a piece of something that has broken; a part broken away [*fragments* of a broken cup]. **2** a part taken from a whole [a *fragment* of a song].

**frag·men·tar·y** (frag′mən ter′ē) ***adj.*** made up of fragments; incomplete [a *fragmentary* report].

**fra·grance** (frā′grəns) ***n.*** a sweet or pleasant smell. *See* SYNONYMS *at* **scent.**

**fra·grant** (frā′grənt) ***adj.*** having a sweet or pleasant smell.

**frail** (frāl) ***adj.*** **1** easily broken or damaged; fragile; weak [a *frail* ladder; a *frail,* sickly child]. **2** easily led to do wrong; morally weak. *See* SYNONYMS *at* **fragile** *and at* **weak.**

**frail·ty** (frāl′tē) ***n.*** **1** the condition of being frail. **2** a weakness in health, character, etc.; fault or flaw. —*pl.* **frail′ties**

**frame** (frām) ***n.*** **1** the support or skeleton around which a thing is built and that gives the thing its shape; framework [the *frame* of a house]. **2** the build of a body [a man with a large *frame*]. **3** the border or case into which a window, door, picture, etc. is set. **4 frames,** *pl.* the framework for a pair of eyeglasses. **5** any of the divisions of a game of bowling. ◆***v.*** **1** to put together according to some plan; make, form, build, compose, etc. [to *frame* laws; to *frame* an excuse]. **2** to put a frame, or border, around [to *frame* a picture]. ☆**3** to make an innocent person seem guilty by a plot: *used only in everyday talk.* —**framed, fram′ing** —**frame of mind,** the way one thinks or feels; mood.

☆**frame-up** (frām′up′) ***n.*** a secret plot to make an innocent person seem guilty: *used only in everyday talk.*

**frame·work** (frām′wurk) ***n.*** the structure or support that holds together the thing built around it [the *framework* of a house]. *See the picture.*

**franc** (frangk) ***n.*** the basic unit of money in France, and also in Belgium, Switzerland, etc.

**France** (frans) a country in western Europe.

**fran·chise** (fran′chīz) ***n.*** **1** a special right or permission given by a government [One must get a *franchise* from the Federal government to operate a TV station.] **2** the right to vote; suffrage. **3** the right given to a dealer to sell the products of a certain company. **293**

**Fran·cis·can** (fran sis′kən) ***adj.*** of the religious order founded by St. Francis of Assisi in 1209. ◆***n.*** a member of this order.

**Fran·cis of As·si·si** (fran′sis əv ə sē′zē), Saint 1181?–1226; an Italian preacher.

**Franck** (fränk), **Cé·sar** (sā zär′) 1822–1890; French composer. He was born in Belgium.

**Frank** (frangk) ***n.*** a member of the German tribes who, by the 9th century, ruled over what is now France, Germany, and Italy.

**frank** (frangk) ***adj.*** open and honest about what one is thinking and feeling; speaking one's mind freely. ◆***v.*** to send mail without having to pay postage [Senators may *frank* official mail.] ◆***n.*** the right to send mail without having to pay postage; also, a mark on the envelope showing this right. —**frank′ly *adv.*** —**frank′ness *n.***

SYNONYMS: To be **frank** is to be honest and blunt in saying what one thinks or feels [a *frank* criticism]. To be **candid** is to be so honest and truthful that one may say things that embarrass other people [Spare me your *candid* opinion!] To be **outspoken** is to speak in a much bolder way than is called for [His *outspoken* attack on the president won him enemies.]

| | | | | | | | |
|---|---|---|---|---|---|---|---|
| **a** | fat | **ir** | here | **ou** | out | **zh** | leisure |
| **ā** | ape | **ī** | bite, fire | **u** | up | **ng** | ring |
| **ä** | car, lot | **ō** | go | **ur** | fur | | a *in* ago |
| **e** | ten | **ô** | law, horn | **ch** | chin | | e *in* agent |
| **er** | care | **oi** | oil | **sh** | she | ə = | i *in* unity |
| **ē** | even | **oo** | look | **th** | thin | | o *in* collect |
| **i** | hit | **ōō** | tool | ***th*** | then | | u *in* focus |

**Frank·en·stein** (frang′kən stīn) the man in a famous novel who builds a monster that destroys him. *See the picture.*

Strictly speaking, the creature built by Dr. Frankenstein should be called "Frankenstein's monster." But many people call the monster itself "Frankenstein."

**Frank·fort** (frangk′fərt) the capital of Kentucky.

**Frank·furt** (frangk′fərt) a city in central West Germany.

☆**frank·furt·er** or **frank·fort·er** (frangk′fər tər) ***n.*** a smoked sausage of beef or beef and pork; wiener: *also* **frank′furt** or **frank′fort.**

**frank·in·cense** (frang′kən sens) ***n.*** a resin from certain trees of Arabia and northeastern Africa. It gives off a spicy smell when burned.

**Frank·ish** (frang′kish) ***adj.*** of the Franks, their language, or culture.

**Frank·lin** (frangk′lin), **Benjamin** 1706–1790; American statesman, inventor, and writer.

☆**Franklin stove** a cast-iron heating stove that looks like an open fireplace. It was invented by Benjamin Franklin.

**fran·tic** (fran′tik) ***adj.*** wild with anger, pain, worry, etc. —**fran′ti·cal·ly *adv.***

**fra·ter·nal** (frə tur′n'l) ***adj.*** of or like brothers; brotherly.

**fra·ter·ni·ty** (frə tur′nə tē) ***n.*** **1** the close tie among brothers; brotherly feeling. **2** a club of men or boys, especially a social club, as in a college. Fraternities usually have letters of the Greek alphabet for their name. **3** a group of people with the same work, interests, beliefs, etc. [Doctors are often called the medical *fraternity.*] —*pl.* **fra·ter′ni·ties**



**frat·er·nize** (frat′ər nīz) ***v.*** to behave in a brotherly way; be friendly. —**frat′er·nized, frat′er·niz·ing**

**Frau** (frou) ***n.*** a married woman; wife: a German word also used as a title meaning "Mrs."

**fraud** (frôd) ***n.*** **1** a cheating, tricking, or lying; dishonesty. **2** something used to cheat or trick. *See* SYNONYMS *at* **deception. 3** a person who cheats or is not what he or she pretends to be.

**fraud·u·lent** (frô′jə lənt) ***adj.*** **1** using fraud; cheating, tricking, or lying [a *fraudulent* scheme]. **2** gained by means of fraud [*fraudulent* wealth].

**fraught** (frôt) ***adj.*** filled or loaded [A pioneer's life is *fraught* with hardships.]

**Frau·lein** (froi′līn) ***n.*** an unmarried woman; young woman or girl: a German word also used as a title meaning "Miss."

**fray**[1] (frā) ***n.*** a noisy quarrel or fight.

**fray**[2] (frā) ***v.*** to wear down so as to become ragged and have loose threads showing [a coat *frayed* at the elbows].

**fraz·zle** (fraz′'l) ***v.*** **1** to wear out until in shreds. **2** to tire out completely. *This word is used only in everyday talk.* —**fraz′zled, fraz′zling**

**freak** (frēk) ***n.*** **1** an animal or plant that is very much different from what is normal [A two-headed calf is a *freak.*] **2** an odd or unusual idea or happening. ☆**3** a person who is devoted to someone or something: *slang in this meaning* [a jazz *freak*]. ◆***adj.*** very different from what is normal; unusual. —**freak out,** to have visions and imagine things as the result of taking certain drugs: *a slang phrase.* —**freak′ish *adj.***

**freck·le** (frek′'l) ***n.*** a small, brownish spot on the skin. Freckles are brought out on the face, arms, etc. by the sun. *See the picture.* ◆***v.*** to make or become spotted with freckles. —**freck′led, freck′ling**

**Fred·er·ick the Great** (fred′ər ik) 1712–1786; the king of Prussia from 1740 to 1786.

**free** (frē) ***adj.*** **1** not under the control of another; not a slave or not in prison. **2** able to vote and to speak, write, meet, and worship as one pleases; having political and civil liberty. **3** not tied up, fastened, or shut in; loose [As soon as the bird was *free,* it flew away. Grab the *free* end of the rope.] **4** not bothered or held down, as by duty, work, worry, etc. [*free* from pain; *free* of debt]. **5** not busy or not in use [The phone booth is *free* now.] **6** not following the usual rules or patterns [*free* verse]. **7** giving readily; generous [You are too *free* with your money.] **8** frank, familiar, or forward [Don't be so *free* with me.] **9** with no charge; without cost [*free* tickets to the ball game]. **10** not needing to pay the usual taxes, etc.; exempt [a package from England *free* of duty]. **11** with no blocking; open or clear [The harbor was *free* of ice all winter.] —**fre′er, fre′est** ◆***adv.*** **1** without cost [We were let in *free.*] **2** in a free manner; without being held back [The wind blows *free.*] ◆***v.*** to make free [The governor *freed* five prisoners by granting pardons.] —**freed, free′ing** —**free from** or **free of, 1** not having; without. **2** let go from. —**free′ly *adv.***

☆**free·bie** or **free·by** (frē′bē) ***n.*** something that has been given to one free of charge, as a theater ticket: *a slang word.* —*pl.* **free′bies**

**free·boot·er** (frē′bo͞ot′ər) ***n.*** a pirate; buccaneer.

**freed·man** (frēd′mən) ***n.*** a man who has been set free from slavery. —*pl.* **freed′men**

**free·dom** (frē′dəm) ***n.*** **1** the condition of being free; liberty; independence. **2** a being able to use or move about in as one wishes [Has your dog been given *freedom* of the house?] **3** easiness, as of action [The tight coat hindered his *freedom* of movement.] **4** frankness or easiness of manner; often, too great frankness, or a being too familiar [Calling her customers "honey" is part of her *freedom* of manner.]

**free·hand** (frē′hand) ***adj.*** drawn by hand, without using a ruler, compasses, etc.

**free lance** a writer, actor, or artist who sells his or her work to different buyers at different times. —**free′-lance′ *adj.***

**free·man** (frē′mən) ***n.*** a person who is not a slave; person free to vote, hold office, own property, etc.; citizen. —*pl.* **free′men**

**Free·ma·son** (frē′mās′'n) ***n.*** a member of a secret social society that has branches all over the world.

**free·stone** (frē′stōn) ***adj.*** having a pit that does not cling to the fruit [a *freestone* peach].

**free·think·er** (frē′thingk′kər) ***n.*** a person who forms his or her own ideas about religion without following established religious teachings.

**free throw** in basketball, a free, or unhindered, throw at the basket from a certain line (**free-throw line**), allowed to a player as a penalty against the other team. If the throw goes in the basket, it counts for one point.

freeway

Frankenstein's monster

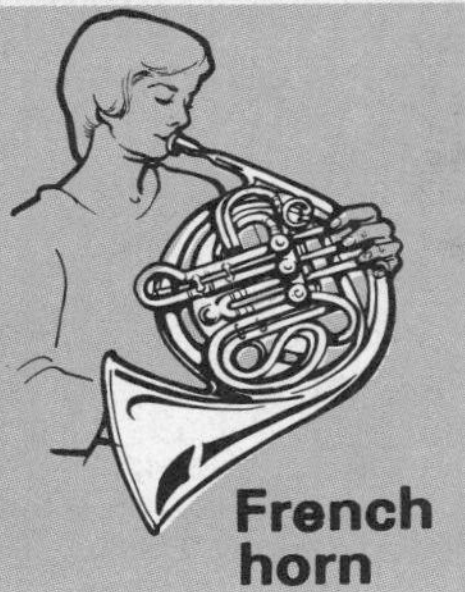
French horn

freckles

☆**free·way** (frē′wā) ***n.*** a highway with many lanes and few, if any, traffic lights, stop signs, etc., so that traffic can move swiftly. *See the picture.*

**free·will** (frē′wil′) ***adj.*** freely given or done; voluntary.

**free will** freedom to act, give, live, etc. as one wishes.

**freeze** (frēz) ***v.*** **1** to harden into ice; make or become solid because of cold [Water *freezes* at 0°C or 32°F.] **2** to make or become filled or covered with ice [The river *froze* over.] **3** to make or become very cold; especially, to kill, die, spoil, etc. with cold [The cold spell *froze* the oranges in the groves.] **4** to stick by freezing [The wheels *froze* to the ground.] **5** to stick or become tight because of overheating, as a piston in a cylinder. **6** to make or become motionless or stunned [to *freeze* with terror]. **7** to make or become unfriendly. **8** to set limits on prices, wages, etc. —**froze, fro′zen, freez′ing** ◆***n.*** **1** a freezing or being frozen. **2** a spell of freezing weather.

☆**freeze-dry** (frēz′drī′) ***v.*** to freeze something quickly and then dry it in a vacuum. Freeze-dried foods can be kept for a long time at room temperature. —**freeze′-dried′, freeze′-dry′ing**

**freez·er** (frēz′ər) ***n.*** **1** a machine for making ice cream. **2** a refrigerator for freezing foods or storing frozen foods.

**freight** (frāt) ***n.*** **1** a load of goods shipped by train, truck, ship, airplane, etc. **2** the cost of shipping such goods. **3** the shipping of goods in this way [Send it by *freight*.] ◆***v.*** **1** to load with freight. **2** to send by freight.

**freight·er** (frāt′ər) ***n.*** a ship for freight.

**French** (french) ***adj.*** of France, its people, etc. ◆***n.*** the language of France. —**the French,** the people of France.

**French** (french), **Daniel Chester** 1850–1931; U.S. sculptor.

**French doors** two matching doors that have glass panes from top to bottom and are hinged at opposite sides of a doorway so that they open in the middle.

☆**French fry** *often* **french fry,** to fry in very hot, deep fat until crisp. French fried potatoes (*in everyday talk,* **French fries**) are first cut into long strips.

**French horn** a brass-wind musical instrument with a long, coiled tube ending in a wide bell. It has a soft, mellow tone. *See the picture.*

**French·man** (french′mən) ***n.*** a person, especially a man, born or living in France. —*pl.* **French′men**

**French Revolution** the revolution in France from 1789 to 1799, which replaced the monarchy with France's first republic.

☆**French toast** bread slices fried after being dipped in an egg batter.

**French·wom·an** (french′woom′ən) ***n.*** a woman born or living in France. —*pl.* **French′wom′en**

**fren·zy** (fren′zē) ***n.*** a wild or mad outburst of feeling or action [a *frenzy* of joy, fear, work, etc.] —*pl.* **fren′zies** —**fren′zied** ***adj.***

**fre·quen·cy** (frē′kwən sē) ***n.*** **1** the fact of being frequent, or happening often. **2** the number of times something is repeated in a certain period [a *frequency* of 1,000 vibrations per second]. The frequency of radio waves is measured in hertz. —*pl.* **fre′quen·cies**

**fre·quent** (frē′kwənt) ***adj.*** happening often or time after time [This airplane makes *frequent* trips.] ◆***v.*** (frē kwent′) to go to again and again; be found in often [They *frequent* theaters.] —**fre′quent·ly** ***adv.***

**fres·co** (fres′kō) ***n.*** **1** the art of painting with watercolors on wet plaster. **2** a painting so made. —*pl.* **fres′coes** or **fres′cos**

**Fresco** comes from the Italian word for "fresh." Watercolors on wet plaster, after they have dried, have a fresh, clear, clean look.



**fresh**[1] (fresh) ***adj.*** **1** newly made, got, or grown; not spoiled, stale, etc. [*fresh* coffee; *fresh* eggs]. *See* SYNONYMS *at* **new. 2** not pickled, canned, etc. [*fresh* meat]. **3** not tired; lively [I feel *fresh* after a nap.] **4** not worn or dirty [*fresh* clothes]. **5** looking youthful or healthy [a *fresh* complexion]. **6** new or different [a *fresh* approach to a problem]. **7** having just arrived [a youth *fresh* from a farm]. **8** cool and clean [*fresh* air]. **9** not salty [Most lakes are *fresh* water.] —**fresh′ly** ***adv.*** —**fresh′ness** ***n.***

☆**fresh**[2] (fresh) ***adj.*** acting too bold; rude or impudent: *a slang word.*

**fresh·en** (fresh′ən) ***v.*** to make or become fresh, or new, clean, etc.

**fresh·et** (fresh′it) ***n.*** ☆**1** a flooding of a stream because of melting snow or heavy rain. **2** a flow of fresh water into the sea.

**fresh·man** (fresh′mən) ***n.*** a student in the ninth grade in high school, or one in the first year of college. —*pl.* **fresh′men**

**fret**[1] (fret) ***v.*** **1** to make or become annoyed or worried [Don't *fret* about things you can't change. Her troubles *fretted* her.] **2** to wear away by gnawing, rubbing, etc. —**fret′ted, fret′ting** ◆***n.*** annoyance or worry [Vacations help us forget our *frets* and cares.]

| | | | | | | | |
|---|---|---|---|---|---|---|---|
| **a** | fat | **ir** | here | **ou** | out | **zh** | leisure |
| **ā** | ape | **ī** | bite, fire | **u** | up | **ng** | ring |
| **ä** | car, lot | **ō** | go | **ur** | fur | | a *in* ago |
| **e** | ten | **ô** | law, horn | **ch** | chin | | e *in* agent |
| **er** | care | **oi** | oil | **sh** | she | **ə =** | i *in* unity |
| **ē** | even | **oo** | look | **th** | thin | | o *in* collect |
| **i** | hit | **ōō** | tool | ***th*** | then | | u *in* focus |

part of a frieze

Frisbee

frets on a guitar

frizzled hair

frog developing from tadpole

frog for a garment

**fret²** (fret) ***n.*** a design made up of short, straight bars or lines joined at right angles. ✦***v.*** to decorate with fretwork. —**fret′ted, fret′ting**



**fret³** (fret) ***n.*** any of the ridges across the fingerboard of a banjo, guitar, etc. *See the picture.*

**fret·ful** (fret′fəl) ***adj.*** annoyed or worried. —**fret′ful·ly** ***adv.*** —**fret′ful·ness** ***n.***

**fret·work** (fret′wurk) ***n.*** a carving or other decoration with a design of frets.

**Freud** (froid), **Sig·mund** (sig′mənd) 1856–1939; an Austrian physician. He was the founder of psychoanalysis. —**Freud′i·an** ***adj.***

**Fri.** *abbreviation for* **Friday.**

**fri·a·ble** (frī′ə b′l) ***adj.*** easily crumbled or broken into bits [*friable* soil].

**fri·ar** (frī′ər) ***n.*** a member of certain religious orders of the Roman Catholic Church.

**fric·as·see** (frik ə sē′) ***n.*** meat cut into pieces, cooked, and served in a sauce of its own gravy. ✦***v.*** to cook meat in this way. —**fric·as·seed′, fric·as·see′ing**

**fric·tion** (frik′shən) ***n.*** **1** a rubbing of one thing against another. **2** arguments or quarrels caused by differences of opinions. **3** the force that slows down the motion of surfaces that touch [Ball bearings lessen *friction* in machines.]

**Fri·day** (frī′dē *or* frī′dā) ***n.*** the sixth day of the week.

**fried** (frīd) *past tense and past participle of* **fry.** ✦***adj.*** cooked by frying.

☆**fried·cake** (frīd′kāk) ***n.*** a small cake fried in deep fat; doughnut or cruller.

**friend** (frend) ***n.*** **1** a person whom one knows well and likes. **2** a person on the same side in a struggle; ally. **3** a person who helps or supports something [a *friend* of the working class]. **4 Friend,** a member of the Society of Friends; Quaker. —**make friends with,** to become a friend of.

**friend·ly** (frend′lē) ***adj.*** **1** of, like, to, or from a friend; kindly [some *friendly* advice]. **2** showing good and peaceful feelings; ready to be a friend [a *friendly* nation]. —**friend′li·er, friend′li·est** ✦***adv.*** in a friendly way [to act *friendly*]. —**friend′li·ness** ***n.***

**friend·ship** (frend′ship) ***n.*** **1** the condition of being friends. **2** friendly feeling.

**frieze** (frēz) ***n.*** a band of designs, drawings, or carvings used as a decoration along a wall or around a room. *See the picture.*

**frig·ate** (frig′it) ***n.*** **1** a fast, sailing warship of the 18th and early 19th centuries. ☆**2** a U.S. warship larger than a destroyer.

**fright** (frīt) ***n.*** **1** sudden fear; alarm. **2** something that looks so strange or ugly as to startle one [That old fur coat is a perfect *fright.*]

**fright·en** (frīt′'n) ***v.*** **1** to make or become suddenly afraid; scare. **2** to force to do something by making afraid [He was *frightened* into confessing.]

**fright·ful** (frīt′fəl) ***adj.*** **1** causing fright; making afraid [a *frightful* dream]. **2** terrible; shocking [a victory won at a *frightful* cost]. **3** great: *used only in everyday talk* [a *frightful* nuisance]. —**fright′ful·ly** ***adv.***

**frig·id** (frij′id) ***adj.*** **1** very cold; freezing [a *frigid* day in January]. *See* SYNONYMS *at* **chilly. 2** not warm or friendly; stiff [a *frigid* welcome]. —**fri·gid·i·ty** (frə jid′ə tē) ***n.***

☆**fri·jol** (frē′hōl) ***n.*** any bean, especially the kidney bean used for food in Mexico and the southwestern U.S.: *also* **fri·jo·le** (frē hō′lē). —*pl.* **fri·jo·les** (frē′hōlz *or* frē hō′lēz)

**frill** (fril) ***n.*** **1** a piece of cloth or lace used as a trimming; ruffle. **2** something useless added just for show [a simple meal without *frills*]. —**frill′y** ***adj.***

**fringe** (frinj) ***n.*** **1** a border of threads for decoration, either hanging loose or tied in bunches. **2** an outside edge; border [We stood at the *fringe* of the crowd.] ✦***v.*** to be or make a fringe for; border [Trees *fringe* the lake.] —**fringed, fring′ing** ✦***adj.*** **1** at the outer edge [a *fringe* area of the city]. ☆**2** additional [*fringe* costs]. ☆**3** less important [*fringe* industries].

☆**fringe benefit** an employee's benefit in addition to wages or salary [A pension or insurance paid for by one's employer is a *fringe benefit.*]

**frip·per·y** (frip′ər ē) ***n.*** **1** cheap, showy clothes or decorations. **2** any silly showing off, as in speech or manners. —*pl.* **frip′per·ies**

☆**Fris·bee** (friz′bē) *a trademark for* a plastic, saucer-shaped disk tossed back and forth in a game. *See the picture.*

**frisk** (frisk) ***v.*** **1** to move or jump about in a lively, playful way; frolic. **2** to search a person quickly, as for hidden weapons: *slang in this meaning.*

**frisk·y** (fris′kē) ***adj.*** lively or playful. —**frisk′i·er, frisk′i·est** —**frisk′i·ly** ***adv.*** —**frisk′i·ness** ***n.***

**frit·ter¹** (frit′ər) ***v.*** to waste bit by bit [to *fritter* away money or time].

**frit·ter²** (frit′ər) ***n.*** a small cake of fried batter filled with fruit, corn, etc.

**fri·vol·i·ty** (fri väl′ə tē) ***n.*** **1** the condition of being frivolous. **2** a frivolous act or thing. —*pl.* **fri·vol′i·ties**

**friv·o·lous** (friv′ə ləs) ***adj.*** not at all serious or important; flighty, silly, etc. [a *frivolous* remark; a *frivolous* student]. —**friv′o·lous·ly** ***adv.***

**friz·zle¹** (friz′'l) ***v.*** to make a sputtering sound, as in frying; sizzle. —**friz′zled, friz′zling**

**friz·zle**[2] (friz′'l) ***v.*** to arrange hair in small, tight curls. *See the picture.* —**friz′zled, friz′zling** —**friz′zly** or **friz′zy** ***adj.***

**fro** (frō) ***adv.*** back: *now used only in the phrase* **to and fro,** *meaning* "back and forth."

**frock** (fräk) ***n.*** **1** a girl's or woman's dress. **2** the robe worn by friars, monks, etc.

**frog** (frôg) ***n.*** **1** a small, coldblooded animal that can live on land and in water. It has long, strong hind legs with which it leaps. *See the picture.* **2** a fancy loop made of braid and used to fasten clothing. *See the picture.* —**frog in the throat,** a hoarseness.

**frol·ic** (fräl′ik) ***n.*** a lively game or party; merry play. ◆***v.*** to play or romp about in a happy and carefree way. —**frol′icked, frol′ick·ing**

**frol·ic·some** (fräl′ik səm) ***adj.*** lively and full of fun; playful.

**from** (frum *or* främ) ***prep.*** **1** starting at [*from* Erie to Buffalo; *from* noon to midnight]. **2** out of [to take clothes *from* a closet; to release a person *from* jail; to keep a child *from* danger]. **3** made, sent, said, etc. by [a letter *from* my cousin]. **4** at a place not near to [Keep away *from* the dog.] **5** out of the whole of [Take 2 *from* 4.] **6** as not being like [I can't tell one car *from* another.] **7** because of [We trembled *from* fear.]

**frond** (fränd) ***n.*** **1** the leaf of a fern. **2** the leaf of a palm. **3** a part like a leaf, as of a seaweed.

**front** (frunt) ***n.*** **1** the part that faces forward; most important side [The *front* of a house usually faces the street.] **2** the part ahead of the rest; first part; beginning [That chapter is toward the *front* of the book.] **3** outward look or behavior [I put on a bold *front* in spite of my fear.] **4** the land alongside a lake, ocean, street, etc. [docks on the water*front*]. **5** in a war, the part where the actual fighting is going on. ☆**6** a person or thing used as a cover to hide the actions of others. **7** the boundary between two large masses of air [a cold *front* advancing from the west]. ◆***adj.*** at, to, in, on, or of the front. ◆***v.*** **1** to face toward [The house *fronts* the lake.] ☆**2** to act as a cover for hiding the actions of others [We *fronted* for the real buyers of the property.]

**Front** comes from a Latin word meaning "forehead." The forehead is a part of the head that faces forward. For many years in English *front* had "forehead" as a meaning, but it no longer has that meaning.

**front·age** (frun′tij) ***n.*** **1** the front part of a building or lot. **2** the length of the front of a lot. **3** land bordering a street, lake, etc.

**fron·tal** (frun′t'l) ***adj.*** of, on, or at the front [The bones of the forehead are called *frontal* bones.]

**fron·tier** (frun tir′) ***n.*** **1** the line or border between two countries. ☆**2** the part of a settled country that lies next to a region that is still a wilderness. **3** any new field of learning or any part of it still to be explored [the *frontiers* of medicine].

☆**fron·tiers·man** (frun tirz′mən) ***n.*** a man who lives on the frontier. —*pl.* **fron·tiers′men**

**fron·tis·piece** (frun′tis pēs) ***n.*** a picture that faces the title page of a book.

**front·let** (frunt′lit) ***n.*** **1** a band or other object worn on the forehead. **2** the forehead of an animal, especially of a bird, when it has colorful markings.

**frost** (frôst) ***n.*** **1** frozen dew or vapor in the form of white crystals [the *frost* on the coils of a refrigerator]. **2** cold weather that can freeze things [*Frost* in the spring may damage fruit trees.] ◆***v.*** **1** to cover with frost or with frosting. **2** to give a surface like frost to [*frosted* glass]. **3** to bleach hair on the head so that it looks streaked.

**Frost** (frôst), **Robert (Lee)** 1874–1963; U.S. poet.

**frost·bite** (frôst′bīt) ***n.*** damage to a part of the body, as the ears or toes, from being out in great cold.

**frost·bit·ten** (frôst′bit″n) ***adj.*** damaged by having been exposed to great cold [*frostbitten* toes].

**frost·ing** (frôs′tiŋ) ***n.*** **1** a mixture of sugar, butter, flavoring, etc. for covering cakes; icing. **2** a dull finish on glass that looks like frost.

**frost·y** (frôs′tē) ***adj.*** **1** cold enough to have frost [a *frosty* day]. **2** covered with frost [the *frosty* ground]. **3** not friendly or cordial [a *frosty* greeting]. —**frost′i·er, frost′i·est**

**froth** (frôth) ***n.*** **1** a white mass of bubbles; foam. **2** anything light and unimportant [The play was an amusing bit of *froth.*] ◆***v.*** to foam or make foam [The dog *frothed* at the mouth.] —**froth′y** ***adj.***

**fro·ward** (frō′wərd) ***adj.*** always going against what is wanted; contrary; stubborn.

**frown** (froun) ***v.*** **1** to wrinkle the forehead and draw the eyebrows together in anger, worry, or deep thought. *See the picture on page 298.* **2** to show that one dislikes or does not approve [The cook *frowned* upon any waste of food.] ◆***n.*** a frowning or the look one has in frowning.



**frow·zy** (frou′zē) ***adj.*** dirty and untidy; slovenly. —**frow′zi·er, frow′zi·est** —**frow′zi·ness** ***n.***

**froze** (frōz) *past tense of* **freeze.**

**fro·zen** (frōz″n) *past participle of* **freeze.** ◆***adj.*** **1** turned into or covered with ice [a *frozen* pond]. **2** hurt or killed by freezing [*frozen* blossoms]. **3** kept fresh by freezing [*frozen* foods]. **4** stunned or shocked [*frozen* with terror]. **5** kept in a fixed place or position [Prices were *frozen.*]

☆**frozen custard** a food that is like ice cream, but not so thick and having less butterfat.

**fru·gal** (froo′g'l) ***adj.*** **1** not wasteful; thrifty or saving [a *frugal* manager]. **2** costing little and very plain [a *frugal* meal]. —**fru·gal·i·ty** (froo gal′ə tē) ***n.*** —**fru′gal·ly** ***adv.***

**fruit** (froot) ***n.*** **1** the parts of certain plants or trees that can be eaten, containing the seeds inside a sweet and juicy pulp, as apples, pears, or grapes. In botany, the seed-bearing part of any plant is called its *fruit,* as a nut, pea pod, tomato, etc. **2** the product of any plant, as grain, flax, cotton, etc. [to harvest the *fruits* of the field]. **3** the result or product of any action [Success can be the *fruit* of hard work.] ◆***v.*** to bear fruit.

| | | | |
|---|---|---|---|
| **a** fat | **ir** here | **ou** out | **zh** leisure |
| **ā** ape | **ī** bite, fire | **u** up | **ŋ** ring |
| **ä** car, lot | **ō** go | **ur** fur | a *in* ago |
| **e** ten | **ô** law, horn | **ch** chin | e *in* agent |
| **er** care | **oi** oil | **sh** she | **ə** = i *in* unity |
| **ē** even | **oo** look | **th** thin | o *in* collect |
| **i** hit | **ōō** tool | ***th*** then | u *in* focus |

**fruit·age** (frōōt′ij) ***n.*** **1** the bearing of fruit. **2** a crop of fruit. **3** a result; product.

**fruit·ful** (frōōt′fəl) ***adj.*** **1** bearing much fruit [a *fruitful* tree]. **2** producing a great deal [Mozart was a *fruitful* composer.] **3** bringing about results; profitable [a *fruitful* scheme]. —**fruit′ful·ly *adv.*** —**fruit′ful·ness *n.***

**fru·i·tion** (frōō ish′ən) ***n.*** **1** the bearing of fruit. **2** a reaching or getting what was planned or worked for [Her book is the *fruition* of years of research.]

**fruit·less** (frōōt′lis) ***adj.*** **1** having no results; not successful [*fruitless* efforts]. **2** bearing no fruit; barren.

**fruit·y** (frōōt′ē) ***adj.*** having the taste or smell of fruit. —**fruit′i·er, fruit′i·est**

**frus·trate** (frus′trāt) ***v.*** to keep a person from getting or doing what that person wants or to keep a thing from being carried out; block; thwart [The rain *frustrated* our plans for a picnic. He is constantly *frustrated* by his lack of skill in sports.] —**frus′trat·ed, frus′trat·ing** —**frus·tra′tion *n.***

**fry**[1] (frī) ***v.*** to cook in hot fat over direct heat. —**fried, fry′ing** ◆***n.*** ☆**1** a kind of picnic at which food is fried and eaten [a fish *fry*]. **2 fries**, *pl.* things fried, as potatoes. —*pl.* **fries**

**fry**[2] (frī) ***n.*** young fish. —*pl.* **fry** —**small fry, 1** children or a child. **2** a person or people who are not important.

298 **ft.** *abbreviation for* **foot** *or* **feet.**

**FTC** Federal Trade Commission.

**fuch·sia** (fyōō′shə) ***n.*** **1** a shrub with pink, red, or purple flowers. *See the picture.* **2** a purplish red.

**fud·dle** (fud′′l) ***v.*** to make stupid or confused, as from drinking alcoholic liquor. —**fud′dled, fud′dling**

**fud·dy-dud·dy** (fud′ē dud′ē) ***n.*** a person who is old-fashioned or fussy and faultfinding: *a slang word.* —*pl.* **fud′dy-dud′dies**

**fudge** (fuj) ***n.*** ☆a soft candy made of butter, sugar, milk, and chocolate or other flavoring. ◆***v.*** ☆**1** to be dishonest or cheat, as in making something. ☆**2** to refuse to give a direct answer; hedge [The senator *fudged* on the issue.] —**fudged, fudg′ing**

**fu·el** (fyōō′′l) ***n.*** **1** anything that is burned to give heat or power [Coal, gas, oil, and wood are *fuels.*] **2** anything that makes a strong feeling even stronger [Their teasing only added *fuel* to her anger.] ◆***v.*** **1** to supply with fuel. **2** to get fuel. —**fu′eled** or **fu′elled, fu′el·ing** or **fu′el·ling**

☆**fuel oil** any oil used for fuel, especially a kind used in diesel engines.

**fu·gi·tive** (fyōō′jə tiv) ***adj.*** **1** running away, as from danger or capture [a *fugitive* criminal]. **2** not lasting long; passing away quickly [*fugitive* pleasures]. ◆***n.*** a person who is running away, as from danger or from officers of the law.

**fugue** (fyōōg) ***n.*** a piece of music in which one part after another takes up a melody and all parts stay in harmony as the melody is repeated in various ways.

**Füh·rer** (fyoor′ər) ***n.*** leader: a German word, used as a title by Adolf Hitler as the head of Nazi Germany.

**Fu·ji** (fōō′jē) a volcano that is no longer active, near Tokyo, Japan: *also called* **Fu·ji·ya·ma** (fōō′jē yä′mə).

**-ful** (fəl) *a suffix meaning:* **1** full of [*Joyful* means full of joy.] **2** likely to [*Forgetful* means likely to forget.] **3** the amount that will fill [A *teaspoonful* is the amount that will fill a teaspoon.] —*pl.* **-fuls 4** having the ways of [*Masterful* means having the ways of a master.]

**ful·crum** (fool′krəm) ***n.*** the support or point that a lever rests on when it is lifting something. *See the picture.* —*pl.* **ful′crums** or **ful·cra** (fool′krə)

**ful·fill** or **ful·fil** (fool fil′) ***v.*** to make happen; carry out, perform, do, complete, etc. [to *fulfill* a promise, a duty, a purpose, a mission]. —**ful·filled′, ful·fill′ing** —**ful·fill′ment** or **ful·fil′ment *n.***

**full** (fool) ***adj.*** **1** having in it all there is space for; filled [a *full* jar]. **2** having much or many in it [a pond *full* of fish; to lead a *full* life]. **3** having eaten all that one wants. **4** whole or complete [a *full* dozen; a *full* load]. **5** clear and strong [the *full* tones of an organ]. **6** filled out; plump; round [a *full* face]. **7** with loose, wide folds [a *full* skirt]. ◆***n.*** the greatest amount or degree [to enjoy life to the *full*]. ◆***adv.*** **1** completely [a *full-grown* animal]. **2** straight; directly [The ball struck her *full* in the face.] **3** very [You know *full* well what we have.] —**full of,** filled with. —**in full, 1** to the complete amount [paid *in full*]. **2** not abbreviated [Write your name *in full.*] —**full′ness *n.***

SYNONYMS: **Full** is used of something that has all the parts that are needed or belong [They put on the *full* play, with nothing cut out.] **Complete** is used of something that has all the parts needed for being whole or perfect [a *complete* set of an author's books].

**full·back** (fool′bak) ***n.*** a football player who is a member of the backfield.

**full-fledged** (fool′flejd′) ***adj.*** completely developed or trained [a *full-fledged* pilot].

**full-length** (fool′lengkth′) ***adj.*** **1** showing the whole length, as of a person's figure: said of a picture or mirror. **2** of the standard length; not shortened [a *full-length* novel; a *full-length* sofa].

**full moon** the moon seen as a full circle.
**full-scale** (fool′skāl′) ***adj.*** **1** exactly the same as the original in size and proportions [a *full-scale* drawing]. **2** complete in every way; to the greatest limit, degree, etc. [*full-scale* war].
**full-time** (fool′tīm′) ***adj.*** being a worker, student, etc. for periods of time that make up a full, regular schedule [a *full-time* employee].
**full time** as a full-time employee, student, etc. [He works *full time* at the shoe factory.]
**full·y** (fool′ē) ***adv.*** in a way that is complete, plentiful, exact, etc.; thoroughly; quite [to understand *fully;* to be *fully* ripe].
**ful·mi·nate** (ful′mə nāt) ***v.*** **1** to protest, argue, or blame in a loud or strong way. **2** to explode. —**ful′mi·nat·ed, ful′mi·nat·ing** —**ful′mi·na′tion *n.***
**ful·some** (fool′səm) ***adj.*** so full of praise, sweetness, etc. as to be sickening; annoying because not sincere [*fulsome* flattery].
**Ful·ton** (fool′t'n), **Robert** 1765–1815; U.S. engineer. He invented a steamboat.
**fum·ble** (fum′b'l) ***v.*** **1** to handle or grope about in a clumsy way [She *fumbled* for the keys in her purse.] **2** to lose one's grasp on something while trying to catch or hold it [to *fumble* a football]. —**fum′bled, fum′bling** ◆***n.*** the act of fumbling.
**fume** (fyōōm) ***n.*** *often* **fumes,** *pl.* a gas, smoke, or vapor, especially if harmful or bad-smelling. ◆***v.*** **1** to give off fumes. **2** to show that one is angry or irritated [He *fumed* at the long delay.] —**fumed, fum′ing**
**fu·mi·gate** (fyōō′mə gāt) ***v.*** to fill a place with fumes so as to get rid of germs, insects, mice, etc. —**fu′mi·gat·ed, fu′mi·gat·ing** —**fu′mi·ga′tion *n.***
**fun** (fun) ***n.*** lively play or joking that lets one enjoy oneself; a happy or joyful time, or something that gives this; amusement. ◆☆***adj.*** giving pleasure; amusing: *used only in everyday talk* [a *fun* party]. —**for fun** or **in fun,** just for amusement; not seriously. —**make fun of,** to make jokes about; ridicule.
**func·tion** (fungk′shən) ***n.*** **1** special or typical work or purpose of a thing or person [The *function* of the brakes is to stop the car.] **2** a formal party or an important ceremony. ◆***v.*** **1** to do its work; act [The motor is not *functioning* properly.] **2** to be used [that table can *function* as a desk.] —**func′tion·al *adj.*** —**func′tion·al·ly *adv.***
**func·tion·ar·y** (fungk′shən er′ē) ***n.*** a person with a certain function; official. —*pl.* **func′tion·ar′ies**
**fund** (fund) ***n.*** **1** an amount of money to be used for a particular purpose [a scholarship *fund*]. **2 funds,** *pl.* money on hand, ready for use. **3** a supply; stock [a *fund* of good will].
**fun·da·men·tal** (fun′də men′t'l) ***adj.*** of or forming a basis or foundation; basic [Freedom of the press is *fundamental* to democracy.] ◆***n.*** a fundamental or basic thing; very necessary part [Mathematics is one of the *fundamentals* of science.] —**fun′da·men′tal·ly *adv.***

> **Fundamental** comes from a Latin word meaning "to put a bottom in." Something that is fundamental is at the bottom and makes a foundation for something else.

**Fun·dy** (fun′dē), **Bay of** a bay of the Atlantic between New Brunswick and Nova Scotia, Canada.
**fu·ner·al** (fyōō′nər əl) ***n.*** the services held when a dead person is buried or cremated. ◆***adj.*** of or for a funeral [a *funeral* march].
**funeral director** a person whose business is taking care of funerals.
**fu·ne·re·al** (fyoo nir′ē əl) ***adj.*** fit for a funeral; sad or gloomy; mournful.
**fun·gous** (fung′gəs) ***adj.*** of, like, or caused by a fungus.
**fun·gus** (fung′gəs) ***n.*** a plant that has no leaves, flowers, or green color. Mildews, molds, mushrooms, and toadstools are forms of fungus. *See the picture.* —*pl.* **fun·gi** (fun′jī *or* fung′gī) or **fun′gus·es**
**funk** (fungk) ***n.*** the condition of being greatly afraid or in a panic: *used only in everyday talk.*
**fun·nel** (fun′'l) ***n.*** **1** a slender tube with a wide cone at one end, used for pouring liquids, powders, etc. into narrow openings. *See the picture.* **2** a smokestack on a steamship. ◆***v.*** **1** to move or pour as through a funnel. **2** to move into a central channel or place [Traffic was *funneled* into a single lane.] —**fun′neled** or **fun′nelled, fun′nel·ing** or **fun′nel·ling**
**fun·ny** (fun′ē) ***adj.*** **1** causing smiles or laughter; amusing; comical. **2** odd or unusual: *used only in everyday talk* [It's *funny* that he's late.] —**fun′ni·er, fun′ni·est** ◆☆***n.*** *usually* **funnies,** *pl.* comic strips: *used only in everyday talk.* —☆**get funny with,** to be rude to: *used only in everyday talk.* —*pl.* **fun′nies** —**fun′ni·ness *n.***



> SYNONYMS: **Funny** is used for anything that causes laughter [a *funny* clown; a *funny* joke]. **Laughable** is usually used for something that is fit to be laughed at, especially with scorn [What a *laughable* excuse!] Something that is **amusing** causes laughter or smiles because it is pleasant or entertains [an *amusing* play].

**fur** (fur) ***n.*** **1** the soft, thick hair that covers many animals. **2** an animal's skin with such hair on it [The trapper traded the *furs* he had for food.] **3** a coat, scarf, etc. made of such skins. **4** a fuzzy coating, as on the tongue during illness. ◆***adj.*** of fur [a *fur* coat]. ◆***v.*** to make, cover, or trim with fur. —**furred, fur′ring**
**fur·be·low** (fur′bə lō) ***n.*** *usually* **furbelows,** *pl.* showy but useless trimmings [frills and *furbelows*].
**fur·bish** (fur′bish) ***v.*** **1** to brighten by rubbing; polish. **2** to put into better condition; clean or freshen up [to *furbish* up an old sofa].
**fu·ri·ous** (fyoor′ē əs) ***adj.*** **1** full of fury or wild anger. **2** very fierce, strong, wild, etc. [*furious* activity]. —**fu′ri·ous·ly *adv.***
**furl** (furl) ***v.*** to roll up tightly around a staff or mast, as a flag or sail. *See the picture.*
**fur·long** (fur′lông) ***n.*** a measure of distance equal to 1/8 of a mile, or 220 yards.

| | | | | | | | |
|---|---|---|---|---|---|---|---|
| a | fat | ir | here | ou | out | zh | leisure |
| ā | ape | ī | bite, fire | u | up | ng | ring |
| ä | car, lot | ō | go | ur | fur | | a *in* ago |
| e | ten | ô | law, horn | ch | chin | | e *in* agent |
| er | care | oi | oil | sh | she | ə = | i *in* unity |
| ē | even | oo | look | th | thin | | o *in* collect |
| i | hit | ōō | tool | *th* | then | | u *in* focus |

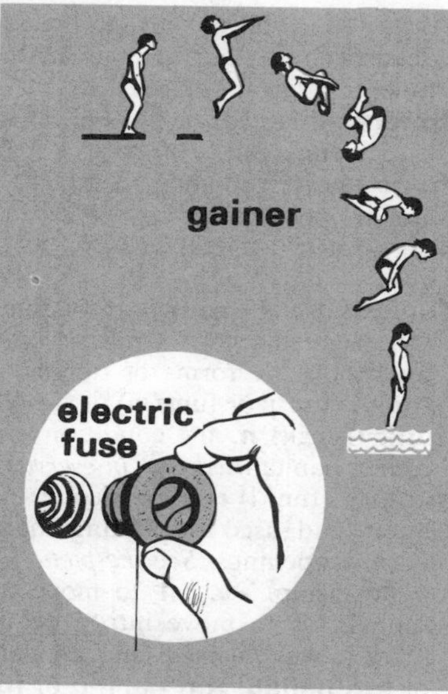


**fur·lough** (fʉr′lō) ***n.*** a vacation given to a soldier or sailor. ➧☆***v.*** to give a furlough to.

**fur·nace** (fʉr′nəs) ***n.*** an enclosed place in which heat is produced, as by burning fuel, for warming a building, melting ores and metals, etc.

**fur·nish** (fʉr′nish) ***v.*** **1** to give whatever is needed; supply [to *furnish* a lawyer with facts]. **2** to put furniture in [to *furnish* a home].



**fur·nish·ings** (fʉr′nish iŋz) ***n.pl.*** **1** furniture, carpets, etc., as for a house. **2** things to wear; clothing [men's *furnishings*].

**fur·ni·ture** (fʉr′ni chər) ***n.*** the things needed for living in a house, as chairs, beds, tables, etc.

**fu·ror** (fyoor′ôr) ***n.*** **1** great excitement or enthusiasm [Her new book has caused quite a *furor*.] **2** wild anger; rage [the *furor* of the mob].

**furred** (fʉrd) ***adj.*** **1** made, trimmed, or lined with fur [a *furred* robe]. **2** having fur [a *furred* animal].

**fur·ri·er** (fʉr′ē ər) ***n.*** a person who deals in furs, especially one who prepares furs for use or who makes and repairs fur garments.

**fur·row** (fʉr′ō) ***n.*** **1** a long groove made in the ground by a plow. **2** anything like this, as a deep wrinkle on the face. ➧***v.*** to make furrows in [Trouble has *furrowed* his brow.]

**fur·ry** (fʉr′ē) ***adj.*** **1** covered with fur [a *furry* kitten]. **2** of or like fur [*furry* cloth]. —**fur′ri·er, fur′ri·est**

**fur·ther** (fʉr′*th*ər) ***adj.*** **1** more; added [I have no *further* news.] **2** more distant. ➧***adv.*** **1** to a greater extent; more [I'll study it *further*.] **2** in addition; moreover; besides [*Further,* I want you to leave at once.] **3** at or to a greater distance. *See the note in color following* **farther**. ➧***v.*** to help onward; promote [to *further* the cause of education]. *See* SYNONYMS *at* **advance.**

**fur·ther·ance** (fʉr′*th*ər əns) ***n.*** a furthering, or helping onward [the *furtherance* of a plan].

**fur·ther·more** (fʉr′*th*ər môr) ***adv.*** besides; also; moreover.

**fur·ther·most** (fʉr′*th*ər mōst) ***adj.*** most distant; furthest.

**fur·thest** (fʉr′*th*ist) ***adj.*** most distant; farthest. ➧***adv.*** to the greatest extent; most [Your ideas are the *furthest* removed from mine.]

**fur·tive** (fʉr′tiv) ***adj.*** done or acting in a sly, sneaky way; stealthy [a *furtive* glance]. —**fur′tive·ly *adv.*** —**fur′tive·ness *n.***

**fu·ry** (fyoor′ē) ***n.*** **1** wild anger; great rage [She is in a *fury* over her wrecked car.] *See* SYNONYMS *at* **anger.** **2** rough or wild force; fierceness [The *fury* of the storm blew down the tall tree.] **3** a wild or raging person. —*pl.* **fu′ries**

**furze** (fʉrz) ***n.*** a prickly evergreen shrub with yellow flowers, growing wild in Europe.

**fuse**[1] (fyo͞oz) ***v.*** **1** to melt or to join by melting, as metals. **2** to join together completely; unite [I was able to *fuse* my interests with theirs.] —**fused, fus′ing**

**fuse**[2] (fyo͞oz) ***n.*** **1** a wick on a bomb, firecracker, etc. that is lighted to set off the explosion. **2** a strip of metal that melts easily, usually set in a plug that is made part of an electric circuit as a safety device. If the current becomes too strong, the fuse melts and breaks the circuit. *See the picture.*

**fu·se·lage** (fyo͞o′sə läzh *or* fyo͞o′zə läj) ***n.*** the body of an airplane, not including the wings, tail, and engines.

**fu·si·ble** (fyo͞o′zə b′l) ***adj.*** that can be fused or melted. —**fu′si·bil′i·ty *n.***

**fu·sil·ier** or **fu·sil·eer** (fyo͞o zə lir′) ***n.*** a soldier of earlier times armed with a light flintlock musket. The name *Fusiliers* is still given to some British regiments.

**fu·sil·lade** (fyo͞o′sə lād *or* fyo͞o′zə läd) ***n.*** **1** a shooting of many guns at the same time. **2** something like this [a *fusillade* of questions].

**fu·sion** (fyo͞o′zhən) ***n.*** a fusing, melting, or joining together: *see also* **nuclear fusion.**

**fuss** (fus) ***n.*** **1** too much bother or worry; nervous or excited action over a small thing [All this *fuss* over some spilled water!] **2** a great display of pleasure: *used only in everyday talk* [They made a big *fuss* over the baby.] ☆**3** a quarrel or argument: *used only in everyday talk.* ➧***v.*** to bustle about or bother with small things.

**fuss·y** (fus′ē) ***adj.*** **1** always fussing; too nervous or too particular about things [a *fussy* parent; to be *fussy* about one's food]. **2** full of many small details that are not needed [a *fussy* painting]. —**fuss′i·er, fuss′i·est** —**fuss′i·ness *n.***

**fus·ty** (fus′tē) ***adj.*** **1** smelling stale or moldy; musty. **2** not up-to-date; old-fashioned. —**fus′ti·er, fus′ti·est**

**fu·tile** (fyo͞ot′'l) ***adj.*** **1** that could not succeed; hopeless; useless [a *futile* attempt to climb the wall]. **2** not important because not likely to have results [a *futile* discussion]. —**fu′tile·ly *adv.*** —**fu·til·i·ty** (fyoo til′ə tē) ***n.***

> SYNONYMS: Something is **futile** if it fails completely [Their attempts to save money were *futile*.] Something is **vain** that fails in what was attempted, but not in the hopeless or useless way that **futile** suggests [The doctor made a *vain* but brave effort to save the dying patient.]

**fu·ture** (fyo͞o′chər) ***adj.*** **1** in the time to come; after the present time [a *future* date; my *future* happiness]. **2** showing time to come ["Shall" and "will" are used with a verb to express *future* tense.] ➧***n.*** **1** the time that is to come [We'll buy a new car sometime in the *future.*] **2** what is going to be [We all have some control over the *future.*] **3** chance to succeed [She has a great *future* as a lawyer.] —**fu′tur·is′tic** ***adj.***

**fu·tur·i·ty** (fyo͞o to͝or′ə tē *or* fyo͞o tyo͝or′ə tē) ***n.*** **1** the future. **2** a future condition or event. —*pl.* **fu·tur′i·ties**

**fuze** (fyo͞oz) ***n.*** *another spelling of* **fuse²**.

**fuzz** (fuz) ***n.*** soft, light hairs or fibers [the *fuzz* on a cheek or on a peach].

**fuzz·y** (fuz′ē) ***adj.*** **1** of, like, or covered with fuzz [a *fuzzy* sweater]. **2** not clear or distinct; blurred [a *fuzzy* picture on TV]. —**fuzz′i·er, fuzz′i·est** —**fuzz′i·ness** ***n.***

**fwd.** *abbreviation for* **forward**.

**-fy** (fī) *a suffix meaning:* **1** to make or become [To *purify* is to make pure. To *putrefy* is to become putrid.] **2** to make have or feel [To *terrify* is to make feel terror.]

**G, g** (jē) ***n.*** the seventh letter of the English alphabet. —*pl.* **G′s, g′s** (jēz)

☆**G** general audience: a movie rating meaning that the film is considered suitable for persons of all ages.

**G.** or **g.** *abbreviation for* **gram** *or* **grams**.

**Ga.** or **GA** *abbreviation for* **Georgia**.

**gab** (gab) ***v.*** to talk a great deal or in an idle way; chatter. —**gabbed, gab′bing** ♦***n.*** idle talk; chatter. *This word is used only in everyday talk.*

**gab·ar·dine** (gab′ər dēn) ***n.*** **1** a closely woven cloth with fine, slanting ribs, used in suits, coats, etc. **2** a garment made of this cloth. *The usual British spelling is* **gaberdine**.

**gab·ble** (gab′′l) ***v.*** to talk rapidly without making any sense; jabber. —**gab′bled, gab′bling** ♦***n.*** rapid talk that does not make any sense [the *gabble* of the crowd leaving the theater].

**gab·by** (gab′ē) ***adj.*** talking too much: *used only in everyday talk.* —**gab′bi·er, gab′bi·est**

**ga·ble** (gā′b′l) ***n.*** the triangle formed in a wall of a building by the sloping ends of a ridged roof. *See the picture.*

**ga·bled** (gā′b′ld) ***adj.*** having or forming a gable or gables [a *gabled* roof].

**Ga·bon** (gä bōn′) a country in west central Africa, on the Atlantic Ocean.

**Ga·bri·el** (gā′brē əl) in the Bible, an angel who acts as God's messenger.

**gad** (gad) ***v.*** to wander about in an idle or restless way, as in looking for excitement. —**gad′ded, gad′ding**

**gad·a·bout** (gad′ə bout) ***n.*** a person who goes about looking for fun and excitement.

**gad·fly** (gad′flī) ***n.*** **1** a large fly that stings cattle and horses. **2** a person who annoys others, especially by trying to stir them to action. —*pl.* **gad′flies**

**gadg·et** (gaj′it) ***n.*** **1** a small, mechanical thing having some special use [a *gadget* for opening cans]. **2** any interesting but not very useful device.

**Gael·ic** (gāl′ik) ***n.*** the Celtic language of the Scottish Highlands and of Ireland. ♦***adj.*** of this language or of the people who speak it.

**gaff** (gaf) ***n.*** **1** a large hook or spear, used in lifting large fish out of the water. **2** a spar or pole holding up the upper edge of a fore-and-aft sail. *See the picture.* ♦***v.*** to hook or pull in a fish with a gaff. —☆**stand the gaff,** to bear up well under trouble: *a slang phrase.*

**gag** (gag) ***v.*** **1** to strain or choke as in vomiting; retch or make retch. **2** to keep from talking or crying out, as by covering the mouth. —**gagged, gag′ging** ♦***n.*** **1** a thing that gags, or keeps one from talking. **2** a joke.



**gage¹** (gāj) ***n.*** **1** a glove thrown down by a knight challenging another to fight. **2** a challenge. **3** something given as a pledge.

**gage²** (gāj) ***n., v.*** *another spelling of* **gauge**.

**gai·e·ty** (gā′ə tē) ***n.*** **1** the condition of being gay; cheerfulness. **2** lively fun; merrymaking. **3** showy brightness. —*pl.* **gai′e·ties**

**gai·ly** (gā′lē) ***adv.*** **1** in a gay manner; happily; merrily. **2** brightly [in a *gaily* decorated hall].

**gain** (gān) ***n.*** **1** a thing or amount added; increase or addition [a *gain* in weight]. **2** *often* **gains,** *pl.* profit or winnings [the *gains* from our business]. **3** the act of getting something, especially money [A love of *gain* can make a person greedy.] ♦***v.*** **1** to get by trying hard or as a reward; win; earn [to *gain* a living; to *gain* first prize]. **2** to get as an increase or advantage [He *gained* ten pounds in two months.] **3** to be fast or go faster by [My watch *gained* two minutes.] **4** to get to; reach [We *gained* our destination after hours of driving.] **5** to become better; improve [She *gained* in health.] —**gain on, 1** to draw nearer to, as in a race. **2** to do better than.

**gain·er** (gā′nər) ***n.*** **1** a person or thing that gains. **2** a fancy dive in which the diver faces forward and does a backward somersault in the air. *See the picture.*

| | | | | | | | |
|---|---|---|---|---|---|---|---|
| **a** | fat | **ir** | here | **ou** | out | **zh** | leisure |
| **ā** | ape | **ī** | bite, fire | **u** | up | **ng** | ring |
| **ä** | car, lot | **ō** | go | **ur** | fur | | a *in* ago |
| **e** | ten | **ô** | law, horn | **ch** | chin | | e *in* agent |
| **er** | care | **oi** | oil | **sh** | she | **ə =** | i *in* unity |
| **ē** | even | **o͝o** | look | **th** | thin | | o *in* collect |
| **i** | hit | **o͞o** | tool | ***th*** | then | | u *in* focus |

**gain·ful** (gān′fəl) ***adj.*** bringing gain or profit [*gainful* employment]. —**gain′ful·ly** ***adv.***

**gain·say** (gān sā′) ***v.*** to deny or contradict [Who could *gainsay* the truth of that statement?] —**gain·said** (gān sed′), **gain·say′ing**

**gait** (gāt) ***n.*** a way of walking or running [The old caretaker had a shuffling *gait.* Pacing and trotting are two different *gaits* used by horses.]

**gai·ter** (gāt′ər) ***n.*** a cloth or leather covering for the lower part of the leg; spat or legging.

**gal** (gal) ***n.*** a girl: *used only in everyday talk.*

**gal.** *abbreviation for* **gallon** *or* **gallons.**

**ga·la** (gā′lə *or* gal′ə) ***adj.*** of, for, or like a joyous or merry celebration; festive [a *gala* occasion]. ◆***n.*** a joyous celebration; festival.

**Gal·a·had** (gal′ə had) the purest knight of King Arthur's Round Table.

**Ga·la·tians** (gə lā′shənz) a book of the New Testament written by the Apostle Paul.

**gal·ax·y** (gal′ək sē) *often* **Galaxy,** *another name for* **Milky Way.** ◆***n.*** **1** any vast group of stars. **2** a group of very famous people. *—pl.* **gal′ax·ies**

> **Galaxy** comes from a Greek word meaning "milk." The *Milky Way* gets its name from the cloudy or milky appearance it has in the sky.

**gale** (gāl) ***n.*** **1** a strong wind. ☆**2** a loud outburst, as of laughter.

**ga·le·na** (gə lē′nə) ***n.*** a gray mineral that is the chief ore in which lead is found.



**Gal·i·le·an** (gal′ə lē′ən) ***adj.*** of Galilee or its people. ◆***n.*** a person born or living in Galilee. —**the Galilean,** Jesus.

**Gal·i·lee** (gal′ə lē) a region of northern Israel.

**Galilee, Sea of** a lake of northeastern Israel, on the Syria border.

**Gal·i·le·o** (gal′ə lē′ō) 1564–1642; an Italian astronomer who proved that the planets move around the sun.

**gall**[1] (gôl) ***n.*** **1** bile, the bitter liquid made by the liver. **2** bitter feeling. **3** rude boldness; impudence: *used only in everyday talk.*

**gall**[2] (gôl) ***n.*** a sore made by rubbing, especially on a horse's back. ◆***v.*** **1** to make sore by rubbing. **2** to annoy or irritate [The thought of losing *galled* Don.] —**gall′ing** ***adj.***

**gall**[3] (gôl) ***n.*** a lump that grows on the parts of a plant hurt by insects, bacteria, etc.

**gal·lant** (gal′ənt) ***adj.*** **1** brave and noble; daring. **2** (*usually* gə lant′) very polite and respectful to women. —**gal′lant·ly** ***adv.***

**gal·lant·ry** (gal′ən trē) ***n.*** **1** great courage. **2** very polite behavior, especially toward women. **3** a polite act or remark. *—pl.* **gal′lant·ries**

**gall·blad·der** (gôl′blad′ər) ***n.*** a small sac attached to the liver: the gall, or bile, is stored in it.

**gal·le·on** (gal′ē ən) ***n.*** a large Spanish sailing ship of olden times, having three or four decks.

**gal·ler·y** (gal′ə rē) ***n.*** **1** a balcony, especially the highest balcony in a theater, etc.: it usually has the cheapest seats. **2** the people who sit in these seats. **3** the public in general; ordinary people. **4** a long hall or corridor, often open or with windows at one side. **5** a room, building, or place for showing or selling works of art. ☆**6** any room used for a special purpose, as for shooting at targets. *—pl.* **gal′ler·ies**

**gal·ley** (gal′ē) ***n.*** **1** a large, low ship of long ago, having both sails and many oars. The oars were usually rowed by slaves or prisoners in chains. *See the picture.* **2** the kitchen of a ship. *—pl.* **gal′leys**

**Gal·lic** (gal′ik) ***adj.*** **1** of ancient Gaul or its people. **2** French [a *Gallic* saying].

**gal·li·vant** (gal′ə vant) ***v.*** to wander about looking for fun or excitement; gad about.

**gal·lon** (gal′ən) ***n.*** a measure of liquids, equal to four quarts or eight pints. One gallon equals 3.785 liters.

**gal·lop** (gal′əp) ***n.*** **1** the fastest gait of a horse, etc. In a gallop, all four feet are off the ground at the same time in each stride. **2** a ride on a galloping animal. ◆***v.*** **1** to go or ride at a gallop. **2** to move very fast; hurry.

**gal·lows** (gal′ōz) ***n.*** **1** a wooden framework with a rope by which people are hanged as a punishment. **2** the punishment of death by hanging. *—pl.* **gal·lows·es** (gal′ō zəz) or **gal′lows**

**ga·lore** (gə lôr′) ***adv.*** in great plenty [to have fun *galore;* to attract crowds *galore*].

**ga·losh** (gə läsh′) ***n.*** a high overshoe worn in wet weather or snow.

**gal·van·ic** (gal van′ik) ***adj.*** of or caused by an electric current, especially from a battery.

**gal·va·nize** (gal′və nīz) ***v.*** **1** to apply an electric current to. **2** to shock or startle someone into doing something. **3** to coat with a layer of zinc [Iron is often *galvanized* to keep it from rusting.] —**gal′va·nized, gal′va·niz·ing**

**Gam·bi·a** (gam′bē ə) a country in western Africa, on the Atlantic Ocean.

**gam·bit** (gam′bit) ***n.*** **1** an opening move in chess in which a pawn or other piece is risked to get some advantage. **2** any action used to get an advantage.

**gam·ble** (gam′b′l) ***v.*** **1** to take part in games in which the players bet, as poker or dice. **2** to bet or wager. **3** to risk losing something in trying to gain something else [Bill is *gambling* that if he drops out of school now he can get a good job.] —**gam′bled, gam′bling** ◆***n.*** an act by which one gambles or risks something [Starting a new business is usually a *gamble.*] —**gamble away,** to lose in gambling. —**gam′bler** ***n.***

**gam·bol** (gam′b′l) ***v.*** to jump and skip about in play, as lambs do; frolic. —**gam′boled** or **gam′bolled, gam′bol·ing** or **gam′bol·ling** ◆***n.*** the act of gamboling; frolic.

☆**gam·brel roof** (gam′brəl) a roof with two slopes on each side. *See the picture.*

**game**[1] (gām) ***n.*** **1** a sport or kind of contest carried on according to rules by persons or teams playing against each other [Baseball and chess are *games.*] **2** any form of play or test of skill [the *game* of love; the *game* of life]. **3** the set of things used in playing a game [Helen received some books and *games* for her birthday.] **4** wild animals or birds hunted for sport or food; also, their flesh used as food. **5** a scheme or plan [We both saw through his *game.*] ◆***adj.*** **1** describing or having to do with wild animals or birds that are hunted [a *game* bird; a *game* warden]. **2** brave in a stubborn way; plucky [a *game* fighter]. —**gam′er, gam′est** ◆***v.*** to gamble. —**gamed, gam′-**

ing —**make game of,** to make fun of; ridicule. —**game'ly** ***adv.*** —**game'ness** ***n.***

**game²** (gām) ***adj.*** lame or injured: *used only in everyday talk* [a *game* leg].

**game·cock** (gām'käk) ***n.*** a rooster bred and trained for fighting other roosters.

**game·some** (gām'səm) ***adj.*** playful; full of fun [in a *gamesome* mood]. —**game'some·ly** ***adv.***

**game·ster** (gām'stər) ***n.*** a person who gambles.

**gam·in** (gam'ən) ***n.*** **1** a child who has no home and roams the streets. **2** a saucy, charming girl.

**gam·ing** (gā'miŋ) ***n.*** the act of gambling.

**gam·ma** (gam'ə) ***n.*** the third letter of the Greek alphabet.

**gam·ut** (gam'ət) ***n.*** **1** the whole musical scale of notes. **2** the full range of anything [the *gamut* of emotions, from joy to grief].

**gam·y** (gā'mē) ***adj.*** **1** having a strong flavor, like that of cooked game. **2** plucky; brave. —**gam'i·er, gam'i·est**

**gan·der** (gan'dər) ***n.*** a male goose.

**Gan·dhi** (gän'dē *or* gan'dē), **Mo·han·das** (mō hän'dəs) **K.** 1869–1948; political leader and reformer in India: *often called* **Mahatma Gandhi.**

**gang** (gaŋ) ***n.*** **1** a group of people who work together or spend much time together [a railroad *gang;* a neighborhood *gang*]. **2** a group of criminals. **3** a set of tools, machines, or parts arranged to work together [A *gang* plow has a number of plowshares fastened side by side.] —☆**gang up on,** to attack or oppose as a group: *used only in everyday talk.*

**Gan·ges** (gan'jēz) a river in northern India.

**gan·gling** (gaŋ'gliŋ) ***adj.*** tall, thin, and awkward; lanky [a *gangling* teen-ager].

☆**gang·plank** (gaŋ'plaŋk) ***n.*** a movable ramp by which people board or leave a ship. *See the picture.*

**gan·grene** (gaŋ'grēn) ***n.*** decay of some part of the body from which the blood is blocked by injury or disease [Frostbite can cause *gangrene* in a toe.] —**gan·gre·nous** (gaŋ'grə nəs) ***adj.***

☆**gang·ster** (gaŋ'stər) ***n.*** a member of a gang of criminals.

**gang·way** (gaŋ'wā) ***n.*** **1** a passageway into or out of a ship. **2** *another name for* **gangplank.** ◆***interj.*** move out of the way!

**gan·net** (gan'it) ***n.*** a large sea bird that looks like a goose.

**gant·let** (gônt'lit *or* gant'lit) ***n.*** a punishment in which a person was made to run between two lines of men who struck him with clubs or switches as he ran past: *this word is very often spelled* **gauntlet.**

**gan·try** (gan'trē) ***n.*** **1** a framework like a bridge, as one on wheels, used for carrying a traveling crane. ☆**2** a framework on wheels with a crane and several platforms, used for getting a rocket in position at its launching site and servicing it. —*pl.* **gan'tries**

**gaol** (jāl) ***n.*** *British spelling of* **jail.** —**gaol'er** ***n.***

**gap** (gap) ***n.*** **1** an opening made by breaking, tearing, etc. [a *gap* in a wall]. **2** a mountain pass. **3** an empty space; break or blank [a *gap* in one's memory].

**gape** (gāp) ***v.*** **1** to open the mouth wide, as in yawning. **2** to stare with the mouth open [The child *gaped* at the elephants.] *See the picture.* **3** to be wide open [a *gaping* hole]. —**gaped, gap'ing** ◆***n.*** the act of gaping.

boy gaping in wonder

gambrel roof

gargoyle

galley

gangplank

**ga·rage** (gə räzh' *or* gə räj') ***n.*** **1** a closed place where automobiles are sheltered. **2** a place where automobiles are repaired.



**garb** (gärb) ***n.*** clothing; style of dress [The ushers were in formal *garb.*] ◆***v.*** to dress or clothe.

**gar·bage** (gär'bij) ***n.*** spoiled or waste food that is thrown away.

**gar·ble** (gär'b'l) ***v.*** to mix up or leave out parts of a story or report, so that what is told is false or not clear. —**gar'bled, gar'bling**

**gar·den** (gär'd'n) ***n.*** a piece of ground where flowers, vegetables, etc. are grown. ◆***v.*** to take care of a garden. —**gar·den·er** (gärd'nər) ***n.***

☆**gar·de·nia** (gär dēn'yə) ***n.*** a flower with waxy, white petals and a very sweet odor.

**Gar·field** (gär'fēld), **James A**(**bram**) 1831–1881; the 20th president of the United States, in 1881. He was assassinated.

**gar·gle** (gär'g'l) ***v.*** to rinse the throat with a liquid that is moved about by forcing the breath out with the head held back. —**gar'gled, gar'gling** ◆***n.*** a liquid used for gargling.

**gar·goyle** (gär'goil) ***n.*** a decoration on a building in the form of a strange, imaginary creature. It usually has a channel to let rain water run off through its mouth. *See the picture.*

**gar·ish** (ger'ish) ***adj.*** bright and showy in an unattractive way; gaudy. —**gar'ish·ly** ***adv.*** —**gar'ish·ness** ***n.***

| | | | | | | | |
|---|---|---|---|---|---|---|---|
| **a** | fat | **ir** | here | **ou** | out | **zh** | leisure |
| **ā** | ape | **ī** | bite, fire | **u** | up | **ŋ** | ring |
| **ä** | car, lot | **ō** | go | **ur** | fur | | a *in* ago |
| **e** | ten | **ô** | law, horn | **ch** | chin | | e *in* agent |
| **er** | care | **oi** | oil | **sh** | she | **ə** = | i *in* unity |
| **ē** | even | **oo** | look | **th** | thin | | o *in* collect |
| **i** | hit | **ōō** | tool | ***th*** | then | | u *in* focus |

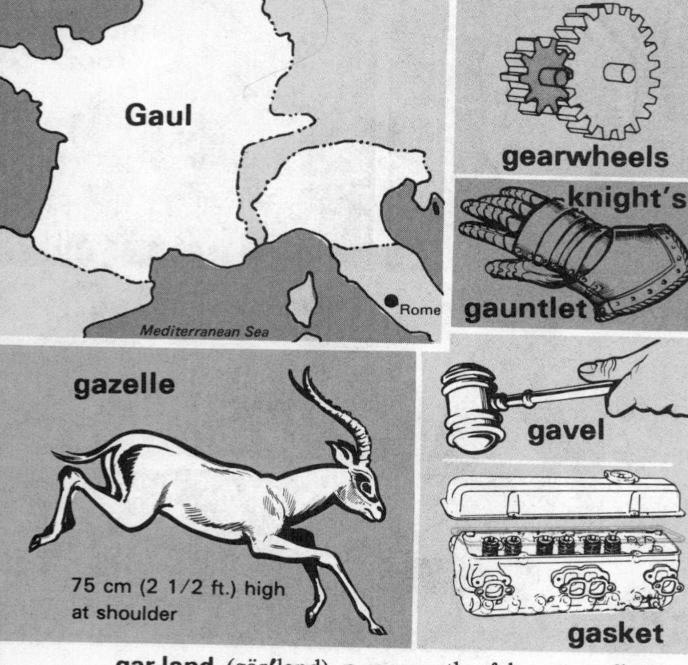


**gar·land** (gär′lənd) ***n.*** a wreath of leaves or flowers. ◆***v.*** to decorate with garlands.

304 **gar·lic** (gär′lik) ***n.*** a plant related to the onion, with a strong-smelling bulb used as a seasoning.

**gar·ment** (gär′mənt) ***n.*** any piece of clothing.

**gar·ner** (gär′nər) ***v.*** to gather and store up, as grain. ◆***n.*** a storehouse for grain.

**gar·net** (gär′nit) ***n.*** **1** a clear, deep-red stone that is used as a jewel. **2** deep red.

**gar·nish** (gär′nish) ***v.*** to decorate; especially, to decorate food to make it look or taste better [to *garnish* ham with parsley]. ◆***n.*** something used in garnishing.

**gar·nish·ee** (gär nə shē′) ***v.*** to hold back wages from someone who owes a debt, so that the money can be used to pay the debt. —**gar·nish·eed′**, **gar·nish·ee′-ing**

**gar·ret** (gar′it) ***n.*** the room or space just below the slanting roof of a house; attic.

**gar·ri·son** (gar′ə s′n) ***n.*** **1** soldiers stationed in a fort or town to protect it. **2** such a place with its soldiers, guns, etc.; military post. ◆***v.*** to put soldiers in a fort, town, etc. to protect it.

**gar·ru·lous** (gar′ə ləs *or* gar′yoo ləs) ***adj.*** talking too much, especially about unimportant things; talkative.

**gar·ter** (gär′tər) ***n.*** an elastic band or strap worn to hold up a stocking or sock.

> **Garter** comes from an old French word meaning "small of the leg behind the knee." Most garters go around the leg just below the knee.

☆**garter snake** a small, striped snake of North America that is not poisonous.

**Gar·vey** (gär′vē), **Marcus** 1880–1940; black political leader in the U.S., born in Jamaica.

**gas** (gas) ***n.*** **1** a substance that has the same form as air and can spread out so as to take up all the space open to it. Gas is a form of matter that is neither liquid nor solid [Oxygen and carbon dioxide are *gases.*] **2** any mixture of gases that will burn easily, used for lighting and heating. **3** any gas used as an anesthetic. **4** any substance used, as in war, to make the air poisonous or very irritating. ☆**5** *a shorter form of* **gasoline**: *used only in everyday talk.* —*pl.* **gas′es** ◆***v.*** **1** to attack, hurt, or kill with poison gas. ☆**2** to talk in an idle or boastful way: *a slang meaning.* —**gassed**, **gas′sing**

**gas·e·ous** (gas′ē əs *or* gas′yəs) ***adj.*** of, like, or in the form of gas.

**gash** (gash) ***v.*** to make a long, deep cut in. ◆***n.*** a long, deep cut.

**gas·ket** (gas′kit) ***n.*** a ring or piece of rubber, metal, etc. fitted tightly around a joint to keep it from leaking. *See the picture.*

**gas mask** a mask with a filter, worn over the face to prevent the breathing in of poisonous gases.

☆**gas·o·line** or **gas·o·lene** (gas ə lēn′ *or* gas′ə lēn) ***n.*** a pale liquid that burns very easily and is used mainly as a fuel in motor engines. It is made from petroleum.

**gasp** (gasp) ***v.*** **1** to breathe in suddenly, as in surprise, or breathe with effort, as in choking. **2** to say or tell with gasps [She *gasped* out her story.] ◆***n.*** the act of gasping [a *gasp* of horror].

☆**gas station** *another name for* **service station.**

**gas·tric** (gas′trik) ***adj.*** of, in, or near the stomach [*gastric* juices; *gastric* pains].

**gas·tron·o·my** (gas trän′ə mē) ***n.*** the art of good eating.

**gate** (gāt) ***n.*** **1** a door in a fence or outside wall, especially one that swings on hinges. **2** *a shorter form of* **gateway**. **3** a door, valve, etc. that controls the flow of water, as in a canal or pipe. **4** the number of people who have paid to see a certain sports contest, exhibition, etc.

☆**gate-crash·er** (gāt′krash′ər) ***n.*** a person who goes to a party, dance, etc. without being invited or who goes to see a play, game, etc. without paying to get in.

**gate·leg table** (gāt′leg) a table with drop leaves that rest on legs that swing out like gates. When the leaves are not in use, the legs are swung back against the frame so that the leaves can drop to the sides.

**gate·way** (gāt′wā) ***n.*** **1** an opening in a wall or fence with a gate fitted into it. **2** a way of getting in, out, or at [St. Louis is called the *gateway* to the West. Study is the *gateway* to knowledge.]

**gath·er** (ga*th*′ər) ***v.*** **1** to bring or come together in one place or group [The child *gathered* her toys together. The families *gathered* for a reunion.] **2** to get or collect gradually; accumulate [to *gather* wealth; to *gather* one's strength; to *gather* news for a paper]. **3** to pick or glean [to *gather* crops]. **4** to get as an idea; conclude [I *gather* that he is rich.] **5** to gain gradually [The train *gathered* speed.] **6** to pull together so as to make folds or pleats [to *gather* cloth]. **7** to fill with pus and come to a head, as a boil. ◆***n.*** a single pleat or fold in cloth. —**gath′er·er** ***n.***

> SYNONYMS: **Gather** is used for any kind of bringing or coming together [We *gathered* fallen leaves. Storm clouds *gathered.*] **Collect** is used of gathering done by choosing or arranging carefully [He *collects* coins.] **Assemble** is used of any special gathering together of persons [Citizens *assembled* in the town hall.]

**gath·er·ing** (ga*th*′ər iŋ) ***n.*** **1** a coming together of people; meeting. **2** a boil or abscess.

**gau·cho** (gou′chō) ***n.*** a cowboy living on the South American pampas. *—pl.* **gau′chos**

**gaud·y** (gôd′ē) ***adj.*** bright and showy in a cheap way; not in good taste. **—gaud′i·er, gaud′i·est —gaud′i·ly *adv.* —gaud′i·ness *n.***

**gauge** (gāj) ***n.*** **1** a standard for measuring size, thickness, etc.; also, a measure according to such a standard [The *gauge* of a railway tells how far apart the rails are. The *gauge* of a wire tells how thick it is.] **2** any device for measuring something, as steam or air pressure, the thickness of wire, etc. ◆***v.*** **1** to measure exactly the size or amount of. **2** to judge or estimate [to *gauge* a person's honesty]. **—gauged, gaug′ing —gaug′er *n.***

**Gau·guin** (gō gan′), **Paul** 1848–1903; French painter, in Tahiti after 1891.

**Gaul** (gôl) a part of the empire of ancient Rome, including mainly what is now France and some regions around it. *See the map.* ◆***n.*** any of the people who lived in Gaul.

**gaunt** (gônt) ***adj.*** **1** so thin that the bones show; worn and lean, as from hunger or illness. **2** looking gloomy and deserted [the *gaunt,* rocky coast of the island]. **—gaunt′ly *adv.* —gaunt′ness *n.***

**gaunt·let**[1] (gônt′lit) ***n.*** **1** a glove worn by knights in armor. It was usually made of leather covered with metal plates. **2** a glove with a long cuff flaring up from the wrist. *See the picture.* **—take up the gauntlet,** to accept a challenge. **—throw down the gauntlet,** to challenge, as to a fight.

**gaunt·let**[2] (gônt′lit) ***n.*** *another spelling of* **gantlet.**

**gauze** (gôz) ***n.*** any thin, light cloth so loosely woven that one can see through it [Cotton *gauze* is used for bandages.]

**gauz·y** (gôz′ē) ***adj.*** thin, light, and easy to see through, like gauze. **—gauz′i·er, gauz′i·est —gauz′i·ness *n.***

**gave** (gāv) *past tense of* **give.**

☆**gav·el** (gav′'l) ***n.*** a small wooden hammer that a chairperson, judge, etc. raps on the table to call for attention or silence. *See the picture.*

**ga·votte** or **ga·vot** (gə vät′) ***n.*** **1** a 17th-century dance like the minuet, but livelier. **2** the music for this.

**gawk** (gôk) ***v.*** to stare in a stupid way.

**gawk·y** (gô′kē) ***adj.*** tall and awkward or clumsy [a *gawky* fellow]. **—gawk′i·er, gawk′i·est —gawk′i·ness *n.***

**gay** (gā) ***adj.*** **1** lively and full of joy; merry; happy. **2** bright and showy [*gay* colors]. ◆☆***n.*** a homosexual. **—gay′ness *n.***

**gay·e·ty** (gā′ə tē) ***n.*** *another spelling of* **gaiety.** *—pl.* **gay′e·ties**

**gay·ly** (gā′lē) ***adv.*** *another spelling of* **gaily.**

**gaze** (gāz) ***v.*** to look in a steady way; stare, as in wonder [The crowd *gazed* at the huge spaceship.] *See* SYNONYMS *at* **look. —gazed, gaz′ing** ◆***n.*** a steady look. **—gaz′er *n.***

**ga·ze·bo** (gə zē′bō *or* gə zā′bō) ***n.*** a small, open building with a roof and seats, from which one can gaze at the scenery, in a garden or park. *—pl.* **ga·ze′bos** or **ga·ze′boes**

**ga·zelle** (gə zel′) ***n.*** a small, graceful antelope of Africa and Asia. It has large, shining eyes and horns that twist back in a spiral. *See the picture.*

**ga·zette** (gə zet′) ***n.*** a newspaper.

> **Gazette** comes from an Italian word for a small coin, which was once the price of a newspaper. **Gazette** is now used mainly as part of the name for certain newspapers [The Phoenix *Gazette*].

**gaz·et·teer** (gaz ə tir′) ***n.*** a dictionary of geographical names, as of cities, countries, mountains, rivers, etc.

**gear** (gir) ***n.*** **1** *often* **gears,** *pl.* a part of a machine consisting of two or more wheels having teeth that fit together so that when one wheel moves the others are made to move [The *gears* pass on the motion of the engine to the wheels of the car.] **2** *a shorter form of* **gearwheel. 3** a certain arrangement of the gears [Shift into low *gear* if you want more power.] **4** tools and equipment needed for doing something [My *gear* for fishing consists of a rod, lines, and flies.] ◆***v.*** **1** to furnish with gear; equip. **2** to connect by gears [The pedals of the bicycle are *geared* to the wheels.] **3** to adjust or make fit [Our new cafeteria is *geared* to handle more students.] —☆**high gear,** the arrangement of gears that gives the greatest speed but little power. **—in gear,** connected to the motor. —☆**low gear,** the arrangement of gears that gives little speed but great power. **—out of gear,** not connected to the motor. —☆**shift gears,** to change from one gear arrangement to another.

**gear·ing** (gir′iŋ) ***n.*** a system of gears or other parts for passing on motion. 

☆**gear·shift** (gir′shift) ***n.*** a part for connecting any of several sets of gears to a motor, or for disconnecting them.

**gear·wheel** (gir′hwēl) ***n.*** any of the toothed wheels in a system of gears. *See the picture.*

**geck·o** (gek′ō) ***n.*** a small lizard that has a soft skin and suction pads on its feet. It eats insects. *—pl.* **geck′os** or **geck′oes**

**gee**[1] (jē) ***interj.*** a word of command to a horse or ox meaning "turn to the right!"

**gee**[2] (jē) ***interj.*** a slang exclamation showing surprise, wonder, etc.

**geese** (gēs) ***n.*** *plural of* **goose.**

☆**ge·fil·te fish** (gə fil′tə) chopped fish, mixed with chopped onion, egg, etc., then shaped into balls or cakes and boiled. It is usually served cold.

> **Gefilte fish** was originally made by boiling a casing of fish skin filled with chopped fish. *Gefilte* is the Yiddish word for "filled."

**Gei·ger counter** (gī′gər) a device used for checking to find radioactivity and for measuring the amount of it when it is found.

**gei·sha** (gā′shə) ***n.*** a Japanese woman whose work is to entertain by singing and dancing. *—pl.* **gei′sha** or **gei′shas**

| | | | | | | | |
|---|---|---|---|---|---|---|---|
| **a** | fat | **ir** | here | **ou** | out | **zh** | leisure |
| **ā** | ape | **ī** | bite, fire | **u** | up | **ŋ** | ring |
| **ä** | car, lot | **ō** | go | **ʉr** | fur | | a *in* ago |
| **e** | ten | **ô** | law, horn | **ch** | chin | | e *in* agent |
| **er** | care | **oi** | oil | **sh** | she | **ə** = | i *in* unity |
| **ē** | even | **oo** | look | **th** | thin | | o *in* collect |
| **i** | hit | **ōō** | tool | ***th*** | then | | u *in* focus |

**gel·a·tin** or **gel·a·tine** (jel'ət 'n) ***n.*** a substance boiled from the bones, hoofs, etc. of animals; also, a vegetable substance like this. Gelatin dissolves in hot water and makes a sort of jelly when it cools. It is used as a food, in photographic film, etc.

**Gelatin** comes from a Latin word meaning "to freeze." Gelatin is often served frozen in a salad or dessert.

**ge·lat·i·nous** (jə lat''n əs) ***adj.*** **1** of or like gelatin or jelly. **2** thick and sticky.

**geld·ing** (gel'diŋ) ***n.*** a male horse whose sex glands have been removed.

**gem** (jem) ***n.*** **1** a precious stone, cut and polished for use as a jewel. **2** a person or thing that is very precious or valuable.

**Gem·i·ni** (jem'ə nī *or* jem'ə nē) the third sign of the zodiac, for the period from May 21 to June 21: *also called* the Twins. *See the picture for* **zodiac.**

**Gen.** *abbreviation for* **General.**

**gen·darme** (zhän'därm) ***n.*** a police officer in France and some other countries. *—pl.* **gen'darmes**

**gen·der** (jen'dər) ***n.*** any of the three classes that nouns, pronouns, and, often, adjectives belong to: these classes are called *masculine, feminine,* and *neuter,* and are more important in the grammars of other languages than in English. In English, such words as *boy, rooster,* and *he* are of the masculine gender; *girl, ship,* and *she* are of the feminine gender; and *baby, ball,* and *it* are of the neuter gender.



☆**gene** (jēn) ***n.*** any of the units for inherited characteristics that are carried by chromosomes: *see* **chromosome.**

**ge·ne·al·o·gy** (jē'nē äl'ə jē *or* jen'ē al'ə jē) ***n.*** **1** a list of a person's ancestors, that shows how they are related to one another; family tree. **2** the study of families and how they are descended. *—pl.* **ge'ne·al'o·gies** —**ge·ne·a·log·i·cal** (jē'nē ə läj'i k'l *or* jen'ē ə läj'i k'l) ***adj.*** —**ge'ne·al'o·gist** ***n.***

**gen·er·a** (jen'ər ə) ***n.*** *plural of* **genus.**

**gen·er·al** (jen'ər əl) ***adj.*** **1** of, for, or from the whole or all, not just a part or some [to promote the *general* welfare]. **2** widespread or common [The *general* opinion of him is unfavorable.] *See* SYNONYMS *at* **common.** **3** having to do with the main parts but not with details [the *general* features of a plan]. **4** not special or specialized [*general* science; a *general* store]. **5** highest in rank; most important [the attorney *general*]. ◆***n.*** any of various military officers ranking above a colonel; especially, such an officer who wears four stars and ranks above a lieutenant general. —**in general,** in the main; usually.

SYNONYMS: Whatever is **general** has to do with all, nearly all, or most of a group or class [*general* attendance is high]. Whatever is **universal** has to do with every individual or case within a group or class [the *universal* need for food].

**general assembly** ☆**1** the lawmaking body of some States of the U.S. **2 General Assembly,** the lawmaking body of the United Nations, in which all member nations are represented.

**gen·er·al·i·ty** (jen'ə ral'ə tē) ***n.*** **1** a statement that is general or vague rather than definite or with details [The mayor offered no exact plan, but spoke only in *generalities.*] **2** the greater number or part; majority [The *generality* of people are friendly.] **3** the fact of being general or common. *—pl.* **gen'er·al'i·ties**

**gen·er·al·ize** (jen'ər ə līz) ***v.*** **1** to form a general rule or idea from particular facts or cases [I have kept several cats, and, to *generalize,* I would say that they make clean, friendly pets.] **2** to talk or write in a general way, without being definite or giving details. —**gen'er·al·ized, gen'er·al·iz·ing** —**gen'er·al·i·za'tion** ***n.***

**gen·er·al·ly** (jen'ər ə lē) ***adv.*** **1** to or by most people; widely [Is it *generally* known that the school will close?] **2** in most cases; usually [I *generally* go straight home from school.] **3** in a general way; without details [Speaking *generally,* I'm happy.]

**gen·er·al-pur·pose** (jen'ər əl pur'pəs) ***adj.*** that can be used in a number of different ways.

☆**general store** a store where many different kinds of things are sold, but not in separate departments.

**gen·er·ate** (jen'ə rāt) ***v.*** to bring into being; cause to be; produce [A dynamo *generates* electricity. Fine service *generates* good will.] —**gen'er·at·ed, gen'er·at·ing**

**gen·er·a·tion** (jen'ə rā'shən) ***n.*** **1** a single stage in the history of a family [Grandmother, mother, and son are three *generations.*] **2** all the people born at about the same time [Most of his *generation* of men spent time in the army.] **3** the average time between the birth of one generation and the birth of the next, about 30 years. **4** a generating, or producing [the *generation* of heat from a fire].

**gen·er·a·tive** (jen'ər ə tiv) ***adj.*** of, or having the power of, producing.

**gen·er·a·tor** (jen'ə rāt'ər) ***n.*** **1** a machine for changing mechanical energy into electricity. **2** any person or thing that generates [His gifts made him a *generator* of much happiness.]

**ge·ner·ic** (jə ner'ik) ***adj.*** **1** of a whole genus, kind, class, etc.; general; inclusive [The word "ship" is a *generic* term for many kinds of large watercraft.] **2** that is not a trademark [A drug can be sold under its *generic* name.] —**ge·ner'i·cal·ly** ***adv.***

**gen·er·os·i·ty** (jen'ə räs'ə tē) ***n.*** **1** the quality of being generous. **2** a generous or unselfish act. *—pl.* **gen'er·os'i·ties**

**gen·er·ous** (jen'ər əs) ***adj.*** **1** willing to give or share; not selfish or stingy; openhanded. **2** large; great in amount [*generous* helpings of dessert]. **3** not mean; noble and forgiving [To forgive your enemy is a *generous* act.] —**gen'er·ous·ly** ***adv.*** —**gen'er·ous·ness** ***n.***

**Generous** comes from a Latin word meaning "born to a noble family." People from noble families were thought to be noble and forgiving, gracious and unselfish. Anyone who has these qualities is generous.

**Gen·e·sis** (jen'ə sis) the first book of the Bible, telling a story of how the world was created by God.

**gen·e·sis** (jen'ə sis) ***n.*** a beginning or origin.

**ge·net·ics** (jə net'iks) ***n.pl.*** the study of the way animals and plants pass on to their offspring such characteristics as size, color, etc.; science of heredity: *used with a singular verb.* —**ge·net'ic** ***adj.***

**Ge·ne·va** (jə nē'və) **1** a city in Switzerland. **2** a lake between Switzerland and France.

geometric design

geodesic dome

**ge·nial** (jēn′yəl) ***adj.*** **1** friendly and cheerful. **2** pleasant and healthful [a *genial* climate]. —**ge·ni·al·i·ty** (jē′nē al′ə tē) ***n.*** —**ge′nial·ly *adv.***

**ge·nie** (jē′nē) ***n.*** *another word for* **jinni.**

**ge·ni·i** (jē′nē ī′) ***n.*** *plural for* **genius** *in meanings* 5 *and* 6.

**gen·i·tals** (jen′ə t'lz) ***n.pl.*** the sex organs. —**gen′i·tal *adj.***

**ge·nius** (jēn′yəs) ***n.*** **1** the special power of mind or the special ability that shows itself in the greatest artists, writers, scientists, etc. **2** a person who has such ability [Leonardo da Vinci was a *genius* in both science and art.] **3** a person with a very high IQ. **4** any special ability [She has a *genius* for making friends.] **5** *often* **Genius,** a spirit that was believed by the ancient Romans to watch over a person or place. **6** a person who has great power over another for good or evil. **7** the special nature or spirit of a nation, time, etc. —*pl. for meanings* 1, 2, 3, 4, *and* 7 **ge′nius·es**, *pl. for meanings* 5 *and* 6 **ge′ni·i′**.

**Gen·o·a** (jen′ə wə) a seaport in northwestern Italy.

**gen·o·cide** (jen′ə sīd) ***n.*** any deliberate attempt to kill, or program planned to destroy, all the people of a certain nation, race, ethnic group, etc.

**gent** (jent) ***n.*** a gentleman or a man: *used only in everyday talk.*

**gen·teel** (jen tēl′) ***adj.*** polite or well-bred; now, especially, trying too hard to seem refined or well-bred. —**gen·teel′ness *n.***

**gen·tian** (jen′shən) ***n.*** a plant with flowers that are usually blue, sometimes with fringed edges.

**gen·tile** or **Gen·tile** (jen′tīl) ***n.*** a person who is not a Jew. ◆***adj.*** not Jewish.

**gen·til·i·ty** (jen til′ə tē) ***n.*** **1** the condition of being born into the upper classes. **2** good manners; politeness; refinement.

**gen·tle** (jent″l) ***adj.*** **1** mild, soft, or easy; not rough [a *gentle* touch; a *gentle* scolding]. **2** tame; easy to handle [a *gentle* horse]. **3** gradual; not sudden [a *gentle* slope]. **4** of or like the upper classes or polite society [They are of *gentle* birth.] **5** courteous, kindly, or patient [a *gentle* nature]. —**gen′tler, gen′tlest** —**gen′tle·ness *n.***

**gen·tle·man** (jent″l mən) ***n.*** **1** a man who is polite, kind, and reliable. **2** a man belonging to a family of high social standing: *no longer used except in talking about earlier times.* **3** any man ["Ladies and *gentlemen,*" the speaker began.] —*pl.* **gen′tle·men** —**gen′tle·man·ly *adj.***

**gent·ly** (jent′lē) ***adv.*** in a gentle way; mildly, softly, easily, etc.

**gen·try** (jen′trē) ***n.*** people of high social standing, but not including nobles.

**gen·u·ine** (jen′yoo wən) ***adj.*** **1** really being what it seems to be; not false; true [a *genuine* diamond]. **2** sincere or honest [*genuine* praise]. —**gen′u·ine·ly *adv.*** —**gen′u·ine·ness *n.***

**Genuine** comes from a Latin word meaning "to be born." Another meaning of *genuine,* but not commonly used, is "of pure breed." A genuine Holstein cow is born from a long line of Holstein cattle and it really is what it seems to be.

**ge·nus** (jē′nəs) ***n.*** a kind, sort, or class. In biology, a genus is a large group of plants or animals that are much alike in certain ways; the large group is divided into smaller groups called species. —*pl.* **gen·er·a** (jen′ər ə) or **ge′nus·es**

**geo-** *a prefix meaning* the earth [*Geology* is the study of the earth's crust.]

**ge·o·des·ic** (jē′ə des′ik *or* jē′ə dē′sik) ***adj.*** ☆having a strong surface made of short, straight bars joined together in a framework [a *geodesic* dome]. *See the picture.*

**ge·o·graph·i·cal** (jē′ə graf′i k'l) or **ge·o·graph·ic** (jē′ə graf′ik) ***adj.*** having to do with geography. —**ge′o·graph′i·cal·ly *adv.***

**ge·og·ra·phy** (jē äg′rə fē) ***n.*** **1** the study of the surface of the earth and how it is divided into continents, countries, seas, etc. Geography also deals with the climates, plants, animals, minerals, etc. of the earth. **2** the natural features of a certain part of the earth [the *geography* of Ohio]. —**ge·og′ra·pher *n.***

**ge·o·log·ic** (jē′ə läj′ik) or **ge·o·log·i·cal** (jē′ə läj′i k'l) ***adj.*** having to do with geology. —**ge′o·log′i·cal·ly *adv.***

**ge·ol·o·gy** (jē äl′ə jē) ***n.*** the study of the earth's crust and of the way in which its layers were formed. It includes the study of rocks and fossils. —**ge·ol′o·gist *n.***

**ge·o·met·ric** (jē′ə met′rik) or **ge·o·met·ri·cal** (jē′ə met′ri k'l) ***adj.*** **1** having to do with geometry. **2** formed of straight lines, triangles, circles, etc. [a *geometric* pattern]. *See the picture.*

**ge·om·e·try** (jē äm′ə trē) ***n.*** the branch of mathematics that deals with lines, angles, surfaces, and solids, and with their measurement.

**George III** (jôrj) 1738–1820; the king of England from 1760 to 1820. He ruled at the time of the American Revolution.

**George,** Saint the patron saint of England, who died probably in 303 A.D.

**Geor·gia** (jôr′jə) **1** a State in the southeastern part of the U.S.: abbreviated **Ga., GA** **2** a republic in the southwestern part of the U.S.S.R. —**Geor′gian *adj., n.***

**Ger.** *abbreviation for* **German** *or* **Germany.**

**ge·ra·ni·um** (jə rā′nē əm) ***n.*** **1** a common garden plant with showy pink, red, or white flowers. **2** a wild plant like this, with pink or purple flowers.

| | | | | | | | |
|---|---|---|---|---|---|---|---|
| **a** | fat | **ir** | here | **ou** | out | **zh** | leisure |
| **ā** | ape | **ī** | bite, fire | **u** | up | **ng** | ring |
| **ä** | car, lot | **ō** | go | **ur** | fur | | a *in* ago |
| **e** | ten | **ô** | law, horn | **ch** | chin | | e *in* agent |
| **er** | care | **oi** | oil | **sh** | she | **ə =** | i *in* unity |
| **ē** | even | **oo** | look | **th** | thin | | o *in* collect |
| **i** | hit | **ōō** | tool | ***th*** | then | | u *in* focus |

**ger·bil** or **ger·bille** (jʉr′b'l) ***n.*** an animal like a mouse but with very long hind legs. It is found in Africa and Asia.

**germ** (jʉrm) ***n.*** **1** a living thing that can cause disease and is too small to be seen except with a microscope; especially, one of the bacteria. **2** a seed, bud, etc. from which a plant or animal develops. **3** that from which something can grow; origin [the *germ* of an idea].

**Ger·man** (jʉr′mən) ***adj.*** of Germany, its people, language, etc. ◆***n.*** **1** a person born or living in Germany. **2** the language of the Germans.

**Ger·man·ic** (jər man′ik) ***adj.*** **1** of Germany or the Germans; German. **2** describing any of a group of languages that are related to German, as Norwegian, Danish, Dutch, and English.

**Ger·ma·ny** (jʉr′mə nē) a former country in north-central Europe: in 1949, it was divided into East Germany and West Germany, each with its own government.

**ger·mi·cide** (jʉr′mə sīd) ***n.*** anything used to kill disease germs. —**ger′mi·ci′dal** ***adj.***

**ger·mi·nate** (jʉr′mə nāt) ***v.*** to start growing or developing; sprout or make sprout, as from a seed, bud, or spore. —**ger′mi·nat·ed, ger′mi·nat·ing** —**ger′mi·na′tion** ***n.***

**Gersh·win** (gʉrsh′win), **George** 1898–1937; U.S. composer.

 **ger·und** (jer′ənd) ***n.*** a verb ending in *-ing* that is used as a noun. A gerund can take an object [In "Playing golf is my only exercise," the word "playing" is a *gerund*.]

**ges·tic·u·late** (jes tik′yoo lāt) ***v.*** to make motions with the hands and arms, as in showing feeling or adding force to what one says. *See the picture.* —**ges·tic′u·lat·ed, ges·tic′u·lat·ing** —**ges·tic′u·la′tion** ***n.***

**ges·ture** (jes′chər) ***n.*** **1** a motion made with some part of the body, especially the hands or arms, to show some idea or feeling. **2** anything said or done to show one's feelings; sometimes, something done just for effect, and not really meant [Our neighbor's gift was a *gesture* of friendship.] ◆***v.*** to make a gesture or gestures. —**ges′tured, ges′tur·ing**

**Ge·sund·heit** (gə zoont′hīt′) ***n.*** a German word meaning "good health!" spoken to a person who has just sneezed.

**get** (get) ***v.*** **1** to become the owner of by receiving, buying, earning, etc.; gain; obtain [We *got* a new car.] **2** to arrive at; reach [They *got* home early.] **3** to reach or receive by telephone, radio, TV, etc. [I *got* a busy signal.] **4** to go and bring [*Get* your books.] **5** to catch; gain hold of [*Get* her attention.] **6** to make willing; persuade [I can't *get* him to leave.] **7** to cause to be [We couldn't *get* the door open. He *got* his hands dirty.] **8** to be or become [She *got* caught in the rain. Don't *get* angry.] **9** to make ready; prepare [It's your turn to *get* dinner.] **10** to be forced or obliged: *used only in everyday talk, with* have *or* has [I've *got* to pass the test.] **11** to own or possess: *used only in everyday talk, with* have *or* has [He's *got* ten dollars.] **12** to become the master of; overpower, kill, puzzle, etc.: *used only in everyday talk* [Such bad habits will *get* you finally. The hunter *got* two birds. This problem *gets* me.] **13** to hit; strike: *used only in everyday talk* [The stone *got* him in the leg.] ☆**14** to understand: *used only in everyday talk* [Did you *get* the joke?] ☆**15** to produce a strong feeling in; annoy, please, thrill, etc.: *slang in this meaning* [Her singing really *gets* me.] ☆**16** to notice: *slang in this meaning* [Did you *get* the look on her face?] —**got, got** or **got′ten, get′ting** —**get along,** *see phrase under* **along.** —**get around, 1** to move from place to place. **2** to become known, as news. ☆**3** to avoid or overcome a difficulty. **4** to flatter in order to gain something. —**get around to,** to find time for. —**get away, 1** to go away. **2** to escape. —☆**get away with,** to manage to do without being found out or punished: *a slang phrase.* —**get by,** to manage to survive or succeed: *used only in everyday talk.* —**get in, 1** to enter. **2** to arrive. **3** to put in. —**get off, 1** to come off or out of. **2** to go away. **3** to take off. **4** to escape or help to escape. **5** to have time off. —**get on, 1** to go on or into. **2** to put on. **3** to grow older. **4** to agree; be friendly. —**get out, 1** to go out. **2** to go away. ☆**3** to become known. **4** to publish. —**get out of,** to escape or avoid. —**get over, 1** to recover from an illness, etc. **2** to forget about. —**get through,** to finish. —**get together,** to bring or come together. —**get up, 1** to rise from a chair, from sleep, etc. **2** to organize.

> SYNONYMS: **Get, obtain,** and **acquire** all describe the action of coming to have or possess something, but **get** is used more often and does not always suggest that any special effort was made to have the thing [to *get* a job; to *get* an idea; to *get* a headache]. **Obtain** suggests that what is got was wanted and that an effort was made to get it [to *obtain* help from city officials]. **Acquire** is used to describe the getting of something little by little over a long period of time [to *acquire* an education].

**get·a·way** (get′ə wā) ***n.*** **1** the act of starting, as in a race. **2** an escape, as from the police.

**Geth·sem·a·ne** (geth sem′ə nē) the garden near Jerusalem where, according to the Bible, Jesus was betrayed and arrested.

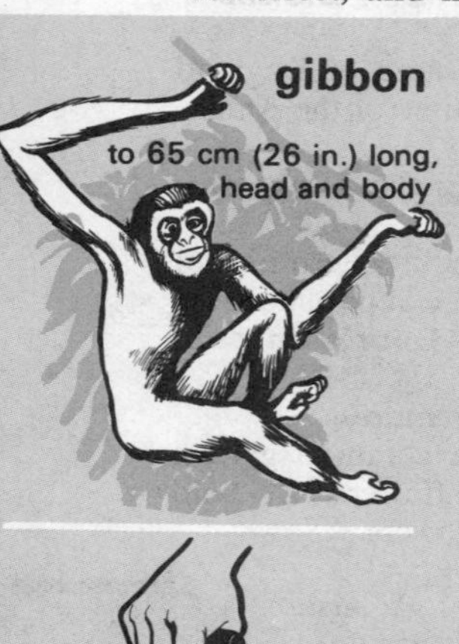

**gibbon**

**gimlet**

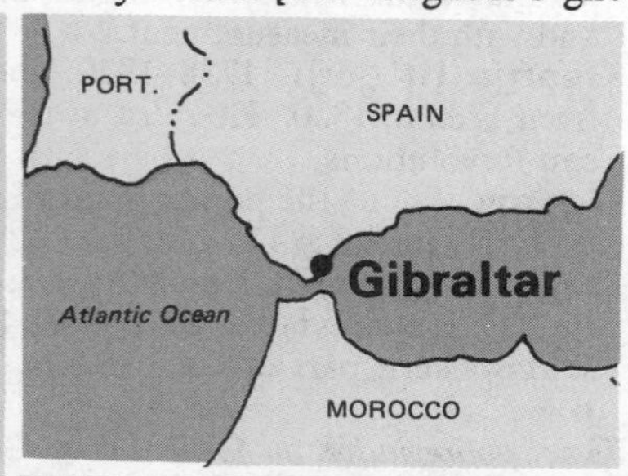


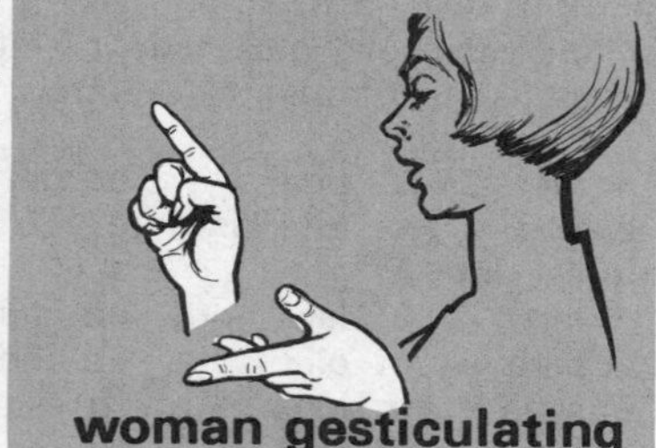
**woman gesticulating**

☆**get·to·geth·er** (get′tə geth′ər) ***n.*** a small meeting or party.

**Get·tys·burg** (get′iz burg′) a town in southern Pennsylvania. An important battle of the Civil War was fought there in 1863.

**get-up** (get′up′) ***n.*** **1** costume or outfit [He wore an old-fashioned *get-up* to the party.] **2** the energy to get things done: *also* **get′-up′-and-go′.** *This word is used only in everyday talk.*

**gew·gaw** (gyōō′gô *or* gōō′gô) ***n.*** something showy but useless and of little value; trinket.

**gey·ser** (gī′zər) ***n.*** a spring that shoots streams of boiling water and steam up into the air from time to time.

**Gha·na** (gä′nə) a country in western Africa.

**ghast·ly** (gast′lē) ***adj.*** **1** horrible or frightening [a *ghastly* crime]. **2** pale and sick [to look *ghastly*]. **3** very bad: *used only in everyday talk* [a *ghastly* mistake]. —**ghast′li·er, ghast′li·est —ghast′li·ness *n.***

**gher·kin** (gur′kin) ***n.*** a small pickled cucumber.

**ghet·to** (get′ō) ***n.*** **1** the section of some European cities where Jews were once forced to live. **2** any section of a city in which a particular group of people live or are forced to live. —*pl.* **ghet′tos** or **ghet′toes**

**ghost** (gōst) ***n.*** **1** a pale, shadowy form that some people think they can see and that is supposed to be the spirit of a dead person. **2** a mere shadow or slight trace [not a *ghost* of a chance]. —**give up the ghost,** to die.

**ghost·ly** (gōst′lē) ***adj.*** of or like a ghost.

☆**ghost·writ·er** (gōst′rīt′ər) ***n.*** a person who writes speeches, articles, etc. for another who pretends to be the author.

**ghoul** (gōōl) ***n.*** **1** a supposed evil spirit that robs graves and feeds on the dead. **2** a person who enjoys things that disgust most people. —**ghoul′ish *adj.*** —**ghoul′ish·ly *adv.*** —**ghoul′ish·ness *n.***

**GHQ** or **G.H.Q.** General Headquarters.

☆**GI** (jē′ī′) ***n.*** an enlisted person in the U.S. Army. —*pl.* **GI's** or **GIs** ◆***adj.*** of or having to do with the army or army life. *This word is used only in everyday talk.*

> **GI** is an abbreviation for *government issue,* which is the term used in the army for clothing and supplies issued, or passed out, to soldiers.

**gi·ant** (jī′ənt) ***n.*** **1** an imaginary being that looks like a person but is many times larger and stronger. **2** a person or thing that is especially large, strong, etc. [Einstein was a mental *giant.*] ◆***adj.*** very great in size or power [*giant* strides].

**gib·ber** (jib′ər) ***v.*** to talk or chatter in a confused or meaningless way [Monkeys *gibber.*]

**gib·ber·ish** (jib′ər ish) ***n.*** confused or meaningless talk or chatter.

**gib·bet** (jib′it) ***n.*** a kind of gallows on which the bodies of criminals were hung after they had been put to death. ◆***v.*** to hang on a gibbet.

**gib·bon** (gib′ən) ***n.*** a small ape of southeastern Asia, with very long arms. *See the picture.*

**gibe** (jīb) ***n.*** a remark used to make fun of someone, often in a scornful way; jeer; taunt. ◆***v.*** to make gibes; jeer; taunt. —**gibed, gib′ing**

**gib·lets** (jib′lits) ***n.pl.*** the parts inside a chicken, turkey, etc. that can be used as food, as the heart, liver, and gizzard.

**Gi·bral·tar** (ji brôl′tər) a British territory on a huge rock in southern Spain at the entrance to the Mediterranean. *See the map.*

**gid·dy** (gid′ē) ***adj.*** **1** feeling as though things were whirling about; dizzy [Climbing ladders makes me *giddy.*] **2** not serious about things; flighty, silly, etc. [a *giddy* youth]. —**gid′di·er, gid′di·est —gid′di·ly *adv.*** —**gid′di·ness *n.***

**gift** (gift) ***n.*** **1** something given to show friendship, thanks, support, etc.; a present [Christmas *gifts;* a *gift* of $5,000 to a museum]. **2** a natural ability; talent [a *gift* for writing catchy tunes]. *See* SYNONYMS *at* **present** *and at* **talent.**

**gift·ed** (gif′tid) ***adj.*** **1** having great natural ability; talented [a *gifted* pianist]. **2** very intelligent [a *gifted* child].

**gig**[1] (gig) ***n.*** a light, open carriage with two wheels, pulled by one horse.

☆**gig**[2] (gig) ***n.*** **1** a job to play or sing jazz, rock, etc. **2** any job. *This is a slang word.*

**gi·gan·tic** (jī gan′tik) ***adj.*** like a giant in size; very big; huge; enormous [a *gigantic* building].

**gig·gle** (gig′′l) ***v.*** to laugh with high, quick sounds in a silly or nervous way, as if trying to hold back. *See* SYNONYMS *at* **laugh.** —**gig′gled, gig′gling** ◆***n.*** such a laugh. —**gig′gly *adj.***

☆**Gi·la monster** (hē′lə) a poisonous lizard of the Southwest. It has a thick body covered with beady scales that are black and orange.

**Gil·bert and Sul·li·van** (gil′bərt ′n sul′ə vən) English writers of many comic operettas in the last part of the 19th century. Gilbert wrote the words and Sullivan wrote the music.

**gild** (gild) ***v.*** **1** to cover with a thin layer of gold. **2** to make something seem better than it really is. —**gild′ed** or **gilt, gild′ing**

**Gil·e·ad** (gil′ē əd) a mountainous region in ancient Palestine, east of the Jordan River.

**gill**[1] (gil) ***n.*** the organ for breathing of most animals that live in water, as fish, lobsters, etc. As water passes through them, the gills remove oxygen from it.

**gill**[2] (jil) ***n.*** a measure of liquids, equal to 1/4 pint. A gill is half a cup.

**gilt** (gilt) *a past tense and past participle of* **gild.** ◆***n.*** a thin layer of gold or a gold-colored paint, used to cover a surface: *also called* **gild′ing.** ◆***adj.*** covered with gilt.

**gim·crack** (jim′krak) ***n.*** a thing that is bright and showy but of little or no use.

**gim·let** (gim′lət) ***n.*** a small tool used to bore holes. *See the picture.*

☆**gim·mick** (gim′ik) ***n.*** a clever gadget, trick, or idea: *a slang word.*

**gin**[1] (jin) ***n.*** a strong alcoholic liquor that is flavored with juniper berries.

| | | | |
|---|---|---|---|
| **a** fat | **ir** here | **ou** out | **zh** leisure |
| **ā** ape | **ī** bite, fire | **u** up | **ng** ring |
| **ä** car, lot | **ō** go | **ur** fur | a *in* ago |
| **e** ten | **ô** law, horn | **ch** chin | e *in* agent |
| **er** care | **oi** oil | **sh** she | ə = i *in* unity |
| **ē** even | **oo** look | **th** thin | o *in* collect |
| **i** hit | **ōō** tool | ***th*** then | u *in* focus |

**gin**[2] (jin) **n.** *a shorter form of* **cotton gin.**

**gin·ger** (jin′jər) **n.** **1** a spice made from the root of a tropical plant. **2** this root.

**ginger ale** a sweet drink made of soda water flavored with ginger.

**gin·ger·bread** (jin′jər bred) **n.** **1** a dark cake flavored with ginger and molasses. **2** showy decoration, such as fancy carvings on furniture, gables, etc.

**gin·ger·ly** (jin′jər lē) **adv.** in a very careful way [walking *gingerly* across the ice]. ◆**adj.** very careful; cautious [taking a *gingerly* step forward].

**gin·ger·snap** (jin′jər snap) **n.** a crisp cookie flavored with ginger and molasses.

**ging·ham** (ging′əm) **n.** a light cotton cloth woven in colored stripes, checks, or plaids.

**gink·go** (ging′kō) **n.** a tree from Asia that has fan-shaped leaves and yellow seeds. *—pl.* **gink′goes**

**gin rummy** (jin) a form of the card game rummy, for two players.

**gin·seng** (jin′seng) **n.** the root of a plant found in China and North America. It has a pleasant smell and is used in medicine by the Chinese.

**gip·sy** (jip′sē) **n.** *another spelling of* **gypsy.**

**gi·raffe** (jə raf′) **n.** a large animal of Africa that chews its cud. It has a very long neck and legs and a spotted coat, and is the tallest animal alive. *See the picture.*

**gird** (gurd) **v.** **1** to put a belt or band around. **2** to fasten with a belt or band [The knight *girded* on a sword.] **3** to form a circle around; surround [Farmland *girded* the castle.] **4** to get ready for action [They are *girding* themselves for the contest.] —**gird′ed** or **girt, gird′ing**



**gird·er** (gur′dər) **n.** a long beam of steel or wood used to support some part in a building, bridge, etc. *See the picture.*

**gir·dle** (gur′d'l) **n.** **1** a belt or sash worn around the waist: *used mostly in talking about earlier times.* **2** anything that surrounds like a belt. ☆**3** a light, elastic corset worn to support the waist and hips. ◆**v.** to surround; encircle [The village was *girdled* by farms.] —**gir′dled, gir′dling**

**girl** (gurl) **n.** **1** a female child or a young, unmarried woman. **2** any woman: *used only in everyday talk.* **3** the sweetheart of a boy or man: *used only in everyday talk.*

☆**girl·friend** (gurl′frend) **n.** **1** a sweetheart of a boy or man. **2** a girl who is one's friend. *This word is used only in everyday talk.*

**girl·hood** (gurl′hood) **n.** the time of being a girl.

**girl·ish** (gurl′ish) **adj.** of, like, or fit for a girl. —**girl′ish·ly adv.** —**girl′ish·ness n.**

☆**girl scout** a member of the **Girl Scouts,** a club for girls that teaches outdoor skills and service to others.

**girt** (gurt) *a past tense and past participle of* **gird.**

**girth** (gurth) **n.** **1** the distance around a person's waist, a tree trunk, etc. **2** a band put around the middle of a horse to hold the saddle in place.

**gist** (jist) **n.** the main point or idea of a story, speech, magazine article, etc.

**give** (giv) **v.** **1** to pass or hand over to another [*Give* me your coat and I'll hang it up.] **2** to hand over to another to keep; make a gift of [My uncle *gave* a book to me for my birthday.] **3** to cause to have [Music *gives* me pleasure.] **4** to be the source of; supply [Cows *give* milk.] **5** to pay a price [I *gave* $20 for that bike.] **6** to part with; sacrifice [He *gave* his life for his country.] **7** to show [She *gave* signs of waking up.] **8** to say or state; utter [She *gave* the right answers.] **9** to perform; present [He is to *give* a concert.] **10** to bend or move because of force or pressure [The floorboards *gave* under our weight.] —**gave, giv′en, giv′ing** ◆**n.** the quality of bending, yielding, or moving because of pressure; a being elastic [a mattress without much *give*]. —**give away, 1** to make a gift of. ☆**2** to make known something that was hidden or secret: *used only in everyday talk.* —**give back,** to return. —**give in,** to stop fighting or working against; surrender. —**give off** or **give forth,** to send out; emit, as a smell. —**give out, 1** to make known. **2** to hand out; distribute. **3** to become worn out or used up. —**give up, 1** to hand over because one must. **2** to stop doing something [to *give up* smoking]. **3** to stop trying; admit that one has failed. —**giv′er n.**

SYNONYMS: **Give** means to hand over something of one's own to someone else. **Grant** suggests that the person to whom the thing is given has asked for it [The judge *granted* the prisoner's request.] **Present** suggests that the thing given is rather valuable and that it is handed over in a fairly formal way, as at a banquet [They *presented* a gold watch to the retiring principal.]

**give·a·way** (giv′ə wā) **n.** ☆**1** the act of making something secret or hidden known to others, without meaning to do so. **2** something given free or sold cheap in order to try to get customers. *This word is used only in everyday talk.*

**giv·en** (giv′'n) *past participle of* **give.** ◆**adj.** **1** in the habit of; accustomed; inclined [an employee *given* to loafing on the job]. **2** that has been mentioned or decided upon [You must finish within the *given* time.]

**given name** a person's first name [Roberta Lutz's *given name* is Roberta.]

**giz·zard** (giz′ərd) **n.** the second stomach of a bird, where the food is ground up again.

**gla·cial** (glā′shəl) **adj.** of or like ice or glaciers [a *glacial* period].

**gla·cier** (glā′shər) **n.** a large mass of ice and snow that moves very slowly down a mountain or across land until it melts. Icebergs are pieces of a glacier that have broken away into the sea.

**glad** (glad) **adj.** **1** feeling or showing joy; happy; pleased [I'm *glad* to be here.] *See* SYNONYMS *at* **happy.** **2** causing joy; pleasing [*glad* news]. **3** very willing [I'm *glad* to help.] —**glad′der, glad′dest** —**glad′ly adv.** —**glad′ness n.**

**glad·den** (glad′'n) **v.** to make glad.

**glade** (glād) **n.** an open space in a forest.

**glad·i·a·tor** (glad′ē āt′ər) **n.** a man, usually a slave or prisoner, who fought against animals or other men in the arenas of ancient Rome, for the entertainment of the public. *See the picture.*

**glad·i·a·to·ri·al** (glad′ē ə tôr′ē əl) **adj.** of or like gladiators or their fights.

**glad·i·o·la** (glad′ē ō′lə) **n.** *another word for* **gladiolus.**

**glad·i·o·lus** (glad′ē ō′ləs) **n.** a plant with sword-shaped leaves and tall spikes of showy flowers. *—pl.* **glad′i·o′lus·es** or **glad·i·o·li** (glad′ē ō′lī)

**glad·some** (glad′səm) ***adj.*** full of joy or giving joy; joyful; cheerful.

**glam·or·ize** (glam′ə rīz) ***v.*** to make glamorous. —**glam′or·ized, glam′or·iz·ing**

**glam·or·ous** or **glam·our·ous** (glam′ər əs) ***adj.*** full of glamour; fascinating. —**glam′or·ous·ly *adv.***

**glam·our** or **glam·or** (glam′ər) ***n.*** ☆mysterious beauty or charm; strange attraction [the *glamour* of faraway lands].

This is a Scottish word that was brought into English and made popular by the famous novelist Sir Walter Scott. When he introduced it, it had the same meaning ("magic" or "a magic spell") it has in Scottish. But not long afterward it began to change and took on the meaning it has today.

**glance** (glans) ***v.*** **1** to strike at a slant and go off at an angle [Hail *glanced* off the roof.] **2** to flash or gleam [Sunlight *glanced* off the metal.] **3** to take a quick look [Just *glance* at this.] ◆***n.*** **1** a glancing off. **2** a quick look. —**glanced, glanc′ing**

**gland** (gland) ***n.*** a part of the body that takes certain things from the blood and changes them into a substance that the body can either use or give off [The liver, kidneys, and thyroid are *glands*. Bile, milk, and sweat are produced by *glands*.]

**glan·du·lar** (glan′jə lər) ***adj.*** of, like, or containing glands.

**glare** (gler) ***v.*** **1** to shine with a light so bright that it hurts the eyes. **2** to stare in an angry way. —**glared, glar′ing** ◆***n.*** **1** a strong, blinding light. **2** an angry stare. **3** a smooth, glassy surface [The streets are a *glare* of ice.]

**glar·ing** (gler′iŋ) ***adj.*** **1** shining so brightly as to hurt the eyes [*glaring* headlights]. **2** too bright and showy [*glaring* colors]. **3** staring in an angry way. **4** standing out so that it cannot be overlooked [a *glaring* mistake]. —**glar′ing·ly *adv.***

**Glas·gow** (glas′kō) city in south central Scotland.

**glass** (glas) ***n.*** **1** a hard substance that breaks easily and that lets light through. It is made by melting together sand, soda or potash, lime, etc. **2** an article made of glass, as a container for drinking, a mirror, or a windowpane. **3 glasses,** *pl.* eyeglasses or binoculars. **4** the amount a drinking glass holds [He drank two *glasses* of milk.] ◆***adj.*** made of glass. —**glass in,** to enclose or cover with panes of glass.

**glass·ful** (glas′fo͝ol) ***n.*** the amount that will fill a drinking glass. —*pl.* **glass′fuls**

**glass·ware** (glas′wer) ***n.*** things made of glass.

**glass·y** (glas′ē) ***adj.*** **1** like glass; smooth, clear, etc. [the *glassy* surface of a lake on a calm day]. **2** having a dull or lifeless look [a *glassy* stare]. —**glass′i·er, glass′i·est** —**glass′i·ness *n.***

**glaze** (glāz) ***v.*** **1** to give a hard, shiny finish to [to *glaze* pottery]. **2** to cover with a sugar coating [to *glaze* doughnuts]. **3** to make or become glassy [with eyes *glazed* from boredom]. **4** to fit with glass, as a window. **5** to cover with a thin layer of ice. —**glazed, glaz′ing** ◆***n.*** **1** a glassy coating, as on pottery. **2** anything used to form such a coating.

**gla·zier** (glā′zhər) ***n.*** a person whose work is fitting glass in windows, etc.

**gleam** (glēm) ***n.*** **1** a faint light or one that lasts only a short time [the *gleam* of dying embers]. **2** brightness thrown back as from a polished surface. **3** a faint show or sign [a *gleam* of hope]. ◆***v.*** to shine with a gleam [Polish the car till it *gleams*.]

giraffe
5.5 m (18 ft.) high

glider

gladiators

girders

**glean** (glēn) ***v.*** **1** to gather the grain left on a field after the reapers are through. **2** to collect facts, information, etc. bit by bit. —**glean′er *n.***

**glee** (glē) ***n.*** lively joy; merriment [shouting out the words in *glee*]. *See* SYNONYMS *at* **mirth.** 

**glee club** a group formed to sing part songs.

**glee·ful** (glē′fəl) ***adj.*** full of glee; merry.

**glen** (glen) ***n.*** a small, narrow valley in a lonely place.

**glen plaid** or **Glen plaid** a plaid pattern or cloth with thin crosswise stripes in black and white and one or more soft colors.

**glib** (glib) ***adj.*** speaking or spoken in a smooth, easy way, often in a way that cannot easily be believed [the politician's *glib* remarks]. —**glib′ber, glib′best** —**glib′ly *adv.*** —**glib′ness *n.***

**glide** (glīd) ***v.*** **1** to move along in a smooth and easy way, as in skating. **2** to go on from one thing to another without a break [Time *glides* by.] —**glid′ed, glid′ing** ◆***n.*** **1** a smooth, easy movement. ☆**2** a small disk or ball, as of nylon, put on the underside of furniture legs, etc. for easy gliding in moving.

**glid·er** (glīd′ər) ***n.*** **1** an aircraft like an airplane except that it has no engine and is carried along by air currents. *See the picture.* ☆**2** a porch seat hung in a frame so that it can swing back and forth.

**glim·mer** (glim′ər) ***v.*** to give a faint and unsteady light [Stars *glimmered* in the sky.] ◆***n.*** **1** a faint, unsteady light. **2** a faint show or sign, as of hope.

**glimpse** (glimps) ***v.*** to get a quick look at [I *glimpsed* a fox as it ran across the trail.] —**glimpsed, glimps′ing** ◆***n.*** a quick look.

| | | | | | | | |
|---|---|---|---|---|---|---|---|
| **a** | fat | **ir** | here | **ou** | out | **zh** | leisure |
| **ā** | ape | **ī** | bite, fire | **u** | up | **ŋ** | ring |
| **ä** | car, lot | **ō** | go | **ur** | fur | | a *in* ago |
| **e** | ten | **ô** | law, horn | **ch** | chin | | e *in* agent |
| **er** | care | **oi** | oil | **sh** | she | **ə =** | i *in* unity |
| **ē** | even | **oo** | look | **th** | thin | | o *in* collect |
| **i** | hit | **ōō** | tool | ***th*** | then | | u *in* focus |

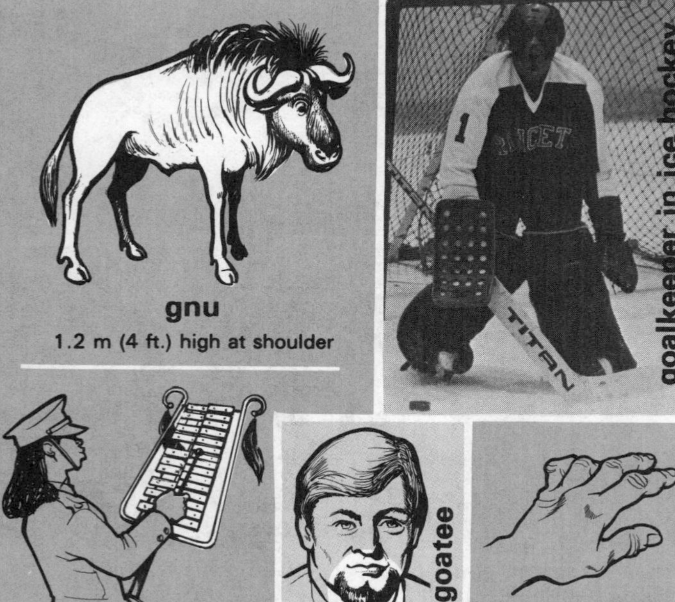

gnu
1.2 m (4 ft.) high at shoulder

goalkeeper in ice hockey

glockenspiel

goatee

gnarled hand

**glint** (glint) ***n.*** a gleam or flash [a *glint* of mischief in his eyes]. ◆***v.*** to gleam or flash [pieces of glass *glinting* in the sunlight].



**glis·ten** (glis′'n) ***v.*** to shine or sparkle, as fresh snow or a well-polished surface.

**glit·ter** (glit′ər) ***v.*** **1** to shine with a sparkling light [The Christmas tree *glittered* with tinsel.] **2** to be showy or attractive [an essay that *glitters* with wit]. ◆***n.*** **1** a sparkling light [the *glitter* of gold]. **2** showy brightness or attractiveness [the *glitter* of a rock concert]. —**glit′ter·y** ***adj.***

**gloam·ing** (glō′miŋ) ***n.*** the dusk of evening.

**gloat** (glōt) ***v.*** to feel a mean or greedy kind of pleasure [to *gloat* over another's bad luck; to *gloat* over one's jewels].

**glob** (gläb) ***n.*** a rounded mass or lump, as of a thick liquid or a partly solid substance.

**glob·al** (glō′b'l) ***adj.*** **1** having the shape of a globe. **2** involving the whole world; worldwide [the author's *global* fame]. —**glob′al·ly** ***adv.***

**globe** (glōb) ***n.*** **1** anything shaped like a ball; sphere. **2** the earth. **3** a round model of the earth showing the continents, oceans, etc.

**glob·u·lar** (gläb′yə lər) ***adj.*** **1** shaped like a globe; round. **2** made up of many globules [Caviar is a *globular* mass of fish eggs.]

**glob·ule** (gläb′yool) ***n.*** a tiny globe or ball; especially, a small drop of liquid.

**glock·en·spiel** (gläk′ən spēl) ***n.*** a musical instrument with tuned metal bars in a frame, played with one or two hammers. *See the picture.*

**gloom** (gloom) ***n.*** **1** dimness of light; gray darkness, as in a cave. **2** deep sadness or hopelessness.

**gloom·y** (gloom′ē) ***adj.*** **1** dark or dim [a *gloomy* dungeon]. **2** having or giving a feeling of deep sadness [a *gloomy* mood; a *gloomy* story]. —**gloom′i·er, gloom′i·est** —**gloom′i·ly** ***adv.*** —**gloom′i·ness** ***n.***

**glo·ri·fy** (glôr′ə fī) ***v.*** **1** to give glory to; cause to be famous and respected [the great names that *glorify* the Victorian Age]. **2** to praise in worship [to *glorify* God]. **3** to make seem better, finer, etc. than is really so [Some old soldiers *glorify* war.] —**glo′ri·fied, glo′ri·fy·ing** —**glo′ri·fi·ca′tion** ***n.***

**glo·ri·ous** (glôr′ē əs) ***adj.*** **1** giving, having, or deserving glory or honor [a *glorious* act of bravery]. **2** beautiful in a splendid way; magnificent [a *glorious* symphony]. **3** very pleasant; delightful: *used only in everyday talk* [a *glorious* vacation].

**glo·ry** (glôr′ē) ***n.*** **1** great honor or fame [to win *glory* as a poet]. **2** worship or praise [*Glory* be to God.] **3** the condition of being very important, successful, etc. [ancient Greece in its *glory*]. **4** great beauty or splendor [the *glory* of the woods in autumn]. —*pl.* **glo′ries** ◆***v.*** to be very proud or happy [to *glory* in one's victory]. —**glo′ried, glo′ry·ing** —**in one's glory,** at one's best, happiest, etc.

**gloss** (glôs *or* gläs) ***n.*** **1** a polish or shine on a surface. **2** a smooth and pleasant look that hides something bad or wrong. ◆***v.*** to pass over or cover up something bad or wrong [to *gloss* over a mistake with a joke].

**glos·sa·ry** (gläs′ə rē *or* glôs′ə rē) ***n.*** a list of hard words with their meanings, often printed at the end of a book. —*pl.* **glos′sa·ries**

> **Glossary** comes from a Greek word meaning "tongue." And since the tongue is so important in forming words when we speak, it is easy to see the connection between that old Greek word and our modern term for a list of words.

**gloss·y** (glôs′ē *or* gläs′ē) ***adj.*** smooth and shiny. —**gloss′i·er, gloss′i·est** —**gloss′i·ness** ***n.***

**glot·tis** (glät′is) ***n.*** the opening between the vocal cords in the larynx.

**glove** (gluv) ***n.*** **1** a covering to protect the hand, with a separate part for each finger and the thumb [Surgeons wear rubber *gloves*. Padded *gloves* are worn in playing baseball.] **2** a padded mitt worn in boxing: *also* **boxing glove.** ◆***v.*** to put gloves on. —**gloved, glov′ing**

**glow** (glō) ***v.*** **1** to give off light because of great heat; be red-hot or white-hot. **2** to give out light without flame or heat [Fireflies *glowed* in the dark.] **3** to show a warm or rosy color [cheeks *glowing* with health]. **4** to show eagerness or excitement [His face *glowed* with delight.] ◆***n.*** **1** light given off as a result of great heat [the *glow* of a blast furnace]. **2** light without flame or heat. **3** warmth or brightness of color. **4** warm or rosy look of the skin. **5** a good or pleasant feeling.

> SYNONYMS: A **glow** is a kind of light that is steady, warm, and soft [the *glow* of the charcoal in the barbecue]. A **blaze**[1] is a fire that is hot, very bright, and somewhat large and steady [the *blaze* of a forest fire].

**glow·er** (glou′ər) ***v.*** to stare in a fierce or angry way; scowl. ◆***n.*** an angry stare.

**glow·worm** (glō′wurm) ***n.*** an insect without wings, or an insect larva, that glows in the dark, as the wingless female or the larva of the firefly.

**glu·cose** (gloo′kōs) ***n.*** **1** a kind of sugar found in plants and animals; dextrose. **2** a sweet syrup containing glucose, made from starch.

**glue** (glo͞o) ***n.*** **1** a thick, sticky substance made by boiling animal hoofs and bones, used for sticking things together. **2** any sticky substance like this. ◆***v.*** **1** to stick together with glue. **2** to keep or hold without moving [The exciting movie kept us *glued* to our seats.] —**glued, glu'ing —glue'y *adj.***

**glum** (glum) ***adj.*** silent in a gloomy or sullen way. —**glum'mer, glum'mest —glum'ly *adv.* —glum'ness *n.***

**glut** (glut) ***v.*** **1** to stuff oneself with food. **2** to supply with much more than is needed or wanted [The market was *glutted* with used cars.] —**glut'ted, glut'ting** ◆***n.*** a supply that is greater than is needed.

**glu·ten** (glo͞ot''n) ***n.*** a gray, sticky protein substance found in wheat flour. —**glu'ten·ous *adj.***

**glu·ti·nous** (glo͞ot''n əs) ***adj.*** sticky; gluey.

**glut·ton** (glut''n) ***n.*** **1** a person who eats too much in a greedy way. **2** a person who is ready and willing to do or receive something [a *glutton* for hard work]. —**glut'ton·ous *adj.* —glut'ton·y *n.***

**glyc·er·in** or **glyc·er·ine** (glis'ər in) ***n.*** a clear, syrupy liquid made from fats and oils and used in skin lotions, explosives, etc.

**gnarl** (närl) ***n.*** a knot or lump on the trunk or branch of a tree.

**gnarled** (närld) ***adj.*** full of gnarls or knobs; twisted and knotty [a *gnarled* tree; *gnarled* hands]. *See the picture.*

**gnash** (nash) ***v.*** to grind or strike the teeth together, as in anger or pain.

**gnat** (nat) ***n.*** a small insect with two wings, that bites or stings.

**gnaw** (nô) ***v.*** **1** to bite and wear away bit by bit with the teeth [The rat *gnawed* the rope in two. The dog *gnawed* on the bone.] **2** to make by gnawing [to *gnaw* a hole]. **3** to keep on troubling for a long time [Jealousy *gnawed* at her heart.]

**gneiss** (nīs) ***n.*** a rock that has a coarse grain and looks like granite.

**gnome** (nōm) ***n.*** a dwarf in folk tales who lives inside the earth and guards the treasures there.

**gnu** (no͞o *or* nyo͞o) ***n.*** a large African antelope with a head like an ox and a long tail. *See the picture.*

**go** (gō) ***v.*** **1** to move along from one place, point, or person to another; pass or proceed [*Go* ten miles down the road. Time *goes* fast. The rumor *went* all over town.] **2** to move away; leave; pass away; depart [The years come and *go*. Has the pain *gone?*] **3** to fail; become worse [My hearing is *going*.] **4** to be given or sold [The prize *goes* to you. The chair *went* for $30.] **5** to turn out; result [Our plans *went* wrong.] **6** to be or become [to *go* hungry for days; to *go* mad]. **7** to work or run, as a clock, machine, etc. does. **8** to be worded, told, sung, etc. [How does that poem *go?*] **9** to make a certain motion, sound, etc. [The gun *went* "bang."] **10** to put oneself [I *went* to a lot of trouble.] **11** to begin or take part in a certain activity [Will you *go* to college? Let's *go* swimming.] **12** to belong in a certain place [The brooms *go* in that closet.] **13** to fit or suit [Does this tie *go* well with my shirt?] ☆**14** to have force or be accepted [That rule still *goes*. Anything *goes*.] —The past tense is **went**, the past participle is **gone**, the present participle is **go'ing**. ◆***n.*** **1** a success [They made a *go* of their marriage.] **2** energy or liveliness: *used only in everyday talk* [You have plenty of *go*.] **3** a try: *used only in everyday talk* [Let me have a *go* at it.] —**go along, 1** to continue. **2** to agree. **3** to accompany. —**go at,** to attack or work at. —☆**go back on, 1** to betray. **2** to break, as a promise. *Used only in everyday talk.* —**go beyond,** to do more than; exceed. —**go by, 1** to pass. **2** to be guided by. **3** to be known by a certain name. —**go for, 1** to try to get. ☆**2** to support. ☆**3** to attack: *used only in everyday talk.* **4** to be attracted by: *used only in everyday talk.* —☆**go in for,** to take part in; engage in: *used only in everyday talk.* —**go in with,** to join. —**go off, 1** to leave. **2** to explode. **3** to happen. —**go on, 1** to continue. **2** to behave. **3** to happen [What's *going on* outside?] —**go out, 1** to come to an end; stop. **2** to go to a party, the theater, etc. **3** to try out [*Go out* for the football team.] —**go over, 1** to examine carefully. **2** to do or look over again. ☆**3** to be successful: *used only in everyday talk.* —☆**go steady,** to date only each other: *used only in everyday talk.* —**go through, 1** to do thoroughly. **2** to undergo; experience. ☆**3** to search. ☆**4** to become accepted. —**go through with,** to complete. —**go together, 1** to suit or fit one another. ☆**2** to date only each other: *used only in everyday talk.* —**go under,** ☆to fail, as in business. —**go without,** to do without. —**let go, 1** to let escape. **2** to stop holding. **3** to give up; abandon. **4** to remove from a job; fire. —**let oneself go,** to stop holding back in one's feelings or actions. —**no go,** not possible; no use: *used only in everyday talk.* —**on the go,** always moving about or doing something: *used only in everyday talk.*

**goad** (gōd) ***n.*** **1** a stick with a sharp point, used in driving oxen. **2** anything that drives a person to do something; spur. ◆***v.*** to drive with a goad; urge on [*goaded* into a rage by insults].

**goal** (gōl) ***n.*** **1** the place at which a race or trip is ended. **2** an end that one tries to reach; aim or purpose [His *goal* was to become a nurse.] **3** the line, net, etc. in certain games over or into which the ball or puck must go to score; also, a score made in this way.

**goal·keep·er** (gōl'kēp'ər) ***n.*** a player who stays at the goal to keep the ball or puck from crossing or entering it: *also* **goal·ie** (gōl'ē). *See the picture.*

**goal post** either of a pair of posts with a crossbar, used as the goal in football, soccer, etc.

**goat** (gōt) ***n.*** **1** an animal that chews its cud, has hollow horns, and is related to the sheep. ☆**2** *a shorter form of* **scapegoat**: *used only in everyday talk.*

☆**goat·ee** (gō tē') ***n.*** a pointed beard on a man's chin. *See the picture.*

**goat·herd** (gōt'hurd) ***n.*** a person who herds or tends goats.

**goat·skin** (gōt'skin) ***n.*** **1** the skin of a goat. **2** leather made from this. **3** a container for wine or water that is made from this leather.

| | | | | | | | |
|---|---|---|---|---|---|---|---|
| **a** | fat | **ir** | here | **ou** | out | **zh** | leisure |
| **ā** | ape | **ī** | bite, fire | **u** | up | **ng** | ring |
| **ä** | car, lot | **ō** | go | **ur** | fur | | a *in* ago |
| **e** | ten | **ô** | law, horn | **ch** | chin | | e *in* agent |
| **er** | care | **oi** | oil | **sh** | she | ə = | i *in* unity |
| **ē** | even | **oo** | look | **th** | thin | | o *in* collect |
| **i** | hit | **o͞o** | tool | ***th*** | then | | u *in* focus |

**gob** (gäb) ***n.*** **1** a lump or mass, as of something soft. **2 gobs,** *pl.* a large amount: *used only in everyday talk* [She has *gobs* of money.]

**gob·ble[1]** (gäb′′l) ***n.*** the throaty sound made by a male turkey. ◆***v.*** to make this sound. —**gob′bled, gob′bling**

**gob·ble[2]** (gäb′′l) ***v.*** **1** to eat quickly and greedily. **2** to grab eagerly; snatch [The land was *gobbled* up quickly.] —**gob′bled, gob′bling**

**gob·bler** (gäb′lər) ***n.*** a male turkey.

**go-be·tween** (gō′bi twēn′) ***n.*** a person who deals with each of two sides in making arrangements between them.

**Go·bi** (gō′bē) a large desert in Mongolia.

**gob·let** (gäb′lit) ***n.*** a drinking glass with a base and stem.

**gob·lin** (gäb′lin) ***n.*** an ugly little elf or spirit in folk tales, that is full of mischief.

**go·cart** (gō′kärt) ***n.*** ☆a small carriage pushed by hand, in which a young child sits to be taken about.

**god** (gäd) ***n.*** **1** a being that is thought of as living forever and having power over people and nature, especially such a being that is male [Odin was the chief Norse *god.* Neptune was the Roman *god* of the sea.] **2** any image or thing that is worshiped as a god; idol. **3** any person or thing that one thinks of as being most important [Money is their *god.*] —**God,** in the Christian, Jewish, and Muslim religions, the all-powerful Being who made and rules the universe and is perfectly good and just.



**god·child** (gäd′chīld) ***n.*** a godson or goddaughter. —*pl.* **god′chil′dren**

**god·daugh·ter** (gäd′dôt′ər) ***n.*** a girl for whom a man or woman acts as godparent.

**god·dess** (gäd′is) ***n.*** **1** a female god. **2** a very beautiful or charming woman.

**god·fa·ther** (gäd′fä′*th*ər) ***n.*** a man who pledges, as at the baptism of a child, that he will be responsible for its religious upbringing.

**god·head** (gäd′hed) ***n.*** **1** the condition of being a god; divinity: *also* **god·hood** (gäd′hood). **2 Godhead,** God.

**god·less** (gäd′lis) ***adj.*** **1** not believing in God. **2** wicked; evil. —**god′less·ness *n.***

**god·like** (gäd′līk) ***adj.*** like or fit for God or a god; very noble or powerful; divine.

**god·ly** (gäd′lē) ***adj.*** serious and faithful in worshiping God; religious. —**god′li·er, god′li·est** —**god′li·ness *n.***

**god·moth·er** (gäd′mu*th*′ər) ***n.*** a woman who pledges, as at the baptism of a child, that she will be responsible for its religious upbringing.

**god·par·ent** (gäd′per′ənt) ***n.*** a godfather or godmother.

**god·send** (gäd′send) ***n.*** something that comes when needed the most, as if sent by God.

**god·son** (gäd′sun) ***n.*** a boy for whom a man or woman acts as godparent.

**God·speed** (gäd′spēd′) ***n.*** success; good luck.

**God·win Aus·ten** (gäd′win ôs′tən) a mountain in northern Jammu and Kashmir. It is the second highest mountain in the world, a little over 8,540 meters (or 28,000 feet).

**Goe·the** (gur′tə *or* gāt′ə), **Jo·hann von** (yō′hän fôn) 1749–1832; German writer of poems and plays.

☆**go-get·ter** (gō′get′ər) ***n.*** a person who works hard in a ruthless, pushing way to get something: *used only in everyday talk.*

**gog·gle** (gäg′′l) ***v.*** to stare with the eyes very wide open [He *goggled* at the odd sight.] —**gog′gled, gog′gling** ◆***adj.*** bulging [*goggle* eyes]. ◆***n.* goggles,** *pl.* large eyeglasses that fit tightly around the eyes to protect them from wind, dust, etc. *See the picture.*

**go·ing** (gō′ing) ***n.*** **1** the act or time of leaving; departure [the *goings* and comings of buses]. **2** the condition of a road or path for traveling [The *going* was difficult through the mud.] **3** conditions as they have an effect on progress [The *going* is rough for a person in a new job.] ◆***adj.*** **1** doing its work or business successfully [a *going* concern]. **2** of the present time; most recent [the *going* rate for plumbers]. —**be going to,** to be planning to; will or shall.

**goi·ter** or **goi·tre** (goit′ər) ***n.*** a swelling in the front of the neck caused by the thyroid gland becoming larger.

**gold** (gōld) ***n.*** **1** a heavy, yellow metal that is a chemical element. Gold is a precious metal and is used in coins and jewelry. It is easily beaten or stretched into different shapes. **2** gold coins; also, money or wealth. **3** a bright or shining yellow. ◆***adj.*** **1** of or containing gold [*gold* coins; a *gold* watch]. **2** having the color of gold.

**gold·en** (gōl′d′n) ***adj.*** **1** made of or containing gold [*golden* earrings]. **2** bright-yellow [*golden* autumn leaves]. **3** very good or favorable; excellent [a *golden* opportunity]. **4** happy and flourishing [the *Golden* Age of Greece]. **5** marking the 50th anniversary [a *golden* wedding].

**golden ag·er** (āj′ər) an elderly person, especially one who is 65 or older and retired: *used only in everyday talk.*

**Golden Fleece** the magic fleece of gold in a Greek myth, that Jason captured from a dragon.

**Golden Gate** the water passage between San Francisco Bay and the Pacific.

**gold·en·rod** (gōl′d′n räd) ***n.*** a common wild plant with small, yellow flowers on long stalks. It blooms at the end of the summer.

**golden rule** the rule that one should treat others in the same way that one wants to be treated by them.

**gold-filled** (gōld′fild′) ***adj.*** covered with a thin layer of gold [a *gold-filled* ring].

**gold·finch** (gōld′finch) ***n.*** ☆a small American finch. The male has a yellow body with black markings on the wings.

**gold·fish** (gōld′fish) ***n.*** a small, yellow or orange fish, often kept in ponds or fish bowls.

**gold·smith** (gōld′smith) ***n.*** a skilled worker who makes things of gold.

**golf** (gôlf *or* gälf) ***n.*** a game played with a small, hard ball and a set of clubs on an outdoor course with 9 or 18 holes. The player tries to hit the ball into each of the holes in turn with the fewest possible strokes. *See the picture.* ◆***v.*** to play this game. —**golf′er *n.***

**Go·li·ath** (gə lī′əth) in the Bible, a giant killed by David with a stone from a sling.

**gol·ly** (gäl′ē) ***interj.*** an exclamation showing pleasure, surprise, wonder, etc.

**Go·mor·rah** or **Go·mor·rha** (gə môr′ə) *see* **Sodom.**
**gon·do·la** (gän′də lə *or* gän dō′lə) ***n.*** **1** a long, narrow boat with high, pointed ends, used on the canals of Venice. *See the picture.* ☆**2** a railroad freight car with low sides and no top. **3** a cabin fastened to the underside of a balloon or airship. ☆**4** a car held from and moved along a cable, for carrying passengers.
**gon·do·lier** (gän də lir′) ***n.*** a man who moves a gondola through the water with a pole or oar.
**gone** (gôn) *past participle of* **go.** ◆***adj.*** **1** moved away; departed. **2** ruined, lost, dead, etc. **3** used up. **4** ago; past [in days long *gone*].
**gong** (gông) ***n.*** a big metal disk that gives a loud, booming sound when struck.
☆**goo** (go͞o) ***n.*** anything sticky, or sticky and sweet: *a slang word.* —**goo′ey** ***adj.***
☆**goo·ber** (go͞o′bər) ***n.*** a peanut: *chiefly a Southern word.*
**good** (go͝od) ***adj.*** **1** better than the usual or average kind [*good* work; a *good* writer; a *good* grade]. **2** not for everyday use; best [Let's use our *good* china.] **3** right for the purpose; satisfactory [a cloth *good* for polishing silver]. **4** pleasing or satisfying; enjoyable or happy [*good* news; a *good* time]. **5** helpful; that benefits [Exercise is *good* for the health.] **6** doing what is right or proper; well-behaved [a *good* child]. **7** kind or friendly [a *good* neighbor]. **8** in good condition; sound, fresh, etc. [*good* health; *good* eggs]. **9** honorable or respected [a *good* name]. **10** thorough; complete [Do a *good* job.] **11** great or large [a *good* many people]. **12** at least; full [She lost a *good* ten pounds.] —The comparative of *good* is **better,** the superlative is **best.** ◆***n.*** **1** that which is good [to know *good* from evil]. **2** benefit [for the *good* of all]. *See also* **goods.** ◆***interj.*** a word spoken to show that one agrees or that one is pleased or satisfied. —**as good as,** nearly; practically. —**for good,** for all time or for the last time. —☆**good and,** very: *used only in everyday talk* [He's *good and* angry.] —**good for, 1** able to last for. **2** able to pay or give. —☆**make good, 1** to repay or replace. **2** to succeed. **3** to carry out, as a promise or boast. —**no good,** useless or worthless. —**to the good,** as a profit or advantage.
**good·by** or **good-by** (go͝od bī′) ***interj., n.*** *other spellings of* **goodbye.** *—pl.* **good·bys′** or **good-bys′**
**good·bye** or **good-bye** (go͝od bī′) ***interj., n.*** a word said when leaving someone; farewell [We said our *goodbyes* quickly and left.] *—pl.* **good·byes′** or **good-byes′**
**Good Friday** the Friday before Easter Sunday. On Good Friday Christians hold services in memory of the Crucifixion of Jesus.
**good-heart·ed** (go͝od′här′tid) ***adj.*** kind and generous.
**Good Hope, Cape of** a cape at the southern tip of Africa.
**good-hu·mored** (go͝od′hyo͞o′mərd) ***adj.*** cheerful and agreeable [a *good-humored* mood].
**good-look·ing** (go͝od′lo͝ok′ing) ***adj.*** pleasing to look at; handsome or beautiful.
**good·ly** (go͝od′lē) ***adj.*** rather large [a *goodly* sum of money].
**good morning, good afternoon, good evening, good day** words of greeting or farewell used at various times of the day.

golfer

goggles
gondola

**good-na·tured** (go͝od′nā′chərd) ***adj.*** pleasant and friendly; easy to get along with.
**good·ness** (go͝od′nis) ***n.*** the condition of being good. ◆***interj.*** an exclamation showing surprise [My *goodness! Goodness* me!]
**good night** words of farewell at night.
**goods** (go͝odz) ***n.pl.*** **1** things made to be sold; wares. **2** personal property that can be moved [household *goods*]. **3** cloth; fabric [dress *goods*].
**good Samaritan** any person who pities and helps others in an unselfish way.

The **good Samaritan** is a man in a Bible story who helps a stranger who was beaten and robbed on the road to Jericho, after other travelers passed the wounded man without stopping.



**good-sized** (go͝od′sīzd′) ***adj.*** big or fairly big; ample [a *good-sized* house].
**good-tem·pered** (go͝od′tem′pərd) ***adj.*** cheerful and patient; not easily made angry.
**good turn** a friendly and helpful act; favor.
**good will 1** a feeling of kindness and friendliness. **2** the extra amount that a business is worth because of its good name and the trade it has built up. *Also* **good·will** (go͝od′wil′) ***n.***
**good·y** (go͝od′ē) ***n.*** a candy, or other sweet thing to eat: *used only in everyday talk.* *—pl.* **good′ies** ◆***interj.*** a child's exclamation showing delight.
**goof** (go͞of) ***n.*** **1** a stupid or silly person. **2** a mistake; blunder. ◆***v.*** **1** to make a mistake; blunder, foil, etc. **2** to waste time, shirk one's duties, etc. [They *goof* off instead of studying.] *This word is slang in all its meanings.*
**goose** (go͞os) ***n.*** **1** a swimming bird that is like a duck but has a larger body and a longer neck; especially, the female of this bird. The male is called a *gander*. **2** the flesh of the goose, used as food. **3** a silly person. *—pl.* **geese** —**cook one's goose,** to spoil one's chances: *used only in everyday talk.*

| | | | |
|---|---|---|---|
| **a** fat | **ir** here | **ou** out | **zh** leisure |
| **ā** ape | **ī** bite, fire | **u** up | **ng** ring |
| **ä** car, lot | **ō** go | **ur** fur | a *in* ago |
| **e** ten | **ô** law, horn | **ch** chin | e *in* agent |
| **er** care | **oi** oil | **sh** she | ə = i *in* unity |
| **ē** even | **o͝o** look | **th** thin | o *in* collect |
| **i** hit | **o͞o** tool | ***th*** then | u *in* focus |

g

**goose·ber·ry** (gōōs′ber′ē) ***n.*** a small, round, sour berry used in making pies, jams, etc. It grows on a prickly shrub. —*pl.* **goose′ber′ries**

**goose flesh** or ☆**goose bumps** or ☆**goose pimples** a bumpy condition of the skin caused by cold or fear.

**GOP** or **G.O.P.** the Grand Old Party: *a name for the* **Republican Party.**

☆**go·pher** (gō′fər) ***n.*** **1** a furry animal like a large rat, with pouches in its cheeks. It lives in tunnels which it digs underground. *See the picture.* **2** a striped ground squirrel of the prairies.

**gore**[1] (gôr) ***n.*** blood from a wound; especially, clotted blood.

**gore**[2] (gôr) ***v.*** to stab or wound with a horn or tusk. —**gored, gor′ing**

**gore**[3] (gôr) ***n.*** a piece of cloth shaped like a triangle, that is sewed into a skirt, sail, etc. to make it fuller.

**gorge** (gôrj) ***n.*** **1** a narrow pass or valley between steep cliffs or walls. **2** the throat or gullet. ◆***v.*** to stuff with food in a greedy way [to *gorge* oneself with cake]. —**gorged, gorg′ing —make one's gorge rise,** to make one disgusted or angry.

**gor·geous** (gôr′jəs) ***adj.*** bright and richly colored; splendid; magnificent [the *gorgeous* tail of a peacock]. *See* SYNONYMS *at* **splendid.** —**gor′geous·ly** ***adv.***

**Gor·gon** (gôr′gən) in Greek myths, any of three sisters who had snakes instead of hair and were so horrible that anyone who looked at them turned to stone.



☆**go·ril·la** (gə ril′ə) ***n.*** the largest and strongest of the apes, found in African jungles. *See the picture.*

**gorse** (gôrs) ***n.*** *another name for* **furze.**

**gor·y** (gôr′ē) ***adj.*** **1** covered with gore; bloody. **2** full of bloodshed or killing [a *gory* movie]. —**gor′i·er, gor′i·est —gor′i·ness** ***n.***

☆**gosh** (gäsh) ***interj.*** an exclamation showing surprise, wonder, etc.

**gos·ling** (gäz′liŋ) ***n.*** a young goose.

**gos·pel** (gäs′p′l) ***n.*** **1** *often* **Gospel,** the teachings of Jesus and the Apostles. **2 Gospel,** any of the first four books of the New Testament: *Matthew, Mark, Luke,* or *John.* **3** anything that is believed to be absolutely true [We accepted the story as *gospel.*]

> **Gospel** comes from an old English word *gōdspel,* which meant "good story or good news." Because this word was written this way, it came to be thought of as meaning "God's story."

**gos·sa·mer** (gäs′ə mər) ***n.*** **1** a fine cobweb or a thin thread from one. **2** a very thin, delicate cloth. ◆***adj.*** light as a cobweb [*gossamer* wings].

**gos·sip** (gäs′əp) ***n.*** **1** small talk or chatter about someone, often about things heard from others but not known to be facts. **2** a person who spends much time in such talk. ◆***v.*** to spread gossip. —**gos′sip·er** ***n.*** —**gos′sip·y** ***adj.***

**got** (gät) *past tense and a past participle of* **get.**

**Goth** (gäth) ***n.*** a member of the German tribes that conquered most of the Western Roman Empire in the 3d, 4th, and 5th centuries A.D.

**Goth·ic** (gäth′ik) ***adj.*** **1** of the Goths or their language. **2** of or describing a style of architecture common in western Europe between the 12th and the 16th centuries. *See the picture.* **3** describing a novel, tale, etc. that has a gloomy setting suggesting horror or mystery. ◆***n.*** **1** the language of the Goths. **2** Gothic architecture.

**got·ten** (gät′'n) *a past participle of* **get.**

**Gou·da cheese** (gou′də *or* gōō′də) a mild, partly soft or hard cheese, usually coated with red wax.

**gouge** (gouj) ***n.*** **1** a chisel with a grooved blade for cutting grooves in wood. **2** a groove cut with such a chisel. ☆**3** the act of charging too high a price or of cheating out of money: *used only in everyday talk.* ◆***v.*** **1** to make grooves in with a gouge. **2** to scoop out [to *gouge* out dirt]. ☆**3** to charge too high a price; also, to cheat out of money: *used only in everyday talk.* —**gouged, goug′ing**

**gou·lash** (gōō′läsh) ***n.*** a beef or veal stew seasoned with paprika.

**Gou·nod** (gōō nō′ *or* gōō′nō), **Charles** (shärl) 1818–1893; French composer.

**gourd** (gôrd *or* goord) ***n.*** **1** a vine with large fruit containing many seeds. Gourds belong to the same family as the squash and pumpkin. **2** the fruit of this vine, not fit for eating but often dried and used for cups, bowls, etc. *See the picture.*

**gour·mand** (goor′mənd *or* goor mänd′) ***n.*** a person who is very fond of eating.

**gour·met** (goor′mā *or* goor mā′) ***n.*** a person who likes fine food and is a good judge of it.

**gout** (gout) ***n.*** a sickness in which there is swelling and pain in the joints, especially in the big toe. —**gout′y** ***adj.***

**gov.** or **Gov.** *abbreviation for* **government, governor.**

**gov·ern** (guv′ərn) ***v.*** **1** to have control over; rule; direct or manage [to *govern* a nation; to *govern* one's feelings]. **2** to influence the action or conduct of; guide [Newspapers help *govern* public opinion.] —**gov′ern·a·ble** ***adj.***

> SYNONYMS: **Govern** suggests that those in power use their power over the people of a country in an orderly and just way and for the good of all [We are *governed* by officials that we elect.] **Rule** suggests that those in power use their power the way a dictator does, in a harsh and unjust way and for their own advantage [That country is *ruled* by a tyrant.]

**gov·ern·ess** (guv′ər nəs) ***n.*** a woman who is hired to teach and train children in a private home.

**gov·ern·ment** (guv′ərn mənt *or* guv′ər mənt) ***n.*** **1** control or rule, as over a country, city, etc. **2** a system of ruling or controlling [a centralized *government;* democratic *governments*]. **3** all the people who control the affairs of a country, city, etc. [The French *government* moved to Vichy during World War II.] —☆**gov′ern·men′tal** ***adj.***

**gov·er·nor** (guv′ər nər) ***n.*** ☆**1** the person elected to be head of a State of the United States. **2** a person appointed to govern a province, territory, etc. **3** any of the persons who direct some organization [the board of *governors* of a hospital]. **4** a device in an engine, etc. that automatically controls its speed. —**gov′er·nor·ship′** ***n.***

> **Governor** comes from a Latin word meaning "pilot." A governor is thought of as directing the business of a government in the same way as a pilot steers the course of a ship.

**govt.** or **Govt.** *abbreviation for* **government.**

**gown** (goun) ***n.*** **1** a woman's dress. **2** a nightgown. **3** *same as* **dressing gown. 4** a long, flowing robe worn by judges, ministers, etc. ◆***v.*** to dress in a gown.

**Go·ya** (gô′yä), **Francisco de** 1746–1828; Spanish painter.

**Gr.** *abbreviation for* **Greece** *or* **Greek.**

**gr.** *abbreviation for* **grain** *or* **grains, gram** *or* **grams.**

**grab** (grab) ***v.*** **1** to seize or snatch suddenly. **2** to take by force or in a selfish way. —**grabbed, grab′-bing** ◆***n.*** **1** the act of grabbing [He made a *grab* for the handle.] **2** something grabbed.

☆**grab bag** a container holding various articles that are wrapped or in bags. Buyers pay a fixed price for each bag without knowing what is in it.

**grab·by** (grab′ē) ***adj.*** eager for all that one can get; greedy. —**grab′bi·er, grab′bi·est**

**grace** (grās) ***n.*** **1** beauty of form, or smoothness and easiness of movement [the *grace* of a statue; to dance with *grace*]. **2** a pleasing quality or manner [She has all the social *graces*.] **3** a sense of what is right and proper [They could have had the *grace* to make their visit brief.] **4** an extra period allowed for doing or paying something [We have a week of *grace* to pay the rent.] **5** a short prayer asking a blessing or giving thanks for a meal. **6 Grace,** a title of respect in speaking to or about an archbishop, duke, or duchess. **7** the love and favor that God shows toward people. **8 Graces,** *pl.* three sister goddesses in Greek myths who brought pleasure and beauty to life. ◆***v.*** **1** to bring honor to [The mayor *graced* our banquet with her presence.] **2** to add grace or charm to; adorn [Paintings *graced* the walls.] —**graced, grac′ing** —**in the bad graces of,** disliked by. —**in the good graces of,** liked by. —**with bad grace,** in an unwilling or sullen way. —**with good grace,** in a willing way.

**grace·ful** (grās′fəl) ***adj.*** having grace, or beauty of form or movement. —**grace′ful·ly** ***adv.*** —**grace′ful-ness** ***n.***

**grace·less** (grās′lis) ***adj.*** **1** not showing any sense of what is right [a *graceless* remark]. **2** without grace; not elegant; clumsy. —**grace′less·ly** ***adv.*** —**grace′-less·ness** ***n.***

**gra·cious** (grā′shəs) ***adj.*** **1** kind, polite, and charming [a *gracious* host and hostess]. **2** full of grace and comfort [*gracious* living]. ◆***interj.*** an expression showing surprise. —**gra′cious·ly** ***adv.*** —**gra′cious·ness** ***n.***

**grack·le** (grak′'l) ***n.*** ☆a kind of blackbird that is a little smaller than a crow.

☆**grad** (grad) ***n.*** *a shorter form of* **graduate**: *used only in everyday talk.*

**grad.** *abbreviation for* **graduate, graduated.**

**gra·da·tion** (grā dā′shən) ***n.*** **1** a gradual change by steps or stages [a *gradation* of color from pink to deep red]. **2** any of the steps or stages in a series.

**grade** (grād) ***n.*** **1** any of the stages or steps in a series [Civil service jobs are usually arranged in *grades*.] **2** a degree in a scale of rank or quality [Which is the best *grade* of oranges?] ☆**3** any of the divisions of a school course, usually equal to one year [Jim is twelve years old and in the seventh *grade*.] ☆**4** a mark or score on a test or in a school course [Her *grades* are mostly B's.] **5** a group of people or class of things that are of the same rank, worth, class, etc. ☆**6** amount of slope, as in a road; also, a sloping part [The train went up a steep *grade*.] ◆***v.*** **1** to arrange in grades; sort [to *grade* apples]. ☆**2** to give a grade to, as on a test. ☆**3** to make ground level or slope it evenly. **4** to change gradually [green *grading* into blue]. —**grad′ed, grad′ing** —☆**make the grade,** to succeed.

gorillas
1.5 m (5 ft.) high

gourds

gopher
30 cm (12 in.) long, including tail

Gothic architecture



☆**grade crossing** the place where railroad tracks cross other tracks or a road on the same level.

☆**grade school** *another name for* **elementary school.**

**grad·u·al** (graj′oo wəl) ***adj.*** taking place by degrees or changes that are so small that they can hardly be seen; little by little [a *gradual* return to health]. —**grad′u·al·ly** ***adv.***

**grad·u·ate** (graj′oo wit) ***n.*** a person who has finished a course of study at a school or college and has been given a diploma or degree. ◆***adj.*** **1** that is a graduate [*Graduate* students work for degrees above the bachelor's.] ☆**2** of or for graduates [*graduate* courses]. ◆***v.*** (graj′oo wāt) **1** to make or become a graduate of a school or college. **2** to mark off with small lines for measuring [A thermometer is a tube *graduated* in degrees.] **3** to arrange in grades or steps [A *graduated* income tax makes the tax higher as the income goes higher.] —**grad′u·at·ed, grad′u·at·ing** —**grad′u·a′tion** ***n.***

**graf·fi·ti** (grə fēt′ē) ***n.pl.*** words, slogans, drawings, etc. crudely scratched or scribbled on a wall in some public place. —*sing.* **graf·fi·to** (grə fēt′ō)

**graft** (graft) ***n.*** **1** a shoot or bud of one plant or tree set into a cut made in another so as to grow there. *See*

| | | | |
|---|---|---|---|
| **a** fat | **ir** here | **ou** out | **zh** leisure |
| **ā** ape | **ī** bite, fire | **u** up | **ŋ** ring |
| **ä** car, lot | **ō** go | **ur** fur | a *in* ago |
| **e** ten | **ô** law, horn | **ch** chin | e *in* agent |
| **er** care | **oi** oil | **sh** she | ə = i *in* unity |
| **ē** even | **oo** look | **th** thin | o *in* collect |
| **i** hit | **ōō** tool | ***th*** then | u *in* focus |

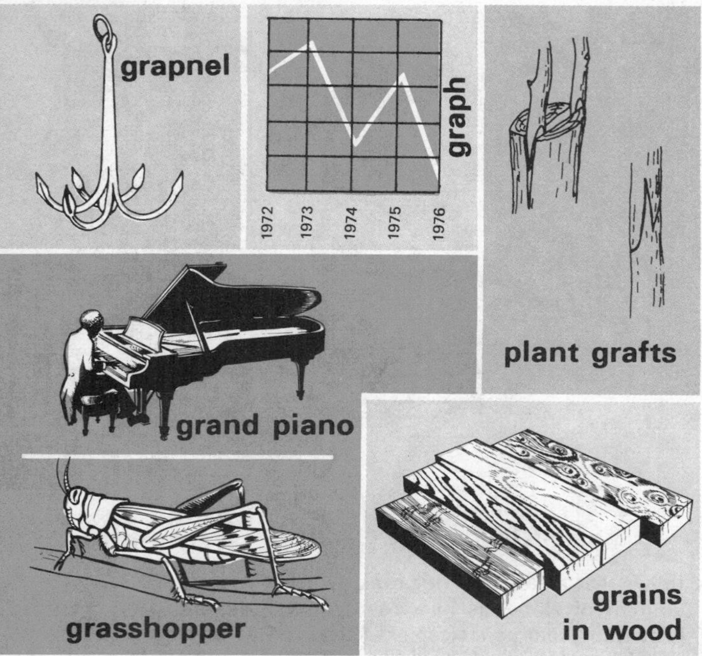




*the picture.* **2** the setting in of such a bud or shoot. **3** a piece of skin, bone, etc. taken from one body, or from a part of a body, and set into another so as to grow there. ☆**4** the dishonest use of one's job, especially by a public official, to get money; also, money got in this way. ➜**v.** **1** to set a graft into a plant or animal [to *graft* skin from the thigh onto the chest]. ☆**2** to get money by graft. —**graft′er** ***n.***

☆**gra·ham** (grā′əm) ***adj.*** made of coarsely ground whole-wheat flour [*graham* crackers].

**Gra·ham** (grā′əm), **Martha** 1893?– ; U.S. dancer.

**Grail** (grāl) in medieval legend, the lost cup from which Jesus had drunk at the Last Supper. It was sought for by the knights of King Arthur.

**grain** (grān) ***n.*** **1** the small, hard seed of any cereal plant, as wheat, corn, or rye. **2** such cereal plants; also, the seeds of cereal plants in general [fields of *grain;* bags of *grain*]. **3** a single, tiny piece of salt, sugar, sand, or the like. **4** a tiny bit [a *grain* of sense]. **5** a very small unit of weight, equal to 0.0648 gram. **6** the markings or pattern formed by the way the layers or fibers are arranged in a piece of wood, stone, etc. *See the picture.* **7** the way one thinks and feels; one's nature [The thought of stealing goes against my *grain.*] ➜**v.** to paint with marks that imitate the grain of wood, etc.

☆**grain elevator** a tall building for storing grain.

**gram** (gram) ***n.*** the basic unit of weight in the metric system. It is the weight of one cubic centimeter of distilled water at 4°C; one gram equals about 1/28 of an ounce.

**-gram** (gram) *a suffix meaning* something written, drawn, or recorded [A *cablegram* is a message written for sending by electric cable.]

**gram·mar** (gram′ər) ***n.*** **1** the study of the forms of words and of the way they are arranged in phrases and sentences. **2** a system of rules for speaking and writing a particular language. **3** a book containing such rules. **4** the way a person speaks or writes, as judged by these rules [His *grammar* is poor.]

**gram·mar·i·an** (grə mer′ē ən) ***n.*** a person who has made a special study of grammar.

**grammar school** ☆*an earlier term for* **elementary school.**

**gram·mat·i·cal** (grə mat′i k'l) ***adj.*** of or according to the rules of grammar ["Between you and I" is a *grammatical* mistake.] —**gram·mat′i·cal·ly** ***adv.***

**gramme** (gram) ***n.*** *a chiefly British spelling of* **gram.**

**gram·pus** (gram′pəs) ***n.*** a small, black, fierce whale related to the dolphins. —*pl.* **gram′pus·es**

**Gra·na·da** (grə nä′də) a city in southern Spain.

**gran·a·ry** (gran′ər ē) ***n.*** a place or building for storing grain. —*pl.* **gran′a·ries**

**grand** (grand) ***adj.*** **1** standing out because of its great size and beauty [a *grand* mansion]. **2** splendid and costly; luxurious [a *grand* banquet]. **3** more important or higher in rank than others [a *grand* duke]. **4** most important; main [the *grand* ballroom of the palace]. **5** very dignified and noble; distinguished [the *grand* old statesman]. **6** complete; full [a *grand* total of $200]. **7** acting too important; haughty [She dismissed us with a *grand* wave of her hand.] **8** very satisfying or pleasing: *used only in everyday talk.* ➜**n.** ☆a thousand dollars: *a slang word.* —*pl.* **grand** —**grand′ly** ***adv.*** —**grand′ness** ***n.***

SYNONYMS: Whatever is **grand** is impressive because of its great size and beauty or splendor [the *Grand* Canyon]. Whatever is **magnificent** has the greatest beauty or splendor [a *magnificent* voice].

**grand·aunt** (grand′ant *or* grand′änt) ***n.*** *another name for* **great-aunt.**

**Grand Canyon** the deep gorge of the Colorado River, in northern Arizona.

**grand·child** (gran′chīld) ***n.*** a child of one's son or daughter. —*pl.* **grand′chil′dren**

**grand·daugh·ter** (gran′dôt′ər) ***n.*** a daughter of one's son or daughter.

**gran·dee** (gran dē′) ***n.*** **1** a nobleman of the highest rank in Spain or Portugal. **2** any man of high rank.

**gran·deur** (gran′jər) ***n.*** **1** great size, beauty, dignity, etc.; splendor [the *grandeur* of the Swiss Alps]. **2** greatness of intellect or moral character [the *grandeur* of his sacrifice].

**grand·fa·ther** (gran′fä′*th*ər *or* grand′fä′*th*ər) ***n.*** **1** the father of one's father or mother. **2** a forefather.

☆**grandfather clock** or **grandfather's clock** a large clock with a pendulum, contained in a tall, upright case.

**gran·dil·o·quent** (gran dil′ə kwənt) ***adj.*** using long words and fancy language that sounds more important than it is. —**gran·dil′o·quence** ***n.***

**gran·di·ose** (gran′dē ōs) ***adj.*** **1** very grand in size, beauty, etc.; magnificent; impressive. **2** seeming or trying to seem very grand or important without really being so.

**grand jury** a special jury with usually more than 12 members that looks into cases of crime and suspected crime, and decides whether there is enough evidence to hold a trial before a regular jury.

**grand·ma** (gran′mä *or* gra′mä) ***n.*** grandmother: *used only in everyday talk.*

**grand·moth·er** (gran′mu*th*′ər *or* grand′mu*th*′ər) ***n.*** the mother of one's father or mother.

**grand·neph·ew** (gran′nef′yo͞o *or* grand′nef′yo͞o) ***n.*** a son of one's nephew or niece.

**grand·niece** (gran′nēs *or* grand′nēs) ***n.*** a daughter of one's nephew or niece.

**grand·pa** (gran′pä *or* gram′pä) ***n.*** grandfather: *used only in everyday talk.*

**grand·par·ent** (gran′per′ənt *or* grand′per′ənt) ***n.*** a grandfather or grandmother.

**grand piano** a large piano with its strings set flat in a case shaped like a harp. *See the picture.*

**Grand Rapids** a city in southwestern Michigan.

**grand·son** (gran′sun *or* grand′sun) ***n.*** a son of one's son or daughter.

**grand·stand** (gran′stand *or* grand′stand) ***n.*** the main seating structure for people watching an outdoor sports event, as at a race track.

**grand·un·cle** (grand′uŋ′k'l) ***n.*** *another name for* **great-uncle.**

**grange** (grānj) ***n.*** **1** a farm with all its buildings. ☆**2 Grange,** a national association of farmers, or any of its local lodges.

**gran·ite** (gran′it) ***n.*** a very hard rock used for buildings and monuments. It is usually gray or pink and can be polished like marble.

**gran·ny** or **gran·nie** (gran′ē) ***n.*** **1** a grandmother. **2** an old woman. *This word is used only in everyday talk.* —*pl.* **gran′nies**

☆**gran·o·la** (grə nō′lə) ***n.*** a breakfast cereal of rolled oats, wheat germ, sesame seeds, honey, bits of dried fruit or nuts, etc.

**grant** (grant) ***v.*** **1** to give what is asked or wanted; let have; agree to [Her parents *granted* her request.] *See* SYNONYMS *at* **give.** **2** to admit as true [I *grant* that you have reason to be angry.] ◆***n.*** **1** the act of granting. **2** something granted or given [a *grant* of $5,000 for study; land *grants* given by Congress for building railroads]. —**take for granted,** to think of as already proved or settled.

**Grant** (grant), **Ulysses S.** 1822–1885; the 18th president of the United States, from 1869 to 1877. He was commander in chief of the Union forces in the Civil War.

**gran·u·lar** (gran′yə lər) ***adj.*** of, like, or containing grains or granules [*granular* sugar].

**gran·u·late** (gran′yə lāt) ***v.*** to form into grains or granules [This sugar is *granulated.*] —**gran′u·lat·ed, gran′u·lat·ing**

**gran·ule** (gran′yo͝ol) ***n.*** a small grain or tiny particle.

**grape** (grāp) ***n.*** **1** a small fruit with a smooth skin, usually purple, red, or green, that grows in bunches on a woody vine. Grapes are eaten raw and are used to make wine and raisins. **2** a grapevine.

**grape·fruit** (grāp′fro͞ot) ***n.*** a large, round citrus fruit with a yellow rind and a juicy, somewhat sour pulp.

**grape·vine** (grāp′vīn) ***n.*** **1** a woody vine that grapes grow on. ☆**2** rumor or gossip [I hear by the *grapevine* that he's leaving town.]

**graph** (graf) ***n.*** a chart or diagram that shows the changes taking place in something, by the use of connected lines, a curve, etc. [a *graph* showing how sales figures vary during the year]. *See the picture.*

**-graph** (graf) *a suffix meaning:* **1** something written or recorded [A *photograph* is a picture recorded by a camera.] **2** something that writes or records [A *seismograph* records earthquakes.]

**graph·eme** (graf′ēm) ***n.*** all the letters or combined letters that stand for the same sound, or a single phoneme [The letters *-ff* in *off, -gh* in *cough,* and *ph-* in *phony* all belong to one *grapheme.*]

**graph·ic** (graf′ik) ***adj.*** **1** shown by a graph [a *graphic* record of the rainfall for a month]. **2** told in a way that makes a sharp picture in the mind; vivid [The announcer gave a *graphic* account of the fire.] **3** having to do with drawing, painting, engraving, etc. [the *graphic* arts]. **4** of or shown in handwriting; written. —**graph′i·cal·ly *adv.***

**graph·ite** (graf′īt) ***n.*** a soft, black carbon used as the writing part of a pencil, as a lubricating powder, etc.

**graph·ol·o·gy** (gra fäl′ə jē) ***n.*** the study of handwriting, especially as a clue to a person's character, abilities, etc. —**graph·ol′o·gist *n.***

**-gra·phy** (grə fē) *a suffix meaning:* **1** a method of writing, recording, picturing, etc. [*photography*]. **2** a science that describes something [*geography*].

**grap·nel** (grap′n'l) ***n.*** **1** a small anchor with several hooks. **2** an iron piece with claws at one end for grasping and holding things. *See the picture.*

**grap·ple** (grap′'l) ***v.*** **1** to fight or struggle in a close or hard way [to *grapple* with a burglar; to *grapple* with a problem]. **2** to grip or seize. —**grap′pled, grap′pling** ◆***n.*** **1** the act of grappling. **2** *same as* **grapnel** *in meaning* 2: *also called* **grappling iron.** 

**grasp** (grasp) ***v.*** **1** to seize firmly with the hand; grip. **2** to take hold of with the mind; understand [Did you *grasp* what the story is about?] ◆***n.*** **1** a grasping; grip of the hand [The fish squirmed from his *grasp* and fell into the water.] **2** control or possession [These towns were in the *grasp* of the enemy.] **3** the ability to seize or reach [It is on the top shelf, beyond the baby's *grasp.*] **4** understanding or knowledge [She has a good *grasp* of the subject.] —**grasp at, 1** to try to seize. **2** to take eagerly [I would *grasp at* the chance to go.]

**grasp·ing** (grasp′iŋ) ***adj.*** eager to get more money, power, etc.; greedy.

**grass** (gras) ***n.*** **1** the common green plants with narrow, pointed leaves that cover lawns and meadows [Grazing animals feed on *grass.*] **2** a plant with narrow leaves, jointed stems, and clusters of seeds [Wheat, oats, bamboo, and sugar cane are *grasses.*] —**grass′y *adj.***

**grass·hop·per** (gras′häp′ər) ***n.*** a leaping insect with two pairs of wings and strong hind legs. It feeds on leafy plants. *See the picture.*

**grass·land** (gras′land) ***n.*** land with grass growing on it; meadow or prairie.

**grass roots** ☆**1** the common people, thought of as having basic or simple opinions on political issues.

| | | | |
|---|---|---|---|
| **a** fat | **ir** here | **ou** out | **zh** leisure |
| **ā** ape | **ī** bite, fire | **u** up | **ŋ** ring |
| **ä** car, lot | **ō** go | **ʉr** fur | a *in* ago |
| **e** ten | **ô** law, horn | **ch** chin | e *in* agent |
| **er** care | **oi** oil | **sh** she | **ə** = i *in* unity |
| **ē** even | **oo** look | **th** thin | o *in* collect |
| **i** hit | **o͞o** tool | ***th*** then | u *in* focus |

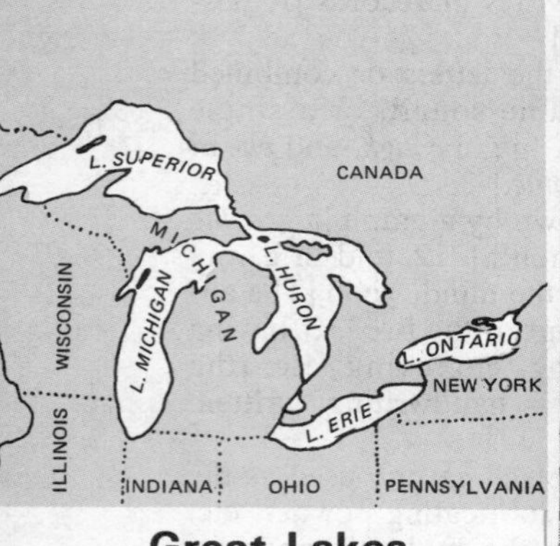


**Great Lakes**

**Great Dane**
75 cm (30 in.) high

**greenhouse**

☆**2** the basic support of a movement. *This term is used only in everyday talk.*

**grate**[1] (grāt) ***v.*** **1** to grind into small bits or shreds by rubbing against a rough surface [to *grate* cabbage]. **2** to make a harsh or rasping sound, as by scraping [The door *grated* on its rusty hinges. His voice *grated.*] **3** to annoy or irritate [His boasting *grated* on us all.] —**grat′ed, grat′ing**

**grate**[2] (grāt) ***n.*** **1** a frame of metal bars for holding fuel, as in a fireplace or furnace. **2** a fireplace. **3** a framework of bars set in a window or door; grating. ◆***v.*** to furnish with a grate. —**grat′ed, grat′ing**



**grate·ful** (grāt′fəl) ***adj.*** **1** feeling thankful or showing thanks; appreciative. **2** pleasing or welcome [a *grateful* blessing]. —**grate′ful·ly** ***adv.*** —**grate′ful·ness** ***n.***

**grat·er** (grāt′ər) ***n.*** a kitchen tool with a rough surface for grating vegetables, cheese, etc.

**grat·i·fy** (grat′ə fī) ***v.*** **1** to make pleased or satisfied [Actors are *gratified* by applause.] **2** to give in to; indulge; humor [One may spoil children by *gratifying* their every wish.] —**grat′i·fied, grat′i·fy·ing** —**grat′i·fi·ca′tion** ***n.***

**grat·ing**[1] (grāt′ing) ***n.*** a framework of bars set in a window or door; grate.

**grat·ing**[2] (grāt′ing) ***adj.*** **1** harsh and rasping in sound. **2** annoying or irritating.

**gra·tis** (grat′is *or* grāt′is) ***adv., adj.*** free of charge [This ticket will admit you *gratis.*]

**grat·i·tude** (grat′ə to͞od *or* grat′ə tyo͞od) ***n.*** the condition of being grateful for some favor; thankfulness.

**gra·tu·i·tous** (grə to͞o′ə təs *or* grə tyo͞o′ə təs) ***adj.*** **1** given or received free [*gratuitous* lessons]. **2** done without any good reason; unnecessary [She told a *gratuitous* lie.] —**gra·tu′i·tous·ly** ***adv.***

**gra·tu·i·ty** (grə to͞o′ə tē *or* grə tyo͞o′ə tē) ***n.*** a gift of money in return for some service; tip [She left a *gratuity* for the waiter.] —*pl.* **gra·tu′i·ties**

**grave**[1] (grāv) ***adj.*** **1** important or serious [*grave* doubts]. **2** full of danger; threatening [a *grave* illness]. **3** dignified; solemn or sedate [The judge had a *grave* manner.] —**grav′er, grav′est** —**grave′ly** ***adv.*** —**grave′ness** ***n.***

**Grave**[1] comes from a Latin word meaning "heavy" or "weighty." Heavy or weighty matters can be a cause for grave, or serious, concern.

**grave**[2] (grāv) ***n.*** **1** a place in the ground where a dead body is buried. It is often marked with a gravestone. **2** any place where a dead body is laid or comes to rest [The sea becomes the *grave* for many sailors.] **3** final end or death. ◆***v.*** to carve out or sculpture. —**graved, grav′en** or **graved, grav′ing**

**grav·el** (grav″l) ***n.*** a mixture of small stones and pebbles, used for paving roads, etc. ◆***v.*** to cover with gravel. —**grav′eled** or **grav′elled, grav′el·ing** or **grav′el·ling**

**graven image** an idol carved from stone, wood, etc.

**grave·stone** (grāv′stōn) ***n.*** a carved stone placed at a grave, telling who is buried there.

**grave·yard** (grāv′yärd) ***n.*** a burial ground; cemetery.

☆**graveyard shift** a work shift that starts during the night, usually at midnight: *used only in everyday talk.*

**grav·i·tate** (grav′ə tāt) ***v.*** **1** to move or be pulled by the force of gravity [The moon *gravitates* toward the earth.] **2** to be attracted and move [The townspeople *gravitated* toward the park for the band concert.] —**grav′i·tat·ed, grav′i·tat·ing**

**grav·i·ta·tion** (grav′ə tā′shən) ***n.*** **1** the act of gravitating. **2** the force by which every particle or mass of matter attracts and is attracted by every other particle or mass. Gravitation keeps all the planets moving around the sun and prevents them from moving off into space. —**grav′i·ta′tion·al** ***adj.***

**grav·i·ty** (grav′ə tē) ***n.*** **1** the condition of being grave, or serious. **2** danger or threat [the *gravity* of her illness]. **3** gravitation, especially the force that tends to draw objects toward the center of the earth [Things fall to the ground because of *gravity.*] **4** weight; heaviness: *see* **center of gravity, specific gravity.**

**gra·vy** (grā′vē) ***n.*** **1** the juice given off by meat in cooking. **2** a sauce made by mixing this juice with flour and seasoning. —*pl.* **gra′vies**

**gray** (grā) ***n.*** a color made by mixing black and white. ◆***adj.*** **1** of the color gray. **2** somewhat dark; dull or dismal [a *gray* day]. **3** having hair that is gray. ◆***v.*** to make or become gray.

**gray·beard** (grā′bird) ***n.*** an old man.

**gray·ish** (grā′ish) ***adj.*** somewhat gray.

**gray matter** **1** the grayish nerve tissue of the brain and spinal cord. **2** brains; intelligence: *used only in everyday talk.*

**graze**[1] (grāz) ***v.*** **1** to feed on growing grass or other plants in pastures [Cows are *grazing* in the meadow.] **2** to put into a pasture to feed [to *graze* livestock]. —**grazed, graz′ing**

The word **graze**[1] comes from the old English word that means "grass." When sheep or cattle graze, they feed on grass.

**graze**[2] (grāz) ***v.*** to rub lightly or scrape in passing [The car swerved and *grazed* the tree. The bullet *grazed* his arm.] —**grazed, graz′ing** ◆***n.*** **1** a grazing. **2** a scratch or scrape caused by grazing.

**grease** (grēs) ***n.*** **1** melted animal fat. **2** any soft, oily substance. ◆***v.*** (grēs *or* grēz) to smear with grease, as in order to make slippery or smooth [to *grease* machine parts; to *grease* a cake pan]. —**greased, greas′ing**

**grease·paint** (grēs′pānt) ***n.*** a mixture of grease and coloring matter used by performers in making up for the stage.

**greas·y** (grē'sē *or* grē'zē) ***adj.*** **1** smeared with grease [*greasy* hands]. **2** full of grease [*greasy* food]. **3** like grease; oily [a *greasy* salve]. —**greas'i·er, greas'i·est** —**greas'i·ly *adv.*** —**greas'i·ness *n.***

**great** (grāt) ***adj.*** **1** much above the average in size, degree, power, etc.; big or very big; much or very much [the *Great* Lakes; a *great* distance; *great* pain]. **2** very much of a [a *great* reader]. **3** very important; noted; remarkable [a *great* composer; a *great* discovery]. **4** older or younger by a generation: *used in words formed with a hyphen* [my *great*-aunt; my *great*-niece]. **5** very able or skillful: *used only in everyday talk* [She's *great* at tennis.] ☆**6** fine or excellent: *used only in everyday talk* [a *great* party]. ◆***adv.*** very well: *used only in everyday talk.* —**great'ly *adv.*** —**great'ness *n.***

SYNONYMS: **Great, large,** and **big** are all used to mean "of more than usual size or extent" [a *great, large,* or *big* oak]. **Large** is used of measurements or quantity [a *large* room; a *large* sum]. **Big** is used of bulk, weight, or scope [a *big* boulder; *big* plans]. **Great** is used of size, extent, or power that impresses or surprises one [a *great* river; a *great* leader].

**great-aunt** (grāt'ant' *or* grāt'änt') ***n.*** an aunt of one's father or mother; grandaunt.

**Great Bear** a constellation whose brightest stars form the Big Dipper.

**Great Britain** England, Wales, and Scotland. Great Britain is the largest of the British Isles.

**great·coat** (grāt'kōt) ***n.*** a heavy overcoat.

**Great Dane** a very large dog with short, smooth hair. *See the picture.*

☆**Great Divide** the Rocky Mountains, which divide the rivers flowing toward the east from those flowing toward the west.

**great-grand·child** (grāt'gran'chīld) ***n.*** a child of one's grandchild (**great'-grand'daugh'ter** or **great'-grand'son**). —*pl.* **great'-grand'chil'dren**

**great-grand·par·ent** (grāt'gran'per'ənt) ***n.*** a parent of one's grandparent (**great'-grand'fa'ther** or **great'-grand'moth'er**).

**great·heart·ed** (grāt'här'tid) ***adj.*** **1** brave; fearless. **2** noble and unselfish.

**Great Lakes** a chain of lakes in Canada and the United States. They are Lakes Superior, Michigan, Huron, Erie, and Ontario. *See the map.*

**great-neph·ew** (grāt'nef'yo͞o) ***n.*** a son of one's nephew or niece.

**great-niece** (grāt'nēs') ***n.*** a daughter of one's nephew or niece.

**Great Plains** the broad, level land that stretches eastward from the base of the Rocky Mountains for about 400 miles in the United States and Canada.

**Great Salt Lake** a shallow salt lake in northern Utah.

**great-un·cle** (grāt'uŋ'k'l) ***n.*** an uncle of one's father or mother; granduncle.

**grebe** (grēb) ***n.*** a water bird related to the loon, with partly webbed feet and a sharp bill.

**Gre·cian** (grē'shən) ***adj.*** *another word for* **Greek.**

**Greece** (grēs) a country in southeastern Europe, on the Mediterranean.

**greed** (grēd) ***n.*** the condition of being greedy [the miser's *greed* for money].

**greed·y** (grēd'ē) ***adj.*** wanting or taking all that one can get with no thought of what others need [The *greedy* girl ate all the cookies.] —**greed'i·er, greed'i·est** —**greed'i·ly *adv.*** —**greed'i·ness *n.***

**Greek** (grēk) ***adj.*** of Greece, its people, etc. ◆***n.*** **1** a person born or living in Greece. **2** the language of the Greeks.

**green** (grēn) ***adj.*** **1** having the color of grass [*green* peas]. **2** not ripe [*green* bananas]. **3** not having had training or experience [a *green* camper]. **4** not yet dried or cured for use [*green* lumber]. **5** fresh; not faded [to keep someone's memory *green*]. ◆***n.*** **1** the color of grass [*Green* is produced by mixing blue and yellow.] **2** a grassy piece of ground, especially the smooth, grassy area around each of the holes on a golf course. **3 greens,** *pl.* green, leafy vegetables, as spinach, turnip leaves, etc. —**green'ness *n.***

☆**green·back** (grēn'bak) ***n.*** a piece of U.S. paper money printed green on the back.

**green·er·y** (grēn'ər ē) ***n.*** green leaves, plants, branches, etc.

**green·horn** (grēn'hôrn) ***n.*** a person who has had no experience doing something; beginner.

**green·house** (grēn'hous) ***n.*** a heated building with glass roof and sides, for growing plants. *See the picture.*

**green·ish** (grēn'ish) ***adj.*** somewhat green.

**Green·land** (grēn'lənd) a Danish island northeast of North America. It is the largest island in the world.

More than 85% of this island is covered with ice, and only a small part of the land is ever green. It was given the name **Greenland** in an attempt to attract settlers.

**green onion** an onion that is not fully grown. It has a long stalk and green leaves and is eaten raw.

☆**green pepper** the green, unripe fruit of the sweet red pepper. It is eaten as a vegetable.

**green·sward** (grēn'swôrd) ***n.*** ground covered with grass.

☆**green thumb** a skill that a person seems to have for growing plants easily.

**Green·wich** (gren'ich; *usually pronounced* grin'ij *by the British*) a section of London, England. Degrees of longitude and zones of time are measured east and west from Greenwich.

**green·wood** (grēn'wood) ***n.*** a green forest, with leaves.

**greet** (grēt) ***v.*** **1** to meet and speak to with polite and friendly words; hail or welcome [Our host *greeted* us with a warm "Hello!"] **2** to meet or receive in a particular way [The speech was *greeted* with cheers.] **3** to come or appear to [A roaring sound *greeted* his ears.]

**greet·ing** (grēt'iŋ) ***n.*** **1** the act or words of one who greets. **2** *often* **greetings,** *pl.* a message of regards from someone not present.



| | | | |
|---|---|---|---|
| **a** fat | **ir** here | **ou** out | **zh** leisure |
| **ā** ape | **ī** bite, fire | **u** up | **ŋ** ring |
| **ä** car, lot | **ō** go | **ur** fur | a *in* ago |
| **e** ten | **ô** law, horn | **ch** chin | e *in* agent |
| **er** care | **oi** oil | **sh** she | **ə** = i *in* unity |
| **ē** even | **oo** look | **th** thin | o *in* collect |
| **i** hit | **o͞o** tool | ***th*** then | u *in* focus |

**gre·gar·i·ous** (grə ger′ē əs) ***adj.*** **1** liking to be with other people; sociable. **2** living in herds or flocks [Seals are *gregarious* animals.]

**Gre·go·ri·an** (grə gôr′ē ən) ***adj.*** **1** of or describing the calendar in common use today. It was established in 1582 by Pope Gregory XIII. **2** describing a kind of chant used in Roman Catholic churches, introduced under Pope Gregory I in the 6th century.

**gre·nade** (grə nād′) ***n.*** a small bomb set off by a fuse and usually thrown by hand.

**gren·a·dier** (gren ə dir′) ***n.*** **1** a soldier in earlier days who threw grenades. **2** a member of a special regiment, as in the British army.

**Gre·no·ble** (grə nō′b'l) a city in southeastern France, in the Alps.

**grew** (gro͞o) *past tense of* **grow.**

**grey** (grā) ***n., adj., v.*** *British spelling of* **gray.**

**grey·hound** (grā′hound) ***n.*** a tall, slender dog with a narrow head. It is a swift runner. *See the picture.*

**grid** (grid) ***n.*** **1** a framework of parallel bars; gridiron or grating. **2** a metallic plate in a storage cell for conducting the electric current. **3** an electrode in the form of a wire spiral or mesh in an electron tube: it controls the flow of electrons or ions in the tube.

**grid·dle** (grid′'l) ***n.*** a heavy, flat, metal plate or pan for cooking pancakes, etc.

**grid·dle·cake** (grid′'l kāk) ***n.*** a thin, flat cake made by pouring batter on a griddle and frying it; pancake.



**grid·i·ron** (grid′ī′ərn) ***n.*** **1** a framework of metal bars or wires for broiling meat or fish; grill. **2** any framework that looks like this. ☆**3** a football field.

**grief** (grēf) ***n.*** **1** deep and painful sorrow, as that caused by someone's death. **2** something that causes such sorrow. —**come to grief,** to fail or be ruined.

**grief-strick·en** (grēf′strik′'n) ***adj.*** stricken with grief; sorrowful.

**Grieg** (grēg), **Ed·vard** (ed′värd) 1843–1907; Norwegian composer.

**griev·ance** (grē′vəns) ***n.*** something that one thinks is unjust and feels hurt and angry about; a real or supposed wrong [The employees stated their *grievances* about working conditions.]

**grieve** (grēv) ***v.*** **1** to fill with grief; sadden deeply [His death *grieved* the whole nation.] **2** to feel grief; be sad [She is *grieving* over her lost kitten.] —**grieved, griev′ing**

**griev·ous** (grē′vəs) ***adj.*** **1** causing grief or deep sorrow [a *grievous* loss]. **2** showing grief [a *grievous* cry]. **3** hard to bear; severe [*grievous* pain]. **4** very cruel or very bad [a *grievous* crime]. —**griev′ous·ly** ***adv.***

**grif·fin** or **grif·fon** (grif′ən) ***n.*** an imaginary animal with the body and hind legs of a lion and the head and wings of an eagle. *See the picture.*

**grill** (gril) ***n.*** **1** a framework of metal bars or wires for broiling meat or fish; gridiron. **2** a large griddle. **3** grilled food. **4** a restaurant that specializes in grilled food: *also called* **grill′room.** ◆***v.*** **1** to cook on a grill. ☆**2** to keep firing questions at, as about a crime [The police *grilled* the suspect.]

**grille** (gril) ***n.*** an open grating of wrought iron, wood, etc. forming a screen to a door, window, etc.

**grim** (grim) ***adj.*** **1** fierce or cruel; savage [War is *grim.*] **2** not giving in; unyielding [*grim* courage]. **3** looking stern or harsh [a *grim* face]. **4** frightful or shocking; ghastly [The gravedigger made *grim* jokes about his *grim* task.] —**grim′mer, grim′mest** —**grim′ly** ***adv.*** —**grim′ness** ***n.***

**gri·mace** (gri mās′ *or* grim′əs) ***n.*** a twisting of the face in fun or in a look of pain, disgust, etc. *See the picture.* ◆***v.*** to make grimaces. —**gri·maced′, gri·mac′ing**

**grime** (grīm) ***n.*** dirt or soot rubbed into a surface, as of the skin. ◆***v.*** to soil with grime. —**grimed, grim′ing**

**grim·y** (grī′mē) ***adj.*** covered with grime; very dirty. —**grim′i·er, grim′i·est** —**grim′i·ness** ***n.***

**grin** (grin) ***v.*** to draw back the lips and show the teeth, as in a big or foolish smile. —**grinned, grin′ning** ◆***n.*** the look on the face when grinning [a broad *grin*].

> **Grin** comes from an old English word meaning "to gnash or bare the teeth," as an animal does in threatening a victim. Because a person shows the teeth while smiling, *grin* came to mean a broad smile.

**grind** (grīnd) ***v.*** **1** to crush into tiny bits or into powder [The miller *grinds* grain between millstones.] **2** to sharpen or smooth by rubbing against a rough surface [to *grind* a knife]. **3** to press down or rub together harshly or with a grating sound [She *ground* her teeth in anger.] **4** to treat in a harsh or cruel way [a people *ground* by tyranny]. **5** to work by turning the crank of [to *grind* a pepper mill]. **6** to work or study hard: *used only in everyday talk.* —**ground, grind′ing** ◆***n.*** **1** the act of grinding. **2** the fineness of the particles ground [The store sells three *grinds* of coffee.] **3** long, hard work or study; drudgery. ☆**4** a student who studies very hard: *used only in everyday talk.* —**grind out,** to produce by hard, steady work [to *grind out* a novel].

**grind·er** (grīn′dər) ***n.*** a person or thing that grinds, as any of the back teeth, or molars.

**grind·stone** (grīnd′stōn) ***n.*** a flat, round stone that is turned on an axle for sharpening or polishing things. *See the picture.*

**grip** (grip) ***v.*** **1** to grasp and hold fast, as with the hand or the teeth. **2** to get and hold the attention of; have control over [The horror movie *gripped* them.] —**gripped, grip′ping** ◆***n.*** **1** a grasping and holding fast, as with the hand or the teeth. **2** any special way of clasping hands [Some fraternities have secret *grips.*] **3** the way one holds a bat, golf club, etc. **4** the ability to understand or deal with something [She has a good *grip* on the situation.] **5** a handle, as of a tool. **6** a small handbag for travelers. —**come to grips,** to fight or struggle.

**gripe** (grīp) ***v.*** **1** to cause or feel sharp pains in the bowels. ☆**2** to annoy or irritate: *slang in this meaning.* ☆**3** to complain: *slang in this meaning.* —**griped, grip′ing** ◆***n.*** **1 gripes,** *pl.* sharp pains in the bowels. ☆**2** a complaint: *slang in this meaning.*

**grippe** (grip) ***n.*** *earlier term for* **influenza.**

**gris·ly** (griz′lē) ***adj.*** very frightening; horrible [a *grisly* tale of ghosts]. —**gris′li·er, gris′li·est**

**grist** (grist) ***n.*** grain that is ready to be ground or that has been ground.

**gris·tle** (gris′'l) ***n.*** a tough, flexible tissue, like soft bone, found in meat; cartilage.

**gris·tly** (gris′lē) ***adj.*** **1** full of gristle. **2** like gristle.

**grist·mill** (grist′mil) ***n.*** a mill for grinding grain.
**grit** (grit) ***n.*** **1** small bits of stone or sand. **2** a coarse kind of sandstone. ☆**3** stubborn courage; pluck. ◆***v.*** to clench or grind together [to *grit* one's teeth in anger]. —**grit′ted, grit′ting**

> SYNONYMS: **Fortitude** is the courage shown by patiently enduring misfortune, pain, etc. [to face a disaster with *fortitude*]. **Grit** is a stubborn courage shown by refusing to give in no matter what happens.

☆**grits** (grits) ***n.pl.*** coarsely ground wheat or corn; especially, in the South, hominy.
**grit·ty** (grit′ē) ***adj.*** **1** full of or like grit. **2** brave or plucky. —**grit′ti·er, grit′ti·est**
**griz·zled** (griz′′ld) ***adj.*** gray or streaked with gray [a *grizzled* beard].
**griz·zly** (griz′lē) ***adj.*** grayish; grizzled. —**griz′zli·er, griz′zli·est** ◆***n.*** *a shorter form of* **grizzly bear**. —*pl.* **griz′zlies**
**grizzly bear** a large, ferocious, brownish, grayish, or yellowish bear found in western North America.
**groan** (grōn) ***v.*** **1** to make a deep sound showing sorrow, pain, etc. [We *groaned* when our team lost.] **2** to make a creaking sound, as from great strain [The heavy gate *groaned* on its hinges.] **3** to be loaded down [The table *groaned* with food.] ◆***n.*** a groaning sound.
**gro·cer** (grō′sər) ***n.*** a storekeeper who sells food and certain household supplies.
**gro·cer·y** (grō′sər ē) ***n.*** ☆**1** a store selling food and household supplies. **2 groceries**, *pl.* the goods sold by a grocer. —*pl.* **gro′cer·ies**
**grog** (gräg) ***n.*** **1** an alcoholic liquor, especially rum, mixed with water. **2** any alcoholic liquor.
**grog·gy** (gräg′ē) ***adj.*** shaky or dizzy, as from being sleepy or drunk. —**grog′gi·er, grog′gi·est** —**grog′gi·ly** ***adv.*** —**grog′gi·ness** ***n.***
**groin** (groin) ***n.*** **1** the hollow or fold where the leg joins the abdomen. **2** the curved line where two ceiling vaults meet. *See the picture.* ◆***v.*** to build with groins [a *groined* vault].
**groom** (gro͞om) ***n.*** **1** a person whose work is taking care of horses. **2** *a shorter form of* **bridegroom**. ◆***v.*** **1** to brush and clean a horse. **2** to make neat and tidy [to *groom* one's hair]. ☆**3** to train for a particular purpose [She was *groomed* to take over the manager's job.]
**groove** (gro͞ov) ***n.*** **1** a long and narrow hollow, cut or worn into a surface. **2** the track cut in a phonograph record for the needle to follow. **3** a regular way of doing something, as by habit [After our vacation we slipped back into our everyday *groove*.] ◆***v.*** to make a groove in. —**grooved, groov′ing** —☆**groove on** or **groove with**, to enjoy or appreciate in a relaxed, unthinking way: *a slang phrase.*
☆**groov·y** (gro͞o′vē) ***adj.*** very pleasing or attractive: *a slang word used to show approval.* —**groov′i·er, groov′i·est**
**grope** (grōp) ***v.*** **1** to feel or search about in a blind or fumbling way [to *grope* for the keys in one's pocket; to *grope* for knowledge]. **2** to seek or find by feeling about [to *grope* one's way in the dark]. —**groped, grop′ing**
**Gro·pi·us** (grō′pē əs), **Walter** 1883–1969; German architect, in the U.S. after 1937.

grindstone

griffin

grotesque costume

groins in vault

68 cm (27 in.) high at shoulder

grimace

greyhound

**gros·beak** (grōs′bēk) ***n.*** a small songbird with a thick beak shaped like a cone.
**gross** (grōs) ***adj.*** **1** very bad; glaring [a *gross* lie; a 323
*gross* error]. **2** vulgar; not refined; coarse [*gross* language; *gross* manners]. **3** big or fat, and coarse-looking [*gross* features]. **4** with nothing taken away; total; entire [What is your *gross* income before you pay taxes?] ◆***n.*** **1** the whole amount; total [We earned a *gross* of $30, but we owed $10 for supplies.] —*pl.* **gross′es** **2** twelve dozen; 144. —*pl.* **gross** ◆***v.*** to earn a certain amount before expenses are subtracted: *used only in everyday talk.* —**gross′ly** ***adv.*** —**gross′ness** ***n.***
**gro·tesque** (grō tesk′) ***adj.*** **1** looking strange and unreal in a wild way; fantastic [*grotesque* drawings of imaginary creatures on Mars]. *See the picture.* **2** so strange, twisted, different, etc. as to be funny; absurd [People often have *grotesque* adventures in their dreams.] ◆***n.*** a grotesque person or thing. —**gro·tesque′ly** ***adv.***
**grot·to** (grät′ō) ***n.*** **1** *another name for* **cave**. **2** any shaded or sheltered place or shrine that is like a cave. —*pl.* **grot′toes, grot′tos**
☆**grouch** (grouch) ***v.*** to be in a bad mood and keep finding fault with everything. ◆***n.*** **1** a person who grouches. **2** a bad or grumbling mood.
☆**grouch·y** (grouch′ē) ***adj.*** in a grouch; cross and complaining. —**grouch′i·er, grouch′i·est** —**grouch′i·ly** ***adv.*** —**grouch′i·ness** ***n.***

| | | | | | | | |
|---|---|---|---|---|---|---|---|
| **a** | fat | **ir** | here | **ou** | out | **zh** | leisure |
| **ā** | ape | **ī** | bite, fire | **u** | up | **ng** | ring |
| **ä** | car, lot | **ō** | go | **ur** | fur | | a *in* ago |
| **e** | ten | **ô** | law, horn | **ch** | chin | | e *in* agent |
| **er** | care | **oi** | oil | **sh** | she | **ə =** | i *in* unity |
| **ē** | even | **oo** | look | **th** | thin | | o *in* collect |
| **i** | hit | **o͞o** | tool | ***th*** | then | | u *in* focus |

**ground**[1] (ground) ***n.*** **1** the solid part of the earth's surface; land; earth. **2** a piece of land of a particular kind [a hunting *ground*]. **3 grounds,** *pl.* the lands around a house, that belong to it. **4** an area of discussion, work, etc. [The two books cover the same *ground*.] **5** a reason, cause, or basis [She hasn't much *ground* for complaint. On what *grounds* are you refusing?] **6 grounds,** *pl.* solid bits that settle to the bottom of a liquid [coffee *grounds*]. **7** the background, as of a painting, flag, etc. **8** the connection of an electrical conductor with the ground. ◆***adj.*** of, on, or near the ground [the *ground* floor of a building]. ◆***v.*** **1** to put on the ground. **2** to run aground [The ship *grounded* on the reef.] **3** to base or establish [On what do you *ground* your argument?] **4** to give good, sound training to in some subject [to *ground* students in science]. **5** to keep from flying [The airplanes were *grounded* by the storm.] **6** to connect an electrical conductor with the ground. —**break ground, 1** to dig or plow. **2** to start building. —**cover ground, 1** to go some distance; travel. **2** to make progress. —**gain ground,** to move ahead; make progress; advance. —☆**get off the ground,** to get something started. —**give ground,** to yield or retreat. —☆**ground out,** to be put out by a grounder in baseball. —**lose ground,** to drop back; fall behind. —☆**run into the ground,** to do too long or too often: *used only in everyday talk.*

 **ground**[2] (ground) *past tense and past participle of* **grind.**

**ground cover** low, dense-growing plants, as ivy or myrtle, used for covering the ground, as in places where it is hard to grow grass.

**ground crew** a group of people whose job it is to maintain and repair aircraft.

**ground·er** (groun′dər) ***n.*** a batted ball in baseball that rolls or bounces along the ground: *also called* **ground ball.**

☆**ground·hog** (ground′hôg) ***n.*** *another name for* **woodchuck.**

☆**Groundhog Day** February 2. There is a legend that the groundhog comes out of its winter hole on this day. If it sees its shadow, it returns to its hole for six more weeks of winter weather.

**ground·less** (ground′lis) ***adj.*** without good cause or reason [a *groundless* rumor].

Guernsey cow

grouse

guava

☆**ground rule 1** in baseball, any of a set of rules made up to suit the playing conditions in a particular ball park. **2** any of a set of rules governing a certain activity.

**ground·work** (ground′wurk) ***n.*** a foundation or basis [This school supplied the *groundwork* of her education.]

**group** (gro͞op) ***n.*** **1** a number of persons or things gathered together. **2** a number of related things that form a class [the woodwind *group* of instruments]. ◆***v.*** to gather together into a group [*Group* yourselves in a circle.]

**grouse**[1] (grous) ***n.*** a wild bird, like a plump chicken, that is hunted as game. *See the picture.* —*pl.* **grouse**

**grouse**[2] (grous) ***v.*** to complain or grumble. —**groused, grous′ing** ◆***n.*** a complaint. *This word is used only in everyday talk.*

**grove** (grōv) ***n.*** a small group of trees.

**grov·el** (gruv′'l *or* gräv′'l) ***v.*** **1** to lie or crawl on the ground with the face down. **2** to act in a very humble or cringing way. —**grov′eled** or **grov′elled, grov′el·ing** or **grov′el·ling** —**grov′el·er** or **grov′el·ler** ***n.***

**grow** (grō) ***v.*** **1** to become larger; increase [Our business has *grown* rapidly.] **2** to become older; develop; mature [to *grow* from childhood into adulthood]. **3** to be found; exist [Oranges *grow* in warm regions.] **4** to make grow; raise [They *grow* wheat on their farm.] **5** to come to be; become [We *grew* tired during the long drive.] —**grew, grown, grow′ing** —**grow into, 1** to develop so as to be [A boy *grows into* a man.] **2** to develop so as to be fit [She *grew into* her job.] —**grow on,** to become gradually more likable or desirable to. —**grow out of, 1** to develop from. **2** to grow too large for. —**grow together,** to become joined by growing. —**grow up,** to become an adult. —**grow′er** ***n.***

**growl** (groul) ***v.*** **1** to make a low, rumbling sound in the throat, as an angry dog does. **2** to grumble or complain. ◆***n.*** the act or sound of growling.

**grown** (grōn) *past participle of* **grow.** ◆***adj.*** finished growing; fully mature [a *grown* man].

**grown-up** (grōn′up′) ***adj.*** **1** fully grown. **2** of or for an adult. ◆***n.*** (grōn′up′) an adult: *also* **grown′up′.**

**growth** (grōth) ***n.*** **1** the act of growing; a becoming larger or a developing. **2** the amount grown; increase [a *growth* of two inches over the summer]. **3** something that grows or has grown [He shaved off the two weeks' *growth* of beard. A tumor is an abnormal *growth* in the body.]

**grub** (grub) ***v.*** **1** to dig or dig up; uproot. **2** to work hard; drudge or plod. —**grubbed, grub′bing** ◆***n.*** **1** a larva, as of the beetle, that looks like a short, fat worm. **2** food: *slang in this meaning.*

**grub·by** (grub′ē) ***adj.*** dirty or untidy. —**grub′bi·er, grub′bi·est** —**grub′bi·ness** ***n.***

☆**grub·stake** (grub′stāk) ***n.*** money or supplies lent to a prospector in return for a share of whatever may be found: *used only in everyday talk.*

**grudge** (gruj) ***v.*** **1** to envy a person because of something that person has; begrudge [They *grudged* her her success.] **2** to give without wanting to [The miser *grudges* his dog its food.] —**grudged, grudg′ing** ◆***n.*** bad feeling against a person who is supposed to have done something wrong [He bore a *grudge* against me all his life.] —**grudg′ing·ly** ***adv.***

**gru·el** (gro͞o′əl) ***n.*** a thin, watery food made by cooking oatmeal or other meal in milk or water. It is often fed to sick people.

**gru·el·ing** or **gru·el·ling** (gro͞o′əl iŋ) ***adj.*** very tiring; exhausting [*grueling* work].

**grue·some** (gro͞o′səm) ***adj.*** causing fear and disgust; horrible [a *gruesome* murder].

> **Gruesome** comes from a Middle English word meaning "to shudder." Something gruesome or horrible often makes us shudder.

**gruff** (gruf) ***adj.*** **1** rough or unfriendly; rude [a *gruff* reply]. **2** harsh; hoarse [*gruff* voices]. —**gruff′ly** ***adv.*** —**gruff′ness** ***n.***

**grum·ble** (grum′b'l) ***v.*** **1** to make a low, growling or rumbling sound. **2** to complain in an angry or sullen way [The soldiers *grumbled* about the food.] —**grum′bled, grum′bling** ◆***n.*** the act of grumbling. —**grum′bler** ***n.***

**grump·y** (grum′pē) ***adj.*** grouchy; peevish. —**grump′i·er, grump′i·est** —**grump′i·ly** ***adv.*** —**grump′i·ness** ***n.***

**grunt** (grunt) ***v.*** **1** to make the short, deep, hoarse sound of a hog. **2** to make a sound like this [Joe *grunted* as he picked up the heavy load.] **3** to say by grunting ["No!" she *grunted*.] ◆***n.*** the sound made in grunting.

☆**G-suit** (jē′so͞ot′) ***n.*** a garment worn by pilots or astronauts that has air pressure built up inside it to protect the body when the aircraft or spacecraft speeds up or slows down very rapidly.

**gt.** *abbreviation for* **great.**

**gtd.** or **guar.** *abbreviations for* **guaranteed.**

**Gua·da·la·ja·ra** (gwä′d'l ə här′ə) a city in western Mexico.

**Guam** (gwäm) an island in the western Pacific, belonging to the United States.

**guar·an·tee** (gar ən tē′) ***n.*** **1** a promise to replace something sold if it does not work or last as it should [a one-year *guarantee* on the clock]. **2** a promise or assurance that something will be done [You have my *guarantee* that we'll be on time.] **3** *same as* **guaranty** *in meanings* 1 *and* 2. **4** a person who gives a guarantee; guarantor. ◆***v.*** **1** to give a guarantee or guaranty for. **2** to promise or assure [I cannot *guarantee* that she will be there.] —**guar·an·teed′, guar·an·tee′ing**

**guar·an·tor** (gar′ən tôr *or* gar′ən tər) ***n.*** a person who gives a guaranty or guarantee.

**guar·an·ty** (gar′ən tē) ***n.*** **1** a promise to pay another's debt, or do some other thing that a person has pledged to do, if the person is unable to do so. **2** something given or kept as security. **3** an agreement that makes sure that something is or will continue. —*pl.* **guar′an·ties** ◆***v.*** *another word for* **guarantee.** —**guar′an·tied, guar′an·ty·ing**

**guard** (gärd) ***v.*** **1** to watch over; protect; defend [The Secret Service *guards* the President.] **2** to keep from escaping [Two sentries *guarded* the prisoners.] **3** to be watchful; take care [Lock the doors to *guard* against burglars.] ◆***n.*** **1** the act of guarding; careful watch; protection [We kept a *guard* against prowlers.] **2** anything that protects against injury or loss [The hilt on a sword usually has a *guard* for the hand.] **3** any person or group that guards or protects [a museum *guard*]. ☆**4** either of two basketball players who set up offensive plays. ☆**5** either of two football players on offense, left and right of the center. —**on one's guard,** careful and watchful.

**guard·ed** (gär′did) ***adj.*** **1** watched over and protected. **2** kept from escaping. **3** cautious; careful [a *guarded* reply]. —**guard′ed·ly** ***adv.***

**guard·house** (gärd′hous) ***n.*** **1** a building used by guards for resting. **2** a building used as a military jail for soldiers who have broken some rules.

**guard·i·an** (gär′dē ən) ***n.*** **1** a person chosen by a court to take charge of a child or of someone else who cannot take care of his or her own affairs. **2** a person who guards or protects; custodian [A sexton is a *guardian* of church property.] —**guard′i·an·ship′** ***n.***

**guard·room** (gärd′ro͞om) ***n.*** a room used by guards for resting.

**guards·man** (gärdz′mən) ***n.*** a member of any military group called a guard; especially, ☆a member of a National Guard. —*pl.* **guards′men**

**Gua·te·ma·la** (gwä′tə mä′lə) a country in Central America, south and east of Mexico.

**gua·va** (gwä′və) ***n.*** the yellowish, pear-shaped fruit of a tropical American tree or shrub. It is used for making jelly. *See the picture.*

**gu·ber·na·to·ri·al** (go͞o′bər nə tôr′ē əl) ***adj.*** of a governor or the office held by a governor.

**Guern·sey** (gurn′zē) a British island in the English Channel. ◆***n.*** a breed of dairy cattle first raised on this island. It is usually light brown with white markings. *See the picture.* —*pl.* **Guern′seys** 

**guer·ril·la** or **gue·ril·la** (gə ril′ə) ***n.*** a member of a small group of fighters who are not part of a regular army. They usually make surprise raids behind the enemy's lines.

**guess** (ges) ***v.*** **1** to judge or decide about something without having enough facts to know for certain [Can you *guess* how old he is?] **2** to judge correctly by doing this [She *guessed* the exact number of beans in the jar.] **3** to think or suppose [I *guess* you're right.] ◆***n.*** a judgment formed by guessing; surmise [Your *guess* is as good as mine.] —**guess′er** ***n.***

**guess·work** (ges′wurk) ***n.*** the act of guessing, or a judgment formed by guessing.

**guest** (gest) ***n.*** **1** a person who is visiting another's home, or who is being treated to a meal, etc. by another. **2** any paying customer of a hotel or restaurant. **3** any person invited to appear on a program. ◆***adj.*** **1** for guests. **2** that has been invited [a *guest* speaker].

**guf·faw** (gə fô′) ***n.*** a loud and rough laugh. ◆***v.*** to laugh with such a laugh.

**Gui·a·na** (gē an′ə *or* gē ä′nə) a region in northern South America.

**guid·ance** (gīd′'ns) ***n.*** **1** a guiding, or directing; leadership [Our school clubs are under the *guidance* of teachers.] **2** something that guides.

| | | | |
|---|---|---|---|
| **a** fat | **ir** here | **ou** out | **zh** leisure |
| **ā** ape | **ī** bite, fire | **u** up | **ŋ** ring |
| **ä** car, lot | **ō** go | **ur** fur | a *in* ago |
| **e** ten | **ô** law, horn | **ch** chin | e *in* agent |
| **er** care | **oi** oil | **sh** she | **ə** = i *in* unity |
| **ē** even | **o͝o** look | **th** thin | o *in* collect |
| **i** hit | **o͞o** tool | ***th*** then | u *in* focus |

**guide** (gīd) ***v.*** **1** to show the way to; conduct or lead [Can you *guide* me through the museum?] **2** to manage or control; steer [to *guide* the affairs of state]. —**guid′ed, guid′ing** ◆***n.*** **1** a person who leads others on a trip or tour. **2** something that controls, directs, or instructs [The *guide* on a typewriter keeps the paper straight. A dictionary is a *guide* to the use of words.] **3** a guidebook.

SYNONYMS: To **guide** is to show the way because one knows the way and is always present to point it out [to *guide* tourists]. To **lead** is to go ahead to show the way, often after offering to do so [He *led* us to victory.] To **pilot** is to guide over a difficult course, with twists and turns or dangerous places [She *piloted* us through the many halls and corridors.]

**guide·book** (gīd′book) ***n.*** a book that has directions and information for tourists.

**guided missile** a war missile or rocket that is guided to its target by radio signals, radar devices, etc.

**guide dog** a dog trained to lead a blind person.

**guide·line** (gīd′līn) ***n.*** ☆a rule or principle set forth as a guide for those who must choose a policy or course of action.

**guide·post** (gīd′pōst) ***n.*** **1** a post along a road, with a sign giving directions to places. **2** anything that can be used as a guide, or principle; guideline.

**guild** (gild) ***n.*** **1** in the Middle Ages, a union of men in the same craft or trade to keep the quality of work high and to protect the members. **2** any group of people joined together in some work or for some purpose [The Ladies' *Guild* of the church is planning a show of religious art.]



**guil·der** (gil′dər) ***n.*** the basic unit of money in the Netherlands.

**guild·hall** (gild′hôl) ***n.*** **1** a hall where a guild meets. **2** a town hall.

**guile** (gīl) ***n.*** slyness and cunning in dealing with others; craftiness. —**guile′ful *adj.***

**guile·less** (gīl′lis) ***adj.*** not having or using guile; honest; frank. —**guile′less·ly *adv.***

**guil·lo·tine** (gil′ə tēn) ***n.*** an instrument for cutting off a person's head by means of a heavy blade dropped between two grooved uprights. The guillotine was introduced in France during the French Revolution. *See the picture.* ◆***v.*** (gil ə tēn′) to cut off a person's head with a guillotine. —**guil·lo·tined′, guil·lo·tin′ing**

**guilt** (gilt) ***n.*** **1** the act or state of having done a wrong or committed a crime [Is there any proof of his *guilt?*] **2** a feeling that one has done something wrong or is to blame for something [She is filled with *guilt* but isn't sure why.] **3** a wrong act; crime; sin.

**guilt·less** (gilt′lis) ***adj.*** not guilty; innocent.

**guilt·y** (gil′tē) ***adj.*** **1** having done something wrong; being to blame for something [She is often *guilty* of telling lies.] **2** judged in court to be a wrongdoer [The jury found him *guilty* of robbery.] **3** caused by a feeling of guilt [a *guilty* look]. —**guilt′i·er, guilt′i·est** —**guilt′i·ly *adv.*** —**guilt′i·ness *n.***

**Guin·ea** (gin′ē) a country on the western coast of Africa.

**guin·ea** (gin′ē) ***n.*** **1** a gold coin used in England in earlier times. **2** *a shorter form of* **guinea fowl.**

**guinea fowl** a bird like a chicken, having a rounded body and dark feathers with white spots. It is hunted and also raised for food.

**guinea hen** a guinea fowl, especially a female.

**guinea pig** **1** a small, fat animal related to the rat, with short ears and a short tail. It is used in experiments in biology. *See the picture.* ☆**2** any person or thing used in an experiment.

**Guin·e·vere** (gwin′ə vir) the wife of King Arthur in the legends about him.

**guise** (gīz) ***n.*** **1** a way or style of dressing; costume. **2** the way something looks; appearance; often, a false appearance [Under the *guise* of friendship he betrayed us.]

**gui·tar** (gi tär′) ***n.*** a musical instrument with six strings. It is played by plucking the strings with the fingers or with a plectrum. *See the picture.* —**gui·tar′·ist *n.***

☆**gulch** (gulch) ***n.*** a narrow valley with steep walls, cut by a swift stream.

**gulf** (gulf) ***n.*** **1** a large area of ocean reaching into land. It is larger than a bay. **2** a wide, deep opening in the earth; large chasm. **3** a wide gap or separation [There is a *gulf* between his beliefs and hers.]

**Gulf Stream** a warm ocean current, about 50 miles wide, that flows from the Gulf of Mexico along the eastern U.S. coast and then across the Atlantic to Europe.

**gull**[1] (gul) ***n.*** a water bird with large wings, webbed feet, and feathers of gray and white.

**gull**[2] (gul) ***n.*** a person who is easily cheated or tricked. ◆***v.*** to cheat or trick.

☆**Gul·lah** (gul′ə) ***n.*** **1** any of a group of black people living on the coast of South Carolina and Georgia. **2** the dialect of English they speak.

**gul·let** (gul′ət) ***n.*** **1** the tube through which the food passes from the mouth to the stomach; esophagus. **2** the throat or neck.

**gul·li·ble** (gul′ə b'l) ***adj.*** that is easily cheated or tricked. *See* SYNONYMS *at* **trusting.** —**gul′li·bil′i·ty *n.***

**gul·ly** (gul′ē) ***n.*** a channel worn by water; small, narrow ravine. —*pl.* **gul′lies**

**gulp** (gulp) ***v.*** **1** to swallow in a hurried or greedy way [She *gulped* her breakfast and ran to school.] **2** to choke back as if swallowing [He *gulped* down his sobs.] **3** to catch one's breath; gasp [The diver came up *gulping* for air.] ◆***n.*** **1** the act of gulping. **2** the amount swallowed at one time [She took two *gulps* of milk.]

**gum**[1] (gum) ***n.*** **1** a sticky substance given off by certain trees and plants. It is used in pastes, jellies, varnishes, etc. **2** *a shorter form of* **gum tree.** ☆**3** *short for* **chewing gum.** ◆***v.*** **1** to stick together or cover with gum. **2** to become sticky or clogged [The drain in the sink is *gummed* up.] —**gummed, gum′·ming**

**gum**[2] (gum) ***n.*** *often* **gums,** *pl.* the firm flesh around the teeth.

☆**gum·bo** (gum′bō) ***n.*** **1** the okra plant or its sticky pods. **2** a soup made thick with okra pods. —*pl.* **gum′bos**

☆**gum·drop** (gum′dräp) ***n.*** a small candy that is like firm and chewy jelly.

**gum·my** (gum′ē) ***adj.*** **1** full of or covered with gum [*gummy* leaves]. **2** thick and sticky. —**gum′mi·er, gum′mi·est**

**gump·tion** (gump′shən) *n.* courage or boldness: *used only in everyday talk.*

☆**gum tree** any of the trees that give gum.

**gun** (gun) *n.* **1** a weapon that has a metal tube from which a bullet, shell, etc. is shot by exploding gunpowder. **2** anything like this that shoots or squirts something [a BB *gun;* a spray *gun*]. **3** a shooting of a gun to signal or salute someone [The President receives a salute of 21 *guns.*] ◆*v.* to shoot or hunt with a gun. —**gunned, gun′ning** —**stick to one's guns,** to refuse to give in or to change one's opinion.

In technical use, a **gun** is only a large, heavy weapon such as a cannon or machine gun, but in common talk, it is also a rifle or pistol.

**gun·boat** (gun′bōt) *n.* a small armed ship used in guarding rivers, harbors, etc.

**gun·cot·ton** (gun′kät″n) *n.* an explosive made of cotton treated with nitric and sulfuric acids.

**gun·fire** (gun′fīr) *n.* the shooting of a gun or guns.

**gun·lock** (gun′läk) *n.* the part by which the charge was fired in early guns.

**gun·man** (gun′mən) *n.* ☆a gangster, robber, etc. who carries a gun. —*pl.* **gun′men**

**gun·ner** (gun′ər) *n.* **1** a soldier, sailor, etc. who helps to fire large guns. **2** a naval officer in charge of a ship's guns.

**gun·ner·y** (gun′ər ē) *n.* the science of making or firing cannon or other large guns.

**gun·ny** (gun′ē) *n.* a coarse, thick material of jute or hemp, used for sacks.

**gun·ny·sack** (gun′ē sak) or **gun·ny·bag** (gun′ē bag) *n.* a sack or bag made of gunny.

**gun·pow·der** (gun′pou′dər) *n.* an explosive powder used in firing guns, for blasting, in fireworks, etc.

**gun·shot** (gun′shät) *n.* **1** shot fired from a gun. **2** the distance a bullet, shell, etc. can be fired; range of a gun [a duck within *gunshot*].

**gun·smith** (gun′smith) *n.* a person who makes or repairs small guns.

**gun·stock** (gun′stäk) *n.* the wooden handle of a gun to which the barrel is attached.

**gun·wale** (gun′'l) *n.* the upper edge of the side of a boat or ship.

**gup·py** (gup′ē) *n.* a tiny tropical fish that lives in fresh water and is kept in home aquariums. —*pl.* **gup′pies**

**gur·gle** (gʉr′g'l) *v.* **1** to flow with a bubbling sound, as water out of a bottle. **2** to make a bubbling sound in the throat [Babies *gurgle* when they are pleased.] —**gur′gled, gur′gling** ◆*n.* a gurgling sound.

**gu·ru** (goor′o͞o *or* goo ro͞o′) *n.* **1** a leader who is highly respected by a group of followers. **2** a Hindu teacher.

**gush** (gush) *v.* **1** to flow out with force and in large amounts; spout [Water *gushed* from the broken pipe.] **2** to talk with too much feeling or enthusiasm in a silly way. ◆*n.* **1** a gushing; sudden, heavy flow [a *gush* of water]. **2** gushing talk. —**gush′y** *adj.*

**gush·er** (gush′ər) *n.* an oil well from which oil gushes without being pumped.

**gus·set** (gus′it) *n.* a small piece shaped like a triangle or diamond, set into a skirt, glove, etc. to make it stronger or roomier. *See the picture.*

**gust** (gust) *n.* **1** a strong and sudden rush of air or of

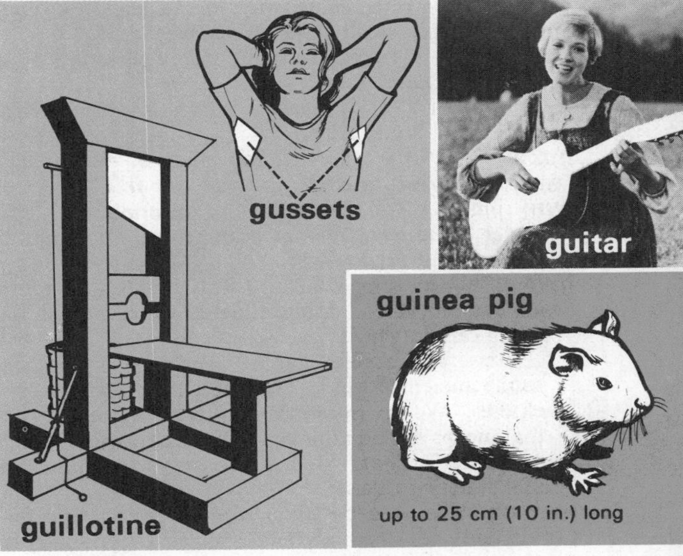


something carried by the air [a *gust* of wind; *gusts* of smoke]. **2** a sudden outburst of laughter, rage, etc. ◆*v.* to blow in gusts. —**gust′y** *adj.*

**gus·to** (gus′tō) *n.* much relish or enjoyment [to eat with *gusto;* to sing with *gusto*].

**gut** (gut) *n.* **1 guts,** *pl.* the intestines or bowels: *now thought by some people to be not a polite use.* **2** tough cord made from the intestines of sheep, goats, etc.: it is used for violin strings, in tennis rackets, etc. **3 guts,** *pl.* courage or daring: *slang in this meaning.* ◆*v.* **1** to take out the intestines, etc. from [to *gut* a fish]. **2** to destroy the inside of [The building had been *gutted* by fire.] —**gut′ted, gut′ting** ◆*adj.* important and basic: *slang in this meaning* [the *gut* issues in the campaign].



**Gu·ten·berg** (go͞ot′'n bʉrg), **Jo·hann** (yō′hän) 1400?–1468; German printer thought to be the first European to use separate pieces of type.

**gut·less** (gut′lis) *adj.* lacking courage; giving up easily: *a slang word.*

**gut·ta-per·cha** (gut′ə pʉr′chə) *n.* a substance like rubber, made from the milky juice of certain tropical trees. It is used inside golf balls, in dentistry, etc.

**gut·ter** (gut′ər) *n.* **1** a narrow channel along the edge of a road or street to carry water, as to a sewer. **2** a narrow channel of metal or tile along the edge of a roof, to carry off rain water. **3** a channel or groove like a gutter, as the groove on either side of a bowling alley. ◆*v.* to melt quickly so that the wax runs off in channels [The wind made the candle *gutter.*]

**gut·tur·al** (gut′ər əl) *adj.* **1** of or made in the throat [The *g* in "go" is a *guttural* sound.] **2** harsh or growling [a *guttural* voice].

| | | | | | | | |
|---|---|---|---|---|---|---|---|
| **a** | fat | **ir** | here | **ou** | out | **zh** | leisure |
| **ā** | ape | **ī** | bite, fire | **u** | up | **ng** | ring |
| **ä** | car, lot | **ō** | go | **ʉr** | fur | | a *in* ago |
| **e** | ten | **ô** | law, horn | **ch** | chin | | e *in* agent |
| **er** | care | **oi** | oil | **sh** | she | ə = | i *in* unity |
| **ē** | even | **oo** | look | **th** | thin | | o *in* collect |
| **i** | hit | **o͞o** | tool | ***th*** | then | | u *in* focus |

**guy**[1] (gī) ***n.*** a rope, chain, wire, etc. fastened to something to keep it steady. *See the picture.*

**guy**[2] (gī) ***n.*** ☆**1** a boy or man. **2** any person [She's a good *guy.*] *This is a slang word.*

**Guy·a·na** (gī an′ə *or* gī än′ə) a country in northeastern South America.

**guz·zle** (guz′'l) ***v.*** to drink too much or in a greedy way. —**guz′zled, guz′zling** —**guz′zler *n.***

**gym** (jim) ***n.*** **1** *a shorter form of* **gymnasium**. ☆**2** *another name for* **physical education**. *This word is used only in everyday talk.*

**gym·na·si·um** (jim nā′zē əm) ***n.*** a building or room with equipment for doing athletic exercises and for playing certain games.

Exercise and athletic games were very important to the ancient Greeks. Their athletes did not wear clothes. We get **gymnasium** from a Greek word that means "to do athletic exercises naked."

**gym·nast** (jim′nast) ***n.*** a person who is trained in doing athletic exercises.

**gym·nas·tics** (jim nas′tiks) ***n.pl.*** exercises that develop and train the body and muscles. —**gym·nas′tic *adj.***

☆**gyp** (jip) ***v., n.*** cheat or swindle: *used only in everyday talk.* —**gypped, gyp′ping**

**gyp·sum** (jip′səm) ***n.*** a calcium mineral in crystal or chalky form, used for making plaster of Paris and as a fertilizer.

**Gyp·sy** (jip′sē) ***n.*** **1** *also* **gypsy,** a member of a wandering people with dark skin and black hair, found throughout the world. They are thought to have come from India many centuries ago. **2 gypsy,** a person who looks like a Gypsy, or who lives a wandering life. *—pl.* **Gyp′sies** or **gyp′sies**

The word **Gypsy** comes from an earlier form of **Egyptian.** It used to be thought that the Gypsies had come from Egypt many centuries ago.

**gypsy moth,** a brownish or white moth common in the eastern United States. Its larvae feed on leaves, damaging trees and plants.

**gy·rate** (jī′rāt) ***v.*** to move in a circle or spiral; revolve. —**gy′rat·ed, gy′rat·ing** —**gy·ra′tion *n.***

**gy·ro·scope** (jī′rə skōp) ***n.*** a wheel set in a ring so that the shaft on which the wheel spins can turn in any direction. When the wheel is spun rapidly, the shaft will stay at a tilt as if free from the law of gravity. The gyroscope is used to help keep ships, airplanes, etc. steady. *See the picture.*

**H, h** (āch) ***n.*** the eighth letter of the English alphabet. *—pl.* **H's, h's** (āch′iz)

**H** *the symbol for the chemical element* hydrogen.

**H.** or **h.** *abbreviation for* **height, hit** *or* **hits** (in baseball), **hour** *or* **hours.**

**ha** (hä) ***interj.*** a sound made in showing surprise, triumph, scorn, etc., or when repeated (**ha-ha**), in laughing.

**ha·be·as cor·pus** (hā′bē əs kôr′pəs) a paper from a court of law ordering officials either to prove that they have a lawful reason for keeping a person in jail or to release that person.

**hab·er·dash·er** (hab′ər dash′ər) ***n.*** a person who sells small articles of men's clothing, as hats, shirts, etc.

**hab·er·dash·er·y** (hab′ər dash′ər ē) ***n.*** **1** a haberdasher's store. **2** the articles sold in such a store. *—pl.* **hab′er·dash′er·ies**

**ha·bil·i·ments** (hə bil′ə mənts) ***n.pl.*** clothing; dress.

**hab·it** (hab′it) ***n.*** **1** a thing that a person has done so often without thinking about it that it becomes hard to stop [the *habit* of biting one's nails]. *See* SYNONYMS *at* **custom. 2** a usual or typical way of doing, being, etc.; practice [It is the *habit* of bears to sleep through the winter.] **3** special clothes, as a religious costume, or clothing for a certain occasion [a nun's *habit;* a riding *habit*]. *See the picture.*

**hab·it·a·ble** (hab′it ə b'l) ***adj.*** fit to be lived in [a *habitable* cottage].

**hab·i·tat** (hab′ə tat) ***n.*** the place where an animal or plant is normally found [Woodland streams are the *habitat* of beavers.]

**hab·i·ta·tion** (hab′ə tā′shən) ***n.*** **1** a place in which to live; dwelling or home. **2** the act of inhabiting, or living in [a slum unfit for *habitation*].

**hab·it-form·ing** (hab′it fôr′miŋ) ***adj.*** causing one to form a habit or become addicted [Watching TV can be *habit-forming.*]

**ha·bit·u·al** (hə bich′o͞o wəl) ***adj.*** **1** done by habit; fixed as a habit [*habitual* kindness]. **2** doing something by habit [a *habitual* smoker]. **3** often used, seen, done, etc.; usual [That easy chair has become my *habitual* seat.] —**ha·bit′u·al·ly *adv.***

**ha·bit·u·ate** (hə bich′o͞o wāt) ***v.*** to make or get used to something; accustom [to *habituate* oneself to a cold climate]. —**ha·bit′u·at·ed, ha·bit′u·at·ing**

☆**ha·ci·en·da** (hä′sē en′də) ***n.*** a large ranch or country home in the southwestern U.S. and Spanish America.

**hack**[1] (hak) ***v.*** **1** to chop or cut roughly, as with an ax [to *hack* one's way through underbrush]. **2** to give harsh, dry coughs. ◆***n.*** **1** a chopping cut. **2** a harsh, dry cough.

**hack**[2] (hak) ***n.*** **1** a horse, or horse and carriage, that can be hired. **2** an old, worn-out horse. **3** a person, especially a writer, who does dull, ordinary work. **4** a taxicab: *used only in everyday talk.* ◆***adj.*** **1** working as a hack [a *hack* writer]. **2** done by a hack [a *hack* job]. ◆***vi.*** ☆to drive a taxicab: *used only in everyday talk.*

**hack·le** (hak′'l) ***n.*** **1** any of the feathers at the neck of a rooster, pigeon, etc. **2 hackles,** *pl.* the hairs on a dog's neck and back that bristle, as when the dog is ready to fight.

**hack·ney** (hak′nē) ***n.*** **1** a horse for driving or riding. **2** a carriage that can be hired. —*pl.* **hack′neys**

**hack·neyed** (hak′nēd) ***adj.*** used so often that it has become stale and dull ["Last but not least" is a *hackneyed* phrase.]

**hack·saw** (hak′sô) ***n.*** a saw with a narrow blade and fine teeth, used for cutting metal. *See the picture.*

**had** (had) *past tense and past participle of* **have.**

> **Had** is also used with certain words of comparison, such as *better, rather, sooner,* etc., to show that something is necessary or preferred ["I *had* better leave now" means "It is necessary that I leave now."]

**had·dock** (had′ək) ***n.*** a small ocean fish used as food. It is related to the cod. —*pl.* **had′dock** or **had′docks**

**Ha·des** (hā′dēz) **1** in Greek myths, the place where the spirits of the dead go, beneath the earth. **2** *often* **hades,** hell: *used only in everyday talk.*

**had·n't** (had′'nt) had not.

**hadst** (hadst) *an older form of* **had,** *used with* thou, *as in the Bible.*

**haft** (haft) ***n.*** the handle of a knife, ax, etc.

**hag** (hag) ***n.*** an ugly old woman, especially one who is mean [Witches were called *hags.*]

**Hag·ga·da** (hä gä dä′ *or* hə gä′də) ***n.*** the story of the Exodus read at the Seder during Passover.

**hag·gard** (hag′ərd) ***adj.*** having a wild but tired look, as from illness, hunger, or grief. *See the picture.*

**hag·gle** (hag′'l) ***v.*** to argue about the price of something or in trying to reach an agreement. —**hag′gled, hag′gling**

**Hague** (hāg), **The** one of the two capitals of the Netherlands. The lawmakers meet there.

**hah** (hä) ***interj.*** *another spelling of* **ha.**

**hai·ku** (hī′ko͞o) ***n.*** a short Japanese poem, usually on a subject in nature. It has three lines that do not rhyme, the first having five syllables, the second, seven, and the third, five.

**hail**[1] (hāl) ***v.*** **1** to welcome or greet with a shout; cheer [The Romans *hailed* Caesar as emperor.] **2** to try to get the attention of, as by shouting [I had to *hail* a cab.] ◆***n.*** **1** the act of hailing or greeting. **2** the distance that a shout can be heard [The boat approached within *hail* of the shore.] ◆***interj.*** a shout of greeting or welcome. —**hail from,** to come from [My family *hails from* Iowa.]

**hail**[2] (hāl) ***n.*** **1** small round pieces of ice that sometimes fall during a thunderstorm; frozen raindrops. **2** anything that comes in large numbers and with force [a *hail* of bullets; a *hail* of curses]. ◆***v.*** **1** to pour down hail [It *hailed* last night.] **2** to come down or throw down in large numbers and with force [Arrows *hailed* down from the castle walls.]

**Hail Mary** *another name for* **Ave Maria.**

**hail·stone** (hāl′stōn) ***n.*** a piece of hail.

**hair** (her) ***n.*** **1** any of the thin growths, like threads, that come from the skin of animals and human beings. **2** the whole number of these growths that cover a person's head, the skin of an animal, etc. [I must comb my *hair.*] **3** a tiny space or amount [You missed the bull's-eye by a *hair.*] **4** a growth like a fine thread on the leaves or stems of some plants. —**let one's hair down,** to talk or act in a free or relaxed way: *a slang phrase.* —**split hairs,** to pay too much attention to small differences that are not important.

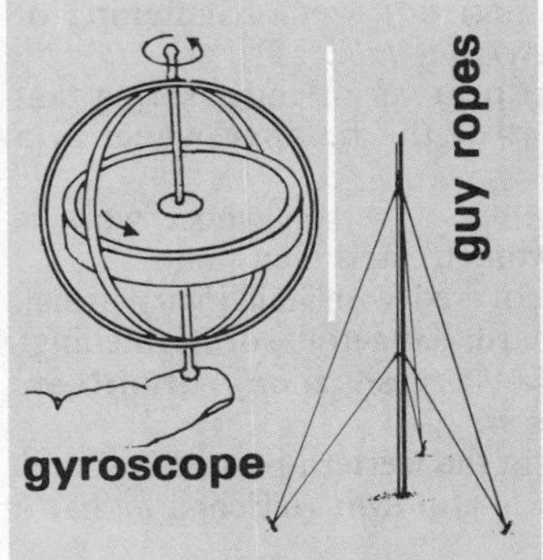

gyroscope

guy ropes

nun's habit

riding habit

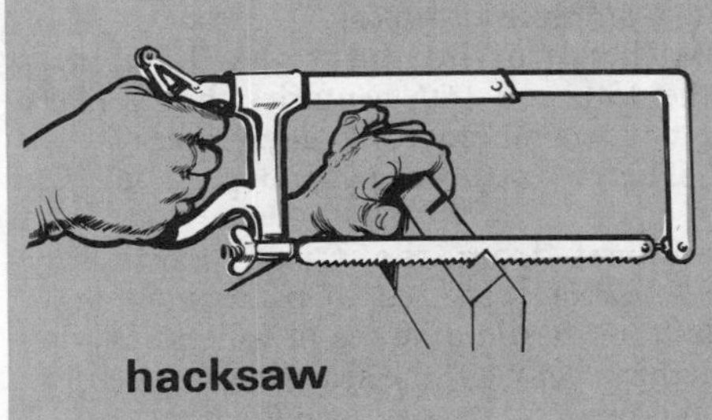

hacksaw

haggard face



**hair·breadth** (her′bredth) ***n.*** a tiny space or amount [Our team won by a *hairbreadth.*] ◆***adj.*** very close; narrow [a *hairbreadth* escape]. *Also* **hairs′breadth** or **hair's′-breadth.**

**hair·cloth** (her′klôth) ***n.*** cloth woven from the hair of a horse or camel. It is used mainly for covering furniture.

**hair·cut** (her′kut) ***n.*** the act or a style of cutting the hair of the head.

☆**hair·do** (her′do͞o) ***n.*** the style in which a woman's hair is arranged.

**hair·dress·er** (her′dres′ər) ***n.*** a person whose work is cutting and arranging women's hair.

**hair·less** (her′lis) ***adj.*** without hair; bald.

**hair·line** (her′līn) ***n.*** **1** a very thin line. **2** the line just above the forehead where the hair begins to grow.

**hair·piece** (her′pēs) ***n.*** **1** a wig or toupee. **2** a bunch of hair, sometimes false hair, used as part of a hairdo.

**hair·pin** (her′pin) ***n.*** a small piece of wire, plastic, etc., shaped like a U, that is used to keep the hair in place. ◆***adj.*** shaped like a hairpin [a *hairpin* curve].

| | | | |
|---|---|---|---|
| **a** fat | **ir** here | **ou** out | **zh** leisure |
| **ā** ape | **ī** bite, fire | **u** up | **ng** ring |
| **ä** car, lot | **ō** go | **ur** fur | a *in* ago |
| **e** ten | **ô** law, horn | **ch** chin | e *in* agent |
| **er** care | **oi** oil | **sh** she | **ə** = i *in* unity |
| **ē** even | **oo** look | **th** thin | o *in* collect |
| **i** hit | **o͞o** tool | ***th*** then | u *in* focus |

**hair·rais·ing** (her′rāz′iŋ) ***adj.*** very frightening or shocking: *used only in everyday talk.*

**hair·spring** (her′spriŋ) ***n.*** a very slender spring that controls the movement of the balance wheel in a watch or clock.

**hair·styl·ist** (her′stīl′ist) ***n.*** a person whose work is cutting and arranging women's and men's hair.

**hair·y** (her′ē) ***adj.*** **1** covered with hair [*hairy* arms]. **2** of or like hair. ☆**3** hard, dangerous, or frightening: *slang in this meaning* [a *hairy* situation]. —**hair′i·er, hair′i·est** —**hair′i·ness *n.***

**Hai·ti** (hā′tē) a country in the western part of Hispaniola, in the West Indies. —**Hai·tian** (hā′shən *or* hāt′ē ən) ***adj., n.***

**hake** (hāk) ***n.*** a sea fish that looks like the cod and is used for food. *—pl.* **hake** or **hakes**

**hal·berd** (hal′bərd) or **hal·bert** (hal′bərt) ***n.*** a weapon of the 15th and 16th centuries that is like a spear and battle-ax combined. *See the picture.*

**hal·cy·on** (hal′sē ən) ***adj.*** happy and peaceful [*halcyon* days].

> **Halcyon** comes from the Greek word for "kingfisher," *alkyon.* It used to be thought that this bird built her nest on the sea in winter. While she was hatching her eggs, the sea was supposed to stay calm and peaceful in some magical way.

**hale**[1] (hāl) ***adj.*** healthy and strong [My grandparents are still *hale* and hearty.] —**hal′er, hal′est**

 **hale**[2] (hāl) ***v.*** to force a person to go [They were *haled* into court.] —**haled, hal′ing**

**Hale** (hāl), **Nathan** 1755–1776; an American soldier in the Revolutionary War, who was hanged by the British as a spy.

**half** (haf) ***n.*** **1** either of the two equal parts of something [Five is *half* of ten.] **2** either of two almost equal parts: *thought by some people to be not a proper use* [Take the smaller *half* of the pie.] **3** a half hour [It is *half* past two.] **4** either of the two parts of an inning in baseball, or of the two main time periods of a game of football, basketball, etc. *—pl.* **halves** ◆***adj.*** **1** being either of the two equal parts [a *half* gallon]. **2** being about a half [A *half* mask covered the eyes.] **3** not complete or perfect; partial [I could barely see it in the *half* light.] ◆***adv.*** **1** to half or about half of the whole amount [*half* full]. **2** to some degree; partly [I was *half* convinced.] —**in half,** into halves. —**not half bad,** rather good.

**half·back** (haf′bak) ***n.*** either of two football players whose position is behind the line.

**half-baked** (haf′bākt′) ***adj.*** **1** only partly baked. **2** not having enough thought, planning, experience, etc.; foolish [a *half-baked* idea].

**half brother** someone who is one's brother through one parent only.

**half dollar** a coin of the U.S. or Canada, worth 50 cents.

**half·heart·ed** (haf′här′tid) ***adj.*** with not much enthusiasm or interest [a *halfhearted* attempt]. —**half′-heart′ed·ly *adv.***

**half-hour** (haf′our′) ***n.*** **1** half of an hour; thirty minutes. **2** the point thirty minutes after any given hour [Take your medicine on the *half-hour.*] ◆***adj.*** lasting for thirty minutes [a *half-hour* program].

**half-mast** (haf′mast′) ***n.*** the position of a flag lowered about halfway down its staff, as in mourning someone who has died.

**half-moon** (haf′mo͞on′) ***n.*** the moon between new moon and full moon, when only half its disk is clearly seen.

**half note** a note in music that is held half as long as a whole note.

**half·pen·ny** (hā′pə nē *or* hāp′nē) ***n.*** a British coin equal to half a penny, that is no longer coined. *—pl.* **half·pence** (hā′pəns) or **half′pen·nies**

**half sister** someone who is one's sister through one parent only.

☆**half time** the rest period between the halves of a football game, basketball game, etc.

**half·way** (haf′wā′) ***adj.*** **1** at the middle between two points or limits [to reach the *halfway* mark]. **2** not complete; partial [to take *halfway* measures]. ◆***adv.*** **1** to the midway point; half the distance [They had gone *halfway* home.] **2** partially [The house is *halfway* built.] —**meet someone halfway,** to try to reach an agreement with someone by having each side give up something.

**half-wit** (haf′wit′) ***n.*** a stupid, silly, or feeble-minded person; fool. —**half′-wit′ted *adj.***

**hal·i·but** (hal′ə bət) ***n.*** a large flatfish of the northern seas, used for food. *See the picture. —pl.* **hal′i·but** or **hal′i·buts**

**Hal·i·fax** (hal′ə faks) the capital of Nova Scotia, Canada.

**hal·ite** (hal′īt *or* hā′līt) ***n.*** *another word for* **rock salt.**

**hall** (hôl) ***n.*** **1** a passageway from which doors open into various rooms. **2** a room or passageway at the entrance of a building. **3** a large room used for meetings, shows, dances, etc. **4** a building containing public offices or a headquarters of some sort [the city *hall*]. **5** any of the buildings of a college, especially a dormitory.

**hal·le·lu·jah** or **hal·le·lu·iah** (hal′ə lo͞o′yə) ***interj.*** praise the Lord! ◆***n.*** a hymn of praise to God.

**hall·mark** (hôl′märk) ***n.*** anything that shows how genuine or pure something is [Fairness is the *hallmark* of a good judge.]

> The **hallmark** was originally a mark stamped on gold and silver articles at Goldsmiths' Hall in London to show how pure the articles were.

**hal·low** (hal′ō) ***v.*** to make or keep holy or sacred [to *hallow* the name of God].

**Hal·low·een** or **Hal·low·e′en** (hal′ə wēn′ *or* häl′ə wēn′) ***n.*** the evening of October 31, celebrated nowadays by children in costumes asking for treats.

**hal·lu·ci·nate** (hə lo͞o′sə nāt) ***v.*** to have hallucinations. —**hal·lu′ci·nat·ed, hal·lu′ci·nat·ing**

**hal·lu·ci·na·tion** (hə lo͞o′sə nā′shən) ***n.*** **1** the seeing or hearing of things around one that are not really there at all [People with very sick minds sometimes have *hallucinations.*] **2** the thing seen or heard in this way.

☆**hall·way** (hôl′wā) ***n.*** a passageway, as between rooms; corridor.

**ha·lo** (hā′lō) ***n.*** **1** a ring of light around the sun, the moon, a street light, etc. **2** a ring of light shown around the head of a saint, angel, etc., as in a painting. It is a symbol of holiness. *See the picture. —pl.* **ha′los** or **ha′loes**

**halt¹** (hôlt) ***n., v.*** stop [I worked all morning without a *halt*. Rain *halted* the game.] —☆**call a halt,** to order a stop.

**halt²** (hôlt) ***v.*** to be unsure; hesitate [to *halt* in one's speech]. ◆***adj.*** lame or crippled; limping.

**hal·ter** (hôl′tər) ***n.*** **1** a rope or strap for leading or tying an animal. *See the picture.* **2** an upper garment without a back, worn by a woman or girl. It is held up by a loop around the neck. **3** a rope for hanging a person.

**halve** (hav) ***v.*** **1** to divide into two equal parts [to *halve* a melon]. **2** to make only half as much, half as large, etc. [This process will *halve* our costs.] —**halved, halv′ing**

**halves** (havz) ***n.*** *plural of* **half.** —**go halves,** to have each one pay half of the expenses.

**hal·yard** (hal′yərd) ***n.*** a rope used to raise or lower a flag, sail, etc.

**ham** (ham) ***n.*** **1** the meat from the upper part of a hog's hind leg, salted, smoked, etc. for eating. **2** the back part of the thigh and the buttock. ☆**3** an amateur radio operator: *used only in everyday talk.* ☆**4** an actor or actress who acts in an awkward or exaggerated way: *slang in this meaning.*

**Ham·burg** (ham′bərg) a city in northern West Germany.

☆**ham·burg·er** (ham′bur′gər) ***n.*** **1** ground beef. **2** a small, flat patty of ground beef, fried or broiled. **3** a sandwich made with such a patty, usually in a round bun. *Also* **ham′burg.**

The **hamburger,** or Hamburg steak as it was once called, gets its name from the city of Hamburg in West Germany.

**Ham·il·ton** (ham′əl t′n), **Alexander** 1757–1804; the first secretary of the U.S. treasury, from 1789 to 1795. He was killed in a duel by Aaron Burr.

**Ham·let** (ham′lit) **1** a tragic play by Shakespeare. **2** the hero of this play, who gets revenge for the murder of his father, the king of Denmark.

**ham·let** (ham′lit) ***n.*** a very small village.

**ham·mer** (ham′ər) ***n.*** **1** a tool for driving in nails, breaking stones, shaping metal, etc. It usually has a metal head and a handle. **2** a thing like this in shape or use, as the part that strikes against the firing pin of a gun or any of the parts that strike the strings of a piano. ◆***v.*** **1** to hit with many blows [They *hammered* on the door with their fists.] **2** to make or shape with a hammer [*Hammer* the metal flat.] **3** to drive or force [to *hammer* an idea into someone's head]. —**hammer away at,** **1** to work hard and steadily at. **2** to keep talking about. —**hammer out,** **1** to shape by hammering. **2** to work out with thought or effort [to *hammer out* a plan].

**ham·mock** (ham′ək) ***n.*** a long piece of canvas that is hung from ropes at each end and is used as a bed or couch. *See the picture.*

**ham·per¹** (ham′pər) ***v.*** to get in the way of; hinder [to be *hampered* by a lack of education].

**ham·per²** (ham′pər) ***n.*** a large basket, usually with a cover [We brought the picnic food in a *hamper*.]

**ham·ster** (ham′stər) ***n.*** a small animal like a mouse, with large cheek pouches. It is often used in scientific experiments or kept as a pet.

**ham·string** (ham′string) ***n.*** **1** one of the tendons at the back of a person's knee. **2** the large tendon at the back of the hock of a horse, ox, etc. ◆***v.*** **1** to make lame by cutting the hamstring. **2** to make less able to do something, as by taking away the power of. —**ham′strung, ham′string·ing**

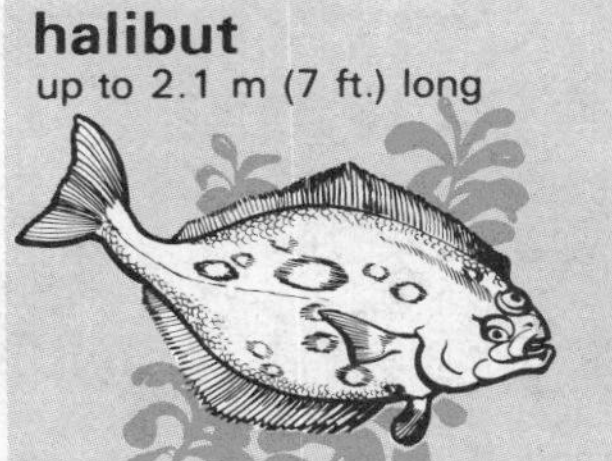

**halibut**
up to 2.1 m (7 ft.) long

**hammock**

**halberd**

**halter**

**halo**

**Han·cock** (han′käk), **John** 1737–1793; a leader in the American Revolution. He was the first to sign the Declaration of Independence.

**hand** (hand) ***n.*** **1** the end of the arm beyond the wrist, including the palm, fingers, and thumb. **2** any of the pointers on a clock or watch. **3** side [The guest of honor will sit at your right *hand*.] **4** a person hired to work with the hands [a farm *hand;* dock *hand*]. **5** skill or ability [These sketches show the *hand* of a master.] **6** control or power [He ruled with an iron *hand*. The matter is now in the *hands* of her lawyer.] **7** a part or share in some action [Take a *hand* in the work.] **8** help [Give me a *hand* with this job.] **9** a clapping of hands; applause [Give the dancer a big *hand*.] **10** handwriting [I recognize your fine *hand*.] **11** the place from which something comes; source [I got the news at first *hand*.] **12** a promise to marry [It used to be common for a man to ask a woman's father for her *hand*.] **13** a handshake used to show agreement or friendship. **14** the breadth of the hand, about four inches [This horse is 15 *hands* high.] **15** the cards held by each player in a card game. **16** a single round of play in a card game. ◆***adj.*** of, for, or worked by the hand or hands [*hand* lotion; a *hand* saw]. ◆***v.*** to give with the hand; pass [*Hand* me the



| | | | | | | | |
|---|---|---|---|---|---|---|---|
| **a** | fat | **ir** | here | **ou** | out | **zh** | leisure |
| **ā** | ape | **ī** | bite, fire | **u** | up | **ng** | ring |
| **ä** | car, lot | **ō** | go | **ur** | fur | | a *in* ago |
| **e** | ten | **ô** | law, horn | **ch** | chin | | e *in* agent |
| **er** | care | **oi** | oil | **sh** | she | **ə** = | i *in* unity |
| **ē** | even | **oo** | look | **th** | thin | | o *in* collect |
| **i** | hit | **ōō** | tool | ***th*** | then | | u *in* focus |

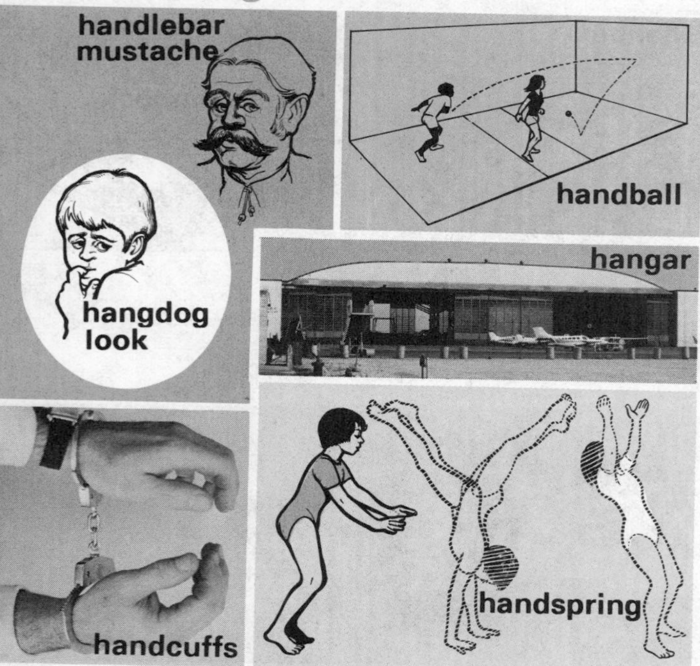


book, please.] —**at hand,** near; close by. —**at the hand of** or **at the hands of,** through the action of
 [They suffered *at the hands of* the dictator.] —**by hand,** with the hands, not by machines. —**change hands,** to pass from one owner to another. —**from hand to mouth,** with nothing left over for future needs. —**hand down,** **1** to pass along, as from generation to generation. ☆**2** to give a verdict, as in court. —**hand in hand,** **1** holding hands. **2** together [Hard work and success go *hand in hand.*] —**hands down,** easily [to win *hands down*]. —**hand to hand,** very close to the opponent [to fight *hand to hand*]. —**in hand,** under control [We now have the flood *in hand.*] —**lay hands on,** **1** to hurt or attack. **2** to get hold of; take. —**on hand,** **1** near. ☆**2** ready or available. ☆**3** present. —**on the other hand,** from the opposite point of view. —**wash one's hands of,** to refuse to have anything to do with.

**hand·bag** (hand′bag) ***n.*** **1** a woman's pocketbook; purse. **2** a small suitcase.

**hand·ball** (hand′bôl) ***n.*** **1** a game in which a small ball is batted against a wall or walls with the hand. *See the picture.* **2** the small rubber ball used in this game.

**hand·bill** (hand′bil) ***n.*** a small, printed advertisement that is passed out by hand.

**hand·book** (hand′bo͝ok) ***n.*** a small book that contains facts or instructions on some subject; manual.

**hand·cuff** (hand′kuf) ***n.*** either of a pair of connected metal rings that can be locked about the wrists, as those of a prisoner. *See the picture.* ◆***v.*** to put handcuffs on.

**Han·del** (han′d'l), **George Frederick** 1685–1759; British composer who was born in Germany.

**hand·ful** (hand′fo͝ol) ***n.*** **1** as much or as many as the hand can hold [a *handful* of popcorn]. **2** a small number; few [a *handful* of people]. **3** a person or thing that is hard to manage: *used only in everyday talk.* —*pl.* **hand′fuls**

**hand·gun** (hand′gun) ***n.*** any small gun that is held and fired with one hand, as a pistol.

**hand·i·cap** (han′dē kap) ***n.*** **1** a race or other contest in which things are made harder for some or easier for others so that all have an equal chance. **2** the harder or easier condition given in such a contest [a *handicap* of extra weight in a horse race or of a shorter distance in running]. **3** something that holds a person back or makes things harder; hindrance [Lack of education can be a great *handicap.*] ◆***v.*** to be or give a handicap; make things harder for. —**hand′i·capped, hand′i·cap·ping**

**hand·i·craft** (han′dē kraft) ***n.*** **1** skill in working with the hands. **2** work that takes this kind of skill, as weaving or pottery.

**hand·i·ly** (han′d'l ē) ***adv.*** in a handy way; without much trouble; easily [to win *handily*].

**hand·i·work** (han′dē wurk) ***n.*** **1** work done by hand. **2** anything made or done by someone [Is this poem your *handiwork?*]

**hand·ker·chief** (haŋ′kər chif) ***n.*** a small piece of cloth for wiping the nose, eyes, or face, or worn as a decoration.

**han·dle** (han′d'l) ***n.*** the part by which a tool, door, cup, etc. can be held, lifted, or turned with the hand. ◆***v.*** **1** to hold or touch with the hand [*Handle* that china cup with care.] **2** to take care of, manage, or control [Police *handled* the traffic.] **3** to deal with; treat [There are many ways to *handle* that problem.] **4** to work or act in a certain way [My new bicycle *handles* well.] ☆**5** to buy or sell as a business; deal in [The drugstore *handles* many items.] —**han′dled, han′dling** —**fly off the handle,** to become very angry and lose one's self-control: *used only in everyday talk.* —**han′dler** ***n.***

**han·dle·bar** (han′d'l bär) ***n.*** **1** a curved metal bar on a bicycle or motorcycle, used for steering. ☆**2** a mustache with long, curved ends: *the full name is* **handlebar mustache.** *See the picture.*

**hand·made** (hand′mād′) ***adj.*** made by hand instead of by machine [*handmade* boots].

**hand·maid·en** (hand′mād′'n) ***n.*** a woman or girl servant: *also* **hand′maid′**. *These words are now seldom used.*

☆**hand organ** *another name for* **barrel organ.**

☆**hand·out** (hand′out) ***n.*** **1** a gift of food, clothing, etc., as to a beggar. **2** a leaflet, folder, etc. handed out free.

**hand·rail** (hand′rāl) ***n.*** a rail that can be used for support, as along a stairway.

**hand·shake** (hand′shāk) ***n.*** the act of holding and shaking another's hand, as in greeting or in making an agreement.

**hand·some** (han′səm) ***adj.*** **1** pleasant to look at; good-looking, especially in a manly or dignified way. **2** large in amount or size [a *handsome* sum of money]. **3** kind and courteous; generous [We were treated in a *handsome* way.] —**hand′some·ly** ***adv.*** —**hand′some·ness** ***n.***

**hand·spring** (hand′spriŋ) ***n.*** a kind of somersault in which only the hands or a hand touches the ground. *See the picture.*

**hand·work** (hand′wurk) ***n.*** work done by hand.

**hand·writ·ing** (hand′rīt′iŋ) ***n.*** **1** writing done by hand, with pen, pencil, etc. **2** a person's way of forming letters and words in writing [His *handwriting* slants to the left.]

**hand·y** (han′dē) ***adj.*** **1** easily reached; nearby [The bus stop is *handy.*] **2** easily used; saving time or work [a *handy* device for opening cans]. **3** clever in using one's hands; deft [She is *handy* with tools.] —**hand′i·er, hand′i·est**

**Han·dy** (han′dē), **W. C.** 1873–1958; U.S. composer of jazz music. His full name was William Christopher Handy.

**hang** (haŋ) ***v.*** **1** to fasten or be fastened to something above, as by pins, hooks, nails, etc. [to *hang* laundry on a clothesline; to *hang* a picture]. **2** to put to death or to die by hanging from a rope tied around the neck. **3** to fasten or be fastened so as to swing freely [The shutters are *hung* on hinges.] **4** to fasten to walls with paste [to *hang* wallpaper]. **5** to decorate by hanging pictures, drapes, etc. [The room was *hung* with oil paintings.] **6** to bend or lean down; droop [a head *hung* in shame]. ☆**7** to keep from coming to a decision [The jury was *hung* because its members couldn't agree on a verdict.] —**hung** (**hanged** *for meaning* 2), **hang′ing** ◆***n.*** the way a thing hangs [the *hang* of the curtains]. —☆**get the hang of, 1** to learn the skill of [to *get the hang of* driving a truck]. **2** to understand the meaning or idea of [I don't *get the hang of* this story.] —☆**hang around** or **hang about,** to loiter or linger in some place: *used only in everyday talk.* —**hang back,** to be unwilling to go forward, as because of shyness. —**hang fire,** to stay undecided. —**hang on, 1** to keep hold. **2** to depend on [It all *hangs on* whether she decides to go.] **3** to lean on. **4** to listen closely to [We were *hanging on* his every word.] —**hang out, 1** to lean out. **2** to spend much of one's time: *a slang phrase.* —**hang over, 1** to stick out over; overhang. **2** to hover over. —**hang together, 1** to stick together. **2** to make sense, as a story. —**hang up, 1** to put on a hanger or hook, as a coat. **2** to put a telephone receiver back in place in ending a call. **3** to delay [We were *hung up* in traffic.]

**hang·ar** (haŋ′ər) ***n.*** a shed in which aircraft are kept for repairs or when not in use. *See the picture.*

**hang·dog** (haŋ′dôg) ***adj.*** ashamed and cringing [a *hangdog* look]. *See the picture.*

**hang·er** (haŋ′ər) ***n.*** **1** a person who hangs things [a paper*hanger*]. **2** a thing on which another thing is hung [a clothes *hanger*].

**hang·er-on** (haŋ′ər än′) ***n.*** a supporter of someone, especially one who hopes to gain something in this way. —*pl.* **hang′ers-on′**

☆**hang glider** a large plastic sail on a metal frame, from which a person hangs in a harness. It is used in the sport of gliding through the air.

**hang·ing** (haŋ′iŋ) ***adj.*** that hangs [a *hanging* lamp]. ◆***n.*** **1** the act of putting to death by hanging. **2** something hung on a wall, window, etc., as a drapery.

**hang·man** (haŋ′mən) ***n.*** a person who hangs those sentenced to die by hanging. —*pl.* **hang′men**

**hang·nail** (haŋ′nāl) ***n.*** a bit of torn skin at the side or base of a fingernail.

**hang·out** (haŋ′out) ***n.*** a place where some person or group spends much time: *a slang word.*

**hang·o·ver** (haŋ′ō′vər) ***n.*** **1** something left over from an earlier time. **2** a headache and a feeling of being sick that comes from drinking too much alcoholic liquor.

☆**hang-up** (haŋ′up′) ***n.*** a problem that a person has and does not seem to be able to work out: *a slang word* [to have a *hang-up* about being tall].

**hank** (haŋk) ***n.*** a loop or coil of hair or yarn.

**hank·er** (haŋ′kər) ***v.*** to have a strong wish or longing; crave [to *hanker* after fame].

**Han·ni·bal** (han′ə bəl) 247?–183? B.C.; a general of Carthage who crossed the Alps to invade Rome.

**Ha·noi** (hə noi′) the capital of Vietnam.

**Han·o·ver** (han′ō′vər) a city in northern West Germany.

**han·som** (han′səm) ***n.*** a covered carriage with two wheels, drawn by one horse. The driver's seat is above and behind the cab. *See the picture on page 335.*

**Ha·nu·ka** (hä′noo kä) ***n.*** a Jewish festival celebrating the restoring of the Temple after the successful revolt against the Syrians in 165 B.C.

**hap** (hap) ***n.*** chance; luck. ◆***v.*** to happen or occur by chance. —**happed, hap′ping**

**hap·haz·ard** (hap′haz′ərd) ***adj.*** not planned; accidental [*haphazard* events]. ◆***adv.*** by chance; in a haphazard way [toys scattered *haphazard* on the floor]. —**hap′haz′ard·ly *adv.***

**hap·less** (hap′lis) ***adj.*** unlucky; unfortunate.

**hap·pen** (hap′′n) ***v.*** **1** to take place, especially by chance; occur [What *happened* at the party? It *happened* to rain that day.] **2** to have the luck, good or bad; chance [I *happened* to see it.] **3** to come by chance [She *happened* along just as I was leaving.] —**happen on** or **happen upon,** to meet or find by chance. —**happen to,** to be done to or be the fate of [What ever *happened to* the story you were writing?]



**hap·pen·ing** (hap′′n iŋ) ***n.*** something that happens; event [the day's *happenings*].

**hap·py** (hap′ē) ***adj.*** **1** feeling or showing pleasure or joy; glad; contented [a *happy* child; a *happy* song]. **2** lucky; fortunate [The story has a *happy* ending.] **3** just right; suitable; fitting [Your dress was a *happy* choice for the dance.] —**hap′pi·er, hap′pi·est** —**hap′pi·ly *adv.*** —**hap′pi·ness *n.***

SYNONYMS: **Happy** is used to show general feelings of great pleasure, contentment, or joy [a *happy* marriage]. **Glad** shows these feelings even more strongly, usually for a particular happening [She is very *glad* to have won the prize.] Both **happy** and **glad** are commonly used in certain polite expressions [I'm *happy,* or *glad,* to meet you.]

**hap·py-go-luck·y** (hap′ē gō luk′ē) ***adj.*** trusting to luck; not worrying; carefree.

**ha·ra-ki·ri** (hä′rə kir′ē *or* har′ə kir′ē) ***n.*** a way of committing suicide by cutting the belly open. It used

| | | | | | | | |
|---|---|---|---|---|---|---|---|
| **a** | fat | **ir** | here | **ou** | out | **zh** | leisure |
| **ā** | ape | **ī** | bite, fire | **u** | up | **ŋ** | ring |
| **ä** | car, lot | **ō** | go | **ur** | fur | | a *in* ago |
| **e** | ten | **ô** | law, horn | **ch** | chin | | e *in* agent |
| **er** | care | **oi** | oil | **sh** | she | **ə =** | i *in* unity |
| **ē** | even | **oo** | look | **th** | thin | | o *in* collect |
| **i** | hit | **ōō** | tool | ***th*** | then | | u *in* focus |

to be done by Japanese of the upper classes when they were in danger of disgrace.

**ha·rangue** (hə rang′) ***n.*** a long speech made in a loud or scolding way. ◆***v.*** to give a harangue or talk to in a harangue. —**ha·rangued′, ha·rangu′ing**

**har·ass** (hə ras′ *or* har′əs) ***v.*** **1** to worry or trouble [He was *harassed* with many debts.] **2** to trouble by attacking again and again [Flies *harassed* the horse.] —**har·ass′ment** ***n.***

> **Harass** comes from an old French word meaning "to set, or sic, a dog on." To have a dog set on one would surely be harassing or troubling.

**har·bin·ger** (här′bin jər) ***n.*** a person or thing that comes to show what will follow [The first frost is a *harbinger* of winter.]

**har·bor** (här′bər) ***n.*** **1** a place where ships may anchor and be safe from storms; port; haven. **2** any place where one is safe; shelter. ◆***v.*** **1** to shelter or hide [to *harbor* an outlaw]. **2** to hold in the mind [Try not to *harbor* ill will.]

**hard** (härd) ***adj.*** **1** firm to the touch; not easy to cut, bend, or crush; not soft; solid [a *hard* rock]. *See* SYNONYMS *at* **firm.** **2** not easy to do, understand, or deal with; difficult [a *hard* job; a *hard* problem]. **3** strong or powerful; violent [a *hard* punch]. **4** not showing kindness, love, etc.; unfeeling or unfriendly [a *hard* heart; *hard* feelings]. **5** harsh or severe; stern [*hard* words; a *hard* look on one's face; a *hard* life]. **6** using energy and steady effort; energetic [a *hard* worker]. **7** containing much alcohol [*hard* liquor]. **8** having minerals in it that keep soap from making a lather [*hard* water]. **9** describing the sound of *g* in *get* or of *c* in *can.* ◆***adv.*** **1** with effort and energy [to work *hard*]. **2** with strength or power [to hit *hard*]. **3** with pain or difficulty [He took the bad news *hard.*] **4** in a firm way [Hold on *hard!*] **5** so as to be solid [to freeze *hard*]. **6** close or near [We lived *hard* by the woods.] —**hard and fast,** strict; that cannot be changed. —**hard of hearing,** not able to hear well. —**hard up,** in great need of money: *used only in everyday talk.*

**hard-boiled** (härd′boild′) ***adj.*** **1** cooked in hot water until the inside is solid [*hard-boiled* eggs]. **2** without gentle feelings or sympathy; tough: *used only in everyday talk.*

**hard-core** (härd′kôr′) ***adj.*** in every way; absolute; thorough [a *hard-core* conservative].

**hard·en** (här′d'n) ***v.*** to make or become hard.

**hard hat** ☆**1** a helmet worn by construction workers, miners, etc. to protect the head. *See the picture.* ☆**2** such a worker: *slang in this meaning.*

**hard·head·ed** (härd′hed′id) ***adj.*** **1** not giving in; stubborn. **2** thinking only in a practical way and not allowing feelings to affect one [a *hardheaded* boss].

**hard·heart·ed** (härd′härt′id) ***adj.*** without pity or sympathy; cruel or unfeeling.

**har·di·hood** (här′dē hood) ***n.*** boldness; daring.

**Har·ding** (här′ding), **Warren G.** 1865–1923; the 29th president of the United States, from 1921 to 1923.

**hard·ly** (härd′lē) ***adv.*** **1** only just; almost not; scarcely [I can *hardly* tell them apart. There is *hardly* any time left.] **2** probably not; not likely [That can *hardly* be the best way.]

**hard·ness** (härd′nis) ***n.*** the condition of being hard.

**hard·ship** (härd′ship) ***n.*** something that is hard to bear; trouble, pain, suffering, etc. *See* SYNONYMS *at* **difficulty.**

**hard·tack** (härd′tak) ***n.*** unraised bread in the form of very hard, large wafers, much used by sailors and soldiers in earlier days.

**hard·ware** (härd′wer) ***n.*** things made of metal, as tools, nails, pots and pans, etc.

**hard·wood** (härd′wood) ***n.*** any wood that is hard and has a close grain, as oak, walnut, maple, etc.

**har·dy** (här′dē) ***adj.*** **1** strong and sturdy; able to hold up under bad conditions [*Hardy* plants can live through frosts.] **2** bold or daring [a *hardy* adventurer]. —**har′di·er, har′di·est** —**har′di·ly** ***adv.*** —**har′di·ness** ***n.***

**hare** (her) ***n.*** a swift animal with long ears, a split upper lip, large front teeth used for gnawing, and long, powerful hind legs. Hares are related to rabbits but are usually larger.

**hare·bell** (her′bel) ***n.*** the bluebell, a plant with blue flowers shaped like bells.

**hare·brained** (her′brānd) ***adj.*** having or showing little sense; silly [a *harebrained* idea].

**hare·lip** (her′lip) ***n.*** a split upper lip that some people are born with.

**ha·rem** (her′əm) ***n.*** **1** that part of a Muslim household in which the women live. **2** the women who live in a harem.

> **Harem** comes from an Arabic word meaning "forbidden" or "prohibited." Strangers were forbidden to enter the harem.

**ha·ri-ka·ri** (her′ē ker′ē) ***n.*** *another spelling of* **hara-kiri.**

**hark** (härk) ***v.*** to listen carefully: *now seldom used except in poetry* ["*Hark!* the herald angels sing."] —**hark back,** to go back, as in thought [to *hark back* to one's childhood].

**hark·en** (här′k'n) ***v.*** *another spelling of* **hearken.**

**Har·le·quin** (här′lə kwin) a comic character in pantomime, who wears tights of many colors and a mask. *See the picture.*

**har·le·quin** (här′lə kwin) ***n.*** a clown; buffoon.

**har·lot** (här′lət) ***n.*** *another word for* **prostitute.**

**harm** (härm) ***n.*** **1** damage or hurt [Too much rain can do *harm* to crops.] **2** wrong [I meant no *harm* by my remark.] ◆***v.*** to do harm to; hurt or damage. *See* SYNONYMS *at* **injure.**

**harm·ful** (härm′fəl) ***adj.*** doing harm or able to do harm [Sugar is *harmful* to the teeth.] —**harm′ful·ly** ***adv.*** —**harm′ful·ness** ***n.***

**harm·less** (härm′lis) ***adj.*** that cannot harm; doing no harm [Most snakes are *harmless.*] —**harm′less·ly** ***adv.*** —**harm′less·ness** ***n.***

**har·mon·ic** (här män′ik) ***adj.*** of or in harmony in music. ◆***n.*** *another word for* **overtone.**

☆**har·mon·i·ca** (här män′i kə) ***n.*** a small musical instrument with a row of reeds that sound tones when the breath is blown out or sucked in across them; mouth organ. *See the picture.*

**har·mo·ni·ous** (här mō′nē əs) ***adj.*** **1** fitting or blending together in an orderly or pleasing way [*harmonious* shades of blue and green]. **2** getting along well together; friendly [*harmonious* partners].

**har·mo·nize** (här′mə nīz) ***v.*** **1** to be, sing, or play in harmony [Those colors *harmonize* well. The voices *harmonized* in a quartet.] **2** to bring into harmony [to *harmonize* the colors in a room; to *harmonize* a melody]. —**har'mo·nized, har'mo·niz·ing**

**har·mo·ny** (här'mə nē) ***n.*** **1** pleasing arrangement of things, parts, colors, etc. **2** peace and friendship; agreement in ideas, feelings, etc. [We work in perfect *harmony*.] **3** the sound of music. **4** the sounding together of tones in a way that is pleasing to hear. **5** the study of chords and their use in music. —*pl.* **har'mo·nies**

**har·ness** (här'nis) ***n.*** **1** the leather straps and metal pieces by which a horse, mule, etc. is fastened to a wagon, plow, carriage, etc. **2** any arrangement of straps like this [the *harness* that fastens a parachute to a person]. ◆***v.*** **1** to put a harness on. **2** to control so as to use the power of [to *harness* the energy of a waterfall so as to produce electricity].

**harp** (härp) ***n.*** a musical instrument having many strings stretched on a large, upright frame. The strings are plucked with the fingers. *See the picture.* ◆***v.*** **1** to talk or write about something so much that it becomes boring [He's always *harping* on his illnesses.] **2** to play on a harp.

**Har·pers Ferry** (här'pərz) a town in West Virginia. John Brown led a raid on a U.S. arsenal there to get weapons for slaves to use in revolting.

**harp·ist** (här'pist) ***n.*** a harp player.

**har·poon** (här po͞on') ***n.*** a spear with a barb at one end and a line attached to the shaft. It is used for spearing whales or other sea animals. ◆***v.*** to strike or catch with a harpoon.

**harp·si·chord** (härp'si kôrd) ***n.*** an early musical instrument like a piano, except that the strings are plucked by points of leather or quill instead of being struck by hammers. *See the picture.*

**Har·py** (här'pē) ***n.*** **1** an ugly monster in Greek myths with the head and body of a woman and the wings, tail, and claws of a bird. **2 harpy,** a greedy or grasping person. —*pl.* **Har'pies** or **har'pies**

**har·ri·er** (har'ē ər) ***n.*** a breed of dog used for hunting rabbits and hares.

**Har·ris·burg** (har'is burg') the capital of Pennsylvania, in the southern part of the State.

**Har·ri·son** (har'ə s'n), **Benjamin** 1833–1901; the 23d president of the United States, from 1889 to 1893.

**Harrison, William Henry** 1773–1841; the ninth president of the United States, in 1841 He was the grandfather of Benjamin Harrison.

**har·row** (har'ō) ***n.*** a heavy frame with metal spikes or sharp discs. It is pulled by a horse or tractor over plowed ground for breaking up the soil and for covering seeds. *See the picture for* **disc harrow.** ◆***v.*** to pull a harrow over.

**har·row·ing** (har'ō iŋ) ***adj.*** causing pain, fear, or discomfort [The fire was a *harrowing* experience.]

**har·ry** (har'ē) ***v.*** **1** to keep on attacking and raiding; plunder [Invaders from Denmark *harried* the early British tribes.] **2** to worry or trouble; harass [*harried* by debts]. —**har'ried, har'ry·ing**

**harsh** (härsh) ***adj.*** **1** rough and not pleasing to one's hearing, sight, taste, or touch; grating, glaring, coarse, etc. [*harsh* music; a *harsh* light; *harsh* medicine; *harsh* woolen cloth]. *See* SYNONYMS *at* **rough. 2** cruel or severe; that hurts [*harsh* punishment]. —**harsh'ly *adv.*** —**harsh'ness *n.***

harmonica

Harlequin

hansom

harp

harpsichord

man wearing hard hat

**hart** (härt) ***n.*** a male deer; especially, the male red deer of Europe after its fifth year.

**Hart·ford** (härt'fərd) the capital of Connecticut.



**har·um-scar·um** (her'əm sker'əm) ***adj.*** acting or done without thinking; reckless; rash. ◆***adv.*** in a reckless or careless way.

**har·vest** (här'vist) ***n.*** **1** the act of gathering a crop of grain, fruit, etc. when it becomes ripe. **2** the time of the year when a crop is gathered. **3** all the grain, fruit, etc. gathered in one season; crop [a large *harvest*]. **4** the results of doing something [She reaped a *harvest* of love for all her good works.] ◆***v.*** **1** to gather in a crop [to *harvest* peaches]. **2** to gather a crop from [to *harvest* a field]. **3** to get as the result of doing something [to *harvest* the fruits of hard work].

**har·vest·er** (här'vis tər) ***n.*** **1** a person who harvests a crop. ☆**2** a machine for harvesting.

**har·vest·man** (här'vist mən) ***n.*** an animal like a spider with very long and slender legs; daddy-longlegs. —*pl.* **har'vest·men**

**has** (haz) *the form of the verb* **have** *showing the present time with singular nouns and with* he, she, *or* it.

**hash** (hash) ***n.*** **1** a dish made of meat and vegetables chopped up into small pieces, mixed together, and baked or fried. **2** a mess or muddle [He made a *hash* of the job.] ◆***v.*** to chop up into small pieces. —**hash over,** to talk about; discuss: *used only in everyday talk.*

**has·n't** (haz''nt) has not.

| | | | | | | | |
|---|---|---|---|---|---|---|---|
| **a** | fat | **ir** | here | **ou** | out | **zh** | leisure |
| **ā** | ape | **ī** | bite, fire | **u** | up | **ŋ** | ring |
| **ä** | car, lot | **ō** | go | **ur** | fur | | a *in* ago |
| **e** | ten | **ô** | law, horn | **ch** | chin | | e *in* agent |
| **er** | care | **oi** | oil | **sh** | she | **ə =** | i *in* unity |
| **ē** | even | **oo** | look | **th** | thin | | o *in* collect |
| **i** | hit | **o͞o** | tool | ***th*** | then | | u *in* focus |

**h**

**hasp** (hasp) ***n.*** a metal piece that swings on a hinge and fits over a staple through which a pin or lock is passed to keep a door, window, or lid closed. *See the picture.*

☆**has·sle** (has′'l) ***n.*** **1** an angry argument; squabble. **2** trouble or bother. ◆***v.*** **1** to have an angry argument. **2** to be a trouble or bother to; annoy. *This word is used only in everyday talk.* —**has′sled, has′sling**

**has·sock** (has′ək) ***n.*** a firm cushion used as a footstool or low seat. *See the picture.*

**hast** (hast) *an older form of* **have,** *used with* thou, *as in the Bible.*

**haste** (hāst) ***n.*** **1** the act of hurrying; quick movement or action [She left in *haste.*] **2** a hurrying in a careless way [*Haste* makes waste.] —**make haste,** to hurry.

**has·ten** (hās′'n) ***v.*** **1** to go or act quickly; hurry [*Hasten* to call the doctor!] **2** to send or bring faster; speed up [to *hasten* one's departure].

**hast·y** (hās′tē) ***adj.*** **1** done or made with haste; hurried [a *hasty* lunch]. **2** done or made too quickly, without enough thought; rash [a *hasty* decision]. —**hast′i·er, hast′i·est** —**hast′i·ly** ***adv.*** —**hast′i·ness** ***n.***

**hat** (hat) ***n.*** a covering for the head, usually with a brim and a crown. —☆**pass the hat,** to take up a collection, as for charity. —**take one's hat off to,** to congratulate. —☆**talk through one's hat,** to talk nonsense: *used only in everyday talk.* —☆**under one's hat,** secret: *used only in everyday talk.*



**hatch**[1] (hach) ***v.*** **1** to bring forth young birds, fish, turtles, etc. from eggs [Birds *hatch* their eggs by keeping them warm.] **2** to come forth from the egg [Our chicks *hatched* this morning.] **3** to think up or plan, often in a secret or bad way [They *hatched* a plot to rob the bank.]

**hawk**
up to 60 cm (2 ft.) long

**hazel and hazelnuts**

**hatchet**

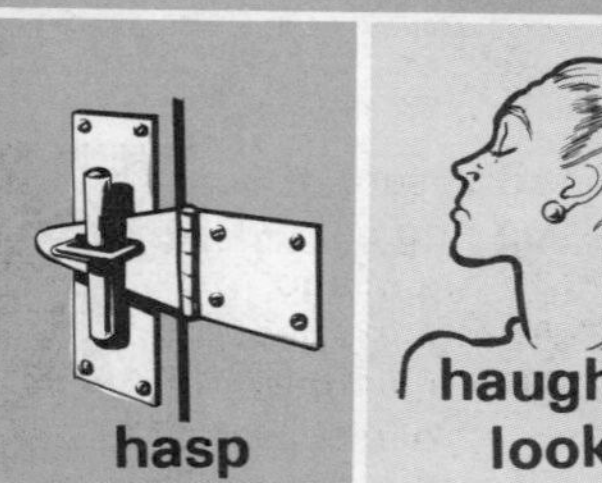

**hasp**

**haughty look**

**hassock**

**hatch**[2] (hach) ***n.*** **1** *a shorter form of* **hatchway. 2** a covering for a hatchway.

☆**hatch·back** (hach′bak) ***n.*** an automobile body with a rear panel that swings up, making a wide opening into a storage area.

**hatch·er·y** (hach′ər ē) ***n.*** a place for hatching eggs, as of fish or hens. —*pl.* **hatch′er·ies**

**hatch·et** (hach′it) ***n.*** a small ax with a short handle. *See the picture.* —**bury the hatchet,** to stop fighting; make peace.

**hatch·way** (hach′wā) ***n.*** **1** an opening in the deck of a ship, as one through which cargo is moved into and out of the hold. **2** an opening like this in the floor or roof of a building.

**hate** (hāt) ***v.*** to have very bad feeling against; dislike very much [to *hate* an enemy; to *hate* to clean house]. —**hat′ed, hat′ing** ◆***n.*** a very strong dislike; hatred [a look full of *hate*]. —**hat′er** ***n.***

**hate·ful** (hāt′fəl) ***adj.*** **1** deserving to be hated [a *hateful* crime; a *hateful* bully]. **2** feeling or showing hate: *now seldom used.* —**hate′ful·ly** ***adv.*** —**hate′ful·ness** ***n.***

**hath** (hath) *the older form of* **has,** *used with* thou, *as in the Bible.*

**ha·tred** (hā′trid) ***n.*** a very strong dislike; hate.

**hat·ter** (hat′ər) ***n.*** a person who makes or sells men's hats.

**Hat·ter·as** (hat′ər əs), **Cape** a cape on an island off the coast of North Carolina.

**haugh·ty** (hôt′ē) ***adj.*** having or showing too much pride in oneself and scorn for others. *See* SYNONYMS *at* **proud.** —**haugh′ti·er, haugh′ti·est** —**haugh′ti·ly** ***adv.*** —**haugh′ti·ness** ***n.***

> **Haughty** comes from the Latin word *altus,* meaning "high." A very proud person carries the head high. *See the picture.* We sometimes say someone haughty is "high and mighty."

**haul** (hôl) ***v.*** **1** to move by pulling; drag or tug [We *hauled* the boat up on the beach.] *See* SYNONYMS *at* **drag. 2** to carry by wagon, truck, etc. [He *hauls* steel for a large company.] **3** to change the course of a ship by setting the sails. ◆***n.*** **1** the act of hauling; pull [Give a *haul* on the rope.] **2** the amount caught, taken, won, etc. at one time; catch [a large *haul* of fish]. **3** the distance that something is hauled [It's a long *haul* to town.] **4** the load hauled. —**haul off,** ☆to draw the arm back before hitting: *used only in everyday talk.*

**haunch** (hônch) ***n.*** **1** the hip, buttock, and upper part of the thigh. **2** an animal's loin and leg together [a *haunch* of mutton].

**haunt** (hônt) ***v.*** **1** to spend much time at; visit often [We like to *haunt* bookstores. A *haunted* house is one that is supposed to be visited by a ghost.] **2** to keep coming back to the mind [Memories *haunt* her.] ◆***n.*** a place often visited [They made the library their *haunt.*]

**hau·teur** (hō tʉr′) ***n.*** a haughty manner or look.

**Ha·van·a** (hə van′ə) the capital of Cuba.

**have** (hav) ***v.*** **1** to be the owner of; possess [She *has* a car. He *has* red hair.] **2** to contain within itself [A week *has* seven days.] **3** to hold in the mind [to *have* an idea]. **4** to go through; undergo or experience [to *have* the measles; to *have* a good time]. **5** to get or take [*Have* an apple.] **6** to be the parent of [Mrs. Moore *has* twins.] **7** to cause to do, go, be, etc. [*Have* the plumber fix the leak. He *had* his shoes shined.] **8** to put up with; allow [I won't *have* any more arguing.] **9** to be forced or obliged [I *have* to go now.] **10** to claim or say [Rumor *has* it that he's rich.] **11** to hold an advantage over: *used only in everyday talk* [She *had* me on that point.] —**had, hav'ing** —**have it good,** to be well-off, rich, etc.: *used only in everyday talk.* —**have it out,** to settle a problem once and for all, as by a full discussion. —**have on,** to be wearing.

**Have** is used as a helping verb with past participles [I *have* eaten. I *had* eaten. I shall *have* eaten.] In the present tense **have** has these forms: I, we, you, or they *have;* he, she, or it *has.*

**ha·ven** (hā'vən) ***n.*** **1** a port or harbor. **2** any place of shelter or safety; refuge.

**have-not** (hav'nät') ***n.*** a person or country that is poor or that has few resources.

**have·n't** (hav''nt) have not.

**hav·er·sack** (hav'ər sak) ***n.*** a canvas bag for carrying food, etc., usually worn over one shoulder by soldiers and hikers.

**hav·oc** (hav'ək) ***n.*** great damage or destruction [The hurricane caused much *havoc.*] —**play havoc with,** to destroy or ruin.

**haw**[1] (hô) ***n.*** **1** the reddish berry of the hawthorn. **2** *a shorter name for* **hawthorn.**

**haw**[2] (hô) ***interj.*** a word of command to a horse or ox meaning "turn to the left!"

**haw**[3] (hô) ***v.*** to make sounds like "haw" or "uh" while searching for the right words in speaking: *usually used in the phrase* **hem and haw.**

**Ha·wai·i** (hə wä'ē *or* hə wä'yē) **1** a State of the U.S., consisting of a group of islands (**Hawaiian Islands**) in the North Pacific: abbreviated **HI** **2** the largest island in this group.

**Ha·wai·ian** (hə wä'yən) ***adj.*** of Hawaii, its people, etc. ◆***n.*** **1** a person born or living in Hawaii. **2** the original language of Hawaii.

**hawk**[1] (hôk) ***n.*** a large bird with a strong, hooked beak and claws, and keen sight. It captures and eats smaller birds and animals. *See the picture.* ◆***v.*** to hunt small game with the help of trained hawks.

**hawk**[2] (hôk) ***v.*** to advertise or offer things for sale in the street by shouting. —**hawk'er** ***n.***

**hawk**[3] (hôk) ***v.*** to clear the throat noisily by coughing up phlegm. ◆***n.*** a noisy clearing of the throat.

**hawk-eyed** (hôk'īd') ***adj.*** having keen sight.

**hawse** (hôz) ***n.*** **1** the part at the front of a ship with holes through which the hawsers and cables go. **2** any of these holes: *also* **hawse'hole.**

**haw·ser** (hô'zər) ***n.*** a large rope or small cable used in anchoring or towing a ship.

**haw·thorn** (hô'thôrn) ***n.*** a shrub or small tree with white or pink, sweet-smelling flowers and small, red berries.

**Haw·thorne** (hô'thôrn), **Nathaniel** 1804–1864; a U.S. writer of novels and stories.

**hay** (hā) ***n.*** grass, clover, etc. cut and dried for use as food for animals. ◆***v.*** to cut down grass, clover, etc. and spread it out to dry. —☆**hit the hay,** to go to bed: *a slang phrase.*

**hay·cock** (hā'käk) ***n.*** a small heap of hay drying in a field.

**Hay·dn** (hīd''n), **Franz Jo·seph** (fränts yō'zef) 1732–1809; an Austrian composer of music.

**Hayes** (hāz), **Ruth·er·ford** (ruth'ər fərd) **B.** 1822–1893; the 19th president of the United States, from 1877 to 1881.

**hay fever** an illness like a cold that makes the eyes water and causes sneezing and coughing. It develops in people who are sensitive to the pollen of ragweed and other plants.

**hay·field** (hā'fēld) ***n.*** a field of grass, clover, etc. grown to make hay.

**hay·loft** (hā'lôft) ***n.*** a loft in a barn or stable, used for storing hay.

**hay·mow** (hā'mou) ***n.*** **1** a pile of hay in a barn. **2** *another word for* **hayloft.**

**hay·rick** (hā'rik) ***n.*** *another word for* **haystack.**

☆**hay·ride** (hā'rīd) ***n.*** a pleasure ride taken by a group of people in a wagon partly filled with hay.

**hay·stack** (hā'stak) ***n.*** a large heap of hay piled up outdoors.

☆**hay·wire** (hā'wīr) ***n.*** wire used to tie up bales of hay. ◆***adj.*** mixed up, confused, crazy, etc.: *a slang word.*

**haz·ard** (haz'ərd) ***n.*** **1** danger or something dangerous; risk; peril [the *hazards* of icy streets]. **2** anything on a golf course that makes it harder to play, as a pond or a pit filled with sand. ◆***v.*** to take a chance on; risk [to *hazard* a guess].

SYNONYMS: A **hazard** is something dangerous that one knows about but has to leave to chance because it cannot be controlled [the *hazards* of driving a racing car]. A **peril** is something very dangerous that is very close or soon to happen [When his brakes failed, he was in *peril* of death.]

**haz·ard·ous** (haz'ər dəs) ***adj.*** dangerous; risky.

**haze**[1] (hāz) ***n.*** **1** thin mist, smoke, or dust in the air, that makes it harder to see. *See* SYNONYMS *at* **mist.** **2** the condition of being confused in the mind; daze.

**haze**[2] (hāz) ***v.*** ☆to play tricks on or make do dangerous or silly things [It is forbidden to *haze* freshmen at our school.] —**hazed, haz'ing**

**ha·zel** (hā'z'l) ***n.*** a shrub or small tree related to the birch. ◆***adj.*** light brown [*Hazel* eyes usually have green or gray flecks.]

**haz·el·nut** (hā'z'l nut) ***n.*** the small, round nut of the hazel, used as food. *See the picture.*

**ha·zy** (hā'zē) ***adj.*** **1** covered by or full of haze; somewhat misty or smoky [a *hazy* autumn day]. **2** not certain; vague [Her future plans are *hazy.*] —**ha'zi·er, ha'zi·est** —**ha'zi·ly** ***adv.*** —**ha'zi·ness** ***n.***

☆**H-bomb** (āch'bäm') ***n.*** *a shorter word for* **hydrogen bomb.**

**hdqrs.** *abbreviation for* **headquarters.**

**he** (hē) ***pron.*** **1** the man, boy, or male animal being talked about [Ivan knew *he* was late.] **2** a person; anyone [*He* who hesitates is lost.] ◆***n.*** a man, boy, or male animal [This cat is a *he.*] —*pl.* **they**

| | | | | | | | |
|---|---|---|---|---|---|---|---|
| **a** | fat | **ir** | here | **ou** | out | **zh** | leisure |
| **ā** | ape | **ī** | bite, fire | **u** | up | **ng** | ring |
| **ä** | car, lot | **ō** | go | **ur** | fur | | a *in* ago |
| **e** | ten | **ô** | law, horn | **ch** | chin | | e *in* agent |
| **er** | care | **oi** | oil | **sh** | she | **ə =** | i *in* unity |
| **ē** | even | **oo** | look | **th** | thin | | o *in* collect |
| **i** | hit | **ōō** | tool | ***th*** | then | | u *in* focus |

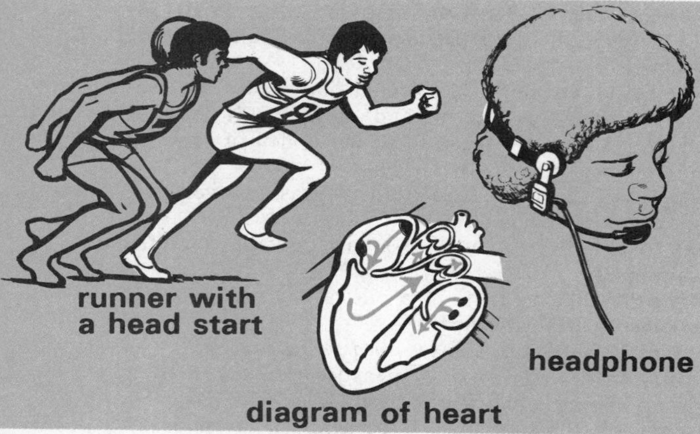


**He** *the symbol for the chemical element* helium.

**head** (hed) ***n.*** **1** the top part or front part of the body, which contains the brain, eyes, ears, nose, and mouth. **2** a person's mind or intelligence [Use your *head.*] **3** a single person or animal of a group: *for animals, the plural is* **head** [dinner at $6.00 a *head;* fifty *head* of cattle]. **4** *often* **heads,** *pl.* the main side of a coin, usually showing a head. **5** the top part of a thing [the *head* of a page; the *head* of a nail]. **6** the front part of a thing [the *head* of a bed; the *head* of a line of people]. **7** the part of something used to hit other things [the *head* of a hammer]. **8** the part of a tape recorder that records or plays back the magnetic signals on the tape. **9** the skin stretched across the end of a drum. **10** a large bud, or round, tight cluster of leaves [a *head* of cabbage]. **11** the place where a river or stream begins; source [The *head* of the Mississippi is in Minnesota.] **12** the person who is in charge; leader, ruler, etc. [the *head* of a committee]. **13** the highest position or rank [She's at the *head* of the class.] **14** the part of a boil where pus is gathered. **15** pressure in a fluid [a *head* of steam]. **16** a turning point or crisis [Their feuding has come to a *head.*] **17** a topic or title [to deal with a subject under several *heads*]. **18** a person who uses marijuana or drugs: *slang in this meaning.* ◆***adj.*** **1** most important; of highest rank; chief [the *head* coach]. **2** at the front or striking against the front [*head* winds]. ◆***v.*** **1** to be in charge of; direct [Who will *head* the new school?] **2** to be at the front or top of; lead [Leo *heads* the class in spelling.] **3** to turn or go in a certain direction [*Head* the horses home. Are you *heading* toward town?] —**by a head,** by just a little [to win *by a head*]. —**come to a head,** to reach a crisis or turning point. —**go to one's head, 1** to make one dizzy or drunk. **2** to make one feel too proud or vain. —**head and shoulders above,** very much better than. —**head off,** to get ahead of and force to stop. —**keep one's head,** to keep control over oneself. —**lose one's head,** to lose control over oneself. —**make head,** to go forward; advance. —**make head or tail of,** to understand. —**one's head off,** very much or too much [to talk *one's head off*]. —**out of one's head,** crazy, mad, or enraged: *used only in everyday talk.* —**over one's head,** too hard for one to understand. —**put heads together,** to talk over plans or a plot together. —**turn one's head,** to make one feel too proud or vain. —**head′less** ***adj.***



**head·ache** (hed′āk) ***n.*** **1** a pain in the head. ☆**2** a cause of worry or trouble: *used only in everyday talk* [This old car has really been a *headache.*]

**head·dress** (hed′dres) ***n.*** a covering or decoration for the head.

**head·er** (hed′ər) ***n.*** a fall or dive with the head first: *used only in everyday talk.*

**head·first** (hed′furst′) ***adv.*** with the head first; headlong [He dived *headfirst* into the water.] *Also* **head·fore·most** (hed′fôr′mōst).

**head·gear** (hed′gir) ***n.*** a hat, cap, helmet, or other covering for the head.

**head·ing** (hed′iŋ) ***n.*** **1** something at the head, top, or front. **2** a title at the top of a paragraph, chapter, etc. **3** a topic or subject.

**head·land** (hed′lənd) ***n.*** a piece or point of land reaching out into the water; cape.

☆**head·light** (hed′līt) ***n.*** any of the lights at the front of an automobile, train, etc., for throwing a bright light ahead at night.

**head·line** (hed′līn) ***n.*** ☆a line or lines in large print at the top of a newspaper article, telling about it in a few words. ◆☆***v.*** **1** to put a headline on an article. **2** to list as the main attraction in a show. —**head′lined, head′lin·ing**

**head·lock** (hed′läk) ***n.*** a hold in wrestling in which one wrestler's head is held tightly between the arm and body of the other.

**head·long** (hed′lôŋ) ***adv., adj.*** **1** with the head first [to fall *headlong;* a *headlong* dive]. **2** with wild speed or force; recklessly or reckless [to rush *headlong* into a fight].

**head·mas·ter** (hed′mas′tər) ***n.*** a man principal, especially of a private school.

**head·mis·tress** (hed′mis′tris) ***n.*** a woman principal, especially of a private school.

☆**head-on** (hed′än) ***adj., adv.*** with the head or front first [a *head-on* crash; to hit *head-on*].

**head·phone** (hed′fōn) ***n.*** a telephone or radio receiver held to the ear by a band over the head. *See the picture.*

**head·piece** (hed′pēs) ***n.*** a helmet, cap, or other covering for the head.

**head·quar·ters** (hed′kwôr′tərz) ***n.pl.*** **1** the main office or center of work of those in command of an army, police force, etc. **2** any main office. *Often used with a singular verb.*

**head·rest** (hed′rest) ***n.*** a support for the head, as on a dentist's chair.

**head·room** (hed′ro͞om) ***n.*** space overhead, as in a doorway or tunnel.

**head·stand** (hed′stand) ***n.*** the act of holding one's body upright while it is resting on the head and both hands.

**head start** an early start ahead of others, as in running a race. *See the picture.*

**head·stone** (hed′stōn) ***n.*** a stone marker placed at the head of a grave.

**head·strong** (hed′strôŋ) ***adj.*** doing just as one pleases, without listening to others; hard to control; stubborn.

**head·wa·ters** (hed′wôt′ərz) ***n.pl.*** the small streams that come together to form a river.

**head·way** (hed′wā) ***n.*** **1** motion ahead or forward [The boat made slow *headway* against the current.] **2** advance or progress [The club has made *headway* in raising money.] **3** *another word for* **headroom.**

**head·y** (hed′ē) ***adj.*** **1** reckless or headstrong. **2** making one dizzy or drunk [a *heady* wine]. —**head′i·er, head′i·est**

**heal** (hēl) ***v.*** to get or bring back to good health or a sound condition; cure or mend [The wound *healed* slowly. Time *heals* grief.] —**heal′er** ***n.***

**health** (helth) ***n.*** **1** the condition of being well in body and mind; freedom from sickness. **2** condition of body or mind [good *health;* bad *health*]. **3** a wish for one's health and happiness, as in drinking a toast.

**health·ful** (helth′fəl) ***adj.*** good for one's health; wholesome [*healthful* food].

**health·y** (hel′thē) ***adj.*** **1** having good health; well [a *healthy* child]. *See* SYNONYMS *at* **well. 2** showing good health [a *healthy* appetite]. **3** good for one's health; healthful [a *healthy* climate]. —**health′i·er, health′i·est —health′i·ness** ***n.***

**heap** (hēp) ***n.*** **1** a group of things lying together in a pile [The leaves were raked into *heaps.*] **2** a large amount: *used only in everyday talk* [a *heap* of money]. ◆***v.*** **1** to pile up in a heap [toys *heaped* in the corner]. **2** to give in large amounts [She *heaped* gifts upon us.] **3** to fill very full; load up [a plate *heaped* with food].

**hear** (hir) ***v.*** **1** to receive sound through the ears [I *hear* music. Pat doesn't *hear* well.] **2** to listen to; pay attention [*Hear* what I tell you.] **3** to hold a hearing, as of a law case. **4** to give what is asked for; grant [Lord, *hear* our prayer.] **5** to learn about; be told [I *hear* prices are going up.] —**heard** (hurd), **hear′ing** —**hear from,** to get a letter, telephone call, etc. from. —**not hear of,** not allow or permit.

**hear·ing** (hir′ing) ***n.*** **1** the act of receiving sound through the ears. **2** the power to hear; sense by which sound is received [His *hearing* is poor.] **3** a chance to be heard [The city council granted them a *hearing.*] **4** the distance that a sound can be heard [Are you within *hearing* of my voice?]

**hearing aid** a small electronic device that makes sounds louder, worn by a person with poor hearing.

**heark·en** (här′kən) ***v.*** to listen carefully; pay attention: *no longer much used.*

**hear·say** (hir′sā) ***n.*** something one has heard but does not know to be true; gossip or rumor.

**hearse** (hurs) ***n.*** a car or carriage for carrying the dead body in a funeral.

**heart** (härt) ***n.*** **1** the hollow muscle that gets blood from the veins and sends it through the arteries by squeezing together and expanding. *See the picture.* **2** the part at the center [*hearts* of celery; the *heart* of the jungle]. **3** the main or most important part [Get to the *heart* of the matter.] **4** the human heart thought of as the part that feels love, kindness, pity, sadness, etc. [a tender *heart;* a heavy *heart*]. **5** courage or spirit [Don't lose *heart!*] **6** a person who is liked or admired [She's a brave *heart.*] **7** a figure or design shaped a little like the heart: ♡ **8** a playing card of a suit marked with this figure in red. —**after one's own heart,** that pleases one perfectly. —**at heart,** in one's truest feelings. —**break one's heart,** to cause one to feel great sorrow or disappointment. —**by heart, 1** by memorizing. **2** from memory. —☆**change of heart,** a change of mind or feeling. —**set one's heart on,** to want very much. —**take heart,** to get courage or confidence; cheer up. —**take to heart,** to be very serious or troubled about. —**with all one's heart, 1** very sincerely. **2** very willingly; gladly.

**heart·ache** (härt′āk) ***n.*** sorrow or grief.

**heart·break·ing** (härt′brāk′ing) ***adj.*** that causes very great unhappiness or sadness [a *heartbreaking* story].

**heart·bro·ken** (härt′brō′k'n) ***adj.*** very unhappy; filled with grief or sorrow [The children were *heartbroken* when their dog died.]

**heart·burn** (härt′burn) ***n.*** a burning feeling in the chest, caused by too much acid in the stomach.

**heart·ed** (här′tid) ***adj.*** having a certain kind of heart or spirit: *used to form compound words* [good*hearted;* stout*hearted*].

**heart·en** (härt′'n) ***v.*** to cheer up; encourage.

**heart·felt** (härt′felt) ***adj.*** with deep feeling; sincere [You have my *heartfelt* thanks.]

**hearth** (härth) ***n.*** **1** the stone or brick floor of a fireplace. **2** the home, or life in the home. **3** the lowest part of a blast furnace, where the melted metal and slag settle.

**hearth·stone** (härth′stōn) ***n.*** **1** the stone forming a hearth. **2** the home, or life in the home.

**heart·i·ly** (härt′'l ē) ***adv.*** **1** in a friendly way; sincerely [to welcome *heartily*]. **2** with eagerness or zest [to work *heartily;* to eat *heartily*]. **3** completely; very [I'm *heartily* sorry I missed the party.]



**heart·less** (härt′lis) ***adj.*** without pity; unkind or cruel [a *heartless* criminal]. —**heart′less·ly** ***adv.*** —**heart′less·ness** ***n.***

**heart-rend·ing** (härt′ren′ding) ***adj.*** causing much grief; very sad [a *heart-rending* story].

**heart·sick** (härt′sik) ***adj.*** very sad or unhappy.

**heart·strings** (härt′stringz) ***n.pl.*** deep feelings of pity or sympathy [His sad tale tugged at my *heartstrings.*]

> The word **heartstrings** comes from the idea people once had that the heart is held in place by strings made of tendons and nerves.

**heart-to-heart** (härt′tə härt′) ***adj.*** private and frank [a *heart-to-heart* talk].

**heart·y** (härt′ē) ***adj.*** **1** warm and friendly [a *hearty* welcome]. **2** deeply felt; strong [a *hearty* dislike]. **3** healthy, lively, strong, etc. [a *hearty* laugh; a *hearty* appetite]. **4** large and satisfying [a *hearty* meal]. —**heart′i·er, heart′i·est** ◆***n.*** a comrade; especially, a fellow sailor: *now seldom used.* —*pl.* **heart′ies** —**heart′i·ness** ***n.***

**heat** (hēt) ***n.*** **1** the condition of being hot; great warmth [the *heat* of the sun]. In physics, heat is thought of as a form of energy caused by a quickened movement of molecules. **2** hot weather or climate [the *heat* of tropical countries]. **3** the warming of a

| | | | | | | | |
|---|---|---|---|---|---|---|---|
| **a** | fat | **ir** | here | **ou** | out | **zh** | leisure |
| **ā** | ape | **ī** | bite, fire | **u** | up | **ng** | ring |
| **ä** | car, lot | **ō** | go | **ur** | fur | | a *in* ago |
| **e** | ten | **ô** | law, horn | **ch** | chin | | e *in* agent |
| **er** | care | **oi** | oil | **sh** | she | ə = | i *in* unity |
| **ē** | even | **oo** | look | **th** | thin | | o *in* collect |
| **i** | hit | **ōō** | tool | ***th*** | then | | u *in* focus |

room, house, etc. [We get our *heat* from a gas furnace.] **4** strong feeling or emotion; excitement [to argue with *heat;* in the *heat* of battle]. **5** a single round, trial, etc.; especially, any of the early trials of a race. The winners of such heats race in the final round. ✦***v.*** **1** to make or become warm or hot [to *heat* water]. **2** to make excited or angry [The argument soon became *heated.*]

**heat·er** (hēt′ər) ***n.*** a stove, furnace, or the like for heating a room, car, water, etc.

**heath** (hēth) ***n.*** **1** an open stretch of land covered with heather, low shrubs, etc., mainly in the British Isles. **2** heather or a plant like it.

**hea·then** (hē′*th*ən) ***n.*** **1** a person who does not believe in the God of the Bible; one who is not a Jew, Christian, or Muslim. **2** a person thought of as uncivilized or as worshiping false gods. —*pl.* **hea′thens** or **hea′then** ✦***adj.*** of or having to do with heathens; pagan. —**hea′then·ish** ***adj.***

**heath·er** (he*th*′ər) ***n.*** a low plant with tiny, purple flowers, found mainly in the British Isles. *See the picture.*

☆**heat wave** a period of very hot weather.

**heave** (hēv) ***v.*** **1** to lift, or to lift and throw, with much effort [We *heaved* the sofa onto the truck.] **2** to make a sound, as if with effort or pain [to *heave* a sigh or groan]. **3** to rise and fall in a regular rhythm [His chest *heaved* with sobs.] **4** to breathe hard; pant. **5**
340 to vomit. **6** to lift or pull with a rope or cable [*Heave* in the anchor!] **7** to move or come [We saw a ship *heave* into view.] —**heaved** or **hove** (mainly in sailors' talk), **heav′ing** ✦***n.*** the act or strain of heaving. —**heave ho!** pull hard! —**heave to,** to stop going forward, as a ship.

**heav·en** (hev′′n) ***n.*** **1** *usually* **heavens,** *pl.* the space in which the sun, moon, and stars move; the sky. **2** the place where God, the angels, and saints are thought to be. **3 Heaven,** God [*Heaven* help me!] **4** any place or condition of great happiness [It's *heaven* to be home again!]

**heav·en·ly** (hev′′n lē) ***adj.*** **1** of or in the heavens or sky [The sun is a *heavenly* body.] **2** of or in heaven [God is called our *heavenly* Father.] **3** very delightful or pleasing [*heavenly* music].

**heav·en·ward** (hev′′n wərd) ***adj., adv.*** to or toward heaven [a *heavenward* glance].

**heav·y** (hev′ē) ***adj.*** **1** hard to lift or move because of its weight; weighing very much [a *heavy* load]. **2** weighing more than is usual for its kind [Lead is a *heavy* metal.] **3** larger, deeper, greater, etc. than usual [a *heavy* vote; a *heavy* sleep; a *heavy* blow]. **4** full of sorrow; sad [a *heavy* heart]. **5** hard to do, bear, etc.; difficult [*heavy* work; *heavy* sorrow]. **6** dark and gloomy [*heavy* skies]. **7** hard to digest [a *heavy* meal]. **8** almost closed, as if weighed down [*heavy* eyelids]. **9** clumsy or awkward [a *heavy* way of walking]. ☆**10** very good, important, intelligent, etc.: *slang in this meaning.* —**heav′i·er, heav′i·est** ✦***adv.*** in a heavy manner [*heavy*-laden]. ✦***n.*** an actor who plays serious roles, especially villains. —*pl.* **heav′ies** —**hang heavy,** to pass in a slow, boring way [Time *hangs heavy* on her hands.] —**heav′i·ly** ***adv.*** —**heav′i·ness** ***n.***

**heav·y-hand·ed** (hev′ē han′did) ***adj.*** **1** without a light touch; clumsy or awkward [a *heavy-handed* joke]. **2** harsh or cruel [a *heavy-handed* ruler].

**heav·y·set** (hev′ē set′) ***adj.*** having a heavy, sturdy build [a *heavyset* football player].

**heav·y·weight** (hev′ē wāt′) ***n.*** **1** a boxer or wrestler who weighs more than 175 pounds. One weighing between 161 and 175 is called a **light heavyweight.** **2** a person or animal that weighs much more than average.

**Heb.** *abbreviation for* **Hebrew** *or* **Hebrews.**

**He·brew** (hē′brōō) ***n.*** **1** a member of the ancient people of the Bible who settled in Canaan; Israelite. The Hebrews were the ancestors of the Jews. **2** the ancient language of the Israelites or the modern form of this language, used in Israel today. It is written in a different alphabet from English. *See the picture.* ✦***adj.*** of the Hebrews or of the Hebrew language.

**He·brews** (hē′brōōz) a book of the New Testament.

**Heb·ri·des** (heb′rə dēz) a group of Scottish islands off the western coast of Scotland.

**heck·le** (hek′′l) ***v.*** to annoy by asking many questions, shouting insults, etc. [The speaker was *heckled* by some people in the audience.] —**heck′led, heck′ling** —**heck′ler** ***n.***

**hec·tare** (hek′ter) ***n.*** a unit of surface measure equal to 100 ares, 10,000 square meters, or 2.471 acres.

**hec·tic** (hek′tik) ***adj.*** **1** having a fever; flushed, as in an illness. **2** full of rush and confusion [a *hectic* day of running errands].

**Hec·tor** (hek′tər) a Trojan hero in Homer's *Iliad,* who was killed by Achilles.

**hec·tor** (hek′tər) ***v.*** to bully or tease.

**he'd** (hēd) **1** he had. **2** he would.

**hedge** (hej) ***n.*** **1** a row of shrubs or bushes planted close together to form a kind of fence. **2** a protection of some kind [Our savings account is a *hedge* against sudden expenses.] ✦***v.*** **1** to plant a hedge around [The yard was *hedged* with roses.] **2** to shut in on all sides; hem in [Switzerland is *hedged* in by mountains.] **3** to get out of giving a straight answer [Julia *hedged* when I asked whether she liked the concert.] —**hedged, hedg′ing**

**hedge·hog** (hej′hôg) ***n.*** **1** a small animal of Europe, with sharp spines on its back, which bristle when the animal curls up to protect itself. *See the picture.* ☆**2** *another name for* **porcupine.**

**hedge·row** (hej′rō) ***n.*** a row of shrubs, bushes, etc. forming a hedge.

**heed** (hēd) ***v.*** to pay careful attention to [*Heed* my advice.] ✦***n.*** careful attention [He paid no *heed* to our warning.] —**heed′ful** ***adj.*** —**heed′ful·ly** ***adv.***

**heed·less** (hēd′lis) ***adj.*** not paying any attention; careless [She went out, *heedless* of the storm.] —**heed′less·ly** ***adv.*** —**heed′less·ness** ***n.***

**hee·haw** (hē′hô) ***n.*** **1** the sound that a donkey makes. **2** a loud, often silly laugh.

**heel**[1] (hēl) ***n.*** **1** the back part of the foot, below the ankle and behind the arch. **2** that part of a stocking or sock which covers the heel. **3** the part of a shoe that is built up to support the heel. **4** anything like a heel in shape, position, etc., as the end of a loaf of bread. ☆**5** a person who acts in a mean or shameful way: *used only in everyday talk.* ✦***v.*** **1** to put heels on [to *heel* shoes]. **2** to follow closely [Did you teach your dog to *heel?*] —**down at the heels,** shabby or run-down. —**take to one's heels,** to run away.

**heel²** (hēl) ***v.*** to lean to one side; list [The ship *heeled* to port under the strong wind.]

**heft** (heft) ***v.*** **1** to lift or heave. **2** to try to guess the weight of by lifting. ◆***n.*** heaviness; weight. *This word is used only in everyday talk.*

**heft·y** (hef′tē) ***adj.*** **1** heavy; weighty. **2** large and strong [a *hefty* wrestler]. **3** big or fairly big [to eat a *hefty* meal]. *This word is used only in everyday talk.* —**heft′i·er, heft′i·est**

**Hei·del·berg** (hīd′'l burg) a city in southwestern West Germany, home of an old university.

**heif·er** (hef′ər) ***n.*** a young cow that has not given birth to a calf.

**height** (hīt) ***n.*** **1** the distance from the bottom to the top; tallness [the *height* of a building; a child four feet in *height*]. **2** the highest point or degree [to reach the *height* of fame]. **3** the distance above the surface of the earth [The plane flew at a *height* of 20,000 feet.] **4** a high place or point [Alpine *heights*].

SYNONYMS: **Height** is used of the distance of anything from bottom to top [a tree 50 feet in *height*]. **Stature** is used for the height of a human being standing up straight [a woman of average *stature*].

**height·en** (hīt′'n) ***v.*** to make or become higher, greater, or stronger; increase [The music helped to *heighten* the excitement of the movie.]

**hei·nous** (hā′nəs) ***adj.*** very evil or wicked [a *heinous* crime]. —**hei′nous·ly** ***adv.***

**heir** (er) ***n.*** a person who gets or has the right by law to get property or a title when the person possessing it dies.

**heir apparent** the person who is sure to be the heir to some property or title by outliving the person holding it [The king's *heir apparent* is his oldest son.]

**heir·ess** (er′is) ***n.*** a woman or girl who has inherited or will inherit much wealth.

**heir·loom** (er′lo͞om) ***n.*** a valuable or valued article handed down in a family over the years.

**heir presumptive** a person who will become the heir to some property or title only if someone with a stronger legal claim is not born in the meantime.

**held** (held) *past tense and past participle of* **hold.**

**Hel·e·na** (hel′i nə) the capital of Montana, in the west-central part.

**Hel·en of Troy** (hel′ən) a beautiful queen of Sparta in Greek legends. The Trojan War began because she was taken away by a prince of Troy.

**hel·i·cop·ter** (hel′ə käp′tər) ***n.*** a kind of aircraft that has a large propeller fixed above in a horizontal way, but no wings. It can be flown backward or forward or straight up and down. *See the picture.*

**he·li·o·trope** (hē′lē ə trōp′) ***n.*** **1** a plant having small, white or purple flowers. **2** reddish purple.

**Heliotrope** comes from two Greek words meaning "to turn toward the sun," the way the blossom of the sunflower does. *Heliotrope* used to be a name for the sunflower.

**hel·i·port** (hel′ə pôrt) ***n.*** a place, often on the roof of a building, where helicopters take off and land.

**he·li·um** (hē′lē əm) ***n.*** a chemical element that is a very light gas. It is used to inflate balloons and dirigibles because it will not burn or explode.

helmets

hedgehogs
25 cm (10 in.) long

heather

Hebrew writing

תפלה ערבית לשבת

helicoptor

**hell** (hel) ***n.*** **1** the place where Christians believe that devils live and wicked people go to be punished after they die. **2** the place according to various religions 
where the spirits of the dead are: *see* **Hades** *and* **Sheol.** **3** any place or condition of evil, pain, or misery ["War is *hell.*"]

**he'll** (hēl *or* hil) **1** he will. **2** he shall.

**hel·le·bore** (hel′ə bôr) ***n.*** **1** a plant that blooms in winter with flowers like buttercups. Its dried root has been used in medicine. **2** a plant related to the lily, having poisonous roots.

**Hel·len·ic** (hə len′ik) ***adj.*** having to do with the Greeks, especially the ancient Greeks.

**hel·lion** (hel′yən) ***n.*** a wild person who causes much mischief: *used only in everyday talk.*

**hell·ish** (hel′ish) ***adj.*** as if from hell; horrible; devilish [a *hellish* plot to commit murder].

**hel·lo** (he lō′ *or* hə lō′) ***interj.*** **1** a word used in greeting someone or in answering the telephone. **2** a word called out to get attention or to show surprise [*Hello!* what's this?] ◆***n.*** a saying or calling of "hello." —*pl.* **hel·los′** ◆***v.*** to say or call "hello." —**hel·loed′, hel·lo′ing**

**helm** (helm) ***n.*** **1** the wheel or tiller by which a ship is steered. **2** the position of a leader or ruler [A new president has taken the *helm.*]

**hel·met** (hel′mət) ***n.*** a hard covering to protect the head, worn by soldiers, certain athletes, motorcycle riders, etc. *See the picture.*

| | | | | | | | |
|---|---|---|---|---|---|---|---|
| **a** fat | **ir** here | **ou** out | **zh** leisure |
| **ā** ape | **ī** bite, fire | **u** up | **ng** ring |
| **ä** car, lot | **ō** go | **ur** fur | a *in* ago |
| **e** ten | **ô** law, horn | **ch** chin | e *in* agent |
| **er** care | **oi** oil | **sh** she | **ə** = i *in* unity |
| **ē** even | **oo** look | **th** thin | o *in* collect |
| **i** hit | **o͞o** tool | ***th*** then | u *in* focus |

**helms·man** (helmz′mən) ***n.*** the person who steers a ship. *—pl.* **helms′men**

**Hel·ot** (hel′ət *or* hē′lət) ***n.*** **1** a serf in ancient Sparta. **2 helot,** any serf or slave.

**help** (help) ***v.*** **1** to give or do something that is needed or useful; make things easier for; aid; assist [We *helped* our poor relatives. *Help* me lift this.] **2** to make better; give relief to; remedy [This medicine will *help* your cold.] **3** to stop or keep from; avoid or prevent [I can't *help* feeling sad.] ◆***n.*** **1** the act of helping or a thing that helps; aid; assistance [Your advice was a great *help*.] ☆**2** a person or persons hired to help, as in housework or farming. **3** a cure or relief [There is no *help* for his problem.] —**cannot help but,** cannot stop oneself from; is obliged to [One *cannot help but* like her.] —**help oneself to, 1** to serve oneself with [*Help yourself to* some fruit.] **2** to take without asking; steal. —**help out,** to help in getting or doing something. —**help′er** ***n.***

SYNONYMS: To **help** someone is to supply that person with what is needed or wanted [She *helped* me weed the garden.] **Aid** and **assist** often suggest that the person helping is under the direction of the person being helped [He *assisted,* or *aided,* her in her scientific experiments.]

**help·ful** (help′fəl) ***adj.*** giving help; useful [*helpful* hints]. —**help′ful·ly** ***adv.*** —**help′ful·ness** ***n.***

**help·ing** (hel′piŋ) ***n.*** the amount of a food served to one person at a time.



**helping word** or **helping verb** *another name for* **auxiliary verb.**

**help·less** (help′lis) ***adj.*** **1** not able to help oneself or take care of one's own needs [a *helpless* invalid]. **2** without help or protection [They were left *helpless* on the desert.] **3** not able to give help; powerless [I am *helpless* to advise you.] —**help′less·ly** ***adv.*** —**help′less·ness** ***n.***

**help·mate** (help′māt) ***n.*** a wife or a husband.

**Hel·sin·ki** (hel′siŋ kē) the capital of Finland.

**hel·ter-skel·ter** (hel′tər skel′tər) ***adv., adj.*** in a wild, disorderly way [clothes thrown *helter-skelter* around the room].

**helve** (helv) ***n.*** the handle of an ax, hatchet, etc.

**hem**[1] (hem) ***n.*** the border on a skirt, curtain, towel, etc., made by folding the edge over and sewing it down. ◆***v.*** **1** to fold back the edge of and sew down [to *hem* a skirt]. **2** to close in on all sides; surround [troops *hemmed* in by the enemy]. —**hemmed, hem′ming**

**hem**[2] (hem) ***interj., n.*** a sound made as if in clearing one's throat. ◆***v.*** **1** to make this sound, as in trying to get attention or in showing doubt. **2** to make this sound while searching for the right words: *usually used in the phrase* **hem and haw.** —**hemmed, hem′ming**

☆**he-man** (hē′man′) ***n.*** a strong, brave man: *used only in everyday talk.*

**hemi-** *a prefix meaning* half [A *hemisphere* is half of a sphere.]

**Hem·ing·way** (hem′iŋ wā′), **Ernest** 1899–1961; U.S. writer of novels and short stories.

**hem·i·sphere** (hem′ə sfir) ***n.*** **1** half of a sphere or globe [The dome of the church was in the shape of a *hemisphere*.] **2** any of the halves into which the earth's surface is divided in geography: *see* **Eastern Hemisphere, Western Hemisphere, Northern Hemisphere, Southern Hemisphere.**

**hem·lock** (hem′läk) ***n.*** **1** an evergreen tree of the pine family, with drooping branches and short, flat needles. **2** a poisonous weed of the parsley family, or a poison made from it.

**he·mo·glo·bin** (hē′mə glō′bin *or* hem′ə glō′bin) ***n.*** the red coloring matter in red blood corpuscles.

**he·mo·phil·i·a** (hē′mə fil′ē ə) ***n.*** a condition that is inherited, in which the blood does not clot in the normal way, so that even a small cut can cause heavy bleeding.

**hem·or·rhage** (hem′ər ij) ***n.*** heavy bleeding. ◆***v.*** to bleed heavily. —**hem′or·rhaged, hem′or·rhag·ing**

**Hemorrhage** comes from two Greek words meaning "blood" and "burst." If a blood vessel bursts, there is much bleeding.

**hem·or·rhoids** (hem′ə roidz) ***n.pl.*** swollen veins in the anus.

**hemp** (hemp) ***n.*** **1** a tall plant having tough fibers in its stalk. **2** this fiber, used for making rope, heavy cloth, etc. —**hemp′en** ***adj.***

**hem·stitch** (hem′stich) ***n.*** a fancy stitch made by pulling out several threads in a piece of cloth and tying the cross threads together in small groups. This stitch is often used to decorate a hem. *See the picture.* ◆***v.*** to put hemstitches in.

**hen** (hen) ***n.*** a female chicken, or the female of certain other birds, as the pheasant.

**hence** (hens) ***adv.*** **1** for this reason; as a result; therefore [He eats too much and is, *hence,* overweight.] **2** from here; away [We shall be ten miles *hence* by dusk.] **3** from this time; after now [A year *hence* things may be different.]

**hence·forth** (hens′fôrth′) ***adv.*** from this time on [We shall *henceforth* be friends.] *Also* **hence·for·ward** (hens′fôr′wərd).

**hench·man** (hench′mən) ***n.*** ☆a person who blindly follows and supports a leader [a gangster and his *henchmen*]. *—pl.* **hench′men**

**hen·na** (hen′ə) ***n.*** **1** a plant from whose leaves a reddish-brown dye is made. **2** this dye, often used to color hair or make it shiny. **3** reddish brown.

**hen·peck** (hen′pek) ***v.*** to rule over one's husband in a nagging way. —**hen′pecked** ***adj.***

**Hen·ry VIII** (hen′rē) 1491–1547; the king of England from 1509 to 1547. He founded the Church of England.

**Henry, O.** 1862–1910; U.S. short-story writer whose real name was William Sydney Porter.

**Henry, Patrick** 1736–1799; one of the leaders of the American Revolution. He was a skillful speaker.

**he·pat·i·ca** (hi pat′i kə) ***n.*** a plant with broad leaves and small white, pink, or purple flowers that bloom early in the spring.

The **hepatica** gets its name from the Latin word for liver. Its large leaves, which have three lobes, are shaped somewhat like the human liver.

**her** (hur) ***pron.*** **1** *the form of* **she** *that is used as the object of a verb or preposition* [I saw *her*. Give it to *her*.] **2** of her or done by her. *This possessive form of* **she** *is used before a noun and thought of as an adjective* [*her* dress; *her* work]. *See also* **hers.**

**He·ra** (hir′ə) the Greek goddess of marriage, who was the wife of Zeus. The Romans called her *Juno*.

**her·ald** (her′əld) ***n.*** **1** an official in earlier times who made public announcements, carried messages for kings or lords, etc. **2** a person or thing that comes to show or tell what will follow [Dark clouds are *heralds* of storms.] ◆***v.*** to be a sign of; announce [The crocus *heralds* spring.]

**he·ral·dic** (hə ral′dik) ***adj.*** having to do with heraldry or heralds.

**her·ald·ry** (her′əl drē) ***n.*** **1** the science in which coats of arms are studied or designed, families are traced back, etc. **2** a coat of arms or coats of arms.

**herb** (ʉrb *or* hʉrb) ***n.*** any plant whose stems and leaves wither after the growing season each year; especially, any such plant used as a medicine, seasoning, etc. [Mint and sage are *herbs*.]

**her·ba·ceous** (hər bā′shəs) ***adj.*** of or like an herb or herbs.

**herb·age** (ʉr′bij *or* hʉr′bij) ***n.*** grass or green plants grown in pastures as food for cattle.

**her·bi·cide** (hʉr′bə sīd *or* ʉr′bə sīd) ***n.*** any poison used to kill plants, especially weeds.

**her·biv·o·rous** (hər biv′ər əs) ***adj.*** feeding mainly on grass or other plants [Cows and deer are *herbivorous*.]

**Her·cu·le·an** (hʉr′kyə lē′ən *or* hər kyo͞o′lē ən) ***adj.*** **1** of Hercules. **2** *usually* **herculean,** very strong, large, and brave; also, needing great strength or courage [a *herculean* task].

**Her·cu·les** (hʉr′kyə lēz) a very strong and powerful hero in Greek and Roman myths.

**herd** (hʉrd) ***n.*** **1** a number of cattle or other large animals feeding or living together [a *herd* of cows; a *herd* of elephants]. **2** the common people; a crowd: *a scornful word.* ◆***v.*** **1** to form into a herd, group, or crowd. **2** to take care of a herd of animals.

**herds·man** (hʉrdz′mən) ***n.*** a person who takes care of a herd of animals. —*pl.* **herds′men**

**here** (hir) ***adv.*** **1** at or in this place [Who lives *here?*] **2** to, toward, or into this place [Come *here*.] **3** at this point; now [The speaker paused *here,* and everyone applauded.] **4** on earth; among the living [No one is *here* forever.] ◆***interj.*** a word called out to get attention, answer a roll call, etc. ◆***n.*** **1** this place [Let's get out of *here*.] **2** this life or time [She cares only about the *here* and now.] —**here and there,** in or to various places. —**here goes!** *an exclamation meaning* I am about to do something new, daring, unpleasant, etc. —**neither here nor there,** beside the point; without real purpose [When you say you don't like milk, that's *neither here nor there;* you have to drink it.]

**here·a·bout** (hir′ə bout′) ***adv.*** about or near here. *Also* **here·a·bouts** (hir′ə bouts′).

**here·af·ter** (hir af′tər) ***adv.*** after this; from now on [*Hereafter* I'll be careful.] ◆***n.*** **1** the future. **2** the time or condition after death.

**here·by** (hir′bī) ***adv.*** by means of this message, paper, etc. [You are *hereby* ordered to appear in court.]

**he·red·i·tar·y** (hə red′ə ter′ē) ***adj.*** **1** inherited from an ancestor [her *hereditary* home]. **2** having a title by inheritance [a *hereditary* king]. **3** that can be passed down to offspring by heredity [a *hereditary* trait].

**he·red·i·ty** (hə red′ə tē) ***n.*** **1** the passing on of certain characteristics from parent to offspring by means of genes in the chromosomes [The color of one's hair is determined by *heredity*.] **2** all the characteristics passed on in this way [Their good health is due to their *heredity*.]

**Hereford**

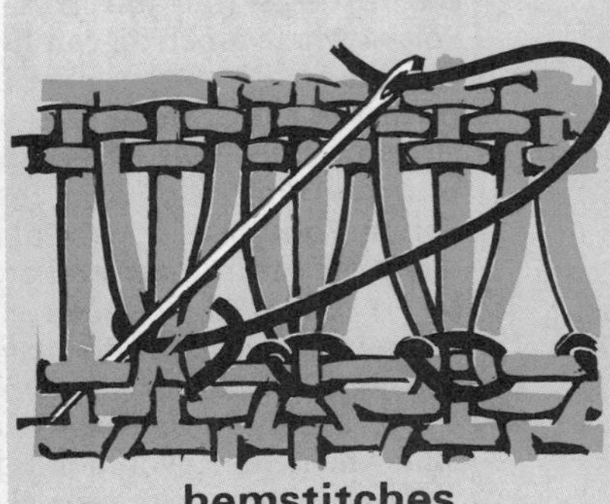

**hemstitches**

**Her·e·ford** (hʉr′fərd *or* her′ə fərd) ***n.*** a breed of beef cattle with a white face and a red body. *See the picture.*

**here·in** (hir in′) ***adv.*** **1** in this place, writing, etc. [Her name is listed *herein*.] **2** in this matter or detail [*Herein* you are right.]

**here·of** (hir uv′) ***adv.*** of this or about this.

**here's** (hirz) here is.

**her·e·sy** (her′ə sē) ***n.*** **1** a religious belief that a particular church considers to be false. **2** any belief that is against a belief held by most people, as in politics, science, etc. **3** the holding of such a belief [guilty of *heresy*]. —*pl.* **her′e·sies**

**her·e·tic** (her′ə tik) ***n.*** a person who believes in something that is regarded by a church or other group as a heresy.

**he·ret·i·cal** (hə ret′i k'l) ***adj.*** **1** of heresy or heretics. **2** that is or contains a heresy [*heretical* writings].

**here·to·fore** (hir′tə fôr′) ***adv.*** until this time; up to now [Bluebirds have not come to this area *heretofore*.]

**here·up·on** (hir ə pän′) ***adv.*** just after this; at this point.

**here·with** (hir *th*with′) ***adv.*** along with this [You will find my check enclosed *herewith*.]

**her·it·age** (her′ət ij) ***n.*** something handed down from one's ancestors or the past, as certain skills or rights, or a way of life [our *heritage* of free speech].

**Her·mes** (hʉr′mēz) a god in Greek myths who was the messenger of the other gods. The Romans called this god *Mercury*.

**her·met·ic** (hər met′ik) ***adj.*** closed so tightly that air cannot get in or out; airtight. *Also* **her·met′i·cal.** —**her·met′i·cal·ly** ***adv.***

**her·mit** (hʉr′mit) ***n.*** a person who lives alone, away from others, often for religious reasons.

| | | | | | | | |
|---|---|---|---|---|---|---|---|
| **a** | fat | **ir** | here | **ou** | out | **zh** | leisure |
| **ā** | ape | **ī** | bite, fire | **u** | up | **ŋ** | ring |
| **ä** | car, lot | **ō** | go | **ʉr** | fur | | a *in* ago |
| **e** | ten | **ô** | law, horn | **ch** | chin | | e *in* agent |
| **er** | care | **oi** | oil | **sh** | she | **ə =** | i *in* unity |
| **ē** | even | **oo** | look | **th** | thin | | o *in* collect |
| **i** | hit | **o͞o** | tool | ***th*** | then | | u *in* focus |

**her·mit·age** (hʉr′mit ij) ***n.*** **1** a hermit's home. **2** a place where a person can live and be away from other people.

**hermit crab** a small crab with a soft body, that lives in empty shells, as of snails. *See the picture.*

**her·ni·a** (hʉr′nē ə) ***n.*** a condition in which an organ of the body, as a part of the intestine, sticks out through a tear in the wall around it; rupture.

**he·ro** (hir′ō) ***n.*** **1** a person, especially a man or boy, who is looked up to for having done something brave or noble [He became a *hero* when he saved his family from a burning house. Washington was the *hero* of the American Revolution.] **2** the most important man in a novel, play, etc., especially if he is good or noble. —*pl.* **he′roes**

**Her·od** (her′əd) the ruler of Judea at the time Jesus was born.

**He·rod·o·tus** (hə räd′ə təs) a Greek historian who lived in the 5th century B.C.

**he·ro·ic** (hi rō′ik) ***adj.*** **1** of or like a hero [a *heroic* life; a *heroic* woman]. **2** showing great bravery or daring [*heroic* deeds]. **3** of or about heroes and their deeds [a *heroic* poem]. —**he·ro′i·cal·ly** ***adv.***

**he·ro·ics** (hi rō′iks) ***n.pl.*** talk or action that seems grand or noble but is really false or foolish.

**her·o·in** (her′ə win) ***n.*** a drug made from morphine that is habit-forming and is illegal in the U.S.

**her·o·ine** (her′ə win) ***n.*** **1** a woman or girl who is looked up to for having done something brave or noble [She became a *heroine* when she saved her brother from drowning. Joan of Arc is one of the great *heroines* of history.] **2** the most important woman in a novel, play, etc., especially if she is good or noble.

**her·o·ism** (her′ə wiz′m) ***n.*** the actions and qualities of a hero or heroine; bravery, nobility, etc. [to receive an award for *heroism*].

**heron**
up to 1.5 m (5 ft.) long, including bill

**hexagon**

**hermit crab**
up to 45 cm (18 in.) long

**hieroglyphics**

**herringbone jacket**

**hickory**

**her·on** (her′ən) ***n.*** a wading bird with long legs, a long neck, and a long, pointed bill. Herons live in marshes or along river banks. *See the picture.*

☆**hero sandwich** a sandwich made of a large roll sliced the long way and filled with cold meats, cheese, lettuce and tomato, etc.

**her·pe·tol·o·gy** (hʉr′pə täl′ə jē) ***n.*** the science that studies reptiles and amphibians.

**Herr** (her) ***n.*** a man; gentleman: *a German word also used as a title meaning* Mr.

**her·ring** (her′iŋ) ***n.*** a small fish of the North Atlantic. The full-grown fish are eaten cooked, dried, salted, or smoked, and the young of some kinds are canned as sardines.

**her·ring·bone** (her′iŋ bōn′) ***n.*** a woven pattern of slanting lines in cloth. ◆***adj.*** having this pattern. *See the picture.*

**hers** (hʉrz) ***pron.*** the one or the ones that belong to her. *This form of* **her** *is used when it is not followed by a noun* [This book is *hers*. *Hers* have not arrived yet.]

**her·self** (hər self′) ***pron.*** **1** her own self. *This form of* **she** *is used when the object is the same as the subject of the verb* [She cut *herself.*] **2** her usual or true self [She's not *herself* today.] *Herself* is also used to give force to the subject [She *herself* told me so.]

**hertz** (hʉrts) ***n.*** a unit for measuring frequency, as of radio waves. —*pl.* **hertz**

**he's** (hēz) **1** he is. **2** he has.

**hes·i·tan·cy** (hez′ə tən sē) ***n.*** the act or state of hesitating, as because of doubt.

**hes·i·tant** (hez′ə tənt) ***adj.*** hesitating; having doubt [I am *hesitant* to lend them money.]

**hes·i·tate** (hez′ə tāt) ***v.*** **1** to stop or hold back, as because of feeling unsure [Never *hesitate* to speak the truth. He *hesitated* at the door before entering.] **2** to feel unwilling [I *hesitate* to ask you for money.] —**hes′i·tat·ed, hes′i·tat·ing**

SYNONYMS: **Hesitate** suggests a stopping for a moment because of being unsure or unwilling [I *hesitated* before entering.] **Waver** is often used of holding back or hesitating after one has decided what to do [She never *wavered* in her plan to become an engineer.]

**hes·i·ta·tion** (hez′ə tā′shən) ***n.*** **1** the act of hesitating, as because of doubt, fear, etc.; unsure or unwilling feeling [I agreed without *hesitation.*] **2** a pausing for a moment [talk filled with *hesitations*].

**Hes·per·us** (hes′pər əs) *another name for* **evening star.**

**Hesse** (hes) a state in West Germany.

**Hes·sian** (hesh′ən) ***adj.*** of Hesse or its people. ◆***n.*** **1** a person born or living in Hesse. **2** any of the Hessian soldiers hired to fight for the British in the Revolutionary War.

**het·er·o·ge·ne·ous** (het′ər ə jē′nē əs) ***adj.*** different in kind; not alike, or made up of parts that are not alike [a *heterogeneous* group of people].

**het·er·o·sex·u·al** (het′ər ə sek′sho͞o wəl) ***adj.*** being attracted sexually to persons of the opposite sex. ◆***n.*** a heterosexual person.

**hew** (hyo͞o) ***v.*** **1** to chop or cut with an ax, knife, etc. [to *hew* wood for a fire]. **2** to make or shape by chopping or cutting [a statue *hewed* from wood]. —**hewed, hewed** or **hewn** (hyo͞on), **hew′ing** —**hew′er** ***n.***

☆**HEW** (hyōō) *abbreviation for* Department of **Health, Education, and Welfare** in the U.S. government.

☆**hex** (heks) ***n.*** something supposed to bring bad luck; jinx. ◆***v.*** to cause bad luck to.

**hex·a·gon** (hek′sə gän) ***n.*** a flat figure with six angles and six sides. *See the picture.*

**hex·ag·o·nal** (hek sag′ə n'l) ***adj.*** having the shape of a hexagon.

**hex·am·e·ter** (hek sam′ə tər) ***n.*** **1** a line of verse having six measures or feet. **2** poetry made up of hexameters.

**hey** (hā) ***interj.*** a word called out to get attention or to show surprise, wonder, etc. or ask a question [*Hey,* watch out! Quite a show tonight, *hey?*]

**hey·day** (hā′dā) ***n.*** the time of greatest success, strength, etc.; prime [Radio was in its *heyday* in the 1930's and 1940's.]

**Hg** *the symbol for the chemical element* mercury.

**hgt.** *abbreviation for* **height.**

☆**hi** (hī) ***interj.*** hello: *an everyday word of greeting.*

**HI** *abbreviation for* **Hawaii.**

**hi·a·tus** (hī āt′əs) ***n.*** a blank space where a part is missing; gap [a *hiatus* in an old manuscript]. —*pl.* **hi·a′tus·es** or **hi·a′tus**

> **Hiatus** comes from a Latin word that means "to gape." When the mouth is opened wide, an empty space, or gap, is formed.

**Hi·a·wa·tha** (hī′ə wô′thə) the Indian hero of Longfellow's poem *The Song of Hiawatha.*

**hi·ba·chi** (hi bä′chē) ***n.*** a small kind of grill that burns charcoal and that was first used by the Japanese. —*pl.* **hi·ba′chis**

**hi·ber·nate** (hī′bər nāt) ***v.*** to spend the winter in a kind of sleep, in which the body temperature is lower than normal [Woodchucks *hibernate* in holes in the ground.] —**hi′ber·nat·ed, hi′ber·nat·ing** —**hi′ber·na′tion *n.***

**hic·cup** (hik′əp) ***n.*** a sudden stopping of the breath with a sharp gulping sound. Hiccups are caused by tightening of the muscles used in breathing and are hard to stop. ◆***v.*** to have hiccups. —**hic′cuped** or **hic′cupped, hic′cup·ing** or **hic′cup·ping** *This word is sometimes spelled* **hic′cough,** *but it is always pronounced* (hik′əp).

**hick·o·ry** (hik′ər ē) ***n.*** **1** a tree related to the walnut, with smooth-shelled nuts that can be eaten. *See the picture.* **2** its hard wood. —*pl.* **hick′o·ries**

**hid** (hid) *past tense and a past participle of* **hide.**

**hid·den** (hid″n) *a past participle of* **hide.** ◆***adj.*** concealed; secret [a *hidden* message].

**hide**[1] (hīd) ***v.*** **1** to put or keep out of sight; conceal [*Hide* the present in the closet.] **2** to keep others from knowing about; keep secret [He tried to *hide* his sorrow.] **3** to keep from being seen; cover up [The billboard *hides* the view.] **4** to keep oneself out of sight [I *hid* behind the large tree.] —**hid, hid′den** or **hid, hid′ing**

> SYNONYMS: **Hide** is used of putting something in a place where it is not easily seen or found [The toy was *hidden* deep in the chest.] **Conceal** more often suggests a hiding of something on purpose [She *concealed* the key under the doormat.]

**hide**[2] (hīd) ***n.*** **1** the skin of an animal, either raw or tanned. **2** a person's skin: *used in a joking or scornful way* [To tan a person's *hide* means to give that person a beating.] —**neither hide nor hair,** nothing whatsoever [I've seen *neither hide nor hair* of them since yesterday.]

**hide-and-seek** (hīd″n sēk′) ***n.*** a children's game in which one player tries to find the other players, who have hidden: *also called* **hide′-and-go-seek′.**

**hide·bound** (hīd′bound) ***adj.*** keeping stubbornly to one's old ideas and opinions; narrow-minded.

**hid·e·ous** (hid′ē əs) ***adj.*** horrible to see, hear, etc.; very ugly or disgusting [a *hideous* sight or a *hideous* sound]. —**hid′e·ous·ly *adv.***

☆**hide-out** (hīd′out′) ***n.*** a hiding place, as for criminals: *used only in everyday talk.*

**hie** (hī) ***v.*** to hurry or hasten: *no longer much used except in a joking way* [You'd better *hie* yourself to school.] —**hied, hie′ing** or **hy′ing**

**hi·er·ar·chy** (hī′ə rär′kē) ***n.*** **1** a system in which a church is ruled by priests of different ranks or grades. **2** all the priests in such a system. **3** any group in which there are higher and lower positions of power. —*pl.* **hi′er·ar′chies** —**hi′er·ar′chi·cal *adj.***

**hi·er·o·glyph·ic** (hī′ər ə glif′ik) ***n.*** **1** a picture or symbol that stands for a word, syllable, or sound. The ancient Egyptians and others used such pictures instead of an alphabet. *See the picture.* **2** *usually* **hieroglyphics,** *pl.* a method of writing that uses such pictures. **3 hieroglyphics,** *pl.* any writing that is hard to read. ◆***adj.*** of or like hieroglyphics.



> **Hieroglyphic** comes from two Greek words meaning "holy carving." Such carving was done by the ancient Egyptian priests. For everyday writing a different system was used. In 1798 a stone was found near the village of Rosetta in Egypt, that had the same message carved in hieroglyphics, popular writing, and Greek. From this Rosetta stone, scholars were able to solve the mystery of hieroglyphics.

☆**hi-fi** (hī′fī′) ***n., adj.*** *a shorter form of* **high fidelity.**

**high** (hī) ***adj.*** **1** reaching a long distance up; tall; lofty [a *high* mountain]. **2** as measured from top to bottom [a fence four feet *high*]. **3** far above the ground [The plane was *high* in the clouds.] **4** upward to or downward from a height [a *high* jump; a *high* dive]. **5** above others, as in rank or position; superior [a *high* official; *high* marks in school]. **6** good; favorable [They have a *high* opinion of you.] **7** main or chief [the *high* priest]. **8** very serious [*high* treason]. **9** greater than usual in amount, cost, power, etc. [*high* prices; *high* voltage]. **10** raised in pitch [a *high* note]. **11** joyful or merry [*high* spirits]. **12** drunk or under the influence of a drug: *slang in this meaning.* ◆***adv.*** in or to a high level, place, degree, etc. [Throw the ball *high.*] ◆***n.*** **1** a high level, place, or degree [Prices

| | | | | | | | |
|---|---|---|---|---|---|---|---|
| **a** | fat | **ir** | here | **ou** | out | **zh** | leisure |
| **ā** | ape | **ī** | bite, fire | **u** | up | **ng** | ring |
| **ä** | car, lot | **ō** | go | **ur** | fur | | a *in* ago |
| **e** | ten | **ô** | law, horn | **ch** | chin | | e *in* agent |
| **er** | care | **oi** | oil | **sh** | she | **ə =** | i *in* unity |
| **ē** | even | **oo** | look | **th** | thin | | o *in* collect |
| **i** | hit | **ōō** | tool | ***th*** | then | | u *in* focus |

reached a new *high.*] ☆**2** an arrangement of gears that gives the greatest speed [I shifted into *high.*] —**high and dry,** alone and helpless, as a boat stranded on the shore. —**high and low,** everywhere [to look *high and low*]. —**on high,** in heaven.

☆**high·ball** (hī′bôl) ***n.*** a drink of whiskey or brandy mixed with soda water or ginger ale.

**high·born** (hī′bôrn) ***adj.*** born into a family of the upper class.

☆**high·brow** (hī′brou′) ***n.*** a person who knows or pretends to know more about literature, music, etc. than most people do: *used only in everyday talk.*

**high·chair** (hī′cher) ***n.*** a baby's chair that is set on long legs and has a tray for food.

**high fidelity** the reproducing of music or speech on a radio, phonograph, etc. so that it sounds very much like the original. This is done by using the full range of sound waves that can be heard by the human ear.

**high-flown** (hī′flōn′) ***adj.*** that sounds grand or important but really has little meaning [a *high-flown* speech].

**high frequency** any radio frequency between 3 and 30 megahertz.

**high-grade** (hī′grād′) ***adj.*** of the very best quality.

**high·hand·ed** (hī′han′did) ***adj.*** acting or done without thought for what others want or think; arrogant.

**high jump** an athletic contest to see who can jump



the highest over a bar that is raised higher and higher. *See the picture.*

**high·land** (hī′lənd) ***n.*** a region of many hills or mountains, that is higher than the land around it. —**the Highlands,** the region of high mountains in northern Scotland. *See the map.* —**high′land·er** or **High′land·er *n.***

**high·light** (hī′līt) ***n.*** **1** a part on which light is brightest; also, the part of a painting on which light is shown as brightest [The artist put *highlights* on the cheeks of the subject.] **2** the most important or interesting part [The trip down the canyon was the *highlight* of our vacation.] ◆***v.*** **1** to give highlights to [*Highlight* the forehead in the picture.] **2** to give an important place to [We will *highlight* these books in our display.]

**high·ly** (hī′lē) ***adv.*** **1** to a high degree; very much [*highly* pleased]. **2** in a kind or friendly way; favorably [They speak *highly* of you.] **3** in a high position [a *highly* placed official]. **4** at a high price [a *highly* paid official].

**high-mind·ed** (hī′mīn′did) ***adj.*** having or showing high ideals or noble feelings [a *high-minded* attitude].

**High·ness** (hī′nis) ***n.*** **1** a title of respect used in speaking to or about a member of a royal family. **2 highness,** height; elevation.

**high-pres·sure** (hī′presh′ər) ***adj.*** **1** that has, or that can resist, a strong pressure [a *high-pressure* steam boiler]. **2** using strong arguments in order to convince [a *high-pressure* salesperson].

☆**high-rise** (hī′rīz′) ***adj.*** describing a tall apartment house or office building that has many stories. ◆***n.*** such a building.

**high school** ☆a school that includes grades 10, 11, and 12, and sometimes grade 9. It prepares students for college or trains them for business or a trade. *See also* **junior high school.**

**high seas** the open parts of the ocean that do not belong to any country.

**high-sound·ing** (hī′soun′diŋ) ***adj.*** sounding important or dignified, often in a false way [a *high-sounding* title].

**high-spir·it·ed** (hī′spir′i tid) ***adj.*** **1** full of energy; lively [a *high-spirited* horse]. **2** full of courage or daring [a *high-spirited* child].

**high-strung** (hī′struŋ′) ***adj.*** very nervous or tense; easily excited.

**high tide** **1** the time when the tide rises highest. **2** the highest level of the tide.

**high time** time after the proper time, but before it is too late [It is *high time* we left.]

**high·way** (hī′wā) ***n.*** a main road.

**high·way·man** (hī′wā mən) ***n.*** a person who robs travelers on a highway. *This term is no longer much used.* —*pl.* **high′way·men**

☆**hi·jack** (hī′jak) ***v.*** to take over by force and direct to a place not originally intended [to *hijack* an airplane; to *hijack* a truck full of goods].

**hike** (hīk) ☆***n.*** **1** a long walk, especially in the country or in woods. **2** a moving upward; rise: *used only in everyday talk* [a *hike* in prices]. ◆***v.*** **1** to take a hike. ☆**2** to pull up or raise: *used only in everyday talk* [to *hike* up one's socks; to *hike* prices]. —**hiked, hik′ing**

**hi·lar·i·ous** (hi ler′ē əs) ***adj.*** noisy and full of fun and laughter; very gleeful.

**hi·lar·i·ty** (hi ler′ə tē) ***n.*** noisy fun; gaiety; glee.

**hill** (hil) ***n.*** **1** a piece of ground that is heaped up higher than the land around it, but not so high as a mountain. **2** any small heap or mound [an ant *hill*]. **3** a small heap of soil piled up around plant roots [a *hill* of potatoes].

☆**hill·bil·ly** (hil′bil′ē) ***n.*** a person who lives in or comes from the mountains or backwoods, especially of the South: *used only in everyday talk, sometimes in an unfriendly way.* —*pl.* **hill′bil′lies**

**hill·ock** (hil′ək) ***n.*** a small hill; mound.

**hill·side** (hil′sīd) ***n.*** the slope of a hill.

**hill·top** (hil′täp) ***n.*** the top of a hill.

**hill·y** (hil′ē) ***adj.*** full of hills; rolling and uneven [*hilly* country]. —**hill′i·er, hill′i·est** —**hill′i·ness *n.***

**hilt** (hilt) ***n.*** the handle of a sword or dagger. *See the picture.*

**him** (him) ***pron.*** *the form of* **he** *that is used as the object of a verb or preposition* [Call *him* back. The dog jumped on *him.*]

**Hi·ma·la·yas** (him′ə lā′əz *or* hi mäl′yəz) a group of very high mountains between India and Tibet. —**Hi′ma·la′yan *adj.***

**him·self** (him self′) ***pron.*** **1** his own self. *This form of* **he** *is used when the object is the same as the subject of the verb* [He hurt *himself.*] **2** his usual or true self [He isn't *himself* today.] *Himself* is also used to give force to the subject [He *himself* told us so.]

**hind**[1] (hīnd) ***adj.*** back; rear [a *hind* leg].

**hind**[2] (hīnd) ***n.*** a full-grown, female red deer.

**hin·der**[1] (hin′dər) ***v.*** to keep back; get in the way of; obstruct; prevent [Heavy snows *hindered* us on our trip.] *See* SYNONYMS *at* **delay.**

**hind·er**[2] (hīn′dər) ***adj.*** hind; back; rear.

**hind·most** (hīnd′mōst) ***adj.*** farthest back; last: *also* **hind·er·most** (hīn′dər mōst).

**hin·drance** (hin′drəns) ***n.*** **1** any person or thing that hinders; obstacle [A poor education can be a *hindrance* to success.] **2** the act of keeping back or hindering [to come and go without *hindrance*].

☆**hind·sight** (hīnd′sīt) ***n.*** an understanding of what one should have done, after it is too late [In *hindsight,* I now know we should have passed the ball more.]

**Hin·du** (hin′do͞o) ***n.*** any member of the largest native group of India, especially one whose religion is Hinduism. ◆***adj.*** of the Hindus.

**Hin·du·ism** (hin′do͝o wiz′m) ***n.*** the main religion of India.

**hinge** (hinj) ***n.*** a joint on which a door, lid, etc. swings open and shut. *See the picture.* ◆***v.*** **1** to put a hinge or hinges on. **2** to swing on a hinge. **3** to depend on in an important way [Our chances of winning *hinge* on whether or not you play.] —**hinged, hing′ing**

**hint** (hint) ***n.*** **1** a slight suggestion that is not made in an open or direct way; inkling [When she began reading again, we took the *hint* and left.] **2** a very small amount [a *hint* of spice]. ◆***v.*** to suggest in a way that is not open or direct [He *hinted* that he would like to go with us.]

**hin·ter·land** (hin′tər land) ***n.*** **1** the land lying behind the land along a coast or river. **2** land that is far from cities or towns.

**hip**[1] (hip) ***n.*** the part between the upper thigh and the waist on either side of the body.

☆**hip**[2] (hip) ***adj.*** knowing or understanding what is going on or what is fashionable; aware: *a slang term.* —**hip′per, hip′pest**

☆**hip·pie** (hip′ē) ***n.*** a young person, especially in the 1960's, who did not want to follow the usual customs and beliefs of society and, as a result, dressed in unusual ways, showed a fondness for unconventional art, took drugs, etc.: *a slang word.*

**Hip·poc·ra·tes** (hi päk′rə tēz) a Greek doctor who lived about 400 B.C. and has been called "the Father of Medicine."

**hip·po·drome** (hip′ə drōm) ***n.*** **1** an oval track with seats around it, used by the ancient Greeks and Romans for horse races and chariot races. **2** an arena for a circus, games, etc.

**hip·po·pot·a·mus** (hip′ə pät′ə məs) ***n.*** a large animal with a thick skin and short legs. It feeds on plants and lives in or near rivers in Africa. *See the picture.* —*pl.* **hip′po·pot′a·mus·es** or **hip·po·pot·a·mi** (hip′ə pät′ə mī′) *Also* **hip·po** (hip′ō), *pl.* **hip′pos:** *used only in everyday talk.*

> To the ancient Greeks, the **hippopotamus** looked like a large horse. Since it also spent so much time in water, they took their word for "horse," which was *hippos,* and put it together with *potamos,* meaning "river," to form a name for the animal, meaning "river horse."

**hire** (hīr) ***v.*** **1** to agree to pay wages to in return for work; employ [She has *hired* a new secretary.] **2** to pay money for the use of; rent [Let's *hire* a hall for the dance.] **3** to allow to be used in return for pay [The ranch *hires* out its horses.] —**hired, hir′ing** ◆***n.*** the amount of money paid to get the services of a person or the use of a thing. —**for hire,** available for work or use in return for pay [Are these bikes *for hire?*]

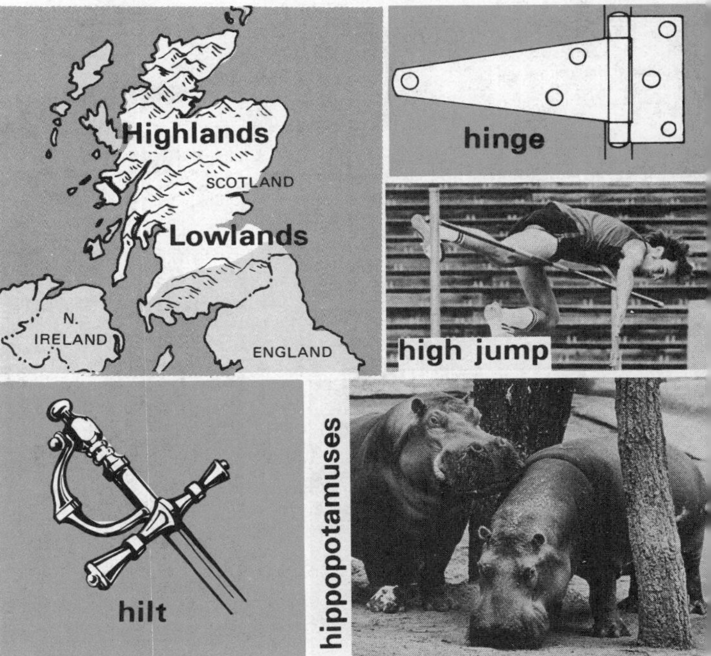


**hire·ling** (hīr′liŋ) ***n.*** a person who will do almost anything for pay, even something improper.



**Hi·ro·shi·ma** (hir′ə shē′mə) a seaport in southwest Japan. On August 6, 1945, it was largely destroyed by an American atomic bomb, the first ever used in war.

**his** (hiz) ***pron.*** **1** the one or the ones that belong to him [This book is *his. His* cost more than mine.] **2** of him or done by him. *When this possessive form of* **he** *is used before a noun, it is thought of as an adjective* [*his* hat; *his* work].

**His·pan·io·la** (his′pən yō′lə) an island in the West Indies, between Cuba and Puerto Rico.

**hiss** (his) ***v.*** **1** to make a sound like the sound of an *s* held for a long time [The snake *hissed.* Gas *hissed* from the stove burner.] **2** to make such a sound in showing dislike [The crowd *hissed* the speaker.] ◆***n.*** the act or sound of hissing.

**hist** (st *or* hist) ***interj.*** a hissing sound made to mean "Be quiet! Listen!"

**his·to·ri·an** (his tôr′ē ən) ***n.*** a writer of histories or an expert in history.

**his·tor·ic** (his tôr′ik) ***adj.*** famous in history; historical [a *historic* invention].

**his·tor·i·cal** (his tôr′i k′l) ***adj.*** **1** of or having to do with history as a science [the *historical* method]. **2** that actually existed or happened in history; not imaginary or fictional [*historical* persons or events]. **3** based on real people or events of the past [a *historical* novel]. **4** *same as* **historic.** —**his·tor′i·cal·ly** ***adv.***

| | | | | | | | |
|---|---|---|---|---|---|---|---|
| **a** | fat | **ir** | here | **ou** | out | **zh** | leisure |
| **ā** | ape | **ī** | bite, fire | **u** | up | **ŋ** | ring |
| **ä** | car, lot | **ō** | go | **ʉr** | fur | | a *in* ago |
| **e** | ten | **ô** | law, horn | **ch** | chin | | e *in* agent |
| **er** | care | **oi** | oil | **sh** | she | **ə** = | i *in* unity |
| **ē** | even | **o͝o** | look | **th** | thin | | o *in* collect |
| **i** | hit | **o͞o** | tool | ***th*** | then | | u *in* focus |

field hockey

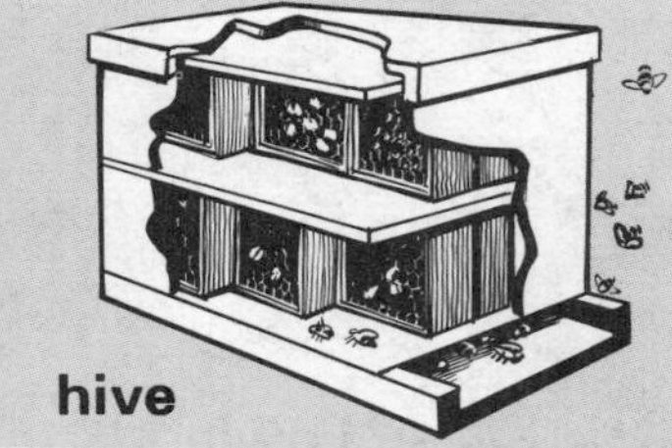

hive

hocks of a horse

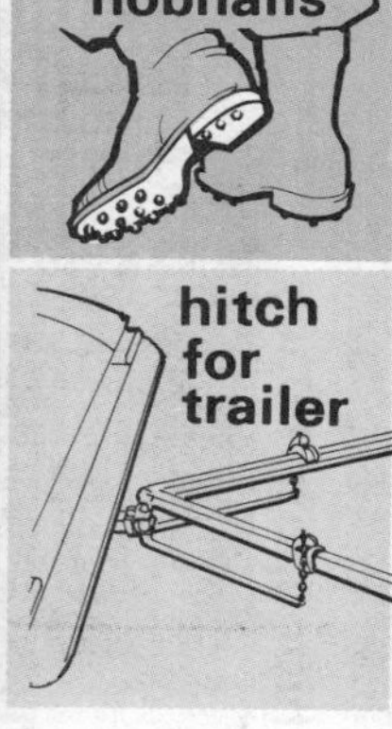

hobnails

hitch for trailer

girl on hobbyhorse

**his·to·ry** (his′tə rē) ***n.*** **1** what has happened in the life of a people, country, science, art, etc.; also, an account of this [the *history* of medicine; a *history* of England]. **2** the record of everything that has happened in the past [Nero was one of the worst tyrants in *history*.] **3** the science or study that keeps a record of past events [How will *history* treat our times?] **4** a story or tale [This hat has a strange *history*.] —*pl.* **his′to·ries**



**his·tri·on·ics** (his′trē än′iks) ***n.pl.*** **1** the art of acting in plays; dramatics. **2** acting that is too emotional or showy.

**hit** (hit) ***v.*** **1** to come against with force; bump or knock [The car *hit* the tree. I *hit* my head on the door.] **2** to give a blow to; strike [The boxer was *hit* on the jaw.] *See* SYNONYMS *at* **strike**. **3** to strike by throwing or shooting something at [She *hit* the bull's-eye with her next shot.] **4** to make suffer; distress [a town *hit* hard by floods]. **5** to find by chance or after searching [He *hit* upon the right answer.] ☆**6** to reach or come to [Prices *hit* a new high.] ☆**7** to get as a hit in baseball [to *hit* a home run]. —**hit, hit′ting** ◆***n.*** **1** a blow or stroke, especially one that strikes its mark. **2** a song, play, record, etc. that is a great success. ☆**3** the successful hitting of a baseball, which lets the batter get on base safely: *also called* **base hit**. —**hit it off,** to get along well together. —**hit or miss,** in an aimless way. —**hit out at, 1** to aim a blow at. **2** to attack in words. —☆**hit the road,** to leave; go away: *a slang phrase.* —**hit′ter *n.***

☆**hit-and-run** (hit″n run′) ***adj.*** speeding away to escape after causing an accident with one's car [a *hit-and-run* driver].

**hitch** (hich) ***v.*** **1** to move with jerks [He *hitched* his chair forward.] **2** to fasten with a hook, knot, strap, etc. [to *hitch* a horse to a fence]. **3** to become fastened or caught, as on a nail or hook. **4** to get a ride by hitchhiking: *slang in this meaning.* ◆***n.*** **1** a quick pull; tug or jerk [Give the rope a *hitch*.] **2** something that gets in the way; hindrance [The parade went off without a *hitch*.] **3** a fastening or catching; also, a part that catches [The *hitch* holding the trailer broke.] *See the picture.* **4** a kind of knot that can be untied easily.

☆**hitch·hike** (hich′hīk) ***v.*** to travel by asking for rides from motorists along the way. —**hitch′hiked, hitch′hik·ing** —**hitch′hik·er *n.***

**hith·er** (hith′ər) ***adv.*** to this place; here: *this word is no longer much used.*

**hith·er·to** (hith′ər to͞o) ***adv.*** until this time; to now [a *hitherto* unknown writer].

**Hit·ler** (hit′lər), **Adolf** 1889–1945; the Nazi dictator of Germany from 1933 to 1945.

☆**hit-skip** (hit′skip′) ***adj.*** *another word for* **hit-and-run.**

**Hit·tite** (hit′īt) ***n.*** a member of a people who lived in Asia Minor and Syria from about 1700 B.C. to about 700 B.C.

**hive** (hīv) ***n.*** **1** a box or other shelter for a colony of bees; beehive. *See the picture.* **2** a colony of bees living in a hive. **3** a place where there are many people busy doing something. ◆***v.*** to gather into a hive, as bees. —**hived, hiv′ing**

**hives** (hīvz) ***n.*** a skin disease caused by an allergy, in which smooth, raised patches form and there is itching.

**H.M.S.** His Majesty's Ship *or* Her Majesty's Ship.

**ho** (hō) ***interj.*** a word called out to get attention or to show surprise, wonder, etc.

☆**hoa·gy** or **hoa·gie** (hō′gē) ***n.*** *another name for* **hero sandwich.** —*pl.* **hoa′gies**

**hoar** (hôr) ***adj.*** *another word for* **hoary.** ◆***n.*** *another word for* **hoarfrost.**

**hoard** (hôrd) ***v.*** to collect and store away, often secretly [A miser *hoards* money.] ◆***n.*** anything that is hoarded [a squirrel's *hoard* of acorns]. —**hoard′er *n.***

**hoar·frost** (hôr′frôst) ***n.*** white, frozen dew on the ground, on leaves, etc.

**hoarse** (hôrs) ***adj.*** sounding rough and husky [the *hoarse* call of a crow; to become *hoarse* from shouting]. —**hoars′er, hoars′est** —**hoarse′ly *adv.*** —**hoarse′ness *n.***

**hoar·y** (hôr′ē) ***adj.*** **1** white or gray [ground *hoary* with frost]. **2** having white or gray hair because of old age [a *hoary* head]. **3** very old; ancient [*hoary* laws]. —**hoar′i·er, hoar′i·est** —**hoar′i·ness *n.***

**hoax** (hōks) ***n.*** something that is meant to trick or fool others, especially a practical joke. ◆***v.*** to play a trick on; fool. —**hoax′er *n.***

**hob** (häb) ***n.*** an elf or goblin. —**play hob with** or **raise hob with,** to make trouble for.

**hob·bit** (häb′it) ***n.*** an imaginary being in stories by J.R.R. Tolkien (1892–1973) of England. A hobbit looks like a small person, but with some features of rabbits. Hobbits are friendly and peaceful.

**hob·ble** (häb″l) ***v.*** **1** to walk in a lame or clumsy way. **2** to keep from moving by tying the legs together [to *hobble* a horse]. **3** to get in the way of; hinder [They were *hobbled* by the many forms they had to fill out.] —**hob′bled, hob′bling** ◆***n.*** **1** a limping walk. **2** a rope or strap used to hobble a horse.

**hob·by** (häb′ē) ***n.*** something that one likes to do, study, etc. for pleasure in one's spare time [Her *hobby* is collecting coins.] —*pl.* **hob′bies**

**hob·by·horse** (häb′ē hôrs′) ***n.*** **1** a toy made up of a horse's head at the end of a stick, that a child can pretend to ride. *See the picture.* **2** *another name for* **rocking horse.**

**hob·gob·lin** (häb′gäb′lin) ***n.*** **1** an elf or goblin. **2** an imaginary being that scares one.

**hob·nail** (häb′nāl) ***n.*** a short nail with a large head, put on the soles of heavy shoes to keep them from slipping or wearing out. *See the picture.*

**hob·nob** (häb′näb) ***v.*** to spend time with in a close, friendly way [The reporter *hobnobbed* with politicians and movie stars.] —**hob′nobbed, hob′nob·bing**

☆**ho·bo** (hō′bō) ***n.*** a person who wanders from place to place, doing odd jobs or begging for a living; tramp. —*pl.* **ho′bos** or **ho′boes**

**hock**[1] (häk) ***n.*** the joint that bends backward in the hind leg of a horse, cow, dog, etc. *See the picture.*

☆**hock**[2] (häk) ***v., n.*** *a slang word for* **pawn**[1].

**hock·ey** (häk′ē) ***n.*** ☆**1** a game played on ice, in which the players wear ice skates and use curved sticks to try to drive a rubber disk (called the *puck*) into the other team's goal: *also called* **ice hockey. 2** a game like this played on a dry field with a small ball: *also called* **field hockey.** *See the picture.*

> **Hockey** probably comes from an older Dutch word meaning "hook," or "crook." Long ago the game was probably played in fields by shepherds, who used their crooks to hit a small, leather-covered ball.

**ho·cus-po·cus** (hō′kəs pō′kəs) ***n.*** words without meaning, supposed to help in doing magic tricks.

**hod** (häd) ***n.*** **1** a wooden trough with a long handle. It is filled with bricks or cement and carried on the shoulder by workers. *See the picture on page 350.* **2** a bucket for carrying coal.

**hodge-podge** (häj′päj) ***n.*** a jumbled mixture of things; mess [The book is a *hodge-podge* of facts and opinions.]

**hoe** (hō) ***n.*** a garden tool with a thin, flat blade on a long handle. It is used for removing weeds, loosening the soil, etc. *See the picture on page 350.* ◆***v.*** to dig, loosen soil, etc. with a hoe. —**hoed, hoe′ing**

☆**hoe·down** (hō′doun) ***n.*** **1** a lively dance, often a square dance. **2** a party at which hoedowns are danced.

**hog** (hôg *or* häg) ***n.*** **1** a pig, especially a full-grown pig raised for its meat. **2** a person who is selfish, greedy, or very dirty: *used only in everyday talk.* ◆***v.*** ☆to take all of or too much of: *a slang meaning* [Don't *hog* all the room on the bench.] —**hogged, hog′ging** —**hog′gish** ***adj.***

**hogs·head** (hôgz′hed *or* hägz′hed) ***n.*** **1** a large barrel or cask. Different hogsheads hold between 63 and 140 gallons. **2** a measure of liquids, especially one equal to 63 gallons.

**hog·wash** (hôg′wôsh *or* häg′wäsh) ***n.*** **1** watery garbage fed to hogs. **2** useless or foolish talk or writing.

**hoist** (hoist) ***v.*** to lift or pull up; raise, especially with a crane, pulley, or rope [to *hoist* a statue into place]. ◆***n.*** **1** a pulley, elevator, etc. used to raise heavy things. **2** an act of hoisting; a lift [Give me a *hoist* over the fence.]

**hold** (hōld) ***v.*** **1** to take and keep in the hands or arms [Please *hold* the baby for a while.] **2** to keep in a certain place or position [*Hold* your head up. They were *held* in jail.] **3** to keep under control; not lose or let go of [*Hold* your temper. The speaker *held* our attention.] **4** to keep or reserve for use later [They will *hold* the motel room for us.] **5** to have or keep as one's own; occupy [She *holds* the office of mayor.] **6** to have or carry on; conduct [Our club *held* a meeting on Friday.] **7** to have room for; contain [This jar *holds* a liter.] **8** to have as one's opinion or belief; decide; consider [The judge *held* that I was at fault.] **9** to stay together or in one piece [That rope won't *hold.*] **10** to stay the same or be true [a rule which still *holds*]. —**held, hold′ing** ◆***n.*** **1** the act of holding or grasping, or the way this is done [Take a firm *hold.* I learned a new *hold* in wrestling.] **2** a strong influence or power [She has a great *hold* over her brother.] **3** the inside of a ship below the deck, where the cargo is put. —**get hold of, 1** to grasp or seize: *also* **catch hold of. 2** to get; acquire. —**hold down, 1** to keep under control. **2** to have and keep (a job): *used only in everyday talk.* —**hold forth, 1** to speak for a long time; lecture or preach. **2** to offer, as a plan. —**hold off, 1** to keep away; keep at a distance. **2** to keep from doing something. —**hold on, 1** to keep on holding. **2** to keep on doing something. **3** wait! stop! —**hold one's own,** to keep one's position in spite of difficulties. —**hold out, 1** to go on; last. **2** to stand up against without giving in. —**hold over, 1** to keep or stay longer than planned. **2** to keep as a threat or advantage over. —**hold up, 1** to keep from falling; prop up. **2** to continue or last. **3** to stop or delay. ☆**4** to rob by using force. —**hold′er** ***n.***



> SYNONYMS: **Hold** means to have something in one's grasp or to have control over it [to *hold* a book; to *hold* the attention of an audience]. **Own** means to have something as one's personal property [to *own* a boat]. **Possess** is a more formal word that means the same thing as **own,** but it also means to have some special quality [to *possess* wisdom].

**hold·ing** (hōl′diŋ) ***n.*** something owned, as land, stocks, or bonds: *usually used in the plural,* **holdings.**

☆**hold·up** (hōld′up) ***n.*** **1** a stopping or delay of something. **2** robbery by someone who is armed.

**hole** (hōl) ***n.*** **1** an opening in or through something; a break or tear [*holes* in the roof; a *hole* in my sweater]. **2** a hollow place; cavity [a *hole* in the ground]. **3** the burrow or den of an animal. **4** any of the small cups sunk into the greens on a golf course, into which the ball is to be hit. **5** a weak point; flaw [*holes* in an argument]. ◆***v.*** to put into a hole, as a ball in golf. —**holed, hol′ing** —**hole up, 1** to spend the winter sleeping, as in a hole [Bears *hole up* in caves.]

| | | | | | | | |
|---|---|---|---|---|---|---|---|
| **a** | fat | **ir** | here | **ou** | out | **zh** | leisure |
| **ā** | ape | **ī** | bite, fire | **u** | up | **ŋ** | ring |
| **ä** | car, lot | **ō** | go | **ur** | fur | | a *in* ago |
| **e** | ten | **ô** | law, horn | **ch** | chin | | e *in* agent |
| **er** | care | **oi** | oil | **sh** | she | **ə** = | i *in* unity |
| **ē** | even | **oo** | look | **th** | thin | | o *in* collect |
| **i** | hit | **ōō** | tool | ***th*** | then | | u *in* focus |

2 to stay some place for a long time. *This phrase is used only in everyday talk.*

**hol·i·day** (häl′ə dā) ***n.*** **1** a day on which most people do not have to work, often one set aside by law [Thanksgiving is a *holiday* in all States.] **2** a religious festival; holy day [Easter is a Christian *holiday*.]

**ho·li·ness** (hō′lē nis) ***n.*** **1** the condition of being holy. **2 Holiness,** a title of the Pope: *used with* His *or* Your.

**Hol·land** (häl′ənd) *another name for the* **Netherlands.**

**hol·ler** (häl′ər) ***v.*** to shout or yell: *used only in everyday talk.*

**hol·low** (häl′ō) ***adj.*** **1** having an empty space on the inside; not solid [a *hollow* log]. **2** shaped like a bowl; concave. **3** sunken in [*hollow* cheeks]. **4** with no real meaning; empty or false [*hollow* praise]. **5** sounding deep and dull, as if echoing out of a large, empty place. ***•n.*** **1** a hollow place; hole or cavity. **2** a small valley. ***•v.*** to make or become hollow. —**hollow out, 1** to make a hollow in. **2** to make by hollowing. —**hol′low·ness *n.***

**hol·low-eyed** (häl′ō īd′) ***adj.*** having the eyes sunken in or having dark areas under the eyes, as from being sick or very tired.

**hol·ly** (häl′ē) ***n.*** a small tree or shrub with shiny leaves and red berries. Its branches are used as Christmas decorations. *See the picture.* —*pl.* **hol′lies**

 **hol·ly·hock** (häl′ē häk′) ***n.*** a tall plant with a hairy stem and large, showy flowers. *See the picture.*

**Hol·ly·wood** (häl′ē wood′) a part of Los Angeles where many movie studios were once located.

**Holmes** (hōmz), **Ol·i·ver Wen·dell** (äl′ə vər wen′d'l) **1** 1809–1894; U.S. writer. **2** 1841–1935; his son, who was a Supreme Court justice from 1902 to 1932.

**Holmes, Sher·lock** (shur′läk) an expert detective in stories by A. Conan Doyle (1859–1930) of England.

hod

hollyhock

Holstein

holly

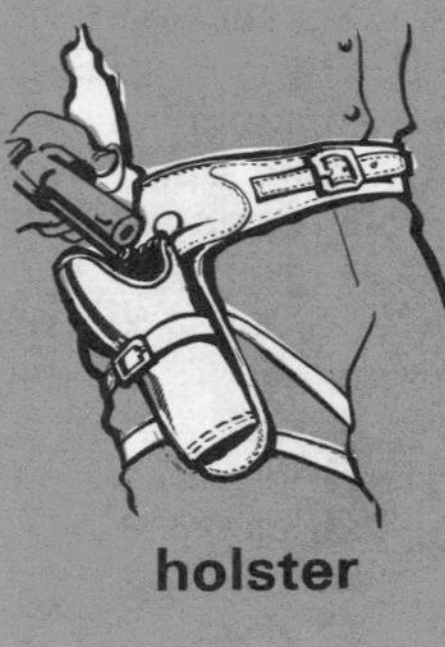
holster

hoe

**hol·o·caust** (häl′ə kôst *or* hō′lə kôst) ***n.*** great destruction of life by fire. —**the Holocaust,** the killing of millions of Jews by Nazi Germany.

**Holocaust** comes from two Greek words, *holos,* meaning "whole" and *kaustos,* meaning "burned." It was originally used of a sacrifice that was burned entirely on an altar. Many of the people killed by the Nazis were burned in furnaces.

**Hol·stein** (hōl′stēn *or* hōl′stīn) ***n.*** ☆ a breed of large, black-and-white dairy cattle. *See the picture.*

**hol·ster** (hōl′stər) ***n.*** a leather case for holding a pistol, usually fastened to a belt. *See the picture.*

**ho·ly** (hō′lē) ***adj.*** **1** set apart for religious use; connected with religion or God; sacred [a *holy* festival; the *Holy* Bible]. **2** very good or very religious; saintly [a *holy* person]. **3** thought of with very deep feeling [The fight for civil rights was a *holy* cause to us.] —**ho′li·er, ho′li·est**

**Holy Communion** a ritual in Christian churches during which bread and wine are blessed and received as the body and blood of Jesus or as symbols of them.

**Holy Ghost** or **Holy Spirit** the third person of the Trinity; spirit of God.

**Holy Grail** *see* **Grail.**

**Holy Land** *another name for* **Palestine.**

**Holy Roman Empire** the empire in central Europe that lasted from 800 A.D. to 1806.

**Holy Scripture** or **Holy Scriptures** *another name for the* **Bible**: *also* **Holy Writ.**

**Holy See** the position or authority of the Pope.

**Holy Week** the week before Easter.

**hom·age** (häm′ij *or* äm′ij) ***n.*** **1** anything done to show honor or respect [Lincoln's speech paid *homage* to the men who fought at Gettysburg.] **2** a pledge of allegiance made by vassals to their lords in the Middle Ages.

☆**hom·bre** (äm′brā) ***n.*** a man; fellow: *a Spanish word used only in everyday talk in English.*

**home** (hōm) ***n.*** **1** the place where one lives; one's house, apartment, etc. **2** the city, country, etc. where one was born or brought up. **3** a family or family life [a *home* broken up by divorce]. **4** a place where orphans or people who are old or helpless are taken care of. **5** the place where a certain plant or animal is normally found [Australia is the *home* of the kangaroo.] **6** the place where something began or where it developed [Detroit is the *home* of the auto industry.] **7** in many games, the base or goal; especially, ☆the home plate in baseball. ***•adj.*** **1** that is or has to do with one's home [my *home* town]. **2** having to do with the home or family [*home* cooking]. **3** that is the headquarters; main or central [the *home* office of a company]. ***•adv.*** **1** at, to, or toward home [Go *home!*] **2** to the point aimed at [to drive a nail *home*]. —**at home, 1** in one's home. **2** at ease; comfortable [She always makes us feel *at home* when we visit her.] **3** willing to receive visitors. —**bring home to,** to make clear to [The accident in the street *brought home to* us the need for a safe playground.] —**home′less *adj.***

☆**home economics** the science of managing a home, including budgeting, cooking, child care, etc.

**home·land** (hōm′land) ***n.*** the country where one was born or where one's home is.

**home·like** (hōm′līk) ***adj.*** like one's home; comfortable, cozy, and making one feel at ease.

**home·ly** (hōm′lē) ***adj.*** **1** plain or simple [a *homely* meal; a *homely* way of speaking]. **2** not very pretty or handsome; plain [a *homely* face]. —**home′li·er, home′li·est** —**home′li·ness** ***n.***

**home·made** (hōm′mād′) ***adj.*** made at home or as if made at home [*homemade* bread].

**home·mak·er** (hōm′māk′ər) ***n.*** a person whose work is managing a home; especially, a housewife.

**home·own·er** (hōm′ō′nər) ***n.*** a person who owns the house he or she lives in.

☆**home plate** in baseball, the slab that a player stands beside when batting. It is the last base that must be touched in scoring a run.

**Ho·mer** (hō′mər) a Greek poet who is thought to have lived in the 8th century B.C. and to have written the *Iliad* and the *Odyssey*. —**Ho·mer·ic** (hō mer′ik) ***adj.***

☆**home·room** (hōm′ro͞om) ***n.*** the room where a class in school meets daily for a short time to have their attendance taken, to get announcements, etc.

☆**home run** in baseball, a hit that allows the batter to touch all bases and score a run: *in everyday talk, also called* **hom·er** (hōm′ər) ***n.***

**home·sick** (hōm′sik) ***adj.*** longing to be home again. —**home′sick·ness** ***n.***

**home·spun** (hōm′spun) ***n.*** cloth made of yarn spun at home or a coarse cloth like this. ◆***adj.*** plain or simple [*homespun* humor].

**home·stead** (hōm′sted) ***n.*** ☆**1** a place where a family makes its home, including the house and the land around it. ☆**2** a piece of public land given by the U.S. government to a settler to develop as a farm. ◆☆***v.*** to become a settler on a homestead. —☆**home′stead·er** ***n.***

☆**home·stretch** (hōm′strech′) ***n.*** **1** the part of a race track from the last turn to the finish line. **2** the last part of any task.

**home·ward** (hōm′wərd) ***adj., adv.*** toward home.

**home·wards** (hōm′wərdz) ***adv.*** *same as* **homeward.**

**home·work** (hōm′wurk) ***n.*** **1** lessons to be studied or schoolwork to be done outside the classroom. **2** any work to be done at home.

**home·y** (hōm′ē) ***adj.*** like home; comfortable, cozy, etc. —**hom′i·er, hom′i·est**

**hom·i·cide** (häm′ə sīd) ***n.*** any killing of one human being by another. —**hom′i·ci′dal** ***adj.***

**homing pigeon** a pigeon trained to find its way home from far-off places.

☆**hom·i·ny** (häm′ə nē) ***n.*** dry corn kernels that have had the hulls removed and have been broken into coarse bits, which are boiled for food.

**ho·mo·ge·ne·ous** (hō′mə jē′nē əs) ***adj.*** alike or made up of parts that are alike [a *homogeneous* group of people].

**ho·mog·e·nize** (hə mäj′ə nīz) ***v.*** to make something the same throughout [Milk is *homogenized* by breaking down and blending the fat particles so that the cream does not separate and go to the top.] —**ho·mog′e·nized, ho·mog′e·niz·ing**

**hom·o·nym** (häm′ə nim) ***n.*** a word that is pronounced like another word but that has a different meaning and is usually spelled differently ["Bore" and "boar" are *homonyms*.]

**ho·mo·sex·u·al** (hō′mə sek′sho͞o wəl) ***adj.*** being attracted sexually to persons of the same sex as one's own. ◆***n.*** a homosexual person.

**Hon.** *abbreviation for* **Honorable, Honorary.**

**Hon·du·ras** (hän do͝or′əs *or* hän dyo͝or′əs) a country in Central America.

**hone** (hōn) ***v.*** to sharpen a razor, knife, etc., as by rubbing on a hard stone that has a fine grain. —**honed, hon′ing**

**hon·est** (än′əst) ***adj.*** **1** that does not steal, cheat, or lie; upright or trustworthy [an *honest* person]. **2** got in a fair way, not by stealing, cheating, or lying [to earn an *honest* living]. **3** sincere or genuine [He made an *honest* effort.] **4** frank and open [an *honest* face].

**hon·est·ly** (än′əst lē) ***adv.*** **1** in an honest way. **2** truly; really [*Honestly,* I meant no harm.]

**hon·es·ty** (än′əs tē) ***n.*** the quality or fact of being honest; uprightness or sincerity.

> SYNONYMS: **Honesty** means a being truthful and trustworthy, a refusing to lie, cheat, or steal [*Honesty* is the best policy.] **Honor** suggests a careful following of the rules about right behavior that members of a certain group, profession, etc. are supposed to follow [Can there be *honor* among thieves?] **Integrity** suggests a being true to one's moral beliefs even when it would be easier to ignore them [We must elect people of *integrity*.]

**hon·ey** (hun′ē) ***n.*** **1** a thick, sweet, yellow syrup that bees make from the nectar of flowers and store in honeycombs. **2** sweet one; darling: *used in talking to someone dear to one* [How are you, *honey?*] **3** something very pleasing or very good: *used only in everyday talk* [a *honey* of an idea]. —*pl.* **hon′eys**



**hon·ey·bee** (hun′ē bē′) ***n.*** a bee that makes honey.

**hon·ey·comb** (hun′ē kōm′) ***n.*** **1** a cluster of wax cells made by bees to hold their honey, eggs, etc. Each cell has six sides. *See the picture on page 353.* **2** anything like this. ◆***v.*** to cause to be filled with holes like a honeycomb [The hill is *honeycombed* with caves.] ◆***adj.*** of or like a honeycomb [a *honeycomb* design].

**hon·ey·dew** (hun′ē do͞o′ *or* hun′ē dyo͞o′) ***n.*** **1** a melon with a smooth, whitish skin and sweet, greenish flesh. *Its full name is* **honeydew melon.** **2** a sweet liquid that comes from the leaves of some plants in summer. **3** a sweet substance made by aphids and other insects that suck juice from plants.

**hon·eyed** (hun′ēd) ***adj.*** **1** sweetened, as with honey. **2** flattering in a loving way [*honeyed* words].

**hon·ey·moon** (hun′ē mo͞on′) ***n.*** the vacation spent together by a couple after their wedding. ◆***v.*** to have a honeymoon [They will *honeymoon* in Florida.] —**hon′ey·moon′er** ***n.***

> There is a story, which may or may not be true, that the **honeymoon** is so called because the sweetness is said to last for one moon, or month. Then, say some sarcastic people, the love begins to wane, or grow dimmer, just as the moon does.

| | | | | | | | |
|---|---|---|---|---|---|---|---|
| **a** | fat | **ir** | here | **ou** | out | **zh** | leisure |
| **ā** | ape | **ī** | bite, fire | **u** | up | **ng** | ring |
| **ä** | car, lot | **ō** | go | **ur** | fur | | a *in* ago |
| **e** | ten | **ô** | law, horn | **ch** | chin | | e *in* agent |
| **er** | care | **oi** | oil | **sh** | she | ə = | i *in* unity |
| **ē** | even | **oo** | look | **th** | thin | | o *in* collect |
| **i** | hit | **o͞o** | tool | ***th*** | then | | u *in* focus |

h

**hon·ey·suck·le** (hun′ē suk′'l) ***n.*** a climbing vine with small flowers that have a sweet smell.

**Hong Kong** (häng′käng′ *or* hông′kông′) a British colony in southeastern China.

**honk** (hôngk *or* hängk) ***n.*** **1** the call of a wild goose. **2** a sound like this, as of an automobile horn. ◆***v.*** to make or cause to make this sound.

**Hon·o·lu·lu** (hän′ə lo͞o′lo͞o) the capital of Hawaii.

**hon·or** (än′ər) ***n.*** **1** great respect given because of worth, noble deeds, high rank, etc. [to pay *honor* to the geniuses of science]. **2** glory or credit, or a person or thing that brings this to others [the *honor* of winning a Nobel prize; to be an *honor* to one's profession]. **3** something done or given as a sign of respect [Madame Curie received many *honors* for her work.] **4 Honor,** a title of respect given to a judge, mayor, etc. [His *Honor,* the Mayor]. **5** good name or reputation [You must uphold the *honor* of the family.] **6** a being true to what is right, honest, etc. [Her sense of *honor* kept her from cheating.] *See* SYNONYMS *at* **honesty. 7 honors,** ***pl.*** special praise given to a student with very high grades [to graduate with *honors*]. ◆***v.*** **1** to have or show great respect for [America *honors* the memory of Lincoln. *Honor* your father and your mother.] **2** to do something in honor of [We *honored* the team with a banquet.] **3** to accept as good for payment, credit, etc. [That store *honors* most credit cards.] ◆***adj.*** of or showing honor [an *honor* roll]. —**do the honors,** to act as a host or hostess.



**hon·or·a·ble** (än′ər ə b'l) ***adj.*** **1** worthy of being honored [an *honorable* trade]. *It is often written with a capital letter and used as a title of respect* [our mayor, the *Honorable* Julia Kline]. **2** honest, upright, and sincere [*honorable* intentions]. **3** bringing honor [*honorable* mention]. —**hon′or·a·bly** ***adv.***

**hon·or·ar·y** (än′ə rer′ē) ***adj.*** **1** given as an honor, without the usual courses, tests, etc. [an *honorary* degree]. **2** holding the office only as an honor, without duties or pay [*honorary* director of a fund drive].

**hon·our** (än′ər) ***n.*** *the British spelling of* **honor.**

**Hon·shu** (hän′sho͞o′) the largest of the islands that form Japan.

**hood** (hood) ***n.*** **1** a covering for the head and neck, often part of a coat or cloak. **2** anything like a hood, as the fold of skin around a cobra's head. ☆**3** the metal cover over the engine of an automobile. ◆***v.*** to cover with a hood. —**hood′ed** ***adj.***

**-hood** (hood) *a suffix meaning:* **1** the condition or time of being [*Childhood* is the time of being a child.] **2** all the members in a group [The *priesthood* is the whole group of priests.]

☆**hood·lum** (ho͞od′ləm) ***n.*** a rough person with no respect for the law, often a member of a gang of criminals: *used only in everyday talk.*

☆**hoo·doo** (ho͞o′do͞o) ***n.*** **1** *another word for* **voodoo. 2** a person or thing that is thought to cause bad luck: *used only in everyday talk.*

**hood·wink** (hood′wingk) ***v.*** to trick or fool; mislead [Don't be *hoodwinked* by their promises.]

**hoof** (hoof *or* ho͞of) ***n.*** **1** the horny covering on the feet of cows, horses, deer, pigs, etc. **2** the whole foot of such an animal. —*pl.* **hoofs** or **hooves** ◆***v.*** to walk: *used only in everyday talk and often followed by* it [We'll have to *hoof* it into town.] —☆**on the hoof,** not butchered; alive [Live cattle are called beef *on the hoof.*]

**hook** (hook) ***n.*** **1** a piece of metal, plastic, etc. that is curved or bent so that it will catch or hold something [a fish*hook;* a coat *hook*]. *See the picture.* **2** something shaped like a hook, as a bend in a river. **3** a sharp blow made with the arm bent at the elbow. **4** in sports, the act of hooking a ball. ◆***v.*** **1** to curve as a hook does. **2** to catch, fasten, etc. with a hook [I *hooked* a fish. *Hook* the screen door.] **3** in sports, to hit a ball so that it curves [When a right-handed golfer *hooks* a ball, it curves to the left.] **4** to steal: *used only in everyday talk.* —**by hook or by crook,** in any way at all, honest or dishonest. —**hook up,** to set up and connect the parts, as of a radio. —**off the hook,** out of trouble or freed from a responsibility: *used only in everyday talk.* —☆**on one's own hook,** by oneself, without help from others: *used only in everyday talk.*

**hook·ah** (hook′ə) ***n.*** a kind of tobacco pipe used in the Orient. It has a long tube by which the smoke is drawn through a vase of water, where it is cooled.

**hooked** (hookt) ***adj.*** **1** curved like a hook. **2** having a hook or hooks. ☆**3** made by drawing strips of cloth or yarn back and forth with a hook through canvas or burlap [a *hooked* rug]. ☆**4** depending so much on something that one cannot easily do without it: *slang in this meaning* [*hooked* on television].

☆**hook·up** (hook′up) ***n.*** the way the parts or circuits are connected, as in a radio network.

☆**hook·worm** (hook′wurm) ***n.*** a small worm with hooks around the mouth, that can live in the intestines and cause fever, weakness, and pain.

☆**hook·y** (hook′ē) ***n.*** *see* **play hooky.**

**hoop** (ho͞op) ***n.*** **1** a round band of metal that holds together the staves of a barrel. **2** anything like this, as a ring in a hoop skirt or the metal rim of the basket in basketball.

☆**hoop skirt** a woman's skirt worn over a framework of hoops to make it spread out. *See the picture.*

**hoo·ray** (hoo rā′) ***interj., n., v.*** *another word for* **hurrah.**

**hoot** (ho͞ot) ***n.*** **1** the sound that an owl makes, or a sound like this. **2** a shout of anger or scorn. ◆***v.*** **1** to make the sound that an owl makes or a sound like this [The train whistle *hooted.*] **2** to show anger or scorn, as by hooting or booing. **3** to chase away by hooting [to *hoot* actors off a stage].

**Hoo·ver** (ho͞o′vər), **Herbert Clark** 1874–1964; the 31st president of the United States, from 1929 to 1933.

**hooves** (hoovz *or* ho͞ovz) ***n.*** *a plural of* **hoof.**

**hop**[1] (häp) ***v.*** **1** to make a short leap or leaps on one foot. **2** to jump over [to *hop* a fence]. **3** to move by jumps, as a bird or frog. ☆**4** to get aboard [to *hop* a bus]. **5** to move or go briskly: *used only in everyday talk* [I *hopped* out of bed to answer the phone.] —**hopped, hop′ping** ◆***n.*** **1** the act of hopping. ☆**2** a bounce, as of a baseball. **3** a short flight in an airplane: *used only in everyday talk.*

**hop**[2] (häp) ***n.*** **1** a climbing vine with small, yellow flowers shaped like cones. **2 hops,** ***pl.*** these flowers, which are dried and used to flavor beer and ale.

**hope** (hōp) ***n.*** **1** a feeling that what one wants will happen [We gave up *hope* of being rescued.] **2** the thing that one wants [It is my *hope* to go to college.] **3**

a person or thing on which one may base some hope [The 1500-meter run is our last *hope* for a victory.] ◆***v.*** **1** to have hope; want and expect [I *hope* to see you soon.] **2** to want to believe [I *hope* I didn't overlook anybody.] —**hoped, hop'ing**

**hope·ful** (hōp'fəl) ***adj.*** **1** feeling or showing hope [a *hopeful* smile]. **2** causing or giving hope [a *hopeful* sign]. —**hope'ful·ness *n.***

**hope·ful·ly** (hōp'fəl ē) ***adv.*** **1** in a hopeful way [to smile *hopefully*]. **2** it is to be hoped: *thought by some people to be not a proper use* [We'll leave early, *hopefully* before six o'clock.]

**hope·less** (hōp'lis) ***adj.*** **1** without hope [a *hopeless* prisoner]. **2** causing one to lose hope; discouraging [a *hopeless* situation]. —**hope'less·ly *adv.*** —**hope'less·ness *n.***

**hop·per** (häp'ər) ***n.*** **1** a person or thing that hops. **2** a container, often shaped like a funnel, from which the contents can be emptied slowly and evenly.

**hop·scotch** (häp'skäch) ***n.*** a children's game in which the players hop from one section to another of a figure drawn on the ground. *See the picture.*

**horde** (hôrd) ***n.*** **1** a wandering tribe, as of early Mongols. **2** a large crowd [a *horde* of picnickers].

**hore·hound** (hôr'hound) ***n.*** **1** a bitter plant of the mint family. **2** a cough medicine or candy flavored with juice got from its leaves.

**ho·ri·zon** (hə rī'z'n) ***n.*** **1** the line where the sky seems to meet the earth [A ship appeared over the *horizon.*] *See the picture.* **2** the limit of one's experience, knowledge, etc. [Travel widens our *horizons.*]

A standing person can see only about three miles before the surface of the earth curves away out of eyesight. No matter how good one's eyes are, the horizon forms a kind of boundary line beyond which one cannot see. Our word **horizon** comes from a Greek word *horos,* which means "boundary."

**hor·i·zon·tal** (hôr'ə zän't'l) ***adj.*** parallel to the horizon; not vertical; level; flat [The top of a table is *horizontal;* its legs are vertical.] ◆***n.*** a horizontal line, plane, etc. —**hor'i·zon'tal·ly *adv.***

**hor·mone** (hôr'mōn) ***n.*** a substance formed in an organ of the body and carried in the blood to some other part, where it has an effect [The pituitary gland makes *hormones* that control growth.]

**horn** (hôrn) ***n.*** **1** a hard, pointed growth on the head of some animals, as cattle and goats. Horns usually grow in pairs. **2** the substance that such horns are made of. **3** anything that sticks out or is curved like a horn, as each end of a crescent. **4** a container made by hollowing out a horn [a powder *horn*]. **5** a musical instrument made of a horn and sounded by blowing. **6** any brass-wind instrument, especially the *French horn.* **7** a device that makes a loud noise as a warning or a signal [a fog*horn*]. ◆***adj.*** made of horn [glasses with *horn* rims]. —☆**horn in,** to meddle in; butt in: *used only in everyday talk.* —**horn'less *adj.***

The antlers of deer are true horns, but they are shed every year, unlike the horns of cattle and goats, which are permanent. The so-called horn of a rhinoceros is not a true horn. It is made up of matted hair.

**Horn, Cape** a cape on an island at the southern tip of South America.

ship on the horizon

hoop skirts

hopscotch

types of hook

horned toad
10 cm (4 in.) long

honeycombs

**horned** (hôrnd) ***adj.*** having a horn or horns.

☆**horned toad** a small lizard with a short tail and spines like horns. *See the picture.* 353

**hor·net** (hôr'nit) ***n.*** a large wasp that lives in colonies and can give a painful sting.

**horn of plenty** *another name for* **cornucopia.**

**horn·pipe** (hôrn'pīp) ***n.*** **1** a lively dance that sailors used to do. *See the picture on page 354.* **2** music for this dance.

**horn·y** (hôr'nē) ***adj.*** **1** of, like, or made of horn. **2** hard like horn; tough and calloused [the carpenter's *horny* hands]. —**horn'i·er, horn'i·est**

**hor·o·scope** (hôr'ə skōp) ***n.*** a chart showing the signs of the zodiac and the positions of the stars and planets at a particular time. Astrologers believe that such a chart for a particular person can be used to predict that person's future.

**hor·ri·ble** (hôr'ə b'l) ***adj.*** **1** causing a feeling of horror; terrible; dreadful [a *horrible* accident]. **2** very bad, ugly, unpleasant, etc.: *used only in everyday talk* [What a *horrible* color!] —**hor'ri·bly *adv.***

**hor·rid** (hôr'id) ***adj.*** **1** causing a feeling of horror; terrible [the *horrid* face of the monster]. **2** very bad, ugly, unpleasant, etc.: *used only in everyday talk* [What a *horrid* thing to say!]

**hor·ri·fy** (hôr'ə fī) ***v.*** **1** to fill with horror [He was *horrified* at the sight of the victims.] **2** to shock or disgust: *used only in everyday talk* [His bad manners *horrified* her.] —**hor'ri·fied, hor'ri·fy·ing**

| | | | | | | | |
|---|---|---|---|---|---|---|---|
| **a** | fat | **ir** | here | **ou** | out | **zh** | leisure |
| **ā** | ape | **ī** | bite, fire | **u** | up | **ng** | ring |
| **ä** | car, lot | **ō** | go | **ur** | fur | | a *in* ago |
| **e** | ten | **ô** | law, horn | **ch** | chin | | e *in* agent |
| **er** | care | **oi** | oil | **sh** | she | **ə =** | i *in* unity |
| **ē** | even | **oo** | look | **th** | thin | | o *in* collect |
| **i** | hit | **ōō** | tool | ***th*** | then | | u *in* focus |

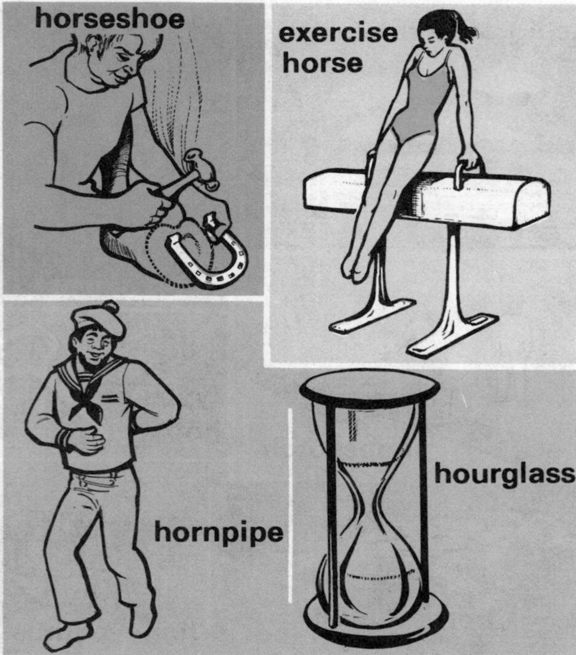


**hor·ror** (hôr′ər) ***n.*** **1** great fear and disgust that makes one shudder [a movie that filled them with *horror*]. **2** strong dislike; loathing [to have a *horror* of being photographed]. **3** the fact of being horrible [the *horror* of starvation]. **4** something that causes horror [the *horrors* of war].



**horse** (hôrs) ***n.*** **1** a large animal with four legs, solid hoofs, and a flowing mane and tail. People have been riding horses and using them to pull loads since ancient times. **2** a frame on legs for supporting something [a saw*horse*]. **3** a padded block on legs, used in doing exercises in a gymnasium. *See the picture.* ◆***v.*** to supply with a horse or horses. —**horsed, hors′ing** —**horse around,** to take part in horseplay: *a slang phrase.*

**horse·back** (hôrs′bak) ***n.*** the back of a horse. ◆***adv.*** on horseback [to ride *horseback*].

**horse chestnut** **1** a tree with large leaves, clusters of white flowers, and glossy brown seeds growing inside burs. **2** this seed.

**horse·fly** (hôrs′flī) ***n.*** a large fly that sucks the blood of horses and cattle. —*pl.* **horse′flies**

**horse·hair** (hôrs′her) ***n.*** **1** hair from the mane or tail of a horse. **2** a stiff cloth made from this hair. ◆***adj.*** made of or stuffed with horsehair.

**horse·hide** (hôrs′hīd) ***n.*** **1** the hide of a horse. **2** leather made from such a hide.

**horse·man** (hôrs′mən) ***n.*** **1** a man who rides on horseback. **2** a man skilled in riding or caring for horses. —*pl.* **horse′men**

**horse·man·ship** (hôrs′mən ship) ***n.*** skill in riding or handling horses.

☆**horse opera** a movie or play about cowboys, cattle rustlers, etc. in the western U.S.: *a slang term.*

**horse·play** (hôrs′plā) ***n.*** rough play in fun.

**horse·pow·er** (hôrs′pou′ər) ***n.*** a unit for measuring the power of motors or engines. One horsepower equals the force needed to raise 550 pounds at the rate of one foot per second.

**horse·rad·ish** (hôrs′rad′ish) ***n.*** **1** a plant with a long, white root, that has a sharp, burning taste. **2** a relish made by grating this root.

☆**horse sense** ordinary common sense: *used only in everyday talk.*

**horse·shoe** (hôrs′shōō) ***n.*** **1** a flat metal plate shaped like a U, nailed to a horse's hoof to protect it. *See the picture.* **2** anything shaped like this. **3** **horseshoes,** *pl.* a game in which the players toss horseshoes at a stake in the ground.

☆**horseshoe crab** a sea animal that is shaped somewhat like the bottom of a horse's foot and that has a long, spiny tail.

**horse·whip** (hôrs′hwip) ***n.*** a whip for driving horses. ◆***v.*** to lash with a horsewhip. —**horse′whipped, horse′whip·ping**

**horse·wom·an** (hôrs′woom′ən) ***n.*** **1** a woman who rides on horseback. **2** a woman skilled in riding or caring for horses. —*pl.* **horse′wom′en**

**hors·y** or **hors·ey** (hôr′sē) ***adj.*** **1** of or like a horse. **2** fond of horses, horse races, etc. —**hors′i·er, hors′i·est**

**hor·ti·cul·ture** (hôr′tə kul′chər) ***n.*** the science of growing flowers, fruits, and vegetables. —**hor′ti·cul′tur·al** ***adj.*** —**hor′ti·cul′tur·ist** ***n.***

**ho·san·na** (hō zan′ə) ***n., interj.*** a shout of praise to God.

**hose** (hōz) ***n.*** **1** a tube of rubber, plastic, etc., through which water or other fluid is sent [a garden *hose*]. **2** an outer garment like tights, once commonly worn by men. ◆***n.pl.*** stockings or socks [These *hose* are torn.] ◆***v.*** to water with a hose [Will you *hose* the lawn?] —**hosed, hos′ing**

**ho·sier·y** (hō′zhər ē) ***n.*** stockings and socks.

**hos·pice** (häs′pis) ***n.*** a kind of inn where travelers can stop for rest and food, especially one run by monks.

**hos·pi·ta·ble** (häs′pi tə b′l *or* häs pit′ə b′l) ***adj.*** **1** liking to have guests in one's home and treating them in a warm and generous way. **2** having an open mind [*hospitable* to new ideas]. —**hos′pi·ta·bly** ***adv.***

**hos·pi·tal** (häs′pi t′l) ***n.*** a place where doctors, nurses, etc. take care of those who are sick or hurt.

> **Hospital** comes from the Latin word for an inn, or place of rest and entertainment. Later certain monks used the word for places where they cared for pilgrims to the Holy Land. Sometimes such pilgrims would be sick and need medical care. Soon **hospitals** stopped being inns and became only places for the sick.

**hos·pi·tal·i·ty** (häs′pə tal′ə tē) ***n.*** a friendly and generous way of treating guests.

**hos·pi·tal·i·za·tion** (häs′pi t′l ə zā′shən) ***n.*** **1** the act of hospitalizing or the condition of being hospitalized. ☆**2** insurance that pays for some or all of the cost of being in a hospital: *the full name is* **hospitalization insurance.**

**hos·pi·tal·ize** (häs′pi t′l īz′) ***v.*** to put in a hospital [I was *hospitalized* for a week when I broke my leg.] —**hos′pi·tal·ized′, hos′pi·tal·iz′ing**

**host**[1] (hōst) ***n.*** a wafer of unleavened bread eaten at Holy Communion: *also* **Host.**

**host**[2] (hōst) ***n.*** **1** a man who has guests in his own home, or who pays for their entertainment away from home. **2** a man who runs a hotel or inn. **3** an animal or plant on or in which another animal or plant (called a *parasite)* lives.

**host**[3] (hōst) ***n.*** **1** a great number [a *host* of friends]. **2** an army.

**hos·tage** (häs′tij) ***n.*** a person given to or taken by an enemy and held prisoner until certain things are done.

**hos·tel** (häs′t'l) ***n.*** an inn or other place for staying overnight; now often, a shelter for use by hikers.

**hos·tel·ry** (häs′t'l rē) ***n.*** a hotel, inn, or other lodging place. *—pl.* **hos′tel·ries**

**host·ess** (hōs′tis) ***n.*** **1** a woman who has guests in her own home, or who pays for their entertainment away from home. **2** a woman hired by a restaurant to welcome people and show them to their tables.

**hos·tile** (häs′t'l) ***adj.*** **1** of or like an enemy; warlike [surrounded by *hostile* tribes]. **2** having or showing hate or dislike; unfriendly [a *hostile* look]. —**hos′tile·ly** ***adv.***

**hos·til·i·ty** (häs til′ə tē) ***n.*** **1** a feeling of hate or dislike; enmity. **2 hostilities,** *pl.* acts of war; warfare. *—pl.* **hos·til′i·ties**

**hos·tler** (häs′lər *or* äs′lər) ***n.*** a person who takes care of horses at an inn or a stable.

**hot** (hät) ***adj.*** **1** having a high temperature, especially one that is higher than that of the human body; very warm [a *hot* day; a *hot* bath]. **2** that causes a burning feeling in the mouth [*hot* pepper]. **3** full of strong feeling or great activity; angry, violent, eager, etc. [a *hot* temper; a *hot* argument]. **4** close behind [We're *hot* on his trail.] **5** fresh or new: *used only in everyday talk* [*hot* news]. ☆**6** recently stolen: *slang in this meaning* [He was arrested for dealing in *hot* jewelry.] —**hot′ter, hot′test** ◆***adv.*** in a hot way [The fire burns *hot*.] —**hot′ly** ***adv.*** —**hot′ness** ***n.***

**hot·bed** (hät′bed) ***n.*** **1** a warm bed of earth in a frame covered with glass, in which plants can be grown quickly. **2** any place where something develops quickly [a *hotbed* of crime].

☆**hot cake** *another name for* **griddlecake.** —**sell like hot cakes,** to be sold quickly in large quantities; be very popular: *used only in everyday talk.*

☆**hot dog** a frankfurter or wiener, especially one served in a long roll: *used only in everyday talk.*

**ho·tel** (hō tel′) ***n.*** a building where travelers may rent rooms, buy meals, etc.

**hot·head·ed** (hät′hed′id) ***adj.*** very easily excited or made angry; hasty; rash.

**hot·house** (hät′hous) ***n.*** *another name for* **greenhouse.**

☆**hot line** a direct telephone or telegraph line, as between the heads of governments, for use in an emergency.

**hot plate** a small device for cooking, usually with only one or two gas or electric burners.

☆**hot rod** an automobile, usually an old one, in which the power of the engine has been increased to produce greater speed: *a slang term.*

**hot-tem·pered** (hät′tem′pərd) ***adj.*** having the kind of temper that is excited quickly; easily made angry.

**Hot·ten·tot** (hät′'n tät) ***n.*** **1** a member of a black people of southwestern Africa. **2** their language.

**hound** (hound) ***n.*** **1** a hunting dog with long, drooping ears and short hair. **2** any dog. ◆***v.*** to chase or keep after closely [She was *hounded* by reporters.]

**hour** (our) ***n.*** **1** any of the 24 equal parts of a day; 60 minutes. **2** a particular time [At what *hour* shall we meet?] **3** *often* **hours,** *pl.* a particular period of time [the dinner *hour;* the doctor's office *hours*]. **4** distance measured by the time it takes to travel it [He lives two *hours* away from us.] —**after hours,** after the regular hours for business, school, etc.

**hour·glass** (our′glas) ***n.*** a device for measuring time by the trickling of sand from one glass bulb through a small opening to another bulb below it. It takes exactly one hour to empty the top bulb. *See the picture.*

**hour·ly** (our′lē) ***adj.*** **1** done, taken, etc. every hour [an *hourly* dose of medicine]. **2** for every hour [an *hourly* wage of $4.00]. **3** continual; never ending [to live in *hourly* dread of disaster]. ◆***adv.*** **1** every hour [Bells ring *hourly*.] **2** soon [We expect her *hourly*.]

**house** (hous) ***n.*** **1** a building for people to live in. **2** a family or household, especially a royal family [the head of the *house;* the *House* of Tudor]. **3** any building, especially one for sheltering or storing something [the elephant *house* at the zoo; a ware*house;* a court*house*]. **4** a place of business, or a business firm. **5** an audience [The actors played to a large *house*.] **6** a group of persons who make the laws, or the place where it meets [the *House* of Representatives]. *—pl.* **hous′es** (hou′ziz) ◆***v.*** (houz) **1** to give shelter or lodging to [The cottage *houses* a family of five.] **2** to store or shelter [We *housed* their furniture in our attic.] —**housed, hous′ing** —**keep house,** to take care of a home; do housework. —☆**on the house,** given free by the owner of the business [You pay for the meal, but the coffee is *on the house*.]

**house·boat** (hous′bōt) ***n.*** a large boat made to be lived in as a home.

**house·break·ing** (hous′brāk′iŋ) ***n.*** the act of forcing one's way into another's house in order to rob or commit some other crime.

☆**house·coat** (hous′kōt) ***n.*** a long, loose robe worn by a woman at home.

**house·fly** (hous′flī) ***n.*** a common fly with two wings, found in and around houses. It feeds on garbage and food and can spread disease. *—pl.* **house′flies**

**house·hold** (hous′hōld) ***n.*** **1** all the persons who live in one house, especially a family. **2** the home and its affairs [to manage a *household*]. ◆***adj.*** **1** of a household [*household* duties]. **2** common; well-known [That's a *household* expression.]

**house·hold·er** (hous′hōl′dər) ***n.*** **1** a person who owns or occupies a house. **2** the head of a household.

**house·keep·er** (hous′kēp′ər) ***n.*** a woman who manages a home, often one who is hired to do so.

**house·maid** (hous′mād) ***n.*** a woman hired to do housework.

**House of Commons** the lower branch of the parliament of the United Kingdom or Canada.

| | | | | | | | |
|---|---|---|---|---|---|---|---|
| **a** | fat | **ir** | here | **ou** | out | **zh** | leisure |
| **ā** | ape | **ī** | bite, fire | **u** | up | **ŋ** | ring |
| **ä** | car, lot | **ō** | go | **ur** | fur | | a *in* ago |
| **e** | ten | **ô** | law, horn | **ch** | chin | | e *in* agent |
| **er** | care | **oi** | oil | **sh** | she | ə = | i *in* unity |
| **ē** | even | **oo** | look | **th** | thin | | o *in* collect |
| **i** | hit | **ōō** | tool | ***th*** | then | | u *in* focus |

**House of Lords** the upper branch of the parliament of the United Kingdom. It is made up of members of the nobility and clergymen of high rank.

☆**House of Representatives** the lower branch of the U.S. Congress or of the lawmaking body of most States.

**house·top** (hous′täp) ***n.*** the roof of a house.

**house·warm·ing** (hous′wôr′ming) ***n.*** a party given by or for someone moving into a new home.

**house·wife** (hous′wīf) ***n.*** a woman, especially a married woman, who manages the home for her family. —*pl.* **house′wives**

**house·work** (hous′wurk) ***n.*** the work done in keeping house, such as cleaning and cooking.

**hous·ing** (houz′ing) ***n.*** **1** the providing of a home or lodging [the problem of *housing* for older people]. **2** houses or lodgings [new *housing* in the area]. **3** a frame or box in which something is protected [the *housing* of an engine].

**Hous·ton** (hyōōs′tən) a city in southeastern Texas.

**Hous·ton** (hyōōs′tən), **Samuel** 1793–1863; U.S. statesman who was president of the Republic of Texas before it became a State.

**hove** (hōv) *a past tense and past participle of* **heave.**

**hov·el** (huv′'l *or* häv′'l) ***n.*** a small house or hut that is old and broken down.

**hov·er** (huv′ər *or* häv′ər) ***v.*** **1** to stay fluttering in the air near one place [The butterfly *hovered* over the

356 flower.] **2** to stay or wait very close by [Eager fans *hovered* about the movie star.] **3** to be uncertain; waver [to *hover* between hope and despair].

**how** (hou) ***adv.*** **1** in what way [*How* do you start the motor? She taught him *how* to dance.] **2** in what condition [*How* is your mother today?] **3** for what reason; why [*How* is it that you don't know?] **4** to what degree or extent [*How* high will it fly?] **How** is also used to make an exclamation stronger [*How* nice!] —**how about,** how do you think or feel about? —**how so?** why?

**how·be·it** (hou bē′it) ***adv.*** however it may be; nevertheless: *now seldom used.*

hub

hula

football huddle

howdah

**how·dah** (hou′də) ***n.*** a seat for riding on the back of an elephant or camel, often with a canopy. *See the picture.*

**how·dy** (hou′dē) ***interj.*** hello; how do you do: *used as a greeting in everyday talk.*

**Howe** (hou), **E·li·as** (i lī′əs) 1819–1867; the U.S. inventor of a sewing machine.

**how·ev·er** (hou ev′ər) ***adv.*** **1** in whatever way; by whatever means [*However* did you find the place?] **2** no matter how; to whatever degree [*However* hard the task, he succeeded.] ◆***conj.*** nevertheless; but [I'll go; *however,* I don't want to.]

**how·itz·er** (hou′it sər) ***n.*** a short cannon that fires shells in a high curve.

**howl** (houl) ***v.*** **1** to make the long wailing cry of wolves, dogs, etc. **2** to make a sound like this [The boy *howled* in pain.] **3** to shout or laugh in scorn, glee, etc. **4** to drive or force by howling [The audience *howled* the actors off the stage.] ◆***n.*** the sound of howling.

**how·so·ev·er** (hou′sō ev′ər) ***adv.*** no matter how; in whatever way; however.

**hoy·den** (hoid′'n) ***n.*** a bold girl who acts in a rough, noisy way; tomboy.

**HP, H.P., hp, h.p.** *abbreviations for* **horsepower.**

**HQ, H.Q., hq, h.q.** *abbreviations for* **headquarters.**

**hr, h.r., HR** *abbreviations for* **home run** *or* **home runs.**

**hr.** *abbreviation for* **hour** *or* **hours.** —*pl.* **hrs.**

**H.R.** *abbreviation for* **House of Representatives.**

**H.R.H.** *abbreviation for* **Her Royal Highness** *or* **His Royal Highness.**

**H.S.** or **h.s.** *abbreviation for* **high school.**

**ht.** *abbreviation for* **heat, height.**

**hub** (hub) ***n.*** **1** the center part of a wheel. It is the part fastened to the axle, or turning on it. *See the picture.* **2** a center of activity or interest [Detroit is the *hub* of the auto industry.]

**hub·bub** (hub′ub) ***n.*** the noise of many voices mixed together; uproar, as of a crowd.

☆**huck·le·ber·ry** (huk′'l ber′ē) ***n.*** **1** a dark-blue berry that looks like the blueberry. **2** the shrub it grows on. —*pl.* **huck′le·ber′ries**

**huck·ster** (huk′stər) ***n.*** a peddler, especially of fruits and vegetables.

☆**HUD** (hud) *abbreviation for* the Department of **Housing and Urban Development,** a government department that decides how Federal money is to be spent on housing and buildings in the cities and towns.

**hud·dle** (hud′'l) ***v.*** **1** to crowd or push close together [Cows often *huddle* together in a storm. Six of us were *huddled* around one small table.] **2** to draw or hunch oneself up [The child *huddled* under the blanket.] —**hud′dled, hud′dling** ◆***n.*** **1** a confused crowd of people or heap of things [Her clothes lay in a *huddle* on the floor.] ☆**2** a huddling together of a football team to get the signals for the next play. *See the picture.* ☆**3** a private talk: *a slang meaning.*

**Hud·son** (hud′s'n) a river in eastern New York. Its mouth is at New York City.

**Hudson Bay** a bay of the Atlantic that reaches into northeastern Canada.

**hue** (hyōō) ***n.*** color, especially a particular shade of color; tint [orange with a reddish *hue*].

**hue and cry** an outcry of alarm or anger [The new tax was greeted by a great *hue and cry*.]

**huff** (huf) ***n.*** a fit of anger, as because of hurt feelings. ◆***v.*** to blow or puff ["The wolf *huffed* and puffed and blew the house down."] —**huff′y *adj.***

**hug** (hug) ***v.*** **1** to clasp in the arms and hold close to one in a loving way. **2** to squeeze tightly with the forelegs, as a bear does. **3** to keep close to [The car *hugged* the curb.] —**hugged, hug′ging** ◆***n.*** a close embrace.

**huge** (hyo͞oj) ***adj.*** very large; immense [the *huge* trunk of the redwood tree]. *See* SYNONYMS *at* **enormous.** —**huge′ly *adv.*** —**huge′ness *n.***

**Hughes** (hyo͞oz), **Lang·ston** (laŋ′stən) 1902–1967; U.S. poet and writer.

**Hu·go** (hyo͞o′gō), **Victor** 1802–1885; French writer.

**Hu·gue·not** (hyo͞o′gə nät) ***n.*** a French Protestant of the 16th and 17th centuries.

**huh** (hu) ***interj.*** a sound made in showing surprise, scorn, etc. or in asking a question.

☆**hu·la** (ho͞o′lə) or **hu·la-hu·la** (ho͞o′lə ho͞o′lə) ***n.*** a Hawaiian dance using flowing movements of the hands and arms to tell a story. *See the picture.*

**hulk** (hulk) ***n.*** **1** an old ship that is no longer sailed on voyages. **2** a deserted wreck. **3** a big, clumsy person or a big thing that is hard to handle.

**hulk·ing** (hul′kiŋ) ***adj.*** big and clumsy.

**hull** (hul) ***n.*** **1** the outer covering of a seed or fruit, as the shell of nuts, the pod of peas, or the husk of grain. **2** the tiny leaves at the base of some berries, as the strawberry. **3** the main body of a ship. ◆***v.*** to take the hulls from [to *hull* peanuts].

**hul·la·ba·loo** (hul′ə bə lo͞o′) ***n.*** a loud noise of many voices and sounds; uproar.

**hum** (hum) ***v.*** **1** to make a low, steady, buzzing sound like that of a bee or a motor. **2** to sing with the lips closed, not saying the words. **3** to be very busy or active: *used only in everyday talk* [Business is *humming*.] —**hummed, hum′ming** ◆***n.*** the act or sound of humming.

**hu·man** (hyo͞o′mən) ***adj.*** **1** that is a person or that has to do with people in general [a *human* being; *human* affairs]. **2** that is typical of or like people in general [It is a *human* failing to gossip.] ◆***n.*** a person: *some people still prefer the full phrase* **human being.**

**hu·mane** (hyo͞o mān′) ***adj.*** kind, gentle, and showing mercy [*humane* treatment of prisoners]. —**hu·mane′ly *adv.***

**hu·man·ist** (hyo͞o′mə nist) ***n.*** a person whose main interest is human ideals and needs rather than religion. —**hu′man·ism *n.***

**hu·man·i·tar·i·an** (hyo͞o man′ə ter′ē ən) ***n.*** a person who spends much time in doing good for others, especially for those who are suffering; philanthropist. ◆***adj.*** that helps mankind; philanthropic [a *humanitarian* plan to end famines]. *See* SYNONYMS *at* **philanthropic.**

**hu·man·i·ty** (hyo͞o man′ə tē) ***n.*** **1** all human beings; the human race [Could *humanity* survive an atomic war?] **2** kindness or sympathy [She showed her *humanity* by caring for the sick.] **3** the special qualities of all human beings; human nature [It is our common *humanity* to be selfish at one time and unselfish at another.] —*pl.* **hu·man′i·ties** —**the humanities,** studies that deal with human relations and human thought, as literature, philosophy, the fine arts, etc., but not the sciences.

**hu·man·ize** (hyo͞o′mə nīz) ***v.*** to make or become human or humane; make kind, gentle, generous, etc.; civilize. —**hu′man·ized, hu′man·iz·ing**

**hu·man·kind** (hyo͞o′mən kīnd) ***n.*** the human race; all people; humanity.

**hu·man·ly** (hyo͞o′mən lē) ***adv.*** by human means or in a human way [Do all that is *humanly* possible to help them.]

**hu·man·oid** (hyo͞o′mə noid) ***adj.*** like a human being. ◆***n.*** in science fiction, a creature of another planet that is able to reason like a human being.

**hum·ble** (hum′b'l) ***adj.*** **1** knowing one's own weaknesses and faults; not proud or bold; modest or meek [He became *humble* and asked her to forgive him.] **2** low in rank or position; plain and simple; lowly ["Be it ever so *humble,* there's no place like home."] —**hum′bler, hum′blest** ◆***v.*** to make humble; take away the pride, fame, or power of [We *humbled* their team by keeping them from scoring.] —**hum′bled, hum′bling** —**hum′ble·ness *n.*** —**hum′bly *adv.***

> SYNONYMS: **Humble** suggests, in a good sense, that one is never proud or demanding or, in a bad sense, that one has no respect for oneself at all. **Modest** suggests that one is not conceited and never brags or boasts about oneself.

**hum·bug** (hum′bug) ***n.*** **1** something said or done to cheat or trick; fraud; hoax. **2** a person who is not what he or she pretends to be; impostor. ◆***v.*** to cheat; trick. —**hum′bugged, hum′bug·ging** ◆***interj.*** nonsense!

**hum·drum** (hum′drum) ***adj.*** dull or boring because always the same [to lead a *humdrum* life].

**hu·mer·us** (hyo͞o′mər əs) ***n.*** the bone of the upper arm, reaching from the shoulder to the elbow. —*pl.* **hu·mer·i** (hyo͞o′mər ī).

> **Humerus** is the Latin word for the upper arm, but because it sounds so much like **humorous,** we sometimes call the bone of the upper arm the "funny bone."

**hu·mid** (hyo͞o′mid) ***adj.*** full of water vapor; damp; moist [the *humid* jungles of Africa].

**hu·mid·i·fy** (hyo͞o mid′ə fī) ***v.*** to make humid; moisten. —**hu·mid′i·fied, hu·mid′i·fy·ing** —**hu·mid′i·fi·er *n.***

**hu·mid·i·ty** (hyo͞o mid′ə tē) ***n.*** dampness; especially, the amount of moisture in the air.

**hu·mil·i·ate** (hyo͞o mil′ē āt) ***v.*** to take away the pride or dignity of; make feel ashamed [I felt *humiliated* when no one would dance with me.] *See* SYNONYMS *at* **embarrass.** —**hu·mil′i·at·ed, hu·mil′i·at·ing** —**hu·mil′i·a′tion *n.***

**hu·mil·i·ty** (hyo͞o mil′ə tē) ***n.*** the condition of being humble, or not proud; modesty.



| | | | | | | | |
|---|---|---|---|---|---|---|---|
| **a** | fat | **ir** | here | **ou** | out | **zh** | leisure |
| **ā** | ape | **ī** | bite, fire | **u** | up | **ŋ** | ring |
| **ä** | car, lot | **ō** | go | **ur** | fur | | a *in* ago |
| **e** | ten | **ô** | law, horn | **ch** | chin | | e *in* agent |
| **er** | care | **oi** | oil | **sh** | she | **ə** = | i *in* unity |
| **ē** | even | **oo** | look | **th** | thin | | o *in* collect |
| **i** | hit | **o͞o** | tool | ***th*** | then | | u *in* focus |

☆**hum·ming·bird** (hum′iŋ bʉrd′) ***n.*** a tiny bird with a long, thin bill, that it uses to suck nectar from flowers. Its wings move very fast, with a humming sound, and it can hover in the air. *See the picture.*

**hum·mock** (hum′ək) ***n.*** a low, rounded hill; mound; knoll.

**hu·mor** (hyo͞o′mər) ***n.*** **1** the quality of being funny or amusing [a story full of *humor*]. **2** the ability to see or express what is funny or amusing [She has no sense of *humor* and rarely laughs.] *See* SYNONYMS *at* **wit**. **3** a state of mind; mood [He was in a bad *humor* and glared at us.] **4** whim or fancy [She ate only when it pleased her *humor*.] ◆***v.*** to give in to; give whatever another wishes; indulge [If you don't *humor* him, he starts to grumble.] *See* SYNONYMS *at* **indulge**. —**out of humor**, in a bad mood; cross.

**Humor** comes from the Latin word *humor*, meaning fluid. Humor is still a medical term for a fluid in the body, such as the blood, lymph, or bile. People used to think that one's mood, or state of mind, was caused by whichever humor in the body was the strongest.

**hu·mor·ist** (hyo͞o′mər ist) ***n.*** a person who says amusing things or tells funny stories well.

**hu·mor·ous** (hyo͞o′mər əs) ***adj.*** funny or amusing; comical. —**hu′mor·ous·ly** ***adv.***

**hu·mour** (hyo͞o′mər) ***n., v.*** *the British spelling of* **humor**.



**hump** (hump) ***n.*** **1** a round lump on the back, as of a camel. **2** a mound; hummock. ◆***v.*** to form into a hump; arch; hunch [A cat often *humps* its back.]

**hump·back** (hump′bak) ***n.*** **1** a person with a hump on the back, caused by a curving of the spine; hunchback. **2** a back with such a hump. —**hump′backed** ***adj.***

**humph** (humf) ***interj., n.*** a snorting sound made to show doubt, surprise, disgust, etc.

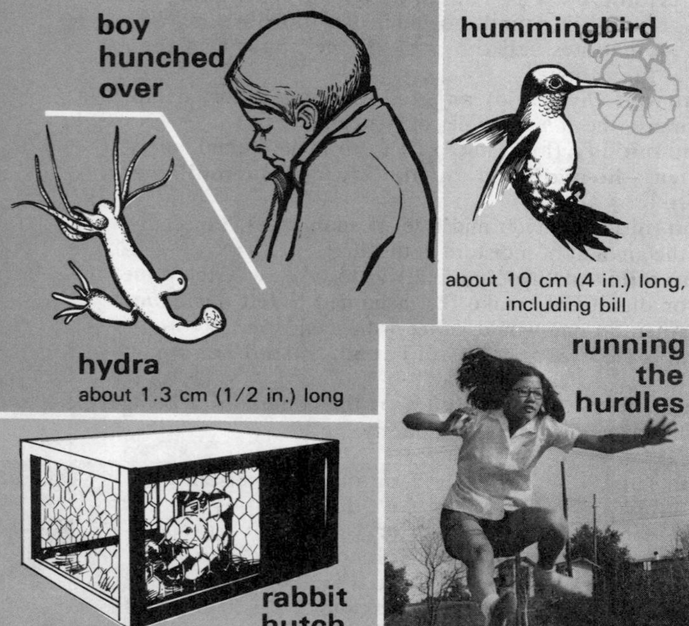


about 10 cm (4 in.) long, including bill

about 1.3 cm (1/2 in.) long

**hu·mus** (hyo͞o′məs) ***n.*** brown or black soil made up of decayed leaves, plants, etc.

**Hun** (hun) ***n.*** a member of an Asian people who invaded Europe in the 4th and 5th centuries A.D.

**hunch** (hunch) ***v.*** **1** to draw one's body up so as to form a hump [She *hunched* herself over her desk.] *See the picture.* **2** to push forward by jerks [He *hunched* his way through the crowd.] ◆***n.*** **1** a hump on the back. **2** a feeling about something not based on known facts: *used only in everyday talk* [I have a *hunch* she'll be there.]

**hunch·back** (hunch′bak) ***n.*** *another word for* **humpback**.

**hun·dred** (hun′drid) ***n., adj.*** ten times ten; the number 100.

**hun·dred·fold** (hun′drid fōld′) ***adj., adv., n.*** a hundred times as much or as many.

**hun·dredth** (hun′dridth) ***adj.*** coming after ninety-nine others; 100th in order. ◆***n.*** **1** the hundredth one. **2** one of 100 equal parts of something; 1/100.

**hun·dred·weight** (hun′drid wāt′) ***n.*** a unit of weight, equal to 100 pounds in the U.S. and 112 pounds in England.

**hung** (huŋ) *past tense and past participle of* **hang**.

**Hung.** *abbreviation for* **Hungarian** *or* **Hungary**.

**Hun·ga·ry** (huŋ′gər ē) a country in central Europe. —**Hun·gar′i·an** (huŋ ger′ē ən) ***adj., n.***

**hun·ger** (huŋ′gər) ***n.*** **1** the discomfort or weakness caused by having little or nothing to eat. **2** an appetite or need for food [The meal satisfied their *hunger*.] **3** any strong desire; craving [a *hunger* for knowledge]. ◆***v.*** **1** to be hungry; need food. **2** to have a strong desire; crave [to *hunger* for love].

**hun·gry** (huŋ′grē) ***adj.*** **1** wanting or needing food [Cold weather makes me *hungry*.] **2** having a strong desire; eager [*hungry* for praise]. —**hun′gri·er, hun′gri·est** —**hun′gri·ly** ***adv.*** —**hun′gri·ness** ***n.***

SYNONYMS: **Hungry** is the general word for wanting or needing food. To be **famished** is to be so hungry that one is weak or in pain. To be **starved** is to have had no food or so little food over a long period of time that one is wasting away and will soon die. Both **famished** and **starved** are sometimes used in an exaggerated way when only **hungry** is meant.

**hunk** (huŋk) ***n.*** a large piece or lump: *used only in everyday talk* [a *hunk* of meat].

**hunt** (hunt) ***v.*** **1** to set out to kill wild animals or birds for food or as a sport. **2** to try to find; search; seek [to *hunt* for buried treasure]. **3** to chase or drive [The mob *hunted* him out of town.] ◆***n.*** **1** the act of hunting; a chase or search [a fox *hunt;* a treasure *hunt*]. **2** a group of people hunting together.

**hunt·er** (hun′tər) ***n.*** **1** a person who hunts. **2** a horse or dog trained for use in hunting.

**hunt·ing** (hun′tiŋ) ***n.*** the act of a person or animal that hunts. ◆***adj.*** used by one who hunts.

**hunt·ress** (hun′tris) ***n.*** a woman who hunts.

**hunts·man** (hunts′mən) ***n.*** **1** a man who hunts. **2** the manager of a hunt, especially a fox hunt. —*pl.* **hunts′men**

**hur·dle** (hʉr′d'l) ***n.*** **1** any of the small fences or frames that runners or horses must jump over in a special race, called **the hurdles**. *See the picture.* **2** something difficult that has to be overcome [Passing the final exams is our last *hurdle.*] ⬥**v.** **1** to jump over [to *hurdle* a fence]. **2** to overcome something difficult. —**hur′dled, hur′dling**

**hur·dy-gur·dy** (hur′dē gur′dē) **n.** *another name for* **barrel organ.** —*pl.* **hur′dy-gur′dies**

**hurl** (hurl) **v.** **1** to throw with great force [to *hurl* a rock]. *See* SYNONYMS *at* **throw.** **2** to say in a strong or angry way [to *hurl* insults]. —**hurl′er n.**

**hurl·y-burl·y** (hur′lē bur′lē) **n.** an uproar or confusion; hubbub.

**Hu·ron** (hyoor′ən), **Lake** one of the Great Lakes, between Lake Michigan and Lake Erie.

**hur·rah** (hə rô′ *or* hə rä′) ***interj., n.*** a word called out to show joy, approval, etc. ⬥**v.** to shout "hurrah"; cheer. *Also* **hur·ray** (hə rā′).

**hur·ri·cane** (hur′ə kān) **n.** a very strong windstorm, often with heavy rain, in which the wind blows in a circle at 73 or more miles per hour. Hurricanes usually start in the West Indies and move northward.

**hur·ried** (hur′ēd) **adj.** done or acting in a hurry; hasty [We ate a *hurried* lunch.] —**hur′ried·ly adv.**

**hur·ry** (hur′ē) **v.** **1** to move, send, or carry quickly or too quickly [You fell because you *hurried.* A taxi *hurried* us home.] **2** to make happen or be done more quickly [Please try to *hurry* those letters.] **3** to try to make move or act faster [Don't *hurry* me when I'm eating.] —**hur′ried, hur′ry·ing** ⬥**n.** **1** the act of hurrying; rush or haste [In my *hurry* I left the door open.] **2** need for hurrying [There's no *hurry* about repaying me.]

**hurt** (hurt) **v.** **1** to cause pain or injury to; wound [The fall *hurt* my leg.] **2** to have pain [My head *hurts.*] **3** to harm or damage in some way [Water won't *hurt* this table top.] **4** to offend or make unhappy [He was *hurt* by the unkind remarks.] —**hurt, hurt′ing** ⬥**n.** pain, injury, or harm [Warm water will ease the *hurt.*]

**hurt·ful** (hurt′fəl) **adj.** causing hurt; harmful.

**hur·tle** (hurt′′l) **v.** to move or throw with great speed or much force [The racing cars *hurtled* through the town.] —**hur′tled, hur′tling**

**hus·band** (huz′bənd) **n.** the man to whom a woman is married. ⬥**v.** to manage carefully so that nothing is wasted [to *husband* one's money].

> **Husband** comes from an Old English word that means "householder." Since most householders were married, the word later came to mean "a married man." The verb still carries the idea of managing something, as a household, in a careful way.

**hus·band·ry** (huz′bən drē) **n.** **1** a careful managing so that nothing is wasted; thrift. **2** the business of running a farm; farming [Animal *husbandry* is the raising of farm animals.]

**hush** (hush) **v.** to make or become quiet [I *hushed* the baby. *Hush,* or you will wake her.] ⬥**n.** silence; quiet [A sudden *hush* fell over the room.] —**hush up, 1** to keep quiet. **2** to keep people from talking about; keep secret [to *hush up* a scandal].

☆**hush puppy** a small, fried ball of cornmeal dough.

**husk** (husk) **n.** the dry covering of certain fruits and seeds, as of an ear of corn. ⬥**v.** to remove the husk from [to *husk* corn]. —**husk′er n.**

☆**hus·ky**[1] (hus′kē) **n.** a strong dog used for pulling sleds in the Arctic. —*pl.* **hus′kies** *Also* **Hus′ky.**

**husk·y**[2] (hus′kē) **adj.** **1** sounding deep and hoarse; rough [a *husky* voice]. ☆**2** big and strong [a *husky* boxer]. —**husk′i·er, husk′i·est** —**husk′i·ly adv.** —**husk′i·ness n.**

**hus·sar** (hoo zär′) **n.** a member of certain European cavalry troops with showy uniforms.

**hus·sy** (huz′ē *or* hus′ē) **n.** **1** a woman of low morals. **2** a bold, saucy girl. —*pl.* **hus′sies**

**hus·tle** (hus′′l) **v.** **1** to push one's way quickly [We *hustled* through the crowd.] **2** to force in a rough and hurried way [The waiter *hustled* the rowdy customer out the door.] **3** to go or do quickly or with much energy: *used only in everyday talk* [You'll have to *hustle* to catch the bus.] ☆**4** to get, sell, etc. by bold, sometimes dishonest, means: *slang in this meaning.* —**hus′tled, hus′tling** ⬥**n.** the act of hustling. —**hus′tler n.**

**hut** (hut) **n.** a little house or cabin of the plainest kind.

**hutch** (huch) **n.** **1** a pen or coop for small animals. *See the picture.* **2** a chest for storing things. **3** a china cabinet with open shelves on top.

**Hwang Ho** (hwäng′ hō′) a river in northern China, flowing into the Yellow Sea.

**Hwy.** or **hwy.** *abbreviation for* **highway.**

**hy·a·cinth** (hī′ə sinth) **n.** a plant of the lily family, with long, narrow leaves and a spike of sweet-smelling flowers shaped like bells.

**hy·brid** (hī′brid) **n.** **1** the offspring of two animals or plants of different species or varieties [The mule is a *hybrid,* being the offspring of a donkey and a horse.] **2** anything of mixed background [The word "hydroplane" is a *hybrid* because "hydro-" comes from Greek and "plane" comes from Latin.] ⬥**adj.** being a hybrid [*hybrid* corn].

**hy·brid·ize** (hī′brə dīz) **v.** to breed or produce hybrids; crossbreed [to *hybridize* corn]. —**hy′brid·ized, hy′brid·iz·ing** —**hy′brid·i·za′tion n.**

**Hy·der·a·bad** (hī′dər ə bad′ *or* hī′dər ə bäd′) a city in south-central India.

**hy·dra** (hī′drə) **n.** a tiny water animal with a body shaped like a tube. Any part that is cut off will grow into a whole new animal. *See the picture.* —*pl.* **hy′dras** or **hy·drae** (hī′drē)

> In Greek myths, the Hydra was a serpent with nine heads. When a head was cut off, two others grew in its place. Hercules killed the Hydra by burning each neck after its head was cut off.

**hy·dran·gea** (hī drān′jə) **n.** a shrub with large balls of white, blue, or pink flowers.

☆**hy·drant** (hī′drənt) **n.** a closed pipe at a street curb, with a spout that can be opened up so as to draw water from a main waterline; fireplug.

**hy·drate** (hī′drāt) **n.** a chemical compound that contains a definite number of water molecules [Plaster of Paris is a *hydrate.*]

**hy·drau·lic** (hī drô′lik) **adj.** **1** worked by the force of a moving liquid [*hydraulic* brakes]. **2** hardening under



| | | | | | | | |
|---|---|---|---|---|---|---|---|
| **a** | fat | **ir** | here | **ou** | out | **zh** | leisure |
| **ā** | ape | **ī** | bite, fire | **u** | up | **ng** | ring |
| **ä** | car, lot | **ō** | go | **ur** | fur | | a *in* ago |
| **e** | ten | **ô** | law, horn | **ch** | chin | | e *in* agent |
| **er** | care | **oi** | oil | **sh** | she | **ə** = | i *in* unity |
| **ē** | even | **oo** | look | **th** | thin | | o *in* collect |
| **i** | hit | **ōō** | tool | ***th*** | then | | u *in* focus |

water [*hydraulic* cement]. **3** having to do with hydraulics. —**hy·drau′li·cal·ly** ***adv.***

**hy·drau·lics** (hī drô′liks) ***n.pl.*** the science that studies how water and other liquids act at rest or in motion and how the force of moving liquids can be used to run machines: *used with a singular verb.*

**hy·dro·car·bon** (hī′drə kär′bən) ***n.*** any compound made up of only hydrogen and carbon [Benzene is a *hydrocarbon.*]

**hy·dro·chlo·ric acid** (hī′drə klôr′ik) a strong acid formed of hydrogen and chlorine.

**hy·dro·e·lec·tric** (hī′drō i lek′trik) ***adj.*** producing electricity by water power or having to do with electricity so produced.

**hy·dro·foil** (hī′drə foil) ***n.*** a blade like a small wing on the hull of some boats. At high speeds the boat skims along on the hydrofoils.

**hy·dro·gen** (hī′drə jən) ***n.*** a gas that has no color or smell and burns very easily. It is a chemical element and the lightest of all known substances.

**hy·dro·gen·ate** (hī′drə jə nāt) ***v.*** to treat with hydrogen [Vegetable oils can be *hydrogenated* to produce a solid fat.] —**hy′dro·gen′at·ed, hy′dro·gen·at·ing**

☆**hydrogen bomb** a very destructive kind of bomb. Its enormous force comes from the energy given off when atoms of a heavy form of hydrogen are fused by explosion of a nuclear-fission unit in the bomb.

**hy·drom·e·ter** (hī dräm′ə tər) ***n.*** an instrument for finding out the weight of any liquid as compared with that of water.



**hy·dro·pho·bi·a** (hī′drə fō′bē ə) ***n.*** *another name for* **rabies.**

> **Hydrophobia** comes from a Greek word that means "fear of water." A person who has rabies is usually unable to swallow water.

**hy·dro·plane** (hī′drə plān) ***n.*** **1** a small motorboat that skims along on the back of its hull at high speeds. **2** *another name for* **seaplane.**

☆**hy·dro·pon·ics** (hī′drə pän′iks) ***n.pl.*** the growing of plants in water with minerals added, instead of in soil: *used with a singular verb.*

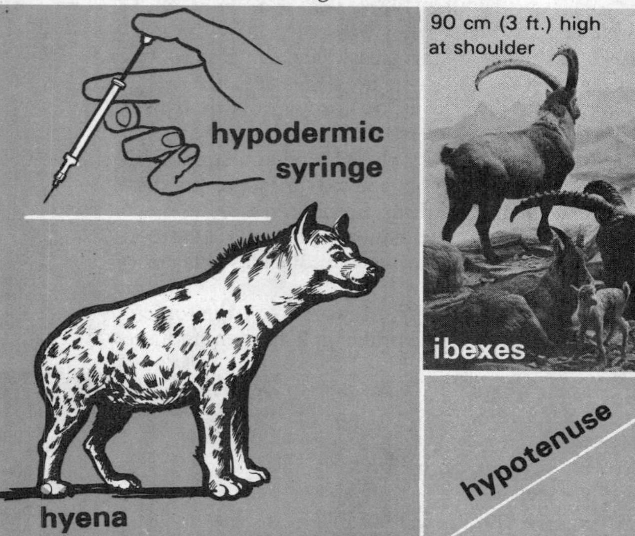


ibexes
90 cm (3 ft.) high at shoulder

hyena
75 cm (30 in.) high at shoulder

**hy·dro·ther·a·py** (hī′drō ther′ə pē) ***n.*** the treatment of bodily disorders or injuries by whirlpool baths, compresses, or other uses of water.

**hy·e·na** (hī ē′nə) ***n.*** a wild animal of Africa and Asia that looks like a large dog. It feeds on the remains of dead animals and has a shrill cry. *See the picture.*

**hy·giene** (hī′jēn) ***n.*** the science that has to do with keeping people healthy; also, a system of rules for keeping healthy and preventing disease.

**hy·gi·en·ic** (hī′jē en′ik *or* hī jē′nik) ***adj.*** **1** free from dirt and germs that might cause disease; sanitary [This farm has *hygienic* dairy equipment.] **2** having to do with hygiene or health. —**hy′gi·en′i·cal·ly** ***adv.***

**hy·gi·en·ist** (hī′jē ə nist *or* hī jē′nist) ***n.*** an expert in hygiene, or the rules of health.

**hy·ing** (hī′iŋ) *a present participle of* **hie.**

**Hy·men** (hī′mən) the Greek god of marriage.

**hymn** (him) ***n.*** **1** a song praising or honoring God. **2** any song of praise.

**hym·nal** (him′n′l) ***n.*** a book of hymns for use in a church: *also* **hymn′book.**

**hyper-** *a prefix meaning* over, more than normal, too much [A *hypercritical* person is too critical.]

**hy·per·ac·tive** (hī′pər ak′tiv) ***adj.*** very active, often more active than is usual or normal [a *hyperactive* child].

**hy·per·bo·le** (hī pur′bə lē) ***n.*** an exaggeration, used to make something seem greater or better than it is [It is *hyperbole* to say "John is as strong as an ox."] —**hy·per·bol·ic** (hī′pər bäl′ik) ***adj.***

> **Hyperbole** comes from a Greek word that means "a throwing over or beyond." If one uses hyperbole, one throws an idea beyond what it originally meant. Hyperbole is used for greater force.

**hy·per·crit·i·cal** (hī′pər krit′i k′l) ***adj.*** too critical; too hard to please.

**hy·per·son·ic** (hī′pər sän′ik) ***adj.*** of or moving at a speed at least five times the speed of sound.

**hy·per·ten·sion** (hī′pər ten′shən) ***n.*** blood pressure that is much higher than normal.

**hy·phen** (hī′f′n) ***n.*** the mark (-), used between the parts of a compound word (as *court-martial),* or between the parts of a word divided at the end of a line. ◆***v.*** to hyphenate.

**hy·phen·ate** (hī′f′n āt) ***v.*** to join or write with a hyphen. —**hy′phen·at·ed, hy′phen·at·ing** —**hy′phen·a′tion** ***n.***

**hyp·no·sis** (hip nō′sis) ***n.*** the condition like sleep into which a hypnotist can put people.

**hyp·not·ic** (hip nät′ik) ***adj.*** **1** causing sleep [*hypnotic* drugs]. **2** of, like, or causing hypnosis [*hypnotic* suggestion; a *hypnotic* trance]. ◆***n.*** **1** any drug that causes sleep. **2** a hypnotized person or one who is easily hypnotized. —**hyp·not′i·cal·ly** ***adv.***

**hyp·no·tism** (hip′nə tiz'm) ***n.*** the act or science of hypnotizing people.

**hyp·no·tist** (hip′nə tist) ***n.*** a person who hypnotizes others.

**hyp·no·tize** (hip′nə tīz) ***v.*** to put someone into a condition like sleep, in which that person will do or say the things suggested by the one who has put the person into this condition. —**hyp′no·tized, hyp′no·tiz·ing**

**hy·po** (hī′pō) ***n.*** ☆*a shorter word for* **hypodermic.** —*pl.* **hy′pos**

**hy·po·chon·dri·a** (hī′pə kän′drē ə) ***n.*** worry or anxiety about one's health that is so great that one may imagine oneself to have some sickness.

**hy·po·chon·dri·ac** (hī′pə kän′drē ak) ***n.*** a person who has hypochondria.

**hy·poc·ri·sy** (hi päk′rə sē) ***n.*** the condition of being a hypocrite or the action of a hypocrite. *—pl.* **hy·poc′ri·sies**

**hyp·o·crite** (hip′ə krit) ***n.*** a person who pretends to be good, pious, sympathetic, etc. without really being so. —**hyp′o·crit′i·cal *adj.***

**hy·po·der·mic** (hī′pə dur′mik) ***n.*** **1** a glass tube with a hollow needle at one end and a plunger, used for forcing a medicine or drug under the skin: *the full name is* **hypodermic syringe**. *See the picture.* **2** the forcing of a medicine or drug under the skin in this way: *the full name is* **hypodermic injection.** ◆***adj.*** under the skin.

**hy·pot·e·nuse** (hī pät′'n ōōs *or* hī pät′'n yōōs) ***n.*** in a triangle having a right angle, the side that is opposite the right angle. *See the picture.*

**hy·poth·e·sis** (hī päth′ə sis) ***n.*** an unproved idea taken for granted for the time being because it may explain certain facts or can be used as the basis for reasoning, study, etc. [the *hypothesis* that sunspots affect our weather].

**hy·po·thet·i·cal** (hī′pə thet′i k'l) ***adj.*** based on a hypothesis; supposed [a *hypothetical* case]. —**hy′po·thet′i·cal·ly *adv.***

**hys·sop** (his′əp) ***n.*** **1** a low shrub with blue flowers. Its leaves are used in medicine and for flavoring. **2** in the Bible, a plant used in ancient Jewish religious ceremonies.

**hys·te·ri·a** (his tir′ē ə) ***n.*** **1** a sickness of the mind in which a person may become blind, paralyzed, etc. without any real, physical cause. **2** a wild fit of laughing, crying, etc. that gets out of control.

**hys·ter·i·cal** (his ter′i k'l) ***adj.*** **1** of or like hysteria. **2** having or likely to have wild fits of laughing, crying, etc. **3** very funny or comical. *Also* **hys·ter′ic.** —**hys·ter′i·cal·ly *adv.***

**hys·ter·ics** (his ter′iks) ***n.pl.*** a wild fit of laughing, crying, etc. that is out of control.

**Hz** or **hz** *abbreviation for* **hertz.**

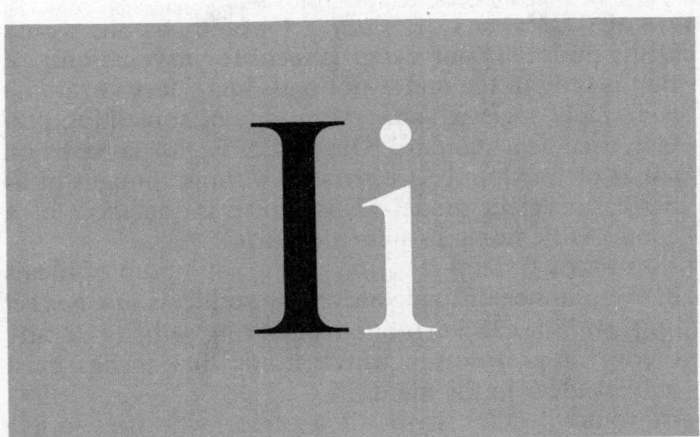

**I, i** (ī) ***n.*** the ninth letter of the English alphabet. *—pl.* **I's, i's** (īz)

**I** (ī) ***n.*** a Roman numeral for the figure 1.

**I** (ī) ***pron.*** the person speaking or writing [*I* like candy. It is *I*.] *—pl.* **we**

**I** *the symbol for the chemical element* iodine.

**I.** or **i.** *abbreviation for* **island** *or* **islands.**

**Ia.** or **IA** *abbreviation for* **Iowa.**

**i·am·bic** (ī am′bik) ***adj.*** describing poetry made up of measures of two syllables each, with the accent on the second syllable ["Whose woods′/ these are′/ I think′/ I know′" is an *iambic* line.]

**-i·an** (ē ən *or* yən) *a suffix meaning:* **1** of or having to do with [*Reptilian* fossils are the fossils of reptiles.] **2** born or living in [An *Italian* is a person born or living in Italy.]

**I·be·ri·a** (ī bir′ē ə) the peninsula in southwestern Europe that includes Spain and Portugal: *a Latin name.* —**I·be′ri·an *adj., n.***

**i·bex** (ī′beks) ***n.*** a wild goat that lives in the mountains of Europe, Asia, and Africa. The male has large horns that curve backward. *See the picture.*

**i·bis** (ī′bis) ***n.*** a large wading bird with long legs and a long, curved bill, usually found in warm regions. The ibis was sacred to the ancient Egyptians.

**-i·ble** (i b'l) *a suffix meaning:* **1** that can be [A *divisible* number can be divided.] **2** tending to [A *sensible* idea tends to make sense.] 

**Ib·sen** (ib′s'n), **Hen·rik** (hen′rik) 1828–1906; Norwegian poet and writer of plays.

**-ic** (ik) *a suffix meaning:* **1** of or like [An *angelic* voice is like that of an angel.] **2** made by or caused by [A *photographic* copy is made by taking a photograph.] **3** made up of or containing [An *alcoholic* drink is one containing alcohol.]

**-i·cal** (i k'l) *a suffix meaning the same as* **-ic.** Some words have a different meaning if the suffix is *-ical* instead of *-ic* [*Economical* means "thrifty," but *economic* does not.]

**ICBM** intercontinental ballistic missile.

**ICC** or **I.C.C.** Interstate Commerce Commission.

**ice** (īs) ***n.*** **1** water frozen solid by cold [Water turns to *ice* at 0°C.] **2** anything that looks like frozen water [Dry *ice* is carbon dioxide made solid.] **3** a frozen dessert, usually made of water, fruit juice, egg white, and sugar. ◆***v.*** **1** to change into ice; freeze [The lake *iced* over.] **2** to cover or fill with ice, especially to cool [to *ice* a drink]. **3** to cover with icing, or frosting [to *ice* a cake]. —**iced, ic′ing**

**Ice.** *abbreviation for* **Iceland** *or* **Icelandic.**

**ice age** any period of time when a large part of the earth was covered with glaciers.

| | | | |
|---|---|---|---|
| **a** fat | **ir** here | **ou** out | **zh** leisure |
| **ā** ape | **ī** bite, fire | **u** up | **ng** ring |
| **ä** car, lot | **ō** go | **ur** fur | a *in* ago |
| **e** ten | **ô** law, horn | **ch** chin | e *in* agent |
| **er** care | **oi** oil | **sh** she | **ə** = i *in* unity |
| **ē** even | **oo** look | **th** thin | o *in* collect |
| **i** hit | **ōō** tool | ***th*** then | u *in* focus |

iceberg

iguana
up to 1.5 m (5 ft.) long, including tail

icebreaker

igloo

**ice·berg** (īs′burg) ***n.*** a mass of ice broken off from a glacier and floating in the sea. The larger part of an iceberg is under water. *See the picture.*

**ice·boat** (īs′bōt) ***n.*** **1** a light frame or boat on runners, with sails, propeller, etc. for moving over ice. **2** *another name for* **icebreaker**.

362 ☆**ice·box** (īs′bäks) ***n.*** a box or cabinet with ice in it for keeping food cold.

☆**ice·break·er** (īs′brā′kər) ***n.*** a sturdy ship for breaking a channel through ice. *See the picture.*

☆**ice cream** a frozen food made of cream or milk, sugar, flavoring, etc.

**ice hockey** *same as* **hockey** *in meaning* 1.

**Ice·land** (īs′lənd) a country on a large island in the North Atlantic, between Norway and Greenland. —**Ice′land·er** ***n.***

**Ice·land·ic** (īs lan′dik) ***adj.*** of Iceland or its people. ◆***n.*** the language of Iceland.

☆**ice milk** a frozen dessert like ice cream, but containing less butterfat.

**ice pack** **1** a large, floating mass of pieces of ice that have broken and then frozen together. **2** a rubber bag or cloth filled with crushed ice, to put on a swollen or bruised part of the body.

☆**ice pick** a metal tool with a sharp point for breaking up ice into pieces.

**ice skate** a skate for skating on ice: *see* **skate**[1]. —**ice′-skate′** ***v.*** —**ice skater**

**i·ci·cle** (ī′si k'l) ***n.*** a hanging stick of ice formed by water freezing as it drips down.

**ic·ing** (ī′siŋ) ***n.*** a mixture of sugar, butter, flavoring, etc. as for covering cakes; frosting.

☆**ick·y** (ik′ē) ***adj.*** **1** unpleasantly sticky or sweet. **2** sickening or disgusting. *This is a slang word.* —**ick′i·er, ick′i·est** —**ick′i·ness** ***n.***

**i·con** (ī′kän) ***n.*** **1** an image or picture. **2** in the Orthodox Eastern Church, a sacred image or picture of Jesus, Mary, a saint, etc.

**i·con·o·clast** (ī kän′ə klast) ***n.*** **1** a person who is against the worship of images. **2** a person who attacks or makes fun of the things most people believe in or accept without questioning. —**i·con′o·clas′tic** ***adj.***

**-ics** (iks) *a suffix meaning:* **1** a study or science [*Dietetics* is the study of proper diets.] **2** practice or system [*Athletics* is the practice or system of athletic sports.]

**i·cy** (ī′sē) ***adj.*** **1** full of or covered with ice [*icy* streets]. **2** like ice; slippery or very cold [*icy* fingers]. **3** cold in feeling; unfriendly [an *icy* look]. —**i′ci·er, i′ci·est** —**i′ci·ly** ***adv.*** —**i′ci·ness** ***n.***

**ID, I.D.** (ī′dē′) ***n.*** ☆a card (**ID card**) or document, as a birth certificate, that serves as identification of a person, proves his age, etc. —*pl.* **ID's, I.D.'s**

**I'd** (īd) **1** I had. **2** I would. **3** I should.

**I·da·ho** (ī′də hō) a State in the northwestern part of the U.S.: abbreviated **Ida., ID**

**i·de·a** (ī dē′ə) ***n.*** **1** something one thinks, knows, imagines, feels, etc.; belief or thought. **2** a plan or purpose [an *idea* for making money].

> SYNONYMS: **Idea** means anything that may be in the mind as an object of knowledge or thought. **Thought** means any idea, whether or not expressed, that occurs to the mind when thinking things out [She rarely speaks her *thoughts*.] An **impression** is an idea that is not quite clear and has been brought to mind by something seen or heard [I had the *impression* that Juan is sad.]

**i·de·al** (ī dē′əl *or* ī dēl′) ***adj.*** **1** exactly as one would wish; perfect [Your camp is *ideal* for a vacation.] **2** that is only in the mind; not real; imaginary [A utopia is an *ideal* society.] ◆***n.*** **1** an idea of something perfect, used as a standard [Our Bill of Rights is based on *ideals* of freedom.] **2** a person or thing thought of as perfect; perfect model [This house is the *ideal* of a comfortable home.] —**i·de′al·ly** ***adv.***

**i·de·al·ism** (ī dē′əl iz'm) ***n.*** **1** the setting up of ideals or the practice of living according to ideals one has set up [*Idealism* can keep one from being selfish.] **2** any theory of philosophy which holds that things exist only as ideas in the mind.

**i·de·al·ist** (ī dē′əl ist) ***n.*** **1** a person who tries to live according to ideals; often, one who follows ideals to the point of not being practical. **2** a person who believes in a philosophy of idealism. —**i′de·al·is′tic** ***adj.*** —**i′de·al·is′ti·cal·ly** ***adv.***

**i·de·al·ize** (ī dē′ə līz) ***v.*** to think of as or make seem ideal or perfect [Some people *idealize* their childhood after they are grown up.] —**i·de′al·ized, i·de′al·iz·ing** —**i·de′al·i·za′tion** ***n.***

**i·den·ti·cal** (ī den′ti k'l) ***adj.*** **1** the very same [This is the *identical* house where I was born.] **2** exactly alike [These two pictures are *identical*.] *See* SYNONYMS *at* **same**. —**i·den′ti·cal·ly** ***adv.***

**i·den·ti·fi·ca·tion** (ī den′tə fi kā′shən) ***n.*** **1** anything that identifies a person or thing [Fingerprints are used as *identification*.] **2** an identifying or being identified.

**i·den·ti·fy** (ī den′tə fī) ***v.*** **1** to think of or treat as the same [The Roman god Jupiter is *identified* with the Greek god Zeus.] **2** to show or prove to be a certain person or thing [She was *identified* by a scar on her chin.] **3** to connect closely [The senator is now *identified* with the new political party.] —**i·den′ti·fied, i·den′ti·fy·ing**

**i·den·ti·ty** (ī den′tə tē) ***n.*** **1** the condition of being the same or exactly alike; sameness [Our two groups are united by an *identity* of interests.] **2** who or what a person or thing is; the fact of being oneself or itself and none other [The *identity* of the thief was hidden by a mask.] —*pl.* **i·den′ti·ties**

**i·de·ol·o·gy** (ī′dē äl′ə jē *or* id′ē äl′ə jē) ***n.*** the teachings, beliefs, or ideas of a person, group, etc. [a political *ideology*]. —*pl.* **i′de·ol′o·gies**

**ides** (īdz) ***n.pl.*** in the ancient Roman calendar, the fifteenth day of March, May, July, or October, or the thirteenth of the other months.

**id·i·o·cy** (id′ē ə sē) ***n.*** **1** great foolishness or stupidity. **2** an idiotic act or remark. —*pl.* **id′i·o·cies**

**id·i·om** (id′ē əm) ***n.*** **1** a phrase or expression that has a meaning different from what the words suggest in their usual meaning ["To catch one's eye," meaning "to get one's attention," is an *idiom.*] **2** the way in which a certain people, writer, group, etc. puts words together to express meaning [the Italian *idiom;* the *idiom* of Shakespeare]. —**id·i·o·mat·ic** (id′ē ə mat′ik) ***adj.*** —**id′i·o·mat′i·cal·ly *adv.***

**id·i·o·syn·cra·sy** (id′ē ə siŋ′krə sē) ***n.*** an unusual or peculiar way of acting or being that a certain person or group has [Wearing only white was an *idiosyncrasy* of Emily Dickinson.] —*pl.* **id′i·o·syn′cra·sies**

> **Idiosyncrasy** comes from two Greek words that mean "to mix together." A person may have a peculiar way of acting, or idiosyncrasy, because of the way things are mixed together to make that person's character.

**id·i·ot** (id′ē ət) ***n.*** **1** a person who is mentally retarded to a severe extent: *psychologists no longer use this word.* **2** a very foolish or stupid person.

**id·i·ot·ic** (id′ē ät′ik) ***adj.*** of or like an idiot; very foolish or stupid. —**id′i·ot′i·cal·ly *adv.***

**i·dle** (ī′d'l) ***adj.*** **1** not working; not busy [*idle* machines]. **2** not wanting to work; lazy [The *idle* bums sat in the park.] **3** having no use or value; worthless; useless [*idle* talk; *idle* rumors]. —**i′dler, i′dlest** •***v.*** **1** to spend time doing nothing or doing useless things [We *idled* away the summer.] **2** to run slowly and out of gear [Let the motor *idle* to warm it up.] **3** to make inactive or unemployed [The strike *idled* thousands of workers.] —**i′dled, i′dling** —**i′dle·ness *n.*** —**i′dly *adv.***

**i·dler** (īd′lər) ***n.*** a lazy person.

**i·dol** (ī′d'l) ***n.*** **1** an image of a god, used as something to be worshiped. **2** a person or thing that is greatly admired or loved [Money is their *idol.*]

**i·dol·a·ter** (ī däl′ə tər) ***n.*** a person who worships idols.

**i·dol·a·trous** (ī däl′ə trəs) ***adj.*** **1** worshiping idols. **2** having to do with idolatry.

**i·dol·a·try** (ī däl′ə trē) ***n.*** **1** the worship of idols. **2** too great love or admiration for some person or thing. —*pl.* **i·dol′a·tries**

**i·dol·ize** (ī′d'l īz) ***v.*** **1** to love or admire very much or too much [Baseball players are often *idolized* by young people.] **2** to make an idol of for worshiping [The Aztecs *idolized* a sun god.] —**i′dol·ized, i′dol·iz·ing**

**i·dyll** or **i·dyl** (ī′d'l) ***n.*** **1** a short poem or story describing a simple, pleasant scene of country life. **2** any scene or happening about which such a story or poem could be written.

**i·dyl·lic** (ī dil′ik) ***adj.*** simple and pleasant, as a scene of country life [an *idyllic* vacation]. —**i·dyl′li·cal·ly *adv.***

**i.e.** *abbreviation for* the Latin phrase *id est,* meaning "that is" or "namely."

**if** (if) ***conj.*** **1** in case that; supposing that [*If* I were you, I'd quit.] **2** whether [I wonder *if* it will rain.] **3** granting that [*If* you were there, I didn't see you.] **4** I wish that [*If* only I had known!]

**ig·loo** (ig′lo͞o) ***n.*** a hut built by Eskimos using blocks of packed snow. *See the picture.* —*pl.* **ig′loos**

**Ig·na·tius Loy·o·la** (ig nā′shəs loi ō′lə), Saint 1491–1556; a Spanish priest who founded the Jesuit order.

**ig·ne·ous** (ig′nē əs) ***adj.*** formed by fire or great heat, especially by the action of volcanoes [Granite is an *igneous* rock.]

**ig·nite** (ig nīt′) ***v.*** **1** to set fire to; make burn [The glowing cigarette *ignited* the dry leaves.] **2** to catch fire; burn [Dry paper *ignites* easily.] —**ig·nit′ed, ig·nit′ing**

**ig·ni·tion** (ig nish′ən) ***n.*** **1** the act of setting on fire or catching fire. **2** the switch, spark plugs, etc. that set fire to the mixture of gases in the cylinders of a gasoline engine.

**ig·no·ble** (ig nō′b'l) ***adj.*** not honorable or respectable; shameful [To betray one's country is an *ignoble* act.] —**ig·no′bly *adv.***

**ig·no·min·i·ous** (ig′nə min′ē əs) ***adj.*** of or causing shame or disgrace; dishonorable [an *ignominious* defeat]. —**ig′no·min′i·ous·ly *adv.***

**ig·no·min·y** (ig′nə min′ē) ***n.*** shame and disgrace; dishonor. —*pl.* **ig′no·min′ies** 

**ig·no·ra·mus** (ig′nə rā′məs *or* ig′nə ram′əs) ***n.*** an ignorant person. —*pl.* **ig′no·ra′mus·es**

> **Ignoramus** was the name of an ignorant lawyer in a 17th-century English play. The word was a legal term used then by a grand jury when it decided to ignore a case. It is a Latin word that means "We take no notice."

**ig·no·rance** (ig′nər əns) ***n.*** lack of knowledge or education.

**ig·no·rant** (ig′nər ənt) ***adj.*** **1** having little or no knowledge or education [an intelligent, but *ignorant,* peasant]. **2** showing a lack of knowledge [an *ignorant* suggestion]. **3** not knowing about; not aware of [*ignorant* of the rules]. —**ig′no·rant·ly *adv.***

**ig·nore** (ig nôr′) ***v.*** to pay no attention to; take no notice of [Try to *ignore* their laughter.] —**ig·nored′, ig·nor′ing**

**i·gua·na** (i gwä′nə) ***n.*** a large lizard of the tropical parts of the Americas. It has a row of spines from neck to tail. *See the picture.*

**il-** *a prefix meaning* not. **Il-** is the form of **in-**[2] used before words beginning with *l* [*Illogical* means not logical and *illegal* means not legal.]

**Il·i·ad** (il′ē əd) a long Greek poem about the Trojan War, thought to have been written by Homer.

| | | | | | | | |
|---|---|---|---|---|---|---|---|
| **a** | fat | **ir** | here | **ou** | out | **zh** | leisure |
| **ā** | ape | **ī** | bite, fire | **u** | up | **ŋ** | ring |
| **ä** | car, lot | **ō** | go | **ur** | fur | | a *in* ago |
| **e** | ten | **ô** | law, horn | **ch** | chin | | e *in* agent |
| **er** | care | **oi** | oil | **sh** | she | **ə =** | i *in* unity |
| **ē** | even | **oo** | look | **th** | thin | | o *in* collect |
| **i** | hit | **o͞o** | tool | ***th*** | then | | u *in* focus |

**-il·i·ty** (il′ə tē) *a suffix used to form nouns from adjectives ending in* -ile, -il, -able, -ible [*Capability* is a noun formed from "capable."]

**ilk** (ilk) ***n.*** family; kind; sort.

> **Ilk** is used now mainly in the phrase **of that ilk**, meaning "of the same kind or sort." This came from a misunderstanding of the phrase *of that ilk* used in Scotland to mean "having the same name as the place from which one comes." In Scotland, "MacDonald of that ilk" means "MacDonald from MacDonald."

**ill** (il) ***adj.*** **1** not healthy; having a disease; sick. **2** harmful or evil; bad; wrong [the *ill* effects of poverty; *ill* fortune]. **3** not proper or right [*ill* manners]. —The comparative of *ill* is **worse**, the superlative is **worst**. ◆***adv.*** **1** in a bad or wrong way; improperly [*ill*-gotten]. **2** in an unkind way; harshly [to speak *ill* of someone]. **3** not easily; hardly [I can *ill* afford to refuse.] ◆***n.*** harm, trouble, pain, sickness, etc. [the *ills* of old age]. —**ill at ease**, not comfortable; uneasy.

**I'll** (īl) **1** I shall. **2** I will.

**Ill.** *abbreviation for* **Illinois.**

**ill-bred** (il′bred′) ***adj.*** not having been taught good manners; not polite; rude.

**il·le·gal** (i lē′gəl) ***adj.*** not legal; not allowed by law; against the law. —**il·le′gal·ly *adv.***

**il·leg·i·ble** (i lej′ə b'l) ***adj.*** hard to read or impossible to read, as because badly written or printed. *See the picture.* —**il·leg′i·bly *adv.***

364 **il·le·git·i·mate** (il′ə jit′ə mit) ***adj.*** **1** born of parents not married to each other. **2** against the laws or rules [the dictator's *illegitimate* seizure of power]. —**il′le·git′i·mate·ly *adv.***

**ill-fat·ed** (il′fāt′id) ***adj.*** sure to come to a bad or unhappy end; unlucky [The *ill-fated* ocean liner struck an iceberg and sank.]

**ill-fa·vored** (il′fā′vərd) ***adj.*** not pleasant to look at; ugly [an *ill-favored* person].

**ill-got·ten** (il′gät′'n) ***adj.*** gotten in an evil or dishonest way [*ill-gotten* gains].

**il·lib·er·al** (i lib′ər əl) ***adj.*** **1** not liberal; narrow-minded. **2** not generous; stingy.

**il·lic·it** (i lis′it) ***adj.*** not allowed; improper or unlawful.

**il·lim·it·a·ble** (i lim′it ə b'l) ***adj.*** without limit or boundary; endless [an *illimitable* supply].

**Il·li·nois** (il′ə noi′ *or* il′ə noiz′) a State in the north central part of the U.S.: abbreviated **Ill., IL**

**il·lit·er·ate** (i lit′ər it) ***adj.*** **1** not educated; especially, not knowing how to read or write. **2** showing a lack of education [an *illiterate* letter]. ◆***n.*** a person who does not know how to read or write. —**il·lit′er·a·cy *n.***

**ill-man·nered** (il′man′ərd) ***adj.*** having bad manners; rude; impolite.

**ill-na·tured** (il′nā′chərd) ***adj.*** having or showing a bad temper; cross; disagreeable.

**ill·ness** (il′nis) ***n.*** the condition of being ill or in poor health; sickness; disease.

**il·log·i·cal** (i läj′i k'l) ***adj.*** not logical; showing poor reasoning. —**il·log′i·cal·ly *adv.***

**ill-tem·pered** (il′tem′pərd) ***adj.*** having or showing a bad temper; cross; irritable.

**ill-timed** (il′tīmd′) ***adj.*** coming or done at the wrong time [an *ill-timed* remark].

**ill-treat** (il′trēt′) ***v.*** to treat in a cruel or unkind way; abuse. —**ill′-treat′ment *n.***

**il·lu·mi·nate** (i lo͞o′mə nāt) ***v.*** **1** to give light to; light up [Candles *illuminated* the room.] **2** to make clear; explain [The teacher *illuminated* the meaning of the poem by discussing the symbols in it.] **3** to decorate, as letters on a page, with fancy designs, colors, etc. *See the picture.* —**il·lu′mi·nat·ed, il·lu′mi·nat·ing** —**il·lu′mi·na′tion *n.***

**il·lu·mine** (i lo͞o′min) ***v.*** to illuminate or light up. —**il·lu′mined, il·lu′min·ing**

**illus.** *abbreviation for* **illustrated** *or* **illustration.**

**ill-us·age** (il′yo͞o′sij *or* il′yo͞o′zij) ***n.*** unfair or cruel treatment; abuse: *also* **ill usage.**

**ill-use** (il′yo͞oz′) ***v.*** to treat in an unkind or cruel way; abuse. —**ill′-used′, ill′-us′ing**

**il·lu·sion** (i lo͞o′zhən) ***n.*** **1** a false idea or mistaken belief [Your cheating on this test has destroyed my *illusion* about your honesty.] **2** the appearance of something that makes one see it in a false way [A large mirror gives the *illusion* of more space in a room.] *See the picture.*

**il·lu·so·ry** (i lo͞o′sər ē) ***adj.*** caused by or having to do with an illusion; deceiving; false; not real: *also* **il·lu·sive** (i lo͞o′siv).

**il·lus·trate** (il′ə strāt *or* i lus′trāt) ***v.*** **1** to make clear or explain by giving examples, making comparisons, etc. [Census figures *illustrate* how the city has grown.] **2** to put drawings or pictures in that explain or decorate [an *illustrated* book]. —**il′lus·trat·ed, il′lus·trat·ing**

**il·lus·tra·tion** (il′ə strā′shən) ***n.*** **1** a picture or drawing used to explain or decorate something. **2** an example, comparison, etc. that helps explain [We need *illustrations* of the way the law works.] **3** the act or process of illustrating.

**il·lus·tra·tive** (i lus′trə tiv *or* il′ə strāt′iv) ***adj.*** that illustrates or explains [The speaker used *illustrative* slides in the talk.]

**il·lus·tra·tor** (il′ə strāt′ər) ***n.*** an artist who makes illustrations for books and magazines.

**il·lus·tri·ous** (i lus′trē əs) ***adj.*** very famous; outstanding [an *illustrious* scientist].

**ill will** unfriendly feeling; hate; dislike.

**I'm** (īm) I am.

**im-** *a prefix meaning:* **1** not [An *imperfect* copy is not perfect.] **2** in or into [To *imprison* is to put into a prison.] **Im-** is the form of **in-**[1] and **in-**[2] used before words beginning with *m, b,* and *p.*

**im·age** (im′ij) ***n.*** **1** a drawing, picture, or especially a statue, of some person or thing [to worship *images*]. **2** that which is seen in a mirror, through a lens, etc. [He saw his own *image* reflected in the pool.] **3** a close likeness or copy [Meg is the *image* of her aunt.] **4** a picture in the mind; idea; impression [*Images* of what might happen frightened us.] ☆**5** a general impression of what a person or thing is, often an idea deliberately created by publicity. **6** a picture in words, especially a simile or metaphor [Homer used the *image* of "rosy-fingered dawn."]

**im·age·ry** (im′ij rē) ***n.*** pictures in words, especially descriptions and figures of speech [A good poem has vivid *imagery*.]

**i·mag·i·na·ble** (i maj′ə nə b'l) ***adj.*** that can be imagined [the worst crime *imaginable*].

**i·mag·i·nar·y** (i maj′ə ner′ē) ***adj.*** that is only in the imagination; not real [Unicorns are *imaginary* beasts.]

**i·mag·i·na·tion** (i maj′ə nā′shən) ***n.*** **1** the act or power of making up pictures or ideas in the mind of what is not present or of how things might be [The flying saucer you thought you saw is just in your *imagination*. It takes great *imagination* to write a play.] **2** the ability to understand and appreciate what others imagine, especially in art and literature [She hasn't enough *imagination* to know what that short story is about.]

SYNONYMS: Imagination is the ability of the mind to call up images and make up happenings, using facts and experiences from the world that one knows, while **fantasy** is a dreaming up of fanciful happenings and creatures that are unreal.

**i·mag·i·na·tive** (i maj′ə nə tiv *or* i maj′ə nāt′iv) ***adj.*** having or showing imagination.

**i·mag·ine** (i maj′in) ***v.*** **1** to make up a picture or idea in the mind; form an idea of [*Imagine* that you are on Mars.] **2** to suppose; guess; think [I *imagine* Terry will be there.] —**i·mag′ined, i·mag′in·ing**

**im·be·cile** (im′bə s'l) ***n.*** **1** a person who is mentally retarded to a moderate extent: *psychologists no longer use this word.* **2** a very foolish or stupid person.

**im·be·cil·i·ty** (im′bə sil′ə tē) ***n.*** **1** great foolishness or stupidity. **2** a stupid act or remark. —*pl.* **im′be·cil′i·ties**

**im·bed** (im bed′) ***v.*** *another spelling for* **embed**. —**im·bed′ded, im·bed′ding**

**im·bibe** (im bīb′) ***v.*** **1** to drink, especially alcoholic liquor. **2** to take into the mind and keep [to *imbibe* new ideas]. —**im·bibed′, im·bib′ing**

**im·bro·glio** (im brōl′yō) ***n.*** a confused situation or disagreement that is hard to clear up [a hopeless *imbroglio* over national boundaries]. —*pl.* **im·bro′glios**

**im·bue** (im byōō′) ***v.*** **1** to fill with ideas or feelings; inspire [Patrick Henry was *imbued* with ideals of liberty.] **2** to fill with a liquid or color [a coat *imbued* with scarlet dye]. —**im·bued′, im·bu′ing**

**im·i·tate** (im′ə tāt) ***v.*** **1** to copy the way someone looks, acts, sounds, etc. [Babies *imitate* their parents. Some birds *imitate* human speech.] **2** to act like in fun; mimic [The comedian *imitated* TV stars.] **3** to look like; resemble [Rhinestones are glass cut to *imitate* diamonds.] —**im′i·tat·ed, im′i·tat·ing** —**im′i·ta·tor** ***n.***

SYNONYMS: To **imitate** is to follow something as an example or model, but not so as to be exactly alike [The child *imitated* the barking dog.] To **copy** is to make as nearly an exact imitation as is possible [to *copy* a painting]. To **mimic** is to imitate something closely, often as a joke or to make fun of it [The comedian *mimicked* the heckler's accent.]

**im·i·ta·tion** (im′ə tā′shən) ***n.*** **1** the act of imitating or copying [The children danced in *imitation* of swaying trees.] **2** a copy or likeness [These jewels are clever *imitations* of precious gems.] ◆***adj.*** made to look like something better; not real [a belt of *imitation* leather].

**im·i·ta·tive** (im′ə tāt′iv) ***adj.*** imitating or copying [the *imitative* sounds of a parrot].

illuminated letter

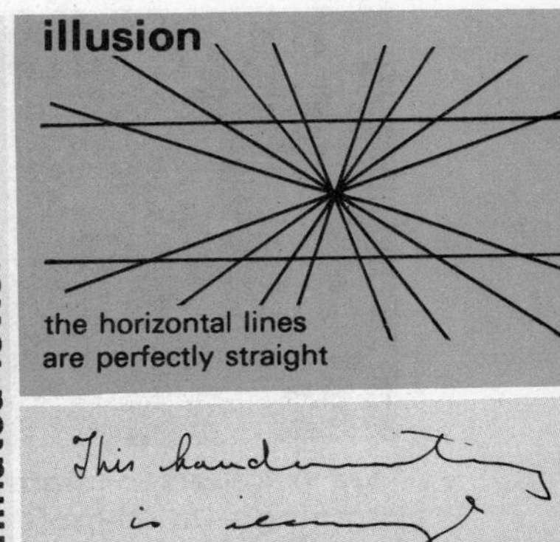


illegible handwriting

**im·mac·u·late** (i mak′yə lit) ***adj.*** **1** perfectly clean; spotless [an *immaculate* kitchen]. **2** without sin; pure [the *immaculate* life of a saint]. —**im·mac′u·late·ly** ***adv.***

**im·ma·te·ri·al** (im′ə tir′ē əl) ***adj.*** **1** of no importance [The cost is *immaterial* if the quality is good.] **2** not made of matter; spiritual.

**im·ma·ture** (im ə toor′ *or* im ə choor′) ***adj.*** not mature; not fully grown or developed [*immature* fruit; *immature* judgment]. —**im′ma·tu′ri·ty** ***n.***

**im·meas·ur·a·ble** (i mezh′ər ə b'l) ***adj.*** too large or too much to be measured [the *immeasurable* space of the universe; an *immeasurable* love]. —**im·meas′ur·a·bly** ***adv.***

**im·me·di·ate** (i mē′dē it) ***adj.*** **1** without delay; happening at once [The medicine had an *immediate* effect.] **2** closest; with nothing coming between [the *immediate* past; one's *immediate* family]. **3** acting in a direct way; direct [What was the *immediate* cause of their quarrel?] —**im·me′di·ate·ly** ***adv.***

**im·me·mo·ri·al** (im′ə môr′ē əl) ***adj.*** reaching back further than all memory or records [customs handed down from time *immemorial*].

**im·mense** (i mens′) ***adj.*** very large; huge; vast [an *immense* territory]. *See* SYNONYMS *at* **enormous**. —**im·mense′ly** ***adv.***

**im·men·si·ty** (i men′sə tē) ***n.*** the fact of being immense; great size; vastness.

**im·merse** (i murs′) ***v.*** **1** to plunge or dip into a liquid. **2** to baptize a person by dipping under water. **3** to get or be deeply in; absorb [*immersed* in study; *immersed* in sadness]. —**im·mersed′, im·mers′ing** —**im·mer·sion** (i mur′shən) ***n.***

☆**im·mi·grant** (im′ə grənt) ***n.*** a person who comes into a foreign country to make a new home.

**im·mi·grate** (im′ə grāt) ***v.*** to come into a foreign country to make one's home [Over 15 million persons *immigrated* into the United States from 1900 to 1955.]

| | | | | | | | |
|---|---|---|---|---|---|---|---|
| **a** | fat | **ir** | here | **ou** | out | **zh** | leisure |
| **ā** | ape | **ī** | bite, fire | **u** | up | **ng** | ring |
| **ä** | car, lot | **ō** | go | **ur** | fur | | a *in* ago |
| **e** | ten | **ô** | law, horn | **ch** | chin | | e *in* agent |
| **er** | care | **oi** | oil | **sh** | she | **ə =** | i *in* unity |
| **ē** | even | **oo** | look | **th** | thin | | o *in* collect |
| **i** | hit | **ōō** | tool | ***th*** | then | | u *in* focus |

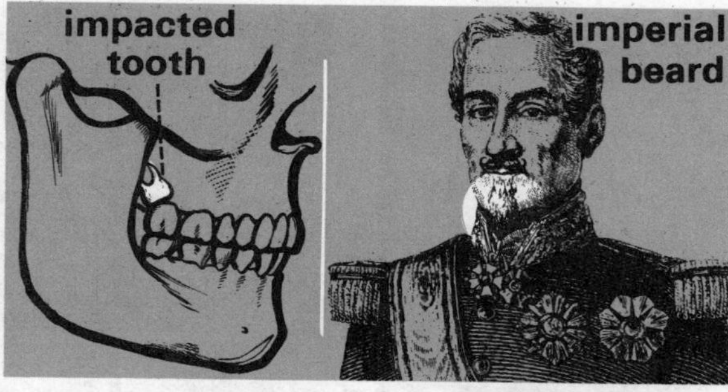


*See* SYNONYMS *at* **migrate.** —**im′mi·grat·ed, im′mi·grat·ing** —**im′mi·gra′tion** *n.*

**im·mi·nent** (im′ə nənt) ***adj.*** likely to take place soon; about to happen [War seemed to be *imminent.*] —**im′mi·nence** *n.* —**im′mi·nent·ly** *adv.*

**im·mo·bile** (i mō′b'l) ***adj.*** not moving or changing; without motion [The frightened deer stood *immobile.*] —**im′mo·bil′i·ty** *n.*

**im·mo·bi·lize** (i mō′bə līz) ***v.*** to make immobile; keep from moving. —**im·mo′bi·lized, im·mo′bi·liz·ing**

**im·mod·er·ate** (i mäd′ər it) ***adj.*** not moderate; too much; too great [an *immoderate* thirst].

**im·mod·est** (i mäd′ist) ***adj.*** **1** not modest or decent [an *immodest* dress]. **2** not shy or humble; bold; forward [an *immodest* boast].

**im·mor·al** (i môr′əl) ***adj.*** against what is right or moral; not good or decent; corrupt, wicked, lewd, etc. —**im·mo·ral·i·ty** (im′ə ral′ə tē) *n.* —**im·mor′al·ly** *adv.*



**im·mor·tal** (i môr′t'l) ***adj.*** **1** never dying; living forever [The Greek gods were thought of as *immortal* beings.] **2** having fame that will last a long time [Shakespeare is an *immortal* poet.] ✦***n.*** **1** a being that lasts forever. **2** a person having lasting fame. —**im·mor·tal·i·ty** (i′môr tal′ə tē) *n.* —**im·mor′tal·ly** *adv.*

**im·mor·tal·ize** (i môr′tə līz) ***v.*** to make immortal; especially, to make famous for a long time [Whistler *immortalized* his mother in a painting.] —**im·mor′tal·ized, im·mor′tal·iz·ing**

**im·mov·a·ble** (i mōō′və b'l) ***adj.*** **1** that cannot be moved; firmly fixed [The ancients thought the earth *immovable.*] **2** not changing; steadfast [an *immovable* purpose].

**im·mune** (i myōōn′) ***adj.*** protected against a bad or unpleasant thing, especially against a disease, as by a vaccine [*immune* to smallpox; *immune* from punishment]. —**im·mu′ni·ty** *n.*

> **Immune** comes from a Latin word meaning "free of public duties." A person who was immune did not have to do certain things, as pay taxes. The word later came to mean being free of anything that was unpleasant.

**im·mu·nize** (im′yə nīz) ***v.*** to make immune, as by vaccination. —**im′mu·nized, im′mu·niz·ing** —**im′mu·ni·za′tion** *n.*

**im·mure** (i myoor′) ***v.*** to shut up inside walls, as in a prison; confine. —**im·mured′, im·mur′ing**

**im·mu·ta·ble** (i myōōt′ə b'l) ***adj.*** never changing; always the same.

**imp** (imp) ***n.*** **1** a child of a devil; a young, small demon. **2** a naughty, mischievous child.

**imp.** *abbreviation for* **imperfect, imperial, import.**

**im·pact** (im′pakt) ***n.*** **1** a hitting together with force; collision [The *impact* of the two cars broke both windshields.] **2** the power of a happening, idea, etc. to cause changes or strong feelings [the *impact* of high prices on our daily lives].

**im·pact·ed** (im pak′tid) ***adj.*** **1** pressed tightly together; wedged in [An *impacted* tooth is wedged so tightly against another tooth that it cannot break through the gum.] *See the picture.* ☆**2** very heavily populated [an *impacted* area].

**im·pair** (im per′) ***v.*** to make worse, less, weaker, etc.; damage [The disease *impaired* her hearing.] —**im·pair′ment** *n.*

**im·pale** (im pāl′) ***v.*** to pierce through with something pointed [to *impale* a dead moth on a pin]. —**im·paled′, im·pal′ing**

**im·pan·el** (im pan″l) ***v.*** **1** to add to a list of those who may be called to serve on a jury. **2** to choose from such a list [to *impanel* a jury]. —**im·pan′eled** or **im·pan′elled, im·pan′el·ing** or **im·pan′el·ling**

**im·part** (im pärt′) ***v.*** **1** to give a part or share of; give [The onion *imparted* its smell to the soup.] **2** to tell; reveal [to *impart* news].

**im·par·tial** (im pär′shəl) ***adj.*** not favoring one side more than another; fair; just [an *impartial* referee]. —**im·par·ti·al·i·ty** (im pär′shē al′ə tē) *n.* —**im·par′tial·ly** *adv.*

**im·pass·a·ble** (im pas′ə b'l) ***adj.*** that cannot be traveled on or across [*impassable* icy roads].

**im·passe** (im′pas *or* im pas′) ***n.*** a difficulty that cannot be solved or an argument where no agreement is possible [Our discussion reached an *impasse.*]

**im·pas·sioned** (im pash′ənd) ***adj.*** having or showing strong feelings or emotions; passionate [an *impassioned* plea for mercy].

**im·pas·sive** (im pas′iv) ***adj.*** not showing any feelings or emotions; calm [Jose's *impassive* face hid his anger.] —**im·pas′sive·ly** *adv.*

**im·pa·tience** (im pā′shəns) ***n.*** the condition of being impatient; lack of patience.

**im·pa·tient** (im pā′shənt) ***adj.*** **1** not patient; not willing to put up with delay, annoyance, etc. [Some parents become *impatient* when their children cry.] **2** eager to do something or for something to happen [Rita is *impatient* to go swimming.] —**im·pa′tient·ly** *adv.*

**im·peach** (im pēch′) ***v.*** **1** to accuse of doing wrong; especially, to try a public official on a charge of wrongdoing [President Andrew Johnson was *impeached* in the U.S. Senate, but was found innocent.] **2** to raise questions or doubts about [This gossip *impeaches* his honor.] —**im·peach′ment** *n.*

**im·pec·ca·ble** (im pek′ə b'l) ***adj.*** without faults or errors; perfect [*impeccable* manners]. —**im·pec′ca·bly** *adv.*

**im·pe·cu·ni·ous** (im′pi kyōō′nē əs) ***adj.*** having no money; poor.

**im·pede** (im pēd′) ***v.*** to get in the way of; delay or obstruct [The accident *impeded* traffic.] —**im·ped′ed, im·ped′ing**

> **Impede** comes from a Latin word meaning "to shackle the feet." Shackles on the feet make it hard to walk or move about. They get in one's way.

**im·ped·i·ment** (im ped′ə mənt) ***n.*** anything that impedes or gets in the way; obstacle [Bad roads are *impediments* to travel. A lisp is an *impediment* in speaking.]

**im·pel** (im pel′) ***v.*** **1** to push or move forward. **2** to force or drive [What *impels* them to lie?] —**im·pelled′, im·pel′ling**

**im·pend** (im pend′) ***v.*** to be about to happen; threaten [Disaster seemed to be *impending*.]

**im·pen·e·tra·ble** (im pen′i trə b′l) ***adj.*** **1** that cannot be penetrated or passed through [an *impenetrable* jungle]. **2** that cannot be understood [the *impenetrable* mystery of death].

**im·pen·i·tent** (im pen′ə tənt) ***adj.*** not feeling shame or regret; not sorry for what one has done. —**im·pen′i·tent·ly *adv.***

**im·per·a·tive** (im per′ə tiv) ***adj.*** **1** that must be done; necessary; urgent [Quick action is *imperative*.] **2** showing power or authority; commanding [The police officer stopped traffic with an *imperative* gesture.] **3** describing the mood of a verb used in giving commands or orders [In "Be careful!", "be" is in the *imperative* mood.] ◆***n.*** an order or command.

**im·per·cep·ti·ble** (im′pər sep′tə b′l) ***adj.*** so small or slight that it is not noticed [an *imperceptible* scar]. —**im′per·cep′ti·bly *adv.***

**im·per·fect** (im pur′fikt) ***adj.*** **1** not perfect; having some fault or flaw. **2** lacking in something; not complete; unfinished [an *imperfect* knowledge of Russian]. —**im·per′fect·ly *adv.***

**im·per·fec·tion** (im′pər fek′shən) ***n.*** **1** the condition of being imperfect. **2** a flaw; fault.

**im·pe·ri·al** (im pir′ē əl) ***adj.*** of an empire, emperor, or empress [an *imperial* army]. ◆***n.*** ☆a small, pointed beard on the chin. *See the picture.*

**im·pe·ri·al·ism** (im pir′ē əl iz′m) ***n.*** the idea or practice of setting up an empire by conquering other countries, forming colonies in other lands, trying to control the wealth or politics of weaker countries, etc. —**im·pe′ri·al·ist *n., adj.*** —**im·pe′ri·al·is′tic *adj.***

**im·per·il** (im per′əl) ***v.*** to put in peril, or danger [Their lives were *imperiled* by the fire.] —**im·per′iled** or **im·per′illed, im·per′il·ing** or **im·per′il·ling**

**im·pe·ri·ous** (im pir′ē əs) ***adj.*** **1** ruling or ordering around in a harsh and bullying way; arrogant or overbearing [In an *imperious* voice she ordered us away.] **2** necessary or urgent [an *imperious* duty]. —**im·pe′ri·ous·ly *adv.***

**im·per·ish·a·ble** (im per′ish ə b′l) ***adj.*** that will not perish or die; lasting a long time or forever [the *imperishable* fame of a hero].

**im·per·son·al** (im pur′s′n əl) ***adj.*** **1** not referring to any particular person [The teacher's remarks about cheating were *impersonal* and meant for all the students.] **2** not existing as a person [Nature is an *impersonal* force.] **3** describing a verb that is used only in the third person singular, usually with *it* as the subject [In the sentence "It is cold in here," "is" is an *impersonal* verb.] —**im·per′son·al·ly *adv.***

**im·per·son·ate** (im pur′sə nāt) ***v.*** **1** to imitate or mimic in fun [The students *impersonated* their teachers in the school play.] **2** to pretend to be in order to cheat or trick [He was arrested for *impersonating* a police officer.] —**im·per′son·at·ed, im·per′son·at·ing** —**im·per′son·a′tion *n.*** —**im·per′son·a′tor *n.***

**im·per·ti·nent** (im pur′t′n ənt) ***adj.*** not showing the right respect; impudent or rude [The reporter was asked to leave for being *impertinent*.] —**im·per′ti·nence *n.*** —**im·per′ti·nent·ly *adv.***

**im·per·turb·a·ble** (im′pər tur′bə b′l) ***adj.*** not easily excited or disturbed; calm.

**im·per·vi·ous** (im pur′vē əs) ***adj.*** **1** not letting something come through it [These tiles are *impervious* to water.] **2** not affected by [a person *impervious* to criticism].

**im·pe·ti·go** (im′pə tī′gō) ***n.*** a contagious disease of the skin in which there are many small swellings filled with a yellowish liquid.

**im·pet·u·ous** (im pech′oo wəs) ***adj.*** **1** moving with great or wild force; rushing [*impetuous* winds]. **2** rushing into action with little thought; rash. —**im·pet·u·os·i·ty** (im pech′oo wäs′ə tē) ***n.*** —**im·pet′u·ous·ly *adv.***

**im·pe·tus** (im′pə təs) ***n.*** **1** the force with which a body moves; momentum. **2** any force that helps something along; stimulus [The new loans gave fresh *impetus* to the building program.]

**im·pi·e·ty** (im pī′ə tē) ***n.*** **1** a lack of respect or reverence for sacred things. **2** an impious act or remark. —*pl.* **im·pi′e·ties**

**im·pinge** (im pinj′) ***v.*** **1** to come in contact with; touch or strike [The sound of trumpets *impinged* on their eardrums.] **2** to break in on; encroach or infringe [Censorship *impinges* on our freedoms.] —**im·pinged′, im·ping′ing** —**im·pinge′ment *n.***

**im·pi·ous** (im′pē əs) ***adj.*** not pious; lacking respect for what one should honor or worship. —**im′pi·ous·ly *adv.***

**imp·ish** (imp′ish) ***adj.*** like an imp; mischievous. —**imp′ish·ly *adv.*** —**imp′ish·ness *n.***

**im·pla·ca·ble** (im plak′ə b′l *or* im plā′kə b′l) ***adj.*** that cannot be made calm or peaceful; relentless [*implacable* anger; *implacable* enemies.] —**im·pla′ca·bly *adv.***

**im·plant** (im plant′) ***v.*** **1** to plant firmly [to *implant* seeds]. **2** to fix firmly in the mind [Respect for the law was *implanted* in them.]

**im·ple·ment** (im′plə mənt) ***n.*** something used in doing some work; tool or instrument [A plow is a farm *implement*.] ◆***v.*** (im′plə ment) to carry out; put into effect [to *implement* a plan].

> SYNONYMS: **Implement** is the word given to any device that is used to carry on some work [A loom is an *implement* for weaving.] **Tool** is the word usually given to implements that are used with the hands, as in carpentry or plumbing [The hammer is a *tool*.] **Utensil** is used for any implement or container for home use, especially a pot, pan, etc.

**im·pli·cate** (im′plə kāt) ***v.*** to show that someone has had a part, especially in something bad; involve [Her

| | | | | | | | |
|---|---|---|---|---|---|---|---|
| **a** | fat | **ir** | here | **ou** | out | **zh** | leisure |
| **ā** | ape | **ī** | bite, fire | **u** | up | **ng** | ring |
| **ä** | car, lot | **ō** | go | **ur** | fur | | a *in* ago |
| **e** | ten | **ô** | law, horn | **ch** | chin | | e *in* agent |
| **er** | care | **oi** | oil | **sh** | she | ə = | i *in* unity |
| **ē** | even | **oo** | look | **th** | thin | | o *in* collect |
| **i** | hit | **ōō** | tool | ***th*** | then | | u *in* focus |

confession *implicated* Gordon in the crime.] —**im′pli·cat·ed, im′pli·cat·ing**

**im·pli·ca·tion** (im′plə kā′shən) ***n.*** **1** an implicating or being implicated. **2** an implying or suggesting. **3** the thing implied [Your *implication* that she lied to us seems to be correct.]

**im·plic·it** (im plis′it) ***adj.*** **1** implied or suggested but not actually said [We gave *implicit* approval by our silence.] **2** without doubting or holding back; absolute [I have *implicit* faith in her honesty.] —**im·plic′it·ly** ***adv.***

**im·plore** (im plôr′) ***v.*** to plead for or beg with much feeling; beseech [The stranded passengers *implored* us to give them a ride.] —**im·plored′, im·plor′ing**

**im·ply** (im plī′) ***v.*** to mean or suggest without openly saying [Your frown *implied* disapproval.] *See note at* **infer.** —**im·plied′, im·ply′ing**

**im·po·lite** (im pə līt′) ***adj.*** not polite; rude. —**im·po·lite′ly** ***adv.*** —**im·po·lite′ness** ***n.***

**im·pol·i·tic** (im päl′ə tik) ***adj.*** not wise or careful; showing poor judgment [It was *impolitic* of you to insult your boss.]

**im·port** (im′pôrt) ***v.*** to bring goods into one country from another [England *imports* much of its food.] ◆***n.*** **1** something imported from another country [Automobiles are one of Canada's chief *imports*.] **2** meaning [the *import* of a remark]. **3** importance [a matter of no *import*].

368 **im·por·tance** (im pôr′t'ns) ***n.*** the fact of being important [news of little *importance*].

SYNONYMS: **Importance** suggests that the worth, meaning, influence, etc. of something is great [a message of *importance*]. **Significance** suggests that the importance of something is due to a special meaning that may or may not be easily understood [an event of *significance*].

**im·por·tant** (im pôr′t'nt) ***adj.*** **1** having much meaning or value [Our wedding anniversary is an *important* date in our lives.] **2** having power or authority, or acting as if one had power [an *important* official]. —**im·por′tant·ly** ***adv.***

**im·por·ta·tion** (im′pôr tā′shən) ***n.*** **1** the importing of goods into a country. **2** something that has been imported into a country.

**im·port·er** (im pôr′tər) ***n.*** a person or company in the business of importing goods.

**im·por·tu·nate** (im pôr′chə nit) ***adj.*** asking or asked again and again in a pestering way [an *importunate* job seeker; *importunate* pleas].

**im·por·tune** (im′pôr to͞on′ *or* im′pôr tyo͞on′ *or* im pôr′chən) ***v.*** to plead for or beg again and again in a pestering way [Tim kept *importuning* his father to take him to the circus.] —**im′por·tuned′, im′por·tun′ing**

**im·pose** (im pōz′) ***v.*** **1** to put on as a duty, burden, penalty, etc. [to *impose* a tax on furs; to *impose* a fine on speeders]. **2** to force one's company or ideas on another or put another to some trouble [Can I *impose* on you to drive me home?] —**im·posed′, im·pos′ing**

**im·pos·ing** (im pō′ziŋ) ***adj.*** grand in size, manner, looks, etc. [an *imposing* statue].

**im·po·si·tion** (im′pə zish′ən) ***n.*** **1** an imposing or imposing on; a taking advantage of friendship, courtesy, etc. [Staying for a meal when you were not invited is an *imposition*.] **2** something imposed, as a tax, fine, or burden.

**im·pos·si·ble** (im päs′ə b'l) ***adj.*** **1** that cannot be, be done, or happen; not possible [He found it *impossible* to lift the crate.] **2** very unpleasant or hard to put up with [You're always asking *impossible* questions!] —**im·pos′si·bil′i·ty** ***n.*** —**im·pos′si·bly** ***adv.***

**im·pos·tor** (im päs′tər) ***n.*** a person who cheats or tricks people, especially by pretending to be someone else or a different sort of person.

**im·pos·ture** (im päs′chər) ***n.*** the act of an impostor; fraud; deception.

**im·po·tent** (im′pə tənt) ***adj.*** not having the strength or power to act; helpless [We were *impotent* against the storm.] —**im′po·tence** ***n.***

**im·pound** (im pound′) ***v.*** **1** to shut up in a pound or enclosure [Stray dogs will be *impounded*.] **2** to take and hold in the care of the law [The police *impounded* the stolen car.]

**im·pov·er·ish** (im päv′ər ish) ***v.*** **1** to make poor [Gambling had *impoverished* me.] **2** to make lose strength or richness [Planting the same crops every year *impoverishes* the soil.] —**im·pov′er·ish·ment** ***n.***

**im·prac·ti·ca·ble** (im prak′ti kə b'l) ***adj.*** that cannot be put into practice or used [*impracticable* plans]. —**im·prac′ti·ca·bly** ***adv.***

**im·prac·ti·cal** (im prak′ti k'l) ***adj.*** not practical; not useful, efficient, etc.

**im·pre·cise** (im′pri sīs′) ***adj.*** not precise, accurate, or definite.

**im·preg·na·ble** (im preg′nə b'l) ***adj.*** that cannot be conquered or overcome; unyielding; firm [an *impregnable* faith]. —**im·preg′na·bil′i·ty** ***n.***

**im·preg·nate** (im preg′nāt) ***v.*** **1** to fill full or mix throughout [Their clothing was *impregnated* with smoke.] **2** to make pregnant; fertilize. —**im·preg′nat·ed, im·preg′nat·ing** —**im′preg·na′tion** ***n.***

**im·pre·sa·ri·o** (im′prə sär′ē ō) ***n.*** the organizer or manager of an opera company, a series of concerts, etc. —*pl.* **im′pre·sa′ri·os**

**im·press**[1] (im pres′) ***v.*** to seize and force to serve in a navy or an army [The British used to *impress* men into their navy.]

**im·press**[2] (im pres′) ***v.*** **1** to affect the thinking or feelings of [Your quick answers *impressed* us all greatly.] **2** to fix firmly in the mind [Let me *impress* on you the importance of fire drills.] **3** to mark by pressing on; stamp [The envelopes were *impressed* with her name.] ◆***n.*** (im′pres) **1** any mark or imprint made by pressing [All letters carry the *impress* of a postmark.] **2** an effect made by some strong influence.

**im·pres·sion** (im presh′ən) ***n.*** **1** the act of impressing. **2** a mark or imprint made by pressing [The police took an *impression* of his fingerprints.] **3** an effect produced on the mind [The play made a great *impression* on us.] *See* SYNONYMS *at* **idea.** **4** the effect produced by some action [Cleaning made no *impression* on the stain.] **5** a vague feeling [I have the *impression* that someone was here.]

**im·pres·sion·a·ble** (im presh′ən ə b'l) ***adj.*** with a mind or feelings that are easily impressed; sensitive.

**im·pres·sive** (im pres′iv) ***adj.*** that impresses or has a strong effect on the mind [an *impressive* display]. —**im·pres′sive·ly** ***adv.***

**im·print** (im print') ***v.*** **1** to mark by pressing or stamping [The paper was *imprinted* with the state seal.] **2** to fix firmly [Her face is *imprinted* in my memory.] ◆***n.*** (im'print) **1** a mark made by pressing; print [the *imprint* of a dirty hand on the wall]. **2** a lasting impression or effect [the *imprint* of starvation on their bodies]. **3** a note, as on the title page of a book, giving the publisher's name and telling where and when the book was published.

**im·pris·on** (im priz''n) ***v.*** **1** to put or keep in prison. **2** to shut up or confine [a bird *imprisoned* in a cage]. —**im·pris'on·ment** ***n.***

**im·prob·a·ble** (im präb'ə b'l) ***adj.*** not probable; not likely to happen or be true [It is *improbable* that we will win again.] —**im·prob'a·bil'i·ty** ***n.*** —**im·prob'a·bly** ***adv.***

**im·promp·tu** (im prämp'to͞o *or* im prämp'tyo͞o) ***adj., adv.*** without preparation or thought ahead of time; offhand [After winning the prize, she gave an *impromptu* speech.]

**im·prop·er** (im präp'ər) ***adj.*** **1** not proper or suitable; unfit [Sandals are *improper* shoes for tennis.] **2** not true; wrong; incorrect [an *improper* street address]. **3** not decent; in bad taste [*improper* jokes]. —**im·prop'er·ly** ***adv.***

**improper fraction** a fraction in which the denominator is less than the numerator [4/3, 8/5, and 9/7 are *improper fractions.*]

**im·pro·pri·e·ty** (im'prə prī'ə tē) ***n.*** **1** the fact of being improper, or something that is not proper. **2** an incorrect use of a word or phrase [The use of "its" for "it's" is an *impropriety.*] —*pl.* **im'pro·pri'e·ties**

**im·prove** (im pro͞ov') ***v.*** **1** to make or become better [Business has *improved.*] **2** to make good use of [She *improved* her spare time by reading.] —**im·proved', im·prov'ing**

SYNONYMS: **Improve** and **better** both suggest making progress in or correcting something that may already be good or all right. **Improve** is used when a lack or want is being taken care of [to *improve* a way of doing something]. **Better** is used when something that is more desirable is being sought [She hopes to *better* herself in a new job.]

**im·prove·ment** (im pro͞ov'mənt) ***n.*** **1** a making or becoming better [Your playing shows *improvement.*] **2** an addition or change that makes something worth more [Our taxes rose because of *improvements* we made to the house.] **3** a person or thing that is better than another [The new choir is an *improvement* over the old one.]

**im·prov·i·dent** (im präv'ə dənt) ***adj.*** not planning carefully for the future; not thrifty. —**im·prov'i·dence** ***n.***

**im·pro·vise** (im'prə vīz) ***v.*** **1** to compose and perform at the same time, without preparation [Calypso singers often *improvise* verses as they sing.] **2** to make quickly with whatever is at hand [We *improvised* a bed by putting some chairs together.] *See the picture.* —**im'pro·vised, im'pro·vis·ing** —**im·prov·i·sa·tion** (im präv'ə zā'shən) ***n.***

**Improvise** comes from a Latin word meaning "not known or seen ahead of time." When we improvise in a situation, we do so because we did not know ahead of time what we would do or what we could plan for.

**improvised bookcase**

**im·pru·dent** (im pro͞od''nt) ***adj.*** not prudent or careful; rash or indiscreet. —**im·pru'dence** ***n.*** —**im·pru'dent·ly** ***adv.***

**im·pu·dent** (im'pyo͝o dənt) ***adj.*** not showing respect; shamelessly rude [an *impudent* sneer]. —**im'pu·dence** ***n.*** —**im'pu·dent·ly** ***adv.***

**im·pugn** (im pyo͞on') ***v.*** to doubt or question [Do you *impugn* my sincerity?]

**im·pulse** (im'puls) ***n.*** **1** a sudden feeling that makes one want to do something [She had an *impulse* to buy some candy.] **2** the force that starts some action; push or thrust [The *impulse* of the propeller drives the ship through the water.] **3** a short surge of electricity in one direction.

**im·pul·sive** (im pul'siv) ***adj.*** **1** acting or likely to act suddenly and without thinking [The *impulsive* child dashed into the street.] **2** done or made on a sudden impulse [an *impulsive* remark]. *See* SYNONYMS *at* **spontaneous.** —**im·pul'sive·ly** ***adv.*** 

**im·pu·ni·ty** (im pyo͞o'nə tē) ***n.*** freedom from the danger of being punished or harmed [You can't ignore the rules of health with *impunity.*]

**im·pure** (im pyo͝or') ***adj.*** **1** not clean; dirty [Smoke made the air *impure.*] **2** mixed with things that do not belong [*impure* gold]. **3** not decent or proper [*impure* thoughts].

**im·pu·ri·ty** (im pyo͝or'ə tē) ***n.*** **1** the condition of being impure [a high level of *impurity*]. **2** something mixed in that makes another thing impure [Strain the oil to remove *impurities.*] —*pl.* **im·pu'ri·ties**

**im·pute** (im pyo͞ot') ***v.*** to think of as being guilty of; blame or charge with [to *impute* a crime to someone]. —**im·put'ed, im·put'ing** —**im·pu·ta·tion** (im'pyo͝o tā'shən) ***n.***

**IN** *abbreviation for* **Indiana.**

**in** (in) ***prep.*** **1** contained by, covered by, or surrounded by [to live *in* town; to dress *in* furs; caught *in* a storm]. **2** during or after [done *in* a day; to leave *in* an hour]. **3** not beyond [still *in* sight]. **4** having or showing [*in* trouble; *in* tears]. **5** having to do with; with regard to [*in* business; *in* my opinion; the best *in* the school]. **6** by means of; using [written *in* ink]. **7** because of [to shout *in* anger]. **8** into [Go *in* the house.] ◆**adv.** **1** inside or toward the inside [Walk *in* slowly.] **2** to or toward a certain place or direction [We flew *in* today.] **3** within a certain place [Keep the cat *in.*] ◆**adj.** **1** that has power or control [the *in* group]. **2** that is inside or leads inside [Use the *in* door.] **3** that is now popular or in fashion: *used only in everyday talk* [an *in* joke]. ◆**n.** **1** *usually* **ins,** *pl.* those who are in power or in office. ☆**2** a way to get special favor: *used only in everyday talk* [Do you have an *in* with the boss?] —**in for,** certain to have [You're *in for* a big surprise.] —**in on,** having a share or part of. —**ins and outs,** all the parts or details. —**in that,** for this reason; because. —**in with,** being friends or partners with.

**in-**[1] *a prefix meaning* in, into, within, on, or toward. It is usually seen in words coming from Latin, such as *induct* and *infer.*

**in-**[2] *a prefix meaning* not [*Incorrect* means not correct.]

**in.** *abbreviation for* **inch** *or* **inches.**

**in·a·bil·i·ty** (in′ə bil′ə tē) **n.** the condition of being unable; lack of ability or power.

**in·ac·ces·si·ble** (in′ək ses′ə b'l) **adj.** impossible or hard to reach or get to [Their cottage is *inaccessible* except by boat.] —**in′ac·ces′si·bil′i·ty n.**

**in·ac·cu·ra·cy** (in ak′yər ə sē) **n.** **1** the condition of being inaccurate, or wrong; incorrectness. **2** an error or mistake [This map has many *inaccuracies.*] —*pl.* **in·ac′cu·ra·cies**

370 **in·ac·cu·rate** (in ak′yər it) **adj.** not accurate or exact; in error; wrong [an *inaccurate* clock]. —**in·ac′cu·rate·ly adv.**

**in·ac·tion** (in ak′shən) **n.** the condition of not moving or acting; lack of action; idleness.

**in·ac·tive** (in ak′tiv) **adj.** not active; idle. —**in·ac′tive·ly adv.** —**in′ac·tiv′i·ty n.**

**in·ad·e·quate** (in ad′ə kwət) **adj.** not adequate; less than is needed. —**in·ad·e·qua·cy** (in ad′ə kwə sē) **n.** —**in·ad′e·quate·ly adv.**

**in·ad·mis·si·ble** (in′əd mis′ə b'l) **adj.** that cannot be admitted or allowed; unacceptable [an *inadmissible* excuse; *inadmissible* evidence].

**in·ad·vert·ent** (in′əd vur′tənt) **adj.** not meant; not on purpose; accidental [an *inadvertent* insult]. —**in′ad·vert′ence n.** —**in′ad·vert′ent·ly adv.**

**in·ad·vis·a·ble** (in′əd vī′zə b'l) **adj.** not advisable; not wise or sensible.

inauguration of President Grant

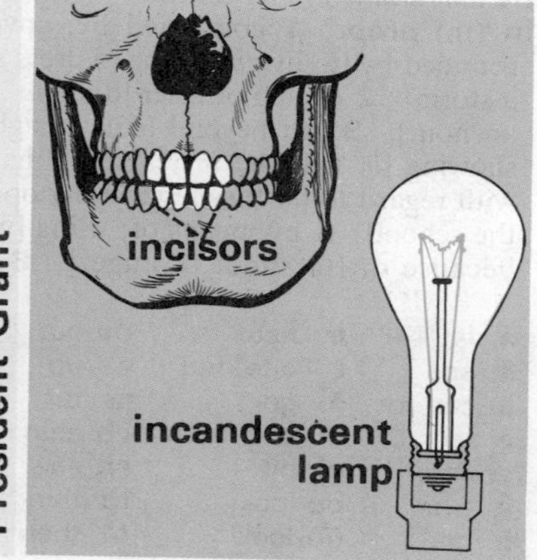

incisors

incandescent lamp

**in·al·ien·a·ble** (in āl′yən ə b'l) **adj.** that cannot be taken away or given away [Freedom of speech is an *inalienable* right.]

**in·ane** (in ān′) **adj.** foolish or silly [an *inane* smile]. —**in·ane′ly adv.**

**in·an·i·mate** (in an′ə mit) **adj.** **1** without life [A rock is an *inanimate* object.] **2** not lively; dull [an *inanimate* style of writing].

**in·an·i·ty** (in an′ə tē) **n.** **1** the condition of being foolish or silly. **2** a foolish or silly act or remark. —*pl.* **in·an′i·ties**

**in·ap·pli·ca·ble** (in ap′li kə b'l) **adj.** that does not apply or is not suitable.

**in·ap·pro·pri·ate** (in′ə prō′prē it) **adj.** not appropriate; not suitable or proper.

**in·apt** (in apt′) **adj.** **1** not apt; not suitable or fitting [an *inapt* remark]. **2** not skillful; awkward; inept. —**in·apt′ly adv.**

**in·ar·tic·u·late** (in′är tik′yə lit) **adj.** **1** not in speech that can be understood [an *inarticulate* cry]. **2** not able to speak or not able to speak clearly [*inarticulate* with rage].

**in·ar·tis·tic** (in′är tis′tik) **adj.** not artistic; without good taste. —**in′ar·tis′ti·cal·ly adv.**

**in·as·much as** (in′əz much′ əz) because; since; seeing that [I couldn't have seen them, *inasmuch as* they weren't there.]

**in·at·ten·tion** (in′ə ten′shən) **n.** a failing to pay attention; carelessness; negligence.

**in·at·ten·tive** (in′ə ten′tiv) **adj.** not attentive; not paying attention; careless; negligent. —**in′at·ten′tive·ly adv.**

**in·au·di·ble** (in ô′də b'l) **adj.** not audible; that cannot be heard. —**in·au′di·bly adv.**

**in·au·gu·ral** (in ô′gyə rəl) **adj.** of an inauguration [an *inaugural* ceremony]. ◆**n.** ☆**1** a speech made at an inauguration. ☆**2** an inauguration.

**in·au·gu·rate** (in ô′gyə rāt) **v.** **1** to place in office with a ceremony; install [The new President will be *inaugurated* on January 20.] *See the picture.* **2** to begin or start [to *inaugurate* a new school year]. **3** to mark the first public use of with a ceremony [to *inaugurate* a new bridge]. —**in·au′gu·rat·ed, in·au′gu·rat·ing** —**in·au′gu·ra′tion n.**

**in·aus·pi·cious** (in′ô spish′əs) **adj.** not auspicious; not favorable to plans or hopes; unlucky [an *inauspicious* beginning].

**in·board** (in′bôrd) **adj.** inside the hull of a ship or boat [an *inboard* motor].

**in·born** (in′bôrn) **adj.** that seems to have been born in one; natural [an *inborn* talent].

**in·bred** (in′bred′) **adj.** **1** bred from parents that are closely related. **2** inborn; natural [an *inbred* curiosity].

**in·breed·ing** (in′brēd′iŋ) **n.** the act of breeding from parents that are closely related.

**inc.** *abbreviation for* **inclosure, included, income, incorporated, increase.**

**In·ca** (iŋ′kə) **n.** a member of the highly civilized Indian people of ancient Peru, who were conquered by the Spanish. —**In′can adj.**

**in·cal·cu·la·ble** (in kal′kyə lə b'l) **adj.** **1** too great to be calculated [*incalculable* damage]. **2** too uncertain to be counted on or predicted [the *incalculable* future]. —**in·cal′cu·la·bly adv.**

**in·can·des·cent** (in'kən des''nt) ***adj.*** **1** glowing with heat. An **incandescent lamp** has a metal filament that gives off light when it is made hot by an electric current. *See the picture.* **2** very bright; gleaming. —**in'can·des'cence** ***n.***

**in·can·ta·tion** (in'kan tā'shən) ***n.*** **1** the chanting of special words that are supposed to have magic power [an *incantation* to drive away demons]. **2** such words.

**in·ca·pa·ble** (in kā'pə b'l) ***adj.*** **1** not capable; not having the ability or power needed [*incapable* of helping]. **2** not able to undergo; not open to [*incapable* of change]. —**in'ca·pa·bil'i·ty** ***n.***

**in·ca·pac·i·tate** (in'kə pas'ə tāt) ***v.*** to make unable or unfit; disable [She was *incapacitated* by a broken leg.] —**in'ca·pac'i·tat·ed, in'ca·pac'i·tat·ing**

**in·ca·pac·i·ty** (in'kə pas'ə tē) ***n.*** lack of ability or fitness; the condition of being unable or unfit.

**in·car·cer·ate** (in kär'sə rāt) ***v.*** to put in prison. —**in·car'cer·at·ed, in·car'cer·at·ing —in·car'cer·a'tion** ***n.***

**in·car·nate** (in kär'nit *or* in kär'nāt) ***adj.*** in human form; being a living example of [He is evil *incarnate.*] ◆***v.*** (in kär'nāt) **1** to give solid form to; make real. **2** to be a living example of; typify [Joan of Arc *incarnates* the spirit of France.] —**in·car'nat·ed, in·car'nat·ing**

**in·car·na·tion** (in'kär nā'shən) ***n.*** **1** a taking on of human form. In Christian belief, the Incarnation is the taking on of human form by Jesus as the Son of God. **2** a living example or symbol of a quality [To him she was the *incarnation* of beauty itself.]

**in·cau·tious** (in kô'shəs) ***adj.*** not cautious; not careful; reckless [an *incautious* driver].

**in·cen·di·ar·y** (in sen'dē er'ē) ***adj.*** **1** having to do with the destroying of property on purpose by setting fire to it. **2** causing fires [an *incendiary* bomb]. **3** stirring up riots, trouble, etc. [*incendiary* speeches]. ◆***n.*** **1** a person who sets fire to property on purpose. **2** a person who stirs up riots, trouble, etc. —*pl.* **in·cen'di·ar'ies**

**in·cense**[1] (in'sens) ***n.*** **1** a substance made of gums, spices, etc., that is burned for the sweet smell it gives off. **2** the smoke or sweet smell from it. **3** any pleasant smell.

**in·cense**[2] (in sens') ***v.*** to make very angry; fill with rage [We are *incensed* at your lies.] —**in·censed', in·cens'ing**

> **Incense**[2] comes from a Latin word meaning "to burn." Thus, to become incensed is to burn with rage or anger. The words **candle, incandescent,** and **incense**[1], all having to do with burning, also come from this Latin word.

**in·cen·tive** (in sen'tiv) ***n.*** the thing that makes one want to work, try, etc.; motive or stimulus [A promise of higher pay is an *incentive* to work hard.] *See* SYNONYMS *at* **motive.**

**in·cep·tion** (in sep'shən) ***n.*** a beginning; start [the *inception* of a new project].

**in·ces·sant** (in ses''nt) ***adj.*** going on without stopping or in a way that seems endless [*incessant* chatter]. —**in·ces'sant·ly** ***adv.***

**in·cest** (in'sest) ***n.*** sexual intercourse between persons too closely related to marry legally.

**in·ces·tu·ous** (in ses'chōō wəs) ***adj.*** of or having to do with incest.

**inch** (inch) ***n.*** a unit for measuring length, equal to 1/12 foot. One inch equals 2.54 centimeters. ◆***v.*** to move a little at a time [Lou *inched* along the narrow ledge.] —**by inches,** slowly or gradually: *also* **inch by inch.** —**within an inch of,** very close to.

**in·ci·dence** (in'si dəns) ***n.*** the range within which something falls or has an effect [The *incidence* of flu was widespread that year.]

**in·ci·dent** (in'si dənt) ***n.*** **1** something that happens in real life or in a story; often, an event of little importance [She told an *incident* of her childhood.] **2** a minor clash or disagreement, as between nations, that may have serious results. ◆***adj.*** likely to happen as part of; incidental [the expenses *incident* to owning a car].

**in·ci·den·tal** (in'si den't'l) ***adj.*** **1** likely to happen along with something else [the duties *incidental* to a job]. **2** minor or of lesser importance [the *incidental* costs of education]. ◆***n.*** **1** something incidental. **2** **incidentals,** *pl.* various small items or expenses.

**in·ci·den·tal·ly** (in'si dent'lē *or* in'si den't'l ē) ***adv.*** **1** in an incidental way; along with something else. **2** by the way [*Incidentally,* who are you?]

**in·cin·er·ate** (in sin'ə rāt) ***v.*** to burn to ashes; burn up. —**in·cin'er·at·ed, in·cin'er·at·ing —in·cin'er·a'tion** ***n.***

**in·cin·er·a·tor** (in sin'ə rāt'ər) ***n.*** a furnace for burning trash.

**in·cip·i·ent** (in sip'ē ənt) ***adj.*** just starting; in the first stage [an *incipient* illness].



**in·cise** (in sīz') ***v.*** to cut into with a sharp tool; carve; engrave [letters *incised* in stone]. —**in·cised', in·cis'ing**

**in·ci·sion** (in sizh'ən) ***n.*** **1** a cut or gash, as one made in surgery. **2** the act of engraving or cutting.

**in·ci·sive** (in sī'siv) ***adj.*** sharp and clear; keen [an *incisive* mind]. —**in·ci'sive·ly** ***adv.*** —**in·ci'sive·ness** ***n.***

**in·ci·sor** (in sī'zər) ***n.*** any of the front teeth with a cutting edge, between the canine teeth. A human being has eight incisors. *See the picture.*

**in·cite** (in sīt') ***v.*** to stir up; rouse; urge [to *incite* a mob to riot]. —**in·cit'ed, in·cit'ing —in·cite'ment** ***n.***

**in·ci·vil·i·ty** (in'sə vil'ə tē) ***n.*** rudeness; lack of courtesy; also, an impolite act. —*pl.* **in'ci·vil'i·ties**

**in·clem·ent** (in klem'ənt) ***adj.*** **1** rough or stormy [*inclement* weather]. **2** lacking mercy; harsh [an *inclement* king]. —**in·clem'en·cy** ***n.***

**in·cli·na·tion** (in'klə nā'shən) ***n.*** **1** a natural liking for or leaning toward something; tendency [an *inclination* to talk]. **2** a bending, leaning, or sloping [the *inclination* of a roof].

**in·cline** (in klīn') ***v.*** **1** to lean, slope, or slant [The flagpole *inclines* toward the left.] **2** to bend or bow, as the head. **3** to have a liking for or leaning toward;

| | | | | | | | |
|---|---|---|---|---|---|---|---|
| **a** | fat | **ir** | here | **ou** | out | **zh** | leisure |
| **ā** | ape | **ī** | bite, fire | **u** | up | **ng** | ring |
| **ä** | car, lot | **ō** | go | **ur** | fur | | a *in* ago |
| **e** | ten | **ô** | law, horn | **ch** | chin | | e *in* agent |
| **er** | care | **oi** | oil | **sh** | she | **ə =** | i *in* unity |
| **ē** | even | **oo** | look | **th** | thin | | o *in* collect |
| **i** | hit | **ōō** | tool | ***th*** | then | | u *in* focus |

tend [Jeff *inclines* to be athletic.] —**in·clined′, in·clin′ing** ✦***n.*** (in′klīn) a sloping surface; slope or slant [a road with a steep *incline*].

**in·close** (in klōz′) ***v.*** *another spelling for* **enclose.** —**in·closed′, in·clos′ing**

**in·clo·sure** (in klō′zhər) ***n.*** *another spelling for* **enclosure.**

**in·clude** (in klo͞od′) ***v.*** to have or take in as part of a whole; contain [Prices *include* taxes.] —**in·clud′ed, in·clud′ing**

**in·clu·sion** (in klo͞o′zhən) ***n.*** **1** a taking in as part of a whole. **2** something taken in, or included.

**in·clu·sive** (in klo͞o′siv) ***adj.*** including; especially, including both limits mentioned [A vacation from the first to the tenth *inclusive* is a vacation of ten days.] —**in·clu′sive·ly *adv.***

**in·cog·ni·to** (in′käg nēt′ō *or* in käg′ni tō′) ***adv., adj.*** using a false name [The king traveled *incognito.*]

**in·co·her·ent** (in′kō hir′ənt) ***adj.*** not clearly connected; confused; rambling [an *incoherent* story]. —**in′co·her′ence *n.*** —**in′co·her′ent·ly *adv.***

**in·com·bus·ti·ble** (in′kəm bus′tə b′l) ***adj.*** that cannot be burned; fireproof.

**in·come** (in′kum) ***n.*** the money that one gets as wages, salary, rent, interest, profit, etc.

**income tax** a tax on a person's income after certain amounts have been subtracted from that income.

**in·com·ing** (in′kum′iŋ) ***adj.*** coming in or about to come in [the *incoming* traffic]. ✦***n.*** a coming in [the *incoming* of the flood waters].



**in·com·mu·ni·ca·ble** (in′kə myo͞o′ni kə b′l) ***adj.*** that cannot be told to others.

☆**in·com·mu·ni·ca·do** (in′kə myo͞o′nə kä′dō) ***adj.*** not able to send messages to others [The prisoners were held *incommunicado.*]

**in·com·pa·ra·ble** (in käm′pər ə b′l) ***adj.*** so much greater or better that it cannot be compared with any other; without an equal; matchless [the *incomparable* genius of Shakespeare]. —**in·com′pa·ra·bly *adv.***

**in·com·pat·i·ble** (in′kəm pat′ə b′l) ***adj.*** **1** not getting along in a friendly or peaceful way; not in agreement [*incompatible* partners]. **2** not going well together; not in harmony [*incompatible* colors]. —**in′com·pat′i·bil′i·ty *n.***

**in·com·pe·tent** (in käm′pə tənt) ***adj.*** **1** not able to do what is needed; without enough skill or knowledge [an *incompetent* typist]. **2** not fit according to the law [Persons who are almost blind are judged to be *incompetent* to drive a car.] ✦***n.*** an incompetent person. —**in·com′pe·tence *n.*** —**in·com′pe·tent·ly *adv.***

**in·com·plete** (in kəm plēt′) ***adj.*** not complete; without all its parts; not whole or finished. —**in·com·plete′ly *adv.***

**in·com·pre·hen·si·ble** (in′käm pri hen′sə b′l) ***adj.*** that cannot be understood; not clear; obscure. —**in′com·pre·hen′si·bly *adv.***

**in·con·ceiv·a·ble** (in′kən sē′və b′l) ***adj.*** that cannot be thought of, imagined, or believed; unthinkable [It is *inconceivable* that Neal would lie.] —**in′con·ceiv′a·bly *adv.***

**in·con·clu·sive** (in′kən klo͞o′siv) ***adj.*** not final; not leading to a definite result [The tests were *inconclusive.*] —**in′con·clu′sive·ly *adv.***

**in·con·gru·i·ty** (in′kən gro͞o′ə tē) ***n.*** **1** the condition of being incongruous; lack of harmony or fitness. **2** something that is incongruous. —*pl.* **in′con·gru′i·ties**

**in·con·gru·ous** (in käŋ′gro͞o wəs) ***adj.*** not going well together; out of place; not fitting or proper. *See the picture.* —**in·con′gru·ous·ly *adv.***

**in·con·se·quen·tial** (in kän′sə kwen′shəl) ***adj.*** of no importance; too small or ordinary to matter; trivial [It cost an *inconsequential* sum.] —**in·con′se·quen′tial·ly *adv.***

**in·con·sid·er·a·ble** (in′kən sid′ər ə b′l) ***adj.*** not worth considering; trivial; small.

**in·con·sid·er·ate** (in′kən sid′ər it) ***adj.*** not thoughtful of other people; thoughtless.

**in·con·sis·ten·cy** (in′kən sis′tən sē) ***n.*** **1** the condition of being inconsistent. **2** an inconsistent thing. —*pl.* **in′con·sis′ten·cies**

**in·con·sis·tent** (in′kən sis′tənt) ***adj.*** **1** not always acting or thinking in the same way; changeable [You can't depend on an *inconsistent* person.] **2** not in agreement or harmony [The excuse he gave you is *inconsistent* with the one he gave me.] —**in′con·sis′tent·ly *adv.***

**in·con·sol·a·ble** (in′kən sōl′ə b′l) ***adj.*** that cannot be comforted or cheered; very sad or unhappy [The children were *inconsolable* when their dog died.] —**in′con·sol′a·bly *adv.***

**in·con·spic·u·ous** (in′kən spik′yo͞o wəs) ***adj.*** hard to see or notice; attracting little attention [an *inconspicuous* stain]. —**in′con·spic′u·ous·ly *adv.***

**in·con·stant** (in kän′stənt) ***adj.*** not constant or steady; changing often; changeable; fickle [an *inconstant* friend]. —**in·con′stan·cy *n.***

**in·con·test·a·ble** (in′kən tes′tə b′l) ***adj.*** that cannot be argued about or questioned [an *incontestable* decision].

**in·con·ven·ience** (in′kən vēn′yəns) ***n.*** **1** the condition of being inconvenient; trouble or bother. **2** anything that causes this. ✦***v.*** to cause trouble or bother to. —**in′con·ven′ienced, in′con·ven′ienc·ing**

**in·con·ven·ient** (in′kən vēn′yənt) ***adj.*** not convenient; causing trouble or bother.

**in·cor·po·rate** (in kôr′pə rāt) ***v.*** **1** to make part of another thing; combine with something else [*Incorporate* these new facts into your report.] **2** to bring together into a single whole; merge [The two churches have been *incorporated* into one.] **3** to form into a corporation [The owner of a store may *incorporate* his business.] —**in·cor′po·rat·ed, in·cor′po·rat·ing** —**in·cor′po·ra′tion *n.***

**in·cor·po·re·al** (in′kôr pôr′ē əl) ***adj.*** not made of matter; not material; spiritual.

**in·cor·rect** (in kə rekt′) ***adj.*** not correct; not right, true, proper, etc.; wrong [an *incorrect* answer; *incorrect* conduct]. —**in·cor·rect′ly *adv.*** —**in·cor·rect′ness *n.***

**in·cor·ri·gi·ble** (in kôr′i jə b′l) ***adj.*** that cannot be made better or cured because so bad or so deeply fixed [an *incorrigible* liar; an *incorrigible* habit]. ✦***n.*** an incorrigible person.

**in·cor·rupt** (in kə rupt′) ***adj.*** not corrupt; sound, pure, upright, honest, etc.

**in·cor·rupt·i·ble** (in′kə rup′tə b′l) ***adj.*** that cannot be corrupted, as by being bribed into doing wrong [an *incorruptible* official].

**in·crease** (in krēs′) ***v.*** to make or become greater, larger, etc.; add to or grow [When she *increased* her wealth, her power *increased*.] —**in·creased′, in·creas′ing** ◆***n.*** (in′krēs) **1** an increasing; addition; growth [an *increase* in population]. **2** the amount by which something increases [a population *increase* of 10%]. —**on the increase,** increasing.

**in·creas·ing·ly** (in krēs′iŋ lē) ***adv.*** more and more [She became *increasingly* happy.]

**in·cred·i·ble** (in kred′ə b'l) ***adj.*** so great, unusual, etc. that it is hard or impossible to believe [an *incredible* story; *incredible* speed]. —**in·cred′i·bly *adv.***

**in·cre·du·li·ty** (in′krə do͞o′lə tē *or* in′krə dyo͞o′lə tē) ***n.*** the state of being unwilling or unable to believe something; doubt.

**in·cred·u·lous** (in krej′oo ləs) ***adj.*** **1** not willing or able to believe; doubting; skeptical. **2** showing doubt or disbelief [an *incredulous* look]. —**in·cred′u·lous·ly *adv.***

**in·cre·ment** (in′krə mənt) ***n.*** **1** the amount by which something increases [a yearly *increment* of $300 in wages]. **2** a growing greater or larger; increase.

**in·crim·i·nate** (in krim′ə nāt) ***v.*** to say or show that someone is guilty [Her fingerprints on the murder weapon tend to *incriminate* her.] —**in·crim′i·nat·ed, in·crim′i·nat·ing** —**in·crim′i·na′tion *n.***

**in·crust** (in krust′) ***v.*** **1** to cover with a crust or layer [The vase is *incrusted* with minerals from water.] **2** to set into all parts of the surface of [a tiara *incrusted* with gems]. —**in′crus·ta′tion *n.***

**in·cu·bate** (iŋ′kyə bāt) ***v.*** **1** to hatch eggs by sitting on them or otherwise keeping them warm. **2** to develop or mature gradually [An idea was *incubating* in my mind.] —**in′cu·bat·ed, in′cu·bat·ing** —**in′cu·ba′tion *n.***

**in·cu·ba·tor** (iŋ′kyə bāt′ər) ***n.*** **1** a container that is kept warm for hatching eggs. **2** a container in which babies who are born too soon are kept warm and protected for a time. *See the picture.*

**in·cu·bus** (iŋ′kyə bəs) ***n.*** **1** a nightmare, or the evil spirit that was once thought to weigh a person down in a nightmare. **2** anything that weighs one down; burden.

**in·cul·cate** (in kul′kāt *or* in′kul kāt) ***v.*** to fix in a person's mind by teaching over and over again [to *inculcate* obedience in children]. —**in·cul′cat·ed, in·cul′cat·ing** —**in′cul·ca′tion *n.***

> **Inculcate** comes from a Latin word that means "to trample underfoot." After a thought or idea has been inculcated in one's mind, one may feel as if one's brain has been trampled over many times.

**in·cum·bent** (in kum′bənt) ***n.*** the person holding a certain office or position. ◆***adj.*** resting upon as a duty [It is *incumbent* upon the strong to help the weak.] —**in·cum′ben·cy *n.***

**in·cur** (in kur′) ***v.*** to bring something bad or unpleasant upon oneself [He *incurred* debts when he was out of work.] —**in·curred′, in·cur′ring**

**in·cur·a·ble** (in kyoor′ə b'l) ***adj.*** that cannot be cured [an *incurable* disease]. —**in·cur′a·bly *adv.***

**in·cu·ri·ous** (in kyoor′ē əs) ***adj.*** not curious or interested; not eager to find out.

**in·cur·sion** (in kur′zhən) ***n.*** a sudden, brief invasion or raid [the *incursions* of armed bands at a border].

**Ind.** *abbreviation for* **India, Indian, Indiana.**

incongruous way to herd cattle

incubator for babies

**ind.** *abbreviation for* **independent, index, industrial.**

**in·debt·ed** (in det′id) ***adj.*** owing money, thanks, etc.; in debt; obliged [I am *indebted* to the doctor for saving my life.]

**in·debt·ed·ness** (in det′id nis) ***n.*** **1** the condition of being indebted. **2** the amount owed; one's debts.

**in·de·cen·cy** (in dē′s'n sē) ***n.*** **1** the condition of being indecent; lack of decency. **2** an indecent act or remark. —*pl.* **in·de′cen·cies**

**in·de·cent** (in dē′s'nt) ***adj.*** **1** not decent, proper, or fitting [*indecent* vanity]. **2** not moral or modest; nasty [to call someone an *indecent* name]. —**in·de′cent·ly *adv.***

**in·de·ci·sion** (in′di sizh′ən) ***n.*** the state of being unable to decide or make up one's mind.

**in·de·ci·sive** (in′di sī′siv) ***adj.*** **1** not able to decide or make up one's mind; hesitating. **2** not deciding or settling anything [an *indecisive* reply]. —**in′de·ci′sive·ly *adv.***



**in·dec·o·rous** (in dek′ər əs) ***adj.*** not proper or fitting; lacking good taste; unbecoming.

**in·deed** (in dēd′) ***adv.*** in fact; truly; really [It is *indeed* warm.] ◆***interj.*** a word used to show surprise, doubt, scorn, etc.

**in·de·fen·si·ble** (in′di fen′sə b'l) ***adj.*** **1** that cannot be defended or protected [an *indefensible* bridge]. **2** that cannot be excused or proved right [Their rudeness was *indefensible*.]

**in·de·fin·a·ble** (in′di fīn′ə b'l) ***adj.*** that cannot be defined or described [an *indefinable* feeling].

**in·def·i·nite** (in def′ə nit) ***adj.*** **1** having no exact limits [an *indefinite* area]. **2** not clear or exact in meaning; vague [*indefinite* instructions]. **3** not sure or positive; uncertain [*indefinite* plans]. —**in·def′i·nite·ly *adv.***

**indefinite article** *see the note at* **article.**

**in·del·i·ble** (in del′ə b'l) ***adj.*** that cannot be erased or rubbed out; permanent [*indelible* ink; an *indelible* impression]. —**in·del′i·bly *adv.***

**in·del·i·ca·cy** (in del′i kə sē) ***n.*** **1** the quality of being indelicate. **2** an indelicate act, remark, etc. —*pl.* **in·del′i·ca·cies**

| | | | | | | | |
|---|---|---|---|---|---|---|---|
| **a** | fat | **ir** | here | **ou** | out | **zh** | leisure |
| **ā** | ape | **ī** | bite, fire | **u** | up | **ŋ** | ring |
| **ä** | car, lot | **ō** | go | **ur** | fur | | a *in* ago |
| **e** | ten | **ô** | law, horn | **ch** | chin | | e *in* agent |
| **er** | care | **oi** | oil | **sh** | she | **ə =** | i *in* unity |
| **ē** | even | **oo** | look | **th** | thin | | o *in* collect |
| **i** | hit | **o͞o** | tool | ***th*** | then | | u *in* focus |

**in·del·i·cate** (in del'i kit) ***adj.*** not refined or polite; improper; coarse [*indelicate* jokes].

**in·dem·ni·fy** (in dem'nə fī) ***v.*** **1** to pay back for some loss or injury [We were *indemnified* for our stolen car.] **2** to protect against loss or damage; insure. **—in·dem'ni·fied, in·dem'ni·fy·ing —in·dem'·ni·fi·ca'tion *n.***

**in·dem·ni·ty** (in dem'nə tē) ***n.*** **1** protection or insurance against loss or damage. **2** payment for loss or damage. *—pl.* **in·dem'ni·ties**

**in·dent** (in dent') ***v.*** **1** to cut notches into the edge of something; make jagged or uneven [The shoreline is *indented* with bays.] **2** to begin a line or lines of typed or written material farther in from the margin than the other material on the page.

**in·den·ta·tion** (in'den tā'shən) ***n.*** **1** the act of indenting. **2** an indented part; notch, bay, dent, etc.

**in·den·ture** (in den'chər) ***n.*** an agreement in writing; especially, a contract that binds a person to work for another for a certain length of time. **◆*v.*** to put under such a contract [an *indentured* servant]. **—in·den'·tured, in·den'tur·ing**

In earlier times, an **indenture** was a contract that had two copies, with edges notched so that they would fit together, proving they were copies of the same document. **Indenture** comes from the Latin word for "tooth." A notched edge looks like a row of teeth.



**in·de·pend·ence** (in'di pen'dəns) ***n.*** the state of being independent; freedom from the control of another or others.

☆**Independence Day** the Fourth of July, a legal holiday. The Declaration of Independence was adopted on July 4, 1776.

**in·de·pend·ent** (in'di pen'dənt) ***adj.*** **1** not ruled or controlled by another; self-governing [Many colonies became *independent* countries after World War II.] **2** not connected with others; separate [an *independent* grocer]. **3** not influenced by others; thinking for oneself [an *independent* voter]. **4** not depending on another for money to live on; supporting oneself. **5** that gives one enough to live on without working [an *independent* income]. **◆*n.*** an independent person; especially, ☆a voter who is not a member of any political party. **—in'de·pend'ent·ly *adv.***

**independent clause** *another name for* **main clause.**

**in-depth** (in'depth') ***adj.*** carefully worked out in detail; thorough [an *in-depth* study].

**in·de·scrib·a·ble** (in'di skrī'bə b'l) ***adj.*** that cannot be described; too beautiful, horrible, etc. to describe. **—in'de·scrib'a·bly *adv.***

**in·de·struct·i·ble** (in'di struk'tə b'l) ***adj.*** that cannot be destroyed; very strong. **—in'de·struct'i·bil'i·ty *n.* —in'de·struct'i·bly *adv.***

**in·de·ter·mi·nate** (in'di tʉr'mi nit) ***adj.*** not having exact limits; not definite; vague.

**in·dex** (in'deks) ***n.*** **1** a list as of names and subjects in alphabetical order at the end of a book, showing on what pages these names and subjects appear. **2** a thing that points out something else; indication [High wages are an *index* of prosperity.] **3** the finger next to the thumb; forefinger: *its full name is* **index finger.** *See the picture.* **4** a pointer, as the needle on a dial. *—pl.* **in'dex·es** or **in·di·ces** (in'də sēz) **◆*v.*** to make an index for [to *index* a book].

**In·di·a** (in'dē ə) **1** a large peninsula of southern Asia. **2** a country in the central and southern part of this peninsula. *See the map.*

**In·di·an** (in'dē ən) ***n.*** **1** a member of any of the peoples living in America when Europeans first came there: *also called* **American Indian. 2** a native person of India or the East Indies. **3** any of the languages of the American Indians. **◆*adj.*** **1** of the American Indians. **2** of India or the East Indies or their people.

**In·di·an·a** (in'dē an'ə) a State in the north central part of the U.S.: abbreviated **Ind., IN**

**In·di·an·ap·o·lis** (in'dē ə nap'ə lis) the capital of Indiana.

☆**Indian club** a wooden club swung in the hand for exercise. *See the picture.*

☆**Indian corn** *same as* **corn[1]** *in meaning* 1.

**Indian Ocean** an ocean south of Asia, between Africa and Australia.

☆**Indian pudding** a cornmeal pudding made with milk and molasses.

☆**Indian summer** a period of warm, hazy weather after the first frosts of late fall.

**in·di·cate** (in'də kāt) ***v.*** **1** to point out; make known; point to; show [*Indicate* with a pointer where India is on the map.] **2** to be or give a sign of [Smoke *indicates* fire.] **—in'di·cat·ed, in'di·cat·ing**

**in·di·ca·tion** (in'də kā'shən) ***n.*** **1** an indicating. **2** something that indicates, or shows; sign [The baby's smile was an *indication* of pleasure.]

**in·dic·a·tive** (in dik'ə tiv) ***adj.*** **1** that shows or is a sign of [Her questions are *indicative* of a keen mind.] **2** describing the mood of a verb used in making a statement of actual fact or in asking a question of fact [In the sentences "I went home" and "Is she here?", "went" and "is" are in the *indicative* mood.]

**in·di·ca·tor** (in'də kāt'ər) ***n.*** a pointer, dial, gauge, etc. that measures or shows something.

**in·di·ces** (in'də sēz) ***n.*** *a plural of* **index.**

**in·dict** (in dīt') ***v.*** to accuse of having committed a crime; especially, to order that a suspect be put on trial after being charged with some crime [A grand jury can *indict* a person if it decides there is enough evidence to do so.] **—in·dict'ment *n.***

**In·dies** (in'dēz) *a shorter form of* **East Indies** *and* **West Indies.**

**in·dif·fer·ence** (in dif'ər əns *or* in dif'rəns) ***n.*** **1** lack of interest or concern [the public's *indifference* to the high rate of crime]. **2** no importance [His election is a matter of *indifference* to me.]

**in·dif·fer·ent** (in dif'ər ənt *or* in dif'rənt) ***adj.*** **1** having or showing no interest or concern; unmoved [He remained *indifferent* to my pleas for help.] **2** neither very good nor very bad; mediocre [an *indifferent* singer]. **3** not taking sides; neutral [to remain *indifferent* in a dispute]. **—in·dif'fer·ent·ly *adv.***

SYNONYMS: To be **indifferent** is to show a lack of interest [Few people are *indifferent* to the kind of food they eat.] To be **disinterested** is to be fair and not take sides or try to benefit oneself [Judges for the contest must be *disinterested* men and women.]

**in·dig·e·nous** (in dij′ə nəs) ***adj.*** growing or living naturally in a certain place; native [The kangaroo is *indigenous* to Australia.]

**in·di·gent** (in′di jənt) ***adj.*** very poor or needy. —**in′·di·gence *n.***

**in·di·gest·i·ble** (in′di jes′tə b'l) ***adj.*** **1** that cannot be digested. **2** hard to digest.

**in·di·ges·tion** (in′di jes′chən) ***n.*** **1** difficulty in digesting food. **2** the discomfort caused by this.

**in·dig·nant** (in dig′nənt) ***adj.*** angry about something that seems unjust, unfair, mean, etc. [He was *indignant* when she said he was a liar.] —**in·dig′nant·ly *adv.***

**in·dig·na·tion** (in′dig nā′shən) ***n.*** anger at something that seems unjust, unfair, mean, etc.

**in·dig·ni·ty** (in dig′nə tē) ***n.*** something that insults or hurts one's pride [The student resented the *indignity* of being scolded in front of the class.] —*pl.* **in·dig′ni·ties**

**in·di·go** (in′di gō) ***n.*** **1** a blue dye that comes from a certain plant of the pea family or is now made artificially. **2** deep violet-blue.

> **Indigo** is a Spanish word that comes from two Greek words that mean "Indian dye." The plant from which the dye was originally made came from India.

**in·di·rect** (in′di rekt′) ***adj.*** **1** not direct or straight; by a longer way; roundabout [an *indirect* route]. **2** not the main one; secondary [an *indirect* benefit]. **3** not straight to the point [an *indirect* reply]. —**in′di·rect′ly *adv.***

**indirect object** the word in a sentence that names the person or thing that something is given to or done for [In "Neal gave me a dime," "dime" is the direct object and "me" is the *indirect object.*] *See also* **direct object.**

**in·dis·creet** (in′dis krēt′) ***adj.*** not discreet; not careful about what one says or does; unwise. —**in′dis·creet′ly *adv.***

**in·dis·cre·tion** (in′dis kresh′ən) ***n.*** **1** lack of good judgment or care in what one says or does. **2** an indiscreet act or remark.

**in·dis·crim·i·nate** (in′dis krim′ə nit) ***adj.*** not paying attention to differences; not showing care in choosing; making no distinctions [*indiscriminate* praise for everyone; an *indiscriminate* buyer of books]. —**in′dis·crim′i·nate·ly *adv.***

**in·dis·pen·sa·ble** (in′dis pen′sə b'l) ***adj.*** that cannot be done without; absolutely necessary [Good brakes are *indispensable* to a car.]

**in·dis·posed** (in′dis pōzd′) ***adj.*** **1** not well; slightly sick. **2** not willing; unwilling.

**in·dis·po·si·tion** (in′dis pə zish′ən) ***n.*** **1** a slight sickness. **2** unwillingness.

**in·dis·pu·ta·ble** (in′dis pyo͞ot′ə b'l) ***adj.*** that cannot be argued against or doubted; certain [an *indisputable* truth]. —**in′dis·pu′ta·bly *adv.***

**in·dis·sol·u·ble** (in′di säl′yoo b'l) ***adj.*** that cannot be dissolved, broken up, etc.; lasting; durable [an *indissoluble* partnership].

**in·dis·tinct** (in′dis tiŋkt′) ***adj.*** not clearly heard, seen, or understood; dim or confused [an *indistinct* signature; an *indistinct* murmur of voices]. —**in′dis·tinct′ly *adv.***

**in·dis·tin·guish·a·ble** (in′dis tiŋ′gwish ə b'l) ***adj.*** that cannot be told apart because very much alike [The twins are *indistinguishable.*]

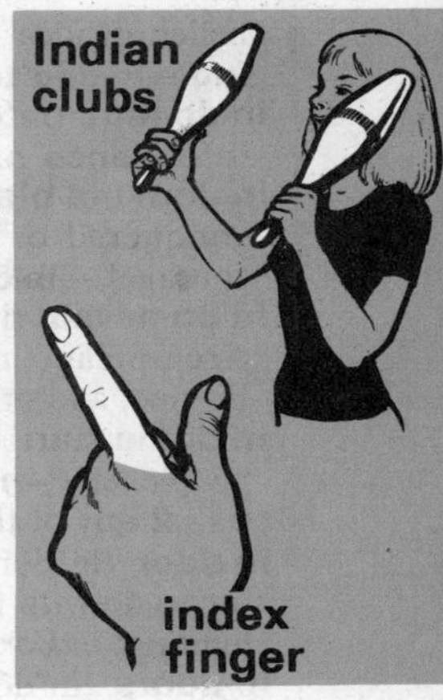

Indian clubs

index finger

**in·di·vid·u·al** (in′di vij′oo wəl) ***adj.*** **1** that is one separate being or thing; single [presents for each *individual* child]. **2** for or from each single person or thing [a dormitory with *individual* rooms; *individual* reports]. **3** different from others; personal or unusual [your *individual* way of signing your name]. *See* SYNONYMS *at* **characteristic.** ◆***n.*** **1** a single being or thing [to fight for the rights of the *individual*]. **2** a person [Rosita is a clever *individual.*]

**in·di·vid·u·al·ism** (in′di vij′oo wəl iz′m) ***n.*** **1** the living of one's life as one wants to live it. **2** the idea that the individual is more important than the state or nation. —**in′di·vid′u·al·ist *n., adj.*** —**in′di·vid′u·al·is′tic *adj.*** 375

**in·di·vid·u·al·i·ty** (in′di vij′oo wal′ə tē) ***n.*** **1** the qualities that make a person different from all others [Her unusual use of color shows her *individuality* as an artist.] **2** the condition of being different from others [Houses in the suburbs often have no *individuality.*]—*pl.* **in′di·vid′u·al′i·ties**

**in·di·vid·u·al·ize** (in′di vij′oo wə līz′) ***v.*** to make individual, or different from all others [to *individualize* one's writing]. —**in′di·vid′u·al·ized′, in′di·vid′u·al·iz′ing**

**in·di·vid·u·al·ly** (in′di vij′oo wəl ē) ***adv.*** in an individual way; one at a time; as individuals [I shall answer each of you *individually.*]

**in·di·vis·i·ble** (in′di viz′ə b'l) ***adj.*** **1** that cannot be divided or broken up [This nation is an *indivisible* union of States.] **2** that cannot be divided by another number without leaving a remainder [The number 17 is *indivisible.*] —**in′di·vis′i·bly *adv.***

**In·do·chi·na** (in′dō chī′nə) **1** a large peninsula in Asia, south of China. **2** a part of this peninsula consisting of Laos, Cambodia, and Vietnam. *Also spelled* **Indo-China** or **Indo China.** —**In·do·chi·nese** (in′dō chī nēz′) ***adj., n.***

**in·doc·tri·nate** (in däk′trə nāt) ***v.*** to teach a doctrine,

| | | | | | | | |
|---|---|---|---|---|---|---|---|
| **a** | fat | **ir** | here | **ou** | out | **zh** | leisure |
| **ā** | ape | **ī** | bite, fire | **u** | up | **ŋ** | ring |
| **ä** | car, lot | **ō** | go | **ur** | fur | | a *in* ago |
| **e** | ten | **ô** | law, horn | **ch** | chin | | e *in* agent |
| **er** | care | **oi** | oil | **sh** | she | **ə** = | i *in* unity |
| **ē** | even | **oo** | look | **th** | thin | | o *in* collect |
| **i** | hit | **o͞o** | tool | ***th*** | then | | u *in* focus |

belief, or idea to. —**in·doc′tri·nat·ed, in·doc′tri·nat·ing** —**in·doc′tri·na′tion** ***n.***

**in·do·lent** (in′də lənt) ***adj.*** not liking work; lazy. —**in′do·lence** ***n.*** —**in′do·lent·ly** ***adv.***

**in·dom·i·ta·ble** (in däm′it ə b'l) ***adj.*** that cannot be conquered or overcome; not yielding [*indomitable* courage]. —**in·dom′i·ta·bly** ***adv.***

**In·do·ne·sia** (in′də nē′zhə) a country in the Malay Archipelago made up of Java, Sumatra, most of Borneo, and other islands.

**In·do·ne·sian** (in′də nē′zhən) ***adj.*** of Indonesia, its people, etc. ◆***n.*** **1** a person born or living in Indonesia. **2** any of the languages spoken in Indonesia.

**in·door** (in′dôr) ***adj.*** being, belonging, done, or having to do with the inside of a house or building [*indoor* lighting; *indoor* sports].

**in·doors** (in′dôrz′) ***adv.*** in or into a house or other building [Let's go *indoors*.]

**in·dorse** (in dôrs′) ***v.*** *another spelling of* **endorse**. —**in·dorsed′, in·dors′ing**

**in·du·bi·ta·ble** (in dōō′bi tə b'l *or* in dyōō′bi tə b'l) ***adj.*** that cannot be doubted; certain [*indubitable* evidence]. —**in·du′bi·ta·bly** ***adv.***

**in·duce** (in dōōs′ *or* in dyōōs′) ***v.*** **1** to lead a person into doing something; persuade [Can't we *induce* you to go with us?] **2** to cause; bring on [Indigestion may be *induced* by overeating.] **3** to come to a general rule or conclusion by studying particular facts. **4** to produce an electric or magnetic effect by induction. —**in·duced′, in·duc′ing**

376

**in·duce·ment** (in dōōs′mənt *or* in dyōōs′mənt) ***n.*** **1** the act of inducing. **2** anything that induces [Your mother's cooking is an *inducement* for me to stay.]

**in·duct** (in dukt′) ***v.*** **1** to place in office with a ceremony; install [The new mayor was *inducted* this morning.] **2** to initiate into a society or club. ☆**3** to take a person into the armed forces, especially as a draftee.

**in·duc·tion** (in duk′shən) ***n.*** **1** an inducting or being inducted, as into office, a society, or the armed forces. **2** the act of coming to a general conclusion from particular facts; also, the conclusion reached. **3** the creating of magnetism or electricity in a body, as by bringing it near to a magnet or a conductor carrying an electric current. —**in·duc′tive** ***adj.***

**in·dulge** (in dulj′) ***v.*** **1** to give in to something one wants or wants to do; let oneself have some pleasure [to *indulge* a craving for sweets; to *indulge* in sports]. **2** to give in to the wishes of; humor [They *indulge* their children too much.] —**in·dulged′, in·dulg′ing**

SYNONYMS: To **indulge** oneself is to let oneself do or have what one wants, often because one has no willpower. To **indulge** another person is to let the person have or do anything, usually because one is eager to please. To **humor** someone is to give in to any wish or whim the person has [They *humored* him by laughing at all his jokes.]

**in·dul·gence** (in dul′jəns) ***n.*** **1** an indulging. **2** a thing indulged in [Playing golf is my one *indulgence*.] **3** a favor or right granted; permission. **4** in the Roman Catholic Church, a freeing from all or part of the punishment due in purgatory for a sin.

**in·dul·gent** (in dul′jənt) ***adj.*** indulging; kind or too kind; not at all strict [*indulgent* parents]. —**in·dul′gent·ly** ***adv.***

**In·dus** (in′dəs) a river in southern Asia, flowing from Tibet into the Arabian Sea.

**in·dus·tri·al** (in dus′trē əl) ***adj.*** having to do with industries or with the people working in industries [an *industrial* city; *industrial* unions]. —**in·dus′tri·al·ly** ***adv.***

**industrial arts** ☆the subjects taught to students in a school to make them skillful in using the tools, machines, etc. used in industry or in a trade.

**in·dus·tri·al·ist** (in dus′trē əl ist) ***n.*** an owner or manager of a large industry.

**in·dus·tri·al·ize** (in dus′trē ə līz′) ***v.*** to build up industries in [to *industrialize* an underdeveloped country]. —**in·dus′tri·al·ized′, in·dus′tri·al·iz′ing**

☆**industrial park** an area zoned for use by business and industry, usually located on the outskirts of a city.

**Industrial Revolution** the change in home life, work, and society that came about as things that had been made by hand, often at home, were made instead by machines and power tools, usually in factories. This revolution began in England in the 18th century.

**in·dus·tri·ous** (in dus′trē əs) ***adj.*** working hard and steadily. —**in·dus′tri·ous·ly** ***adv.***

**in·dus·try** (in′dəs trē) ***n.*** **1** any branch of business or manufacturing [the steel *industry;* the motion-picture *industry*]. **2** all business and manufacturing [Leaders of *industry* met in Chicago.] **3** hard, steady work; diligence. —*pl.* **in′dus·tries**

**-ine** (in) *a suffix meaning:* **1** of or like [A *crystalline* compound is made up of crystals.] **2** female; woman [A *heroine* is a woman hero.]

**in·e·bri·ate** (in ē′brē āt) ***v.*** to make drunk. —**in·e′bri·at·ed, in·e′bri·at·ing** ◆***n.*** (in ē′brē it) a drunkard.

**in·ed·i·ble** (in ed′ə b'l) ***adj.*** not fit to be eaten.

**in·ef·fa·ble** (in ef′ə b'l) ***adj.*** **1** too great to be described [*ineffable* beauty]. **2** too holy to be spoken [the *ineffable* name of God].

**in·ef·fec·tive** (in′i fek′tiv) ***adj.*** not having the result that is wanted; not effective [an *ineffective* punishment]. —**in′ef·fec′tive·ly** ***adv.***

**in·ef·fec·tu·al** (in′i fek′choo wəl) ***adj.*** not having the result wanted or not able to bring it about [an *ineffectual* plan to make money]. —**in′ef·fec′tu·al·ly** ***adv.***

**in·ef·fi·cient** (in′ə fish′ənt) ***adj.*** **1** not having the skill to do what is needed; incapable [an *inefficient* worker]. **2** not bringing the result wanted without wasting time, energy, or material [an *inefficient* motor]. —**in′ef·fi′cien·cy** ***n.*** —**in′ef·fi′cient·ly** ***adv.***

**in·e·las·tic** (in′i las′tik) ***adj.*** not elastic; stiff; rigid; not yielding.

**in·el·e·gant** (in el′ə gənt) ***adj.*** not elegant or refined; in poor taste; crude [*inelegant* manners]. —**in·el′e·gance** ***n.*** —**in·el′e·gant·ly** ***adv.***

**in·el·i·gi·ble** (in el′i jə b'l) ***adj.*** not fit to be chosen according to rules; not qualified [Poor grades made her *ineligible* for a scholarship.] —**in·el′i·gi·bil′i·ty** ***n.***

**in·ept** (in ept′) ***adj.*** **1** not right or suitable; wrong in a foolish and awkward way [*inept* praise]. **2** clumsy or bungling [an *inept* mechanic]. —**in·ept′ly** ***adv.*** —**in·ept′ness** ***n.***

**in·e·qual·i·ty** (in′i kwäl′ə tē) ***n.*** **1** the fact of not being equal in size, amount, position, etc. **2** lack of equality in the way something is available [educational *inequality*]. *—pl.* **in′e·qual′i·ties**

**in·eq·ui·ta·ble** (in ek′wit ə b′l) ***adj.*** not fair or just; unfair. —**in·eq′ui·ta·bly *adv.***

**in·eq·ui·ty** (in ek′wət ē) ***n.*** **1** lack of justice; unfairness. **2** an instance in which there is lack of justice. —*pl.* **in·eq′ui·ties**

**in·ert** (in ʉrt′) ***adj.*** **1** not having the power to move or act [*inert* matter]. **2** very slow in action; sluggish [I tried to rouse the *inert* members of the club.] **3** having no chemical action on other substances [*Inert* gases, as neon and helium, do not combine with other elements.]

**in·er·tia** (in ʉr′shə) ***n.*** **1** the natural force in matter that makes it stay at rest or keep on moving in a fixed direction unless it is acted on by an outside force. **2** a feeling that keeps one from wanting to do things, make changes, etc. [*Inertia* kept her from looking for a new job.]

> **Inertia** comes from a Latin word meaning "having no skill" or "idle." A person who does not know how to do a certain thing tends to be idle and not do anything. Inertia keeps such a person from moving or acting.

**in·es·cap·a·ble** (in′ə skāp′ə b′l) ***adj.*** that cannot be escaped or avoided; inevitable [an *inescapable* duty]. —**in′es·cap′a·bly *adv.***

**in·es·ti·ma·ble** (in es′tə mə b′l) ***adj.*** too great to be measured [a treasure of *inestimable* value].

**in·ev·i·ta·ble** (in ev′ə tə b′l) ***adj.*** that must happen; unavoidable. —**in·ev′i·ta·bly *adv.***

**in·ex·act** (in′ig zakt′) ***adj.*** not exact or accurate; not strictly correct.

**in·ex·cus·a·ble** (in′ik skyo͞o′zə b′l) ***adj.*** that cannot or should not be excused or forgiven; unpardonable. —**in′ex·cus′a·bly *adv.***

**in·ex·haust·i·ble** (in′ig zôs′tə b′l) ***adj.*** **1** too much to be used up or emptied [an *inexhaustible* water supply]. **2** that cannot be tired out; tireless [an *inexhaustible* worker].

**in·ex·or·a·ble** (in ek′sər ə b′l) ***adj.*** that cannot be stopped, altered, checked, etc. [She felt she was pursued by an *inexorable* fate.] —**in·ex′or·a·bly *adv.***

**in·ex·pe·di·ent** (in′ik spē′dē ənt) ***adj.*** not expedient; not right or suitable; unwise.

**in·ex·pen·sive** (in′ik spen′siv) ***adj.*** not expensive; low-priced. *See* SYNONYMS *at* **cheap**. —**in′ex·pen′sive·ly *adv.***

**in·ex·pe·ri·ence** (in′ik spir′ē əns) ***n.*** lack of experience or of the skill that it brings.

**in·ex·pe·ri·enced** (in′ik spir′ē ənst) ***adj.*** without experience or the skill that it brings.

**in·ex·pert** (in ek′spərt *or* in′ik spʉrt′) ***adj.*** not expert; unskilled.

**in·ex·pli·ca·ble** (in eks′pli kə b′l *or* in′ik splik′ə b′l) ***adj.*** that cannot be explained or understood. —**in·ex′pli·ca·bly *adv.***

**in·ex·press·i·ble** (in′ik spres′ə b′l) ***adj.*** that cannot be expressed or described.

**in·ex·tin·guish·a·ble** (in′ik stiŋ′gwish ə b′l) ***adj.*** that cannot be put out or stopped, as a fire or hope.

**in·ex·tri·ca·ble** (in eks′tri kə b′l *or* in′ik strik′ə b′l) ***adj.*** **1** that one cannot get oneself out of [an *inextricable* difficulty]. **2** that cannot be cleared up or straightened out [*inextricable* confusion].

**inf.** *abbreviation for* **infantry, infinitive, information.**

**in·fal·li·ble** (in fal′ə b′l) ***adj.*** **1** that cannot make a mistake; never wrong. **2** not likely to fail or go wrong; sure [*infallible* proof]. —**in·fal′li·bil′i·ty *n.*** —**in·fal′li·bly *adv.***

**in·fa·mous** (in′fə məs) ***adj.*** **1** having a very bad reputation; notorious [an *infamous* thief]. **2** very bad or wicked [an *infamous* crime]. —**in′fa·mous·ly *adv.***

**in·fa·my** (in′fə mē) ***n.*** **1** very bad reputation; disgrace; dishonor [He brought *infamy* on himself by his crime.] **2** great wickedness, or a wicked act. —*pl.* **in′fa·mies**

**in·fan·cy** (in′fən sē) ***n.*** **1** the time of being an infant; babyhood. **2** the earliest stage of anything [In 1900 the automobile industry was in its *infancy*.] —*pl.* **in′fan·cies**

**in·fant** (in′fənt) ***n.*** a very young child; baby. ◆***adj.*** **1** of or for infants [a book on *infant* care]. **2** in a very early stage [an *infant* nation].

> **Infant** comes from a Latin word meaning "not yet speaking." During the first year after birth, infants usually are "not yet speaking," except for a word or two.

**in·fan·tile** (in′fən tīl) ***adj.*** **1** of infants or infancy [*infantile* diseases]. **2** like an infant; babyish [*infantile* behavior].

**infantile paralysis** *another name for* **poliomyelitis.**

**in·fan·try** (in′fən trē) ***n.*** soldiers who are trained and armed for fighting on foot. 

**in·fan·try·man** (in′fən trē mən) ***n.*** a soldier in the infantry. —*pl.* **in′fan·try·men**

**in·fat·u·ate** (in fach′o͝o wāt) ***v.*** to make fall in love in a foolish or shallow way [You'll probably be *infatuated* with someone else next week.] —**in·fat′u·at·ed, in·fat′u·at·ing** —**in·fat′u·a′tion *n.***

**in·fect** (in fekt′) ***v.*** **1** to make diseased with a germ, virus, etc. that can enter the body [The well water is *infected* with bacteria.] **2** to spread to other persons feelings, ideas, etc. that are good or bad [Her gaiety *infected* the whole group.]

**in·fec·tion** (in fek′shən) ***n.*** **1** an infecting or being infected. **2** a disease caused by a germ, virus, etc. **3** anything that infects.

**in·fec·tious** (in fek′shəs) ***adj.*** **1** caused by infection [Shingles is an *infectious* disease, but not contagious.] **2** tending to spread to others [*infectious* laughter]. —**in·fec′tious·ly *adv.***

**in·fer** (in fʉr′) ***v.*** to arrive at a conclusion or opinion by reasoning [I *infer* from your smile that you're happy.] —**in·ferred′, in·fer′ring**

> People who speak carefully use the word **imply**, rather than **infer**, in a sentence like this [He *implied* by his remarks that I was a liar.] The person who is speaking **implies** something in what is

| | | | | | | | |
|---|---|---|---|---|---|---|---|
| **a** | fat | **ir** | here | **ou** | out | **zh** | leisure |
| **ā** | ape | **ī** | bite, fire | **u** | up | **ŋ** | ring |
| **ä** | car, lot | **ō** | go | **ʉr** | fur | | a *in* ago |
| **e** | ten | **ô** | law, horn | **ch** | chin | | e *in* agent |
| **er** | care | **oi** | oil | **sh** | she | **ə =** | i *in* unity |
| **ē** | even | **o͝o** | look | **th** | thin | | o *in* collect |
| **i** | hit | **o͞o** | tool | ***th*** | then | | u *in* focus |

said. The person who is listening **infers** something from what is heard [I *inferred* from his remarks that he thought I was a liar.]

**in·fer·ence** (in′fər əns) ***n.*** **1** the act of inferring. **2** a conclusion or opinion arrived at by inferring.

**in·fe·ri·or** (in fir′ē ər) ***adj.*** **1** not so good as someone or something else [This bread is *inferior* to that bread.] **2** not very good; below average [*inferior* merchandise]. **3** lower in position, rank, etc. [A captain is *inferior* to a major.] ◆***n.*** an inferior person or thing.

**in·fe·ri·or·i·ty** (in fir′ē ôr′ə tē) ***n.*** the condition of being inferior.

**in·fer·nal** (in fʉr′n'l) ***adj.*** of hell or as if from hell; hellish; horrible [*infernal* torture].

**in·fer·no** (in fʉr′nō) ***n.*** **1** *another name for* **hell**. **2** any place that seems like hell [The desert was an *inferno* in the noonday sun.] —*pl.* **in·fer′nos**

**in·fest** (in fest′) ***v.*** to swarm in or over, so as to harm or bother [Mice *infested* the house.]

**in·fi·del** (in′fə d'l) ***n.*** **1** a person who has no religion. **2** a person who does not believe in a certain religion, especially in the main religion of the person's country; among Christians, a non-Christian. ◆***adj.*** that is an infidel or has to do with infidels.

**in·fi·del·i·ty** (in′fə del′ə tē) ***n.*** **1** the state of being untrue to one's promise, duty, etc.; unfaithfulness, especially by committing adultery. **2** lack of belief in religion or in a certain religion. —*pl.* **in′fi·del′i·ties**

378 **in·field** (in′fēld) ***n.*** ☆**1** the part of a baseball field enclosed by the four base lines. ☆**2** all the infielders.

☆**in·field·er** (in′fēld′ər) ***n.*** a baseball player whose position is in the infield; any of the basemen or the shortstop.

**in·fil·trate** (in fil′trāt *or* in′fil trāt) ***v.*** to pass through or into, as if being filtered [Our troops *infiltrated* the enemy lines.] —**in·fil′trat·ed, in·fil′trat·ing —in′fil·tra′tion *n.***

**in·fi·nite** (in′fə nit) ***adj.*** **1** that has no limits; without beginning or end [Is the universe *infinite?*] **2** very great; vast [*infinite* love]. ◆***n.*** something infinite. —**in′fi·nite·ly *adv.***

**in·fin·i·tes·i·mal** (in′fin ə tes′ə məl) ***adj.*** too small to be measured. —**in′fin·i·tes′i·mal·ly *adv.***

**in·fin·i·tive** (in fin′ə tiv) ***n.*** a form of a verb that does not show person, number, or tense, and is usually used with "to" [In "I need to eat" and "I must eat," "eat" is an *infinitive*.]

**in·fin·i·tude** (in fin′ə to͞od *or* in fin′ə tyo͞od) ***n.*** **1** the fact of being infinite. **2** a vast number, extent, etc. [an *infinitude* of details].

**in·fin·i·ty** (in fin′ə tē) ***n.*** **1** the fact of being infinite. **2** space, time, or number without beginning or end. **3** a very great number, extent, etc. —*pl.* **in·fin′i·ties**

**in·firm** (in fʉrm′) ***adj.*** not strong; weak or feeble [*infirm* from old age; an *infirm* will].

**in·fir·ma·ry** (in fʉr′mə rē) ***n.*** a room or building where people who are sick or injured are cared for, especially at a school or other institution. —*pl.* **in·fir′ma·ries**

**in·fir·mi·ty** (in fʉr′mə tē) ***n.*** weakness or sickness. —*pl.* **in·fir′mi·ties**

**in·flame** (in flām′) ***v.*** **1** to make excited or angry. **2** to make greater or stronger [His laughter *inflamed* my rage.] **3** to make or become hot, swollen, red, and sore [a wound *inflamed* by infection]. —**in·flamed′, in·flam′ing**

**in·flam·ma·ble** (in flam′ə b'l) ***adj.*** **1** *another word for* **flammable**. *See the note at* **flammable**. **2** easily excited. —**in·flam′ma·bil′i·ty *n.***

**in·flam·ma·tion** (in′flə mā′shən) ***n.*** **1** a hot, red, sore swelling in some part of the body, caused by disease or injury. **2** an inflaming or being inflamed.

**in·flam·ma·to·ry** (in flam′ə tôr′ē) ***adj.*** **1** likely to stir up anger or trouble [an *inflammatory* speech]. **2** of or caused by inflammation.

**in·flate** (in flāt′) ***v.*** **1** to swell out by putting in air or gas; expand [to *inflate* a balloon]. **2** to make proud or happy [The team is *inflated* by its victory.] **3** to make greater or higher than normal [War *inflates* prices.] —**in·flat′ed, in·flat′ing**

**in·fla·tion** (in flā′shən) ***n.*** **1** an inflating or being inflated. ☆**2** an increase in the amount of money in circulation. It makes the money less valuable and brings prices up.

**in·fla·tion·ar·y** (in flā′shən er′ē) ***adj.*** causing or caused by inflation.

**in·flect** (in flekt′) ***v.*** **1** to change the tone or pitch of the voice. **2** to change the form of a word by inflection.

**in·flec·tion** (in flek′shən) ***n.*** **1** a change in the tone or pitch of the voice [A rising *inflection* at the end of a sentence often means a question.] **2** a change in the form of a word to show case, number, gender, tense, comparison, etc. [The word "he" is changed by *inflection* to "him" or "his," depending on what case is needed.] —**in·flec′tion·al *adj.***

**in·flex·i·ble** (in flek′sə b'l) ***adj.*** not flexible; stiff, rigid, fixed, unyielding, etc. [*inflexible* steel rods; *inflexible* rules]. —**in·flex′i·bil′i·ty *n.*** —**in·flex′i·bly *adv.***

**in·flict** (in flikt′) ***v.*** **1** to cause as by striking; make suffer [to *inflict* a wound; to *inflict* pain]. **2** to impose, or put on [to *inflict* a penalty; to *inflict* a tax]. —**in·flic′tion *n.***

**in·flow** (in′flō) ***n.*** **1** the act of flowing in. **2** anything that flows in.

**in·flu·ence** (in′flo͞o wəns) ***n.*** **1** the power to act on or affect persons or things [under the *influence* of a drug]. **2** a person or thing that has this power [He's a good *influence* on the children.] **3** power that comes from being rich or having a high position [a person of *influence*]. ◆***v.*** to have influence or power over [Her advice *influenced* my decision.] —**in′flu·enced, in′flu·enc·ing**

**Influence** comes from a Latin word meaning "to flow in." Originally, the word was used by astrologers for the power that was supposedly flowing in from the stars to affect human lives.

**in·flu·en·tial** (in′flo͞o wen′shəl) ***adj.*** having or using influence, especially great influence; powerful. —**in′flu·en′tial·ly *adv.***

**in·flu·en·za** (in′flo͞o wen′zə) ***n.*** a disease caused by a virus, like a bad cold only more serious.

**in·flux** (in′fluks) ***n.*** a coming in or pouring in without stopping [an *influx* of tourists from Canada].

**in·fold** (in fōld′) ***v.*** *another spelling of* **enfold**.

**in·form** (in fôrm′) ***v.*** **1** to give facts to; tell [*Inform* us when you plan to move.] **2** to give information or tell secrets that harm another; tattle [The spy *informed* against his friends.]

**in·for·mal** (in fôr′məl) ***adj.*** **1** not following fixed rules or forms; relaxed or familiar [an *informal* letter; an *informal* dinner]. **2** of or in everyday talk; colloquial [*informal* writing]. —**in·for′mal·ly** ***adv.***

**in·for·mal·i·ty** (in′fôr mal′ə tē) ***n.*** **1** the condition of being informal. **2** an informal act. —*pl.* **in′for·mal′i·ties**

**in·form·ant** (in fôr′mənt) ***n.*** a person who gives information or facts about something.

**in·for·ma·tion** (in′fər mā′shən) ***n.*** **1** an informing or being informed [This is for your *information* only.] **2** something told or facts learned; news or knowledge; data [An encyclopedia gives *information* about many things.] **3** a person or service that answers certain questions [Ask *information* for the location of the shoe department.]

SYNONYMS: **Information** is made up of facts that have been gathered by reading, looking, listening, etc. and that may or may not be true [a book full of *information*]. **Knowledge** is the result of gathering and studying the facts about something and drawing conclusions by reasoning based on the facts [our *knowledge* of outer space].

**in·form·a·tive** (in fôr′mə tiv) ***adj.*** that gives information or facts [an *informative* talk].

**in·form·er** (in fôr′mər) ***n.*** a person who secretly accuses another, often for a reward.

**in·frac·tion** (in frak′shən) ***n.*** a breaking of a law, rule, or agreement; violation.

**in·fra·red** (in′frə red′) ***adj.*** describing rays of light that are just beyond red in the spectrum. They cannot be seen but they produce heat deep inside an object.

**in·fre·quent** (in frē′kwənt) ***adj.*** not frequent; rare; uncommon. —**in·fre′quent·ly** ***adv.***

**in·fringe** (in frinj′) ***v.*** **1** to fail to obey; break or violate [to *infringe* a law]. **2** to break in; encroach [to *infringe* on the rights of others]. —**in·fringed′**, **in·fring′ing** —**in·fringe′ment** ***n.***

**in·fu·ri·ate** (in fyoor′ē āt) ***v.*** to make very angry; enrage. —**in·fu′ri·at·ed**, **in·fu′ri·at·ing**

**in·fuse** (in fyo͞oz′) ***v.*** **1** to put or pour in; instill [The teacher *infused* a desire to learn into the students.] **2** to fill or inspire [Your talk *infused* us with hope.] **3** to soak or steep [Tea is made by *infusing* tea leaves in hot water.] —**in·fused′**, **in·fus′ing** —**in·fu·sion** (in fyo͞o′zhən) ***n.***

**-ing** (iŋ) *a suffix used to form the present participle of many verbs* [*eating*]. *It is also used as a suffix meaning:* **1** the act of [A *washing* is the act of one who washes.] **2** something made by or used for [A *painting* is something made by a painter. *Carpeting* is material used for carpets.] **3** something that [A *covering* is something that covers.]

**in·gen·ious** (in jēn′yəs) ***adj.*** **1** clever or skillful, as at inventing things [an *ingenious* designer]. **2** made or done in a clever way [an *ingenious* plan]. —**in·gen′ious·ly** ***adv.***

**in·ge·nu·i·ty** (in′jə no͞o′ə tē *or* in′jə nyo͞o′ə tē) ***n.*** the quality of being ingenious; cleverness.

**in·gen·u·ous** (in jen′yoo wəs) ***adj.*** frank or innocent in an open or natural way [The *ingenuous* fellow believed that everyone liked him.] —**in·gen′u·ous·ly** ***adv.***

**in·glo·ri·ous** (in glôr′ē əs) ***adj.*** **1** bringing shame; disgraceful [an *inglorious* defeat]. **2** without glory; not famous: *used mostly in old poems.*

**in·got** (iŋ′gət) ***n.*** gold, steel, or other metal cast into a bar or other solid shape. *See the picture on page 380.*

**in·grained** (in grānd′) ***adj.*** that cannot be changed; firmly fixed [an *ingrained* habit].

**in·grate** (in′grāt) ***n.*** an ungrateful person.

**in·gra·ti·ate** (in grā′shē āt) ***v.*** to make oneself liked by doing things that please [He tried to *ingratiate* himself by flattering me.] —**in·gra′ti·at·ed**, **in·gra′ti·at·ing**

**in·grat·i·tude** (in grat′ə to͞od *or* in grat′ə tyo͞od) ***n.*** a lack of gratitude; ungratefulness.

**in·gre·di·ent** (in grē′dē ənt) ***n.*** any of the things that a mixture is made of [Sugar is a basic *ingredient* of candy.]

**in·gress** (in′gres) ***n.*** **1** the act of entering or the right to enter. **2** a place for entering; entrance.

**in·grown** (in′grōn) ***adj.*** that has grown inward, as a toenail that curves under at the sides.

**in·hab·it** (in hab′it) ***v.*** to live in or on; occupy [The island is not *inhabited*.]

**in·hab·it·a·ble** (in hab′it ə b′l) ***adj.*** that can be inhabited; fit to live in.

**in·hab·it·ant** (in hab′i tənt) ***n.*** a person or animal that lives in a certain place.

**in·hal·ant** (in hāl′ənt) ***n.*** a medicine that is breathed in as a vapor.



☆**in·ha·la·tor** (in′hə lāt′ər) ***n.*** **1** a device used for inhaling a medicine as a vapor. **2** *another name for* **respirator.**

**in·hale** (in hāl′) ***v.*** to breathe in; draw into the lungs, as air or tobacco smoke. —**in·haled′**, **in·hal′ing** —**in·ha·la·tion** (in′hə lā′shən) ***n.*** —**in·hal′er** ***n.***

**in·har·mo·ni·ous** (in′här mō′nē əs) ***adj.*** not harmonious; not blending well or getting along well together [an *inharmonious* relationship].

**in·her·ent** (in hir′ənt *or* in her′ənt) ***adj.*** being a natural part of someone or something; characteristic [Rudy's *inherent* shyness kept him from speaking.] —**in·her′ent·ly** ***adv.***

**in·her·it** (in her′it) ***v.*** **1** to get from someone when that person dies; receive as an heir [Marie *inherited* her aunt's fortune.] **2** to have or get certain characteristics because one's parents or ancestors had them [Ed *inherited* his father's good looks.] —**in·her′i·tor** ***n.***

**in·her·i·tance** (in her′it əns) ***n.*** **1** the act or right of inheriting. **2** something inherited.

**in·hib·it** (in hib′it) ***v.*** to hold back or keep from some action, feeling, etc.; check [a boy *inhibited* by fear; a spray that *inhibits* sweating].

**in·hi·bi·tion** (in′hi bish′ən) ***n.*** **1** an inhibiting or being inhibited. **2** anything that inhibits; especially, some process in the mind that holds one back from

| | | | | | | | |
|---|---|---|---|---|---|---|---|
| **a** | fat | **ir** | here | **ou** | out | **zh** | leisure |
| **ā** | ape | **ī** | bite, fire | **u** | up | **ŋ** | ring |
| **ä** | car, lot | **ō** | go | **ur** | fur | | a *in* ago |
| **e** | ten | **ô** | law, horn | **ch** | chin | | e *in* agent |
| **er** | care | **oi** | oil | **sh** | she | **ə =** | i *in* unity |
| **ē** | even | **oo** | look | **th** | thin | | o *in* collect |
| **i** | hit | **o͞o** | tool | ***th*** | then | | u *in* focus |

**i**

steel ingot

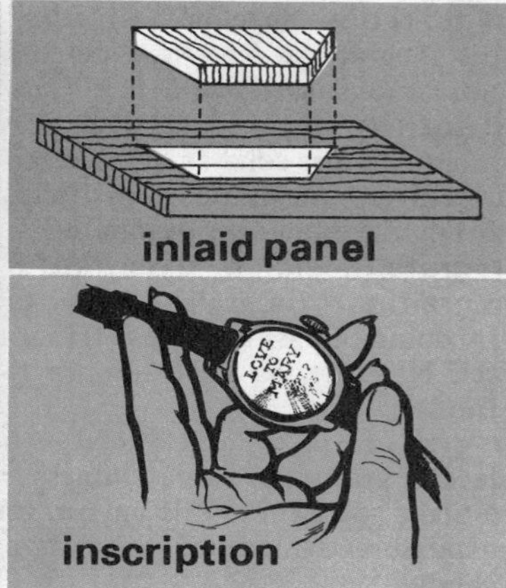
inlaid panel

inscription


some action, feeling, etc. [His *inhibitions* kept him from relaxing.]

**in·hos·pi·ta·ble** (in häs′pi tə b'l) ***adj.*** not hospitable; not kind or generous to visitors.

**in·hu·man** (in hyo͞o′mən) ***adj.*** cruel, heartless, or unfeeling. —**in·hu·man·i·ty** (in′hyo͞o man′ə tē) ***n.***

**in·im·i·cal** (in im′i k'l) ***adj.*** **1** unfriendly; showing hate [*Inimical* nations may go to war.] **2** acting against a thing; harmful [laws *inimical* to free speech; drugs *inimical* to health].

**in·im·i·ta·ble** (in im′ə tə b'l) ***adj.*** that cannot be imitated or copied [Mark Twain's *inimitable* humor.]



**in·iq·ui·tous** (in ik′wə təs) ***adj.*** very wicked or unjust [Jezebel was an *iniquitous* woman.]

**in·iq·ui·ty** (in ik′wə tē) ***n.*** **1** great wickedness or injustice. **2** a very wicked or unjust act. —*pl.* **in·iq′ui·ties**

**in·i·tial** (i nish′əl) ***adj.*** of or at the beginning; first [the *initial* stage of a disease]. ◆***n.*** the first letter of a name [Richard Wright's *initials* were R.W.] ◆***v.*** to mark with one's initials [He *initialed* the letter to show he had read it.] —**in·i′tialed** or **in·i′tialled, in·i′tial·ing** or **in·i′tial·ling**

**in·i·tial·ly** (i nish′əl ē) ***adv.*** at first; at the beginning.

**in·i·ti·ate** (i nish′ē āt) ***v.*** **1** to begin to use, do, make, etc.; start [The company will *initiate* a new line of sporting goods.] **2** to give the first knowledge or experience of something to [I *initiated* Joan into the game of chess.] **3** to take in as a member of a fraternity, sorority, or club, with a special or secret ceremony. —**in·i′ti·at·ed, in·i′ti·at·ing** ◆***n.*** (i nish′ē it) a person who has just been initiated. —**in·i′ti·a′tion** ***n.*** —**in·i′ti·a·tor** ***n.***

**in·i·ti·a·tive** (i nish′ē ə tiv *or* i nish′ə tiv) ***n.*** **1** the first step in bringing something about [Julia took the *initiative* in forming our club.] **2** the ability to get things started or done without needing to be told what to do. **3** the right of citizens to get a new law voted on by means of petitions calling for such a vote.

**in·ject** (in jekt′) ***v.*** **1** to force a fluid in; especially, to force a liquid into some part of the body [The doctor *injected* the serum in Bob's arm with a hypodermic syringe.] **2** to break in with [to *inject* a note of humor into a serious story]. —**in·jec′tion** ***n.*** —**in·jec′tor** ***n.***

**in·ju·di·cious** (in′jo͞o dish′əs) ***adj.*** showing poor judgment; unwise.

**in·junc·tion** (in jungk′shən) ***n.*** an order or command; especially, an order from a court of law forbidding something or ordering something to be done.

**in·jure** (in′jər) ***v.*** to do harm to; hurt or damage [to *injure* a leg; to *injure* one's pride]. —**in′jured, in′jur·ing**

> SYNONYMS: To **injure** is to mar the looks, health, or good condition of [She *injured* her hand when the knife slipped.] To **harm** is to cause much pain or suffering [No one was *harmed* by the explosion.] To **damage** is to make less valuable or useful by injuring [The store was *damaged* by fire.]

**in·ju·ri·ous** (in jo͝or′ē əs) ***adj.*** harmful or damaging [Smoking can be *injurious* to one's health.]

**in·ju·ry** (in′jər ē) ***n.*** harm or damage done to a person or thing [*injuries* received in a fall; *injury* to one's good name]. —*pl.* **in′ju·ries**

**in·jus·tice** (in jus′tis) ***n.*** **1** lack of justice or fairness [the *injustice* of being put in prison without having a trial]. **2** an unjust act; a wrong.

**ink** (ingk) ***n.*** a black or colored liquid or paste used for writing, printing, etc. ◆***v.*** to cover, mark, or color with ink.

**ink·ling** (ingk′ling) ***n.*** a slight hint or suggestion; vague idea [I had no *inkling* he was a thief.]

**ink·well** (ingk′wel) ***n.*** a container for holding ink, usually set into a desk.

**ink·y** (ing′kē) ***adj.*** **1** like ink in color; black or dark. **2** covered, marked, or stained with ink. —**ink′i·er, ink′i·est**

**in·laid** (in′lād *or* in lād′) ***adj.*** **1** set into the surface in small pieces that form a smooth surface [a pine table top with an *inlaid* walnut design]. *See the picture.* **2** having a surface made in this way [an *inlaid* floor].

**in·land** (in′lənd) ***adj.*** not on or near the coast or border; inside a country or region [The Ohio River is an *inland* waterway.] ◆***adv.*** into or toward an inland area.

**in-law** (in′lô) ***n.*** a relative by marriage: *used only in everyday talk.*

**in·lay** (in′lā *or* in lā′) ***v.*** **1** to set into a surface to form a decoration. **2** to decorate in this way [to *inlay* a wood panel with mother-of-pearl]. —**in′laid, in′lay·ing** ◆***n.*** (in′lā) **1** inlaid decoration. **2** a filling of gold, etc. for a tooth, made from a mold and cemented into place. —*pl.* **in′lays**

**in·let** (in′let) ***n.*** **1** a narrow strip of water running into land, as from a river, lake, or ocean. **2** an opening or entrance.

**in·mate** (in′māt) ***n.*** a person kept in a prison, hospital, etc.

**in-mi·grant** (in′mī′grənt) ***adj.*** coming in from another region of the same country [*in-migrant* workers]. ◆***n.*** an in-migrant person.

**in·most** (in′mōst) ***adj.*** *another word for* **innermost.**

**inn** (in) ***n.*** **1** a hotel that has a tavern or restaurant. **2** a tavern or restaurant.

> The word **inn** is really just another spelling of **in.** In earlier times, the owner of a place with rooms to rent would put up a sign reading INN, meaning "Come in if you need a place to stay," just as today some small restaurants put up a sign reading EAT.

**in·nards** (in′ərdz) ***n.pl.*** the internal organs of the body, as the intestines, stomach, etc. *This word is used only in everyday talk.*

**in·nate** (i nāt′ *or* in′āt) ***adj.*** that seems to have been born in one; natural [an *innate* talent for music].

**in·ner** (in′ər) ***adj.*** **1** farther in; interior [the *inner* rooms of the palace]. **2** more secret or private [one's *inner* feelings].

☆**inner city** the sections of a large city in or near its center, especially when they are crowded or in bad condition.

**Inner Mongolia** a region in northeastern China.

**in·ner·most** (in′ər mōst) ***adj.*** **1** farthest in [the *innermost* chamber]. **2** most secret or private [one's *innermost* thoughts].

**in·ning** (in′iŋ) ***n.*** **1** a round of play in which both teams have a turn at bat. In baseball, there are usually nine innings, each team's turn being ended by three outs. **2** a turn at bat. **3** *often* **innings,** *pl.* the time a person or political party is in power.

**inn·keep·er** (in′kē′pər) ***n.*** a person who owns or manages an inn.

**in·no·cence** (in′ə səns) ***n.*** the condition of being innocent; freedom from guilt, trickery, harmfulness, etc.

**in·no·cent** (in′ə sənt) ***adj.*** **1** not guilty of some crime or sin; blameless [If his alibi is true, he is *innocent* of the robbery.] **2** that knows no evil; simple [an *innocent* child]. **3** that does no harm [an *innocent* entertainment]. ◆***n.*** an innocent person. —**in′no·cent·ly** ***adv.***

**in·noc·u·ous** (i näk′yoo wəs) ***adj.*** that cannot harm or hurt; harmless. —**in·noc′u·ous·ly** ***adv.***

**in·no·va·tion** (in′ə vā′shən) ***n.*** a new device or a new way of doing something; change [Lighting by electricity was an *innovation* in 1890.]

**in·no·va·tor** (in′ə vāt′ər) ***n.*** a person who makes changes or thinks of new ways to do things.

**Inns·bruck** (inz′brook) a city in the Alps of western Austria.

**in·nu·en·do** (in′yoo wen′dō) ***n.*** a hint or sly remark, especially one that suggests something bad about someone. —*pl.* **in′nu·en′does** or **in′nu·en′dos**

**in·nu·mer·a·ble** (i nōō′mər ə b'l *or* i nyōō′mər ə b'l) ***adj.*** more than can be counted; countless.

**in·oc·u·late** (i näk′yoo lāt) ***v.*** to inject into the body a serum or vaccine that will cause a mild form of a disease. In this way the body is able to build up its ability to fight off that disease later. —**in·oc′u·lat·ed, in·oc′u·lat·ing —in·oc′u·la′tion** ***n.***

**in·of·fen·sive** (in′ə fen′siv) ***adj.*** not offensive; causing no trouble; harmless.

**in·op·er·a·tive** (in äp′ər ə tiv) ***adj.*** not working; not in effect [an *inoperative* law].

**in·op·por·tune** (in äp′ər tōōn′ *or* in äp′ər tyōōn′) ***adj.*** happening at the wrong time; not suitable or appropriate [It was an *inopportune* time to call him, during the dinner hour.]

**in·or·di·nate** (in ôr′d'n it) ***adj.*** too great or too many; excessive. —**in·or′di·nate·ly** ***adv.***

**in·or·gan·ic** (in′ôr gan′ik) ***adj.*** made up of matter that is not animal or vegetable; not living [Minerals are *inorganic.*]

**in·put** (in′poot) ***n.*** what is put in, as electric power put into a machine to make it work, information fed into a computer to be stored, etc.

**in·quest** (in′kwest) ***n.*** an investigation made by a jury or a coroner in order to decide whether or not someone's death was the result of a crime.

**in·quire** (in kwīr′) ***v.*** to ask a question; ask about in order to learn [The students *inquired* about their grades. We *inquired* the way home.] —**in·quired′, in·quir′ing —in·quir′er** ***n.***

**in·quir·y** (in′kwə rē *or* in kwīr′ē) ***n.*** **1** the act of inquiring. **2** an investigation or examination. **3** a question; query. —*pl.* **in′quir·ies**

**in·qui·si·tion** (in′kwə zish′ən) ***n.*** **1** the act of inquiring; investigation. **2** **Inquisition,** a court for finding and punishing heretics, set up by the Roman Catholic Church in the 13th century and lasting until 1820. **3** strict control by those in power over the beliefs of others.

**in·quis·i·tive** (in kwiz′ə tiv) ***adj.*** asking many questions; curious; especially, too curious about others' affairs. —**in·quis′i·tive·ly** ***adv.***

**in·quis·i·tor** (in kwiz′ə tər) ***n.*** **1** a person who makes an investigation. **2** a harsh questioner. **3** **Inquisitor,** a member of the Inquisition.

**in·road** (in′rōd) ***n.*** **1** a sudden raid or attack. **2** *usually* **inroads,** *pl.* harm or damage [Eating too much will make *inroads* on your health.]

**ins.** *abbreviation for* **inches, insurance.**

**in·sane** (in sān′) ***adj.*** **1** mentally ill; not sane: *no longer much used except as a term in law.* ☆**2** of or for insane people. **3** very foolish; senseless. —**in·sane′ly** ***adv.***



**in·san·i·ty** (in san′ə tē) ***n.*** **1** the condition of being insane, or mentally ill: *no longer much used except as a term in law.* **2** a very foolish action or belief. —*pl.* **in·san′i·ties**

**in·sa·tia·ble** (in sā′shə b'l) ***adj.*** always wanting more; never satisfied; greedy [*insatiable* hunger]. —**in·sa′tia·bly** ***adv.***

**in·scribe** (in skrīb′) ***v.*** **1** to write, print, or engrave [an old tombstone *inscribed* with a verse]. **2** to add to a list [Nagy's name was *inscribed* on the Honor Roll.] **3** to fix firmly in the mind. —**in·scribed′, in·scrib′ing**

**in·scrip·tion** (in skrip′shən) ***n.*** **1** the act of inscribing. **2** something printed, written, or engraved, as on a coin or a monument or in a book. *See the picture.*

**in·scru·ta·ble** (in skrōōt′ə b'l) ***adj.*** that cannot be easily understood; strange; mysterious [an *inscrutable* look]. —**in·scru′ta·bly** ***adv.***

**in·seam** (in′sēm) ***n.*** an inner seam; especially, the seam from the crotch to the bottom of a trouser leg.

**in·sect** (in′sekt) ***n.*** **1** a small animal with six legs, usually two pairs of wings, and a head, thorax, and abdomen [Flies, ants, wasps, and mosquitoes are *insects.*] **2** any small animal somewhat like this, as the

| | | | | | | | |
|---|---|---|---|---|---|---|---|
| a | fat | ir | here | ou | out | zh | leisure |
| ā | ape | ī | bite, fire | u | up | ng | ring |
| ä | car, lot | ō | go | ur | fur | | a *in* ago |
| e | ten | ô | law, horn | ch | chin | | e *in* agent |
| er | care | oi | oil | sh | she | ə = | i *in* unity |
| ē | even | oo | look | th | thin | | o *in* collect |
| i | hit | ōō | tool | *th* | then | | u *in* focus |

spider, centipede, and louse: *this is a popular but not a scientific use.*

An **insect** has a body that is made up of three parts very clearly marked off, almost as if it had been cut into. The Latin word from which *insect* comes means "to cut into."

**in·sec·ti·cide** (in sek′tə sīd) ***n.*** any poison used to kill insects.

**in·se·cure** (in′si kyo͞or′) ***adj.*** **1** not secure or safe; dangerous; not dependable [an *insecure* mountain ledge; an *insecure* partnership]. **2** not feeling safe or confident [A person can feel *insecure* in a new job.] —**in′se·cure′ly *adv.*** —**in·se·cu·ri·ty** (in′si kyo͞or′ə tē) ***n.***

**in·sen·sate** (in sen′sāt) ***adj.*** **1** not having feelings, because not living; inanimate [*insensate* rocks]. **2** without reason or good sense [*insensate* fury].

**in·sen·si·ble** (in sen′sə b′l) ***adj.*** **1** not able to notice or feel [My frozen fingers were *insensible* to pain.] **2** unconscious [I fainted and lay *insensible.*] **3** not noticing or not concerned about; indifferent [Factory workers often become *insensible* to noise.] —**in·sen′si·bil′i·ty *n.*** —**in·sen′si·bly *adv.***

**in·sen·si·tive** (in sen′sə tiv) ***adj.*** not sensitive; not affected by [*insensitive* to music].

**in·sep·a·ra·ble** (in sep′ər ə b′l) ***adj.*** that cannot be separated or parted [*inseparable* friends]. —**in·sep′a·ra·bly *adv.***



**in·sert** (in surt′) ***v.*** to put or fit something into something else [to *insert* a key into a lock]. ✦***n.*** (in′sərt) something inserted or to be inserted, as an extra page or section inserted in a newspaper.

**in·ser·tion** (in sur′shən) ***n.*** **1** the act of inserting. **2** something inserted, as an advertisement in a newspaper.

**in·set** (in′set) ***n.*** something inserted or set in, as a small map set inside the border of a larger one. ✦***v.*** (in set′) to insert; set something into something else. —**in·set′, in·set′ting**

**in·shore** (in′shôr *or* in shôr′) ***adv., adj.*** toward the shore or near the shore.

**in·side** (in′sīd′) ***n.*** **1** the side or part that is within; interior [Wash the windows on the *inside.*] **2 insides,** *pl.* the organs within the body: *used only in everyday talk.* ✦***adj.*** **1** on or in the inside; internal; indoor [*inside* work; an *inside* page]. ☆**2** secret or private [*inside* information]. ✦***adv.*** (*usually* in sīd′) on or in the inside; within [They played *inside.*] ✦***prep.*** (*usually* in sīd′) within; in [*inside* the box]. —**inside out,** with the inside where the outside should be.

**in·sid·er** (in sīd′ər) ***n.*** a person who knows things that are known only to members of the person's group.

**in·sid·i·ous** (in sid′ē əs) ***adj.*** **1** dishonest, sly, or tricky [an *insidious* plot]. **2** more dangerous than it seems to be [an *insidious* disease]. —**in·sid′i·ous·ly *adv.***

**in·sight** (in′sīt) ***n.*** **1** the ability to understand things as they really are, especially by intuition. **2** a clear understanding of some problem or idea.

**in·sight·ful** (in′sīt fəl) ***adj.*** having or showing insight.

**in·sig·ni·a** (in sig′nē ə) ***n.*** a special mark or badge of some organization, rank, etc. *See the picture.* —*pl.* **in·sig′ni·a** or **in·sig′ni·as**

**in·sig·nif·i·cant** (in′sig nif′ə kənt) ***adj.*** not important; of little value [*insignificant* details]. —**in′sig·nif′i·cance *n.***

**in·sin·cere** (in′sin sir′) ***adj.*** not sincere; not meaning what one says or does. —**in′sin·cere′ly *adv.*** —**in·sin·cer·i·ty** (in′sin ser′ə tē) ***n.***

**in·sin·u·ate** (in sin′yo͞o wāt) ***v.*** **1** to get in slowly and in an indirect way, so as to be hardly noticed [to *insinuate* oneself into a group]. **2** to hint at something without actually saying it [Are you *insinuating* that I lied?] —**in·sin′u·at·ed, in·sin′u·at·ing** —**in·sin′u·a′tion *n.***

**in·sip·id** (in sip′id) ***adj.*** **1** having no flavor; tasteless. **2** not interesting; dull [*insipid* talk].

**in·sist** (in sist′) ***v.*** **1** to stick strongly to a belief [I *insist* that I saw them there.] **2** to demand strongly [I *insist* that you come for dinner.]

**in·sist·ent** (in sis′tənt) ***adj.*** **1** insisting or demanding [*insistent* pleas]. **2** that forces and keeps one's attention [an *insistent* pain]. —**in·sist′ence *n.*** —**in·sist′ent·ly *adv.***

**in·sole** (in′sōl) ***n.*** the inside sole of a shoe, especially an extra one put in for comfort. *See the picture.*

**in·so·lent** (in′sə lənt) ***adj.*** not having or showing the proper respect; rude. —**in′so·lence *n.*** —**in′so·lent·ly *adv.***

**in·sol·u·ble** (in säl′yo͞o b′l) ***adj.*** **1** that cannot be solved [an *insoluble* problem]. **2** that cannot be dissolved [an *insoluble* powder].

**in·sol·vent** (in säl′vənt) ***adj.*** not able to pay one's debts; bankrupt. —**in·sol′ven·cy *n.***

**in·som·ni·a** (in säm′nē ə) ***n.*** a condition in which it is difficult to fall asleep or stay asleep.

**in·som·ni·ac** (in säm′nē ak) ***n.*** a person who has insomnia.

**in·so·much** (in′sō much′) ***adv.*** to such a degree; so [She worked fast, *insomuch* that she finished first.] —**insomuch as,** *another phrase for* **inasmuch as.**

**in·spect** (in spekt′) ***v.*** **1** to look at carefully; examine [You should *inspect* the bicycle before you buy it.] **2** to examine officially; review [The major will *inspect* Company B.] —**in·spec′tion *n.***

**in·spec·tor** (in spek′tər) ***n.*** **1** a person who inspects, as in a factory. **2** a police officer who ranks next below a superintendent.

**in·spi·ra·tion** (in′spə rā′shən) ***n.*** **1** an inspiring or being inspired [Our cheers gave *inspiration* to the team.] **2** something that inspires thought or action [The ocean was an *inspiration* to the artist.] **3** an inspired idea, action, etc. [Your bringing the camera was an *inspiration.*] **4** a breathing in; inhaling. —**in′spi·ra′tion·al *adj.***

**in·spire** (in spīr′) ***v.*** **1** to cause, urge, or influence to do something [The sunset *inspired* her to write a poem.] **2** to cause to have a certain feeling or thought [Praise *inspires* us with confidence.] **3** to arouse or bring about [Your kindness *inspired* his love.] **4** to do or make as if guided by some higher power [The Bible is an *inspired* book.] **5** to breathe in; inhale. —**in·spired′, in·spir′ing**

**Inst.** *abbreviation for* **Institute, Institution.**

**in·sta·bil·i·ty** (in′stə bil′ə tē) ***n.*** the condition of being unstable; lack of firmness or steadiness.

**in·stall** (in stôl′) ***v.*** **1** to place in an office or position with a ceremony [We saw the new governor *installed.*]

2 to fix in position for use [to *install* a gas stove]. 3 to put or settle in a place [The cat *installed* itself in the big chair.] —**in·stal·la·tion** (in′stə lā′shən) *n.*

**in·stall·ment** or **in·stal·ment** (in stôl′mənt) *n.* 1 a sum of money that a person pays at regular times until the total amount that is owed has been paid [I paid the debt in nine monthly *installments.*] 2 one of several parts that appear at different times, as of a serial story in a magazine. 3 an installing or being installed.

**in·stance** (in′stəns) *n.* 1 an example; something that shows or proves [This gift is another *instance* of their generosity.] 2 an occasion or case [The fine in the first *instance* is $10.]

**in·stant** (in′stənt) *n.* 1 a very short time; moment [Wait just an *instant.*] 2 a particular moment [At that *instant* the bell rang.] ✦*adj.* 1 with no delay; immediate [an *instant* response]. 2 calling for fast action; urgent [an *instant* need for change]. 3 that can be prepared quickly, as by adding water [*instant* coffee].

**in·stan·ta·ne·ous** (in′stən tā′nē əs) *adj.* done or happening in an instant [an *instantaneous* effect]. —**in′stan·ta′ne·ous·ly** *adv.*

**in·stant·ly** (in′stənt lē) *adv.* with no delay; in an instant; immediately.

**in·stead** (in sted′) *adv.* in place of the other; as a substitute [If you have no cream, use milk *instead.*] —**instead of,** in place of.

**in·step** (in′step) *n.* 1 the upper part of the foot at the arch. *See the picture.* 2 the part of a shoe or stocking that covers this.

**in·sti·gate** (in′stə gāt) *v.* to stir up or urge on, or bring about by urging [to *instigate* a plot]. —**in′sti·gat·ed, in′sti·gat·ing** —**in′sti·ga′tion** *n.* —**in′sti·ga′tor** *n.*

**in·still** or **in·stil** (in stil′) *v.* to put an idea or feeling into someone's mind in a slow but sure way [We must *instill* honesty in our children.] —**in·stilled′, in·still′·ing**

**Instill** comes from a Latin word meaning "to put a liquid in drop by drop," and this was its first meaning in English. From this meaning comes the one we have today, "to put an idea or feeling into the mind little by little."

**in·stinct** (in′stiŋkt) *n.* 1 a way of acting, feeling, etc. that is natural to an animal from birth [the *instinct* of birds for building nests]. 2 a natural ability or knack; talent [an *instinct* for saying the right thing].

**in·stinc·tive** (in stiŋk′tiv) *adj.* caused or done by instinct; seeming to be natural to one since birth [an *instinctive* fear of the dark]. —**in·stinc′tive·ly** *adv.*

**in·sti·tute** (in′stə to͞ot *or* in′stə tyo͞ot) *v.* 1 to set up; bring into being; establish [The modern Olympic games were *instituted* in 1896.] 2 to start; enter upon [The police *instituted* a search.] —**in′sti·tut·ed, in′sti·tut·ing** ✦*n.* a school or organization for some special study or work, as in education, science, art, etc.

**in·sti·tu·tion** (in′stə to͞o′shən *or* in′stə tyo͞o′shən) *n.* 1 an instituting or being instituted. 2 an established law, custom, practice, etc. [the *institution* of marriage]. 3 a school, church, hospital, prison, or other organization for doing some special work. —**in′sti·tu′tion·al** *adj.*

**in·struct** (in strukt′) *v.* 1 to teach or train [The teacher *instructed* me in science.] *See* SYNONYMS *at* teach. 2 to order or direct [The sentry was *instructed* to shoot.] 3 to give certain facts, rules, etc. to; inform [The judge *instructed* the jury.]

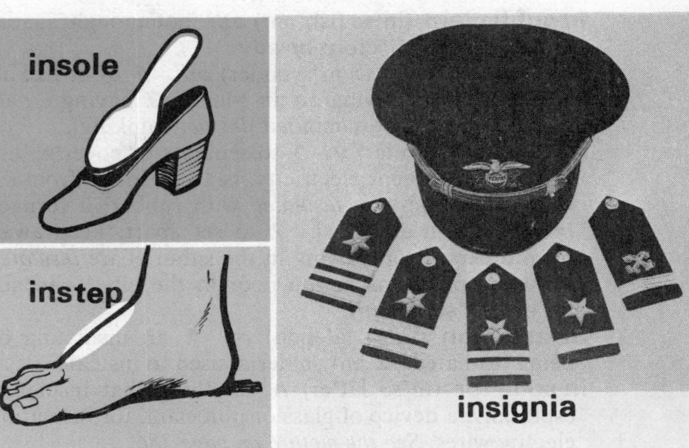


**in·struc·tion** (in struk′shən) *n.* 1 the act of teaching; education [The philosopher spent a lifetime in the *instruction* of others.] 2 something taught; lesson [swimming *instruction*]. 3 **instructions,** *pl.* orders or directions [*instructions* for a test].

**in·struc·tive** (in struk′tiv) *adj.* instructing; giving knowledge [an *instructive* book].

**in·struc·tor** (in struk′tər) *n.* 1 a teacher. ☆2 a college teacher ranking below an assistant professor.



**in·stru·ment** (in′strə mənt) *n.* 1 a person or thing used to get something done; means [People once believed in witches as *instruments* of the devil.] 2 a tool or other device for doing very exact work, for scientific purposes, etc. [surgical *instruments*]. 3 a device used in making musical sound, as a flute, violin, piano, etc. 4 a legal paper by means of which some action is carried out, as a deed or will.

**in·stru·men·tal** (in′strə men′t'l) *adj.* 1 serving as a means; helpful [The librarian was *instrumental* in finding this book for me.] 2 played on or written for musical instruments [Bach wrote both *instrumental* and vocal music.]

**in·stru·men·tal·i·ty** (in′strə men tal′ə tē) *n.* the thing by which something is done; means; agency. —*pl.* **in′stru·men·tal′i·ties**

**in·sub·or·di·nate** (in′sə bôr′d'n it) *adj.* refusing to obey. —**in′sub·or′di·na′tion** *n.*

**in·sub·stan·tial** (in′səb stan′shəl) *adj.* 1 not solid or firm; flimsy [an *insubstantial* foundation]. 2 not real; imaginary [the *insubstantial* dream world].

**in·suf·fer·a·ble** (in suf′ər ə b'l) *adj.* hard to put up with; unbearable [an *insufferable* bore]. —**in·suf′fer·a·bly** *adv.*

**in·suf·fi·cien·cy** (in′sə fish′ən sē) *n.* a lack of something needed; inadequacy.

| | | | |
|---|---|---|---|
| **a** fat | **ir** here | **ou** out | **zh** leisure |
| **ā** ape | **ī** bite, fire | **u** up | **ŋ** ring |
| **ä** car, lot | **ō** go | **ur** fur | a *in* ago |
| **e** ten | **ô** law, horn | **ch** chin | e *in* agent |
| **er** care | **oi** oil | **sh** she | **ə** = i *in* unity |
| **ē** even | **oo** look | **th** thin | o *in* collect |
| **i** hit | **o͞o** tool | ***th*** then | u *in* focus |

**in·suf·fi·cient** (in′sə fish′ənt) ***adj.*** not enough; inadequate. —**in′suf·fi′cient·ly** ***adv.***

**in·su·lar** (in′sə lər *or* in′syoo lər) ***adj.*** **1** of or like an island or people living on an island. **2** having a narrow outlook; narrow-minded [*insular* thinking].

**in·su·late** (in′sə lāt) ***v.*** **1** to separate or cover with a material that keeps electricity, heat, or sound from escaping [electric wire *insulated* with rubber; a furnace *insulated* with asbestos]. **2** to set apart; keep away from others [People living in the suburbs are *insulated* from the problems of the poor in the city.] —**in′su·lat·ed, in′su·lat·ing**

**in·su·la·tion** (in′sə lā′shən) ***n.*** **1** an insulating or being insulated. **2** any material used to insulate.

**in·su·la·tor** (in′sə lāt′ər) ***n.*** anything that insulates; especially, a device of glass or porcelain, for insulating electric wires. *See the picture on page 386.*

**in·su·lin** (in′sə lin) ***n.*** a hormone of the pancreas that helps the body use sugars and starches. People who have diabetes get regular injections of insulin taken from animals.

**in·sult** (in sult′) ***v.*** to say or do something on purpose that hurts a person's feelings or pride [He *insulted* me by ignoring my questions.] *See* SYNONYMS *at* **offend.** ◆***n.*** (in′sult) an insulting act or remark.

> An **insult** is a kind of attack on someone in which one uses words as weapons. A person who has been insulted may feel "jumped upon." The word **insult** comes from a Latin word meaning "to leap upon."



**in·su·per·a·ble** (in sōō′pər ə b'l *or* in syōō′pər ə b'l) ***adj.*** that cannot be overcome [*insuperable* difficulties].

**in·sup·port·a·ble** (in′sə pôrt′ə b'l) ***adj.*** **1** that cannot be put up with or endured, as pain. **2** that cannot be proved [*insupportable* evidence].

**in·sur·ance** (in shoor′əns) ***n.*** **1** an insuring against loss by fire, death, accident, etc. **2** a contract by which a company guarantees a person that a certain sum of money will be paid in case of loss by fire, death, etc. The insured person makes regular payments for this guarantee. **3** the regular sum paid for insurance; premium. **4** the amount for which something is insured [How much *insurance* does she have on her car?] **5** the business of insuring against loss.

**in·sure** (in shoor′) ***v.*** **1** to get or give insurance on [We *insured* our car against theft. Will your company *insure* my house against storms?] **2** *another spelling of* **ensure.** —**in·sured′, in·sur′ing** —**in·sur′a·ble** ***adj.***

**in·sur·gent** (in sur′jənt) ***adj.*** rising up in revolt; rebelling. ◆***n.*** a rebel. —**in·sur′gence** ***n.***

**in·sur·mount·a·ble** (in′sər moun′tə b'l) ***adj.*** that cannot be overcome [*insurmountable* barriers].

**in·sur·rec·tion** (in′sə rek′shən) ***n.*** a revolt or rebellion. —**in′sur·rec′tion·ist** ***n.***

**int.** *abbreviation for* **interest, interior, internal, international, intransitive.**

**in·tact** (in takt′) ***adj.*** kept or left whole; with nothing missing or injured; in one piece [Boyd received his uncle's stamp collection *intact*.]

**in·take** (in′tāk) ***n.*** **1** a taking in [A gasp is a sharp *intake* of breath.] **2** the place in a pipe or channel where water, air, or gas is taken in. **3** the amount or thing that is taken in [She had a small *intake* of food while she was ill.]

**in·tan·gi·ble** (in tan′jə b'l) ***adj.*** that cannot be touched or grasped [Good will is an *intangible* asset in a business.]

**in·te·ger** (in′tə jər) ***n.*** a whole number; a number that is not a fraction [2, 83, and 145 are *integers*.]

**in·te·gral** (in′tə grəl) ***adj.*** **1** necessary to something to make it complete; essential [Wheels are *integral* parts of automobiles.] **2** having to do with integers.

**in·te·grate** (in′tə grāt) ***v.*** **1** to bring together into a whole; unite or unify [to *integrate* the study of history with the study of English]. ☆**2** to do away with the segregation of races, as in schools. —**in′te·grat·ed, in′te·grat·ing** —**in′te·gra′tion** ***n.***

**in·teg·ri·ty** (in teg′rə tē) ***n.*** **1** the quality of being honest and trustworthy; honesty or uprightness [A government official of *integrity* never takes a bribe.] *See* SYNONYMS *at* **honesty.** **2** the condition of being whole, not broken into parts [Wars destroyed the territorial *integrity* of Germany.]

**in·teg·u·ment** (in teg′yoo mənt) ***n.*** an outer covering, as a skin, shell, or rind.

**in·tel·lect** (in′t'l ekt) ***n.*** **1** the ability to understand ideas and to think; understanding. **2** high intelligence; great mental power. **3** a person of high intelligence.

**in·tel·lec·tu·al** (in′t'l ek′choo wəl) ***adj.*** **1** of the intellect or understanding [one's *intellectual* powers]. **2** needing intelligence and clear thinking [Chess is an *intellectual* game.] **3** having or showing high intelligence. ◆***n.*** a person who does intellectual work or has intellectual interests. —**in′tel·lec′tu·al·ly** ***adv.***

**in·tel·li·gence** (in tel′ə jəns) ***n.*** **1** the ability to learn and understand, or to solve problems [Human beings have much greater *intelligence* than any other animals.] **2** news or information [secret *intelligence* about the enemy's plans]. **3** the gathering of secret information [She works in *intelligence* for the CIA.]

**in·tel·li·gent** (in tel′ə jənt) ***adj.*** having or showing intelligence, especially high intelligence. —**in·tel′li·gent·ly** ***adv.***

> SYNONYMS: To be **intelligent** is to be able to learn or understand from experience and to be able to deal with new situations. To be **clever** is to be quick in thinking or learning but not necessarily wise or careful. To be **brilliant** is to be very highly intelligent.

**in·tel·li·gi·ble** (in tel′i jə b'l) ***adj.*** that can be understood; clear [an *intelligible* explanation]. —**in·tel′li·gi·bly** ***adv.***

**in·tem·per·ance** (in tem′pər əns) ***n.*** **1** a lack of control or of self-control. **2** the drinking of too much alcoholic liquor.

**in·tem·per·ate** (in tem′pər it) ***adj.*** **1** having or showing a lack of self-control; not moderate; excessive [*intemperate* language]. **2** harsh or severe [the *intemperate* climate of Antarctica]. **3** drinking too much alcoholic liquor.

**in·tend** (in tend′) ***v.*** **1** to have in mind; plan [I *intend* to leave tomorrow.] **2** to set apart; mean [The cake is *intended* for the party.]

> **Intend** comes from a Latin word meaning "to aim at." When we aim or direct the mind toward some purpose, we are intending that it be done.

**in·tend·ed** (in ten′did) ***adj.*** **1** meant or planned [We set off on our *intended* trip.] **2** expected or future [his *intended* bride]. ◆***n.*** the person whom one has agreed to marry: *used only in everyday talk.*

**in·tense** (in tens′) ***adj.*** **1** very strong or deep; very great; extreme [an *intense* light; *intense* joy]. **2** feeling things strongly and acting with force [an *intense* person]. —**in·tense′ly *adv.***

**in·ten·si·fy** (in ten′sə fī) ***v.*** to make or become more intense; increase [We want to *intensify* our efforts.] —**in·ten′si·fied, in·ten′si·fy·ing** —**in·ten′si·fi·ca′tion *n.***

**in·ten·si·ty** (in ten′sə tē) ***n.*** **1** the quality of being intense; great strength or force [the *intensity* of the battle; to speak with *intensity*]. **2** the amount of a force, as of heat, light, or sound, for each unit of area, volume, etc.

**in·ten·sive** (in ten′siv) ***adj.*** **1** complete and in great detail; deep and thorough [an *intensive* search]. **2** giving force; emphasizing [In "I myself saw them," "myself" is an *intensive* pronoun.] —**in·ten′sive·ly *adv.***

**in·tent** (in tent′) ***adj.*** **1** having the mind or attention fixed; concentrating [They were *intent* on their studies.] **2** firmly fixed or directed [She gave him an *intent* look.] **3** firmly decided; determined [She is *intent* on saving money.] ◆***n.*** something intended; purpose; intention [It was not my *intent* to harm you.] —**in·tent′ly *adv.***

**in·ten·tion** (in ten′shən) ***n.*** anything intended or planned; purpose [She borrowed the chair with the *intention* of returning it.]

**in·ten·tion·al** (in ten′shən ′l) ***adj.*** done on purpose; intended. *See* SYNONYMS *at* **voluntary.** —**in·ten′tion·al·ly *adv.***

**in·ter** (in tʉr′) ***v.*** to put into a grave; bury. —**in·terred′, in·ter′ring**

**inter-** *a prefix meaning:* **1** between or among [An *interstate* highway can be used to travel between states.] **2** with or on each other; together [*Interacting* parts act on each other.]

**in·ter·act** (in tər akt′) ***v.*** to act on each other. —**in′ter·ac′tion *n.***

**in·ter·breed** (in tər brēd′) ***v.*** *another word for* **hybridize.** —**in·ter·bred** (in tər bred′), **in·ter·breed′ing**

**in·ter·cede** (in tər sēd′) ***v.*** **1** to ask or plead in behalf of another [You must *intercede* with the governor to get a pardon for the prisoner.] **2** to interfere in order to bring about an agreement [to *intercede* in another's quarrel]. —**in·ter·ced′ed, in·ter·ced′ing**

**in·ter·cept** (in tər sept′) ***v.*** to stop or seize on the way; cut off [to *intercept* a message]. —**in′ter·cep′tion *n.***

**in·ter·ces·sion** (in′tər sesh′ən) ***n.*** the act of interceding.

**in·ter·ces·sor** (in′tər ses′ər) ***n.*** a person who intercedes.

**in·ter·change** (in tər chānj′) ***v.*** **1** to put two things in one another's place; change about [If you *interchange* the middle letters of "clam," you get "calm."] **2** to give and receive in exchange [to *interchange* ideas]. —**in·ter·changed′, in·ter·chang′ing** ◆***n.*** (in′tər chānj) **1** the act of interchanging. **2** a place on a freeway where traffic can come in or go out, usually by means of a cloverleaf.

**in·ter·change·a·ble** (in′tər chān′jə b′l) ***adj.*** that can be put or used in place of one another [The tires on an automobile are *interchangeable.*]

**in·ter·col·le·giate** (in′tər kə lē′jət) ***adj.*** between colleges [*intercollegiate* sports].

**in·ter·com** (in′tər käm) ***n.*** a system for communicating by radio or telephone between sections of an airplane or ship, or between different rooms in a building.

**in·ter·com·mu·ni·cate** (in′tər kə myo͞o′nə kāt) ***v.*** to communicate with one another. —**in′ter·com·mu′ni·cat·ed, in′ter·com·mu′ni·cat·ing** —**in′ter·com·mu′ni·ca′tion *n.***

**in·ter·con·nect** (in′tər kə nekt′) ***v.*** to connect with one another. —**in′ter·con·nec′tion *n.***

**in·ter·con·ti·nen·tal** (in′tər kän′tə nen′t′l) ***adj.*** **1** between or among continents. **2** able to travel from one continent to another, as a missile launched by a rocket.

**in·ter·course** (in′tər kôrs) ***n.*** **1** dealings between people or countries; exchange of products, ideas, etc. [*Intercourse* in trade between the two nations has improved.] **2** sexual union.

**in·ter·de·pend·ent** (in′tər di pen′dənt) ***adj.*** depending on one another. —**in′ter·de·pend′ence *n.***

**in·ter·dict** (in tər dikt′) ***v.*** **1** to forbid or prohibit. **2** in the Roman Catholic Church, to refuse to allow to take part in certain church services. ◆***n.*** (in′tər dikt) the act of interdicting.



**in·ter·est** (in′trist *or* in′tər ist) ***n.*** **1** a feeling of wanting to know, learn, see, or take part in something; curiosity or concern [an *interest* in mathematics; an *interest* in seeing justice done]. **2** the power of causing this feeling [books of *interest* to children]. **3** something that causes this feeling [My main *interest* is dancing.] **4** a share in something [to buy an *interest* in a business]. **5** what is good for one; benefit; advantage [He has our best *interests* at heart.] **6** *usually* **interests,** *pl.* a group of people taking part or having a share in the same business or industry [the steel *interests*]. **7** money paid for the use of money; also, the rate at which it is paid [We had to pay 15% *interest* on the loan.] ◆***v.*** **1** to stir up the interest or curiosity of [That new movie *interests* me.] **2** to cause to have an interest or take part in; involve [Can I *interest* you in a game of tennis?] —**in the interest of,** for the sake of.

**in·ter·est·ing** (in′trist iŋ *or* in′tər ist iŋ) ***adj.*** stirring up one's interest; exciting attention. —**in′ter·est·ing·ly *adv.***

**in·ter·fere** (in tər fir′) ***v.*** **1** to meddle in another's affairs without being asked [My parents seldom *interfere* in my plans.] **2** to come between for some purpose [The teacher *interfered* in the pupils' fight.] **3** to come against; get in the way of; conflict [Noise *interferes*

| | | | | | | | |
|---|---|---|---|---|---|---|---|
| **a** fat | **ir** here | **ou** out | **zh** leisure |
| **ā** ape | **ī** bite, fire | **u** up | **ŋ** ring |
| **ä** car, lot | **ō** go | **ʉr** fur | a *in* ago |
| **e** ten | **ô** law, horn | **ch** chin | e *in* agent |
| **er** care | **oi** oil | **sh** she | ə = i *in* unity |
| **ē** even | **oo** look | **th** thin | o *in* collect |
| **i** hit | **o͞o** tool | ***th*** then | u *in* focus |

with our work.] **4** to be guilty of interference in football. —**in·ter·fered′, in·ter·fer′ing**

**in·ter·fer·ence** (in′tər fir′əns) ***n.*** **1** an interfering. ☆**2** the act of blocking players in football to clear the way for the ball carrier, or the act of illegally keeping an opponent from catching the ball. *See the picture.*

**in·ter·im** (in′tər im) ***n.*** the time between; meantime [It took a month to get the book, and in the *interim* he lost interest in it.] ◆***adj.*** during an interim; temporary [an *interim* mayor].

**in·te·ri·or** (in tir′ē ər) ***n.*** **1** the inside or inner part [an old house with a modern *interior*]. **2** the inland part of a country. **3** the internal affairs of a country [The U.S. Department of the *Interior*.] ◆***adj.*** of the interior; inside; inner [an *interior* wall].

**interior decorator** a person whose work is the decorating and furnishing of the interior of a room, house, etc.

**interj.** *abbreviation for* **interjection.**

**in·ter·ject** (in tər jekt′) ***v.*** to interrupt with; throw in; insert [to *interject* a question].

**in·ter·jec·tion** (in′tər jek′shən) ***n.*** **1** the act of interjecting. **2** a word or phrase that is exclaimed to show strong feeling; exclamation ["Oh!" and "Good grief!" are *interjections*.] **3** a remark, question, etc. interjected.

**in·ter·lace** (in tər lās′) ***v.*** to join or become joined as by weaving or lacing together [a chair seat made by

386 *interlacing* strips of cane]. *See the picture.* —**in·ter·laced′, in·ter·lac′ing**

**in·ter·line¹** (in tər līn′) ***v.*** to write between the lines of a book, letter, etc. —**in·ter·lined′, in·ter·lin′ing**

**in·ter·line²** (in′tər līn) ***v.*** to put a lining between the outer material and the regular lining of a garment. —**in′ter·lined, in′ter·lin·ing**

**in·ter·lock** (in tər läk′) ***v.*** to fit tightly together [an *interlocking* jigsaw puzzle]. *See the picture.*

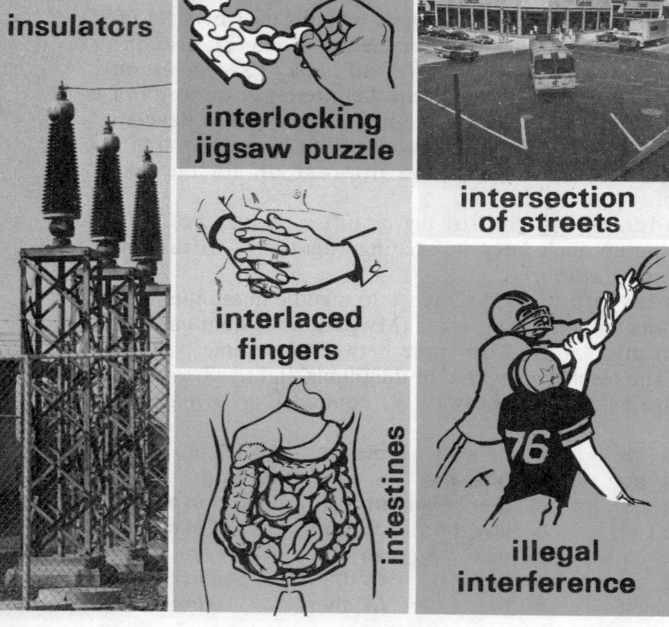

insulators

interlocking jigsaw puzzle

intersection of streets

interlaced fingers

intestines

illegal interference

**in·ter·lop·er** (in′tər lō′pər) ***n.*** a person who meddles in others' affairs without being asked; intruder.

**in·ter·lude** (in′tər lo͞od) ***n.*** **1** anything that fills time between two happenings [Recess is an *interlude* between classes.] **2** any performance between the acts of a play. **3** a piece of music played between the parts of a song, the acts of a play, etc.

**in·ter·mar·ry** (in′tər mar′ē) ***v.*** to marry a person of a different tribe, race, religion, etc. —**in′ter·mar′ried, in′ter·mar′ry·ing** —**in·ter·mar·riage** (in′tər mar′ij) ***n.***

**in·ter·me·di·ar·y** (in′tər mē′dē er′ē) ***n.*** a person who deals with each of two sides in making arrangements between them; go-between. —*pl.* **in′ter·me′di·ar′ies** ◆***adj.*** **1** being or happening between; intermediate. **2** acting as an intermediary.

**in·ter·me·di·ate** (in′tər mē′dē it) ***adj.*** coming between two other things or happenings; in the middle [Adolescence is an *intermediate* stage between being a child and being an adult.]

**in·ter·ment** (in tʉr′mənt) ***n.*** a burial.

**in·ter·mez·zo** (in′tər met′sō) ***n.*** a short piece of music; especially, one played between acts of a play or opera. —*pl.* **in′ter·mez′zos**

**in·ter·mi·na·ble** (in tʉr′mi nə b′l) ***adj.*** that lasts or seems to last forever; endless [an *interminable* talk]. —**in·ter′mi·na·bly** ***adv.***

**in·ter·min·gle** (in′tər miŋ′g′l) ***v.*** to mix together; blend; mingle. —**in′ter·min′gled, in′ter·min′gling**

**in·ter·mis·sion** (in′tər mish′ən) ***n.*** a stopping for a time; rest or pause [a ten-minute *intermission* between the first two acts of the play].

**in·ter·mit·tent** (in′tər mit′′nt) ***adj.*** stopping and starting again from time to time [Malaria causes an *intermittent* fever.] —**in′ter·mit′tent·ly** ***adv.***

**in·ter·mix** (in tər miks′) ***v.*** to mix together; blend.

**in·tern** (in′tərn) ☆***n.*** a doctor who is getting more training, after graduation from medical school, by assisting other doctors in a hospital: *also spelled* **in′terne.** ◆***v.*** (*usually* in tʉrn′) ☆**1** to serve as an intern. **2** to keep from leaving a country, as by putting in special camps [to *intern* aliens in time of war].

**in·ter·nal** (in tʉr′n′l) ***adj.*** **1** of or on the inside; inner [*internal* bleeding]. **2** within a country; domestic [*internal* revenue]. —**in·ter′nal·ly** ***adv.***

**in·ter·nal-com·bus·tion engine** (in tʉr′n′l kəm bus′chən) an engine, as in an automobile, in which the power is built up inside the cylinders by exploding a mixture of air and some fuel, such as gasoline or oil.

☆**internal revenue** money that a government gets by taxing income, profits, luxuries, etc.

**in·ter·na·tion·al** (in′tər nash′ən ′l) ***adj.*** **1** between or among nations [*international* trade]. **2** having to do with the relations between nations [an *international* court]. **3** for the use of all nations [*international* waters]. **4** of, for, or by people in a number of nations [an *international* organization]. —**in′ter·na′tion·al·ly** ***adv.***

**in·ter·na·tion·al·ize** (in′tər nash′ən ′l īz′) ***v.*** to put under the control of a number of nations, or open for the use of all nations. —**in′ter·na′tion·al·ized′, in′ter·na′tion·al·iz′ing**

**in·ter·ne·cine** (in′tər nē′sin) ***adj.*** causing many deaths, especially on both sides in a conflict; destructive [*internecine* warfare].

**in·ter·per·son·al** (in'tər pʉr'sə n'l) ***adj.*** between persons [*interpersonal* relationships].

**in·ter·plan·e·tar·y** (in'tər plan'ə ter'ē) ***adj.*** between planets [*interplanetary* travel].

**in·ter·play** (in'tər plā) ***n.*** action or influence of things on each other; interaction.

**in·ter·pose** (in tər pōz') ***v.*** **1** to interrupt with [to *interpose* a question]. **2** to come between people who can't agree, in order to settle the dispute; intervene. —**in·ter·posed', in·ter·pos'ing**

**in·ter·pret** (in tʉr'prit) ***v.*** **1** to explain the meaning of [to *interpret* a poem]. **2** to translate [Our guides *interpreted* for us what the natives said.] **3** to understand in one's own way; construe; take [I *interpret* his silence as a sign of approval.] **4** to show one's own understanding of a piece of music, a role in a play, etc. by the way one performs it. —**in·ter'pre·tive *adj.***

**in·ter·pre·ta·tion** (in tʉr'prə tā'shən) ***n.*** the act or way of interpreting; explanation [our teacher's *interpretation* of the story].

**in·ter·pret·er** (in tʉr'prə tər) ***n.*** a person who interprets, especially one whose work is translating things said in one language into another language.

**in·ter·ra·cial** (in'tər rā'shəl) ***adj.*** between, among, or for people of different races.

**in·ter·re·lat·ed** (in'tər ri lāt'id) ***adj.*** closely connected with each other or one another. —**in'ter·re·la'tion *n.*** —**in'ter·re·la'tion·ship *n.***

**in·ter·ro·gate** (in ter'ə gāt) ***v.*** to ask questions of in examining [to *interrogate* a witness]. —**in·ter'ro·gat·ed, in·ter'ro·gat·ing** —**in·ter'ro·ga'tion *n.*** —**in·ter'ro·ga'tor *n.***

**in·ter·rog·a·tive** (in'tə räg'ə tiv) ***adj.*** that asks a question [an *interrogative* sentence].

**in·ter·rupt** (in tə rupt') ***v.*** **1** to break in on talk, action, etc. or on a person who is talking, working, etc. [We *interrupt* this program with a news bulletin. Don't *interrupt* me!] **2** to make a break in; cut off [A strike *interrupted* steel production.]

**in·ter·rup·tion** (in'tə rup'shən) ***n.*** **1** the act of interrupting or the condition of being interrupted. **2** anything that interrupts. **3** a break, pause, or halt.

**in·ter·scho·las·tic** (in'tər skə las'tik) ***adj.*** between or among schools [*interscholastic* sports].

**in·ter·sect** (in tər sekt') ***v.*** **1** to divide into two parts by passing through or across [A river *intersects* the plain.] **2** to cross each other [The lines *intersect* and form right angles.]

**in·ter·sec·tion** (in'tər sek'shən) ***n.*** **1** the act of intersecting. **2** the place where two lines, streets, etc. meet or cross. *See the picture.*

**in·ter·sperse** (in tər spʉrs') ***v.*** **1** to put here and there; scatter [Sprigs of mistletoe were *interspersed* in the wreath.] **2** to vary with things scattered here and there [black hair *interspersed* with gray]. —**in·ter·spersed', in·ter·spers'ing**

☆**in·ter·state** (in'tər stāt) ***adj.*** between or among the states of a federal government [an *interstate* highway].

**in·ter·twine** (in tər twīn') ***v.*** to twist together [Strands of hemp are *intertwined* to make rope.] —**in·ter·twined', in·ter·twin'ing**

☆**in·ter·ur·ban** (in'tər ʉr'bən) ***adj.*** between cities or towns [an *interurban* railway].

**in·ter·val** (in'tər v'l) ***n.*** **1** space or time between things [an *interval* of five feet between bookcases; a one-year *interval*]. **2** the difference in pitch between two musical tones. —**at intervals, 1** now and then. **2** here and there.

**in·ter·vene** (in tər vēn') ***v.*** **1** to come or be between [Two days *intervened* between semesters.] **2** to come in so as to help settle, stop, etc. [to *intervene* in a dispute, a war, etc.] **3** to get in the way [If nothing *intervenes,* I'll see you Friday.] —**in·ter·vened', in·ter·ven'ing**

**in·ter·ven·tion** (in'tər ven'shən) ***n.*** **1** an act of intervening. **2** interference, as by one country in the affairs of another.

**in·ter·view** (in'tər vyo͞o) ***n.*** **1** a meeting of one person with another to talk about something [an *interview* with an employer about a job]. ☆**2** a meeting in which a person is asked about his or her opinions, activities, etc., as by a reporter. ◆☆***v.*** to have an interview with. —**in'ter·view·er *n.***

**in·ter·weave** (in tər wēv') ***v.*** **1** to weave together. **2** to mingle or mix together [fact *interwoven* with fiction]. —**in·ter·wove', in·ter·wo'ven, in·ter·weav'ing**

**in·tes·tate** (in tes'tāt) ***adj.*** not having made a will [He died *intestate.*]

**in·tes·ti·nal** (in tes'ti n'l) ***adj.*** of or in the intestines [*intestinal* flu].

**in·tes·tine** (in tes'tin) ***n.*** *usually* **intestines,** *pl.* the tube through which food passes from the stomach. The long, narrow part with many coils is called the **small intestine,** and the shorter and thicker part is called the **large intestine.** Food is digested in the intestines as well as in the stomach. *See the picture.*

**in·ti·ma·cy** (in'tə mə sē) ***n.*** **1** the condition of being intimate; closeness, as in friendship. **2** an intimate act. —*pl.* **in'ti·ma·cies**

**in·ti·mate**[1] (in'tə mit) ***adj.*** **1** most private or personal [one's *intimate* thoughts]. **2** very close or familiar [an *intimate* friend]. **3** deep and thorough [an *intimate* knowledge of physics]. ◆***n.*** an intimate friend. —**in'ti·mate·ly *adv.***

> **Intimate** comes from a Latin word meaning "inside." Our *intimate* feelings are usually kept deep inside us. Our *intimate* friends are people we know so well that we seem to understand what is going on inside their minds.

**in·ti·mate**[2] (in'tə māt) ***v.*** to hint; suggest without openly saying [Mrs. Johnson only *intimated* what she really felt.] —**in'ti·mat·ed, in'ti·mat·ing** —**in'ti·ma'tion *n.***

**in·tim·i·date** (in tim'ə dāt) ***v.*** to make afraid; force to do something or keep from doing something by frightening [a climber *intimidated* by the height of the mountain]. —**in·tim'i·dat·ed, in·tim'i·dat·ing** —**in·tim'i·da'tion *n.***

**intl.** *abbreviation for* **international.**

| | | | |
|---|---|---|---|
| **a** fat | **ir** here | **ou** out | **zh** leisure |
| **ā** ape | **ī** bite, fire | **u** up | **ŋ** ring |
| **ä** car, lot | **ō** go | **ʉr** fur | a *in* ago |
| **e** ten | **ô** law, horn | **ch** chin | e *in* agent |
| **er** care | **oi** oil | **sh** she | **ə** = i *in* unity |
| **ē** even | **o͝o** look | **th** thin | o *in* collect |
| **i** hit | **o͞o** tool | ***th*** then | u *in* focus |

**in·to** (in′to͞o *or* in′tə) ***prep.*** **1** to the inside of [to go *into* the house]. **2** to the form, condition, etc. of [The farm has been turned *into* a park. They got *into* trouble.] **3** so as to strike [to skid *into* a wall]. ☆**4** very interested in: *used only in everyday talk* [I'm *into* old movies.]

**in·tol·er·a·ble** (in täl′ər ə b'l) ***adj.*** too painful, cruel, etc. to bear. —**in·tol′er·a·bly** ***adv.***

**in·tol·er·ant** (in täl′ər ənt) ***adj.*** not tolerant; not willing to put up with ideas or beliefs that are different from one's own, or not willing to put up with people of other races or backgrounds. —**intolerant of,** not willing or able to bear. —**in·tol′er·ance** ***n.*** —**in·tol′er·ant·ly** ***adv.***

**in·to·na·tion** (in′tə nā′shən) ***n.*** **1** the way of singing or playing notes with regard to correct pitch. **2** the way the voice of a person who is talking rises and falls in pitch.

**in·tone** (in tōn′) ***v.*** to speak or recite in a singing tone or chant [to *intone* a prayer]. —**in·toned′, in·ton′ing**

**in·tox·i·cant** (in täk′sə kənt) ***n.*** something that intoxicates; especially, alcoholic liquor.

**in·tox·i·cate** (in täk′sə kāt) ***v.*** **1** to make lose control of oneself as alcoholic liquor does. **2** to make very excited or happy [The team's fans were *intoxicated* by the victory.] —**in·tox′i·cat·ed, in·tox′i·cat·ing**

**in·tox·i·ca·tion** (in täk′sə kā′shən) ***n.*** **1** drunkenness. **2** a feeling of wild excitement. **3** poisoning of the body, as by a drug.



**in·trac·ta·ble** (in trak′tə b'l) ***adj.*** hard to control; stubborn [an *intractable* prisoner].

**in·tra·mur·al** (in′trə myoor′əl) ***adj.*** between or among members of the same school, college, etc. [*intramural* sports].

**in·tran·si·tive** (in tran′sə tiv) ***adj.*** not transitive; describing a verb that does not take a direct object [In "The patient seems to be better," "seems" and "be" are *intransitive* verbs.]

**in·tra·ve·nous** (in′trə vē′nəs) ***adj.*** directly into a vein [an *intravenous* injection].

**in·trep·id** (in trep′id) ***adj.*** very brave; fearless; bold. —**in·trep′id·ly** ***adv.***

**in·tri·ca·cy** (in′tri kə sē) ***n.*** **1** an intricate quality or condition [the *intricacy* of a design]. **2** something that is intricate [a story with a plot full of *intricacies*]. —*pl.* **in′tri·ca·cies**

**in·tri·cate** (in′tri kit) ***adj.*** hard to follow or understand because complicated and full of details [an *intricate* pattern]. —**in′tri·cate·ly** ***adv.***

**in·trigue** (in trēg′) ***v.*** **1** to plot or plan in a secret or sneaky way; scheme [The nobles *intrigued* against the king.] **2** to stir up the interest of; make curious; fascinate [Such unusual beauty *intrigues* me.] —**in·trigued′, in·trigu′ing** ◆***n.*** (*also* in′trēg) **1** a sneaky plot; scheme. **2** a secret love affair.

**in·trin·sic** (in trin′sik) ***adj.*** that has to do with what a thing really is; real; essential [Wealth tells us nothing about a person's *intrinsic* worth.] —**in·trin′si·cal·ly** ***adv.***

**in·tro·duce** (in trə do͞os′ *or* in trə dyo͞os′) ***v.*** **1** to make known; make acquainted; present [Please *introduce* me to them.] **2** to bring into use; make popular or common [Science has *introduced* many new words.] **3** to make familiar with something [They *introduced* me to the music of Bach.] **4** to add or put in [*Introduce* some humor into the play.] **5** to bring to the attention of others in a formal way [to *introduce* a bill into Congress]. **6** to put in; insert [to *introduce* a drain into a wound]. —**in·tro·duced′, in·tro·duc′ing**

> **Introduce** was taken from a Latin word that means "to lead in." Introducing someone or something is a little like leading or guiding that person or thing into a new, unfamiliar place.

**in·tro·duc·tion** (in′trə duk′shən) ***n.*** **1** the act of introducing, especially of making one person known to another or others. **2** the part at the beginning of a book, speech, etc. leading into or explaining what follows. **3** anything that has been introduced, or brought into use [Transistors are a fairly recent *introduction*.]

**in·tro·duc·to·ry** (in′trə duk′tər ē) ***adj.*** that introduces or begins something; preliminary [an *introductory* course in science].

**in·tro·spec·tion** (in′trə spek′shən) ***n.*** a looking into and examining one's own thoughts or feelings. —**in′tro·spec′tive** ***adj.***

**in·tro·vert** (in′trə vurt) ***n.*** a person who is more interested in his or her own thoughts and feelings than in other people and what is happening in the world.

**in·trude** (in tro͞od′) ***v.*** to force oneself or one's thoughts on others without being asked or wanted. —**in·trud′ed, in·trud′ing** —**in·trud′er** ***n.***

**in·tru·sion** (in tro͞o′zhən) ***n.*** the act of intruding. —**in·tru·sive** (in tro͞o′siv) ***adj.***

**in·tu·i·tion** (in′too wish′ən *or* in′tyoo wish′ən) ***n.*** a knowing of something without actually thinking it out or studying; instant understanding [to sense danger by a flash of *intuition*].

**in·tu·i·tive** (in to͞o′i tiv *or* in tyo͞o′i tiv) ***adj.*** knowing or known by intuition [an *intuitive* sense of right and wrong]. —**in·tu′i·tive·ly** ***adv.***

**in·un·date** (in′ən dāt) ***v.*** to cover as with an overflow of water; flood or overwhelm [Creek water *inundated* the road. Angry letters *inundated* the newspaper office.] —**in′un·dat·ed, in′un·dat·ing**

**in·ure** (in yoor′) ***v.*** to make used to something hard or painful; accustom [His term as mayor has *inured* him to criticism.] —**in·ured′, in·ur′ing**

**in·vade** (in vād′) ***v.*** **1** to enter with an army in order to conquer [Napoleon *invaded* Russia.] **2** to crowd into; throng [Tourists *invaded* the beaches.] **3** to break in on; intrude upon [Reporters *invaded* the governor's privacy by asking personal questions.] —**in·vad′ed, in·vad′ing** —**in·vad′er** ***n.***

**in·va·lid**[1] (in′və lid) ***n.*** a person who is sick or injured, especially one who is likely to be so for some time. ◆***adj.*** **1** not well; weak and sick [caring for an *invalid* parent]. **2** of or for invalids [an *invalid* home].

**in·val·id**[2] (in val′id) ***adj.*** not valid; having no force or value [A check with no signature is *invalid.*]

**in·val·i·date** (in val′ə dāt) ***v.*** to make invalid; take away the force or value of [The new will *invalidates* the old one.] —**in·val′i·dat·ed, in·val′i·dat·ing**

**in·val·u·a·ble** (in val′yoo wə b'l *or* in val′yə b'l) ***adj.*** having value too great to measure; priceless.

**in·var·i·a·ble** (in ver′ē ə b'l) ***adj.*** not changing; always the same; constant; uniform [an *invariable* rule]. —**in·var′i·a·bly** ***adv.***

**in·va·sion** (in vā′zhən) ***n.*** the act of invading; an attacking, intruding, etc.

**in·vec·tive** (in vek′tiv) ***n.*** an attack in words; strong criticism, insults, curses, etc.

**in·veigh** (in vā′) ***v.*** to attack strongly in words; talk or write bitterly against.

**in·vei·gle** (in vē′g'l *or* in vā′g'l) ***v.*** to trick or lure into doing something [Tom Sawyer *inveigled* his friends into painting the fence.] —**in·vei′gled, in·vei′gling**

**in·vent** (in vent′) ***v.*** **1** to think out or make something that did not exist before; be the first to do or make [Who *invented* the telephone?] *See* SYNONYMS *at* **create. 2** to create in the mind; think up [to *invent* excuses].

**in·ven·tion** (in ven′shən) ***n.*** **1** the act of inventing [the *invention* of television]. **2** something invented [the many *inventions* of Edison]. **3** the ability to invent [a novelist who shows great *invention* in telling a story]. **4** a falsehood.

**in·ven·tive** (in ven′tiv) ***adj.*** **1** skilled in inventing [an *inventive* person]. **2** of invention [*inventive* powers]. —**in·ven′tive·ness *n.***

**in·ven·tor** (in ven′tər) ***n.*** a person who invents.

**in·ven·to·ry** (in′vən tôr′ē) ***n.*** **1** a complete list of goods or property [The store makes an *inventory* of its stock every year.] **2** the stock of goods on hand [Because of fewer sales this year, dealers have large *inventories.*] —*pl.* **in′ven·to′ries** ◆***v.*** to make an inventory or list of [to *inventory* our books]. —**in′ven·to′ried, in′ven·to′ry·ing**

**in·verse** (in vurs′ *or* in′vurs) ***adj.*** exactly opposite; reversed [The number 237 in *inverse* order becomes 732.] ◆***n.*** the exact opposite; reverse.

**in·ver·sion** (in vur′zhən) ***n.*** **1** an inverting or being inverted ["Said she" is an *inversion* of "she said."] **2** something inverted.

**in·vert** (in vurt′) ***v.*** **1** to turn upside down [The image that falls on the film in a camera is *inverted.*] **2** to change the order of; turn around.

**in·ver·te·brate** (in vur′tə brit *or* in vur′tə brāt) ***adj.*** having no backbone. ◆***n.*** an animal that has no backbone, or spinal column [Worms, insects, clams, crabs, etc. are *invertebrates.*]

**in·vest** (in vest′) ***v.*** **1** to use or lend money for some business, property, stock, etc. in order to get a profit. **2** to spend in order to get something in return [to *invest* much time in a search for a cure]. **3** to cause to have; furnish with [The law *invests* a governor with many powers.] —**in·ves′tor *n.***

**in·ves·ti·gate** (in ves′tə gāt) ***v.*** to search into so as to learn the facts; examine in detail [to *investigate* an accident]. —**in·ves′ti·gat·ed, in·ves′ti·gat·ing** —**in·ves′ti·ga′tion *n.*** —**in·ves′ti·ga′tor *n.***

The Latin word from which we took our word **investigate** means "to search out by following the footprints of." Detectives, including a famous one in stories, Sherlock Holmes, have often followed tracks when investigating a crime.

**in·vest·ment** (in vest′mənt) ***n.*** **1** an investing of money, time, etc. to get something in return. **2** the amount of money invested. **3** something in which money is invested [Is real estate a good *investment?*]

**in·vet·er·ate** (in vet′ər it) ***adj.*** **1** firmly fixed over a long period of time [an *inveterate* custom]. **2** doing a certain thing by habit; habitual [an *inveterate* liar].

**in·vid·i·ous** (in vid′ē əs) ***adj.*** likely to cause bad feeling, as an unfair comparison between things that are not really equal.

**in·vig·or·ate** (in vig′ə rāt) ***v.*** to fill with vigor or energy [A brisk walk will *invigorate* you.] —**in·vig′or·at·ed, in·vig′or·at·ing** —**in·vig′or·a′tion *n.***

**in·vin·ci·ble** (in vin′sə b'l) ***adj.*** that cannot be beaten or overcome [a team that seemed *invincible*]. —**in·vin′ci·bil′i·ty *n.*** —**in·vin′ci·bly *adv.***

**in·vi·o·la·ble** (in vī′ə lə b'l) ***adj.*** that should not be violated or broken; sacred [an *inviolable* promise]. —**in·vi′o·la·bil′i·ty *n.***

**in·vi·o·late** (in vī′ə lit *or* in vī′ə lāt) ***adj.*** not violated or broken; kept sacred.

**in·vis·i·ble** (in viz′ə b'l) ***adj.*** that cannot be seen; not visible [The moon was *invisible* behind the clouds. Oxygen is *invisible.* Most body cells are *invisible* except under a microscope.] —**in·vis′i·bil′i·ty *n.*** —**in·vis′i·bly *adv.***

**in·vi·ta·tion** (in′və tā′shən) ***n.*** **1** the act of inviting to come somewhere or do something. **2** the written or spoken form used in inviting a person.

**in·vi·ta·tion·al** (in′və tā′shən 'l) ***adj.*** with only those taking part who have been invited [an *invitational* golf tournament].

**in·vite** (in vīt′) ***v.*** **1** to ask in a polite way to come somewhere or do something; ask to be one's guest [They *invited* me to dine with them.] **2** to ask for; request [After her talk she *invited* questions from the audience.] **3** to bring on; give the chance for [Doing things like that *invites* gossip.] —**in·vit′ed, in·vit′ing**



**in·vit·ing** (in vīt′iŋ) ***adj.*** tempting or attractive [an *inviting* display of food].

**in·vo·ca·tion** (in′və kā′shən) ***n.*** **1** a prayer calling on God, a god, etc. for blessing or help. **2** magic words used in calling forth evil spirits.

**in·voice** (in′vois) ***n.*** a list of the goods shipped to a buyer, giving the amounts and the prices of the goods sent. ◆***v.*** to list in an invoice. —**in′voiced, in′voic·ing**

**in·voke** (in vōk′) ***v.*** **1** to call on for blessing or help, as in a prayer [to *invoke* God; to *invoke* the power of the law]. **2** to ask for in a serious way [to *invoke* aid]. **3** to call forth by magic [to *invoke* evil spirits]. —**in·voked′, in·vok′ing**

**in·vol·un·tar·y** (in väl′ən ter′ē) ***adj.*** **1** not done by choice; unwilling [the *involuntary* labor of prisoners]. **2** done without thinking about it [Sneezing is *involuntary.*] —**in·vol′un·tar′i·ly *adv.***

**in·volve** (in välv′) ***v.*** **1** to have as a part of it; include or require [Becoming a doctor *involves* years of study.] **2** to make busy; occupy [They are *involved* in scientific research.] **3** to draw into trouble or difficulty [Repairs on the house *involved* us in debt.] **4** to

| | | | | | | | |
|---|---|---|---|---|---|---|---|
| **a** | fat | **ir** | here | **ou** | out | **zh** | leisure |
| **ā** | ape | **ī** | bite, fire | **u** | up | **ŋ** | ring |
| **ä** | car, lot | **ō** | go | **ur** | fur | | a *in* ago |
| **e** | ten | **ô** | law, horn | **ch** | chin | | e *in* agent |
| **er** | care | **oi** | oil | **sh** | she | **ə** = | i *in* unity |
| **ē** | even | **oo** | look | **th** | thin | | o *in* collect |
| **i** | hit | **ōō** | tool | ***th*** | then | | u *in* focus |

make difficult or complicated [an *involved* set of instructions]. —**in·volved′, in·volv′ing**

**in·vul·ner·a·ble** (in vul′nər ə b'l) ***adj.*** that cannot be hurt, destroyed, damaged, etc. [an *invulnerable* fort; an *invulnerable* reputation for honesty].

**in·ward** (in′wərd) ***adj.*** **1** being on the inside; inner. **2** toward the inside [giving the door an *inward* push]. **3** of the mind or feelings [I felt an *inward* calm.] ***•adv.*** toward the inside [boring *inward* through the wall]. —**in′ward·ly *adv.***

**i·o·dide** (ī′ə dīd) ***n.*** a compound of iodine with another element.

**i·o·dine** (ī′ə dīn *or* ī′ə din) ***n.*** a mineral that is a chemical element. It is in the form of dark crystals which can be dissolved in alcohol and used as an antiseptic.

**i·o·dize** (ī′ə dīz) ***v.*** to treat with iodine or an iodide. **Iodized salt** is common table salt with a small amount of an iodide added; it is used by people who need iodine in their diet. —**i′o·dized, i′o·diz·ing**

**i·on** (ī′ən *or* ī′än) ***n.*** an atom or a group of atoms that has an electrical charge. A salt dissolved in water breaks down into ions.

**-ion** *a suffix meaning:* **1** the act or condition of [*Translation* is the act of translating.] **2** the result of [A *correction* is the result of correcting.]

**I·o·ni·an Sea** (ī ō′nē ən) the part of the Mediterranean Sea that lies between Greece, Sicily, and the southern part of Italy.



**I·on·ic** (ī än′ik) ***adj.*** describing a style of Greek architecture in which the columns have decorations like scrolls at the top. *See the picture.*

**i·on·ize** (ī′ə nīz) ***v.*** to change or be changed into ions. A gas can be ionized under the influence of radiation. —**i′on·ized, i′on·iz·ing** —**i′on·i·za′tion *n.***

**i·on·o·sphere** (ī än′ə sfir) ***n.*** the outer part of the earth's atmosphere. It begins at an altitude of about 40 kilometers (25 miles). It is made up of changing layers of ionized gases.

**i·o·ta** (ī ōt′ə) ***n.*** **1** the ninth letter of the Greek alphabet. **2** a very small amount; bit [That story hasn't an *iota* of truth in it.]

**IOU** or **I.O.U.** (ī′ō′yōō′) **1** I owe you. **2** a paper with these letters on it, signed by someone who owes money to someone else [I gave her my *IOU* for $20.]

**I·o·wa** (ī′ə wə) a State in the north central part of the U.S.: abbreviated **Ia., IA**

**IP** innings pitched (in baseball).

☆**ip·e·cac** (ip′ə kak) ***n.*** a medicine made from the roots of a South American plant. It is given to patients to make them vomit, as in cases of poisoning.

**IQ** or **I.Q.** *abbreviation for* **intelligence quotient,** a number that is supposed to show whether a person's intelligence is average, below average, or above average, according to a test.

**ir-** *a prefix meaning* not. **Ir-** is the form of **in-²** used before words beginning with *r* [*Irrational* means "not rational."]

**Ir.** *abbreviation for* **Ireland** *or* **Irish.**

**I.R.A.** or **IRA** Irish Republican Army.

**I·ran** (i ran′ *or* ē rän′) a country in southwestern Asia. Its older name is *Persia.* —**I·ra·ni·an** (i rā′nē ən) ***adj., n.***

**I·raq** (i räk′ *or* i rak′) a country in southwestern Asia. Its older name is *Mesopotamia.* —**I·ra·qi** (i rä′kē) ***adj., n.***

**i·ras·ci·ble** (i ras′ə b'l) ***adj.*** easily made angry; quick-tempered.

**i·rate** (ī rāt′ *or* ī′rāt) ***adj.*** angry. —**i·rate′ly *adv.***

**ire** (īr) ***n.*** anger; wrath.

**Ire·land** (īr′lənd) a large island west of Great Britain. An independent country, the Republic of Ireland, takes up most of the island, but a small part in the north (*Northern Ireland)* is in the United Kingdom.

**ir·i·des·cent** (ir′ə des″nt) ***adj.*** showing many colors that keep shifting and changing [Soap bubbles are often *iridescent.*] —**ir′i·des′cence *n.***

> The Greek word *iris* means "a rainbow." From this word come two English words, both with meanings which stress color. **Iridescent** is an adjective used to describe things that have the colors of the rainbow. **Iris,** taken unchanged from Greek, is our term for the colored part of the eye, and for a plant with flowers in many bright colors.

**i·ris** (ī′ris) ***n.*** **1** the colored part of the eye, around the pupil. *See the picture for* **eye. 2** a plant with long leaves like blades and showy flowers. *See the picture.*

**I·rish** (ī′rish) ***adj.*** of Ireland, its people, etc. ***•n.*** **1** the Celtic language used by some of the Irish. **2** the English dialect of Ireland. —**the Irish,** the people of Ireland.

**I·rish·man** (ī′rish mən) ***n.*** a person, especially a man, born or living in Ireland. —*pl.* **I′rish·men**

**Irish Sea** the part of the Atlantic Ocean between Ireland and Great Britain.

**I·rish·wom·an** (ī′rish woom′ən) ***n.*** a woman born or living in Ireland. —*pl.* **I′rish·wom′en**

**irk** (urk) ***v.*** to annoy, irritate, etc. [That banging door *irks* me.] *See* SYNONYMS *at* **annoy.**

**irk·some** (urk′səm) ***adj.*** tiresome or annoying [*irksome* duties].

**i·ron** (ī′ərn) ***n.*** **1** a strong metal that is a chemical element. It can be molded or stretched into various shapes after being heated, and is much used in the form of steel. **2** a device made of iron or other metal and having a flat, smooth bottom. It is heated and used for pressing clothes, etc. **3 irons,** *pl.* iron shackles or chains. **4** great strength or power [a will of *iron*]. ***•adj.*** **1** of or made of iron [*iron* bars]. **2** like iron; strong [*iron* determination]. ***•v.*** to press clothes, etc. with a hot iron. —☆**iron out,** to smooth out; get rid of [trying to *iron out* their problems]. —**strike while the iron is hot,** to act while there is a good opportunity to do so.

**i·ron·clad** (ī′ərn klad) ***adj.*** **1** covered or protected with iron. **2** hard to change or break [an *ironclad* agreement].

**iron curtain** secrecy and censorship that keep a country cut off from the rest of the world.

**i·ron·i·cal** (ī rän′i k'l) or **i·ron·ic** (ī rän′ik) ***adj.*** **1** meaning just the opposite of what is said [Calling their mansion "a humble home" was an *ironical* remark.] **2** opposite to what might be expected [It was *ironical* that the lifeguard drowned.] —**i·ron′i·cal·ly *adv.***

☆**iron lung** a large machine used to force air into and out of the lungs of a person who cannot breathe without help.

**iron pyrites** *another name for* **pyrite.**

**i·ro·ny** (ī′rən ē) ***n.*** **1** a way of being amusing or sarcastic by saying exactly the opposite of what one means [Using *irony,* I called the stupid plan "very clever."] **2** an event or a result that is the opposite of what might be expected [That the fire station burned down was an *irony.*] *—pl.* **i′ro·nies**

**Ir·o·quois** (ir′ə kwoi) ***n.*** a member of a group of Indian tribes that lived in western and northern New York. *—pl.* **Ir·o·quois** (ir′ə kwoi *or* ir′ə kwoiz)

**ir·ra·di·ate** (i rā′dē āt) ***v.*** **1** to cause X-rays, ultraviolet rays, etc. to act upon, as in treating a disease. **2** to radiate; give out; spread [to *irradiate* joy]. —**ir·ra′di·at·ed, ir·ra′di·at·ing**

**ir·ra·tion·al** (i rash′ən ′l) ***adj.*** that does not make sense; not rational; absurd [an *irrational* fear of the dark]. —**ir·ra′tion·al·ly *adv.***

SYNONYMS: **Irrational** suggests a being unable to think clearly because one's mind is so confused or one's feelings are so out of control [It is *irrational* to believe that everyone is your enemy.] **Unreasonable** suggests a failure to think clearly and logically even though one is able to do so [It is *unreasonable* to ask anyone to pay that much for an old, run-down house.]

**ir·rec·on·cil·a·ble** (i rek′ən sīl′ə b′l) ***adj.*** that cannot be reconciled or made to agree; incompatible [*irreconcilable* enemies].

**ir·re·cov·er·a·ble** (ir′i kuv′ər ə b′l) ***adj.*** that cannot be recovered, regained, or got back [an *irrecoverable* loss].

**ir·re·deem·a·ble** (ir′i dēm′ə b′l) ***adj.*** that cannot be redeemed; especially, that cannot be changed or made better [an *irredeemable* sinner].

**ir·re·duc·i·ble** (ir′i do͞os′ə b′l *or* ir′i dyo͞os′ə b′l) ***adj.*** that cannot be reduced or made smaller.

**ir·ref·u·ta·ble** (i ref′yoo tə b′l *or* ir′i fyo͞ot′ə b′l) ***adj.*** that cannot be denied or proved wrong [an *irrefutable* claim].

☆**ir·re·gard·less** (ir′i gärd′lis) ***adj., adv.*** *a word used by mistake or in a humorous way instead of* **regardless.**

**ir·reg·u·lar** (i reg′yə lər) ***adj.*** **1** not regular; not like the usual rule, way, or custom [an *irregular* diet]. **2** not straight, even, or the same throughout [an *irregular* design]. *See the picture.* **3** not changing its forms in the usual way ["Go" is an *irregular* verb.] —**ir·reg′u·lar·ly *adv.***

**ir·reg·u·lar·i·ty** (i reg′yə lar′ə tē) ***n.*** **1** the condition of being irregular. **2** something irregular. *—pl.* **ir·reg′u·lar′i·ties**

**ir·rel·e·vant** (i rel′ə vənt) ***adj.*** having nothing to do with the subject; not to the point [That remark about the candidate's religion was *irrelevant* to the issues of the campaign.] —**ir·rel′e·vance *n.*** —**ir·rel′e·vant·ly *adv.***

**ir·re·li·gious** (ir′i lij′əs) ***adj.*** not religious.

**ir·rep·a·ra·ble** (i rep′ər ə b′l) ***adj.*** that cannot be repaired, mended, or put right [*irreparable* damage]. —**ir·rep′a·ra·bly *adv.***

**ir·re·place·a·ble** (ir′i plās′ə b′l) ***adj.*** that cannot be replaced [an *irreplaceable* friend].

**ir·re·press·i·ble** (ir′i pres′ə b′l) ***adj.*** that cannot be held back or controlled [*irrepressible* tears].

**ir·re·proach·a·ble** (ir′i prō′chə b′l) ***adj.*** that cannot be blamed or criticized; blameless.

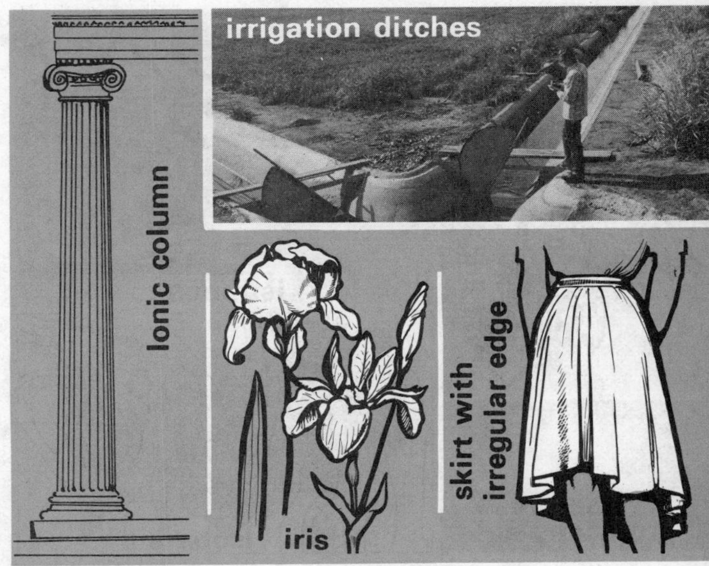


**ir·re·sist·i·ble** (ir′i zis′tə b′l) ***adj.*** that cannot be resisted; too strong to fight against [an *irresistible* force]. —**ir′re·sist′i·bly *adv.***

**ir·res·o·lute** (i rez′ə lo͞ot) ***adj.*** not able to decide or make up one's mind; hesitating. —**ir·res·o·lu·tion** (i rez′ə lo͞o′shən) ***n.***

**ir·re·spec·tive** (ir′i spek′tiv) ***adj.*** regardless [All citizens may vote, *irrespective* of sex.] 

**ir·re·spon·si·ble** (ir′i spän′sə b′l) ***adj.*** not responsible; not showing a sense of duty; doing as one pleases. —**ir′re·spon′si·bly *adv.***

**ir·re·triev·a·ble** (ir′i trēv′ə b′l) ***adj.*** that cannot be recovered or brought back.

**ir·rev·er·ent** (i rev′ər ənt) ***adj.*** not reverent; not showing respect for religion or for things that deserve respect. —**ir·rev′er·ence *n.***

**ir·re·vers·i·ble** (ir′i vur′sə b′l) ***adj.*** that cannot be reversed or changed [the *irreversible* decision of the judge].

**ir·rev·o·ca·ble** (i rev′ə kə b′l) ***adj.*** that cannot be called back, undone, or changed [an *irrevocable* choice]. —**ir·rev′o·ca·bly *adv.***

**ir·ri·gate** (ir′ə gāt) ***v.*** **1** to water by means of canals, ditches, or pipes, or by sprinklers [to *irrigate* desert land so it can bear crops]. *See the picture.* **2** to wash out with a flow of water or other liquid [The doctor *irrigated* the wound.] —**ir′ri·gat·ed, ir′ri·gat·ing —ir′ri·ga′tion *n.***

**ir·ri·ta·ble** (ir′ə tə b′l) ***adj.*** easily annoyed or made angry. —**ir·ri·ta·bil·i·ty** (ir′ə tə bil′ə tē) ***n.*** —**ir′ri·ta·bly *adv.***

**ir·ri·tant** (ir′ə tənt) ***adj.*** that irritates. ◆***n.*** something that irritates.

| | | | | | | | |
|---|---|---|---|---|---|---|---|
| **a** | fat | **ir** | here | **ou** | out | **zh** | leisure |
| **ā** | ape | **ī** | bite, fire | **u** | up | **ng** | ring |
| **ä** | car, lot | **ō** | go | **ur** | fur | | a *in* ago |
| **e** | ten | **ô** | law, horn | **ch** | chin | | e *in* agent |
| **er** | care | **oi** | oil | **sh** | she | **ə =** | i *in* unity |
| **ē** | even | **oo** | look | **th** | thin | | o *in* collect |
| **i** | hit | **o͞o** | tool | ***th*** | then | | u *in* focus |

isthmus

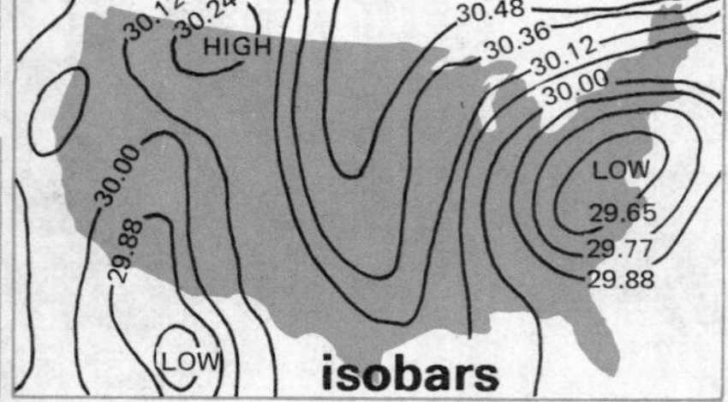


isobars

isosceles triangle

**ir·ri·tate** (ir′ə tāt) ***v.*** **1** to bother or annoy; make impatient or angry [Your bragging *irritates* most of the other students.] **2** to make red, raw, sore, etc. [Harsh soap *irritates* her skin.] —**ir′ri·tat·ed, ir′ri·tat·ing** —**ir′ri·ta′tion** ***n.***



**ir·rup·tion** (i rup′shən) ***n.*** a bursting in or rushing in with wild force [the *irruption* of flood waters into the valley].

**IRS** or **I.R.S.** Internal Revenue Service, the government agency that collects income taxes.

**Ir·ving** (ur′ving), **Washington** 1783–1859; U.S. writer.

**is** (iz) *the form of* **be** *showing the present time with singular nouns and with* he, she, *or* it.

**Is.** or **is.** *abbreviation for* **island** *or* **islands, isle** *or* **isles.**

**I·saac** (ī′zək) in the Bible, the son of Abraham and the father of Jacob and Esau.

**I·sa·iah** (ī zā′ə) **1** a Hebrew prophet of the 8th century B.C. **2** a book of the Bible with his teachings.

**Iscariot** *see* **Judas Iscariot.**

**-ise** (īz) *the usual British spelling of* **-ize.**

**-ish** (ish) *a suffix meaning:* **1** of or belonging to [A *Swedish* citizen is a citizen of Sweden.] **2** like or like that of [A *devilish* person is like a devil.] **3** somewhat; rather [*Warmish* weather is rather warm weather.]

**i·sin·glass** (ī′z'n glas′) ***n.*** **1** a jelly made from fish bladders. It is used in glues, etc. **2** mica, especially in thin sheets.

**I·sis** (ī′sis) a goddess of ancient Egypt.

**Is·lam** (is′läm *or* is′ləm) ***n.*** **1** the Muslim religion, founded by Mohammed, in which God is called Allah. **2** all the Muslims, or all the countries in which mostly Muslims live. —**Is·lam·ic** (is lam′ik *or* is läm′ik) ***adj.***

**Is·lam·a·bad** (is läm′ə bäd) the capital of Pakistan, in the northeastern part of the country.

**is·land** (ī′lənd) ***n.*** **1** a piece of land smaller than a continent and surrounded by water. **2** any place set apart from what surrounds it [The oasis was an *island* of green in the desert.]

**is·land·er** (ī′lənd ər) ***n.*** a person born or living on an island.

**isle** (īl) ***n.*** an island, usually a small island.

**Isle Roy·ale** (īl roi′əl) an island in northern Lake Superior. It is part of the State of Michigan.

**is·let** (ī′lit) ***n.*** a very small island.

**-ism** (iz′m) *a suffix meaning:* **1** doctrine, theory, or belief [*Liberalism* is a belief in liberal ideas.] **2** the act or result of [*Criticism* is the act of or result of criticizing.] **3** the condition, conduct, or qualities of [*Patriotism* is the conduct of a patriot.] **4** an example of [A *witticism* is an example of a witty saying.]

**is·n't** (iz″nt) is not.

**i·so·bar** (ī′sə bär) ***n.*** a line on a weather map connecting places where the air pressure is the same. *See the picture.*

**i·so·late** (ī′sə lāt) ***v.*** to set apart from others; place alone; seclude [The snowstorm *isolated* the village.] —**i′so·lat·ed, i′so·lat·ing** —**i′so·la′tion** ***n.***

☆**i·so·la·tion·ist** (ī′sə lā′shən ist) ***n.*** a person who believes that his or her country should not take part in international affairs. —**i′so·la′tion·ism** ***n.***

**i·sos·ce·les triangle** (ī säs′ə lēz) a triangle that has two equal sides. *See the picture.*

**i·so·therm** (ī′sə thurm) ***n.*** a line on a map connecting places where the average temperature is the same.

**i·so·tope** (ī′sə tōp) ***n.*** any of two or more forms of a chemical element having the same atomic number but different atomic weights.

**Is·ra·el** (iz′rē əl) **1** a country between the Mediterranean Sea and the country of Jordan. **2** the ancient land of the Hebrews, at the southeastern end of the Mediterranean. **3** in the Bible, the name given to Jacob after he wrestled with the angel. **4** the Jewish people, as descendants of Jacob.

**Is·rae·li** (iz rā′lē) ***adj.*** of modern Israel or its people. ◆***n.*** a person born or living in modern Israel.

**Is·ra·el·ite** (iz′rē ə līt′) ***n.*** any of the people of ancient Israel; also, any Jew.

☆**is·su·ance** (ish′oo wəns) ***n.*** the act of issuing.

**is·sue** (ish′ōō) ***n.*** **1** a sending out or giving out [the army *issue* of clothing to the soldiers]. **2** a thing or group of things sent or given out [the July *issue* of a magazine]. **3** a problem to be talked over [The candidates will debate the *issues.*] **4** a flowing out; outflow [*issue* of water from a pipe]. **5** a result; outcome [The *issue* of the battle was in doubt.] **6** a child or children; offspring [Elizabeth I died without *issue.*] ◆***v.*** **1** to put forth or send out [The city *issues* bonds. The general *issued* an order.] **2** to give or deal out; distribute [The teacher *issued* new books.] **3** to go forth or flow out [Blood *issued* from the wound.] **4** to come about as a result [Will anything good *issue* from their research?] —**is′sued, is′su·ing** —**at issue,** still to be decided. —**take issue,** to disagree.

**-ist** (ist) *a suffix meaning:* **1** a person who [A *moralist* is one who moralizes.] **2** a person who is skilled in or who works at [An *artist* is one skilled in art.] **3** a person who believes in [A *socialist* is one who believes in socialism.]

**Is·tan·bul** (is′tan bool′ *or* is′tän bōōl′) a seaport in the northwestern part of Turkey.

**isth·mus** (is′məs) ***n.*** a narrow strip of land with water on each side, that joins two larger bodies of land [the *Isthmus* of Panama]. *See the picture.*

**it** (it) ***pron.*** the animal or thing being talked about [I read that book and liked *it.*] ◆***n.*** the player, as in the game of tag, who must try to touch, catch, or find another. *—pl.* **they**

> **It** is also used as: **1** the subject of a clause to refer to another clause that comes later [*It* is settled that I will go.] **2** a word referring to the condition of the weather or to things in general [*It* is snowing. *It's* all right; no harm was done.]

**It.** or **Ital.** *abbreviations for* **Italian** *or* **Italy.**

**I·tal·ian** (i tal′yən) ***adj.*** of Italy, its people, etc. ◆***n.*** **1** a person born or living in Italy. **2** the language of Italy.

**i·tal·ic** (i tal′ik) ***adj.*** describing printing type in which the letters slant upward to the right: it is used to call attention to words [*This is italic type.*] ◆***n.*** *usually* **italics,** *pl.* italic type: *sometimes used with a singular verb.*

**i·tal·i·cize** (i tal′ə sīz) ***v.*** **1** to print in italic type. **2** to underline something written, to show that it is to be printed in italics. —**i·tal′i·cized, i·tal′i·ciz·ing**

**It·a·ly** (it′'l ē) a country in southern Europe, including the islands of Sicily and Sardinia.

**itch** (ich) ***v.*** **1** to have a tickling feeling on the skin, that makes one want to scratch; also, to cause to have this feeling [The wool shirt *itches* my skin.] **2** to have a restless desire [He's *itching* to leave.] ◆***n.*** **1** an itching feeling on the skin. **2** a restless desire [an *itch* to travel]. —**the itch,** a skin disease in which an itching feeling is very strong.

**itch·y** (ich′ē) ***adj.*** feeling or causing an itch. —**itch′i·er, itch′i·est** —**itch′i·ness *n.***

**-ite** (īt) *a suffix meaning:* **1** a person born or living in [A *Canaanite* was one born in Canaan.] **2** a person who believes in or supports [A *laborite* is a supporter of a labor party.]

**i·tem** (īt′əm) ***n.*** **1** a separate thing; one of a group of things; unit [Check each *item* on this list.] **2** a piece of news or information.

> SYNONYMS: **Item** is used for each separate thing on a list [The third *item* to be auctioned off was a sofa.] **Detail** is used for a single thing or small part that is a piece of a whole or of something larger [the *details* of a story; a *detail* in a painting].

☆**i·tem·ize** (īt′əm īz) ***v.*** to list the items of, one by one [Please *itemize* my purchases.] —**i′tem·ized, i′tem·iz·ing**

**Ith·a·ca** (ith′ə kə) an island off the west coast of Greece: said to be the home of Odysseus.

**i·tin·er·ant** (ī tin′ər ənt) ***adj.*** traveling from place to place, especially in connection with some kind of work [*itinerant* laborers]. ◆***n.*** a person who travels from place to place.

**i·tin·er·ar·y** (ī tin′ə rer′ē) ***n.*** **1** the route for traveling on a journey. **2** a detailed plan for a journey that one intends to take. *—pl.* **i·tin′er·ar′ies**

**it'll** (it′'l) **1** it will. **2** it shall.

**its** (its) ***pron.*** of it or done by it: *the possessive form of* **it,** *thought of as an adjective* [Give the cat *its* dinner. The frost had done *its* damage.]

**it's** (its) **1** it is. **2** it has.

**it·self** (it self′) ***pron.*** **1** its own self. *This form of* **it** *is used when the object is the same as the subject of the verb* [The dog scratched *itself.*] **2** its usual or true self [The bird is not *itself* today.] *Itself* is also used to give force to a noun [The work *itself* is easy.]

**-i·ty** (ə tē) *a suffix meaning* condition *or* quality [*Acidity* is the condition or quality of being acid.]

**IV** or **i.v.** *abbreviation for* **intravenous.**

**I·van** (ī′vən) 1530–1584; the first czar of Russia, from 1547 to 1584. He was called *Ivan the Terrible.*

**I've** (īv) I have.

**-ive** (iv) *a suffix meaning:* **1** of or having to do with [*Instinctive* feelings are feelings having to do with instinct.] **2** likely to; given to [An *instructive* story is a story that is likely to instruct.]

**Ives** (īvz), **Charles Edward** 1874–1954; U.S. composer.

**i·vied** (ī′vēd) ***adj.*** with ivy growing over it [an *ivied* wall].

**i·vo·ry** (ī′vər ē) ***n.*** **1** the hard, white substance that forms the tusks of the elephant, walrus, etc. **2** any substance like ivory, as the white plastic used on piano keys. **3** the color of ivory; creamy white. *—pl.* **i′vo·ries** ◆***adj.*** **1** made of or like ivory. **2** having the color of ivory; creamy-white.

**Ivory Coast** a country on the western coast of Africa.

☆**ivory tower** a place thought of as being more peaceful than the real world and set apart from its problems.

**i·vy** (ī′vē) ***n.*** **1** a climbing vine with a woody stem and shiny, evergreen leaves. *The full name is* **English Ivy.** *See the picture.* **2** any of various plants like this. *—pl.* **i′vies**

**-ize** (īz) *a suffix meaning:* **1** to make or become [*Sterilize* means to make sterile.] **2** to engage in or act in a certain way [*Sympathize* means to act in a sympathetic way.] **3** to treat or unite with [*Oxidize* means to unite with oxygen.]

| | | | | | | | |
|---|---|---|---|---|---|---|---|
| **a** | fat | **ir** | here | **ou** | out | **zh** | leisure |
| **ā** | ape | **ī** | bite, fire | **u** | up | **ŋ** | ring |
| **ä** | car, lot | **ō** | go | **ur** | fur | | a *in* ago |
| **e** | ten | **ô** | law, horn | **ch** | chin | | e *in* agent |
| **er** | care | **oi** | oil | **sh** | she | **ə** = | i *in* unity |
| **ē** | even | **oo** | look | **th** | thin | | o *in* collect |
| **i** | hit | **ōō** | tool | ***th*** | then | | u *in* focus |

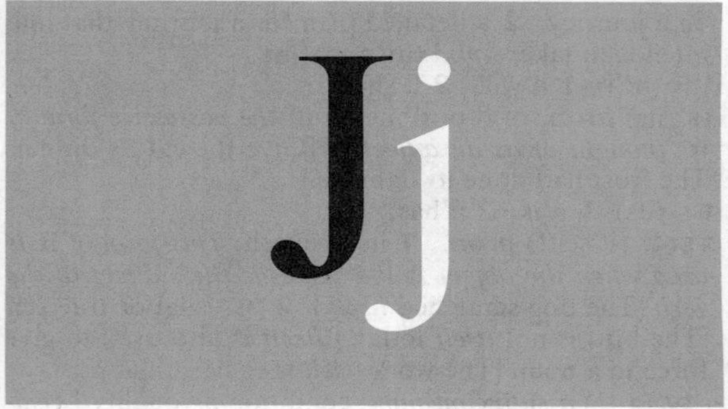

**J, j** (jā) ***n.*** the tenth letter of the English alphabet. *—pl.* **J's, j's** (jāz)

**jab** (jab) ***v.*** **1** to poke with something hard or sharp [Your elbow is *jabbing* my ribs.] **2** to punch with short blows. **—jabbed, jab′bing** **◆*n.*** a poke or punch.

**jab·ber** (jab′ər) ***v.*** to talk fast in a silly, rambling way, or without making sense; chatter. **◆*n.*** talk of this kind. **—jab′ber·er *n.***

**ja·bot** (zha bō′) ***n.*** a broad ruffle or frill worn on the front of a blouse or dress and fastened at the neck.

**jac·a·ran·da** (jak′ə ran′də) ***n.*** a tree grown in the southern U.S., with delicate leaves and lavender flowers.

**jack** (jak) ***n.*** **1** a machine or tool used to lift or move something heavy a short distance [an automobile *jack*]. *See the picture.* **2** a male donkey. **3** a playing card with the picture of a page or servant on it. **4** any of the small pebbles or six-pointed metals pieces used in playing the game of jacks: *the full name is* **jackstone** (jak′stōn). *See the picture.* **5** a small flag flown at the front of a ship as a signal. **6** a device into which a plug is put to make an electric connection. **—jack up, 1** to lift by means of a jack. ☆**2** to raise, as prices: *used only in everyday talk.*

**jack·al** (jak′əl) ***n.*** a wild dog of Asia and Africa, smaller than a wolf. Jackals hunt in packs, often feeding on flesh left uneaten by other animals.



**jack·a·napes** (jak′ə nāps) ***n.*** an impudent young person who is full of mischief; rascal.

**jack·ass** (jak′as) ***n.*** **1** a male donkey. **2** a stupid or foolish person.

**jack·boot** (jak′bo͞ot) ***n.*** a heavy boot reaching above the knee.

**jack·daw** (jak′dô) ***n.*** a black bird like the crow, but smaller. It is found in Europe.

**jack·et** (jak′it) ***n.*** **1** a short coat. **2** an outer covering, as the skin of a potato, or the paper wrapper for a book. ☆**3** a cardboard holder for a phonograph record.

☆**jack·ham·mer** (jak′ham′ər) ***n.*** a noisy kind of heavy drilling tool, worked by air pressure and used in road repairs, breaking up concrete surfaces, etc.

**jack-in-the-box** (jak′in *th*ə bäks′) ***n.*** a toy made up of a box with a little figure in it that jumps up when the lid is lifted.

☆**jack-in-the-pul·pit** (jak′in *th*ə pool′pit) ***n.*** a wildflower that grows in the woods. Its blossom is covered by a kind of hood. *See the picture.*

☆**jack·knife** (jak′nīf) ***n.*** **1** a large pocketknife. **2** a dive in which the diver touches the feet with the hands while in the air. *—pl.* **jack′knives** **◆*v.*** to bend at the middle as in a jackknife dive. **—jack′knifed, jack′knif·ing**

**jack-of-all-trades** (jak′əv ôl′trādz′) ***n.*** a person who can do many kinds of work.

**jack-o′-lan·tern** (jak′ə lan′tərn) ***n.*** a lantern made of a hollow pumpkin cut to look like a face. It is used as a decoration at Halloween.

☆**jack·pot** (jak′pät) ***n.*** any prize that is the highest that can be won: *used only in everyday talk.* **—hit the jackpot, 1** to win the highest prize. **2** to get the highest reward or success. *This is a slang phrase.*

☆**jack rabbit** a large hare of western North America, with long ears and strong hind legs.

**jacks** (jaks) ***n.pl.*** a children's game in which pebbles or small, six-pointed metal pieces are tossed and picked up, especially while bouncing a small ball: *used with a singular verb.*

**Jack·son** (jak′s'n) the capital of Mississippi.

**Jack·son** (jak′s'n), **Andrew** 1767–1845; the seventh president of the United States, from 1829 to 1837.

**Jackson, Thomas J.** 1824–1863; Confederate general in the Civil War. He was also called **Stonewall Jackson.**

**Jack·son·ville** (jak′s'n vil) a city in northeastern Florida.

**jack·straw** (jak′strô) ***n.*** any of the narrow strips of wood, plastic, etc. used in a children's game called **jackstraws.** The strips are tossed in a jumbled heap from which the players try to remove them one at a time without moving the others.

**Ja·cob** (jā′kəb) in the Bible, a son of Isaac and father of the founders of the tribes of Israel.

**jade**[1] (jād) ***n.*** **1** a hard, green stone used in jewelry and artistic carvings. **2** its green color.

> **Jade** comes from a Spanish phrase meaning "stone of the side." In earlier times, it was thought that jade could cure pains in the side of a person's body.

**jade**[2] (jād) ***n.*** **1** an old worn-out horse. **2** a woman of low morals. **◆*v.*** to make tired or worn-out. **—jad′ed, jad′ing**

**jad·ed** (jā′did) ***adj.*** **1** tired; worn-out. **2** made dull or too satisfied, as from having or doing too much [*Jaded* from all the parties, we decided to stay home.]

**jag**[1] (jag) ***n.*** a sharp, rough point, as of rock.

**jag**[2] (jag) ***n.*** **1** a drunken condition or a drunken party. **2** a period of doing something without stopping [a crying *jag*]. *This is a slang word.*

**jag·ged** (jag′id) ***adj.*** having sharp points and notches, as the edge of a saw.

**jag·uar** (jag′wär) ***n.*** a large wildcat that looks like a large leopard. It is yellowish with black spots and is found from the southwestern U.S. to Argentina. *See the picture.*

**jai a·lai** (hī′lī *or* hī′ə lī) a game like handball. Each player has a curved basket fastened to the arm for catching the small, hard ball and hurling it against the wall.

> **Jai alai** is a lively Spanish game that is also very popular in Spanish American countries. Its name comes from Spanish words that mean "merry celebration."

**jail** (jāl) ***n.*** a building where people are locked up who are waiting for a trial or who are serving a short sentence for breaking the law. ◆***v.*** to put or keep in jail.

☆**jail·break** (jāl′brāk) ***n.*** the act of breaking out of jail by force.

**jail·er** or **jail·or** (jāl′ər) ***n.*** a person in charge of a jail or of prisoners in a jail.

**Ja·kar·ta** (jə kär′tə) the capital of Indonesia, on the island of Java.

☆**ja·lop·y** (jə läp′ē) ***n.*** an old, worn-out automobile: *a slang word.* —*pl.* **ja·lop′ies**

**jal·ou·sie** (jal′ə sē) ***n.*** a window, door, or shade made of horizontal slats of metal, wood, or glass. The slats can be moved to control the amount of air or light coming in. *See the picture.*

**jam**[1] (jam) ***v.*** **1** to squeeze or force tightly [to *jam* one's hands into one's pockets]. **2** to injure or crush [His hand was *jammed* in the car door.] **3** to fill or block up by crowding in [Cars *jammed* the parking lot.] ☆**4** to push or shove hard [to *jam* on the brakes]. **5** to wedge in or stick tight so that it cannot move [The door was *jammed* shut.] **6** to keep radio signals from being clearly heard, by sending out others on the same wavelength. —**jammed, jam′ming** ◆***n.*** **1** a jamming or being jammed, or many things jammed together [a traffic *jam*]. ☆**2** a difficult situation: *used only in everyday talk.*

**jam**[2] (jam) ***n.*** a sweet food made by boiling fruit and sugar until it forms a thick paste.

**Ja·mai·ca** (jə mā′kə) a country on an island in the West Indies. —**Ja·mai′can** ***adj., n.***

**jamb** (jam) ***n.*** a side post of an opening for a door, window, etc.

☆**jam·bo·ree** (jam bə rē′) ***n.*** **1** a large gathering of boy scouts from many places or countries. **2** a lively, noisy party, or a gathering with entertainment.

**James·town** (jāmz′toun) the first successful English colony in America, set up in 1607 in what is now Virginia.

**Jam·mu and Kashmir** (jum′o͞o) a state of northern India. Pakistan also claims control of this state. *See the map for* **Kashmir**.

**Jane Doe** (jān dō) a name used in legal papers for any woman whose name is not known.

**jan·gle** (jaŋ′g′l) ***v.*** **1** to make or cause to make a harsh, jarring sound [keys *jangling* together]. **2** to bother or upset very much [to *jangle* one's nerves]. —**jan′gled, jan′gling** ◆***n.*** a harsh sound.

**jan·i·tor** (jan′i tər) ***n.*** a person who takes care of cleaning and repairing a building.

**Jan·u·ar·y** (jan′yoo wer′ē) ***n.*** the first month of the year, which has 31 days: abbreviated **Jan.**

> **January** gets its name from the Roman god *Janus,* who had a face in front and another at the back of his head. He was supposed to keep special watch over the beginnings and ends of things. January marks the beginning of the new year and the end of the old one.

**Jap.** *abbreviation for* **Japan** *or* **Japanese.**

**Ja·pan** (jə pan′) a country east of Korea, made up of many islands.

**Jap·a·nese** (jap ə nēz′) ***n.*** **1** a member of a people whose native country is Japan. —*pl.* **Jap·a·nese′** **2** the language of Japan. ◆***adj.*** of Japan, its people, language, or culture.

cap at a jaunty angle

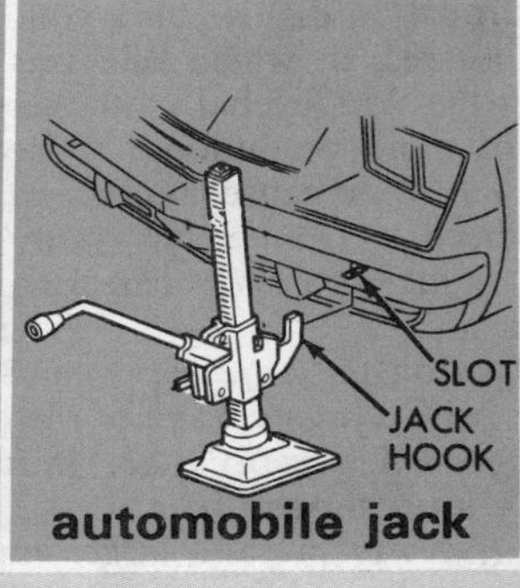


automobile jack

jack-in-the-pulpit

jalousies

jaguar

75 cm (30 in.) high at shoulder

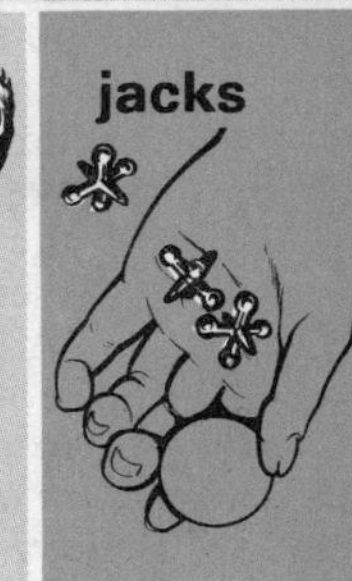

jacks

☆**Japanese beetle** a shiny, green-and-brown beetle that is harmful to crops.

**jar**[1] (jär) ***v.*** **1** to shake up; rattle; jolt [The explosion *jarred* our windows.] **2** to make a harsh sound; grate. **3** to be harsh on the ears, eyes, nerves, etc. [a *jarring* noise; *jarring* news]. **4** to clash; disagree sharply [Her rude remark *jarred* with her refined manners.] —**jarred, jar′ring** ◆***n.*** **1** a shaking or rattling; jolt. **2** a harsh or grating sound. 395

**jar**[2] (jär) ***n.*** **1** a container made of glass, pottery, or stone, having a broad mouth. **2** as much as a jar will hold.

**jar·di·niere** (jär′d′n ir′) ***n.*** a fancy pot or stand for flowers or plants.

**jar·gon** (jär′gən) ***n.*** **1** the special words and phrases used by people in the same kind of work [Sportswriters have a *jargon* of their own, and so do scientists.] **2** talk that makes no sense; gibberish.

> **Jargon** comes from an old French word that meant "the sound of chattering by birds." From this it came to mean the kind of talk that one cannot understand any better than one can understand the sounds that birds make.

**jas·mine** (jaz′min) ***n.*** a plant of warm regions that has sweet-smelling flowers of red, yellow, or white.

**Ja·son** (jās′′n) the prince in a Greek legend who searched for the Golden Fleece.

**jas·per** (jas′pər) ***n.*** a dull kind of quartz, usually yellow, red, or brown.

| | | | |
|---|---|---|---|
| **a** fat | **ir** here | **ou** out | **zh** leisure |
| **ā** ape | **ī** bite, fire | **u** up | **ŋ** ring |
| **ä** car, lot | **ō** go | **ʉr** fur | a *in* ago |
| **e** ten | **ô** law, horn | **ch** chin | e *in* agent |
| **er** care | **oi** oil | **sh** she | **ə** = i *in* unity |
| **ē** even | **oo** look | **th** thin | o *in* collect |
| **i** hit | **o͞o** tool | ***th*** then | u *in* focus |

**jaun·dice** (jôn′dis) ***n.*** **1** a condition caused by various diseases, in which bile gets into the blood and makes the skin, eyeballs, etc. very yellow. **2** a bitterness of mind or outlook, as because of jealousy or hate. ◆***v.*** **1** to cause jaundice in. **2** to make bitter or prejudiced, as from envy. —**jaun′diced, jaun′dic·ing**

**jaunt** (jônt) ***n.*** a short trip for pleasure. ◆***v.*** to take such a trip.

**jaun·ty** (jôn′tē) ***adj.*** happy and carefree; sprightly; perky [with a *jaunty* wave of the hand]. *See the picture on page 395.* —**jaun′ti·er, jaun′ti·est** —**jaun′ti·ly** ***adv.*** —**jaun′ti·ness** ***n.***

**Ja·va** (jä′və *or* jav′ə) a large, important island of Indonesia. —**Jav·a·nese** (jav ə nēz′) ***adj., n.***

**jav·e·lin** (jav′lin *or* jav′ə lin) ***n.*** a light spear; nowadays, one used in an athletic contest to see who can throw it farthest. *See the picture.*

**jaw** (jô) ***n.*** **1** either of the two bony parts that form the frame of the mouth and that hold the teeth. **2** either of two parts that close to grip or crush something [A vise and a pair of pliers have *jaws.*] **3 jaws,** *pl.* the mouth; also, the entrance of a canyon, valley, etc. ◆***v.*** to talk, especially in a boring or insulting way: *slang in this meaning.*

**jaw·bone** (jô′bōn) ***n.*** a bone of the jaw, especially of the lower jaw.

**jay** (jā) ***n.*** **1** any of several brightly colored birds of the crow family. **2** *a shorter name for* **blue jay.**

396 ☆**jay·walk** (jā′wôk) ***v.*** to walk in or across a street carelessly, without obeying traffic rules and signals. *See the picture.* —**jay′walk·er** ***n.***

☆**jazz** (jaz) ***n.*** a kind of American music that originated with Southern blacks and is usually played by small groups. It has strong rhythms and the players or singers usually make up parts as they go along.

**jeal·ous** (jel′əs) ***adj.*** **1** worried or afraid that someone is taking the love or attention one has or wants [a *jealous* child]. **2** resulting from such a feeling [a *jealous* rage]. **3** unhappy because another has something one would like; envious [Are you *jealous* of your playmate's new bicycle?] **4** careful in guarding; watchful [We should be *jealous* of our rights as citizens.] —**jeal′ous·ly** ***adv.*** —**jeal′ous·ness** ***n.***

jaywalker

jerkin

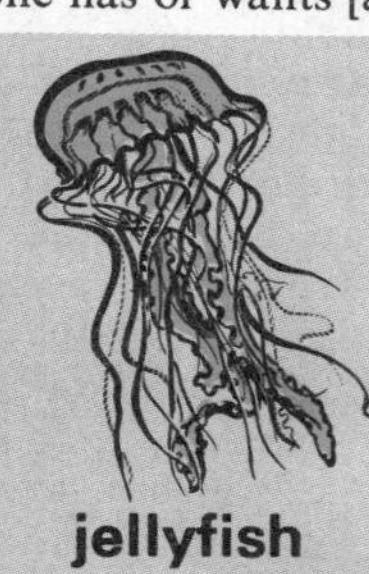
jellyfish
40 cm (16 in.) long

jerboa
25 cm (10 in.) long, including tail

jib

man throwing the javelin

**jeal·ous·y** (jel′əs ē) ***n.*** the condition of being jealous, or a jealous feeling.

**jeans** (jēnz) ***n.pl.*** trousers or overalls made of a heavy, cotton cloth, usually blue.

☆**jeep** (jēp) ***n.*** a small, powerful automobile first made in World War II for army use.

**jeer** (jir) ***v.*** to make fun of in a rude or mocking way [The audience *jeered* at the clumsy dancer.] ◆***n.*** a jeering cry or remark.

**Jef·fer·son** (jef′ər s'n), **Thomas** 1743–1826; the third president of the United States, from 1801 to 1809.

**Jefferson City** the capital of Missouri.

**Je·ho·vah** (ji hō′və) the Hebrew name for God.

☆**jell** (jel) ***v.*** **1** to become, or make into, jelly [The mixture will *jell* when it cools.] **2** to take on or give definite form: *used only in everyday talk* [Plans for the dance have *jelled.*]

☆**Jell-O** (jel′ō) *a trademark for* a flavored gelatin eaten as a dessert or used in molded salads.

**jel·ly** (jel′ē) ***n.*** **1** a soft, firm food that looks smooth and glassy, and is easily cut, spread, etc. Jelly is made from cooked fruit syrup, meat juice, or gelatin. **2** any substance like this. —*pl.* **jel′lies** ◆***v.*** to become, or make into, jelly. —**jel′lied, jel′ly·ing**

☆**jel·ly·bean** (jel′ē bēn′) ***n.*** a small, gummy candy shaped like a bean.

**jel·ly·fish** (jel′ē fish′) ***n.*** a sea animal with a body that feels like jelly. *See the picture.*

**jel·ly·roll** (jel′ē rōl′) ***n.*** a thin layer of sponge cake spread with jelly and rolled up.

**jen·ny** (jen′ē) ***n.*** the female of some animals [a *jenny* wren]. —*pl.* **jen′nies**

**jeop·ard·ize** (jep′ər dīz) ***v.*** to put in danger; risk; endanger [Getting married did not *jeopardize* her career as a singer.] —**jeop′ard·ized, jeop′ard·iz·ing**

**jeop·ard·y** (jep′ər dē) ***n.*** great danger or risk [A firefighter's life is often in *jeopardy.*]

**jer·bo·a** (jər bō′ə) ***n.*** a small animal of Asia and northern Africa, like a mouse: it has long hind legs with which it can jump far. *See the picture.*

**Jer·e·mi·ah** (jer′ə mī′ə) **1** a Hebrew prophet of the 7th and 6th centuries B.C. **2** a book of the Bible with his prophecies.

**Jer·i·cho** (jer′ə kō) a city in Jordan, where an ancient city stood whose walls, according to the Bible, were destroyed by a miracle when trumpets were blown.

**jerk**[1] (jurk) ***n.*** **1** a sudden, sharp pull, lift, twist, or push [The train started with a *jerk* that threw our heads back.] **2** a sudden twitch of a muscle. ☆**3** a person thought of as stupid, foolish, etc. ◆***v.*** **1** to move or pull with a jerk or jerks [He *jerked* the book from my hands.] **2** to twitch.

**jerk**[2] (jurk) ***v.*** to slice meat into strips and dry it in the sun or over a fire [*jerked* beef].

**jer·kin** (jur′kin) ***n.*** a short, tight jacket often with no sleeves, worn by men in the 16th and 17th centuries. *See the picture.*

**jerk·y** (jur′kē) ***adj.*** making sudden, sharp movements; moving by jerks. —**jerk′i·er, jerk′i·est**

**Je·rome** (jə rōm′), Saint 340?–420 A.D.; a monk who translated the Bible into Latin.

**Jer·sey** (jur′zē) a British island in the English Channel. ◆*n.* a breed of small, reddish-brown dairy cattle first raised on this island. *—pl.* **Jer′seys**

**jer·sey** (jur′zē) *n.* a soft, knitted cloth; also, a blouse, shirt, etc. made of this. *—pl.* **jer′seys**

**Jersey City** a city in New Jersey. It is across the Hudson River from New York City.

**Je·ru·sa·lem** (jə rōō′sə ləm) the capital of Israel.

**jest** (jest) *n.* **1** a joke or joking remark. **2** the act of joking or having fun [I spoke only in *jest,* but I hurt his feelings.] **3** something to be made fun of or laughed at. ◆*v.* **1** to say something funny; joke. **2** to make fun; mock or jeer.

> **Jest** comes from an old French word that meant "a story about daring deeds." From that it came to mean a daring deed, and at last, as it does now, a joke.

**jest·er** (jes′tər) *n.* a person who jests; especially, a clown hired by a ruler in the Middle Ages to do tricks and tell jokes.

**Jes·u·it** (jezh′oo wit, jez′yoo wit) *n.* a member of the Society of Jesus, a Roman Catholic religious group begun in 1534. **—Jes′u·it′ic** or **Jes′u·it′i·cal** *adj.*

**Je·sus** (jē′zəs *or* jē′zəz) the founder of the Christian religion: *also called* **Jesus Christ.**

**jet¹** (jet) *n.* **1** a stream of liquid or gas forced from a nozzle or spout. **2** a nozzle or spout for shooting out a jet. **3** a jet-propelled airplane: *its full name is* **jet plane** *or* **jet airplane.** ◆*v.* **1** to spout or shoot out in a stream. **2** to travel or carry by jet plane. **—jet′ted, jet′ting** ◆*adj.* **1** jet-propelled. **2** having to do with jet-propelled aircraft [a *jet* flight; the *jet* age].

**jet²** (jet) *n.* **1** a hard, black mineral that is polished and used in jewelry. **2** a bright, shiny black. ◆*adj.* of or like jet.

**jet-black** (jet′blak′) *adj.* bright, shiny black.

**jet lag** a condition of being tired and upset because one's usual time for meals and sleep has been changed around during a long flight by jet aircraft.

**jet-pro·pelled** (jet′prə peld′) *adj.* driven by jet propulsion.

**jet propulsion** a method of driving an airplane, boat, rocket, etc. forward by forcing a jet of hot gases under pressure through a rear opening.

**jet·sam** (jet′səm) *n.* **1** part of a cargo that is thrown overboard to lighten a ship in danger. *See also* **flotsam. 2** such cargo that is washed ashore.

**jet·ti·son** (jet′ə s′n) *v.* **1** to throw goods overboard to lighten a ship or aircraft in danger. **2** to throw away; get rid of.

**jet·ty** (jet′ē) *n.* **1** a kind of wall built out into the water to protect a harbor, pier, etc. from the force of currents or waves. **2** a landing pier. *—pl.* **jet′ties**

**Jew** (jōō) *n.* **1** a person whose ancestors were the ancient Hebrews. **2** a person whose religion is Judaism.

**jew·el** (jōō′əl) *n.* **1** a precious stone, as a diamond or ruby; gem. **2** a valuable ring, pin, necklace, etc., often set with such stones or gems. **3** a person or thing that is very precious or valuable. ◆*v.* to decorate with jewels [a *jeweled* dagger]. **—jew′eled** or **jew′elled, jew′el·ing** or **jew′el·ling**

**jew·el·er** or **jew·el·ler** (jōō′əl ər) *n.* a person who makes, sells, or repairs jewelry, watches, etc.

**jew·el·ry** (jōō′əl rē) *n.* jewels or ornaments made with jewels.

**Jew·ish** (jōō′ish) *adj.* of or having to do with Jews.

**Jew·ry** (jōō′rē) *n.* the Jewish people; Jews as a group [American *Jewry*].

**Jez·e·bel** (jez′ə bel) **1** a very wicked woman in the Bible, who married a king of Israel. **2** any wicked woman who shows no shame.

**jib** (jib) *n.* a sail shaped like a triangle, set ahead of the foremast. *See the picture.*

**jibe¹** (jīb) *v.* **1** to shift suddenly to the other side of the boat: said of a fore-and-aft sail or its boom. **2** to change the course of a boat so that the sails shift thus. **3** to agree; fit together: *used only in everyday talk* [Their stories don't *jibe.*] **—jibed, jib′ing**

**jibe²** (jīb) *v., n. another spelling of* **gibe.**

**jif·fy** (jif′ē) *n.* a very short time: *used only in everyday talk* [I'll do it in a *jiffy.*] *—pl.* **jif′fies**

**jig** (jig) *n.* **1** a fast, lively dance. **2** the music for this. **3** a weighted fishhook with a part that is jiggled up and down. **4** a device used to guide a tool. ◆*v.* to dance a jig. **—jigged, jig′ging**

**jig·gle** (jig′'l) *v.* to move quickly up and down or back and forth. **—jig′gled, jig′gling** ◆*n.* a jiggling movement.

☆**jig·saw** (jig′sô) *n.* a saw with a narrow blade set in a frame. The blade moves up and down and is used for cutting along curved or irregular lines: *also* **jig saw.** *See the picture on page 399.*

☆**jigsaw puzzle** a puzzle made by cutting up a picture into pieces of uneven shapes, which must be put together to form the picture again.

**jilt** (jilt) *v.* to turn away a lover or sweetheart that one no longer wants.

**jim·my** (jim′ē) *n.* a short metal bar used by burglars to pry open windows, doors, etc. *—pl.* **jim′mies** ◆☆*v.* to pry open with a jimmy or a tool like a jimmy. **—jim′mied, jim′my·ing**

**jin·gle** (jiŋ′g'l) *v.* **1** to make ringing, tinkling sounds, as bits of metal striking together [The pennies *jingled* in my pocket.] **2** to make jingle [She *jingled* her keys.] **3** to have simple rhymes and a regular rhythm, as some poetry and music. **—jin′gled, jin′gling** ◆*n.* **1** a ringing, tinkling sound. **2** a verse that jingles [advertising *jingles* on the radio].

**jin·ni** (ji nē′ *or* jin′ē) *n.* an imaginary being in Muslim legend that can take human or animal form and can either help or harm people. *See the picture on page 399. —pl.* **jinn** (jin)

**jin·rik·i·sha** (jin rik′shô) *n.* a small carriage with two wheels, pulled by one or two men. It was once much used in Oriental countries: *also* **jin·rick′sha.**

☆**jinx** (jiŋks) *v.* to cause bad luck to. ◆*n.* something that brings bad luck. *This word is used only in everyday talk.*



| | | | | | | |
|---|---|---|---|---|---|---|
| **a** fat | **ir** here | **ou** out | **zh** leisure | | | |
| **ā** ape | **ī** bite, fire | **u** up | **ŋ** ring | | | |
| **ä** car, lot | **ō** go | **ur** fur | | a *in* ago | | |
| **e** ten | **ô** law, horn | **ch** chin | | e *in* agent | | |
| **er** care | **oi** oil | **sh** she | **ə** = | i *in* unity | | |
| **ē** even | **oo** look | **th** thin | | o *in* collect | | |
| **i** hit | **ōō** tool | ***th*** then | | u *in* focus | | |

**j**

☆**jit·ter·y** (jit′ər ē) ***adj.*** nervous or restless. —**the jitters,** a nervous feeling. *This word and phrase are used only in everyday talk.*

**jiu·jit·su** (jo͞o jit′so͞o) ***n.*** *another spelling of* **jujitsu.**

**Joan of Arc** (jōn əv ärk), Saint 1412–1431; French heroine who led the French army to victory over the English. She was burned as a witch.

**Job** (jōb) **1** a man in the Bible who kept his faith in God in spite of his many troubles. **2** a book of the Bible telling his story.

**job** (jäb) ***n.*** **1** a piece of work done for pay [We let Brown have the *job* of painting the house.] **2** anything one has to do; task or duty [This week it is my *job* to do the dishes.] ☆**3** a place or kind of work; employment [to look for a new *job*]. ◆***adj.*** done by the job or piece [*job* printing].

**job·ber** (jäb′ər) ***n.*** a person who buys goods wholesale and sells to dealers.

**job·less** (jäb′lis) ***adj.*** **1** without a job; unemployed. **2** having to do with the unemployed. —**the jobless,** those who are unemployed.

**jock** (jäk) ***n.*** an athlete: *a slang word.*

**jock·ey** (jäk′ē) ***n.*** a person whose work is riding horses in races. *See the picture.* —*pl.* **jock′eys** ◆***v.*** **1** to trick into or cheat out of something. **2** to manage things in a skillful way so as to get some advantage [to *jockey* for position in a race]. —**jock′eyed, jock′ey·ing**

**jo·cose** (jō kōs′) ***adj.*** joking or playful [a *jocose* uncle]. —**jo·cose′ly *adv.***

**joc·u·lar** (jäk′yə lər) ***adj.*** full of fun; joking [a *jocular* suggestion]. —**joc·u·lar·i·ty** (jäk′yə lar′ə tē) ***n.*** —**joc′u·lar·ly *adv.***

**joc·und** (jäk′ənd *or* jō′kənd) ***adj.*** merry; jolly.

**jodh·purs** (jäd′pərz) ***n.pl.*** trousers for horseback riding made loose and full above the knees and tight from the knees to the ankles. *See the picture.*

**jog**[1] (jäg) ***v.*** **1** to give a little shake to; jostle or nudge [*Jog* him to see if he's awake.] **2** to shake up or rouse, as the memory or the mind. **3** to move along slowly or steadily, but with a jolting motion. —**jogged, jog′ging** ◆***n.*** **1** a little shake or nudge. **2** a jogging pace; trot. —**jog′ger *n.***

**jog**[2] (jäg) ***n.*** a part, as in a wall or road, that changes direction sharply.

**jog·gle** (jäg′'l) ***v.*** to jolt slightly. —**jog′gled, jog′gling** ◆***n.*** a slight jolt.

**Jo·han·nes·burg** (jō han′is burg *or* yō hän′is burg) a city in South Africa.

**John** (jän) **1** one of the twelve Apostles of Jesus. **2** the fourth book of the New Testament. John is believed to have written this book. **3** a king of England who reigned from 1199 to 1216. He was forced by his barons to sign the Magna Charta in 1215.

**John Bull** (jän bo͝ol) *a name that stands for* England *or* an Englishman.

**John Doe** (jän dō) a name used in legal papers for any person, especially a man, whose name is not known.

☆**john·ny·cake** (jän′ē kāk) ***n.*** a kind of corn bread, originally baked on a griddle.

**John·son** (jän′s'n), **Andrew** 1808–1875; the 17th president of the United States, from 1865 to 1869.

**Johnson, Lyn·don B.** (lin′dən) 1908–1973; the 36th president of the United States, from 1963 to 1969.

**Johnson, Samuel** 1709–1784; English writer and dictionary maker.

**John the Baptist** in the Bible, the cousin and baptizer of Jesus.

**join** (join) ***v.*** **1** to bring together; connect; fasten [We *joined* hands and stood in a circle.] **2** to come together; meet [Where do the Ohio and Mississippi rivers *join?*] **3** to become a part or member of [Paula has *joined* our club.] **4** to go along with; accompany [Will you *join* us in a walk?] **5** to take part along with others [Everyone *joined* in the singing.] —**join battle,** to start fighting.

SYNONYMS: To **join** means to bring or come together, often in close contact or connection [to *join* forces; *join* in marriage]. To **unite** is to join things to form a single whole [the *United* States]. To **connect** means to link by some physical means or in thought or meaning [to *connect* the roads by a bridge; to *connect* germs with disease].

**join·er** (join′ər) ***n.*** **1** a person or thing that joins. **2** a carpenter, especially one who finishes inside woodwork, as doors, molding, etc.

**joint** (joint) ***n.*** **1** a place where two things or parts are joined [Water leaked from the *joint* in the pipe.] **2** a place or part where two bones are joined, usually so that they can move [the elbow *joint*]. **3** a large cut of meat with the bone still in it. ☆**4** a cheap restaurant or drinking place; also, any house, building, etc.: *slang in these meanings.* ◆***v.*** **1** to connect by a joint or joints [Bamboo is *jointed.*] **2** to cut at the joints [The butcher *jointed* the chicken.] ◆***adj.*** **1** done or owned by two or more [a *joint* appeal by several charities for money; the *joint* property of wife and husband]. **2** sharing with someone else [a *joint* owner]. —**out of joint, 1** not in place at the joint; dislocated. **2** out of order. —**joint′ly *adv.***

**joist** (joist) ***n.*** any of the parallel pieces that hold up the boards of a floor or the laths of a ceiling. *See the picture.*

**joke** (jōk) ***n.*** **1** anything said or done to get a laugh, as a funny story. **2** a person or thing to be laughed at. ◆***v.*** **1** to tell or play jokes. **2** to say or do something as a joke; jest. —**joked, jok′ing** —**no joke,** a serious matter. —**jok′ing·ly *adv.***

**jok·er** (jō′kər) ***n.*** **1** a person who jokes. ☆**2** an extra card in a deck of playing cards, used in some games. ☆**3** a tricky section put into a law, contract, etc. to make it different from what it seems to be.

**jol·li·ty** (jäl′ə tē) ***n.*** fun or merriment.

**jol·ly** (jäl′ē) ***adj.*** **1** full of fun; merry; jovial [a *jolly* old man]. **2** pleasant or enjoyable: *used only in everyday talk* [a *jolly* party]. —**jol′li·er, jol′li·est** ◆***adv.*** very: *used mainly in British everyday talk.* —**jol′li·ness *n.***

**Jol·ly Rog·er** (jäl′ē räj′ər) a black flag of pirates, with white skull and crossbones on it.

**jolt** (jōlt) ***v.*** **1** to shake up; jar [We were *jolted* along over the bumpy road.] **2** to move along in a bumpy, jerky manner [The cart *jolted* over the cobblestones.] ◆***n.*** **1** a sudden bump or jerk. **2** a shock or surprise [The news gave us a *jolt.*]

**Jo·nah** (jō′nə) **1** a Hebrew prophet. **2** a book of the Bible telling of this prophet. He was swallowed by a big fish but later was cast up on shore unharmed. **3** any person said to bring bad luck by being present.

**Jon·a·than** (jän′ə thən) a son of Saul in the Bible, and a close friend of David.

**Jones** (jōnz), **John Paul** 1747–1792; American naval officer in the Revolutionary War.

**jon·quil** (jäng′kwil) ***n.*** a narcissus with a yellow or white flower and long, slender leaves.

**Jor·dan** (jôr′dən) **1** a country in the Near East, east of Israel. **2** a river in the Near East that flows into the Dead Sea. —**Jor·dan·i·an** (jôr dā′nē ən) ***adj., n.***

**Jo·seph** (jō′zəf) **1** one of Jacob's sons in the Bible. He was sold into slavery in Egypt but became a high official there. **2** the husband of Mary, the mother of Jesus.

☆**josh** (jäsh) ***v.*** to make fun of or tease in a joking way; banter: *used only in everyday talk.*

**Josh·u·a** (jäsh′oo wə) **1** in the Bible, the man who led the Israelites into the Promised Land after Moses died. **2** a book of the Bible telling about him.

**jos·tle** (jäs′′l) ***v.*** to shove or push in a rough way. —**jos′tled, jos′tling** ◆***n.*** a rough push or shove.

**jot** (jät) ***n.*** the smallest bit [There's not a *jot* of truth in it.] ◆***v.*** to make a brief note of [She *jotted* down the address.] —**jot′ted, jot′ting**

**jounce** (jouns) ***n., v.*** jolt or bounce. —**jounced, jounc′ing**

**jour·nal** (jur′nəl) ***n.*** **1** a daily record of what happens, such as a diary [She kept a *journal* of her trip.] **2** a written record of what happens at the meetings of a legislature, club, etc. **3** a newspaper or magazine. **4** a book in which business accounts are kept. **5** the part of an axle or shaft that turns in a bearing.

> **Journal** comes from the Latin word for "daily." It was first used in English for a book of prayers and worship used in the daytime. **Journey** comes from the same Latin word. An early meaning of *journey* was "the distance that one could travel in one day."

**jour·nal·ism** (jur′nəl iz′m) ***n.*** the work of gathering, writing, or editing the news for publication in newspapers or magazines or for broadcasting on radio or television.

**jour·nal·ist** (jur′n′l ist) ***n.*** a person whose work is journalism, as a reporter, news editor, etc. —**jour′nal·is′tic** ***adj.***

**jour·ney** (jur′nē) ***n.*** a traveling from one place to another; trip. *See* SYNONYMS *at* **trip.** —*pl.* **jour′neys** ◆***v.*** to go on a trip; travel. —**jour′neyed, jour′ney·ing**

**jour·ney·man** (jur′nē mən) ***n.*** a worker who is skilled in a particular trade. —*pl.* **jour′ney·men**

**joust** (joust *or* just) ***n.*** a fight between two knights on horseback using lances. ◆***v.*** to take part in a joust, as for sport.

**Jove** (jōv) *another name for* **Jupiter,** the Roman god.

**jo·vi·al** (jō′vē əl) ***adj.*** friendly and cheerful; playful and jolly. —**jo·vi·al·i·ty** (jō′vē al′ə tē) ***n.*** —**jo′vi·al·ly** ***adv.***

**jowl** (joul) ***n.*** **1** a jaw, especially the lower jaw with the chin. **2** the cheek. **3** *often* **jowls,** *pl.* fleshy parts hanging under the lower jaw. *See the picture.*

**joy** (joi) ***n.*** **1** a very happy feeling; great pleasure; delight [The new baby brought us *joy.*] **2** anything that causes this feeling [This book is a *joy* to read.]

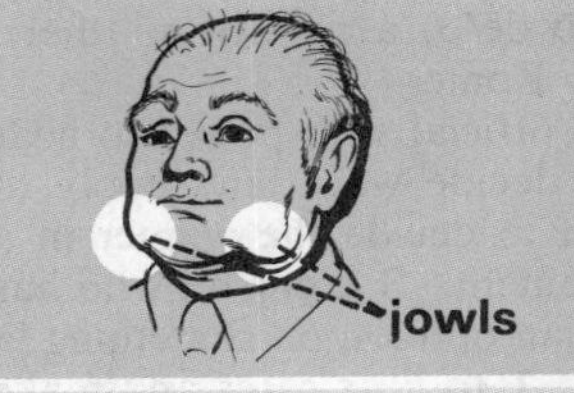
jowls

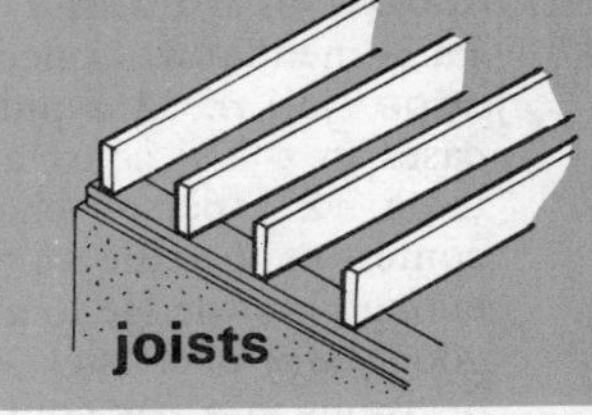
joists

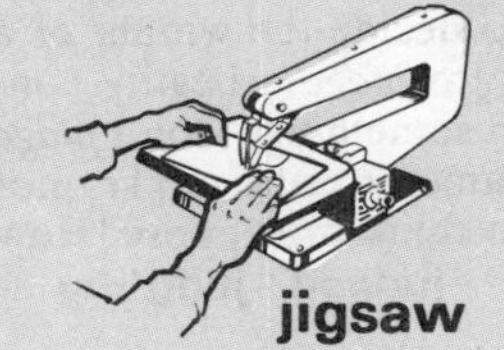
jigsaw

jockey

jodhpurs

jinni

**joy·ful** (joi′fəl) ***adj.*** feeling, showing, or causing joy; glad; happy. —**joy′ful·ly** ***adv.***

**joy·less** (joi′lis) ***adj.*** without joy; unhappy; sad.

**joy·ous** (joi′əs) ***adj.*** full of joy; happy. —**joy′ous·ly** ***adv.***

**J.P.** *abbreviation for* **justice of the peace.**

**Jpn.** *abbreviation for* **Japan** *or* **Japanese.**

**Jr.** *abbreviation for* **Junior.**

**Juá·rez** (hwä′res), **Be·ni·to Pa·blo** (be nē′tō pä′blō) 1806–1872; Mexican statesman and the president of Mexico from 1858 to 1872.

**ju·bi·lant** (jōō′b′l ənt) ***adj.*** joyful and proud; rejoicing [*Jubilant* crowds celebrated the victory.] —**ju′bi·lant·ly** ***adv.***

**ju·bi·la·tion** (jōō′bə lā′shən) ***n.*** the act of rejoicing, as in celebrating a victory.

**ju·bi·lee** (jōō′bə lē) ***n.*** **1** a celebration of an anniversary, especially of a 50th or 25th anniversary. **2** a time or condition of great joy.

**Ju·dah** (jōō′də) **1** in the Bible, one of Jacob's sons, or the tribe descended from him. **2** an ancient kingdom in Palestine formed by the tribes of Judah and Benjamin.

**Ju·da·ism** (jōō′də iz′m) ***n.*** the religion of the Jewish people, which is based on a belief in one God and on the teachings of the Holy Scriptures.

**Ju·das Is·car·i·ot** (jōō′dəs is ker′ē ət) **1** the disciple who betrayed Jesus for money. **2** anyone who betrays another person; informer.



| | | | | | | | |
|---|---|---|---|---|---|---|---|
| **a** | fat | **ir** | here | **ou** | out | **zh** | leisure |
| **ā** | ape | **ī** | bite, fire | **u** | up | **ng** | ring |
| **ä** | car, lot | **ō** | go | **ur** | fur | | a *in* ago |
| **e** | ten | **ô** | law, horn | **ch** | chin | | e *in* agent |
| **er** | care | **oi** | oil | **sh** | she | **ə =** | i *in* unity |
| **ē** | even | **oo** | look | **th** | thin | | o *in* collect |
| **i** | hit | **ōō** | tool | ***th*** | then | | u *in* focus |

**Ju·de·a** or **Ju·dae·a** (jo͞o dē′ə) a part of southern Palestine that was ruled by Rome.

**judge** (juj) ***n.*** **1** a public official with power to hear cases in a law court and decide what laws apply to them. **2** a person chosen to decide the winner in a contest or to settle an argument. **3** a person who has enough knowledge to give an opinion on something [a good *judge* of music]. ◆***v.*** **1** to hear cases and make decisions in a law court. **2** to decide the winner of a contest or settle an argument [to *judge* a beauty contest]. **3** to form an opinion on something [Don't *judge* by first impressions.] **4** to blame or criticize [Try not to *judge* me too harshly.] **5** to think or suppose [How tall do you *judge* her to be?] —**judged, judg′ing** —**judge′ship′** ***n.***

**Judg·es** (juj′iz) a book of the Bible telling the history of the Jews from the death of Joshua to the birth of Samuel.

**judg·ment** (juj′mənt) ***n.*** **1** a judging or deciding. **2** a decision given by a judge or a law court [The *judgment* was for the defendant.] **3** an opinion; the way one thinks or feels about something [In my *judgment*, she will win the election.] **4** criticism or blame [to pass *judgment* on another]. **5** a being able to decide what is right, good, practical, etc.; good sense [a person of clear *judgment*]. *Sometimes spelled* **judgement.**

**Judgment Day** in certain religions, the day on which God gives his final rewards and punishments to all people; doomsday.



**ju·di·cial** (jo͞o dish′əl) ***adj.*** **1** of judges, law courts, or their duties [*judicial* robes; *judicial* duties]. **2** ordered or allowed by a court [a *judicial* decree]. **3** careful in forming opinions or making decisions; fair [a *judicial* mind]. —**ju·di′cial·ly** ***adv.***

**ju·di·ci·ar·y** (jo͞o dish′ē er′ē) ***adj.*** of judges, law courts, or their duties. ◆***n.*** **1** the part of government whose work is seeing that justice is carried out according to law; system of law courts. **2** judges as a group. —*pl.* **ju·di′ci·ar′ies**

**ju·di·cious** (jo͞o dish′əs) ***adj.*** having or showing good judgment; wise. —**ju·di′cious·ly** ***adv.***

**ju·do** (jo͞o′dō) ***n.*** a sport and a method of self-defense without the use of weapons. It is based on jujitsu. *See the picture.*

**jug** (jug) ***n.*** **1** a container for liquids, with a small opening and a handle. **2** the amount that a jug holds.

**jug·gle** (jug′′l) ***v.*** **1** to do skillful tricks with the hands; especially, to keep tossing a number of things up in the air one by one and keep them all moving. *See the picture.* **2** to handle in a tricky way so as to cheat or fool others [The cashier *juggled* the figures so as to show a profit.] —**jug′gled, jug′gling** —**jug′gler** ***n.***

**Ju·go·sla·vi·a** (yo͞o′gō slä′vē ə) *another spelling of* **Yugoslavia.** —**Ju′go·slav** ***adj., n.***

**jug·u·lar** (jug′yoo lər) ***adj.*** of the neck or throat. The **jugular veins** are the two large veins in the neck carrying blood from the head back to the heart.

**juice** (jo͞os) ***n.*** **1** the liquid part of a plant or animal [orange *juice;* gastric *juice;* meat *juice*]. ☆**2** electricity: *slang in this meaning.* ◆***v.*** ☆to squeeze juice from [to *juice* lemons]. —**juiced, juic′ing**

**juic·y** (jo͞o′sē) ***adj.*** **1** full of juice [a *juicy* plum]. **2** full of interest: *used only in everyday talk* [a *juicy* story]. —**juic′i·er, juic′i·est**

**ju·jit·su** (jo͞o jit′so͞o) ***n.*** a kind of Japanese wrestling in which the opponent's strength and weight are used against the opponent.

☆**juke·box** (jo͞ok′bäks) ***n.*** an electric phonograph worked by dropping a coin in a slot: *also written* **juke box.**

**ju·lep** (jo͞o′ləp) ***n.*** ☆*a shorter name for* **mint julep.**

**ju·li·enne** (jo͞o′lē en′) ***adj.*** cut into strips: said of vegetables, etc., as used in salad or soup.

**Ju·li·et** (jo͞ol′yət *or* jo͞o′lē et′) the heroine of Shakespeare's tragedy *Romeo and Juliet.*

**Ju·ly** (jo͞o lī′) ***n.*** the seventh month of the year, which has 31 days: abbreviated **Jul., Jl.**

The month of **July** was named after Julius Caesar by the Roman Senate in 44 B.C., the year in which he died. Julius Caesar was born in this month.

**jum·ble** (jum′b′l) ***v.*** to mix up or put into disorder [The papers were *jumbled* together on the desk.] —**jum′bled, jum′bling** ◆***n.*** a confused heap or a muddle.

☆**jum·bo** (jum′bō) ***n.*** a large thing or animal. —*pl.* **jum′bos** ◆***adj.*** larger than usual [a *jumbo* soda].

**Jumbo** came into American English when it was used as the name for an enormous circus elephant. It came from an African word that means "elephant."

**jump** (jump) ***v.*** **1** to move oneself suddenly from the ground, floor, etc. by using the leg muscles; spring or leap [to *jump* up to catch a ball; to *jump* from a plane; to *jump* on a bus]. **2** to leap over [The child *jumped* the creek.] **3** to make leap or spring [She *jumped* her horse over the fence.] **4** to jerk or bounce; bob [The line *jumped* as the fish took the bait.] **5** to move suddenly, as in surprise [He *jumped* as the door slammed.] **6** to rise or make rise suddenly [The price of milk *jumped* two cents last week.] **7** to change suddenly in thinking, talking, etc. [to *jump* to conclusions; to *jump* to a new subject]. **8** to attack suddenly: *used only in everyday talk.* ◆***n.*** **1** a leap; bound. **2** a distance jumped [a *jump* of ten feet]. **3** a descent from an aircraft by parachute. **4** a sudden rise, as in prices. **5** a sudden, nervous start. **6** a contest in jumping [the high *jump*]. —☆**get the jump on,** to get an advantage over: *a slang phrase.* —☆**jump a claim,** to seize land claimed by someone else. —**jump at,** to take eagerly [He *jumped at* the chance to go.] —**jump on** or **jump all over,** to scold; criticize severely: *a slang phrase.* —**on the jump,** busily moving about: *used only in everyday talk.*

**jump·er**[1] (jum′pər) ***n.*** **1** a person, animal, or thing that jumps. **2** a wire used to make an electrical connection for a short time.

**jump·er**[2] (jum′pər) ***n.*** **1** a dress without sleeves, worn over a blouse or sweater. *See the picture.* **2** a smock, sailor's blouse, child's rompers, etc.

☆**jump suit** **1** a coverall worn by paratroops, garage mechanics, etc. **2** a one-piece suit like this that opens down the front and is worn for lounging.

**jump·y** (jum′pē) ***adj.*** **1** moving in jumps or jerks. **2** nervous; easily startled [Ghost stories make me *jumpy.*] —**jump′i·er, jump′i·est** —**jump′i·ness *n.***

**jun·co** (juŋ′kō) ***n.*** ☆a small American bird with a white breast; snowbird. —*pl.* **jun′cos**

**junc·tion** (juŋk′shən) ***n.*** **1** a place of joining or crossing, as of highways or railroads. **2** a joining or being joined.

**junc·ture** (juŋk′chər) ***n.*** **1** a point or line where things join or connect; joint. **2** a point of time or a state of affairs [At this *juncture,* we changed our plans.] **3** a joining or being joined.

**June** (jo͞on) ***n.*** the sixth month of the year, which has 30 days: abbreviated **Je., Ju.**

**Ju·neau** (jo͞o′nō) the capital of Alaska.

**June bug** ☆any of various large beetles found in the United States.

**jun·gle** (juŋ′g'l) ***n.*** land thickly covered with trees, vines, etc., as in the tropics. Jungles are usually filled with animals that prey on one another.

**jun·ior** (jo͞on′yər) ***adj.*** **1** the younger: a word written after the name of a son who has exactly the same name as his father: abbreviated **Jr.** **2** lower in position or rank [a *junior* executive]. ☆**3** of juniors in a high school or college [the *junior* class]. ◆***n.*** **1** a person who is younger or has a lower rank than another [Her sister is her *junior* by three years.] ☆**2** a student in the next to last year of a high school or college.

☆**junior college** a school offering courses two years beyond the high school level.

☆**junior high school** a school between elementary school and high school. It usually has the 7th, 8th, and 9th grades.

**ju·ni·per** (jo͞o′nə pər) ***n.*** a small evergreen shrub or tree with cones that look like berries.

**junk**[1] (juŋk) ***n.*** **1** old metal, glass, paper, rags, etc. **2** things of little value; rubbish: *used only in everyday talk.* ◆***v.*** ☆to get rid of as worthless: *used only in everyday talk* [I *junked* my old car.]

**junk**[2] (juŋk) ***n.*** a Chinese sailing ship with a flat bottom. *See the picture.*

**jun·ket** (juŋ′kit) ***n.*** **1** milk that has been sweetened, flavored, and thickened into curd. ☆**2** a pleasure trip, especially one paid for out of public funds. **3** a picnic. ◆***v.*** to go on a junket, or pleasure trip.

**junk food** any food eaten as a snack, such as potato chips, candy bars, soda pop, etc., that is high in sugar and fat but low in other food values, as protein.

☆**junk mail** mail, such as advertisements, requests for money, etc., received by many people without their asking for it.

☆**junk·man** (juŋk′man′) ***n.*** a person who buys and sells old metal, glass, paper, rags, etc. —*pl.* **junk′men′**

**Ju·no** (jo͞o′nō) the Roman goddess of marriage and the wife of Jupiter.

**jun·ta** (hoon′tə) ***n.*** **1** a small group of politicians plotting to get more power. **2** a group of military people who put themselves in power after overthrowing a government.

**Ju·pi·ter** (jo͞o′pə tər) **1** the chief Roman god, ruling over all other gods. **2** the largest planet. It is the fifth in distance away from the sun.

**ju·ris·dic·tion** (joor′is dik′shən) ***n.*** **1** authority, as of a judge, court, or official [Juvenile court has *jurisdiction* over children.] **2** the limits or area of one's authority [The suburb is outside the *jurisdiction* of the city police.]

**ju·ris·pru·dence** (joor′is pro͞o′dəns) ***n.*** **1** the science that deals with the principles on which law is based. **2** a system of laws [criminal *jurisprudence*].

**ju·rist** (joor′ist) ***n.*** an expert in law; scholar in the field of law.

**ju·ror** (joor′ər) ***n.*** a member of a jury.

**ju·ry** (joor′ē) ***n.*** **1** a group of people chosen to listen to the evidence in a law trial, and then to reach a decision, or verdict: *see also* **grand jury.** **2** a group of people chosen to decide the winners in a contest. —*pl.* **ju′ries**



**ju·ry·man** (joor′ē mən) ***n.*** *another name for* **juror.** —*pl.* **ju′ry·men**

**just** (just) ***adj.*** **1** that is right or fair [a *just* decision; *just* praise]. **2** doing what is right or honest; righteous [a *just* person]. **3** based on good reasons [*just* suspicions]. **4** true or correct; exact [a *just* measurement]. ◆***adv.*** **1** neither more nor less than; exactly [*just* two o'clock]. **2** almost at the point of; nearly [I was *just* leaving.] **3** no more than; only [The coach is *just* teasing you.] **4** by a very small amount; barely [She *just* missed the bus.] **5** a very short time ago [The plane *just* took off.] **6** quite; really: *used only in everyday talk* [She looks *just* fine.] —**just now,** a very short time ago. —☆**just the same,** nevertheless: *used only in everyday talk.* —**just′ness *n.***

> SYNONYMS: To be **just** is to follow what is right without showing favor to anyone [It is *just* to protect the innocent and punish wrongdoers.] To be **fair** is to be reasonable and honest in treating all equally [It is *fair* for Linda to get the same allowance as her brother.]

**jus·tice** (jus′tis) ***n.*** **1** the condition of being just or fair [There is *justice* in their demand.] **2** reward or punishment as deserved [The prisoner asked only for *justice.*] **3** the upholding of what is just or lawful [a

| | | | | | | | |
|---|---|---|---|---|---|---|---|
| **a** | fat | **ir** | here | **ou** | out | **zh** | leisure |
| **ā** | ape | **ī** | bite, fire | **u** | up | **ŋ** | ring |
| **ä** | car, lot | **ō** | go | **ur** | fur | | a *in* ago |
| **e** | ten | **ô** | law, horn | **ch** | chin | | e *in* agent |
| **er** | care | **oi** | oil | **sh** | she | **ə =** | i *in* unity |
| **ē** | even | **oo** | look | **th** | thin | | o *in* collect |
| **i** | hit | **o͞o** | tool | ***th*** | then | | u *in* focus |

court of *justice*]. **4** a judge [a *justice* of the Supreme Court]. —**bring to justice,** to bring a person who has done wrong into a law court to be tried. —**do justice to,** **1** to treat in a fair or proper way. **2** to enjoy fully [to *do justice to* a meal].

**justice of the peace** a public official with power to decide law cases for offenses less serious than crimes, to send persons to trial in a higher court, to perform marriages, etc.

**jus·ti·fi·a·ble** (jus′tə fī′ə b'l) ***adj.*** that can be shown to be just, right, or free from blame. —**jus′ti·fi′a·bly** ***adv.***

**jus·ti·fi·ca·tion** (jus′tə fi kā′shən) ***n.*** **1** a fact that frees one from blame or guilt [There is no *justification* for such a mistake.] **2** a justifying or being justified.

**jus·ti·fy** (jus′tə fī) ***v.*** **1** to show to be right or fair [Her higher pay is *justified* by her special skills.] **2** to free from blame or guilt [He was *justified* before the court.] **3** to give good reasons for [Can you *justify* that decision?] —**jus′ti·fied, jus′ti·fy·ing**

**just·ly** (just′lē) ***adv.*** **1** in a just way; fairly. **2** in a way that is deserved; rightly [*justly* rewarded].

**jut** (jut) ***v.*** to stick out; project [a *jutting* cliff]. —**jut′-ted, jut′ting**

**jute** (jo͞ot) ***n.*** a strong fiber got from a plant of India. It is used for making burlap, rope, etc.

**ju·ven·ile** (jo͞o′və n'l *or* jo͞o′və nīl) ***adj.*** **1** young or youthful. **2** of, like, or for children or young people [*juvenile* ideas; *juvenile* books]. ◆***n.*** **1** a child or young person. ☆**2** a book for children.

**juvenile delinquent** a young person under a certain age, usually 18, who is guilty of doing things that are against the law, such as stealing or street fighting.

**jux·ta·pose** (juk stə pōz′) ***v.*** to put side by side or close together. —**jux·ta·posed′, jux·ta·pos′ing** —**jux′ta·po·si′tion** ***n.***

402

**K, k** (kā) ***n.*** the eleventh letter of the English alphabet. —*pl.* **K's, k's** (kāz)

**K** *the symbol for the chemical element* potassium.

**K.** or **k.** *abbreviation for* **karat** (carat), **kilo.**

**Kai·ser** (kī′zər) ***n.*** an emperor, especially of Germany or Austria before 1918.

**kale** (kāl) ***n.*** a kind of cabbage with loose, curled leaves instead of a head.

**ka·lei·do·scope** (kə lī′də skōp) ***n.*** **1** a small tube with mirrors and loose bits of colored glass or plastic in it. When the tube is held to the eye and turned, the bits form one pattern after another. **2** anything that is always changing. —**ka·lei·do·scop·ic** (kə lī′də skäp′ik) ***adj.***

**Kam·pu·che·a** (kam′po͝o chē′ə) *the name of* **Cambodia** *since 1976.*

**kan·ga·roo** (kang gə ro͞o′) ***n.*** an animal of Australia with short forelegs and strong, large hind legs, with which it makes long leaps. The female carries her young in a pouch in front. *See the picture.* —*pl.* **kan-ga·roos′**

**Kan·sas** (kan′zəs) a State in the central part of the U.S.: abbreviated **Kans., KS** —**Kan′san** ***adj., n.***

**Kansas City** **1** a city in western Missouri. **2** a city next to it in eastern Kansas.

**ka·o·lin** (kā′ə lin) ***n.*** a fine white clay used in making porcelain.

**ka·pok** (kā′päk) ***n.*** the silky fibers around the seeds of a tropical tree. The fibers are used for stuffing mattresses, sleeping bags, etc.

**Ka·ra·chi** (kə rä′chē) a seaport in southern Pakistan, on the Arabian Sea.

**kar·a·kul** (kar′ə kəl) ***n.*** **1** a kind of sheep of central Asia. **2** the black fur made from the fleece of its lambs, usually having loose, flat curls: *in this sense commonly spelled* **caracul.**

**kar·at** (kar′ət) ***n.*** one 24th part of pure gold [14 *karat* gold is 14 parts pure gold and 10 parts other metal.]

**ka·ra·te** (kə rät′ē) ***n.*** a Japanese form of self-defense, in which sharp, quick blows are given with the hands and feet. *See the picture.*

**Karate** means "open hand" in Japanese. The side of the hand, held open and stiff, is used to strike blows to the opponent.

**kart** (kärt) ***n.*** ☆a small, flat, 4-wheeled vehicle with a motor, seating one person and used for racing **(karting).**

**Kash·mir** (kash′mir) a region in northern India, between Afghanistan and Tibet. It is part of the state of Jammu and Kashmir: *see also* **Jammu and Kashmir.** *See the map.*

☆**ka·ty·did** (kāt′ē did′) ***n.*** a large, green insect that looks like a grasshopper. The male katydid makes a shrill sound with its wings.

**kay·ak** (kī′ak) ***n.*** an Eskimo canoe made of a wooden frame covered with skins all around, except for an opening for the paddler. *See the picture.*

☆**ka·zoo** (kə zo͞o′) ***n.*** a toy musical instrument that is a small, open tube with a hole on top covered by something like paper. It makes a buzzing tone when the player hums through the tube.

**kc** or **kc.** *abbreviation for* **kilocycle** *or* **kilocycles.**

**Keats** (kēts), **John** 1795–1821; English poet.

**ke·bab** (kə bäb′) ***n.*** a dish made up of small pieces of meat stuck on a skewer along with pieces of onion, tomato, etc., and broiled or roasted.

**keel** (kēl) ***n.*** **1** the center timber or steel plate that runs along the lowest part of the bottom of a ship. **2**

anything like this, as beams or girders along the bottom of an airship. —☆**keel over,** **1** to turn over; upset. **2** to fall over suddenly, as in a faint. —**on an even keel,** in an even, steady way; stable.

**keen** (kēn) ***adj.*** **1** having a sharp edge or point [a *keen* knife]. **2** sharp or cutting in force [a *keen* wind; a *keen* appetite]. **3** sharp and quick in seeing, hearing, thinking, etc.; acute [*keen* eyesight; a *keen* mind]. **4** eager or enthusiastic [Are they *keen* about going?] **5** strong or intense [*keen* competition]. **6** good, fine, excellent, etc.: *slang in this meaning.* —**keen'ly** ***adv.*** **keen'ness** ***n.***

**keep** (kēp) ***v.*** **1** to have or hold and not let go [He was *kept* after school. She *kept* her trim figure. Can you *keep* a secret?] **2** to hold for a later time; save [I *kept* the cake to eat later.] **3** to hold back; restrain [I can't *keep* him from talking.] **4** to take care of; look after [He *keeps* house for himself.] **5** to guard or protect [The lifeguard *kept* us from harm.] **6** to write down a regular record in [to *keep* a diary; to *keep* the books]. **7** to have in stock for sale [That drugstore *keeps* soft drinks.] **8** to have in one's service or for one's use [to *keep* an assistant]. **9** to stay or make stay as it is; last; continue [The fish will *keep* a whiie if you pack it in ice. *Keep* your engine running. *Keep* on walking.] **10** to carry out; fulfill; observe [to *keep* a promise; to *keep* the Sabbath]. —**kept, keep'ing** ◆***n.*** **1** food and shelter; support [The cat earned its *keep* by catching mice.] **2** a castle or stronghold of a castle. —☆**for keeps,** **1** with all the winnings kept by the winner. **2** forever. *This phrase is used only in everyday talk.* —**keep at,** to continue doing. —**keep to oneself,** **1** to avoid being with other people. **2** to hold back from telling. —**keep up,** **1** to maintain in good condition. **2** to continue; go on. **3** to not lag or fall behind. **4** to stay informed about something. —**keep up with,** to go or do as fast as; stay even with.

**keep·er** (kēp'ər) ***n.*** a person or thing that keeps, guards, or takes care of something.

**keep·ing** (kēp'iŋ) ***n.*** **1** care or protection [He left his money in her *keeping.*] **2** the observing of a rule, holiday, etc. —**in keeping with,** in agreement or harmony with.

**keep·sake** (kēp'sāk) ***n.*** an object kept in memory of some person or event; memento.

**keg** (keg) ***n.*** a small barrel.

**Kel·ler** (kel'ər), **Helen Adams** 1880–1968; U.S. writer and lecturer. She was blind and deaf from the time she was an infant, but she was taught to speak and read.

**kelp** (kelp) ***n.*** **1** a brown seaweed that is large and coarse. *See the picture.* **2** ashes of burned seaweed.

**ken** (ken) ***n.*** knowledge or understanding [Nuclear physics is beyond my *ken.*] ◆***v.*** to know: *used mainly in Scotland.* —**kenned, ken'ning**

**Ken·ne·dy** (ken'ə dē), **John F.** 1917–1963; the 35th president of the United States, from 1961 to 1963. He was assassinated.

**ken·nel** (ken''l) ***n.*** **1** a doghouse. **2** *often* **kennels,** *pl.* a place where dogs are raised or kept.

**Ken·tuck·y** (kən tuk'ē) a State in the eastern central part of the U.S.: abbreviated **Ky., KY**

**Ken·ya** (ken'yə *or* kēn'yə) a country in east central Africa, on the Indian Ocean.

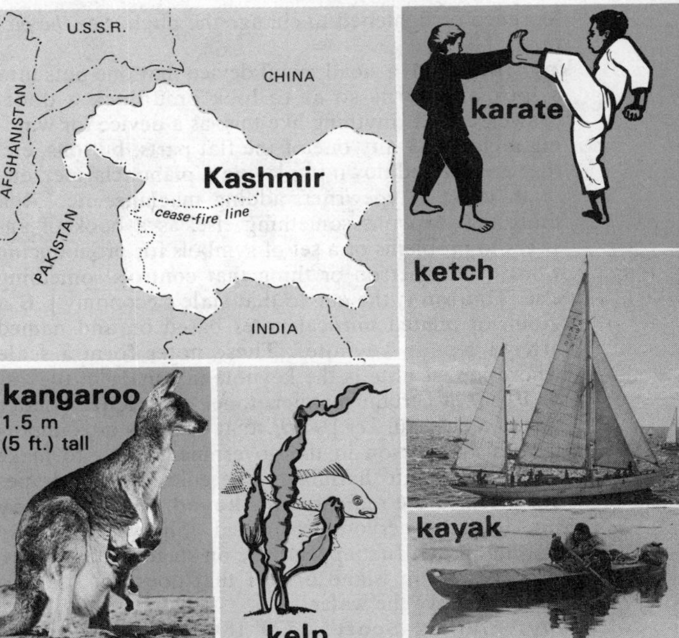


**kept** (kept) *past tense and past participle of* **keep.**

**ker·chief** (kur'chif) ***n.*** **1** a piece of cloth, usually square, worn over the head or around the neck. **2** a handkerchief. 

The *ker-* of **kerchief** is an earlier, different spelling of the word *cover. Chief* comes from the Latin word for "head." Thus the word **kerchief** means "cover the head."

**ker·nel** (kur'n'l) ***n.*** **1** a grain or seed, as of corn or wheat. **2** the soft, inner part of a nut or fruit pit. **3** the most important part; gist.

☆**ker·o·sene** (ker'ə sēn) ***n.*** a thin oil made from coal or petroleum and used in some lamps, stoves, etc.; coal oil.

**ker·o·sine** (ker'ə sēn) ***n.*** *another spelling of* **kerosene**: *used especially in science and industry.*

**ketch** (kech) ***n.*** a small sailing ship with two masts. *See the picture.*

**Ketch** was another form of the word *catch* in early days. The name was originally given to fishing boats because they went out to catch fish. Now it just means a certain kind of sailing ship.

**ketch·up** (kech'əp) ***n.*** a thick sauce made of tomatoes, onion, spices, etc. and used as a flavoring on foods: *its full name is* **tomato ketchup.**

**ket·tle** (ket''l) ***n.*** **1** a metal container for boiling or cooking things. **2** a teakettle.

**ket·tle·drum** (ket''l drum) ***n.*** a drum that is half a hollow, metal globe with a parchment top that can be

| | | | | | | | |
|---|---|---|---|---|---|---|---|
| **a** | fat | **ir** | here | **ou** | out | **zh** | leisure |
| **ā** | ape | **ī** | bite, fire | **u** | up | **ŋ** | ring |
| **ä** | car, lot | **ō** | go | **ur** | fur | | a *in* ago |
| **e** | ten | **ô** | law, horn | **ch** | chin | | e *in* agent |
| **er** | care | **oi** | oil | **sh** | she | **ə =** | i *in* unity |
| **ē** | even | **oo** | look | **th** | thin | | o *in* collect |
| **i** | hit | **ōō** | tool | ***th*** | then | | u *in* focus |

loosened or tightened to change the pitch. *See the picture.*

**key**[1] (kē) ***n.*** **1** a small metal device that one puts into a lock and turns so as to lock or unlock a door, drawer, etc. **2** anything like this, as a device for winding a clock. **3** any one of the flat parts, buttons, etc. that are pressed down in playing a piano, clarinet, etc. or in using a typewriter, adding machine, etc. **4** a thing that explains something else, as a book of answers to problems or a set of symbols for pronouncing words. **5** a person or thing that controls something else [Tourism is the *key* to that state's economy.] **6** a group of related musical notes based on and named after a certain keynote. These notes form a scale whose lowest note is the keynote [a sonata in the *key* of F]. **7** a certain manner, tone, or style [Her letter was in a cheerful *key*.] ◆***adj.*** that controls or is important [a *key* person in the government]. ◆***v.*** to make agree; bring into harmony [The colors in the drapes are *keyed* to the red carpet.] —**keyed, key'ing** —**key up,** to make nervous or excited. [She was *keyed up* waiting for her first appearance on stage.]

**key**[2] (kē) ***n.*** an island or reef that does not stick up very far above the water.

**Key, Francis Scott** 1779–1843; U.S. lawyer. He wrote the words for "The Star-Spangled Banner."

**key·board** (kē'bôrd) ***n.*** the row or rows of keys of a piano, organ, typewriter, etc.

 **key·hole** (kē'hōl) ***n.*** the opening in a lock in which a key is put to lock or unlock it.

**key·note** (kē'nōt) ***n.*** **1** the lowest, basic note of a musical scale, or key. **2** the main idea or principle of a speech, policy, etc.

**key punch** a machine, operated from a keyboard, that records data by punching holes in cards. The punched cards can then be fed into machines for sorting.

**key ring** a metal ring for holding keys.

**key·stone** (kē'stōn) ***n.*** **1** the central stone of an arch at its very top. It is thought of as holding the other stones in place. *See the picture.* **2** the main idea or most important part [Free speech is the *keystone* of our liberties.]

kimono

keystone

kettledrum

kilts

**kg** or **kg.** *abbreviation for* **kilogram** *or* **kilograms.**

**kha·ki** (kak'ē) ***n.*** **1** yellowish brown. **2** a strong, heavy cotton cloth of this color. **3** *often* **khakis,** *pl.* a uniform made of khaki.

> **Khaki** comes from the Hindi word for dust or dirt. The color of dirt or earth is often a yellowish brown.

**khan** (kän) ***n.*** **1** a title used by the Mongol rulers of Asia during the Middle Ages. **2** now, a title given to certain officials in Iran, Afghanistan, etc.

**Khar·kov** (kär'kôf) a city in the Ukraine, in the U.S.S.R.

**Khar·toum** (kär to͞om') the capital of Sudan, on the Nile.

**kHz** *abbreviation for* **kilohertz.**

**kib·ble** (kib''l) ***n.*** coarse particles or bits, as of prepared dog food.

**kib·butz** (ki bo͞ots' *or* ki bo͝ots') ***n.*** a collective farm in Israel. —*pl.* **kib·but·zim** (kē bo͞o tsēm')

☆**kib·itz** (kib'its) ***v.*** to act as a kibitzer: *used only in everyday talk.*

☆**kib·itz·er** (kib'its ər) ***n.*** a person who watches others do something and gives advice that is not wanted: *used only in everyday talk.*

**kick** (kik) ***v.*** **1** to strike out with the foot or feet, as in striking something or in dancing, swimming, etc. **2** to move by striking with the foot [to *kick* a football]. **3** to spring back suddenly, as a gun does when fired. **4** to complain or grumble: *used only in everyday talk.* ☆**5** to get rid of: *slang in this meaning* [to *kick* a habit]. ◆***n.*** **1** a blow with the foot. **2** a way of kicking. **3** a springing back suddenly, as a gun does when fired; recoil. ☆**4** a complaint or protest: *used only in everyday talk.* ☆**5** a thrill, or excited feeling: *used only in everyday talk.* —☆**kick in,** to pay, as one's share: *a slang phrase.* —**kick off, 1** to put a football into play with a place kick. ☆**2** to start, as a campaign. ☆**3** to die: *slang in this meaning.* —**kick out,** to get rid of or put out: *used only in everyday talk.* —**kick'er** ***n.***

☆**kick·back** (kik'bak) ***n.*** a giving back of part of money paid to one, often because one has been forced to; also, the money given back: *slang in these meanings.*

**kick·off** (kik'ôf) ***n.*** a kick in football that begins play, as at the beginning of each half.

☆**kick·stand** (kik'stand) ***n.*** a short metal bar fastened to a bicycle or motorcycle. When it is kicked down, it holds the parked cycle upright.

**kid** (kid) ***n.*** **1** a young goat. **2** leather from the skin of young goats. It is used for gloves, shoes, etc. **3** a child: *used only in everyday talk.* ◆***v.*** to tease, fool, etc.: *used only in everyday talk.* —**kid'ded, kid'ding** ◆***adj.*** **1** made of leather from young goats. **2** younger: *used only in everyday talk* [my *kid* sister].

**Kidd** (kid), Captain 1645?–1701; Scottish pirate. His full name was William Kidd.

**kid·dy** or **kid·die** (kid'ē) ***n.*** a child: *used only in everyday talk.* —*pl.* **kid'dies**

**kid·nap** (kid'nap) ***v.*** to carry off a person by force or trickery, often in order to get a ransom. —**kid'napped** or **kid'naped, kid'nap·ping** or **kid'nap·ing** —**kid'nap·per** or **kid'nap·er** ***n.***

**kid·ney** (kid′nē) ***n.*** **1** either of a pair of organs in the central part of the body that take water and waste products out of the blood and pass them through the bladder as urine. **2** the kidney of an animal, used as food. —*pl.* **kid′neys**

**kidney bean** the kidney-shaped seed of the common bean plant. The seed, or bean, is used for food.

**kid·skin** (kid′skin) ***n.*** leather from the skin of young goats.

**kiel·ba·sa** (kēl bä′sə) ***n.*** a smoked Polish sausage flavored with garlic. —*pl.* **kiel·ba·si** (kēl bä′sē) or **kiel·ba′sas**

**Ki·ev** (kē′ef *or* kē ev′) capital of the Ukraine, in the U.S.S.R.

**Kil·i·man·ja·ro** (kil′ə män jä′rō) a mountain in northeastern Tanganyika. It is the highest mountain in Africa, almost 5,900 meters (19,340 feet).

**kill** (kil) ***v.*** **1** to cause the death of; make die; slay. **2** to put an end to; destroy or ruin [Her defeat *killed* all our hopes.] **3** to keep a bill from becoming law, as by veto or by voting against it. **4** to make time pass in doing unimportant things [an hour to *kill* before my train leaves]. **5** to overcome, as with laughter, surprise, dismay, etc.: *used only in everyday talk.* ☆**6** to stop, as an engine. ☆**7** to muffle, as a sound. **8** to make feel great pain: *used only in everyday talk.* ◆***n.*** **1** the act of killing [to be in at the *kill*]. **2** an animal or animals killed [the lion's *kill*]. —**kill′er *n.***

SYNONYMS: To **kill** is to cause death in any way [Many were *killed* in the war. Butchers *kill* hogs for food. Frost *kills* flowers.] To **murder** is to kill unlawfully, often after deliberate planning [Macbeth *murdered* the king.] To **execute** is to kill someone who has been sentenced to die by a court of law.

☆**kill·deer** (kil′dir) ***n.*** a small wading bird that has a shrill cry.

**kill·joy** (kil′joi′) ***n.*** a person who spoils other people's fun or enjoyment: *also written* **killjoy.**

**kiln** (kil *or* kiln) ***n.*** a furnace or oven for drying or baking bricks, pottery, etc.

**ki·lo** (kē′lō *or* kil′ō) ***n.*** *a shorter word for* **kilogram** *or* **kilometer.** —*pl.* **ki′los**

**kilo-** *a prefix meaning* one thousand [*kilogram*].

**kil·o·cy·cle** (kil′ə sī′k′l) ***n.*** *an earlier name for* **kilohertz.**

**kil·o·gram** (kil′ə gram) ***n.*** a unit of weight, equal to 1,000 grams. *An earlier British spelling is* **kil′o·gramme.**

**kil·o·hertz** (kil′ə hurts) ***n.*** 1,000 hertz: the frequency of radio waves is measured in kilohertz.

**kil·o·li·ter** (kil′ə lēt′ər) ***n.*** a unit of volume, equal to 1,000 liters or one cubic meter. *The usual British spelling is* **kil′o·li′tre.**

**ki·lo·me·ter** (ki läm′ə tər *or* kil′ə mēt′ər) ***n.*** a unit of measure, equal to 1,000 meters, or about 5/8 mile. *The usual British spelling is* **ki·lo′me·tre.**

**kil·o·ton** (kil′ə tun) ***n.*** the explosive force of 1,000 tons of TNT. The power of thermonuclear weapons is measured in kilotons.

**kil·o·watt** (kil′ə wät) ***n.*** a unit of electrical power, equal to 1,000 watts.

**kil·o·watt-hour** (kil′ə wät our′) ***n.*** a unit for measuring electrical energy, equal to work done by one kilowatt acting for one hour.

**kilt** (kilt) ***n.*** a short skirt with pleats worn by men of the Scottish Highlands. *See the picture.*

**kil·ter** (kil′tər) ***n.*** working order: *used only in everyday talk* [Our TV set is out of *kilter*.]

**ki·mo·no** (kə mō′nə) ***n.*** **1** a loose robe with wide sleeves and a sash, that used to be the common outer garment of Japanese men and women and is still sometimes worn. *See the picture.* **2** a woman's dressing gown like this. —*pl.* **ki·mo′nos**

**kin** (kin) ***n.*** relatives or family. One's **next of kin** is one's nearest relative or relatives. ◆***adj.*** related, as by birth [Is she *kin* to you?]

**-kin** (kin) *a suffix meaning* little [A *lambkin* is a little lamb.]

**kind**[1] (kīnd) ***n.*** **1** sort or variety [all *kinds* of books]. **2** a natural grouping, as of plants or animals: sometimes used in compounds [*humankind*]. —**in kind, 1** in the same way. **2** with goods instead of money [payment *in kind*]. —**kind of,** somewhat; rather: *used only in everyday talk* [It's *kind of* cold here.] —**of a kind,** of the same kind; alike [The twins are two *of a kind*.]

**kind**[2] (kīnd) ***adj.*** **1** always ready to help others and do good; friendly, gentle, generous, sympathetic, etc. **2** showing goodness, generosity, sympathy, etc. [*kind* deeds; *kind* regards].

**kin·der·gar·ten** (kin′dər gär′t′n) ***n.*** a school or class for young children about five years old, to get them ready for regular schoolwork by games, exercises, simple handicraft, etc.



**kind·heart·ed** (kīnd′här′tid) ***adj.*** kindly or kind.

**kin·dle** (kin′d′l) ***v.*** **1** to set on fire; light [to *kindle* logs in a fireplace]. **2** to catch fire; start burning [The logs *kindled* quickly.] **3** to stir up; excite [His insulting remarks *kindled* my anger.] **4** to light up; brighten [Her eyes *kindled* with joy.] —**kin′dled, kin′dling**

**kin·dling** (kin′dling) ***n.*** bits of dry wood or the like, for starting a fire.

**kind·ly** (kīnd′lē) ***adj.*** **1** kind, gentle, sympathetic, etc. **2** agreeable or pleasant [a *kindly* climate]. —**kind′li·er, kind′li·est** ◆***adv.*** **1** in a kind or pleasant way [Please treat my cousin *kindly*.] **2** please [*Kindly* shut the door.] —**take kindly to,** to be attracted to. —**kind′li·ness *n.***

**kind·ness** (kīnd′nis) ***n.*** **1** the condition or habit of being kind. **2** a kind act or kind treatment.

**kin·dred** (kin′drid) ***n.*** **1** relatives or family; kin [He and all his *kindred* live in the same town.] **2** family relationship; kinship. ◆***adj.*** **1** related, as by birth. **2** alike or similar [The two girls are *kindred* spirits.]

**ki·net·ic** (ki net′ik) ***adj.*** of or resulting from motion [*kinetic* energy].

**kin·folk** (kin′fōk) ***n.pl.*** family or relatives; kin: *also* **kin·folks** (kin′fōks).

| | | | | | | | |
|---|---|---|---|---|---|---|---|
| **a** | fat | **ir** | here | **ou** | out | **zh** | leisure |
| **ā** | ape | **ī** | bite, fire | **u** | up | **ng** | ring |
| **ä** | car, lot | **ō** | go | **ur** | fur | | a *in* ago |
| **e** | ten | **ô** | law, horn | **ch** | chin | | e *in* agent |
| **er** | care | **oi** | oil | **sh** | she | **ə =** | i *in* unity |
| **ē** | even | **oo** | look | **th** | thin | | o *in* collect |
| **i** | hit | **ōō** | tool | ***th*** | then | | u *in* focus |

**king** (kiŋ) ***n.*** **1** a man who rules a country and whose position is handed down from parent to child. Kings today usually have little power to rule. **2** an important or powerful man in some field [an oil *king*]. **3** a playing card with a picture of a king on it. **4** the chief piece in chess. The game is won when a king is checkmated. **5** a piece in checkers that has moved the length of the board. —**king′ship′** ***n.***

**King** (kiŋ), **Martin Luther, Jr.** 1929–1968; U.S. clergyman and leader in the civil rights movement. He was assassinated.

**king·dom** (kiŋ′dəm) ***n.*** **1** a country ruled by a king or queen; monarchy. **2** the spiritual region where God rules [the *kingdom* of heaven]. **3** any of the three groupings into which all things are placed [the animal, vegetable, and mineral *kingdoms*].

**king·fish·er** (kiŋ′fish′ər) ***n.*** a bright-colored bird with a short tail, a large head, and a strong beak. Many kingfishers eat fish. *See the picture.*

**King Lear** (lir) **1** a tragic play by Shakespeare. **2** the main character of this play.

**king·ly** (kiŋ′lē) ***adj.*** of, like, or fit for a king; royal; regal [*kingly* splendor]. —**king′li·er, king′li·est**

**Kings** (kiŋz) either of two books of the Bible, or in the Roman Catholic Bible, any of four books.

☆**king-size** (kiŋ′sīz′) ***adj.*** larger than the regular kind: *used only in everyday talk* [a *king-size* bed]. *Also* **king-sized.**

**kink** (kiŋk) ***n.*** **1** a short twist or curl, as in a hair or thread. **2** a painful cramp in a muscle. ☆**3** an odd idea or queer notion. ◆***v.*** to form a kink or kinks.

**kink·y** (kiŋ′kē) ***adj.*** ☆**1** full of kinks; tightly curled [*kinky* hair]. **2** peculiar; weird: *slang in this meaning.* —**kink′i·er, kink′i·est** —**kink′i·ness** ***n.***

**kin·ship** (kin′ship′) ***n.*** **1** family relationship. **2** the condition of being related or connected.

**kins·man** (kinz′mən) ***n.*** a relative; especially, a man who is a relative. —*pl.* **kins′men**

**kins·wom·an** (kinz′wo͝om′ən) ***n.*** a woman who is a relative. —*pl.* **kins′wom′en**

**ki·osk** (kē äsk′) ***n.*** a small, open building used as a newsstand, bandstand, etc. *See the picture.*

The word **kiosk** comes to us from French, from Turkish, and then from Persian. In Turkey and Persia, a **kiosk** is a large, one-story building with open sides and richly decorated woodwork. The small kiosks on city streets are sometimes decorated with carved designs on the posts and along the tops.

**Kip·ling** (kip′liŋ), **Rud·yard** (rud′yərd) 1865–1936; English writer and poet, born in India.

**kip·per** (kip′ər) ***v.*** to clean and salt a fish, and then dry or smoke it. ◆***n.*** a kippered fish, especially a herring.

**kirk** (kurk) ***n.*** a church: *a Scottish word.*

**kis·met** (kiz′met *or* kis′met) ***n.*** fate; destiny.

**kiss** (kis) ***v.*** **1** to touch with the lips as a way of showing love, respect, etc. or as a greeting. **2** to touch lightly [Her bowling ball just *kissed* the last pin.] ◆***n.*** **1** a touch or caress with the lips. **2** a light touch. **3** any of various candies.

**kit** (kit) ***n.*** a set of tools or other articles for some special use, a number of parts to be put together, etc.; also, a box or bag for carrying these [a carpenter's *kit;* a model airplane *kit*].

**kitch·en** (kich′ən) ***n.*** a room or place for preparing and cooking food.

☆**kitch·en·ette** or **kitch·en·et** (kich ə net′) ***n.*** a small kitchen with little waste space, as in some apartments.

**kitch·en·ware** (kich′ən wer) ***n.*** utensils used in the kitchen, as pans, bowls, ladles, etc.

**kite** (kīt) ***n.*** **1** a light frame, as of wood, covered with paper or cloth. It is tied to a string and flown in the air when the wind is blowing. *See the picture.* **2** a hawk with long, pointed wings.

**kith** (kith) ***n.*** friends. **Kith** is now used only in the phrase **kith and kin,** meaning "friends and relatives."

**kit·ten** (kit′'n) ***n.*** a young cat.

**kit·ty** (kit′ē) ***n.*** a pet name for a cat or kitten. —*pl.* **kit′ties**

**ki·wi** (kē′wē) ***n.*** a tailless bird of New Zealand. It has undeveloped wings, hairlike feathers, and a long, slender bill. —*pl.* **ki′wis**

**kl** or **kl.** *abbreviation for* **kiloliter** *or* **kiloliters.**

☆**Klee·nex** (klē′neks) *a trademark for* soft paper tissue used as a handkerchief, etc.

**Klon·dike** (klän′dīk) a region in northwestern Canada where gold was found in 1896. *See the map.*

**km** or **km.** *abbreviation for* **kilometer** *or* **kilometers.**

**knack** (nak) ***n.*** a special ability or skill [She has the *knack* of making friends.]

**knack·wurst** (näk′wurst) ***n.*** a thick, highly seasoned sausage.

**knap·sack** (nap′sak) ***n.*** a leather or canvas bag worn on the back, as by hikers, for carrying supplies.

**knave** (nāv) ***n.*** **1** a dishonest or tricky person; rascal. **2** a playing card with a page's picture on it; jack.

**Knave** originally meant simply a boy, and from that a serving boy, then a man of humble birth. And now the present meaning is "a dishonest or tricky person." But the early meaning "a serving boy or page" lives on in the figure on the playing card that is also called the jack.

**knav·er·y** (nāv′ər ē) ***n.*** an act or way of acting that is dishonest or tricky. —*pl.* **knav′er·ies**

**knav·ish** (nāv′ish) ***adj.*** like a knave; dishonest or tricky. —**knav′ish·ly** ***adv.***

**knead** (nēd) ***v.*** **1** to keep pressing and squeezing dough, clay, etc. to make it ready for use. **2** to rub or press with the hands; massage [to *knead* a muscle].

**knee** (nē) ***n.*** **1** the joint between the thigh and the lower leg. **2** anything shaped like a knee, especially like a bent knee. **3** the part of a trouser leg, etc. that covers the knee.

**knee·cap** (nē′kap) ***n.*** the flat, movable bone that forms the front of a person's knee.

**kneel** (nēl) ***v.*** to rest on a knee or knees [Some people *kneel* when they pray.] —**knelt** or **kneeled, kneel′ing**

**knell** (nel) ***n.*** **1** the sound of a bell rung slowly, as at a funeral. **2** a warning that something will end or pass away [The invention of the car sounded the *knell* of the horse and buggy.] ◆***v.*** **1** to ring a bell slowly; toll. **2** to announce or warn as by a knell [The jury's verdict *knelled* the prisoner's death.]

**knelt** (nelt) *a past tense and past participle of* **kneel.**
**knew** (no͞o *or* nyo͞o) *past tense of* **know.**
☆**knick·er·bock·ers** (nik′ər bäk′ərz) ***n.pl.*** short, loose trousers gathered in just below the knees: *also called* **knick·ers** (nik′ərz). *See the picture.*
**knick·knack** (nik′nak) ***n.*** a small, showy, but not valuable article [a table loaded with china figures and other *knickknacks*].
**knife** (nīf) ***n.*** **1** a tool having a flat, sharp blade set in a handle, used for cutting. **2** a cutting blade that is part of a machine. —*pl.* **knives** ◆***v.*** to cut or stab with a knife. —**knifed, knif′ing**
**knight** (nīt) ***n.*** **1** a man in the Middle Ages who was given a military rank of honor after serving as a page and squire. Knights were supposed to be gallant and brave. **2** in Great Britain, a man who has been honored with a high social rank that allows him to use *Sir* before his first name. **3** a chess piece shaped like a horse's head. ◆***v.*** to give the rank of knight to.
**knight-er·rant** (nīt′er′ənt) ***n.*** a knight of the Middle Ages who wandered about seeking adventure. —*pl.* **knights′-er′rant** —**knight′-er′rant·ry** ***n.***
**knight·hood** (nīt′hood) ***n.*** **1** the rank of a knight. **2** politeness and bravery, as of a knight; chivalry. **3** knights as a group.
**knight·ly** (nīt′lē) ***adj.*** of or like a knight; brave, polite, etc. —**knight′li·ness** ***n.***
**knit** (nit) ***v.*** **1** to make by looping yarn or thread together with special needles [to *knit* a scarf]. **2** to join or grow together in a close or firm way; unite [My broken leg *knit* slowly. Our family is close *knit*.] **3** to draw together in wrinkles [to *knit* the brows]. —**knit′ted** or **knit, knit′ting** ◆***n.*** cloth or a garment made by knitting. —**knit′ter** ***n.***
**knives** (nīvz) ***n.*** *plural of* **knife.**
**knob** (näb) ***n.*** **1** a handle that is more or less round, as on a door or drawer, or on a TV set for working some control. **2** a round part that sticks out [a *knob* at the end of a cane]. **3** a hill or mountain with a round top. —**knob′by** ***adj.***
**knock** (näk) ***v.*** **1** to hit as with the fist; especially, to rap on a door [Who is *knocking?*] *See* SYNONYMS *at* **strike. 2** to hit and cause to fall [The dog *knocked* down the papergirl.] **3** to make by hitting [to *knock* a hole in the wall]. **4** to make a pounding or tapping noise [An engine *knocks* when the combustion is faulty.] ☆**5** to find fault with; criticize: *used only in everyday talk.* ◆***n.*** **1** a hard, loud blow, as with the fist; rap, as on a door. **2** a pounding or tapping noise, as in an engine. **3** trouble or misfortune: *used only in everyday talk* [the school of hard *knocks*]. —**knock about** or **knock around,** to wander about; roam: *used only in everyday talk.* —**knock down, 1** to hit and make fall. ☆**2** to take apart so as to be shipped more easily. **3** to earn as pay: *slang in this meaning.* —**knock off, 1** to stop working. **2** to deduct. **3** to do or make. *This phrase is used only in everyday talk.* —**knock out, 1** to score a knockout over in boxing. **2** to make unconscious or very tired. —**knock together,** to put together hastily or crudely.
**knock·er** (näk′ər) ***n.*** a person or thing that knocks; especially, a ring or knob fastened to a door by a hinge and used for knocking.
**knock-kneed** (näk′nēd′) ***adj.*** having legs that bend inward at the knee. *See the picture.*

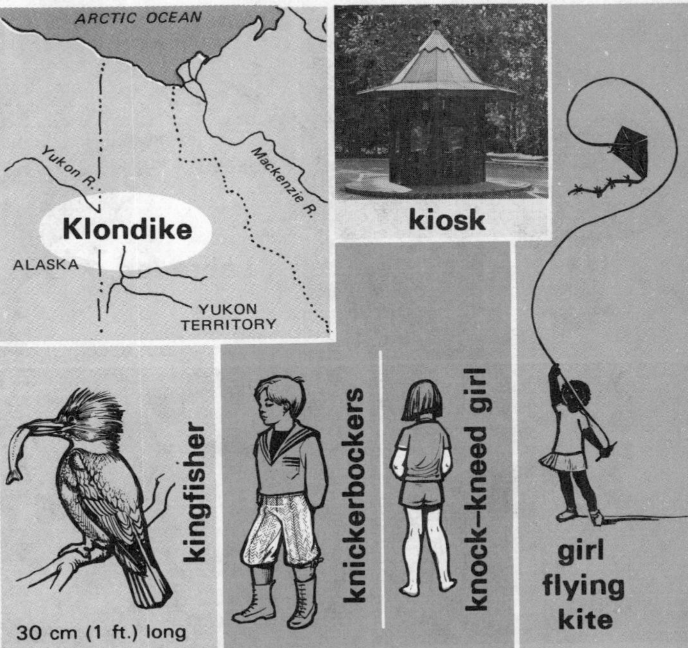


**knock·out** (näk′out) ***n.*** a blow that knocks a boxer down so that he cannot get up and go on fighting before the referee counts to ten.
**knock·wurst** (näk′wurst) ***n.*** *another spelling of* **knackwurst.**
**knoll** (nōl) ***n.*** a little rounded hill; mound.
**knot** (nät) ***n.*** **1** a lump, as in a string or ribbon, formed by a loop or a tangle drawn tight. **2** a fastening made by tying together parts or pieces of string, rope, etc. [Sailors make a variety of *knots*.] **3** a small group [a *knot* of people]. **4** something that joins closely, as the bond of marriage. **5** a problem or difficulty. **6** a hard lump on a tree where a branch grows out, or a cross section of such a lump in a board. **7** a unit of speed of one nautical mile (1,852 meters, or 6,076.12 feet) an hour [The ship averaged 20 *knots*.] ◆***v.*** **1** to tie or fasten with a knot; make a knot in. **2** to become tangled. —**knot′ted, knot′ting**
**knot·hole** (nät′hōl) ***n.*** a hole in a board or tree trunk where a knot has fallen out.
**knot·ty** (nät′ē) ***adj.*** **1** full of knots [*knotty* pine]. **2** hard to deal with [a *knotty* problem]. —**knot′ti·er, knot′ti·est**
**know** (nō) ***v.*** **1** to be sure of or have the facts about [Do you *know* why grass is green? She *knows* the law.] **2** to be aware of; realize [He suddenly *knew* he would be late.] **3** to have in one's mind or memory [The actress *knows* her lines.] **4** to be acquainted with [I *know* your brother well.] **5** to recognize [I'd *know* that



| | | | | | | |
|---|---|---|---|---|---|---|
| **a** fat | **ir** here | **ou** out | **zh** leisure | | | |
| **ā** ape | **ī** bite, fire | **u** up | **ng** ring | | | |
| **ä** car, lot | **ō** go | **ur** fur | | a *in* ago | | |
| **e** ten | **ô** law, horn | **ch** chin | | e *in* agent | | |
| **er** care | **oi** oil | **sh** she | **ə** = | i *in* unity | | |
| **ē** even | **oo** look | **th** thin | | o *in* collect | | |
| **i** hit | **o͞o** tool | ***th*** then | | u *in* focus | | |

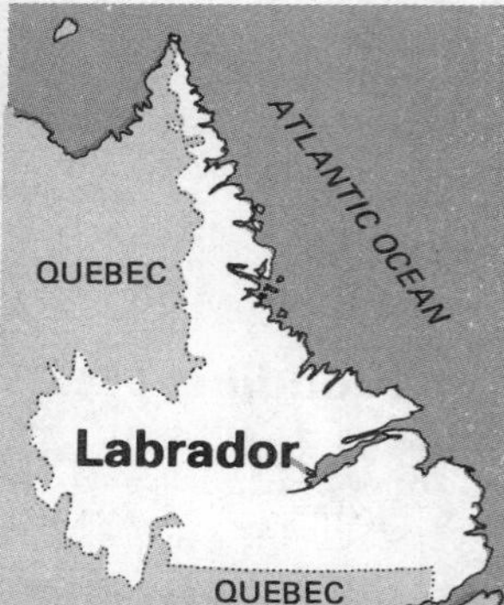


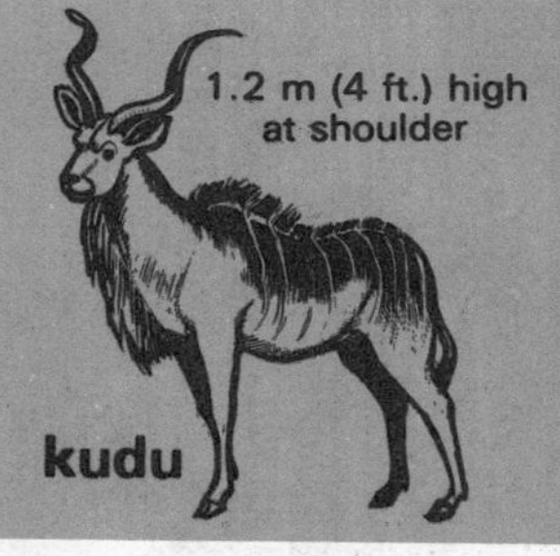

face anywhere.] **6** to be able to tell the difference in [It's not always easy to *know* right from wrong.] —**knew, known, know′ing**



☆**know-how** (nō′hou) ***n.*** knowledge of how to do something well: *used only in everyday talk.*

**know·ing** (nō′ing) ***adj.*** **1** having the facts; well-informed. **2** clever or shrewd. **3** showing shrewd or secret understanding [a *knowing* look].

**know·ing·ly** (nō′ing lē) ***adv.*** **1** in a knowing way. **2** on purpose; knowing clearly what one is doing [She would not *knowingly* hurt your feelings.]

**knowl·edge** (näl′ij) ***n.*** **1** the fact or condition of knowing [*Knowledge* of the murder spread through the town.] **2** what is known or learned, as through study or experience [a scientist of great *knowledge*]. *See* SYNONYMS *at* **information**. **3** all that is known by all people. —**to the best of one's knowledge**, as far as one knows.

**knowl·edge·a·ble** (näl′ij ə b′l) ***adj.*** having or showing knowledge or intelligence.

**known** (nōn) *past participle of* **know**.

**Knox·ville** (näks′vil) a city in eastern Tennessee.

**knuck·le** (nuk″l) ***n.*** **1** a joint of the finger; especially, a joint connecting a finger to the rest of the hand. **2** the knee or hock joint of a pig, calf, etc., used as food. —☆**knuckle down**, to work hard. —**knuckle under**, to give in. —**knuck′led, knuck′-ling**

☆**KO** (kā′ō′) ***v.*** to knock out in boxing. —**KO′d, KO′ing** •***n.*** a knockout in boxing. —*pl.* **KO's** *Also* **K.O., k.o.** *This is a slang term.*

**ko·a·la** (kō ä′lə) ***n.*** an Australian animal that lives in trees and looks like a very small bear. The mother carries her young in a pouch in front. *See the picture.*

**Ko·be** (kō′bā′) a seaport in Honshu, Japan.

**kohl·ra·bi** (kōl rä′bē *or* kōl′rä bē) ***n.*** a kind of cabbage whose leaves grow from a rounded stem that looks like a turnip: the stem is eaten as a vegetable. *See the picture.* —*pl.* **kohl·ra′bies**

☆**kook** (ko͞ok) ***n.*** a person who is thought of as silly, crazy, etc.: *a slang word.* —**kook′y *adj.* kook′i·er, kook′i·est**

**kook·a·bur·ra** (ko͝ok′ə bur′ə) ***n.*** an Australian bird related to the kingfisher. Its cry sounds like someone laughing loudly.

**ko·peck** or **ko·pek** (kō′pek) ***n.*** a small Russian coin. One ruble equals 100 kopecks.

**Ko·ran** (kō ran′ *or* kō rän′) ***n.*** the sacred book of the Muslims.

**Ko·re·a** (kô rē′ə) a country in eastern Asia, divided into two republics, North Korea and South Korea. —**Ko·re′an *adj., n.***

**Kos·ci·us·ko** (käs′ē us′kō), **Thaddeus** 1746–1817; Polish general. He served in the American army in the American Revolution.

**ko·sher** (kō′shər) ***adj.*** clean or fit to eat according to the Jewish laws of diet.

**Ko·sy·gin** (kə sē′gin), **A·lek·sei** (ä lyik sā′) 1904– ; premier of the Soviet Union, from 1964.

**kow·tow** (kou′tou′) ***v.*** to be very humble in showing obedience or respect [The Chinese used to *kowtow* to their lords by kneeling and bringing the forehead to the ground.]

**Kowtow** comes from a Chinese word meaning "knock head." When the Chinese used to kowtow, they often knocked their heads on the ground or floor.

**KP** *abbreviation for* kitchen police, those soldiers given the military duty of working in an army kitchen helping the cooks.

**Kreis·ler** (krīs′lər), **Fritz** (frits) 1875–1962; U.S. violinist and composer. He was born in Austria.

**Krem·lin** (krem′lin) a large fortress in the center of Moscow, where the government offices of the U.S.S.R. used to be.

**KS** *abbreviation for* **Kansas**.

**Kua·la Lum·pur** (kwä′lə lo͝om po͝or′) the capital of Malaysia.

☆**ku·chen** (ko͞o′kən) ***n.*** a cake that is like a sweet bread, covered with sugar and spices and often containing raisins, nuts, etc.

**ku·dos** (ko͞o′däs *or* ko͞o′dōs) ***n.*** praise for something one has done; glory; fame: *used only in everyday talk.*

**Kudos** is sometimes wrongly thought to be the plural of "kudo," but there is no word "kudo."

**ku·du** (ko͞o′do͞o) ***n.*** a large, gray-brown antelope of Africa. *See the picture.*

**kum·quat** (kum′kwät) ***n.*** a fruit like a small orange, used for preserves.

**kung fu** (ko͝ong′ fo͞o′) a Chinese form of self-defense. It is like karate, but blows are delivered with circular as well as straight movements.

**Ku·wait** (ko͞o wāt′) a country in eastern Arabia.

**kw** or **kw.** *abbreviation for* **kilowatt** *or* **kilowatts.**

**Kwang·chow** (kwäng′chō′) a large seaport city in southeastern China.

**kwhr, kwh, K.W.H.** *abbreviations for* **kilowatt-hour** *or* **kilowatt-hours.**

**Ky.** or **KY** *abbreviation for* **Kentucky.**

**Kyo·to** (kyō′tō′) a city in Honshu, Japan.

**Kyu·shu** (kyo͞o′sho͞o′) one of the four main islands of Japan.

**L, l** (el) ***n.*** the twelfth letter of the English alphabet. —*pl.* **L's, l's** (elz)

**L** (el) ***n.*** **1** something shaped like an L. **2** the Roman numeral for 50.

**L., l.** *abbreviation for* **lake, latitude, left, length, line, liter** *or* **liters.**

**L.** *abbreviation for* **Latin.**

**la** (lä) ***n.*** the sixth note of a musical scale.

**La.** or **LA** *abbreviation for* **Louisiana.**

**lab** (lab) ***n.*** a laboratory: *used only in everyday talk.*

**Lab.** *abbreviation for* **Labrador.**

**la·bel** (lā′b'l) ***n.*** a piece of paper, cloth, etc. that is marked and attached to an object to show what it is, what it contains, who owns it, etc. [a *label* on a can or in a suit; a mailing *label* on a package]. ◆***v.*** **1** to attach a label to [to *label* a package]. **2** to name or describe as; call [No one wants to be *labeled* a "coward."] —**la′beled** or **la′belled, la′bel·ing** or **la′bel·ling**

> **Label** comes from an old French word meaning "strip" or "rag." Originally, a label was a narrow strip of ribbon attached to a document to hold a seal on it.

**la·bor** (lā′bər) ***n.*** **1** work; toil. *See* SYNONYMS *at* **work. 2** a piece of work; task [We rested from our *labors.*] **3** workers as a group [an agreement between *labor* and management on wages]. **4** the act of giving birth to a child. ◆***v.*** **1** to work or toil [Coal miners *labor* underground.] **2** to move slowly and with effort [The old car *labored* up the steep hill.]

**lab·o·ra·to·ry** (lab′rə tôr′ē *or* lab′ər ə tôr′ē) ***n.*** a room or building where scientific work or tests are carried on, or where chemicals, drugs, etc. are prepared. —*pl.* **lab′o·ra·to′ries**

☆**Labor Day** the first Monday in September, a legal holiday honoring labor.

**la·bored** (lā′bərd) ***adj.*** done with great effort; strained [a *labored* attempt to be funny].

**la·bor·er** (lā′bər ər) ***n.*** a worker; especially, one who does rough work that takes little skill.

**la·bo·ri·ous** (lə bôr′ē əs) ***adj.*** **1** taking much work or effort [years of *laborious* study]. **2** hard-working.

☆**labor union** a group of workers joined together to protect and further their interests.

**la·bour** (lā′bər) ***n., v.*** *British spelling of* **labor.**

**Lab·ra·dor** (lab′rə dôr) **1** a large peninsula in northeastern North America, between the Atlantic Ocean and Hudson Bay. **2** the eastern part of this peninsula, a part of Newfoundland. *See the map.*

**la·bur·num** (lə bur′nəm) ***n.*** a small tree or shrub with drooping yellow flowers.

**lab·y·rinth** (lab′ə rinth) ***n.*** a place with winding passages, blind alleys, etc. that make it hard to find one's way through; maze.

**lab·y·rin·thine** (lab′ə rin′thin) ***adj.*** like a labyrinth; complicated; hard to follow.

**lace** (lās) ***n.*** **1** a string, ribbon, etc. put through holes or around hooks in a shoe, bodice, etc. for pulling the edges together and fastening them. **2** a fabric of thread woven into fancy designs with many openings like those in a net. ◆***v.*** **1** to pull together and fasten with a lace. **2** to trim with lace. **3** to weave together; intertwine. **4** to beat or whip. —**laced, lac′ing**

**lac·er·ate** (las′ə rāt) ***v.*** **1** to tear in a jagged way [The flesh on his arm was *lacerated* by the barbed wire.] **2** to hurt deeply [Your cruel words *lacerated* his feelings.] —**lac′er·at·ed, lac′er·at·ing —lac′er·a′tion *n.***

**lack** (lak) ***n.*** **1** a need for something that is missing; shortage [*Lack* of money forced him to return home.] **2** the thing that is needed [Our most serious *lack* was fresh water.] ◆***v.*** **1** to be without or not have enough; need [The soil *lacks* nitrogen.] **2** to be missing or not enough [Money is *lacking* to buy new band uniforms.]

> SYNONYMS: To **lack** is not to have any or enough of something necessary or desired [He *lacks* the training needed for the job.] To **need** is to feel strongly that something lacking must be supplied [She *needs* a warm coat for the winter.] To **require** is to need very much something that is really necessary [The baby *requires* frequent feedings.]

**lack·a·dai·si·cal** (lak′ə dā′zi k'l) ***adj.*** showing little or no interest or spirit; listless.

**lack·ey** (lak′ē) ***n.*** **1** a man servant of low rank. **2** a person who carries out another's orders like a servant. —*pl.* **lack′eys**

**lack·lus·ter** (lak′lus′tər) ***adj.*** lacking brightness; dull [*lackluster* eyes].

**la·con·ic** (lə kän′ik) ***adj.*** using few words; brief; terse [a *laconic* reply].

**lac·quer** (lak′ər) ***n.*** **1** a varnish made of shellac, natural or artificial resins, etc. dissolved in alcohol or some other liquid. Coloring matter can be added to lacquer to form a **lacquer enamel. 2** a natural varnish obtained from certain trees in Asia. ◆***v.*** to coat with lacquer.

☆**la·crosse** (lə krôs′) ***n.*** a ball game played by two teams on a field with a goal at each end. The players use webbed rackets with long handles. *See the picture.*

**lac·tic** (lak′tik) ***adj.*** of or got from milk [*Lactic* acid is formed when milk sours.]

**lac·tose** (lak′tōs) ***n.*** a kind of sugar found in milk.

**lac·y** (lā′sē) ***adj.*** of or like lace. —**lac′i·er, lac′i·est**

**lad** (lad) ***n.*** a boy or youth.

| | | | | | | | |
|---|---|---|---|---|---|---|---|
| **a** | fat | **ir** | here | **ou** | out | **zh** | leisure |
| **ā** | ape | **ī** | bite, fire | **u** | up | **ng** | ring |
| **ä** | car, lot | **ō** | go | **ur** | fur | | a *in* ago |
| **e** | ten | **ô** | law, horn | **ch** | chin | | e *in* agent |
| **er** | care | **oi** | oil | **sh** | she | ə = | i *in* unity |
| **ē** | even | **oo** | look | **th** | thin | | o *in* collect |
| **i** | hit | **ōō** | tool | ***th*** | then | | u *in* focus |

**lad·der** (lad′ər) ***n.*** **1** a framework of two long pieces connected by a series of rungs or crosspieces on which a person steps in climbing up or down. **2** anything that helps a person to go higher [to rise on the *ladder* of success].

**lade** (lād) ***v.*** *an earlier word for* **load.** **—lad′ed, lad′ed** or **lad′en, lad′ing**

**lad·en** (lād′'n) ***adj.*** having or carrying a load; burdened [a heart *laden* with sorrow].

**lad·ing** (lā′diŋ) ***n.*** a load or cargo: *usually used in* **bill of lading,** a receipt, as from a shipping company, that lists the goods received for shipping.

**la·dle** (lā′d'l) ***n.*** a cuplike spoon with a long handle, used for dipping liquids out of a container. ◆***v.*** to dip out, as with a ladle. **—la′dled, la′dling**

**la·dy** (lā′dē) ***n.*** **1** a woman, especially one who is polite and refined and has a sense of honor. **2** a woman belonging to a family of high social standing, as the wife of a lord. **3 Lady,** a British title given to some women of high rank, as countesses. *—pl.* **la′dies** ◆***adj.*** that is a woman; female [a *lady* barber]. **—Our Lady,** the Virgin Mary.

**la·dy·bug** (lā′dē bug′) ***n.*** a small, round, flying beetle, brightly colored with dark spots on its back: *also* **la·dy·bird** (lā′dē burd′). *See the picture.*

**la·dy·fin·ger** (lā′dē fiŋ′gər) ***n.*** a small spongecake shaped somewhat like a finger.

**la·dy-in-wait·ing** (lā′dē in wāt′iŋ) ***n.*** a woman who waits upon, or serves, a queen or princess. *—pl.* **la′dies-in-wait′ing**

**la·dy·like** (lā′dē līk′) ***adj.*** like or fit for a lady; polite, cultured, or refined.

**La·dy·ship** (lā′dē ship′) ***n.*** a title of respect used in speaking to or of a Lady [Is your *Ladyship* pleased?]

**la·dy-slip·per** (lā′dē slip′ər) ***n.*** a wild or cultivated orchid with a flower that looks like a slipper: *also* **la′dy's-slip′per.**

**La·fa·yette** (lä′fi yet′), marquis **de** 1757–1834; French general who served in the American Revolutionary army.

**La Fon·taine** (lə fän tān′) 1621–1695; French poet and writer of fables.

**lag** (lag) ***v.*** to move so slowly as to fall behind; loiter [The older hikers *lagged* behind the younger ones.] **—lagged, lag′ging** ◆***n.*** **1** the act of lagging. **2** the amount by which one thing lags behind another [There is a great *lag* between what she can do and what she has done.]

**lag·gard** (lag′ərd) ***n.*** a person who lags behind. ◆***adj.*** slow or late in doing things [a *laggard* pupil].

**la·goon** (lə go͞on′) ***n.*** **1** a shallow lake or pond, especially one that joins a larger body of water. **2** the water that is surrounded by an atoll. **3** shallow salt water cut off from the sea by sand dunes.

**La·hore** (lə hôr′) a city in northeastern Pakistan.

**laid** (lād) *past tense and past participle of* **lay**[1].

**lain** (lān) *past participle of* **lie**[1].

**lair** (ler) ***n.*** the bed or resting place of a wild animal; den.

**la·i·ty** (lā′ət ē) ***n.*** all lay people, as a group.

**lake** (lāk) ***n.*** **1** a large body of water, usually fresh water, surrounded by land. **2** a pool of liquid, as of oil.

**lake trout** ☆a large, gray fish that lives in deep, cold lakes of the northern U.S. and Canada.

**la·ma** (lä′mə) ***n.*** a Buddhist priest or monk in Tibet and Mongolia.

**la·ma·ser·y** (lä′mə ser′ē) ***n.*** a monastery of lamas. —*pl.* **la′ma·ser′ies**

**lamb** (lam) ***n.*** **1** a young sheep. **2** its flesh, used as food. **3** lambskin. **4** a gentle or innocent person, especially a child.

**Lamb** (lam), **Charles** 1775–1834; English writer of essays and, with his sister Mary, of *Tales from Shakespeare.*

**lam·baste** (lam bāst′) ***v.*** **1** to beat or thrash. **2** to scold harshly. *This word is used only in everyday talk.* **—lam·bast′ed, lam·bast′ing**

**lam·bent** (lam′bənt) ***adj.*** **1** playing lightly over a surface [a *lambent* flame]. **2** glowing softly [the *lambent* sky]. **3** light and graceful [*lambent* wit].

**lamb·kin** (lam′kin) ***n.*** a little lamb.

**lamb·skin** (lam′skin) ***n.*** **1** the skin of a lamb, especially with the wool left on it. **2** leather or parchment made from the skin of a lamb.

**lame** (lām) ***adj.*** **1** having a hurt leg or foot that makes one limp. **2** crippled, or stiff and painful [a *lame* leg; a *lame* back]. **3** not good enough; poor [a *lame* excuse]. ◆***v.*** to make lame. **—lamed, lam′ing —lame′ly *adv.* —lame′ness *n.***

**la·mé** (la mā′) ***n.*** a cloth with metal threads woven into it, especially of gold or silver.

**lame duck** a public official serving out a term in office that stretches past the election at which he or she was not reelected.

**la·ment** (lə ment′) ***v.*** to feel or show deep sorrow over something; mourn [to *lament* the death of a friend]. ◆***n.*** **1** weeping or crying that shows sorrow; wail. **2** a poem, song, etc. that mourns some loss or death.

**lam·en·ta·ble** (lam′ən tə b'l *or* lə men′tə b'l) ***adj.*** that should be lamented; regrettable; distressing [a *lamentable* accident]. **—lam′en·ta·bly *adv.***

**lam·en·ta·tion** (lam′ən tā′shən) ***n.*** the act of lamenting; a wailing because of grief.

**lam·i·nate** (lam′ə nāt) ***v.*** **1** to form into or cover with a thin layer. **2** to make by putting together thin layers, as plywood. *See the picture.* **—lam′i·nat·ed, lam′i·nat·ing —lam′i·na′tion *n.***

**lamp** (lamp) ***n.*** **1** a thing for giving light, as an electric bulb, a gas jet, a wick soaked in oil, a fluorescent tube, etc. **2** such a thing with the support or stand that it is set in [a table *lamp;* a floor *lamp*].

**lamp·black** (lamp′blak) ***n.*** fine soot formed by burning oils, tars, etc.: it is used in making black paints and inks.

**lam·poon** (lam po͞on′) ***n.*** a piece of writing that attacks or makes fun of someone. ◆***v.*** to make fun of in a lampoon.

**lamp·post** (lam′pōst) ***n.*** a post that holds a street lamp.

**lam·prey** (lam′prē) ***n.*** a water animal like an eel, with a mouth shaped like a funnel, by which it clings to fishes it feeds on. *See the picture.* *—pl.* **lam′preys**

☆**la·nai** (lə nī′ *or* la nī′) ***n.*** a living room with a wall that opens to the outdoors, common in Hawaii.

**lance** (lans) ***n.*** **1** a weapon made of a long pole with a pointed metal head. *See the picture.* **2** anything that stabs or cuts like a lance, as a fish spear, a surgeon's lancet, etc. ◆*v.* **1** to stab with a lance. **2** to cut open with a lancet [to *lance* a boil]. —**lanced, lanc′ing**

**Lan·ce·lot** (lan′sə lät) the bravest knight of King Arthur's Round Table.

**lanc·er** (lan′sər) *n.* a cavalry soldier armed with a lance.

**lan·cet** (lan′sit) *n.* a small, pointed knife with two cutting edges, used by surgeons.

**land** (land) *n.* **1** the solid part of the earth's surface [by *land* or by sea]. **2** a country, region, etc. [a distant *land;* one's native *land*]. **3** ground or soil [high *land;* fertile *land*]. **4** ground thought of as property [to invest money in *land*]. ◆*v.* **1** to put or go on shore from a ship [The ship *landed* its cargo. The Marines *landed.*] **2** to come to a port or to shore [The Mayflower *landed* in America in 1620.] **3** to bring an aircraft down to the ground or on water. **4** to come down after flying, jumping, or falling [The cat *landed* on its feet.] **5** to bring to or end up at [This bus *lands* you in Reno at midnight. He stole the money and *landed* in jail.] **6** to catch [to *land* a fish]. **7** to get or win: *used only in everyday talk* [to *land* a job]. **8** to strike: *used only in everyday talk* [to *land* a blow to the jaw].

**land·ed** (lan′did) *adj.* **1** owning land [the *landed* gentry]. **2** consisting of land [a *landed* estate].

**land·fill** (land′fil) *n.* **1** the disposal of garbage or rubbish by burying it under a shallow layer of earth. **2** a place used for this purpose.

**land·hold·er** (land′hōl′dər) *n.* a person who owns or holds land. —**land′hold′ing** *adj., n.*

**land·ing** (lan′diŋ) *n.* **1** a coming to shore or a putting on shore [the *landing* of troops]. **2** a place where a ship can land; pier or dock. **3** a platform at the end of a flight of stairs. *See the picture.* **4** a coming down after flying, jumping, or falling.

**landing field** a field with a smooth surface, used by airplanes for landing and taking off.

**landing gear** those parts underneath an aircraft, including wheels, pontoons, etc., that support the aircraft when landing.

**landing strip** *another name for* **airstrip.**

**land·la·dy** (land′lā′dē) *n.* **1** a woman who owns land, houses, etc. that she rents to others. **2** a woman who keeps a rooming house, inn, etc. —*pl.* **land′la′dies**

**land·locked** (land′läkt) *adj.* **1** shut in on all sides or nearly all sides by land, as a bay or country. **2** living in fresh water, cut off from the sea [*landlocked* salmon].

**land·lord** (land′lôrd) *n.* **1** a person, especially a man, who owns land, houses, etc. that are rented out to others. **2** a man who keeps a rooming house, inn, etc.

**land·lub·ber** (land′lub′ər) *n.* a person who has not spent much time on ships and is clumsy when sailing: *a sailor's word.*

**land·mark** (land′märk) *n.* **1** a building, tree, etc. that helps one to find or recognize a place because it is easily seen [The Eiffel Tower is a Paris *landmark.*] **2** a very important happening in the development of something [The invention of the microscope is a *landmark* in science.] **3** a post, rock, etc. that marks the boundary of a piece of land.

**land·own·er** (land′ō′nər) *n.* a person who owns land.

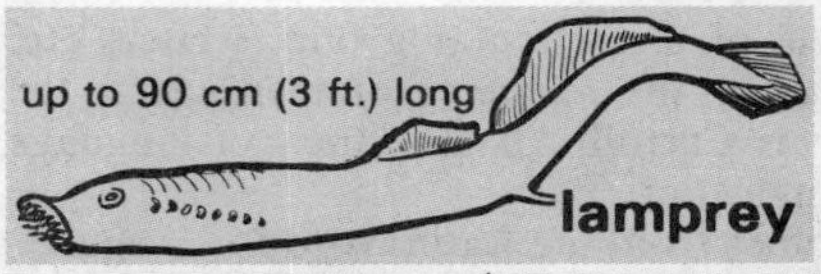

up to 90 cm (3 ft.) long
lamprey

ladybug

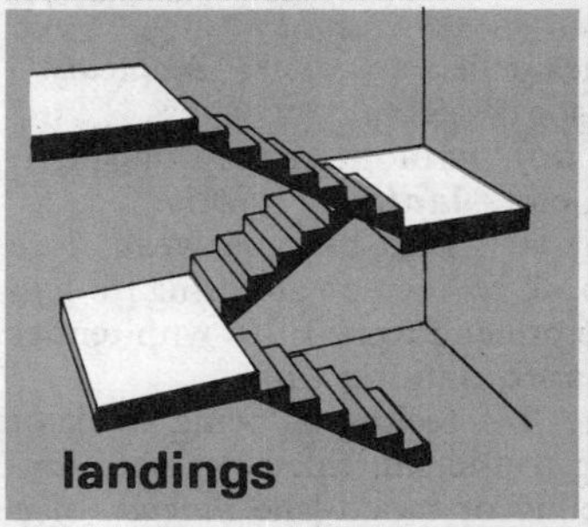

landings

knight with lance

bowling lanes

laminated plywood

**land·scape** (land′skāp) *n.* **1** a stretch of scenery that can be seen in one view [the dull *landscape* of the desert]. **2** a picture of such scenery [to paint a mountain *landscape*]. ◆*v.* to make a piece of ground more attractive by adding trees, shrubs, gardens, etc. —**land′scaped, land′scap·ing —land′scap·er** *n.*

☆**land·slide** (land′slīd) *n.* **1** the sliding of a great mass of rocks and earth down the side of a hill; also, the mass itself. **2** the winning of an election by a great majority of the votes.

**lands·man** (landz′mən) *n.* **1** any person who lives on land and is not a sailor. **2** a person of or from one's own country. —*pl.* **lands′men**

**land·ward** (land′wərd) *adj., adv.* toward the land.

**land·wards** (land′wərdz) *adv.* toward the land.

**lane** (lān) *n.* **1** a narrow path between hedges, walls, etc.; narrow country road or city street. **2** any narrow way through [The police formed a *lane* through the crowd.] **3** a path or route for ships, cars, or airplanes going in the same direction [a highway with two *lanes* on either side]. **4** the long stretch of polished wood along which the balls are rolled in bowling; alley. *See the picture.*

**lan·guage** (laŋ′gwij) *n.* **1** human speech or writing that stands for speech [People communicate by means of *language.*] **2** the speech of a particular nation, tribe, etc. [the Greek *language;* the Navaho *language*]. **3** any means of passing on one's thoughts or feelings to others [sign *language*]. **4** the special words,

| | | | | | | | |
|---|---|---|---|---|---|---|---|
| **a** | fat | **ir** | here | **ou** | out | **zh** | leisure |
| **ā** | ape | **ī** | bite, fire | **u** | up | **ŋ** | ring |
| **ä** | car, lot | **ō** | go | **ur** | fur | | a *in* ago |
| **e** | ten | **ô** | law, horn | **ch** | chin | | e *in* agent |
| **er** | care | **oi** | oil | **sh** | she | **ə =** | i *in* unity |
| **ē** | even | **oo** | look | **th** | thin | | o *in* collect |
| **i** | hit | **ōō** | tool | ***th*** | then | | u *in* focus |

phrases, or style of a particular group, writer, etc. [technical *language;* the *language* of teen-agers; the *language* of Lewis Carroll]. **5** the study of language or languages; linguistics.

**Language** comes from the Latin word for tongue, *lingua.* One could not speak without a tongue. A language is sometimes called a tongue. A *linguist* is a person who can speak several languages.

**lan·guid** (laŋ′gwid) ***adj.*** without energy or spirit; weak, sluggish, listless, etc. —**lan′guid·ly *adv.***

**lan·guish** (laŋ′gwish) ***v.*** **1** to become weak; lose energy or spirit; droop. **2** to keep on suffering [to *languish* in poverty]. **3** to pretend to be filled with tender feelings or sadness. —**lan′guish·ing *adj.***

**lan·guor** (laŋ′gər) ***n.*** **1** a feeling of being weak or tired; weakness [Lying in the sun filled her with *languor.*] **2** a tender feeling or mood [the *languor* of a love song]. **3** the condition of being still and sluggish [the *languor* of the steaming jungle]. —**lan′guor·ous *adj.***

**lank** (laŋk) ***adj.*** **1** tall and slender; lean [a *lank* youth]. **2** straight; not curly [*lank* hair].

**lank·y** (laŋ′kē) ***adj.*** tall and slender in an awkward way [a *lanky* cowboy]. *See the picture.* —**lank′i·er, lank′i·est** —**lank′i·ness *n.***

**lan·o·lin** (lan″l in) ***n.*** a fat got from sheep wool and used in hair oils, face creams, etc.

**Lan·sing** (lan′siŋ) the capital of Michigan.



**lan·tern** (lan′tərn) ***n.*** a case of glass, paper, etc. holding a light and protecting it from wind and rain. *See the picture.*

**lan·yard** (lan′yərd) ***n.*** **1** a short rope or cord used by sailors for holding or fastening something. **2** a cord used in firing some cannons.

**La·os** (lä′ōs *or* lous) a country in a large peninsula south of central China. —**La·o·tian** (lā ō′shən) ***adj., n.***

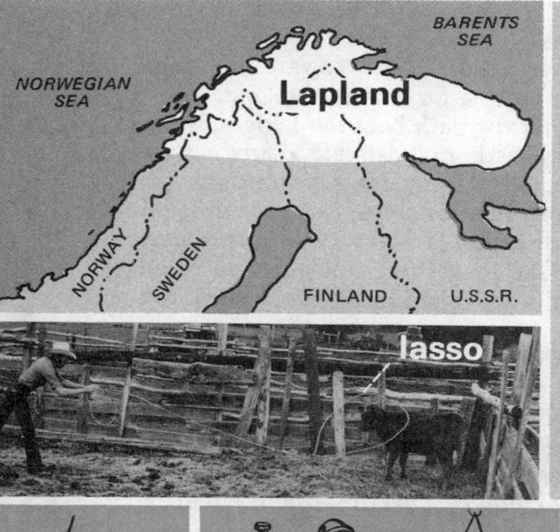

lanky youth

larynx

lanterns

lapwing
30 cm (12 in.) long

**lap**[1] (lap) ***n.*** **1** the front part of a person sitting down, from the waist to the knees; also, the part of the clothing covering this [She caught the spool in her *lap.*] **2** a place where something is held and protected like a baby in a lap [He was raised in the *lap* of luxury.] **3** a part that overlaps or hangs loose [The rug had a three-inch *lap* on one side.] **4** one complete trip around a race track [He fell behind in the third *lap* of the race.] ◆***v.*** **1** to fold or wrap. **2** to put something so that it lies partly on something else [*Lap* each row of shingles over the row before.] **3** to reach beyond, into, or onto something else [The ball game *lapped* over into an extra inning.] —**lapped, lap′ping**

**lap**[2] (lap) ***v.*** **1** to drink by dipping up with the tongue as a dog does. **2** to hit against with a gentle splash [Waves *lapped* the boat.] —**lapped, lap′ping** ◆***n.*** the act or sound of lapping. —**lap up,** to take in or receive eagerly: *used only in everyday talk.*

**La Paz** (lə päz′) a city in western Bolivia. It is one of the two capitals.

**lap dog** a pet dog small enough to hold in the lap.

**la·pel** (lə pel′) ***n.*** either of the front parts of a coat that are folded back.

**lap·i·dar·y** (lap′ə der′ē) ***n.*** a person who cuts and polishes precious stones, either as a job or as a hobby. —*pl.* **lap′i·dar′ies**

**lap·is laz·u·li** (lap′is laz′yoo lī) **1** a bright-blue stone used as a jewel. **2** bright blue.

**Lap·land** (lap′land) a region in northern Norway, Sweden, and Finland, and a northwestern part of the U.S.S.R. *See the map.*

**Lapp** (lap) ***n.*** **1** any of a Mongoloid people who live in Lapland and herd reindeer. **2** their language.

**lap·pet** (lap′it) ***n.*** a small fold or flap, as of a garment or as of flesh.

**lapse** (laps) ***n.*** **1** a small mistake or slip; fault [a *lapse* of memory]. **2** a going by of time [a *lapse* of five years]. **3** a slipping into a worse condition [a *lapse* of health; the store's *lapse* into bankruptcy]. **4** the ending of some right or claim because it was not used, renewed, etc. [the *lapse* of an insurance policy because premiums were not paid]. ◆***v.*** **1** to fall or slip into some condition [She *lapsed* into her old lazy habits.] **2** to come to an end; stop [Our magazine subscription *lapsed.*] —**lapsed, laps′ing**

**lap·wing** (lap′wiŋ) ***n.*** a shore bird of Europe and Asia, with an irregular way of flying. *See the picture.*

**lar·board** (lär′bərd) ***n.*** the left side of a ship as one faces forward; port. ◆***adj.*** on or of this side.

**Larboard** has for the most part been replaced by *port.* This is because "larboard" sounds so much like "starboard" that people got them mixed up. *Starboard* means the right side of a ship, opposite from *larboard.*

**lar·ce·ny** (lär′sə nē) ***n.*** the stealing of another's property; theft. —**lar′ce·nous *adj.***

**larch** (lärch) ***n.*** **1** a kind of pine tree having leaves shaped like needles that are shed yearly. **2** the tough wood of this tree.

**lard** (lärd) ***n.*** the fat of pigs or hogs, melted down for use in cooking. ◆***v.*** **1** to cover or smear with lard or other fat. **2** to scatter throughout; sprinkle [a talk *larded* with puns].

**lard·er** (lär′dər) ***n.*** **1** a place in a home where food is kept. **2** a supply of food.

**large** (lärj) ***adj.*** of great size or amount; big [a *large* house; a *large* sum of money]. *See* SYNONYMS *at* **great**. —**larg'er, larg'est** ◆***adv.*** in a large way [Don't write so *large*.] —**at large, 1** free; not locked up [Bandits roamed *at large* in the countryside.] ☆**2** representing the whole State or district rather than one of its divisions [a delegate *at large*]. —**large'ness** ***n.***

**large·ly** (lärj'lē) ***adv.*** for the most part; mainly [Pat is *largely* to blame for the fight.]

**lar·gess** or **lar·gesse** (lär jes') ***n.*** generous giving or a generous gift.

**lar·go** (lär'gō) ***adj., adv.*** slow and dignified. It is an Italian word used in music to tell how fast a piece should be played.

☆**lar·i·at** (lar'ē it) ***n.*** **1** a rope used for tying horses and other animals while they graze. **2** *another name for* **lasso.**

**lark**[1] (lärk) ***n.*** **1** any of a group of songbirds of Europe, especially the skylark. **2** a bird somewhat like this, as the meadowlark.

**lark**[2] (lärk) ***n.*** a happy or lively time; bit of fun.

**lark·spur** (lärk'spur) ***n.*** *another name for* **delphinium.**

**lar·va** (lär'və) ***n.*** the early form of an insect or of any animal that changes to another form when it becomes an adult [A caterpillar is the *larva* of a butterfly.] —*pl.* **lar·vae** (lär'vē) or **lar'vas** —**lar'val** ***adj.***

**lar·yn·gi·tis** (lar'ən jīt'əs) ***n.*** a condition, as during a cold, in which the larynx is inflamed and the voice is often lost for a while.

**lar·ynx** (lar'ingks) ***n.*** the upper end of the windpipe, that contains the vocal cords. *See the picture.*

**la·sa·gna** (lə zän'yə) ***n.*** an Italian dish of wide, flat noodles baked in layers with cheese, tomato sauce, and ground meat.

**La Salle** (lə sal'), **Robert** 1643–1687; French explorer in North America.

**las·civ·i·ous** (lə siv'ē əs) ***adj.*** showing much interest in sex; lustful. —**las·civ'i·ous·ly** ***adv.***

☆**la·ser** (lā'zər) ***n.*** a device that sends out light waves in a very narrow and strong beam.

**lash** (lash) ***n.*** **1** a whip, especially the part that strikes the blow. **2** a blow or stroke as with a whip. **3** an eyelash. ◆***v.*** **1** to strike or make move as with a whip; flog [The driver *lashed* the horses onward.] **2** to strike with force; beat [Waves *lashed* against the rocks.] **3** to swing back and forth in a quick or angry way; switch [The tiger *lashed* its tail in fury.] **4** to attack or stir up with harsh, bitter words [to *lash* out at critics]. **5** to tie or fasten to something with a rope.

**La Spe·zia** (lä spāt'syä) a seaport in northwestern Italy.

**lass** (las) ***n.*** a young woman; girl.

**las·si·tude** (las'ə to͞od *or* las'ə tyo͞od) ***n.*** a feeling of being tired, weak, and without interest in doing things; weariness.

☆**las·so** (las'ō) ***n.*** a long rope with a sliding loop at one end, used to catch horses or cattle. *See the picture.* —*pl.* **las'sos** or **las'soes** ◆***v.*** to catch with a lasso. —**las'soed, las'so·ing**

**last**[1] (last) ***adj.*** **1** being or coming after all others; final [December is the *last* month. Jane had the *last* word in the argument.] **2** that is the only one left [Don ate the *last* cookie in the jar.] **3** that is the one just before this one; most recent [I was ill *last* week.] **4** that is the least likely or expected [You are the *last* person I would suspect of lying to me.] ◆***adv.*** **1** after all others [Our team came in *last*.] **2** most recently [I saw them *last* in May.] ◆***n.*** **1** the one that is last [The *last* of the guests has left.] **2** the end [They were friends to the *last*.] —**at last,** after a long time. —**see the last of,** to see for the last time.

SYNONYMS: Something is **last** if it comes after a number of other things and nothing else follows it [I was the *last* one to enter.] Something is **final** if it comes at the end and brings about a conclusion or ending [That's my *final* argument.]

**last**[2] (last) ***v.*** **1** to go on; continue [The play *lasts* only an hour.] **2** to stay in good condition; wear well [Stone *lasts* longer than wood.]

**last**[3] (last) ***n.*** a form shaped like a foot, on which shoes are made or repaired.

**last-ditch** (last'dich') ***adj.*** made or done in a final, often desperate attempt to stop or oppose [a *last-ditch* effort to save her life].

**last·ing** (las'ting) ***adj.*** that lasts a long time; enduring; durable [a *lasting* peace].

**last·ly** (last'lē) ***adv.*** at the end; finally [*Lastly*, the speaker discussed the future.]

**Last Supper** the last meal eaten by Jesus with the Apostles before the Crucifixion.

**Las Ve·gas** (läs vā'gəs) a city in southeastern Nevada.

**Lat.** *abbreviation for* **Latin.** 

**lat.** *abbreviation for* **latitude.**

**latch** (lach) ***n.*** a simple fastening for a door or gate. It usually is a bar that falls into a notch fixed to the jamb. A spring lock on a door is now often called a latch. *See the picture on page 415.* ◆***v.*** to fasten with a latch. —☆**latch onto,** to get: *used only in everyday talk.*

**late** (lāt) ***adj.*** **1** happening or coming after the usual or expected time; tardy [*late* for school; a *late* train]. **2** coming toward the end of some period [the *late* Middle Ages]. **3** happening or appearing just before now; recent [a *late* news broadcast]. **4** having been so recently but not now [His *late* partner has opened a new business.] **5** having recently died [my *late* parents]. *See* SYNONYMS *at* **dead.** —**lat'er** or **lat'ter, lat'est** or **last** ◆***adv.*** **1** after the usual or expected time [Roses bloomed *late* last year.] **2** toward the end of some period [They came *late* in the day.] **3** lately; recently [I saw them as *late* as yesterday.] —**lat'er, lat'est** or **last** —**of late,** lately; recently. —**late'ness** ***n.***

**la·teen sail** (la tēn') a sail shaped like a triangle and fastened to a long yard that sticks out from a short mast. *See the picture on page 415.*

**late·ly** (lāt'lē) ***adv.*** just before this time; not long ago; recently.

| | | | | | | | |
|---|---|---|---|---|---|---|---|
| **a** | fat | **ir** | here | **ou** | out | **zh** | leisure |
| **ā** | ape | **ī** | bite, fire | **u** | up | **ng** | ring |
| **ä** | car, lot | **ō** | go | **ur** | fur | | a *in* ago |
| **e** | ten | **ô** | law, horn | **ch** | chin | | e *in* agent |
| **er** | care | **oi** | oil | **sh** | she | **ə** = | i *in* unity |
| **ē** | even | **oo** | look | **th** | thin | | o *in* collect |
| **i** | hit | **o͞o** | tool | ***th*** | then | | u *in* focus |

**la·tent** (lāt′'nt) ***adj.*** present but hidden or not active [*latent* talents].

> **Latent** comes from a Latin word that means "lying hidden." Something that is latent is hidden but may be found or noticed at any time.

**lat·er·al** (lat′ər əl) ***adj.*** of, at, from, or toward the side; sideways [*lateral* movement]. ◆***n.*** ☆*a shorter form of* **lateral pass.** —**lat′er·al·ly** ***adv.***

☆**lateral pass** a short pass in football that is parallel to the goal line or in a slightly backward direction.

**la·tex** (lā′teks) ***n.*** **1** a milky liquid in certain plants and trees, as the rubber tree. **2** water with tiny bits of rubber or plastic in it, used in paints, glues, etc.

**lath** (lath) ***n.*** **1** any of the thin, narrow strips of wood used to build lattices or as the framework on which plaster is put. **2** any framework for plaster, as wire screening. —*pl.* **laths** (la*th*z)

**lathe** (lā*th*) ***n.*** a machine for shaping a piece of wood, metal, etc. by holding and turning it rapidly against the edge of a cutting tool.

**lath·er** (la*th*′ər) ***n.*** **1** foam made by mixing soap and water. **2** foamy sweat, as on a horse after a race. ◆***v.*** **1** to cover with lather [He *lathered* his face and shaved.] **2** to form lather [Few soaps *lather* in salt water.]

**Lat·in** (lat′'n) ***n.*** **1** the language of the ancient Romans. **2** a person whose language developed from Latin, as a Spaniard or Italian. ◆***adj.*** **1** of or in the language of the ancient Romans. **2** having to do with the languages that developed from Latin or with the peoples who speak them, their countries, etc.



**Latin America** all of the Western Hemisphere south of the United States where Spanish, Portuguese, and French are spoken. —**Latin American**

**lat·i·tude** (lat′ə to͞od *or* lat′ə tyo͞od) ***n.*** **1** freedom from strict rules; freedom to do as one wishes [Our school allows some *latitude* in choosing courses.] **2** distance north or south of the equator, measured in degrees [Minneapolis is at 45 degrees north *latitude.*] *See the picture.* **3** a region in relation to its distance from the equator [cold northern *latitudes*].

**la·trine** (lə trēn′) ***n.*** a toilet, privy, etc. for many people to use, as in an army camp.

**lat·ter** (lat′ər) *a comparative of* **late.** ◆***adj.*** **1** nearer the end or last part; later [the *latter* part of May]. **2** being the second of two just mentioned: *often used as a noun with* the [We like football and baseball but prefer the *latter.*]

**lat·tice** (lat′is) ***n.*** a framework made of thin strips of wood or metal crossed and fastened together, and used as a screen or as a support for climbing plants. *See the picture.* ◆***v.*** to form into or furnish with a lattice. —**lat′ticed, lat′tic·ing**

**lat·tice·work** (lat′is wurk′) ***n.*** a lattice or lattices [The old house has *latticework* on all the windows.]

**Lat·vi·a** (lat′vē ə) a republic of the U.S.S.R. in northeastern Europe. —**Lat′vi·an** ***adj., n.***

**laud** (lôd) ***v.*** to praise highly; extol.

**laud·a·ble** (lôd′ə b'l) ***adj.*** deserving praise [a *laudable* performance]. —**laud′a·bly** ***adv.***

**laud·a·num** (lôd′'n əm) ***n.*** opium dissolved in alcohol.

**laud·a·to·ry** (lôd′ə tôr′ē) ***adj.*** that praises.

**laugh** (laf) ***v.*** **1** to make a series of quick sounds with the voice that show one is amused or happy or, sometimes, that show scorn. One usually smiles or grins when laughing. **2** to bring about, get rid of, etc. by means of laughter [*Laugh* your fears away.] ◆***n.*** the act or sound of laughing. —**have the last laugh,** to win after seeming to have lost. —**laugh at, 1** to be amused by. **2** to make fun of. —**laugh off,** to ignore or get rid of by laughing [You can't *laugh off* that mistake.] —**no laughing matter,** a serious matter.

> SYNONYMS: To **laugh** is to make sounds to show that one is happy, amused, etc. [We *laughed* at the circus clowns.] To **chuckle** is to laugh in a soft, quiet way that shows that one is mildly amused [I *chuckled* over the story I was reading.] To **giggle** is to make a number of quick, high-pitched sounds that show that one feels silly or embarrassed [The children *giggled* when they put on the funny hats at the party.]

**laugh·a·ble** (laf′ə b'l) ***adj.*** causing laughter; funny; ridiculous [a *laughable* costume]. *See* SYNONYMS *at* **funny.**

**laugh·ing·stock** (laf′iŋ stäk′) ***n.*** a person or thing laughed at or made fun of by all.

**laugh·ter** (laf′tər) ***n.*** the act or sound of laughing [He shook with *laughter.*]

**launch**¹ (lônch) ***v.*** **1** to throw, hurl, or send off into space [to *launch* a rocket]. **2** to cause to slide into the water; set afloat [to *launch* a new ship]. **3** to start or begin [to *launch* an attack]. ◆***n.*** the act of launching a ship, spacecraft, etc.

**launch**² (lônch) ***n.*** an open, or partly enclosed, motorboat.

**launch pad** the platform from which a rocket, guided missile, etc. is launched: *also called* **launching pad.**

**laun·der** (lôn′dər) ***v.*** to wash, or to wash and iron, clothes, linens, etc. —**laun′der·er** ***n.***

**laun·dress** (lôn′dris) ***n.*** a woman whose work is washing and ironing clothes, etc.

☆**Laun·dro·mat** (lôn′drə mat) *a trademark for* a laundry where a person pays to use machines for washing and drying clothes.

**laun·dry** (lôn′drē) ***n.*** **1** a place where laundering is done. **2** clothes, linens, etc. that have been, or are about to be, washed and ironed. —*pl.* **laun′dries**

**laun·dry·man** (lôn′drē mən) ***n.*** a man who works for a laundry, especially one who picks up and delivers laundry. —*pl.* **laun′dry·men**

**lau·re·ate** (lôr′ē it) ***adj.*** **1** crowned with a wreath of laurel leaves as a sign of honor. **2** famous and honored. *See also* **poet laureate.**

**lau·rel** (lôr′əl) ***n.*** **1** an evergreen tree or shrub of Europe, with large, glossy leaves. The ancient Greeks crowned winners of contests with wreaths of laurel leaves. *See the picture.* ☆**2** a plant similar to this, as the mountain laurel. **3 laurels,** *pl.* honor or victory. —**look to one's laurels,** to beware that another may do better than one has done. —**rest on one's laurels,** to be satisfied with what one has already done.

**la·va** (lä′və *or* lav′ə) ***n.*** **1** hot, melted rock pouring out of a volcano. **2** such rock when cooled and solid.

**lav·a·to·ry** (lav′ə tôr′ē) ***n.*** **1** a bowl or basin for washing the face and hands. It usually has water faucets and a drain. **2** a room with such a basin and a toilet. —*pl.* **lav′a·to′ries**

**lav·en·der** (lav′ən dər) ***n.*** **1** a sweet-smelling plant of the mint family, having pale-purple flowers. **2** the dried flowers and leaves of this plant, placed with stored clothes or linens to make them smell sweet. **3** pale purple.

> **Lavender** comes from a Latin word meaning "to wash." Lavender has been used as a perfume that is added to the water when a person is taking a bath.

**lav·ish** (lav′ish) ***adj.*** **1** very generous or too generous in giving or spending. **2** more than enough; very great or costly [a *lavish* allowance; *lavish* decorations]. ◆***v.*** to give or spend generously [They *lavished* time and money on their dogs.]

**law** (lô) ***n.*** **1** all the rules that tell people what they must or must not do, made by the government of a city, state, nation, etc. [the *law* of the land]. **2** any one of these rules; a statute, ordinance, etc. [a *law* against jaywalking]. **3** the condition that exists when these rules are obeyed [to keep *law* and order on the frontier]. **4** the courts that enforce these rules [to go to *law*]. **5** all such rules that have to do with a particular activity [criminal *law;* maritime *law*]. **6** the profession of lawyers and judges [a career in *law*]. **7** a series of events that will happen in the same way every time conditions are the same [the *law* of gravitation]. **8** any rule that people are expected to obey [the *laws* of health]. —**go to law,** to take a dispute to a law court to have it settled. —**the Law,** the law of Moses, especially as found in the first five books of the Bible.

**law-a·bid·ing** (lô′ə bīd′iŋ) ***adj.*** obeying the law [*law-abiding* citizens].

**law·break·er** (lô′brā′kər) ***n.*** a person who breaks the law. —**law′break′ing** ***n., adj.***

**law·ful** (lô′fəl) ***adj.*** in keeping with the law; permitted or recognized by law; legal [a *lawful* act; a *lawful* heir]. *See* SYNONYMS *at* **legal.** —**law′ful·ly** ***adv.***

**law·giv·er** (lô′giv′ər) ***n.*** a person who draws up a code of laws for a people, as Moses.

**law·less** (lô′lis) ***adj.*** **1** not controlled by law; having no laws [a *lawless* town]. **2** not obeying the law; disorderly or wild [*lawless* bandits].

**law·mak·er** (lô′mā′kər) ***n.*** a person who helps to make laws; especially, a member of a legislature. —**law′mak′ing** ***n., adj.***

**lawn**[1] (lôn) ***n.*** ground covered with grass that is cut short, as around a house.

**lawn**[2] (lôn) ***n.*** a very thin linen or cotton cloth, used for handkerchiefs, blouses, etc.

**lawn mower** a machine with steel blades that turn for cutting the grass of a lawn. It is pushed by hand or driven by a motor. *See the picture.*

**lawn tennis** tennis, especially when it is played on a grass court.

**law·suit** (lô′so͞ot) ***n.*** a case brought before a law court by certain persons to decide which person has the right to something claimed.

**law·yer** (lô′yər) ***n.*** a person whose profession is giving advice on law or acting for others in lawsuits.

**lax** (laks) ***adj.*** **1** not strict or exact; careless [a *lax* parent; *lax* morals]. **2** not tight or firm; loose; slack [a *lax* rope].

**lax·a·tive** (lak′sə tiv) ***adj.*** making the bowels move. ◆***n.*** a medicine that makes the bowels move.

parallels of latitude

laurel wreath

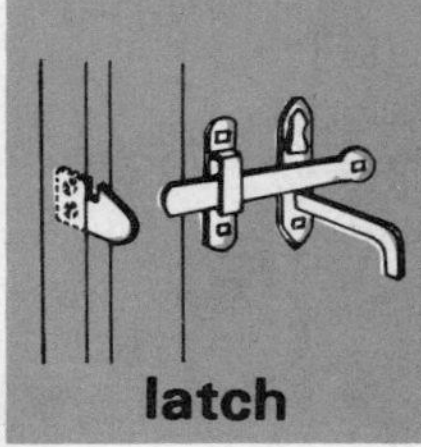

latch

lateen sails

lawn mower

lattice

**lax·i·ty** (lak′sə tē) ***n.*** the condition of being lax; looseness.

**lay**[1] (lā) ***v.*** **1** to put down so as to rest on, in, or against something [*Lay* your books on the shelf.] **2** to knock down [One blow *laid* me low.] **3** to put down in a special way; set in place [to *lay* floor tiles; to *lay* a carpet]. **4** to put or place; set [We *lay* great emphasis on diet. The scene is *laid* in France.] **5** to bring forth an egg, as a hen does. **6** to settle or quiet down; still [Sprinkle water to *lay* the dust. Our fears were *laid* when we knew the children were safe.] **7** to work out; prepare [to *lay* plans]. **8** to present; put forth [She *laid* claim to the property.] **9** to bet [to *lay* a wager]. —**laid, lay′ing** ◆***n.*** the way in which a thing lies or is arranged [the *lay* of the land]. —**lay aside, lay away,** or **lay by,** to put away for future use; save. —**lay down,** to sacrifice, as one's life. —**lay for,** to be waiting to attack: *used only in everyday talk.* —**lay in,** to get and store away for future use. —**lay into,** to attack with words or blows: *a slang phrase.* —**lay off,** ☆**1** to discharge a worker from a job, usually for only a short time. ☆**2** to stop criticizing, teasing, etc.: *slang in this meaning.* —**lay open, 1** to cut open. **2** to leave unprotected, as from attack or blame. —**lay out, 1** to set out clothes, equipment, etc. ready for wear or use. **2** to get a dead body ready for burial. **3** to plan or arrange [to *lay out* a vegetable garden in the spring]. **4** to spend. —**lay over,** ☆to stop for a while in a place before going on with a journey. —**lay**



| | | | | | | | |
|---|---|---|---|---|---|---|---|
| **a** | fat | **ir** | here | **ou** | out | **zh** | leisure |
| **ā** | ape | **ī** | bite, fire | **u** | up | **ŋ** | ring |
| **ä** | car, lot | **ō** | go | **ʉr** | fur | | a *in* ago |
| **e** | ten | **ô** | law, horn | **ch** | chin | | e *in* agent |
| **er** | care | **oi** | oil | **sh** | she | **ə =** | i *in* unity |
| **ē** | even | **oo** | look | **th** | thin | | o *in* collect |
| **i** | hit | **o͞o** | tool | ***th*** | then | | u *in* focus |

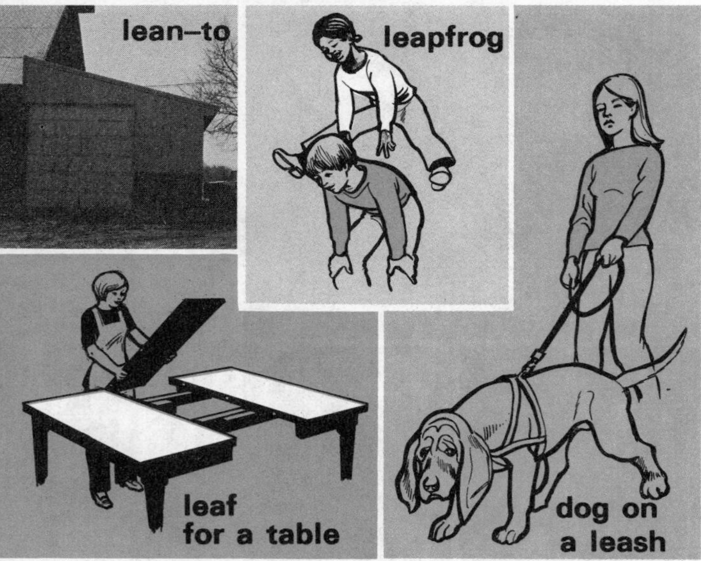


**up,** **1** to store for future use. **2** to make unable to get about because of illness or injury.

**lay²** (lā) *past tense of* **lie¹**.

**lay³** (lā) ***adj.*** **1** having to do with people who are not clergy. **2** of or for people who are not in a certain profession [a legal handbook for *lay* people].

 **lay⁴** (lā) ***n.*** a short poem or song, especially one that tells a story.

**lay·er** (lā′ər) ***n.*** **1** a single thickness, fold, coating, etc. [a cake with two *layers*]. **2** a person or thing that lays [These hens are poor *layers*.]

**lay·ette** (lā et′) ***n.*** a complete outfit of clothes, bedding, etc. for a newborn baby.

**lay·man** (lā′mən) ***n.*** a person who is not a clergyman, or one who does not belong to a certain profession. —*pl.* **lay′men**

☆**lay·off** (lā′ôf) ***n.*** **1** the act of putting a person or persons out of work, usually for only a short time. **2** the period of this.

☆**lay·out** (lā′out) ***n.*** **1** the way in which something is laid out or arranged; plan [the *layout* of a factory]. **2** the thing arranged in this way.

☆**lay·o·ver** (lā′ō′vər) ***n.*** a stopping for a short time before going on with one's journey.

**lay reader** a lay person who has the right to conduct certain religious services, as in the Episcopal Church, or to read parts of the service, as in the Roman Catholic Church.

**Laz·a·rus** (laz′ə rəs) in the Bible, a man raised from the dead by Jesus.

**la·zy** (lā′zē) ***adj.*** **1** not eager or willing to work or try hard [a *lazy* person]. **2** slow or sluggish [a *lazy* river]. —**la′zi·er, la′zi·est** —**la′zi·ly *adv.*** —**la′zi·ness *n.***

**lb.** *abbreviation for* **pound**. —*pl.* **lbs.**

> In Latin, the word for "pound," the unit of weight, is *libra.* The abbreviation for *libra* is **lb.** and that has been carried over into English as the abbreviation for "pound."

**lea** (lē) ***n.*** a meadow: *used in poetry.*

**leach** (lēch) ***v.*** **1** to wash with water that filters through and removes something [People used to *leach* wood ashes to get lye.] **2** to dissolve and wash away [The minerals in this soil have *leached* out.]

**lead¹** (lēd) ***v.*** **1** to show the way for; guide [*Lead* us along the path. The lights *led* me to the house.] *See* SYNONYMS *at* **guide**. **2** to cause to do something as by teaching or setting an example [Your advice *led* me to change jobs.] **3** to go or make go in some direction [This path *leads* to the lake. Drainpipes *lead* the water away.] **4** to be at the head of or be first [He *leads* the band. Their team was *leading* at the half.] **5** to live or spend time [They *lead* a hard life.] **6** to bring one as a result [A bad cold may *lead* to pneumonia.] **7** to go or do first; begin [He *led* with a left jab to the jaw.] —**led, lead′ing** ◆***n.*** **1** position or example of a leader [Let us follow her *lead.*] **2** the first place or position [The bay horse is in the *lead.*] **3** the amount or distance that one is ahead [Our team has a *lead* of six points in the game.] **4** a clue [The police followed up every *lead.*] **5** a going first or the right to go first, as in a game. **6** the most important role in a play. **7** the opening paragraph in a newspaper story. —**lead off,** to begin. —**lead on,** **1** to guide further. **2** to lure or tempt. —**lead up to,** to prepare the way for.

**lead²** (led) ***n.*** **1** a heavy, soft, gray metal that is a chemical element. Lead is easily shaped and is used in making pipe and in many alloys. **2** anything made of this metal, as a weight lowered on a line to find out how deep water is. **3** bullets. **4** a thin stick of graphite or other substance, used in pencils. ◆***adj.*** made of lead. ◆***v.*** **1** to fasten in place with lead [to *lead* windowpanes]. **2** to make heavier by adding lead.

**lead·en** (led′'n) ***adj.*** **1** made of lead. **2** hard to move or lift [a *leaden* weight]. **3** dull gray or gloomy [a *leaden* sky; *leaden* spirits].

**lead·er** (lē′dər) ***n.*** a person or thing that leads, or guides. —**lead′er·ship *n.***

**lead·ing** (lē′diŋ) ***adj.*** **1** that leads; guiding [A *leading* question guides one toward a certain answer.] **2** most important; playing a chief role [She played a *leading* part in our campaign.]

**leaf** (lēf) ***n.*** **1** any of the flat, green parts growing from the stem of a plant or tree. **2** a petal [a rose *leaf*]. **3** a sheet of paper in a book [Each side of a *leaf* is a page.] **4** metal in very thin sheets [a frame covered with gold *leaf*]. **5** a board hinged to a table, or put into a table top, to make it larger. *See the picture.* —*pl.* **leaves** ◆***v.*** **1** to grow leaves, as a tree. **2** to turn the pages of [to *leaf* through a book]. —**in leaf,** having leaves grown. —**turn over a new leaf,** to make a new start. —**leaf′less *adj.***

**leaf·let** (lēf′lit) ***n.*** **1** a small or young leaf. **2** a sheet of printed matter, folded once or twice [advertising *leaflets*].

**leaf·y** (lēf′ē) ***adj.*** made up of many leaves or having many leaves [a *leafy* vegetable; a *leafy* tree]. —**leaf′i·er, leaf′i·est**

**league¹** (lēg) ***n.*** a number of persons, groups, or nations joined together for some purpose, as to help one another. ◆***v.*** to join in a league. —**leagued, leagu′ing** —**in league,** united for a common purpose.

**league²** (lēg) ***n.*** an old measure of distance, usually equal to about 3 miles.

**League of Nations** a union of nations that was formed in 1920 to help keep world peace. It was replaced by the United Nations.

**leak** (lēk) ***v.*** **1** to let water, air, or other fluid in or out by accident [The roof *leaks* when it rains. The oven is *leaking* gas.] **2** to go in or come out by accident [The air in the tire *leaked* out through the valve.] **3** to become known little by little or by accident [The truth *leaked* out.] ◆***n.*** **1** a hole, crack, etc. that lets something in or out by accident [Sand spilled from the *leak* in the bag.] **2** any way by which something gets out. **3** a leaking in or out; leakage [a slow *leak* in one of the tires]. ☆**4** a making something known supposedly by accident but actually on purpose [a news *leak* about the scandal in the Bureau of Highways]. —**leak'y** ***adj.***

**leak·age** (lēk'ij) ***n.*** **1** a leaking in or out. **2** a thing or the amount that leaks.

**lean**[1] (lēn) ***v.*** **1** to bend or slant so as to rest upon something [Pedro *leaned* against the desk. *Lean* the ladder against the house.] **2** to bend to one side; stand at a slant [The old tree *leans* toward the barn.] **3** to depend on for advice, support, etc. [Jean still *leans* on her parents.] **4** to favor a little; tend [to *lean* toward an opposite opinion]. —**leaned** (lēnd) or **leant** (lent), **lean'ing**

**lean**[2] (lēn) ***adj.*** **1** having little or no fat [a *lean* athlete; *lean* meat]. **2** producing very little; meager [a *lean* year for business]. ◆***n.*** meat with little or no fat. —**lean'ness** ***n.***

**Leaning Tower of Pisa** a bell tower in Pisa, Italy. It leans more than 17 feet away from the perpendicular.

**lean-to** (lēn'to͞o') ***n.*** a shed with a roof that slopes up and rests against a wall or building. *See the picture.* —*pl.* **lean'-tos'**

**leap** (lēp) ***v.*** **1** to move oneself suddenly from the ground by using the leg muscles; jump; spring [The cat *leaped* onto my lap.] **2** to move in jumps; bound [The deer were *leaping* across the meadow.] **3** to jump over [to *leap* a brook]. —**leaped** (lēpt) or **leapt** (lept *or* lēpt), **leap'ing** ◆***n.*** a leaping; jump [over the fence in one *leap*]. —**leap at,** to take advantage of eagerly [I'd *leap* at a chance to go to Europe.]

**leap·frog** (lēp'frôg) ***n.*** a game in which each player in turn jumps over the backs of the other players, who are bending over. *See the picture.* ◆***v.*** **1** to move in jumps or skips. **2** to jump or skip over. —**leap'-frogged, leap'frog·ging**

**leap year** a year of 366 days, in which February has 29 days. Every fourth year is a leap year.

**learn** (lurn) ***v.*** **1** to get some knowledge or skill, as by studying or being taught [I have *learned* to knit. Some people never *learn* from experience.] **2** to find out about something; come to know [When did you *learn* of his illness?] **3** to fix in the mind; memorize [*Learn* this poem by tomorrow.] —**learned** (lurnd) or **learnt** (lurnt), **learn'ing**

**learn·ed** (lur'nid) ***adj.*** full of knowledge or learning; scholarly [a *learned* professor; a *learned* book].

**learn·ing** (lur'ning) ***n.*** **1** the getting of some knowledge or skill [A few tumbles are part of a baby's *learning* to walk.] **2** knowledge [a person of great *learning*].

**lease** (lēs) ***n.*** **1** an agreement by which an owner rents property for a certain period of time and for a certain price. **2** the period of time that this lasts [a three-year *lease*]. ◆***v.*** to get or give by means of a lease; rent [I *leased* this car for a week. The owner will not *lease* the apartment to noisy tenants.] —**leased, leas'ing** —**new lease on life,** another chance to be happy, successful, etc. because of a new situation.

**leash** (lēsh) ***n.*** a strap or chain by which a dog, etc. is led or held. *See the picture.* ◆***v.*** **1** to put a leash on. **2** to keep under control; check [to *leash* the energy of a river with a dam]. —**hold in leash,** to control.

**least** (lēst) ***adj.*** smallest in size, amount, or importance [I haven't the *least* interest in the matter.] —*Least* is a superlative of **little.** ◆***adv.*** in the smallest amount or degree [I was *least* impressed by the music.] —*Least* is the superlative of **little.** ◆***n.*** the smallest in amount, degree, etc. [The *least* you can do is apologize. I'm not in the *least* interested.] —**at least,** in any case [*At least* I tried.]

**least·wise** (lēst'wīz) ***adv.*** at least; anyway: *used only in everyday talk.*

**leath·er** (leth'ər) ***n.*** a material made from the skin of cows, horses, goats, etc. by cleaning and tanning it. ◆***adj.*** made of leather.

**leath·er·neck** (leth'ər nek) ***n.*** ☆a U.S. Marine: *a slang word.*

A U.S. Marine is called a **leatherneck** because in earlier times the Marine uniform had a collar lined with leather.

**leath·er·y** (leth'ər ē) ***adj.*** like leather; tough, tan, etc. [a *leathery* skin].



**leave**[1] (lēv) ***v.*** **1** to go away or go from [Rosa *left* early. Jose *leaves* the house at 8:00.] **2** to stop living in or being in [She *left* home at the age of 16. Ten members *left* the club last year.] **3** to let stay or be [*Leave* the door open.] **4** to cause to remain behind one [The invaders *left* a trail of destruction. The heavy boots *left* footprints.] **5** to let be in the care of [They *leave* such decisions to me.] **6** to have remaining after one or more are gone [Five minus two *leaves* three.] **7** to give at one's death; give by a will [The Hunaks *left* all their money to charity.] —**left, leav'-ing** —**leave off,** **1** to stop. **2** to stop doing or using. —**leave out,** to omit; not include. —**leave someone alone,** to stop bothering someone.

**leave**[2] (lēv) ***n.*** **1** permission [May I have your *leave* to go?] **2** permission to be away, as from work, school, the army, navy, etc.: *also called* **leave of absence.** **3** the length of time for which this is given [a three-day *leave*]. —**by your leave,** with your permission. —**take leave of,** to say goodbye to. —**take one's leave,** to go away; depart.

**leave**[3] (lēv) ***v.*** to grow leaves; leaf. —**leaved, leav'-ing**

**leav·en** (lev''n) ***n.*** **1** a small piece of fermenting dough used to make a fresh batch of dough ferment. **2** *another word for* **leavening.** ◆***v.*** **1** to make rise

| | | | | | | | |
|---|---|---|---|---|---|---|---|
| **a** | fat | **ir** | here | **ou** | out | **zh** | leisure |
| **ā** | ape | **ī** | bite, fire | **u** | up | **ng** | ring |
| **ä** | car, lot | **ō** | go | **ur** | fur | | a *in* ago |
| **e** | ten | **ô** | law, horn | **ch** | chin | | e *in* agent |
| **er** | care | **oi** | oil | **sh** | she | **ə =** | i *in* unity |
| **ē** | even | **oo** | look | **th** | thin | | o *in* collect |
| **i** | hit | **o͞o** | tool | ***th*** | then | | u *in* focus |

with a leaven or leavening, as dough. **2** to spread through, slowly causing a change.

**leav·en·ing** (lev′'n iŋ) ***n.*** **1** yeast or another substance that is used to make dough rise. **2** anything that works on something else to make it slowly change [Humor is a welcome *leavening* to conversation.]

**leaves** (lēvz) ***n.*** *plural of* **leaf.**

**leave-tak·ing** (lēv′tāk′iŋ) ***n.*** the act of taking leave, or saying goodbye.

**leav·ings** (lēv′iŋz) ***n.pl.*** things left over, as from a meal; leftovers.

**Leb·a·non** (leb′ə nən) a country at the eastern end of the Mediterranean, north of Israel. —**Leb·a·nese** (leb ə nēz′) ***adj., n.***

**lec·i·thin** (les′ə thin) ***n.*** a fatty substance found in egg yolk and in the cells of animals, and used in medicine, foods, etc.

**Le Cor·bu·sier** (lə kôr byo͞o zyā′) 1887–1965; Swiss architect in France. His real name was Charles-Édouard Jeanneret-Gris.

**lec·tern** (lek′tərn) ***n.*** a stand with a sloping top on which to rest a book, notes, etc. that will be read from, as in a church. *See the picture.*

**lec·ture** (lek′chər) ***n.*** **1** a talk on some subject to an audience or class. **2** a long or tiresome scolding. ◆***v.*** **1** to give a lecture. **2** to scold. —**lec′tured, lec′tur·ing** —**lec′tur·er** ***n.***

**led** (led) *past tense and past participle of* **lead**[1].

418 ☆**LED** a device that gives off light when given an electric charge. It is used in lamps and on digital clocks and watches.

**ledge** (lej) ***n.*** a flat part like a narrow shelf that comes out from a cliff, wall, etc. [a *ledge* of rock; a window *ledge*].

**ledg·er** (lej′ər) ***n.*** a book in which a business keeps a record of all its accounts.

**lee** (lē) ***n.*** **1** a sheltered place, especially one on that side of anything away from the wind [The cows stood in the *lee* of the barn.] **2** the side of a ship away from the wind. ◆***adj.*** of or on the side away from the wind [Parachutists jump from the *lee* side of a plane.]

**Lee** (lē), **Robert E.** 1807–1870; commander in chief of the Confederate army in the Civil War.

**leech** (lēch) ***n.*** **1** a worm that lives in water and sucks blood from animals. Leeches were once used in medicine to draw blood from bruises, etc. **2** a person who stays close to another, trying to get money, help, etc. *See* SYNONYMS *at* **parasite.**

**leek** (lēk) ***n.*** a vegetable like a thick green onion, but with a milder taste.

**leer** (lir) ***n.*** a sly look out of the corner of the eye, together with a wicked or hinting smile. ◆***v.*** to look with a leer.

**leer·y** (lir′ē) ***adj.*** on one's guard; suspicious [I'm *leery* of anyone who promises me something for nothing.] —**leer′i·er, leer′i·est**

**lees** (lēz) ***n.pl.*** dregs, as of wine.

**lee·ward** (lē′wərd *or* lo͞o′ərd) ***adj.*** in the same direction as the wind is blowing [the *leeward* drift of the boat]. ◆***n.*** the lee side [The canoes approached the ship from *leeward.*] ◆***adv.*** toward the lee.

**Lee·ward Islands** (lē′wərd) a group of small islands in the West Indies, east of Puerto Rico. *See the map.*

**lee·way** (lē′wā) ***n.*** **1** the leeward drift of a ship or plane from its course. **2** extra time, money, etc., in addition to what might be needed: *used only in everyday talk* [The weather is bad, so leave early to give yourself plenty of *leeway* to get here on time.]

**left**[1] (left) ***adj.*** **1** on or to the side that is toward the west when one faces north [the *left* hand; a *left* turn]. **2** closer to the left side of a person facing the thing mentioned [the top *left* drawer of the desk]. **3** radical or liberal in politics. ◆***n.*** **1** the left side [Forks are placed at the *left* of the plate.] *See the picture.* **2** a turn toward the left side [Take a *left* when you come to the next intersection.] ◆***adv.*** on or toward the left hand or side [Turn *left* here.] —**have two left feet,** to be very clumsy.

**left**[2] (left) *past tense and past participle of* **leave**[1].

**left-hand** (left′hand′) ***adj.*** **1** on or to the left [a *left-hand* turn]. **2** of, for, or with the left hand [a *left-hand* glove].

**left-hand·ed** (left′han′did) ***adj.*** **1** using the left hand more easily than the right. **2** done with or made for use with the left hand [a *left-handed* throw; *left-handed* scissors]. **3** finding fault while seeming to praise [a *left-handed* compliment]. ◆***adv.*** with the left hand [to write *left-handed*].

**left·ist** (lef′tist) ***n.*** a radical or liberal in politics. ◆***adj.*** radical or liberal.

☆**left·o·ver** (left′ō′vər) ***n.*** something left over, as food not eaten at a meal.

☆**left·y** (lef′tē) ***n.*** a left-handed person: *a slang word.* —*pl.* **left′ies**

**leg** (leg) ***n.*** **1** one of the parts of the body used for standing and walking. **2** the part of a garment that covers a leg. **3** anything like a leg in looks or use [the *legs* of a chair]. **4** a stage, as of a trip. —**on one's last legs,** nearly dead, worn out, etc. —**pull someone's leg,** to fool someone. *These phrases are used only in everyday talk.*

**leg·a·cy** (leg′ə sē) ***n.*** **1** money or property left to someone by a will. **2** anything handed down from an ancestor. —*pl.* **leg′a·cies**

**le·gal** (lē′gəl) ***adj.*** **1** of or based on law [*legal* knowledge; *legal* rights]. **2** allowed by law; lawful [Is it *legal* to park here?] **3** of or for lawyers [*legal* ethics]. —**le′gal·ly** ***adv.***

> SYNONYMS: **Legal** and **lawful** are both used to describe actions that are allowed by law, but **legal** often suggests a very close following of the law in every detail [a *legal* contract]. **Lawful** may suggest not going against the general purpose or spirit of the law [a *lawful* act].

**le·gal·i·ty** (li gal′ə tē) ***n.*** the condition of being legal or lawful.

**le·gal·ize** (lē′gə līz) ***v.*** to make legal or lawful [Some States have *legalized* gambling.] —**le′gal·ized, le′gal·iz·ing**

**legal tender** money that a person to whom a debt is owed must by law accept in payment.

**leg·a·tee** (leg ə tē′) ***n.*** a person to whom money or property is left by a will.

**le·ga·tion** (li gā′shən) ***n.*** **1** a group of officials representing their government in a foreign country. The head of a legation is lower in rank than an ambassador. **2** the headquarters of a legation.

**le·ga·to** (li gät′ō) ***adj., adv.*** in a smooth, even style, with no pauses between notes. It is an Italian word used in music to tell how the notes should be played.

**Legato** comes from a Latin word meaning "to tie." When musical notes are played or sung legato, they come out in a smooth, even flow almost as if they were tied tightly together with no gaps between them.

**leg·end** (lej′ənd) ***n.*** **1** a story handed down through the years and connected with some real events, but probably not true in itself [The story of King Arthur is a British *legend.*] *See* SYNONYMS *at* **myth**. **2** all such stories as a group [famous in Irish *legend*]. **3** a remarkable person who is much talked about while still alive [Babe Ruth was a baseball *legend.*] **4** the writing on a coin, medal, etc. **5** a title or description under a picture, map, etc.

**leg·end·ar·y** (lej′ən der′ē) ***adj.*** of, in, or like a legend [a *legendary* heroine].

**leg·er·de·main** (lej′ər di mān′) ***n.*** **1** the tricks of a stage magician. **2** trickery; deceit.

**leg·gings** (leg′iŋz *or* leg′ənz) ***n.pl.*** **1** coverings of canvas, leather, etc. worn by soldiers, etc. to protect the leg below the knee. **2** a child's outer garment with legs, worn in cold weather.

**Leg·horn** (leg′hôrn *or* leg′ərn) ***n.*** a breed of small chicken: *also written* **leghorn.**

**leg·i·ble** (lej′ə b′l) ***adj.*** clear enough to be read easily [*legible* handwriting]. —**leg·i·bil·i·ty** (lej′ə bil′ə tē) ***n.*** —**leg′i·bly** ***adv.***

**le·gion** (lē′jən) ***n.*** **1** a division of the ancient Roman army, with from 3,000 to 6,000 soldiers. **2** any large group of soldiers, or army. **3** a large number [a *legion* of followers].

**leg·is·late** (lej′is lāt) ***v.*** to make or pass laws. —**leg′is·lat·ed, leg′is·lat·ing**

**leg·is·la·tion** (lej′is lā′shən) ***n.*** **1** the making of laws. **2** the laws made.

**leg·is·la·tive** (lej′is lāt′iv) ***adj.*** **1** having to do with making laws [*legislative* powers]. **2** having the power to make laws [a *legislative* assembly].

**leg·is·la·tor** (lej′is lāt′ər) ***n.*** a lawmaker; member of a congress, parliament, etc.

**leg·is·la·ture** (lej′is lā′chər) ***n.*** a group of people who make laws; congress, parliament, etc.

**le·git·i·mate** (lə jit′ə mit) ***adj.*** **1** allowed by law or custom; lawful [a *legitimate* claim]. **2** reasonable; to be expected [a *legitimate* complaint]. **3** born of parents who are married to each other [a *legitimate* child]. —**le·git·i·ma·cy** (lə jit′ə mə sē) ***n.***

**leg·ume** (leg′yo͞om *or* li gyo͞om′) ***n.*** any plant of a large family with seeds growing in pods, as peas, beans, and lentils. Because they store up nitrates, legumes are often plowed under to fertilize the soil.

**lei** (lā *or* lā′ē) ***n.*** a wreath of flowers, often worn around the neck in Hawaii. *See the picture.* —*pl.* **leis**

**Leib·niz** (līb′nits), **Gottfried Wilhelm von** 1646–1716; German philosopher and mathematician. His name is also spelled **Leibnitz.**

**Leip·zig** (līp′sig) a city in central East Germany.

**lei·sure** (lē′zhər *or* lezh′ər) ***n.*** free time not taken up with work or duty, that a person may use for rest or recreation. ◆***adj.*** free and not busy; spare [*leisure* time]. —**at leisure, 1** having free or spare time. **2** with no hurry. **3** not busy or working. —**at one's leisure,** when one has the time.

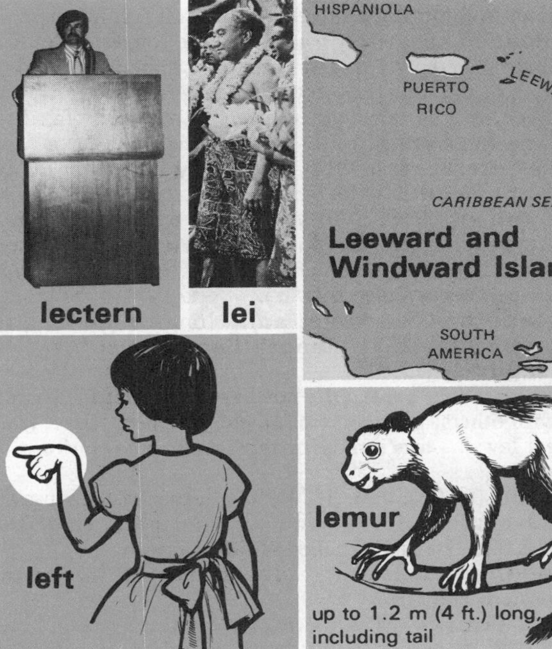


lectern

lei

left

lemur

up to 1.2 m (4 ft.) long, including tail

**lei·sure·ly** (lē′zhər lē *or* lezh′ər lē) ***adj.*** without hurrying; slow [a *leisurely* walk]. ◆***adv.*** in a slow, unhurried way [We talked *leisurely.*] 419

**lem·ming** (lem′iŋ) ***n.*** a small animal like a mouse with a short tail. It lives in the arctic. Some lemmings at times migrate in very large numbers and crowd into the sea, where they drown.

**lem·on** (lem′ən) ***n.*** **1** a small citrus fruit with a yellow skin and a juicy, sour pulp, used to make drinks or to flavor foods. **2** the tree it grows on. **3** pale yellow.

**lem·on·ade** (lem ə nād′) ***n.*** a drink made of lemon juice, sugar, and water.

**le·mur** (lē′mər) ***n.*** a small animal related to the monkey, with large eyes and soft, woolly fur. *See the picture.*

**Le·na** (lē′nə) a river in the U.S.S.R., in east central Siberia.

**lend** (lend) ***v.*** **1** to let someone use something for a while: *opposite of* **borrow** [Will you *lend* me your umbrella until tomorrow?] **2** to give something to someone who must later give back an equal thing, sometimes with interest [to *lend* $100 at 8% interest; to *lend* a cup of sugar]. **3** to give a part or share of; add [The flowers *lend* gaiety to the room.] —**lent, lend′ing** —**lend itself to,** to be useful or suitable for. —**lend′er** ***n.***

**length** (leŋkth) ***n.*** **1** the measure of how long a thing is; distance from one end to the other end or

| | | | | | | | |
|---|---|---|---|---|---|---|---|
| **a** | fat | **ir** | here | **ou** | out | **zh** | leisure |
| **ā** | ape | **ī** | bite, fire | **u** | up | **ŋ** | ring |
| **ä** | car, lot | **ō** | go | **ur** | fur | | a *in* ago |
| **e** | ten | **ô** | law, horn | **ch** | chin | | e *in* agent |
| **er** | care | **oi** | oil | **sh** | she | **ə =** | i *in* unity |
| **ē** | even | **oo** | look | **th** | thin | | o *in* collect |
| **i** | hit | **o͞o** | tool | ***th*** | then | | u *in* focus |

time from beginning to end [a rope 20 feet in *length;* a movie 90 minutes in *length*]. **2** the longest side of a thing [*length,* width, and breadth]. **3** the fact of being long or too long [I object to the *length* of the car.] **4** a piece of a certain length [a *length* of pipe]. —**at full length,** stretched out. —**at length,** **1** after a long time; finally. **2** in full. —**go to any length** or **go to great lengths,** to do whatever is necessary.

**length·en** (leŋkth′'n) ***v.*** to make or become longer.

**length·wise** (leŋkth′wīz) ***adj., adv.*** in the direction of the length [Carry the box in *lengthwise.*] *Also written* **length·ways** (leŋkth′wāz).

☆**length·y** (leŋkth′ē) ***adj.*** long or too long [a *lengthy* speech]. —**length′i·er, length′i·est** —**length′i·ly *adv.***

**len·ient** (lēn′yənt) ***adj.*** not harsh or strict in dealing with others; gentle, merciful, etc. [a *lenient* judge; *lenient* laws]. —**len′ien·cy** or **len′ience *n.*** —**len′ient·ly *adv.***

**Len·in** (len′in), **V. I.** 1870–1924; leader of the Russian Revolution of 1917 and the first premier of the U.S.S.R. He is also called **Nikolai Lenin.**

**Len·in·grad** (len′in grad) a seaport in the northwestern U.S.S.R.

**lens** (lenz) ***n.*** **1** a piece of clear glass, plastic, etc. curved on one or both sides so as to bring together or spread rays of light that pass through it. Lenses are used in eyeglasses, cameras, microscopes, etc. **2** a clear part of the eye that focuses light rays on the retina. *See the picture for* **eye.**



We took this word directly from the Latin word *lens,* meaning "lentil." Why? Because a lens that has both of its sides curved slightly outward looks very much like a lentil seed.

**Lent** (lent) ***n.*** the forty weekdays from Ash Wednesday to Easter, a time of fasting and repenting in Christian churches. —**Lent·en** or **lent·en** (lent′'n) ***adj.***

**lent** (lent) *past tense and past participle of* **lend.**

**len·til** (lent′'l) ***n.*** **1** a plant of the legume family, with small, nearly flat seeds that grow in pods and are used as food. **2** the seed itself.

**Le·o** (lē′ō) the fifth sign of the zodiac, for the period from July 22 to August 21: *also called* the Lion. *See the picture for* **zodiac.**

**le·o·nine** (lē′ə nīn) ***adj.*** of or like a lion.

**leop·ard** (lep′ərd) ***n.*** **1** a large, fierce animal of the cat family, having a tan coat with black spots. It is found in Africa and Asia. *See the picture.* **2** *another name for* **jaguar.**

**le·o·tard** (lē′ə tärd) ***n.*** a tightfitting, one-piece garment worn by dancers, acrobats, etc. *See the picture.*

**lep·er** (lep′ər) ***n.*** a person who has leprosy.

**lep·re·chaun** (lep′rə kôn) ***n.*** an elf in Irish legends who can show a buried crock of gold to anyone who catches him.

**lep·ro·sy** (lep′rə sē) ***n.*** a disease that causes open sores and white scabs and that slowly wastes away parts of the body. —**lep′rous *adj.***

**Les·bos** (lez′bäs *or* lez′bəs) a Greek island in the Aegean Sea, off the coast of Turkey.

**le·sion** (lē′zhən) ***n.*** a hurt or injury, especially a sore or wound in some part of the body.

**Le·sot·ho** (le sut′hō) a country in southern Africa, surrounded by South Africa.

**less** (les) ***adj.*** not so much, so many, so great, etc.; smaller, fewer, etc. [6 is *less* than 8.] *See the note in color at* **few.** ◆***adv.*** not so much; to a smaller or lower degree [Please talk *less* and work more.] —*Less* is a comparative form of **little.** ◆***n.*** a smaller amount [He ate *less* than I did.] ◆***prep.*** minus [She earns $7,000 *less* taxes.] —**less and less,** to an ever smaller degree.

**-less** (lis) *a suffix meaning:* **1** without [A *worthless* thing is without worth.] **2** that does not or cannot be [A *ceaseless* effort does not cease. A *dauntless* person cannot be daunted.]

**les·see** (les ē′) ***n.*** a person to whom property is leased; tenant.

**less·en** (les′'n) ***v.*** to make or become less [Your help *lessens* my work. The rain *lessened.*]

**less·er** (les′ər) ***adj.*** smaller, less, or less important [a *lesser* evil].

**les·son** (les′'n) ***n.*** **1** something to be learned, as by a student; teaching done during one class period [Did you study today's history *lesson?*] **2** something a person needs to learn in order to be safe, happy, etc. [My narrow escape taught me a *lesson.*] **3** a part of the Bible, read during a church service.

**les·sor** (les′ôr) ***n.*** a person who gives a lease on some property; landlord.

**lest** (lest) ***conj.*** **1** for fear that [Speak softly *lest* you be overheard.] **2** that: *used after words that show fear* [I was afraid *lest* he might fall.]

**let** (let) ***v.*** **1** to not keep from doing something; allow; permit [They *let* me help.] **2** to allow to pass, come, or go [*Let* them in.] **3** to rent [We *let* our spare room.] **4** to cause to flow out [to *let* blood]. —**let, let′ting** *Let* may be used as a helping verb with other verbs to give commands or make suggestions or dares [*Let* us give generously. Just *let* them try to stop us.] —**let alone,** **1** to keep away from; not disturb. **2** not to mention; much less [I can't even walk, *let alone* run.] —**let down,** **1** to lower. **2** to disappoint. —**let off,** **1** to give forth [to *let off* steam]. **2** to treat in a mild or gentle way. —**let on,** **1** to pretend. **2** to show that one is aware of something. *This phrase is used only in everyday talk.* —**let out,** **1** to allow to flow or run away; release. **2** to make a garment larger. —**let up,** to slow down or stop. —☆**let up on,** to stop dealing harshly with: *used only in everyday talk.*

SYNONYMS: **Let** is the everyday word for giving someone permission to do something [Will you *let* us go?] but often it suggests simply not doing anything to keep something from happening [I'm *letting* my hair grow.] **Permit** and **allow** are more formal words. **Permit** is used when someone who is in charge says yes to a request [The librarian *permitted* our club to use the meeting room.] **Allow** is used when certain rules that might keep someone from doing something are set aside by those who have the power to do so [Honor students are *allowed* to miss exams.]

**-let** (lit) *a suffix meaning* small [A *booklet* is a small book.]

**le·thal** (lē′thəl) ***adj.*** causing death; deadly; fatal [a *lethal* blow].

**leth·ar·gy** (leth′ər jē) ***n.*** the condition of being very tired or sleepy; lack of energy. —**le·thar·gic** (li thär′jik) ***adj.*** —**le·thar′gi·cal·ly** ***adv.***

**Le·the** (lē′thē) in Greek and Roman myths, a river in Hades that made those who drank from it forget everything.

**let's** (lets) let us.

**let·ter** (let′ər) ***n.*** **1** any of the marks used in writing or printing to stand for a sound of speech; character of an alphabet. **2** a written message, usually sent by mail. **3** the exact or strict meaning, as different from the purpose or spirit [The judge enforced the *letter* of the law.] ☆**4** the first letter of the name of a school or college, given as a prize to students who have done very well in sports, etc. **5 letters,** *pl.* the work of a writer; literature. ◆***v.*** to print letters by hand [Will you *letter* this poster?] —**to the letter,** exactly as written or ordered.

**let·ter·head** (let′ər hed) ***n.*** a printed name and address at the top of a sheet of letter paper.

**let·ter·ing** (let′ər iŋ) ***n.*** **1** the act of printing, stamping, or carving letters on something. **2** letters made in this way.

**let·ter-per·fect** (let′ər pur′fikt) ***adj.*** correct in every detail; perfect.

**let·tuce** (let′is) ***n.*** a plant with crisp, green leaves that are much used in salads.

Our word **lettuce** comes from the Latin word for milk. The root and stems of the lettuce plant contain a white, milky juice.

☆**let·up** (let′up) ***n.*** a becoming slower or less, or a stopping: *used only in everyday talk.*

**leu·ke·mi·a** (lo͞o kē′mē ə) ***n.*** a disease in which too many leukocytes are formed.

**leu·ko·cyte** (lo͞o′kə sīt) ***n.*** any of the small, white cells in the blood that kill germs; white corpuscle.

☆**lev·ee** (lev′ē) ***n.*** **1** a bank built along a river to keep it from overflowing. **2** a landing place for ships, along a river.

**lev·el** (lev′'l) ***adj.*** **1** with no part higher than any other part; flat and even [a *level* plain]. **2** as high as something else; even [Make this pile *level* with the other.] **3** even with the top or rim; not heaping [a *level* cup of sugar]. **4** not excited or confused; calm or sensible [Keep a *level* head on your shoulders.] ◆***n.*** **1** a small tube of liquid in a frame that is placed on a surface to see if the surface is level. A bubble in the liquid moves to the center of the tube when the frame is level. *See the picture.* **2** height [The water in the tank rose to a *level* of five feet.] *See also* **sea level. 3** the same even line or surface [The tops of the pictures are on a *level* with each other.] **4** a stage or degree, as of position or rank [the reading *level* of sixth graders]. ◆***v.*** **1** to make level or flat [to *level* ground with a bulldozer]. **2** to knock to the ground [A storm *leveled* that tree.] **3** to raise and aim [to *level* a gun at a target]. —**lev′eled** or **lev′elled, lev′el·ing** or **lev′el·ling** —**level off, 1** to give a flat, even surface to. **2** to come or bring into a level position [Airplanes *level off* just before landing.] —**one's level best,** the best one can do: *used only in everyday talk.* —☆**on the level,** honest and fair: *a slang phrase.* —**lev′el·er** or **lev′el·ler** ***n.*** —**lev′el·ness** ***n.***

☆**lev·el·head·ed** (lev′'l hed′id) ***adj.*** having or showing good sense and an even temper; sensible.

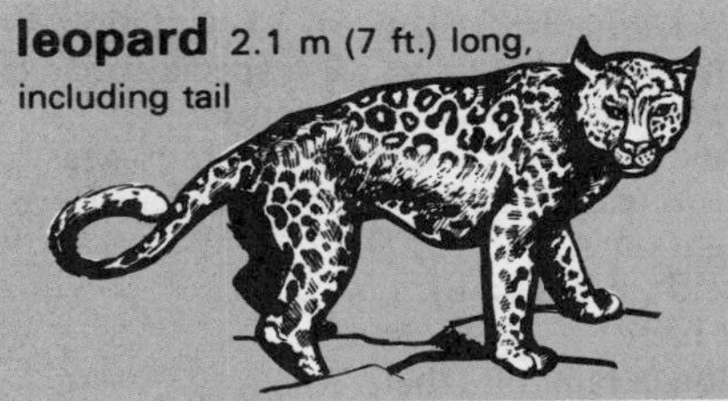
**leopard** 2.1 m (7 ft.) long, including tail

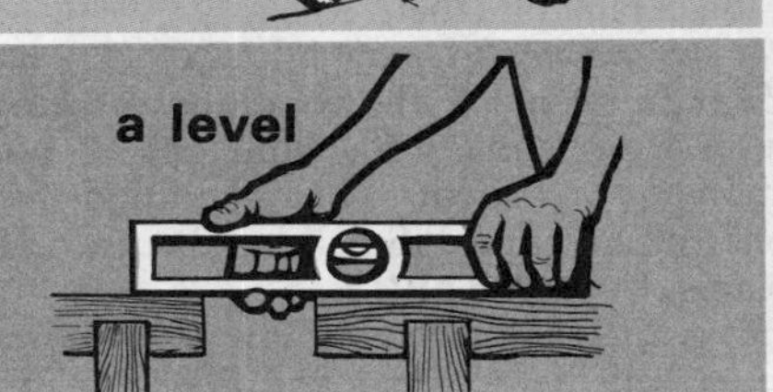
**a level**

**leotards**

**lev·er** (lev′ər *or* lē′vər) ***n.*** **1** a bar that can be rested on a support (the *fulcrum*) and pushed down at one end to lift a weight at the other. *See the picture for* **fulcrum. 2** any bar that can be turned or moved to work something [a gearshift *lever*].

**lev·er·age** (lev′ər ij *or* lē′vər ij) ***n.*** **1** the working of a lever. **2** extra power that comes from using a lever [We put a wedge under the crowbar to get *leverage.*]

**Le·vi** (lē′vī) in the Bible, one of Jacob's sons, or the tribe descended from him.

**le·vi·a·than** (lə vī′ə thən) ***n.*** **1** a large sea animal mentioned in the Bible. **2** anything huge or very powerful.



☆**Le·vi's** (lē′vīz) *a trademark for* tightfitting trousers of heavy denim.

**Le·vite** (lē′vīt) ***n.*** in the Bible, a member of the tribe of Levi. The Levites were chosen to assist the Jewish priests.

**Le·vit·i·cus** (lə vit′i kəs) the third book of the Bible.

**lev·i·ty** (lev′ə tē) ***n.*** lively fun or joking, especially when it is out of place; lack of seriousness.

**lev·y** (lev′ē) ***v.*** **1** to order the payment of [to *levy* a tax]. **2** to force into military service; enlist [to *levy* troops]. **3** to wage; carry on [to *levy* war]. —**lev′ied, lev′y·ing** ◆***n.*** **1** a levying of a tax, of troops, etc. **2** the money, troops, etc. collected by levying. —*pl.* **lev′ies**

**lewd** (lo͞od) ***adj.*** showing interest in sex in a way that is thought to be immoral or improper. —**lewd′ly** ***adv.*** —**lewd′ness** ***n.***

**Lew·is** (lo͞o′is), **Mer·i·weth·er** (mer′ē weth′ər) 1774–1809; U.S. explorer and leader, along with **William Clark,** of the Lewis and Clark expedition (1804–1806) to the northwestern part of the U.S.

**Lewis, Sin·clair** (sin′kler) 1885–1951; U.S. writer of novels.

**lex·i·cog·ra·phy** (lek′sə käg′rə fē) ***n.*** the science or work of writing dictionaries. —**lex′i·cog′ra·pher** ***n.***

| | | | | | | | |
|---|---|---|---|---|---|---|---|
| **a** | fat | **ir** | here | **ou** | out | **zh** | leisure |
| **ā** | ape | **ī** | bite, fire | **u** | up | **ŋ** | ring |
| **ä** | car, lot | **ō** | go | **ur** | fur | | a *in* ago |
| **e** | ten | **ô** | law, horn | **ch** | chin | | e *in* agent |
| **er** | care | **oi** | oil | **sh** | she | ə = | i *in* unity |
| **ē** | even | **oo** | look | **th** | thin | | o *in* collect |
| **i** | hit | **o͞o** | tool | ***th*** | then | | u *in* focus |

**lex·i·con** (lek′si kən *or* lek′si kän) ***n.*** **1** a dictionary, especially of an ancient language. **2** a special vocabulary, as the words used in a certain science.

**Lex·ing·ton** (lek′siŋ tən) a town in eastern Massachusetts, where an early battle of the American Revolution was fought on April 19, 1775.

**lf** or **l.f.** left field (in baseball).

**l.h.** or **LH** left hand.

**Lha·sa** (lä′sə) the capital of Tibet.

**Li** *the symbol for the chemical element* lithium.

**li·a·bil·i·ty** (lī′ə bil′ə tē) ***n.*** **1** the condition of being liable [*liability* to error; *liability* for damages]. **2 liabilities,** *pl.* money owed; debts. **3** a condition that acts against one; disadvantage [Small hands can be a *liability* to a pianist.] —*pl.* **li′a·bil′i·ties**

**li·a·ble** (lī′ə b′l) ***adj.*** **1** obliged by law to pay; responsible [We caused the accident and are *liable* for the damage done.] **2** likely to have or get; subject to [run-down and *liable* to colds]. **3** (*often* lī′b′l) likely to do, cause, etc. something unpleasant or not wanted [The boxes are *liable* to fall.]

**li·ai·son** (lē′ə zän *or* lē ā′zän) ***n.*** a linking up of groups or parts, as of an army, so that they can work together effectively.

**li·ar** (lī′ər) ***n.*** a person who tells lies.

**lib** (lib) ***n.*** *a shorter form of* **liberation.**

**li·ba·tion** (lī bā′shən) ***n.*** **1** the ceremony of pouring out wine or oil in honor of a god. **2** the wine or oil poured out.

422 **li·bel** (lī′b′l) ***n.*** **1** anything written or printed that harms a person's reputation in an unfair way. **2** the act or crime of publishing such a thing. ◆***v.*** to publish a libel against. —**li′beled** or **li′belled, li′bel·ing** or **li′bel·ling** —**li′bel·er** or **li′bel·ler** ***n.***

**li·bel·ous** or **li·bel·lous** (lī′b′l əs) ***adj.*** containing or making a libel against someone.

**lib·er·al** (lib′ər əl) ***adj.*** **1** giving freely; generous [a *liberal* contributor to charity]. **2** more than enough or than might be expected; large [a *liberal* reward]. **3** open to new ideas; broad-minded; tolerant. **4** broad in range; not limited to one subject or field of study [a *liberal* education]. **5** in favor of reform or progress in politics, religion, etc. ◆***n.*** a person who is in favor of reform and progress. —**lib′er·al·ly** ***adv.***

**liberal arts** literature, philosophy, languages, history, etc. as courses of study.

**lifeboat**

**lichens**

**lie detector**

**lib·er·al·ism** (lib′ər əl iz'm) ***n.*** the quality of being liberal, as in politics; liberal beliefs.

**lib·er·al·i·ty** (lib′ə ral′ə tē) ***n.*** the quality of being liberal; generosity, broad-mindedness, etc.

**lib·er·al·ize** (lib′ər ə līz′) ***v.*** to make or become liberal. —**lib′er·al·ized′, lib′er·al·iz′ing** —**lib′er·al·i·za′tion** ***n.***

**lib·er·ate** (lib′ə rāt) ***v.*** to free as from slavery [to *liberate* prisoners of war]. —**lib′er·at·ed, lib′er·at·ing** — **lib′er·a·tor** ***n.***

**lib·er·a·tion** (lib′ə rā′shən) ***n.*** **1** the act of liberating. **2** the condition of being set free [our *liberation* from the grip of winter weather]. ☆**3** a doing away with customs, laws, etc. that keep a certain group of people from being treated fairly [the movement for women's *liberation*].

**Li·ber·i·a** (lī bir′ē ə) a country on the western coast of Africa. —**Li·ber′i·an** ***adj., n.***

**lib·er·tine** (lib′ər tēn) ***n.*** a man of loose morals, who makes love to many women.

**lib·er·ty** (lib′ər tē) ***n.*** **1** the condition of being free from control by others [The slaves fought for their *liberty*.] **2** the right or power to believe and act in the way one thinks is right ["sweet land of *liberty*"]. **3** the area in which one is free to move or go [This pass gives us the *liberty* of the whole library.] **4** permission given a sailor to go ashore. —*pl.* **lib′er·ties** —**at liberty, 1** not shut up; free. **2** allowed; permitted [I am not *at liberty* to say.] **3** not busy; not in use. — **take liberties,** to be too free, bold, or friendly.

☆**Liberty Bell** the bell of Independence Hall in Philadelphia. It was rung on July 8, 1776, to announce the independence of the United States.

**Li·bra** (lē′brə *or* lī′brə) the seventh sign of the zodiac, for the period from September 23 to October 23: *also called* the Scales. *See the picture for* **zodiac.**

**li·brar·i·an** (lī brer′ē ən) ***n.*** **1** a person who is in charge of a library. **2** a person who has had special training in order to work in a library.

**li·brar·y** (lī′brer′ē) ***n.*** **1** a place where a collection of books is kept for reading or borrowing. **2** a collection of books. —*pl.* **li′brar′ies**

> Long ago, people used the inner bark of trees to write on. In Latin, the word for such bark changed in meaning as time went by and became the word for a book. Our word **library** comes from it.

☆**library science** the study of how libraries are organized and run.

**li·bret·to** (li bret′ō) ***n.*** **1** the words of an opera, oratorio, etc. **2** a book containing these words. —*pl.* **li·bret′tos** or **li·bret·ti** (li bret′ē)

**Lib·y·a** (lib′ē ə) a country in northern Africa. —**Lib′y·an** ***adj., n.***

**lice** (līs) ***n.*** *plural of* **louse.**

**li·cense** (līs′'ns) ***n.*** **1** a paper, card, etc. showing that one is permitted by law to do something [a marriage *license;* driver's *license*]. **2** freedom to ignore the usual rules [To take poetic *license* is to ignore, as in a poem, the usual rules of style, logic, etc. in order to gain a special effect.] **3** freedom of action or speech that goes beyond what is right or proper [Booing in a courtroom isn't free speech—it's *license*.] ◆***v.*** to give a license to; permit by law [Are they *licensed* to fish?] — **li′censed, li′cens·ing**

**li·cen·tious** (lī sen′shəs) ***adj.*** living a wild, immoral life. —**li·cen′tious·ly** ***adv.*** —**li·cen′tious·ness** ***n.***

**li·chen** (lī′kən) ***n.*** a plant that looks like dry moss and grows in patches on rocks and trees. *See the picture.*

**lick** (lik) ***v.*** **1** to rub the tongue over [to *lick* one's lips]. **2** to remove by lapping up with the tongue [The dog *licked* the gravy from the floor.] **3** to pass lightly over like a tongue [Flames *licked* the roof of the house.] **4** to whip or spank: *used only in everyday talk.* **5** to defeat: *used only in everyday talk* [Our team can *lick* theirs.] ◆***n.*** **1** the act of licking with the tongue. **2** *a shorter form of* **salt lick.** **3** a small amount; bit [I haven't done a *lick* of work.] **4** a sharp blow: *used only in everyday talk.* —**lick into shape,** to bring into proper condition: *used only in everyday talk.*

**lic·o·rice** (lik′ər ish *or* lik′ər is) ***n.*** **1** a black, sweet flavoring made from the root of a European plant. **2** candy flavored with this.

**lid** (lid) ***n.*** **1** a movable cover for a pot, box, trunk, etc. **2** *a shorter form of* **eyelid.**

**lie**[1] (lī) ***v.*** **1** to stretch one's body in a flat position along the ground, a bed, etc. **2** to be in a flat position; rest [A book is *lying* on the table.] **3** to be or stay in some condition [The treasure *lay* hidden for years.] **4** to be placed or located [Ohio *lies* east of Indiana.] **5** to be or exist [Our best hope *lies* in new laws.] **6** to be buried [Here *lie* the bones of many kings.] —**lay, lain, ly′ing** —☆**lie over,** to stay and wait until later. —**take something lying down,** to take punishment, a wrong, etc. without fighting back or resisting.

**lie**[2] (lī) ***n.*** something said that is not true, especially if it is said on purpose to fool or trick someone. ◆***v.*** **1** to tell a lie; say what is not true. **2** to give a false idea [Your camera *lied;* I'm not that fat.] —**lied, ly′ing**

**Liech·ten·stein** (lēk′tən shtīn) a small country in Europe, west of Austria.

☆**lie detector** an instrument used on persons suspected of lying. It records certain bodily changes, as in pulse rate, blood pressure, etc., that are thought to occur when the suspect tells lies in answering questions. *See the picture.*

**lief** (lēf) ***adv.*** willingly; gladly: *no longer much used* [I would as *lief* die as tell the secret.]

**liege** (lēj) ***adj.*** in the Middle Ages, having a right to the loyal service of one's vassals [a *liege* lord]. Also, owing such service [*liege* subjects]. ◆***n.*** a liege lord or his vassal.

**li·en** (lēn *or* lē′ən) ***n.*** a legal claim that one has on the property of a person who owes one money [The bank has a *lien* on my house until I pay back my loan.]

**lieu** (lo͞o) ***n.*** place. This word is now used only in the phrase **in lieu of,** meaning "instead of" or "in place of."

**Lieut.** *abbreviation for* **Lieutenant.**

**lieu·ten·ant** (lo͞o ten′ənt) ***n.*** **1** an army or air force officer ranking below a captain. A **second lieutenant** is the lowest ranking officer. A **first lieutenant** ranks between a second lieutenant and a captain. **2** a navy officer ranking just above a lieutenant junior grade. **3** a person who assists someone of higher rank [The president of the company isn't here, but one of her *lieutenants* can discuss the matter with you.]

**lieutenant colonel** a military officer ranking just above a major.

**lieutenant commander** a navy officer ranking just above a lieutenant.

**lieutenant general** a military officer ranking just above a major general.

**lieutenant governor** the official of a State who ranks just below the governor and takes the governor's place if the governor dies or is away.

**lieutenant junior grade** a navy officer ranking just above an ensign.

**life** (līf) ***n.*** **1** the quality of plants and animals that makes it possible for them to take in food, grow, produce others of their kind, etc. and that makes them different from rocks, water, etc. [Death is the loss of *life.*] **2** a living thing; especially, a human being [The crash took six *lives.*] **3** living things as a group [the plant *life* in the pond]. **4** the time that a person or thing is alive or lasts [Her *life* has just begun. What is the *life* of a battery?] **5** the story of a person's life; biography [Boswell wrote a *life* of Samuel Johnson.] **6** the way that a person or group lives [a *life* of ease; the military *life*]. **7** liveliness or energy [a person who is full of *life*]. —*pl.* **lives** —**bring to life, 1** to make conscious again. **2** to make lively. —**come to life, 1** to become conscious again. **2** to become lively. —**for dear life,** with a desperate effort. —☆**not on your life,** certainly not: *used only in everyday talk.* —**take one's own life,** to kill oneself. —**true to life,** true to the way things really are.

**life belt** a life preserver in the form of a belt. 

**life·blood** (līf′blud) ***n.*** **1** the blood that one needs to live. **2** the necessary part of anything [Research is the *lifeblood* of science.]

**life·boat** (līf′bōt) ***n.*** **1** any of the small boats carried by a ship for use if the ship must be abandoned. *See the picture.* **2** a sturdy boat kept on a shore, for use in rescuing people in danger of drowning.

**life·guard** (līf′gärd) ***n.*** ☆an expert swimmer hired to keep people from drowning, as at a beach.

**life insurance** insurance by which a certain sum of money is paid to the family or others when the person who is insured dies.

**life jacket** a life preserver that looks like a jacket without sleeves.

**life·less** (līf′lis) ***adj.*** **1** no longer living; dead [the *lifeless* body of the victim]. **2** that never had life [a *lifeless* statue]. **3** that has no living beings [a *lifeless* planet]. **4** dull; not lively [a *lifeless* expression].

**life·like** (līf′līk) ***adj.*** like real life; that looks alive [a *lifelike* photograph].

**life·line** (līf′līn) ***n.*** **1** a rope for saving life, as one thrown to a person in the water. **2** the rope used to raise and lower a diver in the water. **3** a route for trade, supplies, etc. that is very important.

**life·long** (līf′lôŋ′) ***adj.*** lasting or not changing during one's life [a *lifelong* love].

| | | | | | | | |
|---|---|---|---|---|---|---|---|
| **a** | fat | **ir** | here | **ou** | out | **zh** | leisure |
| **ā** | ape | **ī** | bite, fire | **u** | up | **ŋ** | ring |
| **ä** | car, lot | **ō** | go | **ur** | fur | | a *in* ago |
| **e** | ten | **ô** | law, horn | **ch** | chin | | e *in* agent |
| **er** | care | **oi** | oil | **sh** | she | **ə** = | i *in* unity |
| **ē** | even | **oo** | look | **th** | thin | | o *in* collect |
| **i** | hit | **o͞o** | tool | ***th*** | then | | u *in* focus |

**life preserver** a belt, jacket, or large ring that can keep a person afloat in water. *See the picture.*

☆**life·sav·er** (līf′sā′vər) ***n.*** a person or thing that saves people from drowning. —**life′sav′ing *n., adj.***

**life-size** (līf′sīz′) ***adj.*** as big as the person or thing represented [a *life-size* statue of the president]. *Also* **life-sized.**

☆**life style** the way one lives as shown by one's activities, possessions, attitudes, type of home, etc.

**life·time** (līf′tīm) ***n.*** the length of time that someone or something lives or lasts.

**lift** (lift) ***v.*** **1** to bring up to a higher place; raise [Please *lift* that box onto the truck.] **2** to make higher or better in rank, condition, value, etc. [to *lift* oneself up from poverty]. **3** to rise or go up [Our spirits *lifted* when spring came.] **4** to end [to *lift* a blockade, siege, ban, etc.] **5** to rise and vanish [The fog *lifted.*] **6** to carry by aircraft [Supplies were *lifted* to the snowbound crew.] **7** to steal: *slang in this meaning.* ◆***n.*** **1** the act of lifting. **2** the amount lifted, or the distance that something is lifted. **3** a raising of one's spirits [Her kind words gave me a *lift.*] **4** a ride in the direction one is going. **5** help of any kind. **6** a device for carrying people up or down a slope [a ski *lift*]. **7** a device for lifting an automobile for repairs. **8** an elevator: *a British meaning.* —**lift up one's voice,** to speak or sing out loudly. —**lift′er *n.***

> SYNONYMS: To **lift** is to use some effort in bringing something to a higher position [Help me *lift* the TV set.] To **raise** is also to lift something, but **raise** means especially to bring something upright by lifting one end [to *raise* a flagpole].

☆**lift·off** (lift′ôf) ***n.*** **1** the sudden upward movement as of a spacecraft or helicopter when it is launched or takes off. **2** the moment when this takes place.

**lig·a·ment** (lig′ə mənt) ***n.*** a band of strong, tough tissue that joins bones or holds organs of the body in place.

**lig·a·ture** (lig′ə chər) ***n.*** **1** something used for tying or binding; especially, a thread used by a doctor to tie up the end of a bleeding artery or vein. **2** two or more letters joined together as one character in printing.

> Some **ligatures** used in pronunciations in this dictionary are th, sh, ch, zh, ơo, σi, σu, and ŋ.

**light**[1] (līt) ***n.*** **1** the form of energy that acts on the eyes so that one can see [*Light* travels at the speed of nearly 300,000 kilometers per second, or 186,000 miles per second.] **2** brightness or radiance [the *light* of a candle; the *light* of love in his eyes]. **3** something that gives light, as a lamp [Turn off the *light.*] **4** a flame or spark to start something burning [a *light* for a pipe]. **5** helpful information or knowledge [Can you shed *light* on the problem?] **6** public notice [to bring new facts to *light*]. **7** the way something is seen [This report places her in a favorable *light.*] **8** an outstanding person [one of the shining *lights* of our school]. ◆***adj.*** **1** having light; not dark [It's getting *light* outside.] **2** having a pale color; fair [*light* hair]. ◆***adv.*** not brightly; in a pale way [a *light* green dress]. ◆***v.*** **1** to set on fire or catch fire; burn [to *light* a match; the candle *lighted* at once]. **2** to cause to give off light [to *light* a lamp]. **3** to cast light on or in [Lamps *light* the streets.] **4** to guide by giving light [A beacon *lights* the ships to harbor.] **5** to become light, bright, or lively [Her face *lighted* up with joy.] —**light′ed** or **lit, light′ing** —**in the light of,** knowing that; considering. —**strike a light,** to make a flame, as with a match. —**light′ness *n.***

**light**[2] (līt) ***adj.*** **1** having little weight, especially for its size; not heavy [a *light* cargo; a *light* suit]. **2** little or less than usual in force, quantity, etc. [a *light* blow; a *light* rain; a *light* meal]. **3** not serious or important [*light* conversation; *light* reading]. **4** not sad; happy [*light* spirits]. **5** easy to do, put up with, etc.; not hard or severe [*light* work; a *light* tax]. **6** dizzy or silly [to feel *light* in the head]. **7** soft and spongy [a *light* cake]. **8** moving in a quick, easy way; nimble [*light* on her feet]. **9** having small weapons or thin armor [a *light* cruiser]. ◆***v.*** **1** to get down, as from a horse. **2** to come to rest after flying; land [birds *lighting* on the roof]. **3** to come by chance; happen [She *lighted* on the right answer.] —**light′ed** or **lit, light′ing** —☆**light into,** to attack or to scold: *used only in everyday talk.* —☆**light out,** to leave suddenly: *used only in everyday talk.* —**make light of,** to treat as silly or unimportant. —**light′ness *n.***

**light·en**[1] (līt′'n) ***v.*** **1** to make or become light or brighter; brighten. **2** to shine brightly; flash.

**light·en**[2] (līt′'n) ***v.*** **1** to make or become less heavy [to *lighten* a load]. **2** to make or become more cheerful [Lou's jokes *lightened* our spirits.]

**light·er**[1] (līt′ər) ***n.*** a thing that starts something burning [a cigarette *lighter*].

**light·er**[2] (līt′ər) ***n.*** a large, open barge used for loading and unloading ships offshore.

**light-foot·ed** (līt′foot′id) ***adj.*** moving lightly and gracefully on one's feet; nimble.

**light·head·ed** (līt′hed′id) ***adj.*** **1** feeling dizzy. **2** not serious; silly or flighty.

**light·heart·ed** (līt′här′tid) ***adj.*** cheerful; free from care; not sad or worried.

**light·house** (līt′hous) ***n.*** a tower with a bright light on top to guide ships at night or in fog. *See the picture.*

**light·ly** (līt′lē) ***adv.*** **1** with little weight or force; gently [Leaves brushed *lightly* against his face.] **2** to a small degree; very little [She ate *lightly.*] **3** with grace and skill; nimbly [skipping *lightly* along]. **4** cheerfully; merrily. **5** without being concerned; carelessly [taking her responsibility *lightly*].

**light·ning** (līt′niŋ) ***n.*** a flash of light in the sky caused by the passing of electricity from one cloud to another or between a cloud and the earth.

☆**lightning bug** *another name for* **firefly**: *also* **lightning beetle.**

☆**lightning rod** a metal rod placed high on a building and connected to the ground so as to carry off lightning.

**light·some** (līt′səm) ***adj.*** **1** not serious; lighthearted. **2** graceful, lively, or nimble.

**light·weight** (līt′wāt) ***n.*** **1** a boxer or wrestler between a featherweight and a welterweight (in boxing, between 127 and 135 pounds). **2** a person or animal that weighs less than normal.

**light-year** (līt′yir′) ***n.*** the distance that light travels in a year, over 9 1/2 trillion kilometers, or about 6 trillion miles. The distance between stars is measured in light-years.

**lig·nite** (lig′nīt) ***n.*** a soft, dark-brown coal in which the grain of the original wood is seen.

**lik·a·ble** or **like·a·ble** (līk′ə b'l) ***adj.*** easy to like because pleasing, friendly, etc.

**like¹** (līk) ***prep.*** **1** somewhat the same as; similar to [hands *like* claws]. **2** in the same way as [crying *like* a baby]. **3** as one would expect of; typical of [It is not *like* her to be late.] **4** in the mood for [He felt *like* eating.] **5** as if there will be [It looks *like* rain.] ◆***adj.*** the same or nearly the same; equal or similar [a cup of sugar and a *like* amount of flour]. ◆***adv.*** likely: *used only in everyday talk* [*Like* as not, she is already here.] ◆***n.*** a person or thing equal or similar to another [I never saw the *like* of this snow.] ◆***conj.*** **1** the same as [It was just *like* you said.] **2** as if [It looks *like* you'll win.] *Used as a conjunction only in everyday talk.* —**and the like,** and others of the same kind. —**like anything, like crazy, like mad,** etc., with wild energy, great speed, etc.: *used only in everyday talk.* —**nothing like,** not at all like. —**something like,** almost like. —**the likes of,** any person or thing like: *used only in everyday talk.*

Many people who are careful about the way they speak do not use **like** as a conjunction in a sentence such as "She practices every day, *like* a guitarist should." Instead, they use **as**: "She practices every day, *as* a guitarist should."

**like²** (līk) ***v.*** **1** to be fond of or pleased with; enjoy [Neal *likes* dogs. I *like* to write.] **2** to want to have, do, be, etc.; wish [You may leave whenever you *like*. Would you *like* more milk?] —**liked, lik′ing** ◆***n.*** **likes,** *pl.* the things one enjoys or prefers [a list of Pat's *likes* and dislikes].

**-like** (līk) *a suffix meaning* like, like that of, typical of [A *ducklike* waddle is like the waddle of a duck.]

**like·li·hood** (līk′lē hood) ***n.*** the fact of being likely to happen; probability [There is a strong *likelihood* he will win.]

**like·ly** (līk′lē) ***adj.*** **1** apt to be, happen, do, etc.; to be expected [A storm is *likely* before noon.] *See* SYNONYMS *at* **probable. 2** seeming to be true; believable [a *likely* answer]. **3** seeming to be good, suitable, etc.; promising [a *likely* person for the job]. —**like′li·er, like′li·est** ◆***adv.*** probably [I will very *likely* go.]

**lik·en** (līk′'n) ***v.*** to describe as being like something else; compare [to *liken* a baby's smile to sunshine].

**like·ness** (līk′nis) ***n.*** **1** the fact of being like or similar [her *likeness* to her brother]. **2** shape or form [a cloud in the *likeness* of a cow]. **3** something that is like; copy; picture [The photograph is a good *likeness* of you.]

**like·wise** (līk′wīz) ***adv.*** **1** in the same way [They worked hard and we must do *likewise*.] **2** also; too [Jim will sing and Mary *likewise*.]

**lik·ing** (lī′king) ***n.*** the fact of enjoying or being fond of something; preference [a *liking* for sweets].

**li·lac** (lī′lək *or* lī′läk) ***n.*** **1** a shrub with clusters of tiny, sweet-smelling flowers, ranging in color from white to purple. *See the picture.* **2** the flower cluster of this shrub. **3** pale purple.

**lilt** (lilt) ***v.*** to sing or play with a light, graceful rhythm or swing. ◆***n.*** **1** a light, swaying rhythm or movement. **2** a tune or song with such a rhythm.

**lil·y** (lil′ē) ***n.*** **1** a plant that grows from a bulb and has white or colored flowers shaped like a trumpet. **2** any plant somewhat like this [the *waterlily*]. —*pl.* **lil′ies**

lighthouse

lily of the valley

lilac

life preserver

**lily of the valley** a low plant with tiny, sweet-smelling, white flowers growing along a single stem. *See the picture.* —*pl.* **lilies of the valley**

**Li·ma** (lē′mə) the capital of Peru.

**li·ma bean** (lī′mə) a broad, flat bean that grows in pods and is used for food: *also* **Lima bean.** 425

**limb** (lim) ***n.*** **1** an arm, leg, or wing. **2** a large branch of a tree.

**lim·ber** (lim′bər) ***adj.*** bending easily; not stiff; flexible; supple [the *limber* branches of a young tree; the *limber* body of an athlete]. ◆***v.*** to make or become limber [Exercise *limbers* the fingers.]

**lim·bo** (lim′bō) ***n.*** **1** *often* **Limbo,** a place near the borders of hell that some Christians believe in. The souls of unbaptized children and of good people who lived before Jesus are thought to go there after death. **2** the state of those who are forgotten or neglected [the *limbo* of election losers]. —*pl.* **lim′bos**

**Lim·bur·ger cheese** (lim′bər gər) a soft, white cheese with a strong smell.

**lime¹** (līm) ***n.*** a white substance got by burning limestone, shells, etc. It is used in making cement, mortar, and fertilizers. ◆***v.*** to put lime on; treat with lime [to *lime* the soil]. —**limed, lim′ing**

**lime²** (līm) ***n.*** **1** a fruit like a lemon, with a green skin and a sour, juicy pulp, used to make drinks or flavor foods. **2** the tree it grows on.

**lime·light** (līm′līt) ***n.*** **1** a very bright theater light used at one time to throw a beam of light on a part of the stage. **2** the condition of getting much attention from the public [Superstars are often in the *limelight*.]

| | | | | | | | | | |
|---|---|---|---|---|---|---|---|---|---|
| **a** | fat | **ir** | here | **ou** | out | **zh** | leisure | | |
| **ā** | ape | **ī** | bite, fire | **u** | up | **ng** | ring | | |
| **ä** | car, lot | **ō** | go | **ur** | fur | | | | a *in* ago |
| **e** | ten | **ô** | law, horn | **ch** | chin | | | | e *in* agent |
| **er** | care | **oi** | oil | **sh** | she | | **ə** | = | i *in* unity |
| **ē** | even | **oo** | look | **th** | thin | | | | o *in* collect |
| **i** | hit | **ōō** | tool | ***th*** | then | | | | u *in* focus |

**lim·er·ick** (lim′ər ik) ***n.*** a funny poem of five lines, with this kind of rhyme and rhythm:
"A flea and a fly in a flue
Were imprisoned, so what could they do?
Said the flea, 'Let us fly!'
Said the fly, 'Let us flee!'
So they flew through a flaw in the flue."

**lime·stone** (līm′stōn) ***n.*** rock containing calcium carbonate, used to make building stones, lime, etc. Marble is a kind of limestone.

**lim·it** (lim′it) ***n.*** **1** the point or line where something ends or that cannot be passed [There is a *limit* to my patience.] **2 limits,** *pl.* boundary lines; bounds [the city *limits*]. **3** the greatest amount allowed [A catch of ten trout is the *limit*.] ◆***v.*** to set a limit to; restrict [*Limit* your talk to ten minutes.] *See* SYNONYMS *at* **bound**[4]. —**the limit,** ☆any person or thing thought to be absolutely unbearable, remarkable, etc.: *used only in everyday talk.*

**lim·i·ta·tion** (lim′ə tā′shən) ***n.*** **1** something that restricts, holds in, or holds back [His chief *limitation* as a salesman is his shyness.] **2** a limiting or being limited.

**lim·it·ed** (lim′it id) ***adj.*** **1** having a limit or limits; restricted in some way [This offer is good for a *limited* time only.] ☆**2** making only a few stops [a *limited* bus].

**lim·it·less** (lim′it lis) ***adj.*** without limits or without an end; vast; infinite.



**limn** (lim) ***v.*** **1** to paint or draw, as a picture. **2** to describe in words.

**lim·ou·sine** (lim′ə zēn) ***n.*** **1** a large automobile driven by a chauffeur, who is sometimes separated from the passengers by a glass window. ☆**2** a buslike sedan used to carry passengers to or from an airport.

In the old days the people of the French province Limousin wore costumes with hoods, and now the word **limousine** means "hood" in French. Early limousines had the passenger section enclosed, with the top extended over the chauffeur's seat, looking somewhat like a hood.

**limp** (limp) ***v.*** to walk in an uneven way because of a lame leg. ◆***n.*** a lameness in walking. ◆***adj.*** not stiff or firm; flexible [as *limp* as a wet rag].

**limp·et** (lim′pit) ***n.*** a shellfish that clings to rocks and timbers with its thick foot.

**lim·pid** (lim′pid) ***adj.*** so clear that one can see through it [a *limpid* pool of water].

**linch·pin** (linch′pin) ***n.*** a pin that goes through the end of an axle outside the wheel to keep the wheel from coming off.

**Lin·coln** (liŋ′kən) the capital of Nebraska.

**Lin·coln** (liŋ′kən), **Abraham** 1809–1865; 16th president of the United States, from 1861 to 1865. He was assassinated.

**Lind·bergh** (lind′bərg), **Charles Augustus** 1902–1974; U.S. aviator. He made the first nonstop solo flight from New York to Paris, in 1927.

**lin·den** (lin′dən) ***n.*** a tree with yellowish flowers and heart-shaped leaves. *See the picture.*

**line**[1] (līn) ***n.*** **1** a cord, rope, string, etc. [a fishing *line;* a clothes*line*]. **2** a wire or pipe or a system of wires or pipes for carrying water, gas, electricity, etc. **3** a long, thin mark [*lines* made by a pen or pencil; *lines* formed in the face by wrinkles]. ☆**4** a border or boundary [to cross a State *line*]. **5 lines,** *pl.* outline or form in general [This house is built along modern *lines*.] **6** a row of persons or things [a *line* of people waiting to get in; a *line* of words across a page]. **7** a series of persons or things following each other [a *line* of Democratic presidents]. ☆**8** a company that carries people or goods by bus, ship, airplane, etc. **9** the path of something that moves [in the *line* of cannon fire]. **10** a way of thinking, acting, etc. [the *line* of an argument]. **11** a person's business, work, etc. [He's in the hardware *line*.] ☆**12** a supply of goods of a certain kind [This store carries a fine *line* of shoes.] **13** a short letter or note [Drop me a *line*.] **14 lines,** *pl.* all the speeches of a single actor in a play. ☆**15** the football players on a team arranged in a row even with the ball at the start of each play. **16** any of the imaginary circles that divide the earth into zones or parts [the date *line;* the *line* of the equator]. **17** in mathematics, the path of a moving point; especially, a straight line. **18** flattering or insincere talk: *used only in everyday talk.* ◆***v.*** **1** to mark with lines [Age has *lined* her face.] **2** to form a line along [Elms *line* the streets.] —**lined, lin′ing** —**all along the line,** everywhere. —**down the line,** completely; entirely. —**draw a line,** to set a limit. —☆**get a line on,** to find out about: *used only in everyday talk.* —**hold the line,** to stand firm; not allow anyone or anything to get through. —**in line,** in a straight row or in agreement. —**in line for,** being considered for. —**into line,** into a straight row or into agreement [to bring or come *into line*]. —**line of duty,** the work or duties one is expected to do [above and beyond the *line of duty*]. —**line out,** ☆to be put out in baseball by hitting a line drive that is caught by a fielder. —**line up,** to bring or come into a line, or row. —**on a line,** even or level. —**out of line,** **1** not in a straight line, or not in agreement. **2** impudent or rude.

**line**[2] (līn) ***v.*** to cover on the inside with a layer or lining [The coat is *lined* with fur.] —**lined, lin′ing**

**lin·e·age** (lin′ē ij) ***n.*** line of descent; ancestry.

**lin·e·al** (lin′ē əl) ***adj.*** **1** in the direct line of descent, as from parent to child to grandchild [George Washington has no *lineal* descendants.] **2** of a line or lines; linear.

**lin·e·a·ment** (lin′ē ə mənt) ***n.*** a special feature or part, especially of the face.

**lin·e·ar** (lin′ē ər) ***adj.*** **1** of, made of, or using a line or lines [*linear* boundaries]. **2** of length [*linear* measure].

☆**line·back·er** (līn′bak′ər) ***n.*** any of the football players who are placed directly behind the line, in a defensive position.

☆**line drive** a baseball that has been hit hard and moves in a line not far above the ground.

**line·man** (līn′mən) ***n.*** **1** a person whose work is putting up and repairing telephone, telegraph, or electric wires. *See the picture.* ☆**2** a football player in the line. —*pl.* **line′men**

**lin·en** (lin′ən) ***n.*** **1** a thread or cloth made of flax. **2** things made of linen, or of cotton, etc., as tablecloths, sheets, shirts, etc.

**lin·er** (lī′nər) ***n.*** ☆**1** a ship or airplane in regular service for a transportation line. ☆**2** *another name* *for* **line drive.** **3** something that fits inside something else [a helmet *liner*]. ☆**4** the cover of a long-playing record with information (**liner notes**) about the music.

**lines·man** (līnz′mən) ***n.*** **1** *another word for* **lineman.** **2** a football official who keeps track of the yards gained or lost. —*pl.* **lines′men**

☆**line·up** (līn′up′) ***n.*** **1** a number of persons or things in a line, especially a row of persons lined up by the police to be identified. **2** a list of the players on a team, arranged in a certain order.

**-ling** (liŋ) *a suffix meaning:* **1** small [A *duckling* is a small duck.] **2** low in rank or respect [A *hireling,* who can be hired to do almost anything for pay, is not respected.]

**lin·ger** (liŋ′gər) ***v.*** to keep on staying, as if not wanting to leave; loiter [The last guest *lingered.*]

**lin·ge·rie** (län zhə rā′ *or* lan jə rē′) ***n.*** women's underwear.

**lin·go** (liŋ′gō) ***n.*** a language or dialect that sounds strange to one: *used in a joking or mocking way* [the *lingo* of lawyers]. —*pl.* **lin′goes**

**lin·guist** (liŋ′gwist) ***n.*** **1** a person who can speak, read, and write several languages. *See note in color at* **language.** **2** an expert in linguistics.

**lin·guis·tics** (liŋ gwis′tiks) ***n.pl.*** the general study of language, including the sounds of speech, grammar, forms and meanings of words, etc.: *used with a singular verb.* —**lin·guis′tic *adj.***

**lin·i·ment** (lin′ə mənt) ***n.*** a liquid rubbed on the skin to soothe sores, sprains, etc.

**lin·ing** (lī′niŋ) ***n.*** material that covers an inside surface [the *lining* of a coat].

**link** (liŋk) ***n.*** **1** any of the rings or loops that form a chain. **2** any of the joined sections of something like a chain [a *link* of sausage]. *See the picture.* **3** anything that joins or connects [Books are a *link* with the past.] ◆***v.*** to join or connect [We *linked* arms.]

**linking verb** a verb showing a state of being, used to connect a subject and the word or words that tell about the subject ["Are" is a *linking verb* in the sentence "They are stupid."]

**links** (liŋks) ***n.pl.*** a golf course.

> **Links** comes from an old English word for "slope," and is used in Scotland to mean a stretch of rolling, sandy seashore. Gently rolling land with patches of sand is the kind that is used for a golf course.

**lin·net** (lin′it) ***n.*** a small songbird found in Europe, Asia, and Africa.

**li·no·le·um** (li nō′lē əm) ***n.*** a hard, smooth floor covering made of a mixture of ground cork, ground wood, and linseed oil on a backing, as of canvas.

**lin·seed** (lin′sēd) ***n.*** the seed of flax.

**linseed oil** a yellowish oil pressed from linseed and used in oil paints, printer's ink, linoleum, etc.

**lint** (lint) ***n.*** **1** fine bits of thread, fluff, etc. from cloth or yarn. **2** linen scraped and made soft, once used to cover wounds. —**lint′y *adj.***

**lin·tel** (lin′t′l) ***n.*** the piece set lengthwise across the top of a door or window to support the wall above the opening. *See the picture.*

**li·on** (lī′ən) ***n.*** **1** a large, strong animal of the cat family, living in Africa and southwest Asia. Lions have a brownish-yellow coat, and the males have a heavy mane. *See the picture.* **2** a person who is very strong and brave. **3** a person who is famous; celebrity.

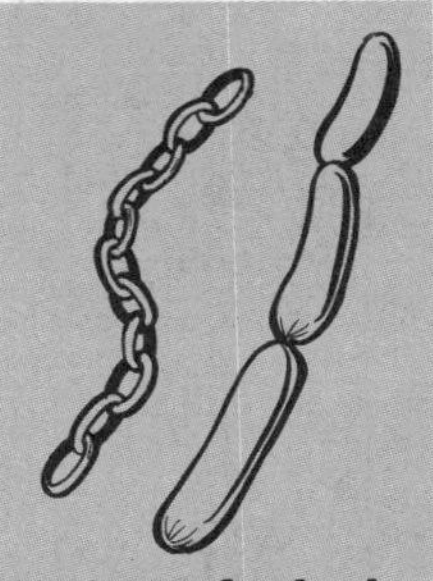
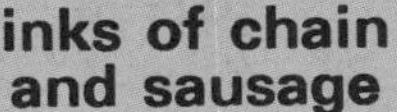

**links of chain and sausage**

**linden**

**lineman**

**lintel**

**lions**
3 m (10 ft.) long, including tail

**li·on·ess** (lī′ən is) ***n.*** a female lion.

**lip** (lip) ***n.*** **1** either the upper or the lower edge of the mouth. **2** anything like a lip, as the edge of a wound or the rim of a cup. ◆***adj.*** spoken, but not sincere or honest; false [to pay *lip* service to an idea one does not believe]. —**bite one's lip,** to keep back one's anger, annoyance, etc. —☆**keep a stiff upper lip,** to remain unafraid and not give up hope: *used only in everyday talk.*

**lip reading** the act or skill of recognizing the words a person speaks by watching that person's lips move. It is often taught to the deaf. —**lip′-read′ *v.***

☆**lip·stick** (lip′stik) ***n.*** a small stick of red paste for coloring the lips.

**liq·ue·fy** (lik′wə fī) ***v.*** to change into a liquid [Gases can be *liquefied.*] —**liq′ue·fied, liq′ue·fy·ing** —**liq·ue·fac·tion** (lik′wə fak′shən) ***n.***

**li·queur** (li kur′) ***n.*** a strong, sweet alcoholic liquor, often with a fruit flavor.

**liq·uid** (lik′wid) ***n.*** a substance that flows easily; matter that is neither a solid nor a gas [Water is a *liquid* when it is not ice or steam.] ◆***adj.*** **1** flowing easily; fluid [Oil is a *liquid* fuel.] **2** moving or flowing in a smooth, musical way [dancing with *liquid* grace]. **3** easily changed into cash [Bonds and stocks are *liquid* assets.]



| | | | |
|---|---|---|---|
| **a** fat | **ir** here | **ou** out | **zh** leisure |
| **ā** ape | **ī** bite, fire | **u** up | **ŋ** ring |
| **ä** car, lot | **ō** go | **ur** fur | a *in* ago |
| **e** ten | **ô** law, horn | **ch** chin | e *in* agent |
| **er** care | **oi** oil | **sh** she | **ə** = i *in* unity |
| **ē** even | **oo** look | **th** thin | o *in* collect |
| **i** hit | **ōō** tool | ***th*** then | u *in* focus |

**l**

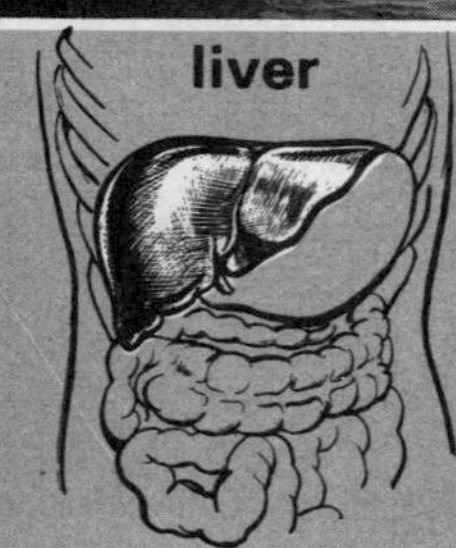

**liq·ui·date** (lik′wə dāt) ***v.*** **1** to settle the affairs of a business that is closing, usually because it is bankrupt. **2** to pay a debt in full. **3** to get rid of, as by killing [The dictator *liquidated* enemies.] —**liq′ui·dat·ed, liq′ui·dat·ing** —**liq′ui·da′tion *n.***

**liquid measure** a system of measuring liquids, especially the system in which 4 gills = 1 pint, 2 pints = 1 quart, 4 quarts = 1 gallon. In the metric system one quart equals 0.9464 liter.



**liq·uor** (lik′ər) ***n.*** **1** a drink that contains alcohol, as whiskey, gin, or rum. **2** any liquid, as sap from trees or juice from meat.

**li·ra** (lir′ə) ***n.*** the basic unit of money in Italy and Turkey. —*pl.* **li·re** (lir′ā) or **li′ras**

**Lis·bon** (liz′bən) the capital of Portugal.

**lisle** (līl) ***n.*** a thin, hard, very strong cotton thread. ◆***adj.*** made of lisle [*lisle* socks].

**lisp** (lisp) ***v.*** **1** to use the sounds (th) and (*th*) in place of the sounds (s) and (z) ["Yeth," he *lisped,* trying to say "yes."] **2** to speak in a way that is childish or not clear. ◆***n.*** the act or sound of lisping.

**lis·some** or **lis·som** (lis′əm) ***adj.*** bending or moving easily and gracefully; supple.

**list**[1] (list) ***n.*** a series of names, words, or numbers set down in order [a grocery *list*]. ◆***v.*** to make a list of; put into a list [Is your name *listed* in the phone book?] *See also* **lists.**

> **List**[1] originally meant a hem or border, then later a boundary or a narrow strip of wood or cloth. From the idea of a narrow strip of paper comes the meaning that we now have, that of a series of words or numbers put down in a column.

**list**[2] (list) ***v.*** to tilt to one side [The ship *listed* in the storm.] *See the picture.* ◆***n.*** the act of listing.

**list**[3] (list) ***v.*** to listen: *now seldom used.*

**lis·ten** (lis′'n) ***v.*** to pay attention in order to hear; try to hear [*Listen* to the rain. *Listen* when the counselor speaks.] —☆**listen in,** to listen to others talking, as on the telephone or radio. —**lis′ten·er *n.***

**Lis·ter** (lis′tər), **Joseph** 1827–1912; English surgeon. He was the first to use antiseptics in surgery.

**list·less** (list′lis) ***adj.*** having no interest in what is going on around one, because one is sick, sad, or tired. —**list′less·ly *adv.***

**lists** (lists) ***n.pl.*** a field where knights fought in tournaments in the Middle Ages. —**enter the lists,** to enter a contest or struggle.

**Liszt** (list), **Franz** (fränts) 1811–1886; Hungarian composer and pianist.

**lit** (lit) *a past tense and past participle of* **light**[1] and **light**[2].

**lit.** *abbreviation for* **liter** *or* **liters, literature.**

**lit·a·ny** (lit′'n ē) ***n.*** a prayer in which the clergyman and the congregation take turns in reciting the parts. —*pl.* **lit′a·nies**

**li·ter** (lēt′ər) ***n.*** the basic unit of capacity in the metric system, equal to 1 cubic decimeter. A liter is equal to a little more than a quart in liquid measure and to a little less than a quart in dry measure.

**lit·er·a·cy** (lit′ər ə sē) ***n.*** the ability to read and write.

**lit·er·al** (lit′ər əl) ***adj.*** **1** following the original, word for word [a *literal* translation of a French poem]. **2** based on the actual words in their usual meaning; not allowing for idiom or exaggeration [The *literal* meaning of "lend an ear" is to let another borrow one's ear.] **3** according to the facts; real; correct [the *literal* truth]. —**lit′er·al·ly *adv.***

**lit·er·ar·y** (lit′ə rer′ē) ***adj.*** **1** having to do with literature, especially in a formal style [*literary* studies]. **2** having to do with writing [*literary* agents].

**lit·er·ate** (lit′ər it) ***adj.*** educated; especially, able to read and write. ◆***n.*** a literate person.

**lit·er·a·ture** (lit′ər ə chər) ***n.*** **1** all the writings of a certain time, country, etc.; especially, those that have lasting value because of their beauty, imagination, etc., as fine novels, plays, and poems. **2** the work or profession of writing such things; also, the study of such writings. **3** all the writings on some subject [medical *literature*].

**lithe** (līth) ***adj.*** bending easily; limber or supple [a *lithe* dancer; *lithe* willow branches]. —**lith′er, lith′est**

**lith·i·um** (lith′ē əm) ***n.*** a soft, silver-white metal that is a chemical element. Lithium is the lightest metal and is used in thermonuclear explosives and in many alloys.

**lith·o·graph** (lith′ə graf) ***n.*** a picture or print made by lithography. ◆***v.*** to make by lithography.

**li·thog·ra·phy** (li thäg′rə fē) ***n.*** the process of printing from a flat stone or metal plate whose surface is treated so that only the parts having the design will hold ink. —**li·thog′ra·pher *n.***

**Lith·u·a·ni·a** (lith′oo wā′nē ə) a republic of the U.S.S.R. in northeastern Europe. —**Lith′u·a′ni·an *adj., n.***

**lit·i·gant** (lit′ə gənt) ***n.*** any of the persons taking part in a lawsuit.

**lit·i·ga·tion** (lit′ə gā′shən) ***n.*** **1** the act of carrying on a lawsuit. **2** a lawsuit.

**lit·mus** (lit′məs) ***n.*** a purple coloring matter got from a certain plant: paper treated with this (called **litmus paper**) turns red in an acid and blue in an alkali.

**li·tre** (lēt′ər) ***n.*** *the usual British spelling of* **liter.**

**lit·ter** (lit′ər) ***n.*** **1** a stretcher for carrying a sick or injured person. **2** a couch joined to long poles by which it can be carried, as on men's shoulders. *See the picture.* **3** straw or hay for animals to lie on. **4** odd bits or scraps lying around in disorder [Pick up your *litter* after a picnic.] **5** all the puppies, kittens, etc. born at one time to a dog, cat, etc. ◆***v.*** **1** to make messy or untidy with things scattered about [The lawn was *littered* with leaves.] **2** to give birth to a number of young animals at one time.

☆**lit·ter·bug** (lit′ər bug) ***n.*** a person who litters highways or other public places with waste paper, cans, etc.

**lit·tle** (lit′'l) ***adj.*** **1** small in size; not large or big [a *little* house]. **2** small in amount or degree; not much [*little* sugar; *little* danger]. **3** short or brief [Wait a *little* while. Go a *little* distance.] **4** not important; trivial [just a *little* error]. *See* SYNONYMS *at* **small. 5** not open to new ideas; not liberal [a person with a *little* mind]. —**lit′tler** or **less** or **less′er, lit′tlest** or **least** ◆***adv.*** **1** to a small degree; not very much [She is a *little* better.] **2** not at all [We *little* knew what lay ahead.] —**less, least** ◆***n.*** **1** a small amount [Have a *little* of this cake.] **2** not much [They have done *little* to help.] **3** a short time or distance [Sit a *little* with me.] —**little by little,** in a slow way; in small amounts; gradually. —**make little of,** to treat as not very important. —**not a little,** very much; very. —**lit′tle·ness** ***n.***

**Little Rock** the capital of Arkansas.

**lit·ur·gy** (lit′ər jē) ***n.*** the form or order of worship in a religious service. —*pl.* **lit′ur·gies** —**li·tur·gi·cal** (li tur′jə k'l) ***adj.***

**liv·a·ble** (liv′ə b'l) ***adj.*** **1** fit or pleasant to live in [a *livable* house]. **2** that can be lived through or endured [Life is barely *livable* in this place.]

**live**[1] (liv) ***v.*** **1** to have life; be alive [No one *lives* forever.] **2** to stay alive; last or endure [He *lived* to be 100 years old.] **3** to pass one's life in a certain way [She *lives* a useful life. They *lived* happily.] **4** to have a full, exciting life [That artist has really *lived*.] **5** to support oneself [She *lives* on a small pension.] **6** to feed [Bats *live* on insects and fruit.] **7** to make one's home; reside [We *live* on a farm.] —**lived, liv′ing** —**live down,** to live in a way that makes people forget something wrong that one has done. —**live high,** to live in luxury. —**live up to,** to act in keeping with one's ideals, promises, etc. —**live with,** to put up with; bear; endure.

**live**[2] (līv) ***adj.*** **1** having life; not dead. **2** full of life or energy; active; vigorous; bright [a *live* person]. ☆**3** of interest now [a *live* topic]. **4** still burning or glowing [*live* coals]. **5** that has not exploded [a *live* bomb]. **6** carrying electrical current [a *live* wire]. **7** that is broadcast while it is taking place; not photographed or recorded [a *live* television or radio program].

**live·li·hood** (līv′lē hood) ***n.*** the means of living, or of supporting oneself [She earns her *livelihood* as a teacher.]

**live·long** (liv′lông) ***adj.*** through the whole length of; entire [the *livelong* day].

**live·ly** (līv′lē) ***adj.*** **1** full of life or energy; active [a *lively* puppy]. **2** full of excitement [a *lively* meeting]. **3** cheerful or bright [a *lively* voice; *lively* colors]. **4** with quick, light movements [a *lively* dance]. ☆**5** having much bounce [a *lively* ball]. —**live′li·er, live′li·est** ◆***adv.*** in a lively way. —**live′li·ness** ***n.***

**liv·en** (lī′vən) ***v.*** to make or become lively, cheerful, bright, etc. [Games *liven* up a party.]

**liv·er**[1] (liv′ər) ***n.*** **1** a large organ of the body, near the stomach. It makes bile and helps break down food into substances that the body can absorb. *See the picture.* **2** the liver of some animals, used as food.

**liv·er**[2] (liv′ər) ***n.*** a person who lives in a certain way [a clean *liver*].

**liv·er·ied** (liv′ər ēd) ***adj.*** wearing livery.

**Liv·er·pool** (liv′ər pōōl) a seaport in northwestern England.

**liv·er·wort** (liv′ər wurt) ***n.*** a small plant that looks like moss.

**liv·er·wurst** (liv′ər wurst) ***n.*** a sausage containing ground liver: *also* **liver sausage.**

**liv·er·y** (liv′ər ē) ***n.*** **1** a uniform worn by servants or by people doing a certain kind of work [the *livery* of a butler]. **2** the work of keeping and feeding horses for pay; also, the business of renting horses and carriages. **3** a stable where horses are kept for these purposes: *also* **livery stable.** —*pl.* **liv′er·ies**

> **Livery** comes from an old French word meaning "to deliver." Later, in early English, *livery* came to mean "a thing delivered" or "a gift of clothes to a servant." The gift of clothes then became a uniform that the servant was required to wear.

**lives** (līvz) ***n.*** *plural of* **life.**

**live·stock** (līv′stäk) ***n.*** animals kept or raised on farms, as cattle, horses, pigs, or sheep.

**liv·id** (liv′id) ***adj.*** **1** black-and-blue from a bruise. **2** grayish-blue or, sometimes, pale or red [a face *livid* with rage].

**liv·ing** (liv′ing) ***adj.*** **1** having life; alive; not dead. **2** still active or in common use among people [a *living* tradition; a *living* language]. **3** of people alive [within *living* memory]. **4** exact in every detail [She is the *living* image of her sister.] **5** of life or of keeping alive [poor *living* conditions]. **6** enough to live on [a *living* wage]. ◆***n.*** **1** the fact of being alive. **2** the means of supporting oneself or one's family [He makes a *living* selling shoes.] **3** the way in which one lives [the standard of *living*]. —**the living,** those who are still alive.

> SYNONYMS: **Living** and **alive** are both used of anything that has life or exists. **Living** is used especially of something that goes on and on existing or being active [The scholarship fund is a *living* memorial.] **Alive** is used to suggest full force or vigor [The hope of being with her kept his love *alive*.]

**living room** ☆a room in a home, with chairs, sofas, etc., used by the family for reading, playing, entertaining guests, etc.

**liz·ard** (liz′ərd) ***n.*** a reptile with a long, slender body and tail, a scaly skin, and four legs, as the chameleon, gecko, and iguana. *See the picture.*

**ll.** *abbreviation for* **lines.**

| | | | | | | | |
|---|---|---|---|---|---|---|---|
| **a** | fat | **ir** | here | **ou** | out | **zh** | leisure |
| **ā** | ape | **ī** | bite, fire | **u** | up | **ng** | ring |
| **ä** | car, lot | **ō** | go | **ur** | fur | | a *in* ago |
| **e** | ten | **ô** | law, horn | **ch** | chin | | e *in* agent |
| **er** | care | **oi** | oil | **sh** | she | **ə =** | i *in* unity |
| **ē** | even | **oo** | look | **th** | thin | | o *in* collect |
| **i** | hit | **ōō** | tool | ***th*** | then | | u *in* focus |

**lla·ma** (lä′mə) ***n.*** a South American animal like the camel, but smaller and without a hump. It is used as a beast of burden, and its wool is made into cloth. *See the picture.*

**lla·no** (lä′nō) ***n.*** any of the flat, grassy plains of Spanish America. *—pl.* **lla′nos**

**lo** (lō) ***interj.*** look! see!: *now used mainly in the phrase* **lo and behold!**

**load** (lōd) ***n.*** **1** something that is carried or to be carried at one time [a heavy *load* on his back]. **2** the usual amount carried at one time [We hauled two *loads* of trash to the dump.] **3** something that makes one worried or anxious [Her safe arrival took a *load* off my mind.] **4** the amount of current or power supplied by a dynamo, engine, etc. **5** a single charge for a gun [a *load* of shot]. **6** *often* **loads**, *pl.* a great amount or number: *used only in everyday talk* [She has *loads* of friends.] ◆***v.*** **1** to put something to be carried into or upon a carrier [to *load* a bus with passengers; to *load* groceries into a cart]. **2** to weigh down with a burden [She is *loaded* with troubles.] **3** to supply in great amounts [to *load* a person with gifts]. **4** to fill with what is needed to make something work [to *load* a gun with bullets; to *load* a camera with film]. **5** to take on a load of passengers, goods, etc. [The bus is now *loading.*] **6** to ask in such a way as to draw out the answer that is wanted [a *loaded* question]. —**load′er** ***n.***

430 **load·stone** (lōd′stōn) ***n.*** *another spelling of* **lodestone.**

**loaf**[1] (lōf) ***n.*** **1** a portion of bread baked in one piece, usually oblong in shape. **2** any food baked in this shape [a meat *loaf*]. *—pl.* **loaves**

☆**loaf**[2] (lōf) ***v.*** to spend time doing little or nothing; idle [to *loaf* on the job].

☆**loaf·er** (lōf′ər) ***n.*** **1** a person who loafs; idler. **2** **Loafer,** *a trademark for* a sport shoe somewhat like a moccasin.

**loam** (lōm) ***n.*** a rich, dark soil with rotting plant matter in it.

**loan** (lōn) ***n.*** **1** the act of lending [Thanks for the *loan* of your pen.] **2** something lent, especially a sum of money. ◆***v.*** to lend, especially a sum of money or something to be returned. —**on loan,** lent for use by another for a certain period of time.

**loan·er** (lōn′ər) ***n.*** **1** a person who loans something. **2** an automobile, radio, etc. on loan to a customer while the customer's is being repaired.

**loath** (lōth) ***adj.*** not willing; reluctant [They were *loath* to go home.]

**loathe** (lō*th*) ***v.*** to feel hate or disgust for. —**loathed, loath′ing**

**loath·ing** (lō*th*′iŋ) ***n.*** hatred or disgust.

**loath·some** (lō*th*′səm) ***adj.*** very disgusting.

**loaves** (lōvz) ***n.*** *plural of* **loaf.**

**lob** (läb) ***v.*** to hit or throw a ball, etc. so that it goes high in the air. —**lobbed, lob′bing** ◆***n.*** the act of lobbing.

**lob·by** (läb′ē) ***n.*** **1** an entrance hall or waiting room, as in a hotel or theater. ☆**2** a group of lobbyists working for the benefit of a special group. *—pl.* **lob′bies** ◆☆***v.*** to try to influence the voting of lawmakers by acting as a lobbyist. —**lob′bied, lob′by·ing**

☆**lob·by·ist** (läb′ē ist) ***n.*** a person who tries to influence lawmakers in voting for or against certain laws, in order to benefit a special group, or lobby.

> **Lobbyists** got their name because they used to stand around in the lobby next to the large hall where the lawmakers met, in order to try to persuade them to vote for or against certain laws.

**lobe** (lōb) ***n.*** a rounded part that sticks out, as the fleshy lower end of the human ear.

**lo·be·li·a** (lō bē′lē ə) ***n.*** a plant with long clusters of blue, red, or white flowers.

**lob·lol·ly** (läb′läl′ē) ***n.*** ☆a pine tree with thick bark, that grows in the southeastern U.S. *—pl.* **lob′lol′lies**

**lob·ster** (läb′stər) ***n.*** **1** a large sea shellfish with five pairs of legs, of which the first pair are large, powerful pincers. Lobsters' shells turn red when boiled. *See the picture.* **2** the flesh of this animal used as food.

**lo·cal** (lō′k'l) ***adj.*** **1** having to do with a particular place; not general [*local* customs]. **2** having an effect on just a certain part of the body [a *local* anesthetic]. ☆**3** making all stops along its run [a *local* bus]. ◆***n.*** ☆**1** a local bus, train, etc. ☆**2** a branch or chapter of a larger organization, as of a labor union.

**lo·cal·ism** (lō′k'l iz'm) ***n.*** a word, custom, pronunciation, etc. used only in a certain region ["Butter bean" is a Southern *localism* for "lima bean."]

**lo·cal·i·ty** (lō kal′ə tē) ***n.*** a place, district, or neighborhood. *—pl.* **lo·cal′i·ties**

**lo·cal·ize** (lō′kə līz) ***v.*** to keep or make stay in a particular part or place [The pain is *localized* in her hand.] —**lo′cal·ized, lo′cal·iz·ing**

**lo·cal·ly** (lō′k'l ē) ***adv.*** within a particular place [The storm did much damage *locally.*]

**lo·cate** (lō′kāt *or* lō kāt′) ***v.*** **1** to set up or place; situate [Their shop is *located* in the new mall.] **2** to find out where something is [Have you *located* the gloves that you lost?] ☆**3** to settle: *used only in everyday talk* [The family *located* in Boston.] —**lo′cat·ed, lo′cat·ing**

**lo·ca·tion** (lō kā′shən) ***n.*** **1** the act of locating. **2** the place where something is or will be; site [a good *location* for a gas station].

**loch** (läk) ***n.*** a lake; also, a long narrow bay, nearly cut off from the sea: *a Scottish word.*

**lock**[1] (läk) ***n.*** **1** a device for fastening a door, safe, etc. by means of a bolt. A lock can usually be opened only by a special key, etc. **2** an enclosed part of a canal, river, etc. with gates at each end. Water can be let in or out of it to raise or lower ships from one level to another. *See the picture.* **3** anything that holds something in place or keeps it from moving [an oar*lock*]. **4** the part of a firearm that fires the charge. ◆***v.*** **1** to fasten or become fastened with a lock. **2** to shut in or out [*Lock* the money in the box. *Lock* the cat out of the house.] **3** to join or become joined together firmly; interlock [The two elks *locked* horns while fighting.] **4** to jam together so that no movement is possible [The gears are *locked.*]

**lock**[2] (läk) ***n.*** a curl, tress, or ringlet of hair.

**lock·er** (läk′ər) ***n.*** a closet, chest, etc., usually of metal, that can be locked; especially, one to be used by one person.

☆**locker room** a room with a number of lockers, as at a gymnasium, factory, etc. for storing one's clothes and equipment.

**lock·et** (läk′it) ***n.*** a small metal case for holding a picture, lock of hair, etc., usually worn around the neck on a chain or ribbon.

**lock·jaw** (läk′jô) ***n.*** *another word for* **tetanus.**

**lock·out** (läk′out) ***n.*** the refusal by a company, corporation, etc. to allow employees to come in to work until they agree to the terms of the company.

**lock·smith** (läk′smith) ***n.*** a person whose work is making or repairing locks and keys.

**lo·co·mo·tion** (lō′kə mō′shən) ***n.*** the act or power of moving from one place to another [Both walking and riding are forms of *locomotion.*]

**lo·co·mo·tive** (lō′kə mō′tiv) ***n.*** a steam, electric, or Diesel engine on wheels, that pulls or pushes railroad trains. ◆***adj.*** moving or able to move from one place to another.

**lo·cust** (lō′kəst) ***n.*** **1** a large insect like a grasshopper, that often travels in great swarms and destroys crops. *See the picture.* ☆**2** a tree with a number of leaflets growing from each stem and clusters of sweet-smelling, white flowers; also, its yellowish, hard wood.

**lo·cu·tion** (lō kyōō′shən) ***n.*** a word or phrase.

**lode** (lōd) ***n.*** a deposit of the ore of some metal which fills a crack or seam in rock.

**lode·star** (lōd′stär) ***n.*** a star to be guided by; especially, the North Star.

**lode·stone** (lōd′stōn) ***n.*** **1** an iron ore that is a strong magnet. **2** anything that attracts strongly.

**lodge** (läj) ***n.*** **1** a place to live in; especially, a small house for some special purpose [a hunting *lodge*]. **2** the local branch of certain societies or clubs, or its meeting place. **3** a beaver's den. ☆**4** the hut or tent of an American Indian. ◆***v.*** **1** to provide with a place to live or sleep in for a time [She agreed to *lodge* the strangers overnight.] **2** to live in a place for a time; be a lodger [Don *lodged* with the Hall family while attending college.] **3** to put, drive, shoot, etc. firmly [The archer *lodged* the arrow in the center of the target.] **4** to come to rest and stick firmly [A fish bone *lodged* in her throat.] **5** to bring before an official [to *lodge* a protest with the mayor]. —**lodged, lodg′ing** —**lodg′ment** ***n.***

**lodg·er** (läj′ər) ***n.*** a person who rents a room in another person's home.

**lodg·ing** (läj′iŋ) ***n.*** **1** a place to live in, especially for a short time. **2 lodgings,** ***pl.*** a room or rooms rented in another's home.

**loft** (lôft) ***n.*** **1** the space just below the roof of a house, barn, etc. [a hay*loft*]. **2** an upper story of a warehouse or factory. **3** a gallery or balcony [a choir *loft*]. ◆***v.*** to send high into the air [The golfer *lofted* the ball over the bunker.]

**loft·y** (lôf′tē) ***adj.*** **1** very high [a *lofty* skyscraper]. **2** high in ideals or noble in feelings [the *lofty* thoughts of the poet]. **3** too proud; haughty [the king's *lofty* manner]. —**loft′i·er, loft′i·est** —**loft′i·ness** ***n.***

**log** (lôg) ***n.*** **1** a part of a tree that has been cut down [Cut the trunk into *logs* for the fireplace.] **2** a device floated at the end of a line to measure the speed of a ship. **3** a daily record of a ship's voyage, giving speed, position, weather, and other important happenings. **4** any record of a trip [the flight *log* of an airplane]. ◆***adj.*** made of logs [a *log* cabin]. ◆***v.*** ☆**1** to cut down trees and take the logs to a sawmill. **2** to record in a log. —**logged, log′ging**

**lobster**
45 cm (18 in.) long

**lock in a canal**

**llama**
1.2 m (4 ft.) high at shoulder

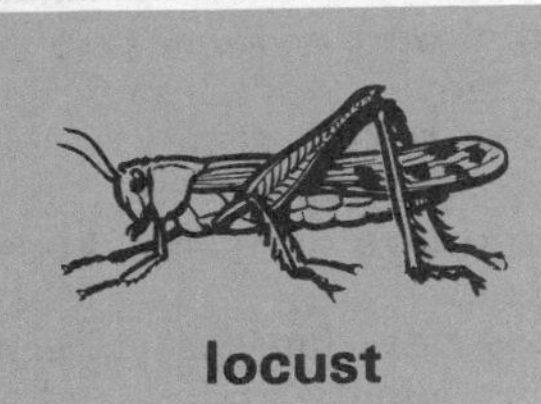

**locust**

☆**lo·gan·ber·ry** (lō′gən ber′ē) ***n.*** a purplish-red berry that is a cross between the blackberry and the red raspberry. —*pl.* **lo′gan·ber′ries**

**log·a·rithm** (lôg′ə rith′m) ***n.*** the figure that tells to what power a certain fixed number, as ten, must be raised to equal a given number [The *logarithm* of 100 is 2, when 10 is taken as the fixed number ($10^2 = 100$).] Such numbers are listed in tables to shorten the working of problems in mathematics.



**log·book** (lôg′book) ***n.*** a book in which the log of a ship or airplane is kept.

☆**log·ger** (lôg′ər) ***n.*** a person whose work is logging.

**log·ger·head** (lôg′ər hed) ***n.*** a sea turtle with a large head, that lives in warm seas. —**at loggerheads,** in a quarrel; arguing; disagreeing.

☆**log·ging** (lôg′iŋ) ***n.*** the work of cutting down trees and taking the logs to a sawmill.

**log·ic** (läj′ik) ***n.*** **1** correct reasoning; sound thinking. **2** the science that deals with the rules of correct reasoning and with proof by reasoning. **3** way of reasoning [poor *logic*].

> **Logic** comes from the Greek word *logos,* which means "word" or "thought." In order to be logical or reason correctly, one must learn to use words properly and to think.

**log·i·cal** (läj′i k′l) ***adj.*** **1** based on logic or using logic [a *logical* explanation]. **2** that is to be expected because of what has gone before [the *logical* result of one's actions]. —**log′i·cal·ly** ***adv.***

**lo·gi·cian** (lō jish′ən) ***n.*** a person who is skilled in logic.

**-lo·gy** (lə jē) *a suffix meaning* the science or study of [*Zoology* is the science of animal life.]

| | | | | | | | |
|---|---|---|---|---|---|---|---|
| **a** | fat | **ir** | here | **ou** | out | **zh** | leisure |
| **ā** | ape | **ī** | bite, fire | **u** | up | **ŋ** | ring |
| **ä** | car, lot | **ō** | go | **ur** | fur | | a *in* ago |
| **e** | ten | **ô** | law, horn | **ch** | chin | | e *in* agent |
| **er** | care | **oi** | oil | **sh** | she | **ə =** | i *in* unity |
| **ē** | even | **oo** | look | **th** | thin | | o *in* collect |
| **i** | hit | **ōō** | tool | ***th*** | then | | u *in* focus |

**loin** (lɔin) ***n.*** **1** the part of an animal between the hip and the ribs; lower back. **2 loins,** *pl.* the hips and lower part of the abdomen. —**gird up one's loins,** to get ready to do something difficult.

**loin·cloth** (lɔin′klôth) ***n.*** a cloth worn about the loins by some people in warm climates.

**Loire** (lwär) a river flowing from southern France north and west into the Atlantic Ocean.

**loi·ter** (lɔit′ər) ***v.*** **1** to spend time in an idle way; linger [Do not *loiter* in the halls.] **2** to walk in a slow, lazy way. —**loi′ter·er** ***n.***

**loll** (läl) ***v.*** **1** to sit or lean back in a lazy way. *See the picture.* **2** to hang or droop [The dog's tongue *lolled* out.]

**lol·li·pop** or **lol·ly·pop** (läl′ē päp) ***n.*** a piece of hard candy on a small stick; sucker.

**Lom·bar·dy** (läm′bər dē) a region of northern Italy. *See the map.*

**Lo·mond** (lō′mənd), **Loch** a lake in west central Scotland.

**Lon·don** (lun′dən) the capital of the United Kingdom, in southeastern England.

**Lon·don** (lun′dən), **Jack** 1876–1916; U.S. writer of novels and short stories. His full name was John Griffith London.

**lone** (lōn) ***adj.*** by itself or by oneself; solitary.

**lone·ly** (lōn′lē) ***adj.*** **1** unhappy because one is alone or away from friends or family [Billy was *lonely* his

432 first day at camp.] *See* SYNONYMS *at* **alone.** **2** without others nearby; alone [a *lonely* cottage]. **3** with few or no people [a *lonely* island]. —**lone′li·er, lone′li·est** —**lone′li·ness** ***n.***

☆**lon·er** (lō′nər) ***n.*** a person who would rather be alone than with other people: *used only in everyday talk.*

**lone·some** (lōn′səm) ***adj.*** **1** having a lonely feeling [a *lonesome* sentry]. *See* SYNONYMS *at* **alone.** **2** causing a lonely feeling [a *lonesome* whistle]. **3** seldom used; remote [a *lonesome* road]. —**lone′some·ness** ***n.***

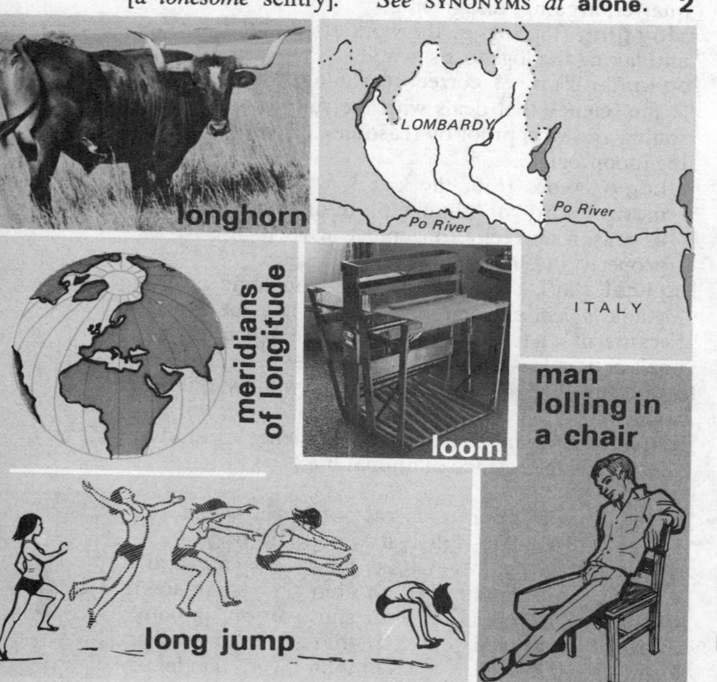


**long**[1] (lông) ***adj.*** **1** measuring much from end to end or from beginning to end; not short [a *long* board; a *long* trip; a *long* wait]. **2** reaching over a certain distance; in length [a rope six feet *long*]. **3** large; big [She took a *long* chance.] **4** taking a longer time to say than other sounds [The "a" in "cave" and the "i" in "hide" are *long*.] ◆***adv.*** **1** for a long time [Don't be gone *long*.] **2** from the beginning to the end [all summer *long*]. **3** at a far distant time [They lived *long* ago.] —**as long as** or **so long as, 1** during the time that. **2** seeing that; since. **3** on the condition that. —**before long,** soon.

**long**[2] (lông) ***v.*** to want very much; feel a strong desire for [We *long* to go home.]

**long.** *abbreviation for* **longitude.**

**long·boat** (lông′bōt) ***n.*** the largest boat carried on a merchant sailing ship.

☆**long distance** a system by which telephone calls can be made between distant places.

**lon·gev·i·ty** (län jev′ə tē) ***n.*** long life.

**Long·fel·low** (lông′fel′ō), **Henry Wads·worth** (wädz′wurth) 1807–1882; U.S. poet.

**long·hand** (lông′hand) ***n.*** ordinary handwriting, with the words written out in full.

**long·horn** (lông′hôrn) ***n.*** ☆**1** a breed of cattle with long horns, raised in the Southwest. *See the picture.* ☆**2** an orange-colored cheddar cheese.

**long·ing** (lông′ing) ***n.*** strong desire; yearning. ◆***adj.*** showing strong desire. —**long′ing·ly** ***adv.***

**Long Island** a large island in southeast New York that is between Long Island Sound and the Atlantic.

**Long Island Sound** an arm of the Atlantic between northern Long Island and southern Connecticut.

**lon·gi·tude** (län′jə to͞od *or* län′jə tyo͞od) ***n.*** distance measured in degrees east or west of a line running north and south through Greenwich, England [Chicago is at 87 degrees west *longitude.*] *See the picture. See also* **meridian.**

**lon·gi·tu·di·nal** (län′jə to͞od′′n əl *or* län′jə tyo͞od′′n əl) ***adj.*** **1** of or in length. **2** running lengthwise or placed lengthwise [*longitudinal* stripes]. **3** of longitude. —**lon′gi·tu′di·nal·ly** ***adv.***

**long jump** an athletic contest to see who can jump the farthest. *See the picture.*

**long-lived** (lông′līvd′ *or* lông′livd′) ***adj.*** living or lasting for a long time.

**long-play·ing** (lông′plā′ing) ***adj.*** having very narrow grooves and turning at a slow speed so as to play for a long time [a *long-playing* record for a phonograph].

**long-range** (lông′rānj′) ***adj.*** reaching over a long distance or time [*long-range* guns, *long-range* plans].

**long·shore·man** (lông′shôr′mən) ***n.*** a person who works on a waterfront loading and unloading ships. —*pl.* **long′shore′men**

**long shot** a try that is not likely to succeed, but that will be very rewarding if it should: *used only in everyday talk.* —☆**not by a long shot,** not at all: *used only in everyday talk.*

**long·stand·ing** (lông′stan′ding) ***adj.*** having continued for a long time.

**long-suf·fer·ing** (lông′suf′ər ing) ***adj.*** bearing trouble, pain, etc. patiently for a long time.

**long·ways** (lông′wāz) ***adv.*** *another word for* **lengthwise.**
**long-wind·ed** (lông′win′did) ***adj.*** speaking or writing so much as to be boring.
**long·wise** (lông′wīz) ***adv.*** *another word for* **lengthwise.**
**look** (look) ***v.*** **1** to turn or aim one's eyes in order to see [Don't *look* back.] **2** to keep one's eyes fixed on [*Look* me in the face.] **3** to bring one's attention [Just *look* at the trouble you've caused.] **4** to search or hunt [Did you *look* in every pocket for the letter?] **5** to seem or appear [Maria *looks* happy.] **6** to face in a certain direction [The hotel *looks* toward the lake.] ◆***n.*** **1** the act of looking; glance [an angry *look*]. **2** the way someone or something seems; appearance [He has the *look* of a beggar.] **3 looks,** *pl.* appearance: *used only in everyday talk* [I don't like the *looks* of this place.] —**look after,** to take care of. —**look back,** to think about the past. —**look down on,** to think of as bad or worthless; despise. —**look for, 1** to search or hunt for. **2** to expect. —**look forward to,** to wait eagerly for. —**look in on,** to pay a brief visit to. —**look into** or **look over,** to examine or inspect. —**look on, 1** to watch what is going on. **2** to consider; regard. —**look out,** to be careful. —**look out for, 1** to be wary about. **2** to take care of. —**look to, 1** to take care of. **2** to rely upon. **3** to expect. —**look up, 1** to search for, as in a dictionary. **2** to pay a visit to: *used only in everyday talk.* —**look up to,** to respect; admire. —**look′er** ***n.***

SYNONYMS: To **look** is to direct one's eyes so as to see something [to *look* at a picture]. To **gaze** is to look steadily at something that arouses interest, delight, or wonder [to *gaze* at the stars]. To **stare** is to look with the eyes fixed and wide-open at something that arouses surprise, curiosity, etc. [It is rude to *stare* at people.]

**look·er-on** (look′ər än′) ***n.*** an onlooker; spectator. —*pl.* **look′ers-on′**
**looking glass** a mirror made of glass.
**look·out** (look′out) ***n.*** **1** a careful watching for someone or something [She's on the *lookout* for a new job.] **2** a person who is supposed to keep watch; guard; sentry. **3** a place, especially a high place, from which to watch. **4** concern or worry: *used only in everyday talk* [That's your *lookout.*]
**loom¹** (lōōm) ***n.*** a machine for weaving thread or yarn into cloth. *See the picture.*
**loom²** (lōōm) ***v.*** to come into sight in a sudden or frightening way [A ship *loomed* out of the fog.]
**loon** (lōōn) ***n.*** a diving bird that looks like a duck but has a pointed bill and a weird cry. *See the picture on page 435.*
**loop** (lōōp) ***n.*** **1** the figure made by a line, string, wire, etc. that curves back to cross itself. **2** anything having or forming a figure like this or like a ring [The letter *g* has a *loop.* The belt goes through *loops* at the waist.] ◆***v.*** **1** to make a loop of or in [to *loop* a rope]. **2** to form a loop or loops [The airplane *looped.*] **3** to fasten with a loop [The curtain was *looped* to one side.]
**loop·hole** (lōōp′hōl) ***n.*** **1** a hole in a wall for looking or shooting through. **2** a way of getting around some law or escaping some trouble.
**loose** (lōōs) ***adj.*** **1** not tied or held back; free [a *loose* end of wire]. **2** not tight or firmly fastened on or in something [*loose* clothing; a *loose* table leg]. **3** not packed down [*loose* soil]. **4** not put up in a special package or box [*loose* salt]. **5** not careful or exact [*loose* talk; a *loose* translation]. **6** not moral [to lead a *loose* life]. ◆***adv.*** in a loose way [My coat hangs *loose.*] ◆***v.*** **1** to make loose, or set free; release [Don't *loose* your anger on me. The heavens *loosed* a downpour.] **2** to let fly; shoot [We *loosed* our arrows into the air.] **3** to make less rigid; loosen [Modern times have *loosed* the old ties of duty.] —**loosed, loos′ing** —**break loose,** to free oneself; escape. —**cast loose,** to unfasten or untie. —**let loose with,** to let go; release. —**on the loose, 1** not confined; free. **2** having fun in a free and easy way: *used only in everyday talk.* —**set loose** or **turn loose,** to make free; release. —**loose′ly** ***adv.*** —**loose′ness** ***n.***
**loose-joint·ed** (lōōs′join′tid) ***adj.*** having loose joints; moving freely; limber.
**loose-leaf** (lōōs′lēf′) ***adj.*** having leaves that can be taken out or put in easily [a *loose-leaf* notebook].
**loos·en** (lōōs′'n) ***v.*** to make or become loose or looser. —☆**loosen up, 1** to talk freely. **2** to give money generously. **3** to relax. *This phrase is used only in everyday talk.*
**loot** (lōōt) ***n.*** something stolen or robbed; plunder; booty. ◆***v.*** to rob or plunder.
**lop¹** (läp) ***v.*** **1** to cut off or chop off [to *lop* a branch]. **2** to trim by cutting off branches [to *lop* a tree]. —**lopped, lop′ping**
**lop²** (läp) ***v.*** to hang down loosely [the *lopping* ears of a spaniel]. —**lopped, lop′ping**
**lope** (lōp) ***v.*** to move along easily with long, jumping steps. —**loped, lop′ing** ◆***n.*** the act of loping.
**lop·sid·ed** (läp′sīd′id) ***adj.*** **1** larger, heavier, or lower on one side than the other. *See the picture on page 435.* **2** not balanced; uneven.
**lo·qua·cious** (lō kwā′shəs) ***adj.*** talking very much; talkative. —**lo·quac·i·ty** (lō kwas′ə tē) ***n.***
**lord** (lôrd) ***n.*** **1** a person with much power or authority; ruler or master. **2** the owner of an estate in the Middle Ages. **3 Lord,** God; also, Jesus Christ. **4 Lords,** *pl.* the upper house in the British Parliament: *usually called the* **House of Lords. 5 Lord,** a British title given to some men of high rank [The Earl of Russell is called *Lord* Russell.] **6** a man with this title. —**lord it over,** to order about in a bullying way.

**Lord** comes from an old English word meaning "loaf keeper," or "one who feeds those who depend on him." In the Middle Ages a lord had many vassals who depended on him.

**lord·ly** (lôrd′lē) ***adj.*** **1** of or fit for a lord; grand. **2** too proud; scornful; haughty. —**lord′li·er, lord′li·est**
**Lord·ship** (lôrd′ship) ***n.*** a title of respect used in speaking to or of a Lord [Is your *Lordship* pleased?]



| | | | | | | | |
|---|---|---|---|---|---|---|---|
| **a** | fat | **ir** | here | **ou** | out | **zh** | leisure |
| **ā** | ape | **ī** | bite, fire | **u** | up | **ng** | ring |
| **ä** | car, lot | **ō** | go | **ur** | fur | | a *in* ago |
| **e** | ten | **ô** | law, horn | **ch** | chin | | e *in* agent |
| **er** | care | **oi** | oil | **sh** | she | ə = | i *in* unity |
| **ē** | even | **oo** | look | **th** | thin | | o *in* collect |
| **i** | hit | **ōō** | tool | ***th*** | then | | u *in* focus |

**Lord's Prayer** the prayer beginning "Our Father," which Jesus taught his disciples.

**Lord's Supper** **1** *another name for* **Last Supper.** **2** *another name for* **Holy Communion.**

**lore** (lôr) ***n.*** knowledge or learning, especially that handed down from earlier times.

**lor·gnette** (lôr nyet′) ***n.*** a pair of eyeglasses, or opera glasses, with a handle. *See the picture.*

**lorn** (lôrn) ***adj.*** forlorn: *now seldom used.*

**Lor·raine** (lô rān′) a region in France. *See* **Alsace-Lorraine.**

**lor·ry** (lôr′ē) ***n.*** **1** a flat wagon without sides. **2** a motor truck: *a British meaning.* —*pl.* **lor′ries**

**Los An·gel·es** (lôs an′jə ləs *or* lôs aŋ′gə ləs) a city on the southwestern coast of California.

**lose** (lo͞oz) ***v.*** **1** to put, leave, or drop, so as to be unable to find; mislay [He *lost* his keys somewhere.] **2** to have taken from one by death, accident, etc. [She *lost* a brother in the war.] **3** to fail to keep [I *lost* my temper.] **4** to fail to win; be defeated in [We *lost* the football game.] **5** to fail to have or make use of; miss or waste [She *lost* her chance. Don't *lose* any time.] **6** to fail to see, hear, or understand [I did not *lose* a word of the lecture.] **7** to destroy or ruin [The ship was *lost* in the storm.] **8** to cause the loss of [His bad manners *lost* him friends.] **9** to wander from and not be able to find [He *lost* his way in the woods.] **10** to get rid of [She has *lost* weight.] —**lost, los′ing** —**lose**

**oneself,** **1** to lose one's way; become confused. **2** to become so interested in something as to notice nothing else. —☆**lose out,** to be unsuccessful: *used only in everyday talk.* —**los′er** ***n.***

**los·ing** (lo͞o′ziŋ) ***adj.*** **1** that loses [the *losing* team]. **2** resulting in loss [a *losing* proposition]. ◆***n.*** **losings,** *pl.* money lost, as in gambling.

**loss** (lôs) ***n.*** **1** a losing or being lost [a *loss* of weight]. **2** the amount, thing, or person lost [The company's *loss* was great.] **3** trouble, damage, etc. caused by losing something [Their absence was no *loss.*] —**at a loss,** puzzled; not certain. —**at a loss to,** not able to; not certain how to [I'm *at a loss to* explain the problem.]

**lost** (lôst) *past tense and past participle of* **lose.** ◆***adj.*** that is mislaid, missing, destroyed, defeated, wasted, etc. [a *lost* hat; a *lost* child; a *lost* ship; a *lost* cause; *lost* time]. —**lost in,** very much interested in; absorbed by [*lost in* thought]. —**lost on,** having no effect on [My advice was *lost on* them.]

**Lot** (lät) in the Bible, Abraham's nephew, who escaped from the doomed city of Sodom. When his wife stopped to look back, she was turned into a pillar of salt.

**lot** (lät) ***n.*** **1** any of a number of counters, slips of paper, etc. that people draw from without looking, in deciding something by chance [Draw *lots* to see who goes first.] **2** the use of such a method in deciding [Ten people were chosen by *lot.*] **3** the decision reached in this way. **4** what comes to a person in this way; one's share by lot. **5** the fate of a person in life [his unhappy *lot*]. **6** a small piece of land [a *lot* to build a house on]. **7** a number of persons or things thought of as a group [the best of the *lot*]. **8** *often* **lots,** *pl.* a great amount: *used only in everyday talk* [a *lot* of cars; *lots* of money]. ◆***adv.*** very much [a *lot* richer]. *Also* **lots** [*lots* richer]. —**cast in one's lot with,** to take one's chances with.

**loth** (lōth) ***adj.*** *another spelling of* **loath.**

**lo·tion** (lō′shən) ***n.*** a liquid rubbed on the skin to keep it soft, to heal it, etc.

**lot·ter·y** (lät′ər ē) ***n.*** a form of gambling in which people buy numbered tickets, and prizes are given to those whose numbers are drawn by lot. —*pl.* **lot′teries**

**lo·tus** or **lo·tos** (lōt′əs) ***n.*** **1** a kind of waterlily found in Egypt and other warm places. *See the picture.* **2** a plant in old Greek legends that made those who ate it dreamy and forgetful.

**loud** (loud) ***adj.*** **1** strong in sound; not soft or quiet [a *loud* noise; a *loud* bell]. **2** noisy [a *loud* party]. **3** so strong as to force attention; forceful [*loud* demands]. **4** too bright or showy: *used only in everyday talk* [a *loud* tie]. ◆***adv.*** in a loud way. —**loud′ly** ***adv.*** —**loud′ness** ***n.***

**loud·speak·er** (loud′spē′kər) ***n.*** a device, as in a radio, that changes electric current into sound waves and makes the sound loud enough to be heard in a room, hall, etc.

**Lou·is XIV** (lo͞o′ē) 1638–1715; the king of France from 1643 to 1715, when French culture reached a high point.

**Louis XVI** 1754–1793; the king of France from 1774 to 1792. He was executed during the French Revolution.

**Lou·i·si·an·a** (lo͝o wē′zē an′ə) a State in the south central part of the U.S.: abbreviated **La., LA**

☆**Louisiana Purchase** land bought by the U.S. from France in 1803 for $15,000,000. The land reached from the Mississippi to the Rocky Mountains and from the Gulf of Mexico to Canada.

**Lou·is·ville** (lo͞o′ē vil *or* lo͞o′ə vəl) a city in northern Kentucky, on the Ohio River.

**lounge** (lounj) ***v.*** to move, sit, or lie in an easy or lazy way; loll. —**lounged, loung′ing** ◆***n.*** **1** a room with comfortable furniture where people can lounge. **2** a couch or sofa. —**loung′er** ***n.***

**lour** (lour) ***v.*** *another spelling of* **lower**[2].

**louse** (lous) ***n.*** **1** a small insect pest that lives in the hair or on the skin of human beings and other animals and sucks their blood. *See the picture.* **2** an insect like this that lives on plants. —*pl.* **lice**

**lous·y** (lou′zē) ***adj.*** **1** covered with lice. **2** dirty, disgusting, poor, bad, etc.: *slang in this meaning* [a *lousy* trick; a *lousy* golfer]. —**lous′i·er, lous′i·est**

**lout** (lout) ***n.*** a clumsy, stupid person; boor. —**lout′ish** ***adj.***

**lou·ver** (lo͞o′vər) ***n.*** **1** an opening in a wall, with sloping boards that let in air and light but keep out rain. *See the picture.* **2** any one of these boards. —**lou′vered** ***adj.***

**Lou·vre** (lo͞o′vrə *or* lo͞ov) a large and famous art museum in Paris. In earlier times it was a royal palace.

**lov·a·ble** or **love·a·ble** (luv′ə b′l) ***adj.*** that deserves to be loved; easily loved.

**love** (luv) ***n.*** **1** a deep and tender feeling of fondness and devotion [parents' *love* for their children; the *love* of Romeo and Juliet]. **2** a strong liking [a *love* of books]. **3** a person that one loves [my own true *love*].

**4** in tennis, a score of zero. ◆*v.* **1** to feel love for [to *love* one's parents; to *love* all people]. **2** to take great pleasure in [I *love* to eat.] —**loved, lov′ing —fall in love,** to begin to love. —**for the love of,** for the sake of. —**in love,** feeling love. —**make love,** to hug, kiss, etc. as lovers do. —**love′less** *adj.*

SYNONYMS: **Love** suggests very great fondness or deep devotion for someone or something [*love* of one's work; *love* for a parent]. **Affection** suggests warm, tender feelings, usually not so strong or so deep as those that go with the word *love* [They have no *affection* for animals.]

**love·bird** (luv′burd) ***n.*** a small parrot that is often kept as a cage bird. The mates seem to show great fondness for each other.

**love·lorn** (luv′lôrn) ***adj.*** sad or lonely because the person one loves does not love in return.

**love·ly** (luv′lē) ***adj.*** **1** very pleasing in looks or character; beautiful [a *lovely* person]. **2** very enjoyable: *used only in everyday talk* [We had a *lovely* time.] —**love′li·er, love′li·est —love′li·ness** ***n.***

**lov·er** (luv′ər) ***n.*** **1** the person who is in love with one; sweetheart. **2** a person who likes something very much [a music *lover*].

**love seat** a small sofa that seats two people. *See the picture on page 436.*

**love·sick** (luv′sik) ***adj.*** so much in love that one cannot act in a normal way.

**lov·ing** (luv′iŋ) ***adj.*** feeling or showing love [a *loving* parent]. —**lov′ing·ly** ***adv.***

**loving cup** a large drinking cup with two handles, given as a prize in contests.

**lov·ing·kind·ness** (luv′iŋ kīnd′nis) ***n.*** kind or tender actions that show love.

**low**[1] (lō) ***adj.*** **1** reaching only a short distance up; not high or tall [a *low* building]. **2** close to the earth; not far above the ground [*low* clouds]. **3** below the usual surface or level [*low* land]. **4** below others, as in rank or position; inferior or humble [*low* marks in school; of *low* birth]. **5** less than usual in amount, cost, power, strength, etc. [*low* prices; *low* voltage]. **6** deep in pitch [the *low* notes of a bass]. **7** not loud; soft [Speak in a *low* voice.] **8** not good or favorable; poor [a *low* opinion of the book]. **9** sad or gloomy [*low* spirits]. **10** rude or vulgar [*low* jokes]. **11** having only a little of [*low* on fuel; *low* in calories]. ◆*adv.* in or to a low level, place, degree, etc. [Pitch the ball *low*. Speak *low*.] ◆*n.* **1** a low level, place, or degree [The temperature hit a new *low*.] ☆**2** an arrangement of gears that gives the lowest speed and greatest power [Shift into *low* on steep hills.] —**lay low,** to overcome or kill. —**lie low,** ☆to stay hidden. —**low′ness** ***n.***

**low**[2] (lō) ***n.*** the sound that a cow makes; moo. ◆*v.* to make this sound.

☆**low·brow** (lō′brou) ***n.*** a person who has little or no interest in literature, music, art, etc.: *used only in everyday talk.*

**Low Countries** the Netherlands, Belgium, and Luxembourg.

☆**low·down** (lō′doun) ***n.*** the important facts; especially, secret information: *a slang word* [We got the *lowdown*.]

**low·er**[1] (lō′ər) ***adj.*** **1** below another in place, rank, etc. [a *lower* berth; the *lower* baseball leagues]. **2** less in amount, value, strength, etc. [a *lower* price]. ◆*v.* **1** to let down or put down [*Lower* the window.] **2** to make or become less in amount, cost, value, etc. [They will *lower* the price. The voice *lowered* to a whisper.] **3** to bring down in respect [You will *lower* yourself by taking a bribe.]

**low·er**[2] (lou′ər) ***v.*** **1.** to frown or scowl. **2** to look dark and threatening [a *lowering* sky].

**lower class** the social class below the middle class; working class.

**low frequency** any radio frequency between 30 and 300 kilohertz.

**low-grade** (lō′grād′) ***adj.*** **1** of poorer quality or value [*low-grade* coal]. **2** of low degree [a *low-grade* infection].

**low·land** (lō′lənd) ***n.*** land that is lower than the land around it. —**the Lowlands,** the region of low land in southern and central Scotland. *See the map at* **Highlands.** —**low′land·er** or **Low′land·er** ***n.***

**low·ly** (lō′lē) ***adj.*** **1** of a low position or rank [a *lowly* job]. **2** not proud; humble or meek [the *lowly* manner of the slave]. —**low′li·er, low′li·est** ◆*adv.* in a humble, meek, or modest way. —**low′li·ness** ***n.***

☆**low-rise** (lō′rīz′) ***adj.*** describing a building, especially an apartment house, having only a few stories. ◆*n.* such a building.

**low-spir·it·ed** (lō′spir′i tid) ***adj.*** full of sadness; unhappy; depressed.

**low tide** **1** the time when the tide sinks lowest. **2** the lowest level of the tide.



| | | | | | | | |
|---|---|---|---|---|---|---|---|
| **a** | fat | **ir** | here | **ou** | out | **zh** | leisure |
| **ā** | ape | **ī** | bite, fire | **u** | up | **ŋ** | ring |
| **ä** | car, lot | **ō** | go | **ur** | fur | | a *in* ago |
| **e** | ten | **ô** | law, horn | **ch** | chin | | e *in* agent |
| **er** | care | **oi** | oil | **sh** | she | **ə =** | i *in* unity |
| **ē** | even | **oo** | look | **th** | thin | | o *in* collect |
| **i** | hit | **ōō** | tool | ***th*** | then | | u *in* focus |

love seat

lute

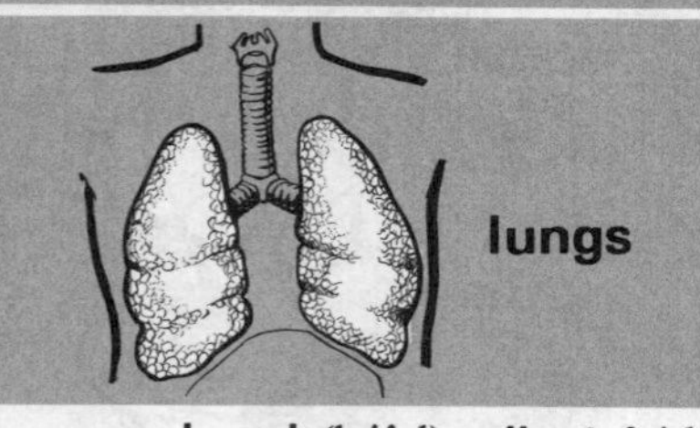
lungs

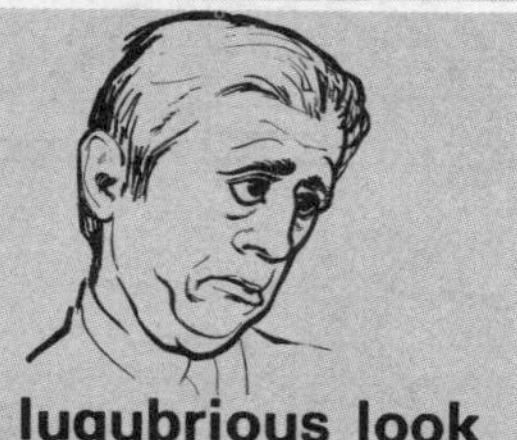
lugubrious look

**loy·al** (loi′əl) ***adj.*** **1** faithful to one's country [a *loyal* citizen]. **2** faithful to one's family, duty, beliefs, etc. [a *loyal* friend; a *loyal* member]. *See* SYNONYMS *at* **faithful.** —**loy′al·ly** ***adv.***

**loy·al·ist** (loi′əl ist) ***n.*** a person who supports the government during a revolt.



**loy·al·ty** (loi′əl tē) ***n.*** the condition of being loyal; faithfulness. *See* SYNONYMS *at* **allegiance.** —*pl.* **loy′al·ties**

**loz·enge** (läz′inj) ***n.*** **1** a figure in the shape of a diamond. **2** a cough drop or hard piece of candy, at one time made in this shape.

**LPN** or **L.P.N.** Licensed Practical Nurse (see **practical nurse**).

**LSD** a drug that makes one imagine amazing or frightening things that are not real.

**Lt.** *abbreviation for* **Lieutenant.**

**Ltd.** or **ltd.** *abbreviation for* **limited.**

**Lu·an·da** (lo͞o än′də) the capital of Angola.

**lu·au** (lo͞o ou′ *or* lo͞o′ou) ***n.*** a Hawaiian feast.

**lub·ber** (lub′ər) ***n.*** **1** a big, clumsy person. **2** a clumsy sailor aboard ship.

☆**lube** (lo͞ob) ***n.*** a lubrication, as of a car: *used only in everyday talk.*

**lu·bri·cant** (lo͞o′brə kənt) ***n.*** an oil, grease, etc. put on parts, as of a machine, to let them move more smoothly against each other.

**lu·bri·cate** (lo͞o′brə kāt) ***v.*** to put a lubricant in or on so as to make the parts more slippery [to *lubricate* a motor]. —**lu′bri·cat·ed, lu′bri·cat·ing** —**lu′bri·ca′tion** ***n.*** —**lu′bri·ca′tor** ***n.***

> **Lubricate** comes from a Latin word meaning "smooth." When a motor is lubricated, it should run smoothly.

**lu·cid** (lo͞o′sid) ***adj.*** **1** clear to the mind; easily understood; not vague or confused [a *lucid* explanation]. **2** that can be seen through; clear [*lucid* water]. **3** thinking clearly; rational [I had a few *lucid* moments during the fever.] —**lu·cid·i·ty** (lo͞o sid′ə tē) ***n.*** —**lu′cid·ly** ***adv.***

**Lu·ci·fer** (lo͞o′sə fər) Satan; the Devil.

☆**Lu·cite** (lo͞o′sīt) *a trademark for* a clear or nearly clear plastic that is cast or molded into sheets, tubes, rods, etc.

**luck** (luk) ***n.*** **1** the things that seem to happen to a person by chance, good or bad; fortune [We started a new business, hoping for a change in *luck.*] **2** good fortune [I had the *luck* to get here first.] —**in luck,** lucky. —☆**luck out,** to have things turn out favorably: *used only in everyday talk.* —**out of luck,** unlucky. —**try one's luck,** to try to do something without being sure what the outcome will be.

**luck·less** (luk′lis) ***adj.*** having no good luck; unlucky. —**luck′less·ly** ***adv.***

**luck·y** (luk′ē) ***adj.*** **1** having good luck [She is *lucky* in games.] **2** having a good result by chance [A *lucky* accident led to the discovery.] **3** thought to bring good luck [a *lucky* rabbit's foot]. —**luck′i·er, luck′i·est** —**luck′i·ly** ***adv.***

**lu·cra·tive** (lo͞o′krə tiv) ***adj.*** bringing wealth or profit; profitable [a *lucrative* business].

**lu·cre** (lo͞o′kər) ***n.*** riches or money: *used chiefly as a scornful word, as in* **filthy lucre.**

**lu·di·crous** (lo͞o′di krəs) ***adj.*** so out of place or silly as to be funny; ridiculous [a *ludicrous* costume—derby, sneakers, and swimming trunks].

**luff** (luf) ***v.*** to turn the bow of a ship toward the wind.

**lug** (lug) ***v.*** to carry or drag with effort [We *lugged* the heavy box upstairs.] —**lugged, lug′ging** ◆***n.*** a part that sticks out, by which something is held or supported.

**lug·gage** (lug′ij) ***n.*** the suitcases, trunks, etc. of a traveler; baggage.

**lug·ger** (lug′ər) ***n.*** a boat with lugsails.

**lug·sail** (lug′s'l *or* lug′sāl) ***n.*** a four-sided sail attached to an upper yard that hangs on the mast in a slanting position.

**lu·gu·bri·ous** (loo go͞o′brē əs) ***adj.*** very sad or mournful, especially in a way that seems exaggerated or ridiculous. *See the picture.*

**Luke** (lo͝ok) **1** an early Christian who was a companion of Paul the Apostle. **2** the third book of the New Testament. Luke is believed to have written this book.

**luke·warm** (lo͞ok′wôrm′) ***adj.*** **1** just barely warm [*lukewarm* water]. **2** not very eager or enthusiastic [*lukewarm* praise].

**lull** (lul) ***v.*** **1** to calm by gentle sound or motion [The baby was *lulled* to sleep in a cradle.] **2** to make or become calm; quiet [The good news *lulled* our fears. The storm *lulled.*] ◆***n.*** a short period when things are quiet or less active [a *lull* in business].

**lull·a·by** (lul′ə bī) ***n.*** a song for lulling a baby to sleep. —*pl.* **lull′a·bies**

**lum·ba·go** (lum bā′gō) ***n.*** a backache in the lower part of the back.

**lum·bar** (lum′bər) ***adj.*** of or near the loins, or lower part of the back.

**lum·ber**[1] (lum′bər) ***n.*** ☆wood that has been sawed into beams, planks, and boards.

**lum·ber**[2] (lum′bər) ***v.*** to move in a heavy, clumsy way [The truck *lumbered* up the hill.]

**lum·ber·ing** (lum′bər iŋ) ***n.*** ☆the work of cutting down trees and sawing them into lumber.

**lum·ber·jack** (lum′bər jak) ***n.*** *another name for* **logger.**

☆**lum·ber·man** (lum′bər mən) ***n.*** **1** *another name for* **logger**. **2** a person whose business is buying and selling lumber. *—pl.* **lum′ber·men**

☆**lum·ber·yard** (lum′bər yärd) ***n.*** a place where lumber is kept for sale.

**lu·mi·nar·y** (lo͞o′mə ner′ē) ***n.*** **1** a body that gives off light, such as the sun or moon. **2** a famous or well-known person. *—pl.* **lu′mi·nar′ies**

**lu·mi·nous** (lo͞o′mə nəs) ***adj.*** **1** giving off light; bright [the *luminous* rays of the sun]. **2** filled with light [a *luminous* room]. **3** glowing in the dark [*luminous* paint]. **4** very clear; easily understood [a *luminous* explanation of the answer]. —**lu·mi·nos·i·ty** (lo͞o′mə näs′ə tē) ***n.***

**lump** (lump) ***n.*** **1** a small, solid mass, with no special shape; hunk [a *lump* of clay]. **2** a raised place; swelling [The bee sting made a *lump* on my neck.] ◆***adj.*** **1** in a lump or lumps [*lump* sugar]. **2** in a single total [We were paid for the work in one *lump* sum.] ◆***v.*** **1** to form into a lump or lumps. **2** to put or group together [They *lumped* all their expenses.] ☆**3** to put up with anyhow: *used only in everyday talk* [If you don't like it, you can *lump* it.] —**lump in one's throat,** a tight feeling in the throat, as when one tries to keep from crying.

**lump·ish** (lump′ish) ***adj.*** **1** like a lump; heavy. **2** dull or stupid.

**lump·y** (lum′pē) ***adj.*** full of lumps [*lumpy* pudding; a *lumpy* old couch]. —**lump′i·er, lump′i·est —lump′i·ness** ***n.***

**Lu·na** (lo͞o′nə) the Roman goddess of the moon.

**lu·na·cy** (lo͞o′nə sē) ***n.*** **1** the condition of being unsound of mind; insanity; madness: *now seldom used.* **2** great foolishness.

☆**luna moth** a large North American moth with light-green wings having crescent marks. The hind pair of wings end in long tails.

**lu·nar** (lo͞o′nər) ***adj.*** **1** of or like the moon [a *lunar* eclipse; a *lunar* crater]. **2** measured by the revolution of the moon around the earth [A *lunar* month is equal to about 29 1/2 days.]

**lu·na·tic** (lo͞o′nə tik) ***adj.*** **1** mentally ill; insane. **2** of or for insane persons. **3** very foolish. ◆***n.*** a person who is mentally ill. *This word is now seldom used.*

> **Lunatic** comes from a Latin word meaning "the moon." People once believed that mental illness was caused by changes of the moon.

**lunch** (lunch) ***n.*** **1** the meal eaten in the middle of the day, between breakfast and dinner. **2** any light meal. ◆***v.*** to eat lunch.

**lunch·eon** (lun′chən) ***n.*** a lunch; especially, a formal lunch with others.

☆**lunch·room** (lunch′ro͞om) ***n.*** a restaurant where lunches are served or, as in schools, where lunches brought from home can be eaten.

**lung** (luŋ) ***n.*** either of the two organs in the chest that are used in breathing. They are like sponges that put oxygen into the blood and take carbon dioxide from it. *See the picture.*

**lunge** (lunj) ***n.*** a sudden, sharp move forward; thrust, as with a sword. ◆***v.*** to make a lunge. —**lunged, lung′ing**

**lu·pine** (lo͞o′pin) ***n.*** a plant with long spikes of white, yellow, rose, or blue flowers and with pods that contain white seeds like beans.

**lurch**[1] (lʉrch) ***v.*** to lean or roll suddenly forward or to one side. ◆***n.*** a lurching movement [The bus started with a *lurch.*]

**lurch**[2] (lʉrch) ***n.*** danger or trouble: used only in the phrase **leave in the lurch,** which means "to leave in trouble and needing help."

**lure** (lo͝or) ***v.*** to attract or lead by offering something that seems pleasant; entice [The sunny day *lured* me from my studies.] —**lured, lur′ing** ◆***n.*** **1** anything that lures [the *lure* of the sea]. **2** an artificial bait used in fishing.

**lu·rid** (lo͝or′id) ***adj.*** **1** so terrible as to shock or startle; sensational [the *lurid* details of the murder]. **2** glowing in a strange or frightening way [the *lurid* sky before a storm].

**lurk** (lʉrk) ***v.*** to stay or be hidden, usually ready to attack or spring out suddenly.

> SYNONYMS: **Lurk** suggests that someone is waiting in hiding or in the background, especially in order to do something evil or harmful [The thief was *lurking* in the shadows.] **Sneak** and **slink** suggest that someone is moving secretly or quietly so as not to be seen or heard, but **sneak** more often suggests a sly or cowardly purpose while **slink** usually suggests fear or guilt [We *sneaked* into the movie without paying. They *slunk* out after stealing some cookies.]

**lus·cious** (lush′əs) ***adj.*** **1** having a delicious taste or smell; full of flavor [a *luscious* steak]. **2** very pleasing to see, hear, etc. [the *luscious* sound of violins]. —**lus′cious·ly** ***adv.***



**lush** (lush) ***adj.*** growing thick and healthy, or covered with thick, healthy growth [*lush* jungle plants; *lush* fields]. —**lush′ly** ***adv.*** —**lush′ness** ***n.***

**lust** (lust) ***n.*** **1** a strong desire [a *lust* for success]. **2** a strong sexual desire. ◆***v.*** to feel a strong desire [The tyrant *lusted* for more power.] —**lust′ful** ***adj.***

**lus·ter** (lus′tər) ***n.*** **1** the brightness of things that reflect light; gloss; brilliance [the *luster* of polished brass]. **2** great fame or glory [Your brave deeds gave new *luster* to your name.]

**lus·trous** (lus′trəs) ***adj.*** having luster; shining; bright [*lustrous* silken robes].

**lust·y** (lus′tē) ***adj.*** strong and full of energy and spirit; robust [The baby gave a *lusty* cry.] —**lust′i·er, lust′i·est —lust′i·ly** ***adv.*** —**lust′i·ness** ***n.***

**lu·ta·nist** (lo͞ot′'n ist) ***n.*** a player on the lute: *also* **lut′ist.**

**lute** (lo͞ot) ***n.*** an early musical instrument played like a guitar. *See the picture.*

**Lu·ther** (lo͞o′thər), **Martin** 1483–1546; German Protestant leader.

**Lu·ther·an** (lo͞o′thər ən) ***n.*** a member of the Protestant church founded by Martin Luther. ◆***adj.*** having to do with this church or its doctrines.

| | | | | | | | |
|---|---|---|---|---|---|---|---|
| **a** | fat | **ir** | here | **ou** | out | **zh** | leisure |
| **ā** | ape | **ī** | bite, fire | **u** | up | **ŋ** | ring |
| **ä** | car, lot | **ō** | go | **ʉr** | fur | | a *in* ago |
| **e** | ten | **ô** | law, horn | **ch** | chin | | e *in* agent |
| **er** | care | **oi** | oil | **sh** | she | **ə =** | i *in* unity |
| **ē** | even | **o͝o** | look | **th** | thin | | o *in* collect |
| **i** | hit | **o͞o** | tool | ***th*** | then | | u *in* focus |

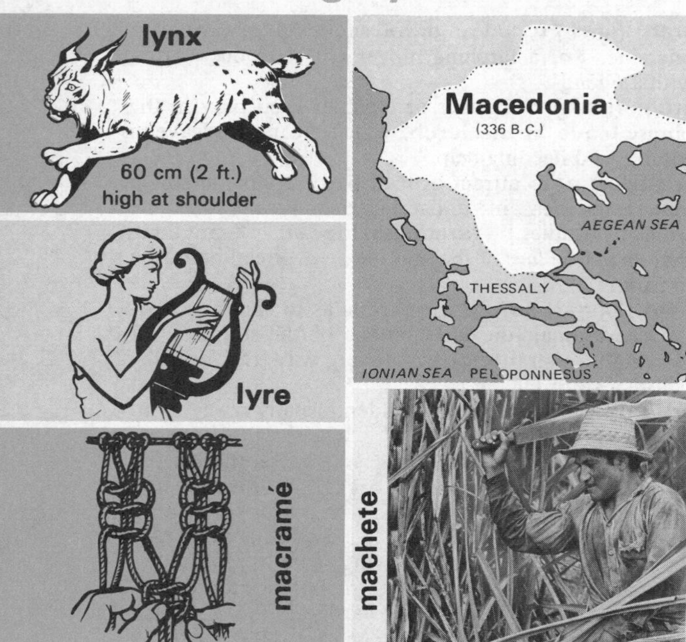


**Lux·em·bourg** (luk′səm burg) **1** a small country in western Europe, surrounded by Belgium, West Germany, and France. **2** its capital.



**lux·u·ri·ant** (lug zho͝or′ē ənt *or* luk sho͝or′ē ənt) ***adj.*** **1** growing thick and healthy; lush [*luxuriant* vines]. **2** full or too full of fancy decorations or ideas; flowery [a *luxuriant* imagination]. —**lux·u′ri·ance *n.*** —**lux·u′ri·ant·ly *adv.***

**lux·u·ri·ate** (lug zho͝or′ē āt *or* luk sho͝or′ē āt) ***v.*** **1** to live in great luxury. **2** to take much pleasure; delight [I *luxuriated* in a hot bath.] —**lux·u′ri·at·ed, lux·u′ri·at·ing**

**lux·u·ri·ous** (lug zho͝or′ē əs *or* luk sho͝or′ē əs) ***adj.*** **1** giving a feeling of luxury; rich, comfortable, etc. [a big, soft, *luxurious* chair]. **2** fond of luxury [*luxurious* tastes]. —**lux·u′ri·ous·ly *adv.***

**lux·u·ry** (luk′shə rē *or* lug′zhə rē) ***n.*** **1** the use and enjoyment of the best and most costly things that give one the most comfort and pleasure [a life of *luxury*]. **2** anything that gives one such comfort, usually something one does not need for life or health [Jewels are *luxuries*.] —*pl.* **lux′u·ries**

**Lu·zon** (lo͞o zän′) the main island of the Philippines.

**-ly** (lē) *a suffix used to form adjectives and adverbs, meaning:* **1** of, like, or suitable to [*Friendly* advice is advice like that a friend would give.] **2** every or each [A *weekly* newspaper appears every week.] **3** in a certain way, or at a certain time or place [To sing *harshly* is to sing in a harsh way.] **4** in or from a certain direction [A *westerly* wind blows from the west.] **5** in a certain order [*Secondly* means second in order.]

**ly·ce·um** (lī sē′əm) ***n.*** **1** a large hall where public lectures are given. **2** an organization that gives public lectures, concerts, etc.

**lye** (lī) ***n.*** any strong alkaline substance, used in cleaning and in making soap. At one time lye was got from wood ashes.

**ly·ing** (lī′iŋ) *present participle of* **lie¹** *or* **lie²**. ◆***adj.*** not telling the truth [a *lying* witness]. ◆***n.*** the telling of a lie or lies.

**lymph** (limf) ***n.*** a clear, slightly yellow liquid that flows through the body in a system of tubes. **Lymph** is somewhat like blood plasma.

**lym·phat·ic** (lim fat′ik) ***adj.*** of or carrying lymph [The *lymphatic* vessels carry lymph to various parts of the body.]

**lymph node** any of the small masses of tissue lying in groups along the course of the lymphatic vessels. Lymph nodes produce lymphocytes. *Also called* **lymph gland.**

**lym·pho·cyte** (lim′fə sīt) ***n.*** any of the colorless cells formed in lymphatic tissue that help in forming antibodies.

☆**lynch** (linch) ***v.*** to kill by the action of a mob, without a lawful trial, as by hanging. —**lynch′er *n.***

The word **lynch** comes from the name of Captain William *Lynch.* He was part of a group in Pittsylvania, Virginia, in 1780 that set itself up to punish people thought to be guilty of crimes.

**lynx** (liŋks) ***n.*** a wildcat of North America, that has long legs, a short tail, and long, silky, yellow fur. *See the picture.*

**Lyon** (lyōn) a city in east central France. *The British spelling is* **Ly·ons** (lī′ənz).

**lyre** (līr) ***n.*** an old instrument like a small harp, used by the ancient Greeks to accompany singers or poets. *See the picture.*

**lyre·bird** (līr′burd) ***n.*** an Australian songbird. The long tail feathers of the male spread out to look like a lyre.

**lyr·ic** (lir′ik) ***adj.*** **1** of or having to do with poetry that describes the poet's feelings and thoughts [Sonnets and odes are *lyric* poems.] **2** like a song or suitable for singing. **3** of or having a high voice that moves lightly and easily from note to note [a *lyric* soprano]. ◆***n.*** **1** a lyric poem. **2** *usually* **lyrics**, *pl.* the words of a song.

**lyr·i·cal** (lir′i k′l) ***adj.*** **1** *another word for* **lyric. 2** very excited, emotional, enthusiastic, etc. [They gave a *lyrical* account of their trip.] —**lyr′i·cal·ly *adv.***

**lyr·i·cist** (lir′ə sist) ***n.*** a writer of lyrics, especially lyrics for popular songs.

**M, m** (em) ***n.*** the thirteenth letter of the English alphabet. *—pl.* **M's, m's** (emz)

**M** (em) ***n.*** the Roman numeral for 1,000.

**M.** *abbreviation for* **Monsieur.** *—pl.* **MM.**

**M.** or **m.** *abbreviation for* **male, mile** *or* **miles, minute** *or* **minutes.**

**m** or **m.** *abbreviation for* **meter** *or* **meters.**

**ma** (mä) ***n.*** mother: *used only in everyday talk.*

**MA** *abbreviation for* **Massachusetts.**

**M.A.** Master of Arts.

**ma'am** (mam) ***n.*** madam: *used only in everyday talk.*

**mac·ad·am** (mə kad′əm) ***n.*** **1** small broken stones used in making roads. **2** a road made by macadamizing with layers of such stones.

**mac·a·dam·i·a nut** (mak′ə dā′mē ə) a round, hard-shelled nut from an Australian tree that is also grown in Hawaii. The nuts are eaten as food.

**mac·ad·am·ize** (mə kad′ə mīz) ***v.*** to make or cover a road with layers of macadam, often mixed with tar or asphalt and rolled until smooth. **—mac·ad′am·ized, mac·ad′am·iz·ing**

**mac·a·ro·ni** (mak′ə rō′nē) ***n.*** long, hollow tubes of dried flour paste, often baked with cheese or meat.

**mac·a·roon** (mak ə ro͞on′) ***n.*** a small, sweet cookie made with crushed almonds or coconut.

**ma·caw** (mə kô′) ***n.*** a large, bright-colored parrot of Central and South America.

**Mac·beth** (mək beth′) **1** a tragic play by Shakespeare. **2** its main character. With the help of his wife, he kills the king so that he himself may become king.

**mace**[1] (mās) ***n.*** **1** a heavy club with a metal head, usually with spikes, used as a weapon in the Middle Ages. **2** a staff carried by or before an official as a symbol of power.

**mace**[2] (mās) ***n.*** a spice made from the dried outer covering of the nutmeg.

**Mace** (mās) *a trademark for* a chemical that is a tear gas and that irritates the skin. It is sprayed from a can to stop an attacker.

**Mac·e·do·ni·a** (mas′ə dō′nē ə) an ancient kingdom in southeastern Europe. It is now divided among Greece, Yugoslavia, and Bulgaria and is a state of Yugoslavia. *See the map.* **—Mac′e·do′ni·an *adj., n.***

**Mach** or **Mach number** (mäk) a number that represents the ratio of the speed of an airplane or missile to the speed of sound [A plane with a speed of *Mach* 1 travels as fast as sound, 1,192 kilometers or about 741 miles per hour.]

**ma·che·te** (mə shet′ē *or* mə chet′ē) ***n.*** a large knife with a heavy blade, used for cutting down sugar cane or underbrush in Central and South America. *See the picture.*

**Mach·i·a·vel·li·an** (mak′ē ə vel′ē ən) ***adj.*** of or like Machiavelli, an Italian statesman of the 16th century, who taught that it was right for rulers to use tricky and dishonest methods to keep power; deceitful; crafty.

**mach·i·na·tion** (mak′ə nā′shən) ***n.*** a secret plot or scheming, especially of a kind meant to cause trouble: *usually used in the plural,* **machinations.**

**ma·chine** (mə shēn′) ***n.*** **1** a thing made up of fixed and moving parts, for doing some kind of work [a sewing *machine*]. **2** a thing that works in a simple way to get the most force from the energy used [Levers, screws, and pulleys are simple *machines.*] **3** a person or group thought of as acting like a machine, without thought. ☆**4** the group of people who control a political party. ◆***adj.*** **1** of machines. **2** made or done by machinery [a *machine* product]. ◆***v.*** to make or shape by machinery. **—ma·chined′, ma·chin′ing**

☆**machine gun** an automatic gun that fires many bullets, one right after the other.

**ma·chin·er·y** (mə shēn′ər ē) ***n.*** **1** machines in general [the *machinery* of a factory]. **2** the working parts of a machine [the *machinery* of a printing press]. **3** the means or system by which something is kept in action [the *machinery* of government]. *—pl.* **ma·chin′er·ies**

☆**machine shop** a factory for making or repairing machines or parts for machines. 439

**machine tool** a tool worked by electricity, steam, etc., as a lathe, drill, or saw.

**ma·chin·ist** (mə shēn′ist) ***n.*** **1** a person who is skilled in working with machine tools. **2** a person who makes, repairs, or runs machinery.

**Mac·ken·zie** (mə ken′zē) a river in northwestern Canada, flowing into the Arctic Ocean.

**mack·er·el** (mak′ər əl) ***n.*** a fish of the North Atlantic, used for food. *—pl.* **mack′er·el** or **mack′er·els**

**Mack·i·nac** (mak′ə nô), **Straits of** a strait joining Lake Huron and Lake Michigan.

**Mack·i·naw coat** (mak′ə nô) a short coat of heavy woolen cloth, often with a plaid design: *also* **mackinaw.**

**mack·in·tosh** or **mac·in·tosh** (mak′in täsh′) ***n.*** a raincoat of waterproof, rubberized cloth.

**mac·ra·mé** (mak′rə mā) ***n.*** a rough fringe or lace of thread or cord knotted so as to form designs. *See the picture.*

**ma·cron** (mā′krən *or* mā′krän) ***n.*** a short, straight mark (¯) used over a vowel to show how it is pronounced, as in *came* (kām).

**mad** (mad) ***adj.*** **1** very sick in the mind; insane. **2** excited in a wild way; frantic [*mad* with fear]. **3** foolish and reckless; unwise [a *mad* scheme]. **4** fond or

| | | | |
|---|---|---|---|
| **a** fat | **ir** here | **ou** out | **zh** leisure |
| **ā** ape | **ī** bite, fire | **u** up | **ng** ring |
| **ä** car, lot | **ō** go | **ur** fur | a *in* ago |
| **e** ten | **ô** law, horn | **ch** chin | e *in* agent |
| **er** care | **oi** oil | **sh** she | **ə** = i *in* unity |
| **ē** even | **oo** look | **th** thin | o *in* collect |
| **i** hit | **o͞o** tool | ***th*** then | u *in* focus |

enthusiastic in a way that is foolish [*mad* about hats]. **5** having rabies [a *mad* dog]. **6** angry [Don't be *mad* at us for leaving.] —**have a mad on,** to be angry: *used only in everyday talk.* —**mad′der, mad′dest**

**Mad·a·gas·car** (mad′ə gas′kər) a country on a large island off the southeastern coast of Africa.

**mad·am** (mad′əm) ***n.*** a woman; lady: *a polite form used in speaking to or of a woman* [May I serve you, *madam? Madam* is not in.] —*pl.* **mes·dames** (mā däm′) or **mad′ams**

**mad·ame** (mad′əm *or* mə däm′) ***n.*** a French word used, like "Mrs.," as a title for a married woman: abbreviated **Mme., Mdme.** —*pl.* **mes·dames** (mā däm′)

**mad·cap** (mad′kap) ***n.*** a lively, reckless person. ◆***adj.*** lively and reckless [*madcap* pranks].

**mad·den** (mad′′n) ***v.*** to make or become insane, angry, or wildly excited.

**made** (mād) *past tense and past participle of* **make.** ◆***adj.*** built; put together; formed [a well-*made* house].

**Ma·deir·a** (mə dir′ə) **1** the main island in a group of Portuguese islands (called **Madeira Islands**), off the coast of Morocco. **2** a strong white wine made on this island.

**ma·de·moi·selle** (mad′ə mə zel′ *or* mam zel′ *or* mäd mwä zel′) ***n.*** a French word used, like "Miss," as a title for an unmarried woman or girl: abbreviated **Mlle., Mdlle.** —*French pl.* **mesde·moi·selles** (mād mwä zel′)

**made-to-or·der** (mād′tə ôr′dər) ***adj.*** made just as the customer ordered; not ready-made.

**made-up** (mād′up′) ***adj.*** **1** invented; false; not true [a *made-up* story]. **2** with lipstick, mascara, etc. on.

**mad·house** (mad′hous) ***n.*** **1** a place for keeping insane people: *no longer used in this meaning.* **2** a place of noise and confusion [The stores are *madhouses* during the Christmas rush.]

**Mad·i·son** (mad′i s′n) the capital of Wisconsin.

**Mad·i·son** (mad′i s′n), **James** 1751–1836; the fourth president of the United States, from 1809 to 1817.

**mad·ly** (mad′lē) ***adv.*** in a way that is insane, wild, foolish, etc.

**mad·man** (mad′man *or* mad′mən) ***n.*** a person who is insane; maniac. —*pl.* **mad′men′**

**mad·ness** (mad′nis) ***n.*** **1** the condition of being mad, or insane. **2** great anger; fury. **3** great foolishness.

**Ma·don·na** (mə dän′ə) ***n.*** **1** Mary, the mother of Jesus. **2** a picture or statue of Mary.

> **Madonna** comes from an Italian word that means "my lady." The Italian word *donna,* meaning "lady," comes in turn from the Latin word *domina,* which means ruler or mistress of a household.

**Ma·dras** (mə dras′ *or* mad′rəs) a city on the southeastern coast of India.

**ma·dras** (mad′rəs *or* mə dras′) ***n.*** a fine cotton cloth, used for shirts, dresses, etc.

**Ma·drid** (mə drid′) the capital of Spain.

**mad·ri·gal** (mad′ri gəl) ***n.*** **1** a short poem, usually about love, which can be set to music. **2** a song with parts for several voices, sung without accompaniment.

**mad·wom·an** (mad′woom′ən) ***n.*** a woman who is insane. —*pl.* **mad′wom′en**

**mael·strom** (māl′strəm) ***n.*** **1** a large or violent whirlpool; especially, **the Maelstrom,** a dangerous whirlpool off the west coast of Norway. **2** a condition or state in which things are very confused or upset.

**ma·es·tro** (mīs′trō *or* mä es′trō) ***n.*** a master. This is an Italian word, especially for a great composer, conductor, or teacher of music. —*pl.* **ma·es′tros** or **ma·es·tri** (mä es′trē)

**Ma·fi·a** or **Maf·fi·a** (mä′fē ə) ***n.*** a secret society of criminals.

**mag.** *an abbreviation for* **magazine, magnitude.**

**mag·a·zine** (mag ə zēn′ *or* mag′ə zēn) ***n.*** **1** a publication that comes out regularly, as weekly or monthly, and contains articles, stories, pictures, etc. **2** a place for storing things, as military supplies. **3** a space, as in a warship, for storing explosives. **4** the space in a gun from which the cartridges are fed. **5** the space in a camera from which the film is fed.

**Ma·gel·lan** (mə jel′ən), **Ferdinand** 1480?–1521; Portuguese explorer who led a voyage that became the first around the world. He died on the way.

**ma·gen·ta** (mə jen′tə) ***n.*** **1** a purplish-red dye. **2** purplish red.

**mag·got** (mag′ət) ***n.*** an insect in an early stage, when it looks like a worm, as the larva of the housefly. Some maggots are found in rotting matter. *See the picture.*

**Ma·gi** (mā′jī) ***n.pl.*** the wise men in the Bible who brought gifts to the baby Jesus.

**mag·ic** (maj′ik) ***n.*** **1** the use of charms, spells, and rituals that are supposed to make things happen in an unnatural way [In fairy tales, *magic* is used to work miracles.] **2** any power or force that seems mysterious or hard to explain [the *magic* of love]. **3** the skill of doing puzzling tricks by moving the hands so fast as to fool those watching and by using boxes with false bottoms, hidden strings, etc.; sleight of hand. ◆***adj.*** of or as if by magic.

**mag·i·cal** (maj′i k′l) ***adj.*** of or like magic. —**mag′i·cal·ly** ***adv.***

**ma·gi·cian** (mə jish′ən) ***n.*** **1** a person, as in fairy tales, who works magic. **2** a person who does magic tricks, or sleight of hand. *See the picture.*

**mag·is·te·ri·al** (maj′is tir′ē əl) ***adj.*** **1** of or fit for a magistrate [*magisterial* robes]. **2** that shows authority [a *magisterial* manner].

**mag·is·tra·cy** (maj′is trə sē) ***n.*** **1** the office or term of a magistrate. **2** magistrates as a group.

**mag·is·trate** (maj′is trāt) ***n.*** **1** an official with the power to put laws into effect, as the president of a republic. **2** a minor official, as a judge in a police court.

**Mag·na Char·ta** or **Mag·na Car·ta** (mag′nə kär′tə) **1** the document that King John was forced by the English barons to sign in 1215, guaranteeing certain rights to them. **2** any constitution that guarantees civil and political rights.

**mag·na·nim·i·ty** (mag′nə nim′ə tē) ***n.*** the state of being magnanimous.

**mag·nan·i·mous** (mag nan′ə məs) ***adj.*** generous in forgiving injury; not mean or petty. —**mag·nan′i·mous·ly** ***adv.***

**mag·nate** (mag′nāt) ***n.*** a very important or powerful person [a business *magnate*].

**mag·ne·sia** (mag nē′zhə *or* mag nē′shə) ***n.*** a white powder with no taste, mixed with water and used as a medicine.

**mag·ne·si·um** (mag nē′zē əm *or* mag nē′zhē əm) ***n.*** a silvery, very light metal that is a chemical element. It burns with a bright light and is used in flashbulbs for taking photographs.

**mag·net** (mag′nit) ***n.*** **1** any piece of iron, steel, or lodestone that has the natural power to draw iron and steel to it. This power may also be given artificially by passing an electric current through wire wrapped around the metal. *See the picture.* **2** a person or thing that attracts.

**mag·net·ic** (mag net′ik) ***adj.*** **1** working like a magnet [a *magnetic* needle]. **2** that can be magnetized. **3** that attracts strongly [*magnetic* eyes].

**magnetic north** the direction toward which the needle of a compass points. In most places it is not true north.

**magnetic tape** a thin plastic ribbon with a magnetized coating, used for recording sound, computer data, etc.

**mag·net·ism** (mag′nə tiz′m) ***n.*** **1** the power that a magnet has. **2** the branch of physics dealing with magnets and their power. **3** the power to attract; personal charm.

**mag·net·ize** (mag′nə tīz) ***v.*** **1** to make magnetic, as iron or steel. **2** to attract or charm [We feel *magnetized* by your personality.] —**mag′net·ized, mag′net·iz·ing**

**mag·ne·to** (mag nēt′ō) ***n.*** a small kind of electric generator, used with some gasoline engines to make the electric spark for the ignition. —*pl.* **mag·ne′tos**

☆**magnet school** a public school that offers new, unconventional courses and specialized training in order to bring together students of many races and backgrounds.

**mag·nif·i·cence** (mag nif′ə s′ns) ***n.*** grand or impressive beauty; grandeur or splendor.

**mag·nif·i·cent** (mag nif′ə s′nt) ***adj.*** rich, fine, noble, beautiful, etc. in a grand way; splendid [a *magnificent* castle; a *magnificent* idea]. *See* SYNONYMS *at* **grand.**

**mag·ni·fy** (mag′nə fī) ***v.*** to make look or seem larger or greater than is really so [This lens *magnifies* an object to ten times its size. He *magnified* the seriousness of his illness.] —**mag′ni·fied, mag′ni·fy·ing**

**magnifying glass** a lens that makes the things seen through it look larger. *See the picture.*

**mag·ni·tude** (mag′nə to͞od *or* mag′nə tyo͞od) ***n.*** **1** greatness, as of size, importance, or power [the *magnitude* of her discovery]. **2** size or importance [a country of lesser *magnitude*].

☆**mag·no·li·a** (mag nō′lē ə *or* mag nōl′yə) ***n.*** a tree or shrub with large, sweet-smelling flowers of white, pink, or purple.

**mag·pie** (mag′pī) ***n.*** **1** a black-and-white bird of the crow family, that chatters noisily. **2** a person who chatters.

**mag·uey** (mag′wā) ***n.*** a desert plant of Mexico and the southwestern U.S., related to the agave. Fibers from it are used in making rope.

**Mag·yar** (mag′yär) ***n.*** **1** a member of the main group of people of Hungary. **2** their language; Hungarian. ◆***adj.*** of the Magyars, their language, customs, etc.

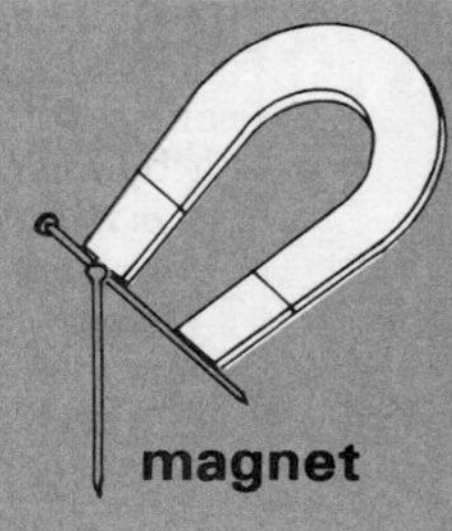


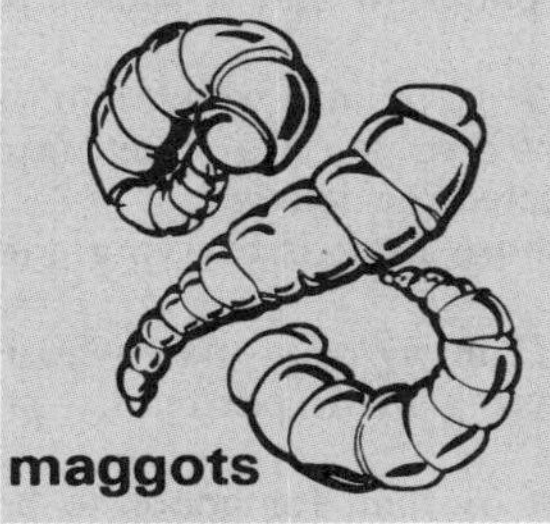

**ma·ha·ra·jah** or **ma·ha·ra·ja** (mä′hə rä′jə) ***n.*** a former prince of India, especially one who in earlier times was a ruler of one of its states.

**ma·ha·ra·ni** *or* **ma·ha·ra·nee** (mä′hə rä′nē) ***n.*** the wife of a maharajah.

**ma·hat·ma** (mə hat′mə *or* mə hät′mə) ***n.*** a very wise and holy person in India.



**mah-jongg** or **mah·jong** (mä′jôŋ) ***n.*** a game that came from China, played with many small tiles.

**ma·hog·a·ny** (mə häg′ə nē *or* mə hôg′ə nē) ***n.*** **1** the hard, reddish-brown wood of a tropical American tree, used in making furniture. **2** this tree. **3** reddish brown. —*pl.* **ma·hog′a·nies**

**Ma·hom·et** (mə häm′it) *another name for* **Mohammed.** —**Ma·hom′et·an** ***adj., n.***

**maid** (mād) ***n.*** **1** a maiden. **2** a girl or woman servant.

**maid·en** (mād′′n) ***n.*** a girl or young woman who is not married. ◆***adj.*** **1** of, like, or fit for a maiden. **2** unmarried [a *maiden* aunt]. **3** first or earliest [a *maiden* voyage]. —**maid′en·ly** ***adv.***

**maid·en·hair** (mād′′n her) ***n.*** a kind of fern with very thin stalks and delicate, fan-shaped leaflets. *The full name is* **maidenhair fern.**

**maid·en·hood** (mād′′n hood) ***n.*** the time or state of being a maiden.

**maiden name** the family name that a woman had before she was married.

**maid of honor** ☆**1** an unmarried woman who is the chief bridesmaid at a wedding. **2** an unmarried woman attending a queen or princess.

**maid·ser·vant** (mād′sʉr′vənt) ***n.*** a girl or woman servant.

| | | | |
|---|---|---|---|
| **a** fat | **ir** here | **ou** out | **zh** leisure |
| **ā** ape | **ī** bite, fire | **u** up | **ŋ** ring |
| **ä** car, lot | **ō** go | **ʉr** fur | a *in* ago |
| **e** ten | **ô** law, horn | **ch** chin | e *in* agent |
| **er** care | **oi** oil | **sh** she | **ə** = i *in* unity |
| **ē** even | **oo** look | **th** thin | o *in* collect |
| **i** hit | **o͞o** tool | ***th*** then | u *in* focus |

**m**

**mail**[1] (māl) ***n.*** **1** letters, packages, etc. carried and delivered by a post office. **2** the system of picking up and delivering letters, papers, etc.; postal system [Send it by *mail.*] ◆***adj.*** having to do with or carrying mail [a *mail* truck]. ◆***v.*** ☆to send by mail; place in a mailbox. —**mail′a·ble** ***adj.***

**Mail**[1] comes from an old German word that at first meant "wallet" and then came to mean "traveling bag." Mail carriers today still use bags that resemble those early traveling bags.

**mail**[2] (māl) ***n.*** armor for the body, made of small metal rings or overlapping plates so that it will bend easily. *See the picture.*

**mail·box** (māl′bäks) ***n.*** ☆**1** a box into which mail is delivered at a home. ☆**2** a box, as on a street, into which mail is put to be collected for delivery.

☆**mail carrier** a person whose work is carrying and delivering mail.

**mail·man** (māl′man *or* māl′mən) ***n.*** a man whose work is carrying and delivering mail; postman. *—pl.* **mail′men′**

☆**mail order** an order sent by mail for goods to be delivered by mail. —**mail′-or′der** ***adj.***

**maim** (mām) ***v.*** to hurt a person so that an arm, leg, etc., or its use, is lost; cripple.

SYNONYMS: To **maim** is to injure a person's body so that some part is lost or can no longer be used [*maimed* in an auto accident]. To **cripple** is to cause to be without a leg or arm or to make unable to move in a normal way [*crippled* by rheumatism]. To **mutilate** is to take away or injure greatly a part of a person or thing so that the person or thing is no longer complete [a statue *mutilated* by vandals].



**Mai·mon·i·des** (mī män′ə dēz) 1135–1204; a Spanish rabbi and philosopher, in Egypt.

**main** (mān) ***adj.*** first in size or importance; chief; principal [the *main* office of a company; the *main* characters in a play]. ◆***n.*** **1** any of the larger pipes from which smaller pipes carry water, gas, etc. to a building. **2** the ocean or sea: *used in poetry.* —**by main force** or **by main strength,** by great force or strength alone. —**in the main,** mostly; chiefly. —**with might and main,** with all one's strength.

**main clause** a clause that could stand alone as a complete sentence.

**Maine** (mān) a New England State of the U.S.: abbreviated **Me., ME**

**main·land** (mān′land *or* mān′lənd) ***n.*** the main part of a country or continent, as apart from its peninsulas or nearby islands.

**main·ly** (mān′lē) ***adv.*** most of all; chiefly.

**main·mast** (mān′məst *or* mān′mast) ***n.*** the highest and most important mast on a ship.

**main·sail** (mān′s'l *or* mān′sāl) ***n.*** the largest sail on a ship, as that set from the mainmast.

**main·spring** (mān′spriŋ) ***n.*** **1** the most important spring in a clock, watch, etc., that keeps it going. *See the picture.* **2** the chief motive, purpose, or cause.

**main·stay** (mān′stā) ***n.*** **1** the line that runs forward from the upper part of the mainmast, helping to hold it in place. **2** the main or chief support [She was the *mainstay* of her family.]

**main·tain** (mān tān′) ***v.*** **1** to keep or keep up; continue in the same condition; carry on [*Maintain* an even speed. Food *maintains* life.] **2** to keep in good repair; preserve [to *maintain* roads]. **3** to support by supplying what is needed [Can you *maintain* a family?] **4** to say in a positive way; declare; assert [He still *maintains* that he's innocent.] **5** to defend, as by argument [They *maintained* the position that slavery was wrong.]

**main·te·nance** (mān′t'n əns) ***n.*** **1** a maintaining or being maintained; upkeep or support [Taxes pay for the *maintenance* of schools.] **2** a means of support; livelihood [a job that barely provides a *maintenance*].

**maize** (māz) ***n.*** *another word for* **corn**[1] *in meaning* 1.

**Maj.** *abbreviation for* **Major.**

**ma·jes·tic** (mə jes′tik) or **ma·jes·ti·cal** (mə jes′ti k'l) ***adj.*** having majesty; grand; stately; dignified [a *majestic* mountain peak]. —**ma·jes′ti·cal·ly** ***adv.***

**maj·es·ty** (maj′is tē) ***n.*** **1** the dignity or power of a king, queen, etc. **2 Majesty,** a title used in speaking to or of a king, queen, etc. [His *Majesty,* the Emperor]. **3** grandeur or stateliness [the *majesty* of the Alps]. —*pl.* **maj′es·ties**

**ma·jor** (mā′jər) ***adj.*** **1** greater in size, importance, amount, etc. [the *major* part of his wealth; a *major* poet]. **2** in music, that is separated from the next tone by a full step instead of a half step [a *major* interval]. **3** that is or has to do with a musical scale with half steps after the third and seventh tones: *see also* **minor.** ◆***n.*** **1** a military officer ranking just above a captain. ☆**2** the main subject that a student is studying [History is my *major.*] ◆***v.*** ☆to have as one's major subject [to *major* in English].

**ma·jor-do·mo** (mā′jər dō′mō) ***n.*** a servant in charge of a royal household. —*pl.* **ma′jor-do′mos**

☆**ma·jor·ette** (mā jər et′) ***n.*** *a shorter form of* **drum majorette.**

**major general** a military officer ranking above a brigadier general. —*pl.* **major generals**

**ma·jor·i·ty** (mə jôr′ə tē) ***n.*** **1** the greater part or number; more than half [A *majority* of the class went to the play.] ☆**2** the amount by which the greater or greatest number of votes is more than all the rest [To get 50 votes of a total of 90 is to have a *majority* of 10.] **3** the age at which a young person is said by law to become an adult [In some States one's *majority* is reached on one's 21st birthday.] —*pl.* **ma·jor′i·ties**

**make** (māk) ***v.*** **1** to bring into being; build, create, produce, put together, etc. [to *make* a dress; to *make* a fire; to *make* plans; to *make* noise]. **2** to cause to be or become [His giggling *makes* me nervous. Lincoln *made* Grant a general.] **3** to turn out to be [The book will *make* a good movie.] **4** to do, perform, carry on, etc. [to *make* a right turn; to *make* a speech]. **5** to get or gain, as by working; earn; acquire [to *make* money; to *make* friends]. **6** to prepare for use; arrange [to *make* the bed]. **7** to amount to; total [Two pints *make* a quart.] **8** to cause or force to [She *made* the engine purr.] **9** to cause to be successful [Good pitching can *make* a baseball team.] **10** to understand [What do you *make* of the poem?] **11** to arrive at; reach [The ship *made* port today.] **12** to go or travel [We *made* 500 miles in a day. The ship can *make* 35 knots.] **13** to succeed in becoming a member of, being mentioned in, etc.: *used only in everyday talk* [Ten of us made the honor roll. The earthquake *made* the headlines.] —**made, mak'ing** ✦*n.* **1** the way something is made or put together [a bicycle of a lighter *make*]. **2** a brand or type of product, as showing where or by whom it is made [a foreign *make* of automobile]. —**make after,** to chase or follow. —**make away with, 1** to steal. **2** to get rid of. **3** to kill. —**make believe,** to pretend. —**make for, 1** to go toward; head for. **2** to help bring about [Respect for the rights of others *makes for* a happy home.] —**make it,** to manage to do a certain thing: *used only in everyday talk.* —☆**make like,** to imitate; pretend to be: *a slang phrase.* —**make off with,** to steal. —**make or break,** to cause the success or failure of. —**make out, 1** to see with difficulty. **2** to understand. **3** to fill out, as a blank form. **4** to prove or try to prove to be [They *made* me *out* to be a loser.] **5** to get along; succeed. —**make over, 1** to change; cause to be different. **2** to hand over the ownership of [My uncle *made over* the car to his daughter.] —**make up, 1** to put together. **2** to form; be the parts of. **3** to invent. **4** to supply what is missing. **5** to give or do in place of; compensate [You can never *make up* the loss.] **6** to become friendly again after a quarrel. **7** to put on lipstick, mascara, etc. **8** to decide [He *made up* his mind to go.] ☆**9** to take, as a test one has missed. —**make up to,** to try to make oneself liked by, as by flattering. —**mak'er** *n.*

**make-be·lieve** (māk'bə lēv') *n.* a pretending or imagining, as in a game. ✦*adj.* pretended; imagined [a *make-believe* playmate].

**make·shift** (māk'shift) *n.* something used for a time in place of the usual thing [We used the sofa as a *makeshift* for a bed.] *See the picture.*

**make·up** or **make-up** (māk'up) *n.* **1** the way a thing is put together; composition [the *makeup* of the atom]. **2** one's nature or disposition [a cheerful *makeup*]. **3** cosmetics; lipstick, mascara, etc. *See the picture.* **4** the greasepaint, wigs, costumes, etc. put on by a person acting in a play. ☆**5** a special test taken by a student to make up for a test that was missed: *used only in everyday talk.*

**mal-** *a prefix meaning* bad or badly [*Maladjustment* is bad adjustment.]

**Ma·lac·ca** (mə lak'ə), **Strait of** a strait between Sumatra and the Malay Peninsula.

**mal·ad·just·ed** (mal'ə jus'tid) *adj.* badly adjusted; especially, not able to fit happily into the life around one. —**mal'ad·just'ment** *n.*

**mal·a·droit** (mal ə droit') *adj.* awkward; clumsy.

**mal·a·dy** (mal'ə dē) *n.* a sickness or disease. —*pl.* **mal'a·dies**

**ma·lar·i·a** (mə ler'ē ə) *n.* a disease in which a person keeps having chills and fever. It is carried to human beings by the bite of a certain kind of mosquito. —**ma·lar'i·al** *adj.*

**Malaria** is a shortened form of two Italian words that mean "bad air." The disease was given this name from the mistaken notion that it was caused by the bad air of swamps.

**Mal·a·wi** (mä'lä wē) a country in southeastern Africa.

**Ma·lay** (mā'lā) *n.* **1** a member of a brown-skinned people of the Malay Peninsula and Archipelago. **2** their language. ✦*adj.* of the Malays, their language, etc. *Also* **Ma·lay·an** (mə lā'ən).

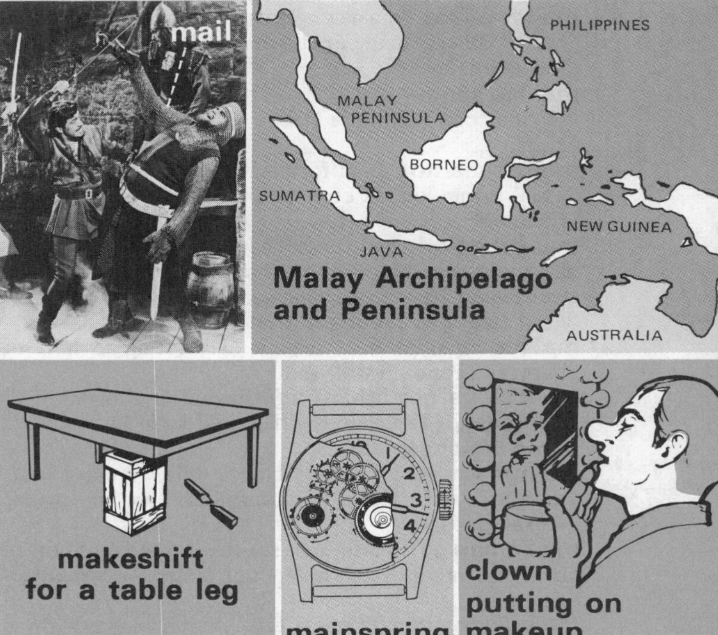

makeshift for a table leg

mainspring

clown putting on makeup

**Ma·lay·a** (mə lā'ə) the Malay Peninsula.

**Malay Archipelago** a large group of islands between the Malay Peninsula and Australia. *See the map.*



**Malay Peninsula** a long, narrow peninsula in southeastern Asia, north of Sumatra. *See the map.*

**Ma·lay·sia** (mə lā'zhə) **1** *another name for* **Malay Archipelago. 2** a country in southeastern Asia, on the Malay Peninsula and part of Borneo. —**Ma·lay'·sian** *adj., n.*

**mal·con·tent** (mal'kən tent) *adj.* not satisfied with the way things are; ready to rebel. ✦*n.* a person who is malcontent.

**Mal·dive Islands** (mal'dīv) a country on a group of islands in the Indian Ocean.

**male** (māl) *adj.* **1** of or belonging to the sex that can make the egg of the female fertile [A *male* goose is called a "gander."] **2** of or for men or boys [a *male* chorus]. ✦*n.* a male person, animal, or plant.

SYNONYMS: **Male** stands for the members of the sex that is different from the female sex and is used of plants and animals as well as human beings. **Masculine** refers to those qualities thought of as making up the special character of men and boys, such as strength. **Manly** suggests the noble qualities of a man who has courage and honesty.

**mal·e·dic·tion** (mal'ə dik'shən) *n.* a calling down of injury or harm on someone; curse.

**mal·e·fac·tor** (mal'ə fak'tər) *n.* a person who does evil or wrong; criminal.

| | | | |
|---|---|---|---|
| **a** fat | **ir** here | **ou** out | **zh** leisure |
| **ā** ape | **ī** bite, fire | **u** up | **ng** ring |
| **ä** car, lot | **ō** go | **ur** fur | a *in* ago |
| **e** ten | **ô** law, horn | **ch** chin | e *in* agent |
| **er** care | **oi** oil | **sh** she | ə = i *in* unity |
| **ē** even | **oo** look | **th** thin | o *in* collect |
| **i** hit | **ōō** tool | ***th*** then | u *in* focus |

**ma·lev·o·lent** (mə lev′ə lənt) ***adj.*** wishing harm or evil to others; malicious. —**ma·lev′o·lence** ***n.*** —**ma·lev′o·lent·ly** ***adv.***

**mal·fea·sance** (mal fē′z'ns) ***n.*** unlawful wrongdoing by someone holding a public office, as the taking of graft.

**mal·for·ma·tion** (mal′fôr mā′shən) ***n.*** a wrong or unusual formation, as of some part of the body. —**mal·formed′** ***adj.***

**mal·func·tion** (mal fuŋk′shən) ***v.*** to fail to work as it should. ◆***n.*** an instance of such failure [The launch was delayed by the *malfunction* of a rocket.]

**Ma·li** (mä′lē) a country in western Africa.

**mal·ice** (mal′is) ***n.*** a feeling of wanting to hurt or harm someone; ill will; spite.

**ma·li·cious** (mə lish′əs) ***adj.*** having or showing malice; spiteful [The jealous girl started *malicious* rumors.] —**ma·li′cious·ly** ***adv.***

**ma·lign** (mə līn′) ***v.*** to say bad or unfair things about; slander. ◆***adj.*** bad, evil, harmful, etc. [*malign* forces]. —**ma·lign′er** ***n.***

**ma·lig·nan·cy** (mə lig′nən sē) ***n.*** **1** the condition of being malignant. **2** a malignant tumor. —*pl.* **ma·lig′nan·cies**

**ma·lig·nant** (mə lig′nənt) ***adj.*** **1** causing or wishing harm to others; evil [a *malignant* gossip]. **2** causing or likely to cause death [a *malignant* tumor]. —**ma·lig′nant·ly** ***adv.***



**ma·lig·ni·ty** (mə lig′nə tē) ***n.*** **1** a very strong desire to harm others; great malice. **2** great harmfulness; deadliness.

**ma·lin·ger** (mə liŋ′gər) ***v.*** to pretend to be sick in order to keep from working or doing one's duty. —**ma·lin′ger·er** ***n.***

**mall** (môl) ***n.*** **1** a broad, often shaded place for the public to walk, as in the center of a city. ☆**2** an enclosed, air-conditioned shopping center with a broad passageway through it and shops on each side of the passageway.

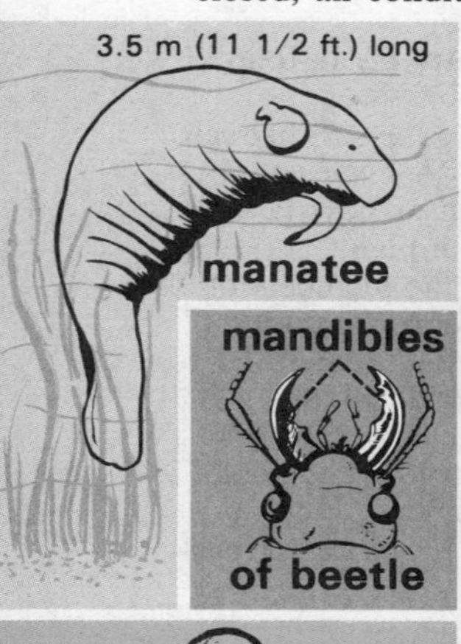


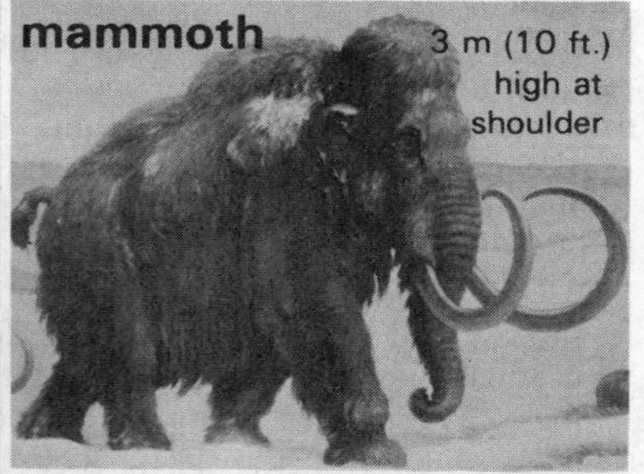

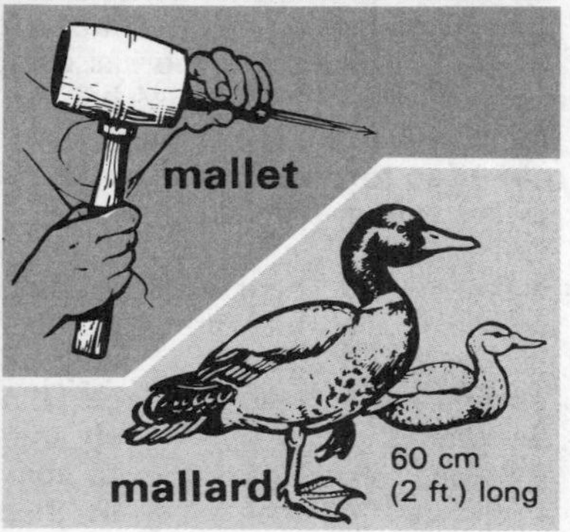


**mal·lard** (mal′ərd) ***n.*** a common wild duck. The male has a dark-green head and a white ring around the neck. *See the picture.*

**mal·le·a·ble** (mal′ē ə b'l) ***adj.*** **1** that can be hammered or pressed into a new shape without breaking, as gold and silver. **2** that can be changed, formed, trained, etc. [a *malleable* child]. —**mal′le·a·bil′i·ty** ***n.***

**mal·let** (mal′it) ***n.*** **1** a wooden hammer made with a short handle for use as a tool. *See the picture.* **2** a wooden hammer made with a long handle for playing croquet or with a long, flexible handle for playing polo.

**mal·low** (mal′ō) ***n.*** a plant with purplish, white, or pink flowers. The leaves and stems of the mallow have a sticky juice.

**mal·nu·tri·tion** (mal′nōō trish′ən) ***n.*** an unhealthy condition of the body caused by not getting enough food, or enough of the right foods; faulty nutrition.

**mal·prac·tice** (mal prak′tis) ***n.*** **1** medical treatment that harms a patient because the doctor has done something wrong or has failed to do the right thing. **2** any wrong practice by a professional person or by an official.

**malt** (môlt) ***n.*** barley or other grain soaked in water until it sprouts, and then dried. It is used in brewing beer, ale, etc. ◆***v.*** **1** to change into malt. **2** to add malt to.

**Mal·ta** (môl′tə) a country on a group of islands in the Mediterranean, south of Sicily. —**Mal·tese** (môl tēz′) ***adj., n.***

☆**malted milk** a drink made by mixing a powder of dried milk and malted cereals with milk and, usually, ice cream and flavoring.

**Maltese cat** a kind of cat with bluish-gray fur.

**Maltese cross** a cross with eight points.

**mal·treat** (mal trēt′) ***v.*** to treat in a rough, unkind, or cruel way; abuse. —**mal·treat′ment** ***n.***

**mam·ma** or **ma·ma** (mä′mə *or now seldom* mə mä′) ***n.*** mother: *mainly a child's word.*

**mam·mal** (mam′əl) ***n.*** any animal with glands in the female that produce milk for feeding its young. —**mam·ma·li·an** (mə mā′lē ən) ***adj., n.***

**mam·mon** (mam′ən) ***n.*** wealth thought of as an evil that makes people selfish and greedy.

**mam·moth** (mam′əth) ***n.*** a type of large elephant that lived long ago. Mammoths had a hairy skin and long tusks that curved upward. *See the picture.* ◆***adj.*** very big; huge.

**mam·my** (mam′ē) ***n.*** **1** mother: *a child's word.* ☆**2** a black woman who takes care of white children, especially as in earlier times in the South. —*pl.* **mam′mies**

**man** (man) ***n.*** **1** an adult male human being. **2** any human being; person ["that all *men* are created equal"]. **3** the human race; mankind [*man's* conquest of space]. **4** a male servant, employee, follower, etc. [giving orders to his *men*]. **5** a husband [*man* and wife]. **6** any of the pieces used in playing chess, checkers, etc. —*pl.* **men** ◆***v.*** **1** to supply with men for work, defense, etc. [to *man* a ship]. **2** to take one's place at, on, or in [to *man* a gun]. —**manned, man′ning** —**as a man** or **as one man,** all together; with everyone united or agreeing. —**to a man,** with all taking part; everyone.

**-man** (mən *or* man) *a suffix meaning:* **1** a person of a certain country [A *Frenchman* is a person born or living in France.] **2** a person doing a certain kind of work [A *mailman* delivers mail.] **3** a person who engages in a certain activity [A *sportsman* takes part in or follows sports.]

**Man.** *abbreviation for* **Manitoba.**

**Man, Isle of** one of the British Isles, between Northern Ireland and England.

**man·a·cle** (man′ə k'l) ***n.*** a handcuff. ◆***v.*** **1** to put handcuffs on. **2** to keep from acting freely; hamper; hinder. —**man′a·cled, man′a·cling**

**man·age** (man′ij) ***v.*** **1** to have charge of; direct the work of [to *manage* a store]. **2** to control the movement or behavior of [Grandmother *manages* the children easily.] **3** to succeed in getting something done [We *managed* to reach shelter.] —**man′aged, man′ag·ing**

**man·age·a·ble** (man′ij ə b'l) ***adj.*** that can be managed, controlled, or done.

**man·age·ment** (man′ij mənt) ***n.*** **1** the act or skill of managing; a controlling or directing [A successful business needs careful *management*.] **2** the persons who manage a certain business; also, managers of businesses as a group [the problems of labor and *management*].

**man·ag·er** (man′ij ər) ***n.*** a person who manages a business, baseball team, etc.

**man·a·ge·ri·al** (man′ə jir′ē əl) ***adj.*** having to do with a manager or management.

**man-at-arms** (man′ət ärmz′) ***n.*** a soldier of the Middle Ages who rode on a horse and carried powerful weapons. —*pl.* **men′-at-arms′**

**man·a·tee** (man ə tē′) ***n.*** a large animal that lives in shallow tropical waters and feeds on plants. It has flippers and a broad, flat tail; sea cow. *See the picture.*

**Man·ches·ter** (man′ches′tər) a city in northwestern England.

**Man·chu** (man cho͞o′ *or* man′cho͞o) ***n.*** **1** a member of a people of Manchuria who ruled China from 1644 to 1912. —*pl.* **Man·chus′** or **Man·chu′** **2** their language.

**Man·chu·ri·a** (man cho͝or′ē ə) a large region in northeastern China. —**Man·chu′ri·an *adj., n.***

**man·da·rin** (man′də rin) ***n.*** **1** a high public official of China under the Empire, before 1911. **2 Mandarin,** the main and most widespread form of the Chinese language. It is the official language of China. **3** a small, sweet orange: *the full name is* **mandarin orange.**

**man·date** (man′dāt) ***n.*** **1** an order or command, especially one in writing. **2** the will of the people as made known by their votes in elections. **3** control over a territory as formerly given by the League of Nations to one of its member nations; also, the territory so controlled.

**man·da·to·ry** (man′də tôr′ē) ***adj.*** ordered or demanded by someone in power; required.

**man·di·ble** (man′də b'l) ***n.*** **1** the jaw; especially, the lower jaw. **2** a part like this, as either part of a bird's beak or either of an insect's biting jaws. *See the picture.*

**man·do·lin** (man′d'l in) ***n.*** a musical instrument with four or five pairs of strings, played with a pick. *See the picture.*

**man·drake** (man′drāk) ***n.*** a poisonous plant with purple or white flowers. Its thick, often forked root was in earlier times used as a narcotic.

**man·drill** (man′dril) ***n.*** a large, strong baboon of western Africa. The male has blue and red patches on the face and rump.

**mane** (mān) ***n.*** the long hair growing along the neck of a horse, male lion, etc.

**Ma·net** (ma nā′), **É·douard** (ā dwär′) 1832–1883; French painter.

**ma·neu·ver** (mə no͞o′vər *or* mə nyo͞o′vər) ***n.*** **1** a carefully directed movement of troops, warships, etc., as in a battle or for practice. **2** any skillful change of movement or direction as in driving a car or flying an airplane. **3** a skillful move or clever trick [a *maneuver* to get control of the business]. ◆***v.*** **1** to carry out maneuvers with [She *maneuvered* her car through the heavy traffic.] **2** to plan or manage in a clever way [Who *maneuvered* this plot?] **3** to move, get, make, etc. by some trick or scheme [I *maneuvered* Lynn into asking the question for me.]

**man·ful** (man′fəl) ***adj.*** brave, determined, etc.; manly. —**man′ful·ly *adv.*** —**man′ful·ness *n.***

**man·ga·nese** (maŋ′gə nēs *or* maŋ′gə nēz) ***n.*** a grayish, brittle metal that is a chemical element. It is used in making alloys.

**mange** (mānj) ***n.*** a skin disease of animals that makes the hair fall out.

**man·ger** (mān′jər) ***n.*** a box or trough in a barn, from which horses or cattle eat. 

**man·gle**[1] (maŋ′g'l) ***v.*** **1** to tear, cut, or crush badly [The toy was *mangled* in the lawn mower.] **2** to botch or spoil [to *mangle* a piano solo]. —**man′gled, man′gling**

**man·gle**[2] (maŋ′g'l) ***n.*** a machine for pressing and smoothing sheets, tablecloths, etc. between rollers. ◆***v.*** to press in a mangle. —**man′gled, man′gling**

**man·go** (maŋ′gō) ***n.*** **1** a slightly sour fruit with a thick, orange rind and a hard stone. **2** the tropical tree that it grows on. —*pl.* **man′goes** or **man′gos**

**man·grove** (maŋ′grōv) ***n.*** a tropical tree with branches that spread and send down roots, which then form new trunks. *See the picture on page 447.*

**man·gy** (mān′jē) ***adj.*** **1** having mange [a *mangy* dog]. **2** dirty and poor; shabby [*mangy* clothing]. **3** mean and low [to play a *mangy* trick]. —**man′gi·er, man′gi·est** —**man′gi·ness *n.***

**man·han·dle** (man′han′d'l) ***v.*** to handle in a rough way. —**man′han′dled, man′han′dling**

**Man·hat·tan** (man hat″n) an island at the mouth of the Hudson River, that is a borough of New York City.

**man·hole** (man′hōl) ***n.*** an opening through which a person can get into a sewer, large pipe, etc., as in order to do repair work.

| | | | | | | | |
|---|---|---|---|---|---|---|---|
| **a** | fat | **ir** | here | **ou** | out | **zh** | leisure |
| **ā** | ape | **ī** | bite, fire | **u** | up | **ŋ** | ring |
| **ä** | car, lot | **ō** | go | **ur** | fur | | a *in* ago |
| **e** | ten | **ô** | law, horn | **ch** | chin | | e *in* agent |
| **er** | care | **oi** | oil | **sh** | she | **ə =** | i *in* unity |
| **ē** | even | **o͝o** | look | **th** | thin | | o *in* collect |
| **i** | hit | **o͞o** | tool | ***th*** | then | | u *in* focus |

**man·hood** (man′hood) ***n.*** **1** the time of being a man. **2** the qualities a man is thought of as having, as strength and courage [a test of one's *manhood*]. **3** men as a group [the *manhood* of a nation].

**man-hour** (man′our′) ***n.*** a time unit used in industry, equal to one hour of work done by one person.

**ma·ni·a** (mā′nē ə) ***n.*** **1** mental illness in which a person acts or talks in a wild way. **2** too much enthusiasm or fondness for something; craze [a *mania* for dancing]. —**man·ic** (man′ik) ***adj.***

**ma·ni·ac** (mā′nē ak) ***n.*** a mentally ill person who behaves in a wild way; lunatic. ◆***adj.*** *same as* **maniacal.**

**ma·ni·a·cal** (mə nī′ə k'l) ***adj.*** having or showing mania; wildly insane [*maniacal* laughter].

**man·ic-de·pres·sive** (man′ik di pres′iv) ***adj.*** of or having a mental illness in which one goes back and forth between periods of mania and periods of depression. ◆***n.*** a person who has this illness.

**man·i·cure** (man′ə kyoor) ***n.*** the care of the hands; especially, the trimming and cleaning of the fingernails. ◆***v.*** to give a manicure to. —**man′i·cured, man′i·cur·ing —man′i·cur′ist *n.***

**man·i·fest** (man′ə fest) ***adj.*** plain to see or understand; clear; evident [a *manifest* lie]. ◆***v.*** **1** to make clear; show plainly; reveal [When did your illness *manifest* itself?] **2** to prove or show [Her kindness to them *manifested* her love.] ◆***n.*** a list of things in a ship's cargo or of passengers and cargo on an airplane. —**man′i·fest·ly *adv.***

446

> **Manifest** comes from a Latin word meaning "struck by the hand." To strike anything with one's hand is to do something that is clearly seen or understood. It is manifest what one is doing.

**man·i·fes·ta·tion** (man′ə fes tā′shən) ***n.*** **1** the act of showing, making clear, or proving. **2** something that shows, proves, etc. [A smile is a *manifestation* of happiness.]

**man·i·fes·to** (man′ə fes′tō) ***n.*** a public statement by a government, political group, etc., telling what its plans, beliefs, policies, etc. are. —*pl.* **man′i·fes′toes**

**man·i·fold** (man′ə fōld) ***adj.*** **1** having many parts or forms [*manifold* wisdom]. **2** of many kinds; many and varied [her *manifold* duties]. ◆***n.*** a pipe with several openings for connecting it to other pipes, as for carrying away exhaust from an engine. *See the picture.*

**man·i·kin** (man′ə k'n) ***n.*** **1** a little man; dwarf. **2** a lifelike model of the human body, used in medical schools, art classes, etc. **3** *another spelling of* **mannequin.**

**Ma·nil·a** (mə nil′ə) the capital of the Philippines, on the island of Luzon.

**Manila hemp** a strong fiber from the stalks of the leaves of a Philippine tree. It is used for making rope, paper, etc.: *also* **manila hemp.**

**Manila paper** a strong, light brown paper, used for envelopes, wrapping paper, etc.: *also* **manila paper.**

**ma·nip·u·late** (mə nip′yə lāt) ***v.*** **1** to work or operate with the hands; use with skill [to *manipulate* the controls of a machine]. **2** to manage or control in a clever or unfair way [to *manipulate* a person by making vague promises]. **3** to change figures, accounts, etc., as in bookkeeping, for some dishonest reasons. —**ma·nip′u·lat·ed, ma·nip′u·lat·ing —ma·nip′u·la′tion *n.* —ma·nip′u·la′tor *n.***

**Man·i·to·ba** (man′ə tō′bə) a province in the south central part of Canada.

**man·kind** (man kīnd′ *or* man′kīnd) ***n.*** **1** all human beings; the human race. **2** (*always* man′kīnd) all human males; men in general.

**man·ly** (man′lē) ***adj.*** **1** strong, brave, bold, etc. in the way that men are generally supposed to be. *See* SYNONYMS *at* **male. 2** fit for a man [*manly* sports]. —**man′li·er, man′li·est —man′li·ness *n.***

**man-made** (man′mād′) ***adj.*** made by man; artificial or synthetic.

**Mann** (män), **Thom·as** (tō′mäs) 1875–1955; German writer of novels in the U.S. and Switzerland.

**man·na** (man′ə) ***n.*** **1** in the Bible, the food provided by a miracle for the Israelites in the wilderness. **2** anything needed badly that comes as a surprise.

> It is thought that when the Israelites found food in the wilderness they called it **manna** from the Hebrew phrase meaning "What is it?" that was said when the food was found.

**man·ne·quin** (man′ə kin) ***n.*** **1** a model of the human body, used by tailors, window dressers, artists, etc. **2** a woman whose work is modeling clothes in stores, etc. for customers to see.

**man·ner** (man′ər) ***n.*** **1** a way in which something happens or is done; style [the *manner* in which an artist sketches a scene]. *See* SYNONYMS *at* **method. 2** a way of acting; behavior [an angry *manner*]. **3 manners,** *pl.* ways of behaving or living, especially polite ways of behaving [It is good *manners* to say "Thank you."] **4** kind; sort [What *manner* of man is he?]

**man·ner·ism** (man′ər iz'm) ***n.*** a special manner or way of doing something that has become a habit [She had a *mannerism* of scratching her ear.]

**man·ner·ly** (man′ər lē) ***adj.*** showing good manners; polite; well-behaved. ◆***adv.*** politely.

**man·ni·kin** (man′ə kin) ***n.*** *another spelling of* **mannequin.**

**man·nish** (man′ish) ***adj.*** like or fit for a man: used of a woman who looks or acts like a man [She walks with a *mannish* stride.]

**ma·noeu·vre** (mə noo′vər *or* mə nyoo′vər) ***n., v.*** *mainly a British spelling of* **maneuver. —ma·noeu′vred, ma·noeu′vring**

**man-of-war** (man′əv wôr′) ***n.*** a ship used in war; warship. —*pl.* **men′-of-war′**

**man·or** (man′ər) ***n.*** **1** land belonging to a lord in the Middle Ages, that was partly divided among peasants who paid rent. **2** any large estate. —**ma·no·ri·al** (mə nôr′ē əl) ***adj.***

**man·pow·er** (man′pou′ər) ***n.*** **1** power supplied by the physical effort of human beings. **2** the total number of people working or able to work in a certain area.

**man·sard** (man′särd) ***n.*** a roof having four sides with two slopes on each side: *also called* **mansard roof.** *See the picture.*

**manse** (mans) ***n.*** the house that a church provides for its minister, especially a Presbyterian minister.

**man·sion** (man′shən) ***n.*** a large, stately house.

**man·slaugh·ter** (man′slôt′ər) ***n.*** the killing of one person by another, especially when it is unlawful but not done on purpose [A driver who hits and kills someone accidentally may be charged with *manslaughter*.]

**man·tel** (man′t'l) ***n.*** **1** the shelf above a fireplace: *also* **man′tel·piece**. **2** the facing of stone, marble, brick, etc. around a fireplace, usually along with such a shelf. *See the picture.*

**man·tis** (man′tis) ***n.*** an insect that holds its front pair of legs as if praying, and eats other insects: *often called* **praying mantis**. *See the picture.*

**man·tle** (man′t'l) ***n.*** **1** a loose cloak without sleeves; cape. **2** anything that covers or hides as a cloak [the night's *mantle* of darkness]. **3** a small tube or hood made of a fine screen that is placed over a flame so that it glows and gives off light. ◆***v.*** **1** to cover or hide as with a mantle. **2** to blush. —**man′tled, man′tling**

**man·u·al** (man′yoo wəl) ***adj.*** made, done, or worked with the hands [*manual* labor; *manual* controls]. ◆***n.*** a small book of facts or instructions; handbook [a stamp collector's *manual*]. —**man′u·al·ly *adv.***

**man·u·fac·ture** (man′yə fak′chər) ***n.*** **1** the making of goods or articles, especially in large amounts and by machinery. **2** the making of something in any way [the *manufacture* of bile by the liver]. ◆***v.*** **1** to make goods, especially in large amounts. **2** to make or make up in any way [to *manufacture* an excuse]. —**man′u·fac′tured, man′u·fac′tur·ing**

**Manufacture** comes from two Latin words that mean "to make with the hands." Before there were machines and factories everything had to be made with the hands.

**man·u·fac·tur·er** (man′yə fak′chər ər) ***n.*** a person or company that manufactures; especially, a factory owner.

**ma·nure** (mə noor′ *or* mə nyoor′) ***n.*** any substance used to fertilize soil; especially, the waste matter of animals. ◆***v.*** to put manure on or into. —**ma·nured′, ma·nur′ing**

**man·u·script** (man′yə skript) ***n.*** a book, article, etc. that is typewritten or in handwriting; especially, the copy of an author's work that is sent to a publisher or printer.

**Manx** (mangks) ***adj.*** of the Isle of Man, its people, or their language. ◆***n.*** the language at one time spoken on the Isle of Man. —**the Manx**, the people of the Isle of Man.

**Manx cat** a kind of cat that has almost no tail: *also* **manx cat**.

**man·y** (men′ē) ***adj.*** a large number of; not few [*many* boxes; *many* times]. —The comparative of *many* is **more**, the superlative is **most**. ◆***n.*** a large number [*Many* of us plan to go.] ◆***pron.*** many persons or things [*Many* came to see our play.] The phrases *many a, many an,* and *many another* followed by a singular noun mean the same as *many* followed by the plural form ["*Many a* person has tried" means the same as "*Many* persons have tried."] —**a good many**, quite a large number: *used with a plural verb.* —**as many**, the same number of [She read ten books in *as many* days.]

SYNONYMS: **Many** is the simple, common word used to mean a large number [*many* cats; *many* dreams; *many* germs]. **Numerous** is more formal and sometimes suggests a crowding of one upon another [We have received *numerous* complaints about the noise.]

**Ma·o·ri** (mou′rē *or* mä′ô rē) ***n.*** **1** a member of a brown-skinned people who live in New Zealand. —*pl.* **Ma′o·ris** or **Ma′o·ri** **2** their language.



**Mao Tse-tung** (mou′ dzu′doong′) 1893–1976; Chinese Communist leader.

**map** (map) ***n.*** **1** a drawing or chart of all or part of the earth's surface, showing where countries, oceans, rivers, cities, etc. are. **2** a drawing of part of the sky, showing where the stars, planets, etc. are. ◆***v.*** **1** to make a map of [Lewis and Clark *mapped* western America.] **2** to plan in a careful way, step by step [to *map* out one's work]. —**mapped, map′ping**

**ma·ple** (mā′p'l) ***n.*** **1** a tree with fruits having two wings, grown for its wood or sap, or as a shade tree. *See the picture.* **2** its hard, light-colored wood. **3** the flavor of the syrup (☆**maple syrup**) or sugar (☆**maple sugar**) made from its sap.

**mar** (mär) ***v.*** to hurt or spoil the looks, value, etc.; damage [The kitten's claws *marred* the table top.] —**marred, mar′ring**

**Mar.** *abbreviation for* **March**.

**ma·ra·ca** (mə rä′kə) ***n.*** a musical instrument made of a gourd or rattle, with loose pebbles in it. It is shaken to beat out a rhythm. *See the picture on page 449.*

**Mar·a·cai·bo** (mar′ə kī′bō) a seaport in northwestern Venezuela.

**mar·a·schi·no cherry** (mar′ə shē′nō *or* mar′ə skē′nō) a cherry preserved in a sweet syrup and used to decorate sundaes, salads, drinks, etc.

| | | | |
|---|---|---|---|
| **a** fat | **ir** here | **ou** out | **zh** leisure |
| **ā** ape | **ī** bite, fire | **u** up | **ng** ring |
| **ä** car, lot | **ō** go | **ur** fur | a *in* ago |
| **e** ten | **ô** law, horn | **ch** chin | e *in* agent |
| **er** care | **oi** oil | **sh** she | **ə** = i *in* unity |
| **ē** even | **oo** look | **th** thin | o *in* collect |
| **i** hit | **ōō** tool | ***th*** then | u *in* focus |

**mar·a·thon** (mar′ə thän) ***n.*** a foot race of 26 miles, 385 yards; also, any contest to test endurance.

The soldiers of Athens defeated the Persians in a battle on the plain of Marathon in 490 B.C. According to legend, a Greek runner ran from Marathon to Athens, 26 miles and 385 yards, to tell the news of the victory. From this comes the name of the **marathon** race and its distance.

**ma·raud·er** (mə rôd′ər) ***n.*** a person or animal that roams about attacking or plundering. —**ma·raud′ing** ***adj.***

**mar·ble** (mär′b'l) ***n.*** **1** a hard kind of limestone that is white or colored, sometimes with streaks. It takes a high polish and is used as a building material and in statues. **2** a little ball of stone, glass, or clay, used in a children's game called **marbles.** ◆***adj.*** made of or like marble. ◆***v.*** to make look like marble that is streaked [*marbled* fat in steak; to *marble* the edges of a book]. —**mar′bled, mar′bling**

**March** (märch) ***n.*** the third month of the year, which has 31 days: abbreviated **Mar.**

**march** (märch) ***v.*** **1** to walk with regular, steady steps, as soldiers do. **2** to move or go in a steady way [Time *marches* on.] **3** to cause to march [He *marched* the children up to bed.] ◆***n.*** **1** a marching [the army's *march* to the sea]. **2** steady movement forward; progress [the *march* of history]. **3** a piece of music with a steady rhythm, to be played while people



march. **4** the distance traveled in marching [The enemy was camped two days' *march* away.] **5** an organized walk as a public show of opinion [a peace *march*]. —**on the march,** marching. —**steal a march on,** to get a secret advantage over. —**march′er** ***n.***

**mar·chion·ess** (mär′shə nis) ***n.*** **1** the wife or widow of a marquess. **2** a lady with the rank of a marquess.

**Mar·co·ni** (mär kō′nē), **Gu·gliel·mo** (goo͞ lyel′mō) 1874–1937; Italian inventor who developed the wireless telegraph.

☆**Mar·di gras** (mär′di grä′) the last day before Lent, celebrated with parties and parades.

**mare** (mer) ***n.*** a female horse, donkey, etc.

**mar·ga·rine** (mär′jə rin) ***n.*** a spread like butter, made of vegetable oils and skim milk.

**mar·gin** (mär′jən) ***n.*** **1** a border or edge [the *margin* of a pond]. **2** the blank space around the writing or printing on a page. **3** an extra amount of time, money, etc. that can be used if needed [Budgets must allow a *margin* for emergencies.]

**mar·gin·al** (mär′jən 'l) ***adj.*** **1** written in the margin of a page. **2** of, at, or near a margin. **3** close to a lower limit [a *marginal* standard of living].

**Ma·rie An·toi·nette** (mə rē′ an′twə net′ *or* an′tə net′) 1755–1793; queen of France who was executed during the French Revolution.

**mar·i·gold** (mar′ə gōld) ***n.*** a plant with red, yellow, or orange flowers. *See the picture.*

☆**ma·ri·jua·na** or **ma·ri·hua·na** (mar′ə wä′nə) ***n.*** the dried leaves and flowers of a hemp plant, smoked in a pipe or like a cigarette.

**ma·rim·ba** (mə rim′bə) ***n.*** a musical instrument somewhat like a xylophone. *See the picture.*

**ma·ri·na** (mə rē′nə) ***n.*** ☆a small harbor where boats can dock, pick up supplies, etc.

**mar·i·nate** (mar′ə nāt) ***v.*** to soak meat, fish, salad, etc. in spiced vinegar, wine, salt water, etc. —**mar′i·nat·ed, mar′i·nat·ing**

**ma·rine** (mə rēn′) ***adj.*** **1** of the sea [Seaweeds are *marine* plants.] **2** having to do with sailing or shipping [*Marine* insurance protects cargo ships.] **3** for use on a ship [a *marine* engine]. ◆***n.*** ☆*usually* **Marine,** a member of the Marine Corps. *See also* **merchant marine.**

☆**Marine Corps** a branch of the U.S. armed forces, trained to fight on land, at sea, and in the air.

**mar·i·ner** (mar′ə nər) ***n.*** a sailor: *now seldom used.*

**mar·i·o·nette** (mar′ē ə net′) ***n.*** a puppet or small jointed doll moved by strings or wires and used in putting on shows on a small stage. *See the picture.*

**mar·i·tal** (mar′ə t'l) ***adj.*** of or having to do with marriage [*marital* bliss].

**mar·i·time** (mar′ə tīm) ***adj.*** **1** on, near, or living near the sea [California is a *maritime* State.] **2** having to do with sailing or shipping on the sea [*maritime* laws].

**Maritime Provinces** the Canadian provinces of Nova Scotia, New Brunswick, and Prince Edward Island.

**mar·jo·ram** (mär′jər əm) ***n.*** a plant related to the mint; especially, **sweet marjoram** grown for its sweet-smelling leaves used in cooking.

**Mark** (märk) **1** an early follower of Jesus. **2** the second book of the New Testament. Mark is believed to have written this book.

**mark**[1] (märk) ***n.*** **1** a spot, stain, scratch, dent, etc. made on a surface. **2** a printed or written sign or label [punctuation *marks;* a trade*mark*]. **3** a sign of some quality [Politeness is the *mark* of good training.] **4** a grade or rating [a *mark* of B in spelling]. **5** a cross or other sign made in place of a signature by a person unable to write. **6** influence or effect [Poverty leaves a *mark* on many people.] **7** a line, dot, or notch that shows a certain position [Fill the cup to this *mark.*] **8** the starting line of a race [On your *mark,* get set, go!] **9** something aimed at; target [The arrow fell short of the *mark.*] **10** something that acts as a sign or guide; landmark. ◆***v.*** **1** to make a mark or marks on. **2** to name or show; make clear [abilities that *mark* a person for success]. **3** to draw or write [*Mark* your name on your gym shoes.] **4** to show by a mark or marks [*Mark* the capitals on the map.] **5** to set off; make different [inventions that *marked* the 19th century]. **6** to pay attention to; note [*Mark* what I say.] **7** to give a grade to [to *mark* test papers]. —**beside the mark, 1** not hitting what was aimed at. **2** not to the point; irrelevant. —**hit the mark, 1** to reach one's goal; succeed. **2** to be right. —**make one's mark,** to become famous. —**mark down, 1** to make a note of; record. ☆**2** to mark for sale at a lower price. —**mark off** or **mark out,** to mark the limits of. —**mark time, 1** to keep time while at a halt by lifting the feet as if marching. **2** to make no progress for a while. —**mark up, 1** to cover with marks. ☆**2** to mark for sale at a higher price. —**miss the mark,** to fail or be wrong. —**mark′er** ***n.***

**Mark**[1] comes from the word in Old English that meant one of the signs put up to mark the boundaries of a piece of land. It is related to the word **margin,** which means a border or edge.

**mark²** (märk) ***n.*** **1** the basic unit of money in East Germany. **2** the basic unit of money in West Germany: *the full name is* **deut·sche mark** (doi′chə märk).

☆**mark·down** (märk′doun) ***n.*** **1** a marking for sale at a lower price. **2** the amount by which the sale price is lowered.

**marked** (märkt) ***adj.*** **1** having a mark or marks on it. **2** very easily noticed; obvious [a *marked* change]. **3** picked out as a suspicious person to be watched [a *marked* man].

**mark·ed·ly** (mär′kid lē) ***adv.*** in a marked way; noticeably; obviously.

**mar·ket** (mär′kit) ***n.*** **1** a gathering of people for buying and selling things; also, the people gathered. **2** an open place, or a building, with stalls where goods are sold. **3** any store where food is sold [a meat *market*]. **4** a place where goods can be sold [England is a good *market* for tea.] **5** a desire by many people to buy; demand [The *market* for used cars is good now.] •***v.*** **1** to take or send to market to sell. **2** to buy food [We *market* on Saturdays.] —**be in the market for,** to want to buy. —**be on the market,** to be offered for sale. —**put on the market,** to offer to sell. —**mar′ket·a·ble *adj.***

**mar·ket·place** (mär′kit plās) ***n.*** **1** an open place where goods are offered for sale. **2** the world of trade, business, etc.

**mark·ing** (mär′king) ***n.*** **1** a mark or marks. **2** a special pattern of marks or colorings, as on fur or feathers.

**marks·man** (märks′mən) ***n.*** a person who shoots well at targets. —*pl.* **marks′men** —**marks′man·ship *n.***

☆**mark·up** (märk′up) ***n.*** **1** a marking for sale at a higher price. **2** the amount by which the sale price is increased.

**mar·lin** (mär′lin) ***n.*** a large, deep-sea fish whose upper jaw sticks out like a spear.

**mar·line·spike** or **mar·lin·spike** (mär′lin spīk) ***n.*** a pointed iron tool used to separate the strands of a rope, as for splicing.

**mar·ma·lade** (mär′mə lād) ***n.*** a sweet food like jam, made from oranges or other fruit.

**Mar·ma·ra** (mär′mə rə), **Sea of** a sea between the part of Turkey in Europe and the part in Asia.

**mar·mo·set** (mär′mə zet *or* mär′mə set) ***n.*** a very small monkey of South and Central America, with a long tail and thick, silky fur. *See the picture.*

**mar·mot** (mär′mət) ***n.*** any of a group of small animals with a thick body and a short, bushy tail, related to rabbits and rats [The woodchuck is a *marmot.*] *See the picture.*

**ma·roon¹** (mə ro͞on′) ***adj., n.*** dark brownish red.

**ma·roon²** (mə ro͞on′) ***v.*** **1** to put ashore and leave someone in a lonely place, as a desert island. **2** to leave helpless and alone [The storm *marooned* us.]

> **Maroon²** comes from an American Spanish word *cimarrón,* which means "wild." A person who is marooned might be put in a wild place, where no one else lives.

**mar·quee** (mär kē′) ***n.*** a small roof built out over an entrance to a theater, store, hotel, etc. *See the picture on page 451.*

**mar·quess** (mär′kwis) ***n.*** a British nobleman ranking above an earl, and below a duke.

**marmoset**

20 cm (8 in.) long, not including tail

**marimba**

**maracas**

**marionettes**

**marmot**

60 cm (2 ft.) long, including tail

**marigold**

**Mar·quette** (mär ket′), **Jacques** (zhäk) 1637–1675; French Jesuit missionary who explored part of the Mississippi River: *called* **Père Marquette.**



**mar·quis** (mär′kwis *or* mär kē′) ***n.*** in some European countries, a nobleman ranking above an earl or count, and below a duke.

**mar·quise** (mär kēz′) ***n.*** **1** the wife or widow of a marquis. **2** a lady with the rank of marquis.

**mar·qui·sette** (mär′ki zet′ *or* mär′kwi zet′) ***n.*** a thin cloth, like net, used for curtains, dresses, etc.

**mar·riage** (mar′ij) ***n.*** **1** the state of being married; married life. **2** the act or ceremony of marrying; wedding.

**mar·riage·a·ble** (mar′i jə b′l) ***adj.*** old enough to get married [a *marriageable* girl].

**mar·ried** (mar′ēd) ***adj.*** **1** being husband and wife [a *married* couple]. **2** having a husband or wife. **3** of marriage [*married* life].

**mar·row** (mar′ō) ***n.*** **1** the soft, fatty substance that fills the hollow centers of most bones. **2** the central or most important part [This book gets to the *marrow* of the problem.]

**mar·ry** (mar′ē) ***v.*** **1** to join a man and a woman as husband and wife [A ship's captain may *marry* people at sea.] **2** to take as one's husband or wife [John Alden *married* Priscilla.] **3** to give in marriage [They have *married* off both their daughters.] **4** to join closely; unite [Gentleness and strength are *married* in him.] —**mar′ried, mar′ry·ing**

| | | | | | | | |
|---|---|---|---|---|---|---|---|
| **a** | fat | **ir** | here | **ou** | out | **zh** | leisure |
| **ā** | ape | **ī** | bite, fire | **u** | up | **ng** | ring |
| **ä** | car, lot | **ō** | go | **ur** | fur | | a *in* ago |
| **e** | ten | **ô** | law, horn | **ch** | chin | | e *in* agent |
| **er** | care | **oi** | oil | **sh** | she | ə = | i *in* unity |
| **ē** | even | **oo** | look | **th** | thin | | o *in* collect |
| **i** | hit | **o͞o** | tool | ***th*** | then | | u *in* focus |

**Mars** (märz) **1** the Roman god of war. **2** the seventh largest planet, known for its reddish color. It is the fourth in distance away from the sun.

**Mar·seil·laise** (mär sə lāz′) the national song of France, composed in 1792.

**Mar·seille** (mär sā′) a seaport in southeastern France, on the Mediterranean.

**marsh** (märsh) ***n.*** low land that is wet and soft; swamp; bog. —**marsh′y** ***adj.***

**mar·shal** (mär′shəl) ***n.*** ☆**1** an officer of a U.S. Federal court, with duties like those of a sheriff. ☆**2** the head of some police or fire departments. **3** a person in charge of a parade or certain ceremonies. **4** a general of the highest rank in certain foreign armies. ◆***v.*** **1** to arrange in order, as troops, ideas, etc. **2** to lead or guide. —**mar′shaled** or **mar′shalled, mar′shaling** or **mar′shal·ling**

A **marshal** was originally a servant, or groom, who took care of horses. This came to be an important position in a royal household, where there were many horses. By the Middle Ages the marshal was a high court official who directed military ceremonies. Today the title of marshal is given to various military or law officers, as well as to a person in charge of a parade.

**Mar·shall** (mär′shəl), **John** 1755–1835; the chief justice of the United States from 1801 to 1835.

**Marshall Islands** a group of islands in the western Pacific Ocean, under U.S. control.



**marsh·mal·low** (märsh′mel′ō *or* märsh′mal′ō) ***n.*** a soft, white, spongy candy made of sugar, gelatin, etc. and covered with powdered sugar.

**marsh mallow** a hairy plant with large, pink flowers, growing in marshes.

**mar·su·pi·al** (mär so͞o′pē əl) ***n.*** an animal whose newly born young are carried by the female in a pouch on the front of her body [Kangaroos are *marsupials.*]

**mart** (märt) ***n.*** a market; place where goods are bought and sold.

**mar·ten** (mär′t′n) ***n.*** **1** an animal like a large weasel, with soft, thick, valuable fur. **2** this fur.

**mar·tial** (mär′shəl) ***adj.*** **1** having to do with war or armies [*martial* music]. **2** showing a readiness or eagerness to fight [*martial* spirit].

**martial law** rule by an army over civilians, as during a war or riots.

**Mar·tian** (mär′shən) ***n.*** an imaginary creature of the planet Mars, as in science fiction. ◆***adj.*** of Mars, especially the planet Mars.

**mar·tin** (mär′t′n) ***n.*** a bird of the swallow family; especially, the **purple martin**, a large, dark-blue swallow of North America. *See the picture.*

**mar·ti·net** (mär t′n et′) ***n.*** a person who believes in very strict discipline; one who forces others to follow rules exactly.

**Mar·ti·nique** (mär tə nēk′) a French island in the southern part of the West Indies.

**mar·tyr** (mär′tər) ***n.*** **1** a person who chooses to suffer or die rather than give up his or her religion, beliefs, etc. **2** a person who suffers silently for a long time. ◆***v.*** to kill or make suffer for not giving up one's religion, beliefs, etc. —**mar′tyr·dom** ***n.***

**mar·vel** (mär′v′l) ***n.*** a wonderful or astonishing thing [the natural *marvels* of Yellowstone National Park]. ◆***v.*** to wonder; be amazed [We *marveled* at the skill of the pianist.] —**mar′veled** or **mar′velled, mar′veling** or **mar′vel·ling**

**mar·vel·ous** (mär′v′l əs) ***adj.*** **1** causing wonder; astonishing [the *marvelous* process of the formation of coal]. **2** very good; fine; splendid: *used only in everyday talk. Also spelled* **mar′vel·lous** —**mar′vel·ous·ly** ***adv.***

**Marx** (märks), **Karl** 1818–1883; German socialist leader and writer.

**Marx·ism** (märk′siz′m) ***n.*** the teachings of Karl Marx and his followers, upon which most systems of communism and socialism are based. —**Marx′ist** ***adj., n.***

**Mar·y** (mer′ē) the mother of Jesus: *often called the* **Virgin Mary.**

**Mar·y·land** (mer′ə lənd) a State on the eastern coast of the U.S.: abbreviated **Md., MD**

**Mary, Queen of Scots** 1542–1587; queen of Scotland from 1542 to 1567. She was beheaded.

**masc.** *abbreviation for* **masculine.**

**mas·ca·ra** (mas kar′ə) ***n.*** a paste put on the eyelashes and eyebrows to darken or color them.

**Mascara** comes from a Spanish word that comes from an Italian word, both of them meaning "mask." The Italian word probably comes from an Arabic word meaning "clown." Short eyelashes can be *masked* with mascara to make them seem longer. Clowns use coloring like mascara on their faces.

**mas·cot** (mas′kät *or* mas′kət) ***n.*** a person, animal, or thing thought to bring good luck by being present [A goat is the *mascot* of the U.S. Naval Academy.]

**mas·cu·line** (mas′kyə lin) ***adj.*** **1** of or having to do with men or boys [*masculine* traits]. **2** having those qualities that men and boys have been thought of as having. *See* SYNONYMS *at* **male. 3** of a class of words in grammar that refer to males or to things thought of as male. —**mas·cu·lin·i·ty** (mas′kyə lin′ə tē) ***n.***

**Mase·field** (mās′fēld), **John** 1878–1967; English writer and poet.

☆**ma·ser** (mā′zər) ***n.*** a device in which atoms of a crystal or gas are made to give off radiation in a very narrow beam.

**mash** (mash) ***n.*** **1** a mixture of bran, meal, etc. for feeding horses, cattle, and poultry. **2** crushed malt or meal soaked in hot water and used in brewing beer. **3** any soft mass. ◆***v.*** **1** to beat or crush into a soft mass [to *mash* potatoes]. **2** to crush and injure [to *mash* one's finger]. —**mash′er** ***n.***

**mask** (mask) ***n.*** **1** something worn over the face to hide or protect it [a Halloween *mask;* a baseball catcher's *mask*]. *See the picture.* **2** anything that hides or disguises [His smile was a *mask* to hide his disappointment.] **3** a copy of a person's face, made of clay, wax, etc. [a death *mask*]. ◆***v.*** **1** to cover or hide with a mask [to *mask* one's face]. **2** to hide or disguise [to *mask* one's fear]. —**mask′er** ***n.***

**masking tape** a sticky tape for covering and protecting margins or borders, as during painting.

**mas·och·ist** (mas′ə kist *or* maz′ə kist) ***n.*** a person who gets pleasure from being hurt by others. —**mas′och·is′tic** ***adj.***

**ma·son** (mā′s'n) ***n.*** **1** a person whose work is building with stone, brick, etc. **2 Mason,** *a shorter form of* **Freemason.**

**Ma·son-Dix·on line** (mā′s'n dik′s'n) **1** an old name for the boundary between Pennsylvania and Maryland. **2** an imaginary line thought of as separating the North from the South.

**Ma·son·ic** (mə sän′ik) ***adj.*** of Freemasons or their society.

**ma·son·ry** (mā′s'n rē) ***n.*** **1** something built of stone, brick, etc. by a mason. **2** the work or skill of a mason. *—pl.* **ma′son·ries**

**masque** (mask) ***n.*** **1** *a shorter form of* **masquerade** *in meaning* 1. **2** a kind of play in verse put on for kings and nobles in the 16th and 17th centuries, using fancy costumes, music, dancing, etc.

**mas·quer·ade** (mas kə rād′) ***n.*** **1** a party or dance where masks and fancy costumes are worn. **2** a costume for such a party. **3** the act of hiding who one is, how one feels, etc.; disguise. ◆***v.*** **1** to take part in a masquerade. **2** to hide who one is by pretending to be someone else. **—mas·quer·ad′ed, mas·quer·ad′ing —mas·quer·ad′er *n.***

**Mass** or **mass** (mas) ***n.*** **1** the service in the Roman Catholic Church and some other churches in which Holy Communion takes place. **2** a setting of music for certain parts of this service.

**mass** (mas) ***n.*** **1** a piece or amount of no definite shape or size [a *mass* of clay; a *mass* of cold air]. **2** a large amount or number [a *mass* of freckles]. **3** bulk or size [We couldn't move the piano because of its *mass.*] *See* SYNONYMS *at* **bulk. 4** the main part; majority [The *mass* of opinion is against the plan.] **5** in physics, the amount of matter in a body. ◆***adj.*** **1** of a large number of persons or things [a *mass* meeting; *mass* production]. **2** of or for the masses [*mass* education]. ◆***v.*** to gather or form into a mass [Crowds were *massing* along the curb.] —**in the mass,** as a whole; taken together. —**the masses,** the great mass of common people; especially, the working people as a class.

**Mas·sa·chu·setts** (mas′ə cho͞o′sits) a New England State of the U.S.: abbreviated **Mass., MA**

**mas·sa·cre** (mas′ə kər) ***n.*** the cruel and violent killing of a large number of people; wholesale slaughter. *See* SYNONYMS *at* **slaughter.** ◆***v.*** to kill in large numbers. **—mas′sa·cred, mas′sa·cr·ing**

**mas·sage** (mə säzh′ *or* mə säj′) ***n.*** a rubbing and kneading of part of the body to loosen up muscles and improve the circulation. ◆***v.*** to give a massage to. **—mas·saged′, mas·sag′ing**

**mas·sive** (mas′iv) ***adj.*** large, solid, heavy, etc. [a *massive* statue]. *See the picture.* **—mas′sive·ly *adv.* —mas′sive·ness *n.***

**mass media** all the ways of informing and influencing large numbers of people, including newspapers, popular magazines, radio, and TV.

**mast** (mast) ***n.*** **1** a tall pole set upright on a ship or boat, for supporting the sails, yards, etc. **2** any upright pole like this [the *mast* for a TV antenna].

**mas·ter** (mas′tər) ***n.*** **1** a man who rules others or has control over something, as an owner of an animal or slave, the head of a household, or the victor in a contest. **2** a man teacher: *used chiefly in Great Britain.* **3** an expert in some work, as a skilled craftsman or great

massive statue

marquee

masks

20 cm (8 in.) long
purple martin

artist. **4** a painting by a great artist. **5 Master,** a title used before the name of a boy too young to be called *Mr.* **6** a person who holds a college degree beyond that of bachelor [He is a *Master* of Arts in music.] ◆***adj.*** **1** being or of a master [The wall was built by a *master* mason.] **2** chief; main; controlling [A *master* switch controls a number of other switches.] ◆***v.*** **1** to become master of; control or conquer [She *mastered* her fear.] **2** to become expert in [Picasso *mastered* the art of painting.]



**mas·ter·ful** (mas′tər fəl) ***adj.*** **1** acting like a master; liking to be in control. **2** very skillful; expert [a *masterful* pianist].

**mas·ter·ly** (mas′tər lē) ***adj.*** showing the skill of a master; expert [You did a *masterly* job of repairing the clock.] ◆***adv.*** in an expert way.

**mas·ter·mind** (mas′tər mīnd) ***n.*** a very intelligent person, especially one who plans and directs the work of a group. ◆***v.*** to be the mastermind of.

**master of ceremonies** ☆a person in charge of an entertainment, who introduces the people on the program, tells jokes, etc.

**mas·ter·piece** (mas′tər pēs) ***n.*** **1** a thing made or done with very great skill; great work of art. **2** the best thing one has ever made or done ["The Divine Comedy" was Dante's *masterpiece.*]

**mas·ter·work** (mas′tər wurk) ***n.*** *another word for* **masterpiece.**

**mas·ter·y** (mas′tər ē) ***n.*** **1** control or power that a master has. **2** victory over another or others. **3** expert skill or knowledge [her *mastery* of tennis].

**mast·head** (mast′hed) ***n.*** **1** the top part of a ship's mast. ☆**2** that part of a newspaper or magazine that

| | | | | | | |
|---|---|---|---|---|---|---|
| **a** fat | **ir** here | **ou** out | **zh** leisure | | | |
| **ā** ape | **ī** bite, fire | **u** up | **ng** ring | | | |
| **ä** car, lot | **ō** go | **ur** fur | | a *in* ago | | |
| **e** ten | **ô** law, horn | **ch** chin | | e *in* agent | | |
| **er** care | **oi** oil | **sh** she | ə = | i *in* unity | | |
| **ē** even | **oo** look | **th** thin | | o *in* collect | | |
| **i** hit | **o͞o** tool | ***th*** then | | u *in* focus | | |

tells who its publisher and editors are, where its offices are, etc.

**mas·ti·cate** (mas′tə kāt) ***v.*** to chew or chew up [*Masticate* your food thoroughly.] —**mas′ti·cat·ed, mas′ti·cat·ing** —**mas′ti·ca′tion *n.***

**mas·tiff** (mas′tif) ***n.*** a large, strong dog with a smooth coat and powerful jaws.

**mas·to·don** (mas′tə dän) ***n.*** a large animal like the elephant, that lived a long time ago. *See the picture.*

**mas·toid** (mas′toid) ***n.*** a small bone behind the ear.

**mas·tur·bate** (mas′tər bāt) ***v.*** to excite oneself in a sexual way. —**mas′tur·bat·ed, mas′tur·bat·ing** —**mas′tur·ba′tion *n.***

**mat**[1] (mat) ***n.*** **1** a flat, rough material made by weaving hemp, straw, rope, etc., often used as a floor covering. **2** a piece of this, or of other rough material, as for wiping the shoes on. **3** a flat piece of cloth, woven straw, etc., put under a vase, hot dish, etc. **4** a thickly padded floor covering, as for wrestling or tumbling on. **5** anything tangled or woven together in a thick mass [a *mat* of hair]. ◆***v.*** **1** to cover with a mat. **2** to weave together or tangle into a thick mass. —**mat′ted, mat′ting**

**mat**[2] (mat) ***n.*** a piece of cardboard used to form a border around a picture. *See the picture.* ◆***v.*** to frame with a mat. —**mat′ted, mat′ting**

**mat·a·dor** (mat′ə dôr) ***n.*** the bullfighter who kills the bull with a sword thrust.



**match**[1] (mach) ***n.*** **1** a slender piece of wood or cardboard having a tip coated with a chemical that catches fire when rubbed on a certain surface. **2** a slowly burning cord or wick once used for firing a gun or cannon.

**match**[2] (mach) ***n.*** **1** any person or thing equal to or like another in some way [Joan met her *match* in chess when she played Joe.] **2** two or more people or things that go well together [That suit and tie are a good *match.*] **3** a game or contest between two persons or teams [a tennis *match*]. **4** a marriage [Did you make a good *match?*] **5** a person thought of as a future husband or wife [Would Dan be a good *match* for their daughter?] ◆***v.*** **1** to go well together [Do your shirt and tie *match?*] **2** to make or get something like or equal to [Can you *match* this cloth?] **3** to be equal to [I could never *match* that lawyer in an argument.] **4** to pit against one another [to *match* two boxers].

**match·less** (mach′lis) ***adj.*** having no equal; best of its kind; peerless.

**match·lock** (mach′läk) ***n.*** **1** an old type of gunlock in which the gunpowder was set off by a burning wick. **2** a musket with such a gunlock.

**mate** (māt) ***n.*** **1** one of a pair [Where is the *mate* to this sock?] **2** a husband or wife. **3** the male or female of a pair of animals. **4** a friend or companion [a school*mate*]. **5** an officer of a merchant ship ranking next below the captain. ☆**6** any of various petty officers in the navy. ◆***v.*** **1** to join as a pair. **2** to join in marriage. —**mat′ed, mat′ing**

**ma·te·ri·al** (mə tir′ē əl) ***adj.*** **1** of or having to do with matter; physical [a *material* object]. **2** having to do with the body and its needs [*material* comforts]. **3** important or necessary [a *material* witness; a fact *material* to the debate]. ◆***n.*** **1** what a thing is made up of [raw *material*]. **2** cloth or other fabric. **3** ideas, notes, etc. that can be worked up [*material* for a story]. **4 materials,** *pl.* things or tools needed to do something [writing *materials*].

**ma·te·ri·al·ism** (mə tir′ē əl iz′m) ***n.*** **1** a tendency to be concerned more with material things than with spiritual values. **2** the belief that nothing exists except matter and that everything can be explained in terms of physical matter. —**ma·te′ri·al·ist *n.***

**ma·te·ri·al·ize** (mə tir′ē ə līz) ***v.*** **1** to become fact; develop into something real [His plan never *materialized.*] **2** to give a physical form to, or take on a physical form [A lovely portrait *materialized* from her sketches.] —**ma·te′ri·al·ized, ma·te′ri·al·iz·ing** —**ma·te′ri·al·i·za′tion *n.***

**ma·te·ri·al·ly** (mə tir′ē ə lē) ***adv.*** **1** as regards the matter or content of something and not its form or spirit; physically [This book, although rewritten, is *materially* the same.] **2** to a great extent; considerably [Her health has *materially* improved.]

**ma·te·ri·el** or **ma·té·ri·el** (mə tir′ē el′) ***n.*** the weapons, supplies, etc. of an army.

**ma·ter·nal** (mə tur′n'l) ***adj.*** **1** of or like a mother; motherly. **2** related to one on one's mother's side [my *maternal* aunt]. —**ma·ter′nal·ly *adv.***

**ma·ter·ni·ty** (mə tur′nə tē) ***n.*** the condition or character of being a mother; motherhood or motherliness. ◆***adj.*** for women who are about to become mothers or women who have just had babies [a *maternity* dress; a *maternity* ward in a hospital].

**math** (math) ***n.*** *a shorter form of* **mathematics.**

**math·e·mat·i·cal** (math′ə mat′i k'l) ***adj.*** **1** having to do with mathematics. **2** accurate; exact; precise. —**math′e·mat′i·cal·ly *adv.***

**math·e·ma·ti·cian** (math′ə mə tish′ən) ***n.*** an expert in mathematics.

**math·e·mat·ics** (math′ə mat′iks) ***n.pl.*** the group of sciences using numbers and symbols in dealing with the relationships and measurements of amounts and forms: *used with a singular verb* [*Mathematics* includes arithmetic, geometry, algebra, and calculus.]

**mat·i·nee** or **mat·i·née** (mat′'n ā′) ***n.*** a performance of a play, movie, etc. in the afternoon.

**mat·ins** (mat′'nz) ***n.pl.*** **1** in the Roman Catholic Church, a daily service held at midnight or at daybreak. **2** in the Church of England, the morning prayer service.

**Ma·tisse** (ma tēs′), **Hen·ri** (än rē′) 1869–1954; French painter.

**ma·tri·arch** (mā′trē ärk) ***n.*** a woman who is the head or ruler of her family or tribe.

**ma·tric·u·late** (mə trik′yoo lāt) ***v.*** to enroll, especially as a student in a college or university. —**ma·tric′u·lat·ed, ma·tric′u·lat·ing** —**ma·tric′u·la′tion** ***n.***

**mat·ri·mo·ny** (mat′rə mō′nē) ***n.*** the condition of being married; marriage. —**mat′ri·mo′ni·al** ***adj.***

**ma·trix** (mā′triks) ***n.*** something within which or from which a thing develops or is formed [A mold for casting is called a *matrix*. Boston was the *matrix* of the Revolution.] —*pl.* **ma·tri·ces** (mā′trə sēz) or **ma′trix·es**

**ma·tron** (mā′trən) ***n.*** **1** a wife or a widow, especially one who is not young. **2** a woman who has charge of others, as in a prison.

**ma·tron·ly** (mā′trən lē) ***adj.*** of, like, or fit for a matron; serious and dignified.

☆**matron of honor** a married woman who is the chief bridesmaid at a wedding.

**mat·ted** (mat′id) ***adj.*** **1** tangled together in a thick mass [*matted* hair]. **2** covered with matting or mats.

**mat·ter** (mat′ər) ***n.*** **1** what all things are made of; anything that takes up space. Science has now shown that matter can be changed into energy, and energy into matter [Solids, liquids, and gases are *matter*.] **2** what a particular thing is made of; material [The hard *matter* of bones is mainly calcium salts.] **3** things sent by mail; mail [first-class *matter*]. **4** something to be talked about, acted upon, etc.; affair [business *matters*]. **5** the contents or meaning of something written or spoken, as apart from its style or form [the subject *matter* of an essay]. **6** an amount or number [We waited a *matter* of hours.] **7** importance [It's of no *matter*.] **8** an unpleasant happening; trouble [What's the *matter*?] **9** pus. ◆***v.*** **1** to be important or have meaning [Your friendship really *matters* to me.] **2** to form pus. —**as a matter of fact,** really; to tell the truth. —**for that matter,** as far as that is concerned. —**matter of course,** a thing that can be expected to happen. —**no matter,** **1** it is not important. **2** in spite of.

**Mat·ter·horn** (mat′ər hôrn) a mountain in the Alps, on the Swiss-Italian border.

**mat·ter-of-fact** (mat′ər əv fakt′) ***adj.*** keeping to the facts; showing no strong feeling or imagination.

**Mat·thew** (math′yōō) **1** one of the twelve Apostles of Jesus. **2** the first book of the New Testament. Matthew is believed to have written this book.

**mat·ting** (mat′ing) ***n.*** a fabric woven of straw, hemp, or other fiber, used for mats, rugs, etc.

**mat·tock** (mat′ək) ***n.*** a tool somewhat like a pickax, for loosening soil, digging up roots, etc. *See the picture.*

**mat·tress** (mat′ris) ***n.*** a casing of strong cloth filled with cotton, foam rubber, coiled springs, etc. and used on a bed.

**mat·u·rate** (mach′oo rāt *or* mat′yoo rāt) ***v.*** to become fully grown or developed; ripen; mature. —**mat′u·rat·ed, mat′u·rat·ing** —**mat′u·ra′tion** ***n.***

**ma·ture** (mə toor′ *or* mə choor′) ***adj.*** **1** fully grown or developed [a *mature* plant; a *mature* person; a *mature* mind]. **2** completely or carefully worked out [a *mature* plan]. **3** due or payable [In ten years this bond will be *mature*.] ◆***v.*** to make or become mature. —**ma·tured′, ma·tur′ing**

**ma·tu·ri·ty** (mə toor′ə tē *or* mə choor′ə tē) ***n.*** **1** the condition of being fully grown or developed. **2** the time when a bond, insurance policy, etc. becomes due or reaches its full value.

**mat·zo** (mät′sə) ***n.*** a thin, crisp bread without leavening, eaten during Passover. *See the picture.* —*pl.* **mat·zot** (mät′sōt) or **mat′zos**

**maud·lin** (môd′lin) ***adj.*** showing sorrow, pity, or love in a foolish, tearful way; too sentimental, as because of being drunk.

**maul** (môl) ***v.*** to handle roughly or injure by being rough [The lion *mauled* its victim.]

**Mau·na Lo·a** (mou′nə lō′ə) an active volcano on the island of Hawaii.

**maun·der** (môn′dər) ***v.*** **1** to talk in a confused or rambling way. **2** to move or act in a confused or dreamy way.

**Maun·dy Thursday** (môn′dē) the Thursday before Easter.

**Mau·pas·sant** (mō′pə sänt), **Guy de** (gē də) 1850–1893; French writer of novels and short stories.

**Mau·ri·ta·ni·a** (môr′ə tā′nē ə) a country in western Africa, on the Atlantic Ocean.



**Mau·ri·ti·us** (mô rish′ē əs) a country on a group of islands in the Indian Ocean.

**mau·so·le·um** (mô′sə lē′əm) ***n.*** a large tomb.

**mauve** (mōv) ***adj., n.*** pale purple.

☆**mav·er·ick** (mav′ər ik) ***n.*** **1** an animal, especially a lost calf, that has not been branded. **2** a person who is independent of any political party or group: *used only in everyday talk.*

A **maverick** gets its name from Samuel Maverick, a Texas rancher of the 19th century who did not brand his cattle.

**maw** (mô) ***n.*** **1** the stomach of an animal. **2** the throat, gullet, jaws, etc. of some animals, as of the alligator.

**mawk·ish** (mô′kish) ***adj.*** **1** showing love, pity, etc. in a foolish or tearful way; so sentimental as to be sickening. **2** having a sweet, weak, sickening taste. —**mawk′ish·ly** ***adv.*** —**mawk′ish·ness** ***n.***

**max.** *abbreviation for* **maximum.**

**max·im** (mak′sim) ***n.*** a short saying that has become a rule of conduct ["Better late than never" is a *maxim*.]

**max·i·mum** (mak′sə məm) ***n.*** **1** the greatest amount or number that is possible or allowed [Forty pounds of luggage is the *maximum* you can take.] **2** the highest degree or point reached [Today's *maximum*

| | | | | | | | |
|---|---|---|---|---|---|---|---|
| **a** | fat | **ir** | here | **ou** | out | **zh** | leisure |
| **ā** | ape | **ī** | bite, fire | **u** | up | **ng** | ring |
| **ä** | car, lot | **ō** | go | **ur** | fur | | a *in* ago |
| **e** | ten | **ô** | law, horn | **ch** | chin | | e *in* agent |
| **er** | care | **oi** | oil | **sh** | she | **ə =** | i *in* unity |
| **ē** | even | **oo** | look | **th** | thin | | o *in* collect |
| **i** | hit | **ōō** | tool | ***th*** | then | | u *in* focus |

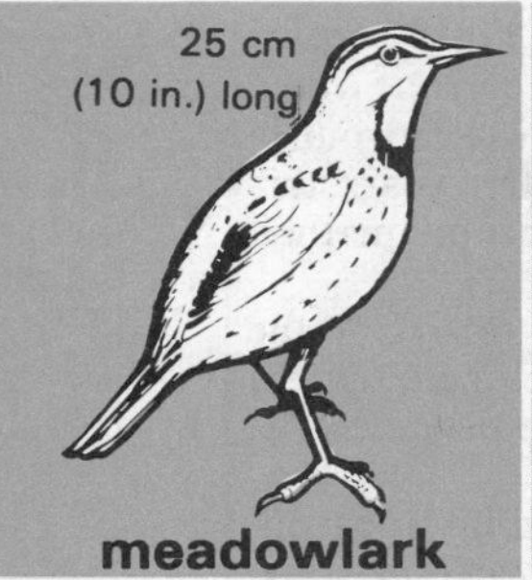

meadowlark

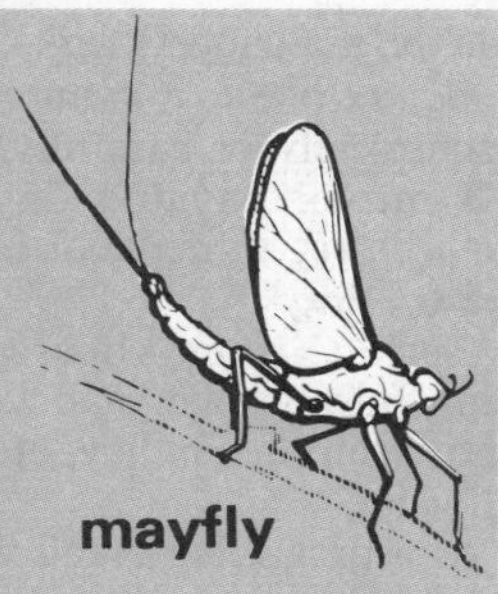
mayfly

Mayan carving

measure

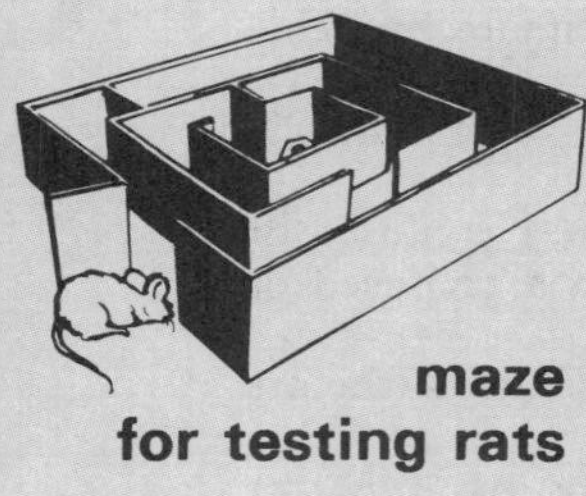
maze
for testing rats

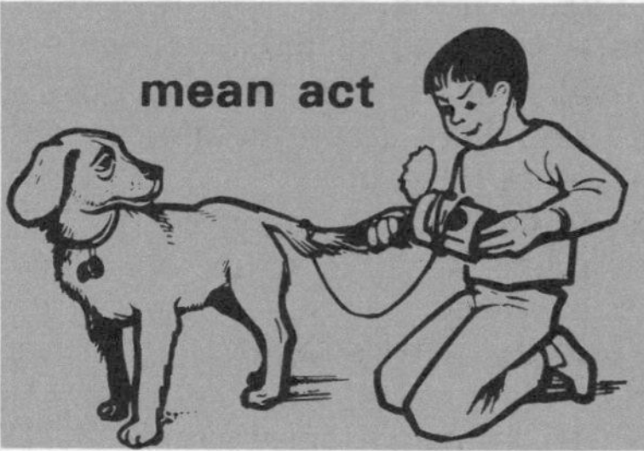
mean act

was 35°C.] *—pl.* **max'i·mums** or **max·i·ma** (mak'sə mə) **◆adj.** greatest possible or allowed [*maximum* speed].



**May** (mā) ***n.*** the fifth month of the year, which has 31 days.

**may** (mā) *a helping verb used with other verbs and meaning:* **1** to be possible or likely [It *may* rain.] **2** to be allowed or have permission [You *may* go.] *See* SYNONYMS *at* **can.** **3** to be able to as a result [Be quiet so that we *may* hear.] *May* is also used in exclamations to mean "I or we hope or wish" [*May* you win!] —The past tense is **might.**

**Ma·ya** (mä'yə) ***n.*** **1** a member of a highly civilized Indian people of southern Mexico and Central America who were conquered by the Spanish in the 16th century. *See the picture.* **2** their language. *—pl.* **Ma'yas** or **Ma'ya** **◆adj.** of the Mayas. —**Ma'yan** ***n., adj.***

☆**May apple** a woodland plant with shield-shaped leaves and a single, large, white, cuplike flower.

**may·be** (mā'bē) ***adv.*** it may be; perhaps.

**May Day** May 1, celebrated in honor of spring by dancing and by crowning a May queen. May Day is also sometimes celebrated as an international labor holiday.

**May·flow·er** (mā'flou'ər) the ship on which the Pilgrims sailed to America in 1620.

**may·flow·er** (mā'flou'ər) ***n.*** any of various early spring flowers, especially the arbutus.

**may·fly** (mā'flī) ***n.*** a slender insect with gauzy wings. The adult lives only a few days. *See the picture. —pl.* **may'flies**

**may·hem** (mā'hem *or* mā'əm) ***n.*** the crime of crippling or maiming a person on purpose.

**may·on·naise** (mā ə nāz' *or* mā'ə nāz) ***n.*** a thick, creamy salad dressing made of egg yolks, olive oil, lemon juice or vinegar, and seasoning.

**may·or** (mā'ər *or* mer) ***n.*** the head of the government of a city or town.

**may·or·al·ty** (mā'ər əl tē *or* mer'əl tē) ***n.*** the position of a mayor or the time of being a mayor.

**May·pole** (mā'pōl) ***n.*** a decorated pole around which people dance on May Day.

**May queen** a girl chosen to be queen of the merrymakers on May Day and crowned with flowers.

**mayst** (māst) *an older form of* **may,** *used with* thou, *as in the Bible.*

**maze** (māz) ***n.*** **1** a series of winding passages, blind alleys, etc. that make it hard to find one's way through. *See the picture.* **2** a condition of confusion.

**ma·zur·ka** or **ma·zour·ka** (mə zur'kə) ***n.*** **1** a fast Polish dance like the polka. **2** music for this dance.

**M·ba·ba·ne** ('m bä bä'nā) the capital of Swaziland.

**MBS** Mutual Broadcasting System.

**M.C.** *abbreviation for* **Master of Ceremonies.**

**Mc·Clel·lan** (mə klel'ən), **George B.** 1826–1885; Union general in the Civil War.

**Mc·Kin·ley** (mə kin'lē), **Mount** a mountain in Alaska that is the highest peak in North America. It is 20,320 ft. high (6,197 meters).

**Mc·Kin·ley** (mə kin'lē), **William** 1843–1901; the 25th president of the United States, from 1897 to 1901. He was assassinated.

**Md.** or **MD** *abbreviation for* **Maryland.**

**M.D.** Doctor of Medicine. This abbreviation is used after the doctor's name.

**Mdlle.** *an abbreviation for* **Mademoiselle.** *—pl.* **Mdlles.**

**Mdme.** *an abbreviation for* **Madame.** *—pl.* **Mdmes.**

**mdse.** *abbreviation for* **merchandise.**

**me** (mē) ***pron.*** *the form of* **I** *that is used as the object of a verb or preposition* [She helped *me.* Send it to *me.*]

> **Me** is often used in everyday talk after the verb *be* [It's *me.*] In formal writing most people prefer "It is I" or "It's I."

**Me.** or **ME** *abbreviation for* **Maine.**

**mead**[1] (mēd) ***n.*** an alcoholic drink made from honey.

**mead**[2] (mēd) ***n.*** *another word for* **meadow:** *used in earlier poetry.*

**Mead** (mēd), **Margaret** 1901–1978; U.S. anthropologist.

**mead·ow** (med'ō) ***n.*** **1** a piece of land where grass is grown for hay. **2** low, level grassland near a stream or lake.

☆**mead·ow·lark** (med'ō lärk') ***n.*** a North American songbird having upper parts streaked with black and brown and a bright yellow breast with a black collar. *See the picture.*

**mea·ger** (mē'gər) ***adj.*** of poor quality or small amount; scanty [a *meager* lunch].

> SYNONYMS: An early meaning of **meager** is "thin, lean, or starved-looking," which suggests the later meaning "of small amount, not rich or full, inadequate" [a *meager* diet]. **Scanty** suggests that there is not enough of something necessary [a *scanty* income].

**meal**[1] (mēl) ***n.*** **1** any of the regular times at which food is eaten, as breakfast, lunch, or dinner. **2** the food eaten at such a time [a delicious *meal*].

**meal**[2] (mēl) ***n.*** **1** grain ground up, but not so fine as flour [corn*meal*]. **2** anything ground up like this.

**meal·time** (mēl′tīm) ***n.*** the usual time for serving or eating a meal.

**meal·y** (mēl′ē) ***adj.*** **1** like meal; dry, crumbly, or pale. **2** of or covered with meal. —**meal′i·er, meal′i·est** —**meal′i·ness *n.***

**meal·y-mouthed** (mēl′ē mouthd′) ***adj.*** not willing to speak frankly or plainly; not sincere.

**mean**[1] (mēn) ***v.*** **1** to have in mind as a purpose; intend [She *meant* to go, but she changed her mind.] **2** to want to make known or understood [He says exactly what he *means.*] **3** to be a sign of; signify or indicate [Falling leaves *mean* winter is near. What does this word *mean?*] **4** to have a certain importance, effect, etc. [Your friendship *means* very much to me.] —**meant, mean′ing** —**mean well,** to have a good purpose in mind.

**mean**[2] (mēn) ***adj.*** **1** poor in looks, quality, etc.; shabby [a shack in a *mean* part of town]. **2** not noble or honorable; petty [Greed is a *mean* motive.] **3** not generous; stingy [A miser is *mean* with money.] ☆**4** dangerous or bad-tempered; hard to control [a *mean* dog]. ☆**5** selfish, unkind, rude, etc. in a shameful way. *See the picture.* ☆**6** in poor health; not well: *used only in everyday talk.* ☆**7** hard to cope with; difficult: *slang in this meaning* [That pitcher throws a *mean* curve.]

**mean**[3] (mēn) ***adj.*** halfway between two limits or extremes [If the highest temperature in May was 85 and the lowest 55, then the *mean* temperature was 70.] ◆***n.*** a point halfway between extremes [The *mean* between 2 and 10 is 6. I bought a compact as a happy *mean* between a big car and a small one.] *See* SYNONYMS *at* **average.**

**me·an·der** (mē an′dər) ***v.*** **1** to go winding back and forth [a *meandering* stream]. **2** to wander in an idle or aimless way.

> **Meander** comes from the ancient Greek name for the river Menderes, which has a twisting, winding course as it crosses Asia Minor to flow into the Aegean.

**mean·ing** (mēn′iŋ) ***n.*** what is meant; what is supposed to be understood; significance [She repeated her words to make her *meaning* clear. What is the *meaning* of this poem?] ◆***adj.*** that has some meaning [a *meaning* smile].

> SYNONYMS: The word **meaning** is used for whatever is intended to be expressed or understood by something [the *meaning* of a message]. The word **significance** is used for whatever is hidden or hinted at in addition to any meaning that is openly expressed [What is the *significance* of his sudden coolness toward us?]

**mean·ing·ful** (mēn′iŋ fəl) ***adj.*** full of meaning [She gave me a *meaningful* look.]

**mean·ing·less** (mēn′iŋ lis) ***adj.*** having no meaning; senseless [The whole letter is a *meaningless* scrawl.]

**mean·ness** (mēn′nis) ***n.*** the condition of being mean, poor, petty, stingy, selfish, unkind, etc.

**means** (mēnz) ***n.pl.*** **1** a way of getting or doing something [Flying is the fastest *means* of travel.] **2** wealth; riches [a person of *means*]. —**by all means,** certainly; of course. —**by any means,** in any way possible. —**by means of,** by using. —**by no means,** certainly not. —**means to an end,** a method of getting what one wants.

**meant** (ment) *past tense and past participle of* **mean.**

**mean·time** (mēn′tīm) ***adv.*** **1** during the time between [She came back in an hour; *meantime,* I had eaten.] **2** at the same time [We watched TV; *meantime,* dinner was cooking.] ◆***n.*** the time between [in the *meantime*].

**mean·while** (mēn′hwīl) ***adv., n.*** *another word for* **meantime.**

**mea·sles** (mē′z′lz) ***n.pl.*** **1** a disease in which there is a fever and red spots form on the skin. It is more common among children than adults. **2** a disease like this but milder, usually called **German measles.** *This word is used with a singular verb* [*Measles* is catching.]

**meas·ur·a·ble** (mezh′ər ə b′l) ***adj.*** large enough to be measured. —**meas′ur·a·bly *adv.***

**meas·ure** (mezh′ər) ***v.*** **1** to find out the size, amount, or extent of, as by comparing with something else [*Measure* the child's height with a yardstick. How do you *measure* a person's worth?] **2** to set apart or mark off a certain amount or length of [*Measure* out three pounds of sugar.] **3** to be of a certain size, amount, or extent [The table *measures* five feet on each side.] **4** to be a thing for measuring [Clocks *measure* time.] **5** to compare [*Measure* her score against the class average.] —**meas′ured, meas′ur·ing** ◆***n.*** **1** the size, amount, or extent of something, found out by measuring [The *measure* of the bucket is 15 liters.] **2** a unit or standard for use in measuring [The meter is a *measure* of length. Is its cost a fair *measure* of its worth?] **3** a system of measuring [Liquid *measure* is a system of measuring liquids.] **4** anything used to measure with [You can use that empty olive jar as a pint *measure.*] **5** a certain amount, extent, or degree [His success is due in some *measure* to his charm.] **6** an action meant to bring something about [The mayor promised to take *measures* to stop crime.] **7** a law [Congress passed a *measure* for flood control.] **8** the notes or rests between two bars on a staff of music. *See the picture.* **9** rhythm or meter, as of a poem or song. —**beyond measure,** so much that it cannot be measured; extremely. —**for good measure,** as a bonus or something extra. —☆**measure up to,** to be as good or satisfying as.

**meas·ured** (mezh′ərd) ***adj.*** **1** set or marked off according to a standard [a *measured* mile]. **2** regular or steady [*measured* steps]. **3** chosen with care [*measured* words].

**meas·ure·less** (mezh′ər lis) ***adj.*** too large or great to be measured; huge; vast.

**meas·ure·ment** (mezh′ər mənt) ***n.*** **1** a measuring or being measured. **2** size, amount, or extent found by measuring [His waist *measurement* is 32 inches.] **3** a system of measuring [liquid *measurement*].

| | | | | | | | |
|---|---|---|---|---|---|---|---|
| **a** | fat | **ir** | here | **ou** | out | **zh** | leisure |
| **ā** | ape | **ī** | bite, fire | **u** | up | **ŋ** | ring |
| **ä** | car, lot | **ō** | go | **ur** | fur | | a *in* ago |
| **e** | ten | **ô** | law, horn | **ch** | chin | | e *in* agent |
| **er** | care | **oi** | oil | **sh** | she | **ə =** | i *in* unity |
| **ē** | even | **oo** | look | **th** | thin | | o *in* collect |
| **i** | hit | **ōō** | tool | ***th*** | then | | u *in* focus |

**meat** (mēt) ***n.*** **1** the flesh of animals used as food. Meat usually does not include fish and often does not include poultry. **2** the part that can be eaten [the *meat* of a nut]. **3** the main part [the *meat* of an argument]. **4** food in general: *now used chiefly in the phrase* **meat and drink.**

☆**meat·pack·ing** (mēt′pak′iŋ) ***n.*** the business of slaughtering animals in large numbers and preparing their meat to be sold to meat markets and butcher shops. —**meat′pack′er** ***n.***

**meat·y** (mēt′ē) ***adj.*** **1** of, like, or full of meat [a rich, *meaty* broth]. ☆**2** full of ideas or meaning [a *meaty* speech]. —**meat′i·er, meat′i·est** —**meat′i·ness** ***n.***

**Mec·ca** (mek′ə) a capital of Saudi Arabia. It is a holy city of Muslims because Mohammed was born there. ◆***n.*** *often* **mecca,** any place that many people visit or want to visit [a *mecca* for tourists].

**mech.** *abbreviation for* **mechanical** *or* **mechanics.**

**me·chan·ic** (mə kan′ik) ***n.*** a worker skilled in using tools or in making, repairing, and using machinery.

**me·chan·i·cal** (mə kan′i k′l) ***adj.*** **1** having to do with machinery, or having skill in its use. **2** made or run by machinery [a *mechanical* toy]. **3** acting or done as if by a machine and without thought; automatic [to greet someone in a *mechanical* way]. —**me·chan′i·cal·ly** ***adv.***

**me·chan·ics** (mə kan′iks) ***n.pl.*** **1** the science that deals with motion and the effect of forces on bodies.
456 **2** knowledge of how to make, run, and repair machinery. **3** the technical part or skills [Spelling and punctuation form part of the *mechanics* of writing.] *This word is used with a singular verb.*

**mech·a·nism** (mek′ə niz′m) ***n.*** **1** the working parts of a machine. **2** any system whose parts work together like the parts of a machine [The human body is not a simple *mechanism.*]

**mech·a·nize** (mek′ə nīz) ***v.*** **1** to bring about the use of machinery in [Henry Ford *mechanized* the making of automobiles.] **2** to supply with tanks, trucks, etc. [to *mechanize* an army]. **3** to make mechanical, or like a machine. —**mech′a·nized, mech′a·niz·ing**

**med.** *abbreviation for* **medical, medicine, medieval, medium.**

**med·al** (med′′l) ***n.*** a small, flat piece of metal with words or a design on it, given as an honor or reward for some great action or service.

**me·dal·lion** (mə dal′yən) ***n.*** **1** a round design, decoration, etc. that looks like a medal. *See the picture.* **2** a large medal.

**med·dle** (med′′l) ***v.*** to touch another's things or take part in another's affairs without being asked or wanted; interfere [Don't *meddle* in my business.] —**med′dled, med′dling** —**med′dler** ***n.***

megaphone

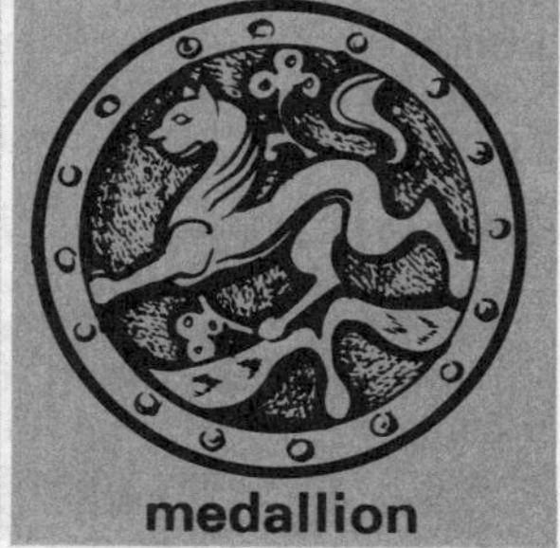
medallion

**med·dle·some** (med′′l səm) ***adj.*** in the habit of meddling; interfering.

**Mede** (mēd) ***n.*** a person of ancient Media.

**Me·de·a** (mi dē′ə) a witch in a Greek myth, who helped Jason get the Golden Fleece.

**Me·di·a** (mē′dē ə) an ancient country in what is now northwestern Iran.

**me·di·a** (mē′dē ə) ***n.*** *a plural of* **medium**: *see meaning* 3 *of* **medium.**

**me·di·ae·val** (mē′dē ē′v′l *or* med′ē ē′v′l) ***adj.*** *another spelling of* **medieval.**

**me·di·al** (mē′dē əl) ***adj.*** **1** of or in the middle; median. **2** average or ordinary.

**me·di·an** (mē′dē ən) ***adj.*** in the middle; halfway between the two ends [7 is the *median* number in the series 1, 4, 7, 25, 48.] ◆***n.*** **1** a median number, point, or line. *See* SYNONYMS *at* **average.** ☆**2** a strip of land in the middle of a divided highway, that separates traffic going in opposite directions: *also called* **median strip.**

**me·di·ate** (mē′dē āt′) ***v.*** **1** to act as a judge or go-between in trying to settle a quarrel between persons or sides. **2** to bring about an agreement by acting as a go-between. —**me′di·at′ed, me′di·at′ing** —**me′di·a′tor** ***n.***

☆**Med·i·caid** (med′i kād′) ***n.*** a public health plan that pays some of the medical expenses of persons with low income or with no income. The money comes from State and Federal funds.

**me·di·a·tion** (mē′dē ā′shən) ***n.*** a mediating, or working to bring about an agreement.

**med·ic** (med′ik) ***n.*** **1** a medical doctor. **2** a soldier whose work is giving first aid in battle. *This word is used only in everyday talk.*

**med·i·cal** (med′i k′l) ***adj.*** having to do with the practice or study of medicine [*medical* care; a *medical* school]. —**med′i·cal·ly** ***adv.***

**Med·i·care** (med′i ker′) ***n.*** a national health program for providing medical and hospital care for older people and the needy from Federal funds.

**med·i·cate** (med′ə kāt) ***v.*** **1** to put medicine in or on [These cough drops are *medicated.*] **2** to treat with medicine [It is often dangerous to *medicate* oneself without a doctor's advice.] —**med′i·cat·ed, med′i·cat·ing**

**med·i·ca·tion** (med′ə kā′shən) ***n.*** **1** the act of medicating. **2** a medicine.

**me·dic·i·nal** (mə dis′in ′l) ***adj.*** that is or acts as a medicine; curing or healing [a *medicinal* cream].

**med·i·cine** (med′ə s′n) ***n.*** **1** any substance used in or on the body to treat disease, lessen pain, heal, etc. **2** the science of treating and preventing disease. **3** the branch of this science that makes use of drugs, diet, etc., especially as separate from surgery. ☆**4** among North American Indians, any thing or action supposed to have magic power to cure illness, keep away evil, etc.; also, such magic power.

☆**medicine man** among North American Indians and certain other peoples, a man who was thought to have magic power in curing disease, keeping away evil, etc.

**me·di·e·val** (mē′dē ē′v′l *or* med′ē ē′v′l) ***adj.*** of, like, or belonging to the Middle Ages.

**me·di·o·cre** (mē′dē ō′kər) ***adj.*** **1** neither very good nor very bad; just ordinary. **2** not good enough. —**me·di·oc·ri·ty** (mē′dē äk′rə tē) ***n.***

**med·i·tate** (med′ə tāt) ***v.*** **1** to pass some time thinking in a quiet way; reflect. **2** to plan or consider [to *meditate* making a change]. *See* SYNONYMS *at* **ponder.** —**med′i·tat·ed, med′i·tat·ing** —**med′i·ta′tion** ***n.*** —**med′i·ta′tive** ***adj.***

**Med·i·ter·ra·ne·an** (med′i tə rā′nē ən) ***adj.*** of the Mediterranean Sea or the regions around it.

**Mediterranean Sea** a large sea surrounded by Europe, Africa, and Asia.

**me·di·um** (mē′dē əm) ***adj.*** in the middle in amount, degree, etc.; average [a *medium* price]. ◆***n.*** **1** a thing or condition in the middle; something that is not an extreme [A temperature of 70° is a happy *medium.*] **2** a thing through which a force acts or an effect is made [Copper is a good *medium* for conducting heat.] **3** any way by which something is done; especially, a way of communicating with the general public, as TV or newspapers: *in this meaning the plural* **media** *is sometimes used as a singular noun* [The *media* is covering the president's inauguration.] **4** the substance, condition, etc. in which something lives. ☆**5** a person through whom messages are supposedly sent from the dead, as at a séance. —*pl.* **me′di·ums** or **me·di·a** (mē′dē ə): **mediums** *is always used with meaning* 5.

**med·ley** (med′lē) ***n.*** **1** a mixture of unlike things. **2** a selection of songs or tunes played as a single piece. —*pl.* **med′leys**

**Me·du·sa** (mə do͞o′sə *or* mə dyo͞o′zə) in Greek myths, one of the Gorgons: *see* **Gorgon.**

**meek** (mēk) ***adj.*** **1** patient and mild; not showing anger. **2** very humble or too humble in one's feelings, actions, etc.; not showing spirit. —**meek′ly** ***adv.*** —**meek′ness** ***n.***

**meer·schaum** (mir′shəm) ***n.*** **1** a soft, white mineral like clay. **2** a tobacco pipe made of this.

**meet**[1] (mēt) ***v.*** **1** to come upon; come face to face with [We *met* two friends walking down the street.] **2** to be introduced to [I *met* you at a party.] **3** to become acquainted [Have you two *met?*] **4** to be present at the arrival of [Please *meet* the bus.] **5** to keep an appointment with [I'll *meet* you at noon.] **6** to come into contact [The cars *met* with a crash.] **7** to come together; assemble [The school board *meets* today.] **8** to be joined [The rivers *meet* below the mill.] **9** to face or deal with [I *met* their questions with honest answers.] **10** to undergo; experience [Their plan will *meet* disaster.] **11** to satisfy, as a demand or need. **12** to pay [to *meet* one's bills]. —**met, meet′ing** ◆***n.*** a meeting, as for some sport [a track *meet*]. —**meet with, 1** to experience; have [to *meet with* an accident]. **2** to come upon.

**meet**[2] (mēt) ***adj.*** fitting or proper: *no longer much used.*

**meet·ing** (mēt′iŋ) ***n.*** **1** a coming together of persons or things. **2** a gathering of people for some purpose; assembly.

**meet·ing·house** (mēt′iŋ hous′) ***n.*** a building used for religious services.

**meg·a·hertz** (meg′ə hurts) ***n.*** one million hertz.

**meg·a·lop·o·lis** (meg′ə läp′ə ləs) ***n.*** a very large, crowded area made up of several cities.

☆**meg·a·phone** (meg′ə fōn) ***n.*** a large tube shaped like a funnel, through which a person speaks or shouts. It sends the voice farther. *See the picture.*

**meg·a·ton** (meg′ə tun) ***n.*** a unit of measure for the power produced by nuclear fusion, equal to the explosive power of a million tons of TNT.

**Me·kong** (mā′käŋ′) a river in southeastern Asia, flowing through China and the Indochinese peninsula.

**mel·an·chol·y** (mel′ən käl′ē) ***n.*** sadness or a tendency to be sad and gloomy. ◆***adj.*** **1** sad and gloomy. **2** causing sadness or gloom [a *melancholy* rain].

> The ancient Greeks thought that there were four body fluids, or humors, that had an effect on a person's health and mood. *See the note in color at* **humor.** One of these fluids they called *melancholia,* meaning "black bile." Having too much of this, they thought, caused a person to be sad and gloomy, or **melancholy.**

**Mel·a·ne·sia** (mel′ə nē′zhə) a group of islands in the South Pacific, northeast of Australia. —**Mel′a·ne′sian** ***adj., n.***

**Mel·bourne** (mel′bərn) a seaport in southeastern Australia.

☆**meld** (meld) ***v.*** in card games, to put a certain grouping of one's cards face up on the table, to be counted for a score. ◆***n.*** **1** the act of melding. **2** the cards melded.

**me·lee** or **mê·lée** (mā′lā *or* mā lā′) ***n.*** a noisy, confused fight or struggle among a number of people; brawl; riot. 

**mel·lif·lu·ous** (mə lif′lo͝o wəs) ***adj.*** sounding sweet and smooth [a *mellifluous* voice].

**mel·low** (mel′ō) ***adj.*** **1** soft, sweet, and juicy; ripe [a *mellow* apple]. **2** having a good flavor from being aged [a *mellow* wine]. **3** rich, soft, and pure; not harsh [the *mellow* tone of a cello]. **4** made gentle and kind by age and experience [a *mellow* teacher]. ◆***v.*** to make or become mellow. —**mel′low·ness** ***n.***

**me·lod·ic** (mə läd′ik) ***adj.*** **1** of or like melody [the *melodic* pattern]. **2** melodious.

**me·lo·di·ous** (mə lō′dē əs) ***adj.*** **1** making pleasant music. **2** pleasing to hear; tuneful.

**mel·o·dra·ma** (mel′ə drä′mə *or* mel′ə dram′ə) ***n.*** **1** a play in which there is much suspense and strong feeling, and a great exaggeration of good and evil in the characters. **2** any exciting action or talk like that in such a play.

> **Melodrama** comes from a Greek word meaning "song" and the French word for "drama." In the original melodramas there were songs sung at various points in the action of the play.

**mel·o·dra·mat·ic** (mel′ə drə mat′ik) ***adj.*** of, like, or fit for melodrama; violent, emotional, etc. —**mel′o·dra·mat′i·cal·ly** ***adv.***

**mel·o·dy** (mel′ə dē) ***n.*** **1** an arrangement of musical tones in a series so as to form a tune; often, the main tune in the harmony of a musical piece [The *melody* is played by the oboes.] **2** any pleasing series of sounds [a *melody* sung by birds]. *—pl.* **mel′o·dies**

**mel·on** (mel′ən) ***n.*** a large, juicy fruit that grows on a vine and is full of seeds [Watermelons, muskmelons, and cantaloupes are *melons.*]

**melt** (melt) ***v.*** **1** to change from a solid to a liquid, as by heat [The bacon fat *melted* in the frying pan.] **2** to dissolve [The candy *melted* in my mouth.] **3** to disappear or go away [Our fear *melted* away.] **4** to blend in slowly [The blue sky seemed to *melt* into the sea.] **5** to make gentle or full of pity [To see someone crying *melts* my heart.]

SYNONYMS: To **melt** something is to change it from a solid to a liquid, usually by heating it [to *melt* butter]. To **thaw** is to change something frozen back to its normal state by raising its temperature [ice *thawing* in the river; to *thaw* frozen steaks].

**melting pot** a country in which immigrants of many nationalities and races are taken in and help to make up the whole culture. This term is often used to describe the U.S.

**Mel·ville** (mel′vil), **Herman** 1819–1891; U.S. writer of novels.

**mem.** *abbreviation for* **member, memorandum, memorial.**

**mem·ber** (mem′bər) ***n.*** **1** any of the persons who make up a church, club, political party, or other group. **2** a leg, arm, or other part of the body. **3** a single part of a thing, as a word in a sentence or a column of a building.

**mem·ber·ship** (mem′bər ship) ***n.*** **1** the condition of being a member. **2** all the members of a group. **3** the number of members.

**mem·brane** (mem′brān) ***n.*** a thin, soft layer of tissue that covers a part of an animal or plant.

**mem·bra·nous** (mem′brə nəs) ***adj.*** of or like membrane.

**me·men·to** (mi men′tō) ***n.*** an object kept to remind one of something; souvenir [This toy is a *memento* of my childhood.] *—pl.* **me·men′tos** or **me·men′toes**

**mem·o** (mem′ō) ***n.*** *a shorter form of* **memorandum.** *—pl.* **mem′os**

**mem·oir** (mem′wär) ***n.*** **1 memoirs,** *pl.* the story of one's life written by oneself; autobiography; also, a written record based on the writer's own experience and knowledge. **2** a written story of someone's life; biography.

**mem·o·ra·ble** (mem′ər ə b′l) ***adj.*** worth remembering; not easily forgotten; remarkable.

**mem·o·ran·dum** (mem′ə ran′dəm) ***n.*** **1** a short note written to help one remember something. **2** an informal note, as from one part of a business office to another. *—pl.* **mem′o·ran′dums** or **mem·o·ran·da** (mem′ə ran′də)

**me·mo·ri·al** (mə môr′ē əl) ***adj.*** held or done in memory of some person or event [a *memorial* service for the dead]. ◆***n.*** anything meant to remind people of some event or person, as a holiday or statue.

☆**Memorial Day** the last Monday in May, a legal holiday for honoring dead members of the armed forces of all wars.

**mem·o·rize** (mem′ə rīz) ***v.*** ☆to fix in one's memory exactly or word for word; learn by heart. **—mem′o·rized, mem′o·riz·ing —mem′o·ri·za′tion *n.***

**mem·o·ry** (mem′ər ē) ***n.*** **1** the act or power of remembering [to have a good *memory*]. **2** all that one remembers. **3** something remembered [The music brought back many *memories.*] **4** the time over which one can remember [It had never happened before within my *memory.*] **5** the part of a computer that stores information. *—pl.* **mem′o·ries —in memory of,** that keeps alive in one's memory [a statue *in memory of* the President].

**Mem·phis** (mem′fis) **1** a city in southwestern Tennessee. **2** a city in ancient Egypt.

**men** (men) ***n.*** *plural of* **man.**

**men·ace** (men′is) ***n.*** a threat or danger; thing likely to cause harm. ◆***v.*** to threaten with harm; be a danger to [Snow *menaced* the crops.] **—men′aced, men′ac·ing**

**me·nag·er·ie** (mə naj′ər ē) ***n.*** a collection of wild animals kept in cages; often, such a collection taken from place to place for public showing.

**mend** (mend) ***v.*** **1** to put back in good condition; repair; fix [to *mend* a broken lamp; to *mend* a torn shirt]. **2** to make or become better; improve [You must *mend* your ways. Her health *mended.*] ◆***n.*** a part that has been mended. **—on the mend,** becoming better, as in health.

**men·da·cious** (men dā′shəs) ***adj.*** not truthful; lying or false. **—men·dac·i·ty** (men das′ə tē) ***n.***

**Men·dels·sohn** (men′d'l sən), **Fe·lix** (fā′liks) 1809–1847; German composer.

**men·di·cant** (men′di kənt) ***adj.*** begging; asking for charity [*mendicant* friars]. ◆***n.*** a beggar.

**men·folk** (men′fōk) ***n.pl.*** men as a group: *used in everyday talk, mainly in the South* [The *menfolk* are out in the yard.] *Also* **men·folks** (men′fōks).

☆**men·ha·den** (men hād′'n) ***n.*** a fish related to the herring, found along the Atlantic coast. It is important for its oil and for its use as fertilizer.

**me·ni·al** (mē′nē əl *or* mēn′yəl) ***adj.*** of or fit for servants; low or humble. ◆***n.*** a servant, especially in the home.

**men·in·gi·tis** (men′in jīt′is) ***n.*** a disease in which the membranes surrounding the brain or spinal cord become inflamed by infection.

**Men·non·ite** (men′ə nīt) ***n.*** a member of a Christian church that is against military service, the taking of oaths, etc. Mennonites dress and live in a very plain way.

**men·o·pause** (men′ə pôz) ***n.*** the period in life when a woman stops menstruating.

**men·o·rah** (mə nō′rə *or* mə nôr′ə) ***n.*** a candlestick with seven branches that is a symbol of the Jewish religion. Menorahs used during Hanuka have nine branches. *See the picture.*

**Me·not·ti** (mə nät′ē), **Gian Car·lo** (jän kär′lō) 1911– ; Italian composer of operas. He has been living in the U.S. since 1928.

**men·stru·ate** (men′stro͞o wāt′ *or* men′strāt) ***v.*** to have the normal flow of blood from the uterus, about every four weeks [Women *menstruate* from the time they become sexually mature until some time in middle age.] **—men′stru·at′ed, men′stru·at′ing — men′stru·a′tion *n.***

**mens·wear** (menz′wer) ***n.*** clothing for men: *also* **men's wear.**

**-ment** (mənt) *a suffix meaning:* **1** the act or result of [*Improvement* is the act or result of improving.] **2** a way of or thing for [An *adornment* is a thing for adorning.] **3** the condition or fact of being [*Disappointment* is the condition or fact of being disappointed.]

**men·tal** (men′t'l) ***adj.*** **1** of, for, by, or in the mind [*mental* ability; *mental* arithmetic]. **2** sick in mind [a *mental* patient]. **3** for the sick in mind [a *mental* hospital].

**men·tal·i·ty** (men tal′ə tē) ***n.*** the ability to think and reason; mind. —*pl.* **men·tal′i·ties**

**men·tal·ly** (men′t'l ē) ***adv.*** in, with, or by the mind [*mentally* ill; *mentally* alert].

**men·thol** (men′thôl) ***n.*** a substance got from oil of peppermint in the form of white crystals that give a cool taste or feeling. It is used in salves, cough drops, etc.

**men·tion** (men′shən) ***v.*** to speak about or name briefly. ✦***n.*** something said or named briefly, without going into detail. —**make mention of,** to mention; remark about.

**men·tor** (men′tər) ***n.*** **1** a wise, loyal adviser. **2** a teacher or coach.

**men·u** (men′yo͞o) ***n.*** a list of the foods served at a meal [a restaurant's dinner *menu*].

**me·ow** (mē ou′) ***n.*** the sound made by a cat. ✦***v.*** to make this sound.

**Meph·i·stoph·e·les** (mef′ə stäf′ə lēz) a devil in an old legend to whom Faust sold his soul: *see also* **Faust.**

**mer·can·tile** (mur′kən til *or* mur′kən tīl) ***adj.*** having to do with merchants, trade, or commerce.

**mer·ce·nar·y** (mur′sə ner′ē) ***adj.*** working or done just for money; greedy [The *mercenary* property owner raised rents steeply.] ✦***n.*** a soldier who fights for any country that will pay. —*pl.* **mer′ce·nar′ies**

**mer·cer·ize** (mur′sə rīz) ***v.*** to treat cotton thread with a chemical that makes it strong and silky. —**mer′cer·ized, mer′cer·iz·ing**

**mer·chan·dise** (mur′chən dīz *or* mur′chən dīs) ***n.*** things bought and sold; goods. ✦***v.*** (mur′chən dīz) to buy and sell; deal in [to *merchandise* hardware]. —**mer′chan·dised, mer′chan·dis·ing**

**mer·chant** (mur′chənt) ***n.*** a person who buys and sells goods for profit, either wholesale or as a storekeeper. ✦***adj.*** of or used in buying and selling goods; commercial [a *merchant* ship].

**mer·chant·man** (mur′chənt mən) ***n.*** a ship for carrying cargo. —*pl.* **mer′chant·men**

**merchant marine** all the ships of a nation that carry cargo, or their crews.

**mer·ci·ful** (mur′si fəl) ***adj.*** having or showing mercy; kind; forgiving. —**mer′ci·ful·ly *adv.***

**mer·ci·less** (mur′si lis) ***adj.*** having or showing no mercy; cruel. —**mer′ci·less·ly *adv.***

**mer·cu·ri·al** (mər kyoor′ē əl) ***adj.*** **1** like mercury; quick, lively, changeable, etc. [a *mercurial* person]. **2** of or having to do with mercury.

**Mer·cu·ry** (mur′kyoo rē) **1** the Roman messenger of the gods, who was also the god of trade and cleverness. *See the picture.* **2** the smallest planet. It is also the one nearest the sun.

menorah

Mercury

**mer·cu·ry** (mur′kyoo rē) ***n.*** a heavy, silvery metal that is a chemical element. It is ordinarily a liquid and is used in thermometers, medicines, etc.

**mer·cy** (mur′sē) ***n.*** **1** kindness, as to a wrongdoer or enemy, that is greater than might be expected. **2** the power to forgive or be kind [Throw yourself on the *mercy* of the court.] **3** a lucky thing; blessing [It's a *mercy* they weren't killed.] —*pl.* **mer′cies** ✦***interj.*** a word showing surprise, slight anger, etc. —**at the mercy of,** completely in the power of.

**mere** (mir) ***adj.*** nothing more than; only [You're a *mere* child.] —The superlative of *mere* is **mer′est.**

**mere·ly** (mir′lē) ***adv.*** no more than; and nothing else; only.

**mer·e·tri·cious** (mer′ə trish′əs) ***adj.*** attractive in a false, showy way; flashy, but cheap [*meretricious* advertising]. 459

**mer·gan·ser** (mər gan′sər) ***n.*** a large duck with a long, slender beak.

**merge** (murj) ***v.*** to combine or unite into one larger thing so as to lose separate character [The two companies *merged.*] —**merged, merg′ing**

**merg·er** (mur′jər) ***n.*** a merging; especially, ☆a combining of several companies into one.

**me·rid·i·an** (mə rid′ē ən) ***n.*** the half circle made by a line passing north and south across the surface of the earth, from one pole to the other. The lines of longitude on a map or globe are a series of such half circles.

**me·ringue** (mə rang′) ***n.*** egg whites mixed with sugar, beaten stiff and baked as a covering for pies, or as separate small cakes.

**me·ri·no** (mə rē′nō) ***n.*** **1** a sheep with long, silky wool. **2** its wool, or a soft yarn made from it. **3** a soft, thin, woolen cloth. —*pl.* **me·ri′nos**

**mer·it** (mer′it) ***n.*** **1** good quality; worth; goodness [a plan of great *merit*]. **2 merits,** *pl.* actual rightness or wrongness [to decide a case on its *merits*]. ✦***v.*** to be worthy of; deserve [to *merit* praise].

**mer·i·to·ri·ous** (mer′ə tôr′ē əs) ***adj.*** deserving reward, praise, etc.

**Mer·lin** (mur′lin) a magician in the legends about King Arthur.

| | | | | | | | |
|---|---|---|---|---|---|---|---|
| **a** | fat | **ir** | here | **ou** | out | **zh** | leisure |
| **ā** | ape | **ī** | bite, fire | **u** | up | **ng** | ring |
| **ä** | car, lot | **ō** | go | **ur** | fur | | a *in* ago |
| **e** | ten | **ô** | law, horn | **ch** | chin | | e *in* agent |
| **er** | care | **oi** | oil | **sh** | she | **ə =** | i *in* unity |
| **ē** | even | **oo** | look | **th** | thin | | o *in* collect |
| **i** | hit | **o͞o** | tool | ***th*** | then | | u *in* focus |

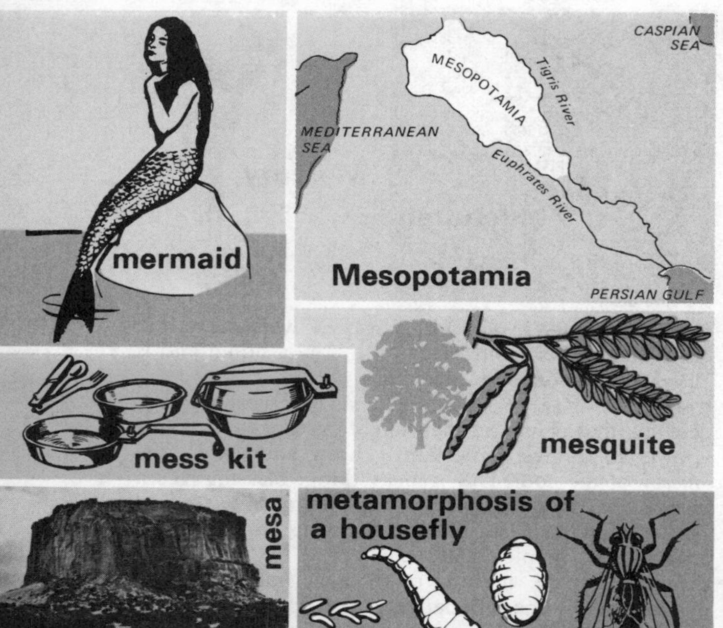


**mer·maid** (mʉr′mād) ***n.*** an imaginary sea creature with the head and upper body of a woman and the tail of a fish. *See the picture.*



**mer·man** (mʉr′mən) ***n.*** an imaginary sea creature with the head and upper body of a man and the tail of a fish. *—pl.* **mer′men**

**mer·ri·ment** (mer′i mənt) ***n.*** laughter and lively fun; merrymaking; mirth. *See* SYNONYMS *at* **mirth.**

**mer·ry** (mer′ē) ***adj.*** filled with fun and laughter; lively and cheerful [a *merry* party]. —**mer′ri·er, mer′ri·est** —**make merry,** to have fun. —**mer′ri·ly** ***adv.*** —**mer′ri·ness** ***n.***

**mer·ry-go-round** (mer′ē gō round′) ***n.*** **1** a platform that is turned around and around by machinery and that has wooden animals and seats on which people ride for amusement; carrousel. **2** an exciting series of parties, dances, etc.

**mer·ry·mak·ing** (mer′ē māk′iŋ) ***n.*** **1** the act of making merry and having fun. **2** a happy and lively party or amusement. ➧***adj.*** lively and filled with fun [a *merrymaking* weekend]. —**mer′ry·mak′er** ***n.***

☆**me·sa** (mā′sə) ***n.*** a large, high rock having steep walls and a flat top. *See the picture.*

> **Mesa** is a Spanish word that came from a Latin word meaning "table." Some mesas looked like tables to the Spanish explorers in what is now the southwestern United States.

**mes·dames** (mā däm′) ***n.*** *plural of* **madame, madam,** *or* **Mrs.**: abbreviated **Mmes.**

**mes·de·moi·selles** (mād mwä zel′) ***n.*** *plural of* **mademoiselle**: abbreviated **Mlles.**

**mesh** (mesh) ***n.*** **1** any of the open spaces of a net, screen, or sieve. **2 meshes,** *pl.* the threads, cords, or wires that form a network [to repair the *meshes* of a fishing net]. **3** a woven material that looks like a net. ➧***v.*** **1** to catch or trap as in a net. ☆**2** to engage or become engaged [The gears *meshed.*] **3** to fit together closely; interlock [Our plans don't *mesh.*] —**in mesh,** with the gears engaged.

**mes·mer·ize** (mez′mər īz) ***v.*** **1** to hypnotize. **2** to fascinate. —**mes′mer·ized, mes′mer·iz·ing**

☆**mes·on** (mes′än *or* mez′än) ***n.*** a particle that has a mass between that of the electron and the proton. Mesons can have a neutral, positive, or negative charge.

**Mes·o·po·ta·mi·a** (mes′ə pə tā′mē ə) an ancient country in southwestern Asia, between the Tigris and Euphrates rivers. *See the map.*

☆**mes·quite** or **mes·quit** (mes kēt′ *or* mes′kēt) ***n.*** a thorny tree or shrub common in the southwestern U.S. and in Mexico. Its sugary beanlike pods are used as fodder. *See the picture.*

**mess** (mes) ***n.*** **1** a heap or mass of things thrown together or mixed up; jumble [clothes in a *mess* on the bed]. **2** a condition of being dirty, untidy, etc. [Your room is in a *mess.*] ☆**3** a person in such a condition: *used only in everyday talk.* **4** a condition of trouble or difficulty [He's in a real *mess* for failing to finish the assignment.] **5** a group of people who regularly eat together, as in the army or navy. **6** a meal eaten by such a group, or the place where they eat. **7** a serving of food. ➧***v.*** **1** to make a mess of; make dirty, confused, etc. [They *messed* up my life.] **2** to putter or meddle [Don't *mess* around with my books.] **3** to eat as one of a mess (*meaning* 5).

**mes·sage** (mes′ij) ***n.*** **1** a piece of news, a request, facts, etc. sent from one person to another, either by speaking or writing. **2** an important idea that a writer, artist, etc. is trying to bring to people.

**mes·sen·ger** (mes′′n jər) ***n.*** a person who carries a message or is sent on an errand.

☆**mess hall** a room or building where a group of people regularly have their meals, especially such a place where soldiers eat.

**Mes·si·ah** (mə sī′ə) ***n.*** **1** in Jewish belief, the person that God will send to save the Jewish people. **2** in Christian belief, Jesus. **3 messiah,** any person expected to save others.

**Mes·si·an·ic** (mes′ē an′ik) ***adj.*** **1** of the Messiah. **2 messianic,** of or like a messiah.

**mes·sieurs** (mes′ərz *or* mā syʉr′) ***n.*** *plural of* **monsieur**: abbreviated **MM.** *See also* **Messrs.**

**mess kit** a set consisting of plates, a fork, a spoon, etc. carried by a soldier or camper for eating. *See the picture.*

**Messrs.** (mes′ərz) *abbreviation for* **Messieurs:** *commonly used as the plural of* **Mr.**

**mess·y** (mes′ē) ***adj.*** in or like a mess; untidy, dirty, etc. —**mess′i·er, mess′i·est** —**mess′i·ly** ***adv.*** —**mess′i·ness** ***n.***

**mes·ti·zo** (mes tē′zō) ***n.*** a person who has one Spanish or Portuguese parent and one American Indian parent. *—pl.* **mes·ti′zos** or **mes·ti′zoes**

**met** (met) *past tense and past participle of* **meet[1].**

**met.** *abbreviation for* **metropolitan.**

**me·tab·o·lism** (mə tab′ə liz′m) ***n.*** the process in all plants and animals by which food is changed into energy, new cells, waste products, etc. —**met·a·bol·ic** (met′ə bäl′ik) ***adj.***

**met·al** (met′′l) ***n.*** **1** a chemical element that is more or less shiny, can be hammered or stretched, and can conduct heat and electricity, as iron, gold, aluminum, lead, and magnesium. **2** a substance of some metal [made of either plastic or *metal*]. **3** material; stuff [You must be made of strong *metal* to bear such trouble.] ◆***adj.*** made of metal.

**me·tal·lic** (mə tal′ik) ***adj.*** **1** of or producing metal [*metallic* ores]. **2** like that of metal [a *metallic* sound].

**met·al·lur·gy** (met′'l ʉr′jē) ***n.*** the science of getting metals from their ores and making them ready for use, by smelting, refining, etc. —**met′al·lur′gi·cal *adj.*** —**met′al·lur′gist *n.***

**met·al·work** (met′'l wʉrk) ***n.*** **1** things made of metal. **2** the making of such things: *also called* **met′al·work′ing.** —**met′al·work′er *n.***

**met·a·mor·phose** (met′ə môr′fōz) ***v.*** to change completely in form; transform [The caterpillar *metamorphosed* into a butterfly.] —**met′a·mor′phosed, met′a·mor′phos·ing**

**met·a·mor·pho·sis** (met′ə môr′fə sis) ***n.*** **1** a change in form; especially, the change that some animals go through in developing, as of tadpole to frog or larva to moth. *See the picture.* **2** a complete change in the way someone or something looks or acts. —*pl.* **met·a·mor·pho·ses** (met′ə môr′fə sēz)

**met·a·phor** (met′ə fôr) ***n.*** the use of a word or phrase in a way that is different from its usual use, to show a likeness to something else ["The curtain of night" is a *metaphor* that likens night to a curtain that hides something.]

**met·a·phor·i·cal** (met′ə fôr′i k'l) ***adj.*** of or using metaphors [*metaphorical* language].

**met·a·phys·ics** (met′ə fiz′iks) ***n.pl.*** a philosophy that tries to answer questions about what really exists and about how the world began: *used with a singular verb.* —**met′a·phys′i·cal *adj.***

**me·tas·ta·size** (mə tas′tə sīz) ***v.*** to spread as disease from one part of the body to another, as when cancer cells travel through the bloodstream. —**me·tas′ta·sized, me·tas′ta·siz·ing**

**mete** (mēt) ***v.*** to deal out in shares or according to what is deserved [The judge *meted* out punishments.] —**met′ed, met′ing**

**me·te·or** (mēt′ē ər) ***n.*** a small solid body that moves with great speed from outer space into the air around the earth, where it is made white-hot by friction and usually burned up; shooting star.

**me·te·or·ic** (mēt′ē ôr′ik) ***adj.*** **1** of a meteor or meteors. **2** bright and swift like a meteor [the actor's *meteoric* rise to fame].

**me·te·or·ite** (mēt′ē ə rīt′) ***n.*** a mass of metal or stone remaining from a meteor that has fallen upon the earth.

**me·te·or·oid** (mēt′ē ə roid′) ***n.*** any of the many small, solid bodies traveling through outer space. When they enter the air around the earth, they become meteors.

**me·te·or·o·log·i·cal** (mēt′ē ər ə läj′i k'l) ***adj.*** **1** of weather or climate [*meteorological* conditions]. **2** of meteorology.

**me·te·or·ol·o·gy** (mēt′ē ə räl′ə jē) ***n.*** the science that studies weather, climate, and the earth's atmosphere. —**me′te·or·ol′o·gist *n.***

**me·ter**[1] (mēt′ər) ***n.*** **1** a measure of length that is the basic unit in the metric system. One meter is equal to 39.37 inches. **2** rhythm in poetry; regular arrangement of accented and unaccented syllables in each line. **3** rhythm in music; arrangement of beats in each measure [Marches are often in 4/4 *meter,* with four equal beats in each measure.]

**me·ter**[2] (mēt′ər) ***n.*** an instrument for measuring and keeping a record of the amount of gas, electricity, water, etc. that passes through it. *See the picture on page 463.*

**meth·ane** (meth′ān) ***n.*** a gas that has neither color nor smell and burns easily. It is formed by rotting plants, as in marshes and swamps, or can be made artificially.

**me·thinks** (mi thingks′) ***v.*** it seems to me: *now seldom used* [*Methinks* thou art brave.]

**meth·od** (meth′əd) ***n.*** **1** a way of doing anything; process [Frying is one *method* of cooking fish.] **2** a way of thinking or doing that is regular and orderly [It is a good *method* to put the names in alphabetical order.]

> SYNONYMS: A **method** is a planned, orderly way to do something [We need a *method* for choosing sides for games.] **Manner** is a personal, individual way [Kim's *manner* of speech]. **Mode** is a customary, familiar method or manner [their *mode* of dress].

**me·thod·i·cal** (mə thäd′i k'l) ***adj.*** working, acting, etc. by a method or system; doing or done in an orderly way. —**me·thod′i·cal·ly *adv.***

**Meth·od·ist** (meth′ə dist) ***n.*** a member of a Protestant church that follows the teachings of John Wesley. ◆***adj.*** of the Methodists. **461**

**me·thought** (mi thôt′) *past tense of* **methinks:** *now seldom used.*

**Me·thu·se·lah** (mə tho͞o′zə lə) in the Bible, a man who lived 969 years.

**me·tic·u·lous** (mə tik′yoo ləs) ***adj.*** very careful or too careful about details; fussy.

**me·tre** (mēt′ər) ***n.*** *the usual British spelling of* **meter**[1].

**met·ric** (met′rik) ***adj.*** **1** of or in the metric system: *see* **metric system. 2** *same as* **metrical.**

**met·ri·cal** (met′ri k'l) ***adj.*** **1** of or written in meter or verse [*metrical* lines]. **2** of or used in measuring; metric.

**met·ri·ca·tion** (met′rə kā′shən) ***n.*** the process of changing from an earlier system of weights and measures to the metric system.

**metric system** a system of weights and measures in which units go up or down by tens, hundreds, etc. The basic unit of length in this system is the meter (39.37 inches). The basic unit of weight is the gram (.035 ounce). The basic unit of volume is the liter (61.025 cubic inches).

**met·ro·nome** (met′rə nōm) ***n.*** an instrument that can be set to make a clicking sound at different rates of speed. It is used to set the tempo for playing a musical piece. *See the picture on page 463.*

| | | | |
|---|---|---|---|
| **a** fat | **ir** here | **ou** out | **zh** leisure |
| **ā** ape | **ī** bite, fire | **u** up | **ng** ring |
| **ä** car, lot | **ō** go | **ʉr** fur | a *in* ago |
| **e** ten | **ô** law, horn | **ch** chin | e *in* agent |
| **er** care | **oi** oil | **sh** she | **ə** = i *in* unity |
| **ē** even | **oo** look | **th** thin | o *in* collect |
| **i** hit | **o͞o** tool | ***th*** then | u *in* focus |

**me·trop·o·lis** (mə träp′'l is) ***n.*** **1** the main city of a state, country, or region. **2** any large or important city. *—pl.* **me·trop′o·lis·es**

**Metropolis** comes from the ancient Greek words for "mother" and "city." For the ancient Greeks a metropolis was the mother city of a colony.

**met·ro·pol·i·tan** (met′rə päl′ə t'n) ***adj.*** **1** of a metropolis [a *metropolitan* park]. ☆**2** making up a metropolis [*Metropolitan* Chicago includes the central city and its suburbs.] ◆***n.*** **1** a person who lives in, or is at home in, a big city. **2** an archbishop over a church province. **3** a bishop ranking just below a patriarch in the Orthodox Eastern Church.

**met·tle** (met′'l) ***n.*** spirit or courage. —**on one's mettle,** prepared to do one's best.

**mew** (myo͞o) ***n., v.*** *another word for* **meow.**

**mewl** (myo͞ol) ***v.*** to cry or whimper like a baby.

**Mex.** *abbreviation for* **Mexican** *or* **Mexico.**

**Mex·i·can** (mek′si kən) ***adj.*** of Mexico, its people, their dialect of Spanish, or their culture. ◆***n.*** a person born or living in Mexico.

**Mexican War** a war between the U.S. and Mexico, from 1846 to 1848.

**Mex·i·co** (mek′si kō) a country in North America, south of the U.S.

**Mexico, Gulf of** a gulf of the Atlantic, east of Mexico and south of the U.S.

**Mexico City** the capital of Mexico.



**mez·za·nine** (mez′ə nēn) ***n.*** **1** a low story between two main stories of a building. It is usually just above the ground floor and sometimes sticks out over it like a balcony. **2** in some theaters, the first few rows of the balcony.

**mez·zo-so·pra·no** (met′sō sə pran′ō) ***n.*** **1** a woman's singing voice between soprano and contralto. **2** a woman singer with such a voice. *—pl.* **mez′zo-so·pra′nos**

**mfg.** *abbreviation for* **manufacturing.**

**mfr.** *abbreviation for* **manufacturer.** *—pl.* **mfrs.**

**Mg** *the symbol for the chemical element* magnesium.

**mg, mg.** *abbreviation for* **milligram** *or* **milligrams.**

**Mgr.** *abbreviation for* **Manager.**

**MHz** or **Mhz** *abbreviation for* **megahertz.**

**mi** (mē) ***n.*** the third note of a musical scale.

**mi.** *abbreviation for* **mile** *or* **miles.**

**MIA** missing in action.

**Mi·am·i** (mī am′ē) a city on the southeastern coast of Florida.

**mi·ca** (mī′kə) ***n.*** a mineral that forms thin layers that are easily separated and are not affected by heat or electricity. When these layers can be seen through, mica is called *isinglass.*

**mice** (mīs) ***n.*** *plural of* **mouse.**

**Mi·chael** (mī′k'l) an archangel in the Bible.

**Mich·ael·mas** (mik″l məs) a church feast on September 29, honoring the archangel Michael.

**Mi·chel·an·ge·lo** (mī′k'l an′jə lō) 1475–1564; Italian artist, architect, and poet.

**Mich·i·gan** (mish′ə gən) **1** a State in the north central part of the U.S.: abbreviated **Mich., MI** **2** one of the Great Lakes, west of Lake Huron: *the full name is* **Lake Michigan.**

**micro-** *a prefix meaning:* **1** little, small, tiny, etc. **2** making small things look larger [A *microscope* makes small things look larger.]

**mi·crobe** (mī′krōb) ***n.*** any living thing too tiny to be seen without a microscope; now, especially, a disease germ.

A **microbe** can be thought of as "a tiny bit of life," for it comes from the Latin words for "tiny" and "life."

**mi·cro·film** (mī′krə film) ***n.*** film on which written or printed pages, pictures, etc. are photographed in a very small size, so that they can be stored in a small space. Large prints can be made from such film, or the film can be viewed with a projector.

**mi·crom·e·ter** (mī kräm′ə tər) ***n.*** a tool for measuring very small distances, angles, etc. *See the picture.*

**Mi·cro·ne·sia** (mī′krə nē′zhə) a group of islands in the Pacific, east of the Philippines. —**Mi′cro·ne′sian** ***adj., n.***

**mi·cro·or·gan·ism** (mī′krō ôr′gə niz'm) ***n.*** any living thing too tiny to be seen without a microscope; especially, any of the bacteria, viruses, protozoans, etc.

**mi·cro·phone** (mī′krə fōn) ***n.*** a device for picking up sound that is to be made stronger, as in a theater, or sent over long distances, as in radio. Microphones change sound into electric waves, which go into electron tubes and are changed back into sound by loudspeakers.

**mi·cro·scope** (mī′krə skōp) ***n.*** a device with a lens or group of lenses for making tiny things look larger so that they can be seen and studied. *See the picture.*

**mi·cro·scop·ic** (mī′krə skäp′ik) ***adj.*** **1** so tiny that it cannot be seen without a microscope. **2** of, with, or like a microscope [*microscopic* examination]. —**mi′cro·scop′i·cal·ly** ***adv.***

**mi·cro·wave** (mī′krə wāv) ***n.*** any radio wave within a certain range, usually between 300,000 and 300 megahertz. Those of a certain wavelength create great heat when they pass through substances such as food. A **microwave oven** uses these waves for fast cooking. Others are used to transmit signals to and from communications satellites.

**mid**[1] (mid) ***adj.*** *a shorter form of* **middle.**

**mid**[2] or **'mid** (mid) ***prep.*** *a shorter form of* **amid:** *used in poetry.*

**mid-** *a prefix meaning* middle or middle part of [*Midweek* means the middle of the week.]

**mid·air** (mid er′) ***n.*** any point in space, not touching the ground or other surface.

**Mi·das** (mī′dəs) a king in Greek legend who was given the power of turning everything he touched into gold.

**mid·day** (mid′dā) ***n., adj.*** *another word for* **noon.**

**mid·dle** (mid″l) ***n.*** the point or part that is halfway between the ends or that is in the center [the *middle* of the morning; an island in the *middle* of the lake]. ◆***adj.*** being in the middle or center [the *middle* toe on a foot].

SYNONYMS: **Middle** means the point or part that is equally far away from all sides or limits and is said of space or time [The performer stood in the *middle* of the stage. Noon is the *middle* of the day.] **Center** means the exact point equally distant from the bounding lines or surfaces of a circle or globe and is also used to mean the most important place or thing [The baby is the *center* of attention.]

**middle age** the time of life when a person is neither young nor old, usually the years from about 40 to about 65. —**mid′dle-aged′** ***adj.***
**Middle Ages** the period of history in Europe between ancient and modern times: the time from about 500 A.D. to about 1450 A.D.
**middle class** the social class between the nobles or very wealthy and the lower working class. Nowadays it includes skilled workers, business and professional people, well-to-do farmers, and those with an average income. —**mid′dle-class′** ***adj.***
**middle ear** the hollow part of the ear just inside the eardrum, containing three small bones.
**Middle East** a region of southwestern Asia, northeastern Africa, etc., including Israel, Egypt, Jordan, Syria, Lebanon, Iran, Iraq, Arabia, Cyprus, and Asiatic Turkey.
**Middle English** the English language as spoken and written between about 1100 and 1500.
**mid·dle·man** (mid′′l man′) ***n.*** **1** a merchant who buys goods from the producer and sells them to storekeepers or directly to the consumer. **2** a go-between. —*pl.* **mid′dle·men′**
**mid·dle·most** (mid′′l mōst′) ***adj.*** *same as* **midmost.**
**middle school** a school between elementary school and high school, having three or four grades, between the 5th and 9th grades.
**mid·dle-sized** (mid′′l sīzd′) ***adj.*** of medium size.
**mid·dle·weight** (mid′′l wāt) ***n.*** **1** a boxer or wrestler between a welterweight and a light heavyweight (in boxing, between 148 and 160 pounds). **2** a person or animal of average weight.
**Middle West** the part of the U.S. between the Rocky Mountains and the eastern border of Ohio, north of the Ohio River and the southern borders of Kansas and Missouri. —**Middle Western**
**mid·dling** (mid′liŋ) ***adj.*** of medium size, quality, grade, etc.; average; ordinary. ◆***n.*** **middlings,** ***pl.*** **1** goods that are middling. **2** coarse bits of ground grain mixed with bran. —**fair to middling,** fairly good or well: *used only in everyday talk.*
**mid·dy** (mid′ē) ***n.*** ☆**1** a loose blouse, with a large, wide collar, worn by women or children: *also* **middy blouse.** *See the picture.* **2** a midshipman: *used only in everyday talk.* —*pl.* **mid′dies**
**midge** (mij) ***n.*** a tiny insect like a gnat.
**midg·et** (mij′it) ***n.*** **1** a very small person. *See* SYNONYMS *at* **dwarf. 2** anything very small of its kind.
**mid·land** (mid′lənd) ***n.*** the middle part of a country, away from its coasts or borders. ◆***adj.*** in or of the midland; inland [*midland* lakes].
**mid·most** (mid′mōst) ***adj.*** exactly in the middle, or nearest to the middle.
**mid·night** (mid′nīt) ***n.*** twelve o'clock at night; the middle of the night. ◆***adj.*** **1** of or at midnight [a *midnight* ride]. **2** like midnight; very dark [*midnight* blue].
**mid·rib** (mid′rib) ***n.*** the middle vein of a leaf.
**mid·riff** (mid′rif) ***n.*** the middle part of the body, between the belly and the chest.
**mid·ship·man** (mid′ship′mən) ***n.*** a student at the U.S. Naval Academy. —*pl.* **mid′ship′men**
**midst**[1] (midst) ***n.*** the middle; part in the center. —**in the midst of, 1** in the middle of; surrounded by. **2** in the course of; during.

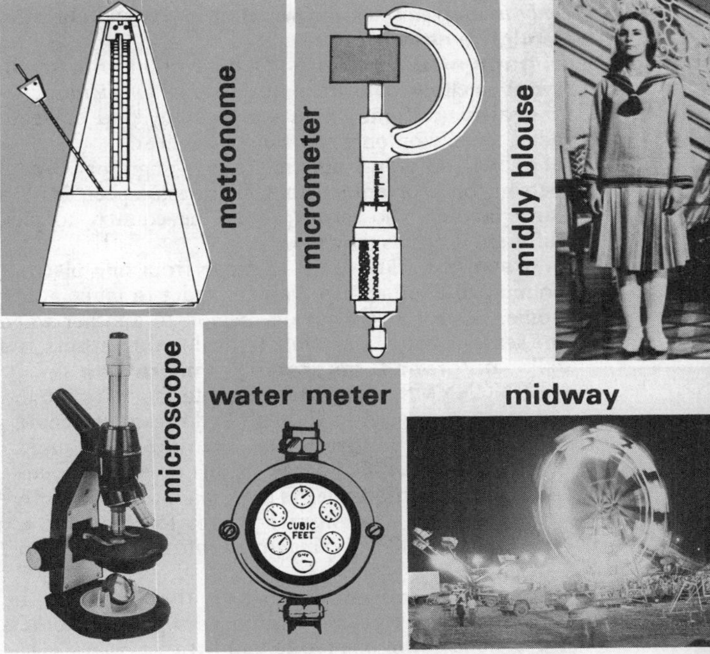


**midst**[2] or **′midst** (midst) ***prep.*** in the middle of; amidst; amid: *used in poetry.*
**mid·stream** (mid′strēm) ***n.*** the middle of a stream. 463
**mid·sum·mer** (mid′sum′ər) ***n.*** **1** the middle of summer. **2** the period around June 21.
**mid·term** (mid′turm) ☆***adj.*** happening in the middle of the term.
**mid·way** (mid′wā) ***adj., adv.*** in the middle; halfway. ◆***n.*** ☆the part of a fair, circus, etc. where sideshows, rides, etc. are located. *See the picture.*
**Mid·west** (mid′west′) ***n.*** *another name for* **Middle West.**
**Mid·west·ern** (mid′wes′tərn) ***adj.*** of, in, or having to do with the Middle West
**mid·wife** (mid′wīf) ***n.*** a woman who takes care of women in childbirth. —*pl.* **mid′wives**
**mid·win·ter** (mid′win′tər) ***n.*** **1** the middle of the winter. **2** the period around December 22.
**mien** (mēn) ***n.*** **1** the way a person looks. **2** a way of carrying oneself; manner; bearing.
**might**[1] (mīt) *past tense of* **may.**

> **Might** is also used as a helping verb with about the same meaning as *may,* but often showing a bit of doubt [It *might* be raining there. I *might* go.]

**might**[2] (mīt) ***n.*** great strength, force, or power [Pull with all your *might.*]
**might·y** (mīt′ē) ***adj.*** **1** very strong; powerful [a *mighty* blow]. **2** great; very large [a *mighty* forest]. —**might′i·er, might′i·est** ◆***adv.*** very; extremely: *used*

| | | | | | | | |
|---|---|---|---|---|---|---|---|
| **a** | fat | **ir** | here | **ou** | out | **zh** | leisure |
| **ā** | ape | **ī** | bite, fire | **u** | up | **ŋ** | ring |
| **ä** | car, lot | **ō** | go | **ur** | fur | | a *in* ago |
| **e** | ten | **ô** | law, horn | **ch** | chin | | e *in* agent |
| **er** | care | **oi** | oil | **sh** | she | **ə =** | i *in* unity |
| **ē** | even | **oo** | look | **th** | thin | | o *in* collect |
| **i** | hit | **ōō** | tool | ***th*** | then | | u *in* focus |

only in everyday talk [mighty tired]. —**might′i·ly** ***adv.*** —**might′i·ness** ***n.***

**mi·gnon·ette** (min yə net′) ***n.*** a plant with small, sweet-smelling, pale green flowers. *See the picture.*

**mi·graine** (mī′grān) ***n.*** a very painful kind of headache, usually on only one side of the head.

**mi·grant** (mī′grənt) ***adj.*** migrating; migratory. ◆***n.*** a person, bird, or animal that migrates; especially, ☆a farm laborer who moves about the country to pick different crops as they ripen.

**mi·grate** (mī′grāt) ***v.*** **1** to move from one place or country to another, especially in order to make a new home. **2** to move from one region to another when the season changes, as some birds do in the spring and fall. —**mi′grat·ed, mi′grat·ing** —**mi·gra′tion** ***n.***

SYNONYMS: **Migrate** means to move from one country or region to another, and is said of people or animals. **Emigrate** and **immigrate** are used only of people. **Emigrate** means to leave a country to settle in another [They *emigrated* from Iran to America.] **Immigrate** means to come into a new country [They *immigrated* into America from Iran.]

**mi·gra·to·ry** (mī′grə tôr′ē) ***adj.*** that migrates, or moves from one place to another [*Migratory* workers travel about from one job to another.]

**mi·ka·do** (mi kä′dō) ***n.*** a title for the emperor of Japan that is no longer used: *also* **Mi·ka′do.** *—pl.* **mi·ka′dos**



☆**mike** (mīk) ***n.*** a microphone: *a slang word.*

**mil.** *abbreviation for* **military, militia.**

**mi·la·dy** or **mi·la·di** (mi lā′dē) ***n.*** a polite title used in speaking to or of an English woman of the upper classes.

**Mi·lan** (mi lan′) a city in northern Italy.

**milch** (milch) ***adj.*** that gives milk; raised for its milk [a *milch* cow].

**mild** (mīld) ***adj.*** **1** gentle; not harsh or severe [a *mild* winter; a *mild* punishment]. **2** having a weak taste; not strong or sharp [a *mild* cheese]. —**mild′ly** ***adv.*** —**mild′ness** ***n.***

**mil·dew** (mil′do͞o *or* mil′dyo͞o) ***n.*** a fungus that appears as a furry, white coating on plants or on damp, warm paper, cloth, etc. ◆***v.*** to become coated with mildew.

**mile** (mīl) ***n.*** a measure of length, equal to 5,280 feet or 1.6093 kilometers. The **nautical mile** is about 6,076 feet or 1.852 kilometers.

The **mile** was figured out as a unit of length by measuring the distance covered in walking one thousand paces. The Latin for "thousand paces" is *milia passuum,* and from that came the English word *mile.*

☆**mile·age** (mīl′ij) ***n.*** **1** total number of miles [What is the *mileage* from Boston to Chicago?] **2** money given for traveling expenses, at the rate of a certain amount for each mile. **3** the average number of miles an automobile or other motor vehicle will go on a gallon of fuel. **4** the amount of use or service one can get from something.

☆**mile·post** (mīl′pōst) ***n.*** a signpost showing the distance in miles to some place or places.

**mile·stone** (mīl′stōn) ***n.*** **1** a stone or pillar showing the distance in miles to some place or places. **2** an important happening in history, in someone's life, etc.

**mi·lieu** (mēl yo͞o′) ***n.*** the kind of society in which a person lives.

**mil·i·tant** (mil′i tənt) ***adj.*** ready to fight, especially for some cause or idea [a *militant* defender of freedom]. ◆***n.*** a militant person. —**mil′i·tan·cy** ***n.*** —**mil′i·tant·ly** ***adv.***

**mil·i·ta·rism** (mil′ə tər iz′m) ***n.*** the policy of keeping strong armed forces and preparing for war; warlike spirit. —**mil′i·ta·rist** ***n.***

**mil·i·ta·ris·tic** (mil′ə tə ris′tik) ***adj.*** fond of war or preparing for war; warlike.

**mil·i·ta·rize** (mil′i tə rīz′) ***v.*** **1** to build up the armed forces of in preparing for war. **2** to fill with warlike spirit. —**mil′i·ta·rized′, mil′i·ta·riz′ing** —**mil′i·ta·ri·za′tion** ***n.***

**mil·i·tar·y** (mil′ə ter′ē) ***adj.*** **1** of, for, or by soldiers or the armed forces [a *military* band; *military* law]. **2** of or for war. ◆***n.*** soldiers; the army [The *military* took charge.]

**military police** soldiers whose work is to carry on the duties of police for the army.

**mil·i·tate** (mil′ə tāt) ***v.*** to have an effect; work; operate [His lack of skill *militated* against him.] —**mil′i·tat·ed, mil′i·tat·ing**

**mil·i·tia** (mə lish′ə) ***n.*** a group of citizens who are not regular soldiers, but who get some military training for service in an emergency.

**milk** (milk) ***n.*** **1** a white liquid formed in special glands of female mammals for suckling their young. The milk that is a common food comes from cows. **2** any liquid or juice like this [*Milk* of magnesia is a white liquid, made of magnesia in water.] ◆***v.*** **1** to squeeze milk out from a cow, goat, etc. **2** to get money, ideas, etc. from, as if by milking. —**milk′er** ***n.*** —**milk′ing** ***n.***

**milk·maid** (milk′mād) ***n.*** a girl or woman who milks cows or who works in a dairy.

**milk·man** (milk′man) ***n.*** a man who sells or delivers milk. *—pl.* **milk′men′**

☆**milk·shake** (milk′shāk) ***n.*** a drink of milk, flavoring, and ice cream, mixed until frothy.

☆**milk snake** a gray or reddish snake with black markings. It is not poisonous.

**milk·sop** (milk′säp) ***n.*** a man or boy who is weak and timid; sissy.

**milk·weed** (milk′wēd) ***n.*** a plant with a milky juice in the stems and leaves. It has large pods holding many seeds with silky fibers on them. *See the picture.*

**milk·y** (mil′kē) ***adj.*** **1** like milk; white as milk. **2** of or containing milk. —**milk′i·er, milk′i·est** —**milk′i·ness** ***n.***

**Milky Way** a broad band of cloudy light seen across the sky at night. It is made up of billions of stars that are very far away.

**mill**[1] (mil) ***n.*** **1** a building with machinery for grinding grain into flour or meal. **2** a machine for grinding, crushing, cutting, etc. [a coffee *mill;* a cider *mill*]. **3** a factory [a steel *mill*]. ◆***v.*** **1** to grind, make, form, etc. in or as in a mill. **2** to put ridges in the edge of a coin to guard against wear. ☆**3** to move slowly in a confused way [The crowd was *milling* around outside the stadium.]

☆**mill²** (mil) ***n.*** one tenth of a cent; $.001: a mill is not a coin but is used in figuring, especially in figuring taxes.

**Mil·lay** (mi lā′), **Edna St. Vincent** 1892–1950; U.S. poet.

**mil·len·ni·um** (mi len′ē əm) ***n.*** **1** a thousand years. **2** in the belief of some Christians, the period of a thousand years during which Christ is expected to return and reign on earth. **3** a period of peace and happiness for everyone. *—pl.* **mil·len′ni·ums** or **mil·len·ni·a** (mi len′ē ə) **—mil·len′ni·al *adj.***

**mill·er** (mil′ər) ***n.*** **1** a person who owns or works in a mill where grain is ground. **2** a moth with wings that look dusty like the clothes of a miller.

**mil·let** (mil′it) ***n.*** **1** a cereal grass grown for hay. **2** its small seeds, or grain, used for food in Asia and Europe.

**mil·li·gram** (mil′ə gram) ***n.*** a unit of weight, equal to one thousandth of a gram. *An earlier British spelling is* **mil′li·gramme.**

**mil·li·li·ter** (mil′ə lēt′ər) ***n.*** a unit of volume, equal to one thousandth of a liter. *The usual British spelling is* **mil′li·li′tre.**

**mil·li·me·ter** (mil′ə mēt′ər) ***n.*** a unit of measure, equal to one thousandth of a meter (.03937 inch). *The usual British spelling is* **mil′li·me′tre.**

**mil·li·ner** (mil′ə nər) ***n.*** a person who designs, makes, or sells women's hats.

> In the old days, any Englishman who sold ribbons, bonnets, and gloves from Milan, Italy, was called a *Milaner,* the name given to natives of that city. After a while, the spelling changed and **milliner** came to mean anyone who sells women's hats.

**mil·li·ner·y** (mil′ə ner′ē) ***n.*** **1** women's hats. **2** the work or business of a milliner.

**mil·lion** (mil′yən) ***n., adj.*** a thousand thousands (1,000,000).

**mil·lion·aire** (mil′yə ner′) ***n.*** a person who has at least a million dollars, pounds, etc.

**mil·lionth** (mil′yənth) ***adj.*** last in a series of a million. ◆***n.*** **1** the millionth one. **2** one of the million equal parts of something.

**mill·pond** (mil′pänd) ***n.*** a pond from which water flows for driving a mill wheel.

**mill·race** (mil′rās) ***n.*** **1** the stream of water that drives a mill wheel. **2** the channel in which it runs.

**mill·stone** (mil′stōn) ***n.*** **1** either of a pair of flat, round stones between which grain is ground. **2** a heavy burden.

**mill wheel** the wheel that drives the machinery in a mill, usually a water wheel.

**Mil·ton** (mil′t′n), **John** 1608–1674; English poet.

**Mil·wau·kee** (mil wô′kē) a city in southeastern Wisconsin, on Lake Michigan.

**mime** (mīm) ***n.*** a clown or mimic. *See the picture.* ◆***v.*** to act as a mime; imitate, usually without speaking. **—mimed, mim′ing**

☆**mim·e·o·graph** (mim′ē ə graf) ***n.*** a machine for making copies of written, drawn, or typewritten matter by using a stencil. ◆***v.*** to make copies of on such a machine.

**mim·ic** (mim′ik) ***v.*** **1** to imitate so as to make fun of. *See the picture.* **2** to copy closely; imitate [Parakeets *mimic* human voices.] *See* SYNONYMS *at* **imitate. —mim′icked, mim′ick·ing** ◆***n.*** a person, especially a

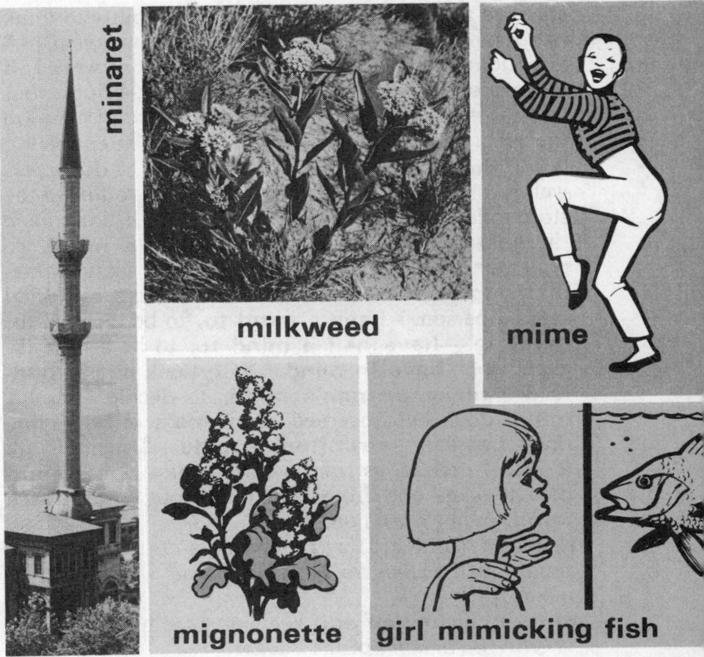


performer, who mimics; imitator. ◆***adj.*** **1** imitative. **2** make-believe; not real.

**mim·ic·ry** (mim′ik rē) ***n.*** **1** the art of imitating, or an example of this. **2** the way in which some living thing looks like another or like some natural object. *—pl.* **mim′ic·ries**



**mi·mo·sa** (mi mō′sə) ***n.*** a tree of warm climates, with white, yellow, or pink flowers.

**min.** *abbreviation for* **minimum, minute** *or* **minutes.**

**min·a·ret** (min ə ret′) ***n.*** a high tower on a mosque with a balcony from which a crier calls Muslims to prayer. *See the picture.*

**mince** (mins) ***v.*** **1** to cut into small pieces; hash [to *mince* onions]. **2** to make weaker or less direct [The director *minced* no words.] **3** to act, move, or say in a way that is too careful or dainty. **—minced, minc′ing** ◆***n.*** *a shorter form of* **mincemeat. —not mince matters,** to speak frankly.

**mince·meat** (mins′mēt) ***n.*** a mixture of chopped apples, raisins, suet, spices, and sometimes meat, used as a filling for a pie (called a **mince pie**).

**minc·ing** (min′siŋ) ***adj.*** **1** with short, dainty steps [a *mincing* walk]. **2** elegant or dainty in an affected way.

**mind** (mīnd) ***n.*** **1** the part of a person that thinks, reasons, feels, decides, etc.; intellect [The *mind* was once thought of as apart from the body.] **2** what one thinks or intends; opinion, desire, purpose, etc. [I've

| | | | | | | | |
|---|---|---|---|---|---|---|---|
| **a** | fat | **ir** | here | **ou** | out | **zh** | leisure |
| **ā** | ape | **ī** | bite, fire | **u** | up | **ŋ** | ring |
| **ä** | car, lot | **ō** | go | **ʉr** | fur | | a *in* ago |
| **e** | ten | **ô** | law, horn | **ch** | chin | | e *in* agent |
| **er** | care | **oi** | oil | **sh** | she | **ə =** | i *in* unity |
| **ē** | even | **oo** | look | **th** | thin | | o *in* collect |
| **i** | hit | **o͞o** | tool | ***th*** | then | | u *in* focus |

changed my *mind* about going.] **3** the ability to think or reason; intelligence [Have you lost your *mind?*] **4** attention; notice [Your *mind* is not on your work.] **5** the act of remembering; memory [That brings your story to *mind.*] **6** a very intelligent person [Who are the great *minds* today?] ✦***v.*** **1** to pay attention to; heed [*Mind* your manners.] **2** to obey [The dog *minds* well.] **3** to take care of; look after [Will you *mind* the store today?] **4** to care about; object to [I don't *mind* the heat.] —**bear in mind** or **keep in mind,** to remember. —**be of one mind,** to agree about something. —**give someone a piece of one's mind,** to scold a person. —**have a mind to,** to be inclined to; intend to. —**have half a mind to,** to be a little inclined to. —**have in mind,** **1** to think of. **2** to intend. —**make up one's mind,** to decide. —**never mind,** don't be concerned. —**on one's mind,** filling one's thoughts. —**out of one's mind,** **1** mentally ill. **2** wildly excited, as from worry. —**take one's mind off,** to stop one from thinking about. —**to one's mind,** in one's opinion.

**mind·ed** (mīn′did) ***adj.*** having a certain kind of mind: *used mainly to form compound words* [strong-*minded*].

**mind·ful** (mīnd′fəl) ***adj.*** keeping something in mind; careful [Be *mindful* of the danger.]

**mind·less** (mīnd′lis) ***adj.*** **1** not using one's mind; thoughtless. **2** careless or heedless.

 **mine**[1] (mīn) ***pron.*** the one or ones that belong to me.

**Mine** is the form of *my* used when it is not followed by a noun [This ball is *mine. Mine* are the red shoes.] **Mine** is sometimes used, especially in poetry, as an adjective meaning "my" ["*Mine* eyes have seen the glory. . . ."]

**mine**[2] (mīn) ***n.*** **1** a large hole made in the earth from which to dig out coal, ores, salt, etc. **2** a large supply or store [a *mine* of information]. **3** an explosive hidden in the ground or in water to blow up enemy troops, ships, etc. ✦***v.*** **1** to dig a mine or ores, coal, etc. **2** to get from a mine [to *mine* copper]. **3** to work in a mine. **4** to place explosive mines under or in [to *mine* a harbor]. —**mined, min′ing**

**min·er** (mī′nər) ***n.*** a person whose work is digging ore, coal, salt, etc. in a mine.

**min·er·al** (min′ər əl) ***n.*** **1** a substance formed in the earth by nature; especially, a solid substance that was never animal or vegetable [Iron, granite, and salt are *minerals.* Coal is sometimes called a *mineral,* too.] **2** any of certain elements, as iron or phosphorus, needed by plants and animals. ✦***adj.*** of or full of minerals [*mineral* water].

Minotaur

miniature of an elephant

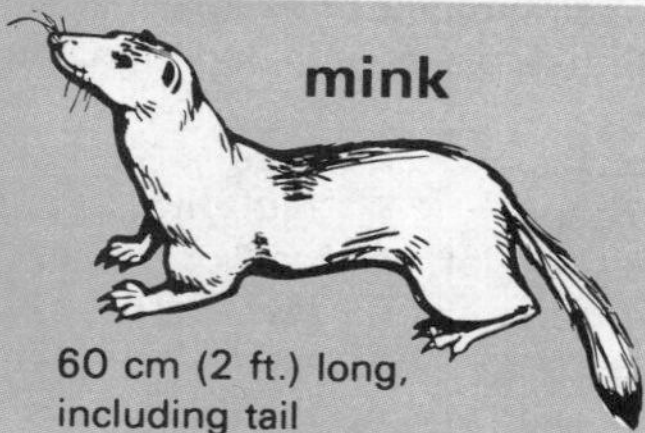
mink

60 cm (2 ft.) long, including tail

**min·er·al·o·gy** (min′ə räl′ə jē) ***n.*** the science of minerals. —**min′er·al′o·gist** ***n.***

**Mi·ner·va** (mi nʉr′və) the Roman goddess of wisdom and of arts and crafts.

**min·gle** (miŋ′g'l) ***v.*** **1** to mix or be mixed together; blend [We had *mingled* feelings of fear and pleasure.] *See* SYNONYMS *at* **mix.** **2** to join with others [We *mingled* with the crowd.] —**min′gled, min′gling**

**mini-** *a prefix meaning* miniature, very small or short.

**Mini-** is used often in words made up and intended to be used just once, or for a particular thing or occasion, meaning "smaller than usual" [*mini*bus; *mini*-conference; *mini*-camera].

**min·i·a·ture** (min′ē ə chər *or* min′i chər) ***n.*** **1** a very small copy or model [a *miniature* of the Liberty Bell]. *See the picture.* **2** a very small painting, especially a portrait. ✦***adj.*** that is a miniature [a *miniature* railroad].

**min·i·a·tur·ize** (min′ē ə chər īz′) ***v.*** to make in a small and compact form. —**min′i·a·tur·ized′, min′i·a·tur·iz′ing**

☆**min·i·bus** (min′ē bus′) ***n.*** a very small bus.

**min·im** (min′im) ***n.*** the smallest liquid measure, about a drop.

**min·i·mal** (min′ə məl) ***adj.*** smallest or least possible.

**min·i·mize** (min′ə mīz) ***v.*** **1** to make as small as possible [Safe storage of gas will *minimize* the danger of fire.] **2** to make seem small or unimportant [The paratroopers *minimized* their bravery.] —**min′i·mized, min′i·miz·ing**

**min·i·mum** (min′ə məm) ***n.*** **1** the smallest amount or number that is possible or allowed [The patient must have a *minimum* of excitement.] **2** the lowest degree or point reached [a *minimum* of 14° temperature]. —*pl.* **min′i·mums** or **min·i·ma** (min′ə mə) ✦***adj.*** smallest or least possible or allowed [a law on *minimum* wages].

**min·ing** (mī′niŋ) ***n.*** the work of digging ores, coal, salt, etc. from mines.

**min·ion** (min′yən) ***n.*** a trusted or faithful follower, often one who serves in a slavish way.

**minion of the law** *another name for* **police officer.**

**min·i·skirt** (min′ē skʉrt′) ***n.*** a very short skirt, ending well above the knees.

**min·is·ter** (min′is tər) ***n.*** **1** a person who is the spiritual head of a church, especially a Protestant church; pastor. **2** a person in charge of some department of government, as in Great Britain [the *Minister* of Housing]. **3** an official sent by a country to represent it in a foreign country. A minister ranks below an ambassador. ✦***v.*** to give help; serve or attend [to *minister* to the poor]. —**min·is·te·ri·al** (min′is tir′ē əl) ***adj.***

**min·is·trant** (min′is trənt) ***n.*** a person who ministers.

**min·is·tra·tion** (min′is trā′shən) ***n.*** the act of helping others; service.

**min·is·try** (min′is trē) ***n.*** **1** the office or duties of a minister, or the time of serving as a minister. **2** church ministers or government ministers as a group. **3** a department of government that has a minister as its head. **4** the act of ministering, or helping others. —*pl.* **min′is·tries**

**mink** (mingk) ***n.*** **1** an animal somewhat like a large weasel, that lives on land and in the water. *See the picture.* **2** its costly, thick, brown fur.

**Min·ne·ap·o·lis** (min′ē ap″l is) a city in eastern Minnesota.

**Min·ne·so·ta** (min′ə sōt′ə) a State in the north central part of the U.S.: abbreviated **Minn., MN**

**min·now** (min′ō) ***n.*** **1** a very small fish of the carp family, found in fresh water and used as bait. **2** any very small fish.

**mi·nor** (mī′nər) ***adj.*** **1** lesser in size, importance, amount, etc. [a *minor* part of one's time; a *minor* baseball league; a *minor* car accident]. **2** in music, that is separated from the next tone by a half step instead of a full step [a *minor* interval]. **3** that is or has to do with either of two musical scales, especially one with half steps after the second and seventh tones going up and after the sixth and third tones going down. *See also* **major.** ◆***n.*** a person under the age at which one is said by law to become an adult: in some States, the age of 21.

**mi·nor·i·ty** (mə nôr′ə tē) ***n.*** **1** the smaller part or number; less than half [A *minority* of the Senate voted for the law.] **2** a small group of people of a different race, religion, etc. from the main group of which it is a part. **3** the time of being a minor, or not yet an adult. —*pl.* **mi·nor′i·ties**

**Min·o·taur** (min′ə tôr) a monster in Greek myths, with the head of a bull and the body of a man. It was kept in a labyrinth in Crete, where it was killed by Theseus. *See the picture.*

**Minsk** (minsk) a city in the western U.S.S.R.

**min·strel** (min′strəl) ***n.*** **1** an entertainer during the Middle Ages, as at the court of a lord, or one who traveled from place to place singing and reciting poems. ☆**2** a performer in a minstrel show.

☆**minstrel show** an earlier type of stage show in the U.S., put on by performers with faces painted black, who told jokes, sang songs, etc.

**min·strel·sy** (min′strəl sē) ***n.*** **1** the art or work of a minstrel. **2** a group of minstrels. **3** a collection of their songs.

**mint**[1] (mint) ***n.*** **1** a place where the government makes coins. **2** a large amount [He made a *mint* of money.] ◆***adj.*** new; never used [a coin in *mint* condition]. ◆***v.*** to make into coins by stamping metal.

**mint**[2] (mint) ***n.*** **1** a plant with a pleasant smell whose leaves are used for flavoring, as peppermint and spearmint. **2** a piece of candy flavored with mint.

☆**mint julep** an iced drink made with whiskey or brandy, sugar, and mint leaves.

**min·u·end** (min′yoo wend′) ***n.*** the number from which another number is to be subtracted [In the problem 9 – 5 = 4, 9 is the *minuend.*]

**min·u·et** (min′yoo wet′) ***n.*** **1** a slow, graceful dance, popular in the 18th century. **2** music for such a dance.

> **Minuet** came into English from a French word that meant "tiny" and was used of the dance because of the small steps taken in it.

**mi·nus** (mī′nəs) ***prep.*** **1** less; made smaller by subtracting [Four *minus* two equals two (4 – 2 = 2).] **2** without: *used only in everyday talk* [This cup is *minus* a handle.] ◆***adj.*** **1** less than zero; negative [The temperature is *minus* 5°, or five degrees below zero.] **2** a little less than [a rating of A *minus*]. ◆***n.*** the sign (–), put before a number or quantity that is to be subtracted or one that is less than zero: *the full name is* **minus sign.**

**mi·nus·cule** (mi nus′kyo͞ol *or* min′ə skyo͞ol) ***adj.*** very small; tiny.

**min·ute**[1] (min′it) ***n.*** **1** any of the sixty equal parts of an hour; 60 seconds. **2** any of the sixty equal parts of a degree of an arc; 60 seconds. **3** a very short period of time; moment [They'll be done in a *minute.*] **4** a particular time [Come home this *minute!*] **5 minutes,** *pl.* a written record of what happened during a meeting [The secretary writes the *minutes.*]

**mi·nute**[2] (mī no͞ot′ *or* mī nyo͞ot′) ***adj.*** **1** very small; tiny. **2** paying attention to small details; exact [She keeps a *minute* account of expenses.] —**mi·nute′ly *adv.*** —**mi·nute′ness *n.***

☆**min·ute·man** or **Min·ute·man** (min′it man′) ***n.*** a member of the American citizen army at the time of the Revolutionary War, who volunteered to be ready to fight at a minute's notice. —*pl.* **min′ute·men′** or **Min′ute·men′**

**mi·nu·ti·ae** (mi no͞o′shi ē *or* mi nyo͞o′shi ē) ***n.pl.*** small or unimportant details.

**minx** (mingks) ***n.*** a bold or saucy girl.

**mir·a·cle** (mir′ə k'l) ***n.*** **1** a happening that seems to be against the known laws of nature or science, thought of as caused by God or a god [the *miracles* in the Bible]. **2** an amazing or remarkable thing; marvel [It will be a *miracle* if we win.]

**mi·rac·u·lous** (mi rak′yoo ləs) ***adj.*** **1** of or having to do with miracles. **2** very remarkable or amazing. —**mi·rac′u·lous·ly *adv.***

**mi·rage** (mi räzh′) ***n.*** an image caused by the reflection of light in such a way that something far away appears to be near. [What seems to be a pool of water often seen up ahead on a hot highway is a *mirage* caused by the reflection of the sky.] *See the picture.*

**mire** (mīr) ***n.*** **1** an area of wet, soft ground; bog. **2** deep mud. ◆***v.*** to sink or get stuck in mire. —**mired, mir′ing**

**mir·ror** (mir′ər) ***n.*** **1** a smooth surface that reflects light; especially, a piece of glass coated with silver on the back; looking glass. **2** anything that gives a true description [A good novel is a *mirror* of life.] ◆***v.*** to reflect as in a mirror [The moon was *mirrored* in the lake.]

**mirth** (murth) ***n.*** joyfulness or happy fun, usually shown by laughter. —**mirth′less *adj.***

> SYNONYMS: **Mirth** suggests gladness or great amusement, especially when shown by laughter [The jokes filled the audience with *mirth.*] **Glee** suggests an open display of joy or it may suggest

| | | | | | | | |
|---|---|---|---|---|---|---|---|
| **a** | fat | **ir** | here | **ou** | out | **zh** | leisure |
| **ā** | ape | **ī** | bite, fire | **u** | up | **ng** | ring |
| **ä** | car, lot | **ō** | go | **ur** | fur | | a *in* ago |
| **e** | ten | **ô** | law, horn | **ch** | chin | | e *in* agent |
| **er** | care | **oi** | oil | **sh** | she | **ə =** | i *in* unity |
| **ē** | even | **oo** | look | **th** | thin | | o *in* collect |
| **i** | hit | **o͞o** | tool | ***th*** | then | | u *in* focus |

delight over another's bad luck [The children greeted the clowns with *glee.*] **Merriment** suggests the mirth or joy of a group having a good time, as at a lively party [Dunking for apples caused great *merriment.*]

**mirth·ful** (murth′fəl) ***adj.*** full of mirth or showing mirth; merry.

**mis-** *a prefix meaning* wrong, wrongly, bad, badly [To *misplace* is to place wrongly. *Misconduct* is bad conduct.]

**mis·ad·ven·ture** (mis′əd ven′chər) ***n.*** an unlucky accident; bad luck; mishap.

**mis·an·thrope** (mis′ən thrōp) ***n.*** a person who hates people or does not trust anybody. —**mis·an·throp·ic** (mis′ən thräp′ik) ***adj.***

**Misanthrope** comes from two Greek words that mean "to hate man or mankind." A misanthrope hates mankind, or all people.

**mis·ap·ply** (mis ə plī′) ***v.*** to use in a wrong or wasteful way [to *misapply* one's energies]. —**mis·ap·plied′, mis·ap·ply′ing** —**mis·ap·pli·ca·tion** (mis′ap lə kā′shən) ***n.***

**mis·ap·pre·hend** (mis′ap rə hend′) ***v.*** to misunderstand. —**mis′ap·pre·hen′sion *n.***

**mis·ap·pro·pri·ate** (mis′ə prō′prē āt) ***v.*** to use in a wrong or dishonest way [The treasurer *misappropriated* the money in our club's account.] —**mis′ap·pro′pri·at·ed, mis′ap·pro′pri·at·ing** —**mis′ap·pro′pri·a′tion *n.***



**mis·be·have** (mis′bi hāv′) ***v.*** to behave in a bad way; do what one is not supposed to do. —**mis′be·haved′, mis′be·hav′ing** —**mis·be·hav·ior** (mis′bi hāv′yər) ***n.***

**misc.** *abbreviation for* **miscellaneous.**

**mis·cal·cu·late** (mis kal′kyə lāt) ***v.*** to make a mistake in figuring or planning; misjudge. —**mis·cal′cu·lat·ed, mis·cal′cu·lat·ing** —**mis′cal·cu·la′tion *n.***

**mis·call** (mis kôl′) ***v.*** to call by a wrong name.

**mis·car·riage** (mis kar′ij) ***n.*** **1** failure to carry out what was intended [Putting an innocent person in prison is a *miscarriage* of justice.] **2** the birth of a baby before it has developed enough to live.

**mis·car·ry** (mis kar′ē) ***v.*** **1** to go wrong; fail [Our careful plans *miscarried.*] **2** to have a miscarriage. —**mis·car′ried, mis·car′ry·ing**

**mis·cel·la·ne·ous** (mis′ə lā′nē əs *or* mis′ə lān′yəs) ***adj.*** of many different kinds; mixed; varied [A *miscellaneous* collection of objects filled the shelf.]

**mis·cel·la·ny** (mis′ə lā′nē) ***n.*** a mixed collection; especially, a book containing various writings. —*pl.* **mis′cel·la′nies**

**mis·chance** (mis chans′) ***n.*** an unlucky accident; bad luck; misfortune.

**mis·chief** (mis′chif) ***n.*** **1** harm or damage [Gossip can cause great *mischief.*] **2** action that causes harm, damage, or trouble. **3** a person, especially a child, who annoys or teases. **4** a playful trick; prank. **5** playful, harmless spirits [a child full of *mischief*].

**mis·chie·vous** (mis′chi vəs) ***adj.*** **1** causing some slight harm or annoyance, often in fun; naughty. *See the picture.* **2** full of playful tricks; teasing; prankish. **3** causing harm or damage; injurious [*mischievous* slander].

**mis·con·ceive** (mis kən sēv′) ***v.*** to get a wrong idea about; misunderstand. —**mis·con·ceived′, mis·con·ceiv′ing**

**mis·con·cep·tion** (mis′kən sep′shən) ***n.*** a misunderstanding; wrong idea.

**mis·con·duct** (mis kän′dukt) ***n.*** bad or wrong conduct or behavior. ◆***v.*** (mis kən dukt′) **1** to behave badly. **2** to manage badly or dishonestly.

**mis·con·struc·tion** (mis′kən struk′shən) ***n.*** the act of judging or explaining in a wrong way; misunderstanding.

**mis·con·strue** (mis kən stro͞o′) ***v.*** to think of or explain in a wrong way; misunderstand [He *misconstrued* her silence as approval.] —**mis·con·strued′, mis·con·stru′ing**

**mis·count** (mis kount′) ***v.*** to count incorrectly. ◆***n.*** (mis′kount) an incorrect count, as of votes in an election.

**mis·cre·ant** (mis′krē ənt) ***n.*** a person who does wrong or commits a crime; villain; criminal. ◆***adj.*** wicked; evil.

**mis·deed** (mis dēd′) ***n.*** a wrong or wicked act; crime, sin, etc.

**mis·de·mean·or** (mis′di mēn′ər) ***n.*** a breaking of the law that is less serious than a felony and brings a lesser penalty [It is a *misdemeanor* to throw litter in the streets.]

**mis·di·rect** (mis də rekt′) ***v.*** to direct wrongly or badly [to *misdirect* a letter].

**mis·do·ing** (mis do͞o′ing) ***n.*** wrongdoing.

**mi·ser** (mī′zər) ***n.*** a greedy, stingy person who saves up money without ever using it. —**mi′ser·ly *adj.***

**mis·er·a·ble** (miz′ər ə b′l *or* miz′rə b′l) ***adj.*** **1** very unhappy; sad; wretched. **2** causing pain, unhappiness, etc. [*miserable* weather]. **3** bad, poor, unpleasant, etc. [a *miserable* play]. —**mis′er·a·bly *adv.***

**mis·er·y** (miz′ər ē) ***n.*** **1** a condition in which one suffers greatly or is very unhappy. **2** something that causes such suffering, as illness or poverty. —*pl.* **mis′er·ies**

**mis·file** (mis fīl′) ***v.*** to file, as papers, in the wrong place or order. —**mis·filed′, mis·fil′ing**

**mis·fire** (mis fīr′) ***v.*** to fail to go off; fail to work right [The rocket *misfired.*] —**mis·fired′, mis·fir′ing**

**mis·fit** (mis′fit) ***n.*** **1** anything that does not fit right, as a suit that is too small. **2** a person who does not get along well at work, with people, etc.

**mis·for·tune** (mis fôr′chən) ***n.*** **1** bad luck; trouble. **2** an accident that brings trouble; mishap.

**mis·give** (mis giv′) ***v.*** to cause fear, doubt, or worry in [His heart *misgave* him.] —**mis·gave′, mis·giv′en, mis·giv′ing**

**mis·giv·ing** (mis giv′ing) ***n.*** *often* **misgivings**, *pl.* a feeling of fear, doubt, worry, etc. [He had *misgivings* about whether he could do the job.]

**mis·gov·ern** (mis guv′ərn) ***v.*** to govern or manage badly. —**mis·gov′ern·ment *n.***

**mis·guid·ed** (mis gīd′id) ***adj.*** led into making mistakes or doing wrong [The *misguided* boy ran away from home.]

**mis·han·dle** (mis han′d′l) ***v.*** to manage or handle badly or roughly; abuse. —**mis·han′dled, mis·han′dling**

**mis·hap** (mis′hap) ***n.*** an accident that brings trouble; bad luck; misfortune.

**mish·mash** (mish′mash) ***n.*** a confused mixture; hodgepodge; jumble.

**mis·in·form** (mis in fôrm′) ***v.*** to give wrong facts or ideas to. —**mis′in·for·ma′tion *n.***

**mis·in·ter·pret** (mis′in tur′prit) ***v.*** to give a wrong meaning to; explain or understand in a wrong way. —**mis′in·ter′pre·ta′tion *n.***

**mis·judge** (mis juj′) ***v.*** to judge unfairly or wrongly. —**mis·judged′, mis·judg′ing**

**mis·lay** (mis lā′) ***v.*** to put something in a place and then forget where it is. —**mis·laid** (mis lād′), **mis·lay′ing**

**mis·lead** (mis lēd′) ***v.*** **1** to lead in a wrong direction [That old road map will *mislead* you.] **2** to cause to believe what is not true; deceive [She *misled* us into thinking she would help.] **3** to lead into wrongdoing [He was *misled* by friends who turned out to be thieves and made him one too.] —**mis·led** (mis led′), **mis·lead′ing**

**mis·man·age** (mis man′ij) ***v.*** to manage in a bad or dishonest way. —**mis·man′aged, mis·man′ag·ing** —**mis·man′age·ment *n.***

**mis·name** (mis nām′) ***v.*** to call by a wrong name or one that does not fit. —**mis·named′, mis·nam′ing**

**mis·no·mer** (mis nō′mər) ***n.*** a wrong name or one that does not fit ["Fish" is a *misnomer* for a whale.]

**mis·place** (mis plās′) ***v.*** **1** to put in a wrong place [He *misplaced* the book of poems in the art section.] **2** to give trust, love, etc. to one who does not deserve it [I *misplaced* my confidence in you.] **3** *another word for* **mislay.** —**mis·placed′, mis·plac′ing**

**mis·play** (mis plā′) ***v.*** to play wrongly or badly, as in a game. ◆☆***n.*** a wrong or bad play.

**mis·print** (mis′print) ***n.*** a mistake in printing.

**mis·pro·nounce** (mis prə nouns′) ***v.*** to pronounce in a wrong way [Some people *mispronounce* "cavalry" as "calvary."] —**mis·pro·nounced′, mis·pro·nounc′ing** —**mis·pro·nun·ci·a·tion** (mis′prə nun′sē ā′shən) ***n.***

**mis·quote** (mis kwōt′) ***v.*** to quote wrongly. —**mis·quot′ed, mis·quot′ing**

**mis·read** (mis rēd′) ***v.*** to read in the wrong way, especially so that one gets the wrong meaning [to *misread* directions]. —**mis·read** (mis red′), **mis·read′ing**

**mis·rep·re·sent** (mis′rep ri zent′) ***v.*** to give a wrong or false idea of something, on purpose. —**mis′rep·re·sen·ta′tion *n.***

**mis·rule** (mis ro͞ol′) ***v.*** to rule in a bad or unfair way. —**mis·ruled′, mis·rul′ing** ◆***n.*** **1** bad or unfair government. **2** disorder or riot.

**miss**[1] (mis) ***v.*** **1** to fail to hit, meet, reach, get, catch, see, hear, etc. [The arrow *missed* the target. We *missed* our plane. I *missed* you at the play last night.] **2** to let go by; fail to take [You *missed* your turn.] **3** to escape; avoid [He just *missed* being hit.] **4** to fail to do, keep, have, attend, etc. [She *missed* a class today.] **5** to notice or feel the absence or loss of [I suddenly *missed* my wallet. Do you *miss* your friends back home?] ◆***n.*** a failure to hit, meet, get, etc.

**miss**[2] (mis) ***n.*** **1 Miss** a title used before the name of a girl or unmarried woman [*Miss* Smith]. **2** a young, unmarried woman or girl [dresses for *misses*]. —*pl.* **miss′es**

**Miss.** *abbreviation for* **Mississippi.**

**mis·sal** (mis′′l) ***n.*** a book of prayers used in celebrating Mass in the Roman Catholic Church.

mischievous act

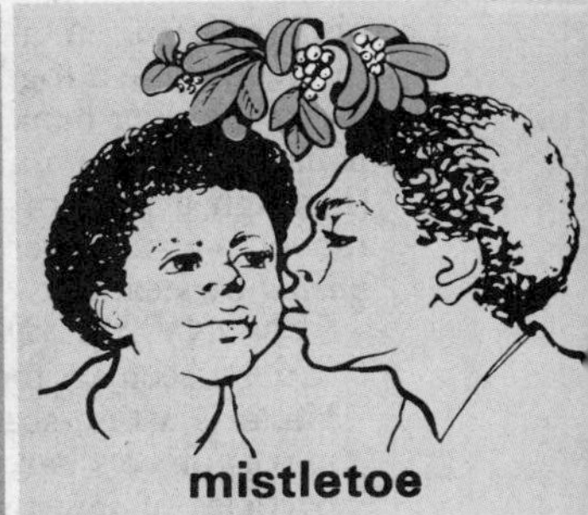
mistletoe

**mis·shap·en** (mis shāp′′n) ***adj.*** badly shaped or formed; deformed.

**mis·sile** (mis′′l) ***n.*** a weapon or other object made to be thrown or shot at a target [Bullets, arrows, some rockets, etc. are *missiles.*]

**mis·sile·ry** or **mis·sil·ry** (mis′′l rē) ***n.*** **1** the science of building and launching guided missiles. **2** guided missiles.

**miss·ing** (mis′iŋ) ***adj.*** absent, lost, gone, lacking, etc. [Pat found the *missing* book.]

**mis·sion** (mish′ən) ***n.*** **1** the special duty or errand that a person or group is sent out to do, as by a church, government, air force, etc. [a *mission* to gain converts; a *mission* to increase trade; a *mission* to bomb a factory]. **2** a group of missionaries, or the place where they live, work, etc. [the foreign *missions* of a church]. **3** a group of persons sent to a foreign government to carry on dealings, as for trade, a treaty, etc. **4** the special task that a person seems to be meant for in life; calling [Joan of Arc's *mission* was to set France free.] 

**mis·sion·ar·y** (mish′ən er′ē) ***n.*** a person sent out by a church to spread its religion in a foreign country. —*pl.* **mis′sion·ar′ies** ◆***adj.*** having to do with religious missions.

**Mis·sis·sip·pi** (mis′ə sip′ē) **1** a river in the U.S., flowing from Minnesota to the Gulf of Mexico. **2** a State in the southeastern part of the U.S.: abbreviated **Miss., MS**

**mis·sive** (mis′iv) ***n.*** a letter or note.

**Mis·sour·i** (mi zoor′ē *or* mi zoor′ə) **1** a river in the U.S., flowing from Montana into the Mississippi River. **2** a State in the central part of the U.S.: abbreviated **Mo., MO**

**mis·spell** (mis spel′) ***v.*** to spell incorrectly. —**misspelled′** or **mis·spelt′, mis·spell′ing**

**mis·spell·ing** (mis spel′iŋ) ***n.*** an incorrect spelling.

**mis·spent** (mis spent′) ***adj.*** spent in a wrong or wasteful way [a *misspent* life].

**mis·state** (mis stāt′) ***v.*** to state wrongly or falsely. —**mis·stat′ed, mis·stat′ing** —**mis·state′ment *n.***

☆**mis·step** (mis step′) ***n.*** **1** a wrong or clumsy step. **2** a mistake in one's behavior.

| | | | | | | | |
|---|---|---|---|---|---|---|---|
| **a** | fat | **ir** | here | **ou** | out | **zh** | leisure |
| **ā** | ape | **ī** | bite, fire | **u** | up | **ŋ** | ring |
| **ä** | car, lot | **ō** | go | **ur** | fur | | a *in* ago |
| **e** | ten | **ô** | law, horn | **ch** | chin | | e *in* agent |
| **er** | care | **oi** | oil | **sh** | she | **ə =** | i *in* unity |
| **ē** | even | **oo** | look | **th** | thin | | o *in* collect |
| **i** | hit | **o͞o** | tool | ***th*** | then | | u *in* focus |

**mist** (mist) ***n.*** **1** a large mass of tiny drops of water in the air, like a fog but not so thick [the morning *mist* along the river bank]. **2** anything that blurs or makes it hard to see or understand something; haze or film [through a *mist* of tears; lost in the *mists* of ignorance]. ◆***v.*** to cover by a mist; blur or dim [windows *misted* by steam].

SYNONYMS: **Mist** is a thin water vapor that can be seen in the air and that blurs the vision. **Haze** is a thin scattering of smoke, dust, etc. that makes objects hard to see. **Fog** is made up of tiny particles of moisture thicker than mist and sometimes impossible to see through.

**mis·take** (mi stāk′) ***n.*** an idea, answer, act, etc. that is wrong; error or blunder. *See* SYNONYMS *at* **error.** ◆***v.*** **1** to get a wrong idea of; misunderstand [You *mistake* his real purpose.] **2** to think that someone or something is some other person or thing [to *mistake* one twin for the other]. —**mis·took′, mis·tak′en, mis·tak′ing**

**mis·tak·en** (mi stāk′′n) ***adj.*** wrong; making or showing a mistake [a *mistaken* idea]. —**mis·tak′en·ly** ***adv.***

**Mis·ter** (mis′tər) ***n.*** a title used before the name of a man or his office, and usually written *Mr.* [*Mr.* Brown; *Mr.* President].

**mis·tle·toe** (mis′′l tō) ***n.*** an evergreen plant with waxy white, poisonous berries, growing as a parasite on certain trees. People kiss under the mistletoe at Christmas. *See the picture on page 469.*



**mis·took** (mi stook′) *past tense of* **mistake.**

**mis·treat** (mis trēt′) ***v.*** to treat badly; abuse. —**mis·treat′ment** ***n.***

**mis·tress** (mis′tris) ***n.*** **1** a woman who rules others or has control over something, as the owner of an animal or slave, the head of a household or school, etc. **2** *sometimes* **Mistress,** a country or thing thought of as a female ruler [England was *Mistress* of the seas.] **3** a woman who lives with a man without being married to him. **4 Mistress,** a title used in earlier times before the name of a woman: now replaced by *Mrs.* or *Miss* or *Ms.*

**mis·trust** (mis trust′) ***n.*** a lack of trust or confidence; suspicion; doubt [He felt *mistrust* of the stranger.] ◆***v.*** to have no trust or confidence in; doubt. —**mis·trust′ful** ***adj.***

**mist·y** (mis′tē) ***adj.*** **1** of, like, or covered by mist. **2** blurred, as if by mist; vague [a *misty* idea]. —**mist′i·er, mist′i·est —mist′i·ness** ***n.***

**mis·un·der·stand** (mis′un dər stand′) ***v.*** to understand in a way that is wrong; give a wrong meaning to. —**mis·un·der·stood** (mis′un dər stood′), **mis′un·der·stand′ing**

**mis·un·der·stand·ing** (mis′un dər stand′iŋ) ***n.*** **1** a failure to understand correctly; wrong idea of the meaning or purpose of something. **2** a quarrel or disagreement.

**mis·use** (mis yo͞oz′) ***v.*** **1** to treat badly; abuse. **2** to use in a wrong way [to *misuse* one's time]. —**mis·used′, mis·us′ing** ◆***n.*** (mis yo͞os′) the use of something in a way that is wrong [the *misuse* of funds by the treasurer].

**Mitch·ell** (mich′əl), **Maria** 1818–1889; U.S. astronomer and teacher.

**mite¹** (mīt) ***n.*** a tiny animal of the spider family that lives as a parasite on plants or animals.

**mite²** (mīt) ***n.*** **1** a very small sum of money. **2** a tiny thing, amount, etc.; bit.

**mi·ter¹** (mīt′ər) ***n.*** a tall cap worn by bishops during certain ceremonies. *See the picture.*

**mi·ter²** (mīt′ər) ***n.*** a corner joint formed by fitting together two pieces cut at an angle. ◆***v.*** to fit together in a miter.

**mit·i·gate** (mit′ə gāt) ***v.*** to make or become milder or less severe [The aspirin helped to *mitigate* her pain.] —**mit′i·gat·ed, mit′i·gat·ing —mit′i·ga′tion** ***n.***

**mitt** (mit) ***n.*** **1** a woman's glove covering the forearm, but only part of the fingers. **2** *a shorter form of* **mitten.** ☆**3** a large, padded glove, with a thumb but usually without separate fingers, worn by baseball players [a catcher's *mitt*]. ☆**4** a padded mitten worn by boxers. ☆**5** a hand: *slang in this meaning.*

**mit·ten** (mit′′n) ***n.*** a glove with a separate pouch for the thumb and another, larger pouch for the four fingers.

**mix** (miks) ***v.*** **1** to put, stir, or come together to form a single, blended thing [*Mix* red and yellow paint to get orange. Oil and water won't *mix.*] **2** to make by stirring together the necessary things [to *mix* a cake]. **3** to join or combine [to *mix* work and play]. **4** to get along in a friendly way; associate [He *mixes* well with all kinds of people.] —**mixed** or **mixt, mix′ing** ◆***n.*** ☆a mixture, or a group of things that are to be mixed together [a cake *mix*]. —**mix up, 1** to mix thoroughly. **2** to confuse. **3** to involve [The mayor is *mixed up* in the scandal.]

SYNONYMS: To **mix** is to combine things in such a way as to make something that is the same throughout [to *mix* paints]. To **mingle** is to bring things together so that we can still see or recognize the separate things [hail *mingled* with rain]. To **blend** is to combine different things so as to get a desired result or special effect [to *blend* light and shade].

**mixed** (mikst) ***adj.*** **1** put or stirred together in a single blend. **2** of different kinds [*mixed* nuts]. **3** made up of both sexes [*mixed* company]. **4** confused [to get one's dates *mixed*].

**mixed marriage** marriage between persons of different religions or races.

**mixed media 1** a show that uses acting, the flashing of colored lights, tape recordings, etc. at the same time. **2** in painting, the use of different kinds of coloring matter, as watercolor and crayon, in the same composition.

**mixed number** a number that is a whole number and a fraction, as 6 7/8.

**mix·er** (mik′sər) ***n.*** **1** a device for mixing things, as foods. ☆**2** a person thought of as getting along with people in a certain way [a poor *mixer*].

**mix·ture** (miks′chər) ***n.*** **1** a mixing. **2** something made by mixing [Punch is a *mixture* of fruit juices.]

**mix-up** (miks′up′) ***n.*** confusion or tangle.

**miz·zen** (miz′′n) ***n.*** **1** a fore-and-aft sail set on the mizzenmast. **2** *a shorter form of* **mizzenmast.**

**miz·zen·mast** (miz′′n məst *or* miz′′n mast) ***n.*** the mast closest to the stern on a ship with two or three masts.

**ml** or **ml.** *abbreviation for* **milliliter** *or* **milliliters.**

**Mlle.** *abbreviation for* **Mademoiselle.** *—pl.* **Mlles.**
**mm** or **mm.** *abbreviation for* **millimeter** *or* **millimeters.**
**MM.** *abbreviation for* **Messieurs.**
**Mme.** *abbreviation for* **Madame.** *—pl.* **Mmes.**
**Mn** *the symbol for the chemical element* manganese.
**MN** *abbreviation for* **Minnesota.**
**Mo** *the symbol for the chemical element* molybdenum.
**Mo.** or **MO** *abbreviation for* **Missouri.**
**mo.** *abbreviation for* **month.** *—pl.* **mos.**
**M.O.** or **m.o.** *abbreviation for* **money order.**
**Mo·ab** (mō′ab) an ancient kingdom mentioned in the Bible, east of the Dead Sea.
**moan** (mōn) ***n.*** **1** a low, long sound of sorrow or of pain. **2** any sound like this [the *moan* of the wind]. ◆***v.*** **1** to make a moan or moans. **2** to say with a moan. **3** to complain.
**moat** (mōt) ***n.*** a deep, wide ditch dug around a castle, to keep enemies out. Moats were often filled with water. *See the picture.*
**mob** (mäb) ***n.*** **1** a large crowd; especially, an excited crowd that pays no attention to law and order. **2** the common people: *an unfriendly use.* **3** a gang of criminals: *slang in this meaning.* ◆***v.*** to crowd around and annoy, attack, admire, etc. —**mobbed, mob′bing**

> **Mob** comes from a Latin phrase that meant "an easily moved crowd." Today *mob* still means a crowd of people whose emotions are so easily moved that they will do anything.

**Mo·bile** (mō bēl′ *or* mō′bēl) a seaport in southwestern Alabama.
**mo·bile** (mō′b'l *or* mō′bīl *or* mō′bēl) ***adj.*** **1** that can be moved quickly and easily [a *mobile* army]. **2** that can change rapidly or easily in response to different moods, conditions, needs, etc. [*mobile* features; *mobile* policies]. ◆***n.*** (mō′bēl) a kind of sculpture made of flat pieces, rods, etc. that hang balanced from wires so as to move easily in air currents. *See the picture.* —**mo·bil·i·ty** (mō bil′ə tē) ***n.***
☆**mobile home** a large trailer furnished as a home and usually parked permanently at one location.
**mo·bi·lize** (mō′bə līz) ***v.*** to make or become organized or ready, as for war [to *mobilize* the armed forces]. —**mo′bi·lized, mo′bi·liz·ing** —**mo′bi·li·za′tion *n.***
☆**moc·ca·sin** (mäk′ə s'n) ***n.*** **1** a slipper made of soft leather, without a heel, as those once worn by North American Indians. *See the picture.* **2** a slipper like this but with a hard sole and heel. **3** a poisonous snake found in the southeastern U.S.: *the full name is* **water moccasin.**
**mo·cha** (mō′kə) ***n.*** a kind of coffee first grown in Arabia. ◆***adj.*** flavored with coffee or with coffee and chocolate.
**mock** (mäk) ***v.*** **1** to make fun of or scoff at; ridicule [Some scientists *mocked* Pasteur's theories.] **2** to make fun of by imitating or mimicking [It is cruel to *mock* a limping person.] **3** to lead on and then disappoint [The weather *mocked* them by changing suddenly.] **4** to defeat or make useless [The high wall *mocked* his hopes of escaping.] ◆***adj.*** not genuine; false; pretended [a *mock* battle]. —**mock′er *n.*** —**mock′ing·ly *adv.***
**mock·er·y** (mäk′ər ē) ***n.*** **1** the act of mocking, or making fun. **2** a person or thing that deserves to be

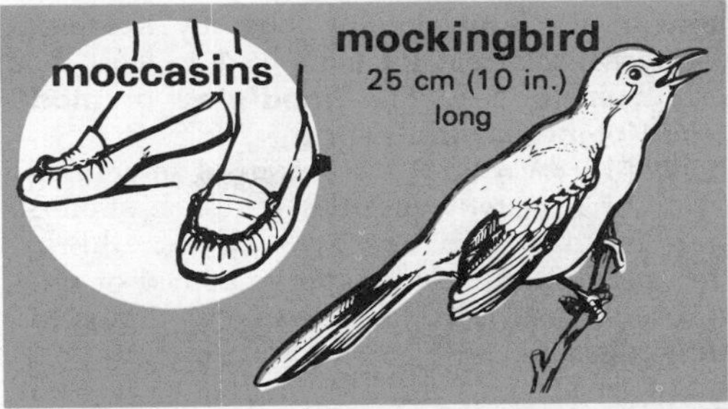


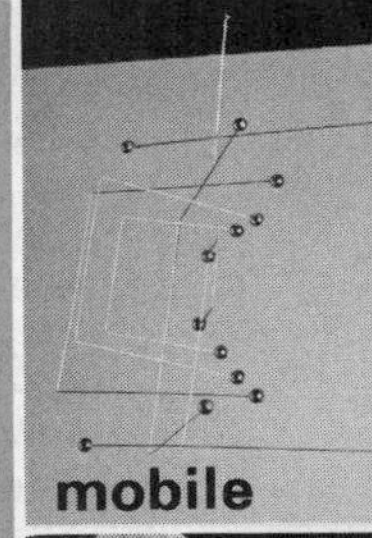

made fun of. **3** a poor imitation or copy [The movie is a *mockery* of the novel.] **4** a useless or disappointing effort [Rain made a *mockery* of our picnic.] *—pl.* **mock′er·ies**
☆**mock·ing·bird** (mäk′iŋ burd′) ***n.*** a small American bird that imitates the calls of other birds. *See the picture.*
**mod** (mäd) ***adj.*** very fashionable, especially in a showy way: *used of certain young people or their clothes.*
**mod.** *abbreviation for* **moderate, modern.**
**mode** (mōd) ***n.*** **1** a way of acting or doing something; method [a *mode* of transportation]. *See* SYNONYMS *at* **method. 2** style or fashion [They always dress in the latest *mode.*] **3** *another word for* **mood²**.
**mod·el** (mäd″l) ***n.*** **1** a small copy of something [a *model* of a ship]. **2** a small object made to serve as the plan for the final, larger thing [a clay *model* for a marble sculpture]. **3** a person or thing that ought to be imitated [He is a very *model* of honesty.] **4** a style or design [Our new car is a two-door *model.*] **5** a person who poses for an artist or photographer. **6** a person whose work is wearing clothes that are for sale, so that customers can see how they look when worn. ◆***adj.*** **1** that is a model [a *model* airplane]. **2** that ought to be imitated; excellent [a *model* student]. ◆***v.*** **1** to plan, form, or make, using a model as a guide [a church *modeled* after a Greek temple]. **2** to make a piece of sculpture [to *model* a figure in clay]. **3** to



| | | | | | | | |
|---|---|---|---|---|---|---|---|
| **a** fat | **ir** here | **ou** out | **zh** leisure | | | | |
| **ā** ape | **ī** bite, fire | **u** up | **ŋ** ring | | | | |
| **ä** car, lot | **ō** go | **ur** fur | a *in* ago | | | | |
| **e** ten | **ô** law, horn | **ch** chin | e *in* agent | | | | |
| **er** care | **oi** oil | **sh** she | ə = i *in* unity | | | | |
| **ē** even | **oo** look | **th** thin | o *in* collect | | | | |
| **i** hit | **ōō** tool | ***th*** then | u *in* focus | | | | |

show how an article of clothing looks by wearing it [Will you *model* this coat for me?] ☆**4** to work as a model (*in meaning* 5 *or* 6). —**mod'eled** or **mod'elled, mod'el·ing** or **mod'el·ling**

SYNONYMS: A **model** is someone or something with fine or excellent qualities that one should copy or imitate. An **example** is something, whether good or bad, that could be copied or imitated. A **pattern** is a model, plan, etc. that is to be followed exactly.

**mod·er·ate** (mäd'ər it) ***adj.*** **1** neither very great, good, strong, etc. nor very small, bad, weak, etc.; reasonable or ordinary [a *moderate* fee; a *moderate* wind]. **2** mild or gentle [a *moderate* reply to an angry letter]. ◆***n.*** a person whose opinions, as in politics or religion, are not strong or extreme. ◆***v.*** (mäd'ə rāt) **1** to make or become less strong or extreme. **2** to serve as chairman of a discussion or debate. —**mod'er·at·ed, mod'er·at·ing** —**mod'er·ate·ly *adv.***

**mod·er·a·tion** (mäd'ə rā'shən) ***n.*** the act or condition of being moderate, or within limits; a keeping away from extremes [This diet makes us follow *moderation* in eating.] —**in moderation,** to a moderate degree [My doctor suggested that I exercise *in moderation.*]

**mod·er·a·tor** (mäd'ə rāt'ər) ***n.*** a person who is in charge of conducting a discussion or debate.

472 **mod·ern** (mäd'ərn) ***adj.*** **1** of or having to do with the present time or the period we live in [a *modern* poet]. **2** of the period after about 1450 [the *modern* history of Europe]. **3** of or having to do with the latest styles, methods, or ideas; up-to-date [He travels the *modern* way, by jet airplane.] ◆***n.*** a person who lives in modern times or has up-to-date ideas.

**Modern** comes originally from a Latin word, *modus,* that meant "a measure" and that came to mean also "a measure of time." The later term, *modern,* is a more limited measure of time and has to do only with recent or present time.

**mod·ern·is·tic** (mäd'ər nis'tik) ***adj.*** modern; of the present time: used in speaking of certain present-day forms of art, music, etc., sometimes in a scornful way. —**mod'ern·is'ti·cal·ly *adv.***

**mod·ern·ize** (mäd'ər nīz) ***v.*** to make or become modern; bring up to date in style, design, etc. —**mod'ern·ized, mod'ern·iz·ing** —**mod'ern·i·za'tion *n.***

**mod·est** (mäd'ist) ***adj.*** **1** not vain or boastful about one's worth, skills, deeds, etc.; humble [a famous, but *modest* person]. *See* SYNONYMS *at* **humble. 2** not bold or forward; shy. **3** behaving, dressing, speaking, etc. in a way that is considered proper or moral; decent. **4** reasonable; not extreme [a *modest* request]. **5** quiet and humble in looks, style, etc. [a *modest* home]. —**mod'est·ly *adv.***

**mod·es·ty** (mäd'is tē) ***n.*** the quality of being modest; humble or proper behavior.

**mod·i·cum** (mäd'i kəm) ***n.*** a small amount; bit [a *modicum* of common sense].

**mod·i·fy** (mäd'ə fī) ***v.*** **1** to make a small or partial change in [Exploration has *modified* our maps of Antarctica.] **2** to make less harsh, strong, etc. [to *modify* a jail term]. **3** to limit the meaning of; describe or qualify [In the phrase "old man" the adjective "old" *modifies* the noun "man."] —**mod'i·fied, mod'i·fy·ing** —**mod'i·fi·ca'tion *n.*** —**mod'i·fi'er *n.***

**mod·ish** (mōd'ish) ***adj.*** in the latest style; fashionable. —**mod'ish·ly *adv.***

**mod·u·late** (mäj'ə lāt) ***v.*** **1** to make a slight change in; adjust [shutters for *modulating* the light coming into the room]. **2** to change the pitch or loudness of the voice in speaking. **3** to vary a radio wave in some way according to the sound being broadcast. *See* **AM, FM** —**mod'u·lat·ed, mod'u·lat·ing** —**mod'u·la'tion *n.***

**mod·ule** (mäj'ōōl) ***n.*** ☆**1** any of a set of units, as wall cabinets, that can be arranged together in various ways. ☆**2** a section of a machine or device that can be detached for some special use [the landing *module* of a spacecraft]. —**mod·u·lar** (mäj'ə lər) ***adj.***

**Mo·gul** (mō'gul) ***n.*** **1** a Mongolian; especially, any of the Mongolian conquerors of India. **2 mogul,** a powerful or important person.

**mo·hair** (mō'her) ***n.*** **1** the silky hair of the Angora goat. **2** a fabric made of this, especially an upholstery fabric with a mohair pile.

**Mo·ham·med** (mō ham'id) 570?–632 A.D.; Arabian prophet. He was the founder of the Muslim religion.

**Mo·ham·med·an** (mō ham'ə dən) ***adj.*** of Mohammed or the Muslim religion. ◆***n.*** *another name for* **Muslim.** —**Mo·ham'med·an·ism *n.***

**Mo·hawk** (mō'hôk) ***n.*** a member of a tribe of Indians who live in Canada and New York State.

**Mo·hi·can** (mō hē'kən) ***n.*** a member of a tribe of Indians who lived in the upper Hudson Valley.

**moi·e·ty** (moi'ə tē) ***n.*** **1** a half. **2** some part or share. —*pl.* **moi'e·ties**

**moist** (moist) ***adj.*** damp or slightly wet. *See* SYNONYMS *at* **wet.**

**mois·ten** (mois''n) ***v.*** to make or become moist.

**mois·ture** (mois'chər) ***n.*** liquid causing a dampness, as fine drops of water in the air.

**mois·tur·ize** (mois'chər īz) ***v.*** to add, supply, or restore moisture to the skin, the air, etc. —**mois'tur·ized, mois'tur·iz·ing** —**mois'tur·iz·er *n.***

**Mo·ja·ve Desert** (mō hä'vē) a desert in southeastern California.

**mo·lar** (mō'lər) ***n.*** any of the back teeth used for grinding food [An adult person has twelve *molars,* three on each side of each jaw.] *See the picture.*

**mo·las·ses** (mə las'iz) ***n.*** a thick, dark syrup that remains after sugar is refined.

**mold**[1] (mōld) ***n.*** **1** a hollow form used to give shape to something soft or melted [Candles are made of wax poured into *molds.*] **2** something shaped in a mold [a *mold* of gelatin]. **3** a special character or kind [Our school needs more teachers of his *mold.*] ◆***v.*** **1** to make or shape in a mold. **2** to give a certain shape or form to [She *molded* the soft clay into a vase.] **3** to have a strong influence on [The newspapers try to *mold* public opinion.]

**mold**[2] (mōld) ***n.*** a fuzzy growth caused by a fungus on vegetable or animal matter that is damp or decaying. ◆***v.*** to become moldy.

**mold**[3] (mōld) ***n.*** loose, soft soil, especially when it is rich and good for growing plants.

**mold·er** (mōl'dər) ***v.*** to crumble into dust; decay slowly [Even iron in time *molders* away.]

**mold·ing** (mōl'diŋ) ***n.*** **1** the act of giving shape or form to [the *molding* of metals]. **2** the act of having a strong influence on [the *molding* of a child's personality]. **3** something molded. **4** a shaped strip of wood, plastic, etc. fastened around the frame of a door, along the upper part of a wall, etc. *See the picture.*

**mold·y** (mōl′dē) ***adj.*** like or covered with a fuzzy growth of mold; stale or musty [a *moldy* smell; *moldy* bread]. —**mold′i·er, mold′i·est**

**mole**[1] (mōl) ***n.*** a small, dark-colored spot on the skin, often one that is there at birth.

**mole**[2] (mōl) ***n.*** a small animal with small eyes and ears and soft fur, that lives mainly underground. *See the picture.*

**mole**[3] (mōl) ***n.*** *another name for* **breakwater.**

**mol·e·cule** (mäl′ə kyo͞ol) ***n.*** **1** the smallest particle of a substance that can exist alone without losing its chemical form. A molecule consists of one or more atoms. **2** a very small piece. —**mo·lec·u·lar** (mə lek′yə lər) ***adj.***

**mole·hill** (mōl′hil) ***n.*** a small ridge of earth formed by a mole burrowing under the ground. —**make a mountain out of a molehill,** to treat a small problem as if it were a large, important one.

**mole·skin** (mōl′skin) ***n.*** **1** a strong cotton fabric with a soft nap, used for work clothes. **2** a soft fabric, often with a sticky backing, used for foot bandages.

**mo·lest** (mə lest′) ***v.*** to meddle with so as to hurt or trouble; bother. —**mo·les·ta·tion** (mō′les tā′shən) ***n.***

**Mo·lière** (mōl yer′) 1622–1673; French writer of plays. His real name was Jean Baptiste Poquelin.

**mol·li·fy** (mäl′ə fī) ***v.*** to soothe; make calm or less violent [We *mollified* the barking dog by giving it a bone.] —**mol′li·fied, mol′li·fy·ing**

**mol·lusk** or **mol·lusc** (mäl′əsk) ***n.*** an animal with a soft body that is usually protected by a shell, as the oyster, clam, snail, etc.

**mol·ly·cod·dle** (mäl′ē käd′'l) ***n.*** a man or boy who is too much pampered or taken care of; sissy. ◆***v.*** to pamper; coddle. —**mol′ly·cod′dled, mol′ly·cod′dling**

**molt** (mōlt) ***v.*** to shed skin, feathers, etc. before getting a new growth, as snakes and birds do. *See the picture.*

**mol·ten** (mōl′t'n) ***adj.*** **1** melted by heat [*molten* iron]. **2** made by being melted and put in a mold [a *molten* statue].

**Mo·luc·cas** (mō luk′əz) a group of islands of Indonesia: *also* **Molucca Islands.**

**mo·lyb·de·num** (mə lib′də nəm) ***n.*** a silver-white metal that is a chemical element, used in alloys.

**mom** (mäm) ***n.*** mother: *used only in everyday talk.*

**mo·ment** (mō′mənt) ***n.*** **1** a very short period of time; instant [to pause for a *moment*]. **2** a particular time [At that *moment* the bell rang.] **3** importance [matters of great *moment*].

**mo·men·tar·i·ly** (mō′mən ter′ə lē) ***adv.*** **1** for a short time [I saw her *momentarily* between classes.] **2** from moment to moment; at any moment [We expect them *momentarily*.]

**mo·men·tar·y** (mō′mən ter′ē) ***adj.*** lasting for only a moment [a *momentary* pain].

**mo·men·tous** (mō men′təs) ***adj.*** very important [a *momentous* occasion].

**mo·men·tum** (mō men′təm) ***n.*** **1** the force with which a body moves, equal to its mass multiplied by its speed [His sled gained *momentum* as it coasted downhill.] **2** strength or force that keeps growing [The peace movement gained *momentum*.]

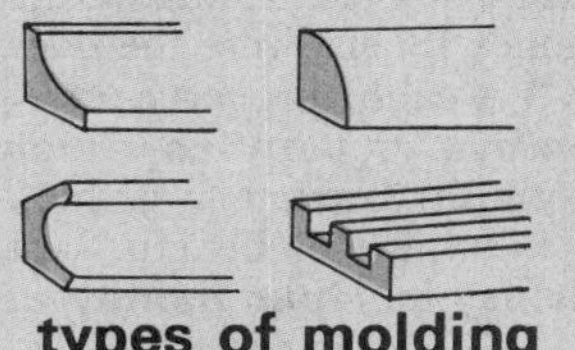
types of molding

mole
18 cm (7 in.) long, including tail

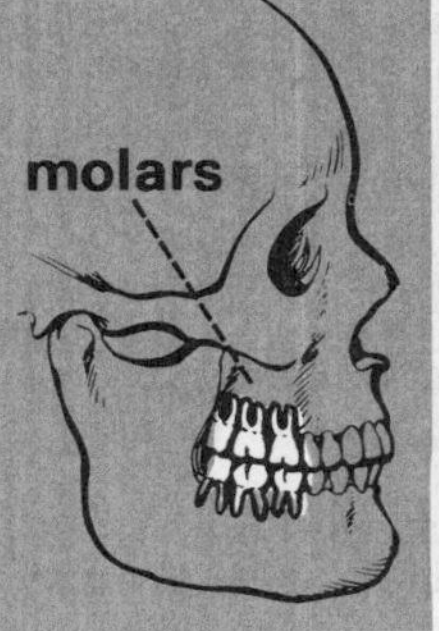

snake molting

**Mon.** *abbreviation for* **Monday.**

**Mon·a·co** (män′ə kō) a small country on the Mediterranean, mostly surrounded by France.

**Mo·na Li·sa** (mō′nə lē′sə) a famous painting of a faintly smiling woman, by Leonardo da Vinci.

**mon·arch** (män′ərk) ***n.*** **1** a ruler, as a king, queen, or emperor. **2** a large North American butterfly, with reddish-brown wings with black edges.

**mo·nar·chi·cal** (mə när′ki k'l) ***adj.*** of or like a monarch or monarchy.

**mon·ar·chist** (män′ər kist) ***n.*** a person who is in favor of government by a monarch.

**mon·ar·chy** (män′ər kē) ***n.*** government by a monarch, or a country with such government. —*pl.* **mon′ar·chies**

**mon·as·ter·y** (män′ə ster′ē) ***n.*** a place where a group of monks live. —*pl.* **mon′as·ter′ies**

**mo·nas·tic** (mə nas′tik) ***adj.*** of or having to do with monks or their way of life. ◆***n.*** *another name for* **monk.**

**Mon·dale** (män′dāl), **Walter Frederick** 1928– ; vice president of the United States (1977– ).

**Mon·day** (mun′dē) ***n.*** the second day of the week.

**Mo·net** (mō nā′), **Claude** 1840–1926; French painter.

**mon·e·tar·y** (män′ə ter′ē) ***adj.*** **1** in money; pecuniary [That old car has little *monetary* value.] **2** of the money used in a country [The *monetary* unit of France is the franc.]

**mon·ey** (mun′ē) ***n.*** **1** coins of gold, silver, or other metal, or paper bills to take the place of these, issued



| | | | | | | | |
|---|---|---|---|---|---|---|---|
| **a** | fat | **ir** | here | **ou** | out | **zh** | leisure |
| **ā** | ape | **ī** | bite, fire | **u** | up | **ŋ** | ring |
| **ä** | car, lot | **ō** | go | **ʉr** | fur | | a *in* ago |
| **e** | ten | **ô** | law, horn | **ch** | chin | | e *in* agent |
| **er** | care | **oi** | oil | **sh** | she | **ə =** | i *in* unity |
| **ē** | even | **o͝o** | look | **th** | thin | | o *in* collect |
| **i** | hit | **o͞o** | tool | ***th*** | then | | u *in* focus |

by a government for use in buying and selling. **2** anything regularly used as money [Shells were the *money* of some Indian tribes.] **3** wealth, property, etc. [a man of *money*]. *—pl.* **mon′eys** or **mon′ies** —**make money,** to earn or get wealth; become wealthy. —**one's money's worth,** full value or benefit. —**put money into,** to invest money in. —**put money on,** to bet on.

**Money** comes from the Latin word *Moneta,* a name given to the goddess Juno, in whose temple the ancient Romans coined money. **Monetary** comes from the same word.

**mon·ey·bags** (mun′ē bagz′) ***n.*** a rich person: *used only in everyday talk.*

**money belt** a belt with a place to hold money.

**mon·ey-chang·er** (mun′ē chān′jər) ***n.*** **1** a person whose business is exchanging sums or kinds of money. ☆**2** a device that holds stacked coins to be used in making change quickly.

**mon·eyed** (mun′ēd) ***adj.*** very rich; wealthy.

**money order** a written order that a certain sum of money be paid to a certain person. It can be bought at a bank or post office as a safe way of sending money to a person, who can cash it at any bank or post office.

**Mon·gol** (mäŋ′gəl) ***adj., n.*** *another name for* **Mongolian** *in meaning* 1.

**Mon·go·li·a** (mäŋ gō′lē ə) a country in east central

474 Asia, north of China. *See the map.*

**Mon·go·li·an** (mäŋ gō′lē ən) ***adj.*** **1** of Mongolia, its people, etc. **2** *another word for* **Mongoloid.** ✦***n.*** **1** a native of Mongolia. **2** *another word for* **Mongoloid.**

**Mon·gol·oid** (mäŋ′gə loid) ***adj.*** having to do with or belonging to the group of human beings that is loosely called the "yellow race." The group includes the Eskimos, the North American Indians, and most Asians. ✦***n.*** a member of this group.

**mon·goose** (mäŋ′go͞os) ***n.*** an animal of India that looks like a ferret and can kill rats and snakes. *See the picture.* *—pl.* **mon′goos·es**

**mon·grel** (muŋ′grəl *or* mäŋ′grəl) ***n.*** an animal or plant produced by crossing different kinds or breeds; especially, a dog of this kind. ✦***adj.*** of mixed breed or origin.

**mon·i·tor** (män′ə tər) ***n.*** **1** in some schools, a student chosen to help keep order, take attendance, etc. **2** something that reminds or warns. **3** a former kind of armored warship with a low deck and heavy guns mounted in turrets. **4** in a radio or TV studio, a receiver for checking on programs in order to tell how they are coming through. ✦***v.*** to listen to or watch in order to check up on [to *monitor* a broadcast].

**mon·i·to·ry** (män′ə tôr′ē) ***adj.*** warning or cautioning [a *monitory* letter].

**monk** (muŋk) ***n.*** a man who has joined a religious order whose members live together in a monastery according to certain rules, after vowing to give up worldly goods, never to marry, etc.

**mon·key** (muŋ′kē) ***n.*** **1** any animal of the group that is closest to man in appearance; especially, any small animal of this group that has a long tail and is not one of the apes. **2** a playful child who is full of mischief. *—pl.* **mon′keys** ✦***v.*** ☆to meddle or fool: *used only in everyday talk* [Don't *monkey* around with the TV set.]

☆**monkey business** foolish or mischievous tricks or behavior: *used only in everyday talk.*

**monkey wrench** a tool with a kind of vise at one end that can be tightened, used for grasping and turning pipes, nuts, etc. *See the picture.*

**monk·ish** (muŋk′ish) ***adj.*** of or like monks: *often used scornfully.*

**monk's cloth** a heavy cloth, as of cotton, with a weave like that used in weaving baskets, used for drapes.

**mon·o** (män′ō) ***adj.*** *a shorter form of* **monophonic.** ✦***n.*** *a shorter form of* **mononucleosis.**

**mono-** *a prefix meaning* one, alone, *or* single [A *monoplane* is an airplane with one pair of wings.]

**mon·o·cle** (män′ə k'l) ***n.*** an eyeglass for one eye only.

**mon·o·cot·y·le·don** (män′ə kät″l ēd′'n) ***n.*** a flowering plant with only one cotyledon, or seed leaf, in the embryo. All flowering plants are either monocotyledons or dicotyledons.

**mo·nog·a·my** (mə näg′ə mē) ***n.*** the practice of being married to only one person at a time. —**mo·nog′a·mous *adj.***

**mon·o·gram** (män′ə gram) ***n.*** initials, especially of a person's name, put together in a design and used on clothing, stationery, etc. *See the picture.*

**mon·o·lith** (män′ə lith) ***n.*** a large block of stone, or a statue, monument, etc. carved from a single, large stone. —**mon′o·lith′ic *adj.***

**mon·o·logue** or **mon·o·log** (män′ə lôg) ***n.*** **1** a long speech by one person during a conversation. **2** a poem, part of a play, etc. in which one person speaks alone. **3** a play, skit, etc. performed by one actor.

**mon·o·ma·ni·a** (män′ə mā′nē ə) ***n.*** too great an interest in something; especially, an interest or concern that is not reasonable; craze. —**mon·o·ma·ni·ac** (män′ə mā′nē ak) ***n.***

**mon·o·nu·cle·o·sis** (män′ə no͞o′klē ō′sis *or* män′ə nyo͞o′klē ō′sis) ***n.*** a disease, especially of young people, in which one has a fever, sore throat, and swollen lymph nodes: *the full name is* **infectious mononucleosis.**

**mon·o·phon·ic** (män′ə fän′ik) ***adj.*** describing or having to do with a way of recording or playing records, tapes, etc. that uses a single channel for the sound.

**mon·o·plane** (män′ə plān) ***n.*** an airplane with only one pair of wings.

**mo·nop·o·list** (mə näp′ə list) ***n.*** a person who has a monopoly or is in favor of monopolies.

**mo·nop·o·lis·tic** (mə näp′ə lis′tik) ***adj.*** that is a monopoly or that has a monopoly.

**mo·nop·o·lize** (mə näp′ə līz) ***v.*** **1** to get or have a monopoly of some product or service. **2** to get or take up all of [to *monopolize* a conversation]. —**mo·nop′o·lized, mo·nop′o·liz·ing**

**mo·nop·o·ly** (mə näp′ə lē) ***n.*** **1** complete control of a product or service in some place by a single person or group. A company with a monopoly has no competition and can set prices as it wishes. **2** such control given and regulated by a government [The city gave the bus company a *monopoly* for ten years.] **3** a company that has a monopoly. **4** the thing that is controlled by a monopoly. **5** the condition of having something all to oneself [No one has a *monopoly* on brains.] —*pl.* **mo·nop′o·lies**

**mon·o·rail** (män′ə rāl) ***n.*** **1** a railway having cars that run on a single rail, or track, and are hung from it or balanced on it. *See the picture.* **2** this track.

**mon·o·syl·la·ble** (män′ə sil′ə b'l) ***n.*** a word of one syllable, as *he* or *thought.* —**mon·o·syl·lab·ic** (män′ə si lab′ik) ***adj.***

**mon·o·the·ism** (män′ə thē iz'm) ***n.*** the belief that there is only one God. —**mon′o·the·ist** ***n.*** —**mon′o·the·is′tic** ***adj.***

**mon·o·tone** (män′ə tōn) ***n.*** **1** a keeping of the same tone or pitch without change, as in talking or singing. **2** a person who sings with few if any changes of tone. **3** sameness of color, style, etc. [The room was decorated in gray *monotones.*]

**mo·not·o·nous** (mə nät′'n əs) ***adj.*** **1** going on and on in the same tone [a *monotonous* voice]. **2** having little or no change; boring or tiresome [a *monotonous* trip; *monotonous* work].

**mo·not·o·ny** (mə nät′'n ē) ***n.*** **1** sameness of tone or pitch. **2** lack of change or variety; tiresome sameness.

**mon·ox·ide** (mə näk′sīd) ***n.*** an oxide with one atom of oxygen in each molecule.

**Mon·roe** (mən rō′), **James** 1758–1831; the fifth president of the United States, from 1817 to 1825.

**Monroe Doctrine** President Monroe's statement that the U.S. would regard as an unfriendly act any move by a European nation to try to control the affairs of American countries or to get more territory on the American continents.

**Mon·ro·vi·a** (mən rō′vē ə) the capital of Liberia.

**mon·sieur** (mə syʉr′) ***n.*** a French word used, like "Mr.," as a title for a man. —*pl.* **mes·sieurs** (mes′ərz)

**Mon·si·gnor** (män sēn′yər) ***n.*** **1** a title given to certain clergymen of high rank in the Roman Catholic Church. **2** *often* **monsignor,** a person who has this title.

**mon·soon** (män so͞on′) ***n.*** **1** a wind of the Indian Ocean and southern Asia, blowing from the southwest from April to October, and from the northeast the rest of the year. **2** the rainy season when this wind blows from the southwest.

**mon·ster** (män′stər) ***n.*** **1** any plant or animal that is not normal in shape or form, as a fish with two heads. **2** an imaginary creature in stories, as a dragon or unicorn, often one that is partly human, as a mermaid or centaur. **3** a very cruel or wicked person. **4** a huge animal or thing [a *monster* of a house]. ◆***adj.*** huge; enormous.

> **Monster** comes from a Latin word meaning "something sent by the gods as a warning that some misfortune will take place." Ancient people thought that a deformed creature was a warning from the gods. **Monitor,** for "something that warns," comes from the same Latin word.

**mon·stros·i·ty** (män sträs′ə tē) ***n.*** **1** the condition of being monstrous. **2** a monstrous thing or creature. —*pl.* **mon·stros′i·ties**

**mon·strous** (män′strəs) ***adj.*** **1** very large; huge. **2** very different from the normal in looks or shape [a *monstrous* face]. **3** very wicked; shocking; horrible [a *monstrous* crime].

**mon·tage** (män täzh′ *or* mōn täzh′) ***n.*** **1** a picture put together from a number of different pictures, as by putting or lapping one over another. **2** the art of making such a picture.

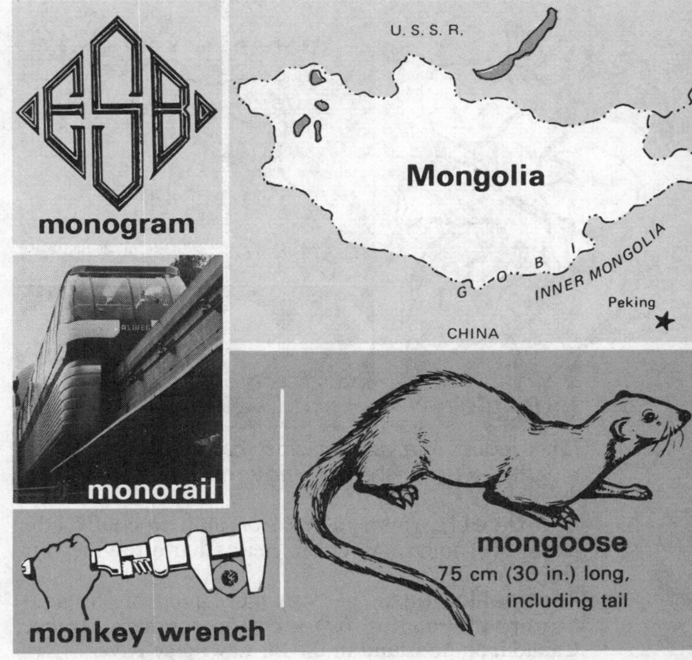

monogram

monorail

mongoose
75 cm (30 in.) long, including tail

monkey wrench

**Mon·tan·a** (män tan′ə) a State in the northwestern part of the U.S.: abbreviated **Mont., MT** 

**Mont Blanc** (mōn blän′) the highest mountain in the Alps, in eastern France on the Italian border. It is a little over 4,813 meters (or 15,781 feet).

**Mon·te Car·lo** (män′ti kär′lō) a town in Monaco that is a gambling resort.

**Mon·tes·so·ri** (män tə sôr′ē), **Maria** 1870–1952; Italian educator.

**Montessori method** a method of teaching young children in which they are trained in using their senses and are guided in what they do rather than rigidly controlled. The method was started by Maria Montessori in 1907.

**Mon·te·vid·e·o** (män′tə vi dā′ō) the capital of Uruguay.

**Mon·te·zu·ma II** (män′tə zo͞o′mə) 1479?–1520; the last Aztec emperor of Mexico, from 1502 to 1520. He was conquered by Cortés.

**Mont·gom·er·y** (mənt gum′ər ē *or* mänt gum′ər ē) the capital of Alabama.

**month** (munth) ***n.*** **1** any of the twelve parts into which the year is divided. **2** the period of one complete revolution of the moon, about 29 1/2 days. **3** any period of four weeks or of 30 days.

**month·ly** (munth′lē) ***adj.*** **1** happening, done, being due, etc. once a month [*monthly* payments]. **2** lasting

| | | | | | | | |
|---|---|---|---|---|---|---|---|
| **a** | fat | **ir** | here | **ou** | out | **zh** | leisure |
| **ā** | ape | **ī** | bite, fire | **u** | up | **ŋ** | ring |
| **ä** | car, lot | **ō** | go | **ʉr** | fur | | a *in* ago |
| **e** | ten | **ô** | law, horn | **ch** | chin | | e *in* agent |
| **er** | care | **oi** | oil | **sh** | she | **ə** = | i *in* unity |
| **ē** | even | **oo** | look | **th** | thin | | o *in* collect |
| **i** | hit | **o͞o** | tool | ***th*** | then | | u *in* focus |

morning glory

moose
1.7 m (5 1/2 ft.) high at shoulder

phases of the moon

for a month. ◆*n.* a magazine that comes out once a month. —*pl.* **month′lies** ◆*adv.* once a month; every month.

**Mon·ti·cel·lo** (män tə sel′ō *or* män tə chel′ō) the home of Thomas Jefferson, near Charlottesville, Virginia.

**Mont·pel·ier** (mänt pēl′yər) the capital of Vermont.

**Mont·re·al** (män′trē ôl′) a city in southern Quebec, Canada, on an island in the St. Lawrence River.

**mon·u·ment** (män′yə mənt) *n.* **1** something put up in memory of a person or happening, as a statue, building, etc. **2** something great or famous, especially from long ago [Shakespeare's plays are *monuments* of English culture.]

**mon·u·men·tal** (män′yə men′t'l) *adj.* **1** that is or has to do with a monument. **2** large, important, and likely to last for a long time [the *monumental* symphonies of Beethoven]. **3** very great; colossal [a *monumental* liar]. —**mon′u·men′tal·ly** *adv.*

**moo** (mo͞o) *n.* the sound made by a cow. —*pl.* **moos** ◆*v.* to make this sound. —**mooed, moo′ing**

**mooch** (mo͞och) *v.* to get by begging or asking, without paying: *a slang word.*

**mood**[1] (mo͞od) *n.* the way one feels; frame of mind [I'm in no *mood* for joking. She's in a happy *mood* today.]

**mood**[2] (mo͞od) *n.* the form of a verb that shows whether it is expressing a fact (*indicative mood*), a wish or possibility (*subjunctive mood*), or a command (*imperative mood*).

**mood·y** (mo͞o′dē) *adj.* having or showing sad, gloomy moods or changes of mood [a *moody* child; a *moody* face]. —**mood′i·er, mood′i·est** —**mood′i·ly** *adv.* —**mood′i·ness** *n.*

**moon** (mo͞on) *n.* **1** the heavenly body that revolves around the earth once in about every 29 1/2 days and shines at night by reflecting the light of the sun. *See the picture.* **2** any small body that spins around a planet. Moons may be natural or artificial. **3** moonlight [the *moon* on the water]. **4** anything shaped like the moon. **5** a month [Hiawatha returned in five *moons.*] ◆*v.* to wander or look about in a dreamy or aimless way.

**moon·beam** (mo͞on′bēm) *n.* a ray of moonlight.

**moon·calf** (mo͞on′kaf) *n.* **1** a fool. **2** a young person who spends time in a dreamy or aimless way.

☆**moon child** a person born under the sign of the zodiac called Cancer. —*pl.* **moon children** *See* **Cancer.**

**moon·light** (mo͞on′līt) *n.* the light of the moon. ◆*adj.* **1** lighted by moonlight; moonlit. **2** done or happening by moonlight, or at night [a *moonlight* ride].

**moon·light·ing** (mo͞on′līt′iŋ) *n.* ☆the practice of working at a second regular job in addition to one's main job. —**moon′light′er** *n.*

**moon·lit** (mo͞on′lit) *adj.* lighted by the moon.

**moon·shine** (mo͞on′shīn) *n.* **1** *another name for* **moonlight. 2** foolish or useless talk, ideas, etc. ☆**3** whiskey made secretly and sold without paying a government tax: *used only in everyday talk.*

☆**moon·shot** (mo͞on′shät) *n.* the launching of a spacecraft to the moon.

**moon·stone** (mo͞on′stōn) *n.* a milky-white, glassy mineral that is used as a gem.

☆**moon·walk** (mo͞on′wôk) *n.* a walking about by an astronaut on the surface of the moon.

**Moor** (mo͝or) *n.* a member of a Muslim people who live in northwestern Africa. Moors invaded Spain and settled there in the 8th century, but were driven out in the late 15th century. —**Moor′ish** *adj.*

**moor**[1] (mo͝or) *n.* an area of open wasteland, usually covered with heather and often swampy: *a British word.*

**moor**[2] (mo͝or) *v.* **1** to hold a ship in place by means of cables to the shore or by anchors. **2** to hold or fix in place [a tent firmly *moored* by strong ropes].

**Moore** (mo͝or *or* môr), **Henry** 1898– ; English sculptor, especially of abstract forms.

**Moore, Marianne** 1887–1972; U.S. poet.

**Moore, Thomas** 1779–1852; Irish poet.

**moor·ings** (mo͝or′iŋz) *n.pl.* **1** the lines, cables, or anchors by which a ship is moored. **2** a place where a ship is moored.

☆**moose** (mo͞os) *n.* a large animal related to the deer, of the northern U.S. and Canada. The male has broad antlers with many points. *See the picture.* —*pl.* **moose**

**moot** (mo͞ot) *adj.* that can be discussed or argued about; debatable [a *moot* point]. ◆*v.* to debate; argue.

> **Moot** comes from an Old English word that means "a meeting or assembly." At these early English meetings certain matters were discussed and settled. Now we say that a *moot point* or a *moot question* is one that should be discussed in order to be settled properly.

**mop** (mäp) *n.* **1** a bundle of rags or yarn, or a sponge, fastened to the end of a stick for washing floors. **2** anything like a mop, as a thick head of hair. ◆*v.* to wash or wipe as with a mop. —**mopped, mop′ping** —**mop up, 1** to finish or end; also, to defeat completely: *used only in everyday talk.* **2** to clear out or round up beaten enemy troops from a town or battle area.

**mope** (mōp) *v.* to be gloomy and dull, without spirit. —**moped, mop′ing**

**mo·ped** (mō′ped) *n.* a bicycle with a small motor to make it go.

**mop·pet** (mäp′it) *n.* a little child: *used only in everyday talk to show affection.*

**mo·raine** (mə rān′) *n.* a mass of rocks, gravel, sand, etc. pushed along or left by a glacier.

**mor·al** (môr′əl) ***adj.*** **1** having to do with right and wrong in conduct [Cheating is a *moral* issue.] **2** good or right according to ideas of being decent and respectable [She was a *moral* woman all her life.] **3** teaching or showing ideas of right and wrong [a *moral* story]. **4** that shows sympathy but gives no active help [She gave *moral* support but no money.] ✦***n.*** **1** a lesson about what is right and wrong, taught by a story or event [the *moral* of a fable]. **2 morals,** *pl.* standards of behavior having to do with right and wrong; ethics. —**moral victory,** a defeat that is thought of as a victory because it has some good results.

SYNONYMS: **Moral** has to do with common standards of what is good or right in the way one lives [our *moral* duty to care for the aged]. **Ethical** has to do with a code of moral principles based on ideals and serious thinking, especially such a code for doctors, lawyers, etc. [It is not *ethical* to give or take a bribe.]

**mo·rale** (mə ral′) ***n.*** the courage, self-control, and confidence that help one to keep up one's spirits in facing hardship or danger [The team was defeated because of its low *morale.*]

**mor·al·ist** (môr′əl ist) ***n.*** a person who moralizes.

**mo·ral·i·ty** (mə ral′ə tē) ***n.*** **1** rightness or wrongness of an action [We discussed the *morality* of getting help on our homework.] **2** good or proper conduct. **3** rules of right and wrong; ethics. —*pl.* **mo·ral′i·ties**

**mor·al·ize** (môr′ə līz) ***v.*** **1** to talk or write about matters of right and wrong. **2** to make morally better. —**mor′al·ized, mor′al·iz·ing**

**mor·al·ly** (môr′əl ē) ***adv.*** **1** in a way that is moral, good, honest, etc. **2** with regard to morals [a *morally* admirable person]. **3** practically [I am *morally* certain that we shall win.]

**mo·rass** (mə ras′) ***n.*** a piece of marshy ground; bog or swamp.

**mor·a·to·ri·um** (môr′ə tôr′ē əm) ***n.*** **1** a time during which a delay is granted, as by law, for paying debts. **2** the granting of such a delay.

**Mo·ra·vi·a** (mô rā′vē ə) a region in Czechoslovakia. —**Mo·ra′vi·an** ***adj., n.***

☆**mo·ray** (môr′ā *or* mô rā′) ***n.*** a brightly colored eel found in warm seas, especially among coral reefs: *the full name is* **moray eel.**

**mor·bid** (môr′bid) ***adj.*** **1** having or showing an interest in gloomy or unpleasant things [a *morbid* imagination]. **2** horrible or disgusting [the *morbid* details of a murder]. **3** of or caused by disease; unhealthy [a *morbid* growth in the body]. —**mor·bid′i·ty** ***n.*** —**mor′bid·ly** ***adv.***

**mor·dant** (môr′d′nt) ***adj.*** sharp and cutting with words; sarcastic [Her novels are full of *mordant* wit.] ✦***n.*** a substance used in dyeing to fix the colors so that they will not fade.

**more** (môr) ***adj.*** **1** greater in amount or degree: *used as the comparative of* **much** [He has *more* free time than I do.] **2** greater in number: *used as the comparative of* **many** [We need *more* helpers.] **3** additional; further [There will be *more* news later.] ✦***n.*** **1** a greater amount or degree [She spends *more* of her time playing than studying.] **2** a greater number: *used with a plural verb* [*More* of us are going this time.] **3** something extra or further [I shall have *more* to say later.] ✦***adv.*** **1** in or to a greater degree or extent [Judy laughs *more* than she used to.] **More** is also used before many adjectives and adverbs to form comparatives just as **most** is used to form superlatives [*more* horrible; *more* quickly]. **2** in addition; again [Do it once *more.*] —**more and more, 1** to an ever greater degree. **2** an amount that keeps on growing. —**more or less, 1** to some extent; somewhat. **2** about; nearly.

**mo·rel** (mə rel′) ***n.*** a kind of mushroom that looks like a sponge on a stalk and can be eaten.

**more·o·ver** (môr ō′vər) ***adv.*** in addition to what has been said; besides; also.

☆**mo·res** (môr′ēz *or* môr′āz) ***n.pl.*** attitudes and ways of behaving that have become so firmly fixed within a group of people that they are followed like laws.

**morgue** (môrg) ***n.*** **1** a place where the bodies of unknown dead and those dead of unknown causes are kept to be examined or identified before being buried. ☆**2** a newspaper office's library of back copies, etc.

**mor·i·bund** (môr′ə bund) ***adj.*** coming to an end or dying.

☆**Mor·mon** (môr′mən) ***n.*** a member of a church founded in the U.S. in 1830 by Joseph Smith. The official name of this church is **Church of Jesus Christ of Latter-day Saints.**

**morn** (môrn) ***n.*** morning: *used mainly in older poetry.*

**morn·ing** (môr′ning) ***n.*** the early part of the day, from midnight to noon or, especially, from dawn to noon.

☆**morning glory** a climbing plant with flowers of lavender, blue, pink, or white, shaped like trumpets. *See the picture.*

**morning star** a planet seen in the eastern sky before sunrise, usually Venus.

**Mo·roc·co** (mə rä′kō) a country in northwestern Africa. —**Mo·roc′can** ***adj., n.***

**mo·roc·co** (mə rä′kō) ***n.*** a fine, soft leather made from goatskins and used for binding books.

☆**mo·ron** (môr′än) ***n.*** **1** a person who is mentally retarded to a mild extent: *psychologists no longer use this word.* **2** a very foolish or stupid person. —**mo·ron·ic** (mô rän′ik) ***adj.***

**mo·rose** (mə rōs′) ***adj.*** gloomy, bad-tempered, sullen, etc. —**mo·rose′ly** ***adv.*** —**mo·rose′ness** ***n.***

**mor·pheme** (môr′fēm) ***n.*** the smallest unit or form that has meaning in a language [The forms *un-* or *-do* in *undo, -ing* in *doing,* and *-s* in *girls* are all *morphemes.*]

**Mor·phe·us** (môr′fē əs) the Greek god of dreams.

**mor·phine** (môr′fēn) ***n.*** a drug got from opium, used in medicine to lessen pain.

**mor·ris dance** (môr′is) an old English folk dance, in which fancy costumes were worn, especially on May Day.



| | | | | | | | |
|---|---|---|---|---|---|---|---|
| **a** | fat | **ir** | here | **ou** | out | **zh** | leisure |
| **ā** | ape | **ī** | bite, fire | **u** | up | **ng** | ring |
| **ä** | car, lot | **ō** | go | **ur** | fur | | a *in* ago |
| **e** | ten | **ô** | law, horn | **ch** | chin | | e *in* agent |
| **er** | care | **oi** | oil | **sh** | she | **ə** = | i *in* unity |
| **ē** | even | **oo** | look | **th** | thin | | o *in* collect |
| **i** | hit | **ōō** | tool | ***th*** | then | | u *in* focus |

**mor·row** (mär′ō *or* môr′ō) ***n.*** **1** morning. **2** the next day. *This word is now seldom used.*

**Morse** (môrs), **Samuel F. B.** 1791–1872; U.S. inventor of the telegraph.

**Morse code** a code or alphabet made up of a system of dots and dashes (or short and long clicks, flashes, etc.) that stand for letters and numbers. It is used in sending messages by telegraph or teletypewriter, or in signaling.

**mor·sel** (môr′s'l) ***n.*** **1** a small bite or bit of food. **2** any small piece or amount.

**mor·tal** (môr′t'l) ***adj.*** **1** that must die at some time [All men are *mortal.*] **2** of people as beings who must die; human [a *mortal* weakness]. **3** causing death of the body or soul [a *mortal* wound; *mortal* sin]. **4** lasting until death [*mortal* combat; *mortal* enemies]. **5** very great; extreme [*mortal* terror]. ◆***n.*** a human being.

**mor·tal·i·ty** (môr tal′ə tē) ***n.*** **1** the condition of being mortal or sure to die. **2** the death of a large number of people, as from war or disease. **3** the number of deaths in relation to the number of people, as in a certain place; death rate.

**mor·tal·ly** (môr′t'l ē) ***adv.*** **1** so as to cause death; fatally [*mortally* wounded]. **2** very; greatly [*mortally* embarrassed].

**mor·tar** (môr′tər) ***n.*** **1** a mixture of cement or lime with sand and water, used to hold bricks or stones together. **2** a small cannon that shoots shells in a high curve. **3** a hard bowl in which materials are ground to a powder with a pestle. *See the picture.*



**mort·gage** (môr′gij) ***n.*** **1** an agreement in which a person borrowing money gives the lender a claim to property as a pledge that the debt will be paid [The bank holds a *mortgage* of $15,000 on our house.] **2** the legal paper by which such a claim is given. ◆***v.*** **1** to pledge by a mortgage in order to borrow money [to *mortgage* a home]. **2** to put a claim on; make risky [He *mortgaged* his future by piling up debts.] —**mort′gaged, mort′gag·ing**

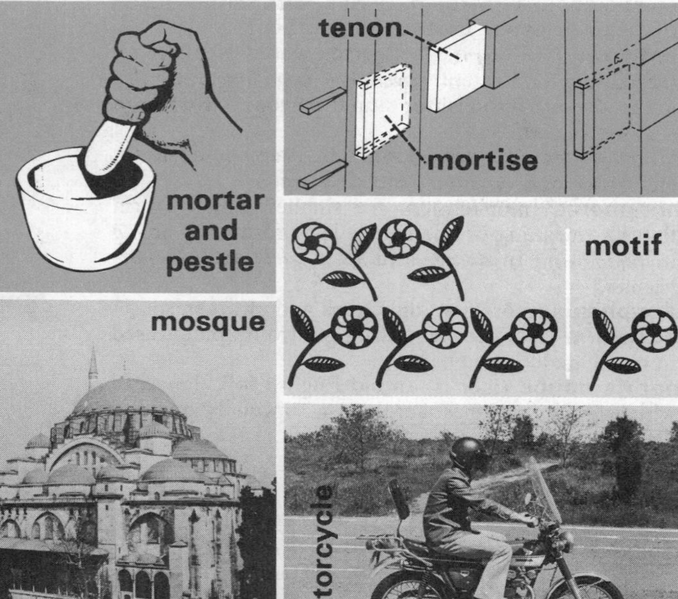


**Mortgage** comes from two words in old French *mort* and *gage* that meant "dead" and "pledge." The pledge would be "dead" to the lender if the borrower paid the debt and kept the property that had been pledged. And the pledge would be "dead" to the borrower if he or she failed to pay the debt and lost the property.

**mort·ga·gee** (môr gə jē′) ***n.*** the lender to whom property is mortgaged.

**mort·ga·gor** or **mort·gag·er** (môr′gi jər) ***n.*** a person who mortgages property.

☆**mor·ti·cian** (môr tish′ən) ***n.*** *another name for* **funeral director.**

**mor·ti·fy** (môr′tə fī) ***v.*** **1** to make ashamed or embarrassed [She was *mortified* when she forgot her speech.] **2** to control one's desires or feelings as by fasting or otherwise giving oneself pain [to *mortify* one's body]. —**mor′ti·fied, mor′ti·fy·ing —mor′ti·fi·ca′tion *n.***

**mor·tise** or **mor·tice** (môr′tis) ***n.*** a hole cut in a piece of wood, etc. so that a part (called a **tenon**) coming out from another piece will fit into it to form a joint. *See the picture.* ◆***v.*** to fasten with a mortise. —**mor′tised** or **mor′ticed, mor′tis·ing** or **mor′tic·ing**

**mor·tu·ar·y** (môr′choo wer′ē) ***n.*** a place where dead bodies are kept before the funeral. *—pl.* **mor′tu·ar′ies** ◆***adj.*** of death or funerals.

**Mo·sa·ic** (mō zā′ik) ***adj.*** of Moses [The code of laws in the Pentateuch, supposedly written down by Moses, is called the *Mosaic* law.]

**mo·sa·ic** (mō zā′ik) ***n.*** **1** a picture or design made by putting together small bits of colored stone, glass, etc. **2** the art of making such pictures and designs. **3** anything like a mosaic. ◆***adj.*** of, like, or forming a mosaic.

**Mos·cow** (mäs′kou *or* mäs′kō) the capital of the U.S.S.R., in the western part.

**Mo·ses** (mō′ziz) in the Bible, the man who led the Israelites out of slavery in Egypt and passed on to them laws from God.

☆**mo·sey** (mō′zē) ***v.*** **1** to stroll or shuffle along. **2** to go away. *This is a slang word.*

**Mos·lem** (mäz′ləm) ***n., adj.*** *another name for* **Muslim.**

**mosque** (mäsk) ***n.*** a Muslim place of worship. *See the picture.*

**mos·qui·to** (mə skēt′ō) ***n.*** a small insect with two wings. The female bites animals to suck their blood. Some mosquitoes spread diseases, as malaria. *—pl.* **mos·qui′toes** or **mos·qui′tos**

☆**mosquito net** a very fine cloth mesh or a curtain made of this, for keeping out mosquitoes: *also* **mosquito netting.**

**moss** (môs) ***n.*** **1** tiny green plants growing in clumps like velvet, on rocks, trees, etc. **2** one of these plants.

**moss·y** (môs′ē) ***adj.*** **1** covered with moss [a *mossy* rock]. **2** like moss [*mossy* green]. —**moss′i·er, moss′i·est —moss′i·ness *n.***

**most** (mōst) ***adj.*** **1** greatest in amount or degree: *used as the superlative of* **much** [Who won the *most* money?] **2** greatest in number; almost all: *used as the* *superlative of* **many** [*Most* children like candy.] ◆***n.*** **1** the greatest amount or degree [We spent *most* of our money.] **2** the greatest number: *used with a plural verb* [*Most* of us are going.] ◆***adv.*** **1** in or to the greatest degree or extent [The music pleased me *most*.] **Most** is also used before many adjectives and adverbs to form superlatives just as **more** is used to form comparatives [*most* horrible; *most* quickly]. **2** very [a *most* beautiful dress]. —**at most** or **at the most,** not more than. —**make the most of,** to use in the best way.

**-most** (mōst) *a suffix used in forming superlatives* [The *topmost* branch is the highest one.]

**most·ly** (mōst′lē) ***adv.*** mainly; chiefly.

**mote** (mōt) ***n.*** a speck, as of dust.

☆**mo·tel** (mō tel′) ***n.*** a hotel for those traveling by car, usually with a parking area easily reached from each room.

**moth** (môth) ***n.*** an insect like a butterfly, but usually smaller and less brightly colored. Moths fly mostly at night. One kind has larvae that eat holes in woolen cloth, fur, etc. —*pl.* **moths** (mô*th*z *or* môths)

**moth·ball** (môth′bôl) ***n.*** a small ball of a substance that gives off fumes which keep moths away from woolen clothes, furs, etc. ◆***adj.*** in storage [a *mothball* fleet]. —**in mothballs,** put into storage.

**moth-eat·en** (môth′ēt″n) ***adj.*** **1** having holes eaten in it by the larvae of moths [a *moth-eaten* coat]. **2** worn-out or out-of-date.

**moth·er** (mu*th*′ər) ***n.*** **1** a woman as she is related to her child or children; a female parent. **2** the origin, source, or cause of something [Virginia is the State known as the *mother* of Presidents.] **3** a nun who is the head of a convent, school, etc.: *the full name is* **mother superior.** ◆***adj.*** of, like, or as if from a mother [*mother* love; one's *mother* tongue]. ◆***v.*** to care for as a mother does. —**moth′er·hood** ***n.*** —**moth′er·less** ***adj.***

**moth·er-in-law** (mu*th*′ər ən lô′) ***n.*** the mother of one's wife or husband. —*pl.* **moth′ers-in-law′**

**moth·er·land** (mu*th*′ər land) ***n.*** **1** the country where one was born. **2** the country that one's ancestors came from.

**moth·er·ly** (mu*th*′ər lē) ***adj.*** of or like a mother [*motherly* care]. —**moth′er·li·ness** ***n.***

**moth·er-of-pearl** (mu*th*′ər əv purl′) ***n.*** the hard, pearly layer on the inside of some sea shells. It is used in making buttons, jewelry, etc.

☆**Mother's Day** the second Sunday in May, a day set aside (in the U.S.) in honor of mothers.

**mo·tif** (mō tēf′) ***n.*** a main theme or idea that is developed, or a figure that is repeated, in a work of art, music, or literature. *See the picture.*

**mo·tion** (mō′shən) ***n.*** **1** a moving from one place to another; movement [the car's forward *motion*]. **2** a moving of the head, a hand, etc., especially in a way that has meaning [He made a beckoning *motion*.] **3** a suggestion made at a meeting for the group to discuss and vote on [a *motion* to adjourn]. ◆***v.*** to move the hand, head, etc. so as to show what one means or wants [I *motioned* them to stop.] —**go through the motions,** to do something one has done over and over again, but without any purpose or meaning. —**in motion,** moving, working, etc.

**mo·tion·less** (mō′shən lis) ***adj.*** not moving.

**motion picture** **1** a series of pictures flashed on a screen quickly, one after another, so that the persons and things in them seem to move. **2** a story told in such pictures.

**motion sickness** sickness in which there is nausea, vomiting, and dizziness. It is caused by the motion of an aircraft, boat, etc.

**mo·ti·vate** (mōt′ə vāt) ***v.*** to give a motive to or be a motive for [Love *motivated* my actions.] —**mo′ti·vat·ed, mo′ti·vat·ing** —**mo′ti·va′tion** ***n.***

**mo·tive** (mō′tiv) ***n.*** **1** a desire, feeling, etc. that makes one do something [What was their *motive* for inviting us?] **2** *same as* **motif.** ◆***adj.*** of or causing motion [Engines supply *motive* power.]

SYNONYMS: **Motive** is used for any feeling or desire that causes one to do something [Greed was their only *motive* for stealing.] **Incentive** is used for something, often a reward, that encourages one to do a certain thing [The chance of getting a scholarship was his *incentive* for studying hard.]

**mot·ley** (mät′lē) ***adj.*** **1** of many colors [The clown wore a *motley* costume.] **2** made up of many different kinds or parts [a *motley* group]. ◆***n.*** a garment of many colors [a clown in *motley*].

**mo·to·cross** (mō′tō krôs′) ***n.*** a race for lightweight motorcycles over a cross-country course that has a number of obstacles.

**mo·tor** (mōt′ər) ***n.*** **1** a machine that uses electricity to make something move or work [the *motor* of an electric fan]. **2** an engine, especially a gasoline engine, as in an automobile. ◆***adj.*** **1** of or run by a motor [a *motor* vehicle]. **2** of, by, or for motor vehicles [a *motor* trip]. **3** causing motion [*Motor* nerves cause the muscles to move.] ◆***v.*** to travel by automobile: *no longer much used.*



☆**mo·tor·bike** (mōt′ər bīk) ***n.*** **1** a bicycle made to go by a motor. **2** a lightweight motorcycle. *This word is used only in everyday talk.*

**mo·tor·boat** (mōt′ər bōt) ***n.*** a boat made to go by a motor.

☆**mo·tor·cade** (mōt′ər kād) ***n.*** a line of automobiles moving along, usually for taking an important person from one place to another.

**Motorcade** is one of those words that are formed by joining together two or more words or parts of words. *Motorcade* was formed by taking *motor* and joining it to the last part of *cavalcade*.

**mo·tor·car** (mōt′ər kär) ***n.*** *another name for* **automobile.**

**mo·tor·cy·cle** (mōt′ər sī′k'l) ***n.*** a kind of very heavy bicycle that is run by a gasoline engine. *See the picture.* ◆***v.*** to ride a motorcycle. —**mo′tor·cy′cled, mo′tor·cy′cling** —**mo′tor·cy′clist** ***n.***

**mo·tor·ist** (mōt′ər ist) ***n.*** a person who drives an automobile or travels by automobile.

| | | | | | | | |
|---|---|---|---|---|---|---|---|
| **a** | fat | **ir** | here | **ou** | out | **zh** | leisure |
| **ā** | ape | **ī** | bite, fire | **u** | up | **ng** | ring |
| **ä** | car, lot | **ō** | go | **ur** | fur | | a *in* ago |
| **e** | ten | **ô** | law, horn | **ch** | chin | | e *in* agent |
| **er** | care | **oi** | oil | **sh** | she | ə = | i *in* unity |
| **ē** | even | **oo** | look | **th** | thin | | o *in* collect |
| **i** | hit | **ōō** | tool | ***th*** | then | | u *in* focus |

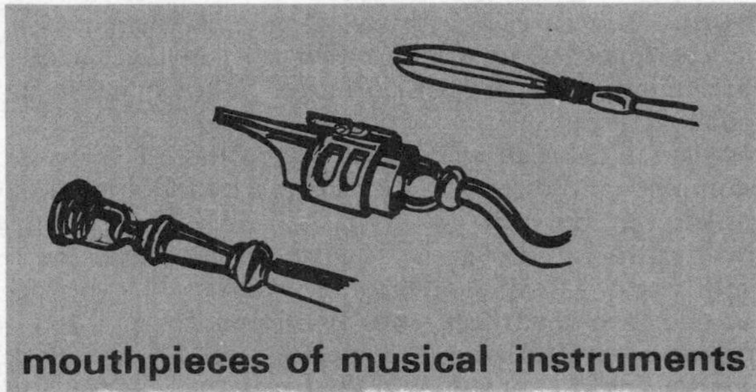
mouthpieces of musical instruments

☆**mo·tor·man** (mōt′ər mən) ***n.*** a person who drives an electric railway car. *—pl.* **mo′tor·men**

**Mott** (mät), **Lu·cre·tia** (lo͞o krē′shə) 1793–1880; U.S. abolitionist and leader in the women's rights movement.

**mot·tle** (mät′'l) ***v.*** to mark with spots or blotches of different colors. **—mot′tled, mot′tling**

**mot·to** (mät′ō) ***n.*** **1** a brief saying used as a rule to live by ["Honesty is the best policy" was his *motto*.] **2** a word or phrase chosen to show the goals or ideals of a nation, club, etc. and marked or written on a seal, flag, coin, etc. ["Don't tread on me!" was the *motto* on the flag.] *—pl.* **mot′toes** or **mot′tos**

**mould** (mōld), **mould·er** (mōl′dər), **mould·ing** (mōl′diŋ), **mould·y** (mōl′dē) *mainly British spelling of* **mold, molder, molding, moldy.**

 **moult** (mōlt) ***v.*** *mainly British spelling of* **molt.**

**mound** (mound) ***n.*** **1** a heap or bank of earth, sand, etc.; little hill. ☆**2** the slightly raised place from which a baseball pitcher throws.

**Mound Builders** the early Indian peoples who built the burial mounds, forts, and other earthworks found in the Middle West and the Southeast.

**mount**[1] (mount) ***n.*** a mountain or hill: *used in poetry or as part of a name* [*Mount* Everest].

**mount**[2] (mount) ***v.*** **1** to climb or go up [to *mount* stairs]. **2** to get up on [to *mount* a bicycle]. **3** to provide with a horse or horses [Troops that are *mounted* are called cavalry.] **4** to increase or rise [The flood waters are *mounting*. Profits *mounted*.] **5** to place, fix, or arrange on or in a support, backing, etc., as a gem in a setting, a picture in a scrapbook, or a cannon on a carriage. **6** to furnish the costumes, settings, etc. for [to *mount* a play]. **7** to get ready and carry on [to *mount* a campaign]. **8** to be armed with [This ship *mounts* six cannon.] ◆***n.*** **1** a horse for riding. **2** the support, setting, etc. on or in which something is mounted.

**moun·tain** (moun′t'n) ***n.*** **1** a part of the earth's surface that rises high into the air; very high hill. **2 mountains,** *pl.* a chain or group of such high hills: *also called* **mountain chain** *or* **mountain range. 3** a large heap [a *mountain* of trash]. ◆***adj.*** of, on, or in mountains.

**mountain ash** a small tree with clusters of white flowers and red or orange berries.

**moun·tain·eer** (moun t'n ir′) ***n.*** **1** a person who lives in a region of mountains. **2** a person who climbs mountains. ◆***v.*** to climb mountains, as for sport.

☆**mountain goat** *another name for* **Rocky Mountain goat.**

☆**mountain laurel** an evergreen shrub with pink and white flowers and shiny leaves, growing in eastern North America.

☆**mountain lion** *another name for* **cougar.**

**moun·tain·ous** (moun′t'n əs) ***adj.*** **1** full of mountains [a *mountainous* region]. **2** very large [a *mountainous* debt].

☆**Mountain Standard Time** *see* **Standard Time.**

**moun·te·bank** (moun′tə baŋk) ***n.*** a person who cheats or tricks people, as by telling them lies; charlatan or quack.

The word **mountebank** was first used of any person who got up on a bench or platform, in a public place, and sold quack medicines, usually attracting an audience by tricks, stories, etc. **Mountebank** comes from Italian words meaning "to mount a bench."

**Mount Ver·non** (vʉr′nən) the home of George Washington, in Virginia, near Washington, D.C.

**mourn** (môrn) ***v.*** to be sad or show sorrow over someone's death, a loss, etc. **—mourn′er *n.***

**mourn·ful** (môrn′fəl) ***adj.*** showing or causing sorrow or grief; sad. **—mourn′ful·ly *adv.***

**mourn·ing** (môr′niŋ) ***n.*** **1** the showing of sorrow, as when someone dies. **2** black clothes, a black armband, etc. worn to show sorrow at someone's death.

☆**mourning dove** a wild dove of the U.S. whose cooing sounds mournful.

**mouse** (mous) ***n.*** **1** a small, gnawing animal found in houses and fields throughout the world. **2** a timid person. *—pl.* **mice** (mīs) ◆***v.*** (mouz) to hunt for mice. **—moused, mous′ing**

**mouse·trap** (mous′trap) ***n.*** a trap for catching mice.

**mousse** (mo͞os) ***n.*** a light chilled or frozen dessert, made of whipped cream, gelatin, etc.

**mous·tache** (mə stash′ *or* mus′tash) ***n.*** *another spelling for* **mustache.**

**mous·y** or **mous·ey** (mou′sē *or* mou′zē) ***adj.*** quiet, timid, shy, etc. **—mous′i·er, mous′i·est**

**mouth** (mouth) ***n.*** **1** the opening in an animal's head through which food is taken in and sounds are made; also, the space behind this opening, which contains the tongue and teeth. **2** any opening thought of as like the mouth [the *mouth* of a river; the *mouth* of a jar]. *—pl.* **mouths** (mouthz) ◆***v.*** (mouth) **1** to say in a showy, unnatural way [to *mouth* speeches in a play]. **2** to hold or rub with the mouth. **—down at the mouth,** depressed; discouraged: *used only in everyday talk.* **—have a big mouth,** to talk too loud, too much, or too boldly: *a slang phrase.*

**mouth·ful** (mouth′fo͝ol) ***n.*** **1** as much as the mouth can hold. **2** as much as is usually put into the mouth at one time. *—pl.* **mouth′fuls**

**mouth organ** ☆*another name for* **harmonica.**

**mouth·part** (mouth′pärt) ***n.*** a part or organ around the mouth in insects, crustaceans, etc. that is used for biting, holding, etc.

**mouth·piece** (mouth′pēs) ***n.*** **1** a part held in or near the mouth [the *mouthpiece* of a trumpet, pipe, or telephone]. *See the picture.* **2** a person, newspaper, etc. that is used by some other person or persons to express their ideas.

**mouth·wash** (mouth′wôsh) ***n.*** a liquid with flavoring, used for rinsing the mouth or gargling. It often has an antiseptic in it.

**mov·a·ble** or **move·a·ble** (mo͞o'və b'l) ***adj.*** **1** that can be moved; not fixed [*movable* shelves]. **2** changing in date from one year to the next [Thanksgiving is a *movable* holiday.] ◆***n.*** **movables,** *pl.* movable things, especially furniture.

**move** (mo͞ov) ***v.*** **1** to change the place or position of [*Move* the lamp closer. Can you *move* your legs?] **2** to change place or position [Please *move* to the left. Your head *moved* a little.] **3** to turn, work, revolve, stir, etc. [The steering wheel *moves* the front wheels of the car.] **4** to change the place where one lives [They *moved* to another city.] **5** to cause; give a reason for [What *moved* you to buy a car?] **6** to cause to have strong feelings [Your plea *moved* me deeply.] **7** to go forward; make progress [This book *moves* slowly.] **8** to begin to act or cause to act [Fresh troops *moved* against the enemy. Laxatives *move* the bowels.] **9** to suggest or propose, as in a meeting [I *move* that we accept their offer.] **10** to change the position of a piece in chess, checkers, etc. —**moved, mov'ing** ◆***n.*** **1** the act of moving; movement [Don't make a *move!*] **2** an action toward getting something done [the city's latest *move* in its housing program]. **3** the act of moving a piece in checkers, chess, etc.; also, a player's turn to move. —☆**get a move on, 1** to start moving. **2** to go faster. *This is a slang phrase.* —**on the move,** moving about from place to place: *used only in everyday talk.*

**move·ment** (mo͞ov'mənt) ***n.*** **1** the act of moving or a way of moving [a *movement* of the branches; the regular *movement* of the stars]. **2** a working together to bring about some result [the *movement* for world peace]. **3** a getting rid of waste matter in the bowels. **4** the moving parts of a watch, clock, etc. **5** one of the main sections of a long piece of music, as of a symphony.

**mov·er** (mo͞ov'ər) ***n.*** a person or thing that moves; especially, ☆one whose work is moving people's furniture from one home to another.

☆**mov·ie** (mo͞ov'ē) ***n.*** *another name for* **motion picture.** —**the movies, 1** the business of making motion pictures. **2** a showing of a motion picture [an evening at *the movies*].

**mov·ing** (mo͞ov'iŋ) ***adj.*** **1** that moves or causes movement [a *moving* car; the *moving* spirit behind the revolt]. **2** that makes one feel sad or full of pity [a *moving* plea for help].

SYNONYMS: Something is **moving** if it arouses or stirs the feelings, especially feelings of pity or sorrow [a *moving* story about the flood victims]. Something is **poignant** if it has a sharp and painful effect on the feelings [the *poignant* cry of a lost child]. Something is **touching** if it arouses tender feelings, as of being sympathetic or grateful [a *touching* gift of food to a poor family].

**moving picture** *another name for* **motion picture.**

**mow**[1] (mō) ***v.*** **1** to cut down grass or grain with a lawn mower, sickle, etc. **2** to cut grass or grain from [to *mow* a lawn]. —**mowed, mowed** or **mown** (mōn), **mow'ing** —**mow down,** to cause to fall like grass or grain being cut; knock down [to *mow down* pins in bowling].

**mow**[2] (mou) ***n.*** **1** a pile of hay, grain, etc., especially in a barn. **2** the part of a barn where hay, grain, etc. is stored.

**mow·er** (mō'ər) ***n.*** a person or machine that mows [a lawn *mower*].

**Mo·zam·bique** (mō zəm bēk') a country in southeastern Africa.

**Mo·zart** (mō'tsärt), **Wolf·gang A·ma·de·us** (vôlf'gäŋk ä'mä dā'oos) 1756–1791; Austrian composer.

**M.P. 1** Member of Parliament. **2** Military Police. **3** Mounted Police.

**mpg** or **m.p.g.** miles per gallon.

**mph** or **m.p.h.** miles per hour.

**Mr.** (mis'tər) mister: *used before the name of a man or his title* [*Mr.* Shapiro; *Mr.* Secretary]. —*pl.* **Messrs.** (mes'ərz)

**Mrs.** (mis'iz) mistress: *used before the name of a married woman.* —*pl.* **Mmes.** (mā däm')

**MS** *abbreviation for* **Mississippi, multiple sclerosis.**

**MS** or **ms.** *abbreviation for* **manuscript.** —*pl.* **MSS** or **mss.**

☆**Ms.** (miz *or* em'es') a title used before the name of a woman instead of either *Miss* or *Mrs.* [*Ms.* Bell].

**M.S.** or **M.Sc.** Master of Science.

**Msgr.** *abbreviation for* **Monsignor.**

**MST, M.S.T.** Mountain Standard Time.

**MT** *abbreviation for* **Montana.**

**Mt.** or **mt.** *abbreviation for* **mount, mountain.** —*pl.* **Mts.** or **mts.**

**mtg.** *abbreviation for* **meeting, mortgage.**

**much** (much) ***adj.*** great in amount or degree [*much* applause; *much* joy]. —The comparative of *much* is **more,** the superlative is **most.** ◆***n.*** **1** a great amount [We learned *much* from the teacher.] **2** something great or important [Our car is not *much* to look at.] ◆***adv.*** **1** to a great extent [I feel *much* happier.] **2** just about; almost [The patient is *much* the same.] —**as much as, 1** to the degree that. **2** nearly; practically; virtually [They *as much as* told us to leave.] —**make much of,** to treat as if very important.



**mu·ci·lage** (myo͞o's'l ij) ***n.*** ☆a sticky substance, such as glue, for making things stick together.

**muck** (muk) ***n.*** **1** black earth with rotting leaves, etc. in it, used as fertilizer. **2** wet earth; mud. **3** moist manure. **4** any dirt or filth.

**muck·rake** (muk'rāk) ***v.*** ☆to search out dishonest acts of public officials, business people, etc. and make them known, as in newspapers. —**muck'raked, muck'rak·ing** —☆**muck'rak·er** ***n.***

**mu·cous** (myo͞o'kəs) ***adj.*** **1** of, having, or giving off mucus. **2** like mucus; slimy.

**mucous membrane** the moist skin that lines body cavities that open to the air, as the mouth, nose, etc.

**mu·cus** (myo͞o'kəs) ***n.*** the thick, slimy substance given off by mucous membranes. Mucus protects the membranes by keeping them moist.

**mud** (mud) ***n.*** wet earth that is soft and sticky.

| | | | | | | | |
|---|---|---|---|---|---|---|---|
| a | fat | ir | here | ou | out | zh | leisure |
| ā | ape | ī | bite, fire | u | up | ŋ | ring |
| ä | car, lot | ō | go | ʉr | fur | | a *in* ago |
| e | ten | ô | law, horn | ch | chin | | e *in* agent |
| er | care | oi | oil | sh | she | ə = | i *in* unity |
| ē | even | oo | look | th | thin | | o *in* collect |
| i | hit | o͞o | tool | *th* | then | | u *in* focus |

**mud·dle** (mud′'l) ***v.*** **1** to mix up; confuse [to *muddle* a discussion]. **2** to act or think in a confused way [to *muddle* through a hard day at work]. **—mud′dled, mud′dling** ✦***n.*** a confused or mixed-up condition; mess.

**mud·dy** (mud′ē) ***adj.*** **1** full of mud or smeared with mud [a *muddy* yard; *muddy* boots]. **2** not clear; cloudy [*muddy* coffee]. **3** confused [*muddy* thinking]. **—mud′di·er, mud′di·est** ✦***v.*** to make or become muddy. **—mud′died, mud′dy·ing**

☆**mud puppy** a North American salamander that lives in mud under water.

**mu·ez·zin** (myo͞o ez′in) ***n.*** a Muslim crier who calls the people to prayer at the proper hours.

**muff** (muf) ***n.*** **1** a covering, as of fur, in the shape of a tube, into which the hands are placed from either end for keeping them warm. *See the picture.* **2** any clumsy or bungling act. ✦***v.*** to do something badly or in a clumsy way; especially, to miss a catch or bungle a play, as in baseball.

**muf·fin** (muf′in) ***n.*** a kind of bread baked in small cups and usually eaten hot.

**muf·fle** (muf′'l) ***v.*** **1** to wrap up or cover closely so as to keep warm, hide, protect, etc. [*muffled* up in a scarf against the cold]. **2** to cover so as to deaden sound [rowing with *muffled* oars to surprise the enemy]. **3** to make less loud or less clear [Heavy shutters *muffled* the sounds from the street.] **—muf′-**



**fled, muf′fling**

**muf·fler** (muf′lər) ***n.*** **1** a scarf worn around the throat for warmth. **2** a thing used to deaden noise, as ☆a part fastened to the exhaust pipe of an automobile engine. *See the picture.*

**muf·ti** (muf′tē) ***n.*** ordinary clothes, especially when worn by one who usually wears a uniform.

**mug** (mug) ***n.*** **1** a heavy drinking cup with a handle. **2** as much as a mug will hold. **3** the face: *slang in this meaning.* ✦***v.*** **1** to assault someone from behind, usually in order to rob. **2** to make faces, as some actors do to make the audience laugh: *slang in this meaning.* **—mugged, mug′ging —mug′ger *n.***

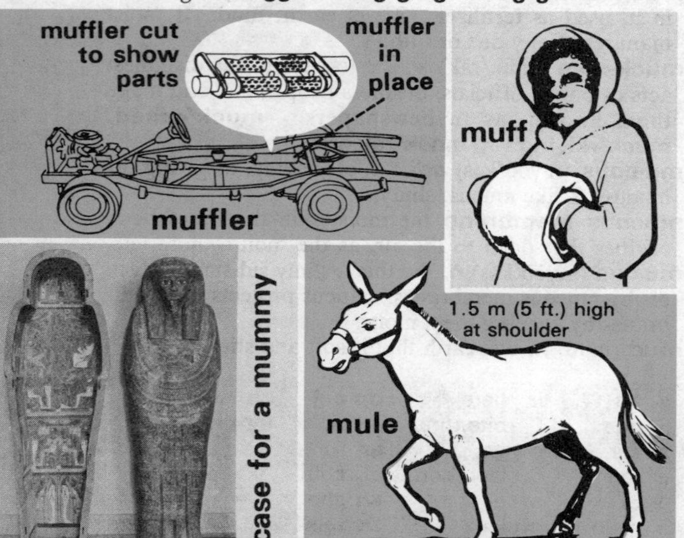


**mug·gy** (mug′ē) ***adj.*** hot and damp, with little or no stirring of the air; close [*muggy* weather]. **—mug′gi·er, mug′gi·est —mug′gi·ness *n.***

☆**mug·wump** (mug′wump) ***n.*** a person who is independent and does not take sides, especially in politics.

**Mu·ham·mad** (mo͞o ham′əd) *same as* **Mohammed.**

☆**muk·luk** (muk′luk) ***n.*** **1** an Eskimo boot made of sealskin or reindeer skin. **2** a boot like this made of canvas and rubber.

**mu·lat·to** (mə lat′ō *or* myo͞o lat′ō) ***n.*** a person who has one black parent and one white parent: *this word is no longer much used.* *—pl.* **mu·lat′toes**

**mul·ber·ry** (mul′ber′ē) ***n.*** **1** a tree that bears fruits that look like the raspberry. **2** the fruit, which can be eaten. **3** purplish red. *—pl.* **mul′ber′ries**

**mulch** (mulch) ***n.*** leaves, straw, peat, etc. spread on the ground around plants to keep the moisture in the soil or to keep the roots from freezing. ✦***v.*** to spread mulch around.

**mulct** (mulkt) ***v.*** **1** to take away from, as by cheating or tricking [The members of the credit union were *mulcted* of their savings.] **2** to punish by a fine. ✦***n.*** a fine or penalty.

**mule**[1] (myo͞ol) ***n.*** **1** the offspring of a donkey and a horse. *See the picture.* **2** a stubborn person: *used only in everyday talk.* **3** a machine that spins cotton fibers into yarn and winds the yarn on spindles.

**mule**[2] (myo͞ol) ***n.*** a slipper that leaves the heel uncovered, for wearing around the house.

**mu·le·teer** (myo͞o lə tir′) ***n.*** a driver of mules.

**mul·ish** (myo͞ol′ish) ***adj.*** like a mule; stubborn.

**mull**[1] (mul) ***v.*** to think over; ponder: *used only in everyday talk* [to *mull* over the plan].

**mull**[2] (mul) ***v.*** to heat cider, wine, etc. and add sugar and spices to it.

**mul·lein** (mul′in) ***n.*** a tall plant with spikes of yellow, lavender, or white flowers.

**mul·let** (mul′it) ***n.*** a fish found both in the sea and in fresh water, used as food. Some kinds have silvery scales and others reddish scales.

**multi-** *a prefix meaning:* **1** having many [A *multicolored* scarf has many colors in it.] **2** more than two [A *multilateral* agreement is one entered into by several nations.] **3** many times more than [A *multimillionaire* has many times more than a million dollars.]

**mul·ti·col·ored** (mul′ti kul′ərd) ***adj.*** having many colors.

**mul·ti·far·i·ous** (mul′tə far′ē əs) ***adj.*** of many kinds; taking many forms; varied.

**mul·ti·lat·er·al** (mul′ti lat′ər əl) ***adj.*** **1** having many sides. **2** among more than two nations [a *multilateral* treaty].

**mul·ti·me·di·a** (mul′ti mē′dē ə) ***n.*** *another name for* **mixed media.**

☆**mul·ti·mil·lion·aire** (mul′ti mil′yə ner′) ***n.*** a person who has at least several million dollars, francs, pounds, etc.; extremely wealthy person.

**mul·ti·na·tion·al** (mul′ti nash′ə n'l) ***adj.*** of or having to do with a number of nations. ✦***n.*** a corporation that has branches in a number of countries.

**mul·ti·ple** (mul′tə p'l) ***adj.*** of or made up of a number of parts, elements, etc. [Twins, triplets, etc. are *multiple* births.] ✦***n.*** a number that contains another number an exact number of times, with no remainder [18 is a *multiple* of 9, and also of 2, 3, and 6.]

☆**mul·ti·ple-choice** (mul′tə p'l chois′) ***adj.*** that is or has to do with a test made up of questions for which only one of several possible answers to be chosen is correct.

**multiple scle·ro·sis** (skli rō′sis) a disease in which the most important nerves of the body are damaged. It causes defects in speech, loss of control of the muscles, etc.

**mul·ti·pli·cand** (mul′tə pli kand′) ***n.*** the number that is to be multiplied by another; number that stands above the multiplier.

**mul·ti·pli·ca·tion** (mul′tə pli kā′shən) ***n.*** a multiplying or being multiplied; especially, a method used to find the result of adding a certain figure to itself a certain number of times.

**mul·ti·plic·i·ty** (mul′tə plis′ə tē) ***n.*** a great number or variety [a *multiplicity* of plans].

**mul·ti·pli·er** (mul′tə plī′ər) ***n.*** **1** the number by which another number is multiplied; number that stands below the multiplicand. **2** a person or thing that multiplies, or increases.

**mul·ti·ply** (mul′tə plī) ***v.*** **1** to become more, greater, etc.; increase [Our troubles *multiplied.*] **2** to repeat a certain figure a certain number of times [If you *multiply* 10 by 4, or repeat 10 four times, you get the product 40.] —**mul′ti·plied, mul′ti·ply·ing**

**mul·ti·stage** (mul′ti stāj′) ***adj.*** having more than one stage, as a rocket or missile that has several systems to propel it. Each system is dropped in stages after it is used.

**mul·ti·tude** (mul′tə to͞od *or* mul′tə tyo͞od) ***n.*** a large number of persons or things; crowd.

**mul·ti·tu·di·nous** (mul′tə to͞od′'n əs *or* mul′tə tyo͞od′'n əs) ***adj.*** very many; numerous.

☆**mum**[1] (mum) ***n.*** *a shorter form of* **chrysanthemum**: *used only in everyday talk.*

**mum**[2] (mum) ***adj.*** not speaking; silent [Keep *mum.*] —**mum's the word,** don't say anything.

**mum·ble** (mum′b'l) ***v.*** to speak or say in a way hard to hear, as with the mouth partly closed. *See* SYNONYMS *at* **murmur.** —**mum′bled, mum′bling** ◆***n.*** mumbled talk or sound.

**mum·ble·ty·peg** (mum′b'l tē peg′) ***n.*** a game in which a jackknife is tossed in various ways to make it land with the blade in the ground.

**mum·mer** (mum′ər) ***n.*** **1** a person who wears a mask or costume for fun, as for acting out pantomimes. **2** any actor.

**mum·mer·y** (mum′ər ē) ***n.*** **1** the acting done by mummers. **2** any foolish ritual that cannot be taken seriously. —*pl.* **mum′mer·ies**

**mum·mi·fy** (mum′ə fī) ***v.*** **1** to make into a mummy. **2** to shrivel or dry up. —**mum′mi·fied, mum′mi·fy·ing**

**mum·my** (mum′ē) ***n.*** a dead body kept from rotting by being treated with chemicals, as was done by the ancient Egyptians. *See the picture.* —*pl.* **mum′mies**

**mumps** (mumps) ***n.pl.*** a disease that causes the swelling of certain glands, especially in the jaw below each ear: *used with a singular verb* [*Mumps* is catching.]

> **Mumps** comes from an old word *mump,* which meant a twisting of the face. The person who has mumps often has a strange, distorted appearance.

**munch** (munch) ***v.*** to chew in a noisy, steady way [Rabbits *munch* carrots.]

**mun·dane** (mun′dān) ***adj.*** of the world, not of heaven, the spirit, etc.; worldly; everyday; ordinary [the *mundane* affairs of business].

**Mu·nich** (myo͞o′nik) a city in southeastern West Germany.

**mu·nic·i·pal** (myoo nis′ə p'l) ***adj.*** of or having to do with a city or town, or its government.

**mu·nic·i·pal·i·ty** (myoo nis′ə pal′ə tē) ***n.*** a city or town that has self-government in local matters. —*pl.* **mu·nic′i·pal′i·ties**

**mu·nif·i·cent** (myoo nif′ə s'nt) ***adj.*** very generous; lavish [a *munificent* reward]. —**mu·nif′i·cence *n.*** —**mu·nif′i·cent·ly *adv.***

**mu·ni·tions** (myoo nish′ənz) ***n.pl.*** war supplies; especially, weapons and ammunition.

**mu·ral** (myoor′əl) ***n.*** a picture or photograph, especially a large one, painted or put on a wall. ◆***adj.*** of or on a wall [a *mural* painting].

**mur·der** (mur′dər) ***n.*** **1** the unlawful killing of one person by another, especially when done on purpose or while committing another crime. **2** something very hard or unsafe to do or deal with: *used only in everyday talk* [Running in this heat is *murder.*] ◆***v.*** **1** to kill in an unlawful way. *See* SYNONYMS *at* **kill. 2** to spoil something as by doing it badly [They *murdered* the song they sang.]

**mur·der·er** (mur′dər ər) ***n.*** a person who is guilty of murder.

**mur·der·ess** (mur′dər əs) ***n.*** a woman who is guilty of murder.



**mur·der·ous** (mur′dər əs) ***adj.*** **1** of or like murder; brutal [a *murderous* act]. **2** guilty of murder or ready to murder [a *murderous* beast]. **3** very difficult, dangerous, etc.: *used only in everyday talk* [a *murderous* trip through snow and ice].

**murk** (murk) ***n.*** darkness; gloom.

**murk·y** (mur′kē) ***adj.*** **1** dark or gloomy [a *murky* cave]. **2** heavy and dim with smoke, fog, mist, etc. [the *murky* air]. —**murk′i·er, murk′i·est** —**murk′i·ness *n.***

**Mur·mansk** (moor mänsk′) a seaport in the northwestern U.S.S.R., on the Barents Sea.

**mur·mur** (mur′mər) ***n.*** **1** a low, steady sound, as of voices far away. **2** a complaint made in a very low voice. ◆***v.*** **1** to make a low, steady sound [The wind *murmured* through the trees.] **2** to speak or complain in a very low voice.

> SYNONYMS: **Murmur** suggests an unbroken flow of words in a low voice and may show that one is pleased or not pleased [to *murmur* prayers]. **Mutter** usually suggests words spoken when one is angry or discontented [to *mutter* curses]. **Mumble** suggests words spoken with the mouth almost closed so that they are hard to hear [We were so sleepy we *mumbled* our farewell.]

| | | | | | | | |
|---|---|---|---|---|---|---|---|
| **a** | fat | **ir** | here | **ou** | out | **zh** | leisure |
| **ā** | ape | **ī** | bite, fire | **u** | up | **ng** | ring |
| **ä** | car, lot | **ō** | go | **ur** | fur | | a *in* ago |
| **e** | ten | **ô** | law, horn | **ch** | chin | | e *in* agent |
| **er** | care | **oi** | oil | **sh** | she | **ə** = | i *in* unity |
| **ē** | even | **oo** | look | **th** | thin | | o *in* collect |
| **i** | hit | **o͞o** | tool | ***th*** | then | | u *in* focus |

**mur·rain** (mur′in) ***n.*** **1** a disease of cattle that is catching. **2** a plague: *now seldom used in this meaning.*

**mus.** *abbreviation for* **museum, music.**

**mus·ca·tel** (mus kə tel′) ***n.*** a rich, sweet wine.

**mus·cle** (mus′′l) ***n.*** **1** the tissue in an animal's body that makes up the fleshy parts. Muscle can be stretched or tightened to move the parts of the body. *See the picture.* **2** any single part or band of this tissue [The biceps is a *muscle* in the upper arm.] **3** strength that comes from muscles that are developed; brawn.

> **Muscle** comes from a Latin word meaning "little mouse." A muscle when it moves was thought to look like a small mouse when it moves.

**mus·cu·lar** (mus′kyoo lər) ***adj.*** **1** of, made up of, or done by a muscle or muscles [*muscular* effort]. **2** with muscles that are well developed; strong [*muscular* legs].

**muscular dys·tro·phy** (dis′trə fē) a disease in which the muscles waste away little by little.

**mus·cu·la·ture** (mus′kyə lə chər) ***n.*** the way in which the muscles of the body or of some part of the body are arranged.

**Muse** (myo͞oz) ***n.*** **1** any one of the nine Greek goddesses of the arts and sciences. **2 muse,** the spirit that is thought to give ideas and feelings to a poet or other artist.



**muse** (myo͞oz) ***v.*** to think about various things in a quiet, slow way. —**mused, mus′ing**

**mu·se·um** (myo͞o zē′əm) ***n.*** a building or room for keeping and showing objects that are important in history, art, or science, as paintings, tools, stuffed animals, machines, etc.

**mush**[1] (mush) ***n.*** **1** cornmeal boiled in water or milk. **2** any thick, soft mass.

**mush**[2] (mush) ***interj.*** in Canada and Alaska, a shout urging sled dogs to start or to go faster. ◆***v.*** to travel over snow, as with a dog sled.

> **Mush**[2] probably comes from the phrase "Mush on!" meaning "Go on!" which is a changing into English of the French word *marchons,* which means "Let's go!"

**mush·room** (mush′ro͞om) ***n.*** a small, fleshy fungus that grows very fast and has a stalk topped with a cap of various shapes. *See the picture.* Some kinds can be eaten, unlike the poisonous ones, which are often called *toadstools.* ◆***adj.*** of or like a mushroom [the *mushroom* cloud of an atom bomb]. ◆***v.*** to grow and spread out rapidly like a mushroom.

**mush·y** (mush′ē) ***adj.*** **1** thick and soft, like mush. **2** showing love or affection in a silly way: *used only in everyday talk.* —**mush′i·er, mush′i·est**

**mu·sic** (myo͞o′zik) ***n.*** **1** the art of putting tones together in various melodies, rhythms, and harmonies to form compositions for singing or playing on instruments [She teaches *music.*] **2** such a composition or compositions, especially as written down in notes [Did you remember to bring your *music?*] **3** any series of pleasing sounds [the *music* of birds]. —☆**face the music,** to accept the results, no matter how unpleasant: *used only in everyday talk.* —**set to music,** to compose music for, as a poem.

**mu·si·cal** (myo͞o′zi k′l) ***adj.*** **1** of music or for making music [a *musical* score; a *musical* instrument]. **2** like music; full of melody, harmony, etc. [Wind has a *musical* sound.] **3** fond of music or skilled in music. **4** containing songs, dances, etc. [a *musical* comedy]. ◆***n.*** ☆a musical comedy. —**mu′si·cal·ly *adv.***

☆**mu·si·cale** (myo͞o zə kal′) ***n.*** a party where the guests listen to music.

**music box** a box that contains a bar with a row of steel teeth that produce a series of tones. These teeth are struck by pins arranged on a roller to produce a certain tune when the roller is turned, as by a clockwork. *See the picture.*

**music hall** an auditorium in which operas, concerts, and other musical productions are held.

**mu·si·cian** (myo͞o zish′ən) ***n.*** a person skilled in music, as a composer or one who plays a musical instrument or sings, especially for a living.

**musk** (musk) ***n.*** **1** a substance got from a gland of the male musk deer. It has a strong smell and is used in making perfumes. **2** the smell of this substance.

**musk deer** a small deer without horns found in central Asia.

☆**mus·kel·lunge** (mus′kə lunj) ***n.*** a very large fish related to the pike, found especially in the Great Lakes: *also called* **mus·kie** (mus′kē). —*pl.* **mus′kel·lunge**

**mus·ket** (mus′kit) ***n.*** a gun with a long barrel, used before the rifle was invented.

> **Musket** comes from an old Italian word that was originally used for another kind of weapon, an arrow with feathers that was shot from a crossbow. The Italian word came from the Latin word for "a fly."

**mus·ket·eer** (mus kə tir′) ***n.*** in earlier times, a soldier armed with a musket.

**mus·ket·ry** (mus′kə trē) ***n.*** **1** the firing of muskets. **2** muskets or musketeers as a group.

**musk·mel·on** (musk′mel′ən) ***n.*** a round melon with a thick, rough rind and sweet, juicy flesh. One kind is called *cantaloupe.*

**musk ox** a sturdy ox that lives in the arctic. It has long hair and long, curved horns.

☆**musk·rat** (musk′rat) ***n.*** **1** a North American animal that is like a large rat. It lives in water and has glossy brown fur. *See the picture.* **2** its fur.

**musk·y** (mus′kē) ***adj.*** of or like musk [a *musky* odor]. —**musk′i·er, musk′i·est** —**musk′i·ness *n.***

**Mus·lim** (muz′lim *or* mooz′lim) ***n.*** a believer in the religion of Islam. ◆***adj.*** of Islam or the Muslims.

**mus·lin** (muz′lin) ***n.*** a strong, often thin, cotton cloth used for sheets, pillowcases, etc.

> Fabrics often get their names from the place of origin. **Muslin** comes from the Arabic name of *Mosul,* a city in Iraq where muslin was originally made.

**muss** (mus) ***v.*** to make untidy, messy, etc. [The wind *mussed* her hair.]

**mus·sel** (mus′′l) ***n.*** a water animal having a soft body enclosed in two shells hinged together. Saltwater mussels are used as food, while the shells of fresh-water mussels were formerly used to make buttons.

**Mus·so·li·ni** (moos′ə lē′nē), **Be·ni·to** (be nē′tō) 1883–1945; Fascist dictator of Italy from 1922 to 1943.

**muss·y** (mus′ē) ***adj.*** messy, untidy, rumpled, etc.: *used only in everyday talk.* —**muss′i·er, muss′i·est**

**must** (must) *a helping verb used with other verbs and meaning:* **1** to be obliged to; to have to [I *must* pay the bill.] **2** to be likely or certain to [It *must* be five o'clock.] ◆***n.*** something that must be done, read, seen, etc.: *used only in everyday talk* [This book is a *must.*]

**mus·tache** (mə stash′ *or* mus′tash) ***n.*** **1** the hair that a man has let grow out on his upper lip. **2** the hair or bristles growing around an animal's mouth.

**mus·ta·chi·o** (məs tä′shō *or* mus tä′shē ō) ***n.*** a man's mustache, especially a large, bushy one. —*pl.* **mus·ta′-chi·os**

☆**mus·tang** (mus′taŋ) ***n.*** a small wild or half-wild horse of the Southwest plains of the U.S.

**mus·tard** (mus′tərd) ***n.*** **1** a plant with yellow flowers and slender pods with round seeds. **2** a dark yellow powder or paste made from its hot-tasting seeds and used as a seasoning for food.

**mus·ter** (mus′tər) ***v.*** **1** to bring or come together; gather [to *muster* troops for roll call]. **2** to gather up; summon [She *mustered* up her strength.] ◆***n.*** **1** a gathering together, as of troops for inspection. **2** the persons or things gathered together. **3** the list of soldiers, sailors, etc. in a unit. —☆**muster out,** to discharge from military service. —**pass muster,** to be approved after being inspected.

**must·n't** (mus′′nt) must not.

**mus·ty** (mus′tē) ***adj.*** **1** having a stale, moldy smell or taste [a *musty* attic; *musty* bread]. **2** worn-out or out-of-date [*musty* ideas]. —**mus′ti·er, mus′ti·est** —**mus′ti·ness *n.***

**mu·ta·ble** (myo͞ot′ə b'l) ***adj.*** that can be changed; liable to change [*mutable* laws]. —**mu′ta·bil′i·ty *n.***

**mu·ta·tion** (myo͞o tā′shən) ***n.*** **1** a change, as in form. **2** the appearance in a plant or animal of a characteristic that has not been found in its species, and that may be passed on by heredity.

**mute** (myo͞ot) ***adj.*** **1** not able to speak. **2** not speaking or making any sounds; silent [He sat there *mute* and unmoving.] **3** not pronounced; silent [The *e* in "mouse" is *mute.*] ◆***n.*** **1** a person who cannot speak; especially, a deaf-mute. **2** a device used to soften or muffle the tone of a musical instrument, as a block placed in the bell of a trumpet. *See the picture.* ◆***v.*** to soften or muffle the sound of, as with a mute. —**mut′ed, mut′ing** —**mute′ly *adv.***

**mu·ti·late** (myo͞ot′′l āt) ***v.*** to hurt or damage seriously by cutting or breaking off a necessary part or parts [to *mutilate* a hand by removing a finger; to *mutilate* a book by tearing out pages]. *See* SYNONYMS *at* **maim.** —**mu′ti·lat·ed, mu′ti·lat·ing** —**mu′ti·la′tion *n.***

**mu·ti·neer** (myo͞ot 'n ir′) ***n.*** a person who takes part in a mutiny.

**mu·ti·nous** (myo͞ot′′n əs) ***adj.*** taking part or likely to take part in a mutiny; rebellious.

**mu·ti·ny** (myo͞ot′′n ē) ***n.*** a resisting or fighting against the leaders of a group; especially, a rebellion by sailors or soldiers against their officers. —*pl.* **mu′ti·nies** ◆***v.*** to take part in a mutiny; revolt. —**mu′ti·nied, mu′ti·ny·ing**

☆**mutt** (mut) ***n.*** a mongrel dog: *a slang word.*

**mut·ter** (mut′ər) ***v.*** **1** to speak or say in low tones, with the lips almost closed, as in talking to oneself. **2** to complain or grumble [People *mutter* about high taxes.] *See* SYNONYMS *at* **murmur.** ◆***n.*** a speaking in low tones; muttering; also, something muttered.

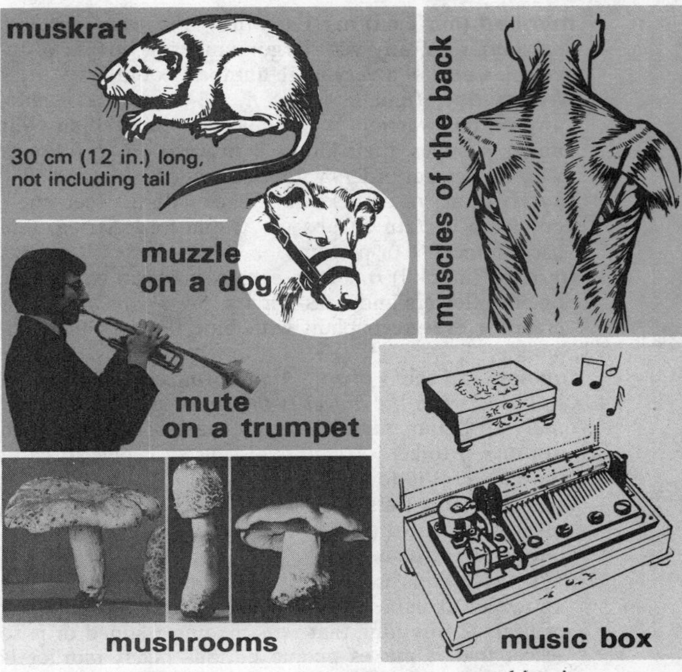


**mut·ton** (mut′′n) ***n.*** the flesh of a sheep, especially a grown sheep, used for food. 485

**mu·tu·al** (myo͞o′cho͞o wəl) ***adj.*** **1** done, felt, etc. by two or more for or toward the other or others [*mutual* admiration]. **2** of each other [The mongoose and snake are *mutual* enemies.] **3** shared together [We have a *mutual* interest in kites.] —**mu′tu·al·ly *adv.***

☆**muu·muu** (mo͞o′mo͞o) ***n.*** a long, loose, brightly colored garment for women, originally worn in Hawaii.

**muz·zle** (muz′′l) ***n.*** **1** the mouth, nose, and jaws of a dog, horse, etc.; snout. **2** a device made of wire, leather, etc. fastened over the mouth of an animal to keep it from biting. *See the picture.* **3** the front end of the barrel of a rifle, pistol, etc. ◆***v.*** **1** to put a muzzle on an animal. **2** to keep a person from talking or giving an opinion [The writer was *muzzled* by censorship.] —**muz′zled, muz′zling**

**my** (mī) ***pron.*** of me or done by me. *This possessive form of* **I** *is used before a noun and thought of as an adjective* [*my* work; *my* school]. *See also note in color at* **mine.** ◆***interj.*** a word said to show surprise, distress, pity, etc. [Oh, *my! My* goodness! *My* eye!]

**my·na** or **my·nah** (mī′nə) ***n.*** a bird of southeastern Asia related to the starling and often kept as a pet. Sometimes this bird can mimic human speech.

**my·o·pi·a** (mī ō′pē ə) ***n.*** the condition of being nearsighted. —**my·op·ic** (mī äp′ik) ***adj.***

| | | | | | | | |
|---|---|---|---|---|---|---|---|
| **a** | fat | **ir** | here | **ou** | out | **zh** | leisure |
| **ā** | ape | **ī** | bite, fire | **u** | up | **ŋ** | ring |
| **ä** | car, lot | **ō** | go | **ur** | fur | | a *in* ago |
| **e** | ten | **ô** | law, horn | **ch** | chin | | e *in* agent |
| **er** | care | **oi** | oil | **sh** | she | **ə** = | i *in* unity |
| **ē** | even | **o͝o** | look | **th** | thin | | o *in* collect |
| **i** | hit | **o͞o** | tool | ***th*** | then | | u *in* focus |

m

**myr·i·ad** (mir'ē əd) ***n.*** **1** ten thousand: *used mostly in old stories.* **2** any very large number [a *myriad* of locusts]. ***•adj.*** of a very large number; countless.

**Myr·mi·don** (mur'mə dän) ***n.*** **1** in Greek legend, any of the warriors who fought in the Trojan War under Achilles, their king. **2 myrmidon,** a follower who carries out orders without question.

**myrrh** (mur) ***n.*** a sticky substance with a sweet smell, got from certain shrubs of Arabia and Africa, and used in incense or perfume.

**myr·tle** (mur't'l) ***n.*** **1** an evergreen shrub with white or pink flowers and dark berries. *See the picture.* **2** a creeping evergreen plant with blue flowers; the periwinkle.

**my·self** (mī self') ***pron.*** **1** my own self. *This form of* **I** *is used when the object is the same as the subject of the verb* [I hurt *myself.*] **2** my usual or true self [I'm not *myself* today.] *Myself* is also used to give force to the subject [I'll do it *myself.*]

**mys·te·ri·ous** (mis tir'ē əs) ***adj.*** full of or suggesting mystery; hard to explain or solve [*mysterious* crimes]. **—mys·te'ri·ous·ly** ***adv.***

**mys·ter·y** (mis'tər ē) ***n.*** **1** something that is not known or explained, or that is kept secret [the *mystery* of life]. **2** anything that remains unexplained or is so secret that it makes people curious [That murder is still a *mystery.*] **3** a story or play about such a happening. **4** the quality of being secret, hard to explain, etc. [She has an air of *mystery.*] **5 mysteries,** *pl.* secret rites, especially religious rites, that are known only to a small group of people. *—pl.* **mys'ter·ies**

> **Mystery** comes from a Greek word that meant "to close the eyes or mouth." A person who was shown secrets of ancient religious ceremonies was not supposed to tell what had been seen and heard.

**mys·tic** (mis'tik) ***n.*** a person who claims to know mysterious things that teach truths not known by ordinary people. ***•adj.*** **1** having to do with mystics or mysticism [*mystic* teachings]. **2** secret, hidden, or mysterious [*mystic* powers].

**mys·ti·cal** (mis'ti k'l) ***adj.*** **1** that is a symbol of some spiritual thing [The *mystical* rose is a symbol of the Virgin Mary.] **2** *same as* **mystic.**

**mys·ti·cism** (mis'tə siz'm) ***n.*** **1** the ideas or beliefs of mystics; especially, the belief that certain people can know God directly or understand mysteries through visions. **2** confused thinking or beliefs.

**mys·ti·fy** (mis'tə fī) ***v.*** to puzzle or bewilder [I was completely *mystified* by her answer.] **—mys'ti·fied, mys'ti·fy·ing —mys'ti·fi·ca'tion** ***n.***

**myth** (mith) ***n.*** **1** an old story handed down through the years, usually meant to explain how something came to be [The *myth* of Prometheus explains how people got fire.] **2** any story that was made up and did not really happen. **3** any imaginary person or thing [The large stamp collection he bragged about was just a *myth.*]

> SYNONYMS: A **myth** usually tells the story of a great deed by a god or goddess and explains some custom, belief, or happening in nature. A **legend** is a story handed down through the years that is thought to be based on something that really happened. A **folk tale** is a story that is passed down over the years by word of mouth rather than being written, and it may sometimes be like a myth or legend.

**myth·i·cal** (mith'i k'l) ***adj.*** **1** of, in, or like a myth [a *mythical* tale; *mythical* creatures]. **2** imaginary; not real [a *mythical* friend].

**my·thol·o·gy** (mi thäl'ə jē) ***n.*** **1** myths as a group; especially, all the myths of a certain people [Roman *mythology*]. *—pl.* **my·thol'o·gies** **2** the study of myths. **—myth·o·log·i·cal** (mith'ə läj'i k'l) ***adj.***

**N, n** (en) ***n.*** the fourteenth letter of the English alphabet. *—pl.* **N's, n's** (enz)

**N** *the symbol for the chemical element* nitrogen.

**N, N., n, n.** *abbreviations for* **north** *or* **northern.**

**N.** or **n.** *abbreviation for* **navy, neuter, new, noon, number.**

**n.** *abbreviation for* **noun.**

**Na** *the symbol for the chemical element* sodium.

**NAACP** or **N.A.A.C.P.** National Association for the Advancement of Colored People.

**nab** (nab) ***v.*** **1** to arrest or catch [The police *nabbed* the robber.] **2** to grab or snatch. *This word is used only in everyday talk.* **—nabbed, nab'bing**

**na·dir** (nā'dər) ***n.*** **1** the point in the heavens directly opposite the zenith and directly beneath where one is standing. **2** the lowest point [He had reached the *nadir* of his hopes.]

**nag**[1] (nag) ***v.*** **1** to annoy by constantly scolding, complaining, or urging. **2** to disturb or trouble [I am *nagged* by doubts.] **3** to cause constant pain or discomfort [a *nagging* toothache]. **—nagged, nag'ging** ***•n.*** a person who nags.

> **Nag**[1] comes from a very old Danish word that is no longer used, meaning "to nibble or gnaw." When someone nags at another person, it is as though the words are nibbling or gnawing.

**nag**[2] (nag) ***n.*** a horse, especially an old one.

**Na·ga·sa·ki** (nä'gə sä'kē) a seaport in southwestern Japan. On Aug. 9, 1945, it was partly destroyed by a U.S. atomic bomb.

**nai·ad** (nā′ad *or* nī′ad) ***n.*** in Greek and Roman myths, a nymph living in a river, lake, etc.

**nail** (nāl) ***n.*** **1** a narrow, pointed piece of metal, often with a flat head. It is hammered into pieces of wood, etc. to hold them together. *See the picture.* **2** the hard, thin substance that grows out from the ends of the fingers and toes. **3** a claw. ◆***v.*** **1** to fasten with nails [*Nail* the box shut. *Nail* the sign on the wall.] **2** to catch or capture: *used only in everyday talk.* —**hit the nail on the head,** to do or say whatever is exactly right or to the point. —**nail down,** to make sure of; make certain.

**Nai·ro·bi** (nī rō′bē) the capital of Kenya.

**na·ive** or **na·ïve** (nä ēv′) ***adj.*** simple in a childlike or, sometimes, foolish way; innocent; not experienced. *See* SYNONYMS *at* **trusting.** —**na·ive′ly *adv.***

**na·ive·té** or **na·ïve·té** (nä ēv tā′) ***n.*** the quality of being naive.

**na·ked** (nā′kid) ***adj.*** **1** without any clothes on; bare; nude. *See* SYNONYMS *at* **bare. 2** without its usual covering [a *naked* sword]. **3** without anything added that hides, changes, decorates, etc.; plain [the *naked* truth; the *naked* eye]. —**na′ked·ness *n.***

**nam·by-pam·by** (nam′bē pam′bē) ***adj.*** weak, foolish, without force, etc. ◆***n.*** a namby-pamby person. —*pl.* **nam′by-pam′bies**

**name** (nām) ***n.*** **1** a word or words by which a person, animal, thing, or place is known; title [Grace, Lopez, Wyoming, and poodle are *names.*] **2** a word or words used instead of the real name, sometimes in order to insult [They were mean and called him names, such as "liar" and "cheat."] **3** reputation [Guard your good *name.*] ◆***v.*** **1** to give a name to [He *named* the child after her mother.] **2** to tell the name or names of [Can you *name* all the Presidents?] **3** to refer to; mention [to *name* an example]. **4** to choose for a certain position; appoint [She was *named* president of the company.] **5** to fix or set, as a date for a meeting, a price, etc. —**named, nam′ing** —**in the name of, 1** for the sake of [*in the name of* good sense]. **2** by the authority of [Open *in the name of* the law!] —**to one's name,** belonging to one.

**name-drop·per** (nām′dräp′ər) ***n.*** a person who mentions famous or important people in a familiar way in order to impress others.

**name·less** (nām′lis) ***adj.*** **1** not having a name. **2** having a name that is not known or given [the *nameless* writer of this article]. **3** that cannot be described [a *nameless* horror].

**name·ly** (nām′lē) ***adv.*** that is to say; to wit [You have a choice of two desserts, *namely,* cake or pie.]

**name·sake** (nām′sāk) ***n.*** a person with the same name as another; especially, a person named after another.

**Na·mib·i·a** (nä mib′ē ə) *another name for* **South West Africa.**

**Nan·king** (nan′kiŋ′) a city in eastern China, on the Yangtze River.

**nan·ny** (nan′ē) ***n.*** *a British word for* a child's nurse. —*pl.* **nan′nies**

**nanny goat** a female goat: *used only in everyday talk.*

**Na·o·mi** (nā ō′mē) in the Bible, the mother-in-law of Ruth: *see* **Ruth.**

**nap**[1] (nap) ***v.*** **1** to sleep for a short time; doze. **2** to be careless or not ready [The attack on the fort caught the settlers *napping.*] —**napped, nap′ping** ◆***n.*** a short sleep; doze.

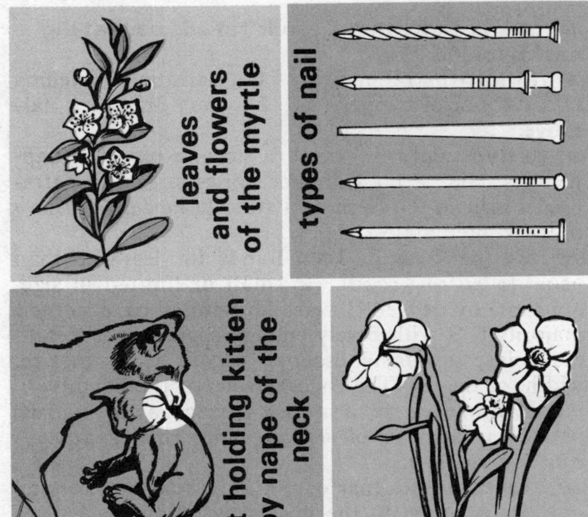


**nap**[2] (nap) ***n.*** the fuzzy or hairy surface of cloth formed by very short fibers.

☆**na·palm** (nā′päm) ***n.*** a jellylike substance shot in flaming streams from special weapons (called *flame throwers*) in warfare. It sticks to the skin of victims, causing severe burns. 

**nape** (nāp) ***n.*** the back of the neck [Cats often carry their kittens by the *nape.*] *See the picture.*

**naph·tha** (naf′thə) ***n.*** an oily liquid got from petroleum, used as a fuel or cleaning fluid.

**nap·kin** (nap′kin) ***n.*** **1** a small piece of cloth or paper used while eating to protect the clothes or to wipe the fingers or lips. **2** any small cloth or towel.

**Na·ples** (nā′p'lz) a city on the southwestern coast of Italy, on the Bay of Naples.

**Na·po·le·on Bo·na·parte** (nə pō′lē ən bō′nə pärt) 1769–1821; French general; emperor of France from 1804–1815. —**Na·po·le·on·ic** (nə pō′lē än′ik) ***adj.***

**Nar·cis·sus** (när sis′əs) a beautiful youth in a Greek legend, who fell in love with his own reflection in a pool and was changed into the narcissus plant.

**nar·cis·sus** (när sis′əs) ***n.*** a plant that grows from a bulb and has white, yellow, or orange flowers. *See the picture.* —*pl.* **nar·cis′sus** or **nar·cis′sus·es**

**nar·cot·ic** (när kät′ik) ***n.*** a drug, as morphine or heroin, that makes one feel dull and can lessen pain. Narcotics are often habit-forming and in large doses can cause death. ◆***adj.*** of, or having the effect of, a narcotic.

**nar·rate** (nar′āt *or* na rāt′) ***v.*** to give the story of in writing or speech; tell what has happened [Our guest

| | | | | | | | |
|---|---|---|---|---|---|---|---|
| **a** | fat | **ir** | here | **ou** | out | **zh** | leisure |
| **ā** | ape | **ī** | bite, fire | **u** | up | **ŋ** | ring |
| **ä** | car, lot | **ō** | go | **ur** | fur | | a *in* ago |
| **e** | ten | **ô** | law, horn | **ch** | chin | | e *in* agent |
| **er** | care | **oi** | oil | **sh** | she | **ə** = | i *in* unity |
| **ē** | even | **oo** | look | **th** | thin | | o *in* collect |
| **i** | hit | **ōō** | tool | ***th*** | then | | u *in* focus |

*narrated* her adventures.] —**nar′rat·ed, nar′rat·ing** —**nar′ra·tor** ***n.***

**nar·ra·tion** (na rā′shən) ***n.*** **1** a narrating, or telling of a story or of happenings. **2** a story or report; narrative.

**nar·ra·tive** (nar′ə tiv) ***n.*** **1** a story; a report of happenings; tale. **2** the telling of stories or events; narration. ◆***adj.*** in the form of a story [a *narrative* history of the United States].

**nar·row** (nar′ō) ***adj.*** **1** small in width; less wide than usual [a *narrow* road]. **2** small or limited in size, amount, or degree [I was the winner by a *narrow* majority.] **3** with barely enough space, time, means, etc.; close [a *narrow* escape]. ◆***v.*** to lessen in size, width, or degree [The road *narrows* at the bend.] ◆***n.*** *usually* **narrows,** *pl.* a narrow passage, as the narrow part of a valley or of a river. —**nar′row·ly** ***adv.*** —**nar′row·ness** ***n.***

**nar·row-mind·ed** (nar′ō mīn′did) ***adj.*** not keeping one's mind open to the beliefs, ways of life, etc. of others; not liberal; prejudiced.

**nar·whal** (när′wəl *or* när′hwəl) ***n.*** a small whale of the arctic. The male has a long tusk sticking out from its upper jaw. *See the picture.*

**nar·y** (ner′ē) ***adj.*** not any; no: *used only in everyday talk* [He had *nary* a doubt.]

**NASA** (nas′ə) National Aeronautics and Space Administration.

488 **na·sal** (nā′z'l) ***adj.*** **1** of the nose [*nasal* passages]. **2** produced by letting air pass through the nose [The *nasal* sounds are (m), (n), and (ŋ). She spoke with a *nasal* twang.]

**Nash·ville** (nash′vil) the capital of Tennessee.

**Nas·sau** (nas′ô) the capital of the Bahamas.

**na·stur·tium** (nə stur′shəm) ***n.*** a plant with a sharp smell and red, yellow, or orange flowers.

> **Nasturtium** comes from two Latin words meaning "to twist the nose." The odor of the flower is so sharp that it can cause one to wrinkle up the nose.

**nas·ty** (nas′tē) ***adj.*** **1** very dirty; filthy [a *nasty,* smelly room]. **2** making one sick [a *nasty* taste]. **3** not decent or proper; disgusting [That was a *nasty* thing to say!] **4** very unpleasant; mean, painful, harmful, etc. [*nasty* weather; a *nasty* temper; a *nasty* fall]. —**nas′ti·er, nas′ti·est** —**nas′ti·ly** ***adv.*** —**nas′ti·ness** ***n.***

**na·tal** (nāt′'l) ***adj.*** of or from one's birth [One's *natal* day is the day of one's birth.]

**na·tion** (nā′shən) ***n.*** **1** a group of people living together in a certain region under the same government; state; country [the Swiss *nation*]. **2** a group of people sharing the same history, language, customs, etc. [the Iroquois *nation*].

**na·tion·al** (nash′ə n'l) ***adj.*** of or having to do with a nation as a whole [a *national* election; the *national* anthem]. ◆***n.*** a citizen of a particular nation [a French *national*].

☆**National Guard** a militia that is organized by each State, but that can be called to service with the U.S. Army or Air Force.

**na·tion·al·ism** (nash′ə n'l iz'm) ***n.*** **1** love of one's nation or country; patriotism. **2** the desire to make one's nation free of control by another country. —**na′tion·al·ist** ***n., adj.*** —**na′tion·al·is′tic** ***adj.***

**na·tion·al·i·ty** (nash′ə nal′ə tē) ***n.*** **1** the condition of belonging to a certain nation by having been born there or by having been made a citizen of it [What was your grandparents' *nationality?*] **2** the condition of being a nation [Israel won *nationality* in 1948.] —*pl.* **na′tion·al′i·ties**

**na·tion·al·ize** (nash′ə nə līz′) ***v.*** **1** to put under the ownership or control of the national government [Coal mines in England were *nationalized* in 1947.] **2** to give a national character to [Mark Twain *nationalized* the American novel.] —**na′tion·al·ized′, na′tion·al·iz′ing** —**na′tion·al·i·za′tion** ***n.***

**na·tion·al·ly** (nash′ə n'l ē) ***adv.*** throughout the nation; by the whole nation [That television show will be seen *nationally.*]

☆**national park** a large area of land that has great beauty or is important in history or science and that is kept by the government for people to visit.

**na·tion·wide** (nā′shən wīd) ***adj.*** by or through the whole nation [A *nationwide* effort must be made to clean up the litter.]

**na·tive** (nāt′iv) ***adj.*** **1** that is or has to do with the place where one was born [Poland is his *native* land. Chinese is her *native* language.] **2** born in or belonging naturally in a certain place or country [a plant *native* to Japan; a *native* New Yorker]. **3** of or having to do with the natives of a place [a *native* custom; *native* dances]. **4** that is part of one from birth; not learned; natural [She has a *native* ability to make friends.] **5** as found in nature; pure or unchanged [*native* ores]. ◆***n.*** **1** a person born in a certain region [a *native* of Ohio]. **2** one of the original people living in a place, not a colonist or invader from some other place [the Indian *natives* of America]. **3** an animal or plant that lives or grows naturally in a certain region [Alligators are *natives* of the southern U.S. and of China.]

**na·tive-born** (nāt′iv bôrn′) ***adj.*** born in a certain region [a *native-born* Canadian].

**na·tiv·i·ty** (nə tiv′ə tē) ***n.*** birth; especially, the place or time of one's birth. —**the Nativity, 1** the birth of Jesus. **2** a painting or other art work showing this. **3** Christmas Day.

**natl.** *abbreviation for* **national.**

**NATO** (nā′tō) North Atlantic Treaty Organization.

**nat·ty** (nat′ē) ***adj.*** neat and in style [a *natty* suit; a *natty* dresser]. —**nat′ti·er, nat′ti·est** —**nat′ti·ly** ***adv.***

**nat·u·ral** (nach′ər əl) ***adj.*** **1** produced by nature; not made by man [*natural* resources; *natural* curls]. **2** of or dealing with nature [Biology and chemistry are *natural* sciences.] **3** that is part of one from birth; native [He has a *natural* ability in music.] **4** of or for all people at all times [*natural* rights]. **5** true to nature; lifelike [The portrait of her is *natural.*] **6** normal or usual; to be expected [It is *natural* for rivers to flood in the spring.] **7** free and easy; not forced or artificial [a *natural* laugh]. **8** in music, that is neither flat nor sharp [B *natural* is a half tone higher than A sharp.] ◆***n.*** **1** a musical note that is neither a sharp nor a flat; also, the sign (♮), used to mark a note that would otherwise be played as a sharp or flat. ☆**2** a person who seems just right for something: *used only in everyday talk* [She's a *natural* for the job.] —**nat′u·ral·ness** ***n.***

**natural gas** a mixture of gases, mostly methane, that is found naturally in the earth and that is taken out through pipes to be used as fuel.

**natural history** the study of physical things in nature, including animals, plants, and minerals, especially in a popular way.

**nat·u·ral·ist** (nach′ər əl ist) ***n.*** a person who makes a special study of plants and animals.

**nat·u·ral·ize** (nach′ər ə līz′) ***v.*** **1** to make a citizen of [Aliens in the U.S. can be *naturalized* after living here a certain time and passing certain tests.] **2** to take over from some other place and make one's own; adopt [The French word "menu" has been *naturalized* in English.] **3** to make a plant or animal used to new surroundings; adapt [Hawaiian farmers *naturalized* the South American pineapple.] —**nat′u·ral·ized′, nat′u·ral·iz′ing** —**nat′u·ral·i·za′tion** ***n.***

**nat·u·ral·ly** (nach′ər əl ē) ***adv.*** **1** in a natural way [to behave *naturally*]. **2** by nature; according to the way one happens to be [He is *naturally* shy.] **3** as one might expect; of course [*Naturally* you will have to pay a fine for the overdue book.]

**natural number** any positive whole number, as 2, 48, or 751.

**na·ture** (nā′chər) ***n.*** **1** all things in the universe; the physical world and everything in it that is not made by man. **2** *sometimes* **Nature,** the power or force that seems to control these things [*Nature* heals an animal's wounds.] **3** scenery that is not artificial, and the plants and animals in it [Are you a *nature* lover?] **4** the special character that makes a thing what it is [the *nature* of light; human *nature*]. **5** the qualities one seems to be born with [a child of a happy *nature*]. **6** kind or type [books, magazines, and other things of that *nature*]. **7** a simple way of life, especially in the outdoors [They are seeking a return to *nature*.]

**naught** (nôt) ***n.*** **1** nothing. **2** the figure zero (0).

**naugh·ty** (nôt′ē) ***adj.*** **1** not behaving; bad, disobedient, mischievous, etc. [*naughty* children]. **2** not nice or proper [*naughty* words]. —**naugh′ti·er, naugh′ti·est** —**naugh′ti·ly** ***adv.*** —**naugh′ti·ness** ***n.***

**nau·se·a** (nô′shə *or* nô′zē ə) ***n.*** **1** a feeling of sickness that makes one want to vomit. **2** great disgust; loathing.

> **Nausea** originally meant "seasickness." This word and **nautical** both come from *naus,* the Greek word for "ship."

**nau·se·ate** (nô′shē āt *or* nô′zē āt) ***v.*** to make feel like vomiting; cause nausea or disgust in [The sight of the accident began to *nauseate* him.] —**nau′se·at·ed, nau′se·at·ing**

**nau·se·ous** (nô′shəs *or* nô′zē əs) ***adj.*** **1** causing nausea; sickening; disgusting. **2** feeling nausea; nauseated: *in this sense used only in everyday talk.*

**nau·ti·cal** (nôt′i k'l) ***adj.*** having to do with sailors, ships, or sailing. —**nau′ti·cal·ly** ***adv.***

**nau·ti·lus** (nôt′'l əs) ***n.*** a small sea animal found in warm seas. The **pearly nautilus** has a spiral shell divided into many chambers. *See the picture.* The **paper nautilus** has eight arms and, in the female, a thin shell like paper.

**Nav·a·ho** or **Nav·a·jo** (nav′ə hō) ***n.*** a member of a tribe of American Indians now mainly in Arizona, New Mexico, and Utah. *See the picture.* —*pl.* **Nav′a·hos** or **Nav′a·jos, Nav′a·hoes** or **Nav′a·joes**

Navaho family

inside view of nautilus

25 cm (10 in.) across the shell

**narwhal** 4.5 m (15 ft.) long, not including tusk

**na·val** (nā′v'l) ***adj.*** **1** of or for a navy, its ships, crews, etc. [*naval* vessels]. **2** having a navy [Some countries are great *naval* powers.]

**nave** (nāv) ***n.*** the main part of a church, in the middle, where the seats are.

**na·vel** (nā′v'l) ***n.*** the small scar in the middle of the belly, that is left when the umbilical cord is separated after birth.

☆**navel orange** an orange without seeds, having a mark at one end that looks like a navel.

**nav·i·ga·ble** (nav′i gə b'l) ***adj.*** **1** wide enough or deep enough for ships to travel on [a *navigable* river]. **2** that can be steered [a *navigable* balloon]. —**nav′i·ga·bil′i·ty** ***n.***

**nav·i·gate** (nav′ə gāt) ***v.*** **1** to steer, or control the course of [to *navigate* a ship or aircraft]. **2** to travel through, on, or over [to *navigate* a river]. —**nav′i·gat·ed, nav′i·gat·ing**

**nav·i·ga·tion** (nav′ə gā′shən) ***n.*** the act or skill of navigating; especially, the science of figuring the course of a ship or aircraft.

**nav·i·ga·tor** (nav′ə gāt′ər) ***n.*** a person who navigates, especially one skilled in figuring the course of a ship or aircraft.

**na·vy** (nā′vē) ***n.*** **1** all the warships of a nation, with their crews, supplies, shipyards, officers, etc. **2** *a shorter form of* **navy blue.** —*pl.* **na′vies**

☆**navy bean** a small, white kidney bean that is dried for use as food.

**navy blue** very dark blue.

**nay** (nā) ***adv.*** **1** not only that, but even more [They are well-off, *nay,* rich.] **2** no: *no longer used in this meaning.* ◆***n.*** a vote of "no" [The count was 57 *nays* and 41 ayes.]

**Naz·a·rene** (naz ə rēn′ *or* naz′ə rēn) ***n.*** a person born or living in Nazareth; especially, **the Nazarene,** Jesus, who grew up there.

**Naz·a·reth** (naz′ər əth) a town in northern Israel.

| | | | | | | | |
|---|---|---|---|---|---|---|---|
| **a** | fat | **ir** | here | **ou** | out | **zh** | leisure |
| **ā** | ape | **ī** | bite, fire | **u** | up | **ng** | ring |
| **ä** | car, lot | **ō** | go | **ur** | fur | | a *in* ago |
| **e** | ten | **ô** | law, horn | **ch** | chin | | e *in* agent |
| **er** | care | **oi** | oil | **sh** | she | **ə =** | i *in* unity |
| **ē** | even | **oo** | look | **th** | thin | | o *in* collect |
| **i** | hit | **ōō** | tool | ***th*** | then | | u *in* focus |

**n**

**Na·zi** (nät′sē *or* nat′sē) ***adj.*** describing or having to do with the fascist political party that ruled Germany under Hitler from 1933 to 1945. ◆***n.*** a member or supporter of this party or of others like it. —**Na·zism** (nät′siz'm) ***n.***

**N.B.** *abbreviation for* **New Brunswick.**

**N.B.** or **n.b.** note well: the abbreviation for *nota bene*, Latin for "note well."

**NBC** National Broadcasting Company.

**NC** or **N.C.** *abbreviation for* **North Carolina.**

**NCO** or **N.C.O.** *abbreviation for* **noncommissioned officer.**

**ND, N.D., N.Dak.** *abbreviations for* **North Dakota.**

**Ne** *the symbol for the chemical element* neon.

**NE** *abbreviation for* **Nebraska.**

**NE, N.E., n.e.** *abbreviations for* **northeast** *or* **northeastern.**

**N.E.** *abbreviation for* **New England.**

**Ne·an·der·thal** (nē an′dər thôl *or* nē an′dər täl) ***adj.*** describing or of an early form of man living in Europe during the Stone Age.

**Ne·a·pol·i·tan** (nē′ə päl′ə t'n) ***adj.*** of Naples. ◆***n.*** a person born or living in Naples.

**neap tide** (nēp) a tide, occurring twice a month, when the difference between high and low tides is the smallest.

**near** (nir) ***adv.*** **1** at or to a short distance in space or time [Spring is drawing *near.*] **2** almost; nearly [I was

*near* frozen by the cold winds.] ◆***adj.*** **1** not distant; not far; close [a house *near* to the school; in the *near* past]. **2** close in relationship or affection [a *near* cousin; his *nearest* friend]. **3** by a small degree; narrow [a *near* escape]. **4** short; direct [She took the *near* way home.] **5** somewhat the same; resembling [a *near* likeness]. ◆***prep.*** close to; not far from [They sat *near* us.] ◆***v.*** to come near to; approach [Slow down as you *near* the curve.] —**near at hand,** very close in time or space. —**near′ness** ***n.***

**near·by** (nir′bī′) ***adj., adv.*** near; close at hand.

**Near East** the area near the eastern end of the Mediterranean. The term includes countries of southwestern Asia, northeastern Africa, and sometimes the Balkans.

**near·ly** (nir′lē) ***adv.*** almost; not quite [We are *nearly* ready.] —**not nearly,** not at all; far from [That's *not nearly* enough.]

negative of photograph

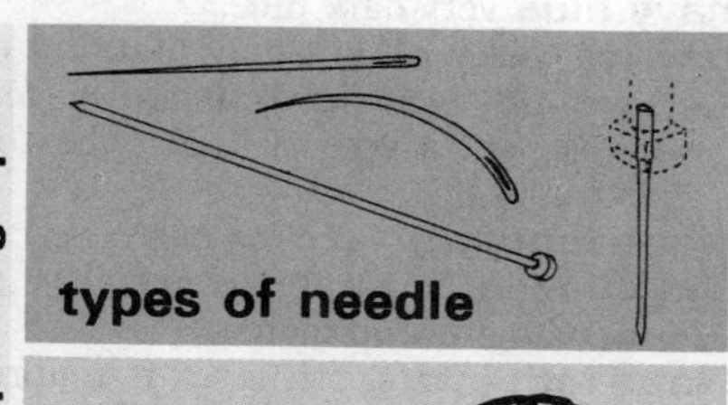
types of needle

neckerchief

**near·sight·ed** (nir′sīt′id) ***adj.*** able to see things that are near more clearly than things far away. —**near′-sight′ed·ness** ***n.***

**neat** (nēt) ***adj.*** **1** clean and in good order; tidy [a *neat* room]. **2** careful and exact [a *neat* worker]. **3** cleverly done or said [That was a *neat* trick.] **4** fine, pleasing, wonderful, etc.: *slang in this meaning.* —**neat′ly** ***adv.*** —**neat′ness** ***n.***

SYNONYMS: **Neat** describes something that is clean and trim, without confusing or unnecessary details [a *neat* pattern; a house that is kept *neat*]. **Tidy** puts more emphasis on having things orderly than on keeping them clean [Try to keep the closet *tidy.*]

**′neath** or **neath** (nēth) ***prep.*** beneath: *used in earlier poetry.*

**Ne·bras·ka** (nə bras′kə) a State in the north central part of the U.S.: abbreviated **Nebr. Neb., NE** —**Ne·bras′kan** ***adj., n.***

**Neb·u·chad·nez·zar** (neb′yə kəd nez′ər) the king of Babylon from about 605 to 562 B.C. He conquered Jerusalem and destroyed the Temple.

**neb·u·la** (neb′yə lə) ***n.*** a cloudlike patch seen in the sky at night. It is either a large mass of thin gas or a group of stars too far away to be seen clearly. —*pl.* **neb·u·lae** (neb′yə lē) or **neb′u·las** —**neb′u·lar** ***adj.***

**neb·u·lous** (neb′yə ləs) ***adj.*** **1** of or like a nebula. **2** not clear; not definite; vague [*nebulous* plans].

**nec·es·sar·i·ly** (nes′ə ser′ə lē) ***adv.*** as a necessary result; always; inevitably [Cloudy skies do not *necessarily* mean rain.]

**nec·es·sar·y** (nes′ə ser′ē) ***adj.*** **1** that is needed or must be done; required; essential [Do only the *necessary* repairs.] **2** that cannot be avoided; inevitable [The accident was a *necessary* result of the driver's carelessness.] ◆***n.*** something necessary. —*pl.* **nec′es·sar′ies**

**ne·ces·si·tate** (nə ses′ə tāt) ***v.*** to make necessary; compel [The hard words in the article *necessitated* her use of a dictionary.] —**ne·ces′si·tat·ed, ne·ces′si·tat·ing**

**ne·ces·si·ty** (nə ses′ə tē) ***n.*** **1** that which is necessary or needed or cannot be done without [Food and shelter are *necessities.*] **2** great need [Call only in case of *necessity.*] **3** poverty; want [to live in great *necessity*]. —*pl.* **ne·ces′si·ties** —**of necessity,** necessarily.

**neck** (nek) ***n.*** **1** the part of a man or animal that joins the head to the body. **2** the part of a garment that goes around the neck. **3** the narrowest part of a bottle, peninsula, etc. —**neck and neck,** very close or even, as in a race. —**neck of the woods,** ☆area or neighborhood [Do you live in this *neck of the woods?*] —**stick one's neck out,** to take the risk of failing, losing, etc.

**neck·er·chief** (nek′ər chif) ***n.*** a handkerchief or scarf worn around the neck. *See the picture.*

**neck·lace** (nek′lis) ***n.*** a string of beads or a fine chain of gold, silver, etc. worn around the neck as an ornament.

**neck·line** (nek′līn) ***n.*** the line formed by the edge of a garment around or near the neck.

**neck·tie** (nek′tī) ***n.*** a band worn around the neck, usually under a collar and knotted in front or tied in a bow.

**neck·wear** (nek′wer) ***n.*** neckties, scarfs, etc.

**nec·ro·man·cy** (nek′rə man′sē) ***n.*** the act of pretending to tell the future by supposedly getting messages from the dead. —**nec′ro·man′cer *n.***

**nec·tar** (nek′tər) ***n.*** **1** the sweet liquid in many flowers, made into honey by bees. **2** the drink of the gods in Greek myths. **3** any delicious drink.

> **Nectar** comes from two Greek words that together mean "to overcome death." In the ancient Greek myths, nectar was the drink that made the gods immortal.

**nec·tar·ine** (nek tə rēn′ *or* nek′tə rēn) ***n.*** a kind of peach that has a smooth skin.

**nee** or **née** (nā) ***adj.*** born: *used before the maiden name of a married woman* [Mrs. Albert Petrov, *nee* Maria Solano.]

**need** (nēd) ***n.*** **1** something that one wants or must have [New shoes are their greatest *need.*] **2** a lack of something useful or wanted [to have *need* of a rest]. **3** a condition that makes something necessary [There is no *need* to worry.] **4** a time or condition when help is wanted [a friend in *need*]. **5** a condition of being very poor [We gave to those in *need.*] ◆***v.*** to have need of; require; want [She *needs* a car.] *See* SYNONYMS *at* **lack.** *Need* is often used as a helping verb meaning "must" or "should" [She *needs* to take a rest. *Need* I tell you?] —**have need to,** to be required to; must. —**if need be,** if it is necessary [*If need be,* I'll type the letter myself.]

**need·ful** (nēd′fəl) ***adj.*** necessary; needed.

**nee·dle** (nē′d'l) ***n.*** **1** a small, slender piece of steel with a sharp point and a hole for thread, used for sewing. *See the picture.* **2** a slender rod of steel, bone, plastic, etc., used in knitting or crocheting. **3** a short, slender piece of metal, often tipped with diamond, that moves in the grooves of a phonograph record to pick up the vibrations. **4** the pointer of a compass, gauge, meter, etc. **5** the thin, pointed leaf of a pine, spruce, etc. **6** the sharp, very slender metal tube at the end of a hypodermic syringe. ◆***v.*** to tease, annoy, or goad: *used only in everyday talk.* —**nee′dled, nee′dling**

**nee·dle·point** (nē′d'l point) ***n.*** embroidery done on canvas, as in making some kinds of tapestry.

**need·less** (nēd′lis) ***adj.*** not needed; unnecessary [That is *needless* worry.] —**need′less·ly *adv.***

**nee·dle·work** (nē′d'l wurk) ***n.*** work done with a needle; embroidery, sewing, etc.

**need·n't** (nēd′'nt) need not.

**need·y** (nēd′ē) ***adj.*** not having enough to live on; in need; very poor. —**need′i·er, need′i·est —need′i·ness *n.***

**ne'er** (ner) ***adv.*** never: *used in earlier poetry.*

**ne'er-do-well** (ner′doo wel′) ***n.*** a lazy person who never does anything worthwhile.

**ne·far·i·ous** (ni fer′ē əs) ***adj.*** very bad or wicked; evil [a *nefarious* plot].

**neg.** *abbreviation for* **negative.**

**ne·ga·tion** (ni gā′shən) ***n.*** **1** the lack or the opposite of something positive [Death is the *negation* of life.] **2** a saying "no" or a denying; negative answer; denial.

**neg·a·tive** (neg′ə tiv) ***adj.*** **1** saying that something is not so or refusing; answering "no" [a *negative* reply]. **2** that does not help, improve, etc. [*negative* criticism]. **3** opposite to or lacking something that is positive [He always takes a *negative* attitude and expects the worst.] **4** showing that a certain disease, condition, etc. is not present [The reaction to her allergy test was *negative.*] ☆**5** describing or of a kind of electricity made in a piece of resin by rubbing it with a wool cloth. It has more electrons than protons. **6** describing a quantity less than zero or one that is to be subtracted. ◆***n.*** **1** a word, phrase, or action showing that one does not approve or agree ["No" and "not" are *negatives.*] **2** the side that argues against the point being debated. **3** the film or plate from which a finished photograph is printed. The negative shows the light areas of the original subject as dark and the dark areas as light. *See the picture.* —**in the negative,** refusing or denying something [She replied *in the negative.*] —**neg′a·tive·ly *adv.***

**neg·lect** (ni glekt′) ***v.*** **1** to fail to do what one should do, as because of carelessness [In her hurry, Sharon *neglected* to lock the door.] **2** to fail to take care of as one should; give too little attention to [He became so busy with work that he began to *neglect* his family.] ◆***n.*** the act of neglecting or the condition of being neglected [The old house suffered from *neglect.*]

**neg·lect·ful** (ni glekt′fəl) ***adj.*** in the habit of neglecting things or people; careless [*neglectful* of her duty].

**neg·li·gee** (neg lə zhā′ *or* neg′lə zhā) ***n.*** a woman's loosely fitting dressing gown of a soft, flowing material.

**neg·li·gent** (neg′li jənt) ***adj.*** in the habit of neglecting things; not being careful; careless. —**neg′li·gence *n.*** —**neg′li·gent·ly *adv.***

**neg·li·gi·ble** (neg′li jə b'l) ***adj.*** that can be ignored because it is small or not important; trifling [a *negligible* error].

**ne·go·ti·a·ble** (ni gō′shē ə b'l *or* ni gō′shə b'l) ***adj.*** **1** that can be sold or passed on to another [A check is *negotiable* if it is endorsed.] **2** that can be crossed, climbed, etc. [Is that hill *negotiable?*]

**ne·go·ti·ate** (ni gō′shē āt) ***v.*** **1** to talk over a problem, business deal, dispute, etc. in the hope of reaching an agreement [to *negotiate* a contract]. **2** to arrange by talking about [to *negotiate* a loan]. **3** to sell or transfer, as stock, bonds, etc. **4** to succeed in crossing, climbing, etc. [to *negotiate* a deep river]. —**ne·go′ti·at·ed, ne·go′ti·at·ing —ne·go′ti·a′tion *n.*** —**ne·go′ti·a′tor *n.***

**Ne·gro** (nē′grō) ***n.*** **1** a member of the largest group of people in Africa, usually having a dark skin and black hair. **2** *another word for* **Negroid.** **3** a person who has some Negro ancestors. —*pl.* **Ne′groes** ◆***adj.*** *another word for* **Negroid.** In the U.S., the term **black** is now preferred by many.

**Ne·groid** (nē′groid) ***adj.*** belonging to the group of human beings that is loosely called the "black race." The group includes most of the peoples of Africa, Melanesia, etc. ◆***n.*** a member of this group.

| | | | | | | | |
|---|---|---|---|---|---|---|---|
| **a** | fat | **ir** | here | **ou** | out | **zh** | leisure |
| **ā** | ape | **ī** | bite, fire | **u** | up | **ng** | ring |
| **ä** | car, lot | **ō** | go | **ur** | fur | | a *in* ago |
| **e** | ten | **ô** | law, horn | **ch** | chin | | e *in* agent |
| **er** | care | **oi** | oil | **sh** | she | **ə** = | i *in* unity |
| **ē** | even | **oo** | look | **th** | thin | | o *in* collect |
| **i** | hit | **o͞o** | tool | ***th*** | then | | u *in* focus |

**Ne·he·mi·ah** (nē′ə mī′ə) **1** a Hebrew leader of the 5th century B.C. **2** a book of the Bible telling about his work.

**Neh·ru** (nā′ro͞o), **Ja·wa·har·lal** (jə wä′hər läl) 1899–1964; the prime minister of India from 1947 to 1964.

**neigh** (nā) ***n.*** the loud cry that a horse makes; whinny. ✦***v.*** to make this cry.

**neigh·bor** (nā′bər) ***n.*** **1** a person who lives near another. **2** a person or thing that is near another [France and Spain are *neighbors.*] **3** another human being; fellow person ["Love thy *neighbor.*"]

**neigh·bor·hood** (nā′bər hood) ***n.*** **1** a small part or district of a city, town, etc. [an old *neighborhood*]. **2** the people in such a district [The whole *neighborhood* helped.] —☆**in the neighborhood of, 1** near; close to [*in the neighborhood of* the zoo]. **2** about; nearly [*in the neighborhood of* $10]. *This phrase is used only in everyday talk.*

**neigh·bor·ing** (nā′bər iŋ) ***adj.*** near or next to each other; adjacent [*neighboring* farms].

**neigh·bor·ly** (nā′bər lē) ***adj.*** friendly, kind, helpful, etc. [It was very *neighborly* of you to shovel the snow from my walk.] —**neigh′bor·li·ness *n.***

**nei·ther** (nē′*th*ər *or* nī′*th*ər) ***adj., pron.*** not one or the other of two; not either [*Neither* boy went. *Neither* of them was invited.] ✦***conj.*** not either; nor yet.

> **Neither** as a conjunction is used before the first of two words or phrases that are separated by *nor* [I could *neither* laugh *nor* cry.] **Neither** is also used after negative words, as *not* and *never* [She *never* smokes, *neither* does she drink.]

**nem·e·sis** (nem′ə sis) ***n.*** **1** punishment that is deserved. **2** the one who brings about such punishment [In Greek myths, *Nemesis* was the goddess of revenge.] **3** anyone or anything by which one is always defeated [A left-handed pitcher is my *nemesis.*]

**ne·on** (nē′än) ***n.*** a chemical element that is a gas without color or smell. It is found in the air in very small amounts.

**neon lamp** a glass tube filled with neon, which glows when an electric current is sent through it.

**ne·o·phyte** (nē′ə fīt) ***n.*** **1** a person who has just been converted to a particular religion. **2** a beginner in some work, craft, etc.; novice.

**Ne·pal** (ni pôl′) a country in the Himalaya Mountains, between India and Tibet.

**neph·ew** (nef′yo͞o) ***n.*** **1** the son of one's brother or sister. **2** the son of one's brother-in-law or sister-in-law.

**nep·o·tism** (nep′ə tiz'm) ***n.*** the giving of jobs, or the showing of special favors, to one's relatives by a person in power.

> **Nepotism** comes to us from the Latin word for "nephew." In the Middle Ages, some Popes, because they had no children of their own, would often show special favors to their nephews. Today, of course, the word covers such favors to any relative.

**Nep·tune** (nep′to͞on *or* nep′tyo͞on) **1** the Roman god of the sea. The Greeks called this god *Poseidon. See the picture.* **2** the fourth largest planet. It is the eighth in distance from the sun.

**Ne·ro** (nir′ō) 37–68 A.D.; the emperor of Rome from 54 to 68 A.D. He was known for his cruelty.

**nerve** (nurv) ***n.*** **1** any of the fibers or bundles of fibers that connect the muscles, glands, organs, etc. with the brain and spinal cord. Nerves carry signals to and from the brain or the nerve centers in controlling activity in the body. **2** the power to control one's feelings in facing danger or risk [The tightrope walker is a person of *nerve.*] **3 nerves,** *pl.* a feeling of being nervous. **4** a rib or vein in a leaf. **5** boldness that is without shame or that shows disrespect: *used only in everyday talk* [She had a lot of *nerve* telling us to leave.] ✦***v.*** to give strength or courage to [to *nerve* oneself for a dangerous task]. —**nerved, nerv′ing** —**get on one's nerves,** to make one annoyed or angry. —**strain every nerve,** to try as hard as possible.

**nerve·less** (nurv′lis) ***adj.*** **1** without strength, courage, etc.; weak [a *nerveless* coward]. **2** not nervous; calm; cool [a *nerveless* daredevil].

**nerve-rack·ing** or **nerve-wrack·ing** (nurv′rak′iŋ) ***adj.*** very hard on one's patience [the *nerve-racking* noise of the machinery].

**nerv·ous** (nur′vəs) ***adj.*** **1** of the nerves [a *nervous* reaction; the *nervous* system]. **2** restless and easily annoyed or upset [The sound of the guns made the horses *nervous.*] **3** feeling fear or expecting trouble [He is *nervous* about seeing a doctor.] **4** showing restlessness or tension [*nervous* energy]. —**nerv′ous·ly *adv.*** —**nerv′ous·ness *n.***

**-ness** (nis *or* nəs) *a suffix meaning:* **1** the condition or quality [*Sadness* is the condition of being sad.] **2** an act or thing that is; an example of being [A *rudeness* is a rude act.]

**nest** (nest) ***n.*** **1** the place built by a bird, as in a tree or field, for laying its eggs and caring for its young. *See the picture.* **2** a place where hornets, ants, fish, mice, etc. live and breed. **3** the birds, insects, etc. in such a place. **4** a cozy or snug place or shelter. **5** a den or hideout, as of thieves, plotters, etc. **6** a set of something in different sizes, each fitting into the one that is a little larger. *See the picture.* ✦***v.*** **1** to build a nest [Swallows often *nest* in chimneys.] **2** to place as in a nest.

**nest egg** money saved for the future; savings.

**nes·tle** (nes′'l) ***v.*** **1** to lie or settle down in a comfortable or snug way [The baby *nestled* in his mother's arms.] **2** to press or hold close for comfort or in fondness; cuddle [She *nestled* the puppy in her lap.] **3** to lie in a sheltered or partly hidden place [a house *nestled* in the hills]. —**nes′tled, nes′tling**

**nest·ling** (nest′liŋ *or* nes′liŋ) ***n.*** a young bird not yet ready to leave the nest.

**net**[1] (net) ***n.*** **1** a fabric of string, cord, etc. woven or knotted together so that open spaces are left between the strands. Nets are used to catch birds, fish, etc. *See the picture.* **2** a trap or snare [a thief caught in the *net* of his own lies]. **3** a piece of fine net used to hold, protect, or mark off something [a hair *net;* a tennis *net*]. **4** a fine cloth like net used to make curtains, trim dresses, etc. ✦***v.*** **1** to make into a net. **2** to catch with a net [I *netted* three fish.] **3** to cover or protect with a net. —**net′ted, net′ting**

**net**[2] (net) ***adj.*** **1** left after certain amounts have been subtracted [*Net* profit is the profit left after expenses.

*Net* weight is the weight of an article without the weight of its container.] **2** after everything has been considered; final [*net* result]. ◆**v.** to get or gain [to *net* a profit]. —**net′ted, net′ting** ◆**n.** a net profit, weight, etc.

**neth·er** (ne*th*′ər) **adj.** lower or under: *no longer much used* [Underwear was once called *nether* garments.]

**Neth·er·lands** (ne*th*′ər ləndz) a country in western Europe, on the North Sea; Holland.

**neth·er·most** (ne*th*′ər mōst) **adj.** lowest.

**net·ting** (net′iŋ) **n.** a netted fabric; net.

**net·tle** (net′′l) **n.** a weed with hairs on its leaves that sting the skin when they are touched. *See the picture.* ◆**v.** to annoy or make angry [She never seems *nettled* by his crude remarks.] —**net′tled, net′tling**

**net·work** (net′wurk) **n.** **1** netting; mesh. **2** any system of things that cross or are connected more or less like the strands in a net [a *network* of roads; a *network* of wires]. **3** a chain of radio or television stations.

**neu·ral·gia** (noo ral′jə *or* nyoo ral′jə) **n.** sharp pain in or along a nerve.

**neu·ri·tis** (noo rīt′əs *or* nyoo rīt′əs) **n.** a condition in which a nerve or nerves are inflamed, causing pain and soreness.

**neu·rol·o·gy** (noo räl′ə jē *or* nyoo räl′ə jē) **n.** the branch of medicine that deals with the nervous system and its diseases. —**neu·rol′o·gist n.**

**neu·ron** (noor′än *or* nyoor′än) **n.** any of the main units that make up the nerves. It consists of a cell body with threadlike parts that carry signals to and from the cells.

**neu·ro·sis** (noo rō′sis *or* nyoo rō′sis) **n.** a condition of the mind in which a person is continually worried, fearful, etc. in a way that is not normal. —*pl.* **neu·ro·ses** (noo rō′sēz *or* nyoo rō′sēz)

**neu·rot·ic** (noo rät′ik *or* nyoo rät′ik) **adj.** like or having a neurosis; too nervous. ◆**n.** a person who has a neurosis. —**neu·rot′i·cal·ly adv.**

**neut.** *abbreviation for* **neuter.**

**neu·ter** (nōōt′ər *or* nyōōt′ər) **adj.** **1** belonging to a class of words in grammar (called **gender**) that refer to things that are thought of as neither masculine nor feminine ["It" is a *neuter* pronoun.] **2** having no sex organs [The amoeba is a *neuter* animal.] **3** having sex organs that never develop fully, as the worker ant. ◆**n.** **1** the neuter gender. **2** a neuter word. **3** a neuter animal or plant.

**neu·tral** (nōō′trəl *or* nyōō′trəl) **adj.** **1** joining neither side in a quarrel or war. **2** neither acid nor alkaline. **3** not strong or definite [Gray and tan are *neutral* colors. The sound of (ə) is *neutral*.] **4** neither negative nor positive [a *neutral* particle in an atom]. ◆**n.** **1** a person or nation not taking part in a quarrel or war. **2** the position of gears when they are not meshed together and therefore cannot pass on power from the engine.

**Neutral** comes from two Latin words that mean "not either." That is still the basic meaning of *neutral*, for something neutral is on neither one side nor the other, but rather in the middle.

**neu·tral·i·ty** (nōō tral′ə tē *or* nyōō tral′ə tē) **n.** the quality or condition of being neutral.

**neu·tral·ize** (nōō′trə līz *or* nyōō′trə līz) **v.** **1** to work against in an opposite way so as to make neutral or weaker [An alkali *neutralizes* an acid.] **2** to declare to be neutral in war [to *neutralize* a seaport]. —**neu′tral·ized, neu′tral·iz·ing** —**neu′tral·i·za′tion n.**

**neu·tron** (nōō′trän *or* nyōō′trän) **n.** one of the particles that make up the nucleus of an atom. A neutron has no electrical charge.



**neutron bomb** a small nuclear bomb or rocket that would send out large numbers of radioactive neutrons which could kill or cripple enemy soldiers but not destroy buildings, vehicles, etc.

**Ne·va·da** (nə vad′ə *or* nə vä′də) a State in the southwestern part of the U.S.: abbreviated **Nev., NV**

**nev·er** (nev′ər) **adv.** **1** at no time; not ever [I *never* saw her again.] **2** not at all; under no conditions [*Never* mind what he says.]

**nev·er·more** (nev′ər môr′) **adv.** never again.

**nev·er·the·less** (nev′ər *th*ə les′) **adv.** in spite of that; however [They were losing the game; *nevertheless*, they kept on trying.]

**new** (nōō *or* nyōō) **adj.** **1** seen, made, thought of, discovered, etc. for the first time [a *new* song; a *new* plan; a *new* star]. **2** different from the earlier one [He's wearing his hair in a *new* way.] **3** that is the more recent or most recent one [This is the *new* library. Sandra is the *new* president of the student council.] **4** having just come recently [I'm *new* to this job.] **5** that has not been worn or used [*new* and used cars]. **6** recently grown; fresh [*new* potatoes]. **7** strange; not familiar [That language is *new* to me.] **8** more; additional [two *new* inches of snow]. **9** beginning again;

| | | | | | | | |
|---|---|---|---|---|---|---|---|
| **a** | fat | **ir** | here | **ou** | out | **zh** | leisure |
| **ā** | ape | **ī** | bite, fire | **u** | up | **ŋ** | ring |
| **ä** | car, lot | **ō** | go | **ur** | fur | | a *in* ago |
| **e** | ten | **ô** | law, horn | **ch** | chin | | e *in* agent |
| **er** | care | **oi** | oil | **sh** | she | **ə =** | i *in* unity |
| **ē** | even | **oo** | look | **th** | thin | | o *in* collect |
| **i** | hit | **ōō** | tool | ***th*** | then | | u *in* focus |

starting once more [the *new* year]. ◆**adv.** newly; recently: *used mainly in words formed with a hyphen* [the *new*-fallen snow]. —**new′ness n.**

SYNONYMS: **New** is used when we want to suggest that something has never existed before or has just come into being or use [a *new* coat, a *new* plan, a *new* book]. **Fresh** is used for something that is so new that it still looks, smells, or tastes the way it did when it first came into being [*fresh* eggs; *fresh* makeup].

**New·ark** (no͞o′ərk *or* nyo͞o′ərk) a city in northeastern New Jersey.

**new·born** (no͞o′bôrn′ *or* nyo͞o′bôrn′) **adj.** **1** just born; born not long ago [a *newborn* calf]. **2** born again; revived [*newborn* courage].

**New Bruns·wick** (brunz′wik) a province of Canada, on the southeastern coast.

**new·com·er** (no͞o′kum′ər *or* nyo͞o′kum′ər) **n.** a person who has come recently; new arrival.

**New Del·hi** (del′ē) the capital of India, right next to Delhi.

**new·el** (no͞o′əl *or* nyo͞o′əl) **n.** a post at the bottom or top of a stairway, that supports the railing: *also called* **newel post.** *See the picture.*

**New England** ☆the six northeastern States of the U.S.: Maine, Vermont, New Hampshire, Massachusetts, Rhode Island, and Connecticut. —**New Eng·land·er** (iŋ′glənd ər)

 **new·fan·gled** (no͞o′faŋ′g′ld *or* nyo͞o′faŋ′g′ld) **adj.** new and strange, but not of much use [It's some kind of *newfangled* gadget.]

**New·found·land** (no͞o′fənd land *or* nyo͞o′fənd lənd) **1** an island off the eastern coast of Canada. **2** a province of Canada, made up of this island and Labrador.

**Newfoundland dog** a large dog with a coat of thick, shaggy hair. *See the picture.*

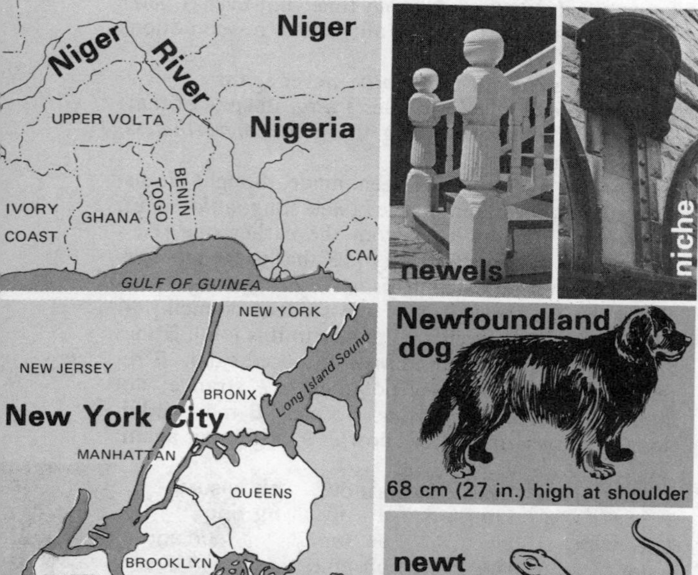


**New Guin·ea** (gin′ē) a large island north of Australia. The western half is part of Indonesia; the eastern half is a country, *Papua New Guinea.*

**New Hamp·shire** (hamp′shir) a New England State of the U.S.: abbreviated **N.H., NH**

**New Ha·ven** (hā′v′n) a city in southern Connecticut, on Long Island Sound.

**New Jer·sey** (jur′zē) a State in the northeastern part of the U.S.: abbreviated **N.J., NJ**

**new·ly** (no͞o′lē *or* nyo͞o′lē) **adv.** a short time ago; recently [a *newly* paved road].

**new·ly·wed** (no͞o′lē wed′ *or* nyo͞o′lē wed′) **n.** a person who has been married only a short time.

☆**new math** (math) a way of teaching mathematics that is based on the use of sets.

**New Mexico** a State in the southwestern part of the U.S.: abbreviated **N.Mex., NM** —**New Mexican**

**new moon** the moon when it cannot be seen at all or when it is seen as a thin crescent curving to the right.

**New Or·le·ans** (ôr′lē ənz *or* ôr lēnz′ *or* ôr′lənz) a city in southeastern Louisiana, on the Mississippi.

**news** (no͞oz *or* nyo͞oz) **n.pl.** **1** happenings that have just taken place, especially as told about in a newspaper, over radio or television, etc. **2** things told that a person has not heard of before; new information [This story about her childhood is *news* to me.] *This word is used with a singular verb.*

**news·boy** (no͞oz′boi *or* nyo͞oz′boi) **n.** a boy who sells or delivers newspapers.

☆**news·cast** (no͞oz′kast *or* nyo͞oz′kast) **n.** a program of news broadcast over radio or television. —**news′cast′er n.**

**news·girl** (no͞oz′gurl *or* nyo͞oz′gurl) **n.** a girl who sells or delivers newspapers.

**news·let·ter** (no͞oz′let′ər *or* nyo͞oz′let′ər) **n.** a regular report with items of news or interest, that is sent to a special group of people.

**New South Wales** a state of southeastern Australia.

**news·pa·per** (no͞oz′pā′pər *or* nyo͞oz′pā′pər) **n.** a daily or weekly publication printed on large, folded sheets of paper and containing news, opinions, advertisements, etc.

☆**news·reel** (no͞oz′rēl *or* nyo͞oz′rēl) **n.** a short motion picture of news events.

☆**news·stand** (no͞oz′stand *or* nyo͞oz′stand) **n.** a stand at which newspapers, magazines, etc. are sold.

**news·y** (no͞oz′ē *or* nyo͞oz′ē) **adj.** full of news: *used only in everyday talk* [a *newsy* letter]. —**news′i·er, news′i·est**

**newt** (no͞ot *or* nyo͞ot) **n.** a small salamander that lives both on land and in water. *See the picture.*

**New Testament** the part of the Christian Bible that tells of the life and teachings of Jesus and his followers.

**New·ton** (no͞ot′′n *or* nyo͞ot′′n), Sir **Isaac** 1642–1727; English mathematician and philosopher, who developed laws of gravity and motion.

**New World** the Western Hemisphere; the Americas. —**new′-world′ adj.**

**New Year's Day** or **New Year's** January 1.

**New York** (yôrk) **1** a State in the northeastern part of the U.S.: abbreviated **N.Y., NY** **2** a seaport in southeastern New York State, on the Atlantic Ocean; the largest city in the U.S.: *often called* **New York City.** *See the map.*

**New Zea·land** (zē′lənd) a country in the southern Pacific, made up of two large islands and some smaller ones.

**next** (nekst) ***adj.*** coming just before or just after; nearest or closest [the *next* person in line; the *next* room; *next* Monday]. ✦***adv.*** **1** in the nearest place, time, etc. [She sits *next* to me in school. Please wait on me *next*.] **2** at the first chance after this [What should I do *next?*] —**next door**, in or at the next house, building, etc.

**next-door** (neks′dôr′) ***adj.*** in or at the next house, building, etc. [a *next-door* neighbor].

**N.F., Nfld., Nfd.** *abbreviations for* **Newfoundland.**

**NH** or **N.H.** *abbreviation for* **New Hampshire.**

**Ni** *the symbol for the chemical element* nickel.

**Ni·ag·a·ra Falls** (nī ag′rə *or* nī ag′ər ə) the large waterfall on the Niagara River, which flows from Lake Erie into Lake Ontario.

**nib** (nib) ***n.*** **1** a bird's beak. **2** a point; especially, the sharp, metal point of some pens.

**nib·ble** (nib′'l) ***v.*** **1** to eat with quick, small bites [The mouse *nibbled* the cheese.] **2** to bite lightly or carefully [The fish *nibbled* at the bait.] —**nib′bled, nib′bling** ✦***n.*** **1** the act of nibbling. **2** a small bite.

**Nic·a·ra·gua** (nik′ə rä′gwə) a country in Central America. —**Nic′a·ra′guan** ***adj., n.***

**Nice** (nēs) a seaport and resort in southeastern France, on the Mediterranean.

**nice** (nīs) ***adj.*** **1** good, pleasant, agreeable, pretty, kind, polite, etc.: *used as a general word showing that one likes something* [a *nice* time; a *nice* dress; a *nice* neighbor]. **2** able to see, hear, or measure small differences [a *nice* ear for musical pitch]. **3** slight and not easily seen; very fine [a *nice* distinction]. —**nice and**, in a pleasing way [We like our tea *nice and* hot.] *This phrase is used only in everyday talk.* —**nic′er, nic′est** —**nice′ly** ***adv.***

**ni·ce·ty** (nī′sə tē) ***n.*** **1** accuracy or exactness [a writer noted for her *nicety* of expression]. **2** a small detail or fine point [the *niceties* of etiquette]. **3** something choice, dainty, or elegant [the *niceties* of life]. —*pl.* **ni′ce·ties** —**to a nicety**, to just the right degree; exactly.

**niche** (nich) ***n.*** **1** a hollow place in a wall, for a statue, bust, or vase. *See the picture.* **2** a place or position for which a person is specially fitted [She found her *niche* in business.]

**Nich·o·las** (nik′ə ləs), Saint, the patron saint of Russia and of young people, who lived in the fourth century.

**nick** (nik) ***v.*** **1** to make a small cut, chip, or notch on or in [to *nick* a cup]. **2** to barely touch [The bat just *nicked* the ball.] ✦***n.*** a small cut, chip, or notch made in an edge or surface. —**in the nick of time**, just before it is too late.

**nick·el** (nik′'l) ***n.*** **1** a silver-white metal that is a chemical element. Nickel is used in alloys and as a plating for other metals. ☆**2** a coin of the U.S. or Canada, made of copper and nickel and worth five cents.

> **Nickel** comes from a German word meaning "goblin." Because its ore is shiny like copper, but contains no copper, early miners thought that goblins were tricking them. *See also the word history at* **cobalt** (which comes from another word for "goblin.")

**nick·name** (nik′nām) ***n.*** **1** a name given to a person or thing in fun or affection, often one that describes in some way ["Shorty" and "Slim" are common *nicknames.*] **2** a familiar, often shorter, form of a person's name ["Tony" is a *nickname* for "Anthony."] ✦***v.*** to give a nickname to. —**nick′named, nick′nam·ing**

**nic·o·tine** (nik′ə tēn) ***n.*** a poisonous, oily liquid found in tobacco leaves. It is used to kill insects.

**niece** (nēs) ***n.*** **1** the daughter of one's brother or sister. **2** the daughter of one's brother-in-law or sister-in-law.

☆**nif·ty** (nif′tē) ***adj.*** good, pleasant, attractive, stylish, etc.: *a slang word.* —**nif′ti·er, nif′ti·est**

**Ni·ger** (nī′jər) **1** a river in western Africa. **2** a country in Africa, north of Nigeria. *See the map.*

**Ni·ger·i·a** (nī jir′ē ə) a country on the western coast of Africa. *See the map.* —**Ni·ger′i·an** ***adj., n.***

**nig·gard** (nig′ərd) ***n.*** a stingy person; miser. ✦***adj.*** stingy; miserly.

**nig·gard·ly** (nig′ərd lē) ***adj.*** **1** stingy; miserly. **2** small or few [a *niggardly* sum]. ✦***adv.*** in a stingy way. —**nig′gard·li·ness** ***n.***

**nigh** (nī) ***adv., adj., prep.*** near: *no longer in common use, except in some regions* [Spring is drawing *nigh.*]

**night** (nīt) ***n.*** **1** the time of darkness between sunset and sunrise. **2** the darkness of this time. **3** any period or condition of darkness or gloom, as a time of sorrow, death, etc. ✦***adj.*** of, for, or at night [*night* school].



**night blindness** poor vision in the dark or in dim light. It is caused by not having enough vitamin A.

**night·cap** (nīt′kap) ***n.*** **1** a cap worn in bed. **2** an alcoholic drink taken just before going to bed: *used only in everyday talk.*

**night·club** (nīt′klub) ***n.*** a place of entertainment open at night for eating, drinking, dancing, etc.

☆**night crawler** any large earthworm that crawls on the ground at night. It is often used as fish bait.

**night·fall** (nīt′fôl) ***n.*** the day's end; dusk.

**night·gown** (nīt′goun) ***n.*** a loose gown worn in bed by women or small children.

**night·hawk** (nīt′hôk) ***n.*** ☆**1** a bird related to the whippoorwill. It is active mostly at night. *See the picture on page 496.* ☆**2** *another name for* **night owl.**

**night·in·gale** (nīt′'n gāl) ***n.*** a small European thrush. The male is known for its sweet singing.

> **Nightingale** comes from the words in Old English for "night" and "sing." At night, during the mating season, the male nightingale sings a beautiful, melodious song.

**Night·in·gale** (nīt′'n gāl), **Florence** 1820–1910; an English nurse who is thought of as the founder of modern nursing.

**night light** a small, dim light kept burning all night, as in a hallway or bathroom.

| | | | |
|---|---|---|---|
| **a** fat | **ir** here | **ou** out | **zh** leisure |
| **ā** ape | **ī** bite, fire | **u** up | **ŋ** ring |
| **ä** car, lot | **ō** go | **ur** fur | a *in* ago |
| **e** ten | **ô** law, horn | **ch** chin | e *in* agent |
| **er** care | **oi** oil | **sh** she | ə = i *in* unity |
| **ē** even | **oo** look | **th** thin | o *in* collect |
| **i** hit | **ōō** tool | ***th*** then | u *in* focus |

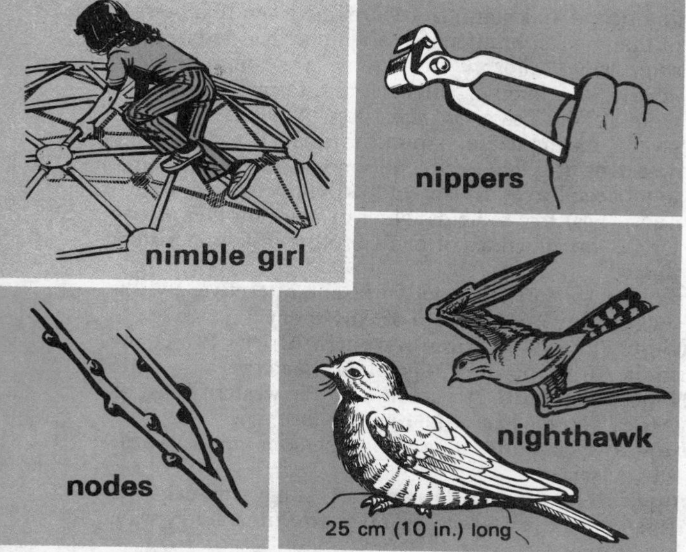


**night·ly** (nīt′lē) ***adj.*** done or happening every night [their *nightly* game of chess]. ◆***adv.*** at night or every night [I read a chapter *nightly.*]

**night·mare** (nīt′mer) ***n.*** **1** a frightening dream. **2** any very frightening experience [The trip during the blizzard was a *nightmare.*]

**night owl** a person who works at night or likes to stay up late.

**night·shade** (nīt′shād) ***n.*** a flowering plant related to the potato and tomato; especially, a poisonous kind, as the belladonna.

**night·shirt** (nīt′shurt) ***n.*** a loose garment like a long shirt, worn in bed by men or boys.

☆**night stand** a small table at the side of a bed.

☆**night stick** a long, heavy club carried by a police officer.

**nil** (nil) ***n.*** nothing [Our chances of winning the game are *nil.*]

**Nile** (nīl) a river in eastern Africa, flowing through Egypt into the Mediterranean.

**nim·ble** (nim′b′l) ***adj.*** **1** moving quickly and lightly; agile [a *nimble* child]. *See the picture.* **2** having or showing mental quickness; clever [a *nimble* mind]. —**nim′bler, nim′blest** —**nim′ble·ness *n.*** —**nim′bly *adv.***

> SYNONYMS: To be **nimble** or **agile** is to move rapidly and easily. To be **nimble** is to be especially quick in doing easily something that takes skill [the *nimble* fingers of a good tailor]. To be **agile** is to be especially quick but graceful in using the limbs and body [an *agile* dancer].

**nim·bus** (nim′bəs) ***n.*** a halo around the head of a god, saint, etc. in a picture.

**nin·com·poop** (nin′kəm po͞op) ***n.*** a stupid, silly person; fool.

**nine** (nīn) ***n., adj.*** one more than eight; the number 9.

**nine·pins** (nīn′pinz) ***n.pl.*** a game like bowling, in which only nine wooden pins are used.

**nine·teen** (nīn′tēn′) ***n., adj.*** nine more than ten; the number 19.

**nine·teenth** (nīn′tēnth′) ***adj.*** coming after eighteen others; 19th in order. ◆***n.*** **1** the nineteenth one. **2** one of nineteen equal parts of something; 1/19.

**nine·ti·eth** (nīn′tē ith) ***adj.*** coming after eighty-nine others; 90th in order. ◆***n.*** **1** the ninetieth one. **2** one of ninety equal parts of something; 1/90.

**nine·ty** (nīn′tē) ***n., adj.*** nine times ten; the number 90. —*pl.* **nine′ties** —**the nineties,** the numbers or years from 90 through 99.

**Nin·e·veh** (nin′ə və) the capital of ancient Assyria.

**nin·ny** (nin′ē) ***n.*** a fool; dolt. —*pl.* **nin′nies**

**ninth** (nīnth) ***adj.*** coming after eight others; 9th in order. ◆***n.*** **1** the ninth one. **2** one of nine equal parts of something; 1/9.

**nip**[1] (nip) ***v.*** **1** to pinch, squeeze, or bite [He *nipped* his finger in the door.] **2** to cut or pinch off; clip [to *nip* dead leaves from a plant]. **3** to hurt or spoil [Frost *nipped* the buds.] —**nipped, nip′ping *n.*** **1** a pinch, squeeze, or bite. **2** stinging cold; chill [There's a *nip* in the air.] —☆**nip and tuck,** so close or even that one cannot tell how it will turn out [It's *nip and tuck* whether the letter will arrive on time.]

**nip**[2] (nip) ***n.*** a small drink of liquor. ◆***v.*** to drink liquor in nips. —**nipped, nip′ping**

**nip·per** (nip′ər) ***n.*** **1** anything that nips, or pinches. **2 nippers,** *pl.* a tool for grasping or cutting, as pliers or pincers. *See the picture.* **3** the claw of a crab or lobster.

**nip·ple** (nip′'l) ***n.*** **1** the part of a breast or udder through which a baby or young animal sucks milk from its mother. **2** anything like this, as a rubber cap for a baby's bottle.

**Nip·pon** (nip′än) *a Japanese name for* **Japan.** —**Nip·pon·ese** (nip ə nēz′) ***adj., n.***

**nip·py** (nip′ē) ***adj.*** cold in a stinging way [a *nippy* breeze]. —**nip′pi·er, nip′pi·est**

**nir·va·na** (nir vä′nə *or* nir van′ə) ***n.*** in Buddhism, perfect happiness, in which the self becomes part of the supreme spirit of the universe.

**nit** (nit) ***n.*** the egg of a louse or similar insect.

**ni·ter** (nīt′ər) ***n.*** potassium nitrate or sodium nitrate, salts that are used in making gunpowder, fertilizers, etc.; saltpeter.

**ni·trate** (nī′trāt) ***n.*** a substance containing nitrogen, especially a salt of nitric acid used as a fertilizer.

**ni·tric acid** (nī′trik) a strong, colorless acid that contains nitrogen and eats into metal, cloth, etc.

**ni·tro·gen** (nī′trə jən) ***n.*** a gas that has no color, taste, or odor, and is a chemical element. It makes up nearly four fifths of the air around the earth, and is found in all living things. —**ni·trog·e·nous** (nī träj′ə nəs) ***adj.***

**nitrogen cycle** the cycle in nature by which nitrogen in the air goes into the soil and is changed into compounds that are used by plants and animals to form proteins. Later, when the plants and animals die and decay, the nitrogen is freed again into the air.

**ni·tro·glyc·er·in** or **ni·tro·glyc·er·ine** (nī′trə glis′ər in) ***n.*** a thick, yellow oil that is a strong explosive. It is used in making dynamite and also as a medicine to treat some forms of heart disease.

**ni·trous oxide** (nī′trəs) a colorless gas used, as by dentists, to lessen pain. It is sometimes called *laughing gas* because it can make one feel giddy.

☆**nit·wit** (nit′wit) ***n.*** a stupid person.

**Nix·on** (nik′s'n), **Richard M.** 1913– ; the 37th president of the United States, from 1969 to 1974. He resigned after a scandal.

**N.J.** or **NJ** *abbreviation for* **New Jersey.**

**NLRB** or **N.L.R.B.** National Labor Relations Board.

**NM, N.M., N.Mex.** *abbreviations for* **New Mexico.**

**no** (nō) ***adv.*** **1** not so; I won't, I can't, I refuse, it isn't, etc.: *opposite of* **yes. 2** not at all [He is *no* worse today.] ◆***adj.*** not in any way; not a [She is *no* dancer.] ◆***n.*** **1** the act of saying "no"; refusal or denial. **2** a vote against something. *—pl.* **noes**

**No.** or **no.** *abbreviation for* **number.**

**No·ah** (nō′ə) a man in the Bible who was told by God to build an ark, so that he and his family and a pair of every kind of creature would be saved during a great flood.

**No·bel prizes** (nō bel′) six international prizes given every year for outstanding work in physics, chemistry, medicine or physiology, literature, and economics, and for promoting peace. They were set up by the will of a Swedish chemist, Alfred Nobel, in 1901.

**no·bil·i·ty** (nō bil′ə tē) ***n.*** **1** the quality of being noble. **2** the class of people who have noble rank, as dukes, duchesses, earls, barons, etc.

**no·ble** (nō′b'l) ***adj.*** **1** having or showing a very good character or high morals; lofty [*noble* ideals]. **2** of or having a high rank or title; aristocratic [a *noble* family]. **3** grand; splendid [a *noble* oak]. ◆***n.*** a person who has noble rank or title. —**no′ble·ness** ***n.*** —**no′bly** ***adv.***

**no·ble·man** (nō′b'l mən) ***n.*** a man who has a noble rank or title; peer. *—pl.* **no′ble·men**

**no·ble·wom·an** (nō′b'l woom′ən) ***n.*** a woman who has a noble rank or title; peeress. *—pl.* **no′ble·wom′en**

**no·bod·y** (nō′bud′ē *or* nō′bäd′ē) ***pron.*** not anybody; no one. ◆***n.*** a person who is thought to be not very important. *—pl.* **no′bod′ies**

**noc·tur·nal** (näk tur′n'l) ***adj.*** **1** of or during the night [a *nocturnal* ride]. **2** active at night [The bat is a *nocturnal* animal.] —**noc·tur′nal·ly** ***adv.***

**noc·turne** (näk′tərn) ***n.*** a piece of music that is romantic or dreamy and is thought to suggest the evening or night.

**nod** (näd) ***v.*** **1** to bend the head forward quickly, as in agreeing or in greeting someone. **2** to let the head fall forward in falling asleep. **3** to sway back and forth, as tree tops or flowers in the wind. —**nod′ded, nod′ding** ◆***n.*** the act of nodding.

**node** (nōd) ***n.*** **1** a swelling; knob. **2** that part of a stem from which a leaf starts to grow. *See the picture.*

**nod·ule** (näj′ōōl) ***n.*** a small node, especially on a stem or root. —**nod·u·lar** (näj′ə lər) ***adj.***

**no·el** or **no·ël** (nō el′) ***n.*** **1** a Christmas carol. **2** **Noel,** *another name for* **Christmas.**

**nog·gin** (näg′in) ***n.*** **1** a small cup or mug. ☆**2** the head: *used only in everyday talk.*

**noise** (noiz) ***n.*** sound, especially a loud, harsh, or confused sound [the *noise* of fireworks; *noises* of a city street]. ◆***v.*** to make public by telling; spread [to *noise* a rumor about]. —**noised, nois′ing**

> SYNONYMS: **Noise** is the word for any sound that is loud and disagreeable. **Din** is the word for any loud, continuing sound that is deafening and painful to hear [the *din* of an auto body shop]. **Racket** is the word for a number of loud, clattering sounds coming together in a way that annoys [Our neighbors made such a *racket* at their party that I couldn't work.] *See also* SYNONYMS *at* **sound[1].**

**noise·less** (noiz′lis) ***adj.*** with little or no noise; silent [a *noiseless* electric fan].

**noi·some** (noi′səm) ***adj.*** having a disgusting or sickening smell [a *noisome* garbage dump].

> **Noisome** has nothing to do with the word **noise.** It is just a shorter way of saying "annoysome." A very foul smell can certainly annoy a person somewhat.

**nois·y** (noi′zē) ***adj.*** **1** making noise [a *noisy* bell]. **2** full of noise [a *noisy* theater]. —**nois′i·er, nois′i·est** —**nois′i·ly** ***adv.*** —**nois′i·ness** ***n.***

**no·mad** (nō′mad) ***n.*** **1** a member of a tribe or people that has no fixed home but keeps moving about looking for food or pasture for its animals. **2** any wanderer who has no fixed home. —**no·mad′ic** ***adj.***

**no·men·cla·ture** (nō′mən klā′chər) ***n.*** a system of names, as those used in studying a certain science [the *nomenclature* of botany].

**nom·i·nal** (näm′i n'l) ***adj.*** **1** in name only, not in fact [The queen is the *nominal* ruler of the country.] **2** very small; slight [There is a *nominal* fee to enter the zoo.] —**nom′i·nal·ly** ***adv.***

**nom·i·nate** (näm′ə nāt) ***v.*** **1** to name as a candidate for an election [Each political party *nominates* a person to run for president.] **2** to appoint to a position [The President *nominates* the members of his Cabinet.] —**nom′i·nat·ed, nom′i·nat·ing**



**nom·i·na·tion** (näm′ə nā′shən) ***n.*** the act of nominating or the fact of being nominated.

**nom·i·na·tive** (näm′ə nə tiv) ***adj.*** showing the subject of a verb or the words that agree with the subject. ◆***n.*** the case in grammar that shows this.

> In Latin and some other languages, nouns, pronouns, and adjectives have special endings to show that they are in the **nominative** case. In English, only a few pronouns, such as *I, she, he,* and *who* are in the nominative case.

**nom·i·nee** (näm ə nē′) ***n.*** a person who is nominated, especially as a candidate for an election.

**non-** *a prefix meaning* not.

> Words beginning with **non-** that are not entered in this dictionary can be understood if "not" is used before the meaning of the base word [*Nonacid* means "not acid." *Nonfiction* is writing that is not fiction.] A hyphen is used after **non-** when it is put before a word beginning with a capital letter [A *non-European* is a person who is not a European.]

**non·al·co·hol·ic** (nän′al kə hôl′ik) ***adj.*** having no alcohol in it [Root beer is a *nonalcoholic* drink.]

| | | | | | | | |
|---|---|---|---|---|---|---|---|
| **a** | fat | **ir** | here | **ou** | out | **zh** | leisure |
| **ā** | ape | **ī** | bite, fire | **u** | up | **ng** | ring |
| **ä** | car, lot | **ō** | go | **ur** | fur | | a *in* ago |
| **e** | ten | **ô** | law, horn | **ch** | chin | | e *in* agent |
| **er** | care | **oi** | oil | **sh** | she | **ə** = | i *in* unity |
| **ē** | even | **oo** | look | **th** | thin | | o *in* collect |
| **i** | hit | **ōō** | tool | ***th*** | then | | u *in* focus |

**nonce** (näns) ***n.*** the present time; right now: *now used mainly in the phrase* **for the nonce**, meaning "for the time being."

**non·cha·lant** (nän shə länt′ *or* nän′shə lənt) ***adj.*** not caring; not showing concern; casual [He is *nonchalant* about his debts.] —**non·cha·lance′** ***n.*** —**non·cha·lant′ly** ***adv.***

**Nonchalant** is a word borrowed from French and comes from two Latin words meaning "to be not warm." A person who is nonchalant does not get warm or passionate about things, but seems always to be cool or lukewarm.

**non·com** (nän′käm) ***n.*** *a shorter form used in everyday talk for* **noncommissioned officer**.

**non·com·bat·ant** (nän käm′bə tənt *or* nän′kəm bat′ənt) ***n.*** **1** a member of the armed forces who does not actually fight, as a nurse or chaplain. **2** a civilian in wartime. ◆***adj.*** not fighting; of noncombatants.

**non·com·mis·sioned officer** (nän′kə mish′ənd) a person in the armed forces who holds a rank higher than the lowest enlisted persons, but without a commission or warrant, as a sergeant or corporal.

☆**non·com·mit·tal** (nän′kə mit″l) ***adj.*** not showing clearly what one thinks or plans to do [She answered with a *noncommittal* smile, instead of a plain "yes" or "no."]

**non·con·duc·tor** (nän′kən duk′tər) ***n.*** something that does not easily conduct electricity, heat, or sound [Glass is a *nonconductor* of electricity.]



**non·con·form·ist** (nän′kən fôr′mist) ***n.*** **1** a person whose beliefs and actions are not like those of most people. **2** a person who does not belong to the official church of a country. —**non′con·form′i·ty** ***n.***

**non·de·script** (nän′di skript′) ***adj.*** hard to describe because not of a definite kind or class [a *nondescript* alley cat].

**none** (nun) ***pron.*** **1** no one; not anyone [*None* of us is ready.] **2** not any [*None* of the money is left. Many letters were received but *none* were answered.] ◆***adv.*** in no way; not at all [We came *none* too soon.]

**non·en·ti·ty** (nän en′tə tē) ***n.*** a person or thing that is not at all important. —*pl.* **non·en′ti·ties**

**non·es·sen·tial** (nän′i sen′shəl) ***adj.*** not essential; of little importance; not absolutely necessary. ◆***n.*** something that is not essential [We won't take *nonessentials* on our trip.]

**none·the·less** (nun *thə* les′) ***adv.*** in spite of that; nevertheless: *also written* **none the less**.

**non·ex·ist·ent** (nän′ig zis′tənt) ***adj.*** not existing; not real [to worry over *nonexistent* dangers]. —**non′ex·ist′ence** ***n.***

**non·pa·reil** (nän pə rel′) ***adj.*** having no equal. ◆***n.*** a person or thing that has no equal.

**non·par·ti·san** (nän pär′tə z'n) ***adj.*** not supporting or controlled by a political party or parties; not partisan [*nonpartisan* candidates for the office of judge].

**non·pay·ment** (nän pā′mənt) ***n.*** a refusing or failing to pay, as one's debts.

**non·plus** (nän plus′) ***v.*** to make so confused that one cannot speak or act; bewilder [The speaker was *nonplused* by the sudden interruption.] —**non·plused′** or **non·plussed′**, **non·plus′ing** or **non·plus′sing**

**non·pro·duc·tive** (nän′prə duk′tiv) ***adj.*** not producing the goods or results wanted [*nonproductive* farmlands; a *nonproductive* plan].

**non·prof·it** (nän präf′it) ***adj.*** not intending to make a profit [a *nonprofit* hospital].

**non·res·i·dent** (nän rez′ə dənt) ***adj.*** not having one's home in the city, State, etc. where one works, goes to school, or the like [*Nonresident* students at the State University pay higher fees.] ◆***n.*** a nonresident person.

**non·re·stric·tive** (nän′ri strik′tiv) ***adj.*** describing a clause, phrase, or word that is not absolutely necessary to the meaning of a sentence and that is set off by commas [In the sentence "John, who is five feet tall, is older than Lois," the clause "who is five feet tall" is a *nonrestrictive* clause.]

**non·sec·tar·i·an** (nän′sek ter′ē ən) ***adj.*** not connected with or controlled by any church or religious sect [a *nonsectarian* college].

**non·sense** (nän′sens) ***n.*** **1** speech or writing that is foolish or has no meaning [I read the letter but it just sounded like *nonsense* to me.] **2** silly or annoying behavior [She is a teacher who will put up with no *nonsense* in the classroom.] ◆***interj.*** how silly! how foolish! indeed not!

**non·sen·si·cal** (nän sen′si k'l) ***adj.*** not making sense; foolish; silly [the *nonsensical* words of the song].

**non·stop** (nän′stäp′) ***adj., adv.*** without making a stop [to fly *nonstop* from New York to Seattle].

**non·un·ion** (nän yo͞on′yən) ***adj.*** **1** not belonging to or having a contract with a labor union. **2** not made or done according to the rules of labor unions.

☆**noo·dle**[1] (no͞o′d'l) ***n.*** a flat, narrow strip of dry dough, usually made with egg and served in soups, baked in casseroles, etc.

**noo·dle**[2] (no͞o′d'l) ***n.*** the head: *a slang word.*

**nook** (no͝ok) ***n.*** **1** a corner of a room, or a part cut off from the main part [a breakfast *nook*]. **2** a small, sheltered spot [a picnic in a shady *nook*].

**noon** (no͞on) ***n.*** twelve o'clock in the daytime: also **noon′day**, **noon′tide**, **noon′time**.

**no one** not anybody; no person; nobody.

**noose** (no͞os) ***n.*** **1** a loop made by putting one end of a rope or cord through a slipknot so that the loop tightens as the rope is pulled. *See the picture.* **2** anything that snares, traps, hampers, etc. —**the noose**, death by hanging.

**nor** (nôr *or* nər) ***conj.*** and not; and not either.

**Nor** is used between two words or phrases when the word *neither* comes before the first word or phrase [Neither Karl *nor* Clara can go.] **Nor** is also used after other negative words, as *not* and *no* [They have no car, *nor* do they want one. I am not hungry, *nor* am I thirsty.]

**Nor·dic** (nôr′dik) ***adj.*** describing or of a type of tall, blond people of northern Europe, esp. Scandinavia.

**norm** (nôrm) ***n.*** **1** a standard for a certain group, usually based on the average for that group [to score higher than the *norm* for a test]. **2** a way of behaving that is usual for a certain group.

**Norm** comes from the Latin word for a carpenter's square. Such a square is an L-shaped tool in the form of a right angle. The tool is used to test whether something is square. It is a standard for square things, as the norm is a standard for a group.

**nor·mal** (nôr′m'l) ***adj.*** **1** agreeing with a standard or norm; natural; usual; regular; average [It is *normal* to make a mistake sometimes.] **2** in good health; not ill or diseased. ◆***n.*** what is normal; the usual condition, amount, level, etc. [His blood pressure is above *normal.*]

**nor·mal·ly** (nôr′mə lē) ***adv.*** **1** in a normal way [They behaved *normally.*] **2** under normal conditions; usually [*Normally* we eat at home.]

**Nor·man** (nôr′mən) ***n.*** **1** a person born or living in Normandy. **2** any of the people of Normandy who settled in England after the Norman Conquest. ◆***adj.*** of Normandy or the Normans.

**Norman Conquest** the conquest of England by the Normans in 1066. They were led by William the Conqueror.

**Nor·man·dy** (nôr′mən dē) a region in northwestern France, on the English Channel.

**Norse** (nôrs) ***adj.*** *an earlier word for* **Scandinavian,** especially for **Norwegian** or **Icelandic.** ◆***n.*** the Scandinavian languages, especially Norwegian. —**the Norse,** the Scandinavians, especially of earlier times.

**Norse·man** (nôrs′mən) ***n.*** any of the people of ancient Scandinavia. *—pl.* **Norse′men**

**north** (nôrth) ***n.*** **1** the direction to the right of a person facing the sunset. **2** a place or region in or toward this direction. ◆***adj.*** **1** in, of, to, or toward the north [the *north* side of the house]. **2** from the north [a *north* wind]. **3 North,** that is the northern part of [*North* Korea]. ◆***adv.*** in or toward the north [Go *north* two miles.] —**the North,** ☆**1** the northern part of the U.S., especially the part north of Maryland, the Ohio River, and southern Missouri. **2** the northern part of the earth, especially the arctic regions.

**North America** the northern continent in the Western Hemisphere. Canada, the United States, Mexico, and the countries of Central America are in North America. —**North American**

**North Carolina** a State in the southeastern part of the U.S.: abbreviated **N.C., NC**

**North Dakota** a State in the north central part of the U.S.: abbreviated **N.Dak., ND**

**north·east** (nôrth ēst′) ***n.*** **1** the direction halfway between north and east. **2** a place or region in or toward this direction. ◆***adj.*** **1** in, of, or toward the northeast [the *northeast* part of the county]. **2** from the northeast [a *northeast* wind]. ◆***adv.*** in or toward the northeast [to sail *northeast*].

☆**north·east·er** (nôrth ēs′tər) ***n.*** a storm or strong wind from the northeast.

**north·east·er·ly** (nôrth ēs′tər lē) ***adj., adv.*** **1** in or toward the northeast. **2** from the northeast.

**north·east·ern** (nôrth ēs′tərn) ***adj.*** **1** in, of, or toward the northeast [*northeastern* Ohio]. **2** from the northeast [a *northeastern* wind].

**north·er·ly** (nôr′*th*ər lē) ***adj., adv.*** **1** in or toward the north. **2** from the north.

**north·ern** (nôr′*th*ərn) ***adj.*** **1** in, of, or toward the north [the *northern* sky]. **2** from the north [a *northern* wind]. **3 Northern,** of the North.

**North·ern·er** (nôr′*th*ər nər) ***n.*** a person born or living in the North.

**Northern Hemisphere** the half of the earth that is north of the equator.

noose

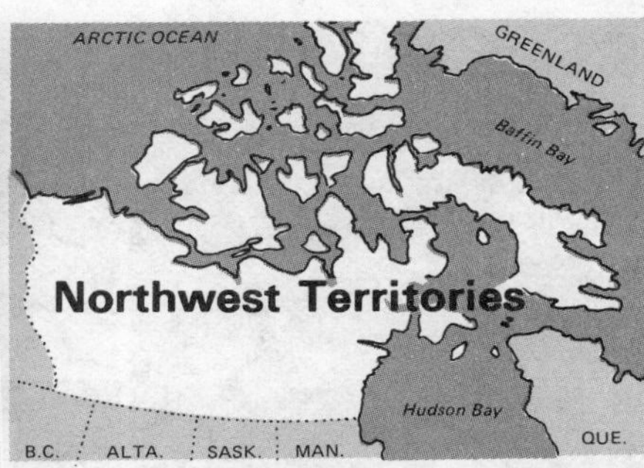



**Northern Ireland** a part of the United Kingdom, in the northeastern part of the island of Ireland.

**northern lights** *another name for* **aurora borealis.**

**north·ern·most** (nôr′*th*ərn mōst) ***adj.*** farthest north.

**North Pole** the spot that is farthest north on the earth; northern end of the earth's axis.

**North Sea** a part of the Atlantic, east of Great Britain and west of Norway and Denmark.

**North Star** the bright star almost directly above the North Pole.

**north·ward** (nôrth′wərd) ***adv., adj.*** toward the north. ◆***n.*** a northward direction or place.

**north·wards** (nôrth′wərdz) ***adv.*** *same as* **northward.**

**north·west** (nôrth west′) ***n.*** **1** the direction halfway between north and west. **2** a place or region in or toward this direction. ◆***adj.*** **1** in, of, or toward the northwest [the *northwest* part of the county]. **2** from the northwest [a *northwest* wind]. ◆***adv.*** in or toward the northwest [to sail *northwest*].



**north·west·er** (nôrth wes′tər) ***n.*** a storm or strong wind from the northwest.

**north·west·er·ly** (nôrth wes′tər lē) ***adj., adv.*** **1** in or toward the northwest. **2** from the northwest.

**north·west·ern** (nôrth wes′tərn) ***adj.*** **1** in, of, or toward the northwest [*northwestern* Utah]. **2** from the northwest [a *northwestern* wind].

**Northwest Territories** a large division of northern Canada, on the Artic Ocean, north and west of Hudson Bay. *See the map.*

**Norw.** *abbreviation for* **Norway** *or* **Norwegian.**

**Nor·way** (nôr′wā) a country in northern Europe, west of Sweden.

**Nor·we·gian** (nôr wē′jən) ***adj.*** of Norway, its people, etc. ◆***n.*** **1** a person born or living in Norway. **2** the language of Norway.

**Nos.** or **nos.** *abbreviation for* **numbers.**

**nose** (nōz) ***n.*** **1** the part of the head that sticks out between the mouth and the eyes and has two openings for breathing and smelling. The nose is part of the muzzle or snout in animals. **2** the sense of smell [a dog with a good *nose*]. **3** the ability to find out things [a reporter with a *nose* for news]. **4** anything like a

| | | | | | | | |
|---|---|---|---|---|---|---|---|
| **a** | fat | **ir** | here | **ou** | out | **zh** | leisure |
| **ā** | ape | **ī** | bite, fire | **u** | up | **ng** | ring |
| **ä** | car, lot | **ō** | go | **ur** | fur | | a *in* ago |
| **e** | ten | **ô** | law, horn | **ch** | chin | | e *in* agent |
| **er** | care | **oi** | oil | **sh** | she | **ə =** | i *in* unity |
| **ē** | even | **oo** | look | **th** | thin | | o *in* collect |
| **i** | hit | **ōō** | tool | ***th*** | then | | u *in* focus |

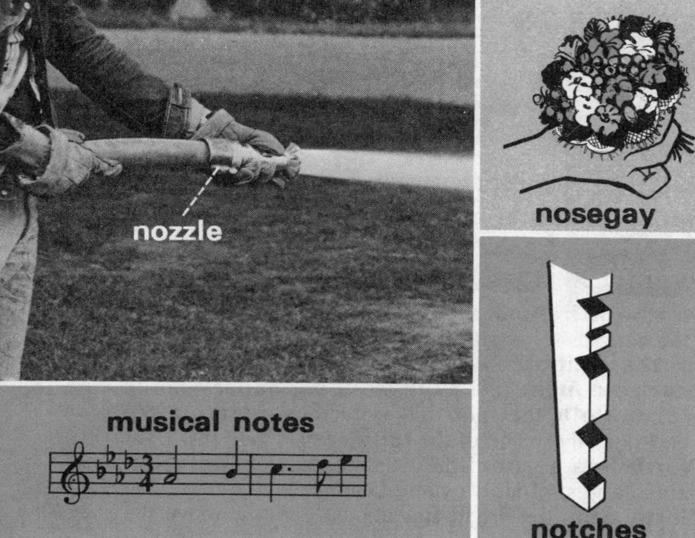


nose in shape or in the way it is placed, as the front of an airplane or the bow of a ship. ◆**v.** **1** to move with the front end forward [The ship *nosed* into the harbor.] **2** to meddle in another's affairs. **3** to smell with the nose. **4** to rub with the nose. —**nosed, nos'ing** —☆**by a nose,** by just a little bit [to win *by a nose*]. —**look down one's nose at,** to be scornful of: *used only in everyday talk.* —**nose out,** to win by just a little bit. —**on the nose,** exactly; precisely: *a slang phrase* [You guessed the score *on the nose.*] —**pay through the nose,** to pay more than something is worth. —**turn up one's nose at,** to sneer at; scorn. —**under one's nose,** in plain view.

**nose·bleed** (nōz'blēd) ***n.*** a bleeding from the nose.

**nose dive** **1** a fast, steep dive of an airplane, with the nose toward the earth. **2** any sudden, sharp drop, as in profits or prices.

**nose-dive** (nōz'dīv') ***v.*** to make a nose dive. —**nose'-dived', nose'-div'ing**

**nose drops** medicine given by putting it into the nose with a dropper.

**nose·gay** (nōz'gā) ***n.*** a small bunch of flowers for carrying in the hand. *See the picture.*

**nos·tal·gia** (näs tal'jə) ***n.*** a wishing for something that happened long ago or is now far away [*nostalgia* for one's home town]. —**nos·tal'gic *adj.***

**nos·tril** (näs'trəl) ***n.*** either of the two openings in the nose through which one breathes and smells.

**nos·trum** (näs'trəm) ***n.*** **1** a medicine that is sold to the public with exaggerated advertising. **2** a favorite scheme or plan for solving some problem: *a word used by those who dislike the plan.*

> **Nostrum** is the Latin word meaning "ours." The people who sold homemade medicines in earlier times would often call them "our special, or secret, remedies."

**nos·y** or **nos·ey** (nō'zē) ***adj.*** too curious about others' affairs; prying: *used only in everyday talk.* —**nos'i·er, nos'i·est** —**nos'i·ness *n.***

**not** (nät) ***adv.*** in no way; to no degree [Do *not* talk. They are *not* happy.]

**no·ta·ble** (nōt'ə b'l) ***adj.*** worth noticing or paying attention to; remarkable [a *notable* pianist; a *notable* success]. ◆***n.*** a notable person. —**no'ta·bly *adv.***

☆**no·ta·rize** (nōt'ə rīz) ***v.*** to sign a legal paper and stamp it with one's seal as a notary public. —**no'ta·rized, no'ta·riz·ing**

**no·ta·ry public** (nōt'ər ē) ***n.*** an official who has the legal power to witness the signing of a deed, will, contract, etc. and to declare that a person has sworn to the truth of something. *The name is often shortened to* **notary.** —*pl.* **no'ta·ries public** or **no'ta·ry publics**

**no·ta·tion** (nō tā'shən) ***n.*** **1** a brief note jotted down, as to remind one of something [She made a *notation* on her calendar to send a letter.] **2** a system of signs or symbols used, as in mathematics, music, or chemistry, to stand for words, numbers, amounts, etc. [In chemical *notation,* $H_2O$ stands for water.] **3** the act of using such symbols or of noting something.

**notch** (näch) ***n.*** **1** a cut in the form of a V, made in an edge or across a surface. *See the picture.* ☆**2** a narrow pass with steep sides, between mountains. **3** a step or degree: *used only in everyday talk* [The price has dropped a *notch.*] ◆***v.*** to cut a notch in.

**note** (nōt) ***n.*** **1** a word, phrase, or sentence written down to help one remember something one has heard, read, thought, etc. [The students kept *notes* on the lecture.] **2** a statement added to a book, as at the back or at the bottom of a page, to explain something or give more information. **3** a short letter. **4** an official letter from one government to another. **5** a written promise to pay money. **6** close attention; notice [Take *note* of what I say.] **7** a musical tone; also, the symbol for such a tone, showing how long it is to be sounded. Where it is placed on the staff tells how high or low it is. *See the picture.* **8** any of the keys of a piano, organ, etc. **9** a cry or call, as of a bird. **10** importance or fame [a person of *note*]. **11** a sign or hint [a *note* of sadness in her voice]. ◆***v.*** **1** to notice; observe [I *noted* that you left early.] **2** to mention. **3** to set down in writing; make a note of [I have *noted* your ideas and put them in my file.] —**not'ed, not'ing** —**compare notes,** to exchange opinions. —**take notes,** to write down notes to remind one of something.

**note·book** (nōt'book) ***n.*** a book in which notes are kept, as in order to help one remember things.

**not·ed** (nōt'əd) ***adj.*** famous; well-known [a *noted* poet].

**note·wor·thy** (nōt'wur'thē) ***adj.*** worth noticing or paying attention to; important; outstanding [a *noteworthy* event].

**noth·ing** (nuth'ing) ***n.*** **1** not anything; no thing [We saw *nothing* to frighten us.] **2** a person or thing not important in any way [A few scratches are *nothing* to an animal trainer.] **3** zero [The score is still *nothing* to *nothing.*] ◆***adv.*** in no way; not at all [It's *nothing* like I thought it would be.] —**for nothing, 1** free [If we help them, they will let us in *for nothing.*] **2** with no effect; uselessly [I'm afraid that our work was all *for nothing.*] —**nothing doing,** no: *used in everyday talk in refusing to do or give something.*

**noth·ing·ness** (nuth'ing nis) ***n.*** **1** the condition of being nothing or not existing [The ancient scroll crumbled to *nothingness.*] **2** the condition of having no value; uselessness.

**no·tice** (nōt′is) ***n.*** **1** an announcement or warning, as in a newspaper or on a sign [a *notice* of a change in bus schedules]. **2** attention; heed; regard [Pay them no *notice.*] **3** an announcement that one plans to end a contract or agreement at a certain time [Did you give your landlord *notice* that you were moving?] **4** a short review or other article about a book, play, etc. [The movie received good *notices.*] ◆***v.*** to pay attention to; observe; take note of [I didn't *notice* the visitor.] —**no′ticed, no′tic·ing** —**serve notice,** to give information or a warning; announce. —**take notice,** to pay attention; look.

**no·tice·a·ble** (nōt′is ə b'l) ***adj.*** easily seen; likely to be noticed; remarkable [*noticeable* improvement]. —**no′tice·a·bly** ***adv.***

SYNONYMS: **Noticeable** is used for that which one cannot help noticing [a *noticeable* change in the weather]. **Remarkable** is used when talking of something which is noticed because it is unusual or extremely good [*remarkable* beauty; *remarkable* strength]. An **outstanding** person or thing is remarkable when it is compared to others of its kind [an *outstanding* artist; an *outstanding* movie].

**no·ti·fi·ca·tion** (nōt′ə fi kā′shən) ***n.*** **1** the act of notifying or the fact of being notified. **2** notice given or received [a *notification* to appear in court].

**no·ti·fy** (nōt′ə fī) ***v.*** to let know; inform; give notice to [Please *notify* me when they arrive.] —**no′ti·fied, no′ti·fy·ing**

**no·tion** (nō′shən) ***n.*** **1** a general idea [Do you have any *notion* of what he meant?] **2** a belief or opinion [She has the *notion* that most people enjoyed the play.] **3** a sudden fancy; whim [I had half a *notion* to call you.] **4** a plan or intention [I have no *notion* of going.] ☆**5 notions,** *pl.* small, useful things, as needles, thread, kitchen gadgets, etc., sold in a store.

**no·to·ri·e·ty** (nōt′ə rī′ə tē) ***n.*** the condition of being notorious; bad reputation.

**no·to·ri·ous** (nō tôr′ē əs) ***adj.*** well-known, especially for something bad [a *notorious* liar]. —**no·to′ri·ous·ly** ***adv.***

**not·with·stand·ing** (nät′with stan′diŋ) ***prep.*** in spite of [We flew on, *notwithstanding* the storm.] ◆***adv.*** all the same; nevertheless [They must be told, *notwithstanding.*]

**nou·gat** (no͞o′gət) ***n.*** a candy made of sugar paste with nuts in it.

**nought** (nôt) ***n.*** **1** nothing [All our dreams came to *nought.*] **2** the figure zero (0).

**noun** (noun) ***n.*** a word that is the name of a person, thing, action, quality, etc. A phrase or a clause can be used in a sentence as a noun ["Boy," "water," and "truth" are *nouns.*]

**nour·ish** (nʉr′ish) ***v.*** **1** to feed; provide with the things needed for life and growth [Water and sunlight *nourished* the plants.] **2** to keep up; make grow; foster; promote [Fair treatment *nourishes* good will.] —**nour′ish·ing** ***adj.***

**nour·ish·ment** (nʉr′ish mənt) ***n.*** **1** the act of nourishing or the condition of being nourished. **2** something that nourishes; food.

**No·va Sco·tia** (nō′və skō′shə) a province of Canada, on the southeastern coast.

**nov·el** (näv′'l) ***adj.*** new and unusual [In the year 1920, flying was still a *novel* way of travel.] ◆***n.*** a long story, usually a complete book about imaginary people and happenings.

**Novel** comes from the Latin word for "new." The meaning of our English noun came by way of the Italian noun *novella,* which means "new things" or "news." A **novel** tells about new things and people that never really existed, whereas a biography tells about the life of a real person.

**nov·el·ette** (näv ə let′) ***n.*** a short novel.

**nov·el·ist** (näv′'l ist) ***n.*** a person who writes novels.

**nov·el·ty** (näv′'l tē) ***n.*** **1** newness and strangeness [The *novelty* of being alone had worn off and I became bored.] **2** something new, fresh, or unusual; change [It was a *novelty* for us to swim in the ocean.] **3** a small, often cheap toy, decoration, souvenir, etc. —*pl.* **nov′el·ties**

**No·vem·ber** (nō vem′bər) ***n.*** the eleventh month of the year, which has 30 days: abbreviated **Nov.**

**November** comes from the Latin word for "nine." It was the ninth month in the ancient Roman year, which began with March.

**nov·ice** (näv′is) ***n.*** **1** a person new at something; beginner [a *novice* at photography]. **2** a person who is going through a test period before taking final vows as a monk, nun, etc.

**no·vi·ti·ate** (nō vish′ē it) ***n.*** the condition or time of being a novice, especially before becoming a nun, monk, etc.

**now** (nou) ***adv.*** **1** at this moment; at the present time [They are eating *now.*] **2** at that time; then; next [*Now* the ninth inning began.] **3** with things as they are [*Now* we'll never know what happened.] ◆***conj.*** since; seeing that [*Now* that you're here, we can leave.] ◆***n.*** this time [That's all for *now.*] —**just now,** only a short while ago [They left *just now.*] —**now and then** or **now and again,** sometimes; occasionally.



**Now** is often used without any definite meaning. It may begin a sentence or be used only to add extra force to what is being said [*Now* look here. *Now* where could it be? *Now, now,* don't cry.]

**now·a·days** (nou′ə dāz) ***adv.*** in these days; at the present time [News travels fast *nowadays.*]

**no·way** (nō′wā) ***adv.*** in no way; not at all. It is now often written and spoken as two words (**no way**) and used to give force to what is being said.

**no·where** (nō′hwer) ***adv.*** not in, at, or to any place [It is *nowhere* to be found.] ◆***n.*** a place that does not exist or is not well-known [lost in the middle of *nowhere*]. —**nowhere near,** not nearly.

**nox·ious** (näk′shəs) ***adj.*** harmful or unhealthy [the *noxious* fumes from the chimneys].

**noz·zle** (näz′'l) ***n.*** a spout at the end of a hose, pipe, etc., through which a stream of liquid or gas is directed. *See the picture.*

**N.S.** *abbreviation for* **Nova Scotia.**

| | | | | | | | |
|---|---|---|---|---|---|---|---|
| **a** | fat | **ir** | here | **ou** | out | **zh** | leisure |
| **ā** | ape | **ī** | bite, fire | **u** | up | **ŋ** | ring |
| **ä** | car, lot | **ō** | go | **ʉr** | fur | | a *in* ago |
| **e** | ten | **ô** | law, horn | **ch** | chin | | e *in* agent |
| **er** | care | **oi** | oil | **sh** | she | **ə** = | i *in* unity |
| **ē** | even | **oo** | look | **th** | thin | | o *in* collect |
| **i** | hit | **o͞o** | tool | ***th*** | then | | u *in* focus |

**NT., NT, N.T.** *abbreviations for* **New Testament.**
**nt. wt.** *abbreviation for* net weight.
**nu·ance** (nōō′äns *or* nyōō′äns) ***n.*** a slight change in color, meaning, tone, etc. [Some words are used with a number of *nuances.*]
**nub** (nub) ***n.*** **1** a knob or lump. ☆**2** the point or main idea of a story, speech, article, etc.; gist: *used only in everyday talk.*
**nub·by** (nub′ē) ***adj.*** having a rough, lumpy surface [a *nubby* cloth]. —**nub′bi·er, nub′bi·est**
**nu·cle·ar** (nōō′klē ər *or* nyōō′klē ər) ***adj.*** **1** of or having to do with a nucleus or nuclei [*nuclear* physics]. **2** of, involving, or using the nuclei of atoms [*nuclear* energy]. **3** of or involving atomic bombs or other nuclear weapons [*nuclear* warfare].
**nuclear fission** the splitting of the nuclei of atoms, with the release of great amounts of energy, as in the atomic bomb.
**nuclear fusion** the combining of the nuclei of atoms, with the release of great amounts of energy, as in the hydrogen bomb.
**nuclear reactor** a device that starts a chain reaction (*see* **chain reaction**) and keeps it going in a material that can undergo nuclear fission. The nuclear reactor is used to produce energy or radioactive substances.
**nu·cle·us** (nōō′klē əs *or* nyōō′klē əs) ***n.*** **1** the thing or part at the center, around which others are grouped. **2** any center around which something grows [His few books became the *nucleus* of a large library.] **3** the small mass at the center of most living cells. It is needed for the plant or animal to grow, reproduce itself, etc. **4** the central part of an atom around which the electrons revolve. It is made up of protons and neutrons. —*pl.* **nu·cle·i** (nōō′klē ī′ *or* nyōō′klē ī′)
**nude** (nōōd *or* nyōōd) ***adj.*** completely without clothing or other covering; naked; bare. *See* SYNONYMS *at* **bare.** ◆***n.*** **1** a nude human figure in painting, sculpture, etc. **2** the condition of being nude [in the *nude*].
**nudge** (nuj) ***v.*** to push or poke gently, as with the elbow, especially so as to get the attention of. —**nudged, nudg′ing** ◆***n.*** a gentle push, as with the elbow.



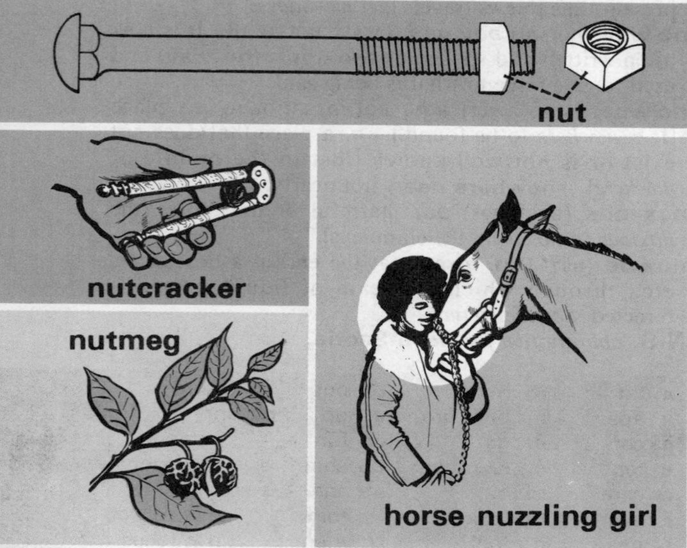


**nu·di·ty** (nōō′də tē *or* nyōō′də tē) ***n.*** the fact or condition of being nude; nakedness.
**nug·get** (nug′it) ***n.*** a lump or rough piece; especially, a lump of gold ore.
**nui·sance** (nōō′s′ns *or* nyōō′s′ns) ***n.*** an act, thing, or person that causes trouble or bother [It's such a *nuisance* to put on boots just to go next door.]
**null** (nul) ***adj.*** having no force or effect; invalid: *usually in the phrase* **null and void,** meaning "having no legal force; not binding."
**nul·li·fy** (nul′ə fī) ***v.*** **1** to cause to have no effect as law; make void [to *nullify* a treaty by ignoring its terms]. **2** to make useless; cancel [Her losses *nullified* her profits.] —**nul′li·fied, nul′li·fy·ing —nul′li·fi·ca′tion *n.***
**numb** (num) ***adj.*** not able to feel, or feeling very little; deadened [My toes were *numb* with cold. He sat *numb* with grief.] ◆***v.*** to make numb. —**numb′ly *adv.* numb′ness *n.***
**num·ber** (num′bər) ***n.*** **1** a symbol or word that is used in counting or that tells how many or which one in a series [Two, 7, 237, and tenth are all *numbers.*] **2** the sum or total of persons or things [a small *number* of people]. **3 numbers,** *pl. an old-fashioned word for* **arithmetic. 4** *often* **numbers,** *pl.* a large group; many [*Numbers* of trees were cut down.] **5** a single issue of a magazine [Was it in the June *number?*] **6** one part of a program of dances, songs, etc. **7** in grammar, the form of a word that shows whether one or more is meant [The word "it" shows singular *number.* The word "are" shows plural *number.*] ◆***v.*** **1** to give a number to [Dollar bills are *numbered.*] **2** to include as one of a group or class [She is *numbered* among our friends.] **3** to have or make up in number; total or contain [My books *number* almost eighty.] **4** to limit the number of; make few [He is very old and his years are *numbered.*] —**a number of,** several or many. —**beyond number** or **without number,** too many to be counted.
**num·ber·less** (num′bər lis) ***adj.*** too many to be counted [the *numberless* stars in the sky].
**Num·bers** (num′bərz) the fourth book of the Bible.
**numb·skull** (num′skul) ***n.*** *another spelling of* **numskull.**
**nu·mer·al** (nōō′mər əl *or* nyōō′mər əl) ***n.*** a figure, letter, or word, or a group of these, standing for a number. *See* **Arabic numerals** *and* **Roman numerals.**
**nu·mer·ate** (nōō′mə rāt *or* nyōō′mə rāt) ***v.*** *another spelling of* **enumerate. —nu′mer·at·ed, nu′mer·at·ing —nu′mer·a′tion *n.***
**nu·mer·a·tor** (nōō′mə rāt′ər *or* nyōō′mə rāt′ər) ***n.*** the number or quantity above or to the left of the line in a fraction. It shows how many of the equal parts of a thing are taken [In the fraction 2/5, 2 is the *numerator.*]
**nu·mer·i·cal** (nōō mer′i k′l *or* nyōō mer′i k′l) ***adj.*** **1** of or having to do with a number or numbers; by numbers [to arrange in *numerical* order]. **2** shown as a number, not as a letter [In the equation x + y = 10, 10 is the only *numerical* quantity.] —**nu·mer′i·cal·ly *adv.***
**nu·mer·ous** (nōō′mər əs *or* nyōō′mər əs) ***adj.*** **1** very many [She has *numerous* friends.] *See* SYNONYMS *at*

many. **2** made up of a large number [a *numerous* collection of animals].

**nu·mis·mat·ics** (no͞o′miz mat′iks *or* nyo͞o′mis mat′iks) ***n.pl.*** the hobby of collecting and studying coins and medals: *used with a singular verb.* —**nu·mis·ma·tist** (no͞o miz′mə tist *or* nyo͞o mis′mə tist) ***n.***

**num·skull** (num′skul) ***n.*** a stupid person.

**nun** (nun) ***n.*** a woman who has joined a religious order whose members live and work together in a convent according to certain rules, after taking vows to give up worldly goods, never to marry, etc.

**nun·ci·o** (nun′shē ō′) ***n.*** the ambassador of the Pope to a foreign government. —*pl.* **nun′ci·os**

**nun·ner·y** (nun′ər ē) ***n.*** a place where nuns live together. *The usual word today is* **convent.** —*pl.* **nun′ner·ies**

**nup·tial** (nup′shəl *or* nup′chəl) ***adj.*** of marriage or a wedding [a *nuptial* feast]. ◆***n.*** **nuptials,** *pl.* a wedding; marriage ceremony.

**nurse** (nurs) ***n.*** **1** a person who has been trained to take care of sick people, help doctors, etc. **2** *a shorter form of* **nursemaid.** ◆***v.*** **1** to take care of sick people, as a nurse does. **2** to treat, or try to cure [I'm *nursing* a cold.] **3** to make grow or develop [to *nurse* a skill]. **4** to use up or spend slowly so as to make last longer [to *nurse* one's allowance]. **5** to give milk to from a breast; suckle. **6** to suck milk from its mother. —**nursed, nurs′ing**

**nurse·maid** (nurs′mād) ***n.*** a woman hired to take care of a child or children.

**nurs·er·y** (nur′sər ē) ***n.*** **1** a room set aside for the special use of children or infants. **2** *a shorter form of* **nursery school** and **day nursery. 3** a place where young trees or plants are raised for study or for sale. —*pl.* **nurs′er·ies**

**nurs·er·y·man** (nur′sər ē mən) ***n.*** a person who owns or works for a nursery that grows trees, plants, etc. —*pl.* **nurs′er·y·men**

**nursery rhyme** a short poem for young children.

**nursery school** a school for children who are too young for kindergarten.

**nursing home** a place to live for those who are too weak or ill to care for themselves.

**nur·ture** (nur′chər) ***n.*** **1** the training, care, or bringing up, as of a child. **2** anything that nourishes; food. ◆***v.*** **1** to bring up with care; help grow or develop; train. **2** to feed or nourish. —**nur′tured, nur′tur·ing**

**nut** (nut) ***n.*** **1** a dry fruit that has a hard or leathery shell and a kernel inside that is often good to eat [Walnuts, pecans, and acorns are *nuts.*] **2** the kernel of such a fruit; nutmeat. **3** a small metal piece that is screwed onto a bolt to hold the bolt in place. *See the picture.* **4** a person who does silly or crazy things: *slang in this meaning.* **5** a person who is greatly interested in something; fan: *slang in this meaning* [a jazz *nut*]. —**hard nut to crack,** a person, problem, or thing that is hard to deal with.

**nut·crack·er** (nut′krak′ər) ***n.*** a tool used to crack the shells of nuts. *See the picture.*

**nut·hatch** (nut′hach) ***n.*** a small bird that has a sharp beak and feeds on nuts, etc.

**nut·meat** (nut′mēt) ***n.*** the kernel of a nut.

**nut·meg** (nut′meg) ***n.*** **1** the hard seed of a tropical tree. It is grated for use as a spice. *See the picture.* **2** the tree it grows on.

☆**nu·tri·a** (no͞o′trē ə *or* nyo͞o′trē ə) ***n.*** **1** a South American animal somewhat like the beaver. **2** its soft, brown fur.

**nu·tri·ent** (no͞o′trē ənt *or* nyo͞o′trē ənt) ***adj.*** nourishing. ◆***n.*** any of the substances in food that are needed for health, such as proteins, minerals, vitamins, etc.

**nu·tri·ment** (no͞o′trə mənt *or* nyo͞o′trə mənt) ***n.*** food that is nourishing; nourishment.

**nu·tri·tion** (no͞o trish′ən *or* nyo͞o trish′ən) ***n.*** **1** the process by which an animal or plant takes in food and uses it in living and growing. **2** food; nourishment. **3** the study of the foods people should eat for health and well-being. —**nu·tri′tion·al *adj.***

**nu·tri·tious** (no͞o trish′əs *or* nyo͞o trish′əs) ***adj.*** having value as food; nourishing.

**nu·tri·tive** (no͞o′trə tiv *or* nyo͞o′trə tiv) ***adj.*** **1** *same as* **nutritious. 2** having to do with nutrition.

**nuts** (nuts) ***adj.*** ☆crazy; foolish. —☆**be nuts about,** to like or love very much [She is *nuts about* football.] *This word and phrase are slang.*

**nut·shell** (nut′shel) ***n.*** the shell of a nut. —**in a nutshell,** in a few words; briefly.

**nut·ty** (nut′ē) ***adj.*** **1** having nuts in it [a *nutty* candy bar]. **2** that tastes like nuts. **3** crazy, silly, very enthusiastic, etc.: *slang in this meaning.* —**nut′ti·er, nut′ti·est** 503

**nuz·zle** (nuz′'l) ***v.*** **1** to push against or rub with the nose [The horse *nuzzled* her gently.] *See the picture.* **2** to lie close; snuggle; nestle. —**nuz′zled, nuz′zling**

**NV** *abbreviation for* **Nevada.**

**NW, N.W., n.w.** *abbreviations for* **northwest** *or* **northwestern.**

**N.W.T.** *abbreviation for* **Northwest Territories.**

**N.Y.** or **NY** *abbreviation for* **New York.**

**N.Y.C.** *abbreviation for* **New York City.**

☆**ny·lon** (nī′län) ***n.*** **1** a very strong, elastic material made from chemicals and used for thread, bristles, etc. **2 nylons,** *pl.* stockings made of nylon yarn.

**nymph** (nimf) ***n.*** **1** any of the nature goddesses of Greek and Roman myths, who lived in trees, woods, rivers, etc. **2** a beautiful young woman. **3** the form of some insects before they become fully adult.

**N.Z.** *abbreviation for* **New Zealand.**

| | | | | | | | |
|---|---|---|---|---|---|---|---|
| **a** | fat | **ir** | here | **ou** | out | **zh** | leisure |
| **ā** | ape | **ī** | bite, fire | **u** | up | **ŋ** | ring |
| **ä** | car, lot | **ō** | go | **ur** | fur | | a *in* ago |
| **e** | ten | **ô** | law, horn | **ch** | chin | | e *in* agent |
| **er** | care | **oi** | oil | **sh** | she | **ə =** | i *in* unity |
| **ē** | even | **oo** | look | **th** | thin | | o *in* collect |
| **i** | hit | **o͞o** | tool | ***th*** | then | | u *in* focus |

**O, o** (ō) ***n.*** the fifteenth letter of the English alphabet. *—pl.* **O's, o's** (ōz)

**O** *the symbol for the chemical element* oxygen.

**O** (ō) ***interj.*** **1** a word used before someone's name or title, in talking to him or her [*O* Lord, help us!] **2** *another spelling for* **oh.**

**o'** (ə *or* ō) ***prep.*** *an abbreviation for* **of** [*o'*clock].

**O.** *abbreviation for* **Ohio.**

**oaf** (ōf) ***n.*** a stupid and clumsy person; dolt; lout. —**oaf'ish** ***adj.***

**O·a·hu** (ō ä'hōō) the main island of Hawaii. Honolulu is on this island.

**oak** (ōk) ***n.*** **1** a large tree with hard wood and nuts called *acorns. See the picture.* **2** the wood of this tree. ◆***adj.*** of oak; oaken.

**oak·en** (ō'kən) ***adj.*** made of the wood of the oak [an *oaken* bucket].

**Oak·land** (ōk'lənd) a city in western California, across a bay from San Francisco.

**oak·um** (ō'kəm) ***n.*** loose, tough fiber got from old ropes. It is used to fill up cracks and seams in wooden boats.

**oar** (ôr) ***n.*** **1** a long pole with a flat blade at one end, used in rowing a boat. **2** a person who uses an oar; rower. —**rest on one's oars,** to stop one's work in order to rest.

**oar·lock** (ôr'läk) ***n.*** a part for holding an oar in place while rowing. It is often shaped like a U.

**oars·man** (ôrz'mən) ***n.*** a person who rows; especially, an expert at rowing. *—pl.* **oars'men**

**OAS** or **O.A.S.** Organization of American States.

**o·a·sis** (ō ā'sis) ***n.*** **1** a place that is fertile in a desert because it has water. **2** any place or thing that gives welcome relief from trouble, dullness, etc. *—pl.* **o·a·ses** (ō ā'sēz)

**oat** (ōt) ***n.*** a cereal grass whose seed, or grain, is used as food; also, this grain. *Usually used in the plural,* **oats.** *See the picture.* —☆**feel one's oats,** to feel or act frisky, lively, or important: *a slang phrase.*

**oat·en** (ōt''n) ***adj.*** of or made of oats.

**oath** (ōth) ***n.*** **1** a serious statement in the name of God or of some sacred thing, as the Bible, that one will speak the truth, keep a promise, etc. **2** the use of the name of God or of some sacred thing to express anger or add force to one's words. Such use shows a lack of respect for God. **3** a curse or swearword. *—pl.* **oaths** (ō*th*z *or* ōths) —**take an oath,** to promise or state with an oath. —**under oath,** bound by an oath or serious promise.

**oat·meal** (ōt'mēl) ***n.*** **1** oats that are ground or rolled into meal or flakes. **2** a soft, cooked cereal made by boiling such oats.

**ob·du·rate** (äb'door ət *or* äb'dyoor ət) ***adj.*** **1** not giving in; stubborn; obstinate [The *obdurate* child would not answer.] **2** not feeling sorry for what one has done; not repenting; hardhearted [an *obdurate* sinner]. —**ob·du·ra·cy** (äb'door ə sē) ***n.***

**o·be·di·ence** (ō bē'dē əns) ***n.*** the act of obeying or a willingness to obey.

**o·be·di·ent** (ō bē'dē ənt) ***adj.*** doing or willing to do what one is told; obeying orders [Our dog was trained to be *obedient.*] —**o·be'di·ent·ly** ***adv.***

**o·bei·sance** (ō bā's'ns *or* ō bē's'ns) ***n.*** **1** a bow, curtsy, or other movement of the body to show respect. **2** deep respect shown; homage. —**o·bei'sant** ***adj.***

**ob·e·lisk** (äb'ə lisk *or* ō'bə lisk) ***n.*** a tall stone pillar with four sides that slope from a pointed top. *See the picture.*

**O·ber·on** (ō'bə rän) the king of fairyland in early folk tales.

**o·bese** (ō bēs') ***adj.*** very fat; stout. —**o·be·si·ty** (ō bē'sə tē) ***n.***

**o·bey** (ō bā') ***v.*** **1** to carry out the orders of [Soldiers must *obey* their officers.] **2** to do as one is told [My dog always *obeys.*] **3** to be controlled or guided by [to *obey* one's conscience; to *obey* the rules of a game]. —**o·bey'er** ***n.***

**o·bi** (ō'bē) ***n.*** a wide sash with a bow in back, worn with a Japanese kimono. *See the picture.*

**o·bit·u·ar·y** (ō bich'oo wer'ē) ***n.*** an announcement, as in a newspaper, that someone has died, usually with a brief story of the person's life. *—pl.* **o·bit'u·ar'ies**

> In talking about unpleasant things, people often try to use softer, or less harsh, words or phrases. Just as we sometimes say of someone who has died that the person "has passed on," the ancient Romans would use the verb *obit,* meaning "has gone forward." From this verb we get **obituary.**

**obj.** *abbreviation for* **object** *or* **objective.**

**ob·ject** (äb'jikt) ***n.*** **1** a thing that can be seen or touched; something that takes up space [That brown *object* is a purse.] **2** a person or thing toward which one turns one's thoughts, feelings, or actions [the *object* of my affection]. **3** what a person is trying to reach; goal; purpose [the *object* of this game; your *object* in life]. **4** a word in a sentence that tells who or what is acted upon. *See* **direct object** *and* **indirect object.** Prepositions are often followed by a noun or pronoun called an *object* [In "the book on the table," "table" is the *object* of the preposition "on."] ◆***v.*** (əb jekt') **1** to dislike or disapprove of something [Bill *objects* to wide neckties.] **2** to tell as a reason for not liking or not approving; protest [Jane *objected* that the prices were too high.] —**ob·jec'tor** ***n.***

**ob·jec·tion** (əb jek'shən) ***n.*** **1** a feeling of dislike or disapproval; protest [I have no *objection* to that plan.] **2** a reason for disliking or disapproving [My main *objection* to this climate is its dampness.]

**ob·jec·tion·a·ble** (əb jek'shən ə b'l) ***adj.*** likely to be objected to; not pleasant or agreeable [an *objectionable* smell].

**ob·jec·tive** (əb jek'tiv) ***adj.*** **1** not having or showing a strong opinion for or against something; without bias [A judge must remain *objective*.] **2** that is or has to do with something real, rather than ideas, feelings, etc.; actually existing [Is pain an *objective* experience?] **3** that shows the object of a verb or of a preposition [In "I gave them to her," "them" and "her" are in the *objective* case.] ◆***n.*** **1** something that one tries to reach; goal; purpose [What are your *objectives* in this job?] **2** the objective case. —**ob·jec′tive·ly** ***adv.*** —**ob·jec·tiv·i·ty** (äb′jek tiv′ə tē) ***n.***

**ob·li·gate** (äb′lə gāt) ***v.*** to hold by means of a contract, promise, or feeling of duty [I feel *obligated* to return the favor she did me.] —**ob′li·gat·ed, ob′li·gat·ing**

**ob·li·ga·tion** (äb′lə gā′shən) ***n.*** **1** the condition of being obligated as by duty or a promise [His kindness put me under *obligation* to him.] **2** a contract, promise, or feeling of duty; also, something one must do because the law, one's conscience, etc. demands it [the *obligations* of a good citizen].

**ob·lig·a·to·ry** (ə blig′ə tôr′ē *or* äb′lig ə tôr′ē) ***adj.*** required by law or one's feeling of duty [Going to school until a certain age is *obligatory*.]

**o·blige** (ə blīj′) ***v.*** **1** to force to do something because the law, one's conscience, etc. demands it [Some religions *oblige* people to fast on certain days.] **2** to make feel as if one owes something because of a favor or kindness received [We are much *obliged* for your help.] **3** to do a favor for [Please *oblige* me by coming along.] —**o·bliged′, o·blig′ing**

**o·blig·ing** (ə blī′jiŋ) ***adj.*** ready to do favors; helpful, friendly, etc. [We have very *obliging* neighbors.] —**o·blig′ing·ly** ***adv.***

**ob·lique** (ə blēk′) ***adj.*** **1** not level or not straight up and down; slanting [An *oblique* angle is any angle other than a right angle.] **2** not going straight ahead; not direct [an *oblique* glance; an *oblique* remark]. —**ob·lique′ly** ***adv.***

**ob·lit·er·ate** (ə blit′ə rāt) ***v.*** to blot out or do away with, leaving no traces; erase or destroy [The spilled ink *obliterated* her signature. The bombs *obliterated* the bridge.] —**ob·lit′er·at·ed, ob·lit′er·at·ing** —**ob·lit′er·a′tion** ***n.***

**ob·liv·i·on** (ə bliv′ē ən) ***n.*** **1** the condition of being forgotten [Many old songs have passed into *oblivion*.] **2** the condition of forgetting; forgetfulness [The *oblivion* of sleep eased his sorrow.]

**ob·liv·i·ous** (ə bliv′ē əs) ***adj.*** **1** forgetting or not noticing; not mindful [She kept on reading, *oblivious* of the time.] **2** causing one to be forgetful [the carefree, *oblivious* days of vacation]. —**ob·liv′i·ous·ly** ***adv.***

**ob·long** (äb′lôŋ) ***adj.*** in the shape of a rectangle and longer in one direction than the other, especially longer horizontally. ◆***n.*** an oblong figure.

**ob·lo·quy** (äb′lə kwē) ***n.*** **1** loud and angry criticism, especially by many people [We shall continue to speak out, in spite of public *obloquy*.] **2** disgrace or dishonor that comes from this. —*pl.* **ob′lo·quies**

**ob·nox·ious** (əb näk′shəs) ***adj.*** very unpleasant; disgusting [an *obnoxious*, noisy neighbor]. —**ob·nox′ious·ly** ***adv.***

The original meaning of **obnoxious** was "liable to be harmed or injured." The Latin word from which it comes had that meaning too. Today, the force of the word has been weakened so that it just means "unpleasant or disagreeable."

oak

obelisk

oboe

oats

obi

**o·boe** (ō′bō) ***n.*** a woodwind instrument whose mouthpiece has a double reed. *See the picture.* —**o′bo·ist** ***n.***

**ob·scene** (äb sēn′) ***adj.*** shocking to one's feelings of modesty or decency; disgusting. —**ob·scene′ly** ***adv.*** **505**

**ob·scen·i·ty** (äb sen′ə tē) ***n.*** **1** the quality of being obscene. **2** something that is obscene. —*pl.* **ob·scen′i·ties**

**ob·scure** (əb skyoor′) ***adj.*** **1** not easily seen or heard; not clear or distinct [an *obscure* figure in the fog; an *obscure* sound in the wall]. **2** not easily understood; not clear to the mind [an *obscure* remark]. **3** dim or dark [the *obscure* night]. **4** not easily noticed; hidden [an *obscure* mountain village]. **5** not famous or well-known [an *obscure* poet]. ◆***v.*** to make obscure; dim, hide, overshadow, confuse, etc. [In an eclipse, the moon *obscures* the sun. That answer only *obscures* the issue.] —**ob·scured′, ob·scur′ing** —**ob·scure′ly** ***adv.*** —**ob·scu′ri·ty** ***n.***

**ob·se·quies** (äb′sə kwēz) ***n.pl.*** funeral services.

**ob·se·qui·ous** (əb sē′kwē əs) ***adj.*** too willing to serve or obey, as in trying to gain favor; servile; fawning. —**ob·se′qui·ous·ly** ***adv.***

**ob·serv·a·ble** (əb zʉr′və b′l) ***adj.*** **1** easily observed, or seen; noticeable [an *observable* change]. **2** that can or should be observed, or kept, as a holiday, rule, etc. —**ob·serv′a·bly** ***adv.***

**ob·serv·ance** (əb zʉr′vəns) ***n.*** **1** the observing, or keeping, of a law, custom, holiday, etc. **2** an act, ceremony, etc. carried out by rule or custom [A St.

| | | | | | | | |
|---|---|---|---|---|---|---|---|
| a | fat | ir | here | ou | out | zh | leisure |
| ā | ape | ī | bite, fire | u | up | ŋ | ring |
| ä | car, lot | ō | go | ʉr | fur | | a *in* ago |
| e | ten | ô | law, horn | ch | chin | | e *in* agent |
| er | care | oi | oil | sh | she | ə = | i *in* unity |
| ē | even | oo | look | th | thin | | o *in* collect |
| i | hit | ōō | tool | *th* | then | | u *in* focus |

observatory

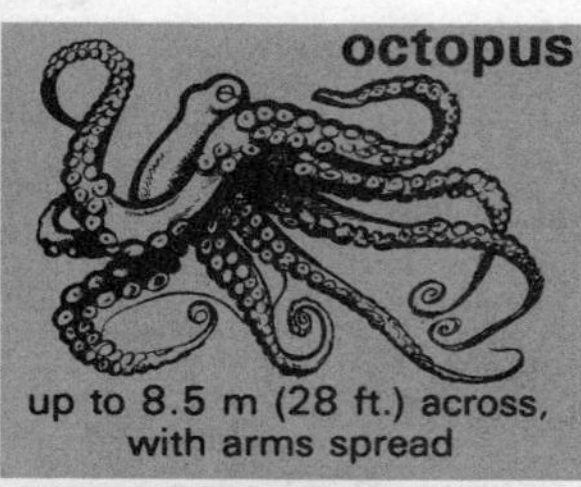
octopus

up to 8.5 m (28 ft.) across, with arms spread

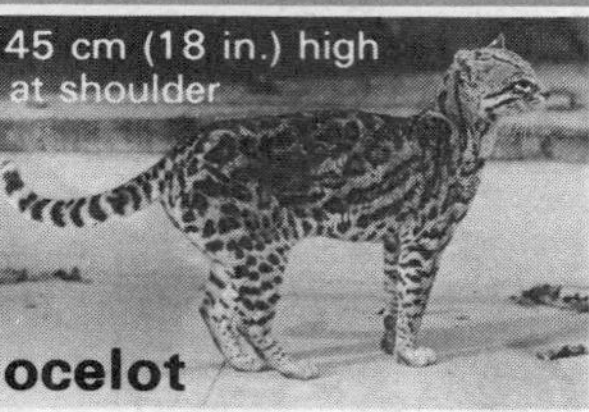
45 cm (18 in.) high at shoulder

ocelot

Patrick's Day parade is a regular *observance* in our city.]

**ob·serv·ant** (əb zur′vənt) ***adj.*** **1** strict in observing, or keeping, a law, custom, etc. [*observant* of the rules of etiquette]. **2** paying careful attention; alert [An *observant* student noticed the wrong spelling.] —**ob·serv′ant·ly *adv.***

**ob·ser·va·tion** (äb′zər vā′shən) ***n.*** **1** the act or power of seeing or noticing [It's a good night for *observation* of the stars.] **2** the fact of being seen or noticed [We came in the back way to avoid *observation.*]

**3** the noting and writing down of some fact; also, the fact written down [Dr. Lopez will publish his *observations* on heart disease.] **4** a remark or comment [the reviewer's *observations* on the novel]. ◆***adj.*** for observing [an *observation* tower].

**ob·serv·a·to·ry** (əb zur′və tôr′ē) ***n.*** a building with telescopes and other equipment in it for studying the stars, weather conditions, etc. *See the picture.* —*pl.* **ob·serv′a·to′ries**

**ob·serve** (əb zurv′) ***v.*** **1** to keep or follow; be guided by [to *observe* the rules of a game]. **2** to celebrate according to custom [We *observe* Thanksgiving with a turkey dinner.] **3** to see, watch, or notice [I *observed* that the child was smiling.] **4** to remark or comment ["It may rain," she *observed.*] **5** to examine and study carefully [to *observe* an experiment]. —**ob·served′, ob·serv′ing —ob·serv′er *n.***

**ob·sess** (əb ses′) ***v.*** to fill the thoughts of; haunt in the mind [She was *obsessed* with dreams of fame.]

**ob·ses·sion** (əb sesh′ən) ***n.*** **1** the condition of being obsessed with an idea, wish, etc. **2** an idea, wish, etc. that fills one's thoughts and cannot be put out of mind [Spending the summer traveling through Europe had become an *obsession* with him.]

**ob·sid·i·an** (əb sid′ē ən) ***n.*** a dark, glassy rock formed from the lava of volcanoes.

**ob·so·les·cent** (äb′sə les′′nt) ***adj.*** becoming obsolete; going out of use or fashion [*obsolescent* machinery]. —**ob′so·les′cence *n.***

**ob·so·lete** (äb sə lēt′ *or* äb′sə lēt) ***adj.*** no longer in use or fashion; out-of-date [an *obsolete* word; an *obsolete* airplane].

**ob·sta·cle** (äb′sti k'l) ***n.*** anything that gets in the way or keeps one from going ahead; obstruction [Lack of an education was the main *obstacle* to his success.]

**ob·ste·tri·cian** (äb′stə trish′ən) ***n.*** a doctor who is an expert in obstetrics.

**ob·stet·rics** (əb stet′riks *or* äb stet′riks) ***n.pl.*** the branch of medicine that deals with the care of women who are giving birth to children: *used with a singular verb.* —**ob·stet′ric** or **ob·stet′ri·cal *adj.***

**ob·sti·na·cy** (äb′stə nə sē) ***n.*** **1** the quality of being obstinate; stubbornness. **2** an obstinate act.

**ob·sti·nate** (äb′stə nit) ***adj.*** **1** not willing to give in or to change one's mind; stubborn [The *obstinate* child refused to answer.] **2** hard to treat or cure [an *obstinate* fever]. —**ob′sti·nate·ly *adv.***

**ob·strep·er·ous** (əb strep′ər əs) ***adj.*** noisy or hard to manage; unruly [The *obstreperous* crowd refused to become quiet.]

**ob·struct** (əb strukt′) ***v.*** **1** to block or stop up; clog [Grease *obstructed* the sink drain.] **2** to hinder or hold back [to *obstruct* progress]. **3** to cut off from being seen [The billboards *obstructed* our view.] —**ob·struc′tive *adj.***

**ob·struc·tion** (əb struk′shən) ***n.*** **1** an obstructing or being obstructed [the *obstruction* of justice]. **2** anything that obstructs; hindrance [to remove an *obstruction* from a pipe].

**ob·tain** (əb tān′) ***v.*** **1** to get by trying [to *obtain* a job; to *obtain* help]. **2** to be in force or in use [That law no longer *obtains.*] *See* SYNONYMS *at* **get.**

**ob·tain·a·ble** (əb tān′ə b'l) ***adj.*** that can be obtained; available [Are tickets for the concert still *obtainable?*]

**ob·trude** (əb trood′) ***v.*** **1** to force oneself, one's opinions, etc. upon others without being asked or wanted [I didn't mean to *obtrude* upon your privacy.] **2** to push out. —**ob·trud′ed, ob·trud′ing**

**ob·tru·sive** (əb troo′siv) ***adj.*** **1** in the habit of obtruding [an *obtrusive* person]. **2** calling attention to itself in an unpleasant way [an *obtrusive* neon sign].

**ob·tuse** (əb toos′ *or* äb tyoos′) ***adj.*** **1** not quick to understand; dull or stupid. **2** more than 90 degrees: said of angles. —**ob·tuse′ness *n.***

**Obtuse** comes from a Latin verb that means "to beat something until it gets blunt or dull." It is hard to beat an idea into the head of an obtuse person.

**ob·verse** (äb′vərs) ***n.*** the main side; front [The *obverse* of a U.S. coin has the date on it.]

**ob·vi·ate** (äb′vē āt) ***v.*** to prevent by acting ahead of time; make unnecessary [Proper care of one's car can *obviate* the need for many repairs.] —**ob′vi·at·ed, ob′vi·at·ing**

**ob·vi·ous** (äb′vē əs) ***adj.*** easy to see or understand; plain; clear [an *obvious* rust stain; an *obvious* danger]. —**ob′vi·ous·ly *adv.*** —**ob′vi·ous·ness *n.***

**O'Ca·sey** (ō kā′sē), **Sean** (shôn) 1880–1964; Irish writer of plays.

**oc·ca·sion** (ə kā′zhən) ***n.*** **1** a suitable time; good chance; opportunity [Did you have *occasion* to visit with them?] **2** a cause or reason [You have no *occasion* to feel sad.] **3** a particular time [We've met on several *occasions.*] **4** a special time or happening [Independence Day is an *occasion* to celebrate.] ◆***v.*** to cause or bring about [Her sudden arrival *occasioned* a change in our plans.] —**on occasion** once in a while [I'll eat ice cream *on occasion.*]

**oc·ca·sion·al** (ə kā′zhən 'l) ***adj.*** **1** happening only once in a while [an *occasional* trip to town]. **2** of or for a special occasion [An *occasional* poem is one written for a birthday, anniversary, etc.] **3** for use only now and then; extra [*occasional* chairs].

**oc·ca·sion·al·ly** (ə kā′zhən ′l ē) ***adv.*** now and then; once in a while.

**Oc·ci·dent** (äk′sə dənt) ***n.*** the part of the world west of Asia; especially, Europe and the Americas.

**Oc·ci·den·tal** (äk′sə den′t′l) ***adj.*** of the Occident; Western [*Occidental* music]. ◆***n.*** a member of any of the peoples who are native to the Occident.

**oc·cult** (ə kult′ *or* ä′kult) ***adj.*** having to do with secret skills or powers that most people do not pretend to have [Magic and astrology are *occult* arts.]

**oc·cu·pan·cy** (äk′yə pən sē) ***n.*** the act of occupying or holding in possession [We will have *occupancy* of the cottage for the whole summer.]

**oc·cu·pant** (äk′yə pənt) ***n.*** a person who occupies land, a house, a position, etc. [a former *occupant* of the White House].

**oc·cu·pa·tion** (äk′yə pā′shən) ***n.*** **1** the work that a person does to earn a living; one's trade, profession, or business; vocation. **2** the act of occupying or the condition of being occupied; possession [the Roman *occupation* of Britain]. —**oc′cu·pa′tion·al *adj.***

**oc·cu·py** (äk′yə pī) ***v.*** **1** to take possession of a place by capturing it or settling in it [The Germans *occupied* much of France during World War II. Pioneers *occupied* the wilderness.] **2** to have or hold [She *occupies* an important post in the government.] **3** to live in [to *occupy* a house]. **4** to take up; fill [The store *occupies* the entire building.] **5** to keep busy; employ [Many activities *occupy* his time.] —**oc′cu·pied, oc′cu·py·ing**

**oc·cur** (ə kur′) ***v.*** **1** to come into one's mind [The idea never *occurred* to me.] **2** to happen; take place [That event *occurred* years ago.] **3** to be found; exist [Fish *occur* in most waters.] —**oc·curred′, oc·cur′·ring**

**oc·cur·rence** (ə kur′əns) ***n.*** **1** the act or fact of occurring [the *occurrence* of rain]. **2** a happening or event [a strange *occurrence*].

**o·cean** (ō′shən) ***n.*** **1** the whole body of salt water that covers more than two thirds of the earth's surface; the sea. **2** any of the five main parts into which it is divided: the Atlantic, Pacific, Indian, Arctic, or Antarctic Ocean.

> **Ocean** comes from *Oceanus,* the name of the Titan who was the god of the sea before Poseidon. The Greeks thought that the earth was flat, and they gave the name *Oceanus* to what they believed was a great river flowing around its edge.

**o·cean·go·ing** (ō′shən gō′iŋ) ***adj.*** made for travel on the ocean [an *oceangoing* yacht].

**O·ce·an·i·a** (ō′shē an′ē ə) islands in the Pacific, including Melanesia, Micronesia, and Polynesia and, sometimes, Australia, New Zealand, and the Malay Archipelago.

**o·ce·an·ic** (ō′shē an′ik) ***adj.*** of, living in, or like the ocean.

**o·cean·og·ra·phy** (ō′shə näg′rə fē) ***n.*** the science that studies the oceans and the animals and plants that live in them. —**o′cean·og′ra·pher *n.***

**o·ce·lot** (äs′ə lät *or* ō′sə lät) ***n.*** a wildcat that is like a small leopard, found in North and South America. *See the picture.*

**o·cher** or **o·chre** (ō′kər) ***n.*** **1** a dark-yellow or light-brown clay, used as a coloring matter in paints. **2** dark yellow.

**o′clock** (ə kläk′ *or* ō kläk′) ***adv.*** of the clock; according to the clock [twelve *o'clock* midnight].

**Oct.** *abbreviation for* **October.**

**oc·ta·gon** (äk′tə gän) ***n.*** a flat figure having eight angles and eight sides.

**oc·tag·o·nal** (äk tag′ə n′l) ***adj.*** having the shape of an octagon.

**oc·tave** (äk′tiv *or* äk′tāv) ***n.*** **1** a musical tone that is the eighth full tone above or below another tone. **2** the difference in pitch between two such tones. **3** the series of tones between two such tones; especially, the eight full steps of a musical scale. **4** two tones an octave apart that are sounded together. **5** a group of eight.

**oc·ta·vo** (äk tā′vō) ***n.*** **1** the page size of a book that is about 6 by 9 inches. **2** a book of such pages. —*pl.* **oc·ta′vos**

**oc·tet** or **oc·tette** (äk tet′) ***n.*** **1** a piece of music for eight voices or eight instruments. **2** the eight people who sing or play it.

**Oc·to·ber** (äk tō′bər) ***n.*** the tenth month of the year, which has 31 days: abbreviated **Oct.**

**oc·to·pus** (äk′tə pəs) ***n.*** **1** a sea animal with a soft body and eight long arms covered with suckers. *See the picture.* **2** anything like an octopus, as a powerful organization that has many branches. —*pl.* **oc′to·pus·es** or **oc·to·pi** (äk′tə pī) 507

**oc·u·lar** (äk′yə lər) ***adj.*** of or having to do with the eye or with eyesight [an *ocular* examination].

**oc·u·list** (äk′yə list) ***n.*** *an earlier name for* **ophthalmologist.**

**odd** (äd) ***adj.*** **1** left over, as from what was once a pair, a set, etc. [an *odd* glove; a few *odd* volumes of an encyclopedia]. **2** having a remainder of one when divided by two; not even [7, 15, and 43 are *odd* numbers.] **3** having an odd number [the *odd* days of the month]. **4** and a little more than what is mentioned; and some extra [forty *odd* years ago; two dollars and some *odd* change]. **5** not regular; occasional [*odd* jobs]. **6** strange or queer [What an *odd* thing to say!] *See* SYNONYMS *at* **strange.** —**odd′ly *adv.*** —**odd′·ness *n.***

**odd·i·ty** (äd′ə tē) ***n.*** **1** strangeness or queerness [the *oddity* of his actions]. **2** a strange or unusual person or thing [A four-leaf clover is an *oddity.*] —*pl.* **odd′i·ties**

**odds** (ädz) ***n.pl.*** **1** a difference that favors one side over the other; advantage [a struggle against great *odds*]. **2** advantage given to a bettor according to the chances that are thought to be against the success of that bet [A bettor who gets *odds* of 10 to 1 will receive 10 times the amount risked if that bet wins.] —**at**

| | | | |
|---|---|---|---|
| **a** fat | **ir** here | **ou** out | **zh** leisure |
| **ā** ape | **ī** bite, fire | **u** up | **ŋ** ring |
| **ä** car, lot | **ō** go | **ur** fur | a *in* ago |
| **e** ten | **ô** law, horn | **ch** chin | e *in* agent |
| **er** care | **oi** oil | **sh** she | **ə** = i *in* unity |
| **ē** even | **oo** look | **th** thin | o *in* collect |
| **i** hit | **ōō** tool | ***th*** then | u *in* focus |

**odds,** having a quarrel; disagreeing. —**by all odds,** by far. —**the odds are,** it is likely [*The odds are* that we won't even be missed.]

**odds and ends** scraps or small bits left over.

**ode** (ōd) ***n.*** a serious poem in a dignified style, usually honoring some person or event.

**O·der** (ō′dər) a river in central Europe, that flows through Czechoslovakia and Poland into the Baltic Sea.

**O·des·sa** (ō des′ə) a seaport of the Ukraine in the U.S.S.R., on the Black Sea.

**O·din** (ō′din) the chief god in Norse myths.

**o·di·ous** (ō′dē əs) ***adj.*** very unpleasant; hateful; disgusting [an *odious* crime].

**o·di·um** (ō′dē əm) ***n.*** **1** hatred or the condition of being hated. **2** the disgrace brought on by hateful or shameful action [Will they ever live down the *odium* of their scandal?]

**o·dom·e·ter** (ō däm′ə tər) ***n.*** an instrument that measures how far a vehicle has traveled.

**o·dor** (ō′dər) ***n.*** any smell, whether pleasant or unpleasant. —**be in bad odor,** to have a bad reputation. —**o′dor·less** ***adj.***

**o·dor·if·er·ous** (ō′də rif′ər əs) ***adj.*** giving off an odor, especially a pleasant odor.

**o·dor·ous** (ō′dər əs) ***adj.*** having an odor, especially a pleasant odor; fragrant.

**o·dour** (ō′dər) ***n.*** *the British spelling of* **odor.**

**O·dys·se·us** (ō dis′yo͞os *or* ō dis′ē əs) a king of Ithaca and a leader of the Greeks in the Trojan War. He is the hero of the *Odyssey*. His Latin name is *Ulysses*.

**Od·ys·sey** (äd′ə sē) a long Greek poem thought to have been written by Homer. It tells about the wanderings of Odysseus for ten years on his way home after the Trojan War. ◆***n.*** *sometimes* **odyssey,** any long journey with many adventures. —*pl.* **Od′ys·seys** or **od′ys·seys**

**OE.** or **O.E.** *abbreviation for* **Old English.**

**Oed·i·pus** (ed′ə pəs *or* ē′də pəs) a king in Greek legend who killed his father and married his mother, not knowing he was their son.

**o'er** (ôr) ***prep., adv.*** over: *used in earlier poetry.*

**of** (uv *or* äv *or* əv) ***prep.*** **1** coming from [men *of* Ohio]. **2** resulting from [to die *of* a fever]. **3** at a distance from [a mile east *of* town]. **4** written or made by [the novels *of* Dickens]. **5** separated from [robbed *of* his money]. **6** from the whole that is or the total number that are [part *of* the time; one *of* his sisters]. **7** made from [a sheet *of* paper]. **8** belonging to [the pages *of* a book]. **9** having or owning [a person *of* property]. **10** containing [a bag *of* nuts]. **11** that is [a height *of* six feet; the State *of* Iowa]. **12** with something mentioned as a goal, object, etc. [a reader *of* books; the education *of* children; a day *of* rest]. **13** concerning; about [Think *of* me when I'm away.] **14** during [They've been away *of* recent months.] **15** before: *used in telling time* [ten *of* four].

**off** (ôf) ***adv.*** **1** away; to some other place [They moved *off* down the road.] **2** so as to be no longer on or attached [Please take *off* your hat. The paint wore *off*.] **3** at a later time [My birthday is only two weeks *off*.] **4** so as to be no longer working, going on, etc. [Turn the motor *off*. They broke *off* their talks.] **5** so as to be less, smaller, etc. [Sales dropped *off*.] **6** so as to be measured, divided, etc. [Mark *off* two meters.] **7** away from one's work [Let's take the day *off*.] ◆***prep.*** **1** not on, not attached to, etc.; away from [a car *off* the road]. **2** branching out from [a lane *off* the main road]. **3** free or released from [*off* duty]. **4** below the usual level or standard of [I was *off* my game today. We sell it at 20% *off* list price.] **5** no longer using, taking part in, etc.: *used only in everyday talk* [I'm *off* candy from now on.] ◆***adj.*** **1** not on or attached [My shoes are *off*.] **2** not working, taking place, etc. [The motor is *off*. Our trip is *off*.] **3** on the way [I'm *off* to bed.] **4** less, smaller, fewer, etc. [Sales are *off*.] **5** slight; not very likely [I'll phone her on the *off* chance that she's home.] **6** taken care of, provided for, etc. [They are well *off*.] **7** wrong; in error [Your figures are a little *off*.] ◆***interj.*** go away! —**be off** or **take off,** to go away. —**off and on,** now and then. —**off with,** take off! remove!

**of·fal** (ôf′′l) ***n.*** **1** the waste parts left over after an animal has been cut up for meat, especially the intestines. **2** rubbish or garbage.

> **Offal** is just a combination of the words *off* and *fall*. That is, *offal* is used of the parts of the animal that fell off and were thrown away when the butcher cut up the animal.

**off·beat** (ôf′bēt) ***adj.*** not of the usual kind; not conventional; unusual, strange, etc.: *used only in everyday talk* [*offbeat* humor].

**of·fence** (ə fens′) ***n.*** *the British spelling of* **offense.**

**of·fend** (ə fend′) ***v.*** **1** to hurt the feelings of; make angry or upset; insult [Her rude answer *offended* him.] **2** to be unpleasant to; displease [The noise *offends* my ears.] **3** to do wrong; commit a crime or sin. —**of·fend′er** ***n.***

> SYNONYMS: To **offend** people is to make them angry or upset by hurting their feelings [He was *offended* by her constant interruptions.] To **insult** people is to treat them in such a rude way as to take away their pride or dignity [I was *insulted* when they made fun of my clothes.] To **outrage** people is to do something so wicked or evil as to cause them to feel the greatest anger or shock [She was *outraged* when vandals destroyed her car.]

**of·fense** (ə fens′) ***n.*** **1** the act of doing wrong or of breaking a law or rule [a traffic *offense*]. **2** the act of making or becoming angry, annoyed, etc. [I really meant no *offense*.] **3** something that causes anger, hurt feelings, etc. [That remark would be an *offense* to anyone.] **4** the act of attacking; assault. **5** the person, army, etc. that is attacking. ☆**6** the side that has the ball or puck and is trying to score in any game. —**give offense,** to offend; anger or annoy. —**take offense,** to become angry or annoyed.

**of·fen·sive** (ə fen′siv) ***adj.*** **1** attacking or used for attacking [*offensive* troops; *offensive* weapons]. ☆**2** being the side that is trying to score in a game. **3** unpleasant; disgusting [an *offensive* odor]. **4** making one angry, annoyed, etc.; insulting [*offensive* comments]. ◆***n.*** an attack or a position for attacking [The army is ready to take the *offensive*.] —**of·fen′sive·ly** ***adv.*** —**of·fen′sive·ness** ***n.***

**of·fer** (ôf′ər) ***v.*** **1** to put forward for someone to take or refuse [to *offer* one's help; to *offer* an opinion]. **2** to give or present in worship [to *offer* a prayer]. **3** to say that one is willing [I *offered* to go with them.] **4** to show or give signs of [The rusty hinges *offered* some resistance.] **5** to suggest as a price one is willing to pay [I *offered* $5 for the book.] **◆*n.*** an act of offering or something that is offered [Will you accept a lower *offer?*]

**of·fer·ing** (ôf′ər iŋ) ***n.*** **1** the act of one who offers. **2** something offered, as money given during a church service.

**of·fer·to·ry** (ôf′ər tôr′ē) ***n.*** **1** the part of Holy Communion when the bread and wine are offered to God. **2** the collection of money at a church service. **3** prayers said or music sung while the collection is made. —*pl.* **of′fer·to′ries**

**off·hand** (ôf′hand′) ***adv.*** without thinking much about it ahead of time [Can you tell us *offhand* how many you will need?] **◆*adj.*** **1** done or said offhand [an *offhand* reply]. **2** sharp or rude; without politeness [an *offhand* refusal].

**of·fice** (ôf′is) ***n.*** **1** the place where a certain kind of business or work is carried on [a lawyer's *office;* the main *office* of a company; a post *office*]. **2** all the people working in such an office. **3** an important position, job, or duty [the *office* of treasurer]. **4** *often* **offices,** *pl.* something done for another person; service [He got the job through his aunt's good *offices.*] **5** a religious ceremony.

**of·fice·hold·er** (ôf′is hōl′dər) ***n.*** a person holding some office, especially in government.

**of·fi·cer** (ôf′ə sər) ***n.*** **1** a person holding some office, as in a business, club, or government. **2** a member of a police force. **3** a person who commands others in an army, navy, etc. [Generals and lieutenants are commissioned *officers.*]

**of·fi·cial** (ə fish′əl) ***n.*** **1** a person who holds an office, especially in government. ☆**2** a person who sees to it that the rules are followed in a game, as a referee or umpire. **◆*adj.*** **1** of or having to do with an office [an *official* record; *official* duties]. **2** coming from a person who has authority [an *official* request]. **3** fit for an important officer; formal [an *official* welcome]. —**of·fi′cial·ly *adv.***

**of·fi·ci·ate** (ə fish′ē āt) ***v.*** **1** to carry out the duties of an office [to *officiate* as mayor]. **2** to act as referee or umpire in a game. **3** to be in charge of a religious service or ceremony [to *officiate* at a wedding]. —**of·fi′ci·at·ed, of·fi′ci·at·ing**

**of·fi·cious** (ə fish′əs) ***adj.*** giving advice or help that is not wanted or needed; meddling. —**of·fi′cious·ly *adv.*** —**of·fi′cious·ness *n.***

**off·ing** (ôf′iŋ) ***n.*** distance or position far away: *now used only in the phrase* **in the offing,** meaning "far away but still in sight" or "at some time or other in the future."

**off-key** (ôf′kē′) ***adj.*** **1** not on the right musical note; flat or sharp. **2** not quite right or proper [an *off-key* remark].

**off·set** (ôf set′) ***v.*** to balance or make up for [The loss on corn was *offset* by the profit on wheat.] —**off·set′, off·set′ting ◆*n.*** (ôf′set) **1** anything that offsets something else. **2** *a shorter form of* **offset printing.**

**offset printing** a way of printing by which the inked impression of a plate is first made on a roller covered with rubber. The roller then transfers the impression onto paper.

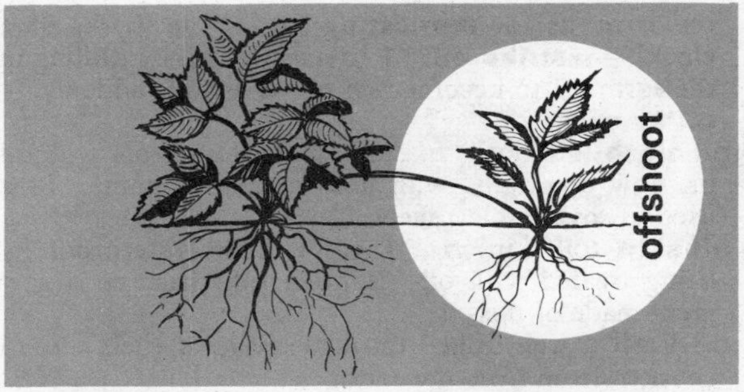


**off·shoot** (ôf′sho͞ot) ***n.*** anything that branches off from a main line; especially, a shoot that grows from the main stem of a plant. *See the picture.*

**off·shore** (ôf′shôr′) ***adj.*** **1** moving away from the shore [an *offshore* current]. **2** at some distance from shore [an *offshore* island]. **◆*adv.*** away from shore [to sail *offshore*].

**off·side** (ôf′sīd′) ***adj.*** not in the proper position for play, as a football player who is ahead of the ball before play begins.

**off·spring** (ôf′spriŋ) ***n.*** a child or animal as related to its parent. —*pl.* **off′spring** or **off′springs**

**off·stage** (ôf′stāj′) ***adj., adv.*** in, from, or to the part of a stage that is not seen by the audience [*offstage* music; to go *offstage*].

**oft** (ôft) ***adv.*** often: *no longer much used except in forming compounds* [an *oft-heard* expression]. 509

**of·ten** (ôf″n *or* ôf′t′n) ***adv.*** many times; frequently.

**of·ten·times** (ôf″n tīmz *or* ôf′t′n tīmz) ***adv.*** often; frequently.

**o·gle** (ō′g'l) ***v.*** to keep looking at boldly in a loving way; flirt. —**o′gled, o′gling ◆*n.*** an ogling look.

**o·gre** (ō′gər) ***n.*** **1** in fairy tales, a giant who eats people. **2** a cruel or evil person.

**oh** (ō) ***interj.*** a sound made in showing surprise, fear, wonder, pain, etc.

**O. Henry** *see* **Henry, O.**

**O·hi·o** (ō hī′ō) **1** a State in the north central part of the U.S.: abbreviated **O., OH** **2** a river that flows along the southern borders of Ohio, Indiana, and Illinois to the Mississippi. —**O·hi′o·an *adj., n.***

**ohm** (ōm) ***n.*** a unit for measuring electrical resistance. It is the resistance of a conductor in which one volt produces a current of one ampere.

**-oid** (oid) *a suffix meaning* like *or* somewhat like [A *spheroid* is a form somewhat like a sphere.]

**oil** (oil) ***n.*** **1** any of certain greasy liquids that come from animal, vegetable, or mineral matter, as whale oil, peanut oil, or petroleum. Oils can be burned and do not mix with water, but float on top. **2** a paint made by mixing some coloring matter with oil: *also called* **oil color, oil paint.** **3** a picture painted with oil colors: *its full name is* **oil painting.** **◆*v.*** to put oil

| | | | |
|---|---|---|---|
| **a** fat | **ir** here | **ou** out | **zh** leisure |
| **ā** ape | **ī** bite, fire | **u** up | **ŋ** ring |
| **ä** car, lot | **ō** go | **ʉr** fur | a *in* ago |
| **e** ten | **ô** law, horn | **ch** chin | e *in* agent |
| **er** care | **oi** oil | **sh** she | **ə** = i *in* unity |
| **ē** even | **oo** look | **th** thin | o *in* collect |
| **i** hit | **o͞o** tool | ***th*** then | u *in* focus |

on or in, as for lubricating [to *oil* the works of a clock]. —☆**strike oil, 1** to discover oil by drilling in the earth. **2** to become rich or successful suddenly. —**oil'er** ***n.***

**oil·cloth** (oil'klôth) ***n.*** cloth made waterproof with oil or, now especially, with heavy coats of paint. It is used to cover tables, shelves, etc.

**oil·skin** (oil'skin) ***n.*** **1** cloth made waterproof by being treated with oil. **2** *often* **oilskins,** *pl.* a garment made of this.

**oil well** a well drilled through layers of rock, etc. to get petroleum from the earth.

**oil·y** (oil'ē) ***adj.*** **1** of or like oil [an *oily* liquid]. **2** full of or covered with oil; greasy [*oily* hair]. **3** too polite or flattering [*oily* compliments]. —**oil'i·er, oil'i·est** —**oil'i·ness** ***n.***

**oint·ment** (oint'mənt) ***n.*** an oily cream rubbed on the skin to heal it or make it soft and smooth; salve.

☆**OK** or **O.K.** (ō'kā') ***adj., adv., interj.*** all right; correct. ◆***n.*** approval. —*pl.* **OK's** or **O.K.'s** ◆***v.*** to put an OK on; approve. —**OK'd** or **O.K.'d, OK'ing** or **O.K.'ing**

510 In the 1830's, some writers would misspell certain words as a joke. For example, "all correct" would be misspelled as "oll korrect," and then abbreviated as "O.K." In 1840, the abbreviation became even more popular, because it was mixed up with the abbreviation for the *Old Kinderhook* Club, which supported Martin Van Buren for president. President Van Buren was born in Kinderhook, N.Y.

☆**o·kay** (ō'kā') ***adj., adv., interj., n., v.*** *an everyday spelling for* **OK.**

**O·kla·ho·ma** (ō'klə hō'mə) a State in the south central part of the U.S.: abbreviated **Okla., OK**

**o·kra** (ō'krə) ***n.*** a plant with green pods that become sticky when cooked, as in soups. *See the picture.*

**old** (ōld) ***adj.*** **1** having lived or existed for a long time [an *old* man; an *old* building]. **2** of a certain age [a car five years *old*]. **3** made some time ago; not new [*old* recordings]. **4** worn out by age or use [*old* shoes]. **5** having been such for a long time [They are *old* friends.] **6** being the earlier or earliest [the *Old* World]. **7** having much experience [an *old* hand at this work]. **8** former; at one time [an *old* teacher of mine]. **9** of or like aged people [*old* for their years]. —**old'er** or **eld'er, old'est** or **eld'est** *Old* is sometimes used in everyday talk to show a warm or friendly feeling [Good *old* Gerry!] ◆***n.*** time long past [days of *old*]. —**the old,** old people. —**old'ness** ***n.***

☆**old country** the country from which an immigrant came, especially a country in Europe.

**old·en** (ōl'd'n) ***adj.*** of long ago; old; ancient [in *olden* times].

**Old English** the language of the Anglo-Saxons. It was spoken in England from about 400 to about 1100.

**old-fash·ioned** (ōld'fash'ənd) ***adj.*** suited to the past more than to the present; out-of-date [an *old-fashioned* dress; *old-fashioned* ideas].

☆**Old Glory** the flag of the United States.

**old·ish** (ōl'dish) ***adj.*** somewhat old.

**old maid** a woman, especially an older woman, who has never married. —**old'-maid'ish** ***adj.***

**Old Testament** the first of the two parts of the Christian Bible. It is the Holy Scriptures of Judaism and contains the history of the Hebrews, the laws of Moses, the writings of the prophets, etc.

**old-time** (ōld'tīm') ***adj.*** of or like past times.

**old-tim·er** (ōld'tīm'ər) ***n.*** a person who has lived or worked at the same place for a long time: *used only in everyday talk.*

**Old World** the Eastern Hemisphere; Europe, Asia, and Africa. —**old'-world'** ***adj.***

**o·le·an·der** (ō'lē an'dər *or* ō'lē an'dər) ***n.*** a poisonous evergreen shrub with sweet-smelling white, pink, or red flowers.

☆**o·le·o·mar·ga·rine** or **o·le·o·mar·ga·rin** (ō'lē ō mär'jə rin) ***n.*** *the full name of* **margarine.**

**ol·fac·to·ry** (äl fak'tər ē *or* ōl fak'tər ē) ***adj.*** of the sense of smell [*olfactory* nerves].

**ol·i·gar·chy** (äl'ə gär'kē) ***n.*** **1** government in which a few persons hold the ruling power. **2** a country with such a government. **3** the persons ruling such a country. —*pl.* **ol'i·gar'chies**

**ol·ive** (äl'iv) ***n.*** **1** the small, oval fruit of an evergreen tree of southern Europe and the Middle East. Olives are eaten green or ripe, or are pressed for their oil. **2** the tree that this fruit grows on, or its wood. *See the picture.* **3** the color of an unripe olive, dull yellowish green.

**olive branch** a branch of the olive tree. It is a symbol of peace.

In ancient times during a war, when a spokesman for one side wanted to talk about peace terms, he would come holding out an olive branch. A king whose reign was a peaceful one would be shown on coins holding an olive branch.

**olive oil** a pale yellow oil pressed from ripe olives and used in cooking, making soap, etc.

**O·lym·pi·a** (ō lim'pē ə) **1** the capital of the State of Washington. **2** a plain in ancient Greece where the Olympic games were held. *See the map.*

**O·lym·pi·an** (ō lim'pē ən) ***adj.*** **1** of Mount Olympus [the *Olympian* gods]. **2** powerful and majestic, like a god [*Olympian* dignity]. ◆***n.*** **1** any of the Greek gods, who were thought to live on Mount Olympus. **2** a person taking part in the Olympic games.

**O·lym·pic** (ō lim'pik) ***adj.*** **1** of or having to do with the Olympic games. **2** *same as* **Olympian.** ◆***n.*** **Olympics,** *pl.* the Olympic games.

**Olympic games** **1** an ancient Greek festival that was held every four years, with contests in athletics, poetry, and music. **2** a contest of modern times, usually held every four years in a different country, in which athletes from all over the world compete in many sports and games.

**O·lym·pus** (ō lim'pəs), **Mount** a mountain in northern Greece. In Greek myths, it was the home of the gods.

**O·ma·ha** (ō'mə hô *or* ō'mə hä) a city in eastern Nebraska, on the Missouri River.

**O·man** (ō män') a country in southeastern Arabia, on the Arabian Sea.

**om·buds·man** (äm'bədz mən) ***n.*** a public official who looks into complaints people have placed against their government. —*pl.* **om'buds·men**

**o·me·ga** (ō mā'gə *or* ō mē'gə) ***n.*** **1** the last letter of the Greek alphabet. **2** the end.

**om·e·let** or **om·e·lette** (äm′lit *or* äm′ə let) ***n.*** eggs beaten up, often with milk or water, and cooked as a pancake in a frying pan. It is sometimes folded over a filling, as of jelly or cheese.

**o·men** (ō′mən) ***n.*** anything that is supposed to be a sign of something to come, whether good or bad [A red sunset is an *omen* of good weather.]

**om·i·nous** (äm′ə nəs) ***adj.*** of or like a bad omen; threatening [an *ominous* silence filled the room.] —**om′i·nous·ly *adv.***

**o·mis·sion** (ō mish′ən) ***n.*** **1** the act of omitting something. **2** anything omitted.

**o·mit** (ō mit′) ***v.*** **1** to leave out [You may *omit* the raisins.] **2** to neglect; fail to do [Don't *omit* to cross your t's.] —**o·mit′ted, o·mit′ting**

**om·ni·bus** (äm′nə bəs) ***n.*** *another name for* **bus.** *—pl.* **om′ni·bus·es** ◆***adj.*** that deals with many things at one time [An *omnibus* bill in the Senate has many parts.]

> **Omnibus** comes from the Latin word *omnis,* meaning "all," with an ending that gives it the meaning "for all." This word was first used for the vehicle in a French phrase *voiture omnibus,* meaning "a carriage for all people." In English it was soon shortened to *bus.* And so the name for one of our most common vehicles today is really just a Latin ending for a word.

**om·nip·o·tent** (äm nip′ə tənt) ***adj.*** having power or authority without limit; all-powerful. —**the Omnipotent,** God. —**om·nip′o·tence *n.***

**om·ni·pres·ent** (äm′ni prez″nt) ***adj.*** present in all places at the same time [an *omnipresent* fear of war]. —**om′ni·pres′ence *n.***

**om·nis·cient** (äm nish′ənt) ***adj.*** knowing all things [People who think they are *omniscient* do not know that they are not.] —**om·nis′cience *n.***

**om·niv·o·rous** (äm niv′ər əs) ***adj.*** **1** eating all kinds of food, whether animal or vegetable [Bears are *omnivorous.*] **2** liking all kinds; taking in everything [an *omnivorous* reader].

**on** (än) ***prep.*** **1** held up by, covering, or attached to [a pack *on* his back; a cloth *on* the table; a picture *on* the wall]. **2** in the surface of [a scratch *on* her arm]. **3** near to; at the side of [You will be seated *on* my right.] **4** at or during the time of [Pay *on* entering.] **5** that is a part of [She is a player *on* our team.] **6** in a condition or state of [The tapes are *on* sale. When will you be *on* vacation?] **7** as a result of [We made $250 *on* the paper sale.] **8** in the direction of; toward [The soldiers crept up *on* the fort.] **9** by using; by means of [Most cars run *on* gasoline.] **10** seen or heard by means of [Have you ever been *on* TV?] **11** having to do with; concerning [a book *on* birds]. ☆**12** using: *slang in this meaning* [None of them is *on* drugs.] ◆***adv.*** **1** in a position of covering, touching, or being held up by something [Put your shoes *on.*] **2** to or toward someone or something [He looked *on* while I worked.] **3** in a forward direction; ahead [Move *on!*] **4** without stopping [The band played *on.*] **5** so that it is acting or working [Turn the light *on.*] ◆***adj.*** **1** in action; working or acting [The radio is *on.*] **2** planned for [Is the party still *on* for tomorrow?] —**on and off,** stopping and starting; from time to time. —**on and on,** without stopping; continuously.

**once** (wuns) ***adv.*** **1** one time [We eat together *once* a week.] **2** at some time in the past; formerly [They were rich *once.*] **3** ever; at any time [She'll succeed if *once* given a chance.] ◆***conj.*** as soon as; whenever [*Once* the horse tires, it will quit.] ◆***n.*** one time [I'll go this *once.*] —**all at once, 1** all at the same time. **2** suddenly. —**at once, 1** immediately. **2** at the same time. —**for once,** for at least one time. —**once and for all,** finally. —**once in a while,** now and then. —**once upon a time,** a long time ago.

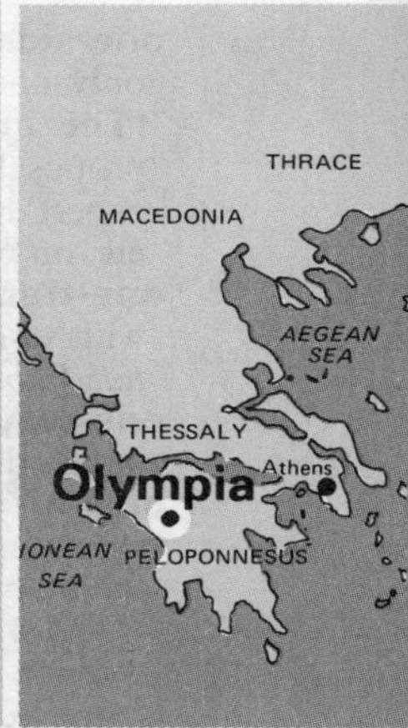


**on·com·ing** (än′kum′ing) ***adj.*** coming nearer; approaching [an *oncoming* train]. ◆***n.*** an approach [the *oncoming* of spring].



**one** (wun) ***adj.*** **1** being a single thing or unit [*one* vote]. **2** forming a whole; united [with *one* accord]. **3** being a certain, but not named, person or thing [Choose *one* road or the other. I went *one* day last week.] **4** single in kind; the same [We are all of *one* mind on the subject.] ◆***n.*** **1** the number that names a single unit; the number 1. **2** a single person or thing [I'll take the blue *one.*] ◆***pron.*** **1** a certain person or thing [*One* of us must go.] **2** any person or thing; anyone or anything [What can *one* do at a time like this?] —**all one,** making no difference; of no importance [It's *all one* to me whether you play or not.] —**at one,** in agreement. —**one and all,** everybody. —**one another,** each person or thing the other; each other [They always help *one another.*] —**one by one,** one following the other.

**O'Neill** (ō nēl′), **Eugene** 1888–1953; U.S. writer of plays.

**one·ness** (wun′nis) ***n.*** the condition of being one or being the same; unity, singleness, or sameness [There is a *oneness* of mind in the group.]

**on·er·ous** (än′ər əs *or* ō′nər əs) ***adj.*** hard to put up with; being a burden [*onerous* tasks].

**one·self** (wun self′) ***pron.*** one's own self [One cannot think only of *oneself.*] *Also written* **one's self.** —**be oneself,** to act naturally. —**by oneself,** alone.

| | | | | | | | |
|---|---|---|---|---|---|---|---|
| **a** | fat | **ir** | here | **ou** | out | **zh** | leisure |
| **ā** | ape | **ī** | bite, fire | **u** | up | **ng** | ring |
| **ä** | car, lot | **ō** | go | **ur** | fur | | a *in* ago |
| **e** | ten | **ô** | law, horn | **ch** | chin | | e *in* agent |
| **er** | care | **oi** | oil | **sh** | she | **ə =** | i *in* unity |
| **ē** | even | **oo** | look | **th** | thin | | o *in* collect |
| **i** | hit | **ōō** | tool | ***th*** | then | | u *in* focus |

**one-sid·ed** (wun′sīd′id) ***adj.*** **1** favoring or showing only one side or one point of view; biased; not fair [The newspaper gave a *one-sided* report of the proposal.] **2** unequal or uneven [A game between an expert and a beginner is *one-sided.*] **3** larger, heavier, etc. on one side; lopsided.

**one-track** (wun′trak′) ***adj.*** ☆able or willing to deal with only one thing at a time: *used only in everyday talk* [a *one-track* mind].

**one-way** (wun′wā′) ***adj.*** that moves or lets one move in one direction only [a *one-way* street].

**on·ion** (un′yən) ***n.*** **1** a plant with a bulb that has a sharp smell and taste and is eaten as a vegetable. **2** the bulb itself. *See the picture.*

The word **onion** is just another spelling of **union,** which comes from a Latin word. The plant was given its name because the bulb is made up of many layers "united" to form a solid growth.

**on·look·er** (än′lo͝ok′ər) ***n.*** a person who watches without taking part; spectator.

**on·ly** (ōn′lē) ***adj.*** **1** without any other or others of the same kind; sole [the *only* suit I own; their *only* friends]. **2** best; finest [This is the *only* soap to use on a baby's skin.] ◆***adv.*** **1** and no other; and no more; just; merely [I have *only* fifty cents. Bite off *only* what you can chew.] **2** as short a time ago as [I was there *only* yesterday.] ◆***conj.*** except that; but: *used only in everyday talk* [I'd go, *only* it's too late.] —**if only,** I wish that [*If only* they would come!] —**only too,** very [I'll be *only too* glad to do it.]

**on·rush** (än′rush) ***n.*** a swift or strong rush forward.

**on·set** (än′set) ***n.*** **1** an attack [The *onset* of enemy troops.] **2** a beginning; start [the *onset* of winter].

**on·slaught** (än′slôt) ***n.*** a fierce attack.

**On·tar·i·o** (än ter′ē ō) **1** the smallest of the Great Lakes, the one farthest east. *The full name is* **Lake Ontario.** **2** a province of south central Canada: abbreviated **Ont.**

**on·to** (än′to͞o *or* än′tə) ***prep.*** **1** to a position on [The cat climbed *onto* the roof.] ☆**2** aware of: *slang in this meaning* [I'm *onto* your tricks.] *Also written* **on to.**

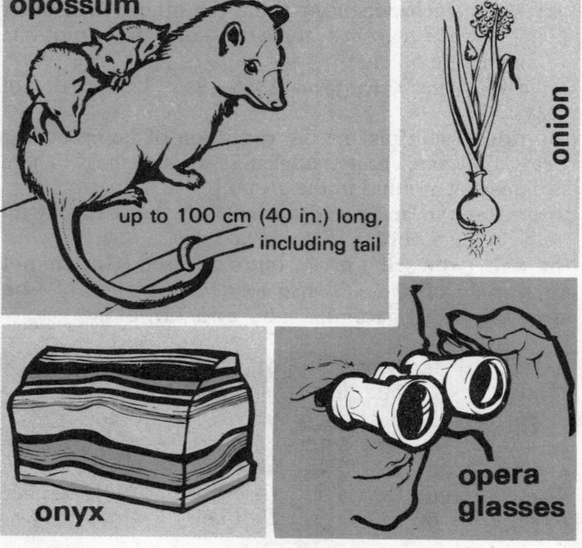


**o·nus** (ō′nəs) ***n.*** a duty or responsibility that is hard for one; burden [The *onus* of cleaning the garage fell upon Jim.]

**on·ward** (än′wərd) ***adv.*** toward or at a place ahead; forward [They marched *onward.*] ◆***adj.*** moving ahead [an *onward* course].

**on·wards** (än′wərdz) ***adv.*** *same as* **onward.**

**on·yx** (än′iks) ***n.*** a stone with layers of different colors, used in jewelry, etc. *See the picture.*

**ooze** (o͞oz) ***v.*** **1** to leak out slowly [Oil *oozed* through the crack.] **2** to disappear little by little [Our hope *oozed* away.] **3** to give forth [a tree that *oozed* sap; a voice that *oozed* friendliness]. —**oozed, ooz′ing** ◆***n.*** **1** the act of oozing or something that oozes [the *ooze* of sap from a tree]. **2** soft, watery mud, as at the bottom of a lake. —**oo′zy** ***adj.***

**o·pac·i·ty** (ō pas′ə tē) ***n.*** the condition of being opaque.

**o·pal** (ō′p'l) ***n.*** a stone of various colors, used as a jewel. Light passing through it seems to make the colors change and move about.

**o·pal·es·cent** (ō′pə les″nt) ***adj.*** having colors that seem to change and move about, as in the opal. —**o′pal·es′cence** ***n.***

**o·paque** (ō pāk′) ***adj.*** **1** that cannot be seen through; not letting light through; not transparent [an *opaque* screen]. **2** not shiny; dull [The desk had an *opaque* surface.] **3** hard to understand [an *opaque* remark].

**o·pen** (ō′p'n) ***adj.*** **1** not closed, shut, covered, or stopped up [*open* eyes; *open* doors; an *open* jar; an *open* drain]. **2** not closed in, fenced in, protected, etc. [an *open* field; an *open* view; an *open* car; *open* to attack]. **3** unfolded; spread out [an *open* book]. **4** having spaces between parts [*open* ranks; cloth with an *open* weave]. **5** that may be entered, taken part in, used, etc. by all [We had an *open* meeting. The store is *open* now.] **6** not settled or decided [an *open* question]. **7** not prejudiced; honest, fair, etc. [an *open* mind]. **8** generous [Give with an *open* heart.] ☆**9** free from strict laws or limits [*open* season in deer hunting]. ☆**10** free from unfair limits having to do with race, religion, etc. [*open* housing]. **11** not already taken or filled; available [The job at the factory is still *open.* There are three courses *open* to us.] **12** not secret; public [an *open* quarrel]. ◆***v.*** **1** to make or become open, or no longer closed [Please *open* that trunk. The door suddenly *opened.*] **2** to spread out; unfold [He *opened* his arms and welcomed us.] **3** to begin or start [We *opened* the program with a song.] **4** to start operating [She *opened* a new store. School will *open* in September.] **5** to be an opening; lead [This door *opens* onto a porch.] —**open to,** willing to listen to or consider [I am *open to* suggestions.] —**the open, 1** any open, clear space; the outdoors. **2** the condition of being known to all. —**o′pen·ly** ***adv.*** —**o′pen·ness** ***n.***

**open air** the outdoors. —**o′pen-air′** ***adj.***

☆**o·pen-and-shut** (ō′p'n 'n shut′) ***adj.*** easily decided because there is no doubt [an *open-and-shut* case].

**o·pen·er** (ō′p'n ər) ***n.*** **1** a person or thing that opens, as a tool for opening cans, bottles, etc. **2** the first game in a series or in a season, the first act in a stage show, etc.

**o·pen-eyed** (ō′p'n īd′) ***adj.*** with the eyes wide open, as in surprise or in careful watching.

**o·pen-faced** (ō′p'n fāst′) ***adj.*** **1** having a frank, honest face. ☆**2** that is a sandwich without a top slice of bread: *also* **o′pen-face′**.

**o·pen·hand·ed** (ō′p'n han′did) ***adj.*** giving freely; generous. —**o′pen·hand′ed·ness** ***n.***

**open house** **1** a party at one's home, with guests coming and going when they wish. **2** a time when a school, business, etc. is open to visitors.

**o·pen·ing** (ō′p'n iŋ) ***n.*** **1** the act of making or becoming open. **2** an open place; hole, clearing, etc. [an *opening* in the wall]. **3** a beginning [the *opening* of a program; the *opening* of a new store]. **4** a good chance; opportunity [At the first *opening* in the conversation, I made a suggestion.] **5** a job that is not filled [The company has no *openings* now.]

**o·pen-mind·ed** (ō′p'n mīn′did) ***adj.*** willing to consider new plans or ideas; not prejudiced or biased. —**o′pen-mind′ed·ness** ***n.***

**o·pen·work** (ō′p'n wurk′) ***n.*** decorations, as in cloth, with openings that are part of the design.

**op·er·a**[1] (äp′ər ə) ***n.*** a play in which all or most of the speeches are sung as solos or by groups. There is usually an orchestra accompanying the singers.

**op·er·a**[2] (ō′pə rə *or* äp′ər ə) ***n.*** *a plural of* **opus**.

**opera glasses** a pair of binoculars, like small field glasses, for use in a theater, etc. *See the picture.*

**op·er·ate** (äp′ə rāt) ***v.*** **1** to keep or be in action; work; run [Can you *operate* a sewing machine? This elevator doesn't *operate* at night.] **2** to have a certain result or effect [a drug that *operates* on the heart]. **3** to do a surgical operation. **4** to control or manage [He *operates* a laundry.] —**op′er·at·ed, op′er·at·ing**

**op·er·at·ic** (äp′ə rat′ik) ***adj.*** of or like opera.

**op·er·a·tion** (äp′ə rā′shən) ***n.*** **1** the act or way of operating [Explain the *operation* of a typewriter.] **2** the condition of being in action or use [The new factory will be in *operation* soon.] **3** any one of a series of actions or movements in some work or plan [Hundreds of *operations* are involved in making automobiles.] **4** a treatment by surgery to heal or correct an injury or illness. **5** any process in mathematics, such as addition or division, that has to do with a change in a quantity.

**op·er·a·tion·al** (äp′ə rā′shən 'l) ***adj.*** **1** having to do with the operation of a system, device, etc. [*operational* costs]. **2** in use or able to be used [The new airplane will be *operational* in a month.]

**op·er·a·tive** (äp′ə rā′tiv *or* äp′ər ə tiv) ***adj.*** **1** working or in operation; in effect [That lease is not yet *operative.*] **2** having to do with the work of people or machines. ◆***n.*** **1** a skilled worker, especially in industry. ☆**2** a detective or spy.

**op·er·a·tor** (äp′ə rāt′ər) ***n.*** ☆**1** a person who operates a machine or device [a telephone *operator*]. **2** an owner or manager of a factory, mine, etc.

**op·er·et·ta** (äp′ə ret′ə) ***n.*** a kind of opera that is light and amusing. Some of the speeches are spoken rather than sung.

**oph·thal·mol·o·gy** (äf′thal mäl′ə jē) ***n.*** the branch of medicine that deals with diseases of the eye. —**oph′thal·mol′o·gist** ***n.***

**o·pi·ate** (ō′pē it) ***n.*** **1** any medicine containing opium or a drug made from opium, used to cause sleepiness or to lessen pain. **2** anything that quiets or soothes.

**o·pine** (ō pīn′) ***v.*** to have or give an opinion; think: *now seldom used except in a joking way.* —**o·pined′, o·pin′ing**

**o·pin·ion** (ə pin′yən) ***n.*** **1** a belief that is not based on what is certain, but on what one thinks to be true or likely [In my *opinion,* it will rain before dark.] **2** what one thinks about how good or valuable something is [What is your *opinion* of that painting?] **3** a judgment made by an expert [It would be better to get several medical *opinions.*]

**o·pin·ion·at·ed** (ə pin′yən ā′tid) ***adj.*** holding to one's opinions in a stubborn way.

**o·pi·um** (ō′pē əm) ***n.*** a drug got from one kind of poppy, used to cause sleep and lessen pain.

☆**o·pos·sum** (ə päs′əm) ***n.*** a small American animal that lives in trees and moves about mostly at night. The female carries its newly born young in a pouch. When it is in danger, the opossum lies perfectly still, as if dead. *See the picture.*

**op·po·nent** (ə pō′nənt) ***n.*** a person against one in a fight, game, debate, etc.; foe; adversary.

**op·por·tune** (äp′ər to͞on′ *or* äp′ər tyo͞on′) ***adj.*** just right for the purpose; suitable; timely [Next Friday would be the most *opportune* time for our talk.]

> **Opportune** comes from a Latin word meaning "at the port." When a ship had arrived safely and was at the mouth of the harbor, that was an opportune time for celebrating.



**op·por·tun·ist** (äp′ər to͞on′ist *or* äp′ər tyo͞on′ist) ***n.*** a person who uses every opportunity for selfish purposes, rather than for doing what is right or proper. —**op′por·tun′ism** ***n.***

**op·por·tu·ni·ty** (äp′ər to͞o′nə tē *or* äp′ər tyo͞o′nə tē) ***n.*** a time or occasion that is right for doing something; good chance [You will have an *opportunity* to ask questions after the talk.] —*pl.* **op′por·tu′ni·ties**

**op·pose** (ə pōz′) ***v.*** **1** to act or be against; fight or resist [The mayor *opposes* raising taxes.] **2** to put opposite or in contrast; set against [To each of his arguments the lawyer *opposed* one of her own.] —**op·posed′, op·pos′ing**

> SYNONYMS: **Oppose** means to take action against something that may cause one harm. **Resist** means to take action against something that is already working against one [One can *oppose* an act before it is passed by a legislature, but one *resists* a law already passed by refusing to obey it.] **Withstand** means to be able to endure something that could harm or destroy one [A politician must be strong enough to *withstand* much criticism.]

**op·po·site** (äp′ə zit) ***adj.*** **1** different in every way; exactly reverse or in contrast [Up is *opposite* to down.] **2** at the other end or side; directly facing or back to

| | | | | | | | |
|---|---|---|---|---|---|---|---|
| **a** | fat | **ir** | here | **ou** | out | **zh** | leisure |
| **ā** | ape | **ī** | bite, fire | **u** | up | **ŋ** | ring |
| **ä** | car, lot | **ō** | go | **ur** | fur | | a *in* ago |
| **e** | ten | **ô** | law, horn | **ch** | chin | | e *in* agent |
| **er** | care | **oi** | oil | **sh** | she | **ə** = | i *in* unity |
| **ē** | even | **oo** | look | **th** | thin | | o *in* collect |
| **i** | hit | **o͞o** | tool | ***th*** | then | | u *in* focus |

back [the *opposite* end of a table; the *opposite* side of a coin]. ◆*n.* anything opposite or opposed [Love is the *opposite* of hate.] ◆*prep.* across from; facing [We sat *opposite* each other.] —**op′po·site·ly** *adv.*

**op·po·si·tion** (äp′ə zish′ən) *n.* **1** the act of opposing or the condition of being opposed; contrast [ideas that are in *opposition*]. **2** a fighting against or resisting [Our plan met *opposition.*] **3** anything that opposes; especially, a political party opposing the party in power.

**op·press** (ə pres′) *v.* **1** to trouble the mind of; worry; weigh down [*oppressed* by a feeling of fear]. **2** to keep down by the cruel use of power; rule in a very harsh way [Pharaoh *oppressed* the Israelite slaves.] —**op·pres′sor** *n.*

**op·pres·sion** (ə presh′ən) *n.* **1** the act of oppressing or the condition of being oppressed; harsh rule. **2** a feeling of being weighed down with problems, worries, etc.

**op·pres·sive** (ə pres′iv) *adj.* **1** hard to put up with; being a burden [the *oppressive* rain of the tropics]. **2** cruel and unjust; harsh [the dictator's *oppressive* laws]. —**op·pres′sive·ly** *adv.*

**op·pro·bri·ous** (ə prō′brē əs) *adj.* showing scorn or dislike; insulting [*opprobrious* names].

**op·pro·bri·um** (ə prō′brē əm) *n.* **1** disgrace that comes from behaving in a shameful way. **2** scorn felt or shown for something or someone thought of as inferior.



**opt** (äpt) *v.* to make a choice [They *opted* for the trip to California rather than a new car.]

**op·tic** (äp′tik) *adj.* of the eye or the sense of sight [the *optic* nerve].

**op·ti·cal** (äp′ti k'l) *adj.* **1** of the sense of sight; visual [an *optical* illusion]. **2** made to give help in seeing [Lenses are *optical* instruments.] **3** of optics. —**op′ti·cal·ly** *adv.*

**op·ti·cian** (äp tish′ən) *n.* a person who makes or sells eyeglasses and other optical supplies.

**op·tics** (äp′tiks) *n.pl.* the science that deals with light and vision: *used with a singular verb* [*Optics* is a branch of physics.]

**op·ti·mism** (äp′tə miz'm) *n.* **1** a bright and hopeful feeling about life, in which one expects things to turn out all right. **2** the belief that there is more good than evil in life. —**op′ti·mis′tic** *adj.* —**op′ti·mis′ti·cal·ly** *adv.*

**op·ti·mist** (äp′tə mist) *n.* a person who is cheerful and hopeful, no matter what happens.

**op·ti·mum** (äp′tə məm) *n.* the condition, amount, etc. that is best or most favorable [Our sales are at the *optimum.*] ◆*adj.* best; most favorable [What is the *optimum* temperature for roasting a turkey?]

**op·tion** (äp′shən) *n.* **1** the act of choosing; choice [I had no *option* but to go.] **2** the right of choosing [They have the *option* of taking a vacation now or in the winter.] *See* SYNONYMS *at* **choice**. **3** the right to buy or sell something at a certain price within a certain period of time.

**op·tion·al** (äp′shən 'l) *adj.* that one may choose to do or not do; not forced [a book list for *optional* reading].

☆**op·tom·e·trist** (äp täm′ə trist) *n.* a person who is skilled in optometry.

**op·tom·e·try** (äp täm′ə trē) *n.* the science or work of examining people's eyes and fitting them with eyeglasses or contact lenses to help them see better. —**op·to·met·ric** (äp′tə met′rik) *adj.*

**op·u·lent** (äp′yə lənt) *adj.* **1** wealthy; rich [an *opulent* nation]. **2** in great amounts; abundant [an *opulent* growth of hair]. —**op·u·lence** (äp′yə ləns) *n.*

**o·pus** (ō′pəs) *n.* a work or composition; especially, any of the musical works of a composer numbered in the order in which they appeared. —*pl.* **o·pe·ra** (ō′pə rə *or* äp′ər ə) or **o′pus·es**

**or** (ôr *or* ər) *conj. a word used before:* **1** the second of two choices or possibilities [Do you want milk *or* cocoa? Answer, *or* I will be angry.] **2** the last of a series of choices [Is the light red, yellow, *or* green?] **3** a word or phrase of the same meaning [botany, *or* the study of plants]. **4** the second of two choices when the first comes after *either* or *whether* [Take *either* this one *or* that one. I don't know *whether* to laugh *or* cry.]

**-or** (ər *or* ôr) *a suffix meaning* a person or thing that [An *inventor* is a person who invents.]

**OR** *abbreviation for* **Oregon.**

**or·a·cle** (ôr′ə k'l) *n.* **1** a place or priest through which the ancient Greeks and Romans believed they could get from the gods the answers to questions. **2** a message coming from such a place or person. **3** a very wise person whose opinions are greatly respected. —**o·rac·u·lar** (ô rak′yoo lər) *adj.*

**o·ral** (ôr′əl) *adj.* **1** spoken, not written [an *oral* report for class]. *See* SYNONYMS *at* **verbal**. **2** of or at the mouth [*oral* surgery]. —**o′ral·ly** *adv.*

**O·ran** (ō ran′) a seaport in northern Algeria.

**or·ange** (ôr′inj *or* är′inj) *n.* **1** a round citrus fruit with a reddish-yellow skin and a sweet, juicy pulp. **2** the evergreen tree it grows on, having shiny leaves and white, sweet-smelling blossoms. **3** reddish yellow. ◆*adj.* reddish-yellow.

**or·ange·ade** (ôr′inj ād′ *or* är′inj ād′) *n.* a drink made of orange juice, water, and sugar.

**o·rang·u·tan** (ô raŋ′oo tan) *n.* a large ape with very long arms and shaggy, reddish hair, found in Borneo and Sumatra. *Also* **o·rang·ou·tang** (ô raŋ′oo taŋ). *See the picture.*

**o·ra·tion** (ô rā′shən) *n.* a public speech of a serious kind, as at some ceremony.

**or·a·tor** (ôr′ət ər) *n.* **1** a person who gives an oration. **2** a skillful speaker.

**or·a·to·ri·o** (ôr′ə tôr′ē ō) *n.* a long musical work for an orchestra, chorus, and solo singers. It is usually on a religious subject and is like an opera except that the singers do not wear costumes or move about. —*pl.* **or′a·to′ri·os**

**or·a·to·ry** (ôr′ə tôr′ē) *n.* the art or skill of speaking in public. —**or′a·tor′i·cal** *adj.*

**orb** (ôrb) *n.* **1** a ball or globe. **2** a heavenly body, as the sun or moon. **3** the eye or eyeball: *used in earlier poetry.*

**or·bit** (ôr′bit) *n.* **1** the path followed by a heavenly body going around another, as the path of a planet around the sun. **2** a single course of a spacecraft or artificial satellite around a heavenly body. ◆*v.* to put or go in an orbit, as an artificial satellite.

**or·chard** (ôr′chərd) *n.* **1** a piece of land where fruit trees or nut trees are grown. **2** such trees.

**or·ches·tra** (ôr′kis trə) ***n.*** **1** a group of musicians playing together, especially with some stringed instruments. **2** the instruments of such a group. **3** the space in front of and below the stage in a theater, where the musicians sit. *The full name is* **orchestra pit.** ☆**4** the main floor of a theater, especially the front part. —**or·ches·tral** (ôr kes′trəl) ***adj.***

**Orchestra** comes from a Greek word meaning "to dance." Originally the orchestra was the place in an outdoor theater where the dancers performed. Later it came to be used of the place for the musicians, and finally it came to mean the group of musicians itself.

**or·ches·trate** (ôr′kis trāt) ***v.*** to arrange a piece of music for the various instruments of an orchestra. —**or′ches·tra·ted, or′ches·trat·ing** —**or′ches·tra′tion *n.***

**or·chid** (ôr′kid) ***n.*** **1** a plant with flowers having three petals, of which the middle one is larger than the others and has the shape of a lip. **2** the flower of such a plant. *See the picture.* **3** the pale purple color of some orchids.

**or·dain** (ôr dān′) ***v.*** **1** to make happen; arrange beforehand; order; establish [to believe that fate *ordains* one's future]. **2** to appoint as a minister, priest, or rabbi, often by a special ceremony.

**or·deal** (ôr dēl′) ***n.*** **1** a way used in earlier times to judge whether a person was guilty of some crime. The person was placed in great danger; if not hurt, the person was supposed to be innocent. **2** any difficult or painful experience [It is an *ordeal* for him to speak to a large audience.]

**or·der** (ôr′dər) ***n.*** **1** the way in which things are placed or follow one another; arrangement [The entries in this dictionary are in alphabetical *order.*] **2** a condition in which everything is in its right place or is working properly [We got the house back in *order.*] **3** the way a thing is; condition [a motor in working *order*]. **4** a peaceful condition in which people obey the rules [The hall guards help to keep *order.*] **5** the rules by which a meeting, debate, etc. is carried out. **6** a direction telling someone what to do, given by a person with authority; command [The general's *orders* were quickly obeyed.] **7** a request for something that one wants to buy or receive [Mail your *order* for flower seeds today.] **8** the things asked for [That store will deliver your *order.*] ☆**9** a single portion of a food in a restaurant [and two *orders* of cole slaw]. **10** a group of related animals or plants, larger than a family [Whales and dolphins belong to the same *order* of mammals.] **11** a class or kind [intelligence of a high *order*]. **12** a group of people joined together because they share the same beliefs, interests, etc. [an *order* of monks; the Fraternal *Order* of Police]. **13** a group of people who have been honored in some way, or a medal or ribbon worn by members of such a group [The *Order* of the Purple Heart is made up of soldiers wounded in action.] **14** a style of ancient building shown by the kind of columns it has [the Doric *order*]. **15 orders,** *pl.* the position of a minister or priest [to take holy *orders*]. **16** *see* **money order.** ◆***v.*** **1** to tell what to do; give an order to [The captain *ordered* the troops to charge.] **2** to command to go [She *ordered* them out of the room.] **3** to put in order; arrange [I must *order* my affairs before I leave.] **4** to ask for something one wants to buy or receive [Please *order* some art supplies for the class.] —**by order of,** according to the command of [*by order of* the Governor]. —**call to order,** to ask to become quiet, as in order to start a meeting. —**in order, 1** in its proper place. **2** working as it should. **3** according to the rules, as of a meeting. —**in order that,** so that. —**in order to,** for the purpose of. —**in short order,** without waiting; quickly. —**on order,** asked for but not yet supplied. —**on the order of,** similar to; rather like. —**out of order, 1** out of its proper place. **2** not working. **3** not according to rules, as of a meeting. —**to order,** in the way asked for by the buyer [a suit made *to order*].

1.4 m (4 1/2 ft.) high

orchid

orderly desk

**or·der·ly** (ôr′dər lē) ***adj.*** **1** neatly arranged; tidy; in order [an *orderly* desk]. *See the picture.* **2** behaving well; obeying the rules [an *orderly* crowd]. ◆***n.*** **1** a soldier who acts as a messenger or servant for an officer or who has a particular task. **2** a man who does general work in a hospital helping the doctors and nurses. —*pl.* **or′der·lies** —**or′der·li·ness *n.***

**or·di·nal number** (ôr′d′n əl) any number used to show where something comes in a series [First, sixth, and 10th are *ordinal numbers.*] *See also* **cardinal number.**

**or·di·nance** (ôr′d′n əns) ***n.*** **1** an order, command, or rule. ☆**2** a law, especially one made by a city government [an *ordinance* forbidding jaywalking].

**or·di·nar·i·ly** (ôr′d′n er′ə lē) ***adv.*** usually; as a rule; generally [I'm *ordinarily* home on Sunday.]

**or·di·nar·y** (ôr′d′n er′ē) ***n.*** **1** usual; regular; normal [The *ordinary* price is $10.] **2** not special in any way; common; average [a person of *ordinary* ability]. —**out of the ordinary,** unusual; extraordinary.

**or·di·na·tion** (ôr′d′n ā′shən) ***n.*** the act or ceremony of ordaining a minister, priest, or rabbi.

**ord·nance** (ôrd′nəns) ***n.*** **1** artillery and cannon. **2** all military weapons and ammunition.

| | | | | | | | |
|---|---|---|---|---|---|---|---|
| **a** | fat | **ir** | here | **ou** | out | **zh** | leisure |
| **ā** | ape | **ī** | bite, fire | **u** | up | **ng** | ring |
| **ä** | car, lot | **ō** | go | **ʉr** | fur | | a *in* ago |
| **e** | ten | **ô** | law, horn | **ch** | chin | | e *in* agent |
| **er** | care | **oi** | oil | **sh** | she | **ə =** | i *in* unity |
| **ē** | even | **oo** | look | **th** | thin | | o *in* collect |
| **i** | hit | **ōō** | tool | ***th*** | then | | u *in* focus |

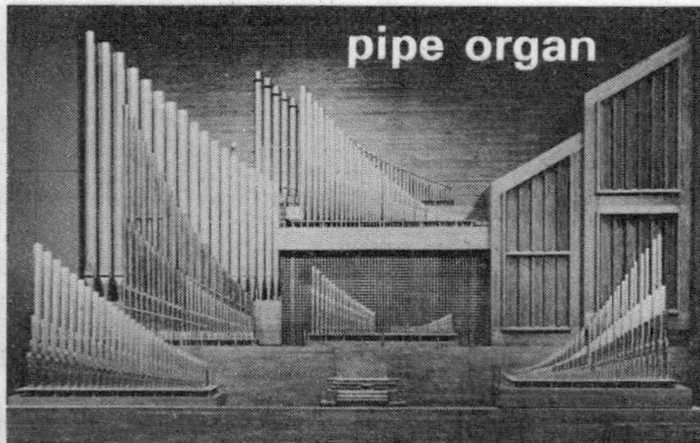

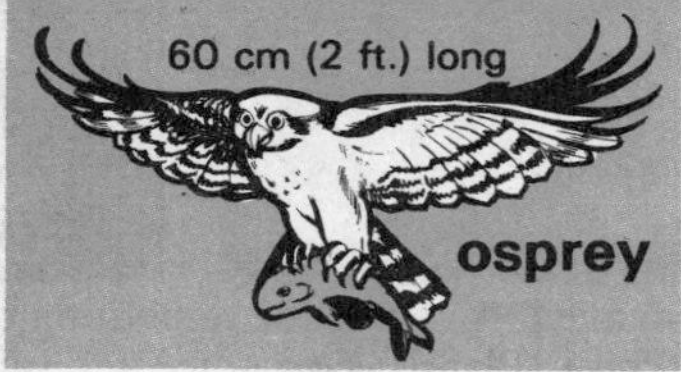

**ore** (ôr) ***n.*** a rock or mineral from which a metal can be got [iron *ore*].



**o·reg·a·no** (ô reg′ə nō) ***n.*** a plant of the mint family, whose pleasant-smelling leaves are used as a seasoning.

**Or·e·gon** (ôr′i gən *or* ôr′i gän′) a State in the northwestern part of the U.S.: abbreviated **Oreg., OR**

**org.** *abbreviation for* **organization.**

**or·gan** (ôr′gən) ***n.*** **1** a musical instrument having sets of pipes that make sounds when keys or pedals are pressed to send air through the pipes. *Also called* **pipe organ.** *See the picture.* **2** an instrument like this, but with reeds or electronic devices instead of pipes. **3** a part of an animal or plant that has some special purpose [The heart, lungs, and eyes are *organs* of the body.] **4** a means by which things are done [The city council is an *organ* of local government.] **5** a means of passing on ideas or opinions, as a newspaper or magazine.

**or·gan·dy** or **or·gan·die** (ôr′gən dē) ***n.*** a very thin, stiff cotton cloth, used for dresses, etc.

**or·gan·ic** (ôr gan′ik) ***adj.*** **1** of or having to do with an organ of the body [An *organic* disease causes some change in a body organ.] **2** arranged according to a system [the *organic* structure of the U.S. government]. **3** of, like, or coming from living matter [Coal is *organic* rather than mineral in origin.] **4** having to do with chemical compounds containing carbon [*organic* chemistry]. ☆**5** grown with only animal or vegetable fertilizers and without the use of chemical sprays [*organic* foods]. —**or·gan′i·cal·ly** ***adv.***

**or·gan·ism** (ôr′gə niz′m) ***n.*** **1** any living thing [Plants, animals, and bacteria are *organisms.*] **2** anything made up of many complicated parts [A nation is a political *organism.*]

**or·gan·ist** (ôr′gə nist) ***n.*** a person who plays the organ.

**or·gan·i·za·tion** (ôr′gə ni zā′shən) ***n.*** **1** the act of organizing or arranging. **2** the way in which the parts of something are organized or arranged [to study the *organization* of a beehive]. **3** a group of persons organized for some purpose.

**or·gan·ize** (ôr′gə nīz) ***v.*** **1** to arrange or place according to a system [The library books are *organized* according to their subjects.] **2** to bring into being by working out the details; start [to *organize* a club; to *organize* a bank]. **3** to make part of a group, especially of a labor union [The coal miners were *organized.*] —**or′gan·ized, or′gan·iz·ing** —**or′gan·iz′er** ***n.***

**or·gy** (ôr′jē) ***n.*** a wild, drunken, uncontrolled merrymaking. —*pl.* **or′gies**

**o·ri·el** (ôr′ē əl) ***n.*** a large window built out from a wall and resting on a bracket. *See the picture.*

**o·ri·ent** (ôr′ē ənt) ***n.*** **Orient,** the East, or Asia, especially the Far East, or eastern Asia. ✦***v.*** (ôr′ē ent′) **1** to put into the right position or direction with respect to something else [to *orient* a map with the directions of the compass]. **2** to make or become used to a certain situation [You will have to take time to *orient* yourself to your new school.]

> The **Orient** gets its name from a Latin word meaning "rising," because it is in the direction of the rising sun. We usually think of Asia as being to the west of us, but to Europe of the early days, the Orient was to the east, or where the sun rises.

**O·ri·en·tal** (ôr′ē en′t′l) ***adj.*** of the Orient, its people, etc.; Eastern. ✦***n.*** a member of any of the peoples whose native country is in the Orient.

**o·ri·en·tate** (ôr′ē ən tāt′) ***v.*** to orient. —**o′ri·en·tat′ed, o′ri·en·tat′ing**

**o·ri·en·ta·tion** (ôr′ē ən tā′shən) ***n.*** the condition or process of being oriented; especially, the act of making or becoming used to a certain situation.

**or·i·fice** (ôr′ə fis) ***n.*** an opening or mouth, as of a tube, cave, etc.

**o·ri·ga·mi** (ôr′ə gä′mē) ***n.*** **1** a Japanese art of folding paper to form flowers, animal figures, etc. **2** an object made in this way. *See the picture.*

**or·i·gin** (ôr′ə jin) ***n.*** **1** the place or point from which something comes; beginning [The word "rodeo" has its *origin* in Spanish.] **2** parentage or ancestors [of French *origin*].

**o·rig·i·nal** (ə rij′ə n′l) ***adj.*** **1** having to do with an origin; first or earliest [the *original* settlers of North America]. **2** that has never been before; not copied; fresh; new [an *original* idea; *original* music]. **3** able to think of new things; inventive [Edison had an *original* mind.] **4** being the one of which there are copies [the *original* letter and three carbon copies]. ✦***n.*** **1** a painting, piece of writing, etc. that is not a copy, reproduction, or translation. **2** the person or thing pictured in a painting, etc. **3** the form from which others have developed [An animal the size of a fox was the *original* of the modern horse.] —**o·rig·i·nal·i·ty** (ə rij′ə nal′ə tē) ***n.***

**o·rig·i·nal·ly** (ə rij′ə n′l ē) ***adv.*** **1** at the start; at first [There were *originally* great herds of bison in America.] **2** in a way that is new, different, or fresh [a room decorated quite *originally*].

**o·rig·i·nate** (ə rij′ə nāt) ***v.*** **1** to bring into being; create; invent [England *originated* the use of government postage stamps.] **2** to begin; come from [Many TV programs *originate* in Los Angeles.] **—o·rig′i·nat·ed, o·rig′i·nat·ing —o·rig′i·na′tor *n.***

**O·ri·no·co** (ôr′ə nō′kō) a river in Venezuela, flowing into the Atlantic.

**o·ri·ole** (ôr′ē ōl) ***n.*** any of a number of songbirds of Europe and America; especially, an American bird that has orange and black feathers and builds a hanging nest. *See the picture.*

**O·ri·on** (ō rī′ən) a constellation that is supposed to form the outline of a hunter's belt and sword.

**Ork·ney Islands** (ôrk′nē) a group of islands north of Scotland.

**Or·lan·do** (ôr lan′dō) a city in central Florida.

**or·na·ment** (ôr′nə mənt) ***n.*** **1** anything added or put on to make something look better; decoration [Christmas-tree *ornaments*]. **2** a person whose character or talent makes the whole group seem better [That teacher is an *ornament* to the profession.] ◆***v.*** (ôr′nə ment′) to add ornaments to; decorate.

**or·na·men·tal** (ôr′nə men′t'l) ***adj.*** serving as an ornament; decorative [an *ornamental* fringe].

**or·na·men·ta·tion** (ôr′nə men tā′shən) ***n.*** **1** the act of decorating or the condition of being decorated. **2** the things used as ornaments; decoration.

**or·nate** (ôr nāt′) ***adj.*** having much or too much decoration; showy. *See the picture.* **—or·nate′ly *adv.***

**or·ner·y** (ôr′nər ē) ***adj.*** mean or bad-tempered; ready to quarrel: *used only in everyday talk.*

**or·ni·thol·o·gy** (ôr′nə thäl′ə jē) ***n.*** the science that studies birds. **—or′ni·thol′o·gist *n.***

**o·ro·tund** (ôr′ə tund) ***adj.*** **1** clear, strong, and deep [an *orotund* voice]. **2** too solemn and dignified; pompous [*orotund* speech].

**or·phan** (ôr′fən) ***n.*** a child whose parents are dead or, sometimes, one of whose parents is dead. ◆***adj.*** **1** being an orphan [an *orphan* child]. **2** of or for orphans [an *orphan* home]. ◆***v.*** to cause to become an orphan [children *orphaned* by war].

**or·phan·age** (ôr′fən ij) ***n.*** a home for taking care of a number of orphans.

**Or·phe·us** (ôr′fē əs *or* ôr′fyo͞os) a musician in a Greek myth, with magic musical skill.

**or·tho·don·tics** (ôr′thə dän′tiks) ***n.pl.*** the branch of dentistry that works to straighten teeth, so that the upper and lower ones will come together properly. *Used with a singular verb. Also called* **or·tho·don·tia** (ôr′thə dän′shə). **—or′tho·don′tist *n.***

**or·tho·dox** (ôr′thə däks) ***adj.*** keeping to the usual or fixed beliefs, customs, etc., as in religion or politics; conventional [*orthodox* political views; *orthodox* Judaism]. **—or′tho·dox′y *n.***

**Orthodox Eastern Church** the main Christian church in eastern Europe, western Asia, and northern Africa.

**or·thog·ra·phy** (ôr thäg′rə fē) ***n.*** **1** correct spelling. **2** any way of spelling [In earlier times, *orthography* was not fixed.] **—or·tho·graph·ic** (ôr′thə graf′ik) ***adj.***

**or·tho·pe·dics** or **or·tho·pae·dics** (ôr′thə pē′diks) ***n.pl.*** the branch of surgery that deals with bones, joints, etc. that are injured, deformed, or diseased. **—or′tho·pe′dic** or **or′tho·pae′dic *adj.***

**or·tho·pe·dist** or **or·tho·pae·dist** (ôr′thə pē′dist) ***n.*** a surgeon who specializes in orthopedics.

**-o·ry** (ôr′ē) *a suffix meaning:* **1** having to do with, or like [*Illusory* means having to do with an illusion.] **2** a place or thing for [An *observatory* is a place for observing the stars.]

**o·ryx** (ôr′iks) ***n.*** a large antelope of Africa and Asia, with long, straight horns that slant backward. *—pl.* **o′ryx·es** or **o′ryx**

**O·sa·ka** (ō sä′kə) a city and seaport of Japan.

**os·cil·late** (äs′ə lāt) ***v.*** **1** to swing or move back and forth [an *oscillating* pendulum]. **2** to shift back and forth, as in trying to decide something. **—os′cil·lat·ed, os′cil·lat·ing —os′cil·la′tion *n.***

**os·cu·late** (äs′kyə lāt) ***v.*** to kiss: *used in a joking way.* **—os′cu·lat·ed, os′cu·lat·ing**

**o·sier** (ō′zhər) ***n.*** a willow tree whose twigs are used in making baskets and furniture.

**O·si·ris** (ō sī′ris) the ancient Egyptian god of the lower world and judge of the dead.

**Os·lo** (äs′lō *or* äz′lō) the capital of Norway.

**os·mo·sis** (äs mō′sis *or* äz mō′sis) ***n.*** the tendency of liquids separated by a thin membrane, as the wall of a living cell, to pass through it, so as to become mixed and equal in strength on both sides.

**os·prey** (äs′prē) ***n.*** a large hawk with a blackish back and a white breast, that feeds only on fish. *See the picture. —pl.* **os′preys**

**os·si·fy** (äs′ə fī) ***v.*** **1** to form or change into bone [The soft spots in a baby's skull *ossify* as it grows.] **2** to make or become fixed or set, not likely to change [a mind *ossified* by prejudice]. **—os′si·fied, os′si·fy·ing —os′si·fi·ca′tion *n.*** 517

**os·ten·si·ble** (äs ten′sə b'l) ***adj.*** seeming, claimed, or pretended, but not real [Her *ostensible* reason for quitting was the low pay, but she really disliked the job.] **—os·ten′si·bly *adv.***

**os·ten·ta·tion** (äs′tən tā′shən) ***n.*** a showing off, as of one's wealth, knowledge, etc. [They spend money with great *ostentation,* especially on parties.]

**os·ten·ta·tious** (äs′tən tā′shəs) ***adj.*** showing off or done in order to get attention [an *ostentatious* monument]. **—os′ten·ta′tious·ly *adv.***

**os·te·o·path** (äs′tē ə path) ***n.*** a doctor of osteopathy.

☆**os·te·op·a·thy** (äs′tē äp′ə thē) ***n.*** a system of treating diseases by working on the joints and muscles with the hands, as well as by the use of medicine and surgery. **—os·te·o·path·ic** (äs′tē ə path′ik) ***adj.***

**os·tra·cism** (äs′trə siz'm) ***n.*** **1** in ancient Greece, a way of punishing someone by voting to send that person out of the country for a time. **2** the action of a group or of society in deciding to have nothing to do with someone who is disliked or disapproved of.

> The words **ostracism** and **ostracize** come from a Greek word for "a broken piece of pottery." When the ancient Greeks voted on whether to banish a person, they would write their vote on such a piece of pottery and place it in a container, the way we put ballots in a ballot box.

| | | | | | | | |
|---|---|---|---|---|---|---|---|
| **a** | fat | **ir** | here | **ou** | out | **zh** | leisure |
| **ā** | ape | **ī** | bite, fire | **u** | up | **ng** | ring |
| **ä** | car, lot | **ō** | go | **ur** | fur | | a *in* ago |
| **e** | ten | **ô** | law, horn | **ch** | chin | | e *in* agent |
| **er** | care | **oi** | oil | **sh** | she | **ə =** | i *in* unity |
| **ē** | even | **oo** | look | **th** | thin | | o *in* collect |
| **i** | hit | **o͞o** | tool | ***th*** | then | | u *in* focus |

**os·tra·cize** (äs′trə sīz) ***v.*** to refuse as a group to have anything to do with; banish or bar [Because he held unpopular opinions, his party *ostracized* him.] —**os′-tra·cized, os′tra·ciz·ing**

**os·trich** (ôs′trich) ***n.*** a very large bird of Africa and southwestern Asia, with a long neck and long legs. It cannot fly, but runs swiftly. *See the picture.*

**OT., OT, O.T.** *abbreviations for* **Old Testament.**

**O·thel·lo** (ə thel′ō) a tragic play by Shakespeare in which the hero, Othello, is made jealous of his faithful wife and kills her.

**oth·er** (u*th*′ər) ***adj.*** **1** not this one or the one just mentioned, but a different one [Stand on one foot and lift the *other* one. Not Karen but some *other* girl called.] **2** being the one or ones remaining; in addition [Al, Ben, and the *other* boys.] **3** additional; extra [I have no *other* coat.] ◆***pron.*** **1** the other one [Each loved the *other*.] **2** some other person or thing [That's what *others* say. I want that seat and no *other*.] ◆***adv.*** in a different way; otherwise [She can't do *other* than go.] —**the other day,** not long ago; recently.

**oth·er·wise** (u*th*′ər wīz) ***adv.*** **1** in some other way; differently [I believe *otherwise*.] **2** in all other ways [Jan has a cough, but *otherwise* feels fine.] **3** if things were different; or else [I'm tired; *otherwise,* I would play.] ◆***adj.*** different [She cannot be *otherwise* than polite.]

**other world** a world that some people believe we go to after we die.

**Ot·ta·wa** (ät′ə wə) the capital of Canada, in eastern Ontario.

**ot·ter** (ät′ər) ***n.*** **1** a furry animal related to the weasel. It has webbed feet used in swimming and a long tail, and it eats small animals and fish. *See the picture.* **2** its soft, thick fur.

**Ot·to·man** (ät′ə mən) ***n.*** **1** *another name for* **Turk.** *—pl.* **Ot′to·mans** **2 ottoman,** a low seat without back or arms; also, a padded footstool. ◆***adj.*** *another word for* **Turkish.**

**Ottoman Empire** the empire of the Turks, from about 1300 to 1918. At one time it included much of southeastern Europe, southwestern Asia, and northeastern Africa.

**ouch** (ouch) ***interj.*** a sound made in showing sudden or sharp pain.

**ought**[1] (ôt) *a helping verb used with infinitives and meaning:* **1** to be forced by what is right, wise, or necessary [He *ought* to pay his debts. You *ought* to eat well-balanced meals.] **2** to be expected or likely [It *ought* to be over soon.]

**ought**[2] (ôt) ***n.*** a nought; the figure zero (0).

**ounce** (ouns) ***n.*** **1** a unit of weight, equal to 1/16 pound in avoirdupois weight and 1/12 pound in troy weight. One avoirdupois ounce equals about 28 grams. One troy ounce equals about 31 grams. **2** a measure of liquids, equal to 1/16 pint. One liquid ounce equals about .03 liter. **3** any small amount.

**our** (our) ***pron.*** of us or done by us. *This possessive form of* **we** *is used before a noun and thought of as an adjective* [*our* car; *our* work]. *See also* **ours.**

**ours** (ourz) ***pron.*** the one or the ones that belong to us. *This form of* **our** *is used when it is not followed by a noun* [This car is *ours*. *Ours* are larger than yours.]

**our·selves** (our selvz′) ***pron.*** **1** our own selves. *This form of* **we** *is used when the object is the same as the subject of the verb* [We hurt *ourselves*.] **2** our usual or true selves [We are not *ourselves* today.] *Ourselves* is also used to give force to the subject [We built it *ourselves*.]

**-ous** (əs) *a suffix meaning* having, full of, *or* like [A *courageous* person is full of courage.]

**oust** (oust) ***v.*** to force out; drive out [The usher *ousted* them from our seats.] *See* SYNONYMS *at* **eject.**

**oust·er** (ou′stər) ***n.*** the act of ousting or the fact of being ousted.

**out** (out) ***adv.*** **1** away from the inside, center, etc. [Open the door and look *out*. Spit it *out*. Come *out* and play.] **2** away from a certain place, as from one's home or office [Let's go *out* for dinner.] **3** into being or action [A fire broke *out*.] **4** to the end; completely; thoroughly [to argue it *out;* tired *out*]. **5** so as to be no more [The fire died *out*.] **6** beyond what is usual or normal [ears that stick *out*]. **7** loudly [Sing *out!*] **8** from among several [to pick *out* a new hat]. ☆**9** so as to make an out in baseball [He struck *out*.] **10** into unconsciousness: *a slang meaning* [She passed *out*.] ◆***adj.*** **1** away from work, school, etc. [He is *out* because of illness] **2** not in the inside, center, usual limits, etc. [Turn off the lights after everyone is *out*.] **3** not right; in error [She is *out* in her estimate.] **4** known or made public [Their secret is *out*.] **5** not possible [That idea is *out*.] **6** not in power [the *out* group]. **7** not working or in use [The lights are *out*.] ☆**8** having made an out in baseball. ☆**9** having had a loss: *used only in everyday talk* [He is *out* ten dollars.] **10** no longer popular: *used only in everyday talk* [Wide cuffs are *out* this year.] ◆***prep.*** out of; through to the outside [She walked *out* the door.] ◆***n.*** **1** *usually* **outs,** *pl.* those who are not in power or in office. ☆**2** in baseball, the act of failing to get on base or to the next base safely. ☆**3** a way of avoiding something; excuse: *slang in this meaning* [He has an *out* and won't have to go.] ◆***v.*** to become known [The truth will *out*.] ◆***interj.*** get out! —**all out,** with all effort; completely. —**on the outs,** no longer friendly; quarreling: *used only in everyday talk.* —**out and away,** by far. —☆**out for,** trying hard to get or do. —**out of, 1** from inside of [He went *out of* the room.] **2** through to the outside [thrown *out of* the window]. **3** from the number of [chosen *out of* a crowd]. **4** past the limits of; beyond [*out of* sight]. **5** from; using [made *out of* bricks]. **6** because of [done *out of* spite]. **7** not having any [*out of* gas]. **8** so as to take away or have taken away [cheated *out of* one's money]. —**out to,** trying hard to [The members of the welcoming committee are *out to* please the visitors.]

**out-** *a prefix meaning:* **1** away from; outside [An *outbuilding* is away from a main building.] **2** going away or forth; outward [The *outbound* traffic goes away from the city.] **3** better or more than [To *outdo* another means to do better than another.]

☆**out·age** (out′ij) ***n.*** a loss of electric power for a time, as because of an accident.

**out-and-out** (out′′n out′) ***adj.*** complete; thorough [an *out-and-out* rascal].

**out·bid** (out bid′) ***v.*** to bid more than another. —**out-bid′, out·bid′ding**

☆**out·board motor** (out′bôrd) a gasoline engine

with a propeller, fixed to the outside of the stern of a boat. *See the picture*.

**out·bound** (out′bound) ***adj.*** headed away from a place; outward bound [an *outbound* ship].

**out·break** (out′brāk) ***n.*** a breaking out, as of disease or rioting among people.

**out·build·ing** (out′bil′ding) ***n.*** a shed, barn, garage, etc. separate from the main building.

**out·burst** (out′burst) ***n.*** a sudden show of strong feeling or energy.

**out·cast** (out′kast) ***adj.*** shunned by people; without a home or friends. ◆***n.*** an outcast person.

**out·class** (out klas′) ***v.*** to be better by far.

**out·come** (out′kum) ***n.*** the way something turns out; result [the *outcome* of the election].

**out·crop** (out′kräp) ***n.*** a coming out at the surface of the earth [an *outcrop* of rock].

**out·cry** (out′krī) ***n.*** **1** a crying out; a scream or shout. **2** a strong protest or objection. —*pl.* **out′cries**

**out·dat·ed** (out dāt′id) ***adj.*** behind the times; out-of-date [*outdated* ideas].

**out·dis·tance** (out dis′təns) ***v.*** to get far ahead of, as in a race. —**out·dis′tanced, out·dis′tanc·ing**

**out·do** (out do͞o′) ***v.*** to do better or more than. —**out·did′, out·done′, out·do′ing —outdo oneself,** to do one's best or better than expected.

**out·door** (out′dôr) ***adj.*** being, belonging, done, etc. outside a house or other building [an *outdoor* pool; *outdoor* exercise].

☆**out·doors** (out′dôrz′) ***adv.*** in or into the open; outside [We went *outdoors* to play.] ◆***n.*** (out dôrz′) the world outside of buildings; the open air.

**out·er** (out′ər) ***adj.*** on or closer to the outside [the *outer* wall; an *outer* coating].

**out·er·most** (out′ər mōst) ***adj.*** farthest out.

**outer space** **1** space beyond the air around the earth. **2** space outside the solar system.

**out·field** (out′fēld) ***n.*** ☆**1** the part of a baseball field beyond the infield. ☆**2** all the outfielders.

☆**out·field·er** (out′fēl′dər) ***n.*** a baseball player whose position is in the outfield.

**out·fit** (out′fit) ***n.*** **1** the clothing or equipment used in some work, activity, etc. [a hiking *outfit*]. ☆**2** a group of people working together, as in a military unit or a business. ◆***v.*** to supply with what is needed [Their store *outfits* campers.] —**out′fit·ted, out′fit·ting**

**out·flank** (out flangk′) ***v.*** to pass around the side or sides of enemy troops.

**out·flow** (out′flō) ***n.*** **1** the act of flowing out. **2** anything that flows out.

**out·go** (out′gō) ***n.*** that which goes out or is paid out; especially, money spent.

**out·go·ing** (out′gō′ing) ***adj.*** **1** going out; departing [the *outgoing* mail]. **2** friendly; sociable [a warm, *outgoing* person].

**out·grow** (out grō′) ***v.*** **1** to grow bigger than [Sandy *outgrew* her older sister.] **2** to lose by growing older [to *outgrow* an interest in dolls]. **3** to grow too large for [Bill has *outgrown* his clothes.] *See the picture*. —**out·grew′, out·grown′, out·grow′ing**

**out·growth** (out′grōth) ***n.*** **1** something that develops from something else; result or offshoot [Chemistry was an *outgrowth* of alchemy.] **2** the act of growing out or that which grows out.

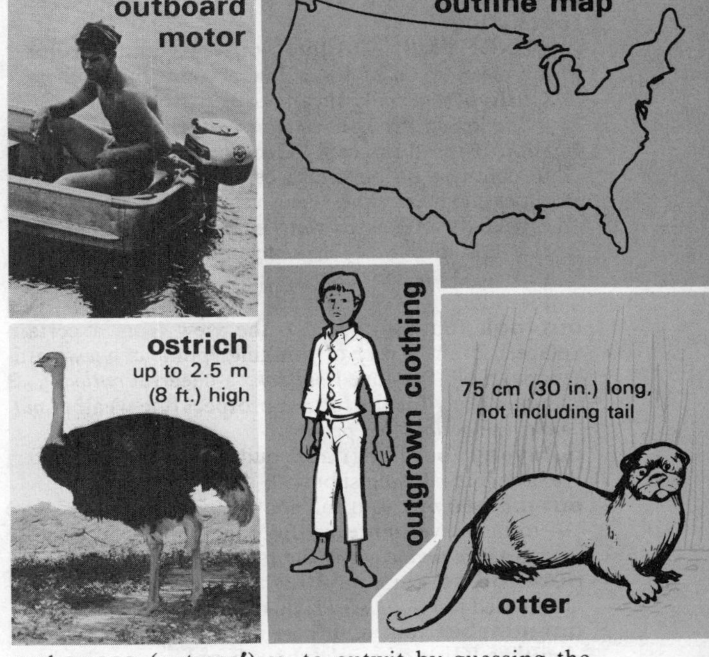


**out·guess** (out ges′) ***v.*** to outwit by guessing the plans of.

**out·house** (out′hous) ***n.*** an outbuilding; especially, ☆an outdoor toilet.

**out·ing** (out′ing) ***n.*** a picnic or other short pleasure trip out-of-doors.

**out·land·ish** (out lan′dish) ***adj.*** very strange or unusual [*outlandish* clothes; *outlandish* ideas].

**out·last** (out last′) ***v.*** to last longer than. *See* SYNONYMS *at* **outlive**.

**out·law** (out′lô) ***n.*** **1** originally, a person who had lost the rights and protection of the law. **2** a criminal, especially one who is being hunted by the police. ◆***v.*** to pass a law against; rule out as not lawful [The city has *outlawed* gambling.]

**out·lay** (out′lā) ***n.*** a spending of money, or the money spent [The trip will need an *outlay* of $500.]

**out·let** (out′let) ***n.*** **1** a means or opening for letting something out [the *outlet* of a river; an electrical *outlet*]. **2** a way of using up [Tennis is an *outlet* for his energy.] **3** a market for goods. **4** a store that sells the goods of a certain manufacturer.

**out·line** (out′līn) ***n.*** **1** a line around the outer edges of an object, showing its shape [the dim *outline* of a ship in the fog]. **2** a drawing that shows only the outer lines, or form, of a thing. *See the picture*. **3** a report or plan giving the main points, but not the details [an *outline* of a speech]. ◆***v.*** to make an outline of. —**out′lined, out′lin·ing**

| | | | |
|---|---|---|---|
| **a** fat | **ir** here | **ou** out | **zh** leisure |
| **ā** ape | **ī** bite, fire | **u** up | **ng** ring |
| **ä** car, lot | **ō** go | **ur** fur | a *in* ago |
| **e** ten | **ô** law, horn | **ch** chin | e *in* agent |
| **er** care | **oi** oil | **sh** she | **ə** = i *in* unity |
| **ē** even | **oo** look | **th** thin | o *in* collect |
| **i** hit | **o͞o** tool | ***th*** then | u *in* focus |

**out·live** (out liv′) ***v.*** to live longer than. —**out·lived′, out·liv′ing**

SYNONYMS: **Outlive, outlast,** and **survive** all mean to exist for a longer time than others. **Outlive** especially means to win or overcome by living longer [They have *outlived* their enemies. He *outlived* the disgrace.] **Outlast** especially means to continue on beyond a certain point [These old shoes have *outlasted* their usefulness.] **Survive** especially means to remain alive after someone else has died or to live through something dangerous [Two sons *survive* her. They *survived* the tornado.]

**out·look** (out′look) ***n.*** **1** the view from a certain place. **2** one's way of thinking; point of view; attitude [an old-fashioned *outlook;* a cheerful *outlook*]. **3** what is likely for the future; prospect [the weather *outlook;* the *outlook* for peace].

**out·ly·ing** (out′lī′iŋ) ***adj.*** quite far from the center; remote [the *outlying* suburbs].

**out·ma·neu·ver** (out′mə nōō′vər *or* out′mə nyōō′vər) ***v.*** to maneuver more skillfully than [We won because our team *outmaneuvered* theirs.]

**out·mod·ed** (out mōd′id) ***adj.*** out-of-date; old-fashioned [an *outmoded* style of shoes].

**out·num·ber** (out num′bər) ***v.*** to be greater in number than [Girls *outnumber* boys here.]

**out-of-date** (out′əv dāt′) ***adj.*** no longer in style or use; old-fashioned [That word is now *out-of-date.*]



**out-of-door** (out′əv dôr′) ***adj.*** *same as* **outdoor.**

**out-of-doors** (out′əv dôrz′) ***adv., n.*** *same as* **outdoors.**

**out-of-the-way** (out′əv *thə* wā′) ***adj.*** **1** away from crowded centers, main roads, etc.; secluded [an *out-of-the-way* cabin]. **2** not common; unusual [an *out-of-the-way* experience].

**out·pa·tient** (out′pā′shənt) ***n.*** a patient who goes to a hospital for treatment or care but does not need to stay there overnight or longer.

**out·play** (out plā′) ***v.*** to play better than [I guess their basketball team just *outplayed* us.]

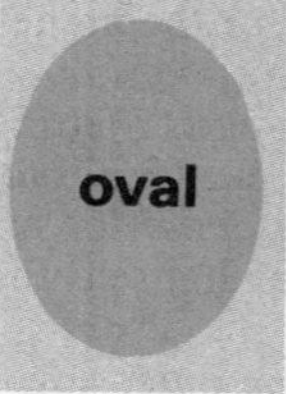
oval

outrigger

overalls

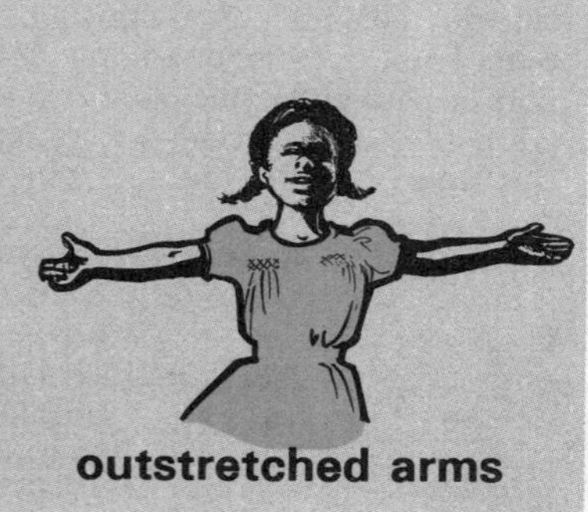
outstretched arms

**out·post** (out′pōst) ***n.*** **1** a small group of soldiers on guard some distance away from the main body of troops. **2** the place where this group is. **3** a small village on a frontier.

**out·put** (out′poot) ***n.*** **1** the amount made or done [the daily *output* of a factory]. **2** the information delivered by a computer. **3** the electric current or power delivered by an electric circuit or by an electric machine, as a generator.

**out·rage** (out′rāj) ***n.*** **1** a cruel or evil act that is shocking in its wickedness [The bombing of the hospital was an *outrage.*] **2** an act, remark, etc. that deeply hurts or angers a person. ◆***v.*** to be an outrage against or do something that is an outrage against. *See* SYNONYMS *at* **offend.** —**out′raged, out′rag·ing**

**Outrage** has nothing to do with the words **out** and **rage.** It comes from an old French word *outre,* which comes from the Latin word *ultra,* both of them meaning "beyond." An outrage is an act so evil, cruel, or shocking that it goes beyond what one may imagine.

**out·ra·geous** (out rā′jəs) ***adj.*** **1** doing great injury or wrong [*outrageous* crimes]. **2** so wrong or bad that it hurts or shocks [an *outrageous* lie]. —**out·ra′geous·ly *adv.***

☆**out·rank** (out raŋk′) ***v.*** to rank higher than [A colonel *outranks* a major.]

**out·rig·ger** (out′rig′ər) ***n.*** **1** a framework built out from the side of a canoe to keep it from tipping. **2** a canoe of this type. *See the picture.*

**out·right** (out′rīt) ***adj.*** thorough, downright, complete, etc. [an *outright* fool; an *outright* denial]. ◆***adv.*** **1** entirely; wholly [The farm was sold *outright.*] **2** without holding back; openly [to laugh *outright*]. **3** at once [He was hired *outright.*]

**out·run** (out run′) ***v.*** **1** to run faster or longer than. **2** to go beyond the limits of; exceed [Expenses *outran* our income.] —**out·ran′, out·run′, out·run′ning**

**out·sell** (out sel′) ***v.*** to sell in greater amounts than [This brand of tea *outsells* that.] —**out·sold′, out·sell′ing**

**out·set** (out′set) ***n.*** a setting out; beginning; start [We had trouble at the *outset.*]

**out·shine** (out shīn′) ***v.*** **1** to shine brighter than. **2** to be better than; surpass [Fran *outshines* the other players.] —**out·shone′** or **out·shined′, out·shin′ing**

**out·side** (out′sīd′) ***n.*** **1** the side or part that faces out; exterior [Wash the windows on the *outside.*] **2** any place not inside; the world beyond [The prisoners got little news from the *outside.*] ◆***adj.*** **1** of or on the outside; outer [the *outside* layer]. **2** from some other person or place [She did it herself without *outside* help.] **3** largest, highest, etc.; extreme [an *outside* estimate]. **4** small; slight [The team has an *outside* chance of winning.] ◆***adv.*** (*usually* out sīd′) on or to the outside [Let's play *outside.*] ◆***prep.*** (*usually* out sīd′) **1** on, to, or near the outside of [Leave it *outside* the door.] **2** beyond the limits of [They live *outside* the city.] —**at the outside,** at the most [It should cost $20 *at the outside.*] —**outside of, 1** outside. **2** except for: *used only in everyday talk.*

**out·sid·er** (out sīd′ər) ***n.*** a person who does not belong to a certain group.

**out·size** (out′sīz) ***adj.*** of a size that is different, especially larger than usual [an *outsize* bed].

**out·skirts** (out′skurts) ***n.pl.*** the districts or parts far from the center, as of a city.

☆**out·smart** (out smärt′) ***v.*** to win out over by being more clever or cunning. —**outsmart oneself,** to fail by trying too hard to be clever or cunning.

**out·spo·ken** (out′spō′k'n) ***adj.*** speaking or spoken in a frank or bold way. *See* SYNONYMS *at* **frank.**

**out·spread** (out′spred) ***adj.*** spread out [the *outspread* branches of the tree].

**out·stand·ing** (out stan′diŋ) ***adj.*** **1** that stands out as very good or important [an *outstanding* lawyer]. *See* SYNONYMS *at* **noticeable. 2** not paid [*outstanding* debts].

**out·stretched** (out′strecht′) ***adj.*** stretched out; extended [She greeted us with *outstretched* arms.] *See the picture.*

**out·strip** (out strip′) ***v.*** to get ahead of; leave behind or do better than; surpass or excel [He *outstripped* the other runners.] —**out·stripped′, out·strip′ping**

**out·ward** (out′wərd) ***adj.*** **1** being on the outside; outer. **2** that can be seen or noticed; visible [She showed no *outward* sign of fear.] **3** toward the outside [an *outward* glance; *outward* traffic]. ◆***adv.*** toward the outside [The door opens *outward*.] —**out′ward·ly** ***adv.***

**out·wards** (out′wərdz) ***adv.*** *same as* **outward.**

**out·wear** (out wer′) ***v.*** **1** to last longer than [These shoes will *outwear* any others.] **2** to wear out or use up. —**out·wore′, out·worn′, out·wear′ing**

**out·weigh** (out wā′) ***v.*** **1** to weigh more than. **2** to be more important, valuable, etc. than [The pleasure we got *outweighed* the cost.]

**out·wit** (out wit′) ***v.*** to win out over by being more clever or cunning [to *outwit* an opponent in chess]. —**out·wit′ted, out·wit′ting**

**out·worn** (out′wôrn′) ***adj.*** **1** worn out [*outworn* shoes]. **2** out-of-date [*outworn* ideas].

**o·va** (ō′və) ***n.*** *plural of* **ovum.**

**o·val** (ō′v'l) ***adj.*** shaped like an egg or like an ellipse. ◆***n.*** anything with such a shape. *See the picture.*

**o·va·ry** (ō′vər ē) ***n.*** **1** the organ in a female in which the eggs are formed. **2** the part of a flower in which the seeds are formed. —*pl.* **o′va·ries**

**o·va·tion** (ō vā′shən) ***n.*** loud and long applause or cheering by a crowd to show welcome or approval.

**ov·en** (uv′ən) ***n.*** a container, or an enclosed space as in a stove, for baking or roasting food or for heating or drying things.

**ov·en·bird** (uv′ən burd) ***n.*** ☆a North American bird that builds a nest on the ground, with a dome on top.

**o·ver** (ō′vər) ***prep.*** **1** in, at, or to a place above [Hang the picture *over* the fireplace.] **2** so as to cover [Put this blanket *over* your legs.] **3** above in rank or power [They have a new police chief *over* them.] **4** along the length of [We've driven *over* this road many times.] **5** to or on the other side of [The deer jumped *over* the fence.] **6** above and beyond [She leaned *over* the edge.] **7** across and down from [The car went *over* the cliff.] **8** through all the parts of [The news spread *over* the whole town.] **9** during; through [*over* the past five years]. **10** more than [It cost *over* ten dollars.] **11** rather than [We chose the brown rug *over* the blue one.] **12** upon, so that it affects [His singing cast a spell *over* us.] **13** concerning; about [Don't fight *over* it.] **14** by means of [We talked *over* the telephone.] ◆***adv.*** **1** above or across [A plane flew *over*.] **2** across the brim or edge [The soup boiled *over*.] **3** more; beyond [The movie will last two hours or *over*.] **4** remaining as something extra [There is much food left *over*.] **5** so as to be covered [The wound healed *over*.] **6** from start to finish [Let's talk it *over*.] **7** from a standing position; down [The stack of blocks fell *over*.] **8** so that the other side is up [Turn the plate *over*.] **9** again [Do the lesson *over*.] **10** at or on the other side of something [They live *over* in France.] **11** from one side or opinion to another [We won her *over*.] **12** from one person to another [Hand *over* the money.] ◆***adj.*** **1** finished; done with [The game is *over*.] **2** having reached the other side [We were barely *over* when the bridge broke.] —**over again,** another time; again. —**over all,** from end to end. —**over and above,** in addition to; more than. —**over and over,** again and again.

**over-** *a prefix meaning:* **1** above or higher [An *overhead* heater is above one's head.] **2** too much [To *overeat* is to eat too much.] **3** across or beyond [To *overshoot* a target is to shoot beyond it.]

> Many words beginning with **over-** that are not entered in this dictionary can be understood if "too" or "too much" is used before the meaning of the base word [Parents who are *overanxious* are too anxious. To *overcook* meat is to cook it too much.]

**o·ver·a·bun·dance** (ō′vər ə bun′dəns) ***n.*** much more than enough; excess. —**o′ver·a·bun′dant** ***adj.***

**o·ver·act** (ō vər akt′) ***v.*** to act a part in a play in an exaggerated way.

**o·ver·all** (ō′vər ôl) ***adj.*** **1** from end to end [the *overall* length of a boat]. **2** including everything; total [the *overall* cost of the car].

☆**o·ver·alls** (ō′vər ôlz) ***n.pl.*** loose-fitting trousers, often with a part that comes up over the chest, worn over other clothes to keep them from getting dirty. *See the picture.*

**o·ver·awe** (ō vər ô′) ***v.*** to overcome by filling with awe [The giant did not *overawe* Jack.] —**o·ver·awed′, o·ver·aw′ing**

**o·ver·bal·ance** (ō′vər bal′əns) ***v.*** **1** to be greater than, as in weight or importance. **2** to throw off balance. —**o′ver·bal′anced, o′ver·bal′anc·ing**

**o·ver·bear·ing** (ō′vər ber′iŋ) ***adj.*** ordering others about in a harsh, bullying way.

**o·ver·board** (ō′vər bôrd) ***adv.*** from a ship into the water [He fell *overboard*.] —**go overboard,** ☆to be too enthusiastic: *used only in everyday talk.*

**o·ver·bur·den** (ō′vər bur′d'n) ***v.*** to be too great a burden for; weigh down.

**o·ver·cast** (ō′vər kast) ***adj.*** cloudy; dark [an *overcast* sky]. ◆***v.*** **1** to cover over with clouds or darkness. **2** to sew over an edge with long, loose stitches to keep it from raveling. —**o′ver·cast, o′ver·cast·ing**

| | | | | | | | |
|---|---|---|---|---|---|---|---|
| a | fat | ir | here | ou | out | zh | leisure |
| ā | ape | ī | bite, fire | u | up | ŋ | ring |
| ä | car, lot | ō | go | ur | fur | | a *in* ago |
| e | ten | ô | law, horn | ch | chin | | e *in* agent |
| er | care | oi | oil | sh | she | ə = | i *in* unity |
| ē | even | oo | look | th | thin | | o *in* collect |
| i | hit | ōō | tool | *th* | then | | u *in* focus |

**o·ver·charge** (ō vər chärj′) ***v.*** **1** to charge too high a price. **2** to fill too full. —**o·ver·charged′, o·ver·charg′ing** ◆***n.*** (ō′vər chärj) too high a charge.

**o·ver·cloud** (ō vər kloud′) ***v.*** **1** to cover over with clouds; darken. **2** to make or become gloomy [Grief *overclouded* his face.]

☆**o·ver·coat** (ō′vər kōt) ***n.*** a heavy coat worn outdoors in cold weather.

**o·ver·come** (ō vər kum′) ***v.*** **1** to get the better of; defeat; master [to *overcome* an enemy; to *overcome* a problem]. **2** to make weak or helpless [We were *overcome* by laughter.] **3** to be victorious; win. —**o·ver·came′, o·ver·come′, o·ver·com′ing**

**o·ver·con·fi·dent** (ō′vər kän′fə dənt) ***adj.*** more confident than one has reason to be; too confident or sure of oneself. —**o′ver·con′fi·dence *n.*** —**o′ver·con′fi·dent·ly *adv.***

**o·ver·crowd** (ō vər kroud′) ***v.*** to crowd with too many people or things.

**o·ver·do** (ō vər do͞o′) ***v.*** **1** to tire oneself out by doing too much. **2** to spoil by exaggerating [Don't *overdo* your praise.] **3** to cook too long. —**o·ver·did′, o·ver·done′, o·ver·do′ing**

**o·ver·dose** (ō′vər dōs) ***n.*** too large a dose. ◆***v.*** (ō vər dōs′) to give or take too large a dose. —**o·ver·dosed′, o·ver·dos′ing**

**o·ver·draw** (ō vər drô′) ***v.*** **1** to write checks for more money than one has in one's bank account. **2** to overdo or exaggerate [Villains are *overdrawn* in melodramas.] —**o·ver·drew′, o·ver·drawn′, o·ver·draw′ing**



**o·ver·dress** (ō vər dres′) ***v.*** to dress in a way that is too showy or too formal.

**o·ver·due** (ō vər do͞o′ *or* ō vər dyo͞o′) ***adj.*** delayed past the time set for payment, arrival, etc. [an *overdue* bill; a bus long *overdue*].

**o·ver·eat** (ō vər ēt′) ***v.*** to eat too much. —**o·ver·ate′, o·ver·eat′en, o·ver·eat′ing**

**o·ver·es·ti·mate** (ō′vər es′tə māt) ***v.*** to put too high an estimate on or for; rate too highly [Don't *overestimate* the chances of our team.] —**o′ver·es′ti·mat·ed, o′ver·es′ti·mat·ing** ◆***n.*** (ō′vər es′tə mit) too high an estimate.

**o·ver·ex·pose** (ō′vər ik spōz′) ***v.*** to expose too much or too long. —**o′ver·ex·posed′, o′ver·ex·pos′ing** —**o′ver·ex·po′sure *n.***

**o·ver·flow** (ō vər flō′) ***v.*** **1** to flow across; flood [Water *overflowed* the streets.] **2** to flow over the bounds of something [The river *overflowed* its banks. The crowd *overflowed* into the hall.] **3** to have its contents flowing over [The sink is *overflowing*.] **4** to be very full [She is *overflowing* with kindness.] ◆***n.*** (ō′vər flō) **1** the act of overflowing. **2** an opening, as at the top of a sink, for draining off liquids that would otherwise overflow.

**o·ver·grow** (ō vər grō′) ***v.*** **1** to grow all over [The lawn is *overgrown* with weeds.] **2** to grow too large or too fast [a youth *overgrown* for his age]. —**o·ver·grew′, o·ver·grown′, o·ver·grow′ing**

**o·ver·hand** (ō′vər hand) ***adj., adv.*** with the hand held higher than the elbow or the arm higher than the shoulder [an *overhand* pitch; to throw a ball *overhand*]. *See the picture.*

**o·ver·hang** (ō vər haŋ′) ***v.*** to hang over and beyond [The roof *overhangs* the house.] —**o·ver·hung′, o·ver·hang′ing** ◆***n.*** (ō′vər haŋ) a part that overhangs.

**o·ver·haul** (ō vər hôl′) ***v.*** **1** to check over carefully and make repairs or changes that are needed [to *overhaul* an engine]. **2** to catch up with; overtake. ◆***n.*** (ō′vər hôl) an overhauling.

**o·ver·head** (ō′vər hed) ***adj.*** **1** above one's head [an *overhead* light]. **2** in the sky [the clouds *overhead*]. ◆***n.*** the regular expenses of running a business, as of rent, heat, light, taxes, etc. ◆***adv.*** (ō vər hed′) above the head; aloft [airplanes flying *overhead*].

**o·ver·hear** (ō vər hir′) ***v.*** to hear something that one is not meant to hear [We *overheard* a quarrel at the next table.] —**o·ver·heard** (ō vər hurd′), **o·ver·hear′ing**

**o·ver·heat** (ō vər hēt′) ***v.*** to make or become too hot [The radiator keeps the engine from *overheating*.]

**o·ver·in·dulge** (ō′vər in dulj′) ***v.*** to indulge too much. —**o′ver·in·dulged′, o′ver·in·dulg′ing** —**o′ver·in·dul′gence *n.*** —**o′ver·in·dul′gent *adj.***

**o·ver·joy** (ō vər joi′) ***v.*** to give great joy to; delight [We were *overjoyed* to hear of your marriage.]

☆**o·ver·kill** (ō′vər kil) ***n.*** the ability of a country to kill with its nuclear bombs many times the total of all the people in another country.

**o·ver·land** (ō′vər land) ***adv., adj.*** by, on, or across land [an *overland* journey].

**o·ver·lap** (ō vər lap′) ***v.*** to lap over part of something or part of each other [The scales on a fish *overlap* one another. The two events *overlapped* in time.] *See the picture.* —**o·ver·lapped′, o·ver·lap′ping** ◆***n.*** (ō′vər lap) **1** the act of overlapping. **2** a part that overlaps.

**o·ver·lay** (ō vər lā′) ***v.*** to cover with a layer or coating of something that decorates [The box was *overlaid* with ivory.] —**o·ver·laid′, o·ver·lay′ing** ◆***n.*** (ō′vər lā) a covering or layer of decoration.

**o·ver·load** (ō vər lōd′) ***v.*** to put too great a load in or on [Don't *overload* the washing machine.] ◆***n.*** (ō′vər lōd) too great a load.

**o·ver·look** (ō vər look′) ***v.*** **1** to give a view of from above; look down on [Your room *overlooks* the ocean.] **2** to fail to notice [I *overlooked* that detail.] **3** to pay no attention to; excuse [Can you *overlook* her rudeness?]

**o·ver·lord** (ō′vər lôrd) ***n.*** a lord who ranks above other lords.

**o·ver·ly** (ō′vər lē) ***adv.*** too or too much [Macbeth was *overly* ambitious.]

**o·ver·much** (ō′vər much′) ***adj., adv., n.*** too much.

**o·ver·night** (ō vər nīt′) ***adv.*** **1** during or through the night [Plan on staying with us *overnight*.] **2** very suddenly [He changed his mind *overnight*.] ◆***adj.*** (ō′vər nīt) **1** done or going on during the night [an *overnight* snow]. **2** staying for the night [an *overnight* guest]. ☆**3** of or for a short trip [an *overnight* bag].

**o·ver·pass** (ō′vər pas) ☆***n.*** a bridge or road over a river, another road, etc. *See the picture.*

**o·ver·pow·er** (ō′vər pou′ər) ***v.*** to get the better of; make helpless; overcome [Samson *overpowered* the lion. My rage nearly *overpowered* me.]

**o·ver·pro·duc·tion** (ō′vər prə duk′shən) ***n.*** the production of more than is needed or wanted.

**o·ver·pro·tect** (ō′vər prə tekt′) ***v.*** to protect more than is necessary or helpful, especially by trying to keep someone from the normal hurts and disappointments of life.

**o·ver·rate** (ō vər rāt′) ***v.*** to rate too highly; think of as better or greater than it really is [That singing group is a little *overrated.*] —**o′ver·rat′ed, o′ver·rat′ing**

**o·ver·reach** (ō vər rēch′) ***v.*** **1** to reach beyond or above. **2** to reach too far and miss. —**overreach oneself,** to fail because of trying too hard or being too clever.

**o·ver·re·act** (ō′vər rē akt′) ***v.*** to respond to something with greater feeling or force than seems necessary.

**o·ver·ride** (ō vər rīd′) ***v.*** **1** to ignore in an unjust or scornful way [The tyrant *overrode* the wishes of the people.] **2** to overrule; set aside [Congress *overrode* the president's veto.] —**o·ver·rode′, o·ver·rid′den, o·ver·rid′ing**

**o·ver·rule** (ō vər ro͞ol′) ***v.*** to rule out or set aside a ruling by someone with less authority [The higher court *overruled* the judge's decision.] —**o·ver·ruled′, o·ver·rul′ing**

**o·ver·run** (ō vər run′) ***v.*** **1** to spread out over [Weeds *overran* the garden.] **2** to swarm over, doing harm [a house *overrun* with mice]. **3** to go over or beyond certain limits [Fran *overran* second base and was tagged out.] —**o·ver·ran′, o·ver·run′, o·ver·run′ning**

**o·ver·seas** (ō′vər sēz′) ***adv.*** over or beyond the sea; abroad [Food was sent *overseas.*] ✦***adj.*** **1** over or across the sea [an *overseas* flight]. **2** of, from, or to countries across the sea; foreign [an *overseas* visitor].

**o·ver·see** (ō vər sē′) ***v.*** to watch over and direct; supervise [Who will *oversee* the work next week?] —**o·ver·saw′, o·ver·seen′, o·ver·see′ing**

**o·ver·se·er** (ō′vər sē′ər) ***n.*** a person who watches over and directs the work of others.

**o·ver·shad·ow** (ō′vər shad′ō) ***v.*** **1** to cast a shadow over. **2** to be or seem more important than [Good times have *overshadowed* our bad ones.]

☆**o·ver·shoe** (ō′vər sho͞o) ***n.*** a shoe or boot, as of rubber, worn over the regular shoe in cold or wet weather.

**o·ver·shoot** (ō vər sho͞ot′) ***v.*** to shoot or go over or beyond [to *overshoot* a target or a turn in the road]. —**o·ver·shot′, o·ver·shoot′ing**

**o·ver·shot** (ō′vər shät) ***adj.*** **1** with the upper part sticking out over the lower part [an *overshot* jaw]. **2** driven by water flowing over the top part [an *overshot* water wheel].

**o·ver·sight** (ō′vər sīt) ***n.*** **1** a failure to notice or do something; careless mistake. **2** the act of overseeing; supervision.

**o·ver·sim·pli·fy** (ō′vər sim′plə fī) ***v.*** to make something seem to be much more simple than it really is. —**o′ver·sim′pli·fied, o′ver·sim′pli·fy·ing**

**o·ver·size** (ō′vər sīz) ***adj.*** larger than is usual or normal [an *oversize* bed]. *Also* **o′ver·sized.**

**o·ver·sleep** (ō vər slēp′) ***v.*** to sleep past the time one meant to get up. —**o·ver·slept′, o·ver·sleep′ing**

**o·ver·spread** (ō vər spred′) ***v.*** to spread over [A faint blush *overspread* his face.] —**o·ver·spread′, o·ver·spread′ing**

**o·ver·state** (ō vər stāt′) ***v.*** to state too strongly; say more than is true about; exaggerate [Don't *overstate* your case.] —**o·ver·stat′ed, o·ver·stat′ing**

**o·ver·stay** (ō vər stā′) ***v.*** to stay beyond the time of [The guests *overstayed* their welcome.]

overpass

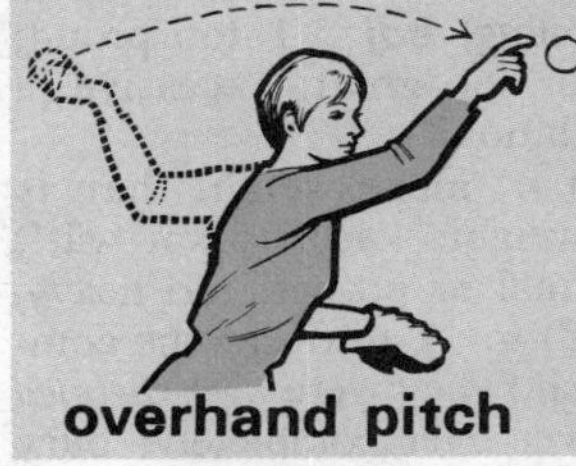
overhand pitch

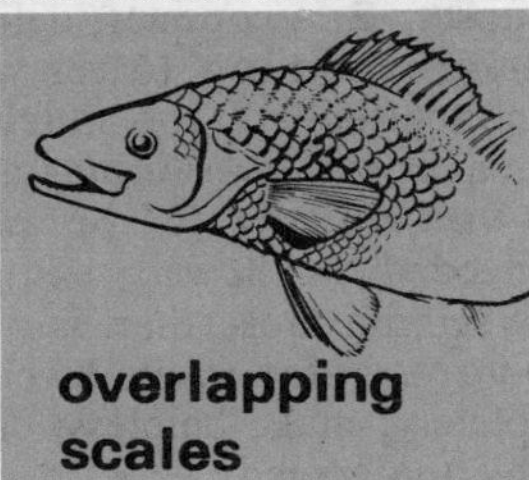
overlapping scales

**o·ver·step** (ō vər step′) ***v.*** to go beyond the limits of; exceed [to *overstep* one's authority]. —**o·ver·stepped′, o·ver·step′ping**

**o·ver·stock** (ō vər stäk′) ***v.*** to stock more of than is needed or can be used. ✦***n.*** (ō′vər stäk) too large a stock, or supply [We have an *overstock* of CB radios.]

**o·ver·sup·ply** (ō′vər sə plī′) ***v.*** to supply with more than is needed. —**o′ver·sup·plied′, o′ver·sup·ply′ing** ✦***n.*** too great a supply. —*pl.* **o′ver·sup·plies′**

**o·vert** (ō vurt′ *or* ō′vurt) ***adj.*** not hidden; open; public [Crying is an *overt* show of grief.] —**o·vert′ly *adv.***

**o·ver·take** (ō vər tāk′) ***v.*** **1** to catch up with and, often, go beyond [The tortoise *overtook* the hare.] **2** to come upon suddenly or by surprise [A sudden storm *overtook* us.] —**o·ver·took′, o·ver·tak′en, o·ver·tak′ing**

**o·ver·tax** (ō vər taks′) ***v.*** **1** to put too great a tax on [an *overtaxed* country]. **2** to put too much strain on [The work *overtaxed* his strength.]

**o·ver·throw** (ō vər thrō′) ***v.*** **1** to put an end to; defeat [The rebels *overthrew* the government.] **2** to throw or turn over; upset. **3** to throw beyond [The catcher *overthrew* first base.] —**o·ver·threw′, o·ver·thrown′, o·ver·throw′ing** ✦***n.*** (ō′vər thrō) **1** an upset; defeat. **2** the act of throwing beyond something.

**o·ver·time** (ō′vər tīm) ***n.*** **1** time beyond the regular time, as for working or playing a game; extra time. **2** pay for working beyond the regular time. ✦***adj., adv.*** of, for, or during a period of overtime.

**o·ver·tone** (ō′vər tōn) ***n.*** **1** a higher tone heard faintly along with a main tone made by a musical instrument. **2** a slight or subtle meaning or hint [Her reply had *overtones* of a threat.]

**o·ver·ture** (ō′vər chər) ***n.*** **1** a piece of music played at the beginning of an opera, musical play, etc.; introduction. **2** an offer to talk something over or do something; proposal [to make peace *overtures*].

| | | | | | | | |
|---|---|---|---|---|---|---|---|
| **a** | fat | **ir** | here | **ou** | out | **zh** | leisure |
| **ā** | ape | **ī** | bite, fire | **u** | up | **ŋ** | ring |
| **ä** | car, lot | **ō** | go | **ur** | fur | | a *in* ago |
| **e** | ten | **ô** | law, horn | **ch** | chin | | e *in* agent |
| **er** | care | **oi** | oil | **sh** | she | **ə =** | i *in* unity |
| **ē** | even | **oo** | look | **th** | thin | | o *in* collect |
| **i** | hit | **o͞o** | tool | ***th*** | then | | u *in* focus |

An **overture** has nothing to do with the word **over**, for it is not played when the rest of the work is over. Actually it comes from a French word which comes from a Latin word, both meaning "opening." An overture is the opening or beginning of a larger musical work.

**o·ver·turn** (ō vər turn′) ***v.*** **1** to turn or tip over; upset. **2** to conquer; defeat; destroy.

**o·ver·ween·ing** (ō′vər wē′niŋ) ***adj.*** **1** too proud; conceited. **2** too much or too great; excessive [a mayor with *overweening* ambition].

**o·ver·weight** (ō′vər wāt) ***n.*** more weight than is needed or allowed; extra weight. ◆***adj.*** (ō vər wāt′) weighing more than is normal or proper; too heavy.

**o·ver·whelm** (ō vər hwelm′) ***v.*** **1** to overcome completely; make helpless; crush [They were *overwhelmed* by the tragedy.] **2** to cover over completely; bury [Floods *overwhelmed* the farm.]

**o·ver·work** (ō vər wurk′) ***v.*** to work or use too hard or too much [to *overwork* a horse; to *overwork* an excuse]. ◆***n.*** too much work.

**o·ver·wrought** (ō vər rôt′) ***adj.*** **1** too nervous or excited; strained; tense. **2** having too much decoration; showy [an *overwrought* design].

**o·vi·duct** (ō′vi dukt) ***n.*** the tube through which the egg cells pass from the ovary to the uterus.

**o·vu·late** (ō′vyə lāt *or* äv′yə lāt) ***v.*** to produce egg cells and release them from the ovary. —**o′vu·lat·ed,**
524 **o′vu·lat·ing**

**o·vule** (ō′vyōōl *or* äv′yōōl) ***n.*** **1** a small ovum that is not yet ready to be fertilized. **2** the part of a plant that develops into a seed.

**o·vum** (ō′vəm) ***n.*** the egg cell in a female that develops into a new animal or human being after it is fertilized. —*pl.* **o′va**

**owe** (ō) ***v.*** **1** to be in debt for a certain amount or thing [I still *owe* the bank $200 on a loan. She *owes* her life to that doctor.] **2** to have or feel the need to do, give, etc., as because of being grateful [I *owe* my aunt a letter. We *owe* respect to our parents.] —**owed, ow′ing**

25 cm (10 in.) long

**ow·ing** (ō′iŋ) ***adj.*** **1** that owes. **2** due; not paid [There is $10 *owing* on your bill.] —**owing to,** because of; as a result of.

**owl** (oul) ***n.*** a bird with a large head, large eyes, a short, hooked beak, and sharp claws. Owls fly mostly at night, hunting small animals and birds. *See the picture.* —**owl′ish *adj.***

**owl·et** (oul′it) ***n.*** a young or small owl.

**own** (ōn) ***adj.*** belonging to or having to do with oneself or itself [I have my *own* pony. Use your *own* judgment.] ◆***n.*** that which belongs to oneself [The car is her *own*.] ◆***v.*** **1** to have for oneself; possess [We *own* that farm.] *See* SYNONYMS *at* **hold. 2** to admit; confess [I *owned* that I was wrong.] —**come into one's own,** to get what one deserves, especially fame and success. —**of one's own,** belonging strictly to oneself [He wants a stereo *of his own*.] —**on one's own,** by one's own efforts; without help: *used only in everyday talk.*

**own·er** (ōn′ər) ***n.*** a person who owns something.

**own·er·ship** (ōn′ər ship) ***n.*** the condition of being an owner; possession.

**ox** (äks) ***n.*** **1** a castrated male of the cattle family, used for pulling heavy loads. **2** any animal of a group that chew their cud and have cloven hoofs, including the buffalo, bison, etc. —*pl.* **ox·en** (äk′s′n)

**ox·bow** (äks′bō) ***n.*** **1** the U-shaped part of a yoke for oxen, which goes under the animal's neck. *See the picture.* ☆**2** a U-shaped bend in a river.

**Ox·ford** (äks′fərd) a city in southern England, the home of Oxford University.

**ox·ford** (äks′fərd) ***n.*** **1** a low shoe that is laced over the instep: *also called* **oxford shoe. 2** a cotton cloth with a loose weave, used for shirts, etc.: *also called* **oxford cloth.**

**ox·i·da·tion** (äk′sə dā′shən) ***n.*** the act of oxidizing or the condition of being oxidized.

**ox·ide** (äk′sīd) ***n.*** a compound of oxygen with some other chemical element or with a radical.

**ox·i·dize** (äk′sə dīz) ***v.*** to unite with oxygen [When iron rusts or paper burns, it is *oxidized*.] —**ox′i·dized, ox′i·diz·ing**

**ox·y·gen** (äk′si jən) ***n.*** a gas that has no color, taste, or odor and is a chemical element. It makes up almost one fifth of the air and combines with nearly all other elements. All living things need oxygen.

**oxygen tent** a small tent into which oxygen is fed, fitted around the bed of a patient to make breathing easier in certain conditions.

**o·yez** (ō′yez′ *or* ō′yes′) ***interj.*** hear ye! attention! This word is called out three times at the opening of a law court to get everyone's attention.

**oys·ter** (oi′stər) ***n.*** a shellfish with a soft body enclosed in two rough shells hinged together. Some are used as food, and pearls are formed inside others.

☆**oyster cracker** a small, round soda cracker.

**oz.** *abbreviation for* **ounce.** —*pl.* **oz.** or **ozs.**

**O·zark Mountains** (ō′zärk) a region of low mountains in southwestern Missouri, northwestern Arkansas, and northeastern Oklahoma. *Also called* **Ozarks.** *See the map.*

**o·zone** (ō′zōn) ***n.*** **1** a pale-blue gas that is a form of oxygen with a sharp smell. It is formed by an electrical discharge in the air and is used as a bleach, water purifier, etc. **2** pure, fresh air: *a slang meaning.*

**P, p** (pē) ***n.*** the sixteenth letter of the English alphabet. —*pl.* **P's, p's** (pēz) —**mind one's p's and q's,** to be careful of what one does and says.

**P** *the symbol for the chemical element* phosphorus.

**P.** or **p.** *abbreviation for* **pitcher, pressure.**

**p.** *abbreviation for* **page, part, participle, penny.**

**pa** (pä) ***n.*** father: *used only in everyday talk.*

**PA** or **Pa.** *abbreviation for* **Pennsylvania.**

**P.A.** *abbreviation for* **public-address system.**

☆**pac** (pak) ***n.*** an insulated, waterproof, laced boot, for wear in very cold weather.

**pace** (pās) ***n.*** **1** a step in walking or running. **2** the length of a step or stride, thought of as about 30 to 40 inches. **3** the rate of speed at which something moves or develops [The scoutmaster set the *pace* in the hike. Science goes forward at a rapid *pace*.] **4** a certain way of walking or running [a halting *pace*]. **5** a way of walking or running of some horses in which both legs on the same side are raised together. ◆***v.*** **1** to walk back and forth across [While waiting for the verdict, I *paced* the floor nervously.] **2** to measure by paces [*Pace* off 30 yards.] **3** to set the rate of speed for a runner. **4** to move at a pace, as a horse does. *See the picture.* —**paced, pac'ing** —**keep pace with,** to keep up with in a race, progress, etc. —**put through one's paces,** to test one's abilities or skills. —**set the pace, 1** to go at a speed that others try to equal. **2** to do or be something for others to equal or improve on. —**pac'er *n.***

**pace·mak·er** (pās'mā'kər) ***n.*** **1** a runner, horse, etc. that sets the pace for others. **2** an electronic device put in the body and connected to the wall of the heart, in order to give regular, mild electric shocks to the heart that keep the heartbeat normal.

**pach·y·derm** (pak'ə durm) ***n.*** a large animal with a thick skin, as the rhinoceros, hippopotamus, or, especially, the elephant.

☆**pach·y·san·dra** (pak ə san'drə) ***n.*** a low, dense-growing evergreen plant, often used for a ground cover in the shade.

**Pa·ci·fic** (pə sif'ik) the largest of the oceans, lying between Asia and the American continents. ◆***adj.*** of, in, on, or near this ocean.

Ferdinand Magellan, the Portuguese explorer, thought that the **Pacific** Ocean looked very calm and peaceful. He gave it this name, which comes from a Latin word meaning "to make peace."

**pa·cif·ic** (pə sif'ik) ***adj.*** **1** making or tending to make peace [a *pacific* agreement]. **2** not warlike; peaceful; quiet. —**pa·cif'i·cal·ly *adv.***

☆**Pacific Standard Time** *see* **Standard Time.**

**pac·i·fi·er** (pas'ə fī'ər) ***n.*** **1** a person or thing that pacifies. ☆**2** a ring, nipple, etc., as of rubber, for babies to chew on while teething.

**pac·i·fism** (pas'ə fiz'm) ***n.*** the principle that quarrels between nations should be settled in a peaceful way, never by war.

**pac·i·fist** (pas'ə fist) ***n.*** a person who believes in pacifism and refuses to take part in war.

**pac·i·fy** (pas'ə fī) ***v.*** to make peaceful or calm; appease [Offering apologies will *pacify* your neighbors.] —**pac'i·fied, pac'i·fy·ing** —**pac·i·fi·ca·tion** (pas'ə fi kā'shən) ***n.***

**pack**[1] (pak) ***n.*** **1** a bundle of things tied or wrapped [a hiker's *pack*]. **2** a package holding a number of items [a *pack* of chewing gum]. *See* SYNONYMS *at* **bundle. 3** a group or set of persons, animals, or things [a *pack* of thieves; a *pack* of wolves; a *pack* of lies]. **4** *a shorter form of* **ice pack.** ◆***v.*** **1** to tie or wrap together in a bundle. **2** to put things together in a box, trunk, can, etc. for carrying or storing [to *pack* away summer clothes; to *pack* a suitcase]. **3** to fill with more than it usually holds; crowd; cram [A huge crowd *packed* the stadium.] **4** to fill or cover tightly in order to protect, keep from leaking, etc. [*Pack* the wheel bearings with grease.] **5** to send [The child was *packed* off to school.] **6** to give or contain: *slang in this meaning* [Your punch *packs* a lot of force. The play *packs* a real message.] —**send packing,** to send away or dismiss in a hurry.



**pack**[2] (pak) ***v.*** to choose as members of a jury, committee, etc. people who will vote in a certain way [The jury was *packed* with friends of the person who won first prize.]

**pack·age** (pak'ij) ***n.*** **1** a thing or things wrapped or tied up, as in a box or in wrapping paper; parcel. *See* SYNONYMS *at* **bundle.** ☆**2** a number of things offered together as one [a retirement *package*]. ◆☆***v.*** to put into a package. —**pack'aged, pack'ag·ing** ◆☆***adj.*** that is or has to do with a plan, offer, etc. by which a number of items are offered together as one [a *package* deal; a *package* tour].

**pack·er** (pak'ər) ***n.*** **1** a person or thing that packs. ☆**2** a person who owns or manages a packing house.

**pack·et** (pak'it) ***n.*** **1** a small package. **2** a boat that travels a regular route, carrying passengers, freight, and mail: *the full name is* **packet boat.**

☆**packing house** a place where meats, vegetables, or fruits are prepared or packed for sale.

**pact** (pakt) ***n.*** an agreement between persons, groups, or nations; compact.

**pad**[1] (pad) ***n.*** the dull sound of a footstep on a soft surface. ◆***v.*** to walk with a soft step. —**pad'ded, pad'ding**

**pad**[2] (pad) ***n.*** **1** anything made of or stuffed with soft material, and used to protect against blows, to give

| | | | | | | | |
|---|---|---|---|---|---|---|---|
| **a** | fat | **ir** | here | **ou** | out | **zh** | leisure |
| **ā** | ape | **ī** | bite, fire | **u** | up | **ŋ** | ring |
| **ä** | car, lot | **ō** | go | **ur** | fur | | a *in* ago |
| **e** | ten | **ô** | law, horn | **ch** | chin | | e *in* agent |
| **er** | care | **oi** | oil | **sh** | she | **ə =** | i *in* unity |
| **ē** | even | **oo** | look | **th** | thin | | o *in* collect |
| **i** | hit | **ōō** | tool | ***th*** | then | | u *in* focus |

comfort, etc.; cushion [a shoulder *pad;* seat *pad*]. **2** the under part of the foot of some animals, as the wolf, lion, etc. ☆**3** the floating leaf of a waterlily. **4** a number of sheets of paper for writing or drawing, fastened together along one edge. **5** a small cushion soaked with ink and used for inking a rubber stamp. ◆***v.*** **1** to stuff or cover with soft material [a *padded* chair]. **2** to make larger or longer by putting in parts not needed [to *pad* a speech with jokes]. ☆**3** to add to an expense account items that are made up. —**pad′ded, pad′ding**

**pad·ding** (pad′iŋ) ***n.*** **1** a soft material, as cotton or felt, used to pad something. **2** something added, as to a speech, to make it longer.

**pad·dle[1]** (pad′′l) ***n.*** **1** a short oar with a wide blade at one or both ends, pulled through the water with both hands to make a canoe go. *See the picture.* **2** something shaped like this and used for beating someone, for washing clothes, for playing table tennis, etc. **3** any of the boards in a water wheel or in a paddle wheel. ◆***v.*** **1** to row with a paddle [to *paddle* a canoe]. **2** to punish by beating with a paddle; spank. —**pad′dled, pad′dling** —**pad′dler *n.***

**pad·dle[2]** (pad′′l) ***v.*** to move the hands or feet about in the water, as in playing; dabble. —**pad′dled, pad′dling**

☆**paddle ball** a game like squash, played with short-handled rackets.

**paddle wheel** a wheel with flat boards set around its rim, that turns in order to move a steamboat through the water.

**pad·dock** (pad′ək) ***n.*** **1** an enclosed place at a race track where horses are gathered before a race. **2** a small field for exercising horses.

**pad·dy** (pad′ē) ***n.*** rice growing in a rice field, or the field in which rice is growing. —*pl.* **pad′dies**

**pad·lock** (pad′läk) ***n.*** a lock with a U-shaped arm that turns on a hinge at one end. The other end snaps into the body of the lock after the arm is passed through a staple, chain, etc. *See the picture.* ◆***v.*** to fasten or keep shut as with a lock.

**pad·re** (pä′drā *or* pä′drē) ***n.*** father. This title is given to a priest in Italy, Spain, Portugal, and the countries of Latin America.

**pae·an** (pē′ən) ***n.*** a song of joy or praise.

**pa·gan** (pā′gən) ***n.*** **1** a person who is not a Christian, Muslim, or Jew; heathen. **2** a person who has no religion. ◆***adj.*** of or having to do with pagans. —**pa′gan·ism *n.***

**page[1]** (pāj) ***n.*** **1** one side of a leaf of paper in a book, newspaper, letter, etc. **2** the printing or writing on such a leaf [the sports *pages*]. **3** an entire leaf in a book, etc. [This *page* is torn.] **4** a record of events [the *pages* of history]. ◆***v.*** **1** to number the pages of. **2** to turn pages in looking quickly [to *page* through a book]. —**paged, pag′ing**

**page[2]** (pāj) ***n.*** **1** a boy, or sometimes a girl, who runs errands and carries messages in a hotel, office building, or legislature. **2** a boy servant who waits upon a person of high rank. **3** in the Middle Ages, a boy in training to become a knight. ◆***v.*** ☆to try to find a person by calling out the name, as a hotel page does. —**paged, pag′ing**

**pag·eant** (paj′ənt) ***n.*** **1** a large, elaborate public show, parade, etc. **2** an elaborate play based on events in history, often performed outdoors.

**pag·eant·ry** (paj′ən trē) ***n.*** large, elaborate show; grand display or spectacle [the *pageantry* of the crowning of a king].

**pa·go·da** (pə gō′də) ***n.*** a temple in the form of a tower with several stories, as in China, India, Japan, etc. *See the picture.*

**Pa·go Pa·go** (päŋ′ō päŋ′ō *or* pä′gō pä′gō) a seaport in American Samoa.

**paid** (pād) *past tense and past participle of* **pay.**

**pail** (pāl) ***n.*** **1** a round, deep container, usually with a handle, for holding and carrying liquids, etc.; bucket. **2** *a shorter name for* **pailful.**

**pail·ful** (pāl′fo͝ol) ***n.*** as much as a pail will hold. —*pl.* **pail′fuls**

**pain** (pān) ***n.*** **1** a feeling of hurting in some part of the body [a sharp *pain* in a tooth]. **2** suffering of the mind; sorrow [The memory of that loss brought us *pain.*] **3 pains,** *pl.* very careful effort; special care [You must take *pains* to do the work correctly.] ◆***v.*** to give pain to; cause to suffer; hurt [The wound *pains* me. Their insults *pained* us.] —**on pain of** or **under pain of,** at the risk of bringing upon oneself [She spoke fearlessly *on pain of* death.]

**Paine** (pān), **Thomas** 1737–1809; American Revolutionary patriot and writer.

**pained** (pānd) ***adj.*** showing hurt feelings [a *pained* expression].

**pain·ful** (pān′fəl) ***adj.*** causing pain; hurting; unpleasant [a *painful* wound; *painful* embarrassment]. —**pain′ful·ly *adv.*** —**pain′ful·ness *n.***

**pain·less** (pān′lis) ***adj.*** causing no pain; without pain [a *painless* operation]. —**pain′less·ly *adv.***

**pains·tak·ing** (pānz′tā′kiŋ) ***adj.*** taking or showing great care; very careful; diligent [*painstaking* work].

**paint** (pānt) ***n.*** a mixture of coloring matter with oil, water, etc., used to coat a surface or to make a picture. ◆***v.*** **1** to make a picture of with paints [The artist *painted* the same scene twice.] **2** to make pictures with paints [I *paint* as a hobby.] **3** to cover or decorate with paint [to *paint* furniture]. **4** to describe in a colorful way; picture in words. **5** to spread medicine, etc. on, as with a brush or swab [The doctor *painted* my throat.]

**paint·brush** (pānt′brush) ***n.*** a brush used in putting on paint.

**paint·er[1]** (pānt′ər) ***n.*** **1** an artist who paints pictures. **2** a person whose work is painting walls, houses, etc.

**paint·er[2]** (pānt′ər) ***n.*** a rope fastened to the bow of a boat, used to tie the boat to a dock, etc.

☆**paint·er[3]** (pānt′ər) ***n.*** *another name for* **cougar.**

**paint·ing** (pānt′iŋ) ***n.*** **1** the work or art of one who paints. **2** a picture made with paints.

**pair** (per) ***n.*** **1** two things of the same kind that are used together; set of two [a *pair* of skates]. **2** a single thing with two parts that are used together [a *pair* of eyeglasses; a *pair* of pants]. **3** two persons or animals that are joined together [a *pair* of oxen; a newly married *pair*]. **4** two legislators on opposing sides of a question who agree not to vote on the question. **5** two playing cards of the same value [a *pair* of aces]. ◆***v.*** to arrange in or form a pair or pairs; match. —**pair off,** to join in or make a pair or pairs.

SYNONYMS: **Pair** is used for two similar things that are thought of together or must be used together to be used properly [a *pair* of socks]. Or a **pair** may be a single thing with two parts that work together [a *pair* of scissors]. **Couple** is used for any two things that are alike and are in some way thought of together [a *couple* of lovebirds]. **Couple** is sometimes used to mean "several" or "a few" [The bus was a *couple* of minutes late.]

**pais·ley** (pāz′lē) ***adj.*** *also* **Paisley**, having an elaborate, colorful pattern of curved figures [a *paisley* necktie].

**pa·ja·mas** (pə jam′əz *or* pə jä′məz) ***n.pl.*** a loosely fitting suit for sleeping. It consists of a jacket, or blouse, and pants. —**pa·ja′ma *adj.***

**Pa·ki·stan** (pä′ki stän′ *or* pak′i stan′) a country in southern Asia, on the Arabian Sea.

**Pa·ki·stan·i** (pä′ki stä′nē *or* pak′i stan′ē) ***adj.*** of Pakistan or its people. ◆***n.*** a person born or living in Pakistan.

**pal** (pal) ***n.*** a close friend; chum. ◆***v.*** to go about together as close friends do. *This word is used only in everyday talk.* —**palled, pal′ling**

**Pal** comes from a word in the language of the Gypsies of England. To the Gypsies the word means "brother."

**pal·ace** (pal′is) ***n.*** **1** the official house of a king or queen, emperor, etc. **2** any large, splendid building.

**pal·at·a·ble** (pal′it ə b′l) ***adj.*** pleasing to the taste or mind [a *palatable* meal or idea].

**pal·ate** (pal′it) ***n.*** **1** the roof of the mouth. The bony front part is called the **hard palate**; the fleshy back part is called the **soft palate**. *See the picture.* **2** taste [The food was delicious to our *palates*.]

**pa·la·tial** (pə lā′shəl) ***adj.*** of, like, or fit for a palace; large and splendid; grand.

**pa·lav·er** (pə lav′ər) ***n.*** **1** talk; especially, idle chatter. **2** smooth or flattering talk. ◆***v.*** to talk in an idle or flattering way.

**pale**[1] (pāl) ***adj.*** **1** having little color in the face; wan [*pale* with fright]. **2** not bright; dim; faint [*pale* blue]. **3** weak [a *pale* imitation]. —**pal′er, pal′est** ◆***v.*** **1** to turn pale [Their faces *paled* at the news.] **2** to seem weaker or less important [My work *paled* beside theirs.] —**paled, pal′ing** —**pale′ness *n.***

**pale**[2] (pāl) ***n.*** **1** any of the pieces used in making a picket fence. *See the picture for* **picket fence**. **2** a boundary or limit [outside the *pale* of the law].

☆**pale·face** (pāl′fās) ***n.*** a white person. This is a word that people suppose American Indians once used.

**Pa·ler·mo** (pə lur′mō) a seaport on the northern coast of Sicily.

**Pal·es·tine** (pal′əs tīn) a region on the eastern coast of the Mediterranean. It was the country of the Jews in Biblical times and is now divided into Arab and Jewish states.

**pal·ette** (pal′it) ***n.*** **1** a surface, as a thin board with a hole for the thumb at one end, on which an artist mixes paints. *See the picture.* **2** the colors used by a particular artist.

**pal·ing** (pāl′ing) ***n.*** **1** a fence made of pales. **2** a pale or pales.

**pal·i·sade** (pal ə sād′) ***n.*** **1** a fence made of large, pointed stakes, set firmly in the ground as a defense against attack. *See the picture.* ☆**2 palisades**, *pl.* a line of steep cliffs, usually along a river.

palette

padlock

**pall**[1] (pôl) ***v.*** to become dull, boring, tiresome, etc. [Those jokes are beginning to *pall* on me.] —**palled, pall′ing** 527

**pall**[2] (pôl) ***n.*** **1** a piece of velvet or other heavy cloth used to cover a coffin, hearse, or tomb. **2** a dark or gloomy covering [a heavy *pall* of smoke].

**Pal·las** (pal′əs) *another name for* **Athena**.

**pall·bear·er** (pôl′ber′ər) ***n.*** one of the persons who carry or walk beside the coffin at a funeral.

**pal·let**[1] (pal′it) ***n.*** **1** a low platform that can be moved around, on which goods can be stored in warehouses or factories. **2** *another word for* **pawl**.

**pal·let**[2] (pal′it) ***n.*** a straw bed or mattress used on the floor.

**pal·li·ate** (pal′ē āt′) ***v.*** **1** to make less painful or severe without actually curing; ease [Aspirin *palliates* a fever.] **2** to make seem less serious; excuse [to *palliate* an error]. —**pal′li·at·ed, pal′li·at·ing**

**pal·li·a·tive** (pal′ē āt′iv *or* pal′ē ə tiv) ***adj.*** that palliates, eases, or excuses. ◆***n.*** something that palliates, as a drug.

**pal·lid** (pal′id) ***adj.*** without much color; pale; wan [a *pallid* face].

**pal·lor** (pal′ər) ***n.*** paleness of the skin, especially of the face, that comes from being sick, tired, afraid, etc.

**palm**[1] (päm) ***n.*** **1** any of various trees that grow in warm climates and have a tall trunk with a bunch of

| | | | | | | | |
|---|---|---|---|---|---|---|---|
| **a** | fat | **ir** | here | **ou** | out | **zh** | leisure |
| **ā** | ape | **ī** | bite, fire | **u** | up | **ng** | ring |
| **ä** | car, lot | **ō** | go | **ur** | fur | | a *in* ago |
| **e** | ten | **ô** | law, horn | **ch** | chin | | e *in* agent |
| **er** | care | **oi** | oil | **sh** | she | **ə =** | i *in* unity |
| **ē** | even | **oo** | look | **th** | thin | | o *in* collect |
| **i** | hit | **ōō** | tool | ***th*** | then | | u *in* focus |

man panning for gold

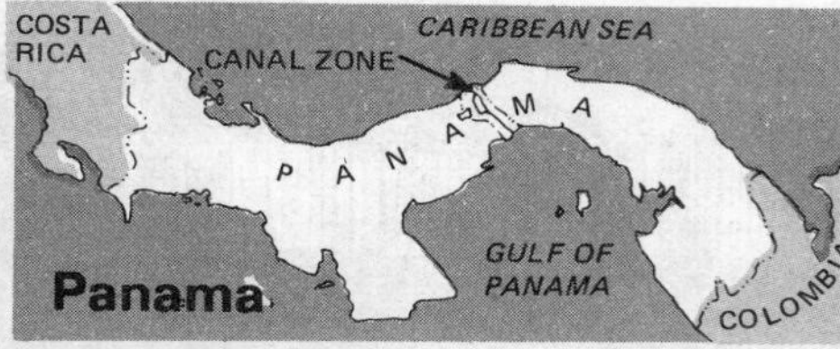

Panama

chickens in panic

Pan

coconut palm

giant pandas
1.5 m (5 ft.) long

large leaves at the top, but no branches. *See* **coconut** *and* **date[2]**. *See the picture.* **2** a leaf of this tree, used as a symbol of victory. —**bear the palm** or **carry off the palm,** to be the winner; take the prize.



**palm[2]** (päm) ***n.*** **1** the inside part of the hand between the fingers and wrist. **2** the part of a glove, etc. that covers the palm. ◆***v.*** to hide in the palm or between the fingers. —**palm off,** to get something sold, accepted, etc. by using trickery.

**palm·er** (päm′ər) ***n.*** a pilgrim who carried a palm leaf as a sign of having visited the Holy Land.

**pal·met·to** (pal met′ō) ***n.*** a small palm tree with leaves shaped like a fan. —*pl.* **pal·met′tos** or **pal·met′toes**

**palm·is·try** (päm′is trē) ***n.*** the practice of pretending to tell a person's future from the lines on the palm of the hand. —**palm′ist** ***n.***

**Palm Sunday** the Sunday before Easter.

**palm·y** (päm′ē) ***adj.*** **1** having many palm trees. **2** successful; prosperous [In their *palmy* days, they were the richest family in the city.] —**palm′i·er, palm′i·est**

☆**pal·o·mi·no** (pal′ə mē′nō) ***n.*** a horse having a pale-yellow coat and a white mane and tail. —*pl.* **pal′o·mi′nos**

**pal·pa·ble** (pal′pə b′l) ***adj.*** **1** that can be touched or felt; tangible [a small but *palpable* lump under the skin]. **2** easy to see, hear, recognize, etc.; clear; obvious [a *palpable* sound; *palpable* lies]. —**pal′pa·bly** ***adv.***

**pal·pi·tate** (pal′pə tāt) ***v.*** **1** to beat rapidly, as the heart does after hard exercise. **2** to shake or tremble. —**pal′pi·tat·ed, pal′pi·tat·ing** —**pal′pi·ta′tion** ***n.***

**pal·sied** (pôl′zēd) ***adj.*** **1** having palsy; paralyzed. **2** shaking; trembling [*palsied* hands].

**pal·sy** (pôl′zē) ***n.*** paralysis in some part of the body, often with a shaking or trembling that cannot be controlled.

**pal·try** (pôl′trē) ***adj.*** very small and almost worthless; trifling; petty [to work for *paltry* wages]. —**pal′tri·er, pal′tri·est**

**pam·pas** (pam′pəz) ***n.pl.*** the large plains, on which there are no trees, in Argentina and some other parts of South America.

**pam·per** (pam′pər) ***v.*** to give in easily to the wishes of; be too gentle with [to *pamper* a child].

**pam·phlet** (pam′flit) ***n.*** a thin booklet with a paper cover.

**pam·phlet·eer** (pam flə tir′) ***n.*** a writer of pamphlets, especially political pamphlets.

**Pan** (pan) a Greek god of nature and of shepherds. He is shown as having a goat's body from the waist down, and sometimes a goat's horns. *See the picture.*

**pan[1]** (pan) ***n.*** **1** a wide, shallow container used for cooking, etc., usually made of metal [a frying *pan*]. **2** a thing or part like this [a *pan* for washing out gold from gravel in mining; the *pan* on either side of a pair of scales]. **3** the part holding the powder in a flintlock. ◆***v.*** ☆**1** in gold mining, to separate gold from gravel by washing in a pan. *See the picture.* ☆**2** to find fault with; criticize: *used only in everyday talk* [to *pan* a new play]. —**panned, pan′ning** —☆**pan out,** to turn out in some way; especially, to turn out well: *used only in everyday talk.*

**pan[2]** (pan) ***v.*** to move a television or movie camera so as to follow a person or thing that is moving, or to get a very wide view. —**panned, pan′ning**

**pan-** *a prefix meaning* of or for all [*Pan-American* means of all the Americas or their people.]

**pan·a·ce·a** (pan′ə sē′ə) ***n.*** something that is supposed to cure all ills; cure-all.

> **Panacea** comes from a Greek word meaning "to cure all." In olden days people used to dream that a wonderful substance would be found that could cure any illness, evil, or bad condition.

**Pan·a·ma** (pan′ə mä *or* pan′ə mô) a country in Central America, on the narrow strip of land (**Isthmus of Panama**) that connects North America and South America. *See the map.*

**Panama Canal** a ship canal built across Panama, joining the Atlantic and Pacific oceans.

**Panama hat** a fine hat woven from the leaves of a Central and South American tree: *the name is sometimes shortened to* **Panama** *or* **panama.**

☆**Pan-A·mer·i·can** (pan′ə mer′ə kən) ***adj.*** of North, Central, and South America.

**pan·cake** (pan′kāk) ***n.*** **1** a thin, flat cake made by pouring batter onto a griddle or into a pan and frying it; flapjack. **2** a landing in which an airplane levels off, stalls, then drops straight down: *the full name is* **pancake landing.**

**pan·chro·mat·ic** (pan′krō mat′ik) ***adj.*** sensitive to light of all colors [*panchromatic* film for a camera].

**pan·cre·as** (pan′krē əs) ***n.*** a large gland behind the stomach that sends a juice into the small intestine to help digestion. —**pan·cre·at·ic** (pan′krē at′ik) ***adj.***

**pan·da** (pan′də) ***n.*** **1** a white-and-black animal of China and Tibet, that looks like a bear: *also called* **giant panda.** *See the picture.* **2** a reddish animal of the Himalayan region, that looks a little like a raccoon: *also called* **lesser panda.**

**pan·de·mo·ni·um** (pan′də mō′nē əm) ***n.*** wild disorder, noise, or confusion, or a place full of this.

**pan·der** (pan′dər) ***n.*** a person who helps another person to satisfy his or her desires, vices, etc.: *also* **pan′der·er.** ◆***v.*** to act as a pander.

**Pan·do·ra** (pan dôr′ə) in Greek myths, the first mortal woman, who let out all human troubles into the world when she became curious and opened a box she had been told not to open.

**pane** (pān) ***n.*** a single sheet of glass set in a frame, as in a window or door.

**pan·e·gyr·ic** (pan′ə jir′ik) ***n.*** **1** a formal speech or writing in which a person or thing is highly praised. **2** high praise.

**pan·el** (pan′'l) ***n.*** **1** a flat section or part of a wall, door, etc., either raised above or sunk below the surfaces around it. **2** a board or section containing dials, controls, etc. as for an airplane or a system of electric wiring. **3** a picture or painting that is long and narrow. **4** a strip of different material sewn lengthwise into a skirt or dress. **5** a group of persons chosen for some purpose, as for serving on a jury or for discussing some subject. ◆***v.*** to cover or decorate with panels [to *panel* a room with pine]. —**pan′eled** or **pan′elled, pan′el·ing** or **pan′el·ling**

**pan·el·ing** or **pan·el·ling** (pan′'l iŋ) ***n.*** a series of panels in a wall or other surface.

**pan·el·ist** (pan′'l ist) ***n.*** a member of a group of persons who join in discussing some subject, answering questions, etc., as on a radio or TV program.

**pang** (paŋ) ***n.*** a sudden, sharp pain or feeling [hunger *pangs;* a *pang* of homesickness].

**pan·go·lin** (paŋ gō′lin) ***n.*** a toothless, scaly animal of Asia and Africa. It can roll into a ball when attacked.

**pan·han·dle**[1] (pan′han′d'l) ***n.*** ☆*also* **Panhandle,** a strip of land that looks on a map like the handle of a pan. The Panhandle of West Virginia is a strip of land between Ohio and Pennsylvania.

☆**pan·han·dle**[2] (pan′han′d'l) ***v.*** to beg from people on the streets: *used only in everyday talk.* —**pan′han′dled, pan′han′dling —pan′han′dler *n.***

**pan·ic** (pan′ik) ***n.*** a sudden, wild fear that is not controlled and can spread quickly [The fire caused *panic* in the theater.] *See the picture.* ◆***v.*** to fill with or show panic [The loud noise *panicked* the hens. The outlaw *panicked* at the sight of the sheriff.] —**pan′icked, pan′ick·ing**

> SYNONYMS: **Panic** is a wild kind of fear that keeps a person from thinking clearly. It often spreads quickly and leads to reckless action [The cry of "fire!" created a *panic.*] **Terror** is a kind of fear that overcomes someone so much that the person can hardly move or act [We waited in *terror* as the monster drew closer.]

**pan·ick·y** (pan′i kē) ***adj.*** **1** like, showing, or caused by panic [frightened soldiers in *panicky* retreat]. **2** likely to be overcome with panic.

**pan·ic-strick·en** (pan′ik strik′'n) ***adj.*** filled with panic; badly frightened.

**pan·nier** or **pan·ier** (pan′yər *or* pan′ē ər) ***n.*** a large basket for carrying loads, especially either of a pair of baskets hung across the back of a donkey, horse, etc.

**pan·o·ply** (pan′ə plē) ***n.*** **1** a complete suit of armor. **2** any complete, splendid covering or display. *—pl.* **pan′o·plies**

**pan·o·ra·ma** (pan′ə ram′ə) ***n.*** **1** an open view in all directions [the *panorama* from the tall building]. **2** a series of sights, events, etc. that keep changing [the *panorama* of the waterfront]. **3** a full view of any subject. —**pan′o·ram′ic *adj.***

> **Panorama** was formed from two Greek words meaning "to see all" by Robert Barker about 1789 as a name for an unusual sort of picture he painted. The picture was painted on a surface that went completely around the person looking at it. From such a picture one may get the idea of a view that is open in all directions.

**pan·sy** (pan′zē) ***n.*** a small flower with flat, velvety petals of various colors. *See the picture on page 530.* —*pl.* **pan′sies**

**pant** (pant) ***v.*** **1** to breathe with quick, deep breaths; gasp, as from running fast. **2** to speak with quick, heavy breaths [A messenger rushed up and *panted* out the news.] **3** to want very much; long for [to *pant* after fame and fortune]. ◆***n.*** any of a series of quick, heavy breaths; gasp.

**pan·ta·lets** or **pan·ta·lettes** (pan t'l ets′) ***n.pl.*** long, loose underpants showing below the skirt, that were worn by women in the 19th century.

**pan·ta·loons** (pan t'l o͞onz′) ***n.pl.*** any kind of trousers.

**pan·the·ism** (pan′thē iz'm) ***n.*** the belief that God is the sum of all beings, things, forces, etc. in the universe. —**pan′the·ist *n.*** —**pan′the·is′tic *adj.***



**Pan·the·on** (pan′thē än′) a temple built in ancient Rome for all the Roman gods. It is now a Christian church.

**pan·ther** (pan′thər) ***n.*** **1** a leopard, especially a black one. **2** *another name for* **cougar.** **3** *another name for* **jaguar.**

☆**pant·ies** (pan′tēz) ***n.pl.*** short underpants worn by women or children: *also* **pant·ie** (pan′tē).

**pan·to·mime** (pan′tə mīm) ***n.*** **1** a play in which actors move and gesture but do not speak. **2** the use of gestures only, without words, to tell something. ◆***v.*** to act or tell by pantomime. —**pan′to·mimed, pan′to·mim·ing**

**pan·try** (pan′trē) ***n.*** a small room near the kitchen where food, dishes, pots, etc. are kept. *—pl.* **pan′tries**

☆**pants** (pants) ***n.pl.*** **1** a garment reaching from the waist to the ankles or the knees and covering each leg separately; trousers. **2** drawers or panties.

> When used as an adjective or with another word, the word *pants* is usually shortened to **pant** [*pant* legs; *pantsuit*].

**pant·suit** (pant′so͞ot) ***n.*** a woman's suit of jacket and pants that match: *also written* **pants suit.**

**panty hose** women's panties joined with hose as a one-piece undergarment: *also written* **pant·y·hose** (pan′tē hōz′) ***n.***

| | | | | | | | |
|---|---|---|---|---|---|---|---|
| a | fat | ir | here | ou | out | zh | leisure |
| ā | ape | ī | bite, fire | u | up | ŋ | ring |
| ä | car, lot | ō | go | ur | fur | | a *in* ago |
| e | ten | ô | law, horn | ch | chin | | e *in* agent |
| er | care | oi | oil | sh | she | ə = | i *in* unity |
| ē | even | oo | look | th | thin | | o *in* collect |
| i | hit | o͞o | tool | *th* | then | | u *in* focus |

**pap** (pap) ***n.*** soft food, as custard or cooked cereal, for babies or sick persons.

**pa·pa** (pä′pə *or now seldom* pə pä′) ***n.*** father: *mainly a child's word.*

**pa·pa·cy** (pā′pə sē) ***n.*** **1** the position or power of the Pope. **2** the period during which a pope rules. **3** the list of all the popes. **4** *also* **Papacy,** the government of the Roman Catholic Church, headed by the Pope. *—pl.* **pa′pa·cies**

**pa·pal** (pā′pəl) ***adj.*** **1** of the Pope [a *papal* crown]. **2** of the papacy [*papal* history]. **3** of the Roman Catholic Church [*papal* rites].

**pa·paw** (pô′pô) ***n.*** ☆**1** a tree of the central and southern U.S., with a yellowish fruit full of seeds. ☆**2** this fruit, used as food.

**pa·pa·ya** (pə pä′yə) ***n.*** **1** a tree of tropical America, a little like the palm, with a yellowish-orange fruit like a small melon. **2** this fruit, used as food. *See the picture.*

**pa·per** (pā′pər) ***n.*** **1** a thin material in sheets, made from wood pulp, rags, etc. and used to write or print on, to wrap or decorate with, etc. **2** a single sheet of this material. **3** something written or printed on paper, as an essay, report, etc. [The teacher is grading a set of *papers*.] **4** *a shorter word for* **newspaper.** **5** *a shorter word for* **wallpaper.** **6** a small paper wrapper holding something [a *paper* of pins]. **7** written promises to pay that can be used as money in
530 business dealings: *the full name is* **commercial paper.** **8** **papers,** *pl.* official documents [Do you have your citizenship *papers* yet?] ◆***adj.*** **1** of, like, or made of paper [*paper* flowers]. **2** written down on paper, but not really existing [*paper* profits]. ◆***v.*** to cover with wallpaper. —**on paper,** **1** in written or printed form. **2** in theory, not in fact.

**pa·per·back** (pā′pər bak) ***n.*** a book bound in paper, instead of cloth, leather, etc.

parapet

papaya

parakeet

up to 21 cm (8 in.) long, including tail

pansies

parallel bars

**pa·per·boy** (pā′pər boi) ***n.*** a boy or man who sells or delivers newspapers.

☆**paper clip** a piece of metal wire bent back on itself in a closed loop to make a clasp for holding papers together.

**pa·per·girl** (pā′pər gurl) ***n.*** a girl or woman who sells or delivers newspapers.

**pa·per·hang·er** (pā′pər haŋ′ər) ***n.*** a person whose work is covering walls with wallpaper.

☆**paper money** printed paper issued by a government to be used as money along with metal coins.

**paper tiger** a person, nation, etc. that seems to present a threat but is actually powerless.

**pa·per·weight** (pā′pər wāt) ***n.*** any small, heavy object placed on papers to keep them from being scattered.

**paper work** the keeping of records, filing of reports, etc. that must be done as a part of some work or task.

**pa·per·y** (pā′pər ē) ***adj.*** thin or light in weight like a sheet of paper.

**pa·pier-mâ·ché** (pā′pər mə shā′) ***n.*** a material made of paper pulp mixed with glue, paste, etc. It can be molded when wet and becomes hard when it dries.

**pa·pil·la** (pə pil′ə) ***n.*** a tiny swelling of flesh, as on the tongue. *—pl.* **pa·pil·lae** (pə pil′ē)

☆**pa·poose** (pa po͞os′) ***n.*** a North American Indian baby.

**pap·py** (pap′ē) ***n.*** father: *used only in some regions in everyday talk. —pl.* **pap′pies**

**pap·ri·ka** (pa prē′kə *or* pap′ri kə) ***n.*** a red seasoning made by grinding certain peppers.

**Pap·u·a New Guinea** (pap′yo͞o wə) a country on the eastern half of the island of New Guinea.

**pa·py·rus** (pə pī′rəs) ***n.*** **1** a tall plant growing in or near water in Egypt. **2** a kind of writing paper made from the pith of this plant by the ancient Egyptians, Greeks, and Romans. **3** any ancient document on papyrus.

**par** (pär) ***n.*** **1** the average or normal condition or quality [His work is above *par.*] **2** the value that is written on stocks, bonds, etc.; face value. **3** the number of strokes thought of as a skillful score in golf for a particular hole or for a certain course. ◆***adj.*** **1** of or at par. **2** average; normal. —**on a par,** equal in quality, rank, etc. [They are *on a par* in ability.]

**par·a·ble** (par′ə b′l) ***n.*** a short, simple story that teaches a moral lesson, as in the Bible.

**pa·rab·o·la** (pə rab′ə lə) ***n.*** a curve formed by cutting through a cone parallel to a sloping side.

**par·a·chute** (par′ə sho͞ot) ***n.*** a large cloth device that opens up like an umbrella and is used for slowing down a person or thing dropping from an airplane. ◆***v.*** to jump with or drop by a parachute. —**par′a·chut·ed, par′a·chut·ing —par′a·chut·ist** ***n.***

**pa·rade** (pə rād′) ***n.*** **1** a ceremony of troops marching, as for review; also, a place for such a ceremony. **2** any march or procession, as to celebrate a holiday [a Fourth of July *parade*]. **3** a public walk; also, people walking along in a crowd [the Easter *parade*]. **4** a showing off; a boastful show [Must you make a *parade* of your knowledge?] **5** a number of persons or things coming one after another [a *parade* of suspects]. ◆***v.*** **1** to march in a parade. **2** to walk about in a showy way. **3** to show off [They *parade* their wealth.] —**pa·rad′ed, pa·rad′ing —on parade,** on display.

**par·a·dise** (par′ə dīs) ***n.*** **1 Paradise,** the garden of Eden. **2** *another name for* **heaven**. **3** any place that is very beautiful or seems exactly as one would wish [a golfer's *paradise*]. **4** any place or condition of great happiness.

**par·a·dox** (par′ə däks) ***n.*** **1** a statement that seems to contradict itself or seems false, but that may be true in fact. Example: "Water, water, everywhere, and not a drop to drink." **2** a statement that contradicts itself and is false. Example: The sun was so hot we nearly froze. **3** a person or thing that seems full of contradictions. —**par′a·dox′i·cal** ***adj.***

**par·af·fin** (par′ə fin) ***n.*** a white, waxy substance got from petroleum and used for making candles, sealing jars, etc.

**par·a·gon** (par′ə gän) ***n.*** a perfect or excellent person or thing that serves as an example.

**par·a·graph** (par′ə graf) ***n.*** **1** a separate section of a piece of writing, that deals with a particular point and is made up of one or more sentences. Each paragraph begins on a new line that is usually moved in from the margin. **2** a short note or item in a newspaper or magazine. ◆***v.*** **1** to write about in paragraphs. **2** to arrange in paragraphs.

**Paragraph** comes from a Greek word meaning "a sign written beside." Originally paragraphs had a mark or line to show where they began.

**Par·a·guay** (par′ə gwā *or* par′ə gwī) a country in central South America. —**Par′a·guay′an** ***adj., n.***

**par·a·keet** (par′ə kēt) ***n.*** a small, slender parrot with a long tail. Parakeets are often kept as pets. *See the picture.*

**par·a·le·gal** (par′ə lē′gəl) ***adj.*** being or having to do with persons trained to aid lawyers but not licensed to practice law. ◆***n.*** a person doing paralegal work.

**par·al·lax** (par′ə laks) ***n.*** **1** the change that seems to take place in the position of an object when the person looking at it moves. **2** the amount of such change, especially in the position of a star as seen from different places.

**par·al·lel** (par′ə lel) ***adj.*** **1** moving out in the same direction and always the same distance apart so as to never meet, as the tracks of a sled in the snow. **2** similar or alike [Their lives followed *parallel* courses.] ◆***n.*** **1** a parallel line, plane, etc. **2** something similar to or like something else [Your experience is a *parallel* to mine.] **3** a comparison showing how things are alike [The teacher drew a *parallel* between the two books.] **4** any of the imaginary circles around the earth parallel to the equator that mark degrees of latitude [New Orleans is on the 30th *parallel* north of the equator.] ◆***v.*** **1** to be in a *parallel* line or plane with [The road *parallels* the river.] **2** to be or find something that is like or similar to; match [Nothing can *parallel* that discovery.] **3** to compare things in order to show likeness. —**par′al·leled** or **par′al·lelled, par′al·lel·ing** or **par′al·lel·ling**

**parallel bars** two bars parallel to each other, set on upright posts about 15 inches apart and used in gymnastic exercises. *See the picture.*

**par·al·lel·ism** (par′ə lel iz′m) ***n.*** **1** the condition of being parallel. **2** close likeness or similarity.

**par·al·lel·o·gram** (par′ə lel′ə gram) ***n.*** a figure having four sides, with the opposite sides parallel and of equal length.

**pa·ral·y·sis** (pə ral′ə sis) ***n.*** **1** a loss of the power to move or feel in any part of the body, as because of injury to the brain or spinal cord. **2** a condition of being powerless or helpless to act [a *paralysis* of industry].

**par·a·lyt·ic** (par′ə lit′ik) ***adj.*** of, having, or causing paralysis. ◆***n.*** a person having paralysis.

**par·a·lyze** (par′ə līz) ***v.*** **1** to cause paralysis in. **2** to make powerless or helpless [Heavy snows *paralyzed* the city.] —**par′a·lyzed, par′a·lyz·ing**

**par·a·me·ci·um** (par′ə mē′shē əm) ***n.*** a tiny water animal made up of one cell, that moves by waving the fine hairs, or cilia, on its body. —*pl.* **par·a·me·ci·a** (par′ə mē′shē ə)

☆**par·a·med·ic** (par′ə med′ik) ***n.*** a person doing paramedical work.

☆**par·a·med·i·cal** (par′ə med′i k'l) ***adj.*** being or having to do with persons whose work is helping doctors and nurses. Paramedical workers, such as midwives or nurses' aides, get special training.

**par·a·mil·i·tar·y** (par′ə mil′ə ter′ē) ***adj.*** being or having to do with forces working along with, or in place of, regular military forces.

**par·a·mount** (par′ə mount) ***adj.*** most important; ranking highest; supreme; chief [of *paramount* concern to us].

**par·a·pet** (par′ə pit) ***n.*** **1** a wall for protecting soldiers from enemy fire. **2** a low wall or railing, as along a balcony or bridge. *See the picture.* 531

**par·a·pher·na·lia** (par′ə fər nāl′yə) ***n.pl.*** **1** personal belongings. **2** all the things used in some activity; equipment [fishing *paraphernalia*]. *This word is often used with a singular verb.*

**par·a·phrase** (par′ə frāz) ***n.*** a putting of something spoken or written into different words having the same meaning. ◆***v.*** to write or say in a paraphrase. —**par′a·phrased, par′a·phras·ing**

**par·a·pro·fes·sion·al** (par′ə prə fesh′ən ′l) ***n.*** a worker trained to do certain things, as in medicine or teaching, but not allowed to do all the things a professional may do.

**par·a·site** (par′ə sīt) ***n.*** **1** a plant or animal that lives on or in another plant or animal and gets food from it [Mistletoe and fleas are *parasites*.] **2** a person who lives at another's expense without paying that person back in any way.

SYNONYMS: A **parasite** is a person who gets help or advantage from another and gives nothing in return. A **leech** is a parasite who holds on tightly to another and takes as much as possible from that person.

**par·a·sit·ic** (par′ə sit′ik) ***adj.*** of, like, or caused by parasites: *also* **par′a·sit′i·cal.**

**par·a·sol** (par′ə sôl) ***n.*** a light umbrella carried to shade oneself from the sun.

| | | | | | | | |
|---|---|---|---|---|---|---|---|
| **a** | fat | **ir** | here | **ou** | out | **zh** | leisure |
| **ā** | ape | **ī** | bite, fire | **u** | up | **ng** | ring |
| **ä** | car, lot | **ō** | go | **ur** | fur | | a *in* ago |
| **e** | ten | **ô** | law, horn | **ch** | chin | | e *in* agent |
| **er** | care | **oi** | oil | **sh** | she | **ə** = | i *in* unity |
| **ē** | even | **oo** | look | **th** | thin | | o *in* collect |
| **i** | hit | **ōō** | tool | ***th*** | then | | u *in* focus |

**par·a·troops** (par′ə tro͞ops) ***n.pl.*** a unit of soldiers trained to parachute from airplanes into an area where fighting is going on. *See the picture.* —**par′a·troop′er *n.***

**par·boil** (pär′boil) ***v.*** to boil until partly cooked, as before roasting.

**par·cel** (pär′s'l) ***n.*** **1** a small, wrapped package; bundle. *See* SYNONYMS *at* **bundle. 2** a piece of land [a *parcel* of ten acres]. ◆***v.*** to divide into parts for giving away or selling [to *parcel* out land to settlers]. —**par′celed** or **par′celled, par′cel·ing** or **par′cel·ling**

**parcel post** a postal service for carrying and delivering parcels.

**parch** (pärch) ***v.*** **1** to roast or dry with great heat [to *parch* corn]. **2** to make or become dry and hot [*parched* fields]. **3** to make very thirsty.

**parch·ment** (pärch′mənt) ***n.*** **1** the skin of a sheep or goat, prepared so that it can be written or painted on. **2** a document written on this. **3** a paper that is made to look like parchment.

**par·don** (pär′d'n) ***v.*** **1** to free from further punishment [A governor may *pardon* a criminal.] **2** to forgive or excuse [*Pardon* me for interrupting.] ◆***n.*** **1** the act of pardoning. **2** an official document granting a pardon. —**par′don·er *n.***

**par·don·a·ble** (pär′d'n ə b'l) ***adj.*** that can be pardoned, forgiven, or excused.

**pare** (per) ***v.*** **1** to cut or trim away the rind or covering of something; peel [to *pare* a potato; to *pare* the bark from a tree]. **2** to make less, bit by bit [to *pare* down expenses]. —**pared, par′ing**



**par·e·gor·ic** (par′ə gôr′ik) ***n.*** a medicine with opium in it, sometimes used for relieving stomach pains, etc.

**par·ent** (per′ənt) ***n.*** **1** a father or mother. **2** any animal or plant as it is related to its offspring. **3** anything from which other things come; source; origin [Latin is the *parent* of various languages.] —**par′ent·hood *n.***

**par·ent·age** (per′ənt ij) ***n.*** one's parents or ancestors; family line.

**pa·ren·tal** (pə ren′t'l) ***adj.*** of or like a parent.

**pa·ren·the·sis** (pə ren′thə sis) ***n.*** **1** a word, phrase, etc. put into a complete sentence as an added note or explanation and set off, as between curved lines, from the rest of the sentence. **2** either or both of the curved lines ( ) used to set off such a word, phrase, etc. —*pl.* **pa·ren·the·ses** (pə ren′thə sēz)

> **Parenthesis** comes from a Greek word meaning "to put beside." Words in parentheses are put beside other words to explain them.

**par·en·thet·i·cal** (par′ən thet′i k'l) ***adj.*** **1** that is or has to do with a word, phrase, etc. put in as an added note or explanation ["We'll win!" I shouted, adding a *parenthetical* "I hope."] **2** marked off by parentheses. *Also* **par′en·thet′ic.** —**par′en·thet′i·cal·ly *adv.***

**par·ent·ing** (per′ənt iŋ) ***n.*** the work or skill of a parent in raising a child or children.

**par·fait** (pär fā′) ***n.*** a frozen dessert of ice cream, syrup, fruit, etc., served in a tall glass. *See the picture.*

**pa·ri·ah** (pə rī′ə) ***n.*** a person whom others will have nothing to do with; outcast.

**par·ing** (per′iŋ) ***n.*** a thin strip of skin, rind, etc., that has been pared off [potato *parings*].

**Par·is**[1] (par′is) a son of the king of Troy in Greek myths. His kidnapping of Helen, wife of the king of Sparta, started the Trojan War.

**Par·is**[2] (par′is) the capital of France. —**Pa·ri·sian** (pə rizh′ən) ***adj., n.***

**par·ish** (par′ish) ***n.*** **1** a church district under the charge of a priest or minister. **2** the people living in such a district who go to its church. ☆**3** in Louisiana, a district like a county.

**pa·rish·ion·er** (pə rish′ə nər) ***n.*** a member of a parish.

**par·i·ty** (par′ə tē) ***n.*** the condition of being the same or equal, especially in value; equality.

**park** (pärk) ***n.*** **1** a piece of land with trees, lawns, benches, etc., where people can come for rest or recreation. Some parks have playing fields, beaches, amusement rides, etc. **2** a place known for its natural scenery, wild animals, etc., that is set apart by a State or country for the enjoyment of the public [Yellowstone National *Park*]. **3** the lawn, woods, etc. belonging to a large house. **4** an arrangement of gears that holds an automobile, truck, etc. in place when it is parked. ◆***v.*** ☆**1** to leave an automobile, truck, etc. in a certain place for a time [You may not *park* here.] ☆**2** to steer an automobile, etc. into a space where it can be left for a time.

☆**par·ka** (pär′kə) ***n.*** a jacket made of fur, wool, etc., with a hood on it. Parkas often have fleece or pile linings. *See the picture.*

☆**parking lot** an area where automobiles, trucks, etc. may be parked.

☆**parking meter** a timing device operated by coins and placed near a parking space. It shows the length of time that a parked vehicle may go on being parked in that space.

☆**park·way** (pärk′wā) ***n.*** a wide road with plantings of trees, grass, and bushes along its edges or in a center strip dividing the road.

**parl·ance** (pär′ləns) ***n.*** a way of speaking or writing; language; talk [military *parlance*].

**par·ley** (pär′lē) ***n.*** a meeting to talk over or settle something [The opposing generals met in a *parley* to discuss a truce.] —*pl.* **par′leys** ◆***v.*** to hold a parley, especially with an enemy.

**Par·lia·ment** (pär′lə mənt) ***n.*** **1** the lawmaking body of Great Britain, that is like our Congress. It consists of the House of Commons and the House of Lords. **2 parliament,** any group like this.

> **Parliament** comes from a French word *parler* that means "to speak." In Parliament or in our Congress one or another of the members is almost always speaking, usually about a law being considered.

**par·lia·men·ta·ry** (pär′lə men′tər ē) ***adj.*** **1** of or like a parliament. **2** of or following the rules of a group like this [*parliamentary* procedure]. **3** governed by a parliament.

**par·lor** (pär′lər) ***n.*** **1** a living room, especially one that was used in earlier times for entertaining guests: *this meaning is old-fashioned.* **2** a kind of business with special services [a beauty *parlor*]. *The usual British spelling is* **parlour.**

**Par·me·san** (pär′mə zän) ***n.*** a very hard, dry Italian cheese usually grated for sprinkling on spaghetti, soup, etc.: *the full name is* **Parmesan cheese.**

**Par·nas·sus** (pär nas′əs) a mountain in southern Greece. In ancient times it was sacred to Apollo and the Muses.

**pa·ro·chi·al** (pə rō′kē əl) ***adj.*** **1** of, in, or run by a church parish [*parochial* schools]. **2** limited; narrow [a *parochial* outlook].

**par·o·dy** (par′ə dē) ***n.*** a piece of writing or music that imitates another in such a way as to make fun of it. —*pl.* **par′o·dies** ◆***v.*** to make fun of by imitating. —**par′o·died, par′o·dy·ing**

**pa·role** (pə rōl′) ***n.*** ☆**1** the freeing of a prisoner before a full sentence has been served, on the condition that the prisoner will obey certain rules of good behavior. **2** a promise made by a prisoner of war not to fight any further if freed. ◆***v.*** ☆to free under the conditions of parole. —**pa·roled′, pa·rol′ing** —**on parole,** free under the conditions of parole.

☆**pa·rol·ee** (pə rō′lē′) ***n.*** a person on parole from a prison.

**par·ox·ysm** (par′ək siz′m) ***n.*** a sudden, sharp outburst; fit, as of laughter, anger, etc.

**par·quet** (pär kā′) ***n.*** **1** a flooring made of pieces of wood fitted together to form a pattern. *See the picture.* **2** the main floor of a theater; orchestra.

**par·ra·keet** (par′ə kēt) ***n.*** *another spelling of* **parakeet.**

**par·rot** (par′ət) ***n.*** **1** a bird with a hooked bill and brightly colored feathers. Some parrots can learn to imitate human speech. **2** a person who just repeats or copies what others do or say without understanding. ◆***v.*** to repeat or copy without full understanding.

**par·ry** (par′ē) ***v.*** **1** to turn aside, as a blow or a lunge with a sword; ward off. **2** to avoid answering, as a question; evade. —**par′ried, par′ry·ing** ◆***n.*** **1** a warding off of a blow, etc. **2** a clever or tricky answer. —*pl.* **par′ries**

**par·si·mo·ni·ous** (pär′sə mō′nē əs) ***adj.*** too careful in spending; too thrifty; miserly; stingy. —**par′si·mo′ni·ous·ly** ***adv.***

**par·si·mo·ny** (pär′sə mō′nē) ***n.*** the condition of being too thrifty; stinginess.

**pars·ley** (pärs′lē) ***n.*** a plant with small, often curly leaves used to flavor and decorate food. *See the picture.*

**pars·nip** (pärs′nip) ***n.*** a plant with a long, thick, white root that is eaten as a vegetable.

**par·son** (pär′s′n) ***n.*** a minister or clergyman.

**par·son·age** (pär′s′n ij) ***n.*** the house provided by a church for the use of its parson.

**part** (pärt) ***n.*** **1** a section, piece, or portion of a whole [the newer *part* of town; *parts* of the body; *part* of our class]. **2** a necessary piece that can be replaced [automobile *parts*]. **3** any of the equal pieces or shares into which a thing can be divided [A cent is a 100th *part* of a dollar.] **4** a share of work or duty [You must do your *part.*] **5 parts,** *pl.* talents or abilities [a person of *parts*]. **6** a role in a play; character [Who will play the *part* of Hamlet?] **7** the music for a certain voice or instrument in a musical piece [Our teacher will play the piano *part.*] **8** *usually* **parts,** *pl.* a region or area [Are you from these *parts?*] **9** a side in an argument, fight, etc. [I'll not take their *part* in the quarrel.] ☆**10** the dividing line formed by combing the hair in opposite directions. ◆***v.*** **1** to break or pull apart; separate [He *parted* the curtains to

look out. The rope *parted* in the middle.] **2** to go away from each other [They *parted* at the crossroads.] **3** to comb the hair so as to form a part [She *parts* her hair in the middle.] ◆***adj.*** less than a whole; not complete [*part* owner of a factory]. ◆***adv.*** not fully or completely; partly [The house is *part* mine.] —**for one's part,** as far as one is concerned. —**for the most part,** mostly; usually. —**in good part,** in a good-natured way. —**in part,** not fully or completely; partly. —**on one's part, 1** as far as one is concerned. **2** by or from one. —**part from,** to go away from; leave. —**part with,** to give up; let go. —**take part,** to have or take a share in something; participate. —**take someone's part,** to support someone in a struggle or disagreement.



**par·take** (pär tāk′) ***v.*** **1** to eat or drink something. **2** to take part; participate. —**partake of, 1** to have or take a share of. **2** to have a trace of; suggest. —**par·took′, par·tak·en** (pär tāk″n), **par·tak′ing** —**par·tak′er** ***n.***

**part and parcel** a necessary part of something.

**Par·the·non** (pär′thə nän) the ancient Greek temple of Athena on the Acropolis in Athens. *See the picture.*

**par·tial** (pär′shəl) ***adj.*** **1** of or in only a part; not complete or total [a *partial* eclipse of the sun]. **2** favoring one person or side more than another; biased [A judge should not be *partial.*] —**be partial to,** to have a special liking for; be fond of. —**par′tial·ly** ***adv.***

| | | | | | | | |
|---|---|---|---|---|---|---|---|
| **a** | fat | **ir** | here | **ou** | out | **zh** | leisure |
| **ā** | ape | **ī** | bite, fire | **u** | up | **ng** | ring |
| **ä** | car, lot | **ō** | go | **ur** | fur | | a *in* ago |
| **e** | ten | **ô** | law, horn | **ch** | chin | | e *in* agent |
| **er** | care | **oi** | oil | **sh** | she | **ə** = | i *in* unity |
| **ē** | even | **oo** | look | **th** | thin | | o *in* collect |
| **i** | hit | **ōō** | tool | ***th*** | then | | u *in* focus |

**partridge**
30 cm (12 in.) long

**par·ti·al·i·ty** (pär′shē al′ə tē) ***n.*** **1** a being partial, or favoring one side unfairly. **2** a strong liking; special fondness [a *partiality* for pickles]. *—pl.* **par′ti·al′i·ties**

**par·tic·i·pant** (pär tis′ə pənt) ***n.*** a person who takes part in something.

**par·tic·i·pate** (pär tis′ə pāt) ***v.*** to take part with others; have a share [Sue *participated* in the school play.] **—par·tic′i·pat·ed, par·tic′i·pat·ing —par·tic′-i·pa′tion *n.* —par·tic′i·pa′tor *n.***

**par·ti·cip·i·al** (pär′tə sip′ē əl) ***adj.*** of, formed with, or like a participle [In "a pouring rain," "pouring" is a *participial* adjective.]

**par·ti·ci·ple** (pär′tə sip′'l) ***n.*** a form of a verb used as both a verb and an adjective. Participles have tense and voice, and can take an object [In "He is humming a tune," "humming" is a present *participle* used as a



verb. In "a man dressed in gray," "dressed" is a past *participle* used as an adjective.]

**par·ti·cle** (pär′ti k'l) ***n.*** a very small piece; tiny bit; speck [*particles* of dust]. Some particles, as in the nucleus of an atom, are so small that they cannot be seen through a microscope.

☆**par·ti·cle·board** (pär′ti k'l bôrd′) ***n.*** a somewhat flexible board made by pressing sawdust or wood particles together with a gluelike resin.

**par·ti·col·ored** (pär′tē kul′ərd) ***adj.*** having different colors in different parts [The pheasant is a *particolored* bird.]

**par·tic·u·lar** (pər tik′yə lər) ***adj.*** **1** of only one person, group, part, or thing; not general; individual [What is your *particular* opinion?] **2** apart from any other; specific [Do you have a *particular* color in mind?] **3** more than ordinary; unusual; special [Pay *particular* attention.] **4** hard to please; very careful [They are *particular* about what movies they see.] ◆***n.*** a detail; fact; item [Give full *particulars* about the robbery to the police.] **—in particular,** particularly; especially.

**par·tic·u·lar·i·ty** (pər tik′yə lar′ə tē) ***n.*** **1** great care or special attention to small details. **2** a particular trait; peculiarity. **3** a small detail. *—pl.* **par·tic′u·lar′-i·ties**

**par·tic·u·lar·ize** (pər tik′yə lə rīz′) ***v.*** to tell or list in detail. **—par·tic′u·lar·ized′, par·tic′u·lar·iz′ing**

**par·tic·u·lar·ly** (pər tik′yə lər lē) ***adv.*** **1** more than usually; especially [a *particularly* hot day]. **2** in a particular way; in detail.

**par·tic·u·late** (pär tik′yə lit) ***adj.*** of or made up of very small, separate particles [soot, ash, and other *particulate* matter in the air]. ◆***n.*** a very small, separate particle.

**part·ing** (pärt′iŋ) ***adj.*** **1** said, given, etc. at the time of leaving [a *parting* remark]. **2** departing or leaving. **3** dividing or separating. ◆***n.*** **1** the act of leaving or saying goodbye ["*Parting* is such sweet sorrow."] **2** a dividing or separating [the *parting* of a frayed rope].

**par·ti·san** or **par·ti·zan** (pär′tə z'n) ***n.*** **1** a strong, often emotional supporter of some party, cause, or person. **2** a guerrilla fighter; especially, a member of a civilian force fighting to drive out enemy troops occupying a country. ◆***adj.*** of or like a partisan. **—par′-ti·san·ship′** or **par′ti·zan·ship′ *n.***

**par·ti·tion** (pär tish′ən) ***n.*** **1** a dividing into parts; separation [the *partition* of Ireland in 1925]. **2** something that separates, as a wall between rooms. ◆***v.*** to divide into parts [to *partition* a basement].

**part·ly** (pärt′lē) ***adv.*** in part; not completely.

**part·ner** (pärt′nər) ***n.*** **1** a person who takes part in something with another or others; especially, one of the owners of a business who shares in its profits and risks. **2** either of two players on the same side or team [my tennis *partner*]. **3** either of two persons dancing together. **4** a husband or wife.

**part·ner·ship** (pärt′nər ship) ***n.*** **1** the condition or relationship of being a partner. **2** a business firm made up of two or more partners.

**part of speech** any of the classes in which words are placed according to the way they are used. The usual names for the parts of speech are: noun, verb, pronoun, adjective, adverb, preposition, conjunction, and interjection.

**par·took** (pär to͝ok′) *past tense of* **partake.**

**par·tridge** (pär′trij) ***n.*** any of several wild birds hunted as game, including the pheasant. *See the picture.*

**part song** a song for several voices singing in harmony, usually without accompaniment.

**part-time** (pärt′tīm′) ***adj.*** being a worker, student, etc. for periods that take less time than a full, regular schedule [a *part-time* college student].

**part time** as a part-time employee, student, etc. [She works *part time* in the store.]

**part·way** (pärt′wā′) ***adv.*** to some point or degree less than full or complete [*partway* done].

**par·ty** (pär′tē) ***n.*** **1** a gathering of people to have a good time [a birthday *party*]. **2** a group of people who share the same political opinions and work together to elect certain people, to promote certain policies, etc. [the Republican *Party*]. **3** a group of people working or acting together [a hunting *party*]. **4** a person connected in some way with an action, plan, lawsuit, etc. [She is a *party* to his crime.] **5** a person: *used only in everyday talk.* *—pl.* **par′ties** ◆***v.*** ☆to go to or give parties or social affairs. **—par′tied, par′ty·ing**

**Pas·a·de·na** (pas′ə dē′nə) a city in southwestern California, near Los Angeles.

**pass**[1] (pas) ***n.*** a narrow opening or way through, especially between mountains.

**pass**[2] (pas) ***v.*** **1** to go by, beyond, over, or through [I *pass* your house every day. The guards won't let anyone *pass*.] **2** to go; move on [The crowd *passed* down the street. The days *passed* quickly.] **3** to go or change from one place, form, condition, owner, etc. to another [The liquid *passed* into solid form when it froze. The property will *pass* to her son when she dies.] **4** to come to an end or go away [The fever passed.] **5** to get through a test, trial, course, etc. successfully [She *passed* the final exam. Will your car *pass* inspection?] **6** to vote for; approve [City Council *passed* the resolution.] **7** to make or let go, move, advance, etc. [He *passed* a comb through his hair. *Pass* the bread to Jean. The teacher *passed* the whole class into the next grade.] **8** to spend [We *passed* the day at the zoo.] **9** to be taken as being; present oneself as being [They look so much alike that they could *pass* for brothers.] **10** to give as a judgment, opinion, etc. [to *pass* sentence on a criminal]. **11** to take place; happen [No one knows what *passed* behind those locked doors.] **12** to make no bid when one's turn comes in certain card games. **13** to throw or hit a ball, puck, etc. to another player. ◆***n.*** **1** an act of passing; passage. **2** a ticket, note, etc. which allows a person to come and go freely or without charge [a movie *pass;* a *pass* to go through the halls of a school]. **3** written permission given a soldier to be absent from duty for a short time [a weekend *pass*]. **4** a state of affairs; condition [Things have come to a sorry *pass,* and we don't speak to each other.] **5** a motion of the hand or hands [The magician made a quick *pass* and the rabbit disappeared.] **6** a throwing or hitting of the ball, puck, etc. to another player. —**bring to pass,** to make happen. —**come to pass,** to happen. —**pass away, 1** to come to an end. **2** to die. —**pass off, 1** to come to an end. **2** to take place. **3** to cause to be accepted by trickery or fraud [to *pass* oneself *off* as a police officer]. —**pass out, 1** to give out; distribute. **2** to faint. —**pass over,** to ignore; leave out. —☆**pass up,** to refuse or let go, as an opportunity: *used only in everyday talk.* —**pass′er** ***n.***

**pass·a·ble** (pas′ə b′l) ***adj.*** **1** that can be traveled over, crossed, etc. [a *passable* trail]. **2** fairly good; adequate [a *passable* meal].

**pas·sage** (pas′ij) ***n.*** **1** the act of passing [the *passage* of day into night; the *passage* of a bill into law]. **2** permission or right to pass [He was given *passage* through the enemy lines.] **3** a voyage [a *passage* to India]. **4** passenger space on a ship, as a berth or cabin [We booked *passage* on the steamer.] **5** a way through which to pass; road, opening, hall, etc. [a *passage* through the mountains]. **6** a part of a speech or writing [to read a *passage* from the Bible]. **7** an exchange, as of blows or words.

**pas·sage·way** (pas′ij wā′) ***n.*** a narrow passage or way, as a hall, corridor, or alley.

**pas·sé** (pa sā′) ***adj.*** old-fashioned; out-of-date.

**pas·sen·ger** (pas′′n jər) ***n.*** a person traveling in a car, bus, plane, ship, etc., but not driving or helping to operate it.

☆**passenger pigeon** a North American wild pigeon, with a long, narrow tail. These pigeons were all killed off by the year 1914.

**pass·er-by** (pas′ər bī′) ***n.*** a person who is passing by. —*pl.* **pass′ers-by′**

**pass·ing** (pas′iŋ) ***adj.*** **1** going by [a *passing* train]. **2** that lasts only a short time; fleeting [a *passing* fancy]. **3** done or made without careful thought; casual [a *passing* remark]. **4** allowing one to pass a test, course, etc. [a *passing* grade]. ◆***adv.*** very; extremely: *no longer much used* [She was *passing* fair.] ◆***n.*** **1** the act of one that passes. **2** death. —**in passing,** without careful thought; casually.

**pas·sion** (pash′ən) ***n.*** **1** any very strong feeling, as of great joy, anger, etc.; especially, strong love between a man and woman. **2** great liking; enthusiasm [her *passion* for books]. **3** that for which one feels a strong desire or liking [Golf is Pat's *passion.*] **4 Passion,** the suffering of Jesus on the cross or after the Last Supper.

> SYNONYMS: **Passion** is an emotion so very strong that it overpowers one [His *passions* make him act like a madman.] **Enthusiasm** is a strong liking for something which is eagerly sought or followed [her *enthusiasm* for golf]. **Zeal** is great enthusiasm for something, as a cause, that one works hard for without tiring or giving up [their *zeal* for improving the schools]. *See also* SYNONYMS *at* **emotion.**

**pas·sion·ate** (pash′ən it) ***adj.*** **1** having or showing strong feelings [a *passionate* speech]. **2** easily worked up, especially to anger. **3** very strong; intense [a *passionate* longing]. —**pas′sion·ate·ly** ***adv.***

**pas·sion·less** (pash′ən lis) ***adj.*** free from passion or emotion; calm.

**pas·sive** (pas′iv) ***adj.*** **1** not active, but acted upon [Spectators have a *passive* interest in sports.] **2** not resisting; yielding; submissive [The *passive* child did as he was told.] **3** having the verb in the form (called *voice*) that shows its subject as being acted upon: opposite of *active* [In the sentence "I was hit by the ball," "was hit" is in the *passive* voice.] —**pas′sive·ly** ***adv.***



**passive resistance** opposition in nonviolent ways to those in power, by refusing to pay certain taxes, obey certain laws, etc. or by fasting, peaceful demonstrations, etc.

**pass·key** (pas′kē) ***n.*** **1** a key that fits a number of different locks. **2** one's own key to something.

**Pass·o·ver** (pas′ō′vər) ***n.*** a Jewish holiday in memory of the freeing of the ancient Hebrews from slavery in Egypt.

**pass·port** (pas′pôrt) ***n.*** **1** an official paper given by a government to a citizen traveling in foreign countries, stating who the person is and giving him or her the right to protection. **2** anything that makes it possible for a person to go somewhere, do something, etc. [Education was her *passport* to a job.]

☆**pass-through** (pas′thro͞o′) ***n.*** an opening in a wall, as between a kitchen and dining room, often with a shelf, for passing food, dishes, etc. through.

**pass·word** (pas′wurd) ***n.*** a secret word or signal that must be given when asked for in order to be allowed to pass by a guard or sentry.

**past** (past) ***adj.*** **1** gone by; ended; over [What is *past* is finished.] **2** of a former time [a *past* president]. **3** that came just before this [the *past* week]. **4** showing time gone by [The *past* tense of "walk" is "walked."]

| | | | | | | | |
|---|---|---|---|---|---|---|---|
| **a** | fat | **ir** | here | **ou** | out | **zh** | leisure |
| **ā** | ape | **ī** | bite, fire | **u** | up | **ŋ** | ring |
| **ä** | car, lot | **ō** | go | **ur** | fur | | a *in* ago |
| **e** | ten | **ô** | law, horn | **ch** | chin | | e *in* agent |
| **er** | care | **oi** | oil | **sh** | she | **ə =** | i *in* unity |
| **ē** | even | **oo** | look | **th** | thin | | o *in* collect |
| **i** | hit | **o͞o** | tool | ***th*** | then | | u *in* focus |

**p**

**◆n.** **1** the time that has gone by [That's all in the *past*.] **2** the history or past life of a person, group, etc. [His *past* was exciting.] **◆prep.** **1** later than or farther than; beyond [ten minutes *past* two; *past* the city limits]. **2** beyond the power or limits of [That story is *past* belief.] **◆adv.** to and beyond; by [The band marched *past*.]

**pas·ta** (päs′tə) ***n.*** **1** dough made of wheat flour and shaped and dried in the form of spaghetti, macaroni, etc. **2** spaghetti, macaroni, etc. cooked in some way.

**paste** (pāst) ***n.*** **1** a mixture of flour, water, etc. used for sticking paper or other light things together. **2** any soft, moist, smooth mixture [tooth*paste*]. **3** a hard, shiny glass used for artificial gems. **4** dough used in making pie crusts, noodles, etc. **◆v.** to make stick, as with paste [to *paste* pictures in a book]. —**past′ed, past′ing**

**paste·board** (pāst′bôrd) ***n.*** a stiff material made by pasting layers of paper together or by pressing and drying paper pulp.

**pas·tel** (pas tel′) ***n.*** **1** a soft, pale shade of some color. **2** a kind of crayon made of ground coloring matter. **3** a picture drawn with such crayons. **◆adj.** **1** soft and pale [*pastel* blue]. **2** drawn with pastels [a *pastel* landscape].

**pas·tern** (pas′tərn) ***n.*** the part of a horse's foot between the fetlock and the hoof. *See the picture.*

**Pas·teur** (pas tʉr′), **Louis** 1822–1895; French scientist who found a way of treating rabies and of killing bacteria in milk.



**pas·teur·ize** (pas′chə rīz *or* pas′tə rīz) ***v.*** to kill harmful bacteria in milk, beer, etc. by heating the liquid to a certain high temperature for a certain period of time. —**pas′teur·ized, pas′teur·iz·ing** —**pas′teur·i·za′tion *n.***

**pas·time** (pas′tīm) ***n.*** a way of spending spare time pleasantly; amusement, recreation, etc.

**pas·tor** (pas′tər) ***n.*** a member of the clergy in charge of a church or congregation; minister or priest.

> **Pastor** comes from the Latin word for "shepherd," which comes from another Latin word meaning "to feed." As a shepherd looks after sheep and feeds the flock, so does a pastor look after a "flock," or congregation, and feed them in a spiritual way.

**pas·to·ral** (pas′tər əl) ***adj.*** **1** of pastors or their duties. **2** of shepherds, their work, their way of life, etc. **3** of life in the country, thought of as peaceful, simple, etc. **◆n.** a poem, play, etc. about life in the country.

**pas·tor·ate** (pas′tər it) ***n.*** the position, duties, or period of service of a pastor.

**past participle** a participle used to show time gone by or an action that took place in the past [In the sentence "She has given much to others," "given" is a *past participle*.]

**pas·tra·mi** (pə strä′mē) ***n.*** highly spiced, smoked beef, especially from a shoulder cut.

**pas·try** (pās′trē) ***n.*** **1** pies, tarts, and other baked goods that have a crust made from flour dough with shortening in it. **2** such dough. **3** all fancy baked goods. —*pl.* **pas′tries**

**pas·tur·age** (pas′chər ij) ***n.*** *another name for* **pasture.**

**pas·ture** (pas′chər) ***n.*** **1** land where grass and other plants grow and where cattle, sheep, etc. can graze. **2** grass and other plants eaten by grazing animals. **◆v.** **1** to put animals in a pasture to graze. **2** to feed in a pasture; graze. —**pas′tured, pas′tur·ing**

**past·y** (pās′tē) ***adj.*** of or like paste; white, thick, or sticky [a *pasty* complexion]. —**past′i·er, past′i·est**

**pat** (pat) ***n.*** **1** a quick, gentle tap or stroke with something flat, as the open hand. **2** the sound made by this. **3** a small lump, as of butter. **◆v.** to touch or stroke with a pat or pats, as to show love, to encourage, etc. —**pat′ted, pat′ting ◆adj.** just right for the time or purpose; suitable; apt [a *pat* answer]. —**have down pat,** to know thoroughly: *used only in everyday talk.* —☆**stand pat,** to refuse to change an opinion, way of acting, etc.

**Pat·a·go·ni·a** (pat′ə gō′nē ə) a region of grassy land in southern Argentina and Chile.

**patch** (pach) ***n.*** **1** a piece of cloth, metal, etc. put on to mend a hole, tear, or worn spot. *See the picture.* **2** a bandage put on a wound, or a pad worn over an injured eye. **3** an area or spot [*patches* of blue sky]. **4** a small piece of ground [a cabbage *patch*]. **5** a small piece; scrap; bit. **◆v.** **1** to put a patch or patches on [to *patch* the worn elbows of a coat]. **2** to make in a hurry as by putting bits together [He *patched* together a speech.] —**patch up,** to settle, as a quarrel.

**patch·work** (pach′wʉrk) ***n.*** **1** a quilt or other needlework sewn together from pieces of cloth of various colors and shapes. *See the picture.* **2** a design like this.

**pate** (pāt) ***n.*** the head, especially the top of the head: *used in a joking way.*

**pat·ent** (pat′'nt) ***n.*** **1** the right given to someone by a government to be the only one who may make and sell a new invention, or use a new method, for a certain number of years. **2** the paper giving such a right. **3** the invention or new method protected by such a right. **◆v.** to get a patent for [to *patent* a new process]. **◆adj.** **1** protected by a patent. **2** (pāt′'nt) easy to see or recognize; plain; evident [a *patent* lie].

**pat·ent·ee** (pat′'n tē′) ***n.*** a person who has been given a patent.

☆**patent leather** leather with a hard, smooth, shiny surface. It is usually black.

**pa·tent·ly** (pāt′'nt lē) ***adv.*** in a patent or obvious way; plainly; clearly [*patently* false].

**patent medicine** a medicine with a trademark, usually made by a secret process.

**pa·ter·nal** (pə tʉr′n'l) ***adj.*** **1** of or like a father; fatherly. **2** related to one on one's father's side [my *paternal* aunt]. —**pa·ter′nal·ly *adv.***

**pa·ter·nal·ism** (pə tʉr′n'l iz'm) ***n.*** a way of ruling a country, handling employees, etc. like that used by a father in dealing with his children. —**pa·ter′nal·is′tic *adj.***

**pa·ter·ni·ty** (pə tʉr′nə tē) ***n.*** **1** the condition of being a father; fatherhood. **2** the fact of who one's father is.

**pa·ter·nos·ter** (pät′ər nôs′tər *or* pat′ər näs′tər) ***n.*** the Lord's Prayer, especially in Latin.

**Pat·er·son** (pat′ər s'n) a city in northeastern New Jersey.

**path** (path) ***n.*** **1** a track worn by the footsteps of people or animals. **2** a way made for people to walk on [a flagstone *path* in a garden]. **3** a course along which something moves [the *path* of a rocket]. **4** a way of behaving [She followed the *path* of duty.]

**pa·thet·ic** (pə thet′ik) ***adj.*** causing or deserving pity, sorrow, etc.; pitiful [a wounded bird's *pathetic* cries]. —**pa·thet′i·cal·ly** ***adv.***

**path·o·log·i·cal** (path′ə läj′i k'l) ***adj.*** **1** of pathology [*pathological* research]. **2** caused by or having to do with disease [a *pathological* thirst]. **3** ruled by a feeling of being compelled; compulsive [a *pathological* liar]. *Also* **path′o·log′ic.** —**path′o·log′i·cal·ly** ***adv.***

**pa·thol·o·gy** (pə thäl′ə jē) ***n.*** the branch of medicine that deals with the causes, symptoms, and results of disease. —**pa·thol′o·gist** ***n.***

**pa·thos** (pā′thäs) ***n.*** the quality in some happening, story, speech, etc. that makes one feel pity, sadness, or sympathy [slow music, filled with *pathos*].

**path·way** (path′wā) ***n.*** *another name for* **path.**

**pa·tience** (pā′shəns) ***n.*** **1** the fact of being patient or the ability to be patient. **2** any card game of solitaire: *mainly British in this meaning.*

SYNONYMS: **Patience** is the ability to bear pain, trouble, waiting, boredom, etc. and at the same time keep calm and not complain [She listened to his long, sad story with *patience*.] **Endurance** is the ability to keep going in spite of suffering or hardship [Their *endurance* helped them get through a life of being poor and hungry.]

**pa·tient** (pā′shənt) ***adj.*** **1** able to put up with pain, trouble, delay, boredom, etc. without complaining [The *patient* children waited in line for the theater to open.] **2** working steadily without giving up [It took the Curies years of *patient* labor to discover radium.] **3** showing that one is patient [a *patient* smile; a *patient* search for the needle]. ◆***n.*** a person under the care of a doctor. —**pa′tient·ly** ***adv.***

**pa·ti·o** (pat′ē ō *or* pät′ē ō) ***n.*** ☆**1** in Spain and Spanish America, a courtyard around which a house is built. ☆**2** a paved area near a house, with chairs, tables, etc. for outdoor lounging, dining, etc. *See the picture.* —*pl.* **pa′ti·os**

**pat·ois** (pat′wä) ***n.*** a form of a language that is different from the standard form, as a dialect of a certain region [the *patois* of a French Canadian]. —*pl.* **pat·ois** (pat′wäz)

**pat. pend.** *abbreviation for* **patent pending,** a patent that has been applied for but not yet granted.

**pa·tri·arch** (pā′trē ärk) ***n.*** **1** the father and head of a family or tribe, as Abraham, Isaac, or Jacob in the Bible. **2** a man who is very old and dignified. **3** a bishop of high rank, as in the Orthodox Eastern Church. —**pa′tri·ar′chal** ***adj.***

**pa·tri·cian** (pə trish′ən) ***n.*** **1** a member of a noble family in ancient Rome. **2** a person of high social rank; aristocrat. ◆***adj.*** of, like, or fit for an aristocrat.

**Pat·rick** (pat′rik), Saint 385?–461? A.D.; a British bishop who became the patron saint of Ireland. His day is celebrated March 17.

**pat·ri·mo·ny** (pat′rə mō′nē) ***n.*** property inherited from one's father or ancestors.

**pa·tri·ot** (pā′trē ət) ***n.*** a person who shows great love for his or her country and is loyal to it.

**pa·tri·ot·ic** (pā′trē ät′ik) ***adj.*** showing great love for one's country and loyalty to it. —**pa′tri·ot′i·cal·ly** ***adv.***

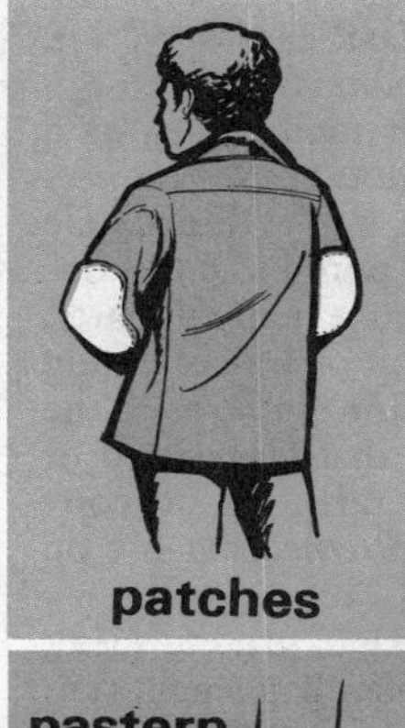
patches

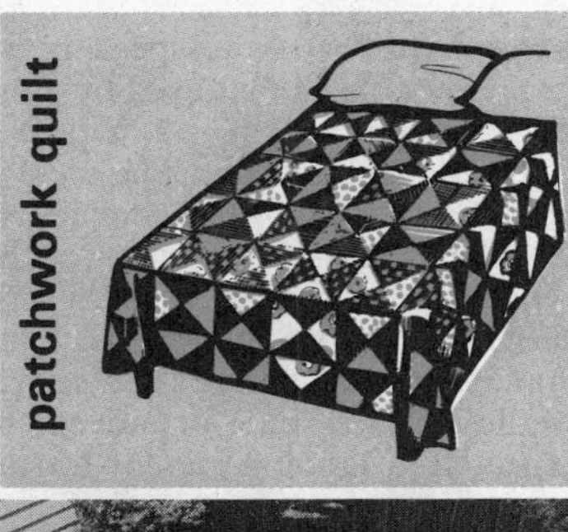
patchwork quilt

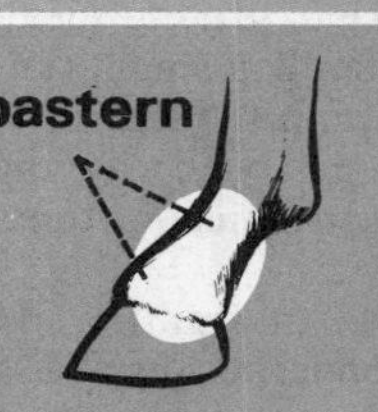
pastern

patio

**pa·tri·ot·ism** (pā′trē ə tiz'm) ***n.*** great love for one's own country and loyalty to it.

**pa·trol** (pə trōl′) ***v.*** to make regular trips around a place in order to guard it. —**pa·trolled′, pa·trol′ling** ◆***n.*** **1** a patrolling. **2** a person or group that patrols. **3** a group of soldiers, ships, or airplanes used to guard an area or to get information about the enemy. **4** a small group of boy scouts or girl scouts, forming part of a troop.



☆**pa·trol·man** (pə trōl′mən) ***n.*** a police officer who patrols a certain area. —*pl.* **pa·trol′men**

☆**patrol wagon** a small, enclosed truck used by the police for carrying prisoners.

**pa·tron** (pā′trən) ***n.*** **1** a rich or important person who helps or supports another person, a group, an institution, etc. [the *patrons* of an orchestra]. **2** a regular customer.

**pa·tron·age** (pā′trən ij *or* pat′rən ij) ***n.*** **1** the help or support given by a patron. **2** customers; also, the regular business or trade of customers. **3** the power to appoint persons to political office or give other political favors.

**pa·tron·ize** (pā′trə nīz *or* pat′rə nīz) ***v.*** **1** to be a patron to; support or sponsor. **2** to be kind to, but in a haughty or snobbish way. **3** to be a regular customer of. —**pa′tron·ized, pa′tron·iz·ing**

**patron saint** a saint looked on as the special protector of some person, group, or place.

**pa·troon** (pə tro͞on′) ***n.*** ☆a man who was given an estate that he could rent to others, in the old Dutch colonies of New York and New Jersey.

**pat·ter**[1] (pat′ər) ***n.*** a series of light, quick taps [the *patter* of rain on the window]. ◆***v.*** to make a patter.

| | | | | | | | |
|---|---|---|---|---|---|---|---|
| **a** | fat | **ir** | here | **ou** | out | **zh** | leisure |
| **ā** | ape | **ī** | bite, fire | **u** | up | **ng** | ring |
| **ä** | car, lot | **ō** | go | **ur** | fur | | a *in* ago |
| **e** | ten | **ô** | law, horn | **ch** | chin | | e *in* agent |
| **er** | care | **oi** | oil | **sh** | she | **ə** = | i *in* unity |
| **ē** | even | **oo** | look | **th** | thin | | o *in* collect |
| **i** | hit | **o͞o** | tool | ***th*** | then | | u *in* focus |

**pat·ter²** (pat′ər) ***v.*** to speak in a fast, easy way. ◆***n.*** fast, easy talk, as that used by comedians.

**pat·tern** (pat′ərn) ***n.*** **1** a plan or model used as a guide for making things [a dress *pattern*]. *See the picture.* **2** a person or thing taken as a model or example [Sir Galahad was the *pattern* of the pure knight.] *See* SYNONYMS *at* **model**. **3** the arrangement of parts; design [wallpaper *patterns*]. **4** a habit or way of acting that does not change [the migration *pattern* of the swallow]. **5** a route or movement that is planned or expected [a landing *pattern* for aircraft]. ◆***v.*** to copy or model as from a pattern [She *patterned* her life on that of her aunt, who was a doctor.]

**pat·ty** (pat′ē) ***n.*** **1** a small, flat cake of ground meat, fish, etc., usually fried. **2** a small pie. **3** a small, flat, round candy [a peppermint *patty*]. *—pl.* **pat′ties**

**patty shell** a shell or cup made of pastry for serving small, individual portions of creamed chicken, tuna, etc.

**pau·ci·ty** (pô′sə tē) ***n.*** smallness in number or amount; scarcity [The team was poor because of a *paucity* of good players.]

**Paul VI** (pôl) 1897–1978; the Pope from 1963 to 1978. His Italian name was Giovanni Montini.

**Paul,** Saint, a Christian Apostle who wrote many of the Epistles of the New Testament.

☆**Paul Bun·yan** (bun′yən) a giant lumberjack in American folk tales, who did amazing things.

538 **paunch** (pônch) ***n.*** the abdomen, or belly; also, a large, fat belly. *See the picture.* —**paunch′y** ***adj.***

**pau·per** (pô′pər) ***n.*** a very poor person, especially one living on charity or welfare. —**pau′per·ism** ***n.***

**pau·per·ize** (pô′pə rīz) ***v.*** to make a pauper of. —**pau′per·ized, pau′per·iz·ing**

**pause** (pôz) ***n.*** **1** a short stop, as in speaking or working. **2** a musical sign (𝄑 or 𝄐) placed below or above a note or rest that is to be held longer. ◆***v.*** to make a pause; stop for a short time [He *paused* to catch his breath.] —**paused, paus′ing**

2.1 m (7 ft.) long, including tail

**pave** (pāv) ***v.*** to cover the surface of a road, walk, etc., as with concrete or asphalt. —**paved, pav′ing** —**pave the way,** to make the way ready for something; prepare.

**pave·ment** (pāv′mənt) ***n.*** a paved road, sidewalk, etc., or the material used in paving.

**pa·vil·ion** (pə vil′yən) ***n.*** **1** a building or part of a building, often with open sides, used for exhibits, dancing, etc., as at a fair or park. **2** a separate part of a group of buildings, as of a large hospital. **3** a large tent, often with a pointed top.

**pav·ing** (pāv′iŋ) ***n.*** *another name for* **pavement.**

**paw** (pô) ***n.*** the foot of a four-footed animal that has claws [Dogs and cats have *paws.*] ◆***v.*** **1** to touch, dig, or hit with the paws or feet [The horse *pawed* the earth.] **2** to handle in a rough and clumsy way [He *pawed* through the drawer looking for a shirt.]

**pawl** (pôl) ***n.*** a device that lets a wheel turn only one way, as a hinged bar that catches in a notch of a ratchet wheel if the wheel starts to turn the other way. *See the picture.*

**pawn¹** (pôn) ***v.*** **1** to leave an article with someone in exchange for a loan. When the loan is paid back, the article is returned [to *pawn* a watch for $20.00]. **2** to wager or risk [to *pawn* one's honor]. ◆***n.*** anything pawned in exchange for a loan. —**in pawn,** being held as pledge that a loan will be repaid.

**pawn²** (pôn) ***n.*** **1** a chess piece of the lowest value. **2** a person used by another as a tool.

> **Pawn²** comes from a Latin word used in the Middle Ages for "foot soldier." A foot soldier has the lowest rank in any army, and a pawn has the lowest value of all the pieces used in playing chess. Soldiers have at times been called pawns in the game of war.

**pawn·bro·ker** (pôn′brō′kər) ***n.*** a person whose business is lending money at interest to people who pawn articles with him or her.

**pawn·shop** (pôn′shäp) ***n.*** a pawnbroker's shop.

**paw·paw** (pô′pô) ***n.*** *another spelling of* **papaw.**

**pay** (pā) ***v.*** **1** to give money to for goods or services [Did you *pay* the cab driver?] **2** to give in exchange [We *paid* ten dollars for our tickets.] **3** to settle or get rid of by giving money [to *pay* a debt]. **4** to give or offer [to *pay* a compliment]. **5** to make [to *pay* a visit]. **6** to bring as wages or salary [The job *pays* $150 a week.] **7** to be worthwhile to [It will *pay* you to listen.] —**paid, pay′ing** ◆***n.*** **1** money paid for work or services [We get our *pay* on Friday.] *See* SYNONYMS *at* **wage.** **2** anything given or done in return [My *pay* was his thanks for my help.] ◆***adj.*** **1** worked by putting in coins [a *pay* telephone]. **2** paid for by special arrangement [*pay* TV]. —**in the pay of,** working for and paid by. —☆**pay as you go,** to pay expenses as they come up. —**pay back,** to repay. —**pay for, 1** to be punished because of. **2** to make up for. —**pay off, 1** to pay all that is owed. **2** to bring about the desired result: *used only in everyday talk.* —**pay one's way,** to pay one's share of the expenses. —**pay out, 1** to give out, as money. **2** to let out, as a rope or cable: *the past tense and past participle for meaning 2 is* **payed out.** —**pay up,** to pay in full or on time. —**pay′er** ***n.***

**pay·a·ble** (pā′ə b'l) ***adj.*** **1** due to be paid [This bill is *payable* on the first of the month.] **2** that can be paid.

☆**pay·check** (pā′chek) ***n.*** a check made out to an employee for wages or salary.

☆**pay·day** (pā′dā) ***n.*** the day on which wages are paid.

**pay·ee** (pā ē′) ***n.*** the person to whom a check, money, etc. is to be paid.

**pay·mas·ter** (pā′mas′tər) ***n.*** the person in charge of paying wages to employees.

**pay·ment** (pā′mənt) ***n.*** **1** a paying or being paid [the *payment* of taxes]. **2** something paid [a monthly rent *payment* of $168].

☆**pay·off** (pā′ôf) ***n.*** **1** the act of paying off, as in making a payment or settlement. **2** that which is paid off; return. **3** a bribe: *used only in everyday talk.* **4** something unexpected or unlikely that comes as the climax to a series of events: *used only in everyday talk* [The *payoff* was that in spite of all his injuries he managed to win.]

☆**pay·roll** (pā′rōl) ***n.*** **1** a list of employees to be paid, with the amount due to each. **2** the total amount needed for this for a certain period.

**Pb** *the symbol for the chemical element* lead.

**PBS** Public Broadcasting Service.

**pct.** *abbreviation for* **percent.**

**pd.** *abbreviation for* **paid.**

**P.D.** Police Department.

**pea** (pē) ***n.*** **1** a climbing plant having green pods with seeds in them. **2** the small, round seed, eaten as a vegetable. *See the picture.*

**peace** (pēs) ***n.*** **1** freedom from war or fighting [a nation that lives in *peace* with all other nations]. **2** an agreement or treaty to end war. **3** law and order [The rioters were disturbing the *peace.*] **4** calm or quiet [to find *peace* of mind]. —**at peace,** free from war, fighting, etc. —**hold one's peace** or **keep one's peace,** to be silent. —**keep the peace,** to make sure that the law is not broken. —**make peace,** to end war, fighting, etc.

**peace·a·ble** (pēs′ə b'l) ***adj.*** fond of peace; not fighting; peaceful. —**peace′a·bly** ***adv.***

**peace·ful** (pēs′fəl) ***adj.*** **1** free from noise or disorder; quiet; calm [the *peaceful* countryside]. **2** fond of peace; not fighting [a *peaceful* people]. **3** of or fit for a time of peace [*peaceful* trade between nations]. —**peace′ful·ly** ***adv.*** —**peace′ful·ness** ***n.***

**peace·mak·er** (pēs′mā′kər) ***n.*** a person who makes peace, as by stopping a fight or quarrel.

☆**peace pipe** *another name for* **calumet.**

**peach** (pēch) ***n.*** **1** a round, juicy, pinkish-yellow fruit, with a fuzzy skin and a rough pit. **2** the tree that it grows on. **3** pinkish yellow.

**pea·cock** (pē′käk) ***n.*** the male of a large bird, having long tail feathers of rich blue, green, bronze, etc. which it can spread out like a fan. *See the picture.* The female is usually called a **pea·hen** (pē′hen).

**pea green** light yellowish green.

☆**pea jacket** a short, heavy coat worn by sailors.

> **Pea jacket** comes from two Dutch words. In Dutch *pij* is the name of a kind of coarse, thick cloth, and *jekker* means "jacket." *Jacket* is a close translation, but *pea* is the result of trying to find a word in English that looks and sounds like the Dutch word *pij.*

**peak** (pēk) ***n.*** **1** the pointed top of a hill or mountain. **2** a hill or mountain with such a top. **3** any pointed top or end, as of a roof or cap. **4** the highest point or degree [The steel mills reached their *peak* of production in May.] *See* SYNONYMS *at* **climax.**

**peaked**[1] (pēkt) ***adj.*** with a peak; pointed [a *peaked* roof].

**peak·ed**[2] (pē′kid) ***adj.*** looking thin and tired, as from being ill [a *peaked* face]. *See the picture.*

**peal** (pēl) ***n.*** **1** the loud ringing of a bell or bells. **2** any loud sound that echoes, as of thunder or laughter. **3** a set of bells, or chimes. ✦***v.*** to ring out loud and long.

☆**pea·nut** (pē′nut) ***n.*** **1** a vine like the pea plant, with yellow flowers and dry pods that ripen underground and contain seeds like nuts that can be eaten. *See the picture on page 540.* **2** the pod or one of its seeds. **3 peanuts,** *pl.* a very small sum of money: *slang in this meaning.*

☆**peanut butter** a food paste or spread made by grinding peanuts that have been roasted.

**pear** (per) ***n.*** **1** a soft, juicy fruit, often yellow or green, that is round at one end and narrows toward the stem. **2** the tree it grows on.

**pearl** (purl) ***n.*** **1** a smooth, hard, roundish stone formed inside oysters and some other shellfish. It is usually white or bluish-gray and is used as a gem. **2** *a shorter form of* **mother-of-pearl.** **3** the color of pearl; bluish gray. **4** anything like a pearl, as in shape, color, or value. ✦***adj.*** **1** of or made with pearls [a *pearl* necklace]. **2** made of mother-of-pearl [*pearl* buttons]. —**pearl′y** ***adj.***

> **Pearl** comes from a Latin word which means "a ham." The sea mussels from which some pearls come are often shaped somewhat like a ham.

**pearl gray** pale bluish gray.

**Pearl Harbor** a harbor in Hawaii, near Honolulu. The U.S. naval base there was bombed by Japan on December 7, 1941.

**Pear·y** (pir′ē), **Robert Edwin** 1856–1920; U.S. explorer of the Arctic. He was the first to reach the North Pole.

**peas·ant** (pez′'nt) ***n.*** any person of the class of farm workers and farmers with small farms, as in Europe and Asia.

**peas·ant·ry** (pez′'n trē) ***n.*** peasants as a group.

**pease** (pēz) ***n.*** *an older plural of* **pea.**

**peat** (pēt) ***n.*** a mass of partly rotted plants and grass, formed in marshes. It is dried for fuel.

**peat moss** *another name for* **sphagnum.**

☆**pea·vey** (pē′vē) ***n.*** a heavy wooden lever with a pointed metal tip and a hinged hook near the end. It is used by lumbermen in handling logs. —*pl.* **pea′veys**

**peb·ble** (peb′'l) ***n.*** a small stone worn smooth and round, as by water running over it.

| | | | |
|---|---|---|---|
| **a** fat | **ir** here | **ou** out | **zh** leisure |
| **ā** ape | **ī** bite, fire | **u** up | **ng** ring |
| **ä** car, lot | **ō** go | **ur** fur | a *in* ago |
| **e** ten | **ô** law, horn | **ch** chin | e *in* agent |
| **er** care | **oi** oil | **sh** she | **ə** = i *in* unity |
| **ē** even | **oo** look | **th** thin | o *in* collect |
| **i** hit | **ōō** tool | ***th*** then | u *in* focus |

pediment

peccary
up to 60 cm (2 ft.) high at shoulder

18 cm (7 in.) high at shoulder
Pekingese

violin pegs

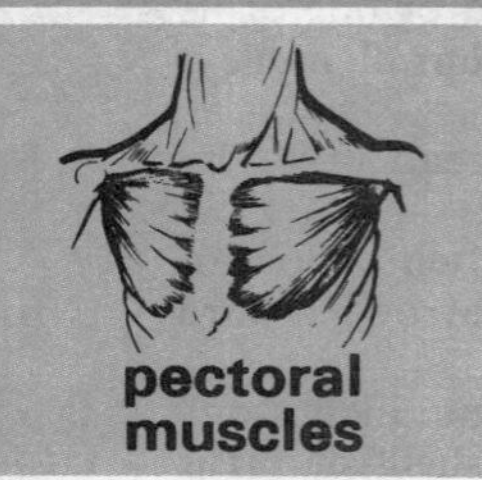
pectoral muscles

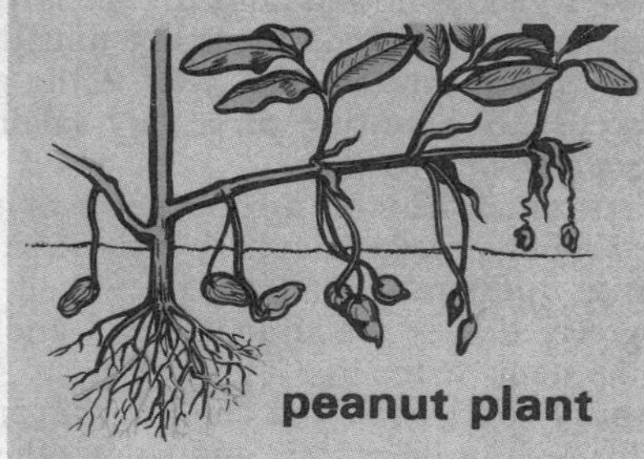
peanut plant

**peb·bly** (peb′lē) ***adj.*** **1** having many pebbles [a *pebbly* stream]. **2** covered with little bumps; uneven [*pebbly* leather].



☆**pe·can** (pi kan′ *or* pi kän′ *or* pē′kän) ***n.*** **1** an oval nut with a thin, smooth shell. **2** the tree it grows on, mainly in the southern U.S.

**pec·ca·dil·lo** (pek′ə dil′ō) ***n.*** a slight fault or mistake that is not important. *—pl.* **pec′ca·dil′loes** or **pec′ca·dil′los**

**pec·ca·ry** (pek′ər ē) ***n.*** a wild animal like a pig with sharp tusks, found in South America and as far north as Arkansas. *See the picture.* *—pl.* **pec′ca·ries**

**peck**[1] (pek) ***v.*** **1** to strike or strike at, as a bird does with its beak. **2** to make by doing this [to *peck* a hole]. **3** to pick up by pecking [Chickens *peck* corn.] ◆***n.*** **1** a stroke or mark made by pecking. **2** a quick, light kiss: *used only in everyday talk.* —**peck at, 1** to eat very little of. **2** to find fault with constantly. *This phrase is used only in everyday talk.*

**peck**[2] (pek) ***n.*** **1** a measure of volume for grain, fruit, vegetables, etc. It is equal to 1/4 bushel or eight quarts. **2** a basket, etc. that holds a peck. **3** a large amount, as of trouble: *used only in everyday talk.*

**Pe·cos** (pā′kōs *or* pā′kəs) a river in the southwestern U.S., flowing into the Rio Grande.

**pec·to·ral** (pek′tər əl) ***adj.*** of, in, or on the breast or chest [a *pectoral* muscle]. *See the picture.*

**pe·cul·iar** (pi kyōōl′yər) ***adj.*** **1** odd; strange; queer [Things look *peculiar* through these dark glasses.] *See* SYNONYMS *at* **strange. 2** of a particular person, thing, or group; special; distinctive [These markings are *peculiar* to this bird.] —**pe·cul′iar·ly** ***adv.***

**pe·cu·li·ar·i·ty** (pi kyōō′lē ar′ə tē) ***n.*** **1** the condition of being peculiar. **2** something peculiar, unusual, or special [a *peculiarity* of speech]. *—pl.* **pe·cu′li·ar′i·ties**

**pe·cu·ni·ar·y** (pi kyōō′nē er′ē) ***adj.*** of or having to do with money [*pecuniary* aid].

**ped·a·gogue** or **ped·a·gog** (ped′ə gäg) ***n.*** a teacher, especially one who is boring and who pays more attention to details than to understanding.

> **Pedagogue** comes from Latin words that mean "to lead a child." Teaching can be thought of as leading a person to knowledge.

**ped·a·go·gy** (ped′ə gō′jē) ***n.*** teaching, or the science of teaching. —**ped·a·gog·ic** (ped′ə gäj′ik) or **ped′a·gog′i·cal** ***adj.***

**ped·al** (ped′'l) ***n.*** a lever worked by the foot, as to turn the wheels of a bicycle, or to control the sound of a piano, organ, etc. ◆***v.*** to move or work by pushing on a pedal or pedals [to *pedal* a bicycle]. —**ped′aled** or **ped′alled, ped′al·ing** or **ped′al·ling** ◆***adj.*** **1** of the foot or feet. **2** of or worked by a pedal.

**ped·ant** (ped′'nt) ***n.*** a person who shows off his or her learning in a boring way, or one who pays too much attention to the unimportant details of a subject. —**pe·dan·tic** (pi dan′tik) ***adj.***

**ped·dle** (ped′'l) ***v.*** **1** to go about from place to place selling small things [to *peddle* magazines]. **2** to give out or hand out [to *peddle* gossip]. —**ped′dled, ped′dling** —**ped′dler** ***n.***

> **Peddle** comes from an old word for "basket." In the old days, a peddler carried in a basket small articles for sale.

**ped·es·tal** (ped′is t'l) ***n.*** **1** the piece at the bottom that holds up a statue, column, lamp, etc. **2** any base, especially a high one.

**pe·des·tri·an** (pə des′trē ən) ***n.*** a person who is walking [a crosswalk for *pedestrians*]. ◆***adj.*** **1** going on foot; walking. **2** without interest or imagination; dull and common [a *pedestrian* lecture].

**pe·di·a·tri·cian** (pē′dē ə trish′ən) ***n.*** a doctor who takes care of babies and children.

**pe·di·at·rics** (pē′dē at′riks) ***n.pl.*** the branch of medicine that has to do with the care and treatment of babies and children: *used with a singular verb.* —**pe′di·at′ric** ***adj.***

☆**ped·i·cure** (ped′i kyoor′) ***n.*** care of the feet, especially a trimming and polishing of the toenails.

**ped·i·gree** (ped′ə grē) ***n.*** **1** a list of one's ancestors. **2** a record of the ancestors of a thoroughbred animal. —**ped′i·greed** ***adj.***

**ped·i·ment** (ped′ə mənt) ***n.*** **1** a part in the shape of a low triangle on the front of an ancient Greek building. *See the picture.* **2** a decoration like this, as over a doorway.

**pe·dom·e·ter** (pi däm′ə tər) ***n.*** an instrument worn by a person who is walking to measure the distance walked.

**peek** (pēk) ***v.*** to take a quick, sly or secret look; peep [to *peek* through a hole in the fence]. ◆***n.*** a quick, sly look.

**peek·a·boo** (pēk′ə bōō) ***n.*** a game to amuse a baby, in which the player's face is hidden behind the hands, then suddenly revealed as the player cries "peekaboo!"

**peel** (pēl) ***v.*** **1** to cut away or pull off the skin or rind of [to *peel* a banana]. **2** to shed skin, bark, etc. [My back is *peeling* from a sunburn.] **3** to come off in flakes [The paint on the house is *peeling.*] ◆***n.*** the rind or skin of fruit.

**peel·ing** (pēl′iŋ) ***n.*** a strip that has been peeled off, as the skin off an apple.

**peep**[1] (pēp) ***n.*** the short, high, thin sound made by a young bird or chicken; chirp. ◆***v.*** to make this sound.

**peep**[2] (pēp) ***v.*** **1** to look through a small opening or from a hiding place; look secretly [to *peep* through a keyhole]. **2** to show partly or briefly [Stars *peeped* through the clouds.] ◆***n.*** **1** a quick or secret look. **2** the first showing [the *peep* of dawn]. —**peep′er** ***n.***

**peep·hole** (pēp′hōl) ***n.*** a hole to peep through.

**peer**[1] (pir) ***n.*** **1** a person or thing of the same value, rank, skill, etc.; an equal [As a poet, she has few *peers.*] **2** a nobleman; especially, a British duke, marquess, earl, viscount, or baron.

**peer**[2] (pir) ***v.*** **1** to look closely or squint in order to see better [to *peer* into a dark room]. **2** to come partly into sight [The moon *peered* over the hill.]

**peer·age** (pir′ij) ***n.*** **1** all the peers, or nobles, of a country. **2** the rank of a peer. **3** a list of peers with their lines of ancestors.

**peer·ess** (pir′is) ***n.*** **1** the wife of a peer. **2** a woman having the rank of peer in her own right.

**peer group** a group of people who are about one's own age and social position and who share more or less the same interests and values.

**peer·less** (pir′lis) ***adj.*** having no equal; better than the rest [her *peerless* beauty].

☆**peeve** (pēv) ***v.*** to make or become cross or annoyed [The teacher will be *peeved* if we are late.] —**peeved, peev′ing** ◆***n.*** a thing that annoys one [a pet *peeve*]. *This word is used only in everyday talk.*

**pee·vish** (pē′vish) ***adj.*** cross or irritable [Illness made the cook *peevish.*] —**pee′vish·ly** ***adv.*** —**pee′vish·ness** ***n.***

☆**pee·wee** (pē′wē) ***n.*** a very small person or thing: *used only in everyday talk.*

**peg** (peg) ***n.*** **1** a thick pin of wood, metal, etc. used to hold parts together, plug up an opening, hang things on, tighten the strings of a musical instrument, fasten ropes to, mark the score in a game, etc. *See the picture.* **2** a step or degree [The promotion moved me up a few *pegs.*] ◆***v.*** to fasten, fix, mark, etc. with pegs. —**pegged, peg′ging** —**peg away at,** to work hard at. —**take down a peg,** to make less proud or less vain; humble.

**Peg·a·sus** (peg′ə səs) a flying horse with wings in Greek myths. It is a symbol of the poet's inspiration.

**peg·board** (peg′bôrd) ***n.*** ☆a board with holes into which pegs or hooks may be put, for holding tools or various articles for display. There is a trademark for this, written **Peg-Board.**

**P.E.I.** *abbreviation for* **Prince Edward Island.**

**Pe·king** (pē′king′ *or* bā′jing′) the capital of China, in the northeastern part.

**Pe·king·ese** or **Pe·kin·ese** (pē kə nēz′) ***n.*** a small dog, with long hair, short legs, and a flat nose. *See the picture. —pl.* **Pe′king·ese′** or **Pe′kin·ese′**

**pe·koe** (pē′kō) ***n.*** a black tea grown in Sri Lanka and India.

**pelf** (pelf) ***n.*** money or wealth looked upon with contempt.

**pel·i·can** (pel′i kən) ***n.*** a large water bird with webbed feet and a pouch that hangs from the lower bill and is used for scooping in fish.

**pel·la·gra** (pə lag′rə *or* pə lā′grə) ***n.*** a disease in which there is a skin rash and nervous disorders, caused by a lack of vitamin B in the diet.

**pel·let** (pel′ət) ***n.*** **1** a little ball, as of clay, paper, etc. rolled between the fingers. **2** a bullet or small lead shot.

**pell-mell** or **pell·mell** (pel′mel′) ***adv., adj.*** **1** in a jumbled mass; in a confused way [She tossed her clothes *pell-mell* into the suitcase.] **2** with reckless speed [Lou ran *pell-mell* down the hill.]

**Pel·o·pon·ne·sus** (pel′ə pə nē′səs) a peninsula that forms the southern part of the mainland of Greece.

**pelt**[1] (pelt) ***v.*** **1** to hit again and again; keep beating [Rain *pelted* the roof.] **2** to throw things at [We *pelted* each other with snowballs.] **3** to rush or hurry [The runners went *pelting* past us.] —**at full pelt,** at full speed.

**pelt**[2] (pelt) ***n.*** the skin of an animal with fur, especially when ready for tanning.

**pel·vic** (pel′vik) ***adj.*** of or near the pelvis.

**pel·vis** (pel′vis) ***n.*** the part of the skeleton formed by the bones of the hip and part of the backbone. It is shaped like a basin. *See the picture on page 543.*

**pem·mi·can** (pem′i kən) ***n.*** **1** dried meat pounded into a paste with fat and pressed into cakes. It was used by North American Indians. **2** dried beef, suet, and dried fruit made into similar cakes of food for use in emergencies, as by arctic explorers.

**pen**[1] (pen) ***n.*** **1** a small yard with a fence for keeping animals [a pig*pen*]. **2** any small, enclosed place [a play*pen* for a baby]. ◆***v.*** to shut up as in a pen. —**penned** or **pent, pen′ning**



**pen**[2] (pen) ***n.*** **1** a device used for writing or drawing with ink, often having a split metal point: *see also* **ball point pen.** **2** the art, skill, or profession of writing ["The *pen* is mightier than the sword."] ◆***v.*** to write. —**penned, pen′ning**

> **Pen**[2] comes from the Latin word for "feather." The first pens were made from quills, or feathers, trimmed to a split point that would hold ink for writing.

**pe·nal** (pē′n'l) ***adj.*** of, having to do with, or bringing punishment [*penal* laws; a *penal* offense].

**pe·nal·ize** (pē′n'l īz *or* pen′'l īz) ***v.*** **1** to set a punishment or penalty for [How shall we *penalize* cheating?] **2** to put a penalty on; punish [to *penalize* a boxer for a foul blow]. —**pe′nal·ized, pe′nal·iz·ing**

**pen·al·ty** (pen′'l tē) ***n.*** **1** punishment for breaking a law. **2** a disadvantage, fine, etc. given to one side in a contest for breaking a rule. **3** any unfortunate result [Indigestion is often the *penalty* for eating fast.] *—pl.* **pen′al·ties**

**pen·ance** (pen′əns) ***n.*** any suffering that one takes on in order to show sorrow for one's sins, wrongdoing, etc.

**pence** (pens) ***n.*** *an older British plural of* **penny.**

**pen·chant** (pen′chənt) ***n.*** a strong liking or fondness [a *penchant* for baseball].

| | | | |
|---|---|---|---|
| **a** fat | **ir** here | **ou** out | **zh** leisure |
| **ā** ape | **ī** bite, fire | **u** up | **ng** ring |
| **ä** car, lot | **ō** go | **ur** fur | a *in* ago |
| **e** ten | **ô** law, horn | **ch** chin | e *in* agent |
| **er** care | **oi** oil | **sh** she | **ə** = i *in* unity |
| **ē** even | **oo** look | **th** thin | o *in* collect |
| **i** hit | **ōō** tool | ***th*** then | u *in* focus |

**pen·cil** (pen′s'l) ***n.*** a long, thin piece of wood, metal, etc. with a center stick of graphite or crayon that is sharpened to a point for writing or drawing. ◆***v.*** to mark, write, or draw with a pencil. —**pen′ciled** or **pen′cilled, pen′cil·ing** or **pen′cil·ling**

> **Pencil** originally meant a small, fine brush and came from *penicillus,* the Latin word for brush. **Penicillin** came from the same word because of the tiny brushlike branches of the mold from which penicillin is made.

**pend·ant** (pen′dənt) ***n.*** an ornament that hangs down, as a locket or earring.

**pend·ent** (pen′dənt) ***adj.*** **1** hanging down or supported from above [a *pendent* lamp]. **2** overhanging [a *pendent* cliff]. **3** pending; undecided.

**pend·ing** (pen′diŋ) ***adj.*** **1** not yet decided or settled [a lawsuit that is *pending*]. **2** about to happen; threatening [*pending* dangers]. ◆***prep.*** **1** during [*pending* this discussion]. **2** while awaiting; until [*pending* her arrival].

**pen·du·lous** (pen′jo͞o ləs) ***adj.*** **1** hanging loosely; free to swing [*pendulous* willow branches]. **2** hanging downward; drooping [*pendulous* jowls].

**pen·du·lum** (pen′jo͞o ləm *or* pen′d'l əm) ***n.*** a weight hung so that it swings freely back and forth, often used to control a clock's movement. *See the picture.*

**Pe·nel·o·pe** (pə nel′ə pē) Odysseus' faithful wife, who waited many years for his return.



**pen·e·tra·ble** (pen′i trə b'l) ***adj.*** that can be penetrated [a *penetrable* wall].

**pen·e·trate** (pen′ə trāt) ***v.*** **1** to pass into or through, as by piercing; enter [The needle *penetrated* my arm.] **2** to spread through [Smoke *penetrated* the whole school.] **3** to understand; find out [I finally *penetrated* the meaning of this riddle.] —**pen′e·trat·ed, pen′e·trat·ing**

**pen·e·trat·ing** (pen′ə trāt iŋ) ***adj.*** that can penetrate; keen or sharp [a *penetrating* mind].

**pen·e·tra·tion** (pen′ə trā′shən) ***n.*** **1** the act of penetrating. **2** keenness of mind; insight.

**pen·guin** (peŋ′gwin) ***n.*** a sea bird mainly of the antarctic region, with webbed feet and flippers for swimming and diving. Penguins cannot fly. *See the picture.*

**pen·i·cil·lin** (pen′ə sil′in) ***n.*** a chemical substance got from a fungus growing as green mold. It is used in treating certain diseases because it can kill or weaken the germs that cause them. *See the word history at* **pencil.**

**pen·in·su·la** (pə nin′sə lə *or* pə nin′syo͞o lə) ***n.*** a long piece of land almost completely surrounded by water [Italy is a *peninsula.*] —**pen·in′su·lar *adj.***

> **Peninsula** comes from Latin words that mean "almost an island." A peninsula would be an island if it were completely surrounded by water.

**pe·nis** (pē′nis) ***n.*** the male sex organ. In male mammals, it is also the organ through which urine leaves the bladder.

**pen·i·tence** (pen′ə təns) ***n.*** a feeling of sorrow for having sinned or done wrong.

**pen·i·tent** (pen′ə tənt) ***adj.*** sorry for having sinned or done wrong. ◆***n.*** a penitent person.

**pen·i·ten·tial** (pen′ə ten′shəl) ***adj.*** of or having to do with penitence or penance.

**pen·i·ten·tia·ry** (pen′ə ten′shə rē) ***n.*** a prison; especially, ☆a State or Federal prison. —*pl.* **pen′i·ten′tia·ries** ◆***adj.*** that can be punished by a term in a penitentiary [a *penitentiary* crime].

**pen·knife** (pen′nīf) ***n.*** a small pocketknife. —*pl.* **pen·knives** (pen′nīvz)

**pen·man** (pen′mən) ***n.*** **1** a person whose work is writing or copying; scribe or author. **2** a person whose handwriting is good. —*pl.* **pen′men**

**pen·man·ship** (pen′mən ship) ***n.*** the art or skill of writing by hand; handwriting.

**Penn** (pen), **William** 1644–1718; English Quaker who founded Pennsylvania.

**pen name** a name used by an author in place of his or her real name. *See* SYNONYMS *at* **pseudonym.**

**pen·nant** (pen′ənt) ***n.*** **1** a long, narrow flag or banner, usually in the shape of a triangle. *See the picture.* **2** such a flag that is the symbol for a championship, as in baseball.

**pen·ni·less** (pen′i lis) ***adj.*** without even a penny; very poor.

**pen·non** (pen′ən) ***n.*** **1** a long, narrow flag once carried by a knight. **2** any flag or pennant.

**Penn·syl·va·ni·a** (pen′səl vān′yə *or* pen′səl vā′nē ə) a State in the northeastern part of the U.S.: abbreviated **Penn., Pa., PA**

☆**Pennsylvania Dutch** **1** people descended from Germans who settled in Pennsylvania. **2** their German dialect.

**pen·ny** (pen′ē) ***n.*** ☆**1** a U.S. or Canadian cent. **2** a British coin equal to 1/100 of a pound. —*pl.* **pen′nies** —**a pretty penny,** a large sum of money: *used only in everyday talk.*

> Before the British changed to a decimal system of money, in 1971, the **penny** was equal to one twelfth of a shilling. There were 240 old pennies in the old pound. The plural of the old penny was **pence.** The full name of the British penny today is the **new penny.**

**pen·ny·weight** (pen′ē wāt) ***n.*** a unit of weight equal to 1/20 of an ounce in troy weight.

**pen·ny-wise** (pen′ē wīz′) ***adj.*** thrifty in small matters. —**penny-wise and pound-foolish,** thrifty in small matters but wasteful in greater ones.

**pen·sion** (pen′shən) ***n.*** money paid regularly by a company or the government to a person who has retired from work, as because of old age, injuries, etc. ◆***v.*** to pay a pension to.

**pen·sion·er** (pen′shən ər) ***n.*** a person who is getting a pension.

**pen·sive** (pen′siv) ***adj.*** thinking deeply in a serious or sad way; thoughtful. *See the picture.* —**pen′sive·ly *adv.***

**pent** (pent) *a past tense and past participle of* **pen**[1]. ◆***adj.*** shut in or kept in; penned [Children love the spring after being *pent* up all winter.]

**pent·a·gon** (pen′tə gän) ***n.*** **1** a flat figure having five sides and five angles. ☆**2 Pentagon,** the five-sided office building of the Defense Department, near Washington, D.C. —**pen·tag·o·nal** (pen tag′ə n'l) ***adj.***

**Pen·ta·teuch** (pen′tə to͞ok *or* pen′tə tyo͞ok) ***n.*** the first five books of the Bible.

**Pen·te·cost** (pen′tə kôst) ***n.*** **1** *another name for* **Shavuot. 2** a Christian festival on the seventh Sunday after Easter; Whitsunday. —**Pen′te·cos′tal *adj.***

**pent·house** (pent′hous) ***n.*** a house or apartment built on the roof of a building.

**pent-up** (pent′up′) ***adj.*** kept under control; held in [*pent-up* anger].

**pe·nu·ri·ous** (pə nyoor′ē əs *or* pə noor′ē əs) ***adj.*** very stingy; like a miser.

**pen·u·ry** (pen′yə rē) ***n.*** the condition of being very poor and in great need.

**pe·on** (pē′än *or* pē′ən) ***n.*** in Spanish America, a person who works at hard labor; often, one who is forced to do this for a certain time to work off a debt. **—pe·on·age** (pē′ən ij) ***n.***

**pe·o·ny** (pē′ə nē) ***n.*** **1** a plant with large, showy flowers of pink, white, red, or yellow. **2** the flower. *See the picture.* *—pl.* **pe′o·nies**

The Greek god Apollo was called *Paion* when he acted as doctor to the other gods. The **peony** was named after him because it was used to make a kind of medicine.

**peo·ple** (pē′p′l) ***n.*** **1** human beings; persons. **2** all the persons of a certain race, religion, nation, language, etc. [the French *people*]. **3** the persons of a certain place, group, or class [country *people;* the *people* of Oregon]. **4** one's family; relatives or ancestors [My *people* came to America from Italy.] **5** the public generally; persons without wealth, special position, etc. [Lee is the *people's* choice for mayor.] *—pl.* **peo′ples** *for meaning* 2; **peo′ple** *for other meanings.* ◆***v.*** to fill with people; populate [The pioneers *peopled* the West.] **—peo′pled, peo′pling**

**Pe·or·i·a** (pē ôr′ē ə) a city in central Illinois.

☆**pep** (pep) ***n.*** energy or vigor. **—pep up,** to make or become livelier; fill with energy. **—pepped, pep′ping** *This word is used only in everyday talk.*

**pep·per** (pep′ər) ***n.*** **1** a plant having green or red pods with many seeds. *See the picture on page 545.* **2** the sweet or hot pod, eaten as a vegetable or relish. **3** a hot-tasting seasoning made from the berries of a tropical plant. *See the picture on page 545. Black pepper* is ground from the dried berries, and *white pepper* is ground from the dried seeds with the coatings removed. **4** *another name for* **cayenne.** ◆***v.*** **1** to sprinkle with ground pepper. **2** to pelt or cover with many small bits [Hailstones *peppered* the lawn.]

**pep·per·corn** (pep′ər kôrn) ***n.*** the dried berry from which black pepper is ground.

**pepper mill** a hand mill used to grind peppercorns.

**pep·per·mint** (pep′ər mint) ***n.*** **1** a plant of the mint family from which an oil with a sharp, cool taste is pressed. **2** this oil, used for flavoring. **3** a candy flavored with this oil.

☆**pep·per·o·ni** (pep′ə rō′nē) ***n.*** a hard, highly spiced Italian sausage. *—pl.* **pep′per·o′nis** or **pep′per·o′ni**

**pep·per·y** (pep′ər ē) ***adj.*** **1** like or full of pepper; hot [*peppery* soup]. **2** showing excitement or anger; fiery [a *peppery* speech].

☆**pep·py** (pep′ē) ***adj.*** full of pep, or energy; vigorous: *used only in everyday talk.* **—pep′pi·er, pep′pi·est**

**pep·sin** (pep′s′n) ***n.*** a substance produced in the stomach, that helps to digest food.

☆**pep talk** a talk, as to an athletic team by its coach, to persuade team members to play their very best.

**pep·tic** (pep′tik) ***adj.*** **1** of or having to do with pepsin. **2** caused to some extent by juices in the stomach for digesting food [a *peptic* ulcer].

**penguins**
90 cm (3 ft.) high

**pennant**

**peony**

**pendulum**

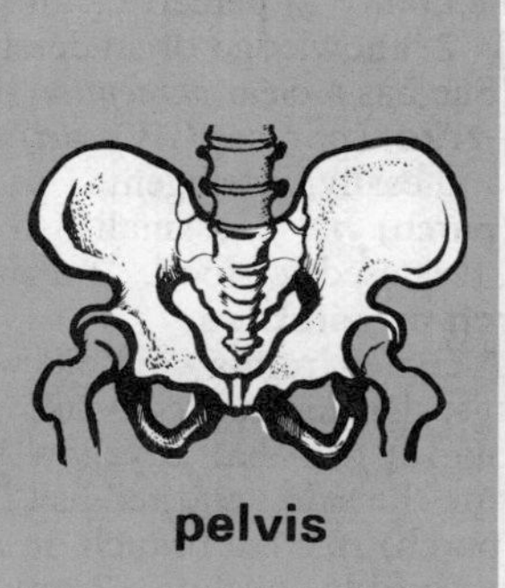

**pelvis**

**pensive man**

**per** (pər) ***prep.*** **1** for each; for every [$2 *per* yard]. **2** during each [50 miles *per* hour]. **3** by means of [delivery *per* messenger]. **4** according to: *used only in everyday talk* [*per* your instructions]. 543

**per·am·bu·late** (pər am′byoo lāt) ***v.*** to walk around, through, or over. **—per·am′bu·lat·ed, per·am′bu·lat·ing —per·am′bu·la′tion *n.***

**per·am·bu·la·tor** (pər am′byoo lāt′ər) ***n.*** a baby carriage: *mainly a British word.*

**per an·num** (pər an′əm) for each year; yearly [Tuition *per annum* is over $3,000.]

**per·cale** (pər kāl′ *or* pər kal′) ***n.*** a fine, closely woven cotton cloth, used for sheets, etc.

**per cap·i·ta** (pər kap′ə tə) for each person [the *per capita* cost of education].

**Per capita** comes directly from Latin, where it means "by heads." *Head* is used to mean a single person in a group. If one counts "heads" in a gathering, one counts the number of persons present.

**per·ceive** (pər sēv′) ***v.*** **1** to become aware of through one of the senses, especially through seeing [to *perceive* the difference between two shades of red]. **2** to take in through the mind [I quickly *perceived* the joke.] **—per·ceived′, per·ceiv′ing**

**per·cent** (pər sent′) ***adv., adj.*** in, to, or for every hundred [A 20 *percent* rate means 20 in every hundred.] *Also written* **per cent.** The symbol for percent is %. ◆***n.*** **1** a hundredth part [Only 10 *percent* of the

| | | | | | | | |
|---|---|---|---|---|---|---|---|
| **a** | fat | **ir** | here | **ou** | out | **zh** | leisure |
| **ā** | ape | **ī** | bite, fire | **u** | up | **ng** | ring |
| **ä** | car, lot | **ō** | go | **ur** | fur | | a *in* ago |
| **e** | ten | **ô** | law, horn | **ch** | chin | | e *in* agent |
| **er** | care | **oi** | oil | **sh** | she | **ə =** | i *in* unity |
| **ē** | even | **oo** | look | **th** | thin | | o *in* collect |
| **i** | hit | **ōō** | tool | ***th*** | then | | u *in* focus |

apples were rotten.] **2** percentage: *used only in everyday talk.*

**per·cent·age** (pər sent′ij) ***n.*** a certain part or amount in every hundred [A large *percentage* of the students won scholarships.]

**per·cen·tile** (pər sen′tīl *or* pər sent′'l) ***n.*** any of the 100 groups into which a series of individuals has been divided according to equal frequency.

**per·cep·ti·ble** (pər sep′tə b'l) ***adj.*** that can be perceived, or noticed [The sound was barely *perceptible.*] —**per·cep′ti·bly *adv.***

**per·cep·tion** (pər sep′shən) ***n.*** **1** the act of perceiving or the ability to perceive [Jan's *perception* of color is poor.] **2** knowledge or understanding got by perceiving [She has a clear *perception* of her duty.]

**per·cep·tive** (pər sep′tiv) ***adj.*** able to perceive quickly and easily; intelligent.

**perch**[1] (pʉrch) ***n.*** **1** a small fish living in lakes and streams. It is used for food. **2** a similar saltwater fish. —*pl.* **perch** or **perch′es**

> **Perch**[1] comes from a very old word in an ancient language, that means "colorful." The *yellow perch* is a colorful fish that is yellow with dark vertical stripes on the sides, and reddish fins.

**perch**[2] (pʉrch) ***n.*** **1** a branch on a tree, or a bar in a cage, for a bird to roost on. **2** any resting place, especially a high one or one that does not look safe. **3** a measure of length, equal to 5 1/2 yards. ◆***v.*** to rest or place as on a perch [Sparrows *perched* on the wires. She *perched* herself on the railing.]

**per·chance** (pər chans′) ***adv.*** possibly; maybe; perhaps: *now seldom used except in poetry.*

**per·co·late** (pʉr′kə lāt) ***v.*** **1** to prepare or be prepared in a percolator, as coffee. **2** to pass slowly through something that has many tiny holes; filter. —**per′co·lat·ed, per′co·lat·ing**

**per·co·la·tor** (pʉr′kə lāt′ər) ***n.*** a coffeepot in which the water boils up through a tube and filters back down through the ground coffee. *See the picture.*

**per·cus·sion** (pər kush′ən) ***n.*** the hitting of one thing against another; blow [A shot from a gun is fired by the *percussion* of the hammer against a cap filled with gunpowder.]

**percussion instrument** a musical instrument in which the tone is made by striking some part of it, as the drums, cymbals, tambourine, bells, xylophone, etc.

**per·di·tion** (pər dish′ən) ***n.*** **1** hell. **2** the loss of one's soul, or of the chance of going to heaven.

**per·e·gri·na·tion** (per′ə gri nā′shən) ***n.*** a traveling about; journey.

**per·e·grine falcon** (per′ə grin) a swift falcon that has been much used in falconry.

**per·emp·to·ry** (pə remp′tər ē) ***adj.*** **1** that may not be refused or questioned [a *peremptory* command]. **2** forcing one's wishes or opinions on another in a bullying way [a *peremptory* tone]. **3** not allowing delay; final [a *peremptory* order by a law court]. —**per·emp′to·ri·ly *adv.***

**per·en·ni·al** (pə ren′ē əl) ***adj.*** **1** that lives for more than two years: said of certain plants. **2** returning or becoming active again and again [Raising money for new sports equipment is a *perennial* problem.] **3** lasting or going on for a long time [to seek *perennial* youth]. ◆***n.*** a plant that lives for more than two years. —**per·en′ni·al·ly *adv.***

**per·fect** (pʉr′fikt) ***adj.*** **1** complete in every way and having no faults or errors [a *perfect* test paper]. **2** being as good as is possible; most excellent [in *perfect* health]. **3** correct or accurate; exact [a *perfect* copy of a drawing]. **4** absolute or complete [*perfect* strangers]. **5** showing that something is completed at the time of speaking or at the time spoken of ["They have eaten" is in the present *perfect* tense; "they had eaten" is in the past *perfect* tense.] ◆***v.*** (pər fekt′) to make perfect or almost perfect [Practice to *perfect* your work.] —**per′fect·ly *adv.***

**per·fect·i·ble** (pər fek′tə b'l) ***adj.*** that can become perfect or be made perfect [Do you believe that human beings are *perfectible?*] —**per·fect′i·bil′i·ty *n.***

**per·fec·tion** (pər fek′shən) ***n.*** **1** the act of making perfect [to work at the *perfection* of a skill]. **2** the condition of being perfect [*Perfection* in spelling is our goal.] **3** a person or thing that is perfect or excellent. —**to perfection,** completely; perfectly.

☆**per·fec·tion·ist** (pər fek′shən ist) ***n.*** a person who is always looking for perfection.

**per·fid·i·ous** (pər fid′ē əs) ***adj.*** showing treachery; betraying trust; faithless; treacherous.

**per·fi·dy** (pʉr′fə dē) ***n.*** the act of betraying others or being false to one's promises; treachery. —*pl.* **per′fi·dies**

**per·fo·rate** (pʉr′fə rāt) ***v.*** **1** to make a hole or holes through [to *perforate* the top of a can of cleaning powder]. **2** to make a row of small holes in for easy tearing [Sheets of stamps are usually *perforated.*] *See the picture.* —**per′fo·ra·ted, per′fo·rat·ing** —**per′fo·ra′tion *n.***

**per·force** (pər fôrs′) ***adv.*** because it must be; through necessity; necessarily.

**per·form** (pər fôrm′) ***v.*** **1** to do or carry out [to *perform* a task; to *perform* a promise]. **2** to do something to entertain an audience; act, play music, sing, etc. —**per·form′er *n.***

**per·form·ance** (pər fôr′məns) ***n.*** **1** the act of performing; a doing [the *performance* of one's duty]. **2** something done; deed. **3** a showing of skill or talent before an audience, as in a play, on a musical instrument, etc.

**per·fume** (pʉr′fyo͞om) ***n.*** **1** a sweet smell; pleasing odor; fragrance [the *perfume* of roses]. *See* SYNONYMS *at* **scent.** **2** a liquid with a pleasing smell, for use on the body, clothing, etc. ◆***v.*** (pər fyo͞om′) to give a pleasing smell to, as with perfume. —**per·fumed′, per·fum′ing**

**per·fum·er·y** (pər fyo͞o′mər ē) ***n.*** **1** a place where perfumes are made or sold. **2** perfume or perfumes. —*pl.* **per·fum′er·ies**

**per·func·to·ry** (pər fuŋk′tər ē) ***adj.*** done or acting without real care or interest; mechanical or careless [a *perfunctory* greeting; a *perfunctory* worker]. —**per·func′to·ri·ly *adv.***

**per·haps** (pər haps′) ***adv.*** possibly; maybe [*Perhaps* it will rain. Did you, *perhaps,* lose it?]

**Per·i·cles** (per′ə klēz) 495?–429 B.C.; Greek statesman and general.

**per·il** (per′əl) ***n.*** **1** a condition in which there could be harm, death, destruction, etc.; danger [The flood put many lives in *peril.*] **2** something that may cause harm [Speeders are a *peril* on the highway.] *See* SYNONYMS *at* **hazard.** ◆*v.* to put in danger; risk; imperil. —**per′iled** or **per′illed, per′il·ing** or **per′il·ling**

**per·il·ous** (per′əl əs) *adj.* dangerous; risky. —**per′il·ous·ly** *adv.*

**pe·rim·e·ter** (pə rim′ə tər) *n.* **1** the boundary or line around a figure or area. **2** the total length of this; distance around an area.

**pe·ri·od** (pir′ē əd) *n.* **1** the time that goes by during which something goes on, a cycle is repeated, etc. [the medieval *period;* a *period* of hot weather]. **2** any of the portions of time into which a game, a school day, etc. is divided. **3** the mark of punctuation (.) used at the end of most sentences or often after abbreviations. **4** an end; finish [Death put a *period* to their plans.]

SYNONYMS: **Period** is the general word for any amount of time. **Era** is used for a period during which something new begins or a basic change takes place [an *era* of revolution]. **Age** is used for a period known for an important person or special quality [the Stone *Age*].

**pe·ri·od·ic** (pir′ē äd′ik) *adj.* happening or done from time to time, in a regular way [*periodic* tests to measure the students' progress].

**pe·ri·od·i·cal** (pir′ē äd′i k′l) *n.* a magazine published every week, month, etc. ◆*adj.* **1** *same as* **periodic. 2** published every week, month, etc. **3** of periodicals [a *periodical* index]. —**pe′ri·od′i·cal·ly** *adv.*

**per·i·pa·tet·ic** (per′i pə tet′ik) *adj.* walking or moving about; not staying in one place.

**pe·riph·er·al** (pə rif′ər əl) *adj.* **1** of or forming a periphery. **2** only connected a little with what is necessary or important [of *peripheral* interest].

**pe·riph·er·y** (pə rif′ər ē) *n.* **1** an outer boundary, especially of something round [The rocket passed the *periphery* of the earth's atmosphere.] **2** the space or area around something; outer parts. —*pl.* **pe·riph′er·ies**

**per·i·scope** (per′ə skōp) *n.* a tube with mirrors or prisms inside it so that a person can look in one end and see the reflection of an object at the other end. Periscopes are used on submarines so that the surface can be seen from under the water. *See the picture.*

**per·ish** (per′ish) *v.* to be destroyed; die [Many animals *perished* in the forest fire.]

**per·ish·a·ble** (per′ish ə b′l) *adj.* that is likely to perish, or spoil, as some foods. ◆*n.* a food, etc. that is likely to spoil.

**per·i·wig** (per′ə wig) *n.* a wig, especially one of the sort worn by men in the 17th and 18th centuries, usually powdered and with the hair tied at the back with a ribbon.

**per·i·win·kle**[1] (per′ə wiŋ′k′l) *n.* a creeping, evergreen plant with blue, white, or pink flowers; myrtle.

**per·i·win·kle**[2] (per′ə wiŋ′k′l) *n.* a small, saltwater snail with a thick shell.

**per·jure** (pʉr′jər) *v.* to make oneself guilty of perjury; lie while under oath to tell the truth, as in a law court. —**per′jured, per′jur·ing** —**per′jur·er** *n.*

**per·ju·ry** (pʉr′jər ē) *n.* the telling of a lie on purpose, after one has taken an oath to tell the truth. —*pl.* **per′ju·ries**

**perk** (pʉrk) *v.* **1** to raise in a quick and lively way [The dog *perked* up its ears at the noise.] **2** to make look fresh or lively [The colorful new drapes *perked* up the living room.] **3** to become lively or get back one's spirits [We *perked* up after hearing the good news.]

perforated stamps

submarine periscope

percolator

pepper pod  pepper berries

**perk·y** (pʉr′kē) *adj.* happy or lively [a *perky* pup]. —**perk′i·er, perk′i·est**

**per·ma·nent** (pʉr′mə nənt) *adj.* lasting or meant to last for a very long time [One's *permanent* teeth should last as long as one lives.] ◆*n.* a hair wave put in by means of chemicals and lasting for months: *the full name is* **permanent wave.** —**per′ma·nence** or **per′ma·nen·cy** *n.* —**per′ma·nent·ly** *adv.*



**per·me·a·ble** (pʉr′mē ə b′l) *adj.* that will let liquids or gases pass through [Blotting paper is a *permeable* material.] —**per′me·a·bil′i·ty** *n.*

**per·me·ate** (pʉr′mē āt′) *v.* to pass through or spread through every part of [The smells of cooking *permeated* the house.] —**per′me·at·ed, per′me·at·ing**

**per·mis·si·ble** (pər mis′ə b′l) *adj.* that can be permitted, or allowed; allowable.

**per·mis·sion** (pər mish′ən) *n.* the act of permitting; consent [You have my *permission* to go.]

**per·mis·sive** (pər mis′iv) *adj.* allowing freedom; not strict; permitting certain things [*permissive* parents]. —**per·mis′sive·ness** *n.*

**per·mit** (pər mit′) *v.* **1** to give consent to; let; allow [Will you *permit* me to help you?] *See* SYNONYMS *at* **let. 2** to give a chance [We'll fly if the weather *permits.*] —**per·mit′ted, per·mit′ting** ◆*n.* (pʉr′mit) a paper, card, etc. showing permission; license [a *permit* to carry a gun].

**per·ni·cious** (pər nish′əs) *adj.* causing great injury, harm, damage, etc. [a *pernicious* disease].

**per·o·ra·tion** (per′ə rā′shən) *n.* the last part of a speech, summing up the main ideas.

| | | | | | | | |
|---|---|---|---|---|---|---|---|
| **a** | fat | **ir** | here | **ou** | out | **zh** | leisure |
| **ā** | ape | **ī** | bite, fire | **u** | up | **ng** | ring |
| **ä** | car, lot | **ō** | go | **ʉr** | fur | | a *in* ago |
| **e** | ten | **ô** | law, horn | **ch** | chin | | e *in* agent |
| **er** | care | **oi** | oil | **sh** | she | **ə** = | i *in* unity |
| **ē** | even | **oo** | look | **th** | thin | | o *in* collect |
| **i** | hit | **ōō** | tool | ***th*** | then | | u *in* focus |

**per·ox·ide** (pə räk′sīd) ***n.*** a chemical compound containing a greater proportion of oxygen than the oxide of the same series [Hydrogen *peroxide* is used as a bleach and disinfectant.]

**per·pen·dic·u·lar** (pʉr′pən dik′yə lər) ***adj.*** **1** at right angles [The wall should be *perpendicular* to the floor.] **2** straight up and down; exactly upright [a *perpendicular* flagpole]. ◆***n.*** a line that is at right angles to the horizon, or to another line or plane [The Leaning Tower of Pisa leans away from the *perpendicular*.] *See the picture.*

**per·pe·trate** (pʉr′pə trāt) ***v.*** to do something bad; be guilty of [to *perpetrate* a crime]. —**per′pe·trat·ed, per′pe·trat·ing** —**per′pe·tra′tion** ***n.*** —**per′pe·tra′tor** ***n.***

**per·pet·u·al** (pər pech′oo wəl) ***adj.*** **1** lasting forever or for a long time. **2** continuing; constant [a *perpetual* bore]. —**per·pet′u·al·ly** ***adv.***

**per·pet·u·ate** (pər pech′oo wāt) ***v.*** to cause to continue or be remembered [The Rhodes scholarships *perpetuate* the memory of Cecil Rhodes.] —**per·pet′u·at·ed, per·pet′u·at·ing** —**per·pet′u·a′tion** ***n.***

**per·pe·tu·i·ty** (pʉr′pə too′ə tē *or* pʉr′pə tyoo′ə tē) ***n.*** the condition of being perpetual; existence forever. —**in perpetuity,** forever.

**per·plex** (pər pleks′) ***v.*** to make unsure of what to do; fill with doubt; confuse or puzzle [Your silence *perplexes* me.]

546 **per·plex·i·ty** (pər plek′sə tē) ***n.*** **1** the condition of being perplexed or in great doubt. *See the picture.* **2** something that confuses or puzzles. —*pl.* **per·plex′i·ties**

**per·qui·site** (pʉr′kwə zit) ***n.*** something in addition to a worker's regular pay, as a tip.

**Per·ry** (per′ē), **Oliver Haz·ard** (haz′ərd) 1785–1819; U.S. naval officer. He commanded the fleet which defeated the British on Lake Erie in 1813.

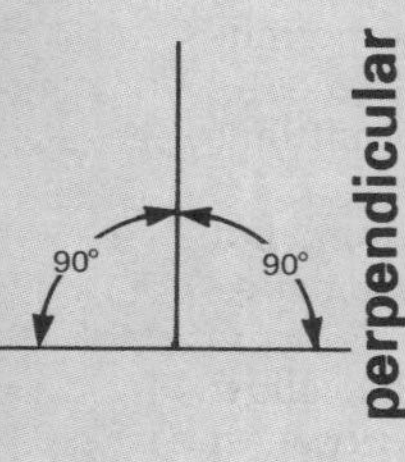

perpendicular

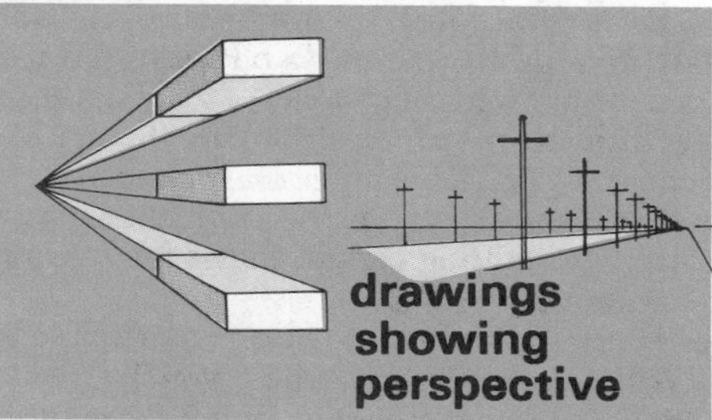
drawings showing perspective

look of perplexity

persimmons

Persian cat

**Pers.** *abbreviation for* **Persia** *or* **Persian.**

**per·se·cute** (pʉr′sə kyoot) ***v.*** to keep on treating in a cruel or harsh way, especially for holding certain beliefs or ideas. —**per′se·cut·ed, per′se·cut·ing** —**per′se·cu′tion** ***n.*** —**per′se·cu′tor** ***n.***

**Per·seph·o·ne** (pər sef′ə nē) *the Greek name for* **Proserpina.**

**per·se·ver·ance** (pʉr′sə vir′əns) ***n.*** **1** the act of persevering; continued, patient effort. **2** persistence; a being steadfast.

**Per·sia** (pʉr′zhə) *the old name for* **Iran.** —**Per′sian** ***adj., n.***

**Persian cat** a kind of cat with long, silky fur. *See the picture.*

**Persian Gulf** the part of the Arabian Sea between Arabia and Iran.

**per·si·flage** (pʉr′sə fläzh) ***n.*** playful or joking talk; banter.

☆**per·sim·mon** (pər sim′ən) ***n.*** **1** an orange-colored fruit that looks like a plum and has several large seeds in it. It is very sour when green, but sweet when ripe. *See the picture.* **2** the tree this fruit grows on. It has white flowers and hard wood.

**per·sist** (pər sist′) ***v.*** **1** to refuse to give up; go on in a stubborn way [The team *persisted* until they won.] **2** to say or do over and over again [Don't *persist* in telling those bad jokes.] **3** to last for some time; continue [The pain *persisted* all day.]

**per·sist·ent** (pər sis′tənt) ***adj.*** **1** refusing to give up; steady and determined [a *persistent* job seeker]. **2** lasting for some time; going on and on [a *persistent* rain]. —**per·sist′ence** or **per·sist′en·cy** ***n.*** —**per·sist′ent·ly** ***adv.***

**per·son** (pʉr′s'n) ***n.*** **1** a human being; man, woman, or child [every *person* in this room]. **2** the body or bodily appearance [He was neat and clean about his *person*.] **3** any of the three sets of pronouns which show who or what the subject is. The **first person** (*I* or *we*) is used for the speaker; the **second person** (*you*) for the one spoken to; the **third person** (*he, she, it,* or *they*) for the one spoken of. Most verbs in English have a special form for the third person singular (he *has,* she *walks,* it *falls*); the verb *to be* has special forms for other persons (I *am,* you *are,* they *were*). —**in person,** actually present, not in a movie, on a record, etc.

> **Person** comes from the Latin word *persona,* which means "an actor's face mask." In the ancient theater, actors wore masks which told the audience what kind of character each was playing. Sometimes we would like to know what a person is really like. Perhaps that person seems to be wearing a mask, like an ancient actor.

**-per·son** (pʉr′s'n) *a suffix meaning* a person (either a man or a woman) who does a certain thing. It is used in place of *-man* where *-man* may suggest only a male person, as chair*person* instead of chair*man.*

**per·son·a·ble** (pʉr′s'n ə b'l) ***adj.*** pleasing in looks and manner; attractive.

**per·son·age** (pʉr′s'n ij) ***n.*** a person; especially, a famous or important person.

**per·son·al** (pʉr′s'n əl) ***adj.*** **1** of one's own; private; individual [a *personal* opinion; a *personal* secretary]. **2** done, made, learned, etc. by oneself, without the help of others [Do you have *personal* knowledge of this matter?] **3** of the body [*personal* fitness]. **4** of or having to do with the way a person looks, acts, etc. [a *personal* remark]. **5** showing person in grammar ["I," "you," and "it" are *personal* pronouns.] **6** describing property that can be moved or is not attached to, or a part of, the land [Furniture is *personal* property.] ◆***n.*** ☆a newspaper advertisement about a personal matter.

**per·son·al·i·ty** (pur′sə nal′ə tē) ***n.*** **1** all the special qualities which make a person different from other people. **2** personal qualities that attract others to one; charm, energy, cleverness, etc. [Your friend is smart, but has no *personality.*] **3** a person; especially, a very unusual or famous person. **4** an impolite remark criticizing the way a certain person looks, acts, etc. [Let's avoid *personalities.*] *—pl.* **per′son·al′i·ties**

**per·son·al·ize** (pur′s'n ə līz′) ***v.*** to make personal; make for one person only [*Personalized* bank checks are printed with one's name.] **—per′son·al·ized′, per′son·al·iz′ing**

**per·son·al·ly** (pur′s'n ə lē) ***adv.*** **1** by oneself, without the help of others [I'll ask them *personally.*] **2** as a person [I dislike the artist *personally,* but I admire her paintings.] **3** speaking for oneself [*Personally,* I think you're right.] **4** as though aimed at oneself [You should not take my remarks *personally.*]

**per·son·i·fy** (pər sän′ə fī) ***v.*** **1** to think of or show some idea or thing as a person [A ship is *personified* when it is referred to as "she."]. **2** to be a good example of some quality, idea, etc. [Tom Sawyer *personifies* the spirit of boyhood.] **—per·son′i·fied, per·son′i·fy·ing —per·son′i·fi·ca′tion *n.***

**per·son·nel** (pur sə nel′) ***n.*** persons employed in any work, service, etc. [office *personnel*].

**per·spec·tive** (pər spek′tiv) ***n.*** **1** the way things look from a given point according to their size, shape, distance, etc. [*Perspective* makes things far away look small.] *See the picture.* **2** the art of picturing things so that they seem close or far away, big or small, etc., just as they look to the eye when viewed from a given point. **3** a certain point of view in understanding or judging things or happenings, especially one that shows them in their true relations to one another [Working in a factory will give you a new *perspective* on labor problems.]

**per·spi·ca·cious** (pur′spə kā′shəs) ***adj.*** able to understand and judge things clearly; wise. **—per·spi·cac·i·ty** (pur′spə kas′ə tē) ***n.***

**per·spic·u·ous** (pər spik′yoo wəs) ***adj.*** easy to understand. **—per·spi·cu·i·ty** (pur′spə kyōō′ə tē) ***n.***

**per·spi·ra·tion** (pur′spə rā′shən) ***n.*** **1** the act of perspiring, or sweating. **2** *another word for* **sweat.**

**per·spire** (pər spīr′) ***v.*** *another word for* **sweat.** **—per·spired′, per·spir′ing**

**per·suade** (pər swād′) ***v.*** to get someone to do or believe something, as by making it seem like a good idea; convince. **—per·suad′ed, per·suad′ing**

**per·sua·sion** (pər swā′zhən) ***n.*** **1** a persuading or being persuaded. **2** the ability to persuade. **3** a belief; often, a particular religious belief [a person of the Muslim *persuasion*].

**per·sua·sive** (pər swā′siv) ***adj.*** able or likely to persuade [a *persuasive* argument]. **—per·sua′sive·ly *adv.* —per·sua′sive·ness *n.***

**pert** (purt) ***adj.*** lively in a way that is too bold; saucy [a *pert* child; a *pert* remark].

**per·tain** (pər tān′) ***v.*** **1** to belong; be connected; be a part [lands *pertaining* to an estate]. **2** to have to do with; be related in some way; have reference [laws that *pertain* to civil rights].

**per·ti·na·cious** (pur′tə nā′shəs) ***adj.*** continuing in a stubborn way to do, believe, or want something; persistent [a *pertinacious* salesperson]. **—per·ti·nac·i·ty** (pur′tə nas′ə tē) ***n.***

**per·ti·nent** (pur′t'n ənt) ***adj.*** having some connection with the subject that is being considered; relevant; to the point [a *pertinent* question]. **—per′ti·nence *n.***

**per·turb** (pər turb′) ***v.*** to make worried or upset; trouble the mind of [I became *perturbed* when they failed to arrive.] **—per·tur·ba·tion** (pur′tər bā′shən) ***n.***

**Pe·ru** (pə rōō′) a country on the western coast of South America. **—Pe·ru·vi·an** (pə rōō′vē ən) ***adj., n.***

**pe·rus·al** (pə rōō′z'l) ***n.*** the act of perusing.

**pe·ruse** (pə rōōz′) ***v.*** to read; especially, to read through carefully. **—pe·rused′, pe·rus′ing**

**per·vade** (pər vād′) ***v.*** to spread through every part of [The smell of cooking *pervaded* the house. Joy *pervades* that poem.] **—per·vad′ed, per·vad′ing**

**per·va·sive** (pər vā′siv) ***adj.*** tending to spread through every part [a *pervasive* odor].

**per·verse** (pər vurs′) ***adj.*** **1** continuing in a stubborn way to do what is wrong or harmful [Only a *perverse* person would continue to smoke against doctor's orders.] **2** turning aside from what is thought to be right or good; wicked [Cruelty to animals is a *perverse* act.] **—per·verse′ly *adv.* —per·verse′ness *n.* —per·ver′si·ty *n.***



**per·ver·sion** (pər vur′zhən) ***n.*** **1** a turning to what is wrong or harmful. **2** a wrong or unhealthy form of something [a *perversion* of the truth].

**per·vert** (pər vurt′) ***v.*** **1** to lead away from what is good or right [Too much candy can *pervert* one's appetite.] **2** to give a wrong meaning to; distort [Our enemies will *pervert* my remarks.] ◆***n.*** (pur′vərt) a perverted person.

**pes·ky** (pes′kē) ***adj.*** annoying or troublesome: *used only in everyday talk.* **—pes′ki·er, pes′ki·est**

**pe·so** (pā′sō) ***n.*** the basic unit of money in Argentina, Colombia, Cuba, Mexico, etc. *—pl.* **pe′sos**

**pes·si·mism** (pes′ə miz'm) ***n.*** **1** a gloomy feeling about life, in which one expects things to turn out badly. **2** the belief that there is more evil than good in life. **—pes·si·mis·tic** (pes′ə mis′tik) ***adj.*** **—pes′si·mis′ti·cal·ly *adv.***

**pes·si·mist** (pes′ə mist) ***n.*** a person who expects things to turn out badly.

**pest** (pest) ***n.*** a person or thing that causes trouble; especially, an insect or small animal that destroys things.

**pes·ter** (pes′tər) ***v.*** to keep on bothering or annoying [to *pester* someone with questions].

| | | | | | | | |
|---|---|---|---|---|---|---|---|
| **a** | fat | **ir** | here | **ou** | out | **zh** | leisure |
| **ā** | ape | **ī** | bite, fire | **u** | up | **ng** | ring |
| **ä** | car, lot | **ō** | go | **ur** | fur | | a *in* ago |
| **e** | ten | **ô** | law, horn | **ch** | chin | | e *in* agent |
| **er** | care | **oi** | oil | **sh** | she | **ə =** | i *in* unity |
| **ē** | even | **oo** | look | **th** | thin | | o *in* collect |
| **i** | hit | **ōō** | tool | ***th*** | then | | u *in* focus |

**pes·ti·cide** (pes′tə sīd) ***n.*** any poison used to kill insects, weeds, etc.

**pes·ti·lence** (pes′t'l əns) ***n.*** a deadly disease that spreads rapidly from person to person; plague.

**pes·ti·lent** (pes′t'l ənt) ***adj.*** likely to cause death; deadly [a *pestilent* disease].

**pes·tle** (pes″l) ***n.*** a tool used to pound or grind something into a powder, as in a mortar. *See the picture for* **mortar.**

**pet**[1] (pet) ***n.*** **1** an animal that is tamed and kept as a companion or treated in a fond way. **2** a person who is liked or treated better than others; favorite [a teacher's *pet*]. ◆***adj.*** **1** kept or treated as a pet [a *pet* turtle]. **2** liked better than others; favorite [a *pet* project of mine]. **3** showing fondness [a *pet* name]. ◆***v.*** to stroke or pat gently [to *pet* a dog]. —**pet′ted, pet′ting**

**pet**[2] (pet) ***n.*** a sulky, cross mood.

**pet·al** (pet″l) ***n.*** any of the brightly colored leaves that make up the flower of a plant. *See the picture.*

**pet·cock** (pet′käk) ***n.*** a small faucet for draining water or air from pipes, etc.

**Pe·ter** (pē′tər) **1** one of the twelve Apostles of Jesus. He is also called **Saint Peter** or **Simon Peter. 2** either of two books of the New Testament believed to have been written by him.

**Peter I** 1672–1725; the czar of Russia from 1682 to 1725. He is also called **Peter the Great.**

548 **pe·ter** (pē′tər) ***v.*** ☆to become smaller or weaker little by little and then disappear: *used only in everyday talk* [The supplies have *petered* out.]

**pet·i·ole** (pet′ē ōl′) ***n.*** the narrow part of a leaf which holds the blade and is attached to the stem. *See the picture.*

**pe·tite** (pə tēt′) ***adj.*** small and dainty: *said of a girl or woman.*

**pe·ti·tion** (pə tish′ən) ***n.*** **1** a strong, serious request, as a prayer. **2** a formal, written request to someone in authority, signed by a number of people. ◆***v.*** to make a petition to or a request for [The mayor of our town has *petitioned* the governor for flood relief.] —**pe·ti′tion·er** ***n.***

**pet·rel** (pet′rəl) ***n.*** a small, dark sea bird with long wings. *See the picture.*

**pet·ri·fy** (pet′rə fī) ***v.*** **1** to change into a substance like stone by replacing the normal cells with minerals [Trees buried under lava for a great many years can become *petrified.*] **2** to make unable to move or act, as because of fear or surprise. —**pet′ri·fied, pet′ri·fy·ing**

**pet·ro·chem·i·cal** (pet′rō kem′i k'l) ***n.*** a chemical that comes from petroleum.

**pet·rol** (pet′rəl) ***n.*** *a British word for* **gasoline.**

**pe·tro·le·um** (pə trō′lē əm) ***n.*** an oily liquid found in the earth in certain layers of rock. We get gasoline, paraffin, fuel oil, etc. from petroleum.

> **Petroleum** comes from two Latin words meaning "rock" and "oil." These Latin words make a very brief definition, since petroleum is an oil found in rock.

**pet·ti·coat** (pet′i kōt′) ***n.*** a kind of skirt worn as an undergarment by women and girls.

**pet·tish** (pet′ish) ***adj.*** cross or peevish.

**pet·ty** (pet′ē) ***adj.*** **1** of little importance; small; minor [*Petty* larceny is the stealing of a small thing or sum.] **2** having or showing a narrow, mean character [full of *petty* spite]. **3** of lower rank [a *petty* official]. —**pet′ti·er, pet′ti·est —pet′ti·ness** ***n.***

> SYNONYMS: To be **petty** is to be small and unimportant or small-minded [*petty* cash; a *petty* grudge]. To be **trivial** is to be ordinary as well as small and unimportant [a *trivial* remark]. To be **trifling** is to be so small and unimportant as to be not worth noticing [a *trifling* matter].

**petty cash** a small sum of money kept on hand in a business to pay minor expenses.

**petty officer** an enlisted person in the navy with the rank of a noncommissioned officer.

**pet·u·lant** (pech′oo lənt) ***adj.*** showing anger or annoyance over little things; peevish. —**pet′u·lance** ***n.***

**pe·tu·nia** (pə to͞on′yə) ***n.*** a plant with flowers of various colors, shaped like funnels. *See the picture.*

**pew** (pyo͞o) ***n.*** any of the benches with a back that are fixed in rows in a church.

☆**pe·wee** (pē′wē) ***n.*** a small bird related to the flycatcher. *See the note at* **bobolink.**

**pew·ter** (pyo͞ot′ər) ***n.*** **1** a grayish alloy of tin with lead, brass, or copper. **2** things made of pewter, especially dishes, tableware, etc. ◆***adj.*** made of pewter.

**Pfc, Pfc., PFC** *abbreviations for* **Private First Class.**

☆**PG** parental guidance suggested: a movie rating meaning that parents may decide that the movie is one that they do not want their children to see.

**pg.** *abbreviation for* **page.**

**pha·e·ton** or **pha·ë·ton** (fā′ət 'n) ***n.*** a light carriage with four wheels, front and back seats, and a top that could be folded back.

> **Phaeton,** the carriage, takes its name from Phaëton, the son of the Greek sun god. When Phaëton tried to drive his father's sun chariot across the sky, he lost control of it. He would have set the world on fire if Zeus had not struck him down with a thunderbolt.

**pha·lanx** (fā′langks *or* fal′angks) ***n.*** **1** in ancient times, a group of soldiers arranged for battle in a very close formation, with shields together. *See the picture.* **2** a group of persons or things massed close together. **3** a group of persons joined together for some purpose. *—pl.* **pha′lanx·es** or **pha·lan·ges** (fə lan′jēz)

**phan·tasm** (fan′taz'm) ***n.*** something that one imagines is real, but that exists only in the mind; especially, a ghost or specter.

**phan·ta·sy** (fan′tə sē) ***n.*** *another spelling of* **fantasy.** *—pl.* **phan′ta·sies**

**phan·tom** (fan′təm) ***n.*** **1** something that one seems to see although it is not really there [the *phantoms* of a dream]. **2** any shadowy or ghostly image; ghost. **3** something feared [the *phantom* of poverty]. **4** a person or thing that is not really what it seems to be or should be [a *phantom* of a leader]. ◆***adj.*** of or like a phantom; unreal [*phantom* ships in the fog].

**Phar·aoh** (fer′ō) ***n.*** the title of the rulers of ancient Egypt.

**phar·ma·ceu·ti·cal** (fär′mə so͞ot′i k'l *or* fär′mə syo͞ot′i k'l) ***adj.*** **1** of or by drugs. **2** of pharmacy or pharmacists. ◆***n.*** a pharmaceutical product; drug.

**phar·ma·cist** (fär′mə sist) ***n.*** a person who is trained to prepare and sell drugs and medicine according to the orders of a doctor; druggist.

**phar·ma·cy** (fär′mə sē) ***n.*** **1** the work of preparing drugs and medicines according to a doctor's orders. **2** a place where this is done; drugstore. —*pl.* **phar′ma·cies**

**phar·yn·gi·tis** (far′in jīt′əs) ***n.*** a condition in which the pharynx is inflamed.

**phar·ynx** (far′iŋks) ***n.*** the place at the back of the mouth where the larynx and esophagus begin. *See the picture.* —*pl.* **phar′ynx·es** or **pha·ryn·ges** (fə rin′jēz)

**phase** (fāz) ***n.*** **1** any of the sides or views of a subject by which it may be looked at, thought about, or shown [We discussed the many *phases* of the problem.] **2** any stage in a series of changes [Adolescence is a *phase* we all go through. The moon is full in its third *phase*.] ◆***v.*** to bring into use or carry out in stages [The new equipment will be *phased* in a little at a time.] —**phased, phas′ing** —☆**phase out,** to bring or come to an end, or take out of use, by stages.

**Ph.D.** Doctor of Philosophy.

**pheas·ant** (fez′′nt) ***n.*** a wild bird with a long, sweeping tail and brightly colored feathers. It is hunted as game. *See the picture on page 550.*

**phe·nom·e·nal** (fi näm′ə n'l) ***adj.*** **1** very unusual; extraordinary [a *phenomenal* success]. **2** of or like a phenomenon or phenomena. —**phe·nom′e·nal·ly** ***adv.***

**phe·nom·e·non** (fi näm′ə nän) ***n.*** **1** any fact, condition, or happening that can be seen, heard, etc. and described in a scientific way, as an eclipse. **2** an unusual or remarkable person or thing [Rain is a *phenomenon* in the desert.] —*pl.* **phe·nom·e·na** (fi näm′ə nə); *for meaning* 2 *sometimes* **phe·nom′e·nons**

**phi·al** (fī′əl) ***n.*** a small glass bottle; vial.

**Phil·a·del·phi·a** (fil′ə del′fē ə) a city in southeastern Pennsylvania.

**phil·an·throp·ic** (fil′ən thräp′ik) ***adj.*** of or showing philanthropy; generous; charitable.

> SYNONYMS: A person who is **philanthropic** shows an interest in the welfare of all people by giving large sums of money to charities, organizations, colleges, etc. A person who is **humanitarian** is directly interested in making life better for everyone, especially by personal efforts to lessen the pain and suffering of others.

**phi·lan·thro·pist** (fi lan′thrə pist) ***n.*** a person who shows a love of other people, especially by giving much money to help them.

**phi·lan·thro·py** (fi lan′thrə pē) ***n.*** **1** a strong wish to help human beings, shown by giving large sums of money to causes that help other people. **2** something done or given by a philanthropist to help others. —*pl.* **phi·lan′thro·pies**

**phi·lat·e·ly** (fi lat′′l ē) ***n.*** the collecting and studying of postage stamps, postmarks, etc., usually as a hobby. —**phi·lat′e·list** ***n.***

**-phile** (fīl *or* fil) *a suffix meaning* a person who likes or loves [An *Anglophile* is a person who likes English people and their ways.]

**phil·har·mon·ic** (fil′här män′ik) ***adj.*** loving music [a *philharmonic* society]. ◆***n.*** a society that supports a symphony orchestra; also, such an orchestra.

**Phil·ip·pine** (fil′ə pēn) ***adj.*** of the Philippine Islands or their people.

petunia

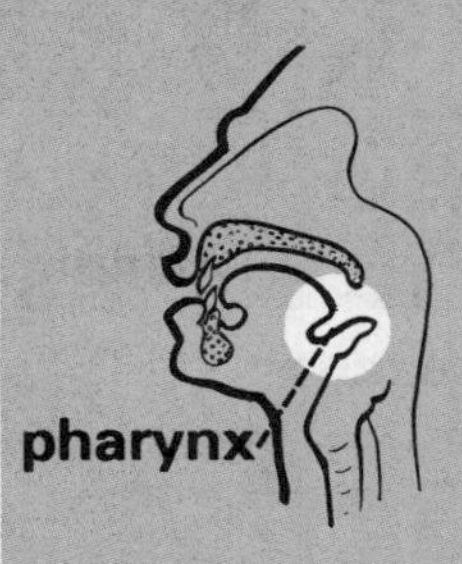

phalanx

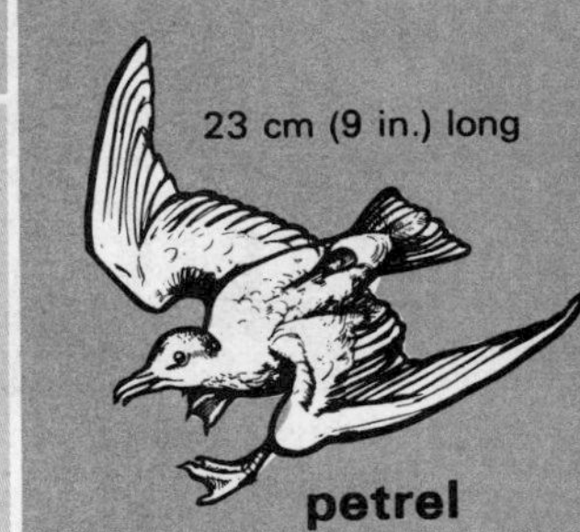


**Phil·ip·pines** (fil′ə pēnz) a country in the Pacific, north of Indonesia, made up of more than 7,000 islands (**Philippine Islands**). 549

**Phil·is·tine** (fil′is tēn′ *or* fi lis′tin) ***n.*** **1** a member of an ancient people in southwestern Palestine who were enemies of the Israelites. **2** *often* **philistine,** a person who is narrow-minded and has very ordinary tastes and ideas; one who does not have and does not want culture and learning.

**phil·o·den·dron** (fil′ə den′drən) ***n.*** a vine of tropical America with heart-shaped leaves. It is popular as a house plant.

**phi·lol·o·gy** (fi läl′ə jē) ***n.*** *an earlier name for* **linguistics.** —**phi·lol′o·gist** ***n.***

**phi·los·o·pher** (fi läs′ə fər) ***n.*** **1** a person who studies philosophy. **2** a person who lives by a certain philosophy. **3** a person who meets difficulties in a calm, brave way.

**phil·o·soph·ic** (fil′ə säf′ik) ***adj.*** **1** of philosophy or philosophers. **2** calm and wise; reasonable [You should try to be *philosophic* about losing your wallet.] *Also* **phil′o·soph′i·cal.** —**phil′o·soph′i·cal·ly** ***adv.***

**phi·los·o·phize** (fi läs′ə fīz) ***v.*** **1** to think or reason like a philosopher. **2** to talk or write about philosophic ideas, matters of right and wrong, etc., especially in a way that is aimless or with little understanding. —**phi·los′o·phized, phi·los′o·phiz·ing** —**phi·los′o·phiz′er** ***n.***

**phi·los·o·phy** (fi läs′ə fē) ***n.*** **1** the study of human

| | | | |
|---|---|---|---|
| **a** fat | **ir** here | **ou** out | **zh** leisure |
| **ā** ape | **ī** bite, fire | **u** up | **ŋ** ring |
| **ä** car, lot | **ō** go | **ʉr** fur | a *in* ago |
| **e** ten | **ô** law, horn | **ch** chin | e *in* agent |
| **er** care | **oi** oil | **sh** she | **ə** = i *in* unity |
| **ē** even | **oo** look | **th** thin | o *in* collect |
| **i** hit | **o͞o** tool | ***th*** then | u *in* focus |

**p**

piccolo

spinet piano

**pheasants**
88 cm (35 in.) long, including tail

phlox

thought about the meaning of life, the relationship of mind to matter, the problems of right and wrong, etc. [*Philosophy* includes ethics, logic, metaphysics, etc.] **2** a system of principles that comes from such study [Plato's *philosophy*]. **3** calmness and wisdom in meeting problems. *—pl.* **phi·los′o·phies**

 **phil·ter** (fil′tər) ***n.*** a magic drink that is supposed to make one fall in love. *The usual British spelling is* **philtre.**

**phlegm** (flem) ***n.*** the thick, stringy substance that is formed in the throat and nose and is coughed up, as during a cold.

**phleg·mat·ic** (fleg mat′ik) ***adj.*** hard to make excited or active; dull and sluggish, or calm and cool [The *phlegmatic* fellow wasn't worried about the coming hurricane.]

**phlox** (fläks) ***n.*** a plant having clusters of small red, pink, blue, or white flowers. *See the picture.*

**-phobe** (fōb) *a suffix meaning* a person who fears or dislikes [An *Anglophobe* is a person who fears or dislikes the English people and their ways.]

**pho·bi·a** (fō′bē ə) ***n.*** a strong and unreasonable fear of something [I have a *phobia* about spiders.]

☆**phoe·be** (fē′bē) ***n.*** a small bird with a gray or brown back, a light-yellow breast, and a short tuft of feathers on its head.

**Phoe·bus** (fē′bəs) *another name for* **Apollo.**

**Phoe·ni·cia** (fə nish′ə *or* fə nē′shə) an ancient country on the eastern coast of the Mediterranean Sea. —**Phoe·ni′cian *adj., n.***

**Phoe·nix** (fē′niks) the capital of Arizona.

**phoe·nix** (fē′niks) ***n.*** a beautiful bird of Arabia in ancient myths that lived about 500 years. Then it burned itself to death and rose out of its own ashes to start another long life. The phoenix is used as a symbol of life that goes on forever.

☆**phone** (fōn) ***n., v.*** *a shorter word for* **telephone**: *used only in everyday talk.* —**phoned, phon′ing**

**pho·neme** (fō′nēm) ***n.*** a set of similar but slightly different sounds in a language that are all shown by the same symbol [In *pin, spin,* and *tip, p* is a *phoneme.*]

**pho·net·ic** (fə net′ik) ***adj.*** **1** of the sounds made in speaking [The letters and marks used to show pronunciations in this dictionary are called *phonetic* symbols.] **2** of phonetics. **3** according to the way something is pronounced ["Tuf" is a *phonetic* spelling of "tough."]

**pho·net·ics** (fə net′iks) ***n.pl.*** the study of speech sounds and of ways to represent them in writing: *used with a singular verb.*

**phon·ics** (fän′iks) ***n.pl.*** **1** the science of sound. **2** the use of a simple system of phonetics in teaching beginners to read. *This word is used with a singular verb.*

**pho·no·graph** (fō′nə graf) ***n.*** ☆an instrument for playing records with grooves on them in which sounds of music, speech, etc. have been recorded.

☆**pho·ny** or **pho·ney** (fō′nē) ***adj.*** not real or genuine; fake; false. —**pho′ni·er, pho′ni·est** ◆***n.*** a person or thing that is not really what it is supposed to be. *—pl.* **pho′nies** *This is a slang word.*

> **Phony** comes from one of the secret words used among British thieves and swindlers. Their secret word for "a gilt ring" was *fawney.* They would sell to a victim a gilt ring that they said was made of gold. But the ring was not real or genuine gold, and the word *phony* came to be used of anything that was fake or not genuine.

**phos·phate** (fäs′fāt) ***n.*** **1** a chemical salt having phosphorus in it. **2** a fertilizer containing such salts. **3** a soft drink made of soda water and flavored syrup.

**phos·pho·res·cence** (fäs′fə res′′ns) ***n.*** **1** the act or power of giving off light without heat or burning, as phosphorus does. **2** such a light. —**phos′pho·res′cent *adj.***

**phos·phor·ic** (fäs fôr′ik) or **phos·pho·rous** (fäs′fər əs) ***adj.*** of, like, or containing phosphorus.

**phos·pho·rus** (fäs′fər əs) ***n.*** a chemical element that in its ordinary pure form is a white or yellow waxy solid. In this form it glows in the dark, starts burning at room temperature, and is very poisonous.

**pho·to** (fōt′ō) ***n.*** *a shorter name for* **photograph**: *used only in everyday talk. —pl.* **pho′tos**

**pho·to·cop·y** (fōt′ə käp′ē) ***n.*** a copy of printed or written material, a drawing, etc. made by a device (**photocopier**) which reproduces the original photographically. *—pl.* **pho′to·cop′ies** ◆***v.*** to make a photocopy of. —**pho′to·cop′ied, pho′to·cop′y·ing**

☆**pho·to·e·lec·tric cell** (fōt′ō i lek′trik) a device that sends out an electric current as long as light falls on it. When the light is cut off, some action takes place, such as the opening of a door or the sounding of a burglar alarm.

**pho·to·en·grav·ing** (fōt′ō in grā′viŋ) ***n.*** **1** a method of copying photographs onto printing plates. **2** a printing plate so made. **3** a print from such a plate.

**photo finish** **1** a race so close that the winner can be known only by means of a photograph taken at the finish line. **2** any close finish of a game, contest, etc.

**pho·to·gen·ic** (fōt′ə jen′ik) ***adj.*** that looks attractive in photographs [a *photogenic* person].

**pho·to·graph** (fōt′ə graf) ***n.*** a picture made with a camera. ◆***v.*** **1** to take a photograph of. **2** to look a certain way in photographs [She *photographs* taller than she is.]

**pho·tog·ra·pher** (fə täg′rə fər) ***n.*** a person who takes photographs, especially for a living.

**pho·to·graph·ic** (fōt′ə graf′ik) ***adj.*** **1** of or like photography [in *photographic* detail]. **2** used in or made by photography [*photographic* equipment]. —**pho′to·graph′i·cal·ly** ***adv.***

**pho·tog·ra·phy** (fə täg′rə fē) ***n.*** the art or method of making pictures by means of a camera. *See* **camera.**

**pho·to·syn·the·sis** (fōt′ə sin′thə sis) ***n.*** the forming of sugars and starches in plants from water and carbon dioxide, when sunlight acts upon the chlorophyll in the plant.

**phrase** (frāz) ***n.*** **1** a group of words that is not a complete sentence, but that gives a single idea, usually as a separate part of a sentence ["Drinking fresh milk," "with meals," and "to be healthy" are *phrases.*] **2** a short, forceful expression ["It's raining cats and dogs" is a well-known *phrase.*] **3** a short passage of music, usually two, four, or eight measures. ◆***v.*** to say or write in a certain way [He *phrased* his answer carefully.] —**phrased, phras′ing**

**phra·se·ol·o·gy** (frā′zē äl′ə jē) ***n.*** the words used and the way they are arranged; way of speaking or writing [legal *phraseology*].

**Phryg·i·a** (frij′ē ə) an ancient country in west central Asia Minor. —**Phryg′i·an** ***adj., n.***

**phys.** *abbreviation for* **physical, physician, physics.**

**phys. ed.** *abbreviation for* **physical education.**

**phys·ic** (fiz′ik) ***n.*** **1** a medicine for making the bowels move. **2** the science of medicine: *an earlier name now seldom used.*

**phys·i·cal** (fiz′i k'l) ***adj.*** **1** of nature or matter; material; natural [the *physical* universe]. **2** of the body rather than the mind [Swimming is good *physical* exercise.] **3** of or having to do with the natural sciences or the laws of nature [the *physical* force that makes an object move]. ◆***n.*** ☆a medical examination of the whole body: *the full name is* **physical examination.**

> SYNONYMS: **Physical** and **bodily** both have to do with the human body, but **bodily** suggests more strongly the flesh and bones of the body apart from the mind or spirit [*bodily* ills]. Usually **physical** suggests the workings of the body as a whole [*physical* exercise].

☆**physical education** a course in the schools that teaches how to exercise and take proper care of the body, as by means of games and sports.

**phys·i·cal·ly** (fiz′i k'l ē) ***adv.*** **1** in regard to the laws of nature [It is *physically* impossible to be in two places at the same time.] **2** in regard to the body [Keep *physically* fit.]

**physical therapy** the treatment of disease or injury by physical means rather than with drugs, as by exercise, massage, heat, baths, etc. —**physical therapist**

**phy·si·cian** (fə zish′ən) ***n.*** a doctor of medicine, especially one who is not mainly a surgeon.

**phys·i·cist** (fiz′ə sist) ***n.*** an expert in physics.

**phys·ics** (fiz′iks) ***n.pl.*** the science that deals with energy and matter, and studies the ways that things are moved and work is done: *used with a singular verb* [*Physics* includes the study of light, heat, sound, electricity, and mechanics.]

**phys·i·og·no·my** (fiz′ē äg′nə mē) ***n.*** the face; especially, the features of a person's face, as they show the person's character [the *physiognomy* of an honest man]. —*pl.* **phys′i·og′no·mies**

**phys·i·ol·o·gy** (fiz′ē äl′ə jē) ***n.*** the science that deals with living things and the ways in which their parts and organs work [the *physiology* of birds; plant *physiology*]. —**phys·i·o·log·i·cal** (fiz′ē ə läj′i k'l) ***adj.*** —**phys′i·ol′o·gist** ***n.***

**phy·sique** (fi zēk′) ***n.*** the form or build of one's body.

**pi** (pī) ***n.*** the symbol $\pi$ that stands for the ratio of the circumference of a circle to its diameter. $\pi$ equals about 3.14159.

**pi·a·nis·si·mo** (pē′ə nis′ə mō) ***adj., adv.*** very soft. This is an Italian word used in music to tell how loud a piece should be played.

**pi·an·ist** (pē an′ist *or* pē′ən ist) ***n.*** a person who plays the piano.

**pi·an·o**[1] (pē an′ō) ***n.*** a large musical instrument with many wire strings in a case and a keyboard. When a key is struck, it makes a small hammer hit a string so that it gives out a tone. *See the picture. See pictures also for* **grand piano** *and* **upright.** —*pl.* **pi·an′os**

**pi·an·o**[2] (pē ä′nō) ***adj., adv.*** soft. This is an Italian word used in music to tell how loud a piece should be played.

**pi·an·o·for·te** (pē an′ə fôrt *or* pē an′ə fôr′tē) ***n.*** *another word for* **piano**[1].

**pi·az·za** (pē az′ə) ***n.*** ☆**1** a long porch with a roof, along the front or side of a building. **2** (*usually* pē at′sə) a public square in Italian towns.

**pi·broch** (pē′bräk) ***n.*** a piece of music, as a march, for playing on the bagpipe.



**Pic·ar·dy** (pik′ər dē) a region in northern France.

**Pi·cas·so** (pi kä′sō), **Pa·blo** (pä′blō) 1881–1973; Spanish artist who lived in France.

☆**pic·a·yune** (pik′ē o͞on′ *or* pik ə yo͞on′) ***adj.*** small and not very important; trivial or petty.

> **Picayune** comes from a French word meaning "small coin." Years ago in Louisiana a certain small Spanish coin was called a *picayune.* The coin had little value. As time went by, anything that had little value or was small and not very important came to be called *picayune.*

**pic·ca·lil·li** (pik′ə lil′ē) ***n.*** a relish made with chopped vegetables, mustard, vinegar, and hot spices.

**pic·co·lo** (pik′ə lō) ***n.*** a small flute that sounds notes an octave higher than an ordinary flute does. *See the picture.* —*pl.* **pic′co·los**

**pick**[1] (pik) ***n.*** **1** a heavy metal tool with a pointed head, used for breaking up rock, soil, etc. **2** any pointed tool for picking or digging at something [a tooth*pick;* an ice *pick*]. **3** *another word for* **plectrum.**

**pick**[2] (pik) ***v.*** **1** to choose or select [The judges *picked* the winner.] **2** to scratch or dig at with the fingers or with something pointed [to *pick* the teeth with a toothpick]. **3** to pluck or gather with the fingers or hands [to *pick* flowers]. **4** to clean or leave bare by taking

| | | | | | | | |
|---|---|---|---|---|---|---|---|
| **a** | fat | **ir** | here | **ou** | out | **zh** | leisure |
| **ā** | ape | **ī** | bite, fire | **u** | up | **ŋ** | ring |
| **ä** | car, lot | **ō** | go | **ur** | fur | | a *in* ago |
| **e** | ten | **ô** | law, horn | **ch** | chin | | e *in* agent |
| **er** | care | **oi** | oil | **sh** | she | **ə** = | i *in* unity |
| **ē** | even | **oo** | look | **th** | thin | | o *in* collect |
| **i** | hit | **o͞o** | tool | ***th*** | then | | u *in* focus |

away something [To *pick* a chicken means to remove its feathers.] **5** to look for and find [to *pick* a fight; to *pick* flaws]. ☆**6** to pluck the strings of [to *pick* a guitar]. **7** to open with a wire, etc. instead of a key [to *pick* a lock]. **8** to steal from [to *pick* pockets]. ◆*n.* **1** the act of choosing, or the thing chosen; choice [Take your *pick* of these books.] **2** the one most wanted; best [This kitten is the *pick* of the litter.] —**pick and choose,** to choose or select carefully. —**pick at, 1** to take little bites of [to *pick at* one's food]. **2** to find fault with: *used only in everyday talk.* —**pick off,** to hit with a carefully aimed shot. —**pick on,** to criticize, tease, or annoy: *used only in everyday talk.* —**pick one's way,** to move slowly and cautiously. —**pick out, 1** to choose. **2** to single out; find [Can you *pick* her *out* in the crowd?] —**pick over,** to examine one by one; sort out. —**pick up, 1** to take hold of and lift. **2** to get, find, or learn in an easy or casual way [She *picks up* languages quickly.] **3** to stop for and take along [They stopped the car to *pick up* a hitchhiker.] **4** to go faster; gain speed. ☆**5** to make tidy, as a room. —**pick'er** *n.*

**pick·a·back** (pik'ə bak) ***adv., adj.*** *another word for* **piggyback.**

**pick·ax** or **pick·axe** (pik'aks) ***n.*** a pick with a point at one end of the head and a blade like that of a chisel at the other end. *See the picture.*

**pick·er·el** (pik'ər əl) ***n.*** a fresh-water fish related to the pike, with a narrow head and sharp teeth. It is used for food. —*pl.* **pick'er·el** or **pick'er·els**



**pick·et** (pik'it) ***n.*** **1** a pointed stake used in a fence, as a marker, etc. **2** a soldier or soldiers used to guard troops from surprise attack. **3** a person, as a member of a labor union on strike, standing or walking outside a factory, store, etc. to show protest. ◆*v.* to place pickets, or act as a picket, at a factory, store, etc.

☆**picket fence** a fence made of pickets. *See the picture.*

**picket line** a line of people serving as pickets.

**pick·ings** (pik'iŋz) ***n.pl.*** something picked; especially, small scraps.

**pick·le** (pik''l) ***n.*** **1** a cucumber or other vegetable preserved in salt water, vinegar, or spicy liquid. **2** a liquid of this kind used to preserve food. **3** an unpleasant or difficult situation; trouble: *used only in everyday talk.* ◆*v.* to preserve in a pickle liquid [*pickled* beets]. —**pick'led, pick'ling**

**pick·pock·et** (pik'päk'it) ***n.*** a thief who steals from the pockets of persons, as in crowds.

**pick·up** (pik'up) ***n.*** **1** the act of picking up [The shortstop made a good *pickup* of the ball.] **2** the act or power of gaining speed [Our old car still has good *pickup*.] ☆**3** a small, open truck, for hauling light loads. **4** a device in a phonograph that changes the vibrations of the needle or stylus into electric current.

**pic·nic** (pik'nik) ***n.*** a pleasure outing during which a meal is eaten outdoors. ◆*v.* to have or go on a picnic. —**pic'nicked, pic'nick·ing** —**pic'nick·er** ***n.***

**pi·cot** (pē'kō) ***n.*** any one of the small loops forming a fancy edge on lace, ribbon, etc.

**pic·to·ri·al** (pik tôr'ē əl) ***adj.*** **1** of or having pictures [the *pictorial* page of a newspaper]. **2** showing something by means of pictures [a *pictorial* graph]. **3** that forms a picture in one's mind; vivid [a *pictorial* description]. —**pic·to'ri·al·ly** ***adv.***

**pic·ture** (pik'chər) ***n.*** **1** a likeness of a person, thing, scene, etc. made by drawing, painting, or photography; also, a printed copy of this. **2** any likeness, image, or good example [Sue is the *picture* of her mother. Joe is the *picture* of health.] **3** anything admired for its beauty [The rose garden was a *picture*.] **4** an idea; image in the mind. **5** a description [The book gives a clear *picture* of life in Peru.] **6** a motion picture. **7** an image on a TV screen. ◆*v.* **1** to make a picture of. **2** to show; make clear [Joy was *pictured* in her face.] **3** to describe or explain [Dickens *pictured* life in England.] **4** to form an idea or picture in the mind; imagine [You can *picture* how pleased I was!] —**pic'tured, pic'tur·ing**

**Picture** comes from a Latin word meaning "to paint." Most of the pictures in art museums were painted in oils.

**pic·tur·esque** (pik chə resk') ***adj.*** **1** like a picture; having natural beauty. **2** pleasant and charming in a strange or unfamiliar way [a *picturesque* village]. **3** giving a clear picture in the mind; vivid [a *picturesque* description].

**picture window** a large window, especially in a living room, that seems to frame the outside view.

**pidg·in English** (pij'in) a form of English mixed with Chinese, etc. and used in Asia and the South Pacific in dealing with foreigners.

**pie** (pī) ***n.*** a dish with a filling made of fruit, meat, etc., baked in a pastry crust.

**pie·bald** (pī'bôld) ***adj.*** covered with large patches of two colors, often black and white, as a horse. ◆*n.* a piebald animal.

**piece** (pēs) ***n.*** **1** a part broken or separated from a whole thing [The glass shattered and I swept up the *pieces*.] **2** a part or section of a whole, thought of as complete by itself [a *piece* of meat; a *piece* of land]. **3** any one of a set or group of things [a dinner set of 52 *pieces;* a chess *piece*]. **4** a work of music, writing, or art [a *piece* for the piano]. **5** a firearm, as a rifle [an old shooting *piece*]. **6** a coin [a fifty-cent *piece*]. **7** a single item or example [a *piece* of information]. **8** a thing or the amount of a thing made up as a unit [to sell cloth by the *piece*]. ◆*v.* **1** to add a piece or pieces to, as in making larger or repairing [to *piece* a pair of trousers]. **2** to join the pieces of, as in mending [to *piece* together a broken jug]. **3** to eat a snack between meals: *used only in everyday talk.* —**pieced, piec'ing** —**go to pieces, 1** to fall apart. **2** to lose control of oneself, as in crying. —**of a piece** or **of one piece,** of the same sort; alike. —☆**speak one's piece,** to say what one really thinks about something.

**piece·meal** (pēs'mēl) ***adv.*** **1** piece by piece; a part at a time. **2** into pieces. ◆***adj.*** made or done piecemeal.

**piece of eight,** the silver dollar of Spain and Spanish America used in earlier times.

**piece·work** (pēs'wurk) ***n.*** work paid for at a fixed rate for each piece of work done. —**piece'work'er** ***n.***

**pied** (pīd) ***adj.*** covered with spots of two or more colors [The *Pied* Piper wore a suit of many colors.]

**Pied·mont** (pēd'mänt) a plateau in the southeastern U.S., between the Atlantic coast and the Appalachian Mountains. *See the map.*

**pier** (pir) ***n.*** **1** a structure built out over water on pillars and used as a landing place, a walk, etc. *See the picture.* **2** a strong support for the arch of a bridge or of a building. **3** the part of a wall between windows or other openings.

**pierce** (pirs) ***v.*** **1** to pass into or through; penetrate [The needle *pierced* her finger. A light *pierced* the darkness.] **2** to have a sharp effect on the senses or feelings [*pierced* by the cold]. **3** to make a hole through; perforate; bore [to *pierce* one's ears for earrings]. **4** to force a way into; break through [The explorer *pierced* the jungle.] **5** to make a sharp sound through [A shriek *pierced* the air.] **6** to understand [The detectives were not able to *pierce* the mystery.] —**pierced, pierc'ing**

**Pierce** (pirs), **Franklin** 1804–1869; the 14th president of the United States, from 1853 to 1857.

**pier glass** a tall mirror set in the pier, or wall section between windows.

**Pierre** (pir) the capital of South Dakota.

**pi·e·ty** (pī'ə tē) ***n.*** **1** the condition of being pious, or devoted in following one's religion. **2** loyalty and a sense of duty toward one's parents, family, etc. **3** a pious act, statement, etc. —*pl.* **pi'e·ties**

**pig** (pig) ***n.*** **1** an animal with a long, broad snout and a thick, fat body covered with coarse bristles; swine; hog. It is raised for its meat. **2** a young hog. **3** a person thought of as like a pig in being greedy, filthy, coarse, etc. **4** a long and narrow casting of iron or other metal that has been poured in a mold from the smelting furnace.

**pi·geon** (pij'ən) ***n.*** a bird with a small head, plump body, and short legs. It is larger than a dove. *See the picture.*

**pi·geon·hole** (pij'ən hōl) ***n.*** **1** a small hole for pigeons to nest in; usually, one of a series of such holes. **2** a small box, open at the front, as in a desk, for filing papers, etc.; usually, one of a series of such boxes. ◆***v.*** **1** to put in a pigeonhole of a desk, etc. **2** to lay aside, where it is likely to be ignored or forgotten [The governor *pigeonholed* the plan for a new hospital.] **3** to arrange according to a system; classify. —**pi'geon·holed, pi'geon·hol·ing**

**pi·geon-toed** (pij'ən tōd') ***adj.*** having the feet turned in toward each other.

**pig·gish** (pig'ish) ***adj.*** like a pig; greedy; filthy; coarse. —**pig'gish·ly *adv.*** —**pig'gish·ness *n.***

**pig·gy** or **pig·gie** (pig'ē) ***n.*** a little pig. —*pl.* **pig'gies** ◆***adj.*** *same as* **piggish.** —**pig'gi·er, pig'gi·est**

**pig·gy·back** (pig'ē bak') ***adv., adj.*** **1** on the shoulders or back [to carry a child *piggyback*]. *See the picture.* ☆**2** of or by a transportation system in which loaded truck trailers are carried on railroad flatcars.

☆**piggy bank** a small bank, often shaped like a pig, with a slot for putting coins into it.

**pig·head·ed** (pig'hed'id) ***adj.*** stubborn; obstinate.

**pig iron** crude iron, as it comes from the blast furnace.

**pig·ment** (pig'mənt) ***n.*** **1** coloring matter, usually a powder, mixed with oil, water, etc. to make paints. **2** the matter in the cells and tissues that gives color to plants and animals.

**Pig·my** (pig'mē) ***adj., n.*** *another spelling of* **Pygmy.** —*pl.* **Pig'mies**

**pig·pen** (pig'pen) ***n.*** a pen where pigs are kept.

**pig·skin** (pig'skin) ***n.*** **1** the skin of a pig. **2** leather made from this. ☆**3** a football: *used only in everyday talk.*

**pig·sty** (pig'stī) ***n.*** *another name for* **pigpen.** —*pl.* **pig'sties**

**pig·tail** (pig'tāl) ***n.*** a long braid of hair hanging at the back of the head.

**pike**[1] (pīk) ***n.*** a turnpike, or road with tollgates.

**pike**[2] (pīk) ***n.*** a long wooden shaft with a sharp metal head, once used as a weapon by soldiers.

**pike**[3] (pīk) ***n.*** a slender, fresh-water fish with a pointed snout and a lower jaw that sticks out.

**Pikes Peak** (pīks) a mountain in central Colorado.

**pi·laf** or **pi·laff** (pi läf' *or* pē'läf) ***n.*** a dish of rice boiled in a seasoned liquid, and usually containing meat or fish.

**pi·las·ter** (pi las'tər) ***n.*** a support that is part of a wall and juts out a bit from it. It looks like a column with a base and capital. *See the picture on page 554.*

**Pi·late** (pī'lət), **Pon·tius** (pän'shəs *or* pän'tē əs) the Roman governor of Judea when Jesus was crucified.

**pile**[1] (pīl) ***n.*** **1** a mass of things heaped together [a *pile* of leaves]. **2** a heap of wood, etc. on which a corpse or sacrifice is burned. **3** a large building or group of buildings. **4** a large amount: *used only in everyday talk* [a *pile* of work]. ☆**5** *an earlier name for* **nuclear reactor.** ◆***v.*** **1** to put or set in a pile; heap up [to *pile* rubbish]. **2** to gather or collect in heaps; accumulate [Letters *piled* up on his desk.] **3** to cover



| | | | | | | | |
|---|---|---|---|---|---|---|---|
| a | fat | ir | here | ou | out | zh | leisure |
| ā | ape | ī | bite, fire | u | up | ŋ | ring |
| ä | car, lot | ō | go | ur | fur | | a *in* ago |
| e | ten | ô | law, horn | ch | chin | | e *in* agent |
| er | care | oi | oil | sh | she | ə = | i *in* unity |
| ē | even | oo | look | th | thin | | o *in* collect |
| i | hit | ōō | tool | *th* | then | | u *in* focus |

with a heap or large amount [We *piled* the cart with hay.] **4** to move together in a confused way; crowd [The football fans *piled* into the stadium.] —**piled, pil′ing**

**pile²** (pīl) ***n.*** **1** the thick, soft nap, as on a rug, made of loops of yarn that are either cut to make a velvety surface, or left uncut. **2** soft, fine hair, as on fur or wool.

**pile³** (pīl) ***n.*** **1** a long, heavy beam driven into the ground, sometimes under water, to support a bridge, dock, etc. **2** any support like this, as of concrete.

**pile driver** a machine with a heavy weight that is raised and then dropped, used to drive piles.

**piles** (pīlz) ***n.pl.*** *another name for* **hemorrhoids.**

**pil·fer** (pil′fər) ***v.*** to steal small sums or things of little value; filch. —**pil′fer·er *n.***

**pil·grim** (pil′grəm) ***n.*** **1** a person who travels to a holy place or shrine. **2** a person who travels about; wanderer. ☆**3 Pilgrim,** any of the group of English Puritans who founded a colony in Plymouth, Massachusetts, in 1620.

**pil·grim·age** (pil′grəm ij) ***n.*** **1** a journey made by a pilgrim to a holy place or shrine. **2** any long journey.

**pill** (pil) ***n.*** a little ball or capsule of medicine to be swallowed whole. ◆***v.*** to form into small balls, as fuzz on a fabric.

**pil·lage** (pil′ij) ***v.*** to rob or plunder with wild force, as in war. —**pil′laged, pil′lag·ing** ◆***n.*** plunder; loot.

 **pil·lar** (pil′ər) ***n.*** **1** a long, slender, upright structure used as a support for a roof, etc. or as a monument; column. **2** any person or thing thought of as like a pillar; a main support [The sponsors of our art museum are *pillars* of society.] —**from pillar to post,** from one difficulty to another.

**pil·lion** (pil′yən) ***n.*** a seat behind the saddle on a horse or motorcycle, for an extra rider.

**pil·lo·ry** (pil′ər ē) ***n.*** a wooden board with holes in which the head and hands can be locked. At one time pillories were set up in public places and used to punish wrongdoers. *See the picture.* —*pl.* **pil′lo·ries** ◆***v.*** **1** to punish by placing in a pillory. **2** to present in such a way that people will be scornful or full of contempt [The mayor was *pilloried* in the newspapers because he had accepted bribes.] —**pil′lo·ried, pil′lo·ry·ing**

**pil·low** (pil′ō) ***n.*** a bag or case filled with feathers, foam rubber, air, etc., used to rest the head on, as in sleeping. ◆***v.*** **1** to rest as on a pillow. **2** to be a pillow for [Roll up a blanket to *pillow* her head.]

**pil·low·case** (pil′ō kās′) ***n.*** a cloth covering for a pillow, that can be taken off for washing. *Also called* **pil·low·slip** (pil′ō slip′)

**pi·lot** (pī′lət) ***n.*** **1** a person who steers a ship; often, one whose job is steering ships in and out of harbors or through difficult waters. **2** a person who flies an aircraft. **3** a guide or leader. ◆***v.*** **1** to act as a pilot of, on, in, or over. **2** to guide or lead [to *pilot* a team to a championship]. *See* SYNONYMS *at* **guide.**

**pilot light** a small gas burner kept burning for use in lighting a main burner when needed.

**pi·men·to** (pi men′tō) ***n.*** a kind of garden pepper or its sweet, red fruit, used as a relish, for stuffing olives, etc. —*pl.* **pi·men′tos**

**pi·mien·to** (pi myen′tō) ***n.*** *another spelling of* **pimento.** —*pl.* **pi·mien′tos**

**pim·per·nel** (pim′pər nel) ***n.*** a plant with scarlet or blue flowers that close in bad weather.

**pim·ple** (pim′p′l) ***n.*** a small swelling of the skin that is red and sore. —**pim′ply *adj.***

**pin** (pin) ***n.*** **1** a short piece of thin, stiff wire with a pointed end and a flat or round head, for fastening things together. **2** an ornament or badge with a pin or clasp for fastening it to the clothing [a fraternity *pin*]. **3** a small, thin rod of wood, metal, etc., used for fastening things together, hanging things on, etc. **4** *a shorter form of* **hairpin, safety pin, cotter pin,** etc. **5** any of the wooden clubs at which the ball is rolled in bowling. **6** *usually* **pins,** *pl.* the legs: *used only in everyday talk.* ◆***v.*** **1** to fasten as with a pin. **2** to hold firmly in one position [One wrestler *pinned* the other to the floor.] —**pinned, pin′ning** —**on pins and needles,** worried or anxious. —**pin someone down,** to get someone to tell what his or her real opinions, plans, etc. are. —**pin something on someone,** to put the blame for something on someone.

**pin·a·fore** (pin′ə fôr) ***n.*** **1** a garment without sleeves, like a kind of apron, worn by little girls over the dress. *See the picture.* **2** a housedress without sleeves, worn by women, usually over a blouse.

☆**pin·ball machine** (pin′bôl) a game machine with a slanting board on which there are many pins, springs, holes, etc. A ball is put in motion by a rod on a spring worked by the player. Each time the ball hits a pin, spring, etc., the machine records a score. The more hits that are made, the higher the total score.

**pince-nez** (pans′nā′ *or* pins′nā′) ***n.*** eyeglasses that are kept in place by a spring that grips the bridge of the nose. *See the picture.* —*pl.* **pince-nez** (pans′nāz′ *or* pins′nāz′)

**pin·cers** (pin′sərz) ***n.pl.*** **1** a tool with two handles and two jaws, used in gripping or nipping things. **2** a large claw of a crab, lobster, etc.

**pinch** (pinch) ***v.*** **1** to squeeze between a finger and the thumb or between two surfaces [He gently *pinched* the baby's cheek. She *pinched* her finger in the door.] **2** to nip off the end of [to *pinch* a plant shoot]. **3** to press upon in a painful way [These new shoes *pinch* my toes.] **4** to make look thin, gaunt, etc. [The illness had *pinched* her face.] **5** to be stingy or thrifty [We *pinched* and saved for years to buy our car.] **6** to steal: *slang in this meaning.* **7** to arrest: *slang in this meaning.* ◆***n.*** **1** a pinching; squeeze; nip [a *pinch* on the arm]. **2** the amount that can be picked up between the finger and thumb [a *pinch* of salt]. **3** hardship; difficulty [the *pinch* of poverty]. **4** an emergency [She will help us in a *pinch*.] **5** an arrest: *slang in this meaning.* —**pinch pennies,** to spend very little money or as little as possible.

**pinch·ers** (pin′chərz) ***n.pl.*** *another spelling of* **pincers.**

☆**pinch-hit** (pinch′hit′) ***v.*** **1** in baseball, to bat in place of the batter whose turn it is. **2** to take the place of, in an emergency. —**pinch′-hit′, pinch′-hit′ting** —**pinch′-hit′ter** ***n.***

**pin·cush·ion** (pin′ko͝osh′ən) ***n.*** a small cushion in which pins and needles are stuck to keep them handy.

**pine**[1] (pīn) ***n.*** **1** an evergreen tree with cones and clusters of leaves shaped like needles. **2** the wood of this tree, used in building.

**pine**[2] (pīn) ***v.*** **1** to become thin or weak through grief, pain, longing, etc. [The jilted lover *pined* away.] **2** to have a strong longing; yearn [to *pine* for the old days]. —**pined, pin′ing**

> **Pine**[2] comes from the Latin word for "punishment." When we pine away because of grief, pain, or longing, we are punishing ourselves.

**pine·ap·ple** (pīn′ap′'l) ***n.*** **1** a juicy tropical fruit that looks a little like a large pine cone. **2** the plant it grows on, having a short stem and curved leaves with prickly edges. *See the picture.*

**pin·ey** (pī′nē) ***adj.*** **1** having many pines [a *piney* woods]. **2** of pines or smelling like pines.

**pin·feath·er** (pin′feth′ər) ***n.*** a feather that has just started to grow through the skin.

**ping** (piŋ) ***n.*** a sharp sound, as that made by a bullet striking, an engine knocking, etc. ◆***v.*** to make such a sound.

**Ping-Pong** (piŋ′pôŋ′) *a trademark for* equipment to be used for the game of **table tennis.**

**pin·head** (pin′hed) ***n.*** **1** the head of a pin. ☆**2** a stupid or silly person.

**pin·hole** (pin′hōl) ***n.*** a tiny hole that might be made by a pin.

**pin·ion**[1] (pin′yən) ***n.*** a small gearwheel which meshes with a larger gearwheel or a rack.

**pin·ion**[2] (pin′yən) ***n.*** **1** the end joint of a bird's wing. **2** a bird's wing. **3** any wing feather. ◆***v.*** **1** to cut off a pinion of a bird or bind its wings, to keep it from flying. **2** to bind the arms to keep a person from moving them.

**pink**[1] (piŋk) ***n.*** **1** a plant with white, pink, or red flowers, often smelling like cloves. **2** pale red. ◆***adj.*** pale-red. —**in the pink,** in very good condition; in fine form: *used only in everyday talk.* —**pink′ish** ***adj.*** —**pink′ness** ***n.***

**pink**[2] (piŋk) ***v.*** **1** to cut cloth with special shears (called **pinking shears**) so that it has a toothed edge, to keep it from unraveling or for decoration. *See the picture.* **2** to decorate with small holes in a pattern. **3** to prick, as with a sword.

**pink·eye** (piŋk′ī) ***n.*** a disease in which the lining of the eyelid becomes red and sore.

**pink·ie** or **pink·y** (piŋ′kē) ***n.*** the smallest finger. —*pl.* **pink′ies**

**pin money** a small sum of money set aside for minor personal expenses.

**pin·na·cle** (pin′ə k'l) ***n.*** **1** a pointed top, as of a mountain; high peak. **2** the highest point [the *pinnacle* of success]. **3** a slender, pointed tower or steeple.

**pin·nate** (pin′āt) ***adj.*** **1** like a feather. **2** with leaflets on each side of the stem [Hickory leaves are *pinnate.*]

☆**pi·noch·le** or **pi·noc·le** (pē′nuk''l *or* pē′näk''l) ***n.*** a game of cards played with a deck of 48 cards, made up of two of every card above the eight.

☆**pi·ñon** (pin′yən *or* pin′yōn) ***n.*** **1** a small pine with large seeds, found in western North America. **2** the seed, which can be eaten.

**pin·point** (pin′point) ***v.*** to show the exact location of something, as on a map.

☆**pin·set·ter** (pin′set′ər) ***n.*** **1** a person who sets up the pins after each frame of bowling and returns the ball to the bowler. **2** a device for doing this automatically.

**pin stripe** **1** a very narrow stripe, as in the fabric of some suits. **2** a pattern of such stripes parallel to one another.



**pint** (pīnt) ***n.*** a measure of volume equal to 1/2 quart [a *pint* of milk; a *pint* of berries].

☆**pin·to** (pin′tō) ***adj.*** marked with patches of two or more colors. ◆***n.*** a pinto horse or pony. —*pl.* **pin′tos**

> A **pinto** is sometimes called a "paint," perhaps because **pinto,** the Spanish word for "spotted," is related to the Portuguese word for "paint." A pinto has patches or spots of color that look as though they may have been painted on the horse's coat.

**pin·up** (pin′up) ***adj.*** that can be fastened to a wall [a *pinup* lamp; a *pinup* picture].

**pin·wale** (pin′wāl) ***adj.*** having fine wales, or narrow ridges, as some corduroy.

**pin·wheel** (pin′hwēl) ***n.*** **1** a small wheel made of pieces of paper, plastic, etc., pinned to a stick so that it spins in the wind. **2** a firework that spins and sends off colored lights.

**pi·o·neer** (pī′ə nir′) ***n.*** ☆a person who goes before, opening up the way for others to follow, as an early settler or a scientist doing original work [Daniel Boone was a *pioneer* in Kentucky. Marie Curie was a *pioneer* in the study of radium.] ◆***v.*** to act as a pioneer; open up the way for others [The Wright brothers *pioneered* in air travel.]

| | | | | | | | |
|---|---|---|---|---|---|---|---|
| **a** | fat | **ir** | here | **ou** | out | **zh** | leisure |
| **ā** | ape | **ī** | bite, fire | **u** | up | **ŋ** | ring |
| **ä** | car, lot | **ō** | go | **ʉr** | fur | | a *in* ago |
| **e** | ten | **ô** | law, horn | **ch** | chin | | e *in* agent |
| **er** | care | **oi** | oil | **sh** | she | **ə =** | i *in* unity |
| **ē** | even | **oo** | look | **th** | thin | | o *in* collect |
| **i** | hit | **o͞o** | tool | ***th*** | then | | u *in* focus |

**pi·ous** (pī'əs) ***adj.*** very devoted in following one's religion. —**pi'ous·ly *adv.*** —**pi'ous·ness *n.***

SYNONYMS: **Pious** suggests a careful sticking to the forms of one's religion, but may also suggest that the person is only pretending or has little deep feeling. **Devout** suggests sincere, worshipful devotion to one's faith or religion.

**pip**[1] (pip) ***n.*** a small seed, as of an apple.

**pip**[2] (pip) ***n.*** a disease of chickens or other birds.

**pipe** (pīp) ***n.*** **1** a long tube of metal, concrete, etc. through which water, gas, oil, etc. can flow. **2** a tube with a small bowl at one end in which tobacco is smoked. **3** a wooden or metal tube through which air is blown for making musical sounds; often, one of a set of such tubes in an organ. **4 pipes,** *pl. a shorter word for* **bagpipe. 5** the call or note of a bird. ◆***v.*** **1** to play on a pipe. **2** to speak or sing in a high, shrill voice ["Good morning," *piped* the children.] ☆**3** to move from one place to another by means of pipes [to *pipe* oil from Alaska]. ☆**4** to put pipes in. —**piped, pip'ing** —**pipe down,** to stop shouting or talking: *a slang phrase.*

☆**pipe·line** (pīp'līn) ***n.*** a long line of connected pipes for moving water, gas, oil, etc.

**pip·er** (pīp'ər) ***n.*** a person who plays on a pipe, especially on a bagpipe.

**pip·ing** (pīp'iŋ) ***n.*** **1** music made by pipes. **2** a high, shrill sound. **3** a cord or narrow fold of cloth used to trim edges or seams. **4** pipes or the material for pipes. ◆***adj.*** sounding high and shrill [a *piping* voice]. ◆***adv.*** so as to sizzle [*piping* hot].

**pip·pin** (pip'in) ***n.*** any of several kinds of apple.

**pip·squeak** (pip'skwēk) ***n.*** any person or thing thought of as small or unimportant: *used only in everyday talk.*

**pi·quant** (pē'kənt) ***adj.*** **1** sharp or spicy in a pleasant way [a *piquant* sauce]. **2** arousing interest or curiosity [a *piquant* remark]. —**pi·quan·cy** (pē'kən sē) ***n.***

**pique**[1] (pēk) ***n.*** hurt feelings caused by being insulted, ignored, etc.; resentment [her *pique* at not being invited]. ◆***v.*** **1** to hurt the feelings of or make resentful [His rudeness *piqued* her.] **2** to arouse or excite [to *pique* one's curiosity]. —**piqued, piqu'ing**

**pi·qué** or **pi·que**[2] (pē kā') ***n.*** a firmly woven cotton cloth with ribs or cords along the length.

**pi·ra·cy** (pī'rə sē) ***n.*** **1** the robbing of ships on the ocean. **2** the use of a copyrighted or patented work without permission. —*pl.* **pi'ra·cies**

**pi·ra·nha** (pi rän'yə) ***n.*** a tiny, fiercely hungry, freshwater fish of South America. In schools, it will attack any animal, including human beings.

**pi·rate** (pī'rət) ***n.*** a person who attacks and robs ships on the ocean. ◆***v.*** to use a copyrighted or patented work without permission of the person who holds the copyright or patent. —**pi'rat·ed, pi'rat·ing** —**pi·rat·i·cal** (pī rat'i k'l) ***adj.***

**pi·ro·gi** (pi rō'gē) ***n.pl.*** small pastry turnovers with a filling, as of meat, cheese, mashed potatoes, etc.: also **pi·rosh·ki** (pi räsh'kē).

**pir·ou·ette** (pir'oo wet') ***n.*** a whirling on the toes in dancing. ◆***v.*** to do a pirouette. —**pir'ou·et'ted, pir'ou·et'ting**

**Pirouette** is a French word that means "a spinning top." A ballet dancer doing a pirouette somewhat resembles one of these spinning toys.

**Pi·sa** (pē'zə) a city in northwestern Italy. It is famous for its Leaning Tower.

**Pis·ces** (pī'sēz *or* pis'ēz) the twelfth sign of the zodiac, for the period from February 20 to March 20: *also called* the Fishes. *See the picture for* **zodiac.**

**pis·ta·chi·o** (pi stä'shē ō *or* pi stash'ē ō) ***n.*** **1** a sweet, greenish nut. **2** the tree it grows on. **3** the flavor of this nut. **4** a light yellowish green. —*pl.* **pis·ta'chi·os**

**pis·til** (pis't'l) ***n.*** the part of a flower in which the seeds grow. *See the picture.* A single pistil is made up of a stigma, style, and ovary. *See also* **carpel.**

**pis·til·late** (pis'tə lit) ***adj.*** having a pistil or pistils, but no stamen.

**pis·tol** (pis't'l) ***n.*** a small gun held and fired in one hand.

**Pistol** comes from a Czech word that originally meant "pipe," perhaps because the barrel of a pistol looks like a pipe.

**pis·ton** (pis't'n) ***n.*** a disk or short cylinder that moves back and forth in a hollow cylinder in which it fits closely. In a water pump, the piston pushes against the water; in a steam engine, the steam pushes against the piston. *See the picture.*

**piston ring** a metal ring around a piston to make it fit the cylinder closely.

**piston rod** a rod fastened to a piston so as to move it or be moved by it.

☆**pit**[1] (pit) ***n.*** the hard stone in the center of a peach, plum, cherry, etc. that holds the seed. ◆***v.*** to take the pit from. —**pit'ted, pit'ting**

**pit**[2] (pit) ***n.*** **1** a hole in the ground, especially one dug deep, as the shaft of a coal mine. **2** a small hollow on a surface, as a scar on the body. **3** a hole covered lightly to catch wild animals that fall into it. **4** a place in which animals are made to fight. **5** the section where the orchestra sits in front of the stage. It is often lower than the main floor. **6** a place off the side of a speedway for servicing racing cars. ◆***v.*** **1** to make pits or scars in [iron *pitted* by rust]. **2** to match or set up against [Which team is *pitted* against ours?] —**pit'ted, pit'ting**

**pitch**[1] (pich) ***n.*** **1** a black, sticky substance formed from coal tar, petroleum, etc. and used to cover roofs, pave streets, etc. **2** a sticky substance found in certain evergreen trees.

pitchfork

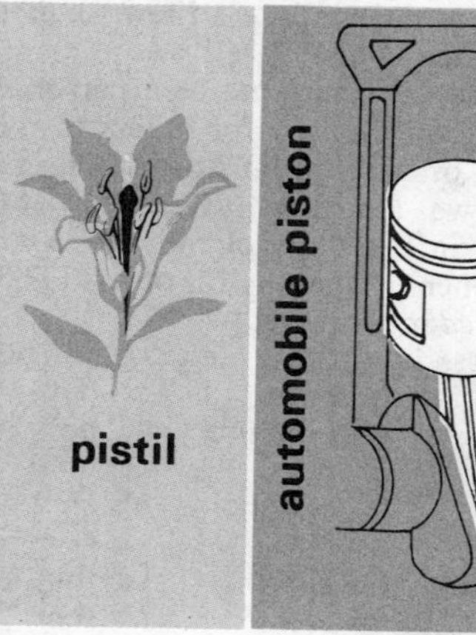

pistil

automobile piston

**pitch²** (pich) ***v.*** **1** to throw or toss [*Pitch* the newspaper on the porch.] ☆**2** in baseball, to throw the ball to the batter. ☆**3** in baseball, to serve as pitcher for [to *pitch* a game]. **4** to set up; make ready for use [to *pitch* a tent]. **5** to fall forward or head first. **6** to slope downward [The roof *pitches* sharply.] **7** to be tossed so that the bow rises and falls rapidly, as a ship in a storm. **8** to be tossed in this way in the air, as an airplane in a storm. **9** to choose a musical key for [You *pitched* the song too high for my voice.] ◆***n.*** **1** a pitching or a way of pitching [a fast *pitch*]. **2** anything pitched or thrown [The wild *pitch* hit the batter.] **3** a certain level, point, or degree [Our excitement was at a high *pitch*.] **4** the amount by which something slopes down [a roof with a steep *pitch*]. **5** the highness or lowness of a musical sound [Some notes have a *pitch* too high for human ears to hear.] ☆**6** a line of talk, such as a salesperson uses to persuade customers: *slang in this meaning.* —**make a pitch for,** to speak in favor of: *slang in this meaning.*—**pitch in,** **1** to begin working hard. **2** to give one's share. *This phrase is used only in everyday talk.* —**pitch into,** to attack: *used only in everyday talk.*

**pitch-black** (pich′blak′) ***adj.*** very black.

**pitch·blende** (pich′blend) ***n.*** a dark brown to black mineral containing radium, uranium, etc.

**pitch·er¹** (pich′ər) ***n.*** **1** a container for holding and pouring water, milk, etc., usually with a handle and a lip for pouring. **2** as much as a pitcher will hold.

**pitch·er²** (pich′ər) ***n.*** the baseball player who pitches the ball to the batters.

**pitcher plant** a plant with leaves that attract and trap insects.

**pitch·fork** (pich′fôrk) ***n.*** a large fork with a long handle, for lifting and tossing hay, etc. *See the picture.*

**pitch pipe** a small metal pipe that sounds a fixed tone to help in tuning a musical instrument or in finding the right pitch.

**pit·e·ous** (pit′ē əs) ***adj.*** causing or deserving pity [*piteous* groans]. —**pit′e·ous·ly** ***adv.***

**pit·fall** (pit′fôl) ***n.*** **1** a pit for trapping animals. **2** any hidden danger.

**pith** (pith) ***n.*** **1** the soft, spongy tissue in the center of some plant stems. **2** the soft center of other things, as of a bone or feather. **3** the spongy fiber lining the rind and around the sections of an orange, grapefruit, etc. **4** the important or necessary part; core.

**pith·y** (pith′ē) ***adj.*** **1** of, like, or full of pith [The orange was too *pithy*.] **2** short and full of meaning or force [a *pithy* saying]. —**pith′i·er, pith′i·est**

**pit·i·a·ble** (pit′ē ə b′l) ***adj.*** causing or deserving pity, sometimes mixed with scorn or contempt [his *pitiable* attempts to be witty]. —**pit′i·a·bly** ***adv.***

**pit·i·ful** (pit′i fəl) ***adj.*** **1** causing or deserving pity [the *pitiful* sobs of the lost child]. **2** causing or deserving contempt or scorn [What a *pitiful* repair job!] —**pit′i·ful·ly** ***adv.***

**pit·i·less** (pit′i lis) ***adj.*** having or showing no pity; cruel. —**pit′i·less·ly** ***adv.***

**pit·tance** (pit′əns) ***n.*** a small amount or share, especially of money.

**pit·ter-pat·ter** (pit′ər pat′ər) ***n.*** a series of light, tapping sounds, as of raindrops.

**Pitts·burgh** (pits′burg) a city in southwestern Pennsylvania.

**pi·tu·i·tar·y** (pi to͞o′ə ter′ē *or* pi tyo͞o′ə ter′ē) ***adj.*** describing or having to do with a small, oval gland at the base of the brain: it gives off hormones which control the body's growth. ◆***n.*** this gland. —*pl.* **pi·tu′i·tar′ies**

**pit·y** (pit′ē) ***n.*** **1** a feeling of sorrow for another's suffering or trouble; sympathy. **2** a cause for sorrow or regret [It's a *pity* that you weren't there.] —*pl.* **pit′ies** ◆***v.*** to feel pity for. —**pit′ied, pit′y·ing** —**have pity on** or **take pity on,** to show pity for.

> SYNONYMS: **Pity** means sorrow felt for another's suffering or bad luck, sometimes hinting at slight contempt because one feels the person being pitied is weak or lower in some way [We felt *pity* for a group so ignorant.] **Compassion** means pity along with an urge to help [Moved by *compassion,* he did not ask for the money they owed him.] **Sympathy** implies such closeness of feeling that one really understands and even shares the sorrow or bad luck of another [He always turned to his wife for *sympathy*.]

**piv·ot** (piv′ət) ***n.*** **1** a point, pin, or rod upon which something turns [A swinging door turns on a *pivot*.] **2** a person or thing on which something depends [This point is the *pivot* of her argument.] **3** a movement made as if turning on a pivot [The soldiers made a quick *pivot* at the corner.] ◆***v.*** **1** to turn as on a pivot [The dancer *pivoted* on one toe.] **2** to furnish with or mount on a pivot.

**piv·ot·al** (piv′ət ′l) ***adj.*** **1** of or acting as a pivot. **2** very important because much depends on it [a *pivotal* battle in the war].



**pix·ie** or **pix·y** (pik′sē) ***n.*** a fairy or elf, especially one that is full of mischief. —*pl.* **pix′ies**

☆**pi·zazz** or **piz·zazz** (pə zaz′) ***n.*** **1** energy, vigor, spirit, etc. **2** style, sparkle, smartness, etc. *This word is slang.*

☆**piz·za** (pēt′sə) ***n.*** an Italian dish made by baking a thin layer of dough covered with tomatoes, spices, cheese, etc.

☆**piz·ze·ri·a** (pēt′sə rē′ə) ***n.*** a place where pizzas are prepared and sold.

**piz·zi·ca·to** (pit′sə kät′ō) ***adj.*** plucked. This is an Italian word used in music to show when the strings of a violin, viola, etc. should be plucked.

☆**pj's** (pē′jāz′) ***n.pl.*** pajamas: *used only in everyday talk.*

**pk.** *abbreviation for* **park, peak, peck.** —*pl.* **pks.**

**pkg.** *abbreviation for* **package** *or* **packages.**

**Pkwy.** or **pkwy.** *abbreviation for* **parkway.**

**pl.** *abbreviation for* **plural.**

**plac·ard** (plak′ärd) ***n.*** a poster or sign put up in a public place. ◆***v.*** to put placards on or in.

**pla·cate** (plā′kāt *or* plak′āt) ***v.*** to stop from being angry; make peaceful; soothe. —**pla′cat·ed, pla′cat·ing**

| | | | |
|---|---|---|---|
| **a** fat | **ir** here | **ou** out | **zh** leisure |
| **ā** ape | **ī** bite, fire | **u** up | **ng** ring |
| **ä** car, lot | **ō** go | **ur** fur | a *in* ago |
| **e** ten | **ô** law, horn | **ch** chin | e *in* agent |
| **er** care | **oi** oil | **sh** she | **ə** = i *in* unity |
| **ē** even | **oo** look | **th** thin | o *in* collect |
| **i** hit | **o͞o** tool | ***th*** then | u *in* focus |

**place** (plās) ***n.*** **1** a space taken up or used by a person or thing [Please take your *places.*] **2** a city, town, or village. **3** a house, apartment, etc. where one lives [Visit me at my *place.*] **4** a building or space set aside for a certain purpose [a *place* of amusement]. **5** a certain point, part, or position [a sore *place* on the leg; an important *place* in history]. **6** rank or position, especially in a series [I finished the race in fifth *place.*] **7** the usual or proper time or position [This is not the *place* for loud talking.] **8** condition or situation [What would you do in my *place?*] **9** a position or job [Lou's new *place* at the bank.] **10** the duties of any position or job [It is the judge's *place* to instruct the jury.] **11** a short city street. ◆***v.*** **1** to put in a certain place, position, etc. [*Place* the pencil on the desk.] **2** to put or let rest [She *placed* her trust in God.] ☆**3** to recognize by connecting with some time, place, or happening [I can't *place* that person's voice.] **4** to finish in a certain position in a contest [Lynn *placed* sixth in the race.] —**placed, plac′ing** —**give place, 1** to make room. **2** to yield. —**in place of,** instead of; rather than. —**take place,** to come into being; happen; occur. —**take the place of,** to be a substitute for. —**place′ment** ***n.***

**place kick** a kick made in football while the ball is held in place on the ground, as in trying to make a field goal.

**place mat** a small mat that serves as a separate table
558 cover for a person at a meal.

☆**plac·er** (plas′ər) ***n.*** a deposit of sand or gravel containing bits of gold, platinum, etc., that can be washed out.

**plac·id** (plas′id) ***adj.*** calm and quiet; peaceful [a *placid* brook; a *placid* child]. —**pla·cid·i·ty** (plə sid′ə tē) ***n.*** —**plac′id·ly** ***adv.***

**plack·et** (plak′it) ***n.*** a slit at the waist of a skirt or dress to make it easy to put on or take off. *See the picture.*

**pla·gia·rize** (plā′jə rīz) ***v.*** to take ideas or writings from someone else and present them as one's own. —**pla′gia·rized, pla′gia·riz·ing** —**pla·gia·rism** (plā′jə riz'm) ***n.*** —**pla′gia·rist** ***n.***

**plague** (plāg) ***n.*** **1** a deadly disease that spreads rapidly from person to person; especially, the bubonic plague. **2** anything that causes suffering or trouble [a *plague* of mosquitoes]. ◆***v.*** to trouble or make suffer [As a child, she was *plagued* with illness.] —**plagued, plagu′ing**

**plaid** (plad) ***n.*** **1** a checkered pattern formed by colored bands and lines crossing each other. *See the picture.* **2** cloth with this pattern, especially a long woolen cloth worn over the shoulder in the Highlands of Scotland.

**plain** (plān) ***adj.*** **1** open; clear; not blocked [in *plain* view]. **2** easy to understand; clear to the mind [The meaning is *plain.*] **3** without holding back what one thinks; frank [*plain* talk]. **4** without luxury [a *plain* way of life]. **5** simple; easy [I can do a little *plain* cooking.] **6** not good-looking; homely. **7** not fancy; not much decorated [a *plain* necktie]. **8** common; ordinary [a *plain* workman]. ◆***n.*** a large stretch of flat land. ◆***adv.*** clearly or simply [just *plain* tired]. —**plain′ly** ***adv.*** —**plain′ness** ***n.***

☆**plains·man** (plānz′mən) ***n.*** a person who lives on the plains. —*pl.* **plains′men**

**plain-spo·ken** (plān′spō′k'n) ***adj.*** speaking or spoken in a plain or frank way.

**plaint** (plānt) ***n.*** **1** a complaint. **2** a wail of sorrow; lament: *used in earlier poetry.*

**plain·tiff** (plān′tif) ***n.*** the person who starts a suit against another in a court of law.

**plain·tive** (plān′tiv) ***adj.*** sad or full of sorrow; mournful. —**plain′tive·ly** ***adv.***

**plait** (plāt *or* plat) ***n.*** **1** a braid of hair, ribbon, etc. **2** *another spelling of* **pleat.** ◆***v.*** **1** to braid. **2** *another spelling of* **pleat.**

**plan** (plan) ***n.*** **1** a method or way of doing something, that has been thought out ahead of time [vacation *plans*]. **2** a drawing that shows how the parts of a building or piece of ground are arranged [floor *plans* of a house; a *plan* of the battlefield]. ◆***v.*** **1** to think out a way of making or doing something [They *planned* their escape carefully.] **2** to make a drawing or diagram of beforehand [An architect is *planning* our new school.] **3** to have in mind; intend [I *plan* to visit Hawaii soon.] —**planned, plan′ning**

**plane**[1] (plān) ***n.*** a large tree with broad leaves much like maple leaves, and bark that comes off in large patches: *also called* **plane tree.**

**plane**[2] (plān) ***adj.*** **1** flat; level; even. **2** of or having to do with flat surfaces or points, lines, etc. on them [*plane* geometry]. ◆***n.*** **1** a flat, level surface. **2** a level or stage of growth or progress. **3** *a shorter form of* **airplane.**

**plane**[3] (plān) ***n.*** a tool used by carpenters for shaving wood in order to make it smooth or level. *See the picture.* ◆***v.*** **1** to make smooth or level with a plane. **2** to take off part of, as with a plane [to *plane* off the top of a door]. —**planed, plan′ing**

**plan·et** (plan′it) ***n.*** any of the large heavenly bodies that revolve around the sun and shine as they reflect the sun's light. The planets, in their order from the sun, are Mercury, Venus, Earth, Mars, Jupiter, Saturn, Uranus, Neptune, and Pluto. —**plan·e·tar·y** (plan′ə ter′ē) ***adj.***

> **Planet** comes from the Greek word for "wanderer." *Planet* originally meant any of the heavenly bodies that seemed to move or "wander," compared to the stars that seemed to stay always in the same place as seen from the earth.

**plan·e·tar·i·um** (plan′ə ter′ē əm) ***n.*** a room with a large dome ceiling on which images of the heavens are cast by a special projector. The natural movements of the sun, moon, planets, and stars can be shown in these images.

**plank** (plangk) ***n.*** **1** a long, wide, thick board. ☆**2** any of the main points in the platform of a political party. ◆***v.*** **1** to cover with planks [to *plank* the deck of a sailboat]. ☆**2** to broil and serve on a plank, as steak. —**plank down, 1** to lay or set down firmly. ☆**2** to pay [to *plank down* $10.00 for a dinner]. *This phrase is used only in everyday talk.* —**walk the plank,** to walk blindfold off a plank sticking out from the side of a ship, and be drowned. Pirates often forced their victims to do this.

**plank·ton** (plangk′tən) ***n.*** the mass of tiny plants and animal life found floating in a body of water, used as food by fish.

**plant** (plant) ***n.*** **1** any living thing that cannot move about by itself, has no sense organs, and usually makes its own food by photosynthesis [Trees, shrubs, and vegetables are *plants.*] **2** a plant with a soft stem, thought of as different from a tree or a shrub [Ivy, grass, and mushrooms are *plants.*] **3** the machinery, buildings, etc. of a factory or business. **4** a factory. ◆***v.*** **1** to put into the ground so that it will grow [to *plant* corn]. **2** to place plants in a piece of land, or fish in a body of water; stock [to *plant* a garden; to *plant* trout in a pond]. **3** to set firmly in place [*Plant* both feet squarely on the ground.] **4** to put or fix in the mind; instill [to *plant* an idea]. **5** to establish or found [to *plant* a colony].

**plan·tain**[1] (plan′tin) ***n.*** a common weed with broad leaves and spikes of tiny, green flowers. *See the picture.*

**plan·tain**[2] (plan′tin) ***n.*** **1** a tropical banana plant bearing a kind of fruit eaten as a cooked vegetable. **2** this fruit.

**plan·ta·tion** (plan tā′shən) ***n.*** **1** a large estate, usually in a warm climate, on which crops are grown by workers who live on the estate [a coffee *plantation* in Brazil]. **2** a large group of trees planted for their product [a rubber *plantation*].

**plant·er** (plan′tər) ***n.*** ☆**1** the owner of a plantation. **2** a person or machine that plants. **3** a decorated container in which house plants are grown.

**plaque** (plak) ***n.*** **1** a thin, flat piece of metal, wood, etc. with decoration or lettering on it. Plaques are hung on walls, set in monuments, etc. **2** a thin film that forms on the teeth. It hardens into tartar if it is not removed.

**plash** (plash) ***n., v.*** *another word for* **splash.**

**plas·ma** (plaz′mə) ***n.*** the fluid part of blood, without the corpuscles; also, the fluid part of lymph.

**plas·ter** (plas′tər) ***n.*** **1** a pasty mixture of lime, sand, and water, used for coating walls, ceilings, etc. It becomes hard when it dries. **2** a soft, sticky substance spread on cloth and put on the body as a medicine [a mustard *plaster*]. **3** *same as* **plaster of Paris.** ◆***v.*** **1** to cover with or as with plaster [to *plaster* walls; to *plaster* one's hair down with hair oil]. **2** to put on like a plaster [to *plaster* posters on a wall]. —**plas′ter·er** ***n.*** —**plas′ter·ing** ***n.***

☆**plas·ter·board** (plas′tər bôrd) ***n.*** a board made of layers of plaster and paper, used for walls.

**plaster of Paris** a thick paste of gypsum and water that hardens quickly. It is used to make statues, casts for broken bones, etc.

**plas·tic** (plas′tik) ***adj.*** **1** that can be shaped or molded [Clay is a *plastic* material.] **2** that gives form or shape to matter [Sculpture is a *plastic* art.] **3** made of plastic [a *plastic* comb]. ◆***n.*** a substance, made from various chemicals, that can be molded and hardened into many useful products. —**plas·tic·i·ty** (plas tis′ə tē) ***n.***

**Plas·ti·cine** (plas′tə sēn) *a trademark for* a pasty substance used for modeling, as wax or clay is used.

**plastic surgery** surgery in which injured parts of the body are repaired, usually by grafting on skin, bone, etc. from other places.

**plat** (plat) ***n.*** **1** a map or plan. **2** a small piece of ground. ◆***v.*** to make a map or plan of. —**plat′ted, plat′ting**

plantain

plaid

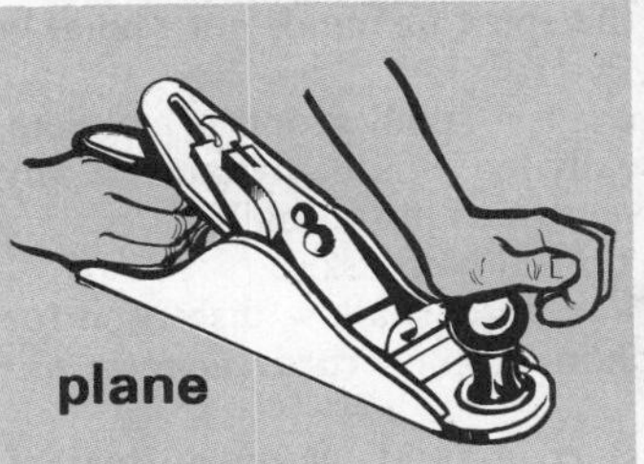
plane

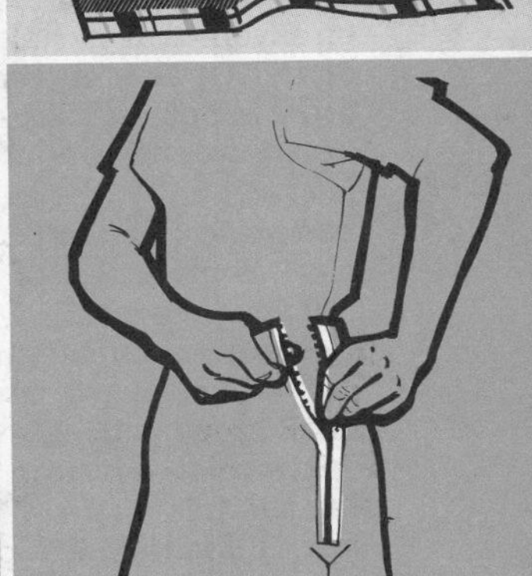
placket

**plate** (plāt) ***n.*** **1** a shallow dish from which food is eaten. **2** the food in a dish or course [Did you finish your *plate?*] **3** a meal for one person [lunch at $3 a *plate*]. **4** dishes, knives, forks, spoons, etc. made of, or coated with, silver or gold. **5** a flat, thin piece of metal, etc., especially one on which something is engraved. **6** an illustration printed from such a plate. **7** a thin, flat or curved piece of metal or other material from which a page is printed on a press. **8** a sheet of metal used on boilers, as armor on ships, etc. **9** a thin layer of bony or horny tissue that forms part of the covering of some reptiles, fish, etc. **10** a thin cut of beef from the breast, near the brisket. ☆**11** in baseball, *same as* **home plate. 12** a set of false teeth. **13** a sheet of glass, metal, etc. coated with a film sensitive to light. It is used in taking photographs. ◆***v.*** **1** to coat with gold, tin, silver, etc. **2** to cover with metal plates, as for armor. —**plat′ed, plat′ing**



**pla·teau** (pla tō′) ***n.*** **1** a broad stretch of high, level land. **2** a period in which progress stops for a while [to reach a *plateau* in learning]. —*pl.* **pla·teaus′**

**plate·ful** (plāt′fool) ***n.*** as much as a plate will hold [I ate a *plateful* of spaghetti.] —*pl.* **plate′fuls**

**plate glass** polished, clear glass in thick sheets, used for large windows, mirrors, etc.

**plat·en** (plat′'n) ***n.*** the roller in a typewriter, against which the keys strike the paper.

**plat·form** (plat′fôrm) ***n.*** **1** a flat surface or stage higher than the ground or floor around it [a *platform* at a railroad station; a speaker's *platform*]. ☆**2** all the plans and principles that a political party says it stands for. ◆***adj.*** describing a shoe with a thick sole, as of cork or leather.

| | | | | | | | |
|---|---|---|---|---|---|---|---|
| **a** | fat | **ir** | here | **ou** | out | **zh** | leisure |
| **ā** | ape | **ī** | bite, fire | **u** | up | **ng** | ring |
| **ä** | car, lot | **ō** | go | **ur** | fur | | a *in* ago |
| **e** | ten | **ô** | law, horn | **ch** | chin | | e *in* agent |
| **er** | care | **oi** | oil | **sh** | she | **ə** = | i *in* unity |
| **ē** | even | **oo** | look | **th** | thin | | o *in* collect |
| **i** | hit | **ōō** | tool | ***th*** | then | | u *in* focus |

**plat·i·num** (plat′'n əm) ***n.*** a white precious metal that is a chemical element. Platinum is easily hammered or bent and does not rust much. It has many important uses in science and industry and is also much used in jewelry.

**plat·i·tude** (plat′ə to͞od *or* plat′ə tyo͞od) ***n.*** a thought or saying that is stale and worn from use, especially one given as if it were new. ["Money doesn't always bring happiness" is a *platitude.*]

**Pla·to** (plā′tō) about 427–347 B.C.; Greek philosopher.

**Pla·ton·ic** (plə tän′ik) ***adj.*** **1** of Plato or his philosophy. **2 platonic,** of the spirit or mind, not sexual [a *platonic* friendship].

**pla·toon** (plə to͞on′) ***n.*** **1** a small group of soldiers, part of a company, usually led by a lieutenant. **2** any small group [a defensive *platoon* in football].

**Platte** (plat) a river in central Nebraska.

**plat·ter** (plat′ər) ***n.*** **1** a large, shallow dish used for serving food. ☆**2** a phonograph record: *slang in this meaning.*

**plat·y·pus** (plat′ə pəs) ***n.*** a small water animal of Australia that has webbed feet, a tail like a beaver's, and a bill like a duck's. It lays eggs, but suckles its young. *Also called* **duckbill** *or* **duckbill platypus.** *See the picture.* —*pl.* **plat′y·pus·es** or **plat·y·pi** (plat′ə pī′)

560 The platypus is a peculiar creature in many ways, but it is the strange webbed feet that give it its name. **Platypus** comes from the Greek word for "flatfooted." In Greek, *platys* means "flat," and *pous* is "foot."

**plau·dit** (plô′dit) ***n.*** a strong show of approval or praise, as by a clapping of hands or cheering: *usually used in the plural,* **plaudits** [The heroine received the *plaudits* of the crowd.]

**plau·si·ble** (plô′zə b'l) ***adj.*** that seems to be true, honest, fair, etc. but may not be [a *plausible* excuse]. —**plau·si·bil·i·ty** (plô′zə bil′ə tē) ***n.***

**play** (plā) ***v.*** **1** to have fun; amuse oneself [children *playing* in the sand]. **2** to do in fun [to *play* a joke on a friend]. **3** to take part in a game or sport [to *play* golf]. **4** to take part in a game against [We *played* West High tonight.] **5** to be at a certain position in a game [Who's *playing* shortstop?] **6** to perform music on [He *plays* the piano.] **7** to give out sounds: said of a phonograph, tape recorder, etc. **8** to perform or be performed [What is *playing* at the movies? The orchestra *played* well.] **9** to act the part of [Who *plays* Hamlet?] **10** to handle in a light or careless way; trifle; toy [She merely *played* with her food.] **11** to act in a certain way [to *play* fair; to *play* dumb]. **12** to move quickly or lightly [A smile *played* across his face.] **13** to make move or keep moving [to *play* a stream of water on a fire; to *play* a fish on a line]. **14** to cause [The storm *played* havoc with our plans.] **15** to bet or gamble on [to *play* the horses]. ◆***n.*** **1** something done just for fun or to amuse oneself; recreation [She has little time for *play.*] **2** fun; joking [Jan said it in *play.*] **3** the playing of a game [Rain halted *play.*] **4** a move or act in a game [It's your *play.* The long forward pass is an exciting *play.*] **5** a story that is acted out, as on a stage, on radio or television, etc.; drama. **6** movement or action, especially when quick and light [bringing his full strength into *play;* the *play* of sunlight on the waves]. **7** freedom of movement or action [This steering wheel has too much *play.*] —**play down,** to make seem not too important. —**played out, 1** tired out; exhausted. **2** finished. —**play into someone's hands,** to let another get an advantage over one, by doing the wrong things. —**play off, 1** to set one against another, as in a fight or contest. ☆**2** to break a tie by playing one more game. —**play on,** to make clever use of another's feelings in order to get what one wants [He's *playing on* our sympathy.] —**play out, 1** to play to the finish; end. **2** to let out little by little, as a rope; pay out. —☆**play up,** to give special attention to; emphasize: *used only in everyday talk.* —**play up to,** to flatter: *used only in everyday talk.*

**play·er** (plā′ər) ***n.*** **1** a person who plays a game or a musical instrument [a baseball *player;* a trumpet *player*]. **2** an actor or actress. ☆**3** a device that gives out sound [a record *player*].

**play·ful** (plā′fəl) ***adj.*** **1** fond of play or fun; lively; frisky [a *playful* puppy]. **2** said or done in fun; joking [She gave her brother a *playful* shove.] —**play′ful·ly** ***adv.*** —**play′ful·ness** ***n.***

**play·ground** (plā′ground) ***n.*** a place, often near a school, for outdoor games and play.

☆**play hook·y** (plā′ ho͝ok′ē) to stay away from school without permission; be a truant.

**Hooky** is thought to come from a Dutch word *hoeckje,* that means "hide-and-seek." When students play hooky, they try to stay out of sight of those who would make them return to school, as though they were playing hide-and-seek.

**play·house** (plā′hous) ***n.*** ☆**1** a small house for children to play in. **2** a theater.

**playing cards** a set of cards used in playing a number of games. They are arranged in four suits: clubs, diamonds, hearts, and spades. The deck used for most games has 52 cards.

**play·mate** (plā′māt) ***n.*** a child who joins with another in playing games and having fun.

**play-off** (plā′ôf′) ***n.*** a game or one of a series of games played to break a tie or decide who is champion.

**play·pen** (plā′pen) ***n.*** a small, enclosed place in which a baby can be left safely to crawl, play, etc.

**play·thing** (plā′thing) ***n.*** a thing to play with; toy.

**play·wright** (plā′rīt) ***n.*** a person who writes plays; dramatist.

**pla·za** (plä′zə *or* plaz′ə) ***n.*** **1** a public square in a city or town. **2** *another name for* **shopping center. 3** a place along a superhighway with a restaurant, service station, etc.: *also* **service plaza.**

**plea** (plē) ***n.*** **1** the act of asking for help; appeal [a *plea* for mercy]. **2** something said to defend oneself; excuse [Illness was his *plea* for being absent.] **3** the answer by a defendant in a law case to a charge of having done wrong or broken the law [a *plea* of not guilty].

**plead** (plēd) ***v.*** **1** to ask in a serious way; beg [to *plead* for help]. **2** to offer as an excuse [to *plead* icy roads as the reason for being late]. **3** to present a case or make a plea in a law court. —**plead′ed** or **pled, plead′ing** *See* SYNONYMS *at* **appeal.**

**pleas·ant** (plez′'nt) ***adj.*** **1** that gives pleasure; bringing happiness; enjoyable [a *pleasant* day in the park]. **2** having a look or manner that gives pleasure; likable [a *pleasant* person]. —**pleas′ant·ly *adv.*** —**pleas′ant·ness *n.***

SYNONYMS: **Pleasant** and **pleasing** are both used of something or someone that makes one feel satisfied or delighted, but **pleasant** stresses the feeling one has [How *pleasant* to see you!] and **pleasing** stresses the ability the person or thing has to cause that feeling [their *pleasing* ways]. **Agreeable** is used of something that suits one's personal likes, mood, taste, etc. [*agreeable* music].

**pleas·ant·ry** (plez′'n trē) ***n.*** **1** a pleasant joke or joking. **2** a polite remark. —*pl.* **pleas′ant·ries**

**please** (plēz) ***v.*** **1** to give pleasure to; satisfy [Few things *please* me more than a good book.] **2** to be kind enough to: *used in asking for something politely* [*Please* pass the salt.] **3** to wish or desire; like [Do as you *please.*] **4** to be the wish of [We would like a recess, if it *please* the court.] —**pleased, pleas′ing**

**pleas·ing** (plēz′iŋ) ***adj.*** giving pleasure; enjoyable [a *pleasing* smile]. *See* SYNONYMS *at* **pleasant.**

**pleas·ur·a·ble** (plezh′ər ə b'l) ***adj.*** giving pleasure; pleasant; enjoyable.

**pleas·ure** (plezh′ər) ***n.*** **1** a feeling of delight or satisfaction; enjoyment [I get *pleasure* from taking long walks.] **2** a thing that gives pleasure [Her voice is a *pleasure* to hear.] **3** one's wish or choice [For dessert, what is your *pleasure?*]

**pleat** (plēt) ***n.*** a flat double fold in cloth, pressed or stitched in place. *See the picture.* ◆***v.*** to fold into pleats. —**pleat′ed *adj.***

**ple·be·ian** (pli bē′ən) ***n.*** **1** a member of the lower class in ancient Rome. **2** one of the common people. ◆***adj.*** of or like plebians; common.

**pleb·i·scite** (pleb′ə sīt) ***n.*** a direct vote of the people to settle an important political question.

**plec·trum** (plek′trəm) ***n.*** a thin piece of plastic, metal, bone, etc., used for plucking the strings of a guitar, mandolin, etc. *See the picture.*

**pled** (pled) *a past tense and past participle of* **plead.**

**pledge** (plej) ***n.*** **1** a promise or agreement [the *pledge* of allegiance to the flag]. **2** something promised, especially money to be given as to a charity. **3** a thing given as a guarantee or token of something [They gave each other rings as a *pledge* of their love.] **4** the condition of being held as a guarantee or token [Articles left in a pawnshop are held in *pledge.*] ◆***v.*** **1** to promise to give [to *pledge* $100 to a building fund]. **2** to bind by a promise [He is *pledged* to marry her.] **3** to give as a guarantee that something will be done, especially that a loan will be paid back; pawn. —**pledged, pledg′ing**

**ple·na·ry** (plē′nə rē *or* plen′ə rē) ***adj.*** **1** full; complete [*plenary* power]. **2** that all members attend [a *plenary* session of a conference].

**plen·i·po·ten·ti·ar·y** (plen′i pə ten′shē er′ē) ***adj.*** that has been given full power [an ambassador *plenipotentiary*]. ◆***n.*** a person who has been given full power to act for his or her country in a foreign land. —*pl.* **plen′i·po·ten′ti·ar′ies**

**plen·i·tude** (plen′ə to͞od *or* plen′ə tyo͞od) ***n.*** fullness or plenty; completeness.

**plen·te·ous** (plen′tē əs) ***adj.*** *same as* **plentiful.**

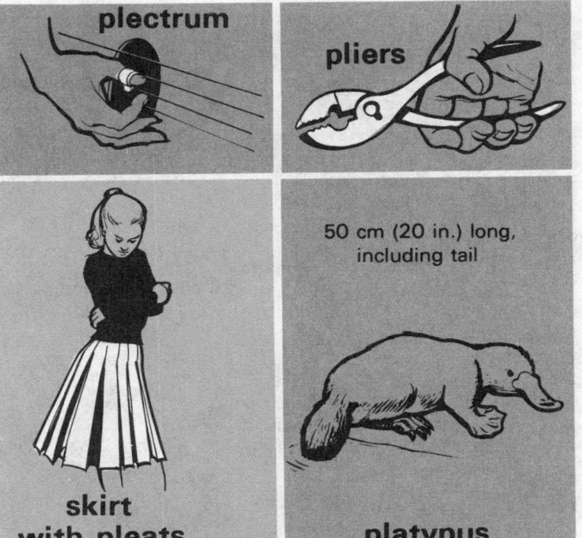


**plen·ti·ful** (plen′ti fəl) ***adj.*** great in amount or number; more than enough [a *plentiful* food supply]. —**plen′ti·ful·ly *adv.***

**plen·ty** (plen′tē) ***n.*** **1** a supply that is large enough; all that is needed [We have *plenty* of help.] **2** a large number [*plenty* of errors]. ◆***adv.*** very; quite: *used only in everyday talk* [It's *plenty* hot.] 561

**pleth·o·ra** (pleth′ə rə) ***n.*** too great an amount or number; excess [a *plethora* of words].

**pleu·ri·sy** (plo͝or′ə sē) ***n.*** a condition in which the membrane lining the chest and covering the lungs is inflamed. It makes breathing painful.

**plex·us** (plek′səs) ***n.*** a network, as of blood vessels, nerves, etc. *See* **solar plexus.**

**pli·a·ble** (plī′ə b'l) ***adj.*** **1** easy to bend; flexible [Copper tubing is *pliable.*] **2** easy to influence or persuade. —**pli′a·bil′i·ty *n.***

**pli·ant** (plī′ənt) ***adj.*** *another word for* **pliable.**

**pli·ers** (plī′ərz) ***n.pl.*** a tool like a small pincers, used for gripping small objects, bending wire, etc. *See the picture.*

**plight**[1] (plīt) ***n.*** a condition or situation, especially a sad or dangerous one [the *plight* of the men trapped in the mine].

**plight**[2] (plīt) ***v.*** to pledge or promise. —**plight one's troth,** to promise to marry.

☆**plink** (pliŋk) ***n.*** a light, sharp, ringing or clinking sound. ◆***v.*** to make such a sound or sounds.

**plinth** (plinth) ***n.*** **1** the square block at the base of a column, pedestal, etc. **2** the base on which a statue rests.

**plod** (pläd) ***v.*** **1** to walk or move heavily and with effort [An old horse *plodded* along the road.] **2** to work

| | | | |
|---|---|---|---|
| **a** fat | **ir** here | **ou** out | **zh** leisure |
| **ā** ape | **ī** bite, fire | **u** up | **ŋ** ring |
| **ä** car, lot | **ō** go | **ur** fur | a *in* ago |
| **e** ten | **ô** law, horn | **ch** chin | e *in* agent |
| **er** care | **oi** oil | **sh** she | **ə =** i *in* unity |
| **ē** even | **oo** look | **th** thin | o *in* collect |
| **i** hit | **o͞o** tool | ***th*** then | u *in* focus |

plumes

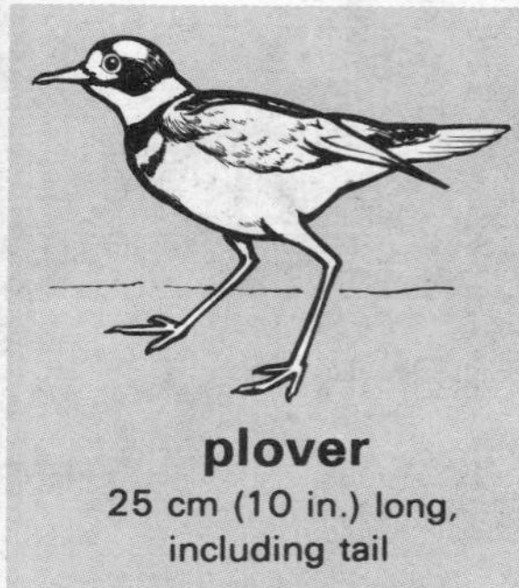
**plover**
25 cm (10 in.) long, including tail

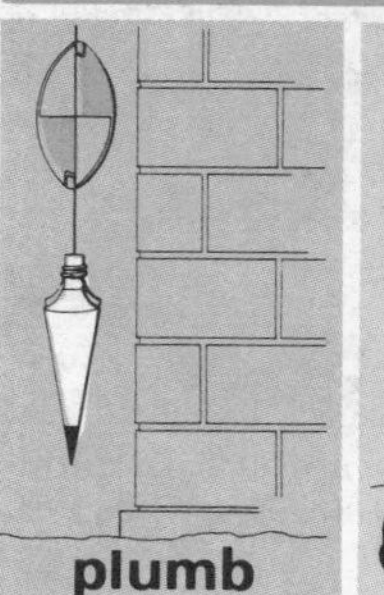
plumb

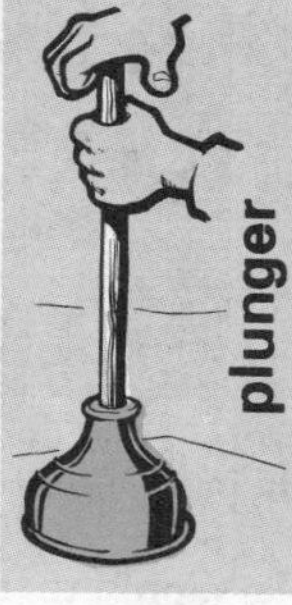
plunger

pneumatic hammer

in a slow, steady way, especially in doing something dull. —**plod′ded, plod′ding** —**plod′der** *n.*

 **plop** (pläp) ***n.*** the sound of something flat falling into water. ◆***v.*** to drop with such a sound. —**plopped, plop′ping**

**plot** (plät) ***n.*** **1** a secret plan, usually to do something bad or unlawful; conspiracy [a *plot* to rob a bank]. **2** all the happenings that form the main story in a novel, play, etc. [a murder mystery with an exciting *plot*]. **3** a small piece of ground [a sunny *plot* for a garden]. ◆***v.*** **1** to plan together secretly [to *plot* against the king]. **2** to make a map, plan, or outline of [to *plot* a ship's course]. —**plot′ted, plot′ting** —**plot′ter** ***n.***

**plough** (plou) ***n., v.*** *the British spelling of* **plow.**

**plov·er** (pluv′ər *or* plō′vər) ***n.*** a shore bird with a short tail and long, pointed wings. *See the picture.*

**plow** (plou) ***n.*** **1** a tool used in farming to cut into the soil and turn it up. It is usually pulled by a tractor or, especially in earlier times, an animal. ☆**2** anything like this; especially, a **snowplow.** ◆***v.*** **1** to turn up soil with a plow [to *plow* a field]. **2** to move, cut, etc. as if by plowing [to *plow* one's way through a crowded room].

**plow·man** (plou′mən) ***n.*** **1** a person who guides a plow. **2** a farm worker. —*pl.* **plow′men**

**plow·share** (plou′sher) ***n.*** the cutting blade of a plow.

**ploy** (ploi) ***n.*** a sly or tricky action that is meant to get the better of another person [His offer to check the furnace was only a *ploy* to get into the house.]

**pluck** (pluk) ***v.*** **1** to pull out or off; pick [to *pluck* an apple from a tree]. **2** to drag or snatch; grab [to *pluck* a burning stick from a fire]. **3** to pull feathers or hair from [to *pluck* a chicken; to *pluck* one's eyebrows]. **4** to pull and let go quickly [to *pluck* the strings of a guitar]. ◆***n.*** **1** the act of pulling; tug. **2** courage to meet danger or difficulty.

**pluck·y** (pluk′ē) ***adj.*** having or showing pluck; brave. —**pluck′i·er, pluck′i·est** —**pluck′i·ness** ***n.***

**plug** (plug) ***n.*** **1** a piece of wood, rubber, or the like used to stop up a hole, drain, etc. **2** a cake of pressed tobacco, used for chewing. **3** a part with prongs or openings that connect an electric circuit with a lamp, iron, radio, etc. **4** *a shorter name for* **fireplug** *or* **spark plug.** ☆**5** a praising remark or advertisement, especially one slipped into the entertainment part of a radio or TV program, a magazine article, etc.: *used only in everyday talk.* ☆**6** an old, worn-out horse: *slang in this meaning.* ◆***v.*** **1** to stop up or close with a plug [to *plug* up a hole]. **2** to work hard and steadily: *used only in everyday talk* [Just keep *plugging* away.] ☆**3** to advertise or praise with a plug: *used only in everyday talk* [The singer *plugged* her new record during the interview.] **4** to shoot a bullet into: *slang in this meaning.* —**plugged, plug′ging** —**plug in,** to connect to an electric circuit.

**plum** (plum) ***n.*** **1** a juicy fruit with a smooth skin and a smooth pit. **2** the tree it grows on. **3** the dark reddish-purple color of some plums. **4** something worth getting [That contract would be quite a *plum* for our company.] **5** a raisin: *now only in* **plum pudding,** a pudding made with raisins, suet, etc. and boiled or steamed.

**plum·age** (plo͞o′mij) ***n.*** a bird's feathers.

**plumb** (plum) ***n.*** a metal weight hung at the end of a line called a **plumb line.** It is used to find out how deep water is or whether a wall is straight up and down. *See the picture.* ◆***adj.*** straight up and down; vertical. ◆***adv.*** completely; entirely: *used only in everyday talk* [*plumb* crazy]. ◆***v.*** **1** to test with a plumb. **2** to get to the bottom of; solve [to *plumb* a mystery]. —**out of plumb** or **off plumb,** not straight up and down.

**plumb·er** (plum′ər) ***n.*** a person whose work is putting in and repairing the pipes and fixtures of water and gas systems in a building.

**plumb·ing** (plum′iŋ) ***n.*** **1** the pipes and fixtures of water and gas systems in a building. **2** the work of a plumber.

**plume** (plo͞om) ***n.*** **1** a feather, especially a large, fluffy one. **2** a decoration of such a feather or feathers, worn on a hat or helmet. *See the picture.* **3** something like a plume, as in shape [a *plume* of smoke]. ◆***v.*** **1** to decorate with plumes. **2** to smooth its feathers with its beak [a bird *pluming* itself]. —**plumed, plum′ing** —**plume oneself on,** to be proud because of; take credit for.

**plum·met** (plum′it) ***n.*** *another name for* **plumb.** ◆***v.*** to fall or drop straight down [The plane *plummeted* to earth.]

**plump**[1] (plump) ***adj.*** full and rounded in form; chubby [a *plump* child]. ◆***v.*** to fill out; puff up [to *plump* up a pillow]. —**plump′ness** ***n.***

**plump**[2] (plump) ***v.*** to drop in a sudden or heavy way [He *plumped* himself down and fell sound asleep.] ◆***n.*** a sudden or heavy fall, or the sound of this. ◆***adv.*** suddenly or heavily [It fell *plump* to the ground.] —**plump for,** to support strongly.

**plun·der** (plun′dər) ***v.*** to rob or take from by force, as during war [Soldiers *plundered* the captured cities.] ◆***n.*** **1** the act of plundering. **2** goods taken by force; loot. —**plun′der·er** ***n.***

**plunge** (plunj) ***v.*** **1** to thrust or force suddenly [I *plunged* my hand into the icy water. The action *plunged* the nation into war.] **2** to dive or rush; throw oneself [She *plunged* into the pool. We *plunged* into our work.] **3** to move downward or forward with great speed and force [The car *plunged* over the cliff.] **4** to gamble recklessly: *used only in everyday talk.* —**plunged, plung'ing** ◆***n.*** **1** a dive or fall. **2** a reckless investment of much money: *used only in everyday talk* [a *plunge* in the stock market].

> **Plunge** suggests the fast, forceful movement of something heavy that has been dropped or thrown. It comes from the Latin word for the metal lead, *plumbum,* from which we also get **plumb**. Lead is a very dense, heavy metal.

**plung·er** (plun'jər) ***n.*** **1** a person who plunges. **2** a rubber suction cup with a long handle, used to clear out drains that are clogged up. *See the picture.* **3** any device that works with a plunging, up-and-down motion, as a piston in an engine.

**plunk** (plungk) ***v.*** **1** to put down or drop suddenly or heavily [She *plunked* down her money. The stone *plunked* into the pond.] **2** to pluck or strum, as on a banjo. **3** to make a twanging sound, as a banjo. ◆***n.*** the act of plunking or the sound made by plunking.

**plu·ral** (ploor'əl) ***adj.*** showing that more than one is meant [The *plural* form of "box" is "boxes."] ◆***n.*** the form of a word which shows that more than one is meant.

> The plurals of most English words are formed by adding *-s* or *-es* (*hat, hats; glass, glasses*), but some plurals are formed in other ways (*foot, feet; child, children*). For some words there is no change for the plural (*sheep, sheep*).

**plu·ral·i·ty** (ploo ral'ə tē) ***n.*** **1** more than half of a total; majority. ☆**2** the number of votes that the winner has over the number received by the next highest candidate, in an election with more than two candidates [If Brown gets 65 votes, Green gets 40, and White gets 35, then Brown has a *plurality* of 25.] —*pl.* **plu·ral'i·ties**

**plus** (plus) ***prep.*** **1** added to [Two *plus* two equals four (2 + 2 = 4).] **2** and in addition [It costs $10 *plus* tax.] ◆***adj.*** **1** more than zero; positive [a *plus* quantity]. **2** a little higher than [a grade of C *plus*]. **3** added and helpful [Having a good school nearby is a *plus* factor.] ◆***n.*** **1** the sign +, put before a number or quantity that is to be added or one that is more than zero. *The full name is* **plus sign**. **2** something extra and helpful.

**plush** (plush) ***n.*** a fabric like velvet, but softer and thicker. ◆***adj.*** very expensive and luxurious: *slang in this meaning* [a *plush* home].

**Plu·to** (plōō'tō) **1** the Greek and Roman god of Hades and the dead. **2** the planet farthest from the sun.

**plu·to·crat** (plōōt'ə krat) ***n.*** a person who has power over others because of being rich.

☆**plu·to·ni·um** (plōō tō'nē əm) ***n.*** a radioactive chemical element, used in producing atomic energy.

**ply**[1] (plī) ***n.*** **1** a thickness or layer, as of plywood, cloth, etc. **2** any of the strands twisted together to make rope, yarn, etc. —*pl.* **plies**

**ply**[2] (plī) ***v.*** **1** to use with force or energy [to *ply* a hammer]. **2** to work at [*plying* the trade of bricklayer for ten years]. **3** to keep supplying [They *plied* their guests with food.] **4** to travel back and forth across, especially at regular times [Boats *ply* the channel.] —**plied, ply'ing**

**Ply·mouth** (plim'əth) **1** a town on the coast of Massachusetts, settled by the Pilgrims in 1620. **2** a seaport in southwestern England.

☆**Plymouth Rock** **1** a large rock at Plymouth, Massachusetts, where the Pilgrims are said to have landed. **2** a breed of chicken with feathers that usually have dark stripes.

**ply·wood** (plī'wood) ***n.*** strong board made of thin layers of wood glued and pressed together.

**P.M.** *abbreviation for* **Postmaster, Prime Minister.**

**P.M.** or **p.m.** in the time from noon to midnight. *P.M.* is the abbreviation of *post meridiem,* a Latin phrase meaning "after noon" [Be here at 7:30 *P.M.*]

**pneu·mat·ic** (nōō mat'ik *or* nyōō mat'ik) ***adj.*** **1** filled with air [a *pneumatic* tire]. **2** worked by air under pressure [a *pneumatic* hammer]. *See the picture.*

**pneu·mo·nia** (noo mōn'yə *or* nyoo mōn'yə) ***n.*** a disease in which the lungs become inflamed and a watery fluid collects in them.

**Po** (pō) a river in northern Italy.

**P.O.** or **p.o.** *abbreviation for* **post office.**

**poach**[1] (pōch) ***v.*** to cook an egg without its shell, in boiling water or in a small cup put over boiling water.

> **Poach** comes from a French word meaning "pocket." When an egg is poached, the white becomes firm, turning into a "pocket" that holds the softer yolk.



**poach**[2] (pōch) ***v.*** to hunt or fish on another person's land without the right to do so. —**poach'er *n.***

**Po·ca·hon·tas** (pō'kə hän'təs) about 1595–1617; an American Indian princess who is said to have saved Captain John Smith from being killed.

**pock** (päk) ***n.*** any of the small blisters caused by smallpox, chicken pox, etc., or the scar sometimes left by one of these.

**pock·et** (päk'it) ***n.*** **1** a small bag or pouch sewed into a garment, for carrying money and small articles. **2** a hollow place, often one filled with something [*pockets* of ore in rock; the *pockets* of a pool table]. **3** a small area or group [*pockets* of poor people in a rich country]. **4** *a shorter form of* **air pocket.** ◆***adj.*** that can be carried in a pocket [a *pocket* watch]. ◆***v.*** **1** to put into a pocket [I *pocketed* my change.] **2** to enclose; shut in [The airport is *pocketed* in fog.] **3** to take dishonestly [He *pocketed* some of the money he had collected for charity.] —**in one's pocket**, completely under one's control.

**pock·et·book** (päk'it book) ***n.*** ☆**1** a purse or small handbag. **2** a billfold or wallet.

**pock·et·ful** (päk'it fool) ***n.*** as much as a pocket will hold. —*pl.* **pock'et·fuls**

| | | | | | | | |
|---|---|---|---|---|---|---|---|
| **a** | fat | **ir** | here | **ou** | out | **zh** | leisure |
| **ā** | ape | **ī** | bite, fire | **u** | up | **ng** | ring |
| **ä** | car, lot | **ō** | go | **ur** | fur | | a *in* ago |
| **e** | ten | **ô** | law, horn | **ch** | chin | | e *in* agent |
| **er** | care | **oi** | oil | **sh** | she | **ə** = | i *in* unity |
| **ē** | even | **oo** | look | **th** | thin | | o *in* collect |
| **i** | hit | **ōō** | tool | ***th*** | then | | u *in* focus |

**pock·et·knife** (päk′it nīf) ***n.*** a small knife with blades that fold into the handle. *See the picture.* —*pl.* **pock′et·knives**

**pock·mark** (päk′märk) ***n.*** a small scar or pit sometimes left on the skin by the sores of smallpox, chicken pox, etc.

**pod** (päd) ***n.*** the case or shell that holds the seeds of certain plants, as the pea and bean.

**po·di·a·trist** (pō dī′ə trist) ***n.*** a person whose work is taking care of feet, as by treating diseases or injuries.

**po·di·um** (pō′dē əm) ***n.*** a low platform, especially one where the conductor of an orchestra stands. *See the picture.*

**Poe** (pō), **Edgar Allan** 1809–1849; U.S. poet and writer of short stories.

**po·em** (pō′əm) ***n.*** a piece of writing having rhythm and, often, rhyme, usually in language that shows more imagination and deep feeling than ordinary speech.

**po·e·sy** (pō′ə sē) ***n.*** *an old-fashioned word for* **poetry.**

**po·et** (pō′ət) ***n.*** a person who writes poems.

**po·et·ess** (pō′ət əs) ***n.*** a woman poet. *This word is no longer much used. Nowadays* **poet** *is used for any person who writes poetry.*

**po·et·ic** (pō et′ik) ***adj.*** **1** of, like, or fit for a poet or poetry [*poetic* talent; *poetic* language]. **2** written in verse [*poetic* drama]. *Also sometimes* **po·et′i·cal.** —**po·et′i·cal·ly** ***adv.***

564 **poetic justice** justice in which good is rewarded and evil is punished, as in some plays.

**poetic license** the freedom to ignore certain rules or facts in order to get a more artistic result.

**poet laureate** the court poet chosen by the ruler of Great Britain to write poems about important events, etc. —*pl.* **poets laureate** or **poet laureates**

**po·et·ry** (pō′ə trē) ***n.*** **1** the art of writing poems. **2** poems [the *poetry* of Keats]. **3** rhythms, deep feelings, imagination, etc., like those of poems [the *poetry* of a dancer's movements].

☆**po·go stick** (pō′gō) a pole with pedals and a spring at one end, used as a toy to bounce along on. *See the picture.*

Some words are just made up by people, without being based on any earlier words. **Pogo** is such a made-up word. Perhaps the bouncing movement of the stick suggested its two syllables.

☆**poi** (poi) ***n.*** a Hawaiian food that is a paste made from cooked taro root, that has been fermented.

**poign·ant** (poin′yənt) ***adj.*** having a sharp and deep effect on the feelings; moving [a *poignant* moment of farewell]. *See* SYNONYMS *at* **moving.** —**poign′an·cy** ***n.*** —**poign′ant·ly** ***adv.***

☆**poin·set·ti·a** (poin set′ē ə *or* poin set′ə) ***n.*** a tropical plant with small, yellow flowers and red leaves that look like petals.

**point** (point) ***n.*** **1** a position or place; location [the *point* where the roads meet]. **2** a dot in printing or writing [a decimal *point*]. **3** an exact time or moment [At that *point* the telephone rang.] **4** a stage or degree reached [the boiling *point* of water]. **5** a unit used in measuring or scoring [A touchdown is worth six *points.*] **6** any of the marks showing direction on a compass. **7** in mathematics, an imaginary mark that has an exact position but no size or shape. **8** a part or detail; item [Explain the plan *point* by *point.*] **9** a special quality [Generosity is one of her good *points.*] **10** a sharp end [the *point* of a needle]. **11** a piece of land sticking out into the water; cape. **12** an important or main idea or fact [the *point* of a joke]. **13** a purpose; object [What's the *point* in crying?] ◆***v.*** **1** to aim [She *pointed* her telescope at Mars.] **2** to aim one's finger [He *pointed* to the book he wanted.] **3** to be directed toward a certain place, condition, result, etc. [Everything *points* to a happy outcome.] **4** to show or call attention to [to *point* the way; to *point* out mistakes]. **5** to show where game is by standing still and facing toward it, as some hunting dogs do. **6** to give extra force to; stress [She raised her voice to *point* up her meaning.] —**at the point of,** very close to [I was *at the point of* leaving when the storm began.] —**beside the point,** having nothing to do with the subject being talked about. —**make a point of,** to insist on [to *make a point of* seeing a movie every week]. —**on the point of,** almost in the act of. —**stretch a point,** to make an exception. —**to the point** or **in point,** having much to do with the subject being talked about.

**point-blank** (point′blangk′) ***adj.*** **1** aimed straight at a target that is very close [a *point-blank* shot]. **2** direct and plain [a *point-blank* answer]. ◆***adv.*** **1** in a direct line; straight [to fire a gun *point-blank*]. **2** in a plain, direct way; bluntly [to refuse *point-blank*].

**point·ed** (poin′tid) ***adj.*** **1** having a point or sharp end [shoes with *pointed* toes]. **2** clearly directed at someone [a *pointed* remark]. **3** easy to see or notice; obvious [a *pointed* lack of interest in what I had to say]. —**point′ed·ly** ***adv.***

**point·er** (poin′tər) ***n.*** **1** a long, thin rod used for pointing to things, as on a map. **2** a hand or needle on a clock, meter, scales, etc. **3** a large hunting dog with a smooth coat, trained to point game. *See the picture.* **4** a helpful hint or suggestion: *used only in ev-*

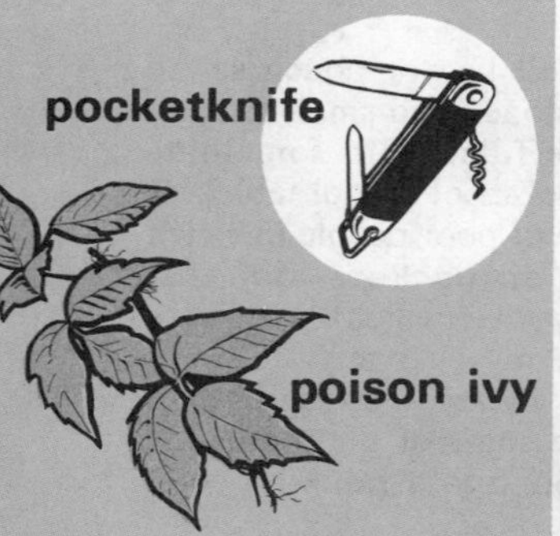

pocketknife

poison ivy

podium

pogo stick

pointer
60 cm (2 ft.) high at shoulder

polar bear 1.5 m (5 ft.) high at shoulder

eryday talk [some *pointers* from the coach on how to hold a bat].

**point·less** (point'lis) ***adj.*** **1** without a point; blunt. **2** without meaning or purpose; senseless [a *pointless* remark].

**point of order** a question of whether a meeting is being conducted according to the rules.

**point of view** the way in which, or the place from which, something is viewed; standpoint [a liberal *point of view*].

**poise** (poiz) ***n.*** **1** balance, as in the way one carries oneself [the perfect *poise* of a tiger that is ready to spring]. **2** calmness and easiness of manner; self-control [I lost my *poise* when they laughed at me.] ◆***v.*** to balance or be held balanced [The stork *poised* itself on one leg. The earth is *poised* in space.] —**poised, pois'ing**

**poi·son** (poi'z'n) ***n.*** **1** a substance that causes illness or death when taken into the body, even in small amounts. **2** anything that harms or destroys [Hatred can be a *poison* that hurts the one who hates.] ◆***v.*** **1** to harm or kill with poison [to *poison* rats]. **2** to put poison on or into [to *poison* bait]. **3** to harm or destroy [a mind *poisoned* by jealousy]. ◆***adj.*** that is or contains a poison [*poison* gas]. —**poi'son·er *n.***

☆**poison ivy** **1** a plant with whitish berries and with leaves that grow in groups of three. It can cause a skin rash if touched. *See the picture.* **2** a rash caused by this plant.

☆**poison oak** *another name for* **poison ivy** *or* **poison sumac.**

**poi·son·ous** (poi'z'n əs) ***adj.*** that is a poison; harming or killing by poison [a *poisonous* berry].

☆**poison sumac** a plant with leaves that grow in groups of 7 to 13. It is found in swamps and can cause a skin rash if touched.

**poke**[1] (pōk) ***v.*** **1** to push or jab, as with a stick, finger, etc. **2** to make by poking [to *poke* a hole in a sack]. **3** to thrust, stick out, push forward, etc. [Don't *poke* your nose into my business.] **4** to search [to *poke* around in the attic]. **5** to move along in a slow or lazy way. **6** to hit with the fist: *slang in this meaning.* —**poked, pok'ing** ◆***n.*** **1** a poking; jab; push. **2** a blow with the fist: *slang in this meaning.* **3** a bonnet with a wide front brim. *The full name is* **poke bonnet.** —**poke fun at,** to make jokes about.

**poke**[2] (pōk) ***n.*** a sack; bag: *now used only in some regions.*

☆**pok·er**[1] (pō'kər) ***n.*** a card game in which one can bet that one holds a better hand than the other players.

**pok·er**[2] (pō'kər) ***n.*** a metal bar for stirring up a fire.

**pok·ey**[1] or **pok·y**[1] (pō'kē) ***n.*** a jail: *a slang word.*

**pok·y**[2] or **pok·ey**[2] (pō'kē) ***adj.*** **1** moving slowly; slow [Don't be so *poky,* or we'll be late.] **2** not lively; dull [a *poky* town]. —**pok'i·er, pok'i·est**

**Po·land** (pō'lənd) a country in central Europe, on the Baltic Sea.

**po·lar** (pō'lər) ***adj.*** **1** of or near the North or South Pole. **2** of a pole or poles.

**polar bear** a large, white bear of the arctic regions. *See the picture.*

**Po·la·ris** (pō lar'is) *another name for* **North Star.**

**po·lar·ize** (pō'lə rīz) ***v.*** **1** to cause to have poles, or opposite ends, that behave in completely opposite ways. **2** to divide into groups that disagree with each other [a political issue that has *polarized* the party]. —**po'lar·ized, po'lar·iz·ing** —**po'lar·i·za'tion *n.***

**Pole** (pōl) ***n.*** a person born or living in Poland.

**pole**[1] (pōl) ***n.*** a long, slender piece of wood, metal, etc. [a tent *pole*]. ◆***v.*** ☆to push along with a pole [to *pole* a raft down a river]. —**poled, pol'ing**

**pole**[2] (pōl) ***n.*** **1** either end of an axis, especially of the earth's axis. *See* **North Pole** *and* **South Pole.** **2** either of two opposite forces, parts, etc., as the ends of a magnet or the terminals of a battery.

**pole·cat** (pōl'kat) ***n.*** ☆**1** *another name for* **skunk.** **2** a small animal of Europe that is like a weasel.

**po·lem·ic** (pə lem'ik) ***adj.*** having to do with argument or dispute. ◆***n.*** an argument or dispute.

**pole·star** (pōl'stär) ***n.*** the North Star; Polaris.

**pole vault** an athletic contest to see who can jump highest over a crossbar, using a long pole to push oneself off the ground.

**po·lice** (pə lēs') ***n.*** **1** the department of a city, state, etc. that keeps order, prevents and discovers crimes, etc. **2** the members of such a department: *used with a plural verb* [The *police* arrest lawbreakers.] ◆***v.*** **1** to keep peaceful and orderly, as with police [to *police* the streets]. ☆**2** to make clean and neat [to *police* the grounds after a picnic]. —**po·liced', po·lic'ing**

**po·lice·man** (pə lēs'mən) ***n.*** a member of a police department. —*pl.* **po·lice'men**

**police officer** *another name for* **policeman.**



Some police departments now use the term **police officer** for any member of the police force, whether man or woman, instead of using the words **policeman** or **policewoman.**

**po·lice·wom·an** (pə lēs'woom'ən) ***n.*** a woman member of a police department. —*pl.* **po·lice'wom'en**

**pol·i·cy**[1] (päl'ə sē) ***n.*** a plan, rule, or way of acting [It is a good *policy* to be honest. A country's foreign *policy* is its way of dealing with other countries.] —*pl.* **pol'i·cies**

**pol·i·cy**[2] (päl'ə sē) ***n.*** the written contract between an insurance company and a person, telling how much the payments to the company are and how much will be paid in case of certain losses. —*pl.* **pol'i·cies**

**po·li·o** (pō'lē ō) ***n.*** *a shorter form of* **poliomyelitis.**

**po·li·o·my·e·li·tis** (pō'lē ō mī'ə līt'əs) ***n.*** a disease in which part of the spinal cord becomes inflamed and sometimes parts of the body are paralyzed. It is most common among young people.

**Pol·ish** (pō'lish) ***adj.*** of Poland, its people, language, etc. ◆***n.*** the language of Poland.

**pol·ish** (päl'ish) ***v.*** **1** to make smooth and bright or shiny, as by rubbing [to *polish* a car with wax]. **2** to make less rough or crude; improve; perfect [to *polish* one's manners; to *polish* a speech one will give]. ◆***n.*** **1** brightness or shine on a surface [a wood floor with

| | | | | | | | |
|---|---|---|---|---|---|---|---|
| **a** | fat | **ir** | here | **ou** | out | **zh** | leisure |
| **ā** | ape | **ī** | bite, fire | **u** | up | **ng** | ring |
| **ä** | car, lot | **ō** | go | **ur** | fur | | a *in* ago |
| **e** | ten | **ô** | law, horn | **ch** | chin | | e *in* agent |
| **er** | care | **oi** | oil | **sh** | she | **ə =** | i *in* unity |
| **ē** | even | **oo** | look | **th** | thin | | o *in* collect |
| **i** | hit | **ōō** | tool | ***th*** | then | | u *in* focus |

a fine *polish*]. **2** a substance used to polish [fingernail *polish;* shoe *polish*]. **3** the condition of being polite or refined, as in speech or manners. —**polish off,** to finish or get rid of completely or quickly: *used only in everyday talk* [They *polished off* their lunch and left.]

**po·lite** (pə līt′) ***adj.*** **1** having or showing good manners; thoughtful of others; courteous [a *polite* note of thanks]. *See* SYNONYMS *at* **civil**. **2** behaving in a way that is considered refined or elegant [Such things aren't done in *polite* society.] —**po·lite′ly *adv.*** —**po·lite′ness *n.***

**pol·i·tic** (päl′ə tik) ***adj.*** **1** wise and clever; sometimes, too clever or sly; crafty [*politic* answers to the reporter's questions]. **2** worked out in a careful or crafty way to fit the situation [a *politic* plan].

**po·lit·i·cal** (pə lit′i k'l) ***adj.*** **1** having to do with government, politics, etc. [*political* parties]. **2** of or like political parties or politicians [a *political* speech]. —**po·lit′i·cal·ly *adv.***

**political science** the study of the principles and methods of government.

**pol·i·ti·cian** (päl′ə tish′ən) ***n.*** a person who is active in politics, usually one holding or running for a political office. *This word is sometimes used of a person who is thought to be active in politics only for selfish reasons.*

**pol·i·tics** (päl′ə tiks) ***n.pl.*** **1** the science of government; political science. **2** the act of taking part in political affairs, often as a profession. **3** the use of schemes to get what one wants, especially power [office *politics*]. **4** the way one thinks or believes in political matters [What are your *politics?*] *This word is used with a singular verb in meanings* 1, 2, *and* 3.



**pol·i·ty** (päl′ə tē) ***n.*** **1** government, or a system for ruling. **2** a group of people under one government; state. —*pl.* **pol′i·ties**

**Polk** (pōk), **James K.** 1795–1849; the 11th president of the United States, from 1845 to 1849.

**pol·ka** (pōl′kə) ***n.*** **1** a fast dance for couples that was first popular in Bohemia. **2** music for this dance. ◆***v.*** to dance the polka.

☆**pol·ka dot** (pō′kə) **1** a pattern of small, round, evenly spaced dots. *See the picture.* **2** any of these dots.

**Polka** is a Czech word meaning "Polish woman." The polka dance was very popular in the late 19th century. The name was later given to many kinds of clothing and material. There were "polka hats" and "polka jackets." A pattern with dots came to be called **polka dots**.

**poll** (pōl) ***n.*** **1** a voting or listing of opinions by persons; also, the counting of these votes or opinions [A *poll* of our class shows that most of us want a party.] **2** the number of votes cast. **3** a list of voters. ☆**4 polls,** *pl.* a place where people go to vote. ◆***v.*** **1** to take and count the votes or opinions of [to *poll* a county]. **2** to get a certain number of votes [Klein *polled* a majority of the votes cast.] **3** to cast one's vote [a *polling* place]. **4** to cut off or trim the wool, hair, horns, or branches of.

**pol·len** (päl′ən) ***n.*** the yellow powder found on the stamens of flowers. It is made up of male cells which fertilize another flower when carried to its pistil, as by bees or the wind.

**pol·li·nate** (päl′ə nāt) ***v.*** to place pollen on the pistil of a flower; fertilize. —**pol′li·nat·ed, pol′li·nat·ing** —**pol′li·na′tion *n.***

**pol·li·wog** (päl′ē wäg′) ***n.*** *another name for* **tadpole**.

☆**poll·ster** (pōl′stər) ***n.*** a person whose work is taking polls of people to get their opinions.

**pol·lu·tant** (pə lo͞ot′'nt) ***n.*** something that pollutes; especially, a harmful chemical or waste material that gets into the air or water.

**pol·lute** (pə lo͞ot′) ***v.*** to make dirty or impure [Smoke from factories *polluted* the air.] *See* SYNONYMS *at* **contaminate**. —**pol·lut′ed, pol·lut′ing**

**po·lo** (pō′lō) ***n.*** a game played on horseback by two teams of four players each. The players try to drive a small wooden ball through the other team's goal, using mallets with long handles. *See the picture.*

**Po·lo** (pō′lō), **Mar·co** (mär′kō) about 1254–1324; a traveler from Venice who went to Asia and wrote a book about his travels.

**po·lo·naise** (päl ə nāz′ *or* pō lə nāz′) ***n.*** **1** a slow, dignified Polish dance. **2** music for this dance.

**pol·troon** (päl tro͞on′) ***n.*** a great coward.

**pol·y·es·ter** (päl′ē es′tər) ***n.*** an artificial resin used in making plastics, fibers for fabrics, etc.

**po·lyg·a·my** (pə lig′ə mē) ***n.*** the practice of being married to more than one person at the same time. —**po·lyg′a·mist *n.*** —**po·lyg′a·mous *adj.***

**pol·y·glot** (päl′i glät′) ***adj.*** **1** speaking and understanding several languages. **2** made up of or written in several languages [a *polyglot* book]. ◆***n.*** a person who can speak and understand several languages.

**pol·y·gon** (päl′i gän′) ***n.*** a flat, closed figure made up of straight lines, especially one having more than four angles and sides.

**Pol·y·ne·sia** (päl′ə nē′zhə) a scattered group of many islands in the central and south Pacific, including Hawaii and Tahiti. —**Pol′y·ne′sian *adj., n.***

**pol·yp** (päl′ip) ***n.*** a small water animal having a body shaped like a tube, with slender tentacles around a mouth at the top, for taking in food. The sea anemone and coral are polyps.

**pol·y·syl·la·ble** (päl′i sil′ə b'l) ***adj.*** a word of four or more syllables ["Elementary" is a *polysyllable*.] —**pol·y·syl·lab·ic** (päl′i si lab′ik) ***adj.***

**pol·y·tech·nic** (päl′i tek′nik) ***adj.*** of or teaching many scientific and technical subjects [a *polytechnic* institute].

**pol·y·the·ism** (päl′i thē iz'm) ***n.*** belief in more than one god [the *polytheism* of the ancient Greeks]. —**pol′y·the·is′tic *adj.***

**pol·y·un·sat·u·rat·ed** (päl′i un sach′ə rāt′id) ***adj.*** describing certain fats and oils that are thought to be better in the diet than some other fats and oils. Polyunsaturated fats and oils remain in liquid form at room temperature.

**po·made** (pä mād′ *or* pə mād′) ***n.*** a perfumed cream for keeping the hair in place.

**Pomade** comes from the Italian word for "apple." At one time it was made with the pulp of apple mixed in to give it a pleasant smell.

**pome·gran·ate** (päm′gran′it *or* pum′gran′it) ***n.*** **1** a round, red fruit with a hard skin and many seeds covered with a red, juicy pulp that can be eaten. **2** the bush or small tree that it grows on.

**pom·mel** (pum′'l) ***n.*** **1** the rounded part that sticks up on the front of a saddle. **2** a round knob at the end of the hilt of a sword. ◆**v.** *another spelling of* **pummel.** —**pom′meled** or **pom′melled, pom′mel·ing** or **pom′mel·ling**

**pomp** (pämp) **n.** dignified or showy display; splendor [the *pomp* of a coronation].

**pom·pa·dour** (päm′pə dôr) **n.** a hair style in which the hair is brushed straight up from the forehead so that it puffs up. *See the picture.*

**Pom·pei·i** (päm pā′ē *or* päm pā′) a city in Italy that was destroyed when Mount Vesuvius erupted in 79 A.D. —**Pom·pei·an** (päm pā′ən) **adj., n.**

**pom·pon** (päm′pän) **n.** **1** a ball of silk, wool, or feathers worn on hats or waved by cheerleaders: *also* **pom-pom** (päm′päm). **2** a chrysanthemum with small, round flowers.

**pom·pos·i·ty** (päm päs′ə tē) **n.** pompous behavior, speech, etc.; self-importance.

**pom·pous** (päm′pəs) **adj.** trying to seem important by acting in a way that is too dignified. —**pom′pous·ly adv.**

**Pon·ce de Le·ón** (pōn′thə *th*ā lā ōn′ *or* päns′ də lē′ən), **Juan** (hwän) about 1460–1521; a Spanish explorer who was the first European to discover Florida.

**pon·cho** (pän′chō) **n.** a cloak like a blanket with a hole in the middle for the head. It is worn as a raincoat, etc., originally in South America. *See the picture.* —*pl.* **pon′chos**

**pond** (pänd) **n.** a small lake, often artificially made.

**pon·der** (pän′dər) **v.** to think deeply about; consider carefully [to *ponder* an offer].

> SYNONYMS: **Ponder** suggests thinking about something very carefully and in all possible ways [to *ponder* over a problem]. **Meditate** can suggest quiet, deep thought [*meditating* on world conditions] or careful thinking about some plan [to *meditate* revenge].

**pon·der·ous** (pän′dər əs) **adj.** **1** large and heavy, often in a clumsy way; massive [The *ponderous* truck lumbered down the road.] **2** dull or tiresome; without a light touch [a *ponderous* joke]. —**pon′der·ous·ly adv.**

☆**pone** (pōn) **n.** a kind of bread. *See* **corn pone.**

**pon·iard** (pän′yərd) **n.** a dagger.

**pon·tiff** (pän′tif) **n.** a bishop; especially **Pontiff,** the Pope.

**pon·tif·i·cal** (pän tif′i k′l) **adj.** **1** having to do with the Pope; papal. **2** acting as if one had the dignity or power of a Pope. —**pon·tif′i·cal·ly adv.**

**pon·tif·i·cate** (pän tif′i kāt) **v.** to speak or act in a very self-confident or pompous way [a writer who often *pontificates* on subjects in the newspaper]. —**pon·tif′i·cat·ed, pon·tif′i·cat·ing**

**pon·toon** (pän to͞on′) **n.** **1** a boat with a flat bottom. **2** such a boat or other floating object, used with others like it to hold up a temporary bridge, called a **pontoon bridge.** **3** a float on an airplane to allow it to land on water.

**po·ny** (pō′nē) **n.** **1** a type of small horse. ☆**2** any horse, especially at a race track: *slang in this meaning.* ☆**3** a translation of something written in a foreign language, used in doing schoolwork, often in a dishonest way. —*pl.* **po′nies**

☆**pony express** a system of riders on swift ponies, once used to carry mail.

polo

poncho

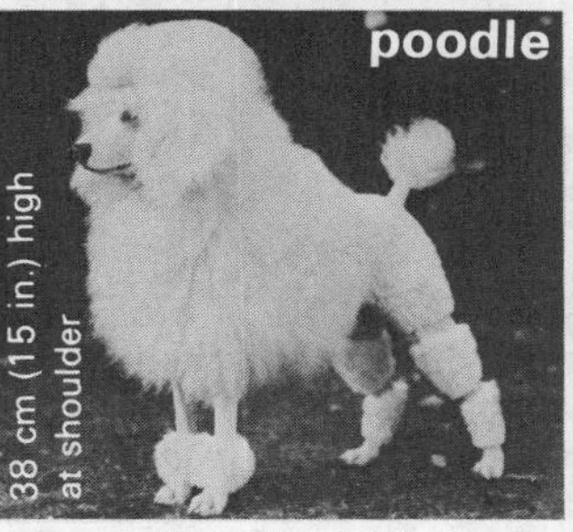
poodle


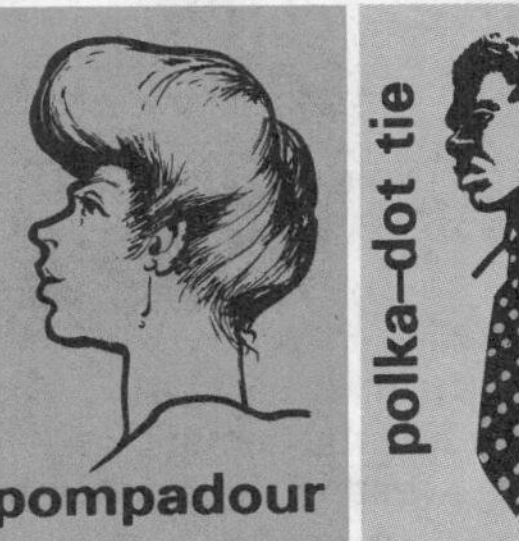
pompadour

polka-dot tie

**po·ny·tail** (pō′nē tāl′) **n.** a hair style in which the hair is pulled back and tied tight high on the back of the head, so that it hangs down like a pony's tail.

**poo·dle** (po͞o′d′l) **n.** a breed of dog with black, white, gray, or brown hair that is sometimes trimmed in patterns. *See the picture.*

**pooh** (po͞o) **interj.** a sound made to show that one is annoyed or does not believe something.

**pooh-pooh** (po͞o′po͞o′) **v.** to treat as unimportant or of little value [to *pooh-pooh* an idea].

**pool¹** (po͞ol) **n.** **1** a small pond. **2** a puddle. **3** *a shorter form of* **swimming pool.** **4** a deep place in a river.

**pool²** (po͞ol) **n.** **1** a game of billiards played on a table, called a **pool table,** having six pockets into which the balls are knocked. **2** an amount of money, a set of things, or a group of skilled people shared by a group [This office has a *pool* of typists who type reports for any of the officers of the company.] **3** a group of persons or companies working together for the benefit of each [a *pool* formed to buy an office building]. **4** all the money that the winner gets from bets made by a number of people, as on the outcome of a game. ◆**v.** ☆to put together for the use of all [We *pooled* our money and rented a cottage.]

**poop** (po͞op) **n.** a deck at the stern of some ships, raised above the main deck and sometimes forming the roof of a cabin. *Also called* **poop deck.**



| | | | | | | | |
|---|---|---|---|---|---|---|---|
| **a** | fat | **ir** | here | **ou** | out | **zh** | leisure |
| **ā** | ape | **ī** | bite, fire | **u** | up | **ng** | ring |
| **ä** | car, lot | **ō** | go | **ur** | fur | | a *in* ago |
| **e** | ten | **ô** | law, horn | **ch** | chin | | e *in* agent |
| **er** | care | **oi** | oil | **sh** | she | **ə** = | i *in* unity |
| **ē** | even | **oo** | look | **th** | thin | | o *in* collect |
| **i** | hit | **o͞o** | tool | ***th*** | then | | u *in* focus |

portico

portcullis

porcupine

90 cm (3 ft.) long, including tail

poplars

**poor** (poor) ***adj.*** **1** having little or no money; not having enough to live on; needy. **2** not good; not what it should be; below average; bad [*poor* health; *poor* grades; a *poor* wheat crop]. **3** not having much skill [a *poor* cook]. **4** deserving pity; unfortunate [The *poor* bird had broken its wing.] —**the poor,** poor people. —**poor'ly** ***adv.*** —**poor'ness** ***n.***



**poor·house** (poor'hous) ***n.*** in earlier times, a place where very poor people stayed, supported by money from the public.

**poor-mouth** (poor'mouth) ***v.*** to complain about not having enough money: *used only in everyday talk.*

**pop**[1] (päp) ***n.*** **1** a sudden, short, bursting sound, as of a pistol shot. **2** soda water that has been flavored and sweetened. ◆***v.*** **1** to make, or burst with, a pop. **2** to make burst open [to *pop* corn]. **3** to move, put, etc. in a quick, sudden way [He *popped* out of bed. She *popped* an unexpected question.] **4** to open wide in a stare; bulge [eyes *popping* with curiosity]. ☆**5** to hit a baseball high in the air, but in the infield. —**popped, pop'ping**

☆**pop**[2] (päp) ***n.*** father: *a slang word.*

**pop**[3] (päp) ***adj.*** *a shorter form of* **popular** [*pop* music].

**pop.** *abbreviation for* **popular, population.**

☆**pop·corn** (päp'kôrn) ***n.*** **1** a kind of corn with hard kernels which pop open into white, puffy masses when heated. **2** the popped kernels.

**Pope** or **pope** (pōp) ***n.*** the bishop who is the head of the Roman Catholic Church.

**Pope** (pōp), **Alexander** 1688–1744; English poet.

**pop·eyed** (päp'īd) ***adj.*** having wide eyes that bulge out.

**pop·gun** (päp'gun) ***n.*** a toy gun that uses air to shoot little corks, etc. with a popping sound.

**pop·in·jay** (päp'in jā) ***n.*** a conceited person who talks a lot.

**pop·lar** (päp'lər) ***n.*** **1** a tall tree that grows fast and has small leaves. *See the picture.* **2** its wood.

**pop·lin** (päp'lin) ***n.*** a strong cloth of silk, cotton, wool, etc. with fine ridges on the surface.

☆**pop·o·ver** (päp'ō'vər) ***n.*** a very light muffin that is puffy and hollow.

**pop·py** (päp'ē) ***n.*** a plant with a milky juice and flowers of various colors. Opium comes from the juice of one kind of poppy. —*pl.* **pop'pies**

☆**pop·py·cock** (päp'ē käk') ***n.*** foolish talk; nonsense.

**poppy seed** the small, dark seed of the poppy, used in baking, etc. as a flavoring.

**pop·u·lace** (päp'yə lis) ***n.*** the public generally; the masses.

**pop·u·lar** (päp'yə lər) ***adj.*** **1** having many friends; very well liked [His quiet humor has made him *popular.*] **2** liked by many people [Pizza is a *popular* food.] **3** of, for, or by all the people or most people [elected by *popular* vote; a *popular* notion]. **4** that most people can afford [goods sold at *popular* prices]. —**pop·u·lar·i·ty** (päp'yə lar'ə tē) ***n.*** —**pop'u·lar·ly** ***adv.***

**pop·u·lar·ize** (päp'yə lə rīz') ***v.*** **1** to make popular [to *popularize* a song by playing it often]. **2** to make something easily understood by the general public [to *popularize* scientific ideas]. —**pop'u·lar·ized', pop'u·lar·iz'ing** —**pop'u·lar·i·za'tion** ***n.***

**pop·u·late** (päp'yə lāt) ***v.*** to fill with people; inhabit [New York is densely *populated.* People from many countries have *populated* the U.S.] —**pop'u·lat·ed, pop'u·lat·ing**

**pop·u·la·tion** (päp'yə lā'shən) ***n.*** **1** the people living in a country, city, etc.; especially, the total number of these. **2** the act of populating or the fact of being populated [The gold rush speeded the *population* of California.]

**pop·u·lous** (päp'yə ləs) ***adj.*** full of people; heavily populated [a *populous* city].

**por·ce·lain** (pôr's'l in) ***n.*** a fine, white, hard earthenware used in making bathtubs, sinks, tiles, etc. Porcelain used for dishes is called **china.**

**porch** (pôrch) ***n.*** **1** a covered entrance to a building, usually with a roof that is held up by posts. **2** a room on the outside of a building, either open or enclosed by screens, etc.

**por·cu·pine** (pôr'kyoo pīn) ***n.*** an animal having coarse hair mixed with long, sharp spines. *See the picture.*

> **Porcupine** comes from two Latin words meaning "pig" and "spine." Porcupines are really rodents, but they look a little like small pigs with long prickly spines.

**pore**[1] (pôr) ***v.*** to study or read carefully [to *pore* over a book]. —**pored, por'ing**

**pore**[2] (pôr) ***n.*** a tiny opening such as in the skin, the leaves of plants, etc. We sweat through pores in the skin.

☆**por·gy** (pôr'gē) ***n.*** a saltwater fish used for food. —*pl.* **por'gies** or **por'gy**

**pork** (pôrk) ***n.*** the flesh of a pig or hog, especially when not cured or salted.

**pork·er** (pôr'kər) ***n.*** a hog, especially a young one, fattened for use as food.

**por·nog·ra·phy** (pôr näg'rə fē) ***n.*** writings, pictures, etc. dealing with sex in a way that is thought to be indecent or immoral.

**po·rous** (pôr'əs) ***adj.*** full of pores or tiny holes through which water, air, etc. may pass [Leather is *porous.*] —**po·ros·i·ty** (pô räs'ə tē) ***n.***

**por·phy·ry** (pôr′fə rē) ***n.*** a rock that was formed by great heat and has large crystals that are plainly seen. —*pl.* **por′phy·ries**

**por·poise** (pôr′pəs) ***n.*** **1** a water animal that is like a small whale. It is dark above and white below and has a blunt snout. **2** *another name for* **dolphin.**

**por·ridge** (pôr′ij) ***n.*** a soft food made of oatmeal or some other cereal boiled in water or milk until it is thick: *mainly a British word.*

**por·rin·ger** (pôr′in jər) ***n.*** a small, shallow bowl for porridge, cereal, etc., especially one used by children in earlier times.

**port**[1] (pôrt) ***n.*** **1** *another word for* **harbor. 2** a city with a harbor where ships can load and unload.

**port**[2] (pôrt) ***n.*** a sweet, dark-red wine.

**port**[3] (pôrt) ***n.*** the left-hand side of a ship or airplane as one faces forward, toward the bow. ◆***adj.*** of or on this side.

**port**[4] (pôrt) ***n.*** **1** *a shorter form of* **porthole. 2** the covering for a porthole. **3** an opening, as in an engine, for letting steam, gas, etc. in or out.

**Port.** *abbreviation for* **Portugal** *or* **Portuguese.**

**port·a·ble** (pôr′tə b′l) ***adj.*** that can be carried; easily carried [a *portable* TV].

**por·tage** (pôr′tij) ***n.*** ☆**1** the act of carrying boats and supplies over land from one river or lake to another. ☆**2** any route over which this is done.

**por·tal** (pôr′t′l) ***n.*** a doorway, gate, or entrance, especially a large and splendid one.

**port·cul·lis** (pôrt kul′is) ***n.*** a large, heavy iron grating that was let down to close off the gateway of an ancient castle or walled town. *See the picture.*

**por·tend** (pôr tend′) ***v.*** to be a sign or warning of; foreshadow [dark clouds that *portend* rain].

**por·tent** (pôr′tent) ***n.*** a sign that something bad is about to happen; omen [The Romans thought comets were *portents* of disaster.]

**por·ten·tous** (pôr ten′təs) ***adj.*** **1** being a sign of something bad about to happen; ominous. **2** amazing; marvelous [a *portentous* discovery].

**por·ter**[1] (pôr′tər) ***n.*** a doorman or gatekeeper.

**por·ter**[2] (pôr′tər) ***n.*** ☆**1** a person whose work is to carry luggage, as at a hotel or railroad station. ☆**2** a person who waits on passengers in a railroad sleeper or parlor car. ☆**3** a person who cleans, does errands, etc., as in a bank or store. **4** a dark-brown beer.

**por·ter·house** (pôr′tər hous) ***n.*** a choice cut of beef from the part of the loin next to the sirloin. *The full name is* **porterhouse steak.**

**port·fo·li·o** (pôrt fō′lē ō) ***n.*** **1** a flat case for carrying loose papers, drawings, etc.; briefcase. **2** things that may be carried in such a case, as a list of stocks and bonds that one owns. **3** the position or rank of certain government officials. —*pl.* **port·fo′li·os**

**port·hole** (pôrt′hōl) ***n.*** a small opening in a ship's side, as for letting in light and air.

**por·ti·co** (pôr′tə kō) ***n.*** a porch or covered walk, having a roof held up by columns. *See the picture.* —*pl.* **por′ti·coes** or **por′ti·cos**

**por·tion** (pôr′shən) ***n.*** a part given to a person or set aside for some purpose; share [a large *portion* of salad; the *portion* of one's time spent in study]. ◆***v.*** to divide or give out in portions [I *portioned* out the food.]

**Port·land** (pôrt′lənd) **1** a seaport on the coast of southern Maine. **2** a city in northwestern Oregon.

**port·ly** (pôrt′lē) ***adj.*** large and heavy in a dignified or stately way [a *portly* judge]. —**port′li·er, port′li·est** —**port′li·ness** ***n.***

**port·man·teau** (pôrt man′tō *or* pôrt′man tō′) ***n.*** a stiff leather suitcase that opens like a book at the middle. —*pl.* **port·man′teaus** or **port·man·teaux** (pôrt man′tōz *or* pôrt′man tōz′)

**por·trait** (pôr′trit *or* pôr′trāt) ***n.*** **1** a drawing, painting, or photograph of a person, especially of the face. **2** a description in a story or play.

**por·trai·ture** (pôr′tri chər) ***n.*** **1** the act or art of making portraits. **2** a portrait or portraits.

**por·tray** (pôr trā′) ***v.*** **1** to make a picture of, as in a painting. **2** to make a picture of in words; describe [The writer *portrays* life in New York.] **3** to play the part of in a play, movie, etc. [The actress *portrayed* a scientist.]

**por·tray·al** (pôr trā′əl) ***n.*** **1** the act of portraying. **2** a portrait or description.

**Por·tu·gal** (pôr′chə gəl) a country in southwestern Europe, west of Spain. It includes the Azores and the Madeira Islands.

**Por·tu·guese** (pôr′chə gēz) ***adj.*** of Portugal, its people, etc. ◆***n.*** **1** a person born or living in Portugal. —*pl.* **Por′tu·guese 2** the language of Portugal and also of Brazil.

**pose** (pōz) ***v.*** **1** to hold oneself in a certain position for a time, as for a photograph. **2** to put in a certain position [The artist *posed* the children around their parents.] **3** to pretend to be what one is not; act [to *pose* as an officer]. **4** to introduce or present [The slums *pose* a serious problem for the city.] —**posed, pos′ing** ◆***n.*** **1** a position of the body held for a picture by an artist, photographer, etc. **2** a way of acting that is meant to fool people; pretense [His gruff manner is just a *pose.*]



**Po·sei·don** (pō sīd′′n) the Greek god of the sea. The Romans called this god *Neptune.*

**po·si·tion** (pə zish′ən) ***n.*** **1** the way in which a person or thing is placed or arranged [a sitting *position*]. **2** the place where a person or thing is; location [The ship radioed its *position.*] **3** what one thinks or believes; stand [What is your *position* on aid to other countries?] **4** the usual or proper place; station [The players are in *position.*] **5** a job or office; post [She has a *position* with the city government.] ◆***v.*** to put in a certain position [They *positioned* themselves around the house.]

SYNONYMS: **Position** is used for any kind of work done for pay, but often only of a white-collar or professional job. **Post**[2] is used of a position to which one has been appointed and which has great responsibilities. **Situation** is now usually used of a position that needs to be filled or one that is wanted [*situation* open for a secretary].

| | | | |
|---|---|---|---|
| **a** fat | **ir** here | **ou** out | **zh** leisure |
| **ā** ape | **ī** bite, fire | **u** up | **ng** ring |
| **ä** car, lot | **ō** go | **ur** fur | a *in* ago |
| **e** ten | **ô** law, horn | **ch** chin | e *in* agent |
| **er** care | **oi** oil | **sh** she | **ə** = i *in* unity |
| **ē** even | **oo** look | **th** thin | o *in* collect |
| **i** hit | **ōō** tool | ***th*** then | u *in* focus |

**pos·i·tive** (päz′ə tiv) ***adj.*** **1** that will not be changed and is not to be questioned; definite [Do you have *positive* evidence that he was there?] **2** perfectly sure; certain [I'm *positive* I locked the front door.] **3** sure of oneself; confident; assured [a very *positive* person]. **4** saying that something is so; answering "yes"; affirmative [a *positive* reply]. **5** that does some good or helps in some way [*positive* criticism; a *positive* attitude toward life]. **6** existing in itself, not just in the absence of other things [a *positive* good]. **7** showing that a certain disease, condition, etc. is present [a *positive* reaction to an allergy test]. **8** being the simple form of an adjective or adverb, not showing comparison ["Good" is the *positive* degree of which "better" and "best" are the comparative and superlative.] ☆**9** describing or of a kind of electricity made on glass by rubbing it with silk. It has more protons than electrons. **10** describing a quantity greater than zero or one that is to be added; plus. **11** complete; downright: *used only in everyday talk* [a *positive* fool]. ◆***n.*** **1** something positive, as a degree, quality, quantity, etc. **2** a photographic print, or a film for use in a projector, in which the light and dark areas are exactly as in the original subject. —**in the positive,** supporting or agreeing to something [She replied *in the positive.*] —**pos′i·tive·ly** ***adv.***

**pos·se** (päs′ē) ***n.*** a group of people called together by a sheriff to help in keeping the peace.



**pos·sess** (pə zes′) ***v.*** **1** to have as something that belongs to one; own [to *possess* great wealth]. **2** to have as part of one [to *possess* wisdom]. *See* SYNONYMS *at* **hold. 3** to get power over; control [Fear suddenly *possessed* us.] —**pos·ses′sor** ***n.***

**pos·ses·sion** (pə zesh′ən) ***n.*** **1** the fact of possessing, holding, or owning; ownership [to have *possession* of secret information]. **2** something that one owns [This vase is my most prized *possession.*] **3** territory ruled by an outside country [Guam is a *possession* of the U.S.]

**pos·ses·sive** (pə zes′iv) ***adj.*** **1** having or showing a strong feeling for owning or keeping things [a *possessive* person]. **2** in grammar, describing the case of words that shows ownership, origin, etc. [The *possessive* case of English nouns is formed by adding 's or ' (the neighbor's dog; Jesus' teachings). "My," "mine," "your," "yours," "its," etc. are *possessive* pronouns.] ◆***n.*** **1** the possessive case. **2** a word in this case. —**pos·ses′sive·ly** ***adv.*** —**pos·ses′sive·ness** ***n.***

girl posting

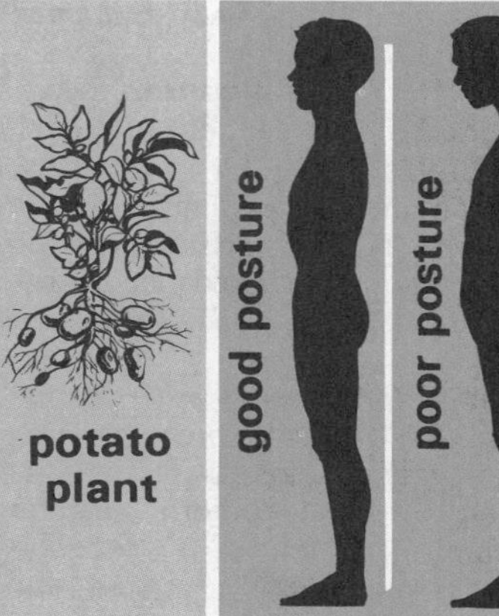
potato plant

good posture

poor posture

**pos·si·bil·i·ty** (päs′ə bil′ə tē) ***n.*** **1** the fact of being possible; chance [There is a *possibility* of rain.] **2** something that is possible [A trip to Niagara Falls is one *possibility* for our vacation.] —*pl.* **pos′si·bil′i·ties**

**pos·si·ble** (päs′ə b′l) ***adj.*** **1** that can be [The highest *possible* score in bowling is 300.] **2** that may or may not happen [colder tomorrow, with *possible* showers]. **3** that can be done, known, got, used, etc. [two *possible* routes to Denver].

SYNONYMS: **Possible** is used for anything that may be or happen or be done depending on the situation [a *possible* solution to a problem]. **Feasible** is used for anything that is likely to be successful when finished and therefore seems worth doing [a *feasible* project]. *See also* SYNONYMS *at* **probable.**

**pos·si·bly** (päs′ə blē) ***adv.*** **1** in any possible way [It can't *possibly* work.] **2** perhaps; maybe [*Possibly* it's true.]

☆**pos·sum** (päs′əm) ***n.*** *a shorter form of* **opossum**: *used only in everyday talk.* —**play possum,** to pretend to be asleep, dead, unconscious, etc.

**post**[1] (pōst) ***n.*** a long, thick piece of wood, metal, etc. set upright for holding something up, as a building, sign, fence, etc. ◆***v.*** **1** to put up on a wall, fence, post, etc. [to *post* a sign]. **2** to announce as by posting signs [A reward is *posted* for their capture.] ☆**3** to put up signs warning strangers to stay out [You should *post* your land during the hunting season.]

**post**[2] (pōst) ***n.*** **1** the place where a soldier, guard, etc. is on duty [The sentry walks a *post* just over the hill.] **2** a place where soldiers are stationed [an army *post*]. **3** the soldiers at such a place. **4** a position or job to which a person is appointed [a government *post*]. *See* SYNONYMS *at* **position. 5** *shorter form of* **trading post.** ◆***v.*** to place at a post [Guards were *posted* at every exit.]

**post**[3] (pōst) ***n.*** **1** mail, or the delivery of mail: *used mainly in Great Britain* [The letter came in this morning's *post.*] **2** in earlier times, any of the stations where riders, horses, etc. were kept as relays along a route. ◆***v.*** **1** to send by mail; place in a mailbox: *used mainly in Great Britain.* ☆**2** to give news to; inform [I will keep you *posted* on my activities.] **3** to travel fast; hurry. **4** to rise and sink back in the saddle when riding a horse, in a way that keeps rhythm with the horse's trot. *See the picture.*

**post-** *a prefix meaning* after *or* following [A *postwar* period is a period after a war.]

**post·age** (pōs′tij) ***n.*** the amount charged for delivering a letter or package by mail.

**postage stamp** a government stamp put on mail to show that postage has been paid.

**post·al** (pōs′t′l) ***adj.*** having to do with mail or post offices [the *postal* service; a *postal* clerk].

☆**postal card** **1** a card with a postage stamp printed on it, used for sending messages by mail. **2** *same as* **post card.**

**post card** **1** a picture card, etc. that can be sent through the mail when a postage stamp is stuck on it. **2** *same as* **postal card.**

**post chaise** a closed carriage with four wheels, that was pulled by fast horses.

**post·er** (pōs′tər) ***n.*** a large sign or notice put up in a public place [a movie *poster*].
**pos·te·ri·or** (päs tir′ē ər) ***adj.*** **1** at or toward the back; rear. **2** coming after; later.
**pos·ter·i·ty** (päs ter′ə tē) ***n.*** **1** the people of future times [This music will be admired by *posterity*.] **2** all the descendants of a person.
☆**post·grad·u·ate** (pōst′graj′o͞o wit) ***adj.*** of or taking a course of study after graduation.
**post·haste** (pōst′hāst′) ***adv.*** in great haste.
**post·hu·mous** (päs′cho͞o məs) ***adj.*** **1** born after its father died [a *posthumous* child]. **2** published after the author died [a collection of *posthumous* poems]. **3** coming after one has died [*posthumous* fame]. —**post′hu·mous·ly** ***adv.***
**pos·til·ion** or **pos·til·lion** (pōs til′yən *or* päs til′yən) ***n.*** a person who rides the front left-hand horse of a team pulling a carriage.
**post·man** (pōst′mən) ***n.*** *another name for* **mail carrier.** —*pl.* **post′men**
**post·mark** (pōst′märk) ***n.*** a mark stamped on mail at the post office of the sender, canceling the postage stamp and showing the place and date. ◆***v.*** to stamp with a postmark.
**post·mas·ter** (pōst′mas′tər) ***n.*** a person in charge of a post office.
**postmaster general** the person in charge of the entire postal system of a country. —*pl.* **postmasters general** or **postmaster generals**
**post-mor·tem** (pōst′môr′təm) ***adj.*** after death [a *post-mortem* examination of a body]. ◆***n.*** **1** an examination of a body after death; autopsy. **2** a careful study of something that has just ended [a *post-mortem* on the last election].
**post office** **1** an office or building where mail is sorted, postage stamps are sold, etc. **2** the department of a government that is in charge of the postal service. —**post′-of′fice** ***adj.***
**post·paid** (pōst′pād′) ***adj.*** with the sender or shipper paying the postage.
**post·pone** (pōst pōn′) ***v.*** to put off until later; delay [I *postponed* my trip because of illness.] —**post·poned′, post·pon′ing** —**post·pone′ment** ***n.***

> **Postpone** comes from two Latin words meaning "to put" and "after." When we postpone something, we are putting it after another thing which is done sooner.

**post road** a road over which mail was carried or along which there were posts for relays of fresh horses, riders, etc.
**post·script** (pōst′skript) ***n.*** a note added below the signature of a letter.
**pos·tu·late** (päs′chə lāt) ***v.*** to suppose to be true or real as the first step in proving an argument; take for granted. —**pos′tu·lat·ed, pos′tu·lat·ing** ◆***n.*** (päs′chə lit) an idea, etc. that is postulated.
**pos·ture** (päs′chər) ***n.*** **1** the way one holds the body in sitting or standing; carriage [good *posture* with the back held straight]. *See the picture.* **2** a special way of holding the body or of acting, as in posing [Doubling up a fist is a *posture* of defiance.] ◆***v.*** to take on a posture; pose. —**pos′tured, pos′tur·ing**
**post·war** (pōst′wôr′) ***adj.*** after the war.
**po·sy** (pō′zē) ***n.*** **1** a flower. **2** a bunch of flowers; bouquet. *This word is old-fashioned.* —*pl.* **po′sies**
**pot** (pät) ***n.*** **1** a round container made of various materials and used for cooking or for certain other purposes [a tea*pot;* a flower*pot*]. **2** as much as a pot will hold. ☆**3** *another name for* **marijuana**: *slang in this meaning.* ◆***v.*** **1** to put into a pot [to *pot* a plant]. **2** to cook or preserve in a pot [*potted* meat]. **3** to shoot, as game. —**pot′ted, pot′ting** —**go to pot,** to become ruined; fall apart. —**pot′ful** ***n.***
**pot·ash** (pät′ash) ***n.*** a white substance containing potassium, got from wood ashes and used in fertilizer, soap, etc.

> **Potash** and **potassium** both come from a Dutch word meaning "pot ash." Potash used to be made by boiling wood ashes in iron pots. Potassium is taken from potash by passing an electric current through the potash.

**po·tas·si·um** (pə tas′ē əm) ***n.*** a soft, silver-white metal that is a chemical element. Its salts are used in fertilizers, glass, etc.
**po·ta·to** (pə tā′tō) ***n.*** **1** a plant whose tuber, or thick, starchy underground stem, is used as a vegetable. **2** this tuber. *See the picture.* —*pl.* **po·ta′toes**
☆**potato chip** a very thin slice of potato, fried until crisp and then salted.
**pot·bel·lied** (pät′bel′ēd) ***adj.*** **1** having a belly that sticks out. **2** having rounded, bulging sides [a *potbellied* stove].
**po·tent** (pōt′'nt) ***adj.*** **1** having great power; mighty [a *potent* monarch]. **2** having a strong effect on the body or mind; very effective or forceful [a *potent* drug; a *potent* argument]. —**po·ten·cy** (pōt′'n sē) ***n.*** 571
**po·ten·tate** (pōt′'n tāt) ***n.*** a person having great power; ruler; monarch.
**po·ten·tial** (pə ten′shəl) ***adj.*** that can be, but is not yet; possible [a *potential* leader; a *potential* source of trouble]. ◆***n.*** **1** power or skill that may be developed [a baseball team with *potential*]. **2** the amount of electrical force in a circuit as measured in volts. —**po·ten′tial·ly** ***adv.***
**po·ten·ti·al·i·ty** (pə ten′shē al′ə tē) ***n.*** a possibility of becoming, developing, etc. [a test that measures one's *potentiality* as a pilot]. —*pl.* **po·ten′ti·al′i·ties**
**poth·er** (päth′ər) ***n.*** noisy confusion; fuss.
**pot·hold·er** (pät′hōl′dər) ***n.*** a thick pad of cloth for handling hot pots, pans, etc.
**pot·hook** (pät′ho͝ok) ***n.*** a hook shaped like the letter S, used to hang a pot over a fire.
**po·tion** (pō′shən) ***n.*** a drink that is supposed to heal, or to poison, do magic, etc.
**pot·luck** (pät′luk′) ***n.*** whatever the family meal happens to be [Stay and take *potluck* with us.]
**Po·to·mac** (pə tō′mək) a river flowing between Virginia and Maryland into Chesapeake Bay.
☆**pot·pie** (pät′pī′) ***n.*** **1** a meat pie baked in a deep dish. **2** a stew with dumplings.

| | | | | | | | |
|---|---|---|---|---|---|---|---|
| a | fat | ir | here | ou | out | zh | leisure |
| ā | ape | ī | bite, fire | u | up | ng | ring |
| ä | car, lot | ō | go | ur | fur | | a *in* ago |
| e | ten | ô | law, horn | ch | chin | | e *in* agent |
| er | care | oi | oil | sh | she | ə = | i *in* unity |
| ē | even | oo | look | th | thin | | o *in* collect |
| i | hit | o͞o | tool | *th* | then | | u *in* focus |

**pot·pour·ri** (pō′po͞o rē′) ***n.*** **1** a mixture of dried flower petals and spices, kept in a jar for its sweet smell. **2** any mixture or medley [a *potpourri* of songs].

> **Potpourri** was first used for a stew of many kinds of meats and vegetables. The word was French and meant "rotten pot." It is thought it was given this name because the meat was cooked until it fell apart, as it would if it were rotten.

**pot roast** a piece of beef cooked slowly in a covered pan with a little liquid.

**pot·shot** (pät′shät) ***n.*** **1** an easy shot, as one fired at close range. **2** a shot or try at something without careful aim or planning.

**pot·tage** (pät′ij) ***n.*** a kind of thick soup.

**pot·ter**[1] (pät′ər) ***n.*** a person who makes pots, dishes, etc. out of clay, shaping them on a wheel that keeps turning (called a **potter's wheel**). *See the picture.*

**pot·ter**[2] (pät′ər) ***v.*** *same as* **putter**[2]. *This spelling is used mainly in Great Britain.*

**Pot·ter** (pät′ər), **Be·a·trix** (bē′ə triks) 1866?–1943; English writer of children's books, including books about Peter Rabbit.

**potter's field** ☆a burial ground for persons who die poor or unknown.

**pot·ter·y** (pät′ər ē) ***n.*** **1** pots, dishes, etc. made of clay and hardened by baking. **2** a place where such things are made. **3** the art or work of a potter. *—pl.* **pot′ter·ies**


**pouch** (pouch) ***n.*** **1** a bag or sack [a tobacco *pouch;* a mail *pouch*]. **2** a loose fold of skin, like a pocket, on the belly of certain female animals, as the kangaroo, in which they carry their newborn young. **3** anything shaped like a pouch [the *pouch* of a pelican's bill]. ◆***v.*** to form a pouch [His cheeks *pouched* out.]

**poul·tice** (pōl′tis) ***n.*** a soft, hot, wet mixture, as of flour or mustard and water, put on a sore or inflamed part of the body.

prairie dog
41 cm (16 in.) long, including tail

powder horn

potter's wheel

prancing horse

boy pouting

**poul·try** (pōl′trē) ***n.*** fowl raised for food; chickens, turkeys, ducks, geese, etc.

**pounce** (pouns) ***v.*** to spring or swoop down, as in order to attack or seize [The cat *pounced* at a bird. The catcher *pounced* on the bunted ball.] **—pounced, pounc′ing** ◆***n.*** a sudden spring or swoop.

**pound**[1] (pound) ***n.*** **1** a unit of weight, equal to 16 ounces in avoirdupois weight or 12 ounces in troy weight. One pound avoirdupois equals 453.59 grams. **2** the basic unit of money in the United Kingdom, equal to 100 pennies; also, the basic unit of money in certain other countries, as Ireland, Israel, Sudan, etc. £ is the symbol for this unit of money.

**pound**[2] (pound) ***v.*** **1** to hit with many heavy blows; hit hard [to *pound* on a door]. *See* SYNONYMS *at* **beat.** **2** to crush into a powder or pulp by beating [to *pound* corn into meal]. **3** to move with loud, heavy steps [He *pounded* down the hall.] **4** to beat in a heavy way; throb [Her heart *pounded* from the exercise.] ◆***n.*** a hard blow or the sound of it. —☆**pound one's ear,** to sleep: *slang in this meaning.*

**pound**[3] (pound) ***n.*** a closed-in place for keeping animals, especially stray ones [a dog *pound*].

**pour** (pôr) ***v.*** **1** to let flow in a steady stream [to *pour* milk into a glass; to *pour* money into a business]. **2** to flow in a steady stream [Wet salt will not *pour.* Fans *poured* out of the stadium.] **3** to rain heavily.

**pout** (pout) ***v.*** **1** to push out the lips as in showing that one is annoyed or has hurt feelings; look sulky. *See the picture.* **2** to be silent and unfriendly; sulk. ◆***n.*** the act of pouting.

**pov·er·ty** (päv′ər tē) ***n.*** **1** the condition of being poor, or not having enough to live on. **2** the condition of being poor in quality or lacking in something [the *poverty* of this writer's imagination].

**pov·er·ty-strick·en** (päv′ər tē strik′'n) ***adj.*** very poor; suffering from great poverty.

**POW** or **P.O.W.** prisoner of war.

**pow·der** (pou′dər) ***n.*** a dry substance in the form of fine particles like dust, made by crushing or grinding [talcum *powder;* baking *powder;* gun*powder*]. ◆***v.*** **1** to sprinkle, dust, or cover as with powder [Snow *powdered* the rooftops.] **2** to make into powder.

**powder blue** pale blue.

**powder horn** a container made of an animal's horn, for carrying gunpowder. *See the picture.*

**powder puff** a soft pad for putting powder on the face or body.

**powder room** ☆a lavatory or restroom for women.

**pow·der·y** (pou′dər ē) ***adj.*** **1** of, like, or in the form of powder [*powdery* snow]. **2** easily crumbled into powder [soft, *powdery* rock]. **3** covered with powder.

**pow·er** (pou′ər) ***n.*** **1** ability to do or act [Lobsters have the *power* to grow new claws.] **2** strength or force [the *power* of a boxer's blows]. *See* SYNONYMS *at* **energy.** **3** force or energy that can be put to work [electric *power*]. **4** the ability to control others; authority [the *power* of the law]. **5** a person, thing, or nation that has control or influence over others. **6** the number of times that a certain figure is to be used as a factor [2 to the fourth *power,* or $2^4$, is equal to 2 x 2 x 2 x 2.] **7** the degree to which a lens can magnify an object [A 300-*power* microscope makes things appear 300 times as large.] ◆***v.*** to supply with power [The machine is *powered* by an engine.] ◆***adj.*** **1** worked by electricity or other kind of power [a *power* saw]. **2** made easier to operate by a special system [*power* brakes]. —**in power,** having control or authority. —**the powers that be,** the persons in control.

SYNONYMS: **Power** means the ability or right to rule, govern, or control others [Our President has limited *power*.] **Authority** is the power that a person has because of rank or position to make decisions, give orders, and make others obey orders [The general has *authority* over the whole army.]

**pow·er·ful** (pou′ər fəl) ***adj.*** having much power; strong or influential [a *powerful* hand; a *powerful* leader]. —**pow′er·ful·ly *adv.***

☆**pow·er·house** (pou′ər hous) ***n.*** **1** a building where electric power is produced. **2** a person, team, etc. with great energy, strength, drive, etc.: *used only in everyday talk.*

**pow·er·less** (pou′ər lis) ***adj.*** without power; weak or helpless [*powerless* against the storm].

**power plant** ☆a building where power, especially electric power, is produced.

☆**pow·wow** (pou′wou) ***n.*** **1** a meeting of or with North American Indians. **2** any meeting held in order to discuss something: *used only in everyday talk.* ◆***v.*** to hold a powwow.

**pox** (päks) ***n.*** a disease in which blisters form on the skin, as smallpox and chicken pox.

**pp.** *abbreviation for* **pages.**

**pr.** *abbreviation for* **pair** *or* **pairs, present, price.**

**P.R.** or **PR** *abbreviation for* **public relations, Puerto Rico.**

**prac·ti·ca·ble** (prak′ti kə b′l) ***adj.*** **1** that can be done or put into use [a *practicable* plan]. **2** that can be used; usable [Flat-bottomed boats are *practicable* in shallow water.] —**prac′ti·ca·bil′i·ty *n.***

**prac·ti·cal** (prak′ti k′l) ***adj.*** **1** that can be put to use; useful and sensible [a *practical* idea; *practical* shoes]. **2** dealing with things in a sensible and realistic way [Wouldn't it be more *practical* to paint it yourself than pay to have it painted?] **3** learned through practice or experience [*practical* nursing]. **4** really so in practice, although not so in law or theory [The *practical* head of England is the prime minister.]

**practical joke** a trick played on someone in fun.

**prac·ti·cal·ly** (prak′tik lē *or* prak′tik ′l ē) ***adv.*** **1** in a practical, useful, or sensible way [Let's look at the problem *practically*.] **2** for practical purposes; virtually; as good as [He is *practically* a dictator.] **3** almost; nearly: *used only in everyday talk* [The game was *practically* over when we left.]

☆**practical nurse** a nurse with less training than a registered nurse, often one licensed by the State (**licensed practical nurse**) to perform certain nursing duties.

**prac·tice** (prak′tis) ***v.*** **1** to do or carry out regularly; make a habit of [to *practice* what one preaches; to *practice* charity]. **2** to do something over and over again in order to become skilled at it [She *practices* two hours a day on the piano.] **3** to work at as a profession or occupation [to *practice* medicine]. —**prac′ticed, prac′tic·ing** ◆***n.*** **1** a usual action or way of acting; habit or custom [It is his *practice* to sleep late.] *See* SYNONYMS *at* **custom. 2** the doing of something over and over again in order to become skilled [batting *practice*]. **3** the skill one gets by doing this [I am out of *practice*.] **4** the work of a profession or occupation [the *practice* of law]. **5** the business built up by a doctor or lawyer [a large *practice*].

SYNONYMS: To **practice** means to repeat a certain action regularly in order to become an expert at it [He *practiced* ballet steps. She *practiced* the swan dive.] To **exercise** is to take part regularly in activities intended to train or develop the body or mind [gymnastic *exercises;* spelling *exercises*].

**prac·ticed** (prak′tist) ***adj.*** skilled; expert [the *practiced* hand of the surgeon].

**prac·tise** (prak′tis) ***v.*** *British spelling of* **practice.** —**prac′tised, prac′tis·ing**

**prac·ti·tion·er** (prak tish′ə nər) ***n.*** a person who practices a profession, art, etc.

**prag·mat·ic** (prag mat′ik) ***adj.*** concerned with actual practice, not with theory; practical: *also* **prag·mat′i·cal.** —**prag·mat′i·cal·ly *adv.***

**Prague** (präg) the capital of Czechoslovakia.

☆**prai·rie** (prer′ē) ***n.*** a large area of level or rolling grassy land without many trees.

☆**prairie chicken** a large, brown and white grouse found on North American prairies.

☆**prairie dog** a small animal of North America, a little like a squirrel. It has a barking cry. *See the picture.*

☆**prairie schooner** a large covered wagon used by pioneers to cross the American prairies.



**praise** (prāz) ***v.*** **1** to say good things about; give a good opinion of [to *praise* someone's work]. **2** to worship, as in song [to *praise* God]. —**praised, prais′ing** ◆***n.*** a praising or being praised; words that show approval. —**sing someone's praises,** to praise someone highly.

**Praise** originally meant to set a price on something or to figure out what that thing is worth. **Praise** comes from the Latin word for "price." When we praise something, we are saying that we put a very high price on it.

**praise·wor·thy** (prāz′wur′*th*ē) ***adj.*** deserving praise; that should be admired.

**pram** (pram) ***n.*** *a British name for* **perambulator**: *used only in everyday talk.*

**prance** (prans) ***v.*** **1** to rise up on the hind legs in a lively way, especially while moving along [*prancing* horses]. *See the picture.* **2** to move about with lively, strutting steps. —**pranced, pranc′ing**

**prank** (prangk) ***n.*** a playful trick, often one causing some mischief. —**prank′ish *adj.***

**prate** (prāt) ***v.*** to talk on and on, in a foolish way. —**prat′ed, prat′ing**

**prat·tle** (prat′′l) ***v.*** **1** to talk in a childish way; babble. **2** to prate; chatter foolishly. —**prat′tled, prat′tling** ◆***n.*** chatter. —**prat′tler *n.***

| | | | | | | | |
|---|---|---|---|---|---|---|---|
| **a** | fat | **ir** | here | **ou** | out | **zh** | leisure |
| **ā** | ape | **ī** | bite, fire | **u** | up | **ng** | ring |
| **ä** | car, lot | **ō** | go | **ur** | fur | | a *in* ago |
| **e** | ten | **ô** | law, horn | **ch** | chin | | e *in* agent |
| **er** | care | **oi** | oil | **sh** | she | **ə =** | i *in* unity |
| **ē** | even | **oo** | look | **th** | thin | | o *in* collect |
| **i** | hit | **ōō** | tool | ***th*** | then | | u *in* focus |

**prawn** (prôn) ***n.*** a shellfish like a large shrimp. *See the picture.*

**pray** (prā) ***v.*** **1** to talk or recite a set of words to God in worship or in asking for something. **2** to beg or ask for seriously ["*Pray* tell me" means "I beg you to tell me."]

**prayer** (prer) ***n.*** **1** the act of praying. **2** something prayed for. **3** a humble and sincere request, as to God. **4** a set of words used in praying to God [morning *prayer;* the Lord's *Prayer*].

**prayer book** a book of prayers.

**prayer·ful** (prer′fəl) ***adj.*** **1** praying often; devout [a *prayerful* monk]. **2** of or like a prayer [a *prayerful* request]. —**prayer′ful·ly** ***adv.***

**praying mantis** *another name for* **mantis.**

**pre-** *a prefix meaning* before [A *prewar* period is a period before a war.]

**preach** (prēch) ***v.*** **1** to speak to people on a religious subject, as in church; give a sermon. **2** to urge or teach as by preaching [to *preach* the word of God; to *preach* peace]. **3** to give moral or religious advice, often in a tiresome way.

**preach·er** (prē′chər) ***n.*** a person who preaches; especially, a clergyman.

**pre·am·ble** (prē′am′b'l) ***n.*** the part at the beginning of a document such as a constitution or law that tells its reason and purpose.

**pre·ar·range** (prē′ə rānj′) ***v.*** to arrange ahead of time
574 [The meeting was *prearranged.*] —**pre′ar·ranged′, pre′ar·rang′ing**

**prec.** *abbreviation for* **preceding.**

**pre·can·cel** (prē kan′s'l) ***v.*** to cancel a postage stamp before use in mailing. —**pre·can′celed** or **pre·can′celled, pre·can′cel·ing** or **pre·can′cel·ling**

**pre·car·i·ous** (pri ker′ē əs) ***adj.*** not safe or sure; uncertain; risky [a *precarious* living; a *precarious* foothold]. *See the picture.* —**pre·car′i·ous·ly** ***adv.***

> **Precarious** comes from a Latin word that means "to get by begging." In English, it originally meant "depending on the kindness of others." Later it came to mean "depending on chance," and therefore "uncertain."

**precast concrete** concrete which has been cast in the form of blocks, pillars, bridge sections, etc. before being put into position.

**pre·cau·tion** (pri kô′shən) ***n.*** care taken ahead of time, as against danger, failure, etc. [She took the *precaution* of locking the door before she left.] —**pre·cau′tion·ar′y** ***adj.***

**pre·cede** (pri sēd′) ***v.*** to go or come before in time, order, rank, etc. [She *preceded* him into the room. A colonel *precedes* a major.] —**pre·ced′ed, pre·ced′ing**

**prec·e·dence** (pres′ə dəns *or* pri sēd′əns) ***n.*** the act, fact, or right of coming before in time, order, rank, etc. [Election of officers will take *precedence* over other business at our next meeting.]

**pre·ced·ent** (pres′ə dənt) ***n.*** an act, ruling, etc. that may be used as an example or rule for one coming later. ◆***adj.*** (pri sēd′ənt) going or coming before; preceding [a *precedent* event].

**pre·ced·ing** (pri sēd′ing) ***adj.*** going or coming before; previous [in the *preceding* paragraph]. *See* SYNONYMS *at* **previous.**

**pre·cept** (prē′sept) ***n.*** a rule that tells how one should behave; maxim ["Look before you leap" is a well-known *precept.*]

**pre·cep·tor** (pri sep′tər) ***n.*** a teacher.

**pre·cinct** (prē′singkt) ***n.*** ☆**1** any of the districts into which a ward or city is divided [a voting *precinct;* a police *precinct*]. **2** *usually* **precincts,** *pl.* the grounds inside the limits of a church, school, etc. **3** a boundary or limit.

**pre·cious** (presh′əs) ***adj.*** **1** having a high price or value [Diamonds are *precious* gems. Freedom is *precious.*] **2** much loved; dear [our *precious* baby]. **3** too delicate or refined; not natural [a *precious* style of writing]. **4** very great [a *precious* liar]. —**pre′cious·ly** ***adv.***

**prec·i·pice** (pres′ə pis) ***n.*** a steep cliff that goes almost straight. *See the picture.*

**pre·cip·i·tant** (pri sip′ə tənt) ***adj.*** *another word for* **precipitate.** ◆***n.*** a substance that causes another substance to separate out as a solid from the liquid in which it is dissolved.

**pre·cip·i·tate** (pri sip′ə tāt) ***v.*** **1** to cause something to happen before one expects it or is ready for it [The floods *precipitated* a crisis.] **2** to separate out as a solid from the liquid in which it is dissolved [Salt was *precipitated* from the solution when acid was added.] **3** to condense and cause to fall as rain, snow, etc. —**pre·cip′i·tat·ed, pre·cip′i·tat·ing** ◆***adj.*** (*also* pri sip′ə tit) acting or done in a very sudden, hasty, or reckless way [Her *precipitate* decision to drop out of school seemed unwise.] ◆***n.*** (*also* pri sip′ə tit) a substance precipitated from a solution.

**pre·cip·i·ta·tion** (pri sip′ə tā′shən) ***n.*** **1** a sudden bringing about of something [the *precipitation* of a cold by getting chilled]. **2** sudden or reckless haste. **3** rain, snow, etc. or the amount of this. **4** the separating out of a solid from the liquid in which it is dissolved.

**pre·cip·i·tous** (pri sip′ə təs) ***adj.*** **1** steep like a precipice. **2** hasty or reckless. —**pre·cip′i·tous·ly** ***adv.***

**pre·cise** (pri sīs′) ***adj.*** **1** exact in every detail; definite; accurate [the *precise* sum of $12.34; *precise* pronunciation]. **2** very careful or strict, especially in following rules; finicky. —**pre·cise′ly** ***adv.*** —**pre·cise′ness** ***n.***

**pre·ci·sion** (pri sizh′ən) ***n.*** exactness; accuracy [the *precision* of a watch].

**pre·clude** (pri klo͞od′) ***v.*** to make impossible; shut out; prevent [His care *precluded* any chance of failure.] —**pre·clud′ed, pre·clud′ing**

**pre·co·cious** (pri kō′shəs) ***adj.*** having or showing much more ability, knowledge, etc. than is usual at such a young age [The *precocious* Mozart composed music at the age of five.] —**pre·co′cious·ly** ***adv.*** —**pre·coc·i·ty** (pri käs′ə tē) ***n.***

> **Precocious** comes from two Latin words that mean either "to cook ahead of time" or "to ripen ahead of time." In English, the word was first used of plants that flowered before the usual time. Now it is usually said of people, especially children, who are ready to perform and do certain things earlier in life than most children.

**pre·con·ceive** (prē kən sēv′) ***v.*** to form an idea or opinion of ahead of time [a *preconceived* notion]. —**pre·con·ceived′, pre·con·ceiv′ing**

**pre·con·cep·tion** (prē kən sep′shən) ***n.*** an idea or opinion formed ahead of time.

**pre·con·di·tion** (prē′kən dish′ən) ***n.*** anything which must exist or is required before something else can occur, be done, etc.

**pre·cur·sor** (pri kʉr′sər) ***n.*** a person or thing that comes before and makes the way ready for what will follow; forerunner [The harpsichord was a *precursor* of the piano.]

**pred·a·to·ry** (pred′ə tôr′ē) ***adj.*** **1** that lives by killing and eating other animals [Eagles are *predatory* birds.] **2** that lives by robbing, stealing, etc. [a *predatory* band of thieves].

**pred·e·ces·sor** (pred′ə ses′ər) ***n.*** a person who held a job or position before another [Hoover was the *predecessor* of Roosevelt as President.]

**pre·des·ti·na·tion** (prē des′tə nā′shən) ***n.*** **1** the belief that God decided in advance everything that would happen. **2** the belief that God decided in advance which souls were to be saved and which to be condemned. **3** one's fate in life; destiny.

**pre·des·tine** (prē des′tin) ***v.*** to order or decide in advance; foreordain [She seemed *predestined* to be a poet.] —**pre·des′tined, pre·des′tin·ing**

**pre·de·ter·mine** (prē′di tʉr′mən) ***v.*** to determine or decide ahead of time [a *predetermined* route]. —**pre′de·ter′mined, pre′de·ter′min·ing**

**pre·dic·a·ment** (pri dik′ə mənt) ***n.*** a bad situation which is hard to work one's way out of [Losing his keys put Lopez in a *predicament*.]

**pred·i·cate** (pred′ə kit) ***n.*** the word or words that say something about the subject of a sentence or clause. A predicate may be a verb, a verb and adverb, a verb and its object, etc. (The wind *blows*. The wind *blows hard*. The wind *blows the leaves down*.) ◆***adj.*** of or in a predicate [In the sentence "Julie is ill," "ill" is a *predicate* adjective.] ◆***v.*** (pred′ə kāt) **1** to base upon certain facts, conditions, etc. [The decisions of the courts are *predicated* upon the Constitution.] **2** to say that something is a quality of something else [Surely honesty can be *predicated* of her character.] —**pred′i·cat·ed, pred′i·cat·ing**

**pre·dict** (pri dikt′) ***v.*** to tell what one thinks will happen in the future [I *predict* that you will win.] *See* SYNONYMS *at* **foretell.** —**pre·dict′a·ble** ***adj.***

**pre·dic·tion** (pri dik′shən) ***n.*** **1** the act of predicting. **2** something predicted or foretold.

**pre·di·lec·tion** (pred″l ek′shən *or* prēd″l ek′shən) ***n.*** a liking or taste; preference.

**pre·dis·pose** (prē′dis pōz′) ***v.*** to make more likely to accept, get, etc.; incline [Being tired *predisposes* a person to illness.] —**pre′dis·posed′, pre′dis·pos′ing** —**pre·dis·po·si·tion** (prē′dis pə zish′ən) ***n.***

**pre·dom·i·nant** (pri däm′ə nənt) ***adj.*** **1** having more power than others; dominating [The judge had the *predominant* voice in the discussion.] **2** most frequent; prevailing [Red is the *predominant* choice of color for warning signs.] —**pre·dom′i·nance** ***n.*** —**pre·dom′i·nant·ly** ***adv.***

**pre·dom·i·nate** (pri däm′ə nāt) ***v.*** to be greater in amount, power, etc.; prevail [Red *predominates* in this pattern.] —**pre·dom′i·nat·ed, pre·dom′i·nat·ing** —**pre·dom′i·na′tion** ***n.***

☆**pree·mie** (prē′mē) ***n.*** a premature baby; a baby that is born before it is fully developed, especially one

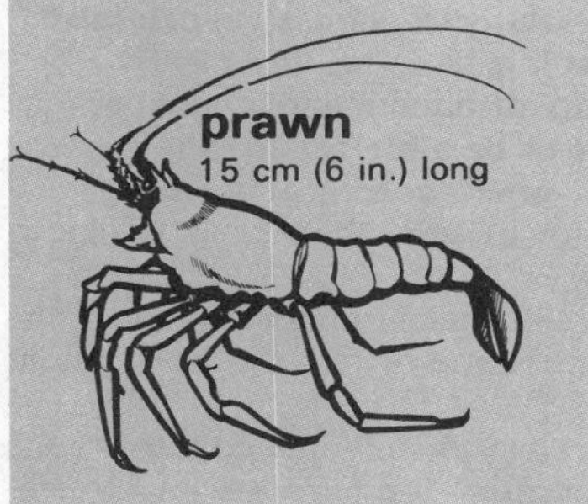

section of a prefab

precipice

bird preening itself

precarious position

that weighs less than 5 1/2 pounds. *This word is used only in everyday talk.*

**pre·em·i·nent** or **pre-em·i·nent** (prē em′ə nənt) ***adj.*** most outstanding in worth, rank, talent, fame, etc. [Marc Chagall is *preeminent* among modern painters.] —**pre·em′i·nence** or **pre-em′i·nence** ***n.*** —**pre·em′i·nent·ly** or **pre-em′i·nent·ly** ***adv.***



☆**pre·empt** or **pre-empt** (prē empt′) ***v.*** **1** to get something before anyone else can [They came early and *preempted* the best seats.] **2** to settle on public land in order to get the right to buy [Each of the settlers *preempted* 160 acres.] **3** on radio or TV, to replace a regularly scheduled program, as with a special. —**pre·emp′tion** or **pre-emp′tion** ***n.***

**preen** (prēn) ***v.*** **1** to clean and smooth the feathers with the beak, as a bird does. *See the picture.* **2** to dress up or make oneself trim and neat.

> **Preen** comes from a very old English word that means "to prick with a pin," because of the pricking motion made by a bird with the sharp point of its beak when it preens its feathers.

**pre·ex·ist** or **pre-ex·ist** (prē′ig zist′) ***v.*** to exist before, or at an earlier time. —**pre′ex·ist′ence** or **pre′-ex·ist′ence** ***n.*** —**pre′ex·ist′ent** or **pre′-ex·ist′ent** ***adj.***

**pre·fab** (prē′fab′) ***n.*** a prefabricated building: *used only in everyday talk. See the picture.*

**pre·fab·ri·cate** (prē fab′rə kāt) ***v.*** to make at a factory in sections that can be put together quickly after

| | | | | | | | |
|---|---|---|---|---|---|---|---|
| **a** | fat | **ir** | here | **ou** | out | **zh** | leisure |
| **ā** | ape | **ī** | bite, fire | **u** | up | **ng** | ring |
| **ä** | car, lot | **ō** | go | **ʉr** | fur | | a *in* ago |
| **e** | ten | **ô** | law, horn | **ch** | chin | | e *in* agent |
| **er** | care | **oi** | oil | **sh** | she | **ə =** | i *in* unity |
| **ē** | even | **oo** | look | **th** | thin | | o *in* collect |
| **i** | hit | **ōō** | tool | ***th*** | then | | u *in* focus |

being shipped [a *prefabricated* house]. —**pre·fab′ri·cat·ed, pre·fab′ri·cat·ing**

**pref·ace** (pref′is) ***n.*** an introduction to a book, article, or speech. ◆***v.*** to give or be a preface to [She *prefaced* her talk with a joke.] —**pref′aced, pref′ac·ing**

**pref·a·to·ry** (pref′ə tôr′ē) ***adj.*** that is, or is like, a preface; introductory.

**pre·fect** (prē′fekt) ***n.*** an official of high rank, as in the government of ancient Rome or of local government in modern France.

**pre·fec·ture** (prē′fek chər) ***n.*** in some countries, one of the divisions of territory for purposes of government.

**pre·fer** (pri fur′) ***v.*** 1 to like better; choose first [He *prefers* baseball to football.] 2 to bring before a law court [She *preferred* charges against the thief who stole her car.] 3 to put in a higher position or office; promote. —**pre·ferred′, pre·fer′ring**

**pref·er·a·ble** (pref′ər ə b′l) ***adj.*** that is to be preferred; more desirable. —**pref′er·a·bly *adv.***

**pref·er·ence** (pref′ər əns) ***n.*** 1 a greater liking; a preferring [She has a *preference* for seafood.] 2 one's choice; something preferred [What is your *preference* in sports?] 3 favor shown to one over another; advantage [They show *preference* for thin girls in modeling.]

**pref·er·en·tial** (pref′ə ren′shəl) ***adj.*** showing, giving, or getting preference [*preferential* treatment].

576 **pre·fer·ment** (pri fur′mənt) ***n.*** the fact of being given a higher rank, office, etc.; promotion.

**pre·fig·ure** (prē fig′yər) ***v.*** 1 to show ahead of time; be a foreshadowing of. 2 to imagine ahead of time. —**pre·fig′ured, pre·fig′ur·ing**

**pre·fix** (prē′fiks) ***n.*** a syllable or group of syllables joined to the beginning of a word to change its meaning. Some common prefixes are *un-, non-, re-, anti-,* and *in-*. ◆***v.*** (*also* prē fiks′) to place before [She *prefixed* a brief introduction to her talk.]

**preg·nan·cy** (preg′nən sē) ***n.*** the condition of being pregnant. —*pl.* **preg′nan·cies**

**preg·nant** (preg′nənt) ***adj.*** 1 having an unborn child or offspring growing in the uterus; with young. 2 filled; rich [a book *pregnant* with ideas]. 3 full of meaning; significant [a *pregnant* silence].

**pre·heat** (prē hēt′) ***v.*** to heat ahead of time.

**pre·his·tor·ic** (prē′his tôr′ik) ***adj.*** of the time before history was written [Dinosaurs were *prehistoric* creatures.] *Also* **pre′his·tor′i·cal.** —**pre′his·tor′i·cal·ly *adv.***

**pre·judge** (prē juj′) ***v.*** to judge in advance or before one knows enough to judge fairly. —**pre·judged′, pre·judg′ing**

**prej·u·dice** (prej′ə dis) ***n.*** 1 an opinion formed without knowing the facts or by ignoring the facts; unfair or unreasonable opinion [Some people have a *prejudice* against modern art.] 2 dislike or distrust of people just because they are of another race, religion, country, etc. 3 harm or damage [He gave evidence to the *prejudice* of the defendant.] ◆***v.*** 1 to fill with prejudice [Joan *prejudiced* her sister against their uncle.] 2 to harm or damage [One low grade *prejudiced* the student's chance for a scholarship.] —**prej′u·diced, prej′u·dic·ing**

SYNONYMS: **Prejudice** means an unjust opinion or judgment marked by hatred or fear [The riot was blamed on race *prejudice*.] **Bias** means a leaning in favor of or against someone or something [Several newspapers showed *bias* against our Representative.]

**prej·u·di·cial** (prej′ə dish′əl) ***adj.*** causing prejudice, or harm; damaging.

**prel·a·cy** (prel′ə sē) ***n.*** 1 the office or rank of a prelate. 2 prelates as a group. 3 church government by prelates. —*pl.* **prel′a·cies**

**prel·ate** (prel′it) ***n.*** a member of the clergy who has a high rank, as a bishop.

**pre·lim·i·nar·y** (pri lim′ə ner′ē) ***adj.*** leading up to the main action; introductory [the *preliminary* matches before the main bout]. ◆***n.*** something that is done first; preliminary step [When the *preliminaries* were over, the meeting began.] —*pl.* **pre·lim′i·nar′ies**

**prel·ude** (prel′yo͞od *or* prē′lo͞od) ***n.*** 1 a part that comes before or leads up to what follows [The calm was a *prelude* to the storm.] 2 a part at the beginning of a piece of music, as of a fugue; also, a short, romantic piece of music.

**pre·mar·i·tal** (prē mar′ə t′l) ***adj.*** before marriage.

**pre·ma·ture** (prē mə to͝or′ *or* prē mə cho͝or′) ***adj.*** before the usual or proper time; too early or too hasty. —**pre·ma·ture′ly *adv.***

**pre·med·i·tate** (pri med′ə tāt) ***v.*** to think out or plan ahead of time [a *premeditated* crime]. —**pre·med′i·tat·ed, pre·med′i·tat·ing —pre′med·i·ta′tion *n.***

**pre·mier** (pri mir′) ***n.*** a chief official; especially, a prime minister. ◆***adj.*** first in importance or position; chief.

**pre·mière** or **pre·miere** (pri myer′ *or* pri myir′) ***n.*** the first performance of a play, motion picture, etc. ◆***v.*** to show for the first time, as a play or movie. —**pre·mièred′** or **pre·miered′, pre·mièr′ing** or **pre·mier′ing**

**prem·ise** (prem′is) ***n.*** 1 a statement or belief that is taken for granted and is used as the basis for a theory, argument, etc. [the democratic *premise* that all citizens have equal rights]. 2 **premises,** *pl.* a building and the land belonging to it [Keep off the *premises*.] ◆***v.*** (*also* pri mīz′) to state as a premise. —**prem′ised, prem′is·ing**

**pre·mi·um** (prē′mē əm) ***n.*** 1 a reward or prize offered to give an added reason for buying or doing something [a valuable *premium* inside the box; extra pay as a *premium* for good work]. 2 an extra amount added to the regular charge. 3 any of the payments made for an insurance policy. 4 very high value [She puts a *premium* on neatness.] ◆***adj.*** rated as very good and higher in price [a *premium* beer]. —**at a premium,** very valuable because hard to get.

**pre·mo·ni·tion** (prē′mə nish′ən) ***n.*** a feeling that something bad will happen; forewarning.

**pre·na·tal** (prē nāt′′l) ***adj.*** before birth.

**pre·oc·cu·py** (prē äk′yə pī) ***v.*** 1 to take up one's attention so that other things are not noticed; absorb [We are *preoccupied* with vacation plans.] 2 to take or occupy before someone else can. —**pre·oc′cu·pied, pre·oc′cu·py·ing —pre·oc′cu·pa′tion *n.***

**pre·or·dain** (prē′ôr dān′) ***v.*** to order or decide beforehand what will happen.

**prep.** *abbreviation for* **preparatory, preposition.**

☆**pre·pack·age** (prē pak′ij) ***v.*** to put foods or other merchandise into packages before selling so that in each package there is a standard weight or number of units. —**pre·pack′aged, pre·pack′ag·ing**

**pre·paid** (prē pād′) *past tense and past participle of* **prepay.**

**prep·a·ra·tion** (prep′ə rā′shən) ***n.*** **1** a getting ready or being ready. **2** something done to prepare, or get ready. **3** something made or put together for some purpose, as a medicine, cosmetic, etc.

**pre·par·a·to·ry** (pri par′ə tôr′ē) ***adj.*** **1** that prepares or helps to prepare [A *preparatory* school prepares students for college.] **2** being prepared.

**pre·pare** (pri par′) ***v.*** **1** to make or get ready [to *prepare* for a test; to *prepare* ground for planting]. **2** to furnish with what is needed; equip [to *prepare* an expedition]. **3** to make or put together out of parts or materials [to *prepare* a medicine]. —**pre·pared′, pre·par′ing**

**pre·pay** (prē pā′) ***v.*** to pay for ahead of time [Postage is normally *prepaid.*] —**pre·paid′, pre·pay′ing**

**pre·pon·der·ant** (pri pän′dər ənt) ***adj.*** greater in amount, power, importance, etc. [the *preponderant* religion of a country]. —**pre·pon′der·ance** ***n.*** —**pre·pon′der·ant·ly** ***adv.***

**pre·pon·der·ate** (pri pän′də rāt) ***v.*** to be greater in amount, power, importance, etc. —**pre·pon′der·at·ed, pre·pon′der·at·ing**

**prep·o·si·tion** (prep′ə zish′ən) ***n.*** a word that connects a noun or pronoun to something else in the sentence, as to a verb (we went *to* the store), to a noun (the sound *of* music), or to an adjective (good *for* you).

**prep·o·si·tion·al** (prep′ə zish′ən ′l) ***adj.*** of, used as, or formed with a preposition.

**pre·pos·sess·ing** (prē′pə zes′iŋ) ***adj.*** making a good impression; pleasing; attractive [The speaker's *prepossessing* manner held our attention.]

**pre·pos·ter·ous** (pri päs′tər əs) ***adj.*** so clearly wrong or against reason as to be laughable; absurd [a *preposterous* idea].

**pre·req·ui·site** (pri rek′wə zit) ***n.*** something that is needed before something else can happen or be done [A college education is a *prerequisite* for a career in teaching.]

**pre·rog·a·tive** (pri räg′ə tiv) ***n.*** a special right that belongs to anyone who is a member of a certain group, has a certain rank or office, etc. [Most governors have the *prerogative* of pardoning prisoners.]

**Pres.** *abbreviation for* **President.**

**pres.** *abbreviation for* **present.**

**pres·age** (pri sāj′) ***v.*** to give a sign or warning of; foretell [dark clouds *presaging* a storm]. —**pres·aged′, pres·ag′ing** ◆***n.*** (pres′ij) **1** a sign or warning of a future happening. **2** a feeling that something is going to happen, especially something bad.

**Pres·by·te·ri·an** (prez′bə tir′ē ən) ***n.*** a member of a Protestant church that is governed by church officials called *elders.* ◆***adj.*** of the Presbyterians.

**pres·by·ter·y** (prez′bə ter′ē) ***n.*** **1** a Presbyterian church council made up of ministers and elders in a certain district. **2** such a district. —*pl.* **pres′by·ter′·ies**

**pre·school** (prē′sko͞ol′) ***adj.*** of or for children who do not yet go to school, usually children between the ages of two and five or six. —**pre·school′er** ***n.***

**pre·sci·ence** (prē′shē əns *or* presh′ē əns) ***n.*** a knowing about things before they happen; foresight. —**pre′sci·ent** ***adj.***

**pre·scribe** (pri skrīb′) ***v.*** **1** to set up as a rule or direction to be followed; order [the penalty *prescribed* by law]. **2** to order or advise to take a certain medicine or treatment [The doctor *prescribed* an antibiotic for her infection.] —**pre·scribed′, pre·scrib′ing**

**pre·scrip·tion** (pri skrip′shən) ***n.*** **1** an order or direction. **2** a doctor's written instructions telling how to prepare and use a medicine; also, a medicine made by following such instructions.

**pres·ence** (prez′′ns) ***n.*** **1** the fact or condition of being present [We need her *presence* at the meeting.] **2** the very place where a certain person is [We came into the king's *presence.*] **3** a person's looks, manner, etc. [a woman of dignified *presence*]. **4** a ghost, spirit, etc. felt to be present.

**presence of mind** the ability to think clearly and act quickly in an emergency.

**pres·ent** (prez′′nt) ***adj.*** **1** being here or at a certain place; not absent [Is everyone *present* today?] **2** of or at this time; for now; not past or future [My *present* needs are few.] **3** showing time now going on. The **present tense** of a verb shows action now taking place (he *goes*), a condition now existing (the plums *are* ripe), action that keeps taking place (she *speaks* with an accent), or action that is always true (living things *die*). ◆***n.*** **1** this time; now [At *present,* I have a job.] **2** something presented, or given; gift [birthday *presents*]. ◆***v.*** (pri zent′) **1** to make known; introduce [John *presented* his friend to me.] **2** to put on view; display; show [to *present* a play on Broadway]. **3** to offer for others to think about [May I *present* my ideas at the meeting?] **4** to give as a gift [to *present* a book to someone]. **5** to give to [She *presented* the school with a piano.] *See* SYNONYMS *at* **give.**

> SYNONYMS: A **present** and a **gift** are both given to show one's friendship, love, or respect for another. But a **present** is more personal, while a **gift** is a more formal sort of thing [birthday *presents;* a *gift* to the library].

**pre·sent·a·ble** (pri zen′tə b′l) ***adj.*** **1** that can be presented; fit to be shown, given, etc. to others [She's rewriting her story to put it in *presentable* form.] **2** properly dressed for meeting people.

**pre·sen·ta·tion** (prē′zen tā′shən *or* prez′′n tā′shən) ***n.*** **1** the act of presenting, or introducing, giving, showing, etc. [a *presentation* of awards]. **2** something that is presented, as a show, gift, etc.

**pres·ent-day** (prez′′nt dā′) ***adj.*** of the present time [*present-day* styles in clothing].

**pre·sen·ti·ment** (pri zen′tə mənt) ***n.*** a feeling that something is going to happen, especially something bad; foreboding.



| | | | | | | | |
|---|---|---|---|---|---|---|---|
| **a** | fat | **ir** | here | **ou** | out | **zh** | leisure |
| **ā** | ape | **ī** | bite, fire | **u** | up | **ŋ** | ring |
| **ä** | car, lot | **ō** | go | **ur** | fur | | a *in* ago |
| **e** | ten | **ô** | law, horn | **ch** | chin | | e *in* agent |
| **er** | care | **oi** | oil | **sh** | she | **ə =** | i *in* unity |
| **ē** | even | **oo** | look | **th** | thin | | o *in* collect |
| **i** | hit | **o͞o** | tool | ***th*** | then | | u *in* focus |

**p**

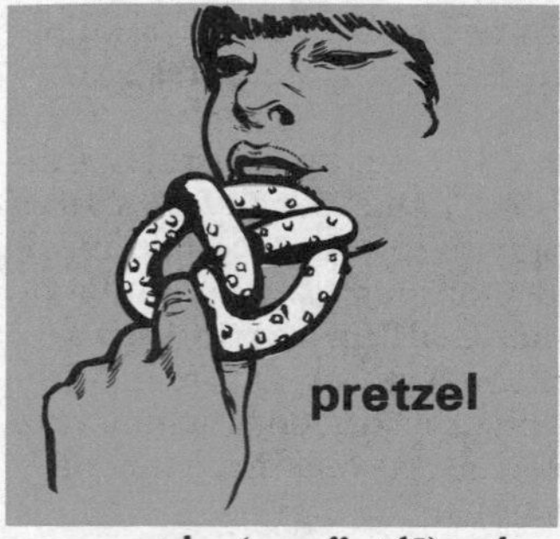
pretzel

cider press

**pres·ent·ly** (prez′'nt lē) ***adv.*** **1** in a little while; soon [The doctor will see you *presently*.] **2** at this time; now [Peg is *presently* on vacation.]

**pre·sent·ment** (pri zent′mənt) ***n.*** the act of presenting; presentation.

**present participle** a participle used to show present time, or action still going on [In the sentence "I am leaving now," "leaving" is a *present participle*.]

**pres·er·va·tion** (prez′ər vā′shən) ***n.*** a preserving or being preserved [*preservation* of food].

**pre·serv·a·tive** (pri zur′və tiv) ***n.*** anything that preserves; especially, a substance added to food to keep it from spoiling.

**pre·serve** (pri zurv′) ***v.*** **1** to protect from harm or damage; save [to *preserve* our national forests]. **2** to keep from spoiling or rotting. **3** to prepare food for later use by canning, pickling, or salting it. **4** to keep in a certain condition; maintain [She behaved politely and *preserved* her dignity.] —**pre·served′, pre·serv′·ing** ◆***n.*** **1** *usually* **preserves,** *pl.* fruit preserved by cooking it with sugar and canning it. **2** a place where fish and wild animals are protected or are kept for controlled hunting and fishing.



**pre-shrunk** (prē′shrungk′) ***adj.*** shrunk by a special process while being made so that it will shrink very little later when it is laundered or dry-cleaned.

**pre·side** (pri zīd′) ***v.*** **1** to be in charge of a meeting; act as chairman [The Vice President *presides* over the U.S. Senate] **2** to be in charge [She *presided* at his birthday party.] —**pre·sid′ed, pre·sid′ing**

**Preside** comes from two Latin words that mean "to sit in front of." A person who presides over a meeting sits in front of those at the meeting.

**pres·i·den·cy** (prez′i dən sē) ***n.*** **1** the office of president. **2** a president's term of office. —*pl.* **pres′i·den·cies**

**pres·i·dent** (prez′i dənt) ***n.*** ☆**1** the highest officer of a company, club, college, etc. **2** *often* **President,** the head of government in a republic.

**pres·i·den·tial** (prez′i den′shəl) ***adj.*** of or having to do with a president or the presidency.

**press**[1] (pres) ***v.*** **1** to act on with steady force or weight; push against, weigh down, squeeze, etc. [to *press* a doorbell]. **2** to push closely together; crowd [Thousands *pressed* into the stadium.] **3** to make clothes smooth by ironing; iron. **4** to squeeze out [to *press* oil from olives]. **5** to hold close; hug; embrace [He *pressed* the child in his arms.] **6** to keep moving forward [The soldiers *pressed* on through the night.] **7** to force [She *pressed* the gift on her friend.] **8** to trouble or worry by a lack of something [to be *pressed* for money]. **9** to keep on asking or urging [The store *pressed* her for the money she owed.] ◆***n.*** **1** a pressing or being pressed; pressure [The *press* of business kept us working overtime.] **2** a crowd. **3** a machine or tool by which something is pressed, smoothed, squeezed, etc. [a cider *press*]. *See the picture.* **4** *a shorter form for* **printing press.** **5** a place where printing is done. **6** newspapers, magazines, etc., or the people who work for them [The President meets the *press* on Tuesday.] —**go to press,** to start to be printed. —**press′er** ***n.***

**press**[2] (pres) ***v.*** to force into some work or service, especially into an army or navy.

☆**press agent** a person whose work is to get publicity for a person, group, etc.

☆**press conference** an interview granted to a group of news reporters by a celebrity or important person.

**press·ing** (pres′ing) ***adj.*** needing quick action; urgent [a *pressing* problem].

**pres·sure** (presh′ər) ***n.*** **1** a pressing or being pressed; force of pushing or of weight [the *pressure* of the foot on the brake]. **2** a condition of trouble, strain, etc. that is hard to bear [She never gave in to the *pressure* of her grief.] **3** influence or force to make someone do something [His friends put *pressure* on him to resign as president.] **4** urgent demands; urgency [She neglected her homework and now has to work under *pressure* of time.] **5** the force pressing against a surface, stated in weight per unit of area [Normal air *pressure* at sea level is 14.69 pounds per square inch.] ◆***v.*** ☆to try to force to do something. —**pres′sured, pres′sur·ing**

☆**pressure cooker** an airtight container made of metal for cooking meat, vegetables, etc. quickly by means of steam under pressure.

**pressure group** any group that puts pressure on lawmakers and the public by lobbying and propaganda for or against certain laws and policies.

**pressure suit** a type of G-suit designed to keep respiration and circulation normal, especially during spaceflights.

**pres·sur·ize** (presh′ər īz) ***v.*** to keep the air pressure close to normal, as inside an airplane. —**pres′sur·ized, pres′sur·iz·ing**

**pres·tige** (pres tēzh′) ***n.*** fame or respect that comes from doing great things, having good character, wealth, success, etc.

**pres·ti·gious** (pres tij′əs *or* pres tē′jəs) ***adj.*** having or giving prestige or fame.

**pres·to** (pres′tō) ***adj., adv.*** fast. This is an Italian word used in music to tell how fast a piece should be played.

**pre·sum·a·ble** (pri zo͞om′ə b'l) ***adj.*** that can be taken to be true; probable. —**pre·sum′a·bly** ***adv.***

**pre·sume** (pri zo͞om′) ***v.*** **1** to be so bold as to; dare [I wouldn't *presume* to tell you what to do.] **2** to take as true; take for granted; suppose [I *presume* you know what you are doing.] **3** to be too bold; take advantage of [Would I be *presuming* on our friendship if I asked you for some money?] —**pre·sumed′, pre·sum′ing**

**pre·sump·tion** (pri zump′shən) ***n.*** **1** the act of presuming. **2** the thing that is presumed or taken for granted [Because they are undefeated, the *presumption* is that they will win this game.] **3** a reason for presuming something. **4** too great boldness [his *presumption* in ordering us to leave].

**pre·sump·tive** (pri zump′tiv) ***adj.*** giving reason for believing something [*presumptive* evidence].

**pre·sump·tu·ous** (pri zump′cho͞o wəs) ***adj.*** too bold or daring; taking too much for granted [How *presumptuous* of her to offer advice without being asked!] —**pre·sump′tu·ous·ly *adv.***

**pre·sup·pose** (prē sə pōz′) ***v.*** **1** to suppose beforehand; take for granted [Her questions *presuppose* that we have read the book.] **2** to need or show as a reason [A healthy body *presupposes* a proper diet.] —**pre·sup·posed′, pre·sup·pos′ing** —**pre·sup·po·si·tion** (prē′sup ə zish′ən) ***n.***

☆**pre·teen** (prē′tēn′) ***n.*** a child who is nearly a teenager.

**pre·tend** (pri tend′) ***v.*** **1** to make believe, as in play [Let's *pretend* we're cowboys.] **2** to claim or act in a false way [She *pretended* to be angry, but she wasn't.] **3** to lay claim [He *pretended* to the throne.] —**pre·tend′ed *adj.***

**pre·tend·er** (pri ten′dər) ***n.*** **1** a person who pretends. **2** a person who claims the right to a title, especially to be a king or queen.

**pre·tense** (pri tens′ *or* prē′tens) ***n.*** **1** a claim [She made no *pretense* to being rich.] **2** a false claim, excuse, or show [a *pretense* of being ill; a *pretense* of honesty]. **3** a pretending, as in a game; make-believe. **4** a showing off; display [a simple person, without *pretense*]. *The usual British spelling is* **pretence.**

**pre·ten·sion** (pri ten′shən) ***n.*** **1** a claim, as to some right or title [He has *pretensions* to the property.] **2** a false claim or excuse. **3** a showing off; display.

**pre·ten·tious** (pri ten′shəs) ***adj.*** claiming or seeming to be very important, fine, etc.; showing off; flashy [a *pretentious* house]. —**pre·ten′tious·ly *adv.*** —**pre·ten′tious·ness *n.***

**pre·ter·nat·u·ral** (prēt′ər nach′ər əl) ***adj.*** different from or beyond what is natural; abnormal or supernatural. —**pre′ter·nat′u·ral·ly *adv.***

**pre·text** (prē′tekst) ***n.*** a false reason given to hide the real one [She was bored but left on the *pretext* of being ill.]

**pret·ty** (prit′ē *or* pur′tē) ***adj.*** **1** pleasant to look at or hear, especially in a delicate, dainty, or graceful way [a *pretty* girl; a *pretty* voice; a *pretty* garden]. **2** fine; good; nice: *often used to mean just the opposite* [You've made a *pretty* mess!] **3** quite large: *used only in everyday talk* [a *pretty* price]. —**pret′ti·er, pret′ti·est** •***adv.*** somewhat; rather [I'm *pretty* tired.] •***n.*** a pretty person or thing. —*pl.* **pret′ties** •***v.*** to make pretty [She *prettied* up her room.] —**pret′tied, pret′ty·ing** —☆**sitting pretty,** in a favorable position: *a slang phrase.* —**pret′ti·ly *adv.*** —**pret′ti·ness *n.***

☆**pret·zel** (pret′s'l) ***n.*** a slender roll of dough, usually twisted in a knot, sprinkled with salt, and baked until hard. *See the picture.*

**pre·vail** (pri vāl′) ***v.*** **1** to be successful or win out [to *prevail* over an enemy]. **2** to be or become more common or widespread, as a custom or practice. —**prevail on** or **prevail upon,** to get to do something; persuade.

**pre·vail·ing** (pri vāl′iŋ) ***adj.*** strongest, most common, or most frequent; leading all others [a *prevailing* wind; a *prevailing* style].

**prev·a·lent** (prev′ə lənt) ***adj.*** that exists, happens, etc. over a wide area; common; general [a *prevalent* belief]. —**prev′a·lence *n.***

**pre·var·i·cate** (pri var′ə kāt) ***v.*** to try to hide the truth; lie. —**pre·var′i·cat·ed, pre·var′i·cat·ing** —**pre·var′i·ca′tion *n.*** —**pre·var′i·ca′tor *n.***

> **Prevaricate** comes from a Latin word that means "to walk crookedly." A person who walks crookedly does not keep to the right or true course. A person who prevaricates does not stick to the truth but goes astray and tells a lie that he or she hopes others will believe as the truth.

**pre·vent** (pri vent′) ***v.*** **1** to stop or hinder [A storm *prevented* us from going.] **2** to keep from happening [Careful driving *prevents* accidents.] —**pre·vent′a·ble** or **pre·vent′i·ble *adj.***

**pre·ven·tion** (pri ven′shən) ***n.*** **1** the act of preventing. **2** a means of preventing: *now seldom used.*

**pre·ven·tive** (pri ven′tiv) ***adj.*** that prevents; especially, that prevents disease [*preventive* medicine]. •***n.*** anything that prevents disease, trouble, etc.

**pre·view** (prē′vyo͞o) ***n.*** ☆a view or showing ahead of time; especially, a private showing of a movie before showing it to the public. •***v.*** to give a preview of.

**pre·vi·ous** (prē′vi əs) ***adj.*** **1** happening before in time or order; earlier [at a *previous* meeting; on the *previous* page]. ☆**2** too early or too quick: *used only in everyday talk* [Weren't you a little *previous,* asking for a raise?] —**previous to,** before. —**pre′vi·ous·ly** 
***adv.***

> SYNONYMS: Anything **previous** comes before something else in time or order [a *previous* meeting]. Anything **prior** not only comes before in time or order but also is more important than something else because it is first [a *prior* claim]. Anything **preceding** comes right before something else [the *preceding* day].

**pre·war** (prē′wôr′) ***adj.*** before the war.

**prey** (prā) ***n.*** **1** an animal hunted for food by another animal [Chickens often are the *prey* of hawks.] **2** a person or thing that becomes the victim of someone or something [These simple folk were the *prey* of swindlers.] **3** the act of seizing other animals for food [The eagle is a bird of *prey.*] •***v.*** **1** to hunt other animals for food. **2** to rob by force; plunder [The pirates *preyed* upon helpless ships.] **3** to get money from, as by cheating [Gamblers *prey* on foolish people.] **4** to harm or weigh down [Debts *prey* upon my mind.]

**price** (prīs) ***n.*** **1** the amount of money asked or paid for something; cost [What is the *price* of that coat?] **2** value or worth [a painting of great *price*]. **3** a reward for the capture or killing as of a criminal [There's a *price* on his head.] **4** what must be done or sacrificed in order to get something [He gained success at the *price* of his health.] •***v.*** **1** to set the price of [The rug

| | | | | | | | |
|---|---|---|---|---|---|---|---|
| **a** | fat | **ir** | here | **ou** | out | **zh** | leisure |
| **ā** | ape | **ī** | bite, fire | **u** | up | **ŋ** | ring |
| **ä** | car, lot | **ō** | go | **ur** | fur | | a *in* ago |
| **e** | ten | **ô** | law, horn | **ch** | chin | | e *in* agent |
| **er** | care | **oi** | oil | **sh** | she | **ə =** | i *in* unity |
| **ē** | even | **oo** | look | **th** | thin | | o *in* collect |
| **i** | hit | **o͞o** | tool | ***th*** | then | | u *in* focus |

was *priced* at $40.] **2** to find out the price of: *used only in everyday talk* [I'll *price* all the models before I buy.] —**priced, pric′ing —at any price,** no matter what the cost. —**beyond price,** very valuable; priceless.

**price control** the setting of ceilings on prices for certain basic things by a government, in order to keep prices from going higher.

**price·less** (prīs′lis) ***adj.*** **1** too valuable to be measured by price [a *priceless* painting]. **2** very amusing or funny: *used only in everyday talk* [She told some *priceless* jokes.]

**prick** (prik) ***v.*** **1** to make a small hole in with a sharp point [I *pricked* my finger with the needle.] **2** to cause or feel sharp pain in; sting [Guilt *pricked* her conscience.] **3** to mark by dots or small holes [to *prick* a design in leather]. ✦***n.*** **1** a tiny hole made by a sharp point. **2** a pricking, or a sharp pain caused as by pricking [the *prick* of a pin]. —**prick up one's ears,** to raise the ears or listen closely.

**prick·le** (prik′'l) ***n.*** **1** a small, sharp point, as a thorn. **2** a stinging feeling; tingle. ✦***v.*** **1** to prick as with a thorn. **2** to sting or tingle. —**prick′led, prick′ling**

**prick·ly** (prik′lē) ***adj.*** **1** full of prickles, or sharp points. **2** that stings or tingles. —**prick′li·er, prick′li·est**

☆**prickly pear** **1** a kind of cactus with a flat stem. **2** its fruit, which is shaped like a pear and can be eaten. *See the picture.*



**pride** (prīd) ***n.*** **1** an opinion of oneself that is too high; vanity [Her *pride* blinded her to her own faults.] **2** proper respect for oneself; dignity; self-respect [He has too much *pride* to go begging.] **3** pleasure or satisfaction in something done, owned, etc. [We take *pride* in our garden.] **4** a person or thing that makes one proud [She is her father's *pride* and joy.] —**pride oneself on,** to be proud of. —**prid′ed, prid′ing**

printing press

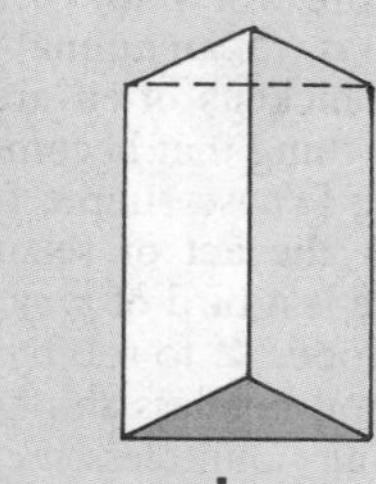
prism

prickly pear

primrose

prim woman

**priest** (prēst) ***n.*** **1** a clergyman in certain Christian churches, especially in the Roman Catholic Church. **2** a person of special rank who performs religious rites in a temple of God or of a god or goddess. —**priest′hood** ***n.***

> **Priest** comes from the Greek word *presbyteros,* meaning "elder." The Presbyterian Church, which also gets its name from this word, is governed by a group of people called "elders."

**priest·ess** (prēs′tis) ***n.*** a woman who is a priest.

**Priest·ley** (prēst′lē), **Joseph** 1733–1804; English scientist. He discovered oxygen.

**priest·ly** (prēst′lē) ***adj.*** of, like, or fit for a priest. —**priest′li·ness** ***n.***

**prig** (prig) ***n.*** an annoying person who acts as though he or she were better than others in manners, morals, etc. —**prig′gish** ***adj.***

**prim** (prim) ***adj.*** very proper in a stiff and narrow way. *See the picture.* —**prim′mer, prim′mest** —**prim′ly** ***adv.*** —**prim′ness** ***n.***

**pri·ma·cy** (prī′mə sē) ***n.*** the position of being first in time, rank, importance, etc.

**pri·ma don·na** (prē′mə dän′ə) **1** the most important woman singer in an opera. **2** a very conceited, excitable person, especially a woman who is such a person: *used only in everyday talk.* —*pl.* **pri′ma don′nas**

**pri·mal** (prī′m'l) ***adj.*** **1** first in time; original. **2** first in importance; chief.

**pri·ma·ri·ly** (prī mer′ə lē *or* prī′mer′ə lē) ***adv.*** **1** at first; originally [*Primarily* fertile land, it later became a desert.] **2** for the most part; mainly [a concert *primarily* for children].

**pri·ma·ry** (prī′mer′ē *or* prī′mər ē) ***adj.*** **1** first in time or order [the *primary* grades in school]. **2** from which others are taken or made; basic [Red, yellow, and blue are the *primary* colors in painting.] **3** first in importance; chief [a matter of *primary* interest]. ✦***n.*** **1** something first in order, importance, etc. ☆**2** an election in which candidates are chosen for a later election. —*pl.* **pri′ma′ries**

**pri·mate** (prī′māt) ***n.*** **1** an archbishop, or the bishop ranking highest in a region. **2** any member of the most highly developed order of animals, including human beings, the apes, and monkeys.

**prime** (prīm) ***adj.*** **1** first in rank or importance [her *prime* concern]. **2** first in quality [*prime* beef]. **3** that can be divided only by itself or by 1 without leaving a fraction [3, 5, 19, and 97 are *prime* numbers.] ✦***n.*** **1** the first or earliest part or stage. **2** the best or most active period in the life of a person or thing [an athlete in his *prime*]. ✦***v.*** to make ready by putting something in or on [to *prime* a gun by putting in an explosive powder; to *prime* a pump by pouring in water; to *prime* a surface for painting by putting on sizing; to *prime* a student for a test by supplying facts]. —**primed, prim′ing**

**prime minister** in countries with a parliament, the chief official of the government.

**prim·er**[1] (prim′ər) ***n.*** **1** a simple book for teaching children to read for the first time. **2** a book that gives the first lessons of any subject.

**prim·er**[2] (prī′mər) ***n.*** a person or thing that primes, as a first coat of paint, sizing, etc.

**prime ribs** a choice cut of beef that includes the seven ribs just before the loin.

☆**prime time** the hours on radio and TV when the largest audience will probably be hearing and viewing programs; especially, the evening hours.

**pri·me·val** (prī mē′v'l) ***adj.*** of earliest times; very ancient [a *primeval* forest of pine trees].

**prim·ing** (prī′miŋ) ***n.*** **1** the explosive used to set off the charge in a gun or in blasting. **2** a first coat of paint, sizing, etc.

**prim·i·tive** (prim′ə tiv) ***adj.*** **1** of or living in earliest times; ancient [Some *primitive* peoples worshiped the sun.] **2** like that of earliest times; crude; simple [*primitive* art]. ◆***n.*** **1** a primitive person or thing. **2** an artist who does primitive work. —**prim′i·tive·ly** ***adv.***

**primp** (primp) ***v.*** to dress up in a fussy way.

**prim·rose** (prim′rōz) ***n.*** **1** a plant that has small, tubelike flowers of various colors. *See the picture.* **2** the light yellow of some primroses.

**prince** (prins) ***n.*** **1** a ruler, especially of a principality. **2** a man or boy of a royal family; especially, a son or grandson of a king or queen. ☆**3** a very important person [a merchant *prince*]. ☆**4** a fine, generous, helpful fellow: *used only in everyday talk.*

**prince consort** the husband of a queen or empress who reigns in her own right.

**Prince Edward Island** an island province of southeastern Canada, north of Nova Scotia.

**prince·ly** (prins′lē) ***adj.*** **1** of or like a prince; royal; noble. **2** fit for a prince; magnificent.

**prin·cess** (prin′sis) ***n.*** **1** a daughter or granddaughter of a king or queen. **2** the wife of a prince. **3** a woman ruler with the rank of a prince.

**prin·ci·pal** (prin′sə pəl) ***adj.*** most important; chief; main [the *principal* crop of a State]. ◆***n.*** **1** a person or thing of first importance. **2** the head of a school. **3** the sum of money owed, invested, etc., not counting the interest.

**prin·ci·pal·i·ty** (prin′sə pal′ə tē) ***n.*** the land ruled by a prince [the *principality* of Monaco]. —*pl.* **prin′ci·pal′i·ties**

**prin·ci·pal·ly** (prin′sə pəl ē) ***adv.*** mainly; chiefly.

**principal parts** the present infinitive, the past tense, the past participle, and, sometimes, the present participle of a verb [The *principal parts* of "drink" are "drink," "drank," "drunk," and, sometimes, "drinking."]

**prin·ci·ple** (prin′sə pəl) ***n.*** **1** a rule, truth, etc. upon which others are based [the basic *principles* of law]. **2** a rule used in deciding how to behave [It is against her *principles* to lie.] **3** the following of the rules of right conduct; honesty and fairness [He is a man of *principle.*] **4** a scientific law that explains how a thing works [Living things grow by the *principle* of cell division.] **5** the way something works [the *principle* of the gasoline engine]. —**on principle,** because of a principle, or rule of conduct.

**print** (print) ***n.*** **1** a mark made on a surface by pressing or stamping [a foot*print*]. **2** cloth stamped with a design, or a dress, shirt, etc. made of this [She wore a floral *print.*] **3** letters or words stamped on paper as with inked type or plates [a book with small *print*]. **4** a picture or design made from an inked plate or block, as an etching or woodcut. **5** a picture made by developing a photographic negative. ◆***v.*** **1** to stamp letters, designs, etc. on a surface as with type or plates. **2** to publish in print [The magazine *printed* her story.] **3** to write in letters that look like printed ones. **4** to make a photograph by passing light through a negative onto a specially treated paper. —**in print,** still for sale by the publisher. —**out of print,** no longer for sale by the publisher.

**print·ing** (print′iŋ) ***n.*** **1** the act of one that prints. **2** the making of printed material, as books, newspapers, etc. **3** printed words. **4** all the copies of a book, etc. printed at one time. —**print′er** ***n.***

**printing press** a machine for printing from inked type, plates, or rolls. *See the picture.*

**print·out** (print′out) ***n.*** the output of a computer printed or typewritten on sheets of paper.

**pri·or**[1] (prī′ər) ***adj.*** coming before in time, order, importance, etc. [at some *prior* time; a *prior* claim to the land]. *See* SYNONYMS *at* **previous.** —**prior to,** before in time.

**pri·or**[2] (prī′ər) ***n.*** the head of a priory.

**pri·or·ess** (prī′ər is) ***n.*** a woman who is the head of a priory of nuns.

**pri·or·i·tize** (prī ôr′ə tīz) ***v.*** to arrange things in order of priority, or of what is more important and less important. —**pri·or′i·tized, pri·or′i·tiz·ing**

**pri·or·i·ty** (prī ôr′ə tē) ***n.*** **1** the fact of being prior [the *priority* of a claim to land]. **2** the right to get, buy, or do something before others. **3** something thought of as being more important than something else [high on our list of *priorities*]. —*pl.* **pri·or′i·ties** 581

**pri·or·y** (prī′ər ē) ***n.*** a monastery headed by a prior, or a convent headed by a prioress. —*pl.* **pri′or·ies**

**prism** (priz′m) ***n.*** **1** a solid figure whose ends are exactly equal and parallel and whose sides are parallelograms. *See the picture.* **2** an object of glass or clear plastic shaped like this, having ends that are triangles. It can break up light rays into the colors of the rainbow.

**pris·mat·ic** (priz mat′ik) ***adj.*** **1** of or like a prism. **2** formed by light rays passing through a prism [The *prismatic* colors are red, orange, yellow, green, blue, indigo, and violet.]

**pris·on** (priz′'n) ***n.*** a place where people are kept shut up, as while waiting for a trial or serving a sentence for breaking the law.

**pris·on·er** (priz′nər *or* priz′'n ər) ***n.*** a person who is kept shut up, as in a prison, or held as a captive, as in war.

**pris·tine** (pris′tēn) ***adj.*** of or like the earliest time or condition; also, fresh and untouched [the *pristine* look of newly fallen snow].

**prith·ee** (prith′ē) ***interj.*** I pray thee; please: *now seldom used.*

**pri·va·cy** (prī′və sē) ***n.*** **1** the condition of being away from the company of others; seclusion [She went to her room for *privacy.*] **2** secrecy [I tell you this in

| | | | |
|---|---|---|---|
| **a** fat | **ir** here | **ou** out | **zh** leisure |
| **ā** ape | **ī** bite, fire | **u** up | **ŋ** ring |
| **ä** car, lot | **ō** go | **ur** fur | a *in* ago |
| **e** ten | **ô** law, horn | **ch** chin | e *in* agent |
| **er** care | **oi** oil | **sh** she | **ə** = i *in* unity |
| **ē** even | **oo** look | **th** thin | o *in* collect |
| **i** hit | **ōō** tool | ***th*** then | u *in* focus |

strictest *privacy.*] **3** one's private life [Printing that story in the paper was an invasion of her *privacy.*]

**pri·vate** (prī′vit) ***adj.*** **1** of or for a particular person or group only; not public [*private* property; one's *private* affairs; a *private* school]. **2** not holding public office [a *private* citizen]. **3** secret; confidential [one's *private* opinion]. **4** working on one's own, not for an organization [a *private* detective]. ◆***n.*** an enlisted person of the lowest rank in the armed forces. —**in private,** secretly. —**pri′vate·ly *adv.***

**pri·va·teer** (prī və tir′) ***n.*** **1** an armed ship owned by a private person, which is put into service by the government to attack enemy ships during war. **2** the captain or a crew member of a privateer.

☆**private eye** a private detective: *a slang word.*

☆**private first class** an enlisted person in the armed forces ranking just below a corporal.

**pri·va·tion** (prī vā′shən) ***n.*** the lack of things needed to live or be comfortable [Washington's troops faced severe *privation* at Valley Forge.]

**priv·et** (priv′it) ***n.*** a shrub with small, shiny leaves, commonly used for hedges.

**priv·i·lege** (priv″l ij) ***n.*** a special right, favor, or advantage given to some person or group [The children have the *privilege* of staying up late tonight.] ◆***v.*** to give a privilege to [Wealthy people are *privileged* in several ways.] —**priv′i·leged, priv′i·leg·ing**



> **Privilege** comes from a Latin word meaning "a special law to or against the advantage of a particular person." Even today a privilege or right may be due to a law that favors one person or group and not another, as tax laws which sometimes favor a small group.

**priv·y** (priv′ē) ***adj.*** private or confidential: *now only in* **privy council,** a group appointed by a ruler to advise him or her. ◆***n.*** a toilet, especially an outdoor one. —*pl.* **priv′ies** —**privy to,** secretly informed about. —**priv′i·ly *adv.***

**prize** (prīz) ***n.*** **1** something offered or given to a winner of a contest, lottery, etc. [The first *prize* is a bicycle.] **2** anything worth trying to get [Her friendship would be a great *prize.*] **3** something captured in a war, especially an enemy warship. ◆***adj.*** **1** that has won or should win a prize; outstanding [*prize* livestock]. **2** given as a prize. ◆***v.*** to think highly of; value [I *prize* your friendship.] *See* SYNONYMS *at* **appreciate.** —**prized, priz′ing**

**prize·fight** (prīz′fīt) ***n.*** a contest between prizefighters.

**prize·fight·er** (prīz′fīt′ər) ***n.*** a fighter who takes part in boxing matches for money; professional boxer.

**pro**[1] (prō) ***adv.*** in a way that is in favor; for: *now only in the phrase* **pro and con,** meaning "for and against" [We discussed the matter *pro and con.*] ◆***prep.*** in favor of; for [They were *pro* war.] ◆***n.*** a reason or vote for [the *pros* and cons of the plan]. —*pl.* **pros**

**pro**[2] (prō) ***adj., n.*** professional: *used only in everyday talk* [*pro* golf; a golf *pro*]. —*pl.* **pros**

**pro-** *a prefix meaning* for *or* in favor of [A *prolabor* speech is a speech in favor of labor unions.]

**prob·a·bil·i·ty** (präb′ə bil′ə tē) ***n.*** **1** the fact of being probable; likelihood; good chance [There is some *probability* of rain today.] **2** something that is probable [His return is thought to be a *probability.*] —**in all probability,** very likely. —*pl.* **prob′a·bil′i·ties**

**prob·a·ble** (präb′ə b'l) ***adj.*** likely to happen or to turn out to be [the *probable* winner of an election].

> SYNONYMS: Something is **probable** if it seems from what is known that there is a strong chance something may turn out a certain way, but not for sure [Smoking is a *probable* cause of lung cancer.] Something is **possible** if it can exist, happen, be done, etc., but it is not probable that it will [It is *possible* you may live to be 100 years old.] Something is **likely** if it is more than just possible and less than probable that something will turn out a certain way [You are *likely* to fail if you don't study harder.]

**prob·a·bly** (präb′ə blē) ***adv.*** very likely; without much doubt [It will *probably* rain.]

**pro·bate** (prō′bāt) ***v.*** **1** to prove officially that the will of someone who has died is genuine and legal. ☆**2** to declare in a probate court that someone should be in a mental hospital. —**pro′bat·ed, pro′bat·ing** ◆***adj.*** having to do with such proving [a *probate* court]. ◆***n.*** ☆such official proof.

**pro·ba·tion** (prō bā′shən) ***n.*** **1** a testing of a person's character or ability, or the time of this [As a new employee, you must pass six months' *probation.*] **2** a system of dealing with certain lawbreakers, in which they are allowed to go free as long as they do nothing else wrong and report regularly to a probation officer.

☆**probation officer** an officer appointed by a court whose work is to watch over lawbreakers who have been placed on probation.

**probe** (prōb) ***n.*** **1** a slender instrument with a blunt end that a doctor uses in examining the inside of a wound or body opening. *See the picture.* **2** a complete investigation [The mayor ordered a *probe* of gambling in the city.] ☆**3** a spacecraft with instruments in it for exploring the upper atmosphere, space, or a heavenly body in order to get information. ◆***v.*** **1** to explore with a probe [to *probe* a wound]. **2** to examine or investigate carefully [to *probe* the secrets of the atom]. —**probed, prob′ing**

**prob·i·ty** (prō′bə tē) ***n.*** the quality of being honest, upright, trustworthy, etc.

**prob·lem** (präb′ləm) ***n.*** **1** a condition, person, etc. that is difficult to deal with or hard to understand [Getting the table through that narrow door will be a *problem.*] **2** a question to be solved or worked out [an arithmetic *problem;* the *problem* of reckless drivers].

**prob·lem·at·ic** (präb′lə mat′ik) ***adj.*** that is a problem; hard to figure out or deal with; not sure; uncertain [Whether we go or stay is *problematic.*] *Also* **prob′lem·at′i·cal.** —**prob′lem·at′i·cal·ly *adv.***

**pro·bos·cis** (prō bäs′is) ***n.*** **1** an elephant's trunk, or any long snout that bends easily. **2** a tubelike part of some insects, used for sucking.

**pro·ce·dure** (prə sē′jər) ***n.*** a way or method of doing something [the correct *procedure* to follow during a fire drill].

**pro·ceed** (prə sēd′) ***v.*** **1** to go on, especially after stopping for a while [After eating, we *proceeded* to the next town.] **2** to begin and go on doing something [I *proceeded* to build a fire.] **3** to move along or go on

[Things *proceeded* smoothly.] **4** to come out; issue [Smoke *proceeded* from the chimney.]

**pro·ceed·ing** (prə sēd′iŋ) ***n.*** **1** an action or series of actions; activity or procedure. **2 proceedings,** *pl.* a record of the things done at a meeting. **3 proceedings,** *pl.* legal action; lawsuit [to start *proceedings* against someone].

**pro·ceeds** (prō′sēdz) ***n.pl.*** the money or profit from some business deal or other activity.

**proc·ess** (präs′es) ***n.*** **1** a series of changes by which something develops [the *process* of growth in a plant]. **2** a method of making or doing something, in which there are a number of steps [the refining *process* used in making gasoline from crude oil]. **3** the act of doing something, or the time during which something is done [I was in the *process* of writing a report when you called.] **4** a written order to appear in a court of law; court summons. A person who delivers such a summons is called a **process server.** **5** a part growing out [a bony *process* on the heel]. ◆***v.*** to prepare by a special process [to *process* cheese].

**pro·ces·sion** (prə sesh′ən) ***n.*** **1** a number of persons or things moving forward in an orderly way. **2** the act of moving in this way.

**pro·ces·sion·al** (prə sesh′ən ′l) ***adj.*** of or having to do with a procession. ◆***n.*** **1** a hymn sung at the beginning of a church service when the clergy come in. **2** any musical work played during a procession.

**pro·claim** (prō klām′) ***v.*** to make known publicly; announce [They *proclaimed* him a hero.]

**proc·la·ma·tion** (präk′lə mā′shən) ***n.*** a proclaiming or being proclaimed; public statement.

**pro·cras·ti·nate** (prō kras′tə nāt) ***v.*** to put off doing something until later; delay. **—pro·cras′ti·nat·ed, pro·cras′ti·nat·ing —pro·cras′ti·na′tion *n.* —pro·cras′ti·na′tor *n.***

**pro·cre·a·tion** (prō′krē ā′shən) ***n.*** the act of producing or bringing into being; especially, the begetting of offspring.

**proc·tor** (präk′tər) ***n.*** an official in a school or college who keeps order, watches over students taking tests, etc.

**pro·cure** (prō kyoor′) ***v.*** to get or bring about by trying; obtain [to *procure* a job; to *procure* supplies]. **—pro·cured′, pro·cur′ing —pro·cur′a·ble *adj.***

**prod** (präd) ***v.*** **1** to poke or jab with something pointed, as a stick. **2** to urge or drive into action; goad [I needed no *prodding* to practice on my guitar.] **—prod′ded, prod′ding** ◆***n.*** **1** a poke or jab. **2** something pointed used for prodding.

**prod·i·gal** (präd′i g′l) ***adj.*** **1** wasteful in a reckless way [We have been *prodigal* with our natural resources.] **2** generous or lavish [He was *prodigal* with his praise.] **3** very plentiful [*prodigal* jungle growth]. ◆***n.*** a person who wastes money, skills, etc. in a reckless way. **—prod·i·gal·i·ty** (präd′i gal′ə tē) ***n.***

**pro·di·gious** (prə dij′əs) ***adj.*** **1** very great; huge; enormous [a *prodigious* appetite]. **2** causing wonder; amazing, especially because grand or large [a *prodigious* display of learning].

**prod·i·gy** (präd′ə jē) ***n.*** a person or thing so remarkable as to cause wonder; especially, a child who is amazingly talented or intelligent. *—pl.* **prod′i·gies**

**pro·duce** (prə do͞os′ *or* prə dyo͞os′) ***v.*** **1** to bring forth; bear; yield [trees *producing* apples; a well that *produces* oil]. **2** to make or manufacture [a company that *produces* bicycles]. **3** to bring out into view; show [*Produce* your fishing license.] **4** to cause; bring about [The flood *produced* misery.] **5** to get ready and bring to the public, as a play, movie, etc. **—pro·duced′, pro·duc′ing** ◆***n.*** (präd′o͞os *or* prō′dyo͞os) something that is produced, especially fruits and vegetables for marketing. **—pro·duc′er *n.***

probe

**prod·uct** (präd′əkt) ***n.*** **1** something produced by nature or by human beings [Wood is a natural *product.* A desk is a manufactured *product.*] **2** result [The story is a *product* of her imagination.] **3** a number that is the result of multiplying [28 is the *product* of 7 multiplied by 4.]

**pro·duc·tion** (prə duk′shən) ***n.*** **1** the act of producing [The new steel plant began *production* last week.] **2** the amount produced [The new machinery increased *production.*] **3** something that is produced, as a play that is staged for the public.



**pro·duc·tive** (prə duk′tiv) ***adj.*** **1** producing much; fertile [*productive* soil; a *productive* mind]. **2** producing goods or wealth [*productive* labor]. **3** marked by satisfying results [a *productive* day]. **4** causing [War is *productive* of much misery.] **—pro·duc·tiv·i·ty** (prō′dək tiv′ə tē) ***n.***

**Prof.** *abbreviation for* **Professor.**

**pro·fane** (prə fān′) ***adj.*** **1** showing disrespect or scorn for sacred things, as by curses or vulgar words [*profane* language]. **2** not connected with religion; not holy [Rembrandt painted both sacred and *profane* subjects.] ◆***v.*** to treat something sacred with disrespect or scorn [to *profane* a Bible by ripping its pages]. **—pro·faned′, pro·fan′ing —prof·a·na·tion** (präf′ə nā′shən) ***n.*** **—pro·fane′ly *adv.***

**Profane** comes from a Latin word meaning "outside of the temple." In ancient times, anything that was not inside the temple, or having to do with religion, was part of the world and therefore not sacred.

**pro·fan·i·ty** (prə fan′ə tē) ***n.*** **1** the quality of being profane. **2** profane language; swearing. *See* SYNONYMS *at* **blasphemy.** *—pl.* **pro·fan′i·ties —pro·fan·a·to·ry** (prə fan′ə tôr′ē) ***adj.***

| | | | | | | | |
|---|---|---|---|---|---|---|---|
| **a** | fat | **ir** | here | **ou** | out | **zh** | leisure |
| **ā** | ape | **ī** | bite, fire | **u** | up | **ŋ** | ring |
| **ä** | car, lot | **ō** | go | **ʉr** | fur | | a *in* ago |
| **e** | ten | **ô** | law, horn | **ch** | chin | | e *in* agent |
| **er** | care | **oi** | oil | **sh** | she | ə = | i *in* unity |
| **ē** | even | **oo** | look | **th** | thin | | o *in* collect |
| **i** | hit | **o͞o** | tool | ***th*** | then | | u *in* focus |

**pro·fess** (prə fes′) ***v.*** **1** to make clearly known; declare openly [They *professed* their love for each other.] **2** to claim to have or be [He *professed* a friendship which he did not really feel.] **3** to declare one's belief in [to *profess* Christianity]. **4** to follow as a profession [to *profess* medicine].

**pro·fessed** (prə fest′) ***adj.*** **1** openly declared; admitted [a *professed* conservative]. **2** falsely declared; pretended [your *professed* sympathy].

**pro·fes·sion** (prə fesh′ən) ***n.*** **1** an occupation for which one must have special education and training [Medicine, law, and teaching are *professions.*] **2** all the people in such an occupation [the legal *profession*]. **3** the act of professing, or openly declaring [a *profession* of love].

**pro·fes·sion·al** (prə fesh′ən ′l) ***adj.*** **1** of or in a profession [the *professional* ethics of a lawyer]. **2** earning one's living from a sport or other activity not usually thought of as an occupation [a *professional* golfer]. **3** engaged in by professional players [*professional* football]. ✦***n.*** **1** a person who is professional. **2** a person who does something with great skill. —**pro·fes′sion·al·ism** ***n.*** —**pro·fes′sion·al·ly** ***adv.***

**pro·fes·sor** (prə fes′ər) ***n.*** a teacher; especially, a college teacher of the highest rank. —**pro·fes·so·ri·al** (prō′fə sôr′ē əl) ***adj.*** —**pro·fes′sor·ship** ***n.***

**prof·fer** (präf′ər) ***v.*** to offer [to *proffer* friendship to a new neighbor]. ✦***n.*** an offer.

584 **pro·fi·cient** (prə fish′ənt) ***adj.*** able to do something very well; skilled; expert [a person *proficient* in many languages]. —**pro·fi′cien·cy** ***n.*** —**pro·fi′cient·ly** ***adv.***

**pro·file** (prō′fīl) ***n.*** **1** a side view of a person's face. *See the picture.* **2** a drawing of this. **3** an outline [the *profile* of the trees against the sky]. ☆**4** a short biography. **5** a graph or summary giving facts about a particular subject.

**prof·it** (präf′it) ***n.*** **1** the amount of money gained in business deals after all expenses have been subtracted [They took in $500, of which $120 was *profit.*] **2** gain of any kind; benefit; advantage [There's no *profit* in arguing about this.] ✦***v.*** **1** to be of advantage to [It will *profit* you to study hard.] **2** to get a benefit; gain [We *profited* by the sale.]

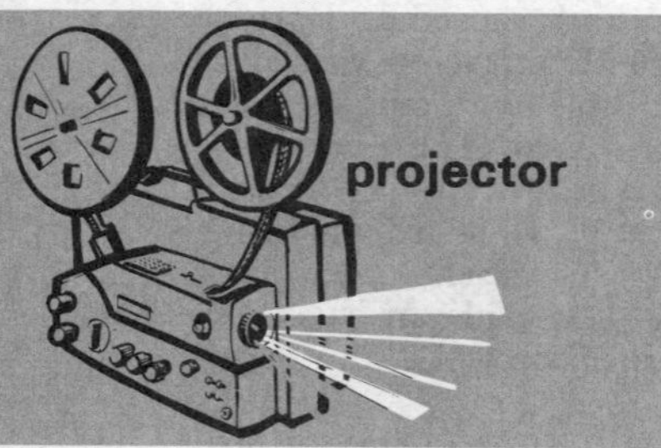
projector

profile

promenade

prominent eyebrows

**prof·it·a·ble** (präf′it ə b′l) ***adj.*** that brings profit or benefit [a *profitable* sale; a *profitable* idea]. —**prof′it·a·bly** ***adv.***

**prof·it·eer** (präf ə tir′) ***n.*** a person who makes an unfair profit by charging very high prices when there is a short supply of something that people need. ✦***v.*** to be a profiteer.

**prof·li·gate** (präf′lə git) ***adj.*** **1** very wasteful; wildly extravagant [a *profligate* spender]. **2** very wicked; immoral [a *profligate* life]. ✦***n.*** a profligate person. —**prof′li·ga·cy** ***n.***

**pro·found** (prə found′) ***adj.*** **1** showing great knowledge, thought, etc. [the *profound* remarks of the judge]. **2** very deep or strong; intense [*profound* sleep; *profound* grief]. **3** thorough [*profound* changes]. —**pro·found′ly** ***adv.***

**pro·fun·di·ty** (prə fun′də tē) ***n.*** **1** the condition of being profound; great depth. **2** something profound, as an idea. —*pl.* **pro·fun′di·ties**

**pro·fuse** (prə fyo͞os′) ***adj.*** **1** very plentiful; abundant [a *profuse* flow of water]. **2** giving freely; generous [They were *profuse* in their praise.] —**pro·fuse′ly** ***adv.*** —**pro·fuse′ness** ***n.***

**pro·fu·sion** (prə fyo͞o′zhən) ***n.*** a great or generous amount; abundance [lilies in *profusion*].

**pro·gen·i·tor** (prō jen′ə tər) ***n.*** an ancestor.

**prog·e·ny** (präj′ə nē) ***n.*** children or offspring.

**prog·no·sis** (präg nō′sis) ***n.*** **1** a foretelling. **2** a prediction of how a disease will probably develop in a person and what the chances are that the person will get well. —*pl.* **prog·no·ses** (präg nō′sēz)

**prog·nos·tic** (präg näs′tik) ***adj.*** that tells or warns of something to come; foretelling.

**prog·nos·ti·cate** (präg näs′tə kāt) ***v.*** to tell what will happen; predict; foretell. —**prog·nos′ti·cat·ed, prog·nos′ti·cat·ing** —**prog·nos′ti·ca′tion** ***n.***

**pro·gram** (prō′gram) ***n.*** **1** the acts, speeches, musical pieces, etc. that make up a ceremony or entertainment [a commencement *program;* a radio *program*]. **2** a printed list of these [May I share your *program?*] **3** a plan for doing something [a government *program* to help farmers]. **4** a series of operations to be performed by an electronic computer, as in solving problems. ✦***v.*** **1** to place in a program; schedule. **2** to set up as a plan or series of operations to be performed by an electronic computer [to *program* instructions]. **3** to furnish with such a plan or series [to *program* a computer]. —**pro′grammed** or **pro′gramed, pro′gram·ming** or **pro′gram·ing**

**prog·ress** (präg′res) ***n.*** **1** a moving forward [the boat's slow *progress* down the river]. **2** a developing or improving [She shows *progress* in learning French.] ✦***v.*** (prə gres′) **1** to move forward; go ahead. **2** to develop or improve; advance [Science has helped us to *progress.*] —**in progress,** going on.

**pro·gres·sion** (prə gresh′ən) ***n.*** **1** a moving forward or ahead; progress. **2** a series, as of acts [A *progression* of events led to our success.] **3** a series of numbers in which each is related to the next in the same way [The *progression* 1, 5, 9, 13, 17 has a difference of 4 between each two numbers. In the *progression* 1, 2, 4, 8, 16, each number is twice as large as the one before.]

**pro·gres·sive** (prə gres′iv) ***adj.*** **1** moving forward; going ahead, as by a series of steps [the *progressive* improvement of our city]. **2** wanting, bringing, or showing progress or improvement, as through political reform [*progressive* laws; a *progressive* senator]. ♦***n.*** a person who is in favor of progress or reform, especially in politics. —**pro·gres′sive·ly** ***adv.***

**pro·hib·it** (prō hib′it) ***v.*** **1** to forbid by law or by an order [Smoking is *prohibited* in this building.] *See* SYNONYMS *at* **forbid.** **2** to stop or hold back; prevent [A high wall *prohibited* us from going farther.]

**pro·hi·bi·tion** (prō′ə bish′ən) ***n.*** **1** a prohibiting or being prohibited. **2** an order or law that prohibits, especially one that prohibits people from making or selling alcoholic liquors. ☆**3 Prohibition,** the period from 1920 to 1933, when there was a Federal law of this kind. —**pro′hi·bi′tion·ist** ***n.***

**pro·hib·i·tive** (prō hib′ə tiv) ***adj.*** that prevents one from doing something [*Prohibitive* prices are prices so high that they prevent people from buying.] *Also* **pro·hib·i·to·ry** (prō hib′ə tôr′ē).

**proj·ect** (präj′ekt) ***n.*** a plan, scheme, or undertaking [Our next *project* is to build a raft.] ♦***v.*** (prə jekt′) **1** to plan or draw up, as a scheme; propose [our *projected* trip next summer]. **2** to throw forward. **3** to stick out [The shelf *projects* from the wall.] **4** to cause a shadow or image to be seen on a surface [to *project* motion pictures on a screen]. **5** to predict by using facts that are already known [to *project* sales for next year].

**pro·jec·tile** (prə jek′t'l) ***n.*** an object made to be shot with force through the air, as a cannon shell, bullet, or rocket.

**pro·jec·tion** (prə jek′shən) ***n.*** **1** a projecting or being projected. **2** something that projects, or sticks out. **3** a prediction made by using facts that are already known.

**pro·jec·tor** (prə jek′tər) ***n.*** a machine for projecting pictures or movies on a screen. *See the picture.*

**pro·le·tar·i·an** (prō′lə ter′ē ən) ***adj.*** of or belonging to the working class. ♦***n.*** a member of the proletariat; worker.

> **Proletarian** and **proletariat** come from a Latin word meaning "children." A person who belonged to the poorest group of people in Rome was called a *proletarius.* This group of people served the government only by having children.

**pro·le·tar·i·at** (prō′lə ter′ē ət) ***n.*** the working class, especially those who work in industry.

**pro·lif·er·ate** (prō lif′ə rāt) ***v.*** to grow or become greater rapidly [The cells *proliferated.* Problems are *proliferating.*] —**pro·lif′er·at·ed, pro·lif′er·at·ing** —**pro·lif′er·a′tion** ***n.***

**pro·lif·ic** (prə lif′ik) ***adj.*** **1** producing many offspring [Mice are *prolific.*] **2** producing much [a *prolific* song writer]. —**pro·lif′i·cal·ly** ***adv.***

**pro·logue** (prō′lôg) ***n.*** **1** an introduction to a poem, play, etc.; especially, lines spoken by an actor before a play begins. **2** any action or happening that serves as an introduction to another, more important happening.

**pro·long** (prə lông′) ***v.*** to make last longer; stretch out [We *prolonged* our visit by another day. Don't *prolong* the suspense.] —**pro·lon·ga·tion** (prō′lông gā′shən) ***n.***

☆**prom** (präm) ***n.*** a ball or dance of a college or school class: *used only in everyday talk.*

**prom·e·nade** (präm′ə nād′ *or* präm′ə näd′) ***n.*** **1** a walk taken for pleasure, to show off one's fine clothing, etc. **2** a public place for such a walk, as an avenue or the deck of a ship. **3** a march that begins a formal dance or comes between two parts of a square dance. *See the picture.* ♦***v.*** to take a promenade or walk. —**prom′e·nad′ed, prom′e·nad′ing** —**prom′e·nad′er** ***n.***

**Pro·me·the·us** (prə mē′thē əs *or* prə mē′thyo͞os) a giant in a Greek myth who stole fire from heaven and taught human beings how to use it. He was punished by being chained to a rock.

**prom·i·nence** (präm′ə nəns) ***n.*** **1** the condition of being prominent, or sticking out. **2** something that is prominent or sticks out, as a hill.

**prom·i·nent** (präm′ə nənt) ***adj.*** **1** standing out from a surface; projecting [*prominent* eyebrows]. *See the picture.* **2** widely known; famous; distinguished [a *prominent* artist]. **3** sure to be seen; conspicuous [*prominent* markings]. —**prom′i·nent·ly** ***adv.***

**pro·mis·cu·ous** (prə mis′kyoo wəs) ***adj.*** **1** taking whatever comes along without care in choosing [A *promiscuous* person makes love casually to many partners.] **2** made up of different kinds [a *promiscuous* collection of cheap and expensive books]. —**prom·is·cu·i·ty** (präm′is kyo͞o′ə tē) ***n.*** —**pro·mis′cu·ous·ly** ***adv.***



**prom·ise** (präm′is) ***n.*** **1** an agreement to do or not to do something; vow [to make and keep a *promise*]. **2** a sign that gives reason for expecting success; cause for hope [She shows *promise* as a singer.] ♦***v.*** **1** to make a promise to [I *promised* them I'd arrive at ten.] **2** to make a promise of [He *promised* his help.] **3** to give a reason to expect [Clear skies *promise* good weather.] **4** to say positively; assure: *used only in everyday talk.* —**prom′ised, prom′is·ing**

**Promised Land** Canaan, the land promised to Abraham by God in the Bible.

**prom·is·ing** (präm′is iŋ) ***adj.*** likely to be successful; showing promise [He is a *promising* poet.]

**prom·is·so·ry** (präm′i sôr′ē) ***adj.*** containing a promise. A **promissory note** is a written promise to pay a certain sum of money on a certain date or when it is demanded.

**prom·on·to·ry** (präm′ən tôr′ē) ***n.*** a peak of high land that juts out into a sea, lake, etc.; headland. —*pl.* **prom′on·to′ries**

**pro·mote** (prə mōt′) ***v.*** **1** to raise to a higher rank, grade, or position [She was *promoted* to manager.] **2** to help to grow, succeed, etc. [New laws were passed to *promote* the general welfare.] *See* SYNONYMS *at* **advance.** ☆**3** to make more popular, increase the sales of, etc. by advertising or giving publicity [to *promote* a

| | | | | | | | |
|---|---|---|---|---|---|---|---|
| **a** | fat | **ir** | here | **ou** | out | **zh** | leisure |
| **ā** | ape | **ī** | bite, fire | **u** | up | **ŋ** | ring |
| **ä** | car, lot | **ō** | go | **ur** | fur | | a *in* ago |
| **e** | ten | **ô** | law, horn | **ch** | chin | | e *in* agent |
| **er** | care | **oi** | oil | **sh** | she | **ə** = | i *in* unity |
| **ē** | even | **oo** | look | **th** | thin | | o *in* collect |
| **i** | hit | **o͞o** | tool | ***th*** | then | | u *in* focus |

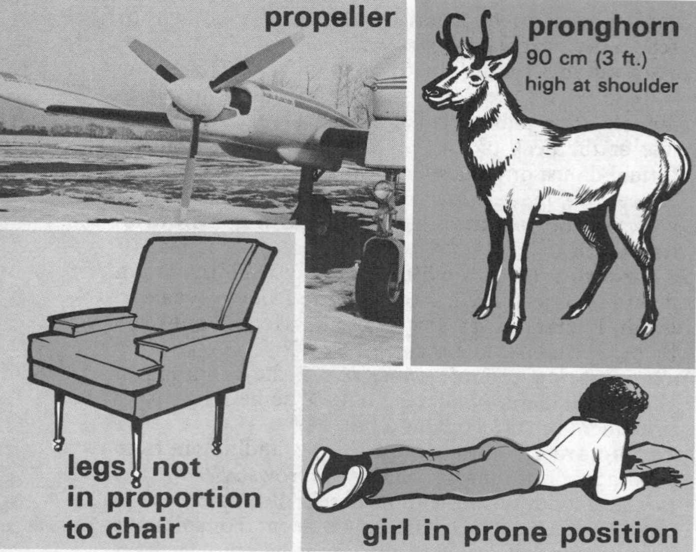


product]. ☆**4** to move a student forward a grade in school. —**pro·mot′ed, pro·mot′ing —pro·mot′er** *n.* —**pro·mo′tion** *n.*

**prompt** (prämpt) ***adj.*** **1** quick in doing what should be done; on time [He is *prompt* in paying his bills.] **2** done, spoken, etc. without waiting [We would like a



*prompt* reply.] *See* SYNONYMS *at* **quick.** ◆***v.*** **1** to urge or stir into action [Tyranny *prompted* them to revolt.] **2** to remind of something that has been forgotten [to *prompt* an actor when a line has been forgotten]. **3** to inspire [Cheerful music *prompts* happy thoughts.] —**prompt′ly** ***adv.*** —**prompt′ness** *n.*

**prompt·er** (prämp′tər) ***n.*** a person whose job is reminding actors, singers, etc. when they forget what they are supposed to say or do.

**prom·ul·gate** (präm′əl gāt *or* prō mul′gāt) ***v.*** **1** to make known in an official way; proclaim [to *promulgate* a law]. **2** to spread over a wide area [to *promulgate* a rumor]. —**prom′ul·gat·ed, prom′ul·gat·ing —prom′ul·ga′tion** *n.* —**prom′ul·ga′tor** *n.*

**pron.** *abbreviation for* **pronoun, pronunciation.**

**prone** (prōn) ***adj.*** **1** apt or likely; inclined [This typist is *prone* to error.] **2** lying face downward. *See the picture.* **3** lying flat. —**prone′ness** *n.*

**prong** (prông) ***n.*** **1** any of the pointed ends of a fork. **2** any pointed part that sticks out, as the tip of an antler. —**pronged** ***adj.***

☆**prong·horn** (prông′hôrn) ***n.*** a small antelope like a goat, found in the western U.S. and Mexico. *See the picture.*

**pro·noun** (prō′noun) ***n.*** a word used in the place of a noun. *I, us, you, they, he, her, it* are some pronouns.

**pro·nounce** (prə nouns′) ***v.*** **1** to say or make the sounds of [How do you *pronounce* "leisure"?] **2** to say or declare in an official or serious way [I now *pronounce* you husband and wife.] —**pro·nounced′, pro·nounc′ing**

**pro·nounced** (prə nounst′) ***adj.*** clearly marked; definite [a *pronounced* change].

**pro·nounce·ment** (prə nouns′mənt) ***n.*** a formal statement of a fact, opinion, etc.

☆**pron·to** (prän′tō) ***adv.*** quickly; at once. *This is a slang word.*

> **Pronto** comes from a Spanish word that means "promptly." *Pronto* was first used as an English word meaning "quickly" in the southwestern part of the United States, where there are many people who speak Spanish.

**pro·nun·ci·a·tion** (prə nun′sē ā′shən) ***n.*** **1** the act or way of forming sounds to say words [Your *pronunciation* is clear.] **2** the way a word is usually pronounced ["Either" has two *pronunciations.*]

**proof** (pro͞of) ***n.*** **1** anything that can be used to show that something is true or correct; evidence [Do they have *proof* of your guilt?] **2** the act of showing that something is true [The scientist was working on the *proof* of a theory.] **3** a test or trial [The *proof* of the pudding is in the eating.] **4** a trial print from the negative of a photograph. **5** a sheet printed from set type, used for checking errors. ◆***adj.*** of tested strength in resisting; able to withstand [The fortress was *proof* against attack.]

> SYNONYMS: **Proof** stands for facts, documents, etc. that make one believe something is true without a doubt [Their business records were clear *proof* of honesty.] **Evidence** means something presented before a court, as an object or the statement of a witness, that helps to prove a fact is true [The bloody knife was *evidence* of the murder.]

**-proof** (pro͞of) *a suffix meaning* resisting *or* protected from [*Waterproof* cloth resists wetting by water.]

☆**proof·read** (pro͞of′rēd) ***v.*** to read in order to correct errors [We *proofread* the printer's proofs before the final printing.] —**proof·read** (pro͞of′red), **proof′read·ing —proof′read′er** *n.*

**prop**[1] (präp) ***n.*** **1** a stake, pole, etc. used to hold something up. **2** a person or thing that gives support or aid. ◆***v.*** **1** to support or hold up, as with a prop [to *prop* up a sagging roof; to *prop* up one's spirits]. **2** to lean against a support [*Prop* that bike up against the wall.] —**propped, prop′ping**

**prop**[2] (präp) ***n.*** *a shorter word for* **propeller.**

**prop·a·gan·da** (präp′ə gan′də) ***n.*** the spreading of information, ideas, etc. in a way meant to make others accept them; also, the idea, etc. so spread. This word now often suggests that the ideas are false or misleading on purpose. —**prop′a·gan′dist** *n.*

**prop·a·gan·dize** (präp′ə gan′dīz) ***v.*** to spread ideas, etc. by propaganda. —**prop′a·gan′dized, prop′a·gan′diz·ing**

**prop·a·gate** (präp′ə gāt) ***v.*** **1** to increase by producing offspring [Animals and plants *propagate* their species.] **2** to cause to reproduce; raise or breed [to *propagate* pine trees]. **3** to spread from one person or place to another [to *propagate* ideas; to *propagate* light]. —**prop′a·gat·ed, prop′a·gat·ing —prop′a·ga′tion** *n.*

**pro·pane** (prō′pān) ***n.*** a kind of gas used commonly as a fuel, as for outdoor cooking grills.

**pro·pel** (prə pel′) ***v.*** to push or drive forward [Some rockets are *propelled* by liquid fuel.] —**pro·pelled′, pro·pel′ling**

**pro·pel·lant** (prə pel′ənt) ***n.*** **1** something that propels. ☆**2** the fuel used to propel a rocket.

**pro·pel·lent** (prə pel′ənt) ***adj.*** that propels or tends to propel. ◆***n.*** *same as* **propellant.**

**pro·pel·ler** (prə pel′ər) ***n.*** a device made up of blades mounted on a shaft, which is turned by an engine for driving an airplane, ship, etc. *See the picture.*

**pro·pen·si·ty** (prə pen′sə tē) ***n.*** a natural leaning or tendency; bent [She has a *propensity* for saving things.] —*pl.* **pro·pen′si·ties**

**prop·er** (präp′ər) ***adj.*** **1** right, correct, or suitable [the *proper* tool for this job; the *proper* clothes for a party]. **2** not to be ashamed of; decent; respectable [*proper* manners]. **3** in its strict or narrow sense; actual [Boston *proper,* not including its suburbs]. **4** that naturally belongs to or goes with [weather *proper* to April]. —**prop′er·ly** ***adv.***

**proper fraction** a fraction in which the numerator is less than the denominator, as 2/5.

**proper noun** a noun that is the name of a particular person, thing, or place and is begun with a capital letter [Some *proper nouns* are "Terry," "Sunday," and "Paris."] *See also* **common noun.**

**prop·er·tied** (präp′ər tēd) ***adj.*** owning property.

**prop·er·ty** (präp′ər tē) ***n.*** **1** something owned, especially land or real estate [There is much loss of *property* because of fire. We have a fence around our *property.*] **2** any of the special qualities by which a thing is known; characteristic [Oxygen has the *properties* of being colorless, odorless, and tasteless.] **3** any of the movable articles used in a play, except costumes and scenery. —*pl.* **prop′er·ties**

**proph·e·cy** (präf′ə sē) ***n.*** **1** the act or power of prophesying. **2** something told about the future, as by a prophet. —*pl.* **proph′e·cies**

**proph·e·sy** (präf′ə sī) ***v.*** **1** to tell what will happen; predict [to *prophesy* a change]. **2** to speak or write as when inspired by God. —**proph′e·sied, proph′e·sy·ing**

**proph·et** (präf′it) ***n.*** **1** a religious leader who is believed to speak for God or a god, as in giving messages or warnings [Isaiah was a *prophet.* The Greek oracles were *prophets.*] **2** a person who claims to tell what will happen in the future.

**proph·et·ess** (präf′it is) ***n.*** a woman prophet.

**pro·phet·ic** (prə fet′ik) ***adj.*** **1** of or like a prophet. **2** like or containing a prophecy [a *prophetic* warning]. —**pro·phet′i·cal·ly** ***adv.***

**pro·phy·lac·tic** (prō′fə lak′tik) ***adj.*** that helps prevent disease. ◆***n.*** a medicine, device, etc. that helps prevent disease.

> **Prophylactic** comes from a Greek word that means "to be on guard." A prophylactic cleaning of the teeth by a dentist or dental hygienist guards against tooth decay or various diseases of the gums.

**pro·pin·qui·ty** (prō piŋ′kwə tē) ***n.*** the fact of being near or close; nearness.

**pro·pi·ti·ate** (prə pish′ē āt) ***v.*** to stop or keep from being angry; win the good will of; appease [The pagans made sacrifices to *propitiate* the gods.] —**pro·pi′ti·at·ed, pro·pi′ti·at·ing** —**pro·pi′ti·a′tion** ***n.***

**pro·pi·tious** (prə pish′əs) ***adj.*** **1** that helps in some way; favorable [Sunny days mean *propitious* weather for golf.] **2** in a mood to help; gracious [The gods were *propitious.*] —**pro·pi′tious·ly** ***adv.***

**pro·po·nent** (prə pō′nənt) ***n.*** a person who proposes or supports a certain idea [Our senator is a *proponent* of lower taxes.]

**pro·por·tion** (prə pôr′shən) ***n.*** **1** the relation of one thing to another in size, amount, etc.; ratio [The *proportion* of girls to boys in our class is three to two; that is, there are three girls to every two boys.] **2** a pleasing or proper arrangement or balance of parts [The small desk and large chair are not in *proportion.*] *See the picture.* **3** a part or portion [A large *proportion* of the earth is covered with water.] **4** a relationship between four numbers, in which the first two are in the same relationship as the last two (Example: 2 is to 6 as 3 is to 9.) **5 proportions,** *pl.* dimensions, as length, width, and height [a house of large *proportions*]. ◆***v.*** **1** to arrange the parts of in a pleasing or balanced way [a well-*proportioned* statue]. **2** to put in proper relation; make fit [*Proportion* the punishment to the crime.]

**pro·por·tion·al** (prə pôr′shən ′l) ***adj.*** in proper proportion [The number of members of Congress from a State is *proportional* to its population.] —**pro·por′tion·al·ly** ***adv.***

**pro·por·tion·ate** (prə pôr′shə nit) ***adj.*** in proper proportion; proportional. —**pro·por′tion·ate·ly** ***adv.***

**pro·pos·al** (prə pō′z′l) ***n.*** **1** the act of suggesting or offering. **2** something proposed, as a plan or scheme [The council approved the mayor's *proposal.*] **3** an offer of marriage.

**pro·pose** (prə pōz′) ***v.*** **1** to suggest for others to think about, approve, etc. [We *propose* that the city build a zoo. I *propose* Robin for treasurer.] **2** to plan or intend [Do you *propose* to leave us?] **3** to make an offer of marriage. —**pro·posed′, pro·pos′ing**



**prop·o·si·tion** (präp′ə zish′ən) ***n.*** **1** something proposed; proposal; plan [I accepted their *proposition* to share expenses.] **2** a subject or idea to be discussed, proved, etc., as in a debate. **3** a problem in mathematics to be solved.

**pro·pound** (prə pound′) ***v.*** to put forth to be considered; propose [to *propound* a new theory].

**pro·pri·e·tar·y** (prə prī′ə ter′ē) ***adj.*** **1** owned by a person or company, as under a patent, trademark, or copyright [A *proprietary* medicine is patented.] **2** owning property [the *proprietary* classes]. **3** of ownership [*proprietary* rights].

**pro·pri·e·tor** (prə prī′ə tər) ***n.*** a person who owns and sometimes also operates a store or business. —**pro·pri′e·tor·ship′** ***n.***

**pro·pri·e·tress** (prə prī′ə tris) ***n.*** a woman proprietor.

**pro·pri·e·ty** (prə prī′ə tē) ***n.*** **1** the polite and correct way of behaving: *often used in the plural,* **proprieties** [We observe the *proprieties* by shaking hands when we first meet.] **2** the fact of being proper or suitable; correctness [People question the *propriety* of a judge accepting gifts from lawyers.] —*pl.* **pro·pri′e·ties**

**pro·pul·sion** (prə pul′shən) ***n.*** **1** a propelling, or driving forward. **2** a force that propels.

| | | | | | | | |
|---|---|---|---|---|---|---|---|
| **a** | fat | **ir** | here | **ou** | out | **zh** | leisure |
| **ā** | ape | **ī** | bite, fire | **u** | up | **ŋ** | ring |
| **ä** | car, lot | **ō** | go | **ur** | fur | | a *in* ago |
| **e** | ten | **ô** | law, horn | **ch** | chin | | e *in* agent |
| **er** | care | **oi** | oil | **sh** | she | ə = | i *in* unity |
| **ē** | even | **oo** | look | **th** | thin | | o *in* collect |
| **i** | hit | **ōō** | tool | ***th*** | then | | u *in* focus |

**pro·sa·ic** (prō zā′ik) ***adj.*** **1** of or like prose, not poetry. **2** dull and ordinary [My neighbor seems to lead a *prosaic* life.] —**pro·sa′i·cal·ly *adv.***

**pro·scribe** (prō skrīb′) ***v.*** **1** to forbid or talk against as being wrong or harmful [Candy is *proscribed* for children by most dentists.] **2** to take away legal rights or protection from; outlaw. —**pro·scribed′, pro·scrib′ing** —**pro·scrip·tion** (prō skrip′shən) ***n.***

**prose** (prōz) ***n.*** speech or writing that is not poetry; ordinary language.

> **Prose** comes from a Latin phrase meaning "direct speech." Prose is the form of language we ordinarily speak and write to each other. It does not have a formal pattern of rhyme or meter, as poetry usually does.

**pros·e·cute** (präs′i kyo͞ot) ***v.*** **1** to put on trial in a court of law on charges of crime or wrongdoing. **2** to carry on; keep at [to *prosecute* one's studies]. —**pros′e·cut·ed, pros′e·cut·ing**

**pros·e·cu·tion** (präs′i kyo͞o′shən) ***n.*** **1** the carrying on of a case in a court of law. **2** the State as the one who starts and carries on such a case against a person [a witness for the *prosecution*]. **3** a prosecuting, or carrying on of something.

**pros·e·cu·tor** (präs′ə kyo͞ot′ər) ***n.*** a person who prosecutes; especially, a lawyer who works for the State in prosecuting persons charged with crime.

**pros·e·lyte** (präs′ə līt) ***n.*** a person who has changed

588 from one religion, political party, etc. to another. ◆***v.*** to change or try to change a person from one religion, political party, etc. to another. —**pros′e·lyt·ed, pros′e·lyt·ing**

**pros·e·lyt·ize** (präs′ə li tīz′) ***v.*** *same as* **proselyte.** —**pros′e·lyt·ized′, pros′e·lyt·iz′ing**

**Pro·ser·pi·na** (prō sur′pi nə) in Roman myths, the daughter of Ceres, kidnapped by Pluto to be his wife in the underworld. The Greeks called her *Persephone.*

**pros·o·dy** (präs′ə dē) ***n.*** the art or rules of poetry, especially of meter and rhythm.

**pros·pect** (präs′pekt) ***n.*** **1** a looking forward to something; anticipation [the happy *prospect* of a party]. **2** *usually* **prospects,** *pl.* the likely chance of succeeding or getting something [a team with no *prospects* of winning the pennant]. **3** a person who is a likely customer, candidate, etc. **4** a wide view that is seen, as from a tower. ◆***v.*** ☆to search or explore for [*prospecting* for uranium in Australia]. —**in prospect,** expected.

**pro·spec·tive** (prə spek′tiv) ***adj.*** that is likely some day to be; expected [*prospective* parents; a *prospective* inheritance].

☆**pros·pec·tor** (präs′pek tər) ***n.*** a person who searches for deposits of valuable ores, oil, etc.

**pro·spec·tus** (prə spek′təs) ***n.*** a report describing a new business, project, etc.

**pros·per** (präs′pər) ***v.*** to succeed, thrive, grow, etc. in a vigorous way [The town *prospered* when oil was discovered nearby.]

**pros·per·i·ty** (prä sper′ə tē) ***n.*** the condition of being prosperous, wealthy, successful, etc.

**pros·per·ous** (präs′pər əs) ***adj.*** successful, well-off, thriving, etc. [a *prosperous* business]. —**pros′per·ous·ly *adv.***

**pros·ti·tute** (präs′tə to͞ot *or* präs′tə tyo͞ot) ***n.*** a person who does immoral things for money; especially, a woman who offers to have intercourse with men for money. ◆***v.*** to use in a wrongful way in order to get money [to *prostitute* one's talents]. —**pros′ti·tut·ed, pros′ti·tut·ing** —**pros′ti·tu′tion *n.***

**pros·trate** (präs′trāt) ***adj.*** **1** lying face downward [worshipers *prostrate* before an idol]. **2** lying flat, either on one's face or on one's back [The boxer was laid *prostrate* by the blow.] **3** completely overcome; weak and helpless [*prostrate* with terror]. ◆***v.*** **1** to lay in a prostrate position. **2** to overcome; make helpless [I was *prostrated* by illness.] —**pros′trat·ed, pros′trat·ing** —**pros·tra′tion *n.***

**pros·y** (prō′zē) ***adj.*** dull and boring; not exciting. —**pros′i·er, pros′i·est**

**pro·tect** (prə tekt′) ***v.*** to guard or defend against harm or danger; shield [armor to *protect* the knight's body]. *See* SYNONYMS *at* **defend.** —**pro·tec′tor *n.***

**pro·tec·tion** (prə tek′shən) ***n.*** **1** a protecting or being protected [The guard carried a club for *protection.*] **2** a person or thing that protects [Being careful is your best *protection* against accidents.]

**pro·tec·tive** (prə tek′tiv) ***adj.*** **1** that protects or helps to protect [The *protective* coloring of the brown bird hides it from its enemies.] *See the picture.* **2** that is meant to protect manufacturers from competing with cheaper products brought in from foreign countries [a *protective* tariff]. —**pro·tec′tive·ly *adv.***

**pro·tec·tor·ate** (prə tek′tər it) ***n.*** **1** a weak country or territory protected and controlled by a stronger country. **2** the relationship of the ruling country to the weaker one.

**pro·té·gé** (prōt′ə zhā) ***n.*** a person who is helped and guided in his or her career by another.

**pro·te·in** (prō′tēn *or* prō′tē in) ***n.*** a substance containing nitrogen and other elements, found in all living things and in such foods as cheese, meat, eggs, beans, etc. It is a necessary part of an animal's diet.

> **Protein** comes from the Greek word for "prime" or "chief," and that came from the word for "first." Protein is the chief substance making up plant and animal bodies.

**pro·test** (prə test′) ***v.*** **1** to speak out against; object [They joined the march to *protest* against injustice.] **2** to say in a positive way; insist [Bill *protested* that he would be glad to help.] ◆***n.*** (prō′test) the act of protesting; objection [They ignored my *protest* and continued hammering.] —**under protest,** without doing so willingly; while objecting. —**pro·test′er** or **pro·tes′tor *n.***

**Prot·es·tant** (prät′is tənt) ***n.*** a member of any of the Christian churches that grew out of the Reformation or developed since then. ◆***adj.*** of Protestants. —**Prot′es·tant·ism *n.***

**prot·es·ta·tion** (prät′is tā′shən) ***n.*** a protest or protesting; especially, an insisting in a positive way [*protestations* of love].

**pro·to·col** (prōt′ə kôl) ***n.*** the manners and forms that are accepted as proper and polite in official dealings, as between the ministers of different countries.

> **Protocol** comes from the Greek words for "first" and "glue," and originally meant the first leaf glued to a document, describing what was in it. From this it came to mean the document telling of

points of agreement reached by countries making a treaty. Later it also came to mean the code of behavior in ceremonies and dealings between high officials.

**pro·ton** (prō′tän) ***n.*** one of the particles that make up the nucleus of an atom. A proton has a single positive electric charge.

**pro·to·plasm** (prōt′ə plaz'm) ***n.*** the clear, thick, liquid substance that is the necessary part of all living animal and plant cells.

**pro·to·type** (prōt′ə tīp) ***n.*** the first one of its kind; original or model [The U.S. Constitution was the *prototype* of other democratic constitutions.]

**pro·to·zo·an** (prōt′ə zō′ən) ***n.*** a tiny, one-celled animal, living chiefly in water, that can be seen only under a microscope.

**pro·tract** (prō trakt′) ***v.*** **1** to draw out in time; prolong [*protracted* arguments]. **2** to thrust out; extend.

**pro·trac·tor** (prō trak′tər) ***n.*** an instrument used for drawing and measuring angles. It is in the form of a half circle marked with degrees. *See the picture.*

**pro·trude** (prō tro͞od′) ***v.*** to stick out; project; extend [*protruding* front teeth]. —**pro·trud′ed, pro·trud′ing** —**pro·tru·sion** (prō tro͞o′zhən) ***n.***

**pro·tu·ber·ance** (prō to͞o′bər əns *or* prō tyo͞o′bər əns) ***n.*** a part or thing that sticks out; bulge; swelling. —**pro·tu′ber·ant *adj.***

**proud** (proud) ***adj.*** **1** having proper respect for oneself, one's work, one's family, etc. [He is too *proud* to ask for help.] **2** thinking too highly of oneself; conceited; vain or haughty [They are too *proud* to say hello to us.] **3** feeling or causing pride or pleasure [his *proud* mother; a *proud* moment]. **4** splendid; magnificent [a *proud* ship]. —**proud of,** very pleased with; feeling pride about. —**proud′ly *adv.***

SYNONYMS: **Proud** ranges in meaning from having ordinary self-respect to having too great a sense of one's importance [too *proud* to beg; *proud* as a peacock]. **Arrogant** means trying to impress others with how much better or more important one is [The *arrogant* landowner ordered the peasants around.] **Haughty** means showing too much pride in oneself and contempt for others [The *haughty* official stalked by rudely.]

**Proust** (pro͞ost), **Mar·cel** (mär sel′) 1871–1922; French writer of novels.

**Prov.** *abbreviation for* **Province.**

**prove** (pro͞ov) ***v.*** **1** to show that something is true or correct [She showed us the method of *proving* our arithmetic problems.] **2** to put to a test or trial; find out about through experiments [A *proving* ground is a place for testing new equipment, as aircraft.] **3** to turn out to be [Your guess *proved* right.] —**proved, proved** or **prov′en, prov′ing**

**Pro·ven·çal** (prō vən säl′) ***n.*** a common language of Provence and nearby regions in southern France, much used in the writings of the Middle Ages.

**Pro·vence** (prō väns′) a region in southeastern France that was once a separate province.

**prov·en·der** (präv′ən dər) ***n.*** dry food for farm animals, as hay, corn, and oats.

**prov·erb** (präv′ərb) ***n.*** an old and familiar saying that tells something wise ["A stitch in time saves nine" is a *proverb.*]

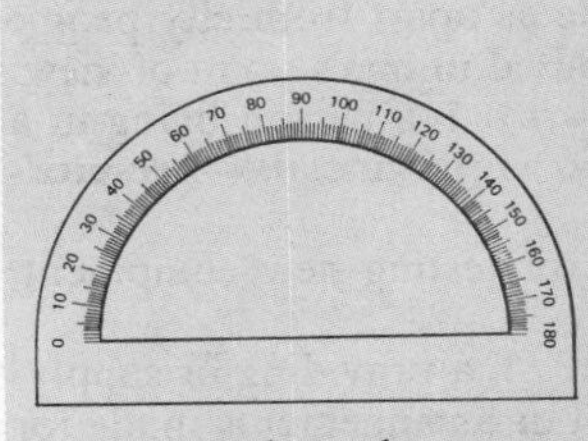

protractor

frog with protective markings

**pro·ver·bi·al** (prə vur′bē əl) ***adj.*** **1** of, like, or as in a proverb [*proverbial* wisdom]. **2** well-known because often mentioned [the *proverbial* glamour of Paris]. —**pro·ver′bi·al·ly *adv.***

**Prov·erbs** (präv′ərbz) a book of the Bible containing many sayings supposed to have been said by Solomon and others.

**pro·vide** (prə vīd′) ***v.*** **1** to give what is needed; supply; furnish [The school *provides* free books.] **2** to furnish the means of support [How large a family do you *provide* for?] **3** to get ready ahead of time; prepare [You'd better *provide* for rain by taking umbrellas.] **4** to set forth as a condition, as in a contract [Our lease *provides* that rent will be paid monthly.] —**pro·vid′ed, pro·vid′ing**

**pro·vid·ed** (prə vīd′id) ***conj.*** on the condition that; with the understanding; if [You may go swimming, *provided* you do your homework first.]



**Prov·i·dence** (präv′ə dəns) the capital of Rhode Island.

**prov·i·dence** (präv′ə dəns) ***n.*** **1** a looking ahead to the future; careful preparation or management [the *providence* of a nation in saving its natural resources]. **2** the care or help of God or fortune [A special *providence* seemed to guide the weary travelers.] **3 Providence,** God.

**prov·i·dent** (präv′ə dənt) ***adj.*** **1** providing for future needs. **2** prudent or economical.

**prov·i·den·tial** (präv′ə den′shəl) ***adj.*** by or as if ordered by the providence of God.

**pro·vid·ing** (prə vīd′iŋ) ***conj.*** on the condition that; with the understanding; if; provided [You may go bicycling, *providing* you come back soon.]

**prov·ince** (präv′ins) ***n.*** **1** a region in or belonging to a country, having its own local government; especially, any of the ten divisions of Canada that are like the States. **2 provinces,** *pl.* the parts of a country away from the large cities. **3** range of duties or work [Enforcing laws falls within the *province* of a police department.] **4** a branch of learning [the *province* of medicine].

**pro·vin·cial** (prə vin′shəl) ***adj.*** **1** of a province [a *provincial* capital]. **2** having the ways, speech, etc. of

| | | | | | | | |
|---|---|---|---|---|---|---|---|
| **a** | fat | **ir** | here | **ou** | out | **zh** | leisure |
| **ā** | ape | **ī** | bite, fire | **u** | up | **ŋ** | ring |
| **ä** | car, lot | **ō** | go | **ur** | fur | | a *in* ago |
| **e** | ten | **ô** | law, horn | **ch** | chin | | e *in* agent |
| **er** | care | **oi** | oil | **sh** | she | ə = | i *in* unity |
| **ē** | even | **oo** | look | **th** | thin | | o *in* collect |
| **i** | hit | **o͞o** | tool | ***th*** | then | | u *in* focus |

**p**

a certain province [the *provincial* customs of Quebec]. **3** of or like country people as apart from city people [*provincial* manners]. **4** limited in one's point of view; thinking in narrow ways. ◆***n.*** **1** a person living in a province. **2** a person who is provincial. —**pro·vin'cial·ism** ***n.***

**proving ground** a place for testing new equipment, new theories, etc.

**pro·vi·sion** (prə vizh'ən) ***n.*** **1** a providing or supplying. **2** something provided or arrangements made for the future [Her savings are a *provision* for her old age.] **3 provisions,** *pl.* a supply or stock of food. **4** a statement, as in a will, that makes a condition [The money was left with the *provision* that it be used for education.] ◆***v.*** to supply with provisions, especially of food [to *provision* an army].

**pro·vi·sion·al** (prə vizh'ən 'l) ***adj.*** for the time being; until a permanent one can be set up; temporary [a *provisional* government]. —**pro·vi'sion·al·ly** ***adv.***

**pro·vi·so** (prə vī'zō) ***n.*** a statement that makes a condition; provision [You may borrow it, with the *proviso* that you return it promptly.] —*pl.* **pro·vi'sos** or **pro·vi'soes**

**prov·o·ca·tion** (präv'ə kā'shən) ***n.*** **1** the act of provoking. **2** something that provokes or angers [Noisy parties are a *provocation* to the neighbors.]

**pro·voc·a·tive** (prə väk'ə tiv) ***adj.*** that arouses one to be angry, curious, amused, thoughtful, etc. [a *provocative* remark]. —**pro·voc'a·tive·ly** ***adv.***



**pro·voke** (prə vōk') ***v.*** **1** to annoy or make angry [It *provoked* me to see litter on the lawn.] **2** to arouse or call forth [The clown's antics *provoked* laughter from the crowd.] —**pro·voked', pro·vok'ing**

> **Provoke** comes from Latin words that mean "to call forth." One might say that to provoke someone is to call forth some kind of reaction, so that the person becomes curious, angry, amused, etc.

**pro·vost marshal** (prō'vō) an officer in charge of military police.

**prow** (prou) ***n.*** the forward part of a ship. *See the picture.*

**prow·ess** (prou'is) ***n.*** **1** very great skill or ability [her *prowess* in archery]. **2** bravery or a brave act, especially in fighting or war.

**prowl** (proul) ***v.*** to roam around in a quiet, secret way, as an animal looking for prey. —**on the prowl,** prowling about. —**prowl'er** ***n.***

☆**prowl car** *another name for* **squad car.**

**prox·im·i·ty** (präk sim'ə tē) ***n.*** the state of being near; nearness; closeness.

**prox·y** (präk'sē) ***n.*** **1** a person who is given the power to act for another, as in voting; agent. **2** a statement in writing giving such power. **3** the action of a proxy [to vote by *proxy*]. —*pl.* **prox'ies**

**prude** (pro͞od) ***n.*** a person who is too modest or too proper in a way that annoys others.

**pru·dent** (pro͞od'ənt) ***adj.*** careful or cautious in a sensible way; not taking chances; wise. —**pru'dence** ***n.*** —**pru'dent·ly** ***adv.***

**pru·den·tial** (pro͞o den'shəl) ***adj.*** of or showing prudence.

**prud·er·y** (pro͞od'ər ē) ***n.*** a being prudish, or too proper or modest.

**prud·ish** (pro͞od'ish) ***adj.*** of or like a prude; too proper or modest. —**prud'ish·ly** ***adv.*** —**prud'ish·ness** ***n.***

**prune**[1] (pro͞on) ***n.*** a plum dried for eating.

**prune**[2] (pro͞on) ***v.*** **1** to cut off or trim branches, twigs, etc. from [to *prune* hedges]. *See the picture.* **2** to make shorter by cutting out parts [to *prune* a novel]. —**pruned, prun'ing**

**Prus·sia** (prush'ə) a former state of northern Germany. *See the map.* —**Prus'sian** ***adj., n.***

**pry**[1] (prī) ***v.*** **1** to raise or move with a lever or crowbar. **2** to get by trying hard [to *pry* money from a miser]. —**pried, pry'ing** ◆***n.*** a lever or crowbar. —*pl.* **pries**

**pry**[2] (prī) ***v.*** to look or search closely, often to satisfy one's curiosity [Don't *pry* into my affairs.] —**pried, pry'ing**

**P.S.** or **PS** *abbreviation for* **postscript.**

**psalm** (säm) ***n.*** a sacred song or hymn, especially one from the Book of Psalms in the Bible.

**psalm·ist** (säm'ist) ***n.*** a person who writes psalms. —**the Psalmist,** King David, who is thought to have written the Book of Psalms.

**Psalms** (sämz) a book of the Bible, made up of 150 psalms: *also called* **Book of Psalms.**

**Psal·ter** (sôl'tər) the Book of Psalms, or a version of this for use in religious services.

**psal·ter·y** (sôl'tər ē) ***n.*** an ancient musical instrument with strings, played by plucking with the fingers or a plectrum. *See the picture.* —*pl.* **psal'ter·ies**

**pseu·do** (so͞o'dō *or* syo͞o'dō) ***adj.*** not really so; false; pretended [He is a *pseudo* liberal.]

**pseu·do·nym** (so͞o'də nim *or* syo͞o'də nim) ***n.*** a name used by a writer or other person in place of the real name [O. Henry is the *pseudonym* of William Sydney Porter.]

> SYNONYMS: **Pseudonym** and **pen name** mean a false name taken by a writer, although *pseudonym* is the more formal word. **Alias** also means a false name but is generally a name taken by a criminal to hide his or her real name.

**pseu·do·sci·ence** (so͞o'dō sī'əns *or* syo͞o'dō sī'əns) ***n.*** any system of methods or theories that pretends to have a basis in science but does not [Astrology is a *pseudoscience.*]

**pshaw** (shô) ***interj.*** a sound made to show that one is disgusted, impatient, etc.

**PST, P.S.T.** Pacific Standard Time.

☆**psych** (sīk) ***v.*** to use clever psychological tricks or methods to outwit, overcome, or control someone: *usually followed by* out. *This word is slang.*

**Psy·che** (sī'kē) a maiden in Roman myths who was loved by Cupid and was made immortal by Jupiter.

**psy·che** (sī'kē) ***n.*** the soul or mind.

☆**psy·che·del·ic** (sī'kə del'ik) ***adj.*** **1** causing one to have strange feelings, to see and hear things that are not there, and to have mistaken notions, like those in mental illness [LSD is a *psychedelic* drug.] **2** having effects like those caused by a psychedelic drug [*psychedelic* art or music].

**psy·chi·a·trist** (sə kī'ə trist *or* sī kī'ə trist) ***n.*** a doctor who takes care of people who are mentally ill.

**psy·chi·a·try** (sə kī'ə trē *or* sī kī'ə trē) ***n.*** the branch of medicine that deals with the treatment of mental illness. —**psy·chi·at·ric** (sī'kē at'rik) ***adj.***

**psy·chic** (sī′kik) ***adj.*** **1** that cannot be explained by natural or physical laws; supernatural [People used to think that an eclipse was due to *psychic* forces.] **2** that seems to be sensitive to supernatural forces [a *psychic* person who seems to read your mind]. **3** of the mind; mental [*psychic* processes]. *Also* **psy′chi·cal.** —**psy′chi·cal·ly *adv.***

**psy·cho·a·nal·y·sis** (sī′kō ə nal′ə sis) ***n.*** a method of treating certain mental illnesses by helping the patient bring to mind unpleasant memories that have been forced into the unconscious. —**psy·cho·an·a·lyst** (sī′kō an′əl ist) ***n.***

**psy·cho·log·i·cal** (sī′kə läj′i k'l) ***adj.*** **1** of or using psychology [*psychological* tests]. **2** of the mind; mental [*psychological* development]. **3** using propaganda and psychology to influence or confuse people [*psychological* warfare]. **4** most favorable or most suitable [the *psychological* moment]. —**psy′cho·log′i·cal·ly *adv.***

**psy·chol·o·gy** (sī käl′ə jē) ***n.*** **1** the science that studies the mind and the reasons for the ways that people think and act. **2** the ways of thinking and acting of a person or group [the *psychology* of the child; mob *psychology*]. —*pl.* **psy·chol′o·gies** —**psy·chol′o·gist *n.***

**psy·cho·path** (sī′kə path) ***n.*** a person with a mental illness, especially one who does cruel or criminal acts without feeling sorry or guilty. —**psy·cho·path·ic** (sī′kə path′ik) ***adj.***

**psy·cho·sis** (sī kō′sis) ***n.*** a severe mental illness. —*pl.* **psy·cho·ses** (sī kō′sēz)

**psy·cho·so·mat·ic** (sī′kō sō mat′ik) ***adj.*** of or having to do with pain or a physical illness that is caused by or made worse by mental or emotional troubles of the patient.

**psy·cho·ther·a·py** (sī′kō ther′ə pē) ***n.*** treatment of mental illness by counseling, discussion, etc.

**psy·chot·ic** (sī kät′ik) ***adj.*** like or having a psychosis; very ill mentally. ➧***n.*** a person who has a psychosis. —**psy·chot′i·cal·ly *adv.***

**Pt** *the symbol for the chemical element* platinum.

**pt.** *abbreviation for* **part, pint, point.** —*pl.* **pts.**

**P.T.A.** Parent-Teacher Association.

**ptar·mi·gan** (tär′mə gən) ***n.*** a grouse with feathers on its legs, found in northern regions.

**pter·o·dac·tyl** (ter′ə dak′t'l) ***n.*** a flying reptile that lived millions of years ago. It was somewhat like a large lizard with huge wings. *See the picture.*

**Ptol·e·ma·ic** (täl′ə mā′ik) ***adj.*** of Ptolemy or his theory that all heavenly bodies revolved around the earth.

**Ptol·e·my** (täl′ə mē) a Greek astronomer who lived in Egypt in the second century A.D.

**pto·maine** (tō′mān) ***n.*** a substance found in decaying animal or vegetable matter.

> **Ptomaine** comes from the Greek word for "corpse." A corpse is a dead and decaying animal. Ptomaines form in corpses and rotten food and other decaying matter.

**ptomaine poisoning** *an earlier name for* **food poisoning.** At one time it was thought that ptomaines cause food poisoning, but they do not.

**Pu** *the symbol for the chemical element* plutonium.

**pub** (pub) ***n.*** a bar or tavern in Great Britain. *The full name is* **public house.**

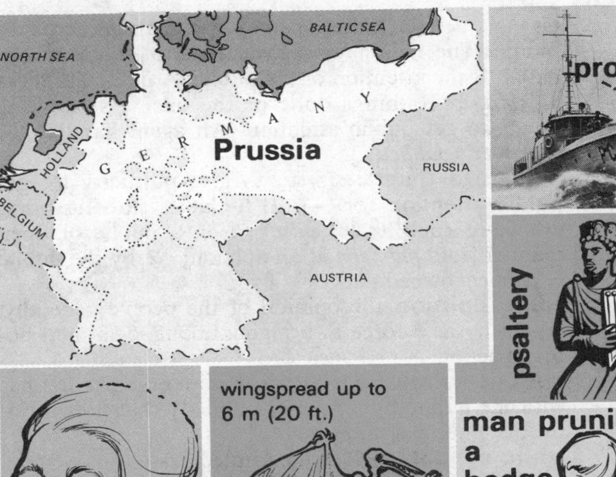


prow

psaltery

puckered lips

wingspread up to 6 m (20 ft.)

pterodactyl

man pruning a hedge

**pu·ber·ty** (pyo͞o′bər tē) ***n.*** the time of life in which boys and girls physically begin to be men and women, and are able to have children. 591

**pub·lic** (pub′lik) ***adj.*** **1** of or having to do with the people as a whole [*public* affairs; *public* opinion]. **2** for the use or the good of everyone [a *public* park]. **3** acting for the people as a whole [a *public* official]. **4** known by all or most people; open [a *public* figure; a *public* scandal]. ➧***n.*** **1** the people as a whole [what the *public* wants]. **2** a particular part of the people [the reading *public*]. —**in public,** openly; where all can see.

☆**pub·lic-ad·dress system** (pub′lik ə dres′) an electronic system, used in auditoriums and theaters, for making speeches, music, etc. sound loud enough to be heard easily by a large audience.

**pub·li·can** (pub′li kən) ***n.*** **1** a tax collector of ancient Rome. **2** a person who keeps an inn or tavern: *used in Great Britain.*

**pub·li·ca·tion** (pub′lə kā′shən) ***n.*** **1** something published, as a book, magazine, etc. **2** the printing and selling of books, magazines, newspapers, etc. **3** a publishing or being published [the *publication* of the facts].

**pub·li·cist** (pub′lə sist) ***n.*** **1** a journalist who writes about politics and public affairs. **2** a person whose work is to bring some person, place, etc. to the attention of the public.

**pub·lic·i·ty** (pə blis′ə tē) ***n.*** ☆**1** information that

| | | | | | | | |
|---|---|---|---|---|---|---|---|
| **a** | fat | **ir** | here | **ou** | out | **zh** | leisure |
| **ā** | ape | **ī** | bite, fire | **u** | up | **ŋ** | ring |
| **ä** | car, lot | **ō** | go | **ʉr** | fur | | a *in* ago |
| **e** | ten | **ô** | law, horn | **ch** | chin | | e *in* agent |
| **er** | care | **oi** | oil | **sh** | she | **ə =** | i *in* unity |
| **ē** | even | **oo** | look | **th** | thin | | o *in* collect |
| **i** | hit | **o͞o** | tool | ***th*** | then | | u *in* focus |

p

brings a person, place, or thing to the attention of the public [The newspapers gave much *publicity* to our play.] **2** the attention of the public [A politician seeks *publicity*.] **3** things done or the business of doing things to get public attention [An agent handles the rock star's *publicity*.]

**pub·li·cize** (pub′lə sīz) ***v.*** to give publicity to; get public attention for. —**pub′li·cized, pub′li·ciz·ing**

**pub·lic·ly** (pub′lik lē) ***adv.*** **1** in a public or open manner [sold *publicly,* at an auction]. **2** by the public [a *publicly* owned park].

**public opinion** the opinion of the people generally, especially as a force in bringing about social and political action.

☆**public relations** relations that an organization has with the public by means of publicity that tries to influence public opinion.

**public school** ☆**1** in the United States, an elementary school or high school that is supported by public taxes. **2** in England, a private boarding school where boys are prepared for college.

**public servant** a person who serves the public, as anyone elected or appointed to a position or work in government.

**pub·lic-spir·it·ed** (pub′lik spir′i tid) ***adj.*** interested in and working for the public welfare.

**public works** ☆works constructed by the government for public use or service, as highways or dams.



**pub·lish** (pub′lish) ***v.*** **1** to prepare and bring out a book, magazine, newspaper, etc., as for sale. **2** to make known to the public; announce [to *publish* a secret].

**pub·lish·er** (pub′lish ər) ***n.*** a person or business that publishes books, magazines, newspapers, printed music, etc.

**Puc·ci·ni** (po͞ot chē′nē), **Gia·co·mo** (jä′kō mō′) 1858–1924; Italian composer of operas.

pumps

water pump

pug nose

pueblo

pulley

puffins
30 cm (12 in.) long

**puck¹** (puk) ***n.*** the hard rubber disk used in ice hockey.

**puck²** (puk) ***n.*** a mischievous elf or fairy in folk tales. —**puck′ish** ***adj.***

**puck·er** (puk′ər) ***v.*** to draw up into wrinkles or small folds [to *pucker* the brow in a frown; to *pucker* up the lips to kiss; to *pucker* cloth by pulling a thread]. *See the picture on page 591.* ◆***n.*** a wrinkle or small fold made by puckering.

**pud·ding** (po͝od′iŋ) ***n.*** a soft, sweet food, usually made with flour or some cereal and eggs, milk, fruit, etc.

**pud·dle** (pud′'l) ***n.*** a small pool of water, or water mixed with earth [*puddles* after the rain; a mud *puddle*].

**pud·dling** (pud′liŋ) ***n.*** the process of making wrought iron by heating and stirring melted pig iron with other substances.

**pudg·y** (puj′ē) ***adj.*** short and fat [*pudgy* fingers]. —**pudg′i·er, pudg′i·est**

☆**pueb·lo** (pweb′lō) ***n.*** **1** a kind of Indian village in the southwestern United States, made up of stone or adobe buildings built one above the other. *See the picture. —pl.* **pueb′los** **2 Pueblo,** an Indian of any of the tribes that live in such villages. *—pl.* **Pueb′los** or **Pueb′lo**

> **Pueblo** is the Spanish word for village or people, and comes from the same Latin word as do the English words *people* and *public.*

**pu·er·ile** (pyo͞o′ər əl) ***adj.*** acting like a child, not as a grown-up should; childish.

**Puer·to Ri·co** (pwer′tō rē′kō) an island in the West Indies that is a commonwealth associated with the United States. —**Puer′to Ri′can**

**puff** (puf) ***n.*** **1** a short, sudden burst, as of wind, breath, smoke, or steam [Try to blow out the candles in one *puff.*] **2** a soft, light shell of pastry filled with a creamy mixture [cream *puff*]. **3** a soft roll of hair on the head. **4** a quilted bed covering with a fluffy filling. **5** *a shorter name for* **powder puff. 6** too great praise, as of a book. ◆***v.*** **1** to blow in a puff or puffs [The wind *puffed* out the flame.] **2** to give out puffs, as while moving [The steam engine *puffed* uphill.] **3** to breathe hard and fast, as after running. **4** to fill or swell as with air [The sails *puffed* out in the wind.] **5** to praise too greatly. **6** to smoke [to *puff* a cigar]. —**puff′er** ***n.***

**puff adder** a large, poisonous snake of Africa. It hisses or puffs loudly when irritated.

**puff·ball** (puf′bôl) ***n.*** a round plant like a mushroom. When it is fully ripe, it bursts if it is touched, and scatters a brown powder.

**puf·fin** (puf′in) ***n.*** a bird of northern seas, with a body like a duck's and a brightly colored beak shaped like a triangle. *See the picture.*

**puff·y** (puf′ē) ***adj.*** **1** puffed up; swollen [*puffy* clouds]. **2** coming in puffs [*puffy* gusts of air]. —**puff′i·er, puff′i·est —puff′i·ness** ***n.***

**pug** (pug) ***n.*** a small dog with short hair, a curled tail, and a short, turned-up nose.

**Pu·get Sound** (pyo͞o′jit) a narrow bay of the Pacific, reaching southward into the State of Washington.

**pu·gil·ism** (pyo͞o′jə liz′m) ***n.*** the skill or sport of fighting with the fists; boxing. —**pu′gil·ist** ***n.*** —**pu′gil·is′tic** ***adj.***

**pug·na·cious** (pug nā′shəs) ***adj.*** eager and ready to fight; quarrelsome. —**pug·na′cious·ly** ***adv.*** —**pug·nac·i·ty** (pug nas′ə tē) or **pug·na′cious·ness** ***n.***

**pug nose** a short, thick, turned-up nose. *See the picture.*

**puke** (pyo͞ok) ***n., v.*** *another word for* **vomit**: *used only in everyday talk.* —**puked, puk′ing**

**pul·chri·tude** (pul′krə to͞od *or* pul′krə tyo͞od) ***n.*** physical beauty.

**pule** (pyo͞ol) ***v.*** to whine or cry, as a sick baby does. —**puled, pul′ing**

**pull** (pool) ***v.*** **1** to use force so as to move or draw something, usually closer or nearer [to *pull* a sled; to *pull* up a sock]. **2** to draw or pluck out [to *pull* a tooth]. **3** to tear or rip [The shutter *pulled* loose in the storm.] **4** to stretch, especially to stretch so much as to hurt; strain [to *pull* a muscle]. **5** to be able to be pulled [This wagon *pulls* easily.] **6** to move or go [Lou *pulled* ahead of the other runners.] **7** to perform; do: *used only in everyday talk* [to *pull* a trick]. ◆***n.*** **1** the act of pulling or the effort made in pulling [It's a long *pull* to the top. One more *pull* brought the car out of the ditch.] **2** something by which to pull, as a handle [a drawer *pull*]. ☆**3** influence or an advantage: *used only in everyday talk.* —**pull apart,** to find fault with. —**pull down, 1** to tear down or overthrow. **2** to humble or disgrace. **3** to get, as a certain wage: *used only in everyday talk.* —☆**pull for,** to hope for the success of: *used only in everyday talk.* —**pull off,** to manage to do: *used only in everyday talk.* —**pull oneself together,** to gather one's courage, self-control, etc. —**pull out,** ☆**1** to leave or retreat. ☆**2** to escape from a contract, etc. **3** in flying an aircraft, to level out from a dive or landing approach. —**pull over,** to drive a car to the curb. —**pull through,** to get safely through an illness or trouble: *used only in everyday talk.* —**pull up, 1** to take out by the roots. **2** to bring or come to a stop. **3** to move ahead. —**pull′er** ***n.***

**pul·let** (pool′it) ***n.*** a young hen, usually not more than one year old.

**pul·ley** (pool′ē) ***n.*** a small wheel with a groove in the rim in which a rope or belt moves. A pulley may be used to lift a thing fastened to one end of the rope by pulling down on the other end. *See the picture.* —*pl.* **pul′leys**

☆**Pull·man car** (pool′mən) a railroad car with small private rooms or seats that can be made into berths for sleeping.

**pull·o·ver** (pool′ō′vər) ***adj.*** that is put on by being pulled over the head. ◆***n.*** a pullover sweater, shirt, etc.

**pull·up** (pool′up) ***n.*** the act of chinning as an athletic exercise.

**pul·mo·nar·y** (pul′mə ner′ē) ***adj.*** of or having to do with the lungs [The *pulmonary* artery carries blood to the lungs.]

**pulp** (pulp) ***n.*** **1** the soft, juicy part of a fruit. **2** the soft, center part of a tooth. It contains nerves and blood vessels. **3** any soft, wet mass, as the mixture of ground-up wood, rags, etc. from which paper is made. —**pulp′y** ***adj.***

**pul·pit** (pool′pit) ***n.*** **1** a platform in a church on which the clergyman stands when giving a sermon. **2** preachers as a group; clergy.

**pul·sar** (pul′sär) ***n.*** any of several small, heavenly objects in the Milky Way that give out radio pulses at regular intervals.

**pul·sate** (pul′sāt) ***v.*** **1** to beat or throb in a regular rhythm, as the heart. **2** to shake; vibrate. —**pul′sat·ed, pul′sat·ing** —**pul·sa′tion** ***n.***

**pulse** (puls) ***n.*** **1** the regular beating in the arteries, caused by the movements of the heart in pumping the blood. **2** any regular beat [the *pulse* of a radio signal]. ◆***v.*** to beat or throb [The music *pulsed* in our ears.] —**pulsed, puls′ing**

**pul·ver·ize** (pul′və rīz) ***v.*** **1** to crush or grind into a powder. **2** to destroy completely; demolish [The bombs *pulverized* the city.] —**pul′ver·ized, pul′ver·iz·ing** —**pul′ver·iz′er** ***n.***

**pu·ma** (pyo͞o′mə *or* po͞o′mə) ***n.*** *another name for* **cougar.**

**pum·ice** (pum′is) ***n.*** a light, spongy rock sometimes formed when lava from a volcano hardens. It is often ground into a powder, which is used for polishing things or taking out stains. *Also called* **pumice stone.**

**pum·mel** (pum″l) ***v.*** to beat or hit again and again, especially with the fists. —**pum′meled** or **pum′melled, pum′mel·ing** or **pum′mel·ling**

**pump¹** (pump) ***n.*** a machine that forces a liquid or gas into or out of something, as by pressure. *See the picture.* ◆***v.*** **1** to raise, move, or force with a pump [to *pump* water from a well; to *pump* air into a tire]. **2** to empty out with a pump [to *pump* out a flooded basement]. **3** to move with the action of a pump [The heart *pumps* blood.] **4** to move up and down like a pump handle [His legs kept *pumping* as the bicycle climbed the hill.] **5** to keep on asking questions in order to get information: *used only in everyday talk* [The police *pumped* the suspect.]

**pump²** (pump) ***n.*** a kind of shoe with low sides and no straps or laces. *See the picture.*

☆**pump·er·nick·el** (pum′pər nik″l) ***n.*** a coarse, dark kind of rye bread.

**pump·kin** (pum′kin *or* pung′kin) ***n.*** a large, round, orange fruit that grows on a vine and has many seeds. *See the picture on page 594.* The pulp is much used as a filling for pies.

> **Pumpkin** comes from a Greek word meaning "cooked by the sun" or "ripe." Thus it meant a gourd not eaten until it is ripe. The pumpkin plant is related to the gourd.

**pun** (pun) ***n.*** the humorous use of words which have the same sound or spelling, but have different meanings; play on words [There is a *pun* in the name of a restaurant called "Dewdrop Inn."] ◆***v.*** to make a pun or puns. —**punned, pun′ning**

**punch¹** (punch) ***n.*** **1** a tool for making holes in something or one for stamping or cutting designs on a surface. **2** a hard blow with the fist. ◆***v.*** **1** to hit



| | | | | | | | |
|---|---|---|---|---|---|---|---|
| **a** | fat | **ir** | here | **ou** | out | **zh** | leisure |
| **ā** | ape | **ī** | bite, fire | **u** | up | **ng** | ring |
| **ä** | car, lot | **ō** | go | **ur** | fur | | a *in* ago |
| **e** | ten | **ô** | law, horn | **ch** | chin | | e *in* agent |
| **er** | care | **oi** | oil | **sh** | she | **ə =** | i *in* unity |
| **ē** | even | **oo** | look | **th** | thin | | o *in* collect |
| **i** | hit | **o͞o** | tool | ***th*** | then | | u *in* focus |

with the fist. **2** to make holes in, stamp, etc. with a punch. ☆**3** to herd or drive cattle.

**punch²** (punch) ***n.*** a sweet drink made by mixing various fruit juices or other liquids together, sometimes with wine or liquor added. It is often served in cups from a large bowl (**punch bowl**).

> **Punch** comes from the Sanskrit word meaning "five." In India punch originally was a mixture of five kinds of juice or liquor.

**Punch-and-Ju·dy show** (punch′'n jo͞o′dē) a puppet show in which the quarrelsome Punch is always fighting with his wife, Judy.

**punch card** a card with holes or notches in certain places so it can be easily sorted. Punch cards contain information and are often used in computer work.

**punch·y** (pun′chē) ***adj.*** ☆forceful; full of energy: *used only in everyday talk* [a *punchy* style of writing]. —**punch′i·er, punch′i·est**

**punc·til·i·ous** (puŋk til′ē əs) ***adj.*** **1** paying strict attention to the small details of good manners, conduct, etc. [a *punctilious* host]. **2** very exact; careful of details [to keep *punctilious* records]. —**punc·til′i·ous·ly** ***adv.***

**punc·tu·al** (puŋk′cho͝o wəl) ***adj.*** coming, or doing something, at the right time; prompt. —**punc′tu·al′i·ty** ***n.*** —**punc′tu·al·ly** ***adv.***

**punc·tu·ate** (puŋk′cho͝o wāt′) ***v.*** **1** to put in commas, periods, question marks, etc. to make the meaning clear [to *punctuate* a sentence]. **2** to break in on here and there; interrupt [a speech *punctuated* with applause]. —**punc′tu·at′ed, punc′tu·at′ing**



**punc·tu·a·tion** (puŋk′cho͝o wā′shən) ***n.*** **1** the use of commas, periods, etc. in writing [rules of *punctuation*]. **2** punctuation marks [What *punctuation* is used to end sentences?]

**punctuation mark** any of the marks used in writing and printing to help make the meaning clear, as the comma, period, question mark, colon, semicolon, exclamation mark, dash, etc.

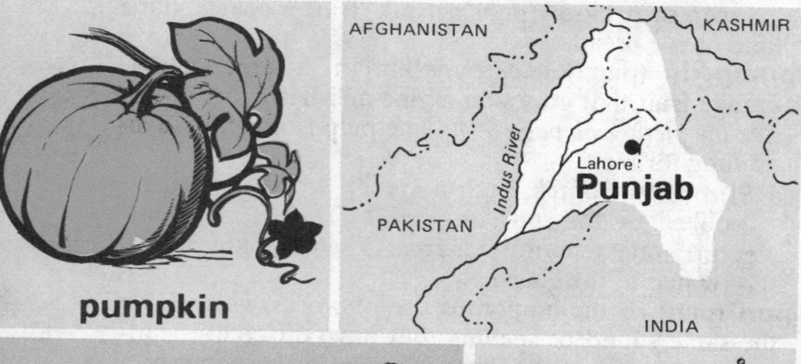

pumpkin

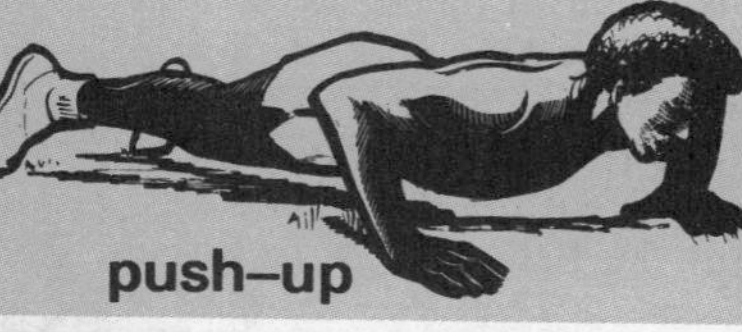
push–up

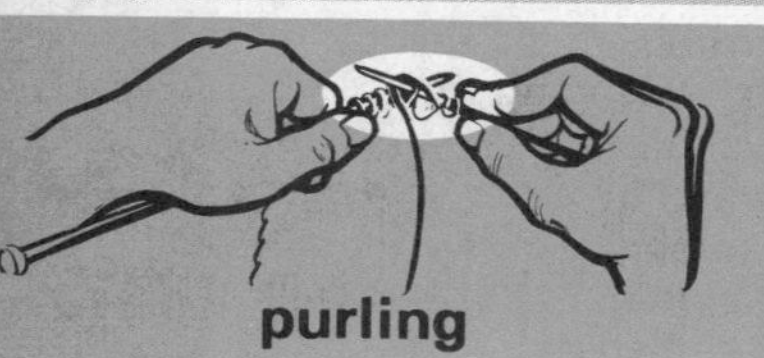
purling

puppets

**punc·ture** (puŋk′chər) ***n.*** a hole made by a sharp point or the act of making such a hole [a *puncture* in a tire caused by a nail]. ◆***v.*** **1** to make a hole with a sharp point; pierce [to *puncture* a balloon]. **2** to put an end to or make smaller, as if by piercing [The criticism *punctured* her pride.] —**punc′tured, punc′tur·ing**

**pun·dit** (pun′dit) ***n.*** a person who has or claims to have great learning; authority or expert.

**pun·gent** (pun′jənt) ***adj.*** **1** having a sharp or stinging taste or smell [a *pungent* chili sauce]. **2** very keen and direct, sometimes in a painful way; biting [*pungent* criticism; *pungent* wit]. —**pun′gen·cy** ***n.*** —**pun′gent·ly** ***adv.***

**pun·ish** (pun′ish) ***v.*** **1** to make suffer pain, loss, etc. for doing something wrong, bad, or against the law. **2** to set as a penalty for [to *punish* murder with death]. **3** to treat roughly or harshly [the *punishing* rays of the sun].

> SYNONYMS: **Punish** suggests making someone who has done something wrong suffer for it by paying a penalty. Usually it also carries the idea that no one will try to reform or correct the person [to *punish* a murderer by hanging]. **Discipline,** however, suggests that punishment will be used to control the person who has done wrong or to help that person gain self-control [to *discipline* a naughty child].

**pun·ish·a·ble** (pun′ish ə b'l) ***adj.*** that can or should be punished [a *punishable* crime].

**pun·ish·ment** (pun′ish mənt) ***n.*** **1** a punishing or being punished. **2** what is done to a person as a penalty for crime, wrongdoing, etc. [A ten-dollar fine was the *punishment* for speeding.]

**pu·ni·tive** (pyo͞o′nə tiv) ***adj.*** punishing or having to do with punishment [*punitive* laws].

**Pun·jab** (pun jäb′ *or* pun′jäb) a region in southern Asia, divided between India and Pakistan. *See the map.*

☆**punk¹** (puŋk) ***n.*** **1** any substance, as rotted wood, that burns very slowly without a flame, used to start fires. **2** a fungous substance shaped into slender sticks. Its glowing tips are often used to light fireworks.

**punk²** (puŋk) ***n.*** ☆**1** a young, reckless person. ☆**2** anyone, especially a young person, thought of as not having much experience or as being unimportant. *This is a slang word.*

**pun·ster** (pun′stər) ***n.*** a person who often makes puns, and is fond of doing this.

**punt¹** (punt) ***v.*** to kick a football after letting it drop from the hands, but before it touches the ground. ◆***n.*** such a kick.

**punt²** (punt) ***n.*** a boat with a flat bottom and square ends. ◆***v.*** to make a punt move by pushing against the bottom of a shallow river or lake with a long pole.

**pu·ny** (pyo͞o′nē) ***adj.*** small or weak; feeble. —**pu′ni·er, pu′ni·est**

**pup** (pup) ***n.*** **1** a young dog; puppy. **2** a young fox, wolf, seal, whale, etc.

**pu·pa** (pyo͞o′pə) ***n.*** an insect in the stage between a larva and an adult [The *pupa* of a moth is enclosed in a cocoon.] —*pl.* **pu·pae** (pyo͞o′pē) or **pu′pas**

**pu·pil** (pyo͞o′p'l) ***n.*** **1** a person being taught by a teacher, as in a school; student. **2** the dark opening in the center of the eye that grows larger or smaller to let in more or less light.

> **Pupil** comes from the Latin word for doll. The pupil of the eye was given this name because we can see our own figure reflected in the eye of another person as though it were a little doll.

**pup·pet** (pup′it) ***n.*** **1** a small figure in the form of a human being, moved by strings or the hands, as in acting out a play (called a **puppet show**) on a small stage. *See the picture.* **2** a person who does, says, and thinks what another orders.

**pup·pet·eer** (pup′i tir′) ***n.*** a person who works the strings that make puppets move or one who puts on puppet shows.

**pup·py** (pup′ē) ***n.*** **1** a young dog. **2** a silly, vain young man. —*pl.* **pup′pies**

**pur·chase** (pʉr′chis) ***v.*** **1** to buy; get for money [to *purchase* a car]. **2** to get by a sacrifice [to *purchase* fame with one's life]. —**pur′chased, pur′chas·ing** ◆***n.*** **1** anything that is bought [I carried my *purchases* home in a bag.] **2** the act of buying [the *purchase* of a house]. **3** a firm hold to keep from slipping or to move something heavy [The tires can't get a good *purchase* on ice.] —**pur′chas·er** ***n.***

**pure** (pyoor) ***adj.*** **1** not mixed with anything else [*pure* maple syrup]. **2** not having anything dirty, unhealthful, etc. in it; clean [*pure* drinking water; *pure* country air]. **3** not bad or evil; morally good; innocent ["Blessed are the *pure* in heart."] **4** nothing else but; mere [*pure* luck]. **5** not for a certain practical use; dealing only with theory [*pure* science]. —**pur′er, pur′est** —**pure′ly** ***adv.*** —**pure′ness** ***n.***

**pu·rée** (pyoo rā′) ***n.*** **1** a thick, moist food made by putting cooked vegetables, fruits, etc. through a sieve or in a blender. **2** a thick soup. ◆***v.*** to make a purée of. —**pu·réed′, pu·rée′ing**

**pur·ga·tive** (pʉr′gə tiv) ***n.*** a medicine that makes the bowels move; cathartic. ◆***adj.*** causing the bowels to move [a *purgative* medicine].

**pur·ga·to·ry** (pʉr′gə tôr′ē) ***n.*** *often* **Purgatory,** a condition or place in which some Christians believe that the souls of dead persons suffer until they have been cleansed of the sins of which they were guilty while alive. —*pl.* **pur′ga·to′ries**

**purge** (pʉrj) ***v.*** **1** to make clean or pure by getting rid of things that are dirty or wrong [The city council vowed to *purge* the city of slums.] **2** to rid of persons or things thought to be harmful, dangerous, disloyal, etc. [to *purge* a political party]. **3** to make the bowels move. —**purged, purg′ing** ◆***n.*** **1** the act of purging, or making clean or pure. **2** anything that purges; especially, a medicine that makes the bowels move.

**pu·ri·fy** (pyoor′ə fī) ***v.*** to make pure, clean, etc. [to *purify* water by filtering it through sand]. —**pu′ri·fied, pu′ri·fy·ing** —**pu′ri·fi·ca′tion** ***n.***

**pur·ist** (pyoor′ist) ***n.*** a person who insists on being very careful or exact in using the rules of grammar, art, etc. [A *purist* in the use of English does not approve of "It's me."] —**pur′ism** ***n.***

**Pu·ri·tan** (pyoor′ə t'n) ***n.*** **1** a member of an English religious group in the 16th and 17th centuries, which wanted to make the Church of England simpler in its services and stricter about morals. Many Puritans came to New England in the 17th century. **2 puritan,** a person thought of as too strict in morals and religion. —**pu·ri·tan·i·cal** (pyoor′ə tan′i k'l) or **pu′ri·tan′ic** ***adj.*** —**Pu′ri·tan·ism** or **pu′ri·tan·ism** ***n.***

**pu·ri·ty** (pyoor′ə tē) ***n.*** the condition of being pure; cleanness, goodness, etc.

**purl** (pʉrl) ***v.*** to make stitches in knitting that are looped opposite to the usual stitches, so as to form ribbing. *See the picture.*

**pur·loin** (pər loin′) ***v.*** to steal.

**pur·ple** (pʉr′p'l) ***n.*** **1** a color that is a mixture of red and blue. **2** crimson clothing worn long ago by royalty and high officials. ◆***adj.*** of the color purple.

> **Purple** comes from a Greek word for a kind of tiny snail of the Mediterranean Sea used to make a dye in ancient times. Thousands of snails were needed to make a small amount of dye. Thus it was expensive, and used only for the robes of royalty or nobles.

☆**Purple Heart** a medal given to U.S. soldiers, sailors, etc. who were wounded in action.

**pur·plish** (pʉr′plish) ***adj.*** slightly purple.

**pur·port** (pər pôrt′) ***v.*** to seem or claim to be, mean, etc., often falsely [This book *purports* to give the true facts.] ◆***n.*** (pʉr′pôrt) meaning; main idea [What is the *purport* of this message?]

**pur·pose** (pʉr′pəs) ***n.*** **1** what one plans to get or do; aim; goal [I came for the *purpose* of speaking to you.] **2** the reason or use for something [a room with no *purpose*]. —**on purpose,** not by accident; intentionally. —**to good purpose,** with a good result. —**to little or no purpose,** with little or no result. —**pur′pose·ful** ***adj.*** —**pur′pose·less** ***adj.***



**pur·pose·ly** (pʉr′pəs lē) ***adv.*** with a purpose; not by chance or by accident; intentionally; deliberately.

**purr** (pʉr) ***n.*** the low, soft rumbling sound made by a cat when it seems to be pleased. ◆***v.*** to make such a sound.

**purse** (pʉrs) ***n.*** **1** a small bag for carrying money. ☆**2** a larger bag of leather, etc. used for carrying money, cosmetics, keys, etc. **3** a sum of money given as a prize or gift [a horse race with a $1,000 *purse*]. ◆***v.*** to draw tightly together; pucker [He *pursed* his lips and began to whistle.] —**pursed, purs′ing**

**purs·er** (pʉr′sər) ***n.*** the officer on a ship who keeps the accounts, checks passengers' tickets, etc.

**pur·su·ance** (pər so͞o′əns *or* pər syo͞o′əns) ***n.*** the act of pursuing, or carrying out, a plan, project, etc.

**pur·su·ant** (pər so͞o′ənt *or* pər syo͞o′ənt) ***adj.*** *same as* **pursuing**: *no longer in common use.* —**pursuant to,** according to [We will leave now, *pursuant to* our plans.]

**pur·sue** (pər so͞o′ *or* pər syo͞o′) ***v.*** **1** to follow in order to catch or catch up to [to *pursue* a runaway horse]. **2** to carry out or follow; go on with [She is

| | | | |
|---|---|---|---|
| **a** fat | **ir** here | **ou** out | **zh** leisure |
| **ā** ape | **ī** bite, fire | **u** up | **ng** ring |
| **ä** car, lot | **ō** go | **ʉr** fur | a *in* ago |
| **e** ten | **ô** law, horn | **ch** chin | e *in* agent |
| **er** care | **oi** oil | **sh** she | **ə** = i *in* unity |
| **ē** even | **oo** look | **th** thin | o *in* collect |
| **i** hit | **o͞o** tool | ***th*** then | u *in* focus |

**p**

python
up to 9 m (30 ft.) long

putter

puttees

pylon for electric lines

catkins of a pussy willow

pyramids

*pursuing* a career in acting.] **3** to try to find; seek [to *pursue* knowledge]. **4** to continue to bother or trouble



[Bad luck still *pursues* us.] —**pur·sued′**, **pur·su′ing** —**pur·su′er** ***n.***

**pur·suit** (pər so͞ot′ *or* pər syo͞ot′) ***n.*** **1** the act of pursuing [the *pursuit* of truth]. **2** an activity, job, sport, etc. to which one gives time and energy [Golf is Pat's favorite *pursuit*.]

**pur·vey** (pər vā′) ***v.*** to supply, as food or provisions. —**pur·vey′ance** ***n.*** —**pur·vey′or** ***n.***

**pus** (pus) ***n.*** the thick, yellowish matter that oozes from a sore or is found in a boil.

**push** (poosh) ***v.*** **1** to press against so as to move; shove [to *push* a stalled car; to *push* a stake into the ground]. **2** to move by using force [We *pushed* through the crowd.] **3** to urge or press forward; force or drive [The supervisor *pushed* the workers to go faster.] **4** to try hard to succeed or go higher [to *push* to the top]. **5** to urge the use, sale, etc. of [The company is *pushing* its new product.] ☆**6** to be near or close to: *used only in everyday talk* [*pushing* sixty years]. •***n.*** **1** the act of pushing; a shove or thrust [One hard *push* opened the door.] **2** the power or energy to get things done: *used only in everyday talk* [a leader with plenty of *push*]. —**push on,** to go forward; proceed. —**push′er** ***n.***

SYNONYMS: To **push** is to use force as in moving something ahead or aside [I *pushed* the baby carriage downtown.] To **shove** is to push something so as to force it to slide along a surface, or to handle something roughly in pushing it [*Shove* the box into the corner.]

☆**push button** a small knob or button that is pushed to operate something, as by electricity.

☆**push·o·ver** (poosh′ō′vər) ***n.*** **1** anything that is very easy to do. **2** a person who is very easy to fool, persuade, defeat, etc. *This is a slang word.*

**push-up** or **push·up** (poosh′up′) ***n.*** an exercise in which one lies face down on the floor and pushes up with the arms. *See the picture on page 594.*

☆**push·y** (poosh′ē) ***adj.*** bold and rude in such a way as to make others angry: *used only in everyday talk.* —**push′i·er**, **push′i·est** —**push′i·ness** ***n.***

**pu·sil·lan·i·mous** (pyo͞o′s′l an′ə məs) ***adj.*** timid or cowardly; not brave. —**pu·sil·la·nim·i·ty** (pyo͞o′s′l ə nim′ə tē) ***n.*** —**pu′sil·lan′i·mous·ly** ***adv.***

**puss** (poos) ***n.*** a pet name for a cat.

**puss·y** (poos′ē) ***n.*** a cat, especially a kitten. —*pl.* **puss′ies**

☆**puss·y·foot** (poos′ē foot′) ***v.*** **1** to move quickly and carefully, as a cat does. **2** to keep from making one's feelings or opinions clear [The candidate *pussyfooted* on the subject of taxes.] *This word is used only in everyday talk.*

☆**pussy willow** a willow that bears soft, furry, grayish catkins. *See the picture.*

**pus·tule** (pus′cho͞ol) ***n.*** a small swelling of the skin that contains pus.

**put** (poot) ***v.*** **1** to make be in a certain place or position; place; set [*Put* soap in the water. *Put* the books side by side.] **2** to make be in a certain condition [The sound of the waves *put* me to sleep.] **3** to say or express; state [Can you *put* the problem in simple words?] **4** to push with force; thrust [to *put* nails in wood]. **5** to bring about; make happen [We *put* a stop to cheating.] **6** to give or assign; attach [The store *put* a price of $10 on the rug. The government *put* a tax on luxuries.] **7** to move or go [The fleet *put* out to sea.] **8** to throw by pushing up and out from the shoulder [to *put* the shot]. —**put**, **put′ting** —**put about,** to change a ship's direction. —**put across,** ☆**1** to make understood or accepted. **2** to carry out with success. *This phrase is used only in everyday talk.* —**put aside** or **put away** or **put by,** to save for later use. —**put back,** **1** to replace. **2** to turn back the hands of a clock to an earlier time. ☆**3** to set a pupil back a grade. —**put down,** **1** to overcome with force; crush, as a revolt. **2** to write down. **3** to make a landing in an aircraft. ☆**4** to find fault with, make little of, or make feel ashamed: *a slang meaning.* —**put forth,** to grow, as leaves or shoots. —**put off,** **1** to leave until later; postpone. **2** to confuse, mislead, make wait, etc. **3** to upset greatly. —**put on,** **1** to dress oneself with. **2** to take on; add [to *put on* a few pounds]. **3** to pretend [to *put on* an air of innocence]. **4** to present, as a play on a stage. ☆**5** to fool or trick: *a slang meaning.* —**put out,** **1** to make leave; send away. **2** to stop from burning; extinguish, as a fire. **3** to annoy or bother. —**put over,** ☆to do something by using tricks; also, to do something that is hard to do: *used only in everyday talk.* —**put through,** ☆**1** to succeed in doing something; carry out [to *put through* a business deal]. **2** to cause to do [I *put* the horse *through* its paces.] —**put up,** **1** to offer; show [to *put up* a house for sale]. **2** to preserve or can, as fruits. **3** to build; erect. **4** to furnish with a place to live. ☆**5** to provide, as money. **6** to get to do something, as by urging: *used only in everyday talk* [My friends *put* me *up* to it.] —**put upon,** to take advantage of. —**put up with,** to tolerate; bear.

☆**put-on** (poot′än′) ***n.*** a made-up story, practical joke, or trick intended to fool someone: *a slang word.*

☆**put·out** (poot′out) ***n.*** a baseball play in which a defensive player catches or stops the ball and causes the batter or runner to be out.

**pu·tre·fy** (pyōō′trə fī) ***v.*** to make or become rotten or decayed. —**pu′tre·fied, pu′tre·fy·ing** —**pu·tre·fac·tion** (pyōō′trə fak′shən) ***n.***

**pu·trid** (pyōō′trid) ***adj.*** **1** rotten and smelling bad [*putrid* garbage]. **2** coming from decay or rottenness [a *putrid* smell].

**putt** (put) ***n.*** a light stroke made in golf in trying to roll the ball into the hole on a green. ◆***v.*** to hit a golf ball with a putt.

**put·tee** (pu tē′ *or* put′ē) ***n.*** a covering for the leg from the ankle to the knee, once worn by soldiers, hikers, etc. It is either a long strip of cloth wound around the leg or a piece of leather or canvas buckled or laced in place. *See the picture.*

When British soldiers went to India, they started using the word **puttee** for the leg covering they wore. **Puttee** comes from a Hindu word for bandage, and that was from an earlier Sanskrit word for a strip of cloth.

**putt·er**[1] (put′ər) ***n.*** **1** a short golf club used in putting. **2** a person who putts. *See the picture.*

**put·ter**[2] (put′ər) ***v.*** to busy oneself without getting anything worthwhile done [She *puttered* around the house most of the day.]

**put·ty** (put′ē) ***n.*** a soft mixture of powdered chalk and linseed oil, used to hold panes of glass in windows, to fill cracks, etc. ◆***v.*** to hold in place or fill with putty. —**put′tied, put′ty·ing**

**puz·zle** (puz″l) ***n.*** **1** a question, problem, etc. that is hard to solve or understand [It's a *puzzle* to me how they got here so quickly.] **2** a toy or problem that tests one's cleverness or skill [a jigsaw *puzzle;* a crossword *puzzle*]. ◆***v.*** **1** to make think hard or to confuse; perplex [Her strange behavior *puzzled* them.] **2** to think hard or be perplexed [He *puzzled* a long time over the first question.] —**puz′zled, puz′zling** —**puzzle out,** to find the answer to by serious thought, study, etc. —**puz′zle·ment** ***n.***

**Pvt.** *abbreviation for* **Private** (military title).

**PX** (pē′eks′) *abbreviation for* **post exchange,** which is a shop or store at an army base, run by the base for the use of military people.

**Pyg·my** (pig′mē) ***n.*** **1** a member of any of several African or Asian peoples who are very short. **2** **pygmy,** any very small or unimportant person or thing. —*pl.* **Pyg′mies** or **pyg′mies** ◆***adj.*** **1** of the Pygmies. **2** **pygmy,** very small; dwarfish.

**Pygmy** comes from a Greek unit of measure, the *pygme,* which was the distance between the elbow and the knuckles or fist. The ancient Greeks wrote down stories about very small people that were about this size.

**py·ja·mas** (pə jam′əz *or* pə jä′məz) ***n.pl.*** *the British spelling of* **pajamas.**

**py·lon** (pī′län) ***n.*** **1** a gateway, as of an Egyptian temple. **2** any high tower, as for holding up electric lines, for marking a course for airplanes, etc. *See the picture.*

**py·or·rhe·a** or **py·or·rhoe·a** (pī′ə rē′ə) ***n.*** a disease of the gums and tooth sockets, in which pus forms and the teeth become loose.

**pyr·a·mid** (pir′ə mid) ***n.*** **1** a solid figure whose sloping sides are triangles that come together in a point at the top. **2** anything having this shape; especially, any of the huge structures with a square base and four sides in which ancient Egyptian rulers were buried. *See the picture.* ◆***v.*** to build up or heap up in the form of a pyramid.

**py·ram·i·dal** (pi ram′ə d′l) ***adj.*** of a pyramid or shaped like a pyramid.

**pyre** (pīr) ***n.*** a pile of wood on which a dead body is burned; funeral pile.

**Pyr·e·nees** (pir′ə nēz) a mountain range between France and Spain.

**py·rite** (pī′rīt) ***n.*** a shiny yellow mineral that is a compound of iron and sulfur.

**py·ri·tes** (pə rīt′ēz *or* pī′rīts) ***n.*** any mineral that is a compound of sulfur and a metal.

**py·ro·ma·ni·a** (pī′rə mā′nē ə) ***n.*** an uncontrollable, intense desire to destroy things by fire.

**Pyromania** comes from two Greek words. In Greek, *pyr* means "fire," while *mania* means "madness." *Mania* means a kind of mental illness in English, but it also means too much enthusiasm for something. A person with pyromania has a wild, abnormal desire to start fires.



**py·ro·ma·ni·ac** (pī′rə mā′nē ak) ***n.*** a person who has pyromania.

**py·ro·tech·nics** (pī′rə tek′niks) ***n.pl.*** **1** the art of making and using fireworks: *used with a singular verb.* **2** a display of fireworks. **3** any brilliant display, as of skill in playing a musical instrument. —**py′ro·tech′nic** or **py′ro·tech′ni·cal** ***adj.***

**Pyr·rhic victory** (pir′ik) a victory that costs too much to win.

An ancient king named Pyrrhus led his army in two battles against the Romans in 280 and 279 B.C. His troops won both battles, but he lost a great many soldiers and much equipment. From this we get the term **Pyrrhic victory.**

**Py·thag·o·ras** (pi thag′ər əs) a Greek philosopher of the 6th century B.C. His special interest was mathematics.

**py·thon** (pī′thän *or* pī′thən) ***n.*** a very large snake found in Asia, Africa, and Australia. It is not poisonous, but twists around its prey and crushes it to death. *See the picture.*

| | | | |
|---|---|---|---|
| **a** fat | **ir** here | **ou** out | **zh** leisure |
| **ā** ape | **ī** bite, fire | **u** up | **ng** ring |
| **ä** car, lot | **ō** go | **ur** fur | a *in* ago |
| **e** ten | **ô** law, horn | **ch** chin | e *in* agent |
| **er** care | **oi** oil | **sh** she | **ə** = i *in* unity |
| **ē** even | **oo** look | **th** thin | o *in* collect |
| **i** hit | **ōō** tool | ***th*** then | u *in* focus |

**Q,q** (kyōō) ***n.*** the seventeenth letter of the English alphabet. *—pl.* **Q's, q's**

**Qa·tar** (gut'ər *or* kä'tär) an independent state on the Arabian peninsula. *See the map for* **Iran.**

**qb** quarterback (in football).

**qt.** *abbreviation for* **quart** *or* **quarts.**

**quack**[1] (kwak) ***n.*** the sound a duck makes. ◆***v.*** to make this sound.

**quack**[2] (kwak) ***n.*** **1** a person without proper training or skill who pretends to be a doctor. **2** any person who falsely pretends to have knowledge or skill; charlatan. ◆***adj.*** that is or has to do with a quack; false; pretended [a *quack* medicine].

**quack·er·y** (kwak'ər ē) ***n.*** the actions or methods of a quack.

**quad·ran·gle** (kwäd'rang'g'l) ***n.*** **1** a flat figure with four angles and four sides. **2** an area, as of a college campus, surrounded by buildings on all four sides. **3** the buildings themselves. —**quad·ran·gu·lar** (kwäd rang'gyə lər) ***n.***

**quad·rant** (kwäd'rənt) ***n.*** **1** one quarter of a circle. *See the picture.* **2** an instrument like the sextant, used for measuring angles and heights.

☆**quad·ra·phon·ic** (kwäd'rə fän'ik) ***adj.*** of or having to do with a way of recording or broadcasting using four channels to bring the sounds to the listener. The sounds come from a number of sources and are heard through separate speakers.



**quad·ren·ni·al** (kwäd ren'ē əl) ***adj.*** **1** happening once every four years. **2** lasting four years. —**quadren'ni·al·ly** ***adv.***

**quad·ri·lat·er·al** (kwäd'rə lat'ər əl) ***adj.*** having four sides. ◆***n.*** a flat figure with four sides and four angles. *See the picture.*

**qua·drille** (kwə dril') ***n.*** **1** a square dance for four couples. **2** music for this dance.

The **quadrille** was originally a French dance, but before that the French word was used for one of four groups of horsemen who took part in a certain exercise. In turn, that word came from a Spanish word that means a four-sided battle square, which comes from *quattuor,* the Latin word for four.

**quad·ru·ped** (kwäd'roo ped) ***n.*** an animal with four feet. ◆***adj.*** having four feet.

**quad·ru·ple** (kwä drōō'p'l *or* kwäd'roo p'l) ***adj.*** **1** made up of four [a *quadruple* alliance of nations]. **2** four times as much or as many. ◆***n.*** an amount four times as much or as many [Forty is the *quadruple* of ten.] ◆***v.*** to make or become four times as much or as many [The population of the city has *quadrupled.*] —**quad·ru'pled, quad·ru'pling**

**quad·ru·plet** (kwä drup'lit *or* kwäd'roo plit) ***n.*** any of four children born at a single birth.

**quaff** (kwäf *or* kwaf) ***v.*** to drink deeply in a thirsty way. ◆***n.*** the act of quaffing.

**quag·mire** (kwag'mīr) ***n.*** **1** soft, wet ground that sinks down under one's feet. **2** a difficult or dangerous situation from which it is hard to escape [stuck in a *quagmire* of debts].

☆**qua·hog** or **qua·haug** (kwô'hôg *or* kō'hôg) ***n.*** a clam used for food, found on the eastern shore of North America. It has a very hard shell.

**quail**[1] (kwāl) ***v.*** to shrink or draw back in fear; lose one's courage.

**quail**[2] (kwāl) ***n.*** a small wild bird hunted for sport or for food. It looks like a partridge. *See the picture.*

**quaint** (kwānt) ***adj.*** unusual or old-fashioned in a pleasing way [We stayed at a *quaint* old inn.] —**quaint'ly** ***adv.*** —**quaint'ness** ***n.***

**quake** (kwāk) ***v.*** **1** to tremble or shake, as the ground does in an earthquake. **2** to shudder or shiver, as with fear or cold. —**quaked, quak'ing** ◆***n.*** **1** *a shorter word for* **earthquake. 2** a shaking or shivering.

**Quak·er** (kwāk'ər) ***n.*** *another name for* **Friend.** *See* **Society of Friends.**

**qual·i·fi·ca·tion** (kwäl'ə fi kā'shən) ***n.*** **1** a qualifying or being qualified. **2** a thing that changes, limits, or holds back [I can recommend the book without any *qualification.*] **3** any skill, experience, special training, etc. that fits a person for some work, office, etc.

**qual·i·fied** (kwäl'ə fīd) ***adj.*** **1** having the qualities that are needed; fit [a person *qualified* to be a leader]. **2** limited [*qualified* approval].

**qual·i·fy** (kwäl'ə fī) ***v.*** **1** to make or be fit or suitable, as for some work or activity [Your training *qualifies* you for the job. Does he *qualify* for the team?] **2** to give or get the right to do something [This license *qualifies* you to drive a car.] **3** to soften or limit; make less strong [to *qualify* a punishment; to *qualify* a statement by adding "perhaps"]. **4** to limit the meaning of a word; modify [Adjectives *qualify* nouns.] —**qual'i·fied, qual'i·fy·ing**

**qual·i·ta·tive** (kwäl'ə tāt'iv) ***adj.*** having to do with quality or qualities, not quantity.

**qual·i·ty** (kwäl'ə tē) ***n.*** **1** any of the features that make a thing what it is; characteristic [Coldness is one *quality* of ice cream.] **2** nature; character [This soap has an oily *quality.*] **3** degree of excellence [a poor *quality* of paper]. **4** excellence [to look for *quality* in a product]. **5** high position in society: *now seldom used* [a person of *quality*]. *—pl.* **qual'i·ties**

**qualm** (kwäm) ***n.*** **1** a slight feeling of guilt; scruple. [The thief had no *qualms* about taking the money.] **2** a sudden anxious or uneasy feeling; misgiving [I felt *qualms* about sailing in rough weather.] **3** a sudden, brief feeling of sickness or faintness.

**Qualm** comes from an Old English word for death or disaster. It is related to a German word for pain and a Swedish word for nausea. As the word came into modern English, its meaning became milder. Now it means a brief feeling of sickness or a slight feeling of anxiety or guilt.

**quan·da·ry** (kwän′drē *or* kwän′də rē) ***n.*** a condition of being doubtful or confused about what to do [in a *quandary* about going]. *—pl.* **quan′da·ries**

**quan·ti·ta·tive** (kwän′tə tāt′iv) ***adj.*** **1** having to do with quantity. **2** that can be measured.

**quan·ti·ty** (kwän′tə tē) ***n.*** **1** an amount or portion [large *quantities* of food]. **2** a large amount [The factory makes toys in *quantity*.] **3** a number or symbol that stands for some amount in mathematics. *—pl.* **quan′ti·ties**

**quan·tum** (kwän′təm) ***n.*** a tiny unit of energy. The **quantum theory** states that radiant energy is taken in or sent out in a series of small, separate bits. *—pl.* **quan·ta** (kwän′tə)

**quar·an·tine** (kwôr′ən tēn) ***n.*** **1** the act of keeping a diseased person, animal, or plant away from others so that the disease will not spread. **2** a place where such persons, animals, or plants are kept. **3** the time during which a ship is kept in port while the passengers, cargo, etc. are inspected for some disease. ◆***v.*** **1** to put in a place of quarantine. **2** to cut off, as a country, from dealings with another or others. —**quar′an·tined, quar′an·tin·ing**

**Quarantine** comes from an Italian word meaning "forty days." Originally a ship was kept in port for forty days when it was suspected of carrying a disease.

**quark** (kwôrk) ***n.*** ☆any one of three proposed particles that are thought to be basic units of matter, smaller than nuclear particles.

**quar·rel** (kwôr′əl) ***n.*** **1** an argument or disagreement, especially an angry one; dispute. **2** a reason for arguing [I have no *quarrel* with the way things are being done.] ◆***v.*** **1** to argue or disagree in an angry way. **2** to find fault; complain [She *quarrels* with his methods, not with his results.] —**quar′reled** or **quar′relled, quar′rel·ing** or **quar′rel·ling**

**Quarrel** comes from a Latin verb meaning "to complain." The Latin word developed from an ancient term that meant "to snort or wheeze." When people quarrel, or speak with anger, they sometimes make snorting noises.

**quar·rel·some** (kwôr′əl səm) ***adj.*** likely to quarrel; fond of fighting or arguing.

**quar·ry¹** (kwôr′ē) ***n.*** **1** an animal that is being chased or hunted down; prey. **2** anything being chased or hunted. *—pl.* **quar′ries**

**quar·ry²** (kwôr′ē) ***n.*** a place where stone, marble, or slate is cut or blasted out of the earth, to be used as in building or for statues. *—pl.* **quar′ries** ◆***v.*** to take from a quarry [to *quarry* marble]. —**quar′ried, quar′ry·ing**

**quart** (kwôrt) ***n.*** **1** a measure of liquids, equal to two pints or 1/4 gallon. **2** a measure of volume for dry things, such as grain, fruit, vegetables, etc., equal to 1/8 peck. **3** a bottle, box, etc. holding a quart. A quart is equal to a little less than a liter in liquid measure and to a little more than a liter in dry measure.

**quar·ter** (kwôr′tər) ***n.*** **1** any of the four equal parts of something; fourth [a *quarter* of a mile; the third *quarter* of a football game]. **2** one fourth of a year; three months. **3** the point fifteen minutes before or after any given hour [It's a *quarter* after five.] **4** a coin of the U.S. or Canada, worth 25 cents; one fourth of a dollar. **5** one leg of a four-legged animal

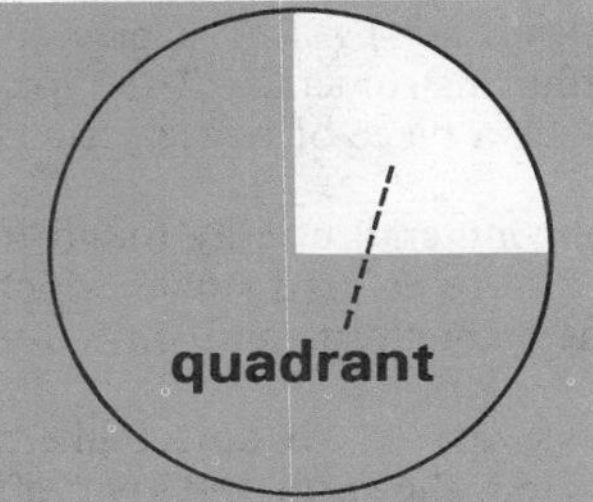


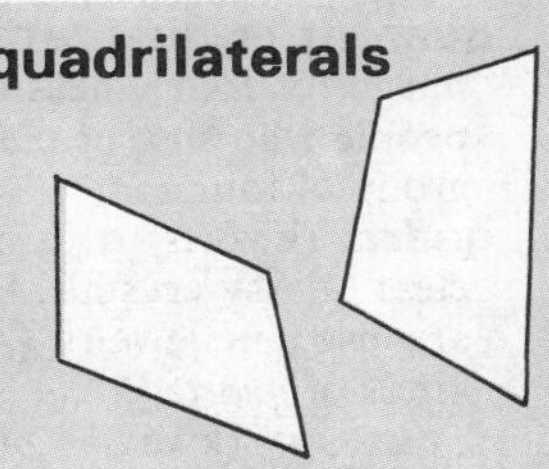

25 cm (10 in.) long

with the parts connected to it [a *quarter* of beef]. **6** any of the four main points of the compass; north, east, south, or west. **7** a certain section of a town [the Chinese *quarter*]. **8** **quarters,** *pl.* a place to live in, often just for a while. **9** a source or origin [news from the highest *quarters*]. **10** the time in which the moon makes one fourth of its circle around the earth, about 7 days. **11** mercy shown to an enemy. ◆***v.*** **1** to divide into four equal parts. **2** to furnish with a place to live or stay [to *quarter* soldiers in barracks]. ◆***adj.*** that is equal to one fourth [a *quarter* share of the profits]. —**at close quarters,** very close together. —**cry quarter,** to beg for mercy.



☆**quar·ter·back** (kwôr′tər bak) ***n.*** the player in football who calls the signals and who usually receives the ball from the center.

**quar·ter·deck** (kwôr′tər dek) ***n.*** the back part of the upper deck of a ship, usually for officers. *See the picture.*

**quar·ter·ly** (kwôr′tər lē) ***adj.*** happening or appearing four times a year [a *quarterly* magazine]. ◆***adv.*** once every quarter of the year [to pay rent *quarterly*]. ◆***n.*** a magazine that comes out four times a year. *—pl.* **quar′ter·lies**

**quar·ter·mas·ter** (kwôr′tər mas′tər) ***n.*** **1** a military officer who is in charge of supplies, quarters, etc. for troops. **2** a petty officer on a ship with special training in navigation, signaling, etc.

**quarter note** a note in music that is held one fourth as long as a whole note.

**quar·ter·staff** (kwôr′tər staf) ***n.*** a long, wooden pole with an iron tip, once used in England as a weapon. —*pl.* **quar·ter·staves** (kwôr′tər stāvz)

| | | | |
|---|---|---|---|
| **a** fat | **ir** here | **ou** out | **zh** leisure |
| **ā** ape | **ī** bite, fire | **u** up | **ng** ring |
| **ä** car, lot | **ō** go | **ur** fur | a *in* ago |
| **e** ten | **ô** law, horn | **ch** chin | e *in* agent |
| **er** care | **oi** oil | **sh** she | **ə** = i *in* unity |
| **ē** even | **oo** look | **th** thin | o *in* collect |
| **i** hit | **o͞o** tool | ***th*** then | u *in* focus |

q

**quar·tet** or **quar·tette** (kwôr tet′) ***n.*** **1** a piece of music for four voices or four instruments. **2** the four people who sing or play such a piece of music. **3** any group of four.

**quartz** (kwôrts) ***n.*** a bright mineral, usually found in clear, glassy crystals, but also as colored stones which are used in jewelry [Agate, amethyst, and onyx are kinds of *quartz*.]

☆**qua·sar** (kwā′sär *or* kwā′zär) ***n.*** an object like a star, that is very far away from the earth and gives off powerful radio waves.

**quash**[1] (kwäsh) ***v.*** to put an end to by law; annul or set aside [to *quash* an order].

This word and the one that comes next are spelled and pronounced the same. But **quash**[1] comes from a Latin word that means "to destroy completely" and **quash**[2] comes from another Latin word that means "to break into pieces."

**quash**[2] (kwäsh) ***v.*** to put down or overcome by force; crush [to *quash* a revolt].

**qua·si** (kwā′sī *or* kwā′zī) ***adj., adv.*** seeming as if it were; not real or not really. *Quasi* is usually used in words formed with a hyphen [a *quasi*-legal document].

**quat·rain** (kwä′trān) ***n.*** a verse of a poem, or a poem, with four lines.

**qua·ver** (kwā′vər) ***v.*** **1** to tremble or shake, as the voice may do when one is afraid. **2** to make a trill in singing or in playing an instrument. ◆***n.*** a trembling or trilling tone.



**Quaver** is thought to come from a very old word that meant both "wobbly" and "tadpole." As a tadpole swims through the water, its tail moves back and forth and the tiny creature wobbles. Trembling is a movement something like wobbling. **Quaver** changed through the years into a verb meaning "to shake or tremble."

**quay** (kē) ***n.*** a wharf for loading and unloading ships, usually one made of stone or concrete.

**Que.** *abbreviation for* **Quebec.**

**quea·sy** (kwē′zē) ***adj.*** **1** feeling as if one might vomit [Sailing makes me *queasy*.] **2** feeling uncomfortable or uneasy. —**quea′si·er, quea′si·est** —**quea′si·ly** ***adv.*** —**quea′si·ness** ***n.***

**Que·bec** (kwi bek′) **1** a province of eastern Canada. **2** its capital.

**queen** (kwēn) ***n.*** **1** a woman who rules a country and whose position is handed down from parent to child. Queens today usually have little power to rule. **2** the wife of a king. **3** a woman who is famous or honored for something [a beauty *queen*]. **4** the female that lays all the eggs for a colony of bees or ants. **5** a playing card with a picture of a queen on it. **6** the most powerful piece in chess.

☆**Queen Anne's lace** a wild plant of the carrot family, with white, lacy flowers. *See the picture.*

**queen·ly** (kwēn′lē) ***adj.*** of, like, or fit for a queen. —**queen′li·er, queen′li·est**

☆**queen-size** (kwēn′sīz′) ***adj.*** larger than usual, but less than king-size [A *queen-size* bed is usually 60 inches wide.]

**queer** (kwir) ***adj.*** **1** different from what is usual or normal; odd; strange [How *queer* to see snow in June!] **2** slightly sick; queasy or faint. **3** doubtful; suspicious: *used only in everyday talk* [That signature looks a little *queer*.] ◆***v.*** to spoil the success of: *slang in this meaning* [a mistake that *queered* our plans]. —**queer′ly** ***adv.*** —**queer′ness** ***n.***

**quell** (kwel) ***v.*** **1** to put an end to; crush [to *quell* a riot]. **2** to quiet [to *quell* their fears].

**quench** (kwench) ***v.*** **1** to put out; extinguish [Use water to *quench* the fire.] **2** to satisfy or make less strong [to *quench* one's thirst].

**quer·u·lous** (kwer′ə ləs) ***adj.*** **1** always complaining or finding fault. **2** showing a cross or irritable outlook [a *querulous* voice]. —**quer′u·lous·ly** ***adv.***

**que·ry** (kwir′ē) ***n.*** **1** a question [I expressed my doubt in the form of a *query*.] **2** a question mark (?). —*pl.* **que′ries** ◆***v.*** **1** to ask or ask about; question [They *queried* my reasons for leaving.] **2** to show doubt about; question the correctness of [to *query* a date in an article]. —**que′ried, que′ry·ing**

**quest** (kwest) ***n.*** **1** a hunt or search [a student in *quest* of knowledge]. **2** a journey in search of adventure, as those taken by knights in the Middle Ages. ◆***v.*** to go in search.

**ques·tion** (kwes′chən) ***n.*** **1** something that is asked in order to learn or know [The athlete refused to answer the reporter's *questions*.] **2** doubt [There is no *question* about his honesty.] **3** a matter to be considered; problem [It's not a *question* of money.] **4** a matter that is being talked over by a group [The *question* is before the committee.] ◆***v.*** **1** to ask questions of [The lawyer started to *question* the witness.] **2** to object to; have doubts about [The batter *questioned* the umpire's decision.] —**beside the question,** not having anything to do with the subject being considered or talked about. —**beyond question,** without any doubt. —**in question,** being considered or talked about. —**out of the question,** impossible. —**ques′tion·er** ***n.***

**ques·tion·a·ble** (kwes′chən ə b′l) ***adj.*** **1** that can or should be doubted [a *questionable* statement]. **2** probably not honest, not moral, etc.; not well thought of [a person of *questionable* character].

**question mark** the mark (?), used after a word or sentence to show that a question is being asked.

**ques·tion·naire** (kwes chə ner′) ***n.*** a written or printed list of questions used in gathering information from people.

**queue** (kyo͞o) ***n.*** **1** a long braid of hair hanging at the back of the head; pigtail. **2** a line of people, cars, etc. waiting for something. ◆***v.*** to form in a line while waiting for something [*Queue* up here for the bus.] —**queued, queu′ing** *The verb and meaning* 2 *of the noun are used mainly in Great Britain.*

A braid of hair hanging down a person's back or a long line of waiting people does look a little like an animal's tail. **Queue** comes from a Latin word meaning "tail."

**quib·ble** (kwib′′l) ***n.*** **1** a keeping away from the main point as by arguing about some unimportant detail. **2** a minor, unimportant point used in arguing. ◆***v.*** to keep away from the main point being discussed by using quibbles. —**quib′bled, quib′bling**

**quick** (kwik) ***adj.*** **1** done with speed; rapid; swift; [We took a *quick* trip.] **2** done or happening at once; prompt [I was grateful for her *quick* reply.] **3** able to learn or understand easily [You have a *quick* mind.] **4**

easily stirred up; touchy [Lynn has a *quick* temper.] ◆***adv.*** with speed; rapidly [Come *quick!*] ◆***n.*** **1** the tender flesh under a fingernail or toenail. **2** a person's deepest feelings [He was hurt to the *quick* by her insult.] **3** people who are alive; the living: *now used only in the phrase* "the quick and the dead." —**quick′ly** ***adv.*** —**quick′ness** ***n.***

SYNONYMS: **Quick** suggests a natural ability to act speedily [An ambulance driver needs to have a *quick* mind.] **Prompt** suggests getting a task done at once and without wasting time because one has learned to do so or wants to do so [An efficient manager sends off *prompt* answers to all letters.] *See also* SYNONYMS *at* **fast.**

**quick·en** (kwik′ən) ***v.*** **1** to move or make move faster; speed up [My pulse *quickened* with fear. The horse *quickened* its pace.] **2** to make or become active or more alive [The news *quickened* my interest. Old trees *quickened* in the spring sun.]

☆**quick·ie** (kwik′ē) ***n.*** anything made or done quickly. *This is a slang word.*

**quick·lime** (kwik′līm) ***n.*** lime, the substance derived from limestone.

**quick·sand** (kwik′sand) ***n.*** deep, wet, loose sand in which a person may be swallowed up.

**quick·sil·ver** (kwik′sil′vər) ***n.*** the metal mercury.

**Quicksilver** uses the old meaning of *quick* for "living," and is a translation of a Latin term, "living silver." Mercury is called *quicksilver* because it is silver in color and is often in liquid form. It was thought that anything that moves, as a liquid does, could be described as living.

**quick-tem·pered** (kwik′tem′pərd) ***adj.*** becoming angry at the slightest thing.

**quick-wit·ted** (kwik′wit′id) ***adj.*** able to learn or understand quickly; alert.

**qui·es·cent** (kwī es′′nt) ***adj.*** quiet; not moving; inactive [Animals are *quiescent* during hibernation.] —**qui·es′cence** ***n.***

**qui·et** (kwī′ət) ***adj.*** **1** not noisy; hushed [a *quiet* motor]. **2** not talking; silent [She was *quiet* during dinner.] **3** not moving; still; calm [a *quiet* pond]. **4** not easily excited or upset; gentle [He has a *quiet* nature.] **5** peaceful and relaxing [We spent a *quiet* evening at home.] **6** not bright or showy [*quiet* colors; a *quiet* tie]. ◆***n.*** the condition of being quiet, hushed, calm, peaceful, etc. [in the *quiet* of the night]. ◆***v.*** to make or become quiet [*Quiet* down and go to sleep.] —**qui′et·ly** ***adv.*** —**qui′et·ness** ***n.***

**qui·e·tude** (kwī′ə to͞od *or* kwī′ə tyo͞od) ***n.*** the condition of being quiet, still, calm, etc.

**qui·e·tus** (kwī ēt′əs) ***n.*** **1** the freeing of someone from a promise, debt, etc. **2** death. **3** anything that kills or ends something [to give the *quietus* to a rumor].

**quill** (kwil) ***n.*** **1** a large, stiff feather. **2** something made from the hollow stem of such a feather, especially a pen for writing. *See the picture.* **3** any of the sharp, stiff spines that stick out on the body of a porcupine or hedgehog.

**quilt** (kwilt) ***n.*** a covering for a bed, made of two layers of cloth filled with down, wool, etc. and stitched together in lines or patterns to keep the filling in place. ◆***v.*** **1** to make in the form of a quilt [a *quilted* potholder]. ☆**2** to make quilts.



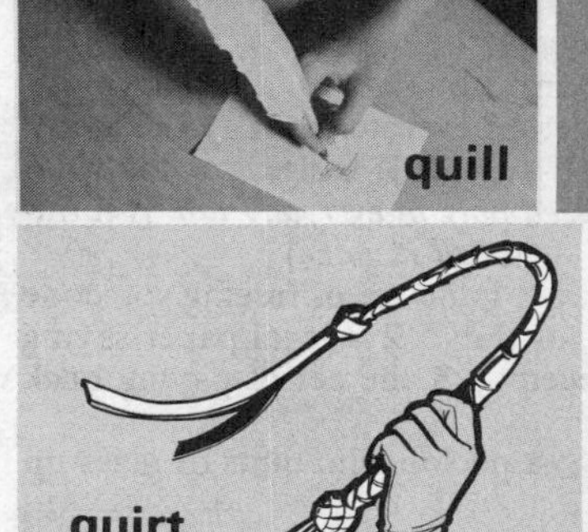

quill

quirt

Queen Anne's lace

**quilt·ing** (kwilt′iŋ) ***n.*** **1** the act of making quilts. **2** material for making quilts.

**quince** (kwins) ***n.*** **1** a hard, yellow fruit shaped like an apple and used in jams and preserves. **2** the tree that it grows on.

**qui·nine** (kwī′nīn) ***n.*** a bitter substance taken from cinchona bark and used in treating malaria.

**quin·tes·sence** (kwin tes′′ns) ***n.*** **1** the essence or most important part of something, in its purest form. **2** the perfect type or example of something [To me, this painting is the *quintessence* of beauty.]

**quin·tet** or **quin·tette** (kwin tet′) ***n.*** **1** a piece of music for five voices or five instruments. **2** the five people who sing or play such a piece of music. **3** any group of five. 

**quin·tu·plet** (kwin tup′lit *or* kwin to͞o′plit *or* kwin′too plit) ***n.*** any of five children born at a single birth.

**quip** (kwip) ***n.*** a clever or witty remark; jest.

**quirk** (kwurk) ***n.*** **1** a strange little habit; peculiarity. **2** a sudden twist or turn [a *quirk* of fate].

☆**quirt** (kwurt) ***n.*** a whip with a short handle and a lash of braided leather, carried by people when they ride horseback. *See the picture.*

**quis·ling** (kwiz′liŋ) ***n.*** a traitor.

This word comes from the name of a Norwegian politician, Vidkun *Quisling,* who betrayed his country to the Nazis during World War II.

**quit** (kwit) ***v.*** **1** to stop doing something [My father *quit* smoking.] **2** to give up; resign from [to *quit* one's job]. **3** to leave; go away from [She decided to *quit* the country and live in Spain.] **4** to stop trying; admit that one has failed. —**quit** or **quit′ted, quit′ting** ◆***adj.*** free; clear [*quit* of all debts].

**quit·claim** (kwit′klām) ***n.*** a legal paper by which one person gives up to another a claim to a certain property or right.

**quite** (kwīt) ***adv.*** **1** completely; entirely [I haven't *quite* finished eating.] **2** really; truly [You are *quite* a

| | | | | | | | |
|---|---|---|---|---|---|---|---|
| **a** | fat | **ir** | here | **ou** | out | **zh** | leisure |
| **ā** | ape | **ī** | bite, fire | **u** | up | **ŋ** | ring |
| **ä** | car, lot | **ō** | go | **ur** | fur | | a *in* ago |
| **e** | ten | **ô** | law, horn | **ch** | chin | | e *in* agent |
| **er** | care | **oi** | oil | **sh** | she | **ə =** | i *in* unity |
| **ē** | even | **oo** | look | **th** | thin | | o *in* collect |
| **i** | hit | **o͞o** | tool | ***th*** | then | | u *in* focus |

musician.] **3** very or somewhat [It's *quite* warm outside.] —☆**quite a few,** more than a few: *used only in everyday talk.* —**quite so!** certainly! I agree!

**Qui·to** (kē′tō) the capital of Ecuador.

**quits** (kwits) ***adj.*** owing nothing, as after paying a debt or getting revenge; on even terms [Pay me a dollar, and we'll be *quits.*] —☆**call it quits,** to stop what one has been doing: *used only in everyday talk* [I'll finish painting this wall, then *call it quits.*]

**quit·tance** (kwit′'ns) ***n.*** **1** the act of freeing someone from a debt, promise, or duty. **2** a legal paper saying this has happened; receipt. **3** the act of paying back or getting revenge.

**quit·ter** (kwit′ər) ***n.*** ☆a person who quits or gives up too easily.

**quiv·er**[1] (kwiv′ər) ***v.*** to shake with little, trembling movements [leaves *quivering* in the breeze]. *See* SYNONYMS *at* **shake.** ◆***n.*** the act of quivering.

**quiv·er**[2] (kwiv′ər) ***n.*** a case for holding arrows. *See the picture.*

**Quixote, Don** *see* **Don Quixote.**

**quix·ot·ic** (kwik sät′ik) ***adj.*** kind and noble, but in a way that is foolish or not practical. —**quix·ot′i·cal·ly *adv.***

**quiz** (kwiz) ***n.*** ☆a questioning; especially, a short test given to find out how much one has learned. —*pl.* **quiz′zes** ◆***v.*** ☆to ask questions of; give a quiz to [to *quiz* a class]. —**quizzed, quiz′zing**

☆**quiz show** or **quiz program** a radio or television program on which people try to win prizes by answering questions correctly.

**quiz·zi·cal** (kwiz′i k'l) ***adj.*** **1** making fun of others; teasing [a *quizzical* smile]. **2** that seems to ask a question [a *quizzical* look on her face]. —**quiz′zi·cal·ly *adv.***

**quoin** (koin *or* kwoin) ***n.*** the outside corner of a building, or any of the stones in such a corner.

**quoit** (kwoit) ***n.*** any of the metal or rope rings which players in a game called **quoits** throw in trying to encircle a peg in the ground. *See the picture.*

**quon·dam** (kwän′dəm) ***adj.*** that was at one time; former [my *quondam* partner].

**quo·rum** (kwôr′əm) ***n.*** the smallest number of members that must be present at a meeting of some group before it can carry on its business.

**quo·ta** (kwō′tə) ***n.*** the share or part of a total that each one of a certain group is asked to give or is allowed to get [What is the *quota* for our class in the paper sale?]

> Our word **quota** was taken directly from Latin with no change in spelling. Its meaning comes from its use in the Latin phrase *quota pars,* meaning "how large a part."

**quot·a·ble** (kwōt′ə b'l) ***adj.*** so well said, so true, etc. as to be worth quoting [Lincoln made many *quotable* remarks.]

**quo·ta·tion** (kwō tā′shən) ***n.*** **1** the act of quoting. **2** the words or section quoted [Sermons often have *quotations* from the Bible.] **3** the present price as of a stock or bond.

**quotation marks** the marks " ", placed before and after words that are quoted.

**quote** (kwōt) ***v.*** **1** to repeat exactly the words of another person or words from a piece of writing [The newspaper *quotes* our principal. The speaker *quoted* from Shakespeare.] **2** to give the price of [Cotton was *quoted* at 50 cents a pound.] —**quot′ed, quot′ing** ◆***n.*** **1** something quoted; quotation. **2 quotes,** *pl. same as* **quotation marks.** *The noun is used only in everyday talk.*

> In giving a quotation when speaking, people often say "quote" at the beginning of the quoted words and "unquote" at the end.

**quoth** (kwōth) ***v.*** said: *used mostly in old stories, poems, etc.* [*Quoth* the raven, "Nevermore."]

**quo·tient** (kwō′shənt) ***n.*** the number got by dividing one number into another [In $32 \div 8 = 4$, the number 4 is the *quotient.*]

**R, r** (är) ***n.*** the eighteenth letter of the English alphabet. —*pl.* **R's, r's** (ärz) —**the three R's,** reading, writing, and arithmetic, thought of as the basic school subjects. They are called "the three R's" because they are sometimes written in a joking way "reading, 'riting, and 'rithmetic."

☆**R** restricted: a movie rating meaning that no one under 17 will be let in unless a parent or guardian goes along.

**r** *the symbol for* **radius** (in mathematics).

**R.** or **r.** *abbreviation for* **right, river, run** *or* **runs** (in baseball).

**Ra** (rä) the sun god and chief god of the ancient Egyptians. He was pictured as having the head of a hawk. *See the picture.*

**Ra** *the symbol for the chemical element* radium.

**rab·bi** (rab′ī) ***n.*** a teacher of the Jewish law, now usually the leader of a synagogue or temple. —*pl.* **rab′bis**

> **Rabbi** comes from the Hebrew word meaning "my master." The word was used in speaking to a teacher of the Jewish law in order to show one's great respect for him.

**rab·bin·i·cal** (rə bin′i k'l) ***adj.*** of rabbis, their teachings, learning, etc.

**rab·bit** (rab′it) ***n.*** **1** an animal having soft fur, long ears, and a very short tail. Rabbits are related to hares but are usually smaller and live in burrows. **2** the fur of a rabbit.

**rab·ble** (rab′'l) ***n.*** a noisy crowd of people that pays no attention to law and order; mob. —**the rabble,** the common people: *used to show scorn.*

**rab·id** (rab′id) ***adj.*** **1** holding certain ideas, opinions, etc. in a strong, unreasonable way; fanatical. **2** of or having rabies [a *rabid* dog].

**ra·bies** (rā′bēz) ***n.*** a disease that can kill dogs and other animals, or people who have been bitten by an animal that has the disease; hydrophobia. It causes choking and makes the muscles tighten and twitch. *See the word history at* **hydrophobia.**

☆**rac·coon** (ra ko͞on′) ***n.*** **1** a furry animal having a long tail with black rings. It climbs trees and is active mostly at night. *See the picture.* **2** its fur.

**race**[1] (rās) ***n.*** **1** a contest, as between runners, swimmers, cars, boats, etc., to see who can go fastest. **2** any contest, as for election [the *race* for mayor]. **3** a strong, swift current of water. ◆***v.*** **1** to take part in a race [How many planes are *racing?*] **2** to cause to take part in a race [Four owners are *racing* their horses.] **3** to have a race with [I'll *race* you to the corner.] **4** to go very fast [Her eye *raced* over the page.] **5** to run an engine at high speed while the gears are not meshed. —**raced, rac′ing**

**race**[2] (rās) ***n.*** **1** any of the major groups into which all human beings are divided based on some physical features, such as the color of hair and skin [The Caucasoid, Negroid, and Mongoloid *races* all belong to one species.] **2** any large group of living creatures [the human *race*]. **3** a group of people who have something in common [The pioneers were a *race* of heroes and heroines.]

Because the word **race** has been misused, as by the Nazis, to suggest false ideas, many scientists today prefer to use some other term, such as "ethnic group."

**ra·ceme** (rā sēm′) ***n.*** a flower stem on which single flowers grow from shorter stems along its length, as in a lily of the valley.

**rac·er** (rās′ər) ***n.*** **1** an animal, car, etc. that takes part in races. ☆**2** any of several snakes that can move swiftly, as the American blacksnake.

**race track** a track laid out for racing, usually in an oval.

**Ra·chel** (rā′chəl) in the Bible, the second wife of Jacob. Her sister **Leah** was his first wife.

**ra·cial** (rā′shəl) ***adj.*** **1** having to do with a race of people. **2** of or between races [*racial* equality]. —**ra′cial·ly** ***adv.***

**rac·ism** (rā′siz'm) ***n.*** **1** the notion that one race is better than another. **2** prejudice against another race, that comes from this notion. —**rac′ist** ***adj., n.***

**rack**[1] (rak) ***n.*** **1** a framework, stand, etc. for holding things [a clothes *rack;* a magazine *rack*]. *See the picture.* **2** a device for lifting an automobile so that it can be repaired from below. **3** a bar having teeth into which the teeth of a gearwheel fit as the wheel moves along. **4** a device used at one time to torture people by stretching their arms and legs out of place. ◆***v.*** to cause pain to [a body *racked* with disease]. —**rack one's brains,** to try hard to think of something.

**rack**[2] (rak) ***n.*** destruction: *now used only in the phrase* **go to rack and ruin,** meaning "to become ruined."

**rack·et**[1] (rak′it) ***n.*** **1** loud, confused noise; clatter; din [A car without a muffler makes a terrible *racket.*] *See* SYNONYMS *at* **noise.** ☆**2** a scheme for getting money in a way that is not honest or legal. 

**rack·et**[2] (rak′it) ***n.*** a light bat for tennis, badminton, etc., having a network as of catgut or nylon strung in a frame attached to a handle. *See the picture.*

This word **racket** comes from an Arabic word meaning "palm of the hand." The first "racket" used in games was certainly the palm of the hand, and it is still the one used in the game of handball.

☆**rack·et·eer** (rak ə tir′) ***n.*** a person who gets money in a way that is not honest or legal, as by cheating others or threatening to harm them.

☆**ra·coon** (ra ko͞on′) ***n.*** *another spelling of* **raccoon.**

**rac·quet** (rak′it) ***n.*** *another spelling of* **racket**[2]**.**

**rac·y** (rās′ē) ***adj.*** **1** lively, or full of spirit [a *racy* style of writing]. ☆**2** not quite proper; slightly indecent [a *racy* story]. —**rac′i·er, rac′i·est** —**rac′i·ness** ***n.***

☆**ra·dar** (rā′där) ***n.*** a device that sends out radio waves and picks them up after they strike some object and bounce back. It is used to find out the distance, direction, and speed of airplanes, ships, storms, etc.

**Radar** is the kind of word called an acronym, made up by using the first letter or syllable of each of two or more words. **Radar** is formed from "**ra**dio **d**etecting **a**nd **r**anging."

**ra·di·al** (rā′dē əl) ***adj.*** like a ray or rays; branching out in all directions from a center.

| | | | | | | | | | |
|---|---|---|---|---|---|---|---|---|---|
| **a** | fat | **ir** | here | **ou** | out | **zh** | leisure | | |
| **ā** | ape | **ī** | bite, fire | **u** | up | **ng** | ring | | |
| **ä** | car, lot | **ō** | go | **ur** | fur | | | a *in* ago | |
| **e** | ten | **ô** | law, horn | **ch** | chin | | | e *in* agent | |
| **er** | care | **oi** | oil | **sh** | she | **ə** = | | i *in* unity | |
| **ē** | even | **oo** | look | **th** | thin | | | o *in* collect | |
| **i** | hit | **o͞o** | tool | ***th*** | then | | | u *in* focus | |

**radial tire** an automobile tire with layers, as of fabric, in strips that pass straight across under the tread from one side of the tire to the other.

**ra·di·ant** (rā′dē ənt) ***adj.*** **1** shining brightly. **2** showing joy, very good health, etc.; beaming [a *radiant* smile]. **3** coming from a source in rays [*radiant* energy from the sun]. —**ra′di·ance *n.*** —**ra′di·ant·ly *adv.***

**ra·di·ate** (rā′dē āt′) ***v.*** **1** to send out in rays [The stove *radiated* heat.] **2** to come forth in rays [Light *radiates* from the sun.] **3** to give forth or show [a face that *radiated* happiness]. **4** to branch out in lines from a center [highways *radiating* from a city]. —**ra′di·at′ed, ra′di·at′ing**

**ra·di·a·tion** (rā′dē ā′shən) ***n.*** **1** the process in which energy is sent out in rays from atoms and molecules because of changes inside them. **2** the energy or rays sent out.

**ra·di·a·tor** (rā′dē āt′ər) ***n.*** ☆**1** a series of pipes through which hot water or steam moves in order to radiate heat into a room, etc. ☆**2** a system of pipes for cooling water that has become hot from passing through an engine. This helps keep the engine cool.

**rad·i·cal** (rad′i k'l) ***adj.*** **1** having to do with the root or source; basic; fundamental [a *radical* difference in their views]. **2** very great; complete [Moving to the farm made a *radical* change in their lives.] **3** in favor of basic or great changes or reforms [a *radical* political party]. ◆***n.*** **1** a person who favors basic or great changes or reforms. **2** a group of two or more atoms that acts as a single atom during a chemical change [$SO_4$ is a *radical* in $H_2SO_4$.] —**rad′i·cal·ism *n.*** —**rad′i·cal·ly *adv.***

**radical sign** the sign ($\surd$ or $\sqrt{\ }$) used before a number or quantity in mathematics to show that a root is to be found by figuring.

**ra·di·i** (rā′dē ī′) ***n.*** *a plural of* **radius.**

rail
up to 45 cm (18 in.) long

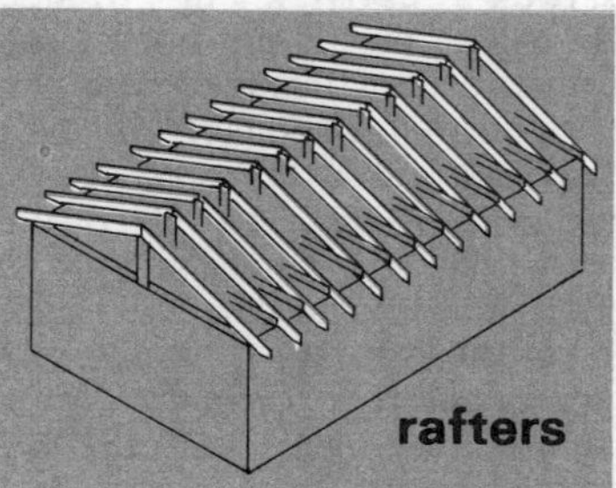
rafters

raglan sleeves

types of rake

ragweed

☆**ra·di·o** (rā′dē ō′) ***n.*** **1** a way of sending sounds through space by changing them into electric waves which are sent and picked up, without wires, by a receiver that changes them back to sounds. **2** such a receiver. **3** the act or business of broadcasting news, music, talks, etc. by radio. —*pl.* **ra′di·os′** ◆***adj.*** of, using, used in, or sent by radio [a *radio* program; a *radio* tube]. ◆***v.*** to send a message by radio [to *radio* for help]. —**ra′di·oed′, ra′di·o′ing**

**ra·di·o·ac·tive** (rā′dē ō ak′tiv) ***adj.*** giving off energy in the form of particles or rays as a result of the breaking up of nuclei of atoms [Radium and uranium are *radioactive* elements.] —**ra·di·o·ac·tiv·i·ty** (rā′dē ō ak tiv′ə tē) ***n.***

**ra·di·ol·o·gy** (rā′dē äl′ə jē) ***n.*** the use of X-rays, radioactive drugs, etc. to discover and treat diseases. —**ra′di·ol′o·gist *n.***

**rad·ish** (rad′ish) ***n.*** **1** a plant with a small, round or long root that has a red or white skin. **2** this root, which has a sharp taste and is eaten raw as a relish or in a salad.

**ra·di·um** (rā′dē əm) ***n.*** a radioactive chemical element that is a metal. It is found in small amounts in pitchblende and other ores and has been used in treating cancer.

**ra·di·us** (rā′dē əs) ***n.*** **1** any straight line that goes from the center to the outside of a circle or sphere. *See the picture for* **circle. 2** a round area as measured by its radius [no houses within a *radius* of five miles]. **3** the thicker of the two bones in the forearm. —*pl.* **ra·di·i** (rā′dē ī′) or **ra′di·us·es**

**raf·fi·a** (raf′ē ə) ***n.*** fiber from the leaves of certain palm trees, used for weaving.

**raf·fle** (raf′'l) ***n.*** a form of gambling in which people buy chances on getting prizes, which are given to winners picked by lot. ◆***v.*** to offer as a prize in a raffle [Our church made money by *raffling* off a new car.] —**raf′fled, raf′fling**

**raft**[1] (raft) ***n.*** **1** a number of logs, boards, etc. fastened together and used as a flatboat. **2** a tube made of rubber, etc., that can be used as a boat when it is filled with air or gas.

**raft**[2] (raft) ***n.*** a large number or amount; lot: *used only in everyday talk* [a *raft* of trouble].

**raft·er** (raf′tər) ***n.*** any of the sloping beams used to hold up a roof. *See the picture.*

**rag**[1] (rag) ***n.*** **1** a piece of cloth that is old, torn, not needed, etc. **2** any small cloth used for dusting, washing, etc. **3 rags,** *pl.* old, worn clothing. **4** a newspaper that is not respected: *slang in this meaning.* ◆***adj.*** made of rags [a *rag* doll].

☆**rag**[2] (rag) ***n.*** a musical piece in ragtime [playing the "Maple Leaf *Rag*"].

**rag·a·muf·fin** (rag′ə muf′in) ***n.*** a poor child wearing torn or dirty clothes.

**rage** (rāj) ***n.*** **1** a short period of great anger; raving fury [He flew into a *rage* and flung the book to the floor.] *See* SYNONYMS *at* **anger. 2** great force or violence, as of the wind. **3** anything that many people are eager to get or do; fad; craze [Very short skirts were the *rage* for a time.] ◆***v.*** **1** to show great anger. **2** to be violent and out of control [a *raging* storm; a fire *raging* through the barn]. —**raged, rag′ing**

**rag·ged** (rag′id) ***adj.*** **1** shabby or torn from being worn a great deal [a *ragged* shirt]. **2** wearing shabby or torn clothes [a *ragged* child]. **3** rough and uneven [the *ragged* edge of a torn sheet of paper]. —☆**run (someone) ragged,** to wear someone out by having too many things for that person to do. —**rag′ged·ness** ***n.***

**rag·lan** (rag′lən) ***n.*** a loose topcoat having sleeves that go straight to the collar with no seam at the shoulder. ◆***adj.*** describing such a sleeve. *See the picture.*

**ra·gout** (ra go͞o′) ***n.*** a stew made of meat, vegetables, and much seasoning.

☆**rag·time** (rag′tīm) ***n.*** an early form of jazz music, first popular from about 1890 to 1915. It is played in fast, even time, but with irregular rhythms in the melody.

**rag·weed** (rag′wēd) ***n.*** a common weed with small, greenish flowers. Its pollen can cause hay fever. *See the picture.*

☆**rah** (rä) ***interj.*** *another word for* **hurrah.**

**raid** (rād) ***n.*** **1** a sudden attack, as by soldiers, bandits, etc. **2** a sudden entering of a place, as by police to arrest people breaking the law. ◆***v.*** to make a raid on [to *raid* a town]. —**raid′er** ***n.***

**rail**[1] (rāl) ***n.*** **1** a bar of wood or metal placed crosswise between standing posts, as in a fence. **2** either of the metal bars forming the track of a railroad. **3** a railroad [Ship it by *rail.*]

**rail**[2] (rāl) ***v.*** to keep on talking or shouting in an angry way; complain strongly [to *rail* at one's bad luck].

**rail**[3] (rāl) ***n.*** a small wading bird that has short wings and tail, long toes, and lives in marshes. *See the picture.*

**rail·ing** (rāl′iŋ) ***n.*** a kind of fence, made of a series of posts and rails [a porch *railing*].

**rail·ler·y** (rāl′ər ē) ***n.*** playful teasing or joking.

**rail·road** (rāl′rōd) ***n.*** **1** a road on which there is a track made up of parallel steel rails along which trains run. **2** a series of such roads managed as a unit, together with the cars, engines, stations, etc. that belong to it. **3** the company that owns such a unit. ◆***v.*** ☆**1** to work on a railroad. ☆**2** to rush through in an unfair way: *used only in everyday talk* [to *railroad* a bill through Congress]. ☆**3** to put in prison on a false charge or after an unfair trial: *slang in this meaning.*

**rail·way** (rāl′wā) ***n.*** **1** *the usual British word for* **railroad. 2** any set of tracks for the wheels of a car [Many cities used to have street *railways.*]

**rai·ment** (rā′mənt) ***n.*** clothing: *an old-fashioned word no longer much used.*

**rain** (rān) ***n.*** **1** water that falls to the earth in drops formed from the moisture in the air. **2** the falling of such drops; a shower [Sunshine followed the *rain.*] **3** a fast falling of many small things or bits [a *rain* of ashes from the volcano]. ◆***v.*** **1** to fall as rain [It is *raining.*] **2** to pour down like rain [Bullets *rained* about them.] **3** to give in large amounts [They *rained* praises on her.]—☆**rain out,** to cause a game, picnic, etc. to be postponed because of rain.

**rain·bow** (rān′bō) ***n.*** a curved band across the sky with all the colors of the spectrum in it. It is seen when the sun's rays pass through falling rain or mist.

☆**rain·coat** (rān′kōt) ***n.*** a waterproof coat that protects a person from the rain.

**rain·drop** (rān′dräp) ***n.*** a single drop of rain.

**rain·fall** (rān′fôl) ***n.*** **1** the amount of water falling as rain or snow over a certain area during a certain time [The annual *rainfall* in Rhode Island is about 40 inches.] **2** a falling of rain; shower.

**Rai·nier** (rā nir′), **Mount** a mountain in the State of Washington.

**rain·storm** (rān′stôrm) ***n.*** a storm in which there is much rain.

**rain·y** (rā′nē) ***adj.*** having much rain [the *rainy* season]. —**rain′i·er, rain′i·est** —**a rainy day,** a future time when there may be great need [to put aside money for *a rainy day*]. —**rain′i·ness** ***n.***

**raise** (rāz) ***v.*** **1** to cause to rise; lift [*Raise* your hand if you have a question. *Raise* the window.] *See* SYNONYMS *at* **lift. 2** to build or put up; construct [The neighbors helped *raise* our barn.] **3** to make larger, greater, higher, louder, etc. [to *raise* prices; to *raise* one's voice]. **4** to bring up; take care of; support [to *raise* a family]. **5** to cause to grow; produce [to *raise* cabbages]. **6** to bring about; cause [They *raised* a storm of protest.] **7** to bring up for thinking about [She *raised* the question of the cost of the repairs.] **8** to bring together; collect [We *raised* money for the flood victims.] **9** to bring to an end; remove [to *raise* a blockade]. **10** to make puffy by using yeast or other leavening [to *raise* dough]. —**raised, rais′ing** ◆***n.*** a making or becoming larger; especially, an increase in salary or wages.

**rai·sin** (rā′z'n) ***n.*** a sweet grape dried for eating.

**ra·jah** or **ra·ja** (rä′jə) ***n.*** in earlier times, a prince or chief in India or in parts of Indonesia. 605

**rake**[1] (rāk) ***n.*** a tool with a long handle having a set of teeth or prongs at one end. It is used for gathering loose grass, leaves, etc. or for smoothing broken ground. *See the picture.* ◆***v.*** **1** to gather together or smooth as with a rake [to *rake* leaves; to *rake* a gravel path]. **2** to look with great care; search carefully [He *raked* through the old papers looking for the letter.] **3** to shoot guns along the whole length of [The deck of the ship was *raked* by cannon.] —**raked, rak′ing** —**rake up,** to discover a fact or gossip from the past and make it known [to *rake up* an old scandal].

**rake**[2] (rāk) ***n.*** a man who leads a wild life, drinking, gambling, etc.

**rak·ish** (rā′kish) ***adj.*** **1** having a lively, careless look; jaunty [a hat worn at a *rakish* angle]. **2** looking as if it can move fast [a *rakish* ship].

**Ra·leigh** (rô′lē) the capital of North Carolina.

**Ra·leigh** (rô′lē), Sir **Walter** about 1552–1618; an English explorer and writer.

**ral·ly**[1] (ral′ē) ***v.*** **1** to gather together so as to bring back into order [The troops retreated, then *rallied* for another charge.] **2** to bring or come together for some purpose [The students *rallied* to cheer the football team.] **3** to come in order to help [to *rally* to the side of a friend in trouble]. **4** to get back health or strength; revive [As the fever left her, she began to

| | | | | | | | |
|---|---|---|---|---|---|---|---|
| **a** | fat | **ir** | here | **ou** | out | **zh** | leisure |
| **ā** | ape | **ī** | bite, fire | **u** | up | **ŋ** | ring |
| **ä** | car, lot | **ō** | go | **ʉr** | fur | | a *in* ago |
| **e** | ten | **ô** | law, horn | **ch** | chin | | e *in* agent |
| **er** | care | **oi** | oil | **sh** | she | **ə =** | i *in* unity |
| **ē** | even | **oo** | look | **th** | thin | | o *in* collect |
| **i** | hit | **o͞o** | tool | ***th*** | then | | u *in* focus |

r

*rally.*] **5** to come from behind and begin to win, as in a game. —**ral′lied, ral′ly·ing** ◆***n.*** the act of rallying or the fact of being rallied; especially, a gathering of people for some purpose [a political *rally*]. —*pl.* **ral′lies**

**ral·ly**[2] (ral′ē) ***v.*** to make fun of; tease playfully. —**ral′lied, ral′ly·ing**

**ram** (ram) ***n.*** **1** a male sheep. **2** *a shorter form of* **battering ram.** ◆***v.*** **1** to hit or drive with force [The car *rammed* into the fence.] **2** to force into place by pressing; stuff or cram [He *rammed* the candy into his pocket.] —**rammed, ram′ming**

**ram·ble** (ram′b'l) ***v.*** **1** to walk or stroll along without any special goal; roam. **2** to talk or write on and on without sticking to any point or subject. **3** to spread in all directions, as a vine. —**ram′bled, ram′bling** ◆***n.*** a rambling; stroll.

**ram·bler** (ram′blər) ***n.*** a person or thing that rambles; especially, any climbing rose.

**ram·i·fi·ca·tion** (ram′ə fi kā′shən) ***n.*** **1** the act of ramifying, or spreading out into branches. **2** any of the results or effects of something [Her decision to sell the company had many *ramifications.*]

**ram·i·fy** (ram′ə fī) ***v.*** to divide or spread out into branches. —**ram′i·fied, ram′i·fy·ing**

**ramp** (ramp) ***n.*** **1** a sloping road, walk, surface, etc. going from a lower to a higher place. ☆**2** a staircase on wheels rolled up to a plane for people to use in getting on or off the plane.



**ram·page** (ram pāj′) ***v.*** to rush about in a wild, angry way; rage. —**ram·paged′, ram·pag′ing** ◆***n.*** (ram′pāj) wild, angry action: *used mainly in the phrase* **on the rampage** *or* **on a rampage,** in a rage; wild and angry.

**ramp·ant** (ram′pənt) ***adj.*** **1** spreading wildly, without control [The plague was *rampant* in Europe in the Middle Ages.] **2** wild in action, speech, etc. **3** standing up on the hind legs, as a lion on a shield. *See the picture.*

**ram·part** (ram′pärt) ***n.*** **1** a bank of earth, often with a wall along the top, surrounding a place to defend it. **2** anything that defends.

**ram·rod** (ram′räd) ***n.*** a metal rod for ramming a charge down the muzzle of a gun, or for cleaning the barrel of a rifle.

**ram·shack·le** (ram′shak′'l) ***adj.*** ready to fall apart; shaky; rickety [a *ramshackle* old barn].

**ran** (ran) *past tense of* **run.**

☆**ranch** (ranch) ***n.*** **1** a large farm, especially in the Western part of the U.S., where cattle, horses, or sheep are raised. **2** any large farm [a fruit *ranch;* a turkey *ranch*]. ◆***v.*** to work on or manage a ranch. —**ranch′er *n.***

**ran·cid** (ran′sid) ***adj.*** having the bad smell or taste of stale fats and oils; spoiled.

**ran·cor** (raŋ′kər) ***n.*** a strong hate or bitter, unfriendly feeling that lasts for a long time; deep spite. —**ran′cor·ous *adj.***

**r & b** or **R & B** rhythm and blues (music).

**R & D** or **R. and D.** research and development.

**ran·dom** (ran′dəm) ***adj.*** made, done, etc. in an aimless way, without planning; chance; haphazard [a *random* choice]. —**at random,** without careful choice, aim, plan, etc. [Pick a card from this deck *at random.*]

**rang** (raŋ) *past tense of* **ring**[1].

**range** (rānj) ***n.*** **1** a row or line, especially of connected mountains [the Appalachian *range*]. **2** the distance that a gun can shoot, a missile can travel, a sound can carry, etc. [a cannon with a twenty-mile *range;* within *range* of my voice]. **3** the distance an airplane can fly on one supply of fuel. **4** a place for practice in shooting [a rifle *range*]. **5** the limits within which there are changes or differences of amount, degree, etc. [a *range* of prices from $20 to $100; a *range* of songs from ballads to rock]. ☆**6** open land over which cattle graze. **7** a cooking stove. ◆***v.*** **1** to wander about; roam [Bears *ranged* the forests.] **2** to stretch or lie [Sand dunes *range* along the seashore.] **3** to be within certain limits [The prices *range* from $5 to $15.] **4** to place in a certain order; especially, to set in a row or rows [Tulips were *ranged* along the path.] **5** to join with [She *ranged* herself with the rebels.] —**ranged, rang′ing**

> SYNONYMS: The **range** of something is the full extent to which it can be seen, heard, felt, known, etc. [The *range* of her knowledge of modern art is unusual.] The **scope** of something is the range that it has within certain set limits [Some very technical words are not within the *scope* of this dictionary.]

**rang·er** (rān′jər) ***n.*** **1** any of a group of special soldiers or police officers who patrol a certain region. ☆**2** a warden who patrols government forests.

**Ran·goon** (raŋ go͞on′) the capital of Burma.

**rang·y** (rān′jē) ***adj.*** ☆tall and thin, and having long legs [a *rangy* cowboy]. —**rang′i·er, rang′i·est**

**rank**[1] (raŋk) ***n.*** **1** a social class; position in society [people from all *ranks* of life]. **2** a high position in society [people of *rank*]. **3** a position or grade, as in the armed forces [the *rank* of captain]. **4** a position as measured by quality [a poet of the first *rank*]. **5** a row or line, as of soldiers, placed side by side. **6 ranks,** *pl.* all the people of some group, as of an army, who are not the officers or leaders [He rose from the *ranks* to become a general.] *Also called* **rank and file.** ◆***v.*** **1** to place in a certain rank [The critics *rank* this movie among the best.] **2** to hold a certain rank [Sarah *ranks* first on our swimming team.] —**pull one's rank,** to use one's higher rank to get others to obey one's commands: *a slang phrase.*

**rank**[2] (raŋk) ***adj.*** **1** growing in a wild, thick, coarse way [*rank* weeds]. **2** having a strong, unpleasant taste or smell [*rank* fish]. **3** of the worst or most extreme kind [*rank* injustice].

**Ran·kin** (raŋ′kin), **Jeannette** 1880–1973; the first U.S. congresswoman.

**rank·ing** (raŋ′kiŋ) ***adj.*** ☆**1** of the highest rank [the *ranking* officer]. ☆**2** outstanding; prominent [one of our *ranking* scholars].

**ran·kle** (raŋ′k'l) ***v.*** to cause an angry or unfriendly feeling that lasts for a long time [Her harsh words *rankled* in my mind for days.] —**ran′kled, ran′kling**

> **Rankle** comes from an old French word meaning "ulcer," and that French word comes from a Latin word meaning "little dragon." An ulcer feels like a little dragon gnawing inside one. And when an insult **rankles,** it is as though one had a dragon or ulcer inside giving one pain.

**ran·sack** (ran′sak) ***v.*** **1** to search through every part of [to *ransack* one's pockets for a key]. **2** to search for loot [Bandits *ransacked* the town.]

**ran·som** (ran′səm) ***n.*** **1** the price asked or paid for freeing a kidnapped person or other captive. **2** the act of freeing a captive by paying the price demanded. ◆***v.*** to pay a price in order to free [to *ransom* a prisoner of war].

**rant** (rant) ***v.*** to talk in a loud, wild way; rave. ◆***n.*** loud, wild speech.

**rap**[1] (rap) ***v.*** **1** to strike or knock sharply [to *rap* on a door]. **2** to say in a sharp, quick way [The captain *rapped* out an order.] ☆**3** to find fault with; criticize: *slang in this meaning* [The critic *rapped* the movie.] ☆**4** to talk or chat: *slang in this meaning.* —**rapped, rap′ping** ◆***n.*** **1** a quick, sharp knock. ☆**2** blame or punishment: *slang in this meaning* [to take the *rap* for a crime]. ☆**3** a talk, or chat: *slang in this meaning.*

**rap**[2] (rap) ***n.*** the least bit: *used only in everyday talk* [She doesn't care a *rap* about what they say.]

**ra·pa·cious** (rə pā′shəs) ***adj.*** **1** taking by force; plundering [a *rapacious* army]. **2** greedy or grasping [a *rapacious* landlord]. **3** living on captured prey [a *rapacious* animal]. —**ra·pa′cious·ly *adv.***

**ra·pac·i·ty** (rə pas′ə tē) ***n.*** the fact or habit of being rapacious; greed.

**rape**[1] (rāp) ***n.*** the crime of forcing a person, especially a woman, to take part in a sexual act. ◆***v.*** to commit rape on; ravish. —**raped, rap′ing**

**rape**[2] (rāp) ***n.*** a plant whose leaves are fed to animals. An oil is pressed from its seeds.

**Raph·a·el** (raf′ē əl *or* rā′fē əl) 1483–1520; an Italian painter.

**rap·id** (rap′id) ***adj.*** very swift or quick [a *rapid* journey]. *See* SYNONYMS *at* **fast.** ◆☆***n.*** **1** *usually* **rapids,** *pl.* a part of a river where the water moves swiftly. ☆**2** a rapid transit train or system. —**rap′id·ly *adv.***

**rap·id-fire** (rap′id fīr′) ***adj.*** **1** that fires shots quickly one after the other [a *rapid-fire* gun]. **2** done, made, etc. rapidly [*rapid-fire* talk].

**ra·pid·i·ty** (rə pid′ə tē) ***n.*** speed or swiftness.

☆**rapid transit** a system for carrying many people in large cities swiftly on electric trains.

**ra·pi·er** (rā′pē ər) ***n.*** a light sword with a sharp point, used only for thrusting. *See the picture.*

**rap·ine** (rap′in) ***n.*** the act of seizing and carrying off things by force; plunder; pillage.

**rap·port** (ra pôr′ *or* ra pôrt′) ***n.*** a relationship in which there is sympathy and understanding on both sides [a coach who has fine *rapport* with the players].

**rap·scal·lion** (rap skal′yən) ***n.*** a person, especially a child, who is full of mischief; rascal; rogue.

**rapt** (rapt) ***adj.*** **1** so completely interested as not to notice anything else; absorbed [She was so *rapt* in study that she didn't hear the bell.] **2** showing rapture, or deep pleasure [a *rapt* look on his face].

**rap·ture** (rap′chər) ***n.*** a deep feeling of joy, love, etc.; ecstasy [The music filled us with *rapture.*] —**rap′turous *adj.***

**rare**[1] (rer) ***adj.*** **1** not often found; not common; scarce [Radium is a *rare* element.] **2** very good; excellent [We had a *rare* time at the party.] **3** not dense; thin [the *rare* air in the mountains]. —**rar′er, rar′est —rare′ly *adv.* —rare′ness *n.***

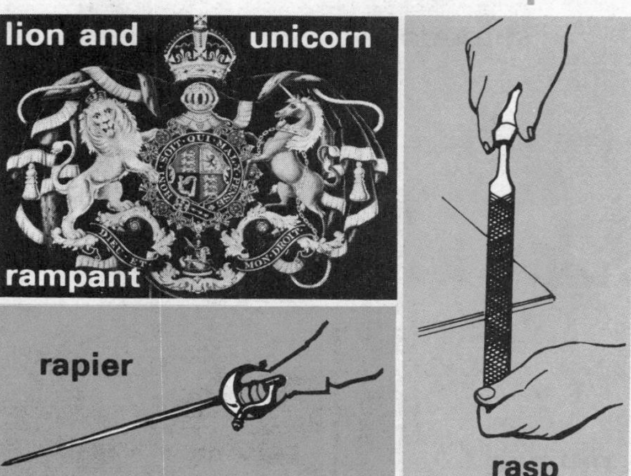


**rare**[2] (rer) ***adj.*** not completely cooked; partly raw [She likes her steak *rare.*] —**rar′er, rar′est —rare′ness *n.***

**rare·bit** (rer′bit) ***n.*** *another name for* **Welsh rabbit.**

**rar·e·fy** (rer′ə fī) ***v.*** **1** to make or become thin, or less dense [The air at high altitudes is *rarefied.*] **2** to make or become refined or subtle [a *rarefied* sense of humor]. —**rar′e·fied, rar′e·fy·ing**

**rare·ly** (rer′lē) ***adv.*** **1** not often; seldom [I *rarely* see them these days.] **2** unusually; remarkably [a *rarely* beautiful vase].

**rar·i·ty** (rer′ə tē) ***n.*** **1** something rare or uncommon [This old coin is a *rarity.*] —*pl.* **rar′i·ties** **2** the condition of being rare; scarcity [the *rarity* of whooping cranes]. **3** the condition of being not dense; thinness [the *rarity* of the air].

**ras·cal** (ras′k'l) ***n.*** **1** a bad or dishonest person; scoundrel. **2** a person, especially a child, who is full of mischief. —**ras·cal·i·ty** (ras kal′ə tē) ***n.***

**rash**[1] (rash) ***adj.*** too hasty or reckless; risky [It would be *rash* to quit your job before you know of a new one.] —**rash′ly *adv.* —rash′ness *n.***

**rash**[2] (rash) ***n.*** **1** a breaking out of red spots on the skin [The measles gave her a *rash.*] **2** a sudden appearance in large numbers [a *rash* of complaints].

**rash·er** (rash′ər) ***n.*** **1** a thin slice of bacon or ham to be fried or broiled. ☆**2** a serving of such slices.

**rasp** (rasp) ***v.*** **1** to scrape or rub as with a file. **2** to say in a rough, harsh tone [The sergeant *rasped* out a command.] **3** to make a rough, grating sound [The old hinges *rasped* as the door opened.] **4** to annoy or irritate [a giggle that *rasped* her nerves]. ◆***n.*** **1** a rough file with sharp points instead of lines. *See the picture.* **2** a rough, grating sound.

**rasp·ber·ry** (raz′ber′ē) ***n.*** **1** a small, juicy, red or black fruit with many tiny seeds. **2** the shrub it grows on. **3** a jeering sound made with the tongue between the lips: *slang in this meaning.* —*pl.* **rasp′ber′ries**



| | | | | | | | |
|---|---|---|---|---|---|---|---|
| **a** | fat | **ir** | here | **ou** | out | **zh** | leisure |
| **ā** | ape | **ī** | bite, fire | **u** | up | **ng** | ring |
| **ä** | car, lot | **ō** | go | **ur** | fur | | a *in* ago |
| **e** | ten | **ô** | law, horn | **ch** | chin | | e *in* agent |
| **er** | care | **oi** | oil | **sh** | she | **ə =** | i *in* unity |
| **ē** | even | **oo** | look | **th** | thin | | o *in* collect |
| **i** | hit | **ōō** | tool | ***th*** | then | | u *in* focus |

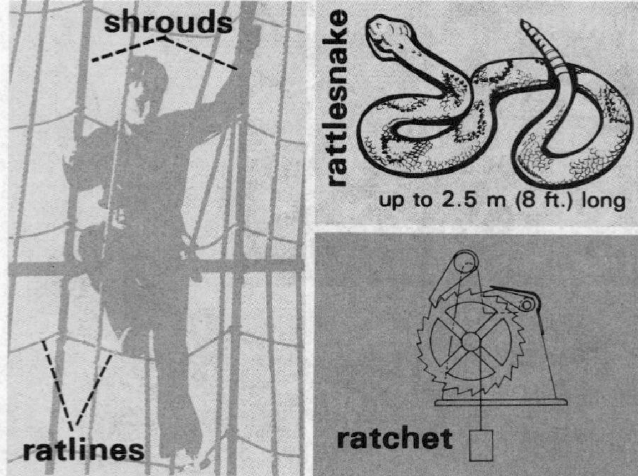


**rat** (rat) ***n.*** **1** a gnawing animal like a mouse but larger, with a long tail and black, brown, or gray fur. Rats are found everywhere and can carry diseases. **2** a mean, sneaky person, especially one who betrays or tells on others: *slang in this meaning.* ◆***v.*** **1** to hunt for rats. **2** to betray or tell on others: *slang in this meaning.* —**rat'ted, rat'ting** —**smell a rat,** to suspect a trick or plot.

**ratch·et** (rach'it) ***n.*** **1** a wheel or bar with slanted teeth that catch on a pawl that keeps the wheel from going backward. **2** the pawl. **3** the wheel or bar together with the pawl. *See the picture.*



**rate**[1] (rāt) ***n.*** **1** the amount or degree of anything in relation to something else [a *rate* of speed measured in kilometers per hour]. **2** a price or charge, as for each unit [Postal *rates* went up again.] **3** speed of moving or acting [He types at a fast *rate.*] **4** class or rank [a painting of the first *rate*]. ◆***v.*** **1** to set a value on; appraise [The dealer *rated* the diamond at $10,000.] **2** to think of or be thought of as in a certain class or rank [Sid is *rated* among the best students.] **3** to deserve: *used only in everyday talk* [She *rates* the best.] —**rat'ed, rat'ing** —**at any rate, 1** in any event; anyhow. **2** at least; anyway.

**rate**[2] (rāt) ***v.*** to find fault; scold; blame. —**rat'ed, rat'ing**

**rath·er** (ra*th*'ər) ***adv.*** **1** in a more willing way; with greater liking; preferably [I would *rather* read than watch TV.] **2** with more justice, reason, etc. [I, *rather* than you, should pay.] **3** more accurately; more truly [a bad storm or, *rather,* a hurricane]. **4** on the contrary [We won't go; *rather,* we'll stay.] **5** to some degree; somewhat [I *rather* liked that show.] ◆***interj.*** certainly; yes: *used as an answer, mainly in Great Britain.* —**had rather** or **would rather,** would prefer that [I *had rather* you said nothing.]

**rat·i·fy** (rat'ə fī) ***v.*** to approve, especially in an official way [The Senate must *ratify* any treaty between the U.S. and another country.] —**rat'i·fied, rat'i·fy·ing** —**rat·i·fi·ca·tion** (rat'ə fi kā'shən) ***n.***

**rat·ing** (rāt'iŋ) ***n.*** **1** a rank or grade [a *rating* of sergeant in the army]. **2** a judgment as to how good or bad the credit of a person or business is. It is based on records of paying bills or debts when due. ☆**3** the popularity of a radio or TV program as compared with others by taking polls or surveys.

**ra·tio** (rā'shō *or* rā'shē ō) ***n.*** **1** the relation of one thing to another in size, amount, etc.; proportion [In our class there is a *ratio* of three girls to every two boys.] **2** the quotient of one number divided by another, usually shown as a fraction [1/3 and 5/15 are equal *ratios.*] —*pl.* **ra'tios**

**ra·tion** (rash'ən *or* rā'shən) ***n.*** **1** a share or portion, especially a daily portion of food, as for a soldier. **2** **rations,** *pl.* food, or a supply of food. ◆***v.*** **1** to give out in rations, as food, clothing, or gasoline, when these are scarce. **2** to give rations to [to *ration* a company of soldiers].

**ra·tion·al** (rash'ən 'l) ***adj.*** **1** able to reason; thinking clearly [She was too angry to be *rational.*] **2** of or based on reasoning; reasonable; sensible [We must prepare a *rational* plan.] **3** in mathematics, describing a number that can be expressed as an integer or as the quotient of integers [8 and 3/8 are *rational* numbers.] —**ra'tion·al·ly** ***adv.***

**ra·tion·ale** (rash ə nal') ***n.*** the main reasons or basis for something [What is the *rationale* for your choice?]

**ra·tion·al·i·ty** (rash'ə nal'ə tē) ***n.*** the condition of being rational; clear thinking.

**ra·tion·al·ize** (rash'ən ə līz') ***v.*** to give a reasonable explanation without seeming to know that it is not the real one [We *rationalized* the small audience by blaming it on the weather.] —**ra'tion·al·ized', ra'tion·al·iz'ing** —**ra'tion·al·i·za'tion** ***n.***

**rat·line** or **rat·lin** (rat'lin) ***n.*** any of the small ropes that join the shrouds of a ship and are used as a ladder by sailors. *See the picture.*

**rat·tan** (ra tan') ***n.*** **1** the long, slender stems of a kind of palm tree, used in making wicker furniture, baskets, etc. **2** a cane or switch made from one of these stems. **3** this palm tree.

**rat·tle** (rat''l) ***v.*** **1** to make or cause to make a series of sharp, short sounds [The shutter *rattled* in the wind. She *rattled* the door handle.] **2** to move with such sounds [The wagon *rattled* over the stones.] **3** to talk in a rapid and thoughtless way; chatter [Joe *rattled* on about his camping trip.] **4** to say or recite quickly [Sue *rattled* off a long list of names.] ☆**5** to confuse or upset [Booing from the audience *rattled* the speaker.] —**rat'tled, rat'tling** ◆***n.*** **1** a baby's toy or other device made to rattle when shaken. **2** a series of sharp, short sounds [What caused the *rattle* in your car?] ☆**3** the series of horny rings at the end of a rattlesnake's tail. The snake shakes these to make a rattling sound when it is disturbed.

**rat·tler** (rat'lər) ***n.*** a person or thing that rattles; especially, ☆a rattlesnake.

☆**rat·tle·snake** (rat''l snāk) ***n.*** a poisonous American snake that has a series of horny rings on its tail, with which it makes a rattling sound when it is disturbed. *See the picture.*

**rau·cous** (rô'kəs) ***adj.*** **1** having a rough, hoarse sound [*raucous* laughter]. **2** loud and rowdy [a *raucous* party]. —**rau'cous·ly** ***adv.***

**rav·age** (rav'ij) ***v.*** to destroy or ruin [Floods had *ravaged* the land.] —**rav'aged, rav'ag·ing** ◆***n.*** great destruction or ruin [the *ravages* of war].

**rave** (rāv) ***v.*** **1** to talk in a wild way that does not make sense [The fever made him *rave.*] **2** to praise greatly or too greatly [She *raved* about the movie.] —**raved, rav'ing** ◆***n.*** the act of raving. ◆☆***adj.*** full of praise: *used only in everyday talk* [The play got *rave* reviews.]

**rav·el** (rav′'l) ***v.*** to separate or undo the threads of something knitted or woven; unravel [The scarf has begun to *ravel* at one end.] —**rav′eled** or **rav′elled, rav′el·ing** or **rav′el·ling**

Although **ravel** and **unravel** mean the same thing today, **ravel** used to have just the opposite meaning, that is, "to make or become tangled."

**Ra·vel** (rə vel′), **Maurice** 1875–1937; French composer.

**rav·el·ing** or **rav·el·ling** (rav′'l iŋ) ***n.*** a thread raveled from a knitted or woven material.

**ra·ven** (rā′vən) ***n.*** a crow of the largest kind, with shiny black feathers and a sharp beak. ◆***adj.*** black and shiny [*raven* hair].

**rav·en·ing** (rav′'n iŋ) ***adj.*** searching for food or prey in a very hungry or greedy way.

**rav·e·nous** (rav′ə nəs) ***adj.*** very hungry or greedy [a *ravenous* appetite]. —**rav′e·nous·ly** ***adv.***

**ra·vine** (rə vēn′) ***n.*** a long, deep hollow worn in the earth by a stream of water; gorge.

**rav·ing** (rā′viŋ) ***adj.*** **1** that raves; raging [a *raving* madman]. **2** remarkable; outstanding: *used only in everyday talk* [a *raving* beauty]. ◆***adv.*** so as to make one rave [*raving* mad].

**ra·vi·o·li** (rav′ē ō′lē) ***n.pl.*** little cases of dough filled with ground meat, cheese, etc. These are boiled and then served in a spicy tomato sauce.

**rav·ish** (rav′ish) ***v.*** **1** to overcome with great joy; delight [We were *ravished* by the beautiful music.] **2** *another word for* **rape[1]**.

**rav·ish·ing** (rav′ish iŋ) ***adj.*** causing great joy or pleasure; enchanting [a *ravishing* voice].

**raw** (rô) ***adj.*** **1** not cooked [*raw* vegetables]. **2** in its natural condition; not changed by some human process [*raw* silk; *raw* milk]. **3** not yet trained; inexperienced [*raw* recruits]. **4** with the skin rubbed off; sore [Scratching made the flesh *raw*.] **5** cold and damp [a *raw* wind]. ☆**6** indecent; bawdy [a *raw* joke]. **7** not fair or too harsh: *used only in everyday talk* [He got a *raw* deal.] —**raw′ness** ***n.***

**raw·boned** (rô′bōnd) ***adj.*** having little fat on the body; very lean.

**raw·hide** (rô′hīd) ***n.*** **1** a cattle hide that is not tanned. **2** a whip made of this.

**ray[1]** (rā) ***n.*** **1** a line or narrow beam of light [the *rays* of the flashlight]. **2** a tiny amount [a *ray* of hope]. **3** a wave or stream of energy thought of as moving in a line [*rays* of heat; X-*rays*]. **4** any of a number of straight, thin parts that come out from a center, as the petals of a daisy. ◆***v.*** to shine or spread out in rays.

**ray[2]** (rā) ***n.*** a fish with a broad, flat body, wide fins at each side, and a long, thin tail. *See the picture for* **stingray**.

☆**ray·on** (rā′än) ***n.*** a fiber made from cellulose, or a fabric woven from such fibers.

**raze** (rāz) ***v.*** to tear down completely; destroy [The city will *raze* the old homes to make room for a new housing project.] —**razed, raz′ing**

**ra·zor** (rā′zər) ***n.*** a tool with a sharp edge or edges, for shaving off hair [Electric shavers are also sometimes called *razors*.]

**ra·zor·back** (rā′zər bak′) ***n.*** a wild hog of the southern U.S., with a ridge along its back.

☆**razz** (raz) ***v.*** to make fun of; tease: *a slang word.*

**rbi, r.b.i., RBI** runs batted in (in baseball).

**R.C.** **1** Red Cross. **2** Roman Catholic.

**Rd.** or **rd.** *abbreviation for* **road.**

**R.D.** Rural Delivery (mail service).

**re[1]** (rā) ***n.*** the second note of a musical scale.

**re[2]** (rē *or* rā) ***prep.*** in the matter of; about [I am writing to you *re* your letter of last week.]

**re-** *a prefix meaning:* **1** again [To *reappear* is to appear again.] **2** back [To *repay* is to pay back.]

A hyphen is used to separate this prefix from a root word when there is another word spelled the same that has a different meaning. For example, *re-sound* means "to sound again," but *resound* means "to echo." Sometimes a hyphen is used to separate the prefix *re-* from a root word beginning with *e* (*re-elect*), but the usual spelling is the solid form (*reelect*). Many words beginning with *re-* that are not entered in this dictionary can be easily understood if *re-* is given the meaning "again." For example, **recheck** means "to check again."

**reach** (rēch) ***v.*** **1** to stretch out one's hand, arm, etc. [He *reached* up and shook the branch.] **2** to touch, as by stretching out [Can you *reach* the top shelf?] **3** to stretch out in time, space, amount, etc. [Her fame *reaches* into all parts of the world.] **4** to get and hand over [Can you *reach* me the salt?] **5** to try to get in one's hand [He *reached* in his pocket for some money.] **6** to go as far as; get to [The climbers *reached* the top of Mt. Everest. The news *reached* us this morning.] **7** to get in touch with [You can *reach* me at this phone number.] **8** to have an influence on; affect [His songs have *reached* the hearts of millions.] ◆***n.*** **1** the act or ability of reaching [A long *reach* helps in playing first base.] **2** the distance or extent covered in reaching [We are out of the *reach* of danger.] **3** a long stretch, as of water.

SYNONYMS: To **reach** is to arrive at some place or goal or point of development [She's *reached* the age of sixteen.] To **achieve** is to use skill in reaching some goal [to *achieve* high scores on tests]. To **attain** is to reach a goal by working very hard [Dickens *attained* fame as a writer.]

**re·act** (rē akt′) ***v.*** **1** to act in response to something [She *reacted* to the drug by getting sleepy.] **2** to act in an opposite way; go back to an earlier condition [After wearing short skirts, women *reacted* by choosing longer ones.] **3** to act with another substance in bringing about a chemical change.

**re·ac·tion** (rē ak′shən) ***n.*** **1** an action, happening, etc. in return or in response to some other action, happening, force, etc. [What was their *reaction* to your suggestion? A rubber ball bounces as a *reaction* to hitting the ground.] **2** the act of going back to an earlier or more backward stage or condition. **3** a change

| | | | | | | | |
|---|---|---|---|---|---|---|---|
| **a** | fat | **ir** | here | **ou** | out | **zh** | leisure |
| **ā** | ape | **ī** | bite, fire | **u** | up | **ŋ** | ring |
| **ä** | car, lot | **ō** | go | **ur** | fur | | a *in* ago |
| **e** | ten | **ô** | law, horn | **ch** | chin | | e *in* agent |
| **er** | care | **oi** | oil | **sh** | she | **ə =** | i *in* unity |
| **ē** | even | **oo** | look | **th** | thin | | o *in* collect |
| **i** | hit | **ōō** | tool | ***th*** | then | | u *in* focus |

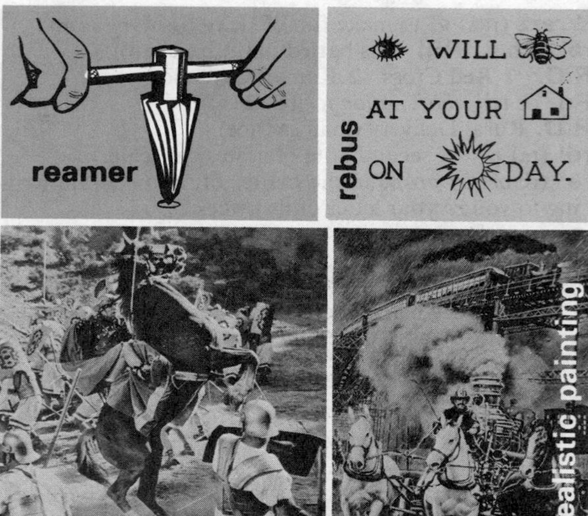

reamer

rebus

horse rearing

realistic painting

caused by chemical action [Gas bubbles are formed by the *reaction* of yeast with starch and sugar.]

**re·ac·tion·ar·y** (rē ak′shə ner′ē) ***adj.*** of, showing, or wanting a return to an earlier or more backward condition, as in politics. ◆***n.*** a person who is in favor of such reaction. *—pl.* **re·ac′tion·ar′ies**



**re·ac·ti·vate** (rē ak′tə vāt) ***v.*** to make active again [Let's *reactivate* the club.] —**re·ac′ti·vat·ed, re·ac′ti·vat·ing —re·ac′ti·va′tion *n.***

**re·ac·tor** (ri ak′tər) ***n.*** **1** a person or thing that reacts. **2** *a shorter form of* **nuclear reactor.**

**read**[1] (rēd) ***v.*** **1** to get the meaning of something written or printed by understanding its letters, signs, or numbers [I *read* the book. She *read* the gas meter. Can you *read* music?] **2** to speak printed or written words aloud [*Read* the story to me.] **3** to learn the true meaning of, as if by reading [I *read* the answer in your face. We can *read* the history of a canyon in its rocks.] **4** to tell ahead of time; predict [to *read* the future]. **5** to study [Lincoln *read* law while still a young man.] **6** to measure and show [The thermometer *reads* 18 degrees.] **7** to be put in certain words [The sentence *reads* as follows.] —**read** (red), **read′ing** —**read into** or **read in,** to interpret or understand in a certain way [You're *reading* things *into* my remarks, that I never meant.] —**read up on,** to learn about by reading.

**read**[2] (red) *past tense and past participle of* **read**[1]. ◆***adj.*** having knowledge got from reading; informed [They are both well-*read.*]

**read·a·ble** (rēd′ə b′l) ***adj.*** **1** that can be read; legible [Your handwriting is quite *readable.*] **2** interesting to read [a very *readable* book].

**read·er** (rēd′ər) ***n.*** **1** a person who reads. **2** a schoolbook with lessons for practicing reading.

**read·i·ly** (red′'l ē) ***adv.*** **1** without hesitation; willingly [He came *readily* when we called.] **2** without difficulty; easily [She writes in a way that is *readily* understood.]

**read·ing** (rēd′iŋ) ***n.*** **1** the act of a person who reads. **2** anything written or printed to be read [This novel is good *reading.*] **3** the amount measured as by a meter [a thermometer *reading*]. **4** the way something is written, read, performed, understood, etc. [I like his *reading* of King Lear.]

**re·ad·just** (rē ə just′) ***v.*** to adjust again; arrange or set as before. —**re·ad·just′ment *n.***

**read·out** (rēd′out) ***n.*** information, as from a computer, shown on a screen or typed on paper.

**read·y** (red′ē) ***adj.*** **1** prepared to act or to be used at once [Is everyone *ready* to leave? Your bath is *ready.*] **2** willing [She is always *ready* to help.] **3** about to; likely or liable; apt [I was so upset, I was *ready* to cry.] **4** quick or prompt [a *ready* answer]. **5** easy to get at and use [*ready* cash]. —**read′i·er, read′i·est** ◆***v.*** to prepare [to *ready* the house for guests]. —**read′ied, read′y·ing —read′i·ness *n.***

**read·y-made** (red′ē mād′) ***adj.*** made so as to be ready for use or sale at once; not made-to-order [a *ready-made* suit].

**re·al**[1] (rē′əl *or* rēl) ***adj.*** **1** being such or happening so in fact; not imagined; true; actual [He could hardly believe that his good luck was *real.*] *See* SYNONYMS *at* **true. 2** genuine [Are these *real* pearls?] ◆***adv.*** very: *used only in everyday talk* [Have a *real* nice time.]

**re·al**[2] (rē′əl *or* re äl′) ***n.*** a Spanish silver coin of earlier times. *—pl.* **re′als** or **re·al·es** (re ä′les)

**real estate** land and anything on it, as buildings, water, trees, etc.

**re·al·ism** (rē′ə liz'm) ***n.*** **1** the seeing of things as they really are, not as one might wish them to be [With his usual *realism,* he recognized that he would never be an opera star.] **2** in art and literature, the picturing of people and things as they really are. —**re′al·ist *n.***

**re·al·is·tic** (rē′ə lis′tik) ***adj.*** **1** facing facts with realism; practical [a *realistic* person]. **2** using realism in art and literature [A *realistic* painting may often look like a photograph.] *See the picture.* —**re′al·is′ti·cal·ly *adv.***

**re·al·i·ty** (rē al′ə tē) ***n.*** **1** the condition of being real [She doubted the *reality* of UFOs.] **2** a person or thing that is real [His dream of fame became a *reality.*] *—pl.* **re·al′i·ties 3** trueness to life, as in art or literature; realism. —**in reality,** in fact; actually.

**re·al·ize** (rē′ə līz) ***v.*** **1** to understand fully [I *realize* that good marks depend upon careful work.] **2** to make real; bring into being [to *realize* one's ambitions]. **3** to change property, rights, etc. into money by selling [The company *realized* its assets.] **4** to get as a profit or price [They *realized* over $60.00 on their garage sale.] —**re′al·ized, re′al·iz·ing —re′al·i·za′tion *n.***

**re·al·ly** (rē′ə lē *or* rēl′ē) ***adv.*** **1** in fact; truly [I am not *really* angry.] **2** indeed [*Really,* you shouldn't do that.]

**realm** (relm) ***n.*** **1** a kingdom. **2** a region or area [the *realm* of the imagination].

**re·al·ty** (rē′əl tē) ***n.*** *another name for* **real estate.**

**ream**[1] (rēm) ***n.*** **1** an amount of paper that varies from 480 to 516 sheets. **2 reams,** *pl.* a large amount: *used only in everyday talk.*

**ream**[2] (rēm) ***v.*** **1** to make a hole or opening larger [to *ream* out the barrel of a gun]. **2** to squeeze the juice from an orange, lemon, etc. **3** to cheat or trick: *slang in this meaning.*

**ream·er** (rēm′ər) ***n.*** **1** a sharp tool for making holes larger. *See the picture.* **2** a device for squeezing the juice from oranges, lemons, etc.

**re·an·i·mate** (rē an′ə māt) ***v.*** to give new life, power, vigor, etc. to. —**re·an′i·mat·ed, re·an′i·mat·ing**

**reap** (rēp) ***v.*** **1** to cut down grain when it is ripe. **2** to gather in after cutting [to *reap* a crop]. **3** to get in return for work, effort, etc. [to *reap* a reward].

**reap·er** (rē′pər) ***n.*** **1** a person who reaps. **2** a machine for reaping grain.

**The Reaper** or **the Grim Reaper** is a fanciful name for death, often pictured as a skeleton wearing a flowing robe with a hood and carrying a scythe. In this way, death is thought of as cutting down its victims, as a harvester cuts down grain with a scythe.

**re·ap·pear** (rē ə pir′) ***v.*** to appear again. —**re′ap·pear′ance *n.***

**re·ap·por·tion** (rē′ə pôr′shən) ***v.*** to apportion again, as in order to make all legislative districts contain about the same number of people. —**re′ap·por′tion·ment *n.***

**re·ap·praise** (rē ə prāz′) ***v.*** to make a fresh appraisal of; reconsider. —**re′ap·prais′al *n.***

**rear**[1] (rir) ***n.*** **1** the back part or place [the *rear* of a house]. **2** the part of an army, navy, etc. farthest from the battle front. ◆***adj.*** of, at, or in the rear [a *rear* entrance]. —**bring up the rear,** to come at the end, as of a parade.

**rear**[2] (rir) ***v.*** **1** to help grow up; bring up [to *rear* children]. **2** to produce or breed [to *rear* sheep]. **3** to set or bring upright; raise [to *rear* a flagpole]. **4** to rise up on the hind legs, as a horse. *See the picture.*

**rear admiral** an officer in the navy who ranks just above a captain.

**re·arm** (rē ärm′) ***v.*** **1** to arm again. **2** to arm with new or more powerful weapons. —**re·ar′ma·ment *n.***

**re·ar·range** (rē ə rānj′) ***v.*** to arrange again or in a different way. —**re·ar·ranged′, re·ar·rang′ing —re′ar·range′ment *n.***

**rear·ward** (rir′wərd) ***adj.*** at, in, or toward the rear. ◆***adv.*** toward the rear.

**rear·wards** (rir′wərdz) ***adv.*** *same as* **rearward.**

**rea·son** (rē′zən) ***n.*** **1** something said to explain or try to explain an act, idea, etc. [Write the *reasons* for your answer.] **2** a cause for some action, feeling, etc.; motive [Noisy neighbors were our *reason* for moving.] **3** the power to think, get ideas, decide things, etc. [Human beings are the only creatures that truly have *reason.*] **4** good thinking or judgment [Maria won't listen to *reason.*] ◆***v.*** **1** to think in a sensible way; come to a conclusion by considering facts [A lawyer learns to *reason* clearly.] **2** to argue in a careful, sensible way [to *reason* with a child who is afraid of the dark]. —**by reason of,** because of. —**stand to reason,** to be logical or sensible. —**within reason,** according to what is reasonable.

**rea·son·a·ble** (rē′zən ə b′l) ***adj.*** **1** using or showing reason; sensible [a *reasonable* person; a *reasonable* decision]. **2** not too high or too low; fair [a *reasonable* price; a *reasonable* salary]. —**rea′son·a·bly *adv.***

**rea·son·ing** (rē′zən iŋ) ***n.*** **1** the act of coming to a conclusion based on facts. **2** reasons or proofs got in this way.

**re·as·sem·ble** (rē′ə sem′b′l) ***v.*** to come or put together again. —**re′as·sem′bled, re′as·sem′bling**

**re·as·sure** (rē ə shoor′) ***v.*** to remove the doubts and fears of; make feel secure again. —**re·as·sured′, re·as·sur′ing —re·as·sur′ance *n.***

**re·bate** (rē′bāt) ***n.*** a part given back from an amount paid [a *rebate* of an overpayment of income tax].

**Re·bec·ca** or **Re·bek·ah** (ri bek′ə) in the Bible, the wife of Isaac.

**reb·el** (reb′′l) ***n.*** a person who fights or struggles against authority or any kind of control [Confederate soldiers in the Civil War were called *Rebels.*] ◆***adj.*** fighting against authority; rebellious [a *rebel* army]. ◆***v.*** (ri bel′) **1** to fight or struggle against authority or control [The peasants *rebelled* against the king.] **2** to have a strong dislike [My mind *rebels* at the idea of leaving.] —**re·belled′, re·bel′ling**

**re·bel·lion** (ri bel′yən) ***n.*** **1** an armed fight against the government; revolt. **2** a fight or struggle against any kind of control.

**re·bel·lious** (ri bel′yəs) ***adj.*** fighting or struggling against authority or any kind of control [*rebellious* colonies]. —**re·bel′lious·ly *adv.***

**re·birth** (rē burth′ *or* rē′burth) ***n.*** a coming back into use again, as if born again; revival [a *rebirth* of freedom].

**re·born** (rē bôrn′) ***adj.*** having new life, spirit, interests, etc., as if born again.

**re·bound** (ri bound′) ***v.*** to bounce back, as after hitting a surface [Aaron caught the ball as it *rebounded* from the fence.] ◆***n.*** (rē′bound) **1** a bouncing or bounding back. **2** an object that bounces back.

**re·buff** (ri buf′) ***n.*** the act of refusing advice, help, etc. in a sharp or rude way [Our offer met with a *rebuff.*] ◆***v.*** to refuse in a sharp or rude way; snub [They *rebuffed* our offer of help.]

**re·build** (rē bild′) ***v.*** to build again, especially something that was damaged, ruined, etc. —**re·built′, re·build′ing**

**re·buke** (ri byook′) ***v.*** to blame or scold in a sharp way; reprimand. —**re·buked′, re·buk′ing** ◆***n.*** a sharp scolding.

**re·bus** (rē′bəs) ***n.*** a puzzle in which words or phrases are shown by means of pictures, signs, etc. *See the picture.*

**re·but** (ri but′) ***v.*** to argue or prove that someone or something is wrong [to *rebut* a claim]. —**re·but′ted, re·but′ting —re·but′tal *n.***

☆**rec** (rek) ***n.*** *a shorter form of* **recreation**: *used in combinations such as* **rec room.**

**re·cal·ci·trant** (ri kal′si trənt) ***adj.*** refusing to obey rules, follow orders, etc.; stubborn and disobedient. —**re·cal′ci·trance *n.***

**Recalcitrant** comes from a Latin word that means "to kick back." People who are recalcitrant or disobedient might be said to be kicking against something they do not like.



| | | | | | | | |
|---|---|---|---|---|---|---|---|
| a | fat | ir | here | ou | out | zh | leisure |
| ā | ape | ī | bite, fire | u | up | ŋ | ring |
| ä | car, lot | ō | go | ur | fur | | a *in* ago |
| e | ten | ô | law, horn | ch | chin | | e *in* agent |
| er | care | oi | oil | sh | she | ə = | i *in* unity |
| ē | even | oo | look | th | thin | | o *in* collect |
| i | hit | ōō | tool | *th* | then | | u *in* focus |

**re·call** (ri kôl′) **v.** **1** to bring back to mind; remember [Can you *recall* how you felt?] *See* SYNONYMS *at* **remember.** **2** to call back; order to return [The ambassador was *recalled* to Washington.] **3** to take back; withdraw or cancel [They *recalled* Stacey's license.] ✦**n.** (*also* rē′kôl) **1** the act of recalling. ☆**2** the right of citizens to vote an official out of office, using petitions to call for such a vote.

**re·cant** (ri kant′) **v.** to take back an opinion or belief; confess that one was wrong. —**re·can·ta·tion** (rē′kan tā′shən) **n.**

**re·cap** (rē kap′) **v.** ☆to put a new tread on a worn automobile tire. —**re·capped′, re·cap′ping** ✦**n.** (rē′-kap) a recapped tire.

**re·ca·pit·u·late** (rē′kə pich′ə lāt) **v.** to tell again in a brief way, as in an outline; summarize. —**re′ca·pit′u·lat·ed, re′ca·pit′u·lat·ing** —**re′ca·pit′u·la′tion n.**

**re·cap·ture** (rē kap′chər) **v.** **1** to capture again; retake. **2** to bring back by remembering [That song helps the old folks *recapture* their youth.] —**re·cap′tured, re·cap′tur·ing**

**re·cast** (rē kast′) **v.** **1** to cast, or shape, again [to *recast* a bronze statue]. **2** to make better by doing over [to *recast* a sentence]. —**re·cast′, re·cast′ing**

**re·cede** (ri sēd′) **v.** to go, move, or slope backward [The flood waters *receded.* Her chin *recedes.*] —**re·ced′ed, re·ced′ing**

**re·ceipt** (ri sēt′) **n.** **1** a receiving or being received [Upon *receipt* of the gift, she thanked him.] **2** a written statement that something has been received [My landlord gave me a *receipt* when I paid my rent.] **3** **receipts,** *pl.* the amount of money taken in, as in a business. **4** *an old-fashioned word for* **recipe.** ✦**v.** to mark "paid" as on a bill for goods.

**re·ceiv·a·ble** (ri sēv′ə b'l) **adj.** due; that must be paid, as a bill [The company will collect $5,000 from accounts *receivable.*]

**re·ceive** (ri sēv′) **v.** **1** to take or get what has been given or sent to one [to *receive* a letter]. **2** to meet with; be given; undergo [to *receive* punishment; to *receive* applause]. **3** to find out about; learn [He *received* the news calmly.] **4** to greet guests and let them come in [Our hostess *received* us at the door.] **5** to have room for or be able to bear [Each wheel *receives* an equal part of the weight.] **6** to change electric waves or signals to sound or light [Our TV set *receives* poorly.] —**re·ceived′, re·ceiv′ing**

> SYNONYMS: To **receive** means to get, as a package or gift, or to hear or experience something [She *received* an award. He *received* a shock when he touched the live wire.] To **accept** is to receive something agreeably [Chris was *accepted* as a club member. Kim *accepted* her injury bravely.]

**re·ceiv·er** (ri sē′vər) **n.** **1** a person who receives. **2** a person appointed to take care of the property involved in a lawsuit. **3** a device that receives electric waves or signals and changes them into sound or light [a TV *receiver;* a telephone *receiver*]. **4** in sports, the player or team receiving the ball, service, etc.

**re·ceiv·er·ship** (ri sē′vər ship) **n.** the condition of being taken care of by a receiver (*meaning* 2) [a bankrupt business in *receivership*].

**re·cent** (rē′sənt) **adj.** of a time just before now; made or happening a short time ago [*recent* news; a *recent* storm]. —**re′cent·ly adv.**

**re·cep·ta·cle** (ri sep′tə k'l) **n.** **1** anything used to keep something in [a trash *receptacle*]. **2** an electrical wall outlet designed to receive a plug.

**re·cep·tion** (ri sep′shən) **n.** **1** a receiving or being received, or the way in which this is done [a friendly *reception*]. **2** a party or gathering at which guests are received [a wedding *reception*]. **3** the receiving of signals on radio or television [Aircraft going over the house can affect *reception.*]

**re·cep·tion·ist** (ri sep′shən ist) **n.** an office employee who receives callers, gives information, etc.

**re·cep·tive** (ri sep′tiv) **adj.** able or ready to receive ideas, requests, etc.

**re·cess** (rē′ses *or* ri ses′) **n.** **1** a hollow place in a wall or other surface. **2** a hidden or inner place [Fish darted through *recesses* in the coral.] **3** (rē′ses) a stopping of work, study, etc. for a short time, to relax. ✦**v.** (ri ses′) **1** to set in a recess; set back [a *recessed* door]. ☆**2** to stop work, study, etc. for a while.

**re·ces·sion** (ri sesh′ən) **n.** **1** a period when business is poor; mild depression. **2** a going or moving back. **3** a departing procession, as of clergy and choir after a church service.

**re·ces·sion·al** (ri sesh′ən 'l) **n.** a hymn sung at the end of a church service when the clergy and the choir march out.

**re·ces·sive** (ri ses′iv) **adj.** that recedes.

**re·charge** (rē chärj′) **v.** to charge again, as a battery. —**re·charged′, re·charg′ing**

**rec·i·pe** (res′ə pē) **n.** **1** a list of ingredients and directions for making something to eat or drink [a *recipe* for cookies]. **2** a way to get or do something [Her *recipe* for success is hard work.]

> **Recipe** originally meant a doctor's prescription for mixing up a particular medicine. Later it also came to mean the instructions for preparing a certain kind of food.

**re·cip·i·ent** (ri sip′ē ənt) **n.** a person or thing that receives.

**re·cip·ro·cal** (ri sip′rə k'l) **adj.** **1** done, felt, or given in return [to lend a hand, hoping for a *reciprocal* favor]. **2** on both sides; mutual [a *reciprocal* treaty]. **3** acting or working together; complementary [*reciprocal* action of the parts of the machine]. ✦**n.** a number related to another number in such a way that the two numbers multiplied together equal 1 [The *reciprocal* of 1/7 is 7, because 1/7 x 7 = 1.] —**re·cip′ro·cal·ly adv.**

**re·cip·ro·cate** (ri sip′rə kāt) **v.** **1** to give and get equally; exchange [The two nations *reciprocated* pledges of peace.] **2** to give, do, or feel something in return for [He *reciprocated* her greeting with a cheery "Hello!"] **3** to move back and forth [*Reciprocating* pistons are used in steam engines.] —**re·cip′ro·cat·ed, re·cip′ro·cat·ing** —**re·cip′ro·ca′tion n.**

**rec·i·proc·i·ty** (res′ə präs′ə tē) **n.** **1** the condition of being reciprocal. **2** the act of reciprocating, or of giving and getting equally [Two nations practice *reciprocity* when each lowers the duty on goods that the other wants to buy.]

**re·cit·al** (ri sīt′'l) **n.** **1** the act of reciting or telling with many details [a long *recital* of his troubles]. **2** the story or report told in this way. **3** a program of music or dances given by a soloist or soloists.

**rec·i·ta·tion** (res′ə tā′shən) ***n.*** **1** a reciting, as of facts, events, etc.; recital. **2** the act of reciting before an audience a poem, story, etc. that one has memorized. **3** the poem, story, etc. recited. ☆**4** a class meeting in which pupils answer aloud questions on the lesson.

**rec·i·ta·tive** (res′ə tə tēv′) ***n.*** a way of singing in which the singer sounds the words quickly, as in speaking, but with musical tones. Recitative is often used in opera for dialogue.

**re·cite** (ri sīt′) ***v.*** **1** to say aloud before an audience, as something that one has memorized [to *recite* the Gettysburg Address]. **2** to tell in detail; give an account of. ☆**3** to answer questions about a lesson in class. —**re·cit′ed, re·cit′ing** —**re·cit′er *n.***

**reck** (rek) ***v.*** to care or heed: *now seldom used* [I *reck* not what others think.]

**reck·less** (rek′lis) ***adj.*** not careful; taking chances; careless; rash [a *reckless* driver]. —**reck′less·ly *adv.*** —**reck′less·ness *n.***

**reck·on** (rek′ən) ***v.*** **1** to count; figure up [to *reckon* one's hotel bill]. **2** to think of as being; consider or judge [I *reckon* him a real friend.] **3** to depend on; count on [I *reckoned* on his being early.] **4** to suppose: *used only in everyday talk.* —**reckon with,** to think about; consider [There are certain things we must *reckon with* in making our plans.]

**reck·on·ing** (rek′ən iŋ) ***n.*** **1** the act of figuring up or finding out [the *reckoning* of a ship's position; a *reckoning* of costs]. **2** payment of an account. **3** a bill, as at a hotel.

**re·claim** (ri klām′) ***v.*** **1** to make fit again for growing things or for living in [to *reclaim* a desert by irrigating it]. **2** to get something useful from waste products [to *reclaim* metal from wrecked cars]. **3** to bring back from a life of sin, crime, etc.; reform.

**rec·la·ma·tion** (rek′lə mā′shən) ***n.*** a reclaiming, as of desert land by irrigation, or of useful materials from waste products.

**re·cline** (ri klīn′) ***v.*** to lie down or lean back. —**reclined′, re·clin′ing**

**re·clin·er** (ri klī′nər) ***n.*** an upholstered armchair with a movable back and seat that can be adjusted for reclining: *also called* **reclining chair.**

**rec·luse** (rek′lōōs *or* ri klōōs′) ***n.*** a person who lives alone, away from others; hermit.

> **Recluse** comes from a Latin word that means "to shut off." A recluse is a person who wants to be shut off from the world.

**rec·og·ni·tion** (rek′əg nish′ən) ***n.*** **1** acceptance; a recognizing or being recognized. **2** attention; notice; approval. **3** the act of showing that one knows a person or thing; also, a greeting [She passed me without a sign of *recognition*.]

**rec·og·niz·a·ble** (rek′əg nī′zə b′l) ***adj.*** that can be recognized.

**re·cog·ni·zance** (ri käg′ni zəns) ***n.*** **1** a promise that a person makes to do a certain thing, as to appear in court [released on one's own *recognizance*]. **2** a sum of money, as a bond, which a person forfeits to a law court for failing to keep such a promise.

**rec·og·nize** (rek′əg nīz) ***v.*** **1** to be aware of as something or someone seen, heard, etc. before; know again [to *recognize* a street; to *recognize* a tune]. **2** to know by a certain feature; identify [to *recognize* a giraffe by its long neck]. **3** to take notice of; show approval of [a ceremony to *recognize* those employees with ten years or more of service]. **4** to admit as true; accept [to *recognize* defeat]. **5** to accept as a new state or government, as by starting to do business with it [The U.S. *recognized* the U.S.S.R. in 1933.] ☆**6** to give the right to speak at a meeting [The chair *recognizes* Ms. Jones.] —**rec′og·nized, rec′og·niz·ing**

**re·coil** (ri koil′) ***v.*** **1** to jump or shrink back suddenly, as because of fear, surprise, etc. [He *recoiled* in horror.] **2** to fly back when let go, as a spring; also, to jump back when fired, as a gun. ◆***n.*** (*also* rē′koil) the act or fact of recoiling.

**rec·ol·lect** (rek ə lekt′) ***v.*** to remember; bring back to mind [She tried to *recollect* the words to the old song.] *See* SYNONYMS *at* **remember.**

**re-col·lect** (rē′kə lekt′) ***v.*** **1** to gather together again [to *re-collect* scattered pearls]. **2** to make calm again [to *re-collect* oneself].

**rec·ol·lec·tion** (rek′ə lek′shən) ***n.*** **1** the act or power of recollecting, or remembering. **2** what is remembered.

**rec·om·mend** (rek ə mend′) ***v.*** **1** to speak of as being good for a certain use, job, etc.; praise [to *recommend* a good plumber; to *recommend* a book]. **2** to make pleasing or worth having [That summer camp has much to *recommend* it.] **3** to give advice; advise [I *recommend* that you study harder.] **4** to turn over; entrust [I *recommend* her to your care.]

613

**rec·om·men·da·tion** (rek′ə mən dā′shən) ***n.*** **1** the act of recommending. **2** anything that recommends, as a letter recommending a person for a job. **3** advice [My *recommendation* is that you return.]

**rec·om·pense** (rek′əm pens) ***v.*** **1** to pay or pay back; reward [Were you *recompensed* for your services?] **2** to make up for; compensate [Insurance *recompensed* her losses.] —**rec′om·pensed, rec′om·pens·ing** ◆***n.*** **1** something given or done in return; reward. **2** something given or done to make up for a loss or injury.

**rec·on·cile** (rek′ən sīl) ***v.*** **1** to make friendly again [to *reconcile* feuding families]. **2** to settle [to *reconcile* a quarrel]. **3** to make agree or fit [I can't *reconcile* my memory of the place with your description.] **4** to help one accept or be content with something unpleasant [Time has *reconciled* us to our loss.] —**rec′on·ciled, rec′on·cil·ing** —**rec·on·cil·i·a·tion** (rek′ən sil′ē ā′shən) ***n.***

**rec·on·dite** (rek′ən dīt *or* ri kän′dīt) ***adj.*** very hard to understand [a *recondite* subject].

**re·con·di·tion** (rē′kən dish′ən) ***v.*** to put back in good condition by cleaning, repairing, etc.

**re·con·nais·sance** (ri kän′ə səns) ***n.*** the act of examining or spying on some area, as in a war, in order to get information.

| | | | | | | | |
|---|---|---|---|---|---|---|---|
| **a** | fat | **ir** | here | **ou** | out | **zh** | leisure |
| **ā** | ape | **ī** | bite, fire | **u** | up | **ŋ** | ring |
| **ä** | car, lot | **ō** | go | **ur** | fur | | a *in* ago |
| **e** | ten | **ô** | law, horn | **ch** | chin | | e *in* agent |
| **er** | care | **oi** | oil | **sh** | she | ə = | i *in* unity |
| **ē** | even | **oo** | look | **th** | thin | | o *in* collect |
| **i** | hit | **ōō** | tool | ***th*** | then | | u *in* focus |

r

**rec·on·noi·ter** (rē′kə noit′ər *or* rek′ə noit′ər) **v.** to examine or spy on an area, as one held by an enemy in a war, in order to get information. *The usual British spelling is* **reconnoitre.**

**re·con·sid·er** (rē′kən sid′ər) **v.** to think about again, as with the idea of changing one's mind.

**re·con·sti·tute** (rē kän′stə to͞ot *or* rē kän′stə tyo͞ot) **v.** to form again or anew; especially, to restore a dehydrated or condensed substance to its full liquid form by adding water. —**re·con′sti·tut·ed, re·con′sti·tut·ing**

**re·con·struct** (rē kən strukt′) **v.** to build up again as it once was; remake.

**re·con·struc·tion** (rē′kən struk′shən) **n.** **1** the act of reconstructing. **2** something reconstructed. ☆**3 Reconstruction,** the process of bringing the Southern States back into the Union after the Civil War, or the time when this took place (1867–1877).

**re·cord** (ri kôrd′) **v.** **1** to write down for future use; keep an account of [to *record* an event in a diary]. **2** to show, as on a dial [We use a thermometer to *record* temperatures.] **3** to put sound in a form in which it can be reproduced again, as on a disc with grooves or a magnetic tape [to *record* music]. ✦**n.** (rek′ərd) **1** something written down and kept as a history; especially, an official account [secret government *records*]. ☆**2** the known facts about something or someone [her fine *record* as mayor; a criminal *record*]. ☆**3** a disc

614 on which sound has been recorded, for playing on a phonograph. **4** the best that has yet been done [the *record* for the high jump]. ✦**adj.** (rek′ərd) being the largest, fastest, etc. of its kind [a *record* wheat crop]. —☆**go on record,** to state one's opinion publicly. —☆**off the record,** not to be published. —**on record,** recorded for all to know.

**re·cord·er** (ri kôr′dər) **n.** **1** a person who records; especially, a public officer who keeps records of deeds and other official papers. **2** *a shorter name for* **tape recorder.** **3** an early form of flute that is held straight up and down when played. *See the picture.*

**re·cord·ing** (ri kôr′diŋ) **n.** **1** what is recorded, as on a phonograph record. **2** such a record.

**re·count** (ri kount′) **v.** to tell about in detail [She *recounted* her adventures.] *See* SYNONYMS *at* **tell.**

**re-count** (rē′kount′) **v.** to count again. ✦**n.** (rē′-kount′) a second count, as of votes [The loser of the election demanded a *re-count.*] *Also written* **recount.**

**re·coup** (ri ko͞op′) **v.** **1** to make up for [to *recoup* a loss]. **2** to pay back; repay.

**re·course** (rē′kôrs *or* ri kôrs′) **n.** **1** a turning for help, protection, etc. [As a last *recourse,* he called the police.] **2** that to which one turns for help, protection, etc. [He is our last *recourse.*]

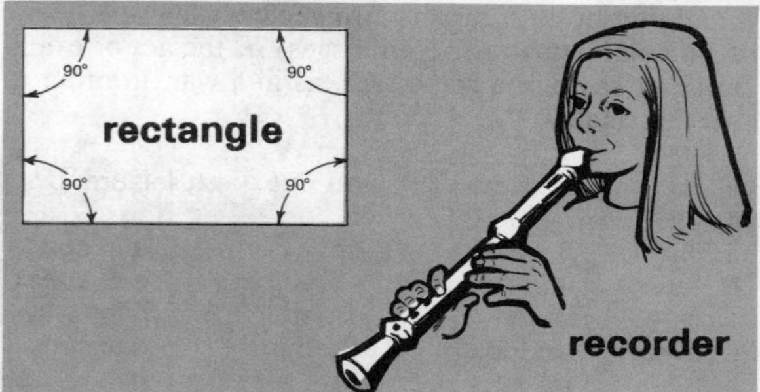


**re·cov·er** (ri kuv′ər) **v.** **1** to get back something lost; regain [to *recover* a stolen car; to *recover* consciousness]. **2** to get well again [Have you *recovered* from your cold?] **3** to save oneself, as from a fall or slip [She stumbled, but was able to *recover* herself.] **4** to make up for [to *recover* losses]. **5** to bring to a useful condition; reclaim [to *recover* land that was under water].

SYNONYMS: **Recover** means to find or get back something that one has lost in any way [to *recover* a lost purse; to *recover* one's self-control]. **Regain** means to win back something that has been taken from one [The team *regained* the pennant. She *regained* her sight after an operation.]

**re-cov·er** (rē′kuv′ər) **v.** to put a new cover on.

**re·cov·er·y** (ri kuv′ər ē) **n.** **1** a getting back of something that was lost or stolen. **2** a return to good health or normal condition. **3** a regaining, as of balance or control. **4** the retrieval as of a spacecraft after a flight in space.

**rec·re·ant** (rek′rē ənt) **n.** **1** a coward. **2** a disloyal person. ✦**adj.** **1** cowardly. **2** disloyal.

**re-cre·ate** (rē′krē āt′) **v.** to create again or in a new way. —**re′-cre·at′ed, re′-cre·at′ing**

**rec·re·a·tion** (rek′rē ā′shən) **n.** **1** the act of refreshing one's body or mind, as after work [He plays chess for *recreation.*] **2** any sport, exercise, hobby, amusement, etc. by which one does this. —**rec′re·a′tion·al** ***adj.***

☆**recreation room** a room, as in a home, where one can play games, dance, have parties, etc. *It is often shortened to* **rec room.**

**re·crim·i·nate** (ri krim′ə nāt) **v.** to accuse in return a person who has accused one. —**re·crim′i·nat·ed, re·crim′i·nat·ing** —**re·crim′i·na′tion n.**

**re·cru·des·cence** (rē′kro͞o des′əns) **n.** a breaking out again, as of a disease, crime, etc. —**re′cru·des′cent** ***adj.***

**re·cruit** (ri kro͞ot′) **n.** **1** a soldier, sailor, etc. who recently joined the armed forces. **2** a new member of any group. ✦**v.** **1** to enlist new members in [to *recruit* an army]. **2** to get to join [Our nature club *recruited* six new members.] **3** to hire or get the services of [We'll need to *recruit* some help.] —**re·cruit′ment n.**

**rec·tal** (rek′t'l) **adj.** of or for the rectum.

**rec·tan·gle** (rek′taŋ′g'l) **n.** any flat figure with four right angles and four sides. *See the picture.*

**rec·tan·gu·lar** (rek taŋ′gyə lər) **adj.** shaped like a rectangle [a *rectangular* field].

**rec·ti·fy** (rek′tə fī) **v.** **1** to put right; correct or adjust [to *rectify* an error]. **2** to change an alternating current of electricity into a direct current. —**rec′ti·fied, rec′ti·fy·ing** —**rec′ti·fi·ca′tion n.** —**rec′ti·fi·er n.**

**rec·ti·tude** (rek′tə to͞od *or* rek′tə tyo͞od) **n.** good moral character; honesty; trustworthiness.

**rec·tor** (rek′tər) **n.** **1** in some churches, the head of a parish. **2** the head of certain schools, colleges, etc.

**rec·to·ry** (rek′tər ē) **n.** the house in which a rector lives. —*pl.* **rec′to·ries**

**rec·tum** (rek′təm) **n.** the lowest or end part of the large intestine.

**re·cum·bent** (ri kum′bənt) **adj.** lying down; reclining [a *recumbent* figure on the sofa].

**re·cu·per·ate** (ri ko͞o′pə rāt *or* ri kyo͞o′pə rāt) ***v.*** **1** to get well again, as after being sick [Lynn is *recuperating* from the flu.] **2** to get back; recover [to *recuperate* one's losses]. —**re·cu′per·at·ed, re·cu′per·at·ing** —**re·cu′per·a′tion** ***n.***

**re·cur** (ri kʉr′) ***v.*** **1** to happen or come again or from time to time [That fever *recurs* every few weeks.] **2** to go back in thought or speech [The speaker *recurred* to his first point.] —**re·curred′, re·cur′ring**

**re·cur·rent** (ri kʉr′ənt) ***adj.*** happening or coming again or from time to time [a *recurrent* dream]. —**re·cur′rence** ***n.***

**re·cy·cle** (rē sī′k'l) ***v.*** to use again and again, as a single supply of water in a fountain or for cooling, metal to be melted down and recast, or paper processed for use again. —**re·cy′cled, re·cy′cling**

**red** (red) ***adj.*** **1** having the color of blood. **2** *often* **Red,** radical in politics; especially, communist. —**red′der, red′dest** ◆***n.*** **1** the color of blood. **2** any red coloring matter. **3** *often* **Red,** a person who is radical in politics; especially, a communist. —☆**in the red,** losing money. —**see red,** to become very angry: *used only in everyday talk.* —**red′ness** ***n.***

**red·bird** (red′bʉrd) ***n.*** any of several birds mostly red-colored, as the cardinal and the scarlet tanager.

**red-blood·ed** (red′blud′id) ***adj.*** high-spirited and strong-willed; vigorous, lusty, etc.

**red·breast** (red′brest) ***n.*** any of several birds with a reddish breast, as the robin.

**red·cap** (red′kap) ***n.*** a porter in a railroad station, bus station, etc.

**red·coat** (red′kōt) ***n.*** a British soldier, as at the time of the American Revolution.

**Red Cross** an international society with branches in different countries, set up to help people in time of war or during other disasters.

**red deer** **1** a kind of deer that is found in Europe and Asia. ☆**2** the American deer, when it has its reddish summer coloring.

**red·den** (red′'n) ***v.*** to make or become red; especially, to blush or flush [He *reddened* with anger.]

**red·dish** (red′ish) ***adj.*** somewhat red.

**re·deem** (ri dēm′) ***v.*** **1** to get or buy back; recover [He *redeemed* his watch from the pawnshop.] **2** to pay off, as a mortgage. **3** to turn in for a prize, premium, etc. [She *redeemed* the coupon for a free bar of soap.] **4** to set free; rescue, as from sin. **5** to carry out; fulfill, as a promise. **6** to make up for [His brave act *redeemed* his faults.] —**re·deem′a·ble** ***adj.*** —**re·deem′er** ***n.***

**re·demp·tion** (ri demp′shən) ***n.*** **1** a buying back, paying off, etc.; a redeeming or being redeemed. **2** rescue or salvation.

**re·de·vel·op** (rē′di vel′əp) ***v.*** **1** to develop again. **2** to rebuild or restore, as an area that is run-down. —**re′de·vel′op·ment** ***n.***

**red-hand·ed** (red′han′did) ***adj.*** while committing a crime [a thief caught *red-handed*].

**red·head** (red′hed) ***n.*** a person who has red hair. —**red′head·ed** ***adj.***

☆**redheaded woodpecker** a North American woodpecker with a bright-red head and neck, a black back, and white underparts.

**red herring** something used to take people's attention away from the important thing.

> A **red herring** is a kind of fish that is sometimes drawn across the trail that hounds are following when hunting. The strong smell of the fish takes the dogs away from the scent of the animal they are supposed to be hunting.

**red-hot** (red′hät′) ***adj.*** **1** hot enough to glow [*red-hot* iron]. **2** very excited, angry, eager, etc. **3** very new, timely, etc. [*red-hot* news]. ◆☆***n.*** a frankfurter; hot dog: *used only in everyday talk.*

**re·dis·cov·er** (rē′dis kuv′ər) ***v.*** to discover again something that was lost or forgotten.

**red-let·ter** (red′let′ər) ***adj.*** worth remembering; important or happy [a *red-letter* day].

> The makers of calendars often print the numbers that stand for Sundays and holidays with red ink rather than the black ink used for ordinary days. When we look at one of these calendars, we can see at once which days are **red-letter** days.

**re·do** (rē do͞o′) ***v.*** **1** to do again. **2** to redecorate, as a room. —**re·did′, re·done′, re·do′ing**

**red·o·lent** (red′'l ənt) ***adj.*** **1** having a sweet smell; fragrant [*redolent* flowers]. **2** giving off a smell [a harbor *redolent* of fish]. **3** suggesting ideas or feelings [a song *redolent* of young love]. —**red′o·lence** ***n.***

**re·dou·ble** (rē dub′'l) ***v.*** **1** to double again; make twice as much; make much greater [to *redouble* one's efforts]. **2** to turn sharply backward [to *redouble* on one's tracks]. —**re·dou′bled, re·dou′bling**

**re·doubt** (ri dout′) ***n.*** a small fort away from the main fort, as for protecting a pass. **615**

**re·doubt·a·ble** (ri dout′ə b'l) ***adj.*** that causes or should cause great fear [a *redoubtable* foe].

**re·dound** (ri dound′) ***v.*** to come back as a result; be reflected back [The Olympic athlete's honors *redounded* to the nation's credit.]

**red pepper** **1** a plant with a red fruit that has many seeds. Some varieties are mild, while others, such as the cayenne, are very hot. **2** the ground fruit or seeds, used for seasoning.

**re·dress** (ri dres′) ***v.*** to correct and make up for [to *redress* a wrong]. ◆***n.*** (rē′dres) something done to make up for a fault, injury, etc. [The citizens petitioned the government for a *redress* of their grievances.]

**Red River** a river flowing along the Texas-Oklahoma border, through Louisiana into the Mississippi.

**Red Sea** a sea between Africa and Arabia. The Suez Canal connects it with the Mediterranean Sea.

**red tape** too great attention to rules and details that slows work or events down in an annoying way.

> The cord or tape used to tie together bundles of official papers is often red. From this, the term **red tape** came to mean a "tying up" or hindrance to work by following official regulations too closely.

| | | | | | | | |
|---|---|---|---|---|---|---|---|
| **a** | fat | **ir** | here | **ou** | out | **zh** | leisure |
| **ā** | ape | **ī** | bite, fire | **u** | up | **ŋ** | ring |
| **ä** | car, lot | **ō** | go | **ʉr** | fur | | a *in* ago |
| **e** | ten | **ô** | law, horn | **ch** | chin | | e *in* agent |
| **er** | care | **oi** | oil | **sh** | she | ə = | i *in* unity |
| **ē** | even | **oo** | look | **th** | thin | | o *in* collect |
| **i** | hit | **o͞o** | tool | ***th*** | then | | u *in* focus |

**re·duce** (ri do͞os′ *or* ri dyo͞os′) ***v.*** **1** to make smaller, less, fewer, etc.; decrease [to *reduce* speed; to *reduce* taxes]. **2** to lose weight, as by dieting. **3** to make lower, as in rank or condition; bring down [to *reduce* a major to the rank of captain; a family *reduced* to poverty]. **4** to change into a different form or condition [to *reduce* peanuts to a paste by grinding]. **5** to change in form without changing in value [to *reduce* 6/8 to 3/4]. **6** to conquer or destroy [The city was *reduced* by the bombing.] —**re·duced′, re·duc′ing** —**re·duc′er *n.*** —**re·duc′i·ble *adj.***

**re·duc·tion** (ri duk′shən) ***n.*** **1** a reducing or being reduced. **2** the amount by which a thing is reduced [a ten-pound *reduction* in weight]. **3** anything reduced, as a lower price.

**re·dun·dan·cy** (ri dun′dən sē) ***n.*** **1** the condition of being redundant. **2** something redundant. **3** the use of more words than are needed to express an idea. *Also* **re·dun′dance.** *—pl.* **re·dun′dan·cies**

**re·dun·dant** (ri dun′dənt) ***adj.*** **1** more than enough; not needed. **2** using more words than are necessary to the meaning [It is *redundant* to say "Take daily doses every day."] —**re·dun′dant·ly *adv.***

> **Redundant** comes from a Latin word that means "to overflow." A redundant expression can be said to overflow with too many words.

☆**red-winged blackbird** (red′wingd′) a North American blackbird with a red patch on each wing in the male: *also called* **redwing.**

616

**red·wood** (red′wood) ***n.*** ☆**1** a giant evergreen of California and Oregon; sequoia. **2** the reddish wood of this tree.

**re·ech·o** (rē ek′ō) ***v.*** to echo back or again [The call echoed and *reechoed* through the valley.] —**re·ech′oed, re·ech′o·ing** ◆***n.*** the echo of an echo. *—pl.* **re·ech′oes** *Also* **re-echo.**

**reed** (rēd) ***n.*** **1** a kind of tall, slender grass growing in wet land; also, the stem of this grass. **2** a musical pipe made from a hollow stem. **3** a thin strip of wood, plastic, or metal in some musical instruments, that vibrates when air is blown against it and produces a tone [The clarinet, oboe, bassoon, saxophone, etc. have a *reed* or *reeds* in the mouthpiece.] *See the picture.*

**reed organ** an organ with a set of metal reeds instead of pipes to make the tones.

**re·ed·u·cate** (rē ej′ə kāt) ***v.*** to educate again, especially so as to prepare for new situations, jobs, etc.: *also* **re-educate.** —**re·ed′u·cat·ed, re·ed′u·cat·ing** —**re·ed′u·ca′tion *n.***

**reed·y** (rēd′ē) ***adj.*** **1** full of reeds. **2** like a reed; slender, delicate, etc. **3** sounding like a reed instrument; thin or shrill [a high, *reedy* voice]. —**reed′i·er, reed′i·est**

**reef**[1] (rēf) ***n.*** a ridge of sand or rock just about even with the surface of the water.

**reef**[2] (rēf) ***n.*** a part of a sail that can be folded up and tied down so that the wind has less to push against. ◆***v.*** to make a sail smaller by taking in part of it.

**reef·er** (rēf′ər) ***n.*** **1** a short, thick coat like a sailor's jacket. **2** a person who reefs.

**reek** (rēk) ***v.*** to have a strong, bad smell; stink. ◆***n.*** a strong, bad smell; stench.

**reel**[1] (rēl) ***v.*** **1** to sway or stagger, as from being struck; totter. *See* SYNONYMS *at* **stagger. 2** to move in an unsteady way, as from dizziness. **3** to spin or whirl [The room seemed to *reel* before my eyes.]

**reel**[2] (rēl) ***n.*** a lively dance or the music for it.

**reel**[3] (rēl) ***n.*** **1** a frame or spool on which film, fishing line, wire, etc. is wound. *See the picture.* **2** the amount of movie film, wire, etc. usually wound on one reel. ◆***v.*** to wind on a reel. —**reel in,** to pull in, as a fish, by winding a line on a reel. —**reel off,** to tell, write, etc. easily and quickly [to *reel off* a long list of names]. —**reel out,** to unwind from a reel. —☆**right off the reel,** without hesitating or pausing.

**re·e·lect** (rē′i lekt′) ***v.*** to elect again: *also* **re-elect.** —**re′e·lec′tion *n.***

**re·en·list** (rē′in list′) ***v.*** to enlist again: *also* **re-enlist.** —**re′en·list′ment *n.***

**re·en·ter** (rē en′tər) ***v.*** to enter a second time or to come back in again: *also* **re-enter.** —**re·en′try *n.***

**re·es·tab·lish** (rē′ə stab′lish) ***v.*** to establish again: *also* **re-establish.** —**re′es·tab′lish·ment *n.***

**re·e·val·u·ate** (rē′i val′yo͞o wāt′) ***v.*** to evaluate again: *also* **re-evaluate.** —**re′e·val′u·at′ed, re′e·val′u·at′ing**

**re·ex·am·ine** (rē′ig zam′ən) ***v.*** to examine again: *also* **re-examine.** —**re′ex·am′ined, re′ex·am′in·ing** —**re′ex·am′i·na′tion *n.***

**re·face** (rē fās′) ***v.*** to put a new face, facing, or surface on. —**re·faced′, re·fac′ing**

**re·fec·to·ry** (ri fek′tər ē) ***n.*** a dining hall, as in a monastery. *—pl.* **re·fec′to·ries**

**re·fer** (ri fur′) ***v.*** **1** to speak of or call attention; mention [You seldom *refer* to your injury.] **2** to go for facts, help, etc. [Columbus had no accurate maps to *refer* to.] **3** to tell to go to a certain person or place for help, service, information, etc. [Our neighbor *referred* me to a good doctor.] **4** to present to, as for help in settling [We *referred* our argument to the teacher.] —**re·ferred′, re·fer′ring**

**ref·er·ee** (ref ə rē′) ***n.*** **1** a person to whom something is presented to be settled [The judge was *referee* in the lawsuit.] **2** a person who is chosen to see to it that the rules are followed in such sports as boxing, basketball, etc. ◆***v.*** to act as referee in [to *referee* a game]. —**ref·er·eed′, ref·er·ee′ing**

**ref·er·ence** (ref′ər əns *or* ref′rəns) ***n.*** **1** the act or fact of referring; mention [They made no *reference* to the accident.] **2** the fact of having to do with; relation; connection [I am writing in *reference* to your letter.] **3** a mention, as in a book, of some other work where information can be found; also, the work so mentioned [Most of the author's *references* are useful.] **4** something that gives information [Look in the encyclopedia and other *references*.] **5** a person who can give information about another; also, a statement about one's character, ability, etc. given by such a person [You have to give three *references* when you apply for this job.]

**ref·er·en·dum** (ref′ə ren′dəm) ***n.*** ☆**1** the placing of a law before the people so that they can vote on it. ☆**2** the right of the people to vote on such a law.

**re·fer·ral** (ri fur′əl) ***n.*** **1** a referring or being referred, as to get help, service, etc. **2** a person who is told to go for help, service, etc. to another person, agency, etc.

**re·fill** (rē fil′) ***v.*** to fill again. ◆***n.*** (rē′fil) **1** something to refill a special container [a *refill* for a ball point pen]. **2** any extra filling of a prescription for medicine. —**re·fill′a·ble** ***adj.***

**re·fi·nance** (rē fə nans′ *or* rē fī′nans) ***v.*** to give or get a new loan or more money for. —**re·fi·nanced′, re·fi·nanc′ing**

**re·fine** (ri fīn′) ***v.*** **1** to remove dirt, unwanted matter, etc. from; make pure [to *refine* sugar]. **2** to make or become less coarse, crude, etc.; improve, polish, etc. [to *refine* one's style of writing]. —**re·fined′, re·fin′ing** —**re·fin′er** ***n.***

**re·fined** (ri fīnd′) ***adj.*** **1** freed from dirt, unwanted matter, etc.; purified [*refined* sugar]. **2** not crude or coarse; cultured, polished, etc. [*refined* manners].

**re·fine·ment** (ri fīn′mənt) ***n.*** **1** the act or result of refining. **2** fineness of manners, tastes, feelings, etc.; cultivation [a person of *refinement*]. **3** a change that improves the details [We made several *refinements* in the plan.]

**re·fin·er·y** (ri fīn′ər ē) ***n.*** a place where some raw material, such as oil or sugar, is refined or purified. —*pl.* **re·fin′er·ies**

**re·fin·ish** (rē fin′ish) ***v.*** to put a new surface on [to *refinish* wood or metal].

**re·fit** (rē fit′) ***v.*** to make fit for use again by repairing, adding new equipment, etc. [a passenger ship *refitted* for use as a freighter]. —**re·fit′ted, re·fit′ting**

**re·flect** (ri flekt′) ***v.*** **1** to throw back or be thrown back, as light, heat, or sound [A polished metal surface *reflects* both light and heat.] **2** to give back an image of [The calm lake *reflected* the trees on the shore.] **3** to bring as a result [Your success *reflects* credit on your teachers.] **4** to bring blame, doubt, etc. [Not paying the money back will *reflect* on your honesty.] **5** to think seriously [You should *reflect* on your past mistakes.] *See* SYNONYMS *at* **consider**. **6** to show [skills that *reflect* years of training].

**re·flec·tion** (ri flek′shən) ***n.*** **1** a reflecting of heat, light, sound, etc. **2** anything reflected; image [one's *reflection* in a mirror]. **3** serious thought; contemplation [After much *reflection,* she began to write.] **4** an idea, remark, etc. that comes from such thought. **5** a remark or an action that brings blame or doubt [That joke was not meant as a *reflection* on your skill.]

**re·flec·tive** (ri flek′tiv) ***adj.*** **1** reflecting. **2** thoughtful; serious [a *reflective* poem].

**re·flec·tor** (ri flek′tər) ***n.*** a surface or part that reflects light, heat, sound, etc. [a *reflector* on a lamp]. *See the picture.*

**re·flex** (rē′fleks) ***n.*** **1** an action of the muscles or glands caused by a stimulus sent through nerves in an automatic way, without being controlled by the mind or by thinking [When a doctor strikes a person's knee to see if the lower leg will jerk, a *reflex* is being tested.] **2 reflexes,** *pl.* the ability to react quickly and with results of a certain kind [a boxer with good *reflexes*]. ◆***adj.*** that is or has to do with a reflex [A sneeze is a *reflex* action.]

**re·flex·ive** (ri flek′siv) ***adj.*** **1** that is or has to do with a verb whose subject and object refer to the same person or thing [In "He cut himself," "cut" is a *reflexive* verb.] **2** that is or has to do with a pronoun used as the object of a reflexive verb [In "I hurt myself," "myself" is a *reflexive* pronoun.]

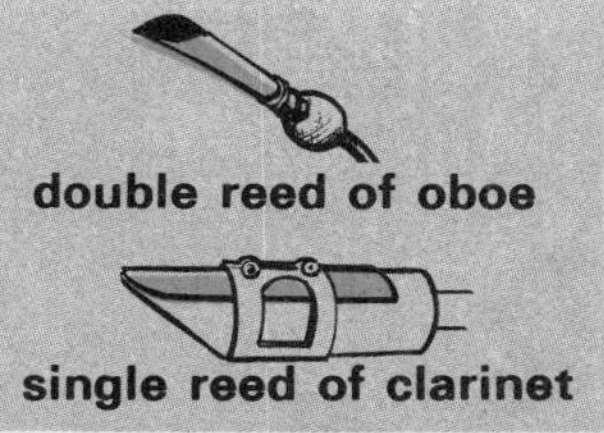

double reed of oboe

single reed of clarinet

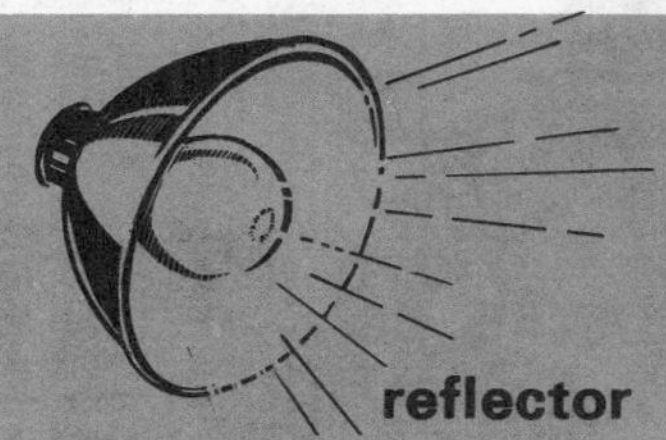

reflector

illusion caused by refraction

fishing reel

**re·for·est** (rē fôr′ist) ***v.*** to plant new trees where a forest once grew. —**re′for·est·a′tion** ***n.***

**re·form** (ri fôrm′) ***v.*** **1** to make better by getting rid of faults, wrongs, etc.; improve [to *reform* working conditions in a factory; to *reform* a criminal]. **2** to become better; give up one's bad ways [The outlaw *reformed* and became a useful citizen.] ◆***n.*** correction of faults or evils, as in government.



**re·form** (rē′fôrm′) ***v.*** to form again.

**ref·or·ma·tion** (ref′ər mā′shən) ***n.*** **1** a reforming or being reformed. **2 Reformation,** the 16th-century religious movement that aimed at reforming the Roman Catholic Church and led to the forming of the Protestant churches.

☆**re·form·a·to·ry** (ri fôr′mə tôr′ē) ***n.*** **1** a kind of prison to which young people who have broken the law are sent for training meant to reform them. **2** a prison for women. —*pl.* **re·form′a·to′ries**

**re·form·er** (ri fôr′mər) ***n.*** a person who tries to bring about reforms, as in government.

**re·fract** (ri frakt′) ***v.*** to bend a ray of light, etc. as it passes from one medium into another [Glass *refracts* light.]

**re·frac·tion** (ri frak′shən) ***n.*** the bending of a ray of light, etc. as it passes on a slant into a medium of a different density, as from air into water. *See the picture.*

**re·frac·to·ry** (ri frak′tər ē) ***adj.*** **1** hard to deal with or control; stubborn [a *refractory* horse; a *refractory* illness]. **2** hard to melt or work, as certain ores or metals.

**re·frain**¹ (ri frān′) ***v.*** to keep from doing something; hold back [Please *refrain* from talking.]

| | | | | | | | |
|---|---|---|---|---|---|---|---|
| **a** | fat | **ir** | here | **ou** | out | **zh** | leisure |
| **ā** | ape | **ī** | bite, fire | **u** | up | **ng** | ring |
| **ä** | car, lot | **ō** | go | **ur** | fur | | a *in* ago |
| **e** | ten | **ô** | law, horn | **ch** | chin | | e *in* agent |
| **er** | care | **oi** | oil | **sh** | she | ə = | i *in* unity |
| **ē** | even | **oo** | look | **th** | thin | | o *in* collect |
| **i** | hit | **ōō** | tool | ***th*** | then | | u *in* focus |

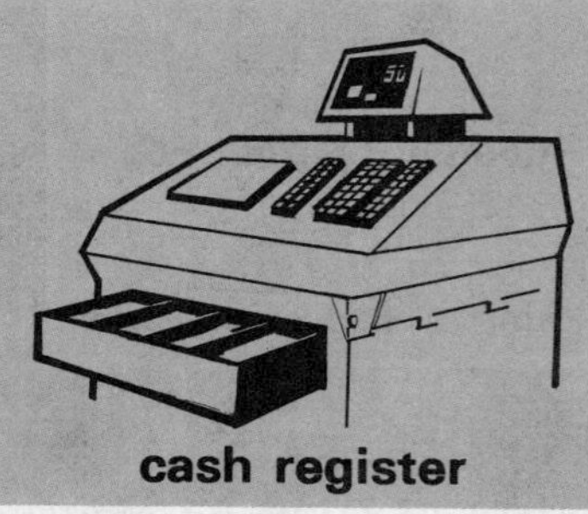
cash register

**re·frain**[2] (ri frān′) ***n.*** a phrase or verse that is repeated from time to time in a song or poem.

**re·fresh** (ri fresh′) ***v.*** to make fresh again; bring back into good condition [A soft rain *refreshed* the wilted plants. She *refreshed* herself with a short nap. *Refresh* my memory by playing the piece again.]

**re·fresh·ing** (ri fresh′iŋ) ***adj.*** **1** that refreshes [a *refreshing* sleep]. **2** pleasant as a change from what is usual [It is *refreshing* to meet a person with new ideas.]

**re·fresh·ment** (ri fresh′mənt) ***n.*** **1** a refreshing or being refreshed. **2** something that refreshes. **3 refreshments,** *pl.* food or drink or both, especially when not a full meal.

**re·frig·er·ate** (ri frij′ə rāt) ***v.*** to make or keep cool or cold [Milk will sour if it is not *refrigerated.*] —**re·frig′er·at·ed, re·frig′er·at·ing —re·frig′er·a′tion** ***n.***

 **re·frig·er·a·tor** (ri frij′ə rāt′ər) ***n.*** a box or room in which the air is kept cool to keep food, etc. from spoiling.

**re·fu·el** (rē fyo͞o′'l) ***v.*** **1** to supply again with fuel. **2** to take on a fresh supply of fuel. —**re·fu′eled** or **re·fu′elled, re·fu′el·ing** or **re·fu′el·ling**

**ref·uge** (ref′yo͞oj) ***n.*** **1** shelter or protection, as from danger [We sought a *refuge* from our enemies.] **2** a safe place to stay; shelter [a wildlife *refuge*]. *See* SYNONYMS *at* **shelter.**

> **Refuge** comes from a Latin word meaning "to flee back." When one is looking for a refuge, one may flee back to a place that has offered safety or shelter.

**ref·u·gee** (ref′yoo jē′ *or* ref′yoo jē′) ***n.*** a person who flees from his or her home or country to seek refuge, as from persecution.

**re·fund** (ri fund′) ***v.*** to give back money, etc.; repay [We will *refund* the full price if you are not satisfied.] ◆***n.*** (rē′fund) the act of refunding or the amount refunded. —**re·fund′a·ble** ***adj.***

**re·fur·bish** (ri fur′bish) ***v.*** to freshen or polish up again; make like new; renovate.

**re·fuse**[1] (ri fyo͞oz′) ***v.*** **1** to say that one will not take something that is offered; reject [to *refuse* a gift; to *refuse* a suggestion]. **2** to say that one will not give, do, or agree to something; turn down [to *refuse* a request; to *refuse* to go]. *See* SYNONYMS *at* **decline.** —**re·fused′, re·fus′ing —re·fus·al** (ri fyo͞o′z'l) ***n.***

**ref·use**[2] (ref′yo͞os *or* ref′yo͞oz) ***n.*** worthless matter; waste; trash; rubbish.

**re·fute** (ri fyo͞ot′) ***v.*** to prove wrong or false; disprove [to *refute* an argument]. —**re·fut′ed, re·fut′ing —ref·u·ta·tion** (ref′yə tā′shən) ***n.***

**reg.** *abbreviation for* **regiment, registered.**

**re·gain** (ri gān′) ***v.*** **1** to get back again; recover [He *regained* his health slowly.] *See* SYNONYMS *at* **recover. 2** to get back to [The boat *regained* the harbor.]

**re·gal** (rē′g'l) ***adj.*** of, like, or fit for a king or queen; royal; stately; splendid. —**re′gal·ly** ***adv.***

**re·gale** (ri gāl′) ***v.*** to entertain or delight; give pleasure to [to *regale* guests with a feast; to *regale* listeners with jokes]. —**re·galed′, re·gal′ing**

**re·ga·li·a** (ri gāl′yə *or* ri gā′lē ə) ***n.pl.*** **1** the symbols of an office or a special group [The crown, scepter, etc. are the *regalia* of a king.] **2** splendid clothes.

**re·gard** (ri gärd′) ***v.*** **1** to think of in a certain way; consider [I *regard* them as friends. All of us *regard* you highly.] **2** to pay attention to; show respect for; heed [Some people never *regard* the feelings of others.] **3** to look carefully at; gaze upon; observe. **4** to have relation to; concern [This *regards* your welfare.] ◆***n.*** **1** attention; concern; care [Have *regard* for your safety.] **2** respect and liking; esteem [She has a high *regard* for her teachers.] **3** a steady look; gaze. **4 regards,** *pl.* good wishes; greetings [Give my *regards* to your parents.] —**as regards,** concerning. —**in regard to** or **with regard to,** in relation to; with respect to. —**without regard to,** without considering.

> SYNONYMS: To **regard** is to judge or decide what the worth or value of someone or something is [This book is highly *regarded* by the critics.] To **respect** is to show honor or courtesy to someone or something that is highly valued [a judge *respected* by lawyers]. To **esteem** is to cherish very much someone or something that is respected [a friend *esteemed* for his loyalty].

**re·gard·ing** (ri gärd′iŋ) ***prep.*** having to do with; concerning; about [*regarding* your letter].

**re·gard·less** (ri gärd′lis) ***adj.*** taking no heed; heedless [*Regardless* of the cost, I'll buy it.] ◆☆***adv.*** anyway: *used only in everyday talk* [We objected but they went *regardless.*] —**re·gard′less·ly** ***adv.***

**re·gat·ta** (ri gät′ə *or* ri gat′ə) ***n.*** a boat race or a series of boat races.

**re·gen·cy** (rē′jən sē) ***n.*** **1** the position or power of a regent or group of regents. **2** a group of regents ruling a country. **3** government by a regent or a group of regents [England was a *regency* from 1811 to 1820.] —*pl.* **re′gen·cies**

**re·gen·er·ate** (ri jen′ə rāt) ***v.*** **1** to give new life or force to; renew [to *regenerate* an old idea]. **2** to open a new life to in a spiritual way. **3** to make better; improve or reform. **4** to grow back anew [If a lizard loses its tail, it can *regenerate* a new one.] —**re·gen′er·at·ed, re·gen′er·at·ing —re·gen′er·a′tion** ***n.***

**re·gent** (rē′jənt) ***n.*** **1** a person chosen to rule while a king or queen is sick, absent, or too young. ☆**2** a member of a governing board, as of a university.

**reg·i·cide** (rej′ə sīd) ***n.*** **1** a person who kills a king. **2** the killing of a king.

**re·gime** or **ré·gime** (rə zhēm′ *or* rā zhēm′) ***n.*** **1** a system of rule or government [a democratic *regime*]. **2** *another word for* **regimen.**

**reg·i·men** (rej′ə mən) ***n.*** a system of diet, exercise, etc. for keeping healthy.

**reg·i·ment** (rej′ə mənt) ***n.*** a unit of soldiers, made up of two or more battalions. ◆***v.*** (rej′ə ment) to organize in a strict system and with strict controls [Life in a prison is *regimented.*] —**reg′i·men′tal** ***adj.*** —**reg′i·men·ta′tion** ***n.***

**re·gion** (rē′jən) ***n.*** **1** a large stretch of land; area or district [an iron mining *region* of Minnesota]. **2** any area, space, realm, etc. [the upper *regions* of the air; the *region* of the liver]. —**re·gion·al** (rē′jən ′l) ***adj.***

**reg·is·ter** (rej′is tər) ***n.*** **1** a record or list of names, events, or things; also, a book in which such a record is kept [a hotel *register; register* of accounts]. **2** a device for counting and keeping a record of [a cash *register*]. *See the picture.* ☆**3** an opening into a room, as from a furnace, that can be opened or closed to control the air passing through. **4** a part of a range of tones of a voice or musical instrument. ◆***v.*** ☆**1** to keep a record of in a register [to *register* a birth]. **2** to put one's name in a register, as of voters. **3** to show on a gauge, scale, etc. [The thermometer *registers* 32°.] **4** to show, as by a look on the face [to *register* surprise]. **5** to protect important mail by paying a fee to have its delivery recorded at a post office.

☆**registered nurse** a nurse who has completed thorough training and has passed a State examination. Such a nurse can perform complete nursing services.

**reg·is·trar** (rej′i strär) ***n.*** a person who keeps records, as in a college.

**reg·is·tra·tion** (rej′i strā′shən) ***n.*** **1** a registering or being registered [the *registration* of an automobile with the State]. **2** an entry in a register. **3** the number of persons registered.

**reg·is·try** (rej′is trē) ***n.*** **1** an office where records are kept. **2** an official record or list; register. **3** the act of registering. —*pl.* **reg′is·tries**

**re·gress** (ri gres′) ***v.*** to go back, as to an earlier condition [The students *regressed* to childish ways of behaving.] —**re·gres′sion** ***n.***

**re·gret** (ri gret′) ***v.*** to be sorry for or feel troubled over something that has happened, that one has done, etc. [to *regret* the loss of a pet; to *regret* a mistake]. —**re·gret′ted, re·gret′ting** ◆***n.*** a feeling of being sorry or troubled, as for something one has done or failed to do. —**one's regrets,** a polite way of saying that one is sorry, as at refusing an invitation. —**re·gret′ful** ***adj.*** —**re·gret′ta·ble** ***adj.***

> **Regret** comes from an old French word that means "to cry for the dead." Regret is often felt when someone dies, as when we feel sad about the loss of someone we have loved.

**reg·u·lar** (reg′yə lər) ***adj.*** **1** formed or arranged in an orderly way; balanced [a *regular* pattern; a face with *regular* features]. **2** according to some rule or habit; usual; customary [Sit in your *regular* place.] **3** steady and even; not changing [a *regular* rhythm]. **4** in grammar, changing form in the usual way in showing tense, number, etc. ["Walk" is a *regular* verb, but "swim" is not.] **5** describing or of an army that is kept up in peace as well as in war. **6** qualified as by training; recognized [a *regular* nurse]. **7** complete; thorough: *used only in everyday talk* [The game was a *regular* battle.] ☆**8** pleasant, friendly, etc.: *used only in everyday talk* [a *regular* fellow]. ◆***n.*** a member of the regular army. —**reg·u·lar·i·ty** (reg′yə lar′ə tē) ***n.*** —**reg′u·lar·ly** ***adv.***

**reg·u·late** (reg′yə lāt) ***v.*** **1** to control according to rules, a system, etc. [What forces *regulate* the weather?] **2** to fix at a certain speed, amount, etc.; adjust to some standard [to *regulate* the heat; to *regulate* a fast clock]. —**reg′u·lat·ed, reg′u·lat·ing** —**reg′u·la′tor** ***n.***

**reg·u·la·tion** (reg′yə lā′shən) ***n.*** **1** the act of regulating or the condition of being regulated [the *regulation* of the sale of alcohol]. **2** a rule or law that regulates [safety *regulations*]. ◆***adj.*** **1** made or done according to rules [a *regulation* uniform]. **2** usual or normal; ordinary.

**re·gur·gi·tate** (ri gur′jə tāt) ***v.*** to bring partly digested food from the stomach back to the mouth, as a cow does. —**re·gur′gi·tat·ed, re·gur′gi·tat·ing** —**re·gur′gi·ta′tion** ***n.***

**re·ha·bil·i·tate** (rē′hə bil′ə tāt) ***v.*** **1** to bring back to a normal or good condition [to *rehabilitate* a slum area]. **2** to bring back to a former rank or reputation. —**re′ha·bil′i·tat·ed, re′ha·bil′i·tat·ing** —**re′ha·bil′i·ta′tion** ***n.***

**re·hash** (rē hash′) ***v.*** to work up again or go over again, with nothing new added [to *rehash* an argument]. ◆***n.*** (rē′hash) the act or result of rehashing [This book is a *rehash* of the author's earlier book.]

**re·hearse** (ri hurs′) ***v.*** **1** to go through a play, speech, etc. for practice, before giving it in public. **2** to repeat in detail [They *rehearsed* all their troubles to me.] —**re·hearsed′, re·hears′ing** —**re·hears′al** ***n.***

> **Rehearse** comes from an old French word which means "to harrow again." The harrow is a device used after plowing to break up land and make it smooth. We rehearse a speech or play to make it smooth the same way a farmer harrows the land.



**Reich** (rīk) *a former name for* Germany *or* the German government.

**reign** (rān) ***n.*** **1** the rule of a king, queen, emperor, etc.; also, the time of ruling [laws made during the *reign* of Victoria]. **2** widespread influence or control [the *reign* of fashion]. ◆***v.*** **1** to rule as a king, queen, etc. [Henry VIII *reigned* for 38 years.] **2** to be widespread; prevail [when peace *reigns*].

**re·im·burse** (rē′im burs′) ***v.*** to pay back money owed, as for services, loss, expenses, etc. [You will be *reimbursed* for your work.] —**re′im·bursed′, re′im·burs′ing** —**re′im·burse′ment** ***n.***

**rein** (rān) ***n.*** **1** a narrow strap of leather attached to each end of a horse's bit. Reins are held by the rider or driver for guiding and controlling the horse. *See the picture.* **2 reins,** *pl.* a means of guiding or controlling [to take up the *reins* of leadership]. ◆***v.*** to guide, control, or check as with reins. —**draw rein** or **draw in the reins,** to slow down or stop. —**give free rein to,** to allow to act freely.

**re·in·car·nate** (rē′in kär′nāt) ***v.*** to give a new body to after death [Souls are *reincarnated,* according to Hindu religious belief.] —**re′in·car′nat·ed, re′in·car′nat·ing** —**re′in·car·na′tion** ***n.***

| | | | | | | | |
|---|---|---|---|---|---|---|---|
| **a** | fat | **ir** | here | **ou** | out | **zh** | leisure |
| **ā** | ape | **ī** | bite, fire | **u** | up | **ng** | ring |
| **ä** | car, lot | **ō** | go | **ur** | fur | | a *in* ago |
| **e** | ten | **ô** | law, horn | **ch** | chin | | e *in* agent |
| **er** | care | **oi** | oil | **sh** | she | **ə =** | i *in* unity |
| **ē** | even | **oo** | look | **th** | thin | | o *in* collect |
| **i** | hit | **ōō** | tool | ***th*** | then | | u *in* focus |

**r**

**rein·deer** (rān′dir) ***n.*** a large deer found in northern regions, where it is tamed and used for work or as food. Both the male and female have antlers. *See the picture.* —*pl.* **rein′deer**

**re·in·force** (rē′in fôrs′) ***v.*** to make stronger, as by adding something [to *reinforce* concrete with steel bars; to *reinforce* a theory with new evidence]. —**re′in·forced′, re′in·forc′ing**

**re·in·force·ment** (rē′in fôrs′mənt) ***n.*** **1** the act of reinforcing or the condition of being reinforced. **2** anything that reinforces. **3 reinforcements,** *pl.* extra troops, ships, etc. to help in a battle.

**re·in·state** (rē′in stāt′) ***v.*** to put back in a former position, rank, etc.; restore [to *reinstate* someone as a member of a club]. —**re′in·stat′ed, re′in·stat′ing** —**re′in·state′ment *n.***

**re·it·er·ate** (rē it′ə rāt) ***v.*** to say over and over again; repeat [The witness *reiterated* the story for the judge and jury.] —**re·it′er·at·ed, re·it′er·at·ing** —**re·it′er·a′tion *n.***

**re·ject** (ri jekt′) ***v.*** **1** to refuse to take, agree to, use, etc. [to *reject* advice]. *See* SYNONYMS *at* **decline. 2** to throw away as worthless; discard [The school *rejected* the old books that were given to it.] **3** to be unable to accept [The body may *reject* an organ transplanted into it.] ✦***n.*** (rē′jekt) something rejected, or thrown away. —**re·jec′tion *n.***

**re·joice** (ri jois′) ***v.*** to be or make glad or happy [We *rejoiced* at the news.] —**re·joiced′, re·joic′ing** —**re·joic′ing *n.***



**re·join** (rē join′) ***v.*** **1** to join again; come or bring together again [to *rejoin* one's class after an illness; to *rejoin* the ends of a torn rope]. **2** to answer ["That's not so!" he *rejoined.*]

**re·join·der** (ri join′dər) ***n.*** an answer, especially to another's reply.

**re·ju·ve·nate** (ri jo͞o′və nāt) ***v.*** to make feel or seem young or fresh again [Our vacation at the lake *rejuvenated* us.] —**re·ju′ve·nat·ed, re·ju′ve·nat·ing** —**re·ju′ve·na′tion *n.***

**re·lapse** (ri laps′) ***v.*** to fall back into an earlier condition, especially into illness after seeming to get better. —**re·lapsed′, re·laps′ing** ✦***n.*** (ri laps′ *or* rē′laps) the act or condition of relapsing.

**re·late** (ri lāt′) ***v.*** **1** to tell about; give an account of [*Relate* to us what you did.] *See* SYNONYMS *at* **tell. 2** to connect, as in thought or meaning [to *relate* one idea to another]. **3** to have to do with; be connected [Proper diet *relates* to good health.] **4** to show sympathy and understanding [not able to *relate* to strangers]. —**re·lat′ed, re·lat′ing**

relief

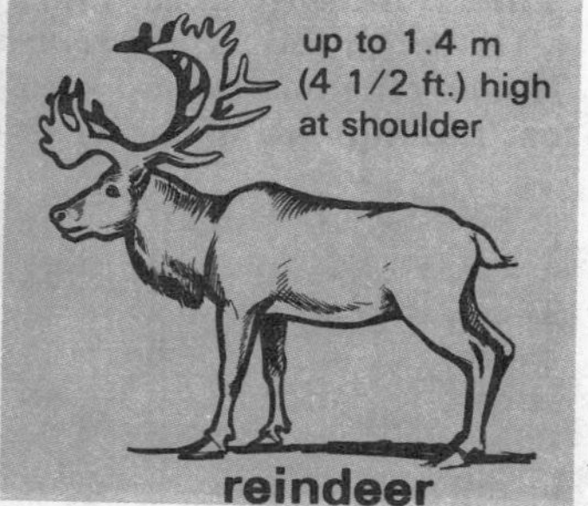


reindeer

**re·lat·ed** (ri lāt′id) ***adj.*** of the same family or kind [oranges, lemons, and *related* fruits; visitors *related* to our boss].

**re·la·tion** (ri lā′shən) ***n.*** **1** a telling, as of a story; account. **2** connection, as in thought or meaning [That remark has no *relation* to the discussion.] **3** connection by being of the same family; kinship. **4** a member of the same family; relative [He is a close *relation.*] **5 relations,** *pl.* the dealings between people, countries, etc. [labor *relations;* foreign *relations*]. —**in relation to** or **with relation to,** concerning; about. —**re·la′tion·ship *n.***

**rel·a·tive** (rel′ə tiv) ***adj.*** **1** having meaning only as related to something ["Cold" is a *relative* term.] **2** as compared with something else; comparative [the *relative* importance of an idea]. **3** having to do with; about [Is your question *relative* to this subject?] **4** related each to the other [We ended in the same *relative* positions.] **5** in grammar, referring to a person or thing mentioned or understood [In "the hat which you bought," "which" is a *relative* pronoun and "which you bought" is a *relative* clause.] ✦***n.*** **1** a relative word or thing. **2** a person of the same family by origin or by marriage. —**relative to, 1** about; concerning. **2** equal or similar to. —**rel′a·tive·ly *adv.***

**rel·a·tiv·i·ty** (rel′ə tiv′ə tē) ***n.*** **1** the condition of being relative. **2** a theory of the universe developed by Albert Einstein, dealing with the relationship of matter, energy, space, and time.

**re·lax** (ri laks′) ***v.*** **1** to make or become less firm, tense, or strict; loosen up [The body *relaxes* in sleep. The parents never *relaxed* their watch over their child.] **2** to rest from work or effort [He *relaxes* by going fishing.] —**re′lax·a′tion *n.***

**re·lax·ant** (ri laks′ənt) ***adj.*** of or causing relaxation, especially a relaxation of tension in the muscles. ✦***n.*** a relaxant drug or medicine.

**re·lay** (rē′lā) ***n.*** **1** a fresh group that takes over some work from another group; shift [The carpenters worked in *relays* to finish the project on time.] **2** a race in which each member of a team runs only a certain part of the whole distance: *the full name is* **relay race.** ✦***v.*** (rē′lā *or* ri lā′) to get and pass on [to *relay* a message]. —**re′layed, re′lay·ing**

> **Relay** comes from an old French word for any group of dogs that was kept ready at points along the path of a hunt. A fresh group could take over for the dogs that became tired. The word has come to be used for any group that comes in to take over for another in completing a job.

**re-lay** (rē′lā′) ***v.*** to lay again [to *re-lay* a cable]. —**re′-laid′, re′-lay′ing**

**re·lease** (ri lēs′) ***v.*** **1** to set free [*Release* the bird from the cage. We were *released* from debt.] **2** to let go; let loose [to *release* an arrow]. ☆**3** to allow to be shown, published, etc. [to *release* information to reporters]. —**re·leased′, re·leas′ing** ✦***n.*** **1** a setting free, as from prison, work, etc. ☆**2** a motion picture, news item, etc. released to the public. **3** a giving up of a right, claim, etc.; also, the legal paper by which this is done. **4** a device to release a catch, etc., as on a machine.

☆**released time** periods during school time when pupils in a public school may leave the school in order to receive religious instruction elsewhere.

**rel·e·gate** (rel′ə gāt) ***v.*** **1** to put in a less important position [The manager of the team was *relegated* to the job of assistant coach.] **2** to hand over; assign [The task was *relegated* to an assistant.] —**rel′e·gat·ed, rel′e·gat·ing**

**re·lent** (ri lent′) ***v.*** to become less harsh or stubborn; soften [Our parents *relented* and let us go.]

**re·lent·less** (ri lent′lis) ***adj.*** **1** not giving in; having no pity; harsh [a *relentless* foe]. **2** going on without stopping; persistent [the *relentless* pounding of the waves on the beach]. —**re·lent′less·ly *adv.***

**rel·e·vant** (rel′ə vənt) ***adj.*** having to do with the matter at hand; to the point [a *relevant* remark]. —**rel′e·vance** or **rel′e·van·cy *n.***

**re·li·a·ble** (ri lī′ə b′l) ***adj.*** that can be trusted; dependable [This barometer gives a *reliable* weather forecast.] —**re·li·a·bil·i·ty** (ri lī′ə bil′ə tē) ***n.*** —**re·li′a·bly *adv.***

**re·li·ance** (ri lī′əns) ***n.*** **1** trust or confidence [Air travelers put complete *reliance* in the pilot.] **2** a thing relied on.

**re·li·ant** (ri lī′ənt) ***adj.*** having or showing trust or confidence; depending [The orphans are *reliant* on our help.] —**re·li′ant·ly *adv.***

**rel·ic** (rel′ik) ***n.*** **1** a thing or part that remains from the past [This cannon is a *relic* of the Civil War.] **2** something kept as sacred because it belonged to a saint or martyr.

**re·lief** (ri lēf′) ***n.*** **1** a lessening of pain, discomfort, worry, etc. [This salve will give *relief* from itching.] **2** anything that lessens pain, worry, etc. or gives a pleasing change [It's a *relief* to get out of that stuffy hall.] **3** help given to poor people, to victims of a flood, etc. **4** a rest from work or duty [Workers get a ten-minute *relief* every morning.] **5** persons who bring such rest by taking over a post [The guard's *relief* arrived at midnight.] **6** sculpture in which the figures stand out from a flat surface. *See the picture.* —**in relief,** carved so as to stand out from a surface. —**on relief,** receiving payments from public funds, as when out of work.

**relief map** a map that shows the difference in height of hills, valleys, etc. by using special lines or colors, or by molding solid material.

**re·lieve** (ri lēv′) ***v.*** **1** to make less or easier, as pain or worry [Cold water *relieves* a swelling.] **2** to free from pain, worry, etc. [We were *relieved* when the danger passed.] **3** to give or bring help to [to *relieve* a besieged city]. **4** to set free from duty or work by replacing [The guard is *relieved* every four hours.] **5** to bring a pleasant change to [a bare wall *relieved* by several pictures]. —**re·lieved′, re·liev′ing**

**re·li·gion** (ri lij′ən) ***n.*** **1** belief in, or the worship of, God or a group of gods. **2** a particular system of belief or worship built around God, moral ideals, a philosophy of life, etc.

**re·li·gious** (ri lij′əs) ***adj.*** **1** having or showing strong belief in a religion; devout; pious. **2** having to do with religion [a *religious* service]. **3** very careful; exact [paying *religious* attention to one's diet]. ◆***n.*** a member of a community of monks, nuns, etc. —**re·li′gious·ly *adv.*** —**re·li′gious·ness *n.***

**re·lin·quish** (ri liŋ′kwish) ***v.*** to give up or let go, as a hold on something, a right or claim, etc. —**re·lin′quish·ment *n.***

**rel·ish** (rel′ish) ***n.*** **1** a pleasing taste; appetizing flavor [Salt adds *relish* to the stew.] **2** enjoyment; zest [He ate the pear with *relish*.] **3** pickles, olives, etc. served with food to add flavor. ◆***v.*** to like or enjoy [to *relish* ice cream; to *relish* a joke].

☆**re·lo·cate** (rē lō′kāt) ***v.*** **1** to locate again. **2** to move to a new location. —**re·lo′cat·ed, re·lo′cat·ing**

**re·luc·tant** (ri luk′tənt) ***adj.*** **1** not wanting to do something; unwilling [He is *reluctant* to ask for help.] **2** showing unwillingness [a *reluctant* agreement]. —**re·luc′tance *n.*** —**re·luc′tant·ly *adv.***

**re·ly** (ri lī′) ***v.*** to trust or depend [You can *rely* on me to be on time.] —**re·lied′, re·ly′ing**

SYNONYMS: We **rely** on people that we trust to go on doing what is expected of them, as they have done in the past [You can *rely* on Sadie to do a good job.] We **depend** on people whose help and support are necessary to us [Should children *depend* on their parents for a college education?]

**re·main** (ri mān′) ***v.*** **1** to stay while others go [Max *remained* at home when they went to the movies.] *See* SYNONYMS *at* **stay**[3]. **2** to be left over after a part is taken or destroyed [Only a few columns of the ancient temple *remain*.] **3** to go on being; continue [She *remained* loyal to her friends.] **4** to be left as not yet done, said, or taken care of [That *remains* to be seen.]

**re·main·der** (ri mān′dər) ***n.*** the part, number, etc. left over [I sold some of my books and gave the *remainder* to the library. When 3 is subtracted from 10, the *remainder* is 7.]

**re·mains** (ri mānz′) ***n.pl.*** **1** what is left after part has been used, destroyed, etc. [the *remains* of last night's dinner]. **2** a dead body.



**re·make** (rē māk′) ***v.*** to make again or in a new way [to *remake* a long coat into a jacket]. —**re·made′, re·mak′ing**

**re·mand** (ri mand′) ***v.*** to send back; especially, to send a prisoner back to jail to await trial.

**re·mark** (ri märk′) ***v.*** **1** to say or comment; mention. **2** to notice or observe [to *remark* a difference in quality]. ◆***n.*** something said briefly; comment [a clever *remark*].

**re·mark·a·ble** (ri märk′ə b′l) ***adj.*** worth noticing because it is very unusual [the *remarkable* strength of Hercules]. *See* SYNONYMS *at* **noticeable.** —**re·mark′a·bly *adv.***

**re·mar·ry** (rē mar′ē) ***v.*** to marry again. —**re·mar′ried, re·mar′ry·ing** —**re·mar′riage *n.***

**Rem·brandt van Rijn** (rem′brant van rīn′) 1606–1669; Dutch painter of pictures.

**re·me·di·a·ble** (ri mē′dē ə b′l) ***adj.*** that can be remedied, cured, or corrected.

**re·me·di·al** (rə mē′dē əl) ***adj.*** that remedies, cures, or corrects [*remedial* reading class].

**rem·e·dy** (rem′ə dē) ***n.*** **1** a medicine or treatment that cures, heals, or relieves [a *remedy* for sunburn]. **2** anything that corrects a wrong or helps make things better [a *remedy* for poor education]. —*pl.* **rem'e·dies** ◆**v.** to cure, correct, make better, etc. [Some money would *remedy* her situation.] —**rem'e·died, rem'e·dy·ing**

**re·mem·ber** (ri mem'bər) ***v.*** **1** to think of again [I suddenly *remembered* I was supposed to mow the lawn.] **2** to bring back to mind by trying; recall [I just can't *remember* your name.] **3** to be careful not to forget [*Remember* to look both ways before crossing.] **4** to mention as sending greetings [*Remember* me to your family.] **5** to keep in mind for a gift, inheritance, etc. [She always *remembers* me on my birthday.]

> SYNONYMS: To **remember** is to bring back to mind something one has kept alive in one's memory [I'll always *remember* this day!] To **recall** or **recollect** is to make an effort to bring something back to mind. **Recall,** in addition, often suggests the telling to another of what is recalled [Let me *recall* for you what was said. Do you *recollect* those happy times we shared?]

**re·mem·brance** (ri mem'brəns) ***n.*** **1** the act of remembering; memory [I had no *remembrance* of what happened.] **2** a souvenir, keepsake, or memento. **3** **remembrances,** *pl.* greetings.

**re·mind** (ri mīnd') ***v.*** to make remember or think of [*Remind* me to pay the gas bill.]

**re·mind·er** (ri mīn'dər) ***n.*** a thing to help one remember something else.

**rem·i·nisce** (rem ə nis') ***v.*** to think, talk, or write about things in one's past. —**rem·i·nisced', rem·i·nisc'ing**

**rem·i·nis·cence** (rem ə nis''ns) ***n.*** **1** the act of remembering past experiences; recollection [The old couple's eyes sparkled in *reminiscence*.] **2** **reminiscences,** *pl.* a story telling about things remembered from one's past.

**rem·i·nis·cent** (rem'ə nis''nt) ***adj.*** **1** remembering past things [At our school reunion we grew *reminiscent*.] **2** causing one to remember [a perfume *reminiscent* of a flower garden]. —**rem'i·nis'cent·ly** ***adv.***

**re·miss** (ri mis') ***adj.*** careless in doing one's work or duty; negligent [The waiter was *remiss* in forgetting our salads.] —**re·miss'ness** ***n.***

**re·mis·sion** (ri mish'ən) ***n.*** **1** forgiveness, as of a sin; pardon. **2** a freeing or being freed from debt, tax, etc. **3** a making or becoming less strong or active [the *remission* of a fever].

**re·mit** (ri mit') ***v.*** **1** to send in payment [*Remit* fifty cents in coin.] **2** to make less or weaker; slacken [to keep working, without *remitting* one's efforts]. **3** to forgive or pardon [to *remit* a sin]. **4** to free someone from [to *remit* a prison sentence; to *remit* a debt]. —**re·mit'ted, re·mit'ting**

**re·mit·tance** (ri mit''ns) ***n.*** **1** money sent in payment. **2** the sending of such money, as by mail.

**rem·nant** (rem'nənt) ***n.*** what is left over, as a piece of cloth at the end of a bolt.

**re·mod·el** (rē mäd''l) ***v.*** to make over; rebuild [to *remodel* a kitchen]. —**re·mod'eled** or **re·mod'elled, re·mod'el·ing** or **re·mod'el·ling**

**re·mon·strance** (ri män'strəns) ***n.*** something said in objecting or complaining; protest.

**re·mon·strate** (ri män'strāt) ***v.*** to say or plead in objecting or protesting [Our teacher *remonstrated* with us for being late.] —**re·mon'strat·ed, re·mon'strat·ing**

**re·morse** (ri môrs') ***n.*** a deep feeling of sorrow or guilt over a wrong one has done [Did you feel any *remorse* after you lied to me?] —**re·morse'ful** ***adj.*** —**re·morse'less** ***adj.***

> **Remorse** comes from two Latin words that mean "to bite again." When one feels very guilty over doing something wrong, the thought of it may bite again and again into one's mind or heart.

**re·mote** (ri mōt') ***adj.*** **1** far off or far away in space or time; distant [a *remote* cabin in the woods]. **2** not closely related [Your question is *remote* from what we've been talking about. They are *remote* cousins.] **3** slight or faint [only a *remote* chance of winning]. —**re·mot'er, re·mot'est** —**re·mote'ly** ***adv.*** —**re·mote'ness** ***n.***

**re·mount** (rē mount') ***v.*** to mount again [to *remount* a horse].

**re·mov·al** (ri mo͞o'v'l) ***n.*** **1** a taking away or being taken away. **2** a dismissing or being dismissed [the *removal* from office of the mayor]. **3** the act of moving [the *removal* of a store to a new location].

**re·move** (ri mo͞ov') ***v.*** **1** to move to another place; take away or take off [*Remove* the rugs so we can dance. They *removed* their coats.] **2** to put out from an office or position; dismiss. **3** to get rid of [to *remove* a stain]. —**re·moved', re·mov'ing** ◆***n.*** a step, or short distance [a remark that was only one *remove* from an insult]. —**re·mov'a·ble** ***adj.*** —**re·mov'er** ***n.***

**re·mu·ner·ate** (ri myo͞o'nə rāt) ***v.*** to pay for work done, a loss suffered, etc.; reward [You will be *remunerated* for your help.] —**re·mu'ner·at·ed, re·mu'ner·at·ing** —**re·mu'ner·a'tion** ***n.***

**re·mu·ner·a·tive** (ri myo͞o'nə rāt'iv *or* ri myo͞o'nər ə tiv) ***adj.*** giving profit or reward [a *remunerative* business].

**Re·mus** (rē'məs) *see* **Romulus.**

**Ren·ais·sance** (ren'ə säns) ***n.*** **1** the great rebirth of art, literature, and learning in Europe in the 14th, 15th, and 16th centuries. **2** **renaissance,** any rebirth or revival like this.

**re·name** (rē nām') ***v.*** to give a new or different name to [Ceylon was *renamed* Sri Lanka.] —**re·named', re·nam'ing**

**re·nas·cence** (ri nas''ns *or* ri nās''ns) ***n.*** **1** a rebirth or revival [a *renascence* of interest in folk songs]. **2** **Renascence,** *another spelling of* **Renaissance.** —**re·nas'cent** ***adj.***

**rend** (rend) ***v.*** to tear, split, or pull apart with great force [The tree was *rent* by lightning.] —**rent, rend'·ing**

**ren·der** (ren'dər) ***v.*** **1** to give or present for someone to consider [to *render* a bill; to *render* an account of one's actions]. **2** to give up; surrender [to *render* up a city to the enemy]. **3** to give in return [to *render* good for evil]. **4** to give or pay as something owed [to *render* thanks]. **5** to cause to be; make [The illness *rendered* him helpless.] **6** to do or perform [to *render* first aid; to *render* a tune on the piano]. **7** to translate [to *render* a French novel into English]. **8** to melt down, as fat.

**ren·dez·vous** (rän'dā vo͞o) ***n.*** **1** a meeting place [The ice cream store is our favorite *rendezvous*.] **2** a place where troops, ships, etc. meet for battle maneuvers. **3** an agreement to meet at a certain time and place. **4** the meeting itself. *—pl.* **ren·dez·vous** (rän′dā vo͞oz) **◆v.** to come together at a rendezvous. —**ren·dez·voused** (rän′dā vo͞od), **ren·dez·vous·ing** (rän′dā vo͞o iŋ)

**ren·di·tion** (ren dish′ən) **n.** a rendering, as of a piece of music, a part in a play, etc.

**ren·e·gade** (ren′ə gād) **n.** a person who gives up his or her religion, political party, etc. and goes over to the opposite side; traitor.

**re·nege** (ri nig′) **v.** **1** to break the rules in a card game by playing a card of the wrong suit. **2** to break a promise. —**re·neged′**, **re·neg′ing**

**re·new** (ri no͞o′ *or* ri nyo͞o′) **v.** **1** to make new or fresh again; restore [*Renew* that old table by painting it.] **2** to begin again; start again after a break [The enemy *renewed* its attack.] **3** to put in a fresh supply of [to *renew* provisions]. **4** to give or get again for a new period of time [It is time to *renew* your subscription.] —**re·new′al n.**

SYNONYMS: To **renew** is to make something new again by replacing what is old, worn out, used up, etc. [The car is *renewed,* with new brakes and tires.] To **restore** is to put something back into its original or normal condition after it has worn out or fallen apart [The White House has been *restored.*]

**ren·net** (ren′it) **n.** a substance got from the stomach of a calf, etc., used to curdle milk, as in making cheese.

**Re·no** (rē′nō) a city in western Nevada.

**Re·noir** (ren′wär), **Pierre Auguste** 1841–1919; French painter.

**re·nounce** (ri nouns′) **v.** **1** to give up, as a claim or right [The king *renounced* the throne.] **2** to refuse to have anything more to do with; disown [He *renounced* his son.] —**re·nounced′**, **re·nounc′ing**

**ren·o·vate** (ren′ə vāt) **v.** to make new or like new; repair; restore [to *renovate* an old house]. —**ren′o·vat·ed**, **ren′o·vat·ing** —**ren′o·va′tion n.**

**re·nown** (ri noun′) **n.** great fame. —**re·nowned′ adj.**

**rent**[1] (rent) **n.** money paid at regular times for the use of a house, office, land, etc. **◆v.** **1** to get or give the use of a house, land, automobile, etc. in return for the regular payment of money. ☆**2** to be let for rent [This room *rents* for $30 a week.] —☆**for rent,** that may be rented. —**rent′er n.**

**rent**[2] (rent) *past tense and past participle of* **rend.** **◆adj.** torn or split. **◆n.** a tear, as in cloth; split.

**rent·al** (ren′t'l) **n.** **1** an amount paid as rent. **2** a house, automobile, etc. for rent. **◆adj.** of or for rent.

**re·nun·ci·a·tion** (ri nun′sē ā′shən) **n.** the act of renouncing a right, claim, etc.

**re·or·der** (rē ôr′dər) **n.** a repeated order for the same goods. **◆v.** **1** to order again. **2** to put in order again. **3** to order goods again.

**re·or·gan·ize** (rē ôr′gə nīz) **v.** to organize again or in a new way [to *reorganize* a company]. —**re·or′gan·ized**, **re·or′gan·iz·ing** —**re·or′gan·i·za′tion n.**

**Rep.** *abbreviation for* **Representative, Republican.**

**re·paid** (ri pād′) *past tense and past participle of* **repay.**

**re·pair**[1] (ri per′) **v.** **1** to put into good condition again; fix; mend [to *repair* a broken toy]. **2** to set right; correct [to *repair* a mistake; to *repair* an injustice]. **◆n.** **1** the act of repairing. **2** *usually* **repairs,** *pl.* work done in repairing [to make *repairs* on a house]. **3** the condition of being fit for use [We try to keep our car in *repair.*] **4** condition in relation to being repaired [a house in bad *repair*]. —**re·pair′a·ble adj.**

**re·pair**[2] (ri per′) **v.** to go: *now seldom used* [They have *repaired* to their cottage for the summer.]

**re·pair·man** (ri per′mən) **n.** a person whose work is repairing things. *—pl.* **re·pair′men**

**rep·a·ra·tion** (rep′ə rā′shən) **n.** **1** a making up for a wrong or injury. **2** something given or done to make up for damage done, especially by a defeated nation for damage done by it in a war.

**rep·ar·tee** (rep ər tē′) **n.** **1** a quick, witty reply. **2** a series of quick, witty replies. **3** skill in making such replies.

**Repartee** comes from a French word meaning "to return quickly a blow given one by another person." To make a quick, witty reply, in repartee, is like hitting back quickly at someone who has hit you.

**re·past** (ri past′) **n.** a meal, or food and drink for a meal.

**re·pa·tri·ate** (rē pā′trē āt) **v.** to send or bring back to one's native country [to *repatriate* prisoners of war]. —**re·pa′tri·at·ed**, **re·pa′tri·at·ing** —**re·pa′tri·a′tion n.**

**re·pay** (ri pā′) **v.** **1** to pay back [to *repay* a loan]. **2** to do or give something to someone in return for some favor, service, etc. received [to *repay* a kindness]. —**re·paid′**, **re·pay′ing** —**re·pay′ment n.**



**re·peal** (ri pēl′) **v.** to do away with; put an end to; cancel [to *repeal* a law]. **◆n.** the act of repealing.

**re·peat** (ri pēt′) **v.** **1** to say again [Will you *repeat* that question?] **2** to say over; recite [to *repeat* a poem]. **3** to tell to others [to *repeat* a secret]. **4** to do or perform again [to *repeat* a success]. **◆n.** **1** the act of repeating. **2** something repeated, as a part of a musical piece. —**repeat oneself,** to say again what one has already said.

**re·peat·ed** (ri pēt′id) **adj.** said, made, or done again or often [*repeated* warnings]. —**re·peat′ed·ly adv.**

**re·pel** (ri pel′) **v.** **1** to drive back [to *repel* an attack]. **2** to hold off; refuse; reject [She *repelled* his offer of help.] **3** to make feel disgusted [The odor *repelled* me.] **4** to make stay away [a spray to *repel* insects]. **5** to keep out; resist [a coating that *repels* water]. —**re·pelled′**, **re·pel′ling**

**re·pel·lent** (ri pel′ənt) **adj.** that repels in any of various ways [a *repellent* smell; a water-*repellent* jacket]. **◆n.** something that repels, as a spray that keeps insects away.

**re·pent** (ri pent′) **v.** **1** to feel sorry for having done wrong [He *repented* and returned the stolen bicycle.]

| | | | | | | | |
|---|---|---|---|---|---|---|---|
| **a** | fat | **ir** | here | **ou** | out | **zh** | leisure |
| **ā** | ape | **ī** | bite, fire | **u** | up | **ŋ** | ring |
| **ä** | car, lot | **ō** | go | **ʉr** | fur | | a *in* ago |
| **e** | ten | **ô** | law, horn | **ch** | chin | | e *in* agent |
| **er** | care | **oi** | oil | **sh** | she | **ə =** | i *in* unity |
| **ē** | even | **oo** | look | **th** | thin | | o *in* collect |
| **i** | hit | **o͞o** | tool | ***th*** | then | | u *in* focus |

**2** to feel regret over something done and change one's mind [He gave away his books, but later *repented* his generosity.]

**re·pent·ance** (ri pent'ʼns) ***n.*** a repenting, or feeling sorry, especially for doing wrong. —**re·pent'ant** ***adj.***

**re·per·cus·sion** (rē'pər kush'ən) ***n.*** **1** the bounding back of sound from a surface; echo. **2** a reaction to some happening, often an indirect one [His death had *repercussions* all over the world.]

**rep·er·toire** (rep'ər twär) ***n.*** all the plays, songs, or other pieces that a company, actor, singer, etc. is ready to perform.

**rep·er·to·ry** (rep'ər tôr'ē) ***n.*** *another word for* **repertoire.** —**rep'er·to'ries**

**rep·e·ti·tion** (rep'ə tish'ən) ***n.*** **1** the act of repeating, or of saying or doing something again. **2** something repeated.

**rep·e·ti·tious** (rep'ə tish'əs) ***adj.*** repeating, especially over and over again in a boring way.

**re·phrase** (rē frāz') ***v.*** to phrase again, especially in a different way. —**re·phrased', re·phras'ing**

**re·pine** (ri pīn') ***v.*** to feel or show that one is not happy or satisfied; complain; fret. —**re·pined', re·pin'ing**

**re·place** (ri plās') ***v.*** **1** to put back in the right place [*Replace* the tools on my bench when you are through.] **2** to take the place of [Many workers have been *replaced* by computers.] **3** to put another in the place of one used, lost, broken, etc. [to *replace* a worn tire]. —**re·placed', re·plac'ing**

**re·place·ment** (ri plās'mənt) ***n.*** **1** a replacing or being replaced. **2** a person or thing that takes the place of another.

**re·plen·ish** (ri plen'ish) ***v.*** to make full or complete again; furnish a new supply for [to *replenish* a wood pile]. —**re·plen'ish·ment** ***n.***

**re·plete** (ri plēt') ***adj.*** supplied with plenty of something; filled or stuffed [a novel *replete* with adventures]. —**re·ple'tion** ***n.***

**rep·li·ca** (rep'li kə) ***n.*** an exact copy, as of a painting, statue, etc.

**re·ply** (ri plī') ***v.*** to answer by saying or doing something [to *reply* to a question; to *reply* to the enemy's fire with a counterattack]. —**re·plied', re·ply'ing** ◆***n.*** an answer. —*pl.* **re·plies'**

**re·port** (ri pôrt') ***v.*** **1** to tell about; give an account of [I *reported* on my trip to the Falls.] **2** to tell as news [The papers *reported* little damage as a result of the storm.] **3** to tell about in a formal way; announce [The committee *reported* on plans for the dance.] **4** to tell a person in charge about a wrongdoer, a wrongdoing, etc. [to *report* a theft to the police]. **5** to be present at a certain place; appear [*Report* for work at 8 o'clock.] ◆***n.*** **1** an account of something, often one in written or printed form [a financial *report*]. **2** rumor or gossip [*Reports* of victory filled the air.] **3** reputation [a person of good *report*]. **4** the noise made by an explosion [the *report* of a gun].

**re·port·age** (ri pôrt'ij) ***n.*** the reporting of news events.

☆**report card** a written report of a student's grades, etc. sent to his or her parents or guardian at certain regular times.

**re·port·ed·ly** (ri pôrt'id lē) ***adv.*** according to report or reports.

**re·port·er** (ri pôrt'ər) ***n.*** a person who reports, especially one who gathers and writes about news for a newspaper or one who reports news on radio or TV.

**re·pose**[1] (ri pōz') ***v.*** **1** to lie at rest [to *repose* on a bed]. **2** to put to rest [to *repose* oneself on a sofa]. —**re·posed', re·pos'ing** ◆***n.*** **1** rest or sleep. **2** calm or peace [*repose* of mind].

**re·pose**[2] (ri pōz') ***v.*** **1** to place, as trust, in someone. **2** to place, as power, in the control of someone. —**re·posed', re·pos'ing**

**re·pos·i·to·ry** (ri päz'ə tôr'ē) ***n.*** a box, room, etc. in which things may be put for safekeeping. —*pl.* **re·pos'i·to'ries**

**re·pos·sess** (rē pə zes') ***v.*** to get possession of again; especially, to take back from a buyer who has failed to keep up payments [The loan company *repossessed* his car.]

**rep·re·hend** (rep'ri hend') ***v.*** **1** to scold or rebuke. **2** to find fault with; blame.

**rep·re·hen·si·ble** (rep'ri hen'sə b'l) ***adj.*** deserving to be scolded, blamed, etc. [a *reprehensible* act or person].

**rep·re·sent** (rep'ri zent') ***v.*** **1** to stand for; be a symbol of [Three dots *represent* "S" in the Morse code.] **2** to show or picture [The artist *represented* America as a woman holding a torch.] **3** to act in place of [My lawyer will *represent* me in court.] **4** to act the part of, as in a play. **5** to serve as or be like [A tent *represents* home to them.] **6** to be an example of [That restaurant *represents* the best the town has to offer.] **7** to describe or set forth [He *represented* himself as an expert.] **8** to act and speak for [She was elected to *represent* us in Congress.]

**rep·re·sen·ta·tion** (rep'ri zen tā'shən) ***n.*** **1** a representing or being represented. **2** a likeness, picture, image, etc. **3 representations,** *pl.* a list of facts, charges, etc. meant to convince someone or to protest something. **4** representatives as a group [our *representation* in Congress]. —**rep're·sen·ta'tion·al** ***adj.***

**rep·re·sent·a·tive** (rep'rə zen'tə tiv) ***adj.*** **1** representing; standing for [a sculptured figure *representative* of Justice]. **2** based on representation of the people by delegates [*representative* government]. **3** being an example; typical [This building is *representative* of modern architecture.] ◆***n.*** **1** a typical example. **2** a person chosen to act or speak for others [Judy is our *representative* on the student council.] ☆**3 Representative,** a member of the lower house of Congress or of a State legislature.

**re·press** (ri pres') ***v.*** **1** to hold back [to *repress* a sigh]. **2** to put or hold down; subdue [to *repress* a revolt]. **3** to force out of one's mind [to *repress* sad thoughts]. **4** to control strictly and keep from behaving naturally [to *repress* a child]. —**re·pres'sion** ***n.***

**re·pres·sive** (ri pres'iv) ***adj.*** that represses or tends to repress [a *repressive* law].

**re·prieve** (ri prēv') ***v.*** **1** to delay the execution of a person sentenced to die. **2** to give relief to for a while, as from trouble or pain. —**re·prieved', re·priev'ing** ◆***n.*** a reprieving or being reprieved; a delay, as in carrying out an execution.

**rep·ri·mand** (rep'rə mand) ***n.*** a harsh or formal scolding, as by a person in authority. ◆***v.*** to scold harshly or in a formal way.

**re·print** (rē print′) ***v.*** to publish again, as a new printing of a book, pamphlet, etc. ◆***n.*** (rē′print) something reprinted.

**re·pris·al** (ri prī′z'l) ***n.*** a harmful thing done to another to get even for some wrong done to one, as in war by one nation to another.

**re·proach** (ri prōch′) ***v.*** to find fault with; blame; rebuke [She *reproached* me for spending too much.] ◆***n.*** **1** shame or a cause of shame [Slums are a *reproach* to a city.] **2** a scolding or blaming; rebuke. —**re·proach′ful** ***adj.*** —**re·proach′ful·ly** ***adv.***

**rep·ro·bate** (rep′rə bāt) ***n.*** a very bad or dishonest person; scoundrel.

**rep·ro·ba·tion** (rep′rə bā′shən) ***n.*** the act of finding fault; strong blame or disapproval.

**re·pro·duce** (rē prə do͞os′ *or* rē prə dyo͞os′) ***v.*** **1** to produce again. **2** to produce others of one's kind; have offspring [Most animals *reproduce* by fertilizing eggs.] **3** to make a copy or imitation of [Tape recorders *reproduce* sound.] —**re·pro·duced′, re·pro·duc′ing**

**re·pro·duc·tion** (rē′prə duk′shən) ***n.*** **1** a reproducing or being reproduced. **2** a copy or imitation [a *reproduction* of an ancient statue]. **3** the process by which animals and plants produce others of their kind. —**re′pro·duc′tive** ***adj.***

**re·proof** (ri pro͞of′) ***n.*** the act of reproving or something said in reproving; blame; rebuke.

**re·prove** (ri pro͞ov′) ***v.*** to find fault with; scold [She *reproved* them for being so rude.] —**re·proved′, re·prov′ing**

**rep·tile** (rep′t'l *or* rep′tīl) ***n.*** **1** a coldblooded animal that has a backbone and crawls on its belly or creeps on very short legs. Snakes, lizards, alligators, and turtles are reptiles. **2** a mean, sneaky person.

**re·pub·lic** (ri pub′lik) ***n.*** a state or nation in which the voters elect officials to make the laws and run the government.

**re·pub·li·can** (ri pub′li kən) ***adj.*** **1** of or having to do with a republic [a *republican* form of government]. ☆**2 Republican,** of or belonging to the Republican Party. ◆***n.*** **1** a person who believes in and supports a republic. ☆**2 Republican,** a member of the Republican Party.

☆**Republican Party** one of the two major political parties in the U.S.

**re·pu·di·ate** (ri pyo͞o′dē āt) ***v.*** **1** to refuse to have anything to do with. **2** to refuse to accept or support [to *repudiate* a belief]. **3** to refuse to pay, as a debt. —**re·pu′di·at·ed, re·pu′di·at·ing** —**re·pu′di·a′tion** ***n.***

> **Repudiate** comes from the Latin word for divorce or separation. Persons who get a divorce or separation usually refuse to have anything more to do with each other.

**re·pug·nant** (ri pug′nənt) ***adj.*** **1** that makes one feel great dislike or distaste; disgusting [a *repugnant* odor]. **2** opposed [conduct *repugnant* to his character]. —**re·pug′nance** ***n.***

**re·pulse** (ri puls′) ***v.*** **1** to drive back; repel, as an attack. **2** to act toward in an unfriendly or impolite way [She *repulsed* her former friends.] —**re·pulsed′, re·puls′ing** ◆***n.*** **1** a repulsing or being repulsed. **2** a refusal or rebuff.

**re·pul·sion** (ri pul′shən) ***n.*** **1** the act of repulsing. **2** strong dislike or disgust.

**re·pul·sive** (ri pul′siv) ***adj.*** causing strong dislike or disgust; disgusting [*repulsive* manners]. —**re·pul′sive·ly** ***adv.***

**rep·u·ta·ble** (rep′yoo tə b'l) ***adj.*** having a good reputation; respected [a *reputable* lawyer].

**rep·u·ta·tion** (rep′yoo tā′shən) ***n.*** **1** what people generally think about the character of a person or thing [She has a *reputation* for being a good doctor.] **2** good character in the opinion of others; good name [Gossip ruined his *reputation.*] **3** fame [Her *reputation* as an artist has grown.]

**re·pute** (ri pyo͞ot′) ***n.*** *same as* **reputation** *in meanings* 1, 3. ◆***v.*** to think or consider generally; suppose [She is *reputed* to be very learned.] —**re·put′ed, re·put′ing**

**re·put·ed** (ri pyo͞ot′id) ***adj.*** generally thought of as such; supposed [the *reputed* author of the book]. —**re·put′ed·ly** ***adv.***

**re·quest** (ri kwest′) ***v.*** **1** to ask for [to *request* a hearing]. **2** to ask to do something [She *requested* him to shut the door.] ◆***n.*** **1** the act of requesting [a *request* for help]. **2** what is asked for [Will you grant our *request?*] **3** the condition of being wanted or asked for; demand [Is this song much in *request?*] —**by request,** in answer to a request [He sang *by request.*]

**Re·qui·em** or **re·qui·em** (rek′wē əm *or* räk′wē əm) ***n.*** **1** a Roman Catholic Mass for a dead person or persons. **2** the music for such a Mass.

**re·quire** (ri kwīr′) ***v.*** **1** to be in need of [Most plants *require* sunlight.] *See* SYNONYMS *at* **lack.** **2** to order, command, or insist upon [He *required* us to leave.] —**re·quired′, re·quir′ing**



**re·quire·ment** (ri kwīr′mənt) ***n.*** **1** the act of requiring. **2** something needed or demanded [Vitamins are a *requirement* in the diet. Does she meet the *requirements* for the job?]

**req·ui·site** (rek′wə zit) ***adj.*** needed for some purpose; required [Has he the training *requisite* for a nurse?] ◆***n.*** something needed [a tent and other *requisites* for camping].

**req·ui·si·tion** (rek′wə zish′ən) ***n.*** **1** an order or request, especially in writing [Do you have a *requisition* for these supplies?] **2** the act of requiring. ◆***v.*** to demand or take, as by authority [The general *requisitioned* trucks for the troops.]

**re·quit·al** (ri kwīt′'l) ***n.*** something given or done in return; repayment, reward, or retaliation.

**re·quite** (ri kwīt′) ***v.*** to pay back; reward [How can we *requite* them for their help?] —**re·quit′ed, re·quit′ing**

**re·route** (rē ro͞ot′ *or* rē rout′) ***v.*** to send by a new or different route. —**re·rout′ed, re·rout′ing**

**re·run** (rē run′) ***v.*** to run again. —**re·ran′, re·run′ning** ◆***n.*** (rē′run) ☆**1** a repeat showing of a movie, taped TV program, etc. ☆**2** the movie, etc. so shown.

| | | | | | | | |
|---|---|---|---|---|---|---|---|
| **a** | fat | **ir** | here | **ou** | out | **zh** | leisure |
| **ā** | ape | **ī** | bite, fire | **u** | up | **ŋ** | ring |
| **ä** | car, lot | **ō** | go | **ʉr** | fur | | a *in* ago |
| **e** | ten | **ô** | law, horn | **ch** | chin | | e *in* agent |
| **er** | care | **oi** | oil | **sh** | she | **ə =** | i *in* unity |
| **ē** | even | **o͝o** | look | **th** | thin | | o *in* collect |
| **i** | hit | **o͞o** | tool | ***th*** | then | | u *in* focus |

**re·scind** (ri sind′) ***v.*** to do away with; set aside; cancel; repeal [to *rescind* a law].

**res·cue** (res′kyo͞o) ***v.*** to free or save from danger, evil, etc. [to *rescue* people from a burning building]. ◆***n.*** the act of rescuing. —**res′cued, res′cu·ing** —**res′cu·er** ***n.***

**re·search** (ri surch′ *or* rē′surch) ***n.*** careful, patient study in order to find out facts and principles about some subject [to carry on *research* into the causes of cancer]. ◆***v.*** to do research.

**re·sem·blance** (ri zem′bləns) ***n.*** the condition or fact of being or looking alike; likeness.

**re·sem·ble** (ri zem′b'l) ***v.*** to be or look like [Rabbits *resemble* hares but are smaller.] —**re·sem′bled, re·sem′bling**

**re·sent** (ri zent′) ***v.*** to feel a bitter hurt and anger about [He *resented* my forgetting our date.] —**re·sent′ful** ***adj.*** —**re·sent′ful·ly** ***adv.***

**re·sent·ment** (ri zent′mənt) ***n.*** a feeling of bitter hurt and anger at being insulted, slighted, etc. [He felt great *resentment* at being left out.]

**res·er·va·tion** (rez′ər vā′shən) ***n.*** **1** the act of reserving or keeping back. **2** an objection or thought that one does not tell [He signed the pledge without any *reservation*.] ☆**3** public land set aside for some special use [an Indian *reservation*]. ☆**4** an arrangement by which a hotel room, plane ticket, etc. is set aside until the buyer calls for it; also, anything set aside in this way.



**re·serve** (ri zurv′) ***v.*** **1** to keep back or set apart for later or special use [to *reserve* part of one's pay for emergencies]. **2** to have set aside for oneself [Call the theater and *reserve* two seats.] **3** to keep back for oneself [I *reserve* the right to refuse.] —**re·served′, re·serv′ing** ◆***n.*** **1** something kept back or stored up, as for later use [a bank's cash *reserve*]. **2** the habit of keeping one's thoughts to oneself; silent manner. **3** **reserves,** *pl.* troops held out of action so that they can be used later; also, units in the armed forces whose members are in civilian life but can be called up for active duty when they are needed. ☆**4** land set apart for a special purpose [a forest *reserve*]. —**in reserve,** reserved for later use or for some person. —**without reserve,** without keeping back anything [She told us everything, *without reserve*.]

**re·served** (ri zurvd′) ***adj.*** **1** set apart for some purpose, person, etc. [*reserved* seats]. **2** keeping one's thoughts to oneself; reticent.

**res·er·voir** (rez′ər vwär *or* rez′ə vôr) ***n.*** **1** a place where something, especially water, is collected and stored for use. **2** a container for a liquid [the ink *reservoir* of a fountain pen]. **3** a large supply [a *reservoir* of workers].

**re·side** (ri zīd′) ***v.*** **1** to make one's home; dwell; live [to *reside* in the suburbs]. **2** to be present or fixed [The power to tax *resides* in Congress.] —**re·sid′ed, re·sid′ing**

**res·i·dence** (rez′i dəns) ***n.*** **1** the place where one resides; home. **2** the fact or time of residing or living in a certain place.

**res·i·dent** (rez′i dənt) ***n.*** a person who lives in a place, not just a visitor. ◆***adj.*** living or staying in a place, as while working [a *resident* physician in a hospital].

**res·i·den·tial** (rez′ə den′shəl) ***adj.*** **1** used for residences, or homes, not businesses [a *residential* area]. **2** of or having to do with residence [a *residential* requirement for voting]. ☆**3** mainly for residents rather than visitors [a *residential* hotel].

**re·sid·u·al** (ri zij′o͝o wəl) ***adj.*** of or being a residue; left over; remaining [a *residual* portion].

**res·i·due** (rez′ə do͞o *or* rez′ə dyo͞o) ***n.*** what is left after part is taken away, burned, dried up, etc.; remainder [a *residue* of ashes].

**re·sign** (ri zīn′) ***v.*** to give up one's office, position, membership, etc. [We *resigned* from the club.] —**resign oneself,** to accept something without complaining; submit.

**res·ig·na·tion** (rez′ig nā′shən) ***n.*** **1** the act of resigning. **2** a written statement that one is resigning. **3** calm or patient acceptance of something without complaining [to endure trouble with *resignation*].

**re·signed** (ri zīnd′) ***adj.*** feeling or showing resignation; accepting patiently what happens.

**re·sil·ient** (ri zil′yənt) ***adj.*** **1** springing back into shape, position, etc.; elastic. **2** getting back strength, spirits, etc. quickly. —**re·sil′ience** or **re·sil′ien·cy** ***n.***

**res·in** (rez′'n) ***n.*** **1** a sticky substance that comes out of certain plants and trees, as the pines. Natural resins are used in medicines, varnish, etc. **2** a similar substance made from chemicals and used in making plastics. **3** *another word for* **rosin.** —**res′in·ous** ***adj.***

**re·sist** (ri zist′) ***v.*** **1** to fight or work against; oppose [to *resist* an invasion]. *See* SYNONYMS *at* **oppose.** **2** to hold off successfully; withstand [Gold *resists* rust.] **3** to refuse to give in to [He *resisted* the temptation and ate no dessert.]

**re·sist·ance** (ri zis′təns) ***n.*** **1** the act of resisting. **2** the power to resist or withstand [Her *resistance* to colds is low.] **3** the opposing of one force or thing to another [the fabric's *resistance* to wear]. **4** the power of a substance to oppose the flow of electrical current and in that way create heat.

**re·sist·ant** (ri zis′tənt) ***adj.*** that offers resistance; resisting [fire-*resistant* paint].

**re·sist·less** (ri zist′lis) ***adj.*** that cannot be resisted; irresistible [a *resistless* force].

**res·o·lute** (rez′ə lo͞ot) ***adj.*** having or showing a fixed purpose; determined; not yielding [with a *resolute* look on her face]. —**res′o·lute·ly** ***adv.***

**res·o·lu·tion** (rez′ə lo͞o′shən) ***n.*** **1** the act of resolving something. **2** something decided upon [his *resolution* to work harder]. **3** a formal statement by a group, giving its opinion or decision. **4** the fact of being resolute; determination [Don't hesitate—act with *resolution*.] **5** the act of solving; answer or solution [the *resolution* of a problem].

**re·solve** (ri zälv′) ***v.*** **1** to decide; make up one's mind [I *resolved* to help them.] **2** to make clear; solve or explain [to *resolve* a problem]. **3** to decide by a vote [It was *resolved* at the meeting to raise club dues.] **4** to change; turn into [The conversation *resolved* itself into an argument.] **5** to break up into separate parts [to *resolve* water into hydrogen and oxygen]. —**re·solved′, re·solv′ing** ◆***n.*** something decided on in a firm way; intention [her *resolve* to be a dancer].

**re·solved** (ri zälvd′) ***adj.*** determined; firm.

**res·o·nance** (rez′ə nəns) ***n.*** **1** the quality of being resonant. **2** the strong, rich effect of a sound when it is reflected or when it causes some object to vibrate [The body of a violin gives the tones *resonance*.]

**res·o·nant** (rez′ə nənt) ***adj.*** **1** rich, full, or deep [the *resonant* sound of a tuba; a *resonant* voice]. **2** making sounds richer or fuller [*resonant* walls].

**re·sort** (ri zôrt′) ***v.*** **1** to turn for help [It would be wrong to *resort* to force to gain our end.] **2** to go, especially often [Folks *resort* to parks in the summer.] ◆***n.*** **1** a place where many people go, as for a vacation [a winter *resort* for skiing]. **2** the act of turning for help. **3** a person or thing that one turns to for help [Sue is our last *resort* for a loan.] *See* SYNONYMS *at* **resource.**

**re·sound** (ri zound′) ***v.*** **1** to echo or be filled with sound [The hall *resounded* with music.] **2** to make a loud, echoing sound; to be echoed [His laughter *resounded* throughout the cave.]

**re·source** (rē′sôrs *or* ri sôrs′) ***n.*** **1** a supply of something to take care of a need [Our main *resource* during illness is insurance. Oil is a valuable natural *resource*.] **2** skill in solving problems or getting out of trouble [It takes great *resource* to survive in the woods.]

**Resource** can be used of any thing, person, or action to which one turns in time of need or emergency [We have several *resources* from whom we can seek a loan.] **Resort** is usually used of a final resource [I'll go by bicycle as a last *resort*.]

**re·source·ful** (ri sôrs′fəl) ***adj.*** skillful at solving problems or getting out of trouble. —**re·source′ful·ly** ***adv.*** —**re·source′ful·ness** ***n.***

**re·spect** (ri spekt′) ***v.*** **1** to feel or show honor for; think highly of; look up to [We *respect* learned people.] *See* SYNONYMS *at* **regard.** **2** to be thoughtful about; have regard for [to *respect* others' rights]. ◆***n.*** **1** a feeling of honor or polite regard [He has great *respect* for his father.] **2** concern; consideration [She had *respect* for our feelings.] **3 respects,** *pl.* a polite showing of respect; regards [We must pay our *respects* to the hostess.] **4** a particular point or detail [In that *respect* he's wrong.] **5** relation or reference [with *respect* to the problem].

**re·spect·a·ble** (ri spek′tə b'l) ***adj.*** **1** having a good reputation; decent, proper, correct, etc. **2** fairly good or large; good enough [a *respectable* score for an amateur; a *respectable* pair of shoes]. —**re·spect′a·bil′i·ty** ***n.*** —**re·spect′a·bly** ***adv.***

**re·spect·ful** (ri spekt′fəl) ***adj.*** feeling or showing respect; polite. —**re·spect′ful·ly** ***adv.***

**re·spect·ing** (ri spek′tiŋ) ***prep.*** about; concerning [I know little *respecting* the plan.]

**re·spec·tive** (ri spek′tiv) ***adj.*** of or for each separately [They went their *respective* ways.]

**re·spec·tive·ly** (ri spek′tiv lē) ***adv.*** in regard to each in the order named [The first and second prizes went to Merle and Sonia, *respectively*.]

**res·pi·ra·tion** (res′pə rā′shən) ***n.*** **1** the act or process of breathing. **2** the process by which a living thing takes in oxygen from the air or water and gives off carbon dioxide, etc.

**res·pi·ra·tor** (res′pə rāt′ər) ***n.*** a device for helping one to breathe, as in giving artificial respiration. *See the picture.*

**res·pi·ra·to·ry** (res′pər ə tôr′ē *or* ri spīr′ə tôr′ē) ***adj.*** having to do with breathing [Emphysema is a *respiratory* disease.]

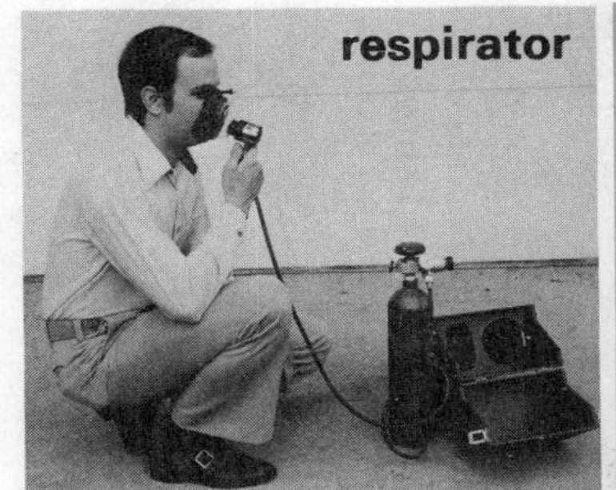

respirator

musical rests

**re·spire** (ri spīr′) ***v.*** to breathe; inhale and exhale. —**re·spired′, re·spir′ing**

**res·pite** (res′pit) ***n.*** **1** a period of relief or rest, as from pain, work, or duty; a pause [The workers kept digging without *respite*.] **2** a delay or postponement, especially in carrying out a sentence of death.

**re·splend·ent** (ri splen′dənt) ***adj.*** shining brightly; dazzling. —**re·splend′ence** ***n.***

**re·spond** (ri spänd′) ***v.*** **1** to answer; reply [You didn't *respond* to my question.] **2** to act as if in answer; react [His infection is *responding* to treatment.]

**re·sponse** (ri späns′) ***n.*** **1** something said or done in answer; reply [We hailed the ship, but got no *response*. I came in *response* to your letter.] **2** words sung or spoken by the congregation or choir in answer to the minister, rabbi, or priest during religious worship.

**re·spon·si·bil·i·ty** (ri spän′sə bil′ə tē) ***n.*** **1** the condition of being responsible [He accepted *responsibility* for the error.] **2** a thing or person that one is supposed to look after, manage, etc. [Her education will be my *responsibility*.] —*pl.* **re·spon′si·bil′i·ties**



**re·spon·si·ble** (ri spän′sə b'l) ***adj.*** **1** supposed or expected to take care of something or do something [Harry is *responsible* for mowing the lawn.] **2** that must get the credit or blame [All of us are *responsible* for our own actions.] **3** having to do with important duties [a *responsible* job]. **4** that can be trusted or depended upon; reliable [a *responsible* person].

**re·spon·sive** (ri spän′siv) ***adj.*** **1** quick to respond; reacting quickly and easily in an understanding way [We had a very *responsive* audience.] **2** containing responses [a *responsive* prayer]. **3** answering [a *responsive* nod].

**rest**[1] (rest) ***n.*** **1** the act or period of taking one's ease after working or being active, as by sleeping, keeping still, etc. **2** freedom from worry, trouble, pain, etc.; peace of mind. **3** the condition of being still, or not moving [Her golf ball came to *rest* near the hole.] **4** a thing or device used to hold something up; support [a foot*rest*]. **5** a fixed pause between musical notes; also, a symbol for such a pause [There are *rests* that are equal to whole notes, half notes, etc.] *See the picture.* ◆***v.*** **1** to take one's ease and become refreshed,

| | | | | | | | | |
|---|---|---|---|---|---|---|---|---|
| **a** fat | **ir** here | **ou** out | **zh** leisure | |
| **ā** ape | **ī** bite, fire | **u** up | **ŋ** ring | |
| **ä** car, lot | **ō** go | **ʉr** fur | | a *in* ago |
| **e** ten | **ô** law, horn | **ch** chin | | e *in* agent |
| **er** care | **oi** oil | **sh** she | **ə =** | i *in* unity |
| **ē** even | **oo** look | **th** thin | | o *in* collect |
| **i** hit | **ōō** tool | ***th*** then | | u *in* focus |

retrorockets

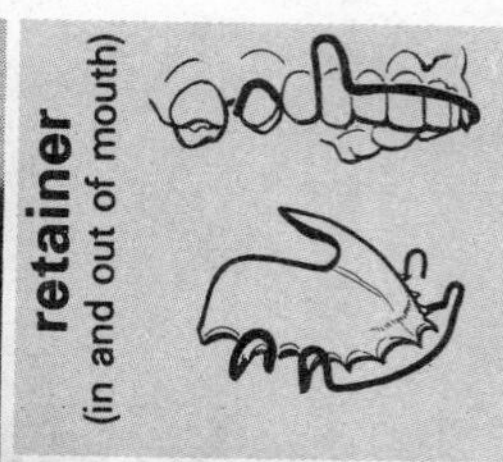
retainer (in and out of mouth)

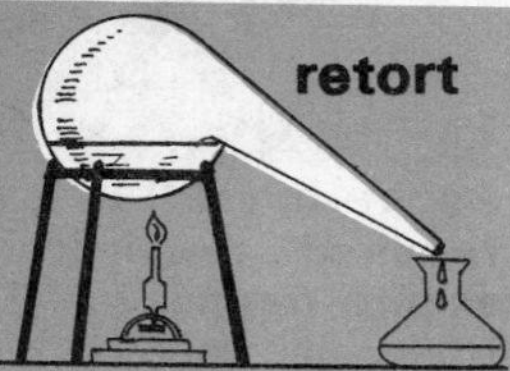
retort

as by sleeping, keeping still, etc. **2** to give rest to; refresh with rest [to *rest* a horse]. **3** to support or be supported; lie or lay; lean [*Rest* your head on the pillow. The hoe *rested* against the fence.] **4** to be at ease; have peace of mind [She couldn't *rest* till she found it.] **5** to be dead [to *rest* in one's grave]. **6** to be or become still or quiet or to stay unchanged [Let the matter *rest*.] **7** to be or lie [The fault *rests* with him.] **8** to be fixed [His eyes *rested* on the picture.] **9** to depend; rely [Success often *rests* on luck.] **10** to finish presenting evidence in a law court. —**lay to**
628 **rest,** to bury a dead body.

**rest²** (rest) ***n.*** **1** the part left over; remainder [Eat what you want and save the *rest* for later.] **2** those that are left; the others: *used with a plural verb* [Some of you take this path; the *rest* follow me.] ✦***v.*** to go on being; remain [*Rest* assured that I'll be there.]

**re·state** (rē stāt′) ***v.*** to state again, especially in a new way [He *restated* the question as a riddle.] —**re·stat′ed, re·stat′ing —re·state′ment *n.***

☆**res·tau·rant** (res′tə rənt *or* res′tə ränt) ***n.*** a place where meals can be bought and eaten.

> **Restaurant** comes from the French word for "restore." When we go to a restaurant to eat, we hope to have our strength and energy restored.

**rest·ful** (rest′fəl) ***adj.*** **1** full of rest or letting one rest [a *restful* vacation]. **2** quiet; peaceful [*restful* music].

**res·ti·tu·tion** (res′tə to͞o′shən *or* res′tə tyo͞o′shən) ***n.*** the act of giving back or paying for what has been lost, taken away, damaged, etc. [The thief made *restitution* for the stolen goods.]

**res·tive** (res′tiv) ***adj.*** **1** hard to control; unruly [a *restive* horse]. **2** restless; nervous [The long wait made us *restive*.]

**rest·less** (rest′lis) ***adj.*** **1** seldom at rest or quiet [the *restless* ocean waves]. **2** unable to rest; moving about fitfully [a *restless* sick child]. **3** without rest; disturbed or disturbing [a *restless* sleep]. —**rest′less·ly *adv.*** —**rest′less·ness *n.***

**res·to·ra·tion** (res′tə rā′shən) ***n.*** **1** the act of restoring or the condition of being restored. **2** something restored, as by rebuilding [This historic 17th-century fort is a *restoration*.]

**re·stor·a·tive** (ri stôr′ə tiv) ***adj.*** able to restore health, strength, etc. [a *restorative* medicine]. ✦***n.*** something that is restorative.

**re·store** (ri stôr′) ***v.*** **1** to give back [She *restored* the lost dog to its owner.] **2** to bring back to an earlier or normal condition, as by rebuilding [to *restore* an old house; to *restore* one's health]. *See* SYNONYMS *at* **renew. 3** to put back in a place, rank, etc. [to *restore* a king to power]. —**re·stored′, re·stor′ing**

**re·strain** (ri strān′) ***v.*** to hold back; keep under control; check [*Restrain* your temper. You can *restrain* that dog by using a leash.]

**re·straint** (ri strānt′) ***n.*** **1** the act of restraining or the condition of being restrained [no *restraint* of action; kept in *restraint*]. **2** something that restrains [The reins on a horse are used as a *restraint*.] **3** control of oneself or one's feelings; reserve [It takes *restraint* to be calm in a crisis.]

**re·strict** (ri strikt′) ***v.*** to keep within certain limits; confine; limit [The use of the pool is *restricted* to members.] —**re·strict′ed *adj.***

**re·stric·tion** (ri strik′shən) ***n.*** **1** something that restricts, as a rule or condition [to place *restrictions* on the sale of drugs]. **2** the act of restricting or the condition of being restricted.

**re·stric·tive** (ri strik′tiv) ***adj.*** **1** that restricts; limiting [*restrictive* laws]. **2** describing a clause, phrase, or word that is necessary to the meaning of a sentence and that is not set off by commas. Example: The person *who wrote the letter* didn't sign it.

☆**rest·room** (rest′ro͞om) ***n.*** a room in a public building, containing toilets and washbowls; lavatory. *Also written* **rest room.**

**re·sult** (ri zult′) ***v.*** **1** to happen because of something else [Floods may *result* from heavy rains.] **2** to end as a result [The argument *resulted* in a fight.] ✦***n.*** **1** anything caused by something else; effect; outcome [The juggler's skill is the *result* of practice.] **2** the answer to a problem in mathematics.

**re·sult·ant** (ri zul′tənt) ***adj.*** resulting; coming as a result [war and its *resultant* agony]. ✦***n.*** a result.

**re·sume** (ri zo͞om′ *or* ri zyo͞om′) ***v.*** **1** to take or occupy again [We *resumed* our seats after the intermission.] **2** to begin again; continue [The baseball game will be *resumed* when the rain stops.] —**re·sumed′, re·sum′ing**

**ré·su·mé** (rez′oo mā′ *or* rā′zoo mā′) ***n.*** **1** a brief report that tells the main points. ☆**2** a record of the work experience and education of a person applying for a job. *Also written* **resumé.**

**re·sump·tion** (ri zump′shən) ***n.*** the act of resuming [the *resumption* of classes after vacation].

**res·ur·rect** (rez′ə rekt′) ***v.*** **1** to bring back to life. **2** to bring back into use [to *resurrect* an old custom].

**res·ur·rec·tion** (rez′ə rek′shən) ***n.*** **1** in religious belief, the act of rising from the dead, or coming back to life. **2** a coming back into use; revival. —**the Resurrection,** the rising of Jesus from the dead.

**re·sus·ci·tate** (ri sus′ə tāt) ***v.*** to bring back to life or consciousness; revive [The firefighters *resuscitated* the baby overcome by smoke.] —**re·sus′ci·tat·ed, re·sus′ci·tat·ing —re·sus′ci·ta′tion *n.***

**re·tail** (rē′tāl) ***n.*** the sale of goods in small amounts to actual users, not to those who will resell them. ✦***adj.*** of or having to do with such sale of goods [a *retail* store; a *retail* price]. ✦***v.*** **1** to sell or be sold in small amounts. **2** (ri tāl′) to repeat to others [to *retail* gossip]. —**re′tail·er *n.***

**Retail** comes from an old French word that means "to cut up in parts." The retailer buys a large lot of goods from a wholesaler, who sells the "whole" lot, then divides, or "cuts," it into units to sell to individual customers.

**re·tain** (ri tān′) ***v.*** **1** to keep or hold [Gerry *retained* a firm grip on the rope. This oven *retains* heat well.] **2** to keep in mind; remember [He *retains* what he reads.] **3** to hire by paying a fee to [to *retain* a lawyer].

**re·tain·er** (ri tā′nər) ***n.*** **1** a fee paid beforehand to get the services of a lawyer, etc. when they are needed. **2** a servant in a rich household. **3** a person or thing that retains, especially a device that holds teeth in place after they have been straightened as by braces. *See the picture.*

**re·take** (rē tāk′) ***v.*** **1** to take again, take back, or recapture. ☆**2** to photograph again. —**re·took′, re·tak′en, re·tak′ing** ✦***n.*** (rē′tāk) ☆a scene in a movie, etc. photographed again.

**re·tal·i·ate** (ri tal′ē āt) ***v.*** to harm or do wrong in return for harm or wrong done [If a bear is hurt, it will *retaliate.*] —**re·tal′i·at·ed, re·tal′i·at·ing** —**re·tal′i·a′tion** ***n.***

**re·tal·i·a·to·ry** (ri tal′ē ə tôr′ē) ***adj.*** retaliating; paying back one wrong with another.

**re·tard** (ri tärd′) ***v.*** to slow down or delay [to *retard* a musical phrase; to *retard* development]. —**re′tar·da′tion** ***n.***

**re·tard·ed** (ri tär′did) ***adj.*** having from the time of birth a slow mind that makes it difficult to learn easily. *The full phrase is* **mentally retarded.**

**retch** (rech) ***v.*** to undergo the straining action of vomiting, especially without bringing anything up.

**re·ten·tion** (ri ten′shən) ***n.*** **1** the act of retaining or the fact of being retained. **2** the ability to retain.

**re·ten·tive** (ri ten′tiv) ***adj.*** able to hold, keep, or remember [a *retentive* mind]. —**re·ten′tive·ness** ***n.***

**ret·i·cent** (ret′ə s′nt) ***adj.*** not saying much, especially about one's thoughts. —**ret′i·cence** ***n.***

**ret·i·na** (ret′'n ə) ***n.*** the part at the back of the eyeball, made up of special cells that react to light. The image picked up by the lens of the eye is formed on the retina. *See the picture for* **eye.**

**Retina** comes from the Latin word for "net," because the retina has a fine network of tiny nerve fibers that help to pick up the image of what is seen by the eye.

**ret·i·nue** (ret′'n ōō *or* ret′'n yōō) ***n.*** the servants or followers of an important person.

**re·tire** (ri tīr′) ***v.*** **1** to give up one's work, business, or career, especially because of age [Dr. Miller is 84, but refuses to *retire.*] **2** to remove from a position or office [to *retire* a general]. **3** to go where it is quieter and more private [He *retired* to the library after dinner.] **4** to go to bed. **5** to retreat, as in battle. **6** to take out of circulation, as bonds. ☆**7** to end the batting turn of a batter or side. —**re·tired′, re·tir′ing** —**re·tire′ment** ***n.***

**re·tired** (ri tīrd′) ***adj.*** **1** that has given up one's work, business, or career, especially because of age [a *retired* teacher]. **2** hidden or private [a *retired* cabin].

**re·tir·ing** (ri tīr′ing) ***adj.*** drawing back from being with others or attracting attention; shy; reserved.

☆**re·tool** (rē tōōl′) ***v.*** to change the machinery of a factory for making a different product.

**re·tort**[1] (ri tôrt′) ***v.*** to answer back, especially in a sharp or clever way. ✦***n.*** a sharp or clever answer.

**re·tort**[2] (ri tôrt′) ***n.*** a container with a long tube, in which substances are distilled or decomposed by heat. *See the picture.*

**re·touch** (rē tuch′) ***v.*** to change some of the details, as in a photograph, in order to make it look better.

**re·trace** (ri trās′) ***v.*** **1** to go over again back to the start [to *retrace* one's steps]. **2** to trace again the story of, from the beginning. —**re·traced′, re·trac′ing**

**re-trace** (rē′trās′) ***v.*** to trace over again, as the lines in a drawing. —**re′-traced′, re′-trac′ing**

**re·tract** (ri trakt′) ***v.*** **1** to draw back or draw in [The turtle can *retract* its head into its shell.] **2** to take back a statement, promise, offer, etc. —**re·tract′a·ble** ***adj.*** —**re·trac′tion** ***n.***

**re·trac·tile** (ri trak′t'l) ***adj.*** that can be drawn back in [A cat's claws are *retractile.*]

**re·tread** (rē tred′; *for n.* rē′tred) ***v., n.*** *another word for* **recap.**

**re·treat** (ri trēt′) ***n.*** **1** the act of going back or backward, as when being attacked [The enemy was in full *retreat.*] **2** a signal for a retreat [The bugle sounded the *retreat.*] **3** the ceremony at sunset when the flag is lowered; also, a signal, as on a bugle, for this ceremony. **4** a safe, quiet place [The cabin was our *retreat* in the woods.] ✦***v.*** to go back; withdraw [The bear *retreated* from the honey when the bees began to swarm.] —**beat a retreat,** to retreat in a hurry. 

**re·trench** (rē trench′) ***v.*** to cut down; reduce [to *retrench* expenses]. —**re·trench′ment** ***n.***

**ret·ri·bu·tion** (ret′rə byōō′shən) ***n.*** punishment that one deserves for having done a wrong. —**re·trib·u·tive** (ri trib′yoo tiv) ***adj.***

**re·trieve** (ri trēv′) ***v.*** **1** to get back; recover [to *retrieve* a kite from a tree]. **2** to find and bring back [The spaniel *retrieved* the wounded duck.] **3** to win, find, or earn again; restore [to *retrieve* a fortune; to *retrieve* one's spirits]. ☆**4** to recover information stored in a computer, files, etc. —**re·trieved′, re·triev′ing**

**re·triev·er** (ri trēv′ər) ***n.*** a dog that is trained to retrieve game in hunting.

**ret·ro·ac·tive** (ret′rō ak′tiv) ***adj.*** going into effect now, but as if it had happened at a certain date in the past [My new salary is *retroactive* to last month.]

**ret·ro·grade** (ret′rə grād) ***adj.*** **1** moving backward. **2** going back to an earlier or worse condition.

**ret·ro·gress** (ret′rə gres) ***v.*** to move backward, especially into an earlier or worse condition. —**ret′ro·gres′sion** ***n.***

☆**ret·ro·rock·et** *or* **ret·ro-rock·et** (ret′rō räk′it) ***n.*** a small rocket on a spacecraft, that produces thrust in a direction opposite to the direction in which the spacecraft is flying, in order to reduce speed, as for landing. *See the picture.*

| | | | |
|---|---|---|---|
| **a** fat | **ir** here | **ou** out | **zh** leisure |
| **ā** ape | **ī** bite, fire | **u** up | **ng** ring |
| **ä** car, lot | **ō** go | **ur** fur | a *in* ago |
| **e** ten | **ô** law, horn | **ch** chin | e *in* agent |
| **er** care | **oi** oil | **sh** she | **ə** = i *in* unity |
| **ē** even | **oo** look | **th** thin | o *in* collect |
| **i** hit | **ōō** tool | ***th*** then | u *in* focus |

**ret·ro·spect** (ret′rə spekt) ***n.*** the act of looking back on or thinking about the past [In *retrospect,* I have decided that you were right.] —**ret′ro·spec′tive** ***adj.***

**re·turn** (ri turn′) ***v.*** **1** to go or come back [When did you *return* from your trip?] **2** to bring, send, carry, or put back [Our neighbor *returned* the ladder.] **3** to pay back by doing the same [to *return* a visit; to *return* a favor]. **4** to give or produce; yield, as a profit. **5** to report back [The jury *returned* a verdict of "not guilty."] **6** to answer; reply ["Never mind," she *returned,* "I'll do it myself."] **7** to throw, hit, or run back a ball. ◆***n.*** **1** the act of coming or going back [the *return* of summer]. **2** the act of bringing, sending, putting, or paying back [the *return* of a favor]. **3** something returned. **4** *often* **returns,** *pl.* an amount received as profit; yield. **5** an official report; account [an income tax *return;* election *returns* from Hawaii]. ◆***adj.*** **1** of or for a return [a *return* ticket; *return* postage]. **2** given, sent, or done in paying back [a *return* visit]. **3** occurring again [a *return* performance]. —**in return,** in exchange.

**re·un·ion** (rē yo͞on′yən) ***n.*** the act of coming together again [Let's have a *reunion* of our graduation class.]

**re·u·nite** (rē′yoo nīt′) ***v.*** to bring or come together again; unite again [The States were *reunited* after the Civil War.] —**re′u·nit′ed, re′u·nit′ing**

**Rev.** *abbreviation for* **Reverend.** —*pl.* **Revs.**

**rev.** *abbreviation for* **revenue, revised, revolution.**

 ☆**re·vamp** (rē vamp′) ***v.*** to make over again; patch up [to *revamp* an old plot for a play].

**re·veal** (ri vēl′) ***v.*** **1** to make known what was hidden or secret [The map *revealed* the spot where the treasure was buried.] **2** to show [She took off her hat, *revealing* her golden hair.]

> SYNONYMS: To **reveal** is to make known something hidden or unknown, as if by drawing back a veil [The stranger *revealed* who she was.] To **disclose** is to bring to attention something that has been concealed on purpose [The newspaper *disclosed* that a secret meeting had taken place.]

**re·veil·le** (rev′ə lē) ***n.*** a signal, usually on a bugle, calling soldiers or sailors to duty in the morning.

**rev·el** (rev″l) ***v.*** **1** to have fun in a noisy way; make merry. **2** to take much pleasure; delight [We *reveled* in our new freedom.] —**rev′eled** or **rev′elled, rev′el·ing** or **rev′el·ling** —**rev′el·er** or **rev′el·ler** ***n.***

**rev·e·la·tion** (rev′ə lā′shən) ***n.*** **1** the act of revealing or making known [the *revelation* of a secret]. **2** something revealed or made known, especially something that comes as a surprise [His talent for painting was a *revelation* to me.] **3 Revelation,** the last book of the New Testament.

**rev·el·ry** (rev″l rē) ***n.*** the act of reveling; noisy merrymaking. —*pl.* **rev′el·ries**

**re·venge** (ri venj′) ***v.*** to do harm or evil in return for a harm or evil received; get even for [Hamlet swore to *revenge* the murder of his father.] —**re·venged′, re·veng′ing** ◆***n.*** **1** the act of revenging or a wish to revenge; vengeance. **2** a chance to get even, as by a return match after having lost the first one. —**be revenged,** to get even for some harm or evil. —**re·venge′ful** ***adj.***

**rev·e·nue** (rev′ə no͞o *or* rev′ə nyo͞o) ***n.*** money got as rent, profit, etc.; income; especially, the money a government gets from taxes, duties, etc.

**re·ver·ber·ate** (ri vur′bə rāt) ***v.*** to bounce back, as sound; echo [The guide's call *reverberated* in the cave.] —**re·ver′ber·at·ed, re·ver′ber·at·ing** —**re·ver′ber·a′tion** ***n.***

**re·vere** (ri vir′) ***v.*** to love and respect greatly [to *revere* the memory of one's grandparents]. —**re·vered′, re·ver′ing**

**Re·vere** (ri vir′), **Paul** 1735–1818; American silversmith and patriot who rode at night to tell the colonists that British troops were coming.

**rev·er·ence** (rev′ər əns *or* rev′rəns) ***n.*** great love and respect, as for something holy. ◆***v.*** to feel reverence for. —**rev′er·enced, rev′er·enc·ing**

**rev·er·end** (rev′ər ənd *or* rev′rənd) ***adj.*** that deserves deep respect. As a title of respect **the Reverend** is used before the name of a member of the clergy.

**rev·er·ent** (rev′ər ənt *or* rev′rənt) ***adj.*** feeling or showing reverence. —**rev′er·ent·ly** ***adv.***

**rev·er·ie** (rev′ər ē) ***n.*** dreamy thinking, especially about pleasant things; daydreaming.

> **Reverie** comes from an old French word that means "raving," or the wild talking or thoughts that a patient with high fever sometimes has. In time, the word came to mean the quieter and more pleasant kind of thinking that is daydreaming.

**re·ver·sal** (ri vur′s'l) ***n.*** the act of reversing or the condition of being reversed [a *reversal* in one's fortune; the *reversal* of a decision].

**re·verse** (ri vurs′) ***adj.*** **1** turned backward or upside down; opposite in position or direction [the *reverse* side of a fabric; in *reverse* order]. **2** causing a car, etc. to move backward [a *reverse* gear]. ◆***n.*** **1** the opposite or contrary [He said "Yes," but meant just the *reverse.*] **2** the back side, as of a coin or rug. **3** a change from good luck to bad; misfortune [Financial *reverses* ruined her.] **4** a reverse gear [Shift into *reverse* and back up.] ◆***v.*** **1** to turn backward, upside down, or inside out [*Reverse* the vest and wear the other side out.] **2** to change so that it is opposite, or completely different [to *reverse* an opinion]. **3** to do away with; revoke [The Supreme Court *reversed* the lower court's decision.] **4** to go or make go in an opposite direction. **5** to transfer the charges for a telephone call to the party being called. —**re·versed′, re·vers′ing**

**re·vers·i·ble** (ri vur′sə b'l) ***adj.*** **1** that can be reversed; made so that either side can be used as the outer side [a *reversible* coat]. *See the picture.* **2** that can be reversed, as some chemical reactions.

**re·ver·sion** (ri vur′zhən) ***n.*** the act of reverting; return to an earlier condition, owner, etc.

**re·vert** (ri vurt′) ***v.*** **1** to go back to an earlier condition, way of acting, etc.; return [Without care, the lawn *reverted* to a field of weeds.] **2** in law, to pass back to a former owner or the heirs of that owner.

**rev·er·y** (rev′ər ē) ***n.*** *another spelling of* **reverie.** —*pl.* **rev′er·ies**

**re·view** (ri vyo͞o′) ***v.*** **1** to go over or study again [to *review* a subject for a test]. **2** to think back on [He *reviewed* the events that led to their quarrel.] **3** to inspect or examine in an official way [to *review* troops]. **4** to tell what a book, play, etc. is about and give one's opinion of it. ◆*n.* **1** the act of reviewing, or studying again, thinking back, etc. [a *review* of yesterday's lesson; a *review* of the week's events]. **2** a talk or piece of writing in which a book, play, etc. is reviewed. **3** an official inspection of soldiers, ships, etc. **4** *another spelling of* **revue.**

**re·view·er** (ri vyōō′ər) ***n.*** a person who reviews books, plays, etc. as in a newspaper or magazine.

**re·vile** (ri vīl′) ***v.*** to say harsh or unkind things to or about; call bad names [The tennis players *reviled* the thieves who stole the net.] —**re·viled′, re·vil′ing**

**re·vise** (ri vīz′) ***v.*** **1** to think about and change; make different [to *revise* one's opinion]. **2** to read carefully and change where necessary in order to make better or bring up to date [to *revise* a history book]. —**re·vised′, re·vis′ing**

**re·vi·sion** (ri vizh′ən) ***n.*** **1** the act or work of revising. **2** something that has been revised, as a new edition of a book.

**re·viv·al** (ri vī′v'l) ***n.*** **1** the act of bringing or coming back into use, being, etc. [the *revival* of an old custom]. **2** a new showing of an earlier movie, play, etc. **3** a meeting at which there is excited preaching for the purpose of stirring up religious feeling.

**re·vive** (ri vīv′) ***v.*** **1** to bring or come back to life or consciousness [to *revive* a person who has fainted]. **2** to bring or come back to a healthy, active condition [A cool shower *revives* me after a hot day.] **3** to bring back or show an earlier play or movie again, or to make something popular again [to *revive* an old song]. —**re·vived′, re·viv′ing**

**rev·o·ca·ble** (rev′ə kə b'l) ***adj.*** that can be revoked.

**re·voke** (ri vōk′) ***v.*** to put an end to, as a law, permit, license, etc.; cancel; repeal. —**re·voked′, re·vok′ing**

**re·volt** (ri vōlt′) ***n.*** **1** the act of rebelling or rising up against the government; rebellion. **2** any refusal to obey rules, customs, authority, etc. ◆***v.*** **1** to rebel or rise up against the government or other authority [The American colonies *revolted* against England.] **2** to disgust or be disgusted [The sight *revolted* her. His stomach *revolted* at the taste.]

**re·volt·ing** (ri vōl′tiŋ) ***adj.*** causing disgust; disgusting [The filthy room was a *revolting* sight.]

**rev·o·lu·tion** (rev′ə lōō′shən) ***n.*** **1** overthrow of a government or a social system, with another taking its place [the American *Revolution;* the Industrial *Revolution*]. **2** a complete change of any kind [The telephone caused a *revolution* in communication.] **3** the act of revolving; movement in an orbit [the *revolution* of the moon around the earth]. **4** a turning motion of a wheel, etc. around a center or axis; rotation. **5** one complete turn [The wheel makes 100 *revolutions* per minute.]

**rev·o·lu·tion·ar·y** (rev′ə lōō′shən er′ē) ***adj.*** **1** of, in favor of, or causing a revolution, especially in a government. **2** bringing about very great change [a *revolutionary* new way to make glass]. **3** revolving or rotating. ◆*n. another name for* **revolutionist.** —*pl.* **rev′o·lu′tion·ar′ies**

☆**Revolutionary War** the war by which the American colonies won their independence from England. It lasted from 1775 to 1783.

**rev·o·lu·tion·ist** (rev′ə lōō′shən ist) ***n.*** a person who is in favor of or takes part in a revolution.

**rev·o·lu·tion·ize** (rev′ə lōō′shən īz) ***v.*** to make a complete change in [Automation has *revolutionized* industry.] —**rev′o·lu′tion·ized, rev′o·lu′tion·iz·ing**

**re·volve** (ri välv′) ***v.*** **1** to move in an orbit or cycle [The earth *revolves* around the sun.] *See* SYNONYMS *at* **turn. 2** to turn around, as a wheel on its axis; rotate. **3** to think about carefully [to *revolve* a problem in one's mind]. **4** to be affected in an important or narrow way [Their lives *revolve* around their children.] —**re·volved′, re·volv′ing**

**re·volv·er** (ri väl′vər) ***n.*** ☆a pistol with a revolving cylinder holding several bullets which can be fired one at a time without reloading. *See the picture.*



☆**revolving door** a door having four panels set upright around an axle. A person who is using the door turns it around by pushing on one of the panels. *See the picture.*

**re·vue** (ri vyōō′) ***n.*** a musical show made up of songs, dances, and skits, often making fun of well-known people and of current events.

**re·vul·sion** (ri vul′shən) ***n.*** a sudden, strong change of feeling; especially, a sudden feeling of disgust [In the middle of the bullfight he was filled with *revulsion.*]

**re·ward** (ri wôrd′) ***n.*** **1** something given in return, especially for good work or a good deed [a *reward* for bravery]. **2** money offered, as for returning something lost. ◆***v.*** to give a reward to or for.

**re·word** (rē wurd′) ***v.*** to change the wording of; put into other words [*Reword* your request for money.]

**re·write** (rē rīt′) ***v.*** to write again or in different words; revise [to *rewrite* a story]. —**re·wrote′, re·writ′ten, re·writ′ing**

**Rey·kja·vik** (rā′kyə vēk) the capital of Iceland.

**Reyn·ard** (ren′ərd *or* rā′nərd) a name for the fox in folk tales and poems.

**rf** or **r.f.** right field (in baseball).

**RFD** or **R.F.D.** Rural Free Delivery (mail service).

**r.h.** or **RH** right hand.

| | | | | | | | |
|---|---|---|---|---|---|---|---|
| **a** | fat | **ir** | here | **ou** | out | **zh** | leisure |
| **ā** | ape | **ī** | bite, fire | **u** | up | **ŋ** | ring |
| **ä** | car, lot | **ō** | go | **ur** | fur | | a *in* ago |
| **e** | ten | **ô** | law, horn | **ch** | chin | | e *in* agent |
| **er** | care | **oi** | oil | **sh** | she | **ə** = | i *in* unity |
| **ē** | even | **oo** | look | **th** | thin | | o *in* collect |
| **i** | hit | **ōō** | tool | ***th*** | then | | u *in* focus |

**r**

**rhap·so·dy** (rap′sə dē) ***n.*** **1** a speech or writing showing very great enthusiasm [The reviewer went into *rhapsodies* over the new play.] **2** a piece of music that has no fixed form and is full of feeling. *—pl.* **rhap′so·dies —rhap·sod·ic** (rap säd′ik) or **rhap·sod′i·cal** ***adj.***

A **rhapsody** in ancient Greece was a long epic poem that was recited without interruption. It came from a word meaning "one who strings songs together," from the Greek word meaning "to stitch." Probably each **rhapsody** was so long as to seem like many songs "stitched together."

**rhe·a** (rē′ə) ***n.*** a large bird of South America that is like the ostrich, but smaller.

**rhe·o·stat** (rē′ə stat) ***n.*** a device for making an electric current stronger or weaker by changing the resistance in the circuit.

**rhe·sus monkey** (rē′səs) a small, brownish monkey of India, often used in medical experiments. *See the picture.*

**rhet·o·ric** (ret′ər ik) ***n.*** **1** the art of using words skillfully in speaking or writing. **2** a book about this. **3** showiness of language. **—rhe·tor·i·cal** (ri tôr′i k'l) ***adj.*** **—rhe·tor′i·cal·ly** ***adv.***

**rhetorical question** a question asked only in order to make a point stand out, not because one expects an answer.

**rhet·o·ri·cian** (ret′ə rish′ən) ***n.*** **1** a person skilled in rhetoric. **2** a person who writes or speaks in a showy way.



**rheum** (ro͞om) ***n.*** watery matter coming from the eyes, nose, or mouth, as during a cold. **—rheum′y** ***adj.***

**rheu·mat·ic** (roo mat′ik) ***adj.*** **1** of or caused by rheumatism [*rheumatic* pain]. **2** having rheumatism. **◆*n.*** a person who has rheumatism.

**rheumatic fever** a disease in which there is fever, the joints ache and swell, and the heart valves sometimes become inflamed.

**rheu·ma·tism** (ro͞o′mə tiz'm) ***n.*** any disease, such as arthritis, in which the joints and muscles become stiff, sore, and swollen: *an old-fashioned word.*

**rheu·ma·toid** (ro͞o′mə toid) ***adj.*** of or like rheumatism.

**rheumatoid arthritis** a disease in which the joints become swollen, inflamed, and painful. Sometimes the joints become twisted out of shape.

**Rh factor** a group of antigens in the red blood cells. People who have this factor are **Rh positive**; those lacking it are **Rh negative.** If blood of one type is transfused into a person with the other type, it can cause a reaction.

**Rh factor** was given its name by scientists, who made it up by using the first two letters of *rhesus monkey.* Laboratory workers first discovered these antigens in the blood of rhesus monkeys.

**Rhine** (rīn) a river flowing from Switzerland through Germany and then through the Netherlands into the North Sea.

**rhine·stone** (rīn′stōn) ***n.*** an artificial gem made of glass, cut to look like a diamond.

**rhi·no** (rī′nō) ***n.*** *a shorter name for* **rhinoceros.** *—pl.* **rhi′nos** or **rhi′no**

**rhi·noc·er·os** (rī näs′ər əs) ***n.*** a large animal with a thick skin, found in Africa and Asia. It has one or two horns on its snout. *See the picture.*

**rhi·zome** (rī′zōm) ***n.*** a creeping stem of a plant, that lies along the ground or slightly under the surface of the ground. The rhizome grows shoots and leaves from its upper side and sends down roots from the lower side.

**Rhode Island** (rōd) a New England State of the U.S.: abbreviated **R.I., RI**

**Rhodes** (rōdz) an island in the Aegean Sea.

**Rho·de·sia** (rō dē′zhə) a country in southern Africa. **—Rho·de′sian** ***adj., n.***

**rho·do·den·dron** (rō′də den′drən) ***n.*** a shrub or small tree, usually an evergreen, that bears flowers of pink, white, or purple.

**Rhone** or **Rhône** (rōn) a river flowing from southwestern Switzerland southward through France to the Mediterranean.

**rhu·barb** (ro͞o′bärb) ***n.*** **1** a plant with large leaves and thick sour stalks used as food. **2** the stalks, cooked as a sauce or baked in a pie. ☆**3** an argument: *slang in this meaning.*

**rhyme** (rīm) ***n.*** **1** likeness of sounds at the ends of words or lines of verse. **2** a word that has the same end sound as another ["Single" is a *rhyme* for "tingle."] **3** poetry or verse using such end sounds. **◆*v.*** **1** to have the same end sound; form a rhyme ["More" *rhymes* with "door."] **2** to use as a rhyme [One could *rhyme* "her king" with "working."] **3** to make verse, especially with rhymes. **4** to have rhymes [Blank verse does not *rhyme.*] **—rhymed, rhym′ing —without rhyme or reason,** without order or sense. **—rhym′er** ***n.***

**rhythm** (rith″'m) ***n.*** **1** movement or flow in which the motions, sounds, etc. follow a regular pattern, with accents or beats coming at certain fixed times [the *rhythm* of the heart, of the waves, of dancing]. **2** the form or pattern of this, as in music, speech, poetry, etc. [waltz *rhythm*].

**rhyth·mi·cal** (rith′mi k'l) ***adj.*** of or having rhythm: *also* **rhyth′mic. —rhyth′mi·cal·ly** ***adv.***

**RI** or **R.I.** *abbreviation for* **Rhode Island.**

**rib** (rib) ***n.*** **1** any of the curved bones that are attached to the backbone and reach around to form the chest. The human body has twelve pairs of such bones. *See the picture.* **2** a raised ridge in cloth or knitted material. **3** a piece like a rib, used to form a frame of some kind [the *ribs* of an umbrella]. **4** a large vein in a leaf. **◆*v.*** **1** to strengthen or form with ribs, or mark with ridges. **2** to tease or make fun of: *slang in this meaning.* **—ribbed, rib′bing**

**rib·ald** (rib′əld) ***adj.*** joking or funny in a coarse or vulgar way.

**rib·ald·ry** (rib′əld rē) ***n.*** ribald language or humor.

**rib·bon** (rib′ən) ***n.*** **1** a narrow strip of silk, velvet, rayon, etc., for tying things or for decoration. **2** anything like such a strip [a *ribbon* of smoke]. **3 ribbons,** *pl.* torn strips or shreds; tatters [His shirt was in *ribbons.*] ☆**4** a narrow strip of cloth with ink on it, for use on a typewriter. **◆*v.*** to decorate with a ribbon or ribbons.

**ri·bo·fla·vin** (rī′bə flā′vin *or* rī′bə flā′vin) ***n.*** one form of vitamin B that is found in milk, eggs, liver, fruits, leafy vegetables, yeast, etc. Lack of riboflavin in the diet causes stunted growth and loss of hair.

**rice** (rīs) ***n.*** **1** the small, starchy seeds or grains of a plant grown in warm climates. Rice is one of the main foods of China, Japan, India, etc. **2** this plant, grown in flooded fields. *See the picture.* **◆*v.*** to make into tiny bits like rice [to *rice* potatoes after cooking them]. —**riced, ric′ing**

**rich** (rich) ***adj.*** **1** having wealth; owning much money or property; wealthy. **2** having much of something; well supplied [Tomatoes are *rich* in vitamin C.] **3** worth much; valuable [a *rich* prize]. **4** full of fats, or fats and sugar [*rich* foods]. **5** full, deep, and brilliant [a *rich* voice; a *rich* blue color]. **6** producing much [*rich* soil]. **7** very funny or amusing: *used only in everyday talk* [a *rich* joke]. —**the rich,** wealthy people as a group. —**rich′ly *adv.*** —**rich′ness *n.***

SYNONYMS: A person is **rich** who has more money or a larger income, as from salary, rent, or interest, than is needed to satisfy the usual, everyday needs for food, shelter, and clothing. Someone who is **wealthy** is rich and also lives in high style and is a leader in the place where he or she lives. Someone who is **well-to-do** is rich enough to live an easy life.

**Rich·ard I** (rich′ərd) 1157–1199; the king of England from 1189 to 1199. He was also called **Richard the Lion-Hearted.**

**rich·es** (rich′iz) ***n.pl.*** much money, property, etc.; wealth.

**Rich·mond** (rich′mənd) the capital of Virginia.

☆**Rich·ter scale** (rik′tər) a scale for measuring how great an earthquake is. The scale has steps graded from 1 to 10. Each step is about 60 times greater than the one before it.

**rick** (rik) ***n.*** a stack of hay, straw, etc. in a field, especially one covered to protect it from rain.

**rick·ets** (rik′its) ***n.*** a children's disease in which the bones become soft, often bent. It is caused by a lack of vitamin D or sunlight.

**rick·e·ty** (rik′it ē) ***adj.*** **1** having rickets. **2** weak and shaky; not firm [a *rickety* old barn].

**rick·shaw** or **rick·sha** (rik′shô) ***n.*** *a shorter name for* **jinrikisha.**

**ric·o·chet** (rik′ə shā) ***n.*** a quick bouncing or skipping, as of a flat stone thrown along the surface of a pond. **◆*v.*** to bounce or skip in this way [The bullet *ricocheted* from the rock.] —**ric·o·cheted** (rik′ə shād), **ric·o·chet·ing** (rik′ə shā ing)

**Ricochet** comes from a French phrase that describes a kind of story in which the person telling the story avoids answering any questions that his listeners may ask. To keep from answering, he may strike out in a new direction in telling the story, the way a bullet strikes off at an angle after hitting something.

**rid** (rid) ***v.*** to clear or free of something not wanted [to *rid* a garden of weeds]. —**rid** or **rid′ded, rid′ding** —**be rid of,** to be made free from. —**get rid of, 1** to get free from. **2** to do away with.

**rid·dance** (rid′′ns) ***n.*** a ridding or being rid of something not wanted. —**good riddance!** I am glad to be rid of this!

**rid·den** (rid′′n) *past participle of* **ride. ◆*adj.*** controlled or ruled over [*ridden* by fear].

**rid·dle**[1] (rid′′l) ***n.*** **1** a puzzle in the form of a question or statement with a tricky meaning or answer that is hard to guess. Example: "What has four wheels and flies?" "A garbage truck." **2** any person or thing that is hard to understand. **◆*v.*** to solve or explain a riddle. —**rid′dled, rid′dling**

**rid·dle**[2] (rid′′l) ***v.*** **1** to make full of holes [Worms *riddled* the apples.] **2** to show many weaknesses in, as an argument. **3** to spread throughout [a report *riddled* with errors]. **4** to sift through a coarse sieve. —**rid′dled, rid′dling ◆*n.*** a coarse sieve.

**ride** (rīd) ***v.*** **1** to sit on and make move along [to *ride* a horse; to *ride* a bicycle]. **2** to move along, as in a car, bus, etc. **3** to be carried along on or by [Army tanks *ride* on treads. The ship *rode* the waves.] **4** to cause to ride; carry [I'll *ride* you to town in my wagon.] **5** to cover or travel by riding [We *rode* ten miles.] **6** to control or rule over [He is *ridden* by doubts.] **7** to keep on teasing or nagging: *used only in everyday talk.* ☆**8** to go on as is, with no action taken: *used only in everyday talk* [Let the matter *ride* for a while.] —**rode, rid′den, rid′ing ◆*n.*** a riding; especially, a trip by horse, car, etc. —**ride down, 1** to knock down by riding against. **2** to overtake or overcome. —**ride out,** to last or stay safe through a storm, time of trouble, etc. —**ride up,** to move upward out of place, as an article of clothing.

**rid·er** (rīd′ər) ***n.*** **1** a person who rides. **2** something added to an official paper, as a clause added to a proposed law before it is voted on.

**ridge** (rij) ***n.*** **1** a top or high part that is long and narrow; crest [the *ridge* of a roof]. **2** a range of hills or mountains. **3** any narrow, raised strip [Waves made tiny *ridges* in the sand.] **◆*v.*** to form into ridges or mark with ridges. —**ridged, ridg′ing**

ribs of a person

rhinoceros

rhesus monkey

rice
(plant and paddy)

| | | | | | | | |
|---|---|---|---|---|---|---|---|
| **a** | fat | **ir** | here | **ou** | out | **zh** | leisure |
| **ā** | ape | **ī** | bite, fire | **u** | up | **ng** | ring |
| **ä** | car, lot | **ō** | go | **ur** | fur | | a *in* ago |
| **e** | ten | **ô** | law, horn | **ch** | chin | | e *in* agent |
| **er** | care | **oi** | oil | **sh** | she | **ə =** | i *in* unity |
| **ē** | even | **oo** | look | **th** | thin | | o *in* collect |
| **i** | hit | **ōō** | tool | ***th*** | then | | u *in* focus |

**ridge·pole** (rij′pōl) ***n.*** the beam along the ridge of a roof, to which the rafters are attached: *also called* **ridge·piece** (rij′pēs). *See the picture.*

**rid·i·cule** (rid′i kyo͞ol′) ***n.*** **1** the act of making a person or thing seem foolish, as by mocking, making fun, laughing, etc. **2** words or actions used in doing this. ◆***v.*** to make fun of or make others laugh at. —**rid′i·culed′, rid′i·cul′ing**

**ri·dic·u·lous** (ri dik′yə ləs) ***adj.*** deserving ridicule; foolish; absurd. —**ri·dic′u·lous·ly *adv.***

**rife** (rīf) ***adj.*** **1** happening often; common or widespread [Gossip is *rife* in our town.] **2** filled [a jungle *rife* with insects].

**riff·raff** (rif′raf) ***n.*** those people thought of as being very low, common, etc.

**ri·fle**[1] (rī′f′l) ***n.*** ☆a shoulder gun having spiral grooves on the inside of the barrel to make the bullet spin. ◆***v.*** to cut spiral grooves on the inside of. —**ri′fled, ri′fling**

**ri·fle**[2] (rī′f′l) ***v.*** to go through wildly in searching and robbing; plunder [Soldiers *rifled* the city. Thieves *rifled* the safe.] —**ri′fled, ri′fling** —**ri′fler *n.***

☆**ri·fle·man** (rī′f′l mən) ***n.*** **1** a soldier armed with a rifle. **2** a person who can shoot well with a rifle. —*pl.* **ri′fle·men**

**rift** (rift) ***n.*** an opening made as by splitting; crack; cleft [a *rift* in a tree hit by lightning; a *rift* in a friendship]. ◆***v.*** to split; crack.

634 **rig** (rig) ***v.*** **1** to put the sails, braces, ropes, etc. of a ship in place [*Rig* the mainsail.] **2** to supply or equip; outfit [Our station wagon is *rigged* for camping.] **3** to put together quickly for use [We *rigged* up a table from boards and boxes.] **4** to arrange in a dishonest way [to *rig* an election]. **5** to dress; clothe: *used only in everyday talk* [boys and girls *rigged* out in blue jeans]. —**rigged, rig′ging** ◆***n.*** **1** the way the sails and masts are arranged on a ship. ☆**2** equipment or gear, as for drilling an oil well. ☆**3** a carriage with its horse or horses. **4** a truck tractor and the trailer attached to it. **5** costume or dress: *used only in everyday talk.* —**rig′ger *n.***

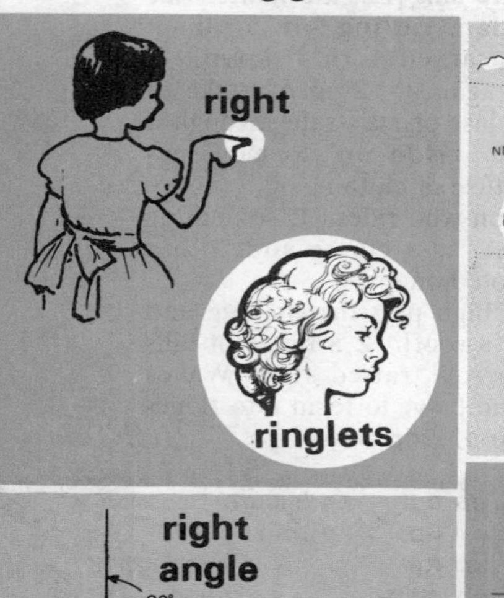


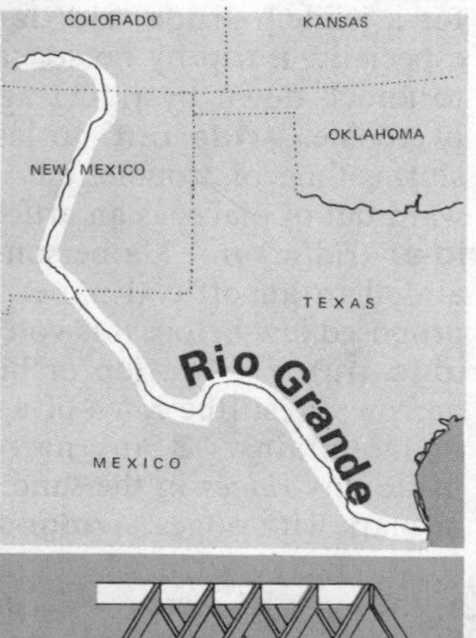


right angle
90°

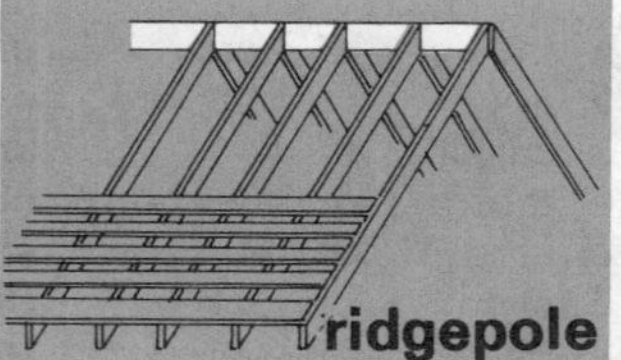


**rig·ging** (rig′iŋ) ***n.*** **1** the chains and ropes used to hold up and work the masts, sails, etc. of a ship. ☆**2** equipment; gear.

**right** (rīt) ***adj.*** **1** that agrees with what is demanded by the law, one's conscience, etc.; just and good [Telling lies is not *right.*] **2** that agrees with the facts; correct or true [a *right* answer; the *right* time]. **3** proper or suitable [the *right* dress for a dance]. **4** having a desired finish and meant to be seen [the *right* side of cloth]. **5** healthy, normal, or well [He doesn't look *right.*] **6** in a good condition or order [She'll make things *right* again.] **7** on or to the side that is toward the east when one faces north [the *right* hand; a *right* turn]. **8** closer to the right side of a person facing the thing mentioned [the lower *right* drawer of the desk]. **9** not curved; straight [a *right* line]. **10** conservative in politics. ◆***n.*** **1** what is just, lawful, proper, etc. [to know *right* from wrong]. **2** something to which a person has a just claim by law or nature [the *right* of all citizens to vote]. **3** the right side [the first door on the *right*]. *See the picture.* **4** a turn toward the right side [Take a *right* at the next intersection.] ◆***adv.*** **1** in a straight line; directly [Go *right* home.] **2** in a correct, proper, or fair way; well [Do it *right.*] **3** completely [The rain soaked *right* through his coat.] **4** exactly [*right* here; *right* now]. ☆**5** immediately [I'll come *right* over.] **6** on or toward the right hand or side [Turn *right* at the next light.] **7** very: *used in certain titles* [The *Right* Honorable Lord Tennyson]. ◆***v.*** **1** to put back in a proper or upright position [We *righted* the boat.] **2** to make right; correct [to *right* a wrong]. **3** to put in order [The maid *righted* the room.] —**by right** or **by rights,** in justice; properly; rightly. —**in one's own right,** without depending on another or others. —**in the right,** on the side that is just and good; right; correct. —**right away** or **right off,** at once; immediately. —☆**right on!** that's right! exactly!: *a slang phrase.* —**to rights,** into a good condition or order: *used only in everyday talk* [Set the room *to rights.*] —**right′ness *n.***

**right angle** an angle of 90 degrees, formed by two lines perpendicular to each other. *See the picture.*

**right·eous** (rī′chəs) ***adj.*** **1** doing what is right; virtuous [a *righteous* person]. **2** fair and just; right [a *righteous* act]. —**right′eous·ly *adv.*** —**right′eous·ness *n.***

**right·ful** (rīt′fəl) ***adj.*** **1** fair and just. **2** having or based on a just claim, or lawful right [the *rightful* owner; his *rightful* share]. —**right′ful·ly *adv.*** —**right′ful·ness *n.***

**right-hand** (rīt′hand′) ***adj.*** **1** on or to the right [Make a *right-hand* turn at the next corner.] **2** of, for, or with the right hand [a *right-hand* glove]. **3** most helpful [the president's *right-hand* man].

**right-hand·ed** (rīt′han′did) ***adj.*** **1** using the right hand more easily than the left. **2** done with or made for use with the right hand [a *right-handed* throw; *right-handed* golf clubs]. ◆***adv.*** with the right hand [to eat *right-handed*].

**right·ist** (rīt′ist) ***n.*** a conservative in politics. ◆***adj.*** conservative.

**right·ly** (rīt′lē) ***adv.*** **1** with justice; fairly. **2** in a fitting or proper way. **3** correctly.

**right of way** **1** the legal right to move in front of others, as at an intersection. **2** the legal right to use a certain route, as over another's land. *Also* **right'-of-way'**

**right triangle** a triangle with a right angle.

**rig·id** (rij'id) ***adj.*** **1** not bending or moving; stiff and firm [a *rigid* steel bar]. *See* SYNONYMS *at* **stiff**. **2** strict; not changing [a *rigid* rule]. —**ri·gid·i·ty** (ri jid'ə tē), **rig'id·ness** ***n.*** —**rig'id·ly** ***adv.***

**rig·ma·role** (rig'mə rōl) ***n.*** confused talk that does not make much sense; nonsense.

**rig·or** (rig'ər) ***n.*** **1** great strictness or harshness [laws enforced with *rigor*]. **2** hardship [the *rigors* of pioneer life]. *The British spelling is* **rigour**.

**rig·or·ous** (rig'ər əs) ***adj.*** **1** very strict or stern [a *rigorous* taskmaster]. **2** severe or harsh [a *rigorous* climate]. **3** very exact; precise [*rigorous* study]. —**rig'or·ous·ly** ***adv.***

**rile** (rīl) ***v.*** **1** to make muddy, as water, by stirring up stuff from the bottom. **2** to make angry; vex. *This word is used only in everyday talk.* —**riled, ril'ing**

**Ri·ley** (rī'lē), **James Whit·comb** (hwit'kəm) 1849–1916; U.S. poet.

**rill** (ril) ***n.*** a little brook.

**rim** (rim) ***n.*** **1** an edge or border, especially of something round [the *rim* of a bowl]. ☆**2** the metal hoop of a basketball net. ◆***v.*** to put or form a rim around. —**rimmed, rim'ming**

**rime**[1] (rīm) ***n., v.*** *another spelling of* **rhyme**. —**rimed, rim'ing**

**rime**[2] (rīm) ***n.*** white frost; hoarfrost.

**rind** (rīnd) ***n.*** a hard or firm outer layer or coating [an orange *rind;* the *rind* of cheese].

**ring**[1] (riŋ) ***v.*** **1** to cause a bell to sound [*Ring* the doorbell.] **2** to make the sound of a bell [The phone *rang*.] **3** to announce or call for as with a bell [*Ring* in the new year. *Ring* for the maid.] **4** to sound loudly or clearly [The room *rang* with laughter.] **5** to seem to be [Your story *rings* true.] **6** to seem to be full of the sound of bells [The blow made his ears *ring*.] —**rang** or rarely **rung, rung, ring'ing** ◆***n.*** **1** the sound of a bell. **2** any sound like this, especially when loud and long [the *ring* of applause]. **3** a sound that shows a certain feeling [a *ring* of pride in his voice]. **4** a telephone call [Give me a *ring* soon.] —**ring a bell,** ☆to sound familiar. —**ring in,** to bring in or put in by a trick: *a slang phrase.* —☆**ring the bell,** to be successful: *used only in everyday talk.* —**ring up,** ☆**1** to record, as a sale on a cash register. **2** to call by telephone. —**ring'er** ***n.***

**ring**[2] (riŋ) ***n.*** **1** a thin band of metal, plastic, etc., shaped like a circle and worn on the finger or used to hold or fasten things [a wedding *ring;* a curtain *ring*]. **2** a line or edge forming a circle [a *ring* around the moon]. **3** a group in a circle [a *ring* of trees]. ☆**4** a group of people joined together, especially to do something wrong or bad [a spy *ring*]. **5** an enclosed space for contests, shows, etc. [the *ring* of a circus; a boxing *ring*]. ◆***v.*** **1** to make a circle around or form in a ring. **2** to fit with a ring [to *ring* a bull's nose]. —**ringed, ring'ing** —**run rings around,** to run much faster than, or do much better than: *used only in everyday talk.* —**ringed** ***adj.*** —**ring'er** ***n.***

**ring·lead·er** (riŋ'lēd'ər) ***n.*** a person who leads a group, as in breaking a law.

**ring·let** (riŋ'lit) ***n.*** **1** a little ring. **2** a curl of hair, especially a long one. *See the picture.*

**ring·side** (riŋ'sīd) ***n.*** the place just outside the ring, as at a boxing match.

**ring·worm** (riŋ'wurm) ***n.*** a skin disease caused by a fungus that forms round patches.

**rink** (riŋk) ***n.*** **1** a smooth area of ice for skating, or a smooth wooden floor for roller-skating. **2** a building having such an area.

**rinse** (rins) ***v.*** **1** to wash lightly, as by running water over or into [to *rinse* off the sand; to *rinse* one's mouth]. **2** to remove soap, scum, etc. from by washing in clear water. —**rinsed, rins'ing** ◆***n.*** **1** the act of rinsing. **2** the liquid used in rinsing.

**Ri·o de Ja·nei·ro** (rē'ō dā zhə ner'ō) a seaport in Brazil, on the Atlantic.

**Ri·o Grande** (rē'ō grand' *or* rē'ō gran'dē) a river that flows from Colorado to the Gulf of Mexico. It forms the boundary between Texas and Mexico. *See the map.*

**ri·ot** (rī'ət) ***n.*** **1** a wild outburst of disorder, especially by a crowd of people disturbing the peace. **2** a very bright show or display [The spring flowers are a *riot* of color.] ☆**3** a very amusing person or thing: *used only in everyday talk.* ◆***v.*** to take part in a riot. —**read the riot act to,** to give very strict orders to so as to make obey; warn sternly. —**run riot, 1** to act in a wild way. **2** to grow wild [The roses along the fence are *running riot*.] —**ri'ot·er** ***n.***

**ri·ot·ous** (rī'ət əs) ***adj.*** **1** of or like a riot; wild; boisterous [a *riotous* celebration]. **2** taking part in a riot. —**ri'ot·ous·ly** ***adv.***



**rip** (rip) ***v.*** **1** to tear apart roughly [to *rip* the hem of a skirt]. **2** to become torn or split apart [My sleeve *ripped* on the nail.] **3** to remove as by tearing roughly [to *rip* a sheet of paper from a tablet]. **4** to move rapidly or violently: *used only in everyday talk* [His car *ripped* past us.] —**ripped, rip'ping** ◆***n.*** the act of ripping or a ripped place. —**rip into,** to attack violently, often with words: *used only in everyday talk.* —**rip off,** ☆to steal, rob, or cheat: *a slang phrase.* —**rip out,** to say quickly or roughly, as when angry: *used only in everyday talk.*

**ripe** (rīp) ***adj.*** **1** ready to be gathered and used for food, as fruit or grain. **2** ready to be used [*ripe* cheese]. **3** fully developed; mature [*ripe* wisdom]. **4** fully prepared; ready [Those two are *ripe* for a fight.] —**rip'er, rip'est** —**ripe'ness** ***n.***

**rip·en** (rī'pən) ***v.*** to get ripe; mature.

☆**rip-off** (rip'ôf') ***n.*** **1** an act of stealing, robbing, cheating, etc. **2** something used to cheat or take advantage of people. *This is a slang word.*

**rip·ple** (rip''l) ***v.*** to form little waves on the surface, as water stirred by a breeze. —**rip'pled, rip'pling** ◆***n.*** **1** a little wave, or a movement like this [*ripples* in a field of grain]. **2** a sound like that of water rippling [a *ripple* of applause].

| | | | | | | | |
|---|---|---|---|---|---|---|---|
| **a** | fat | **ir** | here | **ou** | out | **zh** | leisure |
| **ā** | ape | **ī** | bite, fire | **u** | up | **ŋ** | ring |
| **ä** | car, lot | **ō** | go | **ur** | fur | | a *in* ago |
| **e** | ten | **ô** | law, horn | **ch** | chin | | e *in* agent |
| **er** | care | **oi** | oil | **sh** | she | **ə** = | i *in* unity |
| **ē** | even | **oo** | look | **th** | thin | | o *in* collect |
| **i** | hit | **ōō** | tool | ***th*** | then | | u *in* focus |

**Rocky Mountain goat**
1 m (39 in.) high at shoulder

**Riviera**

**rocking horse**

**rip·saw** (rip′sô) ***n.*** a saw with coarse teeth, for cutting wood along the grain.

**rip·tide** (rip′tīd) ***n.*** a tide that flows against another tide, causing rough waters.

**Rip van Win·kle** (rip′ van wiŋ′k'l) a character in a story with the same name, written by Washington Irving. Rip wakens after sleeping for twenty years and finds everything changed.

**rise** (rīz) ***v.*** **1** to stand up or get up from a lying or sitting position. **2** to get up after sleeping. **3** to move toward or reach a higher place or position [The sun is *rising*. She *rose* to be president of the company.] **4** to slope upward [The hills *rise* steeply from the river.] **5** to become greater, higher, or stronger [The temperature *rose*. Prices are *rising*. Her voice *rose*.] **6** to become larger and puffier, as dough with yeast in it. **7** to rebel; revolt [The miners *rose* against the mine owners.] **8** to come into being; begin [The Mississippi *rises* in northern Minnesota.] **9** in religious belief, to return to life after dying [to *rise* from the grave]. —**rose, ris′en, ris′ing** ◆***n.*** **1** the act of moving to a higher place or position; climb [Lincoln's *rise* to the presidency; the *rise* of the flood waters]. **2** an upward slope, as of land. **3** a piece of ground higher than that around it [There's a good view of the countryside from the top of the *rise*.] **4** the fact of becoming greater, higher, etc.; increase [a *rise* in prices]. **5** a start or beginning; origin. —**give rise to,** to bring about; begin. —**rise to,** to prove oneself able to deal well with [to *rise to* an emergency].



SYNONYMS: **Rise** and **arise** both mean "to begin," but **rise** also means "to go up" [colorful balloons *rising* into the air] and **arise** also means "to come as a result" [Accidents *arise* from carelessness.]

**ris·er** (rīz′ər) ***n.*** **1** a person or thing that rises [I'm an early *riser*.] **2** any of the upright pieces between the steps of a stairway.

**risk** (risk) ***n.*** the chance of getting hurt, or of losing, failing, etc.; danger [He ran into the burning house at the *risk* of his life.] ◆***v.*** **1** to lay open to risk; put in danger [You are *risking* your health by smoking.] **2** to take the chance of [Are you willing to *risk* a fight for your beliefs?]

**risk·y** (ris′kē) ***adj.*** full of risk; dangerous. —**risk′i·er, risk′i·est** —**risk′i·ness *n.***

**rite** (rīt) ***n.*** a formal act or ceremony carried out according to fixed rules [marriage *rites*]. *See* SYNONYMS *at* **ceremony.**

**rit·u·al** (rich′o͝o wəl) ***adj.*** of, like, or done as a rite [*ritual* sacrifices in ancient religions]. ◆***n.*** **1** a system or form of rites, as in a religion. *See* SYNONYMS *at* **ceremony.** **2** anything done at regular intervals, as if it were a rite. —**rit′u·al·ism *n.*** —**rit′u·al·ly *adv.***

**ri·val** (rī′v'l) ***n.*** a person who tries to get the same thing as another, or one who tries to do something better than another; competitor [*rivals* for the championship]. ◆***adj.*** acting as a rival or rivals; competing [*rival* businesses]. ◆***v.*** **1** to equal or be as good as [Her paintings soon *rivaled* her teacher's.] **2** to be a rival of; compete with [They *rivaled* each other for her love.] —**ri′valed** or **ri′valled, ri′val·ing** or **ri′val·ling**

**Rival** comes from a Latin word for river or brook. Persons living along the same river or stream would compete with each other or be **rivals** in using the water.

**ri·val·ry** (rī′v'l rē) ***n.*** the act of rivaling or the fact of being rivals. —*pl.* **ri′val·ries**

**riv·en** (riv′'n) ***adj.*** torn or pulled apart; split [a giant oak *riven* by lightning].

**riv·er** (riv′ər) ***n.*** **1** a large, natural stream of water flowing into an ocean, lake, or another river. **2** any large, flowing stream [a *river* of lava].

**riv·er·side** (riv′ər sīd) ***n.*** the bank of a river. ◆***adj.*** on or near the bank of a river.

**riv·et** (riv′it) ***n.*** a metal bolt with a head on one end, used for fastening metal beams or plates together. It is put through holes in the parts, and then the plain end is hammered into a head. ◆***v.*** **1** to fasten together with rivets. **2** to fix or hold firmly [He stood *riveted* to the spot with fear.]

**Riv·i·er·a** (riv′ē er′ə) a resort area along the Mediterranean, partly in France and partly in Italy. *See the map.*

**riv·u·let** (riv′yo͝o lit) ***n.*** a little stream; brook.

**Ri·yadh** (rē yäd′) a capital of Saudi Arabia.

**RN** or **R.N.** Registered Nurse.

**RNA** an essential part of all living matter, found in every cell. One form carries the pattern of inherited characteristics from the DNA.

☆**roach**[1] (rōch) ***n.*** *a shorter name for* **cockroach.**

**roach**[2] (rōch) ***n.*** a fish like the carp, found in rivers of Europe. —*pl.* **roach** or **roach′es**

**road** (rōd) ***n.*** **1** a way made for cars, trucks, etc. to travel from place to place; highway. **2** a way or course [the *road* to success]. **3** *often* **roads,** *pl.* a protected place near the shore where ships can anchor. —**on the road,** traveling, as a salesman.

**road·bed** (rōd′bed) ***n.*** the foundation on which a road or railroad is built.

**road·block** (rōd′bläk) ***n.*** a blockade set up in a road to keep vehicles from going on.

**road·side** (rōd′sīd) ***n.*** the side of a road. ◆***adj.*** along the side of a road [a *roadside* park].

**road·way** (rōd′wā) ***n.*** a road, especially the part on which cars, trucks, etc. travel.

**roam** (rōm) ***v.*** to travel about with no special plan or purpose; wander [to *roam* the streets].

**roan** (rōn) ***adj.*** reddish-brown, brown, black, etc. thickly sprinkled with white hairs. ◆***n.*** a roan horse.

**roar** (rôr) ***v.*** **1** to make a loud, deep, rumbling sound [A lion *roars.*] **2** to talk or laugh in a loud, noisy way [The crowd *roared* at the clown.] ◆***n.*** a loud, deep, rumbling sound, as of a motor.

**roast** (rōst) ***v.*** **1** to cook with little or no liquid, as in an oven or over an open fire [to *roast* a chicken or a whole ox]. **2** to dry or brown with great heat [to *roast* coffee]. **3** to make or become very hot. **4** to criticize or make fun of in a harsh way: *used only in everyday talk.* ◆***n.*** **1** a piece of roasted meat. **2** a piece of meat for roasting. ☆**3** a picnic at which food is roasted [a steer *roast*]. ◆***adj.*** that has been roasted [*roast* beef].

**roast·er** (rōs′tər) ***n.*** **1** a special oven or pan for roasting meat. **2** a young chicken, pig, etc. fit for roasting.

**rob** (räb) ***v.*** **1** to steal from by using force or threats [to *rob* a bank]. **2** to take from in a wrong way, as by cheating [to *rob* a person of the right to vote]. —**robbed, rob′bing** —**rob′ber *n.***

**rob·ber·y** (räb′ər ē) ***n.*** the act of robbing; theft. —*pl.* **rob′ber·ies**

**robe** (rōb) ***n.*** **1** a long, loose outer garment, as a bathrobe. **2** a garment like this, worn to show one's rank, office, etc. [a judge's *robe*]. ◆***v.*** to dress in a robe. —**robed, rob′ing**

**Robe·son** (rōb′sən), **Paul** 1898–1976; U.S. singer and actor.

**rob·in** (räb′in) ***n.*** ☆**1** a large thrush of North America, with a dull-red breast. **2** a small brown bird of Europe, with a reddish breast.

**Robin Hood** an outlaw in English legend who robbed the rich in order to help the poor.

**Robinson Crusoe** *see* **Crusoe.**

**ro·bot** (rō′bət) ***n.*** **1** a machine made to look and work like a human being. **2** a person who acts or works automatically, like a machine.

**ro·bust** (rō bust′ *or* rō′bust) ***adj.*** strong and healthy; vigorous [a *robust* farmer].

> **Robust** comes from the Latin word for a kind of oak tree with hard, strong wood. A robust person has muscles that are hard and strong like the wood of an oak tree.

**roc** (räk) ***n.*** a huge bird in Arabian and Persian legends, that could carry away large animals.

**Roch·es·ter** (rä′ches′tər *or* räch′is tər) a city in western New York.

**rock**[1] (räk) ***n.*** **1** a large mass of stone. **2** broken pieces of stone [The glacier pushed *rock* and earth before it.] **3** minerals formed into masses in the earth [Granite and salt occur as *rock.*] **4** anything strong or hard like a rock. —**on the rocks, 1** in or into trouble or ruin. **2** served over ice cubes: said of drinks. *This phrase is used only in everyday talk.*

**rock**[2] (räk) ***v.*** **1** to move or swing back and forth or from side to side [to *rock* a cradle]. **2** to sway strongly; shake [The explosion *rocked* the house.] ◆***n.*** **1** a rocking movement. ☆**2** a form of popular music that is a mixture of rock-and-roll with folk music, country music, etc.

☆**rock-and-roll** (räk′′n rōl′) ***n.*** a form of popular music with a strong rhythm. It developed from jazz and the blues.

☆**rock bottom** the lowest level; the very bottom. —**rock′-bot′tom *adj.***

**rock candy** large, hard, clear crystals of sugar.

**Rock·e·fel·ler** (räk′ə fel′ər), **John D.** 1839–1937; U.S. founder of a very large U.S. oil company. He gave large amounts of money to charitable organizations that he set up.

**rock·er** (räk′ər) ***n.*** **1** either of the curved pieces on the bottom of a cradle, rocking chair, etc. ☆**2** *another name for* **rocking chair.**

**rock·et** (räk′it) ***n.*** a device that is shot through the air as a firework, signal, or weapon or into outer space as a spacecraft. When fuel is burned inside the rocket, gases escape in the rear, driving it forward. ◆***v.*** **1** to shoot ahead like a rocket. **2** to rise rapidly [Prices *rocketed.*]

**rock garden** a garden with flowers and plants planted to grow among rocks or on rocky ground.

☆**rocking chair** a chair set on rockers or springs, so that it can rock.

**rocking horse** a toy horse set on rockers or springs, for a child to ride. *See the picture.*

**rock salt** common salt occurring in solid masses.

**rock·y**[1] (räk′ē) ***adj.*** **1** full of rocks [*rocky* soil]. **2** made of rock. **3** firm or hard like rock. —**rock′i·er, rock′i·est**

**rock·y**[2] (räk′ē) ***adj.*** **1** tending to rock or sway; not steady; wobbly [a *rocky* desk]. **2** weak or dizzy: *slang in this meaning.* —**rock′i·er, rock′i·est**

☆**Rocky Mountain goat** a white, goatlike antelope of the mountains of northwestern North America, with a shaggy coat and small black horns that curve backward. *See the picture.*



**Rocky Mountains** a mountain system in western North America. It stretches from New Mexico to Alaska. *Also called* **the Rockies.**

**ro·co·co** (rə kō′kō) ***adj.*** having rich decoration and many fancy designs, such as leaves, shells, scrolls, etc. [*Rococo* architecture was popular in the 18th century.]

**rod** (räd) ***n.*** **1** a straight, thin bar of wood, metal, etc. [a fishing *rod*]. **2** a stick for beating as punishment. **3** punishment. **4** a measure of length equal to 5 1/2 yards. **5** a staff carried as a symbol of position or rank, as by a sovereign.

**rode** (rōd) *past tense of* **ride.**

**ro·dent** (rōd′′nt) ***n.*** an animal having sharp front teeth for gnawing. Rats, mice, rabbits, squirrels, woodchucks, and beavers are rodents.

> **Rodent** comes from a Latin word that means "to gnaw." Animals that are rodents have large, strong biting teeth in front that are used to gnaw roots, nutshells, wood, etc. As the teeth wear down from this use, they continue to grow throughout the animal's lifetime.

☆**ro·de·o** (rō′dē ō *or* rō dā′ō) ***n.*** a contest or show in which cowboys match their skill in riding horses, roping and throwing cattle, etc. —*pl.* **ro′de·os**

| | | | | | | | |
|---|---|---|---|---|---|---|---|
| **a** | fat | **ir** | here | **ou** | out | **zh** | leisure |
| **ā** | ape | **ī** | bite, fire | **u** | up | **ŋ** | ring |
| **ä** | car, lot | **ō** | go | **ur** | fur | | a *in* ago |
| **e** | ten | **ô** | law, horn | **ch** | chin | | e *in* agent |
| **er** | care | **oi** | oil | **sh** | she | **ə** = | i *in* unity |
| **ē** | even | **oo** | look | **th** | thin | | o *in* collect |
| **i** | hit | **ōō** | tool | ***th*** | then | | u *in* focus |

**Ro·din** (rō dan′), **Au·guste** (ō gy͞oost′) 1840–1917; French sculptor.

**roe**[1] (rō) ***n.*** fish eggs.

**roe**[2] (rō) ***n.*** a small, graceful deer found in Asia and Europe: *also called* **roe deer.** *—pl.* **roe** or **roes**

**roe·buck** (rō′buk) ***n.*** the male of the roe deer.

**rogue** (rōg) ***n.*** **1** a dishonest or tricky person; scoundrel; rascal. **2** a person who likes to have fun and play tricks. **3** an elephant or other animal that wanders apart from the herd and is wild and fierce.

**ro·guer·y** (rō′gər ē) ***n.*** the actions of a rogue; trickery or playful mischief. *—pl.* **ro′guer·ies**

**ro·guish** (rō′gish) ***adj.*** **1** dishonest; tricky. **2** playful; mischievous. —**ro′guish·ly *adv.***

**roil** (roil) ***v.*** **1** to make muddy or cloudy, as by stirring up stuff at the bottom [to *roil* a pond]. **2** to make angry; vex; rile.

**Roil** comes from an old French word that means "rust" or "mud." When one roils the waters of a pond, one stirs up the mud on the bottom.

**roist·er** (rois′tər) ***v.*** **1** to be noisy and lively; revel. **2** to brag or show off. —**roist′er·er *n.***

**role** or **rôle** (rōl) ***n.*** **1** the part that an actor takes in a play [the heroine's *role*]. **2** a part that a person plays in life [his *role* as a scoutmaster].

**roll** (rōl) ***v.*** **1** to move by turning over and over [The dog *rolled* on the grass. Workers *rolled* logs to the river.] **2** to move or travel on wheels or rollers [The cars *roll* along. *Roll* the cart over here.] **3** to move smoothly, one after another [Waves *rolled* to the shore. The weeks *rolled* by.] **4** to wrap up or wind into a ball or tube [*Roll* up the rug.] **5** to move or rock back and forth [The ship *rolled* in the heavy seas. Rosita *rolled* her eyes.] **6** to spread, make, or become flat under a roller [to *roll* steel]. **7** to say with a trill [He *rolls* his r's.] **8** to make a loud, echoing sound [The thunder *rolled*.] **9** to beat with light, rapid blows [to *roll* a drum]. **10** to have plenty: *used only in everyday talk* [*rolling* in money]. ◆***n.*** **1** the act of rolling [the *roll* of a ball]. **2** a list of names for checking who is present. **3** something rolled up into a ball or tube [a *roll* of wallpaper]. **4** bread baked in a small, shaped piece. **5** a thin cake or pastry covered with a filling and rolled [jelly*roll*; egg *roll*]. **6** a roller. **7** a rolling motion [the *roll* of the ship]. **8** a loud, echoing sound [a *roll* of thunder]. **9** a series of light, rapid blows on a drum. —**roll in,** to arrive or come in large numbers. —**roll out, 1** to make flat by using a roller on. **2** to spread out by unrolling. **3** to get out of bed: *slang in this meaning.* —**roll up, 1** to get or become more; increase [to *roll up* a big score]. **2** to arrive in a car: *used only in everyday talk* [They *rolled up* to the door.]



☆**roll·a·way** (rōl′ə wā) ***adj.*** having rollers or wheels underneath for easy moving and storage when not in use [a *rollaway* bed].

**roll call** the reading aloud of a list of names, as in a classroom, to find out who is present.

**roll·er** (rō′lər) ***n.*** **1** a tube or cylinder on which something is rolled [the *roller* of a window shade; a hair *roller*]. **2** a heavy cylinder used to roll over something in order to crush, smooth, or spread it [A steam*roller* crushed the gravel on the road.] **3** a cylinder covered with a fuzzy fabric, used for painting walls, etc. **4** a long, heavy wave that breaks on the shoreline. **5** a canary that trills its notes. **6** anything that rolls.

☆**roller coaster** an amusement ride in which cars move on tracks that curve and dip sharply.

☆**roller skate** a skate having wheels instead of a runner, for skating on floors, walks, etc. *See the picture.*

☆**roll·er-skate** (rō′lər skāt′) ***v.*** to move on roller skates. —**roll′er-skat′ed, roll′er-skat′ing**

**rol·lick·ing** (räl′ik iŋ) ***adj.*** lighthearted and carefree; full of fun [a *rollicking* song; a *rollicking* party].

**rolling mill** a factory or machine for rolling metal into sheets and bars.

**rolling pin** a heavy, smooth cylinder of wood, glass, etc., used to roll out dough. *See the picture.*

**rolling stock** all the locomotives and cars of a railroad or the trucks and trailers of a trucking company.

**ro·ly-po·ly** (rō′lē pō′lē) ***adj.*** short and plump; pudgy [a *roly-poly* baby].

**Roly-poly** is a humorous word formed by making the second part rhyme with the first part, but using a different starting letter. Other words formed this way are *hocus-pocus* and *higgledy-piggledy*.

**Rom.** *abbreviation for* **Roman, Romania.**

**ro·maine** (rō mān′ *or* rō′mān) ***n.*** a kind of lettuce with long leaves that form a loose head.

**Ro·man** (rō′mən) ***adj.*** **1** of ancient or modern Rome, its people, etc. **2** of the Roman Catholic Church. **3** *usually* **roman,** describing the ordinary style of printing type, in which the letters do not slant [This is roman type.] ◆***n.*** **1** a person born or living in ancient or modern Rome. **2** *usually* **roman,** roman type.

**Roman Catholic 1** of or belonging to the Christian church that has the Pope as its head. **2** a member of this church.

**ro·mance** (rō mans′ *or* rō′mans) ***n.*** **1** a story or poem of love and adventure, originally one with knights as the heroes. **2** love, adventure, or excitement of the kind found in such stories [a novel full of *romance*]. **3** a love affair. ◆***v.*** (rō mans′) **1** to write or tell romances. **2** to think or talk about romantic things. —**ro·manced′, ro·manc′ing** ◆***adj.*** **Romance,** describing any of the languages that grew out of Latin [French, Spanish, Italian, etc. are *Romance* languages.]

**Romance** comes from the Latin name for the ancient city of Rome. In the Middle Ages, storytellers particularly liked tales of knights and ladies, of adventure and love. These stories were told in the Romance languages, especially French, and so they were called **romances.** Later the spirit of love and adventure in these stories also came to be called **romance.**

**Roman Empire** the empire of ancient Rome, from 27 B.C. to 395 A.D., when it was divided into the **Western Roman Empire,** ending 476 A.D., and the **Eastern Roman Empire,** ending 1453.

**Ro·man·esque** (rō mə nesk′) ***adj.*** describing a style of architecture in Europe in the 11th and 12th centuries, using round arches and vaults.

**Ro·ma·ni·a** (rō mā′nē ə) a country in south central Europe, on the Black Sea. —**Ro·ma′ni·an *adj., n.***

**Roman numerals** letters of the Roman alphabet

used as numerals. In this system, I = 1, V = 5, X = 10, L = 50, C = 100, D = 500, and M = 1,000. These were the only numerals in use until the 10th century A.D.

**Ro·mans** (rō′mənz) a book of the New Testament, a letter from the Apostle Paul to the Christians of Rome.

**ro·man·tic** (rō man′tik) ***adj.*** **1** of, like, or filled with romance, or love and adventure [a *romantic* novel]. *See* SYNONYMS *at* **sentimental**. **2** not practical or realistic; fanciful [a *romantic* scheme]. **3** describing a kind of writing, music, art, etc., especially of the late 18th and 19th centuries, that shows much originality, imagination, strong feeling, etc. [*romantic* poetry; *romantic* music]. **4** suited for romance [a *romantic* night]. ◆***n.*** **1** a romantic, idealistic person. **2** a writer, composer, etc. of the romantic style. —**ro·man′ti·cal·ly *adv.***

**ro·man·ti·cism** (rō man′tə siz′m) ***n.*** the romantic style or outlook in writing, music, etc.

**Rome** (rōm) the capital of Italy. In ancient times it was the capital of the Roman Empire.

**Ro·me·o** (rō′mē ō) the hero of Shakespeare's tragedy *Romeo and Juliet*.

**romp** (rämp) ***v.*** to play in a lively, somewhat rough way; frolic. ◆***n.*** **1** rough, lively play. **2** an easy victory [to win in a *romp*].

**romp·ers** (räm′pərz) ***n.pl.*** a loose, one-piece outer garment for a small child.

**Rom·u·lus** (räm′yoo ləs) in Roman myths, the founder and first king of Rome. He and his twin brother Remus were raised by a she-wolf.

**rood** (ro͞od) ***n.*** **1** a crucifix. **2** a measure of land equal to 1/4 acre.

**roof** (ro͞of *or* ro͝of) ***n.*** **1** the outside top covering of a building. **2** anything like a roof in the way it is placed or used [the *roof* of the mouth; the *roof* of a car]. ◆***v.*** to cover with a roof [a house *roofed* with shingles]. —**roof′less *adj.***

**roof·ing** (ro͞of′iŋ *or* ro͝of′iŋ) ***n.*** materials used for roofs.

**roof·top** (ro͞of′täp *or* ro͝of′täp) ***n.*** the roof of a building.

**rook**[1] (ro͝ok) ***n.*** **1** a European crow that builds its nests in trees around buildings. **2** a cheater, especially in gambling. ◆***v.*** to cheat; swindle.

> The **rook** is a large, noisy crow. It likes to be near people and roosts in huge colonies. The rook is a thieving bird and from that, people who are cheaters or swindlers came to be called **rooks**.

**rook**[2] (ro͝ok) ***n.*** a chess piece that can move straight ahead or to either side across any number of empty squares; castle.

**rook·er·y** (ro͝ok′ər ē) ***n.*** **1** a place where rooks breed in large numbers. **2** the breeding place of certain other birds or animals, as seals or penguins. —*pl.* **rook′er·ies**

**rook·ie** (ro͝ok′ē) ***n.*** **1** a new recruit in the army. ☆**2** any beginner, as on a sports team or police force. *This is a slang word.*

**room** (ro͞om) ***n.*** **1** a space inside a building, set off by walls, doors, etc. **2** enough space [Is there *room* for me at the table?] **3** suitable scope or chance [It leaves little *room* for doubt.] **4** all the people in a room [The whole *room* was silent.] **5 rooms,** *pl.* a

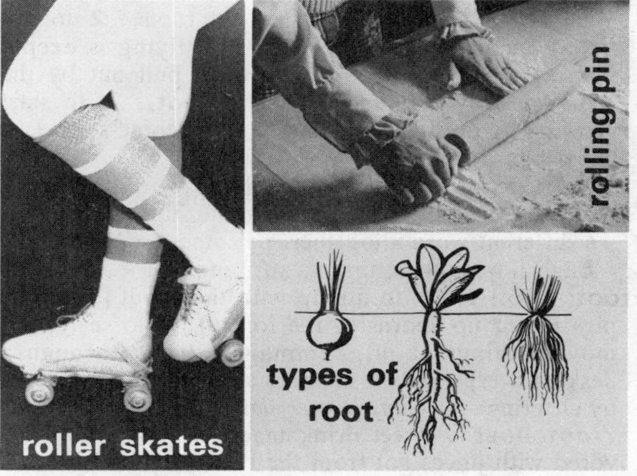


place to live in; lodgings. ◆☆***v.*** to live in a room or rooms; lodge [to *room* with friends].

☆**room·er** (ro͞om′ər) ***n.*** a person who rents a room or rooms to live in; lodger.

**room·ful** (ro͞om′fo͝ol) ***n.*** enough people or things to fill a room. —*pl.* **room′fuls**

☆**rooming house** a house with furnished rooms for people to rent.

☆**room·mate** (ro͞om′māt) ***n.*** a person with whom one shares a room or rooms.

**room·y** (ro͞om′ē) ***adj.*** having plenty of room or space; spacious [a *roomy* car]. —**room′i·er, room′i·est** — **room′i·ness *n.*** 639

**Roo·se·velt, Franklin D.** (rō′zə velt) 1882–1945; 32d president of the United States, from 1933 to 1945.

**Roosevelt, Theodore** 1858–1919; 26th president of the United States, from 1901 to 1909.

**roost** (ro͞ost) ***n.*** **1** a pole, shelf, etc. on which birds can rest or sleep; perch. **2** a place with such roosts, as a hen house. **3** a place to rest or sleep. ◆***v.*** to rest or sleep as on a roost. —**come home to roost,** to have an effect back on the one who began the action; boomerang. —**rule the roost,** to be boss.

**roost·er** (ro͞os′tər) ***n.*** the male of the chicken; cock.

**root**[1] (ro͞ot) ***n.*** **1** the part of a plant that grows into the ground, where it holds the plant in place and takes water and food from the soil. *See the picture.* **2** the part of a tooth, hair, etc. that is attached to the body. **3** a source or cause [This error is the *root* of our trouble.] **4 roots,** *pl.* the close ties one has with some place or people as through birth, upbringing, etc. **5** a number which, when multiplied by itself a certain number of times, gives a certain result [4 is the square *root* of 16 (4 x 4 = 16); 4 is the cube *root* of 64 (4 x 4 x 4 = 64).] **6** a word or part of a word that is used as a base for making other words [The word "body" is the *root* for the words "bodily," "disembodied," etc.] ◆***v.***

| | | | | | | | |
|---|---|---|---|---|---|---|---|
| **a** | fat | **ir** | here | **ou** | out | **zh** | leisure |
| **ā** | ape | **ī** | bite, fire | **u** | up | **ŋ** | ring |
| **ä** | car, lot | **ō** | go | **ur** | fur | | a *in* ago |
| **e** | ten | **ô** | law, horn | **ch** | chin | | e *in* agent |
| **er** | care | **oi** | oil | **sh** | she | **ə** = | i *in* unity |
| **ē** | even | **o͝o** | look | **th** | thin | | o *in* collect |
| **i** | hit | **o͞o** | tool | ***th*** | then | | u *in* focus |

**1** to start to grow by putting out roots. **2** to put firmly in place; settle [Her fear of flying is deeply *rooted.*] —**root up** or **root out,** to pull out by the roots; destroy completely. —**take root, 1** to start growing by putting out roots. **2** to become settled. —**root′less** ***adj.***

> **Root**[1] comes from an old Norse word *rot,* and meant a twig or root right from the start. **Root**[2] is a different word altogether. It comes from an Old English word *wrot,* that meant "snout."

**root**[2] (ro͞ot) ***v.*** **1** to dig up with the snout [The wild pigs *rooted* up acorns in the forest.] **2** to search by moving things about; rummage [to *root* through a desk drawer]. ☆**3** to support a team, player, etc. as by cheering: *used only in everyday talk.*

☆**root beer** a sweet drink made of soda water flavored with juices got from the roots and bark of certain plants.

**root·let** (ro͞ot′lit) ***n.*** a little root.

**rope** (rōp) ***n.*** **1** a thick, strong cord made by twisting fibers or wires together. *See the picture.* **2** a number of things strung together as on a line or thread [a *rope* of pearls]. **3** a sticky, stringy substance [a *rope* of taffy]. ◆***v.*** **1** to fasten or tie together with a rope. **2** to set off or keep apart with a rope [*Rope* off the hole in the ice.] ☆**3** to catch with a lasso [The cowboy *roped* the steer.] —**roped, rop′ing** —**know the ropes,** to know the details of a certain job: *used only in everyday talk.* —☆**rope in,** to trick someone into doing something: *a slang phrase.* —**the end of one's rope,** the end of one's strength, courage, energy, etc.

**rop·y** (rō′pē) ***adj.*** **1** forming sticky, stringy threads, as some liquids. **2** like a rope. —**rop′i·er, rop′i·est**

**Roque·fort cheese** (rōk′fərt) *a trademark for* a strong cheese with a bluish mold, made from goats' and ewes' milk.

**ro·sa·ry** (rō′zər ē) ***n.*** **1** a string of beads used as by Roman Catholics to keep count when saying prayers. **2** the prayers said. —*pl.* **ro′sa·ries**

**rose**[1] (rōz) ***n.*** **1** a bush with prickly stems and sweet-smelling flowers of red, pink, white, yellow, etc. **2** its flower. **3** a pinkish-red color.

**rose**[2] (rōz) *past tense of* **rise.**

**ro·sé** (rō zā′) ***n.*** a light, pink wine.

**ro·se·ate** (rō′zē it) ***adj.*** rose-colored; rosy.

**rose·bud** (rōz′bud) ***n.*** the bud of a rose.

**rose·bush** (rōz′boosh) ***n.*** a shrub that bears roses.

**rose·mar·y** (rōz′mer′ē) ***n.*** an evergreen shrub with sweet-smelling leaves that are used in perfume and as a seasoning in cooking.

> **Rosemary** originally grew along the Mediterranean Sea, and in Latin was called "dew of the sea." In Latin, *ros* means "dew," and *maris* means "of the sea." Later, when it came into English, the spelling was changed as if the word came from *rose,* the flower, and *Mary,* the woman's name.

**ro·sette** (rō zet′) ***n.*** a decoration, as of ribbon, made in the shape of a rose. *See the picture.*

**rose water** a mixture of water with an oil made from rose petals, used as a perfume.

**rose·wood** (rōz′wood) ***n.*** a hard, reddish wood from certain trees that grow in the tropics, used in making fine furniture.

**Rosh Ha·sha·na** (rōsh′ hə shô′nə *or* rōsh′ hə shä′nə) the Jewish New Year. It comes in the fall.

**ros·in** (räz′′n) ***n.*** a hard, yellowish resin made from crude turpentine. It is used in varnishes and is rubbed on violin bows, on athletes' hands and shoes to keep them from slipping, etc.

**Ross** (rôs), **Betsy** 1752–1836; American woman who made the first American flag.

**Ros·si·ni** (rô sē′nē), **Gio·ac·chi·no** (jō′ä kē′nō) 1792–1868; Italian composer.

**ros·ter** (räs′tər) ***n.*** a list of names, as of soldiers or sailors, telling what work each is to do for a certain time.

**ros·trum** (räs′trəm) ***n.*** the platform on which a person stands while making a public speech. —*pl.* **ros′trums** or **ros·tra** (räs′trə)

> Ancient warships had sharp prows shaped much like a bird's beak, used to ram enemy vessels. When such a ship was captured by the ancient Romans, the prow, called a **rostrum** (Latin for "beak"), was displayed on the speaker's platform in the public square, or forum, of Rome. In time the platform itself came to be called a rostrum.

**ros·y** (rō′zē) ***adj.*** **1** like a rose in color; red or pink [*rosy* cheeks]. **2** bright, hopeful, cheerful, etc. [a *rosy* outlook]. —**ros′i·er, ros′i·est** —**ros′i·ly** ***adv.*** —**ros′i·ness** ***n.***

**rot** (rät) ***v.*** **1** to fall apart or spoil, as by the action of bacteria, dampness, etc.; decay [A dead tree will *rot.*] **2** to make this happen to [Water standing in the fields *rots* young plants.] —**rot′ted, rot′ting** ◆***n.*** **1** the act or result of rotting. **2** any rotting disease of plants and animals.

**ro·ta·ry** (rōt′ər ē) ***adj.*** **1** turning around a point or axis in the middle; rotating [the *rotary* motion of a wheel]. **2** having a part or parts that rotate [a *rotary* printing press].

**ro·tate** (rō′tāt) ***v.*** **1** to turn around a center point or axis, as a wheel; revolve [The earth *rotates* on its axis.] *See* SYNONYMS *at* **turn. 2** to change by turns in regular order; alternate [Farmers *rotate* crops to keep soil fertile.] —**ro′tat·ed, ro′tat·ing** —**ro·ta′tion** ***n.***

**rote** (rōt) ***n.*** a fixed way of doing something.

> The word **rote** is now used only in the phrase **by rote,** in speaking of something that has been learned by heart and may then be repeated without thought or understanding [The students recited the poetry *by rote.*]

**Roth·schild** (rôth′chīld *or* räths′chīld) a family of bankers in Europe, originally in Germany.

☆**ro·tis·ser·ie** (rō tis′ər ē) ***n.*** a broiler having a spit that is turned by electricity.

**ro·tor** (rōt′ər) ***n.*** **1** the rotating part of a motor, dynamo, etc. **2** the system of rotating blades in a helicopter.

**rot·ten** (rät′′n) ***adj.*** **1** having rotted; decayed or spoiled [*rotten* apples; a *rotten* floor]. **2** unpleasant or disgusting; putrid [a *rotten* odor]. **3** wicked, dishonest, corrupt, etc. [*rotten* politics]. **4** very bad; disagreeable: *a slang meaning.* —**rot′ten·ly** ***adv.*** —**rot′ten·ness** ***n.***

**Rot·ter·dam** (rät′ər dam) a seaport in the southwestern Netherlands.

**ro·tund** (rō tund′) ***adj.*** rounded out; plump or stout. —**ro·tun′di·ty** ***n.***

**ro·tun·da** (rō tun′də) ***n.*** a round building, hall, or room, especially one with a dome. *See the picture.*

**rou·é** (ro͞o ā′) ***n.*** a man who leads a wild life, as by drinking and gambling; rake.

**rouge** (ro͞ozh) ***n.*** a red powder or paste used to color the cheeks and lips. ◆***v.*** to put rouge on. —**rouged, roug′ing**

**rough** (ruf) ***adj.*** **1** not smooth or level; uneven [a *rough* road; *rough* fur]. **2** wild in force or motion [a *rough* sea]. **3** stormy [*rough* weather]. **4** full of noise and wild action; disorderly [*rough* play]. **5** not gentle or mild, as in manners; rude, harsh, etc. [*rough* language]. **6** having little comfort or luxury [the *rough* life of a pioneer]. **7** not polished or refined; natural, crude, etc. [a *rough* diamond]. **8** not finished; not worked out in detail [a *rough* sketch]. **9** unpleasant or difficult: *used only in everyday talk* [a *rough* time]. ◆***n.*** ☆**1** a rough sketch or draft. **2** any part of a golf course where grass and weeds are allowed to grow uncut. **3** a rowdy person: *used mainly in Great Britain.* ◆***adv.*** in a rough way. ◆***v.*** **1** to make rough; roughen [Use the file to *rough* up the metal.] **2** to treat in a rough or brutal way [The gangsters *roughed* up their victim.] **3** to make or shape in a rough way [He *roughed* in the windows in the sketch of the house.] —**in the rough,** in a rough or crude state. —**rough it,** to live without comforts and conveniences, as in camping.

SYNONYMS: **Rough** is used to describe any surface with points, ridges, bumps, etc. [Her chapped skin was *rough.* The football field was *rough* in the spring.] **Harsh** is used of that which is disagreeably rough to the touch [The *harsh* cloth of the uniform made his neck sore.]

☆**rough·age** (ruf′ij) ***n.*** coarse, rough food, as bran and vegetable peel, that is only partly digested, but helps to move waste products through the intestines.

**rough·en** (ruf′′n) ***v.*** to make or become rough.

**rough-hew** (ruf′hyo͞o′) ***v.*** to hew or form roughly, without the final smoothing: *also* **roughhew.** —**rough′-hewed′, rough′-hewn′, rough′-hew′ing**

**rough·ly** (ruf′lē) ***adv.*** **1** in a rough manner. **2** more or less; about [*Roughly* 50 people came to the party.]

☆**rough·neck** (ruf′nek) ***n.*** a rough person; rowdy: *a slang word.*

**rough·shod** (ruf′shäd′) ***adj.*** having horseshoes with metal points that keep the horse from slipping. —**ride roughshod over,** to show no pity or regard for; treat in a bullying way.

**rou·lette** (ro͞o let′) ***n.*** **1** a gambling game in which players bet on where a ball rolling on a turning wheel (**roulette wheel**) will stop. *See the picture.* **2** a small wheel with sharp teeth for making rows of marks or holes, as between postage stamps.

**Rou·ma·ni·a** (ro͞o mā′nē ə) *another spelling for* **Romania.** —**Rou·ma′ni·an** ***adj., n.***

**round** (round) ***adj.*** **1** shaped like a ball, a circle, or a tube; having an outline that forms a circle or curve [The world is *round.* Wheels are *round.* The ship has a *round* smokestack.] **2** plump; chubby [his *round* cheeks]. **3** done by moving in a circle [The polka is a *round* dance.] **4** pronounced with the lips forming a circle [O is a *round* vowel.] **5** mellow and rich; not harsh [full, *round* tones]. **6** full; complete [a *round* dozen]. **7** large in amount [We paid a good *round* sum for it.] **8** that is a whole number, or is given in even units, as tens, hundreds, thousands, etc. [500 is a *round* number for 498 or 503.] **9** brisk [a *round* pace]. ◆***n.*** **1** something round, as the rung of a ladder. **2** movement in a circle. **3** a dance in which the dancers move in a circle: *the full name is* **round dance. 4** *often* **rounds,** *pl.* a course or route taken regularly; beat [Has the security guard made the *rounds* yet?] **5** a series, as of actions or events [a *round* of parties]. **6** a single shot from a gun, or from several guns fired together. **7** bullets, shells, etc. for such a shot [They passed out one *round* of ammunition.] **8** a single outburst [a *round* of applause]. **9** a single period of action, as one complete game [a *round* of golf]. **10** one of the timed periods in boxing [The champion was knocked out in the third *round.*] **11** a short song for two or more persons or groups, in which the second starts when the first gets to the second phrase, and so on. **12** the thigh of a beef animal: *the full name for this is* **round of beef.** ◆***v.*** **1** to make or become round [*Round* the corners of the board.] **2** to complete; finish (*usually with* out *or* off) [to *round* out the day]. **3** to go around or pass by [The car *rounded* the corner.] **4** to pronounce with the lips forming a circle [to *round* a vowel]. ◆***adv.*** **1** in a circle [The wheels turned *round.*] **2** through a complete cycle of time [They work the whole year *round.*] **3** from one person or place to another [The peddler went *round* from door to door.] **4** for everyone [There was not enough

rotunda

rosette

roulette wheel

rope



| | | | | | | | |
|---|---|---|---|---|---|---|---|
| a | fat | ir | here | ou | out | zh | leisure |
| ā | ape | ī | bite, fire | u | up | ŋ | ring |
| ä | car, lot | ō | go | ur | fur | | a *in* ago |
| e | ten | ô | law, horn | ch | chin | | e *in* agent |
| er | care | oi | oil | sh | she | ə = | i *in* unity |
| ē | even | oo | look | th | thin | | o *in* collect |
| i | hit | o͞o | tool | *th* | then | | u *in* focus |

candy to go *round*.] **5** in circumference; in distance around [The tree trunk is 48 inches *round*.] **6** on all sides [The woods stretched *round*.] **7** about; near [We'll visit all the people *round*.] **8** in a roundabout way [Let's drive *round* by the lake on our way home.] **9** in various places; here and there [They are looking *round* for a new secretary.] **10** in or to the opposite direction [She turned *round*.] ◆***prep.*** **1** in a circle that surrounds [Tie the rope *round* the tree.] **2** on all sides of [The crowd gathered *round* him.] **3** near; in the area of [the towns *round* Cleveland]. **4** to each part or person [She passed the picture *round* the class.] **5** here and there in; about [The child played *round* the room.] **6** so as to turn to the other side of [The water flowed *round* the rock.] *See the note in color at* **around.** —**in the round,** **1** with the people seated all around a central area for a stage or altar, as in a theater or church. **2** in full or rounded form, not coming out from a background, as sculpture. —**round about,** **1** in or to the opposite direction. **2** in every direction around. —**round up,** ☆**1** to drive together into a group or herd, as cattle. ☆**2** to gather or collect: *used only in everyday talk.* —**round′ish** ***adj.*** —**round′ness** ***n.***

**round·a·bout** (round′ə bout) ***adj.*** not straight or direct [a *roundabout* trip; *roundabout* answers].

**roun·de·lay** (roun′də lā) ***n.*** a simple song in which some phrase is repeated over and over.

 **round·house** (round′hous) ***n.*** ☆**1** a building for storing and repairing locomotives. It is usually round, with a turning platform in the center. **2** a cabin at the rear of a ship's upper deck.

**round·ly** (round′lē) ***adv.*** **1** in a round form; in a circle, curve, ball, etc. **2** in a harsh or sharp manner [The lazy student was *roundly* scolded.] **3** fully; completely.

**round-shoul·dered** (round′shōl′dərd) ***adj.*** stooped because the shoulders are not held straight. *See the picture.*

**Round Table** **1** the table around which King Arthur and his knights sat. **2** King Arthur and his knights.

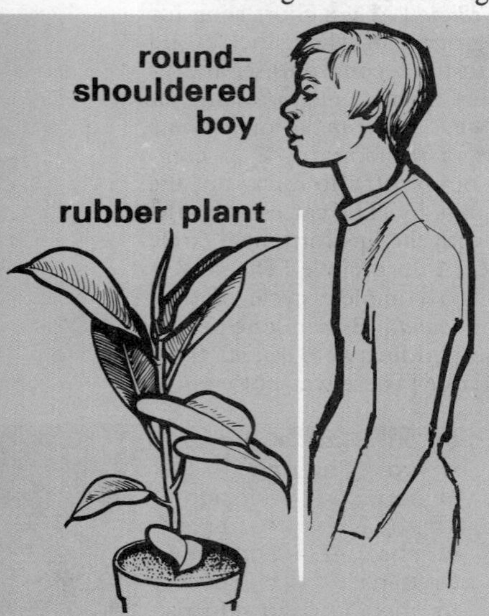

round–shouldered boy

rubber plant

rudder

ruff

**3 round table,** a group of persons gathered together to discuss something.

According to legend, the **Round Table** of King Arthur was made circular because the knights were of equal rank, and thus no seat would be in a more important position than another.

☆**round trip** a trip to a place and back to the starting point. —**round′-trip′** ***adj.***

**round·up** (round′up) ***n.*** ☆**1** the act of driving cattle together into a group, as for branding. ☆**2** the cowboys, horses, etc. that drive the herd together. ☆**3** any act of collecting a group. ☆**4** a summary, as of news on radio or TV.

**rouse** (rouz) ***v.*** **1** to wake; come or bring out of sleep. **2** to stir up; excite [to *rouse* anger]. **3** to flush game birds from cover. —**roused, rous′ing**

**Rous·seau** (ro͞o sō′), **Jean Jacques** (zhän zhäk) 1712–1778; French philosopher and writer.

**roust·a·bout** (roust′ə bout) ***n.*** ☆an unskilled worker on docks, in circuses, on ranches, etc.

**rout**[1] (rout) ***n.*** **1** a confused retreat, as of an army [The enemy was put to *rout*.] **2** a complete, crushing defeat. ◆***v.*** **1** to make retreat in a confused way [to *rout* enemy troops]. **2** to defeat completely.

**Rout**[1] comes from an old French word and first meant a company or band of people or a large party held in the evening. From that it was used to mean a confused, noisy mob, and finally the disorderly retreat of a troop of soldiers.

**rout**[2] (rout) ***v.*** **1** to dig for food with the snout, as a pig does. **2** to search for or get by poking and moving things. **3** to force out. **4** to scoop or gouge out.

**route** (ro͞ot *or* rout) ***n.*** **1** a road or course traveled or to be traveled [We took the scenic *route* west.] ☆**2** a set of customers to whom one delivers something regularly [a mail carrier's *route*]. ◆***v.*** ☆to send by a certain route. —**rout′ed, rout′ing**

**rou·tine** (ro͞o tēn′) ***n.*** **1** a regular way of doing something, fixed by habit, rules, etc. [the *routine* of getting dinner ready]. ☆**2** a series of steps for a dance. **3** a set of coded instructions for a computer. ◆***adj.*** of, using, or done by routine [a *routine* task].

**rove** (rōv) ***v.*** to wander about; roam [We *roved* the woods.] —**roved, rov′ing**

**rov·er** (rō′vər) ***n.*** **1** a person who roves; wanderer. **2** a pirate or pirate ship: *an old-fashioned meaning.*

**row**[1] (rō) ***n.*** a number of people or things in a line [a *row* of poplars; *rows* of seats]. —☆**a hard row to hoe,** a hard or tiring task or duty.

**row**[2] (rō) ***v.*** **1** to move a boat on water by using oars. **2** to carry in a rowboat [I'll *row* you across the lake.] ◆***n.*** a trip made by rowboat [to go for a *row*]. —**row′er** ***n.***

**row**[3] (rou) ***n.*** a noisy quarrel or brawl; uproar or commotion. ◆***v.*** to take part in a row.

**row·boat** (rō′bōt) ***n.*** a boat made to be rowed.

☆**row·dy** (rou′dē) ***n.*** a rough, noisy person who starts fights; hoodlum. —*pl.* **row′dies** ◆***adj.*** rough, noisy, etc. [a *rowdy* party]. —**row′di·er, row′di·est** —**row′di·ly** ***adv.*** —**row′di·ness** ***n.*** —**row′dy·ism** ***n.***

**row·el** (rou′əl) ***n.*** a small wheel with sharp points, forming the end of a spur. *See the picture for* **spur.**

☆**row house** (rō) any of a line of houses that are just alike and are joined along the sides by common walls.

**roy·al** (roi′əl) ***adj.*** **1** of or by a king or queen [a *royal* edict; *royal* power]. **2** that is a king or queen [Her *Royal* Highness]. **3** of a kingdom, its government, etc. [the *royal* fleet]. **4** like or fit for a king or queen; splendid, magnificent, etc. [a *royal* meal]. —**roy'al·ly** ***adv.***

**roy·al·ist** (roi'əl ist) ***n.*** a person who supports a king or a monarchy, as during a civil war or revolution. ◆***adj.*** of royalists.

**roy·al·ty** (roi'əl tē) ***n.*** **1** a royal person, or royal persons as a group [a member of British *royalty*]. **2** the rank or power of a king or queen. **3** royal quality or nature; nobility, splendor, etc. **4** a share of the earnings as from an invention, book, or play, paid to the inventor, writer, etc. for the right to make, use, or publish it. —*pl.* **roy'al·ties**

**rpm** or **r.p.m.** revolutions per minute.

**rps** or **r.p.s.** revolutions per second.

**R.R.** **1** railroad. **2** Right Reverend. **3** Rural Route.

**R.S.F.S.R.** or **RSFSR** Russian Soviet Federated Socialist Republic. *See* **Russia.**

**R.S.V.P.** or **r.s.v.p.** please reply. The initials come from the French words *répondez s'il vous plaît*.

**rub** (rub) ***v.*** **1** to move a hand, cloth, etc. back and forth over something firmly [She *rubbed* her sore leg. *Rub* the wood to make it shine.] **2** to move with pressure and friction [The chair *rubbed* against the wall.] **3** to spread on by rubbing [to *rub* wax on a car]. **4** to make by rubbing [to *rub* oneself dry with a towel]. **5** to make sore by rubbing [This shoe *rubs* my heel.] **6** to remove or be removed by rubbing [*Rub* that mark out with an eraser. This paint will not *rub* off.] —**rubbed, rub'bing** ◆***n.*** **1** the act of rubbing. **2** difficulty or trouble [She may not even know—there's the *rub*.] **3** something that hurts the feelings, as a teasing remark. —**rub down,** to massage. —**rub it in,** to keep mentioning a failure or mistake that someone has made: *a slang phrase.* —**rub the wrong way,** to annoy.

**rub·ber**[1] (rub'ər) ***n.*** **1** a person or thing that rubs. **2** a springy substance made from the milky sap of various tropical plants or from chemicals. It is used in making automobile tires, waterproof material, etc. **3** something made of this substance, as an elastic band (**rubber band**), an eraser, an overshoe, etc. ◆***adj.*** made of rubber [*rubber* gloves]. —**rub'ber·y** ***adj.***

**rub·ber**[2] (rub'ər) ***n.*** **1** a series of games in which two out of three or three out of five must be won to win the whole series. **2** any game played to break a tie.

**rub·ber·ize** (rub'ər īz) ***v.*** to coat or fill with rubber [to *rubberize* cloth]. —**rub'ber·ized, rub'ber·iz·ing**

**rubber plant** an Asian tree with large, glossy, leathery leaves, often used as a house plant. *See the picture.*

**rubber stamp** **1** a stamp made of rubber, inked on a pad and used for printing dates, signatures, etc. ☆**2** a person or group that approves another's plans, decisions, etc. in a routine way, without thought: *used only in everyday talk in this meaning.*

**rub·bish** (rub'ish) ***n.*** **1** anything thrown away as worthless; trash. **2** foolish ideas, statements, etc.; nonsense.

**rub·ble** (rub''l) ***n.*** **1** rough, broken pieces of stone, brick, etc. **2** masonry made up of such pieces. **3** broken pieces from buildings, etc. damaged or destroyed by an earthquake, bombing, etc.

**rub·down** (rub'doun) ***n.*** a massage.

**Ru·bens** (ro͞o'bənz), **Peter Paul** 1577–1640; Flemish painter.

**Ru·bi·con** (ro͞o'bi kän') a small river in northern Italy. Julius Caesar crossed it in 49 B.C. and went on to seize power in Rome. —**cross the Rubicon,** to start to do something important from which one cannot turn back.

**ru·bi·cund** (ro͞o'bi kund') ***adj.*** reddish; ruddy [plump, *rubicund* cheeks].

**ru·ble** (ro͞o'b'l) ***n.*** the basic unit of money in the U.S.S.R.

**ru·bric** (ro͞o'brik) ***n.*** **1** a heading, title, first letter, etc. printed in red or in fancy lettering, as in early books. **2** an agreed-on method of doing something.

**ru·by** (ro͞o'bē) ***n.*** **1** a clear, deep-red, costly jewel. **2** deep red. —*pl.* **ru'bies**

☆**ru·by-throat·ed hummingbird** (ro͞o'bē thrōt'id) a common hummingbird of North America. The male has a shiny green back and a red throat.

**rud·der** (rud'ər) ***n.*** **1** a broad, flat piece of wood or metal attached by hinges to the rear of a boat or ship and used for steering. *See the picture.* **2** a piece like this on an airplane, etc.

**rud·dy** (rud'ē) ***adj.*** **1** red and healthy-looking [a *ruddy* complexion]. **2** red or reddish [the *ruddy* glow of the fire]. —**rud'di·er, rud'di·est** —**rud'di·ness** ***n.***

**rude** (ro͞od) ***adj.*** **1** without respect for others; impolite [It was *rude* of them not to thank you.] **2** rough or crude [a *rude* hut deep in the woods]. **3** not civi- 643
lized or educated [*rude* mountain tribes]. **4** rough or violent [a *rude* awakening]. —**rud'er, rud'est** —**rude'ly** ***adv.*** —**rude'ness** ***n.***

SYNONYMS: **Rude** is used to describe someone who does not show proper respect for others or who behaves in a way that hurts someone's feelings [It was *rude* of you to laugh when I made a mistake in class.] **Discourteous** is a weaker word and suggests simply a failure to be polite or thoughtful of others [It was *discourteous* not to answer the letter.]

**ru·di·ment** (ro͞o'də mənt) ***n.*** **1** something to be learned first, as a basic principle [the *rudiments* of science]. **2** a first slight beginning of something [the *rudiments* of a plan].

**ru·di·men·ta·ry** (ro͞o'də men'tər ē) ***adj.*** **1** to be learned first; elementary [*rudimentary* studies]. **2** not fully developed [A tadpole has *rudimentary* legs].

**rue**[1] (ro͞o) ***v.*** to feel sorry because of something; regret [He *rued* his angry words.] —**rued, ru'ing**

**rue**[2] (ro͞o) ***n.*** a plant with yellow flowers and bitter leaves once used in medicine.

**rue·ful** (ro͞o'fəl) ***adj.*** feeling or showing some sorrow or regret; slightly sad [a *rueful* look]. —**rue'ful·ly** ***adv.***

**ruff** (ruf) ***n.*** **1** a stiff, frilly collar worn by men and women in the 16th and 17th centuries. *See the picture.*

| | | | | | | | |
|---|---|---|---|---|---|---|---|
| **a** | fat | **ir** | here | **ou** | out | **zh** | leisure |
| **ā** | ape | **ī** | bite, fire | **u** | up | **ng** | ring |
| **ä** | car, lot | **ō** | go | **ur** | fur | | a *in* ago |
| **e** | ten | **ô** | law, horn | **ch** | chin | | e *in* agent |
| **er** | care | **oi** | oil | **sh** | she | **ə =** | i *in* unity |
| **ē** | even | **oo** | look | **th** | thin | | o *in* collect |
| **i** | hit | **o͞o** | tool | ***th*** | then | | u *in* focus |

**r**

2 a ring of feathers or fur standing out about the neck of a bird or animal. —**ruffed** ***adj.***

☆**ruffed grouse** a wild bird with neck feathers that it can make stand out in a ruff. It is hunted as a game bird.

**ruf·fi·an** (ruf′ē ən) ***n.*** a rough, brutal person who does not obey the law.

**ruf·fle**[1] (ruf′'l) ***n.*** **1** a strip of cloth, lace, etc. gathered in pleats or puckers and used for trimming. **2** something that disturbs or annoys [The meeting went along without a *ruffle.*] ◆***v.*** **1** to put ruffles on. **2** to fold into ruffles. **3** to disturb the smoothness of [Wind *ruffled* the pond. The bird *ruffled* its feathers.] **4** to disturb or annoy [questions that *ruffled* the speaker]. —**ruf′fled, ruf′fling**

**ruf·fle**[2] (ruf′'l) ***n.*** a low beating of a drum that goes on for some time without any break.

**rug** (rug) ***n.*** a piece of some thick, heavy material used to cover floors.

**Rug·by** (rug′bē) a private school for boys in England. ◆***n.*** a kind of football first played at this school.

**rug·ged** (rug′id) ***adj.*** **1** having an uneven surface; rough [*rugged* ground]. **2** heavy and not regular [the *rugged* features of his face]. **3** stormy or difficult; severe; harsh [*rugged* weather; a *rugged* life]. ☆**4** strong; vigorous; hardy [a *rugged* person].

**Ruhr** (roor) **1** a river in central West Germany. **2** the industrial region along this river.

644 **ru·in** (rōō′in) ***n.*** **1** *often* **ruins,** *pl.* a building, city, etc. that has decayed or been destroyed [We saw the *ruins* of an old castle. The bombed church was a *ruin.*] **2** the condition of being destroyed, decayed, etc. [The unused barn fell into *ruin.*] **3** destruction, decay, or downfall [the *ruin* of our hopes]. **4** anything that causes downfall, destruction, etc. [Gambling was the *ruin* of her.] ◆***v.*** **1** to destroy, or damage greatly [The mud will *ruin* your shoes.] **2** to make poor [Three years of drought *ruined* the farmer.]

An old building that is not taken care of will become a ruin—its roof caved in, its windows and doors missing, its walls tumbled down. The word **ruin** comes from a Latin word meaning "to fall to the ground."

**ru·in·a·tion** (rōō′ə nā′shən) ***n.*** **1** a ruining or being ruined. **2** anything that ruins.

**ru·in·ous** (rōō′ə nəs) ***adj.*** **1** causing ruin; very destructive [*ruinous* floods]. **2** fallen into ruin [an old hotel in a *ruinous* state].

**rule** (rōōl) ***n.*** **1** a statement or law that is meant to guide or control the way one acts or does something [the *rules* of grammar; baseball *rules*]. **2** a usual way of doing something, behaving, etc. [to make it a *rule* never to rush]. **3** the usual or expected thing [Cold winters are the *rule* in North Dakota.] **4** government or reign [the *rule* of Elizabeth I]. **5** *same as* **ruler** *in meaning* 2. ◆***v.*** **1** to have power or control over; govern; manage; guide [to *rule* as king; to be *ruled* by the wishes of one's friends]. *See* SYNONYMS *at* **govern. 2** to decide in an official way [The judge *ruled* that Hodges must pay a fine.] **3** to mark straight lines on, as with a ruler [*ruled* paper]. —**ruled, rul′ing —as a rule,** usually. —**rule out,** to decide to leave out or ignore.

**rul·er** (rōō′lər) ***n.*** **1** a person who rules, as a king or queen. **2** a straight, thin strip of wood, metal, etc. used in drawing lines, measuring, etc.

**rul·ing** (rōō′ling) ***adj.*** that rules; having power or control; governing; chief [a *ruling* monarch; a *ruling* idea]. ◆***n.*** an official decision [a *ruling* by the Supreme Court].

**rum** (rum) ***n.*** **1** an alcoholic liquor made from molasses or sugar cane. ☆**2** any strong liquor.

**Ru·ma·ni·a** (rōō mā′nē ə) *another spelling for* **Romania. —Ru·ma′ni·an *adj., n.***

**rum·ble** (rum′b'l) ***v.*** **1** to make a deep, heavy, rolling sound [Thunder *rumbled* in the distance.] **2** to move with such a sound [Heavy trucks were *rumbling* across the old wooden bridge.] —**rum′bled, rum′bling** ◆***n.*** **1** a deep, heavy, rolling sound. ☆**2** a fight between gangs, especially gangs of teen-agers: *slang in this meaning.*

**ru·mi·nant** (rōō′mə nənt) ***n.*** an animal that chews its cud [Cattle, sheep, goats, deer, and camels are *ruminants.*] ◆***adj.*** **1** of or like such animals. **2** tending to think deeply; thoughtful.

**ru·mi·nate** (rōō′mə nāt) ***v.*** **1** to chew the cud, as a cow does. **2** to think quietly and carefully; ponder [to decide after *ruminating* about the matter for weeks]. —**ru′mi·nat·ed, ru′mi·nat·ing —ru′mi·na′tion *n.* —ru′mi·na′tive *adj.***

**rum·mage** (rum′ij) ***v.*** to search by looking through a place in a thorough way, moving things about [I *rummaged* in the closet, trying to find my boots.] —**rum′maged, rum′mag·ing** ◆***n.*** odds and ends [A *rummage* sale is a sale of odds and ends.]

The word **rummage** comes from an old French word meaning "the hold of a ship." The cargo carried in a ship's hold is often a collection of many different kinds of things.

**rum·my** (rum′ē) ☆***n.*** a card game in which each player tries to match cards into sets or groups.

**ru·mor** (rōō′mər) ***n.*** **1** a story told as news, which may or may not be true and which is passed on from person to person [I heard a *rumor* that they were secretly married.] **2** general talk in which such stories are passed along; gossip [According to *rumor,* they're going to move.] ◆***v.*** to tell as a rumor [It has been *rumored* that Pat is leaving school.] *The usual British spelling is* **rumour.**

**rump** (rump) ***n.*** **1** the hind part of an animal, where the legs and back join. **2** a cut of beef from this part.

**rum·ple** (rum′p'l) ***n.*** an uneven crease; wrinkle. ◆***v.*** **1** to make wrinkles in; crumple. *See the picture.* **2** to make untidy; muss up [*rumpled* hair]. —**rum′pled, rum′pling**

**rum·pus** (rum′pəs) ***n.*** a noisy disturbance; uproar: *used only in everyday talk.*

**run** (run) ***v.*** **1** to go by moving the legs faster than in walking. **2** to move or go swiftly, easily, freely, etc. [A breeze *ran* through the trees.] **3** to make a quick trip [Let's *run* down to Miami.] **4** to go away quickly; flee [*Run* for your life!] **5** to take part in or cause to take part in a race or contest [Lou *ran* in the 100-yard dash. Shannon *ran* for mayor. The Democrats *ran* Meyers for Congress.] **6** to go back and forth [Buses *run* between Omaha and Boise.] **7** to keep on going; continue; extend [The play *ran* for a year. This path *runs* through the woods. Our lease *runs* for two more years.] **8** to put or be in use or action; operate; work [What makes the engine *run?*] **9** to drive into or against something [to *run* a car into a tree]. **10** to flow or make flow [Hot water *runs* through this pipe.] ☆**11** to be in charge of; manage [to *run* a household]. **12** to perform or do as by running [to *run* the mile; to *run* errands]. **13** to bring, pass, force, etc. into a certain condition or position [to *run* the business into debt; to *run* into trouble]. **14** to have a certain size, price, etc. [Apples are *running* large this fall.] **15** to be told, written, etc. [The story *runs* that they were really quite poor.] **16** to spread into other parts [The colors *ran* when the plaid shirt was washed.] **17** to let out mucus, pus, etc. [My nose is *running.*] **18** to come apart or ravel [Her stocking *ran.*] **19** to take upon oneself; incur [to *run* a risk]. ☆**20** to get past or through [to *run* a blockade]. **21** to cost [boots that *run* as much as $30 a pair]. **22** to be affected by; undergo [to *run* a fever]. ☆**23** to publish [We *ran* an ad in the morning newspaper.] —**ran, run, run′ning** ◆***n.*** **1** the act of running [Let's take a *run* around the block.] **2** a running pace [The horses broke into a *run.*] **3** a trip; journey [a plane on a regular *run* to Boston]. **4** a series of happenings, performances, requests, etc. without a change or break [a *run* of good luck; a play that had a long *run;* a *run* on electric fans during the heat wave]. **5** a small stream; brook. **6** the time during which a machine is working; also, the work done [The supervisor says that last *run* of clocks is faulty.] **7** a kind or class [the ordinary *run* of students]. **8** a closed-in place where animals or fowls can move about freely [a chicken *run*]. **9** a sloping path or course [a ski *run*]. **10** freedom to move about as one pleases [We had the *run* of the house.] **11** a large number of fish traveling together [a *run* of salmon]. ☆**12** a place in knitted material where the threads have raveled or come apart [a *run* in a stocking]. ☆**13** a point scored in baseball by touching all the bases in order. **14** a series of musical notes played rapidly. —**a run for one's money, 1** close competition. **2** satisfaction for the money or effort spent. —**in the long run,** in the end; finally. —**on the run,** running or running away. —☆**run across,** to come upon by chance. —**run along,** to leave or depart. —**run away, 1** to leave in a hurry; flee. **2** to go away from one's home or family when one should not leave. —**run away with,** to do much better than all the others in a contest. —**run down, 1** to stop working, as a clock. **2** to hit against and knock down. **3** to chase and catch. **4** to say bad things about. **5** to make or become run-down: *see* **run-down.** —**run for it,** to run to escape something. —**run in,** ☆to arrest: *a slang phrase.* —**run into, 1** to meet or come up against by chance. **2** to bump or crash into. —**run off,** ☆**1** to print, make copies of, etc. **2** to cause to be run, played, etc. **3** to chase away. —**run on,** to go or talk on and on; continue without a break. —**run out,** to come to an end; become used up. —**run out of,** to use up. —**run over, 1** to drive over as with a car. **2** to overflow. **3** to go beyond a limit. **4** to look over or go through rapidly. —**run through, 1** to use up or spend quickly. **2** to look over or go through rapidly. —**run up, 1** to raise or rise quickly. **2** to let go without paying [to *run up* bills]. —**run with,** to spend much time with; be friendly with.

**run·a·way** (run′ə wā) ***n.*** a person or animal that runs away. ◆***adj.*** **1** running away [a *runaway* horse]. **2** easily won [a *runaway* race]. **3** rising rapidly [A shortage of goods caused *runaway* prices.]

**run·down** (run′doun) ***n.*** a brief report [Give us a *rundown* on what happened at the meeting.]

**run-down** (run′doun′) ***adj.*** **1** not working because not wound, as a clock. **2** in poor health, as from overwork. **3** in need of repair; falling apart [a *run-down* house].

**rune** (ro͞on) ***n.*** **1** any of the letters in an alphabet used long ago in northern Europe. **2** something written in such letters. —**ru′nic *adj.***

**rung**[1] (ruŋ) ***n.*** a round stick forming a step of a ladder, a crosspiece on a chair, etc.

**rung**[2] (ruŋ) *a past participle of* **ring**[1].

**run-in** (run′in′) ***n.*** ☆a quarrel or fight: *used only in everyday talk.* 

**run·nel** (run″l) ***n.*** a small stream or channel.

**run·ner** (run′ər) ***n.*** **1** a person who runs, as a racer. **2** a person who runs errands or carries messages. **3** a long, narrow cloth or rug. **4** a long ravel, as in a stocking; run. **5** a long, trailing stem of a plant, that puts out roots along the ground. ☆**6** the blade of a skate. ☆**7** either of the long, narrow pieces on which a sled or sleigh slides. *See the picture.*

**run·ner-up** (run′ər up′) ***n.*** a person or team that finishes second or very close to the winner in a race or contest. —*pl.* **run′ners-up′**

**run·ning** (run′iŋ) ***n.*** the act of one that runs. ◆***adj.*** **1** that runs or moves rapidly. **2** flowing [*running* water]. **3** letting out pus, etc. [a *running* sore]. **4** in operation; working [The motor is *running.*] **5** going on without a break [a *running* report of what is taking place]. **6** done with a run [a *running* jump]. **7** of the run of a train, bus, etc. [The *running* time is two hours.] ◆***adv.*** one after another [It has snowed for five days *running.*] —**in the running,** having a chance to win. —**out of the running,** having no chance to win.

**running knot** *another name for* **slipknot.**

**running lights** the lights that a ship or airplane traveling at night is required to have on.

| | | | | | | | |
|---|---|---|---|---|---|---|---|
| **a** | fat | **ir** | here | **ou** | out | **zh** | leisure |
| **ā** | ape | **ī** | bite, fire | **u** | up | **ŋ** | ring |
| **ä** | car, lot | **ō** | go | **ʉr** | fur | | a *in* ago |
| **e** | ten | **ô** | law, horn | **ch** | chin | | e *in* agent |
| **er** | care | **oi** | oil | **sh** | she | **ə =** | i *in* unity |
| **ē** | even | **o͝o** | look | **th** | thin | | o *in* collect |
| **i** | hit | **o͞o** | tool | ***th*** | then | | u *in* focus |

rustic bench

rye

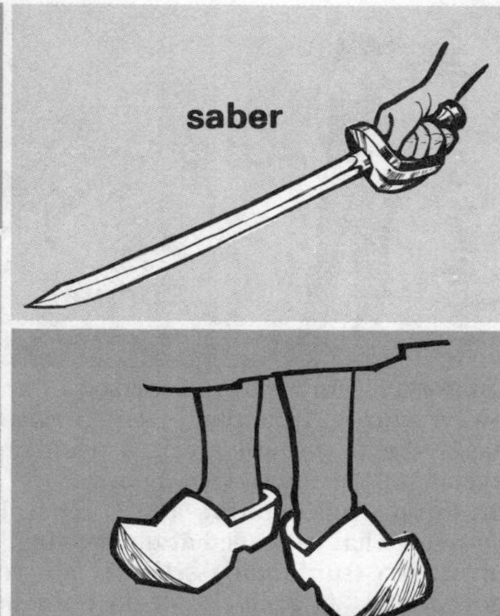
saber

sabots

☆**running mate** a candidate that a political party runs for a less important office, as for the vice-presidency, along with the party's candidate for the more important office.

**run·ny** (run′ē) ***adj.*** **1** that is soft and liquid and flows too freely [The ice cream was not refrigerated and got *runny*.] **2** that keeps on letting out mucus [a *runny* nose].



**run-off** (run′ôf′) ***n.*** ☆**1** something that runs off, as the part of a heavy rain that does not soak into the ground. **2** a final race, election, etc. held to decide who wins, as in case of a tie.

**run-of-the-mill** (run′əv *thə* mil′) ***adj.*** not special in any way; ordinary.

**runt** (runt) ***n.*** an animal or plant that is much smaller than others of its kind.

☆**run·way** (run′wā) ***n.*** a track or path on which something moves, as a paved strip on an airfield used by airplanes in taking off and landing.

**ru·pee** (ro͞o pē′) ***n.*** the basic unit of money in India, and also in Pakistan.

**rup·ture** (rup′chər) ***n.*** **1** a breaking apart or being broken apart [a *rupture* in a gas line]. **2** an ending of friendly relations, as between nations. **3** a pushing out of an organ of the body through a break in the membrane around it; hernia. ◆***v.*** **1** to break or burst [His appendix *ruptured*.] **2** to cause to have a rupture, or hernia [to *rupture* oneself]. —**rup′tured, rup′tur·ing**

**ru·ral** (roor′əl) ***adj.*** having to do with the country or with people who live there, as on farms.

> SYNONYMS: **Rural** is the word we use in talking about life on farms or in the country when it is different from life in the city [*rural* mail delivery]. We use **rustic** when we want to contrast the supposed plainness and simplicity of life in the country and the polish and sophistication of life in the city [They bought a *rustic* picnic table for the patio of their suburban home.]

**ruse** (ro͞oz) ***n.*** a trick or plan for fooling someone [We pretended to be ill as a *ruse* to avoid work.]

**rush**[1] (rush) ***v.*** **1** to move, send, take, etc. with great speed [I *rushed* from the room. We *rushed* him to a hospital.] **2** to act in haste, without thinking carefully [Don't *rush* into marriage.] **3** to do, make, etc. with great haste; hurry [If you *rush* the job, you'll make mistakes.] **4** to attack suddenly [The troops *rushed* the fort.] ◆***n.*** **1** the act of rushing [the *rush* of the wind]. **2** an eager movement of many people to get to a place [the *rush* to California for gold]. **3** hurry; haste [the *rush* and confusion of modern life]. ◆***adj.*** that must be done or sent in a hurry [a *rush* order].

**rush**[2] (rush) ***n.*** a grassy plant that grows in wet places. It has a hollow stem that is used for weaving baskets, chair seats, etc.

☆**rush hour** a time of day when business, traffic, etc. are very heavy.

**rusk** (rusk) ***n.*** a piece of sweet bread or cake toasted in an oven until brown and dry.

**Russ.** *abbreviation for* **Russia** *or* **Russian.**

**rus·set** (rus′it) ***n.*** **1** yellowish brown or reddish brown. **2** coarse, brownish, homemade cloth once used for clothing by country people.

**Rus·sia** (rush′ə) **1** a former empire in eastern Europe and northern Asia, ruled by the czars. Now it forms most of the largest republic of the U.S.S.R.: *the full name of this republic is the* **Russian Soviet Federated Socialist Republic. 2** *a popular name for the* **Union of Soviet Socialist Republics.**

**Rus·sian** (rush′ən) ***n.*** **1** a person born or living in Russia. **2** the chief language of Russia and the U.S.S.R. ◆***adj.*** of Russia, its people, their language, etc.

**rust** (rust) ***n.*** **1** the reddish-brown coating formed on metal, especially iron, by the chemical action of oxygen in the air or in moisture. **2** reddish brown. **3** a disease of plants that makes brownish spots on stems and leaves. ◆***v.*** **1** to make or become coated with rust. **2** to make or become weaker, slower, etc., as through not being used [a mind that has *rusted*].

**rus·tic** (rus′tik) ***adj.*** **1** having to do with the countryside; rural. **2** like country people; plain, simple, natural, unpolished, etc. [*rustic* manners]. **3** made of branches or roots covered with bark [*rustic* furniture]. *See the picture. See* SYNONYMS *at* **rural.** ◆***n.*** a country person, especially one thought of as simple, natural, unpolished, etc.

**rus·tle**[1] (rus′'l) ***v.*** to make or move with soft, rubbing sounds [A breeze *rustled* the leaves.] —**rus′tled, rus′tling** ◆***n.*** soft, rubbing sounds [the *rustle* of papers in the quiet classroom].

**rus·tle**[2] (rus′'l) ***v.*** ☆to steal cattle, etc. —**rus′tled, rus′tling** —☆**rustle up,** to gather together, as by searching [to *rustle up* a meal from leftovers]. *This word is used only in everyday talk.* —**rus′tler *n.***

**rust·proof** (rust′pro͞of) ***v.*** to coat with a material that keeps rust from forming.

**rust·y** (rus′tē) ***adj.*** **1** coated with rust [a *rusty* knife]. **2** not working easily because of rust [a *rusty* lock]. **3** not so good, strong, skillful, etc. as before, as from lack of practice [My golf game is a little *rusty*.] **4** reddish-brown [a *rusty* stain]. —**rust′i·er, rust′i·est** —**rust′i·ness *n.***

**rut** (rut) ***n.*** **1** a groove made in the ground by the wheels of cars, wagons, etc. **2** a way of doing something, thinking, etc. that is always exactly the same

[He was afraid of change and allowed himself to get into a *rut*.] ◆**v.** to make ruts in [The road had become *rutted*.] —**rut'ted, rut'ting**

**ru·ta·ba·ga** (rōōt'ə bā'gə *or* rōōt'ə bā'gə) **n.** a turnip with a large, yellow root.

**Ruth** (rōōth) **1** a woman in the Bible who left her own people in order to live with the people of her mother-in-law, Naomi. **2** a book of the Bible telling her story.

**ruth·less** (rōōth'lis) **adj.** without pity or kindness; cruel. —**ruth'less·ly adv.** —**ruth'less·ness n.**

**Rwan·da** (ur wän'də) a country in east-central Africa.

**Rwy.** or **Ry.** *abbreviation for* **Railway.**

**Rx** *the symbol for* **prescription,** as used on the label for medicine prescribed by a doctor.

**-ry** (rē) *a suffix having the same meanings as* **-ery** [*dentistry, jewelry*].

**rye** (rī) **n. 1** a cereal grass whose seed, or grain, is used in making flour and as feed for farm animals. *See the picture.* **2** this grain.

**rye bread** bread made from rye flour. Caraway seeds are often added to the flour before baking.

**S, s** (es) **n.** the nineteenth letter of the English alphabet. —*pl.* **S's, s's** (es'iz)

**S** *the symbol for the chemical element* sulfur. ◆**n.** something shaped like an S.

**-'s**[1] *an ending that is a short form of:* **1** is [*He's* here.] **2** has [*She's* won.] **3** us [*Let's* go.]

**-'s**[2] the ending that is used to form the possessive of singular nouns [the *child's* toy], of plural nouns that do not end in *s* [the *children's* toys], and of some pronouns [*someone's* toy].

**S, S., s, s.** *abbreviations for* **south** *or* **southern.**

**s.** *abbreviation for* **second** *or* **seconds, son.**

**S.A.** *abbreviation for* **South America.**

**Saar** (sär *or* zär) **1** a river in northeastern France and southwestern West Germany. **2** a region with coal mines in the valley of this river.

**Sab·bath** (sab'əth) **n. 1** the seventh day of the week, Saturday, set aside by Jews and some Christians for rest and worship. **2** Sunday as the usual day for rest and worship by Christians.

**sa·ber** or **sa·bre** (sā'bər) **n.** a heavy sword with a slightly curved blade. *See the picture.*

**sa·ble** (sā'b'l) **n. 1** an animal somewhat like a weasel, with dark, shiny fur. **2** its costly fur. **3** the color black. ◆**adj.** black.

**sa·bot** (sab'ō *or* sa bō') **n. 1** a shoe shaped from a single piece of wood, once worn by peasants in Europe. *See the picture.* **2** a heavy leather shoe with a wooden sole.

**sab·o·tage** (sab'ə täzh) **n. 1** the destroying of railroads, bridges, factories, etc., as by enemy agents or by civilians resisting an invading army. **2** the destroying of machines, tools, etc., as by workers during a strike. **3** any harm done to some effort in order to get it to fail. ◆**v.** to damage or destroy by sabotage. —**sab'o·taged, sab'o·tag·ing**

**sab·o·teur** (sab ə tur') **n.** a person who takes part in sabotage.

**sac** (sak) **n.** in a plant or animal, a part that is shaped like a bag, especially one filled with fluid.

**sac·cha·rin** or **sac·cha·rine**[1] (sak'ə rin) **n.** ☆a very sweet, white substance made from coal tar and used in place of sugar.

**sac·cha·rine**[2] (sak'ə rin) **adj. 1** of or like sugar; sweet. ☆**2** too sweet, or sweet in a false way [a *saccharine* voice].

☆**sa·chem** (sā'chəm) **n.** the chief in certain American Indian tribes. 647

**sa·chet** (sa shā') **n.** a small bag filled with perfumed powder or dried herbs and stored with clothes to make them smell sweet.

**sack**[1] (sak) **n. 1** a bag, especially a large one made of coarse cloth and used to hold grain, food, etc. **2** as much as a sack will hold [We cooked a *sack* of potatoes for the campers.] **3** a loose-fitting jacket or dress. ☆**4** a base in baseball. ◆**v.** to put into sacks [to *sack* corn]. —☆**hit the sack,** to go to bed: *a slang phrase.*

**sack**[2] (sak) **n.** the act of robbing or looting a city or town captured by an army. ◆**v.** to rob or loot a captured city, etc.; plunder.

**sack**[3] (sak) **n.** a dry white wine like light sherry.

**sack·cloth** (sak'klôth) **n. 1** coarse cloth used to make sacks. **2** rough, coarse cloth that used to be worn to show grief or sorrow.

**sack·ful** (sak'fool) **n.** as much as a sack will hold [a *sackful* of apples]. —*pl.* **sack'fuls**

**sack·ing** (sak'ing) **n.** coarse cloth, as burlap, used for making sacks.

**sac·ra·ment** (sak'rə mənt) **n. 1** any of certain very sacred ceremonies in Christian churches, as baptism, Holy Communion, etc. **2** something very sacred. —**the Sacrament,** Holy Communion. —**sac'ra·men'tal adj.**

| | | | | | | | |
|---|---|---|---|---|---|---|---|
| **a** | fat | **ir** | here | **ou** | out | **zh** | leisure |
| **ā** | ape | **ī** | bite, fire | **u** | up | **ng** | ring |
| **ä** | car, lot | **ō** | go | **ur** | fur | | a *in* ago |
| **e** | ten | **ô** | law, horn | **ch** | chin | | e *in* agent |
| **er** | care | **oi** | oil | **sh** | she | **ə** = | i *in* unity |
| **ē** | even | **oo** | look | **th** | thin | | o *in* collect |
| **i** | hit | **ōō** | tool | ***th*** | then | | u *in* focus |

**Sac·ra·men·to** (sak′rə men′tō) the capital of California.

**sa·cred** (sā′krid) ***adj.*** **1** having to do with religion, or set apart for some religious purpose; holy [a *sacred* shrine; a *sacred* song]. **2** given or deserving the greatest respect; hallowed [a place *sacred* to the memory of the Pilgrims]. **3** that must not be broken or ignored [a *sacred* promise].

**sac·ri·fice** (sak′rə fīs) ***n.*** **1** the act of offering something, as the life of a person or animal, to God or a god; also, the thing offered. **2** the act of giving up one thing for the sake of something else; also, the thing given up [the *sacrifice* of one's day off in order to get the job done]. **3** a loss of profit [We are selling last year's cars at a *sacrifice*.] ☆**4** in baseball, a bunt made so that the batter can be put out but a runner will be moved ahead one base: *also called* **sacrifice bunt** or **sacrifice hit.** ◆***v.*** **1** to make a sacrifice of. **2** to sell at a loss. ☆**3** in baseball, to move a base runner ahead by making a sacrifice. —**sac′ri·ficed, sac′ri·fic·ing** —**sac·ri·fi·cial** (sak′rə fish′əl) ***adj.***

☆**sacrifice fly** in baseball, a play in which the batter flies out and a runner scores from third base after the catch.

**sac·ri·lege** (sak′rə lij) ***n.*** an act that shows disrespect for something sacred [Throwing trash on an altar is a *sacrilege*.] —**sac·ri·le·gious** (sak′rə lij′əs *or* sak′rə lē′jəs) ***adj.***



**Sacrilege** comes from a Latin word for a person who stole sacred objects from a temple where the gods of Greece and Rome were worshiped.

**sac·ris·ty** (sak′ris tē) ***n.*** a room in a church where the robes worn by the clergy and articles for the altar are kept. —*pl.* **sac′ris·ties**

**sad** (sad) ***adj.*** **1** feeling unhappy; having or showing sorrow or grief [The cutting down of the beautiful tree made us *sad*.] **2** causing a gloomy or unhappy feeling [a *sad* song]. **3** very bad: *used only in everyday talk* [They're really in *sad* shape financially.] —**sad′der, sad′dest** —**sad′ly *adv.*** —**sad′ness *n.***

SYNONYMS: To be **sad** is to feel unhappy, but the unhappiness may be quite mild and over with quickly or it may be very deep and long-lasting [*sad* because vacation is over; a *sad* and lonely widow]. To be **sorrowful** is to feel more than mildly unhappy over some loss, one's failure to get or do what one wants, etc. [The death of their dog left them *sorrowful*.]

**sad·den** (sad′'n) ***v.*** to make or become sad.

**sad·dle** (sad′'l) ***n.*** **1** a seat, usually of padded leather, for a rider on a horse, bicycle, etc. *See the picture.* **2** a part of a harness worn over a horse's back. **3** anything shaped like a saddle [A ridge between two mountain peaks is called a *saddle*.] **4** a cut of meat including part of the backbone and the two loins [a *saddle* of mutton]. ◆***v.*** **1** to put a saddle on [to *saddle* a horse]. **2** to weigh down, as with a burden or duty [*saddled* with debts]. —**sad′dled, sad′dling** —**in the saddle,** in control.

**sad·dle·bag** (sad′'l bag) ***n.*** one of a pair of bags hung over a horse's back behind the saddle or over the back wheel of a motorcycle or bicycle.

**saddle horse** a horse trained to be ridden.

☆**saddle shoes** shoes with flat heels and a band of different-colored leather across the instep. *See the picture.*

☆**saddle soap** a mild soap used for cleaning and softening leather.

**sad·ist** (sad′ist) ***n.*** a person who gets pleasure from hurting others. —**sa·dis·tic** (sə dis′tik) ***adj.***

**sa·fa·ri** (sə fär′ē) ***n.*** a journey or hunting trip, especially in Africa. —*pl.* **sa·fa′ris**

**safe** (sāf) ***adj.*** **1** free from harm or danger; secure [a *safe* hiding place; *safe* in bed]. **2** not hurt or harmed [We emerged *safe* from the wreck.] **3** that can be trusted [a *safe* investment]. **4** not able to cause trouble or harm; not dangerous [a *safe* toy; *safe* in jail]. **5** taking no risks; careful [a *safe* driver]. ☆**6** in baseball, having reached a base without being put out. —**saf′er, saf′est** ◆***n.*** a strong metal box with a lock, in which to keep money or valuables. *See the picture.* —**safe′ly *adv.***

**safe-con·duct** (sāf′kän′dukt) ***n.*** permission to pass through a dangerous place, as in time of war, without being arrested or harmed.

☆**safe-de·pos·it** (sāf′di päz′it) ***adj.*** describing a box in a bank vault, for keeping jewelry, important papers, etc. safe.

**safe·guard** (sāf′gärd) ***n.*** anything that keeps one safe from danger; protection [Wear gloves as a *safeguard* against frostbite.] ◆***v.*** to protect or guard.

**safe·keep·ing** (sāf′kēp′iŋ) ***n.*** a keeping or being kept safe; protection [Put your money in the bank for *safekeeping*.]

**safe·ty** (sāf′tē) ***n.*** **1** the condition of being safe; freedom from danger or harm [Boats carried them to *safety*.] **2** a device to prevent an accident [a *safety* on a gun to keep it from going off accidentally]. ◆***adj.*** that gives safety or makes something less dangerous [A *safety* match lights only when struck on a special surface. A *safety* belt helps protect passengers in case of a crash.]

**safety pin** a pin that is bent back on itself so as to form a spring. The point is held by a guard, which keeps it from springing free accidentally.

**safety valve** **1** a valve on a steam boiler, etc., that opens and lets out steam when the pressure gets too high. **2** anything that lets a person get rid of strong feeling in a harmless way.

**saf·flow·er** (saf′lou′ər) ***n.*** a plant like a thistle, with large, orange flowers and seeds from which an oil is pressed. The oil (**safflower oil**) is used in food, paint, medicine, etc.

**saf·fron** (saf′rən) ***n.*** **1** a kind of crocus with purple flowers having bright orange center parts. **2** a dye or a seasoning for food, made from the dried orange parts. **3** a bright orange yellow: *also* **saffron yellow.**

**S.Afr.** *abbreviation for* **South Africa** *or* **South African.**

**sag** (sag) ***v.*** **1** to bend or sink, especially in the middle, as from weight [shelves that *sag*]. *See the picture.* **2** to hang down in a loose or uneven way [*sagging* flesh]. **3** to lose strength; weaken [Sales have begun to *sag*.] —**sagged, sag′ging** ◆***n.*** ☆a place where something sags.

**sa·ga** (sä′gə) ***n.*** a long story of brave deeds; especially, such a story told in the Middle Ages about Norse heroes.

**sa·ga·cious** (sə gāʹshəs) ***adj.*** very wise or shrewd. —**sa·gac·i·ty** (sə gasʹə tē) ***n.***

**sage**[1] (sāj) ***adj.*** wise; showing good judgment. —**sagʹer, sagʹest** ♦***n.*** a very wise person; especially, a wise, older man. —**sageʹly *adv.***

**sage**[2] (sāj) ***n.*** **1** a plant related to the mint, with green leaves used as a seasoning in cooking. ☆**2** *a shorter name for* **sagebrush.**

☆**sage·brush** (sājʹbrush) ***n.*** a shrub that smells like sage and has tiny, white or yellow flowers. It grows on the plains in the West.

**Sag·it·ta·ri·us** (saj′i terʹē əs) the ninth sign of the zodiac, for the period from November 23 to December 21: *also called* the Archer. *See the picture for* **zodiac.**

**sa·go** (sāʹgō) ***n.*** **1** a starch made from the soft inside part of certain palm trees. It is used to make puddings and some soups thicker. **2** any of these trees. —*pl.* **saʹgos**

**Sa·ha·ra** (sə harʹə) a very large desert covering much of northern Africa. *See the map.*

**sa·hib** (säʹib *or* säʹhib) ***n.*** master. This word was used in earlier times as a title by natives in India when speaking to a European man.

**said** (sed) *past tense and past participle of* **say.** ♦***adj.*** named or mentioned before [The *said* contract is no longer in force.]

**sail** (sāl) ***n.*** **1** a sheet of heavy cloth such as canvas, used on a ship or boat to move it by catching the wind. **2** a trip in a ship or boat, especially one moved by sails [Let's go for a *sail.*] **3** anything like a sail, as an arm of a windmill. ♦***v.*** **1** to be moved forward by means of sails. **2** to travel on water [This liner *sails* between Miami and New York.] **3** to begin a trip by water [We *sail* at noon for Spain.] **4** to move upon in a boat or ship [to *sail* the seas]. **5** to control or manage, especially a sailboat. **6** to move smoothly [a hawk *sailing* in the sky]. **7** to move or act quickly or with energy: *used only in everyday talk* [He *sailed* through his work.] ☆**8** to attack or criticize with force (*followed by* into): *used only in everyday talk* [She *sailed into* them for being late.] —**set sail** or **make sail, 1** to spread the sails and get ready to leave. **2** to begin a trip by water. —**under sail,** with sails spread out.

**sail·boat** (sālʹbōt) ***n.*** a boat having a sail or sails to make it move. *See the picture.*

**sail·fish** (sālʹfish) ***n.*** a large ocean fish that has a tall fin like a sail on its back. *See the picture on page 650.*

**sail·or** (sālʹər) ***n.*** **1** a person who makes a living by sailing; mariner. **2** an enlisted person in the navy. **3** a person thought of in terms of whether or not he or she gets seasick [a good or bad *sailor*]. **4** a straw hat with a flat crown and brim.

**saint** (sānt) ***n.*** **1** a holy person. **2** a person who is very humble, unselfish, patient, etc. **3** in certain churches, a person said officially to be in heaven as a result of having lived a very holy life. ♦***v.*** to make a saint of; canonize. —**saintʹhood *n.***

Saint **Peter,** Saint **Paul,** etc. are listed in this dictionary under their given names. Names of places beginning with **Saint** are listed among the words following **St.**

**Saint Ber·nard** (bər närdʹ) a large, brown and white dog, at one time used in the Swiss Alps to rescue people lost in the snow.

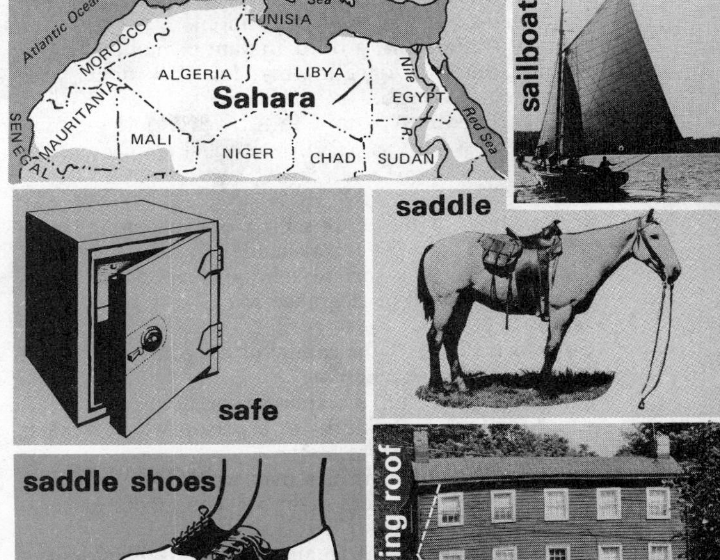


**saint·ed** (sānʹtid) ***adj.*** **1** of, like, or fit for a saint. **2** thought of as a saint. **3** holy; sacred.

**saint·ly** (sāntʹlē) ***adj.*** like or fit for a saint; very good or holy. —**saintʹli·er, saintʹli·est** —**saintʹli·ness *n.*** 649

**Saint Patrick's Day** *see* **Patrick,** Saint.

**Saint Valentine's Day** *see* **Valentine,** Saint.

**saith** (seth; *now also* sāʹith) *old form of* **says,** as in the Bible.

**sake**[1] (sāk) ***n.*** **1** purpose or reason; motive [to cry for the *sake* of getting attention]. **2** benefit or advantage; welfare [for my own *sake*].

**sa·ke**[2] (säʹkē) ***n.*** a Japanese liquor or wine that is made from rice.

**sa·laam** (sə lämʹ) ***n.*** **1** an Arabic word meaning "peace," used as a greeting. **2** a greeting in the Orient, made by bowing low with the right hand placed on the forehead. ♦***v.*** to make a salaam.

**sal·a·ble** or **sale·a·ble** (sālʹə b'l) ***adj.*** that can be sold; fit to buy [*salable* goods].

**sal·ad** (salʹəd) ***n.*** any mixture of vegetables, fruits, fish, eggs, etc., made with a dressing of oil, vinegar, spices, etc. It is usually served cold, often on lettuce leaves.

**sal·a·man·der** (salʹə man′dər) ***n.*** **1** a small animal that looks like a lizard but is related to the frog. It lives in damp, dark places. *See the picture on page 650.* **2** an animal in myths that was said to live in fire.

**sa·la·mi** (sə läʹmē) ***n.*** a spicy, salted sausage made of pork and beef or of beef alone.

| | | | | | | | |
|---|---|---|---|---|---|---|---|
| **a** | fat | **ir** | here | **ou** | out | **zh** | leisure |
| **ā** | ape | **ī** | bite, fire | **u** | up | **ng** | ring |
| **ä** | car, lot | **ō** | go | **ur** | fur | | a *in* ago |
| **e** | ten | **ô** | law, horn | **ch** | chin | | e *in* agent |
| **er** | care | **oi** | oil | **sh** | she | ə = | i *in* unity |
| **ē** | even | **oo** | look | **th** | thin | | o *in* collect |
| **i** | hit | **ōō** | tool | ***th*** | then | | u *in* focus |

**sal·a·ried** (sal′ə rēd) ***adj.*** **1** getting a salary. **2** that gives one a salary [a *salaried* position].

**sal·a·ry** (sal′ə rē) ***n.*** a fixed amount of money paid at regular times, as once a week, for work done. *See* SYNONYMS *at* **wage.** *—pl.* **sal′a·ries**

**Salary** comes from a Latin word that means money for salt, as part of a Roman soldier's pay. To be worth one's salt is to be worth one's salary or wages.

**sale** (sāl) ***n.*** **1** the act of selling, or exchanging something for money [The clerk made ten *sales* today.] **2** an auction. **3** a special selling of goods at prices lower than usual [a clearance *sale*]. —**for sale** or **on sale,** to be sold.

**Sa·lem** (sā′ləm) **1** the capital of Oregon. **2** a city on the coast of Massachusetts.

**Sa·ler·no** (sä ler′nō) a seaport in southern Italy.

☆**sales·clerk** (sālz′klurk) ***n.*** a person whose work is selling goods in a store.

**sales·man** (sālz′mən) ***n.*** a man whose work is selling goods, either in a store or by traveling from place to place. *—pl.* **sales′men**

**sales·man·ship** (sālz′mən ship) ***n.*** skill in selling goods.

☆**sales·peo·ple** (sālz′pē′p'l) ***n.pl.*** people hired to sell goods.

☆**sales·per·son** (sālz′pur′sən) ***n.*** a person hired to sell goods, especially as a clerk in a store: *also* **salesclerk.**



☆**sales·room** (sālz′ro͞om) ***n.*** a room in a store in which things for sale are displayed.

☆**sales tax** a tax on sales and, sometimes, services. It is usually added to the price by the seller.

**sales·wom·an** (sālz′wo͝om′ən) ***n.*** a woman whose work is selling goods, especially in a store. *—pl.* **sales′wom′en** *Also* **sales′girl′** or **sales′la′dy.** *—pl.* **sales′la′dies**

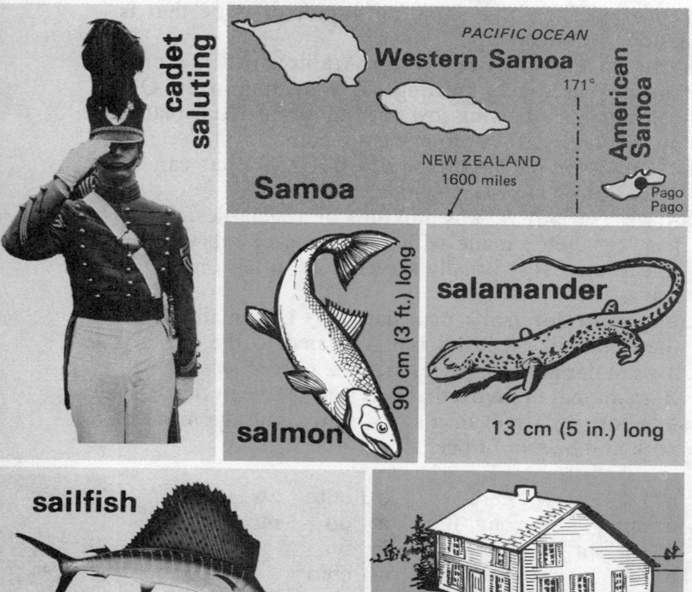


**sa·lient** (sāl′yənt) ***adj.*** standing out; easily seen or noticed [the *salient* idea in the plan].

**Salient,** from the Latin word for "leap," means thrusting or sticking out, as an angle or sharp point. There is also a noun meaning for **salient** for the part of a battle line, trench, or fort that sticks out farthest toward the enemy.

**sa·line** (sā′līn *or* sā′lēn) ***adj.*** of, like, or containing common salt; salty [a *saline* solution]. ◆***n.*** something salty. —**sa·lin·i·ty** (sə lin′ə tē) ***n.***

**Salis·bur·y** (sôlz′ber′ē) the capital of Rhodesia.

☆**Salisbury steak** *another name for* **hamburger** *in meaning* 2.

**sa·li·va** (sə lī′və) ***n.*** the watery liquid produced in the mouth by certain glands; spit. It helps to digest food.

**sal·i·var·y** (sal′ə ver′ē) ***adj.*** of or producing saliva [*salivary* glands].

**Salk** (sôlk), **Jonas E.** 1914– ; U.S. physician. He developed a vaccine to prevent poliomyelitis.

**sal·low** (sal′ō) ***adj.*** pale yellow in a way that looks sickly or unhealthy [a *sallow* complexion].

**sal·ly** (sal′ē) ***n.*** **1** a sudden rush forward [The troops made a *sally* toward the enemy's lines.] **2** a trip or jaunt. **3** a short, witty remark. *—pl.* **sal′lies** ◆***v.*** to start out briskly, as on a trip. —**sal′lied, sal′ly·ing**

**salm·on** (sam′ən) ***n.*** a large food fish with silver scales and flesh that is orange pink when cooked. Salmon live in the ocean but swim up rivers to lay their eggs. *See the picture. —pl.* **salm′on** or **salm′ons**

☆**sal·mo·nel·la** (sal′mə nel′ə) ***n.*** any of a kind of bacteria that cause various diseases in human beings and animals, including typhoid fever, food poisoning, etc. *—pl.* **sal·mo·nel·lae** (sal′mə nel′ē)

**Salmonella** was named after Dr. Daniel E. Salmon (1850–1914), the U.S. scientist who first discovered these bacteria.

**sa·lon** (sə län′) ***n.*** **1** a large drawing room for entertaining guests. **2** a regular meeting of artists, writers, etc., as at a wealthy person's home. **3** a place where works of art are shown; gallery. **4** a business for performing some personal service [a beauty *salon*].

**sa·loon** (sə lo͞on′) ***n.*** ☆**1** a place where alcoholic drinks are bought and drunk; bar: *an old-fashioned word.* **2** a large public room [the dining *saloon* on an ocean liner].

☆**SALT** (sôlt *or* sält) Strategic Arms Limitation Talks.

**salt** (sôlt) ***n.*** **1** a white substance made up of crystals, used to flavor and preserve foods; sodium chloride. **2** any chemical compound formed from an acid by replacing the hydrogen with a metal or a radical, such as ammonium. **3 salts,** *pl.* any of various mineral salts used to help move the bowels (**Epsom salts**), to soften bath water (**bath salts**), or to restore fainting people (**smelling salts**). **4** a sailor: *used only in everyday talk.* ◆***adj.*** **1** containing salt [*salt* water]. **2** preserved with salt [*salt* pork]. **3** tasting or smelling of salt [*salt* breezes]. ◆***v.*** to add salt to for flavoring, preserving, melting, etc. [to *salt* soup; to *salt* meat; to *salt* icy streets]. —**salt away, 1** to preserve with salt. ☆**2** to store away or save, as money: *used only in everyday talk.* —**salt of the earth,** a person or persons thought of as the finest or best. —**with a grain of salt,** with some doubt in believing. —**worth one's salt,** worth one's wages.

**salt·box** (sôlt′bäks) ***n.*** **1** a box for salt. It usually has a sloping lid. ☆**2** a house, as in early New England, having two stories in the front and one in the rear. The gable roof had a longer slope in the rear. *See the picture.*

**salt·cel·lar** (sôlt′sel′ər) ***n.*** a small dish for salt at the table; also, a saltshaker.

☆**salt·ine** (sôl tēn′) ***n.*** a flat, crisp cracker sprinkled with salt.

**Salt Lake City** the capital of Utah.

☆**salt lick** **1** a place where animals go to lick salt that comes naturally from the earth. **2** a block of salt placed in a pasture for cattle, etc. to lick.

**salt·pe·ter** (sôlt′pēt′ər) ***n.*** any of various minerals used in making gunpowder, fertilizers, etc. *The British spelling is* **saltpetre.**

☆**salt·shak·er** (sôlt′shā′kər) ***n.*** a holder for salt, having holes in the top for shaking out the salt.

**salt·wa·ter** (sôlt′wôt′ər *or* sôlt′wät′ər) ***adj.*** of or living in salt water [*saltwater* fish].

**salt water** water with much salt in it, as in the ocean or sea.

**salt·y** (sôl′tē) ***adj.*** **1** tasting of salt or containing salt. **2** smelling of the sea. **3** witty and sharp, or, sometimes, coarse [*salty* talk]. —**salt′i·er, salt′i·est** —**salt′i·ness *n.***

**sa·lu·bri·ous** (sə lo͞o′brē əs) ***adj.*** good for one's health; wholesome [a *salubrious* climate].

**sal·u·tar·y** (sal′yoo ter′ē) ***adj.*** **1** healthful; wholesome [Swimming is a *salutary* pastime.] **2** useful or helpful [a *salutary* lesson].

**sal·u·ta·tion** (sal′yoo tā′shən) ***n.*** **1** an act or words used in greeting or in showing respect [Lynn waved to us in *salutation.*] **2** the words used at the beginning of a letter as "Dear cousin," "Dear friend," etc.

**sa·lute** (sə lo͞ot′) ***v.*** **1** to show honor and respect for, as by raising the hand to the forehead or by firing shots from a gun [A private should *salute* any superior officer. The aircraft carrier *saluted* the President.] *See the picture.* **2** to greet in a friendly way, as by tipping the hat. —**sa·lut′ed, sa·lut′ing** ◆***n.*** an act of saluting or greeting [a twenty-one-gun *salute;* a *salute* to the flag].

**Sal·va·dor** (sal′və dôr) a seaport in eastern Brazil.

**sal·vage** (sal′vij) ***n.*** **1** the act of saving a ship and its cargo from fire, shipwreck, etc.; also, money paid for this. **2** the act of saving any property or goods from damage or complete loss. **3** the property or goods saved, as that brought up from a sunken ship. ◆***v.*** **1** to save from shipwreck, fire, destruction, etc. **2** to use what can be saved from something damaged or destroyed [We *salvaged* two tires from the wreck.] —**sal′vaged, sal′vag·ing**

**sal·va·tion** (sal vā′shən) ***n.*** **1** a saving or being saved from danger, evil, etc.; rescue. **2** a person or thing that saves [The cellar was our *salvation* in the tornado.] **3** in Christian belief, the saving of the soul from sin and death.

**Salvation Army** a Christian organization that works to bring religion and help to the poor.

**salve** (sav) ***n.*** **1** any greasy medicine put on wounds, burns, sores, etc. to soothe or heal them. **2** anything that soothes or heals [Her smile was a *salve* to my anger.] ◆***v.*** to soothe or make quiet; smooth over [We *salved* his wounded pride by praising his courage.] —**salved, salv′ing**

**sal·ver** (sal′vər) ***n.*** a small tray, as of metal.

> **Salver** comes from the Spanish word that meant the testing of food by a taster, and later the tray on which food was placed. In the old days, the food for a sovereign was often tested by a servant to make sure the master would not be poisoned.

**sal·vo** (sal′vō) ***n.*** **1** the firing of a number of guns one after another or at the same time, in a salute or at a target. **2** the release of several bombs or rockets at the same time. **3** a burst of cheers or applause. —*pl.* **sal′vos** or **sal′voes**

**Sa·mar·i·a** (sə mer′ē ə) a region of ancient Palestine, or its main city.

**Sa·mar·i·tan** (sə mer′ə t′n) ***n.*** a person born or living in Samaria. *See also* **good Samaritan.**

**same** (sām) ***adj.*** **1** being the very one, not another [She is the *same* girl who spoke to me.] **2** alike in some way; similar [Both coats are of the *same* color.] **3** without any change; not different [You look the *same* healthy person as always.] ◆***pron.*** the same person or thing [Manuel wants chocolate and I'll have the *same.*] ◆***adv.*** in the same way [Treat her the *same* as us.] —**all the same, 1** of no importance. **2** in spite of that; however.

> SYNONYMS: **Same,** in one meaning, agrees with **very** in speaking of one thing and not two or more different things [That is the *same,* or *very,* car that we owned.] In another meaning, **same** describes things that are really different, but that are alike in kind, amount, etc. [I eat the *same* lunch every day—a sandwich and fruit.] **Identical,** in one meaning, also expresses the first idea [This is the *identical* bed he slept in.] In another meaning, **identical** describes exact sameness in all details [The copies are *identical.*]

**same·ness** (sām′nis) ***n.*** **1** the condition of being the same or just alike. **2** lack of change or variety; monotony.

**Sa·mo·a** (sə mō′ə) a group of islands in the South Pacific. Part of the group (**American Samoa**) belongs to the United States. *See the map.*

**sam·o·var** (sam′ə vär) ***n.*** a metal urn with a tube inside for heating water in making tea. Samovars are used especially in Russia.

**sam·pan** (sam′pan) ***n.*** a small boat used in China and Japan. It is rowed with an oar at the stern, and it often has a sail. *See the picture on page 653.*

**sam·ple** (sam′p′l) ***n.*** a part or piece that shows what the whole group or thing is like; specimen or example [little pieces of wallpaper for *samples;* a *sample* of his typing]. ◆***adj.*** that is a sample [a *sample* page of the book]. ◆***v.*** to test by trying a sample [He *sampled* the basket of grapes.] —**sam′pled, sam′pling**

**sam·pler** (sam′plər) ***n.*** a piece of cloth with designs, mottoes, etc. sewn in fancy stitches.

| | | | |
|---|---|---|---|
| **a** fat | **ir** here | **ou** out | **zh** leisure |
| **ā** ape | **ī** bite, fire | **u** up | **ng** ring |
| **ä** car, lot | **ō** go | **ur** fur | a *in* ago |
| **e** ten | **ô** law, horn | **ch** chin | e *in* agent |
| **er** care | **oi** oil | **sh** she | **ə** = i *in* unity |
| **ē** even | **oo** look | **th** thin | o *in* collect |
| **i** hit | **o͞o** tool | ***th*** then | u *in* focus |

**Sam·son** (sam′s′n) an Israelite in the Bible famous for his great strength.

**Sam·u·el** (sam′yoo wəl) a Hebrew judge and prophet in the Bible. Two books of the Bible are named after him.

**San An·to·ni·o** (san′ ən tō′nē ō) a city in south central Texas.

**san·a·to·ri·um** (san′ə tôr′ē əm) ***n.*** *chiefly British spelling of* **sanitarium.**

**sanc·ti·fy** (sangk′tə fī) ***v.*** **1** to set aside for religious use; consecrate [to *sanctify* a new altar]. **2** to make free from sin; purify. **3** to make seem right; justify [a practice *sanctified* by custom]. —**sanc′ti·fied, sanc′ti·fy·ing** —**sanc′ti·fi·ca′tion** ***n.***

**sanc·ti·mo·ni·ous** (sangk′tə mō′nē əs) ***adj.*** pretending to be very holy or religious.

**sanc·tion** (sangk′shən) ***n.*** **1** approval or permission given by someone in authority; authorization [The club was formed with the *sanction* of the principal.] **2** *usually* **sanctions,** *pl.* an action, as a blockade of shipping, taken by a group of nations against another nation considered to have broken international law. ◆***v.*** to approve or permit [I cannot *sanction* rudeness by anyone.]

**sanc·ti·ty** (sangk′tə tē) ***n.*** **1** saintliness or holiness. **2** the condition of being sacred [the *sanctity* of the cathedral; the *sanctity* of a vow].

**sanc·tu·ar·y** (sangk′choo wer′ē) ***n.*** **1** a place set aside for religious worship, as a church or temple. **2** the main room for services in a house of worship. **3** a place where one can find safety or shelter; also, the safety found there [The criminals found *sanctuary* in a church.] **4** a place where birds and animals are protected from hunters [a wildlife *sanctuary*]. —*pl.* **sanc′tu·ar′ies**



**sanc·tum** (sangk′təm) ***n.*** **1** a sacred place. **2** a private room where one is not to be disturbed.

**sand** (sand) ***n.*** **1** tiny, loose grains worn away from rock and forming the ground of beaches, deserts, etc. **2** *usually* **sands,** *pl.* an area of sand. ☆**3** grit; courage: *slang in this meaning.* ◆***v.*** **1** to make smooth with sand or sandpaper. **2** to cover, mix, or fill with sand. —**sand′er** ***n.***

**san·dal** (san′d′l) ***n.*** **1** a kind of shoe that is just a flat sole fastened to the foot by straps. **2** a kind of open slipper or low shoe. *See the picture.*

**san·dal·wood** (san′d′l wood) ***n.*** the hard, sweet-smelling wood of certain trees of Asia, used for carvings, etc. and burned as incense.

**sand·bag** (sand′bag) ***n.*** **1** a bag filled with sand, used for ballast or to build or strengthen walls against floods or enemy attack. **2** a small bag of sand used as a weapon. ◆***v.*** **1** to put sandbags in or around. ☆**2** to force into doing something: *used only in everyday talk.* —**sand′bagged, sand′bag·ging**

☆**sand bar** a ridge of sand formed in a river or along a shore by currents or tides.

**sand·blast** (sand′blast) ***n.*** a strong stream of air carrying sand, used to etch glass, clean the surface of stone, etc. ◆***v.*** to etch, clean, etc. with a sandblast. —**sand′blast·er** ***n.***

**sand·box** (sand′bäks) ***n.*** a box filled with sand, as for children to play in.

**Sand·burg** (sand′bərg), **Carl** 1878–1967; U.S. poet and writer.

☆**sand·hog** (sand′hôg *or* sand′häg) ***n.*** a laborer who works under compressed air on projects that are underground or under water.

**San Di·e·go** (san′ dē ā′gō) a seaport in southern California.

☆**sand·lot** (sand′lät) ***adj.*** of or having to do with baseball played by amateurs, originally on a sandy lot or field, now usually organized in leagues.

**sand·man** (sand′man) ***n.*** a make-believe man who is supposed to make children sleepy by sprinkling sand in their eyes.

**sand·pa·per** (sand′pā′pər) ***n.*** strong paper with sand glued on one side, used for smoothing and polishing. ◆***v.*** to rub with sandpaper.

**sand·pip·er** (sand′pī′pər) ***n.*** a shore bird having a long bill with a soft tip. *See the picture.*

**sand·stone** (sand′stōn) ***n.*** a kind of rock formed of sand held together by silica, lime, etc. At one time it was much used in building.

**sand·storm** (sand′stôrm) ***n.*** a windstorm in which sand is blown about in large clouds.

**sand·wich** (sand′wich *or* san′wich) ***n.*** slices of bread with a filling of meat, cheese, etc. between them. ◆***v.*** to squeeze in [a shed *sandwiched* between two houses].

> The **sandwich** was named after the 4th Earl of Sandwich (1718–1792). It is said that he ate his bread and meat this way so that he would not have to leave the table where he was gambling in order to eat a regular meal.

**sand·y** (san′dē) ***adj.*** **1** of or full of sand [a *sandy* shore]. **2** of the color of sand; pale reddish-yellow [*sandy* hair]. —**sand′i·er, sand′i·est**

**sane** (sān) ***adj.*** **1** having a normal, healthy mind; rational. **2** showing good sense; sensible [a *sane* policy]. —**san′er, san′est** —**sane′ly** ***adv.***

**San Fran·cis·co** (san′ frən sis′kō) a city on the coast of central California.

**sang** (sang) *past tense of* **sing.**

**san·gui·nar·y** (sang′gwi ner′ē) ***adj.*** **1** with much bloodshed or killing [a *sanguinary* revolt]. **2** bloodthirsty; very cruel.

**san·guine** (sang′gwin) ***adj.*** **1** always cheerful or hopeful; optimistic. **2** bright and red; ruddy.

**san·i·tar·i·um** (san′ə ter′ē əm) ***n.*** a quiet resort or rest home, especially for people who are getting over an illness such as tuberculosis. —*pl.* **san′i·tar′i·ums** or **san·i·tar·i·a** (san′ə ter′ē ə)

**san·i·tar·y** (san′ə ter′ē) ***adj.*** **1** having to do with or bringing about health or healthful conditions [*sanitary* laws]. **2** free from dirt that could bring disease; clean; hygienic [a *sanitary* meat market].

**san·i·ta·tion** (san′ə tā′shən) ***n.*** **1** the science and work of bringing about healthful, sanitary conditions. **2** the system of carrying away and getting rid of sewage.

**san·i·tize** (san′ə tīz) ***v.*** to make sanitary [a *sanitized* water glass in each hotel room]. —**san′i·tized, san′i·tiz·ing**

**san·i·ty** (san′ə tē) ***n.*** **1** the condition of being sane; soundness of mind; mental health. **2** soundness of judgment; sensibleness.

**San Jo·se** (san′ hō zā′) a city in west central California.

**San Jo·sé** (sän′ hō se′) the capital of Costa Rica.
**San Juan** (san hwän′) the capital of Puerto Rico.
**sank** (saŋk) *a past tense of* **sink.**
**San Sal·va·dor** (san sal′və dôr) **1** the capital of El Salvador. **2** an island in the eastern Bahamas: probably the place of Columbus' landing (1492) in the New World.
**San·skrit** (san′skrit) ***n.*** an ancient written language of India. It has given clues to language scholars about the origins of most European languages, which are related to it. *Also spelled* **Sanscrit.**
**San·ta** (san′tə) *same as* **Santa Claus.** ◆***adj.*** holy or saint: *a Spanish or Italian word used in certain names, as* Santa Fe.
**San·ta An·na** (sän′tä ä′nä) 1795?–1876; Mexican general. He was president of Mexico four times between 1833 and 1855.
☆**San·ta Claus** (san′tə klôz′) a fat, jolly old man in popular legends, with a white beard and a red suit, who hands out gifts at Christmas time.

The name **Santa Claus** comes from the Dutch *Sante Klaas,* which comes in turn from *Sant Nikolaas,* the Dutch spelling of Saint **Nicholas.**

**San·ta Fe** (san′tə fā′) the capital of New Mexico.
**San·ti·a·go** (san′tē ä′gō) the capital of Chile.
**San·to Do·min·go** (san′tō dō miŋ′gō) the capital of the Dominican Republic.
**São Pau·lo** (soun pou′loo) a city in southeastern Brazil.
**sap**[1] (sap) ***n.*** the juice that flows through a plant or tree, carrying food, water, etc. to all its parts.
**sap**[2] (sap) ***v.*** **1** to weaken or wear down by digging away at the foundations of; undermine [The flood waters *sapped* the wall of the canal.] **2** to weaken or wear away slowly [A bad cold *sapped* her energy.] —**sapped, sap′ping**
**sa·pi·ent** (sā′pē ənt) ***adj.*** full of knowledge; wise. —**sa′pi·ence *n.*** —**sa′pi·ent·ly *adv.***
**sap·ling** (sap′liŋ) ***n.*** a young tree.
**sap·phire** (saf′īr) ***n.*** **1** a clear, deep-blue, costly jewel. **2** deep blue.
**sap·py** (sap′ē) ***adj.*** **1** full of sap; juicy. **2** foolish; silly: *old slang in this meaning.* —**sap′pi·er, sap′pi·est**
☆**sap·suck·er** (sap′suk′ər) ***n.*** a small American woodpecker that drills holes in trees and drinks the sap. *See the picture.*
**Sar·a·cen** (sar′ə s′n) ***n.*** an Arab or Muslim, especially a Muslim at the time of the Crusades.
**Sar·ah** (ser′ə) in the Bible, the wife of Abraham and mother of Isaac.
☆**sa·ran** (sə ran′) ***n.*** a kind of resin made of chemicals and used to make fabrics, a transparent wrapping material, etc.
**sar·casm** (sär′kaz′m) ***n.*** **1** a mocking or sneering remark meant to hurt or to make someone seem foolish. **2** the making of such remarks ["I only explained it five times," she replied in *sarcasm.*]

**Sarcasm** comes from the Greek word that means "to tear flesh the way dogs do." Sarcastic words are sometimes spoken of as biting words, for they are intended to bite into feelings and hurt, as a dog's teeth would hurt flesh.

**sar·cas·tic** (sär kas′tik) ***adj.*** of, using, or showing sarcasm. —**sar·cas′ti·cal·ly *adv.***

sari

sampans

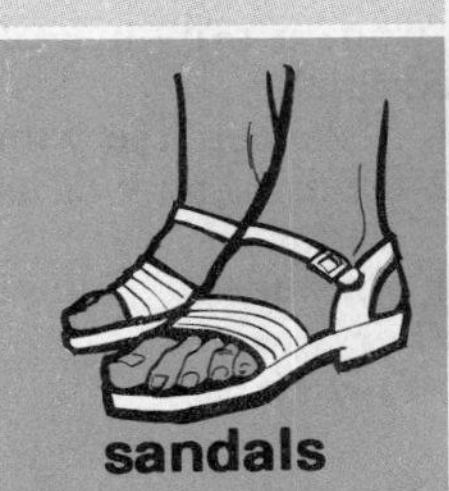
sandals

sandpiper
21 cm (8 in.) long

23 cm (9 in.) long
sapsucker

**sar·co·ma** (sär kō′mə) ***n.*** a cancer that begins in the cells of bones, ligaments, or muscles. —*pl.* **sar·co′mas** or **sar·co·ma·ta** (sär kō′mə tə)



**sar·coph·a·gus** (sär käf′ə gəs) ***n.*** a stone coffin, especially a decorated one set in a tomb. —*pl.* **sar·coph·a·gi** (sär käf′ə jī) or **sar·coph′a·gus·es**
**sar·dine** (sär dēn′) ***n.*** a small fish, as a young herring, preserved in oil and packed in cans.
**Sar·din·i·a** (sär din′ē ə) an Italian island in the Mediterranean. It is just south of the island of Corsica.
**sar·don·ic** (sär dän′ik) ***adj.*** sneering or sarcastic in a bitter or scornful way [a *sardonic* smile]. —**sar·don′i·cal·ly *adv.***
**sar·gas·so** (sär gas′ō) ***n.*** a brownish seaweed floating over large warm areas of the ocean. A part of the northern Atlantic where there is a large amount of this seaweed is called the **Sargasso Sea.**
**Sar·gent** (sär′jənt), **John Sing·er** (siŋ′ər) 1856–1925; U.S. painter. He lived in Europe.
**sa·ri** (sä′rē) ***n.*** an outer garment of Hindu women, formed of a long cloth wrapped around the body with one end forming a long skirt and the other end draped over one shoulder and, sometimes, over the head. *See the picture.*
**sa·rong** (sə rôŋ′) ***n.*** a garment worn by men and women in the Malay Archipelago, the East Indies, etc. It is formed of a long strip of cloth, often brightly colored and printed, worn like a skirt.

| | | | |
|---|---|---|---|
| **a** fat | **ir** here | **ou** out | **zh** leisure |
| **ā** ape | **ī** bite, fire | **u** up | **ŋ** ring |
| **ä** car, lot | **ō** go | **ur** fur | a *in* ago |
| **e** ten | **ô** law, horn | **ch** chin | e *in* agent |
| **er** care | **oi** oil | **sh** she | **ə** = i *in* unity |
| **ē** even | **oo** look | **th** thin | o *in* collect |
| **i** hit | **ōō** tool | ***th*** then | u *in* focus |

S

**sar·sa·pa·ril·la** (sas′pə ril′ə *or* särs′ə pə ril′ə) ***n.*** **1** a tropical American plant with sweet-smelling roots which are dried for use as a flavoring. ☆**2** soda water flavored with sarsaparilla.

**sar·to·ri·al** (sär tôr′ē əl) ***adj.*** **1** having to do with men's clothing [*sartorial* elegance]. **2** of tailors or their work. —**sar·to′ri·al·ly** ***adv.***

**Sar·tre** (sär′tr′), **Jean-Paul** (zhän pôl) 1905– ; French philosopher and writer of novels and plays.

**sash**[1] (sash) ***n.*** a band, ribbon, or scarf worn over the shoulder or around the waist.

**sash**[2] (sash) ***n.*** a sliding frame that holds the glass pane or panes of a window or door.

☆**sa·shay** (sa shā′) ***v.*** **1** to do one of the gliding steps in a square dance. **2** to move or walk in a casual way: *used only in everyday talk.*

**Sas·katch·e·wan** (sas kach′ə wän) a province of southwestern Canada: abbreviated **Sask.**

☆**sas·sa·fras** (sas′ə fras) ***n.*** **1** a slender tree with yellow flowers. *See the picture.* **2** the dried bark of its root, used for flavoring.

**sass·y** (sas′ē) ***adj.*** talking back; impudent; saucy: *used only in everyday talk.* —**sass′i·er, sass′i·est**

**sat** (sat) *past tense and past participle of* **sit.**

**Sat.** *abbreviation for* **Saturday.**

**Sa·tan** (sāt′'n) *another name for* **the Devil.**

> **Satan** comes from the Hebrew word for "enemy." Satan, or the Devil, as the chief evil spirit, is considered in some religions to be the great enemy of humankind and of goodness.



**sa·tan·ic** (sā tan′ik) ***adj.*** like Satan; devilish.

**satch·el** (sach′əl) ***n.*** a small bag of leather, etc. for carrying clothes, books, or the like, sometimes having a shoulder strap.

**sate** (sāt) ***v.*** **1** to satisfy completely [to *sate* a desire]. **2** to supply with so much of something that it becomes unpleasant or disgusting; glut [We were *sated* with all the rich food.] —**sat′ed, sat′ing**

**sa·teen** (sa tēn′) ***n.*** a smooth, glossy cloth, as of cotton, made to look like satin.

**sat·el·lite** (sat′'l īt) ***n.*** **1** a heavenly body that revolves around another, larger one [The moon is a *satellite* of the earth.] **2** an artificial object put into orbit around the earth, the moon, or some other heavenly body. **3** a country that depends on and is controlled by a larger, more powerful one. **4** a follower of an important person.

**sa·ti·ate** (sā′shē āt) ***v.*** to supply with so much of something that it becomes unpleasant or disgusting; glut [*satiated* with flattery]. —**sa′ti·at·ed, sa′ti·at·ing** —**sa′ti·a′tion** ***n.***

**sa·ti·e·ty** (sə tī′ə tē) ***n.*** the feeling of having had more of something than one wants.

**sat·in** (sat′'n) ***n.*** a cloth of nylon, rayon, polyester, silk, or the like having a smooth finish, glossy on the right side and dull on the back. ◆***adj.*** of or like satin. —**sat′in·y** ***adj.***

**sat·in·wood** (sat′'n wood) ***n.*** **1** a smooth, hard wood used in making fine furniture. **2** any of several trees of the East Indies or of the West Indies from which it comes.

**sat·ire** (sa′tīr) ***n.*** **1** the use of irony, sarcasm, and humor to criticize or make fun of something bad or foolish. **2** a novel, story, etc. in which this is done ["Gulliver's Travels" is a *satire* on England of the 18th century.]

**sa·tir·i·cal** (sə tir′i k'l) ***adj.*** of, like, full of, or using satire: *also* **satiric.** —**sa·tir′i·cal·ly** ***adv.***

**sat·i·rist** (sat′ə rist) ***n.*** a person who writes satires or uses satire.

**sat·i·rize** (sat′ə rīz) ***v.*** to criticize or make fun of by using satire. —**sat′i·rized, sat′i·riz·ing**

**sat·is·fac·tion** (sat′is fak′shən) ***n.*** **1** something that satisfies, especially anything that brings pleasure [It was a *satisfaction* to finish the work.] **2** a satisfying or being satisfied. —**give satisfaction,** to satisfy.

**sat·is·fac·to·ry** (sat′is fak′tə rē) ***adj.*** good enough to satisfy, or meet the need or wish. —**sat′is·fac′to·ri·ly** ***adv.***

**sat·is·fy** (sat′is fī) ***v.*** **1** to meet the needs or wishes of; content; please [Only first prize will *satisfy* him.] **2** to make feel sure; convince [The jury was *satisfied* that he was innocent.] **3** to pay off [to *satisfy* a debt]. —**sat′is·fied, sat′is·fy·ing**

> SYNONYMS: **Satisfy** suggests that one's desires and needs are completely fulfilled, while **content** suggests that one is pleased with what one has and does not wish for something more or different [Some days he is *satisfied* only by an enormous meal, while other times he is *contented* with a bowl of soup.]

**sa·trap** (sā′trap *or* sat′rap) ***n.*** **1** the governor of a province in ancient Persia. **2** a ruler of a colony or dependency who is a tyrant.

**sat·u·rate** (sach′ə rāt) ***v.*** **1** to soak through and through [The baby's bib was *saturated* with milk.] **2** to fill so completely or dissolve so much of something that no more can be taken up [to *saturate* water with salt]. —**sat′u·rat·ed, sat′u·rat·ing** —**sat′u·ra′tion** ***n.***

**Sat·ur·day** (sat′ər dē) ***n.*** the seventh and last day of the week.

**Sat·urn** (sat′ərn) **1** the Roman god of farming. **2** the second largest planet, known for the rings seen around it. It is sixth in distance away from the sun. *See the picture.*

**sat·ur·nine** (sat′ər nīn) ***adj.*** quiet and serious, often in a gloomy or solemn way.

**sat·yr** (sāt′ər *or* sat′ər) ***n.*** in Greek myths, a minor god of the woods, with the head and body of a man and the legs, ears, and horns of a goat.

**sauce** (sôs) ***n.*** **1** a liquid or soft dressing served with food to make it tastier [spaghetti with tomato *sauce*]. ☆**2** fruit that has been stewed and, often, mashed [apple*sauce*]. **3** impudence: *used only in everyday talk.*

**sauce·pan** (sôs′pan) ***n.*** a small metal pot with a long handle, used for cooking. *See the picture.*

**sau·cer** (sô′sər) ***n.*** **1** a small, shallow dish, especially one for a cup to rest on. **2** anything round and shallow like this dish.

**sau·cy** (sô′sē) ***adj.*** **1** rude; impudent. **2** lively and bold [a *saucy* smile]. —**sau′ci·er, sau′ci·est** —**sau′ci·ly** ***adv.*** —**sau′ci·ness** ***n.***

**Sa·u·di Arabia** (sä ōō′dē) a kingdom that takes up most of Arabia.

☆**sauer·kraut** (sour′krout) ***n.*** cabbage that has been chopped up, salted, and allowed to turn sour in its own juice.

**Saul** (sôl) in the Bible, the first king of Israel.

**sau·na** (sou′nə *or* sô′nə) ***n.*** **1** a bath in which the air is very hot and fairly dry. Sometimes the people in the bath beat each other lightly with boughs of birch or cedar. **2** the room or shed for such a bath. The Finns were the first to have such baths.

**saun·ter** (sôn′tər) ***v.*** to walk about slowly, not in a hurry; stroll. ◆***n.*** a walk taken in this way [to take a *saunter* through the park].

**sau·sage** (sô′sij) ***n.*** pork or other meat, chopped up and seasoned and, usually, stuffed into a tube made of thin skin.

**sau·té** (sō tā′) ***v.*** to fry quickly in a pan with a little fat. **sau·téed** (sō tād′), **sau·té·ing** (sō tā′iŋ) ◆***adj.*** fried in this way [chicken livers *sauté*].

**sau·terne** (sō turn′ *or* sô turn′) ***n.*** a white, sweet wine.

**sav·age** (sav′ij) ***adj.*** **1** not civilized; primitive [a *savage* tribe]. **2** not tamed; fierce; wild [a *savage* tiger]. **3** cruel; brutal [a *savage* pirate]. ◆***n.*** **1** a person living in a primitive or uncivilized way. **2** a fierce, brutal person. —**sav′age·ly** ***adv.*** —**sav′age·ness** ***n.***

**sav·age·ry** (sav′ij rē) ***n.*** **1** the condition of being savage, wild, or uncivilized. **2** a cruel or brutal act. —*pl.* **sav′age·ries**

**sa·van·na** or **sa·van·nah** (sə van′ə) ***n.*** a flat, open region without trees; plain.

**Sa·van·nah** (sə van′ə) a seaport in Georgia.

**sa·vant** (sə vänt′ *or* sav′ənt) ***n.*** a famous scholar.

**save**[1] (sāv) ***v.*** **1** to rescue or keep from harm or danger [He was *saved* from drowning.] **2** to keep or store up for future use [She *saved* her money for a vacation.] **3** to keep from being lost or wasted [Traveling by plane *saved* many hours.] **4** to prevent or make less [We *saved* the expense by repairing it ourselves.] **5** to keep from being worn out, damaged, etc. [*Save* your dress by wearing this apron.] **6** to avoid expense, loss, waste, etc. [We *save* on meat by buying cheaper cuts.] **7** in religion, to free from sin, death, etc. —**saved, sav′ing** —**sav′er** ***n.***

**save**[2] (sāv) ***prep.*** except; except for; but [I've asked everyone *save* you two.]

**sav·ing**[1] (sā′viŋ) ***adj.*** that saves, rescues, stores up, redeems, etc. [a time-*saving* device; a *saving* virtue]. ◆***n.*** **1** the act of one that saves. **2** *often* **savings,** *pl.* a thing, amount, sum of money, etc. saved [a *saving* of 20%; one's life *savings*].

**sav·ing**[2] (sā′viŋ) ***prep.*** **1** except; save. **2** with due respect for [*Saving* your presence, this must be discussed.] *This word is now seldom used.*

**sav·ior** or **sav·iour** (sāv′yər) ***n.*** a person who saves, or rescues. —**the Saviour** or **the Savior,** Jesus Christ.

**sa·vor** (sā′vər) ***n.*** **1** a special taste or smell; flavor [The salad has a *savor* of garlic.] **2** a special, usually pleasing quality [Golf has lost all its *savor* for her.] ◆***v.*** **1** to taste, enjoy, etc. with relish [He *savored* his success as an actor.] **2** to have a special taste, smell, or quality [Her clever remarks *savor* of rudeness.]

**sa·vor·y**[1] (sā′vər ē) ***adj.*** pleasing to the taste or smell [a *savory* stew].

**sa·vor·y**[2] (sā′vər ē) ***n.*** a kind of herb with a mint flavor, used in cooking.

**saw**[1] (sô) ***n.*** a cutting tool that has a thin metal blade or disk with sharp teeth along the edge. Some saws are worked by hand and others by machinery. *See the picture.* ◆***v.*** **1** to cut or form with a saw [to *saw* wood]. **2** to move the arms through, as if sawing [He *sawed* the air as he argued.] **3** to be sawed [This plank *saws* easily.] —**sawed, sawed** or chiefly British **sawn** (sôn), **saw′ing** 655

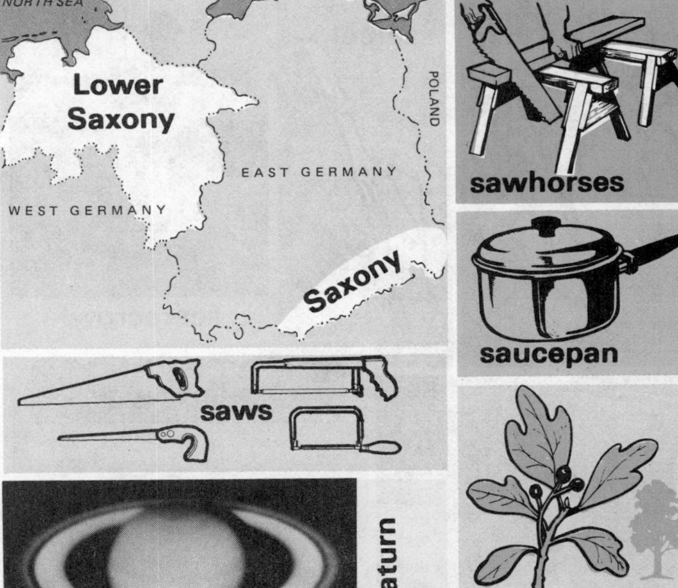


**saw**[2] (sô) ***n.*** an old saying, or proverb.

**saw**[3] (sô) *past tense of* **see**[1].

☆**saw·buck** (sô′buk) ***n.*** *another name for* **sawhorse.**

**saw·dust** (sô′dust) ***n.*** tiny bits of wood formed in sawing wood.

**saw·horse** (sô′hôrs) ***n.*** a rack on which wood is placed while being sawed. *See the picture.*

**saw·mill** (sô′mil) ***n.*** **1** a place where logs are sawed into boards. **2** a large sawing machine.

**saw·yer** (sô′yər) ***n.*** a person whose work is sawing wood.

☆**sax** (saks) ***n.*** *a shorter name for* **saxophone**: *used only in everyday talk.*

**sax·i·frage** (sak′sə frij) ***n.*** a plant with yellow, white, purple, or pink small flowers, and leaves growing in a clump at the base.

**Sax·on** (sak′s′n) ***n.*** a member of a people who lived in northern Germany long ago. Saxons invaded England in the 5th and 6th centuries A.D. ◆***adj.*** of the Saxons, their language, etc.

**Sax·o·ny** (sak′sə nē) **1** a region in the southern part of East Germany. **2** a state in the northern part of West Germany: *the full name is* **Lower Saxony.** *See the map.*

| | | | | | | | |
|---|---|---|---|---|---|---|---|
| **a** | fat | **ir** | here | **ou** | out | **zh** | leisure |
| **ā** | ape | **ī** | bite, fire | **u** | up | **ŋ** | ring |
| **ä** | car, lot | **ō** | go | **ur** | fur | | a *in* ago |
| **e** | ten | **ô** | law, horn | **ch** | chin | | e *in* agent |
| **er** | care | **oi** | oil | **sh** | she | **ə =** | i *in* unity |
| **ē** | even | **oo** | look | **th** | thin | | o *in* collect |
| **i** | hit | **ōō** | tool | ***th*** | then | | u *in* focus |

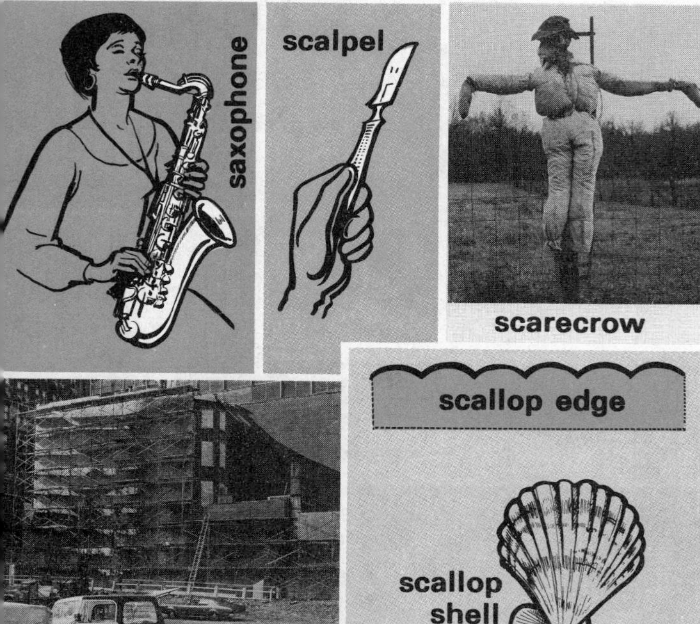


**sax·o·phone** (sak′sə fōn) ***n.*** a woodwind musical instrument with a curved metal body. Its mouthpiece has a single reed. *See the picture.*



**say** (sā) ***v.*** **1** to speak or pronounce; utter ["Hello," he *said.*] **2** to put into words; tell; state [The newspaper *says* it will rain.] **3** to give as an opinion [I cannot *say* which is better.] **4** to recite or repeat [Did you *say* your prayers?] **5** to suppose or guess [He is, I'd *say,* forty.] **6** to show or indicate [The clock *says* ten.] —**said, say′ing** ◆***n.*** **1** a chance to speak [Has the whole class had its *say?*] **2** the power to decide [The coach has the final *say* about who plays.] —**go without saying,** to be so clear that it needs no explaining. —**that is to say,** in other words; that means. —**to say the least,** to say less strongly than the truth allows. —**say′er *n.***

**say·ing** (sā′iŋ) ***n.*** something said, especially a proverb, such as "Waste not, want not."

**says** (sez) *the form of the verb* **say** *showing the present time with singular nouns and with* he, she, *or* it.

**Sb** *the symbol for the chemical element* antimony.

**SC** or **S.C.** *abbreviation for* **South Carolina.**

**scab** (skab) ***n.*** **1** a crust that forms over a sore as it is healing. **2** mange, especially of sheep. **3** a plant disease caused by certain fungi. ☆**4** a worker who keeps on working even though there is a strike, or who takes the place of a striking worker. ◆***v.*** **1** to become covered with a scab. ☆**2** to act as a scab. —**scabbed, scab′bing**

**scab·bard** (skab′ərd) ***n.*** a case or sheath to hold the blade of a sword, dagger, etc.

**scaf·fold** (skaf′'ld) ***n.*** **1** a framework put up to support workers while they are building, repairing, or painting something. *See the picture.* **2** a raised platform on which criminals are hanged or beheaded.

**scaf·fold·ing** (skaf′'l diŋ) ***n.*** **1** the materials that make up a scaffold. **2** *same as* **scaffold.**

**scald** (skôld) ***v.*** **1** to burn with hot liquid or steam. **2** to use boiling liquid on, as to kill germs. **3** to heat until it almost boils [to *scald* milk for a custard]. ◆***n.*** a burn caused by scalding.

**scale**[1] (skāl) ***n.*** **1** a series of marks along a line, with regular spaces in between, used for measuring [A Celsius thermometer has a basic *scale* of 100 degrees.] **2** the way that the size of a map, model, or drawing compares with the size of the thing that it stands for [One inch on a map of this *scale* equals 100 miles of real distance.] **3** a series of steps or degrees based on size, amount, rank, etc. [The passing grade on this *scale* is 70.] **4** a series of musical tones arranged in order from the highest to the lowest or from the lowest to the highest. ◆***v.*** **1** to climb up as by a ladder [to *scale* a wall]. **2** to set according to a scale [The pay is *scaled* according to skill.] —**scaled, scal′ing —on a large scale,** to a large extent.

> **Scale**[1] comes from the Latin word for "ladder" or "flight of stairs." The marks that show the degrees on a thermometer scale look like the rungs of a ladder. The notes showing each tone of a scale on a sheet of music might look like the steps in a flight of stairs.

**scale**[2] (skāl) ***n.*** **1** any of the thin, flat, hard plates that cover and protect certain fish and reptiles. **2** a thin piece or layer; flake [*scales* of rust in a water pipe]. ◆***v.*** **1** to scrape scales from [to *scale* a fish]. **2** to come off in scales [The old, dry paint *scaled* off in the hot sun.] —**scaled, scal′ing**

**scale**[3] (skāl) ***n.*** **1** either of the shallow pans of a balance. **2** *often* **scales,** *pl.* the balance itself; also, any device or machine for weighing. ◆***v.*** to weigh. —**scaled, scal′ing —turn the scales,** to decide or settle.

**scal·lion** (skal′yən) ***n.*** a kind of onion; especially, a young green onion or a leek.

**scal·lop** (skäl′əp *or* skal′əp) ***n.*** **1** a water animal with a soft body enclosed in two hard, ribbed shells hinged together. It has a large muscle, used as food. *See the picture.* **2** any of a series of curves that form a fancy edge on cloth, lace, etc. *See the picture.* ◆***v.*** **1** to bake with a milk sauce and bread crumbs [*scalloped* potatoes]. **2** to cut in scallops [a *scalloped* neckline].

**scal·op·pi·ne** or **scal·lo·pi·ni** (skal′ə pē′nē) ***n.*** thin slices of meat, especially veal, sautéed slowly with herbs and, usually, wine.

**scalp** (skalp) ***n.*** **1** the skin on the top and back of the head, usually covered with hair. **2** a piece of this cut from the head of an enemy. Some American Indians and frontiersmen kept scalps as trophies. ◆☆***v.*** **1** to cut the scalp from. **2** to cheat or rob.

**scal·pel** (skal′pəl) ***n.*** a small, very sharp knife, used by surgeons in operations. *See the picture.*

**scal·y** (skā′lē) ***adj.*** covered with scales [a small, *scaly* lizard]. —**scal′i·er, scal′i·est —scal′i·ness *n.***

**scamp** (skamp) ***n.*** a person who often gets into trouble or mischief; rascal.

**scam·per** (skam′pər) ***v.*** to move quickly or in a hurry [squirrels *scampering* through the trees]. ◆***n.*** a quick run or dash.

**scan** (skan) ***v.*** **1** to look at very carefully; examine [Columbus *scanned* the horizon for land.] ☆**2** to glance at or look over quickly [I *scanned* the list of names to find yours.] **3** to show the pattern of rhythm in the lines of a poem [We can *scan* a line this way: Má rý̆ Má rý̆ quite cŏn trár y̆.] —**scanned, scan′ning** —**scan′ner** ***n.***

**scan·dal** (skan′d'l) ***n.*** **1** someone or something that shocks people and causes shame and disgrace [Years ago, it was a *scandal* for a woman to wear a bikini.] **2** the shame or disgrace caused by this. **3** talk that harms a person's reputation; wicked gossip.

**scan·dal·ize** (skan′də līz) ***v.*** to shock by shameful words or acts [We were *scandalized* at the lies the President told.] —**scan′dal·ized, scan′dal·iz·ing**

**scan·dal·mon·ger** (skan′d'l muŋ′gər) ***n.*** a person who spreads gossip.

**scan·dal·ous** (skan′d'l əs) ***adj.*** **1** causing scandal; shameful; disgraceful [the *scandalous* quarrels of the noisy neighbors]. **2** spreading gossip or slander [a *scandalous* book about movie stars]. —**scan′dal·ous·ly** ***adv.***

**Scan·di·na·vi·a** (skan′də nā′vē ə) **1** a large peninsula of northern Europe, on which Norway and Sweden are located. **2** the countries of Norway, Sweden, Denmark, and Iceland. —**Scan′di·na′vi·an** ***adj., n.***

**scant** (skant) ***adj.*** **1** not as much as is needed; not enough; meager [a *scant* supply of food]. **2** less than full; incomplete [Add a *scant* teaspoon of salt.] ✦***v.*** **1** to limit or make scant. **2** to supply with less than enough. —**scant of,** not having enough of.

**scant·ling** (skant′liŋ) ***n.*** a small beam or timber; especially, a small, upright timber, as in the frame of a structure.

**scant·y** (skan′tē) ***adj.*** not enough or just barely enough; meager [a *scanty* helping of food]. *See* SYNONYMS *at* **meager**. —**scant′i·er, scant′i·est** —**scant′i·ly** ***adv.*** —**scant′i·ness** ***n.***

**scape·goat** (skāp′gōt) ***n.*** a person, group, or thing forced to take the blame for the mistakes or crimes of others.

**scap·u·la** (skap′yoo lə) ***n.*** *another name for* **shoulder blade**. —*pl.* **scap·u·lae** (skap′yoo lē′) or **scap′u·las**

**scar** (skär) ***n.*** **1** a mark left on the skin after a cut, burn, etc. has healed. **2** any mark like this, as the mark on a plant where a leaf has come off. **3** the effect left on the mind by suffering. ✦***v.*** to mark with or form a scar. —**scarred, scar′ring**

**scar·ab** (skar′əb) ***n.*** **1** a beetle of the kind that was sacred to the ancient Egyptians. **2** a likeness of this beetle, used as a charm in earlier times.

**scarce** (skers) ***adj.*** **1** not common; rarely seen [The black bear is *scarce* in settled areas.] **2** not plentiful; hard to get [Gasoline was *scarce* in wartime.] —**scarc′er, scarc′est** —**make oneself scarce,** to go or stay away: *used only in everyday talk.* —**scarce′ness** ***n.***

**scarce·ly** (skers′lē) ***adv.*** **1** only just; barely; hardly [I can *scarcely* taste the pepper in it.] **2** certainly not [You can *scarcely* expect us to believe that.]

**scar·ci·ty** (sker′sə tē) ***n.*** the condition of being scarce; lack, rareness, etc. —*pl.* **scar′ci·ties**

**scare** (sker) ***v.*** to make or become afraid; frighten. —**scared, scar′ing** ✦***n.*** a sudden fear; fright [The loud noise gave me quite a *scare*.] —**scare away** or **scare off,** to drive away or drive off by frightening. —☆**scare up,** to produce or gather quickly: *used only in everyday talk.*

**scare·crow** (sker′krō) ***n.*** a figure of a man made with sticks, old clothes, etc. and set up in a field to scare birds away from crops. *See the picture.*

**scarf** (skärf) ***n.*** **1** a long or broad piece of cloth worn about the head, neck, or shoulders for warmth or decoration. **2** a long, narrow piece of cloth used as a covering on top of a table, bureau, etc. —*pl.* **scarfs** or **scarves** (skärvz)

**scar·la·ti·na** (skär′lə tē′nə) ***n.*** a mild form of scarlet fever.

**scar·let** (skär′lit) ***n.*** very bright red with an orange tinge. ✦***adj.*** of this color.

**scarlet fever** a catching disease, especially of children, that causes a sore throat, fever, and a scarlet rash.

**scarlet tanager** a songbird of the U.S. The male has a scarlet body and black wings and tail.

**scar·y** (sker′ē) ***adj.*** **1** causing fear; frightening. **2** easily frightened. *This word is used only in everyday talk.* —**scar′i·er, scar′i·est** —**scar′i·ness** ***n.***

**scath·ing** (skā′*th*iŋ) ***adj.*** very harsh or bitter, as in showing dislike [a *scathing* reply]. —**scath′ing·ly** ***adv.***

**scat·ter** (skat′ər) ***v.*** **1** to throw here and there; sprinkle [to *scatter* seed over a lawn]. *See* SYNONYMS *at* **sprinkle**. **2** to separate and send or go in many directions; disperse [The wind *scattered* the leaves. The crowd *scattered* after the game.]

**scat·ter·brain** (skat′ər brān) ***n.*** a person who cannot think seriously or pay attention; flighty person. —**scat′ter·brained** ***adj.***

**scat·ter·ing** (skat′ər iŋ) ***n.*** a few here and there [an audience of children with a *scattering* of adults].

☆**scatter rug** any of several small rugs that can be placed here and there in a room.

**scav·eng·er** (skav′in jər) ***n.*** **1** an animal that feeds on rotting meat and garbage [Vultures and hyenas are *scavengers*.] **2** a person who gathers things that others have thrown away.

☆**scavenger hunt** a game played at parties in which persons go out to bring back odd items on a list, without buying them.

**sce·nar·i·o** (si ner′ē ō) ***n.*** ☆**1** the written script from which a movie is made. **2** an outline for the way something might happen or is planned to happen. —*pl.* **sce·nar′i·os**

**scene** (sēn) ***n.*** **1** the place where a thing happens [the *scene* of an accident]. **2** the place and time of a story, play, etc. **3** a division of a play, usually a separate part of an act. **4** a certain event in a play, movie, or story [the *scene* in which the lovers meet]. **5** a view, landscape, etc. [a picture of an autumn *scene*]. **6** a show of anger, bad temper, etc. [He made a *scene* when he wasn't allowed to go.] **7** an area or field in which some people are interested: *used only in everyday talk* [the political *scene*]. —**behind the scenes, 1** backstage. **2** in private or in secrecy.

| | | | | | | | |
|---|---|---|---|---|---|---|---|
| **a** | fat | **ir** | here | **ou** | out | **zh** | leisure |
| **ā** | ape | **ī** | bite, fire | **u** | up | **ŋ** | ring |
| **ä** | car, lot | **ō** | go | **ʉr** | fur | | a *in* ago |
| **e** | ten | **ô** | law, horn | **ch** | chin | | e *in* agent |
| **er** | care | **oi** | oil | **sh** | she | **ə** = | i *in* unity |
| **ē** | even | **oo** | look | **th** | thin | | o *in* collect |
| **i** | hit | **ōō** | tool | ***th*** | then | | u *in* focus |

**sce·ner·y** (sē′nər ē) ***n.*** **1** the way a certain area looks; outdoor views [the *scenery* along the shore]. **2** painted screens, hangings, etc. used on a stage for a play.

**sce·nic** (sē′nik *or* sen′ik) ***adj.*** **1** having to do with scenery or landscapes [the *scenic* wonders of the Rockies]. **2** having beautiful scenery [a *scenic* route along the river]. **3** of the stage and its scenery, lighting, etc. [The *scenic* effects included a garden.] —**sce′ni·cal·ly** ***adv.***

**scent** (sent) ***n.*** **1** a smell; odor [the *scent* of apple blossoms]. **2** the sense of smell [Lions hunt partly by *scent.*] **3** a smell left by an animal [The dogs lost the fox's *scent* at the river.] **4** a liquid with a pleasing smell; perfume. ◆***v.*** **1** to smell [Our dog *scented* a cat.] **2** to get a hint of [We *scented* trouble when he didn't show up.] **3** to put perfume on or in [a *scented* handkerchief].

SYNONYMS: A **scent** is a faint smell that something has and that spreads out around it [the *scent* of freshly cut hay]. A **perfume** is a fairly strong, but usually pleasant, smell [the *perfume* of gardenias]. A **fragrance** is a pleasant, sweet smell, especially of something growing [the *fragrance* of the roses].

**scep·ter** (sep′tər) ***n.*** a rod or staff held by a ruler as a symbol of his power. *See the picture. The usual British spelling is* **sceptre.**



**scep·tic** (skep′tik) ***n.*** *chiefly British spelling of* **skeptic.** —**scep′ti·cal** ***adj.*** —**scep′ti·cism** ***n.***

**sched·ule** (skej′o͞ol) ***n.*** ☆**1** a list of the times at which certain things are to happen; timetable [a *schedule* of the sailings of an ocean liner]. ☆**2** a timed plan for a project [The work is ahead of *schedule.*] **3** a list of details [a *schedule* of postal rates]. ◆***v.*** **1** to make a schedule of [to *schedule* one's hours of work]. ☆**2** to plan for a certain time [to *schedule* a game for 3:00 P.M.] —**sched′uled, sched′ul·ing**

**Sche·he·ra·za·de** (shə her′ə zä′də *or* shə her′ə zäd′) the bride of the Sultan in *The Arabian Nights.* She saves her own life by keeping the Sultan interested in tales that she tells for 1001 nights.

**scheme** (skēm) ***n.*** **1** a plan or system in which things are carefully put together [the color *scheme* of a painting]. **2** a plan or program, often a secret or dishonest one [a *scheme* for getting rich quick]. ◆***v.*** to make secret or dishonest plans; plot [Lee is always *scheming* to get out of work.] —**schemed, schem′ing** —**schem′er** ***n.***

**schem·ing** (skē′miŋ) ***adj.*** forming schemes; sly; tricky.

**Sche·nec·ta·dy** (skə nek′tə dē) a city in eastern New York.

**scher·zo** (sker′tsō) ***n.*** a lively, playful piece of music, often a part of a symphony or sonata. —*pl.* **scher′zos** or **scher·zi** (sker′tsē)

**schism** (siz′'m *or* skiz′'m) ***n.*** a split or division between the members of a church or other group, when they no longer agree on what they believe.

**schis·mat·ic** (siz mat′ik *or* skiz mat′ik) ***adj.*** **1** of or like a schism. **2** tending to cause a schism. ◆***n.*** a person who takes part in a schism.

☆**schmaltz** (shmälts *or* shmôlts) ***n.*** **1** any music, poetry, stories, etc. that appeal to very tender feelings of love, sadness, etc. in ways that have been done over and over again. **2** these very tender feelings.

**schol·ar** (skäl′ər) ***n.*** **1** a person who has learned much through study. **2** a student or pupil. **3** a student who has a scholarship.

**schol·ar·ly** (skäl′ər lē) ***adj.*** **1** of or like scholars. **2** showing much learning [a *scholarly* book]. **3** that likes to study and learn [My sister is a *scholarly* girl.] —**schol′ar·li·ness** ***n.***

**schol·ar·ship** (skäl′ər ship) ***n.*** **1** the knowledge of a learned person; great learning. **2** the kind of knowledge that a student shows [Her paper shows good *scholarship.*] **3** a gift of money to help a student continue his or her education.

**scho·las·tic** (skə las′tik) ***adj.*** having to do with schools, students, teachers, and studies [*scholastic* honors]. —**scho·las′ti·cal·ly** ***adv.***

**school**[1] (sko͞ol) ***n.*** **1** a place, usually a special building, for teaching and learning, as a public school, dancing school, college, etc. **2** the students and teachers of a school [an assembly for the whole *school*]. **3** the time during which students are in classes [*School* starts in September.] **4** the full course of study in a school [He never finished *school.*] **5** any time or situation during which a person learns [the *school* of experience]. **6** a certain part of a college or university [the law *school;* the dental *school*]. **7** a group of people who have the same ideas and opinions [a new *school* of writers]. ◆***v.*** **1** to teach or train; educate [He is *schooled* in auto repair.] **2** to control; discipline [She *schooled* herself to be patient.] ◆***adj.*** of or for a school or schools [our *school* band].

**School**[1] comes from a Greek word that means "leisure or free time" and also "what one does in one's free time." Most young people have the free time to go to school because they are not old enough to work.

**school**[2] (sko͞ol) ***n.*** a large group of fish or water animals of the same kind swimming together [a *school* of porpoises]. ◆***v.*** to swim together in a school.

**school board** a group of people chosen to be in charge of local public schools.

**school·book** (sko͞ol′bo͝ok) ***n.*** a book used for study in schools; textbook.

**school·boy** (sko͞ol′boi) ***n.*** a boy who goes to school.

☆**school bus** a bus for taking children to or from school or on trips related to school.

**school·child** (sko͞ol′chīld) ***n.*** a child who goes to school. —*pl.* **school·chil·dren** (sko͞ol′chil′drən)

**school·fel·low** (sko͞ol′fel′ō) ***n.*** *another name for* **schoolmate.**

**school·girl** (sko͞ol′gurl) ***n.*** a girl who goes to school.

**school·house** (sko͞ol′hous) ***n.*** a building used as a school.

**school·ing** (sko͞ol′iŋ) ***n.*** teaching or training got at school; education [How many years of *schooling* have you had?]

**school·mate** (sko͞ol′māt) ***n.*** a person going to the same school at the same time as another.

**school·room** (sko͞ol′ro͞om) ***n.*** a room in which pupils are taught, as in a school.

**school·teach·er** (sko͞ol′tē′chər) ***n.*** a person whose work is teaching in a school.

**school·work** (sko͞ol′wurk) ***n.*** lessons worked on in classes at school or done as homework.

**school·yard** (sko͞ol′yärd) ***n.*** the ground around a school, often used as a playground.

**school year** the part of a year during which school is held, usually from September to June.

☆**schoon·er** (sko͞o′nər) ***n.*** a ship with two or more masts and sails that are set lengthwise. *See the picture.*

**Schu·bert** (sho͞o′bərt), **Franz** (fränts) 1797–1828; Austrian composer.

**Schu·mann** (sho͞o′män), **Robert** 1810–1856; German composer.

**schwa** (shwä) ***n.*** the sound of a vowel in a syllable that is not accented, as the "a" in "ago"; also, the symbol ə used for this sound.

**sci·ence** (sī′əns) ***n.*** **1** knowledge made up of an orderly system of facts that have been learned from study, observation, and experiments [*Science* helps us to understand how things happen.] **2** a branch of this knowledge [the *science* of astronomy]. *See also* **art** *in meaning* 3. **3** skill based upon training [the *science* of boxing].

**science fiction** stories, novels, etc. that are fantastic and that make use of scientific devices, inventions, etc., such as spacecraft, that are real or imagined.

**sci·en·tif·ic** (sī′ən tif′ik) ***adj.*** **1** having to do with, or used in, science [a *scientific* study; *scientific* equipment]. **2** using the rules and methods of science [*scientific* procedure]. **3** skillful or highly trained [a *scientific* boxer]. —**sci′en·tif′i·cal·ly** ***adv.***

**sci·en·tist** (sī′ən tist) ***n.*** an expert in science, such as a chemist, biologist, etc.

☆**sci-fi** (sī′fī′) ***n.*** *a shorter name for* **science fiction**.

**scim·i·tar** or **scim·i·ter** (sim′ə tər) ***n.*** a curved sword used by Turks, Arabs, etc.

**scin·til·la** (sin til′ə) ***n.*** **1** a spark. **2** a tiny bit; trace [not a *scintilla* of hope].

**scin·til·late** (sin′t'l āt) ***v.*** **1** to sparkle or twinkle. **2** to be very clever and witty [She *scintillates* in conversation.] —**scin′til·lat·ed**, **scin′til·lat·ing** —**scin′til·la′tion** ***n.***

**sci·on** (sī′ən) ***n.*** **1** a bud or shoot of a plant, used for planting or grafting. **2** an heir or descendant.

**scis·sors** (siz′ərz) ***n.pl.*** a tool for cutting, with two blades that are joined so that they slide over each other when their handles are moved: *also used with a singular verb. Also called* **pair of scissors**. *See the picture.*

**scoff** (skôf *or* skäf) ***v.*** to mock or jeer at; make fun of [We *scoffed* at his foolish fears.] ◆***n.*** **1** a rude or mocking remark; jeer. **2** a person or thing scoffed at. —**scoff′er** ***n.***

**scold** (skōld) ***v.*** to find fault with someone in an angry way [I *scolded* her for being late.] ◆***n.*** a person who often scolds, nags, etc.

> **Scold** comes from an old Norse word for a poet who wrote verses pointing out the faults of someone in a scornful way. Sometimes in scolding, we may say someone is "chicken-hearted" or "dumb as an ox," and this is a sort of poetic language.

**scol·lop** (skäl′əp) ***n., v.*** *another spelling of* **scallop**.

**sconce** (skäns) ***n.*** a bracket attached to a wall, for holding a candle, etc. *See the picture.*

**scone** (skōn) ***n.*** a small, flat cake, eaten as a biscuit with butter.

scepter

kitchen scoops

schooner

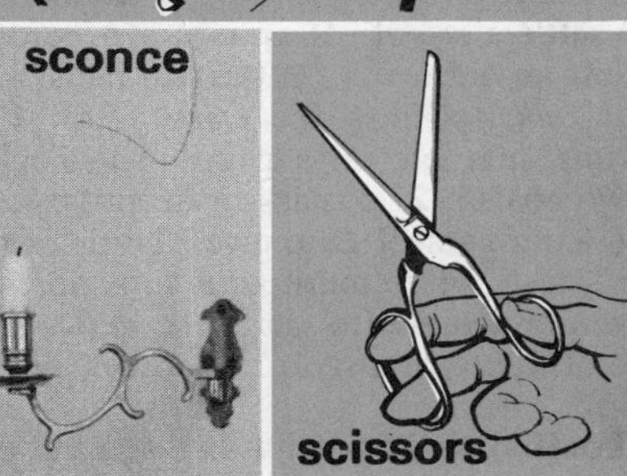

sconce

scissors

**scoop** (sko͞op) ***n.*** **1** a kitchen tool like a small shovel, used to take up sugar, flour, etc., or one with a small, round bowl for dishing up ice cream, etc. *See the picture.* **2** the part of a dredge or steam shovel which takes up the sand, dirt, etc. **3** the act of taking up with a scoop [Every *scoop* of the shovel makes the hole deeper.] **4** the amount taken up at one time by a scoop [three *scoops* of ice cream]. **5** a hollowed-out place; hole. ☆**6** the printing of a news item before other newspapers can print it: *used only in everyday talk.* ◆***v.*** **1** to take up as with a scoop [We *scooped* up water with our hands.] **2** to make a hole, etc. by scooping. ☆**3** to print a news item before others can: *used only in everyday talk.*



**scoot** (sko͞ot) ***v.*** to go quickly; scamper: *used only in everyday talk.*

**scoot·er** (sko͞ot′ər) ***n.*** **1** a child's toy for riding on, having a low board for the foot, with a wheel at each end, and a handlebar for steering. It is moved by pushing the other foot against the ground. **2** a machine like a small motorcycle, run by a motor: *the full name is* **motor scooter**.

**scope** (skōp) ***n.*** **1** the extent of one's ability to understand; the range of one's mind [This problem is beyond my *scope*.] **2** the amount or kind of material that is covered or included [the *scope* of a school dictionary]. *See* SYNONYMS *at* **range**. **3** room for freedom of action or thought; opportunity [plenty of *scope* for new ideas].

| | | | | | | | |
|---|---|---|---|---|---|---|---|
| **a** | fat | **ir** | here | **ou** | out | **zh** | leisure |
| **ā** | ape | **ī** | bite, fire | **u** | up | **ng** | ring |
| **ä** | car, lot | **ō** | go | **ur** | fur | | a *in* ago |
| **e** | ten | **ô** | law, horn | **ch** | chin | | e *in* agent |
| **er** | care | **oi** | oil | **sh** | she | ə = | i *in* unity |
| **ē** | even | **oo** | look | **th** | thin | | o *in* collect |
| **i** | hit | **o͞o** | tool | ***th*** | then | | u *in* focus |

**-scope** (skōp) *a suffix meaning* an instrument for seeing or looking [A *telescope* is an instrument for seeing things far away.]

**scorch** (skôrch) ***v.*** **1** to burn or be burned slightly [I *scorched* the shirt with the iron.] *See* SYNONYMS *at* **burn¹**. **2** to dry up by heat; parch [The sun *scorched* the plants.] ***✦n.*** a slight burn on the surface.

**score** (skôr) ***n.*** **1** the number of points made in a game or contest [The *score* is 2 to 1.] **2** a grade or rating, as on a test [a *score* of 98%]. **3** twenty people or things; set of twenty. **4 scores,** *pl.* very many. **5** a piece of music showing all the parts for the instruments or voices [the *score* of an opera]. **6** a scratch or mark [the *scores* made on ice by skates]. **7** an amount owed; debt [to settle a *score*]. **8** an injury or wrong; grudge [to pay off an old *score*]. **9** the real facts: *used only in everyday talk* [to know the *score*]. ***✦v.*** **1** to make points, runs, hits, etc. in a game [The hockey player *scored* two goals.] **2** to mark or keep the score of [Will you *score* our game?] **3** to give a grade or rating to [to *score* a test]. **4** to mark with cuts, notches, or lines. **5** to win or achieve [to *score* a success]. **6** to arrange a piece of music in a score. —**scored, scor′ing —scor′er** ***n.***

**score·less** (skôr′lis) ***adj.*** not having scored any points.

**scorn** (skôrn) ***n.*** **1** a feeling that one has toward something low, mean, or evil; contempt [We have nothing but *scorn* for a cheater.] **2** the showing of such feeling [the *scorn* in her look]. **3** a person or thing that is treated with scorn. ***✦v.*** **1** to think of and treat as low, mean, etc.; show contempt for [to *scorn* a tattler]. **2** to refuse to do something thought of as wrong or disgraceful [He *scorns* to use a whip on the horse.]

**scorn·ful** (skôrn′fəl) ***adj.*** full of scorn or contempt [a *scornful* laugh]. —**scorn′ful·ly** ***adv.***

**Scor·pi·o** (skôr′pē ō) the eighth sign of the zodiac, for the period from October 24 to November 22: *also called* the Scorpion. *See the picture for* **zodiac.**

**scor·pi·on** (skôr′pē ən) ***n.*** a small animal related to the spider and having a pair of pinching claws in front and a long tail with a poisonous sting at the tip. *See the picture.*

**Scot** (skät) ***n.*** a person born or living in Scotland.

**Scot.** *abbreviation for* **Scotch, Scotland, Scottish.**

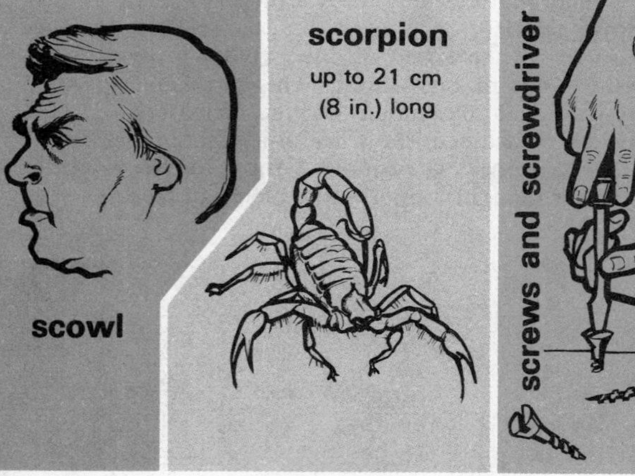


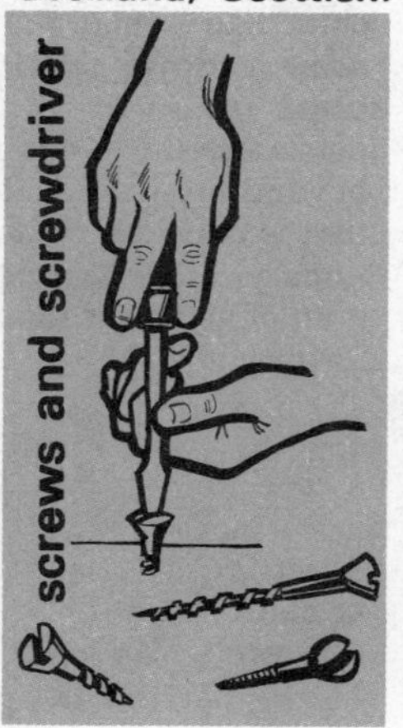


**Scotch** (skäch) ***adj., n.*** *another word for* **Scottish.** *See note at* **Scottish.**

**scotch** (skäch) ***v.*** **1** to stop from causing trouble; put an end to [to *scotch* a rumor]. **2** to wound without killing.

**Scotch·man** (skäch′mən) ***n.*** *another name for* **Scotsman.** *—pl.* **Scotch′men**

☆**Scotch tape** a thin, transparent tape used to make things stick together.

**scot-free** (skät′frē′) ***adj.*** without being punished or hurt; free from penalty; safe.

> **Scot-free** first meant "free from the payment of tax," for the word *scot* is used in some places, especially in Great Britain, to mean "tax."

**Scot·land** (skät′lənd) a part of Great Britain, north of England.

**Scotland Yard** the London police headquarters, especially its detective bureau.

**Scots** (skäts) ***adj., n.*** *another word for* **Scottish.**

**Scots·man** (skäts′mən) ***n.*** a person, especially a man, born or living in Scotland. *—pl.* **Scots′men**

**Scots·wom·an** (skäts′woom′ən) ***n.*** a woman born or living in Scotland. *—pl.* **Scots′wom′en**

**Scott** (skät), Sir **Walter** 1771–1832; Scottish writer of novels and poems.

**Scot·tish** (skät′ish) ***adj.*** of Scotland, its people, etc. ***✦n.*** the dialect of English spoken by the people of Scotland. —**the Scottish,** the people of Scotland.

> **Scottish** is more common than **Scotch** in formal use, as in speaking of the people of Scotland, their language, etc. **Scotch** is used with certain words, as "tweed" and "whisky."

**scoun·drel** (skoun′drəl) ***n.*** a bad or dishonest person; villain; rascal.

**scour¹** (skour) ***v.*** **1** to clean by rubbing hard, especially with something rough or gritty [The cook *scoured* the greasy frying pan with soap and steel wool.] **2** to clear out or cleanse as by a flow of water. ***✦n.*** the act of scouring.

**scour²** (skour) ***v.*** to go about or through in a quick but thorough way, as in searching [Volunteers *scoured* the woods for the lost child.]

**scourge** (skurj) ***n.*** **1** a whip. **2** something that causes great pain, suffering, etc., as war or a plague. ***✦v.*** **1** to whip or flog. **2** to cause much pain or suffering to; punish; torment. —**scourged, scourg′ing**

**scout** (skout) ***n.*** **1** a soldier, ship, or plane sent to spy out the strength, movements, etc. of the enemy. **2** a member of the Boy Scouts or Girl Scouts. **3** a person sent out to get information about a competitor, find people with talent, etc. [a baseball *scout*]. **4** a fellow: *slang in this meaning* [You are really a good *scout!*] ***✦v.*** **1** to go out looking for information, as about an enemy. **2** to go in search of something [*Scout* around for some firewood.]

**scout·mas·ter** (skout′mas′tər) ***n.*** the adult leader of a troop of Boy Scouts.

☆**scow** (skou) ***n.*** a large boat with a flat bottom and square ends, for carrying loads, as of sand or coal.

> **Scow** comes from a Dutch word meaning "boat which is poled along." The flat-bottomed boats of the early days were moved along by pushing poles against the bottom of the river or other body of water on which the boat traveled. Now the scow is often towed by a tugboat.

**scowl** (skoul) ***v.*** to look angry, mean, etc., as by lowering the eyebrows and the corners of the mouth. ◆***n.*** a scowling look. *See the picture.*

**scrab·ble** (skrab′'l) ***v.*** **1** to scratch, scrape, or paw as in looking for something. **2** to struggle. —**scrab′bled, scrab′bling** ◆***n.*** the act of scrabbling.

**scrag·gly** (skrag′lē) ***adj.*** uneven, ragged, irregular, etc. [a *scraggly* beard]. —**scrag′gli·er, scrag′gli·est**

☆**scram** (skram) ***v.*** to leave or get out, especially in a hurry: *a slang word.* —**scrammed, scram′ming**

**scram·ble** (skram′b'l) ***v.*** **1** to climb or crawl in a quick, rough way [The children *scrambled* up the steep hill.] **2** to struggle or scuffle for something [The puppies *scrambled* for the meat.] ☆**3** to cook eggs while stirring the mixed whites and yolks. **4** to get aircraft into the air quickly to fight enemy planes. **5** to mix up electronic signals, as those containing a secret message, so that the message cannot be understood without special equipment. **6** to mix together in a disorderly way. —**scram′bled, scram′bling** ◆***n.*** **1** a climb or crawl over uneven ground. **2** a rough, confused fight or struggle [a *scramble* for the scattered coins]. **3** a quick takeoff of aircraft against enemy planes. **4** a disorderly heap.

**Scran·ton** (skrant′'n) a city in northeastern Pennsylvania.

**scrap**[1] (skrap) ***n.*** **1** a small piece; bit [a *scrap* of paper; a *scrap* of information]. **2** something thrown away because it is useless. **3 scraps,** *pl.* bits of leftover food. ◆***adj.*** in the form of broken bits and pieces [*scrap* metal]. ◆***v.*** **1** to make into scrap or scraps. **2** to get rid of as worthless; discard [He *scrapped* his old habits.] —**scrapped, scrap′ping**

**scrap**[2] (skrap) ***n., v.*** fight or quarrel: *used only in everyday talk.* —**scrapped, scrap′ping**

**scrap·book** (skrap′book) ***n.*** a book of blank pages in which pictures, clippings, etc. are kept.

**scrape** (skrāp) ***v.*** **1** to make smooth or clean by rubbing with a tool or with something rough [to *scrape* the bottom of a ship]. **2** to remove in this way [*Scrape* off the old paint.] **3** to scratch or rub the skin from [He fell and *scraped* his knee.] **4** to rub with a harsh or grating sound [The shovel *scraped* across the sidewalk.] **5** to get together bit by bit, with some effort [They finally *scraped* up enough money to buy the stove.] **6** to get along, but just barely [They *scrape* by on very little money.] —**scraped, scrap′ing** ◆***n.*** **1** the act of scraping. **2** a scraped place. **3** a harsh, grating sound. **4** an unpleasant situation that is hard to get out of [She got into a *scrape* by lying.]

**scrap·er** (skrā′pər) ***n.*** a tool for scraping.

**scratch** (skrach) ***v.*** **1** to mark or cut the surface of slightly with something sharp [Thorns *scratched* her legs. Our cat *scratched* the chair with its claws.] **2** to rub or scrape, as with the nails, to relieve itching [to *scratch* a mosquito bite]. **3** to rub or scrape with a harsh, grating noise [The pen *scratched* when he wrote.] **4** to cross out by drawing lines through [She *scratched* out what he had written.] **5** to write or draw carelessly or in a hurry [to *scratch* off a letter]. **6** to take out of a contest; withdraw [Two horses were *scratched* from the race.] ◆***n.*** **1** a mark or cut made in a surface by something sharp. **2** a slight wound. **3** a harsh, grating sound [the *scratch* of chalk on a blackboard]. ◆***adj.*** ☆**1** used for hasty notes [*scratch* paper]. ☆**2** done or made by chance; lucky [a *scratch* hit in baseball]. —**from scratch,** from little or nothing [She built up a business from *scratch.*] —**up to scratch,** as good as was hoped or expected.

**scratch·y** (skrach′ē) ***adj.*** **1** that scratches, scrapes, itches, etc. [a *scratchy* pen; a *scratchy* sweater]. **2** made as if with scratches [*scratchy* handwriting]. —**scratch′i·er, scratch′i·est**

**scrawl** (skrôl) ***v.*** to write or draw in a hasty, careless way. ◆***n.*** careless or poor handwriting that is hard to read.

**scraw·ny** (skrô′nē) ***adj.*** very thin; skinny. —**scraw′ni·er, scraw′ni·est**

**scream** (skrēm) ***v.*** **1** to give a loud, shrill cry, as in fright or pain [They *screamed* as the roller coaster hurtled downward.] **2** to make a noise like this [The sirens *screamed.* We *screamed* with laughter.] ◆***n.*** **1** a loud, shrill cry or sound; shriek. **2** a very funny person or thing: *used only in everyday talk.*

SYNONYMS: **Scream** is the general word for a loud, high, piercing cry, as in fear, pain, or anger [The *screams* of the burned child were pitiful.] **Shriek** suggests a sharper, more sudden cry than scream [The hiker let out a *shriek* at the sight of the snake.] **Screech** suggests an unpleasantly shrill cry that is painful to the hearer [The owl's *screech* made us shudder.]

**screech** (skrēch) ***v.*** to give a harsh, high shriek. ◆***n.*** a harsh, high shriek. *See* SYNONYMS *at* **scream.**



**screen** (skrēn) ***n.*** **1** a mesh woven loosely of wires so as to leave small openings between them. Screens are used in windows, doors, etc. to keep insects out. **2** a covered frame or curtain used to hide, separate, or protect. **3** anything that hides, separates, or protects [a smoke *screen;* a *screen* of trees]. **4** a sieve for separating smaller pieces of coal, stone, etc. from larger ones. **5** a surface on which movies, television pictures, etc. are shown. ◆***v.*** **1** to hide, shelter, or protect, as with a screen [A hedge *screens* the yard.] **2** to sift coal, stones, etc. through a screen. **3** to test and question in order to separate according to group [to *screen* people applying for jobs].

☆**screen·play** (skrēn′plā) ***n.*** the written script from which a movie is made.

**screw** (skrōō) ***n.*** **1** a piece of metal like a nail with a groove winding around it in a spiral, and usually having a slot across its head. It is forced, by turning, into pieces of wood, etc. to hold them together. *See the picture.* **2** anything that looks or turns like a screw. **3** a turn or twist, as of a screw. **4** a propeller on a ship or plane. ◆***v.*** **1** to turn or twist as or like a screw [*Screw* the lid on tight.] **2** to fasten or be fastened with screws [He *screwed* the shelf to the wall. This hinge *screws* to the door.] **3** to twist out of shape [to *screw* up one's face]. **4** to force [We all must *screw* up our

| | | | |
|---|---|---|---|
| **a** fat | **ir** here | **ou** out | **zh** leisure |
| **ā** ape | **ī** bite, fire | **u** up | **ng** ring |
| **ä** car, lot | **ō** go | **ur** fur | a *in* ago |
| **e** ten | **ô** law, horn | **ch** chin | e *in* agent |
| **er** care | **oi** oil | **sh** she | ə = i *in* unity |
| **ē** even | **oo** look | **th** thin | o *in* collect |
| **i** hit | **ōō** tool | ***th*** then | u *in* focus |

courage.] —**put the screws on,** to use force on. —**screw up,** to bungle; foul up: *a slang phrase.*

☆**screw·ball** (skrōō′bôl) ***n.*** **1** a pitched baseball that curves to the right or the left. **2** a person who seems peculiar: *slang in this meaning.*

**screw·driv·er** (skrōō′drī′vər) ***n.*** a tool used for turning screws. It has an end that fits into the slot on the head of the screw. *See the picture on page 660.*

**screw·y** (skrōō′ē) ***adj.*** ☆**1** mentally ill; crazy. ☆**2** peculiar or odd in a confusing way. *This is a slang word.* —**screw′i·er, screw′i·est** —**screw′i·ness** ***n.***

**scrib·ble** (skrib′′l) ***v.*** **1** to write quickly or carelessly. **2** to make marks that have no meaning [The baby *scribbled* on the wall.] —**scrib′bled, scrib′bling** ◆***n.*** scribbled writing or marks. —**scrib′bler** ***n.***

**scribe** (skrīb) ***n.*** **1** a person who wrote out copies as of books before the invention of printing. **2** a writer or author. **3** a learned Jewish scholar who makes handwritten copies of the Torah.

**scrim·mage** (skrim′ij) ***n.*** **1** a rough, confused fight or struggle. **2** the entire play that follows the pass from center in a football game. ◆***v.*** to take part in a scrimmage. —**scrim′maged, scrim′mag·ing** —**line of scrimmage,** in football, the imaginary line along which the two teams line up before each play.

**scrimp** (skrimp) ***v.*** to spend or use as little as possible [to *scrimp* on food; to *scrimp* to save money].

☆**scrim·shaw** (skrim′shô) ***n.*** an article made from a whale's tooth, walrus tusk, shell, or bone, delicately carved as by a sailor on a long voyage.



**scrip** (skrip) ***n.*** ☆**1** paper money in amounts of less than a dollar, once issued in the United States. **2** a paper giving someone the right to receive something, as a certificate issued by a local government to pay its debts during hard times.

**script** (skript) ***n.*** **1** handwriting. **2** printing type that looks like handwriting. **3** a copy of a play, radio or TV show, etc., used by those putting it on.

**scrip·ture** (skrip′chər) ***n.*** **1** *usually* **Scriptures,** *pl.* the Bible. **2** any sacred writing [The Koran is Muslim *scripture.*] —**scrip′tur·al** ***adj.***

**script·writ·er** (skript′rīt′ər) ***n.*** a person who writes scripts for movies, TV, etc.

**scrive·ner** (skriv′nər) ***n.*** in earlier times, a person who was hired to work as a scribe or clerk.

☆**scrod** (skräd) ***n.*** a young codfish or haddock, especially one split and prepared for cooking.

**scrof·u·la** (skräf′yə lə) ***n.*** a kind of tuberculosis that makes the lymph glands swell up, especially those of the neck. —**scrof′u·lous** ***adj.***

**scroll** (skrōl) ***n.*** **1** a roll of parchment or paper, usually with writing on it. *See the picture.* **2** a decoration or design like a loosely rolled scroll.

**Scrooge** (skrōōj) the mean and miserly old man in Dickens' story *A Christmas Carol.*

**scrounge** (skrounj) ***v.*** **1** to manage to get by hunting around. **2** to get by begging or sponging. **3** to take; pilfer. *This word is used only in everyday talk.* —**scrounged, scroung′ing**

**scrub**[1] (skrub) ***n.*** **1** a growth of short, stubby trees or bushes. **2** any person or thing of less than average size, quality, ability, etc. ☆**3** a football player, etc. not on the regular team. ◆***adj.*** **1** small, stunted, etc. ☆**2** of players that are scrubs [*scrub* practice]. —**scrub′by** ***adj.*** —**scrub′bi·er, scrub′bi·est**

**scrub**[2] (skrub) ***v.*** to clean or wash by rubbing hard [to *scrub* floors]. —**scrubbed, scrub′bing** ◆***n.*** the act of scrubbing.

**scruff** (skruf) ***n.*** the back of the neck, or the loose skin there.

**scruff·y** (skruf′ē) ***adj.*** shabby or untidy; grubby. —**scruff′i·er, scruff′i·est**

**scrump·tious** (skrump′shəs) ***adj.*** very pleasing, especially to the taste; delicious: *used only in everyday talk.* —**scrump′tious·ly** ***adv.***

**scrunch** (skrunch) ***v.*** **1** to crunch or crumple. **2** to hunch or huddle.

**scru·ple** (skrōō′p′l) ***n.*** **1** a doubt or uneasy feeling that may keep one from doing something looked on as bad [Leslie has *scruples* about telling even a small lie.] **2** a very small unit of weight used by druggists. ◆***v.*** to hesitate or hold back because of scruples [She *scrupled* at taking a bribe.] —**scru′pled, scru′pling**

> **Scruple** comes from a Latin word that means "a small, sharp stone." From this it came to be used for a small weight, difficulty, or doubt.

**scru·pu·lous** (skrōō′pyə ləs) ***adj.*** **1** paying strict attention to what is right or proper; very honest [*scrupulous* in her business dealings]. **2** careful about details; exact [a *scrupulous* record of expenses]. —**scru′pu·lous·ly** ***adv.***

**scru·ti·nize** (skrōōt′′n īz) ***v.*** to look at very carefully; examine closely. —**scru′ti·nized, scru′ti·niz·ing**

**scru·ti·ny** (skrōōt′′n ē) ***n.*** a long, careful look; close examination. —*pl.* **scru′ti·nies**

> In earlier days, **scrutiny** meant an examination of ballots to be sure voting had been fair. The word came from a Latin word that meant to search thoroughly, even to look through the trash.

☆**scu·ba** (skōō′bə) ***n.*** equipment worn by divers for breathing under water, usually tanks of compressed air strapped to the back and connected by a hose to a mouthpiece. *See the picture.*

> **Scuba** is an acronym and is formed from the first letters of the parts of the phrase "**s**elf-**c**ontained **u**nderwater **b**reathing **a**pparatus."

**scud** (skud) ***v.*** **1** to move swiftly. **2** to be driven by the wind, as clouds. —**scud′ded, scud′ding** ◆***n.*** **1** the act of scudding. **2** clouds or spray driven by the wind.

**scuff** (skuf) ***v.*** **1** to wear a rough place on the surface of; scrape [The baby *scuffed* the new shoes.] **2** to scrape or drag the feet along the ground in walking. ◆***n.*** **1** the act of scuffing. **2** a worn or rough spot. **3** a loose, flat house slipper.

**scuf·fle** (skuf′′l) ***v.*** **1** to fight or struggle in a rough, confused way. **2** to drag the feet in walking; shuffle. —**scuf′fled, scuf′fling** ◆***n.*** **1** a rough, confused fight. **2** the act or sound of feet shuffling.

**scull** (skul) ***n.*** **1** an oar worked from side to side over the stern of a boat. **2** either of a pair of short, light oars used in rowing. **3** a light, narrow rowboat for racing. *See the picture.* ◆***v.*** to row with a scull or sculls. —**scull′er** ***n.***

**scul·ler·y** (skul′ər ē) ***n.*** a room next to a kitchen, where pots and pans are cleaned and stored or where the rough, dirty kitchen work is done. —*pl.* **scul′ler·ies**

**scul·lion** (skul′yən) ***n.*** a servant who does rough kitchen work: *no longer much used.*

**sculp·tor** (skulp′tər) ***n.*** an artist in sculpture.

**sculp·ture** (skulp′chər) ***n.*** **1** the art of carving wood, chiseling stone, casting or welding metal, modeling clay or wax, etc. into statues, figures, or the like. **2** a statue, figure, etc. made in this way. ✦***v.*** **1** to cut, chisel, form, etc. in making sculptures. **2** to decorate with sculpture. —**sculp′tured, sculp′tur·ing** —**sculp′tur·al** ***adj.***

**scum** (skum) ***n.*** **1** a thin layer of dirt or waste matter that forms on the top of a liquid [an oily *scum* on the lake]. **2** people who are despised as bad or wicked.

**scup·per** (skup′ər) ***n.*** an opening in a ship's side to allow water to run off the deck.

**scurf** (skʉrf) ***n.*** **1** little dry scales shed by the skin, as dandruff. **2** any scaly coating, as on diseased plants.

**scur·ril·ous** (skʉr′ə ləs) ***adj.*** attacking in a coarse or vulgar way [*scurrilous* language]. —**scur·ril·i·ty** (skə ril′ə tē) ***n.*** —**scur′ril·ous·ly** ***adv.***

**scur·ry** (skʉr′ē) ***v.*** to run quickly; scamper. —**scur′ried, scur′ry·ing** ✦***n.*** the act or sound of scurrying.

**scur·vy** (skʉr′vē) ***n.*** a disease that causes weakness and makes the gums swell and bleed. It comes from lack of vitamin C in the diet. ✦***adj.*** low; mean [a *scurvy* trick]. —**scur′vi·er, scur′vi·est** —**scur′vi·ly** ***adv.***

**scut·tle¹** (skut′'l) ***n.*** a bucket for holding or carrying coal: *its full name is* **coal scuttle.** *See the picture.*

**scut·tle²** (skut′'l) ***v.*** to run quickly; scurry, especially away from danger or trouble. —**scut′tled, scut′tling** ✦***n.*** a scurry or scamper; hasty flight.

**scut·tle³** (skut′'l) ***v.*** to sink by cutting holes in the lower hull [to *scuttle* a ship]. —**scut′tled, scut′tling** ✦***n.*** an opening fitted with a cover, as in a roof or a ship's deck or hull.

**scut·tle·butt** (skut′'l but) ***n.*** rumor or gossip: *used only in everyday talk.*

> **Scuttlebutt** is the word used by sailors for a drinking fountain on board a ship. Because sailors waiting for a drink would chat and pass on rumors, the word came to mean "rumor" or "gossip." **Scuttlebutt** is a shorter word for *scuttled butt,* a butt or cask with a hole cut in it for putting in a dipper.

**Scyl·la** (sil′ə) a dangerous rock on the Italian coast, opposite the whirlpool Charybdis off the coast of Sicily. A person who must choose between two dangers is said to be "between Scylla and Charybdis."

**scythe** (sīth) ***n.*** a tool with a long blade on a long, curved handle, for cutting grain or long grass by hand. *See the picture.*

**SD, S.D., S.Dak.** *abbreviations for* **South Dakota.**

**SE, S.E., s.e.** *abbreviations for* **southeast** *or* **southeastern.**

**sea** (sē) ***n.*** **1** the whole body of salt water that covers much of the earth; ocean. **2** a large body of salt water more or less enclosed by land [the Red *Sea*]. **3** a large body of fresh water [the *Sea* of Galilee]. **4** the condition of the ocean's surface [a calm *sea*]. **5** a heavy wave [swamped by the *seas*]. **6** a great amount or number [a *sea* of debt]. —**at sea, 1** sailing on the sea. **2** not sure; confused. —**follow the sea,** to be a sailor. —**go to sea, 1** to become a sailor. **2** to start on a voyage. —**put to sea,** to sail away.

scroll

coal scuttle

scull

scuba divers

scythe

sea horse 16 cm (6 in.) long

**sea anemone** a sea animal that looks like a flower. It is often brightly colored and lives attached to rocks, coral, etc.



**sea·board** (sē′bôrd) ***n.*** land along the sea; seacoast [the Atlantic *seaboard*].

**sea·coast** (sē′kōst) ***n.*** land along the sea.

**sea cow** a large mammal that lives in the sea, as the manatee. *See the picture for* **manatee.**

**sea dog** a sailor, especially one with experience.

**sea·far·er** (sē′fer′ər) ***n.*** a person who travels on the sea; especially, a sailor.

**sea·far·ing** (sē′fer′iŋ) ***n.*** **1** the work of a sailor. **2** travel by sea. ✦***adj.*** of or having to do with life at sea.

☆**sea·food** (sē′fo͞od) ***n.*** saltwater fish or shellfish used as food.

**sea·go·ing** (sē′gō′iŋ) ***adj.*** **1** made for use on the open sea [a *seagoing* ship]. **2** *same as* **seafaring.**

**sea gull** a sea bird with long wings and webbed feet.

**sea horse** **1** a small fish with a slender tail and a head a little like that of a horse. *See the picture.* **2** a creature in myths that is half fish and half horse.

**seal¹** (sēl) ***n.*** **1** a piece of paper, wax, etc. with a design pressed into it, fixed to an official document to show that it is genuine. Such wax designs were once also used to seal letters. **2** a stamp or ring for pressing such a design into wax, on paper, etc. **3** the design itself. **4** something that closes or fastens tightly. **5** a piece of metal, paper, etc. placed over a lid or cap, as of a box or bottle, which cannot be opened without

| | | | |
|---|---|---|---|
| **a** fat | **ir** here | **ou** out | **zh** leisure |
| **ā** ape | **ī** bite, fire | **u** up | **ŋ** ring |
| **ä** car, lot | **ō** go | **ʉr** fur | a *in* ago |
| **e** ten | **ô** law, horn | **ch** chin | e *in* agent |
| **er** care | **oi** oil | **sh** she | ə = i *in* unity |
| **ē** even | **oo** look | **th** thin | o *in* collect |
| **i** hit | **o͞o** tool | ***th*** then | u *in* focus |

S

breaking the metal or paper. ☆**6** a paper stamp used for decoration [a Christmas *seal*]. **7** a sign or token [Their handshake was a *seal* of friendship.] ◆***v.*** **1** to close or fasten tight [to *seal* cracks with putty; to *seal* a letter]. **2** to spread a coating on a surface, as before painting, that will keep the final finish from soaking in [to *seal* wood]. **3** to settle definitely [Pat's fate was *sealed*.] **4** to mark with a seal, as a document, to make it official or genuine. —**seal off, 1** to close completely. **2** to enclose or surround an area with barriers or guards. —**seal′er** ***n.***

**seal**[2] (sēl) ***n.*** **1** a sea animal with four flippers, that lives in cold waters and eats fish. *See the picture.* **2** its short fur. **3** leather made from the skin of the seal. ◆***v.*** to hunt seals. —**seal′er** ***n.***

> **Seal**[2] is probably from a very old word for "pull" or "draw," in reference to the clumsy, awkward way in which the seal moves about while on land.

☆**Sea·lab** (sē′lab) ***n.*** a U.S. Navy undersea laboratory for studying sea life, water currents, etc.

**seal·ant** (sēl′ənt) ***n.*** a substance, as a wax, plastic, silicone, etc., used for sealing.

**sea legs** the ability to walk on a tossing ship without losing one's balance.

**sea level** the level of the surface of the sea, halfway between high and low tide. It is used as the point from which heights of land are measured.

**sea lion** a large seal of the North Pacific.



**seal·skin** (sēl′skin) ***n.*** the skin or fur of the seal, especially with the soft fur dyed dark brown or black. ◆***adj.*** made of sealskin [a *sealskin* coat].

**seam** (sēm) ***n.*** **1** the line formed by sewing or joining together two pieces of material. **2** a line like this, as a scar, wrinkle, etc. **3** a layer of ore, coal, etc. in the ground. ◆***v.*** **1** to join together in a seam. **2** to mark with a line like a seam [a face *seamed* with wrinkles]. *See the picture.*

**sea·man** (sē′mən) ***n.*** **1** a sailor. **2** an enlisted person in the navy, not an officer. —*pl.* **sea′men**

**sea·man·ship** (sē′mən ship) ***n.*** skill as a sailor.

**seam·stress** (sēm′stris) ***n.*** a woman who sews well or who makes her living by sewing.

**seam·y** (sēm′ē) ***adj.*** **1** showing rough, unfinished edges of seams, as the underside of a garment. **2** unpleasant [the *seamy* side of life]. —**seam′i·er, seam′i·est**

**sé·ance** (sā′äns) ***n.*** a meeting at which people try to get messages from the dead.

**sea·plane** (sē′plān) ***n.*** any airplane designed to land on water and take off from water.

**sea·port** (sē′pôrt) ***n.*** a port or harbor for ocean ships, or a town or city with such a port.

**sear** (sir) ***v.*** **1** to dry up; wither [Hot sun *seared* the crops.] **2** to burn or scorch the surface of [Hot grease *seared* his arm.] **3** to brown quickly over high heat before long cooking at a lower heat [to *sear* a roast].

**search** (surch) ***v.*** **1** to look over or through in order to find something [We *searched* the house. The police *searched* the thief for a gun.] **2** to try to find [to *search* for an answer]. **3** to find out or uncover by examining in detail (*usually followed by* out). ◆***n.*** the act of searching. —**in search of,** trying to find. —**search′er** ***n.***

**search·ing** (surch′iŋ) ***adj.*** that searches or looks carefully or thoroughly [a *searching* test].

**search·light** (surch′līt) ***n.*** **1** a light and reflector that can throw a strong beam of light in any direction. *See the picture.* **2** such a strong beam of light.

**search warrant** a written order from a court giving police the right to enter and search a place, as in looking for stolen goods.

**sea·scape** (sē′skāp) ***n.*** **1** a view of the sea. **2** a picture of such a view.

**sea·shell** (sē′shel) ***n.*** the shell of an oyster, clam, etc.

**sea·shore** (sē′shôr) ***n.*** land along the sea.

**sea·sick** (sē′sik) ***adj.*** made sick at the stomach and dizzy by the rolling and pitching of a ship at sea. —**sea′sick·ness** ***n.***

**sea·side** (sē′sīd) ***n.*** land along the sea.

**sea·son** (sē′z′n) ***n.*** **1** any of the four parts into which the year is divided: spring, summer, fall, or winter. **2** a special time of the year [the Easter *season;* the hunting *season*]. **3** a period of time [the busy *season* at a factory]. ◆***v.*** **1** to add to or change the flavor of [to *season* meat with herbs]. **2** to make more fit for use by aging or treating [to *season* lumber]. **3** to make more interesting [to *season* a speech with jokes]. **4** to make used to something; accustom [a *seasoned* traveler]. —**for a season,** for a while. —**in good season,** early enough. —**in season, 1** that can be had fresh for eating [Corn is *in season* in late summer.] **2** allowed to be hunted [Ducks are *in season* now.] —**out of season,** not in season.

> **Season** comes from the Latin word that means the time of year for sowing or planting seeds, which is the time that we call spring. When it came into English, **season** was broadened to mean any of the four parts of the year, spring, summer, fall, or winter.

**sea·son·a·ble** (sē′z′n ə b′l) ***adj.*** **1** that fits the time of year [*seasonable* weather]. **2** at the right time; timely [*seasonable* advice].

**sea·son·al** (sē′z'n əl) ***adj.*** of or depending on a season or the seasons [*seasonal* rains; *seasonal* work]. —**sea′son·al·ly *adv.***

**sea·son·ing** (sē′z'n iŋ) ***n.*** **1** flavoring added to food. **2** anything that adds interest.

**seat** (sēt) ***n.*** **1** a thing to sit on, as a chair, bench, etc. **2** a place to sit or the right to sit [to buy two *seats* for the opera; to win a *seat* in the Senate]. **3** the part of the body or of a garment on which one sits [the *seat* of one's pants]. **4** the part of a chair, bench, etc. on which one sits. **5** a way of sitting, as on a horse. **6** the chief place; center; location [the *seat* of a government]. **7** a residence; especially, a large house that is part of a country estate. ◆***v.*** **1** to cause to sit; put in or on a seat [*Seat* yourself quickly.] **2** to have seats for [This car *seats* six people.] —**be seated, 1** to sit down: *also* **take a seat**. **2** to be sitting. **3** to be located.

**seat belt** a device made up of straps that buckle across the hips of a passenger in a car, airplane, etc. so as to hold the passenger in the seat, as in an accident. *See the picture.*

☆**seat·mate** (sēt′māt) ***n.*** a person in the seat beside one, as in an airplane or bus.

**Se·at·tle** (sē at′'l) a city in Washington.

**sea urchin** a small sea animal with a round body in a shell covered with sharp spines. *See the picture.*

The **sea urchin** has this name because it has sharp spines as does a hedgehog. *Urchin* originally meant "hedgehog," and came from the Latin word for this bristly animal.

**sea wall** a wall made to protect the shore from being washed away by waves.

**sea·ward** (sē′wərd) ***adj.*** **1** toward the sea. **2** from the sea [a *seaward* wind]. ◆***adv.*** toward the sea. ◆***n.*** the direction toward the sea.

**sea·wards** (sē′wərdz) ***adv.*** *same as* **seaward**.

**sea·way** (sē′wā) ***n.*** **1** an inland waterway to the sea for ocean ships, as through connected lakes, rivers, or canals [St. Lawrence *Seaway*]. **2** a route for travel on the sea.

**sea·weed** (sē′wēd) ***n.*** any plant or plants growing in the sea, especially algae. There are some plants like these that grow in fresh water and are also called seaweed.

**sea·wor·thy** (sē′wur′*th*ē) ***adj.*** fit or safe for travel on the sea [a *seaworthy* ship].

**se·ba·ceous** (si bā′shəs) ***adj.*** of or like fat; greasy; especially, referring to certain glands of the skin that give out an oily liquid.

**sec.** *abbreviation for* **second** *or* **seconds, secretary, section.**

**se·cede** (si sēd′) ***v.*** to stop being a member of some group, as of a political union. —**se·ced′ed, se·ced′·ing**

**se·ces·sion** (si sesh′ən) ***n.*** **1** an act of seceding. ☆**2** *often* **Secession,** the withdrawal of the Southern States from the Federal Union at the beginning of the Civil War. —☆**se·ces′sion·ist *n.***

**se·clude** (si klōōd′) ***v.*** **1** to keep away from others; shut off [nuns *secluded* in a convent]. **2** to make private or hidden [a *secluded* cabin]. —**se·clud′ed, se·clud′ing**

**se·clu·sion** (si klōō′zhən) ***n.*** a secluding or being secluded; isolation; privacy [to live in *seclusion*].

**sec·ond**[1] (sek′ənd) ***adj.*** **1** coming next after the first in place or time; 2d or 2nd [the *second* seat; *second* prize]. **2** another, like the first [He thinks he's a *second* Shakespeare.] **3** the forward gear of a motor vehicle after the first. **4** playing or singing the lower part [*second* violin; *second* tenor]. ◆***n.*** **1** the second one [She was the *second* to arrive.] **2** an article that is damaged or not of first quality [a sale on *seconds*]. **3** a person who serves as an assistant or aid, as to a boxer. **4 seconds,** *pl.* a second helping of something to eat: *slang in this meaning.* ◆***v.*** **1** to give help or support to; aid; assist [to *second* a cause by giving money]. **2** to say that one supports a motion so that it can be voted on. ◆***adv.*** in the second place, rank, group, etc.

**sec·ond**[2] (sek′ənd) ***n.*** **1** any of the 60 equal parts of a minute, either of time or of an angle. **2** a very short time; instant [Wait just a *second*.]

**sec·ond·ar·y** (sek′ən der′ē) ***adj.*** **1** next after the first in time or order [*Secondary* schools are high schools.] **2** less important; minor [a matter of *secondary* interest]. **3** coming from something primary or basic; derived [A *secondary* color is made by mixing two primary colors.] —**sec′ond·ar′i·ly *adv.***

**sec·ond-class** (sek′ənd klas′) ***adj.*** **1** next below the highest, best, most expensive, etc. [a *second-class* hotel; a *second-class* cabin on a ship]. **2** of poor quality, standing, etc. [a *second-class* citizen]. ◆***adv.*** in a second-class cabin, etc. [to go *second-class*]. 665

**second cousin** the child of a first cousin of one's parent.

**sec·ond-guess** (sek′ənd ges′) ***v.*** to talk about what should have been done, after it is too late: *used only in everyday talk.*

**sec·ond·hand** (sek′ənd hand′) ***adj.*** **1** not straight from the source; from a second person or thing; indirect [*secondhand* news]. **2** used first by another; not new [a *secondhand* coat]. **3** dealing in goods that are not new [a *secondhand* store].

**sec·ond·ly** (sek′ənd lē) ***adv.*** in the second place.

**second nature** a habit that is fixed so deeply as to seem a part of one's nature [Being polite is *second nature* to her.]

**second person** that form of a pronoun or verb which refers to the person or persons spoken to ["You," "your," and "yours" are in the *second person*.]

**sec·ond-rate** (sek′ənd rāt′) ***adj.*** second in quality; not among the best; inferior. —**sec′ond-rat′er *n.***

**se·cre·cy** (sē′krə sē) ***n.*** **1** the condition of being secret. **2** the practice or habit of keeping things secret [a person often inclined to *secrecy*].

**se·cret** (sē′krit) ***adj.*** **1** kept from being known or seen by others; hidden [a *secret* formula; a *secret* entrance]. **2** acting without others knowing [a *secret* agent; a *secret* society]. ◆***n.*** **1** something hidden or

| | | | | | | | |
|---|---|---|---|---|---|---|---|
| **a** | fat | **ir** | here | **ou** | out | **zh** | leisure |
| **ā** | ape | **ī** | bite, fire | **u** | up | **ŋ** | ring |
| **ä** | car, lot | **ō** | go | **ur** | fur | | a *in* ago |
| **e** | ten | **ô** | law, horn | **ch** | chin | | e *in* agent |
| **er** | care | **oi** | oil | **sh** | she | ə = | i *in* unity |
| **ē** | even | **oo** | look | **th** | thin | | o *in* collect |
| **i** | hit | **ōō** | tool | ***th*** | then | | u *in* focus |

to be kept hidden from the knowledge of others. **2** something not understood or known [nature's *secret*]. —**in secret**, without others knowing. —**se′cret·ly** ***adv.***

SYNONYMS: Something **secret** is kept hidden so that others cannot see it or know about it [a *secret* staircase in the old house]. Something **covert** is kept hidden by lightly covering or disguising it [a *covert* threat to blackmail him]. Something **clandestine** is kept secret because it is morally bad, forbidden, or against the law [a *clandestine* meeting with her boyfriend].

**sec·re·tar·i·at** (sek′rə ter′ē ət) ***n.*** **1** the office or place of work of a secretary of high position, as in government. **2** a staff headed by a secretary-general.

**sec·re·tar·y** (sek′rə ter′ē) ***n.*** **1** a person whose work is keeping records, writing letters, etc. for a person, organization, etc. **2** the head of a department of government [the *Secretary* of State]. **3** a writing desk, especially one with a bookcase built at the top. *See the picture.* —*pl.* **sec′re·tar′ies** —**sec·re·tar·i·al** (sek′rə ter′ē əl) ***adj.***

**sec·re·tar·y-gen·er·al** (sek′rə ter′ē jen′ər əl) ***n.*** the chief officer of an organization, in charge of a secretariat. —*pl.* **sec′re·tar′ies-gen′er·al**

**se·crete** (si krēt′) ***v.*** **1** to put in a secret place; hide. **2** to make and give off into or out of the body [Glands in the skin *secrete* oil.] —**se·cret′ed, se·cret′ing**



**se·cre·tion** (si krē′shən) ***n.*** **1** the act of secreting. **2** something secreted by glands, etc. [Saliva is a *secretion.*]

**se·cre·tive** (sē′krə tiv) ***adj.*** **1** hiding one's feelings, thoughts, etc.; not frank or open. **2** (si krēt′iv) having to do with secretion by glands, etc. —**se′cre·tive·ly** ***adv.***

**secret service** a government office that does special detective work, as hunting down counterfeiters, guarding officials, etc.

**sect** (sekt) ***n.*** a group of people having the same leader, beliefs, etc., especially in religion.

**sec·tar·i·an** (sek ter′ē ən) ***adj.*** **1** of or having to do with a sect. **2** devoted to some sect. **3** narrow-minded; limited; parochial. ◆***n.*** a sectarian person.

**sec·tion** (sek′shən) ***n.*** **1** a part cut off; separate part; division [a *section* of a tangerine; shelves sold in *sections*]. **2** a part of a city, country, etc.; district or region [a hilly *section;* the business *section* of a city]. **3** a division of a book, etc. **4** a numbered paragraph of a writing, etc. **5** a view or drawing of a thing as it would look if cut straight through. ◆***v.*** to cut into sections.

**sec·tion·al** (sek′shən ′l) ***adj.*** **1** of a certain section or region; regional. **2** made up of sections. ◆☆***n.*** a sectional sofa, bookcase, etc.

☆**sec·tion·al·ism** (sek′shən ′l iz′m) ***n.*** a narrow-minded interest in only one section or region at the expense of the whole.

**sec·tor** (sek′tər) ***n.*** **1** a part of a circle formed by two radii and the arc between them [a slice of pie is a *sector*]. **2** any of the areas into which a region is divided for military purposes. **3** a certain part of society, a group, etc. [the public *sector* of the economy]. ◆***v.*** to divide into sectors.

**sec·u·lar** (sek′yə lər) ***adj.*** **1** not connected with the church or religion [*secular* music; *secular* schools]. **2** not living in a monastery, etc. [*secular* clergy].

**sec·u·lar·ize** (sek′yə lə rīz′) ***v.*** to take away the religious quality, influence, etc. of. —**sec′u·lar·ized′, sec′u·lar·iz′ing** —**sec′u·lar·i·za′tion** ***n.***

**se·cure** (si kyoor′) ***adj.*** **1** free from fear, care, worry, etc. [to feel *secure* about the future]. **2** safe from harm, loss, attack, etc. [a *secure* hiding place]. **3** fastened or fixed in a firm way [a *secure* knot]. **4** sure; certain [Our success is now *secure.*] ◆***v.*** **1** to make safe; guard or protect [*Secure* your house against burglars.] **2** to tie or fasten firmly [*Secure* the boat to the dock.] **3** to make sure; guarantee [to *secure* a loan with a pledge]. **4** to get; obtain [to *secure* a job]. —**se·cured′, se·cur′ing** —**se·cure′ly** ***adv.***

**Secure** comes from a Latin word that means "free from care." The meaning in Latin is almost the same as the first meaning given above.

**se·cu·ri·ty** (si kyoor′ə tē) ***n.*** **1** the condition or feeling of being safe or sure; freedom from danger, fear, doubt, etc. **2** something that protects [Insurance is a *security* against loss.] **3** something given or pledged as a guarantee [A car may be used as *security* for a loan.] **4 securities,** *pl.* stocks and bonds. —*pl.* **se·cu′ri·ties**

**Security Council** the council of the United Nations set up for the purpose of maintaining peace and security among the nations of the world.

**secy.** or **sec′y** *abbreviation for* **secretary.**

**se·dan** (si dan′) ***n.*** ☆**1** a closed automobile with front and rear seats and two or four doors. **2** *a shorter name for* **sedan chair.**

**sedan chair** a box with a seat in it for one person, carried on poles by two men. Sedan chairs were used in earlier times. *See the picture.*

**se·date**[1] (si dāt′) ***adj.*** quiet, serious, and without strong feeling. —**se·date′ly** ***adv.***

☆**se·date**[2] (si dāt′) ***v.*** to give an amount of sedative to. —**se·dat′ed, se·dat′ing**

**se·da·tion** (si dā′shən) ***n.*** **1** the lessening of excitement, nervousness, etc. by means of sedatives. **2** the calm condition produced by sedatives.

**sed·a·tive** (sed′ə tiv) ***adj.*** **1** making one calmer. **2** producing sedation. ◆***n.*** a sedative medicine.

**sed·en·tar·y** (sed′'n ter′ē) ***adj.*** **1** in the habit of sitting much of the time [a *sedentary* person]. **2** keeping one seated much of the time [A bookkeeper has a *sedentary* job.]

**Se·der** (sā′dər) ***n.*** the feast held during the Jewish holiday of Passover, at which the Haggada is read.

**sedge** (sej) ***n.*** a plant like coarse grass, usually growing in clumps in wet ground.

**sed·i·ment** (sed′ə mənt) ***n.*** **1** matter that settles to the bottom of a liquid; dregs. **2** any matter set down by wind or water, as sand or soil.

> **Sediment** comes from a Latin word meaning "to sit." Sediment sits at the bottom of a liquid when it comes to rest.

**sed·i·men·ta·ry** (sed′ə men′tər ē) ***adj.*** of, containing, or formed from sediment [*sedimentary* rock].

**se·di·tion** (si dish′ən) ***n.*** a stirring up of rebellion against a government. —**se·di′tious** ***adj.***

**se·duce** (si do͞os′ *or* si dyo͞os′) ***v.*** to get one to do something bad or wrong; tempt; lead astray. —**se·duced′, se·duc′ing** —**se·duc·tion** (si duk′shən) ***n.***

**se·duc·tive** (si duk′tiv) ***adj.*** likely to seduce; very tempting or attractive. —**se·duc′tive·ly** ***adv.***

**sed·u·lous** (sej′oo ləs) ***adj.*** working hard and with care; diligent. —**sed′u·lous·ly** ***adv.***

**see**[1] (sē) ***v.*** **1** to be aware of through the eyes; have or use the sense of sight [We *saw* two birds. I don't *see* so well.] **2** to get the meaning of; understand [Do you *see* the point of the joke?] **3** to find out; learn [*See* what they want.] **4** to make sure [*See* that the door is locked.] **5** to undergo or live through; experience [Our town has *seen* many changes.] **6** to go along with; accompany [I'll *see* you to the door.] **7** to visit with [We stopped to *see* a friend.] **8** to go to for information or advice; consult [*See* a doctor about your cough.] **9** to meet with or receive as a visitor [He's too ill to *see* anyone now.] **10** to think or try to remember [Let me *see,* where did I put that?] —**saw, seen, see′ing** —**see about** or **see after,** to take care of. —**see off,** to go with to the train, ship, etc. to say goodbye. —**see out, 1** to carry out; finish. **2** to wait till the end of. —**see through, 1** to understand the true meaning or nature of. **2** to carry out to the end; finish. **3** to help out during a hard time. —**see to,** to take care of; look after.

**see**[2] (sē) ***n.*** the office or district of a bishop.

**seed** (sēd) ***n.*** **1** the part of a flowering plant that will grow into a new plant under the right conditions. *See the picture.* **2** a large number of seeds [to scatter grass *seed*]. **3** a source or beginning [the *seeds* of knowledge]. **4** children or descendants: *an earlier use, as in the Bible* [the *seed* of Jacob]. —*pl.* **seeds** or **seed** ◆***v.*** **1** to plant with seeds [to *seed* a lawn]. **2** to take the seeds from [to *seed* grapes]. **3** to produce seeds. —**go to seed, 1** to develop seeds from its flowers. **2** to become weak, useless, etc. —**seed′less** ***adj.***

**seed·case** (sēd′kās) ***n.*** a dry, hollow fruit with seeds in it, as the pod of a pea plant.

**seed·ling** (sēd′ling) ***n.*** a young plant grown from a seed, not from a cutting.

**seed·y** (sēd′ē) ***adj.*** **1** full of seeds [a *seedy* grapefruit]. **2** untidy and shabby; not neat [a *seedy* coat]. —**seed′i·er, seed′i·est**

**see·ing** (sē′ing) ***conj.*** in view of the fact; as; since [*Seeing* that they're here, let's begin eating.] ◆***n.*** the sense of sight; vision. ◆***adj.*** having the sense of sight.

☆**Seeing Eye dog** *another name for* **guide dog.** Many guide dogs are trained by Seeing Eye, Inc., of New Jersey.

**seek** (sēk) ***v.*** **1** to try to find; search for [to *seek* gold]. **2** to try to get; aim at [to *seek* a prize]. **3** to try or attempt [They *seek* to please us.] —**sought, seek′ing**

**seem** (sēm) ***v.*** **1** to have the look of being; appear to be [You *seem* happy. The house *seems* empty.] **2** to appear to one's own mind [The speaker's voice *seemed* to falter.] **3** to appear to be true [It *seems* I was right.]

**seem·ing** (sēm′ing) ***adj.*** that seems real, true, etc. but may not be [their *seeming* anger]. —**seem′ing·ly** ***adv.***

**seem·ly** (sēm′lē) ***adj.*** as it should be; right; proper [*seemly* behavior]. —**seem′li·er, seem′li·est** ◆***adv.*** in a right or proper way. —**seem′li·ness** ***n.***

**seen** (sēn) *past participle of* **see.**

**seep** (sēp) ***v.*** to leak through small openings; ooze [Rain *seeped* through the roof.] —**seep′y** ***adj.***

**seep·age** (sēp′ij) ***n.*** **1** the act of seeping. **2** liquid that seeps through.

**seer** (sir) ***n.*** a person who is believed to be able to foretell the future.

**seer·suck·er** (sir′suk′ər) ***n.*** a light, crinkled cloth of cotton, linen, etc., usually with a striped pattern.

**see·saw** (sē′sô) ***n.*** **1** a board balanced on a support at the middle and used by children at play, who ride the ends so that when one goes up the other comes down. *See the picture.* **2** any movement back and forth or up and down [a *seesaw* in prices]. ◆***adj.*** moving back and forth or up and down. ◆***v.*** to move back and forth or up and down.

**seethe** (sē*th*) ***v.*** **1** to bubble or foam as a boiling liquid does [the *seething* waves]. **2** to be very excited or upset [*seething* with rage]. —**seethed, seeth′ing**

**seg·ment** (seg′mənt) ***n.*** **1** any of the parts into which something is divided or can be separated [the *segments* of an earthworm]. **2** a part, as of a circle, cut off by a straight line. ◆***v.*** to divide into segments.

**Se·go·vi·a** (sə gō′vē ə), **An·drés** (än dres′) 1894– ; Spanish guitarist and composer.

**seg·re·gate** (seg′rə gāt) ***v.*** to set apart from others; especially, to keep people of different races separate, as in public schools. —**seg′re·gat·ed, seg′re·gat·ing** —**seg′re·ga′tion** ***n.*** —**seg′re·ga′tion·ist** ***n.***

> **Segregate** comes from a Latin word meaning "to set apart from the flock." In the same way that a shepherd may set apart some of the animals in a flock, some people may try to keep other people apart from themselves by segregating them.

**Seine** (sān *or* sen) a river in northern France. It flows through Paris into the English Channel.

| | | | | | | | |
|---|---|---|---|---|---|---|---|
| **a** | fat | **ir** | here | **ou** | out | **zh** | leisure |
| **ā** | ape | **ī** | bite, fire | **u** | up | **ng** | ring |
| **ä** | car, lot | **ō** | go | **ur** | fur | | a *in* ago |
| **e** | ten | **ô** | law, horn | **ch** | chin | | e *in* agent |
| **er** | care | **oi** | oil | **sh** | she | **ə =** | i *in* unity |
| **ē** | even | **oo** | look | **th** | thin | | o *in* collect |
| **i** | hit | **o͞o** | tool | ***th*** | then | | u *in* focus |

**seine** (sān) ***n.*** a large fishing net with floats along the top edge and weights along the bottom. *See the picture.* ◆***v.*** to fish with a seine. —**seined, sein′ing**

**seis·mic** (sīz′mik) ***adj.*** of or caused by an earthquake, explosion, etc.

**seis·mo·graph** (sīz′mə graf) ***n.*** an instrument that makes a record of the strength of earthquakes, explosions, etc. and how long they last. —**seis′mo·graph′ic *adj.***

**seize** (sēz) ***v.*** **1** to take hold of in a sudden, strong, or eager way; grasp [to *seize* a weapon and fight; to *seize* an opportunity]. **2** to capture or arrest, as a criminal. **3** to take over as by force [The troops *seized* the fort. The city *seized* the property for nonpayment of taxes.] **4** to attack or strike suddenly or harshly [*seized* with a fit of sneezing]. —**seized, seiz′ing** —**seize on** or **seize upon,** to grasp or take eagerly.



**sei·zure** (sē′zhər) ***n.*** **1** the act of seizing or condition of being seized. **2** a sudden attack, as of illness.

**sel·dom** (sel′dəm) ***adv.*** not often; rarely [I *seldom* see my old friends since I've moved.]

**se·lect** (sə lekt′) ***v.*** to choose or pick out [*Select* a tie to go with that suit.] ◆***adj.*** **1** chosen with care; specially picked as being best or choice [Our market sells only *select* cuts of meat.] **2** allowing only certain people in; not open to all [a *select* club]. —**se·lec′tor *n.***

**se·lec·tion** (sə lek′shən) ***n.*** **1** a selecting or being selected; choice. **2** the thing or things chosen; also, things to choose from [a wide *selection* of colors].

**se·lec·tive** (sə lek′tiv) ***adj.*** **1** of or set apart by selection. **2** tending to select. **3** having the power to select [A *selective* radio set brings in each station clearly.] —**se·lec′tive·ly *adv.*** —**se·lec·tiv·i·ty** (sə lek′tiv′ə tē) ***n.***

☆**selective service** a system under which young men are drafted to serve in the armed forces if chosen to do so.

☆**se·lect·man** (sə lekt′mən) ***n.*** any of a board of officers elected in most New England towns to manage the affairs of a town or city. —*pl.* **se·lect′men**

**self** (self) ***n.*** **1** one's own person or being as apart from all others. **2** one's own well-being or advantage [too much concern with *self*]. —*pl.* **selves** ◆***pron.*** myself, himself, herself, or yourself: *used only in everyday talk* [tickets for *self* and family]. ◆***adj.*** of the same kind, material, etc. as the rest [a *self* lining].

**self-** *a prefix meaning:* **1** of oneself [*Self*-restraint is a restraining of oneself.] **2** by oneself [A *self*-taught violinist is one taught by himself or herself to play the violin.] **3** to oneself [A *self*-addressed envelope is addressed to oneself.] **4** in or with oneself [To be *self*-confident is to be confident in oneself.] **5** for oneself [*Self*-pity is pity for oneself.]

**self-ap·point·ed** (self′ə point′tid) ***adj.*** acting as such on one's own, but not appointed as such by others [a *self-appointed* leader].

**self-as·ser·tion** (self′ə sur′shən) ***n.*** boldness in putting forward one's own claims, opinions, etc. —**self′-as·ser′tive *adj.***

**self-as·sur·ance** (self′ə shoor′əns) ***n.*** *same as* **self-confidence.** —**self′-as·sured′ *adj.***

**self-cen·tered** (self′sen′tərd) ***adj.*** thinking mostly of oneself or one's own affairs; selfish.

**self-com·mand** (self′kə mand′) ***n.*** *same as* **self-control.**

**self-con·ceit** (self′kən sēt′) ***n.*** too high an opinion of oneself; conceit.

**self-con·fi·dent** (self′kän′fə dənt) ***adj.*** sure of oneself; confident of one's own ability. —**self′-con′fi·dence *n.*** —**self′-con′fi·dent·ly *adv.***

**self-con·scious** (self′kän′shəs) ***adj.*** **1** too conscious of oneself so that one feels or acts embarrassed when with others. **2** showing that one is embarrassed [a *self-conscious* giggle]. —**self′-con′scious·ly *adv.*** —**self′-con′scious·ness *n.***

**self-con·tained** (self′kən tānd′) ***adj.*** **1** having within itself all that is needed [a *self-contained* radio transmitter]. **2** keeping one's thoughts and feelings to oneself; reserved. **3** showing self-control.

**self-con·trol** (self′kən trōl′) ***n.*** control of oneself or of one's feelings and actions.

**self-de·cep·tion** (self′di sep′shən) ***n.*** the deceiving of oneself concerning what one's true feelings, motives, etc. are.

**self-de·fense** (self′di fens′) ***n.*** defense of oneself or one's property, rights, etc.

**self-de·ni·al** (self′di nī′əl) ***n.*** the act of giving up what one wants or needs, often for the benefit of others. —**self′-de·ny′ing *adj.***

**self-de·struc·tion** (self′di struk′shən) ***n.*** destruction of oneself or itself; especially, suicide. —**self′-de·struc′tive *adj.***

**self-de·ter·mi·na·tion** (self′di tur′mə nā′shən) ***n.*** **1** the act or power of making up one's own mind about what to think or do. **2** the right of the people of a nation to choose their own form of government.

**self-dis·ci·pline** (self′dis′ə plin) ***n.*** the disciplining or controlling of oneself, one's wishes, actions, etc. —**self′-dis′ci·plined *adj.***

**self-ed·u·cat·ed** (self′ej′ə kāt′id) ***adj.*** educated by oneself, with little or no schooling.

**self-em·ployed** (self′im ploid′) ***adj.*** working for oneself, with direct control over work, fees, services, etc. —**self′-em·ploy′ment *n.***

**self-es·teem** (self′ə stēm′) ***n.*** **1** belief in oneself; self-respect. **2** too much pride in oneself.

**self-ev·i·dent** (self′ev′ə dənt) ***adj.*** plain to see or understand without proof or explanation

**self-ex·plan·a·to·ry** (self′ik splan′ə tôr′ē) ***adj.*** explaining itself; that can be understood without being explained.

**self-ex·pres·sion** (self′ik spresh′ən) ***n.*** a bringing out of one's feelings or personality, as through art, music, writing, etc.

**self-ful·fill·ment** (self′fəl fil′mənt) ***n.*** fulfillment of one's hopes, ambitions, etc. through one's own efforts.

**self-gov·ern·ment** (self′guv′ər mənt *or* self′guv′ərn mənt) ***n.*** government of a group by its own members. —**self′-gov′ern·ing *adj.***

**self-help** (self′help′) ***n.*** care or improvement of oneself by one's own efforts, as through study.

**self-im·por·tant** (self′im pôr′t'nt) ***adj.*** having or showing too high an opinion of one's own importance. —**self′-im·por′tance *n.***

**self-im·posed** (self′im pōzd′) ***adj.*** placed on oneself by oneself [*self-imposed* duty].

**self-in·dul·gent** (self′in dul′jənt) ***adj.*** giving in to one's wishes, feelings, etc., without self-control. —**self′-in·dul′gence *n.***

**self-in·ter·est** (self′in′trist *or* self′in′tər ist) ***n.*** **1** one's own interest or advantage. **2** a selfish interest in one's own advantage.

**self·ish** (sel′fish) ***adj.*** caring too much about oneself, with little or no thought or care for others. —**self′ish·ly *adv.*** —**self′ish·ness *n.***

**self·less** (self′lis) ***adj.*** caring more about others than about oneself; unselfish. —**self′less·ly *adv.***

**self-made** (self′mād′) ***adj.*** **1** successful, rich, etc. because of one's own efforts [a *self-made* millionaire]. **2** made by oneself or itself.

**self-pit·y** (self′pit′ē) ***n.*** pity for oneself.

**self-pos·ses·sion** (self′pə zesh′ən) ***n.*** full control over one's own actions and feelings; composure. —**self′-pos·sessed′ *adj.***

**self-pres·er·va·tion** (self′prez ər vā′shən) ***n.*** the act or instinct of keeping oneself safe and alive.

**self-pro·pelled** (self′prə peld′) ***adj.*** moving by its own power.

**self-re·li·ant** (self′ri lī′ənt) ***adj.*** relying or depending on one's own judgment, abilities, efforts, etc. —**self′-re·li′ance *n.***

**self-re·proach** (self′ri prōch′) ***n.*** a feeling of guilt; blame of oneself by oneself.

**self-re·spect** (self′ri spekt′) ***n.*** a proper respect for oneself. —**self′-re·spect′ing *adj.***

**self-re·straint** (self′ri strānt′) ***n.*** *same as* **self-control**. —**self′-re·strained′ *adj.***

**self-right·eous** (self′rī′chəs) ***adj.*** thinking oneself more righteous or moral than others.

**self-sac·ri·fice** (self′sak′rə fīs) ***n.*** sacrifice of oneself or one's interests, usually for the benefit of others. —**self′-sac′ri·fic·ing *adj.***

**self·same** (self′sām) ***adj.*** the very same; identical [We two were born on the *selfsame* day.]

**self-sat·is·fied** (self′sat′is fīd) ***adj.*** satisfied or pleased with oneself or with what one has done. —**self′-sat′is·fac′tion *n.***

**self-seek·ing** (self′sēk′iŋ) ***adj.*** always seeking to benefit oneself; selfish.

☆**self-serv·ice** (self′sur′vis) ***adj.*** set up so that customers serve themselves [a *self-service* gas station].

**self-serv·ing** (self′sur′viŋ) ***adj.*** furthering one's own selfish interests, especially at the expense of others.

**self-styled** (self′stīld′) ***adj.*** so called by oneself [That person is a *self-styled* expert.]

**self-suf·fi·cient** (self′sə fish′ənt) ***adj.*** able to get along without help; independent.

**self-sup·port·ing** (self′sə pôrt′iŋ) ***adj.*** supporting oneself by one's own effort or earnings.

**self-taught** (self′tôt′) ***adj.*** having taught oneself with little or no help from others.

**self-willed** (self′wild′) ***adj.*** stubborn about getting one's own way. —**self′-will′ *n.***

**self-wind·ing** (self′wīn′diŋ) ***adj.*** wound automatically, as certain wristwatches.

**sell** (sel) ***v.*** **1** to give in return for money [Will you *sell* me your skates for $10.00?] **2** to offer for sale; deal in [This store *sells* shoes.] **3** to be on sale [These belts *sell* for $4.00.] **4** to help the sale of [TV *sells* many products.] **5** to betray for money or other gain [to *sell* one's honor]. ☆**6** to win approval from or for: *used only in everyday talk* [to *sell* someone on an idea]. —**sold, sell′ing —sell out, 1** to get rid of completely by selling. ☆**2** to betray, as a cause: *used only in everyday talk.* —☆**sell short,** to value at less than its worth.

> SYNONYMS: To **sell** something is to change its owner to a person who gives money for it to another who has owned it [The Carters will *sell* their house to anyone who will pay $40,000 for it.] To **barter** is to give certain goods or services in return for other goods or services without using money [The farmer *bartered* a bushel of potatoes for a pair of shoes at the general store.] To **trade** is to give something in return for something else [Let's *trade* bicycles. They *traded* jokes.]

**sell·er** (sel′ər) ***n.*** **1** a person who sells. **2** a thing sold, according to how well it has sold [This novel is a best *seller*.]

☆**sell·out** (sel′out) ***n.*** **1** a selling out, or betrayal. **2** a show for which all the seats have been sold. 669

**sel·vage** or **sel·vedge** (sel′vij) ***n.*** a specially woven edge that keeps cloth from raveling.

**selves** (selvz) ***n.*** *plural of* **self**.

**se·man·tics** (sə man′tiks) ***n.pl.*** the study of the meanings of words and ways in which the meanings change and develop: *used with a singular verb* [*Semantics* is a branch of linguistics.] —**se·man′tic *adj.***

**sem·a·phore** (sem′ə fôr) ***n.*** any device or system for signaling, as by lights, flags, etc. *See the picture.* ◆***v.*** to signal by semaphore. —**sem′a·phored, sem′a·phor·ing**

**sem·blance** (sem′bləns) ***n.*** a seeming likeness; outward look or show [a *semblance* of order].

**se·men** (sē′mən) ***n.*** the fluid that is produced by the male sex organs and that contains the cells for fertilizing the eggs of the female.

**se·mes·ter** (sə mes′tər) ***n.*** either of the two terms which usually make up a school year.

☆**sem·i** (sem′ī) ***n.*** a truck tractor and the trailer that is attached to it by a coupling: *used only in everyday talk.*

**semi-** *a prefix meaning:* **1** half [A *semicircle* is a half circle.] **2** partly; not fully [A *semiskilled* worker is only partly skilled.] **3** twice in a certain period [A *semiannual* event takes place twice a year.]

| | | | |
|---|---|---|---|
| **a** fat | **ir** here | **ou** out | **zh** leisure |
| **ā** ape | **ī** bite, fire | **u** up | **ŋ** ring |
| **ä** car, lot | **ō** go | **ur** fur | a *in* ago |
| **e** ten | **ô** law, horn | **ch** chin | e *in* agent |
| **er** care | **oi** oil | **sh** she | **ə** = i *in* unity |
| **ē** even | **oo** look | **th** thin | o *in* collect |
| **i** hit | **ōō** tool | ***th*** then | u *in* focus |

**sem·i·an·nu·al** (sem′i an′yoo wəl) ***adj.*** happening, coming, etc. twice a year [*semiannual* payment of taxes]. —**sem′i·an′nu·al·ly *adv.***

**sem·i·cir·cle** (sem′i sʉr′k′l) ***n.*** a half circle. *See the picture.* —**sem·i·cir·cu·lar** (sem′i sʉr′kyə lər) ***adj.***

**sem·i·co·lon** (sem′i kō′lən) ***n.*** a punctuation mark (;) used to show a pause that is shorter than the pause at the end of a sentence, but longer than the pause marked by the comma [The *semicolon* is often used to separate closely related clauses, especially when they contain commas.]

**sem·i·con·duc·tor** (sem′i kən duk′tər) ***n.*** a substance, as silicon, whose ability to conduct electricity is improved when heat, light, etc. is added to it. Semiconductors are used in transistors and other electronic devices.

**sem·i·fi·nal** (sem′i fī′n′l) ***n.*** a round, match, etc. that comes just before the final one in a contest or tournament. —**sem′i·fi′nal·ist *n.***

☆**sem·i·month·ly** (sem′i munth′lē) ***adj.*** happening, coming, etc. twice a month. ◆***n.*** a magazine that comes out twice a month. ◆***adv.*** twice a month.

**sem·i·nar·y** (sem′ə ner′ē) ***n.*** **1** a school or college where priests, ministers, or rabbis are trained. **2** a private school for young women: *an old-fashioned term.* —*pl.* **sem′i·nar′ies**

**Sem·i·nole** (sem′ə nōl) ***n.*** a member of a tribe of American Indians who settled in Florida. Many Seminoles now also live in Oklahoma.



**sem·i·pre·cious** (sem′i presh′əs) ***adj.*** describing gems, as the garnet or turquoise, that are of less value than the precious gems.

**Sem·ite** (sem′īt) ***n.*** a member of any people speaking a Semitic language, including the Hebrews, Arabs, Phoenicians, etc.

**Se·mit·ic** (sə mit′ik) ***adj.*** **1** of or like the Semites. **2** of or describing a group of languages of southwestern Asia and northern Africa, including Hebrew, Aramaic, Arabic, etc.

**sem·i·trop·i·cal** (sem′i träp′i k′l) ***adj.*** somewhat like the tropics; nearly tropical [Florida has a *semitropical* climate.]

☆**sem·i·week·ly** (sem′i wēk′lē) ***adj.*** happening, coming, etc. twice a week. ◆***n.*** a newspaper coming out twice a week. ◆***adv.*** twice a week.

**sen.** *abbreviation for* **senate, senator.**

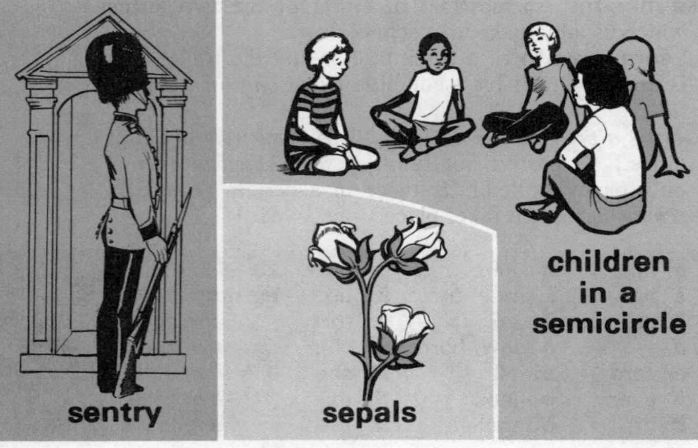

sentry

sepals

children in a semicircle

**sen·ate** (sen′it) ***n.*** **1** an assembly or council. **2 Senate,** the upper and smaller branch of Congress or of a State legislature.

**Senate** comes from a Latin word meaning "old." The senate of ancient Rome was a council of older men who were thought to be wiser and more experienced in ruling a country.

**sen·a·tor** (sen′ə tər) ***n.*** a member of a senate. —**sen·a·to·ri·al** (sen′ə tôr′ē əl) ***adj.***

**send** (send) ***v.*** **1** to cause to go or be carried [*Send* them home for their lunch. Food was *sent* by plane.] **2** to make happen, come, be, etc. [joy *sent* by the gods]. **3** to put into some condition [The noise *sent* me out of my mind.] —**sent, send′ing** —**send for, 1** to call to come; summon. **2** to place an order for. —**send forth,** to cause to appear; produce. —**send off, 1** to mail, as a letter or gift. **2** to cause to go away. **3** to give a send-off to. —**send out, 1** to distribute, issue, mail, etc. from a central point. **2** to send forth. **3** to send someone on an errand [We *sent* Dan *out* for hamburgers.] —**send′er *n.***

☆**send-off** (send′ôf′) ***n.*** **1** something done to show friendly feeling toward someone starting out on a trip, career, etc. **2** a start given to someone or something. *This word is used only in everyday talk.*

**Sen·e·ca** (sen′i kə) ***n.*** a member of a tribe of American Indians who lived in western New York.

**Sen·e·gal** (sen′i gôl′) a country in western Africa, on the Atlantic Ocean.

**se·nile** (sē′nīl) ***adj.*** **1** showing signs of old age; weak in mind and body. **2** of or caused by old age.

**se·nil·i·ty** (sə nil′ə tē) ***n.*** **1** old age. **2** weakness of mind and body caused by old age.

**sen·ior** (sēn′yər) ***adj.*** **1** the older: a word written after the name of a father whose son has exactly the same name: abbreviated **Sr.** **2** of higher rank or longer service [a *senior* partner]. ☆**3** of seniors in a high school or college [the *senior* class]. ◆***n.*** **1** a person who is older or has a higher rank than another [Francis is my *senior* by ten years.] ☆**2** a student in the last year of a high school or college.

**senior citizen** an elderly person, especially one who is retired.

☆**senior high school** a high school (usually grades 10, 11, and 12) following junior high school.

**sen·ior·i·ty** (sēn yôr′ə tē) ***n.*** the condition or fact of being older, higher in rank, or longer in service, which may carry with it some privileges.

**sen·na** (sen′ə) ***n.*** **1** a plant with yellow flowers. **2** the dried leaves of some sennas, used as a medicine to make the bowels move.

**se·ñor** (se nyôr′) ***n.*** a Spanish word used, like "Mr.," as a title for a man. —*pl.* **se·ñor·es** (se nyô′res)

**se·ño·ra** (se nyô′rä) ***n.*** a Spanish word used, like "Mrs.," as a title for a married woman.

**se·ño·ri·ta** (se′nyô rē′tä) ***n.*** a Spanish word used, like "Miss," as a title for an unmarried woman or girl.

**sen·sa·tion** (sen sā′shən) ***n.*** **1** a feeling that comes from the senses, the body, or the mind [a *sensation* of warmth, of dizziness, of joy, etc.] **2** a feeling of great excitement among people [The good news caused a *sensation* at home.] **3** the thing that stirs up such feeling [Her new book will be a *sensation.*]

**sen·sa·tion·al** (sen sā′shən ′l) ***adj.*** **1** stirring up strong feeling or great excitement [a *sensational* new theory]. **2** meant to shock, thrill, excite, etc. [a *sensational* novel]. **3** very good: *used only in everyday talk.* —**sen·sa′tion·al·ism** ***n.*** —**sen·sa′tion·al·ly** ***adv.***

**sense** (sens) ***n.*** **1** any of the special powers of the body and mind that let one see, hear, feel, taste, smell, etc. **2** a feeling or sensation [a *sense* of warmth; a *sense* of guilt]. **3** an understanding or appreciation; special awareness [a *sense* of honor; a *sense* of beauty; a *sense* of rhythm; a *sense* of humor]. **4** judgment or intelligence; reasoning [He showed good *sense* in his decision. There's no *sense* in going there late.] **5** **senses,** *pl.* normal ability to think or reason soundly [Come to your *senses!*] **6** meaning, as of a word [This dictionary lists five *senses* for the word "sensitive."] ◆***v.*** to be or become aware of; feel [I *sensed* something wrong as soon as I saw them.] —**sensed, sens′ing** —**in a sense,** looking at it one way. —**make sense,** to have a meaning that can be understood; be logical.

**sense·less** (sens′lis) ***adj.*** **1** unconscious [knocked *senseless* by a blow]. **2** stupid, foolish, meaningless, etc. [a *senseless* answer].

**sen·si·bil·i·ty** (sen′sə bil′ə tē) ***n.*** **1** the ability to feel or become aware of sensations; power of feeling [the *sensibility* of the skin to heat or cold]. **2** *often* **sensibilities,** *pl.* delicate or refined feelings [That remark wounded my *sensibilities.*] —*pl.* **sen′si·bil′i·ties**

**sen·si·ble** (sen′sə b′l) ***adj.*** **1** having or showing good sense; reasonable; wise [*sensible* advice]. **2** having understanding; aware [She was *sensible* of his unhappiness.] **3** that can be felt or noticed by the senses [a *sensible* change in temperature]. **4** that can receive sensation [The eye is *sensible* to light rays.] —**sen′si·ble·ness** ***n.*** —**sen′si·bly** ***adv.***

**sen·si·tive** (sen′sə tiv) ***adj.*** **1** quick to feel, notice, appreciate, etc. [A dog's ear is *sensitive* to high tones we cannot hear. Poets are *sensitive* to beauty.] **2** quick to change or react when acted on by something [Camera film is *sensitive* to light.] **3** easily hurt, irritated, etc.; touchy [Don't be so *sensitive* about having your manners corrected.] **4** tender or sore [a *sensitive* bruise]. ☆**5** of or having to do with secret or delicate government matters [*sensitive* negotiations]. —**sen′si·tive·ly** ***adv.*** —**sen′si·tive·ness** ***n.***

**sen·si·tiv·i·ty** (sen′sə tiv′ə tē) ***n.*** the condition or degree of being sensitive.

**sen·si·tize** (sen′sə tīz) ***v.*** to make sensitive. —**sen′si·tized, sen′si·tiz·ing**

**sen·so·ry** (sen′sər ē) ***adj.*** of the senses or sensation [*sensory* impressions].

**sen·su·al** (sen′shoo wəl) ***adj.*** **1** of the body and the senses as apart from the mind or spirit [*sensual* pleasures]. **2** giving oneself up to the pleasures of the senses or the body. —**sen·su·al·i·ty** (sen′shoo wal′ə tē) ***n.***

**sen·su·ous** (sen′shoo wəs) ***adj.*** **1** coming from the senses or acting on the senses [*sensuous* pleasures; *sensuous* music]. **2** getting a special pleasure from sights, sounds, tastes, etc. —**sen′su·ous·ly** ***adv.***

**sent** (sent) *past tense and past participle of* **send.**

**sen·tence** (sen′t′ns) ***n.*** **1** a group of words used to tell, ask, command, or exclaim something, usually having a subject and a predicate. A sentence begins with a capital letter and ends with a period, question mark, or exclamation point ["I saw John." is a *sentence.* "An evening spent at home" is not a *sentence.*] **2** the judgment of a court on the punishment to be given to a person found guilty. **3** the punishment itself [He served his *sentence* at the State prison.] ◆***v.*** to pass sentence on [The judge *sentenced* him to ten years in prison.] —**sen′tenced, sen′tenc·ing**

**sen·ten·tious** (sen ten′shəs) ***adj.*** **1** saying much in few words; pithy. **2** using or full of old sayings or proverbs in a way that is high-sounding or boring [a *sententious* sermon].

**sen·tient** (sen′shənt) ***adj.*** having senses or feelings [Dogs and cats are *sentient* creatures.]

**sen·ti·ment** (sen′tə mənt) ***n.*** **1** a feeling about something [Loyalty is a noble *sentiment.*] **2** a thought, opinion, etc. mixed with feeling [What are your *sentiments* about the election?] **3** feelings, especially tender feelings, as apart from reason or judgment [He claims that there is no room for *sentiment* in business.] **4** gentle or tender feelings, sometimes of a weak or foolish kind [a novel full of *sentiment*].

**sen·ti·men·tal** (sen′tə men′t′l) ***adj.*** **1** having or showing tender, gentle feelings, sometimes in a weak or foolish way [a *sentimental* song]. **2** of or caused by sentiment [I'll save this picture for *sentimental* reasons.] —**sen′ti·men′tal·ist** ***n.*** —**sen·ti·men·tal·i·ty** (sen′tə men tal′ə tē) ***n.*** —**sen′ti·men′tal·ly** ***adv.***

SYNONYMS: To be **sentimental** is to have sweet thoughts and tender feelings, as of some happy time or love affair, often in a way that seems foolish or silly to others [She smiled through her tears as she made a *sentimental* journey to her birthplace.] To be **romantic** is to have strong feelings about being a hero or heroine in some great adventure or love affair [The *romantic* youth imagined he was a knight in days of old.]



**sen·ti·nel** (sen′ti n′l) ***n.*** a person or animal set to guard a group; sentry.

**sen·try** (sen′trē) ***n.*** a person, especially a soldier, who keeps watch to guard a group. *See the picture.* —*pl.* **sen′tries**

**Seoul** (sōl) the capital of South Korea.

**se·pal** (sē′p′l) ***n.*** any of the leaves that form the calyx at the base of a flower. *See the picture.*

**sep·a·ra·ble** (sep′ər ə b′l) ***adj.*** that can be separated.

**sep·a·rate** (sep′ə rāt) ***v.*** **1** to set apart; divide into parts or groups [*Separate* the good apples from the bad ones.] **2** to keep apart or divide by being or putting between [A hedge *separates* his yard from ours.] **3** to go apart; stop being together or joined [The friends *separated* at the crossroads.] —**sep′a·rat·ed, sep′a·rat·ing** ◆***adj.*** (sep′ər it *or* sep′rit) **1** set apart from the rest or others; not joined [The garage is *separate* from the house.] **2** not connected with others; distinct [The President has powers *separate* from those of Congress.] **3** not shared; for one only

serape

table set for dinner

serrate leaf and knife

[*separate* bedrooms]. **4** single or individual [the body's *separate* parts]. —**sep′a·rate·ly** ***adv.*** —**sep′a·ra′tion** ***n.***

**sep·a·ra·tor** (sep′ə rāt′ər) ***n.*** a person or thing that separates, as a machine that separates cream from milk.

**se·pi·a** (sē′pē ə) ***n.*** **1** a dark-brown coloring matter made from the inky fluid of cuttlefish. **2** dark, reddish brown.

**Sep·tem·ber** (sep tem′bər) ***n.*** the ninth month of the year, which has 30 days: abbreviated **Sept.**



**sep·tet** or **sep·tette** (sep tet′) ***n.*** **1** a piece of music for seven voices or seven instruments. **2** the seven people who sing or play it.

**sep·tic** (sep′tik) ***adj.*** **1** causing infection. **2** caused by or having to do with infection.

**septic tank** an underground tank into which waste matter from the drains in a house flows and is rotted away by bacteria.

**sep·ul·cher** (sep′'l kər) ***n.*** a tomb or grave. *The British spelling is* **sepulchre.**

**se·pul·chral** (sə pul′krəl) ***adj.*** **1** of tombs, death, or burial. **2** sad or deep and gloomy [a *sepulchral* tone].

**se·quel** (sē′kwəl) ***n.*** **1** something that follows something else, often as a result [Floods came as a *sequel* to the heavy rains.] **2** a book that carries on a story started in an earlier book ["Little Men" is a *sequel* to "Little Women."]

**se·quence** (sē′kwəns) ***n.*** **1** the following of one thing after another; succession [The *sequence* of events in their lives led to marriage.] **2** the order in which things follow one another [Line them up in *sequence* from shortest to tallest.] **3** a series of things that are related [a *sequence* of misfortunes]. *See* SYNONYMS *at* **series.**

**se·quen·tial** (si kwen′shəl) ***adj.*** having or forming a regular sequence of parts.

**se·ques·ter** (si kwes′tər) ***v.*** **1** to hide, or keep away from others; withdraw [He *sequestered* himself in a lonely cabin.] **2** to seize or hold, as until a debt is paid.

**se·quin** (sē′kwin) ***n.*** a small, shiny spangle or disk. Sequins are sewn on cloth as decoration.

☆**se·quoi·a** (si kwoi′ə) ***n.*** a giant evergreen tree of California, as the redwood.

☆**se·ra·pe** (sə rä′pē) ***n.*** a brightly colored woolen blanket worn as an outer garment by men in Spanish-American countries. *See the picture.*

**ser·aph** (ser′əf) ***n.*** an angel of the highest rank. —*pl.* **ser′aphs** or **ser·a·phim** (ser′ə fim)

**se·raph·ic** (sə raf′ik) ***adj.*** of or like a seraph, or angel; angelic.

**Serb** (sʉrb) ***n.*** a member of a Slavic people living in Serbia and nearby areas.

**Ser·bi·a** (sʉr′bē ə) a state of Yugoslavia, formerly a kingdom. —**Ser′bi·an** ***adj., n.***

**sere** (sir) ***adj.*** dried up; withered: *used mainly in older poetry.*

**ser·e·nade** (ser ə nād′) ***n.*** **1** the act of playing or singing music outdoors at night, as by a lover under his sweetheart's window. **2** a piece of music that is right for this. ◆***v.*** to play or sing a serenade to. —**ser·e·nad′ed, ser·e·nad′ing** —**ser·e·nad′er** ***n.***

**se·rene** (sə rēn′) ***adj.*** **1** calm or peaceful [a *serene* look]. **2** bright; clear; without clouds [a *serene* sky]. —**se·rene′ly** ***adv.***

**se·ren·i·ty** (sə ren′ə tē) ***n.*** the fact of being serene; calmness or clearness.

**serf** (sʉrf) ***n.*** a farm worker who was almost like a slave and could be sold along with the land worked on, as in the Middle Ages.

**serge** (sʉrj) ***n.*** a hard, strong cloth, usually wool, with a twill weave. It is used for suits and coats.

**ser·geant** (sär′jənt) ***n.*** ☆**1** in the U.S. armed forces, a noncommissioned officer ranking above a corporal, or any noncommissioned officer whose title includes the word *sergeant*. **2** a police officer ranking below a captain or a lieutenant.

**ser·geant-at-arms** (sär′jənt ət ärmz′) ***n.*** an officer whose duty is to keep order at a meeting, in a law court, etc. —*pl.* **ser′geants-at-arms′**

**se·ri·al** (sir′ē əl) ***adj.*** **1** of or arranged in a series [Dollar bills have *serial* numbers printed on them.] **2** presented in a series of parts, one at a time [a *serial* story]. ◆***n.*** a long story presented one part at a time, at regular times, in a magazine, as a movie in a theater, etc. —**se′ri·al·ly** ***adv.***

**se·ri·al·ize** (sir′ē əl īz′) ***v.*** to present as a serial. —**se′ri·al·ized′, se′ri·al·iz′ing**

**serial number** a number, usually one of a series, given as to engines at the time that they are manufactured so that each one can be identified.

**se·ries** (sir′ēz) ***n.*** **1** a number of like things arranged in a row or coming one after another in regular order [a *series* of arches; a *series* of concerts]. **2** a group of related things; set [a *series* of illustrations for a book]. —*pl.* **se′ries**

SYNONYMS: A **series** is a number of like or related things coming one after another [He had a *series* of operations.] In a **sequence** things are more closely related, as when one thing seems to cause the next [A good plot gives us a *sequence* of events that might take place.] In a **succession** things simply follow one another without being really related [Our club has had a *succession* of good presidents.]

**se·ri·ous** (sir′ē əs) ***adj.*** **1** having or showing deep thought; not frivolous; solemn; earnest [a *serious* student]. **2** not joking or fooling; sincere [Is he *serious* about wanting to help?] **3** needing careful thought; important [a *serious* problem]. **4** that can cause worry; dangerous [a *serious* illness]. —**se′ri·ous·ly** ***adv.*** —**se′ri·ous·ness** ***n.***

**ser·mon** (sʉr′mən) ***n.*** **1** a speech, especially by a clergyman during a worship service, on some religious topic or on morals. **2** any serious or boring talk, as on how one should behave.

**se·rous** (sir′əs) ***adj.*** **1** of or containing serum [the *serous* part of the blood]. **2** like serum; thin and watery [a *serous* fluid].

**ser·pent** (sʉr′pənt) ***n.*** **1** a snake, especially a large or poisonous one. **2** a sneaky person.

> **Serpent** comes from a Latin word meaning "to creep." Serpents and snakes creep along the ground, usually without making any sound. A person who is sneaky and might creep up on us silently is sometimes called a serpent.

**ser·pen·tine** (sʉr′pən tēn *or* sʉr′pən tīn) ***adj.*** **1** of or like a serpent; twisted or winding [a *serpentine* path]. **2** sly or sneaky. ✦***n.*** a green or brownish-red mineral.

**ser·rate** (ser′āt) or **ser·rat·ed** (ser′āt id) ***adj.*** having notches like the teeth of a saw along the edge [a *serrate* leaf; a *serrated* knife]. *See the picture.*

**ser·ried** (ser′ēd) ***adj.*** placed close together [soldiers in *serried* ranks].

**se·rum** (sir′əm) ***n.*** **1** any watery liquid formed in animals. **2** the yellowish liquid that is left after blood clots: *the full name is* **blood serum.** **3** a liquid got from the blood of an animal that has been given a certain disease. It is used as an antitoxin against that disease.

**serv·ant** (sʉr′vənt) ***n.*** **1** a person who is hired to work in another's home as a maid, cook, chauffeur, etc. **2** a person who works for a government [a public *servant*]. **3** a person who works eagerly for a cause [a *servant* of liberty].

**serve** (sʉrv) ***v.*** **1** to work for someone as a servant [I *served* in their household for ten years.] **2** to do services for; aid; help [She *served* her country well.] **3** to hold a certain office [She *served* as mayor for two terms.] **4** to worship [to *serve* God]. **5** to be a member of the armed forces [She *served* in the navy during the war.] **6** to pass or spend in prison [Each of them *served* six years for the robbery.] **7** to offer or pass food, drink, etc. to [May I *serve* you some chicken?] **8** to be useful to; provide with services or goods [One hospital *serves* the town.] **9** to be suitable or enough for [One nail will *serve* to hang the picture. This recipe *serves* four.] **10** to treat [Tess was cruelly *served* by fate.] **11** to deliver or hand over [to *serve* a summons to appear in court]. **12** to start play by hitting the ball, as in tennis. —**served, serv′ing** ✦***n.*** **1** the act or style of serving the ball in tennis, etc. **2** one's turn at doing this. —**serve someone right,** to be what someone deserves, as for doing something wrong.

**serv·er** (sʉr′vər) ***n.*** **1** a person who serves. **2** a thing used in serving, as a tray, cart, etc.

**serv·ice** (sʉr′vis) ***n.*** **1** work done or duty performed for others [the *services* of a doctor; TV repair *service*]. **2** helpful or friendly action; aid [They recognized his *services* on behalf of the blind.] **3** work for the government, or the people who do it [a clerk in the civil *service*]. **4** the armed forces; army, navy, etc. [He was in the *service* four years.] **5** a religious ceremony, especially a regular meeting for public worship [a funeral *service;* Sunday morning *service*]. **6** a set of articles used in serving [a silver tea *service*]. **7** a system or method of providing people with something [telephone *service;* train *service*]. **8** the act of serving a summons, writ, or other legal notice. **9** the act or style of serving the ball in tennis, etc., or one's turn at this. **10** the condition or work of being a servant [He has been in *service* as a cook for many years.] ✦***adj.*** **1** of, for, or in service [the *service* industries]. **2** used by servants or in making deliveries [a *service* entrance]. ✦***v.*** ☆**1** to put into good condition for use; repair or adjust [They *service* radios.] **2** to furnish with a service; supply [One gas company *services* the whole area.] —**serv′iced, serv′ic·ing** —**at one's service, 1** ready to serve one. **2** ready for one's use. —**of service,** helpful; useful.

**serv·ice·a·ble** (sʉr′vis ə b′l) ***adj.*** **1** that will give good or long service; durable [a *serviceable* fabric]. **2** that can be of service; useful [a *serviceable* fellow].

**serv·ice·man** (sʉr′vis man′) ***n.*** **1** a member of the armed forces. **2** a person whose work is servicing or repairing something [a radio *serviceman*]. *Also* **service man.** —*pl.* **serv′ice·men′**

**service station** a place where gasoline and oil and repair service for cars, trucks, etc. are sold.

**ser·vile** (sʉr′v′l *or* sʉr′vīl) ***adj.*** **1** like a slave; too humble [a *servile* flatterer]. **2** of slaves or servants [*servile* employment]. —**ser·vil·i·ty** (sər vil′ə tē) ***n.***

**serv·ing** (sʉr′viŋ) ***n.*** a helping, or single portion, of food. ✦***adj.*** used for serving food [a *serving* spoon]. 

**ser·vi·tor** (sʉr′və tər) ***n.*** a servant or attendant: *an old-fashioned term.*

**ser·vi·tude** (sʉr′və to͞od *or* sʉr′və tyo͞od) ***n.*** slavery or a condition like slavery.

**ses·a·me** (ses′ə mē) ***n.*** **1** a plant of the East Indies or Africa that has flat seeds. **2** its seeds, eaten as food.

**ses·sion** (sesh′ən) ***n.*** **1** the meeting of a court, legislature, class, etc. to do its work. **2** a continuous series of such meetings. **3** the time during which such a meeting or series goes on. **4** a school term or period of study, classes, etc. **5** any meeting with another [a *session* with one's lawyer]. —**in session,** meeting [Congress is *in session.*]

> **Session** comes from a Latin word meaning "to sit." When we say "Congress is in session" or "Congress is sitting," we are saying that the members of Congress are attending meetings for the purpose of making and changing laws.

**set** (set) ***v.*** **1** to put in a certain place or position [*Set* the book on the table.] **2** to cause to be in a certain condition [Who *set* the house on fire?] **3** to put in order or in the right condition, position, etc.; arrange; adjust [to *set* a trap; to *set* a thermostat; to *set* a broken bone; to *set* a table for a meal]. *See the picture.* **4**

| | | | | | | | |
|---|---|---|---|---|---|---|---|
| a | fat | ir | here | ou | out | zh | leisure |
| ā | ape | ī | bite, fire | u | up | ŋ | ring |
| ä | car, lot | ō | go | ʉr | fur | | a *in* ago |
| e | ten | ô | law, horn | ch | chin | | e *in* agent |
| er | care | oi | oil | sh | she | ə = | i *in* unity |
| ē | even | oo | look | th | thin | | o *in* collect |
| i | hit | o͞o | tool | *th* | then | | u *in* focus |

to start [My remark *set* him to thinking.] **5** to make or become rigid, firm, or fixed [He *set* his jaw stubbornly. Has the cement *set?*] **6** to establish or fix, as a time for a meeting, a price, a rule, a limit, etc. **7** to sit or seat on eggs, as a hen, so as to hatch them. **8** to mount in a ring, bracelet, etc., as a gem. **9** to direct or turn [He *set* his face toward home.] **10** to write or fit music to words or words to music [She *set* the poem to an old tune.] **11** to furnish for copying [to *set* an example]. **12** to sink below the horizon [The sun *sets* in the west.] —**set, set'ting** ✦***adj.*** **1** that has been set; fixed, established, firm, rigid, etc. [a *set* time for the party; the *set* rules of a game; a *set* speech; a *set* look on one's face]. **2** stubborn [He is *set* in his ways.] **3** ready [On your mark! Get *set!* Go!] **4** formed; built [a heavy*set* person]. ✦***n.*** **1** a setting or being set. **2** the way in which a thing is set [the *set* of her head]. **3** direction or course, as of the wind. **4** something that is set, as a slip for planting, or the scenery for a play. **5** a group of persons or things that go together [She is not in his social *set*. I bought a *set* of tools.] **6** a number of parts put together, as in a cabinet [a TV *set*]. **7** a group of six or more games of tennis won by a margin of at least two games. **8** in mathematics, any collection of units, points, numbers, etc. —☆**all set,** ready; prepared: *used only in everyday talk.* —**set about,** to start doing; begin. —**set against, 1** to balance or compare. **2** to make an enemy of. —**set aside, 1** to separate and keep for a purpose: *also* **set apart. 2** to get rid of; dismiss, discard, or reject. —**set back,** to hinder the progress of. —**set down, 1** to put down. **2** to put in writing or print. —**set forth, 1** to start out, as on a trip. **2** to make known; state. —**set in,** to begin [Winter has *set in.*] —**set off, 1** to start or start out. **2** to show off by contrast. **3** to make explode. —**set on** or **set upon,** to attack or urge to attack. —**set out, 1** to start out, as on a trip. **2** to display, as for sale. **3** to plant. —**set straight,** to give the correct facts to. —**set to, 1** to get to work; begin. **2** to begin fighting. —**set up, 1** to raise to power, a high position, etc. **2** to build; erect. **3** to establish; found. **4** to start.

**set·back** (set'bak) ***n.*** **1** the condition of being set back, or hindered; reversal; upset; defeat. **2** an upper part of a wall or building, set back so as to form a section like a step.

**Se·ton** (sēt''n), Saint **Elizabeth Ann** 1774–1821; the first American-born woman to be named a saint (1975).

**set·tee** (se tē') ***n.*** **1** a seat or bench with a back. **2** a small or medium-sized sofa. *See the picture.*

**set·ter** (set'ər) ***n.*** **1** a person or thing that sets [a *setter* of rules; an automatic *setter* of bowling pins]. **2** a hunting dog with long hair. Setters are trained to find birds and point them out by standing in a stiff position. *See the picture.*

**set·ting** (set'iŋ) ***n.*** **1** the act of one that sets. **2** the thing in which something is set [a ruby in a gold *setting*]. **3** the time, place, and circumstances of an event, story, play, etc. **4** actual surroundings or scenery, whether real or on a stage. **5** the music written for a set of words, as for a poem.

**set·ting-up exercises** (set'iŋ up') exercises, such as push-ups and sit-ups, done to develop a strong, trim body; calisthenics.

**set·tle**[1] (set''l) ***n.*** a long wooden bench with a back and armrests and sometimes a chest under the seat. *See the picture.*

**set·tle**[2] (set''l) ***v.*** **1** to bring or come to an agreement or decision; decide [Did you *settle* on which route to take? We *settled* our argument by splitting the cost of the dinner.] **2** to put in order; arrange, as one's affairs. **3** to set in place firmly or comfortably [He *settled* himself in the chair to read.] **4** to calm or quiet [This medicine will *settle* your stomach.] **5** to come to rest [The bird *settled* on the branch. The pain *settled* in her back.] **6** to make a home for or go to live in [Mr. Gomez *settled* his family in the country. The Dutch *settled* New York.] **7** to move downward; sink or make sink [The car *settled* in the mud. The rain *settled* the dust.] **8** to clear as by having the dregs sink to the bottom [Let the coffee *settle* before you pour it.] **9** to pay, as a bill or debt. **10** to cast itself [Fog *settled* over the city. Gloom *settled* over her.] —**set'tled, set'tling** —**settle down, 1** to become settled, as in a fixed place or regular way of life. **2** to begin to work or act in a serious and steady way. —☆**settle for,** to accept without question [He will *settle for* any kind of work.] —**settle upon** or **settle on,** to give to someone by law, as money or property.

**set·tle·ment** (set''l mənt) ***n.*** **1** a settling or being settled. **2** the settling of people in a new land, a frontier region, etc. **3** a place where people have gone to settle; colony [early English *settlements* in Virginia]. **4** a small village or hamlet [A *settlement* grew up where the rivers met.] **5** an agreement or understanding [to reach a *settlement* in a dispute]. **6** payment, as of a claim. **7** an amount that a person pays or agrees to pay to another, as at marriage, divorce, or death. **8** a place in a poor, crowded neighborhood where people can go to get advice, take classes, play games, etc.

**set·tler** (set'lər) ***n.*** **1** a person or thing that settles. ☆**2** one who settles in a new country.

**set·up** (set'up) ***n.*** the way something is set up, as the plan or makeup of an organization, or the details of a situation.

**sev·en** (sev''n) ***n., adj.*** one more than six; the number 7.

**seven seas** all the oceans of the world.

**sev·en·teen** (sev''n tēn') ***n., adj.*** seven more than ten; the number 17.

**sev·en·teenth** (sev''n tēnth') ***adj.*** coming after sixteen others; 17th in order. ✦***n.*** **1** the seventeenth one. **2** one of seventeen equal parts of something; 1/17.

**sev·enth** (sev''nth) ***adj.*** coming after six others; 7th in order. ✦***n.*** **1** the seventh one. **2** one of the seven equal parts of something; 1/7.

**seventh heaven** complete happiness.

**sev·en·ti·eth** (sev''n tē ith) ***adj.*** coming after sixty-nine others; 70th in order. ✦***n.*** **1** the seventieth one. **2** one of seventy equal parts of something; 1/70.

**sev·en·ty** (sev''n tē) ***n., adj.*** seven times ten; the number 70. —*pl.* **sev'en·ties** —**the seventies,** the numbers or years from 70 through 79.

**sev·er** (sev'ər) ***v.*** **1** to cut off or break off [to *sever* a limb from a tree; to *sever* a friendship]. **2** to separate or divide [The war *severed* many men and women from their families.] **3** to cut in two [to *sever* a cable]. —**sev′er·ance** ***n.***

**sev·er·al** (sev′ər əl *or* sev′rəl) ***adj.*** **1** more than two but not many; a few [*Several* people called while you were out.] **2** separate or different [We parted and went our *several* ways.] ◆***pron., n.*** not many; a small number [Most of them left, but *several* stayed. *Several* of the windows were broken.]

**se·vere** (sə vir′) ***adj.*** **1** strict or harsh; stern; not gentle or kind [*severe* punishment; a *severe* critic]. **2** serious or grave; forbidding. **3** very plain and simple; with little or no decoration [a *severe* black dress]. **4** causing great damage, pain, etc.; violent [a *severe* headache; a *severe* storm]. **5** hard to bear; difficult [a *severe* test of courage]. —**se·ver′er, se·ver′est** —**se·vere′ly** ***adv.*** —**se·vere′ness** ***n.***

SYNONYMS: To be **severe** is to be very strict or simple and not soft, gentle, or easy [To be put in prison for life was a *severe* penalty.] To be **stern** is to be harsh and firm and to look grim or forbidding [We stopped talking when we saw the *stern* look the teacher gave us.]

**se·ver·i·ty** (sə ver′ə tē) ***n.*** **1** the condition of being severe; strictness, seriousness, plainness, etc. **2** something severe. —*pl.* **se·ver′i·ties**

**Se·ville** (sə vil′) a city in southwestern Spain.

**sew** (sō) ***v.*** **1** to fasten with stitches made with needle and thread [to *sew* buttons on a coat]. **2** to mend, make, etc. by sewing [The tailor *sewed* me a fine suit.] **3** to work with needle and thread or at a sewing machine [Can you *sew?*] —**sewed, sewn** or **sewed, sew′ing** —**sew up, 1** to fasten the edges together with stitches. ☆**2** to get or have complete control over or success in: *used only in everyday talk.* —**sew′er** ***n.***

**sew·age** (so͞o′ij *or* syo͞o′ij) ***n.*** the waste matter carried off by sewers or drains.

**sew·er** (so͞o′ər *or* syo͞o′ər) ***n.*** an underground pipe or drain for carrying off water and waste matter.

**sew·er·age** (so͞o′ər ij *or* syo͞o′ər ij) ***n.*** **1** the removal of surface water and waste matter by sewers. **2** a system of sewers. **3** *same as* **sewage.**

**sew·ing** (sō′iŋ) ***n.*** **1** the act or skill of a person who sews [The *sewing* in this suit is poor.] **2** something that is to be sewed [a basket for one's *sewing*].

☆**sewing machine** a device for sewing with a needle that is worked by machinery.

**sewn** (sōn) *a past participle of* **sew.**

**sex** (seks) ***n.*** **1** either of the two groups, male or female, into which persons, animals, or plants are divided. **2** the character of being male or female. **3** sexual intercourse.

☆**sex·ism** (sek′siz′m) ***n.*** a way of thinking and behaving as though one sex were better than the other; especially, unfair treatment of women by men, caused by such thinking. —**sex′ist** ***adj., n.***

**sex·tant** (seks′tənt) ***n.*** an instrument used to measure distance in degrees of an angle. It is used at sea to find out a ship's position by measuring the angle between a star, the sun, etc. and the horizon. *See the picture.*

**sex·tet** or **sex·tette** (seks tet′) ***n.*** **1** a piece of music for six voices or six instruments. **2** the six people who sing or play it. **3** any group of six.

settee

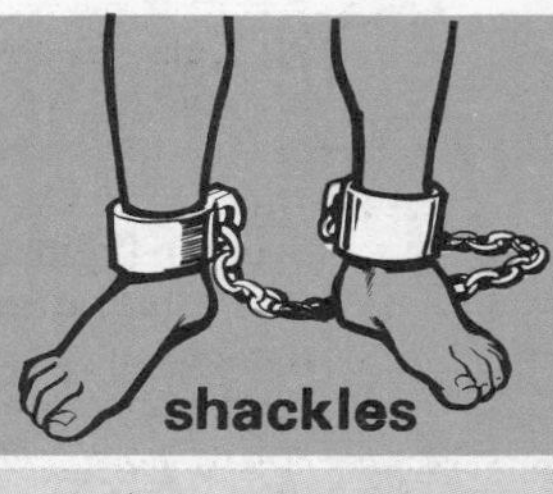
shackles

setter
60 cm (2 ft.) high at shoulder

settle

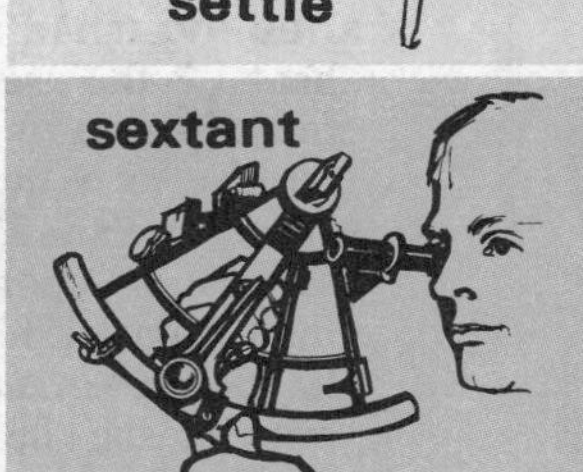
sextant

**sex·ton** (seks′tən) ***n.*** a person whose work is to take care of a church, ring the church bells, etc.

**sex·u·al** (sek′sho͞o wəl) ***adj.*** having to do with sex or the sexes or with the drives, desires, etc. related to sex. —**sex′u·al·ly** ***adv.*** 

**sex·y** (sek′sē) ***adj.*** causing or intended to cause sexual desire; erotic: *used only in everyday talk.* —**sex′i·er, sex′i·est**

**Sgt** or **Sgt.** *abbreviation for* **Sergeant.**

**shab·by** (shab′ē) ***adj.*** **1** that shows much wear; old and worn out [*shabby* clothing]. **2** wearing shabby clothes. **3** poorly taken care of; run-down [a *shabby* neighborhood]. **4** not proper; disgraceful; mean [a *shabby* way to treat guests]. —**shab′bi·er, shab′bi·est** —**shab′bi·ly** ***adv.*** —**shab′bi·ness** ***n.***

☆**shack** (shak) ***n.*** a small house or hut built in a rough, crude way; shanty.

**shack·le** (shak′'l) ***n.*** **1** a metal loop put around the wrist or ankle of a prisoner, usually in pairs joined by a chain; fetter. *See the picture.* **2** anything that keeps one from moving or acting in a free way [the *shackles* of poverty]. **3** any device used in fastening or connecting. ◆***v.*** to bind or hinder as with a shackle or shackles. —**shack′led, shack′ling**

**shad** (shad) ***n.*** a food fish related to the herring. Shad live in the ocean, but swim up rivers to lay their eggs. —*pl.* **shad** or **shads**

**shade** (shād) ***n.*** **1** darkness caused by cutting off rays of light, as from the sun [the deep *shade* of the

| | | | | | | | |
|---|---|---|---|---|---|---|---|
| **a** | fat | **ir** | here | **ou** | out | **zh** | leisure |
| **ā** | ape | **ī** | bite, fire | **u** | up | **ŋ** | ring |
| **ä** | car, lot | **ō** | go | **ur** | fur | | a *in* ago |
| **e** | ten | **ô** | law, horn | **ch** | chin | | e *in* agent |
| **er** | care | **oi** | oil | **sh** | she | **ə** = | i *in* unity |
| **ē** | even | **oo** | look | **th** | thin | | o *in* collect |
| **i** | hit | **o͞o** | tool | ***th*** | then | | u *in* focus |

jungle]. **2** an area with less light than other areas around it [We sat in the *shade* of an awning.] **3** any device for screening from light or for directing light [a window *shade;* a lamp *shade*]. **4** degree of darkness of a color [light and dark *shades* of green]. *See* SYNONYMS *at* **color.** **5** a small amount or degree [There's a *shade* of anger in his voice.] **6** a small difference [Our paper presents all *shades* of opinion.] **7** a ghost; spirit: *now seldom used.* ☆**8 shades,** *pl.* sunglasses: *slang in this meaning.* ◆*v.* **1** to protect or screen from light or heat [The trees *shade* the house.] **2** to change little by little [The drapes *shade* from purple to lavender.] **3** to darken or dim [The awnings *shade* the sun's rays.] **4** to use lines or dark colors in a picture to show shade or shadow. —**shad'ed, shad'ing**

**shad·ing** (shād'ing) *n.* **1** protection against light and heat. **2** the use of lines or dark colors to give the effect of shade or shadow in a picture. **3** any small difference, as in quality.

**shad·ow** (shad'ō) *n.* **1** the darkness or the dark shape cast upon a surface by something cutting off light from it [Her large hat put her face in *shadow.* His hand cast a *shadow* on the wall.] **2 shadows,** *pl.* the growing darkness after sunset. **3** gloom or sadness; also, something that causes gloom or sadness [The *shadow* of her illness hung over them.] **4** a small amount; trace; suggestion [The *shadow* of a smile crossed his face.] **5** something imagined, not real [Is fame a mere *shadow?*] ☆**6** a person who follows another person around, especially as a detective or spy. **7** the shaded part in a picture. **8** a ghost; spirit. ◆*v.* **1** to make a shadow or shadows upon [Hills *shadowed* the valley.] **2** to make dark or gloomy [A frown *shadowed* his face.] **3** to follow closely in a secret way. —**in the shadow of,** very close to.



**shad·ow·y** (shad'ə wē) *adj.* **1** shaded or full of shadow [a *shadowy* corner of the room]. **2** not clear or real; dim [a *shadowy* figure in the fog; a *shadowy* hope].

**shad·y** (shād'ē) *adj.* **1** giving shade [a *shady* tree]. **2** shaded, as from the sun [a *shady* path]. **3** not clearly honest, proper, etc.; doubtful: *used only in everyday talk* [a *shady* business deal]. —**shad'i·er, shad'i·est** —**shad'i·ness** *n.*

**shaft** (shaft) *n.* **1** the long, slender stem or handle of an arrow or spear. **2** an arrow or spear. **3** something that seems to be hurled like an arrow or spear [a *shaft* of light; *shafts* of wit]. **4** a long, slender thing or part, as a column or a long handle [the *shaft* of a golf club]. **5** either of the two poles between which an animal is harnessed to a wagon, carriage, etc. **6** a bar that supports moving parts of a machine, or that makes them move [the drive *shaft* of an engine]. **7** a long, narrow opening dug down into the earth [a mine *shaft*]. **8** an opening going up through the floors of a building [an elevator *shaft*].

shagbark

shamrock

**shag** (shag) *n.* **1** a long, heavy nap, as on some rugs. **2** a rug with such a nap.

☆**shag·bark** (shag'bärk) *n.* a hickory tree with gray bark that peels off in long shreds. *See the picture.*

**shag·gy** (shag'ē) *adj.* **1** having long, thick, rough hair or wool [a *shaggy* dog]. **2** long, coarse, and uneven [*shaggy* eyebrows]. **3** having a long, heavy nap, as some carpeting. —**shag'gi·er, shag'gi·est** —**shag'gi·ness** *n.*

**shah** (shä) *n.* a title of the ruler of Iran.

**shake** (shāk) *v.* **1** to move quickly up and down, back and forth, or from side to side [to *shake* one's head in approval]. **2** to clasp another's hand, as in greeting. **3** to bring, force, throw, stir up, etc. by short, quick movements [I'll *shake* salt on the popcorn. *Shake* the medicine well before taking it.] **4** to tremble or make tremble [His voice *shook* with fear. Chills *shook* his body.] **5** to weaken, disturb, upset, etc. [He was *shaken* by the news.] ☆**6** to get away from: *used only in everyday talk* [He *shook* his pursuers.] —**shook, shak·en** (shāk''n), **shak'ing** ◆*n.* **1** an act of shaking [a *shake* of the fist]. **2** a trembling movement or sound [a *shake* in her voice]. ☆**3** *a shorter name for* **milkshake.** —**no great shakes,** not outstanding; ordinary: *used only in everyday talk.* —**shake down, 1** to make fall by shaking, as fruit from a tree. **2** to make settle by shaking. ☆**3** to get money from, as by blackmailing: *slang in this meaning.* —**shake off,** to get away from or get rid of. —**shake out,** to empty or straighten out by shaking. —**shake up, 1** to shake so as to mix up. **2** to jar or shock. **3** to change greatly.

SYNONYMS: To **shake** is to move up and down or back and forth with quick, short motions [He *shook* his cane at us.] To **tremble** is to have one's body shake without being able to control it [When she got out of the icy water, she *trembled* all over.] To **quiver** is to shake with very rapid, very slight motions [He was so upset his lips *quivered* when he tried to speak.] To **shudder** is to have a sudden, uncontrollable fit of quivering, as from shock [We *shuddered* when we saw the speeding car flip over.]

**shake·down** (shāk'doun) *n.* ☆**1** the getting of money in an illegal way, as by blackmail. ☆**2** a thorough search of a person or place. ◆☆*adj.* for testing the way something new works, getting the crew to know their work, etc. [The ship has had its *shakedown* cruise.] *This word is used only in everyday talk.*

**shak·er** (shā'kər) *n.* **1** a person or thing that shakes. **2** a device used in shaking [a salt*shaker*]. ☆**3 Shaker,** a member of a former religious sect whose members lived and worked together in communes.

**Shake·speare** (shāk'spir), **William** 1564–1616; English poet and writer of plays. —**Shake·spear'e·an, Shake·spear'i·an** *adj.*

**shake-up** (shāk'up') *n.* ☆a great and sudden change, as in an organization.

**shak·y** (shā'kē) *adj.* **1** not firm or steady; weak [a *shaky* bridge]. **2** shaking; trembling [a *shaky* hand].

3 not to be trusted or relied on [*shaky* evidence]. —**shak'i·er, shak'i·est** —**shak'i·ly** ***adv.*** —**shak'i·ness** ***n.***

**shale** (shāl) ***n.*** a rock formed of hardened clay. It splits into thin layers when broken.

**shall** (shal) *a helping verb used with other verbs in speaking of the future* [I *shall* leave tomorrow. *Shall* we eat?] *See the note in color at* **will**. *See also* **should.**

**shal·lot** (shə lät') ***n.*** **1** a small onion that tastes like garlic but is milder. **2** *another name for* **green onion.**

**shal·low** (shal'ō) ***adj.*** **1** not deep [a *shallow* lake]. **2** not serious in thinking or strong in feeling [a *shallow* mind]. ◆***n.*** a shallow place, as in a river.

**sha·lom** (shä lōm') ***n., interj.*** the Hebrew word for "peace," used as a Jewish greeting or farewell.

**shalt** (shalt) *an older form of* **shall**, *used with* thou, *as in the Bible.*

**sham** (sham) ***n.*** something false or fake; fraud [His bravery is a *sham*.] ◆***adj.*** not genuine or real; false; fake [a string of *sham* pearls]. ◆***v.*** to fake; pretend [She's not asleep; she's only *shamming*.] —**shammed, sham'ming**

**sham·ble** (sham'b'l) ***v.*** to walk in a lazy or clumsy way, barely lifting the feet; shuffle. —**sham'bled, sham'bling** ◆***n.*** a lazy or clumsy, shuffling walk.

**sham·bles** (sham'b'lz) ***n.*** **1** a slaughterhouse. **2** a place where there has been much bloodshed. **3** a place where there is much destruction or disorder [The children left the room a *shambles*.]

In some parts of England, **shambles** means a butcher's stall or shop, where meat is sold. From this the word came also to mean the slaughterhouse, or place where animals are killed for food.

**shame** (shām) ***n.*** **1** a painful feeling of having lost the respect of others because of something wrong done by oneself or another. **2** loss of honor or respect; disgrace [to bring *shame* to one's family]. **3** something that brings shame. **4** a thing to feel sorry about [It's a *shame* that you missed the party.] ◆***v.*** **1** to give a feeling of shame to; make ashamed. **2** to make lose honor or respect; disgrace [The actions of a few *shamed* the whole school.] **3** to force into something because of a feeling of shame [Joe's hurt look *shamed* Ted into apologizing.] —**shamed, sham'ing** —**for shame!** you ought to be ashamed! —**put to shame, 1** to make ashamed. **2** to do much better than; surpass. —**shame on,** shame should be felt by.

**shame·faced** (shām'fāst) ***adj.*** **1** showing shame; ashamed. **2** bashful; shy.

**shame·ful** (shām'fəl) ***adj.*** **1** bringing shame or disgrace. **2** not moral or decent. —**shame'ful·ly** ***adv.***

**shame·less** (shām'lis) ***adj.*** feeling or showing no shame; brazen [a *shameless* liar]. —**shame'less·ly** ***adv.***

**sham·poo** (sham po͞o') ***v.*** **1** to wash with foamy suds, as hair or a rug. **2** to wash the hair of. —**shampooed', sham·poo'ing** ◆***n.*** **1** the act of shampooing. **2** a special soap, or soaplike product, that makes suds.

**sham·rock** (sham'räk) ***n.*** a kind of clover with three leaflets. It is the emblem of Ireland. *See the picture.*

☆**sha·mus** (shä'məs) ***n.*** a private detective: *a slang word.*

**Shang·hai** (shaŋ'hī) a seaport in eastern China.

**shang·hai** (shaŋ'hī) ☆***v.*** to kidnap and force to work as a sailor on board a ship. —**shang'haied, shang'hai·ing**

The verb **shanghai** is thought to have been first used about 1850 in San Francisco. Young men were sometimes drugged there in waterfront saloons and taken aboard ships bound for Shanghai.

**shank** (shaŋk) ***n.*** **1** the part of the leg between the knee and the ankle. **2** the whole leg. **3** a cut of beef from the upper part of the leg. **4** the part of a tool or instrument between the handle and the working part; shaft. —**shank of the evening,** the early part of the evening.

**shan't** (shant) shall not.

**Shan·tung** (shan'tuŋ') a province of northeastern China. ◆***n.*** *sometimes* **shantung,** a fabric with an uneven surface, made of silk, rayon, cotton, etc.

☆**shan·ty** (shan'tē) ***n.*** a small house or hut built in a crude way; shack. —*pl.* **shan'ties**

**shape** (shāp) ***n.*** **1** the way a thing looks because of its outline; outer form; figure [The cloud had the *shape* of a lamb.] *See* SYNONYMS *at* **form. 2** definite or regular form [The class is getting the play into *shape*.] ☆**3** condition: *used only in everyday talk* [in bad *shape* financially]. ◆***v.*** **1** to give a certain shape to; form [The potter *shaped* the clay into a bowl.] **2** to prepare or develop in a certain way [I am *shaping* an answer to the letter. The campaign is *shaping* up well.] —**shaped, shap'ing** —☆**shape up, 1** to develop in a definite or favorable way. **2** to do what is expected of one. *This phrase is used only in everyday talk.* —**take shape,** to develop or show a definite form.



**shape·less** (shāp'lis) ***adj.*** without a definite or well-formed shape. —**shape'less·ness** ***n.***

**shape·ly** (shāp'lē) ***adj.*** having a good shape or form; pleasing to look at. —**shape'li·er, shape'li·est**

**shard** (shärd) ***n.*** a fragment or broken piece, especially of pottery.

**share** (sher) ***n.*** **1** a part that each one of a group gets or has [your *share* of the cake; my *share* of the blame]. **2** any of the equal parts into which the ownership of a company is divided, as by stock. ◆***v.*** **1** to divide and give out in shares [The owners *shared* the profits with their employees.] **2** to have a share of with others; have or use together [The three of you will *share* the back seat.] **3** to take part; have a share [We all *shared* in the gift for the teacher.] —**shared, shar'ing** —**go shares,** to take part together; share. —**share and share alike,** with each having an equal share.

☆**share·crop·per** (sher'kräp'ər) ***n.*** a person who farms land owned by another and gets part of the crop in return for the work done.

| | | | | | | | |
|---|---|---|---|---|---|---|---|
| **a** fat | **ir** here | **ou** out | **zh** leisure | | | | |
| **ā** ape | **ī** bite, fire | **u** up | **ŋ** ring | | | | |
| **ä** car, lot | **ō** go | **ur** fur | a *in* ago | | | | |
| **e** ten | **ô** law, horn | **ch** chin | e *in* agent | | | | |
| **er** care | **oi** oil | **sh** she | ə = i *in* unity | | | | |
| **ē** even | **oo** look | **th** thin | o *in* collect | | | | |
| **i** hit | **o͞o** tool | ***th*** then | u *in* focus | | | | |

sheath

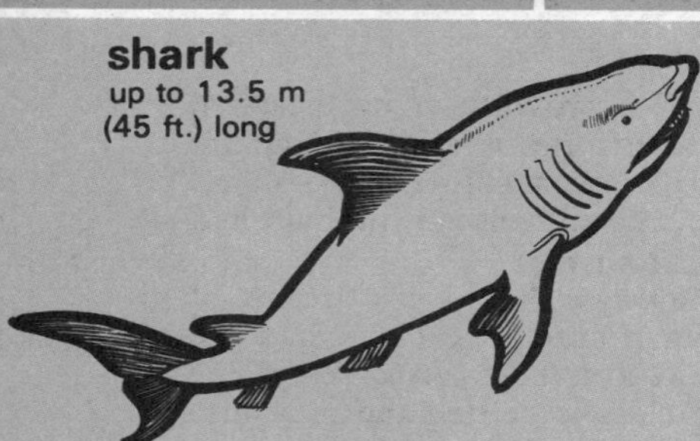

☆**shared time** an arrangement by which pupils from parochial schools or other private schools attend certain classes in public schools.



**share·hold·er** (sher′hōl′dər) ***n.*** a person who owns one or more shares of stock, as in a company.

**shark** (shärk) ***n.*** a large ocean fish that eats other fish and sometimes attacks people in the water. *See the picture.*

**shark·skin** (shärk′skin) ***n.*** **1** leather made from the skin of a shark. ☆**2** a cloth of cotton, wool, rayon, etc. with a smooth, silky surface.

**sharp** (shärp) ***adj.*** **1** having a thin edge for cutting, or a fine point for piercing [a *sharp* knife; a *sharp* needle]. **2** having an edge or point; not round or blunt [a *sharp* ridge; a *sharp* nose]. **3** not gradual; abrupt [a *sharp* turn]. **4** easily seen; distinct; clear [a *sharp* contrast]. **5** very clever or shrewd [a *sharp* mind]. **6** keen in seeing or noticing; alert [*sharp* eyes; a *sharp* lookout]. **7** severe or harsh [a *sharp* reply]. **8** sudden or forceful; violent [a *sharp* blow]. **9** very strong; intense; stinging [a *sharp* wind; *sharp* pain]. **10** strong in odor or taste [*sharp* cheese]. **11** in music, above the true pitch; also, higher in pitch by a half tone. **12** attractive or stylish: *slang in this meaning.* ◆***n.*** a musical tone or note one half step above another; also, the sign (♯) used to mark such a note. ◆***adv.*** **1** exactly or promptly [She gets up at 6:30 *sharp*.] **2** in a sharp manner; keenly, alertly, briskly, etc. [Look *sharp* when crossing streets.] **3** in music, above the true pitch. ◆***v.*** in music, to make or become sharp [to *sharp* a note]. —**sharp′ly** ***adv.*** —**sharp′ness** ***n.***

**sharp·en** (shär′p′n) ***v.*** to make or become sharp or sharper. —**sharp′en·er** ***n.***

**sharp·shoot·er** (shärp′sho͞ot′ər) ***n.*** a person who shoots a gun with skill; good shot.

**sharp-tongued** (shärp′tuŋd′) ***adj.*** using harsh or rude words [a *sharp-tongued* critic].

**sharp-wit·ted** (shärp′wit′id) ***adj.*** having or showing a quick and clever mind [a *sharp-witted* reply].

**shat·ter** (shat′ər) ***v.*** **1** to break into many pieces; smash [Our ball *shattered* the window.] **2** to ruin or destroy; damage badly [The storm *shattered* our plans.]

**shat·ter·proof** (shat′ər pro͞of) ***adj.*** that will resist shattering [*shatterproof* glass].

**shave** (shāv) ***v.*** **1** to cut off hair with a razor, close to the skin. **2** to cut off the hair of [He carefully *shaved* his chin.] **3** to cut off the beard of [The barber will *shave* you.] **4** to cut or scrape away a thin slice from [to *shave* ham]. **5** to barely touch in passing; graze [The car *shaved* the side of the tree.] **6** to lower slightly: *used only in everyday talk* [to *shave* prices or costs]. —**shaved, shaved** or **shav′en, shav′ing** ◆***n.*** the act of cutting off hair, especially the beard, with a razor.

**shav·er** (shā′vər) ***n.*** **1** an instrument used in shaving [an electric *shaver*]. **2** one who shaves. **3** a young boy; lad: *used only in everyday talk.*

**shav·ing** (shā′viŋ) ***n.*** **1** the act of one who shaves. **2** a thin piece of wood, metal, etc. shaved off a larger piece.

**Sha·vu·ot** (shä vo͞o′ōt *or* shə vo͞o′ōs) ***n.*** a Jewish holiday, in honor of the giving of the Mosaic law, or Ten Commandments, at Mount Sinai.

**Shaw** (shô), **George Bernard** 1856–1950; British writer of plays, born in Ireland.

**shawl** (shôl) ***n.*** a large piece of cloth worn, especially by women, over the shoulders or head. *See the picture.*

**shay** (shā) ***n.*** a light carriage: *used in some regions.*

**she** (shē) ***pron.*** the woman, girl, or female animal being talked about [Annette thought *she* heard a noise.] ◆***n.*** a woman, girl, or female animal [This dog is a *she*.] —*pl.* **they**

**sheaf** (shēf) ***n.*** **1** a bunch of cut stalks of wheat, rye, straw, etc. tied up together in a bundle. **2** a number of things gathered together [a *sheaf* of papers]. —*pl.* **sheaves**

**shear** (shir) ***v.*** **1** to cut as with shears or scissors [to *shear* one corner off a sheet of metal]. **2** to clip the hair, wool, etc. from [to *shear* a sheep]. **3** to move as if by cutting [The plane *sheared* through the clouds.] —**sheared, sheared** or **shorn, shear′ing**

**shears** (shirz) ***n.pl.*** any tool like large scissors, used to cut cloth, metal, etc. or to prune plants.

**sheath** (shēth) ***n.*** **1** a case for the blade of a knife, sword, etc. *See the picture.* **2** any covering like this, as the membrane around a muscle. —*pl.* **sheaths** (shēthz *or* shēths)

> **Sheath** comes from a word in an ancient language meaning "to split." The earliest kind of sheath was probably a split stick into which a knife was slipped to protect its sharp blade.

**sheathe** (shēth) ***v.*** **1** to put into a sheath [to *sheathe* a sword]. **2** to cover with something that protects [wire *sheathed* with rubber insulation]. —**sheathed, sheath′ing**

**sheave** (shēv) ***v.*** to gather in sheaves, as grain. —**sheaved, sheav′ing**

**sheaves** (shēvz) ***n.*** *plural of* **sheaf.**

**She·ba** (shē′bə) an ancient country in southern Arabia [The Queen of *Sheba* visited King Solomon to find out how wise he was.]

**shed**[1] (shed) ***n.*** a building or lean-to for storing and protecting things. Sheds are often small and crudely built, or open on one or more sides.

**shed**[2] (shed) ***v.*** **1** to let or make flow or fall; pour out [to *shed* tears; to *shed* blood]. **2** to make flow off without going through [Raincoats *shed* water.] **3** to lose or drop [Maples *shed* their leaves each year.] **4** to get rid of [to *shed* a few pounds]. **5** to send out or give forth [to *shed* confidence; to *shed* light]. —**shed, shed′ding** —**shed blood,** to kill in a violent way.

**she'd** (shēd) **1** she had. **2** she would.

**sheen** (shēn) ***n.*** brightness or shininess [the *sheen* of well-brushed hair].

**sheep** (shēp) ***n.*** **1** an animal that chews its cud and is related to the goat. Its body is covered with heavy wool and its flesh is used as food, called mutton. **2** a stupid or timid person. —*pl.* **sheep** —**make sheep's eyes at,** to look at in a shy, loving way.

**sheep dog** a dog trained to help herd sheep.

**sheep·fold** (shēp′fōld) ***n.*** a pen in which sheep are kept.

☆**sheep·herd·er** (shēp′hur′dər) ***n.*** a person who herds a large flock of grazing sheep.

**sheep·ish** (shēp′ish) ***adj.*** shy or embarrassed in an awkward way [a *sheepish* grin]. *See the picture.* —**sheep′ish·ly *adv.***

**sheep·skin** (shēp′skin) ***n.*** **1** the skin of a sheep, especially with the wool left on it, as for a coat. **2** a parchment or leather made from the skin of a sheep. ☆**3** *another name for* **diploma**: *used only in everyday talk.*

> A diploma is sometimes called a **sheepskin** in fun because in the old days a diploma from a university was printed on parchment made from the skin of a sheep.

**sheer**[1] (shir) ***v.*** to turn aside; swerve.

**sheer**[2] (shir) ***adj.*** **1** very fine; thin enough to be seen through [*sheer* stockings]. **2** absolute; utter [*sheer* luxury]. **3** straight up or down, or almost so; very steep, as the face of a cliff. ◆***adv.*** **1** completely; utterly. **2** very steeply.

**sheet** (shēt) ***n.*** **1** a large piece of cloth, used on a bed, usually in pairs, one under and one over the body. **2** a single piece of paper. **3** a newspaper: *used only in everyday talk* [a scandal *sheet*]. **4** a surface or piece that is broad and thin [a *sheet* of ice; a *sheet* of glass]. **5** a flat baking pan [a cookie *sheet*].

**sheet·ing** (shēt′ing) ***n.*** **1** cloth, usually of cotton, used for bed sheets. **2** material used to cover or line a surface [copper *sheeting*].

**sheet metal** metal rolled thin in the form of a sheet.

**sheet music** music printed and sold on separate sheets of paper, not in a book.

**sheik** or **sheikh** (shēk) ***n.*** the chief or leader of an Arab family, tribe, or village. —**sheik′dom** or **sheikh′dom *n.***

**shek·el** (shek″l) ***n.*** a gold or silver coin of the ancient Hebrews.

**shel·drake** (shel′drāk) ***n.*** **1** a large wild duck of Europe. **2** *another name for* **merganser**.

**shelf** (shelf) ***n.*** **1** a thin, flat length of wood, metal, etc. fastened against a wall or built into a frame so as to hold things [the top *shelf* of a bookcase]. **2** something like a shelf, as a ledge of rock. —*pl.* **shelves** —**on the shelf,** out of use.

**shell** (shel) ***n.*** **1** a hard outer covering, as of eggs, nuts, turtle, clams, snails, etc. **2** material of or like animal shell, used in making things [eyeglasses with *shell* rims]. **3** something like a shell in being hollow, light, an outer part, etc. [the *shell* of a burned house; a pie *shell*]. **4** a shy manner [Come out of your *shell.*] ☆**5** a long, light racing boat, rowed by a team. *See the picture.* **6** a case or cartridge holding an explosive, chemicals, shot, a bullet, etc., to be fired from a large or small gun. ◆***v.*** **1** to take off the shell from [to *shell* peas]. **2** to separate from the ear or cob, as kernels of corn. **3** to fire shells at from large guns. —**shell out,** to pay out money: *used only in everyday talk.*

**she'll** (shēl) **1** she will. **2** she shall.

**shel·lac** (shə lak′) ***n.*** **1** a kind of flaky resin. **2** a thin varnish made from this resin and alcohol. ◆***v.*** **1** to coat with shellac. ☆**2** to beat or defeat soundly: *slang in this meaning.* —**shel·lacked′, shel·lack′ing**

**Shel·ley** (shel′ē), **Mary Woll·stone·craft** (wool′stən kraft) 1797–1851; English author and the wife of Percy Bysshe Shelley. She wrote the novel *Frankenstein.*

**Shelley, Per·cy Bysshe** (pur′sē bish) 1792–1822; English poet.

**shell·fire** (shel′fīr) ***n.*** the firing of large shells; an attack by artillery.

**shell·fish** (shel′fish) ***n.*** an animal that lives in water and has a shell, especially such an animal used as food, as the clam or lobster.



**shel·ter** (shel′tər) ***n.*** **1** a place or thing that covers or protects, as from the weather, danger, etc. **2** the condition of being covered or protected; protection [Give us *shelter.*] ◆***v.*** **1** to give shelter to; protect [This barn will *shelter* us from the rain.] **2** to take shelter, or cover.

> SYNONYMS: **Shelter** refers to the protection of something that covers, as a roof that shields people from bad weather or danger [They huddled under the umbrella for *shelter.*] **Refuge** suggests a place of safety to which a person may flee to escape danger [He came to America for political *refuge.*]

**shelve** (shelv) ***v.*** **1** to fit with shelves. **2** to put on shelves [The librarian *shelved* the books.] **3** to put aside or stop discussing [We *shelved* plans for a new school.] —**shelved, shelv′ing**

**shelves** (shelvz) ***n.*** *plural of* **shelf.**

**shelv·ing** (shel′ving) ***n.*** **1** material for shelves. **2** shelves.

**Shen·an·do·ah** (shen′ən dō′ə) a river in Virginia flowing into the Potomac.

☆**she·nan·i·gans** (shi nan′i g'nz) ***n.pl.*** mischief or trickery: *used only in everyday talk.*

> **Shenanigans** is thought to have come from an Irish word that means "I play the fox." The fox is often thought of as a tricky, sly animal.

| | | | | | | | |
|---|---|---|---|---|---|---|---|
| **a** | fat | **ir** | here | **ou** | out | **zh** | leisure |
| **ā** | ape | **ī** | bite, fire | **u** | up | **ng** | ring |
| **ä** | car, lot | **ō** | go | **ur** | fur | | a *in* ago |
| **e** | ten | **ô** | law, horn | **ch** | chin | | e *in* agent |
| **er** | care | **oi** | oil | **sh** | she | **ə** = | i *in* unity |
| **ē** | even | **oo** | look | **th** | thin | | o *in* collect |
| **i** | hit | **ōō** | tool | ***th*** | then | | u *in* focus |

S

**She·ol** (shē′ōl) ***n.*** a place mentioned in the Bible where the dead are believed to go. It is thought of as a very deep place in the earth.

**shep·herd** (shep′ərd) ***n.*** **1** a person who herds and takes care of sheep. **2** a religious leader or minister. ◆***v.*** to take care of, herd, lead, etc. like a shepherd.

**shep·herd·ess** (shep′ərd is) ***n.*** a girl or woman who is a shepherd.

**sher·bet** (shur′bət) ***n.*** a frozen dessert of fruit juice, sugar, and water, milk, etc.

**sher·iff** (sher′if) ***n.*** ☆the chief officer of the law in a county.

**Sher·lock Holmes** (shur′läk hōmz′) a British detective in many stories by A. Conan Doyle. His great powers of reasoning help him to solve the mysteries in the stories.

**Sher·man** (shur′mən), **William Te·cum·seh** (ti kum′sə) 1820–1891; a Union general in the Civil War.

**sher·ry** (sher′ē) ***n.*** **1** a strong, yellow or brownish wine from Spain. **2** any wine like this.

**Sher·wood Forest** (shur′wood) a forest in England, made famous in the Robin Hood stories.

**she's** (shēz) **1** she is. **2** she has.

**Shet·land pony** (shet′lənd) a breed of sturdy pony, with a rough coat and long, thick tail and mane. *See the picture.*

**shew** (shō) ***n., v.*** *an old spelling of* **show,** *now seldom used.* —**shewed, shewn** or **shewed, shew′ing**



**shib·bo·leth** (shib′ə ləth) ***n.*** something said or done that is a sign or test of belonging to a certain group, party, or class.

**shied** (shīd) *past tense and past participle of* **shy.**

**shield** (shēld) ***n.*** **1** a piece of armor carried on the arm to ward off blows in battle. **2** something that guards or protects, as a safety guard over machinery. **3** anything shaped like a shield, as a coat of arms. ◆***v.*** to guard or protect [Trees *shield* our house from the sun.]

shocks of grain

Shetland pony

shins

shirring

shingles

child shinning up a pole

**shift** (shift) ***v.*** **1** to move or change from one person, place, direction, etc. to another [Don't try to *shift* the blame. He *shifted* his feet. The wind is *shifting*. *Shift* into reverse.] **2** to get along; manage [She *shifts* for herself.] ◆***n.*** **1** the act of shifting; change [a *shift* of public opinion; a *shift* in the wind]. **2** a group of workers taking turns with other groups at the same jobs [The night *shift* will soon take over.] **3** time or turn at work. **4** something turned to in place of the usual means; especially, a trick or scheme [He invented a *shift* to keep himself home from school.] —**make shift,** to manage or do the best one can with whatever means are at hand.

**shift·less** (shift′lis) ***adj.*** lazy or careless.

**shift·y** (shif′tē) ***adj.*** having or showing a nature that is not to be trusted; tricky. —**shift′i·er, shift′i·est**

**shil·ling** (shil′iŋ) ***n.*** a silver coin of Great Britain equal to five (new) pennies or 1/20 of a pound. This coin is no longer minted.

**shil·ly-shal·ly** (shil′ē shal′ē) ***v.*** to be unable to make up one's mind; hesitate. —**shil′ly-shal′lied, shil′ly-shal′ly·ing**

**shim·mer** (shim′ər) ***v.*** to shine with an unsteady or wavering light [The lake *shimmers* in the moonlight.] ◆***n.*** a shimmering light. —**shim′mer·y *adj.***

**shim·my** (shim′ē) ***n.*** ☆a shaking or wobbling, as in the front wheels of a car. ◆☆***v.*** to shake or wobble. —**shim′mied, shim′my·ing**

> **Shimmy** was first used as a slang word for *chemise,* a loose, short dress that women and girls wore in the 1920's. Then a jazz dance in which there is much shaking of the body was called *shimmy* because the girls wore this kind of dress while dancing. The word then came to mean the wobbling or shaking of a car's wheels.

**shin** (shin) ***n.*** the front part of the leg between the knee and ankle. *See the picture.* ◆***v.*** to climb, as a pole or rope, by gripping with the hands and legs. *See the picture.* —**shinned, shin′ning**

**shin·bone** (shin′bōn) ***n.*** the large bone of the lower leg; tibia.

**shine** (shīn) ***v.*** **1** to give off light or reflect light; be bright [The sun *shines.* Her hair *shone.*] **2** to make give off light [to *shine* a flashlight]. **3** to do especially well [She *shines* in arithmetic.] **4** to show itself clearly or brightly [Love *shone* from her eyes.] **5** to make bright by polishing [to *shine* shoes]. —**shone** or **shined, shin′ing** *The past tense and past participle for meaning* 5 *is* **shined.** ◆***n.*** **1** the condition of being shiny. **2** the act of polishing, as shoes.

**shin·er** (shīn′ər) ***n.*** **1** a person or thing that shines. ☆**2** *another name for* **black eye:** *slang in this meaning.*

**shin·gle**[1] (shiŋ′g′l) ***n.*** pebbles or small stones lying on a beach: *mainly a British word.* —**shin′gly *adj.***

**shin·gle**[2] (shiŋ′g′l) ***n.*** **1** a thin, flat piece of wood or a material made of asbestos, asphalt, etc., laid with others to form overlapping rows, as in covering a roof. *See the picture.* ☆**2** a short haircut in which the hair in back is shaped close to the head. ☆**3** a small signboard, as of a doctor: *used only in everyday talk.* ◆***v.*** **1** to cover with shingles, as a roof. **2** to cut hair in a shingle. —**shin′gled, shin′gling**

**shin·gles** (shing′g'lz) ***n.*** a virus disease causing pain and skin sores along the line of a nerve.

**shin·guard** (shin′gärd) ***n.*** a padded guard worn to protect the shins, as by a baseball catcher.

**shin·ing** (shīn′ing) ***adj.*** **1** giving off light; radiant; bright. *See* SYNONYMS *at* **bright**. **2** splendid; remarkable [A *shining* example was set by our champion runner.]

☆**shin·ny** (shin′ē) ***v.*** *same as* **shin**: *used only in everyday talk.* —**shin′nied, shin′ny·ing**

**shin·splints** (shin′splints) ***n.*** painful strain of the lower leg muscles, caused by running on a hard surface: *used with a singular verb.*

**Shin·to** (shin′tō) ***n.*** a religion of Japan, with worship of nature and of ancestors and ancient heroes.

**shin·y** (shīn′ē) ***adj.*** **1** bright; shining. **2** highly polished. —**shin′i·er, shin′i·est** —**shin′i·ness** ***n.***

**ship** (ship) ***n.*** **1** any vessel, larger than a boat, for traveling on deep water. **2** the crew of a ship. **3** an aircraft or spaceship. ◆***v.*** **1** to put, take, go, or send in a ship or boat [The cargo was *shipped* from New York.] **2** to take in water over the side of a ship or boat, as in a storm. ☆**3** to send by any means; transport [to *ship* coal by rail]. **4** to fix in its proper place on a ship or boat [to *ship* the oars]. **5** to hire or be hired for work on a ship. **6** to send away; get rid of: *used only in everyday talk.* —**shipped, ship′ping** —**when one's ship comes in,** when one's fortune is made.

The basic sense for the Old English word from which **ship** comes is "a hollowed-out tree trunk," because the first ships were made by splitting tree trunks and hollowing out the inside.

**-ship** (ship) *a suffix meaning:* **1** the quality or state of [*Friendship* is the state of being friends.] **2** the rank or office of [A *professorship* is the rank of a professor.] **3** skill as [*Leadership* is skill as a leader.]

**ship·board** (ship′bôrd) ***n.*** a ship: *used only in the phrase* **on shipboard,** on or in a ship. ◆***adj.*** happening, done, used, etc. aboard a ship [a *shipboard* romance].

**ship·build·er** (ship′bil′dər) ***n.*** a person whose business or work is building ships. —**ship′build′ing** ***n., adj.***

**ship·load** (ship′lōd) ***n.*** a full load of a ship; cargo.

**ship·mate** (ship′māt) ***n.*** a fellow sailor on the same ship.

**ship·ment** (ship′mənt) ***n.*** **1** the shipping of goods by any means. **2** the goods shipped.

**ship·own·er** (ship′ō′nər) ***n.*** an owner of a ship or ships.

**ship·per** (ship′ər) ***n.*** one who ships goods.

**ship·ping** (ship′ing) ***n.*** **1** the sending or carrying of goods from place to place. **2** all the ships of a nation or port, or their tonnage.

**ship·shape** (ship′shāp) ***adj., adv.*** in good order; in a neat or trim condition or manner.

**ship·wreck** (ship′rek) ***n.*** **1** the remains of a wrecked ship. **2** the loss or ruin of a ship, as in a storm or crash. ◆***v.*** to wreck or destroy a ship.

**ship·yard** (ship′yärd) ***n.*** a place where ships are built and repaired.

**shire** (shīr *or* shər *when part of a name*) ***n.*** a county in England. Many of the county names end in *-shire,* as *Berkshire.*

**shirk** (shurk) ***v.*** to get out of doing or leave undone what should be done [She *shirked* her homework to go swimming.] —**shirk′er** ***n.***

**Shirk** is probably related to the German word for scoundrel or rascal. One who avoids any work or duty might be called a rascal or scoundrel.

☆**shirr** (shur) ***n.*** *same as* **shirring.** ◆***v.*** **1** to make shirring in. **2** to bake eggs with crumbs in small buttered dishes.

☆**shir·ring** (shur′ing) ***n.*** a gathering made in cloth by drawing the material up on parallel rows of short stitches. *See the picture.*

**shirt** (shurt) ***n.*** **1** the common garment worn by a boy or man on the upper part of the body, usually having a collar and a buttoned opening down the front. A shirt is often worn with a necktie. **2** a similar garment for a girl or woman. **3** *a shorter name for* **undershirt.**

☆**shirt·tail** (shurt′tāl) ***n.*** the part of a shirt below the waist.

☆**shirt·waist** (shurt′wāst) ***n.*** a blouse for a woman or girl that is tailored more or less like a shirt.

**shish ke·bab** (shish′ kə bäb′) a dish made up of small pieces of meat stuck on a skewer along with pieces of onion, tomato, etc., and broiled or roasted.

**shiv** (shiv) ***n.*** a knife, especially one with a narrow blade used as a weapon: *a slang word.*

**shiv·er**[1] (shiv′ər) ***v.*** to shake or tremble, as from fear or cold. ◆***n.*** a shaking or trembling. —**shiv′er·y** ***adj.*** 

**Shiver**[1] comes from the Old English word for "jaw" and had as its original meaning "to have chattering teeth."

**shiv·er**[2] (shiv′ər) ***n.*** a thin, sharp, broken piece, as of glass; sliver. ◆***v.*** to shatter, splinter, etc.

**shoal**[1] (shōl) ***n.*** a large group; especially, a school of fish.

**shoal**[2] (shōl) ***n.*** **1** a shallow place in a river, sea, etc. **2** a sand bar or rise of ground causing a shallow place in a body of water. ◆***v.*** to become shallow.

**shoat** (shōt) ***n.*** a young hog weighing between 100 and 180 pounds.

**shock**[1] (shäk) ***n.*** **1** a sudden, powerful blow, shake, or jar [the *shock* of an earthquake]. **2** a sudden and strong upsetting of the mind or feelings; also, the thing that causes this [Her accident was a *shock* to us.] **3** the feeling or effect caused by an electric current passing through the body. **4** a condition of the body caused by injury, loss of blood, severe infection, etc., in which there is a drop in blood pressure, great weakness, rapid pulse, etc. ◆***v.*** **1** to upset the mind or feelings of with sudden force; astonish, horrify, disgust, etc. [His crime *shocked* us.] **2** to give an electrical shock to. —**shock′er** ***n.***

**shock**[2] (shäk) ***n.*** bundles of grain stacked in a pile to dry. *See the picture.* ◆***v.*** to gather and pile in shocks.

| | | | | | | | |
|---|---|---|---|---|---|---|---|
| **a** | fat | **ir** | here | **ou** | out | **zh** | leisure |
| **ā** | ape | **ī** | bite, fire | **u** | up | **ng** | ring |
| **ä** | car, lot | **ō** | go | **ur** | fur | | a *in* ago |
| **e** | ten | **ô** | law, horn | **ch** | chin | | e *in* agent |
| **er** | care | **oi** | oil | **sh** | she | **ə** = | i *in* unity |
| **ē** | even | **oo** | look | **th** | thin | | o *in* collect |
| **i** | hit | **ōō** | tool | ***th*** | then | | u *in* focus |

**shock**[3] (shäk) ***n.*** a thick, bushy mass, as of hair.

**shock·ing** (shäk′iŋ) ***adj.*** causing great surprise, horror, disgust, etc. [a *shocking* disaster]. —**shock′ing·ly** ***adv.***

☆**shock·proof** (shäk′pro͞of) ***adj.*** able to stand shock without being damaged [a *shockproof* watch].

**shod** (shäd) *a past tense and past participle of* **shoe.**

**shod·dy** (shäd′ē) ***n.*** cloth made from used or waste wool. ◆***adj.*** **1** made of shoddy or other poor material. **2** not as good as it seems or claims to be [*shoddy* imitation jewelry]. **3** low or mean [a *shoddy* trick]. —**shod′di·er, shod′di·est**

**shoe** (sho͞o) ***n.*** **1** an outer covering for the foot, usually of leather. **2** *a shorter word for* **horseshoe. 3** something like a shoe in shape or use, as the part of a brake that presses against a wheel. ◆***v.*** to furnish with shoes; put shoes on [to *shoe* a horse]. —**shod** or **shoed, shoe′ing** —**fill one's shoes,** to take one's place. —**in another's shoes,** in another's position. —**where the shoe pinches,** what is really causing the trouble.

**shoe·horn** (sho͞o′hôrn) ***n.*** a small, curved piece of metal, plastic, etc. for helping to slip one's heel into a shoe. *See the picture.*

**shoe·lace** (sho͞o′lās) ***n.*** a lace of cord, leather, etc. used for fastening a shoe.

**shoe·mak·er** (sho͞o′māk′ər) ***n.*** a person whose work is making or repairing shoes.



**shoe·shine** (sho͞o′shīn) ***n.*** the cleaning and polishing of a pair of shoes.

**shoe·string** (sho͞o′striŋ) ***n.*** **1** *another word for* **shoelace.** ☆**2** very little money [They started the business on a *shoestring.*] ◆☆***adj.*** near or around the ankles [The fielder made a *shoestring* catch of a ball.]

☆**shoestring potatoes** potatoes cut into long, narrow strips and fried crisp in deep fat.

**shoe tree** a form put inside a shoe to stretch the shoe or keep it in shape. *See the picture.*

**shone** (shōn) *a past tense and past participle of* **shine.**

**shoo** (sho͞o) ***interj.*** go away! get out! ◆***v.*** to drive away, as by waving or crying "shoo" [to *shoo* chickens away]. —**shooed, shoo′ing**

☆**shoo-in** (sho͞o′in) ***n.*** someone or something expected to win easily in an election, race, etc.: *used only in everyday talk.*

**shook** (sho͝ok) *past tense of* **shake.** —☆**shook up,** upset; disturbed: *a slang phrase.*

**shoot** (sho͞ot) ***v.*** **1** to send out with force from a gun, bow, etc. [to *shoot* bullets or arrows]. **2** to send a bullet, arrow, etc. from [to *shoot* a gun]. **3** to be fired or discharged [This gun won't *shoot.*] **4** to wound or kill with a bullet, etc. **5** to send out or throw swiftly and with force [to *shoot* out rays of heat; to *shoot* insults at someone]. **6** to move out, by, over, etc. swiftly and with force [The horses *shot* out of the barn. The oil *shot* up out of the ground. He *shot* the rapids in a canoe.] ☆**7** to take a picture or film a movie of with a camera. **8** to score a goal or points in certain games [She *shot* six baskets in the basketball game.] **9** to play, as certain games [We hope to *shoot* nine holes of golf.] **10** to push forth, as a growing part [The plant *shoots* out its new leaves.] **11** to grow fast [He *shot* up in his early teens.] **12** to scatter with streaks of another color [red hair *shot* with gray]. **13** to be felt suddenly and sharply [A pain *shot* across my back.] **14** to stick out; project upward or outward [skyscrapers *shooting* up in the air]. **15** to use up or waste time, money, etc.: *used only in everyday talk* [She *shot* a week's pay on the trip.] —**shot, shoot′ing** ◆***n.*** **1** a shooting trip, contest, etc. [a turkey *shoot*]. **2** a new growth; sprout. ☆**3** a sloping channel; chute. —**shoot′er** ***n.***

**shooting star** *another name for* **meteor.**

**shop** (shäp) ***n.*** **1** a place where things are sold; store [a book *shop*]. **2** a place where a certain kind of work is done [a machine *shop*]. ☆**3** in some schools, a class in which students learn to use tools and machines in making and repairing things. ◆***v.*** to go to shops to look over and buy things. —**shopped, shop′ping** —**set up shop,** to start a business. —**talk shop,** to talk about one's work. —**shop′per** ***n.***

**shop·keep·er** (shäp′kēp′ər) ***n.*** a person who owns or runs a shop, or small store. —**shop′keep′ing** ***n.***

**shop·lift·er** (shäp′lif′tər) ***n.*** a person who steals things from stores during the time the stores are open for business. —**shop′lift′ing** ***n.***

**shopping center** a group of stores, restaurants, etc. with one large parking lot for all.

**shop·worn** (shäp′wôrn) ***adj.*** **1** worn or dirty from having been displayed in a store. **2** no longer fresh or interesting; dull or trite [a *shopworn* joke].

**shore**[1] (shôr) ***n.*** **1** land at the edge of a sea or lake. **2** land, not water [The retired sailor lives on *shore.*]

**shore**[2] (shôr) ***n.*** a beam, timber, etc. placed under or against something as a support. *See the picture.* ◆***v.*** to support with shores; prop [to *shore* up a sagging wall]. —**shored, shor′ing**

**shore·line** (shôr′līn) ***n.*** the edge of a body of water.

**shore·ward** (shôr′wərd) ***adj., adv.*** toward the shore [Two boats were headed *shoreward.*]

**shorn** (shôrn) *a past participle of* **shear.**

**short** (shôrt) ***adj.*** **1** not measuring much from end to end or from beginning to end; not long [a *short* stick; a *short* trip; a *short* novel; a *short* wait]. **2** not tall; low [a *short* tree]. **3** brief and rude [a *short* answer]. **4** less or having less than what is enough or correct [Our supply of food is *short.* We are *short* ten dollars.] **5** that tends to break or crumble; flaky [*short* pastry]. **6** taking a shorter time to say than other sounds [The "e" in "bed" and the "i" in "rib" are *short.*] ◆***n.*** **1** something short, especially a short movie. **2 shorts,** *pl.* short trousers reaching down part way to the knee; also, ☆a garment like this worn by men as underwear. **3** *same as* **short circuit.** ◆***adv.*** **1** suddenly [The car stopped *short.*] **2** in a brief or rude manner [I was cut off *short* by the next question.] **3** so as to be short [Cut your speech *short.* We fell *short* of our goal.] **4** by surprise; unawares [We were caught *short* by their sudden marriage.] ◆***v.*** **1** to give less than what is needed, usual, etc. [The cashier *shorted* the customer a dollar.] **2** *same as* **short-circuit.** —**for short,** as a shorter form [Thomas is called Tom *for short.*] —**in short,** in a few words; briefly. —**short for,** being a shorter form of ["Gym" is *short for* "gymnasium."] —**short of,** less than; not equal to [Nothing *short of* perfection will satisfy her.] —**short′ness** ***n.***

☆**short·age** (shôrt′ij) ***n.*** a lack in the amount that is needed or expected [a *shortage* of help].

**short·bread** (shôrt′bred) ***n.*** a rich, crumbly cake or cookie made with much shortening.
**short·cake** (shôrt′kāk) ***n.*** a dessert made with a light biscuit or sweet cake covered with fruit and whipped cream [strawberry *shortcake*].
☆**short·change** (shôrt′chānj′) ***v.*** to give less money than is due in change. —**short′changed′, short′-chang′ing**
**short-cir·cuit** (shôrt′sur′kit) ***v.*** to make a short circuit in.
**short circuit** an electric circuit that has a lower resistance than is normal, causing too much current to flow. A short circuit is most often accidental, and so to avoid a fire or other damage, it usually causes a fuse to melt, thus breaking the circuit.
**short·com·ing** (shôrt′kum′ing) ***n.*** a fault or weakness, as in one's character.
**short cut** **1** a shorter way of getting to a place. **2** any way of saving time, money, etc.
**short·en** (shôrt′'n) ***v.*** **1** to make or become short or shorter [to *shorten* a skirt]. **2** to add shortening to, as pastry.
**short·en·ing** (shôrt′'n ing) ***n.*** **1** the act of making or becoming short or shorter. **2** butter, vegetable oil, or other fat used in pastry to make it flaky.
**short·hand** (shôrt′hand) ***n.*** any system for writing fast by using special symbols in place of letters, words, and phrases. ◆***adj.*** written in or using shorthand. *See the picture.*
**short-hand·ed** (shôrt′han′did) ***adj.*** not having enough workers or helpers.
**short·horn** (shôrt′hôrn) ***n.*** a breed of cattle with short horns, raised for beef and milk.
**short-lived** (shôrt′līvd′ *or* shôrt′livd′) ***adj.*** living or lasting only a short time [a *short-lived* TV show].
**short·ly** (shôrt′lē) ***adv.*** **1** in a short time; soon [I'll leave *shortly*.] **2** in a few words; briefly [to put it *shortly*]. **3** briefly and rudely [to answer *shortly*].
**short-range** (shôrt′rānj′) ***adj.*** **1** having a range of only a short distance [a *short-range* missile]. **2** not looking far into the future [*short-range* plans].
**short shrift** very little care or attention, as from a lack of patience or sympathy [We were given *short shrift* at the information booth.]
**short·sight·ed** (shôrt′sīt′id) ***adj.*** **1** *another word for* **nearsighted**. **2** not looking ahead or planning for the future. —**short′sight′ed·ness** ***n.***
☆**short·stop** (shôrt′stäp) ***n.*** a baseball player whose position is between second and third base.
**short story** a kind of story that is shorter than a novel. It usually has only a few characters and takes place over a short period of time.
**short-tem·pered** (shôrt′tem′pərd) ***adj.*** easily made angry; tending to lose one's temper.
**short·wave** (shôrt′wāv′) ***n.*** a radio wave 60 meters or less in length. Overseas broadcasts are sent by shortwaves.
**short-wind·ed** (shôrt′win′did) ***adj.*** breathing hard or easily put out of breath [I am *short-winded* from running.]
**shot**[1] (shät) ***n.*** **1** the act or sound of shooting a gun or cannon [I heard a *shot*.] **2** the distance that a sound, a bullet, etc. travels or can travel [We were no longer within ear*shot*.] **3** an attempt to hit something, as with a bullet or rocket [The first *shot* missed. They

**shoe tree**

"This is a sample of shorthand writing"

**shoehorn**

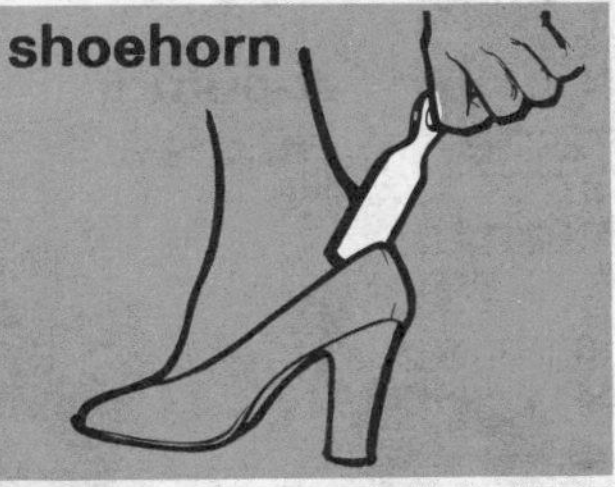

**shot–putter**

**shores**

will try another moon*shot*.] **4** any attempt or try; also, a guess [Take a *shot* at answering the riddle.] **5** an unkind remark [a parting *shot*]. **6** a throw, drive, etc., as of a ball, in certain games [He got two free *shots* at the basket.] **7** something to be fired from a gun, as a bullet or small metal ball; also, a number of such balls in a casing [gun*shot*]. **8** the ball used in the shot put: *see* **shot put**. **9** a person who shoots [She's a good *shot*.] ☆**10** a single photograph. ☆**11** an injection, as of a vaccine. ☆**12** a single drink of liquor. —**like a shot**, quickly or suddenly.



**shot**[2] (shät) *past tense and past participle of* **shoot**. ◆***adj.*** **1** streaked with another color [a green dress *shot* with blue]. ☆**2** worn out or ruined: *used only in everyday talk* [I think this radio is *shot*.]
☆**shot·gun** (shät′gun) ***n.*** a gun for firing cartridges filled with shot, or little metal balls.
**shot put** (shät′ poot′) a contest in which athletes throw a heavy metal ball from above the height of the shoulder, to see who can throw it the farthest. *See the picture.* —**shot′-put′ter** ***n.***
**should** (shood) *past tense of* **shall** [I thought I *should* never see her again.]

**Should** is also used as a helping verb in speaking of something that is likely to happen or might happen [It *should* rain tomorrow. If I *should* go, would you care?] or of something that one ought to do [We *should* obey the law.] *Would* is sometimes used in place of *should*.

| | | | |
|---|---|---|---|
| **a** fat | **ir** here | **ou** out | **zh** leisure |
| **ā** ape | **ī** bite, fire | **u** up | **ng** ring |
| **ä** car, lot | **ō** go | **ur** fur | a *in* ago |
| **e** ten | **ô** law, horn | **ch** chin | e *in* agent |
| **er** care | **oi** oil | **sh** she | **ə** = i *in* unity |
| **ē** even | **oo** look | **th** thin | o *in* collect |
| **i** hit | **ōō** tool | ***th*** then | u *in* focus |

shuffleboard

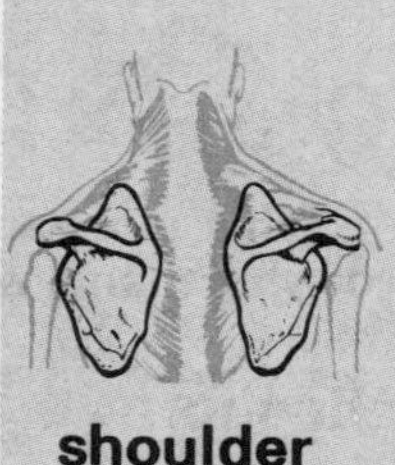
shoulder blades

girl shrugging her shoulders

16 cm (6 in.) long, including tail

shrew

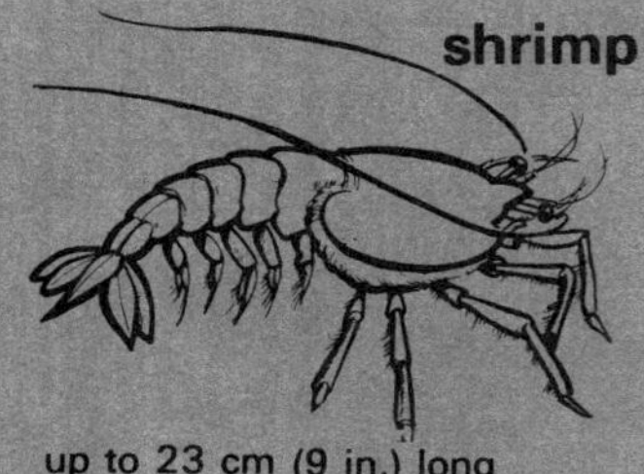
shrimp

up to 23 cm (9 in.) long

**shoul·der** (shōl′dər) ***n.*** **1** the part of the body to which an arm or foreleg is connected. **2 shoulders,** the two shoulders and the part of the back between them. **3** a cut of meat including the upper part of an animal's foreleg and the parts near it. **4** the part of a garment that covers the shoulder. **5** a part that sticks



out like a shoulder. ☆**6** the edge of a road. ◆***v.*** **1** to push with the shoulder [I had to *shoulder* my way into the room.] **2** to carry on the shoulder. **3** to take on the responsibility of [to *shoulder* a task]. —**give someone the cold shoulder,** to snub or be unfriendly to someone. —**put one's shoulder to the wheel,** to start working hard; use extra effort. —**shoulder arms,** to rest a rifle against the shoulder, holding the butt with the hand. —**shoulder to shoulder, 1** side by side and close together. **2** working together. —**straight from the shoulder,** directly to the point; without holding back; frankly.

**shoulder blade** either of two flat bones in the upper back. *See the picture.*

**shoulder strap** a strap worn over the shoulder as for holding up a garment or carrying a purse.

**should·n't** (shood′′nt) should not.

**shouldst** (shoodst) *an older form of* **should,** *used with* thou, *as in the Bible.*

**shout** (shout) ***n.*** a sudden, loud cry or call. ◆***v.*** to say or cry out in a loud voice. —**shout someone down,** to make someone be quiet by shouting at that person. —**shout′er *n.***

**shove** (shuv) ***v.*** **1** to push, as along a surface [*Shove* the chair across the room.] **2** to push roughly [to *shove* others aside]. *See* SYNONYMS *at* **push.** —**shoved, shov′ing** ◆***n.*** a push or thrust. —**shove off, 1** to push a boat away from shore. ☆**2** to start off; leave: *used only in everyday talk.*

**shov·el** (shuv′′l) ***n.*** **1** a tool with a broad scoop and a handle, for lifting and moving loose material. **2** *a shorter form of* **shovelful. 3** a machine with a part like a shovel, used for digging or moving large amounts of loose material [a steam *shovel*]. ◆***v.*** **1** to lift and move with a shovel [to *shovel* coal]. **2** to dig out with a shovel [When the snowstorm stopped, they all began to *shovel* their walks.] **3** to put in large amounts [to *shovel* food into one's mouth]. —**shov′eled** or **shov′elled, shov′el·ing** or **shov′el·ling**

**shov·el·ful** (shuv′′l fool) ***n.*** as much as a shovel will hold. —*pl.* **shov′el·fuls**

**show** (shō) ***v.*** **1** to bring in sight; allow to be seen; display; reveal [*Show* us the new fashions. His red face *showed* his anger.] **2** to be or become seen; appear [Daylight began to *show* in the sky.] **3** to guide or lead [*Show* her to her room.] **4** to point out [We *showed* them the sights of the city. A thermometer *shows* the temperature.] **5** to be easily noticed [The stain won't *show*.] **6** to make clear; explain, prove, or teach [He *showed* how it could be done.] **7** to give or grant; bestow [She has *shown* many favors to us.] **8** to come or arrive as expected: *used only in everyday talk* [They haven't *shown* yet.] —**showed, shown** or **showed, show′ing** ◆***n.*** **1** the act of showing [a *show* of anger; a *show* of hands]. **2** a collection of things shown publicly; display [an art *show*]. **3** a performance of a play or movie, a radio or TV program, etc. **4** something false or pretended [Her sorrow is a mere *show*.] **5** something meant to attract attention [a great *show* of wealth]. —**for show,** in order to attract attention. —**show off, 1** to make a display of [to *show off* one's new clothes]. **2** to do something meant to attract attention [He likes to *show off* by quoting from many writers.] —**show up, 1** to make easily seen; expose, as faults. **2** to be clearly seen; stand out. **3** to come or arrive.

SYNONYMS: **Show** suggests a putting or bringing something into view so that it can be seen or looked at [*Show* us the garden.] To **display** something is to spread it out so that it can be shown in a way that will get the result that is wanted [jewelry *displayed* on a sales counter].

☆**show·boat** (shō′bōt) ***n.*** a boat with a theater and actors, giving shows in river towns.

☆**show business** the theater, movies, TV, etc. thought of as a business or industry.

☆**show·case** (shō′kās) ☆***n.*** a glass case in which things are put on display, as in a store.

☆**show·down** (shō′doun) ***n.*** the act of laying open all the true facts, so as to force a final settlement: *used only in everyday talk.*

**show·er** (shou′ər) ***n.*** **1** a short fall of rain or hail. **2** a sudden, very full fall or flow, as of sparks, praise, etc. ☆**3** a party at which gifts are given to the guest of honor [a *shower* for the bride]. ☆**4** a bath in which the body is sprayed with fine streams of water. *The full name is* **shower bath.** ☆**5** a device that sprays water for such a bath. ◆***v.*** **1** to spray or sprinkle with water. **2** to give much or many of [They *showered* praise upon her.] **3** to fall or come in a shower. **4** to bathe under a shower.

**show·ing** (shō′ing) ***n.*** **1** a display or exhibit [a *showing* of sculpture]. ☆**2** an appearance or result [He made a good *showing* in the music contest.]

**show·man** (shō′mən) ***n.*** a person whose business is giving shows to entertain people. —*pl.* **show′men** —**show′man·ship *n.***

**shown** (shōn) *a past participle of* **show.**

**show·off** (shō′ôf) ***n.*** a person who shows off, or does things to attract attention.

☆**show window** a store window in which things for sale are displayed.

**show·y** (shō′ē) ***adj.*** **1** bright or colorful in an attractive way [a *showy* flower]. **2** too bright or flashy; gaudy. —**show′i·er, show′i·est** —**show′i·ly** ***adv.*** —**show′i·ness** ***n.***

**shrank** (shrangk) *a past tense of* **shrink.**

**shrap·nel** (shrap′n′l) ***n.*** **1** an artillery shell filled with an explosive and with many small metal balls that scatter in the air when the shell explodes. **2** such metal balls or pieces of a shell case scattered by an exploding shell.

Many things get their names from the persons who developed them. **Shrapnel** is such a thing. It is named after a British general, Henry Shrapnel, who invented it in 1784.

**shred** (shred) ***n.*** **1** a long, narrow strip or piece cut or torn off [My shirt was torn to *shreds.*] **2** a tiny piece or amount; fragment [a story without a *shred* of truth]. ◆***v.*** to cut or tear into shreds [*shredded* coconut]. —**shred′ded** or **shred, shred′ding**

**shrew** (shro͞o) ***n.*** **1** a tiny animal like a mouse, but smaller, with soft, brown fur and a long snout. *See the picture.* **2** a woman who is always scolding and nagging. —**shrew′ish** ***adj.***

**shriek** (shrēk) ***n.*** a loud, sharp, shrill cry; screech; scream. *See* SYNONYMS *at* **scream.** ◆***v.*** to cry out with a shriek [to *shriek* in terror].

**shrift** (shrift) *see* **short shrift.**

**shrike** (shrīk) ***n.*** a bird with a shrill cry and a hooked beak. Shrikes catch insects, small birds, frogs, etc., often hanging them on thorns or branches before eating them.

**shrill** (shril) ***adj.*** having or making a sharp, high sound [a *shrill* voice; a *shrill* whistle]. ◆***v.*** to make a sharp, high sound. —**shrill′ness** ***n.*** —**shril′ly** ***adv.***

**shrimp** (shrimp) ***n.*** **1** a small shellfish with a long tail, used as food. *See the picture.* **2** a small or short person: *used only in everyday talk.*

**shrine** (shrīn) ***n.*** **1** something with sacred relics inside it, as the tomb of a saint. **2** a place of worship, usually one whose center is a sacred scene or object. **3** a place or thing held in honor because of someone or something important connected with it [Mount Vernon is an American *shrine.*]

**shrink** (shringk) ***v.*** **1** to make or become smaller by drawing the parts together [Wool often *shrinks* when it is washed.] **2** to become fewer in number or less in worth [The value of the dollar has been *shrinking.*] **3** to draw back, as from fear. —**shrank** or **shrunk, shrunk** or **shrunk′en, shrink′ing**

**shrink·age** (shringk′ij) ***n.*** **1** the act or process of shrinking. **2** the amount of shrinking.

**shrive** (shrīv) ***v.*** **1** to listen to a confession and then give absolution, as a priest does. **2** to show that one is sorry for one's sins in order to get absolution. *This word is no longer much used.* —**shrived** or **shrove** (shrōv), **shriv·en** (shriv″n) or **shrived, shriv′ing**

**shriv·el** (shriv″l) ***v.*** to curl up and shrink or wither [Without water, the flowers *shriveled* up and died.] —**shriv′eled** or **shriv′elled, shriv′el·ing** or **shriv′el·ling**

**shroud** (shroud) ***n.*** **1** a sheet in which a dead person is sometimes wrapped before being buried. **2** something that covers or hides; veil. **3** any of the ropes stretched from a ship's side to the top of a mast to help keep the mast straight. *See the picture at* **ratline.** ◆***v.*** **1** to wrap a dead person in a shroud. **2** to hide from view; cover; screen [The town is *shrouded* in darkness.]

**shrove** (shrōv) *a past tense of* **shrive.**

**Shrove Tuesday** the day before Ash Wednesday.

**shrub** (shrub) ***n.*** a woody plant that is smaller than a tree and has a number of stems instead of a single trunk; bush.

**shrub·ber·y** (shrub′ər ē) ***n.*** a group or heavy growth of shrubs, as around a house.

**shrub·by** (shrub′ē) ***adj.*** **1** covered with shrubs [*shrubby* land]. **2** like a shrub [a *shrubby* plant]. —**shrub′bi·er, shrub′bi·est**

**shrug** (shrug) ***v.*** to draw up the shoulders, as in showing that one does not care or does not know. —**shrugged, shrug′ging** ◆***n.*** the act of shrugging. *See the picture.* —**shrug off,** to put out of one's mind in a carefree way [He simply *shrugs off* his troubles.]

**Shrug** comes from an Old English word meaning "to shiver." When we shiver because of the cold or from fear, the shoulders are often drawn up in the same way as when we shrug.

**shrunk** (shrungk) *a past tense and past participle of* **shrink.**

**shrunk·en** (shrungk″n) *a past participle of* **shrink.**

**shuck** (shuk) ***n.*** a shell, pod, or husk. ◆***v.*** **1** to remove the shucks of [to *shuck* corn]. **2** to remove like a shuck [I *shucked* my coat upon entering.] 

**shud·der** (shud′ər) ***v.*** to shake or tremble in a sudden and violent way [I *shuddered* with fear.] *See* SYNONYMS *at* **shake.** ◆***n.*** the act of shuddering; a sudden, strong trembling.

**shuf·fle** (shuf″l) ***v.*** **1** to move the feet with a dragging motion, as in walking or dancing. **2** to mix playing cards so as to change their order. **3** to push or mix together in a jumbled way [He *shuffled* his clothes into a bag.] **4** to keep shifting from one place to another [She *shuffled* the papers about on her desk.] —**shuf′fled, shuf′fling** ◆***n.*** **1** the act of shuffling, as playing cards. **2** one's turn to shuffle playing cards. —**shuffle off,** to get rid of [Try to *shuffle off* your worry.] —**shuf′fler** ***n.***

**shuf·fle·board** (shuf″l bôrd) ***n.*** a game in which the players use long sticks to slide disks along a smooth lane, trying to get them on numbered sections. *See the picture.*

**shun** (shun) ***v.*** to keep away from; avoid [A hermit *shuns* other people.] —**shunned, shun′ning**

**shunt** (shunt) ***v.*** **1** to move or turn to one side; turn out of the way. **2** to switch a train from one track to another. ◆***n.*** **1** the act of shunting. **2** a railroad switch. **3** a wire connecting two points in an electric circuit and turning aside part of the current.

| | | | | | | | |
|---|---|---|---|---|---|---|---|
| **a** | fat | **ir** | here | **ou** | out | **zh** | leisure |
| **ā** | ape | **ī** | bite, fire | **u** | up | **ng** | ring |
| **ä** | car, lot | **ō** | go | **ur** | fur | | a *in* ago |
| **e** | ten | **ô** | law, horn | **ch** | chin | | e *in* agent |
| **er** | care | **oi** | oil | **sh** | she | **ə =** | i *in* unity |
| **ē** | even | **oo** | look | **th** | thin | | o *in* collect |
| **i** | hit | **o͞o** | tool | ***th*** | then | | u *in* focus |

**shush** (shush) ***interj.*** hush! be quiet! ◆***v.*** to tell to be quiet, as by saying "hush!" or "shush!"

**shut** (shut) ***v.*** **1** to move so as to close an opening [to *shut* a door or window]. **2** to fasten securely, as with a bolt. **3** to close the lid, doors, etc. of [to *shut* a chest]. **4** to fold up or close the parts of [to *shut* an umbrella]. **5** to stop or close, as a business or school. —**shut, shut′ting** ◆***adj.*** closed, fastened, locked up, etc. [Keep the lid *shut.*] —**shut down, 1** to close by lowering. **2** to stop work in, often just for a time [to *shut down* a factory]. —**shut in,** to surround or enclose; keep inside. —**shut off, 1** to keep from moving, flowing, etc. [to *shut off* the water]. **2** to stop movement into or out of [to *shut off* a street]. —**shut out, 1** to keep out; exclude [The curtains *shut out* the light.] ☆**2** to keep from scoring even once in a game. —**shut up, 1** to enclose or lock up, as in prison. **2** to close all ways of getting in. **3** to stop talking or make stop talking: *used only in everyday talk.*

☆**shut·down** (shut′doun) ***n.*** a stopping of work or activity for a time, as in a factory.

**shut-in** (shut′in′) ☆***n.*** a person who is too ill, weak, etc. to go out. ◆***adj.*** not able to go out.

**shut·ter** (shut′ər) ***n.*** **1** a cover for a window, usually swinging on hinges. *See the picture.* **2** a part on a camera that opens and closes in front of the lens to control the light going in. **3** a person or thing that shuts. ◆***v.*** to close or cover with shutters.

**shut·tle** (shut′′l) ***n.*** **1** a device in weaving that carries a thread back and forth between the threads that go up and down. *See the picture.* **2** a device on a sewing machine that carries the lower thread back and forth. ☆**3** a bus, train, or airplane that makes frequent trips back and forth over a short route. ◆***v.*** to move rapidly to and fro. —**shut′tled, shut′tling**

> **Shuttle** comes from an Old English word meaning "to shoot." The shuttle in weaving got its name because it is "shot" to and fro between the threads that are stretched up and down on a frame.

**shut·tle·cock** (shut′′l käk) ***n.*** a cork or plastic piece with feathers in one end, used in playing badminton.

**shy**[1] (shī) ***adj.*** **1** easily frightened; timid [a *shy* animal]. **2** not at ease with other people; bashful [a *shy* child]. **3** not having; lacking; short: *slang in this meaning* [It costs ten dollars, and I am *shy* two dollars.] —**shi′er** or **shy′er, shi′est** or **shy′est** ◆***v.*** **1** to move or pull back suddenly; start [The horse *shied* when the gun went off.] **2** to be cautious or unwilling [John *shied* at going in the deep water.] —**shied, shy′ing** —**shy′ly *adv.*** —**shy′ness *n.***

**shy**[2] (shī) ***v.*** to throw or toss with a jerk [*shying* stones at a target]. —**shied, shy′ing**

**si** (sē) ***n.*** *another name for* **ti.**

**Si** *the symbol for the chemical element* silicon.

**Si·am** (sī am′) *an earlier name for* **Thailand.** —**Si·a·mese** (sī ə mēz′) ***adj., n.***

**Siamese cat** a breed of cat with blue eyes and light-colored, short hair that is darker at the face, ears, paws, and tail. *See the picture.*

**Siamese twins** any pair of twins born joined to each other. A famous pair came from Siam.

**Si·ber·i·a** (sī bir′ē ə) a part of the U.S.S.R. in northern Asia, from the Ural Mountains to the Pacific. *See the map.* —**Si·ber′i·an *adj., n.***

**sib·ling** (sib′liŋ) ***n.*** a sister or brother.

**sib·yl** (sib′′l) ***n.*** any of certain women in ancient Greece and Rome who acted as prophets.

**sic**[1] (sik) ***v.*** to urge to attack [He *sicked* his dog on the burglar.] —**sicked, sick′ing**

**sic**[2] (sik) ***adv.*** thus; so.

> This Latin word is used in brackets, [*sic*], to show that a word or phrase in something that is being quoted is shown exactly as it appears and is not the quoter's mistake. Example: She wrote in her diary, "I will keep it as a momento [*sic*] of the trip."

**Sic·i·ly** (sis′′l ē) a large Italian island off the southwestern tip of Italy. —**Si·cil·ian** (si sil′yən) ***adj., n.***

**sick**[1] (sik) ***adj.*** **1** suffering from disease or illness; not well; ill [a *sick* baby; *sick* with the flu]. **2** having a feeling that makes one vomit or want to vomit; nauseated. **3** of or for people who are ill [*sick* leave]. **4** troubled by a feeling of sorrow or longing [*sick* over the loss of his dog]. **5** disgusted by too much of something; tired [I'm *sick* of your foolish excuses.] **6** unpleasant, disgusting, cruel, etc.: *used only in everyday talk* [a *sick* joke]. —**the sick,** sick people. —**sick′ness *n.***

**sick**[2] (sik) ***v.*** *another spelling of* **sic**[1].

**sick·en** (sik′′n) ***v.*** to make or become sick.

**sick·en·ing** (sik′′n iŋ) ***adj.*** causing sickness; making one want to vomit [a *sickening* smell].

**sick·ish** (sik′ish) ***adj.*** **1** somewhat sick or nauseated. **2** somewhat sick or sickening.

**sick·le** (sik′′l) ***n.*** a tool with a curved blade and a short handle, for cutting tall grass, weeds, etc. *See the picture.*

**sick·ly** (sik′lē) ***adj.*** **1** sick much of the time; in poor health [a *sickly* child]. **2** of or caused by sickness [a face having a *sickly* paleness]. **3** faint, weak, pale, dull, etc. [a *sickly* smile]. **4** sickening [a *sickly* smell]. —**sick′li·er, sick′li·est**

**side** (sīd) ***n.*** **1** the right or left half of the body [a pain in one's *side*]. **2** the position beside one [She never left my *side.*] **3** any of the lines or surfaces that bound something [A triangle has three *sides.* A cube has six *sides.*] **4** a surface of an object that is not the back or front, nor the top or bottom [a door at the *side* of a house]. **5** either of the two surfaces of paper, cloth, etc. [You may write on both *sides* of the sheet.] **6** a surface or part of a surface in a certain position [the inner *side* of a vase; the visible *side* of the moon]. **7** the sloping part [a house on the *side* of a hill]. **8** a place or direction as it is related in position to the person speaking [this *side* of the street; the other *side* of the lake]. **9** any area or place as it is related to a central line [the east *side* of town]. **10** a particular part or quality of a person or thing [his cruel *side;* the bright *side* of life]. **11** any of the groups against each other in a fight, argument, contest, etc. [The judges voted for our *side* in the debate.] **12** the ideas, opinions, or position of one person or group against another [My *side* of the quarrel is easy to explain.] **13** all the relatives of either one's mother or one's father [an uncle on my mother's *side*]. ◆***adj.*** **1** of, at, or on a side [a *side* door]. **2** to or from one side [a *side* glance]. **3** done, happening, etc. as something in addition [a *side* effect]. **4** not main or most important [a *side* issue]. ◆***v.*** to take the same position or hold the same views in an argument or quarrel [The council *sided* with the mayor.] —**sid′ed, sid′ing** —☆**on the side,** as extra work, activity, etc. —**side by side,** beside one another; together. —**take sides,** to give help or support to one person or group in a fight or argument.

☆**side·arm** (sīd′ärm) ***adj., adv.*** with the arm sweeping forward from the side of the body [a *sidearm* pitch].

**side·board** (sīd′bôrd) ***n.*** a piece of furniture, as in a dining room, with drawers and shelves for holding dishes, silverware, linen, etc.

☆**side·burns** (sīd′burnz) ***n.pl.*** the hair on the sides of a man's face, just in front of the ears.

**sid·ed** (sīd′id) ***adj.*** having sides: *used in words formed with a hyphen* [six-*sided*].

**side·line** (sīd′līn) ***n.*** **1** either of the lines that mark the side limits of a playing area, as in football. **2 sidelines,** *pl.* the space just outside these lines [Reporters stood on the *sidelines.*] **3** an extra line of goods or work apart from the main one [Dr. Yen raises orchids as a *sideline.*] —☆**on the sidelines,** not taking part in an active way.

**side·long** (sīd′lông) ***adj., adv.*** toward or to the side [a *sidelong* glance]. *See the picture.*

**si·de·re·al** (sī dir′ē əl) ***adj.*** **1** of the stars or constellations. **2** measured by what seems to be the motion of the stars [a *sidereal* day].

☆**side·show** (sīd′shō) ***n.*** a small, separate show in connection with a main show, as of a circus.

☆**side·step** (sīd′step) ***v.*** to keep away from as by stepping aside. —**side′stepped, side′step·ping**

☆**side·swipe** (sīd′swīp) ***v.*** to hit along the side in passing [Another car must have *sideswiped* yours to make that dent.] —**side′swiped, side′swip·ing**

☆**side·track** (sīd′trak) ***v.*** **1** to switch a train from a main track to a siding. **2** to turn away from the main subject [I got *sidetracked* by all that talk about food.] ◆***n.*** a railroad siding.

☆**side·walk** (sīd′wôk) ***n.*** a path for walking, usually paved, along the side of a street.

**side·ways** (sīd′wāz) ***adv.*** **1** from the side [Seen *sideways,* it looks quite thin.] **2** with one side toward the front [He turned his head *sideways* to show his profile.] **3** toward one side [The car skidded *sideways* on the ice.] ◆***adj.*** toward one side [a *sideways* glance].

**side·wise** (sīd′wīz) ***adj., adv.*** *same as* **sideways.**

**sid·ing** (sīd′ing) ***n.*** ☆**1** a covering, especially of overlapping boards, etc., for an outside wall. **2** a short railroad track onto which cars can be switched from the main track. *See the picture on page 689.*

**si·dle** (sī′d′l) ***v.*** to move sideways, especially in a shy or sneaky way [She *sidled* past the guard.] —**si′dled, si′dling**

**siege** (sēj) ***n.*** **1** the surrounding of a city, fort, etc. by an enemy army trying to capture it. **2** any stubborn and continued effort to win or control something. ☆**3** a long, difficult period [a *siege* of illness]. —**lay siege to,** to force a siege on.

**si·en·na** (sē en′ə) ***n.*** **1** a kind of clay used as a yellowish-brown or reddish-brown coloring matter in paints. **2** either of these colors.

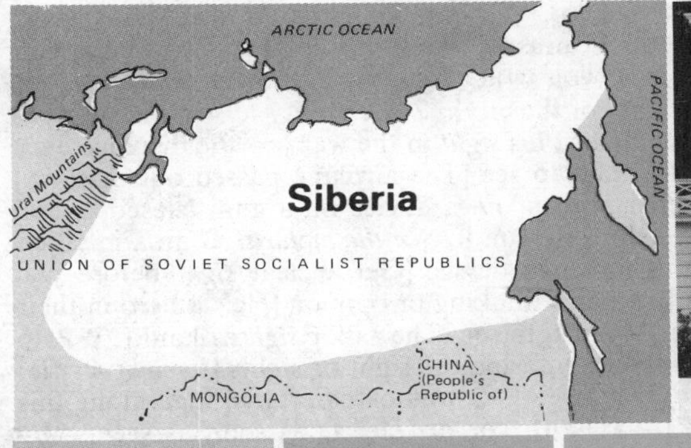

shutters

Siamese cat

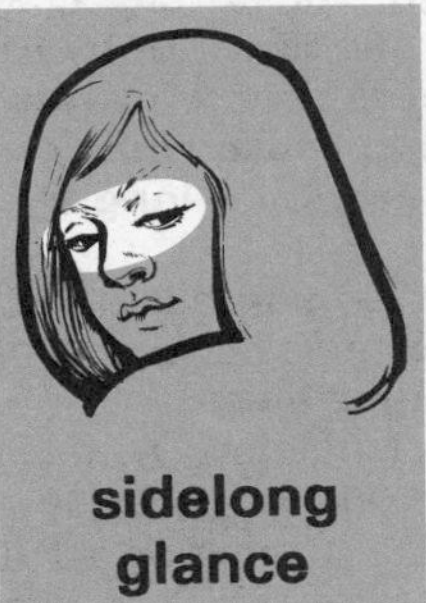
sidelong glance

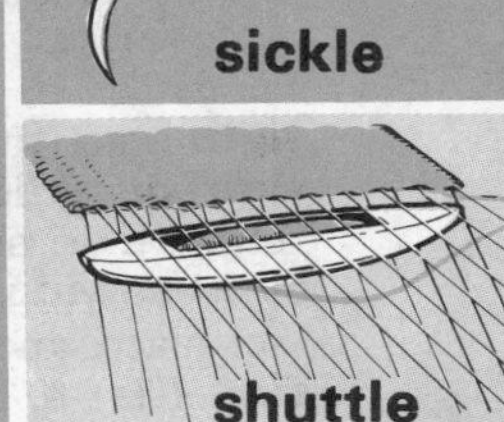
sickle

shuttle

**si·er·ra** (sē er′ə) ***n.*** a chain of mountains whose peaks look like the edge of a saw.

**Si·er·ra Le·one** (sē er′ə lē ōn′) a country on the western coast of Africa. 

**Sierra Nevada** a mountain range in eastern California. *Also called* **the Si·er·ras** (sē er′əz).

**si·es·ta** (sē es′tə) ***n.*** a short nap or rest taken after the noon meal, as in Spain or Mexico.

> **Siesta** is a Spanish word that comes from a Latin phrase, *sexta hora,* meaning "the sixth hour" after sunrise. This is about noon, usually the hottest part of the day in Spain and many Latin American countries.

**sieve** (siv) ***n.*** a strainer for separating liquids from solids or tiny pieces from large ones.

**sift** (sift) ***v.*** **1** to pass through a sieve so as to separate the large pieces from the tiny ones [to *sift* sand so as to remove pebbles]. **2** to come down as if through a sieve [Sunshine *sifted* through the clouds.] **3** to examine with care so as to separate the true from the false [The jury *sifted* the evidence.] **4** to scatter or sprinkle as through a sieve [*Sift* flour over the bottom of the pan.] —**sift′er** ***n.***

**sigh** (sī) ***v.*** **1** to let out a long, deep, sounded breath, usually to show that one is sad, tired, relieved, etc. **2** to make a sound like a sigh [trees *sighing* in the wind]. **3** to feel sadness or longing [He *sighed* for the old days.] ◆***n.*** the act or sound of sighing [She breathed a *sigh* of relief.]

| | | | | | | | |
|---|---|---|---|---|---|---|---|
| **a** | fat | **ir** | here | **ou** | out | **zh** | leisure |
| **ā** | ape | **ī** | bite, fire | **u** | up | **ng** | ring |
| **ä** | car, lot | **ō** | go | **ur** | fur | | a *in* ago |
| **e** | ten | **ô** | law, horn | **ch** | chin | | e *in* agent |
| **er** | care | **oi** | oil | **sh** | she | **ə =** | i *in* unity |
| **ē** | even | **oo** | look | **th** | thin | | o *in* collect |
| **i** | hit | **ōō** | tool | ***th*** | then | | u *in* focus |

**S**

**sight** (sīt) ***n.*** **1** something that is seen; especially, something unusual worth seeing [The Grand Canyon is a *sight* you won't forget.] **2** the act of seeing [our first *sight* of the city]. **3** the ability to see; vision; eyesight [He lost his *sight* in the war.] **4** the distance over which one can see [The airplane passed out of *sight*.] **5** *often* **sights,** *pl.* a device on a gun, telescope, etc. that helps one aim it. *See the picture.* **6** an aim taken through such a device [Get a clear *sight* before you fire.] **7** one's thinking or opinion [He's a hero in their *sight*.] ◆***v.*** **1** to see [The sailor *sighted* land.] ☆**2** to aim carefully, using the sight or sights [to *sight* a rifle; to *sight* a target]. **3** to look carefully [*Sight* along this line.] —**at sight** or **on sight,** as soon as seen. —**by sight,** by having seen, not by having known [I know her only *by sight*.] —**catch sight of,** to see, especially briefly; glimpse. —**lose sight of,** **1** to see no longer. **2** to forget. —**not by a long sight,** not nearly or not at all.

**sight·less** (sīt′lis) ***adj.*** blind; unable to see.

**sight·ly** (sīt′lē) ***adj.*** pleasing to look at; attractive. —**sight′li·er, sight′li·est**

**sight·see·ing** (sīt′sē′iŋ) ***n.*** the act of going about to see places and things of interest. —**sight′se′er** ***n.***

**sign** (sīn) ***n.*** **1** a thing or act that stands for something else; symbol [Black is worn as a *sign* of grief. She saluted the flag as a *sign* of respect. The *sign* + means "add."] **2** a board, card, etc. put up in a public place, with information, a warning, etc. on it [The *sign* said, "Do not enter."] **3** anything that tells of the existence or coming of something else [Red spots on the face may be a *sign* of measles.] ◆***v.*** **1** to write one's name on [to *sign* a contract to make it legal]. **2** to hire by getting to sign a contract [The baseball club *signed* five new players.] —**sign off,** **1** in radio and TV, to stop broadcasting, especially for the night. **2** to stop talking: *slang in this meaning.* —**sign up,** **1** to hire or be hired: *also* **sign on.** **2** to enlist, as in the army.

SYNONYMS: **Sign** is used broadly to mean an action, event, or condition that points to a fact or carries a meaning [Flowers are a *sign* of spring. Spots on apples are *signs* of decay.] **Token** suggests something used as a symbol or sign of some feeling, value, etc. [The gift is a *token* of good will.] A **symptom** is an outward sign of some disease or disorder [A cough is a *symptom* of a cold. Feeling persecuted may be a *symptom* of mental illness.]

**sig·nal** (sig′n'l) ***n.*** **1** something that tells when some action is to start or end, or is used as a warning or direction [A loud bell is the *signal* for a fire drill. The traffic *signal* is green, telling us to go.] **2** the electrical waves sent out or received as sounds or pictures in radio and television. ◆***adj.*** **1** used as a signal [a *signal* light]. **2** not ordinary; remarkable [The discovery of radium was a *signal* achievement.] ◆***v.*** **1** to make a signal or signals to [The driver *signaled* for a turn. The police officer *signaled* us to drive on.] **2** to make known by means of signals [The ship *signaled* it was sinking.] —**sig′naled** or **sig′nalled, sig′nal·ing** or **sig′nal·ling**

**signal corps** the part of an army in charge of communications, as by radio.

**sig·nal·ize** (sig′n'l īz) ***v.*** to make known or worth noticing [Rodin's career was *signalized* by great achievements.] —**sig′nal·ized, sig′nal·iz·ing**

**sig·nal·ly** (sig′n'l ē) ***adv.*** in an unusual or outstanding way [She was *signally* honored.]

**sig·na·ture** (sig′nə chər) ***n.*** **1** a person's name as he or she has written it. **2** a sign in music placed at the beginning of a staff to give the key or the time.

**sign·board** (sīn′bôrd) ***n.*** a board on which a sign with advertising has been painted or pasted.

**sig·net** (sig′nit) ***n.*** **1** a seal or other mark stamped on a paper to make it official. **2** a device used to make such a mark.

**signet ring** a finger ring with a signet engraved on it, often in the form of an initial or monogram.

**sig·nif·i·cance** (sig nif′ə kəns) ***n.*** **1** meaning or sense [I don't understand the *significance* of her remark.] *See* SYNONYMS *at* **meaning.** **2** importance [Gettysburg was a battle of great *significance*.] *See* SYNONYMS *at* **importance.**

**sig·nif·i·cant** (sig nif′ə kənt) ***adj.*** **1** important; full of meaning [The President gave a *significant* speech.] **2** having a meaning, especially a hidden one [She gave him a *significant* wink.] —**sig·nif′i·cant·ly** ***adv.***

**sig·ni·fy** (sig′nə fī) ***v.*** **1** to be a sign of; mean [What does the sign ÷ *signify*?] **2** to make known by a sign, words, etc. [*Signify* your approval by saying "aye."] —**sig′ni·fied, sig′ni·fy·ing**

**sign language** communication of thoughts by means of gestures with the fingers, hands, and arms.

**si·gnor** (sē nyôr′) ***n.*** an Italian word used, like "Mr.," as a title for a man.

**si·gno·ra** (sē nyô′rä) ***n.*** an Italian word used, like "Mrs.," as a title for a married woman.

**si·gno·ri·na** (sē′nyô rē′nä) ***n.*** an Italian word used, like "Miss," as a title for an unmarried woman or girl.

**sign·post** (sīn′pōst) ***n.*** a post with a sign on it, as for showing a route or direction.

**Sikh** (sēk) ***n.*** a member of a religious sect of India.

**si·lage** (sī′lij) ***n.*** green cornstalks, grasses, etc. stored in a silo as food for cattle; ensilage.

**si·lence** (sī′ləns) ***n.*** **1** a keeping still and not speaking, making noise, etc. [His *silence* meant he agreed.] **2** absence of any sound or noise; stillness [There was complete *silence* in the deep forest.] **3** failure to keep in touch, write letters, etc. ◆***v.*** **1** to make silent; to still [*Silence* the dog's barking.] **2** to put down; overcome [The army *silenced* the rebellion against the government.] —**si′lenced, si′lenc·ing** ◆***interj.*** be silent! keep still! —**si′lenc·er** ***n.***

**si·lent** (sī′lənt) ***adj.*** **1** not speaking or not talking much. **2** with no sound or noise; noiseless [Find a *silent* place to study. We went to a *silent* movie.] **3** not spoken or told [*silent* grief; the *silent* "b" in "debt"]. **4** not active [a *silent* partner]. —**si′lent·ly** ***adv.***

**Si·le·sia** (sī lē′shə) a region in eastern Europe, mainly in what is now southwestern Poland. —**Si·le′sian** ***n., adj.***

**sil·hou·ette** (sil′o͞o wet′) ***n.*** **1** an outline drawing, in black or some solid color, especially of a profile. *See the picture.* **2** any dark shape seen against a light background. ◆***v.*** to show as a silhouette [birds *silhouetted* against the sky]. —**sil′hou·et′ted, sil′hou·et′ting**

**sil·i·ca** (sil′i kə) ***n.*** a glassy mineral found in various forms, as sand, quartz, etc.

**sil·i·cate** (sil′i kit) ***n.*** any of certain compounds containing silicon [Asbestos is a *silicate* of calcium and magnesium.]

**sil·i·con** (sil′i kən *or* sil′i kän′) ***n.*** a chemical element that is not a metal and is always found combined with something else, as with oxygen in silica. Silicon is, except for oxygen, the most common element found in nature.

**sil·i·cone** (sil′i kōn′) ***n.*** a substance containing silicon, used in polishes, oils, salves, etc.

**sil·i·co·sis** (sil′ə kō′sis) ***n.*** a lung disease caused in miners, stonecutters, etc. by breathing in silica dust over a long period of time.

**silk** (silk) ***n.*** **1** the fine, soft fiber spun by silkworms to form their cocoons. **2** thread or cloth made from this fiber. **3** anything like silk, as the fibers in the tassels of corn or in milkweed pods. ◆***adj.*** of or like silk; silken.

**silk·en** (sil′k′n) ***adj.*** **1** made of silk [a *silken* gown]. **2** like silk; shiny, soft, smooth, etc. [*silken* hair; *silken* words].

**silk·worm** (silk′wurm) ***n.*** a moth caterpillar that spins silk fiber to make its cocoon.

**silk·y** (sil′kē) ***adj.*** of or like silk; soft, smooth, etc. [*silky* fur; a *silky* voice]. —**silk′i·er, silk′i·est** —**silk′i·ness** ***n.***

**sill** (sil) ***n.*** a board or a slab of stone that forms the bottom of the frame in a door or window.

**sil·ly** (sil′ē) ***adj.*** **1** not having or showing good sense; foolish; unwise. **2** dazed or stunned: *used only in everyday talk* [The blow on his head knocked him *silly*.] —**sil′li·er, sil′li·est** ◆***n.*** a silly person. —*pl.* **sil′lies** —**sil′li·ness** ***n.***

> **Silly** comes from an Old English word that meant "happy" or "blessed." In Chaucer's time it came to mean "good" or "innocent." In other early senses no longer used, it meant "feeble and helpless" or "feebleminded." Now the most common sense is "foolish."

**si·lo** (sī′lō) ***n.*** an airtight tower for storing silage, or green fodder. *See the picture.* —*pl.* **si′los**

**silt** (silt) ***n.*** tiny particles of sand or soil, floating in or left by water. ◆***v.*** to fill up or choke with silt, as a river bottom. —**silt′y** ***adj.***

**sil·ver** (sil′vər) ***n.*** **1** a white precious metal that is a chemical element. Silver is soft and easy to mold and polish. **2** silver coins [two dollars in *silver*]. **3** tableware made of silver, as spoons, forks, dishes, etc. **4** the grayish-white color of silver. **5** something like silver in color, value, etc. [Her hair has turned to *silver*.] ◆***adj.*** **1** of or containing silver [a *silver* tray; *silver* thread]. **2** having the color of silver. **3** having a silvery tone. **4** marking the 25th anniversary [a *silver* wedding]. ◆***v.*** **1** to cover with silver or something like silver [to *silver* a mirror]. **2** to make or become silvery in color.

**sil·ver·smith** (sil′vər smith) ***n.*** a skilled worker who makes things of silver.

☆**sil·ver·ware** (sil′vər wer) ***n.*** things, especially tableware, made of or plated with silver.

**sil·ver·y** (sil′vər ē) ***adj.*** **1** having the color of silver [the *silvery* moon]. **2** soft and clear like the sound of a silver bell.

silo

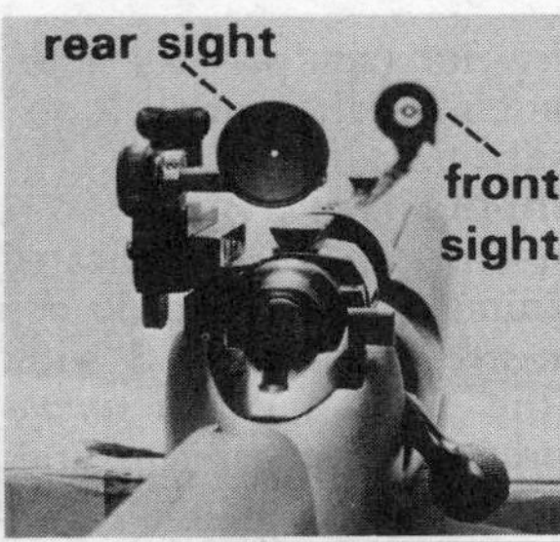


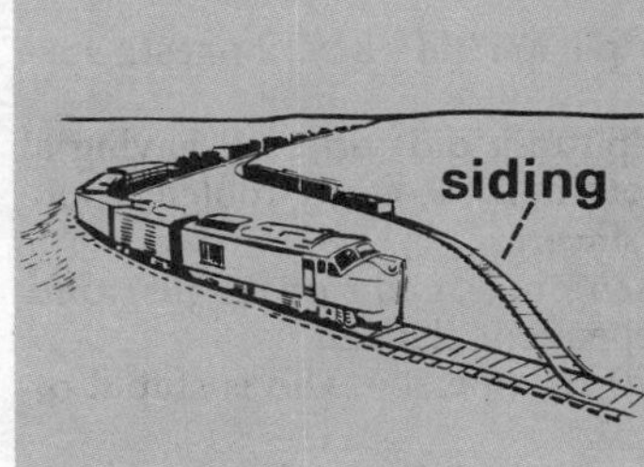

silhouette

**sim·i·an** (sim′ē ən) ***adj.*** of or like an ape or monkey. ◆***n.*** an ape or monkey.

> **Simian** is thought to come from a Latin word that means "flat-nosed," because of the flat noses that most apes and monkeys have.

**sim·i·lar** (sim′ə lər) ***adj.*** almost but not exactly the same; alike [Your ideas are *similar* to mine.] —**sim′i·lar·ly** ***adv.***



**sim·i·lar·i·ty** (sim′ə lar′ə tē) ***n.*** **1** the state of being similar; likeness. **2** a similar point or feature. —*pl.* **sim′i·lar′i·ties**

**sim·i·le** (sim′ə lē) ***n.*** a figure of speech in which two things that are different in most ways are said to be alike, by using either the word *as* or *like* [He's as thin as a rail" and "She sings like a bird" are *similes*.] —*pl.* **sim′i·les**

**si·mil·i·tude** (sə mil′ə to͞od *or* sə mil′ə tyo͞od) ***n.*** likeness or similarity.

**sim·mer** (sim′ər) ***v.*** **1** to keep at or just below the boiling point, usually forming tiny bubbles with a murmuring sound [*Simmer* the stew about two hours.] **2** to be about to lose control of oneself [I *simmered* with rage because I had been cheated.] ◆***n.*** the condition of simmering [Keep the meat at a *simmer*.] —**simmer down, 1** to simmer until little is left. ☆**2** to become calm; cool off.

**Si·mon** (sī′mən) *another name for* **Peter,** the Apostle.

**si·mo·ny** (sī′mə nē *or* sim′ə nē) ***n.*** the buying or selling of sacred things, as an office in a church or pardon for a sin.

**si·moom** (si mo͞om′) ***n.*** a very strong, hot wind blowing sand in the deserts of Africa or Asia: *also* **si·moon** (si mo͞on′).

| | | | | | | | |
|---|---|---|---|---|---|---|---|
| **a** | fat | **ir** | here | **ou** | out | **zh** | leisure |
| **ā** | ape | **ī** | bite, fire | **u** | up | **ŋ** | ring |
| **ä** | car, lot | **ō** | go | **ur** | fur | | a *in* ago |
| **e** | ten | **ô** | law, horn | **ch** | chin | | e *in* agent |
| **er** | care | **oi** | oil | **sh** | she | **ə =** | i *in* unity |
| **ē** | even | **oo** | look | **th** | thin | | o *in* collect |
| **i** | hit | **o͞o** | tool | ***th*** | then | | u *in* focus |

**sim·per** (sim′pər) ***v.*** **1** to smile in a silly way that is not natural; smirk. **2** to say with a simper. ◆***n.*** a silly, unnatural smile.

**sim·ple** (sim′p'l) ***adj.*** **1** having only one part or a few parts; not complicated [The amoeba is a *simple* animal.] **2** easy to do or understand [a *simple* task; *simple* directions]. **3** without anything added; plain [the *simple* facts; a *simple* dress]. **4** not showy or pretended; sincere; natural [her easy, *simple* ways]. **5** of low rank; humble; common [*simple* peasants]. **6** having a weak mind; foolish or stupid. —**sim′pler, sim′plest**

**sim·ple-heart·ed** (sim′p'l här′tid) ***adj.*** honest; sincere.

**sim·ple-mind·ed** (sim′p'l mīn′did) ***adj.*** **1** having a weak mind; mentally retarded. **2** easily fooled; foolish. **3** simple-hearted; sincere.

**simple sentence** a sentence made up of just one main clause, with no dependent clauses.

**sim·ple·ton** (sim′p'l tən) ***n.*** a person who is stupid or easily fooled; fool.

**sim·plic·i·ty** (sim plis′ə tē) ***n.*** **1** the fact of being simple, not complicated, not difficult, etc. **2** a sincere or natural quality. **3** the condition of being plain, not fancy, etc.

**sim·pli·fy** (sim′plə fī) ***v.*** to make more simple; make easier. —**sim′pli·fied, sim′pli·fy·ing —sim′pli·fi·ca′tion *n.***



**sim·plis·tic** (sim plis′tik) ***adj.*** making complicated problems seem simple when they are not; oversimplifying. —**sim·plis′ti·cal·ly *adv.***

**sim·ply** (sim′plē) ***adv.*** **1** in a simple way; plainly [to speak *simply*]. **2** merely; just [I'm *simply* trying to help.] **3** completely; absolutely [I'm *simply* delighted to hear that.]

**sim·u·late** (sim′yoo lāt) ***v.*** **1** to pretend to have or feel [to *simulate* anger]. **2** to look or act like; imitate [The insect *simulated* a twig.] —**sim′u·lat·ed, sim′u·lat·ing —sim′u·la′tion *n.***

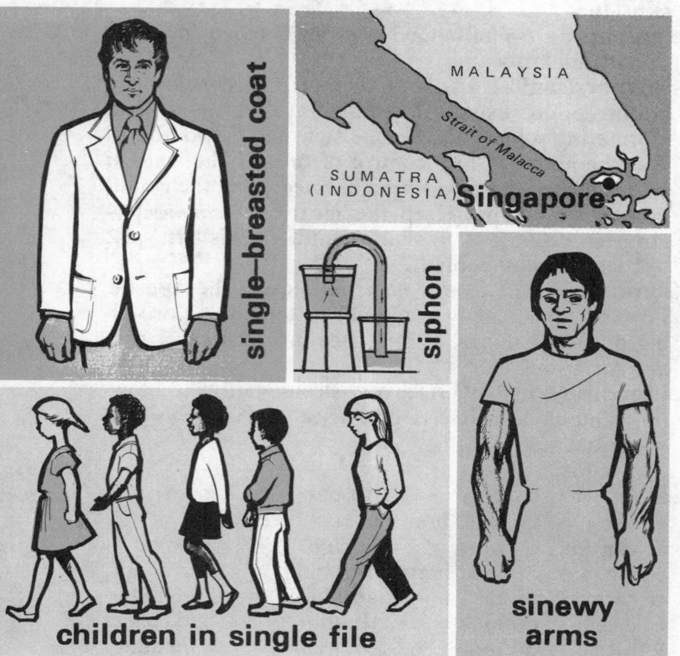

single-breasted coat

siphon

children in single file

sinewy arms

☆**si·mul·cast** (sī′m'l kast) ***v.*** to broadcast, as a program or event, at the same time on both radio and television. —**si′mul·cast** or **si′mul·cast·ed, si′mul·cast·ing** ◆***n.*** a program, event, etc. that is simulcast.

**si·mul·ta·ne·ous** (sī′m'l tā′nē əs) ***adj.*** done or happening together or at the same time. —**si′mul·ta′ne·ous·ly *adv.***

**sin** (sin) ***n.*** **1** the breaking of a religious law, especially when done on purpose. **2** a wrong or fault [a *sin* against good taste]. ◆***v.*** to commit a sin. —**sinned, sin′ning**

**Si·nai** (sī′nī), **Mount** in the Bible, the mountain where Moses received the Law from God.

**Sinai Peninsula** a broad peninsula in northeastern Egypt. *See the map for* **Suez Canal.**

**Sin·bad the Sailor** (sin′bad) a merchant in *The Arabian Nights* who made seven voyages.

**since** (sins) ***adv.*** **1** from then until now [Lynn came Monday and has been here ever *since*.] **2** at a time between then and now [Pat was sick last week but has *since* recovered.] **3** before now; ago [They are long *since* gone.] ◆***prep.*** from or during the time given until now [I've been up *since* dawn.] ◆***conj.*** **1** after the time that [It's been two years *since* I saw you.] **2** because [You may have these tools, *since* I no longer need them.]

**sin·cere** (sin sir′) ***adj.*** **1** not pretending or fooling; honest; truthful [Are you *sincere* in wanting to help?] **2** real; not pretended [*sincere* grief]. —**sin·cer′er, sin·cer′est —sin·cere′ly *adv.***

**sin·cer·i·ty** (sin ser′ə tē) ***n.*** the condition of being sincere; honesty; good faith.

**si·ne·cure** (sī′nə kyo͝or *or* sin′ə kyo͝or) ***n.*** a job or position for which one is paid well without having to do much work.

**sin·ew** (sin′yo͞o) ***n.*** **1** a tendon. **2** power of the muscles; strength. **3** *often* **sinews,** *pl.* anything from which power or strength comes [Schools are the *sinews* of democracy.]

**sin·ew·y** (sin′yo͞o wē) ***adj.*** **1** like or having sinews; tough [*sinewy* meat]. **2** strong and powerful [*sinewy* arms]. *See the picture.*

**sin·ful** (sin′fəl) ***adj.*** full of sin; wicked. —**sin′ful·ly *adv.* —sin′ful·ness *n.***

**sing** (siŋ) ***v.*** **1** to make musical sounds with the voice [She *sings* well.] **2** to perform by singing [to *sing* a song; to *sing* an opera]. **3** to make musical sounds, as a bird does. **4** to hum, buzz, whistle, etc., as an insect, the wind, etc. **5** to tell or tell about in a song or verse ["Of thee I *sing*." We *sing* his praises.] **6** to bring or put by singing [*Sing* the baby to sleep.] —**sang** or **sung, sung, sing′ing** ◆***n.*** a gathering of people to sing songs: *used only in everyday talk.* —**sing out,** to call out loudly; shout: *used only in everyday talk.*

**Sin·ga·pore** (siŋ′gə pôr) **1** a country on an island near the Malay Peninsula. **2** its capital city. *See the map.*

**singe** (sinj) ***v.*** **1** to burn slightly, especially at the ends [The moth *singed* its wings at the candle flame.] *See* SYNONYMS *at* **burn**[1]. **2** to hold in or near a flame so as to burn off feathers, etc. [to *singe* a chicken]. —**singed, singe′ing** ◆***n.*** a slight burn.

**sing·er** (siŋ′ər) ***n.*** **1** a person that sings. **2** a bird that sings.

**sin·gle** (siŋ′g'l) ***adj.*** **1** one only; one and no more [a carriage drawn by a *single* horse]. **2** of or for one person, one family, etc. [a *single* bed; a *single* house]. **3** not married [a club for *single* persons]. **4** having only one set of petals [a *single* daffodil]. **5** between two persons only [*single* combat]. ◆***v.*** **1** to select from others [The teacher *singled* Terry out for praise.] ☆**2** to make a single in baseball. —**sin′gled, sin′gling** ◆***n.*** **1** a single person or thing. ☆**2** a hit in baseball by which the batter reaches first base only. **3** **singles,** *pl.* a game, as in tennis, with only one player on each side. —**sin′gle·ness** ***n.***

> SYNONYMS: **Single** simply refers to one that is not connected or matched with another [There is a *single* lamp in the room. The store has a *single* clerk.] **Sole** means the only one of its kind in a certain situation or discussion [His daughter is his *sole* dependent. That poem is Su Ling's *sole* effort for the school paper.] **Solitary** means all alone [There is a *solitary* tree in the meadow.]

**sin·gle-breast·ed** (siŋ′g'l bres′tid) ***adj.*** overlapping the front of the body just enough to fasten [a *single-breasted* coat]. *See the picture.*

**single file** a single line of persons or things, one behind another. *See the picture.*

**sin·gle-hand·ed** (siŋ′g'l han′did) ***adj.*** without help [He won the fight *single-handed.*]

**sin·gle-heart·ed** (siŋ′g'l här′tid) ***adj.*** honest; faithful; sincere.

**sin·gle-mind·ed** (siŋ′g'l mīn′did) ***adj.*** **1** *same as* **single-hearted**. **2** sticking to one purpose.

☆**sin·gle·tree** (siŋ′g'l trē) ***n.*** the crossbar at the front of a wagon or carriage, to which the traces of a horse's harness are hooked.

**sin·gly** (siŋ′glē) ***adv.*** **1** as a single, separate person or thing; alone [We'll deal with each problem *singly.*] **2** one at a time [They entered the hall *singly.*] **3** without help; single-handed.

**sing·song** (siŋ′sôŋ) ***n.*** a rising and falling of the voice in a steady, boring rhythm. ◆***adj.*** in or like a singsong.

**sin·gu·lar** (siŋ′gyə lər) ***adj.*** **1** more than ordinary; exceptional [the *singular* beauty of her voice]. **2** strange; queer; unusual [a man of *singular* habits]. **3** being the only one of its kind; unique [a *singular* specimen]. **4** showing that only one is meant [The *singular* form of "geese" is "goose."] ◆***n.*** the singular form of a word in grammar. —**sin·gu·lar·i·ty** (siŋ′gyə lar′ə tē) ***n.*** —**sin′gu·lar·ly** ***adv.***

**sin·is·ter** (sin′is tər) ***adj.*** **1** that threatens something bad [dark, *sinister* clouds]. **2** wicked, evil, or dishonest [a *sinister* plot].

> **Sinister** in earlier times had the same meaning, "on the left-hand side," that it had in Latin. When the augurs of ancient Rome watched for omens, as in the flight of birds, they stood facing north, and the side to their left was west and unlucky. A flight of birds on the left would foretell bad luck; a flight on the right, good luck.

**sink** (siŋk) ***v.*** **1** to go or put down below the surface, as of water, earth, etc. [The boat is *sinking*. He *sank* the spade into the ground.] ☆**2** to put a basketball through the basket, a golf ball into the hole, etc. **3** to go down slowly; fall, settle, etc. [The balloon *sank* to the earth.] **4** to seem to come down [The sun is *sinking* in the west.] **5** to make or become lower in level, value, amount, force, etc.; drop [Her voice *sank* to a whisper. Profits *sank* to a new low.] **6** to become hollow, as the cheeks. **7** to go gradually into a certain condition [to *sink* into despair]. **8** to become weaker and closer to death [The patient is *sinking* rapidly.] **9** to go into deeply and firmly [The lesson *sank* into his memory.] **10** to make by digging, drilling, etc. [to *sink* a well]. **11** to invest or to lose by investing [They *sank* a fortune into gold stock.] **12** to defeat or ruin [After the fifth inning we were *sunk.*] —**sank** or **sunk, sunk, sink′ing** ◆***n.*** **1** a basin, as in a kitchen, with a drain and water faucets. **2** a drain, sewer, or cesspool. ☆**3** a sunken place where water collects.

**sink·er** (siŋk′ər) ***n.*** something that sinks, as a lead weight put on the end of a fishing line.

**sink·hole** (siŋk′hōl) ***n.*** a hollow in the earth, into which water from the surface flows and then becomes part of an underground river.

**sin·less** (sin′lis) ***adj.*** without sin; innocent.

**sin·ner** (sin′ər) ***n.*** a person who sins.

**sin·u·ous** (sin′yoo wəs) ***adj.*** **1** twisting or winding in and out [a *sinuous* river]. **2** not straightforward or honest; crooked. —**sin·u·os·i·ty** (sin′yoo wäs′ə tē) ***n.***

**si·nus** (sī′nəs) ***n.*** a hollow place; especially, any of the cavities in the bones of the skull that open into the nose. 

**si·nus·i·tis** (sī′nə sīt′əs) ***n.*** a condition in which the sinuses of the skull become sore and clogged or runny with mucus.

**-sion** (shən *or* zhən) *a suffix meaning* the act, condition, or result of [*Confusion* means the act, condition, or result of confusing.]

**Siou·an** (so͞o′ən) ***n.*** a family of languages of North American Indians, including the Sioux.

**Sioux** (so͞o) ***n.*** a member of a group of Indian tribes living in the northern United States. —*pl.* **Sioux** (so͞o *or* so͞oz)

**sip** (sip) ***v.*** to drink a little at a time. —**sipped, sip′ping** ◆***n.*** **1** the act of sipping. **2** a small amount sipped.

**si·phon** (sī′fən) ***n.*** **1** a bent tube for carrying liquid out over the edge of a container down to a container below, by the force of air pressure. The tube must be filled, as by suction, before flow will start. *See the picture.* **2** a bottle for soda water with a tube inside. When a valve outside is opened, pressure forces the water out through the tube. *Also called* **siphon bottle.** ◆***v.*** to draw off through a siphon [to *siphon* gasoline from a tank].

**sir** (sur) ***n.*** **1** a word used to show respect in talking to a man [Thank you, *sir*. "Dear *Sir*" is often used to

| | | | | | | | |
|---|---|---|---|---|---|---|---|
| **a** | fat | **ir** | here | **ou** | out | **zh** | leisure |
| **ā** | ape | **ī** | bite, fire | **u** | up | **ŋ** | ring |
| **ä** | car, lot | **ō** | go | **ur** | fur | | a *in* ago |
| **e** | ten | **ô** | law, horn | **ch** | chin | | e *in* agent |
| **er** | care | **oi** | oil | **sh** | she | **ə =** | i *in* unity |
| **ē** | even | **oo** | look | **th** | thin | | o *in* collect |
| **i** | hit | **o͞o** | tool | ***th*** | then | | u *in* focus |

begin a letter.] **2 Sir,** a title used before the name of a knight or baronet [*Sir* Walter Raleigh].

**sire** (sīr) ***n.*** **1** the male parent of a horse, dog, cow, etc. **2** a father or male ancestor: *used mostly in earlier poetry.* **3** a title of respect used in talking to a king. ◆***v.*** to be the male parent of [This horse has *sired* two racing champions.] —**sired, sir′ing**

**si·ren** (sī′rən) ***n.*** **1** a device that makes a wailing sound and is used as a warning signal, as on a fire engine. **2** any of the sea nymphs in Greek and Roman myths, whose sweet singing lured sailors to their death on rocky coasts. **3** any woman who attracts and tempts men. ◆***adj.*** of or like a siren; tempting.

**Sir·i·us** (sir′ē əs) the brightest star in the sky: *also called* Dog Star.

**sir·loin** (sur′loin) ***n.*** a fine cut of beef from the loin, next to the rump.

**si·roc·co** (sə räk′ō) ***n.*** any hot, stifling wind, especially one blowing from the deserts of northern Africa into southern Europe. *—pl.* **si·roc′cos**

**sir·up** (sir′əp *or* sur′əp) ***n.*** *another spelling for* **syrup.**

☆**sis** (sis) ***n.*** sister: *used only in everyday talk.*

**si·sal** (sī′s′l) ***n.*** **1** a strong fiber obtained from the leaves of a tropical plant, used in making rope. **2** this plant, a kind of agave.

☆**sis·sy** (sis′ē) ***n.*** **1** a boy or man who acts in a way that is considered not manly. **2** a timid person or coward. *This word is used only in everyday talk. —pl.*
692 **sis′sies**

☆**sissy bar** a metal bar shaped like an upside-down U, attached behind the seat of a motorcycle or bicycle to keep the rider from sliding backward: *a slang term.*

**sis·ter** (sis′tər) ***n.*** **1** a girl or woman as she is related to the other children of her parents. **2** a girl or woman who is close to one in some way; especially, a fellow member of the same race, religion, club, etc. **3** a nun.

**sis·ter·hood** (sis′tər hood) ***n.*** **1** the tie between sisters or between women who feel a close relationship. **2** a group of women joined together in some interest, work, belief, etc.

**sis·ter-in-law** (sis′tər in lô′) ***n.*** **1** the sister of one's husband or wife. **2** the wife of one's brother. *—pl.* **sis′ters-in-law′**

**sis·ter·ly** (sis′tər lē) ***adj.*** **1** of or like a sister. **2** friendly, loyal, kindly, etc. [*sisterly* advice]. —**sis′ter·li·ness *n.***

**sit** (sit) ***v.*** **1** to rest the weight of the body upon the buttocks or haunches [She is *sitting* on a bench. The dog *sat* still.] **2** to make sit; seat [*Sit* yourself down.] **3** to keep one's seat on [He *sits* his horse well.] **4** to perch, rest, lie, etc. [A bird *sat* on the fence. Cares *sit* lightly on him.] **5** to have a seat; be a member [to *sit* in the Senate]. **6.** to meet, as a court. **7.** to pose, as for a picture. **8.** to fit [This coat *sits* loosely.] **9.** to cover eggs with the body to hatch them [a *sitting* hen]. —**sat, sit′ting** —**sit back, 1.** to relax. **2.** to not take an active part. —**sit down,** to take a seat. —**sit in,** to take part. —**sit on** or **sit upon, 1.** to be a member of, as a jury or committee. **2.** to hold or keep something back; squelch: *used only in everyday talk.* —**sit out, 1.** to stay until the end of. **2.** to stay out of for a while, as a dance or game. —**sit up, 1.** to rise to a sitting position. **2.** to sit with the back straight. **3.** to put off going to bed. **4.** to become suddenly alert: *used only in everyday talk.* —**sit well with,** to be agreeable to; please [It didn't *sit well with* the coach when we skipped practice.]

**si·tar** (si tär′) ***n.*** a musical instrument of India with a long neck, and strings that vibrate along with those being played. *See the picture.*

**site** (sīt) ***n.*** **1** a piece of land for a special purpose [This is a good *site* for a shopping center.] **2** the place where something is or was [Gettysburg was the *site* of a Civil War battle.]

**sit·ter** (sit′ər) ***n.*** one that sits; especially, ☆*a shorter name for* **baby sitter.**

**sit·ting** (sit′iŋ) ***n.*** **1** the act or position of one that sits, as for a picture. **2** a meeting, as of a court or a council. **3** a period of being seated [I read the book in one *sitting.*]

**Sitting Bull** 1834?–1890; a Sioux Indian chief and medicine man.

**sitting room** *another name for* **living room.**

**sit·u·ate** (sich′oo wāt) ***v.*** to put or place; locate [The cabin is *situated* in the woods.] —**sit′u·at·ed, sit′u·at·ing**

**sit·u·a·tion** (sich′oo wā′shən) ***n.*** **1** a place or position; location; site. **2** condition or state, as caused by things that have happened [Her election as mayor has created an interesting *situation.*] **3** a job or place to work [He's looking for a *situation* as a keypunch operator.] *See* SYNONYMS *at* **position.**

☆**sit-up** or **sit·up** (sit′up′) ***n.*** an exercise in which a person lying flat on the back rises to a sitting position without using the hands.

**six** (siks) ***n., adj.*** one more than five; the number 6. —**at sixes and sevens, 1** confused. **2** not in agreement. *This phrase is used only in everyday talk.*

☆**six-pack** (siks′pak′) ***n.*** a package containing six units of a product, as six bottles of pop.

☆**six-shoot·er** (siks′shōōt′ər) ***n.*** a revolver that holds six shots: *used only in everyday talk.*

**six·teen** (siks′tēn′) ***n., adj.*** six more than ten; the number 16.

**six·teenth** (siks′tēnth′) ***adj.*** coming after fifteen others; 16th in order. ◆***n.*** **1** the sixteenth one. **2** one of sixteen equal parts of something; 1/16.

**sixteenth note** a note in music that is held one sixteenth as long as a whole note.

**sixth** (siksth) ***adj.*** coming after five others; 6th in order. ◆***n.*** **1** the sixth one. **2** one of the six equal parts of something; 1/6.

**six·ti·eth** (siks′tē ith) ***adj.*** coming after fifty-nine others; 60th in order. ◆***n.*** **1** the sixtieth one. **2** one of the sixty equal parts of something; 1/60.

**six·ty** (siks′tē) ***n., adj.*** six times ten; the number 60. *—pl.* **six′ties —the sixties,** the numbers or years from 60 through 69.

**siz·a·ble** or **size·a·ble** (sī′zə b′l) ***adj.*** fairly large [a *sizable* fortune].

**size**[1] (sīz) ***n.*** **1** the amount of space taken up by a thing; how large or how small a thing is [Tell me the *size* of your room. He is strong for his *size.*] **2** any of a series of measures, often numbered, for grading things [She wears a *size* 12 dress. These are jumbo *size* peanuts.] **3** extent or amount [I couldn't believe the *size* of her fortune.] ➡*v.* to arrange according to size. —**sized, siz'ing** —**of a size,** of the same size. —☆**size up,** to form a judgment of: *used only in everyday talk.*

**size**[2] (sīz) *n.* a substance like a thin paste, used to glaze or stiffen paper, cloth, etc.: *also* **siz'ing.** ➡*v.* to put size on. —**sized, siz'ing**

**siz·zle** (siz''l) *v.* to make a hissing sound, as water on hot metal or something frying. —**siz'zled, siz'zling** ➡*n.* a sizzling sound.

> **Sizzle** is a word that was made up to sound like the hissing of hot grease in a frying pan or of drops of water when they hit hot metal. *Hiss* is such a word too. There are many words like *sizzle* and *hiss,* such as *buzz* and *whiz,* that were made up to sound like what the word describes.

☆**siz·zler** (siz'lər) *n.* something hot, as a very hot day: *used only in everyday talk.*

**S.J.** Society of Jesus: *see* **Jesuit.**

**skate**[1] (skāt) *n.* **1** a long, narrow metal blade, or runner, in a frame that can be fastened to a shoe for gliding on ice; also, a shoe with such a blade built onto it: *also called* **ice skate. 2** a frame or shoe like this with wheels instead of a blade, used for gliding on floors, sidewalks, etc.: *also called* **roller skate.** ➡*v.* to move along on skates. —**skat'ed, skat'ing** —**skat'er** *n.*

**skate**[2] (skāt) *n.* an ocean fish with a broad, flat body and a long, slender tail.

☆**skate·board** (skāt'bôrd) *n.* a short, oblong board with two wheels at each end, on which a person rides, as down an incline, usually while standing. *See the picture.* ➡*v.* to ride or coast on a skateboard. —**skate'board·er** *n.*

☆**skeet** (skēt) *n.* trapshooting in which the shooter fires from several different angles.

**skein** (skān) *n.* a loose, thick coil of yarn or thread.

**skel·e·tal** (skel'ə t'l) *adj.* of a skeleton or like a skeleton.

**skel·e·ton** (skel'ə t'n) *n.* **1** the framework of bones of an animal body. *See the picture.* **2** anything like a skeleton, as a very thin creature, the framework of a ship, an outline of a book, etc. —**skeleton in the closet,** some fact, as about one's family, kept secret because one is ashamed of it.

**skeleton key** a key that can open many simple locks.

**skep·tic** (skep'tik) *n.* **1** a person who questions things most people believe in; doubter. **2** a person who doubts religious doctrines.

**skep·ti·cal** (skep'ti k'l) *adj.* having or showing doubt; not believing easily; questioning. —**skep'ti·cal·ly** *adv.*

**skep·ti·cism** (skep'ti siz'm) *n.* a state of mind in which one doubts or questions things; disbelief.

**sketch** (skech) *n.* **1** a simple, rough drawing or design, usually done quickly and with little detail. **2** a short outline, giving the main points. **3** a short, light story, scene in a show, etc. ➡*v.* to make a sketch of; draw sketches.

> **Sketch** comes from a Latin word for a poem that is made up offhand, without thinking it out ahead of time.

**sketch·y** (skech'ē) *adj.* like a sketch; not detailed; not complete [a *sketchy* report]. —**sketch'i·er, sketch'i·est**

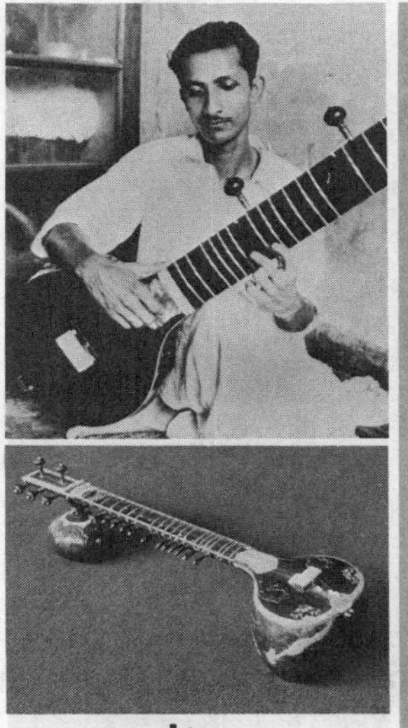

sitar

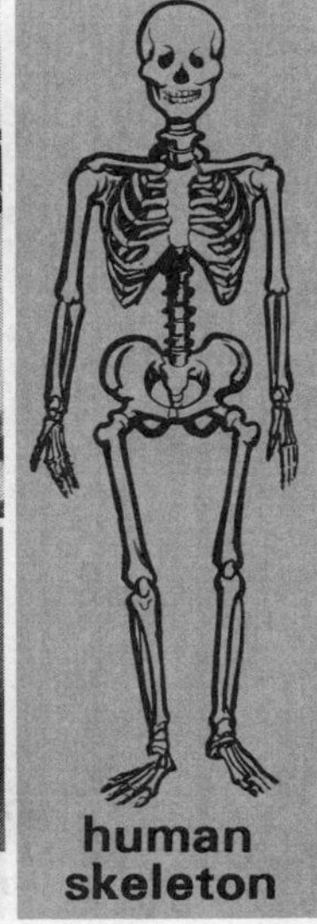

human skeleton

skateboard

skewer

**skew** (skyo͞o) *v.* to twist or slant. ➡*adj.* turned to one side; slanting.

**skew·er** (skyo͞o'ər) *n.* **1** a long pin used to hold meat together while cooking. **2** a similar but longer pin used to hold chunks of meat and vegetables for broiling, as for shish kebab. *See the picture.* ➡*v.* to fasten or pierce with or as with skewers.



**ski** (skē) *n.* one of a pair of long, wooden runners fastened to the shoes for gliding over snow. ➡*v.* to glide on skis, as down snow-covered hills. —**skied** (skēd), **ski'ing** —**ski'er** *n.*

**skid** (skid) *n.* ☆**1** a plank, log, etc. used as a support or as a track on which to slide something heavy. **2** a sliding wedge used as a brake on a wheel. **3** the act of skidding. ➡*v.* **1** to slide without turning, as a wheel does on ice when it is held by a brake. **2** to slide sideways, as a car on ice. **3** to slide on a skid or skids. —**skid'ded, skid'ding** —☆**on the skids,** losing one's power or influence, becoming a failure, etc.: *a slang phrase.*

**skies** (skīz) *n. plural of* **sky.**

**skiff** (skif) *n.* a light rowboat, especially one with a small sail.

**skill** (skil) *n.* **1** ability that comes from training, practice, etc. [He plays the violin with *skill.*] **2** an art, craft, or science, especially one that calls for use of the hands or body [Weaving is a *skill* often taught to the blind.] *See* SYNONYMS *at* **art.**

**skilled** (skild) *adj.* **1** having skill; skillful. **2** needing a special skill got by training [Repairing watches is *skilled* work.]

**skil·let** (skil'it) *n.* a shallow pan with a handle, for frying food; frying pan.

| | | | | | | | |
|---|---|---|---|---|---|---|---|
| **a** | fat | **ir** | here | **ou** | out | **zh** | leisure |
| **ā** | ape | **ī** | bite, fire | **u** | up | **ng** | ring |
| **ä** | car, lot | **ō** | go | **ur** | fur | | a *in* ago |
| **e** | ten | **ô** | law, horn | **ch** | chin | | e *in* agent |
| **er** | care | **oi** | oil | **sh** | she | **ə** = | i *in* unity |
| **ē** | even | **oo** | look | **th** | thin | | o *in* collect |
| **i** | hit | **o͞o** | tool | ***th*** | then | | u *in* focus |

skylights

skittles

skin diving

skunk

60 cm (2 ft.) long, including tail

**skill·ful** or **skil·ful** (skil′fəl) ***adj.*** having or showing skill; expert [a *skillful* cook; her *skillful* performance on the piano]. —**skill′ful·ly** or **skil′ful·ly** ***adv.***

**skim** (skim) ***v.*** **1** to take off floating matter from the top of a liquid [to *skim* cream from milk; to *skim* molten lead]. **2** to look through a book, magazine, etc. quickly without reading carefully. **3** to glide lightly, as over a surface [bugs *skimming* over the water]. —**skimmed, skim′ming**



**skim·mer** (skim′ər) ***n.*** **1** a person or thing that skims. **2** any utensil for skimming liquids.

**skim milk** milk from which cream has been removed: *also* **skimmed milk.**

**skimp** (skimp) ***v.*** to spend or use as little as possible; allow less than enough; scrimp [They *skimped* on clothes to save for a new home.]

**skimp·y** (skim′pē) ***adj.*** barely or not quite enough; scanty [a *skimpy* meal]. —**skimp′i·er, skimp′i·est**

**skin** (skin) ***n.*** **1** the tissue covering the body of persons and animals. **2** the hide or pelt of an animal [Early settlers made coats from beaver *skins*.] **3** the outer covering of some fruits and vegetables [tomato *skin*]. **4** something like skin in looks or use. ◆***v.*** **1** to remove the skin from [to *skin* a rabbit; to *skin* one's elbow by falling]. **2** to cheat or swindle: *used only in everyday talk.* —**skinned, skin′ning** —**by the skin of one's teeth,** by the smallest possible margin; barely. —**have a thick skin,** to pay little attention to blame, insults, etc. —**have a thin skin,** to be easily hurt by blame, insults, etc. —**save one's skin,** to keep oneself from getting killed or hurt: *used only in everyday talk.* —**skin′less** ***adj.***

**skin diving** the act or sport of swimming about under water, especially for a long time by breathing from a tank of air fastened to the body. *See the picture.*

**skin·flint** (skin′flint) ***n.*** a stingy person; miser.

> **Skinflint** comes from a very old saying that a mean, stingy person would manage to take skin off the very hard stone called flint if some money could be saved or earned by doing this. The word **skinflint** was made up about 300 years ago.

**skin·ny** (skin′ē) ***adj.*** very thin or lean. —**skin′ni·er, skin′ni·est**

**skip** (skip) ***v.*** **1** to move along by hopping lightly on first one foot and then the other. **2** to leap lightly over [to *skip* a brook]. **3** to bound or make bounce across a surface [We *skipped* flat stones across a pond.] **4** to pass from one point to another leaving out what is between; pass over; omit [*Skip* from page 56 to 64. I *skipped* lunch.] ☆**5** to leave in a hurry: *used only in everyday talk* [to *skip* town]. —**skipped, skip′ping** ◆***n.*** **1** a light leap or jump. **2** the act of passing over or leaving out. —**skip′per** ***n.***

**skip·per** (skip′ər) ***n.*** **1** the captain of a ship. **2** any person who leads or manages.

**skir·mish** (skur′mish) ***n.*** a brief fight between small groups, usually a part of a battle. ◆***v.*** to take part in a skirmish.

**skirt** (skurt) ***n.*** **1** the part of a dress, coat, etc. that hangs below the waist. **2** a woman's or girl's garment that hangs from the waist, worn with a blouse, sweater, etc. **3** something hanging like a skirt [a *skirt* on a slipcover]. **4 skirts,** ***pl.*** the outer parts; outskirts. ◆***v.*** **1** to go along the edge of; pass around rather than through [The new highway will *skirt* our town.] **2** to avoid [to *skirt* a problem].

**skit** (skit) ***n.*** a short, usually funny sketch or scene, as in a show.

**skit·tish** (skit′ish) ***adj.*** **1** easily frightened or very nervous [a *skittish* horse]. **2** lively or playful, especially in a coy way.

**skit·tles** (skit′′lz) ***n.pl.*** a game like ninepins, played with a wooden disk instead of a ball. *See the picture.*

☆**skul·dug·ger·y** or **skull·dug·ger·y** (skul dug′ər ē) ***n.*** sneaky, dishonest behavior: *used only in everyday talk.*

**skulk** (skulk) ***v.*** to move about or hide in a sneaky, cowardly, or threatening way [a hyena *skulking* in the shadows]. —**skulk′er** ***n.***

**skull** (skul) ***n.*** the bony framework of the head, that encloses and protects the brain.

**skull and crossbones** a picture of a human skull with two crossed bones below. It was used on pirates' flags and is now used to label poisons.

**skull·cap** (skul′kap) ***n.*** a light, closefitting cap with no brim, usually worn indoors.

☆**skunk** (skungk) ***n.*** **1** an animal having a bushy tail and black fur with white stripes down its back. It sprays out a very bad-smelling liquid when frightened or attacked. *See the picture.* **2** its fur. **3** a nasty, mean person: *used only in everyday talk.*

**sky** (skī) ***n.*** **1** *often* **skies,** ***pl.*** the upper part of the air around the earth; the dome that seems to cover the earth [a *cloudy* sky; blue *skies*]. **2** heaven. —*pl.* **skies** —**out of a clear blue sky,** suddenly; without warning.

> **Sky** comes from an old Norse word *sky* meaning "cloud," which in turn came from an earlier word meaning "to cover." When we look at a clear sky, it is sometimes hard to believe we are gazing into unlimited space. To our eyes, the sky appears to cover the earth.

**sky blue** the blue color of a clear sky.

☆**sky diving** the sport of jumping from an airplane and falling freely for some time before opening the parachute.

☆**sky·jack** (skī′jak) ***v.*** to hijack an airplane: *used only in everyday talk.* —**sky′jack·er *n.***

**sky·lark** (skī′lärk) ***n.*** the European lark, famous for the song it sings as it rises high into the air. ◆***v.*** to play or frolic.

**sky·light** (skī′līt) ***n.*** a window in a roof or ceiling. *See the picture.*

**sky·line** (skī′līn) ***n.*** **1** the line where the sky seems to touch the earth; horizon. **2** the outline, as of the buildings of a city, as seen against the sky.

**sky·rock·et** (skī′räk′it) ***n.*** a firework that explodes high in the air in a shower of colored sparks. ◆☆***v.*** to rise rapidly [Meat prices *skyrocketed.*]

**sky·scrap·er** (skī′skrā′pər) ***n.*** ☆a very tall building.

**sky·ward** (skī′wərd) ***adv., adj.*** toward the sky.

**sky·wards** (skī′wərdz) ***adv.*** *same as* **skyward.**

**slab** (slab) ***n.*** a piece that is flat, broad, and fairly thick [a *slab* of concrete].

**slack** (slak) ***adj.*** **1** loose; not tight; relaxed [a *slack* tennis net; a *slack* jaw]. **2** careless; lax [a *slack* worker]. **3** not busy or active; dull [a *slack* season for business]. **4** slow; sluggish; without energy or force [The old dog ambled along at a *slack* pace.] ◆***n.*** **1** a part that is slack or hangs loose [Take in the *slack* of the rope.] **2 slacks,** *pl.* long trousers not made as part of a suit, worn by men or women. —**slack off,** to slacken. —**slack up,** to go or work more slowly. —**slack′ly *adv.*** —**slack′ness *n.***

**slack·en** (slak′'n) ***v.*** **1** to make or become slower or less full of energy [*Slacken* your pace so that I can keep up.] **2** to loosen or relax; make or become less tight [to *slacken* one's grip].

**slack·er** (slak′ər) ***n.*** a person who tries to keep from doing work or carrying out duties.

**slag** (slag) ***n.*** **1** the waste matter that is left after metal has been melted down from ore. **2** lava that looks like this.

**slain** (slān) *past participle of* **slay.**

**slake** (slāk) ***v.*** **1** to satisfy or make less strong [to *slake* one's thirst with water]. **2** to cause a chemical change in lime by adding water to it. —**slaked, slak′ing**

**slam** (slam) ***v.*** **1** to shut or close with force and noise [to *slam* a door]. **2** to put, hit, or throw with force and noise [to *slam* a baseball over the fence]. —**slammed, slam′ming** ◆***n.*** **1** the act or sound of slamming. **2** the winning of all the tricks in a hand of bridge (**grand slam**) or of all but one (**little slam**).

**slan·der** (slan′dər) ***n.*** **1** anything spoken that harms a person's reputation in an unfair way and makes others laugh at or hate the person. **2** the act or crime of saying such a thing. ◆***v.*** to speak slander against. —**slan′der·er *n.***

**slan·der·ous** (slan′dər əs) ***adj.*** containing or speaking slander against someone.

**slang** (slaŋ) ***n.*** words and phrases that are used in everyday talk but are out of place in fine or serious speech or writing.

> Slang words are usually popular for only a short time. A few slang words and meanings that have been in use for a longer time are included in this dictionary. "Crummy" is slang, and so are "rocky" when used to mean "weak or dizzy" and "grub" when used to mean "food."

**slang·y** (slaŋ′ē) ***adj.*** of, like, or full of slang.

**slant** (slant) ***v.*** **1** to turn or lie in a direction that is not straight up and down or straight across; slope [The picture is hanging so that it *slants* to the left.] ☆**2** to write or tell so as to lean in favor of or against something [This newspaper *slants* its news coverage.] ◆***n.*** **1** a surface or line that slants; slope [The ramp goes up at a *slant.*] ☆**2** an attitude or opinion [Your advice gave me a new *slant* on life.] —**slant′ing *adj.***

**slant·ways** (slant′wāz) ***adv.*** *same as* **slantwise.**

**slant·wise** (slant′wīz) ***adv., adj.*** in a direction that slants.

**slap** (slap) ***n.*** **1** a blow with something flat, as the palm of the hand. **2** the sound of this, or a sound like it. ◆***v.*** **1** to hit with something flat. **2** to put or throw carelessly or with force [I *slapped* the hat on my head.] —**slapped, slap′ping**

**slap·stick** (slap′stik) ***n.*** **1** an implement made of two flat pieces of wood that slap together loudly when hit against something, used by clowns and comedians to strike each other with loud, harmless slaps. **2** a kind of comedy that depends on fast, foolish activity for its humor.

**slash** (slash) ***v.*** **1** to cut by striking with something sharp [The knife slipped and I *slashed* my finger.] **2** to whip or lash. **3** to make cuts in cloth or a garment so as to show the material underneath. **4** to make much less or much lower [The store manager decided to *slash* prices.] **5** to speak or criticize harshly. ◆***n.*** a sweeping blow or stroke, or a cut made with such a stroke.

**slat** (slat) ***n.*** a thin, narrow strip of wood or metal [the *slats* of a Venetian blind].

**slate** (slāt) ***n.*** **1** a hard rock that splits easily into thin, smooth layers. **2** the bluish-gray color of this rock. **3** a thin piece of slate used in covering roofs or as something to write on with chalk. ☆**4** a list of candidates as in an election. ◆***v.*** **1** to cover with slate [to *slate* a roof]. ☆**2** to be among those chosen [You are *slated* to speak at the assembly.] —**slat′ed, slat′ing** —**a clean slate,** a record that shows no faults, mistakes, etc.

**slat·tern** (slat′ərn) ***n.*** a woman who is dirty and untidy in her looks, habits, etc. —**slat′tern·ly *adj., adv.***

**slaugh·ter** (slôt′ər) ***n.*** **1** the killing of animals for food; butchering. **2** the killing of people in a cruel way or in large numbers, as in battle. ◆***v.*** **1** to kill for food; butcher [to *slaughter* a hog]. **2** to kill people in a cruel way or in large numbers.

> SYNONYMS: **Slaughter** suggests the killing of large numbers of people in a cruel and violent way, such as in battle. **Massacre** brings to mind the widespread and often complete destruction of those who cannot defend themselves or fight back.

**slaugh·ter·house** (slôt′ər hous) ***n.*** a place where animals are killed for food.

| | | | | | | | |
|---|---|---|---|---|---|---|---|
| **a** | fat | **ir** | here | **ou** | out | **zh** | leisure |
| **ā** | ape | **ī** | bite, fire | **u** | up | **ng** | ring |
| **ä** | car, lot | **ō** | go | **ur** | fur | | a *in* ago |
| **e** | ten | **ô** | law, horn | **ch** | chin | | e *in* agent |
| **er** | care | **oi** | oil | **sh** | she | **ə =** | i *in* unity |
| **ē** | even | **oo** | look | **th** | thin | | o *in* collect |
| **i** | hit | **ōō** | tool | ***th*** | then | | u *in* focus |

**Slav** (släv) ***n.*** a member of a group of peoples of eastern Europe. Russians, Poles, Czechs, Slovaks, Serbs, etc. are Slavs. ◆***adj.*** *same as* **Slavic.**

**slave** (slāv) ***n.*** **1** a person who is owned by another person and has no freedom at all. **2** a person who is completely controlled by a habit, an influence, etc. [They are *slaves* to fashion—always dressed in the latest style.] **3** a person who works hard like a slave; drudge. ◆***v.*** to work hard like a slave; toil [I *slaved* in the kitchen all day.] —**slaved, slav′ing**

**slave·hold·er** (slāv′hōl′dər) ***n.*** a person who owns slaves. —**slave′hold′ing *adj., n.***

**slav·er**[1] (slav′ər) ***v.*** to let saliva drip from the mouth. ◆***n.*** saliva dripping from the mouth.

**slav·er**[2] (slā′vər) ***n.*** **1** a ship in earlier times that carried people to another country to be sold as slaves. **2** a person who deals in slaves.

**slav·er·y** (slā′və rē) ***n.*** **1** the practice of owning slaves [The 13th Amendment abolished *slavery* in the U.S.] **2** the condition of being a slave; bondage [Joseph was sold into *slavery*.] **3** hard work like that of a slave; drudgery.

**Slav·ic** (slä′vik) ***adj.*** of the Slavs, their languages, etc. ◆***n.*** the group of languages spoken by Slavs.

**slav·ish** (slā′vish) ***adj.*** **1** of or like a slave; too humble. **2** of or like slavery [*slavish* work]. **3** not free or independent [a *slavish* imitation of others]. —**slav′ish·ly *adv.*** —**slav′ish·ness *n.***



☆**slaw** (slô) ***n.*** *a shorter word for* **coleslaw.**

**slay** (slā) ***v.*** to kill in a violent way [Hundreds of soldiers were *slain* in the battle.] —**slew, slain, slay′ing** —**slay′er *n.***

**slea·zy** (slē′zē) ***adj.*** **1** thin and easily torn; flimsy [*sleazy* cloth]. **2** low in quality; shabby, shoddy, cheap, etc. [a *sleazy* rooming house; a *sleazy* novel]. —**slea′zi·er, slea′zi·est** —**slea′zi·ness *n.***

**sled** (sled) ***n.*** a low platform on runners, used for riding or carrying things over snow or ice. ◆☆***v.*** to carry, ride, or coast on a sled. —**sled′ded, sled′ding**

**sledge**[1] (slej) ***n.*** *a shorter word for* **sledgehammer.**

**sledge**[2] (slej) ***n.*** a large, heavy sled for carrying loads over ice, snow, etc.

**sledge·ham·mer** (slej′ham′ər) ***n.*** a long, heavy hammer, usually held with both hands. *See the picture.*

**sleek** (slēk) ***adj.*** **1** smooth and shiny; glossy [the *sleek* fur of a seal]. **2** looking healthy and well-groomed [fat, *sleek* pigeons]. **3** speaking or acting in a smooth but insincere way [a *sleek* villain]. ◆***v.*** to make sleek; smooth down, as the hair. —**sleek′ly *adv.*** —**sleek′ness *n.***

**sleep** (slēp) ***n.*** **1** a condition of rest for the body and mind in which the eyes stay closed. In sleep, which comes at regular times, the mind does not control the body but may dream. **2** any condition like this, as death, hibernation, etc. ◆***v.*** **1** to be in the condition of sleep [to *sleep* ten hours each night]. **2** to be in a condition like sleep [Bears *sleep* through the winter.] **3** to put off deciding on something: *used only in everyday talk* [Let me *sleep* on the matter and I'll give you an answer tomorrow.] —**slept, sleep′ing** —**sleep away,** to pass or spend in sleep [to *sleep away* the morning]. —**sleep off,** to get over the effect of by sleeping.

**sleep·er** (slēp′ər) ***n.*** **1** one who sleeps, especially in a certain way [a light *sleeper*]. ☆**2** a railroad car that has berths for sleeping: *also called* **sleeping car. 3** a heavy beam or timber laid flat for supporting something.

☆**sleeping bag** a large bag with a warm lining for sleeping in outdoors. *See the picture.*

☆**sleeping pill** a pill or capsule holding a drug that helps put one to sleep.

**sleeping sickness** a disease that makes one weak and sleepy or unconscious. One type, as in Africa, is caused by the bite of a certain fly.

**sleep·less** (slēp′lis) ***adj.*** with little or no sleep [a *sleepless* night].

**sleep·walk·ing** (slēp′wôk′iŋ) ***n.*** the act or habit of walking while asleep. —**sleep′walk′er *n.***

**sleep·y** (slēp′ē) ***adj.*** **1** ready or likely to fall asleep; drowsy. **2** not very active; dull; quiet [a *sleepy* little town]. —**sleep′i·er, sleep′i·est** —**sleep′i·ly *adv.*** —**sleep′i·ness *n.***

**sleet** (slēt) ***n.*** **1** rain that is partly frozen. **2** a mixture of rain and snow. ◆***v.*** to shower in the form of sleet. —**sleet′y *adj.***

**sleeve** (slēv) ***n.*** the part of a garment that covers all or part of an arm. —**up one's sleeve,** hidden but ready at hand. —**sleeve′less *adj.***

☆**sleigh** (slā) ***n.*** a carriage with runners instead of wheels, for travel over snow or ice. *See the picture.* ◆***v.*** to ride in or drive a sleigh.

**sleight of hand** (slīt) **1** skill in moving the hands so fast as to fool those watching, as in doing magic tricks. **2** tricks done in this way.

**slen·der** (slen′dər) ***adj.*** **1** small in width as compared with the length; long and thin. *See* SYNONYMS *at* **thin. 2** small in amount, size, etc.; slight [a *slender* chance].

**slen·der·ize** (slen′dər īz) ***v.*** **1** to make or cause to seem slender. **2** to become slender. —**slen′der·ized, slen′der·iz·ing**

**slept** (slept) *past tense and past participle of* **sleep.**

**sleuth** (slo͞oth) ***n.*** ☆*another name for* **detective.**

> **Sleuth** is a shorter form of "sleuthhound," a dog that can follow a trail by smelling. Sleuth comes from an old Norse word meaning "trail." From this idea of following a trail came the modern use of the word to mean a detective, as Sherlock Holmes, who follows a trail of clues to catch a criminal.

**slew**[1] (slo͞o) *past tense of* **slay.**

**slew**[2] (slo͞o) ***n.*** a large number or amount; a lot: *used only in everyday talk.*

**slice** (slīs) ***n.*** **1** a thin, broad piece cut from something [a *slice* of cheese; a *slice* of bread]. **2** in sports, the act of slicing a ball. ◆***v.*** **1** to cut into slices [to *slice* a cake]. **2** to cut off as a slice [*Slice* off the crust.] **3** to cut as with a knife [The plow *sliced* through the soft earth.] **4** in sports, to hit a ball so that it curves [When a right-handed golfer *slices* a ball, it curves to the right.] —**sliced, slic′ing** —**slic′er *n.***

**slick** (slik) ***adj.*** **1** smooth and shiny; sleek [*slick* hair]. **2** slippery [a road *slick* with oil]. **3** clever or skillful, often in a sly or tricky way [a *slick* salesperson]. ◆***v.*** to make smooth and shiny [*Slick* down your hair with oil.] ◆***n.*** ☆a smooth area on water, as one caused by a film of oil.

**slide** (slīd) ***v.*** **1** to move easily and smoothly along the length of a surface; glide [Children run and *slide* on the ice. The window won't *slide* up. *Slide* the note under the door.] **2** to shift from a position; slip [The wet glass *slid* from my hand.] **3** to pass, move, get, etc. gradually or without being noticed [to *slide* into bad habits]. —**slid** (slid), **slid'ing** ✦***n.*** **1** an act of sliding. **2** a smooth surface, usually slanting, down which a person or thing slides [a playground *slide*]. **3** something that works by sliding [Move this *slide* to open the camera.] **4** the fall of a mass of rock or earth down a hill, cliff, etc. **5** a small, framed piece of film with a photograph on it that can be thrown on a screen by a projector. **6** a small piece of glass on which things are placed for study under a microscope. ☆**slide fastener** a device used to fasten and unfasten two edges of material by means of interlocking teeth worked by a sliding part.

**slide rule** an instrument for quick figuring, made up of a ruler with a central sliding piece, both marked with scales. *See the picture.*

**sliding scale** a standard or schedule, as of costs or wages, that is supposed to change according to certain conditions [The union wants a *sliding scale* for wages, so that wages go up or down as the cost of living goes up or down.]

**slight** (slīt) ***adj.*** **1** small in amount or degree; not great, strong, important, etc. [a *slight* change in temperature; a *slight* advantage; a *slight* bruise]. **2** light in build; slender [Most jockeys are short and *slight*.] *See* SYNONYMS *at* **thin.** ✦***v.*** to pay little or no attention to; neglect, snub, etc. [to *slight* one's homework; to *slight* a neighbor]. ✦***n.*** the act of slighting a person. —**slight'ly *adv.***

**slim** (slim) ***adj.*** **1** slender or thin. *See* SYNONYMS *at* **thin.** **2** small or slight [a *slim* crowd; *slim* hope]. —**slim'mer, slim'mest** ✦***v.*** to make or become slim [You will have to diet to *slim* down.] —**slimmed, slim'ming**

**slime** (slīm) ***n.*** any soft, moist, slippery matter that is often thought of as filthy or disgusting [*slime* in a cesspool].

**slim·y** (slīm'ē) ***adj.*** **1** of, like, or covered with slime. **2** filthy or disgusting. —**slim'i·er, slim'i·est** —**slim'i·ness *n.***

**sling** (sliŋ) ***n.*** **1** a weapon of ancient times, made of a piece of leather tied to cords and used for hurling stones. **2** *a shorter word for* **slingshot.** **3** a strap, rope, etc. used for holding or lifting a heavy object [a rifle *sling*]. **4** a loop of cloth hanging down from around the neck, for holding an injured arm. ✦***v.*** **1** to throw as with a sling; cast, fling, hurl, etc. **2** to carry, hold, or hang as in a sling [The hammock was *slung* between two trees.] —**slung, sling'ing**

☆**sling·shot** (sliŋ'shät) ***n.*** a stick shaped like a Y with a rubber band tied to the upper tips. It is used for shooting stones. *See the picture.*

**slink** (sliŋk) ***v.*** to move in a fearful or sneaky way, or as if ashamed. *See* SYNONYMS *at* **lurk.** —**slunk, slink'ing**

**slip**[1] (slip) ***v.*** **1** to go or pass quietly or without being noticed; escape [We *slipped* out the door. It *slipped* my mind. Time *slipped* by.] **2** to pass slowly into a certain condition [to *slip* into bad habits]. **3** to move, shift, or drop, as by accident [The plate *slipped* from

sledgehammer

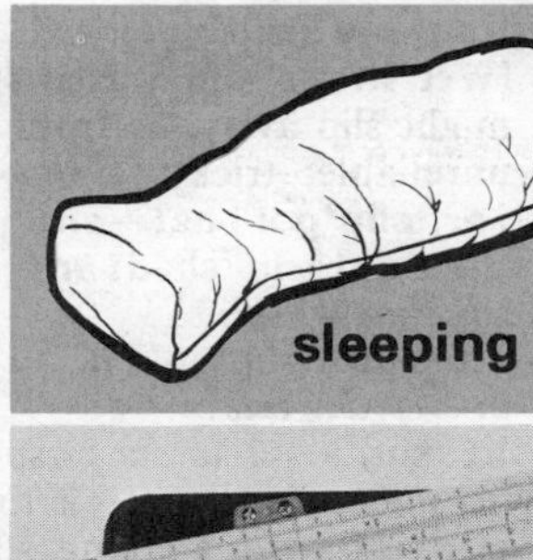
sleeping bag

slide rule

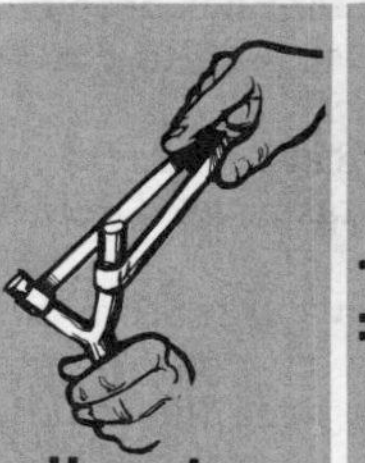
slingshot

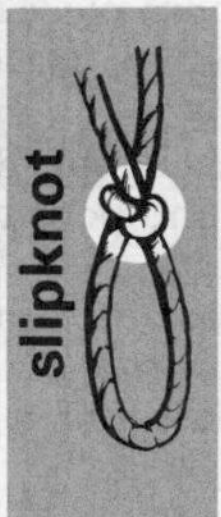
slipknot

sleigh

my hand.] **4** to slide by accident [He *slipped* on the ice.] **5** to make a mistake [I *slipped* when I told you that.] **6** to put or move smoothly, easily, or quickly [*Slip* the bolt through the hole. She *slipped* her shoes off.] **7** to become worse, weaker, lower, etc. [My memory is *slipping*. Prices have *slipped*.] —**slipped, slip'ping** ✦***n.*** ☆**1** a space between piers, where ships can dock. **2** an undergarment worn by women, about the length of a dress or skirt. **3** a pillowcase. **4** the act of slipping or falling down. **5** a mistake or accident [a *slip* of the tongue]. —**give someone the slip,** to escape from someone. —**let slip,** to say without meaning to. —☆**slip one over on,** to trick; fool: *used only in everyday talk.* —☆**slip up,** to make a mistake.



**slip**[2] (slip) ***n.*** **1** a stem, root, etc. cut off from a plant, used for starting a new plant. **2** a young, slim person [a *slip* of a girl]. **3** a small piece of paper, as for a special use [a sales *slip*].

**slip·cov·er** (slip'kuv'ər) ***n.*** a fitted cover for a chair, sofa, etc. that can be taken off for washing.

**slip·knot** (slip'nät) ***n.*** a knot made so that it will slip along the rope around which it is tied. *See the picture.*

**slip-on** (slip'än) ***adj.*** easily put on or taken off, as shoes without laces, or a garment to be slipped on or off over the head.

**slip·per** (slip'ər) ***n.*** a light, low shoe that can be slipped on easily, especially one made to be worn indoors. —**slip'pered *adj.***

| | | | | | | | |
|---|---|---|---|---|---|---|---|
| **a** | fat | **ir** | here | **ou** | out | **zh** | leisure |
| **ā** | ape | **ī** | bite, fire | **u** | up | **ŋ** | ring |
| **ä** | car, lot | **ō** | go | **ur** | fur | | a *in* ago |
| **e** | ten | **ô** | law, horn | **ch** | chin | | e *in* agent |
| **er** | care | **oi** | oil | **sh** | she | ə = | i *in* unity |
| **ē** | even | **oo** | look | **th** | thin | | o *in* collect |
| **i** | hit | **ōō** | tool | ***th*** | then | | u *in* focus |

**slip·per·y** (slip′ər ē) ***adj.*** **1** that can cause slipping [Wet streets and waxed floors are *slippery*.] **2** that might slip away, as from a hold [a *slippery* dish]. **3** unreliable; tricky [a *slippery* politician]. —**slip′per·i·er, slip′per·i·est —slip′per·i·ness *n.***

**slip·shod** (slip′shäd) ***adj.*** careless; not careful or neat [*slipshod* work].

☆**slip-up** (slip′up′) ***n.*** an error or mistake: *used only in everyday talk.*

**slit** (slit) ***v.*** **1** to cut or split open; make a long cut in [to *slit* an envelope]. **2** to cut into long strips. —**slit, slit′ting** ◆***n.*** **1** a long, straight cut or tear. **2** a long, narrow opening.

**slith·er** (sli*th*′ər) ***v.*** to slide or glide, as a snake does. ◆***n.*** a slithering motion.

**sliv·er** (sliv′ər) ***n.*** a thin, sharp piece that has been cut or split off; splinter [a *sliver* of glass]. ◆***v.*** to cut or break into slivers.

**slob** (släb) ***n.*** a person who is not neat or careful, or one who has bad manners and poor taste: *used only in everyday talk.*

**slob·ber** (släb′ər) ***v.*** **1** to let saliva run from the mouth; drool. **2** to speak, write, etc. in a foolish and sentimental way. ◆***n.*** saliva running from the mouth. —**slob′ber·y *adj.***

**sloe** (slō) ***n.*** **1** a dark blue fruit like a small plum. **2** the thorny bush it grows on.

**sloe-eyed** (slō′īd′) ***adj.*** **1** having large, dark eyes. **2** having almond-shaped eyes.



**slog**[1] (släg) ***v.*** to hit hard; slug. —**slogged, slog′ging —slog′ger *n.***

**slog**[2] (släg) ***v.*** **1** to make one's way with great effort; plod. **2** to work hard; toil. —**slogged, slog′ging**

**slo·gan** (slō′gən) ***n.*** a word or phrase used by a political party, business, etc. to get attention or to advertise a product.

> **Slogan** comes from a Gaelic word used by Scottish Highland and Irish clans as a battle cry or to call the clan together. Now the word **slogan** has little to do with war, but it is used to get people to rally around a political candidate or party.

**sloop** (slo͞op) ***n.*** a small sailboat with one mast, a mainsail, and a jib.

**slop** (släp) ***n.*** **1** very wet snow or mud; slush. **2** a puddle of spilled liquid. **3** watery food that is thin and tasteless. **4** *often* **slops,** *pl.* liquid waste or garbage. ◆***v.*** **1** to spill or splash. **2** to walk through slush. —**slopped, slop′ping —slop over,** to overflow or spill; splash.

**slope** (slōp) ***n.*** **1** land that slants up or down, as a hillside [to ski on a *slope*]. **2** a surface, line, etc. that slants or the amount of this slant [The roof has a *slope* of 30 degrees.] ◆***v.*** to have a slope; slant [The lawn *slopes* down to a lake.] —**sloped, slop′ing**

sluice

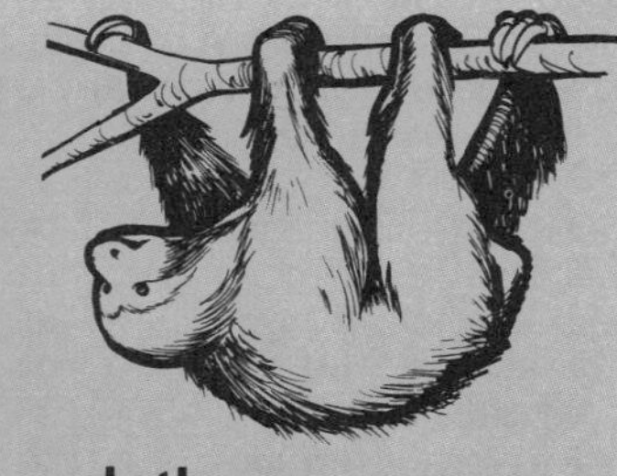

sloth 60 cm (2 ft.) long

**slop·py** (släp′ē) ***adj.*** **1** wet and likely to splash; slushy [a *sloppy* road]. **2** not neat or careful; messy [*sloppy* clothes; a *sloppy* piece of work]. —**slop′pi·er, slop′pi·est —slop′pi·ly *adv.* —slop′pi·ness *n.***

☆**sloppy Joe** ground meat cooked with tomato sauce, spices, etc. and served on a bun.

**slosh** (släsh) ***v.*** **1** to splash through mud, water, etc. in a clumsy way. **2** to splash about, as a liquid. **3** to shake or stir up, as a liquid or something in a liquid.

**slot** (slät) ***n.*** **1** a narrow opening, as in a mailbox. ☆**2** a position in a group, series, etc.: *used only in everyday talk* [Our next game is in the third *slot* on our schedule.] ◆***v.*** **1** to make a slot in. ☆**2** to place in a series: *used only in everyday talk.* —**slot′ted, slot′ting**

**sloth** (slôth *or* slōth) ***n.*** **1** the condition of not liking to work or be active; laziness. **2** an animal of South America that moves very slowly and lives in trees, often hanging upside down from the branches. *See the picture.*

**sloth·ful** (slôth′fəl *or* slōth′fəl) ***adj.*** not liking to work or act; lazy. —**sloth′ful·ly *adv.* —sloth′ful·ness *n.***

**slot machine** a machine, especially a gambling device, worked by putting a coin in a slot.

**slouch** (slouch) ***v.*** to sit, stand, or walk with the head drooping and the shoulders slumping. ◆***n.*** **1** the act or position of slouching. ☆**2** a person who is awkward or lazy. ☆**3** a person who lacks skill: *used only in everyday talk* [She's no *slouch* at golf.] —**slouch′y *adj.***

**slough**[1] (sluf) ***v.*** to shed or get rid of [Snakes *slough* their skins at least once a year. I've *sloughed* off my cold.] ◆***n.*** something that is cast off, as a snake's skin.

**slough**[2] (slou) ***n.*** **1** a place full of soft, deep mud. ☆**2** (slo͞o) a swamp, bog, or marsh.

**Slo·va·ki·a** (slō vä′kē ə *or* slō vak′ē ə) one of the two main parts of Czechoslovakia. —**Slo′vak** or **Slo·va′ki·an *adj., n.***

**slov·en** (sluv′ən) ***n.*** a person who is careless in appearance, habits, work, etc.; dirty or untidy person.

**Slo·ve·ni·a** (slō vē′nē ə) a state of Yugoslavia. —**Slo′vene** or **Slo·ve′ni·an *n., adj.***

**slov·en·ly** (sluv′ən lē) ***adj.*** careless in looks, habits, work, etc.; untidy. ◆***adv.*** in a slovenly way. —**slov′en·li·ness *n.***

**slow** (slō) ***adj.*** **1** not fast or quick in moving, working, etc. [a *slow* train; a *slow* reader]. **2** that makes high speed difficult [a *slow* track]. **3** taking a longer time than is usual [*slow* to answer]. **4** not quick in understanding [a *slow* learner]. **5** not lively, active, or interesting; dull; sluggish [This book has a *slow* plot. Business is *slow*.] **6** showing a time that is behind the real time [Your watch is *slow*.] ◆***v.*** to make, become, or go slow or slower: *often used with* up *or* down. ◆***adv.*** in a slow way; slowly. —**slow′ly *adv.* —slow′ness *n.***

**slow-mo·tion** (slō′mō′shən) ***adj.*** describing a movie or television tape in which the action is made to seem much slower than the real action.

**slow·poke** (slō′pōk) ***n.*** a person who moves or acts slowly: *a slang word.*

**sludge** (sluj) ***n.*** **1** soft mud or mire. **2** any heavy, slimy waste, as thick, dirty oil. —**sludg'y** ***adj.***

**slue** (slo͞o) ***v.*** to turn or swing around, as on a pivot. —**slued, slu'ing** ◆***n.*** the act of sluing.

**slug**[1] (slug) ***n.*** **1** a small, slow-moving animal like a snail, but having no outer shell. Slugs live in damp places and feed on plants. **2** any smooth larva like this.

**slug**[2] (slug) ***n.*** **1** a small piece or lump of metal, as a bullet. ☆**2** a small, round piece of metal used in place of a coin in a coin-operated machine. Slugs are sometimes used in order to cheat.

**slug**[3] (slug) ***n.*** a drink of alcoholic liquor, especially one that is gulped down in one swallow: *a slang word.*

**slug**[4] (slug) ***v.*** to hit hard, as with the fist. —**slugged, slug'ging** ◆***n.*** a hard blow. *This word is used only in everyday talk.* —☆**slug'ger** ***n.***

**slug·gard** (slug'ərd) ***n.*** a lazy person.

**slug·gish** (slug'ish) ***adj.*** **1** not having much energy or vigor; lazy; not active [a *sluggish* mind]. **2** slow or slow-moving [a *sluggish* engine]. —**slug'gish·ly** ***adv.*** —**slug'gish·ness** ***n.***

**sluice** (slo͞os) ***n.*** **1** a channel for water with a gate to control the flow. *See the picture.* **2** the water held back by such a gate. **3** such a gate; floodgate. **4** any channel, as a trough for washing gold, carrying logs, etc. ◆***v.*** **1** to let out or flow out by means of a sluice. **2** to wash with a flow of water [to *sluice* gravel for gold; to *sluice* a ship's deck with hoses]. —**sluiced, sluic'ing**

**slum** (slum) ***n.*** a part of a city which is dirty and rundown and crowded with poor people. ◆***v.*** to visit slums. —**slummed, slum'ming**

**slum·ber** (slum'bər) ***v.*** **1** to sleep. **2** to be quiet or inactive [The volcano has *slumbered* for years.] ◆***n.*** **1** sleep. **2** a quiet or inactive condition.

**slum·ber·ous** (slum'bər əs) ***adj.*** **1** sleepy; drowsy. **2** causing sleep [*slumberous* music]. **3** calm; quiet [a *slumberous* little town]. *Also* **slum·brous** (slum'brəs).

**slump** (slump) ***v.*** **1** to fall, sink, or drop suddenly or heavily [She *slumped* to the floor in a faint. Sales have *slumped.*] **2** to have a drooping posture; slouch. ◆***n.*** **1** a fall or drop, as in value or amount. ☆**2** a period when business is slow or the way one performs is not as good as usual.

**slung** (slung) *past tense and past participle of* **sling.**

**slunk** (slungk) *past tense and past participle of* **slink.**

**slur** (slur) ***v.*** **1** to pass over quickly or carelessly [to *slur* over a point in a talk]. **2** to pronounce in an unclear way, as by combining or dropping sounds [We *slur* "Gloucester" by pronouncing it (gläs'tər).] **3** to sing or play two or more notes by gliding from one to another without a break. **4** to speak badly of; insult. —**slurred, slur'ring** ◆***n.*** **1** the act of slurring. **2** something slurred, as a pronunciation. **3** a remark that hurts someone's reputation; insult. **4** a group of slurred notes in music; also, a mark, (⌒) or (‿), connecting such notes.

**slurp** (slurp) ***v.*** to drink or eat in a noisy way. ◆***n.*** a loud sipping or sucking sound. *This is a slang word.*

**slush** (slush) ***n.*** **1** snow that is partly melted. **2** soft mud. ☆**3** talk or writing that shows tender feelings in a weak or foolish way. ☆**4** shaved or crushed ice with a fruit-flavored syrup poured over it. —**slush'i·ness** ***n.*** —**slush'y** ***adj.***

**slut** (slut) ***n.*** **1** a dirty, untidy woman. **2** an immoral woman.

**sly** (slī) ***adj.*** **1** able to fool or trick others; cunning; crafty [the *sly* fox]. **2** tricking or teasing in a playful way [*sly* humor]. —**on the sly,** secretly [She lent him the money *on the sly.*] —**sli'er** or **sly'er, sli'est** or **sly'est** —**sly'ly** or **sli'ly** ***adv.***

**smack**[1] (smak) ***n.*** **1** a slight taste or flavor. **2** a small amount; trace. ◆***v.*** to have a flavor or trace [Her offer *smacks* of bribery.]

**smack**[2] (smak) ***n.*** **1** a sharp noise made by parting the lips suddenly, as in showing one likes a certain taste. **2** a loud kiss. **3** a sharp slap. ◆***v.*** **1** to make a smack with [to *smack* one's lips]. **2** to kiss or slap loudly. **3** to make a sharp noise, as in hitting [He *smacked* into the desk.] ◆***adv.*** sharply or violently [The car ran *smack* into the wall.]

**smack**[3] (smak) ***n.*** **1** a small sailboat. ☆**2** a fishing boat with a well for keeping fish alive.

**small** (smôl) ***adj.*** **1** little in size; not large or big [a *small* city; a *small* business]. **2** soft and weak [a *small* voice]. **3** not important; trivial [a *small* matter; *small* talk]. **4** mean or selfish [It would be *small* of you not to leave a tip.] **5** young [a book for *small* children]. ◆***n.*** the small or narrow part [the *small* of the back]. —**feel small,** to feel ashamed or humble. —**small'ness** ***n.***

SYNONYMS: **Small** and **little** can often be used in place of each other, but **small** is usually used of something one can see or touch that is less than the usual size, amount, number, etc. [a *small* box; a *small* audience]. **Little** is more often used of something one cannot see or touch [*little* faults] or in showing tenderness [a cute *little* baby] or in describing something unimportant, mean, petty, etc. [of *little* value].

**small arms** firearms that are held in the hand or hands when fired, as pistols, rifles, shotguns, etc.

**small change** **1** coins of low value, as pennies, nickels, and dimes. **2** something of little importance.

**small fry** **1** small fish. **2** young children.

**small letter** a letter that is not a capital letter.

**small-mind·ed** (smôl'mīn'did) ***adj.*** selfish, mean, or narrow-minded.

**small·pox** (smôl'päks) ***n.*** a disease causing a high fever and sores on the skin that often leave pitted scars. It is very contagious, but vaccination has made it rare in most parts of the world.

**small talk** light, easy talk about things that are not very important.

**smart** (smärt) ***adj.*** **1** intelligent or clever [a *smart* student]. **2** neat, clean, and well-groomed. **3** of the newest fashion; stylish [a *smart* new hat]. **4** sharp; strong; intense [a *smart* pain]. **5** causing sharp pain [a *smart* rap on the knuckles]. **6** quick or lively; brisk



| | | | | | | | |
|---|---|---|---|---|---|---|---|
| **a** | fat | **ir** | here | **ou** | out | **zh** | leisure |
| **ā** | ape | **ī** | bite, fire | **u** | up | **ng** | ring |
| **ä** | car, lot | **ō** | go | **ur** | fur | | a *in* ago |
| **e** | ten | **ô** | law, horn | **ch** | chin | | e *in* agent |
| **er** | care | **oi** | oil | **sh** | she | **ə** = | i *in* unity |
| **ē** | even | **oo** | look | **th** | thin | | o *in* collect |
| **i** | hit | **o͞o** | tool | ***th*** | then | | u *in* focus |

**S**

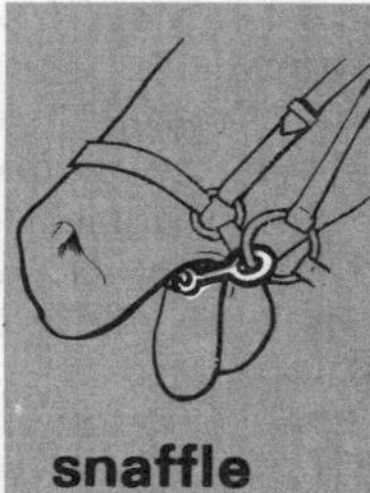


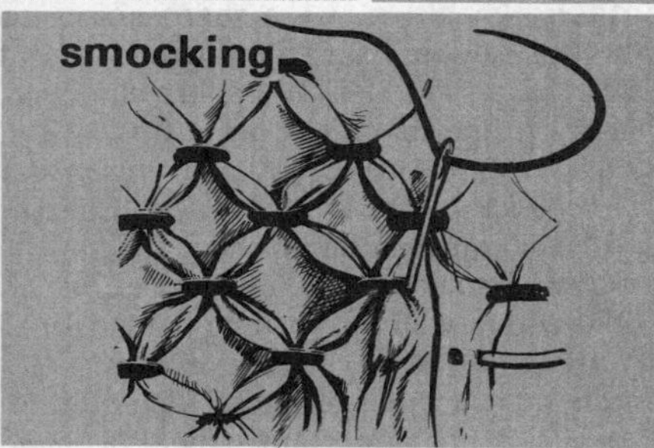


[We jogged at a *smart* pace.] **7** talking back in a way that is not respectful; impudent: *used only in everyday talk* [You'd better not get *smart* with her!] **◆v.** **1** to cause a sharp, stinging pain [A bee sting *smarts.*] **2** to feel such a pain [The smoke from the fire is making my eyes *smart.*] **3** to feel troubled or upset, as from being hurt, angry, etc. [Their insults left him *smarting.*] **◆n.** a sharp, stinging pain or feeling. **—smart'ly** ***adv.*** **—smart'ness** ***n.***



☆**smart al·eck** (al'ik) a person who acts or talks in a cocky, conceited way: *used only in everyday talk.*

**smart·en** (smärt''n) ***v.*** to make or become smart, neat, stylish, brisk, etc.

**smash** (smash) ***v.*** **1** to break into many pieces with noise or force [The plate *smashed* as it hit the floor. The firefighter *smashed* the door with an ax.] *See* SYNONYMS *at* **break**. **2** to move or send with much force; crash [The car *smashed* into a tree.] **3** to destroy completely [to *smash* one's hopes]. **◆n.** **1** the act or sound of smashing. **2** a wreck or collision [Both drivers were hurt in the *smash.*] **◆☆*adj.*** very successful: *used only in everyday talk* [The play is a *smash* hit.]

**smash·up** (smash'up) ***n.*** **1** a very bad wreck or collision. **2** complete failure; ruin [the *smashup* of one's plans].

**smat·ter·ing** (smat'ər iŋ) ***n.*** a little knowledge [I have only a *smattering* of French.]

**smear** (smir) ***v.*** **1** to cover with something greasy, sticky, etc. [to *smear* a face with cold cream]. **2** to rub or spread [*Smear* some grease on the wheel.] **3** to make a mark or streak that is not wanted [He *smeared* the wet paint with his sleeve.] **4** to harm the reputation of in an unfair way; slander [She claims that he *smeared* her in his book.] **◆n.** **1** a mark or streak made by smearing. **2** the act of smearing; especially, slander.

**smell** (smel) ***v.*** **1** to be aware of something through a special sense in the nose; notice the odor or scent of [I *smell* something burning.] **2** to breathe in the odor of [You'll know whether it's gasoline when you *smell* it.] **3** to give off a certain scent [This perfume *smells* of violets.] **4** to give off an unpleasant odor [The fish began to rot and *smell.*] **5** to become aware of [I can *smell* trouble in that crowd.] **—smelled** or **smelt** (smelt), **smell'ing** **◆n.** **1** the power to smell; sense in the nose by which one becomes aware of things. **2** that quality of a thing which is noticed by the nose; odor; scent; aroma [the *smell* of coffee]. **3** an act of smelling [One *smell* told me he was baking bread.]

**smelling salts** a compound of ammonia that has a sharp smell. It is sniffed by people to relieve faintness, headaches, etc.

**smell·y** (smel'ē) ***adj.*** having a bad smell. **—smell'i·er, smell'i·est**

**smelt**[1] (smelt) ***n.*** a small, silvery fish of northern seas, used as food.

**smelt**[2] (smelt) ***v.*** **1** to melt in order to get the pure metal away from the waste matter [to *smelt* iron ore]. **2** to make pure by melting and removing the waste matter [to *smelt* tin].

**smelt·er** (smel'tər) ***n.*** **1** a place or furnace where smelting is done. **2** a person whose work or business is smelting.

☆**smidg·en** (smij'ən) ***n.*** a small amount; a bit: *used only in everyday talk* [Add just a *smidgen* of salt.]

**smile** (smīl) ***v.*** **1** to show that one is pleased, happy, amused, etc., or sarcastic or scornful, by making the corners of the mouth turn up. **2** to show with a smile [She *smiled* her thanks.] **—smiled, smil'ing** **◆n.** **1** the act of smiling or the look on one's face when one smiles. **2** a cheerful, pleasant outlook [to face the future with a *smile*]. **—smile on,** to show approval of [Fortune seems to have *smiled on* them.]

**smirch** (smurch) ***v.*** **1** to stain or make dirty, as by smearing. **2** to dishonor or disgrace [Ugly rumors had *smirched* her good name.] **◆n.** a smear, stain, or dirty spot.

**smirk** (smurk) ***v.*** to smile in a silly, conceited way. *See the picture.* **◆n.** such a silly smile.

**smite** (smīt) ***v.*** **1** to hit or strike hard, especially so as to kill or destroy: *no longer much used in this meaning.* **2** to affect in a sudden and strong way [He was *smitten* with love.] **—smote, smit'ten** or **smote, smit'ing**

**smith** (smith) ***n.*** **1** a person who makes or repairs metal objects [a silver*smith;* a lock*smith*]. **2** *a shorter form of* **blacksmith.**

**Smith** (smith), Captain **John** 1580–1631; English explorer who settled a colony in Virginia. *See the entry for* **Pocahontas.**

**Smith, Joseph** 1805–1844; U.S. religious leader who founded the Mormon Church.

**smith·er·eens** (smith ə rēnz') ***n.pl.*** small pieces or bits: *used only in everyday talk* [The vase was broken to *smithereens.*]

**smith·y** (smith'ē) ***n.*** the workshop of a smith, especially of a blacksmith. *—pl.* **smith'ies**

**smit·ten** (smit''n) *past participle of* **smite.**

**smock** (smäk) ***n.*** a loose outer garment like a long shirt, worn over other clothes to protect them, as by an artist. *See the picture.* **◆v.** to decorate with smocking.

**smock·ing** (smäk'iŋ) ***n.*** fancy stitching used to gather cloth and make it hang in even folds. *See the picture.*

**smog** (smôg *or* smäg) ***n.*** a mixture of fog and smoke.

**Smog** is a word formed by putting together parts from two other words: *sm* from *smoke* and *og* from *fog*. A word formed in this way is called a "blend."

**smoke** (smōk) ***n.*** **1** the gas and bits of carbon that rise from something burning [*smoke* from a campfire]. **2** any cloud or mist that looks like smoke. ☆**3** the act of smoking a cigarette, cigar, etc. **4** a cigarette, cigar, etc. ♦***v.*** **1** to give off smoke [a *smoking* volcano]. **2** to cause smoke to go in the wrong place [This fireplace *smokes.*] **3** to breathe smoke from a cigar, cigarette, etc. into the mouth and blow it out again. **4** to treat with smoke in order to flavor and keep from spoiling [to *smoke* a ham]. **5** to force out as with smoke [We *smoked* the bees from the hollow tree.] —**smoked, smok′ing**

**smoke·house** (smōk′hous) ***n.*** a building where meats, fish, etc. are cured and flavored with smoke.

**smoke·less** (smōk′lis) ***adj.*** giving off little or no smoke [*smokeless* gunpowder].

**smok·er** (smōk′ər) ***n.*** **1** a person who smokes tobacco. ☆**2** a party for men only.

**smoke screen** **1** a cloud of smoke spread to hide the movements of troops, ships, etc. **2** anything said or done to keep something from being found out.

☆**smoke·stack** (smōk′stak) ***n.*** a tall pipe that is a chimney for carrying away the smoke from a factory, steamship, etc.

**smok·y** (smō′kē) ***adj.*** **1** giving off smoke, especially too much smoke [a *smoky* fireplace]. **2** of, like, or having the color or taste of smoke [a *smoky* blue haze; *smoky* cheese]. **3** filled with smoke [a *smoky* room]. **4** made dirty by smoke [a *smoky* wall]. —**smok′i·er, smok′i·est** —**smok′i·ness** ***n.***

**smol·der** (smōl′dər) ***v.*** **1** to burn and smoke without flame. **2** to be present but kept under control [a *smoldering* feeling of revenge]. **3** to feel anger or hate but keep it under control [She *smoldered* after the insult but said nothing.]

**smooth** (smo͞oth) ***adj.*** **1** having an even surface, with no bumps or rough spots [as *smooth* as marble; *smooth* water on the lake]. **2** without lumps [a *smooth* paste]. **3** even or gentle in movement; not jerky or rough [a *smooth* airplane flight; a *smooth* ride; *smooth* sailing]. **4** with no trouble or difficulty [*smooth* progress]. **5** pleasing in taste, sound, etc.; not harsh or sharp [a *smooth* flavor; *smooth* dance music]. ☆**6** speaking or spoken easily and politely, often in a way that seems false or not sincere [a *smooth* talker; *smooth* words]. ♦***v.*** **1** to make smooth or even [*Smooth* the board with sandpaper.] **2** to make easy by taking away troubles, difficulties, etc. [She *smoothed* our way by introducing us to the other guests.] **3** to make less crude; polish or refine [The lessons *smoothed* his dancing style.] ♦***adv.*** in a smooth way [The engine is running *smooth* now.] —**smooth down,** to make even, level, calm, etc. —**smooth over,** to make seem less serious or less bad [She *smoothed* over the criticism by adding a compliment.] —**smooth′ly** ***adv.*** —**smooth′ness** ***n.***

☆**smooth·bore** (smo͞oth′bôr) ***adj.*** not grooved on the inside of the barrel [a *smoothbore* gun].

☆**smor·gas·bord** (smôr′gəs bôrd) ***n.*** **1** a large variety of tasty foods, as cheeses, fishes, meats, etc., on a table where people help themselves. **2** a restaurant where such foods are served in this way.

**smote** (smōt) *past tense of* **smite.**

**smoth·er** (smuth′ər) ***v.*** **1** to keep or be kept from getting enough air to breathe; often, to kill or die in this way; suffocate [I nearly *smothered* in the smoky room.] **2** to keep air from so as to stop burning [We *smothered* the fire with sand.] **3** to cover with a thick layer [liver *smothered* in onions]. **4** to hold back or hide; suppress [He *smothered* a yawn.] ♦***n.*** heavy, choking smoke, dust, etc.

**smoul·der** (smōl′dər) ***v.*** *the British spelling of* **smolder.**

**smudge** (smuj) ***n.*** **1** a dirty spot; stain; smear. **2** a fire made to give off a thick smoke, as for driving away insects or protecting plants from frost. ♦***v.*** to streak with dirt; smear [They came up from the mine *smudged* with coal dust.] —**smudged, smudg′ing** —**smudg′y** ***adj.***

**smug** (smug) ***adj.*** so pleased with oneself as to be annoying to others; too self-satisfied ["No one will beat my score," he said with a *smug* smile.] —**smug′ger, smug′gest** —**smug′ly** ***adv.*** —**smug′ness** ***n.***

**Smug** comes from a German word meaning "neat or trim." People who always look neat and trim may come to have such a good opinion of themselves as to seem smug to other people.

**smug·gle** (smug′'l) ***v.*** **1** to bring into or take out of a country in a way that is secret and against the law [They were arrested for *smuggling* drugs into the country.] **2** to bring or take in a secret way [His sister *smuggled* out letters for him when he was in jail.] —**smug′gled, smug′gling** —**smug′gler** ***n.***

**smut** (smut) ***n.*** **1** soot or dirt, or a dirty mark or smear. **2** disgusting or dirty talk or writing. **3** a fungus disease of plants, especially of grain, in which the plant becomes covered with black dust.

**smut·ty** (smut′ē) ***adj.*** **1** made dirty, as with soot. **2** disgusting or indecent [*smutty* talk or writing]. —**smut′ti·er, smut′ti·est**

**Sn** *the symbol for the chemical element* tin.

**snack** (snak) ***n.*** a small amount of food; often, a light meal eaten between regular meals. ♦***v.*** to eat a snack or snacks.

**snaf·fle** (snaf′'l) ***n.*** a bit for a horse's mouth, having a joint in the middle and no curb. *See the picture.*

**snag** (snag) ***n.*** **1** a sharp part that sticks out and may catch on things. **2** a tear in cloth made by this [The nail made a *snag* in my sweater.] ☆**3** an underwater tree stump or branch that is dangerous to boats. ☆**4** anything hidden or not expected that gets in the way [Our vacation plans hit a *snag* when I became sick.] ♦***v.*** **1** to tear or catch on a snag [I *snagged* my sleeve on a bramble.] **2** to get in the way of; hinder. —**snagged, snag′ging**



| | | | |
|---|---|---|---|
| **a** fat | **ir** here | **ou** out | **zh** leisure |
| **ā** ape | **ī** bite, fire | **u** up | **ng** ring |
| **ä** car, lot | **ō** go | **ur** fur | a *in* ago |
| **e** ten | **ô** law, horn | **ch** chin | e *in* agent |
| **er** care | **oi** oil | **sh** she | **ə** = i *in* unity |
| **ē** even | **oo** look | **th** thin | o *in* collect |
| **i** hit | **o͞o** tool | ***th*** then | u *in* focus |

**snail** (snāl) ***n.*** a slow-moving animal with a soft body and a spiral shell into which it can draw back for protection. Snails live on land or in the water.

**snake** (snāk) ***n.*** **1** a crawling reptile with a long, thin body covered with scales and no legs. A few kinds of snake have a poisonous bite. **2** a person who cannot be trusted, especially one who betrays others. **3** a long, bending rod used by plumbers to clear blocked pipes. ◆***v.*** to move, twist, or turn like a snake. —**snaked, snak′ing**

**snak·y** (snā′kē) ***adj.*** **1** of or like a snake or snakes [*snaky* hair]. **2** winding or twisting [a *snaky* river]. —**snak′i·er, snak′i·est**

**snap** (snap) ***v.*** **1** to bite or grasp suddenly [The frog *snapped* at the fly. We *snapped* up her offer at once.] **2** to speak or say in a short, sharp way [The boss *snapped* out orders. She was so angry she *snapped* back at me.] **3** to break suddenly with a sharp, cracking sound [The cord *snapped* in two when I pulled it tight.] **4** to give way suddenly [His nerves *snapped* under the strain.] **5** to make or cause to make a sharp, cracking sound [She *snapped* her fingers.] **6** to close, fasten, let go, etc. with a sound like this [The lock *snapped* shut.] **7** to move in a quick, lively way [The soldiers *snapped* to attention.] ☆**8** to take a snapshot of [Let me *snap* the children first.] —**snapped, snap′ping** ◆***n.*** **1** a sudden bite, grasp, etc. **2** a sharp, cracking or clicking sound [The purse closed with a *snap.*] **3** a fastening that closes with such a sound. ☆**4** a quick, sharp or lively way of speaking, moving, etc. **5** a short period, as of cold weather. **6** a hard, thin cookie [ginger*snaps*]. **7** *a shorter form of* **snapshot.** ☆**8** an easy job, problem, etc.: *slang in this meaning* [That math test was no *snap.*] ◆***adj.*** ☆**1** made or done quickly without much thought [a *snap* decision]. ☆**2** easy; simple: *slang in this meaning* [Chemistry is not a *snap* course.] —**not a snap,** not at all. —☆**snap out of it,** to recover suddenly, as one's normal ways, feelings, etc.



**snap bean** *another name for* **string bean.**

**snap·drag·on** (snap′drag′ən) ***n.*** a plant with spikes of red, white, or yellow flowers. *See the picture.*

**snap·per** (snap′ər) ***n.*** **1** a food fish of warm oceans; especially, the ☆**red snapper,** which has a reddish body. ☆**2** *a shorter name for* **snapping turtle. 3** a person or thing that snaps.

☆**snapping turtle** a large turtle of North America that lives in ponds and rivers. It has powerful jaws that snap with force.

**snap·pish** (snap′ish) ***adj.*** **1** likely to snap or bite [a *snappish* dog]. **2** easily made angry; cross; irritable. —**snap′pish·ly *adv.*** —**snap′pish·ness *n.***

**snap·py** (snap′ē) ***adj.*** **1** snappish; cross. **2** brisk or lively: *used only in everyday talk* [music with a *snappy* tempo]. —**snap′pi·er, snap′pi·est**

**snap·shot** (snap′shät) ***n.*** a picture taken quickly by snapping the shutter of a hand camera.

**snare** (sner) ***n.*** **1** a trap for catching animals, usually made of a noose that jerks tight about the animal's body. **2** anything by which a person is caught or trapped [That question was a *snare* to get him to admit he was wrong.] ◆***v.*** to catch in a snare; trap. —**snared, snar′ing**

**snare drum** a small drum with strings of wire or gut stretched across the bottom to make more vibration when the drum is struck. *See the picture.*

**snarl**[1] (snärl) ***v.*** **1** to growl in a fierce way, showing the teeth [a *snarling* dog]. **2** to speak or say in a harsh or angry tone ["Go away!" she *snarled.*] ◆***n.*** the act or sound of snarling.

**snarl**[2] (snärl) ***v.*** to make or become tangled or confused [I *snarled* the fishing line while reeling it in. Traffic is *snarled* on the freeway.] ◆***n.*** **1** a tangle or knot [hair full of *snarls*]. **2** a confused condition [These files are in a *snarl.*]

**snatch** (snach) ***v.*** to reach for or seize suddenly; grab; grasp [The thief *snatched* the purse and ran.] ◆***n.*** **1** the act of snatching; a grab. **2** a short time [to sleep in *snatches*]. **3** a small amount; bit [I remember a *snatch* of the tune.] —**snatch at, 1** to try to get. **2** to be eager for.

**sneak** (snēk) ***v.*** **1** to move or act in a quiet or secret way to keep from being noticed [They *sneaked* out of the room while we were talking.] *See* SYNONYMS *at* **lurk. 2** to give, put, carry, etc. in this way [Try to *sneak* the presents into the closet.] ◆***n.*** a dishonest, cheating person. ◆***adj.*** done without warning [a *sneak* attack].

**sneak·er** (snē′kər) ***n.*** ☆a cloth shoe with a flat, rubber sole and no heel, worn for play and for sports.

**sneak·ing** (snē′kiŋ) ***adj.*** **1** moving or acting like a sneak [a person with *sneaking* ways]. **2** secret or hidden [a *sneaking* desire for candy]. —**sneaking suspicion,** a suspicion that is getting stronger.

**sneak·y** (snē′kē) ***adj.*** of or like a sneak; dishonest; cheating. —**sneak′i·er, sneak′i·est** —**sneak′i·ly *adv.***

**sneer** (snir) ***v.*** **1** to look scornful or sarcastic, as by curling the upper lip. *See the picture.* **2** to show scorn or sarcasm in speaking or writing [Many people *sneered* at the first automobiles.] ◆***n.*** a sneering look or remark.

**sneeze** (snēz) ***v.*** to blow out breath from the mouth and nose in a sudden, uncontrolled way, when one has a cold or something irritates the inside of the nose. —**sneezed, sneez′ing** ◆***n.*** an act of sneezing. —**not to be sneezed at,** not to be thought of as unimportant [She earned $70 mowing lawns, and that's *not to be sneezed at.*]

> The word **sneeze** was originally spelled *fnese.* In earlier times there was a long form of s that looked like an f. Some scribes probably copied the word wrongly and *fnese* became *snese.* The number of words in English that have been changed by mistake is not to be sneezed at.

**snick·er** (snik′ər) ***v.*** to give a sly or silly laugh that is partly held back and that shows scorn or ridicule. ◆***n.*** such a laugh.

**sniff** (snif) ***v.*** **1** to make a noise in drawing air in through the nose, as when trying to smell something. **2** to smell in this way [I *sniffed* the milk to see if it was fresh.] **3** to show dislike or doubt by sniffing [He just *sniffed* when I said hello.] ◆***n.*** **1** the act or sound of sniffing. **2** something sniffed; odor; smell.

**snif·fle** (snif″l) ***v.*** to sniff again and again as in trying to keep mucus from running out of the nose. —**snif′fled, snif′fling** ◆***n.*** the act or sound of sniffling. —**the sniffles, 1** a cold in the head. **2** the sniffling

snapdragon

snare drum

woman sneering

snow blower

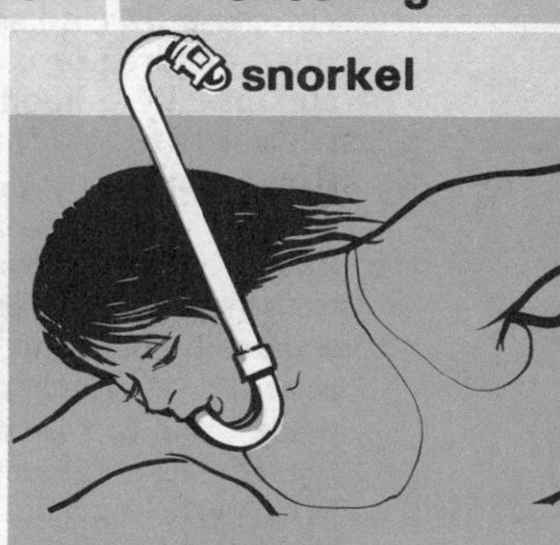

snorkel

that goes along with a crying spell. *This phrase is used only in everyday talk.*

**snig·ger** (snig'ər) ***v., n.*** *another word for* **snicker**.

**snip** (snip) ***v.*** to cut or cut off with a short, quick stroke, as of scissors [*Snip* off the ends of the threads.] —**snipped, snip'ping** ◆***n.*** **1** a small cut made as with scissors. **2** a small piece cut off by snipping. **3** **snips,** *pl.* strong shears for cutting sheet metal. **4** a young or small person, especially one thought of as rude or impudent: *used only in everyday talk.*

**snipe** (snīp) ***n.*** a wading bird with a long bill, that lives mainly in marshes. ◆***v.*** **1** to hunt for snipe. **2** to shoot from a hidden place, as at enemy soldiers, one at a time. **3** to speak or write against a rival in a sly or sneaky way. —**sniped, snip'ing**

**snip·er** (snī'pər) ***n.*** a person, especially a soldier, who shoots from a hidden place.

**snitch** (snich) ***v.*** **1** to steal something of little value [They *snitched* some cookies from the kitchen.] **2** to be a tattletale. ◆***n.*** a tattletale. *This is a slang word.*

**sniv·el** (sniv''l) ***v.*** **1** to cry and sniffle. **2** to cry or complain in a whining way. —**sniv'eled** or **sniv'elled, sniv'el·ing** or **sniv'el·ling**

**snob** (snäb) ***n.*** **1** a person who thinks that people who have money and social position are very important and who ignores or looks down on those who he or she thinks are not important. **2** a person who acts as though his or her taste or intelligence is much higher than that of other people. —**snob'bish** ***adj.*** —**snob'bish·ly** ***adv.***

**snob·ber·y** (snäb'ər ē) ***n.*** the way a snob thinks or behaves. —*pl.* **snob'ber·ies**

**snood** (sno͞od) ***n.*** a net like a bag worn at the back of the head to hold the hair in place.

☆**snoop** (sno͞op) ***v.*** to look about or pry in a sneaking way; spy. ◆***n.*** a person who snoops. *This word is used only in everyday talk.*

> **Snoop** comes from a Dutch word meaning "to eat snacks when no one is looking." A person who is trying to eat snacks in secret would probably be looking about all the time in a sneaking way.

☆**snoot·y** (sno͞ot'ē) ***adj.*** acting in a snobbish or haughty way: *used only in everyday talk.* —**snoot'i·er, snoot'i·est** —**snoot'i·ness** ***n.***

**snooze** (sno͞oz) ***n.*** a short sleep; nap. ◆***v.*** to take a nap. —**snoozed, snooz'ing** *This word is used only in everyday talk.*

**snore** (snôr) ***v.*** to breathe with noisy, rough sounds while sleeping. —**snored, snor'ing** ◆***n.*** the act or sound of snoring.

☆**snor·kel** (snôr'k'l) ***n.*** **1** a device on a submarine for taking in fresh air and letting out stale air. **2** a short tube held in the mouth by swimmers for breathing under water. *See the picture.* ◆***v.*** to swim using a snorkel. —**snor'keled, snor'kel·ing**

**snort** (snôrt) ***v.*** **1** to force breath from the nose in a sudden and noisy way, as a horse does. **2** to make a noise like a snort. **3** to show anger, scorn, etc. by snorting. ◆***n.*** the act or sound of snorting.

**snout** (snout) ***n.*** **1** the nose and jaws of an animal when they stick out, as on a pig or dog. **2** something that looks like this, as a nozzle.

**snow** (snō) ***n.*** **1** soft, white flakes formed from drops of water that freeze in the upper air and fall to the earth. **2** a fall of snow [We are expecting a heavy *snow* tonight.] ◆***v.*** **1** to shower down snow [It is *snowing*.] ☆**2** to cover or shut in with snow or as if with snow [The whole town is *snowed* in. I've been *snowed* under by work.] 

**snow·ball** (snō'bôl) ***n.*** **1** a mass of snow packed into a firm ball. ☆**2** a bush with large, round clusters of small, white flowers. ◆***v.*** **1** to throw snowballs at. **2** to grow larger rapidly like a rolling ball of snow [Her debts began to *snowball*.]

**snow·bank** (snō'baŋk) ***n.*** a large mound of snow.

**snow·bird** (snō'burd) ***n.*** **1** a North American junco with a white belly. **2** *another name for* **snow bunting.**

**snow-blind** (snō'blīnd') ***adj.*** blinded for a short time by the glare of the sun shining on fallen snow. —**snow blindness**

☆**snow blower** a machine driven by a motor for removing snow from walks, driveways, etc. *See the picture.*

**snow·bound** (snō'bound) ***adj.*** shut in or blocked off by snow.

**snow bunting** a small finch living in cold regions.

**snow·drift** (snō'drift) ***n.*** a bank or pile of snow heaped up by the wind.

**snow·drop** (snō'dräp) ***n.*** a small plant with a drooping white flower that blooms in early spring.

**snow·fall** (snō'fôl) ***n.*** **1** a fall of snow. **2** the amount of snow that falls over a certain area during a certain time [a 3-inch *snowfall* on March 3].

| | | | | | | | |
|---|---|---|---|---|---|---|---|
| **a** | fat | **ir** | here | **ou** | out | **zh** | leisure |
| **ā** | ape | **ī** | bite, fire | **u** | up | **ng** | ring |
| **ä** | car, lot | **ō** | go | **ur** | fur | | a *in* ago |
| **e** | ten | **ô** | law, horn | **ch** | chin | | e *in* agent |
| **er** | care | **oi** | oil | **sh** | she | **ə** = | i *in* unity |
| **ē** | even | **oo** | look | **th** | thin | | o *in* collect |
| **i** | hit | **o͞o** | tool | ***th*** | then | | u *in* focus |

**snow·flake** (snō′flāk) ***n.*** a flake of snow. Snowflakes are crystals.
**snow·mo·bile** (snō′mō bēl′) ***n.*** a motor vehicle for traveling on snow. It has runners in front that move so that it can be steered. *See the picture.*
☆**snow·plow** (snō′plou) ***n.*** a machine used to clear snow off a road, etc.
☆**snow·shoe** (snō′sho͞o) ***n.*** a wooden frame strung with leather strips and worn on the shoes to keep one from sinking in deep snow. *See the picture.*
☆**snow·storm** (snō′stôrm) ***n.*** a storm with a heavy snowfall.
☆**snow·suit** (snō′so͞ot) ***n.*** an outer garment worn by small children in cold weather. It has a heavy lining and, usually, a hood.
**snow-white** (snō′hwīt′) ***adj.*** white as snow.
**snow·y** (snō′ē) ***adj.*** **1** having snow [a *snowy* day]. **2** covered with snow [a *snowy* playground]. **3** like snow [*snowy* hair]. —**snow′i·er, snow′i·est**
**snub** (snub) ***v.*** **1** to treat in an unfriendly or scornful way, as by ignoring; slight. **2** to stop from moving [to *snub* a rope attached to a boat, by looping it around a post]. ☆**3** to stop a cigarette from burning by pressing the end against something. —**snubbed, snub′bing** ◆***n.*** scornful or unfriendly treatment. ◆***adj.*** short and turned up [a *snub* nose].
**snuff**[1] (snuf) ***v.*** **1** to put out the flame of [to *snuff* a candle]. **2** to trim off the burned end of a candle's

wick. —**snuff out,** to end suddenly [The accident *snuffed out* three lives.]
**snuff**[2] (snuf) ***v.*** **1** to draw up into the nose by sniffing. **2** to smell or sniff. ◆***n.*** tobacco in powdered form snuffed up into the nose or put on the gums. —**up to snuff,** as good as might be expected: *used only in everyday talk* [not feeling *up to snuff*].
**snuff·box** (snuf′bäks) ***n.*** a small box for snuff.
**snuf·fer** (snuf′ər) ***n.*** **1** a cone at the end of a handle, for putting out the flame of a candle. **2 snuffers,** *pl.* a device like shears, for snuffing a candle.
**snuf·fle** (snuf′'l) ***v.*** to breathe in a noisy way, as when the nose is stopped up with a cold. —**snuf′fled, snuf′fling** ◆***n.*** the act or sound of snuffling.
**snug** (snug) ***adj.*** **1** warm and comfortable; cozy [We lay *snug* in our beds.] **2** small but well-arranged and neat [a *snug* kitchen]. **3** fitting in a tight way [a *snug* vest]. —**snug′ger, snug′gest** —**snug′ly** ***adv.***

snowmobile
snowshoes

soccer player

**snug·gle** (snug′'l) ***v.*** to lie close or hold close in a warm, cozy way; cuddle [The kittens *snuggled* together. He *snuggled* the baby in his arms.] —**snug′gled, snug′gling**
**so** (sō) ***adv.*** **1** to such a degree [She is not *so* tall as I. Why are you *so* late?] **2** as a result; therefore [He couldn't swim and *so* was drowned.] **3** very [They are *so* happy.] **4** also; in the same way [I am hungry and *so* is she.] **5** more or less; just about [I spent a dollar or *so* on candy.] **6** after all; then [*So* you really don't care.] **7** as shown, told, etc.; in such a way [Hold your pencil just *so*.] **8** very much: *used only in everyday talk* [He loves his garden *so*.] ◆***conj.*** **1** for the reason that; in order that [Talk louder *so* that I may hear you.] **2** with the result that: *used only in everyday talk* [She didn't study, *so* she failed the test.] ◆***pron.*** the same [I am his friend and will remain *so*.] ◆***interj.*** a word used to show surprise, dislike, approval or disapproval, doubt, etc. [*So!* I caught you!] ◆***adj.*** **1** being a fact; true [I guess it's really *so*.] **2** in proper order [Everything must be just *so*.] —**and so on** or **and so forth,** and the rest; and others. —**so as,** in order; for the purpose [She left early *so as* to be on time.]
**SO** or **S.O.** strikeout *or* strikeouts (in baseball).
**So.** *abbreviation for* **south** *or* **southern.**
**soak** (sōk) ***v.*** **1** to make or become completely wet by keeping or staying in a liquid [She *soaked* her sore hand in hot water. Let the beans *soak* overnight to soften them.] **2** to suck up or absorb [Use a sponge to *soak* up that water.] **3** to take into the mind [to *soak* up information from books]. **4** to pass or go through [The rain *soaked* through his coat.] ◆***n.*** the act of soaking.

SYNONYMS: To **soak** something is to let it stay in a liquid long enough for it to take in the liquid, become soft, become completely wet, etc. [*Soak* the bread in milk.] To **drench** something is to make it thoroughly wet as by a heavy rain or with water from a hose or bucket [Let the sprinkler run till the garden is *drenched*.]

**so-and-so** (sō′ən sō′) ***n.*** a certain person whose name is not mentioned or not remembered: *used only in everyday talk.* —*pl.* **so′-and-sos′**
**soap** (sōp) ***n.*** a substance used with water to make suds for washing things. Soaps are usually made of an alkali, as potash, and a fat. ◆***v.*** to rub or wash with soap.
☆**soap opera** a radio or TV drama presented in the daytime day after day. The story goes on from one episode to the next and is told in a sentimental and very emotional way.

This sort of drama came to be called a **soap opera** because many of the original sponsors of these programs were soap companies.

**soap·stone** (sōp′stōn) ***n.*** a kind of rock that feels soft and smooth.
**soap·suds** (sōp′sudz) ***n.pl.*** water with soap stirred in until it is foamy.
**soap·y** (sōp′ē) ***adj.*** **1** covered with soapsuds or full of soap [*soapy* water]. **2** of or like soap or soapsuds [*soapy* foam on ocean waves]. —**soap′i·er, soap′i·est**
**soar** (sôr) ***v.*** **1** to rise or fly high in the air [The plane *soared* out of sight.] **2** to rise above what is usual [Prices *soared* after the war.]

**sob** (säb) ***v.*** **1** to cry or weep with a break in the voice and short gasps. **2** to bring or put by sobbing [to *sob* oneself to sleep]. **3** to make a sound like that of a person sobbing [The wind *sobbed* in the trees.] —**sobbed, sob′bing** ◆***n.*** the act or sound of sobbing.

**so·ber** (sō′bər) ***adj.*** **1** showing self-control, especially in not drinking too much alcoholic liquor; temperate. **2** not drunk. **3** serious, quiet, plain, sensible, etc. [a *sober* look on one's face; the *sober* truth; *sober* colors]. ◆***v.*** to make or become sober [The sad news *sobered* us up.] —**so′ber·ly *adv.***

**so·bri·e·ty** (sə brī′ə tē) ***n.*** the condition of being sober.

**Soc.** or **soc.** *abbreviation for* **socialist, society.**

**so-called** (sō′kôld′) ***adj.*** called by this name, but usually not correctly so [Your *so-called* friends tricked you.]

**soc·cer** (säk′ər) ***n.*** a football game in which a round ball is moved by kicking or by using any part of the body except the hands and arms. *See the picture.*

**so·cia·ble** (sō′shə b′l) ***adj.*** **1** enjoying the company of others; friendly [Tracy is a *sociable* person.] **2** full of pleasant talk and friendliness [a *sociable* evening]. ◆***n.*** ☆*another word for* **social.** —**so′cia·bil′i·ty *n.*** —**so′cia·bly *adv.***

**so·cial** (sō′shəl) ***adj.*** **1** of or having to do with human beings as they live together in a group or groups [*social* problems; *social* forces]. **2** living in groups or colonies [Ants are *social* insects.] **3** liking to be with others; sociable [A hermit is not a *social* person.] **4** of or having to do with society, especially with the upper classes [Our party was the *social* event of the year.] **5** of or for companionship [a *social* club]. ◆***n.*** a friendly gathering; party [a church *social*]. —**so′cial·ly *adv.***

**so·cial·ism** (sō′shəl iz′m) ***n.*** any of various systems in which the means of producing goods are publicly owned, with all people sharing in the work and the goods produced.

**so·cial·ist** (sō′shəl ist) ***n.*** **1** a person who is in favor of socialism. **2 Socialist,** a member of a political party that seeks to set up socialism. ◆***adj.*** of or having to do with socialism or socialists: *also* **so′cial·is′tic.**

**so·cial·ize** (sō′shə līz) ***v.*** **1** to make fit for living and getting along in a group; make social. **2** to set up or manage under a system of socialism [to *socialize* industry]. ☆**3** to take part in social activity, parties, etc. [They *socialize* only with members of their club.] —**so′cial·ized, so′cial·iz·ing**

**socialized medicine** any system that uses public funds to give complete medical and hospital care to all the people in a state or nation.

**social science** the study of people living together in groups, their customs, activities, etc. Sociology, history, etc. are social sciences.

☆**social security** a system of government insurance for making payments to those who are retired, unable to work, out of work, etc.

☆**social studies** a course of study, especially in elementary and secondary schools, that includes history, geography, etc.

**social welfare** the welfare of society, especially of those who are poor, out of work, etc.

**social work** work for improving the condition of the people in a community, as by clinics, playgrounds, help for the needy or troubled, etc. —**social worker**

**so·ci·e·ty** (sə sī′ə tē) ***n.*** **1** people living together as a group, or forming a group, with the same way of life; also, their way of life [a primitive *society;* urban *society*]. **2** all people [a law for the good of *society*]. **3** company or companionship [to seek the *society* of others]. **4** a group of people joined together for some common purpose [a medical *society*]. **5** the wealthy, upper class. —*pl.* **so·ci′e·ties**

**Society of Friends** a Christian religious sect that believes in a plain way of life and worship and is against violence of any kind, including war. Its members are often called *Quakers.*

**so·ci·ol·o·gy** (sō′sē äl′ə jē) ***n.*** the study of people living together in groups; study of the history, problems, and forms of human society. —**so·ci·o·log·i·cal** (sō′sē ə läj′i k′l) ***adj.*** —**so′ci·ol′o·gist *n.***

**sock**[1] (säk) ***n.*** a short stocking. —*pl.* **socks** or **sox**

> **Sock** comes from a Latin word meaning "a type of light, low-heeled shoe." Comic characters in ancient Greek and Roman drama wore such light shoes.

**sock**[2] (säk) ***v.*** to hit hard, especially with the fist. ◆***n.*** a hard blow. *This is a slang word.* —☆**sock away,** to set aside money, especially as savings.

**sock·et** (säk′it) ***n.*** a hollow part into which something fits [a *socket* for an electric bulb; the eye *socket*].

**sock·eye** (säk′ī) ***n.*** a salmon of the northern Pacific with red flesh which is used as food and is often canned.



**Soc·ra·tes** (säk′rə tēz) 470?–399 B.C.; Greek philosopher and teacher. —**So·crat·ic** (sə krat′ik) ***adj., n.***

**sod** (säd) ***n.*** **1** the top layer of earth containing grass with its roots; turf. **2** a piece of this layer. ◆***v.*** to cover with sod or sods. —**sod′ded, sod′ding**

**so·da** (sō′də) ***n.*** **1** any of certain substances containing sodium, as baking soda. **2** *a shorter name for* **soda water.** ☆**3** a drink made of soda water, syrup, and ice cream.

☆**soda cracker** a light, crisp cracker made from a dough of flour, water, and leavening. It is usually salted. The leavening originally included baking soda.

☆**soda fountain** a counter for making and serving soft drinks, sodas, sundaes, etc.

**so·dal·i·ty** (sō dal′ə tē) ***n.*** a society of Roman Catholic Church members formed for religious or charitable purposes. —*pl.* **so·dal′i·ties**

**soda water** water filled with carbon dioxide gas to make it bubble.

**sod·den** (säd′′n) ***adj.*** **1** completely wet; soaked through [a lawn *sodden* with rain]. **2** heavy or soggy [*sodden* bread].

**so·di·um** (sō′dē əm) ***n.*** a soft, silver-white metal that is a chemical element. It is found in nature only in

| | | | | | | | |
|---|---|---|---|---|---|---|---|
| **a** | fat | **ir** | here | **ou** | out | **zh** | leisure |
| **ā** | ape | **ī** | bite, fire | **u** | up | **ng** | ring |
| **ä** | car, lot | **ō** | go | **ur** | fur | | a *in* ago |
| **e** | ten | **ô** | law, horn | **ch** | chin | | e *in* agent |
| **er** | care | **oi** | oil | **sh** | she | **ə =** | i *in* unity |
| **ē** | even | **oo** | look | **th** | thin | | o *in* collect |
| **i** | hit | **ōō** | tool | ***th*** | then | | u *in* focus |

compounds. Salt, baking soda, lye, etc. contain sodium.

**sodium ben·zo·ate** (ben′zō āt) a sweet, white powder that is put in food to preserve it.

**sodium bicarbonate** *another name for* **baking soda.**

**sodium chloride** the common salt that is used to flavor and preserve food.

**Sod·om** (säd′əm) a city told about in the Bible as being destroyed by fire from heaven together with a neighboring city, Gomorrah, because the people were wicked.

**so·ev·er** (sō ev′ər) ***adv.*** in any way or of any kind; at all. *Soever* is usually used as a suffix with certain words [who*soever*, what*soever*, where*soever*, how*soever*, when*soever*].

**so·fa** (sō′fə) ***n.*** an upholstered couch with a back and arms.

**So·fi·a** (sō′fē ə *or* sō fē′ə) the capital of Bulgaria.

**soft** (sôft) ***adj.*** **1** not hard or firm; easy to bend, crush, cut, etc. [This pillow is *soft*. Lead is a *soft* metal.] **2** smooth to the touch; not rough [*soft* skin]. **3** not bright or sharp [*soft* gray; a *soft* line]. **4** weak; not strong or powerful [*soft* muscles; a *soft* wind]. **5** not difficult; easy to do [a *soft* job]. **6** filled with pity, kindness, etc. [a *soft* heart]. **7** not harsh or severe [*soft* words; a *soft* life]. **8** weak or low in sound [a *soft* chime]. **9** containing no alcohol [a *soft* drink]. **10** containing no minerals that keep soap from making a lather [*soft* water]. **11** describing the sound of *c* in *cent* or of *g* in *germ.* ◆***adv.*** in a soft or quiet way; gently. —**soft′ly** ***adv.*** —**soft′ness** ***n.***



☆**soft·ball** (sôft′bôl) ***n.*** **1** a form of baseball played on a smaller diamond with a ball that is larger and slightly softer than an ordinary baseball. **2** the ball used in this game.

**soft-boiled** (sôft′boild′) ***adj.*** boiled only a short time so that the yolk is still soft [*soft-boiled* eggs].

**soft drink** a drink that contains no alcohol and is usually carbonated.

**sof·ten** (sôf′′n) ***v.*** to make or become soft or softer. —**sof′ten·er** ***n.***

**soft·wood** (sôft′wood) ***n.*** **1** wood that is light and easy to cut. **2** a tree with such wood. **3** the wood of any tree with cones, as pine.

**sog·gy** (säg′ē) ***adj.*** very wet and heavy; soaked. —**sog′gi·er, sog′gi·est** —**sog′gi·ness** ***n.***

**soil**[1] (soil) ***n.*** **1** the top layer of earth, in which plants grow; ground [fertile *soil*]. **2** land; country [our native *soil*].

**soil**[2] (soil) ***v.*** **1** to make or become dirty; stain; spot. **2** to disgrace [to *soil* one's honor]. ◆***n.*** the act of soiling or a soiled spot; stain.

**soi·ree** or **soi·rée** (swä rā′) ***n.*** a party or gathering in the evening.

**so·journ** (sō′jurn) ***n.*** a short stay; visit. ◆***v.*** (*also* sō jurn′) to stay for a while, as on a visit [We *sojourned* in Italy.] —**so′journ·er** ***n.***

> **Sojourn** comes from a Latin word that means "under a day." Originally a sojourn was a short visit or trip that would take less than a day. **Sojourn, journal,** and **journey** all come to us from the same Latin word for "day."

**Sol** (säl) **1** the sun god of the ancient Romans. **2** the sun represented as a person.

**sol** (sōl) ***n.*** the fifth note of a musical scale.

**sol·ace** (säl′is) ***n.*** comfort or relief [Your kind words gave *solace* to my sorrow.] ◆***v.*** to comfort or give solace to [We attempted to *solace* the survivors.] —**sol′aced, sol′ac·ing**

**so·lar** (sō′lər) ***adj.*** **1** of or having to do with the sun [a *solar* eclipse; *solar* energy]. **2** depending on light or energy from the sun [*solar* heating]. **3** measured by the motion of the earth around the sun [a *solar* day].

**so·lar·i·um** (sō ler′ē əm) ***n.*** a room with glass walls, where people can sit in the sun; sunroom.

**solar plexus** a network of nerves in the abdomen, behind the stomach.

**solar system** the sun and all the planets, asteroids, comets, etc. that move around it.

**sold** (sōld) *past tense and past participle of* **sell.**

**sol·der** (säd′ər) ***n.*** a metal alloy that is melted and used to join or patch metal parts. ◆***v.*** to join or patch as with solder.

**soldering iron** (säd′ər iŋ) a pointed metal tool heated so that it can be used in soldering. *See the picture.*

**sol·dier** (sōl′jər) ***n.*** **1** a person in an army, especially one who is not a commissioned officer. **2** a person who works for a cause [a *soldier* for peace]. ◆***v.*** **1** to serve as a soldier. **2** to pretend to work, without doing much. —**sol′dier·ly** ***adj.***

**soldier of fortune** a man who will serve in any army for money or for adventure.

**sole**[1] (sōl) ***n.*** **1** the bottom surface of the foot. **2** the bottom surface of a shoe, sock, etc. ◆***v.*** to fasten a sole to, as a shoe. —**soled, sol′ing**

**sole**[2] (sōl) ***adj.*** **1** without others; one and only [the *sole* owner of a store]. *See* SYNONYMS *at* **single. 2** of or having to do with only one person or group; only [They are the *sole* inhabitants of the town.]

**sole**[3] (sōl) ***n.*** a kind of flatfish used as food. *See the picture.*

**sol·e·cism** (säl′ə siz′m) ***n.*** **1** a mistake in writing or speaking ["I seen them" is a *solecism*.] **2** a mistake in etiquette.

**sole·ly** (sōl′lē) ***adv.*** **1** alone; without others [We are *solely* to blame.] **2** only; merely [I read *solely* for pleasure.]

**sol·emn** (säl′əm) ***adj.*** **1** serious; grave; very earnest [a *solemn* face; a *solemn* oath]. **2** according to strict rules; formal [a *solemn* ceremony]. **3** set apart for religious reasons; sacred [a *solemn* holy day]. **4** dark in color; somber. —**sol′emn·ly** ***adv.***

**so·lem·ni·ty** (sə lem′nə tē) ***n.*** **1** a solemn ceremony or ritual. **2** solemn feeling or quality; seriousness. —*pl.* **so·lem′ni·ties**

**sol·em·nize** (säl′əm nīz) ***v.*** **1** to celebrate in a formal way, as a holy day. **2** to carry out the ceremony of [to *solemnize* a marriage]. —**sol′em·nized, sol′em·niz·ing**

**so·lic·it** (sə lis′it) ***v.*** to seek or ask in a serious way [to *solicit* money for charity; to *solicit* friends for help]. —**so·lic′i·ta′tion** ***n.***

**so·lic·i·tor** (sə lis′ə tər) ***n.*** **1** a person who tries to get customers for a business, money for a charity, etc. ☆**2** a lawyer for a city, State, etc. **3** in England, any lawyer who is not a barrister.

**so·lic·i·tous** (sə lis′ə təs) ***adj.*** **1** showing care, interest, or worry; concerned [Your parents are *solicitous* about your safety.] **2** anxious or eager [*solicitous* to get praise]. —**so·lic′i·tous·ly** ***adv.***

**so·lic·i·tude** (sə lis′ə to͞od *or* sə lis′ə tyo͞od) ***n.*** care, worry, or concern.

**sol·id** (säl′id) ***adj.*** **1** keeping its shape instead of flowing or spreading out like a liquid or gas; quite firm or hard [Ice is water in a *solid* form.] **2** filled with matter throughout; not hollow [a *solid* block of wood]. **3** that has length, width, and thickness [A prism is a *solid* figure.] **4** strong, firm, sound, dependable, etc. [*solid* thinking; a *solid* building]. **5** serious or deep [*solid* reading]. **6** with no breaks, stops, or rests; continuous [a *solid* wall around the castle; two *solid* hours of work]. **7** written or printed without a space or hyphen between the parts ["Trademark" is now a *solid* word.] **8** of one color, material, etc. throughout [a tray of *solid* silver]. ☆**9** strongly united [The President had the *solid* support of Congress.] **10** healthful and filling: *used only in everyday talk* [a *solid* meal]. ◆***n.*** **1** something that is solid, not a liquid or gas [Iron and glass are *solids*.] **2** anything that has length, width, and thickness [A cube is a *solid*.] —**sol′id·ly** ***adv.***

**sol·i·dar·i·ty** (säl′ə dar′ə tē) ***n.*** the condition of being strongly united, as in action or feeling.

**so·lid·i·fy** (sə lid′ə fī) ***v.*** **1** to make or become solid or firm [Butter *solidifies* as it cools.] **2** to make or become solid, strong, or united [The speeches *solidified* the Senator's support among voters.] —**so·lid′i·fied, so·lid′i·fy·ing** —**so·lid′i·fi·ca′tion** ***n.***

**so·lid·i·ty** (sə lid′ə tē) ***n.*** the condition of being solid; firmness, hardness, etc.

**sol·id-state** (säl′id stāt′) ***adj.*** having electronic devices, as semiconductors, that control electric current without heated filaments.

**so·lil·o·quize** (sə lil′ə kwīz) ***v.*** to talk to oneself; speak a soliloquy. —**so·lil′o·quized, so·lil′o·quiz·ing**

**so·lil·o·quy** (sə lil′ə kwē) ***n.*** **1** the act of talking to oneself. **2** a speech in a play in which a character tells his or her thoughts to the audience by talking aloud, as if to himself or herself. —*pl.* **so·lil′o·quies**

**sol·i·taire** (säl′ə ter) ***n.*** **1** a card game played by one person. **2** a diamond or other gem set by itself, as in a ring.

**sol·i·tar·y** (säl′ə ter′ē) ***adj.*** **1** living or being alone; lonely [a *solitary* hermit; a *solitary* lighthouse]. **2** single; only [a *solitary* example]. *See* SYNONYMS *at* **single.**

**sol·i·tude** (säl′ə to͞od *or* säl′ə tyo͞od) ***n.*** the condition of being solitary, or alone; loneliness.

**so·lo** (sō′lō) ***n.*** a piece of music that is sung or played by one person. —*pl.* **so′los** ◆***adj.*** **1** for or by one singer or one instrument. **2** made or done by one person [a *solo* flight in an airplane]. ◆***adv.*** without another or others; alone [She flew *solo*.] ◆***v.*** **1** to fly an airplane alone. **2** to play or sing a musical solo. —**so′loed, so′lo·ing** —**so′lo·ist** ***n.***

**Sol·o·mon** (säl′ə mən) a king of Israel in the 10th century B.C., famous for his wisdom.

**So·lon** (sō′lən) a lawgiver of ancient Athens, who lived from about 640 to about 559 B.C. ◆***n.*** *sometimes* **solon,** a wise lawmaker.

**sol·stice** (säl′stis) ***n.*** the time of the year when the sun reaches either the point farthest north of the equator (June 21 or 22) or the point farthest south (December 21 or 22). In the Northern Hemisphere, the first is the **summer solstice** and the second, the **winter solstice.**

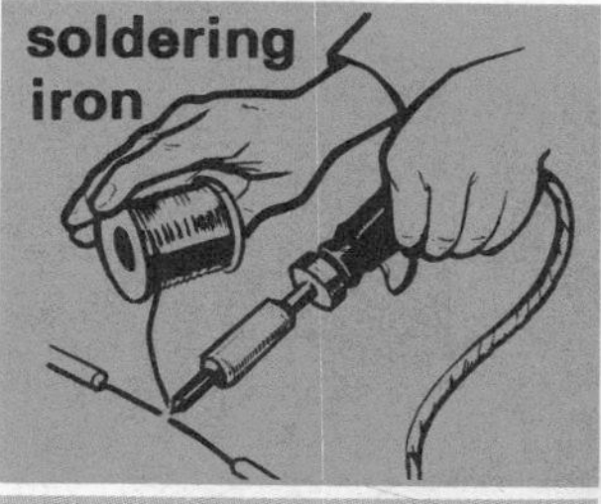
soldering iron

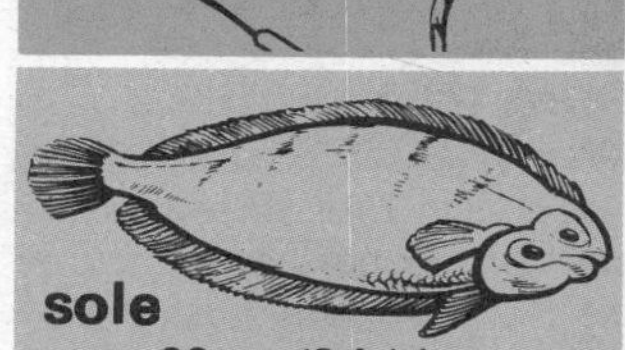
sole
up to 60 cm (2 ft.) long

sombreros

**sol·u·ble** (säl′yoo b'l) ***adj.*** **1** that can be dissolved in a liquid [Iodine is *soluble* in alcohol.] **2** that can be solved or explained [a *soluble* problem]. —**sol′u·bil′i·ty** ***n.***

**so·lu·tion** (sə lo͞o′shən) ***n.*** **1** the solving of a problem. **2** an answer or explanation [to find the *solution* to a mystery]. **3** the dissolving of something in a liquid. **4** a mixture formed in this way [Make a *solution* of sugar and vinegar.]



**solve** (sälv) ***v.*** to find the answer to; make clear; explain [to *solve* a problem in arithmetic]. —**solved, solv′ing**

**sol·vent** (säl′vənt) ***adj.*** **1** able to pay all one's debts [a *solvent* store owner]. **2** able to dissolve a substance. ◆***n.*** a substance that can dissolve another [Turpentine can be used as a *solvent* to clean paint from brushes.] —**sol′ven·cy** ***n.***

**So·ma·li·a** (sō mä′lē ə) a country on the eastern coast of Africa.

**som·ber** (säm′bər) ***adj.*** **1** dark and gloomy or dull [*somber* shadows]. **2** sad or serious [*somber* thoughts on a rainy day]. —**som′ber·ly** ***adv.***

> **Somber** and **sombrero** both come from two Latin words that mean "under shade." Something somber is dark as if it were in a shaded area. The sombrero shades the face from the bright sun.

☆**som·bre·ro** (säm brer′ō) ***n.*** a large hat with a wide brim, worn in Mexico, the southwestern U.S., etc. *See the picture.* —*pl.* **som·bre′ros**

**some** (sum) ***adj.*** **1** being a certain one or ones not named or not known [*Some* people were playing ball.] **2** being of a certain but not a definite number or amount [Have *some* candy.] ☆**3** outstanding or

| | | | |
|---|---|---|---|
| **a** fat | **ir** here | **ou** out | **zh** leisure |
| **ā** ape | **ī** bite, fire | **u** up | **ng** ring |
| **ä** car, lot | **ō** go | **ur** fur | a *in* ago |
| **e** ten | **ô** law, horn | **ch** chin | e *in* agent |
| **er** care | **oi** oil | **sh** she | ə = i *in* unity |
| **ē** even | **oo** look | **th** thin | o *in* collect |
| **i** hit | **o͞o** tool | ***th*** then | u *in* focus |

sorghum

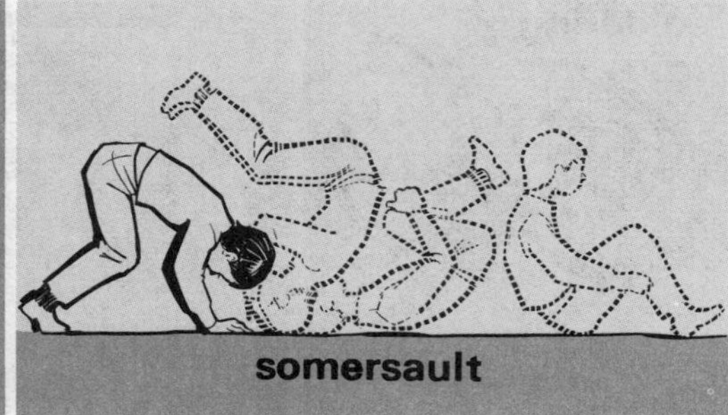
somersault

remarkable: *used only in everyday talk* [It was *some* party.] ◆***pron.*** **1** a certain one or ones not named or not known [*Some* agree.] **2** a certain number or amount, but not all [Take *some*.] ◆***adv.*** **1** about [*Some* ten people were hired.] **2** to some degree or limit: *used only in everyday talk* [I slept *some*.] ☆**3** to a great degree, at a great rate, etc.: *used only in everyday talk* [You must run *some* to catch up.] —☆**and then some,** and more than that: *used only in everyday talk.*

**-some¹** (səm) *a suffix meaning* tending to *or* tending to be [A *tiresome* story tends to tire the listener.]

**-some²** (səm) *a suffix meaning* group of [A *threesome* is a group of three.]

**some·bod·y** (sum′bud′ē *or* sum′bäd′ē) ***pron.*** a certain person not known or named; someone [*Somebody* left the door open.] ◆***n.*** a person who is important. —*pl.* **some′bod′ies**



**some·day** (sum′dā) ***adv.*** at some future time.

**some·how** (sum′hou) ***adv.*** in a way not known or explained; by some means [*Somehow* the pilot managed to land the plane.]

**some·one** (sum′wun) ***pron.*** *same as* **somebody.**

**som·er·sault** (sum′ər sôlt) ***n.*** a stunt in which one turns the body completely over forward or backward, heels over head. *See the picture.* ◆***v.*** to do a somersault.

**some·thing** (sum′thing) ***n.*** **1** a certain thing not named or known [I have *something* to tell you. I'd like *something* to eat.] **2** a thing not definitely known or understood [*Something* is wrong with my car.] **3** an important person or thing: *used only in everyday talk.* ◆***adv.*** somewhat; a little [You look *something* like your cousin.] —**make something of, 1** to find a use for. **2** to treat as very important. ☆**3** to get into a fight or quarrel about: *used only in everyday talk.*

**some·time** (sum′tīm) ***adv.*** **1** at some future time [Come see us *sometime* soon.] **2** at some time not known or named [I saw them *sometime* last week.] ◆***adj.*** **1** former [my *sometime* friend]. **2** happening only once in a while; not regular [My wit is a *sometime* thing.]

**some·times** (sum′tīmz) ***adv.*** once in a while; occasionally [*Sometimes* we go to plays.]

**some·what** (sum′hwut) ***adv.*** to some degree; a little [They are *somewhat* late.] ◆***n.*** a certain part, amount, or degree [You are being *somewhat* of a fool.]

**some·where** (sum′hwer) ***adv.*** **1** in, to, or at some place not known or named [They live *somewhere* near here.] **2** at some time, degree, age, etc. [Be there *somewhere* around ten o'clock.]

**som·nam·bu·lism** (säm nam′byoo liz'm) ***n.*** the act of walking in one's sleep. —**som·nam′bu·list** ***n.***

**som·no·lent** (säm′nə lənt) ***adj.*** **1** ready to sleep; sleepy; drowsy. **2** making one sleepy [a *somnolent* summer day].

**son** (sun) ***n.*** **1** a boy or man as he is related to a parent or to both parents. **2** a boy or man who is influenced by something in the way that a child is by a parent [*sons* of France]. —**the Son,** *another name for* **Jesus Christ.**

**so·nar** (sō′när) ***n.*** a device that sends sound waves through water and picks them up after they strike some object and bounce back. It is used to locate submarines, find depths of oceans, etc.

**so·na·ta** (sə nät′ə) ***n.*** a piece of music for one or two instruments, usually divided into two to five movements with different moods, tempos, keys, etc.

**so·na·ti·na** (sän′ə tē′nə) ***n.*** a short or very simple sonata.

**song** (sông) ***n.*** **1** a piece of music for singing. **2** the act of singing [They broke into *song*.] **3** a poem that is or can be set to music, as a ballad. **4** a musical sound like singing [the *song* of a canary]. —**for a song,** for very little money; cheaply.

**song·bird** (sông′burd) ***n.*** a bird that makes sounds that are like music.

☆**song·fest** (sông′fest) ***n.*** a gathering of people for singing songs, especially folk songs.

**song·ster** (sông′stər) ***n.*** **1** *another word for* **singer.** **2** *another word for* **songbird.**

**song·stress** (sông′stris) ***n.*** a woman singer.

**son·ic** (sän′ik) ***adj.*** of or having to do with sound or the speed of sound.

**sonic boom** an explosive sound caused by the building up of pressure in a wave going ahead of an aircraft moving at or above the speed of sound.

**son-in-law** (sun′in lô′) ***n.*** the husband of one's daughter. —*pl.* **sons′-in-law′**

**son·net** (sän′it) ***n.*** a poem of fourteen lines that rhyme in a certain pattern.

**son·ny** (sun′ē) ***n.*** a pet name or friendly name used in talking to a young boy.

**so·no·rous** (sə nôr′əs *or* sän′ər əs) ***adj.*** **1** making loud, deep, or mellow sounds; resonant [the *sonorous* bass viol]. **2** loud, deep, or mellow [a *sonorous* voice]. **3** sounding important [*sonorous* language].

**soon** (sōōn) ***adv.*** **1** in a short time; before much time has passed [Spring will *soon* be here.] **2** fast or quickly [as *soon* as possible]. **3** ahead of time; early [She left too *soon*.] **4** in a willing way; readily [I would as *soon* go as stay.] —**sooner or later,** in the end; finally.

**soot** (soot) ***n.*** a black powder formed when some things burn. It is mostly carbon and makes smoke gray or black.

**soothe** (sōō*th*) ***v.*** **1** to make quiet or calm by being gentle or friendly [The clerk *soothed* the angry customer with helpful answers.] **2** to take away some of the pain or sorrow of; ease [I hope this lotion will *soothe* your sunburn.] —**soothed, sooth′ing** —**sooth′ing·ly** ***adv.***

**sooth·say·er** (sōōth′sā′ər) ***n.*** a person who claims to be able to tell what is going to happen.

**soot·y** (soot′ē) ***adj.*** covered or dirty with soot. —**soot′i·er, soot′i·est**

**sop** (säp) ***n.*** **1** a piece of food soaked in milk, soup, etc. **2** something given to keep someone calm or satisfied. ◆***v.*** **1** to suck up or absorb [I used the bread to *sop* up the gravy.] **2** to make very wet; soak [Our clothes were *sopped* through.] —**sopped, sop'ping**

**soph·ist** (säf'ist) ***n.*** a person whose reasons seem clever and correct but are really false.

**so·phis·ti·cate** (sə fis'tə kit) ***n.*** a sophisticated person.

**so·phis·ti·cat·ed** (sə fis'tə kāt'id) ***adj.*** **1** not simple, natural, or innocent; wise in the ways of the world. **2** very complicated and based on the latest ideas, techniques, etc. [*sophisticated* electronic equipment]. —**so·phis'ti·ca'tion** ***n.***

**soph·is·try** (säf'is trē) ***n.*** reasoning or an argument that seems clever and correct but is really false or misleading. —*pl.* **soph'is·tries**

**Soph·o·cles** (säf'ə klēz) a Greek writer of tragic plays. He lived from about 496 to 406 B.C.

**soph·o·more** (säf'ə môr) ***n.*** a student in the tenth grade or in the second year of college.

**sop·py** (säp'ē) ***adj.*** very wet; soaked. —**sop'pi·er, sop'pi·est**

**so·pra·no** (sə pran'ō) ***n.*** **1** the highest kind of singing voice of women, girls, or young boys. **2** a singer with such a voice, or an instrument with a range like this. —*pl.* **so·pra'nos** ◆***adj.*** of or for a soprano.

> **Soprano** is an Italian word which comes from the Latin word *supra,* that means "above." The soprano part or voice is above all the others in range.

**sor·cer·er** (sôr'sər ər) ***n.*** a person who works magic or sorcery, as in fairy tales; magician; wizard.

**sor·cer·y** (sôr'sər ē) ***n.*** the supposed use of magical power by means of charms or spells, usually for a bad or harmful purpose; witchcraft. —*pl.* **sor'cer·ies**

**sor·did** (sôr'did) ***adj.*** **1** dirty, filthy, disgusting, etc. [*sordid* slums]. **2** low, mean, selfish, etc. [a *sordid* scheme]. —**sor'did·ly** ***adv.***

**sore** (sôr) ***adj.*** **1** giving pain; aching; painful [a *sore* toe]. **2** feeling pain, as from bruises [I am *sore* all over.] **3** filled with sadness or grief [*sore* at heart]. **4** causing sadness, misery, etc. [a *sore* task]. **5** making one angry or irritated [Losing the game was a *sore* point for them.] ☆**6** angry or irritated: *used only in everyday talk.* —**sor'er, sor'est** ◆***n.*** a place on the body where tissue is injured, as by a cut, burn, boil, etc. —**sore'ness** ***n.***

**sore·ly** (sôr'lē) ***adv.*** greatly or strongly [Help is *sorely* needed.]

**sor·ghum** (sôr'gəm) ***n.*** **1** a tall grass with sweet, juicy stalks, grown for grain, fodder, syrup, etc. *See the picture.* ☆**2** a syrup made from the juice of a type of sorghum.

**so·ror·i·ty** (sə rôr'ə tē) ***n.*** a club of women or girls, especially a social club, as in a college. —*pl.* **so·ror'i·ties**

**sor·rel**[1] (sôr'əl) ***n.*** a plant with sour, fleshy leaves used in salads.

**sor·rel**[2] (sôr'əl) ***n.*** **1** light reddish brown. **2** a horse of this color.

**sor·row** (sär'ō) ***n.*** **1** a sad or troubled feeling; sadness; grief. **2** a loss, death, or trouble causing such a feeling [Our grandmother's illness is a great *sorrow* to us.] ◆***v.*** to feel or show sorrow [We are *sorrowing* over his loss.]

**sor·row·ful** (sär'ə fəl) ***adj.*** feeling, showing, or causing sorrow; sad [a *sorrowful* face; a *sorrowful* duty]. *See* SYNONYMS *at* **sad.** —**sor'row·ful·ly** ***adv.***

**sor·ry** (sär'ē) ***adj.*** **1** full of sorrow, pity, etc. or often just mild regret [We were *sorry* to leave.] **2** low in worth or quality; poor [a *sorry* performance]. **3** causing suffering; deserving pity [a *sorry* sight].

**sort** (sôrt) ***n.*** **1** a group of things that are alike in some way; kind; class [various *sorts* of toys]. **2** quality or type [phrases of a noble *sort*]. ◆***v.*** to separate or arrange according to class or kind [*Sort* out the clothes that need mending.] —**after a sort,** in some way but not very well. —**of sorts** or **of a sort,** of a kind that is not very good [a movie of *sorts*]. —**out of sorts,** not in a good humor or not feeling well: *used only in everyday talk.* —**sort of,** somewhat: *used only in everyday talk.*

**sor·tie** (sôr'tē) ***n.*** **1** a sudden attack made from a place surrounded by enemy troops. **2** one battle flight by one military airplane.

**SOS** (es'ō es') a signal calling for help, used by ships at sea, aircraft, etc.

**so-so** (sō'sō') ***adj., adv.*** neither too good nor too bad; fair or fairly well.

**sot** (sät) ***n.*** a person who is often drunk.

**sou** (so͞o) ***n.*** a French coin no longer in use. It was equal to 1/20 of a franc.

**souf·flé** (so͞o flā') ***n.*** a baked food made light and fluffy by adding beaten egg whites before baking [a cheese *soufflé*].



**sought** (sôt) *past tense and past participle of* **seek.**

**soul** (sōl) ***n.*** **1** the part of one's being that is thought of as the center of feeling, thinking, will, etc., separate from the body. In some religions, the soul is believed to continue on after death. **2** warmth and force of feeling or spirit [That painting has no *soul.*] **3** the most important part, quality, or thing ["Brevity is the *soul* of wit."] **4** something or someone that is a perfect example of some quality [the very *soul* of kindness]. **5** a person [Not a *soul* left the room.] ☆**6** among black Americans, a feeling of being strongly united, along with a feeling of pride in black culture.

☆**soul food** kinds of food popular originally in the South especially among blacks, as chitterlings, ham hocks, yams, turnip greens, etc.

**soul·ful** (sōl'fəl) ***adj.*** full of or showing deep feeling [a *soulful* look].

**soul·less** (sōl'lis) ***adj.*** without tender feelings.

**sound**[1] (sound) ***n.*** **1** the form of energy that acts on the ears so that one can hear. Sound consists of waves of vibrations carried in the air, water, etc. [In air, *sound* travels at a speed of about 332 meters per second, or 1,088 feet per second.] **2** anything that can be heard; noise, tone, etc. [the *sound* of bells]. **3** any of the noises made in speaking [a vowel *sound*]. **4** the

| | | | | | | | |
|---|---|---|---|---|---|---|---|
| **a** | fat | **ir** | here | **ou** | out | **zh** | leisure |
| **ā** | ape | **ī** | bite, fire | **u** | up | **ng** | ring |
| **ä** | car, lot | **ō** | go | **ur** | fur | | a *in* ago |
| **e** | ten | **ô** | law, horn | **ch** | chin | | e *in* agent |
| **er** | care | **oi** | oil | **sh** | she | **ə =** | i *in* unity |
| **ē** | even | **oo** | look | **th** | thin | | o *in* collect |
| **i** | hit | **o͞o** | tool | ***th*** | then | | u *in* focus |

distance within which something may be heard [within *sound* of her voice]. ◆**v.** **1** to make a sound [Your voice *sounds* hoarse.] **2** to cause to sound [*Sound* your horn.] **3** to seem; appear [The plan *sounds* all right.] **4** to make known or announce [*Sound* the alarm.] **5** to say clearly [He doesn't *sound* his r's.]

SYNONYMS: **Sound** is the general word for anything that can be heard [the *sound* of footsteps]. **Noise** is usually used for a sound that is unpleasant because it is too loud, harsh, etc. [the *noise* of a factory]. **Tone** is generally used for a sound thought of as pleasant or musical [the range of *tones* in a violin].

**sound**[2] (sound) ***adj.*** **1** in good condition; not damaged or rotted [*sound* timber]. **2** normal and healthy [a *sound* mind in a *sound* body]. **3** firm, safe, secure, etc. [Put your savings in a *sound* bank.] **4** full of good sense; sensible; wise [a *sound* plan]. **5** deep and not disturbed [a *sound* sleep]. **6** thorough; complete [a *sound* defeat]. ◆**adv.** in a sound way; completely; deeply [They are *sound* asleep.] —**sound'ly *adv.*** —**sound'ness *n.***

**sound**[3] (sound) ***n.*** **1** a channel of water connecting two large bodies of water or separating an island from the mainland. **2** a long arm of the sea.

**sound**[4] (sound) ***v.*** **1** to measure the depth of water, as by lowering a weight fastened to a line. **2** to try to find out the opinions of [Let's *sound* out the members on the subject.] **3** to dive suddenly downward through water, as a whale.



**sound·ing** (soun'diŋ) ***n.*** **1** the act of measuring the depth of water by lowering a weighted line. **2** depth as measured in this way. **3** a probe of space, as with a rocket.

**sound·less** (sound'lis) ***adj.*** without sound; quiet; noiseless. —**sound'less·ly *adv.***

**sound·proof** (sound'pro͞of) ***adj.*** that keeps sound from coming through [*soundproof* walls]. ◆**v.** to make soundproof.

**sound track** the area along one side of a movie film, carrying the sound recording of the film.

**soup** (so͞op) ***n.*** a liquid food made by cooking meat, vegetables, etc. as in water or milk.

**sour** (sour) ***adj.*** **1** having the sharp, acid taste of lemon juice, vinegar, etc. **2** made acid or spoiled by fermenting [*sour* milk]. **3** cross; bad-tempered; disagreeable [He is in a *sour* mood.] **4** below normal; bad [Her writing has gone *sour*.] **5** off pitch or sounding wrong [a *sour* note]. **6** having too much acid [*sour* soil]. ◆**v.** to make or become sour. —**sour'ly *adv.*** —**sour'ness *n.***

SYNONYMS: To be **sour** is to be unpleasantly sharp in taste, especially after spoiling or going bad [The milk turned *sour*.] To be **acid** is to be sour in a way that is normal or natural [A lemon is an *acid* fruit.] To be **tart** is to have a slightly stinging sharpness or sourness that is pleasant to the taste [a *tart* cherry pie].

**sour·ball** (sour'bôl) ***n.*** a small ball of tart, hard candy.

**source** (sôrs) ***n.*** **1** a spring or fountain that is the starting point of a stream. **2** a thing or place from which something comes or is got [The sun is our *source* of energy. This book is the *source* of my information.]

**sour·dough** (sour'dō) ***n.*** **1** fermented dough used in making bread, especially in the far West. **2** a prospector in the western U.S. or Canada.

**Sou·sa** (so͞o'zə *or* so͞o'sə), **John Philip** 1854–1932; U.S. bandmaster and composer of marches.

**souse** (sous) ***v.*** **1** to make or become soaking wet. **2** to plunge or dip in a liquid. **3** to soak or pickle in vinegar, brine, etc. —**soused, sous'ing** ◆***n.*** **1** the act of sousing. **2** liquid for pickling; brine. **3** food that has been pickled, as pigs' feet.

**south** (south) ***n.*** **1** the direction to the left of a person facing the sunset. **2** a place or region in or toward this direction. **3** *often* **South,** the southern part of the earth, especially the antarctic regions. ◆***adj.*** **1** in, of, to, or toward the south [the *south* end of town]. **2** from the south [a *south* wind]. **3 South,** that is the southern part of [*South* Korea]. ◆***adv.*** in or toward the south [Go *south* four miles.] —**the South,** ☆the southern part of the U.S., especially the part south of Pennsylvania, the Ohio River, and northern Missouri.

**South Africa** a country in southern Africa. —**South African**

**South America** the southern continent in the Western Hemisphere. —**South American**

**South·amp·ton** (sou thamp'tən) a seaport in southern England.

**South Carolina** a State in the southeastern part of the U.S.: abbreviated **S.C., SC**

**South Dakota** a State in the north central part of the U.S.: abbreviated **S.Dak., SD**

**south·east** (south ēst') ***n.*** **1** the direction halfway between south and east. **2** a place or region in or toward this direction. ◆***adj.*** **1** in, of, or toward the southeast [the *southeast* part of the county]. **2** from the southeast [a *southeast* wind]. ◆***adv.*** in or toward the southeast [to sail *southeast*].

**south·east·er** (south ēs'tər) ***n.*** a storm or strong wind from the southeast.

**south·east·er·ly** (south ēs'tər lē) ***adj., adv.*** **1** in or toward the southeast. **2** from the southeast.

**south·east·ern** (south ēs'tərn) ***adj.*** **1** in, of, or toward the southeast [*southeastern* Illinois]. **2** from the southeast [a *southeastern* wind].

**south·er·ly** (su*th*'ər lē) ***adj., adv.*** **1** in or toward the south. **2** from the south.

**south·ern** (su*th*'ərn) ***adj.*** **1** in, of, or toward the south [the *southern* sky]. **2** from the south [a *southern* wind]. **3 Southern,** of the South.

**South·ern·er** (su*th*'ər nər) ***n.*** a person born or living in the South.

**Southern Hemisphere** the half of the earth that is south of the equator.

**south·ern·most** (su*th*'ərn mōst) ***adj.*** farthest south.

**south·paw** (south'pô) ***n.*** a person who is left-handed; especially, a left-handed baseball pitcher: *a slang word.*

**Southpaw** came into use in the Chicago baseball park about 1885, where the pitcher's left arm was toward the south.

**South Pole** the spot that is farthest south on the earth; southern end of the earth's axis.

**South Sea Islands** the islands in the South Pacific.

**south·ward** (south′wərd) ***adv., adj.*** toward the south. ◆***n.*** a southward direction or place.

**south·wards** (south′wərdz) ***adv.*** *same as* **southward.**

**south·west** (south west′) ***n.*** **1** the direction halfway between south and west. **2** a place or region in or toward this direction. ◆***adj.*** **1** in, of, or toward the southwest [the *southwest* corner]. **2** from the southwest [a *southwest* wind]. ◆***adv.*** in or toward the southwest [to sail *southwest*].

**South West Africa** a territory in southern Africa, on the Atlantic Ocean.

**south·west·er** (south wes′tər *or* sou wes′tər) ***n.*** **1** a storm or strong wind from the southwest. **2** a sailor's waterproof hat, with a broad brim in the back to protect the neck. *See the picture.*

**south·west·er·ly** (south wes′tər lē) ***adj., adv.*** **1** in or toward the southwest. **2** from the southwest.

**south·west·ern** (south wes′tərn) ***adj.*** **1** in, of, or toward the southwest. **2** from the southwest [a *southwestern* wind].

**sou·ve·nir** (sōō və nir′) ***n.*** an object kept to remind one of something; memento [We save our programs as *souvenirs* of plays we've seen.]

**sou′·west·er** (sou wes′tər) ***n.*** *another spelling of* **southwester.**

**sov·er·eign** (säv′rən *or* säv′ər in) ***adj.*** **1** highest in power or rank; supreme [a *sovereign* prince]. **2** not controlled by others; independent [Indonesia became a *sovereign* republic in 1949.] **3** greater than all others; highest; chief [a problem of *sovereign* importance]. ◆***n.*** **1** a ruler; king, queen, emperor, etc. **2** a British gold coin of earlier times, worth 20 shillings, or one pound.

**sov·er·eign·ty** (säv′rən tē *or* säv′ər in tē) ***n.*** **1** the rank or power of a sovereign. **2** the condition of having independent political power [We must respect the *sovereignty* of other nations.]

**so·vi·et** (sō′vē it) ***n.*** any of the councils, or groups of people, chosen to govern a certain area in the U.S.S.R., ranging from the small soviets of villages and towns to the **Supreme Soviet,** the national congress. ◆***adj.*** **Soviet,** of or having to do with the U.S.S.R.

**Soviet Union** *a shorter name for* **Union of Soviet Socialist Republics.**

**sow**[1] (sou) ***n.*** a full-grown female pig.

**sow**[2] (sō) ***v.*** **1** to scatter or plant seed for growing [to *sow* wheat]. **2** to plant seed in or on [*Sow* the lawn with clover.] **3** to spread or scatter [to *sow* hate by telling lies]. —**sowed, sown** (sōn) or **sowed, sow′ing** —**sow′er *n.***

**sow bug** (sou) a tiny animal with a flat, oval body and a hard shell, found in damp soil, under rocks, in decaying wood, etc.

**sox** (säks) ***n.*** *a plural of* **sock**[1].

**soy·bean** (soi′bēn) ***n.*** **1** the seed, or bean, of a plant of Asia, now grown throughout the world. The beans are ground into flour, pressed for oil, etc. **2** the plant itself. *See the picture.*

**soy sauce** a dark, salty sauce made from soybeans, used especially as a flavoring in Chinese and Japanese dishes.

**spa** (spä) ***n.*** a mineral spring, or a place that has such a spring, to which people go for their health.

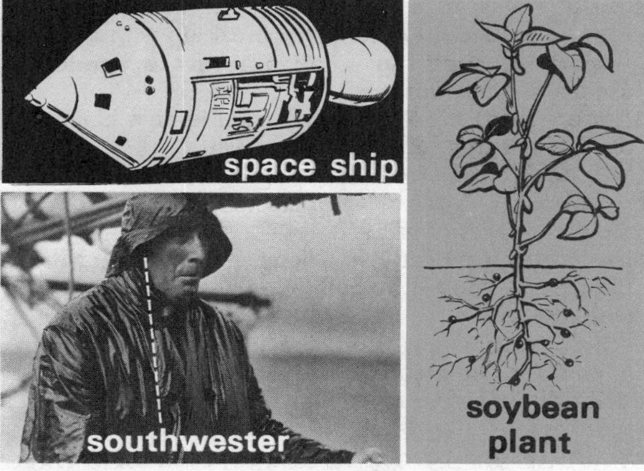

space ship

southwester

soybean plant

**space** (spās) ***n.*** **1** the area that stretches in all directions, has no limits, and contains all things in the universe [The earth, the sun, and all the stars exist in *space.*] **2** the distance or area between things or inside of something, especially as used for some purpose [a closet with much *space;* parking *space*]. **3** a length of time; period [We visited there for the *space* of a week.] **4** *a shorter name for* **outer space.** ◆***v.*** to arrange with spaces in between [The trees are evenly *spaced.*] —**spaced, spac′ing**

**Space Age** or **space age** the period that began in 1957 when the first artificial satellite of the earth was launched. Many satellites have been put into space since, and human beings have traveled in outer space in spacecraft.



**space·craft** (spās′kraft) ***n.*** any spaceship or satellite designed for use in outer space. —*pl.* **space′craft**

☆**space·flight** (spās′flīt) ***n.*** a flight through outer space.

**space heater** a small heating unit for warming the air of a single, small area, as a room.

**space·ship** (spās′ship) ***n.*** a vehicle for travel in outer space. Its movement is controlled by rockets. *See the picture.*

☆**space shuttle** a spacecraft for carrying people and supplies between earth and an orbiting space station.

**space station** a structure put into space as a satellite from which other spacecraft can be launched. It can also be used as a base for making scientific studies.

☆**space·suit** (spās′sōōt) ***n.*** *another name for* **G-suit,** especially one used in spaceflights.

☆**space·walk** (spās′wôk) ***n.*** any act of astronauts in moving about in space outside of their spacecraft.

**spac·ing** (spās′iŋ) ***n.*** **1** the way that something is spaced. **2** space or spaces.

**spa·cious** (spā′shəs) ***adj.*** having much space or room; very large; vast [a *spacious* hall]. —**spa′cious·ly *adv.*** —**spa′cious·ness *n.***

| | | | | | | | |
|---|---|---|---|---|---|---|---|
| **a** | fat | **ir** | here | **ou** | out | **zh** | leisure |
| **ā** | ape | **ī** | bite, fire | **u** | up | **ŋ** | ring |
| **ä** | car, lot | **ō** | go | **ur** | fur | | a *in* ago |
| **e** | ten | **ô** | law, horn | **ch** | chin | | e *in* agent |
| **er** | care | **oi** | oil | **sh** | she | ə = | i *in* unity |
| **ē** | even | **oo** | look | **th** | thin | | o *in* collect |
| **i** | hit | **ōō** | tool | ***th*** | then | | u *in* focus |

**spade**[1] (spād) ***n.*** a tool for digging, like a shovel but with a flat blade. ◆***v.*** to dig or break up with a spade. —**spad′ed, spad′ing —call a spade a spade,** to use plain, blunt words.

**spade**[2] (spād) ***n.*** **1** the mark ♠, used on a black suit of playing cards. **2** a card of this suit.

> **Spade**[2] comes from the Spanish word *espada,* for "sword." A sword is used as the figure on Spanish playing cards of this suit.

**spa·ghet·ti** (spə get′ē) ***n.*** long, thin strings of dried flour paste, cooked by boiling or steaming and served with a sauce.

> **Spaghetti** comes from the plural of the Italian word for "little cord." Spaghetti looks very much like little cords, or strings, especially after it is cooked.

**Spain** (spān) a country on a large peninsula in southwestern Europe.

**spake** (spāk) *a past tense of* **speak**: *used in earlier times.*

**span** (span) ***n.*** **1** the distance between the tip of the thumb and the tip of the little finger when the hand is fully spread, thought of as equal to 9 inches. **2** the part of a bridge, beam, arch, etc. between two supports. **3** a certain period of time [the *span* of a person's life]. ☆**4** a team of two animals used together. ◆***v.*** to stretch or reach across [The bridge *spans* the river.] —**spanned, span′ning**

 **span·gle** (spaŋ′g′l) ***n.*** a small, shiny piece of metal, especially any of a number of these sewn or glued on cloth for decoration. ◆***v.*** to cover or decorate with spangles or other bright objects [the Star-*Spangled* Banner]. —**span′gled, span′gling**

**Span·iard** (span′yərd) ***n.*** a person born or living in Spain.

**span·iel** (span′yəl) ***n.*** a dog with long silky hair, large drooping ears, and short legs. *See the picture.*

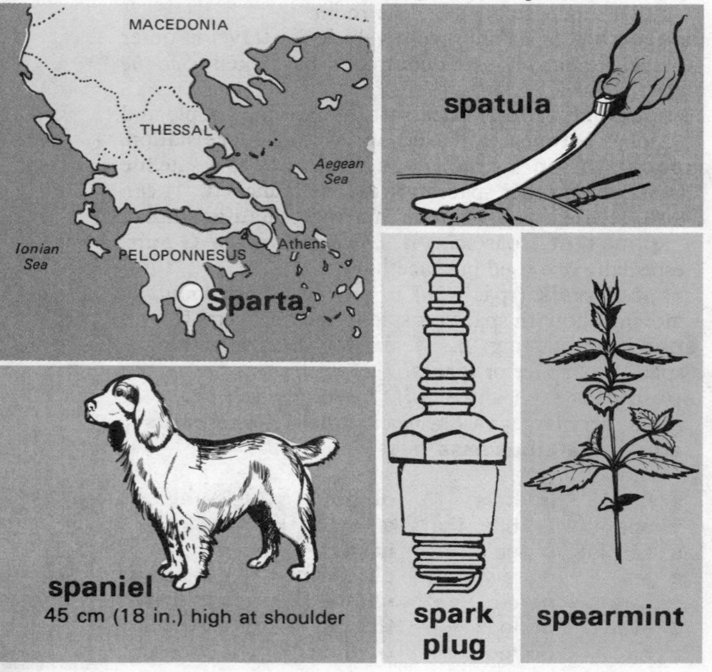


**spaniel**
45 cm (18 in.) high at shoulder

**Span·ish** (span′ish) ***adj.*** of Spain, its people, etc. ◆***n.*** the language of Spain and Spanish America. —**the Spanish,** the people of Spain.

**Spanish America** Mexico and those countries in Central and South America and the West Indies in which Spanish is the chief language.

**Span·ish-A·mer·i·can** (span′ish ə mer′ə kən) ***adj.*** **1** of both Spain and America. **2** of Spanish America or its people. ◆***n.*** a person born or living in Spanish America, especially one with Spanish ancestors.

**Spanish-American War** the war between the U.S. and Spain, in 1898.

**Spanish Main** **1** in earlier times, the northern coast of South America. **2** the Caribbean Sea.

☆**Spanish moss** a rootless plant often found growing in long, graceful strands from the branches of trees in the southeastern U.S.

☆**Spanish rice** boiled rice cooked with tomatoes and chopped onions, green peppers, etc.

**spank** (spaŋk) ***v.*** to slap on the buttocks as a way of punishing. ◆***n.*** the act of spanking.

**spank·ing** (spaŋk′iŋ) ***adj.*** strong and brisk [a *spanking* breeze]. ◆***adv.*** very; completely: *used only in everyday talk* [*spanking* new]. ◆***n.*** a series of sharp slaps, especially on the buttocks, given in punishing someone.

**spar**[1] (spär) ***n.*** a strong, heavy pole for holding up the sails on a ship. Masts, yards, and booms are spars.

**spar**[2] (spär) ***v.*** **1** to box in a skillful and careful way. **2** to exchange remarks, as in arguing. —**sparred, spar′ring**

**spare** (sper) ***v.*** **1** to save or free from something [*Spare* us the trouble of listening to that story again.] **2** to keep from using or use with care [*Spare* no effort to save the sinking ship.] **3** to get along without; give up [We can't *spare* the money or the time for a vacation trip.] **4** to hold back from hurting or killing; show mercy to [Try to *spare* the speaker's feelings.] —**spared, spar′ing** ◆***adj.*** **1** kept for use when needed [a *spare* room; a *spare* tire]. **2** not taken up by regular work or duties; free [*spare* time]. **3** small in amount; meager; scanty [The explorers had to live on *spare* rations.] **4** lean and thin; not fat [a *spare* old horse]. —**spar′er, spar′est** ◆***n.*** **1** an extra part or thing. ☆**2** in bowling, the act of knocking down all ten pins with two rolls of the ball. —**spare′ly *adv.***

**spare·ribs** (sper′ribz) ***n.pl.*** a cut of meat that is the thin end of pork ribs with most of the meat cut away.

**spar·ing** (sper′iŋ) ***adj.*** using or giving little; saving; frugal [She was *sparing* in her praise.] —**spar′ing·ly *adv.***

**spark** (spärk) ***n.*** **1** a small bit of burning matter, as one thrown off by a fire. **2** any flash of light like this [the *spark* of a firefly]. **3** a bit or trace [We hoped they would show a *spark* of enthusiasm.] **4** the small flash of light that takes place when an electric current jumps across an open space, as in a spark plug. ◆***v.*** **1** to make or give off sparks. **2** to stir into action [to *spark* one's interest].

**spar·kle** (spär′k′l) ***v.*** **1** to give off sparks or flashes of light; glitter; glisten [A lake *sparkles* in sunlight.] **2** to be lively and witty [There was much *sparkling* talk at the party.] **3** to bubble as ginger ale does. —**spar′kled, spar′kling** ◆***n.*** **1** a spark. **2** glitter [the *sparkle* of sequins].

**spar·kler** (spär′klər) ***n.*** **1** a firework that is a thin, light stick that burns with bright sparks. **2** a diamond: *used only in everyday talk.*

☆**spark plug** a piece fitted into the cylinder of a gasoline engine to make sparks that explode the fuel mixture. *See the picture.*

**spar·row** (spar′ō) ***n.*** a small gray and brown songbird with a short beak. The common sparrow seen on city streets is the **English sparrow.**

**sparse** (spärs) ***adj.*** thinly spread or scattered; not thick or crowded [a *sparse* crowd; *sparse* hair]. —**sparse′ly *adv.*** —**spar′si·ty *n.***

**Spar·ta** (spär′tə) a powerful city of ancient Greece. It was a rival city to Athens. *See the map.*

**Spar·tan** (spär′t′n) ***adj.*** **1** of Sparta. **2** like the people of Sparta; brave, not complaining, not needing luxuries, etc. ◆***n.*** **1** a citizen of Sparta. **2** a person who is brave, uncomplaining, etc.

**spasm** (spaz″m) ***n.*** **1** any sudden tightening of a muscle or muscles, that cannot be controlled. **2** any short, sudden burst of action or feeling [a *spasm* of coughing; a *spasm* of pity].

**spas·mod·ic** (spaz mäd′ik) ***adj.*** of or like spasms; sudden, sharp, and irregular [a *spasmodic* twitch, pain, etc.] —**spas·mod′i·cal·ly *adv.***

**spas·tic** (spas′tik) ***adj.*** **1** of, like, or affected by spasm. **2** having spastic paralysis.

**spastic paralysis** a condition, as in cerebral palsy, in which certain muscles stay tightened, causing some trouble in moving parts of the body.

**spat**[1] (spat) ***n.*** a small quarrel or argument: *used only in everyday talk.*

**spat**[2] (spat) ***n.*** a heavy cloth covering for the instep and ankle.

**spat**[3] (spat) *a past tense and past participle of* **spit**[2].

**spa·tial** (spā′shəl) ***adj.*** **1** of or in space. **2** happening in space. —**spa′tial·ly *adv.***

**spat·ter** (spat′ər) ***v.*** **1** to spot or splash with small drops [The hot fat *spattered* the stove.] **2** to fall or strike in drops or in a shower [rain *spattering* on the sidewalk]. ◆***n.*** **1** the act of spattering. **2** a mark or wet spot made by spattering.

**spat·u·la** (spach′oo lə) ***n.*** a tool with a broad, flat blade that bends easily, used in various ways, as for spreading and mixing food, paint, etc. *See the picture.*

**spav·in** (spav′in) ***n.*** a disease of horses that attacks the hock joint and causes lameness. —**spav′ined *adj.***

**spawn** (spôn) ***n.*** **1** the eggs or newly hatched young of fish, clams, lobsters, frogs, etc. **2** any offspring, especially if numerous: *an unfriendly or sarcastic use.* ◆***v.*** **1** to produce eggs in large numbers as a fish does. **2** to bring into being [This popular TV show *spawned* many imitations.]

**SPCA** or **S.P.C.A.** Society for the Prevention of Cruelty to Animals.

**speak** (spēk) ***v.*** **1** to say something with the voice; talk [They *spoke* to each other on the phone.] **2** to tell or make known, as one's ideas or opinions [*Speak* your mind freely. He *spoke* well of Juanita.] **3** to make a speech [Who *speaks* first on the program?] **4** to know how to talk in a certain language [Do you *speak* French?] —**spoke** or earlier **spake, spo′ken** or earlier **spoke, speak′ing** —**so to speak,** that is to say. —**speak for, 1** to say something in behalf of [*Speak for* yourself, John.] **2** to ask for. —**speak out** or **speak up,** to speak loudly or openly. —**speak well for,** to show to be good, proper, etc. [This cake *speaks well for* your cooking.]

SYNONYMS: **Speak** and **talk** are often used to mean the same thing, but at times **speak** suggests making a formal speech [The President *spoke* at the inauguration.], while **talk** suggests informal conversation [We were *talking* at dinner.]

**speak·er** (spē′kər) ***n.*** **1** a person who speaks or makes speeches. **2** the person who serves as chairman of a group of lawmakers, especially ☆**Speaker,** the chairman of the U.S. House of Representatives: *the full name is* **Speaker of the House. 3** a device that changes electric current into sound waves, used as part of a hi-fi system, radio, etc.

**spear** (spir) ***n.*** **1** a weapon made up of a long shaft with a sharp head. It is thrust or thrown by hand. **2** a long blade or shoot, as of grass. ◆***v.*** to pierce or stab as with a spear.

**spear·head** (spir′hed) ***n.*** **1** the head of a spear. **2** the person, part, or group that leads, as in an attack. ◆***v.*** to take the lead in [to *spearhead* an attack].

**spear·mint** (spir′mint) ***n.*** a common plant of the mint family, used for flavoring. *See the picture.*

**Spearmint** was given this name a very long time ago because its purple flowers are pointed and shaped like tiny spears.

**spe·cial** (spesh′əl) ***adj.*** **1** not like others; different; distinctive [The cook has a *special* recipe for tacos.] **2** unusual; extraordinary [Your idea has *special* merit.] **3** more than others; chief; main [her *special* friend]. **4** of or for a particular use, purpose, or occasion [a *special* meeting of the club]. ◆***n.*** **1** a special person or thing, as something featured in a sale. ☆**2** a somewhat unusual television program not part of a regular series. —**spe′cial·ly *adv.***



☆**special delivery** the delivery of mail quickly by a special messenger, for an extra fee.

**spe·cial·ist** (spesh′əl ist) ***n.*** a person who has made a special study of something or works in only one branch of some profession, etc. [Dr. Roderiguez is a *specialist* in children's diseases.]

**spe·cial·ize** (spesh′ə līz) ***v.*** **1** to make a special study of something or work only in a special branch of some profession, etc. [The scientist *specialized* in the study of atomic energy.] **2** to fit to a special use or purpose [The word "hound" has become *specialized* to mean a certain kind of dog, though it once meant "any dog."] —**spe′cial·ized, spe′cial·iz·ing** —**spe′cial·i·za′tion *n.***

**spe·cial·ty** (spesh′əl tē) ***n.*** **1** a special interest, study, work, etc. [Painting portraits is this artist's *specialty.*] **2** a special article, product, etc. [Steaks are the *specialty* of this restaurant.] **3** a special quality, feature, etc. —*pl.* **spe′cial·ties**

| | | | |
|---|---|---|---|
| **a** fat | **ir** here | **ou** out | **zh** leisure |
| **ā** ape | **ī** bite, fire | **u** up | **ng** ring |
| **ä** car, lot | **ō** go | **ur** fur | a *in* ago |
| **e** ten | **ô** law, horn | **ch** chin | e *in* agent |
| **er** care | **oi** oil | **sh** she | ə = i *in* unity |
| **ē** even | **oo** look | **th** thin | o *in* collect |
| **i** hit | **ōō** tool | ***th*** then | u *in* focus |

S

Sphinx

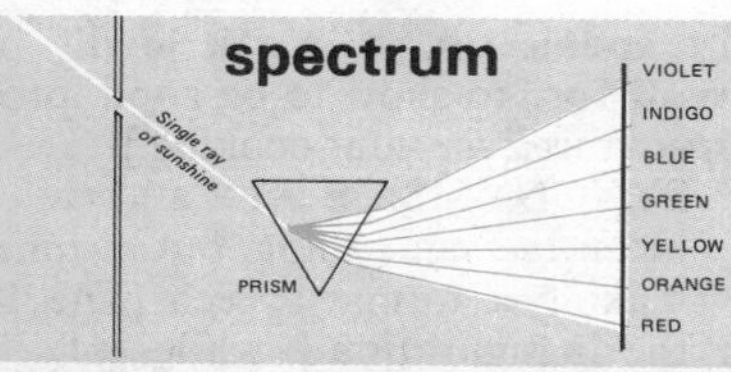

spectrum

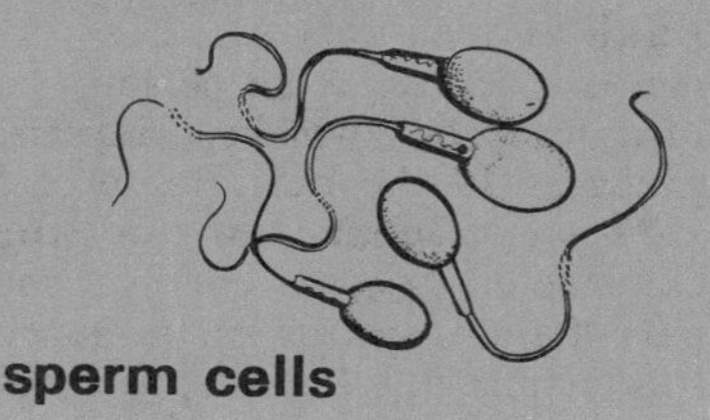
sperm cells

**spe·cie** (spē′shē) ***n.*** money made of metal, not paper; coin [Dimes and quarters are *specie.*]

**spe·cies** (spē′shēz) ***n.*** **1** a group of plants or animals that are alike in certain ways [The lion and tiger are two different *species* of cat.] **2** a kind or sort [a *species* of bravery]. —*pl.* **spe′cies** —**the species,** the human race.

**spe·cif·ic** (spi sif′ik) ***adj.*** **1** definite; exact [We made *specific* plans for our trip.] **2** having to do with or like a particular thing [the *specific* symptoms of an illness]. **3** of a special sort [a *specific* statement of policy]. **4** used to cure a particular disease [Streptomycin is a *specific* remedy for tuberculosis.] ◆***n.*** **1** a specific cure or remedy. **2** *usually* **specifics,** a particular or detail [What are the *specifics* of the new campaign against crime?] —**spe·cif′i·cal·ly *adv.***



**spec·i·fi·ca·tion** (spes′ə fi kā′shən) ***n.*** **1** the act of specifying; detailed mention. **2** something specified; a specific item. **3** *usually* **specifications,** *pl.* a statement or a description of all the necessary details, as of sizes, materials, etc. [the *specifications* for a new building].

**specific gravity** the weight of a given volume of a substance compared with the weight of an equal volume of another substance used as a standard. Water is the standard for liquids and solids; air or hydrogen is the standard for gases [The *specific gravity* of silver is 10.5, which means it weighs 10.5 times as much as water.]

**spec·i·fy** (spes′ə fī) ***v.*** **1** to mention or tell in detail; state definitely [She *specified* the time and place for the meeting.] **2** to call for specifically [The architect *specified* hardwood floors for the house.] —**spec′i·fied, spec′i·fy·ing**

**spec·i·men** (spes′ə mən) ***n.*** **1** a part of a whole, or one thing of a group, used as a sample of the rest [I need a *specimen* of her handwriting.] **2** a sample of urine, blood, etc. taken for medical analysis.

**spe·cious** (spē′shəs) ***adj.*** seeming to be good, correct, sensible, etc. without really being so [The speaker's *specious* reasoning fooled us for a while.] —**spe′cious·ly *adv.***

**speck** (spek) ***n.*** **1** a small spot or mark [A few *specks* of paint got on the rug.] **2** a very small bit; particle [There's not a *speck* of food in the house.] ◆***v.*** to mark with specks; spot.

**speck·le** (spek′'l) ***n.*** a small mark; speck. ◆***v.*** to mark with speckles [The walls are white *speckled* with green.] —**speck′led, speck′ling**

**specs** (speks) ***n.pl.*** **1** spectacles; eyeglasses. ☆**2** *a shorter word for* **specifications.** *This word is used only in everyday talk.*

**spec·ta·cle** (spek′tə k'l) ***n.*** **1** something to look at, especially an unusual sight or a grand public show [The fireworks display was a *spectacle.*] **2 spectacles,** *pl.* a pair of eyeglasses: *an old-fashioned meaning.* —**make a spectacle of oneself,** to behave foolishly or improperly in public.

> **Spectacle, spectacular, spectator, specter, spectroscope,** and **spectrum** all come from the Latin word *spectare,* meaning "to behold." All of these words have to do with someone seeing or with something seen or used in seeing.

**spec·tac·u·lar** (spek tak′yə lər) ***adj.*** of or like a spectacle; showy; striking [a *spectacular* display of roses]. —**spec·tac′u·lar·ly *adv.***

**spec·ta·tor** (spek′tāt′ər) ***n.*** a person who watches something without taking part; onlooker [We were *spectators* at the last game of the World Series.]

**spec·ter** (spek′tər) ***n.*** a ghost or phantom.

**spec·tral** (spek′trəl) ***adj.*** **1** of or like a specter; ghostly. **2** of or caused by a spectrum [*spectral* colors].

**spec·tro·scope** (spek′trə skōp) ***n.*** an instrument for breaking up light into the colors of a spectrum so that they can be studied.

**spec·trum** (spek′trəm) ***n.*** a series of colored bands formed when light is broken up by being passed through a prism or in some other way. All the colors of the spectrum are found in a rainbow, ranging from red to violet. *See the picture.* —*pl.* **spec·tra** (spek′trə) or **spec′trums**

**spec·u·late** (spek′yə lāt) ***v.*** **1** to think about or make guesses; ponder; meditate [Scientists *speculate* on the kinds of life there may be on distant planets.] **2** to make risky business deals with the hope of making large profits. —**spec′u·lat·ed, spec′u·lat·ing** —**spec′u·la′tion *n.*** —**spec′u·la′tor *n.***

**spec·u·la·tive** (spek′yə lāt′iv *or* spek′yə lə tiv) ***adj.*** **1** of, like, or taking part in speculation. **2** having to do with theory only; not practical.

**sped** (sped) *a past tense and past participle of* **speed.**

**speech** (spēch) ***n.*** **1** the act or way of speaking [We knew from their *speech* that they were from the South.] **2** the power to speak [She lost her *speech* from a stroke.] **3** something spoken; remark, utterance, etc. **4** a talk given in public [political *speeches* on TV]. **5** the language of a certain people.

**speech·less** (spēch′lis) ***adj.*** **1** not able to speak because of injury, shock, etc. [*speechless* with rage]. **2** that cannot be put into words [*speechless* terror].

**speed** (spēd) ***n.*** **1** fast motion; swiftness. **2** rate of motion; velocity [a *speed* of 10 miles per hour]. **3** swiftness of any action [reading *speed*]. **4** an arrangement of gears for the drive of an engine [The truck has five forward *speeds.*] **5** the length of time a camera shutter is open to take a picture; also, the sensitivity to light of photographic film. ◆***v.*** **1** to go or move fast or too fast [The arrow *sped* to its mark.] **2** to make go or move fast [He *sped* the letter on its way.] **3** to help to succeed; aid [Your gifts will *speed* the building program.] —**sped** or **speed'ed, speed'ing** —**speed up,** to go or make go faster.

**Speed** comes from an Old English word meaning "wealth" or "power." At one time it meant "to have good luck" or "to wish good luck to." It is still used in that way in the word *Godspeed.* People used to say "God speed you," meaning "God give you good luck."

**speed·boat** (spēd'bōt) ***n.*** a fast motorboat.

**speed·er** (spēd'ər) ***n.*** ☆a person or thing that speeds, especially a person who drives a car, etc. faster than is safe or lawful.

**speed·om·e·ter** (spi däm'ə tər) ***n.*** a device in a car, etc. to show how fast it is going.

☆**speed·ster** (spēd'stər) ***n.*** *another name for* **speeder.**

☆**speed trap** a strip of road where hidden police cars, radar devices, etc. are used to catch and arrest speeders.

**speed·up** (spēd'up) ***n.*** an increase in speed, as in the rate of work.

☆**speed·way** (spēd'wā) ***n.*** a track for racing cars or motorcycles.

**speed·y** (spēd'ē) ***adj.*** **1** fast; swift [*speedy* runners]. **2** without delay; prompt [Please send a *speedy* reply.] —**speed'i·er, speed'i·est** —**speed'i·ly** ***adv.*** —**speed'i·ness** ***n.***

**spell**[1] (spel) ***n.*** **1** a word or words supposed to have some magic power. **2** power or control that seems magical; charm; fascination [His talk cast a *spell* over us.]

**spell**[2] (spel) ***v.*** **1** to say or write in order the letters that make up a word [Can you *spell* "seize"? He *spells* badly.] **2** to make up; form [What word do these letters *spell?*] **3** to mean; signify [Hard work *spells* success.] —**spelled** or **spelt, spell'ing** —**spell out, 1** to read or make out with difficulty. ☆**2** to explain exactly or in detail.

**spell**[3] (spel) ***v.*** to work in place of another for a time; relieve: *used only in everyday talk* [I'll *spell* you at mowing the lawn.] —**spelled, spell'ing** ◆***n.*** **1** a period of time during which something is done or happens [a *spell* of sickness; a hot *spell*]. **2** a turn of working in place of another.

☆**spell·bind·er** (spel'bīn'dər) ***n.*** a speaker who holds an audience spellbound.

**spell·bound** (spel'bound) ***adj.*** held fast as if by a spell; fascinated; enchanted.

☆**spell·down** (spel'doun) ***n.*** a spelling match in which a contestant sits down or leaves when he or she misspells a word or a certain number of words.

**spell·er** (spel'ər) ***n.*** **1** a person who spells [a poor *speller*]. ☆**2** a book with exercises to teach spelling.

**spell·ing** (spel'iŋ) ***n.*** **1** the act of telling or writing the letters of a word in proper order. **2** the way in which a word is spelled.

☆**spelling bee** a contest in spelling words; spelldown.

**spelt** (spelt) *a past tense and past participle of* **spell**[2]**.**

**spend** (spend) ***v.*** **1** to pay out or give up, as money, time, or effort [He *spent* $50 for food. Try to *spend* some time with me.] **2** to pass [She *spent* the summer at camp.] **3** to use up; exhaust [His fury was *spent.*] —**spent, spend'ing** —**spend'er** ***n.***

**spend·thrift** (spend'thrift) ***n.*** a person who wastes money by spending carelessly; squanderer. ◆***adj.*** wasteful with money; extravagant.

**spent** (spent) *past tense and past participle of* **spend.** ◆***adj.*** tired out; used up.

**sperm** (spurm) ***n.*** **1** the fluid from the male sex glands that contains the cells for fertilizing the eggs of the female. **2** any of these cells. *See the picture.*

**sperm whale** a large, toothed whale of warm seas, valuable for its oil.

**spew** (spyoo͞) ***v.*** **1** to throw up from the mouth; vomit. **2** to gush forth [The volcano *spews* lava.]

**sp. gr.** *abbreviation for* **specific gravity.**

**sphag·num** (sfag'nəm) ***n.*** a spongelike, grayish moss found in bogs. It is gathered in masses and used to improve soil and to pack and pot plants.

**sphere** (sfir) ***n.*** **1** any round object whose curved surface is the same distance from the center at all points; ball; globe. **2** a star or planet. **3** the heavens seen as a dome or pictured as a globe. **4** the place or range of action or being [Our country has a wide *sphere* of influence.] **5** place in society; walk of life [She moves in a different *sphere* now that she's rich.]

**spher·i·cal** (sfer'i k'l *or* sfir'i k'l) ***adj.*** of or shaped like a sphere; globular. —**spher'i·cal·ly** ***adv.***

**sphe·roid** (sfir'oid) ***n.*** an object shaped almost but not quite like a sphere.

**sphinc·ter** (sfiŋk'tər) ***n.*** a ring-shaped muscle around a natural opening in the body, such as the mouth. This muscle can open or close the opening by becoming loose or tight. 715

**sphinx** (sfiŋks) ***n.*** **1** any ancient Egyptian statue having a lion's body and the head of a man, ram, or hawk [the famous *Sphinx* near Cairo, Egypt]. *See the picture.* **2** a monster of Greek myths that asked riddles. It had a lion's body with wings, and a woman's head. **3** a person who is hard to know or understand.

**Sphinx** is the Greek word for "strangler." In ancient Greek myths, the Sphinx or monster at Thebes asked a riddle of those people who passed by, and strangled those who were unable to give the right answer.

**spice** (spīs) ***n.*** **1** any of certain vegetable substances used to give a special flavor or smell to food, as cinnamon, nutmeg, or pepper. **2** an interesting touch or detail [Humor added *spice* to her talk.] ◆***v.*** **1** to season or flavor with spice. **2** to add interest to. —**spiced, spic'ing**

**spick-and-span** (spik''n span') ***adj.*** **1** new or fresh. **2** neat and clean.

**spic·y** (spī'sē) ***adj.*** **1** seasoned with spice or spices. **2** having the flavor or smell of spice [a *spicy* flower]. **3** interesting; lively [a *spicy* bit of gossip]. —**spic'i·er, spic'i·est** —**spic'i·ness** ***n.***

**spi·der** (spī'dər) ***n.*** a small animal with eight legs and a body made up of two parts. The back part of the

| | | | | | | | |
|---|---|---|---|---|---|---|---|
| **a** | fat | **ir** | here | **ou** | out | **zh** | leisure |
| **ā** | ape | **ī** | bite, fire | **u** | up | **ŋ** | ring |
| **ä** | car, lot | **ō** | go | **ur** | fur | | a *in* ago |
| **e** | ten | **ô** | law, horn | **ch** | chin | | e *in* agent |
| **er** | care | **oi** | oil | **sh** | she | **ə =** | i *in* unity |
| **ē** | even | **oo** | look | **th** | thin | | o *in* collect |
| **i** | hit | **o͞o** | tool | ***th*** | then | | u *in* focus |

**S**

body has organs that spin silk threads into webs to trap insects. *See the picture.* —**spi′der·y** ***adj.***

> The **spider** gets it name from what it does, for this creature spins threads into a web or a nest. The name comes from an Old English word meaning "to spin."

**spied** (spīd) *past tense and past participle of* **spy.**

☆**spiel** (spēl) ***n.*** a talk or speech, often long and persuasive, as in trying to coax people to buy something. *This is a slang word.*

**spies** (spīz) ***n.*** *plural of* **spy.**

**spig·ot** (spig′ət) ***n.*** **1** a plug used to stop up the hole in a cask. **2** *another name for* **faucet.**

**spike**[1] (spīk) ***n.*** **1** a pointed piece of metal, etc., as any of the sharp pieces along the top of an iron fence or on the soles of shoes used in certain sports. **2** a large, strong nail. ◆***v.*** **1** to fasten a spike or spikes to. **2** to pierce or hurt with a spike or spikes. **3** to stop or block, as a scheme. ☆**4** to jump up at the net and hit the ball forcefully into the court of the other team in the game of volleyball. —**spiked, spik′ing**

**spike**[2] (spīk) ***n.*** **1** a long cluster of flowers attached right to the stalk. *See the picture.* **2** an ear of grain.

**spill** (spil) ***v.*** **1** to let flow over or run out [Who *spilled* water on the floor? Try not to *spill* any sugar.] **2** to flow over or run out [Tears *spilled* from my eyes.] **3** to shed, as blood. **4** to make fall; throw off: *used only in everyday talk* [My horse *spilled* me.] **5** to make known, as a secret: *used only in everyday talk.* —**spilled** or **spilt, spill′ing** ◆***n.*** **1** the act of spilling. **2** a fall or tumble, as from a horse: *used only in everyday talk.*

☆**spill·way** (spil′wā) ***n.*** a channel to carry off an overflow of water, as from a dam.

**spin** (spin) ***v.*** **1** to draw out the fibers of and twist into thread [to *spin* cotton, wool, flax, etc.] **2** to make in this way [to *spin* yarn]. **3** to make from a thread given out by the body [Spiders *spin* webs.] **4** to tell slowly, with many details [to *spin* out a story]. **5** to whirl around swiftly [The earth *spins* in space. *Spin* the wheel.] **6** to seem to be whirling [My head is *spinning.*] **7** to move along swiftly and smoothly [Cars *spun* past us.] **8** to turn freely without holding [wheels *spinning* on ice]. —**spun, spin′ning** ◆***n.*** **1** a whirling movement. **2** a fast ride or drive, as in a car. —**spin off,** to bring forth or grow out of as a new or extra product, benefit, etc. —**spin′ner** ***n.***

**spin·ach** (spin′ich) ***n.*** a vegetable whose large, dark-green leaves are usually cooked before they are eaten.

**spi·nal** (spī′n'l) ***adj.*** of the spine or spinal cord.

**spinal column** the long row of connected bones that form the backbone; spine. *See the picture.*

**spinal cord** the thick cord of nerve tissue inside the spinal column.

**spin·dle** (spin′d'l) ***n.*** **1** a slender rod used to twist and hold thread in spinning. **2** something long and slender like a spindle. **3** a rod or shaft that turns, or on which something turns, as an axle. ◆***v.*** to grow long and thin, as a stalk or stem. —**spin′dled, spin′dling**

**spin·dly** (spin′dlē) ***adj.*** long or tall and very thin, often so much so as to seem weak [The legs of the table are *spindly.*]

**spin·drift** (spin′drift) ***n.*** spray blown from a rough sea.

**spine** (spīn) ***n.*** **1** a thin, sharp, stiff part that sticks out on certain plants and animals, as the cactus or porcupine; thorn or quill. **2** the backbone; spinal column. **3** anything thought of as like a backbone, as the back of a book.

**spine·less** (spīn′lis) ***adj.*** **1** having no backbone. **2** having no courage or willpower. **3** having no spines or thorns.

**spin·et** (spin′it) ***n.*** **1** a type of small harpsichord. **2** a short upright piano. *See the picture for* **piano.**

> The kind of harpsichord called a **spinet** got its name from the pointed quills used to pluck its strings and produce music. The Latin word for quill or thorn is *spina,* which is also the source of the word **spine.**

**spin·na·ker** (spin′ə kər) ***n.*** a large, extra sail shaped like a triangle, used on some racing yachts.

**spinning wheel** a spinning machine with one spindle that is turned by a large wheel. *See the picture.*

**spin·off** (spin′ôf) ***n.*** something that grows out of something else, as a television series built around a character in an earlier series.

**spin·ster** (spin′stər) ***n.*** an unmarried woman, especially an older one; old maid.

**spin·y** (spīn′ē) ***adj.*** **1** covered with spines or thorns. **2** shaped like a spine. —**spin′i·er, spin′i·est**

**spi·ral** (spī′rəl) ***adj.*** circling around a center in a flat or rising curve that keeps growing larger or smaller, as the thread of a screw, or that stays the same, as the thread of a bolt. ◆***n.*** a spiral curve or coil [The mainspring of a watch is a *spiral.*] *See the picture.* ◆***v.*** to move in or form into a spiral. —**spi′raled** or **spi′ralled, spi′ral·ing** or **spi′ral·ling** —**spi′ral·ly** ***adv.***

**spire** (spīr) ***n.*** **1** the tip of something that comes to a gradual point, as a mountain peak. **2** anything that tapers to a point [the *spire* on a steeple]. *See the picture.*

spinning wheel

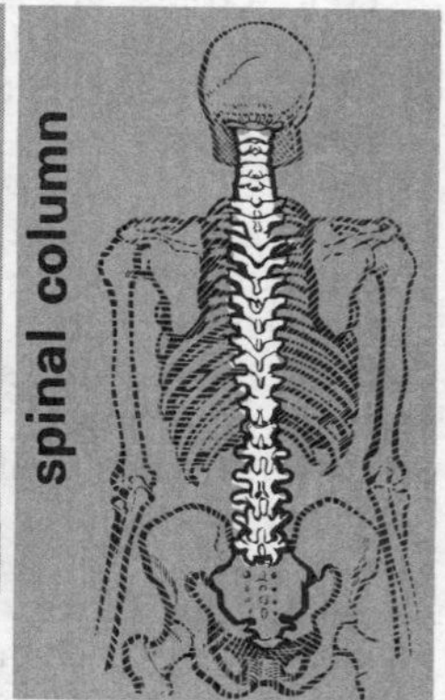

spire

spinal column

flower spikes

spirals

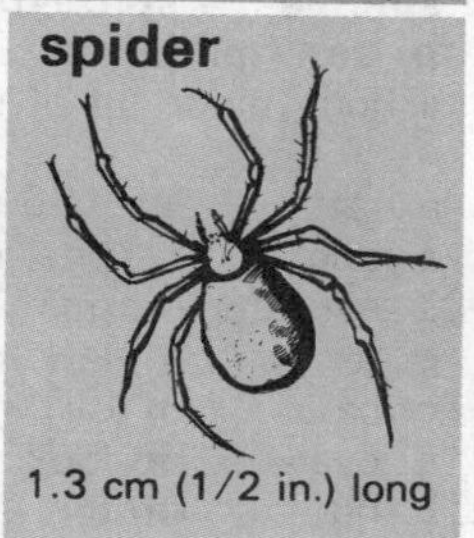

spider

1.3 cm (1/2 in.) long

**spir·it** (spir′it) ***n.*** **1** the soul. **2** a being that is not of this world, as a ghost, angel, fairy, etc. **3** a person [The early pioneers were brave *spirits.*] **4** *often* **spir·its,** *pl.* state of mind; mood [The teacher is in good *spirits.*] **5** vigor, courage, liveliness, etc. [She answered with *spirit.*] **6** enthusiasm and loyalty [school *spirit*]. **7** the true meaning [He follows the *spirit* if not the letter of the law.] **8** the main principle, quality, or influence [the *spirit* of the Western frontier]. **9 spirits,** *pl.* strong alcoholic liquor; also, a solution in alcohol, as of camphor. ◆***v.*** to carry away secretly and swiftly [The fox *spirited* off two chickens.] ◆***adj.*** **1** of spirits or spiritualism [the *spirit* world]. **2** that burns alcohol [a *spirit* lamp]. —**out of spirits,** sad; unhappy. —**spir′it·less *adj.***

**spir·it·ed** (spir′i tid) ***adj.*** **1** having a certain nature or mood [low-*spirited*]. **2** full of spirit; lively [a *spirited* argument; *spirited* horses].

**spir·it·u·al** (spir′i choo wəl) ***adj.*** **1** of the spirit or soul as apart from the body or material things. **2** having to do with religion or the church; sacred. ◆***n.*** ☆a religious folk song of the kind created by black Americans. —**spir·it·u·al·i·ty** (spir′i choo wal′ə tē) ***n.*** —**spir′it·u·al·ly *adv.***

**spir·it·u·al·ism** (spir′i choo wəl iz′m) ***n.*** ☆**1** the belief that the spirits of the dead can send messages to the living, especially with the help of a person called a "medium." **2** the quality of being spiritual. —**spir′it·u·al·ist *n.*** —**spir′it·u·al·is′tic *adj.***

**spit**[1] (spit) ***n.*** **1** a thin, pointed rod on which meat is fixed for roasting over a fire. *See the picture on page 719.* **2** a narrow point of land stretching out into a body of water. ◆***v.*** to fix on a spit; pierce. —**spit′ted, spit′ting**

> **Spit**[1] and **spit**[2] come from different sources. **Spit**[1] comes from a very old word that meant "sharp," and is used to mean a sharp stick or a point of land. **Spit**[2] always had the meaning of saliva from the mouth, even in its earliest spelling centuries ago. The form the word took may have been in imitation of the noise one makes when spitting.

**spit**[2] (spit) ***v.*** **1** to force out saliva or other matter from the mouth. **2** to send out with sudden force [He *spit* out an oath. The radiator is *spitting* steam.] **3** to make an angry, hissing noise, as a cat. —**spit** or, especially in Great Britain, **spat, spit′ting** ◆***n.*** **1** the act of spitting. **2** *another name for* **saliva.** —**spit and image** or **spitting image,** an exact likeness: *used only in everyday talk.*

**spit·ball** (spit′bôl) ***n.*** a piece of paper chewed up into a wad for throwing.

**spite** (spīt) ***n.*** a mean feeling toward another that makes one want to hurt or annoy that person; ill will; malice. ◆***v.*** to show one's spite for by hurting, annoying, etc. [She played her radio loud to *spite* her neighbors.] —**spit′ed, spit′ing** —**in spite of,** regardless of. —**spite′ful *adj.***

**spit·fire** (spit′fīr) ***n.*** a person, especially a woman or girl, who has a quick and violent temper.

**spit·tle** (spit′'l) ***n.*** spit; saliva.

☆**spit·toon** (spi to͞on′) ***n.*** a container to spit into.

**splash** (splash) ***v.*** **1** to make a liquid scatter and fall in drops [to *splash* water or mud about]. **2** to dash a liquid on, so as to wet or soil [The car *splashed* my coat.] **3** to move, fall, or hit with a splash [We *splashed* through the swamp.] ◆***n.*** **1** the act or sound of splashing. **2** water, mud, etc. splashed. **3** a spot or mark made as if by splashing. —**make a splash,** to get much attention: *used only in everyday talk.* —**splash′y *adj.***

☆**splash·down** (splash′doun) ***n.*** the landing of a spacecraft on water.

**splat·ter** (splat′ər) ***n., v.*** spatter or splash.

**splay** (splā) ***n.*** a sloping surface or angle. ◆***adj.*** flat and spreading out [*splay* feet]. ◆***v.*** **1** to spread outward. **2** to make sloping.

**spleen** (splēn) ***n.*** **1** an organ of the body, near the stomach, having something to do with the way the blood is made up. It was once thought of as the cause of bad temper and mean feelings. **2** bad temper; spite; anger.

**splen·did** (splen′did) ***adj.*** **1** very bright, brilliant, showy, magnificent, etc. [a *splendid* display; a *splendid* gown]. **2** deserving high praise; glorious; grand [your *splendid* courage]. **3** very good; excellent; fine: *used only in everyday talk* [a *splendid* trip]. —**splen′did·ly *adv.***

> SYNONYMS: **Splendid** is used for something which affects the mind with its brilliance, magnificence, or greatness [a *splendid* palace; a *splendid* sunrise]. **Gorgeous** is used for that which is unusual or remarkable for its brilliance or many colors [a *gorgeous* display of flowers]. **Superb** is used for something which is greater than all others in brilliance, magnificence, etc. [a *superb* musical performance]. All these words are now used in an exaggerated way in everyday talk and so have a weaker effect.

**splen·dor** (splen′dər) ***n.*** **1** great brightness; brilliance [the *splendor* of a diamond]. **2** glory or magnificence [the *splendor* of his reputation]. *The usual British spelling is* **splendour.**

**sple·net·ic** (spli net′ik) ***adj.*** easily made angry; bad-tempered; irritable; spiteful.

**splice** (splīs) ***v.*** **1** to join ropes or cables by weaving together untwisted strands at the ends. **2** to join pieces of wood by overlapping and fastening the ends. **3** to fasten together the ends of, as motion-picture film, sound tape, etc. —**spliced, splic′ing** ◆***n.*** the act or place of splicing. *See the picture on page 719.*

**splint** (splint) ***n.*** **1** a thin, stiff piece of wood, metal, etc. set along a broken bone to hold the parts in place. *See the picture on page 719.* **2** any of the thin strips of wood or cane used to weave baskets, chair seats, etc.

**splin·ter** (splin′tər) ***v.*** to break or split into thin, sharp pieces [Soft pine *splinters* easily.] ◆***n.*** a thin, sharp piece of wood, bone, etc. broken off. ◆***adj.*** describing a group that separates from a main group because of its different ideas.

| | | | |
|---|---|---|---|
| **a** fat | **ir** here | **ou** out | **zh** leisure |
| **ā** ape | **ī** bite, fire | **u** up | **ng** ring |
| **ä** car, lot | **ō** go | **ur** fur | a *in* ago |
| **e** ten | **ô** law, horn | **ch** chin | e *in* agent |
| **er** care | **oi** oil | **sh** she | ə = i *in* unity |
| **ē** even | **oo** look | **th** thin | o *in* collect |
| **i** hit | **o͞o** tool | ***th*** then | u *in* focus |

**split** (split) ***v.*** **1** to separate or divide along the length into two or more parts [to *split* a wiener bun]. **2** to break apart by force; burst [The board *split* when I hammered in the nail.] **3** to divide into parts or shares [We *split* the cost of our trip.] **4** to separate because of not being able to agree [The club *split* up after big disagreements.] ☆**5** to leave a place: *slang in this meaning.* —**split, split′ting** ◆***n.*** **1** the act of splitting. **2** a break, crack, or tear [a *split* in the seam of a dress]. **3** a division in a group [The argument caused a *split* in our club.] **4** *often* **splits,** *pl.* an acrobatic act in which the legs are spread flat on the floor in a straight line. **5** an arrangement of bowling pins left standing after the ball is rolled the first time, separated so widely that a spare is unlikely. ◆***adj.*** broken into parts; divided.

**split-lev·el** (split′lev′'l) ***adj.*** describing a house that has each floor level a half story above or below the level next to it.

**split·ting** (split′iŋ) ***adj.*** very painful [a *splitting* headache].

**splotch** (spläch) ***n.*** a spot or stain. ◆***v.*** to make a splotch on. —**splotch′y** ***adj.***

☆**splurge** (splurj) ***v.*** to spend much money or effort on something, often just to show off [to *splurge* on a big wedding]. —**splurged, splurg′ing** ◆***n.*** the act of splurging. *This word is used only in everyday talk.*

**splut·ter** (splut′ər) ***v.*** **1** to make hissing or spitting sounds [The kettle *spluttered* on the stove.] **2** to talk in a fast, confused way, as when angry or embarrassed [She *spluttered* out an excuse.] ◆***n.*** the act of spluttering.



**spoil** (spoil) ***v.*** **1** to make or become useless, worthless, rotten, etc.; damage; ruin [Ink stains *spoiled* the paper. Illness *spoiled* my attendance record. Meat *spoils* fast in warm weather.] **2** to cause a person to ask for or expect too much by giving in to all of that person's wishes [to *spoil* a child]. —**spoiled** or **spoilt, spoil′ing** ◆***n.*** *usually* **spoils,** *pl.* **1** goods taken by force in war; loot; booty. ☆**2** jobs or offices to which the political party that wins can appoint people. —**spoil′er** ***n.***

> The first meaning of **spoil** was from the Latin *spolium,* meaning the weapons taken away from a defeated enemy. The plural **spoils** then came to mean any goods or land taken by force in war. From that came the verb, meaning to plunder or seize whatever one could. Later on *spoil* was used to mean simply to destroy or ruin something.

**Spo·kane** (spō kan′) a city in eastern Washington.

**spoke**[1] (spōk) ***n.*** any of the braces reaching from the hub of a wheel to the rim.

**spoke**[2] (spōk) *past tense of* **speak.**

**spo·ken** (spō′kən) *past participle of* **speak.** ◆***adj.*** **1** said aloud; oral [a *spoken* order]. **2** speaking or said in a certain kind of voice [a soft-*spoken* person].

**spokes·man** (spōks′mən) ***n.*** a person who speaks for another or for a group. —*pl.* **spokes′men** *Many people prefer to use the word* **spokes·per·son** (spōks′pur′s'n).

**sponge** (spunj) ***n.*** **1** a sea animal that is like a plant and grows fixed to surfaces under water. *See the picture.* **2** the light, elastic skeleton of such an animal, that is full of holes and can soak up much water. Sponges are used for washing, bathing, etc. **3** any artificial substance like this, as of plastic or rubber, used in the same way. ◆***v.*** **1** to wipe, clean, make wet, or soak up as with a sponge [to *sponge* up gravy with a crust of bread]. **2** to depend on others for food, money, etc. although able to support oneself: *used only in everyday talk* [They are always trying to *sponge* off us.] —**sponged, spong′ing** —**spong′er** ***n.***

**sponge bath** a bath taken by using a wet sponge or cloth without getting into water.

**sponge·cake** (spunj′kāk) ***n.*** a soft, light cake made with flour, eggs, sugar, etc., but no shortening. *Also written* **sponge cake.**

**spon·gy** (spun′jē) ***adj.*** **1** light, elastic, full of holes, etc., like a sponge. **2** soft and wet [*spongy* ground]. —**spon′gi·er, spon′gi·est**

**spon·sor** (spän′sər) ***n.*** **1** a person who agrees to be responsible for another person, as in paying expenses. ☆**2** a person or business that pays the cost of a radio or TV program on which it advertises something. **3** *another name for* **godparent.** ◆***v.*** to be a sponsor for. —**spon′sor·ship** ***n.***

**spon·ta·ne·i·ty** (spän′tə nē′ə tē) ***n.*** the condition of being spontaneous.

**spon·ta·ne·ous** (spän tā′nē əs) ***adj.*** **1** acting or done in a free, natural way, without effort or much thought [We broke into a *spontaneous* song.] **2** caused or brought about by its own force, without outside help [Chemical changes in the oily rags caused fire by *spontaneous* combustion.] —**spon·ta′ne·ous·ly** ***adv.***

> SYNONYMS: **Spontaneous** means acting naturally, without planning ahead of time [The crowd at the football game gave a *spontaneous* cheer.] **Impulsive** means acting according to one's mood, suddenly and without thinking carefully [I was ashamed that I hurt her by my *impulsive* remark.]

**spoof** (spo͞of) ***n., v.*** trick; joke: *a slang word.*

☆**spook** (spo͞ok) ***n.*** a ghost. ◆***v.*** to frighten or be frightened suddenly. *This word is used only in everyday talk.*

☆**spook·y** (spo͞ok′ē) ***adj.*** of, like, or suggesting a ghost or ghosts; weird; eerie: *used only in everyday talk* [a *spooky* old house]. —**spook′i·er, spook′i·est** —**spook′i·ness** ***n.***

**spool** (spo͞ol) ***n.*** a small roller, with a rim at either end, on which thread, wire, etc. is wound.

**spoon** (spo͞on) ***n.*** a tool made up of a small, shallow bowl with a handle, used for eating or stirring food and drink. ◆***v.*** to take up with a spoon.

**spoon·bill** (spo͞on′bil) ***n.*** a wading bird with a flat bill shaped like a spoon at the tip. *See the picture.*

**spoon·ful** (spo͞on′fo͝ol) ***n.*** the amount that a spoon will hold. —*pl.* **spoon′fuls**

**spoor** (spo͝or) ***n.*** the track, trail, or scent of a wild animal.

**spo·rad·ic** (spô rad′ik) ***adj.*** happening from time to time; not regular [*sporadic* gunfire]. —**spo·rad′i·cal·ly** ***adv.***

**spore** (spôr) ***n.*** a tiny cell produced by mosses, ferns, some one-celled animals, etc., that can grow into a new plant or animal.

**sport** (spôrt) ***n.*** **1** active play, a game, etc. taken up for exercise or pleasure and, sometimes, as a profession [Football, golf, bowling, swimming, etc. are *sports.*] **2** fun or play [They thought it was great *sport* to fool others on the telephone.] **3** a person judged by the way he or she takes loss, defeat, teasing, etc.: *used only in everyday talk* [Be a good *sport* if you lose. Let's not be poor *sports* if it rains.] **4** a person who is lively, generous, willing to take chances, etc.: *used only in everyday talk.* **5** a plant or animal different from the normal type [A white robin is a *sport.*] ◆***v.*** **1** to play or have fun [to *sport* on a beach]. **2** to wear or display: *used only in everyday talk* [to *sport* a new tie]. ◆***adj.*** for play, relaxing, etc. [a *sport* coat]. —**in sport** or **for sport,** in fun or jest. —**make sport of,** to make fun of; ridicule.

**sport·ing** (spôrt′iŋ) ***adj.*** **1** of, for, or enjoying sports [a store that sells *sporting* goods]. **2** like a sportsman; fair. ☆**3** having to do with gambling or betting on games, races, etc.

**sporting chance** a fair or even chance: *used only in everyday talk.*

**spor·tive** (spôr′tiv) ***adj.*** **1** playful. **2** done in fun or play.

**sports** (spôrts) ***adj.*** *same as* **sport.**

**sports car** a low, small automobile that usually has a powerful engine and seats for only two.

☆**sports·cast** (spôrts′kast) ***n.*** a broadcast about sports, especially about sports news, on radio or TV. —**sports′cast·er *n.***

**sports·man** (spôrts′mən) ***n.*** **1** a man who takes part in or is interested in sports. **2** a person who plays fair and does not complain about losing or boast about winning. —*pl.* **sports′men** —**sports′man·like *adj.*** —**sports′man·ship *n.***

**sports·wear** (spôrts′wer) ***n.*** clothes worn while taking part in sports or when relaxing or being informal.

**sports·wom·an** (spôrts′woom′ən) ***n.*** a woman who takes part in or is interested in sports. —*pl.* **sports′wom′en**

**sports·writ·er** (spôrts′rīt′ər) ***n.*** a reporter who writes about sports or sports events.

**spot** (spät) ***n.*** **1** a small part that is different in color, feeling, etc. from the parts around it [a leopard's *spots;* a sore *spot* on the skin]. **2** a stain, mark, blemish, etc. [an ink *spot;* a *spot* on one's reputation]. **3** a place [a quiet *spot* in the country]. ◆***v.*** **1** to mark or become marked with spots. **2** to place [Let's *spot* two guards at the entrance.] **3** to see or recognize [I can *spot* our house from here.] ☆**4** to give the advantage of: *used only in everyday talk* [Frieda *spotted* Norman fifty feet and still won the race.] —**spot′ted, spot′ting** ◆***adj.*** **1** ready; on hand [*spot* cash]. **2** made at random [a *spot* check]. —**hit the spot,** to be exactly as wanted: *used only in everyday talk.* —☆**in a bad spot,** in trouble: *a slang phrase.* —**on the spot, 1** at the very place and time. **2** in trouble or in danger: *slang in this meaning.* —**spot′less *adj.***

**spot-check** (spät′chek′) ***v.*** to check or examine by taking samples from time to time. ◆***n.*** an act of such checking.

☆**spot·light** (spät′līt) ***n.*** **1** a strong beam of light shone on a particular person or thing, as on a stage. **2** a lamp used to throw such a beam. **3** public notice [The President is always in the *spotlight.*]

**spot·ty** (spät′ē) ***adj.*** **1** marked with spots; spotted. **2** not regular, even, or steady; not uniform [Their attendance at our meetings has been *spotty.*]

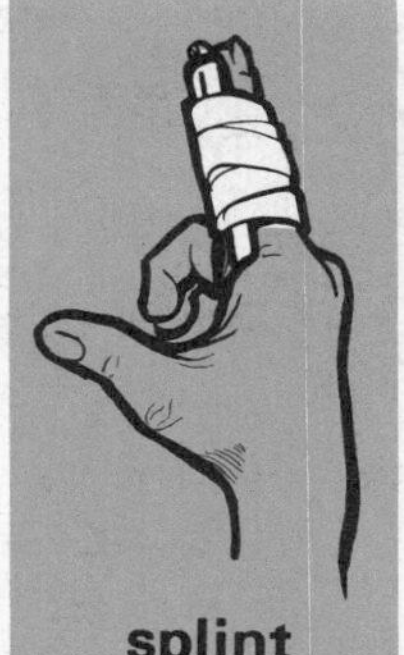
splint

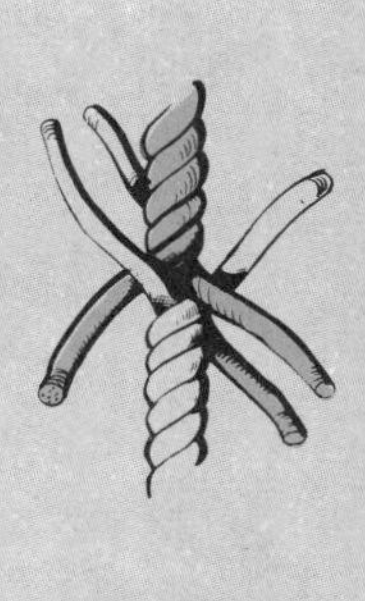
rope splice

sponges

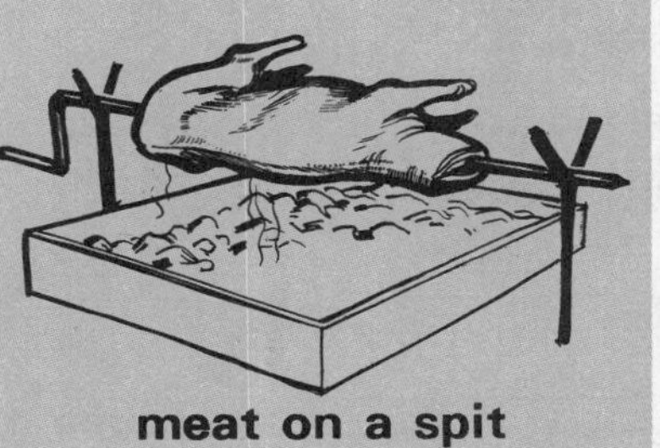
meat on a spit

spoonbill

**spouse** (spous *or* spouz) ***n.*** a husband or wife.

**spout** (spout) ***n.*** **1** a pipe, tube, or lip by which a liquid pours, as from a container. **2** a stream or jet of liquid [Water shot up from the fountain in a high *spout.*] ◆***v.*** **1** to shoot out with force [The well began to *spout* oil. Water *spouted* from the cracked hose.] **2** to talk on and on in a loud, forceful way [He kept *spouting* poems he had learned as a youth.]



**sprain** (sprān) ***v.*** to twist a muscle or ligament in a joint without putting the bones out of place [to *sprain* one's wrist]. ◆***n.*** an injury caused by this.

**sprang** (spraŋ) *a past tense of* **spring.**

**sprat** (sprat) ***n.*** a small kind of herring.

**sprawl** (sprôl) ***v.*** **1** to sit or lie with the arms and legs spread out in a relaxed or awkward way. **2** to spread out in an awkward or uneven way [Your handwriting *sprawls* across the page.] ◆***n.*** a sprawling position [My first attempt to ice skate ended in a *sprawl.*]

**spray**[1] (sprā) ***n.*** **1** a mist of tiny drops, as of water thrown off from a waterfall. **2** a stream of such tiny drops, as from a spray gun or a spray can. **3** something like this [a *spray* of buckshot]. ◆***v.*** **1** to put something on in a spray [to *spray* a car with paint]. **2** to shoot out in a spray [She *sprayed* perfume on herself.] —**spray′er *n.***

**spray**[2] (sprā) ***n.*** a small branch of a tree or plant with leaves, flowers, etc. on it.

**spray can** a can in which gas under pressure is used to make what is inside come out as a spray.

| | | | | | | | |
|---|---|---|---|---|---|---|---|
| **a** | fat | **ir** | here | **ou** | out | **zh** | leisure |
| **ā** | ape | **ī** | bite, fire | **u** | up | **ŋ** | ring |
| **ä** | car, lot | **ō** | go | **ur** | fur | | a *in* ago |
| **e** | ten | **ô** | law, horn | **ch** | chin | | e *in* agent |
| **er** | care | **oi** | oil | **sh** | she | **ə** = | i *in* unity |
| **ē** | even | **oo** | look | **th** | thin | | o *in* collect |
| **i** | hit | **o͞o** | tool | ***th*** | then | | u *in* focus |

**S**

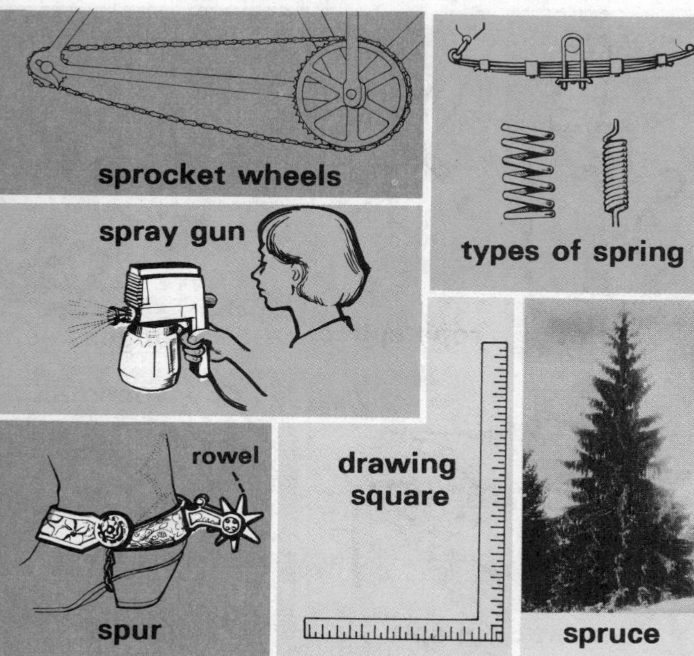


☆**spray gun** a gunlike device that shoots out a spray of liquid, as of paint or of an insect poison. *See the*

*picture.*

**spread** (spred) ***v.*** **1** to open out or stretch out, in space or time [*Spread* out the tablecloth. The eagle *spread* its wings. Our trip *spread* out over two weeks.] **2** to lay or place over so as to cover, be seen, etc. [*Spread* out your paintings on the floor.] **3** to lie or extend [A beautiful valley *spread* out before us.] **4** to go, pass, scatter, etc. [The rumors *spread* quickly.] **5** to make go, pass, etc. [Flies *spread* disease.] **6** to put or cover in a thin layer [to *spread* bread with jelly]. **7** to set the things for a meal on [to *spread* a table]. ◆***n.*** **1** the act of spreading. **2** the amount or distance something can be spread [The *spread* of its wings is six feet.] ☆**3** a cloth cover, as for a table or bed. ☆**4** any soft substance, as jam or butter, that can be spread in a layer. **5** a meal, especially one with many kinds of food: *used only in everyday talk.* —☆**spread oneself thin,** to try to do too many things at once. —**spread'er** ***n.***

**spree** (sprē) ***n.*** **1** a lively, noisy time, especially with much drinking of alcoholic liquor. **2** a space of time in which one does something very freely [Yesterday we went on a shopping *spree.*]

**sprig** (sprig) ***n.*** a little twig or branch, with leaves, flowers, etc. on it.

**spright·ly** (sprīt'lē) ***adj.*** lively; full of energy [a *sprightly* dance, tune, etc.] —**spright'li·er, spright'li·est** —**spright'li·ness** ***n.***

**spring** (spriŋ) ***v.*** **1** to move suddenly and quickly; leap; jump up [I *sprang* to my feet.] **2** to snap back into position or shape, as a rubber band that is stretched and then let go. **3** to make snap shut [to *spring* a trap]. **4** to come into being [A town *sprang* up at that site. The plant *springs* from a seed.] **5** to make known suddenly [to *spring* a surprise]. **6** to make or become split, bent, cracked, warped, etc. [The door has *sprung.*] —**sprang** or **sprung, sprung, spring'ing** ◆***n.*** **1** the act of springing; jump or leap. **2** a device, as a coil of wire, that returns to its original shape when pressure on it is released. Springs are used in beds and automobiles to take up shock, or in clocks, etc. to make them go. *See the picture.* **3** the ability to snap back into position or shape [This elastic belt has no *spring* left.] **4** water flowing up from the ground. **5** a source or beginning. **6** the season when plants begin to grow, between winter and summer. ◆***adj.*** **1** of the season spring [*spring* flowers]. **2** having springs [a *spring* mattress]. **3** coming from a spring [*spring* water]. —**spring a leak,** to begin to leak suddenly.

**spring·board** (spriŋ'bôrd) ***n.*** a board that gives a springing motion to someone jumping from it, as a diving board.

**spring·bok** (spriŋ'bäk) ***n.*** a South African gazelle that can jump high in the air. —*pl.* **spring'bok** or **spring'boks**

**Spring·field** (spriŋ'fēld) **1** a city in Massachusetts. **2** a city in Missouri. **3** the capital of Illinois.

**spring·time** (spriŋ'tīm) ***n.*** the season of spring.

**spring·y** (spriŋ'ē) ***adj.*** full of spring or bounce [*springy* wood for a bow]. —**spring'i·er, spring'i·est**

**sprin·kle** (spriŋ'k'l) ***v.*** **1** to scatter in drops or bits [to *sprinkle* salt on an egg]. **2** to scatter drops or bits on [to *sprinkle* a lawn with water]. **3** to rain lightly. —**sprin'kled, sprin'kling** ◆***n.*** **1** the act of sprinkling. **2** a light rain. —**sprin'kler** ***n.***

SYNONYMS: To **sprinkle** is to cause to fall in small drops or bits [to *sprinkle* water; to *sprinkle* sugar over berries]. To **scatter** is to spread the parts of a group in different directions, usually in an uneven way [The wind *scattered* the papers on the desk.]

**sprin·kling** (spriŋ'kliŋ) ***n.*** a small number or amount [a *sprinkling* of people].

**sprint** (sprint) ***v.*** to run or move very fast, as in a short race. ◆***n.*** a short run or race at full speed. —**sprint'er** ***n.***

**sprit** (sprit) ***n.*** a pole that stretches up at a slant from a mast to help hold a sail.

**sprite** (sprīt) ***n.*** an elf, pixie, fairy, etc.

**sprock·et** (spräk'it) ***n.*** **1** any of a number of teeth, as on a rim of a wheel, that fit into the links of a chain, as on a bicycle. **2** a wheel with such teeth: *the full name is* **sprocket wheel**. *See the picture.*

**sprout** (sprout) ***v.*** **1** to begin to grow [Buds are *sprouting* on the roses. Weeds began to *sprout* in the garden.] **2** to grow or develop rapidly [Our youngest child *sprouted* up this summer.] **3** to make grow [Rain will *sprout* the grass.] ◆***n.*** a young, new growth from a plant, bud, seed, etc.

**spruce**[1] (spro͞os) ***n.*** **1** an evergreen tree with thin needles. *See the picture.* **2** the soft wood of this tree.

**spruce**[2] (spro͞os) ***adj.*** neat and trim; smart. ◆***v.*** to make or become neat, trim, etc. [New drapes will *spruce* up the room.] —**spruced, spruc'ing**

**sprung** (spruŋ) *a past tense and the past participle of* **spring.**

**spry** (sprī) ***adj.*** moving with quickness and ease; lively; agile. —**spri'er** or **spry'er, spri'est** or **spry'est** —**spry'ly** ***adv.***

**spud** (spud) ***n.*** **1** a sharp spade for digging out weeds. **2** a potato: *used only in everyday talk.*

**spume** (spyo͞om) ***n., v.*** foam; froth. —**spumed, spum′ing**

**spu·mo·ni** or **spu·mo·ne** (spə mō′nē) ***n.*** an Italian dessert of ice cream in layers of several flavors and colors, often containing bits of nuts and fruits.

**spun** (spun) *past tense and past participle of* **spin.** ◆***adj.*** formed by or as if by spinning [*spun* glass].

**spun glass** fine glass fiber, made by forming liquid glass into a thread.

**spunk** (spuŋk) ***n.*** courage or a brave spirit; pluck: *used only in everyday talk.*

**spunk·y** (spuŋ′kē) ***adj.*** having spunk, or courage; brave: *used only in everyday talk.* —**spunk′i·er, spunk′i·est**

**spur** (spur) ***n.*** **1** a metal piece with sharp points, worn on the heel by horsemen to urge the horse forward. *See the picture.* **2** something that sticks out like a point on a spur, as a ridge coming out from a mountain, or a sharp spine on the wing or leg of some birds. **3** a short sidetrack connected with the main track of a railroad. **4** anything that urges one on [Fear was the *spur* that kept us going.] ◆***v.*** **1** to prick with spurs. **2** to urge on [The prize money *spurred* us to greater efforts.] —**spurred, spur′ring** —**on the spur of the moment,** quickly, without planning. —**win one's spurs,** to gain honor.

**spu·ri·ous** (spyoor′ē əs) ***adj.*** not true or genuine; false [a *spurious* report].

**spurn** (spurn) ***v.*** **1** to refuse in a scornful way [They *spurned* my friendship.] **2** to drive away as with the foot [to *spurn* a cat].

**spurt** (spurt) ***v.*** **1** to shoot forth suddenly in a stream; squirt [Juice *spurted* from the grapefruit.] **2** to show a sudden, short burst of energy, as near the end of a race. ◆***n.*** **1** a sudden, short stream or jet [The ketchup came out in *spurts.*] **2** a sudden, short burst of energy [to work in *spurts*].

**sput·nik** (spoot′nik *or* sput′nik) ***n.*** an artificial satellite of the earth; especially, **Sputnik,** any of those put into orbit by the U.S.S.R., beginning in 1957.

**sput·ter** (sput′ər) ***v.*** **1** to spit out drops, bits of food, etc. from the mouth, as when talking too fast. **2** to talk in a fast, confused way [He *sputtered* out an excuse.] **3** to make hissing or spitting sounds [The hamburgers *sputtered* over the fire.] ◆***n.*** **1** the act or sound of sputtering. **2** confused talk, as in excitement.

**spu·tum** (spyo͞ot′əm) ***n.*** saliva or spit, often mixed with matter coughed up from the lungs.

**spy** (spī) ***n.*** **1** a person who watches others secretly and carefully. **2** a person sent by a government to find out military secrets, etc. of another country, as in wartime. —*pl.* **spies** ◆***v.*** **1** to act as a spy. **2** to see; catch sight of [Can you *spy* the ship yet?] **3** to find out by watching carefully [She *spied* out our plans.] —**spied, spy′ing**

**spy·glass** (spī′glas) ***n.*** a small telescope.

**sq.** *abbreviation for* **square.**

**squab** (skwäb) ***n.*** a very young pigeon.

**squab·ble** (skwäb′′l) ***v.*** to quarrel in a noisy way about something not important. —**squab′bled, squab′bling** ◆***n.*** a noisy quarrel about something not important.

**squad** (skwäd) ***n.*** **1** a small group of soldiers, often part of a platoon. ☆**2** any small group of people [a police *squad;* a football *squad*].

☆**squad car** a police patrol car, usually with a radio for talking to headquarters.

**squad·ron** (skwäd′rən) ***n.*** **1** a group of warships on a special mission. **2** a group of cavalry soldiers, made up of from two to four troops. **3** a group of airplanes that fly together. **4** any group organized to work together.

**squal·id** (skwäl′id) ***adj.*** **1** dirty; filthy [a *squalid* house]. **2** wretched [a *squalid* life].

**squall¹** (skwôl) ***n.*** a short, violent windstorm, usually with rain or snow. ◆***v.*** to storm for a short time. —**squall′y** ***adj.***

**squall²** (skwôl) ***v.*** to cry or scream loudly. ◆***n.*** a loud, harsh cry or scream. —**squall′er** ***n.***

**squal·or** (skwäl′ər) ***n.*** a squalid condition; filth; misery; wretchedness.

**squan·der** (skwän′dər) ***v.*** to spend or use wastefully [to *squander* money or time].

**square** (skwer) ***n.*** **1** a flat figure with four equal sides and four right angles. **2** anything shaped like this [Arrange the chairs in a *square.*] **3** an area in a city, with streets on four sides, often used as a public park, etc. **4** a tool having two sides that form a right angle, used in drawing or testing right angles. *See the picture.* **5** the result got by multiplying a number by itself [The *square* of 3 is 9 (3 x 3 = 9).] ◆***adj.*** **1** having the shape of a square. **2** forming a right angle [a *square* corner]. **3** straight, level, or even. **4** fair; honest [a *square* deal]. **5** having measure in two directions [A *square* foot is the area of a square that is one foot long and one foot wide.] ☆**6** satisfying; filling: *used only in everyday talk* [a *square* meal]. ☆**7** old-fashioned; conservative: *a slang meaning.* —**squar′er, squar′est** ◆***v.*** **1** to make square [to *square* a stone; to *square* a wall]. **2** to make straight, level, or even [*Square* your shoulders.] **3** to settle [to *square* accounts]. **4** to mark off in squares, as a checkerboard. **5** to multiply by itself [5 *squared* is 25.] **6** to fit; agree [His story *squares* with mine.] —**squared, squar′ing** —**on the square, 1** at right angles. **2** honestly; fairly: *used only in everyday talk.* —☆**square off,** to get into position for attacking or for defending, as in boxing. —☆**square oneself,** to make up for a wrong that one has done: *used only in everyday talk.* —**square′ly** ***adv.*** —**square′ness** ***n.***

**square dance** a lively group dance for couples, with various steps, figures, etc.

**square-rigged** (skwer′rigd′) ***adj.*** having four-sided sails that are set straight across the masts. *See the picture on page 722.*

**square root** the number that is multiplied by itself to produce a given number [The *square root* of 9 is 3.]

| | | | | | | | |
|---|---|---|---|---|---|---|---|
| **a** | fat | **ir** | here | **ou** | out | **zh** | leisure |
| **ā** | ape | **ī** | bite, fire | **u** | up | **ŋ** | ring |
| **ä** | car, lot | **ō** | go | **ur** | fur | | a *in* ago |
| **e** | ten | **ô** | law, horn | **ch** | chin | | e *in* agent |
| **er** | care | **oi** | oil | **sh** | she | **ə** = | i *in* unity |
| **ē** | even | **oo** | look | **th** | thin | | o *in* collect |
| **i** | hit | **o͞o** | tool | ***th*** | then | | u *in* focus |

**squash**[1] (skwäsh) ***v.*** **1** to crush or be crushed into a soft or flat mass [Grapes *squash* easily.] **2** to put down or suppress, as a revolt. **3** to press, crowd, or squeeze. ◆***n.*** **1** the act or sound of squashing [The tomatoes hit the floor with a *squash.*] **2** a game like handball, but played with rackets.

☆**squash**[2] (skwäsh) ***n.*** a fleshy fruit that grows on a vine and is cooked as a vegetable. There are many kinds of squash, differing in color, size, and shape. *See the picture.*

> **Squash**[2] comes from an American Indian word, *askootasquash.* The plant is native to America, and was cultivated by the Indians long before European settlers came. Different kinds of squash often have names that describe their shapes, as butternut, acorn, or crookneck.

**squash·y** (skwäsh′ē) ***adj.*** **1** soft and wet; mushy [*squashy* mud]. **2** easy to squash or crush, as fruit that is too ripe. —**squash′i·er, squash′i·est**

**squat** (skwät) ***v.*** **1** to sit on the heels with the knees bent. **2** to crouch close to the ground, as an animal. ☆**3** to settle on land without any right or title to it. ☆**4** to settle on public land in order to get title to it from the government. —**squat′ted, squat′ting** ◆***adj.*** **1** crouching. **2** short and heavy or thick [a *squat* figure]. ◆***n.*** the act or position of squatting. —**squat′ly *adv.*** —**squat′ness *n.*** —**squat′ter *n.***

☆**squaw** (skwô) ***n.*** a North American Indian woman, especially a wife.



**squawk** (skwôk) ***n.*** **1** a loud, harsh cry such as a chicken or parrot makes. ☆**2** a loud complaining: *used only in everyday talk.* ◆***v.*** **1** to let out a squawk. ☆**2** to complain loudly: *used only in everyday talk.* —**squawk′er *n.***

**squeak** (skwēk) ***n.*** a short, high, thin cry or sound [the *squeak* of a mouse]. ◆***v.*** to make a squeak [His new shoes *squeaked.*] —**narrow squeak** or **close squeak,** a narrow escape: *used only in everyday talk.* —**squeak′i·ness *n.*** —**squeak′y *adj.***

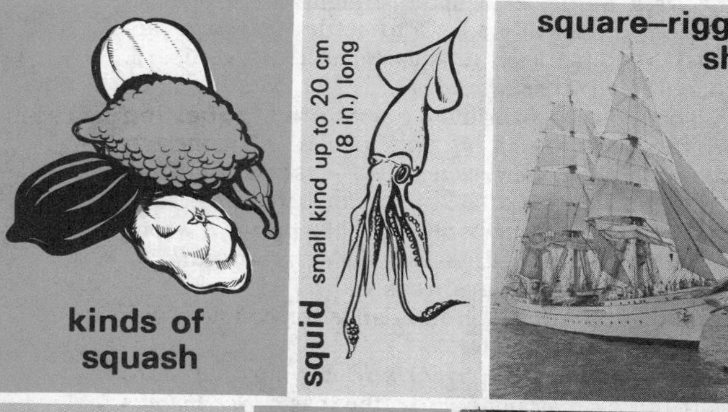
kinds of squash

squid small kind up to 20 cm (8 in.) long

square–rigged ship

squeegee

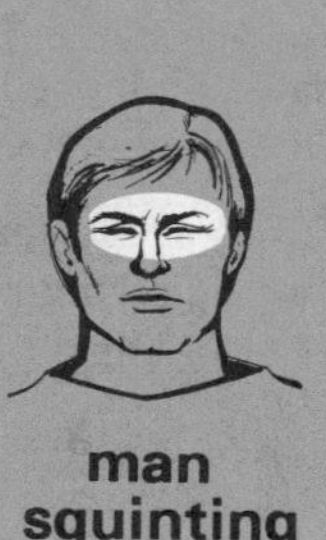
man squinting

stadium

**squeal** (skwēl) ***n.*** a long, high, shrill cry or sound. ◆***v.*** **1** to make a squeal [The baby pigs *squeal.* The tires *squealed* going around a corner.] **2** to tell on someone; tattle: *slang in this meaning.*

**squeam·ish** (skwēm′ish) ***adj.*** **1** easily made sick at the stomach; queasy [I am *squeamish* at the sight of blood.] **2** easily shocked or too easily shocked; prudish. —**squeam′ish·ly *adv.*** —**squeam′ish·ness *n.***

**squee·gee** (skwē′jē) ***n.*** a T-shaped tool with a rubber blade set across a handle, for scraping water from a window, etc. *See the picture.*

**squeeze** (skwēz) ***v.*** **1** to press hard or force together [*Squeeze* the sponge to get rid of the water.] **2** to get by pressing or by force [to *squeeze* juice from an orange; to *squeeze* money from poor people]. **3** to force by pressing [He *squeezed* his hand into the jar.] **4** to hug. **5** to force one's way by pushing or pressing [She *squeezed* through the narrow window.] **6** to give way to pressure [Foam rubber *squeezes* easily.] —**squeezed, squeez′ing** ◆***n.*** a squeezing or being squeezed; hard press. —**squeez′er *n.***

**squelch** (skwelch) ***v.*** to force to be silent; suppress [The ushers *squelched* the hecklers at the rally.]

**squib** (skwib) ***n.*** **1** a kind of firecracker that burns with a hissing noise before it explodes. **2** a short, witty writing that criticizes.

**squid** (skwid) ***n.*** a long, slender sea animal with ten arms, two of them longer than the rest. *See the picture.*

**squint** (skwint) ***v.*** **1** to look with the eyes partly closed, as in strong light. *See the picture.* **2** to look sideways. **3** to be cross-eyed. ◆***n.*** **1** a squinting. **2** the condition of being cross-eyed. **3** a quick glance: *used only in everyday talk.* ◆***adj.*** **1** squinting; looking sideways. **2** cross-eyed.

**squire** (skwīr) ***n.*** **1** in England, a country gentleman who owns much land. ☆**2** a title of respect for a justice of the peace. **3** a man who escorts a lady. **4** a young man who attended a knight. ◆***v.*** to escort a lady. —**squired, squir′ing**

**squirm** (skwurm) ***v.*** **1** to twist and turn the body as a snake does; wriggle; writhe. **2** to feel ashamed or embarrassed. —**squirm′y *adj.***

**squir·rel** (skwur′əl) ***n.*** **1** a small animal with a long, bushy tail, that lives in trees. **2** its fur.

> **Squirrel** comes from a combination of the Greek words for "shadow" and "tail." The squirrel's bushy tail looks like the shadow of its body.

**squirt** (skwurt) ***v.*** **1** to shoot out in a jet; spurt. **2** to wet with liquid shot out in a jet [Lynn *squirted* us with the hose.] ◆***n.*** **1** the act of squirting. **2** a small jet of liquid.

☆**squirt gun** a toy gun that shoots a stream of water.

**squish** (skwish) ***v.*** to make a soft, splashing sound when squeezed, walked on, etc.

**Sr** *the symbol for the chemical element* strontium.

**Sr.** *abbreviation for* **Senior, Sister.**

**Sri Lan·ka** (srē läng′kə) a country on an island south of India. It was formerly called *Ceylon.*

**S.R.O.** standing room only.

**SS** or **S.S.** *abbreviation for* **social security, steamship, Sunday School.**

**SS.** *abbreviation for* **Saints.**

**ss** or **ss.** shortstop (in baseball).

**St.** *abbreviation for* **Saint, Strait, Street.**

**stab** (stab) ***v.*** **1** to pierce or wound with a knife, dagger, etc. **2** to thrust into something [The farmer *stabbed* the pitchfork into the hay.] **3** to hurt very sharply [a *stabbing* pain; *stabbed* by insults]. —**stabbed, stab′bing** ◆***n.*** **1** a wound made by stabbing. **2** a thrust, as with a knife. **3** a sharp hurt or pain. —☆**make a stab at** or **take a stab at,** to make an attempt at.

**sta·bil·i·ty** (stə bil′ə tē) ***n.*** the condition of being stable; steadiness; firmness.

**sta·bi·lize** (stā′bə līz) ***v.*** **1** to make stable, or firm. **2** to keep from changing [to *stabilize* prices]. —**sta′bi·lized, sta′bi·liz·ing** —**sta′bi·li·za′tion** ***n.***

**sta·bi·liz·er** (stā′bə lī′zər) ***n.*** a person or thing that stabilizes; especially, a device used to keep an airplane steady while flying, or one that steadies a ship in rough seas.

**sta·ble**[1] (stā′b'l) ***adj.*** **1** not likely to break down, fall over, or give way; firm; steady [The chair is braced to make it *stable.*] **2** not likely to change; lasting [a *stable* business]. —**sta′bler, sta′blest**

**sta·ble**[2] (stā′b'l) ***n.*** **1** a building in which horses or cattle are sheltered and fed. **2** all the race horses belonging to one owner. ◆***v.*** to put or keep in a stable. —**sta′bled, sta′bling**

**stac·ca·to** (stə kät′ō) ***adj., adv.*** **1** in music, cut short, with sharp breaks between the tones. **2** made up of short, sharp sounds [a *staccato* burst of gunfire].

**stack** (stak) ***n.*** **1** a large pile of hay, straw, etc. stored outdoors. **2** any neat pile, as of boxes or books. ☆**3 stacks,** *pl.* a series of bookshelves in a library, or the main area for these. **4** a part of a computer memory for temporary storage of information. **5** a chimney or smokestack. **6** a number of rifles leaned against each other on end to form a cone. ◆***v.*** **1** to arrange in a stack. **2** to load with stacks of something [We *stacked* the truck with boxes.] **3** to assign aircraft to different altitudes for circling while waiting for a turn to land at an airport. **4** to arrange in a secret and unfair way [to *stack* a deck of cards]. —**stack up,** ☆to be compared with something else.

**sta·di·um** (stā′dē əm) ***n.*** a place for outdoor games, meetings, etc., with rising rows of seats around the open field. *See the picture.*

> In ancient Rome, a **stadium** was a measure of length of about 600 feet. The word was also used for a track for footraces, usually 600 feet in length, with tiers of seats for spectators.

**staff** (staf) ***n.*** **1** a stick, rod, or pole used for support in walking, for holding a flag, or as a weapon, a sign of authority, etc. [a bishop's *staff*]. **2** a group of people working together under a manager, chief, military officer, etc. [the teaching *staff* of a school]. **3** the five lines and the spaces between them on which music is written. *See the picture on page 724.* —*pl.* **staffs** *The plural for meanings* 1 *and* 3 *is sometimes* **staves.** ◆***v.*** to supply with a staff, as of workers.

**staff of life** bread, thought of as the basic food.

**stag** (stag) ***n.*** **1** a full-grown male deer. ☆**2** a man who goes to a dance, party, etc. without a woman. ◆***adj.*** ☆for men only [a *stag* party].

**stage** (stāj) ***n.*** **1** a raised platform or other area on which plays, speeches, etc. are given. **2** the profession of acting; the theater [He left the *stage* to write.] **3** a platform or dock [a landing *stage*]. **4** the place where something takes place; scene [Belgium has been the *stage* of many battles.] **5** a place where a stop is made on a journey. **6** the distance between two such stops. **7** *a shorter name for* **stagecoach. 8** a period or step in growth or development [She has reached a new *stage* in her career.] **9** any of the separate systems that work one at a time in getting a rocket into outer space. ◆***v.*** **1** to present on a stage, as a play. ☆**2** to plan and carry out [The army corps *staged* an attack.] —**staged, stag′ing** —**by easy stages,** a little at a time, with many stops.

**stage·coach** (stāj′kōch) ***n.*** a coach pulled by horses that traveled a regular route, carrying passengers, mail, etc. *See the picture on page 724.*

**stag·ger** (stag′ər) ***v.*** **1** to walk or stand in an unsteady way, as if about to fall; sway; reel [The tired boxer *staggered* from the ring.] **2** to make stagger [The blow *staggered* him.] **3** to shock, confuse, etc. [*staggering* news]. **4** to arrange in a zigzag way. **5** to arrange so as to come at different times [to *stagger* vacations]. ◆***n.*** the act of staggering. —**the staggers,** a nervous disease of horses, cattle, etc., causing them to stagger: *used with a singular verb.*

> SYNONYMS: To **stagger** is to move unsteadily, unable to keep going straight [The donkey *staggered* under the heavy load.] To **reel** is to sway or lurch, as if one were about to fall [She spun around, then *reeled* dizzily down the hall.] To **totter** is to walk with uncertain steps, as a feeble old person may do, or a baby learning to walk.



**stag·nant** (stag′nənt) ***adj.*** **1** not flowing and therefore stale and dirty [The water in the pond is *stagnant.*] **2** not active; sluggish [Business is *stagnant.*]

**stag·nate** (stag′nāt) ***v.*** to become or make stagnant. —**stag′nat·ed, stag′nat·ing** —**stag·na′tion** ***n.***

**staid** (stād) *an earlier form of* **stayed** (remained). ◆***adj.*** quiet, dignified, and serious [a *staid* old man].

**stain** (stān) ***v.*** **1** to spoil with dirt or a patch of color; soil or spot [The rug was *stained* with ink.] **2** to shame or disgrace [to *stain* one's reputation by shoplifting]. **3** to change the color of; dye [Let's *stain* the wood to look like walnut.] ◆***n.*** **1** a dirty or colored spot [grass *stains*]. **2** a shame or disgrace [He died without a *stain* on his character.] **3** a dye for staining wood, glass, etc.

**stained glass** glass colored in any of various ways and used as for church windows. —**stained′-glass′** ***adj.***

**stain·less** (stān′lis) ***adj.*** **1** that has no stains; spotless. **2** that will not easily rust, stain, etc. [*Stainless* steel is an alloy of steel and chromium.] ◆***n.*** flatware made of stainless steel.

**stair** (ster) ***n.*** **1** one of a series of steps going up or down. **2** *usually* **stairs,** *pl.* a flight of steps; staircase.

| | | | |
|---|---|---|---|
| **a** fat | **ir** here | **ou** out | **zh** leisure |
| **ā** ape | **ī** bite, fire | **u** up | **ng** ring |
| **ä** car, lot | **ō** go | **ur** fur | a *in* ago |
| **e** ten | **ô** law, horn | **ch** chin | e *in* agent |
| **er** care | **oi** oil | **sh** she | ə = i *in* unity |
| **ē** even | **oo** look | **th** thin | o *in* collect |
| **i** hit | **ōō** tool | ***th*** then | u *in* focus |

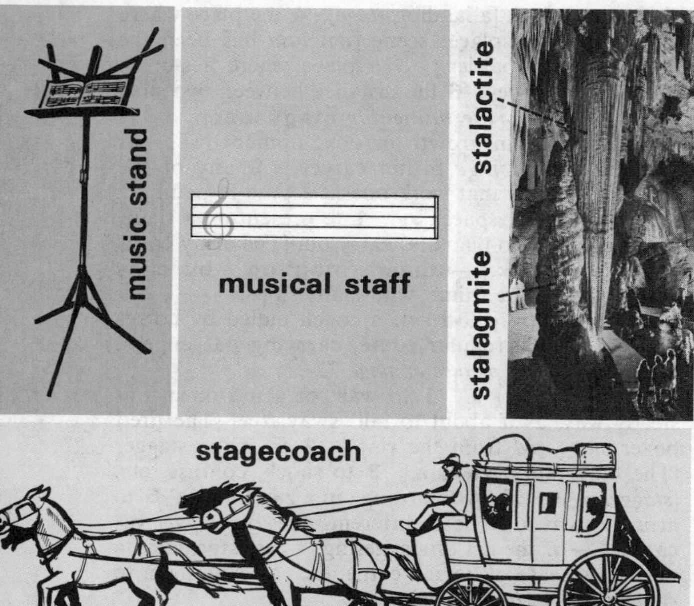


**stair·case** (ster′kās) or **stair·way** (ster′wā) ***n.*** a flight of steps, usually with a handrail.



**stair·well** (ster′wel) ***n.*** a vertical shaft in a building, containing a staircase.

**stake** (stāk) ***n.*** **1** a pointed stick or metal rod for driving into the ground. **2** the post to which a person was tied when being burned to death as a punishment. **3** *often* **stakes,** *pl.* the money, etc. risked in a bet or game [They played cards for high *stakes.*] **4** the winner's prize, as in a race. **5** a share or interest [She has a *stake* in the business.] ◆***v.*** **1** ☆to mark the boundaries of, as with stakes [The prospector *staked* out the claim.] **2** to support with a stake [*Stake* up the tomato plants.] **3** to risk or bet. **4** to give or lend money to for some reason: *used only in everyday talk* [She *staked* us to a meal.] —**staked, stak′ing** —**at stake,** being risked. —☆**pull up stakes,** to change the place where one lives, has a business, etc.: *used only in everyday talk.* —**stake out,** to put a place or a suspected criminal under close watch by the police.

**sta·lac·tite** (stə lak′tīt) ***n.*** a stick of lime shaped like an icicle and hanging from the roof of a cave. It is formed by water dropping down through the rocks above. *See the picture.*

**sta·lag·mite** (stə lag′mīt) ***n.*** a stick like a stalactite, but built up on the floor of a cave. *See the picture.*

**stale** (stāl) ***adj.*** **1** no longer fresh; made bad, dry, flat, etc. from being kept too long [*stale* bread; *stale* air]. **2** no longer new or interesting [a *stale* joke; *stale* gossip]. **3** out of condition, as from too much or too little practice [I haven't played the piano for years and I've grown *stale.*] ◆***v.*** to make or become stale. —**staled, stal′ing**

**stale·mate** (stāl′māt) ***n.*** **1** a position in chess in which a player cannot move without placing his or her king in check. It results in a draw. **2** a halt in a struggle because both sides are equally strong and neither side will give in; deadlock. ◆***v.*** to bring into a stalemate. —**stale′mat·ed, stale′mat·ing**

**Sta·lin** (stä′lin), **Joseph** 1879–1953; Communist dictator of the U.S.S.R. from 1922 to 1953.

**Sta·lin·grad** (stä′lin grad′) a city in the southeastern U.S.S.R.: *now called* Volgograd.

**stalk**[1] (stôk) ***v.*** **1** to walk in a stiff, haughty way; stride. **2** to spread through [Terror *stalked* the streets.] **3** to track secretly so as to catch or kill [The hunters *stalked* the tigers.] ◆***n.*** the act of stalking.

**stalk**[2] (stôk) ***n.*** **1** the stem of a plant. **2** any part like this.

**stall**[1] (stôl) ***n.*** **1** a section for one animal in a stable. **2** a booth, table, etc. at which goods are sold as at a market. **3** an enclosed seat in the choir of a church. **4** a space closed in, as for taking a shower. **5** a space marked off, as in a garage, for parking a car. ◆***v.*** **1** to put or keep in a stall. **2** to bring or come to a stop without meaning to [The car *stalled* when the motor got wet.]

**stall**[2] (stôl) ***v.*** to hold off by sly or clever means; delay by evading [We *stalled* off our creditors. He *stalled* for time.] ◆***n.*** anything said or done in order to stall.

> In earlier times **stall**[2] had the same meaning as *decoy,* a person or thing used to lure someone into a trap. In time its meaning became nearly the opposite, something said or done to keep someone away.

**stal·lion** (stal′yən) ***n.*** a full-grown male horse that can be used for breeding.

**stal·wart** (stôl′wərt) ***adj.*** **1** strong and well-built; robust; sturdy [a *stalwart* athlete]. **2** brave; fearless [a *stalwart* police officer]. **3** not giving in easily; firm [the *stalwart* defense of a cause]. ◆***n.*** a stalwart person.

> **Stalwart** comes from an Old English word meaning "having a firm foundation." A stalwart person is thought of as being very firm and steady.

**sta·men** (stā′mən) ***n.*** the part of a flower in which the pollen grows, including the anther and its stem.

**stam·i·na** (stam′ə nə) ***n.*** the strength to carry on or endure; vigor; endurance.

**stam·mer** (stam′ər) ***v.*** to speak in a halting way, often repeating certain sounds, as in fear, embarrassment, etc. ◆***n.*** stammering talk.

**stamp** (stamp) ***v.*** **1** to bring one's foot down with force ["No!" she cried, *stamping* on the floor.] **2** to walk with loud, heavy steps [The angry boy *stamped* out of the room.] **3** to beat, press, or crush as with the foot [to *stamp* out a fire; to *stamp* out a revolt]. **4** to press or print marks, letters, a design, etc. on something [He *stamped* his initials on all his books.] **5** to cut out or make by pressing with a sharp metal form [This machine can *stamp* out a hundred car fenders an hour.] **6** to mark with a certain quality [His courage *stamped* him as a hero.] **7** to put a postage stamp, official seal, etc. on an envelope, document, etc. ◆***n.*** **1** the act of stamping the foot. **2** a machine, tool, or die used for stamping. **3** a mark or form made by stamping. **4** any official mark, seal, etc. put on papers. **5** a small piece of paper printed and sold by a government for sticking on letters, packages, etc. as proof that the proper postage or taxes have been paid. **6** any piece of paper like this, given to customers, who turn them in for premiums. **7** a sign or mark [the *stamp* of truth]. **8** kind or class [Singers of her *stamp* are rare.]

☆**stam·pede** (stam pēd′) ***n.*** a sudden rush or flight, as of a herd of cattle or of a crowd of frightened or confused people. ◆***v.*** to move in or cause a stampede. —**stam·ped′ed, stam·ped′ing**

> **Stampede** is one of the words that came into the American language in the Southwest, where many Americans have Spanish ancestors. *Stampede* was originally *estampido,* and came from a Spanish word for "crash" or "uproar." When cattle stampede, they make a great deal of noise.

**stance** (stans) ***n.*** **1** the way a person stands; position of one's feet [The batter uses an open *stance,* with feet far apart.] ☆**2** the attitude taken in dealing with a certain situation [The principal took a firm *stance* about punishing those who stole the books.]

**stanch** (stônch *or* stanch) ***adj., v.*** *another spelling of* **staunch.**

**stan·chion** (stan′chən) ***n.*** **1** a post or bar placed upright and used as a support. ☆**2** a loose collar fitted around a cow's neck to keep it in its stall.

**stand** (stand) ***v.*** **1** to be or get in an upright position on one's feet [*Stand* by your desk.] **2** to be or place in an upright position on its base, bottom, etc. [Our trophy *stands* on the shelf. *Stand* the broom in the corner.] **3** to hold a certain opinion, belief, etc. [I *stand* with you in this matter.] **4** to be placed or situated [Our house *stands* on a hill.] **5** to be at a certain rank, degree, etc. [Where do you *stand* in your class?] **6** to be in a certain condition [They *stand* convicted of cruelty.] **7** to gather and stay [Sweat *stood* in drops on his forehead.] **8** to stay without change [My orders *stand* until I cancel them.] **9** to stop or halt. **10** to try to fight off or hold back [One squadron *stood* alone against the enemy.] **11** to put up with; endure; bear [The boss can't *stand* noise.] **12** to withstand with little or no damage or change [This suitcase will *stand* years of hard wear.] **13** to be forced to go through [He must *stand* trial for his crime.] **14** to pay for a dinner, etc., as when treating someone: *used only in everyday talk* [We *stood* them to dinner.] —**stood, stand′ing** ◆***n.*** **1** the act of standing. **2** a stop or halt, as in making a defense [The retreating soldiers made one last *stand* at the bridge.] ☆**3** a stop made by a group of touring actors to give a performance [a one-night *stand*]. **4** a place where a person stands [Take your *stand* at the door.] **5** an opinion, belief, or attitude [What is the Senator's *stand* on higher taxes?] **6** a platform to stand or sit on [a band*stand;* the witness *stand* in a courtroom]. **7** *often* **stands,** *pl.* seats in rising rows, as in a stadium, from which to watch games, races, etc. ☆**8** a booth or counter where goods are sold [a popcorn *stand*]. **9** a rack, framework, etc. for holding something [a music *stand*]. *See the picture.* ☆**10** a group of growing trees or plants [a *stand* of willows]. —**stand a chance,** to have a chance. —**stand by, 1** to be near and ready if needed. **2** to help or support. —**stand for, 1** to be a sign for; represent [The mark & *stands for* the word "and."] ☆**2** to put up with; tolerate: *used only in everyday talk.* —**stand in for,** to take the place of; act for. —**stand off,** to keep at a distance. —**stand out, 1** to stick out; project. **2** to be easily noticed because unusual or outstanding. —**stand up, 1** to take a standing position. **2** to prove to be true, good, lasting, etc. [That idea won't *stand up* under examination.] ☆**3** to fail to keep a date with: *slang in this meaning.* —**stand up for,** to support or defend.

**stand·ard** (stan′dərd) ***n.*** **1** something set up as a rule or model with which other things like it are to be compared [The government sets the *standards* for pure food and drugs.] **2** a flag, banner, etc., as of a military group or a nation [The tricolor is the *standard* of France.] **3** an upright support [Flagpoles are often called *standards.*] ◆***adj.*** **1** that is a standard, rule, or model [The *standard* gauge for railroad track is 4 feet, 8 1/2 inches between the rails.] **2** not special or extra; ordinary [Headlights are *standard* equipment on all cars.] **3** accepted as good or proper [Both "catalog" and "catalogue" are *standard* spellings.]

**stand·ard·ize** (stan′dər dīz) ***v.*** to make according to a standard; make the same in form, quality, size, etc. [Radio and television have begun to *standardize* American speech.] —**stand′ard·ized, stand′ard·iz·ing** —**stand′ard·i·za′tion** ***n.***

☆**Standard Time** the official time for any of the twenty-four time zones in which the world is divided, starting at Greenwich, England. The four time zones of the mainland United States are Eastern, Central, Mountain, and Pacific. When it is noon Eastern Standard Time, it is 11:00 A.M. Central, 10:00 A.M. Mountain, and 9:00 A.M. Pacific.

**stand·by** (stand′bī) ***n.*** **1** a person or thing that can always be depended on if needed. **2** a person without a reservation waiting to board an airplane, etc. if a seat becomes available. —*pl.* **stand′bys**



☆**stand·ee** (stan dē′) ***n.*** a person who is standing because there are no empty seats, as in a theater or on a bus.

☆**stand-in** (stand′in′) ***n.*** a person who takes the place of another for a short time; substitute.

**stand·ing** (stan′diŋ) ***adj.*** **1** that stands; upright or erect. **2** done from a standing position [a *standing* long jump; a *standing* ovation]. **3** not flowing; stagnant [*standing* water in the fields]. **4** going on regularly without change [a *standing* order for coffee every morning]. ◆***n.*** **1** position, rank, or reputation [She is a lawyer of high *standing.*] **2** the time that something lasts; duration [a custom of long *standing*].

**Stan·dish** (stan′dish), Captain **Miles** (mīlz) about 1584–1656; the English military leader of the Pilgrims at Plymouth, Massachusetts.

**stand·off** (stand′ôf) ***n.*** a tie in a game or contest.

**stand·off·ish** (stand ôf′ish) ***adj.*** cold and aloof; not friendly and pleasant.

**stand·point** (stand′point) ***n.*** the position from which something is seen or judged; point of view.

**stand·still** (stand′stil) ***n.*** a stop or halt.

**stank** (staŋk) *a past tense of* **stink.**

| | | | | | | | |
|---|---|---|---|---|---|---|---|
| **a** fat | **ir** here | **ou** out | **zh** leisure |
| **ā** ape | **ī** bite, fire | **u** up | **ŋ** ring |
| **ä** car, lot | **ō** go | **ur** fur | a *in* ago |
| **e** ten | **ô** law, horn | **ch** chin | e *in* agent |
| **er** care | **oi** oil | **sh** she | **ə** = i *in* unity |
| **ē** even | **oo** look | **th** thin | o *in* collect |
| **i** hit | **ōō** tool | ***th*** then | u *in* focus |

**Stan·ton** (stan′t'n), **Elizabeth Cady** 1815–1902; U.S. worker for women's right to vote.

**stan·za** (stan′zə) ***n.*** a group of lines forming one of the sections of a poem or song; verse.

> **Stanza** is an Italian word for "stopping place." A poem or song stops between the stanzas, each of which has a further thought about the poem's subject.

**sta·ple**[1] (stā′p'l) ***n.*** **1** the main product of a certain place [Coffee is the *staple* of Brazil.] **2** any article of food or other common item that is regularly used and is kept in large amounts [Flour, sugar, and soap are *staples.*] **3** the fiber of cotton, wool, flax, etc. [Egyptian cotton has a very long *staple.*] ◆***adj.*** **1** kept on hand because regularly used [*staple* office supplies]. **2** most important; chief; main [Steel is a *staple* U.S. industry.]

**sta·ple**[2] (stā′p'l) ***n.*** **1** a piece of metal shaped like a U with sharp, pointed ends. It is driven into a surface to hold a wire, hook, etc. in place. **2** a thin piece of wire like this, that is driven through papers or other materials so that the ends bend over as a binding. ◆***v.*** to fasten with a staple or staples. —**sta′pled, sta′pling**

**sta·pler** (stā′plər) ***n.*** a device for driving staples to hold papers together, to hold upholstery fabric in place, etc. *See the picture.*

**star** (stär) ***n.*** **1** a heavenly body seen as a small point of light in the night sky; especially, such a body that is actually a far-off sun. **2** a planet, etc. imagined in astrology as having a control over people's lives. **3** a flat figure with five or more points, used as a symbol or decoration. **4** *another word for* **asterisk. 5** a person who is outstanding, as in some sport or in acting. ◆***v.*** **1** to play an important part as an actor or actress [She has *starred* in four movies.] **2** to decorate or mark with stars or asterisks [Some names on the list are *starred.*] **3** to perform in an outstanding way [He *stars* at basketball.] —**starred, star′ring** ◆***adj.*** showing great skill; outstanding [a *star* athlete].

**star·board** (stär′bərd) ***n.*** the right-hand side of a ship or airplane as one faces forward, toward the bow. ◆***adj.*** of or on this side.

> **Starboard** is a combination of two very old English words, *steoran* meaning "steer," and *bord* meaning "the side of a ship." In the old days, the ship's rudder, used for steering, was a large oar on the right side of the ship.

**starch** (stärch) ***n.*** **1** a white food substance found in most plants, especially in potatoes, beans, grain, etc. **2** a powder made from this substance. It is mixed with water and used to make cloth stiff. **3** a food that contains much starch. **4** a stiff, formal way of behaving. ◆***v.*** to make stiff with starch [The laundry *starched* the collar.]

**starch·y** (stär′chē) ***adj.*** **1** of, like, or full of starch. **2** stiffened with starch. **3** stiff or formal. —**starch′i·er, starch′i·est** —**starch′i·ness *n.***

**stare** (ster) ***v.*** to look steadily with the eyes wide open, as in wonder, curiosity, fear, etc. *See* SYNONYMS *at* **look.** —**stared, star′ing** ◆***n.*** a long, steady look. —**stare down,** to stare back at another person until he or she looks away.

**star·fish** (stär′fish) ***n.*** a small sea animal that has a hard covering and five or more arms arranged like the points of a star. *See the picture.*

**stark** (stärk) ***adj.*** **1** lonely and bleak [The picture showed a *stark* landscape.] **2** complete; utter [We felt *stark* terror.] **3** stiff; rigid, as a dead body. ◆***adv.*** completely; entirely [*stark* naked]. —**stark′ly *adv.***

**star·light** (stär′līt) ***n.*** light from the stars. ◆***adj.*** lighted by the stars; starlit.

**star·ling** (stär′liŋ) ***n.*** a bird with black feathers that shine in a greenish or purplish way. *See the picture.*

**star·lit** (stär′lit) ***adj.*** lighted by the stars.

**Star of David** a six-pointed star formed of two triangles. It is a symbol of Judaism and of the country Israel. *See the picture.*

**star·ry** (stär′ē) ***adj.*** **1** of the stars [*starry* light]. **2** full of stars [a *starry* sky]. **3** shining like stars [*starry* eyes]. —**star′ri·er, star′ri·est**

☆**Stars and Stripes** the red, white, and blue flag of the United States. It has thirteen stripes (for the thirteen original colonies) and fifty stars (for the fifty States).

☆**Star-Spangled Banner 1** the United States flag. **2** the national anthem of the United States. The words were written by Francis Scott Key in 1814.

**start** (stärt) ***v.*** **1** to begin to go, do, act, be, etc. [We *start* for Toledo today. The show *starts* at 8:30.] **2** to cause to begin; set in motion or action [*Start* the car. Who *started* the fight?] **3** to move suddenly, as when surprised; jump or jerk [The noise made the baby *start.*] **4** to cause to move suddenly; rouse [The dog *started* a bird.] **5** to put or be put among those starting in a race, game, etc. [What pitcher will you *start* in the second game?] ◆***n.*** **1** the act of starting, or beginning. **2** a sudden jump or jerk, as in surprise [When I coughed, he awoke with a *start.*] **3** a lead or other advantage, as at the beginning of a race. **4** the time or place that something begins [She was ahead from the *start.*] *See also the phrase* **by fits and starts** *at* **fit**[2]. —☆**start in,** to begin to do something. —**start out,** to begin a trip, action, etc. —**start up, 1** to spring up. **2** to cause to begin running [to *start up* an engine].

**start·er** (stärt′ər) ***n.*** **1** a person or thing that starts. **2** the first in a series. **3** one who gives the signal to start, as in a race. **4** a device for starting the engine of a motor vehicle.

**star·tle** (stärt″l) ***v.*** to frighten suddenly or surprise; cause to move or jump [The ring of the telephone *startled* me.] —**star′tled, star′tling**

**star·tling** (stärt′liŋ) ***adj.*** causing sudden fright or surprise [The huge bear was a *startling* sight.]

**star·va·tion** (stär vā′shən) ***n.*** the act of starving or the condition of being starved.

**starve** (stärv) ***v.*** **1** to die or suffer from lack of food. *See* SYNONYMS *at* **hungry. 2** to kill or make suffer with hunger. **3** to be very hungry: *used only in everyday talk.* —**starve for,** to need or want very much [a person *starving for* affection]. —**starved, starv′ing**

> In earlier days, **starve** meant to die slowly from any cause, as from a disease, grief, or cold. Because so many people in those days "starved of hunger," the last two words were dropped from the phrase and **starve** came to mean "to die of hunger."

**starve·ling** (stärv′liŋ) ***n.*** a person or animal that is thin and weak from lack of food.

☆**stash** (stash) ***v.*** to hide, as money, in a secret or safe place: *used only in everyday talk.*

**state** (stāt) ***n.*** **1** the condition in which a person or thing is [The accident put me in a nervous *state.* Things are in a *state* of change.] **2** a rich and showy style; pomp [We dined in *state.*] **3** a group of people united under one government; nation. ☆**4** *usually* **State,** any of the political units that form a federal government, as in the United States [the *State* of Ohio]. **5** the territory or government of a state. ◆***v.*** **1** to fix or settle [Let's *state* a time and place for meeting.] **2** to tell in a definite or formal way [The coach *stated* the rules.] —**stat′ed, stat′ing** —**the States,** the United States.

SYNONYMS: **State** or **condition** are both used for the particular way a person or thing is [the President's annual speech on the *state* of the nation], but **condition** is more often used when there is some connection to a cause or result [Her *condition* is caused by a poor diet.]

**stat·ed** (stāt′id) ***adj.*** fixed; set [a *stated* purpose].

**State·house** (stāt′hous) ***n.*** ☆the building in which a State legislature meets; capitol.

**state·ly** (stāt′lē) ***adj.*** grand or dignified [a *stately* dance]. —**state′li·er, state′li·est** —**state′li·ness *n.***

**state·ment** (stāt′mənt) ***n.*** **1** the act of stating. **2** something stated or said [May we quote your *statement?*] **3** a report or record, as of money owed [The customers receive monthly *statements.*]

**state·room** (stāt′ro͞om) ***n.*** a private cabin or room on a ship or in a railroad car.

**states·man** (stāts′mən) ***n.*** a person who is wise and skillful in the business of government. —*pl.* **states′men** —**states′man·ship *n.***

**stat·ic** (stat′ik) ***adj.*** **1** at rest; not active; not moving or changing [A *static* mind produces no new ideas.] **2** having to do with masses or forces at rest or in balance [*static* equilibrium]. **3** acting through weight only, without motion [*static* pressure]. **4** describing or of electrical charges produced by friction. ◆***n.*** ☆any of the electrical disturbances in the air that are picked up by a radio receiver and cause crackling sounds.

**sta·tion** (stā′shən) ***n.*** **1** the place where a person or thing stands or is located, as one's post when on duty, a building for a special purpose, etc. [a sentry's *station;* a police *station*]. **2** a regular stopping place, as for a bus or train; also, a building at such a place. **3** a place with equipment for sending out radio or television programs. **4** social position or rank [She was able to change her *station* in life.] ◆***v.*** to place at a station, or post.

**sta·tion·ar·y** (stā′shə ner′ē) ***adj.*** **1** not to be moved; fixed [*stationary* seats]. **2** not changing in condition, value, etc. [*stationary* prices].

**sta·tion·er** (stā′shə nər) ***n.*** a person who sells writing or office supplies, some books, etc.

**sta·tion·er·y** (stā′shə ner′ē) ***n.*** paper, envelopes, etc. for writing letters.

☆**station wagon** an automobile with rear seats that can be folded down and a back end that opens for easy loading and unloading.

**sta·tis·ti·cal** (stə tis′ti k′l) ***adj.*** having to do with statistics. —**sta·tis′ti·cal·ly *adv.***

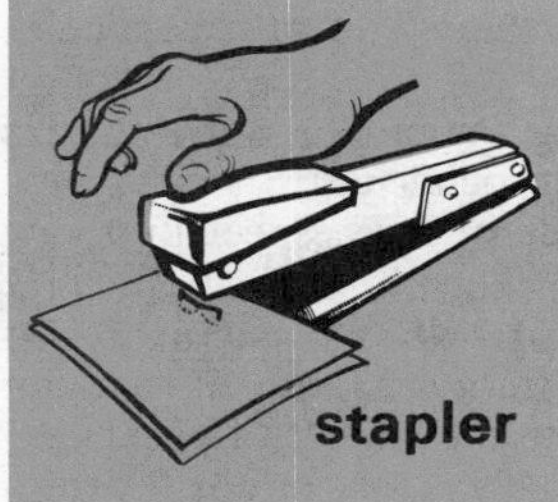
stapler

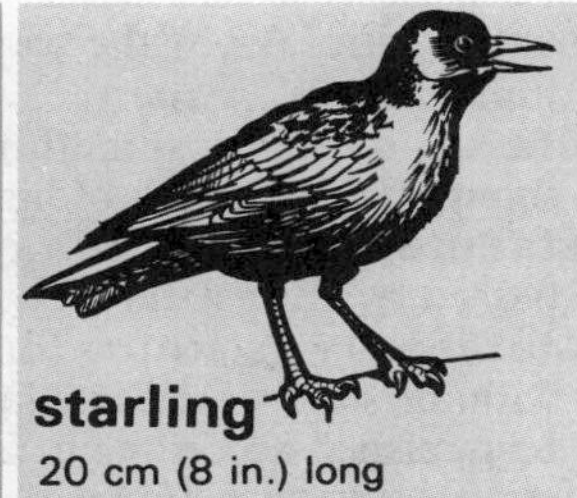
starling
20 cm (8 in.) long

Star of David

starfish
23 cm (9 in.) across

**stat·is·ti·cian** (stat′is tish′ən) ***n.*** an expert in statistics; person who works with statistics.

**sta·tis·tics** (stə tis′tiks) ***n.pl.*** **1** facts in the form of numbers, collected and arranged so as to show certain information [census *statistics*]. **2** the science of collecting and arranging such facts: *used with a singular verb.*



The word **statistics** is actually connected with the word **state.** It was borrowed into English from the German word *statistik,* which first meant the study of the supplies, population, military strength, etc. of the state, or government. Later it came to mean any study of facts in the form of numbers.

**stat·u·ar·y** (stach′o͝o wer′ē) ***n.*** a group of statues.

**stat·ue** (stach′o͞o) ***n.*** the form or likeness of a person or animal carved in wood, stone, etc., modeled in clay, or cast in plaster or a metal.

☆**Statue of Liberty** a huge bronze statue of a woman wearing a crown and holding a torch high. It represents liberty and stands on an island in the harbor of New York City. It was a gift to the U.S. from France.

**stat·u·esque** (stach′o͝o wesk′) ***adj.*** like a statue, as in being tall, or looking graceful, dignified, etc.

**stat·u·ette** (stach′o͝o wet′) ***n.*** a small statue.

**stat·ure** (stach′ər) ***n.*** **1** the height of a person [a man of short *stature*]. *See* SYNONYMS *at* **height. 2** a level of some good quality that one has reached [a person of high moral *stature*].

**sta·tus** (stāt′əs *or* stat′əs) ***n.*** **1** position or rank; standing [A doctor has high *status* in our society.] **2** state or condition, with regard to law [The title "Ms." does not tell the marital *status* of a woman.]

| | | | |
|---|---|---|---|
| **a** fat | **ir** here | **ou** out | **zh** leisure |
| **ā** ape | **ī** bite, fire | **u** up | **ŋ** ring |
| **ä** car, lot | **ō** go | **ur** fur | a *in* ago |
| **e** ten | **ô** law, horn | **ch** chin | e *in* agent |
| **er** care | **oi** oil | **sh** she | **ə** = i *in* unity |
| **ē** even | **o͝o** look | **th** thin | o *in* collect |
| **i** hit | **o͞o** tool | ***th*** then | u *in* focus |

**status quo** (kwō) the way things are at a particular time: *a Latin phrase.*

**status symbol** something owned or done that is thought of as a mark of high social status.

**stat·ute** (stach′o͞ot) ***n.*** a rule or law, especially a law passed by a legislature.

**stat·u·to·ry** (stach′o͝o tôr′ē) ***adj.*** **1** having to do with, or set by, a statute [a *statutory* fine]. **2** that can be punished according to law [a *statutory* offense].

**St. Au·gus·tine** (ô′gəs tēn) a seaport in northeastern Florida. It is the oldest city in the U.S.

**staunch** (stônch *or* stänch) ***v.*** to stop or slow down the flow of blood from a wound. ◆***adj.*** **1** strong, firm, loyal, etc. [*staunch* friendship]. **2** watertight [a *staunch* ship]. —**staunch′ly *adv.***

**stave** (stāv) ***n.*** **1** any of the curved strips of wood that form the wall of a barrel, cask, etc. *See the picture.* **2** a stick or staff. **3** a set of lines of a poem or song; stanza. **4** *another word for* **staff** (in music). ◆***v.*** **1** to make a hole, especially by breaking in staves. **2** to fit with staves. —**staved** or **stove, stav′ing** —**stave in,** to break a hole in [to *stave in* the top of a carton]. —**stave off,** to hold off or put off [She *staved off* her hunger by nibbling raisins.]

**staves** (stāvz) ***n.*** **1** *a plural of* **staff. 2** *the plural of* **stave.**

**stay**[1] (stā) ***n.*** a strong rope or cable used as a brace, as for a mast of a ship.

728 **stay**[2] (stā) ***n.*** **1** a support or prop. **2** a thin strip of bone, plastic, etc. used to stiffen a shirt collar, corset, etc. ◆***v.*** to support; prop up.

**stay**[3] (stā) ***v.*** **1** to keep on being in some place or condition; remain [*Stay* at home. The weather *stayed* bad all day.] **2** to live for a time; dwell [I am *staying* with friends.] **3** to stop or halt; end [*Stay* your anger.] **4** to hold back or put off for a time [These carrots will *stay* your appetite.] **5** to be able to last; hold out or keep up [That horse won't *stay* the distance in a long race.] —**stayed** or earlier **staid, stay′ing** ◆***n.*** **1** a stopping or being stopped; a halt, check, or delay [The prisoner won a *stay* of execution.] **2** the act of remaining, or the time spent, in a place [a long *stay* in the hospital].

SYNONYMS: **Stay** means to continue in a certain place [*Stay* in your seat until recess.] **Remain** suggests especially a staying behind while others go [The cheerleaders *remained* until the very end.]

steamroller

steeplechase

stave

steelyard

**staying power** ability to last; endurance.

**Ste.** *abbreviation for* **Sainte** (the French word for a woman saint).

**stead** (sted) ***n.*** the place of a person or thing as filled by a substitute [If you can't come, send someone in your *stead.*] —**stand someone in good stead,** to give good use or service to someone.

**stead·fast** (sted′fast) ***adj.*** firm or fixed; not changing [a *steadfast* friendship]. —**stead′fast·ly *adv.***

**stead·y** (sted′ē) ***adj.*** **1** firm; not shaky [a *steady* chair]. **2** not changing or letting up; regular [a *steady* gaze; a *steady* worker]. **3** not easily excited; calm [*steady* nerves]. **4** serious and sensible; reliable [a *steady* young person]. —**stead′i·er, stead′i·est** ◆***v.*** to make or become steady. —**stead′ied, stead′y·ing** —**stead′i·ly *adv.*** —**stead′i·ness *n.***

**steak** (stāk) ***n.*** a slice of meat or fish, especially of beef, for broiling or frying.

**Steak** comes from a very old word that means "to roast on a spit," for that was usually the way in which this cut of meat was cooked in the old days.

**steal** (stēl) ***v.*** **1** to take away secretly and without right something that does not belong to one. **2** to take or do in a sly, secret way [to *steal* a look]. **3** to get or win in a tricky or skillful way [He *stole* her heart.] **4** to move in a quiet or secret way [She *stole* out of the house.] **5** in baseball, to get to the next base safely without the help of another's hit or error. —**stole, stol′en, steal′ing** ◆***n.*** something got for a very low price: *used only in everyday talk.*

**stealth** (stelth) ***n.*** a secret, quiet way of moving or acting.

**stealth·y** (stel′thē) ***adj.*** quiet or secret, so as not to be seen or heard [the *stealthy* approach of a cat]. —**stealth′i·er, stealth′i·est** —**stealth′i·ly *adv.***

**steam** (stēm) ***n.*** **1** water changed into a vapor or gas by being heated to the boiling point. Steam is used for heating, to give power in running engines, etc. **2** such a vapor turned to mist by cooling [the *steam* that forms on windows in cold weather]. **3** energy; vigor: *used only in everyday talk* [I ran out of *steam* by noon.] ◆***adj.*** **1** using steam; heated, run, moved, etc. by the power of steam [a *steam* engine]. **2** used for carrying steam [a *steam* pipe]. ◆***v.*** **1** to give off steam [The teakettle is *steaming.*] **2** to become covered with mist [His eyeglasses *steamed* up in the warm room.] **3** to move by the power of steam under pressure [The ship *steamed* out of the harbor.] **4** to cook, soften, or remove with steam [to *steam* asparagus; to *steam* wallpaper off the walls]. —**let off steam** or **blow off steam,** to show strong feeling that had been held back.

☆**steam·boat** (stēm′bōt) ***n.*** a steamship, especially a small one.

**steam engine** an engine run by the power of steam under pressure.

**steam·er** (stēm′ər) ***n.*** something run by the power of steam under pressure, as a steamship.

**steam fitter** a person whose work is putting in and repairing steam pipes, boilers, etc.

**steam·roll·er** (stēm′rōl′ər) ***n.*** **1** a machine run by steam power, with heavy rollers used to pack down and smooth the surface of roads. *See the picture.* **2** a power that crushes anything in its way.

**steam·ship** (stēm′ship) ***n.*** a ship driven by steam power.

☆**steam shovel** a large machine run by steam power and used for digging.

**steam·y** (stē′mē) ***adj.*** **1** filled or covered with steam or mist [a *steamy* bathroom]. **2** of or like steam [his *steamy* breath in the cold air]. —**steam′i·er, steam′i·est** —**steam′i·ness *n.***

**steed** (stēd) ***n.*** a horse; especially, a lively riding horse: *seldom used except in stories, poems, etc.*

**steel** (stēl) ***n.*** **1** a hard, tough metal made of iron mixed with a little carbon. **2** something made of steel, as a sharp weapon. **3** great strength or hardness [muscles of *steel*]. ◆***adj.*** of or like steel. ◆***v.*** to make strong or tough like steel [She *steeled* herself for the shock.]

**steel wool** long, thin shavings of steel in a pad, used for cleaning, smoothing, and polishing.

**steel·work·er** (stēl′wur′kər) ***n.*** a person who works in a factory where steel is made.

**steel·y** (stē′lē) ***adj.*** of or like steel, as in hardness or toughness [a *steely* look]. —**steel′i·er, steel′i·est**

**steel·yard** (stēl′yärd) ***n.*** a scale made up of a metal bar hanging from a hook. The thing to be weighed is hung from the shorter end of the bar and a weight is moved along the longer end until the bar is level. *See the picture.*

**steep**[1] (stēp) ***adj.*** **1** slanting sharply up or down; having a sharp slope. **2** too high; greater than normal: *used only in everyday talk* [a *steep* price]. —**steep′ly *adv.*** —**steep′ness *n.***

**steep**[2] (stēp) ***v.*** to soak in liquid [to *steep* tea leaves]. —**steeped in,** completely filled with or absorbed in [*steeped in* a subject].

**stee·ple** (stē′p'l) ***n.*** a high tower, as on a church, usually having a spire.

**stee·ple·chase** (stē′p'l chās) ***n.*** a horse race on a course that has hedges, ditches, etc., which must be jumped. *See the picture.*

> In the 18th century, horseback riders, for sport, would pick out a church steeple seen in the distance and race toward it. Since that would be a cross-country race, they often had to jump over hedges and ditches, as in the modern **steeplechase.**

**stee·ple·jack** (stē′p'l jak) ***n.*** a person who climbs steeples, smokestacks, etc. to paint or repair them.

**steer**[1] (stir) ***v.*** **1** to guide by means of a rudder or wheel; direct the movement of [A helmsman *steers* a ship. She *steered* the car into the garage.] **2** to be steered [This car *steers* easily.] **3** to set and follow [to *steer* a straight course]. **4** to direct or guide [The coach *steered* the team to victory.] —☆***n.*** a suggestion or tip: *used only in everyday talk.* —**steer clear of,** to avoid; keep away from.

**steer**[2] (stir) ***n.*** any male of cattle raised for its beef, especially a young ox with its sex glands removed.

**steer·age** (stir′ij) ***n.*** in earlier times, the part of a ship for passengers paying the lowest fare.

> The **steerage** section of a ship was down in the hold, near the steering mechanism. The fare for this section was cheap because the area was apt to be noisy, hot, and dirty.

**steers·man** (stirz′mən) ***n.*** a person who steers a ship or boat; helmsman. —*pl.* **steers′men**

**stein** (stīn) ***n.*** a beer mug.

**Stein** (stīn), **Gertrude** 1874–1946; U.S. writer who lived in France.

**Stein·beck** (stīn′bek), **John** 1902–1968; U.S. writer.

**stel·lar** (stel′ər) ***adj.*** **1** of or like a star. **2** by or for a star actor; most important; leading [a *stellar* role in a play].

**stem** (stem) ***n.*** **1** the main part of a plant or tree that grows up from the ground and bears the leaves, flowers, etc.; trunk or stalk. **2** any part that grows from this main part and has a flower, leaf, etc. at its end. **3** any part like a stem [the *stem* of a goblet; a pipe *stem*]. **4** the front part of a ship; bow. **5** the root or base of a word. ◆***v.*** **1** to remove the stem from [to *stem* cherries]. **2** to move forward against [We rowed upstream, *stemming* the current.] **3** to stop; check [to *stem* the bleeding from a cut]. **4** to come or derive [Your troubles *stem* from past mistakes.] —**stemmed, stem′ming** 729

**stench** (stench) ***n.*** a very bad smell; stink.

**sten·cil** (sten′s'l) ***n.*** **1** a thin sheet of paper, metal, etc. with holes cut through in the shape of letters or designs. When ink or paint is spread over the stencil, the letters or designs are marked on the surface beneath. *See the picture.* **2** the design or letters marked in this way. ◆***v.*** to mark with a stencil [I *stenciled* our name on the mailbox.] —**sten′ciled** or **sten′cilled, sten′cil·ing** or **sten′cil·ling**

☆**ste·nog·ra·pher** (stə näg′rə fər) ***n.*** a person whose work is stenography.

**ste·nog·ra·phy** (stə näg′rə fē) ***n.*** the work of writing down in shorthand something that is being said and then copying it out in full, as on a typewriter. —**sten·o·graph·ic** (sten′ə graf′ik) ***adj.***

**sten·to·ri·an** (sten tôr′ē ən) ***adj.*** very loud and strong [a *stentorian* voice].

**step** (step) ***n.*** **1** the act of moving and placing the foot forward, backward, sideways, up, or down, as in walking, dancing, or climbing. **2** the distance covered by such a movement [They stood three *steps* apart.] **3** a way of stepping; gait [light, skipping *steps*]. **4** the sound of stepping; footfall [I hear *steps* outside.] **5** a footprint [The waves wiped out our *steps* in the sand.] **6** a place to rest the foot in going up or down, as a stair or the rung of a ladder. **7 steps,** *pl.* a flight of

| | | | | | | | |
|---|---|---|---|---|---|---|---|
| **a** | fat | **ir** | here | **ou** | out | **zh** | leisure |
| **ā** | ape | **ī** | bite, fire | **u** | up | **ng** | ring |
| **ä** | car, lot | **ō** | go | **ur** | fur | | a *in* ago |
| **e** | ten | **ô** | law, horn | **ch** | chin | | e *in* agent |
| **er** | care | **oi** | oil | **sh** | she | **ə =** | i *in* unity |
| **ē** | even | **oo** | look | **th** | thin | | o *in* collect |
| **i** | hit | **ōō** | tool | ***th*** | then | | u *in* focus |

S

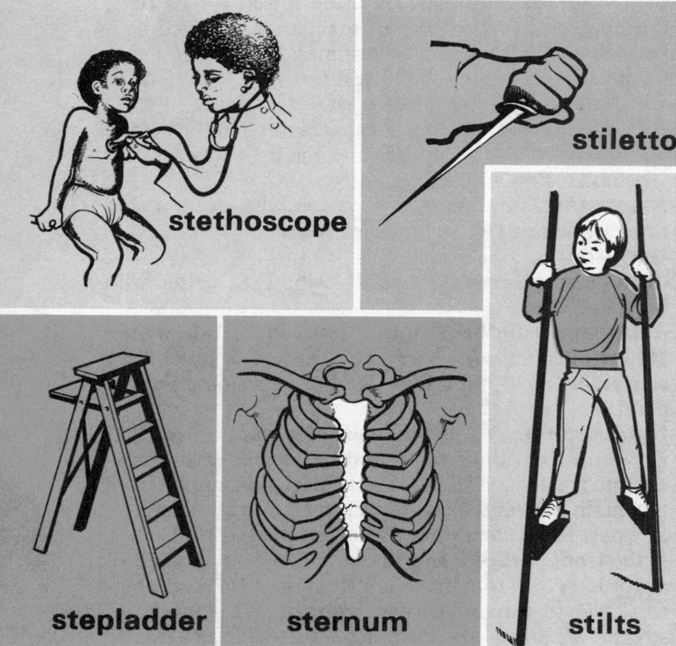


stairs. **8** a degree, rank, grade, etc. [A major is one *step* above a captain.] **9** an act or process in a series [After giving first aid, the next *step* is to call the doctor.] **10** any pattern of movements in a dance [the waltz *step*]. **11** the difference in pitch between two notes next to each other in a musical scale. ◆***v.*** **1** to move by taking a step or steps. **2** to walk a short distance [*Step* outside.] **3** to measure by taking steps [The referee *stepped* off five yards.] **4** to press the foot down [to *step* on the brake]. **5** to move quickly [That horse can really *step* along.] **6** to enter or come [She *stepped* into a fortune.] —**stepped, step′ping** —**in step,** marching, dancing, etc. with the rhythm of others or of music. —**keep step,** to stay in step. —**out of step,** not in step. —**step by step,** gradually; slowly but surely. —**step down,** ☆to resign, as from an office. —**step up, 1** to go or come near. ☆**2** to make greater, faster, etc. [to *step up* production]. —**take steps,** to do the things needed. —☆**watch one's step,** to be careful: *used only in everyday talk.*



**step·broth·er** (step′bru*th*′ər) ***n.*** one's stepparent's son by a former marriage.

**step·child** (step′chīld) ***n.*** a stepson or stepdaughter. —*pl.* **step·chil·dren** (step′chil′drən)

**step·daugh·ter** (step′dôt′ər) ***n.*** one's husband's or wife's daughter by a former marriage.

**step·fa·ther** (step′fä′*th*ər) ***n.*** the man who has married one's mother after the death or divorce of one's father.

**step·lad·der** (step′lad′ər) ***n.*** a ladder with broad, flat steps, made of two frames joined at the top with a hinge so that it stands on four legs. *See the picture.*

**step·moth·er** (step′mu*th*′ər) ***n.*** the woman who has married one's father after the death or divorce of one's mother.

**step·par·ent** (step′per′ənt) ***n.*** one's stepfather or stepmother.

**steppe** (step) ***n.*** any of the great plains of southeastern Europe and Asia, having few trees.

**step·ping·stone** (step′iŋ stōn′) ***n.*** **1** a stone used to step on, as in crossing a stream. **2** a means of reaching some goal [Education is a *steppingstone* to success.] *Also written* **stepping stone.**

**step·sis·ter** (step′sis′tər) ***n.*** one's stepparent's daughter by a former marriage.

**step·son** (step′sun) ***n.*** one's husband's or wife's son by a former marriage.

**ster·e·o** (ster′ē ō′) ***n.*** a stereophonic record player, radio, sound system, etc. —*pl.* **ster′e·os′**

**ster·e·o·phon·ic** (ster′ē ə fän′ik) ***adj.*** describing or having to do with a way of recording or broadcasting so that a listener, using two or more speakers, hears sounds in a natural way from the directions in which they were picked up by two or more microphones.

**ster·e·o·scope** (ster′ē ə skōp′) ***n.*** a device with two eyepieces for looking at two slightly different pictures of the same scene placed side by side, so that one sees a single picture that seems to have depth instead of looking flat. —**ster·e·o·scop·ic** (ster′ē ə skäp′ik) ***adj.***

**ster·e·o·type** (ster′ē ə tīp′) ***n.*** **1** a metal plate from which a page is printed. **2** a way of thinking about a person, group, etc. that follows a fixed, common pattern, paying no attention to individual differences [the *stereotype* of a professor as a mild, absent-minded person].

A **stereotype** printing plate is made by casting a mold of a page of type that has been set by hand or by machine. The plate is used to turn out a great many pages, all exactly alike in every detail. From this, **stereotype** came to mean a way of thinking about people who belong to some group as being alike in all ways.

**ster·e·o·typed** (ster′ē ə tīpt′) ***adj.*** following a fixed, common pattern, without change; not fresh or original [a *stereotyped* excuse].

**ster·ile** (ster′′l) ***adj.*** **1** not able to produce offspring, fruit, plants, etc.; not fertile; barren [a *sterile* animal; *sterile* soil]. **2** free from living germs [A dentist's tools must be kept *sterile.*] —**ste·ril·i·ty** (stə ril′ə tē) ***n.***

**ster·i·lize** (ster′ə līz) ***v.*** to make sterile [*Sterilize* the baby's bottles by putting them in boiling water.] —**ster′i·lized, ster′i·liz·ing** —**ster·i·li·za·tion** (ster′ə li zā′shən) ***n.***

**ster·ling** (stur′liŋ) ***adj.*** **1** describing silver that is at least 92.5% pure. **2** made of such silver [*sterling* candlesticks]. **3** of British money [ten pounds *sterling*]. **4** very fine; excellent [a person of *sterling* character]. ◆***n.*** **1** sterling silver. **2** British money.

**stern**[1] (sturn) ***adj.*** **1** strict or harsh; not gentle, tender, easy, etc. [*stern* parents; *stern* treatment]. *See* SYNONYMS *at* **severe. 2** not changing; fixed; certain [*stern* reality]. —**stern′ly *adv.*** —**stern′ness *n.***

**stern**[2] (sturn) ***n.*** the rear end of a ship or boat.

**ster·num** (stur′nəm) ***n.*** the bone to which most of the ribs are joined in the front. *See the picture.*

**steth·o·scope** (steth′ə skōp) ***n.*** an instrument used by doctors for listening to sounds in the chest, as of the heart or lungs. *See the picture.*

**ste·ve·dore** (stē′və dôr) ***n.*** a person who works on a dock, loading and unloading ships.

**Ste·ven·son** (stē′vən s′n), **Robert Louis** 1850–1894; Scottish poet and writer of novels.

**stew** (stōō *or* styōō) ***v.*** **1** to cook by boiling slowly, usually for a long time. **2** to worry or fret. ◆***n.*** **1** a dish of meat and vegetables cooked by slow boiling. **2** a mood of worrying or fretting [He was in a *stew.*]

**stew·ard** (stōō′ərd *or* styōō′ərd) ***n.*** **1** a person hired to manage a large estate. **2** a person in charge of the property or affairs of another. **3** an attendant, as on a ship or airplane, who looks after the passengers' comfort. *See* **stewardess. 4** the person on a ship in charge of the food supplies. —**stew′ard·ship *n.***

> **Steward** comes from the two early English words from which we get **sty**[1] and **warden.** The first stewards were actually pigsty keepers, who guarded a rich person's herds of pigs against thieves. Later, stewards got more and more responsibility until they became the managers of large estates.

**stew·ard·ess** (stōō′ər dis *or* styōō′ər dis) ***n.*** a woman whose work is to look after the passengers' comfort on a ship or airplane. On airplanes, the usual title today for both men and women is *flight attendant.*

**St. He·le·na** (hə lē′nə) a British island in the southern Atlantic Ocean off the west coast of Africa. Napoleon was sent there in exile.

**stick** (stik) ***n.*** **1** a twig or branch broken or cut off. **2** any long, thin piece of wood, with a special shape for use as a cane, club, etc. [a walking *stick;* a hockey *stick*]. **3** a long, thin piece [a *stick* of celery; a *stick* of chewing gum]. **4** a dull, stupid person: *used only in everyday talk.* ◆***v.*** **1** to press a sharp point into; pierce; stab [He *stuck* his finger with a needle.] **2** to fasten or be fastened as by pinning or gluing [I *stuck* my name tag on my coat. The stamp *sticks* to the paper.] **3** to thrust or push; extend [*Stick* your hands in your pockets. Her ears *stick* out.] **4** to hold back or become caught so that it cannot move [The wheels *stuck* in the mud.] **5** to keep close or hold fast; cling [*Stick* to your job until you finish. Friends *stick* together.] **6** to stop or hesitate because of fear, doubt, etc. [He will *stick* at nothing to get what he wants.] **7** to puzzle: *used only in everyday talk* [Here's a riddle that will *stick* you.] —**stuck, stick′ing —stick by,** to stay loyal to. —**stick up,** to rob by using a gun or other weapon: *a slang phrase.* —**stick up for,** to defend or support: *used only in everyday talk.* —☆**the sticks,** country places away from the cities and towns: *used only in everyday talk.*

**stick·er** (stik′ər) ***n.*** ☆a label with glue on the back.

**stick·le·back** (stik′'l bak) ***n.*** a small fish having sharp spines on its back and no scales. The male builds a nest for the female's eggs.

**stick·ler** (stik′lər) ***n.*** a person who insists on having things done in a certain way [She is a *stickler* for following rules.]

☆**stick·pin** (stik′pin) ***n.*** a pin often with a jewel at the head, for sticking in a necktie, scarf, lapel, etc.

**stick·y** (stik′ē) ***adj.*** **1** that sticks; gluey; clinging [His fingers were *sticky* with candy.] **2** hot and damp; humid: *used only in everyday talk* [a *sticky* August day]. —**stick′i·er, stick′i·est —stick′i·ness *n.***

**stiff** (stif) ***adj.*** **1** that does not bend easily; firm [*stiff* cardboard]. **2** not able to move easily [*stiff* muscles]. **3** not flowing easily; thick [Beat the egg whites until they are *stiff.*] **4** strong; powerful [a *stiff* breeze]. **5** not easy; difficult or hard [*stiff* punishment; a *stiff* test]. **6** not relaxed; tense or formal [a *stiff* smile]. —**stiff′ly *adv.* —stiff′ness *n.***

> SYNONYMS: **Stiff** is used to describe a thing that is firm enough to resist a bending force to some extent, or a person who is formal [a *stiff* collar; a *stiff* manner]. **Rigid** is used to describe a thing that resists a bending force up to the point of breaking, or a person who is strict and severe [a *rigid* framework; a *rigid* taskmaster].

**stiff·en** (stif′'n) ***v.*** to make or become stiff or stiffer.

**stiff-necked** (stif′nekt′) ***adj.*** not giving in; stubborn.

**sti·fle** (stī′f'l) ***v.*** **1** to kill by cutting off the supply of air; smother. **2** to suffer or die from lack of air. **3** to hold back; check [to *stifle* a sob]. —**sti′fled, sti′fling**

**stig·ma** (stig′mə) ***n.*** **1** a bad mark on one's record; sign of disgrace [the *stigma* of having been in jail]. **2** the upper tip of the pistil of a flower, where pollen settles to make seeds grow.

**stig·ma·tize** (stig′mə tīz) ***v.*** to give a bad name to; mark as disgraceful [His accident *stigmatized* him as a reckless driver.] —**stig′ma·tized, stig′ma·tiz·ing**

**stile** (stīl) ***n.*** one or more steps built beside a fence or wall for use in climbing over it.

**sti·let·to** (sti let′ō) ***n.*** a small, thin, sharp dagger. *See the picture.* —*pl.* **sti·let′tos** or **sti·let′toes**

**still**[1] (stil) ***adj.*** **1** without sound; quiet; silent [The empty house is *still.*] **2** not moving or excited; calm [The air is *still* before a storm. Sit *still!*] **3** describing a single photograph or a single frame of a motion-picture film. ◆***n.*** **1** silence; quiet [in the *still* of the night]. **2** a still photograph. ◆***adv.*** **1** at or up to the time talked about; until then or now [Is she *still* talking?] **2** even; yet [It became *still* colder.] **3** in spite of that; nevertheless [He is rich, but *still* unhappy.] ◆***conj.*** nevertheless; yet [I admire her bravery; *still* I think she was foolish.] ◆***v.*** to make or become still, quiet, or calm [The audience *stilled* as the play began. The police *stilled* the riot.] —**still′ness *n.***

**still**[2] (stil) ***n.*** a device used to distill liquids, especially alcoholic liquors.

> **Still**[2] comes from a Latin word meaning "to drip or trickle." The apparatus of a still passes the steam from a boiling impure liquid through a tube enclosed in a jacket of cold water. The cold makes the steam condense, and the distilled pure liquid drips into a container.

**still·born** (stil′bôrn′) ***adj.*** dead at birth.

**still life** **1** an arrangement of objects, as fruit in a bowl or flowers in a vase, used as something to be painted, drawn, etc. **2** a painting, drawing, etc. of this. —*pl.* **still lifes**

**stilt** (stilt) ***n.*** **1** a long pole with a support for the foot part way up it. One can walk high above the ground on a pair of stilts. *See the picture.* **2** any tall pole used as a support, as for a dock over water.

| | | | | | | | |
|---|---|---|---|---|---|---|---|
| **a** | fat | **ir** | here | **ou** | out | **zh** | leisure |
| **ā** | ape | **ī** | bite, fire | **u** | up | **ng** | ring |
| **ä** | car, lot | **ō** | go | **ur** | fur | | a *in* ago |
| **e** | ten | **ô** | law, horn | **ch** | chin | | e *in* agent |
| **er** | care | **oi** | oil | **sh** | she | ə = | i *in* unity |
| **ē** | even | **oo** | look | **th** | thin | | o *in* collect |
| **i** | hit | **ōō** | tool | ***th*** | then | | u *in* focus |

**stilt·ed** (stil′tid) ***adj.*** acting important or dignified in a way that is not natural.

**stim·u·lant** (stim′yə lənt) ***n.*** something that stimulates or excites one, as coffee or any of certain drugs.

**stim·u·late** (stim′yə lāt) ***v.*** to make more active; arouse; excite [Smells of cooking *stimulate* my appetite.] —**stim′u·lat·ed, stim′u·lat·ing —stim′u·la′tion *n.***

**stim·u·lus** (stim′yə ləs) ***n.*** anything that causes some action or activity [The *stimulus* of light makes a sunflower turn toward the sun. Wanting a new car is a *stimulus* to work.] —*pl.* **stim·u·li** (stim′yə lī)

**sting** (stiŋ) ***v.*** **1** to hurt by pricking [Wasps can *sting* you.] **2** to cause or feel sharp pain [The cold wind *stung* her cheeks.] **3** to make unhappy; pain [He was *stung* by her criticism.] **4** to cheat: *slang in this meaning.* —**stung, sting′ing** ◆***n.*** **1** the act or power of stinging [The *sting* of a bee may be dangerous.] **2** a pain or wound caused by stinging. **3** a pointed part as in some insects that can be used to sting.

☆**sting·ray** (stiŋ′rā) ***n.*** a large flat fish with a sharp spine or spines on its long, thin tail, that can cause serious wounds. *See the picture.*

**stin·gy** (stin′jē) ***adj.*** not willing to give or spend money; like a miser; grudging. —**stin′gi·er, stin′gi·est —stin′gi·ly *adv.* —stin′gi·ness *n.***

**stink** (stiŋk) ***v.*** **1** to give off a strong, bad smell. **2** to be no good, or worth nothing: *slang in this meaning*



[His last novel *stinks.*] —**stank** or **stunk, stunk, stink′ing** ◆***n.*** a strong, bad smell; stench. —**stink up,** to cause to stink [Cooking cabbage *stinks up* the house.]

**stint** (stint) ***v.*** to give only a small amount to; limit to a small share [He *stinted* himself on meals to buy a watch.] ◆***n.*** **1** the act of stinting; limit [to help without *stint*]. **2** a task or share of work to be done [We each did our *stint* of housework.]

**sti·pend** (stī′pend) ***n.*** regular pay for work done.

**stip·ple** (stip′'l) ***v.*** to paint or draw with small dots or spots. *See the picture.* —**stip′pled, stip′pling**

**stip·u·late** (stip′yə lāt) ***v.*** to tell or state as a necessary condition, as in a contract [She *stipulated* that the college use her gift for a new library.] —**stip′u·lat·ed, stip′u·lat·ing —stip′u·la′tion *n.***

**stip·ule** (stip′yo͞ol) ***n.*** one of a pair of little leaves at the base of the stem of a leaf. *See the picture.*

**stir** (stur) ***v.*** **1** to move or shake slightly [Not a leaf *stirred* in the quiet air.] **2** to move around or be active ["Not a creature was *stirring.*"] **3** to make move or be active [He *stirred* himself to finish the work.] **4** to mix by moving a spoon, fork, etc. around [*Stir* the paint well.] **5** to cause strong feelings in; excite [Her speech *stirred* the crowd.] —**stirred, stir′ring** ◆***n.*** **1** the act of stirring [Give the fire a *stir.*] **2** the condition of being excited [That movie has caused quite a *stir.*] —**stir′rer *n.***

**stir·ring** (stur′iŋ) ***adj.*** that stirs one's feelings; exciting [*stirring* music].

**stir·rup** (stur′əp) ***n.*** either of two rings with a flat bottom, hung by straps from the sides of a saddle. The feet of a rider fit into them. *See the picture.*

**stitch** (stich) ***n.*** **1** one complete movement of a needle and thread into and out of the material in sewing. **2** one complete movement done in various ways in knitting, crocheting, etc. **3** a loop made by stitching [Tight *stitches* pucker the cloth.] **4** a sudden, sharp pain, as in the side. **5** a bit or piece [They didn't do a *stitch* of work. I haven't a *stitch* to wear.] ◆***v.*** to sew or fasten with stitches [to *stitch* a seam]. —**in stitches,** laughing loudly and noisily.

**St. Law·rence** (lôr′əns) a river that flows from Lake Ontario into the Atlantic Ocean.

**St. Lawrence Seaway** a waterway for large ships between the Great Lakes and the Atlantic Ocean, made up of the St. Lawrence River, canals, etc.

**St. Lou·is** (lo͞o′is *or* lo͞o′ē) a city in eastern Missouri, on the Mississippi River.

**stock** (stäk) ***n.*** **1** a supply on hand for use or for sale [Our *stock* of food is low.] **2** livestock; cattle, horses, sheep, pigs, etc. **3** shares in a business [They own *stock* in several companies.] **4** ancestry or family [We are of Polish *stock.*] **5** a particular breed of animal or plant. **6** water in which meat or fish has been boiled, used to make soup, gravy, etc. **7** the part that serves as a handle or body for the working parts [The *stock* of a rifle holds the barrel in place.] **8** a tree trunk or stump. **9 stocks,** *pl.* a wooden frame with holes for locking around a person's ankles and, sometimes, wrists, used in earlier times as a punishment. ◆***v.*** **1** to furnish with stock or a supply [to *stock* a farm with cattle; to *stock* a store with new goods]. **2** to put in or keep a supply of [This shop *stocks* the kind of shirt you want. We *stocked* up on food for the winter.] ◆***adj.*** **1** always kept on hand as for sale [The lumberyard has *stock* sizes of door frames.] **2** common or trite [a *stock* joke]. —**in stock,** on hand for sale or use. —**out of stock,** not on hand for sale or use. —**take stock, 1** to make a list of goods in stock. **2** to look the situation over before deciding or acting. —☆**take stock in** or **put stock in,** to believe in or have faith in.

**stock·ade** (stä kād′) ***n.*** **1** a wall of tall stakes built around a place for defense, as in early American forts. ☆**2** such a fort. *See the picture.*

**stock·bro·ker** (stäk′brō′kər) ***n.*** a person in the business of buying and selling stocks and bonds for other people.

☆**stock car** a passenger automobile of standard make that has been changed in various ways so that it can be used in racing.

**stock company** a company of actors who put on a series of plays over a period of time.

**stock exchange 1** a place where stocks and bonds are bought and sold. **2** the brokers who do business there.

**stock·hold·er** (stäk′hōl′dər) ***n.*** a person who owns stock or shares in a company.

**Stock·holm** (stäk′hōm *or* stäk′hōlm) the capital of Sweden, on the Baltic Sea.

**stock·ing** (stäk′iŋ) ***n.*** a knitted covering for the foot and, usually, most of the leg.

**stock market 1** a place where stocks and bonds are bought and sold. **2** the buying and selling done there, or the prices listed there.

**stock·pile** (stäk′pīl) ***n.*** a supply of goods, raw materials, etc. stored up for use when needed. ◆***v.*** to collect a stockpile of [to *stockpile* steel]. —**stock′piled, stock′pil·ing**

**stock·room** (stäk′ro͞om) ***n.*** a room where goods, materials, etc. are stored.

**stock-still** (stäk′stil′) ***adj.*** not moving at all; motionless.

**stock·y** (stäk′ē) ***adj.*** having a short, heavy build. —**stock′i·er, stock′i·est —stock′i·ness *n.***

**stock·yard** (stäk′yärd) ***n.*** ☆an enclosed place with pens where cattle, hogs, sheep, etc. are kept until they can be sent to market or slaughtered: *usually used in the plural.*

**stodg·y** (stäj′ē) ***adj.*** heavy and dull; stuffy, uninteresting, etc. [*stodgy* thinking]. —**stodg′i·er, stodg′i·est —stodg′i·ness *n.***

**sto·ic** (stō′ik) ***n.*** a person who stays calm and patient under pain, suffering, trouble, etc. —**sto′i·cal** or **sto′ic *adj.* —sto′i·cal·ly *adv.***

In ancient Greece, a **Stoic** was a member of a school of philosophy which said that the wise person should always stay calm and be guided by reason. Zeno, who started this school, taught under a "porch," or covered walk. The word **stoic** comes from the Greek word for porch.

**stoke** (stōk) ***v.*** to stir up and add fuel to [to *stoke* a fire; to *stoke* a furnace]. —**stoked, stok′ing**

**stoke·hold** (stōk′hōld) ***n.*** the furnace and boiler room of a steamship.

**stok·er** (stōk′ər) ***n.*** **1** a person who stokes a furnace, as of a boiler on a ship. **2** a machine that puts fuel into a furnace as it is needed.

**Sto·kow·ski** (stə kôf′skē *or* stə kou′skē), **Leopold** 1882–1977; U.S. orchestra conductor, born in England.

**stole**[1] (stōl) ***n.*** **1** a woman's long scarf of cloth or fur worn with the ends hanging down in front. *See the picture.* **2** a long strip of cloth worn like a scarf by clergy in some churches.

**stole**[2] (stōl) *past tense of* **steal.**

**stol·en** (stō′lən) *past participle of* **steal.**

**stol·id** (stäl′id) ***adj.*** having or showing little feeling; not easily excited. —**sto·lid·i·ty** (stə lid′ə tē) ***n.*** —**stol′id·ly *adv.***

**stom·ach** (stum′ək) ***n.*** **1** the large, hollow organ into which food goes after it is swallowed. Food is partly digested in the stomach. *See the picture on page 734.* **2** the belly, or abdomen [The fighter was hit in the *stomach.*] **3** appetite or desire [I have no *stomach* for fighting.] ◆***v.*** to bear or put up with [We could not *stomach* such foolishness.]

**stomp** (stämp) ***v.*** to hurt or kill by stamping on.

**stone** (stōn) ***n.*** **1** hard mineral matter that is found in the earth but is not metal; rock [a monument built of *stone*]. **2** a small piece of this [Don't throw *stones.* Rubies are precious *stones.*] **3** a piece of this shaped for some purpose, as a gravestone or grindstone. **4** the hard seed of certain fruits [the *stone* of a peach]. **5** a British unit of weight equal to 14 pounds. —*pl.* **stone** **6** a small, hard mass that may form in the kidney or gall bladder and cause illness. ◆***v.*** **1** to throw stones at or kill with stones. **2** to remove the stone, or seed, from [to *stone* cherries]. —**stoned, ston′ing** ◆***adj.*** of stone or stoneware. —**leave no stone unturned,** to do everything possible.

**Stone** (stōn), **Lucy** 1818–1893; U.S. worker for women's right to vote and the right of a married woman to keep her own name.

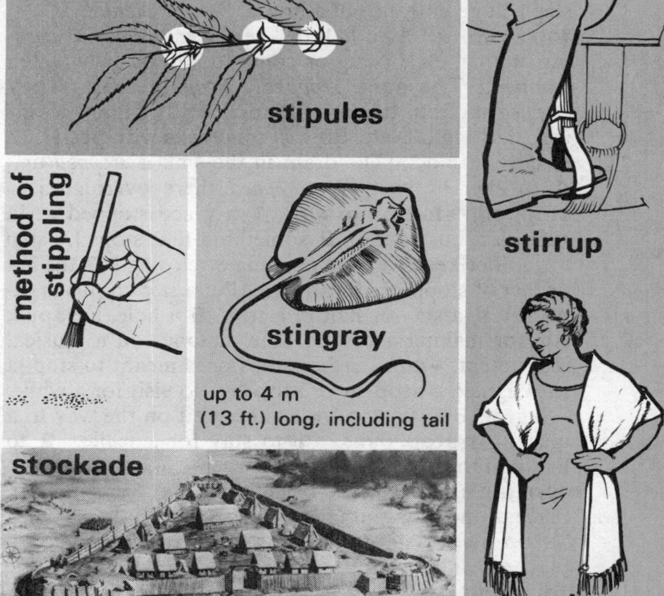


**Stone Age** a very early period in the history of human beings when stone tools and weapons were used.



**stone-blind** (stōn′blīnd′) ***adj.*** completely blind.

**stone·cut·ter** (stōn′kut′ər) ***n.*** a person or machine that cuts stone and makes it smooth.

**stone-deaf** (stōn′def′) ***adj.*** completely deaf.

**Stone·henge** (stōn′henj) a group of huge blocks of stone arranged in a circle on a plain in southern England. They were probably set up late in the Stone Age.

**stone·ware** (stōn′wer) ***n.*** a heavy kind of pottery containing much silica or sand and flint.

**stone·work** (stōn′wurk) ***n.*** **1** the work of building things of stone. **2** something built of stone.

**ston·y** (stō′nē) ***adj.*** **1** covered with stones [a *stony* road]. **2** like stone; hard, cold, etc. [a *stony* heart; a *stony* look]. —**ston′i·er, ston′i·est —ston′i·ly *adv.***

**stood** (stood) *past tense and past participle of* **stand.**

**stool** (sto͞ol) ***n.*** **1** a single seat with no back or arms. **2** *a shorter word for* **footstool.**

☆**stool pigeon** a person who acts as a spy for the police or who informs on others to the police: *used only in everyday talk.*

**stoop**[1] (sto͞op) ***v.*** **1** to bend the body forward or in a crouch [He *stooped* to tie his shoes.] **2** to stand or walk with the head and shoulders bent forward. **3** to lower one's dignity or character [Would you *stoop* to taking bribes?] ◆***n.*** the act or position of stooping.

| | | | | | | | |
|---|---|---|---|---|---|---|---|
| a | fat | ir | here | ou | out | zh | leisure |
| ā | ape | ī | bite, fire | u | up | ng | ring |
| ä | car, lot | ō | go | ur | fur | | a *in* ago |
| e | ten | ô | law, horn | ch | chin | | e *in* agent |
| er | care | oi | oil | sh | she | ə = | i *in* unity |
| ē | even | oo | look | th | thin | | o *in* collect |
| i | hit | o͞o | tool | *th* | then | | u *in* focus |

☆**stoop**[2] (sto͞op) ***n.*** a small porch or platform with steps, at an entrance of a house. *See the picture.*

**stop** (stäp) ***v.*** **1** to halt or keep from going on, moving, acting, etc.; bring or come to an end [My watch *stopped.* The noise *stopped.* *Stop* the car. They *stopped* us from talking.] **2** to close by filling, covering, shutting off, etc. [to *stop* up cracks with putty]. **3** to clog or block [The drain in the sink is *stopped* up.] **4** to stay or visit [We *stopped* there overnight.] —**stopped, stop′ping** ◆***n.*** **1** a place stopped at [a *stop* on a bus route]. **2** something that stops [A *stop* for a door keeps it from opening or closing.] **3** the act or fact of stopping; finish; end [Put a *stop* to this argument.] **4** a stay or halt in a trip. **5** a hole, key, pull, etc. for making a certain tone or tones on a musical instrument. ◆***adj.*** ☆that stops or is meant to stop [a *stop* signal]. —**stop in** or **stop by,** to visit for a while. —☆**stop off,** to stop for a short visit on the way to a place. —☆**stop over,** **1** to stay for a while. **2** to halt a journey, as for rest.

**stop·gap** (stäp′gap) ***n.*** something used for a time in place of the usual thing.

☆**stop·o·ver** (stäp′ō′vər) ***n.*** a stop for a time at a place while on a trip.

**stop·page** (stäp′ij) ***n.*** a stopping or being stopped or stopped up [a *stoppage* in the pipe].

**stop·per** (stäp′ər) ***n.*** something put into an opening to close it; plug [A cork is a bottle *stopper.*]



**stop watch** a watch with a hand that can be started and stopped instantly so as to measure exactly the time taken for a race or other event.

**stor·age** (stôr′ij) ***n.*** **1** a storing or being stored. **2** a place or space for storing things. **3** the cost of keeping goods stored.

**storage battery** a battery with cells in it in which electricity can be stored for use as needed.

**store** (stôr) ***n.*** ☆**1** a place of business where things are sold [a candy *store;* a department *store*]. **2** a supply or stock for use as needed [a *store* of coal]. **3** a place where supplies are kept; storehouse. **4** a great amount [a *store* of knowledge]. ◆***v.*** **1** to put aside for safekeeping until needed [*Store* the extra chairs in the attic.] **2** to fill with a supply or store [to *store* a cabin with provisions]. —**stored, stor′ing** —**in store,** set aside; waiting to be used, to happen, etc. —☆**mind the store,** to tend to business. —**set store by,** to have a good opinion of; value.

☆**store·front** (stôr′frunt) ***n.*** a small retail store that can be walked into from the street. It usually has display windows. ◆***adj.*** housed in what was a storefront [a *storefront* church].

**store·house** (stôr′hous) ***n.*** a place where things are stored, especially a warehouse.

**store·keep·er** (stôr′kēp′ər) ***n.*** ☆a person who owns or manages a retail store.

**store·room** (stôr′ro͞om) ***n.*** a room where things are stored.

**sto·ried**[1] (stôr′ēd) ***adj.*** famous in stories or in history [*storied* Rome].

**sto·ried**[2] (stôr′ēd) ***adj.*** having stories, or floors [many-*storied* buildings].

**stork** (stôrk) ***n.*** a large wading bird with long legs and a long neck and bill. *See the picture.*

**storm** (stôrm) ***n.*** **1** a strong wind along with a heavy rain, snow, etc. and, often, thunder and lightning. **2** a heavy fall of rain, snow, etc. **3** any strong outburst or shower of objects [a *storm* of bullets; a *storm* of criticism]. **4** a sudden, strong attack by soldiers [They took the city by *storm.*] ◆***v.*** **1** to blow violently and rain, snow, etc. **2** to be angry; rage; rant. **3** to rush violently [They *stormed* out of the house.] **4** to attack strongly [to *storm* a fort].

**storm·y** (stôr′mē) ***adj.*** **1** of or having storms [*stormy* weather; a *stormy* day]. **2** wild, rough, angry, etc. [a *stormy* debate].—**storm′i·er, storm′i·est**

**sto·ry**[1] (stôr′ē) ***n.*** **1** a telling of some happening, whether true or made-up [the *story* of the first Thanksgiving]. **2** a made-up tale, written down, that is shorter than a novel [the *stories* of Poe]. **3** a lie or falsehood: *used only in everyday talk.* —*pl.* **sto′ries**

**sto·ry**[2] (stôr′ē) ***n.*** the space or rooms making up one level of a building, from a floor to the ceiling above it [a building with ten *stories*]. —*pl.* **sto′ries**

**stoup** (sto͞op) ***n.*** a basin for holy water in a church.

**stout** (stout) ***adj.*** **1** having a fat body. **2** strong and firm; sturdy [a *stout* wall]. **3** powerful [They put up a *stout* fight.] **4** brave; full of courage [She has a *stout* heart.] ◆***n.*** a strong, dark beer. —**stout′ly** ***adv.*** —**stout′ness** ***n.***

**stout-heart·ed** (stout′här′tid) ***adj.*** brave; courageous.

**stove**[1] (stōv) ***n.*** a device for cooking or heating by the use of gas, oil, electricity, etc.

**stove**[2] (stōv) *a past tense and past participle of* **stave.**

**stove·pipe** (stōv′pīp) ***n.*** **1** a wide pipe used to carry off smoke from a stove. ☆**2** a man's tall silk hat: *used only in everyday talk.*

**stow** (stō) ***v.*** **1** to pack in a close, orderly way [to *stow* luggage in a car trunk]. **2** to fill by packing [to *stow* a box with books]. —**stow away,** **1** to store or hide away. **2** to be a stowaway. **3** to drink up or eat up, especially in large amounts.

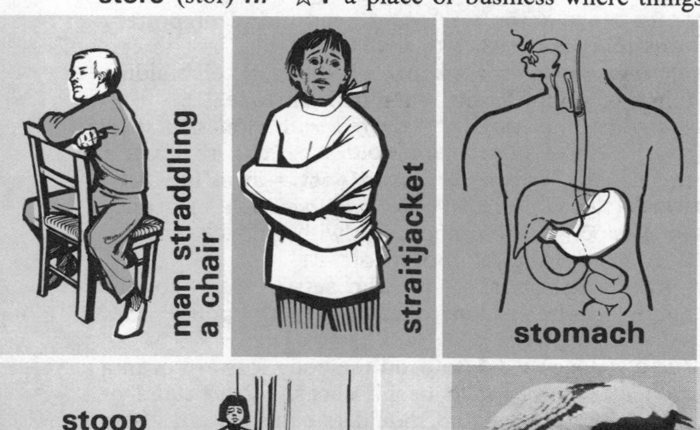

**man straddling a chair**

**straitjacket**

**stomach**

**stoop**

**stork** 107 cm (3 1/2 ft.) long

**stow·a·way** (stō′ə wā) ***n.*** a person who hides aboard a ship, plane etc. for a free or secret ride.

**Stowe** (stō), **Harriet Beecher** 1811–1896; U.S. author. She wrote *Uncle Tom's Cabin.*

**St. Paul** the capital of Minnesota, on the Mississippi River.

**St. Pe·ters·burg** (pēt′ərz burg) **1** an old name for the city of Leningrad in the U.S.S.R. **2** a city in west central Florida.

**strad·dle** (strad′'l) ***v.*** **1** to stand or sit with a leg on either side of [to *straddle* a horse]. *See the picture.* **2** to sit, stand, or walk with the legs wide apart. ☆**3** to take, or seem to take, both sides of an argument, issue, etc.; hedge. —**strad′dled, strad′dling** ◆***n.*** the act or position of straddling.

**strag·gle** (strag′'l) ***v.*** **1** to wander away from the path, course, or main group. **2** to be scattered or spread out in a careless or uneven way [old rambler roses *straggling* on a trellis]. —**strag′gled, strag′gling** —**strag′gler** ***n.*** —**strag′gly** ***adj.***

**straight** (strāt) ***adj.*** **1** having the same direction all the way; not crooked, curved, wavy, etc. [a *straight* line; *straight* hair]. **2** upright or erect [*straight* posture]. **3** level or even [a *straight* hemline]. **4** direct; staying right to the point, direction, etc. [a *straight* course; a *straight* answer]. **5** in order; not in confusion, error, etc. [Put your room *straight.* Is his figuring *straight?*] **6** honest and sincere [*straight* dealing]. **7** not mixed or divided [voting a *straight* ticket]. ◆***adv.*** **1** in a straight line. **2** in a way that is straight, direct, right, etc. [Go *straight* home. Put the picture *straight.*] —**straight away** or **straight off,** at once; without delay.

**straight·en** (strāt′'n) ***v.*** **1** to make or become straight [He *straightened* his tie.] **2** to put in order [to *straighten* a room]. —**straighten out, 1** to make or become less confused, easier to deal with, etc. ☆**2** to make or become better in behavior; reform.

**straight-faced** (strāt′fāst′) ***adj.*** showing no amusement or other feeling.

**straight·for·ward** (strāt′fôr′wərd) ***adj.*** **1** moving or leading straight ahead; direct. **2** honest; frank. ◆***adv.*** directly.

**straight·way** (strāt′wā) ***adv.*** at once.

**strain**[1] (strān) ***v.*** **1** to draw or stretch tight [Samson *strained* his chains and broke them.] **2** to use or explain in a way that is forced and not right [She *strained* the rules to suit herself.] **3** to use to the utmost [He *strained* every nerve to win.] **4** to hurt or weaken by too much force, effort, etc. [to *strain* a muscle]. **5** to try very hard [She *strained* to hear him.] **6** to pull with force [The horse *strained* at the harness.] **7** to put or pass through a screen, sieve, etc. [to *strain* soup]. **8** to hug [to *strain* a child to one's bosom]. ◆***n.*** **1** a straining or being strained. **2** hard, tiring effort of the body or mind, or the hurt caused by this [The funeral was quite a *strain* on her.] **3** great force or pressure [The *strain* of the weight on the bridge made it collapse.] **4** an injury to part of the body as a result of too much effort [heart *strain*].

**strain**[2] (strān) ***n.*** **1** family line; race, stock, breed, etc. **2** a quality that seems to be inherited [There is a *strain* of genius in that family.] **3** a trace or streak [There is a *strain* of sadness in those poems.] **4** *often* **strains,** *pl.* a passage of music; tune.

**strained** (strānd) ***adj.*** not natural or relaxed; forced [a *strained* laugh].

**strain·er** (strān′ər) ***n.*** a thing used for straining, as a sieve, filter, etc.

**strait** (strāt) ***n.*** *often* **straits,** *pl.* **1** a narrow body of water joining two larger ones. **2** trouble or need [to be in desperate *straits*].

**strait·en** (strāt′'n) ***v.*** to bring into difficulties, trouble, etc. *Straiten* is now usually used in the phrase **in straitened circumstances,** meaning "not having enough money to live on."

**strait·jack·et** (strāt′jak′it) ***n.*** a kind of coat tied around one to keep the arms from being moved. It is sometimes used, as in hospitals, to keep people who are acting wild from doing harm. *See the picture.*

**strait-laced** (strāt′lāst′) ***adj.*** very strict or limited in the way one behaves or in what one thinks about right and wrong.

**strand**[1] (strand) ***n.*** a shore, especially along an ocean. ◆***v.*** **1** to run aground [to *strand* a ship]. **2** to leave or be put in a difficult, helpless position [*stranded* in a city, with no money].

**strand**[2] (strand) ***n.*** **1** any of the threads, fibers, or wires that are twisted together to make a string, rope, or cable. **2** anything like a string or rope [a *strand* of hair].

**strange** (strānj) ***adj.*** **1** not known, seen, or heard before; not familiar [I saw a *strange* person at the door.] **2** different from what is usual; peculiar; odd [wearing a *strange* costume]. **3** not familiar; without experience [She is *strange* to this job.] —**strang′er, strang′est** ◆***adv.*** in a strange way [You have been acting very *strange* lately.] —**strange′ly** ***adv.***

SYNONYMS: **Strange** is the word for something unusually different, not ordinary or familiar, etc. [*strange* customs, a *strange* idea, a *strange* voice]. **Odd** is for something unusual or unfamiliar that is queer or fantastic [an *odd* way of acting]. **Peculiar** is for anything strange or odd, especially if it is hard to understand or explain [a *peculiar* smell].

**stran·ger** (strān′jər) ***n.*** **1** a person who is new to a place; outsider; foreigner. **2** a person not known to one [The children were warned not to speak to *strangers.*] **3** a person not used to something [He is a *stranger* to good music.]

**stran·gle** (straŋ′g'l) ***v.*** **1** to kill by squeezing the throat so as to stop the breathing. **2** to choke in any way; suffocate [*strangled* by the thick smoke]. **3** to hold back; stop [I *strangled* a desire to scream.] —**stran′gled, stran′gling** —**stran′gler** ***n.***

**strap** (strap) ***n.*** **1** a narrow strip of leather, canvas, etc., often with a buckle, for tying or holding things together. **2** any narrow strip like a strap [a shoulder *strap*]. ◆***v.*** **1** to fasten with a strap [*Strap* the boxes

| | | | | | | | |
|---|---|---|---|---|---|---|---|
| **a** | fat | **ir** | here | **ou** | out | **zh** | leisure |
| **ā** | ape | **ī** | bite, fire | **u** | up | **ŋ** | ring |
| **ä** | car, lot | **ō** | go | **ur** | fur | | a *in* ago |
| **e** | ten | **ô** | law, horn | **ch** | chin | | e *in* agent |
| **er** | care | **oi** | oil | **sh** | she | ə = | i *in* unity |
| **ē** | even | **oo** | look | **th** | thin | | o *in* collect |
| **i** | hit | **ōō** | tool | ***th*** | then | | u *in* focus |

streamers

streetcar

stretcher

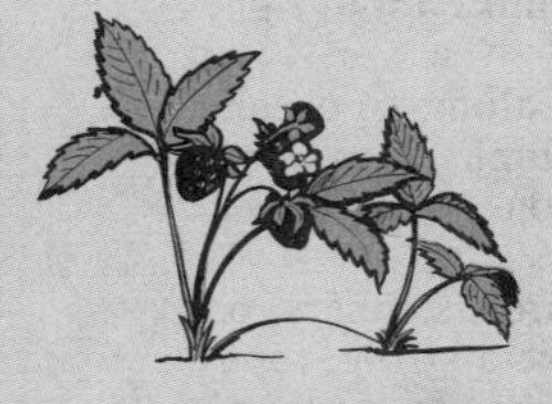

strawberry plant

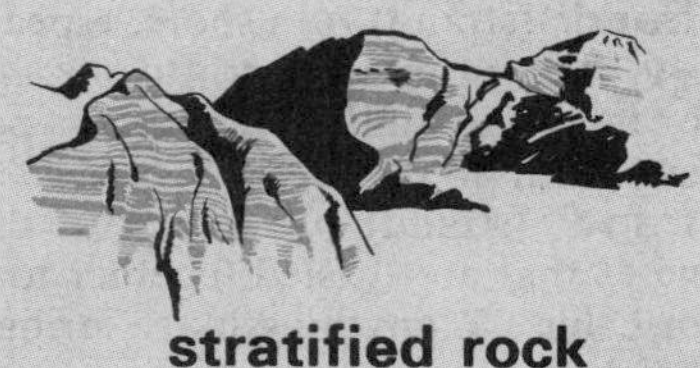

stratified rock

together.] **2** to beat with a strap. —**strapped, strap′ping** —**strap′less** ***adj.***



☆**strapped** (strapt) ***adj.*** in great need of money: *used only in everyday talk.*

**strap·ping** (strap′iŋ) ***adj.*** tall and strong; robust: *used only in everyday talk.*

**Stras·bourg** (stras′bʉrg) a city in northeastern France, on the Rhine River.

**stra·ta** (strāt′ə *or* strat′ə) ***n.*** *a plural of* **stratum.**

**strat·a·gem** (strat′ə jəm) ***n.*** a trick or scheme, as one used in war to deceive an enemy.

**stra·te·gic** (strə tē′jik) ***adj.*** **1** of or having to do with strategy [*strategic* problems]. **2** showing sound planning; useful or important in strategy [a *strategic* retreat].

**strat·e·gist** (strat′ə jist) ***n.*** a person who is skilled in strategy.

**strat·e·gy** (strat′ə jē) ***n.*** **1** the science of planning and directing military movements and operations. **2** skill in managing any matter, especially by using tricks and schemes [It took *strategy* to get them to come with us.] —*pl.* **strat′e·gies**

**Strat·ford-on-A·von** (strat′fərd än ā′vän) a town in central England, where Shakespeare was born: *also called* **Strat′ford-up·on-A′von.**

**strat·i·fy** (strat′ə fī) ***v.*** to arrange in layers [*stratified* rock]. *See the picture.* —**strat′i·fied, strat′i·fy·ing**

**strat·o·sphere** (strat′ə sfir) ***n.*** the part of the earth's atmosphere from about six miles to about fifteen miles above the surface of the earth.

**stra·tum** (strāt′əm *or* strat′əm) ***n.*** **1** a layer of matter, especially any of several layers, as of rock or earth, lying one upon another. **2** a section or level of society [the upper *stratum*]. —*pl.* **stra′ta** or **stra′tums**

**Strauss** (strous), **Jo·hann** (yō′hän) 1825–1899; Austrian composer, especially of waltzes.

**Strauss, Richard** 1864–1949; German composer.

**Stra·vin·sky** (strə vin′skē), **I·gor** (ē′gôr) 1882–1971; U.S. composer, born in Russia.

**straw** (strô) ***n.*** **1** hollow stalks, as of wheat or rye, after the grain has been threshed out. Straw is used as stuffing or is woven into hats, etc. **2** a single one of such stalks. **3** a tube, as of plastic, used for sucking a drink. ◆***adj.*** **1** of the color of straw; yellowish. **2** made of straw [a *straw* hat].

**straw·ber·ry** (strô′ber′ē) ***n.*** **1** the small, red, juicy fruit of a low plant of the rose family. **2** this plant. *See the picture.* —*pl.* **straw′ber′ries**

☆**straw vote** an unofficial poll to find out what people think about some matter.

**stray** (strā) ***v.*** **1** to wander from a certain place, path, etc.; roam [Don't *stray* from the camp. My thoughts *strayed* from the test.] **2** to go away from what is right [to *stray* from truth]. ◆***n.*** a lost or wandering person or animal. ◆***adj.*** **1** that has strayed and is lost [a *stray* dog]. **2** occasional; here and there [a few *stray* cars on the streets].

**streak** (strēk) ***n.*** **1** a long, thin mark, stripe, or smear [a *streak* of dirt]. **2** a layer, as of a mineral in the earth or of fat in meat. **3** a certain amount of some quality [He has a mean *streak* in him.] ☆**4** a period or spell [a *streak* of bad luck]. ◆***v.*** **1** to mark with streaks. **2** to go fast; hurry [to *streak* down the road]. —☆**like a streak,** at high speed; swiftly: *used only in everyday talk.*

**stream** (strēm) ***n.*** **1** a flow of water; especially, a small river. **2** a steady flow of anything [a *stream* of cold air; a *stream* of light; a *stream* of cars]. ◆***v.*** **1** to flow in a stream. **2** to pour out or flow [eyes *streaming* with tears]. **3** to move steadily or swiftly [The crowd *streamed* out of the stadium.] **4** to float or fly [a flag *streaming* in the breeze].

**stream·er** (strē′mər) ***n.*** **1** a long, narrow flag. **2** any long, narrow, flowing strip of material. *See the picture.*

**stream·line** (strēm′līn) ***v.*** to make streamlined. —**stream′lined, stream′lin·ing** ◆***adj.*** *same as* **streamlined.**

**stream·lined** (strēm′līnd) ***adj.*** **1** having a shape that allows it to move smoothly and easily through air, water, etc. [a *streamlined* boat]. ☆**2** arranged so as to be more efficient [a *streamlined* program].

**street** (strēt) ***n.*** **1** a road in a city or town; also, such a road with its sidewalks and buildings. **2** the people who live or work on a certain street [Our whole *street* gave money to the fund.] ◆***adj.*** **1** of, in, on, or near the street [the *street* floor]. **2** proper for wearing everyday in public [*street* clothes].

☆**street·car** (strēt′kär) ***n.*** a large car on rails for carrying people along the streets. *See the picture.*

**strength** (streŋkth *or* streŋth) ***n.*** **1** the quality of being strong; force, power, ability to last or resist, etc. [the *strength* of a blow, of a steel girder, or of a nation]. *See* SYNONYMS *at* **energy.** **2** the degree to which something has an effect [the *strength* of a drug, or of a color, light, sound, taste, etc.] **3** force as measured in numbers [an army at full *strength*]. **4** something that gives strength. —**on the strength of,** depending on or relying on.

**strength·en** (streŋkth′′n *or* streŋth′′n) ***v.*** to make or become stronger. —**strength′en·er** ***n.***

**stren·u·ous** (stren′yoo wəs) ***adj.*** **1** needing much energy or effort [Chopping wood is a *strenuous* task.] **2**

very active or vigorous [a *strenuous* worker; *strenuous* efforts]. —**stren′u·ous·ly** ***adv.***

☆**strep throat** (strep) a sore throat caused by a streptococcus: *used only in everyday talk.*

**strep·to·coc·cus** (strep′tə käk′əs) ***n.*** a kind of bacteria shaped like a ball. Some forms cause disease. —*pl.* **strep·to·coc·ci** (strep′tə käk′sī)

☆**strep·to·my·cin** (strep′tə mī′sin) ***n.*** a chemical substance got from a soil fungus. It is an antibiotic used in treating certain diseases, as tuberculosis.

**stress** (stres) ***n.*** **1** strain or pressure [the *stress* on the wings of an airplane; under the *stress* of a crisis]. **2** special attention; emphasis [Our doctor puts *stress* on good health habits.] **3** special force given a syllable, word, or note in speaking or in music; accent. ◆***v.*** **1** to put stress or strain on. **2** to accent or emphasize [Let me *stress* the importance of fire drills.]

**stretch** (strech) ***v.*** **1** to reach out or hold out, as a hand, object, etc. **2** to draw out to full length, to a greater size, to a certain distance, etc.; extend [She *stretched* out on the sofa. Will this material *stretch? Stretch* the rope between two trees. The road *stretches* for miles through the hills.] **3** to pull or draw tight; strain [to *stretch* a muscle]. **4** to draw out too far, as by exaggerating [to *stretch* a rule; to *stretch* the truth]. ◆***n.*** **1** a stretching or being stretched [a *stretch* of the arms]. **2** the ability to be stretched [This elastic band has lost its *stretch.*] **3** an unbroken space, as of time or land; extent [a *stretch* of two years; a long *stretch* of beach].

**stretch·er** (strech′ər) ***n.*** **1** a person or thing that stretches, as a frame for stretching curtains. **2** a light frame covered with canvas, etc., used for carrying people who are sick or hurt. *See the picture.*

**strew** (stro͞o) ***v.*** **1** to scatter; spread about here and there [clothes *strewn* on the floor]. **2** to cover as by scattering [The street was *strewn* with litter.] —**strewed, strewed** or **strewn** (stro͞on), **strew′ing**

**stri·at·ed** (strī′āt id) ***adj.*** marked with parallel lines or bands; striped.

**strick·en** (strik′'n) *a past participle of* **strike.** ◆***adj.*** **1** struck or wounded. **2** suffering, as from pain, trouble, etc.

**strict** (strikt) ***adj.*** **1** keeping to rules in a careful, exact way [a *strict* supervisor]. **2** never changing; rigid [a *strict* rule]. **3** perfect; exact or absolute [a *strict* translation; *strict* silence]. —**strict′ly** ***adv.*** —**strict′ness** ***n.***

> **Strict** comes from a Latin word meaning "to draw tight" or "to press together." A strict teacher may make students feel as if they are being held tight by rules and regulations.

**stric·ture** (strik′chər) ***n.*** **1** strong criticism. **2** a narrowing of a tube, etc. in the body, as in a disease.

**stride** (strīd) ***v.*** **1** to walk with long steps. **2** to cross with one long step [She *strode* over the puddle.] **3** to sit or stand with a leg on either side of; straddle [to *stride* a horse]. —**strode, strid·den** (strid′'n), **strid′ing** ◆***n.*** **1** a long step in walking or running, or the distance covered by it. **2** *usually* **strides,** *pl.* progress [great *strides* in industry]. —☆**hit one's stride,** to reach one's normal level of skill or speed. —**take in one's stride,** to deal with easily.

**stri·dent** (strīd′'nt) ***adj.*** harsh in sound; shrill or grating [a *strident* voice]. —**stri′dent·ly** ***adv.***

**strife** (strīf) ***n.*** the act or condition of fighting or quarreling; struggle; conflict. *See* SYNONYMS *at* **discord.**

**strike** (strīk) ***v.*** **1** to hit by giving a blow, coming against with force, etc. [Pat *struck* him in anger. The car *struck* the curb.] **2** to make a sound by hitting some part [The clock *struck* one. *Strike* middle C on the piano.] **3** to set on fire as by rubbing [to *strike* a match]. **4** to make by stamping, printing, etc. [The mint *strikes* coins.] **5** to attack [A rattlesnake makes a noise before it *strikes.*] **6** to catch or reach [A sound of music *struck* my ear.] ☆**7** to come upon; find [They drilled and *struck* oil.] **8** to hit one's mind or feelings [The idea just *struck* me. It *strikes* me as silly.] **9** to bring about [The scream *struck* terror to my heart.] **10** to overcome as by a blow [Flu *struck* the entire family.] **11** to make or reach, as by planning [We *struck* a bargain.] **12** to take down or take apart [We *struck* camp at noon. *Strike* the sails.] **13** to go; proceed [We *struck* northward.] **14** to take on; assume [to *strike* a pose]. **15** to stop working until certain demands have been met [The workers are *striking* for shorter hours.] —**struck, struck** or **strick′en, strik′ing** ◆***n.*** **1** the act of striking; a blow. **2** the act of stopping work in order to get higher wages, better working conditions, etc. ☆**3** a sudden or lucky success, as the act of finding oil. ☆**4** in baseball, a fairly pitched ball which the batter does not hit into fair territory according to the rules of the game. Three strikes put the batter out. ☆**5** in bowling, the act of knocking down all ten pins with the first roll of the ball. —**on strike** or **out on strike,** striking; refusing to work. —**strike dumb,** to amaze; astonish. —**strike home,** to have an effect [That speech *struck home.*] —☆**strike it rich,** to have sudden success, as by discovering oil. —**strike off,** to remove, as from a list. —**strike out, 1** to cross out; erase. **2** to start out. ☆**3** in baseball, to be put out by three strikes; also, to put out by pitching three strikes. ☆**4** to be a failure. —**strike up,** to begin, as a friendship.

> SYNONYMS: **Strike** and **hit** can both mean to give a blow to [The batter *struck,* or *hit,* the ball.] However, for some things **strike** is more likely to be used [Lightning *struck* the barn.] and **hit** is more likely to be used for others [He *hit* the bull's-eye.] **Knock** suggests a striking or hitting of something so as to move it from its usual or proper place [He *knocked* the vase off the table.] or it suggests a striking or hitting several times [She *knocked* on the door.]

**strike·break·er** (strīk′brā′kər) ***n.*** a person who tries to break up a strike, as by taking the place of a striking worker, threatening the strikers, etc.

**strik·er** (strī′kər) ***n.*** a worker who is on strike.

| | | | | | | | |
|---|---|---|---|---|---|---|---|
| **a** | fat | **ir** | here | **ou** | out | **zh** | leisure |
| **ā** | ape | **ī** | bite, fire | **u** | up | **ng** | ring |
| **ä** | car, lot | **ō** | go | **ur** | fur | | a *in* ago |
| **e** | ten | **ô** | law, horn | **ch** | chin | | e *in* agent |
| **er** | care | **oi** | oil | **sh** | she | **ə =** | i *in* unity |
| **ē** | even | **oo** | look | **th** | thin | | o *in* collect |
| **i** | hit | **o͞o** | tool | ***th*** | then | | u *in* focus |

**strik·ing** (strī′kiŋ) ***adj.*** getting attention because unusual or remarkable [That's a *striking* hat you have on.] —**strik′ing·ly *adv.***

**string** (striŋ) ***n.*** **1** a thick thread or thin strip of cloth, leather, etc., used for tying or pulling; cord. **2** a number of objects on a string [a *string* of pearls]. **3** a number of things in a row [a *string* of lights]. **4** a thin cord of wire, gut, etc. that is bowed, plucked, or struck to make a musical sound, as on a violin or piano. **5** **strings,** *pl.* stringed musical instruments played with a bow. **6** a plant fiber like a thread, as along the seam in a pod of a string bean. ☆**7** a condition or limit: *used only in everyday talk* [an offer with no *strings* attached]. ◆***v.*** **1** to put strings on [to *string* a tennis racket]. **2** to put on a string [to *string* beads]. **3** to tie, hang, etc. with a string. **4** to stretch like a string; extend [to *string* telephone wires on poles; to *string* out a speech]. **5** to remove the strings from [to *string* beans]. —**strung, string′ing** —**pull strings,** to use influence to get what one wants or to control others. —☆**string along,** **1** to go along or agree. **2** to fool or trick, as by making promises. *This phrase is used only in everyday talk.* —**string up,** to kill by hanging: *used only in everyday talk.*

**string band** a band of stringed instruments, as guitar, banjo, violin, etc., playing folk music or country music. —**string′-band′ *adj.***

☆**string bean** **1** a bean with thick pods eaten as a vegetable before they ripen. **2** the pod. *See the picture.*



**stringed** (striŋd) ***adj.*** having strings [Harps, violins, etc. are *stringed* instruments.]

**strin·gent** (strin′jənt) ***adj.*** **1** strict; severe [a *stringent* rule]. ☆**2** with little money for loans [a *stringent* market]. **3** forceful; convincing [*stringent* reasons]. —**strin′gen·cy *n.*** —**strin′gent·ly *adv.***

**string·er** (striŋ′ər) ***n.*** a long piece of timber used as a support or to connect upright posts.

**string·y** (striŋ′ē) ***adj.*** **1** like a string; long and thin. **2** having tough fibers, as celery. **3** forming strings [*stringy* honey]. —**string′i·er, string′i·est**

**strip**[1] (strip) ***v.*** **1** to take off one's clothes; undress. **2** to take the covering from; skin, peel, etc. [to *strip* a tree of bark]. **3** to take off; remove [to *strip* husks from corn]. **4** to make bare by taking things away; clear or rob [to *strip* a room of furniture]. **5** to take apart [to *strip* down a motor]. **6** to break off, as the thread of a screw or the teeth of a gear. —**stripped, strip′ping** —**strip′per *n.***

**strip**[2] (strip) ***n.*** a long, narrow piece, as of land, material, etc.

**stripe** (strīp) ***n.*** **1** a narrow band of a different color or material from the part around it [The flag has red and white *stripes.*] **2** kind or sort [a man of his *stripe*]. ◆***v.*** to mark with stripes. —**striped, strip′ing**

**strip·ling** (strip′liŋ) ***n.*** a grown boy; youth.

**strip mining** a method of mining, especially for coal, by laying bare a mineral deposit near the earth's surface.

**strive** (strīv) ***v.*** **1** to make great efforts; try very hard [We must *strive* to win.] **2** to struggle or fight [We *strive* against disease.] —**strove, striv·en** (striv′'n), **striv′ing**

**strobe** (strōb) ***n.*** an electronic tube that can send out very quick, short, and bright flashes of light. Strobes are used in photography. *Also called* **strobe light.**

**strode** (strōd) *past tense of* **stride.**

**stroke** (strōk) ***n.*** **1** the act of striking; a blow [a tree felled with six *strokes*]. **2** the sound of striking, as of a clock. **3** a single strong effort [You haven't done a *stroke* of work.] **4** a sudden action or event [a *stroke* of lightning; a *stroke* of luck]. **5** a sudden attack of illness, as of paralysis. **6** a single movement, as with some tool [a *stroke* of a pen; a backhand *stroke* in tennis]. **7** a mark made in writing, painting, etc. **8** one of a series of repeated motions, as in swimming. **9** a rubbing with the hand in a gentle way. ◆***v.*** **1** to rub gently with one's hand, a brush, etc. **2** to hit a ball, as in tennis, pool, etc. —**stroked, strok′ing**

**stroll** (strōl) ***v.*** **1** to walk in a slow, easy way. **2** to wander from place to place [a *strolling* musician]. ◆***n.*** a slow, easy walk.

**stroll·er** (strōl′ər) ***n.*** **1** a person who strolls. ☆**2** a light baby carriage that is like a chair. *See the picture.*

**strong** (strôŋ) ***adj.*** **1** having great force or power; not weak; powerful [a *strong* person; *strong* winds]. **2** able to last; durable; tough [a *strong* wall; *strong* rope]. **3** having a powerful effect on the senses or mind; not mild [a *strong* taste, smell, light, sound, liking, etc.] **4** having a certain number [an army 50,000 *strong*]. ◆***adv.*** in a strong way; with force. —**strong′ly *adv.*** —**strong′ness *n.***

SYNONYMS: Someone or something that is **strong** has the power or energy to do things or to hold off an attack [a *strong* body; a *strong* fort]. Something that is **sturdy** is solidly made or developed and is hard to weaken or destroy [*sturdy* oaks; *sturdy* faith]. Something that is **tough** is so strong and firm that it will not, usually, break or give way.

**strong·hold** (strôŋ′hōld) ***n.*** a place made strong against attack; fortified place.

**strong-mind·ed** (strôŋ′mīn′did) ***adj.*** having a strong, firm mind or will; determined.

**strong-willed** (strôŋ′wild′) ***adj.*** having a strong or stubborn will.

**stron·ti·um** (strän′shē əm) ***n.*** a chemical element that is a pale-yellow metal. A deadly radioactive form, **strontium 90,** occurs in the fallout of nuclear explosions.

**strop** (sträp) ***n.*** a leather strap on which razors are sharpened. ◆***v.*** to sharpen on a strop. —**stropped, strop′ping**

**stro·phe** (strō′fē) ***n.*** a stanza of a poem.

**strove** (strōv) *past tense of* **strive.**

**struck** (struk) *past tense and a past participle of* **strike.**

**struc·tur·al** (struk′chər əl) ***adj.*** **1** used in building [*structural* steel]. **2** of structure [*structural* design]. —**struc′tur·al·ly *adv.***

**struc·ture** (struk′chər) ***n.*** **1** something built; a building, bridge, dam, etc. **2** the way in which something is built or put together; construction, plan, design, etc. [the *structure* of a novel].

**stru·del** (strōō′d'l) ***n.*** a kind of pastry made of a very thin sheet of dough filled with apple slices, cheese, etc., rolled up, and baked.

**strug·gle** (strug′'l) ***v.*** **1** to fight hard [The wrestlers *struggled* with one another.] **2** to try very hard;

strive; labor [She *struggled* to learn French.] **3** to make one's way with great effort [He *struggled* through the thicket.] —**strug'gled, strug'gling** ◆**n.** **1** a great effort [the *struggle* for women's rights]. **2** a fight; conflict; strife.

**strum** (strum) **v.** to play with long strokes across the strings, as a guitar. —**strummed, strum'ming** ◆**n.** the act or sound of strumming.

**strung** (struŋ) *past tense and past participle of* **string.**

**strut** (strut) **v.** to walk in a self-confident way, usually as if to attract attention. —**strut'ted, strut'ting** ◆**n.** **1** a strutting walk. **2** a rod or brace set in a framework, often at an angle, as a support. *See the picture.*

**strych·nine** (strik'nīn) **n.** a poisonous drug got from certain plants. It is given by doctors in small doses as a stimulant.

**Stu·art** (sto͞o'ərt) the ruling family of England from 1603 to 1714.

**stub** (stub) **n.** **1** a short piece that is left after the main part has been used up or cut off [a pencil *stub*]. ☆**2** a short piece of a leaf in a checkbook, kept as a record. **3** any part or thing that is short and blunt [a mere *stub* of a tail]. **4** a tree stump. ◆**v.** to strike against something [He *stubbed* his toe on the rock.] —**stubbed, stub'bing**

**stub·ble** (stub''l) **n.** **1** the short stumps of grain left standing after the harvest. **2** any short, uneven growth [a *stubble* of beard]. *See the picture.* —**stub'bly** ***adj.***

**stub·born** (stub'ərn) **adj.** **1** set on having one's way; not willing to give in; obstinate. **2** hard to treat or deal with [a *stubborn* rash]. —**stub'born·ly adv.** —**stub'born·ness n.**

**stub·by** (stub'ē) **adj.** **1** covered with stubs or stubble [*stubby* land]. **2** short and dense [a *stubby* beard]. **3** short and thick [*stubby* fingers]. —**stub'bi·er, stub'bi·est**

**stuc·co** (stuk'ō) **n.** plaster for coating inside or outside walls, often in a rough or wavy finish. ◆**v.** to cover with stucco. —**stuc'coed, stuc'co·ing**

**stuck** (stuk) *past tense and past participle of* **stick.**

**stuck-up** (stuk'up') **adj.** snobbish or conceited: *used only in everyday talk.*

**stud**[1] (stud) **n.** **1** a small knob or a nail with a round head, used to decorate a surface, as of leather. **2** a kind of removable button used to fasten a collar, shirt, etc. **3** one of the upright pieces to which boards or laths are nailed, as in making a wall. ◆**v.** **1** to decorate as with studs [a crown *studded* with rubies]. **2** to be set thickly on [Rocks *stud* the hillside.] —**stud'ded, stud'ding**

**stud**[2] (stud) **n.** **1** a number of horses kept especially for breeding. ☆**2** any male animal used especially for breeding.

**stu·dent** (sto͞od''nt *or* styo͞od''nt) **n.** a person who studies, as at a school or college.

**stud·ied** (stud'ēd) **adj.** carefully thought out or planned; done on purpose [Her clothes are simple in a *studied* way.]

**stu·di·o** (sto͞o'dē ō *or* styo͞o'dē ō) **n.** **1** a room or a building where an artist or photographer works. **2** a place where movies are made. **3** a place from which radio or TV programs are broadcast or where recordings are made. —*pl.* **stu'di·os**

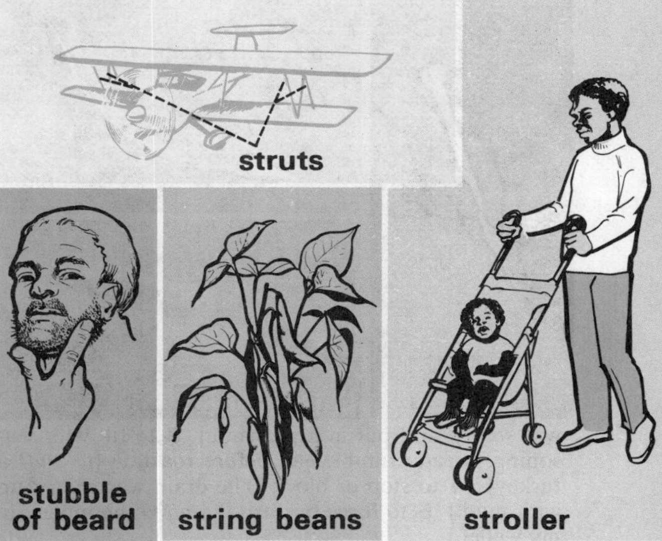

struts

stubble of beard

string beans

stroller

☆**studio couch** a kind of couch that can be opened up into a full bed.

**stu·di·ous** (sto͞o'dē əs *or* styo͞o'dē əs) **adj.** **1** fond of studying [a *studious* pupil]. **2** paying or showing careful attention [a *studious* look]. —**stu'di·ous·ly adv.** —**stu'di·ous·ness n.**

**stud·y** (stud'ē) **v.** **1** to try to learn by reading, thinking, etc. [to *study* law]. **2** to look at or into carefully; examine or investigate [We must *study* the problem of crime.] **3** to read so as to understand and remember [to *study* a lesson]. **4** to give thought to [We will be *studying* possible changes.] **5** to take a course in [All seniors must *study* history.] —**stud'ied, stud'y·ing** ◆**n.** **1** the act of reading, thinking, etc. in order to learn something. **2** careful and serious examination [a *study* of traffic problems]. **3** a branch of learning; subject [the *study* of medicine]. **4 studies,** *pl.* education; schooling [I continued my *studies* at college.] **5** a piece of writing, a picture, etc. dealing with a subject in great detail. **6** a piece of music for practice in certain skills; etude. **7** deep thought [You seemed lost in *study*.] **8** a room used for studying, reading, etc. —*pl.* **stud'ies** —☆**study up on,** to make a careful study of: *used only in everyday talk.*



**stuff** (stuf) **n.** **1** what anything is made of; material; substance. **2** that which makes a thing what it is; character [a person made of stern *stuff*]. **3** a collection of objects, belongings, etc. [I emptied the *stuff* from my bag.] **4** foolish things or ideas [*stuff* and nonsense]. ☆**5** special skill or knowledge: *used only in everyday talk* [She really knows her *stuff*.] ◆**v.** **1** to fill or pack [pockets *stuffed* with candy]. **2** to fill the skin of a dead animal to make it look alive [The bear

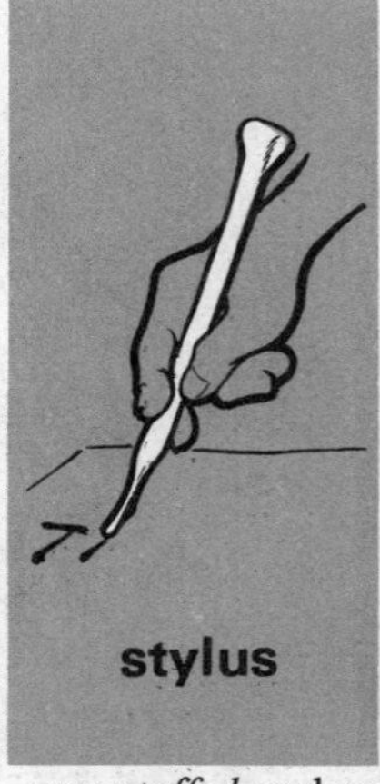


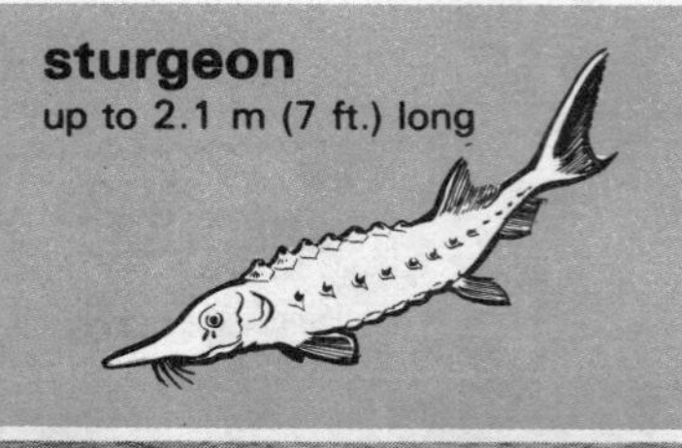

was *stuffed* and put in a museum.] **3** to fill with seasoning, bread crumbs, etc. before roasting [to *stuff* a turkey]. **4** to stop or block [The drain was *stuffed* up with mud.] **5** to force or push [I *stuffed* the money in my wallet.]

**stuff·ing** (stuf′iŋ) ***n.*** something used to stuff, as the soft, springy material used as padding in cushions, some furniture, etc. or the seasoned mixture used to stuff a chicken.

**stuff·y** (stuf′ē) ***adj.*** **1** having little fresh air; close [a *stuffy* room]. **2** stopped up or stuffed full [My head feels *stuffy*.] **3** dull, old-fashioned, pompous, etc.: *used only in everyday talk* [a *stuffy* book, person, etc.] —**stuff′i·er, stuff′i·est —stuff′i·ness *n.***



**stul·ti·fy** (stul′tə fī) ***v.*** to cause to seem or be foolish, dull, useless, etc. —**stul′ti·fied, stul′ti·fy·ing**

**stum·ble** (stum′b′l) ***v.*** **1** to trip or almost fall, as by stubbing the toe against something. **2** to walk in an unsteady way [The tired boy *stumbled* off to bed.] **3** to find or come by chance [We *stumbled* upon a clue to the mystery.] **4** to speak or act in a confused way [She forgot her speech and began to *stumble*.] **5** to do wrong or make mistakes. —**stum′bled, stum′bling** ◆***n.*** **1** the act of stumbling. **2** a mistake or blunder.

**stumbling block** something that gets in the way; obstacle or difficulty.

**stump** (stump) ***n.*** **1** the part of a tree or plant left in the ground after the main part has been cut down. **2** the part of an arm, leg, etc. left after the rest has been removed. **3** a butt; stub [the *stump* of a pencil]. ☆**4** the place where a political speech is made. ◆***v.*** ☆**1** to travel about, making political speeches [The candidate *stumped* the West.] ☆**2** to puzzle; make unable to answer: *used only in everyday talk* [Her question *stumped* the expert.] **3** to walk in a heavy, clumsy way.

**stun** (stun) ***v.*** **1** to make unconscious or dazed, as by a blow. **2** to shock deeply [The news *stunned* us.] —**stunned, stun′ning**

> **Stun** comes from a Latin word meaning "to thunder." In addition to meaning "to daze or shock," *stun* is used in speaking of the way a person can be overcome or bewildered by a loud noise.

**stung** (stuŋ) *past tense and past participle of* **sting.**

**stunk** (stuŋk) *past participle and a past tense of* **stink.**

**stun·ning** (stun′iŋ) ***adj.*** **1** that stuns, as a blow. **2** very attractive, beautiful, etc.: *used only in everyday talk.* —**stun′ning·ly *adv.***

**stunt**[1] (stunt) ***v.*** to keep from growing or developing [Poor soil *stunted* the plants.]

☆**stunt**[2] (stunt) ***n.*** something done for a thrill, to get attention, show off one's skill, etc. ◆***v.*** to do a stunt.

**stu·pe·fac·tion** (stōō′pə fak′shən *or* styōō′pə fak′shən) ***n.*** **1** the condition of being stupefied or dazed. **2** great amazement; astonishment.

**stu·pe·fy** (stōō′pə fī *or* styōō′pə fī) ***v.*** **1** to make dull, senseless, or dazed [The drug *stupefied* me.] **2** to amaze; astonish [We were *stupefied* by the bloody sight.] —**stu′pe·fied, stu′pe·fy·ing**

**stu·pen·dous** (stōō pen′dəs *or* styōō pen′dəs) ***adj.*** **1** astonishing; overwhelming [a *stupendous* development]. **2** amazing because very great or large [a *stupendous* success]. —**stu·pen′dous·ly *adv.***

**stu·pid** (stōō′pid *or* styōō′pid) ***adj.*** **1** slow to learn or understand; not intelligent. **2** foolish or silly [a *stupid* idea]. **3** dull; boring [a *stupid* party]. —**stu′pid·ly *adv.***

**stu·pid·i·ty** (stōō pid′ə tē *or* styōō pid′ə tē) ***n.*** **1** the condition of being stupid. **2** a stupid remark or act. —*pl.* **stu·pid′i·ties**

**stu·por** (stōō′pər *or* styōō′pər) ***n.*** a condition, as of shock, in which one can barely think, act, feel, etc.; dazed condition.

**stur·dy** (stur′dē) ***adj.*** **1** strong and hardy [a *sturdy* oak]. *See* SYNONYMS *at* **strong. 2** not giving in; firm [*sturdy* defiance]. —**stur′di·er, stur′di·est** —**stur′di·ly *adv.*** —**stur′di·ness *n.***

**stur·geon** (stur′jən) ***n.*** a large food fish with a long snout and rows of hard plates on the skin. Fine caviar is got from sturgeon. *See the picture.*

**stut·ter** (stut′ər) ***v.*** to speak with short stops that one cannot control, often repeating certain sounds, as in fear, embarrassment, etc.; stammer. ◆***n.*** stuttering talk. —**stut′ter·er *n.***

**sty**[1] (stī) ***n.*** **1** a pen for pigs. **2** any filthy or disgusting place. —*pl.* **sties**

**sty**[2] or **stye** (stī) ***n.*** a swollen, sore gland on the rim of the eyelid. —*pl.* **sties**

> The word **sty** came about because of a mistake in understanding. It comes from a very old word, *styany,* that meant "swelling." It was pronounced (stī′ə nī′), so that people thought what was being said was "sty on eye." Later it was shortened to **sty.**

**Styg·i·an** (stij′ē ən) ***adj.*** dark or gloomy, like the river Styx.

**style** (stīl) ***n.*** **1** the way in which anything is made, done, written, spoken, etc.; manner; method [pointed arches in the Gothic *style*]. **2** the way in which people generally dress, act, etc. at any particular period; fashion; mode [*Styles* in clothing keep changing.] **3** a fine, original way of writing, painting, etc. [This author lacks *style*.] **4** the part of a flower's pistil between the stigma and the ovary. **5** *same as* **stylus.** ◆***v.*** **1** to name; call [Lincoln was *styled* "Honest Abe."] ☆**2** to design the style of [Those gowns are *styled* in Paris.] **3** to cut and arrange hair in a certain way. —**styled, styl′ing**

**styl·ish** (stī′lish) ***adj.*** in keeping with the latest style; fashionable; smart [She wore a *stylish* coat.] —**styl′·ish·ly *adv.*** —**styl′ish·ness *n.***

**sty·lus** (stī′ləs) ***n.*** **1** a phonograph needle. **2** a pointed tool, as one used long ago for writing on wax. *See the picture.* —*pl.* **sty′lus·es** or **sty·li** (stī′lī)

**sty·mie** (stī′mē) ***n.*** a situation in which a person is frustrated or held back from a desired action. ◆***v.*** to hinder or hold back a person from doing something. —**sty′mied, sty′mie·ing**

**styp·tic** (stip′tik) ***adj.*** that stops bleeding by tightening the body tissues [A *styptic* pencil is a stick of alum, etc., used on small cuts.]

**Styx** (stiks) in Greek myths, a river crossed by dead souls before entering Hades.

**suave** (swäv) ***adj.*** polite or gracious in a smooth way. —**suave′ly *adv.*** —**suav·i·ty** (swä′və tē) ***n.***

**sub** (sub) ***n.*** *a short form of some words that begin with* sub-, as **submarine, subscription,** and **substitute.** ◆***v.*** to be a substitute for someone: *used only in everyday talk.* —**subbed, sub′bing**

**sub-** *a prefix meaning:* **1** under or below [*Subsoil* is soil under the topsoil.] **2** not quite; somewhat [A *subtropical* region is somewhat tropical in climate.] **3** forming or being a division [A *subcommittee* is one of the divisions of a main committee.]

**sub·al·tern** (səb ôl′tərn) ***n.*** any officer in the British army below the rank of captain.

**sub·a·tom·ic** (sub′ə täm′ik) ***adj.*** of or having to do with the inner part of an atom or any particle smaller than an atom.

**sub·com·mit·tee** (sub′kə mit′ē) ***n.*** any of the small committees chosen from the members of a main committee to carry out special tasks.

**sub·com·pact** (sub käm′pakt) ***n.*** a model of automobile that is smaller than a compact.

**sub·con·scious** (sub kän′shəs) ***adj.*** in or of the mind without one's being openly aware of it [a *subconscious* wish to be smarter than anyone else]. —**the subconscious,** the part of one's mind where subconscious feelings, wishes, etc. are stored. —**sub·con′scious·ly *adv.***

**sub·di·vide** (sub də vīd′) ***v.*** **1** to divide again the parts into which something is already divided. **2** to divide land into small sections for sale. —**sub·di·vid′ed, sub·di·vid′ing** —**sub·di·vi·sion** (sub də vizh′ən) ***n.***

**sub·due** (səb do͞o′ *or* səb dyo͞o′) ***v.*** **1** to conquer or overcome; get control over [to *subdue* an invading army; to *subdue* a bad habit]. **2** to make less strong or harsh; soften [*subdued* anger; *subdued* light; *subdued* colors]. —**sub·dued′, sub·du′ing**

**sub·freez·ing** (sub′frē′ziŋ) ***adj.*** below freezing.

**subj.** *abbreviation for* **subject, subjunctive.**

**sub·ject** (sub′jikt) ***adj.*** **1** under the power or control of another [The *subject* peoples in colonies often revolt.] **2** likely to have; liable [He is *subject* to fits of anger.] **3** depending on some action or condition [Our treaties are *subject* to the approval of the Senate.] ◆***n.*** **1** a person under the power or control of a ruler, government, etc. **2** a person or thing being discussed, examined, dealt with, etc. [Lincoln has been the *subject* of many books. Guinea pigs are used as the *subject* of many experiments.] **3** the word or group of words in a sentence about which something is said [In the sentence "Boys and girls enjoy sports," "boys and girls" is the *subject*.] **4** a course of study, as in a school [What is your favorite *subject?*] ◆***v.*** (səb jekt′) **1** to bring under some power or control. **2** to lay open; make liable [Her poor health *subjected* her to disease.] **3** to make undergo [The suspect was *subjected* to much questioning.] —**sub·jec′tion *n.***

SYNONYMS: **Subject** is the general word for whatever is dealt with in talking, study, writing, art, etc. [War was the *subject* of his speech. The *subject* of the Degas painting is a ballet dancer.] A **theme** is a subject that has been worked out in a very careful way in a book, work of art, etc. [Helping people was the *theme* of the sermon.] A **theme** may also be an idea that is repeated in a number of different works of art [The paintings at the show had the *theme* of city life.]

**sub·jec·tive** (səb jek′tiv) ***adj.*** of or resulting from one's own feelings or thinking rather than from the plain facts [Most likes and dislikes are *subjective.*]

**sub·ju·gate** (sub′jə gāt) ***v.*** to bring under control; conquer or subdue. —**sub′ju·gat·ed, sub′ju·gat·ing**

**Subjugate** comes from a Latin word meaning "to bring under the yoke." Someone who has been subjugated is completely controlled in the same way that oxen are when they have been joined together by a yoke.

**sub·junc·tive** (səb juŋk′tiv) ***adj.*** describing the mood of a verb used in stating a wish, possibility, or condition [In the phrase "if I were king," "were" is in the *subjunctive* mood.]

**sub·lease** (sub′lēs) ***n.*** a lease for property given by a person who is leasing it from the owner. ◆***v.*** (sub lēs′) to give or receive a sublease of. —**sub·leased′, sub·leas′ing** 

**sub·let** (sub′let′) ***v.*** **1** *same as* **sublease. 2** to give someone part of the work that one has a contract to do [The builder of the house *sublet* the contract for the plumbing.] —**sub′let′, sub′let′ting**

**sub·li·mate** (sub′lə māt) ***v.*** **1** to sublime a solid. **2** to purify or refine. —**sub′li·mat·ed, sub′li·mat·ing** —**sub′li·ma′tion *n.***

**sub·lime** (sə blīm′) ***adj.*** of the highest kind; great, noble, lofty, etc. [*sublime* beauty]. ◆***v.*** to make a solid substance pure by heating it until it becomes a gas, and then condensing the gas back to a solid form. —**sub·limed′, sub·lim′ing** —**the sublime,** something which causes a feeling of awe because it is so noble, grand, etc. —**sub·lim·i·ty** (sə blim′ə tē) ***n.***

**sub·ma·rine** (sub′mə rēn) ***n.*** a kind of warship that can travel under the surface of water. *See the picture.* ◆***adj.*** (sub mə rēn′) that lives, grows, happens, etc. under the surface of the sea [Sponges are *submarine* animals.]

☆**submarine sandwich** *another name for* **hero sandwich.**

**sub·merge** (səb murj′) ***v.*** to put, go, or stay under water [Whales can *submerge* for as long as half an

| | | | | | | | |
|---|---|---|---|---|---|---|---|
| a | fat | ir | here | ou | out | zh | leisure |
| ā | ape | ī | bite, fire | u | up | ŋ | ring |
| ä | car, lot | ō | go | ur | fur | | a *in* ago |
| e | ten | ô | law, horn | ch | chin | | e *in* agent |
| er | care | oi | oil | sh | she | ə = | i *in* unity |
| ē | even | oo | look | th | thin | | o *in* collect |
| i | hit | o͞o | tool | *th* | then | | u *in* focus |

hour.] —**sub·merged′, sub·merg′ing —sub·mer′gence** ***n.***

**sub·mer·sion** (səb mʉr′zhən *or* səb mʉr′shən) ***n.*** the act of putting, going, or staying under water.

**sub·mis·sion** (səb mish′ən) ***n.*** **1** the act of submitting or giving up; surrender [They brought the rebels to *submission.*] **2** the condition of being obedient or humble [The queen's subjects knelt in *submission.*] **3** the act of submitting something to someone [the *submission* of a petition to the mayor].

**sub·mis·sive** (səb mis′iv) ***adj.*** willing to give in to or obey another; humble; obedient.

**sub·mit** (səb mit′) ***v.*** **1** to give or offer to others for them to look over, decide about, etc.; refer [A new tax law was *submitted* to the voters.] **2** to give in to the power or control of another; surrender [We will never *submit* to the enemy.] —**sub·mit′ted, sub·mit′ting**

**sub·nor·mal** (sub nôr′m′l) ***adj.*** below normal; less than normal, as in intelligence.

**sub·or·di·nate** (sə bôr′də nit) ***adj.*** **1** low or lower in rank; less important; secondary [a *subordinate* job]. **2** under the power or control of another [The firefighters are *subordinate* to their chief.] ◆***n.*** a subordinate person. ◆***v.*** (sə bôr′də nāt) to place in a lower position; treat as less important [We *subordinated* our wishes to theirs.] —**sub·or′di·nat·ed, sub·or′di·nat·ing —sub·or′di·na′tion** ***n.***

**subordinate clause** a clause that cannot stand alone as a complete sentence [In "They will visit us if they can," the words "if they can" form a *subordinate clause.*]



**sub·poe·na** (sə pē′nə) ***n.*** an official paper ordering a person to appear in a court of law. ◆***v.*** to order with such a paper. —**sub·poe′naed, sub·poe′na·ing** *Also spelled* **sub·pe′na.**

**sub·scribe** (səb skrīb′) ***v.*** **1** to agree to take and pay for [We *subscribed* to the magazine for a year.] **2** to promise to give [She *subscribed* $100 to the campaign for a new museum.] **3** to agree with or approve of [I *subscribe* to the principles in the Constitution.] **4** to sign one's name as to a petition. —**sub·scribed′, sub·scrib′ing —sub·scrib′er** ***n.***

**sub·script** (sub′skript) ***n.*** a figure or letter written below and to the side of another, as the 2 in $H_2O$.

**sub·scrip·tion** (səb skrip′shən) ***n.*** **1** the act of subscribing or something that is subscribed. **2** an agreement to take and pay for a magazine, theater tickets, etc. for a particular period of time.

**sub·se·quent** (sub′si kwənt) ***adj.*** coming after; later; following [The candidate lost the election but won a *subsequent* one.] —**sub′se·quent·ly** ***adv.***

**sub·ser·vi·ent** (səb sʉr′vē ənt) ***adj.*** very obedient and eager to please; too polite; slavish [He is annoyed by *subservient* waiters.] —**sub·ser′vi·ence** ***n.***

**sub·set** (sub′set) ***n.*** in mathematics, a set whose elements are all contained in a given set [If all the elements of set Y are contained in set M, then Y is a *subset* of M.]

**sub·side** (səb sīd′) ***v.*** **1** to sink to a lower level; go down [In June the river began to *subside.*] **2** to become quiet or less active [The angry waves *subsided.* The teacher's temper *subsided.*] —**sub·sid′ed, sub·sid′ing**

**sub·sid·i·ar·y** (səb sid′ē er′ē) ***adj.*** **1** helping or useful, especially in a lesser way. **2** of less importance; secondary. ◆***n.*** **1** a person or thing that helps or gives aid. **2** a company that is controlled by another company [The bus company's *subsidiary* operates the lunchrooms in the stations.] —*pl.* **sub·sid′i·ar′ies**

**sub·si·dize** (sub′sə dīz) ***v.*** to help by means of a subsidy [Some college students are *subsidized* by government funds.] —**sub′si·dized, sub′si·diz·ing**

**sub·si·dy** (sub′sə dē) ***n.*** a grant or gift of money, as one made by a government to a private company [The airlines get a *subsidy* because they carry mail.] —*pl.* **sub′si·dies**

**sub·sist** (səb sist′) ***v.*** **1** to live or exist [The lost children *subsisted* on berries.] **2** to go on or continue to be [Our school cannot *subsist* without taxes.]

**sub·sist·ence** (səb sis′təns) ***n.*** **1** the act or fact of living or staying alive; existence. **2** a way to stay alive and support oneself; especially, no more means than enough to stay alive [The job paid only enough for our *subsistence.*]

**sub·soil** (sub′soil) ***n.*** the layer of soil just beneath the surface layer of the earth.

**sub·stance** (sub′stəns) ***n.*** **1** the material of which something is made; physical matter [a plastic *substance* much like leather]. **2** the real or important part [The movie is not changed in *substance* from the novel.] **3** the main point or central meaning, as of a speech. **4** wealth or property [a family of *substance*].

**sub·stand·ard** (sub stan′dərd) ***adj.*** below some standard or rule set by law or custom [a *substandard* dwelling].

**sub·stan·tial** (səb stan′shəl) ***adj.*** **1** of or having substance; material; real or true [Your fears turned out not to be *substantial.*] **2** strong; solid; firm [The bridge didn't look very *substantial.*] **3** more than average or usual; large [a *substantial* share; a *substantial* meal]. **4** wealthy or well-to-do [a *substantial* farmer]. **5** with regard to the main or basic parts [We are in *substantial* agreement.] —**sub·stan′tial·ly** ***adv.***

**sub·stan·ti·ate** (səb stan′shē āt) ***v.*** to prove to be true or real [The experiments *substantiated* my theory.] —**sub·stan′ti·at·ed, sub·stan′ti·at·ing**

**sub·stan·tive** (sub′stən tiv) ***n.*** a noun, or any word or words used as a noun in a sentence. ◆***adj.*** **1** of or used as a substantive. **2** substantial or large. —**sub′stan·tive·ly** ***adv.***

**sub·sta·tion** (sub′stā′shən) ***n.*** a branch station, as of a post office.

**sub·sti·tute** (sub′stə to͞ot *or* sub′stə tyo͞ot) ***n.*** a person or thing that takes the place of another [He is a *substitute* for the regular teacher.] ◆***v.*** to use as or be a substitute [to *substitute* vinegar for lemon juice; to *substitute* for an injured player]. —**sub′sti·tut·ed, sub′sti·tut·ing —sub′sti·tu′tion** ***n.***

**sub·stra·tum** (sub′strāt′əm *or* sub′strat′əm) ***n.*** a layer, part, etc. that supports another above it [This land rests on a *substratum* of solid rock.] —*pl.* **sub·stra·ta** (sub′strāt′ə *or* sub′strat′ə) or **sub′stra′tums**

☆**sub·teen** (sub′tēn′) ***n.*** a child nearly a teen-ager.

**sub·ter·fuge** (sub′tər fyo͞oj) ***n.*** any plan or action used to hide one's true purpose, get out of something unpleasant, etc.

**sub·ter·ra·ne·an** (sub′tə rā′nē ən) ***adj.*** underground [a *subterranean* river].

**sub·tle** (sut′'l) ***adj.*** **1** having or showing a keenness about small differences in meaning, etc. [a *subtle* thinker; *subtle* reasoning]. **2** hard to see or understand [a *subtle* problem]. **3** not open or direct; sly, clever, crafty, etc. [a *subtle* hint; *subtle* criticism]. **4** having or showing delicate skill [a *subtle* design in lace]. **5** not sharp or strong; delicate [a *subtle* shade of red; a *subtle* perfume]. —**sub′tly** ***adv.***

> **Subtle** comes from a Latin word meaning "closely woven," used to describe delicate fabrics. *Subtle* first meant "delicate" but later came to mean "made with skill." Something subtle then is "finely woven" or "delicate and skillful."

**sub·tle·ty** (sut′'l tē) ***n.*** **1** the quality of being subtle, or being able to see or tell small differences, as in meaning. **2** a subtle thing, as a slight difference or a clever hint. —*pl.* **sub′tle·ties**

**sub·tract** (səb trakt′) ***v.*** to take away, as a part from a whole or one number from another [If 3 is *subtracted* from 5, the remainder is 2.]

**sub·trac·tion** (səb trak′shən) ***n.*** the act of subtracting one part, number, etc. from another.

**sub·tra·hend** (sub′trə hend) ***n.*** a number to be subtracted from another number [In the problem 5 – 3 = 2, the *subtrahend* is 3.]

**sub·trop·i·cal** (sub träp′i k'l) ***adj.*** near the tropics; nearly tropical in climate, features, etc. [Southern Florida has a *subtropical* climate.]

**sub·urb** (sub′ərb) ***n.*** a district, town, etc. on the outskirts of a city.

> The word for city in ancient Rome was *urbs*. The *sub-* in **suburb** means "near," so the word itself means literally "near the city."

**sub·ur·ban** (sə bur′bən) ***adj.*** **1** of or living in a suburb. **2** typical of suburbs or of those who live in them [a *suburban* style of living].

**sub·ur·ban·ite** (sə bur′bən īt) ***n.*** a person who lives in a suburb.

**sub·ver·sive** (səb vur′siv) ***adj.*** tending or trying to overthrow an existing government, law, custom, belief, etc. ◆***n.*** a subversive person.

**sub·vert** (səb vurt′) ***v.*** **1** to overthrow something established. **2** to make weaker or corrupt, as in morals. —**sub·ver·sion** (səb vur′zhən) ***n.***

**sub·way** (sub′wā) ***n.*** ☆**1** an underground electric railway in some large cities. **2** any underground way or passage.

**suc·ceed** (sək sēd′) ***v.*** **1** to manage to do or be what was planned; do or go well [I *succeeded* in convincing them to come with us.] **2** to come next after; follow [Carter *succeeded* Ford as President.]

**suc·cess** (sək ses′) ***n.*** **1** the result that was hoped for; satisfactory outcome [Did you have *success* in training your dog?] **2** the fact of becoming rich, famous, etc. [Her *success* did not change her.] **3** a successful person or thing [Our play was a *success*.]

**suc·cess·ful** (sək ses′fəl) ***adj.*** **1** having success; turning out well [a *successful* meeting]. **2** having become rich, famous, etc. [a *successful* architect]. —**suc·cess′ful·ly** ***adv.***

**suc·ces·sion** (sək sesh′ən) ***n.*** **1** a number of persons or things coming one after another [a *succession* of sunny, warm days]. *See* SYNONYMS *at* **series**. **2** the act of coming after another [the *succession* of a new king to the throne]. **3** the right to succeed to an office, rank, etc. **4** the order in which persons succeed to an office [If the President dies, the first in *succession* to that office is the Vice President.] —**in succession**, one after another.

**suc·ces·sive** (sək ses′iv) ***adj.*** coming in regular order without a break; consecutive [I won six *successive* games.] —**suc·ces′sive·ly** ***adv.***

**suc·ces·sor** (sək ses′ər) ***n.*** a person who succeeds another to an office, rank, etc.

**suc·cinct** (sək siŋkt′) ***adj.*** said clearly in just a few words; concise [The speaker gave a *succinct* explanation.] —**suc·cinct′ly** ***adv.***

**suc·cor** (suk′ər) ***v.*** to give badly needed help to; aid. ◆***n.*** help; relief. *The British spelling is* **succour**.

☆**suc·co·tash** (suk′ə tash) ***n.*** lima beans and kernels of corn cooked together.

> **Succotash** is an example of how New England settlers would borrow Indian words and then shorten them. This one comes from an Indian word, *misickquatash*, meaning "ear of corn."

**suc·cu·lent** (suk′yoo lənt) ***adj.*** full of juice; juicy [a *succulent* peach]. —**suc′cu·lence** ***n.***

**suc·cumb** (sə kum′) ***v.*** **1** to give in; yield [We *succumbed* to curiosity and opened the door.] **2** to die.

**such** (such) ***adj.*** **1** of this or that kind; like those mentioned or meant [*Such* rugs are expensive. It was on just *such* a night that I left.] **2** so much, so great, etc. [We had *such* fun that nobody left.] **3** not named; some [at *such* time as you see fit]. ◆***pron.*** **1** such a person or thing [All *such* as are hungry may eat here.] **2** that which has been mentioned or suggested [*Such* is the price of fame.] —**as such**, **1** as being what is mentioned or meant [She is the editor and *as such* will decide.] **2** in itself [A name, *as such,* means nothing.] —**such as**, **1** for example [She speaks several Romance languages, *such as* Spanish and Italian.] **2** like; similar to [I enjoy poets *such as* Poe.]

> An article is never used before the adjective **such**, but "a" or "an" may be used between the adjective and the noun it modifies [That is *such a* beautiful song.]

**suck** (suk) ***v.*** **1** to draw into the mouth by pulling with the lips, etc. [to *suck* the juice from an orange]. **2** to draw in as if by sucking; absorb, inhale, etc. [to *suck* air into one's lungs]. **3** to suck liquid from [to *suck* a lemon]. **4** to hold in the mouth and lick with the tongue [to *suck* a candy]. ◆***n.*** the act of sucking.

**suck·er** (suk′ər) ***n.*** **1** a person or thing that sucks. **2** a fish like a carp with large, soft lips. **3** a part or organ on a leech, octopus, etc. used for sucking or holding tight to something. *See the picture on page 745.* **4** a shoot growing from the roots or lower stem of a plant. ☆**5** a piece of hard candy on the end of a small stick; lollipop. ☆**6** a person easily fooled or cheated: *a slang meaning.*



| | | | | | | | |
|---|---|---|---|---|---|---|---|
| **a** | fat | **ir** | here | **ou** | out | **zh** | leisure |
| **ā** | ape | **ī** | bite, fire | **u** | up | **ŋ** | ring |
| **ä** | car, lot | **ō** | go | **ur** | fur | | a *in* ago |
| **e** | ten | **ô** | law, horn | **ch** | chin | | e *in* agent |
| **er** | care | **oi** | oil | **sh** | she | **ə** = | i *in* unity |
| **ē** | even | **oo** | look | **th** | thin | | o *in* collect |
| **i** | hit | **ōō** | tool | ***th*** | then | | u *in* focus |

**suck·le** (suk′'l) ***v.*** **1** to give milk to from a breast; nurse [to *suckle* a baby]. **2** to suck milk from its mother. —**suck′led, suck′ling**

**suck·ling** (suk′liŋ) ***n.*** a baby or young animal that is still suckling.

**su·crose** (so͞o′krōs) ***n.*** a sugar found in sugar cane, sugar beets, etc.

**suc·tion** (suk′shən) ***n.*** **1** the act of drawing air out of a space to make a vacuum that will suck in air or liquid surrounding it. **2** the act of sucking. ◆***adj.*** that works or is worked by means of suction [a *suction* pump].

**Su·dan** (so͞o dan′) a country in northeastern Africa. —**Su·da·nese** (so͞o də nēz′) ***adj., n.***

**sud·den** (sud′'n) ***adj.*** **1** happening or appearing without warning; not expected [A *sudden* storm came up.] **2** done or taking place quickly; hasty [He made a *sudden* change in his plans.] —**all of a sudden,** without warning; quickly. —**sud′den·ly** ***adv.*** —**sud′-den·ness** ***n.***

**suds** (sudz) ***n.pl.*** soapy water or the foam on its surface. —☆**suds′y** ***adj.***

**sue** (so͞o *or* syo͞o) ***v.*** **1** to begin a lawsuit in court against [to *sue* a person for damages caused by carelessness]. **2** to make an appeal; ask in a formal way [The weary enemy *sued* for peace.] —**sued, su′ing**

**suede** (swād) ***n.*** **1** tanned leather with the flesh side rubbed until it is soft like velvet. **2** cloth that looks



like this: *also called* **suede cloth.**

> **Suede** comes from the French word for Sweden, used in the phrase *gants de Suede,* meaning "gloves of Sweden." It is thought that gloves of this leather were first made in Sweden.

**su·et** (so͞o′it *or* syo͞o′it) ***n.*** hard fat from around the kidneys and loins of cattle and sheep. It is used in cooking and to feed birds in winter.

**Su·ez** (so͞o ez′ *or* so͞o′ez) **1** a seaport in Egypt on the Suez Canal. **2** a strip of land in Egypt (**Isthmus of Suez**) connecting Asia and Africa.

**Suez Canal** a ship canal of Egypt joining the Mediterranean and Red seas. *See the map.*

**suf·fer** (suf′ər) ***v.*** **1** to feel or have pain, discomfort, etc. [to *suffer* from a headache]. **2** to experience or undergo [The team *suffered* a loss when Sal was hurt.] **3** to become worse or go from good to bad [Her grades *suffered* when she didn't study.] **4** to put up with; bear [He won't *suffer* criticism.]

**suf·fer·ance** (suf′ər əns *or* suf′rəns) ***n.*** consent given by not stopping or forbidding something. —**on sufferance,** allowed but not really supported.

**suf·fer·ing** (suf′ər iŋ *or* suf′riŋ) ***n.*** pain, sorrow, loss, etc. [War causes great *suffering*.]

**suf·fice** (sə fīs′) ***v.*** to be enough [One cake should *suffice* for all of us.] —**suf·ficed′, suf·fic′ing**

**suf·fi·cien·cy** (sə fish′ən sē) ***n.*** an amount that is enough [We have a *sufficiency* of funds.]

**suf·fi·cient** (sə fish′ənt) ***adj.*** as much as is needed; enough [Do you have *sufficient* supplies to last through the week?] —**suf·fi′cient·ly** ***adv.***

**suf·fix** (suf′iks) ***n.*** a syllable or group of syllables, joined to the end of a word to change its meaning. Some common suffixes are *-ness, -ed, -ly, -ory,* and *-able.* ◆***v.*** (sə fiks′) to add at the end.

**suf·fo·cate** (suf′ə kāt) ***v.*** **1** to kill by cutting off the supply of oxygen; smother. **2** to die from this cause. **3** to keep from breathing freely. **4** to have trouble breathing. —**suf′fo·cat·ed, suf′fo·cat·ing** —**suf′fo·ca′tion** ***n.***

**suf·frage** (suf′rij) ***n.*** ☆**1** the right to vote in political elections. **2** a vote or the act of voting.

**suf·fra·gist** (suf′rə jist) ***n.*** a person, especially a woman, who worked for women's right to vote.

**suf·fuse** (sə fyo͞oz′) ***v.*** to spread over [The evening sky was *suffused* with a rosy glow.] —**suf·fused′, suf·fus′ing** —**suf·fu·sion** ***n.***

**sug·ar** (shoog′ər) ***n.*** any of certain sweet substances in the form of crystals that dissolve in water. Glucose, lactose, and sucrose are different kinds of sugar. Sucrose is the common sugar used to sweeten food. ◆***v.*** **1** to sweeten or sprinkle with sugar [*sugared* cookies]. **2** to make seem pleasant or less bad [*sugared* criticism]. **3** to form crystals of sugar [The grape jelly *sugared.*]

**sugar beet** a beet with a white root from which common sugar is got.

**sugar cane** a tall grass grown in hot countries. Most of our common sugar comes from sugar cane. *See the picture.*

**sug·ar·coat** (shoog′ər kōt) ***v.*** **1** to cover or coat with sugar, as pills. **2** to make seem more pleasant [She *sugarcoated* the bad news.]

**sug·ar·plum** (shoog′ər plum) ***n.*** a round or oval piece of candy.

**sug·ar·y** (shoog′ər ē) ***adj.*** **1** of, like, or full of sugar; very sweet. **2** flattering in a sweet, but often false, way [*sugary* words].

**sug·gest** (səg jest′) ***v.*** **1** to mention as something to think over, act on, etc. [I *suggest* we meet again.] **2** to bring to mind as something similar or in some way connected [The white dunes *suggested* snow-covered hills. Clouds *suggest* rain.]

**sug·ges·tion** (səg jes′chən) ***n.*** **1** the act of suggesting [It was done at your *suggestion*.] **2** something suggested. **3** a faint hint; trace [A *suggestion* of a smile crossed his face.]

**sug·ges·tive** (səg jes′tiv) ***adj.*** suggesting or likely to suggest thoughts or ideas, sometimes of an indecent kind. —**sug·ges′tive·ly** ***adv.***

**su·i·cide** (so͞o′ə sīd) ***n.*** **1** the act of killing oneself on purpose. **2** harm or ruin brought about by one's own actions [It would be political *suicide* for the governor to ask for a higher sales tax.] **3** a person who commits suicide. —**su′i·ci′dal** ***adj.***

**suit** (so͞ot) ***n.*** **1** a set of clothes to be worn together, especially a coat with trousers or a skirt of the same material, and sometimes a vest. **2** any of the four sets of playing cards in a deck; clubs, diamonds, hearts, or spades. **3** *a shorter form of* **lawsuit. 4** the act of suing, pleading, or wooing. ◆***v.*** **1** to meet the needs of; be right for [This color *suits* your complexion.] **2** to make fit; adapt [a dance *suited* to the music]. —**follow suit, 1** to play a card of the same suit as the card led. **2** to follow the example set [She chose the peach pie and the others *followed suit.*] —**suit oneself,** to do as one pleases.

**suit·a·ble** (so͞ot′ə b'l) ***adj.*** right for the purpose; fitting; proper [a *suitable* gift]. *See* SYNONYMS *at* **fit.** —**suit′a·bil′i·ty** ***n.*** —**suit′a·bly** ***adv.***

**suit·case** (so͞ot′kās) ***n.*** a case for carrying clothes, etc. when traveling, shaped like a long, narrow box.

**suite** (swēt) ***n.*** **1** a group of connected rooms used together [a hotel *suite*]. **2** (*sometimes* so͞ot) a set of matched furniture for a room [a bedroom *suite*]. **3** a piece of music made up of several movements, or, in earlier times, dances. **4** a group of attendants or servants.

**suit·or** (so͞ot′ər) ***n.*** **1** a man who is courting a woman. **2** a person who is suing, appealing, etc.

☆**su·ki·ya·ki** (so͞o′kē yä′kē) ***n.*** a Japanese dish made of thinly sliced meat and vegetables cooked quickly, often at the table.

**Suk·kot** or **Suk·koth** (so͝o kōt′ *or* so͝ok′ōs) ***n.*** a Jewish thanksgiving festival in early fall.

**sul·fa** (sul′fə) ***adj.*** naming or of a group of drugs made from coal tar and used in treating certain infections.

**sul·fate** (sul′fāt) ***n.*** a salt of sulfuric acid.

**sul·fide** (sul′fīd) ***n.*** a chemical compound of sulfur and another element or elements.

**sul·fur** (sul′fər) ***n.*** a pale-yellow solid substance that is a chemical element. It burns with a blue flame, giving off choking fumes, and is used in making gunpowder, in medicine, etc.

**sul·fu·ric** (sul fyo͝or′ik) ***adj.*** of or containing sulfur.

**sulfuric acid** an oily, colorless, very strong acid formed of hydrogen, sulfur, and oxygen.

**sul·fu·rous** (sul′fər əs) ***adj.*** **1** (*usually* sul fyo͝or′əs) of or containing sulfur. **2** like sulfur in color, smell, etc. **3** like the flames of hell; fiery.

**sulk** (sulk) ***v.*** to be sulky. ◆***n.*** *often* **sulks,** *pl.* a sulky mood.

**sulk·y** (sul′kē) ***adj.*** sullen in a pouting or peevish way. —**sulk′i·er, sulk′i·est** ◆***n.*** a light, two-wheeled carriage for one person, now used especially in racing. *See the picture.* —*pl.* **sulk′ies**

A person who is **sulky** often turns away and is aloof from others. It is thought that the carriage which seats only one person is called a **sulky** because the rider is alone and aloof.

**sul·len** (sul′ən) ***adj.*** **1** silent and keeping to oneself because one feels angry, bitter, hurt, etc. **2** gloomy or dismal [a *sullen* day]. —**sul′len·ly** ***adv.*** —**sul′len·ness** ***n.***

**sul·ly** (sul′ē) ***v.*** to soil or damage; besmirch [to *sully* one's honor]. —**sul′lied, sul′ly·ing**

**sul·phur** (sul′fər) ***n.*** *another spelling of* **sulfur.**

**sul·tan** (sul′t′n) ***n.*** a ruler of a Muslim country, especially in earlier times.

**sul·tan·a** (sul tan′ə *or* sul tä′nə) ***n.*** the wife, mother, sister, or daughter of a sultan.

**sul·tan·ate** (sul′t′n it) ***n.*** the territory, power, reign, etc. of a sultan.

**sul·try** (sul′trē) ***adj.*** hot and damp, without a breeze; sweltering [a *sultry* summer day]. —**sul′tri·er, sul′tri·est** —**sul′tri·ness** ***n.***

**sum** (sum) ***n.*** **1** the result got by adding together two or more numbers or quantities; total. **2** a problem in arithmetic: *an old-fashioned meaning* [The pupils did their *sums*.] **3** an amount of money [We paid the *sum* they asked for.] **4** the whole amount [the *sum* of one's experiences]. ◆***v.*** to add up and get the sum of. —**summed, sum′ming** —**sum up,** to tell the main points of in a few words.

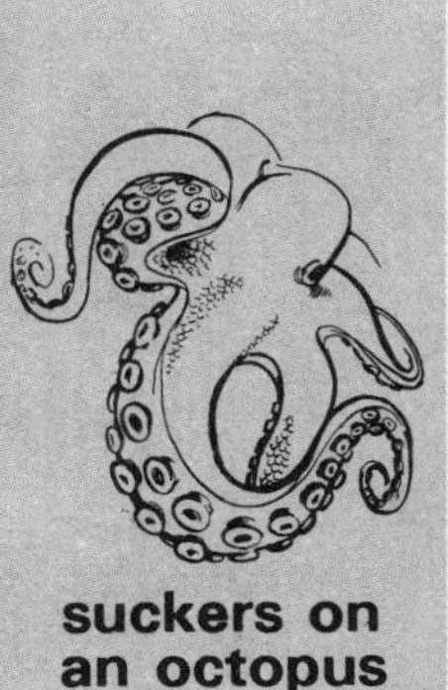
suckers on an octopus

sugar cane

sulky

sumac leaves and berries

**su·mac** or **su·mach** (sho͞o′mak *or* so͞o′mak) ***n.*** a bush with long, narrow leaves that turn red in the fall and clusters of hairy, red berries. *See the picture.*



**Su·ma·tra** (so͝o mä′trə) a large island of Indonesia, south of the Malay Peninsula.

**sum·ma·rize** (sum′ə rīz) ***v.*** to make a summary of; tell in a few words [Let me *summarize* the plot of the movie.] —**sum′ma·rized, sum′ma·riz·ing**

**sum·ma·ry** (sum′ə rē) ***n.*** a brief report that tells the main points in a few words; digest. —*pl.* **sum′ma·ries** ◆***adj.*** **1** done quickly without attention to forms or details [*summary* justice]. **2** brief; concise [a *summary* report]. —**sum·mar·i·ly** (sə mer′ə lē) ***adv.***

**sum·mer** (sum′ər) ***n.*** the warmest season of the year, following spring. ◆***adj.*** of summer [a *summer* day]. ◆***v.*** to spend the summer [We often *summer* in New Hampshire.]

**sum·mer·time** (sum′ər tīm) ***n.*** the season of summer.

**sum·mit** (sum′it) ***n.*** the highest point; top [the *summit* of a hill; the *summit* of one's career]. *See* SYNONYMS *at* **climax.** ◆***adj.*** ☆of the heads of government [They held a *summit* meeting.]

**sum·mon** (sum′ən) ***v.*** **1** to call together; call or send for [The President *summoned* the Cabinet.] **2** to call forth; rouse; gather [*Summon* up your strength.] **3** to order to appear in a court of law.

**sum·mons** (sum′ənz) ***n.*** **1** a call or order to come or attend. **2** an official order to appear in a law court [A traffic ticket is a *summons*.] —*pl.* **sum′mons·es**

| | | | | | | | | |
|---|---|---|---|---|---|---|---|---|
| **a** | fat | **ir** | here | **ou** | out | **zh** | leisure | |
| **ā** | ape | **ī** | bite, fire | **u** | up | **ng** | ring | |
| **ä** | car, lot | **ō** | go | **ur** | fur | | a *in* ago | |
| **e** | ten | **ô** | law, horn | **ch** | chin | | e *in* agent | |
| **er** | care | **oi** | oil | **sh** | she | **ə =** | i *in* unity | |
| **ē** | even | **oo** | look | **th** | thin | | o *in* collect | |
| **i** | hit | **o͞o** | tool | ***th*** | then | | u *in* focus | |

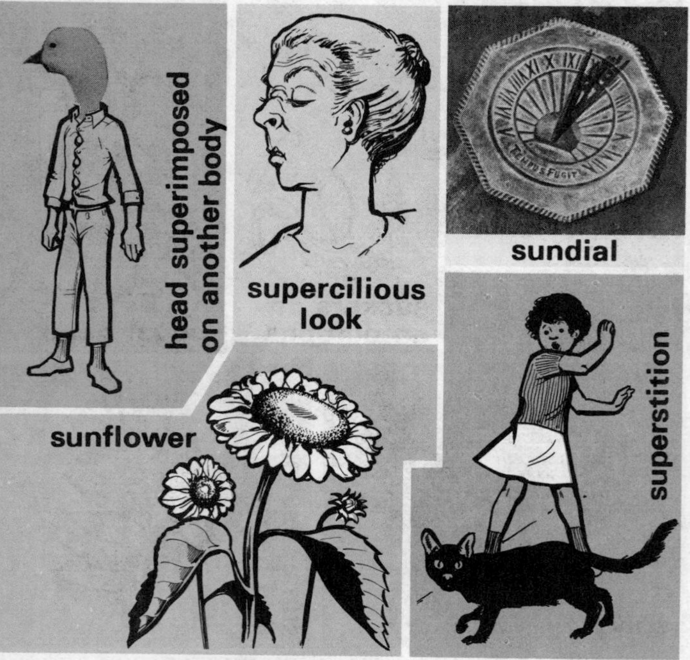


**sump·tu·ous** (sump′choo wəs) ***adj.*** costing a great deal; costly; lavish [a *sumptuous* feast].



**sun** (sun) ***n.*** **1** the very hot, bright star around which the earth and the other planets revolve. Our light, heat, and energy come from the sun. The sun is about 150,000,000 kilometers (or 93,000,000 miles) from the earth. It has a diameter of about 1,391,000 kilometers (or 864,000 miles). **2** the heat or light of the sun [The *sun* is in my eyes.] **3** any heavenly body that is the center of a system of planets. ***•v.*** to warm, dry, tan, etc. in the sunlight [We *sunned* ourselves on the roof.] **—sunned, sun′ning**

**Sun.** *abbreviation for* **Sunday.**

**sun·bathe** (sun′bāth) ***v.*** to expose one's body to sunlight or to light from a sunlamp. **—sun′bathed, sun′bath·ing**

**sun·beam** (sun′bēm) ***n.*** a beam of sunlight.

**sun·bon·net** (sun′bän′it) ***n.*** an old-fashioned bonnet with a large brim in front and a flap at the back for shading the face and neck from the sun.

**sun·burn** (sun′burn) ***n.*** a condition in which the skin is red and sore from being in the sun or under a sunlamp too long. ***•v.*** to give or get a sunburn. **—sun′burned** or **sun′burnt, sun′burn·ing**

☆**sun·dae** (sun′dē) ***n.*** a serving of ice cream covered with syrup, fruit, nuts, etc.

> **Sundae** is just another way of spelling **Sunday.** There is a story that some small American towns in the 1890s had laws that would not allow ice-cream sodas to be sold on Sunday, and so some ice-cream parlor created the **sundae** to get around the law.

**Sun·day** (sun′dē) ***n.*** the first day of the week. Most Christian churches observe Sunday as a day of rest and worship.

**Sunday school** a school held on Sunday for teaching religion.

**sun·der** (sun′dər) ***v.*** to break apart; separate; split [The ship *sundered* on the rock.] **—in sunder,** into pieces or parts; apart.

**sun·di·al** (sun′dī′əl) ***n.*** an instrument that shows time by the position of a shadow cast by a pointer across a dial marked in hours. *See the picture.*

**sun·down** (sun′doun) ***n.*** *another word for* **sunset.**

**sun·dries** (sun′drēz) ***n.pl.*** various articles; miscellaneous items [That store sells drugs and *sundries.*]

**sun·dry** (sun′drē) ***adj.*** various; of different kinds [He asked *sundry* questions.]

**sun·fish** (sun′fish) ***n.*** ☆**1** a small fresh water fish of North America. **2** a large ocean fish with a short, thick body and long fins: *also* **ocean sunfish.**

**sun·flow·er** (sun′flou′ər) ***n.*** a tall plant with large, yellow flowers that look like daisies. An oil is got from the seeds, which can also be eaten. *See the picture.*

**sung** (sung) *past participle and a past tense of* **sing.**

**sun·glass·es** (sun′glas′əz) ***n.pl.*** eyeglasses with dark or tinted lenses to shade the eyes.

**sunk** (sungk) *past participle and a past tense of* **sink.**

**sunk·en** (sungk′ən) ***adj.*** **1** sunk in water or other liquid [a *sunken* boat]. **2** below the level of the surface around it [a *sunken* patio; a *sunken* room]. **3** in or forming a hollow [*sunken* eyes].

☆**sun·lamp** (sun′lamp) ***n.*** an electric lamp that gives off ultraviolet rays like those of sunlight.

**sun·less** (sun′lis) ***adj.*** without sun or sunlight; dark [Monday was a *sunless* day.]

**sun·light** (sun′līt) ***n.*** the light of the sun.

**sun·lit** (sun′lit) ***adj.*** lighted by the sun.

**sun·ny** (sun′ē) ***adj.*** **1** bright with sunlight [Today is a *sunny* day.] **2** like or from the sun [A *sunny* beam shone through.] **3** cheerful; bright [Lynn has a *sunny* smile.] **—sun′ni·er, sun′ni·est**

**sun·rise** (sun′rīz) ***n.*** **1** the daily rising of the sun in the eastern sky. **2** the time when this happens. **3** the color of the sky at this time.

**sun·set** (sun′set) ***n.*** **1** the daily setting of the sun in the western sky. **2** the time when this happens. **3** the color of the sky at this time.

**sun·shine** (sun′shīn) ***n.*** **1** the shining of the sun. **2** the light and heat from the sun. **3** cheerfulness, happiness, etc. **—sun′shin·y *adj.***

**sun·spot** (sun′spät) ***n.*** any of the dark spots sometimes seen on the sun. They are thought to have some connection with the earth's weather.

**sun·stroke** (sun′strōk) ***n.*** an illness caused by being out in the hot sun too long.

**sun·up** (sun′up) ***n.*** *another word for* **sunrise.**

**Sun Yat-sen** (soon′ yät′sen′) 1866–1925; Chinese political leader.

**sup**[1] (sup) ***v., n.*** *same as* **sip. —supped, sup′ping**

**sup**[2] (sup) ***v.*** to eat the evening meal; have supper. **—supped, sup′ping**

**su·per** (sōō′pər) ***n.*** **1** a superintendent of an apartment building. **2** *a shorter form of* **supernumerary.** ***•adj.*** excellent; outstanding: *used only in everyday talk.*

**su·per-** (sōō′pər) *a prefix meaning:* **1** over or above; on top of [A *superstructure* is a structure built on top of another.] **2** very or very much; more than normal [A *supersensitive* person is one who is more sensitive than a normal person.] **3** greater than others of its kind [A *supermarket* is bigger than other markets.] **4** extra [A *supernumerary* is an extra person.]

**su·per·a·bun·dant** (so͞o′pər ə bun′dənt) ***adj.*** much more than is usual or needed [to give someone *superabundant* praise]. —**su′per·a·bun′dance** ***n.***

**su·per·an·nu·at·ed** (su′pər an′yoo wāt′id) ***adj.*** **1** retired from work on a pension. **2** too old for work or use.

**su·perb** (soo purb′) ***adj.*** **1** grand, majestic, splendid, etc. *See* SYNONYMS *at* **splendid. 2** of the finest kind; excellent [a *superb* meal]. —**su·perb′ly** ***adv.***

**su·per·car·go** (so͞o′pər kär′gō) ***n.*** an officer on a ship who has charge of the cargo and business matters connected with it. *—pl.* **su′per·car′goes** or **su′per·car′gos**

**su·per·charge** (so͞o′pər chärj) ***v.*** to increase the power of a gasoline engine by forcing more air into the cylinder with a device called a **su′per·charg·er.** —**su′per·charged, su′per·charg·ing**

**su·per·cil·i·ous** (so͞o′pər sil′ē əs) ***adj.*** proud and scornful; looking down on others; haughty [She gave him a *supercilious* look.] *See the picture.*

> **Supercilious** comes from *supercilium,* the Latin word for eyebrow, and that word was formed from *super-,* meaning "above," and *cilium,* meaning "eyelid." When people look haughty or scornful, they often raise an eyebrow.

**su·per·fi·cial** (so͞o′pər fish′əl) ***adj.*** **1** of or on the surface; not deep [a *superficial* cut; a *superficial* likeness]. **2** with little attention, understanding, feeling, etc.; shallow, hasty, etc. [a *superficial* mind; a *superficial* reading of a book]. —**su·per·fi·ci·al·i·ty** (so͞o′pər fish′ē al′ə tē) ***n.*** —**su′per·fi′cial·ly** ***adv.***

**su·per·fine** (so͞o pər fīn′) ***adj.*** **1** made up of very fine, or tiny, particles or grains [*superfine* sugar]. **2** too fine, subtle, delicate, etc. [a *superfine* distinction].

**su·per·flu·i·ty** (so͞o′pər flo͞o′ə tē) ***n.*** **1** an amount that is more than is needed; excess. **2** something not needed. *—pl.* **su′per·flu′i·ties**

**su·per·flu·ous** (soo pur′floo wəs) ***adj.*** more than is needed; unnecessary [*superfluous* motions; a *superfluous* remark]. —**su·per′flu·ous·ly** ***adv.***

☆**su·per·high·way** (so͞o′pər hī′wā) ***n.*** *another name for* **expressway.**

**su·per·hu·man** (so͞o′pər hyo͞o′mən) ***adj.*** **1** thought of as having a nature above that of human beings; divine [Angels are *superhuman* beings.] **2** greater than that of a normal person [He had *superhuman* strength.]

**su·per·im·pose** (so͞o′pər im pōz′) ***v.*** to put over or above something else. *See the picture.* —**su′per·im·posed′, su′per·im·pos′ing**

**su·per·in·tend** (so͞o′pər in tend′) ***v.*** to direct or manage; supervise. —**su′per·in·tend′ence** ***n.***

**su·per·in·tend·ent** (so͞o′pər in ten′dənt) ***n.*** **1** a person in charge of an institution, school system, etc. **2** the manager of a building; custodian.

**su·pe·ri·or** (sə pir′ē ər) ***adj.*** **1** higher in rank, position, etc. [Soldiers salute their *superior* officers.] **2** above average in quality, value, skill, etc.; excellent [a *superior* grade of cotton]. **3** placed higher up. **4** showing a feeling of being better than others; haughty. —**superior to,** better or greater than [This cloth is *superior to* the other.] ◆***n.*** **1** a person of higher rank, greater skill, etc. **2** the head of a monastery or convent. —**su·pe·ri·or·i·ty** (sə pir′ē ôr′ə tē) ***n.***

**Superior, Lake** the largest of the Great Lakes. It is the one farthest west.

> **Lake Superior** was named by the French settlers of the region because of its location above, or north of, Lake Huron. The meaning of *superior* in this case is "higher than."

**su·per·la·tive** (sə pur′lə tiv) ***adj.*** **1** of the highest sort; supreme [She is a *superlative* cellist.] **2** being the form of adjectives and adverbs that shows the greatest degree in meaning ["Best" is the *superlative* degree of "good."] ◆***n.*** **1** the highest degree; height. **2** the superlative degree ["Softest" and "most elegant" are the *superlatives* of "soft" and "elegant."] —**su·per′la·tive·ly** ***adv.***

**su·per·man** (so͞o′pər man) ***n.*** a man who seems to have greater powers than those of a normal human being. *—pl.* **su′per·men**

☆**su·per·mar·ket** (so͞o′pər mär′kit) ***n.*** a large food store in which shoppers serve themselves from open shelves and pay at the exit.

**su·per·nat·u·ral** (so͞o′pər nach′ər əl) ***adj.*** outside or beyond the known laws of nature [A ghost is a *supernatural* being.] —**the supernatural,** supernatural beings, forces, etc. —**su′per·nat′u·ral·ly** ***adv.***

**su·per·nu·mer·ar·y** (so͞o′pər no͞o′mə rer′ē) ***adj.*** more than is usual or needed; extra. ◆***n.*** an extra person or thing, as an actor with no lines to speak, usually part of a crowd. *—pl.* **su′per·nu′mer·ar′ies**

**su·per·pow·er** (so͞o′pər pou′ər) ***n.*** any one of the few very powerful countries in the world that are rivals for influence over smaller countries.

**su·per·script** (so͞o′pər skript) ***n.*** a figure or letter written above, as the 3 in $x^3$.

**su·per·sede** (so͞o pər sēd′) ***v.*** to take the place of; replace or succeed [The car *superseded* the horse and buggy. Ms. Gomez *superseded* Mr. Dickens as principal.] —**su·per·sed′ed, su·per·sed′ing**

**su·per·son·ic** (so͞o′pər sän′ik) ***adj.*** **1** of or moving at a speed greater than the speed of sound. *See the entry for* **sound**[1]. **2** *another word for* **ultrasonic.**

☆**su·per·star** (so͞o′pər stär) ***n.*** a very well-known athlete or entertainer who is more talented than most.

**su·per·sti·tion** (so͞o′pər stish′ən) ***n.*** a belief or practice that comes from fear and ignorance and that is against the known laws of science [It is a *superstition* that a black cat walking across someone's path brings bad luck.] *See the picture.*

**su·per·sti·tious** (so͞o′pər stish′əs) ***adj.*** of, caused by, or believing in superstitions. —**su′per·sti′tious·ly** ***adv.***

**su·per·struc·ture** (so͞o′pər struk′chər) ***n.*** **1** a structure built on top of another. **2** that part of a building above the foundation. **3** that part of a ship above the main deck.

**su·per·vene** (so͞o pər vēn′) ***v.*** to happen as something

| | | | | | | | |
|---|---|---|---|---|---|---|---|
| **a** | fat | **ir** | here | **ou** | out | **zh** | leisure |
| **ā** | ape | **ī** | bite, fire | **u** | up | **ng** | ring |
| **ä** | car, lot | **ō** | go | **ur** | fur | | a *in* ago |
| **e** | ten | **ô** | law, horn | **ch** | chin | | e *in* agent |
| **er** | care | **oi** | oil | **sh** | she | ə = | i *in* unity |
| **ē** | even | **oo** | look | **th** | thin | | o *in* collect |
| **i** | hit | **o͞o** | tool | ***th*** | then | | u *in* focus |

added or not expected [We were all set to leave, but the storm *supervened* and delayed us.] —**su·per·vened′, su·per·ven′ing**

**su·per·vise** (so͞o′pər vīz) ***v.*** to direct or manage, as a group of workers; be in charge of. —**su′per·vised, su′per·vis·ing**

**su·per·vi·sion** (so͞o′pər vizh′ən) ***n.*** direction or management; the act of supervising.

**su·per·vi·sor** (so͞o′pər vī′zər) ***n.*** a person who supervises; director. —**su′per·vi′so·ry *adj.***

**su·pine** (so͞o pīn′) ***adj.*** **1** lying on the back, with the face up. **2** not active; lazy; listless. —**su·pine′ly *adv.***

**sup·per** (sup′ər) ***n.*** **1** the last meal of the day, eaten in the evening. **2** a party at which such a meal is served [a church *supper*].

**sup·plant** (sə plant′) ***v.*** to take the place of, especially through force or plotting [Mary of Scotland schemed to *supplant* Elizabeth I.]

**sup·ple** (sup′'l) ***adj.*** **1** bending easily; not stiff; flexible [*supple* leather; a *supple* body]. **2** that can change easily to suit new conditions [a *supple* mind].

**sup·ple·ment** (sup′lə mənt) ***n.*** **1** something added, as to make up for something missing [Vitamin pills are a *supplement* to a poor diet.] **2** a section added to a book or newspaper, to give extra or more up-to-date information, special articles, etc. ◆***v.*** (sup′lə ment) to be or give a supplement to; add to. —**sup′ple·men′tal *adj.***

 **sup·ple·men·ta·ry** (sup′lə men′tər ē) ***adj.*** **1** supplying what is missing; extra; additional [a *supplementary* income]. **2** describing two angles that add up to exactly 180°. *See the picture.*

**sup·pli·ant** (sup′lē ənt) ***n.*** a person who begs for something in a humble way, as in praying. ◆***adj.*** asking in a humble way; beseeching; imploring [He gave her a *suppliant* look.]

**sup·pli·cant** (sup′lə kənt) ***adj.*** supplicating; suppliant. ◆***n.*** one who supplicates; suppliant.

**sup·pli·cate** (sup′lə kāt) ***v.*** to ask or beg someone in a humble way to do something; implore. —**sup′pli·cat·ed, sup′pli·cat·ing** —**sup′pli·ca′tion *n.***

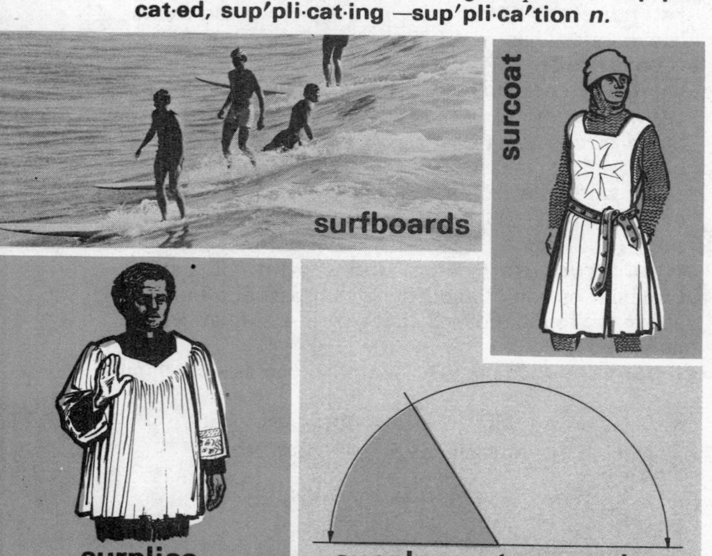

surfboards

surcoat

surplice

supplementary angles

**Supplicate** comes from a Latin word that means "to kneel down in order to pray." That word was a combination of two parts, *sub-*, meaning "under," and *plicare,* meaning "to fold, or double up." One doubles up the knees in order to kneel.

**sup·ply** (sə plī′) ***v.*** **1** to give what is needed; furnish [The camp *supplies* sheets and towels. The book *supplied* us with the facts.] **2** to take care of the needs of [to *supply* workers with tools]. **3** to make up for; fill [These pills *supply* a deficiency of iron.] —**sup·plied′, sup·ply′ing** ◆***n.*** **1** the amount at hand; store; stock [I have a small *supply* of money but a large *supply* of books.] **2 supplies,** *pl.* things needed; materials; provisions [school *supplies*]. —*pl.* **sup·plies′**

**sup·port** (sə pôrt′) ***v.*** **1** to carry the weight or burden of; hold up [Will that old ladder *support* you?] **2** to take the side of; uphold or help [She worked to *support* our cause.] **3** to earn a living for; provide for [He *supports* a large family.] **4** to help prove [Use examples to *support* your argument.] **5** to act in a minor part in a play. ◆***n.*** **1** a supporting or being supported [This wall needs *support*.] **2** a person or thing that supports. —**sup·port′er *n.***

SYNONYMS: **Support** suggests taking the side of a person or cause either by actually helping or just by giving approval [She *supported* the candidate for mayor.] **Uphold** suggests that what is being supported is under attack [I will *uphold* your right to speak at the meeting.]

**sup·pose** (sə pōz′) ***v.*** **1** to take to be true for the sake of argument; assume [Let's *suppose* that the rumor is true.] **2** to believe or guess; think [I *suppose* you're right.] **3** to expect [It's *supposed* to snow today.] **4** to consider as a possibility [*Suppose* she says "no."] —**sup·posed′, sup·pos′ing**

**sup·posed** (sə pōzd′) ***adj.*** thought of as true or possible, without really being known [their *supposed* wealth]. —**sup·pos·ed·ly** (sə pōz′id lē) ***adv.***

**sup·po·si·tion** (sup′ə zish′ən) ***n.*** **1** the act of supposing. **2** something supposed; theory.

**sup·press** (sə pres′) ***v.*** **1** to put down by force or power; crush [The ship's captain acted quickly to *suppress* the mutiny.] **2** to keep back; hide; conceal [to *suppress* a laugh; to *suppress* the truth; to *suppress* a news story]. —**sup·pres·sion** (sə presh′ən) ***n.***

**sup·pu·rate** (sup′yoo rāt′) ***v.*** to become filled with pus, as a wound. —**sup′pu·rat′ed, sup′pu·rat′ing** —**sup′pu·ra′tion *n.***

**su·prem·a·cy** (sə prem′ə sē) ***n.*** supreme power or rank.

**su·preme** (sə prēm′) ***adj.*** highest in power, rank, quality, or degree; greatest, strongest, etc. [The President is *supreme* commander of the armed forces. They succeeded by a *supreme* effort.] —**su·preme′ly *adv.***

**Supreme Being** *another name for* **God.**

**Supreme Court** ☆**1** the highest court in the U.S., made up of a chief justice and eight associate justices. ☆**2** the highest court in most States.

**Supt.** or **supt.** *abbreviation for* **Superintendent.**

**sur·charge** (sur′chärj) ***n.*** **1** an extra charge, as for some special service. **2** an overcharge or overload. **3** a new value printed over the face of a postage stamp. ◆***v.*** (sur chärj′) to put a surcharge on or in something. —**sur·charged′, sur·charg′ing**

**sur·cin·gle** (sʉr′siŋg′g'l) ***n.*** a strap around a horse's body to hold on a saddle, pack, etc.

**sur·coat** (sʉr′kōt) ***n.*** an outer coat; especially, a short cloak worn over a knight's armor. *See the picture.*

**sure** (shoor) ***adj.*** **1** that will not fail; safe, certain, reliable, etc. [a *sure* cure; a *sure* friend]. **2** firm or steady [Be careful to have a *sure* footing on the ladder.] **3** without doubt; certain; positive [I'm *sure* they did it.] **4** that cannot be avoided; bound to happen [The army moved on to *sure* defeat.] **5** bound to do, be, etc. [We are *sure* to win the fight.] —**sur′er, sur′est** ◆***adv.*** surely; certainly: *used only in everyday talk* [*Sure,* I'll go.] —**for sure** or **to be sure,** surely; certainly. —**make sure,** to be or cause to be certain. —**sure′ness *n.***

**sure-foot·ed** (shoor′foot′id) ***adj.*** not likely to stumble, slip, or fall.

**sure·ly** (shoor′lē) ***adv.*** **1** in a sure way; firmly. **2** certainly; without doubt [*Surely* you won't leave!]

☆**sure thing** **1** something certain to win, succeed, etc. **2** all right! O.K.! *This phrase is used only in everyday talk.*

**sur·e·ty** (shoor′ə tē *or* shoor′tē) ***n.*** **1** sureness or certainty. **2** something that makes sure; security, as for a loan. **3** a person who agrees to pay the debts of another, if the other fails to pay them.

**surf** (sʉrf) ***n.*** the waves of the sea breaking on a shore or reef, or the foam of such waves. ◆***v.*** to take part in the sport of surfing. —**surf′er *n.***

**sur·face** (sʉr′fis) ***n.*** **1** the outside or outer face of a thing [the *surface* of the earth]. **2** any side of a thing having several sides [the *surfaces* of a box]. **3** outward look or features [She was all smiles on the *surface* but angry within.] ◆***adj.*** of, on, or at the surface [the *surface* temperature of the lake]. ◆***v.*** **1** to give a surface to, as in paving. **2** to rise to the surface of water, as a submarine. **3** to become known, especially after being hidden. —**sur′faced, sur′fac·ing**

**surf·board** (sʉrf′bôrd) ***n.*** a long, narrow board used in the sport of surfing. *See the picture.*

**sur·feit** (sʉr′fit) ***n.*** **1** too much, especially of food, drink, etc. **2** sickness or disgust from eating or drinking too much. ◆***v.*** to make feel sick or disgusted by giving too much of something to [He was *surfeited* with idle pleasures.]

**surf·ing** (sʉr′fiŋ) ***n.*** the sport of riding in toward shore on the top of a wave, especially on a surfboard.

**surge** (sʉrj) ***n.*** **1** a large wave of water, or its violent rushing motion. **2** any sudden, strong rush [a new *surge* of energy; the *surge* of immigrants to America]. ◆***v.*** to move in a surge [The crowd *surged* over the football field.] —**surged, surg′ing**

**sur·geon** (sʉr′jən) ***n.*** a doctor who specializes in surgery.

**sur·ger·y** (sʉr′jər ē) ***n.*** **1** the treating of disease or injury by operations with the hands or tools, as in setting broken bones, cutting out tonsils, etc. **2** an operation of this kind. **3** the room in a hospital where doctors do such operations. —*pl.* **sur′ger·ies**

> **Surgery** comes from a Greek word meaning "a working with the hands." The doctor who does surgery must be skillful in using the hands to treat patients.

**sur·gi·cal** (sʉr′ji k'l) ***adj.*** of, in, or for surgery [*surgical* experience; *surgical* gauze].

**Su·ri·nam** (soor′i näm′) a country in northeast South America.

**sur·ly** (sʉr′lē) ***adj.*** having or showing a bad temper; rude and unfriendly [The *surly* child ignored our greeting.] —**sur′li·er, sur′li·est** —**sur′li·ness *n.***

> Sometimes people in a high position are rude and haughty to people of lower social rank. The word **surly** was spelled *sirly* in the early days because it described the way a "sir," or master, often acted toward the servants or serfs under his control.

**sur·mise** (sər mīz′) ***n.*** an idea or opinion that is only a guess, based on a few facts [My *surmise* is that they were delayed by the storm.] ◆***v.*** to form such an idea; guess. —**sur·mised′, sur·mis′ing**

**sur·mount** (sər mount′) ***v.*** **1** to get the better of; overcome; defeat [to *surmount* a difficulty]. **2** to climb up and across [to *surmount* an obstacle]. **3** to lie at the top of [A crown *surmounted* his head.]

**sur·name** (sʉr′nām) ***n.*** **1** the family name, or last name [Adams was the *surname* of two of our presidents.] **2** a special name added to a person's name, often to describe that person [The czar Ivan IV of Russia had the *surname* "the Terrible."] ◆***v.*** to give a surname to. —**sur′named, sur′nam·ing**

**sur·pass** (sər pas′) ***v.*** **1** to be better or greater than; excel [The winner *surpassed* the other contestants.] **2** to go beyond the limit of [riches *surpassing* belief].

**sur·plice** (sʉr′plis) ***n.*** a loose, white gown with wide sleeves, worn over other garments by the clergy or members of a church choir. *See the picture.*



> **Surplice** is formed from the Latin words *super,* for "over," and *pelliceum,* for "fur robe." The surplices in the old days were full-length and were worn over fur robes, needed in the unheated churches of the Middle Ages as protection against the cold.

**sur·plus** (sʉr′plus) ***n.*** an amount more than what is needed; that which is left over; excess [The farmers store a grain *surplus* in silos.] ◆***adj.*** that is a surplus; excess [*surplus* profits; *surplus* material left over from making drapes].

**sur·prise** (sər prīz′) ***v.*** **1** to cause to feel wonder by being unexpected [Her sudden anger *surprised* us.] **2** to come upon suddenly or unexpectedly [I *surprised* him in the act of stealing the watch.] **3** to attack or capture suddenly. —**sur·prised′, sur·pris′ing** ◆***n.*** **1** the act of surprising [The news took them by *surprise.*] **2** the condition of being surprised; amazement [Much to our *surprise,* it began to snow.] **3** something that causes wonder because it is not expected [Your answer was quite a *surprise.*] —**take by surprise, 1** to come upon suddenly. **2** to cause to feel wonder or astonishment.

**sur·pris·ing** (sər prīz′iŋ) ***adj.*** causing surprise; strange. —**sur·pris′ing·ly *adv.***

| | | | | | | | |
|---|---|---|---|---|---|---|---|
| **a** | fat | **ir** | here | **ou** | out | **zh** | leisure |
| **ā** | ape | **ī** | bite, fire | **u** | up | **ŋ** | ring |
| **ä** | car, lot | **ō** | go | **ʉr** | fur | | a *in* ago |
| **e** | ten | **ô** | law, horn | **ch** | chin | | e *in* agent |
| **er** | care | **oi** | oil | **sh** | she | **ə** = | i *in* unity |
| **ē** | even | **oo** | look | **th** | thin | | o *in* collect |
| **i** | hit | **ōō** | tool | ***th*** | then | | u *in* focus |

S

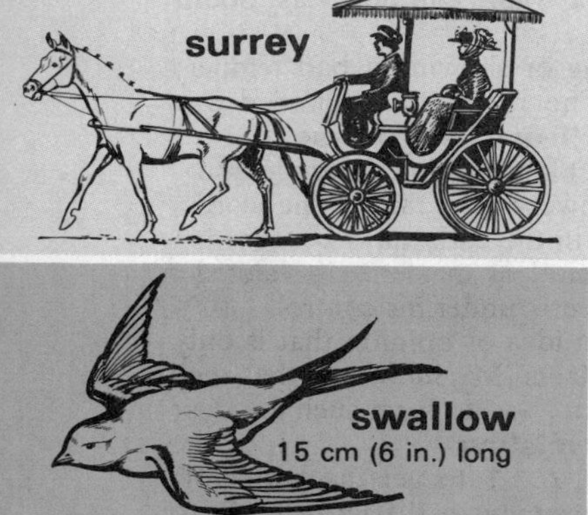

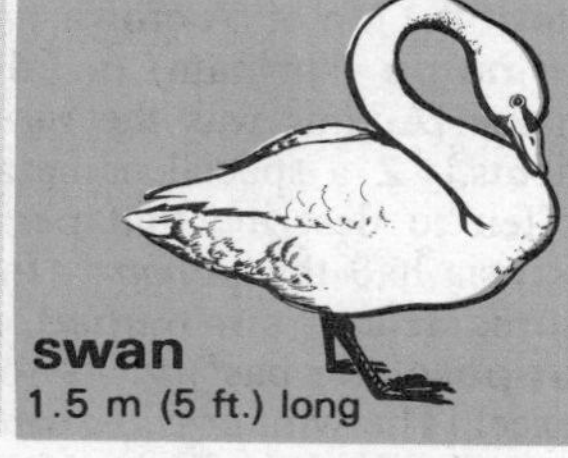




**sur·ren·der** (sə ren′dər) ***v.*** **1** to give oneself up, especially as a prisoner; yield [The troops *surrendered.*] **2** to give up; let go of; abandon [We *surrendered* hope that our dog would come back. The army *surrendered* the town to the enemy.] **3** to give in to [I *surrendered* to temptation.] ◆***n.*** the act of surrendering.

**sur·rep·ti·tious** (sʉr′əp tish′əs) ***adj.*** done in a quiet or secret way; stealthy [He gave the pretty girl a *surreptitious* wink.] —**sur′rep·ti′tious·ly *adv.***

**sur·rey** (sʉr′ē) ***n.*** ☆a light carriage with two seats and a flat top. *See the picture.* —*pl.* **sur′reys**

**sur·ro·gate** (sʉr′ə gāt) ***n.*** **1** a substitute or deputy for another person. ☆**2** a judge of a probate court in some States.

**sur·round** (sə round′) ***v.*** to form or arrange around on all or nearly all sides; enclose [The police *surrounded* the criminals. The house is *surrounded* with trees.]

**sur·round·ings** (sə roun′diŋz) ***n.pl.*** the things or conditions around a place or person; environment [They work in fine *surroundings*.]

**sur·tax** (sʉr′taks) ***n.*** an extra tax on something that is already taxed.

**sur·veil·lance** (sər vā′ləns) ***n.*** close watch kept over someone [We kept the enemy under *surveillance*.]

**sur·vey** (sər vā′) ***v.*** **1** to look over in a careful way; examine; inspect [The lookout *surveyed* the horizon.] **2** to measure the size, shape, boundaries, etc. of a piece of land by the use of special instruments [to *survey* a farm]. ◆***n.*** (sʉr′vā) **1** a general study covering the main facts or points [The *survey* shows that we need more schools. This book is a *survey* of American poetry.] **2** the act of surveying a piece of land, or a record of this [He was hired to make a *survey* of the lake shore.] —*pl.* **sur′veys**

**sur·vey·ing** (sər vā′iŋ) ***n.*** the act, work, or science of one who surveys land.

**sur·vey·or** (sər vā′ər) ***n.*** a person whose work is surveying land.

**sur·viv·al** (sər vī′v'l) ***n.*** **1** the act or fact of surviving, or continuing to exist [Nuclear war threatens the *survival* of all nations.] **2** something surviving from an earlier time, as a custom.

**sur·vive** (sər vīv′) ***v.*** **1** to continue to live or exist [Thanksgiving is a Pilgrim custom that *survives* today.] **2** to live or last longer than; outlive [Most people *survive* their parents.] *See* SYNONYMS *at* **outlive.** **3** to continue to live or exist in spite of [We *survived* the fire.] —**sur·vived′, sur·viv′ing**

**sus·cep·ti·ble** (sə sep′tə b'l) ***adj.*** having feelings that are easily affected; very sensitive [Sad stories make a *susceptible* child cry.] —**susceptible of,** that gives a chance for or allows [That answer is *susceptible of* being understood in two different ways.] —**susceptible to,** easily affected by; open to [*susceptible to* flattery; *susceptible to* colds]. —**sus·cep′ti·bil′i·ty *n.***

**sus·pect** (sə spekt′) ***v.*** **1** to think of as probably guilty, although there is little proof [The detective *suspected* the butler of the murder.] **2** to have no trust in; doubt; distrust [I *suspect* her honesty.] **3** to guess or suppose [I *suspect* that they really don't want to come.] ◆***n.*** (sus′pekt) a person suspected of wrongdoing [The stranger was a *suspect* in the robbery.] ◆***adj.*** (sus′pekt) that should be thought of with suspicion [Your excuse remains *suspect*.]

**sus·pend** (sə spend′) ***v.*** **1** to hang by a support from above [The keys were *suspended* by a chain from his belt.] **2** to hold in place as though hanging [In homogenized milk, the fat particles are *suspended* in the milk.] **3** to keep out for a while as a punishment [She was *suspended* from school for misbehaving.] **4** to stop from operating for a time [to *suspend* bus service; to *suspend* a rule]. **5** to hold back or put off [The judge *suspended* her sentence.]

**sus·pend·ers** (sə spen′dərz) ***n.pl.*** a pair of bands passed over the shoulders to hold up trousers.

**sus·pense** (sə spens′) ***n.*** **1** the condition of being anxious and uncertain [We waited in *suspense* for the jury's verdict.] **2** the growing excitement felt as a story, play, etc. builds to a high point or climax [a movie full of *suspense*].

**sus·pen·sion** (sə spen′shən) ***n.*** **1** the act of suspending or condition of being suspended [the *suspension* of a policeman from the force; the *suspension* of dust in the air]. **2** the springs, etc. that hold up the body of a car.

**suspension bridge** a bridge held up by large cables that run between a series of towers. *See the picture.*

**sus·pi·cion** (sə spish′ən) ***n.*** **1** the act of suspecting guilt, a wrong, etc. with little or no proof [Everyone here is above *suspicion*.] **2** the feeling or idea of one who suspects [I have a *suspicion* you are right.] **3** a very small amount; trace; bit [a salad with just a *suspicion* of garlic].

**sus·pi·cious** (sə spish′əs) ***adj.*** **1** causing or likely to cause suspicion [*suspicious* behavior]. **2** feeling or showing suspicion [She gave the stranger a *suspicious* look.] —**sus·pi′cious·ly *adv.***

**Sus·que·han·na** (sus′kwi han′ə) a river flowing through New York, Pennsylvania, and Maryland into Chesapeake Bay.

**sus·tain** (sə stān′) ***v.*** **1** to hold up or support [Heavy piers *sustain* the bridge.] **2** to keep up; maintain [The soft music *sustained* the mood.] **3** to give courage or strength to [Hope of rescue *sustained* the shipwrecked sailors.] **4** to undergo; suffer [I *sustained* injuries in the accident.] **5** to uphold as true, right, etc. [The Supreme Court *sustained* the verdict.]

**sus·te·nance** (sus′ti nəns) ***n.*** that which sustains life; food or nourishment.

**sut·ler** (sut′lər) ***n.*** a person who followed an army to sell things to its soldiers.

**su·ture** (so͞o′chər) ***n.*** **1** the stitching together of the edges of a wound. **2** any of the stitches of gut or thread used for this. **3** the line where two parts, as the bones of the skull, grow together. ◆***v.*** to join together as with sutures. —**su′tured, su′tur·ing**

**Su·wan·nee** (sə wôn′ē) a river that flows across the northern part of Florida into the Gulf of Mexico. *See word story in color at* **Swanee.**

**su·ze·rain** (so͞o′zə rin) ***n.*** **1** a feudal lord in the Middle Ages. **2** a country having political control over another country.

**su·ze·rain·ty** (so͞o′zə rin tē) ***n.*** the position or power of a suzerain. —*pl.* **su′ze·rain·ties**

**SW, S.W., s.w.** *abbreviations for* **southwest** *or* **southwestern.**

**swab** (swäb) ***n.*** **1** a small piece of cotton, etc., often fixed to a small stick, used to clean a wound, the ears, etc. It is also used to put medicine on wounds. **2** a mop used with water to clean decks, floors, etc. ◆***v.*** to put medicine on, or clean, with a swab. —**swabbed, swab′bing**

**swad·dle** (swäd′′l) ***v.*** to wrap in long, narrow bands of cloth, bandages, etc. Newborn babies were once wrapped in such bands, called **swaddling clothes.** —**swad′dled, swad′dling**

**swag** (swag) ***n.*** stolen money or goods; loot; plunder: *a slang word.*

**swag·ger** (swag′ər) ***v.*** **1** to walk in a showy, strutting way. **2** to boast, brag, or show off. ◆***n.*** a swaggering walk or manner.

**Swa·hi·li** (swä hē′lē) ***n.*** a Bantu language widely used in eastern and central Africa.

**S.W.A.K.** sealed with a kiss: an abbreviation written on the flap of an envelope holding a letter from a sweetheart or a child. *Also written* **SWAK** *or* **swak.**

**swal·low**[1] (swäl′ō) ***n.*** a small, swift-flying bird with long, pointed wings and a forked tail. *See the picture.*

**swal·low**[2] (swäl′ō) ***v.*** **1** to let food, drink, etc. go through the throat into the stomach. **2** to move the muscles of the throat as in swallowing something [I *swallowed* hard to keep from crying.] **3** to take in; engulf [The waters of the lake *swallowed* him up.] **4** to put up with; bear with patience [We refused to *swallow* their insults.] **5** to keep from showing; hold back [to *swallow* one's pride]. **6** to take back, as one's own words. **7** to believe without questioning: *used only in everyday talk* [Surely you won't *swallow* that story.] ◆***n.*** **1** the act of swallowing. **2** the amount swallowed at one time.

**swal·low·tail** (swäl′ō tāl′) ***n.*** a large butterfly with long points on the lower wings.

**swallow-tailed coat** a man's formal suit coat with two long tails at the back. *See the picture.*

**swam** (swam) *past tense of* **swim.**

**swa·mi** (swä′mē) ***n.*** **1** a Hindu title of respect for a Hindu religious leader. The word means "master." **2** a very wise man.

**swamp** (swämp) ***n.*** a piece of wet, spongy land; marsh; bog: *also called* ☆**swamp′land.** ◆***v.*** **1** to plunge in a swamp, in deep water, etc. **2** to flood as with water [The street was *swamped* in the flood.] **3** to fill, or sink by filling, with water [High waves *swamped* the boat.] **4** to overwhelm [The poor family was *swamped* with debts.] —**swamp′y** ***adj.***

**swan** (swän) ***n.*** a large water bird with webbed feet, a long, graceful neck, and, usually, white feathers. *See the picture.*

☆**swan dive** a forward dive in which the legs are held straight and together, the back is arched, and the arms are stretched out to the sides. The arms are brought forward and together just before the diver enters the water.

**Swa·nee** (swô′nē) *another spelling of* **Suwannee.**

> Stephen Foster's song "Old Folks at Home" has as its first line "Way down upon the **Swanee** River." The spelling now used for the name of this river is *Suwannee,* thought to be either from an Indian word that means "echo river" or from the Spanish *San Juan,* for "St. John."

**swank** (swangk) or **swank·y** (swang′kē) ***adj.*** stylish in a showy way: *used only in everyday talk* [a *swank* or *swanky* hotel]. —**swank′i·er, swank′i·est**

> **Swank** was originally a slang word that meant "limber" or "bending easily." It was used to describe the way a stylish person might swing the body when walking.



**swan's-down** or **swans·down** (swänz′doun′) ***n.*** **1** the soft, fine feathers, or down, of the swan, used for trimming clothes. **2** a soft, thick fabric of cotton, wool, etc., used for making baby clothes.

**swan song** **1** the song supposed in old stories to be sung by a dying swan. **2** the final piece of work of an artist, writer, etc.

**swap** (swäp) ***n., v.*** exchange, barter, or trade: *used only in everyday talk.* —**swapped, swap′ping**

> **Swap** comes from an old English word meaning "to strike or hit." It probably suggests the sound of hitting. Today's meaning of **swap** is connected to the ancient custom of clapping hands together to complete a bargain.

**sward** (swôrd) ***n.*** grassy ground; turf.

**swarm** (swôrm) ***n.*** **1** a large number of bees, led by a queen, leaving a hive to start a new colony. **2** a colony of bees in a hive. **3** any large, moving mass or crowd [a *swarm* of flies; a *swarm* of visitors]. ◆***v.*** **1** to fly off in a swarm, as bees do. **2** to move, gather, etc. in large numbers [Shoppers *swarmed* into the store.] **3** to be filled with a crowd [The beach is *swarming* with people.]

| | | | | | | | |
|---|---|---|---|---|---|---|---|
| **a** | fat | **ir** | here | **ou** | out | **zh** | leisure |
| **ā** | ape | **ī** | bite, fire | **u** | up | **ng** | ring |
| **ä** | car, lot | **ō** | go | **ur** | fur | | a *in* ago |
| **e** | ten | **ô** | law, horn | **ch** | chin | | e *in* agent |
| **er** | care | **oi** | oil | **sh** | she | ə = | i *in* unity |
| **ē** | even | **oo** | look | **th** | thin | | o *in* collect |
| **i** | hit | **o͞o** | tool | ***th*** | then | | u *in* focus |

**swarth·y** (swôr′*thē*) ***adj.*** having a dark skin. —**swarth′i·er, swarth′i·est**

**swash** (swäsh) ***v.*** to strike, dash, etc. with a splashing sound; splash [The waves *swashed* against the pier.] ◆***n.*** a splashing of water.

**swash·buck·ler** (swäsh′buk′lər) ***n.*** a fighting man who brags and swaggers. —**swash′buck′ling *n., adj.***

**swas·ti·ka** (swäs′ti kə) ***n.*** an ancient design that was used as a magic symbol in various parts of the world. One form was used as the symbol of the Nazis in Germany.

**swat** (swät) ***v.*** to hit or strike with a quick, sharp blow. —**swat′ted, swat′ting** ◆***n.*** a quick, sharp blow. —**swat′ter *n.***

**swatch** (swäch) ***n.*** a small piece of cloth or other material used as a sample.

**swath** (swäth) ***n.*** **1** the space or width covered by one cut of a scythe, etc. **2** the strip or band of grass, wheat, etc. cut in a single trip across a field by a mower, etc.

**swathe** (swā*th*) ***v.*** **1** to wrap around with a cloth or bandage [My head was *swathed* in a turban for the costume party.] **2** to surround or cover completely [a city *swathed* in fog]. —**swathed, swath′ing**

**sway** (swā) ***v.*** **1** to swing or bend back and forth or from side to side [The flowers *swayed* in the breeze.] *See* SYNONYMS *at* **swing. 2** to lean or go to one side; veer [The car *swayed* to the right on the curve.] **3** to

752 change the thinking or actions of; influence [We will not be *swayed* by their promises.] ◆***n.*** **1** a swinging, leaning, etc. **2** influence or control [under the *sway* of emotion].

**sway·backed** (swā′bakt) ***adj.*** having a spine that sags more than is normal. *See the picture.*

**Swa·zi·land** (swä′zē land′) a country in southeastern Africa.

**swear** (swer) ***v.*** **1** to make a serious statement, supporting it with an appeal to God or to something held sacred [She *swore* on her honor that it was true.] **2** to say or promise in a serious way or with great feeling; vow [She *swore* that she would always love him.] **3** to use bad or profane language; curse. *See* SYNONYMS *at* **blasphemy. 4** to make take an oath, as when putting into office [The President was *sworn* in by the Chief Justice. The bailiff *swore* in the witness.] —**swore, sworn, swear′ing —swear by, 1** to name something sacred in taking an oath. **2** to have great faith in [The cook *swears by* this recipe.] —**swear off,** to promise to give up [to *swear off* smoking]. —☆**swear out,** to get by making a charge under oath [I *swore out* a warrant for his arrest.] —**swear′er *n.***

☆**swear·word** (swer′wurd) ***n.*** a word or phrase used in swearing or cursing.

**sweat** (swet) ***v.*** **1** to give out a salty liquid through the pores of the skin; perspire [Running fast made me *sweat.*] **2** to form little drops of water on its surface [A glass full of iced tea will *sweat* in a warm room.] **3** to work so hard as to cause sweating [I was *sweating* over an examination.] **4** to make work long hours at low wages under bad conditions. **5** to be very worried, nervous, etc.: *used only in everyday talk* [We were *sweating* until the money arrived.] —**sweat** or **sweat′ed, sweat′ing** ◆***n.*** **1** the salty liquid given out through the pores of the skin. **2** the little drops of water that form on a cold surface. **3** the act or condition of sweating [The long run left me in a *sweat.*] **4** a condition of eagerness, great worry, etc. [I was in a *sweat* over car payments that were due.] —☆**sweat out, 1** to suffer through something [to *sweat out* a bad storm]. **2** to wait in an anxious way for. *This phrase is slang.*

**sweat·er** (swet′ər) ***n.*** a knitted outer garment for the upper part of the body.

☆**sweat shirt** a heavy cotton shirt like a T-shirt with long sleeves, worn to soak up sweat. It is sometimes worn with loose trousers (**sweat pants**) of the same material, forming a combination (**sweat suit**). *See the picture.*

☆**sweat·shop** (swet′shäp) ***n.*** a shop or factory where workers are forced to work long hours at low wages under bad conditions.

**sweat·y** (swet′ē) ***adj.*** **1** wet with sweat; sweating. **2** of sweat [a *sweaty* odor]. **3** causing sweat [*sweaty* work]. —**sweat′i·er, sweat′i·est**

**Swed.** or **Sw.** *abbreviations for* **Sweden** *or* **Swedish.**

**Swede** (swēd) ***n.*** a person born or living in Sweden.

**Swe·den** (swē′d′n) a country in northern Europe, east of Norway.

**Swed·ish** (swē′dish) ***adj.*** of Sweden or the Swedes. ◆***n.*** the language of the Swedes.

**sweep** (swēp) ***v.*** **1** to clean as by brushing with a broom [to *sweep* a floor]. **2** to clear away as with a broom [*Sweep* the dirt from the porch.] **3** to carry away or destroy with a quick, strong motion [The tornado *swept* the shed away.] **4** to carry along with a sweeping movement [He *swept* the cards into a pile.] **5** to touch in moving across [Her dress *sweeps* the ground.] **6** to pass swiftly over [His glance *swept* the crowd.] **7** to move in a quick, steady, important way [She *swept* down the aisle to the stage.] **8** to reach in a long curve or line [The road *sweeps* up the hill.] —**swept, sweep′ing** ◆***n.*** **1** the act of sweeping, as with a broom. **2** a steady, sweeping movement [the *sweep* of their oars]. **3** the space covered; range [beyond the *sweep* of their guns]. **4** an unbroken stretch [a *sweep* of flat country]. **5** a line or curve [the graceful *sweep* of the curtains]. **6** a person whose work is sweeping [Chimney *sweeps* clean the soot from chimneys.] *See the picture.* **7** a long oar. **8** a long pole with a bucket on one end, for raising water from a well. —**sweep′er *n.***

**sweep·ing** (swēp′iŋ) ***adj.*** **1** reaching over a wide area [a *sweeping* look]. **2** including a great deal; very broad [The ad made *sweeping* claims.] ◆***n.*** **1** the act or work of a sweeper. **2 sweepings,** *pl.* things swept up, as dirt from the floor.

**sweep·stakes** (swēp′stāks) or **sweep·stake** (swēp′stāk) ***n.*** **1** a lottery in which each person taking part puts money into a fund from which the money for the winners comes. **2** a horse race or other contest which decides the winners of such a lottery.

The money risked in gambling is called the "stakes." A person gambling by taking part in a lottery hopes to win a grand prize and "sweep in" a big share of the stakes. Therefore, a lottery in which there will be a grand winner is often called a **sweepstakes**.

**sweet** (swēt) ***adj.*** **1** having the taste of sugar; having sugar in it [a *sweet* apple]. **2** pleasant in taste, smell, sound, manner, etc. [*sweet* perfume; *sweet* music; a *sweet* child]. **3** not salty [*sweet* butter; *sweet* water]. **4** not spoiled, sour, etc. [*sweet* milk]. ◆***n.*** **1** something sweet, as a candy. **2** a sweet or beloved person; darling. ◆***adv.*** in a sweet manner. —**sweet′ish** ***adj.*** —**sweet′ly** ***adv.*** —**sweet′ness** ***n.***

**sweet·bread** (swēt′bred) ***n.*** the pancreas or thymus of a calf or other animal, used as food.

**sweet·bri·er** or **sweet·bri·ar** (swēt′brī′ər) ***n.*** a rose with sharp thorns and single pink flowers.

☆**sweet corn** a kind of corn with soft, sweet kernels cooked for eating, often on the cob.

**sweet·en** (swēt′'n) ***v.*** to make or become sweet.

**sweet·en·er** (swēt′'n ər) ***n.*** something used to make food sweeter, especially an artificial substance such as saccharin.

**sweet·en·ing** (swēt′'n iŋ) ***n.*** **1** the act of making something sweet. **2** something used to make food sweeter, as sugar or honey.

**sweet·heart** (swēt′härt) ***n.*** **1** a person with whom one is in love. **2** a very nice person or wonderful thing: *slang in this meaning*.

**sweet·meat** (swēt′mēt) ***n.*** a bit of sweet food; especially, a candy, candied fruit, etc.

**sweet pea** a climbing plant with sweet-smelling flowers of many colors.

☆**sweet potato** **1** the sweet, yellow, thick root of a tropical vine, eaten as a vegetable. **2** the vine itself. *See the picture.*

**sweet Wil·liam** or **sweet wil·liam** (wil′yəm) a plant with clusters of small flowers of many colors.

**swell** (swel) ***v.*** **1** to make or become larger, greater, stronger, etc. [buds *swelling* in the early spring; music *swelling* to a grand climax]. *See* SYNONYMS *at* **expand.** **2** to bulge or make bulge; curve out [The wind *swelled* the sails.] **3** to fill or be filled with pride, greed, anger, etc. [My heart *swelled* with joy.] —**swelled, swelled** or **swol′len, swell′ing** ◆***n.*** **1** a part that swells, as a large, rolling wave or a piece of rising ground. **2** a swelling or being swollen [a recent *swell* of orders for new cars]. **3** an increase in size, force, loudness, etc. [the *swell* of the organ]. ◆***adj.*** fine, enjoyable, etc.: *slang in this meaning.*

**swell·ing** (swel′iŋ) ***n.*** **1** an increase in size, force, etc. [a *swelling* of profits]. **2** a swollen part, as on the body [a *swelling* from a bump].

**swel·ter** (swel′tər) ***v.*** to become sweaty, weak, etc. from great heat. ◆***n.*** sweltering condition.

**swel·ter·ing** (swel′tər iŋ) ***adj.*** very hot, damp, sticky, etc.

**swept** (swept) *past tense and past participle of* **sweep.**

**swerve** (swʉrv) ***v.*** to turn aside from a straight line or path [I *swerved* the car to avoid hitting a dog.] —**swerved, swerv′ing** ◆***n.*** a swerving motion.

**swift** (swift) ***adj.*** **1** moving or able to move very fast [a *swift* runner]. **2** coming, happening, or done quickly [a *swift* reply]. **3** acting quickly; prompt [They were *swift* to help us.] ◆***n.*** a brown, swift-flying bird that looks like the swallow. —**swift′ly** ***adv.*** —**swift′ness** ***n.***

**swig** (swig) ***v.*** to drink in large gulps. —**swigged, swig′ging** ◆***n.*** a large gulp of liquid. *This word is used only in everyday talk.*

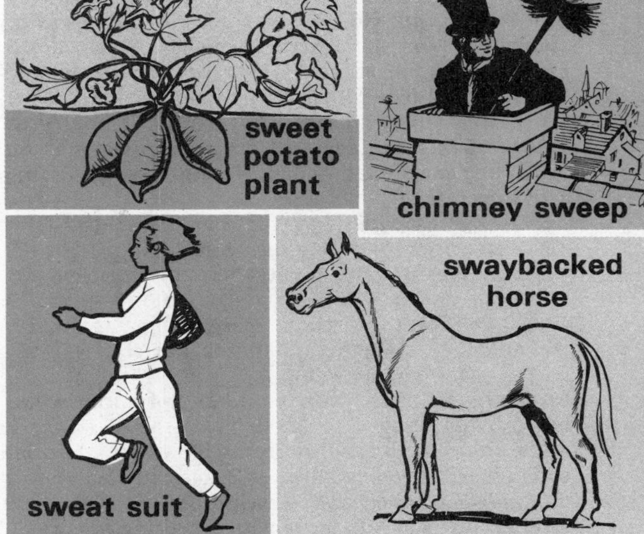


**swill** (swil) ***n.*** garbage, often mixed with liquid and fed to pigs. ◆***v.*** to drink or gulp greedily.

**swim** (swim) ***v.*** **1** to move in water by working the arms, legs, fins, etc. **2** to cross by swimming [to *swim* a river]. **3** to move along smoothly; glide. **4** to float or be dipped in a liquid [food *swimming* in butter]. **5** to overflow [eyes *swimming* with tears]. **6** to be dizzy [The ride made her head *swim.*] **7** to seem to be whirling [The room *swam* before his eyes.] —**swam, swum, swim′ming** ◆***n.*** **1** an act, time, or distance of swimming. **2** a dizzy feeling. —**in the swim,** taking part in what is popular at the moment. —**swim′mer** ***n.***

**swim·ming·ly** (swim′iŋ lē) ***adv.*** easily and with success [Everything went *swimmingly* at the party.]

☆**swimming pool** a pool or tank of water for swimming.

**swin·dle** (swin′d'l) ***v.*** to cheat or trick out of money or property. —**swin′dled, swin′dling** ◆***n.*** an act of swindling; fraud. —**swin′dler** ***n.***

**swine** (swīn) ***n.*** **1** a pig or hog. **2** a mean or disgusting person. —*pl.* **swine**

**swine·herd** (swīn′hʉrd) ***n.*** a person who looks after, or tends, swine.

**swing** (swiŋ) ***v.*** **1** to move or sway back and forth, as something hanging loosely [The pendulum *swings* in the clock.] **2** to walk, trot, etc. with loose, swaying movements [They *swung* down the road.] **3** to turn, as on a hinge or pivot [The door *swung* open. He *swung* the chair around to face the table.] **4** to hang; suspend. **5** to be put to death by hanging: *used only in everyday talk.* **6** to move with a sweeping motion [She *swung* the bat at the ball. I *swung* the bag onto my



| | | | | | | | |
|---|---|---|---|---|---|---|---|
| a | fat | ir | here | ou | out | zh | leisure |
| ā | ape | ī | bite, fire | u | up | ŋ | ring |
| ä | car, lot | ō | go | ʉr | fur | | a *in* ago |
| e | ten | ô | law, horn | ch | chin | | e *in* agent |
| er | care | oi | oil | sh | she | ə = | i *in* unity |
| ē | even | oo | look | th | thin | | o *in* collect |
| i | hit | ōō | tool | *th* | then | | u *in* focus |

back.] ☆**7** to manage to get, do, win, etc.: *used only in everyday talk* [to *swing* an election]. —**swung, swing′ing** ◆*n.* **1** the act of swinging. **2** the curved path of something swinging [the *swing* of a pendulum]. **3** a sweeping blow or stroke [He took a *swing* at my jaw.] **4** a strong, steady rhythm, as of poetry or music. **5** a seat hanging from ropes or chains on which one can sit and swing. —**in full swing,** in full, active operation.

SYNONYMS: **Swing** suggests the to-and-fro movement of something that is hanging so that it is free to turn at the point where it is attached [a *swinging* door]. **Sway** suggests the slow, graceful, back-and-forth movement of something that can bend, often something standing upright [willow trees *swaying* in the wind].

**swin·ish** (swīn′ish) ***adj.*** of, like, or fit for swine; beastly; disgusting.

**swipe** (swīp) ***n.*** a hard, sweeping blow. ◆***v.*** **1** to hit with a hard, sweeping blow. ☆**2** to steal. *This word is used only in everyday talk.* —**swiped, swip′ing**

**swirl** (swurl) ***v.*** **1** to move with a twisting or curving motion; whirl [The snow kept *swirling* down.] **2** to be dizzy [The fever made my head *swirl.*] ◆***n.*** **1** a swirling motion; whirl [a *swirl* of water down the drain]. **2** a twist or curl.

**swish** (swish) ***v.*** **1** to move with a sharp, hissing sound [He *swished* his cane through the air.] **2** to rus-

tle [Her skirts *swished* as she walked.] ◆***n.*** a hissing or rustling sound, or a movement that makes such a sound.

**Swiss** (swis) ***adj.*** of Switzerland or its people. ◆***n.*** a person born or living in Switzerland. —*pl.* **Swiss**

**Swiss cheese** a pale-yellow, hard cheese with many large holes, first made in Switzerland. *See the picture.*

**switch** (swich) ***n.*** **1** a thin twig or stick used for whipping. **2** a sharp stroke, as with a whip. **3** a device used to open, close, or change the path of an electric circuit. **4** a section of railroad track that can be moved to shift a train from one track to another. **5** a change; shift [She had a *switch* in attitude.] ◆***v.*** **1** to whip as with a switch. **2** to jerk or swing sharply [The horse *switched* its tail.] **3** to shift; change [Let's *switch* the party to my house.] ☆**4** to move a train from one track to another by means of a switch. **5** to turn on or off, as a light, radio, etc.

☆**switch-blade knife** (swich′blād′) a large jackknife that snaps open when a button on the handle is pressed.

☆**switch·board** (swich′bôrd) ***n.*** a board that has switches and other devices for controlling or connecting a number of electric circuits [a telephone *switchboard*].

☆**switch-hit·ter** (swich′hit′ər) ***n.*** a baseball player who bats sometimes right-handed and sometimes left-handed.

**Switz.** *abbreviation for* **Switzerland.**

**Switz·er·land** (swit′sər lənd) a country in western Europe, in the Alps.

**swiv·el** (swiv′'l) ***n.*** a fastening that allows any part joined to it to turn freely, or a fastening in two parts, each of which can turn freely. ◆***v.*** to turn as on a swivel [She *swiveled* in her seat.] —**swiv′eled** or **swiv′elled, swiv′el·ing** or **swiv′el·ling**

☆**swivel chair** a chair whose seat turns freely around on a swivel or pivot. *See the picture.*

**swol·len** (swō′lən) *a past participle of* **swell.**

**swoon** (swo͞on) ***n., v.*** *another word for* **faint.**

**swoop** (swo͞op) ***v.*** **1** to sweep down or pounce upon suddenly, as a bird in hunting. **2** to snatch suddenly [He *swooped* up the change.] ◆***n.*** the act of swooping.

**sword** (sôrd) ***n.*** **1** a weapon having a long, sharp blade, with a handle, or hilt, at one end. **2** warfare, or the profession of a soldier ["The pen is mightier than the *sword.*"] —**at swords' points,** ready to quarrel or fight. —**cross swords,** to fight or argue.

**sword·fish** (sôrd′fish) ***n.*** a large ocean fish with an upper jawbone like a long, pointed sword. *See the picture.*

**sword·play** (sôrd′plā) ***n.*** the act or skill of using a sword, as in fighting or in sport.

**swords·man** (sôrdz′mən) ***n.*** **1** a person who uses a sword, as in fencing. **2** a person skilled in using a sword. —*pl.* **swords′men**

**swore** (swôr) *past tense of* **swear.**

**sworn** (swôrn) *past participle of* **swear.** ◆***adj.*** bound as by an oath [*sworn* friends].

**swum** (swum) *past participle of* **swim.**

**swung** (swung) *past tense and past participle of* **swing.**

**syc·a·more** (sik′ə môr) ***n.*** ☆**1** an American shade tree with large leaves and bark that flakes off. **2** a maple tree of Europe and Asia. **3** a kind of fig tree of Egypt and Asia.

**syc·o·phant** (sik′ə fənt) ***n.*** a person who flatters others in order to get things from them.

**Syd·ney** (sid′nē) a seaport in southeastern Australia.

**syl·lab·ic** (si lab′ik) ***adj.*** that is or has to do with a syllable or syllables.

**syl·lab·i·fy** (si lab′ə fī) ***v.*** to divide into syllables. [How is "especially" *syllabified*?] —**syl·lab′i·fied, syl·lab′i·fy·ing** —**syl·lab′i·fi·ca′tion *n.***

**syl·la·ble** (sil′ə b'l) ***n.*** **1** a word or part of a word spoken with a single sounding of the voice ["Moon" is a word of one *syllable.* "Moonlight" is a word of two *syllables.*] **2** any of the parts into which a written word is divided to show where it may be broken at the

Swiss cheese

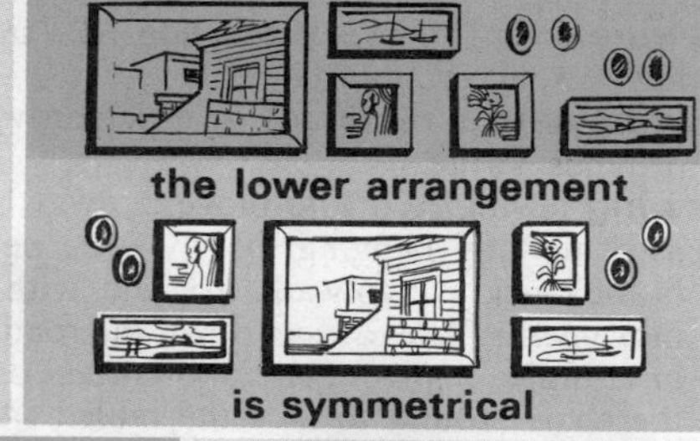
the lower arrangement is symmetrical

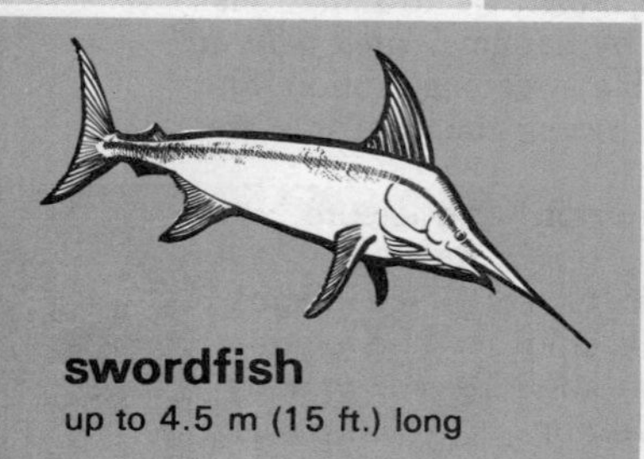
swordfish
up to 4.5 m (15 ft.) long

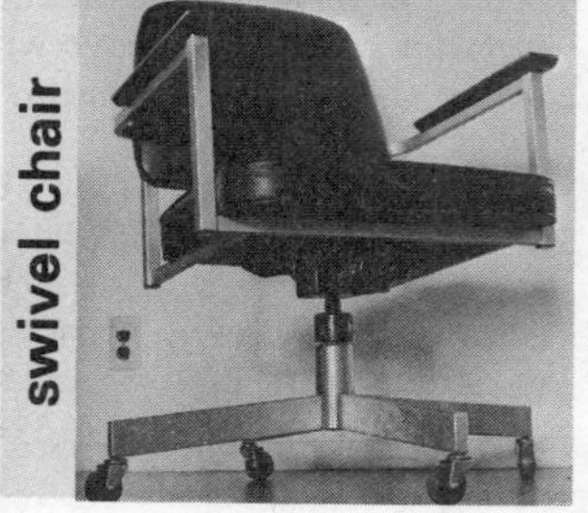
swivel chair

end of a line [The *syllables* of the entry words in this dictionary are divided by tiny dots.]

**Syllable** comes from a Greek word that means "to put or hold together." Syllables are put together to form words.

**syl·la·bus** (sil′ə bəs) ***n.*** an outline or summary, especially of a course of study. *—pl.* **syl′la·bus·es** or **syl·la·bi** (sil′ə bī)

**syl·lo·gism** (sil′ə jiz'm) ***n.*** a form of reasoning in which two statements are made from which a logical conclusion can be drawn.

Here is an example of a **syllogism:**
All mammals have warm blood.
Whales are mammals.
Therefore, whales have warm blood.

**sylph** (silf) ***n.*** **1** an imaginary being, or spirit, supposed to live in the air. **2** a slender, graceful woman or girl.

**syl·van** (sil′vən) ***adj.*** **1** of, like, or found in the woods [Dryads are *sylvan* creatures.] **2** covered with trees; wooded [We came upon a *sylvan* valley.]

**sym·bol** (sim′b'l) ***n.*** an object, mark, sign, etc. that stands for another object, or for an idea, quality, etc. [The dove is a *symbol* of peace. The mark $ is the *symbol* for dollar or dollars.]

**sym·bol·ic** (sim bäl′ik) ***adj.*** **1** of or expressed by a symbol; using symbols [*symbolic* writings]. **2** that is a symbol [Green is *symbolic* of springtime.] *Also* **sym·bol′i·cal.** **—sym·bol′i·cal·ly *adv.***

**sym·bol·ism** (sim′b'l iz'm) ***n.*** **1** the use of symbols to stand for things, especially in art or literature. **2** a set of symbols, standing for a group of ideas.

**sym·bol·ist** (sim′b'l ist) ***n.*** a person who uses symbols, especially in art or literature.

**sym·bol·ize** (sim′b'l īz) ***v.*** **1** to be a symbol of; stand for [A heart *symbolizes* love.] **2** to represent by a symbol [This artist *symbolizes* the human spirit by means of figures with wings.] **—sym′bol·ized, sym′bol·iz·ing**

**sym·met·ri·cal** (si met′ri k'l) ***adj.*** having symmetry; balanced [This is a *symmetrical* design.] *Also* **sym·met′ric.** *See the picture.* **—sym·met′ri·cal·ly *adv.***

**sym·me·try** (sim′ə trē) ***n.*** **1** an arrangement in which the parts on opposite sides of a center line are alike in size, shape, and position [The human body has *symmetry*.] **2** balance or harmony that comes from such an arrangement.

**sym·pa·thet·ic** (sim′pə thet′ik) ***adj.*** **1** feeling, showing, or caused by sympathy; sympathizing [He spoke *sympathetic* words to her.] **2** that suits one's tastes, mood, etc.; agreeable [It pleases me to be in *sympathetic* surroundings.] **3** showing favor or approval [He's *sympathetic* to our plans.] **—sym′pa·thet′i·cal·ly *adv.***

**sym·pa·thize** (sim′pə thīz) ***v.*** to share the feelings or ideas of another; feel or show sympathy [I *sympathize* with my friend who lost her dog.] **—sym′pa·thized, sym′pa·thiz·ing —sym′pa·thiz·er *n.***

**sym·pa·thy** (sim′pə thē) ***n.*** **1** a sharing of feelings, as by feeling sorry for another's suffering [He wept out of *sympathy* for my loss.] *See* SYNONYMS *at* **pity. 2** a feeling or condition that is the same as another's; agreement [Our tastes in furniture are in *sympathy*.] **3** favor; support [She is in *sympathy* with the strikers.] *—pl.* **sym′pa·thies**



**sym·pho·ny** (sim′fə nē) ***n.*** **1** a long piece of music for a full orchestra, usually divided into four movements with different rhythms and themes. **2** a large orchestra for playing such works: *its full name is* **symphony orchestra. 3** harmony, as of sounds, color, etc. [The dance was a *symphony* in motion.] *—pl.* **sym′pho·nies —sym·phon·ic** (sim fän′ik) ***adj.*** **—sym·phon′i·cal·ly *adv.***

**sym·po·si·um** (sim pō′zē əm) ***n.*** **1** a meeting for discussing some subject. **2** a group of writings or opinions on a particular subject. *—pl.* **sym·po′si·ums** or **sym·po·si·a** (sim pō′zē ə)

**symp·tom** (simp′təm) ***n.*** something showing that something else exists; sign [Spots on the skin may be a *symptom* of chicken pox.] *See* SYNONYMS *at* **sign. —symp·to·mat·ic** (simp′tə mat′ik) ***adj.***

**syn.** *abbreviation for* **synonym.**

**syn·a·gogue** (sin′ə gäg *or* sin′ə gôg) ***n.*** a building where Jews gather for worship and religious study.

**syn·chro·nize** (siŋ′krə nīz) ***v.*** **1** to move or happen at the same time or speed [The gears must *synchronize* when you shift.] **2** to make agree in time or rate of speed [Let's *synchronize* our watches. The movie film should be *synchronized* with the sound track.] **—syn′chro·nized, syn′chro·niz·ing**

**Synchronize** comes from two Greek words that mean "to be together in time." The shutter and flashbulb of a camera are synchronized so that they will both operate at the same time.



**syn·chro·nous** (siŋ′krə nəs) ***adj.*** happening at the same time or moving at the same rate of speed [The drum beats were *synchronous*.]

**syn·co·pate** (siŋ′kə pāt) ***v.*** in music, to shift the accent by putting the beat at a place that would normally not be accented and holding it into the next accented beat [Much jazz is *syncopated*.] **—syn′co·pat·ed, syn′co·pat·ing —syn′co·pa′tion *n.***

**syn·di·cate** (sin′də kit) ***n.*** **1** a group of bankers, large companies, etc. formed to carry out some project that needs much money. ☆**2** an organization that sells articles, stories, comic strips, etc. to a number of newspapers. ◆***v.*** (sin′di kāt) **1** to form into a syndicate. **2** to publish through a syndicate in a number of newspapers. **—syn′di·cat·ed, syn′di·cat·ing —syn′di·ca′tion *n.***

**syn·od** (sin′əd) ***n.*** a council of churches or church officials, acting as a governing body.

**syn·o·nym** (sin′ə nim) ***n.*** a word having the same or almost the same meaning as another ["Big" and "large" are *synonyms*.]

**syn·on·y·mous** (si nän′ə məs) ***adj.*** of the same or almost the same meaning.

**syn·op·sis** (si näp′sis) ***n.*** a short outline or review of the main points, as of a story; summary. *—pl.* **syn·op·ses** (si näp′sēz)

| | | | | | | | |
|---|---|---|---|---|---|---|---|
| **a** | fat | **ir** | here | **ou** | out | **zh** | leisure |
| **ā** | ape | **ī** | bite, fire | **u** | up | **ŋ** | ring |
| **ä** | car, lot | **ō** | go | **ur** | fur | | a *in* ago |
| **e** | ten | **ô** | law, horn | **ch** | chin | | e *in* agent |
| **er** | care | **oi** | oil | **sh** | she | **ə** = | i *in* unity |
| **ē** | even | **oo** | look | **th** | thin | | o *in* collect |
| **i** | hit | **ōō** | tool | ***th*** | then | | u *in* focus |

**syn·tax** (sin′taks) ***n.*** the way words are put together and related to one another in sentences; sentence structure. —**syn·tac′ti·cal** or **syn·tac′tic *adj.***

**syn·the·sis** (sin′thə sis) ***n.*** the putting together of parts or elements so as to make a whole [Plastics are made by chemical *synthesis.*] —*pl.* **syn·the·ses** (sin′thə sēz)

**syn·the·siz·er** (sin′thə sī′zər) ***n.*** ☆an electronic musical instrument that makes sounds that cannot be made by ordinary instruments. *See the picture.*

**syn·thet·ic** (sin thet′ik) ***adj.*** **1** of, by, or using synthesis. **2** made by putting together chemicals rather than by using natural products [The tires are made of *synthetic* rubber.] **3** artificial; not real [She gave a *synthetic* excuse.] ◆***n.*** something synthetic [Nylon is a *synthetic.*] —**syn·thet′i·cal·ly *adv.***

**syph·i·lis** (sif′ə lis) ***n.*** a disease that can be passed on to another during sexual intercourse. —**syph·i·lit·ic** (sif′ə lit′ik) ***adj.***

**Syr·a·cuse** (sir′ə kyo͞os) **1** a city in central New York. **2** a town in Sicily, once an important city of the ancient Greeks.

**Syr·i·a** (sir′ē ə) a country in southwestern Asia at the eastern end of the Mediterranean, south of Turkey. —**Syr′i·an *adj., n.***

**sy·rin·ga** (sə ring′gə) ***n.*** a garden shrub with sweet-smelling, white flowers.

**sy·ringe** (sə rinj′ *or* sir′inj) ***n.*** a device made up of a narrow tube with a rubber bulb or a plunger at one end, for drawing in a liquid and then pushing it out in a stream. Syringes are used to inject fluids into the body, to wash out wounds, etc. *See the picture. See also* **hypodermic.** ◆***v.*** to wash out with a syringe. —**sy·ringed′, sy·ring′ing**

**syr·up** (sir′əp *or* sʉr′əp) ***n.*** **1** a sweet, thick liquid made by boiling sugar with water, usually with some flavoring [chocolate *syrup*]. **2** a sweet, thick liquid made by boiling the juice of certain plants [maple *syrup;* corn *syrup*]. —**syr′up·y *adj.***

**sys·tem** (sis′təm) ***n.*** **1** a group of things or parts working together or connected in some way so as to form a whole [a school *system;* the solar *system;* a *system* of highways; the nervous *system*]. **2** a set of facts, rules, ideas, etc. that make up an orderly plan [We have a democratic *system* of government.] **3** an orderly way of doing things; method [a new *system* for losing weight]. **4** the body as a whole [She had poison in her *system.*]

**sys·tem·at·ic** (sis′tə mat′ik) ***adj.*** **1** having or done by a system, method, or plan; orderly [We put on a *systematic* search.] **2** orderly in planning or doing things [a *systematic* person]. —**sys′tem·at′i·cal·ly *adv.***

**sys·tem·a·tize** (sis′təm ə tīz′) ***v.*** to form into a system; arrange in a systematic way; make orderly. —**sys′tem·a·tized′, sys′tem·a·tiz′ing**

**T, t** (tē) ***n.*** the twentieth letter of the English alphabet. —*pl.* **T's, t's** (tēz)

**T** (tē) ***n.*** something shaped like a T. ◆***adj.*** shaped like T. —**to a T,** perfectly; exactly.

**T.** *abbreviation for* **tablespoon** *or* **tablespoons, Tuesday.**

**t.** *abbreviation for* **teaspoon** *or* **teaspoons, ton** *or* **tons.**

**tab** (tab) ***n.*** **1** a small loop, flap, or tag fastened to something [He hung his jacket up by the *tab.* Cards for filing have *tabs* lettered A to Z.] ☆**2** a record of money owed; bill: *used only in everyday talk.* —☆**keep tabs on** or **keep a tab on,** to keep a check on. —☆**pick up the tab,** to pay the bill. *These phrases are used only in everyday talk.*

**tab·ard** (tab′ərd) ***n.*** **1** a short coat worn by a herald, decorated with his king's or lord's coat of arms. **2** a cloak with short sleeves worn by knights over their armor. *See the picture.*

**tab·by** (tab′ē) ***n.*** **1** a gray or brown cat with dark stripes. **2** any pet cat, especially a female. —*pl.* **tab′-bies**

**Tabby** was first used in English as the name for a kind of heavy silk cloth with stripes or wavy markings. The name comes from the Arabic word for a certain part of the city of Baghdad where the cloth was originally made. A cat called a *tabby* has stripes that make it look like this cloth.

**tab·er·nac·le** (tab′ər nak′'l) ***n.*** **1** in early times, a temporary shelter, as a tent. **2 Tabernacle,** the shelter which the Jews carried with them during their wanderings under Moses, for use as a place of worship; also, later, the Jewish Temple. **3** any large place of worship. **4** a container for something considered holy.

**ta·ble** (tā′b'l) ***n.*** **1** a piece of furniture made up of a flat top set on legs. **2** such a table set with food; also, the food served [They set a good *table.*] **3** the people seated at a table [Our *table* played bridge.] **4** an orderly list [a *table* of contents in a book]. **5** an orderly arrangement of facts, figures, etc. [multiplication *tables*]. **6** *a shorter name for* **tableland. 7** a flat, thin piece of metal, stone, or wood, with words, etc. cut into it; tablet. ◆***v.*** ☆to put off discussing; set aside [Congress *tabled* the bill.] —**ta′bled, ta′bling** —**at table,** at a meal. —**turn the tables,** to make a situation just the opposite of what it was. —**under the table,** secretly, as a bribe: *used only in everyday talk.*

**tab·leau** (tab′lō *or* ta blō′) ***n.*** a picture or scene, as of an event in history, made by persons posing in costume [a *tableau* of the landing of the Pilgrims]. *—pl.* **tab·leaux** (tab′lōz) or **tab′leaus**

**ta·ble·cloth** (tā′b′l klôth) ***n.*** a cloth for covering a table, especially at meals.

**ta·ble·land** (tā′b′l land) ***n.*** a high, broad, usually flat region; plateau.

**ta·ble·spoon** (tā′b′l spo͞on) ***n.*** **1** a large spoon for serving food, for eating soup, or for measuring things in cooking. **2** *same as* **tablespoonful.**

**ta·ble·spoon·ful** (tā′b′l spo͞on′fo͝ol) ***n.*** as much as a tablespoon will hold, usually 1/2 fluid ounce. *—pl.* **ta′ble·spoon′fuls**

**tab·let** (tab′lit) ***n.*** **1** sheets of writing paper fastened at one end to form a pad. **2** a small, flat, hard cake, as of medicine [an aspirin *tablet*]. **3** a flat, thin piece of metal, stone, etc. with words, etc. written on it or cut into it [A *tablet* on the museum wall lists the names of the founders.]

**table tennis** a game like tennis, played on a table with a small, hollow ball and small, solid paddles with short handles. *See the picture.*

**ta·ble·ware** (tā′b′l wer) ***n.*** dishes, forks, spoons, etc., used at the table for eating.

**tab·loid** (tab′loid) ***n.*** a newspaper on small sheets, with many pictures and short articles.

**ta·boo** (ta bo͞o′ *or* tə bo͞o′) ***n.*** **1** the act or practice of making certain persons and things sacred so that they cannot be touched or talked about. **2** any rule that makes something forbidden [There is a *taboo* against using certain words on radio and TV.] *—pl.* **ta·boos′** ◆***adj.*** forbidden by taboo. ◆***v.*** to put under taboo; forbid. **—ta·booed′, ta·boo′ing**

**ta·bu** (ta bo͞o′ *or* tə bo͞o′) ***n., adj., v.*** *another spelling of* **taboo.** *—pl.* **ta·bus′ —ta·bued′, ta·bu′ing**

**tab·u·lar** (tab′yə lər) ***adj.*** **1** of or arranged in columns in a table or list [The names are in *tabular* form.] **2** flat like a table [*tabular* rock].

**tab·u·late** (tab′yə lāt) ***v.*** to arrange in tables or columns [to *tabulate* numbers]. **—tab′u·lat·ed, tab′u·lat·ing —tab′u·la′tion *n.* —tab′u·la′tor *n.***

**ta·chom·e·ter** (ta käm′ə tər) ***n.*** a device that shows or measures the speed of a revolving shaft, as the shaft that makes the axle and wheels of a car move. The speed is shown in revolutions per minute.

**tac·it** (tas′it) ***adj.*** **1** understood or meant, but not openly said [Her smile gave *tacit* approval.] **2** making no sound; silent. **—tac′it·ly *adv.***

**tac·i·turn** (tas′ə turn) ***adj.*** not liking to talk; usually silent. **—tac′i·tur′ni·ty *n.***

**tack** (tak) ***n.*** **1** a short nail with a sharp point and a somewhat large, flat head. **2** the direction a ship goes in relation to the position of the sails. **3** a change of a ship's direction. **4** a zigzag course. **5** a way of doing something; course of action [He is on the wrong *tack*.] **6** a long, loose stitch used in sewing, as to baste a hem. **7** a horse's equipment; saddles, bridles, etc. ◆***v.*** **1** to fasten with tacks [She *tacked* down the carpet.] **2** to add or attach as something extra [*Tack* a new ending on the story.] **3** to change the course of a ship. **4** to sail in a zigzag course. *See the picture.* **5** to sew together loosely with long, loose stitches.

**tack·le** (tak′′l) ***n.*** **1** the tools or equipment needed for doing something; gear [fishing *tackle*]. **2** a set of ropes and pulleys for moving heavy things. **3** the act of tackling, as in football. ☆**4** either of two football players next to the ends. ◆***v.*** **1** to try to do or solve; undertake [He *tackled* the job.] **2** to seize and stop or throw to the ground, as a player carrying the ball in football. **3** to fasten by means of tackle. **—tack′led, tack′ling**

table tennis

synthesizer

tabard

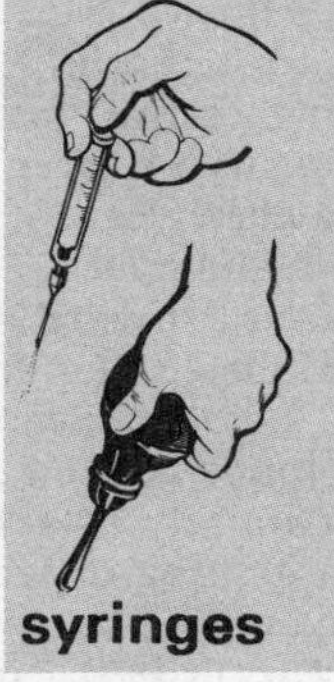
syringes

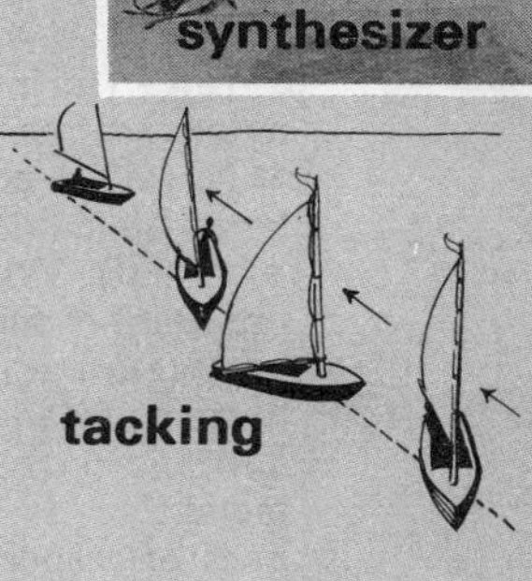
tacking

☆**tack·y** (tak′ē) ***adj.*** **1** worn-out; out of style; shabby [*tacky* clothing]. **2** not proper; in bad taste; coarse; vulgar. *This word is used only in everyday talk.* **—tack′i·er, tack′i·est**

☆**ta·co** (tä′kō) ***n.*** a Mexican food made of a tortilla folded over chopped meat, lettuce, etc. *—pl.* **ta′cos**

> **Taco** comes from an American Spanish word that first meant "a bung for a keg of wine," then later "a drink of wine," and finally "a light lunch, or snack," such as a **taco.**

**Ta·co·ma** (tə kō′mə) a seaport in western Washington.

**tact** (takt) ***n.*** a sense of what is the right thing to do or say without causing anger or hurt feelings; skill in dealing with people.

**tact·ful** (takt′fəl) ***adj.*** having or showing tact. **—tact′ful·ly *adv.* —tact′ful·ness *n.***

**tac·ti·cal** (tak′ti k′l) ***adj.*** **1** of tactics; especially, having to do with the movement of armed troops or ships in battle. **2** skillful or clever in the tactics used. **—tac′ti·cal·ly *adv.***

**tac·ti·cian** (tak tish′ən) ***n.*** a person who is skilled in tactics.

| | | | | | | | |
|---|---|---|---|---|---|---|---|
| **a** | fat | **ir** | here | **ou** | out | **zh** | leisure |
| **ā** | ape | **ī** | bite, fire | **u** | up | **ng** | ring |
| **ä** | car, lot | **ō** | go | **ur** | fur | | a *in* ago |
| **e** | ten | **ô** | law, horn | **ch** | chin | | e *in* agent |
| **er** | care | **oi** | oil | **sh** | she | **ə =** | i *in* unity |
| **ē** | even | **oo** | look | **th** | thin | | o *in* collect |
| **i** | hit | **o͞o** | tool | ***th*** | then | | u *in* focus |

**tac·tics** (tak′tiks) ***n.pl.*** **1** the science of moving armed troops or ships about in battle in trying to get the advantage: *used with a singular verb* [*Tactics* is studied at West Point.] **2** any skillful methods used to bring something about [The Senator knew all about the *tactics* of a political campaign.]

**tact·less** (takt′lis) ***adj.*** not showing tact. —**tact′less·ly** ***adv.*** —**tact′less·ness** ***n.***

**tad·pole** (tad′pōl) ***n.*** a young toad or frog when it still has a tail and lives only in water.

> **Tadpole** comes from two much older English words, one meaning "toad" and the other meaning "head." Put together, it means a toad that seems to be all head, for this is the way a tadpole looks.

**taf·fe·ta** (taf′i tə) ***n.*** a fine, rather stiff fabric of silk, nylon, acetate, etc., with a sheen.

**taf·fy** (taf′ē) ***n.*** a chewy candy made of sugar or molasses boiled down and pulled.

**Taft** (taft), **William Howard** 1857–1930; the 27th president of the United States, from 1909 to 1913.

**tag** (tag) ***n.*** ☆**1** a card, paper, etc. attached to something as a label [price *tags* on merchandise]. **2** any hanging part or loosely attached end. **3** a tip of metal, etc. as on a string or lace. **4** the last line or lines of a speech, story, etc. **5** a children's game in which one player, called "it," chases the others until he or she touches one of them, making that one "it." ◆***v.*** **1** to put a tag on. ☆**2** to touch in the game of tag. ☆**3** in baseball, to touch, as a base runner, with the ball, thus putting the runner out. **4** to follow close behind: *used only in everyday talk* [When they go fishing, the dog *tags* along.] ☆**5** to put a traffic ticket on a car or give a driver a ticket for breaking a traffic law: *used only in everyday talk.* —**tagged, tag′ging**

**Ta·hi·ti** (tə hēt′ē) a French island in the South Pacific, south of Hawaii.

**tail** (tāl) ***n.*** **1** the part at the rear of an animal's body that sticks out beyond the backbone. **2** any thing or part like this [the *tail* of a shirt; a pig*tail*]. **3** the hind or last part [the *tail* of a parade]. **4** *often* **tails,** *pl.* the side of a coin opposite the head, or main side. ☆**5 tails,** *pl.* a man's formal evening suit having a swallow-tailed coat. ◆***v.*** ☆to follow close behind: *used only in everyday talk* [A detective was *tailing* us.] ◆***adj.*** **1** at the rear; hind [We saw the *tail* end of the show.] **2** from the rear [a *tail* wind]. —**turn tail,** to run from danger or trouble. —**tail′less** ***adj.***

☆**tail·gate** (tāl′gāt) ***n.*** a board at the back of a truck, station wagon, etc. that can be taken off or lowered. *See the picture.* ◆***v.*** to follow another vehicle too closely. —**tail′gat·ed, tail′gat·ing**

**tailgate**

**tambourine**

**tail·light** (tāl′līt) ***n.*** a light, usually red, at the back of an automobile, truck, etc. to warn other vehicles that are following.

**tai·lor** (tā′lər) ***n.*** a person who makes or repairs suits, coats, etc. *See the word history in color at* **detail.** ◆***v.*** **1** to work as a tailor or make as a tailor does [suits *tailored* for stout people]. **2** to make or change so as to fit a certain need [That movie was *tailored* to please children.]

☆**tail·pipe** (tāl′pīp) ***n.*** an exhaust pipe at the rear of an automobile, truck, etc.

**tail·spin** (tāl′spin) ***n.*** **1** a downward plunge of an airplane out of control, with the tail up and spinning in circles: *also written* **tail spin.** **2** a state of confusion or gloominess that gets worse rapidly.

**taint** (tānt) ***n.*** a trace of something that spoils, rots, or poisons. ◆***v.*** to spoil, rot, or poison [This food is *tainted.*]

**Tai·wan** (tī′wän′) an island off the southeastern coast of China. On this island is a country that is called the Republic of China.

**take** (tāk) ***v.*** **1** to get hold of; grasp [*Take* my hand as we cross the street.] **2** to get by force or skill; capture; seize; win [Our team *took* the game. The soldiers *took* the town.] **3** to delight or charm [We were *taken* by the comic's wit.] **4** to get as one's own; obtain, select, assume, etc. [She *took* the job. "The farmer *takes* a wife." When does the Senator *take* office?] **5** to eat, drink, etc. [She is too sick to *take* food.] **6** to buy, rent, subscribe for, etc. [We *take* the daily paper.] **7** to be used with [The verb "hit" *takes* an object.] **8** to travel by or on [She *took* a short cut. He *took* a bus.] **9** to deal with; consider [She *took* her studies seriously. *Take* this for an example.] **10** to use up [It *took* all day.] **11** to call for; require; need [It *takes* courage to jump.] **12** to get or draw from a source [He *took* the quotation from the Bible.] **13** to get by observing, studying, etc. [We *take* geography in school. They are *taking* an opinion poll.] **14** to write down; copy [*Take* notes on the lecture.] **15** to photograph [She *took* our picture.] **16** to receive or accept [He *took* my advice. She *took* her punishment.] **17** to be affected by [He *took* cold. The cloth *took* the dye.] **18** to understand [He *took* her remarks as praise.] **19** to have or feel [*Take* pity on me.] **20** to do, make, use, etc. [We'll *take* a walk. *Take* a look. *Take* care.] **21** to remove or steal from some person or place [Someone *took* my wallet.] **22** to carry [*Take* your skis with you.] **23** to subtract [*Take* a dollar off the price.] **24** to lead or bring [I *took* Pat to the movie. This road *takes* us to the park.] **25** to begin growing, taking effect, etc. [The roses *took* in our yard. That dye *takes* well.] **26** to catch [The fire *took* quickly.] **27** to head for; go [They *took* to the hills.] **28** to become: *used only in everyday talk* [He *took* sick.] **29** to cheat or trick: *slang in this meaning.* —**took, tak′en, tak′ing** ◆***n.*** **1** the act of taking. **2** the amount taken or received [a day's *take* of fish]. **3** a movie scene, tape, or record filmed or recorded at one time. —☆**on the take,** willing to take bribes: *a slang phrase.* —**take after,** to be, act, or look like. —**take back,** **1** to withdraw something said, promised, etc. **2** to return something as to a store. —**take down,** **1** to write down; record. **2** to make humble. —**take for,** to think to be; mistake for [I *took* her *for* her sister.] —**take in,** **1** to admit or receive [They *take in* lodgers.] **2** to make smaller by drawing in cloth at a seam. **3** to understand. ☆**4** to visit [We *took in* all the sights.] **5** to cheat or fool. **6** to include. —**take it,** **1** to suppose or believe. ☆**2** to stand up under trouble, criticism, etc.: *a slang phrase.* —**take off,** **1** to rise from the ground or water in an aircraft. **2** to imitate or mimic in fun: *used only in everyday talk.* —**take on,** **1** to get. **2** to hire. **3** to undertake. **4** to play against, as in a game. **5** to show strong feeling: *used only in everyday talk.* —**take one's time,** to be in no hurry. —**take over,** to begin managing. —**take to,** **1** to become fond of. **2** to apply oneself to studies, etc. —**take up,** **1** to make tighter or shorter, as a rope. **2** to absorb, as a liquid. **3** to become interested in. **4** to fill, as space or time. —**take up with,** to become a friend or companion of: *used only in everyday talk.* —**tak'er** *n.*

**take·off** (tāk'ôf) *n.* **1** the act of rising from the ground, as in an aircraft or by jumping. **2** an amusing imitation as done in making fun of someone: *used only in everyday talk.*

**tak·ing** (tāk'iŋ) *adj.* attractive; charming. ◆*n.* **1** the act of one that takes [the *taking* of the census]. **2 takings,** *pl.* money earned; profits.

**talc** (talk) *n.* **1** a soft mineral ground up to make talcum powder. **2** *same as* **talcum powder.**

**tal·cum powder** (tal'kəm) a powder for the face and body made of talc, often with perfume added: *often shortened to* **talcum** *or* **talc.**

**tale** (tāl) *n.* **1** a story, especially about things that are imagined or made up [The sitter read the child both folk *tales* and fairy *tales.*] **2** a lie or false story. **3** gossip, especially when it may do harm.

**tale·bear·er** (tāl'ber'ər) *n.* a person who gossips, tells secrets, informs on others, etc.

**tal·ent** (tal'ənt) *n.* **1** a natural skill that is unusual [She has *talent* as an artist.] **2** people with talent [He helps young *talent* along.] **3** a unit of weight or money used in ancient times.

SYNONYMS: **Talent** means an ability with which one is born, and that may be developed by study and practice [She had a *talent* for writing.] **Gift** is a special ability that is given to one as by nature, and not gained by effort [He has a *gift* for making plants grow.] **Aptitude** means a natural liking for a certain kind of work and suggests that one may be successful at it [*Aptitude* tests can help one in choosing a career.]

**tal·ent·ed** (tal'ən tid) *adj.* having an unusually fine natural skill; gifted.

**tal·is·man** (tal'is mən) *n.* **1** a ring, stone, etc. carved with designs supposed to bring good luck. **2** anything supposed to have magic power. —*pl.* **tal'is·mans**

**talk** (tôk) *v.* **1** to say words or put ideas in words; speak [The baby is learning to *talk.*] *See* SYNONYMS *at* **speak.** **2** to make, bring about, etc. by talking [He *talked* himself hoarse. We *talked* her into going.] **3** to pass on ideas in some way other than with spoken words [We *talked* in sign language.] **4** to speak about; discuss [Let's *talk* business.] **5** to chatter or gossip. **6** to use in speaking [He *talks* French.] ◆*n.* **1** the act of talking; conversation. **2** a speech [He gave a *talk* on cooking.] **3** a conference [*talks* between the company and the union]. **4** gossip; a rumor [There is *talk* that they are engaged.] **5** a person or thing that is being talked about [Her new play is the *talk* of the town.] —☆**talk back,** to answer in a way that is not respectful. —**talk down to,** to talk to in a simple way, as if one must do this in order to be understood. —**talk over,** **1** to have a talk about; discuss. **2** to win to one's view by talking. —**talk something out,** to discuss something at length in an effort to agree or understand. —**talk'er** *n.*

**talk·a·tive** (tôk'ə tiv) *adj.* talking a great deal, or fond of talking.

☆**talking book** a recording of a reading of a book for use especially by the blind.

**tall** (tôl) *adj.* **1** reaching a long way up; not low or short [a *tall* building]. **2** of a certain height [He is six feet *tall.*] ☆**3** large in size; big: *used only in everyday talk* [a *tall* drink]. ☆**4** hard to believe; exaggerated: *used only in everyday talk* [a *tall* tale].

**Tal·la·has·see** (tal'ə has'ē) the capital of Florida.

**tal·low** (tal'ō) *n.* the hard fat of cows, sheep, etc., melted for use in candles, soap, etc.

**tal·ly** (tal'ē) *n.* **1** a record, account, score, etc. [Keep a *tally* of the money you spend.] **2** a paper, pad, etc. on which such a record is kept. **3** a tag or label. —*pl.* **tal'lies** ◆*v.* **1** to put on a tally; record; score [The team *tallied* two runs this inning.] **2** to count; add [*Tally* up the score.] **3** to match or agree [His story of what happened doesn't *tally* with hers.] —**tal'lied,** **tal'ly·ing**



A **tally** was originally a stick with notches cut in it that stood for the amount of money owed or paid. The stick was usually split lengthwise, half for the person who owed the money and half for the one to whom the money was owed.

**tal·ly·ho** (tal'ē hō') *interj.* the cry of a fox hunter when first seeing the fox. ◆*n.* (tal'ē hō') a coach pulled by four horses. —*pl.* **tal'ly·hos'**

**Tal·mud** (täl'mood *or* tal'mood) *n.* the collection of writings that make up the Jewish civil and religious law.

**tal·on** (tal'ən) *n.* the claw of a bird that kills other animals for food, as the eagle.

**tam** (tam) *n. a shorter word for* **tam-o'-shanter.**

☆**ta·ma·le** (tə mä'lē) *n.* a Mexican food of chopped meat and red peppers rolled in cornmeal, wrapped in corn husks, and baked or steamed.

☆**tam·a·rack** (tam'ə rak) *n.* a kind of larch tree usually found in swamps.

**tam·a·rind** (tam'ə rind) *n.* **1** a tropical tree with yellow flowers and brown fruit pods. **2** its fruit, used in foods, medicine, etc.

**tam·bou·rine** (tam bə rēn') *n.* a small, shallow drum with only one head and with jingling metal disks in the rim. It is shaken, struck with the hand, etc. *See the picture.*

| | | | | | | | |
|---|---|---|---|---|---|---|---|
| **a** | fat | **ir** | here | **ou** | out | **zh** | leisure |
| **ā** | ape | **ī** | bite, fire | **u** | up | **ŋ** | ring |
| **ä** | car, lot | **ō** | go | **ur** | fur | | a *in* ago |
| **e** | ten | **ô** | law, horn | **ch** | chin | | e *in* agent |
| **er** | care | **oi** | oil | **sh** | she | **ə** = | i *in* unity |
| **ē** | even | **oo** | look | **th** | thin | | o *in* collect |
| **i** | hit | **ōō** | tool | ***th*** | then | | u *in* focus |

**tame** (tām) ***adj.*** **1** no longer wild, but trained for use by human beings or as a pet [Would you like a *tame* skunk?] **2** gentle, easy to control, and not afraid of human beings [The bronco soon became quite *tame.*] **3** not lively or forceful; dull [a *tame* boxing match]. —**tam′er, tam′est** ◆***v.*** **1** to make tame, or train to obey [to *tame* wild animals for a circus]. **2** to make more gentle or easier to manage; subdue [Kind treatment helped *tame* down the child.] —**tamed, tam′ing** —**tame′ly *adv.*** —**tame′ness *n.*** —**tam′er *n.***

**tam-o′-shan·ter** (tam′ə shan′tər) ***n.*** a Scottish cap with a round, flat top. *See the picture.*

**tamp** (tamp) ***v.*** to pack or pound down with blows or taps [to *tamp* down tobacco in a pipe].

**Tam·pa** (tam′pə) a city in west central Florida.

**tam·per** (tam′pər) ***v.*** to meddle or interfere, especially in a way that is not right or honest or that makes things worse [It is not legal to *tamper* with a witness. I *tampered* with the clock and now it won't run.]

**tan** (tan) ***n.*** **1** *same as* **tanbark.** **2** yellowish brown. **3** the brown color that fair skin gets from being much in the sun. ◆***adj.*** yellowish-brown. —**tan′ner, tan′nest** ◆***v.*** **1** to make into leather by soaking in tannic acid [to *tan* cowhides]. **2** to make or become brown, as from being much in the sun [My skin *tans* quickly.] **3** to whip or flog: *used only in everyday talk.* —**tanned, tan′ning**

**tan·a·ger** (tan′ə jər) ***n.*** a small American songbird. The male is usually brightly colored.

760

**tan·bark** (tan′bärk) ***n.*** any tree bark that contains tannic acid. The acid is used to tan hides, and the bark with the acid removed is used to cover circus rings, race tracks, etc.

**tan·dem** (tan′dəm) ***adv.*** one behind another; in single file [five dogs hitched *tandem* to a sled]. ◆***n.*** **1** a team, as of horses, harnessed one behind the other. **2** a carriage with two wheels, pulled by a tandem of horses. **3** a bicycle with two seats and two sets of pedals, one behind the other: *its full name is* **tandem bicycle.**

**tang** (taŋ) ***n.*** **1** a sharp, strong taste or smell [a spicy *tang*]. **2** a point or prong on a chisel, file, etc. that fits into the handle.

**Tan·gan·yi·ka** (taŋ′gan yē′kə), **Lake** a lake in east central Africa.

☆**tan·ge·lo** (tan′jə lō) ***n.*** a fruit produced by crossing a tangerine with a grapefruit. —*pl.* **tan′ge·los**

> **Tangelo** is a word made by putting together parts of two different words, just as this kind of orange is made by crossing two different fruits. *Tang-* is taken from *tangerine* and *-elo* from *pomelo,* another name for grapefruit.

**tan·gent** (tan′jənt) ***adj.*** touching a curved line or surface at only one point and not cutting across it [a line *tangent* to a circle]. *See the picture.* ◆***n.*** a tangent curve, line, or surface. —**go off at a tangent** or **fly off on a tangent,** to change suddenly from one subject or line of action to another.

**tan·ge·rine** (tan jə rēn′) ***n.*** a small orange with sections that come apart easily and a loose skin that peels off easily.

**tan·gi·ble** (tan′jə b′l) ***adj.*** **1** that can be touched or felt; real or solid [A house is *tangible* property.] **2** that can be understood; definite; not vague [I was frightened for no *tangible* reason.] —**tan′gi·bly *adv.***

**Tan·gier** (tan jir′) a seaport in Morocco.

**tan·gle** (taŋ′g′l) ***v.*** **1** to make or become knotted, confused, etc. [Our fishing lines are *tangled.*] **2** to catch or hold back, as in a snare [His feet became *tangled* in the garden hose.] —**tan′gled, tan′gling** ◆***n.*** **1** a mass of thread, branches, hair, etc. twisted or knotted together [a *tangle* of underbrush]. **2** a confused or mixed-up condition; muddle [Her affairs are in a *tangle.*]

**tank** (taŋk) ***n.*** **1** any large container for liquid or gas [a swimming *tank;* a fuel *tank*]. **2** a military car covered with armor and carrying heavy guns. It moves on endless metal belts that let it travel over rough ground. ◆***v.*** to put in a tank. —**tank up,** to supply with or get a full tank of gasoline: *used only in everyday talk.* —**tank′ful *adj.***

> The military **tank** got its name because it was a military secret when such tanks were first being made. When the parts for these tanks were put in large boxes to be shipped elsewhere, the boxes were stamped "tank" or "tanks" so that anyone who saw the labels would think that the boxes held some kind of containers. By the time the secret became known, the secret name became the real name, **tank.**

**tank·ard** (taŋk′ərd) ***n.*** a large drinking cup with a handle, and a lid joined by a hinge.

**tank·er** (taŋk′ər) ***n.*** a ship with large tanks in the hull for carrying oil or other liquids.

**tan·ner** (tan′ər) ***n.*** a person whose work is making leather by tanning hides.

**tan·ner·y** (tan′ər ē) ***n.*** a place where leather is made by tanning hides. —*pl.* **tan′ner·ies**

**tan·nic acid** (tan′ik) an acid got from oak bark, used in tanning, dyeing, and medicine.

**tan·nin** (tan′in) ***n.*** *another name for* **tannic acid.**

**tan·sy** (tan′zē) ***n.*** a plant with a strong smell and small, yellow flowers. —*pl.* **tan′sies**

**tan·ta·lize** (tan′tə līz) ***v.*** to tease or disappoint by showing or promising something wanted and then holding it back [Dreams of food *tantalized* the starving person.] —**tan′ta·lized, tan′ta·liz·ing**

> **Tantalize** comes from the name of Tantalus, a king in Greek myths. He made the gods angry, and they punished him by placing him in water up to his chin. The water moved away when he tried to drink it, and there were branches of fruit over his head that moved away when he tried to reach them.

**tan·ta·mount** (tan′tə mount) ***adj.*** almost the same as; equal [The king's wishes were *tantamount* to orders.]

**tan·trum** (tan′trəm) ***n.*** a fit of bad temper.

**Tan·za·ni·a** (tan′zə nē′ə) a country on the eastern coast of Africa and on Zanzibar.

**tap**[1] (tap) ***v.*** **1** to hit lightly [She *tapped* my shoulder.] **2** to hit something lightly with [He *tapped* the chalk against the blackboard.] **3** to make or do by tapping [to *tap* out a rhythm]. ☆**4** to choose, as for membership in a club. —**tapped, tap′ping** ◆***n.*** a light blow, or the sound made by it.

**tap**[2] (tap) ***n.*** **1** a device for turning the flow of liquid on or off, as from a pipe; faucet. **2** a plug or cork for stopping a hole in a cask. **3** a place in a pipe, wire, etc. where a connection is made. ◆*v.* **1** to drill a hole in, pull the plug from, etc., so as to draw off liquid [to *tap* a rubber tree; to *tap* a barrel]. **2** to draw out, as from a container [to *tap* wine from a cask]. **3** to make use of [to *tap* wealth from a treasury]. **4** to make a connection with [to *tap* a telephone line]. —**tapped, tap′ping** —**on tap,** ready for use, as liquid in a cask that has been tapped.

**tap dance** a dance done by making sharp, loud taps with the foot, heel, or toe at each step.

**tape** (tāp) *n.* **1** a strong, narrow strip of cloth, paper, plastic, etc. used for binding or tying [adhesive *tape*]. **2** a narrow strip of plastic, steel, etc. on which something is recorded [recording *tape;* a measuring *tape*]. **3** a strip of cloth stretched above the finishing line of a race. ◆*v.* **1** to bind or tie with tape. **2** to record on tape. —**taped, tap′ing**

☆**tape deck** a device for recording sound on magnetic tape and for playing it back when connected to an amplifier and speakers.

**tape measure** a tape marked off in inches and feet for measuring: *also called* **tape′line.**

**ta·per** (tā′pər) *v.* **1** to make or become less wide or less thick little by little [A sword *tapers* to a point.] **2** to lessen little by little [The voice *tapered* off to a whisper.] ◆*n.* **1** the fact or amount of tapering, or becoming gradually thinner [the *taper* of a pyramid]. **2** a slender candle.

**tape recorder** a device for recording sound on magnetic tape and for playing it back after it has been recorded.

**tap·es·try** (tap′is trē) *n.* a heavy cloth with designs and pictures woven into it, for hanging on walls, covering furniture, etc. —*pl.* **tap′es·tries**

**tape·worm** (tāp′wurm) *n.* a long, flat worm sometimes found in the intestines of human beings and animals.

**tap·i·o·ca** (tap′ē ō′kə) *n.* a starchy substance from cassava roots, used in puddings, etc.

**ta·pir** (tā′pər) *n.* a large animal like a pig, with a long snout that can bend. It lives in the forests of Central and South America. *See the picture.*

**tap·room** (tap′ro͞om) *n. another name for* **barroom.**

**tap·root** (tap′ro͞ot) *n.* a main root growing downward, from which small roots branch out.

**taps** (taps) *n.* ☆a bugle call to put out lights and go to bed, as in an army camp. It is also sounded at military burials.

**tar**[1] (tär) *n.* **1** a thick, sticky, brown to black liquid distilled from wood or coal. **2** any of the solid substances in smoke, as from tobacco. ◆*v.* to cover or smear with tar. —**tarred, tar′ring**

**tar**[2] (tär) *n. another name for* **sailor**: *used only in everyday talk.*

**tar·an·tel·la** (tar′ən tel′ə) *n.* **1** a fast, whirling Italian folk dance. **2** music for this.

**ta·ran·tu·la** (tə ran′cho͞o lə) *n.* a large hairy spider of tropical regions, whose bite is slightly poisonous. *See the picture.*

**tar·dy** (tär′dē) *adj.* **1** not on time; late; delayed [to be *tardy* for class]. **2** moving slowly. —**tar′di·er, tar′di·est** —**tar′di·ly** *adv.* —**tar′di·ness** *n.*

**tare**[1] (ter) *n.* **1** a kind of vetch grown as food for cattle. **2** a weed mentioned in the Bible.

tam-o'-shanter

tarantula
6.5 cm (2 1/2 in.) long

tapir
90 cm (3 ft.) high at shoulder

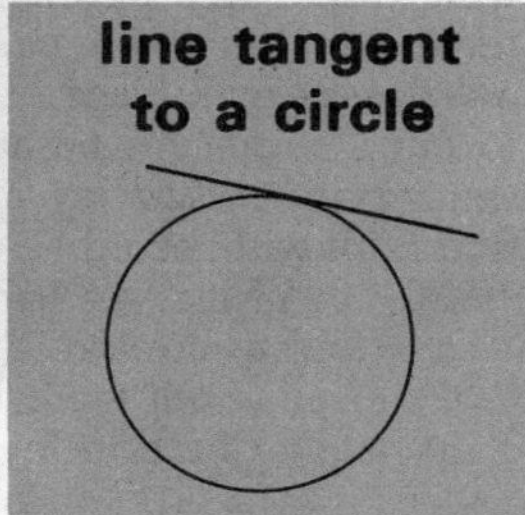
line tangent to a circle

**tare**[2] (ter) *n.* the weight of a container, wrapper, etc. taken from the total weight in figuring the weight of the contents.

**tar·get** (tär′git) *n.* **1** a thing aimed at, as in shooting a rifle or arrow; especially, a board with circles on it, one inside the other. **2** a person or thing that is attacked, made fun of, etc. [to be the *target* of someone's hatred].



**tar·iff** (tar′if) *n.* **1** a list of taxes on goods imported or, sometimes, on goods exported. **2** such a tax or its rate. **3** any list of prices or charges.

**tar·nish** (tär′nish) *v.* **1** to dull, stain, or discolor, as silver. **2** to bring dishonor to [to *tarnish* one's reputation]. ◆*n.* **1** the condition of being tarnished; dullness. **2** the dull coating on a tarnished surface.

**ta·ro** (tä′rō) *n.* a tropical plant with a starchy root that is eaten as food.

☆**tar paper** a heavy paper soaked with tar, used in roofing, etc.

**tar·pau·lin** (tär pô′lin *or* tär′pə lin) *n.* **1** canvas made waterproof with a special coating. **2** a sheet of this for protecting something.

**tar·pon** (tär′pən) *n.* a large, silvery fish found in the western Atlantic.

**tar·ry**[1] (tar′ē) *v.* **1** to stay for a time [We *tarried* in the park till sundown.] **2** to put off; delay [Don't *tarry;* mail the letter now.] —**tar′ried, tar′ry·ing**

**tar·ry**[2] (tär′ē) *adj.* **1** of or like tar. **2** covered with tar. —**tar′ri·er, tar′ri·est** —**tar′ri·ness** *n.*

**tart**[1] (tärt) *adj.* **1** sharp in taste; sour; acid [*tart* grapes]. *See* SYNONYMS *at* **sour.** **2** sharp in meaning; cutting [a *tart* answer]. —**tart′ly** *adv.* —**tart′ness** *n.*

| | | | |
|---|---|---|---|
| **a** fat | **ir** here | **ou** out | **zh** leisure |
| **ā** ape | **ī** bite, fire | **u** up | **ng** ring |
| **ä** car, lot | **ō** go | **ur** fur | a *in* ago |
| **e** ten | **ô** law, horn | **ch** chin | e *in* agent |
| **er** care | **oi** oil | **sh** she | **ə** = i *in* unity |
| **ē** even | **oo** look | **th** thin | o *in* collect |
| **i** hit | **o͞o** tool | ***th*** then | u *in* focus |

**tart²** (tärt) ***n.*** **1** a small, open shell of pastry filled with jam, jelly, etc. **2** in England, a small pie filled with fruit or jam and often having a top crust.

**tar·tan** (tär′t'n) ***n.*** **1** woolen cloth with a woven plaid pattern, worn in the Scottish Highlands. Each clan has its own pattern. **2** any plaid cloth or pattern.

**Tar·tar** (tär′tər) ***n.*** **1** *another spelling of* **Tatar. 2 tartar,** a bad-tempered person who is hard to deal with.

**tar·tar** (tär′tər) ***n.*** **1** a hard substance that forms on the teeth. **2** a reddish, salty crust that forms inside wine casks. In a purified form it is the acid substance (**cream of tartar**) in baking powder.

**task** (task) ***n.*** a piece of work that one must do. ◆***v.*** to put a strain on; be hard for; burden [Reading the small print *tasked* my eyesight.] —**take to task,** to find fault with; scold.

> SYNONYMS: A **task** is something one has to do or is told to do and is usually hard work [the *task* of shoveling out the driveway]. A **chore** is a task that has to be done every day or at regular intervals, as on a farm or in the home [*chores* like doing the dishes and washing clothes].

☆**task force** **1** a specially trained military unit given a certain task to carry out. **2** any group that has a certain project to carry out.

**task·mas·ter** (task′mas′tər) ***n.*** a person who gives tasks or hard work to others to do.

762 **Tas·ma·ni·a** (taz mā′nē ə) an island that is part of Australia. —**Tas·ma′ni·an** ***adj., n.***

**tas·sel** (tas′'l) ***n.*** **1** a bunch of threads, cords, etc. hanging from a knob. *See the picture.* **2** something like this, as the silk that hangs from an ear of corn. ◆***v.*** to put tassels on or have tassels. —**tas′seled** or **tas′selled, tas′sel·ing** or **tas′sel·ling**

**taste** (tāst) ***v.*** **1** to be aware of something by a special sense in the mouth; notice the flavor of [I *taste* garlic in the salad.] **2** to test the flavor of by putting some in one's mouth [*Taste* this sauce to see if it's too sweet.] **3** to eat or drink very little of [She just *tasted* her food.] **4** to have a certain flavor [The milk *tastes* sour.] **5** to have the experience of [to *taste* success]. —**tast′ed, tast′ing** ◆***n.*** **1** the power to taste; the sense in the taste buds of the tongue by which one can tell the flavor of things. **2** that quality of a thing which is noticed by the tongue; flavor [Candy has a sweet *taste.*] **3** a small amount, especially of food or drink; sample; bit [Give me a *taste* of the cake. He had a short *taste* of fame.] **4** the ability to know and judge what is beautiful, proper, etc. [Her simple dress showed her good *taste.*] **5** a style or way that shows such ability to judge what is beautiful, proper, etc. [That remark was in bad *taste.*] **6** a liking; preference [He has no *taste* for sports.] —**tast′er** ***n.***

**taste bud** any of the cells in the tongue that tell whether something is sweet, sour, salty, or bitter.

**taste·ful** (tāst′fəl) ***adj.*** having or showing good taste (*in noun meaning* 4). —**taste′ful·ly** ***adv.***

**taste·less** (tāst′lis) ***adj.*** **1** without taste or flavor [*tasteless* food]. **2** lacking good taste (*in noun meaning* 4). —**taste′less·ly** ***adv.***

**tast·y** (tās′tē) ***adj.*** that tastes good; full of flavor [a *tasty* meal]. —**tast′i·er, tast′i·est** —**tast′i·ness** ***n.***

**tat** (tat) ***v.*** to do tatting or make by tatting. —**tat′ted, tat′ting**

**Ta·tar** (tät′ər) ***n.*** any of the Mongols or Turks who invaded western Asia and eastern Europe in the Middle Ages.

**tat·ter** (tat′ər) ***n.*** **1** a torn and hanging piece or shred, as of cloth; rag. **2 tatters,** *pl.* torn, ragged clothes.

**tat·tered** (tat′ərd) ***adj.*** **1** torn and ragged [*tattered* clothes]. **2** wearing torn and ragged clothes [a *tattered* child].

**tat·ting** (tat′iŋ) ***n.*** **1** the act of making lace by looping and knotting thread with a small shuttle held in the hand. *See the picture.* **2** this kind of lace.

**tat·tle** (tat′'l) ***v.*** **1** to talk in a foolish way; chatter. **2** to tell others' secrets; tell tales [You *tattled* to the teacher.] —**tat′tled, tat′tling** ◆***n.*** foolish talk; chatter. —**tat′tler** ***n.***

☆**tat·tle·tale** (tat′'l tāl) ***n.*** a person who tells the secrets of others; informer.

**tat·too¹** (ta to͞o′) ***v.*** to make marks or designs on the skin by pricking it with needles and putting colors in. —**tat·tooed′, tat·too′ing** ◆***n.*** a mark or design made in this way. *See the picture.* —*pl.* **tat·toos′**

**tat·too²** (ta to͞o′) ***n.*** **1** a signal on a drum or bugle ordering soldiers or sailors to go to their quarters at night. **2** a loud tapping or rapping [The teacher's fingers beat a *tattoo* on the desk.] —*pl.* **tat·toos′**

**taught** (tôt) *past tense and past participle of* **teach.**

**taunt** (tônt *or* tänt) ***v.*** to make fun of with scornful words; jeer at; tease. ◆***n.*** a scornful or jeering remark.

**taupe** (tōp) ***n., adj.*** dark, brownish gray.

**Tau·rus** (tôr′əs) the second sign of the zodiac, for the period from April 20 to May 20: *also called* the Bull. *See the picture for* **zodiac.**

**taut** (tôt) ***adj.*** **1** tightly stretched, as a rope. **2** showing strain; tense [a *taut* smile].

**tav·ern** (tav′ərn) ***n.*** **1** a place where beer, whiskey, etc. are sold and drunk; bar. **2** an inn.

**taw·dry** (tô′drē) ***adj.*** cheap and showy; gaudy. —**taw′dri·er, taw′dri·est**

> At the fair of St. Audrey that used to be held each year in England, one could buy cheap, showy things, especially a lace called *St. Audrey's lace.* That name was shortened to *Tawdry lace,* from which we get our word **tawdry.**

**taw·ny** (tô′nē) ***adj., n.*** brownish yellow; tan [Lions have a *tawny* coat.] —**taw′ni·er, taw′ni·est**

**tax** (taks) ***n.*** **1** money that one must pay to help support a government. It is usually a percentage of one's income or of the value of something bought or owned. **2** a heavy burden or strain [The illness was a *tax* on my health.] ◆***v.*** **1** to put a tax on [to *tax* gasoline]. **2** to make pay a tax [Congress has the power to *tax* the people.] **3** to put a burden or strain on [These pranks are beginning to *tax* my patience.] **4** to find fault with; accuse [They *taxed* him with being unfair.] —**tax′a·ble** ***adj.***

**tax·a·tion** (tak sā′shən) ***n.*** **1** the act or a system of taxing. **2** the amount collected in taxes.

☆**tax·i** (tak′sē) ***n.*** *a shorter form of* **taxicab.** —*pl.* **tax′is** ◆***v.*** **1** to go in a taxicab. **2** to move along the ground or water as an airplane does before taking off or after landing. —**tax′ied, tax′i·ing** or **tax′y·ing**

☆**tax·i·cab** (tak′sē kab) ***n.*** an automobile in which

passengers are carried for a fare. It usually has a meter that shows the amount owed.

**tax·i·der·my** (tak′si dur′mē) ***n.*** the art of stuffing and mounting the skins of animals so that they look alive. —**tax′i·der′mist** ***n.***

**tax·pay·er** (taks′pā′ər) ***n.*** a person who pays a tax or taxes.

**Tay·lor** (tā′lər), **Zach·a·ry** (zak′ər ē) 1784–1850; 12th president of the United States, from 1849 to 1850.

**TB** or **T.B.** *abbreviation for* **tuberculosis.**

**T-bar** (tē′bär′) ***n.*** ☆a T-shaped bar hung from a moving endless cable. It is used to pull skiers up a slope as they hold it and stand on their skis.

**tbs.** or **tbsp.** *abbreviations for* **tablespoon** *or* **tablespoons.**

**Tchai·kov·sky** (chī kôf′skē), **Peter Il·ich** (il′yich) 1840–1893; Russian composer.

**TD** or **td** *abbreviation for* **touchdown.**

**tea** (tē) ***n.*** **1** a plant grown in warm parts of Asia for its leaf buds and young leaves, which are prepared by drying, etc. for use in making a common drink. *See the picture.* **2** the dried leaves and leaf buds. **3** the drink made by steeping these in hot water. **4** a meal in the late afternoon, as in England, at which tea is the usual drink. **5** an afternoon party at which tea, coffee, etc. are served. **6** a drink like tea, made from some other plant or from meat [sassafras *tea;* beef *tea*].

☆**tea bag** a small bag of cloth or paper containing tea leaves, put into hot water to make tea.

**teach** (tēch) ***v.*** **1** to show or help to learn how to do something; train [She *taught* us to skate.] **2** to give lessons to or in [Who *teaches* your class? He *teaches* French.] **3** to be a teacher [I plan to *teach.*] **4** to make or help to know or understand [The accident *taught* her to be careful.] —**taught, teach′ing** —**teach′a·ble** ***adj.***

> SYNONYMS: **Teach** is the word used most often for the act of passing on knowledge or showing how to do something [He *taught* how to play the guitar.] **Instruct** suggests a system of teaching, usually in a particular subject [She *instructs* in chemistry.] **Train** suggests the developing of a skill, especially one that can be used in a certain job [I was *trained* as a mechanic.]

**teach·er** (tēch′ər) ***n.*** a person who teaches, especially in a school or college.

**teach·ing** (tēch′iŋ) ***n.*** **1** the work or profession of a teacher. **2** *usually* **teachings,** *pl.* something taught [the *teachings* of a religion].

**tea·cup** (tē′kup) ***n.*** a cup for drinking tea.

**teak** (tēk) ***n.*** **1** a large tree of the East Indies, with hard, golden-brown wood. **2** this wood, used for making furniture, ships, etc.

**tea·ket·tle** (tē′ket″l) ***n.*** a kettle with a spout, used to boil water as for making tea.

**teal** (tēl) ***n.*** **1** a wild duck with a short neck. *See the picture.* **2** a dark greenish blue.

**team** (tēm) ***n.*** **1** two or more horses, oxen, etc. harnessed together as for pulling a plow or wagon. **2** a group of people working together, or playing together in a contest against another such group [a *team* of scientists; a baseball *team*]. ●***v.*** to join together in a team [Let's *team* up with them.]

**team·mate** (tēm′māt) ***n.*** a fellow member of a team.

tattoo

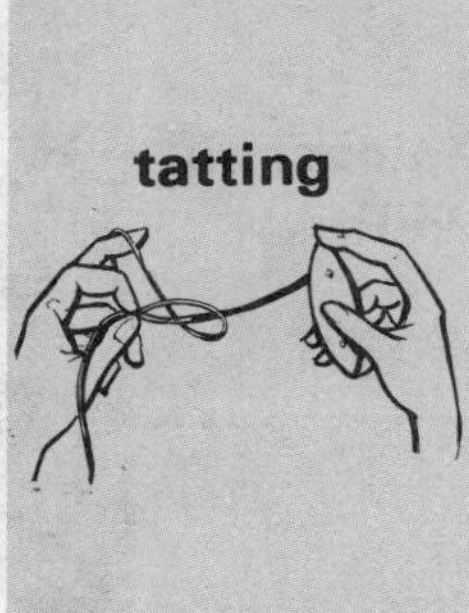

tatting

tassel

teal
36 cm (14 in.) long

tea leaves and plant

☆**team·ster** (tēm′stər) ***n.*** a person whose work is hauling loads with a team or truck.

**team·work** (tēm′wurk) ***n.*** the action or effort of people working together as a group.

**tea·pot** (tē′pät) ***n.*** a pot with a spout, handle, and lid, for making and pouring tea.

**tear**[1] (ter) ***v.*** **1** to pull apart by force; rip [Paper *tears* easily. *Tear* the cloth into strips.] **2** to make by tearing [The nail *tore* a hole in her coat.] **3** to pull up, down, out, at, away, etc. with force [The wind *tore* up trees by their roots.] **4** to divide by struggle, fighting, etc. [The country was *torn* by civil war.] **5** to make suffer very much [*torn* by grief]. **6** to move with force or speed [We *tore* home.] —**tore, torn, tear′ing** ●***n.*** **1** the act of tearing. **2** a torn place; rip [to mend a *tear* in a shirt]. —**tear down,** to take apart; wreck [to *tear down* a building]. —**tear into,** to attack or find fault with in a harsh way: *used only in everyday talk.*

**tear**[2] (tir) ***n.*** a drop of the salty liquid that flows from the eye, as in weeping: *also called* **tear′drop.** ●***v.*** to flow with tears [Onions make my eyes *tear.*] —**in tears,** weeping.

**tear·ful** (tir′fəl) ***adj.*** **1** in tears; weeping. **2** causing tears; sad [a *tearful* tale]. —**tear′ful·ly** ***adv.***

**tear gas** (tir) a gas that makes the eyes sore and blinds them with tears.

**tease** (tēz) ***v.*** **1** to bother or annoy by joking or mocking talk, playful fooling, etc. *See* SYNONYMS *at* **annoy.** **2** to beg in an annoying way [The child kept

| | | | | | | | |
|---|---|---|---|---|---|---|---|
| **a** | fat | **ir** | here | **ou** | out | **zh** | leisure |
| **ā** | ape | **ī** | bite, fire | **u** | up | **ŋ** | ring |
| **ä** | car, lot | **ō** | go | **ur** | fur | | a *in* ago |
| **e** | ten | **ô** | law, horn | **ch** | chin | | e *in* agent |
| **er** | care | **oi** | oil | **sh** | she | **ə =** | i *in* unity |
| **ē** | even | **oo** | look | **th** | thin | | o *in* collect |
| **i** | hit | **ōō** | tool | ***th*** | then | | u *in* focus |

**t**

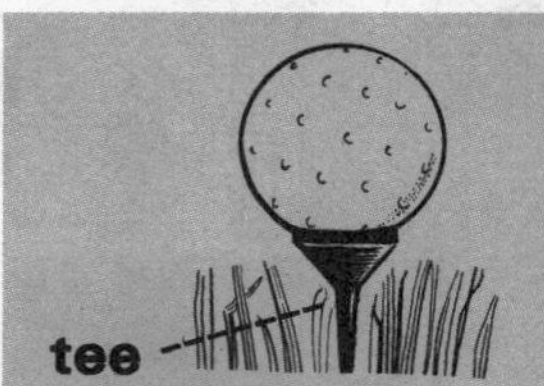

*teasing* for candy.] **3** to fluff the hair by brushing or combing from the ends toward the scalp. —**teased, teas′ing** ◆***n.*** a person who teases.

**tea·spoon** (tē′spoon) ***n.*** **1** a spoon for stirring tea, coffee, etc. and eating some soft foods. **2** *a shorter form of* **teaspoonful.**

**tea·spoon·ful** (tē′spōōn fool) ***n.*** as much as a teaspoon will hold [Three *teaspoonfuls* equal one tablespoonful.] —*pl.* **tea′spoon·fuls**

**teat** (tēt) ***n.*** the nipple of a breast or udder.

**tech.** *abbreviation for* **technical** *or* **technology.**

**tech·ni·cal** (tek′ni k′l) ***adj.*** **1** having to do with the useful or industrial arts or skills [A *technical* school has courses in mechanics, welding, etc.] **2** of or used in a particular science, art, profession, etc. [*technical* words; *technical* skill]. **3** according to the rules of some science, art, sport, etc. [There are *technical* differences between football and Rugby.] —**tech′ni·cal·ly *adv.***

**tech·ni·cal·i·ty** (tek′nə kal′ə tē) ***n.*** **1** a technical point, detail, etc. [the *technicalities* of radio repair]. **2** a small point or detail related to a main issue [She was found guilty on a legal *technicality.*] —*pl.* **tech′ni·cal′i·ties**

**tech·ni·cian** (tek nish′ən) ***n.*** a person who has skill in the technique of some art or science.

**tech·nique** (tek nēk′) ***n.*** a way of using tools, materials, etc. and following rules in doing something artistic, in carrying out a scientific experiment, etc. [a violinist with good bowing *technique*].

**tech·nol·o·gy** (tek näl′ə jē) ***n.*** **1** the study of the industrial arts or applied sciences, as engineering, mechanics, etc. **2** science as it is put to use in practical work [medical *technology*]. **3** a method or process for dealing with a technical problem. —**tech·no·log·i·cal** (tek′nə läj′i k′l) ***adj.*** —**tech′no·log′i·cal·ly *adv.*** —**tech·nol′o·gist *n.***

☆**ted·dy bear** (ted′ē ber′) a child's stuffed toy that looks like a bear cub. *See the picture.*

President Theodore Roosevelt, whose nickname was Teddy, liked to hunt big game. A newspaper once printed a cartoon of him sparing the life of a bear cub. Then a toy company made such a toy bear cub, which it called the **teddy bear.**

**te·di·ous** (tē′dē əs *or* tē′jəs) ***adj.*** long and boring [a *tedious* play]. —**te′di·ous·ly *adv.***

**te·di·um** (tē′dē əm) ***n.*** the condition of being boring or tiresome; monotony.

**tee** (tē) ***n.*** **1** a small holder made of wood or plastic, on which a golf player places the ball before hitting it. *See the picture.* **2** the place from which a golf player makes the first stroke on each hole. ◆***v.*** to place on a tee [to *tee* up a golf ball]. —**teed, tee′ing** —**tee off,** to hit a golf ball from a tee.

**teem** (tēm) ***v.*** to be very full; swarm; abound [a cabin *teeming* with flies].

**teen** (tēn) ***n.*** **1** *a shorter form of* **teen-ager.** **2 teens,** *pl.* the years of one's age from 13 through 19. ◆***adj.*** *a shorter form of* **teen-age.**

**teen-age** (tēn′āj′) ***adj.*** **1** in one's teens. **2** of or for persons in their teens [*teen-age* clothing].

☆**teen-ag·er** (tēn′āj′ər) ***n.*** a person who is 13 through 19 years of age.

**tee·ny** (tē′nē) ***adj.*** *another word for* **tiny,** *used only in everyday talk.* —**tee′ni·er, tee′ni·est** *Also* **teen·sy** (tēn′sē).

☆**tee·pee** (tē′pē) ***n.*** *another spelling of* **tepee.**

☆**tee shirt** *another spelling of* **T-shirt.**

**tee·ter** (tēt′ər) ***v.*** to move in an unsteady way; totter, wobble, etc.

**tee·ter-tot·ter** (tēt′ər tät′ər) ***n., v.*** *another name for* **seesaw.**

**teeth** (tēth) ***n.*** *plural of* **tooth.**

**teethe** (tē*th*) ***v.*** to grow teeth; cut one's teeth. —**teethed, teeth′ing**

**tee·to·tal·er** (tē tōt′′l ər) ***n.*** a person who never drinks alcoholic liquor.

☆**Tef·lon** (tef′län) *a trademark for* a tough chemical substance used to coat surfaces, as of pans or bearings, to keep things from sticking.

**Teh·ran** (te rän′) or **Te·he·ran** (te ə rän′) the capital of Iran.

**Tel A·viv-Jaf·fa** (tel′ä vēv′yäf′ə *or* tel′ə vēv′jaf′ə) a seaport in western Israel. *It is usually called just* **Tel Aviv.**

**tel·e·cast** (tel′ə kast) ***v.*** to broadcast by television. ◆***n.*** a television broadcast. —**tel′e·cast** or **tel′e·cast·ed, tel′e·cast·ing** —**tel′e·cast·er *n.***

☆**tel·e·gram** (tel′ə gram) ***n.*** a message sent by telegraph.

**tel·e·graph** (tel′ə graf) ***n.*** a device or system for sending messages by a code of electrical signals that are sent either over wire or by radio. ◆***v.*** **1** to send by telegraph, as a message. **2** to send a telegram to.

**tel·e·graph·ic** (tel′ə graf′ik) ***adj.*** of or sent by telegraph. —**tel′e·graph′i·cal·ly *adv.***

**te·leg·ra·phy** (tə leg′rə fē) ***n.*** the sending of messages by telegraph. —**te·leg′ra·pher *n.***

**tel·e·me·ter** (tel′ə mēt′ər *or* tə lem′ə tər) ***n.*** an electronic device for making a record of scientific data and sending it over great distances, as from a spaceship.

**te·lep·a·thy** (tə lep′ə thē) ***n.*** the supposed sending of messages from one mind to another, without the help of speech, sight, etc. —**tel·e·path·ic** (tel′ə path′ik) ***adj.***

**tel·e·phone** (tel′ə fōn) ***n.*** ☆**1** a way of sending sounds over distances by changing them into electric signals which are sent through a wire and then changed back into sounds. ☆**2** a device for sending and receiving sounds in this way. ◆***v.*** ☆**1** to talk over a telephone. **2** to send by telephone, as a message. **3** to speak to by telephone. —**tel'e·phoned, tel'e·phon·ing** —**tel·e·phon·ic** (tel'ə fän'ik) ***adj.***

**Telephone** comes from two Greek words, *tele,* meaning "far off," and *phone,* meaning "a sound." Alexander G. Bell took the word *telephone* for his invention in 1876 after the word had been used for other devices.

**tel·e·scope** (tel'ə skōp) ***n.*** a device for making far-off things seem closer and larger, used especially in astronomy. It consists of one or more tubes containing lenses and, often, mirrors. ◆***v.*** **1** to slide together, one part into another, as the tubes of some telescopes. **2** to force or crush together in this way [The crash *telescoped* the whole front end of the car.] —**tel'e·scoped, tel'e·scop·ing**

**tel·e·scop·ic** (tel'ə skäp'ik) ***adj.*** **1** of a telescope [*telescopic* lenses]. **2** seen or got only by means of a telescope [*telescopic* photographs of the stars]. **3** able to see far; farseeing. **4** having sections that slide one inside another [a *telescopic* drinking cup]. *See the picture.*

☆**tel·e·thon** (tel'ə thän) ***n.*** a television program over many hours, to raise money for some cause or charity. People call in pledges by telephone.

☆**Tel·e·type** (tel'ə tīp) *a trademark for* a form of teletypewriter.

☆**tel·e·type·writ·er** (tel'ə tīp'rīt'ər) ***n.*** a form of telegraph in which the message is typed on a keyboard that sends electric signals to a machine that prints the words.

**tel·e·vise** (tel'ə vīz) ***v.*** to send pictures of by television [to *televise* a baseball game]. —**tel'e·vised, tel'e·vis·ing**

**tel·e·vi·sion** (tel'ə vizh'ən) ***n.*** **1** a way of sending pictures through space by changing the light rays into electric waves which are picked up by a receiver that changes them back to light rays shown on a screen. The sound that goes with the picture is sent by radio at the same time. **2** such a receiver, usually in a cabinet. **3** the act, business, etc. of broadcasting by television. ◆***adj.*** of, using, used in, or sent by television [a *television* program; a *television* tube].

**tell** (tel) ***v.*** **1** to put into words; say [*Tell* the facts.] **2** to give the story; report; narrate [The book *tells* of their travels.] **3** to make clear or make known; show [A smile *tells* joy better than words.] **4** to let know; inform [*Tell* me how to get there.] **5** to know by seeing, hearing, etc.; recognize [I can *tell* the difference between them.] **6** to order or command [She *told* us to leave.] **7** to have a definite effect [Our efforts are beginning to *tell.*] **8** to count off one by one [to *tell* one's beads in saying prayers with a rosary]. —**told, tell'ing** —**tell off,** to scold or criticize sharply: *used only in everyday talk.* —**tell on,** **1** to tire [The hard work is beginning to *tell on* him.] **2** to tattle; tell secrets about: *used only in everyday talk.*

SYNONYMS: **Tell** is the simple, general word that means to pass on the facts about something [*Tell* me what you learned.] **Relate** means to tell of something that one has personally seen or lived through [George *related* his dream.] **Recount** means to tell of a series of events in the order in which they happened [The pilot *recounted* her adventures.]

**Tell** (tel), **William** a hero in a Swiss legend, who was forced by a tyrant to shoot an apple off his son's head with an arrow.

**tell·er** (tel'ər) ***n.*** **1** a person who tells a story, etc. **2** a clerk in a bank who receives and pays out money.

**tell·ing** (tel'iŋ) ***adj.*** having a sharp effect; forceful [That last punch was a *telling* blow.]

**tell·tale** (tel'tāl) ***n.*** *another word for* **tattletale.** ◆***adj.*** telling what is meant to be kept secret or hidden [She knew he had been outside, by the *telltale* mud on his shoes.]

**te·mer·i·ty** (tə mer'ə tē) ***n.*** foolish or reckless boldness; rashness.

**temp.** *abbreviation for* **temperature.**

**tem·per** (tem'pər) ***n.*** **1** state of mind; mood [She's in a bad *temper.*] **2** calmness of mind; self-control [Keep your *temper.* He lost his *temper.*] **3** anger or rage; also, quickness to anger [He flew into a *temper.* She has quite a *temper.*] **4** hardness or toughness, as of a metal. ◆***v.*** **1** to make less strong by adding something else; moderate [to *temper* boldness with caution]. **2** to bring to the right condition by treating in some way [Steel is *tempered* by heating and sudden cooling to make it hard and tough.]

**tem·per·a·ment** (tem'prə mənt *or* tem'pər ə mənt) ***n.*** **1** one's usual nature or mood; disposition [a person of calm *temperament*]. **2** a moody nature that makes one easily excited or upset [Some opera singers are known for their *temperament.*] 765

**tem·per·a·men·tal** (tem'prə men't'l *or* tem'pər ə men't'l) ***adj.*** **1** of or caused by temperament [Pat had a *temperamental* burst of anger.] **2** easily excited or upset; moody. —**tem'per·a·men'tal·ly** ***adv.***

**tem·per·ance** (tem'pər əns) ***n.*** **1** care in keeping one's actions, appetites, feelings, etc. under proper control; moderation [*Temperance* in eating would help him lose weight.] **2** the drinking of little or no alcoholic liquor.

**tem·per·ate** (tem'pər it) ***adj.*** **1** using or showing temperance in one's actions, appetites, etc.; moderate [Although she was angry, she made a *temperate* reply.] **2** neither very hot nor very cold [a *temperate* climate]. —**tem'per·ate·ly** ***adv.***

**Temperate Zone** either of two zones of the earth that have a temperate climate. One zone lies between the arctic and the Tropic of Cancer, and the other lies between the antarctic and the Tropic of Capricorn.

**tem·per·a·ture** (tem'prə chər *or* tem'pər ə chər) ***n.*** **1** the degree of hotness or coldness, as of air, liquids, the body, etc., usually as measured by a thermometer. **2** a body heat above the normal, which is about 37°C or 98.6°F; fever.

**tem·pered** (tem'pərd) ***adj.*** having a certain kind of temper: *used in words formed with a hyphen* [Kim is a sweet-*tempered* child.]

| | | | | | | | |
|---|---|---|---|---|---|---|---|
| **a** | fat | **ir** | here | **ou** | out | **zh** | leisure |
| **ā** | ape | **ī** | bite, fire | **u** | up | **ŋ** | ring |
| **ä** | car, lot | **ō** | go | **ur** | fur | | a *in* ago |
| **e** | ten | **ô** | law, horn | **ch** | chin | | e *in* agent |
| **er** | care | **oi** | oil | **sh** | she | **ə** = | i *in* unity |
| **ē** | even | **oo** | look | **th** | thin | | o *in* collect |
| **i** | hit | **ōō** | tool | ***th*** | then | | u *in* focus |

**t**

**tem·pest** (tem′pist) ***n.*** **1** a wild storm with high winds and, often, rain. **2** a wild outburst of feeling, action, etc.

**tem·pes·tu·ous** (tem pes′choo wəs) ***adj.*** of or like a tempest; stormy, wild, raging, etc.

**tem·ple**[1] (tem′p'l) ***n.*** **1** a building for the worship of God or a god. **2 Temple,** any of the three buildings for the worship of God built at different times by the Jews in ancient Jerusalem. Each was in turn destroyed by enemies. **3** *another name for* **synagogue. 4** a building of great size, beauty, etc. for some special purpose [a *temple* of art].

**tem·ple**[2] (tem′p'l) ***n.*** the flat area at either side of the forehead, above and behind the eye.

**tem·po** (tem′pō) ***n.*** the rate of speed for playing a certain piece of music ["America, the Beautiful" is usually played at a slow *tempo.*] *—pl.* **tem′pos** or **tem·pi** (tem′pē)

**tem·po·ral**[1] (tem′pər əl) ***adj.*** **1** having to do with time. **2** having to do with everyday life; worldly; not spiritual. **3** having to do with the laws of a state rather than of a church or religion; civil.

**tem·po·ral**[2] (tem′pər əl) ***adj.*** having to do with the temples of the head.

**tem·po·rar·y** (tem′pə rer′ē) ***adj.*** lasting only for a short time; not permanent [She's serving as *temporary* chairperson.] **—tem′po·rar′i·ly *adv.***

**tem·po·rize** (tem′pə rīz) ***v.*** **1** to talk or act in a way that one thinks will be popular or give an advantage, rather than in the right way. **2** to put off making a decision, or to agree for a while, in order to gain time or avoid trouble. **—tem′po·rized, tem′po·riz·ing**

**tempt** (tempt) ***v.*** **1** to try to get a person to do or want something that is wrong or forbidden [The old sailor's tales *tempted* the boy to run away from home.] **2** to be attractive to; entice [I'm afraid the cat will be *tempted* by the goldfish bowl.] **—tempt fate,** to do something reckless [You *tempt fate* by driving with a bad tire.]

**temp·ta·tion** (temp tā′shən) ***n.*** **1** something that tempts [The fresh cookies were a *temptation* to us all.] **2** the act of tempting or the fact of being tempted.

**tempt·er** (temp′tər) ***n.*** a person who tempts.

**tempt·ing** (temp′tiŋ) ***adj.*** that tempts; attractive [The *tempting* odors of cooking made us go in.]

**tempt·ress** (temp′tris) ***n.*** a woman who tempts.

**ten** (ten) ***n., adj.*** one more than nine; the number 10.

**ten·a·ble** (ten′ə b'l) ***adj.*** that can be held, defended, or believed [The theory that the sun goes around the earth is no longer *tenable.*]

**te·na·cious** (tə nā′shəs) ***adj.*** **1** that grips firmly or clings tightly [the *tenacious* ivy on the walls]. **2** holding fast; stubborn [a person of *tenacious* courage]. **3** that keeps or holds on to something for a long time [She has a *tenacious* memory.] **—te·na′cious·ly *adv.***

**te·nac·i·ty** (tə nas′ə tē) ***n.*** the condition or quality of being tenacious.

**ten·an·cy** (ten′ən sē) ***n.*** **1** the condition of living on land or in a building by renting it; being a tenant. **2** the length of time that one is a tenant.

**ten·ant** (ten′ənt) ***n.*** **1** a person who pays rent to use land, live in a building, etc. **2** one that lives in a certain place [These owls are *tenants* of barns.]

**tenant farmer** a person who farms land owned by another and pays rent in cash or in a share of the crops.

**Ten Commandments** in the Bible, the ten laws that God gave to Moses on Mount Sinai.

**tend**[1] (tend) ***v.*** to take care of; watch over [Shepherds *tend* sheep. I'll *tend* the store.]

**tend**[2] (tend) ***v.*** **1** to be likely or apt; be inclined [We *tend* to eat too much.] **2** to move or go in a certain way; lead [a river *tending* east].

**tend·en·cy** (ten′dən sē) ***n.*** the fact of being likely or apt to move or act in a certain way [There is a *tendency* for prices to go up. Pat has a *tendency* to complain.] *—pl.* **tend′en·cies**

**ten·der**[1] (ten′dər) ***adj.*** **1** soft or delicate and easily chewed, cut, etc. [*tender* meat; *tender* blades of grass]. **2** that is hurt or feels pain easily; sensitive [My sprained ankle still feels *tender.*] **3** warm and gentle; loving [a *tender* smile]. **4** young [at the *tender* age of five]. **—ten′der·ly *adv.* —ten′der·ness *n.***

**ten·der**[2] (ten′dər) ***v.*** **1** to offer as payment for a debt. **2** to give or offer for someone to take [to *tender* an invitation or an apology]. **◆*n.*** **1** an offer, especially a formal offer [a *tender* of marriage]. ☆**2** something offered in payment, especially money: *see* **legal tender.**

**tend·er**[3] (ten′dər) ***n.*** **1** a boat that carries people, supplies, etc. between a large ship and shore. **2** the railroad car behind a steam locomotive for carrying its coal, water, etc. **3** a person who tends, or takes care of, something.

☆**ten·der·foot** (ten′dər foot) ***n.*** **1** a person who is not used to rough or outdoor life, as a newcomer to a ranch in the West. **2** a beginner in the Boy Scouts. *—pl.* **ten′der·foots** or **ten′der·feet**

> **Tenderfoot** is an American word, first used in 1849, when there was a great rush of people to California looking for gold. Many of the new arrivals were not used to wearing Western boots and soon had sore feet.

**ten·der·heart·ed** (ten′dər här′tid) ***adj.*** having a tender heart; quick to feel pity.

**ten·der·ize** (ten′də rīz) ***v.*** to make tender [You can *tenderize* tough meat by pounding it before cooking.] **—ten′der·ized, ten′der·iz·ing —ten′der·iz·er *n.***

☆**ten·der·loin** (ten′dər loin) ***n.*** a cut of beef or pork from the most tender part of the loin.

**ten·don** (ten′dən) ***n.*** the cord of tough fiber that fastens a muscle to a bone, etc.

**ten·dril** (ten′drəl) ***n.*** any of the small, curly stems that hold up a climbing plant by coiling around something [Grapevines have *tendrils.*] *See the picture.*

**ten·e·ment** (ten′ə mənt) ***n.*** **1** a suite of rooms, or an apartment, that is rented. **2** an old, crowded apartment house, as in a city slum: *also called* ☆**tenement house.**

**ten·et** (ten′it) ***n.*** a principle or belief that is held as a truth by some person or group [religious *tenets*].

**Ten·nes·see** (ten ə sē′) **1** a State in the east central part of the U.S.: abbreviated **Tenn., TN 2** a river flowing through Tennessee, Alabama, and Kentucky, into the Ohio.

**ten·nis** (ten′is) ***n.*** a game in which players on each side of a net dividing a court hit a ball back and forth over the net with rackets.

**Ten·ny·son** (ten′ə s'n), **Alfred** 1809–1892; English poet: *called* **Alfred, Lord Tennyson.**

**ten·on** (ten′ən) ***n.*** a part of a piece of wood, etc. cut to stick out so that it will fit into a hole (called a **mortise**) in another piece in order to form a joint. *See the picture for* **mortise.** ◆***v.*** to fasten with a tenon.

**ten·or** (ten′ər) ***n.*** **1** the highest kind of man's singing voice. **2** a singer with such a voice, or an instrument with a range like this [a *tenor* saxophone]. **3** general course [Her happy life had an even *tenor.*] **4** general meaning [What was the *tenor* of his remarks?] ◆***adj.*** of or for a tenor.

**Tenor** comes from a Latin word meaning "to hold." In earlier music, the tenor voice usually "held" the melody, while the other voices sang the harmony to go with it.

**ten·pins** (ten′pinz) ***n.pl.*** **1** the game of bowling: *used with a singular verb.* **2** the pins used in bowling.

**tense**[1] (tens) ***adj.*** **1** stretched tight; taut [a *tense* rope; *tense* muscles]. **2** feeling or showing nervous strain; anxious [a *tense* silence]. **3** causing a nervous feeling [a *tense* situation]. —**tens′er, tens′est** ◆***v.*** to make or become tense; tighten, as muscles. —**tensed, tens′ing** —**tense′ly** ***adv.***

**tense**[2] (tens) ***n.*** any of the forms of a verb that show the time of the action or condition [Present, past, and future *tenses* of "sail" are "sail" or "sails," "sailed," and "will sail."]

**ten·sile** (ten′s'l) ***adj.*** **1** of or under tension [the *tensile* strength of a cable]. **2** that can be stretched.

**ten·sion** (ten′shən) ***n.*** **1** a stretching or being stretched, so as to put or be under strain. **2** nervous strain; tense or anxious feeling [Actors may feel *tension* before a play.] **3** voltage, or electric force [Those poles carry high-*tension* wire.]

**tent** (tent) ***n.*** a shelter of canvas, etc. stretched over poles and fixed to stakes. ◆***v.*** to live or camp out in a tent.

**ten·ta·cle** (ten′tə k'l) ***n.*** **1** a long, slender part growing around the head or mouth of some animals, used for feeling, gripping, or moving [The octopus has eight *tentacles.*] **2** a sensitive hair on a plant.

**ten·ta·tive** (ten′tə tiv) ***adj.*** made or done as a test or for the time being; not definite or final [We made *tentative* plans to move.] —**ten′ta·tive·ly** ***adv.***

**tenth** (tenth) ***adj.*** coming after nine others; 10th in order. ◆***n.*** **1** the tenth one. **2** one of ten equal parts of something; 1/10.

**ten·u·ous** (ten′yo͞o wəs) ***adj.*** **1** slender or fine [the *tenuous* threads of a cobweb]. **2** not dense; thin, as air high up. **3** not solid; flimsy [The evidence is a little *tenuous.*] —**ten′u·ous·ly** ***adv.***

**ten·ure** (ten′yər) ***n.*** **1** the condition or right of holding property, a title, etc. **2** the length of time something is held [A Senator's *tenure* of office is six years.] **3** the condition of holding a job permanently, granted to some teachers and civil service workers after certain requirements are met.

☆**te·pee** (tē′pē) ***n.*** a tent made of animal skins and shaped like a cone, used by some American Indians. *See the picture.*

**tep·id** (tep′id) ***adj.*** slightly warm; lukewarm.

☆**te·qui·la** (tə kē′lə) ***n.*** an alcoholic liquor made from the juice of a desert plant growing in Mexico and Central America.

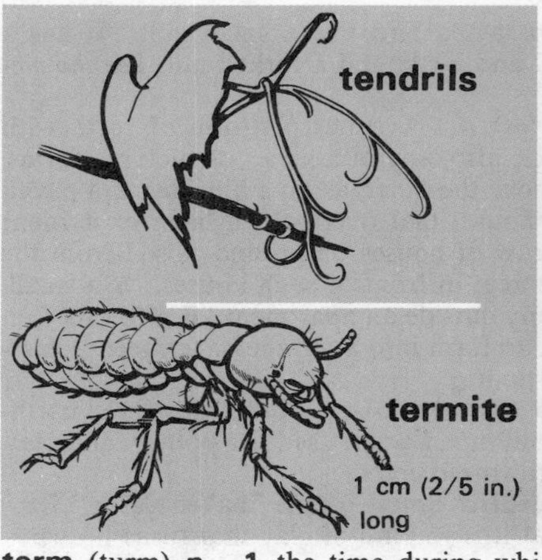

**term** (tʉrm) ***n.*** **1** the time during which something lasts; time fixed by law, agreement, etc. [a *term* of office]. **2** a division of a school year, as a semester [the spring *term*]. **3 terms,** *pl.* the conditions of a contract, agreement, will, etc. **4 terms,** *pl.* relations between persons [Are you two still on speaking *terms?*] **5** a word or phrase, especially as used with a special meaning in some science, art, etc. ["Radical" is a chemical *term* for a cluster of atoms that act as a single atom.] **6 terms,** *pl.* language of a certain kind [He spoke of you in friendly *terms.*] **7 terms,** *pl.* an agreement in dealings [Let's try to come to *terms.*] **8** a quantity in mathematics forming a part of a fraction, ratio, equation, etc. ◆***v.*** to call by a term; name [She is *termed* efficient by all who work with her.]



**ter·mi·na·ble** (tʉr′mi nə b'l) ***adj.*** that can be ended or that ends after a certain time [a *terminable* contract].

**ter·mi·nal** (tʉr′mə n'l) ***adj.*** **1** of, at, or forming the end [a *terminal* bud on a branch; the *terminal* payment of a loan]. **2** describing the last stages of a disease that will soon cause death [*terminal* cancer]. ◆***n.*** **1** an end or end part. **2** either end of an electric circuit. **3** a main station of a railroad, bus line, or airline, where many trips begin or end.

**ter·mi·nate** (tʉr′mə nāt) ***v.*** **1** to bring or come to an end; stop; end [The contract was *terminated.*] **2** to form the end or limit of. —**ter′mi·nat·ed, ter′mi·nat·ing** —**ter′mi·na′tion** ***n.***

**ter·mi·nol·o·gy** (tʉr′mə näl′ə jē) ***n.*** the special words and phrases used in some art, science, work, etc. [Lawyers use legal *terminology.*]

**ter·mi·nus** (tʉr′mə nəs) ***n.*** **1** either end of a railroad line, bus line, or airline. **2** an end, limit, goal, boundary, etc. —*pl.* **ter·mi·ni** (tʉr′mə nī) or **ter′mi·nus·es**

**ter·mite** (tʉr′mīt) ***n.*** a small, pale insect like an ant, that eats wood and damages wooden buildings. Termites live in colonies. *See the picture.*

| | | | | | | | |
|---|---|---|---|---|---|---|---|
| **a** | fat | **ir** | here | **ou** | out | **zh** | leisure |
| **ā** | ape | **ī** | bite, fire | **u** | up | **ŋ** | ring |
| **ä** | car, lot | **ō** | go | **ʉr** | fur | | a *in* ago |
| **e** | ten | **ô** | law, horn | **ch** | chin | | e *in* agent |
| **er** | care | **oi** | oil | **sh** | she | ə = | i *in* unity |
| **ē** | even | **o͝o** | look | **th** | thin | | o *in* collect |
| **i** | hit | **o͞o** | tool | ***th*** | then | | u *in* focus |

**tern** (tʉrn) ***n.*** a sea bird like a small gull. It has a slender body and beak, and a forked tail. *See the picture.*

**ter·race** (ter′əs) ***n.*** **1** a flat platform of earth with sloping banks; also, any of a series of such platforms, rising one above the other, as on a hillside. **2** a paved area near a house, that overlooks a lawn or garden; patio. **3** a row of houses on ground raised from the street. **4** a street in front of such houses. **5** a small, roofed balcony outside an apartment. **6** a flat roof on a house. ◆***v.*** to form into a terrace or terraces. —**ter′raced, ter′rac·ing**

**ter·ra cot·ta** (ter′ə kät′ə) **1** a dull, brown-red earthenware, usually not glazed, used for pottery and statues. **2** its brown-red color.

> In Italian, **terra cotta** means "baked earth," for that is what it is—a kind of clay that turns brown-red when baked.

**terra fir·ma** (fʉr′mə) solid ground [He was glad to return to *terra firma* after his first airplane flight.]

**ter·rain** (tə rān′) ***n.*** ground or an area of land [a farm with hilly *terrain*].

☆**ter·ra·pin** (ter′ə pin) ***n.*** **1** an American turtle that lives in or near fresh water or tidewater. **2** its flesh used as food.

**ter·rar·i·um** (tə rer′ē əm) ***n.*** a glass container holding a garden of small plants, or one used for raising small land animals. *See the picture.* —*pl.* **ter·rar′i·ums** or **ter·rar·i·a** (tə rer′ē ə)



**ter·raz·zo** (tə raz′ō *or* tə rät′sō) ***n.*** flooring of small chips of marble set in cement and polished.

**ter·res·tri·al** (tə res′trē əl) ***adj.*** **1** of the earth [a *terrestrial* globe]. **2** made up of land, not water [the *terrestrial* parts of the world]. **3** living on land [Toads are mainly *terrestrial;* frogs are aquatic.]

**ter·ri·ble** (ter′ə b′l) ***adj.*** **1** causing great fear or terror; dreadful [a *terrible* flood]. **2** very great; severe [*terrible* suffering]. **3** very bad or unpleasant: *used only in everyday talk* [Our guest had *terrible* manners.] —**ter′ri·bly *adv.***

**ter·ri·er** (ter′ē ər) ***n.*** any of several small, lively dogs, as the Scottish terrier, fox terrier, etc.

> **Terrier** comes from the French term *chien terrier,* meaning "hunting dog." *Terrier* was a word for "burrow." These small dogs were taught to burrow into the earth after small game such as rabbits.

**ter·rif·ic** (tə rif′ik) ***adj.*** **1** causing great fear; dreadful [A *terrific* hurricane hit the island.] **2** very great or unusual: *used only in everyday talk* [We saw a *terrific* movie.] —**ter·rif′i·cal·ly *adv.***

**ter·ri·fy** (ter′ə fī) ***v.*** to fill with terror; frighten greatly [They were *terrified* by the lightning and thunder.] —**ter′ri·fied, ter′ri·fy·ing**

**ter·ri·to·ri·al** (ter′ə tôr′ē əl) ***adj.*** **1** of territory or land [the *territorial* expansion of the U.S. in the 19th century]. **2** of or limited to a certain area [fishing rights in the *territorial* waters of another country]. —**ter′ri·to′ri·al·ly *adv.***

**ter·ri·to·ry** (ter′ə tôr′ē) ***n.*** **1** the land ruled by a nation or state. **2 Territory,** a large division of a country or empire, that does not have the full rights of a province or state, as in Canada or Australia [the Northwest *Territories*]. **3** any large stretch of land; region. **4** the particular area chosen as its own by an animal or group of animals. ☆**5** a particular area to travel or work in, as of a traveling salesperson. —*pl.* **ter′ri·to′ries**

**ter·ror** (ter′ər) ***n.*** **1** great fear. *See* SYNONYMS *at* **panic. 2** a person or thing that causes great fear.

**ter·ror·ism** (ter′ər iz′m) ***n.*** the use of force and threats to frighten people into obeying completely. —**ter′ror·ist *n.***

**ter·ror·ize** (ter′ər īz) ***v.*** **1** to fill with terror [The tiger *terrorized* the village.] **2** to keep power over a person or group of people by force or threats. —**ter′ror·ized, ter′ror·iz·ing**

**ter·ry** (ter′ē) ***n.*** a cotton cloth covered with loops of thread that have not been cut. It is used for towels, bathrobes, etc. *Also called* **terry cloth.**

**terse** (tʉrs) ***adj.*** using only a few words but clear and to the point [She gave a *terse* reply.] —**ters′er, ters′est** —**terse′ly *adv.*** —**terse′ness *n.***

> **Terse** comes from a Latin word that means "wiped off" or "clean." A terse expression or manner of speaking is clean and free of words that are not needed to make its meaning clear.

**ter·ti·ar·y** (tʉr′shē er′ē *or* tʉr′shə rē) ***adj.*** of the third rank, order, importance, etc.; third.

**test** (test) ***n.*** **1** an examination or trial to find out what something is like, what it contains, how good it is, etc. [an eye *test;* a *test* of one's courage]. *See* SYNONYMS *at* **trial. 2** a set of questions, problems, etc. for finding out how much someone knows or how skilled the person is [a spelling *test;* a driver's *test*]. ◆***v.*** to put to a test, or examine by a test. —**test′er *n.***

**tes·ta·ment** (tes′tə mənt) ***n.*** **1 Testament,** either of the two parts of the Christian Bible, the **Old Testament** and the **New Testament. 2 Testament,** a copy of the New Testament: *used only in everyday talk.* **3** a statement of beliefs. **4** in law, a will: *used mainly in the phrase* **last will and testament.**

**tes·ta·men·ta·ry** (tes′tə men′tə rē) ***adj.*** having to do with a testament, or will.

**tes·ta·tor** (tes′tāt′ər) ***n.*** a person who has died leaving a will.

**test ban** an agreement between powerful nations to stop testing nuclear weapons, especially in the atmosphere.

**tes·ti·cle** (tes′ti k′l) ***n.*** the gland in a male in which the sperm is formed.

**tes·ti·fy** (tes′tə fī) ***v.*** **1** to tell or give as proof, especially under oath in a court [The witnesses *testified* that they saw the robbery.] **2** to be or give a sign of; indicate [Her look *testified* to her impatience.] —**tes′ti·fied, tes′ti·fy·ing**

**tes·ti·mo·ni·al** (tes′tə mō′nē əl) ***n.*** **1** a statement telling about or praising some person, product, etc. **2** something given to show thanks or to honor someone.

**tes·ti·mo·ny** (tes′tə mō′nē) ***n.*** **1** a statement made by one who testifies, especially under oath in a court. **2** any declaration. **3** a sign or indication. —*pl.* **tes′ti·mo′nies**

**test tube** a tube of thin, clear glass closed at one end, used in chemical experiments, etc. *See the picture.*

**tes·ty** (tes′tē) ***adj.*** easily angered; cross; touchy. —**tes′ti·er, tes′ti·est** —**tes′ti·ly *adv.*** —**tes′ti·ness *n.***

**tet·a·nus** (tet″n əs) ***n.*** a disease that causes spasms of the body, stiffening of the muscles, as of the jaw, and often death; lockjaw. It is caused by a germ that gets into the blood stream through an open wound.

**tête-à-tête** (tāt′ə tāt′) ***n.*** a private talk between two people. ◆***adv.*** two together and in private [They spoke *tête-à-tête.*] ◆***adj.*** of or for two people in private.

> **Tête-à-tête** is French for "head to head," brought over into English to describe two people talking together in private, often with their heads together.

**teth·er** (te*th*′ər) ***n.*** a rope or chain tied to an animal to keep it from roaming. ◆***v.*** to tie to a place with a tether. —**at the end of one's tether,** not able to bear or do any more.

☆**teth·er·ball** (te*th*′ər bôl) ***n.*** a game played by two people who hit with the hand or a paddle a ball hanging by a cord from a pole. The object is to make the cord coil completely around the pole.

**Teu·ton** (to͞ot′'n *or* tyo͞ot′'n) ***n.*** **1** a member of an ancient German people. **2** a member of a group of northern Europeans, including the Germans, Swedes, Dutch, etc.; especially, a German. —**Teu·ton·ic** (to͞o tän′ik *or* tyo͞o tän′ik) ***adj.***

**Tex·as** (tek′səs) a State in the south central part of the U.S.: abbreviated **Tex., TX** —**Tex′an *adj., n.***

**text** (tekst) ***n.*** **1** the main part of the printed matter on a page, not including notes, pictures, etc. **2** the actual words used in a book, speech, etc. by its writer. **3** *a shorter word for* **textbook. 4** a line or sentence from the Bible used as the subject for a sermon. **5** any topic or subject.

**text·book** (tekst′bo͝ok) ***n.*** a book used in teaching a subject, especially one used in a school or college.

**tex·tile** (teks′tīl *or* teks′t'l) ***n.*** a fabric made by weaving; cloth. ◆***adj.*** **1** having to do with weaving or woven fabrics [He works in the *textile* industry.] **2** woven [Linen is a *textile* fabric.]

**tex·tu·al** (teks′cho͞o wəl) ***adj.*** of, found in, or based on a text.

**tex·ture** (teks′chər) ***n.*** **1** the look and feel of a fabric as caused by the arrangement, size, and quality of its threads [Corduroy has a ribbed *texture.*] **2** the general look and feel of any other kind of material; structure; makeup [Stucco has a rough *texture.*] ◆***v.*** to cause to have a particular texture. —**tex′tured, tex′tur·ing**

**-th**[1] a suffix used to form numbers showing order, or place in a series [*fourth, fifth, sixth,* etc.] The suffix **-eth** is used after a vowel [*twentieth, thirtieth, fortieth,* etc.]

**-th**[2] an old-fashioned ending for the present tense of verbs used with *he, she,* or *it* ["He *hath*" is an older way of saying "he has."]

**Thai** (tī) ***n.*** **1** a person born or living in Thailand. —*pl.* **Thais** or **Thai** **2** the language of Thailand. ◆***adj.*** of Thailand, its people, etc.

**Thai·land** (tī′land) a country in southeastern Asia. Its older name is **Siam.**

**Thames** (temz) a river in southern England, flowing through London to the North Sea.

**than** (*th*an *or th*ən) ***conj.*** **1** compared to. *Than* is used before the second part of a comparison [I am taller *than* you.] **2** besides; except [What could I do other *than* stop?] ◆***prep.*** compared to. As a preposition *than* is used only in the phrases *than which* and *than whom* [a poet *than whom* there is no finer].

terrarium

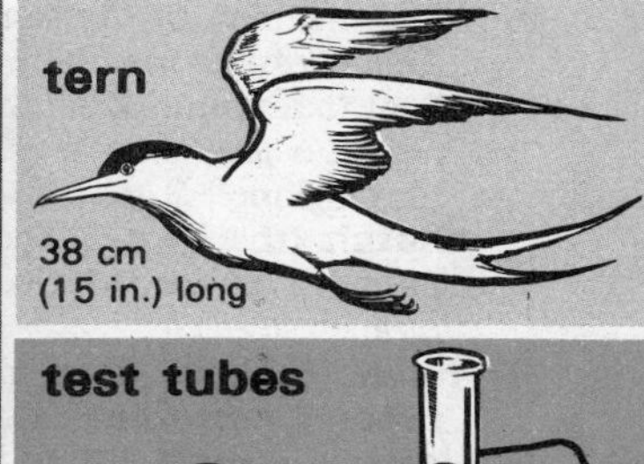

tern

38 cm (15 in.) long

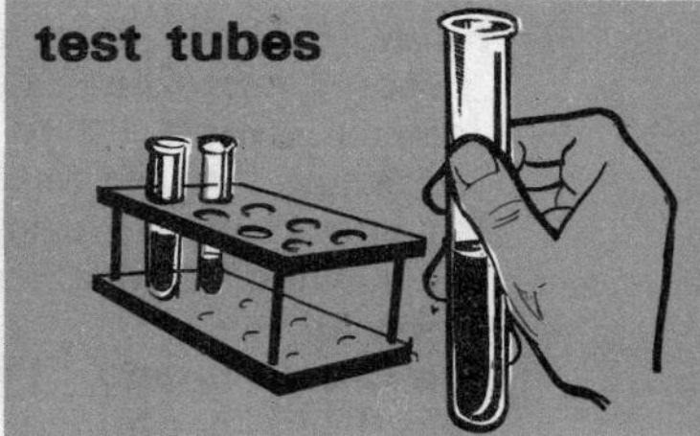

test tubes

**thank** (thaŋk) ***v.*** **1** to say that one is grateful to another for a kindness [We *thanked* her for her help.] **2** to blame [We have him to *thank* for this trouble.]

> **Thank you** means "I thank you" or "We thank you" and is what we usually say to show that we appreciate something. **Thanks** is a briefer way of saying *thank you* and is less formal.

**thank·ful** (thaŋk′fəl) ***adj.*** feeling or showing thanks; grateful. —**thank′ful·ly *adv.***

**thank·less** (thaŋk′lis) ***adj.*** **1** not feeling or showing thanks. **2** not appreciated [a *thankless* task]. —**thank′less·ly *adv.***



**thanks** (thaŋks) ***n.pl.*** the act or fact of thanking someone for something [I owe you *thanks.*] ◆***interj.*** I thank you. —**thanks to, 1** because of. **2** thanks be given to.

**thanks·giv·ing** (thaŋks′giv′iŋ) ***n.*** **1** the act of giving thanks, especially a formal act of public thanks to God. ☆**2 Thanksgiving,** a U.S. holiday, held on the fourth Thursday in November, for feasting and giving thanks: *the full name is* **Thanksgiving Day.**

**that** (*th*at *or th*ət) ***pron.*** **1** the person or thing mentioned [*That* is José.] **2** the thing farther away or in some way different [This is smaller than *that.*] **3** who, whom, or which [She's the one *that* I saw. Here's the book *that* I borrowed.] **4** when [It snowed the day *that* we left.] —*pl.* **those** ◆***adj.*** **1** being the one mentioned [*That* girl is Sue.] **2** being the one farther away or different in some way [This bicycle cost more than *that* one.] —*pl.* **those** ◆***conj.*** *that* is used: **1** before a noun clause [I know *that* you are wrong.] **2** before a clause showing purpose [They died *that* we might live.] **3** before a clause showing result [I ate so much *that* I was sick.] **4** before a clause showing cause [I'm sorry *that* you fell.] **5** before an incomplete sentence showing surprise, desire, anger, etc. [Oh, *that* it were spring!] ◆***adv.*** to such a degree; so [I can't see *that* far.] —**all that, 1** so very [They are not *all that* rich.]

| | | | | | | | |
|---|---|---|---|---|---|---|---|
| a | fat | ir | here | ou | out | zh | leisure |
| ā | ape | ī | bite, fire | u | up | ŋ | ring |
| ä | car, lot | ō | go | ʉr | fur | | a *in* ago |
| e | ten | ô | law, horn | ch | chin | | e *in* agent |
| er | care | oi | oil | sh | she | ə = | i *in* unity |
| ē | even | oo | look | th | thin | | o *in* collect |
| i | hit | o͞o | tool | *th* | then | | u *in* focus |

2 everything of the same sort [baseball and *all that*]. *This phrase is used only in everyday talk.* —☆**at that,** **1** at that point. **2** all things considered; even so. *This phrase is used only in everyday talk.* —**that's that! 1** that is done! **2** that is settled!

**thatch** (thach) ***n.*** a roof or roofing of straw, rushes, palm leaves, etc. ◆***v.*** to cover with thatch. *See the picture.*

**thaw** (thô) ***v.*** **1** to melt [The snow *thawed.*] **2** to become unfrozen: said of frozen foods. *See* SYNONYMS *at* **melt. 3** to become warm enough to melt snow and ice [The forecast says it will *thaw* today.] **4** to stop acting in a cold or formal way. ◆***n.*** **1** the act of thawing. **2** weather that is warm enough to melt snow and ice.

**the** (*thə or thi*) ***adj.*** **1** that one which is here or which has been mentioned [*The* day is hot. *The* story ended.] **2** one and only [*the* universe]. **3** that one of a number or group [Open *the* front door. Take *the* one on top.] **4** that one thought of as best, outstanding, etc. [*the* football player of the year]. **5** any one of a certain kind [*The* goat is a mammal.] **The** is also called the *definite article: see the note at* **article.** ◆***adv.*** **1** that much; to that degree [*the* better to see you with]. **2** by that much [*the* sooner *the* better].

**the·a·ter** or **the·a·tre** (thē′ə tər) ***n.*** **1** a place where plays, movies, etc. are shown. **2** any place like this, with rows of seats, as for those watching surgery in a

770 hospital. **3** any place where certain things happen [She served in the European *theater* in World War II.] **4** the art or business of acting or of producing plays; drama. **5** all the people who write, produce, or act in plays.

**the·at·ri·cal** (thē at′ri k'l) ***adj.*** **1** having to do with the theater, plays, actors, etc. [a *theatrical* company]. **2** like the theater; dramatic; artificial; not natural [She waved her arms in a *theatrical* way.] *Also* **the·at′ric.** —**the·at′ri·cal·ly *adv.***

**the·at·ri·cals** (thē at′ri k'lz) ***n.pl.*** plays presented on the stage, especially by amateurs.

**Thebes** (thēbz) **1** an ancient city in Egypt on the Nile. **2** an ancient city in Greece. —**The·ban** (thē′bən) ***adj., n.***

**thee** (*th*ē) ***pron.*** *an older form of* **you,** *used as the object of a verb or preposition, as in the Bible.*

**theft** (theft) ***n.*** the act of stealing another's property; larceny.

**their** (*th*er) ***adj.*** of them or done by them. *This possessive form of* **they** *is used before a noun and thought of as an adjective* [*their* house; *their* work]. *See also* **theirs.**

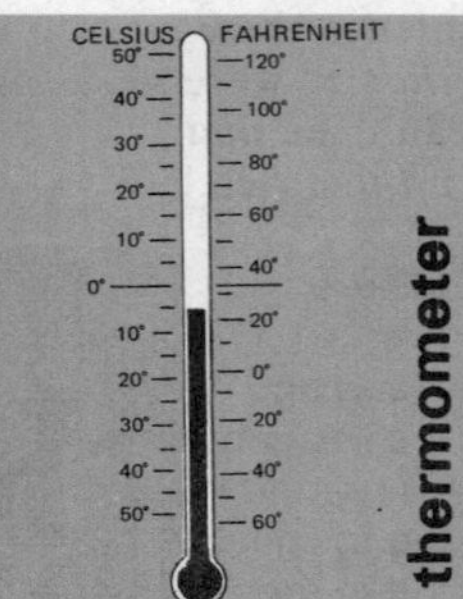

thermometer

thatched roof

**theirs** (*th*erz) ***pron.*** the one or the ones that belong to them. *This form of* **their** *is used when it is not followed by a noun* [This house is *theirs. Theirs* are nicer than ours.]

**them** (*th*em) ***pron.*** the form of **they** that is used as the object of a verb or preposition [I met *them* at the airport. Give the flowers to *them.*]

**theme** (thēm) ***n.*** **1** a topic or subject, as of an essay. *See* SYNONYMS *at* **subject. 2** a short essay or piece of writing on a single subject, written as a school exercise. **3** a short melody that is the subject of a piece of music. ☆**4** the main tune or song of a play, movie, television series, etc.: *also* **theme song.** —**the·mat·ic** (thē mat′ik) ***adj.***

**Theme** comes from a Greek word meaning "what is laid down." A theme can be thought of as having been put in place or laid down as the foundation of a piece of writing or music.

**them·selves** (*th*em selvz′) ***pron.*** **1** their own selves. *This form of* **they** *is used when the object is the same as the subject of the verb* [They hurt *themselves.*] **2** their usual or true selves [They are not *themselves* today.] *Themselves* is also used to give force to the subject [They built it *themselves.*]

**then** (*th*en) ***adv.*** **1** at that time [We were young *then.*] **2** soon afterward; next in time [The party ended, and *then* we left.] **3** next in order [Our house is on the corner and *then* comes the Garcias'.] **4** in that case; therefore [If you read it, *then* you'll know.] **5** besides; also [I like to swim, and *then* it's good exercise.] **6** at another time [Now it's warm, *then* it's cold.] ◆***adj.*** being such at that time [the *then* mayor]. ◆***n.*** that time [They were gone by *then.*] —**but then,** but on the other hand. —**then and there,** at once. —**what then?** what would happen in that case?

**thence** (*th*ens) ***adv.*** from that place; from there [We flew to Boston and *thence* to Maine.]

**thence·forth** (*th*ens′fôrth′) ***adv.*** from that time on [We were *thenceforth* friends.]

**thence·for·ward** (*th*ens′fôr′wərd) ***adv.*** *same as* **thenceforth.**

**the·oc·ra·cy** (thē äk′rə sē) ***n.*** **1** government of a country by a church. **2** a country governed in this way. —*pl.* **the·oc′ra·cies**

**the·o·log·i·cal** (thē′ə läj′i k'l) ***adj.*** of or having to do with theology [a *theological* school]. —**the′o·log′i·cal·ly *adv.***

**the·ol·o·gy** (thē äl′ə jē) ***n.*** **1** the study of God and of religious beliefs. **2** a system of religious beliefs. —*pl.* **the·ol′o·gies** —**the·o·lo·gian** (thē′ə lō′jən) ***n.***

**the·o·rem** (thē′ə rəm) ***n.*** **1** something that can be proved from known facts and so is taken to be a law or principle, as of a science. **2** something in mathematics that is to be proved or has been proved.

**the·o·ret·ic** (thē′ə ret′ik) ***adj.*** *same as* **theoretical.**

**the·o·ret·i·cal** (thē′ə ret′i k'l) ***adj.*** **1** of or based on theory, not on practice or experience [a *theoretical* explanation]. **2** forming theories [a *theoretical* mind]. —**the′o·ret′i·cal·ly *adv.***

**the·o·rize** (thē′ə rīz) ***v.*** to form a theory or theories; guess at causes, reasons, etc. —**the′o·rized, the′o·riz·ing** —**the′o·rist *n.***

**the·o·ry** (thē′ə rē) ***n.*** **1** an explanation of how or why something happens, especially one based on scientific study and reasoning [Charles Darwin's *the-*

*ory* of evolution]. **2** the general principles on which an art or science is based [music *theory*]. **3** an idea, opinion, guess, etc. [My *theory* is that the witness lied.] *—pl.* **the′o·ries**

**ther·a·peu·tic** (ther′ə pyo͞ot′ik) ***adj.*** having to do with or used in treating or curing diseases. **—ther′a·peu′ti·cal·ly *adv.***

**ther·a·peu·tics** (ther′ə pyo͞ot′iks) ***n.pl.*** the branch of medicine that deals with the treating and curing of diseases: *used with a singular verb.*

**ther·a·py** (ther′ə pē) ***n.*** any method of treating disease [drug *therapy;* heat *therapy*]. *—pl.* **ther′a·pies** —☆**ther′a·pist *n.***

**there** (*th*er) ***adv.*** **1** at or in that place [Who lives *there?*] **2** to, toward, or into that place [Go *there.*] **3** at that point; then [I read to page 51 and *there* I stopped.] **4** in that matter [*There* you are wrong.] **5** right now [*There* goes the whistle.] ◆***interj.*** a word used to show dismay, satisfaction, sympathy, etc. [*There!* See what you've done. *There, there!* Don't worry.] ◆***n.*** that place [We left from *there* at six.]

> **There** may be used in other ways as well as those given in the definition. *There* may be used to show approval [*There's* a fine dog!] It may be used to start sentences in which the real subject follows the verb [*There* are three persons here.] *There* is sometimes also used in place of the name in greeting a person [Hi *there!*]

**there·a·bouts** (*th*er′ə bouts) or **there·a·bout** (*th*er′ə bout) ***adv.*** **1** near that place. **2** near that time. **3** near that number or amount.

**there·af·ter** (*th*er af′tər) ***adv.*** after that; from then on.

**there·at** (*th*er at′) ***adv.*** **1** at that place; there. **2** at that time. **3** for that reason. *This word is no longer in common use.*

**there·by** (*th*er bī′) ***adv.*** **1** by that means. **2** connected with that [*Thereby* hangs a tale.]

**there·for** (*th*er fôr′) ***adv.*** for this or that; for it [I enclose a check and request a receipt *therefor.*]

**there·fore** (*th*er′fôr) ***adv.*** for this or that reason; as a result of this or that; hence. *This word is often used as a conjunction* [We missed the bus; *therefore,* we were late.]

**there·from** (*th*er frum′) ***adv.*** from this or that.

**there·in** (*th*er in′) ***adv.*** **1** in there; in that place [the box and all the contents *therein*]. **2** in that matter or detail [*Therein* you are wrong.]

**there·of** (*th*er uv′) ***adv.*** **1** of that; of it [I lifted the cup and drank *thereof.*] **2** from that as a cause or reason.

**there·on** (*th*er än′) ***adv.*** **1** on that. **2** *same as* **thereupon.**

**there's** (*th*erz) there is.

**there·to** (*th*er to͞o′) ***adv.*** to that place, thing, etc.

**there·to·fore** (*th*er′tə fôr′) ***adv.*** up to that time; until then; before that.

**there·un·to** (*th*er un′to͞o *or th*er′un to͞o′) ***adv.*** *same as* **thereto.**

**there·up·on** (*th*er′ə pän′) ***adv.*** **1** just after that. **2** because of that. **3** upon or about that.

**there·with** (*th*er with′) ***adv.*** **1** along with that. **2** by that method. **3** just after that.

**there·with·al** (*th*er′with ôl′) ***adv.*** in addition; besides.

**ther·mal** (thur′m'l) ***adj.*** **1** having to do with heat. **2** warm or hot. ☆**3** made of a loosely knitted material with air spaces to help hold in body heat [*thermal* underwear].

**ther·mom·e·ter** (thər mäm′ə tər) ***n.*** a device for measuring temperature, as a glass tube, marked off in degrees, in which mercury, colored alcohol, etc. rises or falls with changes in temperature. *See also* **Celsius** *and* **Fahrenheit**. *See the picture.*

**ther·mo·nu·cle·ar** (thur′mō no͞o′klē ər *or* thur′mō nyo͞o′klē ər) ***adj.*** describing, of, or using the heat energy set free in nuclear fission.

**Ther·mop·y·lae** (thər mäp′ə lē) a mountain pass on the eastern coast of Greece, where a small force of Spartans in 480 B.C. held off the Persian army but were finally defeated.

**ther·mos** (thur′məs) ***n.*** a container for keeping liquids at almost the same temperature for several hours: *the full name is* **thermos bottle.**

**ther·mo·stat** (thur′mə stat) ***n.*** a device for keeping temperature even, especially one that automatically controls a furnace, etc. **—ther′mo·stat′ic *adj.***

**the·sau·rus** (thi sôr′əs) ***n.*** a book containing lists of synonyms or related words. *—pl.* **the·sau·ri** (thi sôr′ī) or **the·sau′rus·es**

**these** (*th*ēz) ***pron., adj.*** *plural of* **this.**

**The·seus** (thē′so͝os *or* thē′sē əs) a hero of Greek legend, who killed the Minotaur.

**the·sis** (thē′sis) ***n.*** **1** a statement or idea to be defended in an argument. **2** a long essay based on research, prepared by a candidate for a university degree. *—pl.* **the·ses** (thē′sēz)

**Thes·pi·an** (thes′pē ən) ***adj.*** *often* **thespian,** having to do with the theater. ◆***n.*** *often* **thespian,** an actor or actress: *often used in a humorous way.*

> **Thespian** comes from the name of the ancient Greek poet *Thespius.* It is believed that he wrote the first tragic plays for the Greek theater.

**Thes·sa·ly** (thes′ə lē) an ancient region in northeastern Greece. *See the map for* **Macedonia.**

**thews** (thyo͞oz) ***n.pl.*** **1** muscles or sinews. **2** bodily strength; muscular power.

**they** (*th*ā) ***pron.*** **1** the persons, animals, or things being talked about [The players knew *they* had won. Put the keys back where *they* were.] **2** people in general [*They* say it can't happen.] *They* is the plural of *he, she,* or *it.*

**they'd** (*th*ād) **1** they had. **2** they would.

**they'll** (*th*āl) **1** they will. **2** they shall.

**they're** (*th*er) they are.

**they've** (*th*āv) they have.

**thi·a·mine** (thī′ə mēn *or* thī′ə min) ***n.*** one form of vitamin B, called vitamin $B_1$, found in cereal grains, egg yolk, liver, etc. Lack of thiamine may cause beriberi. *Also written* **thi·a·min** (thī′ə min).

| | | | | | | | |
|---|---|---|---|---|---|---|---|
| **a** | fat | **ir** | here | **ou** | out | **zh** | leisure |
| **ā** | ape | **ī** | bite, fire | **u** | up | **ng** | ring |
| **ä** | car, lot | **ō** | go | **ur** | fur | | a *in* ago |
| **e** | ten | **ô** | law, horn | **ch** | chin | | e *in* agent |
| **er** | care | **oi** | oil | **sh** | she | **ə =** | i *in* unity |
| **ē** | even | **o͝o** | look | **th** | thin | | o *in* collect |
| **i** | hit | **o͞o** | tool | ***th*** | then | | u *in* focus |

thimble

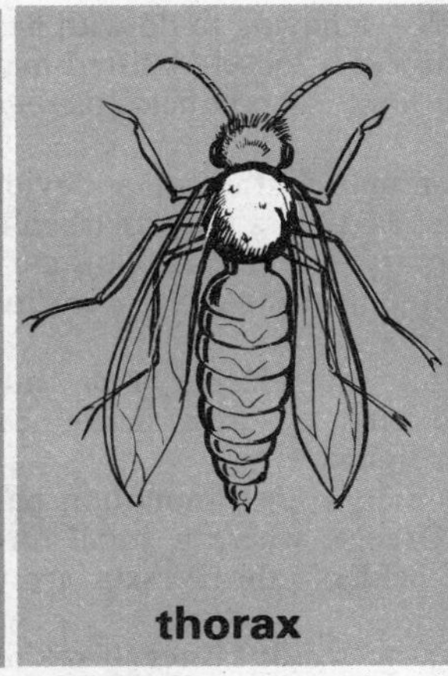
thorax

thistle

**thick** (thik) ***adj.*** **1** great in width or depth from side to side; not thin [a *thick* board]. **2** as measured from one side through to the other [a wall ten inches *thick*]. **3** growing or set close together; dense; heavy [*thick* hair; a *thick* crowd]. **4** flowing or pouring slowly; not watery [*thick* soup]. **5** not clear [a *thick* voice; air *thick* with smoke]. **6** stupid; dull: *used only in everyday talk.* **7** very friendly: *used only in everyday talk.* •***adv.*** in a thick way. •***n.*** the most active part [in the *thick* of a fight]. —**through thick and thin,** in good times and bad times. —**thick′ly *adv.***

**thick·en** (thik′ən) ***v.*** **1** to make or become thick or thicker. **2** to make or become more complicated [The plot *thickened.*]

**thick·et** (thik′it) ***n.*** a place where shrubs, underbrush, or small trees grow close together.

**thick·head·ed** (thik′hed′id) ***adj.*** stupid or dull.

**thick·ness** (thik′nis) ***n.*** **1** the fact or condition of being thick. **2** the distance from one side through to the other [a *thickness* of four inches]. **3** a layer [three *thicknesses* of cloth].

**thick·set** (thik′set′) ***adj.*** **1** planted closely [*thickset* trees]. **2** thick in body; stocky.

**thick-skinned** (thik′skind′) ***adj.*** **1** having a thick skin. **2** not easily hurt by criticism, insults, etc.; unfeeling.

**thief** (thēf) ***n.*** a person who steals, especially secretly. —*pl.* **thieves** (thēvz)

**thieve** (thēv) ***v.*** to steal. —**thieved, thiev′ing**

**thiev·er·y** (thēv′ər ē) ***n.*** the act of stealing; theft. —*pl.* **thiev′er·ies**

**thiev·ish** (thēv′ish) ***adj.*** **1** in the habit of stealing. **2** of or like a thief; stealthy; sneaky.

**thigh** (thī) ***n.*** the part of the leg between the knee and the hip.

**thigh·bone** (thī′bōn) ***n.*** the largest and longest bone in the body, which extends from the hip to the knee; femur: *also written* **thigh bone.**

**thim·ble** (thim′b′l) ***n.*** a small cap of metal, plastic, etc. worn as a protection on the finger that pushes the needle in sewing. *See the picture.*

**thin** (thin) ***adj.*** **1** small in width or depth from side to side; not thick [a *thin* board]. **2** having little fat or flesh; lean; slender. **3** not growing or set close together; not dense; sparse [*thin* hair; a *thin* crowd]. **4** flowing or pouring quickly; watery [*thin* soup]. **5** not deep and strong; weak [*thin* colors; a *thin* voice]. **6** seen through easily; flimsy [*thin* cloth; a *thin* excuse]. —**thin′ner, thin′nest** •***adv.*** in a thin way. •***v.*** to make or become thinner. —**thinned, thin′ning** —**thin′ly *adv.*** —**thin′ness *n.***

SYNONYMS: **Thin** suggests that there is not much width from one side of something to the other or that a thing or person is not full or plump [a *thin* body]. **Slender** and **slim** suggest a thinness that is pleasing [a *slender* or *slim* waist], but may also suggest that there is not enough of what is wanted [a *slender* income; a *slim* possibility]. **Slight** suggests smallness and lightness in the way something is shaped [a *slight* figure] or smallness in amount, importance, etc. [a *slight* difference].

**thine** (*th*īn) ***pron.*** *an older form of* **yours:** *used in the Bible, prayers, etc.* **Thine** is used as an adjective instead of *thy* before a vowel sound [*Thine* eyes are like stars.]

**thing** (thiŋ) ***n.*** **1** that which exists; a real object or substance, not a quality, idea, etc. [A stone is a *thing.* I like pretty *things.*] **2** a happening, act, event, step, etc. [What a *thing* to do! The next *thing* is to clean house.] **3** any matter or affair [How are *things* with you?] **4 things,** *pl.* belongings, as clothes, equipment, etc. [Pick up your *things.*] **5** a person or creature [Poor *thing!*] —**the thing,** what one should have or do because it is needed, in style, etc.

**think** (thiŋk) ***v.*** **1** to use the mind; reason [*Think* before you act.] **2** to form or have in the mind [She was *thinking* happy thoughts.] **3** to consider or judge [I *think* her charming.] **4** to believe, expect, or imagine [They *think* they can come.] **5** to work out, or solve, by reasoning [*Think* the problem through.] **6** to remember [to *think* of the past; to *think* about the old days]. **7** to give thought or be thoughtful [He *thinks* about the future. She *thinks* of the problems of others.] **8** to discover or invent [They *think* of new things to make all the time.] —**thought, think′ing** •***n.*** the act of thinking: *used only in everyday talk* [Give it a *think.*] —**think better of, 1** to form a new and better opinion of. **2** to decide more wisely after thinking again. —**think nothing of,** to think of as easy or not important. —**think over,** to give thought to; consider. —**think through,** to think about so as to solve, understand, etc. —**think twice,** to think over carefully. —**think up,** to invent, plan, etc. by thinking. —**think′er *n.***

**thin-skinned** (thin′skind′) ***adj.*** **1** having a thin skin. **2** easily hurt by criticism or insults.

**third** (thurd) ***adj.*** coming after two others; 3d in order. •***n.*** **1** the third one. **2** one of three equal parts of something; 1/3.

**third degree** ☆harsh questioning or torture by the police to make a prisoner confess: *used only in everyday talk.*

**third·ly** (thurd′lē) ***adv.*** in the third place.

**third person** that form of a pronoun or verb which refers to the person or thing spoken of ["He," "him," "she," "her," "it," "they," "them," etc. are in the *third person.*]

**third world** *often* **Third World** the nations of the world that are new or somewhat poor and weak and are thought of as forming a group separate from the large, powerful nations.

**thirst** (thurst) ***n.*** **1** the feeling of dryness and discomfort caused by a need for water; strong desire to drink. **2** any strong desire; craving [a *thirst* for fame]. ◆***v.*** **1** to have a strong desire to drink; feel thirst. **2** to have a strong desire or craving [We *thirst* for knowledge.]

**thirst·y** (thur′stē) ***adj.*** **1** wanting to drink; feeling thirst [The spicy food made me *thirsty*.] **2** needing water; dry [*thirsty* fields]. **3** having a strong desire [*thirsty* for power]. —**thirst′i·er, thirst′i·est** —**thirst′i·ly** ***adv.*** —**thirst′i·ness** ***n.***

**thir·teen** (thur′tēn′) ***n., adj.*** three more than ten; the number 13.

**thir·teenth** (thur′tēnth′) ***adj.*** coming after twelve others; 13th in order. ◆***n.*** **1** the thirteenth one. **2** one of thirteen equal parts of something; 1/13.

**thir·ti·eth** (thur′tē ith) ***adj.*** coming after twenty-nine others; 30th in order. ◆***n.*** **1** the thirtieth one. **2** one of thirty equal parts of something; 1/30.

**thir·ty** (thurt′ē) ***n., adj.*** three times ten; the number 30. —*pl.* **thir′ties** —**the thirties,** the numbers or years from 30 through 39.

**this** (*th*is) ***pron.*** **1** the person or thing mentioned or understood [*This* is Juan. *This* tastes good.] **2** the thing that is present or nearer [*This* is prettier than that.] **3** the fact, idea, etc. about to be told [Now hear *this!*] —*pl.* **these** (*th*ēz) ◆***adj.*** **1** being the one that is mentioned or understood [Copy down *this* rule.] **2** being the one that is present or nearer [*This* house is newer than that one.] ◆***adv.*** to such a degree; so [It was *this* big.]

**this·tle** (this′′l) ***n.*** a plant with prickly leaves and flower heads of purple, white, etc. *See the picture.*

**this·tle·down** (this′′l doun) ***n.*** the down or fluff from the flower of a thistle.

**thith·er** (thi*th*′ər *or* *th*i*th*′ər) ***adv.*** to that place; there: *no longer much used.*

**tho** or **tho′** (*th*ō) ***conj., adv.*** *another spelling of* **though.**

**thole** (thōl) ***n.*** a pin, often one of a pair, set into the side of a boat for the oar to turn against in rowing: *also* **thole·pin** (thōl′pin).

**Thom·as** (täm′əs) in the Bible, the Apostle who at first doubted that Jesus had risen from the dead.

**thong** (thông) ***n.*** a narrow strip of leather, used as a lace, strap, rein, lash, etc.

**Thor** (thôr) the god of war and thunder in Norse myths.

**tho·rac·ic** (thô ras′ik) ***adj.*** of, in, or near the thorax.

**tho·rax** (thôr′aks) ***n.*** **1** the part of the body between the neck and the abdomen, enclosed by the ribs; chest. **2** the middle one of the three parts of an insect's body. *See the picture.*

**Thor·eau** (thôr′ō *or* thə rō′), **Henry David** 1817–1862; U.S. writer of essays and books about nature.

**thorn** (thôrn) ***n.*** **1** a short, sharp point growing out of a plant stem. **2** a plant full of thorns. **3** anything that keeps troubling or worrying one [That debt has been a *thorn* in my side for years.] —**thorn′y** ***adj.***

**thor·ough** (thur′ō) ***adj.*** **1** complete in every way; with nothing left out, undone, etc. [a *thorough* search; a *thorough* knowledge of the subject]. **2** being wholly such; absolute [a *thorough* rascal]. **3** very careful and exact [a *thorough* worker]. —**thor′ough·ly** ***adv.***

A long time ago **thorough** was a more forceful way of saying *through.* Later **thorough** came to mean "passing through." Today this meaning of *thorough* is mostly found when it is joined to another word, as in *thoroughfare,* a main street on which cars can "pass through" a city.

**thor·ough·bred** (thur′ə bred) ***adj.*** of pure breed. ◆***n.*** **1** a thoroughbred animal. **2** **Thoroughbred,** any of a breed of race horses. **3** a cultured, well-bred person.

**thor·ough·fare** (thur′ə fer) ***n.*** a public street open at both ends; especially, a main highway.

**thor·ough·go·ing** (thur′ə gō′ing) ***adj.*** very thorough [a *thoroughgoing* investigation; a *thoroughgoing* scoundrel].

**those** (*th*ōz) ***adj., pron.*** *plural of* **that.**

**thou** (*th*ou) ***pron.*** *an older form of* **you** *(in the singular), used as the subject of a verb, as in the Bible.*

**though** (*th*ō) ***conj.*** **1** in spite of the fact that; although [*Though* it rained, we went.] **2** and yet; however [They will probably win, *though* no one thinks so.] **3** even if [*Though* you may fail, you will have tried.] ◆***adv.*** however; nevertheless [I must leave; I'll be back, *though.*]

**thought**[1] (thôt) ***n.*** **1** the act or process of thinking [When deep in *thought,* he doesn't hear.] **2** what one thinks; idea, opinion, plan, etc. [a penny for your *thoughts*]. *See* SYNONYMS *at* **idea.** **3** the way of thinking of a particular group, time, etc. [ancient Greek *thought*]. **4** attention or care [Give this matter some *thought.*] **5** a little; trifle [Be a *thought* less hasty.]



**thought**[2] (thôt) *past tense and past participle of* **think.**

**thought·ful** (thôt′fəl) ***adj.*** **1** full of thought or showing thought; serious [a *thoughtful* book]. **2** showing care or paying attention to others; considerate [It was *thoughtful* of you to remember her birthday.] —**thought′ful·ly** ***adv.*** —**thought′ful·ness** ***n.***

SYNONYMS: A **thoughtful** person is one who thinks of the comfort or well-being of others, as by planning out ahead of time what they might need or want [It was *thoughtful* of you to call.] A **considerate** person is one who cares about how other people feel by putting them at ease and keeping them from being worried, embarrassed, or uncomfortable [a *considerate* host].

**thought·less** (thôt′lis) ***adj.*** **1** not stopping to think; careless [The *thoughtless* driver passed the red light.] **2** showing little care for others; not considerate [Our *thoughtless* neighbors are very noisy.] —**thought′less·ly** ***adv.*** —**thought′less·ness** ***n.***

**thou·sand** (thou′z′nd) ***n., adj.*** ten times one hundred; the number 1,000.

**thou·sandth** (thou′z′ndth) ***adj.*** coming after nine hundred and ninety-nine others; 1,000th in order. ◆***n.***

| | | | | | | | |
|---|---|---|---|---|---|---|---|
| **a** | fat | **ir** | here | **ou** | out | **zh** | leisure |
| **ā** | ape | **ī** | bite, fire | **u** | up | **ng** | ring |
| **ä** | car, lot | **ō** | go | **ur** | fur | | a *in* ago |
| **e** | ten | **ô** | law, horn | **ch** | chin | | e *in* agent |
| **er** | care | **oi** | oil | **sh** | she | **ə =** | i *in* unity |
| **ē** | even | **oo** | look | **th** | thin | | o *in* collect |
| **i** | hit | **ōō** | tool | ***th*** | then | | u *in* focus |

**t**

1 the thousandth one. 2 one of the thousand equal parts of something; 1/1000.

**Thrace** (thrās) an ancient region in the Balkan Peninsula.

**thrall** (thrôl) ***n.*** 1 a slave: *no longer used in this meaning.* 2 the condition of being enslaved; slavery; bondage [in the *thrall* of smoking].

**thrash** (thrash) ***v.*** 1 to give a severe beating to; flog, as with a stick or whip. 2 to move about in a violent or jerky way [a bird *thrashing* its wings]. 3 *same as* **thresh.** —**thrash out,** to discuss fully, as a problem, until it is settled. —**thrash'er** ***n.***

**thrash·er** (thrash'ər) ***n.*** ☆an American songbird like the thrush, but with a long, stiff tail.

**thread** (thred) ***n.*** 1 a very thin cord used in sewing and made of strands of spun cotton, silk, etc. twisted together. 2 anything like a thread, as a slender strand of metal or glass, a fine line or vein, etc. 3 the way that a number of ideas, events, etc. are joined together in a single line of thought [I can't follow the *thread* of that story.] 4 the ridge that winds in a sloping way around a screw, in a nut, etc. *See the picture.* ◆***v.*** 1 to put a thread through the eye of [to *thread* a needle]. 2 to string on a thread [to *thread* beads]. 3 to get through, following a winding course [We *threaded* our way through the crowd.] 4 to make a thread, or ridge, on [to *thread* a screw]. 5 to weave or mix together with threads [a red tapestry *threaded* with gold]. —

774 **thread'like** ***adj.***

**thread·bare** (thred'ber) ***adj.*** 1 with the nap worn down so that the threads show [a *threadbare* rug]. 2 wearing worn clothes; shabby [a *threadbare* beggar]. 3 used so often that it is stale [a *threadbare* joke].

**threat** (thret) ***n.*** 1 a warning that one plans to harm another, especially if a certain thing is done or not done [In spite of the bully's *threats* to beat him, Tom continued on his way.] 2 a sign of something dangerous or harmful about to happen [the *threat* of war].

**threat·en** (thret''n) ***v.*** 1 to make a threat; say that one plans to harm or punish [The umpire *threatened* to stop the game if we kept on arguing.] 2 to be a sign of something dangerous or harmful about to happen [Those odd sounds *threaten* engine trouble.] 3 to be a possible danger to [A forest fire *threatened* the cabin.]

**three** (thrē) ***n., adj.*** one more than two; the number 3.

**three·fold** (thrē'fōld) ***adj.*** 1 having three parts. 2 having three times as much or as many. ◆***adv.*** three times as much or as many.

**three·score** (thrē'skôr') ***adj., n.*** three times twenty; sixty.

**three·some** (thrē'səm) ***n.*** a group of three people, as three people playing golf together.

**thresh** (thresh) ***v.*** 1 to separate the seed, or grain, from wheat, rye, etc. by beating. 2 to move about in a violent or jerky way; thrash. —**thresh out,** *same as* **thrash out.**

**thresh·er** (thresh'ər) ***n.*** 1 a person who threshes. 2 a large machine used on farms for threshing grain: *also called* **threshing machine.** 3 a large shark with a long tail.

**thresh·old** (thresh'ōld *or* thresh'hōld) ***n.*** 1 the sill, or piece of wood, stone, etc., placed beneath a door. 2 the point where something begins; entrance [at the *threshold* of a new career].

**threw** (thrōō) *past tense of* **throw.**

**thrice** (thrīs) ***adv.*** three times [The cock crowed *thrice.* She paid *thrice* what it is worth.]

**thrift** (thrift) ***n.*** a careful managing of one's money, income, etc. so that there is no waste; economy [By practicing *thrift,* we could have a long vacation.] — **thrift'less** ***adj.***

**thrift·y** (thrif'tē) ***adj.*** practicing or showing thrift; economical [a *thrifty* shopper; *thrifty* habits]. —**thrift'i·er, thrift'i·est** —**thrift'i·ly** ***adv.*** —**thrift'i·ness** ***n.***

**thrill** (thril) ***v.*** 1 to feel or make greatly excited; shiver or tingle with strong feeling [She *thrilled* at the praise. That movie *thrilled* us.] 2 to quiver or tremble [a voice that *thrilled* with pleasure]. ◆***n.*** 1 a strong feeling of excitement that makes one shiver [Seeing a lion gave me a *thrill.*] 2 something that causes such a feeling [My first airplane ride was a real *thrill.*]

> **Thrill** comes to us from an Old English word meaning "to pierce." An earlier meaning of *thrill,* no longer used, was "to pierce with something pointed." Nowadays when we are thrilled it is as if some strong feeling, as of joy, had pierced us.

**thrill·er** (thril'ər) ***n.*** something that thrills, as an exciting book, movie, etc.

**thrive** (thrīv) ***v.*** 1 to become successful, rich, etc.; prosper [a *thriving* business]. 2 to grow in a strong, healthy way [Plants *thrive* under her care.] —**thrived** or **throve, thrived** or **thriv·en** (thriv''n), **thriv'ing**

**throat** (thrōt) ***n.*** 1 the front part of the neck. 2 the upper part of the passage from the mouth to the stomach or lungs [I have a sore *throat.*] 3 any narrow passage [the *throat* of a bottle]. —**jump down someone's throat,** to attack or criticize someone suddenly and violently: *used only in everyday talk.*

**throat·y** (thrōt'ē) ***adj.*** 1 describing sounds formed in the throat. 2 that makes such sounds; husky [a deep, *throaty* voice]. —**throat'i·er, throat'i·est**

**throb** (thräb) ***v.*** to beat or vibrate hard or fast, as the heart does when one is excited. —**throbbed, throb'bing** ◆***n.*** the act of throbbing; a strong beat.

**throe** (thrō) ***n.*** a sharp, sudden pain; pang [the *throes* of childbirth; death *throes*]. —**in the throes of,** in the act of struggling with some problem, task, etc.

**throne** (thrōn) ***n.*** 1 the raised chair on which a king, cardinal, etc. sits during ceremonies. 2 the power or rank of a monarch [The king lost his *throne* in the revolution.]

**throng** (thrôŋ) ***n.*** a great number gathered together; crowd. ◆***v.*** to crowd together or into [The people *thronged* into the ball park to see the game.]

**throt·tle** (thrät''l) ***n.*** 1 a valve used to control the flow of steam or of air and gasoline into an engine [Opening the *throttle* makes a car go faster.] *See the picture.* 2 the handle or pedal that works this valve. ◆***v.*** 1 to cut down the flow of fuel or slow down by closing a throttle [to *throttle* an engine]. 2 to choke, strangle, or suppress [to *throttle* freedom]. —**throt'tled, throt'tling**

**through** (thrōō) ***prep.*** 1 in one side and out the other side of; from end to end of [The nail went *through* the board. We drove *through* the tunnel.] 2 from one part of to another [Birds fly *through* the air.] 3 by way of [a route to Boston *through* New York]. 4

here and there in; to many places in; around [We toured *through* Utah.] **5** from the beginning to the end of [We stayed in Maine *through* the summer.] ☆**6** up to and including [This sale is on *through* Friday.] **7** by means of [We heard the news *through* friends.] **8** as a result of; because of [He won out *through* sheer courage.] **9** without making a stop for [He went *through* a red light.] ◆***adv.*** **1** in one side and out the other [The target was pierced *through* by the arrow.] **2** from the beginning to the end [to see a job *through*]. **3** in a complete and thorough way; entirely [We were soaked *through* by the rain.] ◆***adj.*** **1** leading from one place to another; open [a *through* street]. **2** going on to the end without a stop or change [a *through* plane to Seattle]. **3** finished [Are you *through* with your homework?]

**through·out** (thrōō out′) ***prep.*** all the way through; in every part of [The fire spread *throughout* the barn. It rained *throughout* the day.] ◆***adv.*** **1** in every part; everywhere [painted white *throughout*]. **2** from start to finish [staying hopeful *throughout*].

☆**through·way** (thrōō′wā) ***n.*** *another name for* **expressway.**

**throve** (thrōv) *a past tense of* **thrive.**

**throw** (thrō) ***v.*** **1** to send through the air by a fast motion of the arm; hurl, toss, etc. [to *throw* a ball]. **2** to make fall down; upset [to *throw* someone in wrestling]. **3** to send or cast in a certain direction, as a glance, light, shadow, etc. **4** to put suddenly into some condition or place [to *throw* into confusion; to *throw* into prison]. **5** to move, as a switch, so as to connect or disconnect. ☆**6** to lose a contest, race, etc. on purpose: *used only in everyday talk.* **7** to confuse or upset: *used only in everyday talk* [The question *threw* me.] —**threw, thrown, throw′ing** ◆***n.*** **1** the act of throwing [The fast *throw* put the runner out at first base.] **2** the distance that something is or can be thrown [It's a stone's *throw* from here.] —**throw away, 1** to get rid of; discard. **2** to waste or fail to make use of [to *throw away* a chance]. —**throw in, 1** to add extra or free. **2** to join with in doing something: *used only in everyday talk.* —**throw off, 1** to rid oneself of [to *throw off* a cold]. **2** to send forth [to *throw off* sparks]. —**throw out, 1** to get rid of. **2** to offer; suggest [to *throw out* a hint]. ☆**3** to put out in baseball by throwing the ball to a base. —**throw over, 1** to give up; abandon. **2** *same as* **jilt.** —**throw together,** to put together in a hurry. —**throw up, 1** to give up or abandon. **2** *same as* **vomit.**

SYNONYMS: To **throw** something is to make it go through the air by moving the arm quickly [to *throw* a stone into the water]. To **toss** something is to throw it lightly or carelessly and usually up or to the side [to *toss* a coin]. To **hurl** something is to throw it with force or violence so that it moves swiftly for a fairly long distance [to *hurl* a spear].

**throw·a·way** (thrō′ə wā) ***n.*** a leaflet, handbill, etc. handed out, as by someone going from house to house. ◆***adj.*** ☆made in such a way that it can be thrown away after being used [a *throwaway* bottle].

**throw·back** (thrō′bak) ***n.*** a return to an earlier or more primitive type or condition.

☆**throw rug** *another name for* **scatter rug.**

**thru** (thrōō) ***prep., adv., adj.*** *a shorter spelling of* **through.**

**thrush** 19 cm (7 1/2 in.) long

**thread of a nut and of a bolt**

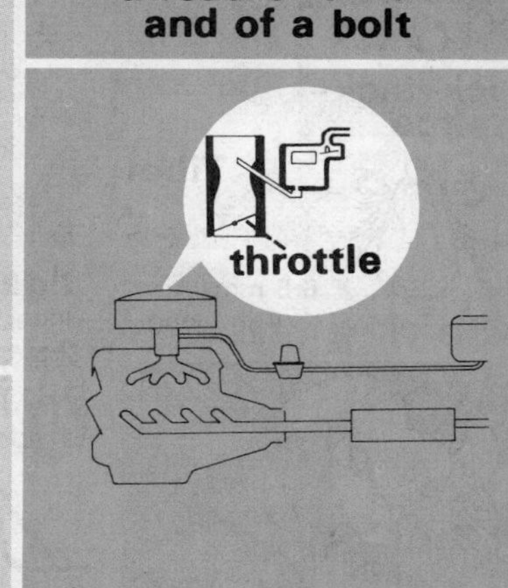

**throttle**

**thumbscrew**

**thrum** (thrum) ***v.*** **1** to pluck at the strings of; strum [to *thrum* a guitar]. **2** to drum or tap with the fingers [to *thrum* on a table]. —**thrummed, thrum′ming**

**thrush** (thrush) ***n.*** any of a large group of songbirds, some plain in color, others having a spotted or bright breast. The wood thrush, robin, and bluebird are thrushes. *See the picture.*

**thrust** (thrust) ***v.*** **1** to push with sudden force [He *thrust* the book into her hand. She *thrust* forward through the crowd.] **2** to stab or pierce, as with a sword. —**thrust, thrust′ing** ◆***n.*** **1** a sudden push or shove. **2** a stab, as with a sword. **3** the forward force produced by the propeller of an airplane or by the gases forced from a jet plane or rocket. ☆**4** the basic meaning or purpose [the *thrust* of a speech].

☆**thru·way** (thrōō′wā) ***n.*** *another name for* **expressway.**

**thud** (thud) ***n.*** a dull sound, as of something heavy dropping on the ground. ◆***v.*** to hit with a thud. —**thud′ded, thud′ding**

**thug** (thug) ***n.*** a rough, violent criminal.

**thumb** (thum) ***n.*** **1** the short, thick finger nearest the wrist. **2** the part of a glove that covers the thumb. ◆***v.*** **1** to handle, turn, soil, etc. with the thumb [to *thumb* the pages of a book]. **2** to ask for or get a ride in hitchhiking by signaling with the thumb: *used only in everyday talk.* —**all thumbs,** clumsy; awkward. —**under one's thumb,** under one's power or influence.

**thumb·nail** (thum′nāl) ***n.*** the nail of the thumb. ◆***adj.*** very small or brief [a *thumbnail* sketch].

**thumb·screw** (thum′skrōō) ***n.*** a screw that can be turned by the thumb and forefinger. *See the picture.*

| | | | |
|---|---|---|---|
| **a** fat | **ir** here | **ou** out | **zh** leisure |
| **ā** ape | **ī** bite, fire | **u** up | **ng** ring |
| **ä** car, lot | **ō** go | **ur** fur | a *in* ago |
| **e** ten | **ô** law, horn | **ch** chin | e *in* agent |
| **er** care | **oi** oil | **sh** she | **ə** = i *in* unity |
| **ē** even | **oo** look | **th** thin | o *in* collect |
| **i** hit | **ōō** tool | ***th*** then | u *in* focus |

**t**

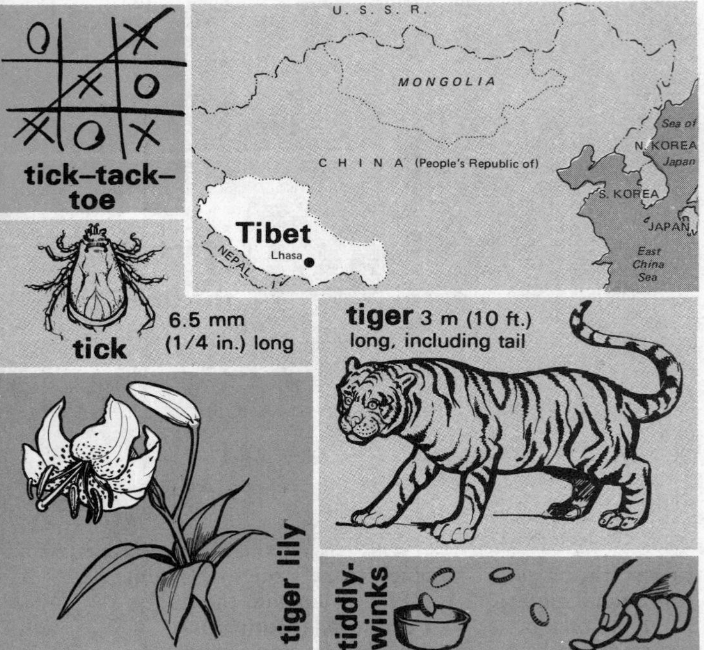


☆**thumb·tack** (thum′tak) ***n.*** a tack with a wide, flat head, that can be pressed into a board, etc. with the thumb.



**thump** (thump) ***n.*** **1** a blow with something heavy and blunt. **2** the dull sound made by such a blow. ◆***v.*** to hit, fall, or pound with a thump [My heart was *thumping*.]

**thun·der** (thun′dər) ***n.*** **1** the loud noise that comes after a flash of lightning. It is caused when the discharge of electricity disturbs the air. **2** any loud, rumbling noise like this [We heard the *thunder* of stampeding cattle.] ◆***v.*** **1** to cause thunder or a sound like thunder [The crowd *thundered* down the steps.] **2** to shout in a loud, forceful way.

**thun·der·bolt** (thun′dər bōlt) ***n.*** **1** a flash of lightning with the thunder that follows it. **2** something sudden and shocking, as bad news.

**thun·der·clap** (thun′dər klap) ***n.*** **1** a loud crash of thunder. **2** anything that happens in a shocking way.

**thun·der·cloud** (thun′dər kloud) ***n.*** a storm cloud that has electricity in it and makes lightning and thunder.

**thun·der·ous** (thun′dər əs) ***adj.*** making a loud, rumbling noise like thunder.

**thun·der·show·er** (thun′dər shou′ər) ***n.*** a shower along with thunder and lightning.

**thun·der·storm** (thun′dər stôrm) ***n.*** a storm along with thunder and lightning.

**thun·der·struck** (thun′dər struk) ***adj.*** amazed or shocked as if struck by a thunderbolt.

**Thurs.** or **Th.** *abbreviations for* **Thursday.**

**Thurs·day** (thurz′dē) ***n.*** the fifth day of the week.

> **Thursday** was originally "Thor's Day." Thor was the god of war, thunder, and strength in the Norse myths of ancient times.

**thus** (*th*us) ***adv.*** **1** in this way or in the following way [Do it *thus*.] **2** to this or that degree; so [*Thus* far he has done well.] **3** as a result; therefore [She is ill and *thus* absent.]

**thwack** (thwak) ***v.*** to hit with something flat; whack. ◆***n.*** a blow with something flat.

**thwart** (thwôrt) ***v.*** to keep from doing or from being done; block; hinder [The guards *thwarted* his attempt to escape.] ◆***n.*** a seat across a boat, for a rower. ◆***adj.*** lying across.

**thy** (*th*ī) ***pron.*** *an older form of* **your,** *used as in the Bible.*

**thyme** (tīm) ***n.*** a plant of the mint family, with sweet-smelling leaves used to flavor food.

**thy·mus** (thī′məs) ***n.*** a small gland near the lower part of the throat.

**thy·roid** (thī′roid) ***n.*** **1** a large gland near the windpipe. It makes a hormone that controls the growth of the body. **2** a substance made from the thyroid gland of certain animals, used in treating goiter. ◆***adj.*** of this gland.

**thy·self** (*th*ī self′) ***pron.*** *an older form of* **yourself,** *used as in the Bible.*

**ti** (tē) ***n.*** the seventh note of a musical scale.

**Ti** *the symbol for the chemical element* titanium.

**ti·ar·a** (tē er′ə) ***n.*** **1** an ornament for a woman's head, like a small crown with jewels, flowers, etc. **2** the Pope's triple crown, worn at some special times.

**Ti·ber** (tī′bər) a river in Italy, flowing through Rome into the Mediterranean Sea.

**Ti·bet** (ti bet′) a region on a high plateau in southwestern China. It has its own government. *See the map.* —**Ti·bet′an** ***adj., n.***

**tib·i·a** (tib′ē ə) ***n.*** the long, thick inner bone of the leg, between the knee and the ankle. —*pl.* **tib·i·ae** (tib′i ē) or **tib′i·as**

**tic** (tik) ***n.*** a twitch of a muscle, especially of the face, that cannot be controlled.

**tick**[1] (tik) ***n.*** **1** a light clicking sound, as that made by a clock. **2** a mark made in checking off things, as the check mark ✓. ◆***v.*** **1** to make a tick or ticks, as a clock. **2** to count by ticks [The watch *ticked* away the seconds.] **3** to mark with a tick, or check [*Tick* off the names on the list.] **4** to work or behave so: *used only in everyday talk* [Find out what makes him *tick*.]

**tick**[2] (tik) ***n.*** any of various insects that suck the blood of human beings, cattle, etc. *See the picture.*

**tick**[3] (tik) ***n.*** the cloth case or cover of a mattress or pillow.

**tick·et** (tik′it) ***n.*** **1** a printed card or piece of paper that one buys to get a certain right, as to a seat in a theater, train, etc. **2** a label or tag on an article, giving its size, price, color, etc. ☆**3** the list of candidates of a political party in an election. ☆**4** a written order to appear in court for breaking a traffic law; traffic summons: *used only in everyday talk.* ◆***v.*** to put a ticket on.

**tick·ing** (tik′ing) ***n.*** a strong, heavy cloth, often striped, used for making ticks for mattresses or pillows.

**tick·le** (tik′'l) ***v.*** **1** to touch or stroke lightly, as with a finger or feather, so as to cause twitching, laughter, etc. **2** to have such a scratching or twitching feeling [The dust makes my nose *tickle*.] **3** to give pleasure to; amuse; delight [The joke really *tickled* her.] —**tick′led, tick′ling** ◆***n.*** a tickling or a feeling of being tickled. —**tick′ler** ***n.***

**tick·lish** (tik′lish) ***adj.*** **1** easily made to laugh or squirm by tickling [He is *ticklish* under the arms.] **2** easily upset; touchy [Sonia is *ticklish* on the subject of her grades.] **3** needing careful handling; delicate [The teachers' strike has made a *ticklish* situation.]

**tick-tack-toe** or **tic-tac-toe** (tik′tak tō′) ***n.*** a game in which players take turns marking either X's or O's in a block of nine squares, trying to get three of the same marks in a line. *See the picture.*

**tid·al** (tīd′'l) ***adj.*** of, having, or caused by a tide [*tidal* current; *tidal* basin].

**tidal wave** a very large, damaging wave, caused by an earthquake or very strong wind.

**tid·bit** (tid′bit) ***n.*** a pleasing or choice bit of food, news, gossip, etc.

**tid·dly·winks** (tid′lē wiŋks′) ***n.*** a game in which players try to snap little disks into a cup by pressing the disks' edges with larger disks. *See the picture.*

**tide** (tīd) ***n.*** **1** the regular rise and fall of the ocean's surface, about every twelve hours, caused by the attraction of the moon and sun. *See the word history in color after* **time**. **2** something that rises and falls like the tide [Her *tide* of popularity is ebbing.] **3** a current, flow, trend, etc. [the *tide* of public opinion]. ◆***v.*** to help in overcoming a time of trouble [Will ten dollars *tide* you over till Monday?] —**tid′ed, tid′ing**

**tide·wa·ter** (tīd′wôt′ər) ***n.*** ☆**1** water, as in some streams along a seacoast, that rises and falls with the tide. ☆**2** a seacoast region with such streams.

**ti·dings** (tī′diŋz) ***n.pl.*** news; information.

**ti·dy** (tī′dē) ***adj.*** **1** neat and orderly [She is a *tidy* person. This is a *tidy* desk.] *See* SYNONYMS *at* **neat**. **2** quite large: *used only in everyday talk* [He donated a *tidy* sum of money.] —**ti′di·er, ti′di·est** ◆***v.*** to make tidy [*Tidy* up your room.] —**ti′died, ti′dy·ing**

**tie** (tī) ***v.*** **1** to bind together or fasten with string, rope, cord, etc. [They *tied* his hands together. *Tie* the boat to the pier.] *See* SYNONYMS *at* **bind**. **2** to tighten and knot the laces or strings of [*Tie* your shoes.] **3** to make, as a knot or bow. **4** to make a knot or bow in [He *tied* his necktie.] **5** to bind in any way [She is *tied* to her work.] **6** to equal, as in a score [Pablo *tied* with Carmela for first place.] —**tied, ty′ing** ◆***n.*** **1** a string, lace, cord, etc. used for tying. **2** something that joins or binds [We have strong family *ties*.] **3** *a shorter word for* **necktie**. ☆**4** a timber, beam, etc. holding parts together or in place [Rails of a railroad are fastened to wooden *ties*.] **5** the fact of being equal, as in score; also, a contest in which scores are equal. **6** a curved line joining two musical notes of the same pitch, and showing that the tone is to be held without a break. —*pl.* **ties** —**tie down,** to hold back or make less free; confine. —☆**tie in,** to bring into harmony or agreement. —**tie up, 1** to tie tightly. **2** to wrap up and tie. ☆**3** to hinder; stop. **4** to cause to be already in use, busy, etc.

**tie-dye** (tī′dī′) ***n.*** **1** a method of dyeing designs on cloth by tightly tying bunches of it with waxed thread so that only the part not tied up will be dyed. **2** cloth dyed this way. ◆***v.*** to dye in this way. —**tie′-dyed′, tie′-dye′ing**

**Tien·tsin** (tin′tsin′) a seaport in northeastern China.

**tier** (tir) ***n.*** any of a series of rows, as of seats, set one above another.

**Tier·ra del Fue·go** (tē er′ə del′ fo͞o ā′gō) a group of islands, belonging to Chile and Argentina, at the southern tip of South America.

**tie-up** (tī′up′) ***n.*** ☆**1** a stopping of action or movement for a time [a traffic *tie-up*]. **2** connection or relation.

**tiff** (tif) ***n.*** a slight quarrel; spat.

**ti·ger** (tī′gər) ***n.*** a large, fierce animal of the cat family, living in Asia. Tigers have a tawny coat with black stripes. *See the picture.*

**tiger lily** a kind of lily having orange flowers with dark purple spots. *See the picture.*

**tight** (tīt) ***adj.*** **1** made so that water, air, etc. cannot pass through [a *tight* boat]. **2** put together firmly or closely [a *tight* knot]. **3** fitting too closely [a *tight* shirt]. **4** stretched and strained; taut [a *tight* wire; *tight* nerves]. **5** hard to manage, do, etc. [a *tight* situation]. **6** almost even; close in score [a *tight* game]. **7** hard to get; scarce [Money was *tight* in 1930.] **8** stingy: *used only in everyday talk*. ◆***adv.*** in a tight way; tightly. —**sit tight,** to keep one's place or position and not budge. —**tight′ly** ***adv.*** —**tight′ness** ***n.***

**tight·en** (tīt′'n) ***v.*** to make or become tight or tighter.

**tight·fist·ed** (tīt′fis′tid) ***adj.*** stingy; miserly.

**tight·fit·ting** (tīt′fit′iŋ) ***adj.*** fitting very tight.

**tight-lipped** (tīt′lipt′) ***adj.*** not saying much; keeping secrets.

**tight·rope** (tīt′rōp) ***n.*** a rope stretched tight, on which acrobats do balancing tricks. 777

**tights** (tīts) ***n.pl.*** a garment that fits tightly over the legs and lower half of the body, worn by acrobats, dancers, and others.

**ti·gress** (tī′gris) ***n.*** a female tiger.

**Ti·gris** (tī′gris) a river in southeastern Turkey and Iraq. It joins with the Euphrates.

**tike** (tīk) ***n.*** *another spelling of* **tyke**.

**til·de** (til′də) ***n.*** in Spanish, the mark ũ, used over an *n* to show that it has the sound of *ny*, as in "señor" (se nyôr′).

**tile** (tīl) ***n.*** **1** a thin piece of baked clay, stone, plastic, etc., used for covering roofs, floors, walls, etc. **2** a pipe of baked clay used for a drain. **3** any of the oblong pieces used in playing mah-jongg. ◆***v.*** to cover with tiles. —**tiled, til′ing**

**till**[1] (til) ***prep., conj.*** *same as* **until**.

**till**[2] (til) ***v.*** to work land by plowing, planting, etc.; cultivate. —**till′a·ble** ***adj.*** —**till′er** ***n.***

**till**[3] (til) ***n.*** a drawer for keeping money, as behind the counter in a store.

**till·age** (til′ij) ***n.*** the tilling of land.

**till·er** (til′ər) ***n.*** a bar or handle for turning the rudder of a boat. *See the picture on page 778.*

**Tiller** comes from an old French word for either of the two large rollers on a weaving loom. When it first came into English, it meant the stock, or

| | | | | | | | |
|---|---|---|---|---|---|---|---|
| **a** | fat | **ir** | here | **ou** | out | **zh** | leisure |
| **ā** | ape | **ī** | bite, fire | **u** | up | **ŋ** | ring |
| **ä** | car, lot | **ō** | go | **ʉr** | fur | | a *in* ago |
| **e** | ten | **ô** | law, horn | **ch** | chin | | e *in* agent |
| **er** | care | **oi** | oil | **sh** | she | ə = | i *in* unity |
| **ē** | even | **oo** | look | **th** | thin | | o *in* collect |
| **i** | hit | **o͞o** | tool | ***th*** | then | | u *in* focus |

t

handle, of a crossbow. Its meaning was influenced by another early English word, *tillen,* meaning "to pull." In our day, it means the handle of a rudder, for steering a boat.

**tilt** (tilt) ***v.*** **1** to slope or tip [The deck *tilted* suddenly. He *tilted* his head to one side.] **2** to fight with lances as knights did; joust. ◆***n.*** **1** a contest in which two knights on horseback tried to unseat each other by thrusting with lances. **2** any lively contest. **3** a tilting, or sloping; slant. —**at full tilt,** at full speed; with full force.

**tim·ber** (tim′bər) ***n.*** **1** wood for building houses, boats, etc. **2** a large, thick piece of such wood; beam. **3** trees or forests. ◆***v.*** to provide, build, etc. with timbers. ◆***interj.*** a warning shout by a lumberman that a cut tree is about to fall.

**tim·bered** (tim′bərd) ***adj.*** **1** made of or showing timbers. **2** covered with trees or forests.

☆**tim·ber·land** (tim′bər land) ***n.*** land having trees on it fit for timber; wooded land.

**tim·bre** (tim′bər *or* tam′bər) ***n.*** the quality of sound, apart from pitch or loudness, that makes one's voice or musical instrument different from others.

**time** (tīm) ***n.*** **1** the passing hours, days, years, etc.; every moment there has ever been or ever will be ["*Time* and tide wait for no man."] **2** a system of measuring the passing of hours [standard *time*]. **3** the period between two events or during which something exists, happens, etc. [an hour's *time;* a *time* of joy; to serve *time* in prison]. **4** *usually* **times,** *pl.* a period of history; age, era, etc. [in ancient *times*]. **5** *usually* **times,** *pl.* conditions as they are; state of affairs [*Times* are getting better.] **6** the exact or proper instant, hour, day, year, etc. [The *time* is 2:17 P.M. It's *time* for lunch.] **7** any one of a series of moments at which the same thing happens, is done, etc. [I read it four *times.*] **8** the period that an employee works; also, the pay for this [We get double *time* for working on holidays.] **9** the rate of speed for marching, playing a piece of music, etc.; tempo; rhythm [waltz *time;* march *time*]. ◆***interj.*** a signal during a game that play is to stop. ◆***v.*** **1** to arrange or choose a proper time for something [We *timed* our visit so as to find her home.] **2** to set, play, etc. something so as to agree in time with something else [*Time* your marching with the music.] **3** to measure or record the speed of [The coach *timed* the runners.] —**timed, tim′ing** ◆***adj.*** **1** having to do with time. **2** set to work, go off, etc. at a given time [a *time* bomb]. ☆**3** describing a series of payments made over a period of time [*time* payments]. —**against time,** trying to finish in a certain time. —☆**ahead of time,** early. —**at one time, 1** together. **2** earlier; formerly. —**at the same time,** however. —**at times,** sometimes. —**behind the times,** out-of-date; old-fashioned. —**behind time,** late. —**for the time being,** for the present time. —**from time to time,** now and then. —**in no time,** very quickly. —**in time, 1** in the end; eventually. **2** before it is too late. **3** keeping the tempo, rhythm, etc. —**make time,** ☆to travel, work, etc. at a fast rate of speed. —**on time,** ☆**1** at the set time; not late. ☆**2** to be paid for over a period of time [She bought the car *on time.*] —**time after time** or **time and again,** again and again.

Both **time** and **tide** come from an ancient word that means "to divide up." Human beings long ago kept track of the way nature divides time up into night and day and the seasons, and the way the sun and moon cause tides to rise and fall. From these things they figured out ways to measure time.

**time-hon·ored** (tīm′än′ərd) ***adj.*** respected because it is very old or in use for a long time.

**time·keep·er** (tīm′kē′pər) ***n.*** a person who keeps track of time, as in some games, or one who keeps a record of hours worked by employees.

**time·less** (tīm′lis) ***adj.*** **1** never ending; eternal. **2** not limited to a particular time. —**time′less·ness** ***n.***

**time·ly** (tīm′lē) ***adj.*** coming at the right time or at a suitable time [a *timely* remark]. —**time′li·er, time′li·est** —**time′li·ness** ***n.***

**time·piece** (tīm′pēs) ***n.*** a clock or watch.

**times** (tīmz) ***prep.*** multiplied by: *the symbol for* times *is* x [Two *times* ten equals twenty or 2 x 10 = 20.]

**time·ta·ble** (tīm′tā′b'l) ***n.*** a schedule of the times when trains, planes, etc. arrive and leave.

**tim·id** (tim′id) ***adj.*** feeling or showing fear or shyness. —**ti·mid·i·ty** (tə mid′ə tē) ***n.***

**tim·ing** (tīm′iŋ) ***n.*** the act of arranging or setting the speed or time of doing something so as to get the best results [A batter needs good *timing* to hit a home run.]

**tim·or·ous** (tim′ər əs) ***adj.*** full of fear or easily frightened; timid; shy.

**tim·o·thy** (tim′ə thē) ***n.*** ☆a grass with long leaves and spikes, grown as food for cattle.

**Timothy** is named after Timothy Hanson, an American farmer. He took some of the seed for this grass from New York to the Carolinas about 1720. It grew as well there as it did farther north, and has become one of the most popular grasses that is grown for hay to be fed to farm animals.

**tim·pa·ni** (tim′pə nē) ***n.pl.*** a set of kettledrums of different pitches played by one performer in an orchestra: *often used with a singular verb.* —**tim′pa·nist** ***n.***

**tin** (tin) ***n.*** **1** a soft, silver-white metal that is a chemical element. Tin is easy to bend or shape. **2** *a shorter*

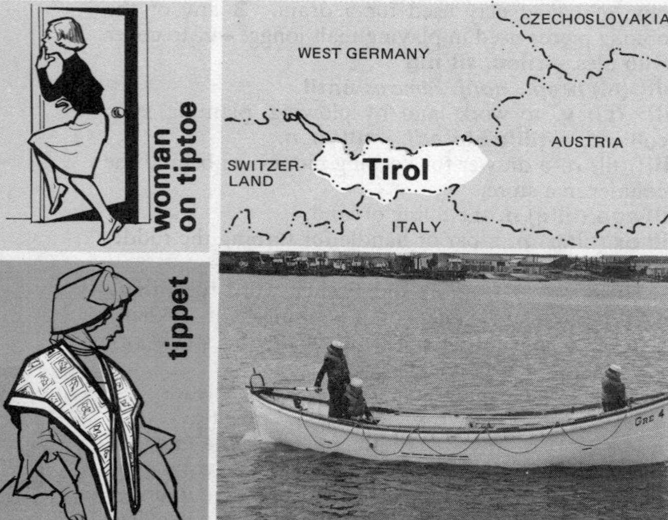


woman on tiptoe

tippet

tiller

*name for* **tin plate**. **3** a can in which food is sealed so that it will keep: *a British meaning.* ◆**v.** **1** to cover with tin. **2** to seal in tins; can: *a British meaning.* —**tinned, tin'ning**

**tinc·ture** (tiŋk'chər) **n.** **1** a solution of a medicine in alcohol [*tincture* of iodine]. **2** a slight trace, hint, or tint. ◆**v.** to give a slight trace or tint to. —**tinc'tured, tinc'tur·ing**

**tin·der** (tin'dər) **n.** any dry material that catches fire easily, used for starting a fire from the sparks of a flint, etc.

**tin·der·box** (tin'dər bäks) **n.** **1** a box for holding tinder, flint, and steel for starting a fire, as used in earlier times. **2** anything that catches fire easily.

**tine** (tīn) **n.** a sharp point that sticks out; prong [An ordinary table fork has four *tines.*]

**tin·foil** (tin'foil) **n.** a very thin sheet of tin, used to wrap food, tobacco, etc. to keep it fresh.

**ting** (tiŋ) **n.** a light, ringing sound, as of a small bell. ◆**v.** to make such a sound.

**tinge** (tinj) **v.** **1** to color slightly; tint [The sunset *tinged* the sky.] **2** to give a slight trace to [Our joy was *tinged* with sorrow.] —**tinged, tinge'ing** or **ting'ing** ◆**n.** **1** a slight coloring; tint. **2** a slight trace.

**tin·gle** (tiŋ'g'l) **v.** to have or give a prickling or stinging feeling, such as that caused by cold, a slap, excitement, etc. —**tin'gled, tin'gling** ◆**n.** such a feeling.

**tin·ker** (tiŋ'kər) **n.** a person who mends pots, pans, etc., often one who travels about doing this. ◆**v.** **1** to work as a tinker. **2** to mend or try to mend in a clumsy way. **3** to fuss with something in a useless or careless way; putter.

**tin·kle** (tiŋ'k'l) **v.** **1** to make a series of light, ringing sounds, like those of a small bell. **2** to cause to tinkle. —**tin'kled, tin'kling** ◆**n.** the act or sound of tinkling.—**tin'kly adj.**

**tin·ny** (tin'ē) **adj.** **1** of or containing tin. **2** like tin, as in looks, sound, value, etc. [*tinny* jewelry; *tinny* music]. —**tin'ni·er, tin'ni·est**

**tin plate** thin sheets of iron or steel plated with tin.

**tin·sel** (tin's'l) **n.** **1** thin, shiny strips or threads of tin, metal foil, etc., used for decoration, as on Christmas trees. **2** anything that looks showy and fine but is really cheap and of little value. ◆**adj.** **1** of or decorated with tinsel. **2** showy; gaudy. ◆**v.** to decorate or make glitter as with tinsel. —**tin'seled** or **tin'selled, tin'sel·ing** or **tin'sel·ling**

**tin·smith** (tin'smith) **n.** a person who works with tin or tin plate; maker of tinware.

**tint** (tint) **n.** **1** a light or pale color; tinge. *See* SYNONYMS *at* **color**. **2** a shading of a color [several *tints* of green]. ◆**v.** to give a tint to.

**tin·ware** (tin'wer) **n.** pots, pans, dishes, etc. made of tin plate.

**ti·ny** (tī'nē) **adj.** very small; minute. —**ti'ni·er, ti'ni·est**

**-tion** (shən) *a suffix meaning:* **1** the act of [*Correction* is the act of correcting.] **2** the condition of being [*Elation* is the condition of being elated.] **3** a thing that is [A *creation* is a thing that is created.]

**tip**[1] (tip) **n.** **1** the rounded or pointed end of something [the *tip* of the nose; a spear *tip*]. **2** something attached to the end [a rubber *tip* on a cane]. ◆**v.** to make or put a tip on. —**tipped, tip'ping**

**tip**[2] (tip) **v.** **1** to hit lightly and sharply; tap. **2** to give a small gift of money to for some service [Be sure to *tip* the waitress.] **3** to give secret information to: *used only in everyday talk* [She *tipped* off the police about the robbery.] —**tipped, tip'ping** ◆**n.** **1** a light, sharp blow; tap. **2** a piece of secret information. **3** a suggestion, hint, warning, etc. **4** a small gift of money given to a waiter, porter, etc. for some service. —**tip'per n.**

**tip**[3] (tip) **v.** **1** to overturn; upset [He *tipped* over his glass.] **2** to tilt or slant. **3** to raise slightly in greeting, as one's hat. —**tipped, tip'ping** ◆**n.** a tipping or being tipped; tilt; slant.

**tip·pet** (tip'it) **n.** **1** a long scarf for the neck and shoulders, with ends that hang down in front. *See the picture.* **2** in olden times, a long, hanging part of a hood, cape, or sleeve.

**tip·ple** (tip''l) **v.** to drink alcoholic liquor often. —**tip'pled, tip'pling** —**tip'pler n.**

**tip·sy** (tip'sē) **adj.** **1** that tips easily; not steady. **2** somewhat drunk. —**tip'si·er, tip'si·est** —**tip'si·ly adv.**

**tip·toe** (tip'tō) **n.** the tip of a toe. ◆**v.** to walk on one's tiptoes in a quiet or careful way. —**tip'toed, tip'toe·ing** —**on tiptoe,** **1** on one's tiptoes. **2** quietly or carefully. *See the picture.*

**tip·top** (tip'täp') **n.** the highest point; very top. ◆**adj., adv.** **1** at the highest point, or top. **2** very best; excellent: *used only in everyday talk.* 

**ti·rade** (tī'rād *or* tī rād') **n.** a long, angry or scolding speech; harangue.

**tire**[1] (tīr) **v.** **1** to make or become unable to go on because of a need for rest; exhaust [The hike *tired* me.] **2** to make or become bored. —**tired, tir'ing**

**tire**[2] (tīr) **n.** a hoop of iron or rubber, or a rubber tube filled with air, fixed around the rim of a wheel to serve as a tread.

**tired** (tīrd) **adj.** worn out; weary.

> SYNONYMS: **Tired** describes a person who is bored or has done something that takes a lot of energy [We are *tired* of listening to dull sermons. She was *tired* after playing volleyball.] **Weary** is used of a person who wants to quit because of having very little energy or interest left [She was *weary* of studying every night.] **Exhausted** describes a person who has completely lost all strength or energy, as after a long, hard climb.

**tire·less** (tīr'lis) **adj.** that does not become tired. —**tire'less·ly adv.**

**tire·some** (tīr'səm) **adj.** **1** tiring; boring. **2** annoying. —**tire'some·ly adv.** —**tire'some·ness n.**

**Tir·ol** (tir'äl *or* tī'rōl) a region in the Alps of western Austria and northern Italy. *See the map.* —**Ti·ro·le·an** (ti rō'lē ən) or **Tir·o·lese** (tir ə lēz') **adj., n.**

**'tis** (tiz) it is.

| | | | | | | | |
|---|---|---|---|---|---|---|---|
| **a** | fat | **ir** | here | **ou** | out | **zh** | leisure |
| **ā** | ape | **ī** | bite, fire | **u** | up | **ŋ** | ring |
| **ä** | car, lot | **ō** | go | **ur** | fur | | a *in* ago |
| **e** | ten | **ô** | law, horn | **ch** | chin | | e *in* agent |
| **er** | care | **oi** | oil | **sh** | she | ə = | i *in* unity |
| **ē** | even | **oo** | look | **th** | thin | | o *in* collect |
| **i** | hit | **ōō** | tool | ***th*** | then | | u *in* focus |

**tis·sue** (tish′o͞o) ***n.*** **1** any material, made up of cells, that forms some part of a plant or animal [muscle *tissue;* nerve *tissue*]. **2** any light, thin cloth, as gauze. **3** a tangled mass or series; mesh [a *tissue* of lies]. **4** a thin, soft paper, formed into pieces or rolls for use as handkerchiefs, toilet paper, etc. **5** a thin, almost transparent paper used for wrapping things: *its full name is* **tissue paper.**

**tit** (tit) ***n.*** a small bird, as a titmouse.

**Ti·tan** (tīt′'n) any one of a race of giant gods in Greek myths, who were overthrown by the gods of Olympus. ◆***n.*** **titan,** a person or thing that is very large or powerful; giant.

**ti·tan·ic** (tī tan′ik) ***adj.*** very large, strong, or powerful.

**ti·ta·ni·um** (tī tā′nē əm) ***n.*** a dark-gray, shiny metal that is a chemical element. It is used in making steel.

**Titanium** was named after the powerful giants of Greek myths called Titans because it can be mixed with iron to make a very strong steel. This steel is used to make airplanes intended for flights faster than the speed of sound.

**tit for tat** blow for blow; this for that.

**tithe** (tīth) ***n.*** **1** one tenth of one's income, paid to support a church. **2** a tenth part or any small part. **3** any tax. ◆***v.*** to pay a tithe. —**tithed, tith′ing**

**tit·il·late** (tit′'l āt) ***v.*** to excite in a pleasant way. —**tit′il·lat·ed, tit′il·lat·ing** —**tit′il·la′tion** ***n.***

**ti·tle** (tīt′'l) ***n.*** **1** the name of a book, chapter, poem,
780 picture, piece of music, etc. **2** a word showing the rank, occupation, etc. of a person ["Baron," "Ms.," and "Dr." are *titles.*] **3** a claim or right; especially, a legal right to own something, or proof of such a right [The *title* to the car is in my name.] **4** a championship [Our team won the football *title.*] ◆***v.*** to give a title to; name. —**ti′tled, ti′tling**

**ti·tled** (tīt′'ld) ***adj.*** having a title, especially the title of a knight, lord, lady, etc.

**tit·mouse** (tit′mous) ***n.*** a small bird found in most parts of the world; especially, ☆the **tufted titmouse,** with a crest on the head, common in the eastern U.S. *See the picture.* —*pl.* **tit·mice** (tit′mīs)

**tit·ter** (tit′ər) ***v.*** to laugh in a silly or nervous way, as if trying to hold back the sound; giggle. ◆***n.*** such a laugh; giggle.

**tit·tle** (tit′'l) ***n.*** a very small bit; jot.

**tit·u·lar** (tich′ə lər) ***adj.*** **1** in name only, not in fact [Most modern kings are only *titular* heads of government.] **2** of a title. **3** having a title.

**TKO** or **T.K.O.** (tē′kā′ō) *abbreviation for* **technical knockout,** a boxing victory won when the referee stops the fight because the losing boxer is badly hurt.

**TLC** or **T.L.C.** tender, loving care.

**TN** *abbreviation for* **Tennessee.**

**TNT** or **T.N.T.** a powerful explosive, used in blasting, in shells for large guns, etc.

**to** (to͞o *or* too *or* tə) ***prep.*** **1** in the direction of [Turn *to* the right.] **2** as far as [We got *to* Akron before dark. They fought *to* the death.] **3** until [There is no left turn from seven *to* nine.] **4** on, onto, against, etc. [Put your hand *to* your mouth. Apply the lotion *to* the skin.] **5** for the purpose of [Come *to* lunch.] **6** having to do with; involving [It's nothing *to* me.] **7** causing or resulting in [torn *to* pieces; *to* my surprise]. **8** with; along with [Add this *to* the others.] **9** belonging with [Here's the coat *to* that suit.] **10** compared with [The score was 8 *to* 0.] **11** in agreement with [That's not *to* my taste.] **12** in or for each [2 pints *to* a quart]. *To* is often used before an indirect object of a verb [Give the book *to* me.] *To* is also used as a sign of the infinitive form of verbs [That was easy *to* read.] ◆***adv.*** **1** forward [His hat was on wrong side *to.*] **2** shut or closed [The door was blown *to.*] *To* is used in many phrases entered in this dictionary. These phrases may be found under their main words. Examples are *come to, bring to, fall to.* —**to and fro,** back and forth; from side to side.

**toad** (tōd) ***n.*** a small animal that is much like a frog, but usually lives on land after an early stage in the water. *See the picture.*

**toad·stool** (tōd′sto͞ol) ***n.*** a mushroom, especially one that is poisonous.

**toad·y** (tōd′ē) ***n.*** a person who flatters others in order to get things from them. —*pl.* **toad′ies** ◆***v.*** to be a toady to; flatter. —**toad′ied, toad′y·ing**

**Toady** comes from *toadeater,* a name for the assistant to an old-time, quack doctor who sold fake medicine made from colored water and flavoring. The assistant would pretend to eat a toad, thought to be poisonous in those days. Then the *toadeater* would take the medicine and be "cured" at once.

**toast**[1] (tōst) ***v.*** **1** to brown the surface of by heating, as bread. **2** to warm [*Toast* yourself by the fire.] ◆***n.*** toasted bread. —**toast′er** ***n.***

**toast**[2] (tōst) ***n.*** **1** a person, thing, idea, etc. in honor of which people raise their glasses and drink. **2** the act of suggesting or taking such a drink. ◆***v.*** to suggest or drink a toast to.

**toast·mas·ter** (tōst′mas′tər) ***n.*** the person at a banquet who offers toasts, introduces speakers, etc.

**to·bac·co** (tə bak′ō) ***n.*** **1** a plant with pink or white flowers and large leaves. **2** the dried leaves of this plant, prepared for smoking, chewing, or snuffing. —*pl.* **to·bac′cos**

**Tobacco** comes from the word that the Indians in the West Indies used for the pipe in which they smoked the plant. When the Spanish explorers who came to the West Indies heard this word, they used it for the plant itself.

**to·bog·gan** (tə bäg′ən) ***n.*** a long, flat sled without runners, for coasting down hills. *See the picture.* ◆***v.*** **1** to coast downhill on a toboggan. **2** to go down rapidly, as in value. —**to·bog′gan·er** ***n.***

**toc·sin** (täk′sin) ***n.*** **1** a bell rung to give an alarm. **2** its sound. **3** any alarm, or sound of warning.

**to·day** (tə dā′) ***adv.*** **1** on or during this day. **2** in these times; nowadays [We are making great strides in medicine *today.*] ◆***n.*** **1** this day [*today's* game]. **2** the present time or period [fashions of *today*].

**tod·dle** (täd′'l) ***v.*** to walk with short, unsteady steps, as a child does. —**tod′dled, tod′dling** —**tod′dler** ***n.***

**to-do** (tə do͞o′) ***n.*** a fuss: *used only in everyday talk.*

**toe** (tō) ***n.*** **1** any of the five parts at the end of the foot. **2** the part of a shoe, stocking, etc. that covers the toes. **3** anything like a toe in position, shape, etc. ◆***v.*** to touch with the toes [The runners *toed* the starting line.] —**toed, toe′ing** —**on one's toes,** alert; ready: *used only in everyday talk.* —**toe the line** or **toe the mark,** to follow orders strictly.

**toe·nail** (tō′nāl) ***n.*** **1** the hard, tough cover on the top of the end of each toe. **2** a nail driven into wood slantingly.

**tof·fee** or **tof·fy** (tôf′ē) ***n.*** a kind of taffy.

**to·ga** (tō′gə) ***n.*** a loose outer garment worn in public by citizens of ancient Rome. *See the picture.*

**to·geth·er** (tə ge*th*′ər) ***adv.*** **1** in or into one gathering, group, or place [The reunion brought the whole family *together.*] **2** with one another [They arrived *together.*] **3** so as to hit, be joined, etc. [The cars skidded *together.*] **4** at the same time [The shots were fired *together.*] **5** in or into agreement [Let's get *together* on this deal.]

**To·go** (tō′gō) a country on the western coast of Africa.

**togs** (tägz) ***n.pl.*** clothes: *used only in everyday talk.*

**toil** (toil) ***v.*** **1** to work hard; labor. **2** to go slowly with pain or effort [to *toil* up a hill]. ◆***n.*** hard work. *See* SYNONYMS *at* **work.** —**toil′er *n.***

**toi·let** (toi′lit) ***n.*** **1** the act of dressing or grooming oneself. ☆**2** a bowl-shaped fixture with a drain, used for ridding the body of waste. ☆**3** a room with such a fixture; bathroom. ◆***adj.*** **1** of or for grooming oneself [*toilet* articles]. ☆**2** for a toilet (*meaning* 2) [a *toilet* brush].

**toilet paper** or **toilet tissue** soft, absorbent paper, usually in a roll, used for cleaning oneself after using a toilet (*meaning* 2).

**toi·let·ry** (toi′lə trē) ***n.*** soap, lotion, cologne, etc. used in cleaning and grooming oneself. —*pl.* **toi′let·ries**

**toilet water** a perfumed liquid, as cologne, for putting on the skin.

**toil·some** (toil′səm) ***adj.*** that takes toil, or hard work; laborious [a *toilsome* task].

**to·ken** (tō′kən) ***n.*** **1** a sign or symbol [This gift is a *token* of my love.] *See* SYNONYMS *at* **sign. 2** a keepsake or souvenir. **3** a piece of stamped metal to be used in place of money, as for fare on a bus or subway. ◆***adj.*** done as a pretended sign of agreement to a principle or practice [*token* integration].

**To·ky·o** (tō′kē ō) the capital of Japan.

**told** (tōld) *past tense and past participle of* **tell.**

**To·le·do** (tə lē′dō) **1** a city in northwestern Ohio. **2** a city in central Spain.

**tol·er·a·ble** (täl′ər ə b′l) ***adj.*** **1** that can be tolerated or put up with; bearable [a *tolerable* burden]. **2** not too bad and not too good; fair [a *tolerable* dinner]. —**tol′er·a·bly *adv.***

**tol·er·ance** (täl′ər əns) ***n.*** **1** a willingness to let others have their own beliefs, ways, etc., even though these are not like one's own. **2** the power of the body to keep a drug or poison from working [My body has built up a *tolerance* for penicillin, so that it can no longer help me.]

**tol·er·ant** (täl′ər ənt) ***adj.*** having or showing tolerance; tolerating. —**tol′er·ant·ly *adv.***

**tol·er·ate** (täl′ə rāt) ***v.*** **1** to let something be done or go on without trying to stop it [I won't *tolerate* such talk.] **2** to put up with; endure; bear [We can't *tolerate* cats.] **3** to have tolerance, as for a drug. —**tol′er·at·ed, tol′er·at·ing**

**tol·er·a·tion** (täl′ə rā′shən) ***n.*** tolerance; especially, willingness to let others worship as they please.

**Tol·kien** (täl′kēn), **J. R. R.** 1892–1973; English writer.

**toll**[1] (tōl) ***n.*** **1** a tax or charge paid for the use of a bridge, highway, etc. **2** a charge made for some service, as for a long-distance telephone call. **3** the number lost, taken, etc. [The storm took a heavy *toll* of lives.]

toga

**tufted titmouse**
16 cm (6 in.) long

**tomahawk**

**toad**
up to 23 cm (9 in.) long

**toboggan**



**toll**[2] (tōl) ***v.*** **1** to ring a bell with slow, regular strokes, as when someone dies. **2** to announce by such ringing [The bell *tolled* ten o'clock.] ◆***n.*** the sound of tolling a bell.

**toll·gate** (tōl′gāt) ***n.*** a gate, as on a highway, that cannot be passed until a toll is paid.

☆**tom·a·hawk** (täm′ə hôk) ***n.*** a light ax used by North American Indians as a tool and a weapon. *See the picture.* ◆***v.*** to hit, cut, or kill with a tomahawk.

**to·ma·to** (tə māt′ō *or* tə mät′ō) ***n.*** **1** a red or yellow, round fruit, with a juicy pulp, used as a vegetable. **2** the plant it grows on. —*pl.* **to·ma′toes**

**tomb** (to͞om) ***n.*** a grave, vault, etc. for the dead. —**the tomb,** death. —**tomb′like *adj.***

**tom·boy** (täm′boi) ***n.*** a girl who behaves or plays like an active boy.

**tomb·stone** (to͞om′stōn) ***n.*** a stone put on a tomb telling who is buried there; gravestone.

**tom·cat** (täm′kat) ***n.*** a male cat.

**tome** (tōm) ***n.*** a book, especially a large one.

An older meaning of **tome** is "any volume, or book, of a work of several volumes." This meaning came from the Greek word *tomos* meaning "a piece cut off." A tome then was a book that was part of a larger book and was "cut off" from it.

| | | | |
|---|---|---|---|
| **a** fat | **ir** here | **ou** out | **zh** leisure |
| **ā** ape | **ī** bite, fire | **u** up | **ng** ring |
| **ä** car, lot | **ō** go | **ur** fur | a *in* ago |
| **e** ten | **ô** law, horn | **ch** chin | e *in* agent |
| **er** care | **oi** oil | **sh** she | **ə** = i *in* unity |
| **ē** even | **oo** look | **th** thin | o *in* collect |
| **i** hit | **o͞o** tool | ***th*** then | u *in* focus |

**t**

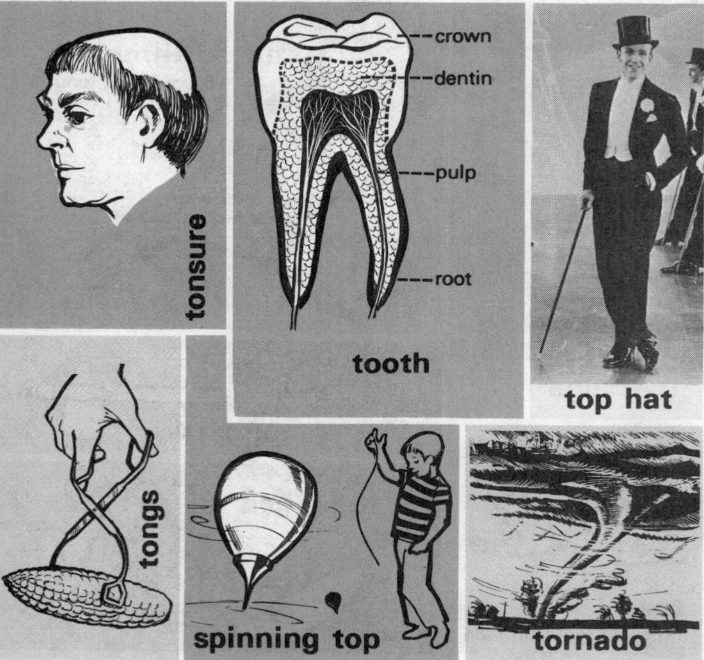


**tom·fool·er·y** (täm′fo͞ol′ər ē) ***n.*** a foolish or silly way of acting. *—pl.* **tom′fool′er·ies**

 **to·mor·row** (tə mär′ō *or* tə môr′ō) ***adv.*** on the day after today. ◆***n.*** **1** the day after today. **2** some future time.

**tom-tom** (täm′täm) ***n.*** a simple kind of drum, usually beaten with the hands.

**ton** (tun) ***n.*** **1** a measure of weight equal to 2,000 pounds, used in the United States. It is often called the **short ton** to tell it from the **long ton**, which is equal to 2,240 pounds and has been used in Great Britain. **2** a metric ton, equal to 1,000 kilograms.

**ton·al** (tō′n′l) ***adj.*** of a tone or tones.

**tone** (tōn) ***n.*** **1** a sound, especially one that is pleasant or musical [the clear *tones* of an oboe]. *See* SYNONYMS *at* **sound**. **2** one of a series of such sounds arranged in a musical scale; note. **3** the difference in pitch of one full step in the scale between musical notes [A is two *tones* below C.] **4** a way of speaking or writing that shows a certain feeling [Her answer had a friendly *tone.*] **5** the style, character, etc. of a place or period [Their many paintings gave the house a cultured *tone.*] **6** a color, shade, or tint [His suit had several *tones* of brown.] **7** the normal, healthy condition of an organ, muscle, etc. [Exercise will improve the *tone* of your muscles.] ◆***v.*** to give a certain tone to, as of color or sound. **—toned, ton′ing —tone down,** to make or become less bright or sharp; soften. **—tone in with,** to blend or harmonize with [Your green hat *tones in with* your red hair.] **—tone up,** to make or become brighter or stronger.

**Ton·ga** (täŋ′gə) a country on a group of islands in the South Pacific, east of Fiji.

**tongs** (tôŋz) ***n.pl.*** a device for seizing or lifting things, usually made with two long arms hinged together. *See the picture.*

**tongue** (tuŋ) ***n.*** **1** the movable muscle attached to the floor of the mouth. It is used in tasting, eating, and speaking. **2** an animal's tongue used as food. **3** the act or power of speaking [Have you lost your *tongue?*] **4** a way of speaking [a smooth *tongue*]. **5** a language [the French *tongue*]. **6** something like a tongue in shape, motion, etc., as the flap under the laces of a shoe, a long, narrow flame, the clapper of a bell, or a narrow strip of land in a lake or sea. **—hold one's tongue,** to keep from speaking. **—on the tip of one's tongue,** almost said or remembered. **—speak in tongues,** to say sounds that cannot be understood, as while in a religious trance.

**tongue-tied** (tuŋ′tīd′) ***adj.*** **1** not able to move the tongue or speak properly, because the membrane fastening the tongue to the mouth is too short. **2** not able to speak because one is amazed, embarrassed, etc.

**ton·ic** (tän′ik) ***adj.*** **1** giving strength or energy; stimulating [Swimming has a *tonic* effect.] **2** of or having to do with a keynote in music [a *tonic* chord]. ◆***n.*** **1** anything that stimulates or gives energy, as a tonic medicine. **2** the keynote of a musical scale.

**to·night** (tə nīt′) ***adv.*** on or during this night or the night of today. ◆***n.*** this night or the night of today.

**ton·nage** (tun′ij) ***n.*** **1** the amount in tons that a ship can carry. **2** the total amount of shipping of a country or port, figured in tons. **3** a tax or duty on ships, based on tons carried. **4** total weight in tons.

**ton·sil** (tän′s′l) ***n.*** either of two soft, oval masses of tissue at the back of the mouth.

**ton·sil·lec·to·my** (tän′sə lek′tə mē) ***n.*** an operation by which a surgeon removes a person's tonsils. *—pl.* **ton′sil·lec′to·mies**

**ton·sil·li·tis** (tän′sə līt′əs) ***n.*** a diseased condition of a person's tonsils in which they become swollen and inflamed.

**ton·so·ri·al** (tän sôr′ē əl) ***adj.*** of a barber or the work of a barber: *now used in a humorous way* [a *tonsorial* artist].

**ton·sure** (tän′shər) ***n.*** **1** the act of shaving a man's head, especially on top, when he becomes a priest or monk. **2** the part of the head left bare by doing this. *See the picture.*

**too** (to͞o) ***adv.*** **1** in addition; besides; also [You come, *too.*] **2** more than enough [This hat is *too* big.] **3** very [You are *too* kind.]

> **Too** is often used just to give force to what is said [I did *too* see them!] **Too** is also used as an adjective with *much* or *many* [We have *too* much to see.]

**took** (to͝ok) *past tense of* **take.**

**tool** (to͞ol) ***n.*** **1** any instrument held in the hand or driven by a motor and used in doing some work [Knives, saws, drills, etc. are *tools.*] *See* SYNONYMS *at* **implement.** **2** any person or thing used as a means to get something done [Books are *tools* of education.] ◆***v.*** **1** to shape, work, or put designs on with a tool [to *tool* leather]. **2** to furnish tools or machinery for [to *tool* up a factory]. **3** to go in an automobile, etc. [We *tooled* along the highway in our new car.]

**tool·mak·er** (to͞ol′mā′kər) ***n.*** a person who makes and repairs machine tools.

**toot** (to͞ot) ***n.*** a short blast of a horn, whistle, etc. ◆***v.*** to sound in short blasts, as a horn or whistle.

**tooth** (to͞oth) ***n.*** **1** any of the white, bony parts growing from the jaws and used for biting and chewing.

*See the picture.* **2** any part more or less like a tooth, as on a saw, comb, gearwheel, etc. **3** an appetite or taste for something [a sweet *tooth*]. **4** *pl.* **teeth,** a way of giving force to something [We must put *teeth* into the law.] *—pl.* **teeth** (tēth) **—get one's teeth into something,** to have one's complete attention taken by something. **—in the teeth of,** going straight against the force of. **—tooth and nail,** with all one's strength. **—tooth'less** *adj.*

**tooth·ache** (to͞oth'āk) *n.* pain in or near a tooth.

**tooth·brush** (to͞oth'brush) *n.* a small brush for cleaning the teeth.

**toothed** (to͞otht *or* to͞othd) *adj.* **1** having teeth, especially of a certain kind [sharp-*toothed;* buck*toothed*]. **2** having notches [a *toothed* leaf].

**tooth·paste** (to͞oth'pāst) *n.* a paste used in cleaning the teeth with a toothbrush.

**tooth·pick** (to͞oth'pik) *n.* a small, pointed stick for getting bits of food free from between the teeth.

**tooth·some** (to͞oth'səm) *adj.* pleasing to the taste; tasty.

**top**[1] (täp) *n.* **1** the highest part or point [the *top* of a hill; the *top* of a page]. **2** the part of a plant growing above ground [carrot *tops*]. **3** the head or the crown of a head [My hair is cut short on *top.*] **4** a part that covers or is uppermost, as a lid or cover [a box *top*]. **5** the highest degree or pitch [He shouted at the *top* of his voice.] **6** the highest rank, position, etc. [Sue is at the *top* of her class.] **7** the best part; pick [the *top* of the crop]. **8** the upper part of a two-piece garment [She mislaid the *top* of her pajamas.] **9** the platform around the head of the lowest section of mast on a sailing ship. ◆*adj.* of or at the top; highest; uppermost [a *top* student]. ◆*v.* **1** to put a top on [to *top* a cake with icing]. **2** to cut or trim the top of, as a plant or tree. **3** to be at the top of [Snow *topped* the mountain.] **4** to reach or go over the top of [We *topped* the hill after a long climb.] **5** to be more than in amount, height, etc. [The fish *topped* 75 pounds.] **6** to do or be better than; surpass [She *tops* them all at golf.] **7** to be at the top of; head; lead [Bill *topped* his class.] **—topped, top'ping —**☆**off the top of one's head,** speaking without first thinking carefully. **—on top,** at the top; successful. **—on top of, 1** resting upon. **2** in addition to; besides. **3** controlling successfully. **—over the top,** beyond the goal set. **—top off,** to finish by adding a final touch.

**top**[2] (täp) *n.* a child's toy shaped like a cone. It is spun on its pointed end. *See the picture.*

**to·paz** (tō'paz) *n.* a clear, crystal stone, usually yellow, used as a gem.

☆**top·coat** (täp'kōt) *n.* a light overcoat.

**To·pe·ka** (tə pē'kə) the capital of Kansas.

**top·gal·lant** (täp'gal'ənt *or* tə gal'ənt) *adj.* next above the topmast on a sailing ship. ◆*n.* a topgallant mast or sail.

**top hat** a tall, black hat with a flat top, worn by men in formal clothes. *See the picture.*

**top-heav·y** (täp'hev'ē) *adj.* so heavy at the top that it may fall over.

**top·ic** (täp'ik) *n.* the subject of a talk, piece of writing, debate, etc.

**top·i·cal** (täp'i k'l) *adj.* **1** dealing with topics of the day; of special interest because timely [*topical* jokes]. **2** having to do with topics [a *topical* outline].

**top·knot** (täp'nät) *n.* a tuft of hair or feathers on the top of the head.

**top·mast** (täp'məst *or* täp'mast) *n.* the section of a mast next to the lowest section, on a sailing ship.

**top·most** (täp'mōst) *adj.* at the very top; highest.

☆**top-notch** (täp'näch') *adj.* of the highest class or quality; first-rate; excellent: *used only in everyday talk.*

**to·pog·ra·phy** (tə päg'rə fē) *n.* **1** the surface features of a region, as hills, rivers, roads, etc. **2** the science of showing these on maps and charts. **—to·pog'ra·pher** *n.* **—top·o·graph·i·cal** (täp'ə graf'i k'l) *adj.*

**top·ple** (täp''l) *v.* **1** to fall over; fall top forward [The tall pile of books *toppled* over.] **2** to make topple; overturn. **3** to defeat or overthrow [The government was *toppled* by a revolution.] **—top'pled, top'pling**

**top·sail** (täp's'l *or* täp'sāl) *n.* the sail next above the lowest sail on a mast.

☆**top·soil** (täp'soil) *n.* the top layer of soil, usually richer than the soil underneath.

**top·sy-tur·vy** (täp'sē tur'vē) *adv., adj.* upside down, or in confusion or disorder [The tornado left many houses *topsy-turvy.*]

**To·rah** or **To·ra** (tō'rə *or* tō rä') *n.* in Judaism, the first five books of the Bible, especially in the form of a parchment scroll written by hand: *a Hebrew word.*

**torch** (tôrch) *n.* **1** a flaming light that can be carried in the hand, as a piece of burning wood with resin in it. **2** something that inspires or sheds the light of truth, reason, etc. [the *torch* of science]. **3** any device that makes a very hot flame, as a blowtorch. **4** *another name for* **flashlight**: *a British meaning.*

**torch·light** (tôrch'līt) *n.* the light of a torch or torches. ◆☆*adj.* done or carried on by torchlight [a *torchlight* parade].

**tore** (tôr) *past tense of* **tear**[1].

**tor·e·a·dor** (tôr'ē ə dôr') *n.* *another name for* **bullfighter**. *This word is no longer used in bullfighting.*

**tor·ment** (tôr'ment) *n.* **1** great pain or suffering of the body or mind. **2** something that causes pain, worry, etc. ◆*v.* (tôr ment') **1** to make suffer in body or mind. **2** to annoy or worry; harass. **—tor·men'tor** or **tor·ment'er** *n.*

SYNONYMS: **Torment** suggests being worried or troubled because one has been bothered or treated harshly again and again [We were *tormented* by the mosquitoes.] **Torture** suggests causing such great pain that the body or mind can hardly stand it [I was *tortured* by old memories.]

**torn** (tôrn) *past participle of* **tear**[1].

**tor·na·do** (tôr nā'dō) *n.* a high, narrow column of air that is whirling very fast. It is often seen as a slender cloud shaped like a funnel, that usually destroys everything in its narrow path. *See the picture.* *—pl.* **tor·na'does** or **tor·na'dos**



| | | | | | | | |
|---|---|---|---|---|---|---|---|
| **a** | fat | **ir** | here | **ou** | out | **zh** | leisure |
| **ā** | ape | **ī** | bite, fire | **u** | up | **ng** | ring |
| **ä** | car, lot | **ō** | go | **ur** | fur | | a *in* ago |
| **e** | ten | **ô** | law, horn | **ch** | chin | | e *in* agent |
| **er** | care | **oi** | oil | **sh** | she | **ə =** | i *in* unity |
| **ē** | even | **oo** | look | **th** | thin | | o *in* collect |
| **i** | hit | **o͞o** | tool | ***th*** | then | | u *in* focus |

**To·ron·to** (tə rän′tō) the capital of Ontario, Canada.

**tor·pe·do** (tôr pē′dō) ***n.*** a large, exploding missile shaped like a cigar. It is fired under water, where it moves under its own power to blow up enemy ships. —*pl.* **tor·pe′does** ◆***v.*** to attack or destroy with a torpedo. —**tor·pe′doed, tor·pe′do·ing**

☆**torpedo boat** a small, fast warship used for firing torpedoes.

**tor·pid** (tôr′pid) ***adj.*** moving, feeling, thinking, etc. slowly or not at all; dull; sluggish [A hibernating animal is *torpid.*] —**tor′pid·ly *adv.***

**tor·por** (tôr′pər) ***n.*** the condition of being torpid; dullness; sluggishness.

**torque** (tôrk) ***n.*** a force that gives a twisting or rotating motion.

**tor·rent** (tôr′ənt) ***n.*** **1** a swift, rushing stream of water. **2** any wild, rushing flow [a *torrent* of insults]. **3** a heavy fall of rain.

**tor·ren·tial** (tô ren′shəl) ***adj.*** of or like a torrent; overwhelming [*torrential* rains].

**tor·rid** (tôr′id) ***adj.*** very hot and dry; scorching or scorched [a *torrid* desert].

**Torrid Zone** the part of the earth's surface between the Tropic of Cancer and the Tropic of Capricorn and divided by the equator. The Torrid Zone has a hot climate.

**tor·sion** (tôr′shən) ***n.*** a twisting or being twisted, especially along the length of an axis, as when a wire is twisted at one end while the other end is held firm or twisted in the opposite direction.



**tor·so** (tôr′sō) ***n.*** **1** the human body, not including the head, arms, and legs; trunk. **2** a statue of the human trunk. —*pl.* **tor′sos**

> **Torso** comes from a Greek word meaning "a stem." A torso is like the stem of a flower in that the arms, legs, and head seem to grow out from it.

☆**tor·til·la** (tôr tē′ə) ***n.*** a kind of very thin pancake made of cornmeal or now sometimes of flour. Tortillas are eaten as a basic food throughout Mexico.

**tor·toise** (tôr′təs) ***n.*** a turtle, especially one that lives on land.

man without a toupee

man with a toupee

tourniquet

toucan
up to 60 cm (2 ft.) long

totem pole

**tor·tu·ous** (tôr′cho͝o wəs) ***adj.*** full of twists, turns, etc.; winding; crooked [a *tortuous* river; *tortuous* thinking].

**tor·ture** (tôr′chər) ***n.*** **1** the act of greatly hurting someone on purpose, as to punish or cause to confess. **2** any great pain; agony [the *torture* of a toothache]. ◆***v.*** **1** to use torture on someone. **2** to cause great pain or agony to someone [I was *tortured* by doubts.] *See* SYNONYMS *at* **torment.** **3** to twist the meaning or form of something. —**tor′tured, tor′tur·ing** —**tor′tur·er *n.***

**To·ry** (tôr′ē) ***n.*** **1** in former times, a member of one of the main political parties of England. This party is now called the *Conservative Party.* **2** an American colonist who favored Great Britain during the American Revolution. **3** *often* **tory,** any very conservative person. —*pl.* **To′ries**

**toss** (tôs) ***v.*** **1** to throw from the hand in a light, easy way [to *toss* a ball]. *See* SYNONYMS *at* **throw.** **2** to throw about; fling here and there [The waves *tossed* the boat.] **3** to be thrown or flung about [The kite *tossed* in the wind.] **4** to lift quickly; jerk upward [to *toss* one's head]. **5** to flip a coin into the air in order to decide something according to which side lands up. ◆***n.*** the act of tossing. —**toss off, 1** to make, write, etc. quickly and easily. **2** to drink quickly, all at once.

**tot** (tät) ***n.*** a young child.

**to·tal** (tōt′'l) ***n.*** the whole amount; sum. ◆***adj.*** **1** making up the whole amount; entire [The *total* amount of your bill is $3.50.] **2** complete [a *total* eclipse of the moon]. ◆***v.*** **1** to find the sum or total of; add [to *total* a column of figures]. **2** to add up to; reach a total of [My golf score *totals* 89.] **3** to wreck completely: *a slang meaning* [The crash *totaled* our car.] —**to′taled** or **to′talled, to′tal·ing** or **to′tal·ling** —**to′tal·ly *adv.***

**to·tal·i·tar·i·an** (tō tal′ə ter′ē ən) ***adj.*** describing or having to do with a government in which one political party has complete control and outlaws all others. ◆***n.*** a person who is in favor of such a government. —**to·tal′i·tar′i·an·ism *n.***

**to·tal·i·ty** (tō tal′ə tē) ***n.*** the total amount. —*pl.* **to·tal′i·ties**

**tote** (tōt) ***v.*** to carry or haul: *used only in everyday talk.* —**tot′ed, tot′ing** ◆***n.*** *same as* **tote bag.**

> The word **tote** is probably of African origin. It is thought to come from a Bantu dialect of a people who live in parts of Angola and Zaire. There the word *tota* means "to pick up."

**tote bag** ☆a large handbag made of cloth, etc. in which one can carry shoes, small packages, etc.

**to·tem** (tōt′əm) ***n.*** **1** an animal or other natural object, taken by a family, tribe, etc. as its symbol, especially among certain North American Indians. **2** an image of this, often carved or painted on poles called **totem poles.** *See the picture.*

**tot·ter** (tät′ər) ***v.*** **1** to rock or sway back and forth as if about to fall. **2** to walk in an unsteady way; stagger. *See* SYNONYMS *at* **stagger.**

**tou·can** (to͞o′kan) ***n.*** a brightly colored bird of tropical America, with a very large beak that curves downward. *See the picture.*

**touch** (tuch) ***v.*** **1** to put the hand, finger, etc. on something in order to feel it [He *touched* the fence to see if the paint was wet.] **2** to tap lightly [She *touched* the horse with a whip.] **3** to handle, use, or disturb [Don't *touch* the papers on my desk.] **4** to eat or drink [He won't *touch* carrots.] **5** to injure slightly [Frost *touched* these plants.] **6** to bring or come into contact with something else [She *touched* a match to the candle. The bumpers of the cars *touched*.] **7** to make feel pity, sympathy, gratitude, etc. [Your kindness *touches* me.] **8** to talk about briefly; mention [The speaker *touched* on many subjects.] **9** to have to do with; concern [a subject that *touches* our welfare]. **10** to be a match for; equal; rival [His boat can't *touch* mine for speed.] ◆***n.*** **1** a touching or being touched; light tap or stroke [I felt the *touch* of a hand on my arm.] **2** the sense in the skin, especially of the fingers, by which one becomes aware of the size, shape, hardness, and smoothness of a thing; power to feel. **3** the feeling one gets from touching something [The cloth has a soft, smooth *touch*.] **4** a small, skillful change in a painting, story, etc. [With a few *touches* she made the joke really funny.] **5** a very small amount or degree [Add a *touch* of salt.] **6** a mild form [a *touch* of the flu]. **7** the way in which a person strikes the keys or strings of a musical instrument [a delicate *touch*]. **8** contact or communication [I try to keep in *touch* with friends. You are out of *touch* with reality.] —**touch off,** **1** to make explode; fire. **2** to cause to begin [Your speech *touched off* a violent reaction.] —**touch up,** to improve by making small changes in.

☆**touch·down** (tuch′doun) ***n.*** **1** a goal scored in football by putting the ball across the opponent's goal line. **2** a score of six points made in this way.

**touch·ing** (tuch′ing) ***adj.*** that makes one feel pity, sympathy, etc. [a *touching* sight]. *See* SYNONYMS *at* **moving.**

**touch·stone** (tuch′stōn) ***n.*** **1** a black stone used at one time to test the purity of gold or silver by rubbing the touchstone with the precious metal and studying the streak made. **2** any test or standard.

**touch·y** (tuch′ē) ***adj.*** **1** easily hurt, annoyed, made angry, etc.; irritable. **2** very risky; dangerous [a *touchy* situation]. —**touch′i·er, touch′i·est**

**tough** (tuf) ***adj.*** **1** that will bend or twist without tearing or breaking [*tough* rubber]. **2** that cannot be cut or chewed easily [*tough* meat]. **3** strong and healthy; robust [a *tough* pioneer]. *See* SYNONYMS *at* **strong.** **4** very difficult or hard [a *tough* job]. ☆**5** rough or brutal [Don't get *tough* with me.] **6** not favorable; bad: *used only in everyday talk* [a *tough* break]. ◆☆***n.*** a rough, brutal person; thug. —**tough′ness *n.***

**tough·en** (tuf′′n) ***v.*** to make or become tough or tougher.

**tou·pee** (tōō pā′) ***n.*** a man's wig for covering a bald spot on the head. *See the picture.*

**tour** (toor) ***n.*** **1** a long trip, as for pleasure and sightseeing. **2** any round trip, as by actors going from city to city to perform. ◆***v.*** **1** to go on a tour. **2** to take a tour through [to *tour* New England].

**tour·ism** (toor′iz′m) ***n.*** the travel of tourists, especially when thought of as a business.

**tour·ist** (toor′ist) ***n.*** a person who tours or travels for pleasure. ◆***adj.*** of or for tourists.

**tour·ma·line** (toor′mə lin *or* toor′mə lēn) ***n.*** a mineral of various colors. Some varieties are used as gems.

**tour·na·ment** (toor′nə mənt) ***n.*** **1** a contest in which knights on horseback tried to knock each other off the horses with lances. **2** a series of contests in some sport or game in which a number of people or teams take part, trying to win the championship.

**tour·ney** (toor′nē) ***n.*** *another name for* **tournament.** —*pl.* **tour′neys**

**tour·ni·quet** (toor′nə kit) ***n.*** anything used to stop bleeding from a wound by closing off a blood vessel, as a bandage twisted tight with a stick and then loosened from time to time. *See the picture.*

**tou·sle** (tou′z'l) ***v.*** to make untidy, or muss up; rumple [*tousled* hair]. —**tou′sled, tou′sling**

**tow**[1] (tō) ***v.*** to pull by a rope or chain [A horse *towed* the canal boat.] *See* SYNONYMS *at* **drag.** ◆***n.*** **1** a towing or being towed. **2** something towed. **3** a rope, etc. for towing. —**in tow,** **1** in one's company or following one [with several friends *in tow*]. **2** under one's control or charge.

**tow**[2] (tō) ***n.*** the coarse, broken fibers of flax, hemp, etc. before spinning.

**toward** (tôrd) ***prep.*** **1** in the direction of [The house faces *toward* the park.] **2** leading to [steps *toward* peace]. **3** having to do with; about [What is your feeling *toward* them?] **4** just before; near [It became cold *toward* morning.] **5** for [to save *toward* a new car].

**towards** (tôrdz) ***prep.*** *same as* **toward.**

**tow·el** (tou′'l *or* toul) ***n.*** a piece of soft paper or cloth for drying things by wiping.

**tow·el·ing** or **tow·el·ling** (tou′'l ing *or* toul′ing) ***n.*** material for making towels.

**tow·er** (tou′ər) ***n.*** **1** a building that is much higher than it is wide or long, either standing alone or as part of another building [a water *tower;* the bell *tower* of a church]. **2** such a building, used as a fort or prison. ◆***v.*** to stand or rise high above the others [The giraffe *towers* over other animals.]

**tow·er·ing** (tou′ər ing) ***adj.*** very high, great, strong, etc. [a *towering* steeple; a *towering* rage].

☆**tow·head** (tō′hed) ***n.*** a person having very light yellow hair. —**tow′head·ed *adj.***

**town** (toun) ***n.*** **1** a place where there are a large number of houses and other buildings, larger than a village but smaller than a city. **2** *another name for* **city.** **3** the business center of a city or town. **4** the people of a town [a friendly *town*].

**town hall** a building in which there are the offices of a town government.

☆**town meeting** a meeting of the voters of a town, as in New England, to act on town business.

**town·ship** (toun′ship) ***n.*** **1** a part of a county having some powers of government, as control over its schools and roads. **2** in United States land surveys, a division six miles square. **3** in Canada, a subdivision of a province.

| | | | | | | | |
|---|---|---|---|---|---|---|---|
| **a** | fat | **ir** | here | **ou** | out | **zh** | leisure |
| **ā** | ape | **ī** | bite, fire | **u** | up | **ng** | ring |
| **ä** | car, lot | **ō** | go | **ur** | fur | | a *in* ago |
| **e** | ten | **ô** | law, horn | **ch** | chin | | e *in* agent |
| **er** | care | **oi** | oil | **sh** | she | ə = | i *in* unity |
| **ē** | even | **oo** | look | **th** | thin | | o *in* collect |
| **i** | hit | **ōō** | tool | ***th*** | then | | u *in* focus |



**t**

**towns·man** (tounz′mən) ***n.*** **1** a person who lives in a town. **2** a person who lives in the same town where one lives. —*pl.* **towns′men**

**towns·peo·ple** (tounz′pē′p'l) ***n.pl.*** the people of a town: *also called* **towns·folk** (tounz′fōk).

☆**tow truck** a truck with equipment for towing away automobiles, etc. that are not able to operate, are not legally parked, etc.

**tox·ic** (täk′sik) ***adj.*** of or caused by a toxin, or poison [the *toxic* effects of some berries].

> **Toxic** comes from a Greek word for a poison in which arrows were dipped before they were used. In turn, the word for this poison comes from the Greek word *toxon,* for the bow from which an arrow is shot.

**tox·in** (täk′sin) ***n.*** **1** a poison produced by some bacteria, viruses, etc., causing certain diseases. **2** any poison produced by an animal or plant [Snake venom is a *toxin.*]

**toy** (toi) ***n.*** **1** a thing to play with; especially, a plaything for children. **2** anything small and of little value. ◆***adj.*** **1** like a toy in size or use [a *toy* dog]. **2** made for use as a toy; especially, made as a small model [a *toy* train]. ◆***v.*** to play or trifle [The child just *toyed* with the food.]

**trace**[1] (trās) ***n.*** **1** a mark, track, sign, etc. left by someone or something [no human *trace* on the island]. **2** a very small amount [a *trace* of garlic in the dressing]. ◆***v.*** **1** to follow the trail of; track [The hunter *traced* the lions to their den.] **2** to follow or study the course of [We *traced* the history of Rome back to Caesar.] **3** to copy a picture, drawing, etc. by following its lines on a thin piece of paper placed over it. **4** to draw, sketch, outline, etc. —**traced, trac′ing**



**trace**[2] (trās) ***n.*** either of two straps, chains, etc. by which a horse is fastened to the wagon, cart, or other vehicle that it pulls.

**trac·er** (trā′sər) ***n.*** **1** a person who tries to find lost or missing things or persons. ☆**2** a request sent out to try to find a letter, package, etc. lost while being carried from one place to another.

**trac·er·y** (trā′sər ē) ***n.*** any graceful design, as in carving, of lines that come together in various ways. *See the picture.* —*pl.* **trac′er·ies**

**tra·che·a** (trā′kē ə) ***n.*** *another name for* **windpipe.** —*pl.* **tra·che·ae** (trā′kē ē′) or **tra′che·as**

**trac·ing** (trā′siŋ) ***n.*** **1** the action of one that traces. **2** something traced, as a copy of a picture or drawing.

**track** (trak) ***n.*** **1** a mark left in passing, as a footprint or wheel rut. **2** a path or trail. **3** steel rails, usually in pairs, on which the wheels of trains, etc. run. **4** a path or course, often in an oval, laid out for racing. ☆**5** sports performed on such a track, as running or hurdling; also, such sports together with those held in the **field** (*meaning* 8). **6** a course of action; way of doing something [You're on the right *track* to solve the problem.] **7** any of the divided parts on a phonograph record; also, any of the parallel recording surfaces along a magnetic tape. ◆***v.*** **1** to follow the tracks of [We *tracked* the fox to its den.] **2** to make tracks or dirty marks [The children *tracked* up the clean floor.] ☆**3** to make tracks with [The dog *tracked* snow into the house.] —☆**in one's tracks,** where one is at the moment. —**keep track of,** to go on knowing or being informed about. —**lose track of,** to stop knowing or being informed about. —**track′er** ***n.***

**track and field** a sport, as in schools, in which a series of contests in running, jumping, etc. is held on a track and on a field.

**track·less** (trak′lis) ***adj.*** **1** without a track or path [a *trackless* wilderness]. **2** not running on rails [a *trackless* trolley].

**tract**[1] (trakt) ***n.*** **1** a large stretch of land, etc. **2** a number of organs in the body that work together in carrying out some function [the digestive *tract*].

**tract**[2] (trakt) ***n.*** a booklet or pamphlet, especially one on a religious subject.

**trac·ta·ble** (trak′tə b'l) ***adj.*** **1** easy to control, train, etc.; not stubborn or disobedient [a *tractable* horse]. **2** easy to shape or work with [a *tractable* metal].

**trac·tion** (trak′shən) ***n.*** **1** the power to grip or hold to a surface while moving, without slipping [The tires lost *traction* on the icy hill, and the car slid backward.] **2** the act of pulling or drawing a load over a surface. **3** the condition of having a leg, arm, etc. pulled by some device, as to bring a dislocated bone back into place. **4** the pulling power of a locomotive, etc.

☆**trac·tor** (trak′tər) ***n.*** **1** a powerful motor vehicle for pulling farm machinery, heavy loads, etc. *See the picture.* **2** a kind of truck with a driver's cab and no body, used to haul large trailers.

**trade** (trād) ***n.*** **1** any work done with the hands that needs special skill got by training [the plumber's *trade*]. **2** all those in a certain business or kind of work [the book *trade*]. **3** buying and selling; commerce [Tariffs restrict *trade* between nations.] **4** customers [This sale will bring in *trade.*] **5** the act of giving one thing for another; exchange [an even *trade* of my comic books for your football]. **6 trades,** *pl.* the trade winds. ◆***v.*** **1** to carry on a business; buy and sell [This company *trades* in tea. Our country *trades* with other countries.] *See* SYNONYMS *at* **sell. 2** to exchange [I *traded* my stamp collection for a camera.] **3** to be a customer: *used only in everyday talk* [We *trade* at the corner supermarket.] —**trad′ed, trad′ing** —☆**trade in,** to give an old or used thing as part of the payment for a new one. —**trade on** or **trade upon,** to take advantage of [He *traded on* his war record to get votes.]

**trade·mark** (trād′märk) ***n.*** a special picture, mark, word, etc. placed on a product to show who its maker or dealer is. Trademarks are usually protected by law.

**trade name** **1** a name used as a trademark. **2** the name used for a certain article by those who deal in it. **3** the business name of a company.

**trad·er** (trā′dər) ***n.*** **1** a person who trades; merchant. **2** a ship used in trade.

**trade school** a school where trades are taught.

**trades·man** (trādz′mən) ***n.*** a person in business; especially, a storekeeper: *mainly a British word.* —*pl.* **trades′men**

**trade union** *another name for* **labor union.**

**trade wind** a wind that blows without stopping from the northeast or southeast toward the equator.

☆**trading post** (trā′diŋ) a store in a frontier town, etc., where trading is done.

**tra·di·tion** (trə dish′ən) ***n.*** **1** the handing down of customs, beliefs, etc. from generation to generation by word of mouth rather than in written records. **2** a custom, belief, etc. handed down in this way [It's a *tradition* to eat turkey at Thanksgiving.]

**tra·di·tion·al** (trə dish′ən ′l) ***adj.*** of or handed down by tradition; customary [a *traditional* costume]. —**tra·di′tion·al·ly** ***adv.***

**tra·duce** (trə do͞os′ *or* trə dyo͞os′) ***v.*** to say false things so as to harm the reputation of; slander. —**tra·duced′, tra·duc′ing** —**tra·duc′er** ***n.***

**traf·fic** (traf′ik) ***n.*** **1** the movement or number of automobiles, persons, ships, etc. along a road or route of travel [to direct *traffic* on city streets; the heavy *traffic* on weekends]. **2** the amount of business done by a railroad, airline, etc. **3** buying and selling, often of a wrong or unlawful kind; trade; commerce [*traffic* in drugs]. **4** dealings or business [I'll have no *traffic* with such people.] ✦***adj.*** of, for, or controlling traffic [a *traffic* light]. ✦***v.*** to carry on traffic, or trade, often of an unlawful kind. —**traf′ficked, traf′fick·ing**

☆**traffic light** a set of signal lights for traffic, as where streets meet, that tell cars or walkers to go (green light), get ready to stop (yellow light), or stop (red light): *also* **traffic signal.**

**tra·ge·di·an** (trə jē′dē ən) ***n.*** an actor or writer of tragedy, mainly of earlier times.

**trag·e·dy** (traj′ə dē) ***n.*** **1** a serious play with a sad ending. **2** a very sad or tragic happening. —*pl.* **trag′e·dies**

> **Tragedy** comes from a Greek word meaning "song of the goat." It was so named probably because of the goatskin dress of actors in Greek plays who played the part of satyrs.

**trag·ic** (traj′ik) ***adj.*** **1** of, like, or having to do with tragedy [a *tragic* actor; a *tragic* tale]. **2** bringing great harm, suffering, etc.; dreadful [a *tragic* accident; a *tragic* misunderstanding]. —**trag′i·cal·ly** ***adv.***

**trail** (trāl) ***v.*** **1** to drag or bring along behind [The bride's veil *trailed* on the floor. He *trailed* dirt into the house.] **2** to flow or drift behind, as smoke. **3** to follow or lag behind [The children *trailed* along after us. She is *trailing* in the race.] **4** to follow the trail of, as in hunting; track. **5** to grow along the ground, etc., as some plants. **6** to become less or weaker [Her voice *trailed* off into a whisper.] ✦***n.*** **1** something that trails behind [a *trail* of dust]. **2** a mark, scent, etc. left behind. ☆**3** a path through woods, etc.

**trail·er** (trāl′ər) ***n.*** **1** a person or animal that trails another. ☆**2** a wagon, van, cart, etc. made to be pulled by an automobile, truck, or tractor. Some trailers are outfitted as homes.

**train** (trān) ***n.*** **1** something that drags along behind, as a trailing skirt. *See the picture.* **2** a group of followers or attendants, as of a king. **3** a group of persons, cars, etc. moving in a line; procession [a wagon *train* heading West]. **4** a series of connected things [a *train* of thought; a gear *train*]. **5** a line of connected railroad cars pulled by a locomotive. ✦***v.*** **1** to develop the mind, character, etc. of; rear [They *trained* their children to be kind.] **2** to teach, or give practice in, some skill [to *train* airplane pilots; to *train* animals to do tricks]. *See* SYNONYMS *at* **teach.** **3** to make or become fit for some sport, as by exercise, practice, etc. **4** to make grow in a certain direction [to *train* roses along a trellis]. **5** to aim [Four guns were *trained* on the target.] —**train′er** ***n.***

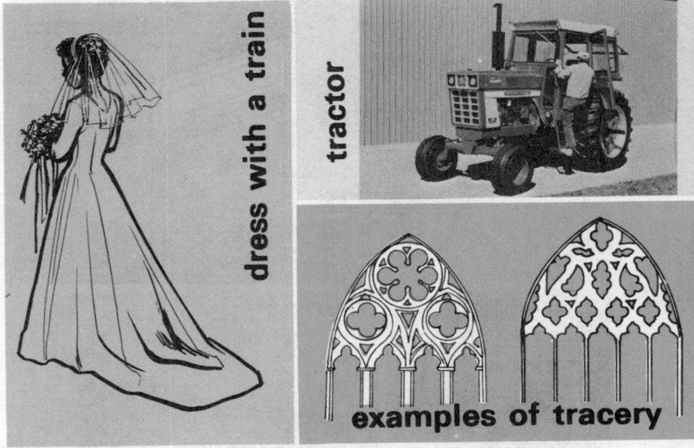

dress with a train

tractor

examples of tracery

**train·ee** (trā nē′) ***n.*** a person who is being trained in something.

**train·ing** (trān′iŋ) ***n.*** **1** the practice, drills, etc. given by one who trains or received by one who is being trained. **2** the condition of being trained for some sport, as by exercise, practice, etc.

☆**train·man** (trān′mən) ***n.*** a person who works on a railroad train, especially as an assistant to a conductor. —*pl.* **train′men**

**traipse** (trāps) ***v.*** to walk or wander in an aimless or lazy way: *used only in everyday talk.* —**traipsed, traips′ing** 

**trait** (trāt) ***n.*** a special quality, as of one's character [A sense of humor is her finest *trait.*]

**trai·tor** (trāt′ər) ***n.*** a person who betrays his or her country, friends, a cause, etc.

**trai·tor·ous** (trāt′ər əs) ***adj.*** of or like a traitor or treason; treacherous.

**tra·jec·to·ry** (trə jek′tər ē) ***n.*** the curved path followed by something thrown or shot through space, as a bullet. —*pl.* **tra·jec′to·ries**

**tram** (tram) ***n.*** **1** an open railway car used in mines for carrying loads. **2** a streetcar: *a British meaning.*

**tram·mel** (tram′′l) ***n.*** **1** anything that holds back, hinders, etc., as a shackle for a horse. **2** a net for catching birds or fish. **3** a device with links, etc. for hanging a pothook in a fireplace. ✦***v.*** to keep from acting or moving freely; restrain, hinder, etc. [*trammeled* by harsh laws]. —**tram′meled** or **tram′melled, tram′mel·ing** or **tram′mel·ling**

**tramp** (tramp) ***v.*** **1** to walk with heavy steps. **2** to step heavily; stamp [The horse *tramped* on my foot.] **3** to walk; roam about on foot [We *tramped* through the woods.] ✦***n.*** **1** a person who wanders from place to place, doing odd jobs or begging; vagrant. **2** a journey on foot; hike [a *tramp* through the woods]. **3** the sound of heavy steps. **4** a freight ship that has no regular route, but picks up cargo wherever it can.

| | | | | | | | |
|---|---|---|---|---|---|---|---|
| **a** | fat | **ir** | here | **ou** | out | **zh** | leisure |
| **ā** | ape | **ī** | bite, fire | **u** | up | **ŋ** | ring |
| **ä** | car, lot | **ō** | go | **ʉr** | fur | | a *in* ago |
| **e** | ten | **ô** | law, horn | **ch** | chin | | e *in* agent |
| **er** | care | **ɔi** | oil | **sh** | she | **ə =** | i *in* unity |
| **ē** | even | **oo** | look | **th** | thin | | o *in* collect |
| **i** | hit | **o͞o** | tool | ***th*** | then | | u *in* focus |

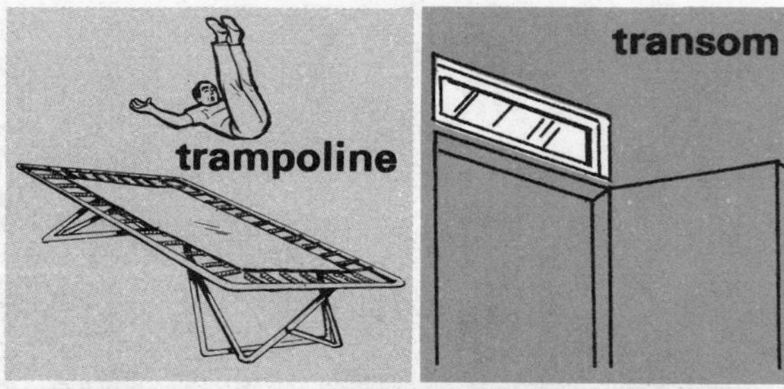


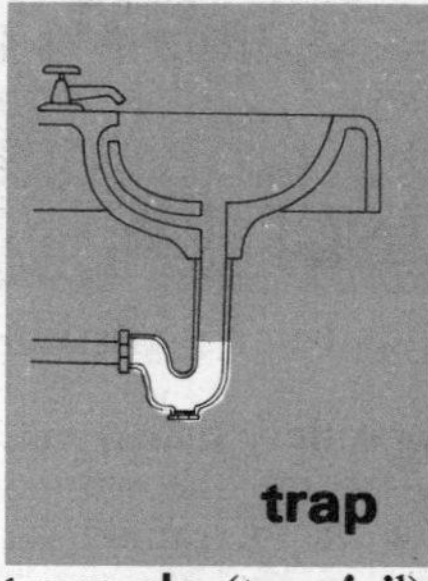

**tram·ple** (tram′p'l) ***v.*** **1** to tread or step hard on. **2** to crush, hurt, etc., as by stepping on [A herd of buffaloes *trampled* the crops.] —**tram′pled, tram′pling**

**tram·po·line** (tram′pə lēn *or* tram′pə lin) ***n.*** ☆a strong piece of canvas stretched tightly on a frame, used as a kind of springboard in acrobatic tumbling. *See the picture.*



**tram·way** (tram′wā) ***n.*** a streetcar line: *a British word.*

**trance** (trans) ***n.*** **1** a condition like sleep brought on by shock, hypnosis, etc., in which one seems to be conscious but is unable to move or act of one's own will. **2** the condition of being completely lost in thought.

**tran·quil** (traŋ′kwəl) ***adj.*** calm, quiet, peaceful, etc. [*tranquil* waters; a *tranquil* mood]. —**tran·quil′li·ty** or **tran·quil′i·ty *n.*** —**tran′quil·ly *adv.***

**tran·quil·ize** or **tran·quil·lize** (traŋ′kwə līz) ***v.*** to make or become tranquil. —**tran′quil·ized** or **tran′quil·lized, tran′quil·iz·ing** or **tran′quil·liz·ing**

**tran·quil·iz·er** or **tran·quil·liz·er** (traŋ′kwə lī′zər) ***n.*** a drug used to calm the nerves.

**trans-** *a prefix meaning* over, across, *or* beyond [A *transatlantic* cable is a cable that extends across the Atlantic.]

**trans·act** (tran sakt′ *or* tran zakt′) ***v.*** to carry on, do, complete, etc. [I have business to *transact* in the city.]

**trans·ac·tion** (tran sak′shən *or* tran zak′shən) ***n.*** **1** a transacting, as of business. **2** something transacted, as a piece of business. **3 transactions,** *pl.* the minutes of a meeting.

**trans·at·lan·tic** (trans′ət lan′tik) ***adj.*** **1** crossing the Atlantic [Lindbergh's *transatlantic* flight]. **2** on the other side of the Atlantic.

**tran·scend** (tran send′) ***v.*** **1** to go beyond the limits of; exceed [Your story *transcends* belief.] **2** to be better or greater than; surpass [Her beauty *transcends* that of others.]

**tran·scend·ent** (tran sen′dənt) ***adj.*** far beyond the usual or ordinary; superior; extraordinary [her *transcendent* wisdom].

**tran·scen·den·tal** (tran′sen den′t'l) ***adj.*** **1** *same as* **transcendent. 2** *another word for* **supernatural.**

☆**trans·con·ti·nen·tal** (trans′kän tə nen′t'l) ***adj.*** that goes from one side of a continent to the other [a *transcontinental* airplane flight].

**tran·scribe** (tran skrīb′) ***v.*** **1** to write out or type out in full [He took down her speech in shorthand and then *transcribed* his notes.] **2** to make a transcription of for radio or TV. —**tran·scribed′, tran·scrib′ing**

**tran·script** (tran′skript) ***n.*** **1** a copy, especially one made by writing or typing. ☆**2** a copy of a student's record in school or college, showing the grades received in courses.

**tran·scrip·tion** (tran skrip′shən) ***n.*** **1** the act of transcribing. **2** something transcribed; copy. **3** a recording made for broadcasting later on radio or TV.

**tran·sept** (tran′sept) ***n.*** in a church shaped like a cross, the part that forms the arms across the long, main part.

**trans·fer** (trans fʉr′ *or* trans′fər) ***v.*** **1** to move, carry, send, or change from one person or place to another [He *transferred* his notes to another notebook. Jill has *transferred* to a new school.] **2** to move a picture, design, etc. from one surface to another, as by making wet and pressing. ☆**3** to change from one bus, train, etc. to another. —**trans·ferred′, trans·fer′ring** ◆***n.*** (trans′fər) **1** the act of transferring. **2** a thing or person that is transferred [They are *transfers* from another school.] ☆**3** a ticket that allows one to change from one bus, train, etc. to another. —**trans·fer′a·ble** or **trans·fer′ra·ble *adj.***

**trans·fer·ence** (trans fʉr′əns) ***n.*** a transferring or being transferred.

**trans·fig·u·ra·tion** (trans fig′yoo rā′shən) ***n.*** **1** a change in form or looks. **2 Transfiguration,** in the Bible, the change that appeared in Jesus on the mountain.

**trans·fig·ure** (trans fig′yər) ***v.*** **1** to change the form or looks of; transform [A new dress and hairdo *transfigured* her.] **2** to make seem splendid or glorious [He was *transfigured* by his deep love.] —**trans·fig′ured, trans·fig′ur·ing**

**trans·fix** (trans fiks′) ***v.*** **1** to pierce through, as with an arrow. **2** to make unable to move, as if pierced through [*transfixed* with horror].

**trans·form** (trans fôrm′) ***v.*** **1** to change the form or looks of [A vase of roses *transformed* the drab room.] **2** to change the nature or condition of [The barn was *transformed* into a house.] —**trans′for·ma′tion *n.***

SYNONYMS: To **transform** something is to change the way it looks or the sort of thing it is [Regular exercise *transformed* him into a new man.] To **convert** something is to change it in certain ways so that it has a new use [The church lawn was *converted* into a parking lot.]

**trans·form·er** (trans fôr′mər) ***n.*** **1** a person or thing that transforms. **2** a device that changes the voltage of an electric current.

**trans·fuse** (trans fyo͞oz′) ***v.*** **1** to pass blood, blood plasma, etc. that has been taken from one person into a vein of another. **2** to pour in or spread through; instill [Victory *transfused* courage into the team.] —**trans·fused′, trans·fus′ing** —**trans·fu′sion *n.***

**trans·gress** (trans gres′) ***v.*** **1** to break a law or rule; do wrong; sin. **2** to pass over or go beyond [Your guest's remark *transgressed* the limits of decency.] —**trans·gres′sor** ***n.***

**trans·gres·sion** (trans gresh′ən) ***n.*** the act of transgressing or breaking a law; a sin.

**tran·sient** (tran′shənt) ***adj.*** **1** passing quickly [*transient* pleasures]. ☆**2** staying for only a short time [*transient* guests at a hotel]. ◆***n.*** ☆a person who stays for only a short time [*transients* at a hotel].

☆**tran·sis·tor** (tran zis′tər *or* tran sis′tər) ***n.*** an electronic device, made up of semiconductor material, that controls the flow of electric current. Transistors are small and last a long time.

☆**tran·sis·tor·ize** (tran zis′tə rīz *or* tran sis′tə rīz) ***v.*** to equip with transistors [a *transistorized* portable radio]. —**tran·sis′tor·ized, tran·sis′tor·iz·ing**

**trans·it** (tran′sit) ***n.*** **1** travel or passage through or across. **2** the act of carrying things from one place to another [A box was lost in *transit*.] **3** an instrument used by surveyors to measure angles. *See the picture.*

**tran·si·tion** (tran zish′ən *or* tran sish′ən) ***n.*** the act or process of passing from one condition, form, or place to another [the *transition* from war to peace]. —**tran·si′tion·al** ***adj.***

**tran·si·tive** (tran′sə tiv) ***adj.*** describing a verb that takes a direct object [In the sentence "He saved money for a car," "saved" is a *transitive* verb.]

**tran·si·to·ry** (tran′sə tôr′ē) ***adj.*** lasting only a short time; temporary [*transitory* fame].

**trans·late** (trans lāt′ *or* trans′lāt) ***v.*** **1** to put into words of a different language [to *translate* a Latin poem into English]. **2** to change into another form [to *translate* ideas into action]. **3** to change from one place or condition to another; especially, to carry up to heaven. —**trans·lat′ed, trans·lat′ing**

**trans·la·tion** (trans lā′shən) ***n.*** **1** the act of translating [He is good at *translation*.] **2** writing or speech translated into a different language.

**trans·la·tor** (trans lāt′ər) ***n.*** a person who translates from one language into another.

**trans·lu·cent** (trans lo͞o′s′nt) ***adj.*** letting light pass through but not allowing things on the other side to be seen clearly [Tissue paper is *translucent*.] —**trans·lu′cence** or **trans·lu′cen·cy** ***n.***

**trans·mi·gra·tion** (trans′mī grā′shən) ***n.*** **1** the act of moving from one region, country, etc. to another. **2** in some religions, the passing of the soul into another body after one dies.

**trans·mis·sion** (trans mish′ən) ***n.*** **1** the act of transmitting or passing something along [the *transmission* of messages by telegraph]. **2** something transmitted. **3** the part of a car that sends the power from the engine to the wheels. **4** the moving of radio waves through space.

**trans·mit** (trans mit′) ***v.*** **1** to send from one person or place to another; pass on; transfer [to *transmit* a disease; to *transmit* a letter; to *transmit* power from an engine by means of gears]. **2** to hand down as by heredity [Color blindness may be *transmitted*.] **3** to pass or let pass, as light, heat, etc. [Water *transmits* sound.] **4** to send out radio or TV signals. —**trans·mit′ted, trans·mit′ting**

**trans·mit·ter** (trans mit′ər) ***n.*** **1** a person or thing that transmits. **2** the part of a telegraph or telephone that sends out sounds or signals. **3** the apparatus for sending out electric waves in radio and TV.

**trans·mute** (trans myo͞ot′) ***v.*** to change from one form, kind, thing, etc. into another [Alchemists tried to *transmute* lead into gold.] —**trans·mut′ed, trans·mut′ing** —**trans′mu·ta′tion** ***n.***

**tran·som** (tran′səm) ***n.*** **1** a small window just above a door or other window. It is usually hinged to the crossbar below it, to allow it to be opened. *See the picture.* **2** this crossbar.

**tran·son·ic** or **trans·son·ic** (tran sän′ik) ***adj.*** of or having to do with a range of speeds just above and below the speed of sound.

**trans·par·en·cy** (trans per′ən sē) ***n.*** **1** a transparent quality or condition. **2** a positive film or slide having a picture, etc. that can be seen when light shines through it or that can be shown on a screen with a projector. —*pl.* **trans·par′en·cies**

**trans·par·ent** (trans per′ənt) ***adj.*** **1** so clear or so fine it can be seen through [*transparent* glass; a *transparent* veil]. *See* SYNONYMS *at* **clear**. **2** plain to see or understand; clear [a *transparent* lie].

**tran·spire** (tran spīr′) ***v.*** **1** to give off vapor, moisture, etc., as through pores. **2** to become known. ☆**3** to take place; happen: *thought of by some people as a loose or incorrect meaning* [What *transpired* while I was gone?] —**tran·spired′, tran·spir′ing**

**trans·plant** (trans plant′) ***v.*** **1** to dig up from one place and plant in another. **2** to move tissue or an organ by surgery from one person or part of the body to another; graft. ◆***n.*** (trans′plant) something transplanted, as a body organ or seedling. 789

**trans·port** (trans pôrt′) ***v.*** **1** to carry from one place to another [to *transport* goods by train or truck]. **2** to cause strong feelings in [*transported* with delight]. **3** to send to a place far away as a punishment. ◆***n.*** (trans′pôrt) **1** the act of carrying from one place to another. **2** a ship, airplane, etc. used for transporting freight, soldiers, etc. **3** a strong feeling, as of delight.

**trans·por·ta·tion** (trans′pər tā′shən) ***n.*** **1** the act of transporting. **2** a system or business of transporting things. ☆**3** fare or a ticket for being transported.

**trans·pose** (trans pōz′) ***v.*** **1** to change about in order or position; interchange [Don't *transpose* the *e* and the *i* in "weird."] **2** to change the key of a piece of music. —**trans·posed′, trans·pos′ing** —**trans·po·si·tion** (trans′pə zish′ən) ***n.***

**trans·verse** (trans vurs′) ***adj.*** lying or placed across; set crosswise [*transverse* beams].

**trap** (trap) ***n.*** **1** any device for catching animals, as one that snaps shut tightly when it is stepped on. **2** a trick used to fool or catch someone [That question was a *trap* to make the witness tell the truth.] **3** a bend in a drainpipe, shaped like a U, where some water stays to hold back bad-smelling gases coming from the sewer. *See the picture.* **4** a device for throwing targets into the air in the sport of trapshooting. **5**

| | | | | | | | |
|---|---|---|---|---|---|---|---|
| **a** | fat | **ir** | here | **ou** | out | **zh** | leisure |
| **ā** | ape | **ī** | bite, fire | **u** | up | **ng** | ring |
| **ä** | car, lot | **ō** | go | **ur** | fur | | a *in* ago |
| **e** | ten | **ô** | law, horn | **ch** | chin | | e *in* agent |
| **er** | care | **oi** | oil | **sh** | she | **ə =** | i *in* unity |
| **ē** | even | **oo** | look | **th** | thin | | o *in* collect |
| **i** | hit | **o͞o** | tool | ***th*** | then | | u *in* focus |

a light carriage with two wheels. ☆**6 traps,** *pl.* the cymbals, blocks, etc. attached to a set of drums, as in a jazz band. **7** the mouth: *a slang meaning.* ✦**v. 1** to catch in a trap. **2** to set traps to catch animals. —**trapped, trap'ping**

**trap·door** (trap'dôr) **n.** a door in a roof or floor.

**tra·peze** (tra pēz') **n.** a short crossbar hung by two ropes, on which acrobats do stunts. *See the picture.*

**trap·e·zoid** (trap'ə zoid) **n.** a flat figure with four sides, two of which are parallel.

**trap·per** (trap'ər) **n.** a person who traps wild animals, especially for their furs.

**trap·pings** (trap'iŋz) **n.pl. 1** highly decorated coverings for a horse. **2** highly decorated clothing or ornaments. **3** the things that go along with something and are an outward sign of it [They have a large, new house in the suburbs and all the *trappings* of success.]

**trap·shoot·ing** (trap'sho͞ot'iŋ) **n.** the sport of shooting at clay targets tossed in the air.

**trash** (trash) **n. 1** anything thrown away as worthless; rubbish. **2** something worthless, disgusting, or foolish [This book is nothing but *trash*.] ✦**v.** to destroy property on purpose: *a slang meaning.* —**trash'y adj.**

**trav·ail** (trav'āl *or* trə vāl') **n. 1** very hard work. **2** the pains of childbirth. **3** great pain; agony. ✦**v. 1** to work hard. **2** to suffer the pains of childbirth.

790 **Travail** comes from a Latin word for a device with three stakes used to torture people. Such a device would cause great pain or agony, a meaning the word now has in English.

**trav·el** (trav''l) **v. 1** to go from one place to another [He *traveled* around the world.] **2** to make a journey over or through [to *travel* a road]. **3** to move or pass [A train *travels* on tracks. Light *travels* faster than sound.] —**trav'eled** or **trav'elled, trav'el·ing** or **trav'el·ling** ✦**n. 1** the act of traveling. **2 travels,** *pl.* trips, journeys, etc. —**trav'el·er** or **trav'el·ler n.**

**trav·eled** or **trav·elled** (trav''ld) **adj. 1** that has traveled. **2** used by those who travel [a well-*traveled* road].

☆**traveler's check** one of a set of checks that a bank, etc. sells to a traveler, who signs it and then signs it again when it is exchanged for money.

☆**trav·e·logue** or **trav·e·log** (trav'ə lôg) **n. 1** a lecture describing travels, usually given with pictures. **2** a movie about travels.

**trav·erse** (tra vurs' *or* trav'ərs) **v.** to pass over, across, or through; cross [Pioneers *traversed* the plains in covered wagons.] —**trav·ersed', trav·ers'ing** ✦**n.** (trav'ərs) something that traverses or crosses, as a crossbar. ✦**adj.** (trav'ərs) **1** lying across. **2** describing drapes hung in pairs so that they can be drawn by pulling cords.

**trav·es·ty** (trav'is tē) **n. 1** an imitation of something done in such a way as to make it seem ridiculous; burlesque. **2** a crude or ridiculous example of something [a *travesty* of justice]. —*pl.* **trav'es·ties** ✦**v.** to imitate so as to make seem ridiculous. —**trav'es·tied, trav'es·ty·ing**

**trawl** (trôl) **n. 1** a large fishing net dragged by a boat along the bottom of a shallow part of the sea. ☆**2** a long line held up by buoys, from which baited fishing lines are hung. ✦**v.** to fish with a trawl.

**trawl·er** (trôl'ər) **n.** a boat used in trawling.

**tray** (trā) **n.** a flat piece of wood, metal, etc., often with a low rim, for carrying food or other things.

**treach·er·ous** (trech'ər əs) **adj. 1** not loyal or faithful; betraying or likely to betray. **2** seeming safe, reliable, etc. but not really so [*treacherous* rocks]. —**treach'er·ous·ly adv.**

**treach·er·y** (trech'ər ē) **n. 1** the act of betraying those who have their trust or faith in one. **2** an act of disloyalty or treason. —*pl.* **treach'er·ies**

**trea·cle** (trē'k'l) **n.** *a British name for* **molasses.**

**tread** (tred) **v. 1** to walk on, in, along, or over [We *trod* the dusty road for hours.] **2** to beat or press with the feet; trample [to *tread* grapes in making wine]. —**trod, trod'den** or **trod, tread'ing** ✦**n. 1** a way or sound of treading [We heard a heavy *tread* on the stairs.] **2** the part on which a person or thing treads or moves, as the upper surface of a stair, or the part of a wheel that touches the ground. **3** the thick, outer layer of an automobile tire. —**tread water,** to keep the body upright and the head above water by kicking the legs. — *The past tense and past participle for this phrase is* **tread'ed.**

**trea·dle** (tred''l) **n.** a lever worked by the foot, as to turn a wheel. *See the picture.* ✦**v.** to work a treadle. —**trea'dled, trea'dling**

**tread·mill** (tred'mil) **n. 1** a mill or other device worked by persons or animals walking on steps about the rim of a wheel or treading on an endless belt. **2** any monotonous series of tasks that never seems to end.

**treas.** *abbreviation for* **treasurer** *or* **treasury.**

**trea·son** (trē'z'n) **n.** the act of betraying one's country, especially by helping the enemy in time of war.

**trea·son·a·ble** (trē'z'n ə b'l) **adj.** of or having to do with treason: *also* **trea·son·ous** (trē'z'n əs).

**treas·ure** (trezh'ər) **n. 1** money, jewels, etc. collected and stored up. **2** a person or thing that is loved or held dear. ✦**v. 1** to love or hold dear; cherish [I *treasure* their friendship.] **2** to store away or save up, as money; hoard. —**treas'ured, treas'ur·ing**

**treas·ur·er** (trezh'ər ər) **n.** a person in charge of a treasury, as of a government, company, club, etc.

**treas·ure-trove** (trezh'ər trōv') **n.** treasure found hidden, whose owner is not known.

**treas·ur·y** (trezh'ər ē) **n. 1** the money or funds of a country, company, club, etc. **2 Treasury,** the department of a government in charge of issuing money, collecting taxes, etc. **3** a place where money is kept. **4** a collection of treasures in art, literature, etc. —*pl.* **treas'ur·ies**

**treat** (trēt) **v. 1** to deal with or act toward in a certain way [We were *treated* with respect. Don't *treat* this matter lightly.] **2** to try to cure or heal, as with medicine [The doctor *treated* my cuts.] **3** to act upon, as by adding something [The water is *treated* with chlorine.] **4** to pay for the food, entertainment, etc. of [My aunt and uncle *treated* us to the movies.] **5** to deal with a subject in speaking or writing; discuss [The talk *treated* of gambling in the U.S.] **6** to discuss business or terms; negotiate. ✦**n. 1** the act of treating another, as to food or entertainment. **2** the food, entertainment, etc. paid for by another. **3** anything that gives pleasure [It was a *treat* to hear the children sing.]

**trea·tise** (trēt′is) ***n.*** a book or long article dealing with some subject in a detailed way.

**treat·ment** (trēt′mənt) ***n.*** **1** act or way of dealing with a person or thing [kind *treatment*]. **2** the use of medicine, surgery, etc. to try to cure or heal.

**trea·ty** (trēt′ē) ***n.*** an agreement between two or more nations, having to do with peace, trade, etc. —*pl.* **trea′ties**

**tre·ble** (treb′'l) ***n.*** **1** the highest part in musical harmony; soprano. **2** a singer or instrument that takes this part. **3** a high-pitched voice or sound. ◆***adj.*** **1** of or for the treble. **2** high-pitched; shrill. **3** triple; threefold. ◆***v.*** to make or become three times as much or as many; triple. —**tre′bled, tre′bling**

**treble clef** a sign on a musical staff showing that the notes on the staff are above middle C.

**tre·bly** (treb′lē) ***adv.*** three times; triply.

**tree** (trē) ***n.*** **1** a large, woody plant with a long trunk having many branches in the upper part. **2** a wooden beam, bar, post, etc. [a clothes *tree*]. **3** anything like a tree, as in having many branches [A family *tree* is a diagram of a family line.] ◆***v.*** ☆to chase up a tree [The pack of dogs *treed* a possum.] —**treed, tree′ing** —☆**up a tree,** in some trouble that is hard to get out of: *used only in everyday talk.* —**tree′less *adj.***

**tre·foil** (trē′foil) ***n.*** **1** a plant with leaves divided into three leaflets, as the clover. **2** a design or decoration shaped like such a leaf. *See the picture.*

**trek** (trek) ***v.*** **1** to travel slowly or with difficulty. **2** to go, especially on foot: *used only in everyday talk.* —**trekked, trek′king** ◆***n.*** **1** a long, slow journey. **2** a short trip, especially on foot: *used only in everyday talk.*

**Trek** comes to us from South Africa where it meant "to travel by ox wagon." Traveling by ox wagon is slow and difficult.

**trel·lis** (trel′is) ***n.*** a frame of crossed strips, as of wood, on which vines or other climbing plants are grown; lattice.

**trem·ble** (trem′b'l) ***v.*** **1** to shake from cold, fear, weakness, excitement, etc. [Your hand is *trembling.*] *See* SYNONYMS *at* **shake.** **2** to quiver or shake [The earth *trembled* from the shock wave.] —**trem′bled, trem′bling** ◆***n.*** the act or a fit of trembling. —**trem′bly *adj.***

**tre·men·dous** (tri men′dəs) ***adj.*** **1** very large or great; enormous [a *tremendous* building]. **2** wonderful, very fine, amazing, etc.: *used only in everyday talk* [a *tremendous* opportunity]. —**tre·men′dous·ly *adv.***

**Tremendous** comes from a Latin word meaning "to tremble." An earlier meaning of **tremendous** in English was "so great or dreadful as to make one tremble." In time the idea of trembling was lost but that of great size stayed.

**trem·or** (trem′ər) ***n.*** **1** a shaking or trembling [an earth *tremor*]. **2** a quivering or tingling feeling of excitement; nervous thrill [in a *tremor* of delight].

**trem·u·lous** (trem′yoo ləs) ***adj.*** **1** trembling or quivering [a *tremulous* voice]. **2** fearful or timid. —**trem′u·lous·ly *adv.***

**trench** (trench) ***n.*** **1** a ditch; deep furrow. **2** a long ditch with earth banked in front, used to protect soldiers in battle. ◆***v.*** to dig a trench in.

**trench·ant** (tren′chənt) ***adj.*** sharp and clear; keen; to the point [She gave a *trenchant* argument.]

trapeze acrobats

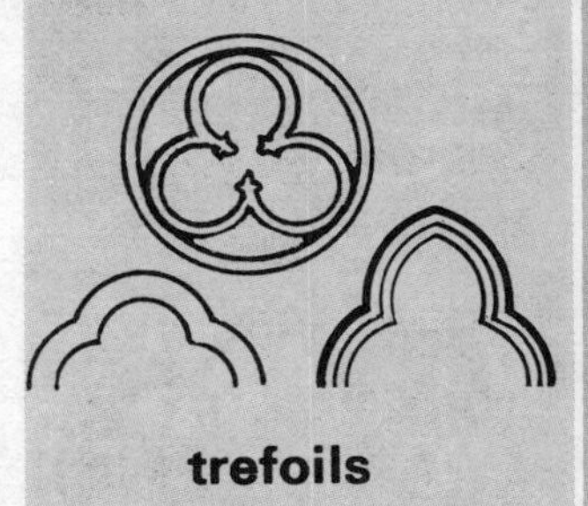

trefoils

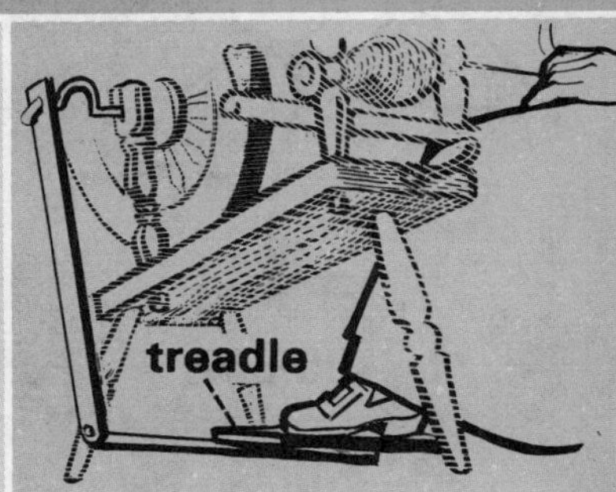

treadle

**trench coat** a belted raincoat like the sort that soldiers wear.

**trench·er·man** (tren′chər mən) ***n.*** a heavy eater who seems to enjoy food a great deal. —*pl.* **trench′er·men**

**trench mouth** a catching disease in which there are open sores in the mouth and throat.

**trend** (trend) ***n.*** the general direction or course; drift [The present *trend* is to make smaller cars.] ◆***v.*** to take a certain direction or course; tend. 

**trend·y** (trend′ē) ***adj.*** of or in the latest style, or trend; faddish: *used only in everyday talk.* —**trend′i·er, trend′i·est**

**Tren·ton** (tren′tən) the capital of New Jersey.

**trep·i·da·tion** (trep′ə dā′shən) ***n.*** **1** a fearful feeling; dread. **2** a trembling or tremor.

**tres·pass** (tres′pəs *or* tres′pas) ***v.*** **1** to go on another's property without permission or right ["No *trespassing*" means "keep out."] **2** to break in on; intrude [Don't *trespass* on my privacy.] **3** to do wrong; sin. ◆***n.*** **1** the act of trespassing. **2** a sin or wrong. —**tres′pass·er *n.***

**tress** (tres) ***n.*** **1** a lock of hair. **2 tress′es,** *pl.* a woman's or girl's hair, especially when long and falling loosely.

**tres·tle** (tres′'l) ***n.*** **1** a frame like a sawhorse, used to support a table top, etc. **2** a framework of uprights and crosspieces, supporting a bridge, etc.

**tri-** *a prefix meaning:* **1** having three [A *triangle* is a figure having three angles.] **2** three times; into three [To *trisect* an angle is to divide it into three equal parts.] **3** happening every three [A *triweekly* event takes place once every three weeks.]

**tri·ad** (trī′ad) ***n.*** a group of three.

| | | | | | | | |
|---|---|---|---|---|---|---|---|
| **a** | fat | **ir** | here | **ou** | out | **zh** | leisure |
| **ā** | ape | **ī** | bite, fire | **u** | up | **ng** | ring |
| **ä** | car, lot | **ō** | go | **ur** | fur | | a *in* ago |
| **e** | ten | **ô** | law, horn | **ch** | chin | | e *in* agent |
| **er** | care | **oi** | oil | **sh** | she | **ə =** | i *in* unity |
| **ē** | even | **oo** | look | **th** | thin | | o *in* collect |
| **i** | hit | **ōō** | tool | ***th*** | then | | u *in* focus |

trillium

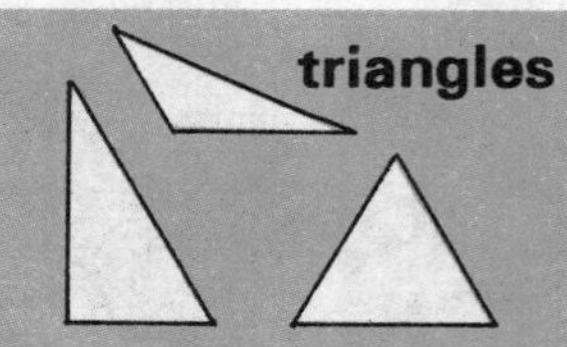
triangles

tricycle

**tri·al** (trī′əl) ***n.*** **1** the act of hearing a case in a law court to decide whether the claim or charge is true [The *trial* proved that the accused person was innocent.] **2** the act of trying; effort; try [She was allowed two *trials* at the high jump.] **3** the act of trying or testing; test [the *trial* of a new rocket]. **4** a test of one's faith, patience, etc. [Job had many *trials.*] **5** something that troubles or annoys one [Our neighbors' barking dog is a great *trial* to us.] ◆***adj.*** **1** of or for a trial or test [a *trial* run; a *trial* sample]. **2** of or having to do with a law court [a *trial* lawyer]. —**on trial,** in the process of being tried.



SYNONYMS: A **trial** is a trying of something in order to see how well it works out in actual practice [She bought it on *trial.*] A **test** is a trying of something under controlled conditions and using strict standards [The new jet plane has been put through many *tests.*]

**trial and error** a trying or testing over and over again until the right result is found.

**tri·an·gle** (trī′aŋ′g'l) ***n.*** **1** a flat figure with three sides and three angles. *See the picture.* **2** anything shaped like this. **3** a musical instrument that is a steel rod bent in a triangle. It makes a high, tinkling sound when struck with a metal rod.

**tri·an·gu·lar** (trī aŋ′gyə lər) ***adj.*** of or shaped like a triangle; having three corners.

**tribe** (trīb) ***n.*** **1** a group of people or families living together under a leader or chief [a North American Indian *tribe;* the *tribes* of ancient Israel]. **2** any group of people having the same work or interests [the *tribe* of newspaper writers]. **3** any group or class, as of animals or plants. —**trib′al** ***adj.***

**Tribe** comes from *tribus,* the Latin word for any one of the three groups into which the ancient Romans were divided. And *tribus* comes from the Latin word for "three."

**tribes·man** (trībz′mən) ***n.*** a member of a tribe. —*pl.* **tribes′men**

**trib·u·la·tion** (trib′yə lā′shən) ***n.*** great misery or trouble [The poor have many *tribulations.*]

**tri·bu·nal** (trī byōō′n'l *or* tri byōō′n'l) ***n.*** a court of justice.

**trib·une** (trib′yōōn) ***n.*** **1** an official in ancient Rome whose duty was to protect the rights and interests of the lower classes. **2** (*often* tri byōōn′) a defender of the people: *often used in the names of newspapers.*

**trib·u·tar·y** (trib′yoo ter′ē) ***n.*** **1** a stream or river that flows into a larger one. **2** a nation that pays tribute or is under the power of another nation. —*pl.* **trib′u·tar′ies** ◆***adj.*** **1** flowing into a larger one [a *tributary* stream]. **2** paying tribute to another, or under another's power [a *tributary* nation].

**trib·ute** (trib′yōōt) ***n.*** **1** something given, done, or said to show thanks or respect [The city put up a statue as a *tribute* to the mayor.] **2** money that one nation is forced to pay to another, more powerful nation. **3** any forced payment.

**trice** (trīs) ***n.*** a moment: *now used only in the phrase* **in a trice,** meaning "in a very short time."

**trick** (trik) ***n.*** **1** something that is done to fool, outwit, cheat, etc. [A *trick* in the contract made us pay more than we expected to.] **2** a piece of playful mischief; prank. **3** a clever or skillful act [Can you do any card *tricks?*] **4** the right or skillful way; knack [I know the *trick* of throwing a Frisbee.] **5** a personal habit [He had a *trick* of tugging at his ear.] **6** a time or turn at work; shift [She's on the morning *trick.*] **7** the cards played in a single round of a card game. ◆***v.*** to work a trick on; fool, outwit, cheat, etc. ◆***adj.*** **1** done by a trick [*trick* photography]. **2** that tricks [a *trick* question]. **3** not always working right [a *trick* knee]. —**do the trick,** to bring about what is wanted. —**trick out** or **trick up,** to dress up.

**trick·er·y** (trik′ər ē) ***n.*** the act of tricking or cheating. —*pl.* **trick′er·ies**

**trick·le** (trik′'l) ***v.*** **1** to flow slowly in a thin stream or fall in drops [Rain *trickled* down the window.] **2** to move little by little [The crowd *trickled* away.] —**trick′led, trick′ling** ◆***n.*** a thin flow or drip.

☆**trick or treat!** give me a treat or I will play a trick on you! This phrase is used by children going from door to door in costume on Halloween asking for treats.

**trick·ster** (trik′stər) ***n.*** a person who tricks; cheat.

**trick·y** (trik′ē) ***adj.*** **1** using tricks; fooling or cheating [He used a *tricky* scheme.] **2** hard or difficult [This is a *tricky* problem.] —**trick′i·er, trick′i·est** —**trick′i·ness** ***n.***

**tri·col·or** (trī′kul′ər) ***n.*** a flag having three colors, especially the flag of France. ◆***adj.*** having three colors. —**tri′col′ored** ***adj.***

**tri·cy·cle** (trī′si k'l) ***n.*** a vehicle for children to ride on that has three wheels, one in front and two in back. It is moved by foot pedals and steered by a handlebar. *See the picture.*

**tri·dent** (trīd′'nt) ***n.*** a spear with three prongs. *See the picture for* **Neptune.** ◆***adj.*** having three prongs.

One might say that a **trident** has three teeth. The word comes from the Latin *tri-* for "three" and *dens* for "tooth."

**tried** (trīd) *past tense and past participle of* **try.** ◆***adj.*** tested or trustworthy [I have a *tried* recipe for cherry pie. He is a friend, *tried* and true.]

**tri·en·ni·al** (trī en′ē əl) ***adj.*** **1** happening once every three years [a *triennial* convention]. **2** lasting for three years. ◆*n.* something that happens every three years. —**tri·en′ni·al·ly** ***adv.***

**tri·er** (trī′ər) ***n.*** a person who tries.

**Tri·este** (trē est′) a city in northeastern Italy, on the Adriatic Sea.

**tri·fle** (trī′f′l) ***n.*** **1** something of little value or importance. **2** a small amount; bit. **3** a small sum of money. ◆***v.*** **1** to talk or act in a joking way; deal lightly [She's not a person to *trifle* with.] **2** to play or toy [Don't *trifle* with your food.] **3** to spend in an idle way; waste [He *trifles* time away.] —**tri′fled, tri′fling** —**tri′fler** ***n.***

**tri·fling** (trī′fliŋ) ***adj.*** **1** of little value or importance; trivial. *See* SYNONYMS *at* **petty**. **2** not at all serious; fickle.

**trig·ger** (trig′ər) ***n.*** **1** the lever that is pressed by the finger in firing a gun. **2** any part like this that releases a catch or spring to set off some action, when it is pressed or pulled. ◆***v.*** to set off [The fight *triggered* a riot.]

**trig·o·nom·e·try** (trig′ə näm′ə trē) ***n.*** the branch of mathematics dealing with the relations between the sides and angles of triangles.

**trill** (tril) ***n.*** **1** a wavering or trembling sound made by playing or singing two close notes back and forth rapidly. **2** a speech sound made by vibrating the tongue or uvula rapidly, as *r* in some languages. **3** a bird's warble. ◆***v.*** to speak, sing, or play with a trill.

**tril·lion** (tril′yən) ***n., adj.*** a thousand billions (1,000,000,000,000).

**tril·li·um** (tril′ē əm) ***n.*** a wildflower with three leaves and a blossom of three petals. *See the picture.*

**tri·lo·bite** (trī′lə bīt) ***n.*** a sea animal that lived millions of years ago. Its body is divided by two furrows into three parts. *See the picture for* **fossil**.

**tril·o·gy** (tril′ə jē) ***n.*** a set of three plays, novels, etc. which form a related group, although each is a complete work [Louisa May Alcott's "Little Women," "Little Men," and "Jo's Boys" make up a *trilogy*.] —*pl.* **tril′o·gies**

**trim** (trim) ***v.*** **1** to make neat or tidy, especially by clipping, smoothing, etc. [She had her hair *trimmed.*] **2** to cut, clip, etc. [He *trimmed* dead branches off the tree.] ☆**3** to decorate [Help *trim* the Christmas tree.] **4** to balance a ship, as by shifting cargo. **5** to put in order for sailing [She helped *trim* the sails.] **6** to take a middle position, as in trying to please both sides. **7** to beat or defeat: *used only in everyday talk.* —**trimmed, trim′ming** ◆***n.*** **1** good condition or order [An athlete must keep in *trim.*] **2** the act of trimming, as by clipping or cutting. **3** the decorative woodwork of a building, especially around windows and doors. **4** any decorative trimming, as chrome on a car, lace on a dress, etc. **5** the condition of being ready to sail; also, the position of a ship in the water. ◆***adj.*** **1** neat, tidy, in good condition, etc. **2** well designed [The boat had *trim* lines.] —**trim′mer, trim′mest** —**trim′ly** ***adv.*** —**trim′ness** ***n.***

**tri·mes·ter** (trī mes′tər) ***n.*** **1** a period of three months. **2** in some colleges, any of the three periods into which the school year is divided.

**trim·ming** (trim′iŋ) ***n.*** **1** something used to trim, as decorations. **2 trimmings,** *pl.* the side dishes of a meal [turkey with all the *trimmings*]. **3 trimmings,** *pl.* parts trimmed off.

**Trin·i·dad and To·ba·go** (trin′ə dad ′n tō bā′gō) a country on islands in the West Indies.

**trin·i·ty** (trin′ə tē) ***n.*** **1** a set of three persons or things that make up a unit. —*pl.* **trin′i·ties** **2 Trinity,** in the belief of most Christians, the three divine persons (Father, Son, and Holy Ghost) that are united in one divine being.

**trin·ket** (triŋ′kit) ***n.*** **1** a small ornament, piece of jewelry, etc. **2** a trifle or toy.

**tri·o** (trē′ō) ***n.*** **1** a piece of music for three voices or three instruments. **2** the three people who sing or play it. **3** any group of three. —*pl.* **tri′os**

**trip** (trip) ***v.*** **1** to stumble or make stumble [She *tripped* over the rug. Bill put out his foot and *tripped* me.] **2** to make or cause to make a mistake [She *tripped* on the spelling of "rhythm." That question *tripped* us all.] **3** to walk, run, or dance with light, rapid steps [She *tripped* happily about the room.] —**tripped, trip′ping** ◆***n.*** **1** a traveling from one place to another and returning; journey, especially a short one. **2** a stumble. **3** the act of tripping someone, as by catching the person's foot. **4** a mistake. ☆**5** the strange, sometimes terrifying, feelings of a person who is under the effects of a psychedelic drug: *a slang meaning.* ☆**6** an activity or experience that is exciting or unusual: *a slang meaning.*

SYNONYMS: **Trip** means traveling a short distance from one place to another and returning [We took a vacation *trip.*] **Journey** means traveling a fairly long distance, usually over land, and not always with the idea of returning [Our *journey* took us from France to China.] **Voyage** usually means a long journey over water [He took a *voyage* across the Pacific.]



**tripe** (trīp) ***n.*** **1** part of the stomach of a cow, ox, etc., used as food. **2** anything worthless, disgusting, etc.; nonsense: *slang in this meaning.*

☆**trip·ham·mer** (trip′ham′ər) ***n.*** a heavy hammer driven by power from electricity, steam, etc. It is lifted and then let fall over and over again: *also* **trip hammer**.

**tri·ple** (trip′′l) ***adj.*** **1** made up of three [A *triple* cone has three dips of ice cream.] **2** three times as much or as many. ◆***n.*** **1** an amount three times as much or as many. ☆**2** a hit in baseball on which the batter gets to third base. ◆***v.*** **1** to make or become three times as much or as many. ☆**2** to hit a triple in baseball. —**tri′pled, tri′pling**

☆**triple play** in baseball, a single play in which three players are put out.

**tri·plet** (trip′lit) ***n.*** **1** any of three children born at a single birth. **2** any group of three.

**trip·li·cate** (trip′lə kit) ***adj.*** made in three copies exactly alike [a *triplicate* receipt]. —**in triplicate,** in three copies exactly alike.

**tri·pod** (trī′päd) ***n.*** a stand, frame, etc. with three legs. Cameras and small telescopes are often held up by tripods. *See the picture.*

**Trip·o·li** (trip′ə lē) **1** a region in northern Africa, now a part of Libya. **2** a seaport on the northwestern coast of Libya.

**trip·ping** (trip′ing) ***adj.*** moving in a quick and easy way; nimble. —**trip′ping·ly *adv.***

**tri·reme** (trī′rēm) ***n.*** an ancient Greek or Roman warship with three rows of oars on each side, one above the other.

**tri·sect** (trī sekt′) ***v.*** to divide into three parts.

**trite** (trīt) ***adj.*** used so much that it is no longer fresh or new; stale ["Happy as a lark" is a *trite* expression.] —**trit′er, trit′est** —**trite′ly *adv.***

> **Trite** comes from a Latin word that means "to wear out." A trite phrase or saying has been used so much that it is worn out.

**tri·umph** (trī′əmf) ***n.*** **1** a victory, as in a battle; success [His *triumph* over illness inspired us.] **2** great joy over a victory or success [She grinned in *triumph* when she won the race.] ◆***v.*** **1** to be the winner; win victory or success [to *triumph* over an enemy]. **2** to rejoice over a victory or success. —**tri·um·phal** (trī um′f'l) ***adj.***

**tri·um·phant** (trī um′fənt) ***adj.*** **1** having won victory or success; victorious [Our team was *triumphant.*] **2** happy or joyful over a victory [We could hear their *triumphant* laughter.] —**tri·um′phant·ly *adv.***



**tri·um·vir** (trī um′vər) ***n.*** in ancient Rome, any one of a ruling group of three officials.

**tri·um·vi·rate** (trī um′vər it) ***n.*** **1** government by a group of three persons, or the period of their rule. **2** any group of three who hold control together.

**triv·et** (triv′it) ***n.*** **1** a small stand with three legs, for holding pots or kettles over or near a fire. **2** a small stand with short legs, for holding hot dishes on a table.

**triv·i·a** (triv′ē ə) ***n.pl.*** small, unimportant matters: *often used with a singular verb* [Their conversation was full of *trivia.*]

**triv·i·al** (triv′ē əl) ***adj.*** not important; trifling [She owes me a *trivial* sum.] *See* SYNONYMS *at* **petty.**

> **Trivial** comes from Latin *tri-* for "three" and *via* for "a road." These two parts make a Latin word that means "a place where three roads meet." To come to any crossroads is a common or ordinary thing in traveling. An earlier sense of **trivial** in English was "ordinary" or "commonplace." Later it came to mean "not important."

**triv·i·al·i·ty** (triv′ē al′ə tē) ***n.*** **1** the state of being trivial. **2** something trivial; trifle. —*pl.* **triv′i·al′i·ties**

**trod** (träd) *the past tense and a past participle of* **tread.**

**trod·den** (träd″n) *a past participle of* **tread.**

**Tro·jan** (trō′jən) ***adj.*** of ancient Troy or its people. ◆***n.*** **1** a person who was born or lived in Troy. **2** a person who is strong and hard-working.

**Trojan horse** a huge, hollow wooden horse in a Greek legend, filled with Greek soldiers and left at the gates of Troy. When the Trojans brought it into the city, the soldiers came out at night and opened the gates to the Greek army. *See the picture.*

**Trojan War** in Greek legends, the war that the Greeks fought with Troy to get back Helen, who had been kidnapped by Paris, a prince of Troy.

**troll**[1] (trōl) ***v.*** **1** to fish by pulling a line through the water, usually behind a moving boat. **2** to sing loudly. **3** to sing as a round: *see* **round** (*meaning* 11).

**troll**[2] (trōl) ***n.*** in fairy stories, a giant or dwarf that lives in a cave or underground.

**trol·ley** (träl′ē) ***n.*** ☆**1** a device that sends electric current from a wire overhead to the motor of a streetcar, trolley bus, etc. ☆**2** an electric streetcar: *also* **trolley car.** —*pl.* **trol′leys**

**trolley bus** a bus that is run by electricity from a trolley on an overhead wire.

**trom·bone** (träm bōn′ *or* träm′bōn) ***n.*** a large, brass-wind musical instrument with a long, bent tube that slides in and out to change the tones: *also called* **slide trombone.** *See the picture.*

**troop** (tro͞op) ***n.*** **1** a company of soldiers in the cavalry. **2 troops,** *pl.* soldiers. **3** a group of Boy Scouts or Girl Scouts under an adult leader. **4** any group of persons or animals [There goes a *troop* of children.] ◆***v.*** to gather or move in a group or crowd [The students *trooped* into the hall.]

**troop·er** (tro͞o′pər) ***n.*** **1** a soldier in the cavalry. **2** a member of the mounted police. ☆**3** a member of a State police force: *used only in everyday talk.*

**troop·ship** (tro͞op′ship) ***n.*** a ship used for carrying soldiers.

**tro·phy** (trō′fē) ***n.*** anything kept as a token of victory or success, as a deer's head from a hunting trip, a silver cup from a sports contest, or a sword from a battle. —*pl.* **tro′phies**

**trop·ic** (träp′ik) ***n.*** **1** either of two imaginary circles around the earth, parallel to the equator. The one about 23 1/2 degrees north of the equator is called the **Tropic of Cancer;** the other, about 23 1/2 degrees south of the equator, is called the **Tropic of Capricorn.** **2 tropics** or **Tropics,** *pl.* the region of the earth that is between these two lines, noted for its hot climate. ◆***adj.*** of the tropics; tropical.

**trop·i·cal** (träp′i k'l) ***adj.*** of, in, or like the tropics [heavy *tropical* rains; *tropical* heat].

**trot** (trät) ***v.*** **1** to step along, as a horse sometimes does, by moving a front leg and the opposite hind leg at the same time. *See the picture.* **2** to ride at a trot. **3** to run slowly, with a loose, easy motion [The boys *trotted* to school.] —**trot′ted, trot′ting** ◆***n.*** **1** the movement of a trotting horse. **2** a slow, jogging run.

**troth** (trôth) ***n.*** **1** a promise, especially to marry; betrothal: *see the verb* **plight**[2]. **2** truth. *This word is now seldom used.*

**Trot·sky** (trät′skē), **Le·on** (lē′än) 1879–1940; Russian revolutionist and writer. —**Trot′sky·ist** *or* **Trot′sky·ite′ *adj., n.***

**trot·ter** (trät′ər) ***n.*** a horse that trots, especially one trained for special trotting races. *See the picture.*

**trou·ba·dour** (tro͞o′bə dôr) ***n.*** any of the poets of the late Middle Ages in France and Italy who wrote and sang poems and ballads of love and knighthood.

**trou·ble** (trub″l) ***n.*** **1** worry, care, annoyance, suffering, etc. [My mind is free of *trouble.*] **2** a difficult or unhappy situation; disturbance [We've had no *trouble* with our neighbors.] **3** a person or thing causing worry, annoyance, difficulty, etc. **4** effort; bother; great care [He took the *trouble* to thank us.] **5** a sick condition [She has heart *trouble.*] ◆***v.*** **1** to be or give trouble to; worry, annoy, pain, disturb, etc. [He was *troubled* by the bad news. Her back *troubles* her.] **2** to put or go to extra work; bother [May I *trouble* you for a ride home? Don't *trouble* to return the pen.] **3** to stir up [The waters were *troubled.*] —**trou'bled, trou'bling**

**trou·ble·some** (trub''l səm) ***adj.*** giving trouble; disturbing [A smoker may have a *troublesome* cough.]

**trough** (trôf) ***n.*** **1** a long, narrow, open container, especially one from which animals eat or drink. **2** a gutter under the edges of a roof, for carrying off rain water. **3** a long, narrow hollow, as between waves.

**trounce** (trouns) ***v.*** **1** to beat or thrash. **2** to defeat soundly: *used only in everyday talk.* —**trounced, trounc'ing**

☆**troupe** (trōōp) ***n.*** a band or company, especially of actors, singers, etc. —**troup'er *n.***

**trou·sers** (trou'zərz) ***n.pl.*** an outer garment with two legs, especially for men and boys, reaching from the waist usually to the ankles; pants.

**trous·seau** (trōō'sō *or* trōō sō') ***n.*** a bride's outfit of clothes, linen, etc. —*pl.* **trous·seaus** or **trous·seaux** (trōō'sōz *or* trōō sōz')

**trout** (trout) ***n.*** a small food fish of the salmon family, found mainly in fresh water.

**trow·el** (trou'əl) ***n.*** **1** a tool with a flat blade for smoothing plaster, laying mortar between bricks, etc. **2** a tool with a pointed scoop, used for digging in a garden. *See the picture.*

**Troy** (troi) **1** an ancient city in Asia Minor. **2** a city in eastern New York.

**troy weight** (troi) a system of weights used for gold, silver, jewels, etc. in which 12 ounces equal 1 pound. *See also* **avoirdupois weight.**

> **Troy weight** got its name from the city of *Troyes,* France. This system of weighing precious metals and jewels was used at fairs in this city back in the Middle Ages.

**tru·ant** (trōō'ənt) ***n.*** a pupil who stays away from school without permission to do so. ◆***adj.*** **1** that is a truant. **2** having to do with truants [a *truant* officer]. —**tru·an·cy** (trōō'ən sē) ***n.***

**truce** (trōōs) ***n.*** a stop in warfare or fighting for a time, because both sides have agreed to stop fighting.

**truck**[1] (truk) ***n.*** ☆**1** a large motor vehicle for carrying loads on highways, streets, etc. Some large trucks are made up of a driver's cab and a trailer that can be taken off. **2** an open frame on wheels for moving heavy things. **3** a frame with two or more pairs of wheels under each end of a railroad car. ◆***v.*** **1** to carry on a truck. **2** to drive a truck.

**truck**[2] (truk) ***n.*** ☆**1** vegetables raised for sale in markets. **2** rubbish; trash: *used only in everyday talk.* —**have no truck with,** to have no dealings with: *used only in everyday talk.*

☆**truck farm** a farm where vegetables are grown for sale in markets. —**truck farmer —truck farming**

**truck·ing** (truk'iŋ) ***n.*** the business of carrying goods by truck. —**truck'er *n.***

**truck·le** (truk''l) ***v.*** to give in or yield too easily; submit [It's disgusting the way he *truckles* to the boss.] —**truck'led, truck'ling**

**truc·u·lent** (truk'yoo lənt) ***adj.*** fierce, violent, and ready to fight. —**truc'u·lence *n.***

Trojan horse

trombone

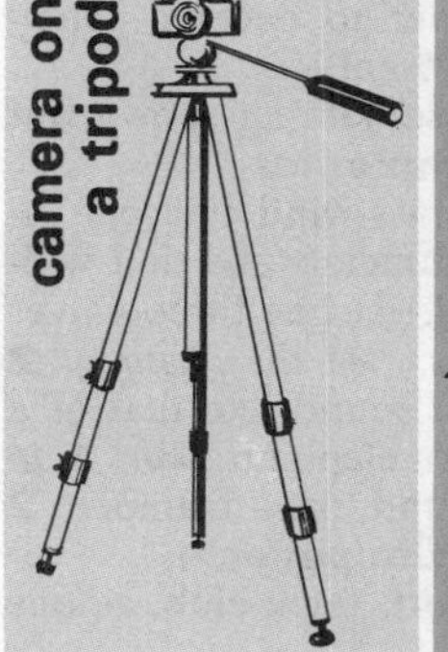

camera on a tripod

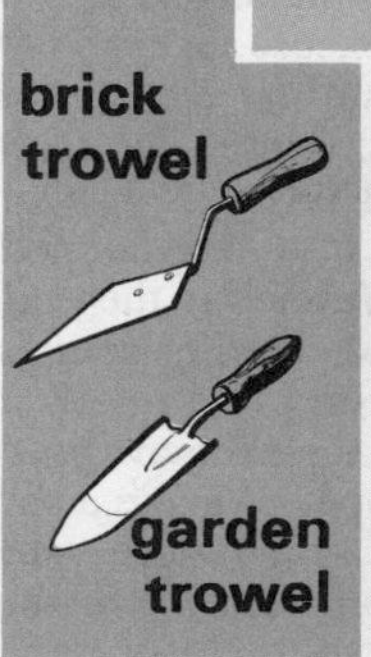

brick trowel

garden trowel

horse trotting

**Tru·deau** (trōō'dō *or* trōō dō'), **Pierre** 1921– ; the prime minister of Canada from 1968.

**trudge** (truj) ***v.*** to walk, especially in a tired way or with effort. —**trudged, trudg'ing** ◆***n.*** a long or tiring walk.

**true** (trōō) ***adj.*** **1** that agrees with fact; not false [a *true* story]. **2** as it should be; real; genuine [a *true* ruby; *true* love]. **3** that can be trusted; faithful; loyal [a *true* friend]. **4** exact or accurate [a *true* copy]. **5** right in form, fit, etc. [The door is not *true* with the frame.] **6** according to law; rightful [the *true* heirs]. —**tru'er, tru'est** ◆***adv.*** truly; exactly [The arrow was shot *true* to the mark.] ◆***n.*** that which is true [Can you tell the *true* from the false?] —**come true,** to happen as expected or hoped for. —**in true,** fitting or set properly. —**out of true,** not fitting or set properly.

> SYNONYMS: **True** is what agrees with fact or a standard or an ideal [Mozart was a *true* genius.] **Actual** is what exists or is happening, rather than just thought of [The party she planned was far different from the *actual* party.] **Real** is what it should be, not a substitute and not pretended [Use *real* lemons to make the lemonade. It took *real* courage to make the high dive.]

☆**true-false test** (trōō'fôls') a test that is a list of statements which the person being tested must mark as being either "true" or "false."

**truf·fle** (truf''l) ***n.*** a fungus that grows underground and is used as food.

| | | | | | | | |
|---|---|---|---|---|---|---|---|
| **a** | fat | **ir** | here | **ou** | out | **zh** | leisure |
| **ā** | ape | **ī** | bite, fire | **u** | up | **ŋ** | ring |
| **ä** | car, lot | **ō** | go | **ur** | fur | | a *in* ago |
| **e** | ten | **ô** | law, horn | **ch** | chin | | e *in* agent |
| **er** | care | **oi** | oil | **sh** | she | **ə =** | i *in* unity |
| **ē** | even | **oo** | look | **th** | thin | | o *in* collect |
| **i** | hit | **ōō** | tool | ***th*** | then | | u *in* focus |

**t**

**tru·ism** (tro͞o′iz′m) ***n.*** a statement so commonly known to be true that it seems unnecessary to say it, such as "You're only young once."

**tru·ly** (tro͞o′lē) ***adv.*** **1** in a true way; exactly, faithfully, etc. [I love you *truly.*] **2** in fact; really [Are you *truly* sorry?]

**Tru·man** (tro͞o′mən), **Harry S.** 1884–1972; the 33d president of the United States, from 1945 to 1953.

**trump** (trump) ***n.*** **1** any playing card of a suit that ranks higher than any other suit during the playing of a hand. **2** *sometimes* **trumps,** *pl.* this suit. ◆***v.*** to take a trick in a card game by playing a trump. —**trump up,** to make up in order to deceive [They *trumped up* an excuse for being absent.]

**trump·er·y** (trum′pər ē) ***n.*** **1** something showy but worthless. **2** nonsense. —*pl.* **trump′er·ies**

**trum·pet** (trum′pit) ***n.*** **1** a brass-wind musical instrument made of a long, looped metal tube that widens out like a funnel at the end. It has three valves and makes loud, blaring sounds. *See the picture.* **2** something shaped like this. **3** a sound like that of a trumpet, especially as made by an elephant. ◆***v.*** **1** to blow on a trumpet or make a sound like a trumpet. **2** to announce in a loud voice. —**trum′pet·er** ***n.***

**trun·cheon** (trun′chən) ***n.*** a short, thick club, as one carried by some police officers.

**trun·dle** (trun′d'l) ***n.*** a small wheel or caster. ◆***v.*** to roll along. —**trun′dled, trun′dling**



**trundle bed** a low bed on wheels, that can be rolled under another bed when not in use. *See the picture.*

**trunk** (trungk) ***n.*** **1** the main stem of a tree. **2** a body, not including the head, arms, and legs; torso. **3** a long snout, as of an elephant. **4** the main line, as of a blood vessel. **5** a large, strong box for storing things or for holding clothes, etc. while traveling. ☆**6** a space in an automobile, usually at the rear, for carrying luggage, a spare tire, etc. ☆**7** **trunks,** *pl.* very short pants worn by men for sports, especially for swimming or boxing.

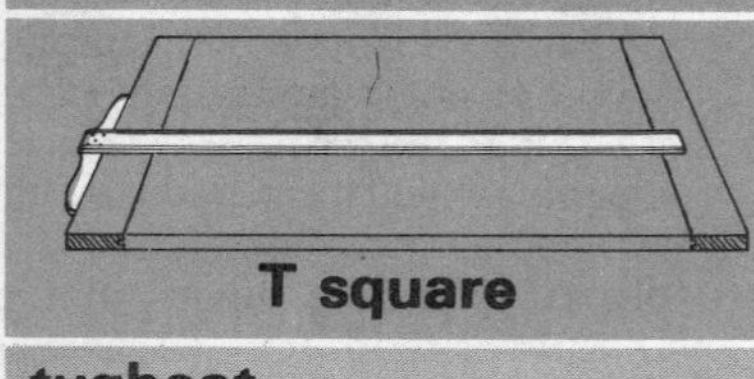

☆**trunk line** a main line of a railroad, telephone system, etc.

**truss** (trus) ***n.*** **1** a framework as of beams and struts for holding up a roof, bridge, etc. **2** a kind of belt worn to support a hernia or rupture. ◆***v.*** to tie, fasten, or tighten; especially, to bind the arms of a person or wings of a bird to the sides.

**trust** (trust) ***n.*** **1** a strong belief that some person or thing is honest or can be depended on; faith [You can put your *trust* in that bank.] **2** the one that is trusted [The Lord is our *trust.*] **3** something that has been put in one's care or charge; duty [The children's welfare is their sacred *trust.*] **4** confidence that a person will be able and willing to pay later; credit [to sell on *trust*]. **5** property that is held and managed by a person, bank, etc. for the benefit of another. **6** a group of businesses joined together to form a monopoly. ◆***v.*** **1** to have or put trust in; rely; depend [I *trust* him to be on time. Don't *trust* that rickety ladder.] **2** to put something in the care of [Her mother *trusted* her with the car.] **3** to expect; hope [I *trust* that you are well.] **4** to believe [I *trust* her story.] **5** to give credit to someone on something bought [The service station would not *trust* him for a new tire.] ◆***adj.*** **1** of a trust or held in trust [a *trust* fund]. **2** acting as trustee [a *trust* company]. —**in someone's trust,** entrusted to someone's care. —**trust to,** to rely on [We can't *trust to* luck.]

**trus·tee** (trus tē′) ***n.*** **1** a person who is put in charge of the property or affairs of another person. **2** any of a group of people (*board of trustees*) that manages the affairs of a college, hospital, etc.

**trus·tee·ship** (trus tē′ship) ***n.*** **1** the position or work of a trustee. **2** the right that has been given by the United Nations to a country to manage the affairs of a certain territory, called a **trust territory.**

**trust·ful** (trust′fəl) ***adj.*** full of trust or confidence; trusting. —**trust′ful·ly** ***adv.***

**trust·ing** (trus′ting) ***adj.*** that trusts others; trustful. —**trust′ing·ly** ***adv.***

SYNONYMS: **Trusting** means having faith in someone [The child looked up in a *trusting* way at his big sister.] **Gullible** means having trust in someone who may try to cheat or trick one [She was *gullible* when she bought the used car from a stranger.] **Naive** means being trusting because one does not have experience or know much about trickery [I came from a small town and was *naive* in the big city.]

**trust·wor·thy** (trust′wur′*th*ē) ***adj.*** deserving to be trusted; reliable. —**trust′wor′thi·ness** ***n.***

**trust·y** (trus′tē) ***adj.*** that can be trusted; reliable [a *trusty* worker]. —**trust′i·er, trust′i·est** ◆***n.*** ☆a convict in a prison who is given special privileges because of good behavior. —*pl.* **trust′ies**

**truth** (tro͞oth) ***n.*** **1** the quality or fact of being true, honest, sincere, accurate, etc. **2** that which is true; the real facts [Did the newspaper print the *truth* about you?] **3** a fact or principle that has been proved, as in science. —*pl.* **truths** (tro͞o*th*z *or* tro͞oths) —**in truth,** truly; in fact.

**truth·ful** (tro͞oth′fəl) ***adj.*** **1** telling the truth; honest [a *truthful* person]. **2** that is the truth; accurate [to give a *truthful* report]. —**truth′ful·ly** ***adv.*** —**truth′ful·ness** ***n.***

**try** (trī) ***v.*** **1** to make an effort; attempt [We must *try* to help them.] **2** to seek to find out about, as by experimenting; test [Please *try* my recipe. *Try* the other window, which may not be locked.] **3** to carry on the trial of in a law court [The judge *tried* the case. They *tried* him and found him innocent.] **4** to test the faith, patience, etc. of [She was sorely *tried.*] **5** to put to a severe test or strain [Such exercise *tried* my strength.] —**tried, try′ing** ◆***n.*** an effort; attempt; trial [He made a successful jump on his third *try.*] —*pl.* **tries** —**try on,** to put on, as a garment, to see how it fits and looks. —**try out,** ☆**1** to test, as by putting into use. ☆**2** to test one's fitness, as for a place on a team, a part in a play, etc. [I *tried out* for the marching band.]

> SYNONYMS: **Try** is the general word for making an effort to do something [*Try* to keep your room neat.] *Try* is also used especially to mean testing or experimenting [I'll *try* your way of skateboarding.] **Attempt** is a more formal word that means to set out to do something, but may suggest failure [I *attempted* twice to call her by telephone.]

**try·ing** (trī′iŋ) ***adj.*** hard to bear; annoying [Those were very *trying* times.]

☆**try·out** (trī′out) ***n.*** a test of one's fitness, as for a place on a team or a part in a play: *used only in everyday talk.*

**tryst** (trist) ***n.*** **1** an appointment to meet at a certain time and place, as one made by lovers. **2** the place of meeting: *also* **tryst′ing place.**

**tsar** (tsär *or* zär) ***n.*** *another spelling of* **czar.**

**tset·se fly** (tset′sē *or* tsēt′sē) a small fly found in central and southern Africa. One kind carries the germ that causes sleeping sickness.

☆**T-shirt** (tē′shurt) ***n.*** a knitted sport shirt or undershirt, usually with short sleeves and no collar. It is pulled on over the head.

**tsp.** *abbreviation for* **teaspoon** *or* **teaspoons.**

**T square** a T-shaped ruler for drawing parallel lines. The crosspiece can slide along the edge of the drawing board. *See the picture.*

**tub** (tub) ***n.*** **1** a round, open, wooden container, like a large bucket. **2** any large, open container, as for washing clothes. **3** as much as a tub will hold. **4** *a shorter name for* **bathtub.**

**tu·ba** (tōō′bə *or* tyōō′bə) ***n.*** a large brass-wind instrument with a full, deep tone. *See the picture.*

**tub·by** (tub′ē) ***adj.*** **1** shaped like a tub. **2** short and fat. —**tub′bi·er, tub′bi·est**

**tube** (tōōb *or* tyōōb) ***n.*** **1** a long, slender, hollow piece of material or tissue in which gases and liquids can flow or be kept [a fluorescent light *tube;* the bronchial *tubes*]. **2** a long, slender container made of soft metal, etc., with a screw cap at one end, from which toothpaste, glue, etc. can be squeezed out. ☆**3** *a shorter name for* **electron tube. 4** a hollow ring of rubber put inside some automobile tires and filled with air. **5** an underground tunnel for an electric railroad. —☆**the tube,** *another name for* **television:** *used only in everyday talk.*

**tu·ber** (tōō′bər *or* tyōō′bər) ***n.*** a short, thick part of an underground stem, as a potato.

**tu·ber·cle** (tōō′bər k'l *or* tyōō′bər k'l) ***n.*** **1** a small, rounded part growing out from a bone, a plant root, etc. **2** a hard swelling that is not normal [Tuberculosis causes *tubercles* in the lungs.]

**tu·ber·cu·lar** (too bur′kyə lər *or* tyoo bur′kyə lər) ***adj.*** **1** having tuberculosis. **2** of, like, or having tubercles.

**tu·ber·cu·lo·sis** (too bur′kyə lō′sis *or* tyoo bur′kyə lō′sis) ***n.*** a disease caused by a germ, in which tubercles form in the body, especially in the lungs, and tissues waste away.

**tu·ber·cu·lous** (too bur′kyə ləs *or* tyoo bur′kyə ləs) ***adj.*** *another word for* **tubercular.**

**tube·rose** (tōōb′rōz *or* tyōōb′rōz) ***n.*** a plant with a tuberous root and white, sweet-smelling flowers.

**tu·ber·ous** (tōō′bər əs *or* tyōō′bər əs) ***adj.*** **1** covered with rounded swellings; knobby. **2** of, like, or having a tuber or tubers.

**tub·ing** (tōōb′iŋ *or* tyōōb′iŋ) ***n.*** **1** tubes or a series of tubes. **2** material in the form of a tube [glass *tubing*]. **3** a piece of tube.

**Tub·man** (tub′mən), **Harriet** about 1820–1913; a black woman who was one of the leaders in the fight against slavery in the U.S.

**tu·bu·lar** (tōō′byə lər *or* tyōō′byə lər) ***adj.*** **1** of or shaped like a tube [*tubular* steel]. **2** made of or with tubes [*Tubular* furniture has legs made of tubes.]

**tuck** (tuk) ***v.*** **1** to gather in folds, so as to make shorter [She *tucked* up her dress to wade the stream.] **2** to push the edges of something in or under [He *tucked* in the sheets of the bed.] **3** to cover or wrap snugly [to *tuck* a baby in bed]. **4** to press snugly into a small space [to *tuck* shoes in a suitcase]. **5** to make tucks in a garment. ◆***n.*** a sewn fold in a garment. —**tuck away,** to put aside, as for future use.

**tuck·er**[1] (tuk′ər) ***n.*** a piece of lace or fine cloth once worn by women to cover the neck and shoulders. —**one's best bib and tucker,** one's finest clothes: *used only in everyday talk.*

☆**tuck·er**[2] (tuk′ər) ***v.*** to make tired: *used only in everyday talk* [I'm all *tuckered* out.]

**Tuc·son** (tōō′sän) a city in southern Arizona.

**Tu·dor** (tōō′dər *or* tyōō′dər) the ruling family of England from 1485 to 1603.

**Tues·day** (tōōz′dē *or* tyōōz′dē) ***n.*** the third day of the week: *abbreviated* **Tues.** *or* **Tu.**

**tuft** (tuft) ***n.*** a bunch of hairs, feathers, grass, threads, etc. growing or tied closely together. ◆***v.*** **1** to put tufts on or decorate with tufts. **2** to keep the padding of a quilt, mattress, etc. in place by putting tufts of threads through at various points.

**tug** (tug) ***v.*** **1** to pull with force or effort; drag; haul [He *tugged* the trunk out of the locker.] **2** to tow with a tugboat. —**tugged, tug′ging** ◆***n.*** **1** a hard pull [A *tug* on the old shoelace broke it.] **2** *a shorter name for* **tugboat.**

**tug·boat** (tug′bōt) ***n.*** a small, powerful boat used for towing or pushing ships and barges. *See the picture.*

| | | | | | | | |
|---|---|---|---|---|---|---|---|
| **a** | fat | **ir** | here | **ou** | out | **zh** | leisure |
| **ā** | ape | **ī** | bite, fire | **u** | up | **ŋ** | ring |
| **ä** | car, lot | **ō** | go | **ur** | fur | | a *in* ago |
| **e** | ten | **ô** | law, horn | **ch** | chin | | e *in* agent |
| **er** | care | **oi** | oil | **sh** | she | **ə** = | i *in* unity |
| **ē** | even | **oo** | look | **th** | thin | | o *in* collect |
| **i** | hit | **ōō** | tool | ***th*** | then | | u *in* focus |

**t**

**tug of war** a contest in which two teams pull at opposite ends of a rope. Each team tries to drag the other across a center line. *See the picture.*

**tu·i·tion** (to͞o ish′ən *or* tyo͞o ish′ən) ***n.*** money paid for being taught in a college or private school.

**tu·lip** (to͞o′lip *or* tyo͞o′lip) ***n.*** a plant that grows from a bulb and has long, pointed leaves and a large flower shaped like a cup.

**Tulip** comes from a Turkish word meaning "turban." The flower of this plant is thought to look a little like a turban.

**tulle** (to͞ol) ***n.*** a thin, fine, net cloth of silk, rayon, nylon, etc., used for veils or scarfs.

**Tul·sa** (tul′sə) a city in Oklahoma.

**tum·ble** (tum′b'l) ***v.*** **1** to do somersaults, handsprings, or other tricks of an acrobat. **2** to fall in a sudden or clumsy way [He slipped and *tumbled* down the steps.] **3** to toss or roll about [The dryer *tumbles* the clothes.] **4** to move in a quick, disorderly way [The children *tumbled* out of the house into the yard.] —**tum′bled, tum′bling** ◆***n.*** **1** a fall [She took a nasty *tumble* from the horse.] **2** a messy or confused condition [His clothes lay on the floor all in a *tumble*.]

**tum·ble·down** (tum′b'l doun) ***adj.*** that looks ready to fall down; ramshackle [a *tumbledown* shack].

**tum·bler** (tum′blər) ***n.*** **1** an ordinary drinking glass, without a stem. **2** an acrobat who does somersaults, handsprings, etc. **3** a part of a lock that must be moved, as by a key, to open the lock.



☆**tum·ble·weed** (tum′b'l wēd) ***n.*** a plant that breaks off near the ground in autumn and is blown about by the wind. *See the picture.*

**tum·brel** or **tum·bril** (tum′brəl) ***n.*** a cart, especially one that was used to carry prisoners to the guillotine during the French Revolution.

**tu·mid** (to͞o′mid *or* tyo͞o′mid) ***adj.*** **1** swollen; bulging. **2** sounding important but not really so; pompous [a *tumid* style of writing].

**tu·mor** (to͞o′mər *or* tyo͞o′mər) ***n.*** a growth of extra tissue on some part of the body. Tumors have no useful purpose and are sometimes harmful.

**tu·mult** (to͞o′mult *or* tyo͞o′mult) ***n.*** **1** loud noise or uproar, as from a crowd. **2** an excited or confused condition; disturbance [The news left us in a *tumult*.]

**tu·mul·tu·ous** (too mul′choo wəs *or* tyoo mul′choo wəs) ***adj.*** full of tumult; very noisy or confused [The city gave a *tumultuous* greeting to the hero.]

**tun** (tun) ***n.*** a large cask, especially one for wine, beer, or ale.

☆**tu·na** (to͞o′nə *or* tyo͞o′nə) ***n.*** a large ocean fish whose oily flesh is used as food and is usually canned: *also called* **tuna fish.** *—pl.* **tu′na** or **tu′nas**

**tun·dra** (tun′drə *or* toon′drə) ***n.*** a large, flat plain without trees in the arctic regions.

**tune** (to͞on *or* tyo͞on) ***n.*** **1** a series of musical tones with a regular rhythm; melody; song [The music of "America" is a very old *tune*.] **2** the condition of having correct musical pitch [Every instrument was in *tune*.] **3** harmony; agreement [He is out of *tune* with the times.] ◆***v.*** to put in the condition of correct musical pitch [to *tune* a piano]. —**tuned, tun′ing** —**to the tune of,** to the sum or amount of: *used only in everyday talk.* —**tune in,** to set a radio or TV to receive a certain station or program. —**tune up, 1** to put into good working condition by adjusting the parts [to *tune up* an engine]. **2** to adjust musical instruments to the same pitch. —**tune′less** ***adj.*** —**tun′er** ***n.***

**tune·ful** (to͞on′fəl *or* tyo͞on′fəl) ***adj.*** full of tunes or melody; pleasing to hear ["Carmen" is a *tuneful* opera.]

**tung·sten** (tung′stən) ***n.*** a hard, heavy metal that is a chemical element. It is used in steel alloys, the filaments of electric lights, etc.

**tu·nic** (to͞o′nik *or* tyo͞o′nik) ***n.*** **1** a garment like a loose gown worn by men and women in ancient Greece and Rome, or one like this worn in medieval Europe. **2** a blouse or jacket that reaches to the hips, often worn with a belt.

**tuning fork** a steel piece with two prongs, that sounds a certain fixed tone when it is struck. It is used as a guide in tuning instruments. *See the picture.*

**Tu·nis** (to͞o′nis *or* tyo͞o′nis) the capital of Tunisia.

**Tu·ni·sia** (to͞o nē′zhə *or* tyo͞o nē′zhə *or* to͞o nish′ə) a country in northern Africa, on the Mediterranean Sea.

**tun·nel** (tun′'l) ***n.*** **1** a passage under the ground for automobiles, trains, etc. **2** a way or place in the ground like this, as the burrow of an animal. ◆***v.*** to make a tunnel. —**tun′neled** or **tun′nelled, tun′nel·ing** or **tun′nel·ling**

**tun·ny** (tun′ē) ***n.*** *another word for* **tuna.** *—pl.* **tun′nies** or **tun′ny**

☆**tu·pe·lo** (to͞o′pə lō) ***n.*** **1** a gum tree of the southern U.S. **2** the wood of this tree, which is used for mallets, furniture, etc. *—pl.* **tu′pe·los**

**Tupelo** comes from two American Indian words, *ito* for "tree," and *opilwa* for "swamp." The tupelo is a tree that was first found in the swamps of the South.

**tur·ban** (tur′bən) ***n.*** **1** a covering for the head worn by Muslims, etc. and made up of a scarf wound around and around, often over a cap. *See the picture.* **2** any head covering or hat like this.

**tur·bid** (tur′bid) ***adj.*** **1** not clear; full of dirt or mud; cloudy [a *turbid* pond]. **2** confused or muddled, as in thought.

**tur·bine** (tur′bin *or* tur′bīn) ***n.*** an engine in which the driving shaft is made to turn by the pressure of steam, water, or air against the vanes of a wheel fixed to it.

**tur·bo·jet** (tur′bō jet′) ***n.*** a jet airplane engine in which the energy of the jet works a turbine which in turn works the air compressor.

**tur·bo·prop** (tur′bō präp′) ***n.*** a jet airplane engine in which the energy of the jet works a turbine which drives the propeller.

**tur·bot** (tur′bət *or* tur′bō) ***n.*** a kind of flounder or halibut used for food.

**tur·bu·lent** (tur′byə lənt) ***adj.*** **1** very excited, upset, etc.; wild or disorderly [*turbulent* feelings; a *turbulent* crowd]. **2** full of violent motion [*turbulent* rapids]. —**tur′bu·lence** ***n.*** —**tur′bu·lent·ly** ***adv.***

**tu·reen** (too rēn′) ***n.*** a large deep dish with a lid, used for serving soup, etc.

**turf** (turf) ***n.*** **1** a top layer of earth containing grass with its roots; sod. **2** a piece of this. *—pl.* **turfs** —**the turf, 1** a track for horse racing. **2** horse racing.

**tur·gid** (tur′jid) ***adj.*** **1** swollen or puffed up. **2** so full of long words and hard language that the meaning is not clear.

**Turk** (turk) ***n.*** a person born or living in Turkey.

**Turk.** *abbreviation for* **Turkey** *or* **Turkish.**

**Tur·key** (tur′kē) a country mostly in western Asia, but partly in southeastern Europe.

**tur·key** (tur′kē) ***n.*** ☆**1** a large, wild or tame bird, originally of North America, with a small head and spreading tail. ☆**2** its flesh, used as food. ☆**3** someone or something that has failed: *a slang meaning* [That play was a *turkey*.] *—pl.* **tur′keys** or **tur′key**

☆**turkey buzzard** a dark-colored vulture with a naked, reddish head. *See the picture.*

**Turk·ish** (tur′kish) ***adj.*** of Turkey, its people, etc. ◆***n.*** the language of Turkey.

**tur·mer·ic** (tur′mər ik) ***n.*** the root of a plant of the East Indies ground into a spicy powder.

**tur·moil** (tur′moil) ***n.*** a noisy, excited, or confused condition; commotion.

**turn** (turn) ***v.*** **1** to move around a center point or axis; revolve; rotate [The wheels *turn*. *Turn* the key.] **2** to do by moving in a circle [*Turn* a somersault.] **3** to seem to be whirling [It made my head *turn*.] **4** to move around or partly around [I tossed and *turned* in bed.] **5** to change in position or direction [*Turn* your chair around. *Turn* to the left. The tide has *turned*.] **6** to change so that the part that was underneath is on top; reverse [*Turn* the page. *Turn* over the soil.] **7** to change in feelings, attitudes, etc. [The news *turned* her family against her.] **8** to shift one's attention [He *turned* to music for relaxing.] **9** to change from one form or condition to another [The leaves *turn* color in the fall. The milk *turned* sour.] **10** to drive, set, let go, etc. in some way [The cat was *turned* loose.] **11** to attack suddenly [The dog *turned* on her.] **12** to depend [The outcome *turns* on whether he will agree.] **13** to go to for help [She *turned* to her teacher for advice.] **14** to upset or unsettle [The smell *turned* my stomach.] **15** to reach or pass [She has just *turned* 21.] **16** to give a round shape to [to *turn* the legs of a table on a lathe]. **17** to give a graceful form to [This writer knows how to *turn* a pretty phrase.] ◆***n.*** **1** the act of turning around or revolving [a *turn* of the wheel]. **2** a change in direction or position [a *turn* to the right; the *turn* of the tide]. **3** a short walk, ride, etc. [Let's take a *turn* around the block.] **4** the place where there is a change in direction; bend [a *turn* in the road]. **5** a twist, coil, etc. [Make one more *turn* with the rope.] **6** the right, duty, or chance to do something in regular order [It's your *turn* to wash dishes.] **7** an action or deed [to do someone a good *turn*]. **8** a change in condition [a *turn* for the worse]. **9** style, form, etc. [an odd *turn* of speech]. **10** the time of change [the *turn* of the century]. **11** a sudden surprise; shock [That shout gave me quite a *turn*.] —**by turns,** one after the other. —**in turn,** in the proper order. —**out of turn,** **1** not in the proper order. **2** at the wrong time, especially unwisely [to talk *out of turn*]. —**take turns,** to say or do something one after the other in a regular order. —**to a turn,** to just the right degree; perfectly. —**turn down,** ☆to refuse or reject. —**turn in,** **1** to make a turn into; enter [*Turn in* that driveway.] ☆**2** to hand over; deliver [*Turn in* your homework.] ☆**3** to inform on or hand over, as to the police. **4** to go to bed: *used only in everyday talk.* —**turn off,** **1** to leave, as a road. **2** to shut off [*Turn off* the water.] ☆**3** to make bored, annoyed, etc.: *a slang meaning.* —**turn on,** **1** to make go on, flow, etc. [*Turn on* the radio.] **2** to attack suddenly. ☆**3** to make or become happy, excited, etc.: *a slang meaning.* —**turn out,** **1** to shut off or put out, as a light. **2** to put outside. **3** to come or gather [Many people *turned out* for the picnic.] **4** to make; produce [She *turns out* good pies.] **5** to result or become [How did it all *turn out?* They *turned out* to be good workers.] —**turn over,** **1** to hand over; give. **2** to think about; ponder. —**turn to,** to start to work. —**turn up,** to happen or arrive. —**turn′er** ***n.***

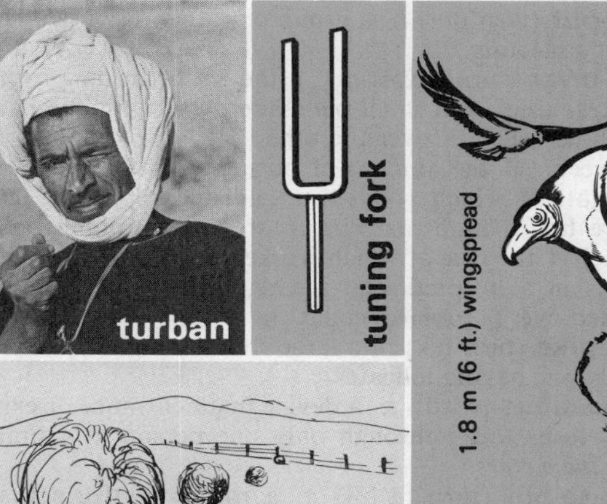

SYNONYMS: **Turn** is the general word that means something is moving around, or partly around, a center [A wheel *turns*. He *turned* on his heel.] **Rotate** means that something is moving around its own center or axis [The earth *rotates* on its axis.] **Revolve** suggests that something moves around a center or axis that is outside itself [The earth *revolves* around the sun.]

**turn·coat** (turn′kōt) ***n.*** a person who goes over to the opposite side or party; traitor.

**Tur·ner** (tur′nər), **Nat** 1800–1831; a U.S. black slave who led a revolt in 1831.

**turning point** a point in time at which a very important change takes place; crisis.

**tur·nip** (tur′nip) ***n.*** a plant with a round, white or yellow root that is eaten as a vegetable.

**turn·key** (turn′kē) ***n.*** a person in charge of the keys of a prison; jailer. *—pl.* **turn′keys**



| | | | |
|---|---|---|---|
| **a** fat | **ir** here | **ou** out | **zh** leisure |
| **ā** ape | **ī** bite, fire | **u** up | **ŋ** ring |
| **ä** car, lot | **ō** go | **ur** fur | a *in* ago |
| **e** ten | **ô** law, horn | **ch** chin | e *in* agent |
| **er** care | **oi** oil | **sh** she | **ə** = i *in* unity |
| **ē** even | **oo** look | **th** thin | o *in* collect |
| **i** hit | **ōō** tool | ***th*** then | u *in* focus |

**t**

**turn·out** (turn′out) ***n.*** a group or gathering of people, as at a meeting.

**turn·o·ver** (turn′ō′vər) ***n.*** **1** the act of turning over, or upsetting. **2** a small pie made by turning one half of the crust back over the other half, with a filling in between. **3** the amount of business done, shown by the rate at which goods are sold and replaced [The store had a high *turnover* in stereo equipment last year.] **4** the rate at which workers in a company, patients in a hospital, etc. are replaced. ◆***adj.*** that is turned over [a *turnover* collar].

**turn·pike** (turn′pīk) ***n.*** a large road, or highway, especially one having tollgates.

**turn·stile** (turn′stīl) ***n.*** a device in an entrance or exit, that turns to let through only one person at a time. *See the picture.*

**turn·ta·ble** (turn′tā′b'l) ***n.*** a round platform that turns, as for playing phonograph records.

**tur·pen·tine** (tur′pən tīn) ***n.*** a colorless oil made from the sap of pines and certain other trees, and used in paints and varnishes.

**tur·pi·tude** (tur′pə tōōd *or* tur′pə tyōōd) ***n.*** the condition of being wicked or evil.

**tur·quoise** (tur′koiz *or* tur′kwoiz) ***n.*** **1** a greenish-blue stone used as a jewel. **2** a greenish blue.

**Turquoise** comes from an old French word meaning "Turkish." The first turquoise stones were brought to western Europe through Turkey and were thus thought to be Turkish although they really had come from Persia.



**tur·ret** (tur′it) ***n.*** **1** a small tower on a building, usually at a corner. **2** a dome or low tower, often one that revolves, from which guns are fired, as on a warship, tank, or airplane. **3** a part of a lathe that holds several cutting tools. It can be turned to change the tool in use. —**tur′ret·ed** ***adj.***

**tur·tle** (tur′t'l) ***n.*** an animal with a soft body covered by a hard shell into which it can pull its head, tail, and four legs. Turtles live on land and in the water and some kinds are used as food. The turtles that live on the land are usually called *tortoises.* —**turn turtle,** to turn upside down.

**tur·tle·dove** (tur′t'l duv) ***n.*** a wild dove known for its sad cooing and the love that the mates seem to show for each other.

**tur·tle·neck** (tur′t'l nek) ***n.*** ☆**1** a high collar that turns down and fits closely around the neck on some sweaters, shirts, etc. ☆**2** a sweater, shirt, etc. with such a neck. *See the picture.*

**Tus·ca·ny** (tus′kə nē) a region in western Italy. *See the map.*

**tusk** (tusk) ***n.*** a very long, pointed tooth, usually one of a pair, that sticks out of the mouth, as in elephants, wild boars, and walruses.

**tus·sle** (tus′'l) ***v.*** to struggle or wrestle; scuffle. —**tus′sled, tus′sling** ◆***n.*** a short but rough struggle or fight.

**tus·sock** (tus′ək) ***n.*** a thick tuft or clump of grass, twigs, etc.

**tut** (tut) ***interj.*** a sound made to show that one is impatient, annoyed, angry, etc.

**tu·te·lage** (tōōt′'l ij *or* tyōōt′'l ij) ***n.*** **1** teaching; instruction. **2** care and protection, as of a guardian.

**tu·te·lar·y** (tōōt′'l er′ē *or* tyōōt′'l er′ē) ***adj.*** watching over or protecting a person or thing [Each Roman family had its *tutelary* gods.]

**tu·tor** (tōōt′ər *or* tyōōt′ər) ***n.*** a teacher who teaches one student at a time; private teacher. ◆***v.*** to act as a tutor to; especially, to teach students one at a time. —**tu·to·ri·al** (tōō tôr′ē əl *or* tyōō tôr′ē əl) ***adj.***

☆**tut·ti-frut·ti** (tōōt′ē frōōt′ē) ***n.*** ice cream or other sweet food that is made or flavored with bits of candied fruits.

**tu·tu** (tōō′tōō) ***n.*** a short or very short, full skirt worn by ballerinas. *See the picture.*

☆**tux·e·do** (tək sē′dō) ***n.*** **1** a man's jacket worn at formal dinners, dances, etc. It was often black, with satin lapels, and had no tails. Today tuxedos have many patterns and colors. **2** a suit with such a jacket, worn with a dark bow tie. *See the picture.* —*pl.* **tux·e′dos**

**TV** (tē′vē′) ***n.*** television or a television receiving set. —*pl.* **TVs** or **TV's**

☆**TV dinner** a dinner that has been cooked, then frozen and put in a tray for heating and serving. The metal tray has a separate compartment for each food of the meal.

**twad·dle** (twäd′'l) ***n.*** silly or foolish talk or writing; nonsense.

**twain** (twān) ***n.*** two: *used mainly in older poetry* [broken in *twain*].

**Twain** (twān), **Mark** 1835–1910; U.S. writer. His real name was *Samuel Langhorne Clemens.*

**twang** (twang) ***n.*** **1** a sharp, vibrating sound, as of a plucked string on a banjo. **2** a way of making speech sounds by letting air pass through the nose. ◆***v.*** **1** to make or cause to make a twang. **2** to speak with a twang.

**'twas** (twuz *or* twäz) it was.

**tweak** (twēk) ***v.*** to give a sudden, twisting pinch to [to *tweak* someone's cheek]. ◆***n.*** a sudden, twisting pinch.

**tweed** (twēd) ***n.*** **1** a rough wool cloth in a weave of two or more colors. **2 tweeds,** *pl.* clothes of tweed.

**Tweed** came into being when someone made a mistake in reading the word *tweel,* which was the Scottish way of writing "twill." Later *tweed* brought to mind the Tweed River in Scotland and it was thought to come from that.

**twee·dle·dum and twee·dle·dee** (twēd′'l dum′'n twēd′'l dē′) two persons or things so much alike that it is hard to tell them apart.

**tweet** (twēt) ***n.*** the high, chirping sound of a small bird. ◆***v.*** to make this sound.

**tweez·ers** (twē′zərz) ***n.pl.*** small pincers for plucking out hairs, handling small things, etc. *See the picture.*

**Tweezers** comes from an old French word, now no longer used, that means a set of surgical instruments. That word came in turn from *etuis,* plural of a word for a small case used to hold needles or other small implements.

**twelfth** (twelfth) ***adj.*** coming after eleven others; 12th in order. ◆***n.*** **1** the twelfth one. **2** one of twelve equal parts of something; 1/12.

**Twelfth Night** the evening of Epiphany. Epiphany is the twelfth day after Christmas.

**twelve** (twelv) ***n., adj.*** two more than ten; the number 12.

**twen·ti·eth** (twen′tē ith) ***adj.*** coming after nineteen others; 20th in order. ◆*n.* **1** the twentieth one. **2** one of twenty equal parts of something; 1/20.

**twen·ty** (twen′tē) ***n., adj.*** two times ten; the number 20. —*pl.* **twen′ties —the twenties,** the numbers or years from 20 through 29.

**twice** (twīs) ***adv.*** **1** two times [Don't make me ask you *twice.*] **2** two times as much or as many; doubly [She is *twice* the student you are.]

**twid·dle** (twid′′l) ***v.*** to twirl or play with lightly. —**twid′dled, twid′dling —twiddle one's thumbs, 1** to twirl one's thumbs idly around one another. **2** to be idle.

**twig** (twig) ***n.*** a small branch or shoot of a tree or shrub.

**twi·light** (twī′līt) ***n.*** **1** the dim light just after sunset or, sometimes, just before sunrise. **2** the time between sunset and dark.

**twill** (twil) ***n.*** **1** a cloth woven with parallel slanting lines or ribs. **2** the pattern of this weave. ◆***v.*** to weave with such a pattern.

**'twill** (twil) it will.

**twin** (twin) ***n.*** **1** either of two born at the same time to the same mother. **2** either of two persons or things very much alike or forming a pair [It is the *twin* of a chair I bought yesterday.] ◆***adj.*** being a twin or twins [*twin* sisters; *twin* gables on the house].

**twine** (twīn) ***n.*** a strong string or cord made of two or more strands twisted together. ◆***v.*** **1** to twist together. **2** to wind or grow in a winding way [The ivy *twined* around the post.] —**twined, twin′ing**

**twinge** (twinj) ***n.*** **1** a sudden, short pain. **2** a sudden, short feeling of guilt, shame, etc.; qualm [She felt a *twinge* of conscience.] ◆***v.*** to have or give a twinge. —**twinged, twing′ing**

**twin·kle** (twiŋ′k′l) ***v.*** **1** to shine with quick flashes of light, as some stars; sparkle. **2** to light up, as with laughter [*twinkling* eyes]. **3** to move about quickly and lightly, as a dancer's feet. —**twin′kled, twin′kling** ◆***n.*** **1** a quick flash of light; sparkle. **2** a quick look of amusement in the eye.

**twirl** (twurl) ***v.*** to turn around rapidly; spin, twist, whirl, etc. ◆***n.*** **1** the act of twirling or condition of being twirled. **2** a twist, coil, curl, etc.

**twist** (twist) ***v.*** **1** to wind or twine together or around something [to *twist* wool fibers into yarn]. **2** to force out of its usual shape or position [I tripped and *twisted* my ankle.] **3** to give the wrong meaning to on purpose [He *twisted* my compliment into an insult.] **4** to turn around [*Twist* the lid to take it off.] **5** to move or turn around in a spiral or curves [Dough is *twisted* to make pretzels. The road *twists* up the hill.] **6** to break off by turning the end [to *twist* the stem from an apple]. ◆***n.*** **1** something twisted, as a bread roll made by twisting the dough. **2** the act of twisting or condition of being twisted [a *twist* to the left]. **3** a knot, etc. made by twisting. **4** a special meaning or slant [He gave a new *twist* to the old joke.]

**twist·er** (twis′tər) ***n.*** **1** a person or thing that twists. ☆**2** a tornado or cyclone.

**twit** (twit) ***v.*** to tease or taunt, as by pointing out a fault or mistake. —**twit′ted, twit′ting**

**twitch** (twich) ***v.*** to move or pull with a sudden jerk [A rabbit's nose *twitches.*] ◆***n.*** a sudden, quick motion or pull, often one that cannot be controlled [a *twitch* of the mouth].

turnstile

tweezers

tuxedo

tutu

turtleneck sweater

**twit·ter** (twit′ər) ***v.*** **1** to make a series of chirping sounds, as birds do. **2** to tremble with excitement. ◆***n.*** **1** the act or sound of twittering. **2** a condition of great excitement [She's in a *twitter.*]



**two** (to͞o) ***n., adj.*** one more than one; the number 2. —**in two,** in two parts.

**two-edged** (to͞o′ejd′) ***adj.*** **1** that has two edges, as for cutting. **2** that can have two different meanings [a *two-edged* remark].

**two-faced** (to͞o′fāst′) ***adj.*** **1** having two faces. **2** not sincere or honest; false.

**two·fold** (to͞o′fōld) ***adj.*** **1** having two parts; double. **2** having two times as much or as many. ◆***adv.*** two times as much or as many.

**two·leg·ged** (to͞o′leg′id) ***adj.*** having two legs.

**two-sid·ed** (to͞o′sīd′id) ***adj.*** **1** having two sides. **2** that can be understood in two ways [a *two-sided* question].

**two·some** (to͞o′səm) ***n.*** two people; a couple.

**two-way** (to͞o′wā′) ***adj.*** **1** that moves or lets one move in either direction [a *two-way* street]. **2** used for both sending and receiving [a *two-way* radio]. **3** that has to do with two persons, groups, etc. [a *two-way* political race]. **4** that can be used in two ways [a *two-way* raincoat].

**twp.** *abbreviation for* **township.**

**TX** *abbreviation for* **Texas.**

**-ty**[1] (tē) *a suffix meaning* the quality or condition of being [*Safety* is the quality or condition of being safe.]

| | | | |
|---|---|---|---|
| **a** fat | **ir** here | **ou** out | **zh** leisure |
| **ā** ape | **ī** bite, fire | **u** up | **ŋ** ring |
| **ä** car, lot | **ō** go | **ur** fur | a *in* ago |
| **e** ten | **ô** law, horn | **ch** chin | e *in* agent |
| **er** care | **oi** oil | **sh** she | **ə** = i *in* unity |
| **ē** even | **oo** look | **th** thin | o *in* collect |
| **i** hit | **o͞o** tool | ***th*** then | u *in* focus |

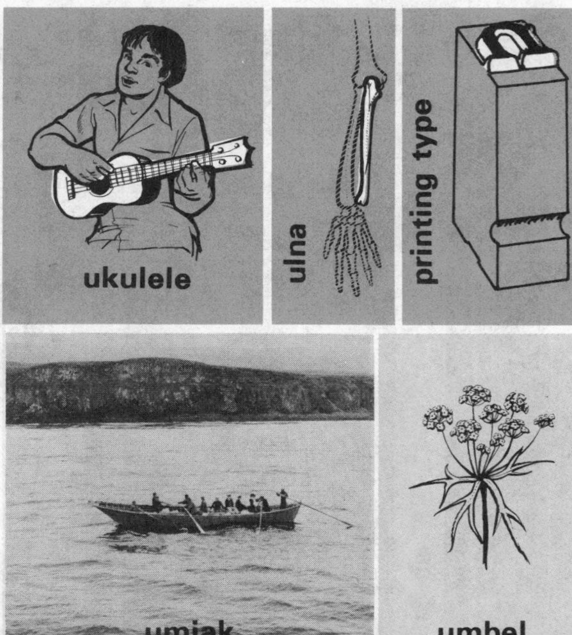
ukulele ulna printing type umiak umbel

**-ty²** (tē) *a suffix meaning* tens *or* times ten [Six times ten is *sixty.*]

☆**ty·coon** (tī ko͞on′) ***n.*** a businessman with much money and power.

> **Tycoon** comes from a Japanese word which comes from Chinese words meaning "great prince." This word was used by foreigners as a title for the military governors that once ruled Japan.

**ty·ing** (tī′iŋ) *present participle of* **tie**.

**tyke** (tīk) ***n.*** a small child: *used only in everyday talk.*

**Ty·ler** (tī′lər), **John** 1790–1862; 10th president of the United States, from 1841 to 1845.

**tym·pan·ic membrane** (tim pan′ik) *another name for* **eardrum.**

**tym·pa·num** (tim′pə nəm) ***n.*** **1** the middle ear. **2** the eardrum. **3** a drum.

**type** (tīp) ***n.*** **1** a group or class of people or things that are alike in some way; kind; sort [people of the bravest *type;* several *types* of insurance]. **2** the general form, character, or style of a particular kind or class [That's not the *type* of shoe I wanted.] **3** a particular person or thing pointed to as an example or model [The Greek temple has been the *type* for many public buildings.] **4** a piece of wood or metal with a raised letter or mark on its top, used in printing. *See the picture.* **5** a set of such pieces. **6** the letters, etc. printed or photographed from such pieces [Small *type* is hard to read.] ◆***v.*** **1** to find the type or class of [to *type* a sample of blood]. **2** to write with a typewriter. —**typed, typ′ing**

> In meaning 1 of the noun, **type** is usually followed by *of* [a new *type of* airplane]. In everyday talk *of* is often left out [a new *type* airplane].

☆**type·write** (tīp′rīt) ***v.*** to write with a typewriter: *now usually shortened to* **type.** —**type′wrote, type′-writ·ten, type′writ·ing**

☆**type·writ·er** (tīp′rīt′ər) ***n.*** a machine with a keyboard for making printed letters or figures on paper.

**ty·phoid** (tī′foid) ***n.*** a serious disease that is spread as by infected food or drinking water, and causing fever, sores in the intestines, etc. *The full name is* **typhoid fever.**

**ty·phoon** (tī fo͞on′) ***n.*** any violent tropical cyclone that starts in the western Pacific.

**ty·phus** (tī′fəs) ***n.*** a serious disease whose germ is carried to human beings by fleas, lice, etc. It causes fever and red spots on the skin. *The full name is* **typhus fever.**

**typ·i·cal** (tip′i k'l) ***adj.*** **1** being a true example of its kind [The church is *typical* of Gothic style.] **2** of its type; characteristic [The snail moved with *typical* slowness.] —**typ′i·cal·ly *adv.***

> SYNONYMS: **Typical** is used for something which has the qualities that can be found in any one of its type or class [We drove through a *typical* American town.] **Usual** is used for something which is in agreement with what is done or used everywhere [Our schoolroom has the *usual* desks and chalkboards.]

**typ·i·fy** (tip′ə fī) ***v.*** to have all the usual qualities or features of; be a true example of [At one time Tom Sawyer *typified* the American boy.] —**typ′i·fied, typ′-i·fy·ing**

**typ·ist** (tīp′ist) ***n.*** a person who uses a typewriter; especially, one whose work is typing.

**ty·pog·ra·phy** (tī päg′rə fē) ***n.*** **1** the work or skill of setting type for printing. **2** the style, design, or appearance of material printed from type. —**ty·pog′ra-pher *n.*** —**ty·po·graph·i·cal** (tī′pə graf′i k'l) ***adj.***

**ty·ran·ni·cal** (ti ran′i k'l *or* tī ran′i k'l) ***adj.*** of or like a tyrant; harsh, cruel, unjust, etc.: *also* **ty·ran′nic.** —**ty·ran′ni·cal·ly *adv.***

**tyr·an·nize** (tir′ə nīz) ***v.*** to rule or act as a tyrant; use power in a harsh or cruel way. —**tyr′an·nized, tyr′-an·niz·ing**

**tyr·an·nous** (tir′ə nəs) ***adj.*** tyrannical; cruel, harsh, unjust, etc.

**tyr·an·ny** (tir′ə nē) ***n.*** **1** the government or power of a tyrant; harsh and unjust government. **2** very cruel and unjust use of power. **3** a tyrannical act. —*pl.* **tyr′-an·nies**

**ty·rant** (tī′rənt) ***n.*** **1** a ruler having complete power, as in some ancient Greek cities. **2** a ruler who is cruel and unjust. **3** a person who uses power in a cruel or unjust way [Your boss is a *tyrant.*]

**Tyre** (tīr) a seaport in ancient Phoenicia. —**Tyr·i·an** (tir′ē ən) ***adj., n.***

**ty·ro** (tī′rō) ***n.*** a beginner in learning something; novice. —*pl.* **ty′ros**

**Tyr·ol** (tir′äl *or* tī′rōl) *another spelling of* **Tirol.** —**Ty-ro·le·an** (ti rō′lē ən) or **Tyr·o·lese** (tir ə lēz′) ***adj., n.***

**tzar** (tsär *or* zär) ***n.*** *another spelling of* **czar.**

**tza·ri·na** (tsä rē′nə *or* zä rē′nə) ***n.*** *another spelling of* **czarina.**

**U, u** (yo͞o) ***n.*** the twenty-first letter of the English alphabet. —*pl.* **U's, u's** (yo͞oz)

**U** *the symbol for the chemical element* uranium.

**U.** *abbreviation for* **union, united, university.**

**u·biq·ui·tous** (yo͞o bik′wə təs) ***adj.*** being everywhere at the same time, or seeming to be so. —**u·biq′ui·ty *n.***

**ud·der** (ud′ər) ***n.*** the gland of a cow, goat, etc. from which milk comes.

☆**UFO** (yo͞o′fō *or* yo͞o′ef ō′) ***n.*** any of a number of objects that people claim to have seen flying at different heights and speeds. No one knows what these things are or if they really exist. UFO stands for **unidentified flying object.** —*pl.* **UFOs** or **UFO's**

**U·gan·da** (yo͞o gan′də *or* o͞o gän′dä) a country in east central Africa.

**ugh *interj.*** a sound made in the throat to show disgust or horror.

**ug·ly** (ug′lē) ***adj.*** **1** unpleasing to look at [an *ugly* shack]. **2** bad, unpleasant, disgusting, etc. [an *ugly* lie; an *ugly* habit]. **3** dangerous; threatening [a wolf with *ugly* fangs]. **4** cross; in a bad temper: *used only in everyday talk.* —**ug′li·er, ug′li·est —ug′li·ness *n.***

**UHF** or **U.H.F.** *abbreviation for* **ultrahigh frequency.**

**U.K.** *abbreviation for* **United Kingdom.**

**U·kraine** (yo͞o krān′) a republic in the southwestern part of the U.S.S.R. —**U·krain′i·an *adj., n.***

☆**u·ku·le·le** (yo͞o′kə lā′lē) ***n.*** a musical instrument with four strings, like a small guitar. *See the picture.*

**UL** or **U.L.** Underwriters' Laboratories.

**ul·cer** (ul′sər) ***n.*** **1** an open sore with pus, as on the skin or stomach lining. **2** any condition that is rotten or corrupting [Slums are the *ulcers* of our cities.] —**ul′cer·ous *adj.***

**ul·cer·ate** (ul′sə rāt) ***v.*** to have or cause to have an ulcer or ulcers [an *ulcerated* stomach]. —**ul′cer·at·ed, ul′cer·at·ing**

**ul·na** (ul′nə) ***n.*** the larger of the two bones of the forearm, on the side opposite the thumb. *See the picture.* —*pl.* **ul·nae** (ul′nē) or **ul′nas**

**Ul·ster** (ul′stər) a region in northern Ireland.

**ul·ster** (ul′stər) ***n.*** a long, loose, heavy overcoat.

**ul·te·ri·or** (ul tir′ē ər) ***adj.*** **1** beyond what is openly said or made known [We suspect that there was an *ulterior* purpose in agreeing to help us.] **2** lying beyond or on the farther side. **3** later, following, or future.

**ul·ti·mate** (ul′tə mit) ***adj.*** **1** most distant; farthest [the *ultimate* limits of space]. **2** final; last [an *ultimate* decision]. **3** most basic; fundamental; primary [the *ultimate* goodness of human beings]. **4** greatest possible; maximum [The flood water reached its *ultimate* level at noon.] ✦***n.*** something ultimate [the *ultimate* in pleasure].

**ul·ti·ma·tum** (ul′tə māt′əm) ***n.*** a final offer or demand presented to another in a dispute, especially with a threat to break off dealings, use force, or take other harsh action if the offer is refused.

**ul·tra** (ul′trə) ***adj.*** going beyond the usual limits; extreme [She is an *ultra* liberal.]

**ul·tra-** *a prefix meaning:* **1** beyond [*Ultraviolet* rays lie beyond the violet end of the spectrum.] **2** beyond what is usual or reasonable; to an extreme; very [An *ultramodern* house is a very modern house.]

**ul·tra·high frequency** (ul′trə hī′) any radio frequency between 300 and 3,000 megahertz.

**ul·tra·ma·rine** (ul′trə mə rēn′) ***adj.*** deep-blue. ✦***n.*** deep blue, or a deep-blue coloring matter.

> **Ultramarine** comes from a Latin word meaning "from beyond the sea." Ultramarine coloring matter was made from a crushed stone, called lapis lazuli. This stone was imported from Asia, "beyond the sea." The name for the coloring matter was soon given to the color itself. Today this color may be made by chemical means.

**ul·tra·son·ic** (ul′trə sän′ik) ***adj.*** describing or having to do with sounds too high for human beings to hear.

**ul·tra·vi·o·let** (ul′trə vī′ə lit) ***adj.*** lying just beyond the violet end of the spectrum [*Ultraviolet* rays are invisible rays of light that help to form vitamin D in plants and animals and can kill certain germs.] 

**U·lys·ses** (yoo lis′ēz) *another name for* **Odysseus.**

**um·bel** (um′b'l) ***n.*** a cluster of flowers on stalks of about the same length that grow out from the end of the main stem. *See the picture.*

**um·ber** (um′bər) ***n.*** **1** a kind of earth used as a coloring matter. **2** yellowish brown **(raw umber)** or reddish brown **(burnt umber).**

**um·bil·i·cal cord** (um bil′i k'l) the cord that connects a pregnant woman with her unborn baby. Through it the baby gets nourishment, and at the point where it is cut at birth the baby's navel is formed.

**um·brage** (um′brij) ***n.*** a feeling of hurt and anger over what one takes to be an insult or slight; offense [to take *umbrage* at a remark].

**um·brel·la** (um brel′ə) ***n.*** cloth, plastic, etc. stretched over a folding frame at the top of a stick, used to protect one from the rain or sun.

**u·mi·ak** or **u·mi·ack** (o͞o′mē ak′) ***n.*** a large, open boat made of skins stretched on a wooden frame, used by Eskimos. *See the picture.*

**um·pire** (um′pīr) ***n.*** **1** a person who rules on the plays of a game, as in baseball. **2** a person chosen to settle an argument. ✦***v.*** to be an umpire in a game or dispute. —**um′pired, um′pir·ing**

**un-** **1** *a prefix meaning* not *or* the opposite of [An *unhappy* person is one who is not happy, but sad.] **2** *a*

| | | | | | | | |
|---|---|---|---|---|---|---|---|
| **a** | fat | **ir** | here | **ou** | out | **zh** | leisure |
| **ā** | ape | **ī** | bite, fire | **u** | up | **ng** | ring |
| **ä** | car, lot | **ō** | go | **ur** | fur | | a *in* ago |
| **e** | ten | **ô** | law, horn | **ch** | chin | | e *in* agent |
| **er** | care | **oi** | oil | **sh** | she | **ə =** | i *in* unity |
| **ē** | even | **oo** | look | **th** | thin | | o *in* collect |
| **i** | hit | **o͞o** | tool | ***th*** | then | | u *in* focus |

*prefix meaning* to reverse or undo the action of [To *untie* a shoelace is to reverse the action of tying it.]

Many words beginning with **un-** that are not entered in this dictionary can be easily understood if "not" is used before the meaning of the root word [*Unaccented* means "not accented." *Unconnected* means "not connected."]

**UN** or **U.N.** *abbreviation for* **United Nations.**

**un·a·ble** (un ā′b'l) ***adj.*** not able; not having the means or power to do something.

**un·a·bridged** (un ə brijd′) ***adj.*** not abridged or shortened [A large dictionary that is not shortened from a still larger dictionary is often called *unabridged.*]

**un·ac·cept·a·ble** (un′ək sep′tə b'l) ***adj.*** not acceptable; unsatisfactory.

**un·ac·com·pa·nied** (un′ə kum′pə nēd) ***adj.*** not accompanied, as a choir or musical performer.

**un·ac·count·a·ble** (un′ə koun′tə b'l) ***adj.*** **1** that cannot be explained; strange [an *unaccountable* accident]. **2** not responsible [They are *unaccountable* to you.] —**un′ac·count′a·bly *adv.***

**un·ac·cus·tomed** (un′ə kus′təmd) ***adj.*** **1** not accustomed or used [*unaccustomed* to wealth]. **2** not usual; strange [an *unaccustomed* action].

**un·af·fect·ed** (un′ə fek′tid) ***adj.*** **1** not affected or influenced. **2** sincere and natural; simple.

**un·a·fraid** (un ə frād′) ***adj.*** not afraid; not feeling fear; not frightened.

804 **un-A·mer·i·can** (un′ə mer′ə kən) ***adj.*** not American; especially, thought of as not agreeing to the principles, policies, etc. of the U.S.

**u·na·nim·i·ty** (yo͞o′nə nim′ə tē) ***n.*** the condition of being unanimous; complete agreement.

**u·nan·i·mous** (yoo nan′ə məs) ***adj.*** showing complete agreement; with no one opposed [a *unanimous* vote; *unanimous* in their decision]. —**u·nan′i·mous·ly *adv.***

**Unanimous** comes from two Latin words meaning "one" and "the mind." When a vote or decision is unanimous, it means that everyone is of "one mind," or everyone thinks the same and agrees completely.

**un·ap·pe·tiz·ing** (un ap′ə tī′ziŋ) ***adj.*** looking, smelling, or tasting so bad as to spoil the appetite.

**un·ap·proach·a·ble** (un′ə prōch′ə b'l) ***adj.*** **1** hard to be friendly with; aloof. **2** having no equal; superior [*unapproachable* skill].

**un·armed** (un ärmd′) ***adj.*** having no weapons; especially, having no gun.

**un·a·shamed** (un ə shāmd′) ***adj.*** not feeling shame or guilt; proud.

**un·as·sum·ing** (un′ə so͞o′miŋ *or* un′ə syo͞o′miŋ) ***adj.*** not bold or forward; modest.

**un·at·tached** (un ə tacht′) ***adj.*** **1** not attached or fastened. **2** not engaged or married.

**un·at·trac·tive** (un′ə trak′tiv) ***adj.*** not attractive; not pleasing, pretty, etc.

**un·a·vail·a·ble** (un′ə vā′lə b'l) ***adj.*** that cannot be got, used, or reached [This book is now *unavailable.*]

**un·a·vail·ing** (un′ə vā′liŋ) ***adj.*** not bringing success; useless; futile [our *unavailing* efforts].

**un·a·void·a·ble** (un′ə voi′də b'l) ***adj.*** that cannot be avoided; inevitable [an *unavoidable* accident]. —**un′a·void′a·bly *adv.***

**un·a·ware** (un ə wer′) ***adj.*** not aware; not knowing or noticing [We were *unaware* of the danger in going there.] ◆***adv.*** *same as* **unawares.**

**un·a·wares** (un ə werz′) ***adv.*** by surprise; in a way not expected [to sneak up on someone *unawares*].

**un·bal·anced** (un bal′ənst) ***adj.*** **1** not balanced or equal [an *unbalanced* budget]. **2** not sane or normal in mind.

**un·bar** (un bär′) ***v.*** to open; unlock; unbolt. —**un·barred′, un·bar′ring**

**un·bear·a·ble** (un ber′ə b'l) ***adj.*** that cannot be put up with or endured [The pain was *unbearable.*] —**un·bear′a·bly *adv.***

**un·beat·a·ble** (un bēt′ə b'l) ***adj.*** **1** that cannot be defeated. **2** that cannot be improved on.

**un·beat·en** (un bēt′'n) ***adj.*** **1** not hit, pounded, etc. **2** not walked on or traveled over [an *unbeaten* path]. **3** not defeated or improved upon [an *unbeaten* team].

**un·be·com·ing** (un′bi kum′iŋ) ***adj.*** not becoming; not fitting or proper [an *unbecoming* dress; *unbecoming* behavior].

**un·be·lief** (un bə lēf′) ***n.*** a lack of belief, especially in matters of religion.

**un·be·liev·a·ble** (un′bə lēv′ə b'l) ***adj.*** that cannot be believed; astounding; incredible.

**un·be·liev·er** (un′bə lē′vər) ***n.*** a person who does not believe, especially one who does not believe in the teachings of some religion.

**un·be·liev·ing** (un′bə lē′viŋ) ***adj.*** not believing; doubting; skeptical.

**un·bend** (un bend′) ***v.*** **1** to make or become straight again. **2** to relax or become natural [After the interview, the senator was able to *unbend* and tell some jokes.] —**un·bent** (un bent′) or **un·bend′ed, un·bend′ing**

**un·bend·ing** (un ben′diŋ) ***adj.*** **1** not bending; stiff. **2** not giving in or yielding; firm.

**un·bi·ased** or **un·bi·assed** (un bī′əst) ***adj.*** without bias or prejudice; fair.

**un·bid·den** (un bid′'n) ***adj.*** without being asked or ordered; uninvited [They walked in *unbidden.*]

**un·bind** (un bīnd′) ***v.*** to let loose or free; unfasten [*Unbind* these prisoners!] —**un·bound′, un·bind′ing**

**un·blessed** or **un·blest** (un blest′) ***adj.*** **1** not blessed. **2** not happy; wretched.

**un·blush·ing** (un blush′iŋ) ***adj.*** **1** not blushing. **2** without feeling any shame.

**un·bolt** (un bōlt′) ***v.*** to open by pulling back the bolt or bolts of; unbar.

**un·born** (un bôrn′) ***adj.*** **1** not born. **2** not yet born; yet to be; future [*unborn* generations].

**un·bos·om** (un booz′əm) ***v.*** to tell or make known, as a secret. —**unbosom oneself,** to tell or reveal one's feelings, etc.

**un·bound** (un bound′) *past tense and past participle of* **unbind.** ◆***adj.*** **1** unfastened or let loose. **2** without a binding, as a book.

**un·bound·ed** (un boun′did) ***adj.*** **1** without bounds or limits. **2** not held back; not controlled [with *unbounded* enthusiasm].

**un·break·a·ble** (un brāk′ə b'l) ***adj.*** that cannot be broken or is not likely to be broken.

**un·bri·dled** (un brī′d'ld) ***adj.*** **1** having no bridle on, as a horse. **2** showing no control [You have an *unbridled* temper.]

**un·bro·ken** (un brō′k'n) ***adj.*** **1** not broken; all in one piece; whole. **2** not tamed, as a wild horse. **3** without any interruption; continuous [an *unbroken* silence]. **4** that has not been bettered or gone beyond [an *unbroken* record].

**un·buck·le** (un buk′'l) ***v.*** to unfasten the buckle or buckles of. —**un·buck′led, un·buck′ling**

**un·bur·den** (un bur̶d′'n) ***v.*** to free from a burden, guilt, anxious feeling, etc.

**un·but·ton** (un but′'n) ***v.*** to unfasten the button or buttons of.

**un·called-for** (un kôld′fôr′) ***adj.*** not needed or asked for; out of place [an *uncalled-for* act].

**un·can·ny** (un kan′ē) ***adj.*** **1** mysterious and unnatural; weird [The empty house had an *uncanny* look.] **2** so good, keen, etc. as to seem unnatural [an *uncanny* sense of hearing].

**un·cap** (un kap′) ***v.*** to remove the cap, as from a bottle. —**un·capped′, un·cap′ping**

**un·cen·sored** (un sen′sərd) ***adj.*** that has not been censored, as a book, movie, etc.

**un·cer·tain** (un sur̶t′'n) ***adj.*** **1** not certain or sure; full of doubt [He looked *uncertain* of what to do.] **2** not definite; vague [an *uncertain* number]. **3** not steady or constant; likely to change [*uncertain* weather].

**un·cer·tain·ty** (un sur̶t′'n tē) ***n.*** **1** lack of sureness; doubt. **2** something uncertain. —*pl.* **un·cer′tain·ties**

SYNONYMS: **Uncertainty** may be a state of mind in which one is not absolutely sure about something [the *uncertainty* about the date of his birth] or a situation which is so vague that one can only guess about it [the *uncertainty* of the future]. **Doubt** comes from being so unsure that one cannot make up one's mind or decide something [There is *doubt* about her guilt.]

**un·chain** (un chān′) ***v.*** to free from chains; set loose.

**un·char·i·ta·ble** (un char′i tə b'l) ***adj.*** harsh or strict, as in judging or dealing with others; unkind, tending to find fault, etc.

**un·chart·ed** (un chär′tid) ***adj.*** not marked on a chart or map; not explored or known.

**un·chris·tian** (un kris′chən) ***adj.*** **1** not having or practicing a Christian religion. **2** not worthy of a Christian or any decent, civilized person.

**un·civ·il** (un siv′'l) ***adj.*** not civil or polite; rude.

**un·civ·i·lized** (un siv′ə līzd) ***adj.*** **1** not civilized; barbarous; primitive. **2** cruel, brutal, etc.

**un·clad** (un klad′) ***adj.*** wearing no clothes; naked.

**un·clasp** (un klasp′) ***v.*** **1** to open or loosen the clasp of [to *unclasp* a string of pearls]. **2** to free from a clasp or grip.

**un·clas·si·fied** (un klas′ə fīd) ***adj.*** not classified; not secret, as certain government documents.

**un·cle** (uŋ′k'l) ***n.*** **1** the brother of one's father or mother. **2** the husband of one's aunt.

**un·clean** (un klēn′) ***adj.*** **1** dirty; filthy. **2** not pure in a moral or religious way.

**un·clean·ly** (un klen′lē) ***adj.*** not clean; dirty [an *uncleanly,* unhealthful room].

**un·clear** (un klir′) ***adj.*** not clear; hard to see or understand.

☆**Uncle Sam** the U.S. government, pictured as a tall man with whiskers, dressed in a red, white, and blue suit. *See the picture.*

Uncle Sam

**un·clothe** (un klōth′) ***v.*** to take off the clothes of; uncover. —**un·clothed′** or **un·clad′, un·cloth′ing**

**un·coil** (un koil′) ***v.*** to unwind; take out of a coiled condition.

**un·com·fort·a·ble** (un kumf′tər b'l *or* un kum′fər tə b'l) ***adj.*** not comfortable; having or giving an uneasy or unpleasant feeling [*uncomfortable* new shoes; *uncomfortable* with strangers]. —**un·com′fort·a·bly *adv.***

**un·com·mit·ted** (un′kə mit′id) ***adj.*** **1** not committed or pledged, as to certain ideas or principles. **2** not having taken a position [an *uncommitted* candidate].

**un·com·mon** (un käm′ən) ***adj.*** **1** rare; unusual; not often seen, used, etc. [an *uncommon* visitor]. **2** strange; remarkable; extraordinary [an *uncommon* experience]. —**un·com′mon·ly *adv.***

**un·com·mu·ni·ca·tive** (un′kə myo͞o′nə kāt′iv *or* un′kə myo͞o′ni kə tiv) ***adj.*** not communicative; keeping one's opinions, feelings, etc. to oneself. **805**

**un·com·pro·mis·ing** (un käm′prə mī′ziŋ) ***adj.*** not giving in at all; firm or strict.

**un·con·cern** (un kən sur̶n′) ***n.*** lack of interest or worry; indifference.

**un·con·cerned** (un kən sur̶nd′) ***adj.*** not concerned, interested, worried, etc.; indifferent.

**un·con·di·tion·al** (un′kən dish′ən 'l) ***adj.*** not depending on any conditions; absolute [an *unconditional* guarantee]. —**un′con·di′tion·al·ly *adv.***

**un·con·scious** (un kän′shəs) ***adj.*** **1** not conscious; not able to feel and think [He is *unconscious* from a blow on the head.] **2** not aware [She is *unconscious* of her mistake.] **3** not doing or done on purpose [an *unconscious* habit]. —**the unconscious,** the part of the mind in which are stored the feelings, desires, etc. that one is not aware of. —**un·con′scious·ly *adv.*** —**un·con′scious·ness *n.***

**un·con·sti·tu·tion·al** (un′kän stə to͞o′shən 'l *or* un′kän stə tyo͞o′shən 'l) ***adj.*** not allowed by the constitution of a nation, etc. [an *unconstitutional* law].

**un·con·ven·tion·al** (un′kən ven′shən 'l) ***adj.*** not agreeing with the ways things are usually done or with the usual rules [an *unconventional* tennis serve].

**un·co·op·er·a·tive** (un′kō äp′ər ə tiv *or* un′kō äp′rə tiv) ***adj.*** not willing to cooperate; not helpful.

| | | | | | | | |
|---|---|---|---|---|---|---|---|
| **a** | fat | **ir** | here | **ou** | out | **zh** | leisure |
| **ā** | ape | **ī** | bite, fire | **u** | up | **ŋ** | ring |
| **ä** | car, lot | **ō** | go | **ur** | fur | | a *in* ago |
| **e** | ten | **ô** | law, horn | **ch** | chin | | e *in* agent |
| **er** | care | **oi** | oil | **sh** | she | **ə =** | i *in* unity |
| **ē** | even | **oo** | look | **th** | thin | | o *in* collect |
| **i** | hit | **o͞o** | tool | ***th*** | then | | u *in* focus |

**un·co·or·di·nat·ed** (un′kō ôr′də nāt′id) ***adj.*** not coordinated; not working together smoothly; lacking good coordination.

**un·cork** (un kôrk′) ***v.*** **1** to pull the cork out of. **2** to let out, let loose, etc.: *used only in everyday talk* [She *uncorked* a loud yell.]

**un·count·ed** (un koun′tid) ***adj.*** **1** not counted. **2** too many to be counted; innumerable.

**un·cou·ple** (un kup′′l) ***v.*** to disconnect or unfasten [to *uncouple* railroad cars]. —**un·cou′pled, un·cou′pling**

**un·couth** (un kōōth′) ***adj.*** clumsy, rough, or crude in manners, speech, etc.

> **Uncouth** comes from an old English word meaning "not known." Today's meaning probably developed from the idea of someone who did not know the polite ways of behaving and was therefore thought to be rough or crude.

**un·cov·er** (un kuv′ər) ***v.*** **1** to remove the cover or covering from. **2** to make known; disclose, as a hidden fact. **3** to take off one's hat, as in showing respect.

**unc·tion** (ungk′shən) ***n.*** **1** the act of putting oil, ointment, etc. on a person, as for a religious purpose. **2** the oil, ointment, etc. used in this way. **3** anything that soothes or comforts. **4** the showing of deep or earnest feeling, often in a false way.

**unc·tu·ous** (ungk′chōō wəs) ***adj.*** **1** oily or greasy. **2** making a false show of deep or earnest feeling; too smooth in speech, manners, etc.



**un·curl** (un kurl′) ***v.*** to straighten out, as something that has been curled up.

**un·daunt·ed** (un dôn′tid) ***adj.*** not afraid or discouraged [a team *undaunted* by its losses].

**un·de·ceive** (un′di sēv′) ***v.*** to cause to be no longer deceived, mistaken, or misled. —**un′de·ceived′, un′de·ceiv′ing**

**un·de·cid·ed** (un′di sīd′id) ***adj.*** **1** not having made up one's mind [*undecided* whether to go or stay]. **2** that is not decided or settled [The date for the dance is *undecided.*]

**un·de·ni·a·ble** (un′di nī′ə b′l) ***adj.*** so true, right, good, etc. that it cannot be questioned or doubted [an *undeniable* fact]. —**un′de·ni′a·bly *adv.***

**un·der** (un′dər) ***prep.*** **1** in or to a place, position, amount, value, etc. lower than; below [He sang *under* her window. It rolled *under* the table. It weighs *under* a pound.] **2** below and to the other side of [We drove *under* the bridge.] **3** beneath the surface of [oil wells *under* the sea]. **4** covered or hidden by [I wore a sweater *under* my coat. She goes *under* an assumed name.] **5** controlled, led, bound, etc. by [*under* orders from the President; *under* oath]. **6** receiving the effect of [to work *under* a strain; a bridge *under* repair]. **7** being the subject of [the question *under* discussion]. **8** because of [*under* the circumstances]. **9** in a certain class, group, section, etc.; with [List your rent *under* fixed expenses.] ◆***adv.*** **1** in or to a lower position or condition [to pass *under*]. **2** so as to be covered or hidden [The car was snowed *under.*] **3** less in amount, value, etc. [It cost two dollars or *under.*] ◆***adj.*** lower in position, rank, amount, etc. [the *under* part].

underhand pitch

undershot water wheel

**under-** *a prefix meaning:* **1** lower than; below or beneath [*Underclothes* are worn beneath a suit, dress, etc. An *undersecretary* is lower in rank than the main secretary.] **2** too little; less than usual or proper [An *underpaid* worker is paid too little.]

> Many words beginning with **under-** that are not entered in this dictionary can be easily understood if **under-** is given the meaning of "below" or "less than usual."

☆**un·der·a·chieve** (un′dər ə chēv′) ***v.*** to fail to do as well as might be expected. —**un′der·a·chieved′, un′der·a·chiev′ing** —**un′der·a·chiev′er *n.***

**un·der·age** (un dər āj′) ***adj.*** below the age required, as by law.

**un·der·arm** (un′dər ärm) ***adj.*** under the arm; especially, in the armpit.

**un·der·bid** (un dər bid′) ***v.*** to bid lower than; offer to do or sell for less money than. —**un·der·bid′, un·der·bid′ding**

☆**un·der·brush** (un′dər brush) ***n.*** small trees, bushes, etc. under large trees, as in a forest.

**un·der·charge** (un dər chärj′) ***v.*** to charge too low a price to. —**un·der·charged′, un·der·charg′ing**

**un·der·clothes** (un′dər klōz *or* un′dər klōthz) ***n.pl.*** *another name for* **underwear.**

**un·der·cloth·ing** (un′dər klōth′ing) ***n.*** *another name for* **underwear.**

☆**un·der·cov·er** (un′dər kuv′ər) ***adj.*** acting or done in secret [*undercover* work as a spy].

**un·der·cur·rent** (un′dər kur′ənt) ***n.*** **1** a current beneath a surface current [a river with a strong *undercurrent*]. **2** a feeling, opinion, etc. that is not out in the open [an *undercurrent* of anger about the new policies of the company].

**un·der·de·vel·op** (un′dər di vel′əp) ***v.*** to develop less than is needed or proper.

**un·der·de·vel·oped** (un′dər di vel′əpt) ***adj.*** having few or no businesses or industries [the *underdeveloped* nations].

☆**un·der·dog** (un′dər dôg) ***n.*** a person, team, etc. that is losing or is expected to lose, as in a contest.

**un·der·done** (un dər dun′) ***adj.*** not cooked enough, as meat.

**un·der·es·ti·mate** (un′dər es′tə māt) ***v.*** to make an estimate or guess about size, amount, cost, etc. that is too low. —**un′der·es′ti·mat·ed, un′der·es′ti·mat·ing** ◆***n.*** an estimate that is too low.

**un·der·feed** (un dər fēd′) ***v.*** to feed less than is needed or too little. —**un·der·fed′, un·der·feed′ing**

**un·der·foot** (un dər foot′) ***adv., adj.*** **1** under one's foot or feet [to trample young grass *underfoot*]. ☆**2** in the way, as of one walking.

**un·der·gar·ment** (un′dər gär′mənt) ***n.*** a piece of underwear.

**un·der·go** (un dər gō′) ***v.*** to go through; have happen to one; often, to suffer or endure [to *undergo* years of poverty]. —**un·der·went′, un·der·gone′, un·der·go′·ing**

**un·der·grad·u·ate** (un′dər graj′oo wit) ***n.*** a student at a university or college who does not yet have a bachelor's degree.

**un·der·ground** (un′dər ground′) ***adj.*** **1** beneath the surface of the earth [an *underground* lake]. **2** done in secret; undercover [an *underground* revolt]. **3** of or describing newspapers, movies, etc. that try to present news and ideas that are radical and not to be found in the usual newspapers, etc. ◆***adv.*** **1** beneath the surface of the earth [Moles burrow *underground.*] **2** in or into hiding [The hunted criminal went *underground.*] ◆***n.*** (un′dər ground) **1** the space beneath the surface of the earth. **2** a group of people working secretly against the government or against an enemy occupying their country.

**un·der·growth** (un′dər grōth) ***n.*** *another name for* **underbrush.**

**un·der·hand** (un′dər hand) ***adj.*** **1** done with the hand kept lower than the elbow or shoulder [an *underhand* pitch in softball]. *See the picture.* **2** *same as* **underhanded.** ◆***adv.*** **1** with an underhand motion [to toss a ball *underhand*]. **2** in a sly or secret way.

**un·der·hand·ed** (un′dər han′did) ***adj.*** not honest, fair, etc.; secret; sly [*underhanded* dealings in business]. —**un′der·hand′ed·ly *adv.***

**un·der·lie** (un dər lī′) ***v.*** **1** to lie beneath [Solid rock *underlies* this topsoil.] **2** to form the basis for; support [Hard work *underlies* their success.] —**un·der·lay′, un·der·lain′, un·der·ly′ing**

**un·der·line** (un′dər līn) ***v.*** **1** to draw a line under [He *underlined* the word "now."] **2** to call attention to; emphasize [The speaker *underlined* her main points by repeating them.] —**un′der·lined, un′der·lin·ing**

**un·der·ling** (un′dər liŋ) ***n.*** a person who must carry out the orders of others of higher rank; inferior.

**un·der·ly·ing** (un′dər lī′iŋ) ***adj.*** **1** lying under; placed beneath [an *underlying* layer of clay]. **2** basic; fundamental [the *underlying* causes of the Civil War].

**un·der·mine** (un dər mīn′) ***v.*** **1** to dig or make a tunnel under [to *undermine* a fort]. **2** to wear away and weaken the supports of [Erosion is *undermining* the wall.] **3** to injure or weaken in a slow or sneaky way [False rumors and gossip had *undermined* their confidence in us.] —**un·der·mined′, un·der·min′ing**

**un·der·most** (un′dər mōst) ***adj., adv.*** lowest in place, position, rank, etc.

**un·der·neath** (un dər nēth′) ***adv., prep.*** under; below; beneath.

**un·der·nour·ished** (un′dər nur′isht) ***adj.*** not getting the food needed to grow or stay healthy.

☆**un·der·pants** (un′dər pants) ***n.pl.*** short or long pants worn as an undergarment.

☆**un·der·pass** (un′dər pas) ***n.*** a passageway or road under a railway or highway.

**un·der·pin·ning** (un′dər pin′iŋ) ***n.*** supports placed under a wall, etc. to strengthen it.

**un·der·priv·i·leged** (un′dər priv″l ijd) ***adj.*** kept from enjoying one's basic social rights, as because of being poor.

**un·der·rate** (un dər rāt′) ***v.*** to rate too low; underestimate. —**un·der·rat′ed, un·der·rat′ing**

**un·der·score** (un dər skôr′) ***v.*** *another word for* **underline.** —**un·der·scored′, un·der·scor′ing**

**un·der·sea** (un dər sē′) ***adj., adv.*** beneath the surface of the sea.

**un·der·seas** (un dər sēz′) ***adv.*** *same as* **undersea.**

**un·der·sell** (un dər sel′) ***v.*** to sell at a lower price than [to *undersell* a competitor]. —**un·der·sold** (un dər sōld′), **un·der·sell′ing**

☆**un·der·shirt** (un′dər shurt) ***n.*** a shirt without a collar and usually without sleeves, worn as an undergarment, especially by men and boys.

☆**un·der·shorts** (un′dər shôrts) ***n.pl.*** short underpants worn by men and boys.

**un·der·shot** (un′dər shät) ***adj.*** **1** having the lower part sticking out past the upper [an *undershot* jaw]. **2** turning by water flowing along the lower part [an *undershot* water wheel]. *See the picture.*

**un·der·side** (un′dər sīd) ***n.*** the side underneath.

**un·der·sign** (un dər sīn′) ***v.*** to sign one's name at the end of, as a letter or document. —**the undersigned,** the person or persons undersigning.

**un·der·stand** (un dər stand′) ***v.*** **1** to get the meaning of; know what is meant by something or someone [Do you *understand* my question?] **2** to get an idea or notion from what is heard, known, etc.; gather [I *understand* that you like to fish.] **3** to take as the meaning; interpret [He *understood* my silence to be a refusal.] **4** to take for granted; take as a fact [It is *understood* that no one is to leave.] **5** to have knowledge 807
of [Do you *understand* French?] **6** to know the feelings of and have sympathy toward [She felt that no one *understood* her.] **7** to fill in with the mind in order to make the grammar clear [In the sentence "She is taller than I," the word "am" is *understood* at the end.] —**un·der·stood′, un·der·stand′ing** —**un·der·stand′a·ble *adj.***

SYNONYMS: To **understand** or **comprehend** something is to be aware of its meaning, but to **understand** is to be more fully aware of something [You may *comprehend* each word in the phrase "walking on air," but do you *understand* that the whole phrase means "feeling very happy"?]

**un·der·stand·ing** (un dər stan′diŋ) ***n.*** **1** the fact of knowing what is meant; knowledge [a full *understanding* of the subject]. **2** the ability to think, learn, judge, etc.; intelligence [a person of keen *understanding*]. **3** a meaning or explanation [What is your *understanding* of this poem?] **4** an agreement, especially one that settles a dispute [The feuding families have reached an *understanding*.] ◆***adj.*** that understands; having sympathy and good judgment [an *understanding* friend].

**un·der·state** (un dər stāt′) ***v.*** **1** to say less or less strongly than the truth allows or demands [Don't *understate* your case.] **2** to say or show in a way that is

| | | | | | | | |
|---|---|---|---|---|---|---|---|
| a | fat | ir | here | ou | out | zh | leisure |
| ā | ape | ī | bite, fire | u | up | ŋ | ring |
| ä | car, lot | ō | go | ur | fur | | a *in* ago |
| e | ten | ô | law, horn | ch | chin | | e *in* agent |
| er | care | oi | oil | sh | she | ə = | i *in* unity |
| ē | even | oo | look | th | thin | | o *in* collect |
| i | hit | ōō | tool | *th* | then | | u *in* focus |

calm or controlled [*understated* grief]. —**un·der·stat'ed, un·der·stat'ing —un'der·state'ment** ***n.***

**un·der·stood** (un dər sto͝od') *past tense and past participle of* **understand.**

**un·der·stud·y** (un'dər stud'ē) ***n.*** an actor or actress who learns the part of another and stands ready to play the part when it becomes necessary. —*pl.* **un'der·stud'ies** ◆***v.*** to learn a part as an understudy. —**un'der·stud'ied, un'der·stud'y·ing**

**un·der·take** (un dər tāk') ***v.*** **1** to enter into or upon, as a task, journey, etc. **2** to agree, promise, pledge, etc. [I *undertook* to lend them the money.] —**un·der·took', un·der·tak'en, un·der·tak'ing**

**un·der·tak·er** (un'dər tā'kər) ***n.*** *an older word for* **funeral director.**

**un·der·tak·ing** (un'dər tā'kiŋ *or* un'dər tā'kiŋ) ***n.*** **1** something undertaken, as a task. **2** a promise or pledge.

**un·der·tone** (un'dər tōn) ***n.*** **1** a low tone of voice [speaking in an *undertone*]. **2** a quality, color, etc. in the background [There is an *undertone* of worry in her letter.]

**un·der·took** (un dər to͝ok') *past tense of* **undertake.**

**un·der·tow** (un'dər tō) ***n.*** a strong current beneath the surface of water and in a different direction; especially, the flow of water back to the sea under the waves breaking on a shore.

**un·der·val·ue** (un'dər val'yo͞o) ***v.*** to value at less than the real worth. —**un'der·val'ued, un'der·val'u·ing**



**un·der·wa·ter** (un'dər wôt'ər) ***adj., adv.*** under the surface of the water

**un·der·wear** (un'dər wer) ***n.*** clothing worn under one's outer clothes, as undershirts, slips, etc.

**un·der·weight** (un'dər wāt) ***adj.*** not weighing enough; less than normal in weight.

**un·der·went** (un dər went') *past tense of* **undergo.**

**un·der·world** (un'dər wʉrld) ***n.*** **1** the class of people who live by crime; criminals, gangsters, etc. as a group. **2** *another name for* **Hades.**

**un·der·write** (un'dər rīt') ***v.*** **1** to agree to pay the cost of, as an undertaking. **2** to agree to buy the unsold part of an issue of stocks, bonds, etc. **3** to write an insurance policy for. —**un'der·wrote', un'der·writ'ten, un'der·writ'ing —un'der·writ'er** ***n.***

**un·de·sir·a·ble** (un'di zīr'ə b'l) ***adj.*** not desirable or pleasing; not wanted. ◆***n.*** an undesirable person.

**un·de·vel·oped** (un'di vel'əpt) ***adj.*** **1** not developed. **2** not put to use [Much *undeveloped* natural gas lies under those fields.]

**un·dis·ci·plined** (un dis'ə plind) ***adj.*** not having proper discipline; hard to control or keep in order.

**un·di·vid·ed** (un'də vīd'id) ***adj.*** not divided; whole; complete [Give me your *undivided* attention.]

**un·do** (un do͞o') ***v.*** **1** to open, untie, or unfasten [*Undo* the knot. I *undid* the package.] **2** to get rid of the effect of; cancel; reverse [You cannot *undo* the damage done by your remark.] **3** to ruin or destroy [*I* was *undone* by my own mistakes.] **4** to upset; make nervous or troubled [He was *undone* by her criticism.] —**un·did', un·done', un·do'ing**

**un·do·ing** (un do͞o'iŋ) ***n.*** **1** the act of reversing something that has been done. **2** ruin or the cause of ruin [His greed was his *undoing.*]

**un·done** (un dun') *past participle of* **undo.** ◆***adj.*** **1** not done; not finished. **2** ruined. **3** greatly upset.

**un·doubt·ed** (un dout'id) ***adj.*** that cannot be doubted; certain [the *undoubted* truth of what she said.]

**un·doubt·ed·ly** (un dout'id lē) ***adv.*** without doubt; certainly [It is *undoubtedly* a ruby.]

**un·dreamed-of** (un drēmd'uv') ***adj.*** not even dreamed of or imagined [*undreamed-of* wealth]. *Also* **un·dreamt-of** (un dremt'uv').

**un·dress** (un dres') ***v.*** to take the clothes off; strip.

**un·due** (un do͞o' *or* un dyo͞o') ***adj.*** more than is proper or right; too much [Don't give *undue* attention to the way you look. *Undue* haste can cause mistakes.]

**un·du·late** (un'jo͝o lāt *or* un'dyo͝o lāt) ***v.*** **1** to rise and fall in waves; also, to twist or wind in and out. **2** to have a wavy look [*undulating* fields of grain]. —**un'du·lat·ed, un'du·lat·ing**

Our word **undulate** comes from a Latin word for a wave that moves along the surface of an ocean, lake, or other body of water.

**un·du·la·tion** (un'jo͝o lā'shən *or* un'dyo͝o lā'shən) ***n.*** **1** the act of undulating. **2** an undulating motion, as of a snake. **3** a wavy, curving line or form.

**un·du·ly** (un do͞o'lē *or* un dyo͞o'lē) ***adv.*** beyond what is proper or right; too much [I was *unduly* alarmed.]

**un·dy·ing** (un dī'iŋ) ***adj.*** not dying or ending; lasting forever.

**un·earned** (un ʉrnd') ***adj.*** **1** not earned by work [Interest on savings is *unearned* income.] **2** not deserved.

**un·earth** (un ʉrth') ***v.*** **1** to dig up from the earth [to *unearth* fossils]. **2** to discover or find [She *unearthed* some old books in the attic.]

**un·earth·ly** (un ʉrth'lē) ***adj.*** **1** not of this world; supernatural. **2** mysterious; weird [an *unearthly* shriek].

**un·eas·y** (un ē'zē) ***adj.*** **1** having or giving no ease; not comfortable [an *uneasy* conscience; an *uneasy* position]. **2** not natural or poised; awkward [an *uneasy* smile]. **3** worried; anxious [Dad felt *uneasy* when Bud was late with the car.] —**un·eas'i·er, un·eas'i·est —un·eas'i·ly** ***adv.*** —**un·eas'i·ness** ***n.***

**un·e·mo·tion·al** (un'i mō'shən 'l) ***adj.*** **1** lacking emotion or strong feeling [an *unemotional* reply]. **2** having feelings that are not easily stirred; slow to cry, be angry, etc. [an *unemotional* person].

**un·em·ployed** (un'im ploid') ***adj.*** **1** having no job or work. **2** not being used; idle [*unemployed* skills]. —**the unemployed,** people who are out of work.

**un·em·ploy·ment** (un'im ploi'mənt) ***n.*** **1** the condition of being unemployed, or without work. **2** the number of people out of work [Is *unemployment* increasing?]

**un·e·qual** (un ē'kwəl) ***adj.*** not equal, as in amount, size, strength, value, or rank [We were given *unequal* shares.] —**unequal to,** not having enough power, skill, or courage for [They were *unequal to* the task of halting the fire.] —**un·e'qual·ly** ***adv.***

**un·e·qualed** or **un·e·qualled** (un ē'kwəld) ***adj.*** better than any other; without equal; unmatched; supreme [Shakespeare's *unequaled* skill as a poet].

**un·e·quiv·o·cal** (un'i kwiv'ə k'l) ***adj.*** very clear in meaning; plain [an *unequivocal* answer of "No!"] —**un'e·quiv'o·cal·ly** ***adv.***

**un·err·ing** (un ʉr′iŋ *or* un er′iŋ) ***adj.*** without error; making no mistake; certain; sure [She took *unerring* aim at the target.]

**UNESCO** (yoo nes′kō) United Nations Educational, Scientific, and Cultural Organization.

**un·e·ven** (un ē′vən) ***adj.*** **1** not even, level, or smooth; irregular [*uneven* ground]. **2** not equal in size, amount, etc. [pencils of *uneven* length]. **3** that leaves a remainder when divided by two; odd [Five is an *uneven* number.] **—un·e′ven·ly *adv.* —un·e′ven·ness *n.***

**un·e·vent·ful** (un′i vent′fəl) ***adj.*** with no unusual or important happenings [an *uneventful* vacation].

**un·ex·cep·tion·a·ble** (un′ik sep′shə nə b′l) ***adj.*** having no errors or faults.

**un·ex·cep·tion·al** (un′ik sep′shən ′l) ***adj.*** not unusual; ordinary.

**un·ex·cit·ing** (un′ik sīt′iŋ) ***adj.*** not exciting; ordinary or dull.

**un·ex·pect·ed** (un′ik spek′tid) ***adj.*** not expected; surprising; sudden. **—un′ex·pect′ed·ly *adv.***

**un·fail·ing** (un fāl′iŋ) ***adj.*** never failing or stopping; always dependable; certain [*unfailing* courage].

**un·fair** (un fer′) ***adj.*** not fair, just, or honest. **—un·fair′ly *adv.* —un·fair′ness *n.***

**un·faith·ful** (un fāth′fəl) ***adj.*** not loyal or trustworthy; faithless.

**un·fal·ter·ing** (un fôl′tər iŋ) ***adj.*** not shaky or unsure; steady [*unfaltering* trust].

**un·fa·mil·iar** (un′fə mil′yər) ***adj.*** **1** not familiar or well-known; strange [an *unfamiliar* face]. **2** not knowing about or acquainted with [I'm *unfamiliar* with Mark Twain's travel books.]

**un·fas·ten** (un fas′′n) ***v.*** to open or make loose; untie, unlock, etc.

**un·fa·vor·a·ble** (un fā′vər ə b′l) ***adj.*** not favorable; opposed or harmful [an *unfavorable* review of a movie]. **—un·fa′vor·a·bly *adv.***

**un·feel·ing** (un fēl′iŋ) ***adj.*** without pity or sympathy; hardhearted [an *unfeeling* refusal to help].

**un·feigned** (un fānd′) ***adj.*** not false or pretended; real; genuine [*unfeigned* joy].

**un·fet·tered** (un fet′ərd) ***adj.*** able to act, move, or think with complete freedom.

**un·fin·ished** (un fin′isht) ***adj.*** **1** not finished or completed. **2** having no finish, or final coat, as of paint.

**un·fit** (un fit′) ***adj.*** not fit or suitable [food *unfit* to eat]. ✦***v.*** to make unfit. **—un·fit′ted, un·fit′ting**

**un·flinch·ing** (un flin′chiŋ) ***adj.*** not giving in or yielding; steadfast; firm.

**un·fold** (un fōld′) ***v.*** **1** to open and spread out something that has been folded [to *unfold* a map]. **2** to make or become known [to *unfold* one's plans].

**un·forced** (un fôrst′) ***adj.*** without strain; relaxed, natural, genuine, etc. [an *unforced* smile].

**un·fore·seen** (un′fôr sēn′) ***adj.*** not known or thought about before it happens; unexpected.

**un·for·get·ta·ble** (un′fər get′ə b′l) ***adj.*** so important, beautiful, shocking, etc. that it cannot be forgotten.

**un·for·tu·nate** (un fôr′chə nit) ***adj.*** **1** not fortunate; unlucky, unhappy, etc. **2** unsuitable, unwise, undesirable, etc. [It turned out to be an *unfortunate* choice.] ✦***n.*** a person who is unlucky, unhappy, etc. **—un·for′tu·nate·ly *adv.***

**un·found·ed** (un foun′did) ***adj.*** not based on fact or truth [*unfounded* rumors].

**un·freeze** (un frēz′) ***v.*** to melt or thaw something frozen. **—un·froze′, un·fro′zen, un·freez′ing**

**un·friend·ly** (un frend′lē) ***adj.*** not friendly.

**un·furl** (un fʉrl′) ***v.*** to open or spread out, as a flag or sail.

**un·fur·nished** (un fʉr′nisht) ***adj.*** without furniture [She has rented an *unfurnished* apartment.]

**un·gain·ly** (un gān′lē) ***adj.*** clumsy; awkward.

**un·god·ly** (un gäd′lē) ***adj.*** **1** not religious. **2** wicked; sinful. **3** very bad, unpleasant, etc.: *used only in everyday talk* [What *ungodly* weather!]

**un·gov·ern·a·ble** (un guv′ər nə b′l) ***adj.*** that cannot be controlled; unruly.

**un·grate·ful** (un grāt′fəl) ***adj.*** not feeling thankful or showing thanks.

**un·guard·ed** (un gärd′id) ***adj.*** **1** not guarded; unprotected. **2** showing a lack of caution; careless; thoughtless [The secret slipped out in an *unguarded* moment.]

**un·guent** (uŋ′gwənt) ***n.*** a salve or ointment.

**un·hand** (un hand′) ***v.*** to stop holding; let go of ["*Unhand* me, you brute!"]

**un·hand·y** (un han′dē) ***adj.*** **1** not easy to use or reach; inconvenient [an *unhandy* location]. **2** not clever in using one's hands; clumsy.

**un·hap·py** (un hap′ē) ***adj.*** **1** full of sorrow; sad. **2** not lucky or fortunate [an *unhappy* result]. **3** not suitable [an *unhappy* choice of words]. **—un·hap′pi·er, un·hap′pi·est —un·hap′pi·ly *adv.* —un·hap′pi·ness *n.***

**un·health·ful** (un helth′fəl) ***adj.*** bad for one's health; unwholesome [an *unhealthful* diet].

**un·health·y** (un hel′thē) ***adj.*** **1** having or showing poor health; not well; sickly. **2** bad for one's health [*unhealthy* habits]. **—un·health′i·er, un·health′i·est**

**un·heard** (un hʉrd′) ***adj.*** not heard or listened to [My warning went *unheard.*]

**un·heard-of** (un hʉrd′uv′) ***adj.*** not heard of before; never known or done before.

**un·hinge** (un hinj′) ***v.*** **1** to remove from its hinges, as a door. **2** to confuse, unbalance, upset, etc. [a mind *unhinged* by grief]. **—un·hinged′, un·hing′ing**

**un·hitch** (un hich′) ***v.*** to free from being hitched; unfasten [We parked and *unhitched* the trailer.]

**un·ho·ly** (un hō′lē) ***adj.*** **1** not holy or sacred. **2** wicked; sinful. **—un·ho′li·er, un·ho′li·est**

**un·hook** (un hook′) ***v.*** **1** to set loose from a hook [to *unhook* a fish]. **2** to unfasten the hooks of [to *unhook* a dress].

**un·horse** (un hôrs′) ***v.*** to make fall from a horse. **—un·horsed′, un·hors′ing**

**un·hur·ried** (un hʉr′ēd) ***adj.*** done or acting without haste; leisurely [a relaxed, *unhurried* lunch].

| | | | |
|---|---|---|---|
| **a** fat | **ir** here | **ou** out | **zh** leisure |
| **ā** ape | **ī** bite, fire | **u** up | **ŋ** ring |
| **ä** car, lot | **ō** go | **ʉr** fur | a *in* ago |
| **e** ten | **ô** law, horn | **ch** chin | e *in* agent |
| **er** care | **oi** oil | **sh** she | **ə** = i *in* unity |
| **ē** even | **oo** look | **th** thin | o *in* collect |
| **i** hit | **ōō** tool | ***th*** then | u *in* focus |

**uni-** *a prefix meaning* of or having only one [A *unicycle* is a vehicle having only one wheel.]

**UNICEF** (yōō′nə sef) United Nations International Children's Emergency Fund.

**u·ni·corn** (yōō′nə kôrn) ***n.*** an imaginary animal like a horse with one long horn in the center of its forehead. *See the picture.*

☆**u·ni·cy·cle** (yōō′nə sī′k'l) ***n.*** a riding device that has only one wheel and pedals like a bicycle. It is used for trick riding, as in a circus. *See the picture.*

**un·i·den·ti·fied** (un′ī den′tə fīd) ***adj.*** not identified; not known or recognized.

**u·ni·fi·ca·tion** (yōō′nə fi kā′shən) ***n.*** the act of unifying or the condition of being unified.

**u·ni·form** (yōō′nə fôrm) ***adj.*** **1** always the same; never changing [Driving at a *uniform* speed saves gas.] **2** all alike; not different from one another [a row of *uniform* houses]. ◆***n.*** the special clothes worn by the members of a certain group [a nurse's *uniform*]. —**u′ni·form·ly *adv.***

**u·ni·formed** (yōō′nə fôrmd) ***adj.*** wearing a uniform [a *uniformed* guard].

**u·ni·form·i·ty** (yōō′nə fôr′mə tē) ***n.*** the condition of being uniform; sameness.

**u·ni·fy** (yōō′nə fī) ***v.*** to make into one; unite. —**u′ni·fied, u′ni·fy·ing**

**u·ni·lat·er·al** (yōō′nə lat′ər əl) ***adj.*** having to do with or done by only one of several persons, nations, etc. [a *unilateral* decision].



**un·i·mag·i·na·ble** (un′i maj′ə nə b'l) ***adj.*** that cannot be imagined [*unimaginable* poverty].

**un·i·mag·i·na·tive** (un′i maj′ə nə tiv) ***adj.*** not having or showing imagination [an *unimaginative* writer].

**un·im·peach·a·ble** (un′im pēch′ə b'l) ***adj.*** that cannot be questioned or doubted [a person of *unimpeachable* honesty].

**un·im·por·tant** (un′im pôr′t'nt) ***adj.*** not important; minor [an *unimportant* remark].

**un·in·formed** (un′in fôrmd′) ***adj.*** not having the needed information [an *uninformed* voter].

**un·in·hab·it·ed** (un′in hab′it id) ***adj.*** not inhabited; not lived in [an *uninhabited* desert].

**un·in·hib·it·ed** (un′in hib′it id) ***adj.*** not inhibited; not held back from some action, feeling, etc. [a person *uninhibited* by fear].

**un·in·tel·li·gi·ble** (un′in tel′i jə b'l) ***adj.*** that cannot be understood [an *unintelligible* mumble].

**un·in·ten·tion·al** (un′in ten′shən 'l) ***adj.*** not done or said on purpose; not intended.

**un·in·ter·est·ed** (un in′trist id *or* un in′tər ist id) ***adj.*** having or showing no interest or concern.

**un·in·ter·est·ing** (un in′trist iŋ *or* un in′tər ist iŋ) ***adj.*** not interesting; dull.

**un·in·ter·rupt·ed** (un′in tə rup′tid) ***adj.*** not interrupted; continuous [a program of *uninterrupted* music].

**un·in·vit·ed** (un′in vīt′id) ***adj.*** not invited; having no invitation [*uninvited* guests at the party].

**un·ion** (yōōn′yən) ***n.*** **1** the act of uniting or the condition of being united; combination [a large corporation formed by the *union* of four companies]. **2** a group of nations, people, etc. joined together in a larger unit. *See* SYNONYMS *at* **unity.** **3** marriage. **4** a device for joining together parts, especially the ends of pipes. **5** *a shorter name for* **labor union.** —☆**the Union,** the United States of America, especially during the Civil War.

**un·ion·ize** (yōōn′yən īz) ***v.*** **1** to organize into a labor union [to *unionize* farm workers]. **2** to form labor unions in [to *unionize* an industry]. —**un′ion·ized, un′ion·iz·ing**

**union jack** **1** a flag used as a symbol of national union, as a blue United States naval flag with fifty white stars. **2 Union Jack** the national flag of the United Kingdom.

**Union of Soviet Socialist Republics** a country made up of fifteen republics in eastern Europe and northern Asia, including Russia.

**u·nique** (yōō nēk′) ***adj.*** **1** that is the only one; having nothing like it [Mercury is a *unique* metal in that it is liquid at ordinary temperatures.] **2** unusual; remarkable [It is a very *unique* motion picture.]

> Meaning 2 of **unique** is a common one, but some people think it is incorrect. They believe the word should be used only to describe something that is completely different from anything else, not something that is merely unusual.

**u·ni·son** (yōō′nə sən) ***n.*** sameness of musical pitch, as of two or more voices or tones. —**in unison,** singing or playing the same notes, or saying the same words, at the same time [Let's recite the poem *in unison*.]

> **Unison** comes from two Latin words meaning "one sound." When a choir sings in unison, you hear what sounds like one full sound rather than a number of separate voices.

**u·nit** (yōō′nit) ***n.*** **1** a single person or group, especially as a part of a whole [an army *unit*]. **2** a single part with some special use [the lens *unit* of a camera]. **3** a fixed amount or measure used as a standard [The ounce is a *unit* of weight.] **4** the smallest whole number; one.

**U·ni·tar·i·an** (yōō′nə ter′ē ən) ***n.*** a member of a Christian church that does not believe in the Trinity and that allows differing religious views.

**u·nite** (yoo nīt′) ***v.*** **1** to put or join together so as to make one; combine [The two churches *united* to form a new church.] *See* SYNONYMS *at* **join.** **2** to bring or join together in doing something [Let us *unite* in the search for peace.] —**u·nit′ed, u·nit′ing**

**u·nit·ed** (yoo nīt′id) ***adj.*** **1** joined together in one; combined [the *united* efforts of many people]. **2** in agreement [They were *united* in wanting to stay.]

**United Arab E·mir·ates** (i mir′its) a country in eastern Arabia, on the Persian Gulf.

**United Kingdom** a country made up of Great Britain and Northern Ireland.

☆**United Nations** an organization set up in 1945 to work for world peace and security. Most of the nations of the world belong to it. Its headquarters are in New York City.

**United States of America** a country, mostly in North America, made up of 50 States and the District of Columbia: *also called* **United States** or **America.**

**u·nit·ize** (yōō′nə tīz) ***v.*** to make into a single unit, all of one piece [a *unitized* automobile body]. —**u′nit·ized, u′nit·iz·ing**

**u·ni·ty** (yōō′nə tē) ***n.*** **1** the condition of being united or combined; oneness. **2** the condition of being in agreement; harmony [Our team plays well because it has *unity*.] **3** the number one. *—pl.* **u′ni·ties**

SYNONYMS: **Unity** suggests a feeling of oneness when many people who make up a large group share the same aims, interests, feelings, etc. [national *unity*]. **Union** suggests a being joined into one group for some purpose [a labor *union*].

**u·ni·ver·sal** (yo͞o′nə vur′s′l) ***adj.*** **1** of, for, or by all people; concerning everyone [a *universal* human need]. *See* SYNONYMS *at* **general**. **2** present everywhere [*universal* pollution of the air we breathe]. —**u·ni·ver·sal·i·ty** (yo͞o′nə vər sal′ə tē) ***n.***

**universal joint** a joint that allows the parts joined to swing in any direction, as in the drive shaft of an automobile. *See the picture.*

**u·ni·ver·sal·ly** (yo͞o′nə vur′s′l ē) ***adv.*** **1** in every case [*universally* true]. **2** in every part or place; everywhere [used *universally*].

**u·ni·verse** (yo͞o′nə vurs) ***n.*** all space and everything in it; earth, the sun, stars, and all things that exist.

**u·ni·ver·si·ty** (yo͞o′nə vur′sə tē) ***n.*** a school of higher education, made up of a college or colleges and, usually, professional schools, as of law and medicine. *—pl.* **u′ni·ver′si·ties**

**un·just** (un just′) ***adj.*** not just or right; unfair [an *unjust* rule]. —**un·just′ly *adv.***

**un·kempt** (un kempt′) ***adj.*** not tidy; messy.

Long ago in English there was a word *kempt* meaning "combed." Later the word **unkempt** was formed by adding the prefix *un-*. It was used to describe uncombed hair that was untidy.

**un·kind** (un kīnd′) ***adj.*** not kind; hurting the feelings of others. —**un·kind′ly *adv.*** —**un·kind′ness *n.***

**un·known** (un nōn′) ***adj.*** **1** not known, seen, or heard before [a song *unknown* to me]. **2** not discovered, identified, etc. [an *unknown* writer]. ◆***n.*** an unknown person or thing.

**un·lace** (un lās′) ***v.*** to untie the laces of [to *unlace* one's shoes]. —**un·laced′, un·lac′ing**

**un·latch** (un lach′) ***v.*** to open by releasing a latch.

**un·law·ful** (un lô′fəl) ***adj.*** against the law; illegal. —**un·law′ful·ly *adv.*** —**un·law′ful·ness *n.***

**un·lead·ed** (un led′id) ***adj.*** describing gasoline that has not been mixed with lead.

**un·learn** (un lurn′) ***v.*** to manage to forget something that one has learned [to *unlearn* a bad habit].

**un·learn·ed** (un lur′nid) ***adj.*** **1** not educated; ignorant. **2** (un lurnd′) known or done without having been learned [Sneezing is an *unlearned* response.]

**un·leash** (un lēsh′) ***v.*** to let loose from a leash or as if from a leash [to *unleash* power].

**un·leav·ened** (un lev′′nd) ***adj.*** made without a leaven such as yeast [Matzo is *unleavened* bread.]

**un·less** (ən les′) ***conj.*** in any case other than; except if [I won't go *unless* you do.]

**un·let·tered** (un let′ərd) ***adj.*** **1** not educated; ignorant. **2** not knowing how to read or write.

**un·like** (un līk′) ***adj.*** not alike; different [They are sisters but quite *unlike* in personality.] ◆***prep.*** not like [It's *unlike* you to cry.] —**un·like′ness *n.***

**un·like·ly** (un līk′lē) ***adj.*** **1** not likely to happen or be true [an *unlikely* story]. **2** not likely to be right or successful [an *unlikely* place to dig for gold].

**un·lim·it·ed** (un lim′it id) ***adj.*** without limits or bounds [*unlimited* power].

unicycle

unicorn

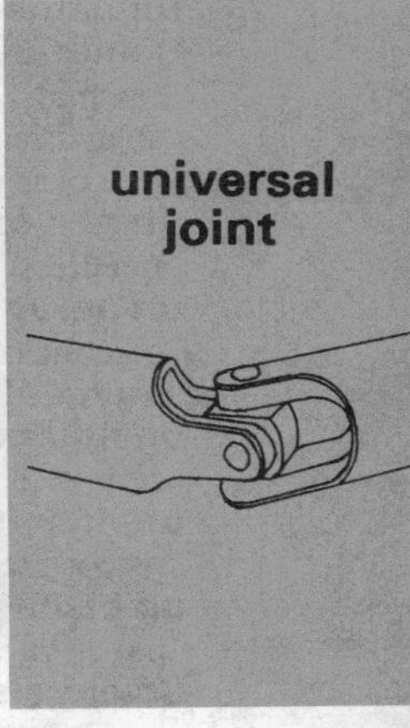
universal joint

**un·load** (un lōd′) ***v.*** **1** to take a load or cargo from a truck, ship, etc. **2** to take the charge out of [to *unload* a gun]. **3** to get rid of [The store is trying to *unload* its extra stock.]

**un·lock** (un läk′) ***v.*** **1** to open by undoing a lock. **2** to make known; reveal [to *unlock* a secret].

**un·looked-for** (un lo͝okt′fôr′) ***adj.*** not expected.

**un·loose** (un lo͞os′) ***v.*** to make or let loose; set free, unfasten, etc. —**un·loosed′, un·loos′ing**

**un·loos·en** (un lo͞os′′n) ***v.*** *another word for* **unloose.**

**un·luck·y** (un luk′ē) ***adj.*** having or bringing bad luck; not lucky; unfortunate [There is a superstition that breaking a mirror is *unlucky*.] —**un·luck′i·er, un·luck′i·est —un·luck′i·ly *adv.***



**un·man** (un man′) ***v.*** to make lose nerve or courage; make weaker [The horrible sight *unmanned* him for a moment.] —**un·manned′, un·man′ning**

**un·manned** (un mand′) ***adj.*** ☆without people on board and working automatically [an *unmanned* spacecraft].

**un·man·ner·ly** (un man′ər lē) ***adj.*** having bad manners; rude. ◆***adv.*** in a rude way; rudely.

**un·mask** (un mask′) ***v.*** **1** to take off a mask or disguise, as at a masquerade. **2** to show the true nature of; expose [They *unmasked* the spy.]

**un·men·tion·a·ble** (un men′shən ə b′l) ***adj.*** not fit to be mentioned; not proper to talk about.

**un·mer·ci·ful** (un mur′si fəl) ***adj.*** having or showing no mercy; cruel. —**un·mer′ci·ful·ly *adv.***

**un·mis·tak·a·ble** (un′mis tāk′ə b′l) ***adj.*** that cannot be mistaken or misunderstood; clear [smiling with *unmistakable* pleasure]. —**un′mis·tak′a·bly *adv.***

**un·mit·i·gat·ed** (un mit′ə gāt′id) ***adj.*** **1** not lessened or eased [*unmitigated* suffering]. **2** complete; absolute [an *unmitigated* fool].

**un·moved** (un mo͞ovd′) ***adj.*** **1** not moved from its place. **2** firm or unchanged in purpose. **3** not feeling pity or sympathy [*unmoved* by their suffering].

| | | | | | | | |
|---|---|---|---|---|---|---|---|
| **a** | fat | **ir** | here | **ou** | out | **zh** | leisure |
| **ā** | ape | **ī** | bite, fire | **u** | up | **ŋ** | ring |
| **ä** | car, lot | **ō** | go | **ur** | fur | | a *in* ago |
| **e** | ten | **ô** | law, horn | **ch** | chin | | e *in* agent |
| **er** | care | **oi** | oil | **sh** | she | **ə =** | i *in* unity |
| **ē** | even | **o͝o** | look | **th** | thin | | o *in* collect |
| **i** | hit | **o͞o** | tool | ***th*** | then | | u *in* focus |

**un·named** (un nāmd′) ***adj.*** not named or identified.

**un·nat·u·ral** (un nach′ər əl) ***adj.*** **1** not natural or normal; abnormal [an *unnatural* craving for sweets]. **2** artificial or pretended [an *unnatural* smile]. **3** very evil or cruel. —**un·nat′u·ral·ly *adv.***

**un·nec·es·sar·y** (un nes′ə ser′ē) ***adj.*** not necessary; needless. —**un·nec′es·sar′i·ly *adv.***

**un·nerve** (un nʉrv′) ***v.*** to make lose nerve, courage, or control [The accident *unnerved* him.] —**un·nerved′, un·nerv′ing**

**un·no·tice·a·ble** (un nōt′is ə b′l) ***adj.*** not easily seen or noticed [a small, *unnoticeable* scar].

**un·num·bered** (un num′bərd) ***adj.*** **1** not numbered or counted. **2** too many to count; countless.

**un·oc·cu·pied** (un äk′yə pīd) ***adj.*** **1** having no occupant; vacant [an *unoccupied* house]. **2** not busy; idle.

**un·or·gan·ized** (un ôr′gə nīzd) ***adj.*** not having or following any regular order or plan.

**un·or·tho·dox** (un ôr′thə däks) ***adj.*** not keeping to the usual or fixed beliefs, customs, etc.

**un·pack** (un pak′) ***v.*** **1** to open and empty out [I'll *unpack* the suitcase.] **2** to take from a crate, trunk, etc. [*Unpack* the books.]

**un·paid** (un pād′) ***adj.*** not receiving pay [an *unpaid* helper].

**un·par·al·leled** (un par′ə leld) ***adj.*** that has no parallel or equal; matchless [*unparalleled* skill].

**un·pin** (un pin′) ***v.*** to unfasten by removing a pin or pins from. —**un·pinned′, un·pin′ning**



**un·pleas·ant** (un plez′'nt) ***adj.*** not pleasant or agreeable; offensive; disagreeable [an *unpleasant* taste]. —**un·pleas′ant·ly *adv.*** —**un·pleas′ant·ness *n.***

**un·pop·u·lar** (un päp′yə lər) ***adj.*** not popular; not liked by most people or by the public. —**un·pop·u·lar·i·ty** (un′päp yə lar′ə tē) ***n.***

**un·prac·ticed** (un prak′tist) ***adj.*** **1** not done or used often or regularly. **2** without skill or experience; not expert [an *unpracticed* speaker].

**un·prec·e·dent·ed** (un pres′ə den′tid) ***adj.*** without a precedent; not done or known before; novel [She received an *unprecedented* award for her discovery.]

**un·prej·u·diced** (un prej′ə dist) ***adj.*** not showing prejudice or bias; fair [A judge must be *unprejudiced.*]

**un·pre·pared** (un′pri pard′) ***adj.*** not prepared or ready [We are still *unprepared* for the visitors.]

**un·prin·ci·pled** (un prin′sə p'ld) ***adj.*** without good morals or principles; unscrupulous.

**un·print·a·ble** (un prin′tə b'l) ***adj.*** not fit to be printed [He called me an *unprintable* name.]

**un·prof·it·a·ble** (un präf′it ə b'l) ***adj.*** not giving profit or gain; useless [an *unprofitable* discussion].

**un·prom·is·ing** (un präm′i siŋ) ***adj.*** not likely to be good or successful [The rain was an *unpromising* beginning to our trip.]

**un·pro·nounce·a·ble** (un′prə noun′sə b'l) ***adj.*** hard to pronounce [a long, *unpronounceable* word].

**un·qual·i·fied** (un kwäl′ə fīd) ***adj.*** **1** not having the qualities that are needed [a person *unqualified* to be mayor]. **2** complete; not limited [The performance was an *unqualified* success.]

**un·quench·a·ble** (un kwen′chə b'l) ***adj.*** that cannot be quenched, or stopped [an *unquenchable* fire; an *unquenchable* thirst].

**un·ques·tion·a·ble** (un kwes′chən ə b'l) ***adj.*** not to be questioned or doubted; certain [a person of *unquestionable* honesty]. —**un·ques′tion·a·bly *adv.***

**un·quote** (un′kwōt) *see the note at* **quote.**

**un·rav·el** (un rav′'l) ***v.*** **1** to separate or undo the threads of something woven, knitted, or tangled [to *unravel* a scarf]. **2** to make clear; solve [to *unravel* a mystery]. *See the note at* **ravel.** —**un·rav′eled** or **un·rav′elled, un·rav′el·ing** or **un·rav′el·ling**

**un·read** (un red′) ***adj.*** **1** not read, as a book. **2** having read little; not educated [an *unread* person].

**un·read·a·ble** (un rēd′ə b'l) ***adj.*** **1** badly written or printed [an *unreadable* signature]. **2** too boring or hard to read [an *unreadable* novel].

**un·read·y** (un red′ē) ***adj.*** not ready or prepared.

**un·re·al** (un rē′əl *or* un rēl′) ***adj.*** not real; imaginary or made up. —**un·re·al·i·ty** (un′rē al′ə tē) ***n.***

**un·rea·son·a·ble** (un rē′z'n ə b'l) ***adj.*** **1** not showing reason; not reasonable [He is in an *unreasonable* mood.] *See* SYNONYMS *at* **irrational.** **2** beyond the limits of what is reasonable; not moderate [an *unreasonable* price]. —**un·rea′son·a·bly *adv.***

**un·reel** (un rēl′) ***v.*** to unwind as from a reel.

**un·re·lent·ing** (un′ri len′tiŋ) ***adj.*** **1** refusing to give in or relent. **2** without mercy; cruel. **3** not relaxing or slowing up [an *unrelenting* effort].

**un·re·mit·ting** (un′ri mit′iŋ) ***adj.*** not stopping or slowing down; continuing [with *unremitting* enthusiasm].

**un·rest** (un rest′) ***n.*** a troubled or disturbed condition; restlessness.

**un·re·strained** (un′ri strānd′) ***adj.*** not held back or kept under control [*unrestrained* praise].

**un·right·eous** (un rī′chəs) ***adj.*** wicked, sinful, unjust, etc. —**un·right′eous·ness *n.***

**un·ripe** (un rīp′) ***adj.*** **1** not ripe or mature; green [*unripe* fruit]. **2** not yet fully developed [*unripe* plans].

**un·ri·valed** or **un·ri·valled** (un rī′v'ld) ***adj.*** having no rival; without one to equal or match it [a scene of *unrivaled* splendor].

**un·roll** (un rōl′) ***v.*** **1** to open or spread out, as something rolled up. **2** to show; display.

**un·ruf·fled** (un ruf′'ld) ***adj.*** not ruffled or disturbed; smooth; calm; serene [the *unruffled* lake; a person of *unruffled* temper].

**un·rul·y** (un rōō′lē) ***adj.*** hard to control or keep in order; not obedient or orderly [an *unruly* horse; *unruly* hair].—**un·rul′i·er, un·rul′i·est**

**un·sad·dle** (un sad′'l) ***v.*** **1** to take the saddle off a horse. **2** to make fall from the saddle of a horse; unhorse. —**un·sad′dled, un·sad′dling**

**un·safe** (un sāf′) ***adj.*** not safe; dangerous [an *unsafe,* rickety ladder].

**un·said** (un sed′) ***adj.*** not said or expressed [That is something better left *unsaid.*]

**un·sat·is·fac·to·ry** (un′sat is fak′tə rē) ***adj.*** not good enough to satisfy, or meet needs or wishes [an *unsatisfactory* meal].

**un·sa·vor·y** (un sā′vər ē) ***adj.*** **1** having little or a poor flavor or smell [an *unsavory* stew]. **2** unpleasant or disgusting [an *unsavory* scandal].

**un·say** (un sā′) ***v.*** to take back something said; retract. —**un·said′, un·say′ing**

**un·scathed** (un skā*th*d′) ***adj.*** not hurt; unharmed [We got out of the accident *unscathed.*]

☆**un·scram·ble** (un skram′b'l) ***v.*** to make no longer mixed up; put back in order; especially, to make scrambled electronic signals clear and understandable at the receiver. —**un·scram′bled, un·scram′bling**

**un·screw** (un skro͞o′) ***v.*** **1** to unfasten or loosen by taking out screws [to *unscrew* the hinges on a door]. **2** to take out, off, etc. or loosen by turning [to *unscrew* a bolt, a jar lid, etc.] **3** to become unscrewed [The cap on this tube does not *unscrew* easily.]

**un·scru·pu·lous** (un skro͞o′pyə ləs) ***adj.*** paying no attention to what is right or proper; not honest [*unscrupulous* business practices].

**un·seal** (un sēl′) ***v.*** to open by breaking a seal.

**un·search·a·ble** (un surch′ə b'l) ***adj.*** that cannot be understood or searched into; mysterious.

**un·seat** (un sēt′) ***v.*** **1** to make fall from one's seat, as from a saddle. **2** to force out of office, as by an election.

**un·seem·ly** (un sēm′lē) ***adj.*** not proper, fitting, or decent; unbecoming [*unseemly* behavior]. ◆***adv.*** in an unseemly way.

**un·sel·fish** (un sel′fish) ***adj.*** not selfish; putting the good of others above one's own interests. —**un·self′ish·ly *adv.*** —**un·self′ish·ness *n.***

**un·set·tle** (un set′'l) ***v.*** to make shaky, troubled, upset, etc. [The news *unsettled* her.] —**un·set′tled, un·set′tling**

**un·set·tled** (un set′'ld) ***adj.*** **1** not fixed; changing or likely to change [*unsettled* weather]. **2** not calm, quiet, or peaceful. **3** not paid [an *unsettled* debt]. **4** not decided or determined [an *unsettled* argument]. ☆**5** not lived in; having no settlers [*unsettled* lands].

**un·shak·a·ble** or **un·shake·a·ble** (un shāk′ə b'l) ***adj.*** that cannot be shaken; firm; steady [an *unshakable* faith].

**un·sheathe** (un shēth′) ***v.*** to take, as a sword or knife, from a sheath or case. —**un·sheathed′, un·sheath′ing**

**un·shod** (un shäd′) ***adj.*** not wearing shoes.

**un·sight·ly** (un sīt′lē) ***adj.*** not pleasant to look at; ugly.

**un·skilled** (un skild′) ***adj.*** not having or needing a special skill or training [Digging ditches is *unskilled* labor.]

**un·skill·ful** (un skil′fəl) ***adj.*** having little or no skill; clumsy; awkward.

**un·snap** (un snap′) ***v.*** to unfasten by opening the snaps of. —**un·snapped′, un·snap′ping**

**un·snarl** (un snärl′) ***v.*** to remove the snarls from; untangle.

**un·so·cia·ble** (un sō′shə b'l) ***adj.*** not sociable or friendly; staying away from others.

**un·so·lic·it·ed** (un′sə lis′it id) ***adj.*** not asked for; given without being requested [*unsolicited* advice].

**un·so·phis·ti·cat·ed** (un′sə fis′tə kāt′id) ***adj.*** simple or innocent; not wise in the ways of the world.

**un·sound** (un sound′) ***adj.*** **1** not sound; not healthy, whole, safe, etc. [an *unsound* mind; an *unsound* ship]. **2** not sensible [an *unsound* plan].

**un·spar·ing** (un sper′ing) ***adj.*** **1** not sparing; generous; lavish [*unsparing* charity]. **2** without mercy; harsh [*unsparing* criticism]. —**un·spar′ing·ly *adv.***

**un·speak·a·ble** (un spēk′ə b'l) ***adj.*** hard to describe or speak about because so great, bad, etc. [*unspeakable* joy; *unspeakable* tortures]. —**un·speak′a·bly *adv.***

**un·sta·ble** (un stā′b'l) ***adj.*** **1** not stable, firm, steady, etc. [an *unstable* foundation]. **2** likely to change; changeable [the *unstable* weather of spring].

**un·stead·y** (un sted′ē) ***adj.*** **1** not steady or firm; shaky. **2** likely to change; changeable.

**un·stick** (un stik′) ***v.*** to loosen or free, as something stuck. —**un·stuck′, un·stick′ing**

**un·stop** (un stäp′) ***v.*** **1** to pull the stopper or cork from. **2** to clear from being blocked. —**un·stopped′, un·stop′ping**

**un·strung** (un strung′) ***adj.*** **1** nervous or upset. **2** having the string or strings loosened or off.

**un·sub·stan·tial** (un′səb stan′shəl) ***adj.*** not substantial; not solid, firm, real, etc.; flimsy [made of *unsubstantial* material; our *unsubstantial* hopes].

**un·suit·a·ble** (un so͞ot′ə b'l *or* un syo͞ot′ə b'l) ***adj.*** not suitable or proper; inappropriate.

**un·sung** (un sung′) ***adj.*** **1** not sung. **2** not honored or praised, as in song or poetry [*unsung* heroes of the Revolutionary War].

**un·sus·pect·ed** (un′sə spek′tid) ***adj.*** **1** not believed guilty, bad, harmful, etc. **2** not thought to exist, be likely, etc. [an *unsuspected* danger].

**un·tan·gle** (un tang′g'l) ***v.*** to free from tangles, or confusion; straighten out [to *untangle* a knot; to *untangle* a mystery]. —**un·tan′gled, un·tan′gling**

**un·taught** (un tôt′) ***adj.*** **1** not taught or educated; ignorant. **2** got without being taught; natural [an *untaught* skill].

**un·think·a·ble** (un thingk′ə b'l) ***adj.*** that cannot be thought about or imagined [It is *unthinkable* that anyone could be so cruel.]

**un·think·ing** (un thingk′ing) ***adj.*** showing no care or thought for others; thoughtless [an *unthinking* remark].

**un·thought-of** (un thôt′uv′) ***adj.*** not thought of or imagined before.

**un·ti·dy** (un tī′dē) ***adj.*** not tidy or neat; messy. —**un·ti′di·er, un·ti′di·est —un·ti′di·ness *n.***

**un·tie** (un tī′) ***v.*** to loosen or unfasten something that is tied or knotted. —**un·tied′, un·ty′ing**

**un·til** (un til′) ***prep.*** **1** up to the time of; till [Wait *until* noon.] **2** before [Don't leave *until* tomorrow.] ◆***conj.*** **1** up to the time when [He was lonely *until* he met her.] **2** to the point, degree, or place that [She ate *until* she was full.] **3** before [Don't stop *until* he does.]

**un·time·ly** (un tīm′lē) ***adj.*** coming at the wrong time, especially too soon [an *untimely* remark; an *untimely* death]. ◆***adv.*** too soon or at the wrong time.

**un·to** (un′to͞o) ***prep.*** *same as* **to:** *now used only in poetry, prayers, etc.* [Give thanks *unto* the Lord.]

**un·told** (un tōld′) ***adj.*** **1** not told or made known [a story left *untold*]. **2** too much to be counted; very great [*untold* wealth].

| | | | | | | | |
|---|---|---|---|---|---|---|---|
| **a** | fat | **ir** | here | **ou** | out | **zh** | leisure |
| **ā** | ape | **ī** | bite, fire | **u** | up | **ng** | ring |
| **ä** | car, lot | **ō** | go | **ur** | fur | | a *in* ago |
| **e** | ten | **ô** | law, horn | **ch** | chin | | e *in* agent |
| **er** | care | **oi** | oil | **sh** | she | **ə =** | i *in* unity |
| **ē** | even | **oo** | look | **th** | thin | | o *in* collect |
| **i** | hit | **o͞o** | tool | ***th*** | then | | u *in* focus |

upright piano

**un·toward** (un tôrd′) ***adj.*** **1** causing trouble; unfortunate; unlucky [*Untoward* delays made us miss the bus.] **2** not proper or suitable [*untoward* remarks].

**un·true** (un tro͞o′) ***adj.*** **1** not correct; false. **2** not faithful or loyal. —**un·tru′ly *adv.***

**un·truth** (un tro͞oth′) ***n.*** **1** a statement that is not true; lie. **2** the fact of being untrue or false; lack of truth.

**un·truth·ful** (un tro͞oth′fəl) ***adj.*** **1** telling lies often [an *untruthful* child]. **2** that is not the truth [*untruthful* reports]. —**un·truth′ful·ly *adv.***

**un·tu·tored** (un to͞ot′ərd *or* un tyo͞ot′ərd) ***adj.*** not educated; ignorant.

**un·twist** (un twist′) ***v.*** to turn in the opposite direction so as to loosen or separate.

**un·used** (un yo͞ozd′) ***adj.*** **1** not in use or never having been used [*unused* space; *unused* clothing]. **2** not accustomed; not familiar with [I am *unused* to traveling.]



**un·u·su·al** (un yo͞o′zho͝o wəl) ***adj.*** not usual or common; rare; remarkable. —**un·u′su·al·ly *adv.***

**un·ut·ter·a·ble** (un ut′ər ə b′l) ***adj.*** that cannot be spoken, described, or talked about; unspeakable. —**un·ut′ter·a·bly *adv.***

**un·var·nished** (un vär′nisht) ***adj.*** **1** not varnished. **2** plain; simple [the *unvarnished* truth].

**un·veil** (un vāl′) ***v.*** **1** to take a veil or covering from so as to show or reveal [to *unveil* a statue]. **2** to remove a veil that one is wearing.

**un·war·y** (un wer′ē) ***adj.*** not watchful; not on one's guard [the *unwary* victims of a fraud].

**un·well** (un wel′) ***adj.*** not well; ill; sick.

**un·whole·some** (un hōl′səm) ***adj.*** **1** harmful to body or mind [an *unwholesome* food]. **2** unhealthy or looking unhealthy [an *unwholesome* appearance].

**un·wield·y** (un wēl′dē) ***adj.*** hard to handle, use, or control because it is very large, heavy, etc. [an *unwieldy* crate]. —**un·wield′i·ness *n.***

**un·will·ing** (un wil′iŋ) ***adj.*** **1** not willing or ready [*unwilling* to take the blame]. **2** done, given, etc. against one's will [*unwilling* permission]. —**un·will′ing·ly *adv.*** —**un·will′ing·ness *n.***

**un·wind** (un wīnd′) ***v.*** **1** to undo something wound by turning or rolling in the opposite direction; also, to become undone in this way [to *unwind* thread from a spool]. **2** to relax or become relaxed. —**un·wound** (un wound′), **un·wind′ing**

**un·wise** (un wīz′) ***adj.*** not wise; not showing good sense; foolish. —**un·wise′ly *adv.***

**un·wit·ting** (un wit′iŋ) ***adj.*** **1** not knowing or aware [*unwitting* of the danger around her]. **2** not done on purpose; not intended [an *unwitting* insult]. —**un·wit′ting·ly *adv.***

**un·wont·ed** (un wun′tid *or* un wôn′tid) ***adj.*** not common or usual [His *unwonted* politeness surprised us.]

**un·wor·thy** (un wur′thē) ***adj.*** **1** not deserving [I am *unworthy* of such honors.] **2** not fit or suitable [That remark is *unworthy* of so fine a person.] —**un·wor′thi·er, un·wor′thi·est** —**un·wor′thi·ly *adv.*** —**un·wor′thi·ness *n.***

**un·wrap** (un rap′) ***v.*** to open by taking off the wrapping; also, to become opened in this way. —**un·wrapped′, un·wrap′ping**

**un·wrin·kled** (un riŋ′k'ld) ***adj.*** not wrinkled; smooth.

**un·writ·ten** (un rit′'n) ***adj.*** **1** not in writing [an *unwritten* agreement]. **2** practiced or observed because it is the custom, but not part of a written code [an *unwritten* law or rule].

**un·yoke** (un yōk′) ***v.*** **1** to remove the yoke from, as oxen. **2** to disconnect; separate. —**un·yoked′, un·yok′ing**

☆**un·zip** (un zip′) ***v.*** to open the zipper, as of a garment. —**un·zipped′, un·zip′ping**

**up** (up) ***adv.*** **1** to, in, or on a higher place [to climb *up;* to stay *up* in the air]. **2** in or to a place thought of as higher [The sun comes *up* at dawn. He has come *up* in the world.] **3** to a later time [from childhood *up*]. **4** to a larger amount, size, etc. [to go *up* in price; to swell *up*]. **5** in or into an upright position [to stand *up*]. **6** into action, discussion, or view [Who brought *up* that question? I put *up* a new sign.] **7** aside; away [to lay *up* grain]. **8** so as to be even with [Run to keep *up* with her!] **9** completely [He ate *up* all our food. Don't use *up* the paste.] **10** apiece; each [The score is six *up*.] ◆***adj.*** **1** put, brought, going, or gone up [Her hand is *up*. The sun is *up*. Prices are *up*. Is the sign *up* yet?] **2** out of bed [Aren't you *up* yet?] **3** above the ground [The new grass is *up*.] **4** at an end; over [Time's *up*.] ☆**5** at bat in baseball [You're *up* next.] **6** going on; happening: *used only in everyday talk* [What's *up?*] ◆***prep.*** up to, toward, along, through, into, or upon [We climbed *up* the hill. We rowed *up* the river.] ◆***v.*** to get up, put up, lift up, raise, etc.: *used only in everyday talk* [The supermarket manager *upped* all the prices.] —**upped, up′ping** ◆***n.*** a time or condition of being successful, having good luck, etc. [We have our *ups* and downs.] —☆**up against,** faced with: *used only in everyday talk.* —**up for, 1** that is a candidate; nominated [*up for* class president]. **2** before a court of law for trial [*up for* murder]. —**up front,** ☆very honest and open: *used only in everyday talk.* —**up to, 1** doing or getting ready to do [That child is *up to* some mischief.] **2** capable of doing. **3** as many as [*Up to* four may play.] **4** as far as [*up to* here]. ☆**5** to be decided by. ☆**6** resting upon as a duty [It's *up to* you to keep your room clean.] *This phrase is used only in everyday talk.*

The adverb **up** is also used after many verbs in order to give special meanings to them. See the phrases following such verbs as **cut, catch, keep, look,** etc.

**up·braid** (up brād′) ***v.*** to scold; find fault with in an angry way.

**up·bring·ing** (up′briŋ′iŋ) ***n.*** the care and training one gets while growing up.

**up·com·ing** (up′kum′iŋ) ***adj.*** coming soon.

**up·coun·try** (up′kun′trē) ***adj., adv.*** in or toward the inner regions of a country.

**up·date** (up dāt′) ***v.*** to bring up to date; make agree with the latest facts, ideas, etc. —**up·dat′ed, up·dat′ing**

**up·end** (up end′) ***v.*** to set or stand on end.

☆**up·grade** (up′grād) ***n.*** an upward slope, especially in a road. ◆***v.*** (up grād′) to raise in importance, value, position, rank, etc. —**up·grad′ed, up·grad′ing** —**on the upgrade,** becoming higher, stronger, or more important.

**up·heav·al** (up hē′v′l) ***n.*** **1** a forceful lifting up from beneath [the *upheaval* of ground in an earthquake]. **2** a sudden, violent change [the *upheaval* begun by the French Revolution].

**up·hill** (up′hil′) ***adj., adv.*** **1** toward the top of a hill; upward. **2** needing or using much effort; with difficulty [an *uphill* battle against illness].

**up·hold** (up hōld′) ***v.*** **1** to hold up; keep from falling. **2** to agree with and support against attack by others [to *uphold* the right of every citizen to vote]. *See* SYNONYMS *at* **support.** —**up·held** (up held′), **up·hold′ing**

☆**up·hol·ster** (up hōl′stər *or* ə pōl′stər) ***v.*** to put springs and padding in, and cover with material, as a chair, sofa, etc. —**up·hol′ster·er** ***n.***

**up·hol·ster·y** (up hōl′stər ē *or* ə pōl′stər ē) ***n.*** the work of upholstering or materials used for this.

**up·keep** (up′kēp) ***n.*** the act of keeping something in good working condition, or the cost of this [the *upkeep* of a car].

**up·land** (up′land) ***n.*** land higher than the land around it. ◆***adj.*** of or in such land.

**up·lift** (up lift′) ***v.*** **1** to lift up; elevate [trees with *uplifted* branches]. **2** to raise to a higher or better level [Her heart was *uplifted* by the good news.] ◆☆***n.*** (up′lift) the act of uplifting, or of making better or more moral.

**up·on** (ə pän′) ***prep., adv.*** on, or up and on [He climbed *upon* the fence. We were set *upon* by bandits.]

> **Upon** can usually be used in place of *on.* Deciding which to use depends on which sounds better in the sentence.

**up·per** (up′ər) ***adj.*** **1** above another [the *upper* lip; an *upper* floor]. **2** of greater importance, rank, etc. [the *upper* house of a legislature]. ◆***n.*** the part of a shoe above the sole.

**upper hand** the position of advantage or control [Our enemy has the *upper hand.*]

**up·per·most** (up′ər mōst) ***adj.*** highest in place, importance, etc. [Safety was *uppermost* in my mind.] ◆***adv.*** in or to the highest place or position.

**Upper Vol·ta** (väl′tə) a country in western Africa, north of Ghana.

**up·raise** (up rāz′) ***v.*** to raise up; lift [marching with banners *upraised*]. —**up·raised′, up·rais′ing**

**up·right** (up′rīt) ***adj.*** **1** standing or pointing straight up; erect [*upright* pickets in a fence]. **2** honest and just [an *upright* judge]. **3** describing a piano in which the strings are mounted straight up and down in a rectangular box. *See the picture.* ◆***adv.*** in an upright position [to stand *upright*]. ◆***n.*** **1** an upright pole, beam, etc. [a lake house built on *uprights*]. **2** an upright piano.

**up·ris·ing** (up′rīz′iŋ) ***n.*** the act of rising up, or rebelling; revolt.

**up·roar** (up′rôr) ***n.*** **1** a noisy, confused condition; commotion [Her remark threw the meeting into an *uproar.*] **2** a loud, confused noise.

**up·roar·i·ous** (up rôr′ē əs) ***adj.*** **1** making an uproar. **2** loud and noisy [*uproarious* laughter].

**up·root** (up ro͞ot′) ***v.*** **1** to pull by the roots [to *uproot* a tree]. **2** to get rid of completely [to *uproot* crime].

**up·set** (up set′) ***v.*** **1** to turn or tip over; overturn [The frightened horse *upset* the wagon.] **2** to disturb the order or working of [to *upset* a busy schedule]. **3** to win a surprising victory over [Our swimming team *upset* the champions.] **4** to make nervous or troubled [The news *upset* our parents.] —**up·set′, up·set′ting** ◆***n.*** (up′set) **1** the act of upsetting. **2** a surprising victory. ◆***adj.*** (up′set) **1** tipped over; overturned [an *upset* bowl of flowers]. **2** disturbed; out of order [*upset* plans].

**up·shot** (up′shät) ***n.*** the result; conclusion.

> The **upshot** was the last shot in an archery match. This meaning led to today's meaning, which has to do with the last thing to happen after a series of other things have happened.

**up·side down** (up′sīd) **1** with the top side or part underneath; with the wrong side up [Turn the glasses *upside down* to drain them.] **2** in disorder or confusion [We turned the room *upside down* looking for the book.] —**up′side-down′** ***adj.***



**up·stairs** (up′sterz′) ***adv., adj.*** to or on an upper floor [to go *upstairs;* an *upstairs* room]. ◆***n.*** an upper floor or floors.

**up·stand·ing** (up stan′diŋ) ***adj.*** honest; honorable [a fine, *upstanding* young person].

**up·start** (up′stärt) ***n.*** a person who has just become rich or important; especially, such a person who is bold and pushing in a way that bothers others.

**up·stream** (up′strēm′) ***adv., adj.*** in the direction against the current or flow of a stream.

☆**up·tight** (up′tīt′) ***adj.*** very nervous, anxious, or tense: *a slang word.*

**up-to-date** (up′tə dāt′) ***adj.*** **1** having the latest facts, ideas, etc. [an *up-to-date* report]. **2** of the newest or latest kind, as in style.

**up·town** (up′toun′) ***adj., adv.*** in or toward the upper part of a city, usually the part away from the main business section.

**up·turn** (up′turn) ***n.*** a turn or move toward a higher place or better condition [Business took a sharp *upturn.*] ◆***v.*** to turn up or over.

**up·ward** (up′wərd) ***adv., adj.*** toward a higher place, position, degree, price, etc. —**upward of,** more than. —**up′ward·ly** ***adv.***

**up·wards** (up′wərdz) ***adv.*** *same as* **upward.** —**upwards of,** more than.

| | | | |
|---|---|---|---|
| **a** fat | **ir** here | **ou** out | **zh** leisure |
| **ā** ape | **ī** bite, fire | **u** up | **ŋ** ring |
| **ä** car, lot | **ō** go | **ur** fur | a *in* ago |
| **e** ten | **ô** law, horn | **ch** chin | e *in* agent |
| **er** care | **oi** oil | **sh** she | ə = i *in* unity |
| **ē** even | **oo** look | **th** thin | o *in* collect |
| **i** hit | **o͞o** tool | ***th*** then | u *in* focus |

**Ur** *the symbol for the chemical element* uranium.
**U·ral** (yoor′əl) **1** a river flowing from the Ural Mountains into the Caspian Sea. **2 Urals,** *pl. same as* **Ural Mountains.**
**Ural Mountains** a mountain system in the U.S.S.R., between Europe and Asia.
**u·ra·ni·um** (yoo rā′nē əm) ***n.*** a very hard, heavy metal that is a radioactive chemical element. It is used in producing atomic energy.
**U·ra·nus** (yoor′ə nəs *or* yoo rā′nəs) **1** a Greek god who was the symbol of heaven. **2** the third largest planet. It is the seventh in distance from the sun.
**ur·ban** (ur′bən) ***adj.*** of, living in, or having to do with cities or towns [*urban* dwellers].
**ur·bane** (ur bān′) ***adj.*** polite and courteous in a smooth, polished way; refined. —**ur·bane′ly *adv.***

> **Urbane** comes from a Latin word meaning "city." It was thought that people living in the city were more polite and less rough than those who lived in the country.

**ur·ban·i·ty** (ur ban′ə tē) ***n.*** the quality of being urbane; refined politeness.
**urban renewal** the fixing up of those areas of a city where there are slums or the buildings are old and run-down, as by clearing the land and building new housing projects.
**ur·chin** (ur′chin) ***n.*** a small boy, or a young child, especially one who is full of mischief.
**-ure** (ər) *a suffix meaning:* **1** act or result [An *enclosure* is the act or result of enclosing.] **2** condition of being [*Exposure* is the condition of being exposed.] **3** a thing or group that [A *legislature* is a group that legislates.]
**u·re·a** (yoo rē′ə) ***n.*** a substance found in urine or made artificially. It is used in making plastics, etc.
**u·re·thra** (yoo rē′thrə) ***n.*** the canal through which urine is passed from the bladder out of the body. In males, semen is also passed through the urethra.
**urge** (urj) ***v.*** **1** to plead with or encourage strongly to do something [We *urged* Sue to finish college.] **2** to force forward; drive [He *urged* his mule up the hill.] **3** to speak in favor of; recommend [to *urge* caution]. —**urged, urg′ing** ◆***n.*** a sudden feeling that makes one want to do something; impulse [an *urge* to sneeze; the *urge* to become a writer].
**ur·gen·cy** (ur′jən sē) ***n.*** **1** the condition of being urgent; need for quick action [the *urgency* of their need]. **2** a strong demand [The *urgency* of public opinion forced the President to resign.] —*pl.* **ur′gen·cies**
**ur·gent** (ur′jənt) ***adj.*** **1** needing quick action [an *urgent* situation]. **2** demanding in a strong and serious way; insistent [an *urgent* call for help]. —**ur′gent·ly *adv.***

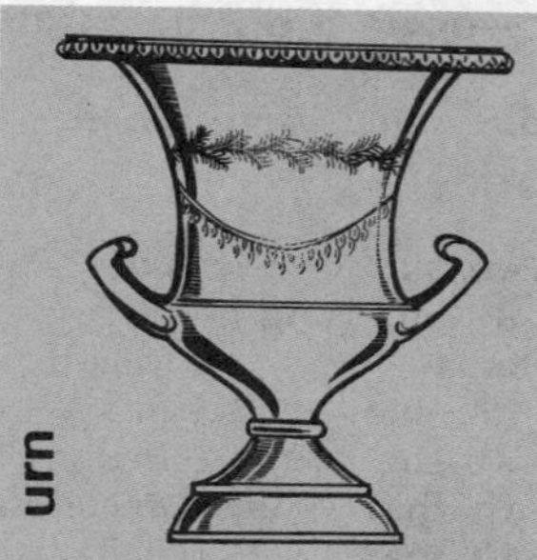
urn

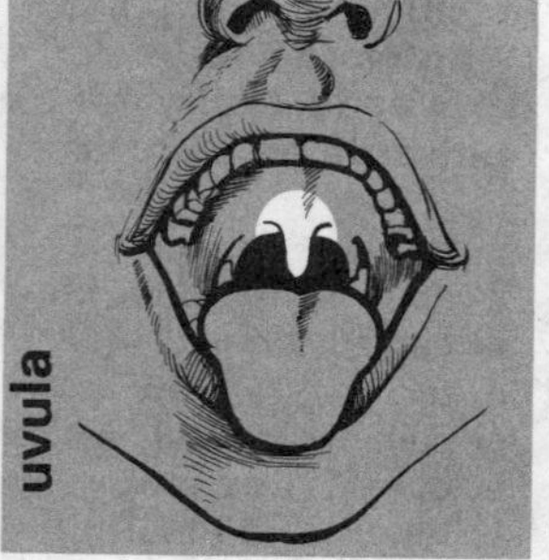
uvula

**u·ri·nal** (yoor′ə n′l) ***n.*** a fixture with a drain, used for urinating.
**u·ri·nar·y** (yoor′ə ner′ē) ***adj.*** of the organs that make and carry off urine.
**u·ri·nate** (yoor′ə nāt) ***v.*** to get rid of urine from the body. —**u′ri·nat·ed, u′ri·nat·ing**
**u·rine** (yoor′in) ***n.*** the liquid with waste products of the body that is passed by the kidneys into the bladder, from which it passes out of the body.
**urn** (urn) ***n.*** **1** a vase with a flat base or pedestal. *See the picture.* **2** a container for keeping the ashes of a cremated body. **3** a metal container with a faucet, for making and serving coffee or tea.
**U·ru·guay** (yoor′ə gwā) a country in southeastern South America. —**U′ru·guay′an *adj., n.***
**us** (us) ***pron.*** the form of **we** that is used as the object of a verb or preposition [They warned *us.* Write a letter to *us.*]
**U.S.** or **US** *abbreviation for* **United States.**
**USA** or **U.S.A.** **1** United States of America. **2** United States Army.
**us·a·ble** or **use·a·ble** (yōō′zə b′l) ***adj.*** that can be used; fit or ready for use.
**USAF** or **U.S.A.F.** United States Air Force.
**us·age** (yōō′sij *or* yōō′zij) ***n.*** **1** the act or way of using; treatment [His shoes were scuffed from hard *usage.*] **2** a practice followed for a long time; custom; habit. **3** the way in which a word or phrase is used ["A turkey" meaning "a failure" is a slang *usage.*]
**USCG** or **U.S.C.G.** United States Coast Guard.
**USDA** United States Department of Agriculture.
**use** (yōōz) ***v.*** **1** to put or bring into service or action [*Use* the vacuum cleaner on the rugs. What kind of toothpaste do you *use?*] **2** to deal with; treat [He *used* us badly.] **3** to do away with by using; consume [She *used* up all the soap. Don't *use* up your energy.] —**used, us′ing** ◆***n.*** (yōōs) **1** the act of using or condition of being used [the *use* of atomic energy for power; old tools still in *use*]. **2** the power to use [He lost the *use* of his hand.] **3** the right or permission to use [May I have the *use* of your car?] **4** the chance or need to use [Give away what you have no *use* for.] **5** a way of using [to be taught the *use* of the typewriter]. **6** benefit or advantage; usefulness [What's the *use* of your worrying?] —**make use of** or **put to use,** to use. —**used to,** **1** did in an earlier time; did once [I *used to* live in El Paso.] **2** accustomed to; familiar with [She's *used to* hard work.] —**us′er *n.***
**used** (yōōzd) ***adj.*** that has been used; not new; secondhand [*used* cars].
**use·ful** (yōōs′fəl) ***adj.*** that can be used; of service; helpful [*useful* advice]. —**use′ful·ly *adv.*** —**use′ful·ness *n.***
**use·less** (yōōs′lis) ***adj.*** having no use; worthless [It is *useless* for you to complain.] —**use′less·ly *adv.*** —**use′less·ness *n.***
**ush·er** (ush′ər) ***n.*** a person who shows people to their seats in a church, theater, etc. ◆***v.*** to show the way or bring in [He *ushered* us to our seats. The landing on the moon *ushered* in a new age.]
**U.S.M.** or **USM** United States Mail.
**USMC** or **U.S.M.C.** United States Marine Corps.
**USN** or **U.S.N.** United States Navy.

**U.S.S.R.** or **USSR** *abbreviation for* **Union of Soviet Socialist Republics.**

**u·su·al** (yo͞o′zhoo wəl) ***adj.*** such as is most often seen, heard, used, etc.; common; ordinary; normal. —**as usual,** in the usual way. —**u′su·al·ly *adv.***

SYNONYMS: We use **usual** in speaking of something that we have learned from experience is the normal or common thing to expect [We got the *usual* results. They gave their *usual* greeting.] We use **customary** for something which fits in with the usual ways of doing things or with the customs of a group [I had my *customary* coffee break at 10. It was *customary* for everyone to dress up for a party.] *See also* SYNONYMS *at* **typical.**

**u·surp** (yo͞o surp′ *or* yo͞o zurp′) ***v.*** to take and hold by force or without right [to *usurp* another's power or position]. —**u′sur·pa′tion *n.*** —**u·surp′er *n.***

**u·su·ry** (yo͞o′zhoo rē) ***n.*** **1** the act or practice of lending money at a rate of interest that is too high or against the law. **2** such a rate of interest. —**u′su·rer *n.*** —**u·su·ri·ous** (yo͞o zhoor′ē əs) ***adj.***

**U·tah** (yo͞o′tô *or* yo͞o′tä) a State in the southwestern part of the U.S.: abbreviated **Ut., UT**

**u·ten·sil** (yo͞o ten′s'l) ***n.*** a container, tool, etc. used for a special purpose [Pots, pans, egg beaters, can openers, etc. are kitchen *utensils.*] *See* SYNONYMS *at* **implement.**

**u·ter·us** (yo͞ot′ər əs) ***n.*** a hollow organ of female mammals in which the young grow before birth; womb. —*pl.* **u·ter·i** (yo͞ot′ər ī) —**u·ter·ine** (yo͞ot′ər in) ***adj.***

**u·til·i·tar·i·an** (yoo til′ə ter′ē ən) ***adj.*** **1** of or having utility; useful; practical. **2** stressing usefulness over beauty, etc.

**u·til·i·ty** (yoo til′ə tē) ***n.*** **1** the quality of being useful; usefulness. **2** something useful to the public, as the service of gas, water, etc.; also, a company that provides such a service: *also called* **public utility.** —*pl.* **u·til′i·ties** ✦***adj.*** useful or used in a number of different ways [a *utility* knife].

☆**utility room** a room containing various household appliances and equipment, as for heating, laundry, or cleaning.

**u·ti·lize** (yo͞o′t'l īz) ***v.*** to put to use; make practical use of [to *utilize* atomic power for peaceful purposes]. —**u′ti·lized, u′ti·liz·ing** —**u′ti·li·za′tion *n.***

**ut·most** (ut′mōst) ***adj.*** **1** most distant; farthest [the *utmost* regions of the earth]. **2** greatest or highest [a meeting of the *utmost* importance]. ✦***n.*** the most that is possible [He strained his muscles to the *utmost.*]

**U·to·pi·a** or **u·to·pi·a** (yoo tō′pē ə) ***n.*** **1** any imaginary place where life is perfect and everyone is happy. **2** any scheme for such a perfect society, that is not really practical or possible. —**U·to′pi·an** or **u·to′pi·an *adj., n.***

**Utopia** is an imaginary island described in a book of the same name by Sir Thomas More in 1516. The people on the island had a perfect way of life. More made the name up from two Greek words meaning "not a place."

**ut·ter¹** (ut′ər) ***adj.*** complete; total; absolute [*utter* joy; an *utter* fool]. —**ut′ter·ly *adv.***

**ut·ter²** (ut′ər) ***v.*** to make or express with the voice [to *utter* a cry; to *utter* a thought].

**ut·ter·ance** (ut′ər əns) ***n.*** **1** the act or way of uttering [to give *utterance* to an idea]. **2** a word or words uttered; something said.

**ut·ter·most** (ut′ər mōst) ***adj., n.*** *same as* **utmost.**

**U-turn** (yo͞o′turn′) ***n.*** a turning completely around, especially of a car or truck within the width of a street, so as to head in the opposite direction.

**u·vu·la** (yo͞o′vyə lə) ***n.*** the small part of the soft palate hanging down above the back of the tongue. *See the picture.* —*pl.* **u′vu·las** or **u·vu·lae** (yo͞o′vyə lē)

# V v

**V, v** (vē) ***n.*** the twenty-second letter of the English alphabet. —*pl.* **V's, v's** (vēz)

**V** (vē) ***n.*** the Roman numeral for five.

**V** *the symbol for the chemical element* vanadium.

**V** or **v** *abbreviation for* **velocity, volt** *or* **volts.**

**v.** *abbreviation for* **verb, verse, versus.**

**VA** or **V.A.** Veterans Administration.

**Va.** or **VA** *abbreviation for* **Virginia.**

**va·can·cy** (vā′kən sē) ***n.*** **1** a job or position for which someone is needed. **2** a place to live in that is for rent. **3** the condition of being vacant; emptiness. **4** lack of interest or thought. —*pl.* **va′can·cies**

**va·cant** (vā′kənt) ***adj.*** **1** having nothing or no one in it; empty [a *vacant* lot; a *vacant* seat; a *vacant* house]. **2** free from work; leisure [a *vacant* period in the day]. **3** without interest or thought [a *vacant* stare; a *vacant* mind]. —**va′cant·ly *adv.***

**va·cate** (vā′kāt) ***v.*** to make a place empty, as by leaving [You must *vacate* your room by noon.] —**va′cat·ed, va′cat·ing**

**va·ca·tion** (və kā′shən *or* vā kā′shən) ***n.*** ☆a period of time when one stops working, going to school, etc.

| | | | | | | | |
|---|---|---|---|---|---|---|---|
| **a** | fat | **ir** | here | **ou** | out | **zh** | leisure |
| **ā** | ape | **ī** | bite, fire | **u** | up | **ŋ** | ring |
| **ä** | car, lot | **ō** | go | **ur** | fur | | a *in* ago |
| **e** | ten | **ô** | law, horn | **ch** | chin | | e *in* agent |
| **er** | care | **oi** | oil | **sh** | she | **ə =** | i *in* unity |
| **ē** | even | **oo** | look | **th** | thin | | o *in* collect |
| **i** | hit | **o͞o** | tool | ***th*** | then | | u *in* focus |

in order to rest and have recreation. ◆*v.* to take one's vacation.

☆**va·ca·tion·er** (və kā′shən ər *or* vā kā′shən ər) ***n.*** a person taking a vacation: *also* **va·ca′tion·ist.**

**vac·ci·nate** (vak′sə nāt) ***v.*** to inject a vaccine into, in order to keep from getting a certain disease, as smallpox. —**vac′ci·nat·ed, vac′ci·nat·ing**

**vac·ci·na·tion** (vak′sə nā′shən) ***n.*** **1** the act of vaccinating. **2** the scar on the skin where a vaccine has been injected.

**vac·cine** (vak sēn′) ***n.*** any substance, made up of bacteria, a virus, etc. that has been killed or weakened, put into the body to keep away a disease. The substance causes a mild form of the disease and the body builds up the ability to fight off the disease later.

> **Vaccine** comes from the Latin word for "cow." The word *vaccine* was used at first to mean only the kind of substance used to prevent smallpox. It was made from a mild virus of cowpox.

**vac·il·late** (vas′ə lāt) ***v.*** **1** to be unable to decide; keep changing one's mind [to *vacillate* between going and staying]. **2** to sway to and fro; waver [The pointer on the scales *vacillated.*] —**vac′il·lat·ed, vac′il·lat·ing —vac′il·la′tion *n.***

**va·cu·i·ty** (va kyōō′ə tē) ***n.*** **1** the condition of being empty; emptiness. **2** empty space; vacuum. **3** emptiness of mind; stupidity. —*pl.* **va·cu′i·ties**

**vac·u·ous** (vak′yoo wəs) ***adj.*** **1** showing little intelligence; stupid. **2** with nothing in it; empty.

818 **vac·u·um** (vak′yoo wəm *or* vak′yoom) ***n.*** **1** a space, as in a bottle or tube, from which most of the air or gas has been taken. **2** a space that has nothing at all in it. ☆**3** *a shorter name for* **vacuum cleaner.** ◆***v.*** to clean with a vacuum cleaner.

**vacuum bottle** a bottle with a vacuum between its inner and outer walls, keeping liquids at almost the same temperature for a time; thermos.

**vacuum cleaner** a machine that cleans rugs, furniture, etc. by sucking up the dirt.

**vacuum tube** an electron tube from which as much air has been taken out as possible.

**vag·a·bond** (vag′ə bänd) ***n.*** **1** a person who moves from place to place. **2** *another name for* **tramp.** ◆***adj.*** **1** wandering from place to place [a *vagabond* tribe]. **2** of or having to do with a drifting, carefree life [*vagabond* habits].

**va·gar·y** (və ger′ē *or* vā′gər ē) ***n.*** an odd or unexpected idea or act; whim. —*pl.* **va·gar′ies**

**va·gi·na** (və jī′nə) ***n.*** the canal leading into the uterus. —**vag·i·nal** (vaj′ə n′l *or* və jī′n′l) ***adj.***

**va·gran·cy** (vā′grən sē) ***n.*** the condition of being a vagrant.

**va·grant** (vā′grənt) ***n.*** a person who wanders from place to place, doing odd jobs or begging; tramp. ◆***adj.*** wandering from place to place, or living the life of a vagrant.

**vague** (vāg) ***adj.*** not clear, definite, or distinct, as in form, meaning, or purpose [*vague* figures in the fog; a *vague* answer]. —**va′guer, va′guest —vague′ly *adv.* —vague′ness *n.***

**vain** (vān) ***adj.*** **1** having too high an opinion of oneself; conceited [He is *vain* about his looks.] **2** with little or no result; not successful [a *vain* attempt to climb the mountain]. *See* SYNONYMS *at* **futile. 3** worthless; having no real value or meaning [*vain* promises]. —**in vain, 1** without success [I pleaded *in vain* for help.] **2** without the proper respect; in a profane way [to use the name of God *in vain*]. —**vain′ly *adv.***

**vain·glo·ri·ous** (vān′glôr′ē əs) ***adj.*** feeling or showing pride in a boastful way.

**vain·glo·ry** (vān′glôr′ē *or* vān glôr′ē) ***n.*** boastful pride.

**val·ance** (val′əns) ***n.*** **1** a short curtain hanging from the edge of a bed, shelf, etc. **2** a short drapery or a covering of wood or metal across the top of a window. *See the picture.*

**vale** (vāl) ***n.*** *another word for* **valley:** *used mainly in older poetry.*

☆**val·e·dic·to·ri·an** (val′ə dik tôr′ē ən) ***n.*** a student, usually the one with the highest grades, who gives the farewell speech at graduation.

**val·e·dic·to·ry** (val′ə dik′tər ē) ☆***n.*** a farewell speech, especially one given at graduation. —*pl.* **val′e·dic′to·ries** ◆***adj.*** saying farewell.

**va·lence** (vā′ləns) ***n.*** the power of an element or radical to combine with another to form molecules. It is measured by the number of hydrogen or chlorine atoms which one radical or one atom of the element will combine with [Oxygen has a *valence* of two, so that one atom of oxygen combines with two hydrogen atoms to form the water molecule, $H_2O$.]

**Val·en·tine** (val′ən tīn), Saint, a Christian martyr of the 3d century A.D., whose day is February 14. It is the custom to send valentines on this day.

**val·en·tine** (val′ən tīn) ***n.*** **1** a greeting card or gift sent on Saint Valentine's Day. **2** a sweetheart to whom one sends a valentine.

**val·et** (val′it *or* val′ā) ***n.*** a man who works as a servant to another man, taking care of his clothes, helping him dress, etc. ◆***adj.*** describing a service, as in a hotel, for cleaning and pressing clothes, etc.

**Val·hal·la** (val hal′ə) the great hall in Norse myths, where Odin feasts the souls of heroes killed in battle.

**val·iant** (val′yənt) ***adj.*** brave; full of courage [a *valiant* struggle for freedom]. —**val′iant·ly *adv.***

**val·id** (val′id) ***adj.*** **1** based on facts or good reasoning; true or sound [a *valid* argument]. **2** binding under law; having legal force [a *valid* deed or will].

**val·i·date** (val′ə dāt) ***v.*** **1** to make valid in law, as a will. **2** to prove to be valid, or sound, true, etc.; confirm [A witness to the accident *validated* my story.] —**val′i·dat·ed, val′i·dat·ing**

**va·lid·i·ty** (və lid′ə tē) ***n.*** the quality or fact of being valid, as in law.

**va·lise** (və lēs′) ***n.*** a piece of hand luggage; suitcase: *an old-fashioned word.*

**Val·kyr·ie** (val kir′ē) any of the maidens in Norse myths who lead the souls of heroes killed in battle to Valhalla.

**val·ley** (val′ē) ***n.*** **1** low land lying between hills or mountains. **2** the land that is drained or watered by a large river and its branches [the Mississippi *valley*]. —*pl.* **val′leys**

**Valley Forge** a village in southeastern Pennsylvania, where Washington and his troops camped in the winter of 1777–1778.

**val·or** (val′ər) ***n.*** courage or bravery, as in battle. —**val′or·ous *adj.***

**Val·pa·rai·so** (val′pə rā′zō *or* val′pə rī′sō) a seaport in central Chile.

**val·u·a·ble** (val′yoo b'l *or* val′yoo wə b'l) ***adj.*** **1** having value or worth; especially, worth much money [a *valuable* diamond]. **2** thought of as precious, useful, worthy, etc. [*valuable* knowledge]. ◆***n.*** something of value, as a piece of jewelry.

**val·u·a·tion** (val′yoo wā′shən) ***n.*** **1** the act of deciding the value of something; appraisal [We took the pearls to a jeweler for a *valuation.*] **2** the value set on something [The car was sold for less than its *valuation.*]

**val·ue** (val′yo͞o) ***n.*** **1** the quality of a thing that makes it wanted or desirable; worth [the *value* of true friendship]. **2** the worth of a thing in money or in other goods [The *value* of our house has gone up.] **3** buying power [the changing *value* of the dollar]. **4** a fair or proper exchange [I'm willing to pay for *value* received.] **5 values,** *pl.* beliefs or ideals [the moral *values* of a nation]. ◆***v.*** **1** to set or estimate the value of [The property was *valued* at $20,000.] **2** to think of or rate, as compared with other things [I *value* health above wealth.] **3** to think highly of [I *value* your friendship.] *See* SYNONYMS *at* **appreciate.** —**val′ued, val′u·ing** —**val′ue·less *adj.***

**val·ued** (val′yo͞od) ***adj.*** **1** having been given a price, value, etc. [a hat *valued* at $10]. **2** highly thought of [a *valued* friend].

**valve** (valv) ***n.*** **1** a device, as in a pipe, that controls the flow of a gas or liquid by means of a flap, lid, or plug that closes off the pipe. *See the picture.* **2** a membrane in the body that acts in this way [The *valves* of the heart let the blood flow in one direction only.] **3** a device, as in a trumpet, that opens a branch to the main tube so as to change the pitch. **4** one of the parts making up the shell of a clam, oyster, etc.

**vamp** (vamp) ***n.*** **1** the top part of a shoe or boot covering the front of the foot. **2** something patched up to look new. ◆***v.*** to repair, as with a new vamp.

**vam·pire** (vam′pīr) ***n.*** **1** in folk tales, a dead body that moves about at night and sucks the blood of sleeping persons. **2** a person who gets things from others in a wicked or evil way. **3** a tropical American bat that lives on the blood of other animals: *the full name is* **vampire bat.**

**van**[1] (van) ***n.*** *a shorter word for* **vanguard.**

**van**[2] (van) ***n.*** a closed truck for moving furniture, carrying freight or people, etc.

**va·na·di·um** (və nā′dē əm) ***n.*** a silver-white metal that is a chemical element. It is used in making a steel alloy (**vanadium steel**) that is especially hard.

**Van Bu·ren** (van byoor′ən), **Martin** 1782–1862; the eighth president of the United States, from 1837 to 1841.

**Van·cou·ver** (van ko͞o′vər) **1** a seaport in British Columbia, Canada. **2** an island of British Columbia, off the southwestern coast.

**Van·dal** (van′d'l) ***n.*** **1** a member of a Germanic tribe that invaded Italy and plundered Rome in 455 A.D. **2 vandal,** a person who destroys or damages things on purpose, especially works of art, public property, etc. ◆***adj.*** of the Vandals.

**van·dal·ism** (van′d'l iz'm) ***n.*** the actions or attitudes of a vandal; brutal destruction.

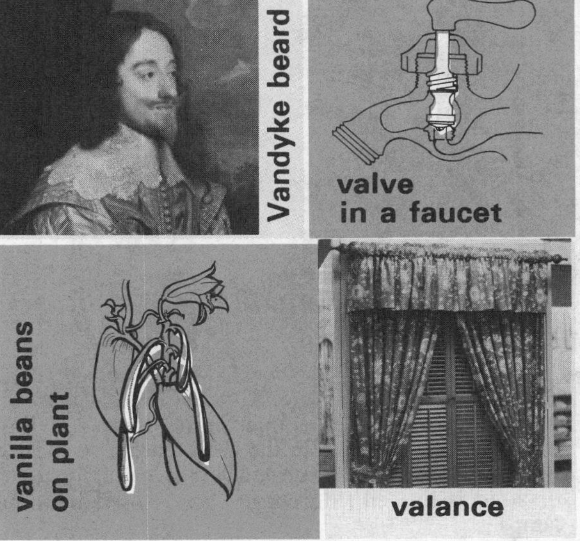

Vandyke beard

valve in a faucet

vanilla beans on plant

valance

**van·dal·ize** (van′d'l īz) ***v.*** to destroy or damage as a vandal does. —**van′dal·ized, van′dal·iz·ing**

**Van·dyke beard** (van dīk′) a closely trimmed beard that comes to a point. *See the picture.*

**vane** (vān) ***n.*** **1** a flat metal object on a pole, that swings with the wind to show which way it is blowing; weather vane. **2** any of the blades of a windmill, elec- **819**
tric fan, propeller, etc.

**van Gogh** (van gō′), **Vincent** 1853–1890; Dutch painter.

**van·guard** (van′gärd) ***n.*** **1** the front part of an army going forward. **2** the leaders of a movement, or the leading position in a movement.

**va·nil·la** (və nil′ə) ***n.*** **1** a flavoring made from the pods of an orchid that twines around trees, etc. **2** this plant, or any of its pods, called **vanilla beans.** *See the picture.*

**van·ish** (van′ish) ***v.*** **1** to go suddenly out of sight; disappear [The sun *vanished* beneath the horizon.] *See* SYNONYMS *at* **disappear. 2** to stop existing; come to an end [The passenger pigeon has *vanished.*]

**van·i·ty** (van′ə tē) ***n.*** **1** the quality of being vain or conceited about oneself, one's looks, etc. **2** the condition of being vain or worthless, or any worthless thing. —*pl.* **van′i·ties**

**van·quish** (vaŋ′kwish) ***v.*** to overcome or defeat; conquer.

**van·tage** (van′tij) ***n.*** **1** a favorable position; advantage [Capturing the hill gave our troops a point of *vantage.*] **2** a position that allows a clear and broad view: *also called* **vantage point.**

**vap·id** (vap′id) ***adj.*** **1** having no taste or flavor; flat [a *vapid* drink]. **2** not exciting; dull [*vapid* talk].

| | | | | | | | |
|---|---|---|---|---|---|---|---|
| **a** | fat | **ir** | here | **ou** | out | **zh** | leisure |
| **ā** | ape | **ī** | bite, fire | **u** | up | **ŋ** | ring |
| **ä** | car, lot | **ō** | go | **ʉr** | fur | | a *in* ago |
| **e** | ten | **ô** | law, horn | **ch** | chin | | e *in* agent |
| **er** | care | **oi** | oil | **sh** | she | **ə =** | i *in* unity |
| **ē** | even | **oo** | look | **th** | thin | | o *in* collect |
| **i** | hit | **o͞o** | tool | ***th*** | then | | u *in* focus |

V

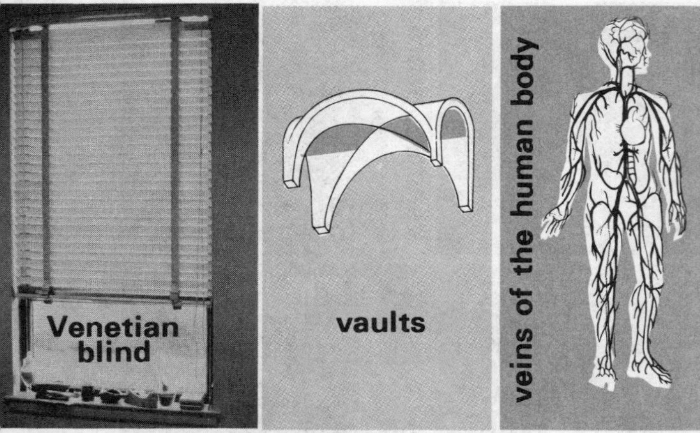


**va·por** (vā′pər) ***n.*** **1** a thick mist or mass of tiny drops of water floating in the air, as steam or fog. **2** the gas formed when a substance that is usually liquid or solid is heated [Mercury *vapor* is used in some lamps.]

**va·por·ize** (vā′pə rīz) ***v.*** to change into vapor, as by spraying or being heated [Atomizers are used to *vaporize* perfume. The water *vaporized* in the sun.] —**va′por·ized, va′por·iz·ing** —**va′por·iz·er** ***n.***

**va·por·ous** (vā′pər əs) ***adj.*** **1** forming or full of vapor [a *vaporous* marsh]. **2** like vapor. **3** imaginary or fanciful [*vaporous* ideas].



☆**va·que·ro** (vä ker′ō) ***n.*** a man who herds cattle; cowboy: *a word used in the Southwest.* —*pl.* **va·que′ros**

**var·i·a·ble** (ver′ē ə b'l) ***adj.*** **1** likely to change or vary; changeable [in a *variable* mood]. **2** that can be changed or varied [a *variable* price]. ◆***n.*** anything that changes or varies, as a shifting wind. —**var·i·a·bil·i·ty** (ver′ē ə bil′ə tē) ***n.***

**var·i·ance** (ver′ē əns) ***n.*** the act or amount of varying, or changing. —**at variance,** disagreeing; differing.

**var·i·ant** (ver′ē ənt) ***adj.*** different in some way from others of the same kind ["Theatre" is a *variant* spelling of "theater."] ◆***n.*** a variant form, spelling, etc.

**var·i·a·tion** (ver′ē ā′shən) ***n.*** **1** the act of varying, changing, or differing [a *variation* in style]. **2** the amount of a change [a *variation* of ten feet]. **3** the repeating of a tune or musical theme, with changes as in rhythm or key.

**var·i·col·ored** (ver′i kul′ərd) ***adj.*** of several or many colors.

**var·i·cose** (ver′ə kōs) ***adj.*** swollen at irregular places [*varicose* veins].

**var·ied** (ver′ēd) ***adj.*** **1** of different kinds [a program of *varied* entertainment]. **2** showing differences, as of color. **3** changed; altered.

**var·i·e·gat·ed** (ver′ē ə gāt′id *or* ver′ə gāt′id) ***adj.*** **1** marked with different colors in spots, streaks, or patches [*variegated* tulips]. **2** having variety; varied. —**var′i·e·ga′tion** ***n.***

**va·ri·e·ty** (və rī′ə tē) ***n.*** **1** change; lack of sameness [I like *variety* in my meals.] **2** any of the various forms of something; sort; kind [many *varieties* of cloth; a cat of the striped *variety*]. **3** a number of different kinds [a *variety* of fruits at the market]. —*pl.* **va·ri′e·ties**

**variety show** a show, as on TV, made up of different kinds of acts, as comic skits, songs, dances, etc.

**var·i·ous** (ver′ē əs) ***adj.*** **1** of several different kinds [We planted *various* seeds.] **2** several or many [*Various* people have said so.] —**var′i·ous·ly** ***adv.***

**var·let** (vär′lit) ***n.*** a rascal or knave; scoundrel: *now seldom used.*

**var·nish** (vär′nish) ***n.*** **1** a liquid made of gums or resins mixed in oil, alcohol, or turpentine and spread over a surface to give it a hard and glossy coat. **2** this hard and glossy coat. **3** an outward show or look of smoothness or polish; gloss [a *varnish* of politeness]. ◆***v.*** **1** to cover with varnish. **2** to smooth over in a false way [to *varnish* a lie with an innocent look].

**var·si·ty** (vär′sə tē) ***n.*** the team that represents a college or school in games or contests against others. —*pl.* **var′si·ties**

**var·y** (ver′ē) ***v.*** **1** to change; make or become different [She *varies* her hair style. The weather has *varied* from day to day.] **2** to be different; differ [Opinions *vary* on this matter.] **3** to give variety to [*Vary* your reading.] —**var′ied, var′y·ing**

**vas·cu·lar** (vas′kyə lər) ***adj.*** of or having vessels for carrying blood, lymph, or sap.

**vase** (vās *or* vāz) ***n.*** an open container used for decoration or for holding flowers.

☆**Vas·e·line** (vas′ə lēn) *a trademark for* a white or yellow jelly made from petroleum and used as a salve or ointment.

**vas·sal** (vas″l) ***n.*** **1** a person in the feudal system who held land in return for military or other help to an overlord. **2** a person or country that owes service or loyalty to another; servant, dependent, subject, etc. ◆***adj.*** of or like a vassal. —**vas′sal·age** ***n.***

**vast** (vast) ***adj.*** very great or very large [a *vast* desert; a matter of *vast* importance]. —**vast′ly** ***adv.*** —**vast′ness** ***n.***

**vat** (vat) ***n.*** a large tank, tub, or cask for holding liquids.

**Vat·i·can** (vat′i k'n) **1** the palace of the Pope in Vatican City. **2** the office, power, or government of the Pope.

**Vatican City** a state inside the city of Rome, with the Pope as its head.

**vaude·ville** (vōd′vil *or* vôd′vil) ***n.*** ☆a stage show made up of different kinds of acts, as comic skits, songs, dances, etc.

> The word **vaudeville** was French to begin with. It comes to us from *Vau-de-Vire,* the name of a valley in Normandy, France. The people of the valley have been famous for their light, merry songs.

**vault**[1] (vôlt) ***n.*** **1** an arched ceiling or roof. *See the picture.* **2** a room with such a ceiling, or a space that seems to have an arch [the *vault* of the sky]. ☆**3** a room for keeping money, valuable papers, etc. safe, as in a bank. **4** a burial chamber. **5** a room in a cellar for storing things. ◆***v.*** **1** to cover with a vault [to *vault* a passageway]. **2** to build in the form of a vault [to *vault* a roof]. **3** to curve like a vault [The bridge *vaults* above the river.]

**vault**[2] (vôlt) ***v.*** to jump or leap over, as a fence or bar, by resting one's hands on the fence, etc. or by using a long pole to push oneself from the ground. *See also* **pole vault.**

**vault·ing** (vôl′ting) ***adj.*** **1** that vaults or leaps. **2** reaching too far or beyond one's abilities [*vaulting* ambition].

**vaunt** (vônt) ***v., n.*** boast or brag. —**vaunt′ed *adj.***

**VD** or **V.D.** venereal disease.

**veal** (vēl) ***n.*** the flesh of a calf, used as meat.

**veer** (vir) ***v.*** **1** to change direction; shift; turn [*Veer* to the left at the fork in the road.] **2** to change the course of; turn [to *veer* a ship]. ✦***n.*** a change of direction.

**veg·e·ta·ble** (vej′tə b'l *or* vej′ə tə b'l) ***n.*** **1** a plant or part of a plant that is eaten raw, as in a salad, or cooked and served with meat, etc. [Tomatoes, potatoes, peas, and lettuce are all *vegetables.*] **2** any plant [Is seaweed an animal, *vegetable,* or mineral?] **3** a person thought of as like a vegetable, as because of having lost the use of the mind. ✦***adj.*** **1** of, like, or from vegetables [*vegetable* oil]. **2** having to do with plants in general [the *vegetable* kingdom].

**veg·e·tar·i·an** (vej′ə ter′ē ən) ***n.*** a person who chooses to eat no meat and eats mainly vegetables. ✦***adj.*** **1** having to do with vegetarians or their ways of eating. **2** made up only of vegetables. —**veg′e·tar′i·an·ism *n.***

**veg·e·tate** (vej′ə tāt) ***v.*** to live or grow as a plant does; especially, to lead a dull life with little action or thought. —**veg′e·tat·ed, veg′e·tat·ing**

**veg·e·ta·tion** (vej′ə tā′shən) ***n.*** **1** things growing from the ground; plant life [thick *vegetation* in the jungle]. **2** the act of vegetating.

**veg·e·ta·tive** (vej′ə tāt′iv) ***adj.*** **1** having to do with plants, or growing as plants do [*vegetative* forms of life]. **2** dull and not very active [a *vegetative* life].

**ve·he·ment** (vē′ə mənt) ***adj.*** **1** full of deep, strong feeling; intense [a *vehement* argument]. **2** acting or moving with great force; violent [a *vehement* storm]. —**ve′he·mence *n.*** —**ve′he·ment·ly *adv.***

**ve·hi·cle** (vē′ə k'l) ***n.*** **1** a means of carrying persons or things, especially over land or in space, as an automobile, bicycle, spacecraft, etc. **2** a means by which something is expressed, passed along, etc. [TV is a *vehicle* for advertising.] **3** a liquid, as oil or water, with which pigments are mixed to make paint.

**veil** (vāl) ***n.*** **1** a piece of thin cloth, as net or gauze, worn especially by women over the face or head to hide the features, as a decoration, or as part of a uniform [a bride's *veil;* a nun's *veil*]. **2** something that covers or hides [a *veil* of mist over the valley; a *veil* of silence]. ✦***v.*** to cover, hide, etc. with or as if with a veil. —**take the veil,** to become a nun.

**vein** (vān) ***n.*** **1** any blood vessel that carries blood back to the heart from some part of the body. *See the picture and also the entry for* **artery**. **2** any of the fine lines, or ribs, in a leaf or in an insect's wing. **3** a layer of mineral, rock, etc. formed in a crack in different rock [a *vein* of silver or of coal]. **4** a streak of a different color or material, as in marble. **5** a state of mind; mood [She spoke in a serious *vein.*] **6** a trace or quality [His writing has a *vein* of humor.] ✦***v.*** to mark as with veins [a cheese heavily *veined* with mold].

**veld** or **veldt** (velt) ***n.*** any grassy region in South Africa with few bushes or trees.

**vel·lum** (vel′əm) ***n.*** **1** the best kind of parchment, used for writing on or for binding books. **2** paper made to look like this.

**ve·loc·i·ty** (və läs′ə tē) ***n.*** **1** rate of motion; speed [a wind *velocity* of 15 miles per hour]. **2** quickness of motion; swiftness [to move with great *velocity*].

**ve·lour** or **ve·lours** (və loor′) ***n.*** a cloth with a soft nap like velvet. It is used for upholstery, drapes, hats, etc. —*pl.* **ve·lours** (və loorz′)

**vel·vet** (vel′vit) ***n.*** a cloth of silk, rayon, nylon, etc. with a soft, thick nap on one side. It is used for clothing, drapes, etc. ✦***adj.*** **1** made of velvet. **2** soft or smooth like velvet. —**vel′vet·y *adj.***

**vel·vet·een** (vel və tēn′) ***n.*** a cotton cloth with a short, thick nap, like velvet.

**ve·nal** (vē′n'l) ***adj.*** **1** that is easily bribed; willing to do wrong things for payment [a *venal* senator]. **2** marked by bribery; corrupt [*venal* politics]. —**ve·nal·i·ty** (vē nal′ə tē) ***n.***

> **Venal** comes from a Latin word meaning "for sale." A venal person is "for sale" to anyone willing to pay the price. **Venal** is sometimes mistaken for **venial,** which comes from a totally different Latin word meaning "forgivable."

**vend** (vend) ***v.*** to sell, especially by peddling.

**ven·det·ta** (ven det′ə) ***n.*** a feud in which the family of a person who has been killed or harmed tries to get revenge on the family of the person who caused the harm.

**vending machine** a machine for selling small things, as candy, fruit, notions, etc. It is worked by putting coins in a slot.



**ven·dor** or **vend·er** (ven′dər) ***n.*** a person who sells; seller [She is a *vendor* of drinks at baseball games.]

**ve·neer** (və nir′) ***v.*** to cover a common material with a thin layer of fine wood or costly material [piano keys *veneered* with ivory]. ✦***n.*** **1** a thin layer of fine wood or costly material put over a common material [a walnut *veneer* on a pine chest]. **2** an outward look or show that hides what is below [a coarse person with a thin *veneer* of culture].

**ven·er·a·ble** (ven′ər ə b'l) ***adj.*** that should be respected or honored because of old age, fine character, etc. [a *venerable* scholar].

**ven·er·ate** (ven′ə rāt) ***v.*** to feel or show great respect for; revere [The children *venerated* their aunt.] —**ven′er·at·ed, ven′er·at·ing** —**ven′er·a′tion *n.***

**ve·ne·re·al** (və nir′ē əl) ***adj.*** describing any of certain diseases that can be passed on during sexual intercourse, as syphilis.

**Ve·ne·tian** (və nē′shən) ***adj.*** of Venice. ✦***n.*** a person born or living in Venice.

**Venetian blind** or **venetian blind** a window blind made of a number of thin slats that can be set at any angle, by pulling cords, to control the amount of light or air passing through. *See the picture.*

**Ven·e·zue·la** (ven′i zwā′lə *or* ven′i zwē′lə) a country in northern South America. —**Ven′e·zue′lan *adj., n.***

| | | | | | | | |
|---|---|---|---|---|---|---|---|
| **a** | fat | **ir** | here | **ou** | out | **zh** | leisure |
| **ā** | ape | **ī** | bite, fire | **u** | up | **ng** | ring |
| **ä** | car, lot | **ō** | go | **ur** | fur | | a *in* ago |
| **e** | ten | **ô** | law, horn | **ch** | chin | | e *in* agent |
| **er** | care | **oi** | oil | **sh** | she | ə = | i *in* unity |
| **ē** | even | **oo** | look | **th** | thin | | o *in* collect |
| **i** | hit | **o͞o** | tool | ***th*** | then | | u *in* focus |

**venge·ance** (ven′jəns) ***n.*** the act of getting even for a wrong or injury; punishment in return for harm done; revenge. —**with a vengeance,** **1** with great force or fury. **2** very much or too much [She started in eating *with a vengeance.*]

**venge·ful** (venj′fəl) ***adj.*** wanting or trying to get revenge. —**venge′ful·ly** ***adv.***

**ve·ni·al** (vē′nē əl *or* vēn′yəl) ***adj.*** that can be forgiven or excused; not serious; minor [a *venial* fault]. *See the note at* **venal.**

**Ven·ice** (ven′is) a seaport in northeastern Italy, built on many small islands, with canals running between them.

**ven·i·son** (ven′i s'n *or* ven′i z'n) ***n.*** the flesh of a deer, used as meat.

**ven·om** (ven′əm) ***n.*** **1** the poison of some snakes, spiders, scorpions, etc. **2** bitter feeling; spite; malice [a look full of *venom*].

**ven·om·ous** (ven′əm əs) ***adj.*** **1** full of venom; poisonous [a *venomous* snake]. **2** full of spite or ill will; hurtful [a *venomous* reply].

**vent**[1] (vent) ***n.*** **1** an opening or passage for gas, air, etc. to pass through or escape. **2** a way of letting something out; outlet [He gave *vent* to his good spirits by laughing.] ◆***v.*** **1** to make a vent in or for [to *vent* a clothes dryer to let the steam escape]. **2** to let out at an opening [to *vent* fumes from a room]. **3** to let out freely, as in words or action [She *vented* her wrath upon us.]



**vent**[2] (vent) ***n.*** a slit in a garment, as at the back or sides of a coat. *See the picture.*

**ven·ti·late** (ven′t'l āt) ***v.*** **1** to get fresh air to move into or through [Open the windows to *ventilate* the room.] **2** to bring into full and open discussion [to *ventilate* a problem]. —**ven′ti·lat·ed, ven′ti·lat·ing** —**ven′ti·la′tion** ***n.***

**ven·ti·la·tor** (ven′t'l āt ər) ***n.*** an opening or device for bringing in fresh air and driving out stale air.

**ven·tral** (ven′trəl) ***adj.*** of, on, or near the side of the body where the belly is.

**ven·tri·cle** (ven′tri k'l) ***n.*** either of the two lower sections of the heart. The blood flows from these into the arteries.

**ven·tril·o·quism** (ven tril′ə kwiz'm) ***n.*** the art or act of speaking without moving the lips much, so that the voice seems to come from another point, as from a puppet or dummy held by the speaker. —**ven·tril′o·quist** ***n.*** *See the picture.*

> The word **ventriloquism** comes from two Latin words which together mean "to speak from the belly." The ancient Romans thought that a ventriloquist's voice came from the stomach.

**ven·ture** (ven′chər) ***n.*** an activity or undertaking in which there is a risk of losing something [a business *venture*]. ◆***v.*** **1** to place in danger; risk the loss of [to *venture* one's life, a fortune, etc.] **2** to dare to say or do [She *ventured* the opinion that we were wrong.] **3** to go in spite of some risk [They *ventured* out on the ice.] —**ven′tured, ven′tur·ing**

**ven·ture·some** (ven′chər səm) ***adj.*** **1** ready to take chances; daring; bold [a *venturesome* explorer]. **2** full of risks or danger; risky [a *venturesome* trip through a swamp]. *Also* **ven·tur·ous** (ven′chər əs).

**Ve·nus** (vē′nəs) **1** the Roman goddess of love and beauty. **2** the sixth largest planet, that is the brightest in the skies. It is the second in distance away from the sun.

☆**Ve·nus′ fly·trap** (vē′nəs flī′trap) a plant that grows in swampy regions of North and South Carolina. It has leaves with two hinged parts that snap shut to trap insects, which are absorbed by the plant. *See the picture.*

**ve·ra·cious** (və rā′shəs) ***adj.*** **1** telling the truth; truthful; honest [a *veracious* witness]. **2** true; accurate [a *veracious* report].

**ve·rac·i·ty** (və ras′ə tē) ***n.*** the quality of being veracious, or truthful, accurate, etc.

**Ver·a·cruz** (ver ə kro͞oz′) a seaport in eastern Mexico, on the Gulf of Mexico.

**ve·ran·da** or **ve·ran·dah** (və ran′də) ***n.*** an open porch, usually with a roof, along the side of a building. *See the picture.*

**verb** (vʉrb) ***n.*** a word that shows action or a condition of being [In the sentence "The children ate early and were asleep by seven o'clock," the words "ate" and "were" are *verbs.*]

**ver·bal** (vʉr′b'l) ***adj.*** **1** of, in, or by means of words [the author's great *verbal* skill]. **2** in speech; oral, not written [a *verbal* agreement]. **3** of, having to do with, or formed from a verb [a *verbal* noun; a *verbal* ending]. ◆***n.*** a word formed from a verb and often used as a noun or adjective [Gerunds, infinitives, and participles are *verbals.*] —**ver′bal·ly** ***adv.***

> SYNONYMS: **Verbal** and **oral** are sometimes used the same way, but careful speakers use only **oral** for something which is spoken rather than written [an *oral* promise]. They use **verbal** when they mean that words, whether written or spoken, and not pictures, music, etc., are the means of telling ideas or feelings [a *verbal* description of a scene].

**ver·bal·ize** (vʉr′bə līz) ***v.*** to express in words [It is hard to *verbalize* my feelings.] —**ver′bal·ized, ver′bal·iz·ing**

**ver·ba·tim** (vər bāt′əm) ***adv., adj.*** in exactly the same words; word for word [to copy a speech *verbatim;* a *verbatim* report].

**ver·be·na** (vər bē′nə) ***n.*** a plant with clusters of red, white, or purplish flowers. *See the picture.*

**ver·bi·age** (vʉr′bē ij) ***n.*** the use of more words than are needed to be clear; wordiness.

**ver·bose** (vər bōs′) ***adj.*** using too many words; wordy. —**ver·bos·i·ty** (vər bäs′ə tē) ***n.***

**ver·dant** (vʉr′d'nt) ***adj.*** **1** green [*verdant* grass]. **2** covered with green plants [the *verdant* plain].

**Verde, Cape** (vʉrd) a cape at the point farthest west on the African coast.

**Ver·di** (ver′dē), **Giu·sep·pe** (jo͞o zep′e) 1813–1901; Italian composer of operas.

**ver·dict** (vʉr′dikt) ***n.*** **1** the decision reached by a jury in a law case [a *verdict* of "not guilty"]. **2** any decision or opinion.

**ver·di·gris** (vʉr′di grēs′) ***n.*** a greenish coating that forms like rust on brass, bronze, or copper.

**ver·dure** (vʉr′jər) ***n.*** a growth of green plants and trees, or their fresh green color.

**verge** (vʉrj) ***n.*** **1** the edge, border, or brink [the *verge* of a forest]. **2** the point at which something begins to happen [He was on the *verge* of tears.] ◆***v.*** to come close to the edge or border; tend [a comedy that *verges* on tragedy]. —**verged, verg′ing**

**Ver·gil** (vʉr′jəl) *another spelling of* **Virgil**.

**ver·i·fi·ca·tion** (ver′ə fi kā′shən) ***n.*** the act of verifying, or something that helps to verify [to seek *verification* of a theory].

**ver·i·fy** (ver′ə fī) ***v.*** **1** to prove to be true; confirm [New research has *verified* that theory.] **2** to test or check the accuracy of; make sure of [Will you please *verify* these figures?] —**ver′i·fied, ver′i·fy·ing**

**ver·i·ly** (ver′ə lē) ***adv.*** in fact; truly: *an older use, as in the Bible* ["*Verily* thou shalt be fed."]

**ver·i·ta·ble** (ver′i tə b′l) ***adj.*** being such truly or in fact; actual [That meal was a *veritable* feast.]

**ver·i·ty** (ver′ə tē) ***n.*** **1** truth; reality [I doubt the *verity* of that rumor.] **2** something that is thought to be true for all times [the *verities* of a religion]. —*pl.* **ver′i·ties**

**ver·mi·cel·li** (vʉr′mə sel′ē *or* vʉr′mə chel′ē) ***n.*** a food like spaghetti, but in thinner strings.

> **Vermicelli** comes from an Italian word meaning "little worm." The strings of vermicelli look somewhat like thin worms.

**ver·mi·form** (vʉr′mə fôrm) ***adj.*** shaped like a worm [The full name of the human appendix is the "*vermiform* appendix."]

**ver·mil·ion** (vər mil′yən) ***n.*** **1** bright-red coloring matter. **2** a bright red.

**ver·min** (vʉr′min) ***n.*** **1** small animals or insects, such as rats and flies, that cause harm or are troublesome to people. **2** a disgusting person. —*pl.* **ver′min**

**Ver·mont** (vər mänt′) a New England State of the U.S.: abbreviated **Vt., VT**

**ver·mouth** (vər mo͞oth′) ***n.*** a white wine flavored with herbs and used in making some cocktails.

**ver·nac·u·lar** (vər nak′yə lər) ***n.*** **1** the native language of a country or place. **2** the everyday language of ordinary people. **3** the special words and phrases used in a particular work, by a particular group, etc. [In the *vernacular* of sailors, "deck" is the word for "floor."] ◆***adj.*** of, using, or based on the everyday speech of ordinary people in a certain country or place [James Whitcomb Riley was a *vernacular* poet.]

**ver·nal** (vʉr′n′l) ***adj.*** **1** of, or happening in, the spring [the *vernal* equinox]. **2** like that of spring; fresh, warm, and mild [a *vernal* breeze].

**Ver·sailles** (vər sī′ *or* vər sālz′) a city in France, near Paris. The large palace of Louis XIV is there.

**ver·sa·tile** (vʉr′sə t′l) ***adj.*** **1** able to do a number of things well [She is a *versatile* musician who can play five instruments.] **2** that can be used in a number of ways [a *versatile* piece of furniture]. —**ver·sa·til·i·ty** (vʉr′sə til′ə tē) ***n.***

**verse** (vʉrs) ***n.*** **1** poems or the form of writing found in poems [French *verse;* to write in *verse.*] **2** a certain kind of poetry [free *verse*]. **3** a group of lines forming one of the sections of a poem or song; stanza. **4** a single line of poetry: *an older use in this meaning.* **5** any of the short, numbered divisions of a chapter in the Bible.

**versed** (vʉrst) ***adj.*** knowing something because of training, study, etc.; skilled [He is well *versed* in languages.]

**ver·si·fi·ca·tion** (vʉr′sə fi kā′shən) ***n.*** **1** the act or

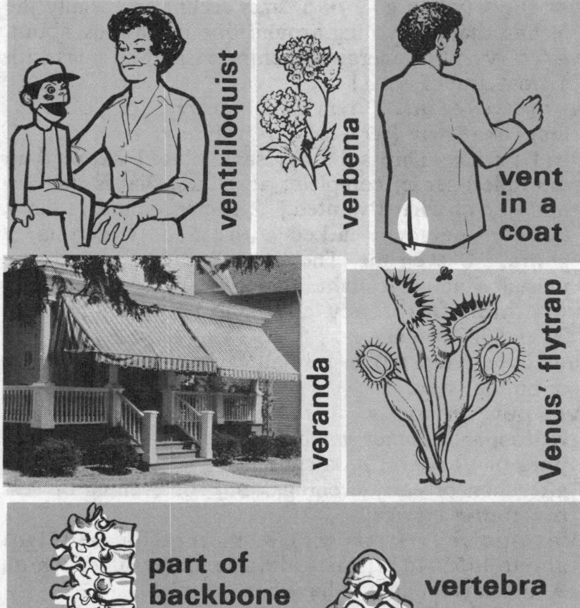


art of writing poems. **2** the way in which a poem is written, in terms of rhythm, rhyme, etc. [the *versification* of a sonnet]. 823

**ver·si·fy** (vʉr′sə fī) ***v.*** **1** to write poems. **2** to tell in verse; make a poem about [to *versify* the story of Paul Bunyan]. —**ver′si·fied, ver′si·fy·ing** —**ver′si·fi·er *n.***

**ver·sion** (vʉr′zhən) ***n.*** **1** something translated from the original language [an English *version* of the Bible]. **2** a report or description from one person's point of view [Give us your *version* of the accident.] **3** a particular form of something [an abridged *version* of a novel; the movie *version* of a play].

**ver·sus** (vʉr′səs) ***prep.*** **1** in a contest against [a softball game of students *versus* the teachers]. **2** in contrast to; as an alternative to [peace *versus* war].

**ver·te·bra** (vʉr′tə brə) ***n.*** any of the bones that make up the spinal column, or backbone. *See the picture.* —*pl.* **ver·te·brae** (vʉr′tə brē) or **ver′te·bras** —**ver′te·bral *adj.***

**ver·te·brate** (vʉr′tə brit *or* vʉr′tə brāt) ***adj.*** having a backbone. ◆***n.*** an animal that has a backbone [Mammals, birds, reptiles, and fishes are *vertebrates.*]

**ver·tex** (vʉr′teks) ***n.*** **1** the highest point; top. **2** any corner point of a triangle, square, cube, etc. —*pl.* **ver′tex·es** or **ver·ti·ces** (vʉr′tə sēz)

**ver·ti·cal** (vʉr′ti k′l) ***adj.*** straight up and down; perpendicular to a horizontal line [The walls of a house are *vertical.*] ◆***n.*** a vertical line, plane, etc. —**ver′ti·cal·ly *adv.***

| | | | | | | | |
|---|---|---|---|---|---|---|---|
| **a** fat | **ir** here | **ou** out | **zh** leisure |
| **ā** ape | **ī** bite, fire | **u** up | **ŋ** ring |
| **ä** car, lot | **ō** go | **ʉr** fur | a *in* ago |
| **e** ten | **ô** law, horn | **ch** chin | e *in* agent |
| **er** care | **oi** oil | **sh** she | **ə** = i *in* unity |
| **ē** even | **oo** look | **th** thin | o *in* collect |
| **i** hit | **o͞o** tool | ***th*** then | u *in* focus |

**ver·ti·go** (vʉr′ti gō′) ***n.*** a dizzy feeling, especially the feeling that everything around one is whirling about.

**verve** (vʉrv) ***n.*** energy and enthusiasm [She sings with a great deal of *verve.*]

**ver·y** (ver′ē) ***adv.*** **1** in a high degree; to a great extent; extremely [*very* cold; *very* funny; *very* sad]. **2** truly; really [This is the *very* same place.] ◆***adj.*** **1** in the fullest sense; complete; absolute [That is the *very* opposite of what I wanted.] **2** same; identical [She is the *very* person I talked with.] *See* SYNONYMS *at* **same.** **3** even the [The *very* rafters shook with the noise.] **4** actual [caught in the *very* act].

**very high frequency** any radio frequency between 30 and 300 megahertz.

**ves·i·cle** (ves′i k′l) ***n.*** a small cavity, sac, or blister in or on the body.

**ves·per** (ves′pər) ***n.*** **1** *an earlier name for* **evening.** **2 Vesper,** *another name for* **evening star.** **3 vespers** or **Vespers,** *pl.* a church service held in the late afternoon or early evening. ◆***adj.*** of evening or vespers [*vesper* service].

**Ves·puc·ci** (ves po͞o′chē), **A·me·ri·go** (ä′me rē′gō) about 1451–1512; an Italian explorer after whom America is thought to have been named.

**ves·sel** (ves″l) ***n.*** **1** anything hollow for holding something; container [Bowls, kettles, tubs, etc. are *vessels.*] **2** a ship or large boat. **3** any of the tubes in the body through which a fluid flows [a blood *vessel*].



**vest** (vest) ***n.*** **1** a short garment without sleeves, worn usually under a suit coat. *See the picture.* **2** *a British word for* **undershirt.** ◆***v.*** **1** to dress or clothe [*vested* in the robes of a priest]. **2** to give some power or right to [The power to levy taxes is *vested* in Congress.]

**Ves·ta** (ves′tə) the Roman goddess of the hearth and the hearth fire.

**ves·tal** (ves′t′l) ***n.*** any of a small group of virgins who kept the sacred fire burning in the temple of Vesta in ancient Rome. ◆***adj.*** pure or chaste.

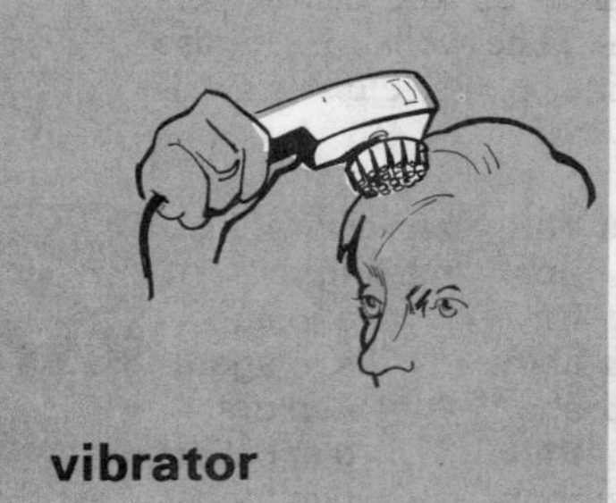

**vest·ed** (ves′tid) ***adj.*** **1** dressed, especially in church robes. **2** that has a vest [a *vested* suit]. **3** held by law in a fixed way that does not depend on anything else; absolute [to have a *vested* interest in an estate].

**ves·ti·bule** (ves′tə byo͞ol) ***n.*** **1** a small hall through which one enters a building or a room. ☆**2** the enclosed passage between passenger cars of a train.

**ves·tige** (ves′tij) ***n.*** **1** a trace or mark left of something that no longer exists as such [*Vestiges* of the ancient wall still stand. Not a *vestige* of hope is left.] **2** a part of the body that is not so fully developed as it once was in the species [The human appendix is a *vestige.*] —**ves·tig·i·al** (ves tij′ē əl *or* ves tij′əl) ***adj.***

> **Vestige** comes from a Latin word that means "footprint." In the same way that footprints are signs that someone has been in a place, **vestiges** are traces of something that was once in that place. *See also the word history at* **investigate.**

**vest·ment** (vest′mənt) ***n.*** a garment; especially, any of the garments worn by clergy during religious services.

**ves·try** (ves′trē) ***n.*** **1** a room in a church where vestments and articles for the altar are kept. **2** a room in a church, where prayer meetings, Sunday school, etc. are held. **3** a group of members who manage the business affairs in certain churches. —*pl.* **ves′tries**

**ves·try·man** (ves′trē mən) ***n.*** a member of a vestry. —*pl.* **ves′try·men**

**Ve·su·vi·us** (və so͞o′vē əs) a live volcano near Naples, Italy. It destroyed Pompeii when it erupted in 79 A.D.

**vet** (vet) ***n.*** *a shorter form of* **veteran** *or of* **veterinarian.**

**vetch** (vech) ***n.*** a plant related to the pea plant, grown as fodder for animals or plowed under to make the soil richer. *See the picture.*

**vet·er·an** (vet′ər ən) ***n.*** **1** a person who has served in the armed forces. **2** a person with much experience in some kind of work. ◆***adj.*** having had long experience in some work or service [*veteran* troops; a *veteran* diplomat].

☆**Veterans Day** November 11, a legal holiday honoring all veterans of the armed forces. This holiday was formerly called Armistice Day, which celebrated the armistice of World War I.

**vet·er·i·nar·i·an** (vet′ər ə ner′ē ən) ***n.*** a doctor who treats the diseases and injuries of animals.

**vet·er·i·nar·y** (vet′ər ə ner′ē) ***adj.*** having to do with the medical care of animals. ◆***n.*** *another name for* **veterinarian.** —*pl.* **vet′er·i·nar′ies**

**ve·to** (vē′tō) ***n.*** ☆**1** the power of the President, a governor, etc. to keep a bill from becoming law by refusing to sign it after the lawmaking body has passed it. ☆**2** the use of this right [Congress can overrule the President's *veto* by a two-thirds vote.] **3** the act or power of preventing something from being done by forbidding it. —*pl.* **ve′toes** ◆***v.*** to use the power of veto on [to *veto* a bill]. —**ve′toed, ve′to·ing**

**vex** (veks) ***v.*** to disturb, annoy, or trouble, often in little ways [I shall be *vexed* if you are late.]

**vex·a·tion** (vek sā′shən) ***n.*** **1** the condition of being vexed [Our *vexation* grew as we waited.] **2** something that vexes [He was a great *vexation* to his sisters.]

**vex·a·tious** (vek sā′shəs) ***adj.*** that vexes or disturbs; annoying [their *vexatious* chatter].

**VHF** or **V.H.F.** *abbreviation for* **very high frequency.**

**VI** or **V.I.** *abbreviation for* **Virgin Islands.**

**vi·a** (vī′ə *or* vē′ə) ***prep.*** **1** by way of or passing through [from Rome to London *via* Paris]. **2** by means of [Send it *via* special delivery.]

**vi·a·ble** (vī′ə b'l) ***adj.*** **1** able to live or exist, especially after being born too soon. **2** likely to work or to continue to exist [a *viable* plan; a *viable* business].

**vi·a·duct** (vī′ə dukt) ***n.*** a bridge held up by a series of piers or towers, usually for carrying a road or railroad over a valley or gorge. *See the picture.*

**vi·al** (vī′əl) ***n.*** a small bottle, usually of glass, for holding medicine or some other liquid.

**vi·and** (vī′ənd) ***n.*** **1** an article of food. **2 viands,** *pl.* food, especially fine, costly food.

**vi·brant** (vī′brənt) ***adj.*** **1** that vibrates or quivers [*vibrant* strings of a harp]. **2** full and rich; resounding [*vibrant* tones]. **3** full of energy [a *vibrant* person]. —**vi′bran·cy *n.***

**vi·brate** (vī′brāt) ***v.*** **1** to move rapidly back and forth; quiver [A guitar string *vibrates* when plucked.] **2** to echo; resound [The hall *vibrated* with their cheers.] —**vi′brat·ed, vi′brat·ing**

**vi·bra·tion** (vī brā′shən) ***n.*** rapid motion back and forth; quivering [The *vibration* of the motor shook the bolts loose.] —**vi·bra·to·ry** (vī′brə tôr′ē) ***adj.***

**vi·bra·to** (vi brät′ō) ***n.*** a slight throbbing in the sound of a singer's voice or of a musical instrument. It is produced by rapid, slight changes of the pitch back and forth.

**vi·bra·tor** (vī′brāt′ər) ***n.*** something that vibrates or causes vibration, as an electrical machine that massages the body. *See the picture.*

**vi·bur·num** (vī bur′nəm) ***n.*** a shrub or small tree with large clusters of small white flowers, as the snowball.

**vic·ar** (vik′ər) ***n.*** **1** a parish priest in the Church of England who is paid a salary from the tithes. **2** a Roman Catholic official who serves in place of a bishop. **3** any person who acts in place of another.

**vic·ar·age** (vik′ər ij) ***n.*** **1** the house where a vicar lives. **2** the duties or salary of a vicar.

**vi·car·i·ous** (vī ker′ē əs) ***adj.*** **1** felt as if one were actually taking part in what is happening to another [to get a *vicarious* thrill from a movie]. **2** given or got by one person in place of another [*vicarious* punishment]. **3** taking the place of another [a *vicarious* ruler]. —**vi·car′i·ous·ly *adv.***

**vice**[1] (vīs) ***n.*** **1** bad or evil behavior; wickedness [to lead a life of *vice*]. **2** a bad or evil habit [Greed is her worst *vice*.]

**vice**[2] (vīs) ***n.*** *the British spelling of* **vise.**

**vice-** *a prefix meaning* substitute *or* one who acts in the place of. *It is usually written with a hyphen* [A *vice*-consul is a substitute for a consul.]

**vice admiral** an officer in the navy ranking just below an admiral.

☆**vice-pres·i·den·cy** (vīs′prez′i dən sē) ***n.*** the office or term of a vice-president.

**vice-pres·i·dent** (vīs′prez′i dənt) ***n.*** **1** an officer next in rank to a president, who takes the place of the president if the president should die, be absent, etc. ☆**2 Vice-President,** such an officer in the United States government, who is also president of the Senate: *usually written* **Vice President.**

**vice·roy** (vīs′roi) ***n.*** a person sent by a king, queen, etc. to rule a region or another country under the control of that sovereign.

**vi·ce ver·sa** (vī′sē vur′sə *or* vīs′vur′sə) the other way around; turning the order around [We like them and *vice versa*—that is, they like us.]

**vi·cin·i·ty** (və sin′ə tē) ***n.*** **1** a nearby or surrounding region; neighborhood [suburbs in the *vicinity* of the city]. **2** the condition of being close by [the *vicinity* of our house to a public library].

**vi·cious** (vish′əs) ***adj.*** **1** wicked or evil [*vicious* habits]. **2** likely to attack or bite one [a *vicious* dog]. **3** meant to harm; spiteful; mean and cruel [a *vicious* rumor]. **4** very severe, sharp, etc. [a *vicious* pain]. —**vi′cious·ly *adv.*** —**vi′cious·ness *n.***

**vicious circle** a condition in which solving one problem brings on another, and solving that one brings back the first problem, etc.

> An example of a **vicious circle** might be the following. To stay on the football team, Bill must pass his chemistry course. To study for the chemistry test, he must miss football practice. If he misses practice, he will be dropped from the team.

**vi·cis·si·tude** (vi sis′ə tōōd *or* vi sis′ə tyōōd) ***n.*** any of a series of changes in conditions; any of one's ups and downs [The *vicissitudes* of life brought Mozart both fame and poverty.]



**vic·tim** (vik′tim) ***n.*** **1** someone or something killed, hurt, sacrificed, etc. [a *victim* of the storm; the *victims* of prejudice]. **2** a person who is cheated or tricked [a *victim* of swindlers].

**vic·tim·ize** (vik′tə mīz) ***v.*** to make a victim of [*victimized* by blackmail]. —**vic′tim·ized, vic′tim·iz·ing**

**vic·tor** (vik′tər) ***n.*** the winner in a battle, struggle, or contest.

**Vic·to·ri·a** (vik tôr′ē ə) **1** 1819–1901; queen of England from 1837 to 1901. **2** a lake in east central Africa. **3** the capital of British Columbia, Canada.

**vic·to·ri·a** (vik tôr′ē ə) ***n.*** a low carriage with four wheels and a single seat for passengers. It has a folding top and a high seat for the driver. *See the picture.*

**Vic·to·ri·an** (vik tôr′ē ən) ***adj.*** **1** of or in the time when Victoria was queen of England. **2** like the ideas, customs, styles, etc. of this time, thought of as being prudish, fussy, stuffy, etc. ◆***n.*** a person, especially a British writer, of the time of Queen Victoria.

**vic·to·ri·ous** (vik tôr′ē əs) ***adj.*** having won a victory; winning or conquering.

**vic·to·ry** (vik′tə rē) ***n.*** the winning of a battle, struggle, or contest; success in defeating an enemy or rival. —*pl.* **vic′to·ries**

**vict·uals** (vit′'lz) ***n.pl.*** *another name for* **food**: *used only in everyday talk, in some regions.*

| | | | | | | | |
|---|---|---|---|---|---|---|---|
| **a** | fat | **ir** | here | **ou** | out | **zh** | leisure |
| **ā** | ape | **ī** | bite, fire | **u** | up | **ng** | ring |
| **ä** | car, lot | **ō** | go | **ur** | fur | | a *in* ago |
| **e** | ten | **ô** | law, horn | **ch** | chin | | e *in* agent |
| **er** | care | **oi** | oil | **sh** | she | **ə =** | i *in* unity |
| **ē** | even | **oo** | look | **th** | thin | | o *in* collect |
| **i** | hit | **ōō** | tool | ***th*** | then | | u *in* focus |

**vi·cu·ña** (vī kōōn′yə *or* vī kyōō′nə) ***n.*** **1** an animal related to the llama, found in the mountains of South America. Its soft, shaggy wool is made into costly cloth. *See the picture.* **2** a fabric made from its wool or made to look like this wool.

**vid·e·o** (vid′ē ō′) ***adj.*** having to do with television, especially with the part of a broadcast that is seen: *see also* **audio.** ◆***n.*** *another name for* **television.**

**vid·e·o·tape** (vid′ē ō tāp′) ***n.*** a thin magnetic tape on which both the sound and picture signals of a TV program are recorded by electronics, as for broadcast at a later time.

**vie** (vī) ***v.*** to be a rival or rivals; compete as in a contest [They *vied* with us for first place.] —**vied, vy′ing**

**Vi·en·na** (vē en′ə) the capital of Austria, on the Danube. —**Vi·en·nese** (vē′ə nēz′) ***adj., n.***

**Vi·et·nam** (vē′ət näm′ *or* vyet′näm′) a country in southeastern Asia. —**Vi·et·nam·ese** (vē′et nə mēz′ *or* vē′et nə mēs′) ***adj., n.***

**view** (vyōō) ***n.*** **1** the act of seeing or looking; examination [On closer *view,* I saw it was a robin.] **2** the distance over which one can see; sight [The parade marched out of *view.*] **3** that which is seen; scene [We admired the *view* from the bridge.] **4** a picture of such a scene [He showed *views* of Niagara Falls.] **5** an idea or thought [The facts will help you get a clear *view* of the situation.] **6** a way of thinking about something; opinion [What are your *views* on this mat-



ter?] ◆***v.*** **1** to look at with great care; inspect [The landlord *viewed* the damage.] **2** to see [A crowd gathered to *view* the fireworks.] **3** to think about; consider [Her plan was *viewed* with scorn.] —**in view,** **1** in sight. **2** being thought over, or considered. **3** as a goal, hope, or wish. —**in view of,** because of; considering. —**on view,** placed where the public can see. —**with a view to,** with the purpose or hope of.

**view·er** (vyōō′ər) ***n.*** **1** a person who views a scene, TV show, etc.; spectator. **2** a device for allowing a person to look at photographic slides, filmstrips, etc.

**view·point** (vyōō′point) ***n.*** a way of thinking about something; attitude; point of view.

**vig·il** (vij′əl) ***n.*** **1** the act or a time of staying awake during the usual hours of sleep; watch [The nurse kept a *vigil* by the patient's bed.] **2** the day or evening before a religious festival.

**vig·i·lant** (vij′ə lənt) ***adj.*** wide-awake and ready for danger; watchful. —**vig′i·lance** ***n.***

☆**vig·i·lan·te** (vij′ə lan′tē) ***n.*** a member of a group that sets itself up without authority to seek out and punish crime.

**vi·gnette** (vin yet′) ***n.*** **1** a photograph that fades away into the background, with no clear border. *See the picture.* **2** a short sketch or description written in a skillful way.

> **Vignette** is French for "young vine." The word was first used in English to mean an ornamental design as of vine leaves and grapes. Such a design was often used on the page of a book at the beginning or end of a chapter. It was inserted in the blank space on such a page and had no border.

**vig·or** (vig′ər) ***n.*** **1** strength and energy of the body or mind [He walked with *vigor.*] **2** great strength or force [We were insulted at the *vigor* of her refusal.]

**vig·or·ous** (vig′ər əs) ***adj.*** **1** full of vigor, or energy; energetic [a *vigorous* public official]. *See* SYNONYMS *at* **active.** **2** forceful; powerful [a *vigorous* writing style].

**vik·ing** (vī′king) ***n.*** *also* **Viking,** any of the Scandinavian pirates who raided the coasts of Europe during the 8th, 9th, and 10th centuries.

**vile** (vīl) ***adj.*** **1** very evil or wicked [*vile* crimes]. **2** very unpleasant or disgusting [*vile* language]. **3** poor, lowly, mean, etc. [*vile* conditions in prison]. **4** very bad or unpleasant [*vile* weather].

**vil·i·fy** (vil′ə fī) ***v.*** to speak to or about in a foul or insulting way; defame. —**vil′i·fied, vil′i·fy·ing**

**vil·la** (vil′ə) ***n.*** a large, showy house in the country or on the outskirts of a city.

**vil·lage** (vil′ij) ***n.*** **1** a group of houses in the country, smaller than a town. **2** the people of a village. —**vil′lag·er** ***n.***

**vil·lain** (vil′ən) ***n.*** an evil or wicked person, or such a character in a play, novel, etc. *See the picture.*

> **Villain** comes from the Latin word *villa,* meaning "farm." At first it meant "a farm worker," then "a coarse, ignorant person," and finally "a wicked or evil person."

**vil·lain·ous** (vil′ən əs) ***adj.*** of or like a villain; evil; wicked [*villainous* plots].

**vil·lain·y** (vil′ən ē) ***n.*** **1** the quality of being a villain; wickedness. **2** an act of a villain; crime. —*pl.* **vil′lain·ies**

**vil·lein** (vil′ən) ***n.*** an English serf in the Middle Ages who was a freeman to all persons except his lord, to whom he was still a slave.

☆**vim** (vim) ***n.*** energy; vigor.

**Vinci, Leonardo da** *see* **da Vinci.**

**vin·di·cate** (vin′də kāt) ***v.*** **1** to free from blame, guilt, suspicion, etc. [Lacy's confession completely *vindicated* Klein.] **2** to show to be true or right; justify [Can the company *vindicate* its claims for its product?] —**vin′di·cat·ed, vin′di·cat·ing**

**vin·di·ca·tion** (vin′də kā′shən) ***n.*** **1** the act of vindicating. **2** a fact or happening that shows something to be true or right [Our success was the *vindication* of their faith.]

**vin·dic·tive** (vin dik′tiv) ***adj.*** **1** wanting to get revenge; ready to do harm in return for harm [He was not *vindictive,* but readily forgave his enemies.] **2** said or done in revenge [*vindictive* punishment]. —**vin·dic′tive·ly** ***adv.***

**vine** (vīn) ***n.*** **1** *same as* **grapevine** *in meaning* 1. **2** any plant with a long, thin stem that grows along the ground or climbs walls, trees, etc. by fastening itself to them [Pumpkins and melons grow on *vines.*]

**vin·e·gar** (vin′i gər) ***n.*** a sour liquid made by fermenting cider, wine, malt, etc. It is used to flavor or preserve foods.

**vine·yard** (vin′yərd) ***n.*** a piece of land where grapevines are grown.

**vi·nous** (vī′nəs) ***adj.*** of, like, or having to do with wine.

**vin·tage** (vin′tij) ***n.*** **1** the crop of grapes from a certain region in a single season, or the wine from such a crop. **2** a model from an earlier time [He has an automobile of ancient *vintage.*] ◆***adj.*** **1** of a good vintage; choice [*vintage* wine]. **2** coming from a time long ago [*vintage* clothes].

**Vintage** comes from the Latin words meaning "to take from the vine." The grapes taken from the vine at a particular time are the *vintage* of that season.

**vint·ner** (vint′nər) ***n.*** a merchant who sells wine.

**vi·nyl** (vī′n′l) ***n.*** having to do with a group of chemical compounds used in forming certain plastics that are made into phonograph records, floor tiles, etc.

**vi·ol** (vī′əl) ***n.*** any of a group of early stringed instruments that were replaced by the violin family. *See the picture.*

**vi·o·la** (vē ō′lə) ***n.*** a stringed instrument like the violin, but a little larger and lower in pitch. —**vi·o′list** ***n.***

**vi·o·late** (vī′ə lāt) ***v.*** **1** to break or fail to keep, as a law, rule, or promise [to *violate* a treaty]. **2** to treat something sacred in a way that is not respectful [Robbers *violated* the grave by digging it up.] **3** to break in upon; disturb [to *violate* one's privacy]. —**vi′o·lat·ed, vi′o·lat·ing** —**vi′o·la′tion** ***n.*** —**vi′o·la·tor** ***n.***

**vi·o·lence** (vī′ə ləns) ***n.*** **1** force used to cause injury or damage [The prisoners attacked their guards with *violence*.] **2** great strength or force [They were frightened by the *violence* of the tornado. He took part in the argument with *violence*.] **3** the harm done by a lack of proper respect [Those insults did *violence* to our sense of decency.]

**vi·o·lent** (vī′ə lənt) ***adj.*** **1** showing or acting with great force that causes damage or injury [*violent* blows of the fists]. **2** caused by such force [a *violent* death]. **3** showing strong feelings [*violent* language]. **4** very strong; severe [a *violent* headache]. —**vi′o·lent·ly** ***adv.***

**vi·o·let** (vī′ə lit) ***n.*** **1** a small, short plant with white, blue, purple, or yellow flowers. *See the picture.* **2** bluish purple. ◆***adj.*** bluish-purple.

**vi·o·lin** (vī ə lin′) ***n.*** the smallest of a group of musical instruments having four strings played with a bow. *See the picture.* The viola, cello, and double bass belong to the same group, called the **violin family**. —**vi·o·lin′ist** ***n.***

**vi·o·lon·cel·lo** (vē′ə län chel′ō *or* vī′ə lən chel′ō) ***n.*** *another name for* **cello.**

**VIP** or **V.I.P.** very important person. *This abbreviation is used only in everyday talk.*

**vi·per** (vī′pər) ***n.*** **1** a poisonous snake, especially such a snake of Europe and Africa, as the adder. **2** a mean person who cannot be trusted. —**vi′per·ous** ***adj.***

☆**vir·e·o** (vir′ē ō′) ***n.*** a small songbird with olive-green or gray feathers. —*pl.* **vir′e·os′**

**Vir·gil** (vʉr′jəl) 70–19 B.C.; Roman poet who wrote the *Aeneid: also spelled* **Vergil.**

**vir·gin** (vʉr′jin) ***n.*** a person, especially a woman, who has not had sexual intercourse; maiden. ◆***adj.*** **1** being a virgin. **2** chaste or modest. **3** pure and fresh; not touched, used, etc. [*virgin* snow; a *virgin* forest]. —**the Virgin,** Mary, the mother of Jesus. —**vir′gin·al** ***adj.***

**vir·gin·al** (vʉr′ji n′l) ***n.*** a small kind of harpsichord without legs, that was set on a table or held on the lap to be played. *See the picture on page 828.*

**Vir·gin·ia** (vər jin′yə) a State on the eastern coast of the U.S.: abbreviated **Va., VA** —**Vir·gin′ian** ***adj., n.***

**Virgin Islands** a group of islands in the West Indies, some of which belong to the U.S. and some to Great Britain.

vignette

villain in an old play

violin

viol

violet

vicuña

80 cm (2 1/2 ft.) high at shoulder

**vir·gin·i·ty** (vər jin′ə tē) ***n.*** the condition or fact of being a virgin.

**Vir·go** (vʉr′gō) the sixth sign of the zodiac, for the period from August 22 to September 22: *also called* the Virgin. *See the picture for* **zodiac.** 

**vir·ile** (vir′əl) ***adj.*** **1** of or having to do with a man; male. **2** like a man is supposed to be; strong, forceful, etc.; manly. —**vi·ril·i·ty** (vi ril′ə tē) ***n.***

**vir·tu·al** (vʉr′choo wəl) ***adj.*** being so practically or in effect, although not in actual fact or name [Although we have met, they are *virtual* strangers to me.]

**vir·tu·al·ly** (vʉr′choo wəl ē) ***adv.*** in effect, although not in fact; really, practically, nearly, etc. [These gloves are *virtually* identical.]

**vir·tue** (vʉr′chōō) ***n.*** **1** goodness; right action and thinking; morality [*Virtue* is its own reward.] **2** a particular moral quality thought of as good [Courage is her greatest *virtue*.] **3** chastity or purity, especially in a woman. **4** a good quality or qualities; merit [There is *virtue* in planning ahead. Your plan has certain *virtues*.] —**by virtue of** or **in virtue of,** because of.

**vir·tu·o·so** (vʉr′choo wō′sō) ***n.*** a person having great skill in the practice of some art, especially in playing music. —*pl.* **vir′tu·o′sos** or **vir·tu·o·si** (vʉr′choo wō′sē) —**vir·tu·os·i·ty** (vʉr′choo wäs′ə tē) ***n.***

**vir·tu·ous** (vʉr′choo wəs) ***adj.*** having virtue; good, moral, chaste, etc. —**vir′tu·ous·ly** ***adv.***

**vir·u·lent** (vir′yoo lənt *or* vir′oo lənt) ***adj.*** **1** very harmful or poisonous; deadly [a *virulent* disease]. **2**

| | | | | | | | |
|---|---|---|---|---|---|---|---|
| **a** | fat | **ir** | here | **ou** | out | **zh** | leisure |
| **ā** | ape | **ī** | bite, fire | **u** | up | **ng** | ring |
| **ä** | car, lot | **ō** | go | **ʉr** | fur | | a *in* ago |
| **e** | ten | **ô** | law, horn | **ch** | chin | | e *in* agent |
| **er** | care | **oi** | oil | **sh** | she | **ə** = | i *in* unity |
| **ē** | even | **oo** | look | **th** | thin | | o *in* collect |
| **i** | hit | **ōō** | tool | ***th*** | then | | u *in* focus |

full of hate; very bitter or spiteful [a *virulent* speech]. —**vir′u·lence** ***n.*** —**vir′u·lent·ly** ***adv.***

**vi·rus** (vī′rəs) ***n.*** a form of matter smaller than any of the bacteria, that can multiply in living cells and cause disease in animals and plants. Smallpox, measles, the flu, etc. are caused by viruses.

> **Virus** comes from a Latin word meaning "poison." *Virus* was used long ago in English to mean "venom," such as the poison of some snakes. Later it came to mean the small forms of matter that, like snake venom, could sometimes bring death.

**vi·sa** (vē′zə) ***n.*** something written or stamped on a passport by an official of a country to show that the passport holder has permission to enter that country.

**vis·age** (viz′ij) ***n.*** the face, especially as showing one's feelings [his stern *visage*].

**vis·cer·a** (vis′ər ə) ***n.pl.*** the organs inside the body, as the heart, lungs, intestines, etc.

**vis·cid** (vis′id) ***adj.*** thick and sticky, like syrup or glue; viscous.

**vis·cos·i·ty** (vis käs′ə tē) ***n.*** the condition or quality of being viscous.

**vis·count** (vī′kount) ***n.*** a nobleman ranking above a baron and below an earl or count.

**vis·count·ess** (vī′koun tis) ***n.*** **1** the wife or widow of a viscount. **2** a woman having the same rank as a viscount.

**vis·cous** (vis′kəs) ***adj.*** thick and sticky, like syrup or glue; viscid.

**vise** (vīs) ***n.*** a device having two jaws opened and closed by a screw, used for holding an object firmly while it is being worked on. *See the picture.*

**vis·i·bil·i·ty** (viz′ə bil′ə tē) ***n.*** **1** the condition of being visible. **2** the distance within which things can be seen [Fog reduced the *visibility* to 500 feet.]

**vis·i·ble** (viz′ə b'l) ***adj.*** that can be seen or noticed; evident [a barely *visible* scar; a *visible* increase in crime]. —**vis′i·bly** ***adv.***

**Vis·i·goth** (viz′ə gäth) ***n.*** any of the western tribes of Goths who captured Rome in 410 A.D.

**vi·sion** (vizh′ən) ***n.*** **1** the act or power of seeing; sight [She wears glasses to improve her *vision*.] **2** something seen in the mind, or in a dream, trance, etc. ["while *visions* of sugarplums danced in their heads"]. **3** the ability to imagine or foresee what cannot actually be seen [a leader of great *vision*]. **4** a person or thing of unusual beauty [She was a *vision* in her new gown.]

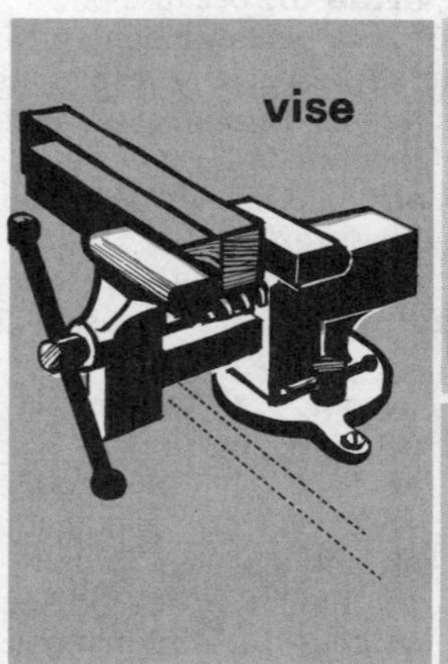

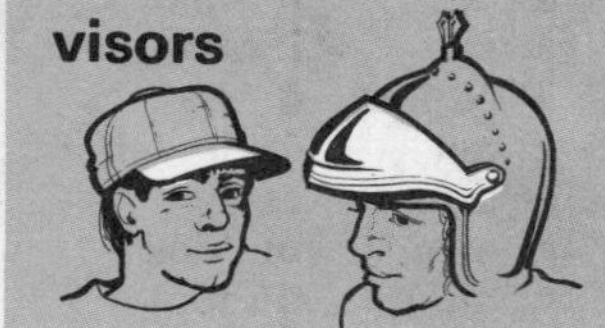


**vi·sion·ar·y** (vizh′ən er′ē) ***adj.*** **1** like or seen in a vision. **2** imaginary or not practical [a *visionary* scheme]. ◆***n.*** **1** a person who sees visions. **2** a person whose ideas or ideals are not practical. —*pl.* **vi′sion·ar′ies**

**vis·it** (viz′it) ***v.*** **1** to go or come to see; call on out of friendship, for business, etc. [We *visit* our cousins at least once a year.] **2** to stay with as a guest [They *visited* us for two days.] **3** to come upon in a harmful way [The valley was *visited* by a drought.] ◆***n.*** an act of visiting, as a social call, a stay as a guest, etc.

**vis·it·ant** (viz′it ənt) ***n.*** **1** a visitor, especially one from a strange or foreign place. **2** a ghost or phantom.

**vis·it·a·tion** (viz′ə tā′shən) ***n.*** **1** the act of visiting, especially an official visit as for inspecting or examining. **2** trouble looked on as punishment sent by God.

**vis·i·tor** (viz′it ər) ***n.*** a person making a visit; caller or guest.

**vi·sor** (vī′zər) ***n.*** **1** a part of a helmet that can be pulled down to cover the face. ☆**2** the brim of a cap, sticking out in front to shade the eyes. *See the picture.* **3** any device, as over the windshield of a car, for shading the eyes.

☆**VISTA** (vis′tə) a U.S. government program of volunteers to help the very poor improve their living conditions. The word VISTA comes from the first letters of *Volunteers in Service to America.*

**vis·ta** (vis′tə) ***n.*** **1** a view, especially one seen through a long passage, as between rows of houses [The street lined with trees gave us a *vista* of the river.] **2** a view in the mind of happenings that one remembers or looks forward to [This book gives a sweeping *vista* of ancient history.]

**Vis·tu·la** (vis′chꝏ lə) a river in Poland, flowing into the Baltic Sea.

**vis·u·al** (vizh′ꝏ wəl) ***adj.*** **1** having to do with sight or used in seeing [*visual* aids]. **2** that can be seen; visible [*visual* proof]. —**vis′u·al·ly** ***adv.***

**visual aids** motion pictures, slides, charts, etc., but not books, used in teaching, lectures, etc.

**vis·u·al·ize** (vizh′ꝏ wə līz′) ***v.*** to form in the mind a picture of [Try to *visualize* the room as it will look after the changes are made.] —**vis′u·al·ized′**, **vis′u·al·iz′ing**

**vi·tal** (vīt′'l) ***adj.*** **1** of or having to do with life [*vital* energy]. **2** necessary to life [the *vital* organs]. **3** full of life and energy [a *vital* personality]. **4** very important [Her help is *vital* to the success of our plan.] **5** destroying life; fatal [a *vital* wound]. ◆***n.*** **vitals**, *pl.* **1** the vital organs of the body, as the brain, heart, and liver. **2** the necessary parts of anything. —**vi′tal·ly** ***adv.***

**vi·tal·i·ty** (vī tal′ə tē) ***n.*** **1** energy or strength of mind or body; vigor. **2** the power to keep on living or existing [The Constitution has shown great *vitality*.]

**vi·tal·ize** (vīt′'l īz) ***v.*** to make vital or lively; give life or energy to. —**vi′tal·ized**, **vi′tal·iz·ing**

**vi·ta·min** (vīt′ə min) ***n.*** any of certain substances needed by the body to keep healthy. Vitamin A is found in fish-liver oil, yellow vegetables, egg yolk, etc. One kind of vitamin B, called vitamin $B_1$, is found in cereals, green peas, beans, liver, etc. Vitamin C is found in citrus fruits, tomatoes, etc. Vitamin D is found in fish-liver oil, milk, eggs, etc. Lack of these vitamins or others can cause certain diseases.

**vi·ti·ate** (vish′ē āt′) ***v.*** **1** to spoil the goodness of; make bad or faulty [His character was *vitiated* by laziness.] **2** to take away the legal force of [The lack of a signature *vitiated* the contract.] —**vi′ti·at′ed, vi′ti·at′ing** —**vi′ti·a′tion** ***n.***

**vit·re·ous** (vit′rē əs) ***adj.*** of or like glass; glassy [*vitreous* china].

**vitreous body** the clear substance like jelly that fills the eyeball behind the lens: *also called* **vitreous humor.** *See the picture for* **eye.**

**vit·ri·fy** (vit′rə fī) ***v.*** to change into glass or a substance like glass, as by heating. —**vit′ri·fied, vit′ri·fy·ing**

**vit·ri·ol** (vit′rē əl) ***n.*** **1** *another name for* **sulfuric acid. 2** a salt formed by the action of sulfuric acid on certain metals [Green *vitriol* is iron sulfate.]

**vit·ri·ol·ic** (vit′rē äl′ik) ***adj.*** **1** having to do with or like vitriol. **2** very sharp, biting, or sarcastic [*vitriolic* talk].

**vi·tu·per·ate** (vī to͞o′pə rāt *or* vī tyo͞o′pə rāt) ***v.*** to scold or talk about in a harsh way; berate. —**vi·tu′per·at·ed, vi·tu′per·at·ing** —**vi·tu′per·a′tion** ***n.*** —**vi·tu′per·a·tive** ***adj.***

**vi·va·cious** (vi vā′shəs *or* vī vā′shəs) ***adj.*** full of life and energy; spirited; lively. —**vi·va′cious·ly** ***adv.*** —**vi·va′cious·ness** ***n.***

**vi·vac·i·ty** (vi vas′ə tē *or* vī vas′ə tē) ***n.*** the quality of being vivacious; liveliness.

**vive** (vēv) ***interj.*** long may he, or she, live!: *a French word shouted in welcome or approval.*

**viv·id** (viv′id) ***adj.*** **1** bright and strong [*vivid* colors]. **2** forming or giving a clear picture in the mind [a *vivid* imagination; a *vivid* description]. **3** full of life or energy; striking; lively [a *vivid* personality]. —**viv′id·ly** ***adv.*** —**viv′id·ness** ***n.***

**viv·i·fy** (viv′ə fī) ***v.*** to give life to; make lively or active. —**viv′i·fied, viv′i·fy·ing**

**viv·i·sec·tion** (viv′ə sek′shən) ***n.*** medical experiments on living animals in studying diseases and trying to find cures for them.

**vix·en** (vik′s′n) ***n.*** **1** a female fox. **2** a spiteful, bad-tempered woman; shrew.

**viz.** or **viz** (viz) that is; namely; by name. *Viz.* is the abbreviation of a Latin word, *videlicet* [You have a choice of two desserts, *viz.,* ice cream or pie.]

**vi·zier** or **vi·zir** (vi zir′) ***n.*** a title used in earlier times for a high official in Muslim states.

**vi·zor** (vī′zər) ***n.*** *another spelling of* **visor.**

**Vla·di·vos·tok** (vlad′i väs′täk) a seaport on the eastern coast of the U.S.S.R.

**vo·cab·u·lar·y** (vō kab′yə ler′ē) ***n.*** **1** all the words of a language, or all those used by a certain person or group [Jan's *vocabulary* is large. The word "fracture" is part of the medical *vocabulary.*] **2** a list of words, usually in alphabetical order with their meanings, as in a dictionary. —*pl.* **vo·cab′u·lar′ies**

**vo·cal** (vō′k′l) ***adj.*** **1** of or made by the voice; in or for singing or speech [the *vocal* cords; *vocal* music]. **2** able to speak or make sounds. **3** speaking openly or strongly [She was very *vocal* in the fight for women's rights.]—**vo′cal·ly** ***adv.***

**vocal cords** the folds at the upper end of the windpipe that vibrate and make voice sounds when air from the lungs passes through.

**vo·cal·ist** (vō′k′l ist) ***n.*** a person who sings; singer.

**vo·cal·ize** (vō′k′l īz) ***v.*** to make sounds with the voice; speak or sing. —**vo′cal·ized, vo′cal·iz·ing**

**vo·ca·tion** (vō kā′shən) ***n.*** one's profession, occupation, trade, or career [He found his *vocation* in social work.] —**vo·ca′tion·al** ***adj.***

> A **vocation** is sometimes referred to as a "calling," and there is a connection between these words. The word **vocation** comes from a Latin word meaning "to call." People often feel as though they have been called upon to follow a certain kind of work.

☆**vocational guidance** the work of testing and interviewing persons in order to help them choose a type of job that fits their abilities and interests.

**vo·cif·er·ous** (vō sif′ər əs) ***adj.*** loud and noisy in making one's feelings known; clamorous [a *vociferous* crowd; *vociferous* complaints].

**vod·ka** (väd′kə) ***n.*** an alcoholic liquor made from grain. It is colorless.

**vogue** (vōg) ***n.*** **1** the general fashion or style [Powdered wigs were in *vogue* in the 18th century.] **2** popularity; popular approval [Rock music has had a great *vogue* in recent years.]

> **Vogue** is a French word which comes from an earlier word *voguer,* meaning "to row or sail a ship." When people follow a vogue, they are going with the current, the way a ship might. We also say of such people that they are "in the swim."



**voice** (vois) ***n.*** **1** sound made through the mouth, especially by human beings in talking, singing, etc. **2** the ability to make such sounds [She lost her *voice* in terror.] **3** anything thought of as like speech or the human voice [the *voice* of the sea; the *voice* of one's conscience]. **4** the right to say what one wants, thinks, or feels [Each voter has a *voice* in the government.] **5** the act of putting into words what one thinks or feels [He gave *voice* to his doubts.] **6** the quality of the sounds made in speaking or singing [He has a fine *voice* for radio. She has a soprano *voice.*] **7** a form of a verb that shows its connection with the subject as active (with the subject doing the action) or passive (with the subject acted upon) ["Give" in "They give freely" is in the active *voice;* "am given" in "I am given presents" is in the passive *voice.*] ◆***v.*** **1** to put into words, as an idea, feeling, etc.; utter. **2** to pronounce by letting the voice sound through the vocal cords [The sounds of "b," "v," and "z" are *voiced.*] —**voiced, voic′ing** —**voice′less** ***adj.***

**voice-o·ver** (vois′ō′vər) ***n.*** the voice talking off camera, as for a TV commercial.

| | | | | | | | |
|---|---|---|---|---|---|---|---|
| **a** | fat | **ir** | here | **ou** | out | **zh** | leisure |
| **ā** | ape | **ī** | bite, fire | **u** | up | **ng** | ring |
| **ä** | car, lot | **ō** | go | **ur** | fur | | a *in* ago |
| **e** | ten | **ô** | law, horn | **ch** | chin | | e *in* agent |
| **er** | care | **oi** | oil | **sh** | she | **ə =** | i *in* unity |
| **ē** | even | **oo** | look | **th** | thin | | o *in* collect |
| **i** | hit | **o͞o** | tool | ***th*** | then | | u *in* focus |

**void** (void) ***adj.*** **1** having nothing in it; empty; vacant [A vacuum is a *void* space.] **2** being without; lacking [a heart *void* of kindness]. **3** having no legal force; not valid [The contract is *void.*] ◆***n.*** **1** an empty space [The craters of the moon are huge *voids.*] **2** a feeling of loss or emptiness [Bill's death left a *void* in our social group.] ◆***v.*** **1** to make empty; empty out. **2** to cause to be without legal force; cancel [to *void* an agreement]. —**void'a·ble** ***adj.***

**voile** (voil) ***n.*** a thin, fine cloth as of cotton, used for dresses, curtains, etc.



**vol.** *abbreviation for* **volume.** —*pl.* **vols.**

**vol·a·tile** (väl'ə t'l) ***adj.*** **1** changing readily into a gas; evaporating quickly [Alcohol is a *volatile* liquid.] **2** changing often in one's feelings or interests; fickle. **3** that might get out of control suddenly.

**vol·can·ic** (väl kan'ik) ***adj.*** **1** of or from a volcano [*volcanic* rock]. **2** like a volcano; violent; likely to explode [a *volcanic* temper].

**vol·ca·no** (väl kā'nō) ***n.*** **1** an opening in the earth's surface through which molten rock from inside the earth is thrown up. **2** a hill or mountain of ash and molten rock built up around such an opening. *See the picture.* —*pl.* **vol·ca'noes** or **vol·ca'nos**

**vole** (vōl) ***n.*** a small animal like the mouse or rat, that has a fat body and short tail.

**Vol·ga** (väl'gə *or* vōl'gə) a river in the western U.S.S.R., flowing into the Caspian Sea.

**vo·li·tion** (vō lish'ən) ***n.*** the act or power of using one's own will in deciding or making a choice [Of his own *volition* he apologized.]

**vol·ley** (väl'ē) ***n.*** **1** the act of shooting a number of guns or other weapons at the same time. **2** the bullets, arrows, etc. shot at one time. **3** a sudden pouring out of a number of things [a *volley* of curses]. **4** in certain sports, the flight or return of a ball, etc. before it touches the ground. —*pl.* **vol'leys** ◆***v.*** **1** to shoot or be shot in a volley. **2** in certain sports, to return the ball, etc. as a volley.

☆**vol·ley·ball** (väl'ē bôl') ***n.*** **1** a game played by two teams who hit a large, light ball back and forth over a high net with their hands. **2** the ball used in this game. *See the picture.*

**volt** (vōlt) ***n.*** a unit for measuring the force of an electric current. One volt causes a current of one ampere to flow through a resistance of one ohm.

**volt·age** (vōl'tij) ***n.*** the force that produces electric current. It is measured in volts.

**vol·ta·ic cell** (väl tā'ik *or* vōl tā'ik) a device for making an electric current by placing two plates of different metals in an electrolyte.

**Vol·taire** (vōl ter') 1694–1778; French writer and philosopher.

**volt·me·ter** (vōlt'mēt'ər) ***n.*** a device for measuring the voltage of an electric current.

**vol·u·ble** (väl'yoo b'l) ***adj.*** talking very much and easily; talkative. —**vol'u·bil'i·ty** ***n.*** —**vol'u·bly** ***adv.***

**vol·ume** (väl'yoom) ***n.*** **1** a book [You may borrow four *volumes* at a time.] **2** one of the books of a set [*Volume* III of the encyclopedia]. **3** the amount of space inside something, measured in cubic inches, feet, etc. [The *volume* of this box is 27 cubic feet, or .756 cubic meter.] **4** an amount, bulk, or mass [a large *volume* of sales]. *See* SYNONYMS *at* **bulk.** **5** loudness of sound [Lower the *volume* of your radio.]

> **Volume** comes to us from the Latin word *volumen* which meant the long roll or scroll of pieces of parchment which were glued together to make a book. **Volume** was used in early English to mean the same thing, but later came to be used for a book which was made up of pieces of paper cut, folded, and sewn together, such as we have today.

**vo·lu·mi·nous** (və lōō'mə nəs) ***adj.*** **1** writing, or made up of, enough to fill volumes [the *voluminous* works of Dickens]. **2** large; bulky; full [a *voluminous* skirt].

**vol·un·tar·y** (väl'ən ter'ē) ***adj.*** **1** acting, done, or given of one's own free will; by choice [*voluntary* workers; *voluntary* gifts]. **2** controlled by one's mind or will [*voluntary* muscles]. —**vol'un·tar'i·ly** ***adv.***

> SYNONYMS: **Voluntary** suggests that a person is using free choice or will in doing something, whether or not outside forces are involved [Most clubs depend upon the *voluntary* work of their members.] **Intentional** is used for something which is done on purpose for a particular reason and is not in any way an accident [My cranky neighbor gave me an *intentional* snub.]

**vol·un·teer** (väl ən tir') ***n.*** a person who offers to do something of his or her own free will, as one who enlists in the armed forces by choice. ◆***adj.*** of or done by volunteers [a *volunteer* regiment; *volunteer* help]. ◆***v.*** **1** to do or give of one's own free will [She *volunteered* some information. Sarah *volunteered* to write the letter.] **2** to enter into a service of one's own free will [The soldier *volunteered* for service overseas.]

**vo·lup·tu·ar·y** (və lup'choo wer'ē) ***n.*** a person who is mainly interested in rich living and personal pleasures. —*pl.* **vo·lup'tu·ar'ies**

**vo·lup·tu·ous** (və lup'choo wəs) ***adj.*** **1** having, giving, or seeking pleasure through the senses [a *voluptuous* feast]. **2** having a full, shapely figure [a *voluptuous* woman].

**vom·it** (väm'it) ***v.*** **1** to be sick and have matter from the stomach come back up through the mouth; throw up. **2** to throw out or be thrown out with force [The cannons *vomited* smoke and fire.] ◆***n.*** the matter thrown up from the stomach.

☆**voo·doo** (vōō'dōō) ***n.*** **1** a primitive religion based on a belief in magic, witchcraft, and charms, that began in Africa and is still practiced in some parts of the West Indies. **2** a person who practices voodoo. —*pl.* **voo'doos** —**voo'doo·ism** *n.*

**vo·ra·cious** (vô rā'shəs) ***adj.*** **1** eating large amounts of food rapidly; greedy. **2** very eager for much of something [a *voracious* reader]. —**vo·ra'cious·ly** ***adv.*** —**vo·rac·i·ty** (vô ras'ə tē) ***n.***

**vor·tex** (vôr'teks) *n.* a whirling or spinning mass as of water or air; whirlpool or whirlwind. —*pl.* **vor'tex·es** or **vor·ti·ces** (vôr'tə sēz)

**vo·ta·ry** (vōt'ə rē) ***n.*** **1** a person who is bound by a vow, as a monk or nun. **2** a person who is devoted to something, as to a cause or interest [a *votary* of music]. —*pl.* **vo'ta·ries**

**vote** (vōt) *n.* **1** one's decision on some plan or idea, or one's choice between persons running for office, shown on a ballot, by raising one's hand, etc. **2** the ballot, raised hand, etc. by which a person shows the choice [to count the *votes*]. **3** all the votes together [A heavy *vote* is expected.] **4** the act of choosing by a vote [I call for a *vote.*] **5** the right to take part in a vote [The 19th Amendment gave the *vote* to women.] **6** a particular group of voters, or their votes [the farm *vote*]. ◆***v.*** **1** to give or cast a vote [For whom did you *vote?*] **2** to decide, elect, or bring about by vote [Congress *voted* new taxes.] **3** to declare as a general opinion [We *voted* the party a success.] **4** to suggest: *used only in everyday talk* [I *vote* we leave now.] —**vot'ed, vot'ing**

**vot·er** (vōt'ər) ***n.*** a person who has the right to vote, especially one who actually votes.

☆**voting machine** a machine on which the votes in an election are made, recorded, and counted.

**vo·tive** (vōt'iv) ***adj.*** given or done because of a promise or vow [*votive* offerings].

**vouch** (vouch) ***v.*** to give a guarantee; give one's word in backing [Her friends *vouch* for her honesty. He has references *vouching* for his ability.]

**vouch·er** (vou'chər) ***n.*** **1** a paper that serves as proof, as a receipt for the payment of a debt. **2** a person who vouches for something, as for the truth of a statement.

**vouch·safe** (vouch sāf') ***v.*** to be kind enough to give or grant [He did not *vouchsafe* an answer.] —**vouch-safed', vouch·saf'ing**

**vow** (vou) ***n.*** a solemn promise or pledge, as one made to God, or with God as one's witness [marriage *vows*]. ◆***v.*** **1** to make a vow or solemn promise [She *vowed* to love him always.] **2** to say in a forceful or earnest way [She *vowed* that she had never heard such noise. We *vowed* revenge.]

**vow·el** (vou'əl) ***n.*** **1** any speech sound made by letting the voiced breath pass through without stopping it with the tongue, teeth, or lips. **2** any of the letters used to show these sounds. The vowels are *a, e, i, o,* and *u,* and sometimes *y,* as in the word "my."

**voy·age** (voi'ij) ***n.*** **1** a journey by water [an ocean *voyage*]. **2** a journey through the air or through outer space [a *voyage* by rocket]. *See* SYNONYMS *at* **trip.** ◆***v.*** to make a voyage. —**voy'aged, voy'ag·ing** —**voy'ag·er** ***n.***

**V.P.** or **VP** *abbreviation for* **Vice-President.**

**vs.** *abbreviation for* **versus.**

**VT** or **Vt.** *abbreviation for* **Vermont.**

**Vul·can** (vul'k'n) the Roman god of fire and of metalworking.

**vul·can·ize** (vul'kə nīz) ***v.*** to add sulfur to crude rubber and heat it in order to make it stronger and more elastic. —**vul'can·ized, vul'can·iz·ing** —**vul'can·i·za'tion** ***n.***

**vul·gar** (vul'gər) ***adj.*** **1** showing bad taste or bad manners; crude; coarse [a *vulgar* joke]. *See* SYNONYMS *at* **coarse. 2** of or common among people in general; of the common people [The Italian language developed from *Vulgar* Latin. The belief that a rabbit's foot brings good luck is nothing more than a *vulgar* superstition.] —**vul'gar·ly** ***adv.***

**vul·gar·ism** (vul'gər iz'm) ***n.*** a word or phrase heard in everyday talk, but thought of as improper or not standard ["He don't" is a *vulgarism.*]

**vul·gar·i·ty** (vul gar'ə tē) ***n.*** **1** the condition of being vulgar or coarse. **2** a vulgar act, habit, or remark. — *pl.* **vul·gar'i·ties**



**vul·gar·ize** (vul'gə rīz) ***v.*** to make vulgar. —**vul'gar-ized, vul'gar·iz·ing**

**Vul·gate** (vul'gāt) ***n.*** a translation of the Bible into Latin, made in the 4th century and used in the Roman Catholic Church.

**vul·ner·a·ble** (vul'nər ə b'l) ***adj.*** **1** that can be hurt, destroyed, attacked, etc. [The wolf looked for a *vulnerable* spot into which to sink its fangs.] **2** likely to be hurt; sensitive [A vain person is *vulnerable* to criticism.] —**vul'ner·a·bil'i·ty** ***n.***

**vul·ture** (vul'chər) *n.* **1** a large bird related to eagles and hawks, that eats the remains of dead animals. *See the picture.* **2** a greedy, ruthless person.

**vy·ing** (vī'iŋ) ***adj.*** that vies; that competes.

| | | | | | | | |
|---|---|---|---|---|---|---|---|
| **a** | fat | **ir** | here | **ou** | out | **zh** | leisure |
| **ā** | ape | **ī** | bite, fire | **u** | up | **ŋ** | ring |
| **ä** | car, lot | **ō** | go | **ur** | fur | | a *in* ago |
| **e** | ten | **ô** | law, horn | **ch** | chin | | e *in* agent |
| **er** | care | **oi** | oil | **sh** | she | **ə** = | i *in* unity |
| **ē** | even | **oo** | look | **th** | thin | | o *in* collect |
| **i** | hit | **ōō** | tool | ***th*** | then | | u *in* focus |

**W, w** (dub′'l yo͞o) ***n.*** the twenty-third letter of the English alphabet. —*pl.* **W's, w's** (dub′'l yo͞oz)

**W** *the symbol for the chemical element* tungsten.

**W** or **w** *abbreviation for* **watt** *or* **watts.**

**W, W., w, w.** *abbreviations for* **west** *or* **western.**

**WA** *abbreviation for* **Washington** (State).

**WAC** Women's Army Corps.

**wad** (wäd *or* wôd) ***n.*** **1** a small, soft mass or ball [a *wad* of cotton]. **2** a lump or small, firm mass [a *wad* of chewing gum]. **3** a plug stuffed into a gun to keep the charge in place. ◆***v.*** **1** to roll up into a tight wad [to *wad* a paper in a ball]. **2** to stuff as with padding. —**wad′ded, wad′ding**



**wad·ding** (wäd′iŋ *or* wôd′iŋ) ***n.*** any soft material for use in padding, packing, stuffing, etc.; especially, cotton made up into loose, fluffy sheets.

**wad·dle** (wäd′'l *or* wôd′'l) ***v.*** to walk with short steps, swaying from side to side, as a duck. —**wad′dled, wad′dling** ◆***n.*** the act of waddling. —**wad′dler** ***n.***

**wade** (wād) ***v.*** **1** to walk through water, mud, or anything that slows one down. **2** to get through with difficulty [to *wade* through a long, dull report]. **3** to cross by wading [to *wade* a stream]. —**wad′ed, wad′ing** —☆**wade in** or **wade into,** to start or attack with force or energy: *used only in everyday talk.*

**wad·er** (wād′ər) ***n.*** **1** one that wades, as a bird with long legs that wades in water for food. **2 waders,** *pl.* waterproof trousers with boots attached, worn for wading in deep water. *See the picture.*

**WAF** Women in the Air Force.

**wa·fer** (wā′fər) ***n.*** **1** a thin, flat, crisp cracker or cookie. **2** a very thin, flat, crisp piece of bread used in Holy Communion. **3** a thin, flat piece of candy. **4** a small disk of sticky paper, used to seal letters, etc.

☆**waf·fle** (wäf′'l *or* wôf′'l) ***n.*** a crisp cake with small, square hollows, baked in a waffle iron.

☆**waffle iron** a device for baking waffles by pressing batter between its two heated plates. *See the picture.*

**waft** (waft *or* wäft) ***v.*** to carry or move lightly over water or through the air [Cooking odors *wafted* through the hallway.] ◆***n.*** **1** a smell, sound, etc. carried through the air. **2** a gust of wind. **3** a wafting movement.

**wag** (wag) ***v.*** to move rapidly back and forth or up and down [The dog *wagged* its tail.] —**wagged, wag′ging** ◆***n.*** **1** the act of wagging. **2** a person who makes jokes.

**wage** (wāj) ***v.*** to take part in; carry on [to *wage* war]. —**waged, wag′ing** ◆***n.*** **1** *often* **wages,** *pl.* money paid to an employee for work done. **2** *usually* **wages,** *pl.* what is given in return: *an older use, with a singular verb* ["The *wages* of sin is death."]

SYNONYMS: **Wage,** or **wages,** is used when we talk about money paid to an employee at regular times, such as at a rate for each hour worked. This use is especially true for skilled labor or for work done with the hands. **Salary** is used for fixed amounts usually paid once or twice each month, especially to clerks or professional workers. The word **pay** can be used in place of either *wages* or *salary*.

**wag·er** (wā′jər) ***n.*** the act of betting or something bet. ◆***v.*** to bet.

**wag·ger·y** (wag′ər ē) ***n.*** the act of joking, or a joke. —*pl.* **wag′ger·ies**

**wag·gish** (wag′ish) ***adj.*** **1** fond of joking [a *waggish* person]. **2** playful; joking [a *waggish* remark].

**wag·gle** (wag′'l) ***v.*** to wag with short, quick movements. —**wag′gled, wag′gling** ◆***n.*** the act of waggling.

**Wag·ner** (väg′nər), **Richard** 1813–1883; German composer, especially of operas.

**wag·on** (wag′ən) ***n.*** a vehicle with four wheels, especially one for carrying heavy loads.

**wag·on·er** (wag′ən ər) ***n.*** a wagon driver.

**waif** (wāf) ***n.*** **1** a person without a home or friends, especially a lost or deserted child. **2** an animal that has strayed from its owner.

**Waif** comes to us from an old Norse word meaning "anything that loosely flaps about." Later the word meant someone or something wandering, and not tied down. The word today adds to this idea of wandering the meaning of being without a home and so a "waif" is someone wandering about without a home.

**wail** (wāl) ***v.*** **1** to show that one is sad or hurt by making long, loud cries. **2** to make a sad, crying sound [The wind *wailed* in the trees.] ◆***n.*** a long cry of sadness or pain, or a sound like this. —**wail′er** ***n.***

**wain·scot** (wān′skət *or* wān′skät) ***n.*** **1** panels of wood on walls of a room, often only on the lower part. **2** the lower part of the wall of a room when it is covered with a different material from the upper part. *See the picture.* ◆***v.*** to cover with a wainscot. —**wain′scot·ed** or **wain′scot·ted, wain′scot·ing** or **wain′scot·ting**

**wain·scot·ing** or **wain·scot·ting** (wān′skət iŋ *or* wān′skät iŋ) ***n.*** *same as* **wainscot.**

**waist** (wāst) ***n.*** **1** the part of the body between the ribs and the hips. **2** the part of a garment that covers the body from the shoulders to the waistline. **3** *same as* **waistline** *in meaning* 2. **4** a garment like a shirt, worn by women or children; blouse. **5** the middle, narrow part of something [the *waist* of a violin].

**waist·band** (wāst′band) ***n.*** a band that fits around the waist, as at the top of a skirt or pair of trousers.

**waist·coat** (wes′kət *or* wāst′kōt) ***n.*** **1** a man's vest: *the usual British word.* **2** a garment worn by women that is like this.

**waist·line** (wāst′līn) ***n.*** **1** the line of the waist, between the ribs and the hips. **2** the narrow part of a woman's dress, etc., worn at the waist or above or below it as styles change. *See the picture.* **3** the distance around the waist.

**wait** (wāt) *v.* **1** to stay in a place or do nothing while expecting a certain thing to happen [*Wait* for the signal. I *waited* until six o'clock, but they never arrived.] **2** to remain undone for a time [Let it *wait* until next week.] **3** to serve food at a meal [He *waits* on table. She *waits* on me.] **4** to keep expecting, or look forward to; await [I'm *waiting* my chance.] **5** to put off serving: *used only in everyday talk* [We'll *wait* dinner for you.] ◆*n.* the act or time of waiting [We had an hour's *wait* for the train.] —**lie in wait,** to keep hidden in order to make a surprise attack. —**wait on** or **wait upon, 1** to act as a servant to. **2** to work as a clerk, waiter, or waitress in a store or restaurant [to *wait on* customers]. **3** to visit a person of higher rank in order to pay one's respects, ask a favor, etc. **4** to wait for: *used in this meaning only in some regions.* —**wait table,** to serve food to people at a table, as in a restaurant.

**wait·er** (wāt′ər) *n.* **1** a man who waits on table, as in a restaurant. **2** one who waits.

**wait·ing** (wāt′iŋ) *adj.* that waits. ◆*n.* the act of one that waits, or the time that one waits. —**in waiting,** serving someone of high rank [a lady *in waiting* to the queen].

**waiting room** a room where people wait, as in a railroad station, a dentist's office, etc.

**wait·ress** (wā′tris) *n.* a woman who waits on table, as in a restaurant.

**waive** (wāv) *v.* to give up as a right, claim, or advantage. —**waived, waiv′ing**

**waiv·er** (wā′vər) *n.* the act of giving up a right or claim, or a paper showing this [to sign a *waiver* of all claims after an accident].

**wake**[1] (wāk) *v.* **1** to come or bring out of a sleep; awake [*Wake* up! Time to *wake* your sister!] **2** to make or become active; stir up [His cruelty *woke* our anger.] **3** to be alert or become aware of [to *wake* to a danger]. —**woke** or **waked, waked, wak′ing** ◆*n.* a watch kept all night over a dead body before the funeral.

**wake**[2] (wāk) *n.* **1** the trail left in water by a moving boat or ship. **2** any track left behind [The storm left wreckage in its *wake.*] —**in the wake of,** following close behind.

**wake·ful** (wāk′fəl) *adj.* **1** not sleeping; watchful [*wakeful* guards]. **2** not able to sleep. **3** sleepless [a *wakeful* night]. —**wake′ful·ness** *n.*

**wak·en** (wāk′'n) *v.* to become awake or cause to wake; wake up.

**wale** (wāl) *n.* **1** a raised line on the skin, as one made by a whip; welt. **2** a ridge on the surface of cloth, as corduroy.

**Wales** (wālz) a part of Great Britain, west of England.

**walk** (wôk) *v.* **1** to move along on foot at a normal speed [*Walk,* do not run, to the nearest exit.] **2** to go through, over, or along by walking [I *walk* this path twice a day.] **3** to cause a horse, dog, etc. to walk. **4** to go along with on foot [I'll *walk* you home.] ☆**5** in baseball, to move to first base as a result of four pitched balls (*meaning* 5) [The pitcher *walked* three players. I *walked* on my first time at bat.] ◆*n.* **1** the act of walking, often for pleasure or exercise; stroll; hike [an afternoon *walk*]. **2** a way of walking [We knew her by her *walk.*] **3** a sidewalk or path for walking on [The park has gravel *walks.*] **4** a distance walked, often measured in time [a two-mile *walk;* an hour's *walk*]. **5** a way of living, a kind of work, a position in society, etc. [people of all *walks* of life]. ☆**6** in baseball, the act of walking a batter or of being walked. —**walk all over, 1** to defeat completely. **2** to rule over in a harsh or bullying way. *This phrase is used only in everyday talk.* —**walk away with** or **walk off with, 1** to steal. **2** to win easily.

waistlines

waders

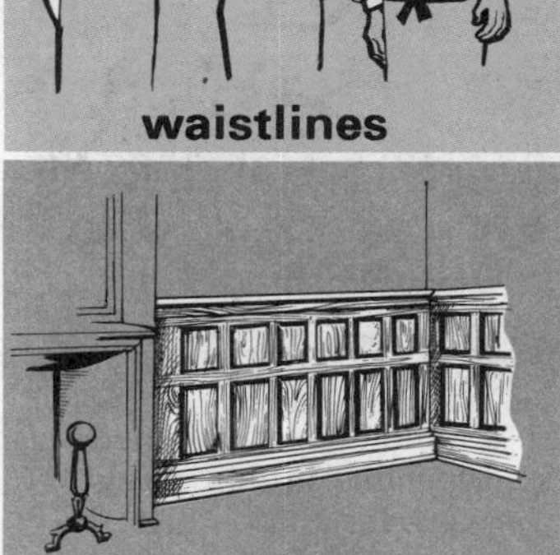

wainscot

waffle iron

**walk·er** (wôk′ər) *n.* **1** a person or animal that walks. ☆**2** a frame with or without wheels for use by babies in learning to walk or by people who have trouble walking because of injuries or disease.

☆**walk·ie-talk·ie** (wôk′ē tôk′ē) *n.* a radio set for sending and receiving messages, that can be carried about by one person.

**walking stick 1** a stick carried when walking; cane. **2** an insect that looks like a twig.

☆**walk·out** (wôk′out) *n.* **1** a strike of workers. **2** a sudden leaving of people, as from a meeting, in a show of protest.

**wall** (wôl) *n.* **1** a structure of wood, brick, plaster, etc. that forms the side of a building or shuts off a space [a stone *wall* around the town; a picture on the bedroom *wall*]. **2** anything like a wall, as in shutting something in [a *wall* of secrecy; the *walls* of the chest]. ◆*v.* **1** to close in, divide, etc. with a wall [to *wall* off an unused room]. **2** to close up with a wall [The windows have been *walled* up.] —**drive up the wall,** to make wild with anger, pain, worry, etc.: *used only in everyday talk.* —**go to the wall, 1** to be defeated. **2** to fail in business.

**wal·la·by** (wäl′ə bē) *n.* a small animal related to the kangaroo. —*pl.* **wal′la·bies** or **wal′la·by**

| | | | |
|---|---|---|---|
| **a** fat | **ir** here | **ou** out | **zh** leisure |
| **ā** ape | **ī** bite, fire | **u** up | **ŋ** ring |
| **ä** car, lot | **ō** go | **ur** fur | a *in* ago |
| **e** ten | **ô** law, horn | **ch** chin | e *in* agent |
| **er** care | **oi** oil | **sh** she | ə = i *in* unity |
| **ē** even | **oo** look | **th** thin | o *in* collect |
| **i** hit | **ōō** tool | ***th*** then | u *in* focus |

warming pan

walrus up to 3.7 m (12 ft.) long

wart hog 75 cm (30 in.) high at shoulder

**wall·board** (wôl′bôrd) ***n.*** a building material made of fibers, sawdust, etc. pressed together in thin sheets. It is used for making or covering walls and ceilings.

**wal·let** (wäl′it *or* wôl′it) ***n.*** ☆a thin, flat case for carrying money, cards, etc. in the pocket.

**wall·eye** (wôl′ī) ***n.*** a fish with large, staring eyes, as the walleyed pike.

**wall·eyed** (wôl′īd) ***adj.*** **1** having large, staring eyes, as some fishes. **2** having one or both eyes turned outward, showing much white.

**wall·flow·er** (wôl′flou′ər) ***n.*** **1** a plant with clusters of red, yellow, or orange flowers. **2** a shy or unpopular person who looks on, as at a dance, without taking part: *used only in everyday talk.*



**wal·lop** (wäl′əp *or* wôl′əp) ***v.*** **1** to hit with a very hard blow. **2** to defeat completely. ◆***n.*** a hard blow or the power to strike a hard blow. *This word is used only in everyday talk.*

**wal·low** (wäl′ō *or* wôl′ō) ***v.*** **1** to roll about in mud, dust, or filth, as pigs do. **2** to take too much pleasure in some feeling, way of life, etc. [to *wallow* in self-pity; to *wallow* in riches]. ◆***n.*** ☆a place in which animals wallow.

**wall·pa·per** (wôl′pā′pər) ***n.*** a kind of paper, usually printed with colored patterns, for covering walls or ceilings. ◆***v.*** to put wallpaper on.

**wal·nut** (wôl′nut) ***n.*** **1** a round nut with a hard, crinkled shell and a seed that is eaten. **2** the tree it grows on. **3** the wood of this tree.

> **Walnut** comes to us from an Old English word that means "foreign nut." That word was probably related to an old German word meaning the same thing, but by "foreign" the Germans meant the Roman lands in France and Italy.

**wal·rus** (wôl′rəs *or* wäl′rus) ***n.*** a large sea animal like the seal, found in northern oceans. It has two tusks and a thick layer of blubber. *See the picture.*

**waltz** (wôlts *or* wôls) ***n.*** **1** a dance for couples, with three beats to the measure. **2** music for this dance. ◆***v.*** **1** to dance a waltz. **2** to move lightly and quickly [She *waltzed* into the room.] **3** to move with success and without effort: *used only in everyday talk* [He *waltzed* through life.]

☆**wam·pum** (wäm′pəm) ***n.*** small beads made of shells and used by North American Indians as money or in belts, bracelets, etc.

**wan** (wän *or* wôn) ***adj.*** **1** having a pale, sickly color [a *wan* complexion]. **2** weak or halfhearted, as of one who is sick, sad, or tired [a *wan* smile].

**wand** (wänd *or* wônd) ***n.*** a slender rod, as one supposed to have magic power.

**wan·der** (wän′dər *or* wôn′dər) ***v.*** **1** to go from place to place in an aimless way; ramble; roam [to *wander* about a city]. **2** to go astray; drift [The ship *wandered* off course. The speaker *wandered* from the subject.] —**wan′der·er** ***n.***

**wan·der·lust** (wän′dər lust *or* wôn′dər lust) ***n.*** a strong feeling of wanting to travel.

**wane** (wān) ***v.*** **1** to get smaller, weaker, dimmer, etc. [The moon waxes and *wanes.* My interest in sports has *waned.*] **2** to draw near to the end [The day is *waning.*] —**waned, wan′ing** ◆***n.*** the act of waning. —**on the wane,** waning; getting smaller, weaker, etc.

> SYNONYMS: **Wane** suggests a fading or weakening of something which has reached a high point [The actor's fame *waned* as he grew older.] **Ebb** is used when we are talking about something that may rise and fall, at a time when it is going down [her *ebbing* fortunes].

**wan·gle** (waŋ′g′l) ***v.*** to get or bring about by sly or tricky means: *used only in everyday talk* [We *wangled* some passes to the theater.] —**wan′gled, wan′gling**

**want** (wänt *or* wônt) ***v.*** **1** to feel that one would like to have, do, get, etc.; wish or long for; desire [Do you *want* dessert? I *want* to visit Tokyo.] *See* SYNONYMS *at* **desire**. **2** to have a need for; need: *mainly a British meaning* [Your coat *wants* mending.] **3** to wish to see or speak to [Your mother *wants* you.] **4** to wish to capture, as for arrest [That man is *wanted* by the police.] **5** to lack; be short of [They *want* a little kindness. It *wants* two minutes of noon.] **6** to be poor ["Waste not, *want* not."] **Want** is also used in everyday talk to mean *ought* or *should* [You *want* to be careful.] ◆***n.*** **1** a lack or need [to starve for *want* of food]. **2** the condition of being very poor or needy [a family in *want*]. **3** a wish or desire.

☆**want ad** an advertisment, as in a newspaper, for something wanted, as a job, an employee, an apartment, etc.: *used only in everyday talk.*

**want·ing** (wän′tiŋ *or* wôn′tiŋ) ***adj.*** **1** missing or lacking [Two forks are *wanting* in this set.] **2** not up to what is needed or expected [given a chance and found *wanting*]. ◆***prep.*** **1** lacking; without [a watch *wanting* a minute hand]. **2** minus; less [The fund is *wanting* $500 of the goal set.]

**wan·ton** (wän′t′n *or* wôn′t′n) ***adj.*** **1** without reason, sense, or mercy [the *wanton* killing by the guerrillas]. **2** paying no attention to what is right [*wanton* disregard of the law]. **3** sexually loose [a *wanton* woman]. **4** playful; lively; unruly [*wanton* breezes]. ◆***n.*** a wanton person or thing; especially, a sexually loose woman.

> **Wanton** comes to us from an Old English word meaning "to bring up lacking," that is, to raise someone without the proper controls. The earliest use in today's English is to describe someone who does not have discipline or cannot be controlled.

☆**wap·i·ti** (wäp′ə tē) ***n.*** the elk of North America. *See the picture for* **elk**.

**war** (wôr) ***n.*** **1** fighting with weapons between countries or parts of a country. **2** any fight or struggle [the *war* against disease and poverty]. **3** the work or science of fighting a war [a general skilled in modern *war*]. ◆*v.* to carry on a war. —**warred, war'ring**

**war·ble** (wôr'b'l) *v.* to sing with trills, runs, etc. as some birds do. —**war'bled, war'bling** ◆*n.* the act or sound of warbling.

**war·bler** (wôr'blər) *n.* **1** a bird or person that warbles. **2** any of various songbirds.

**ward** (wôrd) *n.* **1** a person under the care of a guardian or a law court. **2** a division of a hospital [the children's *ward*]. **3** a district of a city or town, as for purposes of voting. ◆*v.* to turn aside; fend off [to *ward* off a blow, a disaster, etc].

**-ward** (wərd) *a suffix meaning* in the direction of *or* toward [*Backward* means toward the back.]

**war·den** (wôr'd'n) *n.* **1** a person who guards or takes care of something [a game *warden*]. **2** the chief official of a prison.

**ward·er** (wôr'dər) *n.* a person who guards or watches.

**ward·robe** (wôrd'rōb) *n.* **1** a closet or cabinet in which clothes are hung. **2** one's supply of clothes [a spring *wardrobe*].

**-wards** (wərdz) *same as* **-ward.**

**ware** (wer) *n.* **1** a thing or things for sale; a piece or kind of goods for sale [the *wares* of a store; hard*ware*]. **2** pottery or earthenware [dishes of fine white *ware*].

**ware·house** (wer'hous) *n.* a building where goods are stored; storehouse.

**war·fare** (wôr'fer) *n.* war or any conflict.

**war·head** (wôr'hed) *n.* the front part of a torpedo, self-propelled missile, etc., carrying the explosive.

**war·i·ly** (wer'ə lē) *adv.* in a wary, or careful, way; cautiously.

**war·i·ness** (wer'ē nis) *n.* the condition of being wary.

**war·like** (wôr'līk) *adj.* **1** that likes to make war; ready to start a fight [a *warlike* general]. **2** having to do with war [a *warlike* expedition]. **3** threatening war [a *warlike* editorial].

**warm** (wôrm) *adj.* **1** having or feeling a little heat; not cool but not hot [*warm* weather; exercise to keep *warm*]. **2** making one heated [Chopping wood is *warm* work.] **3** that keeps the body heat in [a *warm* coat]. **4** showing strong feeling; lively or enthusiastic [a *warm* welcome; a *warm* argument]. **5** full of love, kindness, etc. [*warm* friends; a *warm* heart]. **6** that suggests warmth [Yellow and orange are *warm* colors.] **7** close to guessing or finding out: *used only in everyday talk.*. ◆*v.* **1** to make or become warm [*Warm* yourself by the fire.] **2** to make or become more interested, pleased, friendly, etc. [Your kind words *warmed* my heart. She *warmed* to him after only a few meetings.] —**warm up, 1** to make or become warm; heat or reheat [*Warm up* the food from the refrigerator.] **2** to practice or exercise, as before playing in a game. —**warm'ly** *adv.* —**warm'ness** *n.*

**warm·blood·ed** (wôrm'blud'id) *adj.* **1** having a body heat that stays the same and is usually warmer than that of the surroundings [Mammals and birds are *warmblooded* animals; fish are not.] **2** having strong feelings; eager or lively; ardent.

☆**warmed-o·ver** (wôrmd'ō'vər) *adj.* **1** heated again [*warmed-over* hash]. **2** presented again, without important change [*warmed-over* ideas].

**warm·heart·ed** (wôrm'här'tid) *adj.* kind, friendly, loving, etc.

**warming pan** a covered pan for holding hot coals, used at one time to warm beds. *See the picture.*

**warmth** (wôrmth) *n.* **1** the condition of being warm [the sun's *warmth*]. **2** strong feeling; ardor, anger, love, etc. [to reply with *warmth*].

☆**warm-up** (wôrm'up') *n.* the act of practicing or exercising before playing in a game, giving a performance, etc.

**warn** (wôrn) *v.* **1** to tell of a danger; advise to be careful [I *warned* him not to play with matches.] **2** to let know in advance [She signaled to *warn* us that she would turn.]

**warn·ing** (wôr'niŋ) *n.* something that warns [Pain in the body is a *warning* of trouble.]

**War of 1812** the war from 1812 to 1815 between the U.S. and Great Britain.

**warp** (wôrp) *v.* **1** to bend or twist out of shape [Rain and heat had *warped* the boards.] **2** to turn from what is right, natural, etc.; distort [Bad companions had *warped* his character.] ◆*n.* **1** a twist or bend as in a piece of wood. **2** a quirk or odd twist of the mind. **3** the threads running lengthwise in a weaver's loom. They are crossed by the woof.

**war·rant** (wôr'ənt) *n.* **1** a good reason for something; justification [She has no *warrant* for such a belief.] **2** something that makes sure; guarantee [His wealth is no *warrant* of happiness.] **3** an official paper that gives the right to do something [The police must have a *warrant* to search a house.] ◆*v.* **1** to be a 
good reason for; justify [Her good work *warrants* our praise.] **2** to give the right to do something [His arrest was not *warranted.*] **3** to give a warranty for [This appliance is *warranted.*] **4** to say in a positive way: *used only in everyday talk* [I *warrant* they'll be late.]

**warrant officer** an officer in the armed forces ranking above an enlisted person but below a commissioned officer.

**war·ran·ty** (wôr'ən tē) *n.* a guarantee; especially, a guarantee of something in a contract. Such a guarantee is often made to someone who has bought something. The one who makes or sells the thing promises to repair or replace it if something goes wrong within a limited space of time. —*pl.* **war'ran·ties**

**war·ren** (wôr'ən *or* wär'ən) *n.* an area in which rabbits breed or are raised.

**War·ren** (wôr'ən *or* wär'ən), **Earl** 1891–1974; chief justice of the United States from 1953 to 1969.

**war·ri·or** (wôr'ē ər) *n.* a soldier: *not often used today.*

**War·saw** (wôr'sô) the capital of Poland.

**war·ship** (wôr'ship) *n.* any ship for use in war, as a destroyer, cruiser, submarine, etc.

**wart** (wôrt) *n.* **1** a small, hard growth on the skin. **2** a small growth on a plant.

**wart hog** a wild African hog with curved tusks, and warts below the eyes. *See the picture.*

| | | | | | | | | |
|---|---|---|---|---|---|---|---|---|
| **a** | fat | **ir** | here | **ou** | out | **zh** | leisure | |
| **ā** | ape | **ī** | bite, fire | **u** | up | **ŋ** | ring | |
| **ä** | car, lot | **ō** | go | **ur** | fur | | | a *in* ago |
| **e** | ten | **ô** | law, horn | **ch** | chin | | | e *in* agent |
| **er** | care | **oi** | oil | **sh** | she | | ə = | i *in* unity |
| **ē** | even | **oo** | look | **th** | thin | | | o *in* collect |
| **i** | hit | **ōō** | tool | ***th*** | then | | | u *in* focus |

**war·time** (wôr′tīm) ***n.*** any period of war.
**war·y** (wer′ē) ***adj.*** **1** on one's guard; cautious [a *wary* patrol]. **2** showing caution or suspicion [a *wary* look]. —**war′i·er, war′i·est** —**wary of,** careful of.
**was** (wuz *or* wäz) *the form of* **be** *showing the past time with singular nouns and with* I, he, she, *or* it.
**wash** (wôsh *or* wäsh) ***v.*** **1** to clean with water or other liquid, often with soap [*Wash* your face. I plan to *wash* the car.] **2** to wash clothes [She *washes* on Mondays.] **3** to carry away by the action of water [*Wash* the dirt off your hands. The bridge was *washed* out.] **4** to wear away by flowing over [The flood *washed* out the road.] **5** to flow over or against [The sea *washed* the shore.] **6** to pass water through in order to get something out [The miners *washed* the gravel for gold.] **7** to cover with a thin coating, as of paint or metal [silverware *washed* with gold]. **8** to make clean in spirit [*washed* of all guilt]. **9** to be washed without being damaged [Good muslin *washes* well.] ◆***n.*** **1** the act of washing [Your car needs a *wash*.] **2** a load of clothes, etc. that has been washed or is to be washed [to hang out the *wash*]. **3** the flow or sound of water rushing [the *wash* of the waves]. **4** an eddy made in water by a propeller, oars, etc. **5** the current of air pushed back by an airplane propeller. **6** a special liquid for washing [mouth*wash*]. **7** a thin coating, as of paint or metal. **8** watery garbage, as for feeding hogs. **9** silt, mud, etc. carried and dropped by flowing water. ◆***adj.*** that can be washed without damage [a *wash* dress]. —**wash down,** to take a drink along with food to help in swallowing.
**Wash.** *abbreviation for* **Washington** (State).
**wash·a·ble** (wôsh′ə b'l *or* wäsh′ə b'l) ***adj.*** that can be washed without being damaged.
☆**wash-and-wear** (wôsh″n wer′ *or* wäsh″n wer′) ***adj.*** of or describing cloth or clothing that needs little or no ironing after washing.
**wash·board** (wôsh′bôrd *or* wäsh′bôrd) ***n.*** ☆a board with ridges for scrubbing laundry. *See the picture.*
**wash·bowl** (wôsh′bōl *or* wäsh′bōl) ***n.*** ☆a bowl or basin for washing the hands and face; often, a bathroom sink.
☆**wash·cloth** (wôsh′klôth *or* wäsh′klôth) ***n.*** a small cloth used in washing the face or body.
**washed-out** (wôsht′out′ *or* wäsht′out′) ***adj.*** **1** faded in color, especially from washing. **2** tired-looking; pale and wan: *used only in everyday talk.*
**wash·er** (wôsh′ər *or* wäsh′ər) ***n.*** **1** a machine for washing [an automatic clothes *washer*]. **2** a disk or flat ring of metal, rubber, etc., used to help bolts, faucet valves, etc. fit more tightly. *See the picture.* **3** a person who washes [a car *washer*].
**wash·er·wom·an** (wôsh′ər woom′ən *or* wäsh′ər woom′ən) ***n.*** a woman whose work is washing clothes, etc. —*pl.* **wash′er·wom′en**
**wash·ing** (wôsh′iŋ *or* wäsh′iŋ) ***n.*** **1** the act of one that washes. **2** a load of clothes, etc. washed or to be washed.
**washing machine** a machine for washing clothes, linens, etc., now usually one working automatically.
**Wash·ing·ton** (wôsh′iŋ tən *or* wäsh′iŋ tən) **1** a State in the northwestern part of the U.S.: abbreviated **Wash., WA** **2** the capital of the U.S., in the District of Columbia.
**Wash·ing·ton** (wôsh′iŋ tən *or* wäsh′iŋ tən), **Book·er** (book′ər) **T.** 1856–1915; U.S. Negro educator and author.
**Washington, George** 1732–1799; first president of the United States, from 1789 to 1797. He was commander in chief of the American army in the Revolutionary War.
**wash·out** (wôsh′out *or* wäsh′out) ***n.*** ☆**1** the washing away of earth, a road, etc. as by a flood; also, the place washed away. **2** a failure: *slang in this meaning.*
☆**wash·room** (wôsh′ro͞om *or* wäsh′ro͞om) ***n.*** *another word for* **restroom.**
**wash·stand** (wôsh′stand *or* wäsh′stand) ***n.*** **1** a bathroom fixture with a sink. **2** a table holding a bowl and pitcher, for washing the face and hands.
**wash·tub** (wôsh′tub *or* wäsh′tub) ***n.*** a tub or deep sink for washing clothes.
**was·n't** (wuz″nt *or* wäz″nt) was not.
**wasp** (wäsp *or* wôsp) ***n.*** a flying insect with a slender body. Some wasps have a sharp sting.
**wasp·ish** (wäs′pish *or* wôs′pish) ***adj.*** **1** of or like a wasp. **2** bad-tempered; snappish.
**was·sail** (wäs″l *or* wäs′āl) ***n.*** **1** a toast of earlier times in drinking to a person's health. **2** the liquor drunk at this toast. **3** a party with much drinking.
**wast** (wäst *or* wəst) *an older form of* **were** *used with* thou, *as in the Bible.*
**wast·age** (wās′tij) ***n.*** what is wasted, as by spoiling, leaking out, etc.
**waste** (wāst) ***v.*** **1** to use up or spend without real need or purpose; make bad use of [to *waste* money or time]. **2** to fail to take advantage of [She *wasted* her chance for an education.] **3** to wear away; use up [soil *wasted* away by erosion]. **4** to lose or make lose strength, health, etc. [In his old age, he *wasted* away.] **5** to destroy or ruin [Swarms of locusts *wasted* the fields.] —**wast′ed, wast′ing** ◆***n.*** **1** the act of wasting, or loss by wasting [Prevent *waste* by using less.] **2** matter left over or thrown out as useless; refuse, scrap, etc. [Sewers carry away *waste*.] **3** matter given off by the body, as feces. **4** bits of cotton fiber or yarn, used to wipe machinery, etc. **5** a desert or wilderness. ◆***adj.*** **1** barren or wild, as land. **2** left over or thrown out as useless [*wastepaper*]. **3** used to carry off or hold waste [*waste* pipes]. —**go to waste,** to be wasted. —**lay waste,** to destroy or ruin. —**wast′er *n.***

SYNONYMS: **Waste** is a general word for any stretch of land that cannot be used to grow crops or to live on. **Wilderness** is used for a stretch of land thickly covered with trees and bushes, where no one lives and where there are no paths or trails by which to find one's way.

**waste·bas·ket** (wāst′bas′kit) ***n.*** a container for wastepaper, bits of trash, etc.
**waste·ful** (wāst′fəl) ***adj.*** using more than is needed; extravagant [a *wasteful* person; *wasteful* habits]. —**waste′ful·ly *adv.***
**waste·land** (wāst′land) ***n.*** land that is barren, empty, ruined, etc.
**waste·pa·per** (wāst′pā′pər) ***n.*** paper thrown away because it is thought to have no further use.
**watch** (wäch *or* wôch) ***v.*** **1** to keep one's sight on; look at [We *watched* the parade.] **2** to pay attention

to; observe [I've *watched* her career with interest.] **3** to take care of; look after; guard [The shepherd *watched* his flock.] **4** to stay awake or keep vigil, as in taking care of a sick person. **5** to be looking or waiting [*Watch* for the signal.] **6** to be alert or on guard [*Watch* that you don't drop the plate.] ◆***n.*** **1** the act of watching or guarding [The dog keeps *watch* over the house.] **2** a person or group that guards. **3** the time that a guard is on duty [Her *watch* ends at 8 o'clock.] **4** a device for telling time that is like a clock but small enough to be worn, as on the wrist, or carried in the pocket. **5** any of the periods of duty on shipboard, usually four hours. **6** the part of a ship's crew on duty during such a period. —**on the watch,** watching. —☆**watch oneself,** to be careful or cautious. —☆**watch out,** to be alert or on guard.

☆**watch·band** (wäch′band *or* wôch′band) ***n.*** a band of leather, cloth, etc. for holding a watch on the wrist.

**watch·dog** (wäch′dôg *or* wôch′dôg) ***n.*** a dog kept to guard a building, grounds, etc.

**watch·ful** (wäch′fəl *or* wôch′fəl) ***adj.*** watching closely; alert [a *watchful* guard]. —**watch′ful·ly** ***adv.***

**watch·mak·er** (wäch′mā′kər *or* wôch′mā′kər) ***n.*** a person who makes or repairs watches.

**watch·man** (wäch′mən *or* wôch′mən) ***n.*** a person hired to guard a building, etc., especially at night. —*pl.* **watch′men**

**watch·tow·er** (wäch′tou′ər *or* wôch′tou′ər) ***n.*** a high tower from which watch is kept, as for forest fires. *See the picture.*

**watch·word** (wäch′wurd *or* wôch′wurd) ***n.*** **1** a secret word that must be spoken to a guard in order to pass; password. **2** the slogan of some group.

**wa·ter** (wôt′ər) ***n.*** **1** the colorless liquid that falls as rain, is found in springs, rivers, lakes, and oceans, and forms a large part of the cells of all living things. It is made up of hydrogen and oxygen, with the chemical formula $H_2O$. **2 waters,** *pl.* the water in a spring, river, lake, or ocean. **3** a liquid like water or containing water [*water* from a blister; soda *water*]. **4** the degree of clearness or brightness [a diamond of the first *water*]. **5** a wavy finish put on silk, linen, etc. or on metal. ◆***v.*** **1** to give water to [to *water* a horse]. **2** to supply with water, as by sprinkling [to *water* a lawn]. **3** to make weaker by adding water [to *water* milk]. **4** to fill with tears [The onion made her eyes *water.*] **5** to fill with saliva [The smell made his mouth *water.*] **6** to put a wavy finish on [*watered* silk]. ◆***adj.*** **1** of or for water [*water* pipes]. **2** in or on water [*water* sports]. **3** found in or near water [*water* plants]. —**by water,** by ship or boat. —**hold water,** to be sound, true, accurate, etc. [His theory just won't *hold water.*]

☆**water bed** a bed that is a plastic bag filled with water and held in a frame.

**wa·ter·buck** (wôt′ər buk) ***n.*** an African antelope with long horns, that lives near water. *See the picture.* —*pl.* **wa′ter·buck** or **wa′ter·bucks**

**water buffalo** a slow, strong buffalo of Asia, Malaya, and the Philippine Islands, used for pulling loads. *See the picture.*

**water chestnut** ☆**1** an Asian plant that grows in clumps in water. ☆**2** its underground stem that is shaped like a button and is used in cooking.

**water clock** a device for measuring time by the fall or flow of water.

1.2 m (4 ft.) high at shoulder

**waterbuck**

**waterlily**

**watchtower**

**washboard**

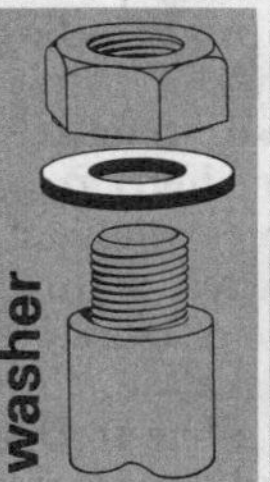

**washer**

**water buffalo**

1.5 m (5 ft.) high at shoulder

**water closet** a toilet or a bathroom.

**wa·ter·col·or** (wôt′ər kul′ər) ***n.*** **1** a paint made by mixing coloring matter with water instead of oil. **2** a picture painted with watercolors. ◆***adj.*** painted with watercolors.



**wa·ter·course** (wôt′ər kôrs) ***n.*** **1** a stream of water; river, brook, etc. **2** a channel for water, as a canal.

**wa·ter·craft** (wôt′ər kraft) ***n.*** a boat, ship, or other water vehicle. —*pl.* **wa′ter·craft**

**wa·ter·cress** (wôt′ər kres) ***n.*** a plant with leaves that are used in salads, etc. It grows usually in running water, as from springs.

**wa·ter·fall** (wôt′ər fôl) ***n.*** a steep fall of water, as from a high cliff.

**wa·ter·fowl** (wôt′ər foul) ***n.*** a bird that lives on or near the water, especially one that swims.

☆**wa·ter·front** (wôt′ər frunt) ***n.*** **1** land at the edge of a river, harbor, etc. **2** an area of such land in a city, often with docks, wharves, etc.

**wa·ter·ing place** (wôt′ər iŋ) **1** a place where animals come to drink. **2** *another name for* **spa.**

**wa·ter·lil·y** (wôt′ər lil′ē) ***n.*** a water plant with large, flat, floating leaves and flowers in many colors. *See the picture.* —*pl.* **wa′ter·lil′ies**

**wa·ter·line** (wôt′ər līn) ***n.*** the line to which the surface of the water comes on the side of a ship or boat, depending on the weight of its load.

**wa·ter·logged** (wôt′ər lôgd) ***adj.*** soaked or filled with water so that it can hardly float.

| | | | | | | | |
|---|---|---|---|---|---|---|---|
| **a** | fat | **ir** | here | **ou** | out | **zh** | leisure |
| **ā** | ape | **ī** | bite, fire | **u** | up | **ng** | ring |
| **ä** | car, lot | **ō** | go | **ur** | fur | | a *in* ago |
| **e** | ten | **ô** | law, horn | **ch** | chin | | e *in* agent |
| **er** | care | **oi** | oil | **sh** | she | **ə =** | i *in* unity |
| **ē** | even | **oo** | look | **th** | thin | | o *in* collect |
| **i** | hit | **ōō** | tool | ***th*** | then | | u *in* focus |

**W**

**Wa·ter·loo** (wôt′ər lo͞o) a village in Belgium, where Napoleon met his final defeat in 1815. ◆***n.*** any complete defeat.

**water main** a main pipe in a system of pipes that carry water.

**wa·ter·mark** (wôt′ər märk) ***n.*** **1** a mark that shows the water level of a river, etc. **2** a design pressed into paper while it is being made.

**wa·ter·mel·on** (wôt′ər mel′ən) ***n.*** a large melon with a green rind and juicy, red pulp with many seeds.

☆**water moccasin** a large, brownish, poisonous snake of the southern U.S.; cottonmouth.

**water polo** a game played with a large ball by two teams of seven swimmers each. *See the picture.*

**water power** the power of water falling or flowing, used to run machinery or to produce electricity.

**wa·ter·proof** (wôt′ər pro͞of) ***adj.*** treated with rubber, plastic, etc. so that water cannot come through [a *waterproof* raincoat]. ◆***v.*** to make waterproof.

**wa·ter·shed** (wôt′ər shed) ***n.*** **1** a ridge of high ground dividing one area whose streams flow into one river from another area whose streams flow into another river. ☆**2** one of these areas.

☆**wa·ter-ski** (wôt′ər skē′) ***v.*** to be towed over water on boards like skis by a line from a speedboat. *See the picture.* —**wa′ter-skied′, wa′ter-ski′ing**

**wa·ter·spout** (wôt′ər spout) ***n.*** **1** a pipe or spout from which water runs. **2** a tornado that moves over water and is seen as a whirling column of spray.

**wa·ter·tight** (wôt′ər tīt) ***adj.*** **1** so tight that no water can get through [a *watertight* hatch on a ship]. **2** perfectly thought out, with no weak points [a *watertight* plan].

**wa·ter·way** (wôt′ər wā) ***n.*** **1** a channel through which water runs. **2** any body of water on which boats or ships can travel, as a canal or river.

**water wheel** a wheel turned by flowing or falling water, used to give power and run machinery.

**wa·ter·works** (wôt′ər wurks) ***n.pl.*** **1** a system of reservoirs, pumps, pipes, etc. for supplying a town or city with water. **2** a building with machinery for pumping water in such a system.

**wa·ter·y** (wôt′ər ē) ***adj.*** **1** of or made up of water [the fish in its *watery* home]. **2** full of water [*watery* soil]. **3** weak, tasteless, soft, etc., as from too much water [*watery* soup].

water–skiing

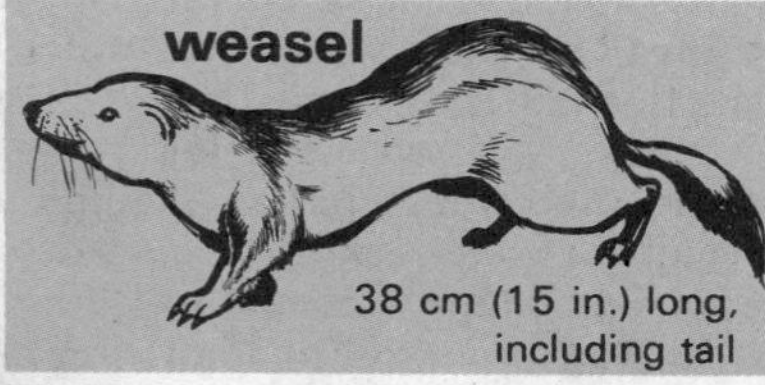

weasel

38 cm (15 in.) long, including tail

water polo

**watt** (wät *or* wôt) ***n.*** a unit for measuring electrical power. It is equal to a current of one ampere under one volt of pressure.

The **watt** was named after James Watt, a Scottish inventor who lived from 1736 to 1819. He is famous for his development of the steam engine.

**wat·tle** (wät′'l *or* wôt′'l) ***n.*** **1** the loose flap of skin hanging from the throat of a turkey, chicken, etc. **2** sticks woven together with twigs or branches and used on walls, roofs, etc. ◆***v.*** **1** to weave sticks, branches, etc. together. **2** to build of wattle. —**wat′tled, wat′tling**

**wave** (wāv) ***v.*** **1** to move up and down or back and forth; flap or sway [The flag *waved* in the breeze.] **2** to wave the hand, a handkerchief, etc., or to signal by doing this [The crowd *waved* as we drove past. I *waved* a goodbye to them.] **3** to arrange in a pattern of curves [to *wave* hair]. —**waved, wav′ing** ◆***n.*** **1** a curving swell of water moving along the surface of an ocean, lake, etc. **2** something with a motion like this [a light *wave;* a sound *wave*]. **3** a curve or pattern of curves [His hair has a natural *wave.*] **4** a waving movement as of the hand in signaling. **5** a sudden increase or rise that builds up, then goes down [a crime *wave;* a *wave* of anger; a *wave* of new settlers].

**wave·length** (wāv′leŋkth) ***n.*** the distance from any point in a wave, as of light or sound, to the same point in the next wave of the series.

**wa·ver** (wā′vər) ***v.*** **1** to show doubt or be uncertain [She never *wavered* in her decision to study law.] *See* SYNONYMS *at* **hesitate**. **2** to flutter, quiver, tremble, flicker, etc. [His voice *wavered.* The candlelight *wavered.*] ◆***n.*** the act of wavering.

**wav·y** (wā′vē) ***adj.*** having or moving in waves [*wavy* hair; fields of *wavy* grain]. —**wav′i·er, wav′i·est** —**wav′i·ness *n.***

**wax**[1] (waks) ***n.*** **1** a yellow substance that bees make and use for building honeycombs; beeswax. **2** any substance like this, as paraffin. Wax is used to make candles, polishes, etc. ◆***v.*** to put wax or polish on.

**wax**[2] (waks) ***v.*** **1** to get larger, stronger, fuller, etc. [The moon *waxes* and wanes every month.] **2** to become or grow [She began to *wax* angry.]

**wax·en** (wak′s'n) ***adj.*** **1** made of wax [a *waxen* candle]. **2** like wax [his *waxen* face].

**wax·wing** (waks′wiŋ) ***n.*** a brown bird with a crest and with red, waxy tips on its wings.

**wax·y** (wak′sē) ***adj.*** **1** covered with wax or made of wax. **2** that looks like wax [*waxy* blossoms]. —**wax′i·er, wax′i·est** —**wax′i·ness *n.***

**way** (wā) ***n.*** **1** a road, street, path, etc. [The Appian *Way* is a famous Roman road.] **2** room to pass through [Make *way* for the fire engine.] **3** a route or course from one place to another [We took the long *way* home.] **4** a ship's movement through the water [The wind died and the sailboat slowly lost *way.*] **5** distance [a long *way* off]. **6** direction [Go that *way.*] **7** a method of doing something [What's the best *way* to make a kite?] **8** manner or style [She smiled in a friendly *way.*] **9** a usual or typical manner of living, acting, etc. [to study the *ways* of ants]. **10** what one wishes; desire [He's happy when he gets his *way.*] **11** a point or detail; particular [a bad idea in some *ways*]. **12 ways,** *pl.* a framework of timber on which a ship is built and down which it slides in launching. **13** a condition: *used only in everyday talk* [She's in a bad *way* as far as money is concerned.] ◆**adv.** away; far: *used only in everyday talk* [*way* behind in the race]. —**by the way,** as a new but related point; incidentally [*By the way,* who will be there?] —**by way of, 1** going through; via [to Rome *by way of* Paris]. **2** as a way of [He did it *by way of* showing his thanks.] —**give way, 1** to go back or give up; yield. **2** to break down [The stand *gave way* under the weight of the load.] —**in the way,** so as to keep from passing, going on, etc. —**lead the way,** to be a guide or example. —**make one's way, 1** to move ahead. **2** to be successful. —**out of the way, 1** not in the way. **2** taken care of; settled. **3** not on the direct or usual route. —**the way,** how; as [with things *the way* they are]. —**under way,** moving ahead; going on.

**way·far·er** (wā'fer'ər) **n.** a person who travels, especially on foot. —**way'far'ing adj., n.**

**way·lay** (wā lā') **v. 1** to lie in wait for and attack; ambush [Robbers *waylaid* the stagecoach at the pass.] **2** to wait for and stop so as to speak with. —**way·laid** (wā lād'), **way·lay'ing**

**-ways** (wāz) *a suffix meaning* in a certain direction, position, or manner [To look *sideways* is to look in a direction to one side.]

**way·side** (wā'sīd) **n.** the land along the side of a road. ◆**adj.** on, near, or along the side of a road. —**go by the wayside,** to be put aside or thrown away.

**way·ward** (wā'wərd) **adj. 1** insisting on having one's own way; willful or disobedient [a *wayward* youth]. **2** not regular or steady; changeable; erratic [*wayward* breezes]. —**way'ward·ly adv.** —**way'ward·ness n.**

**we** (wē) **pron.** the persons speaking or writing [Here *we* are!]

> **We** is also used in speaking for oneself and the person spoken to [Are *we* still friends?] or in speaking for a group. Sometimes monarchs, editors, etc. use **we** in speaking of themselves ["*We* have so ordered," said Queen Victoria.]

**weak** (wēk) **adj. 1** having little strength, force, or power; not strong, firm, effective, etc. [*weak* from illness; a *weak* character; a *weak* team; a *weak* argument]. **2** not able to last under strain, use, etc.; not sound [a *weak* railing]. **3** not having the usual strength or power [*weak* tea; *weak* eyes]. **4** not having the needed skill [I am *weak* in arithmetic.]

> SYNONYMS: **Weak** is the general word used to mean having very little strength or power [a *weak* muscle; *weak* character]. **Feeble** means so weak as to cause pity [a *feeble* old woman; a *feeble* joke]. **Frail** is used of someone or something that is very weak or delicate [his *frail* body; a *frail* prop].

**weak·en** (wēk''n) **v.** to make or become weak or weaker [The fever had *weakened* him.]

☆**weak·fish** (wēk'fish) **n.** an ocean fish used for food, found along the Atlantic coast.

**weak-kneed** (wēk'nēd') **adj.** timid or cowardly.

**weak·ling** (wēk'liŋ) **n.** a person who is weak in body, will, character, etc.

**weak·ly** (wēk'lē) **adj.** weak or sickly; feeble. —**weak'li·er, weak'li·est** ◆**adv.** in a weak way.

**weak·ness** (wēk'nis) **n. 1** a lack of strength, force, or power. **2** a weak point; fault, as in one's character. **3** a special liking that is hard to control [I have a *weakness* for pickles.]

**weal** (wēl) **n.** a mark or ridge raised on the skin, as by a whip; welt.

**wealth** (welth) **n. 1** much money or property; riches. **2** a large amount [a *wealth* of ideas]. **3** any valuable thing or things [the *wealth* of the oceans].

> **Wealth** in its earlier usage meant "well-being" or "happiness." But as people came to think that being happy meant being rich, the word began to be used of the money and property that supposedly made people happy.

**wealth·y** (wel'thē) **adj.** having wealth; rich. *See* SYNONYMS *at* **rich.** —**wealth'i·er, wealth'i·est**

**wean** (wēn) **v. 1** to get a baby or young animal gradually trained away from suckling. **2** to make draw away gradually, as from some habit [We used good books to *wean* her away from TV.]

**weap·on** (wep'ən) **n. 1** a thing used for fighting, as a club, sword, gun, bomb, etc. **2** any means of attack or defense [A cat's claws are its *weapons.* His best *weapon* was silence.]

**wear** (wer) **v. 1** to have or carry on the body [*Wear* your coat. Do you *wear* glasses?] **2** to have or show in the way one appears [She *wore* a frown. He *wears* his hair long.] **3** to make or become damaged, used up, etc. by use or friction [She *wore* her jeans to rags. The water is *wearing* away the river bank.] **4** to make by use or friction [He *wore* a hole in his sock.] **5** to last in use [This cloth *wears* well.] **6** to pass gradually [The year *wore* on.] —**wore, worn, wear'ing** ◆**n. 1** the act of wearing or the condition of being worn [a dress for holiday *wear*]. **2** clothes; clothing [men's *wear*]. **3** the damage or loss from use or friction [These shoes show a little *wear.*] **4** the ability to last in use [There's a lot of *wear* left in that tire.] —**wear down, 1** to become less in height or thickness by use or friction. **2** to overcome by continuing to try [to *wear down* an enemy]. —**wear off,** to pass away gradually [The effects of the medicine *wore off.*] —**wear out, 1** to make or become useless from much use or friction. **2** to tire out; exhaust. —**wear'er n.**



**wear and tear** loss and damage that comes from being used.

**wear·ing** (wer'iŋ) **adj.** that tires one out.

**wea·ri·some** (wir'ē səm) **adj.** tiring or tiresome.

**wea·ry** (wir'ē) **adj. 1** tired; worn out [*weary* after a day's work]. *See* SYNONYMS *at* **tired. 2** having little or no patience or interest left; bored [I grew *weary* of listening to them.] **3** that makes a person tired; tiring [a *weary* trip]. **4** tiresome; boring [a *weary* speech]. —**wea'ri·er, wea'ri·est** ◆**v.** to make or become weary. —**wea'ried, wea'ry·ing** —**wea'ri·ly adv.** —**wea'ri·ness n.**

**wea·sel** (wē'z'l) **n.** a small animal with a long body and tail, and short legs. Weasels feed on rats, mice, birds, etc. *See the picture.*

| | | | | | | | |
|---|---|---|---|---|---|---|---|
| **a** | fat | **ir** | here | **ou** | out | **zh** | leisure |
| **ā** | ape | **ī** | bite, fire | **u** | up | **ŋ** | ring |
| **ä** | car, lot | **ō** | go | **ur** | fur | | a *in* ago |
| **e** | ten | **ô** | law, horn | **ch** | chin | | e *in* agent |
| **er** | care | **oi** | oil | **sh** | she | **ə =** | i *in* unity |
| **ē** | even | **oo** | look | **th** | thin | | o *in* collect |
| **i** | hit | **ōō** | tool | ***th*** | then | | u *in* focus |

**weath·er** (we*th*′ər) ***n.*** the conditions outside at any particular time with regard to temperature, sunshine, rainfall, etc. [We have good *weather* today for a picnic.] ◆***v.*** **1** to pass through safely [to *weather* a storm]. **2** to lay open to the weather; to season, dry, harden, etc. in the open air [a face *weathered* by outdoor living]. —☆**under the weather,** not feeling well; ill: *used only in everyday talk.*

**weath·er-beat·en** (we*th*′ər bēt′'n) ***adj.*** worn or damaged by the weather [a *weather-beaten* shack].

**weath·er·cock** (we*th*′ər käk) ***n.*** a weather vane in the form of a cock, or rooster. *See the picture.*

☆**weath·er·strip** (we*th*′ər strip) ***n.*** a strip of metal, felt, etc. put along the edges of a door or window to keep out drafts, rain, etc.: *also called* **weath′er·strip·ping.** ◆***v.*** to put weatherstrips on. —**weath′er·stripped, weath′er·strip·ping**

**weather vane** a device that swings in the wind to show the direction from which the wind is blowing.

**weave** (wēv) ***v.*** **1** to make by passing threads, strips, etc. over and under one another, as on a loom [to *weave* cloth; to *weave* a straw mat]. **2** to form into a fabric or something woven [to *weave* grass into a basket]. **3** to twist into or through [She *wove* flowers into her hair.] **4** to put together; form [to *weave* events into a story]. **5** to spin, as a spider does its web. **6** to move from side to side or in and out [a car *weaving* through traffic]. —**wove, wo′ven** or **wove** (**weaved** *is a past tense and past participle for meaning* 6), **weav′ing** ◆***n.*** a method or pattern of weaving [Burlap has a rough *weave.*] —**weav′er *n.***



**web** (web) ***n.*** **1** a woven fabric, especially one still on a loom or just taken off. **2** the network of threads spun by a spider or other insect. **3** anything put together in a careful or complicated way [a *web* of lies; the *web* of fate]. **4** the skin joining the toes of a duck, frog, or other swimming animal.

**webbed** (webd) ***adj.*** **1** having the toes joined by a web [*webbed* feet]. *See the picture.* **2** formed like a web or made of webbing.

**web·bing** (web′iŋ) ***n.*** a strong cloth woven in strips, used for belts, in furniture framework, etc.

**web-foot·ed** (web′foot′id) ***adj.*** having webbed feet.

**Web·ster** (web′stər), **Daniel** 1782–1852; U.S. statesman who was a famous orator.

**Webster, Noah** 1758–1843; U.S. writer who prepared the first important American dictionary.

**wed** (wed) ***v.*** **1** to marry; take as one's husband or wife. **2** to join closely; unite [Science and art are *wedded* in this project.] —**wed′ded, wed′ded** or **wed, wed′ding**

**we'd** (wēd) **1** we had. **2** we should. **3** we would.

**Wed.** *abbreviation for* **Wednesday.**

**wed·ded** (wed′id) ***adj.*** **1** married. **2** having to do with marriage [*wedded* bliss]. **3** devoted [She's *wedded* to her work.] **4** united; joined [They are *wedded* by common interests.]

**wed·ding** (wed′iŋ) ***n.*** **1** marriage or the marriage ceremony. **2** an anniversary of a marriage [A silver *wedding* is the 25th wedding anniversary.]

**wedge** (wej) ***n.*** **1** a piece of wood, metal, etc. narrowing to a thin edge that can be driven into a log or the like to split it. *See the picture.* **2** anything shaped like this [a *wedge* of pie]. **3** anything that gradually opens the way for some action, change, etc. ◆***v.*** **1** to split or force apart as with a wedge. **2** to fix in place with a wedge [to *wedge* a door open]. **3** to force or pack tightly [Eight people were *wedged* into the car.] —**wedged, wedg′ing**

**wed·lock** (wed′läk) ***n.*** the condition of being married; marriage.

**Wednes·day** (wenz′dē) ***n.*** the fourth day of the week.

**wee** (wē) ***adj.*** **1** very small; tiny. **2** very early [in the *wee* hours of the morning]. —**we′er, we′est**

**weed** (wēd) ***n.*** a plant that springs up where it is not wanted, as in a lawn. ◆***v.*** **1** to take out weeds, as from a garden. **2** to pick out and get rid of as useless [to *weed* out faded pictures from an album].

**weeds** (wēdz) ***n.pl.*** black clothes worn while in mourning, as by a widow.

**weed·y** (wēd′ē) ***adj.*** **1** full of weeds. **2** of or like a weed. **3** thin, tall, and awkward.

**week** (wēk) ***n.*** **1** a period of seven days, especially one beginning with Sunday and ending with Saturday. **2** the hours or days one works each week [a 35-hour *week;* a five-day *week*].

**week·day** (wēk′dā) ***n.*** **1** any day of the week except Sunday, or sometimes Saturday. **2** any day not in the weekend.

**week·end** or **week-end** (wēk′end′) ***n.*** the period from Friday night or Saturday to Monday morning, as a time for rest and recreation: *also written* **week end.** ◆***v.*** to spend the weekend [to *weekend* at home].

**week·ly** (wēk′lē) ***adj.*** **1** done, happening, appearing, etc. once a week or every week [a *weekly* visit]. **2** of a week, or of each week [a *weekly* wage]. ◆***adv.*** once a week; every week. ◆***n.*** a newspaper or magazine that comes out once a week. —*pl.* **week′lies**

**weep** (wēp) ***v.*** **1** to shed tears, as in grief; cry. **2** to let flow; shed [to *weep* bitter tears]. **3** to shed tears for; mourn. —**wept, weep′ing** —**weep′y *adj.***

**weep·ing** (wēp′iŋ) ***adj.*** **1** that weeps. **2** having graceful, drooping branches [a *weeping* willow]. ◆***n.*** the act of one that weeps.

**wee·vil** (wē′v'l) ***n.*** any of certain small beetles whose larvae destroy trees, cotton, grain, fruits, and nuts.

**weft** (weft) ***n.*** the threads woven across the warp in a loom; woof.

**weigh** (wā) ***v.*** **1** to use a scales, balance, etc. to find out how heavy a thing is [to *weigh* oneself]. **2** to have a certain weight [The suitcase *weighs* six pounds.] **3** to have importance [Her words *weighed* heavily with the jury.] **4** to measure out as by weight [to *weigh* out two pounds of candy]. **5** to think about carefully before choosing; ponder [to *weigh* one plan against another]. *See* SYNONYMS *at* **consider.** **6** to bear down heavily upon, or be a burden [He is *weighed* down with worry. The theft *weighs* on her mind.] **7** to lift up, as an anchor, before sailing.

**weight** (wāt) ***n.*** **1** heaviness; the quality a thing has because of the pull of gravity on it. **2** amount of heaviness [What is your *weight?*] **3** a piece of metal used in weighing [Put the two-ounce *weight* on the balance.] **4** any solid mass used for its heaviness [to lift *weights* for exercise; a paper *weight*]. *See the picture.* **5** any unit of heaviness, as a pound, kilogram, etc.; also, any system of such units. *See* **avoirdupois weight, troy weight.** **6** a burden, as of sorrow, worry, etc. **7** importance or influence [a matter of great *weight;* to throw one's *weight* to the losing side]. ◆***v.*** **1** to add weight to [to *weight* a ship with ballast]. **2** to burden [He is *weighted* down with sorrow.] **3** to control so as to give a particular side an advantage [The evidence was *weighted* in her favor.] —**carry weight,** to be important, have influence, etc. —**pull one's weight,** to do one's share.

**weight·less** (wāt′lis) ***adj.*** seeming to have little or no weight, especially because of being beyond the pull of gravity [Astronauts are *weightless* on spaceflights.]

**weight·y** (wāt′ē) ***adj.*** **1** very heavy. **2** hard to bear; being a burden [*weighty* responsibilities]. **3** very important; serious [a *weighty* problem]. —**weight′i·er, weight′i·est**

**weir** (wir) ***n.*** **1** a low dam built in a river. **2** a fence built across a stream to catch fish.

**weird** (wird) ***adj.*** **1** strange or mysterious in a ghostly way [*Weird* sounds came from the cave.] **2** very odd, strange, etc. [She wore a *weird* hat. That was *weird* behavior for a trusted friend.] —**weird′ly** ***adv.*** —**weird′ness** ***n.***

**Weird** comes to us from an old English word meaning "fate." The earliest meaning of *weird* is that of "having to do with fate or destiny." When we don't understand why certain things happen, they seem mysterious, brought about by fate.

**wel·come** (wel′kəm) ***adj.*** **1** that one is glad to get [a *welcome* guest; *welcome* news]. **2** gladly allowed or invited [You are *welcome* to use our library.] **3** under no obligation for a favor given ["You're *welcome*" is the usual reply to "thank you."] ◆***n.*** words or action used in greeting [We'll give them a hearty *welcome*.] ◆***v.*** to greet or receive with pleasure [I *welcome* your advice. We *welcomed* the guests.] —**wel′comed, wel′com·ing** ◆***interj.*** I am glad you have come!: *a greeting.* —☆**wear out one's welcome,** to come too often or stay too long.

**weld** (weld) ***v.*** **1** to join pieces of metal by heating until they melt together or can be hammered or pressed together. **2** to join together; unite [We *welded* the facts into an interesting story.] **3** to be capable of being welded [This metal *welds* easily.] ◆***n.*** **1** the act of welding. **2** the joint formed by welding. —**weld′er** ***n.***

**wel·fare** (wel′fer) ***n.*** **1** health, happiness, etc.; well-being. **2** aid by government agencies for the poor, those out of work, etc. —**on welfare,** getting help from the government because of being poor, out of work, etc.

**well**[1] (wel) ***n.*** **1** a natural flow of water from the earth; spring. **2** a deep hole dug in the earth to get water, gas, oil, etc. **3** a supply or store [The book is a *well* of information.] **4** a shaft in a building, as for a staircase. **5** a container for liquid, as an inkwell. ◆***v.*** to flow or gush [Pity *welled* up in her heart.]

**well**[2] (wel) ***adv.*** **1** in a way that is pleasing, wanted, good, right, etc. [The work is going *well*. Treat him *well*. She sings *well*.] **2** in comfort and plenty [They live *well*.] **3** with good reason [You may *well* ask for a raise.] **4** to a large degree; much [They are *well* tanned.] **5** with certainty [You know very *well* why it was done.] **6** in a thorough way; completely [Stir it *well*.] **7** in a familiar way; closely [I know him *well*.] **8** properly, fully, etc.: *often used in words formed with*

*a hyphen* [*well*-fed; *well*-worn]. —The comparative of *well* is **better**, the superlative is **best**. ◆***adj.*** **1** in good health; having no illness [to be *well* again]. **2** comfortable, satisfactory, etc. [Things are *well* with us.] **3** proper, fit, right, etc. [It is *well* that you came.] ◆***interj.*** a word used to show surprise, relief, agreement, etc. —**as well, 1** besides; in addition. **2** equally [You could *as well* stay home.] —**as well as, 1** just as good or as much as. **2** in addition to [for pleasure *as well as* profit].



SYNONYMS: To be **well** means simply to be free from illness [She is at last getting *well*.] To be **healthy** is to be free from illness and also to have normal strength and energy [He has been *healthy* all his life.]

**we'll** (wēl) **1** we shall. **2** we will.

**well-bal·anced** (wel′bal′ənst) ***adj.*** **1** having the needed parts in the right amounts [a *well-balanced* meal]. **2** showing good sense; reasonable.

**well-be·ing** (wel′bē′iŋ) ***n.*** the condition of being well, happy, wealthy, etc.; welfare.

**well·born** (wel′bôrn′) ***adj.*** coming from a family of high social position.

**well-bred** (wel′bred′) ***adj.*** having or showing good manners; polite.

**well-done** (wel′dun′) ***adj.*** **1** done with skill [a job *well-done*]. **2** thoroughly cooked [a *well-done* steak].

**well-fed** (wel′fed′) ***adj.*** showing the results of eating much good food; plump or fat.

**well-found·ed** (wel′foun′did) ***adj.*** based on facts or good judgment [a *well-founded* belief].

**well-groomed** (wel′grōōmd′) ***adj.*** **1** clean and neat. **2** carefully cared for, as a horse.

| | | | | | | | |
|---|---|---|---|---|---|---|---|
| **a** | fat | **ir** | here | **ou** | out | **zh** | leisure |
| **ā** | ape | **ī** | bite, fire | **u** | up | **ŋ** | ring |
| **ä** | car, lot | **ō** | go | **ʉr** | fur | | a *in* ago |
| **e** | ten | **ô** | law, horn | **ch** | chin | | e *in* agent |
| **er** | care | **oi** | oil | **sh** | she | **ə** = | i *in* unity |
| **ē** | even | **oo** | look | **th** | thin | | o *in* collect |
| **i** | hit | **ōō** | tool | ***th*** | then | | u *in* focus |

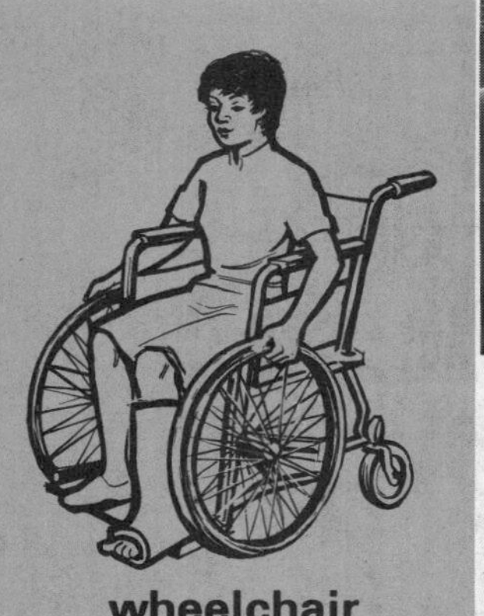
wheelchair

whales
up to 18 m (60 ft.) long

wheat

**well-ground·ed** (wel'groun'did) ***adj.*** **1** having good training in the basic facts of a subject. **2** based on facts or well-founded, as a theory.

**well-in·formed** (wel'in fôrmd') ***adj.*** **1** knowing very much about a subject [*well-informed* on music]. **2** knowing much about many subjects.

**Wel·ling·ton** (wel'iŋ tən), Duke of 1769–1852; British general who defeated Napoleon at Waterloo.

**well-known** (wel'nōn') ***adj.*** **1** widely known; famous [a *well-known* actor]. **2** fully known; familiar [I heard a *well-known* voice behind me.]



**well-man·nered** (wel'man'ərd) ***adj.*** having or showing good manners; polite; courteous.

**well-mean·ing** (wel'mē'niŋ) ***adj.*** showing an intention to help or to do the right thing, but often with bad results.

**well-nigh** (wel'nī') ***adv.*** almost; very nearly.

**well-off** (wel'ôf') ***adj.*** **1** in a good or fortunate condition. **2** wealthy; well-to-do.

**well-pre·served** (wel'pri zurvd') ***adj.*** in good condition or looking good, in spite of age.

**well-read** (wel'red') ***adj.*** having read much.

**well-round·ed** (wel'roun'did) ***adj.*** **1** well planned for proper balance [a *well-rounded* program]. **2** showing interest, ability, etc. in many fields.

**well·spring** (wel'spriŋ) ***n.*** **1** a spring or fountainhead. **2** a supply that is always full.

**well-thought-of** (wel'thôt'uv') ***adj.*** having a good reputation.

**well-to-do** (wel'tə dōō') ***adj.*** wealthy; well-off. *See* SYNONYMS *at* **rich**.

**well-wish·er** (wel'wish'ər) ***n.*** a person who wishes well to another, or to a cause, etc.

**well-worn** (wel'wôrn') ***adj.*** **1** much worn; much used [a *well-worn* sweater]. **2** used too often; no longer fresh or new [a *well-worn* joke].

**Welsh** (welsh) ***adj.*** of Wales, its people, etc. ◆***n.*** the Celtic language spoken by some of the people in Wales. —**the Welsh,** the people of Wales.

**Welsh·man** (welsh'mən) ***n.*** a person born or living in Wales. —*pl.* **Welsh'men**

**Welsh rabbit** a dish made with melted cheese, served on toast: *also called* **Welsh rarebit.**

**welt** (welt) ***n.*** **1** a strip of leather used in a shoe to strengthen the seam where the sole and top part are joined. **2** a ridge raised on the skin, as by a whip.

**wel·ter** (wel'tər) ***v.*** **1** to roll about or wallow [The pigs *weltered* in the mud.] **2** to be soaked, stained, etc. [to *welter* in blood]. ◆***n.*** **1** a tossing and tumbling, as of waves. **2** a confusion; jumble [fighting through a *welter* of bargain hunters].

**wel·ter·weight** (wel'tər wāt) ***n.*** a boxer or wrestler between a lightweight and a middleweight (in boxing, between 136 and 147 pounds)

**wen** (wen) ***n.*** a harmless growth under the skin, especially on the scalp.

**wench** (wench) ***n.*** a girl or young woman: *now seldom used except in a joking or scornful way.*

**wend** (wend) ***v.*** to go; travel [We *wended* our way home.]

**went** (went) *past tense of* **go.**

**wept** (wept) *past tense and past participle of* **weep.**

**were** (wur *or* wər) *the form of the verb* **be** *that is used to show the past time with* we, you, *and* they, *and with plural nouns* [*Were* you pleased? We *were,* and our parents *were,* too.] *Were* is also used with all persons in supposing, wishing, etc. [If I *were* rich, I'd buy a boat.]

**we're** (wir) we are.

**weren't** (wurnt) were not.

**were·wolf** or **wer·wolf** (wir'woolf *or* wur'woolf) ***n.*** in folk tales, a person changed into a wolf, or one who can change into a wolf at any time. —*pl.* **were'-wolves** or **wer'wolves**

**Werewolf** comes to us from two Old English words meaning "man" and "wolf." In earlier times, the people believed that some men could change into wolves and then change back again.

**Wes·ley** (wes'lē), **John** 1703–1791; English minister who founded the Methodist Church.

**west** (west) ***n.*** **1** the direction toward the point where the sun sets. **2** a place or region in or toward this direction. ◆***adj.*** **1** in, of, to, or toward the west [the *west* side of the house]. **2** from the west [a *west* wind]. **3** **West,** that is the western part of [*West* Africa]. ◆***adv.*** in or toward the west ["Go *west,* young man."] —**the West,** ☆**1** the western part of the U.S., especially the part west of the Mississippi River. **2** the Western Hemisphere, or the Western Hemisphere and Europe. **3** the U.S. and its allies in Europe and the Western Hemisphere.

**west·er·ly** (wes'tər lē) ***adj., adv.*** **1** toward the west. **2** from the west.

**west·ern** (wes'tərn) ***adj.*** **1** in, of, or toward the west [the *western* sky]. **2** from the west [a *western* wind]. **3** **Western,** of the West. ◆***n.*** ☆a story, movie, etc. about cowboys or pioneers in the western U.S.

**West·ern·er** (wes'tər nər) ***n.*** a person born or living in the West.

**Western Hemisphere** that half of the earth that includes North and South America.

**west·ern·most** (wes'tərn mōst) ***adj.*** farthest west.

**Western Samoa** a country mainly on two large islands in the South Pacific. *See the map for* **Samoa.**

**West Germany** a country in north-central Europe.

**West Indies** a large group of islands in the Atlantic between North America and South America, including the Bahamas and the Antilles.

**West·min·ster Abbey** (west'min'stər) a church in London where British monarchs are crowned.

**West Point** a military post in New York State on the

Hudson River. The U.S. Military Academy is located there.

**West Virginia** a State in the northeastern part of the U.S.: abbreviated **W.Va., WV**

**west·ward** (west′wərd) ***adv., adj.*** toward the west.

**west·wards** (west′wərdz) ***adv.*** *same as* **westward.**

**wet** (wet) ***adj.*** **1** covered or soaked with water or some other liquid [Wipe it off with a *wet* rag.] **2** rainy [a *wet* day]. **3** not dry yet [*wet* paint]. ☆**4** allowing alcoholic liquor to be sold [a *wet* town]. —**wet′ter, wet′test** ◆***n.*** water, rain, moisture, etc. [They are out there working in the *wet.*] ◆***v.*** to make or become wet [She *wet* her lips.] —**wet** or **wet′ted, wet′ting** —**wet′ness** ***n.***

SYNONYMS: Something is **wet** when it is covered or soaked with water or some other liquid [*wet* hands or clothes] or is not yet dry [*wet* cement]. Something is **damp** when it is wet in a way that is uncomfortable [a *damp* basement]. Something is **moist** when it is a little wet and it is wanted to be so [*moist* air].

**we've** (wēv) we have.

**wh-** these letters at the beginning of a word or syllable are pronounced (hw) or (w), although only the first pronunciation is shown for them. For example, **when** is pronounced either (hwen) or (wen).

**whack** (hwak) ***v.*** to hit or slap with a sharp sound. ◆***n.*** a blow that makes a sharp sound; also, this sound. *This word is used only in everyday talk.* —☆**out of whack,** not in proper working condition: *used only in everyday talk.*

**whale**[1] (hwāl) ***n.*** a very large mammal that lives in the sea and looks like a fish. Whales are valued for their oil. *See the picture.* ◆***v.*** to hunt for whales. —**whaled, whal′ing**

**whale**[2] (hwāl) ***v.*** to beat or thrash: *used only in everyday talk.* —**whaled, whal′ing**

☆**whale·boat** (hwāl′bōt) ***n.*** a long boat used in whaling, or a boat like this, as a ship's lifeboat.

**whale·bone** (hwāl′bōn) ***n.*** the tough, elastic substance that hangs in fringed sheets from the upper jaw of some whales. It strains out the tiny sea animals on which the whale feeds.

**whal·er** (hwāl′ər) ***n.*** **1** a ship used in whaling. **2** a person whose work is whaling.

**whal·ing** (hwāl′iŋ) ***n.*** the hunting and killing of whales for their blubber, whalebone, oil, etc.

**wharf** (hwôrf) ***n.*** a long platform built out over water so that ships can dock beside it to load and unload. —*pl.* **wharves** (hwôrvz) or **wharfs**

**what** (hwut *or* hwät) ***pron.*** **1** which thing, happening, condition, etc. [*What* is that object? *What* did he ask you? *What* is your address?] **2** that which or those which [I heard *what* she said.] ◆***adj.*** **1** which or which kind of [*What* dog is your favorite? I know *what* cookies you like.] **2** as much as or as many as [Borrow *what* books you need.] **3** how great! so much! [*What* nonsense he's talking!] ◆***adv.*** **1** in what way; how [*What* does it help to complain?] **2** in some way; partly [*What* with singing and joking, the time passed quickly.] ◆***conj.*** that [Never doubt but *what* she loves you.] ◆***interj.*** a word used to show surprise, anger, etc. ["*What!* Late again?"] —**and what not,** and other things of all sorts. —**what for?** for what reason? why? —**what if,** what would happen if; suppose. —**what's what,** the real facts of the matter: *used only in everyday talk.*

**what·ev·er** (hwət ev′ər) ***pron.*** **1** anything that [Tell her *whatever* you wish.] **2** no matter what [*Whatever* you do, don't hurry.] **3** anything at all: *used only in everyday talk* [She reads novels, biographies, or *whatever.*] *Whatever* is also used in questions in place of *what* for extra force [*Whatever* can it be?] ◆***adj.*** **1** of any type or kind [I have no plans *whatever.*] **2** no matter what [*Whatever* game we play, I never win.]

**what·not** (hwut′nät *or* hwät′nät) ***n.*** a set of open shelves for small art objects, books, etc.

**what's** (hwuts *or* hwäts) what is.

**what·so·ev·er** (hwut′sō ev′ər *or* hwät′sō ev′ər) ***pron., adj.*** *same as* **whatever.**

**wheat** (hwēt) ***n.*** **1** the cereal grass whose grain is used in making the most common type of flour. **2** this grain. *See the picture.*

**wheat·en** (hwēt′′n) ***adj.*** made of wheat.

☆**wheat germ** a substance got from wheat seeds, that has vitamins and can be added to other food.

**Wheat·ley** (hwēt′lē), **Phillis** 1753?–1784; American poet. She was born in Africa and was brought to America as a slave.

**whee·dle** (hwē′d'l) ***v.*** **1** to coax or flatter into doing something. **2** to get in this way [He tried to *wheedle* a promise out of me.] —**whee′dled, whee′dling**

**wheel** (hwēl) ***n.*** **1** a round disk or frame that turns on an axle fixed at its center [a wagon *wheel*]. **2** any- 
thing like a wheel or having a wheel as its main part [the steering *wheel* of a car; a spinning *wheel*]. ☆**3 wheels,** *pl.* an automobile; car: *slang in this meaning.* **4** *usually* **wheels,** *pl.* the forces or machines that move or control something [the *wheels* of progress]. ☆**5** a person who is important or has influence: *also called* **big wheel**: *slang in this meaning.* ◆***v.*** **1** to move on wheels or in a vehicle with wheels [to *wheel* a grocery cart]. **2** to turn around; revolve, rotate, pivot, etc. [The deer *wheeled* to face the dogs.] —**at the wheel,** steering a car, ship, etc. —☆**wheel and deal,** to act in a bold and forceful way, as in a business deal: *a slang phrase.*

**wheel·bar·row** (hwēl′bar′ō) ***n.*** a small kind of cart pushed or pulled by hand and having a single wheel. *See the picture.*

**wheel·chair** (hwēl′cher) ***n.*** ☆a chair on wheels, used by the sick or injured in moving about. *See the picture.*

**wheel·wright** (hwēl′rīt) ***n.*** a person who makes and repairs wheels, wagons, etc.

**wheeze** (hwēz) ***v.*** **1** to breathe hard with a whistling or rasping sound, as in asthma. **2** to make a sound like this [The old organ *wheezed.*] —**wheezed, wheez′ing** ◆***n.*** the act or sound of wheezing. —**wheez′y** ***adj.***

| | | | | | | | |
|---|---|---|---|---|---|---|---|
| **a** | fat | **ir** | here | **ou** | out | **zh** | leisure |
| **ā** | ape | **ī** | bite, fire | **u** | up | **ŋ** | ring |
| **ä** | car, lot | **ō** | go | **ur** | fur | | a *in* ago |
| **e** | ten | **ô** | law, horn | **ch** | chin | | e *in* agent |
| **er** | care | **oi** | oil | **sh** | she | ə = | i *in* unity |
| **ē** | even | **oo** | look | **th** | thin | | o *in* collect |
| **i** | hit | **ōō** | tool | ***th*** | then | | u *in* focus |

**whelk** (hwelk) ***n.*** a large sea snail with a spiral shell. Some kinds are used for food. *See the picture.*

**whelp** (hwelp) ***n.*** **1** a young dog; puppy. **2** a young lion, tiger, wolf, etc.; cub. ◆***v.*** to give birth to whelps.

**when** (hwen) ***adv.*** at what time? [*When* did they leave?] ◆***conj.*** **1** at what time [They told us *when* to eat.] **2** at which time [The rooster crowed at six, *when* the sun rose.] **3** at or during the time that [*When* I was your age, I couldn't swim.] **4** although [She's reading *when* she might be playing.] **5** if [How can we finish, *when* you don't help?] ◆***pron.*** what time or which time [Until *when* will you be here?]

**whence** (hwens) ***adv.*** from what place, person, or source; from where [*Whence* did he come? *Whence* does she get her strength?]

**when·ev·er** (hwen ev′ər) ***conj.*** at whatever time; at any time that [Visit us *whenever* you can.] ◆***adv.*** when?: *used in everyday talk for extra force* [*Whenever* will you stop teasing?]

**when·so·ev·er** (hwen′sō ev′ər) ***adv., conj.*** *same as* **whenever.**

**where** (hwer) ***adv.*** **1** in or at what place? [*Where* is the car?] **2** to what place [*Where* did he go next?] **3** in what way? how? [*Where* is she at fault?] **4** from what place, person, or source? [*Where* did you find out?] ◆***conj.*** **1** at what place [I know *where* it is.] **2** at the place in which [Stay home *where* you belong. Moss grows *where* there is shade.] **3** to the place to

844 which [We'll go *where* you go.] ◆***pron.*** **1** what place? [*Where* are you from?] **2** the place at which [It is a mile to *where* I live.]

**where·a·bouts** (hwer′ə bouts) ***n.*** the place where a person or thing is [I don't know her *whereabouts.*] ◆***adv.*** at what place? where? [*Whereabouts* are we?]

**where·as** (hwer az′) ***conj.*** **1** in view of the fact that; because [*Whereas* the club needs more money, we hereby raise the dues.] **2** while on the other hand [We had good luck, *whereas* they had none.]

**where·by** (hwer bī′) ***adv.*** with which; by which [a scheme *whereby* to make money].

**where·fore** (hwer′fôr) ***adv.*** for what reason? why?: *no longer much used* [*Wherefore* did you leave?] ◆***conj.*** **1** for which [the reason *wherefore* we have met]. **2** because of which; therefore [We are victorious, *wherefore* let us be glad.] ◆***n.*** the reason; cause [Let me explain the whys and *wherefores* of the plan.]

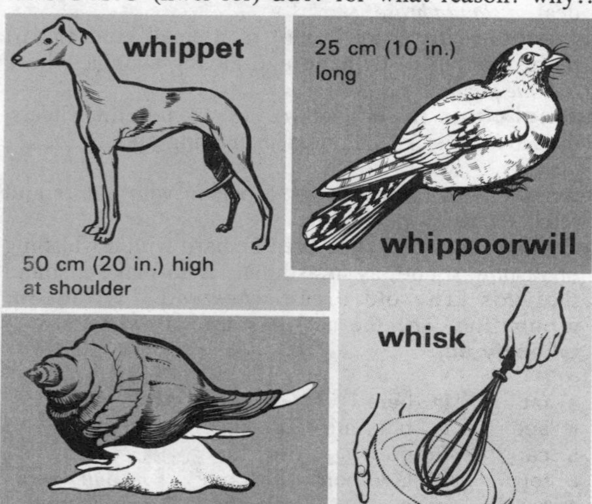


**where·in** (hwer in′) ***conj.*** in which [the room *wherein* she lay].

**where·of** (hwer uv′) ***adv., conj.*** of what, which, or whom [the things *whereof* I spoke].

**where·on** (hwer än′) ***conj.*** on which [the hill *whereon* we stand].

**where·so·ev·er** (hwer′sō ev′ər) ***adv., conj.*** *same as* **wherever.**

**where·to** (hwer to͞o′) ***conj.*** to which [the place *whereto* they hurry].

**where·up·on** (hwer ə pän′) ***conj.*** **1** at which; after which [He ended his speech, *whereupon* everyone cheered.] **2** upon which [the ground *whereupon* she had fallen].

**wher·ev·er** (hwer ev′ər) ***conj.*** in, at, or to whatever place [I'll go *wherever* you tell me.] ◆***adv.*** where?: *used in everyday talk for extra force* [*Wherever* have you been?]

**where·with** (hwer with′ *or* hwer wi*th*′) ***conj.*** with which [lacking the money *wherewith* to pay her].

**where·with·al** (hwer′wi*th* ôl′) ***n.*** what is needed to get something done, especially money [Do you have the *wherewithal* to travel?]

**whet** (hwet) ***v.*** **1** to sharpen by grinding or rubbing, as the edge of a knife. **2** to make stronger; stimulate [to *whet* the appetite]. —**whet′ted, whet′ting**

**wheth·er** (hwe*th*′ər) ***conj.*** **1** if it is true or likely that [I don't know *whether* I can go.] **2** in either case that [It makes no difference *whether* he comes or not.]

**whet·stone** (hwet′stōn) ***n.*** a stone with a rough surface, for sharpening knives and tools.

**whew** (hyo͞o *or* hwyo͞o) ***interj.*** a sound made by blowing out breath through the half-open mouth, to show surprise, relief, disgust, etc.

**whey** (hwā) ***n.*** the thin, watery part of milk, that separates from the curd when cheese is made.

**which** (hwich) ***pron.*** **1** what one or what ones of those being talked about or suggested [*Which* will you choose?] **2** the one or the ones that [I know *which* I like best.] **3** that [the story *which* we all know]. ◆***adj.*** what one or ones [*Which* apples are best for baking?]

**which·ev·er** (hwich ev′ər) ***pron., adj.*** **1** any one [Choose *whichever* desk you like.] **2** no matter which [*Whichever* you choose, you won't like it.]

**whiff** (hwif) ***n.*** **1** a light puff of air or wind. **2** a faint smell [a *whiff* of garlic]. ◆***v.*** to blow in puffs.

**Whig** (hwig) ***n.*** **1** in former times, a member of one of the main political parties of England. ☆**2** an American colonist who favored the Revolution against England. ☆**3** a member of an earlier political party in the U.S., that opposed the Democratic Party.

**while** (hwīl) ***n.*** a period of time [I waited a short *while.*] ◆***conj.*** **1** during the time that [I read a book *while* I waited.] **2** in spite of the fact that; although [*While* the car isn't large, it will hold four people.] **3** and on the other hand [She likes concerts, *while* I like plays.] ◆***v.*** to spend or pass in a pleasant way [to *while* away a few hours]. —**whiled, whil′ing** —**the while,** during the same time. —**worth one's while,** worth the time it takes one.

**whi·lom** (hwī′ləm) ***adj.*** former [their *whilom* friends].

**whilst** (hwīlst) ***conj.*** *same as* **while**: *mainly a British word.*

**whim** (hwim) ***n.*** a sudden thought or wish to do something, without any particular reason [On a *whim,* he climbed aboard the bus for Chicago.]

**whim·per** (hwim′pər) ***v.*** to make low, broken crying sounds [The dog *whimpered* in fear of the bear.] ◆***n.*** the act or sound of whimpering.

**whim·si·cal** (hwim′zi k'l) ***adj.*** **1** full of whims or whimsy; having odd notions [a *whimsical* inventor of useless machines]. **2** different in an odd way [a *whimsical* costume for the party]. —**whim′si·cal·ly** ***adv.***

**whim·sy** (hwim′zē) ***n.*** **1** an odd notion or wish that comes to one suddenly; whim. **2** an odd or fanciful kind of humor [poems full of *whimsy*]. —*pl.* **whim′sies** *Also spelled* **whim′sey.** —*pl.* **whim′seys**

**whine** (hwīn) ***v.*** **1** to make a long, high, feeble sound or cry, as in complaining [a *whining* child]. **2** to say or beg in a whining way [Please stop *whining* about your troubles.] —**whined, whin′ing** ◆***n.*** the act or sound of whining.

**whin·ny** (hwin′ē) ***n.*** the low neighing sound made by a horse when it is comfortable. —*pl.* **whin′nies** ◆***v.*** to make this sound. —**whin′nied, whin′ny·ing**

**whip** (hwip) ***n.*** **1** a thing for striking or beating a person or animal, usually a rod with a lash at one end. **2** a blow or stroke as with a whip. **3** a dessert made of sugar and whipped cream, beaten egg whites, etc., and often fruit. ◆***v.*** **1** to strike as with a whip, strap, etc.; beat; lash. **2** to move, pull, throw, etc. suddenly [He *whipped* off his hat.] **3** to beat into a froth [to *whip* cream]. **4** to flap about [a sail *whipping* in the wind]. —**whipped, whip′ping**

**whip·lash** (hwip′lash) ***n.*** **1** the lash of a whip. ☆**2** a sudden, sharp jolting of the neck backward and then forward, done to a person in a car hit from the rear.

**whip·per·snap·per** (hwip′ər snap′ər) ***n.*** a young or unimportant person who is thought to show lack of respect for those who are older or in a higher position.

**whip·pet** (hwip′it) ***n.*** a swift dog like a small greyhound, used in racing. *See the picture.*

**whipping cream** sweet cream with a large amount of butterfat, that can be whipped until stiff.

☆**whip·poor·will** (hwip′ər wil) ***n.*** a grayish North American bird whose call sounds a little like its name. It is active only at night. *See the picture.*

**whir** or **whirr** (hwur) ***v.*** to move swiftly with a sound like that of a wheel or propeller turning rapidly. —**whirred, whir′ring** ◆***n.*** this sound.

**whirl** (hwurl) ***v.*** **1** to turn rapidly around and around; spin fast [The dancers *whirled* around the room.] **2** to move or carry rapidly [The car *whirled* up the hill.] **3** to seem to be spinning; reel [My head is *whirling.*] ◆***n.*** **1** the act of whirling or a whirling motion [Give the crank a *whirl.*] **2** a series of parties, etc. [in the social *whirl*]. **3** a dizzy or confused condition [My head's in a *whirl.*] —☆**give it a whirl,** to make an attempt: *used only in everyday talk.*

**whirl·i·gig** (hwur′li gig) ***n.*** **1** a child's toy that whirls or spins, as a pinwheel. **2** a whirling motion.

**whirl·pool** (hwurl′po͞ol) ***n.*** water whirling swiftly around and around. A whirlpool sucks floating things in toward its center.

☆**whirlpool bath** a bath, such as one that is used in hydrotherapy, in which a device causes a current of warm water to swirl around.

**whirl·wind** (hwurl′wind) ***n.*** a current of air whirling violently around and around in an upward spiral and moving forward, causing a storm. ◆***adj.*** carried on as fast as possible [a *whirlwind* political campaign].

**whisk** (hwisk) ***v.*** **1** to move, brush, etc. with a quick, sweeping motion [He *whisked* the lint from his coat with a brush.] **2** to move quickly [The cat *whisked* under the sofa.] ◆***n.*** **1** the act of whisking or a whisking motion. **2** a small broom with a short handle, for brushing clothes: *the full name is* **whisk broom. 3** a kitchen tool made up of wire loops fixed in a handle, for whipping eggs, etc. *See the picture.*

**whisk·er** (hwis′kər) ***n.*** **1 whiskers,** *pl.* the hair growing on a man's face, especially the beard on the cheeks. **2** a single hair of a man's beard. **3** any of the long, stiff hairs on the upper lip of a cat, rat, etc. —**whisk′ered** ***adj.***

**whis·key** (hwis′kē) ***n.*** a strong alcoholic liquor made from certain kinds of grain, as wheat, corn, or rye. —*pl.* **whis′keys** or **whis′kies**

> The word **whiskey** comes from the old Irish language. It is a shorter form of *usquebaugh,* an Irish Gaelic word meaning "water of life."

**whis·ky** (hwis′kē) ***n.*** *another spelling of* **whiskey**: *used mainly in Great Britain and Canada.* —*pl.* **whis′kies**



**whis·per** (hwis′pər) ***v.*** **1** to speak or say in a low, soft voice, especially without vibrating the vocal cords. **2** to make a soft, rustling sound [The breeze *whispered* in the tall grass.] **3** to tell as a secret or gossip [It has been *whispered* that they will marry.] ◆***n.*** **1** soft, low tone of voice [to speak in a *whisper*]. **2** something whispered, as a secret or rumor. **3** a soft, rustling sound.

**whist** (hwist) ***n.*** a card game like bridge, usually for two pairs of players.

**whis·tle** (hwis′'l) ***v.*** **1** to make a high, shrill sound as by forcing breath through puckered lips or by sending steam through a small opening. **2** to move with a high, shrill sound [The arrow *whistled* past her ear.] **3** to blow a whistle. **4** to produce by whistling [to *whistle* a tune]. —**whis′tled, whis′tling** ◆***n.*** **1** a device for making whistling sounds. **2** the act or sound of whistling. —**whis′tler** ***n.***

**whit** (hwit) ***n.*** the least bit; jot [He hasn't changed a *whit.* They are not a *whit* the wiser.]

**white** (hwīt) ***adj.*** **1** of the color of pure snow or milk. Although we speak of white as a color, it is really the blending of all colors. A surface is white only when it reflects all the light rays that make color. **2** of a light or pale color [*white* meat; *white* wine]. **3** pale or wan [He turned *white* with fear.] **4** pure or innocent; spotless. **5** having a light-colored skin;

| | | | | | | | |
|---|---|---|---|---|---|---|---|
| **a** | fat | **ir** | here | **ou** | out | **zh** | leisure |
| **ā** | ape | **ī** | bite, fire | **u** | up | **ng** | ring |
| **ä** | car, lot | **ō** | go | **ur** | fur | | a *in* ago |
| **e** | ten | **ô** | law, horn | **ch** | chin | | e *in* agent |
| **er** | care | **oi** | oil | **sh** | she | **ə =** | i *in* unity |
| **ē** | even | **oo** | look | **th** | thin | | o *in* collect |
| **i** | hit | **o͞o** | tool | ***th*** | then | | u *in* focus |

Caucasoid [the *white* people]. —**whit′er, whit′est** ◆*n.* **1** white color, white paint, white dye, etc. **2** white clothes [The bride wore *white.*] **3** a person with light-colored skin; Caucasoid. **4** a white or light-colored part or thing [the *white* of an egg; the *whites* of the eyes]. —**white′ness** *n.*

**white·cap** (hwīt′kap) *n.* a wave with its crest broken into white foam.

**white-col·lar** (hwīt′käl′ər) *adj.* ☆describing or having to do with people who hold jobs as clerks, salespeople, professional workers, etc.

**white elephant** something that has little use or value although it costs a lot to keep up.

**white·fish** (hwīt′fish) *n.* a white or silvery lake fish that is valued as food.

**white flag** a white banner or cloth held up as a sign that one wants a truce or is willing to surrender.

**white gold** gold alloy that looks like platinum.

**white-hot** (hwīt′hät′) *adj.* glowing white with heat.

**White House, the** ☆**1** the building where the President of the U.S. lives, in Washington, D.C.: *also called the* **Executive Mansion.** *See the picture.* ☆**2** the executive branch of the U.S. government.

**white lie** a lie about something unimportant, often one told to keep from hurting someone's feelings.

**whit·en** (hwīt′′n) *v.* to make or become white.

☆**white·wall** (hwīt′wôl) *n.* an automobile tire with a round white strip on the outer side.

 **white·wash** (hwīt′wôsh *or* hwīt′wäsh) *n.* **1** a white liquid made of lime, powdered chalk, and water, used to whiten walls. **2** the act of covering up someone's faults or mistakes so that the person will not be blamed. **3** something said or done for this purpose. ◆*v.* **1** to cover with whitewash. **2** to cover up the faults, etc. of. **3** to defeat an opponent in a game, etc. without allowing a score: *used only in everyday talk.*

**whith·er** (hwi*th*′ər) *adv.* to what place, condition, etc.? where? *Where* is now almost always used in place of *whither.*

**whit·ing**[1] (hwīt′ing) *n.* any of various ocean fishes used for food, such as several of the hakes.

**whit·ing**[2] (hwīt′ing) *n.* powdered chalk, used in making paints, inks, etc.

**whit·ish** (hwīt′ish) *adj.* somewhat white.

**Whit·man** (hwit′mən), **Walt** 1819–1892; U.S. poet.

**Whit·ney** (hwit′nē), **E·li** (ē′lī) 1765–1825; U.S. inventor of the cotton gin.

**Whit·ney** (hwit′nē), **Mount** a mountain in eastern California, 4,418 meters (or 14,494 feet) high.

**Whit·sun·day** (hwit′sun′dē) *n.* the seventh Sunday after Easter; Pentecost.

> **Whitsunday** comes from two words in Old English meaning "white Sunday." It was called this because those who were baptized on this day wore special white clothes.

**Whit·ti·er** (hwit′ē ər), **John Green·leaf** (grēn′lēf) 1807–1892; U.S. poet.

**whit·tle** (hwit′′l) *v.* **1** to cut thin shavings from wood with a knife. **2** to carve by doing this [to *whittle* a doll's head]. **3** to make less bit by bit [to *whittle* down costs]. —**whit′tled, whit′tling** —**whit′tler** *n.*

**whiz** or **whizz** (hwiz) *v.* **1** to make the buzzing or hissing sound of something moving swiftly through the air. **2** to rush with this sound [The bus *whizzed* by us.] —**whizzed, whiz′zing** ◆*n.* a whizzing sound.

**who** (ho͞o) *pron.* **1** what person or persons? [*Who* helped you?] **2** which person or persons [I know *who* she is.] **3** that [the girl *who* lives next door]. **4** any person that ["*Who* steals my purse steals trash."]

> Many people use **who** as the object of a verb when **who** comes at the beginning of a sentence [*Who* did you see?] But some people think that only **whom** should be used in such a sentence [*Whom* did you see?]

**whoa** (hwō) *interj.* a word spoken to a horse, meaning "stop!"

**who·ev·er** (ho͞o ev′ər) *pron.* **1** any person that [*Whoever* wins gets a prize.] **2** no matter what person [*Whoever* told you that, it isn't true.] *Whoever* is also used in questions in place of *who* for extra force [*Whoever* is that knocking?]

**whole** (hōl) *adj.* **1** not divided or cut up; in one piece [Put *whole* carrots in the stew.] **2** having all its parts; complete [The *whole* opera is on two records.] **3** not broken or damaged [Not one dish was left *whole* when the shelf broke.] **4** being the entire amount of; all of [We spent the *whole* $5.] **5** not a fraction or a mixed number [7 and 12 are *whole* numbers; 4 3/4 is not.] ◆*n.* **1** the total amount [He saved the *whole* of his allowance.] **2** something complete in itself [Our 50 States form a *whole.*] —**on the whole,** considering everything; in general. —**whole′ness** *n.*

☆**whole·heart·ed** (hōl′här′tid) *adj.* with all one's energy or interest [my *wholehearted* support].

**whole note** a note in music held four times as long as a quarter note.

**whole·sale** (hōl′sāl) *n.* the sale of goods in large amounts, especially to retail stores that resell them to actual users. ◆*adj.* **1** of or having to do with such sale of goods [a *wholesale* dealer; a *wholesale* price]. **2** widespread or general [*wholesale* destruction by the volcano]. ◆*adv.* **1** in wholesale amounts or at wholesale prices [We are buying the clothes *wholesale.*] **2** in a widespread or general way [The members refused to obey the new rules *wholesale.*] ◆*v.* to sell or be sold in large amounts, usually at lower prices. —**whole′saled, whole′sal·ing** —**whole′sal·er** *n.*

**whole·some** (hōl′səm) *adj.* **1** good for one's health; healthful [a *wholesome* climate]. **2** that tends to improve one's mind or character [a *wholesome* book]. **3** suggesting good health of body and mind; healthy [There is a *wholesome* look about her.] —**whole′some·ness** *n.*

☆**whole-wheat** (hōl′hwēt′) *adj.* made of the whole kernels of wheat [*whole-wheat* flour or bread].

**who'll** (ho͞ol) **1** who shall. **2** who will.

**whol·ly** (hō′lē) *adv.* to the whole amount or degree; altogether; completely [You are *wholly* right. The building was *wholly* destroyed.]

**whom** (ho͞om) *pron. the form of* **who** *that is used as the object of a verb or preposition* [*Whom* did you see? They are the people to *whom* I wrote.] *See the note at* **who** *on the use of* who *and* whom.

**whoop** (ho͞op) *n.* **1** a loud shout or cry, as of joy. **2** a long, loud, gasping breath after a fit of coughing in whooping cough. ◆*v.* to shout with whoops.

**whoop·ing cough** (ho͞o′ping) a children's disease in which there are fits of coughing that end in a whoop.

**whop·per** (hwäp′ər) ***n.*** **1** anything that is very large. **2** a great lie. *This word is used only in everyday talk.*
**whore** (hôr) ***n.*** *another name for* **prostitute**.
**whorl** (hwôrl *or* hwurl) ***n.*** anything arranged in a circle or circles, as the ridges that form a fingerprint or a group of leaves or petals at the same point on a stem.
**who's** (hōōz) **1** who is. **2** who has.
**whose** (hōōz) ***pron.*** the one or the ones belonging to whom [*Whose* are these books?]

**Whose** is the possessive form of *who* and is also used as an adjective meaning "of whom" or "of which" [the man *whose* car I bought; the tree *whose* branches shaded me].

**who·so·ev·er** (hōō′sō ev′ər) ***pron.*** *same as* **whoever**.
**why** (hwī) ***adv.*** for what reason or purpose? [*Why* did he go?] ◆***conj.*** **1** because of which [There is no reason *why* you should go.] **2** the reason for which [That is *why* we went.] ◆***n.*** the reason, cause, etc. [Never mind the *why* of it.] —*pl.* **whys** ◆***interj.*** a word used to show surprise, annoyance, etc., or when pausing to think [*Why,* I didn't know it was so late!]
**WI** *abbreviation for* **Wisconsin**.
**Wich·i·ta** (wich′ə tô) a city in southern Kansas.
**wick** (wik) ***n.*** a piece of cord or a bundle of threads in a candle, oil lamp, etc. It soaks up the fuel and burns with a steady flame when it is lighted.
**wick·ed** (wik′id) ***adj.*** **1** bad or harmful on purpose; evil [a *wicked* scheme]. *See* SYNONYMS *at* **bad**. **2** causing pain or trouble [a *wicked* blow on the head]. **3** naughty or full of mischief. ☆**4** having a great deal of skill: *a slang meaning* [She plays a *wicked* game of golf.] —**wick′ed·ly** ***adv.*** —**wick′ed·ness** ***n.***
**wick·er** (wik′ər) ***n.*** **1** thin twigs or long, woody strips that bend easily and are woven together to make baskets or furniture. *See the picture.* **2** articles made in this way; wickerwork. ◆***adj.*** made of wicker.
**wick·er·work** (wik′ər wurk) ***n.*** **1** baskets, furniture, or other articles made of wicker. **2** *same as* **wicker**.
**wick·et** (wik′it) ***n.*** ☆**1** any of the small wire hoops through which the balls must be hit in croquet. **2** a set of sticks at which the ball is thrown in cricket. **3** a small window, as at a ticket office. **4** a small door or gate, especially one in or near a larger one.
**wide** (wīd) ***adj.*** **1** great in width; measuring much from side to side; broad [a *wide* street]. *See* SYNONYMS *at* **broad**. **2** reaching over a certain distance from side to side [four feet *wide*]. **3** large or not limited in size, amount, or degree [a *wide* variety of foods]. **4** opened as far as possible [eyes *wide* with surprise]. **5** far from the point or goal aimed at [The arrow was *wide* of the mark.] —**wid′er**, **wid′est** ◆***adv.*** **1** over a large area [The news spread far and *wide*.] **2** so as to be wide [Open your mouth *wide*. Their shots went *wide*.] —**wide′ly** ***adv.***
**-wide** (wīd) *a suffix meaning* being or reaching throughout [*Nationwide* means reaching throughout the whole nation.]
**wide-a·wake** (wīd′ə wāk′) ***adj.*** **1** completely awake. **2** watchful and ready; alert.
**wide-eyed** (wīd′īd′) ***adj.*** with the eyes wide open, as in wonder or surprise.
**wid·en** (wīd′'n) ***v.*** to make or become wider.
**wide·spread** (wīd′spred′) ***adj.*** **1** spread out widely [*widespread* wings]. **2** spread, scattered, happening, etc. over a large area [*widespread* damage from fire].

wicker chair

wigwam

White House

**widg·eon** (wij′ən) ***n.*** a duck found near rivers and lakes, having a head that is white on top.
**wid·ow** (wid′ō) ***n.*** a woman whose husband has died and who has not married again. ◆***v.*** to make a widow of [*widowed* late in life].
**wid·ow·er** (wid′ə wər) ***n.*** a man whose wife has died and who has not married again.
**width** (width) ***n.*** **1** distance or measure from side to side; breadth; wideness [a river 500 yards in *width*]. **2** a piece of material of a certain width [Sew two *widths* of cloth together.]
**wield** (wēld) ***v.*** **1** to handle and use, especially with skill [to *wield* a scythe]. **2** to have and use with effect; exercise [to *wield* power in a town]. 
☆**wie·ner** (wē′nər) ***n.*** a smoked sausage of beef or of beef and pork, etc.; frankfurter.

**Wiener** is short for *wienerwurst,* which comes from German *Wiener wurst* meaning "Vienna sausage." This was only one of several kinds of sausage that Europeans brought to America.

**wife** (wīf) ***n.*** the woman to whom a man is married; married woman. —*pl.* **wives**
**wig** (wig) ***n.*** a false covering of hair for the head, worn as part of a costume, to hide baldness, etc.
**Wig·gin** (wig′in), **Kate Douglas** 1856–1923; U.S. teacher and author of children's books.
**wig·gle** (wig′'l) ***v.*** to twist and turn from side to side [The polliwog moves by *wiggling* its tail.] —**wig′gled**, **wig′gling** ◆***n.*** a wiggling motion.
**wig·gly** (wig′lē) ***adj.*** **1** that wiggles [a *wiggly* worm]. **2** wavy [a *wiggly* line]. —**wig′gli·er**, **wig′gli·est**
**wig·wag** (wig′wag) ***v.*** to move back and forth; especially, to signal by waving flags, lights, etc. according to a code. —**wig′wagged**, **wig′wag·ging** ◆***n.*** the sending of messages in this way.
☆**wig·wam** (wig′wäm) ***n.*** a kind of tent used by some American Indians, shaped in a dome or cone and covered with bark, leaves, etc. *See the picture.*

| | | | | | | | |
|---|---|---|---|---|---|---|---|
| **a** | fat | **ir** | here | **ou** | out | **zh** | leisure |
| **ā** | ape | **ī** | bite, fire | **u** | up | **ŋ** | ring |
| **ä** | car, lot | **ō** | go | **ur** | fur | | a *in* ago |
| **e** | ten | **ô** | law, horn | **ch** | chin | | e *in* agent |
| **er** | care | **oi** | oil | **sh** | she | **ə =** | i *in* unity |
| **ē** | even | **oo** | look | **th** | thin | | o *in* collect |
| **i** | hit | **ōō** | tool | ***th*** | then | | u *in* focus |

willow

winch

wimple

windmill



**wild** (wīld) ***adj.*** **1** living or growing in nature; not tamed or cultivated by human beings [*wild* animals; *wild*flowers]. **2** not lived in or used for farming, etc. [*wild* land]. **3** not civilized; savage [*wild* tribes]. **4** not controlled; unruly, rough, noisy, etc. [*wild* children]. **5** very excited or showing great interest [*wild* with delight, *wild* about French food]. **6** violent or stormy [*wild* seas]. **7** reckless, fantastic, crazy, etc. [a *wild* plan to get rich]. **8** missing the target [a *wild* shot]. ◆***adv.*** in a wild way; without aim or control [to shoot *wild;* to run *wild*]. ◆***n.*** *usually* **wilds,** *pl.* a wilderness or wasteland [the *wilds* of Africa]. —**wild′ly** ***adv.*** —**wild′ness** ***n.***

**wild·cat** (wīld′kat) ***n.*** **1** a wild animal of the cat family, larger than a house cat, as the lynx. **2** a person who is fierce in temper and always ready to fight. ☆**3** a successful oil well drilled in a region not known before to have oil. ◆***adj.*** ☆**1** wild or reckless [a *wildcat* scheme]. ☆**2** without official permission [a *wildcat* strike].

**Wil·der** (wīl′dər), **Laura In·galls** (iŋ′g′lz) 1867–1957; U.S. author of children's books.

**wil·der·ness** (wil′dər nis) ***n.*** a wild region; wasteland or overgrown land with no settlers. *See* SYNONYMS *at* **waste.**

**wild·fire** (wīld′fīr) ***n.*** a fire that spreads fast, causes much damage, and is hard to put out [The rumors spread like *wildfire.*]

**wild·flow·er** (wīld′flou′ər) ***n.*** any plant having flowers, that grows wild in fields, woods, etc.: *also written* **wild flower.**

**wild-goose chase** (wīld′go͞os′) any search or action that is as hopeless as trying to catch a wild goose by chasing it.

**wild·life** (wīld′līf) ***n.*** wild animals and birds.

☆**Wild West** or **wild West** the western U.S. in its early frontier days.

**wile** (wīl) ***n.*** a clever trick used to fool or lure someone [The swindler uses flattery and other *wiles* to gain a victim's confidence.] ◆***v.*** to use wiles on in order to lure. —**wiled, wil′ing**

**will**[1] (wil) ***n.*** **1** the power that the mind has to choose, decide, control one's own actions, etc. [a weak *will;* a strong *will;* free *will*]. **2** something wished or ordered; wish; desire [What is your *will?*] **3** strong and fixed purpose; determination ["Where there's a *will,* there's a way."] **4** the way one feels about others [ill *will;* good *will*]. **5** a legal paper in which a person tells what should be done with his or her money and property after the person dies. ◆***v.*** **1** to decide or choose [Let her do as she *wills.*] **2** to control or bring about by the power of the will [He *willed* her to do as he wished.] **3** to leave to someone by a will, as property. —**at will,** when one wishes.

**will**[2] (wil) *a helping verb used with other verbs in speaking of the future* [She *will* be here soon. *Will* you ever learn?]

It has been the rule to use **shall** with *I* and *we* and to use **will** with *you, he, she, it,* and *they,* but now **will** is ordinarily used with all of them, except in the most formal writing. **Will** sometimes means "can" [This jar *will* hold three pints.] or "am, is, or are willing to" [*Will* you open the door?] *See also* **would.**

**will·ful** or **wil·ful** (wil′fəl) ***adj.*** **1** always wanting one's own way; doing as one pleases; stubborn [his *willful* daughter]. **2** done or said on purpose [*willful* lies]. —**will′ful·ly** or **wil′ful·ly** ***adv.*** —**will′ful·ness** or **wil′ful·ness** ***n.***

**Wil·liam I** (wil′yəm) 1027?–1087; a Norman duke who conquered England in 1066 and was king of England from 1066 to 1087: *called* **William the Conqueror.**

**will·ing** (wil′iŋ) ***adj.*** **1** ready or agreeing to do something [Are you *willing* to try?] **2** doing, giving, etc. or done, given, etc. readily or gladly [a *willing* helper; *willing* service]. —**will′ing·ly** ***adv.*** —**will′ing·ness** ***n.***

**will-o′-the-wisp** (wil′ə *th*ə wisp′) ***n.*** **1** a light seen at night moving over swamps or marshy places. **2** any hope or goal that leads one on but is difficult or impossible to reach.

**wil·low** (wil′ō) ***n.*** **1** a tree with narrow leaves and long spikes of flowers. Its twigs can be bent easily for weaving baskets, etc. *See the picture.* **2** the wood of this tree.

**wil·low·y** (wil′ə wē) ***adj.*** **1** covered or shaded with willows [a *willowy* river bank]. **2** slender and graceful [She has a *willowy* figure.]

**will·pow·er** (wil′pou′ər) ***n.*** strength of will, mind, or purpose; self-control [Use *willpower* to break a bad habit.]

**wil·ly-nil·ly** (wil′ē nil′ē) ***adv.*** whether one wishes it or not [He will do his chores *willy-nilly.*]

**Wil·son** (wil′s′n), **Wood·row** (wood′rō) 1856–1924; the 28th president of the United States, from 1913 to 1921.

**wilt** (wilt) ***v.*** **1** to become limp; wither; droop [Water the flowers so they won't *wilt.*] **2** to lose strength or energy; become weak [We *wilted* under the tropical sun.]

**wil·y** (wī′lē) ***adj.*** full of sly tricks; cunning; crafty. —**wil′i·er, wil′i·est** —**wil′i·ness** ***n.***

**wim·ble** (wim′b′l) ***n.*** a tool used for boring.

**wim·ple** (wim′p′l) ***n.*** a cloth worn at one time by women for covering the head and neck, with just the face showing. It is now worn only by certain nuns. *See the picture.*

**win** (win) ***v.*** **1** to get by work, struggle, skill, etc. [to *win* a prize; to *win* applause]. **2** to get the victory in a contest, debate, etc. [Our team *won.* You *win* the argument.] **3** to get the approval or favor of; persuade [I *won* them over to our side. She *won* new friends.] **4** to get to after some effort [The climbers *won* the top of the hill.] —**won, win'ning** ◆***n.*** an act of winning; victory, as in a contest: *used only in everyday talk.*

**wince** (wins) ***v.*** to draw back slightly, usually twisting the face, as in pain or fear. —**winced, winc'ing** ◆***n.*** the act of wincing.

**winch** (winch) ***n.*** a machine for hoisting or pulling, having a drum turned by a crank or by a motor. A rope or chain tied to the load is wound on this drum. *See the picture.*

**wind**[1] (wīnd) ***v.*** **1** to turn or coil something around itself or around something else [to *wind* yarn in a ball; to *wind* a bandage around one's hand]. **2** to grow or pass by turning or coiling [The grapevine *wound* around the tree.] **3** to cover by circling with something [*Wind* the spool with thread.] **4** to tighten the spring of, as by turning a stem [Did you *wind* your watch?] **5** to move or go in a twisting or curving course [The river *winds* through the valley.] —**wound, wind'ing** ◆***n.*** a turn or twist [a *wind* in the road]. —**wind up, 1** to bring or come to an end; finish [to *wind up* the day's work]. **2** to excite very much. ☆**3** to swing the arm before pitching a baseball.

**wind**[2] (wind) ***n.*** **1** air that is moving [Some seeds are carried by the *wind.*] **2** a strong current of air; gale [A *wind* blew the tree down.] **3** breath or the power of breathing [The blow knocked the *wind* out of me.] **4** foolish or boastful talk. **5** a smell or scent in the air [The dogs lost the *wind* of the fox.] **6 winds,** *pl.* the wind instruments of an orchestra. ◆***v.*** to cause to be out of breath [The older people were *winded* from climbing.] —**get wind of,** to find out something about; get a hint of. —**in the wind,** about to happen.

☆**wind·break** (wind'brāk) ***n.*** a fence, hedge, or row of trees that shields a place from the wind.

**wind·burn** (wind'burn) ***n.*** a rough, red, sore condition of the skin, caused by being exposed to the wind too much.

**wind·fall** (wind'fôl) ***n.*** **1** fruit blown down from a tree by the wind. **2** money or gain that one gets without expecting it.

**wind·flow·er** (wind'flou'ər) ***n.*** *another name for* **anemone** *in meaning* 1.

**wind·ing** (wīn'diŋ) ***n.*** **1** a coiling, turning, turn, bend, etc. **2** something that is wound around an object. ◆***adj.*** that winds, turns, coils, etc. [a *winding* road].

**wind instrument** (wind) any musical instrument played by blowing air, especially breath, through it, as a flute, oboe, trombone, or tuba.

☆**wind·jam·mer** (wind'jam'ər) ***n.*** a sailing ship, especially a large one.

**wind·lass** (wind'ləs) ***n.*** a kind of winch, especially one for lifting up an anchor on a ship.

**wind·mill** (wind'mil) ***n.*** a machine getting its power from the wind turning a wheel of vanes at the top of a tower. Windmills are used to grind grain, pump water, etc. *See the picture.*

**win·dow** (win'dō) ***n.*** **1** an opening in a building, car, etc. for letting in light and air. **2** a frame with a pane or panes of glass, set in such an opening.

> **Window** comes from a word in the old Norse language meaning "eye of the wind." Centuries ago, windows were only holes in the wall of a house. The wind could come right in, unless shutters were closed to keep it out.

**window box** a long, narrow box set on or near a window ledge, for growing plants.

**win·dow·pane** (win'dō pān') ***n.*** a pane of glass in a window.

**win·dow-shop** (win'dō shäp') ***v.*** to look at things shown in store windows without going into the stores to buy. —**win'dow-shopped', win'dow-shop'ping**

**wind·pipe** (wind'pīp) ***n.*** the tube from the back of the mouth to the lungs, through which the air passes in breathing; trachea.

**wind·row** (wind'rō) ***n.*** hay, grain, etc. raked into a low ridge to dry before being put into heaps.

☆**wind·shield** (wind'shēld) ***n.*** the window of glass, plastic, etc. in front of the driver's seat of a car, motorcycle, speedboat, etc.

**Wind·sor** (win'zər) the name of the ruling family of Great Britain since 1917.

**Windsor Castle** a castle in southern England that has been a residence of English monarchs since the time of William the Conqueror.

**wind·storm** (wind'stôrm) ***n.*** a storm with a strong wind but little or no rain. 

☆**wind tunnel** a passage through which air is forced for testing models of airplanes, etc. against the effects of wind pressure.

**wind·up** (wīnd'up) ***n.*** **1** the close or end. ☆**2** the swinging movements of a baseball pitcher's arm when getting ready to throw the ball.

**wind·ward** (wind'wərd *or* win'dərd) ***n.*** the direction or side from which the wind is blowing. ◆***adv.*** in the direction from which the wind is blowing; toward the wind. ◆***adj.*** **1** moving windward. **2** on the side from which the wind is blowing.

**Windward Islands** a group of islands in the West Indies, extending south from the Leeward Islands to Trinidad. *See the map for* **Leeward Islands.**

**wind·y** (win'dē) ***adj.*** **1** with much wind [a *windy* day; a *windy* city]. **2** talking too much. —**wind'i·er, wind'i·est —wind'i·ness** ***n.***

**wine** (wīn) ***n.*** **1** the juice of grapes that has fermented and has alcohol in it. **2** the juice of other fruits or plants fermented like this [dandelion *wine*]. ◆***v.*** to drink wine, or serve wine to [We were *wined* and dined last night.] —**wined, win'ing**

**wine-colored** (wīn'kul'ərd) ***adj.*** having the color of red wine; dark purplish-red.

**wing** (wiŋ) ***n.*** **1** either of the pair of feathered parts

| | | | | | | | |
|---|---|---|---|---|---|---|---|
| **a** | fat | **ir** | here | **ou** | out | **zh** | leisure |
| **ā** | ape | **ī** | bite, fire | **u** | up | **ŋ** | ring |
| **ä** | car, lot | **ō** | go | **ur** | fur | | a *in* ago |
| **e** | ten | **ô** | law, horn | **ch** | chin | | e *in* agent |
| **er** | care | **oi** | oil | **sh** | she | **ə** = | i *in* unity |
| **ē** | even | **oo** | look | **th** | thin | | o *in* collect |
| **i** | hit | **ōō** | tool | ***th*** | then | | u *in* focus |

which a bird spreads out from its sides in flying. **2** any of the paired parts used like this for flying, in other creatures [Bats' *wings* are formed of a webbing of skin. Most insects have two pairs of *wings*.] **3** anything like a wing in shape or use [the *wings* of an airplane]. **4** a part that sticks out from a main part [The *wing* of a building is often a part added later. The *wings* of a stage are at the sides out of sight of the audience.] **5** the right or left section of an army, fleet, etc. **6** a political group holding certain views, as of a leftist or rightist kind. ◆***v.*** **1** to fly, or make by flying [The bird *winged* its way across the lake.] **2** to send swiftly [The archer *winged* an arrow at the target.] **3** to wound in the wing or in the arm. —**on the wing,** in flight. —**take wing,** to fly away. —**under one's wing,** under one's protection. —**wing'less** ***adj.***

**winged** (wiŋd *or* wiŋ'id) ***adj.*** **1** having wings. **2** moving as if on wings; swift; fast.

**wing·span** (wiŋ'span) ***n.*** the distance between the ends of an airplane's wings.

**wing·spread** (wiŋ'spred) ***n.*** **1** the distance between the ends of a pair of outspread wings. **2** *same as* **wingspan.**

**wink** (wiŋk) ***v.*** **1** to close and open the eyes quickly; especially, to do this with one eye, for a signal, etc. [He *winked* to show he was joking.] **2** to give off quick flashes of light; twinkle [the *winking* stars]. ◆***n.*** **1** the act of winking. **2** a very short time; instant [I'll be there in a *wink*. She didn't sleep a *wink*.] **3** a signal given by winking. —**wink at,** to pretend not to see [to *wink at* wrongdoing].



SYNONYMS: When we **wink,** we close and then open the eyes or an eye quickly one or more times [He *winked* at me knowingly.] When we **blink,** we close and then open the eyes quickly a number of times, usually without thinking about it [I *blinked* in the bright sunlight.]

**win·ner** (win'ər) ***n.*** **1** one that wins. **2** a person who seems very likely to win or be successful: *used only in everyday talk.*

**win·ning** (win'iŋ) ***adj.*** **1** that wins; having won a victory [the *winning* team]. **2** attractive; charming [a *winning* smile]. ◆***n.*** **1** the act of one that wins. **2** **winnings,** *pl.* something won, especially money won at gambling.

**Win·ni·peg** (win'ə peg) **1** the capital of Manitoba, Canada. **2 Lake,** a large lake in Manitoba.

**win·now** (win'ō) ***v.*** **1** to blow away the chaff from grain [to *winnow* barley after it is threshed]. **2** to sort out or sift, as if by winnowing [to *winnow* useful facts from a report].

**win·some** (win'səm) ***adj.*** attractive in a sweet, pleasant way; charming [a *winsome* girl].

**win·ter** (win'tər) ***n.*** the coldest season of the year, following fall. ◆***adj.*** of or done in winter [*winter* weather; *winter* sports]. ◆***v.*** to spend or cause to spend winter [We *winter* in Florida. They *winter* the circus in the South.]

**win·ter·green** (win'tər grēn) ***n.*** ☆**1** an evergreen plant with small, rounded leaves and white flowers. ☆**2** an oil made from these leaves or from birch bark or artificially, used in medicine and as a flavoring. ☆**3** its sharp flavor.

**win·ter·ize** (win'tər īz) ***v.*** to make ready for winter, as an automobile. —**win'ter·ized, win'ter·iz·ing**

**win·ter·time** (win'tər tīm) ***n.*** the season of winter.

**win·try** (win'trē) ***adj.*** of or like winter; cold, snowy, or gloomy [a *wintry* day; a *wintry* stare]. —**win'tri·er, win'tri·est**

**wipe** (wīp) ***v.*** **1** to clean or dry by rubbing, as with a cloth or on a mat [to *wipe* dishes; to *wipe* one's shoes]. **2** to remove by rubbing, as with a cloth [to *wipe* dust off a table]. —**wiped, wip'ing** ◆***n.*** the act of wiping. —**wipe out, 1** to remove; erase. **2** to kill or destroy. —**wip'er** ***n.***

**wire** (wīr) ***n.*** **1** metal that has been pulled into a very long, thin thread; also, a piece of this [*Wire* is used for carrying electric current, for making fences, for tying bales, etc.] **2** telegraph or a telegram [Reply by *wire*. Send a *wire*.] ◆***v.*** **1** to fasten with wire [to *wire* a vine to a stake]. **2** to furnish with wires for electric current [The cottage is *wired*.] **3** to telegraph. —**wired, wir'ing**

**wire-haired** (wīr'herd') ***adj.*** having stiff and coarse, or wiry, hair.

**wire·less** (wīr'lis) ***adj.*** without wires; sending or sent by radio waves instead of by electric current in wires. ◆***n.*** **1** a wireless telegraph or telephone system. **2** *another name for* **radio**: *mainly a British use.* **3** a message sent by wireless.

☆**wire·tap** (wīr'tap) ***v.*** to make a connection with a telephone line and secretly listen to a private conversation. —**wire'tapped, wire'tap·ping** ◆***n.*** **1** the act of wiretapping. **2** a device used in wiretapping.

**wir·ing** (wīr'iŋ) ***n.*** a system of wires, as for carrying electric current.

**wir·y** (wīr'ē) ***adj.*** **1** like wire; stiff [*wiry* hair]. **2** slender and strong [a *wiry* young man]. —**wir'i·er, wir'i·est**

**Wis·con·sin** (wis kän's'n) a State in the north central part of the U.S.: abbreviated **Wis., Wisc., WI**

**wis·dom** (wiz'dəm) ***n.*** **1** the quality of being wise; good judgment, that comes from knowledge and experience in life [She had the *wisdom* to save money for her old age.] **2** learning; knowledge [a book filled with the *wisdom* of India].

**wisdom tooth** the back tooth on each side of each jaw. The wisdom teeth do not usually appear until the person is fully grown.

**wise**[1] (wīz) ***adj.*** **1** having or showing good judgment [a *wise* judge; a *wise* decision]. **2** having knowledge or information; informed; learned [I was no *wiser* after reading the article.] **3** disrespectful; rude: *slang in this meaning.* —**wis'er, wis'est** —**wise'ly** ***adv.*** —**wise'ness** ***n.***

**wise**[2] (wīz) ***n.*** manner or way [She is in no *wise* at fault.]

**-wise** (wīz) *a suffix meaning:* **1** in a certain way, position, etc. [*Likewise* means in a like way.] **2** in the same way or direction as [To move *clockwise* is to move in the same direction as the hands of a clock.] **3** with regard to [*Weatherwise* means with regard to the weather.]

**wise·a·cre** (wīz'ā'kər) ***n.*** a person who pretends to be much wiser than he or she really is.

☆**wise·crack** (wīz'krak) ***n.*** a joke or clever remark, often one that shows a lack of respect or of seriousness: *a slang word.*

**wish** (wish) ***v.*** **1** to have a longing for; want; desire [You may have whatever you *wish.*] *See* SYNONYMS *at* **desire**. **2** to have or express a desire about [I *wish* you were here. We *wished* her good luck.] **3** to ask or order [I *wish* you to leave now.] ◆***n.*** **1** a desire or longing [I have no *wish* to hear it.] **2** something wanted or hoped for [He got his *wish.*] **3** a request or order [We obeyed her *wishes.*] **4 wishes,** *pl.* a desire for another to have health and happiness [I send you my best *wishes.*] —**make a wish,** to think or tell what one wants.

**wish·bone** (wish′bōn) ***n.*** the bone in front of the breastbone of most birds.

There is a game in which two people make wishes and snap a dried **wishbone** in two. The one holding the longer piece is supposed to have the wish come true. *See the picture.*

**wish·ful** (wish′fəl) ***adj.*** having or showing a wish; longing or hopeful [a *wishful* look].

**wish·y-wash·y** (wish′ē wôsh′ē *or* wish′ē wäsh′ē) ***adj.*** not strong or definite; weak: *used only in everyday talk* [*wishy-washy* ideas].

**wisp** (wisp) ***n.*** **1** a small bunch or tuft [a *wisp* of hair]. **2** a thin, hazy bit or puff [a *wisp* of smoke]. **3** something thin or frail [a *wisp* of a girl]. —**wisp′y** ***adj.***

☆**wis·te·ri·a** (wis tir′ē ə) or **wis·tar·i·a** (wis ter′ē ə) ***n.*** a shrub with clusters of blue, white, or purple flowers, that grows as a vine. *See the picture.*

**wist·ful** (wist′fəl) ***adj.*** showing a wish or longing [The memory brought a *wistful* smile to her face.] —**wist′ful·ly** ***adv.*** —**wist′ful·ness** ***n.***

**wit**[1] (wit) ***n.*** **1** the ability to say clever things in a sharp, amusing way. **2** a person who says such things. **3 wits,** *pl.* the power to think and reason [frightened out of his *wits*].

SYNONYMS: **Wit** is shown by seeing what is strange or odd and making quick, sharp remarks about it so as to amuse people. **Humor** is shown by seeing and expressing what is funny or ridiculous. **Humor** is usually kindly, but **wit** is often biting.

**wit**[2] (wit) ***v.*** to know or learn: *now used only in the phrase* **to wit,** *meaning* "that is to say; namely" [Only one person knows, *to wit,* my father.]

**witch** (wich) ***n.*** **1** a person, now especially a woman, who is imagined to have magic power with the help of the devil. **2** an ugly and mean old woman.

**witch·craft** (wich′kraft) ***n.*** the magic power of a witch.

**witch·er·y** (wich′ər ē) ***n.*** **1** witchcraft; sorcery. **2** great charm; fascination. —*pl.* **witch′er·ies**

**witch hazel** **1** a shrub with yellow flowers and woody fruit. **2** a lotion made from the bark and leaves of this shrub.

**with** (w*i*th *or* with) ***prep.*** **1** in the care or company of [Leave the baby *with* me. Did Mary leave *with* her father?] **2** as part of; into [Mix blue *with* yellow to get green.] **3** in the service of; as a member of [He has been *with* the company for years. She sings *with* the choir.] **4** against; opposed to [Don't argue *with* them.] **5** in regard to; concerning [Deal *with* that problem yourself.] **6** in the opinion of [It's all right *with* me.] **7** as a result of [pale *with* fear]. **8** by means of [Paint *with* a large brush.] **9** by [a pail filled *with* sand]. **10** having got [*With* their help we finished on time.] **11** having or showing [She met him *with* a smile. She has a coat *with* a fur collar.] **12** in spite of [*With* all his faults, I love him still.] **13** at the same time as [*With* the coming of spring, the birds returned.] **14** to or onto [Join this end *with* that one.] **15** as well as [She can run *with* the best.] **16** from [I parted *with* him in June.] **17** after [*With* that remark, I left.]

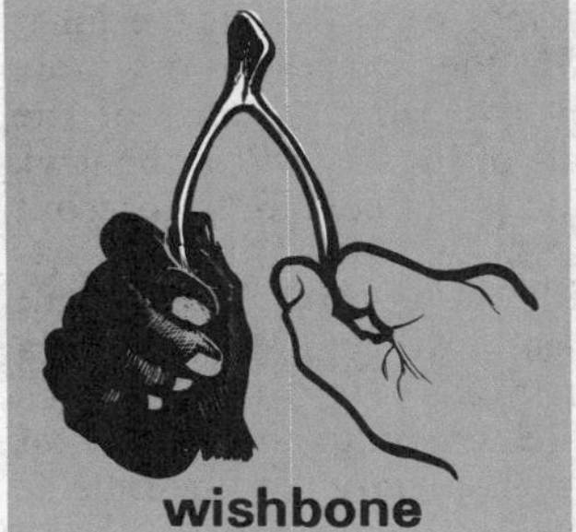

wishbone

wisteria

**with·al** (w*i*th ôl′ *or* with ôl′) ***adv.*** besides; as well as [a strong person and brave *withal*].

**with·draw** (w*i*th drô′ *or* with drô′) ***v.*** **1** to take or pull out; remove [to *withdraw* one's hand from a pocket]. **2** to move back; go away; retreat [She *withdrew* behind the curtain.] **3** to leave; retire or resign [to *withdraw* from school]. **4** to take back; recall [I *withdraw* my statement.] —**with·drew′, with·drawn′, with·draw′ing** 851

**with·draw·al** (w*i*th drô′əl *or* with drô′əl) ***n.*** **1** the act or fact of withdrawing, as money from the bank. **2** a giving up of the use of a narcotic drug by an addict.

**with·drawn** (w*i*th drôn′ *or* with drôn′) *past participle of* **withdraw.** ◆***adj.*** shy, or thinking quietly.

**withe** (with *or* w*i*th) ***n.*** a tough twig, as of willow, that is easily bent and is used for tying things.

**with·er** (w*i*th′ər) ***v.*** **1** to dry up; shrivel [The hot sun *withered* the grass.] **2** to lose strength [Our hopes soon *withered.*] **3** to make lose courage or be ashamed [her *withering* scorn].

**Wither** comes from an earlier English word which means "to expose to the weather." When a plant is exposed to great heat from the sun without getting water, it soon withers and dies.

**with·ers** (w*i*th′ərz) ***n.pl.*** the highest part of a horse's back, between the shoulder blades.

**with·hold** (with hōld′) ***v.*** **1** to keep from giving or granting; refuse [She *withheld* her approval of the plan.] **2** to hold back; keep back; check [He *withheld* his anger.] ☆**3** to take out or subtract from wages or salary, as taxes. —**with·held′, with·hold′ing**

☆**withholding tax** the amount of income tax that is held back from a person's pay by an employer, who then pays it to the government.

| | | | |
|---|---|---|---|
| **a** fat | **ir** here | **ou** out | **zh** leisure |
| **ā** ape | **ī** bite, fire | **u** up | **ŋ** ring |
| **ä** car, lot | **ō** go | **ur** fur | a *in* ago |
| **e** ten | **ô** law, horn | **ch** chin | e *in* agent |
| **er** care | **oi** oil | **sh** she | ə = i *in* unity |
| **ē** even | **oo** look | **th** thin | o *in* collect |
| **i** hit | **ōō** tool | ***th*** then | u *in* focus |

**with·in** (with in′ *or* with in′) ***prep.*** **1** in the inner part of; inside [Stay *within* the house.] **2** not more than; not beyond [They live *within* a mile of the school.] **3** inside the limits of [to stay *within* the law]. ◆***adv.*** in or to the inside [It is cold outdoors but warm *within.*]

**with·out** (with out′ *or* with out′) ***prep.*** **1** free from; not having [a person *without* a worry; a cup *without* a saucer]. **2** in a way that avoids [We passed by each other *without* speaking.] **3** on or to the outside of [They stood *without* the gates.] ◆***adv.*** on the outside [The apples were sound within but wrinkled *without.*]

**with·stand** (with stand′) ***v.*** to stand strongly against; resist or survive [These trees can *withstand* cold winters.] *See* SYNONYMS *at* **oppose.** —**with·stood′, with·stand′ing**

**wit·less** (wit′lis) ***adj.*** without wit or intelligence; foolish; stupid.

**wit·ness** (wit′nis) ***n.*** **1** a person who saw, or can give a firsthand account of, something that happened [A *witness* told the police how the fire started.] **2** a person who gives evidence in a law court. **3** a person who watches a contract, will, etc. being signed and then, as proof that this was done, signs it as well. **4** the statement made by a witness; testimony [to bear false *witness*]. ◆***v.*** **1** to be present at; see [to *witness* a sports event]. **2** to act as a witness of a contract, will, etc. **3** to be or give proof of [Her tears *witnessed* her sadness.] —**bear witness,** to be or give proof, or evidence.



**wit·ti·cism** (wit′ə siz′m) ***n.*** a witty remark.

**wit·ting·ly** (wit′iŋ lē) ***adv.*** on purpose.

**wit·ty** (wit′ē) ***adj.*** showing wit; clever in an amusing way [a *witty* person; a *witty* remark]. —**wit′ti·er, wit′ti·est** —**wit′ti·ly** ***adv.*** —**wit′ti·ness** ***n.***

**wives** (wīvz) ***n.*** *plural of* **wife.**

**wiz·ard** (wiz′ərd) ***n.*** **1** a magician; sorcerer. **2** a person who is very gifted or clever at a particular activity: *used only in everyday talk* [a *wizard* at doing math problems].

**wiz·ard·ry** (wiz′ərd rē) ***n.*** witchcraft; magic.

**redheaded woodpecker** 23 cm (9 in.) long

**wolverine** 90 cm (3 ft.) long, including tail

**woodchuck** 70 cm (28 in.) long, including tail

**wombat** 90 cm (3 ft.) long

**wiz·ened** (wiz′′nd) ***adj.*** dried up and wrinkled; withered; shriveled [the old man's *wizened* face].

**wk.** *abbreviation for* **week.** *—pl.* **wks.**

**wob·ble** (wäb′′l) ***v.*** **1** to move from side to side in an unsteady way. **2** to be uncertain, as in making up one's mind; waver. —**wob′bled, wob′bling** ◆***n.*** a wobbling motion. —**wob′bly** ***adj.***

**woe** (wō) ***n.*** **1** great sorrow; grief [a tale of *woe*]. **2** a cause of sorrow; trouble [the *woes* of the poor]. ◆***interj.*** alas!

**woe·be·gone** (wō′bi gôn′) ***adj.*** showing woe; looking sad or mournful.

**woe·ful** (wō′fəl) ***adj.*** **1** full of woe; mournful; sad. **2** causing or having to do with woe [*woeful* neglect]. **3** making one feel pity; pitiful; miserable [*woeful* poverty]. —**woe′ful·ly** ***adv.***

**wok** (wäk *or* wôk) ***n.*** a metal cooking pan with a bottom shaped like a bowl. It is usually placed on a ringlike stand over a burner.

**woke** (wōk) *a past tense of* **wake**[1].

**wold** (wōld) ***n.*** a high, hilly land without trees.

**wolf** (woolf) ***n.*** **1** a wild animal that looks like a dog. It kills other animals for food. **2** a person who is fierce, cruel, greedy, etc. *—pl.* **wolves** ◆***v.*** to eat in a greedy way: *often used with* down [She *wolfed* down her dinner.] —**cry wolf,** to give a false alarm. —**keep the wolf from the door,** to manage to have enough to live on. —**wolf′ish** ***adj.***

**wolf·hound** (woolf′hound) ***n.*** a large dog of a breed once used for hunting wolves.

**wol·ver·ine** (wool və rēn′) ***n.*** a strong, stocky animal found in northern North America, Europe, and Asia. The wolverine kills other animals for food. *See the picture.*

**wolves** (woolvz) ***n.*** *plural of* **wolf.**

**wom·an** (woom′ən) ***n.*** **1** an adult, female human being. **2** women as a group ["*Woman's* work is never done."] **3** a female servant. *—pl.* **wom′en**

SYNONYMS: **Woman** is the general word used for the adult human being of the sex that bears children. **Female** is used of both plants and animals, in regard to their sex; but when **female** is used instead of **woman,** it shows a lack of respect.

**wom·an·hood** (woom′ən hood) ***n.*** **1** the time or condition of being a woman. **2** womanly qualities. **3** women as a group.

**wom·an·ish** (woom′ən ish) ***adj.*** like or fit for a woman [*womanish* frills].

**wom·an·kind** (woom′ən kīnd) ***n.*** all women; women in general.

**wom·an·like** (woom′ən līk) ***adj.*** *same as* **womanly.**

**wom·an·ly** (woom′ən lē) ***adj.*** like or fit for a woman [a *womanly* figure]. *See* SYNONYMS *at* **female.** —**wom′an·li·ness** ***n.***

**womb** (wōōm) ***n.*** a hollow organ of female mammals in which the young grow before birth; uterus.

**wom·bat** (wäm′bat) ***n.*** a burrowing animal of Australia that looks like a small bear. The female carries her young in a pouch. *See the picture.*

**wom·en** (wim′in) ***n.*** *plural of* **woman.**

**wom·en·folk** (wim′in fōk′) ***n.pl.*** women as a group: *used only in everyday talk, mainly in the South* [The *womenfolk* joined the menfolk in the garden.] *Also* **wom·en·folks** (wim′in fōks′).

**won** (wun) *past tense and past participle of* **win.**

**won·der** (wun′dər) ***n.*** **1** something so unusual that it causes surprise, amazement, etc.; marvel [The Colossus of Rhodes was one of the Seven *Wonders* of the ancient world.] **2** the feeling caused by something strange and remarkable; awe [We gazed in *wonder* at the northern lights.] ◆***v.*** **1** to feel wonder or surprise; marvel [I *wonder* that you were able to do it.] **2** to have doubt and curiosity about; want to know [I *wonder* why they came.]

**won·der·ful** (wun′dər fəl) ***adj.*** **1** that causes wonder; marvelous; amazing. **2** very good; excellent: *used only in everyday talk.* —**won′der·ful·ly** ***adv.***

**won·der·land** (wun′dər land) ***n.*** an imaginary land or place full of wonders, or a real place like this.

**won·der·ment** (wun′dər mənt) ***n.*** wonder or amazement.

**won·drous** (wun′drəs) ***adj.*** wonderful; marvelous. ◆***adv.*** unusually [a maiden *wondrous* fair]. *This word is now seldom used.*

**wont** (wōnt *or* wônt) ***adj.*** having the habit; accustomed [He was *wont* to rise early.] ◆***n.*** usual practice; habit [It is her *wont* to dine late.]

**won't** (wōnt) will not.

**wont·ed** (wōn′tid *or* wôn′tid) ***adj.*** usual; accustomed [in his *wonted* manner].

**woo** (wo͞o) ***v.*** **1** to try to get the love of in order to marry; court [to *woo* a young woman]. **2** to try to get; seek [She *wooed* fame.] —**woo′er** ***n.***

**wood** (wood) ***n.*** **1** the hard material of a tree or shrub, under the bark. **2** trees cut and prepared for use; lumber or firewood. **3** *usually* **woods,** *pl.* a thick growth of trees; forest or grove. **4 woods,** *pl.* woodwind instruments. ◆***adj.*** **1** of wood; wooden. **2** growing or living in woods. —☆**out of the woods,** no longer in trouble or danger: *used only in everyday talk.*

**wood alcohol** a poisonous alcohol distilled from wood and used in paints, as a fuel, etc.

**wood·bine** (wood′bīn) ***n.*** **1** a climbing honeysuckle vine found in Europe. ☆**2** a climbing vine growing in eastern North America.

☆**wood·chuck** (wood′chuk) ***n.*** a North American animal with a thick body and coarse fur, related to rabbits, rats, etc.; groundhog. It burrows in the ground and sleeps all winter. *See the picture.*

**wood·cock** (wood′käk) ***n.*** a small game bird with short legs and a long bill.

**wood·craft** (wood′kraft) ***n.*** **1** knowledge or skills that can help one in the woods, as in camping or hunting. **2** *another word for* **woodworking.**

**wood·cut** (wood′kut) ***n.*** **1** a block of wood with a picture or design carved into it. **2** a print made from this.

☆**wood·cut·ter** (wood′kut′ər) ***n.*** a person who chops down trees and cuts wood. —**wood′cut′ting** ***n.***

**wood·ed** (wood′id) ***adj.*** covered with trees or woods.

**wood·en** (wood′′n) ***adj.*** **1** made of wood. **2** stiff, clumsy, or lifeless [a *wooden* expression on his face]. **3** dull; stupid.

**wood·en·head·ed** (wood′′n hed′id) ***adj.*** dull; stupid: *used only in everyday talk.*

**wooden horse** *another name for* **Trojan horse.**

**wood·land** (wood′land *or* wood′lənd) ***n.*** land covered with trees; forest. ◆***adj.*** of or having to do with the woods [*woodland* creatures].

**wood louse** *another name for* **sow bug.**

**wood·man** (wood′mən) ***n.*** *same as* **woodsman.** —*pl.* **wood′men**

**wood nymph** a nymph living in the woods.

**wood·peck·er** (wood′pek′ər) ***n.*** a bird having a strong, pointed bill, with which it pecks holes in bark to get insects. *See the picture.*

**wood·pile** (wood′pīl) ***n.*** a pile of wood, especially of firewood.

**wood·shed** (wood′shed) ***n.*** a shed for storing firewood.

**woods·man** (woodz′mən) ***n.*** a person who lives or works in the woods, as a hunter, trapper, or woodcutter. —*pl.* **woods′men**

☆**woods·y** (wood′zē) ***adj.*** of or like the woods, or forest. —**woods′i·er, woods′i·est**

**wood thrush** ☆a brown bird of eastern North America, having a strong, clear song.

**wood·wind** (wood′wind) ***n.*** **1 woodwinds,** *pl.* musical instruments made at one time of wood, but now often of metal, and having a mouthpiece into which the player blows [The clarinet, bassoon, oboe, and flute are *woodwinds.*] **2** any of these instruments. ◆***adj.*** of or for such instruments.

**wood·work** (wood′wurk) ***n.*** **1** things made of wood, especially the moldings, doors, stairs, etc. inside a house. **2** work done in wood.

**wood·work·ing** (wood′wur′kiŋ) ***n.*** the art or work of making things out of wood. 853

**wood·y** (wood′ē) ***adj.*** **1** covered with trees; wooded [a *woody* hillside]. **2** made up of wood [the *woody* stem of a shrub]. **3** like wood. —**wood′i·er, wood′i·est** —**wood′i·ness** ***n.***

**woof¹** (woof *or* wo͞of) ***n.*** **1** the threads woven from side to side in a loom, crossing the warp. **2** a woven fabric; cloth.

**woof²** (woof) ***n.*** a harsh barking sound that a dog makes. ◆***v.*** to make such a sound.

**wool** (wool) ***n.*** **1** the soft, curly hair of sheep, or the hair of some other animals, as the goat or llama. **2** yarn, cloth, or clothing made from such hair. **3** anything that looks or feels like wool. ◆***adj.*** of wool. —☆**pull the wool over someone's eyes,** to fool or trick someone.

**wool·en** (wool′ən) ***adj.*** **1** made of wool. **2** having to do with wool or woolen cloth. ◆***n.*** **woolens,** *pl.* clothing or other goods made of wool. *The usual British spelling is* **woollen.**

**wool·gath·er·ing** (wool′gath′ər iŋ) ***n.*** the condition of being absent-minded or of daydreaming.

> The word **woolgathering** comes from the practice of wandering around to gather tufts of wool that have been caught on thorns and hedges. When daydreamers wander in their minds, they remind us of people gathering such tufts of wool.

| | | | | | | | |
|---|---|---|---|---|---|---|---|
| **a** | fat | **ir** | here | **ou** | out | **zh** | leisure |
| **ā** | ape | **ī** | bite, fire | **u** | up | **ŋ** | ring |
| **ä** | car, lot | **ō** | go | **ur** | fur | | a *in* ago |
| **e** | ten | **ô** | law, horn | **ch** | chin | | e *in* agent |
| **er** | care | **oi** | oil | **sh** | she | **ə** = | i *in* unity |
| **ē** | even | **oo** | look | **th** | thin | | o *in* collect |
| **i** | hit | **o͞o** | tool | ***th*** | then | | u *in* focus |

**wool·ly** (wool′ē) ***adj.*** **1** of, like, or covered with wool. ☆**2** crude, rough, and uncivilized [wild and *woolly*]. **3** confused; fuzzy [*woolly* ideas]. —**wool′li·er, wool′li·est** ✦☆***n.*** a woolen garment, especially **woollies,** *pl.* long underwear. —*pl.* **wool′lies** —**wool′li·ness** ***n.***

**wool·y** (wool′ē) ***adj., n.*** *another spelling of* **woolly.** —**wool′i·er, wool′i·est** —*pl.* **wool′ies**

**Worces·ter** (woos′tər) a city in central Massachusetts.

**word** (wʉrd) ***n.*** **1** a spoken sound or group of sounds having meaning and used as a single unit of speech. **2** a letter or group of letters standing for such sounds and used in writing and printing. **3** a brief statement [a *word* of advice]. **4** news; information [Send *word* of yourself.] **5** a signal; order or password [We got the *word* to go ahead.] **6** a promise [Give me your *word.*] **7 words,** *pl.* a quarrel. ✦***v.*** to put into words [How shall I *word* this request?] —**by word of mouth,** by speech, not by writing. —**have a word with,** to have a short talk with. —**in so many words,** exactly and plainly. —**man of his word** or **woman of her word,** one who keeps promises. —**the word** or **Word of God,** the Bible. —**upon my word,** indeed! really! —**word for word,** in exactly the same words.

**word·ing** (wʉrd′ing) ***n.*** the way something is put into words; choice and arrangement of words.

**Words·worth** (wʉrdz′wərth), **William** 1770–1850; English poet.

 **word·y** (wʉr′dē) ***adj.*** having or using too many words; not brief. —**word′i·er, word′i·est** —**word′i·ness** ***n.***

**wore** (wôr) *past tense of* **wear.**

**work** (wʉrk) ***n.*** **1** the use of energy or skill in doing or making something; labor [Chopping wood is hard *work.*] **2** what one does to earn a living; occupation, trade, profession, etc. [His *work* is teaching.] **3** something to be done; task [She had to bring some *work* home from the office.] **4** an act or deed [good *works*]. **5** something made, done, written, etc. [the *works* of Charles Dickens]. **6 works,** *pl.* a place where work is done; factory; plant: *used with a singular verb* [The steel *works* is shut down.] **7** workmanship [The expensive car shows superior *work.*] ✦***v.*** **1** to use effort or energy to do or make something; labor; toil. **2** to have a job for pay; be employed [She *works* in a laboratory.] **3** to cause to work [He *works* himself too hard.] **4** to perform as it should; operate [My watch doesn't *work.*] **5** to cause to operate; manage [Can you *work* this can opener?] **6** to cause; bring about [Her plan *worked* wonders.] **7** to come or bring slowly to a certain condition [He *worked* up to a better job. She *worked* her tooth loose.] **8** to make or shape [*Work* the clay into a ball.] **9** to solve, as a problem. **10** to do one's work in [This salesperson *works* Ohio.] —**worked** *or, now only for some meanings,* **wrought, work′ing** —**at work,** working. —**in the works,** being planned or done: *used only in everyday talk.* —**out of work,** without a job. —**the works, 1** the working parts of a watch, clock, etc. ☆**2** everything that can be included: *used only in everyday talk.* —**work in,** to put in. —**work off,** to get rid of. —**work on,** to try to persuade. —**work out, 1** to make its way out. **2** to solve [to *work out* a crossword puzzle]. **3** to develop or come to some end [We *worked out* a plan.] **4** to have a workout. —**work up,** ☆**1** to advance; move up. **2** to plan or develop [to *work up* a new course]. **3** to excite or arouse.

SYNONYMS: **Work** is the using of energy to do or make something. **Work** may be physical or mental, easy or hard, pleasant or unpleasant, etc. **Labor** more often suggests hard physical work [sentenced to three years at hard *labor*]. **Toil** means long, tiring work, whether physical or mental [years of *toil* in a factory].

**work·a·ble** (wʉr′kə b′l) ***adj.*** that can be worked, done, carried out, etc. [a machine in *workable* condition; a *workable* plan].

**work·a·day** (wʉr′kə dā) ***adj.*** **1** of or fit for workdays [*workaday* clothes]. **2** ordinary; not interesting or unusual [a *workaday* style of writing].

**work·bench** (wʉrk′bench) ***n.*** a table at which work is done, as by a machinist or carpenter.

**work·book** (wʉrk′book) ***n.*** ☆a book that has questions and exercises that are to be worked out by students.

**work·day** (wʉrk′dā) ***n.*** **1** a day on which work is done, usually a weekday. ☆**2** the part of a day during which work is done [a 7-hour *workday*].

**work·er** (wʉr′kər) ***n.*** **1** a person who works for a living. **2** any of the ants, bees, etc. that do the work for the colony.

**work·horse** (wʉrk′hôrs) ***n.*** **1** a horse used for working, as for pulling a plow. **2** a steady, dependable worker who does much work.

**work·house** (wʉrk′hous) ***n.*** ☆a kind of jail where the prisoners are put to work while serving short sentences for minor crimes.

**work·ing** (wʉr′king) ***adj.*** **1** that works [a *working* woman]. **2** of, for, or used in work [a *working* day; *working* clothes]. **3** enough to get work done [a *working* majority]. ✦***n.*** **1** the act of one that works, or the way that a thing works. **2** *usually* **workings,** *pl.* a part of a mine, quarry, etc. where work is or has been done.

**work·ing·man** (wʉr′king man′) ***n.*** a person who works, especially one who works with the hands, as in industry. —*pl.* **work′ing·men′**

**work·ing·wom·an** (wʉr′king woom′ən) ***n.*** a woman worker, especially one who works with her hands, as in industry. —*pl.* **work′ing·wom′en**

**work·load** (wʉrk′lōd) ***n.*** the amount of work that a person or group is required to complete within a particular period of time.

**work·man** (wʉrk′mən) ***n.*** a worker; laborer. —*pl.* **work′men**

**work·man·like** (wʉrk′mən līk) ***adj.*** done carefully and well [a *workmanlike* repair job].

**work·man·ship** (wʉrk′mən ship) ***n.*** **1** skill as a workman, or the quality of work shown. **2** something made by this skill.

☆**work·out** (wʉrk′out) ***n.*** exercise or practice to develop one's body or improve one's skill in a sport, etc.

**work·shop** (wʉrk′shäp) ***n.*** **1** a room or building in which work is done. **2** a series of meetings for special study, work, etc. [a summer *workshop* in writing].

**world** (wʉrld) ***n.*** **1** the earth [a cruise around the *world*]. **2** the whole universe. **3** any planet or place thought of as like the earth [Are there other *worlds* in space?] **4** all people [He thinks the *world* is against him.] **5** some part of the world, some period of history, some special group of people, things, etc. [the Old *World;* the *world* of ancient Rome; the business *world;* the plant *world*]. **6** the everyday life of people, as apart from a life given over to religion and spiritual matters [She retired from the *world* to enter a convent.] **7** *often* **worlds,** *pl.* a large amount; great deal [Your visit did me *worlds* of good.] —**for all the world,** in every way; exactly [She looks *for all the world* like her mother.]

**world·ly** (wurld′lē) ***adj.*** **1** of this world; not heavenly or spiritual [our *worldly* cares]. *See* SYNONYMS *at* **earthly. 2** wise in the ways of the world; sophisticated. —**world′li·ness** ***n.***

☆**World Series** a series of baseball games played every year between the winning teams in the two major leagues to decide the championship.

☆**World War I** a war from 1914 to 1918, between Great Britain, France, Russia, the United States, etc. on the one side and Germany, Austria-Hungary, etc. on the other.

☆**World War II** a war from 1939 to 1945, between Great Britain, France, the Soviet Union, the United States, etc. on the one side and Germany, Italy, Japan, etc. on the other.

**world-wea·ry** (wurld′wir′ē) ***adj.*** bored with living; tired of the world.

**world·wide** (wurld′wīd′) ***adj.*** throughout the world [a *worldwide* reputation].

**worm** (wurm) ***n.*** **1** a small, creeping animal with a soft, slender body, usually jointed, and no legs. **2** any small animal like this, as the larva of an insect. **3** a person looked down on as being too meek, wretched, etc. **4** something that suggests a worm, as the spiral thread of a screw. **5 worms,** *pl.* a disease caused by worms in the intestines, etc. ◆***v.*** **1** to move like a worm, in a winding or creeping way [The hunter *wormed* his way through the underbrush.] **2** to get, bring, make, etc. in a sneaky or roundabout way [He *wormed* the secret out of her.]

**worm-eat·en** (wurm′ēt″n) ***adj.*** **1** eaten into by worms, termites, etc. [*worm-eaten* wood]. **2** worn-out, out-of-date, etc. [*worm-eaten* ideas].

**worm·wood** (wurm′wood) ***n.*** **1** a strong-smelling plant from which a bitter oil is obtained. **2** any bitter, unpleasant experience.

**worm·y** (wur′mē) ***adj.*** **1** having a worm or worms; eaten into by worms; worm-eaten [*wormy* apples]. **2** like a worm. —**worm′i·er, worm′i·est** —**worm′i·ness** ***n.***

**worn** (wôrn) *past participle of* **wear.** ◆***adj.*** **1** showing signs of wear; damaged by use or wear [*worn* soles; a *worn* thread on a screw]. **2** tired or looking tired [a *worn* face].

**worn-out** (wôrn′out′) ***adj.*** **1** used until it is no longer useful [a *worn-out* tire]. **2** very tired; tired out [You look *worn-out* from your travels.]

**wor·ri·some** (wur′ē səm) ***adj.*** **1** causing worry [a *worrisome* child]. **2** always worrying.

**wor·ry** (wur′ē) ***v.*** **1** to be or make troubled in mind; feel or make uneasy or anxious [Don't *worry.* Her absence *worried* us.] **2** to annoy, bother, etc. [Stop *worrying* me with such unimportant matters.] **3** to bite at and shake about with the teeth [The dog *worried* an old shoe.] —**wor′ried, wor′ry·ing** ◆***n.*** **1** a troubled feeling; anxiety; care [sick with *worry*]. **2** a cause of this [He has many *worries.*] —*pl.* **wor′ries**

**Worry** comes from an Old English word meaning "to strangle." A worried person feels as though he or she is being choked to death by the troubled feelings.

**worse** (wurs) ***adj.*** **1** more evil, harmful, bad, unpleasant, etc.; less good [an even *worse* crime]. **2** of poorer quality or condition [cheaper but *worse* equipment]. **3** in poorer health; more ill [The patient is *worse* today.] —*Worse* is the comparative of **bad** and **ill.** ◆***adv.*** in a worse way [He acted *worse* than ever.] ◆***n.*** a person or thing that is worse [I have *worse* to report.] —**for the worse,** to a worse condition. —**worse off,** in a worse condition.

**wors·en** (wur′s'n) ***v.*** to make or become worse.

**wor·ship** (wur′ship) ***n.*** **1** a prayer, church service, etc. showing honor and respect for God or a god [to attend *worship*]. **2** very great love or admiration [our *worship* of heroes]. **3** a title of respect given to certain officials, especially in England [May it please your *worship.*] ◆***v.*** **1** to show religious reverence for [to *worship* God]. **2** to have very great love or admiration for [They *worship* their parents.] **3** to take part in a religious service [Where do you *worship?*] —**wor′shiped** or **wor′shipped, wor′ship·ing** or **wor′ship·ping** —**wor′ship·er** or **wor′ship·per** ***n.***

**worst** (wurst) ***adj.*** most evil, harmful, bad, unpleasant, etc.; least good [the *worst* cold I've ever had]. — 855
*Worst* is the superlative of **bad** and **ill.** ◆***adv.*** in the worst way; to the worst degree [Of the three, he played *worst.*] ◆***n.*** **1** that which is worst [The *worst* of it is that she never told me.] **2** the most wrong that a person can do [The villain did his *worst.*] ◆***v.*** to win out over; defeat [Our team was *worsted.*] —**at worst,** as the worst that can be expected. —**if worst comes to worst,** if the worst possible thing happens. —☆**in the worst way,** very much: *a slang phrase.*

**wor·sted** (woos′tid *or* wur′stid) ***n.*** **1** a smooth thread or yarn made from wool. **2** fabric made from this, with a smooth, hard surface.

**worth** (wurth) ***n.*** **1** the quality of a thing that makes it have value; merit [I know his worth as a friend.] **2** the value of a thing in money or in other goods [What is its *worth* to you?] **3** the amount to be had for a certain sum [a quarter's *worth* of candy]. ◆***adj.*** **1** deserving or worthy of [a movie *worth* seeing]. **2** equal in value to [It's not *worth* a nickel.] **3** having wealth amounting to [She's *worth* a million dollars.]

**worth·less** (wurth′lis) ***adj.*** having no worth, use, value, etc. —**worth′less·ness** ***n.***

**worth·while** (wurth′hwīl′) ***adj.*** worth the time or effort needed for it [a *worthwhile* book].

**wor·thy** (wur′*th*ē) ***adj.*** **1** having worth or merit [a

| | | | | | | | |
|---|---|---|---|---|---|---|---|
| a | fat | ir | here | ou | out | zh | leisure |
| ā | ape | ī | bite, fire | u | up | ng | ring |
| ä | car, lot | ō | go | ur | fur | | a *in* ago |
| e | ten | ô | law, horn | ch | chin | | e *in* agent |
| er | care | oi | oil | sh | she | ə = | i *in* unity |
| ē | even | oo | look | th | thin | | o *in* collect |
| i | hit | ōō | tool | *th* | then | | u *in* focus |

*worthy* cause]. **2** deserving; good enough for [not *worthy* of her love]. —**wor′thi·er, wor′thi·est** ◆***n.*** a very important person: *often used in a joking way* [the village *worthies*]. —*pl.* **wor′thies** —**wor′thi·ly *adv.***

**would** (wood) *the past tense of* **will²** [He promised that he *would* return.]

> **Would** is also used as a helping verb in speaking of something that depends on something else [She *would* have helped if you had asked her.] or in expressing a wish [*Would* that he were here!] or in asking something in a polite way [*Would* you please leave?] *See also* **should.**

**would-be** (wood′bē′) ***adj.*** **1** wishing or pretending to be [a *would-be* actor]. **2** meant to be [Her *would-be* helpfulness was a bother.]

**would·n't** (wood′′nt) would not.

**wouldst** (woodst) *an older form of* **would,** *used with* thou, *as in the Bible.*

**wound¹** (wo͞ond) ***n.*** **1** an injury in which some part of the body is cut, torn, broken, etc. **2** any hurt to the feelings, honor, etc. ◆***v.*** to give a wound to; injure; hurt [Your cruel words *wounded* me.]

**wound²** (wound) *past tense and past participle of* **wind¹.**

**wove** (wōv) *past tense and a past participle of* **weave.**

**wo·ven** (wōv′′n) *a past participle of* **weave.**

**wow** (wou) ***interj.*** an exclamation showing surprise, pleasure, pain, etc.

**wrack¹** (rak) ***n.*** **1** ruin; destruction: *used mainly in the phrase* **wrack and ruin. 2** seaweed, etc. washed up on shore.

**wrack²** (rak) ***v.*** to cause pain or suffering to [a body *wracked* with pain].

**wraith** (rāth) ***n.*** *another word for* **ghost.**

**wran·gle** (raŋ′g′l) ***v.*** **1** to quarrel in an angry, noisy way. ☆**2** to round up in a herd, as saddle horses. —**wran′gled, wran′gling** ◆***n.*** an angry, noisy quarrel. —**wran′gler *n.***

**wrap** (rap) ***v.*** **1** to wind or fold around something [She *wrapped* a scarf around her head.] **2** to cover in this way [They *wrapped* the baby in a blanket.] **3** to cover with paper, etc. [to *wrap* a present]. **4** to hide; conceal [a town *wrapped* in fog]. —**wrapped** or **wrapt** (rapt), **wrap′ping** ◆***n.*** an outer covering or outer garment [Put your *wraps* in the closet.] —**wrapped up in,** giving much time or attention to.

wreath

wren
12 cm (5 in.) long

wrestling

**wrap·a·round** (rap′ə round) ***adj.*** **1** that is wrapped around the body [a *wraparound* skirt]. **2** that is formed so that it curves [a *wraparound* windshield].

**wrap·per** (rap′ər) ***n.*** **1** a person or thing that wraps. **2** a covering or cover [a newspaper mailed in a paper *wrapper*]. **3** a woman's dressing gown.

**wrap·ping** (rap′iŋ) ***n.*** *often* **wrappings,** *pl.* the paper or other material in which something is wrapped.

**wrath** (rath) ***n.*** great anger; rage; fury.

**wrath·ful** (rath′fəl) ***adj.*** full of wrath; very angry. —**wrath′ful·ly *adv.***

**wreak** (rēk) ***v.*** **1** to let out in words or acts [He *wreaked* his fury on me.] **2** to put into effect [to *wreak* vengeance on someone].

**wreath** (rēth) ***n.*** **1** a ring of leaves, flowers, etc. twisted together. *See the picture.* **2** something like this [*wreaths* of smoke]. —*pl.* **wreaths** (rēthz)

**wreathe** (rēth) ***v.*** **1** to coil or twist into a wreath [to *wreathe* flowers and leaves]. **2** to twist or wind around; encircle [Wrinkles *wreathed* her brow.] **3** to decorate with or as with wreaths [His face was *wreathed* in smiles.] —**wreathed, wreath′ing**

**wreck** (rek) ***n.*** **1** the loss of a ship, or of a building, car, etc. through storm, accident, etc. **2** the remains of something that has been destroyed or badly damaged [an old *wreck* stranded on the reef]. **3** a person in very poor health. **4** the act of destroying or ruining [the *wreck* of all our hopes]. ◆***v.*** **1** to destroy or damage badly; ruin [to *wreck* a car in an accident; to *wreck* one's plans for a picnic]. **2** to tear down; raze [to *wreck* an old house].

**wreck·age** (rek′ij) ***n.*** **1** the act of wrecking. **2** the condition of being wrecked. **3** the remains of something that has been wrecked.

**wreck·er** (rek′ər) ***n.*** **1** a person or thing that wrecks. **2** a person, truck, etc. that clears away wrecks. **3** a person whose work is tearing down old buildings, etc.

**wreck·ing** (rek′iŋ) ***n.*** the act or work of a wrecker. ◆***adj.*** used in or taking part in the tearing down of old buildings, the removal of wrecks, etc. [a *wrecking* bar; a *wrecking* crew].

**wren** (ren) ***n.*** a small songbird with a long bill and a stubby tail that tilts up. *See the picture.*

**wrench** (rench) ***n.*** **1** a sudden, sharp twist or pull [With one *wrench,* he loosened the lid.] **2** an injury, as to the back or an arm, caused by a twist. **3** a sudden feeling of sadness, as at parting with someone. **4** a tool for holding and turning nuts, bolts, pipes, etc. ◆***v.*** **1** to twist or pull sharply [She *wrenched* the keys from my grasp.] **2** to injure with a twist [She *wrenched* her knee when she fell.] **3** to twist or distort, as the meaning of a remark.

**wrest** (rest) ***v.*** **1** to pull away with a sharp twist [He *wrested* the pistol from the robber's hand.] **2** to take by force [Rebels *wrested* control of the government from the king.]

**wres·tle** (res′′l) ***v.*** **1** to struggle with, trying to throw or force to the ground without striking blows with the fists. **2** to struggle hard, as with a problem; contend.

—**wres′tled, wres′tling** ◆***n.*** **1** the action or a bout of wrestling. **2** a struggle or contest. —**wres′tler *n.***

> **Wrestle** comes from an Old English word meaning "to twist violently." **Wrest** also comes from this word. When two people wrestle, they twist and turn, trying to force each other to the ground.

**wres·tling** (res′liŋ) ***n.*** a sport in which two people wrestle with each other. *See the picture.*

**wretch** (rech) ***n.*** **1** someone who is miserable or very unhappy. **2** a person looked down on as bad or wicked.

**wretch·ed** (rech′id) ***adj.*** **1** very unhappy or troubled; miserable [She is feeling *wretched* because she lost her job.] **2** causing misery [*wretched* slums]. **3** hateful; vile [a *wretched* tyrant]. **4** bad in quality; very poor; unsatisfactory [a *wretched* meal]. —**wretch′ed·ly *adv.*** —**wretch′ed·ness *n.***

**wrig·gle** (rig′'l) ***v.*** **1** to twist and turn; squirm [to *wriggle* in one's seat]. **2** to move along with such a motion, as a worm does. **3** to manage by shifty or tricky means [He *wriggled* out of his promise.] —**wrig′gled, wrig′gling** ◆***n.*** a wriggling motion. —**wrig′gler *n.***

**wright** (rīt) ***n.*** a person who makes or builds something: *now used mainly as a suffix* [A ship*wright* is one who builds ships.]

**Wright** (rīt), **Frank Lloyd** 1869–1959; U.S. architect.

**Wright, Orville** 1871–1948; U.S. inventor who, with his brother **Wilbur** (1867–1912), built the first airplane to have a successful flight.

**wring** (riŋ) ***v.*** **1** to squeeze and twist with force [to *wring* out wet clothes]. **2** to force out by squeezing, twisting, etc. [to *wring* water from a wet towel]. **3** to get by force, threats, etc. [to *wring* a confession from someone]. **4** to bring painful feelings of pity, distress, etc. to [Her sad story *wrung* our hearts.] —**wrung, wring′ing** ◆***n.*** the act of wringing.

**wring·er** (riŋ′ər) ***n.*** a machine with rollers that squeeze water from wet clothes.

**wrin·kle** (riŋ′k'l) ***n.*** **1** a small or uneven crease or fold [*wrinkles* in a coat; *wrinkles* in skin]. **2** a clever trick, idea, etc.: *used only in everyday talk.* ◆***v.*** **1** to make wrinkles in [a brow *wrinkled* with care]. **2** to form wrinkles [This cloth *wrinkles* easily.] —**wrin′kled, wrin′kling**

**wrist** (rist) ***n.*** the joint or part of the arm between the hand and forearm.

**wrist·band** (rist′band) ***n.*** a band around the wrist, as on the cuff of a sleeve, or a strap for a wristwatch.

**wrist·watch** (rist′wäch *or* rist′wôch) ***n.*** a watch worn on a strap or band that fits around the wrist.

**writ** (rit) ***n.*** a written order by a court of law [a *writ* of habeas corpus].

**write** (rīt) ***v.*** **1** to form words, letters, etc., as with a pen or pencil. **2** to form the words, letters, etc. of [*Write* your address here.] **3** to be the author or composer of [Dickens *wrote* novels. Mozart *wrote* symphonies.] **4** to fill in or cover with writing [to *write* a check; to *write* ten pages]. **5** to send a message in writing; write a letter [*Write* me every week. He *wrote* that he was ill.] **6** to show signs of [Joy was *written* all over her face.] —**wrote, writ′ten, writ′ing** —**write down,** to put into writing. —**write off,** to cancel, as a debt. —**write up,** to write an account of [to *write up* a news story].

**writ·er** (rīt′ər) ***n.*** a person who writes, especially one whose work is writing books, essays, articles, etc.; author.

☆**write-up** (rīt′up′) ***n.*** a written report, often a favorable one, as in a newspaper or magazine: *used only in everyday talk.*

**writhe** (rī*th*) ***v.*** **1** to twist and turn, as in pain; squirm. **2** to suffer from disgust, shyness, etc. —**writhed, writh′ing**

**writ·ing** (rīt′iŋ) ***n.*** **1** the act of one who writes. **2** something written, as a letter, article, poem, book, etc. [the *writings* of Thomas Jefferson]. **3** written form [to put a request in *writing*]. **4** handwriting [Can you read her *writing?*] **5** the art or work of writers.

**writ·ten** (rit′'n) *past participle of* **write.**

**wrong** (rôŋ) ***adj.*** **1** not right, just, or good; unlawful, wicked, or bad [It is *wrong* to steal.] **2** not the one that is true, correct, wanted, etc. [the *wrong* answer]. **3** in error; mistaken [He's not *wrong.*] **4** not proper or suitable [Purple is the *wrong* color for her.] **5** not working properly; out of order [What's *wrong* with the TV?] **6** having a rough finish and not meant to be seen [the *wrong* side of the rug]. ◆***n.*** something wrong; especially, a wicked or unjust act [Does she know right from *wrong?* You do them a *wrong* to accuse them.] ◆***adv.*** in a wrong way, direction, etc.; incorrectly [You did it *wrong.*] ◆***v.*** to treat badly or unjustly [They *wronged* her by telling lies.] —**go wrong, 1** to turn out badly. **2** to change from being good to being bad. —**in the wrong,** at fault; wrong. —**wrong′ly *adv.*** —**wrong′ness *n.***

**wrong·do·ing** (rôŋ′do͞o′iŋ) ***n.*** any act or behavior that is wrong, wicked, unlawful, unjust, etc. —**wrong′do′er *n.***

**wrong·ful** (rôŋ′fəl) ***adj.*** wrong in a way that is unjust, unfair, unlawful, etc.

**wrong·head·ed** (rôŋ′hed′id) ***adj.*** stubborn in sticking to wrong opinions, ideas, etc.

**wrote** (rōt) *past tense of* **write.**

**wroth** (rôth) ***adj.*** full of wrath; angry.

**wrought** (rôt) *a past tense and past participle of* **work.** ◆***adj.*** **1** formed or made [a beautifully *wrought* design]. **2** shaped by hammering or beating, as metals.

**wrought iron** a kind of iron that contains very little carbon. It is tough and hard to break but easy to work or shape.

**wrought-up** (rôt′up′) ***adj.*** very upset or excited.

**wrung** (ruŋ) *past tense and past participle of* **wring.**

**wry** (rī) ***adj.*** **1** turned or bent to one side; twisted [a *wry* face; a *wry* smile]. **2** ironic or bitter [*wry* humor]. —**wri′er, wri′est** —**wry′ly *adv.*** —**wry′ness *n.***

**wt.** *abbreviation for* **weight.**

**WV** or **W.Va.** *abbreviations for* **West Virginia.**

**Wy·o·ming** (wī ō′miŋ) a State in the northwestern part of the United States: abbreviated **Wyo., WY**

| | | | | | | | | |
|---|---|---|---|---|---|---|---|---|
| **a** fat | **ir** here | **ou** out | **zh** leisure | | | | | |
| **ā** ape | **ī** bite, fire | **u** up | **ŋ** ring | | | | | |
| **ä** car, lot | **ō** go | **ʉr** fur | a *in* ago | | | | | |
| **e** ten | **ô** law, horn | **ch** chin | e *in* agent | | | | | |
| **er** care | **oi** oil | **sh** she | **ə** = i *in* unity | | | | | |
| **ē** even | **oo** look | **th** thin | o *in* collect | | | | | |
| **i** hit | **o͞o** tool | ***th*** then | u *in* focus | | | | | |

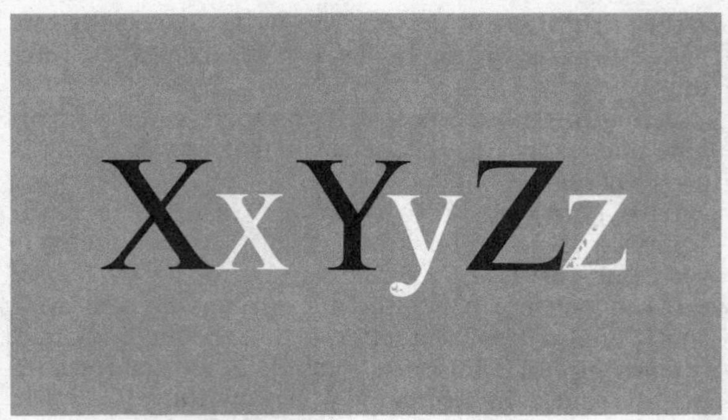


**X, x** (eks) ***n.*** the twenty-fourth letter of the English alphabet. *—pl.* **X's, x's** (eks′iz)

**X** (eks) ***n.*** **1** the Roman numeral for 10. **2** something shaped like an X, as a mark used to show a place on a map, to stand for a kiss in letters, etc. **3** a person or thing that is not known.

☆**X** a motion-picture rating meaning that no one under the age of 17 is to be admitted.

**xe·bec** (zē′bek) ***n.*** a small ship with three masts, at one time common on the Mediterranean.

☆**Xe·rox** (zir′äks) *a trademark for* a machine that copies printed or written material, etc. The machine uses light to transfer an image to paper. The image attracts dry ink particles electrically to form the copy. ◆***n.*** a copy made by such a machine. ◆***v.*** to make copies by using a Xerox.



**Xer·xes I** (zurk′sēz) 519?–465? B.C.; king of Persia from about 486 to about 465 B.C.

**XL** extra large.

**Xmas** (kris′məs *or* eks′məs) ***n.*** *another word for* **Christmas.**

**X-ray** (eks′rā′) ***n.*** **1** an invisible ray that can go through solid substances. X-rays are used to study the bones, organs, etc. inside the body and to treat certain diseases. **2** a photograph made by means of X-rays. ◆***adj.*** of, by, or having to do with X-rays. ◆***v.*** to examine, treat, or photograph with X-rays. *Also written* **X ray, X-ray, x ray.**

**xy·lem** (zī′ləm) ***n.*** the woody tissue of a plant.

**xy·lo·phone** (zī′lə fōn) ***n.*** a musical instrument made up of a row of wooden bars of different sizes, that are struck with wooden hammers. *See the picture.*

**Y,y** (wī) ***n.*** **1** the twenty-fifth letter of the English alphabet. **2** something shaped like a Y. *—pl.* **Y's, y's** (wīz)

**-y**[1] (ē) *a suffix meaning* little *or* dear [A *dolly* is a little doll.]

**-y**[2] (ē) *a suffix meaning:* **1** having; full of; covered with [*Dirty* hands are covered with dirt.] **2** somewhat; rather [A *chilly* room is somewhat chilled.] **3** apt to [*Sticky* fingers are apt to stick to things.] **4** somewhat like [*Wavy* hair looks somewhat like waves.]

**-y**[3] (ē) *a suffix meaning:* **1** the quality or condition of being [*Villainy* is the condition of being a villain.] **2** the act or action of [An *inquiry* is the act of inquiring.]

**y.** *abbreviation for* **yard, year.**

**yacht** (yät) ***n.*** a large boat or small ship for racing, taking pleasure cruises, etc. ◆***v.*** to sail in a yacht. —**yacht′ing** ***n.***

> **Yacht** comes from a Dutch word which means "ship for chasing in order to catch." The Dutch used small, fast ships to hunt down pirate ships. Today's yachts are also small and fast.

**yachts·man** (yäts′mən) ***n.*** a person who owns or sails a yacht. *—pl.* **yachts′men**

**yak**[1] (yak) ***n.*** an ox with long hair, found wild or raised in Tibet and central Asia. *See the picture.*

☆**yak**[2] (yak) ***v.*** to talk much or idly; chatter. —**yakked, yak′king** ◆***n.*** **1** idle talk or chatter. **2** a loud laugh. *This is a slang word.*

**yam** (yam) ***n.*** **1** the starchy root of a climbing plant grown in tropical countries. It is used as food. **2** this plant. ☆**3** the sweet potato: *the name used in some parts of the U.S., especially the South.*

**Yang·tze** (yaŋ′sē) the longest river in China, flowing from Tibet to the China Sea.

**yank** (yaŋk) ***n.*** ☆a sudden, strong pull; jerk. ◆***v.*** to pull or jerk. *This word is used only in everyday talk.*

**Yan·kee** (yaŋ′kē) ***n.*** ☆**1** a person born or living in the United States. ☆**2** a person born or living in one of the Northern States, especially in New England. ◆☆***adj.*** of or like Yankees.

**yap** (yap) ***n.*** a short, sharp bark, as of a small dog. ◆***v.*** **1** to bark with yaps. **2** to talk noisily and stupidly: *a slang meaning.* —**yapped, yap′ping**

**yard**[1] (yärd) ***n.*** **1** a measure of length, equal to three feet, or 36 inches. One yard equals .9144 meter. **2** a long pole fastened across a mast to support a sail.

**yard**[2] (yärd) ***n.*** **1** the ground around or next to a house or other building [a church*yard*]. **2** a place in the open used for a special purpose, work, etc. [a lumber*yard;* a navy *yard*]. **3** a rail center where trains are made up, switched, etc.

**yard·age** (yär′dij) ***n.*** **1** measurement in yards. **2** the length of something in yards.

**yard·arm** (yärd′ärm) ***n.*** either end of the yard supporting a square sail.

☆**yard·stick** (yärd′stik) ***n.*** **1** a measuring stick one yard long. **2** a standard used in judging.

**yarn** (yärn) ***n.*** **1** fibers of wool, silk, nylon, cotton, etc. spun into strands, as for weaving or knitting. **2** a tale or story: *used only in everyday talk.*

**yar·row** (yar′ō) ***n.*** a plant with hairy leaves, clusters of small flowers, and a strong smell.

**yaw** (yô) ***v.*** to swing back and forth across its course, as a ship pushed by high waves. ◆***n.*** an act of yawing.

**yawl** (yôl) ***n.*** **1** a sailboat with the mainmast toward the bow and a short mast toward the stern. *See the picture.* **2** a ship's boat, rowed by oars.

**yawn** (yôn) ***v.*** **1** to open the mouth wide and breathe in deeply in a way that is not controlled, as when one is sleepy or tired. *See the picture.* **2** to open wide; gape [a *yawning* hole]. ◆***n.*** the act of yawning.

**yaws** (yôz) ***n.pl.*** a serious skin disease of tropical regions, caused by a germ.

**yd.** *abbreviation for* **yard.** *—pl.* **yd.** or **yds.**

**ye**[1] (*th*ə *or th*i) ***adj.*** *an older form of* **the.**

> Early English printers used the letter *y* in place of an older letter of the alphabet that looked like a *y* and was called a "thorn." That letter stood for the sound (*th*) or (th), and so *the* was written *ye. Ye* now is often incorrectly pronounced (yē).

**ye**[2] (yē) ***pron.*** *an older form of* **you**, *as in the Bible.*
**yea** (yā) ***adv.*** **1** yes: *used to show that one agrees.* **2** indeed; truly. ◆***n.*** an answer or vote of "yes."
**yeah** (ya *or* ye) ***adv.*** yes: *used only in everyday talk.*
**year** (yir) ***n.*** **1** a period of 365 days, or, in leap year, 366, divided into 12 months and beginning January 1. It is based on the time taken by the earth to go completely around the sun, about 365 1/4 days. **2** any period of twelve months starting at any time [She was six *years* old in July.] **3** a part of a year during which certain things take place [the school *year*]. **4 years,** *pl.* age [He is old for his *years.*] —**year after year,** every year.
**year·book** (yir′book) ***n.*** a book published each year, with information about the year just ended.
**year·ling** (yir′ling) ***n.*** an animal one year old or in its second year.
**year·long** (yir′lông′) ***adj.*** going on for a full year [a *yearlong* celebration].
**year·ly** (yir′lē) ***adj.*** **1** happening, done, etc. once a year, or every year [He sent his *yearly* greetings.] **2** of or for a year [her *yearly* income]. ◆***adv.*** once a year; every year [We have returned *yearly* to the same place for our vacation.]
**yearn** (yurn) ***v.*** **1** to be filled with longing or desire [to *yearn* for fame]. **2** to be filled with pity, sympathy, etc.
**yearn·ing** (yur′ning) ***n.*** deep longing, desire, etc.
**yeast** (yēst) ***n.*** **1** a yellow, frothy substance made up of tiny fungi, used in baking to make dough rise. **2** this substance dried in flakes or tiny grains, or made up in small cakes.
**yell** (yel) ***v.*** to cry out loudly; scream. ◆***n.*** **1** a loud shout. **2** a cheer by a crowd, usually in rhythm, as at a football game.
**yel·low** (yel′ō) ***adj.*** **1** having the color of ripe lemons, or of an egg yolk. **2** having a skin that is more or less yellow. ☆**3** cowardly: *used only in everyday talk.* ◆***n.*** **1** a yellow color. **2** a yellow paint or dye. **3** the yolk of an egg. ◆***v.*** to make or become yellow [linens *yellowed* with age]. —**yel′low·ish *adj.***
☆**yellow fever** a tropical disease that causes fever, vomiting, and yellowing of the skin. Its virus is carried to man by certain mosquitoes.
☆**yellow jack** **1** *another name for* **yellow fever.** **2** a yellow flag used as a signal of quarantine.
☆**yellow jacket** a wasp or hornet having bright-yellow markings.
**Yellow River** *another name for* **Hwang Ho.**
**Yellow Sea** a part of the Pacific Ocean, between China and Korea.
**Yel·low·stone National Park** (yel′ō stōn′) a national park mainly in northwestern Wyoming, famous for its geysers, boiling springs, etc.
**yel·low·y** (yel′ə wē) ***adj.*** somewhat yellow.
**yelp** (yelp) ***n.*** a short, sharp cry, as of a dog in pain. ◆***v.*** to make such a cry or cries.
**Yem·en** (yem′ən) **1** a country in southern Arabia, on the Red Sea. **2** a country east of this, on the Arabian Sea.
**yen**[1] (yen) ***n.*** the basic unit of money in Japan.
**yen**[2] (yen) ***n.*** ☆a deep longing or desire: *used only in everyday talk.*
**yeo·man** (yō′mən) ***n.*** **1** a petty officer in the U.S. Navy, who works as a clerk. **2** a person who owns a

small amount of land: *a British meaning.* —*pl.* **yeo′men**
**yes** (yes) ***adv.*** **1** it is so; I will, I can, I agree, I allow, etc.: *opposite of* **no.** **2** not only that, but more [I am ready, *yes,* eager to help you.] ◆***n.*** **1** the act of saying "yes"; agreement or consent. **2** a vote for something. —*pl.* **yes′es** 859
**yes·ter·day** (yes′tər dē *or* yes′tər dā) ***adv.*** on the day before today. ◆***n.*** **1** the day before today. **2** some time in the past.
**yes·ter·year** (yes′tər yir′) ***n., adv.*** last year: *now seldom used.*
**yet** (yet) ***adv.*** **1** up to now; so far [He has not gone *yet.*] **2** now; at the present time [We can't leave just *yet.*] **3** still; even now [There is *yet* some hope.] **4** at some time to come [We'll get there *yet.*] **5** in addition; even [She was *yet* kinder.] **6** now, after a long time [Haven't you finished *yet?*] **7** but; nevertheless [He is comfortable, *yet* lonely.] ◆***conj.*** nevertheless; however [She seems happy, *yet* she is worried.] —**as yet,** up to now.
**yew** (yōō) ***n.*** **1** an evergreen tree or shrub of Europe, Asia, and America. *See the picture.* **2** the wood of this tree, once much used in making bows for archers.
**Yid·dish** (yid′ish) ***n.*** a language spoken by many Jews in Europe and elsewhere. It developed from old German, but is written with the Hebrew alphabet.
**yield** (yēld) ***v.*** **1** to give up; surrender [to *yield* to a demand; to *yield* a city]. **2** to give or grant [to *yield*

| | | | | | | | |
|---|---|---|---|---|---|---|---|
| **a** | fat | **ir** | here | **ou** | out | **zh** | leisure |
| **ā** | ape | **ī** | bite, fire | **u** | up | **ng** | ring |
| **ä** | car, lot | **ō** | go | **ur** | fur | | a *in* ago |
| **e** | ten | **ô** | law, horn | **ch** | chin | | e *in* agent |
| **er** | care | **oi** | oil | **sh** | she | ə = | i *in* unity |
| **ē** | even | **oo** | look | **th** | thin | | o *in* collect |
| **i** | hit | **ōō** | tool | ***th*** | then | | u *in* focus |

the right of way; to *yield* a point]. **3** to give way [The gate would not *yield* to our pushing.] **4** to bring forth or bring about; produce; give [The orchard *yielded* a good crop. The business *yielded* high profits.] **5** to give place [I *yield* to the Senator from Utah.] ◆***n.*** the amount yielded or produced.

**yield·ing** (yēl′diŋ) ***adj.*** that yields or gives in easily.

**Y.M.C.A.** or **YMCA** Young Men's Christian Association.

**Y.M.H.A.** or **YMHA** Young Men's Hebrew Association.

**yo·del** (yō′d'l) ***v.*** to sing with sudden changes back and forth between one's usual voice and a high, shrill voice. —**yo′deled** or **yo′delled, yo′del·ing** or **yo′del·ling** ◆***n.*** the act or sound of yodeling. —**yo′del·er** or **yo′del·ler** ***n.***

**yo·ga** (yō′gə) ***n.*** a system of exercising by using specials ways of breathing, holding the body, etc. In the Hindu religion yoga is used in trying to reach a condition of oneness with the universal soul.

**yo·gi** (yō′gē) ***n.*** a person who uses yoga. —*pl.* **yo′gis**

**yo·gurt** or **yo·ghurt** (yō′goort) ***n.*** a thick, soft food made from fermented milk.

**yoke** (yōk) ***n.*** **1** a wooden frame that fits around the necks of a pair of oxen, etc. to join them. *See the picture.* **2** a pair joined with a yoke [a *yoke* of oxen]. **3** the condition of being under another's power or control; slavery; bondage [The peasants threw off their *yoke*.] **4** something that binds or unites [a *yoke* of friendship]. **5** something like a yoke, as a frame that fits over the shoulders for carrying pails. **6** a part of a garment fitted closely around the shoulders, or sometimes the hips [the *yoke* of a shirt]. ◆***v.*** **1** to put a yoke on. **2** to fasten with a yoke [to *yoke* oxen to a plow]. **3** to join together. —**yoked, yok′ing**



**yo·kel** (yō′k'l) ***n.*** a person who lives in the country: *used in an unfriendly way.*

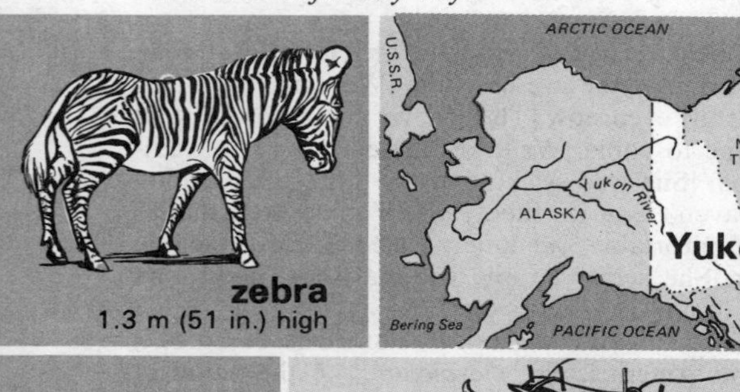


**zebra**
1.3 m (51 in.) high

**yucca**

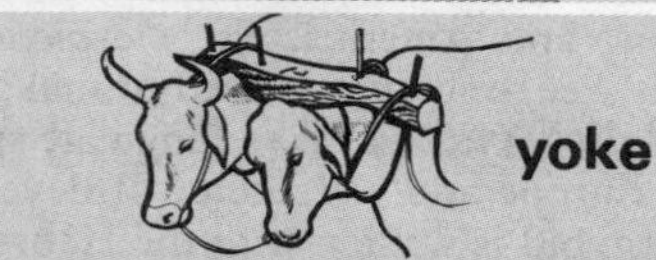

**yoke**

**zebu**
1.6 m (63 in.) high at shoulder

**Yo·ko·ha·ma** (yō′kə hä′mə) a city in Japan.

**yolk** (yōk) ***n.*** the yellow part of an egg.

**Yom Kip·pur** (yäm kip′ər) a Jewish holiday and day of fasting.

**yon** (yän) or **yond** (yänd) ***adj., adv.*** *same as* **yonder**: *now seldom used.*

**yon·der** (yän′dər) ***adj.*** at a distance, but within sight [Go to *yonder* village.] ◆***adv.*** at or in that place; over there.

**yore** (yôr) ***n.*** time long ago: *now used only in the phrase* **of yore,** *meaning* "of long ago."

**York·shire** (yôrk′shir) a former large county in England.

**Yorkshire pudding** a batter of flour, eggs, and milk baked with the juices of roasted meat.

**York·town** (yôrk′toun) a town in Virginia, where Cornwallis surrendered to Washington.

**Yo·sem·i·te National Park** (yō sem′ə tē) a national park in east central California.

**you** (yo͞o) ***pron. sing. & pl.*** **1** the person or persons spoken or written to. *You* is used as the subject of a verb or as the object of a verb or preposition [*You* are right. I told *you* so.] **2** a person; one [*You* seldom see a horse and buggy now.]

**you'd** (yo͞od) **1** you had. **2** you would.

**you'll** (yo͞ol) **1** you will. **2** you shall.

**young** (yuŋ) ***adj.*** **1** being in an early part of life or growth; not old [a *young* actor; a *young* tree]. **2** of or like a young person; fresh; vigorous [She is *young* for her age.] **3** not so old as another of the same name or family [Do you mean *young* Bill or his father?] ◆***n.*** young offspring [The bear defended her *young*.] —**the young,** young people. —**with young,** pregnant. —**young′ish** ***adj.*** —**young′ness** ***n.***

SYNONYMS: Someone who is **young** is in an early period of life and usually not mature [a *young* man or *young* woman]. Someone who is **youthful** is young or seems to be young because he or she is strong and full of energy and shows no sign of aging [my *youthful* grandmother].

**young·ster** (yuŋ′stər) ***n.*** a child or youth.

**your** (yoor) ***pron.*** of you or done by you. *This possessive form of* **you** *is used before a noun and thought of as an adjective* [*your* book; *your* work]. *See also* **yours.**

**you're** (yoor *or* yo͞or) you are.

**yours** (yoorz) ***pron.*** the one or the ones that belong to you. *This form of* **your** *is used when it is not followed by a noun* [Is this pen *yours?* *Yours* cost more than ours.] *Yours* is used as a polite closing of a letter, often with *truly, sincerely,* etc.

**your·self** (yər self′) ***pron.*** **1** your own self. *This form of* **you** *is used when the object is the same as the subject of the verb* [Did you cut *yourself?*] **2** your usual or true self [You are not *yourself* today.] *Yourself* is also used to give force to the subject [You *yourself* told me so.] —*pl.* **your·selves** (yər selvz′)

**youth** (yo͞oth) ***n.*** **1** the time when one is no longer a child but not yet an adult. **2** an early stage of life or growth, as of a country. **3** young people [a club for the *youth* of our city]. **4** a young person; especially, a young man. **5** the quality of being young, fresh, lively, etc. [to restore one's *youth*].

**youth·ful** (yo͞oth′fəl) ***adj.*** **1** young; not yet old [a youthful *widow*]. *See* SYNONYMS *at* **young.** **2** of, like, or fit for a young person [*youthful* styles]. **3** fresh; vigorous; active [still *youthful* at eighty].

**you've** (yo͞ov) you have.

**yowl** (youl) ***v.*** to make a long, sad cry; howl. ◆***n.*** such a cry.

☆**yo-yo** (yō′yō′) ***n.*** a toy like a spool that is fastened to one end of a string. The yo-yo can be made to spin up and down on the string. —*pl.* **yo′-yos′**

**yr.** *abbreviation for* **year** *or* **years, younger, yours.**

**yrs.** *abbreviation for* **years, yours.**

**Yu·ca·tán** or **Yu·ca·tan** (yo͞o′kə tan′) a peninsula at the southeastern end of Mexico.

**yuc·ca** (yuk′ə) ***n.*** a tall plant with long, stiff, pointed leaves and large white flowers. *See the picture.*

**Yu·go·slav** (yo͞o′gō släv′) ***n.*** a person born or living in Yugoslavia. ◆***adj.*** of Yugoslavia or its people. *Also* **Yu′go·sla′vi·an.**

**Yu·go·sla·vi·a** (yo͞o′gō slä′vē ə) a country in southeastern Europe, on the Balkan Peninsula.

**Yu·kon** (yo͞o′kän) **1** a territory of northwestern Canada, east of Alaska: *the full name is* **Yukon Territory.** **2** a river flowing through this territory and Alaska into the Bering Sea. *See the map.*

**yule** (yo͞ol) ***n.*** Christmas or Christmas time.

**yule·tide** (yo͞ol′tīd) ***n.*** Christmas time.

**yum·my** (yum′ē) ***adj.*** very tasty [a *yummy* cake]. *Used only in everyday talk.* —**yum′mi·er, yum′mi·est**

**Y.W.C.A.** or **YWCA** Young Women's Christian Association.

**Y.W.H.A.** or **YWHA** Young Women's Hebrew Association.

**Z, z** (zē) ***n.*** the twenty-sixth and last letter of the English alphabet. —*pl.* **Z's, z's** (zēz)

**Za·ire** or **Za·ïre** (zä ir′) a country in central Africa, on the equator.

**Zam·be·zi** (zam bē′zē) a river in southern Africa, flowing into the Indian Ocean.

**Zam·bi·a** (zam′bē ə) a country in southern Africa.

**za·ny** (zā′nē) ***n.*** **1** a clown, or a person who acts like a clown. **2** a silly or foolish person; fool. —*pl.* **za′nies** ◆***adj.*** funny, foolish, crazy, etc. —**za′ni·er, za′ni·est**

**Zan·zi·bar** (zan′zə bär) an island off the eastern coast of Africa. It is part of Tanzania.

☆**zap** (zap) ***v.*** to move, strike, stun, kill, etc. with sudden speed and force. —**zapped, zap′ping** ◆***n.*** energy, liveliness, pep, etc. *This is a slang word.*

**zeal** (zēl) ***n.*** strong, eager feeling, as in working for a cause; great interest; enthusiasm. *See* SYNONYMS *at* **passion.**

**zeal·ot** (zel′ət) ***n.*** a person who shows zeal for something, especially too much zeal; fanatic.

**zeal·ous** (zel′əs) ***adj.*** full of or showing zeal; very eager; enthusiastic [a *zealous* patriot]. —**zeal′ous·ly** ***adv.*** —**zeal′ous·ness** ***n.***

**ze·bra** (zē′brə) ***n.*** a wild animal of Africa, related to the horse. It has dark stripes on a white or tan body. *See the picture.*

**ze·bu** (zē′byo͞o) ***n.*** a farm animal of Asia and Africa, like an ox with a hump. *See the picture.*

**Zen** (zen) ***n.*** a form of Japanese Buddhism that seeks what is truly real by deep thought without any reasoning or study.

**ze·nith** (zē′nith) ***n.*** **1** the point in the sky directly above one. **2** the highest point; peak [at the *zenith* of her career]. *See also* **nadir.**

**zeph·yr** (zef′ər) ***n.*** **1** a soft, gentle breeze. **2** the west wind. **3** a soft, fine yarn or cloth.

**zep·pe·lin** (zep′ə lin *or* zep′lin) ***n.*** a type of airship with a rigid framework, made around 1900.

**ze·ro** (zir′ō) ***n.*** **1** the number or symbol 0; cipher; naught. **2** a point marked 0, from which something is measured in degrees [It is ten below *zero* on the thermometer.] **3** nothing [Four minus four equals *zero.*] **4** the lowest point [His chances fell to *zero.*] —*pl.* **ze′ros** or **ze′roes** ◆***adj.*** of or at zero. —**zero in on,** to fix attention on; focus on.

**zero hour** the time set for beginning something, as an attack by an army.

**zest** (zest) ***n.*** **1** exciting or interesting quality; relish [Danger adds *zest* to an acrobat's work.] **2** keen enjoyment [a *zest* for life; to work with *zest*]. —**zest′ful** ***adj.***

> **Zest** comes from a French word for a piece of orange peel used to give flavor to a food. **Zest** in English came to mean anything that might add flavor or excitement.

**Zeus** (zo͞os) the chief Greek god, ruling over all other gods. The Romans called this god *Jupiter.*

**zig·zag** (zig′zag) ***n.*** **1** a series of short slanting lines, connected by sharp turns or angles. **2** a design, path, etc. that looks like this [The lightning made a *zigzag* in the sky.] ◆***adj., adv.*** in a zigzag [*zigzag* stitching]. ◆***v.*** to form or move in a zigzag. —**zig′zagged, zig′zag·ging**



**zinc** (zingk) ***n.*** a bluish-white metal that is a chemical element. It is used to coat iron, and in making certain alloys, medicines, etc.

**zing** (zing) ***n.*** **1** a high, whistling sound, like that made by something moving very fast. **2** liveliness, energy, zest, etc. *This is a slang word.*

**zin·ni·a** (zin′ē ə) ***n.*** a garden plant with brightly colored flowers having many petals.

**Zi·on** (zī′ən) **1** a hill in Jerusalem where Solomon's temple and David's palace were built. **2** the Jewish people. **3** heaven; the heavenly city.

**Zi·on·ism** (zī′ən iz′m) ***n.*** the movement for setting up a Jewish nation again in Palestine, that resulted in the state of Israel. —**Zi′on·ist** ***n., adj.***

**zip** (zip) ☆***v.*** **1** to make a short, sharp, hissing sound [A bullet *zipped* past.] **2** to move fast: *used only in everyday talk* [We *zipped* through our work.] **3** to fasten with a zipper. —**zipped, zip′ping** ◆***n.*** **1** a zipping sound. **2** force or energy: *used only in everyday talk.*

☆**ZIP code** (zip) a system for speeding up the delivery of mail. Under this system the post office has assigned a special code number to each area and place in the country.

| | | | | | | | |
|---|---|---|---|---|---|---|---|
| **a** | fat | **ir** | here | **ou** | out | **zh** | leisure |
| **ā** | ape | **ī** | bite, fire | **u** | up | **ng** | ring |
| **ä** | car, lot | **ō** | go | **ur** | fur | | a *in* ago |
| **e** | ten | **ô** | law, horn | **ch** | chin | | e *in* agent |
| **er** | care | **oi** | oil | **sh** | she | **ə** = | i *in* unity |
| **ē** | even | **oo** | look | **th** | thin | | o *in* collect |
| **i** | hit | **o͞o** | tool | ***th*** | then | | u *in* focus |

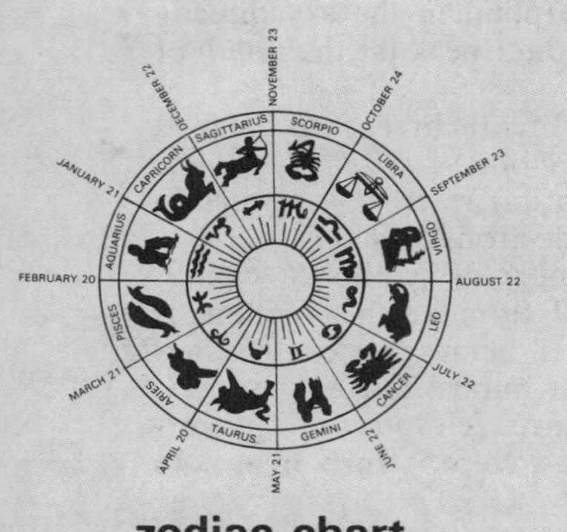

zodiac chart

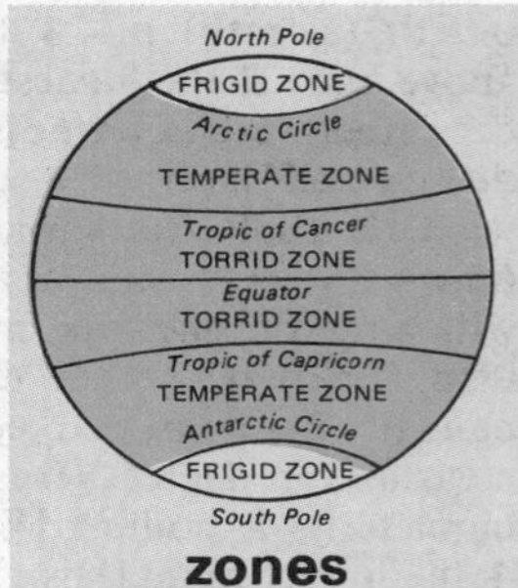

zones

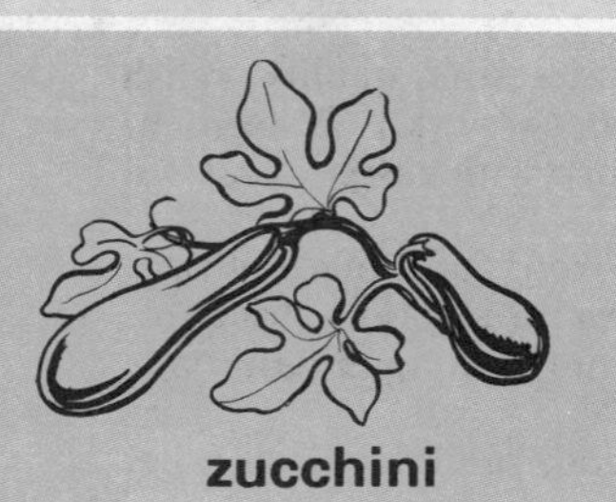
zucchini

zither

☆**zip·per** (zip′ər) ***n.*** a device used to fasten and unfasten two edges of material. It consists of two rows of interlocking teeth worked by a part that slides up or down.



**zir·con** (zʉr′kän) ***n.*** a clear mineral colored yellow, brown, red, orange, etc., often used as a jewel.

**zith·er** (zith′ər *or* zith′ər) ***n.*** a musical instrument made up of a flat, hollow board with 30 to 40 strings stretched across it. It is played by plucking the strings. *See the picture.*

**Zn** *the symbol for the chemical element* zinc.

**zo·di·ac** (zō′dē ak′) ***n.*** an imaginary belt across the sky, along the path that the sun seems to travel. It is divided into twelve parts, each named after a different constellation. A chart showing this is used in astrology. *See the picture.* —**zo·di·a·cal** (zō dī′ə k′l) ***adj.***

☆**zom·bie** (zäm′bē) ***n.*** **1** a dead person supposedly brought back to life by magic power and made to do things by another person. Some people in the West Indies believe that zombies really exist. *Also spelled* **zom′bi**. **2** a person like a zombie as in seeming to be without energy, feelings, or desires. **3** a weird or eccentric person. *Slang in meanings* 2 *and* 3.

**zone** (zōn) ***n.*** **1** any of the five areas into which the earth's surface is marked off by imaginary lines. They are named according to the general climate in each. *See the picture.* **2** an area that is set apart in some special way [the Canal *Zone;* 20 miles per hour in a school *zone*]. **3** a section of a city set apart by law for a particular use, as for homes or for businesses. **4** any of the numbered sections into which a city is divided for the purpose of addressing mail; also, any of the areas marked off around a mailing point, each having a different postage rate for goods sent from that point. ◆***v.*** to mark off into zones, as for a particular purpose [an area *zoned* for industry]. —**zoned, zon′ing**

**zoo** (zo͞o) ***n.*** a place where wild animals are kept for the public to see.

**zo·o·log·i·cal** (zō′ə läj′i k′l) ***adj.*** having to do with zoology or with animals. —**zo′o·log′i·cal·ly *adv.***

**zoological garden** *another name for* **zoo.**

**zo·ol·o·gy** (zō äl′ə jē) ***n.*** the science that studies animals and animal life. —**zo·ol′o·gist *n.***

**zoom** (zo͞om) ***v.*** **1** to move with a loud, humming sound [The cars were *zooming* past us on the highway.] **2** to climb suddenly and sharply, as an airplane. **3** to rise rapidly [Prices *zoomed* last month.] ◆***n.*** the act or sound of zooming.

**zoom lens** a system of lenses in a camera that can be adjusted very quickly so that the camera can be switched from taking a close-up picture to taking a distant picture and have the subject in focus for each picture.

☆**zuc·chi·ni** (zo͞o kē′nē) ***n.*** a type of squash with a green skin, shaped like a cucumber. *See the picture.*

**Zui·der Zee** or **Zuy·der Zee** (zī′dər zē′) an arm of the North Sea that once reached into the Netherlands. It is now shut off by dikes, and much of the land that it covered has been drained.

**Zu·lu** (zo͞o′lo͞o) ***n.*** **1** a member of a cattle-owning people who live in Natal, in South Africa. —*pl.* **Zu′lus** or **Zu′lu** **2** their language. ◆***adj.*** of the Zulus, their language, etc.

**Zu·lu·land** (zo͞o′lo͞o land′) a region of Natal in South Africa.

**Zur·ich** or **Zür·ich** (zoor′ik) a city in northern Switzerland.

☆**zwie·back** (swē′bak *or* swī′bak *or* zwē′bäk) ***n.*** a kind of bread or biscuit made from a baked loaf cut into slices that are toasted brown in an oven.

**Zwieback** comes from two German words meaning "to bake twice." Zwieback is bread that has been baked and that is then sliced and toasted in an oven until it is crisp.

# PICTURE CREDITS FOR THE DICTIONARY

The following credits are arranged alphabetically by the entry words, which appear in boldface type. The boldface numeral following the credit is the number of the page on which that photograph appears. Uncredited photographs are by John T. Westlake.

**abreast** U.S. Military Academy **3** —**abstract sculpture** Princeton University, John B. Putnam Memorial Collection **4** —**Acropolis** Greek National Tourist Office **6** —**adobe** Arizona Historical Society **11** —**aerie** Photo Researchers, Inc. **12** —**Afro** Timothy Olney **15** —**ship aground** U.S. Naval Institute **16** —**aircraft carrier** U.S. Naval Institute **16** —**Airedale** W. Roman **16** —**alligator** Florida State News Bureau **21** —**alpaca** Zoological Society of San Diego **22** —**amphibious vehicle** U.S. Naval Institute **24** —**amphitheater** Greek National Tourist Office **24** —**angel** The Art Museum, Princeton University, gift of Henry W. Cannon, Jr. '10 in memory of his father **27** —**Annunciation** Cleveland Museum of Art, Mr. & Mrs. William H. Marlatt Fund **28** —**antelope** U.S. Forest Service **31** —**anvil** National Park Service **31** —**suit of armor** Cleveland Museum of Art, gift of Mr. & Mrs. John L. Severance **38** —**atoll** Navy Department in National Archives **44** —**austere** Anita Rogoff, Shaker Community **48** —**autograph** Warner Brothers, Inc. **48** —**avalanche** U.S. Forest Service **48** —**baboon** Zoological Society of San Diego **50** —**balance** W. Roman **54** —**barge** U.S. Naval Institute **58** —**bassoon** Indiana University School of Music **60** —**battlement** British Tourist Authority **62** —**beetling cliff** U.S. Forest Service **64** —**belt** U.S. Forest Service **66** —**beret** W. Roman **69** —**bighorn sheep** U.S. Forest Service **72** —**billy** W. Roman **72** —**bleachers** Cleveland Indians Baseball Club **76** —**blockhouse** Museum of West Point **78** —**bloodhounds** United Artists **78** —**bobsled** F. K. MacNeill photo, Olympic Bobrun, Lake Placid, N.Y. **87** —**breakwater** U.S. Coast Guard **89** —**Buddha** Cleveland Museum of Art, purchase, Leonard C. Hanna bequest **94** —**buggy** National Archives **94** —**buoys** U.S. Coast Guard **96** —**burnoose** USIA in National Archives **99** —**cactus** National Park Service, U.S. Forest Service **101** —**calliope** Circus World Museum **102** —**camouflage** National Park Service **104** —**canoe** U.S. Forest Service **107** —**capstan** U.S. Coast Guard **108** —**cart** World Bank photo by Paul Conklin **111** —**cells** American Cancer Society **116** —**chairlift** U.S. Forest Service **119** —**chamois** Swiss National Tourist Office **119** —**cheetah** N.Y. Zoological Society **124** —**chow** USIA in National Archives **129** —**clarinet** Indiana University School of Music **133** —**cloverleaf** Pennsylvania Department of Transportation **136** —**cobra** N.Y. Zoological Society **139** —**collie** Metro Goldwyn Mayer **142** —**Colosseum** British Airways **142** —**combine** John Deere **145** —**composite photo** Florida Division of Tourism **151** —**condor** U.S. Fish & Wildlife Service **153** —**confetti** NASA **153** —**confluence of rivers** Soil Conservation Service **154** —**conning tower** Compix (UPI) **156** —**Continental** National Park Service **160** —**contour plowing** USDA **160** —**coral** Bermuda News Bureau **165** —**cougar** Zoological Society of San Diego **166** —**crow's-nest** National Archives **178** —**crutches** Timothy Olney **179** —**cypress** U.S. Forest Service **183** —**dam** Soil Conservation Service **184** —**date palm** World Bank photo by W. Graham **187** —**davits** U.S. Naval Institute **187** —**decoy** USDA photo by H. P. Moore **190** —**deer** U.S. Forest Service **193** —**defile** U.S. Forest Service **193** —**delta** U.S. Geological Service, photo by A. Lope **194** —**animal den** Photo Researchers, Inc., photo by Leonard Lee Rue III **197** —**destroyer** U.S. Naval Institute **200** —**devilfish** W. Roman **203** —**dickey** W. Roman **204** —**dike** Consulate General of the Netherlands **206** —**dinosaur** W. Roman **206** —**dirigible** U.S. Naval Institute **208** —**discus** Princeton University Sports Information **210** —**divers** U.S. Naval Institute **216** —**dolphins** Marine World of the Pacific **218** —**donkey** World Bank photo by Mary M. Hill **221** —**doublet** Rank Organization Ltd. **221** —**drawbridge** National Park Service **225** —**dredge** U.S. Naval Institute **225** —**dry dock** U.S. Naval Institute **226** —**dulcimer** National Park Service **229** —**dump truck** W. Roman **229** —**bald eagle** British Columbia Government **230** —**echelon** U.S. Air Force **233** —**elk (wapiti)** Government of Alberta **238** —**emu** USIA in National Archives **241** —**epaulets** Paramount Pictures **246** —**excavation** Los Alamos Scientific Laboratory **254** —**facade** National Park Service **263** —**falcon** U.S. Fish & Wildlife Service **264** —**fencing** Princeton University Sports Information **270** —**Ferris wheel** Great Adventure **270** —**festoon** Metro Goldwyn Mayer **272** —**figurehead** U.S. Bureau of Ships National Archives **275** —**fingerprint** W. Roman **276** —**fiord** Norwegian Tourist Bureau **276** —**fishing rod** USDA **278** —**flippers of a seal** USIA in National Archives **282** —**flukes of a whale** USIA in National Archives **284** —**footstool** W. Roman **287** —**forklift** Clarke Equipment Co. **290** —**fossils** U.S. Forest Service **290** —**freeway** Pennsylvania Department of Transportation **295** —**furled sail** U.S. Coast Guard **298** —**gaff** U.S. Coast Guard **300** —**galley** Metro Goldwyn Mayer **303** —**gargoyle** French Government Tourist Office **303** —**geodesic dome** American Society for Metals **307** —**girder** W. Roman **311** —**glider** U.S. Naval Institute **311** —**goalkeeper** Princeton University Sports Information **312** —**golf** Princeton University Sports Information **315** —**gondola** Italian State Tourist Agency **315** —**Gothic architecture** French Government Tourist Office **317** —**gourds** W. Roman **317** —**Great Dane** Champion Baldur Von Schenk, owned by E. M. Schenk, photo by W. Roman **320** —**greyhound** USIA in National Archives **323** —**griffin** Cleveland Museum of Art, gift of the John Huntington Art & Polytechnic Trust **323** —**grouse** U.S. Forest Service **324** —**Guernsey** Agri-Graphic Services **324** —**guitar** 20th Century Fox Pictures Inc. **327** —**religious habit** 20th Century Fox Pictures, Inc. **329** —**riding habit** Miller's, New York **329** —**halberd** Philadelphia Museum of Art, from the collection of Stephen Joseph Herben, given by his wife, Caroline **331** —**halo** reproduced with the permission of the Art Museum, Princeton University **331** —**handcuffs** W. Roman **332** —**helicopter** U.S. Naval Institute **341** —**Hereford** USDA **343** —**heron** U.S. Fish & Wildlife Service **344** —**high jump** Princeton University Sports Information **347** —**hippopotamuses** San Diego Zoological Society **347** —**hockey** IDA photo by Mary M. Hill **348** —**Holstein** Holstein-Friesian Association of America **350** —**hoop skirt** Metro Goldwyn Mayer **353** —**howdah** Information Service of India **356** —**hurdle** George Abbott, advisor, Shasta High School, Redding, Calif. **358** —**ibex** Berne Tourist Association **360** —**icebreaker** U.S. Naval Institute **362** —**igloo** USIA in National Archives **362** —**inauguration** National Archives **370** —**ingot** Weirton Steel Co. **380** —**insignia** National Archives **383** —**javelin** Princeton University Sports Information **396** —**jib** U.S. Forest Service **396** —**jockey** Monmouth Park Track photo by Jim Rafferty **399** —**junk** U.S. Naval Institute **400** —**kangaroo** Australian Information Service **403** —**kayak** Alaska Historical Library **403** —**ketch** U.S. Coast Guard **403** —**kilt** National Archives **404** —**lacrosse** Princeton University Sports Information **408** —**lance** Magasin Pittoresque 1852 **411** —**lateen sail** Direzione Belle Arte del Commune di Genova **415** —**lawn mower** International Harvester **415** —**lei** Edward Small Productions, Inc. **419** —**lighthouse** Bermuda News Bureau **425** —**lineman** AT&T **427** —**lion** John Hatfield III **427** —**listing ship** U.S. Coast Guard **428** —**lizard** U.S. Fish & Wildlife Service **428** —**llama** FAO **431** —**lock** St. Lawrence Seaway Authority **431** —**longhorn** Houston Chamber of Commerce **432** —**love seat** Philadelphia Museum of Art, bequest of Mrs. Alexander Hamilton Rice **436** —**lute** Universal Pictures **436** —**machete** World Bank photo by Larry Daughters **438** —**mail armor** Metro Goldwyn Mayer **443** —**mammoth** copyright Field Museum of Natural History painting by Charles R. Knight **444** —**mangrove** U.S. Fish & Wildlife Service **449** —**maraca** Indiana University School of Music **451** —**marimba** Indiana University School of Music **451** —**Mercury** Alinari **459** —**mesa** U.S. Forest Service **460** —**microscope** Bausch and Lomb **463** —**middy blouse** 20th Century Fox Pictures Inc. **463** —**midway** USDA **463** —**milkweed** U.S. Forest Service **465** —**minaret** IDA **465** —**Minotaur** Gustav Dore **466** —**miter** Rank Organization Inc. **471** —**mosque** Turkish Government Tourist Office **478** —**motorcycle** Bruce Hunter **478** —**mummy case** Cleveland Museum of Art, gift of the John Huntington Art & Polytechnic Trust **482** —**mushrooms** USDA **485** —**mute** Indiana University School of Music **485** —**Navaho** Utah State Historical Society **489** —**noose** U.S. Coast Guard **499** —**oak** U.S. Forest Service **505** —**obelisk** National Park Service **505** —**observatory** U.S. Naval Institute **506** —**olive** U.S. Forest Service & USDA **511** —**orangutan** N.Y. Zoological Society **515** —**organ** Cleveland Museum of Art **516** —**outboard motor** U.S. Fish & Wildlife Service **519** —**outrigger** David Small Productions **520** —**overalls** U.S. Forest Service **520** —**overpass** U.S. Forest Service **523** —**pagoda** British Airways **527** —**pandas** N.Y. Zoological Society **528** —**parallel bars** The Ohio State University, photo by Brian Lewis **530** —**parapet** British Tourist Authority **530** —**paratroops** UPI **533** —**Parthenon** Greek National

Tourist Office **533** —**peacock** USIA in National Archives **538** —**Pekingese** USIA in National Archives **540** —**pendulum** United Metal Goods Mfg. Co., Inc. **543** —**penguins** Office of Territories in National Archives **543** —**periscope** U.S. Naval Institute **545** —**pheasant** U.S. Fish & Wildlife Service **550** —**pier** Port of Cleveland **553** —**pineapple** FAO **554** —**pitchfork** World Bank photo by K. Muldoon **556** —**platypus** USIA in National Archives **561** —**pneumatic hammer** W. Roman **562** —**pointer** USIA in National Archives **564** —**polo** U.S. Polo Association **567** —**poodle** USIA in National Archives **567** —**poplar** U.S. Forest Service **568** —**prairie dog** U.S. Fish & Wildlife Service **572** —**precipice** U.S. Forest Service **575** —**prickly pear** U.S. Forest Service **580** —**printing press** American Type Founders **580** —**prow** U.S. Navy **591** —**pueblo** USIA in National Archives **592** —**puffin** U.S. Fish & Wildlife Service photo by James C. Leupold **592** —**putter** W. Roman **596** —**pyramid** Egyptian Government Tourist Office **597** —**raccoon** U.S. Fish & Wildlife Service **604** —**rampant lion** British Tourist Authority **607** —**ratlines, shrouds** U.S. Coast Guard **608** —**realistic painting** reprinted from Jan. 1977 issue of *Fire Engineering*, M. Bolden painting **610** —**rearing horse** Metro Goldwyn Mayer **610** —**respirator** Timothy Olney **627** —**retrorocket** NASA **628** —**rhesus monkey** Zoological Society of San Diego **633** —**roller skates** Dale R. Evans **639** —**roulette wheel** Las Vegas News Bureau **641** —**ruff** Rank Organization Inc. **642** —**saddle** U.S. Forest Service **649** —**sailfish** W. Roman **650** —**salute** U.S. Army **650** —**sampans** United Nations **653** —**sandpiper** U.S. Fish & Wildlife Service **653** —**Saturn** NASA **655** —**scuba** Bahama News Bureau **663** —**scythe** International Harvester **663** —**seal** Office of Territories in National Archives **664** —**searchlight** U.S. Naval Institute **664** —**secretary** Williamsburg Furniture reproduction by Kittinger **666** —**seine** FAO **668** —**serape** National Archives **672** —**settee** Philadelphia Museum of Art, purchased from the John D. McIlhenny Fund **675** —**shell** Princeton University Sports Information **678** —**Shetland pony** USDA **680** —**shocks of grain** World Bank **680** —**shot-putter** Princeton University Sports Information **683** —**sights on rifle** W. Roman **689** —**silo** N.Y. State Department of Commerce **689** —**sitar** (2) Information Service of India; Stearns Collection of Musical Instruments, University of Michigan, Ann Arbor **693** —**skin diving** Bermuda News Bureau **694** —**skylight** W. Roman **694** —**sleigh** Canadian Pacific Hotels **697** —**slide rule** Pickett **697** —**sluice** USDA **698** —**snowmobile** British Columbia Government **704** —**snowshoes** photo by W. T. Thomson, Fort Snelling State Park, St. Paul, Minn. **704** —**sombrero** USIA **707** —**southwester** USIA **711** —**Sphinx** British Airways **714** —**spinning wheel** National Park Service **716** —**sponges** Bahama News Bureau **719** —**spruce** U.S. Forest Service **720** —**square-rigged** U.S. Naval Institute **722** —**stadium** Princeton University Sports Information **722** —**stalactite, stalagmite** Luray Caverns, Va. **724** —**starfish** W. Roman **727** —**steelyard** Shelburne Museum, Vt. **728** —**stockade** National Park Service **733** —**stretcher** Timothy Olney **736** —**submarine** U.S. Naval Institute **740** —**sulky** U.S. Trotting Association **745** —**surfboard** American Airlines **748** —**suspension bridge** Delaware River Port Authority photo by Carlton Read **750** —**swan** USIA **750** —**synthesizer** Columbia-Princeton Electronic Music Studios **757** —**tapir** N.Y. Zoological Society **761** —**tassel** American University News Bureau **763** —**teal** U.S. Fish & Wildlife Service **763** —**thatched roof** British Tourist Authority **770** —**thrush** U.S. Forest Service painting by Fuertes **775** —**tiller** U.S. Coast Guard **778** —**toga** Metro Goldwyn Mayer **781** —**top hat** RKO Pictures **782** —**totem pole** U.S. Forest Service **784** —**tractor** International Harvester **787** —**transit** World Bank photo by Pamela Johnson **788** —**trotting horse** Darrel E. Wallen **795** —**tugboat** U.S. Naval Institute **796** —**turban** IDA photo by Kay Muldoon **799** —**tuxedo** A. Goodheart **801** —**umiak** Alaska Historical Society **802** —**unicorn** (detail) 60. 178 TIME tapestry, France ca. 1500–1510, Cleveland Museum of Art, Leonard C. Hanna Jr., bequest **811** —**Vandyke beard** Cleveland Museum of Art, J. H. Wade Collection **819** —**Venetian blind** W. Roman **820** —**vest** W. Roman **824** —**viaduct** World Bank photo by Philip Boucas **824** —**virginal** signed Giorlamo Domenico, Italian, early 17th century, Leslie Kinsey Mason 17, 1791, courtesy Museum of Fine Arts, Boston **828** —**volleyball** Princeton University Sports Information **830** —**water buffalo** USIA **837** —**water skis** Soil Conservation Service **838** —**weasel** U.S. Forest Service **838** —**weathercock** National Gallery of Art **841** —**Westminster Abbey** British Airways **842** —**whale** U.S. Fish & Wildlife Service **842** —**White House** National Park Service **847** —**wigwam** Jamestown Foundation **847** —**wimple** Rank Organization Inc. **848** —**woodchuck** U.S. Forest Service **852** —**yak** FAO photo by W. Schulthess **859** —**yoke** United Nations **860**.



# PICTURE CREDITS FOR "A STORY OF SOME AMERICAN WORDS"

The following credits are arranged in the order in which they appear in the prefatory material.

**clipper** The Granger Collection **3** —**Boeing 747** Boeing Commercial Airplane Company, Public Relations **3** —**sequoia tree** Monkmeyer Press (Sumner) **6** —**Chief Sequoya** The Granger Collection **6** —**B. Franklin** The Granger Collection **8** —**T. Jefferson** The Bettmann Archive, Inc. **8** —**gerrymander** New York Public Library Picture Collection **9** —**Christmas tree** The Bettmann Archive, Inc. **9** —**clipper** The Granger Collection **9** —**Burnside** New York Public Library Picture Collection **10** —**Eskimo children** C. Bonington **11** —**scene** North Carolina Collection, University of North Carolina Library, Chapel Hill **11** —**scene (top)** The Bettmann Archive, Inc. **12** —**scene (center)** The Bettman Archive, Inc. **12** —**tortillas** DPI photo by Jerry Frank **12** —**fish** Photo Media Ltd. **12** —**Chicago building** Culver Pictures, Inc. **13** —**skyscrapers** DPI photo by Alex Langley **13** —**convention** Black Star photo by Shelly Katz **13** —**scene (top)** Ford Motor Company News Bureau **14** —**scene (center)** Geoffrey Clements, Collection of Whitney Museum of American Art, gift of William Benton **14** —**trimotor** Wide World Photos, Inc. **14** —**radar** Frederick Lewis photo by Erling Larsen **15** —**battleship** Frederick Lewis photo by Erling Larsen **15** —**Pollock painting** The Neuberger Museum photo by Jackson Pollock **15** —**Country Joe** Magnum Photos, Inc. photo by Elliott Landy **15** —**Boeing 747** Boeing Commercial Airplane Company, Public Relations **16** —**spaceshuttle** National Aeronautics and Space Administration **16**

The type for this dictionary was created on the Fototronic CRT Typesetter, controlled by a Univac 1108 computer at Chi Corporation in Cleveland, Ohio. The typefaces used were 10 point Univers 65 and 9 point Times Roman. The database for the dictionary was created and maintained by the publisher's staff in his own office using a video editing terminal connected via phone line to the Univac computer.

# THE SOLAR SYSTEM

**(a) Mercury**
distance from sun: 46,700,000–69,200,000 km
diameter: 4,990 km
relative size: 2/5 earth's diameter
temperature range: 27°C to 329°C
rotation: 59 earth days
revolution: 88 earth days
satellites: 0

**(b) Venus**
distance from sun: 107,500,000–109,000,000 km
diameter: 12,180 km
relative size: 95/100 earth's diameter
temperature range: 316°C to 527°C
rotation: 243 earth days
revolution: 225 earth days
satellites: 0

**(c) Earth**
distance from sun: 147,100,000–152,100,000 km
diameter: 12,735 km
temperature range: −88.29°C to 58°C
rotation: 23 hours, 56 minutes, 4.09 seconds
revolution: 365¼ days
satellites: 1

**(d) Mars**
distance from sun: 206,000,000–250,000,000 km
diameter: 6,760 km
relative size: 53/100 earth's diameter
temperature range: −101°C to 27°C
rotation: 24 hours, 37 minutes
revolution: 687 earth days
satellites: 2

**(e) Jupiter**
distance from sun: 628,000,000–970,000,000 km
diameter: 142,700 km
relative size: 11 times earth's diameter
temperature range: −145°C at top of clouds to ca. 30,000°C at core
rotation: 9 hours, 55 minutes
revolution: 4,333 earth days
satellites: 13

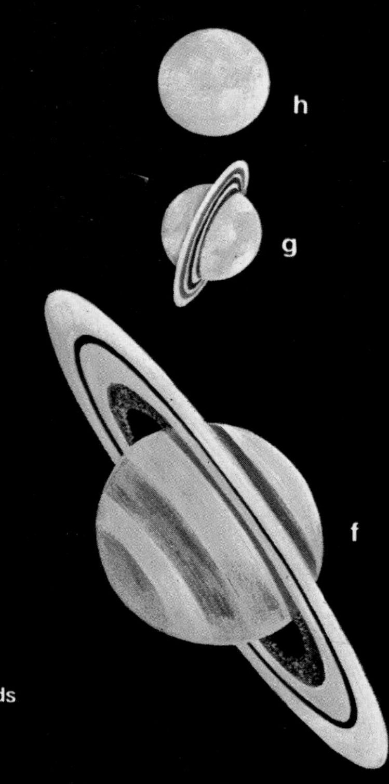

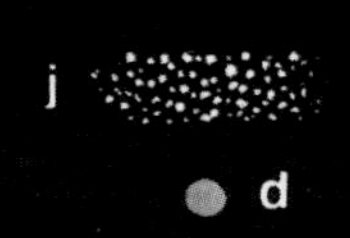


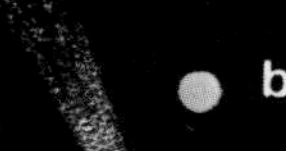

**(f) Saturn**
distance from sun: 1,276,000,000–1,658,000,000 km
diameter: 120,900 km
relative size: ca. 10 times earth's diameter
temperature range: unknown
rotation: 10 hours, 14 minutes
revolution: 10,759 earth days
satellites: 10

**(g) Uranus**
distance from sun: 2,740,000,000–3,009,000,000 km
diameter: 46,700 km
relative size: ca. 4 times earth's diameter
temperature range: unknown
rotation: 10 hours, 49 minutes
revolution: ca. 84 earth years
satellites: 5

**(h) Neptune**
distance from sun: 4,459,500,000–4,536,700,000 km
diameter: 49,500 km
relative size: ca. 4 times earth's diameter
temperature range: unknown
rotation: 15 hours, 40 minutes
revolution: ca. 165 earth years
satellites: 2

**(i) Pluto**
distance from sun: 4,458,000,000–7,371,000,000 km
diameter: ca. 6,400 km
relative size: ½ earth's diameter
temperature range: unknown
rotation: ca. 6 earth days
revolution: ca. 248 earth years
satellites: 1

(j) Asteroids are the thousands of small planets that circle the sun between the orbits of Mars and Jupiter. The largest, called Ceres, has a diameter of 772 km. Icarus, one of the smallest asteroids, has a diameter of 1 km.

(k) Comets are thought to be made of frozen gases and water mixed with particles of dust. As a comet approaches the sun, some of the comet evaporates and forms a hazy cloud. Reflecting sunlight, this cloud appears in the sky as a tail that points away from the sun.

**Sun**
diameter: 1,392,000 km
relative size: 109 times earth's diameter
temperature range: 5500°C at surface to 15,000,000°C at core
rotation: 25 earth days at equator; 35 earth days near poles

# FIRSTS IN SPACE

With the launching of the first artificial satellite in 1957, competition between the United States and Russia, known as the space race, began. Some of the events of this great race are highlighted here.

a **Oct. 4, 1957:** USSR launches **Sputnik I,** first artificial satellite.

**Nov. 3, 1957:** Launched aboard **Sputnik II,** Laika, a dog, is the first animal in space.

**Jan. 31, 1958:** US launches its first satellite, **Explorer I.**

**Apr. 12, 1961:** Yuri Gagarin, first Russian cosmonaut, makes 1 orbit around earth.

**May 5, 1961:** Alan Shepard, first American astronaut, makes suborbital flight aboard the **Mercury** craft **Freedom 7.**

b **Feb. 20, 1962:** John H. Glenn, Jr., is first American to orbit earth, aboard **Friendship 7.**

c **Jul. 10, 1962: Telstar I** launched, first communications satellite to send television between US and Europe.

**June 16, 1963:** Russian cosmonaut Valentina Tereshkova is the first woman in space.

d **June 5, 1965:** Edward H. White II, aboard **Gemini 4,** makes first US spacewalk.

**Feb. 3, 1966:** Russia's **Luna 9** makes first unmanned soft landing on moon.

**Oct. 18, 1967:** Russia's probe **Venera 4** is first to send back data on Venus' atmosphere.

e **Jul. 20, 1969:** US astronauts Neil Armstrong and Edwin Aldrin of **Apollo 11** are first men on the moon.

**Apr. 19, 1971:** Russia's **Salyut I** is first space station.

f **Nov. 13, 1971:** United States' **Mariner IX,** first probe to orbit Mars.

**Dec. 3, 1973:** United States' **Pioneer X** passes Jupiter and sends back data.

**Mar. 29, 1974: Mariner X** passes Mercury and sends back data.

g **Jul. 17, 1975:** Three-man US **Apollo** craft and two-man USSR **Soyuz** craft dock during first joint space mission.

**Jul. 20, 1976:** US probe, **Viking I,** lands on Mars to sample soil, take photos, and search for life.

**Mar. 1978:** Russians aboard **Salyut 6** set new endurance record of 140 days in space, far surpassing 1974 US record of 84 days, set aboard **Skylab** space station.

h **1980's:** US space shuttle to begin regular missions.

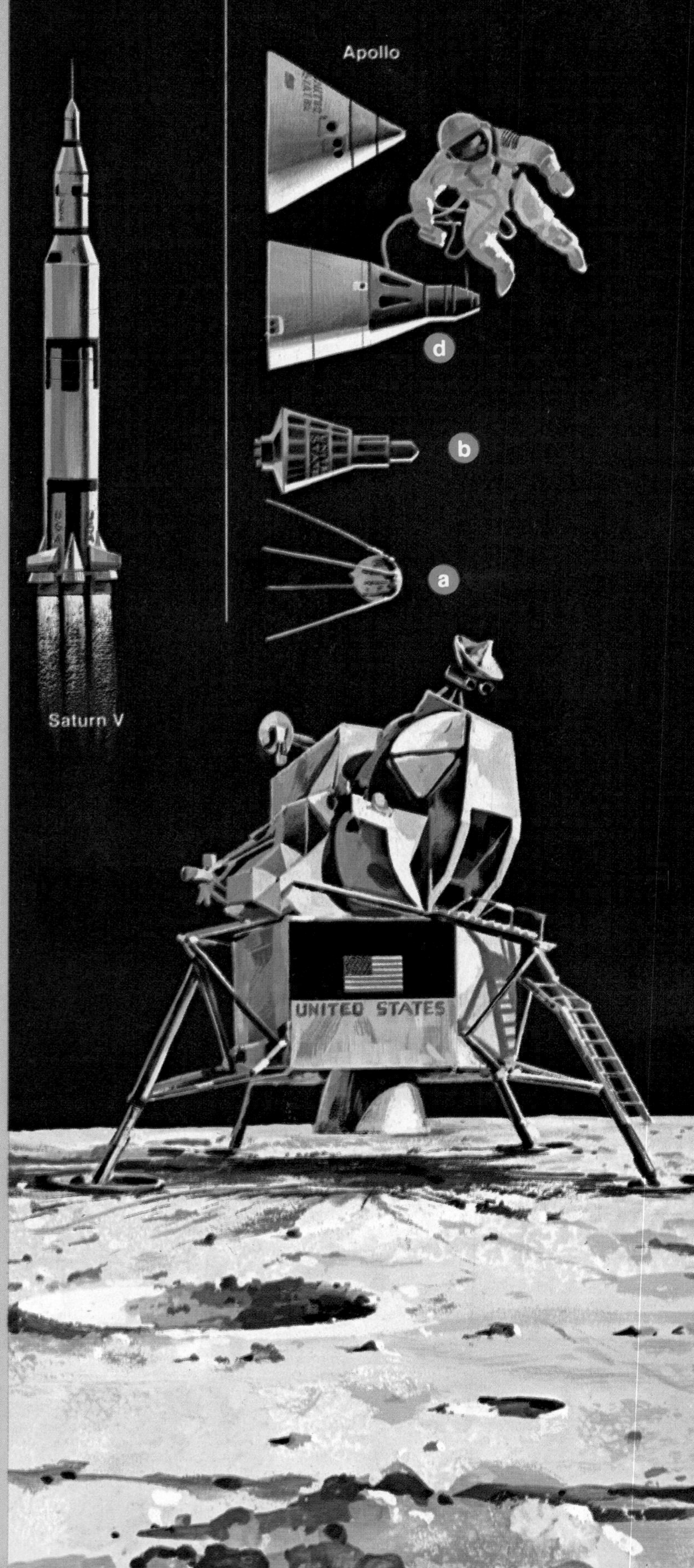

c
f
g
h
e
Pucci

## WEATHER AND CLOUD PATTERNS

A **front** is the area between two air masses. The passing of a front over a location brings a change in the weather.

A **cold front** is the narrow edge of an approaching mass of cold air. Since cold air is heavier and denser than warmer air, a cold front pushes its way forward beneath the warmer air. Clouds form along the cold front, quickly bringing showers, thunderstorms, or, sometimes, tornadoes.

A **warm front** is the wide leading edge of an approaching mass of warm air. As a warm front pushes forward, it moves on top of the colder air and gradually replaces it. Warm fronts bring much cloudiness and snow or steady rain.

a **Tornadoes** are brief violent storms that scientists believe can begin when some of the air from a cold front moves *over* the warmer air. As the cold air sinks through the warmer air, tornadoes may form.

b **Lightning** is the discharge of electricity from one cloud to another or between a cloud and the earth. **Thunder** is the sound made as lightning quickly heats the air along the path it travels.

c A **rainbow** is sunlight broken up through falling rain or mist and reflected in the colors of the spectrum. Rainbows may be seen when the sun is low in one part of the sky while it is raining or misty in the opposite part of the sky.

d **Rain** happens after water from the surface of the earth (1) evaporates in the form of invisible vapor, (2) cools as it rises in the air, (3) forms clouds, and (4) condenses. This water then falls to earth in the form of drops.

e **Hailstones** are balls of ice formed in some thunderstorms. Updrafts of air keep tiny hailstones many miles up in the clouds. There, in the freezing air, they collect layer upon layer of ice until they become heavy enough to fall.

f **Snow** is frozen water vapor that falls in the form of crystals, called snowflakes. All snowflakes have six sides, but no two snowflakes are exactly the same. Sometimes rain freezes around falling snowflakes and forms bits of ice, called **sleet.**

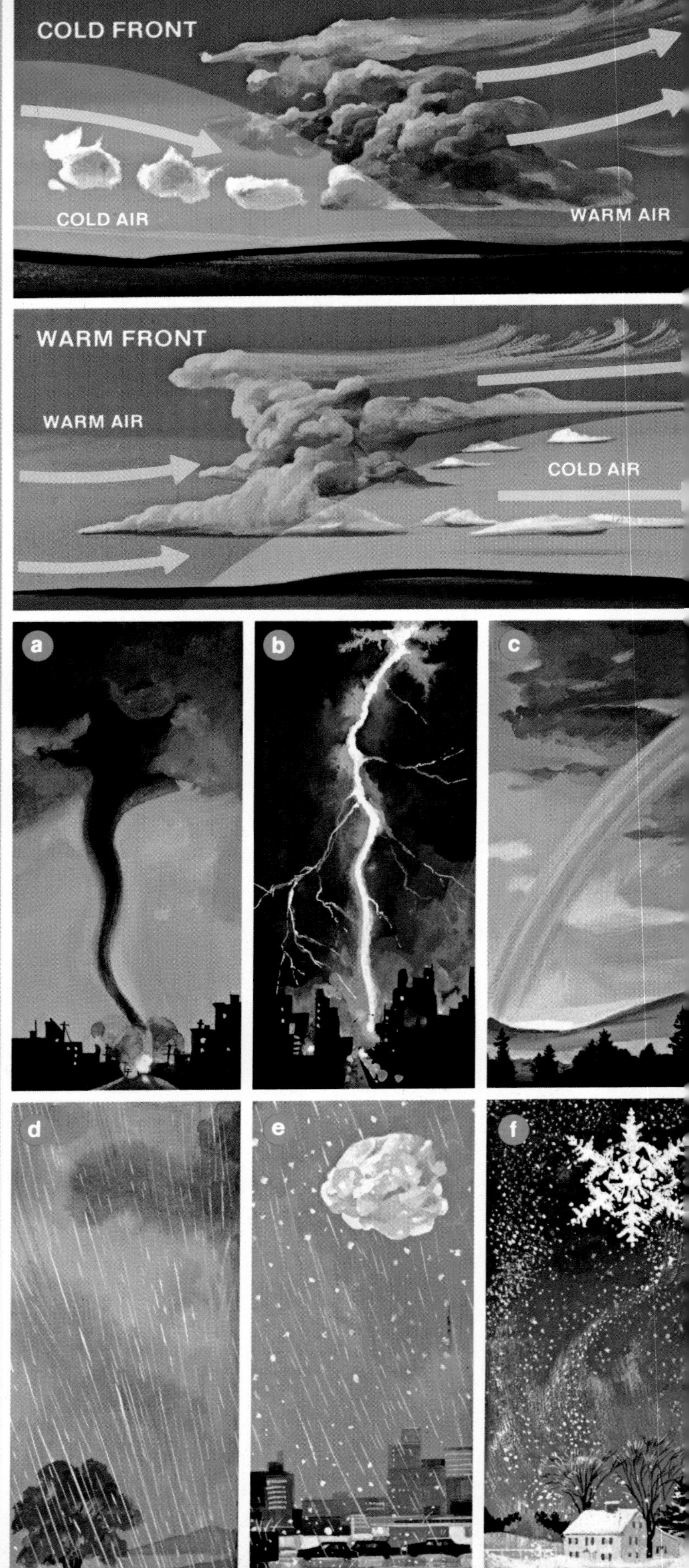

cirrus

cumulonimbus

altocumulus

cumulus congestus

cumulus

stratocumulus

nimbostratus

stratus

# GEOLOGICAL TIME CHART

**How to Read This Time Chart** The two parts of the Geological Time Chart show you the main divisions of the earth's history. The information on the left side (**1**) is arranged from top to bottom, moving in time from the most recent time (top) to the oldest time (bottom).

## MAIN DIVISIONS OF GEOLOGICAL TIME

| ERAS | PERIODS | | | Epochs |
|---|---|---|---|---|
| CENOZOIC | QUATERNARY | | A | Recent 12,000* |
| | | | B | Pleistocene 600,000 |
| | TERTIARY | | C | Pliocene 10 Million |
| | | | D | Miocene 25 Million |
| | | | E | Oligocene 35 Million |
| | | | F | Eocene 55 Million |
| | | | G | Paleocene 65 Million |
| MESOZOIC | CRETACEOUS 135 Million | | H | |
| | JURASSIC 180 Million | | I | |
| | TRIASSIC 230 Million | | J | |
| PALEOZOIC | PERMIAN 280 Million | | K | |
| | CARBONIFEROUS | PENNSYLVANIAN 310 Million | L | |
| | | MISSISSIPPIAN 345 Million | M | |
| | DEVONIAN 405 Million | | N | |
| | SILURIAN 425 Million | | O | |
| | ORDOVICIAN 500 Million | | P | |
| | CAMBRIAN 600 Million | | Q | |
| LATE PRECAMBRIAN 2 Billion | | | R | |
| EARLY PRECAMBRIAN 4.5 Billion | | | S | |

*approximate number of years ago.

Egyptian

**A.** Antarctica and Greenland are the only land masses still largely covered by glaciers; modern human culture develops and spreads.

**B.** Great glaciers covered much of N North America & NW Europe; modern human beings appeared late in this epoch.

Mammoth

**H.** Rocky Mountains began to rise; dinosaurs reached their largest size & then died out completely; mammals were small and primitive.

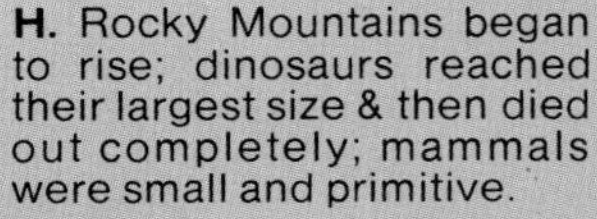

Tyrannosaurus

Therapsid

**K.** Trees of coal-forming forests declined; ferns became abundant; conifers were present; certain primitive marine animals died out completely; reptiles became more abundant than amphibians.

**L.** Mountains formed along E coast of North America & in C Europe; great coal-forming swamp forests flourished in N Hemisphere; seed-bearing ferns were abundant; cockroaches & first reptiles appeared.

Cockroach

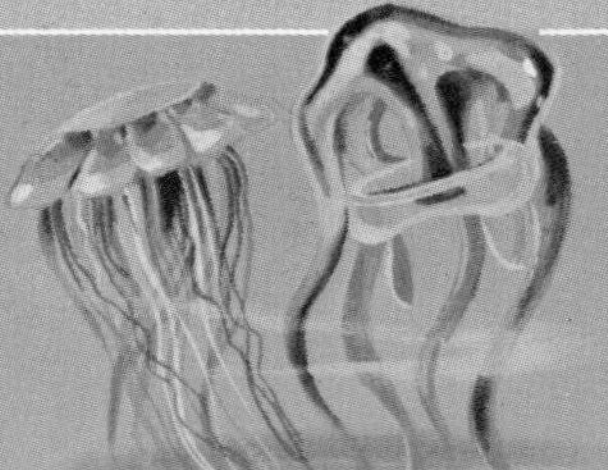

**R.** Layered rocks and granite were formed; first living organisms appeared, as algae & jellyfish.

Jellyfish

In the other part of the chart (**2**), you will find pictures and descriptions of the earth's history. You can find examples for each era by matching the letters in both parts. The information in each colored panel on this side is arranged from left to right, moving from the more recent time in the era (left) to the older time (right).

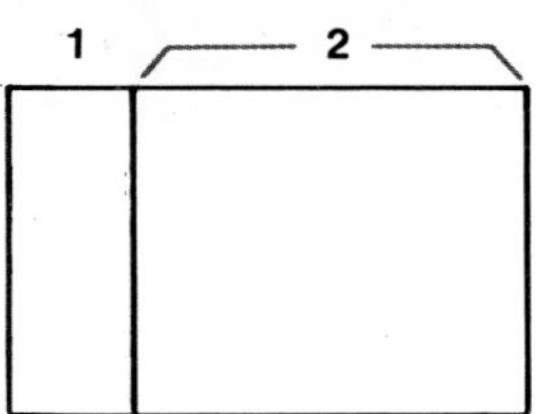


**C.** W North America became highest part of continent; mammals continued to develop.

**D.** Rockies and other mountains were raised higher; mammals began to take on present-day characteristics; dogs and solid-hoofed horses appeared.

**E.** Many earlier types of mammals died out completely; mastodons, first monkeys, and apes appeared.

**F.** Mountains were raised up in Rockies, Andes, Alps & Himalayas; early mammals developed and increased; primitive horses appeared.

**G.** Primitive mammals showed great development; flowering plants became plentiful.

**I.** Sierra Nevada Mountains were raised up; conifers & tropical palms were the principal and most numerous plants; primitive birds appeared.

Archaeopteryx (first bird)

Stegosaurus

Thecodont

**J.** Modern corals appeared & some insects of types found today; reptiles including earliest dinosaurs increased greatly.

**M.** Many different kinds of land plants developed; sharks related to modern types appeared; very few land animals existed.

**N.** Land plants evolved rapidly, large trees appeared; many kinds of primitive fishes existed; first sharks, insects & amphibians appeared.

**O.** Great mountains formed in NW Europe; first small land plants appeared; mollusks with shells were abundant; first fish with jaws appeared.

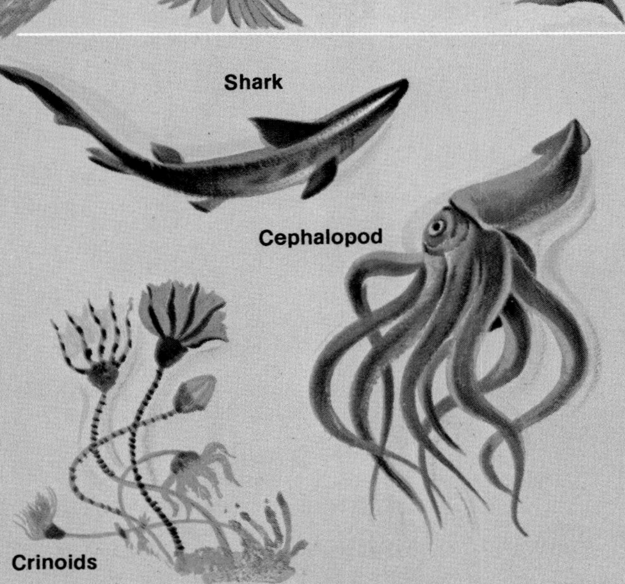


Jawless fish

**P.** Large deposits of limestone formed in shallow seas; many kinds of invertebrate ocean animals developed; first jawless fish appeared.

**Q.** Shallow seas covered parts of continents; various sea animals appeared.

Trilobite

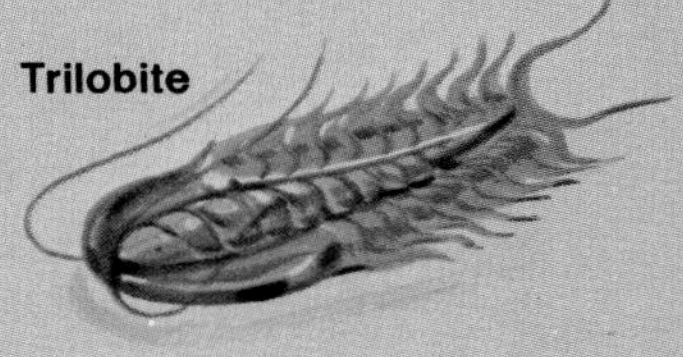

**S.** Crust formed on molten earth; rocks underwent much disturbance; history unknown.

# CHRONOLOGY OF AMERICAN EVENTS

**ca. 20,000 B.C.** First people cross into North America from Asia.

**250-900 A.D.** Mayan civilization flourishes in Yucatán.

**ca. 1000** Vikings settle briefly in Vinland, present-day Newfoundland; Pueblo Indians flourish in Southwest.

**ca. 1200** Aztecs establish empire in central and southern Mexico.

**1492** Columbus lands on San Salvador.

**1521** Hernando Cortes defeats the Aztecs at Mexico City.

**1565** Spanish settle St. Augustine, Florida.

**1607** Founding of Jamestown, Virginia, first permanent British settlement.

**1619** First Africans brought to Virginia as slaves.

**1620** Pilgrims found Plymouth Colony in Massachusetts.

**1624** Dutch settle New Amsterdam (New York).

**1638** Swedes settle New Sweden (Delaware).

**1647** Massachusetts establishes public school system.

**1664** England takes over Dutch and Swedish colonies.

**1682** William Penn founds Philadelphia.

**1692** Nineteen persons executed as witches in Salem, Massachusetts.

**1718** French settle New Orleans.

**1754-63** British wage war against French and Indians.

**1765** British Parliament passes the Stamp Act to tax printed matter in the Colonies.

**1768** British troops sent to Boston and New York.

**1770** British troops kill five Bostonians in the "Boston Massacre."

**1773** Bostonians dump British tea into Boston Harbor.

**1775** American Revolution begins.

**1776** Declaration of Independence.

**1781** Americans, with French help, defeat British at Yorktown, Virginia.

**1783** Treaty of Paris officially ends American Revolution.

**1787** Constitution of the United States written.

**1803** President Thomas Jefferson purchases Louisiana Territory.

**1812** U.S. declares war on Britain.

**1814** British capture Washington, D.C., and burn government buildings; Treaty of Ghent ends War of 1812.

**1819** Spain cedes Florida to U.S.

**1820** Missouri Compromise bans slavery north of Missouri's southern border except in Missouri itself.

**1823** Monroe Doctrine warns Europeans not to interfere in affairs in Western Hemisphere.

**1830** Congress passes Indian Removal Act; by 1840, 70,000 Indians are forced to give up their lands and move west of the Mississippi.

**1836** Americans in Texas proclaim independence from Mexico.

**1845** U.S. annexes Texas and makes it a State.

**1846** Britain cedes Oregon to U.S.

**1848** Treaty of Guadalupe Hildago; U.S. takes over Mexican land between Texas and the Pacific; gold discovered in California; Woman's Rights Convention organized in Seneca Falls, N.Y.

**1854** Kansas-Nebraska Act violates Missouri Compromise.

**1857** Supreme Court rules in the Dred Scott Decision that blacks are not citizens.

**1859** John Brown seizes the Federal arsenal in Harpers Ferry, West Virginia, hoping to start a slave revolt and thus end slavery.

**1860-61** Eleven Southern States form the Confederacy.

**1861** Confederate troops fire on Fort Sumter; Civil War begins.

**1863** Lincoln issues Emancipation Proclamation.

**1865** Lee surrenders to Grant at Appomattox; Civil War ends; Lincoln assassinated.

**1867** U.S. purchases Alaska from Russia.

**1868** Fourteenth Amendment grants blacks citizenship.

**1869** Transcontinental Railroad completed.

**1876** Alexander Graham Bell invents telephone.

**1882** Congress passes first Exclusion Act to stop immigration of Asians, especially Chinese.

**1886** American Federation of Labor founded.

**1890** Congress passes Sherman Antitrust Act.

**1898** U.S. defeats Spain in Spanish-American War; U.S. annexes Hawaii.

**1906** Upton Sinclair's novel *The Jungle*, about unsanitary meatpacking practices, results in federal regulation of food and drug processing.

**1913** Henry Ford begins using assembly line to build Model T cars.

**1914** U.S. completes building of Panama Canal.

**1915** U.S. protests deaths of 128 Americans aboard the British ship *Lusitania*, sunk by a German submarine.

**1917** U.S. declares war on Germany.

**1918** End of World War I.

**1920** U.S. fails to join League of Nations; women win the right to vote when Nineteenth Amendment is added to the Constitution.

**1924** Congress passes Indian Citizenship Act.

**1925** Scopes Trial affirms a state's right to ban the teaching of evolution in public schools.

**1927** Charles Lindbergh makes first solo flight between New York and Paris; first talking motion picture.

**1929** Stock Market crashes; beginning of the Great Depression.

**1933** Thirteen million American workers unemployed; President Franklin D. Roosevelt begins the New Deal, a program for reform and economic recovery.

**1941** Japan bombs Pearl Harbor; U.S. enters World War II.

**1942** 110,000 Japanese-Americans imprisoned in U.S.

**1945** Germany surrenders to Allied forces; U.S. drops atomic bombs on Hiroshima and Nagasaki; Japan surrenders; World War II ends.

**1948** Marshall Plan aids Europe in economic recovery after World War II.

**1950-53** U.S. involved in Korean War.

**1954** Supreme Court rules that compulsory segregation in public schools is illegal.

**1957** "Space Race" between U.S. and Russia begins.

**1962** Russia removes missiles from Cuba after U.S. protests.

**1963** Over 200,000 Americans demonstrate in Washington, D.C., against racial discrimination; President John F. Kennedy assassinated.

**1964** Congress, under President Lyndon B. Johnson, passes many civil rights laws.

**1965** U.S. sends combat troops to Vietnam.

**1968** Rev. Martin Luther King, Jr., assassinated; opposition to Vietnam War grows.

**1973** U.S. removes combat troops from Vietnam; Vice-President Spiro Agnew resigns after being charged with graft.

**1974** Watergate Scandal causes President Richard M. Nixon to resign to avoid impeachment.

**1978** U.S. Senate votes to give control of Panama Canal to Panama in 2000.

# METRIC CONVERSION TABLE

This table can help you change measurements *to* and *from* the metric system. You can change traditional measures to metrics by using the **GOLD** part of the table. You can change metrics to traditional measures by using the **BLUE** part.

Approximate conversions to metric measures

## Length

| When you know | multiply by | to find |
|---|---|---|
| inches (in) | 25 | millimeters (mm) |
| inches (in) | 2.5 | centimeters (cm) |
| feet (ft) | 30 | centimeters (cm) |
| feet (ft) | 0.3 | meters (m) |
| yards (yd) | 0.9 | meters (m) |
| miles (mi) | 1.6 | kilometers (km) |

## Area

| When you know | multiply by | to find |
|---|---|---|
| sq. inches ($in^2$) | 6.5 | sq. centimeters ($cm^2$) |
| sq. feet ($ft^2$) | 0.09 | sq. meters ($m^2$) |
| sq. yards ($yd^2$) | 0.8 | sq. meters ($m^2$) |
| sq. miles ($mi^2$) | 2.6 | sq. kilometers ($km^2$) |
| acres | 0.4 | hectares (ha) |

## Mass (weight)

| When you know | multiply by | to find |
|---|---|---|
| ounces (oz) | 28 | grams (g) |
| pounds (lb) | 0.45 | kilograms (kg) |
| tons (2000 lb) | 0.9 | metric tons (t) |

## Volume

| When you know | multiply by | to find |
|---|---|---|
| teaspoons (tsp) | 5 | milliliters (mL) |
| tablespoons (tbsp) | 15 | milliliters (mL) |
| fluid ounces (fl oz) | 30 | milliliters (mL) |
| cups (c) | 0.24 | liters (L) |
| pints (pt) | 0.47 | liters (L) |
| quarts (qt) | 0.95 | liters (L) |
| gallons (gal) | 3.8 | liters (L) |
| cubic inches ($in^3$) | 16.4 | cubic centimeters ($cm^3$) |
| cubic feet ($ft^3$) | 0.03 | cubic meters ($m^3$) |
| cubic yards ($yd^3$) | 0.76 | cubic meters ($m^3$) |

## Temperature

| When you know | multiply by | to find |
|---|---|---|
| Fahrenheit (°F) | 5/9 (after subtracting 32) | Celsius (°C) |

Approximate conversions from metric measures

## Length

| When you know | multiply by | to find |
|---|---|---|
| millimeters (mm) | 0.04 | inches (in) |
| centimeters (cm) | 0.4 | inches (in) |
| centimeters (cm) | 0.03 | feet (ft) |
| meters (m) | 3.3 | feet (ft) |
| meters (m) | 1.1 | yards (yd) |
| kilometers (km) | 0.6 | miles (mi) |

## Area

| When you know | multiply by | to find |
|---|---|---|
| sq. centimeters ($cm^2$) | 0.16 | sq. inches ($in^2$) |
| sq. meters ($m^2$) | 11.1 | sq. feet ($ft^2$) |
| sq. meters ($m^2$) | 1.2 | sq. yards ($yd^2$) |
| sq. kilometers ($km^2$) | 0.4 | sq. miles ($mi^2$) |
| hectares (ha) | 2.5 | acres |

## Mass (weight)

| When you know | multiply by | to find |
|---|---|---|
| grams (g) | 0.035 | ounces (oz) |
| kilograms (kg) | 2.2 | pounds (lb) |
| metric tons (t) | 1.1 | tons (2000 lb) |

## Volume

| When you know | multiply by | to find |
|---|---|---|
| milliliters (mL) | 0.18 | teaspoons (tsp) |
| milliliters (mL) | 0.06 | tablespoons (tbsp) |
| milliliters (mL) | 0.03 | fluid ounces (fl oz) |
| liters (L) | 4.2 | cups (c) |
| liters (L) | 2.1 | pints (pt) |
| liters (L) | 1.06 | quarts (qt) |
| liters (L) | 0.26 | gallons (gal) |
| cubic centimeters ($cm^3$) | 0.06 | cubic inches ($in^3$) |
| cubic meters ($m^3$) | 35 | cubic feet ($ft^3$) |
| cubic meters ($m^3$) | 1.3 | cubic yards ($yd^3$) |

## Temperature

| When you know | multiply by | to find |
|---|---|---|
| Celsius (°C) | 9/5 (then add 32) | Fahrenheit (°F) |

## METRIC EXERCISES

The following examples give the conversion *to* and *from* metrics for the five different kinds of measurement shown in the pictures. The figures in parentheses are rounded to the nearest unit.

**A. Length** How many meters is a long jump measuring 6 feet?

(to metrics) 6 ft    6 x 0.3 = 1.8 m

How many feet is a long jump measuring 1.8 meters?

(from metrics) 1.8 m    1.8 x 3.3 = 5.94 ft (6 ft)

**B. Area** How many square meters is a window with an area of 30 square feet?

(to metrics) 30 $ft^2$    30 x 0.09 = 2.7 $m^2$

How many square feet is a window with an area of 2.7 square meters?

(from metrics) 2.7 $m^2$    2.7 x 11.1 = 29.97 $ft^2$ (30 $ft^2$)

**C. Mass** (weight) How many kilograms is a bag of peanuts weighing 1 pound?

(to metrics) 1 lb    1 x 0.45 = 0.45 kg

How many pounds is a bag of peanuts weighing 0.45 kilogram?

(from metrics) 0.45 kg    0.45 x 2.2 = 0.99 lb (1 lb)

**D. Volume** How many liters is a gallon of milk?

(to metrics) 1 gal    1 x 3.8 = 3.8 L

How many gallons is 3.8 liters of milk?

(from metrics) 3.8 L    3.8 x 0.26 = 0.988 gal (1 gal)

**E. Temperature** What is the temperature in Celsius when the thermometer reads 50° Fahrenheit?

(to metrics) 50°F    50—32 = 18
18 x $\frac{5}{9}$ = 10°C

What is the temperature in Fahrenheit when the thermometer reads 10° Celsius?

(from metrics) 10°C    10 x $\frac{9}{5}$ = 18
18 + 32 = 50°F

inches 1 2 3 4 5 6

centimeters 1 2 3 4 5 6 7 8 9 10 11 12 13 14 15

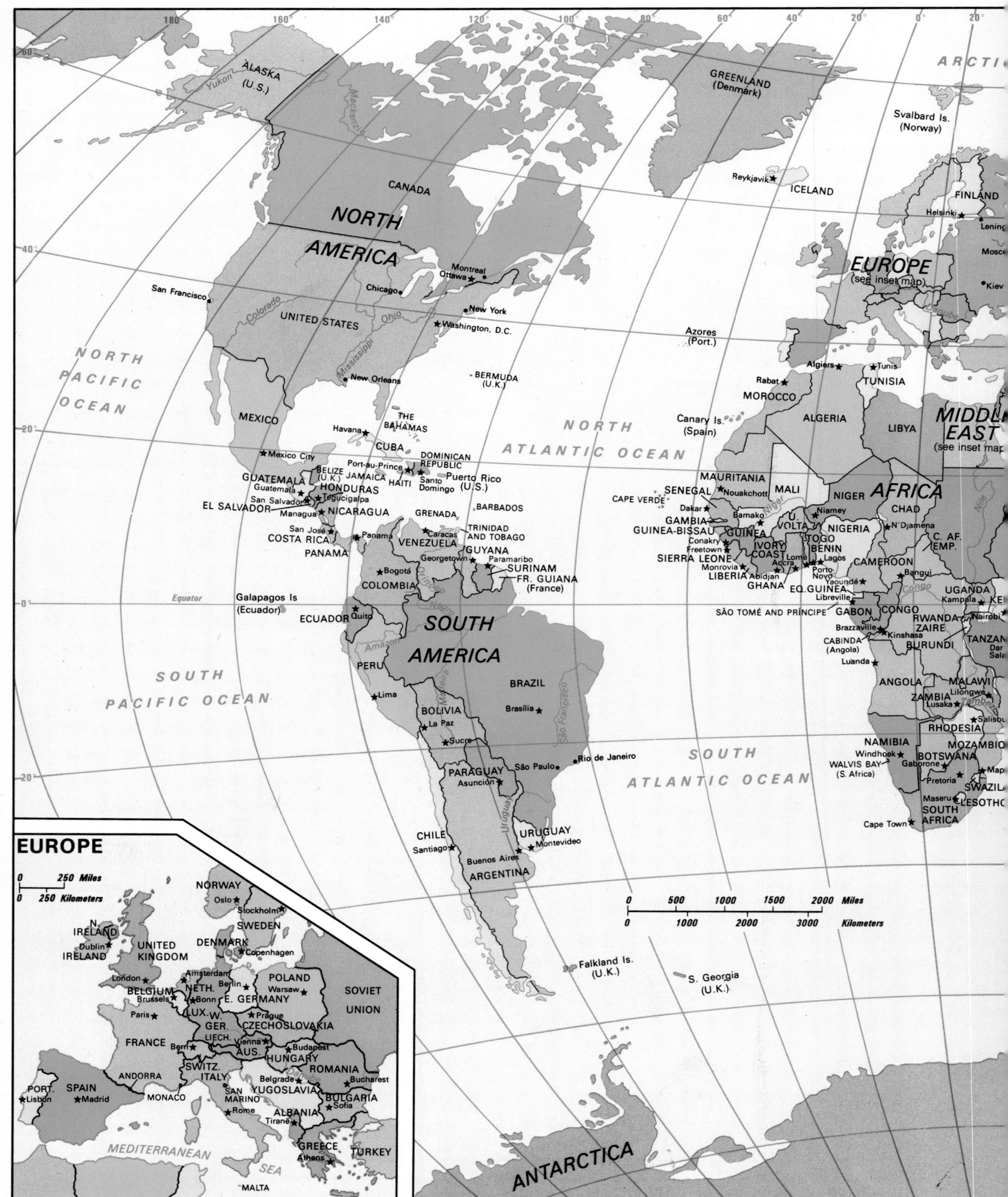

ALASKA
(U.S.)
CANADA
NORTH
AMERICA
GREENLAND
(Denmark)
Svalbard Is.
(Norway)
Reykjavik
ICELAND
FINLAND
Helsinki
EUROPE
(see inset map)
San Francisco
Chicago
Montreal
Ottawa
New York
Washington, D.C.
UNITED STATES
Azores
(Port.)
NORTH
PACIFIC
OCEAN
New Orleans
BERMUDA
(U.K.)
Algiers
Tunis
TUNISIA
Rabat
MOROCCO
MEXICO
THE
BAHAMAS
Havana
CUBA
NORTH
ATLANTIC OCEAN
Canary Is.
(Spain)
ALGERIA
LIBYA
MIDDLE
EAST
Mexico City
DOMINICAN
REPUBLIC
Port-au-Prince
BELIZE
(U.K.)
JAMAICA
HAITI
Santo
Domingo
Puerto Rico
(U.S.)
GUATEMALA
Guatemala
HONDURAS
Tegucigalpa
San Salvador
EL SALVADOR
Managua
NICARAGUA
MAURITANIA
SENEGAL
Nouakchott
MALI
NIGER
AFRICA
CAPE VERDE
Dakar
GAMBIA
GUINEA-BISSAU
GUINEA
Bamako
Niamey
CHAD
N'Djamena
U.
VOLTA
NIGERIA
GRENADA
BARBADOS
San José
COSTA RICA
Panama
PANAMA
Caracas
VENEZUELA
TRINIDAD
AND TOBAGO
GUYANA
Georgetown
Paramaribo
SURINAM
FR. GUIANA
(France)
Conakry
Freetown
SIERRA LEONE
Monrovia
LIBERIA
IVORY
COAST
Abidjan
Accra
GHANA
Lomé
TOGO
BENIN
Porto
Novo
Lagos
C. AF.
EMP.
CAMEROON
Yaoundé
Bangui
EQ. GUINEA
Bogotá
COLOMBIA
Equator
Galapagos Is
(Ecuador)
Quito
ECUADOR
SOUTH
AMERICA
SÃO TOMÉ AND PRINCIPE
Libreville
GABON
CONGO
UGANDA
Kampala
Nairobi
RWANDA
ZAIRE
Brazzaville
Kinshasa
BURUNDI
CABINDA
(Angola)
TANZANIA
Dar
Luanda
PERU
Lima
SOUTH
PACIFIC OCEAN
BRAZIL
Brasília
BOLIVIA
La Paz
Sucre
ANGOLA
ZAMBIA
MALAWI
Lilongwe
Lusaka
Salisbury
RHODESIA
NAMIBIA
Windhoek
WALVIS BAY
(S. Africa)
BOTSWANA
Gaborone
MOZAMBIQUE
Rio de Janeiro
São Paulo
PARAGUAY
Asunción
SOUTH
ATLANTIC OCEAN
Pretoria
SWAZILAND
Maseru
LESOTHO
SOUTH
AFRICA
Cape Town
CHILE
Santiago
URUGUAY
Montevideo
Buenos Aires
ARGENTINA
0 500 1000 1500 2000 Miles
0 1000 2000 3000 Kilometers
Falkland Is.
(U.K.)
S. Georgia
(U.K.)
ANTARCTICA
EUROPE
0 250 Miles
0 250 Kilometers
NORWAY
Oslo
Stockholm
SWEDEN
N.
IRELAND
Dublin
IRELAND
UNITED
KINGDOM
DENMARK
Copenhagen
London
Amsterdam
NETH.
Berlin
POLAND
Warsaw
SOVIET
UNION
BELGIUM
Brussels
Bonn
E. GERMANY
LUX.
W.
GER.
Paris
Prague
CZECHOSLOVAKIA
FRANCE
Bern
LIECH.
Vienna
AUS.
Budapest
HUNGARY
SWITZ.
ITALY
ROMANIA
Bucharest
ANDORRA
Belgrade
YUGOSLAVIA
PORT.
Lisbon
SPAIN
Madrid
MONACO
SAN
MARINO
Rome
BULGARIA
Sofia
ALBANIA
Tirane
GREECE
Athens
TURKEY
MEDITERRANEAN
SEA
MALTA

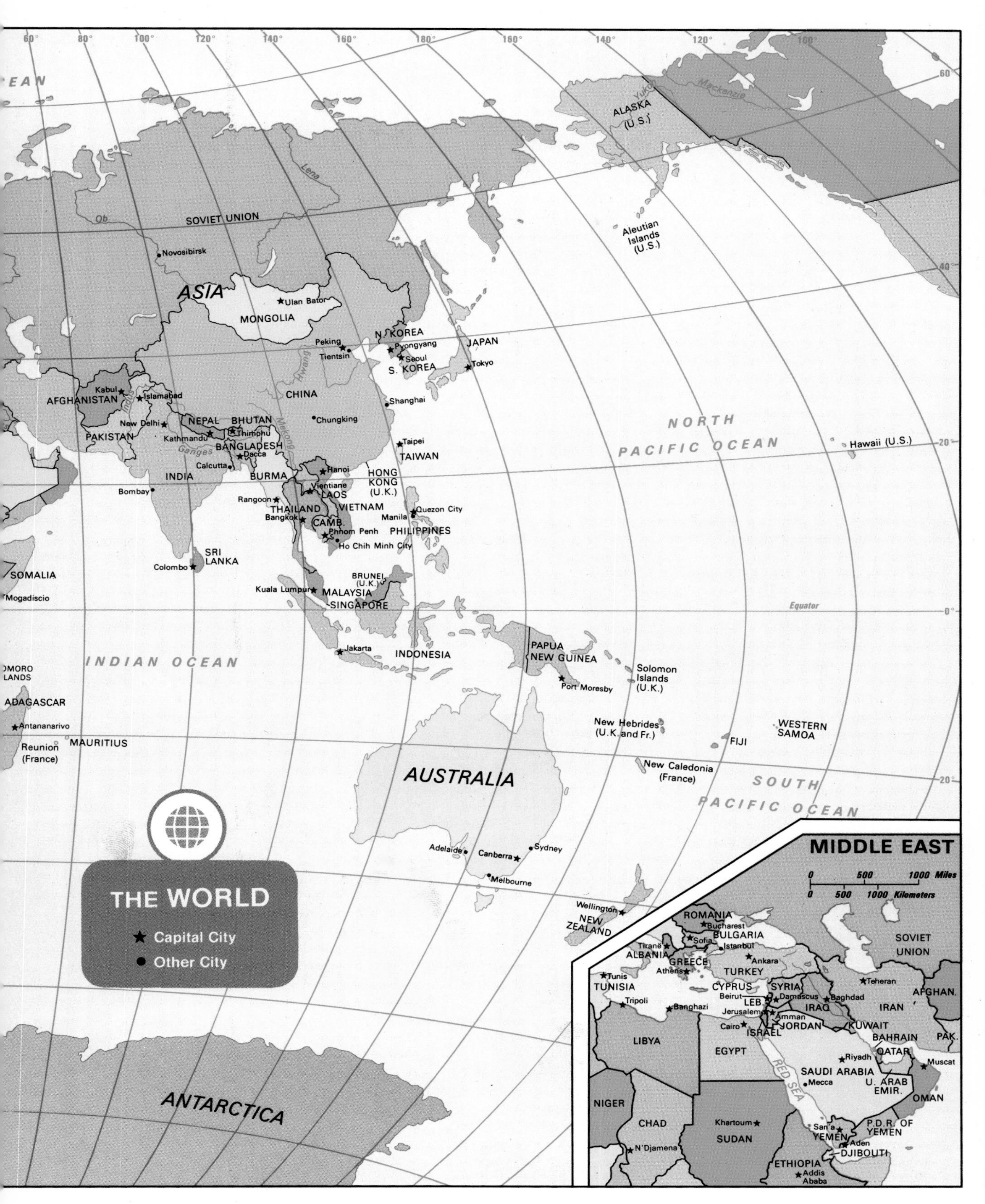

THE WORLD
Capital City
Other City
60° 80° 100° 120° 140° 160° 180° 160° 140° 120° 100°
60° 40° 20° 0° 20°
ASIA
SOVIET UNION
Ob
Lena
Novosibirsk
MONGOLIA
Ulan Bator
N. KOREA
Pyongyang
Seoul
S. KOREA
JAPAN
Tokyo
Peking
Tientsin
Hwang
CHINA
Shanghai
Chungking
AFGHANISTAN
Kabul
Islamabad
Indus
PAKISTAN
New Delhi
NEPAL
BHUTAN
Thimphu
Kathmandu
BANGLADESH
Dacca
Ganges
Mekong
Calcutta
INDIA
Bombay
BURMA
Rangoon
THAILAND
Bangkok
Hanoi
Vientiane
LAOS
VIETNAM
CAMB.
Phnom Penh
Ho Chih Minh City
HONG KONG (U.K.)
Taipei
TAIWAN
Quezon City
Manila
PHILIPPINES
SRI LANKA
Colombo
BRUNEI (U.K.)
Kuala Lumpur
MALAYSIA
SINGAPORE
Jakarta
INDONESIA
PAPUA NEW GUINEA
Port Moresby
Solomon Islands (U.K.)
New Hebrides (U.K. and Fr.)
FIJI
WESTERN SAMOA
New Caledonia (France)
AUSTRALIA
Adelaide
Canberra
Sydney
Melbourne
Wellington
NEW ZEALAND
ANTARCTICA
INDIAN OCEAN
NORTH PACIFIC OCEAN
SOUTH PACIFIC OCEAN
Equator
Hawaii (U.S.)
Aleutian Islands (U.S.)
ALASKA (U.S.)
Yukon
Mackenzie
SOMALIA
Mogadiscio
ADAGASCAR
Antananarivo
Reunion (France)
MAURITIUS
MIDDLE EAST
0 500 1000 Miles
0 500 1000 Kilometers
ROMANIA
Bucharest
BULGARIA
Sofia
Istanbul
Tirane
ALBANIA
GREECE
Athens
Ankara
TURKEY
SOVIET UNION
Tunis
TUNISIA
CYPRUS
SYRIA
Beirut
Damascus
LEB.
Teheran
Baghdad
IRAQ
IRAN
AFGHAN.
Tripoli
Banghazi
Jerusalem
Amman
JORDAN
Cairo
ISRAEL
KUWAIT
BAHRAIN
PAK.
LIBYA
EGYPT
QATAR
Riyadh
Muscat
SAUDI ARABIA
Mecca
RED SEA
U. ARAB EMIR.
OMAN
NIGER
CHAD
Khartoum
SUDAN
San'a
YEMEN
Aden
P.D.R. OF YEMEN
DJIBOUTI
N'Djamena
ETHIOPIA
Addis Ababa

Seattle
Olympia
WASHINGTON
Spokane
Columbia
Portland
Salem
Eugene
CASCADE
RANGE
OREGON
IDAHO
Boise
Snake
Pocatello
ROCKY
MOUNTAINS
Missouri
Great Falls
Helena
MONTANA
Billings
WYOMING
Casper
Cheyenne
Minot
NORTH DAKOTA
Bismarck
GREAT
PLAINS
SOUTH DAKOTA
Rapid City
Pierre
NEBRASKA
Platte
GREAT
NEVADA
BASIN
Reno
Carson City
Sacramento
San Francisco
Oakland
San Jose
SIERRA NEVADA
CALIFORNIA
Ogden
Great Salt Lake
Salt Lake City
Green
UTAH
Denver
Colorado Springs
COLORADO
KANSAS
Arkansas
Wichita
Las Vegas
Los Angeles
Long Beach
Salton Sea
San Diego
Colorado
ARIZONA
Phoenix
Gila
Tucson
San Pedro
Santa Fe
Albuquerque
NEW MEXICO
LLANO ESTACADO
Las Cruces
El Paso
Oklahoma City
Ft. Worth
TEXAS
Austin
San Antonio
Rio Grande
MT. WAIALEALE
Honolulu
HAWAII
PRINCIPAL ISLANDS OF HAWAII
BROOKS RANGE
Yukon
Fairbanks
ALASKA
ALASKA RANGE
Anchorage
Juneau
ALASKA

THE UNITED STATES
Capital City
Other City
Lake of the Woods
Lake Superior
Lake Michigan
Lake Huron
Lake Ontario
Lake Erie
St. Lawrence
Hudson
Ohio
Tennessee
Mississippi
Lake Pontchartrain
Lake Okeechobee
APPALACHIAN MOUNTAINS
OUACHITA MTS.
MINNESOTA
WISCONSIN
MICHIGAN
IOWA
ILLINOIS
INDIANA
OHIO
MISSOURI
KENTUCKY
TENNESSEE
ARKANSAS
MISSISSIPPI
ALABAMA
GEORGIA
LOUISIANA
FLORIDA
SOUTH CAROLINA
NORTH CAROLINA
VIRGINIA
WEST VIRGINIA
PENNSYLVANIA
NEW YORK
NEW JERSEY
MD.
DEL.
CONN.
R.I.
MASS.
VT.
N.H.
MAINE
Duluth
Minneapolis
St. Paul
Green Bay
Milwaukee
Madison
Chicago
Gary
Fort Wayne
Grand Rapids
Lansing
Detroit
Toledo
Cleveland
Akron
Columbus
Cincinnati
Indianapolis
Peoria
Springfield
Des Moines
Kansas City
St. Louis
Jefferson City
Springfield
Louisville
Frankfort
Lexington
Charleston
Huntington
Pittsburgh
Harrisburg
Buffalo
Rochester
Albany
Burlington
Montpelier
Concord
Manchester
Augusta
Lewiston
Bangor
Portland
Boston
Providence
Hartford
New York
Newark
Jersey City
Trenton
Philadelphia
Wilmington
Baltimore
Dover
Washington
Annapolis
Richmond
Norfolk
Winston-Salem
Greensboro
Raleigh
Charlotte
Knoxville
Nashville
Memphis
Little Rock
Fort Smith
Columbia
Atlanta
Macon
Columbus
Birmingham
Montgomery
Jackson
Charleston
Savannah
Jacksonville
Tallahassee
Mobile
Pensacola
Baton Rouge
New Orleans
Shreveport
Houston
Tampa
Miami
0 100 200 300 Miles
0 200 400 Kilometers

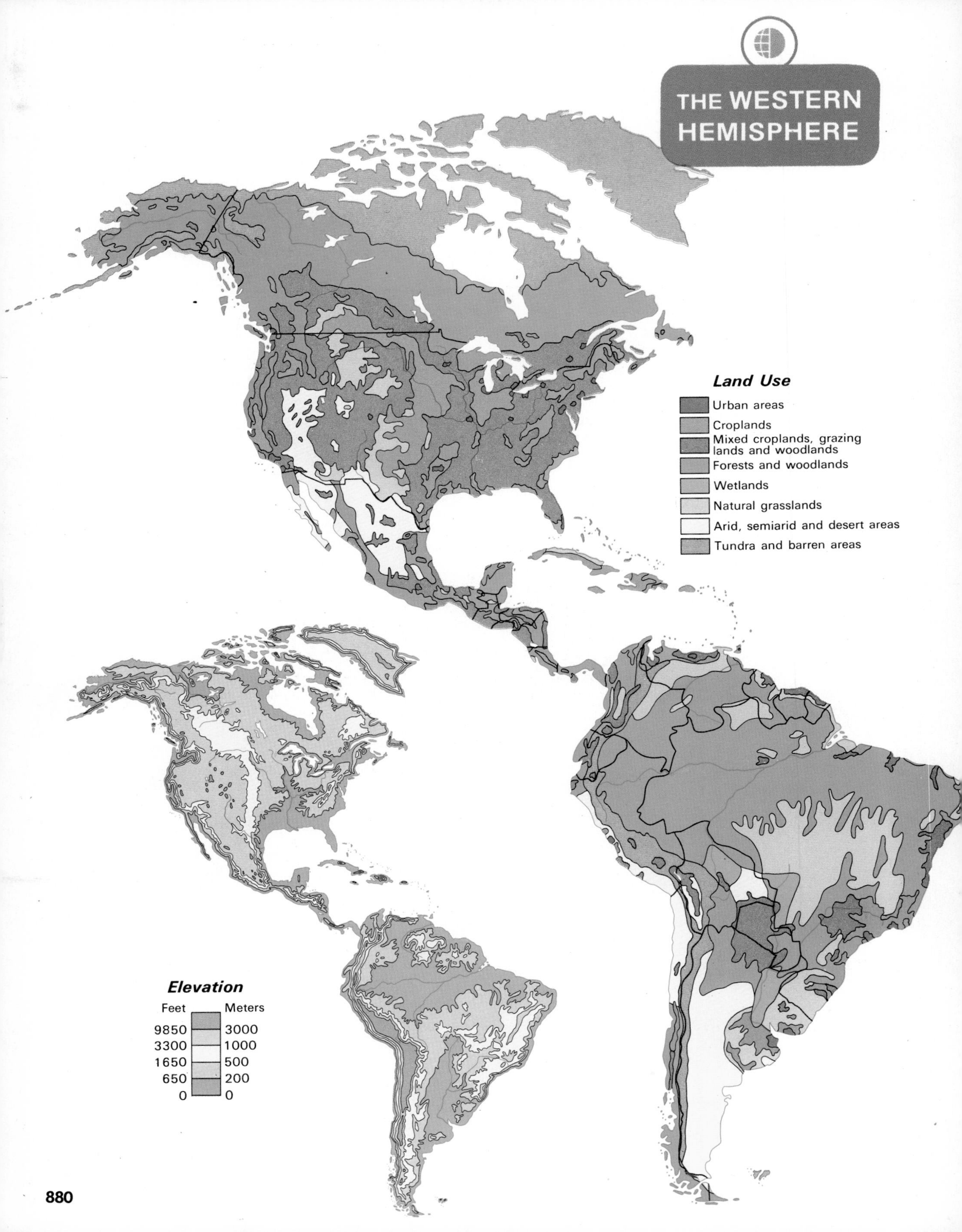
THE WESTERN HEMISPHERE
Land Use
Urban areas
Croplands
Mixed croplands, grazing lands and woodlands
Forests and woodlands
Wetlands
Natural grasslands
Arid, semiarid and desert areas
Tundra and barren areas
Elevation
Feet
Meters
9850
3000
3300
1000
1650
500
650
200
0
0

# Pronunciation Key

| SYMBOL | KEY WORDS |
|---|---|
| a | **a**sk, f**a**t |
| ā | **a**pe, d**a**te |
| ä | c**a**r, l**o**t |
| e | **e**lf, t**e**n |
| er | b**e**rry, c**are** |
| ē | **e**ven, m**ee**t |
| i | **i**s, h**i**t |
| ir | m**ir**ror, h**ere** |
| ī | **i**ce, f**i**re |
| ō | **o**pen, g**o** |
| ô | l**aw**, h**o**rn |
| ơi | **oi**l, p**oi**nt |
| ơo | l**oo**k, p**u**ll |
| $\overline{\text{oo}}$ | **oo**ze, t**oo**l |
| yơo | **u**nite, c**u**re |
| y$\overline{\text{oo}}$ | c**u**te, f**ew** |
| ơu | **ou**t, cr**ow**d |
| u | **u**p, c**u**t |
| ʉr | f**ur**, f**er**n |
| ə | **a** in **a**go |
| | **e** in ag**e**nt |
| | **e** in fath**e**r |
| | **i** in un**i**ty |
| | **o** in c**o**llect |
| | **u** in foc**u**s |

| SYMBOL | KEY WORDS |
|---|---|
| b | **b**ed, du**b** |
| d | **d**id, ha**d** |
| f | **f**all, o**ff** |
| g | **g**et, do**g** |
| h | **h**e, a**h**ead |
| j | **j**oy, **j**ump |
| k | **k**ill, ba**k**e |
| l | **l**et, ba**ll** |
| m | **m**et, tri**m** |
| n | **n**ot, to**n** |
| p | **p**ut, ta**p** |
| r | **r**ed, dea**r** |
| s | **s**ell, pa**ss** |
| t | **t**op, ha**t** |
| v | **v**at, ha**v**e |
| w | **w**ill, al**w**ays |
| y | **y**et, **y**ard |
| z | **z**ebra, ha**z**e |
| ch | **ch**in, ar**ch** |
| ŋ | ri**ng**, si**ng**er |
| sh | **sh**e, da**sh** |
| th | **th**in, tru**th** |
| *th* | **th**en, fa**th**er |
| zh | **s** in plea**s**ure |
| ' | as in (ā'b'l) |

A heavy stress mark **'** is placed after a syllable that gets a strong accent, as in **con·sid·er** (kən sid**'**ər).

A light stress mark ' is placed after a syllable that also gets an accent, but of a weaker kind, as in **dic·tion·ar·y** (dik**'**shə ner'ē).

See also the explanation of how to use the pronunciation key, beginning on page 32 of the introduction.